W9-CAE-609

United States Presidential Primary Elections

1968-1996

CQ Press
A Division of Congressional Quarterly Inc.
1414 22nd Street, N.W.
Washington, D.C. 20037
(202) 822-1475; (800) 638-1710

www.cqpress.com

Cover designer: Rich Pottern

Printed in the United States of America

04 03 02 01 00 5 4 3 2 1

The paper used in this publication meets the minimum requirements of the American National Standard for Information Science—Permanence of Paper for Printed Library Materials, ANSI Z39.48-1984.

Library of Congress Cataloging-in-Publication Data

Cook, Rhodes.
United States presidential primary elections, 1968–1996: a handbook of election statistics / Rhodes Cook.
p. cm.
ISBN: 1-56802-451-7 (alk. paper)
1. Presidents—United States—Nomination. 2. Primaries—United States—Statistics.

JK522.C66 2000
324.5'4'097309045—dc21

99-462083

United States Presidential Primary Elections 1968-1996

A Handbook of Election Statistics

Rhodes Cook

A Division of Congressional Quarterly Inc.
Washington, D.C.

CONTENTS

PREFACE

The purpose of this book is to pull together under one cover the official, county-by-county results for all contested Democratic and Republican presidential primary elections from 1968 through 1996.

Such detailed results for 1992 and 1996 have been published by CQ Press in separate editions of *U.S. Primary Elections.* But to the author's knowledge, never before has such a wide array of county-by-county material on the critical opening stage of the presidential election process been published in a single volume.

Presidential primaries have been a part of the nominating process since the early twentieth century. In a perfect world, this book would have started at the beginning, presenting detailed results from their inception in 1912.

Several other starting points would have also made sense—1952, for instance, when Dwight D. Eisenhower and Ohio Sen. Robert A. Taft put the first-in-the-nation New Hampshire primary on the map with a spirited contest there; or 1960, when John F. Kennedy made the primaries the prescribed route to the nomination for a new era of photogenic and media-savvy candidates.

But for several reasons, 1968 was chosen as the starting point to begin this collection of data. First and foremost, 1968 was an important transition year in presidential politics—the last hurrah for the conventions as the decisive stage of the nominating process and the launching point for the current era in which millions of voters in the myriad primary states decide their party's nominees.

A less significant reason for starting with 1968, but a reason nonetheless, is that it is recent enough that detailed returns from state election boards were, by and large, still readily obtainable. And for many in the author's generation that tumultuous time has special meaning because it is when many of us came of age.

The presidential primaries still played only an advisory role in the nominating process in 1968 because there were so few of them (little more than a baker's dozen). But the number increased rapidly. By 1976, a majority of states held presidential primaries; by 1996, there were more than 40.

The total has fluctuated from year to year. But after 1968, the basic dynamic of presidential nominating politics has remained the same—candidates must compete and win in the primaries, for without exception that is where nominations have been decided.

The introduction to this book seeks to explain the evolution of the presidential nominating process into its present primary-dominated form. Particular emphasis is paid to the years since 1968, an era when voters in each party have replaced party leaders as the true kingmakers.

At the end of the introduction are several sets of summary tables designed to illustrate various aspects of voting behavior in the presidential primaries. First are tables listing Democratic and Republican primary winners by state since 1968. These tables are followed by others listing primary winners over the years in key counties and population centers—representing cities, suburbs and an assorted array of other constituencies that play a visible role in the nominating process.

The introduction concludes with a one-page overview of each Democratic and Republican presidential nominating contest since 1968. There is a national map with each contest illustrating the presidential primary winners in each state, a brief text summarizing the campaign and a box with nationwide primary vote data for the leading candidates.

Following the introduction is the heart of the book, an arrangement of the presidential primary results alphabetically by state. Each state section begins with a brief essay that highlights the recent history of the presidential nominating process in that state. References to various counties are included to illustrate the political geography and internal voting patterns of the state, as well as to give some context to the county-by-county vote tables that follow.

Accompanying the essay is a table summarizing the state's presidential primary results since 1968. The turnout for each Democratic and Republican primary is given, along with the vote share for all candidates who received at least 10 percent of their party's primary vote. Each state section also includes a state map that shows its counties and major population centers.

Following this overview material are the year-by-year tables of presidential primary returns, broken down by county in all but a few New England states, where results are presented for major cities and towns. Democratic results are listed first for each year; the Republican results follow.

In all, there are more than 420 tables for 46 states. Only Alaska, Hawaii, Iowa, Utah and Wyoming did not hold at least one presidential primary in the period from 1968 through 1996, although Iowa Republicans compile their caucus results like a primary vote and they are included in this book because of the importance of Iowa in the nominating process.

Presidential primaries come in various forms. Most states have presidential preference primaries, which provide a direct vote for candidates. A few states, though, accent the election of delegates and do not have a direct vote for the candidates themselves. Most presidential preference primaries elect or allocate delegates, the coin of the realm in the nominating process. Some do not. They are nonbinding "beauty contests," which measure the popularity of candidates without electing delegates.

Tables are included for every presidential primary since 1968, with the following exceptions: (1) where a candidate was running unopposed and, at most, scattered write-ins were the only other votes cast; (2) where no candidates were listed on the ballot and, at most, a comparatively small number of write-in votes were cast; (3) where none of the major candidates was entered; and (4) where there was a primary for delegates only and no vote for presidential candidates could be aggregated on a statewide basis.

Included in the county tables are all candidates who received at least 10 percent of their party's statewide primary vote; their names are listed in alphabetical order. Also included are candidates who went on to win their party's nomination regardless of their vote percentage in a particular primary. Democratic nominees George McGovern in 1972 and Michael Dukakis in 1988, for instance, fell below 10 percent of the vote in several Southern primary states but were included in all the county tables that year in which they were on the ballot.

The county tables are based on official returns from the states, although the numbers in the tables do not always add up to the certified totals from the states. In that case, both sets of totals are listed at the end of the table. The numbers certified by the state are used in other summary tables.

Often where there is a discrepancy, the term "Certified Totals" is used to indicate the vote totals as reported by the state. The term "Published Totals" is used to indicate vote totals that may or may not have been certified by the state but that have appeared in other publications of election data, such as *America at the Polls.*

County votes are reported as certified, although occasionally there is a peculiar result that is at odds with the normal voting behavior of that county. In that case, a note is posted at the end of the table noting the oddity.

In many respects, this book was a labor of love. But in any book this size, it was also labor. It would not have been possible without the assistance of state election boards across the country, who invariably were helpful in providing needed material for this book.

Thanks also are in order to the staff at CQ Press: executive editor David Tarr, who gracefully shepherded this book from its start in early 1998 to its completion in late 1999; senior editor Jon Preimesberger, who managed the editing; and Paul Pressau, who handled the design, graphics and composition.

And a particular debt of gratitude is owed my wife, Memrie McKay-Cook, whose support and forbearance were not only deeply appreciated but vitally important to the completion of this book.

Rhodes Cook
December 1999

United States Presidential Primary Elections 1968-1996

INTRODUCTION

If there is one rule of thumb to describe the presidential nominating process, it is that the constant is change.

The process of nominating presidential candidates is constantly evolving—from congressional caucuses in the early nineteenth century, through the heyday of the national conventions over the next century and a half, to the present, where conventions merely ratify the decisions made earlier by Democratic and Republican primary voters.

That is because the presidential primaries are now where the action is, and they have been since the Democrats' tumultuous convention in Chicago in 1968 encouraged both parties—but the Democrats in particular—to look for ways to open the presidential nominating process to greater grassroots participation.

The principal way to more voter involvement has been through the proliferation of presidential primaries. A product of the Progressive era in the early twentieth century, primaries were few and far between until 1968. But after that, they quickly mushroomed in number—from 15 in 1968, to 36 in 1980, to more than 40 in 1996.

As the number of primaries grew, power in the nominating process quickly shifted from party kingmakers at the national conventions to voters in the primary states. And it has stayed that way.

Long gone are the days when candidates could win their party's nomination without entering the primaries. No Democratic or Republican nominee has done so since Hubert Humphrey in 1968.

And long gone are the days when candidates could be nominated without first proving broad-based popularity among millions of their party's primary voters. Since Democrat George McGovern in 1972, every major-party nominee has been their party's highest vote-getter in the primaries.

In the process, the once climactic conventions have become little more than giant pep rallies, ratifying the choices of Democratic and Republican primary voters made months earlier.

Front-Loaded Process

In recent years, the nominations have been settled earlier and earlier, as more and more states have moved their primaries forward to dates near the beginning of the election year in a bid to heighten their influence (a process that is known as "front-loading.")

In 1968, only one presidential primary (New Hampshire's) was held before the end of March. In 1980, 10 states held primaries so early. By 1988, the number surpassed 20, and by 1996, more than half the country had voted by the end of March.

The result in recent years has been an increasingly truncated nominating process that has followed a clear pattern. Early votes in Iowa and New Hampshire have winnowed the field to a handful of candidates. Then, after a short period of unpredictability, one candidate has scored a knockout in the glut of March primaries, with their victory ratified by a string of votes at the end of the nominating process.

That is what happened in 1992. The first five Democratic primaries that year produced four different winners. But Bill Clinton broke from the pack with a sweep of the early March primaries in his native South and ended up winning all but two of the primaries that followed.

The story was similar on the Republican side in 1996. Bob

Primary Wins Bring Convention Success

No candidate since Hubert Humphrey in 1968 has won the nomination of a major party without first entering its presidential primaries. And no candidate since George McGovern in 1972 has won the Democratic or Republican nomination without being the top vote-getter in his party's primaries; Humphrey won more votes in the Democratic primaries that year.

The chart below compares each nominee's share of his party's primary vote with the share of the delegate votes he won on the first ballot at his party's convention; not since 1952 has a convention taken more than one ballot to settle a presidential nomination. An asterisk (*) indicates an incumbent president.

	DEMOCRATS			REPUBLICANS		
Election Year	Nominee	% of Primary Vote	% of Convention Vote	Nominee	% of Primary Vote	% of Convention Vote
1968	Hubert Humphrey	2	67	Richard Nixon	38	52
1972	George McGovern	25	57	Richard Nixon*	92	99.9
1976	Jimmy Carter	39	74	Gerald Ford*	53	53
1980	Jimmy Carter*	51	64	Ronald Reagan	61	97
1984	Walter Mondale	38	56	Ronald Reagan*	99	99.9
1988	Michael Dukakis	43	69	George Bush	68	100
1992	Bill Clinton	52	79	George Bush*	72	99
1996	Bill Clinton*	89	99.7	Bob Dole	59	97

Dole struggled through a series of primary and caucus contests scattered across the opening weeks of the nominating process, losing as many as he won.

But once the calendar flipped to March and the primaries began to occur in large groupings, Dole's advantages of widespread party support, a large campaign chest and high name familiarity kicked in. He did not lose another primary and had amassed the delegate majority he needed to nail down the GOP nomination by the end of March.

Neither party has had an elongated tug-of-war since 1984, when Walter Mondale and Gary Hart battled for the Democratic nomination into the final week of the primary season. And neither party has had a nominating contest that was even vaguely competitive by the time of its national convention since the 1976 Republican race between President Gerald R. Ford and Ronald Reagan.

Starting Points

Even though much of the primary calendar has changed dramatically over the last few decades, the accepted starting points have remained Iowa and New Hampshire (even though other states have occasionally voted before them).

Both states have made their early events into cottage industries, but the candidates and the media have helped make them so. More than ever, Iowa and New Hampshire are about the only places left where candidates have some control over their destinies. They can woo voters one-on-one, whether in bowling alleys, coffee shops or the frequent gatherings in neighborhood living rooms.

For if there is one thing that has become certain in recent years, once the New Hampshire primary is over, there is a frenetic burst of tarmac-to-tarmac campaigning heavily dependent on media advertising.

Occasionally, candidates have tried to skip Iowa or New Hampshire, or both, and launch their campaigns on terrain more to their choosing. Democrat George Wallace did that in 1976. So, to a degree, did Democrat Al Gore in 1988. But that streak of independence did not yield visible benefits for either of them.

With one exception, every presidential nominee since 1976 has won either Iowa or New Hampshire, and finished no lower than third in the other. The exception was Clinton in 1992, who did not seriously contest Iowa in deference to the home-state appeal of Sen. Tom Harkin and finished second in New Hampshire behind former Massachusetts Sen. Paul Tsongas.

The two states illustrate the two different types of delegate-selection processes that states have to choose from. Iowa is a caucus. New Hampshire is a primary. Primaries require voters only to cast a ballot, an exercise that usually takes just a few minutes. The deliberative nature of a neighborhood caucus, though, often requires the commitment of an afternoon or evening.

A Small Slice of the Electorate

Voter turnout is usually much higher in a primary than a caucus, but even in primaries the turnout is much lower than a general election. In New Hampshire, for instance, where interest in the presidential primary is probably greater than any other state, 300,000 voters turned out in February 1996 for the presidential primary, while 500,000 cast ballots in the general election that fall.

The disparity is much greater in many other states. When both parties last held competitive nominating contests in the same year (1992), fewer than 33 million votes were cast in the presidential primaries—20.2 million on the Democratic side, 12.7 million on the Republican. Activity in the handful of states that held caucuses involved about one million more voters.

By comparison, nearly 105 million voters turned out for the November general election that year, roughly three times the number that took part in the nominating process.

Rules governing voter participation play a role in the comparatively low turnouts for the nominating process. Every primary is not as open as a general election, where any registered voter can participate. A number of states limit participation to registered Democratic and Republican voters. Some others allow independents to participate, but list them on the voting rolls afterward as members of the party in which they cast their primary ballot.

Still, the vast majority of registered voters across the country can participate in a presidential primary or caucus if they want. The fact that more do not has generated the conventional wisdom that the nominating process is dominated by ideological activists—liberals on the Democratic side, conservatives on the Republican.

That is debatable in the primaries, where the winners in recent years have been from the mainstreams of both parties. An ideological bent is more evident in the low-turnout world of the caucuses, where a small cadre of dedicated voters can dominate the outcome.

When religious broadcaster Pat Robertson tried for the Republican presidential nomination in 1988, for instance, he won first-round caucus voting in three states and finished second in three others, including Iowa. But Robertson did not come close that year to winning a presidential primary.

Primary Clues

It has been a matter of debate within the political community whether the current primary-dominated nominating process is better than the old system, in which party leaders controlled the selection process.

But it is a fact that the increased number of primaries helps provide valuable clues about the vote-getting potential of candidates in the general election. Nominees that have exhibited broad-based appeal among the diverse array of primary voters

And the Last Shall Be First

The importance of states in the fall presidential election are closely related to population. The major battlegrounds are nearly always the eight to ten largest states.

But the connection between size and clout is more tenuous in the presidential nominating process. Leadoff spots on the calendar and the weight of political tradition have ensured Iowa and New Hampshire an importance that far outweighs any of the larger, vote-rich states that hold their primaries later. Of the roughly 14 million votes that were cast in the Republican presidential nominating process in 1996 (there was no contest on the Democratic side), approximately 60 percent were cast in the nation's ten most populous states; only 2 percent in Iowa and New Hampshire.

Following is a comparison of voter turnout in the GOP nominating contest that year in each of the ten largest states with that in Iowa and New Hampshire. Each state's primary (or in the case of Iowa, precinct caucus) date in 1996 is given, as well as the proportion of the nationwide GOP primary vote that the state's turnout represented.

The Republican primary in 1996 in New York was for the selection of delegates only; turnout there is an estimate. In parentheses is each state's national ranking according to 1998 population estimates. Iowa, for instance, is the thirtieth most populous state in the country; New Hampshire is forty-second.

	1996 Date	Republican Turnout	Percentage of National GOP Primary Vote
Iowa (30)	Feb. 12	96,451	0.7
New Hampshire (42)	Feb. 20	208,938	1.5
Georgia (10)	March 5	559,067	4.0
New York (3)	March 7	400,000	2.9
Florida (4)	March 12	898,516	6.4
Texas (2)	March 12	1,019,803	7.3
Illinois (5)	March 19	818,364	5.8
Michigan (8)	March 19	524,161	3.7
Ohio (7)	March 19	963,422	6.9
California (1)	March 26	2,452,312	17.5
Pennsylvania (6)	April 23	684,204	4.9
New Jersey (9)	June 4	218,812	1.6
National GOP Primary Vote		13,991,649	

Presidential Primary Turnouts Since 1968

From the inception of presidential primaries in 1912 through 1968, there were never more than twenty primaries in one year. But since then, the number of presidential primaries has grown steadily to the point that in 1996 there were more than forty.

The most votes cast in the presidential primaries came in 1988 when more than 35 million were cast. Nearly 23 million voters turned out for the Democratic presidential primaries in 1988, the most in any election before or since. The Republican high was in 1996, when nearly 14 million ballots were cast in the GOP presidential primaries.

Through much of the first half of the twentieth century, starting with the contest between former president Theodore Roosevelt and President William Howard Taft in 1912, more votes were cast in Republican presidential primaries than Democratic. But that was not the case in the last half of the century. Republicans had a higher turnout only twice—in 1952, when Dwight D. Eisenhower and Robert Taft had a vigorous contest for the GOP nomination—and in 1996, when President Bill Clinton ran virtually unopposed for the Democratic nomination.

Year	Number of States Holding Primaries	Democratic Vote	Republican Vote	Total Vote
1968	14 and D.C.	7,535,069	4,473,551	12,008,620
1972	20 and D.C.	15,993,965	6,188,281	22,182,246
1976	26 and D.C.	16,052,652	10,374,125	26,426,777
1980	35 and D.C.	18,747,825	12,690,451	31,438,276
1984	29 and D.C.	18,009,192	6,575,651	24,584,843
1988	36 and D.C.	22,961,936	12,165,115	35,127,051
1992	38 and D.C.	20,239,385	12,696,547	32,935,932
1996	41 and D.C.	10,947,364	13,991,649	24,939,013

Note: The number of primary states is those in which at least one of the major parties held a primary that allowed a direct vote for presidential candidates, or there was an aggregated statewide vote for delegates. The vote tally, though, does not include the 1996 New York Republican primary for the election of delegates only.

in the winter and spring have gone on to be quite competitive in the fall, while those nominees who have struggled through the primaries showing limited appeal among one or two of their party's major constituency groups have usually been buried under landslides in November.

A less reliable indicator of what will happen in the fall is the number of votes cast in each party's primaries. In every year from 1956 through 1992, more ballots were cast in Democratic than Republican primaries. In part, it was due to the simple fact that through much of this period, Democrats outnumbered Republicans.

But it also reflected the fact that the Democratic primaries drew more voter interest because they often exhibited more conflict between competing constituencies within the party. That kind of political drama and angst was good for primary turnout, but not for the party's chances in the fall elections, as Republicans won most of the presidential contests in this period.

One Election: Two Systems

The quadrennial process of electing a president has two distinct parts—the nominating process and the general election. The latter is straightforward: a one-day nationwide vote on the first Tuesday after the first Monday in November between the Democratic and Republican nominees and any independent and third-party candidates that have met the various state ballot requirements. All registered voters may participate in the general election and the winner is the candidate that wins a majority of the state electoral votes.

By contrast, the presidential nominating process can seem like Alice in Wonderland. Primaries and caucuses are scattered across the calendar from January to June, culminating with party conventions in the summer. A nomination is won by a candidate attaining a majority of delegates, an honor which is formally bestowed at the conventions but for years has informally occurred months earlier during the primary season.

Size is less important in determining a state's importance in the nominating process than its tradition and place on the calendar (early is best). Hence, the quadrennial starring roles for Iowa and New Hampshire, and the bit parts frequently handed out to California and New York.

States have different ground rules in the nominating process. Some have caucuses, many more have primaries. Most primaries allocate a state's delegates, but in some it is a nonbinding "beauty contest." And rules on voter participation can vary from state to state.

The parties themselves also have different playing fields. Democrats do not allow any states but Iowa and New Hampshire to hold a primary or caucus before the first Tuesday in March. Republicans do.

Democrats require states to distribute delegates among the candidates in proportion to their vote, statewide and in congressional districts, with 15 percent required to win a share. Republicans allow a variety of allocation systems, including winner-take-all, where the top vote-getter in a state is awarded all the delegates.

Democrats reserve nearly 20 percent of their delegate seats for high-level party and elected officials (such as Democratic governors, members of Congress and members of the party's national committee), who are free agents and do not have to declare a presidential preference. Republicans have no such automatic delegates.

Then, there is the business of campaign financing. In the wake of the Watergate scandal, a system of public financing was instituted in 1976. Participation is optional for candidates in the nominating process. Those who opt to take part must raise much of their money in small chunks and have it matched by federal funds up to a certain amount in exchange for acceptance of spending limits. Over the years, most candidates have participated in the system, although a few conspicuously have not and spent as much as they wanted.

An Evolutionary Process

But if there is a basic difference between the nominating process and the general election, it is that the latter is generally static in form while the former is constantly changing.

During the early years of the Republic, presidential nominations were decided by party caucuses in Congress (derided by their critics as "King Caucus"). At the dawn of the Jacksonian era in the 1830s, though, the nominating role shifted to national conventions, a broader-based venue where party leaders from around the country held sway.

In the early twentieth century, presidential primaries appeared on the scene, adding a new element of grass-roots democracy and voter input. But for the next half century, the primaries were relatively few in number and played a limited advisory role. Nominations continued to be decided in the party conventions.

Yet after World War II, as the society became more mobile and media oriented, and once-powerful party organizations began to lose their clout, more presidential aspirants saw the primaries as a way to generate popular support that might overcome the resistance of party leaders. Both Dwight D. Eisenhower in 1952 and John F. Kennedy in 1960 scored a string of primary victories that demonstrated their vote-getting appeal and made their nominations possible.

The conventions continued to reign supreme through the 1960s, though 1968 proved to be a watershed year in the evolution of the nominating process. Sens. Eugene McCarthy of Minnesota and Robert F. Kennedy of New York used the handful of Democratic primaries that spring to protest the war in Vietnam, together taking more than two-thirds of the primary vote and driving President Lyndon B. Johnson from the race.

History might have been different if Kennedy had not been gunned down after his victory in the California primary in June. But without Kennedy on the scene, the party's embattled leadership was able to maintain a tenuous control of the con-

The Electorate: Primaries and General

It is often said that Republican primary voters are more conservative and that Democratic primary voters are more liberal than the electorate as a whole.

If true, it is due to the basic fact that only a fraction of those who participate in the November general election participate in the presidential nominating process. As the number of primaries has grown since 1968 and voter participation in the nominating process has increased, the difference has been reduced, although the total vote in the presidential primaries has never surpassed 40 percent of the turnout for the general election.

Following is a comparison of the vote in presidential primaries with those in general elections since 1968. The number of primaries includes those where at least one of the major parties featured a vote for presidential candidates, or there was an aggregated statewide vote for delegates. The total number includes the District of Columbia.

The total primary vote includes both Democratic and Republican primaries. Not included is the voter turnout for primaries for delegates only such as that held by New York Republicans in 1996 or for nonprimary states where caucuses were held. That usually does not total more than several hundred thousand votes for both parties combined in an election year.

Year	Presidential Primaries	Voter Turnout: Primaries	Voter Turnout: General Election	Primary Vote as Percent of General Election Vote
1968	15	12,008,620	73,211,875	16.4
1972	21	22,182,246	77,718,554	28.5
1976	27	26,426,777	81,555,889	32.4
1980	36	31,438,276	86,515,221	36.3
1984	30	24,584,843	92,652,842	26.5
1988	37	35,127,051	91,594,809	38.4
1992	39	32,935,932	104,425,014	31.5
1996	42	24,939,013	96,277,872	25.9

Presidential Primaries: A Brief History

1912: The first presidential primaries are held in 13 states. Most votes are cast in the Republican contests, nine of them won by former president Theodore Roosevelt. But President William Howard Taft retains control of the party machinery and wins renomination at the GOP convention. In his annual message the following year, President Woodrow Wilson includes a call for the overhaul of the nominating process so primaries across the country would determine each party's presidential nominee.

1916: The number of presidential primaries grows to twenty, before declining once the Progressive era is over. It the largest number of primaries until the 1970s.

1924: Democrats nominate John W. Davis on the one-hundred-third ballot to culminate the longest convention ever held. In what was normal for the period, Davis had not competed in any of the presidential primaries.

1944: Wendell Willkie, the GOP's dark-horse nominee in 1940, tries to mount a comeback in 1944 in the Republican presidential primaries. Willkie's distant fourth-place finish in Wisconsin, though, dashes his presidential ambitions.

1948: New York Gov. Thomas E. Dewey and former Minnesota Gov. Harold E. Stassen go head-to-head in the Oregon GOP primary, the high point of which is a coast-to-coast radio debate on the question of whether the Communist Party should be outlawed in the United States. Dewey wins the primary over Stassen by barely 10,000 votes and goes on to win the Republican nomination.

1952: Former Gen. Dwight D. Eisenhower uses the Republican presidential primaries to demonstrate his broad vote-getting appeal to party leaders. Eisenhower wins the newly important, first-in-the-nation New Hampshire primary over Ohio Sen. Robert A. Taft and goes on to win the GOP nomination. Sen. Estes Kefauver of Tennessee also follows the primary route on the Democratic side. But Illinois Gov. Adlai E. Stevenson wins the Democratic nomination on the third ballot, the last time that any major-party convention takes more than a single roll call to decide its presidential nomination.

1960: Sen. John F. Kennedy of Massachusetts enters the Democratic primaries to show his electability. Kennedy scores a pivotal primary victory in heavily Protestant West Virginia that demonstrates his Catholicism is not a disqualifying liability.

1968: Vice President Hubert H. Humphrey becomes the last presidential candidate to win a major party nomination without entering the presidential primaries. Humphrey is nominated at a tumultuous Democratic convention in Chicago, where delegates approve a review of the party's nominating rules that would ensure a more open process in the future.

1972: Democratic rules reforms encourage more grass-roots participation in the presidential nominating process, with a growth in primaries one result. Sen. George McGovern of South Dakota, who headed the party's rules commission for a time, mounts a long-shot, anti–Vietnam War candidacy that wins the Democratic nomination. McGovern, though, is the last nominee of either party not to win at least a plurality of his party's primary vote.

1976: The presidential nominating process continues to evolve quickly. For the first time, a majority of states hold presidential primaries. For the first time, public money is made available to candidates through a system of matching federal funds. And for the first time, Democrats ban statewide winner-take-all primaries, used for years in California. (Republicans continue to allow winner-take-all contests.)

1980: After winning some attention but no victories, Rep. John B. Anderson of Illinois quits the Republican primaries, bolts the party and runs as an independent presidential candidate in the fall campaign. He follows in the footsteps of Theodore Roosevelt, who after losing the Republican nomination in 1912, left the GOP to run on the Progressive Party ticket.

1984: Democrats create a large new category of delegates for party and elected officials that prove to be a key component in former Vice President Walter F. Mondale's successful bid for the Democratic nomination. The new category comes to be known as "superdelegates."

1988: Super Tuesday is at its zenith. All the Southern states except South Carolina hold primaries on the second Tuesday in March. Vice President George Bush sweeps the Republican voting and essentially wraps up the GOP nomination. The Democratic results are more muddled. Rev. Jesse Jackson, Sen. Al Gore of Tennessee, and the eventual nominee, Massachusetts Gov. Michael S. Dukakis, all win primaries in the South.

1996: For the first time, the number of states holding presidential primaries breaks forty, more than two-thirds of which are held before the end of March. Seeking to unclog the "front-loaded" primary calendar, the Republican convention approves awarding bonus delegates in 2000 to states that vote after the ides of March.

vention that August in Chicago, nominating Vice President Humphrey, who had not competed in any primary state.

But Humphrey's nomination came at a price. For the first time in several generations, the legitimacy of the convention itself was thrown into question. And as an outgrowth, a series of Democratic rules review commissions began to overhaul the presidential nominating process to encourage much greater grass-roots participation.

Change Comes Rapidly

The immediate result was a dramatic increase in presidential primaries that enhanced the chances of long-shot outsiders, such as George McGovern and Jimmy Carter, who captured the Democratic nomination in 1972 and 1976, respectively.

In the 1970s, the primary season started slowly, giving little-known candidates the time to raise money and momentum after doing well in the early rounds. Most of the primaries then were held in May and June.

But the layout of the nominating process has been less favorable to dark horses since then. In the 1980s, Democrats reinserted party and elected officials into the process, creating a new category of automatic delegate seats for them that have come to be known as "superdelegates."

And states began to move forward on the calendar in a bid to increase their influence. Democrats sought to put a brake on the calendar sprawl toward New Year's Day by instituting the "window," which prohibited any of the party's primaries or caucuses from being held before early March, with the exception of Iowa, New Hampshire, and for a time, Maine.

With the creation of that early March firewall, many states parked their primary in March—gradually at first, but then in tidal wave proportions in 1988, with the creation of a full-scale primary vote across the South on the second Tuesday in March that came to be known as "Super Tuesday."

The event did not have the effect that its Democratic sponsors had hoped for, in terms of steering the nomination toward a centrist son of the South, such as then-Sen. Al Gore of Tennessee. And in the 1990s, the early March Southern primary lost some of its members.

But the concept of early regional primaries took hold elsewhere. In 1996, all of New England except New Hampshire voted on the first Tuesday in March. Six Southern states, led by Texas and Florida, voted on the second Tuesday. Four states in the industrial Midwest—Illinois, Michigan, Ohio and Wisconsin—voted on the third Tuesday in March. And California anchored a three-state Western primary on the fourth Tuesday.

The upshot in recent years has been both a shorter and earlier nominating season in which only well-financed and well-known candidates have been able to effectively compete.

But it is a process that increasingly has drawn the ire of leaders in both parties. And for once, the Republicans have appeared as concerned as the Democrats.

When they were regularly winning the White House in the 1970s and 1980s, the GOP showed little interest in tinkering with the nominating process. But once they began to lose presidential elections in the 1990s, many Republicans began to decry the "front-loaded" primary calendar that produced nominees within a few weeks of voting.

At their convention in San Diego in 1996, Republicans approved a rules change designed to help spread out the calendar, by offering states bonus delegates the later they held their primary or caucus. It did not get many takers, though, in 2000.

Yet both parties have begun studying changes that could overhaul the nominating process for 2004. If they do take action, the process will obviously be different. But even if the parties opt not to make changes, the process will still be different, because when it comes to the presidential nominating process, the constant is change.

Growth of Presidential Primaries . . .

The Primaries: A Front-Loaded Process

Over the years, there have been more and more states holding primaries earlier and earlier in the presidential election year. The result is that a nominating system that once featured primaries sprinkled across the spring is now front-loaded with the bulk of the primaries held during the winter months of February and March.

Following is a list of primaries held in each month of every nominating season from 1968 through 1996. Primaries included are those in the fifty states and the District of Columbia in which at least one of the parties permitted a direct vote for presidential candidates, or there was an aggregated statewide vote for delegates.

	1968	1972	1976	1980	1984	1988	1992	1996
February	0	0	1	1	1	2	2	5
March	1	3	5	9	8	20	15	24
April	3	3	2	4	3	3	5	1
May	7	11	13	13	11	7	10	8
June	4	4	6	9	7	5	7	4
TOTAL	15	21	27	36	30	37	39	42

1968

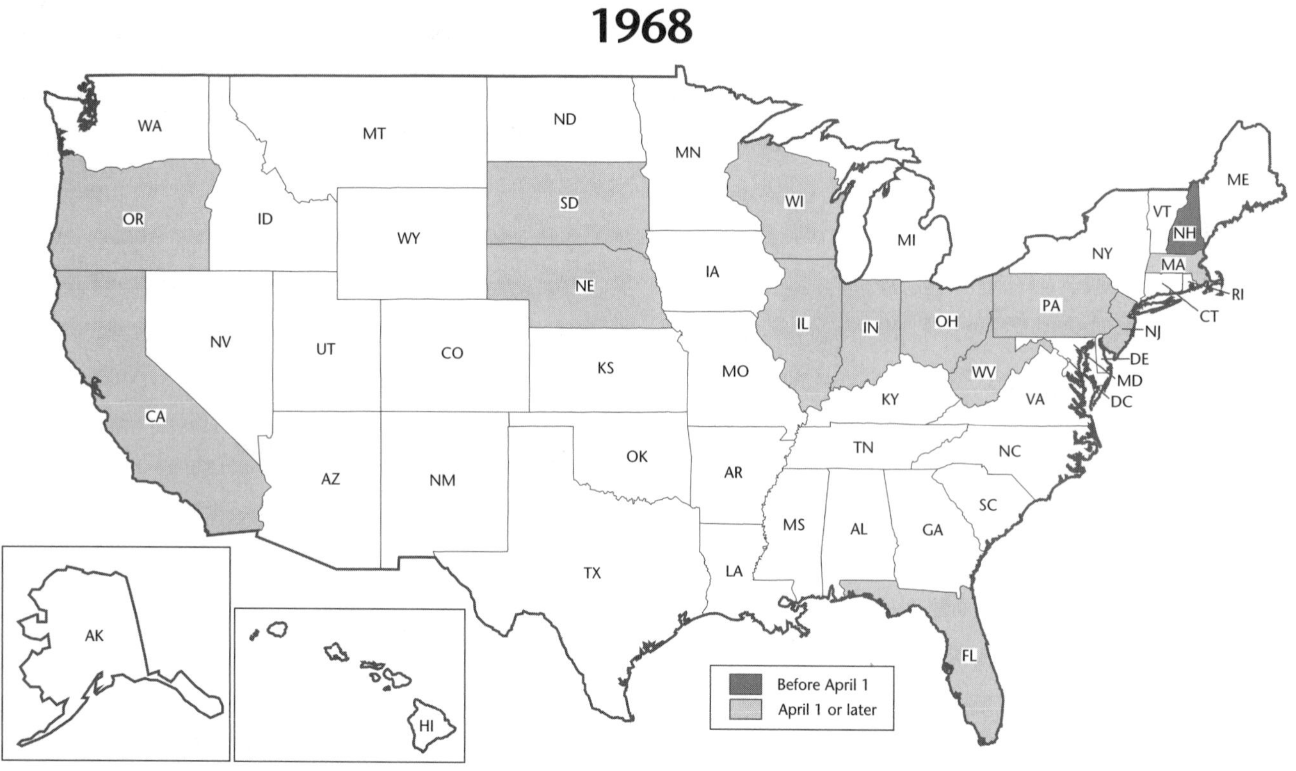

. . . More and More, Earlier and Earlier

1980

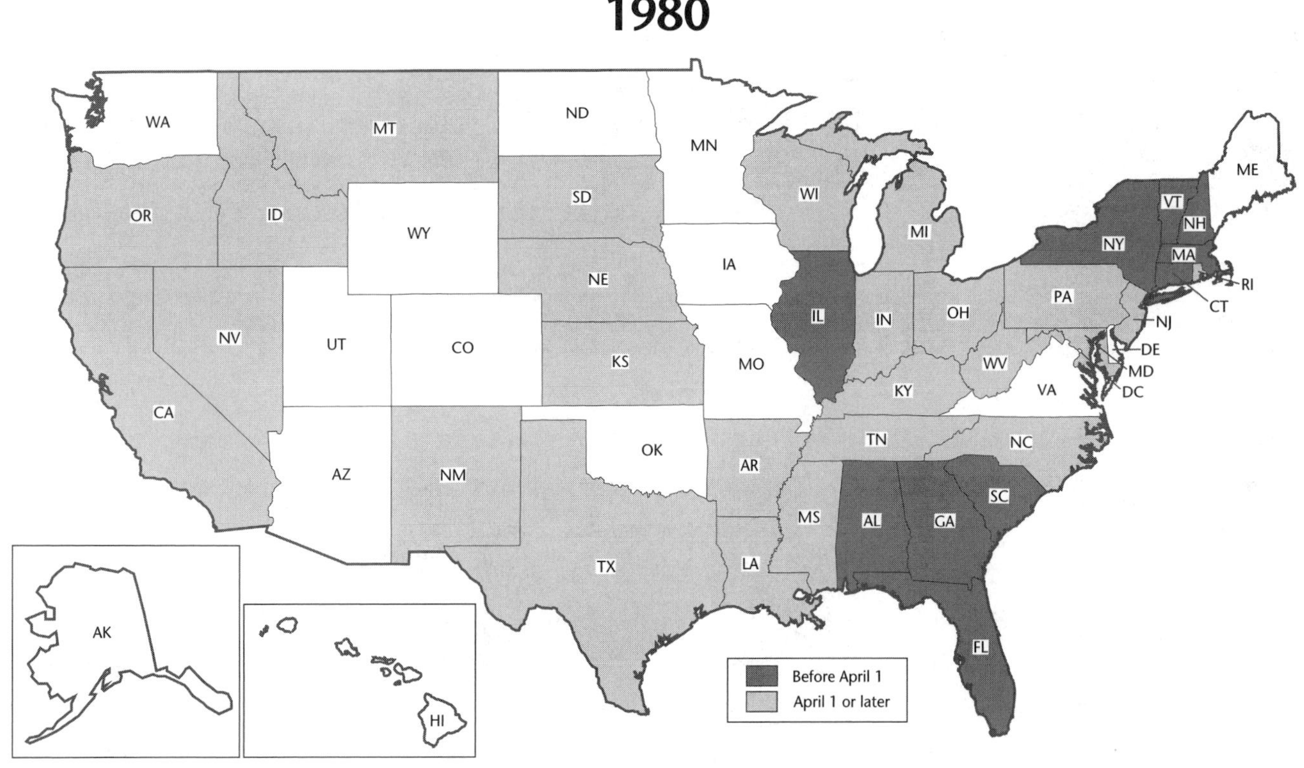

1996

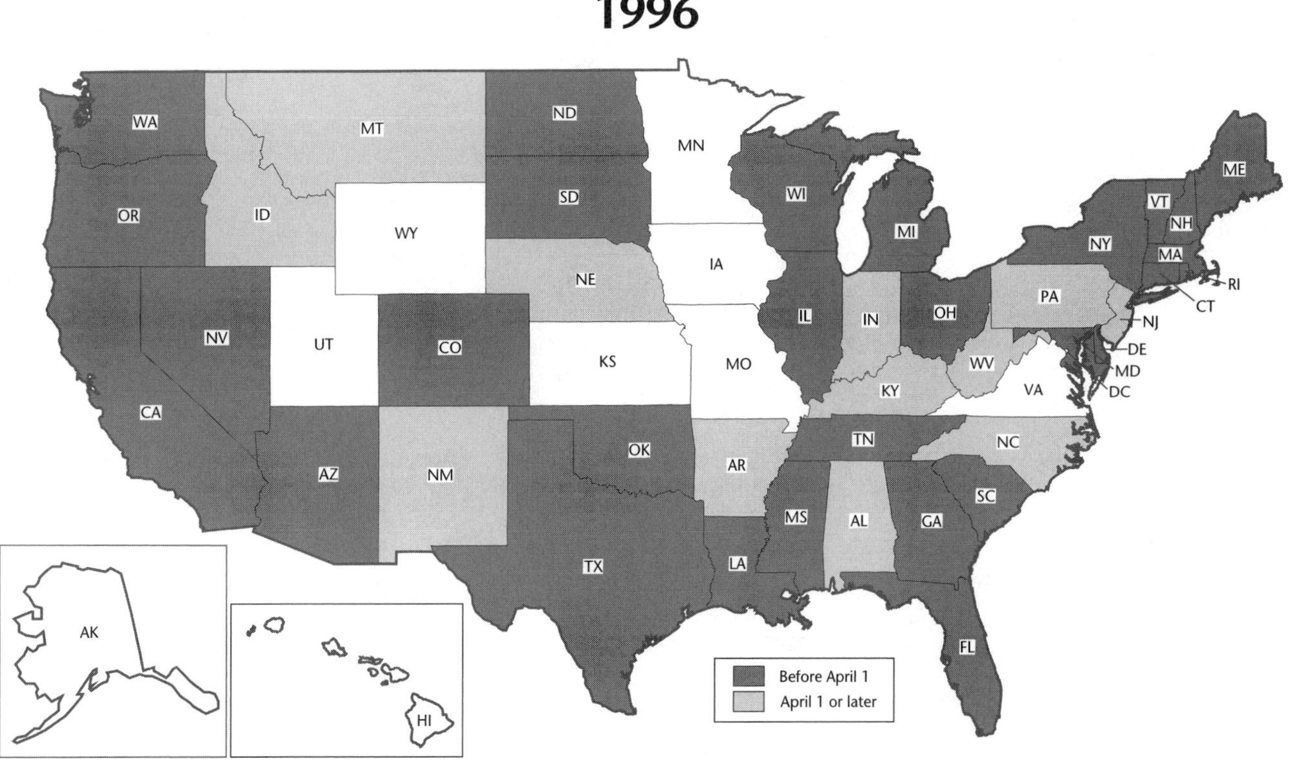

DEMOCRATIC PRESIDENTIAL PRIMARY WINNERS

1968–1996

Nominee	1968 Humphrey	%	1972 McGovern	%	1976 Carter	%	1980 Carter	%	1984 Mondale	%	1988 Dukakis	%	1992 Clinton	%	1996 Clinton	%
EAST																
Connecticut							E. Kennedy	47%	Hart	53%	Dukakis	58%	Brown	37%		
Delaware															Clinton	90%
District of Col.	R. Kennedy	62%	Fauntroy	72%	Carter	32%	E. Kennedy	62%	J. Jackson	67%	J. Jackson	80%	Clinton	74%	Clinton	98%
Maine															Clinton	88%
Maryland			Wallace	39%	Brown	48%	Carter	47%	Mondale	42%	Dukakis	46%	Tsongas	41%	Clinton	84%
Massachusetts	McCarthy	49%	McGovern	53%	H. Jackson	22%	E. Kennedy	65%	Hart	39%	Dukakis	59%	Tsongas	66%	Clinton	87%
New Hampshire	Johnson	50%	Muskie	46%	Carter	28%	Carter	47%	Hart	37%	Dukakis	36%	Tsongas	33%	Clinton	84%
New Jersey	McCarthy	36%	Chisholm	67%	Carter	58%	E. Kennedy	56%	Mondale	45%	Dukakis	63%	Clinton	62%	Clinton	95%
New York							E. Kennedy	59%	Mondale	45%	Dukakis	51%	Clinton	41%		
Pennsylvania	McCarthy	72%	Humphrey	35%	Carter	37%	E. Kennedy	46%	Mondale	45%	Dukakis	66%	Clinton	57%	Clinton	92%
Rhode Island			McGovern	41%	Unpledged	32%	E. Kennedy	68%	Hart	45%	Dukakis	70%	Tsongas	53%	Clinton	89%
Vermont					Carter	42%	Carter	73%	Hart	70%	Dukakis	56%			Clinton	97%
West Virginia	Unpledged	100%	Humphrey	67%	Byrd	89%	Carter	62%	Mondale	54%	Dukakis	75%	Clinton	74%	Clinton	87%
MIDWEST																
Illinois	McCarthy	39%	Muskie	63%	Carter	48%	Carter	65%	Mondale	40%	Simon	42%	Clinton	52%	Clinton	96%
Indiana	R. Kennedy	42%	Humphrey	47%	Carter	68%	Carter	68%	Hart	42%	Dukakis	70%	Clinton	63%	Clinton	100%
Iowa																
Kansas							Carter	57%					Clinton	51%		
Michigan			Wallace	51%	Carter	43%	Uncom.	46%					Clinton	51%	Uncom.	87%
Minnesota													Clinton	31%		
Missouri											Gephardt	58%				
Nebraska	R. Kennedy	52%	McGovern	41%	Church	38%	Carter	47%	Hart	58%	Dukakis	63%	Clinton	46%	Clinton	87%
North Dakota									Hart	85%	Dukakis	85%	Perot	29%	Riemers	41%
Ohio	Young	100%	Humphrey	41%	Carter	52%	Carter	51%	Hart	42%	Dukakis	63%	Clinton	61%	Clinton	92%
South Dakota	R. Kennedy	50%	McGovern	100%	Carter	41%	E. Kennedy	49%	Hart	51%	Gephardt	44%	Kerrey	40%		
Wisconsin	McCarthy	56%	McGovern	30%	Carter	37%	Carter	56%	Hart	44%	Dukakis	48%	Clinton	37%	Clinton	98%

DEMOCRATIC PRESIDENTIAL PRIMARY WINNERS (cont.)

1968–1996

Nominee	1968 Humphrey	%	1972 McGovern	%	1976 Carter	%	1980 Carter	%	1984 Mondale	%	1988 Dukakis	%	1992 Clinton	%	1996 Clinton	%
SOUTH																
Alabama							Carter	82%	Mondale	35%	J. Jackson	44%	Clinton	68%	Clinton	81%
Arkansas					Carter	63%	Carter	60%			Gore	37%	Clinton	68%	Clinton	79%
Florida	Smathers	46%	Wallace	42%	Carter	35%	Carter	61%	Hart	39%	Dukakis	41%	Clinton	51%		
Georgia					Carter	83%	Carter	88%	Mondale	30%	J. Jackson	40%	Clinton	57%	Clinton	100%
Kentucky					Carter	59%	Carter	67%			Gore	46%	Clinton	56%	Clinton	77%
Louisiana							Carter	56%	J. Jackson	43%	J. Jackson	35%	Clinton	69%	Clinton	81%
Mississippi											J. Jackson	45%	Clinton	73%	Clinton	92%
North Carolina			Wallace	50%	Carter	54%	Carter	70%	Mondale	36%	Gore	35%	Clinton	64%	Clinton	81%
Oklahoma											Gore	41%	Clinton	70%	Clinton	76%
South Carolina													Clinton	63%		
Tennessee			Wallace	68%	Carter	78%	Carter	75%	Mondale	41%	Gore	72%	Clinton	67%	Clinton	89%
Texas							Carter	56%			Dukakis	33%	Clinton	66%	Clinton	86%
Virginia											J. Jackson	45%				
WEST																
Alaska																
Arizona																
California	R. Kennedy	46%	McGovern	44%	Brown	59%	E. Kennedy	45%	Hart	39%	Dukakis	61%	Clinton	47%	Clinton	93%
Colorado													Brown	29%	Clinton	89%
Hawaii																
Idaho					Church	79%	Carter	62%	Hart	58%	Dukakis	73%	Clinton	49%	Clinton	88%
Montana					Church	59%	Carter	51%	No Pref.	83%	Dukakis	69%	Clinton	47%	Clinton	90%
Nevada					Brown	53%	Carter	38%								
New Mexico			McGovern	33%			E. Kennedy	46%	Hart	47%	Dukakis	61%	Clinton	53%	Clinton	90%
Oregon	McCarthy	44%	McGovern	50%	Church	34%	Carter	57%	Hart	58%	Dukakis	57%	Clinton	45%	Clinton	95%
Utah																
Washington													Clinton	42%	Clinton	99%
Wyoming																

Note: The percentages represent the winning candidates' share of their party's primary vote. A blank indicates that either no primary was held or there was not a direct vote for presidential candidates.

REPUBLICAN PRESIDENTIAL PRIMARY WINNERS

1968–1996

NOMINEE	1968 Nixon	%	1972 Nixon	%	1976 Ford	%	1980 Reagan	%	1984 Reagan	%	1988 Bush	%	1992 Bush	%	1996 Dole	%
EAST																
Connecticut							Bush	39%			Bush	71%	Bush	67%	Dole	54%
Delaware															Forbes	33%
District of Col.	Nixon-Rockefeller	90%					Bush	66%	Reagan	100%	Bush	88%	Bush	81%	Dole	76%
Maine															Dole	46%
Maryland			Nixon	86%	Ford	58%	Reagan	48%	Reagan	100%	Bush	53%	Bush	70%	Dole	53%
Massachusetts	Rockefeller	30%	Nixon	81%	Ford	61%	Bush	31%	Reagan	89%	Bush	59%	Bush	66%	Dole	48%
New Hampshire	Nixon	78%	Nixon	68%	Ford	49%	Reagan	50%	Reagan	86%	Bush	38%	Bush	53%	Buchanan	27%
New Jersey	Nixon	81%	Unpledged	100%	Ford	100%	Reagan	81%	Reagan	100%	Bush	100%	Bush	78%	Dole	82%
New York																
Pennsylvania	Nixon	60%	Nixon	83%	Ford	92%	Bush	50%	Reagan	99%	Bush	79%	Bush	77%	Dole	64%
Rhode Island			Nixon	88%	Ford	65%	Reagan	72%	Reagan	91%	Bush	65%	Bush	63%	Dole	64%
Vermont					Ford	84%	Reagan	30%	Reagan	99%	Bush	49%			Dole	40%
West Virginia	Unpledged	100%	Unpledged	100%	Ford	57%	Reagan	84%	Reagan	92%	Bush	77%	Bush	81%	Dole	69%
MIDWEST																
Illinois	Nixon	78%	Nixon	97%	Ford	59%	Reagan	48%	Reagan	100%	Bush	55%	Bush	76%	Dole	65%
Indiana	Nixon	100%	Nixon	100%	Reagan	51%	Reagan	74%	Reagan	100%	Bush	80%	Bush	80%	Dole	71%
Iowa																
Kansas							Reagan	63%					Bush	62%		
Michigan			Nixon	96%	Ford	65%	Bush	57%					Bush	67%	Dole	51%
Minnesota													Bush	64%		
Missouri											Bush	42%				
Nebraska	Nixon	70%	Nixon	92%	Reagan	54%	Reagan	76%	Reagan	100%	Bush	68%	Bush	81%	Dole	76%
North Dakota									Reagan	100%	Bush	94%	Bush	83%	Dole	42%
Ohio	Rhodes	100%	Nixon	100%	Ford	55%	Reagan	81%	Reagan	100%	Bush	81%	Bush	83%	Dole	67%
South Dakota	Nixon	100%	Nixon	100%	Reagan	51%	Reagan	82%			Dole	55%	Bush	69%	Dole	45%
Wisconsin	Nixon	80%	Nixon	97%	Ford	55%	Reagan	40%	Reagan	95%	Bush	82%	Bush	76%	Dole	52%

REPUBLICAN PRESIDENTIAL PRIMARY WINNERS (cont.)

1968–1996

NOMINEE	1968 Nixon	%	1972 Nixon	%	1976 Ford	%	1980 Reagan	%	1984 Reagan	%	1988 Bush	%	1992 Bush	%	1996 Dole	%
SOUTH																
Alabama							Reagan	70%			Bush	65%	Bush	74%	Dole	76%
Arkansas					Reagan	63%					Bush	47%	Bush	87%	Dole	76%
Florida	Unpledged	100%	Nixon	87%	Ford	53%	Reagan	56%	Reagan	100%	Bush	62%	Bush	68%	Dole	57%
Georgia					Reagan	68%	Reagan	73%	Reagan	100%	Bush	54%	Bush	64%	Dole	41%
Kentucky					Ford	51%	Reagan	82%			Bush	59%	Bush	75%	Dole	74%
Louisiana							Reagan	75%	Reagan	90%	Bush	58%	Bush	62%	Dole	48%
Mississippi							Reagan	89%			Bush	66%	Bush	72%	Dole	60%
North Carolina			Nixon	95%	Reagan	52%	Reagan	68%			Bush	45%	Bush	71%	Dole	71%
Oklahoma											Bush	37%	Bush	70%	Dole	59%
South Carolina							Reagan	55%			Bush	49%	Bush	67%	Dole	45%
Tennessee			Nixon	96%	Ford	50%	Reagan	74%	Reagan	91%	Bush	60%	Bush	73%	Dole	51%
Texas							Reagan	51%	Reagan	97%	Bush	64%	Bush	70%	Dole	56%
Virginia											Bush	54%				
WEST																
Alaska																
Arizona															Forbes	33%
California	Reagan	100%	Nixon	90%	Reagan	65%	Reagan	80%	Reagan	100%	Bush	83%	Bush	74%	Dole	66%
Colorado													Bush	68%	Dole	44%
Hawaii																
Idaho					Reagan	74%	Reagan	83%	Reagan	92%	Bush	81%	Bush	63%	Dole	62%
Montana					Reagan	63%	Reagan	87%	Reagan	92%	Bush	73%	Bush	72%	Dole	61%
Nevada					Reagan	66%	Reagan	83%							Dole	52%
New Mexico			Nixon	88%			Reagan	64%	Reagan	95%	Bush	78%	Bush	64%	Dole	76%
Oregon	Nixon	65%	Nixon	82%	Ford	50%	Reagan	54%	Reagan	98%	Bush	73%	Bush	67%	Dole	51%
Utah																
Washington													Bush	67%	Dole	63%
Wyoming																

Note: The percentages represent the winning candidates' share of their party's primary vote. A blank indicates that either no primary was held or there was not a direct vote for presidential candidates (as has been the case for Republicans in New York). A joint Nixon-Rockefeller slate won the 1968 Republican primary in the District of Columbia.

DEMOCRATIC PRESIDENTIAL PRIMARY WINNERS

Major Urban Centers

Because most of the nation's cities have a Democratic character, they tend to be more important in primary voting for the Democrats than the Republicans. As such, they have provided a significant toehold in the Democratic nominating process for contenders with a strong appeal to urban voters, such as Edward Kennedy in 1980 and Jesse Jackson in 1984 and 1988. But no recent Democrat has been more dominant in the cities than Bill Clinton, who used them as a springboard to win the party's nomination in 1992.

Following is a selection of major urban centers around the country, with the winners (and their share of the party's primary vote) in competitive Democratic nominating contests since 1968. The results are from cities except for cases in which the abbreviation for county ("Co.") is indicated, in which case the vote is from the entire county in which the city is located. This methodology also pertains to the tables that follow.

NOMINEE	1968 Humphrey	%	1972 McGovern	%	1976 Carter	%	1980 Carter	%	1984 Mondale	%	1988 Dukakis	%	1992 Clinton	%
EAST														
Baltimore, Md			Humphrey	39%	Brown	51%	Carter	48%	J. Jackson	42%	J. Jackson	53%	Clinton	45%
Boston, Mass.			McGovern	47%	Wallace	29%	E. Kennedy	60%	Hart	28%	Dukakis	47%	Tsongas	59%
New York City, N.Y.							E. Kennedy	63%	Mondale	45%	J. Jackson	46%	Clinton	46%
Philadelphia, Pa.	McCarthy	80%	Humphrey	41%	H. Jackson	37%	E. Kennedy	60%	J. Jackson	38%	J. Jackson	56%	Clinton	63%
Washington, D.C.	R. Kennedy	62%	Fauntroy	72%	Carter	32%	E. Kennedy	62%	J. Jackson	67%	J. Jackson	80%	Clinton	74%
MIDWEST														
Chicago, Ill.			Muskie	62%	Carter	44%	Carter	62%	Mondale	38%	J. Jackson	52%	Clinton	55%
Marion Co. (Indianapolis), Ind.	R. Kennedy	48%	Humphrey	59%	Carter	74%	Carter	67%	J. Jackson	35%	Dukakis	52%	Clinton	56%
Wayne Co. (Detroit), Mich.			Wallace	47%	Carter	44%							Clinton	61%
Cuyahoga Co. (Cleveland), Ohio			Humphrey	42%	Carter	41%	E. Kennedy	54%	Mondale	40%	Dukakis	56%	Clinton	53%
Milwaukee Co., Wis.	Johnson	50%	McGovern	27%	Udall	34%	Carter	55%	Mondale	44%	Dukakis	44%	Clinton	39%
SOUTH														
Dade Co. (Miami), Fla.	McCarthy	40%	Wallace	27%	H. Jackson	37%	Carter	50%	Mondale	39%	Dukakis	41%	Clinton	54%
Fulton Co. (Atlanta), Ga.					Carter	89%	Carter	82%	J. Jackson	36%	J. Jackson	65%	Clinton	51%
Orleans Parish (New Orleans), La.							Carter	48%	J. Jackson	67%	J. Jackson	64%	Clinton	73%
Shelby Co. (Memphis), Tenn.			Wallace	64%	Carter	76%	Carter	62%	J. Jackson	59%	J. Jackson	60%	Clinton	82%
Harris Co. (Houston), Texas							Carter	59%			J. Jackson	47%	Clinton	65%
WEST														
Los Angeles Co., Calif.	R. Kennedy	50%	Humphrey	45%	Brown	60%	E. Kennedy	49%	Mondale	37%	Dukakis	55%	Clinton	51%
San Francisco, Calif.	R. Kennedy	48%	McGovern	53%	Brown	61%	E. Kennedy	54%	Hart	35%	J. Jackson	51%	Brown	50%
Denver, Colo.													Brown	32%
Bernalillo Co. (Albuquerque), N.M.			McGovern	42%			E. Kennedy	51%	Hart	47%	Dukakis	62%	Clinton	47%
Multnomah Co. (Portland), Ore	McCarthy	44%	McGovern	54%	Church	37%	Carter	56%	Hart	54%	Dukakis	54%	Clinton	44%

Note: A blank indicates that either no primary was held, there was not a direct vote for presidential candidates, or the primary did not feature any of the major candidates on the ballot.

REPUBLICAN PRESIDENTIAL PRIMARY WINNERS

Major Urban Centers

By and large, the urban vote is less decisive in Republican presidential primaries and has tended to reflect the political sentiment of the state in which it is located. In the closely contested GOP nominating battle in 1976, for instance, President Gerald Ford ran well in the Frost Belt, including its major cities, while Ronald Reagan swept most of the Sun Belt, including its major urban centers.

In this table and other Republican vote tables that follow, it should be noted that since 1968 the Republicans have had fewer competitive presidential primary contests than the Democrats. And those the GOP has had have often been settled before the primary season is over. As a result, there can often be a wide disparity between a candidate's winning percentage in states that vote early in the process and those that vote later.

NOMINEE	1976 Ford	%	1980 Reagan	%	1988 Bush	%	1992 Bush	%	1996 Dole	%
EAST										
Baltimore, Md.	Ford	65%	Bush	48%	Bush	50%	Bush	67%	Dole	44%
Boston, Mass.	Ford	61%	Anderson	40%	Bush	54%	Bush	58%	Dole	41%
New York City, N.Y.										
Philadelphia, Pa.	Ford	99%	Reagan	47%	Bush	82%	Bush	72%	Dole	53%
Washington, D.C.			Bush	66%	Bush	88%	Bush	81%	Dole	76%
MIDWEST										
Chicago, Ill.	Ford	65%	Anderson	56%	Bush	63%	Bush	75%	Dole	62%
Marion Co. (Indianapolis), Ind.	Reagan	54%	Reagan	74%	Bush	83%	Bush	79%	Dole	70%
Wayne Co. (Detroit), Mich.	Ford	60%	Bush	57%			Bush	65%	Dole	43%
Cuyahoga Co. (Cleveland), Ohio	Ford	54%	Reagan	80%	Bush	85%	Bush	84%	Dole	65%
Milwaukee Co., Wis.	Ford	56%	Reagan	33%	Bush	85%	Bush	76%	Dole	48%
SOUTH										
Dade Co. (Miami), Fla.	Reagan	57%	Reagan	66%	Bush	75%	Bush	82%	Dole	79%
Fulton Co. (Atlanta), Ga.	Reagan	61%	Reagan	60%	Bush	57%	Bush	72%	Dole	47%
Orleans Parish (New Orleans), La.			Reagan	60%	Bush	68%	Bush	66%	Dole	54%
Shelby Co. (Memphis), Tenn.	Reagan	52%	Reagan	74%	Bush	62%	Bush	76%	Dole	55%
Harris Co. (Houston), Texas			Bush	63%	Bush	74%	Bush	74%	Dole	56%
WEST										
Los Angeles Co., Calif.	Reagan	69%	Reagan	82%	Bush	84%	Bush	70%	Dole	64%
San Francisco, Calif.	Ford	52%	Reagan	64%	Bush	82%	Bush	80%	Dole	70%
Denver, Colo.							Bush	69%	Dole	49%
Bernalillo Co. (Albuquerque), N.M.			Reagan	61%	Bush	80%	Bush	64%	Dole	77%
Multnomah Co. (Portland), Ore	Ford	58%	Reagan	47%	Bush	73%	Bush	63%	Dole	51%

Note: A blank indicates that either no primary was held, there was not a direct vote for presidential candidates, or the primary did not feature any of the major candidates on the ballot.

DEMOCRATIC PRESIDENTIAL PRIMARY WINNERS

Leading Suburban Counties

More and more, the United States is becoming a suburban nation. But in the Democratic primary in many states, the urban vote trumps the suburban. Still, from Eugene McCarthy to Paul Tsongas, the suburbs have provided a building block for Democratic candidates with a cerebral manner and independent streak.

The chart below and the one on the next page features presidential primary results from 28 counties that have a 1990 population exceeding 500,000 but lack a dominant urban center and are predominantly suburban in character.

NOMINEE	1968 Humphrey	%	1972 McGovern	%	1976 Carter	%	1980 Carter	%	1984 Mondale	%	1988 Dukakis	%	1992 Clinton	%
EAST														
Fairfield, Conn.													Brown	41%
Baltimore, Md.*			Wallace	44%	Brown	54%	Carter	54%	Mondale	52%	Dukakis	62%	Tsongas	44%
Montgomery, Md.			McGovern	42%	Brown	50%	E. Kennedy	48%	Mondale	48%	Dukakis	51%	Tsongas	50%
Prince George's, Md.			Wallace	42%	Brown	45%	E. Kennedy	47%	J. Jackson	43%	J. Jackson	51%	Clinton	41%
Middlesex, Mass.													Tsongas	70%
Bergen, N.J.					Carter	61%	E. Kennedy	63%	Mondale	50%	Dukakis	77%	Clinton	62%
Middlesex, N.J.					Carter	59%	E. Kennedy	52%	Mondale	52%	Dukakis	77%	Clinton	60%
Monmouth, N.J.					Carter	61%	E. Kennedy	58%	Mondale	48%	Dukakis	68%	Clinton	56%
Nassau, N.Y.							E. Kennedy	67%	Mondale	51%	Dukakis	65%	Clinton	39%
Suffolk, N.Y.							E. Kennedy	57%	Mondale	46%	Dukakis	58%	Tsongas	35%
Westchester, N.Y.							E. Kennedy	61%	Mondale	43%	Dukakis	55%	Clinton	40%
Bucks, Pa.	McCarthy	78%	McGovern	34%	Carter	32%	E. Kennedy	53%	Hart	47%	Dukakis	80%	Clinton	49%
Delaware, Pa.	McCarthy	66%	McGovern	38%	Carter	31%	E. Kennedy	53%	Mondale	41%	Dukakis	71%	Clinton	47%
Montgomery, Pa.	McCarthy	77%	McGovern	43%	Udall	33%	E. Kennedy	56%	Mondale	44%	Dukakis	77%	Clinton	54%
MIDWEST														
Du Page, Ill			Muskie	54%	Carter	52%	Carter	71%	Hart	51%	Simon	54%	Tsongas	42%
Lake, Ill.			Muskie	56%	Carter	51%	Carter	67%	Hart	45%	Simon	51%	Tsongas	41%
Macomb, Mich.			Wallace	67%	Udall	48%							Clinton	47%
Oakland, Mich.			Wallace	54%	Udall	59%							Clinton	44%
St. Louis, Mo.*											Gephardt	57%		
SOUTH														
Broward, Fla.	Smathers	45%	Wallace	34%	H. Jackson	39%	Carter	42%	Mondale	43%	Dukakis	57%	Clinton	54%
De Kalb, Ga.					Carter	88%	Carter	87%	Mondale	29%	J. Jackson	45%	Clinton	45%
Fairfax, Va.											Dukakis	44%		
WEST														
Contra Costa, Calif.	McCarthy	44%	McGovern	47%	Brown	60%	E. Kennedy	45%	Hart	42%	Dukakis	62%	Clinton	48%
Orange, Calif.	McCarthy	46%	Humphrey	43%	Brown	61%	E. Kennedy	43%	Hart	44%	Dukakis	71%	Clinton	46%
Riverside, Calif.	R. Kennedy	46%	McGovern	42%	Brown	56%	E. Kennedy	43%	Mondale	43%	Dukakis	71%	Clinton	56%
San Bernardino, Calif.	McCarthy	44%	Humphrey	42%	Brown	59%	E. Kennedy	46%	Mondale	41%	Dukakis	67%	Clinton	50%
San Mateo, Calif.	McCarthy	45%	McGovern	49%	Brown	64%	E. Kennedy	45%	Hart	40%	Dukakis	65%	Brown	46%
Ventura, Calif.	R. Kennedy	44%	Humphrey	42%	Brown	60%	E. Kennedy	45%	Hart	45%	Dukakis	69%	Clinton	46%

Note: A blank indicates that either no primary was held, there was not a direct vote for presidential candidates, or the primary did not feature any of the major candidates on the ballot. An asterisk (*) indicates that the county does not include the city of the same name. No county results were available for Connecticut or Massachusetts before 1992.

REPUBLICAN PRESIDENTIAL PRIMARY WINNERS

Leading Suburban Counties

By and large, moderate Republican candidates such as Gerald Ford and George Bush (in 1980) have run well in the suburbs of the Frost Belt, while conservative Republicans such as Ronald Reagan have shown greater appeal in the suburbs of the Sun Belt.

Yet it is also the case that since the hotly contested Ford-Reagan contest of 1976, Republican nominating contests have been decided before many of the states with large suburban counties have had a chance to vote.

NOMINEE	1976 Ford	%	1980 Reagan	%	1988 Bush	%	1992 Bush	%	1996 Dole	%
EAST										
Fairfield, Conn.							Bush	70%	Dole	56%
Baltimore, Md.*	Ford	58%	Bush	45%	Bush	52%	Bush	72%	Dole	51%
Montgomery, Md.	Ford	63%	Bush	45%	Bush	53%	Bush	70%	Dole	61%
Prince George's, Md.	Ford	55%	Reagan	51%	Bush	54%	Bush	68%	Dole	55%
Middlesex, Mass.							Bush	65%	Dole	48%
Bergen, N.J.			Reagan	82%			Bush	76%	Dole	84%
Middlesex, N.J.			Reagan	86%			Bush	79%	Dole	81%
Monmouth, N.J.			Reagan	86%			Bush	79%	Dole	84%
Nassau, N.Y.										
Suffolk, N.Y.										
Westchester, N.Y.										
Bucks, Pa.	Ford	100%	Bush	55%	Bush	80%	Bush	74%	Dole	60%
Delaware, Pa.	Ford	98%	Bush	53%	Bush	83%	Bush	73%	Dole	55%
Montgomery, Pa.	Ford	95%	Bush	59%	Bush	80%	Bush	75%	Dole	60%
MIDWEST										
Du Page, Ill	Ford	62%	Reagan	42%	Bush	54%	Bush	77%	Dole	67%
Lake, Ill.	Ford	61%	Anderson	45%	Bush	55%	Bush	77%	Dole	67%
Macomb, Mich.	Ford	54%	Bush	57%			Bush	62%	Dole	45%
Oakland, Mich.	Ford	66%	Bush	62%			Bush	67%	Dole	53%
St. Louis, Mo.*					Bush	51%				
SOUTH										
Broward, Fla.	Reagan	51%	Reagan	60%	Bush	63%	Bush	69%	Dole	54%
De Kalb, Ga.	Reagan	63%	Reagan	62%	Bush	54%	Bush	69%	Dole	46%
Fairfax, Va.					Bush	53%				
WEST										
Contra Costa, Calif.	Reagan	57%	Reagan	73%	Bush	82%	Bush	80%	Dole	70%
Orange, Calif.	Reagan	70%	Reagan	85%	Bush	86%	Bush	72%	Dole	65%
Riverside, Calif.	Reagan	71%	Reagan	85%	Bush	85%	Bush	74%	Dole	66%
San Bernardino, Calif.	Reagan	72%	Reagan	85%	Bush	84%	Bush	70%	Dole	63%
San Mateo, Calif.	Reagan	53%	Reagan	70%	Bush	81%	Bush	77%	Dole	71%
Ventura, Calif.	Reagan	68%	Reagan	82%	Bush	84%	Bush	72%	Dole	63%

Note: A blank indicates that either no primary was held, there was not a direct vote for presidential candidates (as in New York), or the primary did not feature any of the major candidates on the ballot. An asterisk (*) indicates that the county does not include the city of the same name. No county results were available for Connecticut or Massachusetts before 1992.

DEMOCRATIC PRESIDENTIAL PRIMARY WINNERS

Assorted Constituencies

One of the most compelling features of Bill Clinton's drive to the Democratic nomination in 1992 was his appeal to a broad variety of constituency groups—minorities, blue-collar voters, retirees. About the only major slice of the primary electorate in which Clinton did not show much appeal was the academic community, which tended to prefer Paul Tsongas and Jerry Brown.

The charts on this page and the next two pages feature a collection of towns, cities and counties (designated with "Co.") that represent various voting constituencies, with the winners and their share of their party's primary vote in competitive nominating contests since 1968.

NOMINEE	1968 Humphrey	%	1972 McGovern	%	1976 Carter	%	1980 Carter	%	1984 Mondale	%	1988 Dukakis	%	1992 Clinton	%
ACADEMIC INFLUENCE														
Boulder Co., Colo. (U. of Colorado)													Brown	43%
Alachua Co., Fla. (U. of Florida)	Smathers	45%	Wallace	31%	Carter	45%	Carter	70%	Hart	45%	Dukakis	32%	Tsongas	40%
Clarke Co., Ga. (U. of Georgia)					Carter	85%	Carter	87%	Hart	29%	J. Jackson	34%	Tsongas	37%
Champaign Co., Ill. (U. of Illinois)			McCarthy	50%	Carter	54%	Carter	65%	Hart	53%	Simon	50%	Tsongas	38%
Amherst, Mass. (Amherst, U. of Mass.)			McGovern	79%	Udall	39%	E. Kennedy	56%	Hart	33%	J. Jackson	49%	Tsongas	50%
Cambridge, Mass. (Harvard, M.I.T.)			McGovern	58%	Udall	31%	E. Kennedy	65%	McGovern	33%	Dukakis	47%	Tsongas	56%
Washtenaw Co., Mich. (U. of Michigan)			McGovern	54%	Udall	69%							Brown	36%
Hanover, N.H. (Dartmouth)	McCarthy	81%	McGovern	76%	Udall	54%	Carter	52%	Hart	38%	Dukakis	42%	Tsongas	48%
Tompkins Co., N.Y. (Cornell)							Carter	51%	Hart	47%	Dukakis	51%	Brown	35%
Orange Co., N.C. (U. of North Carolina)			Sanford	62%	Carter	49%	Carter	61%	Hart	33%	Dukakis	34%	Clinton	56%
Benton Co., Ore. (Oregon State)	McCarthy	49%	McGovern	64%	Brown	37%	Carter	59%	Hart	59%	J. Jackson	55%	Brown	41%
Centre Co., Pa. (Penn State)	McCarthy	61%	McGovern	36%	Udall	36%	Carter	59%	Hart	50%	Dukakis	69%	Clinton	50%
Dane Co., Wis. U. of Wisconsin)	McCarthy	68%	McGovern	43%	Udall	59%	Carter	45%	Hart	47%	Dukakis	44%	Brown	36%
BLACK MAJORITY														
Macon Co., Ala.							Carter	68%	J. Jackson	43%	J. Jackson	92%	Clinton	77%
Lee Co., Ark.					Carter	54%	Carter	54%			J. Jackson	51%	Clinton	75%
Hancock Co, Ga.					Carter	75%	Carter	80%	J. Jackson	66%	J. Jackson	80%	Clinton	69%
Jefferson Co., Miss.											J. Jackson	81%	Clinton	76%
Northampton Co., N.C.			Sanford	48%	Carter	64%	Carter	59%	J. Jackson	41%	J. Jackson	55%	Clinton	68%
HISPANIC MAJORITY														
Imperial Co., Calif.	R. Kennedy	51%	McGovern	42%	Brown	50%	E. Kennedy	46%	Hart	37%	Dukakis	66%	Clinton	50%
Costilla Co., Colo.													Clinton	72%
Mora Co., N.M.			McGovern	50%			E. Kennedy	63%	Hart	51%	Dukakis	55%	Clinton	72%
Starr Co., Texas							E. Kennedy	72%			Dukakis	41%	Clinton	72%
NATIVE AMERICAN MAJORITY														
Big Horn Co, Mont.					Church	47%	E. Kennedy	46%			Dukakis	48%	Clinton	50%
Shannon Co., S.D.	R. Kennedy	92%			Carter	59%	E. Kennedy	81%	Hart	52%	J. Jackson	47%	Kerrey	66%

DEMOCRATIC PRESIDENTIAL PRIMARY WINNERS (cont.)

Assorted Constituencies

NOMINEE	1968 Humphrey	%	1972 McGovern	%	1976 Carter	%	1980 Carter	%	1984 Mondale	%	1988 Dukakis	%	1992 Clinton	%
RESORT/ RETIREMENT														
Baxter Co. (Mountain Home), Ark.					Carter	61%	Carter	65%			Dukakis	29%	Clinton	81%
Pinellas Co. (St. Petersburg), Fla.	Smathers	49%	Wallace	27%	Carter	43%	Carter	66%	Hart	45%	Dukakis	56%	Clinton	49%
Beaufort Co. (Hilton Head), S.C.													Clinton	47%
INDUSTRIAL HERITAGE														
Waterbury, Conn.							E. Kennedy	55%	Hart	50%	Dukakis	56%	Brown	42%
Calcasieu Parish (Lake Charles), La.							Carter	60%	Mondale	33%	J. Jackson	30%	Clinton	68%
Lowell, Mass.			McGovern	47%	H. Jackson	26%	E. Kennedy	71%	Hart	42%	Dukakis	62%	Tsongas	81%
Genesee Co. (Flint), Mich.			Wallace	52%	Carter	54%							Clinton	56%
Mahoning Co. (Youngstown), Ohio			Humphrey	43%	Carter	60%	E. Kennedy	55%	Hart	44%	Dukakis	58%	Clinton	60%
"TEST MARKET"														
Peoria Co, Ill.			Muskie	64%	Carter	54%	Carter	72%	Mondale	42%	Simon	53%	Clinton	56%

Note: A blank indicates that either no primary was held, there was not a direct vote for presidential candidates, or the primary did not feature any of the major candidates on the ballot.

REPUBLICAN PRESIDENTIAL PRIMARY WINNERS

Assorted Constituencies

One thing that can be said about recent Republican presidential nominees: They have played well in Peoria. At least, they have carried Peoria Co. in Illinois' GOP primary. Following is a collection of counties that represent various voting constituencies, from academic communities to the political "test market" of Peoria. By and large, the turnout for Republican primaries in academic, minority and blue-collar venues is less than the turnout for Democratic primaries.

NOMINEE	1976 Ford	%	1980 Reagan	%	1988 Bush	%	1992 Bush	%	1996 Dole	%
ACADEMIC INFLUENCE										
Boulder, Co., Colo. (U. of Colorado)							Bush	67%	Dole	44%
Alachua Co., Fla. (U. of Florida)	Ford	58%	Bush	40%	Bush	49%	Bush	63%	Dole	50%
Clarke Co., Ga. (U. of Georgia)	Reagan	63%	Reagan	57%	Bush	45%	Bush	65%	Dole	46%
Champaign Co., Ill. (U. of Illinois)	Ford	62%	Anderson	43%	Bush	44%	Bush	74%	Dole	68%
Johnson Co., Iowa (U. of Iowa)*			Bush	41%	Dole	41%			Dole	25%
Amherst, Mass. (Amherst, U. of Mass.)	Ford	65%	Anderson	62%	Bush	45%	Bush	70%	Dole	55%
Cambridge, Mass. (Harvard, M.I.T.)	Ford	72%	Anderson	65%	Bush	45%	Bush	60%	Dole	44%
Washtenaw Co., Mich. (U. of Michigan)	Ford	70%	Bush	66%			Bush	69%	Dole	55%
Hanover, N.H. (Dartmouth)	Ford	81%	Bush	44%	Dole	42%	Bush	62%	Dole	39%
Orange Co., N.C. (U. of North Carolina)	Ford	57%	Bush	38%	Dole	51%	Bush	63%	Dole	67%

REPUBLICAN PRESIDENTIAL PRIMARY WINNERS (cont.)

Assorted Constituencies

NOMINEE	1976 Ford	%	1980 Reagan	%	1988 Bush	%	1992 Bush	%	1996 Dole	%
Benton Co., Ore. (Oregon State)	Ford	55%	Reagan	46%	Bush	69%	Bush	72%	Dole	55%
Centre Co. , Pa. (Penn State)	Ford	85%	Bush	53%	Bush	77%	Bush	79%	Dole	69%
Dane Co., Wis. (U. of Wisconsin)	Ford	68%	Anderson	56%	Bush	80%	Bush	78%	Dole	55%
BLACK MAJORITY										
Macon Co., Ala.			Reagan	76%	Bush	62%	Bush	90%	Dole	75%
Lee Co., Ark.	Reagan	38%			Dole	39%	Buchanan	100%	Dole	70%
Hancock Co, Ga.	Reagan	81%	Reagan	96%	Bush	72%	Bush	59%	Dole	44%
Jefferson Co., Miss.			Reagan	99%	Bush	62%	Bush	79%	Dole	71%
Northampton Co., N.C.	Reagan	67%	Reagan	60%	Bush	53%	Bush	59%	Dole	65%
HISPANIC MAJORITY										
Imperial Co., Calif.	Reagan	75%	Reagan	88%	Bush	85%	Bush	81%	Dole	69%
Costilla Co., Colo.							Bush	62%	Forbes	57%
Mora Co., N.M.			Reagan	57%	Bush	66%	Bush	78%	Dole	72%
Starr Co., Texas			Reagan	68%	Bush	55%	Bush	71%	Dole	36%
NATIVE AMERICAN MAJORITY										
Big Horn Co, Mont.	Reagan	62%	Reagan	85%	Bush	71%	Bush	81%	Dole	63%
Shannon Co., S.D.	Reagan	69%	Reagan	83%	Dole	57%	Bush	60%	Dole	44%
RESORT/RETIREMENT										
Baxter Co. (Mountain Home), Ark.	Reagan	56%			Bush	53%	Bush	81%	Dole	77%
Pinellas Co. (St. Petersburg), Fla.	Ford	59%	Reagan	50%	Bush	57%	Bush	63%	Dole	53%
Beaufort Co. (Hilton Head), S.C.			Connally	38%	Bush	55%	Bush	73%	Dole	47%
INDUSTRIAL HERITAGE										
Waterbury, Conn.			Reagan	43%	Bush	72%	Bush	55%	Dole	39%
Calcasieu Parish (Lake Charles), La.			Reagan	75%	Bush	45%	Bush	69%	Buchanan	48%
Lowell, Mass.	Ford	54%	Reagan	39%	Bush	61%	Bush	59%	Buchanan	42%
Genesee Co. (Flint), Mich.	Ford	61%	Bush	58%			Bush	64%	Dole	47%
Mahoning Co. (Youngstown), Ohio	Ford	62%	Reagan	80%	Bush	80%	Bush	84%	Dole	56%
"TEST MARKET"										
Peoria Co, Ill.	Ford	61%	Reagan	52%	Bush	52%	Bush	79%	Dole	69%

Note: A blank indicates that either no primary was held, there was not a direct vote for presidential candidates, or the primary did not feature any of the major candidates on the ballot. An asterisk (*) indicates that the vote is from the Iowa precinct caucuses.

NATIONAL PRIMARY MAPS AND VOTE SUMMARIES, 1968–1996

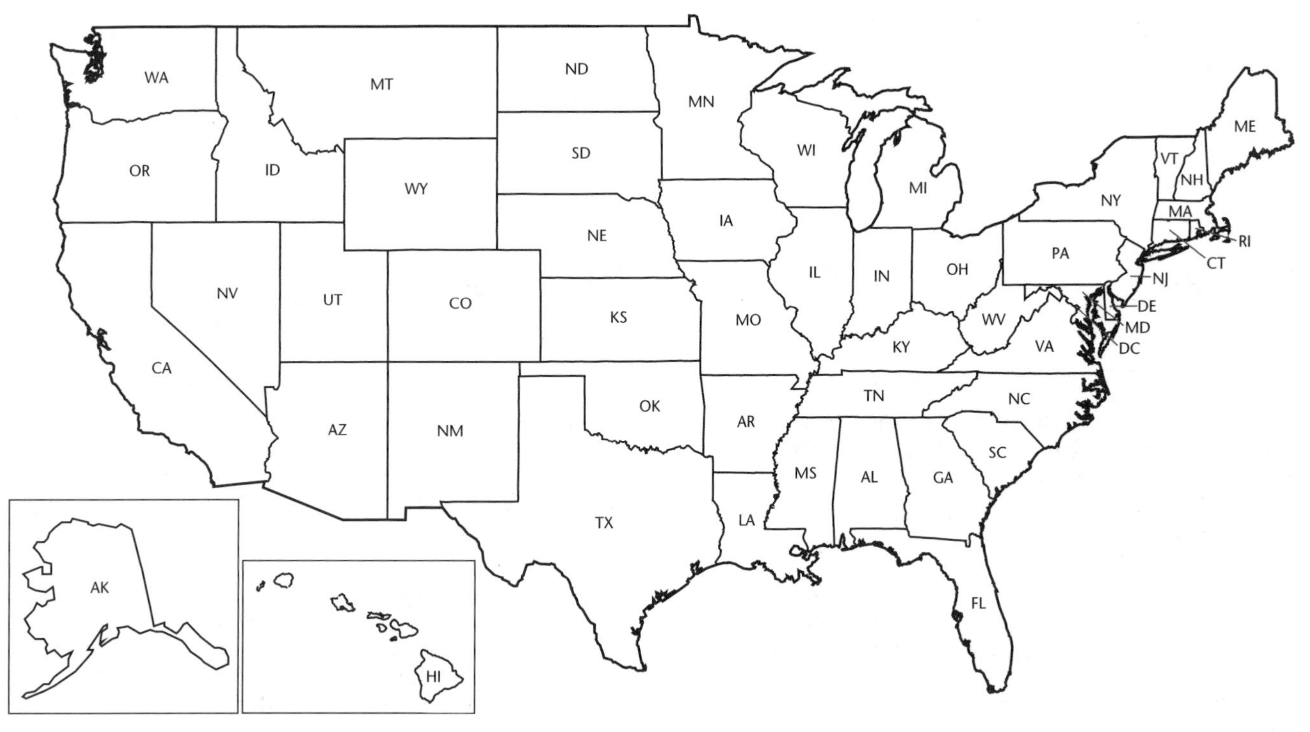

1968 DEMOCRATIC PRIMARIES

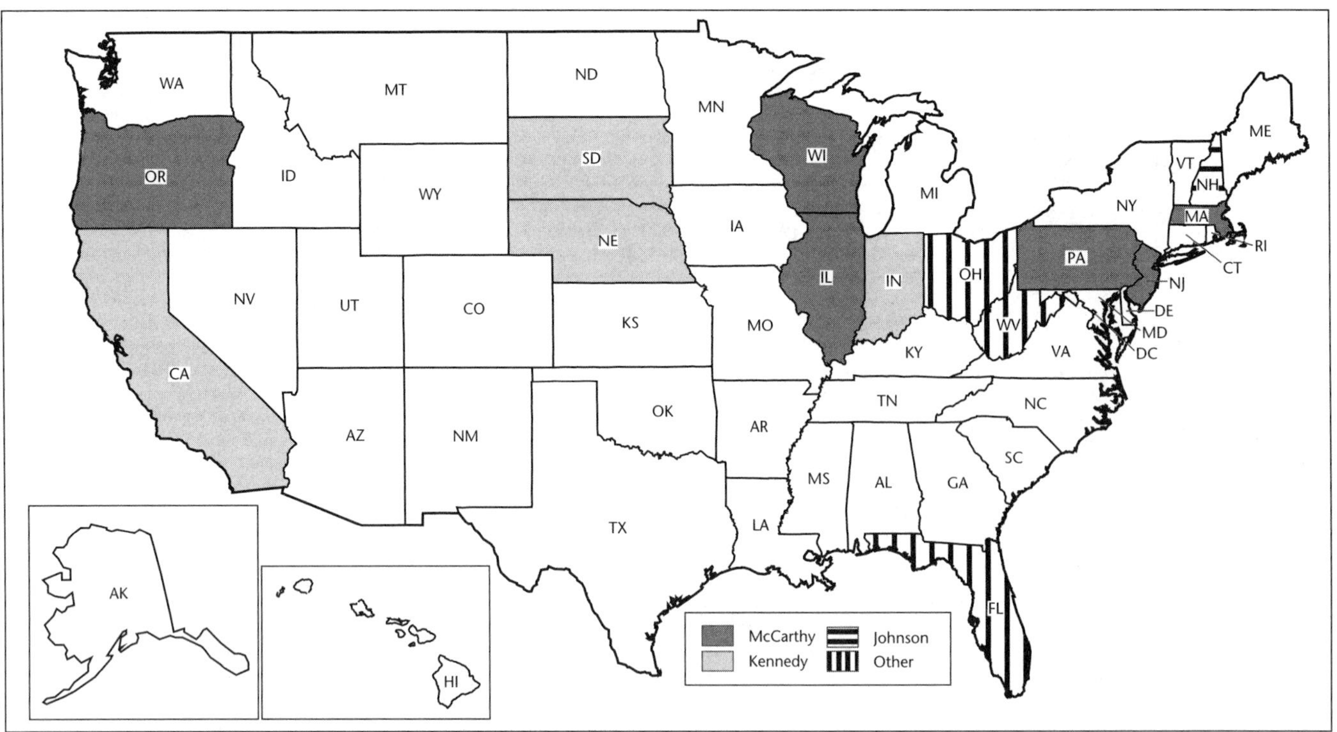

There were only a few presidential primaries in 1968. But nearly every one of them had significance, with the first-in-the-nation primary in New Hampshire March 12 setting the tone.

President Lyndon Johnson won on an organized write-in vote, but with less than a majority, while Minnesota Sen. Eugene McCarthy's grass-roots effort, focused around opposition to the Vietnam War, exceeded all expectations.

On March 16, New York Sen. Robert Kennedy entered the race. On March 31, the embattled president left it. Beginning in Wisconsin April 2, McCarthy registered a series of primary victories before he and Kennedy went head-to-head for the first time May 7 in Indiana.

Kennedy won Indiana, and beat McCarthy in three of four other primaries down the stretch, culminating with a victory in California June 4. But after claiming victory that night in Los Angeles, Kennedy was shot and died less than two days later.

Vice President Hubert Humphrey, who had not run in the primaries, was subsequently nominated that August at a tumultuous Democratic convention in Chicago. He was the last nominee of either major party to win its nomination without having first competed in the primaries.

	Total Vote	Percentage	Primary States Won
Eugene McCarthy (Minn.)	2,914,933	38.7	6
Robert Kennedy (N.Y.)	2,304,542	30.6	4
Lyndon Johnson (Texas)*	383,048	5.1	1
Others	1,932,546	25.6	3
TOTAL	7,535,069		

Note: In this chart and those that follow, all candidates are listed that drew at least 5 percent of their party's nationwide primary vote and were on the ballot in more than one state. The vote for "Others" includes other candidates, miscellaneous write-ins, and any derivation of "Uncommitted" that appeared on the primary ballots. An asterisk (*) indicates an incumbent president. Each candidate's home state is in parentheses. The source for vote data is Congressional Quarterly's *America at the Polls 1960–1996* and *Guide to U.S. Elections.* Results from the primary in the District of Columbia are included in the vote totals, but not territories such as Puerto Rico. The primary winners are shaded on the maps.

1968 REPUBLICAN PRIMARIES

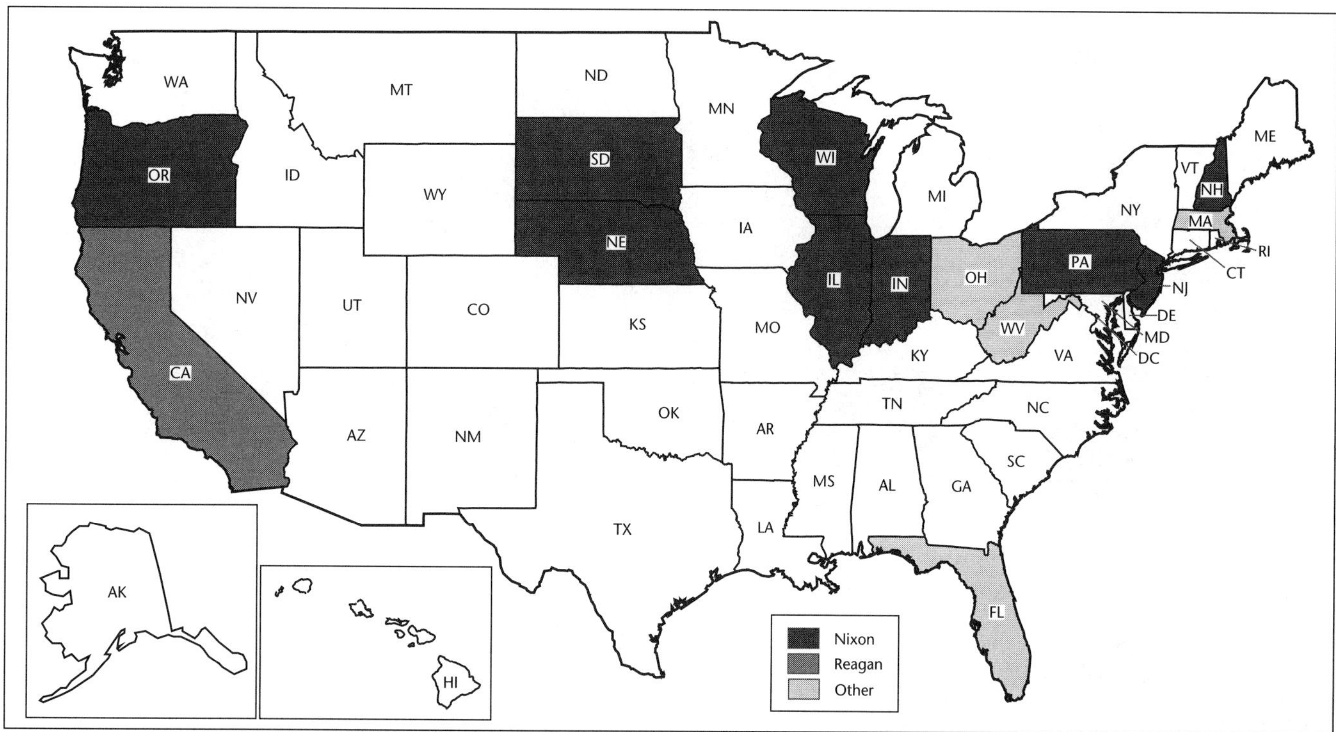

Unlike the Democrats, the Republican primaries in 1968 were like marking time before the August convention. Michigan Gov. George Romney dropped out of the race before the primaries began. New York Gov. Nelson Rockefeller entered too late to compete. And California Gov. Ronald Reagan did not formally announce his candidacy until the eve of the convention, although he was on several primary ballots in the spring, including California, where he ran as an unopposed favorite son.

Elsewhere, former Vice President Richard Nixon was virtually unopposed during the primary season. The only primaries he did not win were those he was not on the ballot. Still, Nixon did not have the nomination locked up when the convention in Miami Beach began. But the ideological gulf between the more liberal Rockefeller and the more conservative Reagan made it difficult for them to agree on a common strategy to stop Nixon, who ultimately prevailed on the first ballot.

	Total Vote	Percentage	Primary States Won
Ronald Reagan (Calif.)	1,696,270	37.9	1
Richard Nixon (N.Y.)	1,679,443	37.5	9
Others	1,097,838	24.5	4
TOTAL	4,473,551		

Note: Richard Nixon lived in New York during the 1968 campaign, although his political career is more associated with California.

1972 DEMOCRATIC PRIMARIES

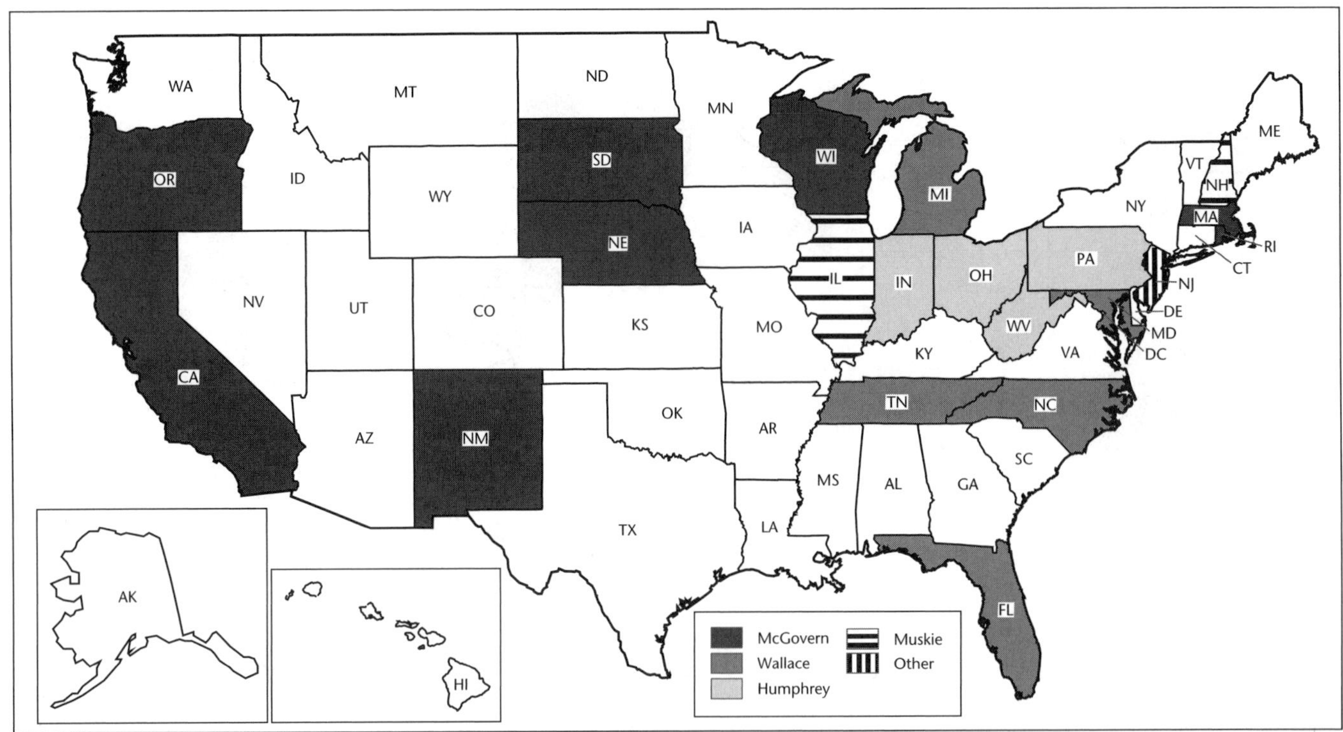

The presidential campaign of 1972 began a new era of nominating politics, where there were more primaries and candidates had to compete in them. Sen. George McGovern of South Dakota was the immediate beneficiary of the new system, mounting a long-shot candidacy that ultimately won the Democratic nomination.

McGovern had some of the same advantages that Eugene McCarthy had in 1968—an issue (opposition to the Vietnam War) and an army of volunteers. And McGovern burst onto the scene in much the same way that McCarthy had, with a stronger-than-expected showing in New Hampshire against a front-runner (Sen. Edmund Muskie from neighboring Maine) who did not do as well as expected.

McGovern carefully picked his way from there to the Democratic nomination, gaining momentum by winning high-profile primary states with progressive traditions, such as Wisconsin, Nebraska, Oregon and California. But he fared poorly in several regions that augured poorly for his chances that fall. He lost all the major industrial states—Pennsylvania and Ohio to former Vice President Hubert Humphrey, and Michigan to Alabama Gov. George Wallace. And he was a nonfactor in the Southern primaries, where Wallace dominated.

Altogether, McGovern received fewer primary votes than Humphrey, and not many more than Wallace. Since McGovern, every major-party nominee has first emerged from the primaries as his party's top vote-getter.

	Total Vote	Percentage	Primary States Won
Hubert Humphrey (Minn.)	4,121,372	25.8	4
George McGovern (S.D.)	4,053,451	25.3	8
George Wallace (Ala.)	3,755,424	23.5	5
Edmund Muskie (Maine)	1,840,217	11.5	2
Others	2,223,501	13.9	1
TOTAL	15,993,965		

1972 REPUBLICAN PRIMARIES

One point that has become clear during the modern era of presidential primaries is that sitting presidents that face little or no opposition for renomination are in great shape to win another term in the fall. On the other hand, every recent president that has struggled through his party's primaries has lost in November.

The first example of the upside of this dynamic was Richard Nixon. He faced minimal opposition for renomination in 1972 from a pair of little-known congressmen—Paul McCloskey of California, who mounted an anti-war challenge, and John Ashbrook of Ohio, who claimed that Nixon was too liberal for the GOP.

The contest was over quickly, as Nixon beat both easily in New Hampshire. Late in the spring, McCloskey did win a delegate in the New Mexico primary; it was the only vote cast against Nixon's renomination at the Republican convention that August.

	Total Vote	Percentage	Primary States Won
Richard Nixon (Calif.)*	5,378,704	86.9	18
John Ashbrook (Ohio)	311,543	5.0	0
Others	498,034	8.0	2
TOTAL	6,188,281		

1976 DEMOCRATIC PRIMARIES

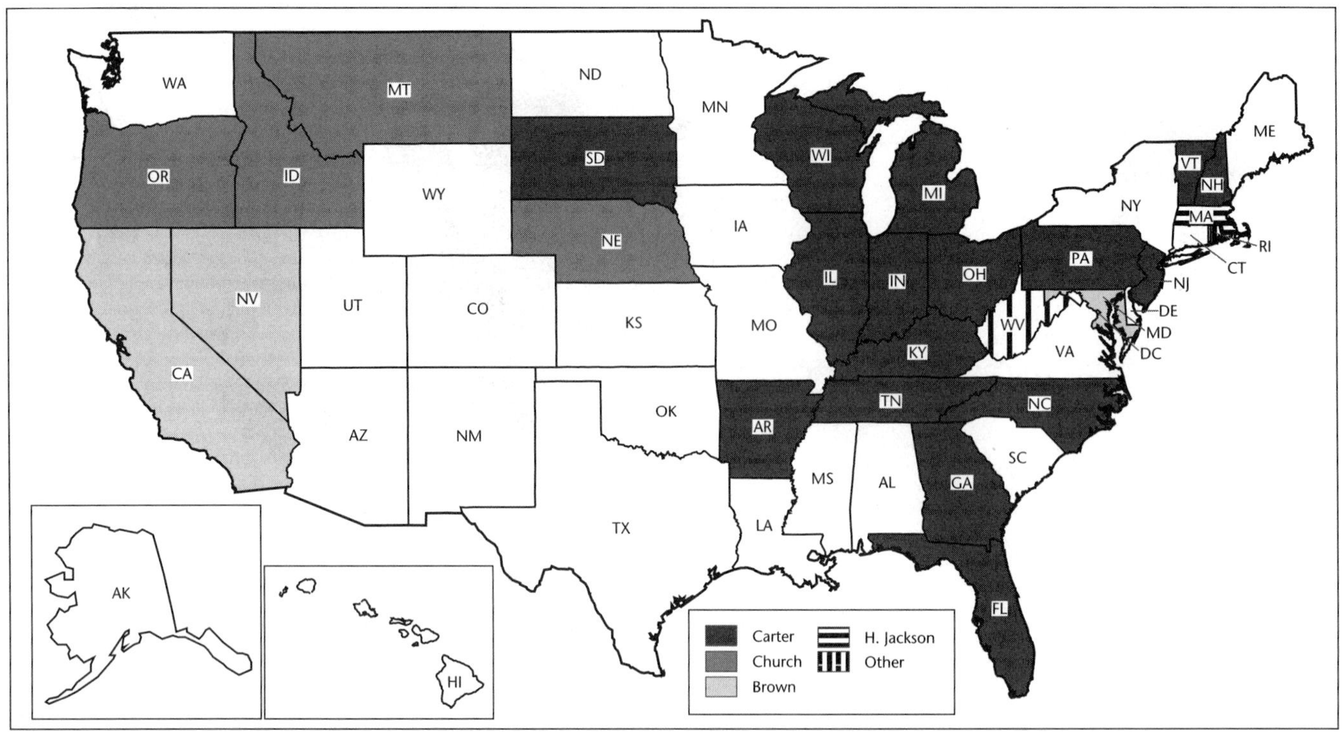

For the second straight election, a dark-horse candidate won the Democratic nomination. But unlike George McGovern four years earlier, former Georgia Gov. Jimmy Carter broke fast from the gate.

Carter established himself as a national candidate with victory in the New Hampshire primary, dispatched George Wallace in their home region with primary triumphs in Florida and North Carolina, eliminated Washington Sen. Henry Jackson in a key industrial state contest in Pennsylvania, and outpolled Rep. Morris Udall of Arizona at every turn, to the point that Udall became known as "Second Place Mo."

Carter lost some late primaries to two late entries from the West—California Gov. Jerry Brown and Sen. Frank Church of Idaho. But by then, Carter was comfortably ahead in the delegate count.

	Total Vote	Percentage	Primary States Won
Jimmy Carter (Ga.)	6,235,609	38.8	16
Jerry Brown (Calif.)	2,449,374	15.3	3
George Wallace (Ala.)	1,995,388	12.4	0
Morris Udall (Ariz.)	1,611,754	10.0	0
Henry Jackson (Wash.)	1,134,375	7.1	1
Frank Church (Idaho)	830,818	5.2	4
Others	1,795,334	11.2	2
TOTAL	16,052,652		

1976 REPUBLICAN PRIMARIES

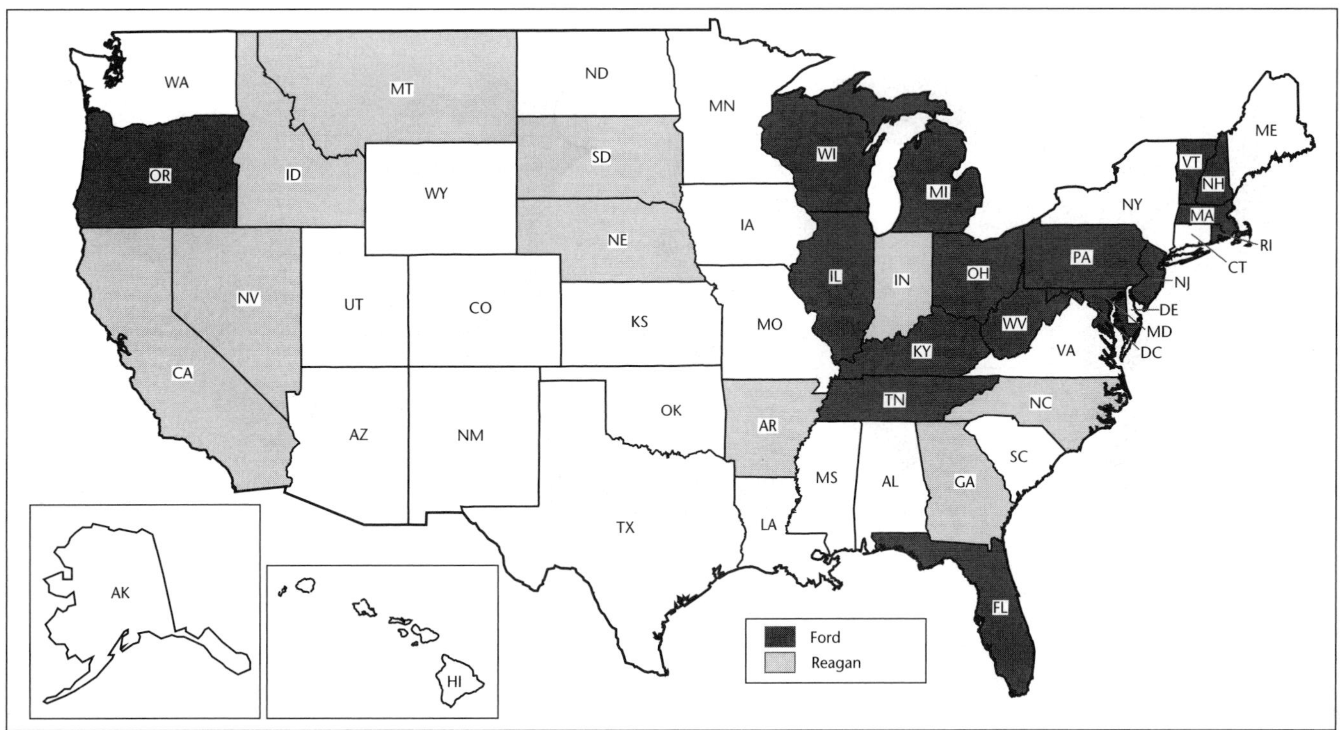

Since presidential primaries were instituted in the early twentieth century, no president who wanted another term has been denied his party's nomination. But in 1976, Gerald Ford found himself more closely challenged in the Republican primaries than any sitting president since William Howard Taft in 1912.

In former California Gov. Ronald Reagan, Ford had a challenger with both strong appeal to the burgeoning conservative wing of the Republican Party and a base in the nation's largest state. The closeness of the challenge was evident from the start, as Ford defeated Reagan by just 1 percentage point in New Hampshire. Ford followed with a string of primary victories that nearly knocked Reagan out of the race. But Reagan steadied himself with a late March victory in North Carolina.

As the primaries unfolded, Ford dominated in the Northeast and major states of the industrial Frost Belt. Reagan had the upper hand in much of the South and West. The only primary state that Ford was able to carry west of the Mississippi River was Oregon.

But Ford prevailed, in large part because he able to pick off some states in the South, including Florida, while Reagan was unable to deeply penetrate Ford's base in the major states of the Frost Belt.

	Total Vote	Percentage	Primary States Won
Gerald Ford (Mich.)*	5,529,899	53.3	16
Ronald Reagan (Calif.)	4,758,325	45.9	10
Others	85,901	0.8	0
TOTAL	10,374,125		

1980 DEMOCRATIC PRIMARIES

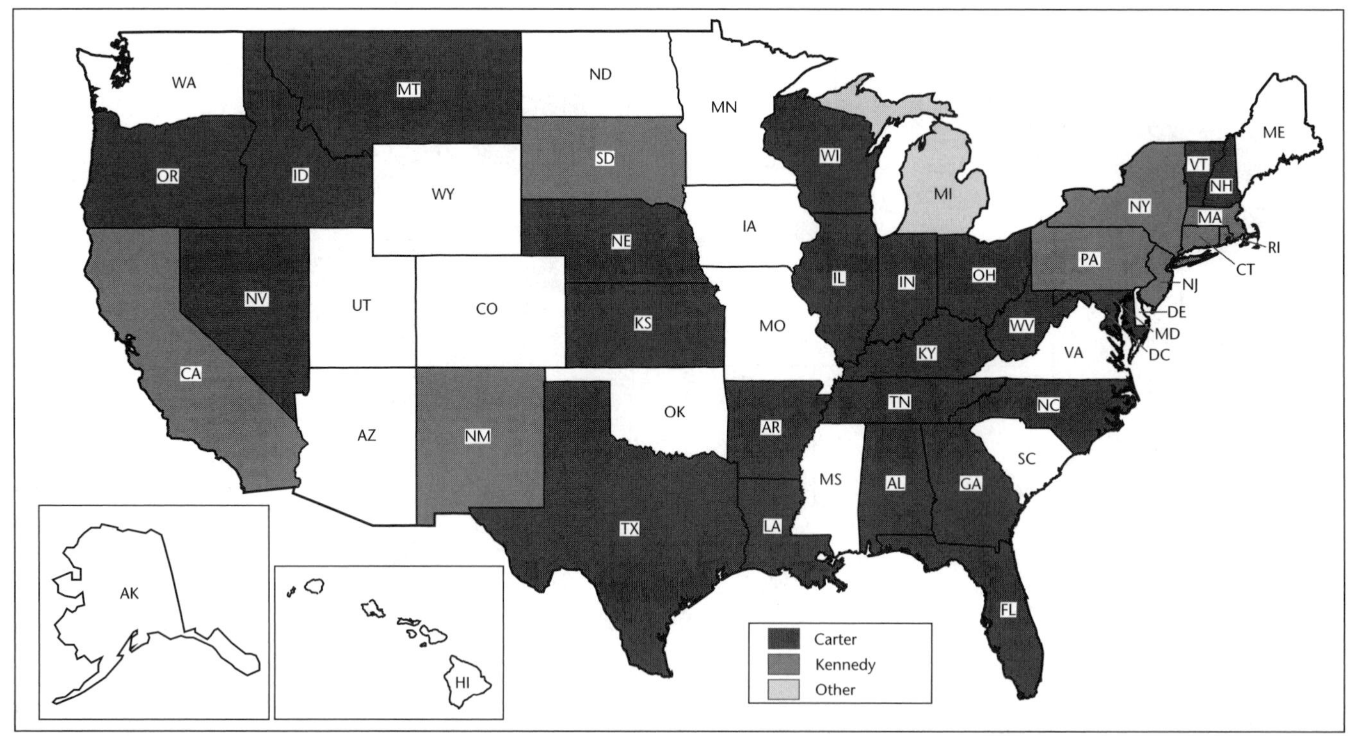

The Democrats had an intra-party brawl of their own in 1980 between an incumbent president (Jimmy Carter) and a well-regarded challenger (Sen. Edward Kennedy of Massachusetts) from the liberal wing of the party. Some polls taken in 1979 showed Kennedy ahead. But a series of events, including the Iranian hostage crisis, shifted sentiment to Carter before the primaries even began.

Carter got off to a fast start, with victories in New Hampshire, Illinois and across the South that removed any suspense about who would win the nomination. But as the primaries proceeded, Kennedy was able to fashion a bicoastal coalition that gave strong hints of Carter's vulnerability in the general election to come. Kennedy won primaries in New York, Pennsylvania and New Jersey on the East Coast and California on the West.

Yet there was also clear evidence that many Democratic voters would have preferred another choice beyond Carter and Kennedy, as more than 1 million votes were cast in the Democratic primaries for ballot lines that indicated "No preference."

	Total Vote	Percentage	Primary States Won
Jimmy Carter (Ga.)*	9,593,335	51.2	23
Edward Kennedy (Mass.)	6,963,625	37.1	9
Others	2,190,865	11.7	1
TOTAL	18,747,825		

1980 REPUBLICAN PRIMARIES

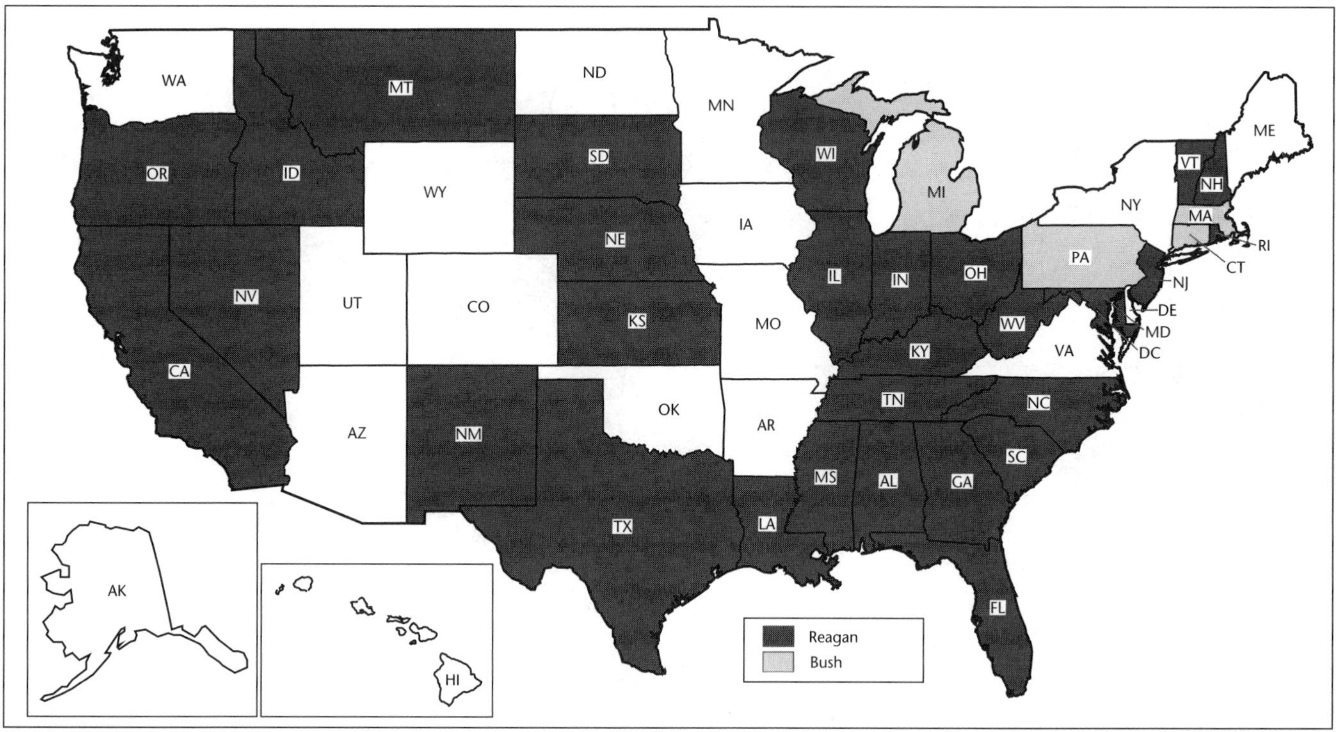

Ronald Reagan's strong showing in the 1976 Republican primaries made him the front-runner for the GOP nomination in 1980. But he got off to a stumbling start, losing the Iowa caucuses to dark-horse challenger, George Bush, who courted the state in a way that Reagan had not.

Bush claimed that he had "Big Mo" after the Iowa vote, but Reagan quickly reestablished his hegemony with a decisive victory in New Hampshire. Bush managed several primary wins in his native New England, and Rep. John Anderson of Illinois briefly was a factor in the race with near-misses in early March voting in Massachusetts and Vermont.

But after losing to Reagan in Illinois and Wisconsin, Anderson quit the Republican race in April in favor of an independent presidential bid. Meanwhile, Bush had fallen far behind after a string of Reagan primary victories in the South and Midwest. But Bush hung around, winning late primaries in Pennsylvania and Michigan that ultimately led to his choice as Reagan's running mate.

	Total Vote	Percentage	Primary States Won
Ronald Reagan (Calif.)	7,709,793	60.8	29
George Bush (Texas)	2,958,093	23.3	4
John Anderson (Ill.)	1,572,174	12.4	0
Others	450,391	3.5	0
TOTAL	12,690,451		

1984 DEMOCRATIC PRIMARIES

Former Vice President Walter Mondale entered the 1984 Democratic primaries with an array of endorsements from Democratic-related interest groups, including the AFL-CIO. But while the early support tended to serve Mondale well in his head-to-head maneuvering against Ohio Sen. John Glenn, it left Mondale open to an anti-establishment challenge from Sen. Gary Hart.

Hart, who had been campaign manager of George McGovern's 1972 presidential campaign, broke fast from the gate. His second-place finish in the Iowa caucuses put him in contention in New Hampshire, where an upset victory produced two weeks worth of momentum that left Mondale on the ropes. Only by winning Georgia and Alabama on Super Tuesday (March 13) was Mondale able to stabilize his campaign.

Mondale victories in the industrial states of Illinois, New York and Pennsylvania followed. But he could not shake Hart, as the senator from Colorado posted a succession of primary triumphs in the Midwest and West. On the final big day of primary voting in early June, Hart won California while Mondale took New Jersey, giving the former vice president just enough delegates to claim the nomination.

Although the Rev. Jesse Jackson won primaries only in Louisiana (and the District of Columbia), he was a factor throughout the primary season. Jackson ran well across the South and in urban centers of the Frost Belt by tapping the minority vote.

	Total Vote	Percentage	Primary States Won
Walter Mondale (Minn.)	6,811,214	37.8	10
Gary Hart (Colo.)	6,503,968	36.1	16
Jesse Jackson (Ill.)	3,282,380	18.2	1
Others	1,411,630	7.8	1
TOTAL	18,009,192		

1984 REPUBLICAN PRIMARIES

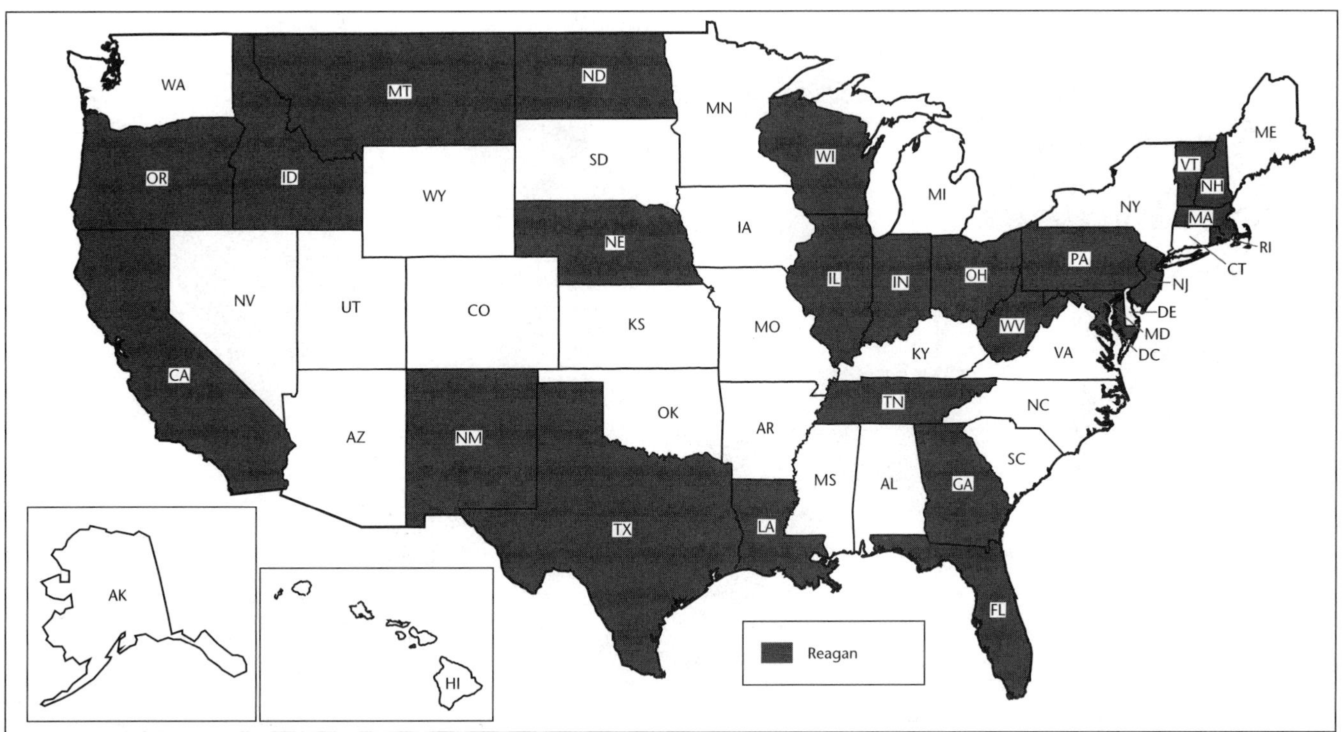

The 1984 GOP nominating process was more notable for what did not happen than what did. After two straight elections in which incumbent presidents faced serious primary challenges within their own party, President Ronald Reagan cruised to renomination over token opposition in 1984. It proved to be the precursor of an easy reelection victory for Reagan that fall.

	Total Vote	Percentage	Primary States Won
Ronald Reagan (Calif.)*	6,484,987	98.6	24
Others	90,664	1.4	0
TOTAL	6,575,651		

1988 DEMOCRATIC PRIMARIES

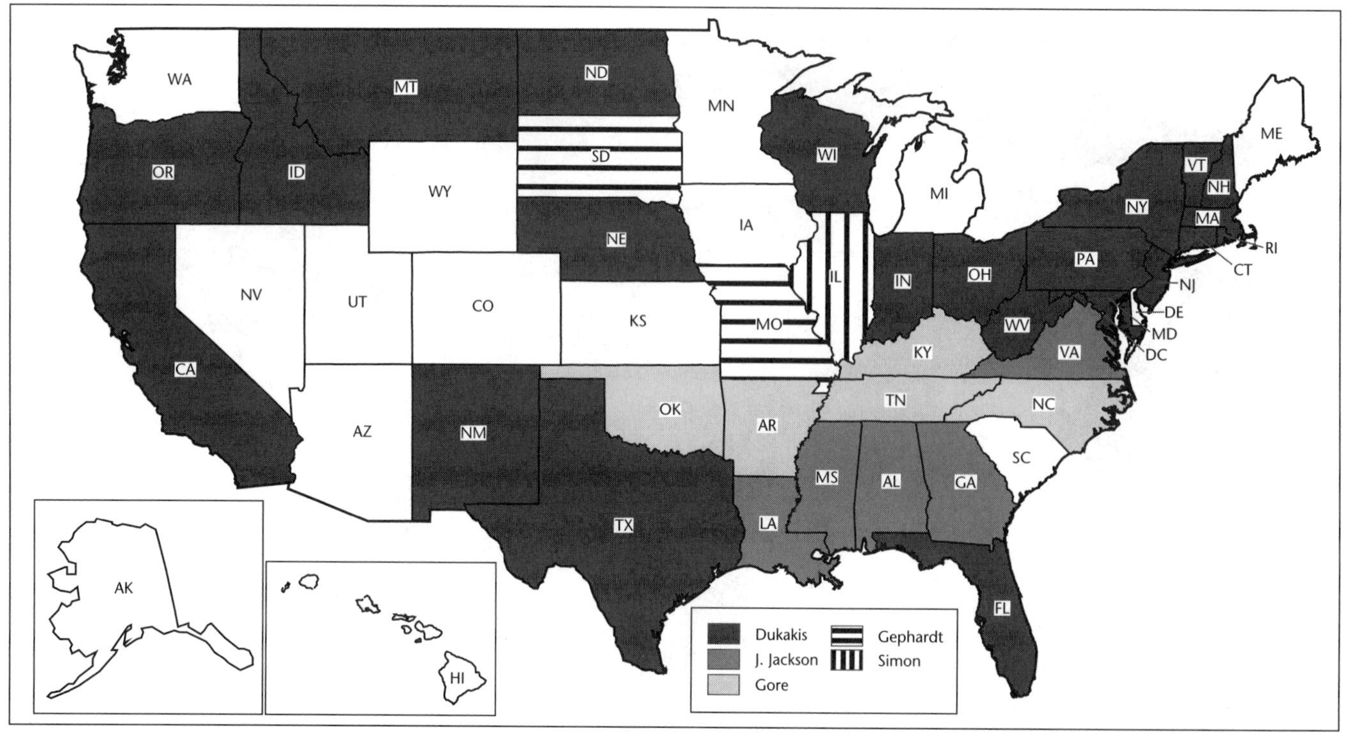

The Democratic nominating process was slow to take shape in 1988. Rep. Richard Gephardt of Missouri won the lead-off caucuses in neighboring Iowa. Gov. Michael Dukakis of Massachusetts won the first-in-the-nation primary in neighboring New Hampshire.

The huge Super Tuesday vote across Dixie in early March was a wash. Dukakis won the two big states on the fringes, Texas and Florida. Jesse Jackson swept five states from the Deep South to Virginia. Sen. Al Gore of Tennessee won five states across the middle of the South from North Carolina to Oklahoma. And Gephardt won his home state of Missouri. The Democratic race got even more convoluted the following week when Sen. Paul Simon won the primary in his home state of Illinois.

But as fast as one could say "brokered convention," the situation began to clear. Gephardt dropped out, and Dukakis began to win decisively across the industrial Frost Belt, with April victories in Wisconsin and New York sending Simon and Gore to the sidelines and relegating Jackson to also-ran status. In the three months of primary voting after Super Tuesday, Jackson could win only in Puerto Rico and the District of Columbia.

	Total Vote	Percentage	Primary States Won
Michael Dukakis (Mass.)	9,817,185	42.8	22
Jesse Jackson (Ill.)	6,685,699	29.1	5
Al Gore (Tenn.)	3,134,516	13.7	5
Richard Gephardt (Mo.)	1,388,356	6.0	2
Others	1,936,180	8.4	1
TOTAL	22,961,936		

1988 REPUBLICAN PRIMARIES

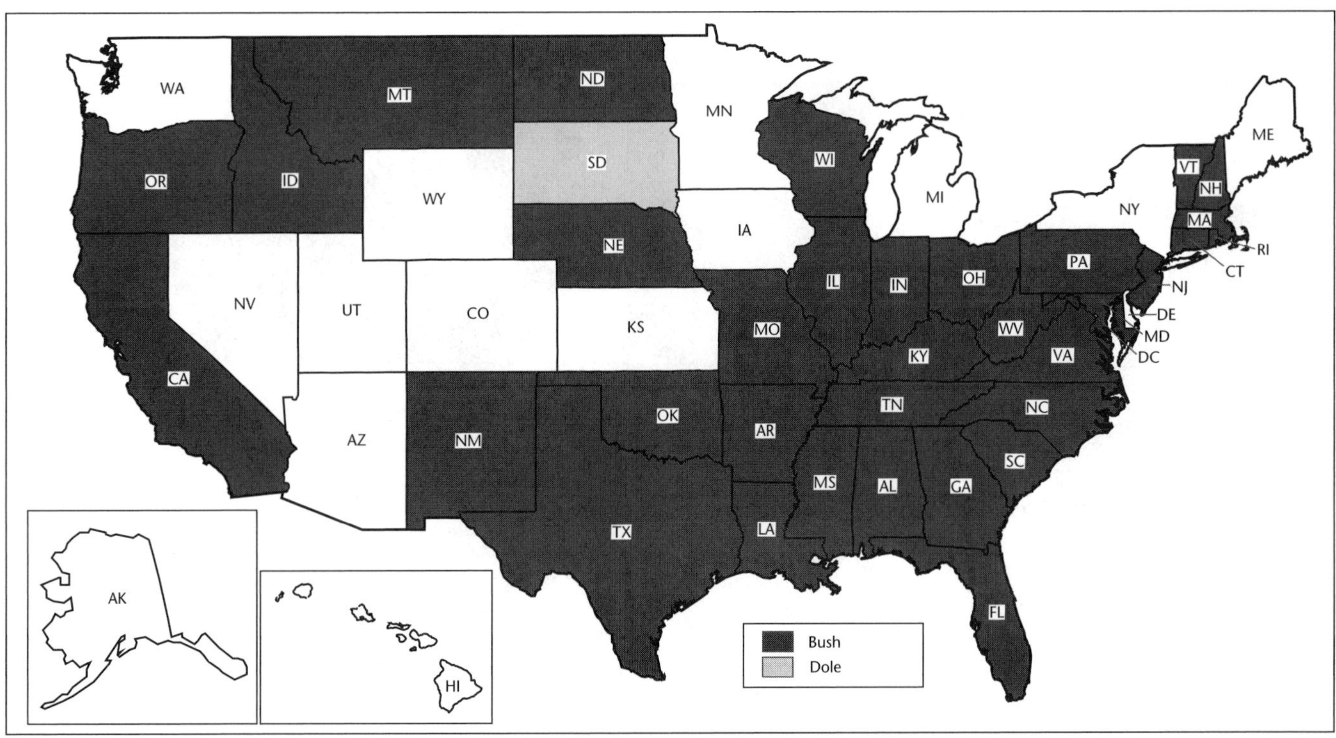

Like the Democrats in 1988, the Republicans began the year with a crowded field. But unlike the Democrats, the Republican picture cleared quickly.

Vice President George Bush could muster only a third-place finish in the first big event of the year, the Iowa precinct caucuses, where he trailed both Kansas Sen. Bob Dole and religious broadcaster Pat Robertson. But Bush rebounded quickly, beating Dole by nearly 10 percentage points in New Hampshire.

From there, Bush's momentum snowballed. A pivotal victory in the early March primary in South Carolina opened the door to a Bush sweep of the Super Tuesday GOP voting three days later, in which all of the remaining Southern states participated.

The results sent New York Rep. Jack Kemp to the sidelines. A week later, Bush's decisive win in Illinois drove Dole out of the race as well. Robertson lingered on, but was a factor only in a handful of caucus states where his small, but dedicated, cadre of supporters had gained a toehold.

In the end, Bush won every Republican primary but one, that a February event in South Dakota that he had essentially conceded to Dole.

	Total Vote	Percentage	Primary States Won
George Bush (Texas)	8,254,654	67.9	34
Bob Dole (Kan.)	2,333,268	19.2	1
Pat Robertson (Va.)	1,097,442	9.0	0
Others	479,751	3.9	0
TOTAL	12,165,115		

1992 DEMOCRATIC PRIMARIES

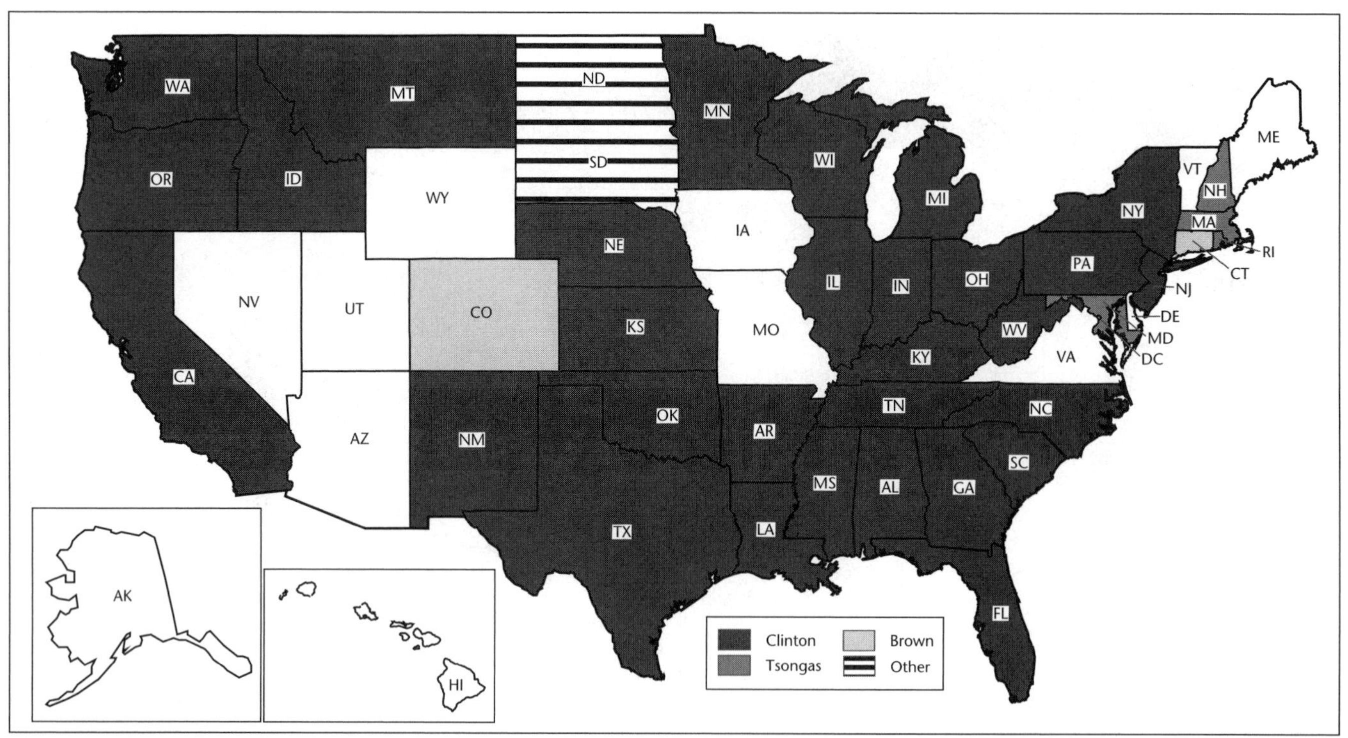

The 1992 Democratic presidential nominating contest had two phases. The first, pre-primary phase, focused on whether New York Gov. Mario Cuomo would run. He decided not to.

With Cuomo out of the race, Arkansas Gov. Bill Clinton was well positioned for the second phase, the primaries themselves. But it began for Clinton on a tenuous note. Hit with charges of womanizing and draft evasion (during the Vietnam War), Clinton did well to survive with a second-place finish in the New Hampshire primary behind former Sen. Paul Tsongas of neighboring Massachusetts.

But survival was enough. Clinton's home region, the South, was the first region to vote en masse and Clinton dominated the early March primaries there. Big victories followed for Clinton in mid-March in Illinois and Michigan that drove Tsongas from the race. Former California Gov. Jerry Brown briefly established himself as a challenger to Clinton with a late March victory in Connecticut. But Clinton swept all the primaries that followed, including a pivotal early April primary in New York that left his route clear to the nomination.

Clinton ended up with 52 percent of the vote in the primaries, the highest vote share for any Democratic nominee since 1956.

	Total Vote	Percentage	Primary States Won
Bill Clinton (Ark.)	10,482,411	51.8	30
Jerry Brown (Calif.)	4,071,232	20.1	2
Paul Tsongas (Mass.)	3,656,010	18.1	4
Others	2,029,732	10.0	2
TOTAL	20,239,385		

1992 REPUBLICAN PRIMARIES

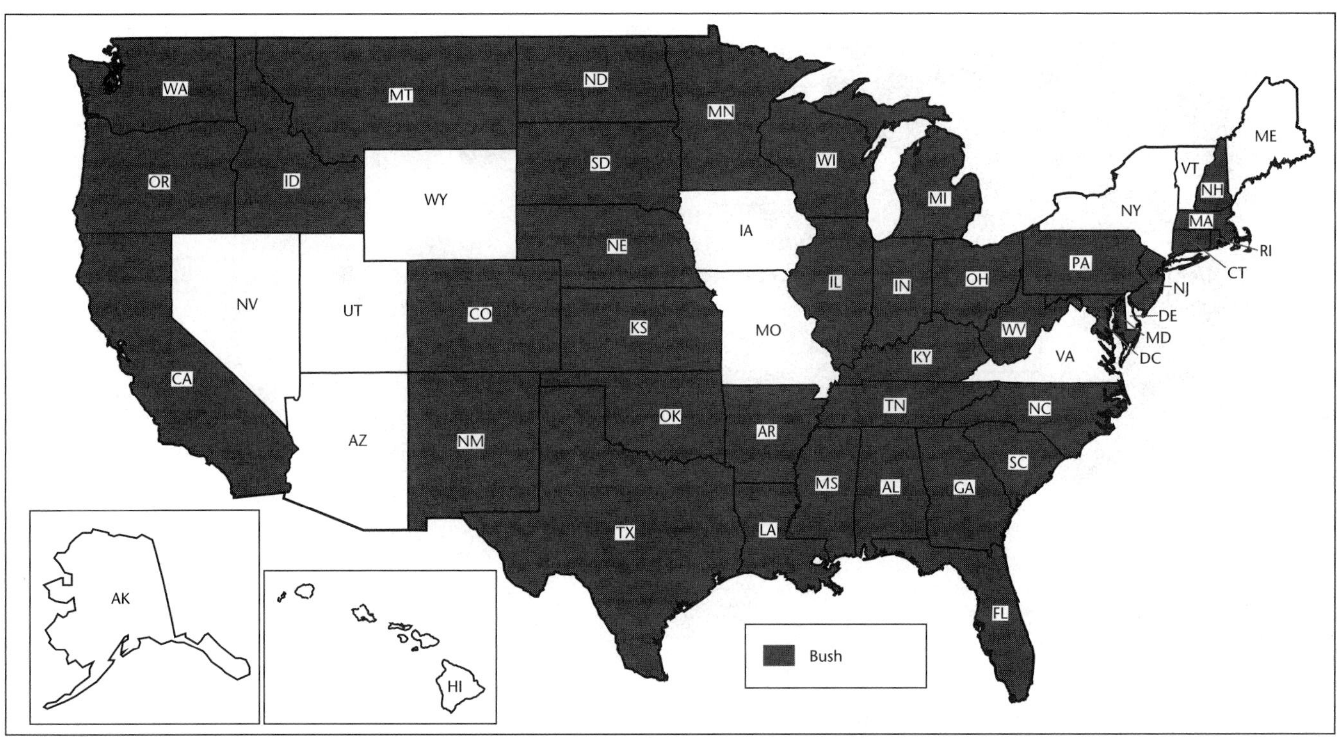

For the third time since 1976, an incumbent president struggled through his party's primaries and ended up a loser at the ballot box in the fall.

In reality, President George Bush was not as closely contested during the Republican primaries in 1992 as Gerald Ford had been in 1976 or Jimmy Carter in the Democratic primaries of 1980. But both Ford and Carter faced more serious challengers than Bush, who was opposed by television commentator Pat Buchanan.

Buchanan came no closer to beating Bush than his 37 percent share of the primary vote in the first-in-the-nation primary in New Hampshire. But Buchanan hung around, sounding a vocal challenge to Bush administration foreign and economic policy and serving as an outlet for anti-Bush protest votes throughout the primary season. Louisiana's David Duke briefly vied with Buchanan for that mantle, but failed to win more than 10 percent of the vote in any Republican primary except Mississippi.

	Total Vote	Percentage	Primary States Won
George Bush (Texas)*	9,199,463	72.5	37
Pat Buchanan (Va.)	2,899,488	22.8	0
Others	597,596	4.7	0
TOTAL	12,696,547		

1996 DEMOCRATIC PRIMARIES

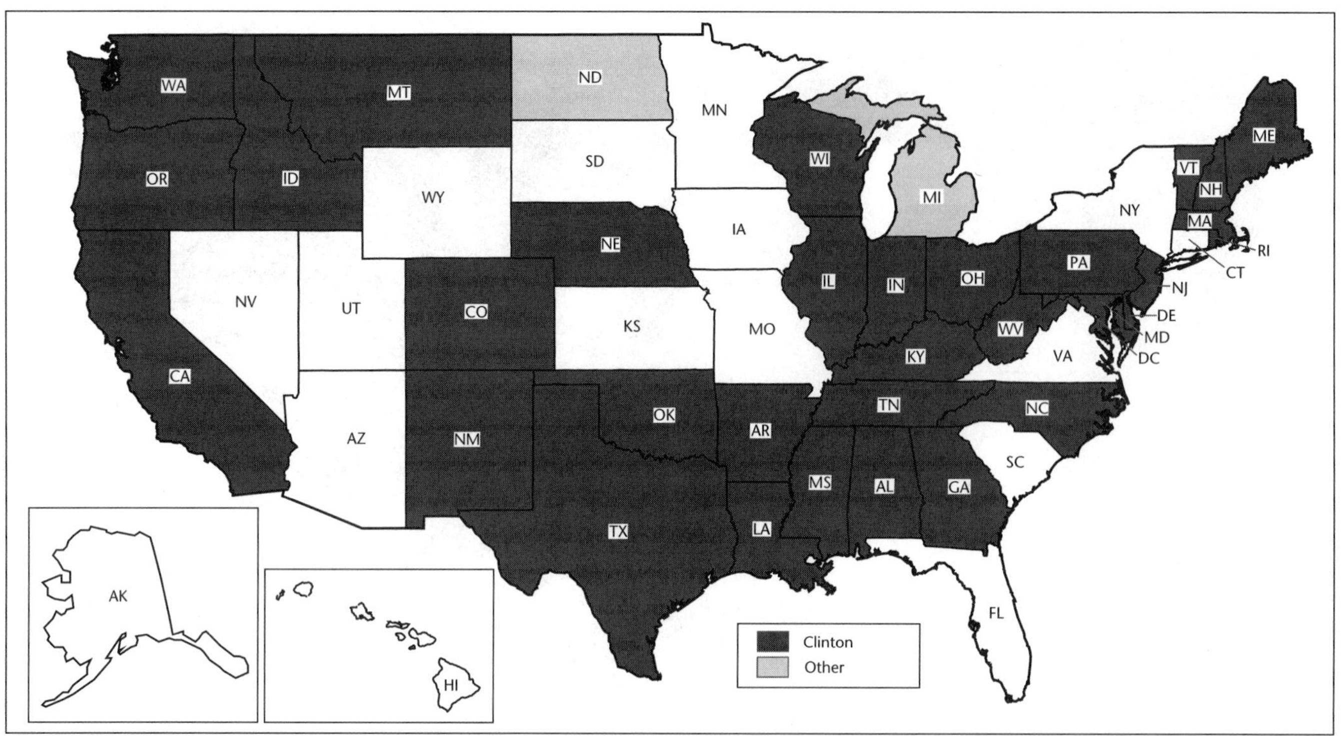

By the time the 1996 Democratic presidential primaries were to begin, President Bill Clinton had already won, as no more than token opposition filed against him. Clinton's most persistent challenge came from perennial presidential aspirant Lyndon LaRouche, but it was opposition the incumbent could safely ignore.

Clinton won easily in every primary that he was on the ballot. And when all the votes were tallied, he had made the best primary showing of any Democratic president since Franklin D. Roosevelt in 1936. That year, FDR took 93 percent of the Democratic primary ballots.

	Total Vote	Percentage	Primary States Won
Bill Clinton (Ark.)*	9,694,499	88.6	32
Lyndon LaRouche (Va.)	596,422	5.4	0
Others	656,443	6.0	2
TOTAL	10,947,364		

1996 REPUBLICAN PRIMARIES

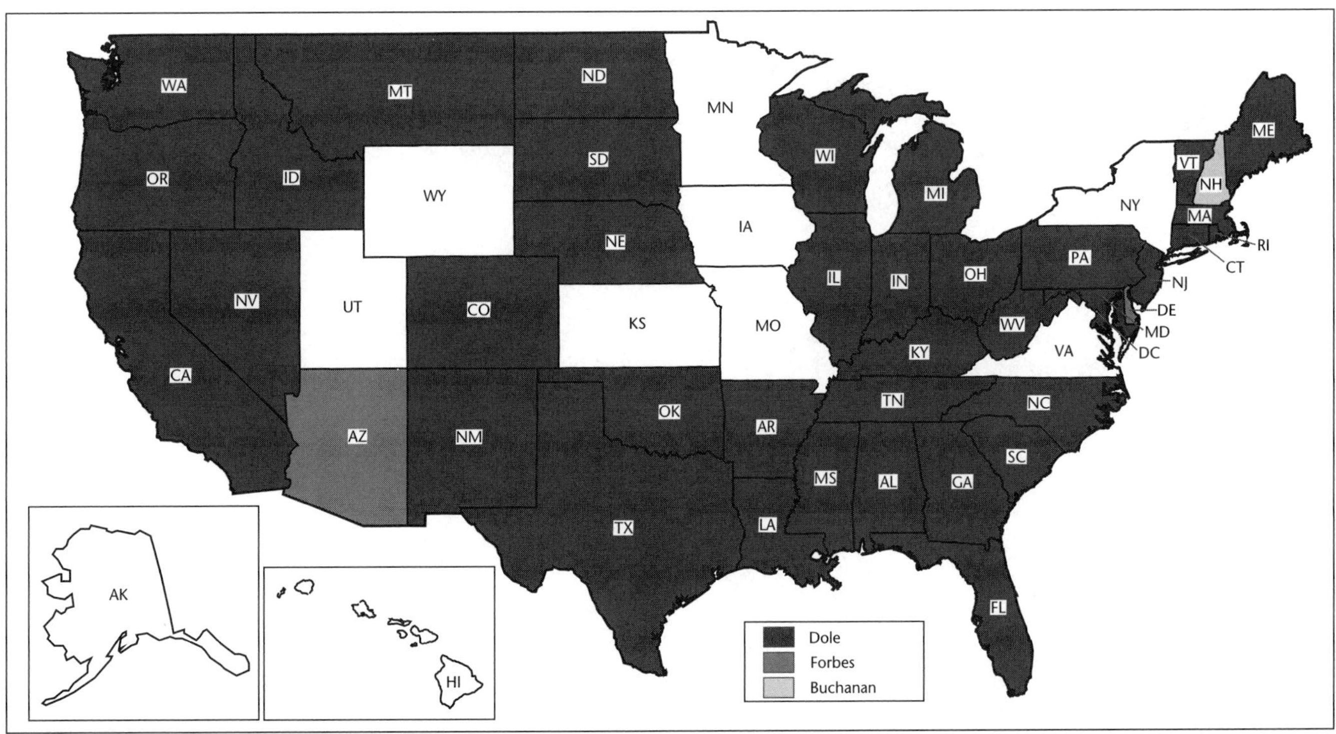

Once former Gen. Colin Powell decided not to seek the Republican nomination in 1996, Bob Dole was the clear front-runner. But he had to survive a turbulent month of February before establishing his hegemony in the myriad primaries that filled the month of March.

Dole basically played ".500 ball" in the opening round of events in February. He won the Iowa caucuses by a small margin, narrowly lost New Hampshire to Pat Buchanan, lost primaries in Delaware and Arizona to Steve Forbes, and won primaries in North and South Dakota.

But once the calendar flipped to March and there was a staccato of primaries on multiple fronts, Dole's considerable assets paid off—a hefty campaign chest, support from much of the Republican establishment and a broad acceptability to GOP voters.

Starting with his pivotal victory in South Carolina March 2, Dole did not lose another primary. He swept all eight primaries on March 5 (including all of New England outside New Hampshire), a New York delegate-selection event on March 7, all seven primaries on March 12 (most in the South), four contests in the industrial Midwest on March 19, and three Western primaries, anchored by California, on March 26. By the end of the month, Dole had won all the delegates he needed to assure himself the Republican nomination.

It marked a reversal of fortune for Dole, who had not won a primary *after* February when he ran in 1988.

	Total Vote	Percentage	Primary States Won
Bob Dole (Kan.)	8,191,239	58.5	37
Pat Buchanan (Va.)	3,020,746	21.6	1
Steve Forbes (N.J.)	1,424,898	10.2	2
Others	1,354,766	9.7	0
TOTAL	13,991,649		

1968–1996
PRESIDENTIAL PRIMARY
RETURNS BY STATE

ALABAMA

By joining with Florida and Georgia to hold a presidential primary in early March 1980, Alabama helped form the embryo of the Southern regional vote that had developed by 1988 into "Super Tuesday." But Alabama voters never turned out in large numbers for the March primary, certainly when compared to the state's midterm gubernatorial primary. In the 1990s, the presidential primary was returned to June, when party nominations for Congress are also settled.

Those that did vote in Alabama's Democratic presidential primaries in the 1980s disproportionately represented the liberal wing of the party. They handed Walter Mondale a critical victory in 1984 and gave Jesse Jackson a clear-cut primary win in 1988.

Mondale, rocked in early 1984 by an upset loss to Gary Hart in New Hampshire, regained his footing with a narrow victory in Georgia and a decisive triumph the same day in Alabama. With support from organized labor Mondale rode to a large lead in Alabama's major industrial centers—Birmingham, Gadsden, Anniston and the Quad Cities of the Tennessee River Valley.

But Mondale also relied on the support of blacks. Exit polls showed him splitting the white vote almost evenly with Hart and John Glenn. But with help from Birmingham Mayor Richard Arrington Jr. and other black leaders, Mondale picked off an estimated one-third to one-half of the black vote. Jackson won virtually all the rest.

The Democratic primary vote was even more racially polarized in 1988. Blacks cast about one-third of the ballots, and Jackson won nearly all of them. Sen. Al Gore of neighboring Tennessee took a majority of the white vote.

The pattern was visible on the map. Except for a pocket of white-majority counties near the Florida panhandle, Jackson swept every county in the southern half of the state. In the rural black-majority counties, his margins were huge. He won by nearly 40-to-1 in Macon County (Tuskegee), which had a population 86 percent black in the 1990 census.

Meanwhile, Gore swept virtually every county in Alabama's hilly and overwhelmingly white northern half. Jackson won statewide by 25,000 votes by virtue of his urban strength. Of the state's five most populous counties, he carried four, losing only Madison (Huntsville), along the Tennessee border, to Gore.

Although after the 1998 elections Republicans held both of Alabama's Senate seats and a majority of the House delegation, the GOP's primary electorate has been comparatively small and centered on the state's major metropolitan areas. More than half the vote in the 1996 GOP presidential primary was cast in four counties—Jefferson (Birmingham), Madison,

Recent Alabama Primary Results

Alabama held its first presidential primary in 1928 to select delegates, but did not include a direct vote for presidential candidates until 1980.

	DEMOCRATS			REPUBLICANS		
Year	Turnout	Candidates	%	Turnout	Candidates	%
1996 (June 4)	302,038	BILL CLINTON* Uncommitted	81 15	211,933	BOB DOLE Pat Buchanan	76 16
1992 (June 2)	450,899	BILL CLINTON Uncommitted	68 20	165,121	GEORGE BUSH* Uncommitted	74 18
1988 (March 8)	405,642	JESSE JACKSON Al Gore	44 37	213,561	GEORGE BUSH Bob Dole Pat Robertson	65 16 14
1984 (March 13)	428,283	WALTER MONDALE John Glenn Gary Hart Jesse Jackson	35 21 21 20		NO PRIMARY	
1980 (March 11)	237,464	JIMMY CARTER* Edward Kennedy	82 13	211,353	RONALD REAGAN George Bush	70 26

Note: All candidates are listed that drew at least 10 percent of their party's primary vote. The names of winning candidates are capitalized. An asterisk (*) indicates an incumbent president.

Mobile and Shelby (a fast-growing suburban county outside Birmingham).

Whether balloting in March or June, Republican primary voters have overwhelmingly endorsed the front-runner: Ronald Reagan in 1980, George Bush in 1988 and 1992, and Bob Dole in 1996. Conservative Christian activists have had only modest success in spite of Alabama's location in the midst of the Bible Belt. Evangelist Pat Robertson drew just 14 percent of the vote in the 1988 GOP primary.

Yet sometimes it takes an election or two for even establishment candidates to make good in Alabama. Dole was beaten badly by Bush in the 1988 primary. Bush was swamped by Reagan in 1980. Bush's loss that time was not from lack of effort. His TV ads featured an endorsement from former Vietnam prisoner of war Jeremiah Denton (who was on his way to election to the Senate that fall). And Bush's state campaign manager, who was also the national president of the Bass Anglers Sportsman Society, sought to organize Alabama fishermen for Bush. The effort, though, did not land many voters.

ALABAMA DEMOCRATIC

1980

County	Total Vote	Carter	E. Kennedy	Other	Winner	Percentage of Total Vote: Carter	E. Kennedy	Other
AUTAUGA	1,669	1,353	222	94	Carter	81.1%	13.3%	5.6%
BALDWIN	3,529	2,997	302	230	Carter	84.9%	8.6%	6.5%
BARBOUR	1,806	1,331	354	121	Carter	73.7%	19.6%	6.7%
BIBB	1,295	1,092	184	19	Carter	84.3%	14.2%	1.5%
BLOUNT	4,177	3,714	257	206	Carter	88.9%	6.2%	4.9%
BULLOCK	1,819	1,155	554	110	Carter	63.5%	30.5%	6.0%
BUTLER	1,463	1,260	125	78	Carter	86.1%	8.5%	5.3%
CALHOUN	8,012	6,337	1,402	273	Carter	79.1%	17.5%	3.4%
CHAMBERS	3,810	3,204	369	237	Carter	84.1%	9.7%	6.2%
CHEROKEE	1,248	1,075	117	56	Carter	86.1%	9.4%	4.5%
CHILTON	1,454	1,314	114	26	Carter	90.4%	7.8%	1.8%
CHOCTAW	1,115	967	137	11	Carter	86.7%	12.3%	1.0%
CLARKE	2,211	1,906	197	108	Carter	86.2%	8.9%	4.9%
CLAY	631	556	59	16	Carter	88.1%	9.4%	2.5%
CLEBURNE	1,692	1,371	237	84	Carter	81.0%	14.0%	5.0%
COFFEE	2,288	1,928	195	165	Carter	84.3%	8.5%	7.2%
COLBERT	4,372	3,565	511	296	Carter	81.5%	11.7%	6.8%
CONECUH	1,157	980	161	16	Carter	84.7%	13.9%	1.4%
COOSA	664	576	59	29	Carter	86.7%	8.9%	4.4%
COVINGTON	1,797	1,647	131	19	Carter	91.7%	7.3%	1.1%
CRENSHAW	759	678	69	12	Carter	89.3%	9.1%	1.6%
CULLMAN	3,485	3,133	283	69	Carter	89.9%	8.1%	2.0%
DALE	1,825	1,571	168	86	Carter	86.1%	9.2%	4.7%
DALLAS	3,927	3,082	563	282	Carter	78.5%	14.3%	7.2%
DE KALB	2,993	2,777	167	49	Carter	92.8%	5.6%	1.6%
ELMORE	2,114	1,767	225	122	Carter	83.6%	10.6%	5.8%
ESCAMBIA	2,001	1,761	187	53	Carter	88.0%	9.3%	2.6%
ETOWAH	7,228	6,372	639	217	Carter	88.2%	8.8%	3.0%
FAYETTE	925	797	116	12	Carter	86.2%	12.5%	1.3%
FRANKLIN	1,362	1,223	102	37	Carter	89.8%	7.5%	2.7%
GENEVA	1,880	1,690	159	31	Carter	89.9%	8.5%	1.6%
GREENE	1,454	1,020	429	5	Carter	70.2%	29.5%	0.3%
HALE	1,601	1,270	211	120	Carter	79.3%	13.2%	7.5%
HENRY	913	801	99	13	Carter	87.7%	10.8%	1.4%
HOUSTON	2,553	2,178	292	83	Carter	85.3%	11.4%	3.3%
JACKSON	2,304	2,029	164	111	Carter	88.1%	7.1%	4.8%
JEFFERSON	39,636	30,504	6,654	2,478	Carter	77.0%	16.8%	6.3%
LAMAR	893	826	58	9	Carter	92.5%	6.5%	1.0%
LAUDERDALE	5,062	4,313	409	340	Carter	85.2%	8.1%	6.7%
LAWRENCE	2,493	2,181	247	65	Carter	87.5%	9.9%	2.6%
LEE	4,234	3,249	649	336	Carter	76.7%	15.3%	7.9%
LIMESTONE	2,755	2,373	218	164	Carter	86.1%	7.9%	6.0%
LOWNDES	1,199	670	452	77	Carter	55.9%	37.7%	6.4%
MACON	2,315	1,575	581	159	Carter	68.0%	25.1%	6.9%
MADISON	13,533	11,003	1,855	675	Carter	81.3%	13.7%	5.0%
MARENGO	2,023	1,618	305	100	Carter	80.0%	15.1%	4.9%
MARION	1,180	1,089	60	31	Carter	92.3%	5.1%	2.6%
MARSHALL	3,076	2,681	191	204	Carter	87.2%	6.2%	6.6%
MOBILE	16,492	12,880	2,716	896	Carter	78.1%	16.5%	5.4%
MONROE	1,911	1,669	196	46	Carter	87.3%	10.3%	2.4%

ALABAMA DEMOCRATIC

1980

County	Total Vote	Carter	E. Kennedy	Other	Winner	Percentage of Total Vote Carter	E. Kennedy	Other
MONTGOMERY	10,750	8,245	1,905	600	Carter	76.7%	17.7%	5.6%
MORGAN	13,142	10,660	1,208	1,274	Carter	81.1%	9.2%	9.7%
PERRY	2,125	1,994	129	2	Carter	93.8%	6.1%	0.1%
PICKENS	1,466	1,221	232	13	Carter	83.3%	15.8%	0.9%
PIKE	1,615	1,340	199	76	Carter	83.0%	12.3%	4.7%
RANDOLPH	1,090	873	134	83	Carter	80.1%	12.3%	7.6%
RUSSELL	2,430	1,781	452	197	Carter	73.3%	18.6%	8.1%
ST. CLAIR	1,600	1,330	132	138	Carter	83.1%	8.3%	8.6%
SHELBY	3,364	2,876	296	192	Carter	85.5%	8.8%	5.7%
SUMTER	948	762	183	3	Carter	80.4%	19.3%	0.3%
TALLADEGA	3,012	2,380	489	143	Carter	79.0%	16.2%	4.7%
TALLAPOOSA	1,919	1,578	212	129	Carter	82.2%	11.0%	6.7%
TUSCALOOSA	7,049	5,594	1,070	385	Carter	79.4%	15.2%	5.5%
WALKER	3,678	3,276	352	50	Carter	89.1%	9.6%	1.4%
WASHINGTON	1,759	1,474	244	41	Carter	83.8%	13.9%	2.3%
WILCOX	1,669	1,458	201	10	Carter	87.4%	12.0%	0.6%
WINSTON	771	730	35	6	Carter	94.7%	4.5%	0.8%
TOTAL	238,722	194,680	31,624	12,418	Carter	81.6%	13.2%	5.2%
Certified Totals	237,464	193,734	31,382	12,348	Carter	81.6%	13.2%	5.2%

ALABAMA REPUBLICAN

1980

County	Total Vote	Bush	Reagan	Other	Winner	Percentage of Total Vote Bush	Reagan	Other
AUTAUGA	1,833	397	1,376	60	Reagan	21.7%	75.1%	3.3%
BALDWIN	6,450	1,809	4,444	197	Reagan	28.0%	68.9%	3.1%
BARBOUR	1,420	269	1,104	47	Reagan	18.9%	77.7%	3.3%
BIBB	674	96	558	20	Reagan	14.2%	82.8%	3.0%
BLOUNT	2,977	504	2,332	141	Reagan	16.9%	78.3%	4.7%
BULLOCK	530	53	464	13	Reagan	10.0%	87.5%	2.5%
BUTLER	1,116	212	873	31	Reagan	19.0%	78.2%	2.8%
CALHOUN	5,829	1,167	4,285	377	Reagan	20.0%	73.5%	6.5%
CHAMBERS	1,719	275	1,358	86	Reagan	16.0%	79.0%	5.0%
CHEROKEE	465	73	368	24	Reagan	15.7%	79.1%	5.2%
CHILTON	1,522	281	1,194	47	Reagan	18.5%	78.4%	3.1%
CHOCTAW	539	80	443	16	Reagan	14.8%	82.2%	3.0%
CLARKE	1,350	326	976	48	Reagan	24.1%	72.3%	3.6%
CLAY	478	52	412	14	Reagan	10.9%	86.2%	2.9%
CLEBURNE	1,013	150	826	37	Reagan	14.8%	81.5%	3.7%
COFFEE	1,939	307	1,568	64	Reagan	15.8%	80.9%	3.3%
COLBERT	1,826	239	1,498	89	Reagan	13.1%	82.0%	4.9%
CONECUH	896	114	759	23	Reagan	12.7%	84.7%	2.6%
COOSA	444	60	374	10	Reagan	13.5%	84.2%	2.3%
COVINGTON	1,722	307	1,364	51	Reagan	17.8%	79.2%	3.0%

ALABAMA REPUBLICAN

1980

County	Total Vote	Bush	Reagan	Other	Winner	Percentage of Total Vote Bush	Reagan	Other
CRENSHAW	589	97	485	7	Reagan	16.5%	82.3%	1.2%
CULLMAN	2,586	404	2,084	98	Reagan	15.6%	80.6%	3.8%
DALE	2,132	330	1,730	72	Reagan	15.5%	81.1%	3.4%
DALLAS	2,692	605	1,987	100	Reagan	22.5%	73.8%	3.7%
DE KALB	2,253	480	1,720	53	Reagan	21.3%	76.3%	2.4%
ELMORE	2,724	540	2,094	90	Reagan	19.8%	76.9%	3.3%
ESCAMBIA	1,650	337	1,215	98	Reagan	20.4%	73.6%	5.9%
ETOWAH	3,902	809	2,944	149	Reagan	20.7%	75.4%	3.8%
FAYETTE	728	99	606	23	Reagan	13.6%	83.2%	3.2%
FRANKLIN	814	157	617	40	Reagan	19.3%	75.8%	4.9%
GENEVA	1,127	165	922	40	Reagan	14.6%	81.8%	3.5%
GREENE	340	80	243	17	Reagan	23.5%	71.5%	5.0%
HALE	653	104	477	72	Reagan	15.9%	73.0%	11.0%
HENRY	737	52	666	19	Reagan	7.1%	90.4%	2.6%
HOUSTON	3,758	609	3,051	98	Reagan	16.2%	81.2%	2.6%
JACKSON	790	170	581	39	Reagan	21.5%	73.5%	4.9%
JEFFERSON	49,201	15,535	31,316	2,350	Reagan	31.6%	63.6%	4.8%
LAMAR	369	33	321	15	Reagan	8.9%	87.0%	4.1%
LAUDERDALE	3,009	631	2,230	148	Reagan	21.0%	74.1%	4.9%
LAWRENCE	791	146	602	43	Reagan	18.5%	76.1%	5.4%
LEE	4,072	1,409	2,394	269	Reagan	34.6%	58.8%	6.6%
LIMESTONE	1,242	222	919	101	Reagan	17.9%	74.0%	8.1%
LOWNDES	523	90	410	23	Reagan	17.2%	78.4%	4.4%
MACON	479	69	363	47	Reagan	14.4%	75.8%	9.8%
MADISON	11,806	3,945	7,034	827	Reagan	33.4%	59.6%	7.0%
MARENGO	1,281	247	978	56	Reagan	19.3%	76.3%	4.4%
MARION	881	113	742	26	Reagan	12.8%	84.2%	3.0%
MARSHALL	2,081	502	1,485	94	Reagan	24.1%	71.4%	4.5%
MOBILE	24,492	7,553	16,142	797	Reagan	30.8%	65.9%	3.3%
MONROE	1,232	319	853	60	Reagan	25.9%	69.2%	4.9%
MONTGOMERY	13,345	4,442	8,481	422	Reagan	33.3%	63.6%	3.2%
MORGAN	7,065	1,628	5,026	411	Reagan	23.0%	71.1%	5.8%
PERRY	718	127	571	20	Reagan	17.7%	79.5%	2.8%
PICKENS	840	146	671	23	Reagan	17.4%	79.9%	2.7%
PIKE	1,645	297	1,283	65	Reagan	18.1%	78.0%	4.0%
RANDOLPH	832	116	679	37	Reagan	13.9%	81.6%	4.4%
RUSSELL	1,024	133	843	48	Reagan	13.0%	82.3%	4.7%
ST. CLAIR	1,918	315	1,525	78	Reagan	16.4%	79.5%	4.1%
SHELBY	4,853	1,486	3,096	271	Reagan	30.6%	63.8%	5.6%
SUMTER	519	168	334	17	Reagan	32.4%	64.4%	3.3%
TALLADEGA	2,330	418	1,814	98	Reagan	17.9%	77.9%	4.2%
TALLAPOOSA	1,470	309	1,133	28	Reagan	21.0%	77.1%	1.9%
TUSCALOOSA	5,780	1,524	3,916	340	Reagan	26.4%	67.8%	5.9%
WALKER	2,209	414	1,741	54	Reagan	18.7%	78.8%	2.4%
WASHINGTON	963	206	726	31	Reagan	21.4%	75.4%	3.2%
WILCOX	746	103	624	19	Reagan	13.8%	83.6%	2.5%
WINSTON	1,420	275	1,102	43	Reagan	19.4%	77.6%	3.0%
TOTAL	211,353	54,730	147,352	9,271	Reagan	25.9%	69.7%	4.4%

ALABAMA DEMOCRATIC

1984

County	Total Vote	Glenn	Hart	J. Jackson	Mondale	Other	Winner	Percentage of Total Vote Glenn	Hart	J. Jackson	Mondale	Other
AUTAUGA	3,061	904	781	390	801	185	Glenn	29.5%	25.5%	12.7%	26.2%	6.0%
BALDWIN	5,659	1,898	1,663	568	1,282	248	Glenn	33.5%	29.4%	10.0%	22.7%	4.4%
BARBOUR	2,910	586	550	720	904	150	Mondale	20.1%	18.9%	24.7%	31.1%	5.2%
BIBB	1,892	443	366	278	797	8	Mondale	23.4%	19.3%	14.7%	42.1%	0.4%
BLOUNT	2,994	861	877	37	1,145	74	Mondale	28.8%	29.3%	1.2%	38.2%	2.5%
BULLOCK	2,721	384	357	920	839	221	J. Jackson	14.1%	13.1%	33.8%	30.8%	8.1%
BUTLER	4,544	896	1,304	588	1,449	307	Mondale	19.7%	28.7%	12.9%	31.9%	6.8%
CALHOUN	12,645	2,010	3,273	1,921	3,767	1,674	Mondale	15.9%	25.9%	15.2%	29.8%	13.2%
CHAMBERS	3,156	734	780	466	996	180	Mondale	23.3%	24.7%	14.8%	31.6%	5.7%
CHEROKEE	1,995	298	662	94	763	178	Mondale	14.9%	33.2%	4.7%	38.2%	8.9%
CHILTON	2,673	708	754	168	956	87	Mondale	26.5%	28.2%	6.3%	35.8%	3.3%
CHOCTAW	2,463	187	417	1,188	663	8	J. Jackson	7.6%	16.9%	48.2%	26.9%	0.3%
CLARKE	4,680	915	985	893	1,600	287	Mondale	19.6%	21.0%	19.1%	34.2%	6.1%
CLAY	1,198	333	380	91	339	55	Hart	27.8%	31.7%	7.6%	28.3%	4.6%
CLEBURNE	1,311	249	442	39	429	152	Hart	19.0%	33.7%	3.0%	32.7%	11.6%
COFFEE	3,386	824	907	499	1,006	150	Mondale	24.3%	26.8%	14.7%	29.7%	4.4%
COLBERT	7,908	1,514	1,384	1,630	2,969	411	Mondale	19.1%	17.5%	20.6%	37.5%	5.2%
CONECUH	1,567	235	264	204	805	59	Mondale	15.0%	16.8%	13.0%	51.4%	3.8%
COOSA	1,581	337	354	208	658	24	Mondale	21.3%	22.4%	13.2%	41.6%	1.5%
COVINGTON	2,387	663	652	153	823	96	Mondale	27.8%	27.3%	6.4%	34.5%	4.0%
CRENSHAW	1,773	332	578	184	630	49	Mondale	18.7%	32.6%	10.4%	35.5%	2.8%
CULLMAN	8,579	1,921	2,750	78	3,441	389	Mondale	22.4%	32.1%	0.9%	40.1%	4.5%
DALE	2,965	992	714	459	674	126	Glenn	33.5%	24.1%	15.5%	22.7%	4.2%
DALLAS	7,293	1,248	1,047	3,192	1,523	283	J. Jackson	17.1%	14.4%	43.8%	20.9%	3.9%
DE KALB	5,007	821	1,644	57	2,423	62	Mondale	16.4%	32.8%	1.1%	48.4%	1.2%
ELMORE	4,884	1,689	1,363	368	1,177	287	Glenn	34.6%	27.9%	7.5%	24.1%	5.9%
ESCAMBIA	2,046	403	561	419	551	112	Hart	19.7%	27.4%	20.5%	26.9%	5.5%
ETOWAH	13,606	2,565	3,401	863	5,895	882	Mondale	18.9%	25.0%	6.3%	43.3%	6.5%
FAYETTE	1,956	462	473	96	888	37	Mondale	23.6%	24.2%	4.9%	45.4%	1.9%
FRANKLIN	6,330	1,531	1,929	277	2,419	174	Mondale	24.2%	30.5%	4.4%	38.2%	2.7%
GENEVA	6,074	1,627	2,088	455	1,649	255	Hart	26.8%	34.4%	7.5%	27.1%	4.2%
GREENE	3,125	195	181	2,293	443	13	J. Jackson	6.2%	5.8%	73.4%	14.2%	0.4%
HALE	2,340	372	365	1,138	357	108	J. Jackson	15.9%	15.6%	48.6%	15.3%	4.6%
HENRY	1,860	378	273	609	496	104	J. Jackson	20.3%	14.7%	32.7%	26.7%	5.6%
HOUSTON	5,665	1,469	1,130	1,465	1,503	98	Mondale	25.9%	19.9%	25.9%	26.5%	1.7%
JACKSON	4,081	752	1,145	203	1,779	202	Mondale	18.4%	28.1%	5.0%	43.6%	4.9%
JEFFERSON	88,069	16,689	12,446	18,448	37,980	2,506	Mondale	18.9%	14.1%	20.9%	43.1%	2.8%
LAMAR	1,503	370	460	102	559	12	Mondale	24.6%	30.6%	6.8%	37.2%	0.8%
LAUDERDALE	9,160	1,915	1,842	1,223	3,597	583	Mondale	20.9%	20.1%	13.4%	39.3%	6.4%
LAWRENCE	3,603	603	770	407	1,765	58	Mondale	16.7%	21.4%	11.3%	49.0%	1.6%
LEE	5,945	1,417	1,529	977	1,645	377	Mondale	23.8%	25.7%	16.4%	27.7%	6.3%
LIMESTONE	4,308	1,211	1,008	355	1,493	241	Mondale	28.1%	23.4%	8.2%	34.7%	5.6%
LOWNDES	2,386	194	235	1,249	583	125	J. Jackson	8.1%	9.8%	52.3%	24.4%	5.2%
MACON	4,220	203	334	1,819	1,450	414	J. Jackson	4.8%	7.9%	43.1%	34.4%	9.8%
MADISON	24,095	7,536	5,477	3,732	6,787	563	Glenn	31.3%	22.7%	15.5%	28.2%	2.3%
MARENGO	3,351	512	621	1,351	730	137	J. Jackson	15.3%	18.5%	40.3%	21.8%	4.1%
MARION	2,715	671	716	44	1,259	25	Mondale	24.7%	26.4%	1.6%	46.4%	0.9%
MARSHALL	5,193	1,289	1,701	71	1,924	208	Mondale	24.8%	32.8%	1.4%	37.0%	4.0%
MOBILE	27,796	5,188	4,331	8,940	8,497	840	J. Jackson	18.7%	15.6%	32.2%	30.6%	3.0%
MONROE	2,137	372	362	902	442	59	J. Jackson	17.4%	16.9%	42.2%	20.7%	2.8%

ALABAMA DEMOCRATIC

1984

County	Total Vote	Glenn	Hart	J. Jackson	Mondale	Other	Winner	Percentage of Total Vote Glenn	Hart	J. Jackson	Mondale	Other
MONTGOMERY	23,925	4,646	4,403	6,164	7,896	816	Mondale	19.4%	18.4%	25.8%	33.0%	3.4%
MORGAN	9,080	2,528	2,529	572	3,003	448	Mondale	27.8%	27.9%	6.3%	33.1%	4.9%
PERRY	3,030	280	299	1,548	725	178	J. Jackson	9.2%	9.9%	51.1%	23.9%	5.9%
PICKENS	2,806	437	634	912	774	49	J. Jackson	15.6%	22.6%	32.5%	27.6%	1.7%
PIKE	2,358	581	589	361	690	137	Mondale	24.6%	25.0%	15.3%	29.3%	5.8%
RANDOLPH	1,760	329	515	189	528	199	Mondale	18.7%	29.3%	10.7%	30.0%	11.3%
RUSSELL	5,732	638	1,298	879	2,293	624	Mondale	11.1%	22.6%	15.3%	40.0%	10.9%
ST. CLAIR	3,119	981	808	168	953	209	Glenn	31.5%	25.9%	5.4%	30.6%	6.7%
SHELBY	5,750	2,040	1,394	287	1,765	264	Glenn	35.5%	24.2%	5.0%	30.7%	4.6%
SUMTER	3,248	128	223	2,554	323	20	J. Jackson	3.9%	6.9%	78.6%	9.9%	0.6%
TALLADEGA	6,282	1,353	1,236	846	2,659	188	Mondale	21.5%	19.7%	13.5%	42.3%	3.0%
TALLAPOOSA	3,140	859	867	403	817	194	Hart	27.4%	27.6%	12.8%	26.0%	6.2%
TUSCALOOSA	11,806	2,382	2,500	3,061	3,035	828	J. Jackson	20.2%	21.2%	25.9%	25.7%	7.0%
WALKER	6,383	1,146	1,374	152	3,219	492	Mondale	18.0%	21.5%	2.4%	50.4%	7.7%
WASHINGTON	2,447	381	454	717	865	30	Mondale	15.6%	18.6%	29.3%	35.3%	1.2%
WILCOX	3,066	353	221	2,132	345	15	J. Jackson	11.5%	7.2%	69.5%	11.3%	0.5%
WINSTON	1,555	318	495	11	725	6	Mondale	20.5%	31.8%	0.7%	46.6%	0.4%
TOTAL	428,283	89,286	88,465	83,787	148,165	18,580	Mondale	20.8%	20.7%	19.6%	34.6%	4.3%

ALABAMA DEMOCRATIC

1988

County	Total Vote	Dukakis	Gore	J. Jackson	Other	Winner	Percentage of Total Vote Dukakis	Gore	J. Jackson	Other
AUTAUGA	2,662	273	731	1,005	653.00	J. Jackson	10.3%	27.5%	37.8%	24.5%
BALDWIN	5,990	800	2,397	1,604	1,189	Gore	13.4%	40.0%	26.8%	19.8%
BARBOUR	2,923	123	632	1,766	402	J. Jackson	4.2%	21.6%	60.4%	13.8%
BIBB	1,788	99	940	605	144	Gore	5.5%	52.6%	33.8%	8.1%
BLOUNT	2,719	213	2,087	130	289	Gore	7.8%	76.8%	4.8%	10.6%
BULLOCK	2,387	70	196	1,953	168	J. Jackson	2.9%	8.2%	81.8%	7.0%
BUTLER	2,142	139	297	1,197	509	J. Jackson	6.5%	13.9%	55.9%	23.8%
CALHOUN	9,226	1,161	4,261	2,717	1,087	Gore	12.6%	46.2%	29.4%	11.8%
CHAMBERS	3,691	271	1,190	1,454	776	J. Jackson	7.3%	32.2%	39.4%	21.0%
CHEROKEE	2,220	395	1,302	270	253	Gore	17.8%	58.6%	12.2%	11.4%
CHILTON	2,690	142	1,594	642	312	Gore	5.3%	59.3%	23.9%	11.6%
CHOCTAW	2,526	94	532	1,774	126	J. Jackson	3.7%	21.1%	70.2%	5.0%
CLARKE	3,650	127	892	2,322	309	J. Jackson	3.5%	24.4%	63.6%	8.5%
CLAY	1,453	115	724	251	363	Gore	7.9%	49.8%	17.3%	25.0%
CLEBURNE	1,093	128	713	112	140	Gore	11.7%	65.2%	10.2%	12.8%
COFFEE	2,948	223	1,177	746	802	Gore	7.6%	39.9%	25.3%	27.2%
COLBERT	8,032	366	4,581	2,178	907	Gore	4.6%	57.0%	27.1%	11.3%
CONECUH	2,169	113	510	1,277	269	J. Jackson	5.2%	23.5%	58.9%	12.4%
COOSA	1,607	90	586	760	171	J. Jackson	5.6%	36.5%	47.3%	10.6%
COVINGTON	2,970	321	1,144	727	778	Gore	10.8%	38.5%	24.5%	26.2%

ALABAMA DEMOCRATIC

1988

County	Total Vote	Dukakis	Gore	J. Jackson	Other	Winner	Percentage of Total Vote Dukakis	Gore	J. Jackson	Other
CRENSHAW	1,515	88	381	708	338	J. Jackson	5.8%	25.1%	46.7%	22.3%
CULLMAN	5,368	498	3,845	238	787	Gore	9.3%	71.6%	4.4%	14.7%
DALE	2,548	211	1,175	710	452	Gore	8.3%	46.1%	27.9%	17.7%
DALLAS	6,807	255	923	4,872	757	J. Jackson	3.7%	13.6%	71.6%	11.1%
DE KALB	5,194	403	4,070	221	500	Gore	7.8%	78.4%	4.3%	9.6%
ELMORE	3,332	348	1,076	1,077	831	J. Jackson	10.4%	32.3%	32.3%	24.9%
ESCAMBIA	3,133	228	1,332	1,110	463	Gore	7.3%	42.5%	35.4%	14.8%
ETOWAH	11,536	718	6,739	2,660	1,419	Gore	6.2%	58.4%	23.1%	12.3%
FAYETTE	2,122	129	1,120	576	297	Gore	6.1%	52.8%	27.1%	14.0%
FRANKLIN	2,844	184	1,743	437	480	Gore	6.5%	61.3%	15.4%	16.9%
GENEVA	2,060	161	1,059	420	420	Gore	7.8%	51.4%	20.4%	20.4%
GREENE	3,070	60	303	2,640	67	J. Jackson	2.0%	9.9%	86.0%	2.2%
HALE	2,263	69	618	1,401	175	J. Jackson	3.0%	27.3%	61.9%	7.7%
HENRY	1,698	77	401	1,031	189	J. Jackson	4.5%	23.6%	60.7%	11.1%
HOUSTON	5,372	385	2,169	2,260	558	J. Jackson	7.2%	40.4%	42.1%	10.4%
JACKSON	3,929	335	2,818	376	400	Gore	8.5%	71.7%	9.6%	10.2%
JEFFERSON	81,420	6,060	20,312	49,940	5,108	J. Jackson	7.4%	24.9%	61.3%	6.3%
LAMAR	1,393	88	669	271	365	Gore	6.3%	48.0%	19.5%	26.2%
LAUDERDALE	9,239	594	6,025	1,489	1,131	Gore	6.4%	65.2%	16.1%	12.2%
LAWRENCE	3,683	97	2,295	926	365	Gore	2.6%	62.3%	25.1%	9.9%
LEE	6,393	841	1,716	2,938	898	J. Jackson	13.2%	26.8%	46.0%	14.0%
LIMESTONE	4,907	247	3,355	824	481	Gore	5.0%	68.4%	16.8%	9.8%
LOWNDES	2,141	41	152	1,750	198	J. Jackson	1.9%	7.1%	81.7%	9.2%
MACON	4,909	73	119	4,499	218	J. Jackson	1.5%	2.4%	91.6%	4.4%
MADISON	23,014	2,442	11,517	6,691	2,364	Gore	10.6%	50.0%	29.1%	10.3%
MARENGO	3,363	102	533	2,479	249	J. Jackson	3.0%	15.8%	73.7%	7.4%
MARION	2,846	201	1,978	144	523	Gore	7.1%	69.5%	5.1%	18.4%
MARSHALL	5,047	396	3,763	248	640	Gore	7.8%	74.6%	4.9%	12.7%
MOBILE	27,229	2,794	6,622	14,009	3,804	J. Jackson	10.3%	24.3%	51.4%	14.0%
MONROE	3,089	126	733	1,852	378	J. Jackson	4.1%	23.7%	60.0%	12.2%
MONTGOMERY	23,798	1,785	4,189	15,071	2,753	J. Jackson	7.5%	17.6%	63.3%	11.6%
MORGAN	9,824	661	6,636	1,471	1,056	Gore	6.7%	67.5%	15.0%	10.7%
PERRY	2,825	97	695	1,881	152	J. Jackson	3.4%	24.6%	66.6%	5.4%
PICKENS	2,710	103	889	1,492	226	J. Jackson	3.8%	32.8%	55.1%	8.3%
PIKE	1,973	131	368	1,098	376	J. Jackson	6.6%	18.7%	55.7%	19.1%
RANDOLPH	2,200	198	1,023	639	340	Gore	9.0%	46.5%	29.0%	15.5%
RUSSELL	5,033	371	1,176	2,791	695	J. Jackson	7.4%	23.4%	55.5%	13.8%
ST. CLAIR	2,940	154	1,745	658	383	Gore	5.2%	59.4%	22.4%	13.0%
SHELBY	6,670	836	3,603	1,393	838	Gore	12.5%	54.0%	20.9%	12.6%
SUMTER	4,015	75	325	3,482	133	J. Jackson	1.9%	8.1%	86.7%	3.3%
TALLADEGA	6,984	438	2,324	3,246	976	J. Jackson	6.3%	33.3%	46.5%	14.0%
TALLAPOOSA	3,302	282	1,168	1,205	647	J. Jackson	8.5%	35.4%	36.5%	19.6%
TUSCALOOSA	14,487	1,804	5,488	5,824	1,371	J. Jackson	12.5%	37.9%	40.2%	9.5%
WALKER	6,325	479	4,033	909	904	Gore	7.6%	63.8%	14.4%	14.3%
WASHINGTON	2,551	118	915	1,213	305	J. Jackson	4.6%	35.9%	47.5%	12.0%
WILCOX	2,443	41	119	2,065	218	J. Jackson	1.7%	4.9%	84.5%	8.9%
WINSTON	1,413	119	996	39	259	Gore	8.4%	70.5%	2.8%	18.3%
TOTAL	405,843	31,206	151,739	176,764	46,134	J. Jackson	7.7%	37.4%	43.6%	11.4%
Certified Totals	405,642	31,306	151,739	176,764	45,833	J. Jackson	7.7%	37.4%	43.6%	11.3%

ALABAMA REPUBLICAN

1988

County	Total Vote	Bush	Dole	Robertson	Other	Winner	Percentage of Total Vote Bush	Dole	Robertson	Other
AUTAUGA	1,727	1,147	241	264	75	Bush	66.4%	14.0%	15.3%	4.3%
BALDWIN	8,213	5,456	1,179	1,180	398	Bush	66.4%	14.4%	14.4%	4.8%
BARBOUR	645	396	74	158	17	Bush	61.4%	11.5%	24.5%	2.6%
BIBB	556	391	66	80	19	Bush	70.3%	11.9%	14.4%	3.4%
BLOUNT	1,830	1,182	254	253	141	Bush	64.6%	13.9%	13.8%	7.7%
BULLOCK	127	88	21	13	5	Bush	69.3%	16.5%	10.2%	3.9%
BUTLER	547	357	71	107	12	Bush	65.3%	13.0%	19.6%	2.2%
CALHOUN	4,048	2,607	581	703	157	Bush	64.4%	14.4%	17.4%	3.9%
CHAMBERS	651	328	84	217	22	Bush	50.4%	12.9%	33.3%	3.4%
CHEROKEE	421	284	66	58	13	Bush	67.5%	15.7%	13.8%	3.1%
CHILTON	1,667	1,215	226	173	53	Bush	72.9%	13.6%	10.4%	3.2%
CHOCTAW	212	135	29	40	8	Bush	63.7%	13.7%	18.9%	3.8%
CLARKE	935	716	132	63	24	Bush	76.6%	14.1%	6.7%	2.6%
CLAY	477	345	59	53	20	Bush	72.3%	12.4%	11.1%	4.2%
CLEBURNE	194	143	30	15	6	Bush	73.7%	15.5%	7.7%	3.1%
COFFEE	1,469	882	251	276	60	Bush	60.0%	17.1%	18.8%	4.1%
COLBERT	1,572	769	396	322	85	Bush	48.9%	25.2%	20.5%	5.4%
CONECUH	332	208	69	35	20	Bush	62.7%	20.8%	10.5%	6.0%
COOSA	562	404	73	70	15	Bush	71.9%	13.0%	12.5%	2.7%
COVINGTON	1,007	714	90	174	29	Bush	70.9%	8.9%	17.3%	2.9%
CRENSHAW	270	163	76	28	3	Bush	60.4%	28.1%	10.4%	1.1%
CULLMAN	2,013	1,412	290	210	101	Bush	70.1%	14.4%	10.4%	5.0%
DALE	1,673	1,146	235	240	52	Bush	68.5%	14.0%	14.3%	3.1%
DALLAS	1,879	1,282	243	311	43	Bush	68.2%	12.9%	16.6%	2.3%
DE KALB	2,724	1,827	447	321	129	Bush	67.1%	16.4%	11.8%	4.7%
ELMORE	2,227	1,534	320	272	101	Bush	68.9%	14.4%	12.2%	4.5%
ESCAMBIA	1,048	676	135	194	43	Bush	64.5%	12.9%	18.5%	4.1%
ETOWAH	2,800	1,809	445	365	181	Bush	64.6%	15.9%	13.0%	6.5%
FAYETTE	539	366	93	68	12	Bush	67.9%	17.3%	12.6%	2.2%
FRANKLIN	772	471	188	88	25	Bush	61.0%	24.4%	11.4%	3.2%
GENEVA	684	457	82	117	28	Bush	66.8%	12.0%	17.1%	4.1%
GREENE	48	32	10	6	0	Bush	66.7%	20.8%	12.5%	
HALE	145	94	32	17	2	Bush	64.8%	22.1%	11.7%	1.4%
HENRY	250	165	37	38	10	Bush	66.0%	14.8%	15.2%	4.0%
HOUSTON	4,248	3,230	702	159	157	Bush	76.0%	16.5%	3.7%	3.7%
JACKSON	1,006	501	305	146	54	Bush	49.8%	30.3%	14.5%	5.4%
JEFFERSON	57,361	39,510	7,710	6,456	3,685	Bush	68.9%	13.4%	11.3%	6.4%
LAMAR	327	190	68	69	0	Bush	58.1%	20.8%	21.1%	
LAUDERDALE	2,650	1,231	814	482	123	Bush	46.5%	30.7%	18.2%	4.6%
LAWRENCE	283	171	45	41	26	Bush	60.4%	15.9%	14.5%	9.2%
LEE	3,635	2,104	650	697	184	Bush	57.9%	17.9%	19.2%	5.1%
LIMESTONE	1,403	761	396	168	78	Bush	54.2%	28.2%	12.0%	5.6%
LOWNDES	179	147	25	3	4	Bush	82.1%	14.0%	1.7%	2.2%
MACON	153	95	23	23	12	Bush	62.1%	15.0%	15.0%	7.8%
MADISON	16,548	8,498	4,431	2,552	1,067	Bush	51.4%	26.8%	15.4%	6.4%
MARENGO	538	140	30	360	8	Robertson	26.0%	5.6%	66.9%	1.5%
MARION	956	606	167	144	39	Bush	63.4%	17.5%	15.1%	4.1%
MARSHALL	2,327	1,345	497	311	174	Bush	57.8%	21.4%	13.4%	7.5%
MOBILE	25,841	16,984	3,613	4,019	1,225	Bush	65.7%	14.0%	15.6%	4.7%
MONROE	603	426	100	66	11	Bush	70.6%	16.6%	10.9%	1.8%

ALABAMA REPUBLICAN

1988

County	Total Vote	Bush	Dole	Robertson	Other	Winner	Percentage of Total Vote Bush	Dole	Robertson	Other
MONTGOMERY	15,327	10,304	2,343	2,083	597	Bush	67.2%	15.3%	13.6%	3.9%
MORGAN	5,149	2,619	1,283	909	338	Bush	50.9%	24.9%	17.7%	6.6%
PERRY	250	203	26	12	9	Bush	81.2%	10.4%	4.8%	3.6%
PICKENS	858	520	135	190	13	Bush	60.6%	15.7%	22.1%	1.5%
PIKE	230	114	4	75	37	Bush	49.6%	1.7%	32.6%	16.1%
RANDOLPH	688	452	116	96	24	Bush	65.7%	16.9%	14.0%	3.5%
RUSSELL	1,490	920	199	309	62	Bush	61.7%	13.4%	20.7%	4.2%
ST. CLAIR	2,356	1,649	336	254	117	Bush	70.0%	14.3%	10.8%	5.0%
SHELBY	10,114	6,439	1,674	1,304	697	Bush	63.7%	16.6%	12.9%	6.9%
SUMTER	91	73	9	6	3	Bush	80.2%	9.9%	6.6%	3.3%
TALLADEGA	2,374	1,497	397	349	131	Bush	63.1%	16.7%	14.7%	5.5%
TALLAPOOSA	1,026	665	113	207	41	Bush	64.8%	11.0%	20.2%	4.0%
TUSCALOOSA	6,586	3,627	1,381	1,278	300	Bush	55.1%	21.0%	19.4%	4.6%
WALKER	1,494	1,158	139	149	48	Bush	77.5%	9.3%	10.0%	3.2%
WASHINGTON	361	248	44	58	11	Bush	68.7%	12.2%	16.1%	3.0%
WILCOX	307	239	41	19	8	Bush	77.9%	13.4%	6.2%	2.6%
WINSTON	1,785	1,246	336	129	74	Bush	69.8%	18.8%	7.2%	4.1%
TOTAL	212,808	137,113	34,777	29,652	11,266	Bush	64.4%	16.3%	13.9%	5.3%
Published Totals	213,561	137,807	34,733	29,772	11,249	Bush	64.5%	16.3%	13.9%	5.3%

Note: There are at least two sets of returns for the 1988 Alabama Republican primary, with the major discrepancy in Marengo County. The set used here gives Robertson 360 votes; the other set lists his total as 36.

ALABAMA DEMOCRATIC

1992

County	Total Vote	Clinton	Uncommitted	Other	Winner	Percentage of Total Vote Clinton	Uncommitted	Other
AUTAUGA	3,249	1,938	501	810	Clinton	59.6%	15.4%	24.9%
BALDWIN	3,334	2,076	541	717	Clinton	62.3%	16.2%	21.5%
BARBOUR	2,623	1,668	425	530	Clinton	63.6%	16.2%	20.2%
BIBB	3,037	1,935	756	346	Clinton	63.7%	24.9%	11.4%
BLOUNT	3,410	2,313	745	352	Clinton	67.8%	21.8%	10.3%
BULLOCK	1,888	1,454	118	316	Clinton	77.0%	6.3%	16.7%
BUTLER	2,421	1,730	213	478	Clinton	71.5%	8.8%	19.7%
CALHOUN	6,102	4,291	995	816	Clinton	70.3%	16.3%	13.4%
CHAMBERS	3,507	2,419	752	336	Clinton	69.0%	21.4%	9.6%
CHEROKEE	2,314	1,596	429	289	Clinton	69.0%	18.5%	12.5%
CHILTON	5,826	3,945	1,365	516	Clinton	67.7%	23.4%	8.9%
CHOCTAW	3,825	2,884	579	362	Clinton	75.4%	15.1%	9.5%
CLARKE	2,845	1,931	411	503	Clinton	67.9%	14.4%	17.7%
CLAY	1,932	1,238	266	428	Clinton	64.1%	13.8%	22.2%
CLEBURNE	2,107	1,392	459	256	Clinton	66.1%	21.8%	12.1%
COFFEE	3,562	2,562	433	567	Clinton	71.9%	12.2%	15.9%
COLBERT	10,459	7,012	2,525	922	Clinton	67.0%	24.1%	8.8%
CONECUH	1,671	1,252	89	330	Clinton	74.9%	5.3%	19.7%
COOSA	1,187	839	237	111	Clinton	70.7%	20.0%	9.4%
COVINGTON	3,721	2,630	74	1,017	Clinton	70.7%	2.0%	27.3%

ALABAMA DEMOCRATIC

1992

County	Total Vote	Clinton	Uncommitted	Other	Winner	Percentage of Total Vote: Clinton	Uncommitted	Other
CRENSHAW	1,012	751	109	152	Clinton	74.2%	10.8%	15.0%
CULLMAN	9,113	5,610	2,543	960	Clinton	61.6%	27.9%	10.5%
DALE	3,275	2,105	570	600	Clinton	64.3%	17.4%	18.3%
DALLAS	7,073	5,217	896	960	Clinton	73.8%	12.7%	13.6%
DE KALB	4,291	3,013	917	361	Clinton	70.2%	21.4%	8.4%
ELMORE	3,457	2,049	561	847	Clinton	59.3%	16.2%	24.5%
ESCAMBIA	3,227	2,008	581	638	Clinton	62.2%	18.0%	19.8%
ETOWAH	10,812	7,909	2,027	876	Clinton	73.2%	18.7%	8.1%
FAYETTE	3,705	2,328	1,002	375	Clinton	62.8%	27.0%	10.1%
FRANKLIN	4,946	3,639	882	425	Clinton	73.6%	17.8%	8.6%
GENEVA	2,825	1,881	429	515	Clinton	66.6%	15.2%	18.2%
GREENE	3,769	3,214	277	278	Clinton	85.3%	7.3%	7.4%
HALE	1,830	1,361	226	243	Clinton	74.4%	12.3%	13.3%
HENRY	2,583	1,652	481	450	Clinton	64.0%	18.6%	17.4%
HOUSTON	8,292	4,595	2,471	1,226	Clinton	55.4%	29.8%	14.8%
JACKSON	4,974	3,743	701	530	Clinton	75.3%	14.1%	10.7%
JEFFERSON	94,673	70,779	16,364	7,530	Clinton	74.8%	17.3%	8.0%
LAMAR	3,649	2,256	1,027	366	Clinton	61.8%	28.1%	10.0%
LAUDERDALE	14,970	9,509	4,121	1,340	Clinton	63.5%	27.5%	9.0%
LAWRENCE	2,049	1,637	154	258	Clinton	79.9%	7.5%	12.6%
LEE	4,207	2,685	618	904	Clinton	63.8%	14.7%	21.5%
LIMESTONE	6,457	3,832	1,947	678	Clinton	59.3%	30.2%	10.5%
LOWNDES	2,013	1,551	131	331	Clinton	77.0%	6.5%	16.4%
MACON	2,630	2,035	107	488	Clinton	77.4%	4.1%	18.6%
MADISON	25,083	13,979	8,198	2,906	Clinton	55.7%	32.7%	11.6%
MARENGO	3,559	2,624	445	490	Clinton	73.7%	12.5%	13.8%
MARION	4,942	3,418	1,137	387	Clinton	69.2%	23.0%	7.8%
MARSHALL	3,879	2,288	871	720	Clinton	59.0%	22.5%	18.6%
MOBILE	25,050	18,612	3,571	2,867	Clinton	74.3%	14.3%	11.4%
MONROE	2,123	1,513	186	424	Clinton	71.3%	8.8%	20.0%
MONTGOMERY	20,661	13,509	4,095	3,057	Clinton	65.4%	19.8%	14.8%
MORGAN	11,898	6,682	3,758	1,458	Clinton	56.2%	31.6%	12.3%
PERRY	2,883	2,339	237	307	Clinton	81.1%	8.2%	10.6%
PICKENS	2,215	1,521	416	278	Clinton	68.7%	18.8%	12.6%
PIKE	2,338	1,676	241	421	Clinton	71.7%	10.3%	18.0%
RANDOLPH	2,400	1,596	351	453	Clinton	66.5%	14.6%	18.9%
RUSSELL	3,249	2,403	371	475	Clinton	74.0%	11.4%	14.6%
ST. CLAIR	3,588	2,332	927	329	Clinton	65.0%	25.8%	9.2%
SHELBY	4,310	2,903	1,010	397	Clinton	67.4%	23.4%	9.2%
SUMTER	4,514	3,440	710	364	Clinton	76.2%	15.7%	8.1%
TALLADEGA	4,910	3,179	795	936	Clinton	64.7%	16.2%	19.1%
TALLAPOOSA	2,101	1,482	231	388	Clinton	70.5%	11.0%	18.5%
TUSCALOOSA	21,774	12,705	6,815	2,254	Clinton	58.3%	31.3%	10.4%
WALKER	14,824	9,873	3,742	1,209	Clinton	66.6%	25.2%	8.2%
WASHINGTON	5,149	3,567	986	596	Clinton	69.3%	19.1%	11.6%
WILCOX	2,546	2,107	228	211	Clinton	82.8%	9.0%	8.3%
WINSTON	2,051	1,409	487	155	Clinton	68.7%	23.7%	7.6%
TOTAL	450,899	307,621	90,863	52,415	Clinton	68.2%	20.2%	11.6%

ALABAMA REPUBLICAN

1992

County	Total Vote	Buchanan	Bush	Uncommitted	Winner	Percentage of Total Vote Buchanan	Bush	Uncom.
AUTAUGA	1,243	148	910	185	Bush	11.9%	73.2%	14.9%
BALDWIN	7,888	763	5,470	1,655	Bush	9.7%	69.3%	21.0%
BARBOUR	139	25	92	22	Bush	18.0%	66.2%	15.8%
BIBB	304	23	251	30	Bush	7.6%	82.6%	9.9%
BLOUNT	1,363	103	1,037	223	Bush	7.6%	76.1%	16.4%
BULLOCK	35	2	27	6	Bush	5.7%	77.1%	17.1%
BUTLER	182	21	145	16	Bush	11.5%	79.7%	8.8%
CALHOUN	2,461	205	1,881	375	Bush	8.3%	76.4%	15.2%
CHAMBERS	586	48	461	77	Bush	8.2%	78.7%	13.1%
CHEROKEE	106	11	82	13	Bush	10.4%	77.4%	12.3%
CHILTON	1,484	67	1,149	268	Bush	4.5%	77.4%	18.1%
CHOCTAW	62	5	53	4	Bush	8.1%	85.5%	6.5%
CLARKE	117	15	92	10	Bush	12.8%	78.6%	8.5%
CLAY	60	5	55		Bush	8.3%	91.7%	
CLEBURNE	72	11	57	4	Bush	15.3%	79.2%	5.6%
COFFEE	1,518	146	1,138	234	Bush	9.6%	75.0%	15.4%
COLBERT	211	19	167	25	Bush	9.0%	79.1%	11.8%
CONECUH	95	15	77	3	Bush	15.8%	81.1%	3.2%
COOSA	239	9	188	42	Bush	3.8%	78.7%	17.6%
COVINGTON	233	24	208	1	Bush	10.3%	89.3%	0.4%
CRENSHAW	160	12	143	5	Bush	7.5%	89.4%	3.1%
CULLMAN	1,286	81	999	206	Bush	6.3%	77.7%	16.0%
DALE	1,103	124	979		Bush	11.2%	88.8%	
DALLAS	303	36	240	27	Bush	11.9%	79.2%	8.9%
DE KALB	517	25	427	65	Bush	4.8%	82.6%	12.6%
ELMORE	1,642	185	1,210	247	Bush	11.3%	73.7%	15.0%
ESCAMBIA	99	8	74	17	Bush	8.1%	74.7%	17.2%
ETOWAH	2,346	178	1,787	381	Bush	7.6%	76.2%	16.2%
FAYETTE	202	12	168	22	Bush	5.9%	83.2%	10.9%
FRANKLIN	103	12	76	15	Bush	11.7%	73.8%	14.6%
GENEVA	438	35	343	60	Bush	8.0%	78.3%	13.7%
GREENE	12	3	8	1	Bush	25.0%	66.7%	8.3%
HALE	67	5	52	10	Bush	7.5%	77.6%	14.9%
HENRY	155	15	112	28	Bush	9.7%	72.3%	18.1%
HOUSTON	2,965	188	2,273	504	Bush	6.3%	76.7%	17.0%
JACKSON	125	13	90	22	Bush	10.4%	72.0%	17.6%
JEFFERSON	71,481	4,579	53,670	13,232	Bush	6.4%	75.1%	18.5%
LAMAR	21	2	16	3	Bush	9.5%	76.2%	14.3%
LAUDERDALE	540	71	394	75	Bush	13.1%	73.0%	13.9%
LAWRENCE	122	20	89	13	Bush	16.4%	73.0%	10.7%
LEE	1,686	208	1,233	245	Bush	12.3%	73.1%	14.5%
LIMESTONE	586	76	381	129	Bush	13.0%	65.0%	22.0%
LOWNDES	90	7	75	8	Bush	7.8%	83.3%	8.9%
MACON	52	2	47	3	Bush	3.8%	90.4%	5.8%
MADISON	8,643	872	5,572	2,199	Bush	10.1%	64.5%	25.4%
MARENGO	129	14	92	23	Bush	10.9%	71.3%	17.8%
MARION	279	19	222	38	Bush	6.8%	79.6%	13.6%
MARSHALL	607	76	426	105	Bush	12.5%	70.2%	17.3%
MOBILE	18,529	1,517	14,257	2,755	Bush	8.2%	76.9%	14.9%
MONROE	478	24	420	34	Bush	5.0%	87.9%	7.1%

ALABAMA REPUBLICAN

1992

County	Total Vote	Buchanan	Bush	Uncommitted	Winner	Percentage of Total Vote Buchanan	Bush	Uncom.
MONTGOMERY	4,913	402	3,826	685	Bush	8.2%	77.9%	13.9%
MORGAN	2,267	213	1,642	412	Bush	9.4%	72.4%	18.2%
PERRY	12	2	9	1	Bush	16.7%	75.0%	8.3%
PICKENS	623	33	507	83	Bush	5.3%	81.4%	13.3%
PIKE	506	60	401	45	Bush	11.9%	79.2%	8.9%
RANDOLPH	141	16	107	18	Bush	11.3%	75.9%	12.8%
RUSSELL	374	51	281	42	Bush	13.6%	75.1%	11.2%
ST. CLAIR	1,838	133	1,358	347	Bush	7.2%	73.9%	18.9%
SHELBY	13,994	956	9,713	3,325	Bush	6.8%	69.4%	23.8%
SUMTER	20	1	17	2	Bush	5.0%	85.0%	10.0%
TALLADEGA	1,277	155	954	168	Bush	12.1%	74.7%	13.2%
TALLAPOOSA	601	71	462	68	Bush	11.8%	76.9%	11.3%
TUSCALOOSA	2,359	203	1,691	465	Bush	8.6%	71.7%	19.7%
WALKER	671	44	534	93	Bush	6.6%	79.6%	13.9%
WASHINGTON	21	1	18	2	Bush	4.8%	85.7%	9.5%
WILCOX	45		45		Bush		100.0%	
WINSTON	2,295	163	1,723	409	Bush	7.1%	75.1%	17.8%
TOTAL	165,121	12,588	122,703	29,830	Bush	7.6%	74.3%	18.1%

ALABAMA DEMOCRATIC

1996

County	Total Vote	Clinton	LaRouche	Uncommitted	Winner	Percentage of Total Vote Clinton	LaRouche	Uncom.
AUTAUGA	1,837	1,740	97		Clinton	94.7%	5.3%	
BALDWIN	3,018	2,716	74	228	Clinton	90.0%	2.5%	7.6%
BARBOUR	2,561	2,204	126	231	Clinton	86.1%	4.9%	9.0%
BIBB	2,786	1,840	163	783	Clinton	66.0%	5.9%	28.1%
BLOUNT	3,063	2,282	176	605	Clinton	74.5%	5.7%	19.8%
BULLOCK	2,496	2,211	92	193	Clinton	88.6%	3.7%	7.7%
BUTLER	3,517	2,503	207	807	Clinton	71.2%	5.9%	22.9%
CALHOUN	6,630	5,621	352	657	Clinton	84.8%	5.3%	9.9%
CHAMBERS	4,312	3,038	254	1,020	Clinton	70.5%	5.9%	23.7%
CHEROKEE	3,072	2,435	173	464	Clinton	79.3%	5.6%	15.1%
CHILTON	4,000	3,041	195	764	Clinton	76.0%	4.9%	19.1%
CHOCTAW	1,375	1,200	32	143	Clinton	87.3%	2.3%	10.4%
CLARKE	5,029	3,058	1,092	879	Clinton	60.8%	21.7%	17.5%
CLAY	2,751	1,724	202	825	Clinton	62.7%	7.3%	30.0%
CLEBURNE	2,242	1,419	215	608	Clinton	63.3%	9.6%	27.1%
COFFEE	1,548	1,413	46	89	Clinton	91.3%	3.0%	5.7%
COLBERT	6,680	5,001	309	1,370	Clinton	74.9%	4.6%	20.5%
CONECUH	2,865	2,146	127	592	Clinton	74.9%	4.4%	20.7%
COOSA	1,968	1,457	108	403	Clinton	74.0%	5.5%	20.5%
COVINGTON	2,989	2,181	258	550	Clinton	73.0%	8.6%	18.4%

ALABAMA DEMOCRATIC

1996

County	Total Vote	Clinton	LaRouche	Uncommitted	Winner	Percentage of Total Vote Clinton	LaRouche	Uncom.
CRENSHAW	679	624	16	39	Clinton	91.9%	2.4%	5.7%
CULLMAN	6,627	4,786	313	1,528	Clinton	72.2%	4.7%	23.1%
DALE	2,090	1,534	95	461	Clinton	73.4%	4.5%	22.1%
DALLAS	6,339	5,018	275	1,046	Clinton	79.2%	4.3%	16.5%
DE KALB	5,083	3,616	366	1,101	Clinton	71.1%	7.2%	21.7%
ELMORE	3,185	2,289	174	722	Clinton	71.9%	5.5%	22.7%
ESCAMBIA	2,107	1,737	144	226	Clinton	82.4%	6.8%	10.7%
ETOWAH	6,220	5,243	165	812	Clinton	84.3%	2.7%	13.1%
FAYETTE	3,243	2,137	188	918	Clinton	65.9%	5.8%	28.3%
FRANKLIN	5,845	3,954	379	1,512	Clinton	67.6%	6.5%	25.9%
GENEVA	1,362	1,048	110	204	Clinton	76.9%	8.1%	15.0%
GREENE	2,747	2,496	64	187	Clinton	90.9%	2.3%	6.8%
HALE	1,760	1,505	61	194	Clinton	85.5%	3.5%	11.0%
HENRY	2,174	1,589	130	455	Clinton	73.1%	6.0%	20.9%
HOUSTON	2,779	2,198	123	458	Clinton	79.1%	4.4%	16.5%
JACKSON	5,749	4,586	371	792	Clinton	79.8%	6.5%	13.8%
JEFFERSON	33,214	31,086	334	1,794	Clinton	93.6%	1.0%	5.4%
LAMAR	2,921	1,911	162	848	Clinton	65.4%	5.5%	29.0%
LAUDERDALE	9,073	6,744	412	1,917	Clinton	74.3%	4.5%	21.1%
LAWRENCE	5,268	3,671	340	1,257	Clinton	69.7%	6.5%	23.9%
LEE	5,258	4,153	196	909	Clinton	79.0%	3.7%	17.3%
LIMESTONE	4,181	3,027	188	966	Clinton	72.4%	4.5%	23.1%
LOWNDES	1,748	1,695	28	25	Clinton	97.0%	1.6%	1.4%
MACON	3,847	3,702	76	69	Clinton	96.2%	2.0%	1.8%
MADISON	11,907	10,430	242	1,235	Clinton	87.6%	2.0%	10.4%
MARENGO	2,301	2,136	69	96	Clinton	92.8%	3.0%	4.2%
MARION	2,554	1,945	97	512	Clinton	76.2%	3.8%	20.0%
MARSHALL	2,994	2,615	137	242	Clinton	87.3%	4.6%	8.1%
MOBILE	14,575	13,612	218	745	Clinton	93.4%	1.5%	5.1%
MONROE	2,373	1,827	93	453	Clinton	77.0%	3.9%	19.1%
MONTGOMERY	7,689	7,100	145	444	Clinton	92.3%	1.9%	5.8%
MORGAN	7,046	5,366	331	1,349	Clinton	76.2%	4.7%	19.1%
PERRY	2,909	2,696	85	128	Clinton	92.7%	2.9%	4.4%
PICKENS	2,148	1,507	111	530	Clinton	70.2%	5.2%	24.7%
PIKE	2,807	2,149	135	523	Clinton	76.6%	4.8%	18.6%
RANDOLPH	4,037	2,470	268	1,299	Clinton	61.2%	6.6%	32.2%
RUSSELL	4,545	3,730	182	633	Clinton	82.1%	4.0%	13.9%
ST. CLAIR	1,856	1,584	47	225	Clinton	85.3%	2.5%	12.1%
SHELBY	5,482	4,591	91	800	Clinton	83.7%	1.7%	14.6%
SUMTER	4,322	3,700	112	510	Clinton	85.6%	2.6%	11.8%
TALLADEGA	3,848	3,263	103	482	Clinton	84.8%	2.7%	12.5%
TALLAPOOSA	3,771	2,723	238	810	Clinton	72.2%	6.3%	21.5%
TUSCALOOSA	8,050	7,006	169	875	Clinton	87.0%	2.1%	10.9%
WALKER	11,621	8,185	511	2,925	Clinton	70.4%	4.4%	25.2%
WASHINGTON	4,722	3,269	253	1,200	Clinton	69.2%	5.4%	25.4%
WILCOX	1,412	1,372	18	22	Clinton	97.2%	1.3%	1.6%
WINSTON	831	733	23	75	Clinton	88.2%	2.8%	9.0%
TOTAL	302,038	243,588	12,686	45,764	Clinton	80.6%	4.2%	15.2%

ALABAMA REPUBLICAN

1996

County	Total Vote	Buchanan	Dole	Other	Winner	Percentage of Total Vote Buchanan	Dole	Other
AUTAUGA	3,130	575	2,287	268	Dole	18.4%	73.1%	8.6%
BALDWIN	11,602	1,737	8,838	1,027	Dole	15.0%	76.2%	8.9%
BARBOUR	256	55	193	8	Dole	21.5%	75.4%	3.1%
BIBB	532	125	373	34	Dole	23.5%	70.1%	6.4%
BLOUNT	1,985	543	1,289	153	Dole	27.4%	64.9%	7.7%
BULLOCK	24	5	14	5	Dole	20.8%	58.3%	20.8%
BUTLER	394	50	318	26	Dole	12.7%	80.7%	6.6%
CALHOUN	3,947	785	2,918	244	Dole	19.9%	73.9%	6.2%
CHAMBERS	629	116	463	50	Dole	18.4%	73.6%	7.9%
CHEROKEE	142	22	106	14	Dole	15.5%	74.6%	9.9%
CHILTON	2,262	440	1,699	123	Dole	19.5%	75.1%	5.4%
CHOCTAW	495	63	426	6	Dole	12.7%	86.1%	1.2%
CLARKE	505	84	398	23	Dole	16.6%	78.8%	4.6%
CLAY	501	100	360	41	Dole	20.0%	71.9%	8.2%
CLEBURNE	137	25	103	9	Dole	18.2%	75.2%	6.6%
COFFEE	961	142	743	76	Dole	14.8%	77.3%	7.9%
COLBERT	1,263	304	844	115	Dole	24.1%	66.8%	9.1%
CONECUH	97	21	70	6	Dole	21.6%	72.2%	6.2%
COOSA	260	42	198	20	Dole	16.2%	76.2%	7.7%
COVINGTON	804	157	581	66	Dole	19.5%	72.3%	8.2%
CRENSHAW	290	38	232	20	Dole	13.1%	80.0%	6.9%
CULLMAN	4,096	859	2,897	340	Dole	21.0%	70.7%	8.3%
DALE	2,036	344	1,484	208	Dole	16.9%	72.9%	10.2%
DALLAS	592	83	477	32	Dole	14.0%	80.6%	5.4%
DE KALB	1,413	188	1,143	82	Dole	13.3%	80.9%	5.8%
ELMORE	3,787	774	2,720	293	Dole	20.4%	71.8%	7.7%
ESCAMBIA	606	121	443	42	Dole	20.0%	73.1%	6.9%
ETOWAH	4,033	662	3,131	240	Dole	16.4%	77.6%	6.0%
FAYETTE	307	57	228	22	Dole	18.6%	74.3%	7.2%
FRANKLIN	299	53	228	18	Dole	17.7%	76.3%	6.0%
GENEVA	862	246	558	58	Dole	28.5%	64.7%	6.7%
GREENE	21	9	11	1	Dole	42.9%	52.4%	4.8%
HALE	311	45	252	14	Dole	14.5%	81.0%	4.5%
HENRY	288	53	216	19	Dole	18.4%	75.0%	6.6%
HOUSTON	3,251	558	2,494	199	Dole	17.2%	76.7%	6.1%
JACKSON	389	72	282	35	Dole	18.5%	72.5%	9.0%
JEFFERSON	41,027	6,313	31,959	2,755	Dole	15.4%	77.9%	6.7%
LAMAR	174	45	121	8	Dole	25.9%	69.5%	4.6%
LAUDERDALE	2,229	454	1,608	167	Dole	20.4%	72.1%	7.5%
LAWRENCE	283	55	213	15	Dole	19.4%	75.3%	5.3%
LEE	3,892	589	2,865	438	Dole	15.1%	73.6%	11.3%
LIMESTONE	2,443	369	1,783	291	Dole	15.1%	73.0%	11.9%
LOWNDES	297	46	233	18	Dole	15.5%	78.5%	6.1%
MACON	111	18	83	10	Dole	16.2%	74.8%	9.0%
MADISON	22,427	2,352	16,640	3,435	Dole	10.5%	74.2%	15.3%
MARENGO	831	131	660	40	Dole	15.8%	79.4%	4.8%
MARION	786	138	594	54	Dole	17.6%	75.6%	6.9%
MARSHALL	2,590	404	2,013	173	Dole	15.6%	77.7%	6.7%
MOBILE	21,381	3,060	16,917	1,404	Dole	14.3%	79.1%	6.6%
MONROE	617	93	501	23	Dole	15.1%	81.2%	3.7%

ALABAMA REPUBLICAN

1996

County	Total Vote	Buchanan	Dole	Other	Winner	Percentage of Total Vote Buchanan	Dole	Other
MONTGOMERY	8,643	1,474	6,664	505	Dole	17.1%	77.1%	5.8%
MORGAN	5,724	725	4,388	611	Dole	12.7%	76.7%	10.7%
PERRY	78	15	50	13	Dole	19.2%	64.1%	16.7%
PICKENS	314	44	245	25	Dole	14.0%	78.0%	8.0%
PIKE	1,313	188	1,033	92	Dole	14.3%	78.7%	7.0%
RANDOLPH	276	65	188	23	Dole	23.6%	68.1%	8.3%
RUSSELL	492	62	403	27	Dole	12.6%	81.9%	5.5%
ST. CLAIR	3,431	681	2,552	198	Dole	19.8%	74.4%	5.8%
SHELBY	21,607	3,125	16,108	2,374	Dole	14.5%	74.5%	11.0%
SUMTER	56	5	47	4	Dole	8.9%	83.9%	7.1%
TALLADEGA	3,133	584	2,322	227	Dole	18.6%	74.1%	7.2%
TALLAPOOSA	1,406	269	1,039	98	Dole	19.1%	73.9%	7.0%
TUSCALOOSA	6,765	1,170	4,999	596	Dole	17.3%	73.9%	8.8%
WALKER	1,387	302	991	94	Dole	21.8%	71.4%	6.8%
WASHINGTON	211	53	149	9	Dole	25.1%	70.6%	4.3%
WILCOX	543	56	468	19	Dole	10.3%	86.2%	3.5%
WINSTON	4,959	971	3,244	744	Dole	19.6%	65.4%	15.0%
TOTAL	211,933	33,409	160,097	18,427	Dole	15.8%	75.5%	8.7%

ALASKA

Alaska is one of the few states in the country that has never held a presidential primary, although it dabbled with one during its territorial days in 1956 that produced victories for the eventual nominees, Adlai Stevenson on the Democratic side and President Dwight Eisenhower on the Republican.

While Alaska has not held a presidential primary since then, the state's Republicans have sought ways to offset the state's small delegate prize and remote location. In 1996, the answer was late January precinct caucuses accompanied by a statewide straw poll. The timing made Alaska the first event of the nominating season, ahead of both Iowa and New Hampshire, and it attracted more than 9,000 caucus participants, far more than the usual number.

The two top vote-getters in Alaska, Pat Buchanan, with 33 percent, and Steve Forbes, with 31 percent, both made campaign forays to the nation's frigid northern frontier. Front-runner, Bob Dole, though, did not, and finished third in the straw vote with 17 percent, in spite of endorsements from much of the state Republican hierarchy.

The ability to surprise has always been a part of the Alaska delegate-selection process. In 1988, it was the only state in the country to buck the political mainstream and give first-round caucus victories to the two preachers who were running, Democrat Jesse Jackson and Republican Pat Robertson.

Robertson's success reflected the rise of social conservatives within the Alaska GOP in recent years. But it has not always been that way. In 1964, Alaska Republicans broke with the rest of the West to give most of its delegates to Pennsylvania Gov. William Scranton, rather than Arizona's Barry Goldwater. And in 1976, Alaska had one of the few Republican delegations from the West that supported President Gerald Ford, rather than Ronald Reagan.

Meanwhile, Alaska Democrats have a penchant for taking their time in deciding whom to support. In much of the last quarter century, the winner of the Democratic mass meetings has been "uncommitted."

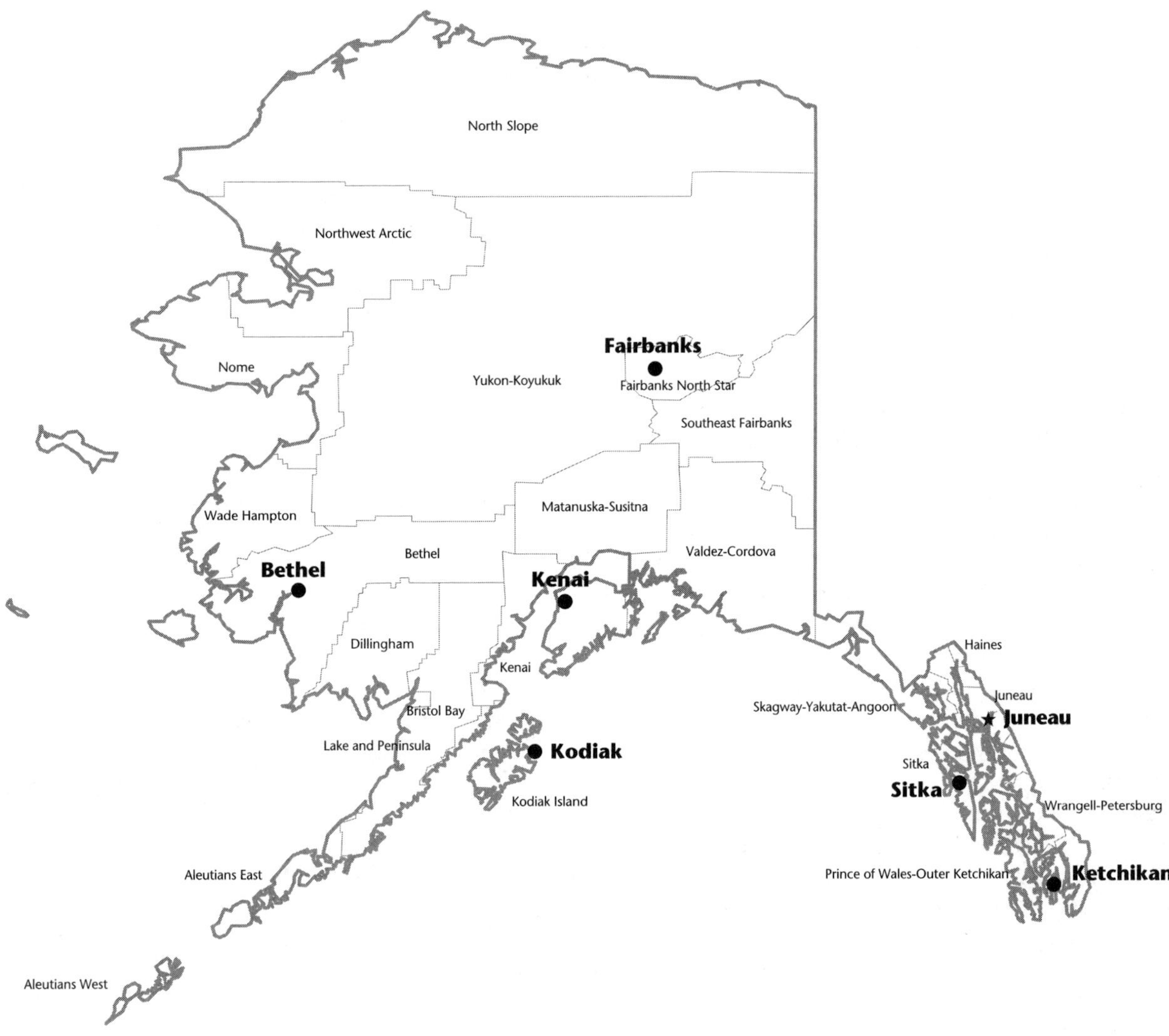
North Slope
Northwest Arctic
Fairbanks
Nome
Yukon-Koyukuk
Fairbanks North Star
Southeast Fairbanks
Matanuska-Susitna
Wade Hampton
Bethel
Bethel
Valdez-Cordova
Kenai
Dillingham
Kenai
Haines
Skagway-Yakutat-Angoon
Juneau
Juneau
Bristol Bay
Lake and Peninsula
Kodiak
Sitka
Sitka
Kodiak Island
Wrangell-Petersburg
Aleutians East
Prince of Wales-Outer Ketchikan
Ketchikan
Aleutians West
Adak Station

ARIZONA

Every dozen years since 1964, Arizona has fielded a presidential candidate—Republican Barry Goldwater in 1964, Democrat Morris Udall in 1976, Democrat Bruce Babbitt in 1988 and Republican John McCain in 2000.

What Arizona did not have until 1996 was a presidential primary. And that it has one at all is due in no small part to McCain, who lobbied hard for the creation of the February event. Travelling in Asia when the legislation was being debated, he reportedly made a call from Hanoi to a wavering state legislator.

That first primary did not go as McCain had hoped. As national chairman of Texas senator Phil Gramm's presidential campaign, McCain saw his candidate drop out of the race before Arizona even voted. But the primary proved a success—attracting candidates to Arizona and voters to the polls.

Steve Forbes mounted a lavish media campaign that accented his flat tax proposal and outsider image. Pat Buchanan and Bob Dole seemed at times to engage in a battle of photo opportunities. Dole was photographed visiting Goldwater, his most famous Arizona supporter. Buchanan cultivated a frontier image, culminating with a visit to the O.K. Corral in Tombstone where he dressed in cowboy garb.

Buchanan came into Arizona fresh from an upset victory over Dole in New Hampshire. And the state's decision to save money by opening barely one-quarter of the usual polling places seemed to favor Buchanan and his energetic cadre of supporters.

Yet the turnout was larger than expected. More Republican ballots were cast in Maricopa County (Phoenix) alone (roughly 215,000) than had been cast the previous week in the entire state of New Hampshire. Maricopa was one of only two counties that Forbes won statewide, but he carried it decisively enough to win the state by more than 10,000 votes over Dole.

Buchanan finished a close third by winning much of rural Arizona, including the two major Native American counties, Apache and Navajo. But his tough stance on immigration did not serve him well in voting along the Mexican border. Dole carried three of the four counties that border Mexico, including populous Pima (Tucson).

According to exit polling, Dole had the edge among Arizona's large contingent of voters age 60 and older (which cast more than four out of every ten GOP primary ballots). Buchanan showed a narrow lead among middle-aged voters. But neither could overcome the consistency of Forbes, who took about one-third of the Arizona primary ballots among all age groups and both sexes. Yet for Forbes, it was his second and last victory of the 1996 primary season.

Arizona Democrats have expressed interest in joining the Republicans on their February primary date. But with national Democratic rules preventing states from establishing primaries so early, they have had to content themselves with a small, party-run preference vote at a limited number of polling places around the state.

Turnout for the Democratic event has been comparatively light. The last competitive contest in 1992 drew barely 35,000 voters—slightly more than 10 percent of the turnout for the Republican presidential primary in 1996.

Arizona's sizable Hispanic and Native American presence has given the Democratic voting a liberal hue, with the result that three of the four winners from 1980 to 1992 were Massachusetts Democrats.

Many of the Southern Democrats who have fared well nationally have had less success in Arizona. Bill Clinton lost the party-run primary to Paul Tsongas in 1992 by 5 percentage points. Meanwhile, Al Gore drew a total of 5 percent of the vote in 1988, hitting double digits only in a few rural counties.

Recent Arizona Primary Results

Arizona held its first presidential primary in 1996.

	DEMOCRATS			REPUBLICANS		
Year	Turnout	Candidates	%	Turnout	Candidates	%
1996 (Feb. 27)	—	NO PRIMARY		347,482	STEVE FORBES	33
					Bob Dole	30
					Pat Buchanan	28

Note: All candidates are listed that drew at least 10 percent of their party's primary vote. The names of winning candidates are capitalized.

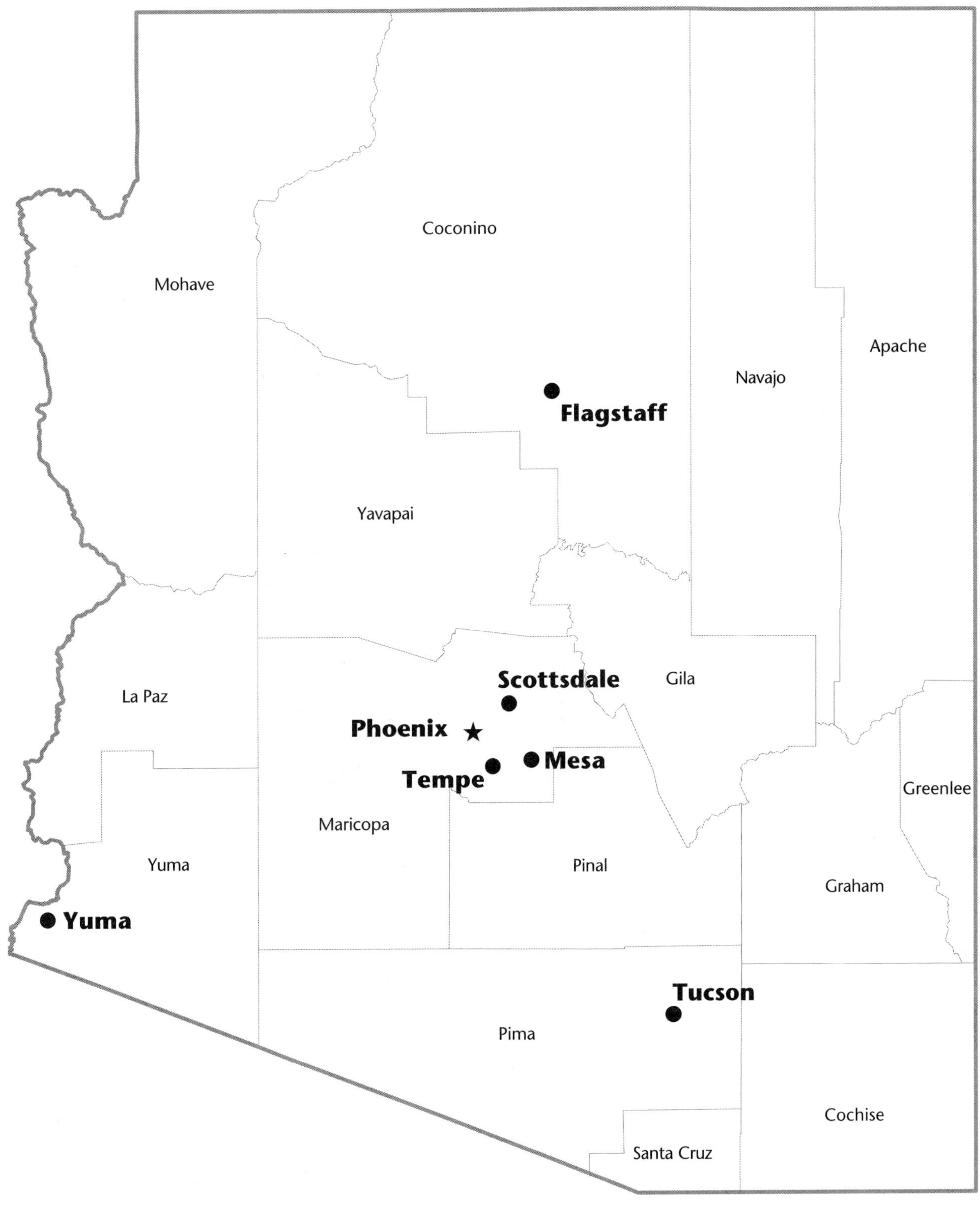
Coconino
Mohave
Apache
Navajo
Flagstaff
Yavapai
Scottsdale
Gila
La Paz
Phoenix
Mesa
Tempe
Greenlee
Maricopa
Yuma
Pinal
Graham
Yuma
Tucson
Pima
Cochise
Santa Cruz

ARIZONA REPUBLICAN

1996

County	Total Vote	Buchanan	Dole	Forbes	Other	Winner	Percentage of Total Vote			
							Buchanan	Dole	Forbes	Other
APACHE	1,673	648	468	324	233	Buchanan	38.7%	28.0%	19.4%	13.9%
COCHISE	7,043	2,098	2,387	1,712	846	Dole	29.8%	33.9%	24.3%	12.0%
COCONINO	6,049	1,665	1,810	1,797	777	Dole	27.5%	29.9%	29.7%	12.8%
GILA	3,345	1,295	693	1,042	315	Buchanan	38.7%	20.7%	31.2%	9.4%
GRAHAM	1,841	881	391	439	130	Buchanan	47.9%	21.2%	23.8%	7.1%
GREENLEE	327	125	79	89	34	Buchanan	38.2%	24.2%	27.2%	10.4%
LA PAZ	1,011	378	262	289	82	Buchanan	37.4%	25.9%	28.6%	8.1%
MARICOPA	215,246	58,562	57,725	79,776	19,183	Forbes	27.2%	26.8%	37.1%	8.9%
MOHAVE	11,752	4,554	2,701	3,505	992	Buchanan	38.8%	23.0%	29.8%	8.4%
NAVAJO	4,320	1,775	1,036	1,093	416	Buchanan	41.1%	24.0%	25.3%	9.6%
PIMA	62,178	12,745	26,681	16,064	6,688	Dole	20.5%	42.9%	25.8%	10.8%
PINAL	6,952	2,065	1,949	2,321	617	Forbes	29.7%	28.0%	33.4%	8.9%
SANTA CRUZ	1,070	228	425	299	118	Dole	21.3%	39.7%	27.9%	11.0%
YAVAPAI	18,855	6,353	4,486	6,316	1,700	Buchanan	33.7%	23.8%	33.5%	9.0%
YUMA	5,820	2,370	1,887	896	667	Buchanan	40.7%	32.4%	15.4%	11.5%
TOTAL	347,482	95,742	102,980	115,962	32,798	Forbes	27.6%	29.6%	33.4%	9.4%

ARKANSAS

Bill Clinton may be Arkansas' most famous politician ever. But at times, the state's Democrats have given him little more than a passing grade.

Running for a fifth term as governor in 1990, Clinton was renominated with a lackluster 55 percent of the primary vote. In the state's presidential primary two years later, he took a more impressive 68 percent. Still, his home-state percentage was less than the share of the vote he won in six other primaries in 1992. And in 1996, running essentially unopposed for renomination, his 79 percent share in Arkansas was his third-lowest percentage in any Democratic primary in the country.

To know him may not have been to love him, particularly to a significant swath of Arkansas Democrats. But Clinton's presidential primary victories in the 1990s reflected the coalition he had put together to dominate the state for more than a decade. He won by large margins in the Little Rock area, the heavily black counties of rural eastern Arkansas, and rural white-majority counties such as Hempstead (Hope), where he was born.

Meanwhile, Republicans have had a slow time constructing a base in Arkansas, and the presidential primary has been of little help. Before 1996, each party conducted its own, with Republicans lacking enough workers in some counties to open more than one polling place. The frequent result: minimal interest in the GOP contest, to the point that in 1992, just one vote was cast in the Republican presidential primary in all of Lee County (it was for Pat Buchanan).

Even with the state operating the primary for the first time in 1996, more than seven times as many ballots were cast in the Democratic primary—the largest ratio of Democratic to Republican ballots in any state in the nation.

The largest concentration of GOP primary voters is in the historically Republican Ozarks in the northwest quadrant of the state. George Bush handily won the region in the party's most competitive primary in 1988. Pat Robertson showed strength in eastern and southern Arkansas, where Republican turnout was light, and his cadre of supporters, though small, was enough to carry 19 counties.

On the Democratic side that year, Al Gore won in dominating fashion, leaving little more than beachheads for Michael Dukakis, Jesse Jackson and Richard Gephardt.

Gephardt and Dukakis each won a handful of counties in northern Arkansas near the Missouri border, an area loaded with retirees. Jackson carried a cluster of counties with a significant black population, most of them hugging the west bank

Recent Arkansas Primary Results

Arkansas held its first presidential primary in 1976.

	DEMOCRATS			REPUBLICANS		
Year	Turnout	Candidates	%	Turnout	Candidates	%
1996 (May 21)	300,389	BILL CLINTON* Uncommitted	79 10	42,814	BOB DOLE Pat Buchanan	76 24
1992 (May 26)	502,617	BILL CLINTON Uncommitted Jerry Brown	68 18 11	52,141	GEORGE BUSH* Pat Buchanan	87 13
1988 (March 8)	497,544	AL GORE Michael Dukakis Jesse Jackson Richard Gephardt	37 19 17 12	68,305	GEORGE BUSH Bob Dole Pat Robertson	47 26 19
1984	—	NO PRIMARY		—	NO PRIMARY	
1980 (May 27)	448,290	JIMMY CARTER* Uncommitted Edward Kennedy	60 18 18	—	NO PRIMARY	
1976 (May 25)	501,800	JIMMY CARTER George Wallace Uncommitted	63 17 11	32,541	RONALD REAGAN Gerald Ford*	63 35

Note: All candidates are listed that drew at least 10 percent of their party's primary vote. The names of winning candidates are capitalized. An asterisk (*) indicates an incumbent president.

of the Mississippi River. Gore won the rest of the state.

No presidential primaries before or since then have been so compelling for either party. Ronald Reagan swamped President Gerald Ford in Republican voting in 1976, as Reagan did in many other parts of the South. But in 1980, Arkansas Republicans did not conduct a presidential primary at all. Instead, they positioned themselves on the calendar between Iowa and New Hampshire with a controversial caucus process that was open only to local party officials. GOP candidates that year were encouraged to fill vacant party positions with their supporters.

Former Texas Gov. John Connally made the most lavish effort, at one point hosting likely caucus participants at an Ozarks resort. But his effort did not pay off. Connally took only one delegate, a conspicuous failure in his expensive, but short-lived, presidential campaign.

ARKANSAS DEMOCRATIC

1976

County	Total Vote	Carter	Wallace	Uncommitted	Other	Winner	Percentage of Total Vote Carter	Wallace	Uncom.	Other
ARKANSAS	5,293	3,061	1,004	793	435	Carter	57.8%	19.0%	15.0%	8.2%
ASHLEY	6,944	4,259	1,771	303	611	Carter	61.3%	25.5%	4.4%	8.8%
BAXTER	5,444	3,333	1,060		1,051	Carter	61.2%	19.5%		19.3%
BENTON	5,001	3,117	517	582	785	Carter	62.3%	10.3%	11.6%	15.7%
BOONE	5,453	3,201	728	696	828	Carter	58.7%	13.4%	12.8%	15.2%
BRADLEY	3,967	2,648	947	3	369	Carter	66.8%	23.9%	0.1%	9.3%
CALHOUN	2,618	1,536	733	221	128	Carter	58.7%	28.0%	8.4%	4.9%
CARROLL	4,236	2,473	493	813	457	Carter	58.4%	11.6%	19.2%	10.8%
CHICOT	4,976	3,189	868	605	314	Carter	64.1%	17.4%	12.2%	6.3%
CLARK	7,023	4,601	990	866	566	Carter	65.5%	14.1%	12.3%	8.1%
CLAY	4,818	3,477	521	572	248	Carter	72.2%	10.8%	11.9%	5.1%
CLEBURNE	6,720	4,048	1,095	1,075	502	Carter	60.2%	16.3%	16.0%	7.5%
CLEVELAND	2,830	1,784	691	247	108	Carter	63.0%	24.4%	8.7%	3.8%
COLUMBIA	5,831	3,351	1,488	538	454	Carter	57.5%	25.5%	9.2%	7.8%
CONWAY	6,524	4,106	1,021	897	500	Carter	62.9%	15.6%	13.7%	7.7%
CRAIGHEAD	11,200	7,804	1,284	1,047	1,065	Carter	69.7%	11.5%	9.3%	9.5%
CRAWFORD	7,097	4,448	880	1,369	400	Carter	62.7%	12.4%	19.3%	5.6%
CRITTENDEN	6,493	4,592	1,294		607	Carter	70.7%	19.9%		9.3%
CROSS	4,791	3,051	882	539	319	Carter	63.7%	18.4%	11.3%	6.7%
DALLAS	3,992	2,308	867	528	289	Carter	57.8%	21.7%	13.2%	7.2%
DESHA	4,564	3,180	682	314	388	Carter	69.7%	14.9%	6.9%	8.5%
DREW	5,108	2,999	1,085	645	379	Carter	58.7%	21.2%	12.6%	7.4%
FAULKNER	12,358	8,005	1,728	1,306	1,319	Carter	64.8%	14.0%	10.6%	10.7%
FRANKLIN	4,901	3,226	796	636	243	Carter	65.8%	16.2%	13.0%	5.0%
FULTON	2,608	1,466	559	391	192	Carter	56.2%	21.4%	15.0%	7.4%
GARLAND	14,437	8,721	2,087	2,005	1,624	Carter	60.4%	14.5%	13.9%	11.2%
GRANT	3,903	2,713	926		264	Carter	69.5%	23.7%		6.8%
GREENE	7,597	5,367	855	926	449	Carter	70.6%	11.3%	12.2%	5.9%
HEMPSTEAD	6,442	4,072	1,228	696	446	Carter	63.2%	19.1%	10.8%	6.9%
HOT SPRING	7,910	4,705	1,563	1,050	592	Carter	59.5%	19.8%	13.3%	7.5%
HOWARD	4,340	3,103	869		368	Carter	71.5%	20.0%		8.5%
INDEPENDENCE	7,700	5,030	1,103	909	658	Carter	65.3%	14.3%	11.8%	8.5%
IZARD	4,128	2,459	881	435	353	Carter	59.6%	21.3%	10.5%	8.6%
JACKSON	6,162	3,958	1,119	701	384	Carter	64.2%	18.2%	11.4%	6.2%
JEFFERSON	19,631	10,993	3,184	3,406	2,048	Carter	56.0%	16.2%	17.4%	10.4%
JOHNSON	5,174	3,350	732	708	384	Carter	64.7%	14.1%	13.7%	7.4%
LAFAYETTE	3,223	1,804	764	514	141	Carter	56.0%	23.7%	15.9%	4.4%
LAWRENCE	5,672	3,745	804	790	333	Carter	66.0%	14.2%	13.9%	5.9%
LEE	4,022	2,162	984	572	304	Carter	53.8%	24.5%	14.2%	7.6%
LINCOLN	2,944	1,974	586	194	190	Carter	67.1%	19.9%	6.6%	6.5%
LITTLE RIVER	3,302	2,049	650	411	192	Carter	62.1%	19.7%	12.4%	5.8%
LOGAN	6,191	4,180	942	695	374	Carter	67.5%	15.2%	11.2%	6.0%
LONOKE	8,000	5,112	1,486	871	531	Carter	63.9%	18.6%	10.9%	6.6%
MADISON	2,197	1,572	257	204	164	Carter	71.6%	11.7%	9.3%	7.5%
MARION	3,557	1,876	566	765	350	Carter	52.7%	15.9%	21.5%	9.8%
MILLER	8,062	4,470	1,610	1,451	531	Carter	55.4%	20.0%	18.0%	6.6%
MISSISSIPPI	11,322	7,381	1,717	1,649	575	Carter	65.2%	15.2%	14.6%	5.1%
MONROE	3,589	2,233	788	379	189	Carter	62.2%	22.0%	10.6%	5.3%
MONTGOMERY	2,836	1,953	499	209	175	Carter	68.9%	17.6%	7.4%	6.2%
NEVADA	3,970	2,395	905	417	253	Carter	60.3%	22.8%	10.5%	6.4%

ARKANSAS DEMOCRATIC

1976

County	Total Vote	Carter	Wallace	Uncommitted	Other	Winner	Percentage of Total Vote Carter	Wallace	Uncom.	Other
NEWTON	1,382	1,025	161	112	84	Carter	74.2%	11.6%	8.1%	6.1%
OUACHITA	9,215	5,761	1,861	670	923	Carter	62.5%	20.2%	7.3%	10.0%
PERRY	2,511	1,666	472	205	168	Carter	66.3%	18.8%	8.2%	6.7%
PHILLIPS	7,512	5,050	998	1,008	456	Carter	67.2%	13.3%	13.4%	6.1%
PIKE	3,332	1,965	703	394	270	Carter	59.0%	21.1%	11.8%	8.1%
POINSETT	6,371	4,332	1,095	660	284	Carter	68.0%	17.2%	10.4%	4.5%
POLK	4,685	2,577	905	801	402	Carter	55.0%	19.3%	17.1%	8.6%
POPE	9,192	5,886	1,205	1,340	761	Carter	64.0%	13.1%	14.6%	8.3%
PRAIRIE	2,814	1,693	706	240	175	Carter	60.2%	25.1%	8.5%	6.2%
PULASKI	57,076	33,150	7,792	6,009	10,125	Carter	58.1%	13.7%	10.5%	17.7%
RANDOLPH	5,256	3,363	718	801	374	Carter	64.0%	13.7%	15.2%	7.1%
ST. FRANCIS	8,109	4,346	2,104	1,161	498	Carter	53.6%	25.9%	14.3%	6.1%
SALINE	13,322	8,358	2,147	1,681	1,136	Carter	62.7%	16.1%	12.6%	8.5%
SCOTT	3,703	2,810	592	19	282	Carter	75.9%	16.0%	0.5%	7.6%
SEARCY	986	754	167		65	Carter	76.5%	16.9%		6.6%
SEBASTIAN	13,840	9,163	1,502	1,976	1,199	Carter	66.2%	10.9%	14.3%	8.7%
SEVIER	4,482	2,721	686	826	249	Carter	60.7%	15.3%	18.4%	5.6%
SHARP	4,055	2,345	706	552	452	Carter	57.8%	17.4%	13.6%	11.1%
STONE	3,392	2,201	605	331	255	Carter	64.9%	17.8%	9.8%	7.5%
UNION	8,601	4,648	1,960	1,281	712	Carter	54.0%	22.8%	14.9%	8.3%
VAN BUREN	4,046	2,772	800	51	423	Carter	68.5%	19.8%	1.3%	10.5%
WASHINGTON	10,791	6,701	929	1,062	2,099	Carter	62.1%	8.6%	9.8%	19.5%
WHITE	10,869	8,141	1,694		1,034	Carter	74.9%	15.6%		9.5%
WOODRUFF	3,125	1,958	627	305	235	Carter	62.7%	20.1%	9.8%	7.5%
YELL	6,032	4,280	781	724	247	Carter	71.0%	12.9%	12.0%	4.1%
TOTAL	501,800	314,306	83,005	57,152	47,337	Carter	62.6%	16.5%	11.4%	9.4%

ARKANSAS REPUBLICAN

1976

County	Total Vote	Ford	Reagan	Uncommitted	Winner	Percentage of Total Vote Ford	Reagan	Uncom.
ARKANSAS	87	29	58		Reagan	33.3%	66.7%	
ASHLEY	58	25	32	1	Reagan	43.1%	55.2%	1.7%
BAXTER	1,678	732	946		Reagan	43.6%	56.4%	
BENTON	2,832	1,181	1,586	65	Reagan	41.7%	56.0%	2.3%
BOONE	631	249	382		Reagan	39.5%	60.5%	
BRADLEY	23	9	14		Reagan	39.1%	60.9%	
CALHOUN	16	2	13	1	Reagan	12.5%	81.3%	6.3%
CARROLL	391	138	243	10	Reagan	35.3%	62.1%	2.6%
CHICOT	4		4		Reagan		100.0%	
CLARK	89	32	57		Reagan	36.0%	64.0%	
CLAY	42	12	30		Reagan	28.6%	71.4%	
CLEBURNE	105	43	61	1	Reagan	41.0%	58.1%	1.0%
CLEVELAND	15	7	8		Reagan	46.7%	53.3%	
COLUMBIA	157	22	134	1	Reagan	14.0%	85.4%	0.6%
CONWAY	60	25	35		Reagan	41.7%	58.3%	
CRAIGHEAD	536	152	381	3	Reagan	28.4%	71.1%	0.6%
CRAWFORD	421	81	339	1	Reagan	19.2%	80.5%	0.2%
CRITTENDEN	176	56	119	1	Reagan	31.8%	67.6%	0.6%
CROSS	61	23	36	2	Reagan	37.7%	59.0%	3.3%
DALLAS	14	5	9		Reagan	35.7%	64.3%	
DESHA	32	8	24		Reagan	25.0%	75.0%	
DREW	37	8	27	2	Reagan	21.6%	73.0%	5.4%
FAULKNER	159	63	95	1	Reagan	39.6%	59.7%	0.6%
FRANKLIN	157	34	122	1	Reagan	21.7%	77.7%	0.6%
FULTON	62	31	31			50.0%	50.0%	
GARLAND	2,395	957	1,405	33	Reagan	40.0%	58.7%	1.4%
GRANT	24	8	16		Reagan	33.3%	66.7%	
GREENE	119	45	74		Reagan	37.8%	62.2%	
HEMPSTEAD	163	42	121		Reagan	25.8%	74.2%	
HOT SPRING	105	31	74		Reagan	29.5%	70.5%	
HOWARD	25	2	23		Reagan	8.0%	92.0%	
INDEPENDENCE	134	60	73	1	Reagan	44.8%	54.5%	0.7%
IZARD	58	20	38		Reagan	34.5%	65.5%	
JACKSON	34	9	25		Reagan	26.5%	73.5%	
JEFFERSON	533	176	350	7	Reagan	33.0%	65.7%	1.3%
JOHNSON	271	126	137	8	Reagan	46.5%	50.6%	3.0%
LAFAYETTE	12	3	7	2	Reagan	25.0%	58.3%	16.7%
LAWRENCE	77	30	47		Reagan	39.0%	61.0%	
LEE	13	4	5	4	Reagan	30.8%	38.5%	30.8%
LINCOLN	16	3	13		Reagan	18.8%	81.3%	
LITTLE RIVER	58	10	48		Reagan	17.2%	82.8%	
LOGAN	236	78	158		Reagan	33.1%	66.9%	
LONOKE	99	26	70	3	Reagan	26.3%	70.7%	3.0%
MADISON	240	120	119	1	Ford	50.0%	49.6%	0.4%
MARION	134	47	87		Reagan	35.1%	64.9%	
MILLER	294	37	256	1	Reagan	12.6%	87.1%	0.3%
MISSISSIPPI	124	31	93		Reagan	25.0%	75.0%	
MONROE	61	32	29		Ford	52.5%	47.5%	
MONTGOMERY	15	4	11		Reagan	26.7%	73.3%	
NEVADA	32	9	23		Reagan	28.1%	71.9%	

ARKANSAS REPUBLICAN

1976

County	Total Vote	Ford	Reagan	Uncommitted	Winner	Percentage of Total Vote Ford	Reagan	Uncom.
NEWTON	373	225	146	2	Ford	60.3%	39.1%	0.5%
OUACHITA	40	12	28		Reagan	30.0%	70.0%	
PERRY	33	12	21		Reagan	36.4%	63.6%	
PHILLIPS	73	20	53		Reagan	27.4%	72.6%	
PIKE	21	4	17		Reagan	19.0%	81.0%	
POINSETT	66	20	46		Reagan	30.3%	69.7%	
POLK	358	62	290	6	Reagan	17.3%	81.0%	1.7%
POPE	338	116	215	7	Reagan	34.3%	63.6%	2.1%
PRAIRIE	49	21	27	1	Reagan	42.9%	55.1%	2.0%
PULASKI	5,646	2,029	3,528	89	Reagan	35.9%	62.5%	1.6%
RANDOLPH	59	18	40	1	Reagan	30.5%	67.8%	1.7%
ST. FRANCIS	48	11	37		Reagan	22.9%	77.1%	
SALINE	200	64	132	4	Reagan	32.0%	66.0%	2.0%
SCOTT	23	10	12	1	Reagan	43.5%	52.2%	4.3%
SEARCY	596	247	349		Reagan	41.4%	58.6%	
SEBASTIAN	6,451	1,952	4,375	124	Reagan	30.3%	67.8%	1.9%
SEVIER	8	4	4			50.0%	50.0%	
SHARP	190	86	99	5	Reagan	45.3%	52.1%	2.6%
STONE	29	11	17	1	Reagan	37.9%	58.6%	3.4%
UNION	614	132	480	2	Reagan	21.5%	78.2%	0.3%
VAN BUREN	146	57	88	1	Reagan	39.0%	60.3%	0.7%
WASHINGTON	3,677	1,324	2,266	87	Reagan	36.0%	61.6%	2.4%
WHITE	348	106	240	2	Reagan	30.5%	69.0%	0.6%
WOODRUFF	No Votes							
YELL	40	10	30		Reagan	25.0%	75.0%	
TOTAL	32,541	11,430	20,628	483	Reagan	35.1%	63.4%	1.5%

ARKANSAS DEMOCRATIC

1980

County	Total Vote	Carter	Finch	E. Kennedy	Uncommitted	Winner	Percentage of Total Vote Carter	Finch	E. Kennedy	Uncom.
ARKANSAS	5,852	3,696	161	943	1,052	Carter	63.2%	2.8%	16.1%	18.0%
ASHLEY	6,454	3,984	349	876	1,245	Carter	61.7%	5.4%	13.6%	19.3%
BAXTER	4,247	2,753	631	863		Carter	64.8%	14.9%	20.3%	
BENTON	4,487	3,022	96	701	668	Carter	67.4%	2.1%	15.6%	14.9%
BOONE	3,350	2,116	175	630	429	Carter	63.2%	5.2%	18.8%	12.8%
BRADLEY	3,061	2,223	304	534		Carter	72.6%	9.9%	17.4%	
CALHOUN	2,390	1,451	120	499	320	Carter	60.7%	5.0%	20.9%	13.4%
CARROLL	3,299	1,892	155	443	809	Carter	57.4%	4.7%	13.4%	24.5%
CHICOT	5,009	2,844	174	1,219	772	Carter	56.8%	3.5%	24.3%	15.4%
CLARK	5,906	4,004	130	945	827	Carter	67.8%	2.2%	16.0%	14.0%
CLAY	3,140	2,193	190	409	348	Carter	69.8%	6.1%	13.0%	11.1%
CLEBURNE	6,234	3,789	165	1,090	1,190	Carter	60.8%	2.6%	17.5%	19.1%
CLEVELAND	2,843	1,704	95	523	521	Carter	59.9%	3.3%	18.4%	18.3%
COLUMBIA	5,566	3,936	702	928		Carter	70.7%	12.6%	16.7%	
CONWAY	6,004	3,301	208	1,444	1,051	Carter	55.0%	3.5%	24.1%	17.5%
CRAIGHEAD	10,075	5,548	702	1,472	2,353	Carter	55.1%	7.0%	14.6%	23.4%
CRAWFORD	6,451	3,290	276	980	1,905	Carter	51.0%	4.3%	15.2%	29.5%
CRITTENDEN	4,309	2,228	196	980	905	Carter	51.7%	4.5%	22.7%	21.0%
CROSS	4,988	3,067	221	761	939	Carter	61.5%	4.4%	15.3%	18.8%
DALLAS	4,518	2,603	194	1,129	592	Carter	57.6%	4.3%	25.0%	13.1%
DESHA	4,756	2,844	184	1,078	650	Carter	59.8%	3.9%	22.7%	13.7%
DREW	3,889	2,599	84	641	565	Carter	66.8%	2.2%	16.5%	14.5%
FAULKNER	9,558	5,834	529	1,532	1,663	Carter	61.0%	5.5%	16.0%	17.4%
FRANKLIN	5,240	2,742	331	1,003	1,164	Carter	52.3%	6.3%	19.1%	22.2%
FULTON	2,931	1,851	66	518	496	Carter	63.2%	2.3%	17.7%	16.9%
GARLAND	15,630	9,321	476	2,437	3,396	Carter	59.6%	3.0%	15.6%	21.7%
GRANT	4,551	3,060	143	578	770	Carter	67.2%	3.1%	12.7%	16.9%
GREENE	7,149	4,787	297	1,034	1,031	Carter	67.0%	4.2%	14.5%	14.4%
HEMPSTEAD	7,264	4,536	170	1,240	1,318	Carter	62.4%	2.3%	17.1%	18.1%
HOT SPRING	7,324	4,918	241	943	1,222	Carter	67.1%	3.3%	12.9%	16.7%
HOWARD	3,112	1,896	102	457	657	Carter	60.9%	3.3%	14.7%	21.1%
INDEPENDENCE	7,322	4,847	748	1,441	286	Carter	66.2%	10.2%	19.7%	3.9%
IZARD	2,710	1,726	82	416	486	Carter	63.7%	3.0%	15.4%	17.9%
JACKSON	4,543	2,657	151	979	756	Carter	58.5%	3.3%	21.5%	16.6%
JEFFERSON	17,024	10,430	894	3,571	2,129	Carter	61.3%	5.3%	21.0%	12.5%
JOHNSON	5,163	2,791	205	975	1,192	Carter	54.1%	4.0%	18.9%	23.1%
LAFAYETTE	3,432	2,072	140	612	608	Carter	60.4%	4.1%	17.8%	17.7%
LAWRENCE	4,568	2,837	199	716	816	Carter	62.1%	4.4%	15.7%	17.9%
LEE	4,330	2,347	193	1,196	594	Carter	54.2%	4.5%	27.6%	13.7%
LINCOLN	2,605	1,716	106	430	353	Carter	65.9%	4.1%	16.5%	13.6%
LITTLE RIVER	3,417	2,048	72	514	783	Carter	59.9%	2.1%	15.0%	22.9%
LOGAN	4,918	2,807	225	891	995	Carter	57.1%	4.6%	18.1%	20.2%
LONOKE	6,524	3,903	280	1,136	1,205	Carter	59.8%	4.3%	17.4%	18.5%
MADISON	2,087	1,375	41	316	355	Carter	65.9%	2.0%	15.1%	17.0%
MARION	2,470	1,286	96	393	695	Carter	52.1%	3.9%	15.9%	28.1%
MILLER	8,260	4,258	137	1,197	2,668	Carter	51.5%	1.7%	14.5%	32.3%
MISSISSIPPI	9,316	5,869	255	1,587	1,605	Carter	63.0%	2.7%	17.0%	17.2%
MONROE	3,643	2,007	212	760	664	Carter	55.1%	5.8%	20.9%	18.2%
MONTGOMERY	1,789	1,091	59	291	348	Carter	61.0%	3.3%	16.3%	19.5%
NEVADA	3,951	2,404	111	732	704	Carter	60.8%	2.8%	18.5%	17.8%

ARKANSAS DEMOCRATIC

1980

County	Total Vote	Carter	Finch	E. Kennedy	Uncommitted	Winner	Percentage of Total Vote Carter	Finch	E. Kennedy	Uncom.
NEWTON	1,230	621	86	262	261	Carter	50.5%	7.0%	21.3%	21.2%
OUACHITA	8,975	5,631	461	1,760	1,123	Carter	62.7%	5.1%	19.6%	12.5%
PERRY	2,459	1,404	130	519	406	Carter	57.1%	5.3%	21.1%	16.5%
PHILLIPS	3,237	1,835	106	745	551	Carter	56.7%	3.3%	23.0%	17.0%
PIKE	3,054	1,946	116	399	593	Carter	63.7%	3.8%	13.1%	19.4%
POINSETT	5,844	3,262	357	1,055	1,170	Carter	55.8%	6.1%	18.1%	20.0%
POLK	4,037	2,265	167	524	1,081	Carter	56.1%	4.1%	13.0%	26.8%
POPE	8,074	4,538	274	1,712	1,550	Carter	56.2%	3.4%	21.2%	19.2%
PRAIRIE	3,496	1,886	146	668	796	Carter	53.9%	4.2%	19.1%	22.8%
PULASKI	47,104	27,989	1,506	8,435	9,174	Carter	59.4%	3.2%	17.9%	19.5%
RANDOLPH	4,282	2,674	114	802	692	Carter	62.4%	2.7%	18.7%	16.2%
ST. FRANCIS	7,792	4,263	364	1,873	1,292	Carter	54.7%	4.7%	24.0%	16.6%
SALINE	11,036	6,917	440	1,574	2,105	Carter	62.7%	4.0%	14.3%	19.1%
SCOTT	3,806	2,154	173	574	905	Carter	56.6%	4.5%	15.1%	23.8%
SEARCY	1,051	667	47	204	133	Carter	63.5%	4.5%	19.4%	12.7%
SEBASTIAN	13,864	7,122	521	2,141	4,080	Carter	51.4%	3.8%	15.4%	29.4%
SEVIER	3,527	2,071	89	489	878	Carter	58.7%	2.5%	13.9%	24.9%
SHARP	4,196	2,593	95	676	832	Carter	61.8%	2.3%	16.1%	19.8%
STONE	3,189	1,833	125	622	609	Carter	57.5%	3.9%	19.5%	19.1%
UNION	9,756	5,894	518	1,050	2,294	Carter	60.4%	5.3%	10.8%	23.5%
VAN BUREN	4,287	2,550	166	760	811	Carter	59.5%	3.9%	17.7%	18.9%
WASHINGTON	8,664	5,260	447	1,559	1,398	Carter	60.7%	5.2%	18.0%	16.1%
WHITE	10,188	6,761	255	1,385	1,787	Carter	66.4%	2.5%	13.6%	17.5%
WOODRUFF	2,575	1,638	59	595	283	Carter	63.6%	2.3%	23.1%	11.0%
YELL	4,908	3,098	634	1,176		Carter	63.1%	12.9%	24.0%	
TOTAL	448,290	269,375	19,469	78,542	80,904	Carter	60.1%	4.3%	17.5%	18.0%

ARKANSAS DEMOCRATIC

1988

County	Total Vote	Dukakis	Gephardt	Gore	J. Jackson	Other	Winner	Dukakis	Gephardt	Gore	J. Jackson	Other
								Percentage of Total Vote				
ARKANSAS	5,513	1,168	624	2,406	819	496	Gore	21.2%	11.3%	43.6%	14.9%	9.0%
ASHLEY	6,585	898	843	2,407	1,367	1,070	Gore	13.6%	12.8%	36.6%	20.8%	16.2%
BAXTER	3,773	1,085	1,074	692	255	667	Dukakis	28.8%	28.5%	18.3%	6.8%	17.7%
BENTON	5,695	1,686	724	2,192	449	644	Gore	29.6%	12.7%	38.5%	7.9%	11.3%
BOONE	2,972	650	957	626	238	501	Gephardt	21.9%	32.2%	21.1%	8.0%	16.9%
BRADLEY	3,356	502	314	1,357	799	384	Gore	15.0%	9.4%	40.4%	23.8%	11.4%
CALHOUN	2,739	490	221	889	502	637	Gore	17.9%	8.1%	32.5%	18.3%	23.3%
CARROLL	3,971	799	1,073	846	382	871	Gephardt	20.1%	27.0%	21.3%	9.6%	21.9%
CHICOT	4,458	413	338	1,105	1,844	758	J. Jackson	9.3%	7.6%	24.8%	41.4%	17.0%
CLARK	4,937	914	458	1,916	1,079	570	Gore	18.5%	9.3%	38.8%	21.9%	11.5%
CLAY	4,243	908	931	1,366	169	869	Gore	21.4%	21.9%	32.2%	4.0%	20.5%
CLEBURNE	6,635	1,358	1,081	2,758	315	1,123	Gore	20.5%	16.3%	41.6%	4.7%	16.9%
CLEVELAND	2,738	425	280	1,369	297	367	Gore	15.5%	10.2%	50.0%	10.8%	13.4%
COLUMBIA	7,236	1,123	591	2,721	1,445	1,356	Gore	15.5%	8.2%	37.6%	20.0%	18.7%
CONWAY	8,276	1,309	998	3,490	1,225	1,254	Gore	15.8%	12.1%	42.2%	14.8%	15.2%
CRAIGHEAD	13,723	2,710	2,162	5,643	899	2,309	Gore	19.7%	15.8%	41.1%	6.6%	16.8%
CRAWFORD	8,140	1,586	849	3,828	360	1,517	Gore	19.5%	10.4%	47.0%	4.4%	18.6%
CRITTENDEN	10,824	935	651	3,694	4,142	1,402	J. Jackson	8.6%	6.0%	34.1%	38.3%	13.0%
CROSS	4,440	654	492	1,727	925	642	Gore	14.7%	11.1%	38.9%	20.8%	14.5%
DALLAS	4,109	482	293	1,473	1,264	597	Gore	11.7%	7.1%	35.8%	30.8%	14.5%
DESHA	4,438	573	507	1,550	1,471	337	Gore	12.9%	11.4%	34.9%	33.1%	7.6%
DREW	4,508	673	376	1,850	931	678	Gore	14.9%	8.3%	41.0%	20.7%	15.0%
FAULKNER	10,591	2,218	1,613	4,371	1,038	1,351	Gore	20.9%	15.2%	41.3%	9.8%	12.8%
FRANKLIN	4,678	859	528	2,162	198	931	Gore	18.4%	11.3%	46.2%	4.2%	19.9%
FULTON	2,770	618	681	848	136	487	Gore	22.3%	24.6%	30.6%	4.9%	17.6%
GARLAND	14,117	3,400	1,960	5,042	1,590	2,125	Gore	24.1%	13.9%	35.7%	11.3%	15.1%
GRANT	3,789	763	444	2,029	220	333	Gore	20.1%	11.7%	53.5%	5.8%	8.8%
GREENE	8,892	1,692	1,170	3,979	455	1,596	Gore	19.0%	13.2%	44.7%	5.1%	17.9%
HEMPSTEAD	4,407	801	484	1,436	1,235	451	Gore	18.2%	11.0%	32.6%	28.0%	10.2%
HOT SPRING	7,061	1,303	830	2,923	734	1,271	Gore	18.5%	11.8%	41.4%	10.4%	18.0%
HOWARD	2,832	484	394	1,061	501	392	Gore	17.1%	13.9%	37.5%	17.7%	13.8%
INDEPENDENCE	7,030	1,527	1,181	3,237	439	646	Gore	21.7%	16.8%	46.0%	6.2%	9.2%
IZARD	3,646	788	686	1,289	207	676	Gore	21.6%	18.8%	35.4%	5.7%	18.5%
JACKSON	4,896	990	624	1,920	747	615	Gore	20.2%	12.7%	39.2%	15.3%	12.6%
JEFFERSON	21,653	2,745	1,315	7,387	8,136	2,070	J. Jackson	12.7%	6.1%	34.1%	37.6%	9.6%
JOHNSON	5,457	1,019	989	1,967	282	1,200	Gore	18.7%	18.1%	36.0%	5.2%	22.0%
LAFAYETTE	3,181	634	316	790	919	522	J. Jackson	19.9%	9.9%	24.8%	28.9%	16.4%
LAWRENCE	5,533	1,057	970	2,108	227	1,171	Gore	19.1%	17.5%	38.1%	4.1%	21.2%
LEE	3,710	228	163	1,113	1,905	301	J. Jackson	6.1%	4.4%	30.0%	51.3%	8.1%
LINCOLN	3,865	491	273	1,492	1,050	559	Gore	12.7%	7.1%	38.6%	27.2%	14.5%
LITTLE RIVER	4,820	1,045	756	1,211	856	952	Gore	21.7%	15.7%	25.1%	17.8%	19.8%
LOGAN	5,091	1,064	779	2,125	246	877	Gore	20.9%	15.3%	41.7%	4.8%	17.2%
LONOKE	6,820	1,166	785	3,301	729	839	Gore	17.1%	11.5%	48.4%	10.7%	12.3%
MADISON	2,260	648	256	978	149	229	Gore	28.7%	11.3%	43.3%	6.6%	10.1%
MARION	3,570	728	1,043	694	276	829	Gephardt	20.4%	29.2%	19.4%	7.7%	23.2%
MILLER	9,326	1,646	1,470	2,320	1,852	2,038	Gore	17.6%	15.8%	24.9%	19.9%	21.9%
MISSISSIPPI	9,578	1,120	942	3,602	2,387	1,527	Gore	11.7%	9.8%	37.6%	24.9%	15.9%
MONROE	3,385	439	272	1,195	1,118	361	Gore	13.0%	8.0%	35.3%	33.0%	10.7%
MONTGOMERY	2,129	554	367	811	122	275	Gore	26.0%	17.2%	38.1%	5.7%	12.9%
NEVADA	3,292	862	330	1,115	776	209	Gore	26.2%	10.0%	33.9%	23.6%	6.3%

ARKANSAS DEMOCRATIC

1988

County	Total Vote	Dukakis	Gephardt	Gore	J. Jackson	Other	Winner	Percentage of Total Vote: Dukakis	Gephardt	Gore	J. Jackson	Other
NEWTON	842	199	232	168	122	121	Gephardt	23.6%	27.6%	20.0%	14.5%	14.4%
OUACHITA	8,899	1,242	749	3,000	2,587	1,321	Gore	14.0%	8.4%	33.7%	29.1%	14.8%
PERRY	2,744	560	408	1,154	198	424	Gore	20.4%	14.9%	42.1%	7.2%	15.5%
PHILLIPS	8,969	826	490	2,692	3,891	1,070	J. Jackson	9.2%	5.5%	30.0%	43.4%	11.9%
PIKE	3,487	614	457	1,551	215	650	Gore	17.6%	13.1%	44.5%	6.2%	18.6%
POINSETT	5,563	897	849	2,496	475	846	Gore	16.1%	15.3%	44.9%	8.5%	15.2%
POLK	3,834	793	553	1,640	178	670	Gore	20.7%	14.4%	42.8%	4.6%	17.5%
POPE	10,100	2,291	1,241	3,748	680	2,140	Gore	22.7%	12.3%	37.1%	6.7%	21.2%
PRAIRIE	3,291	569	391	1,620	368	343	Gore	17.3%	11.9%	49.2%	11.2%	10.4%
PULASKI	59,594	13,470	5,085	20,135	14,819	6,085	Gore	22.6%	8.5%	33.8%	24.9%	10.2%
RANDOLPH	4,491	1,255	898	1,225	219	894	Dukakis	27.9%	20.0%	27.3%	4.9%	19.9%
ST. FRANCIS	8,357	708	399	3,060	3,225	965	J. Jackson	8.5%	4.8%	36.6%	38.6%	11.5%
SALINE	12,086	2,670	1,323	5,392	751	1,950	Gore	22.1%	10.9%	44.6%	6.2%	16.1%
SCOTT	3,665	676	590	1,707	150	542	Gore	18.4%	16.1%	46.6%	4.1%	14.8%
SEARCY	615	136	166	165	78	70	Gephardt	22.1%	27.0%	26.8%	12.7%	11.4%
SEBASTIAN	10,721	2,754	1,088	4,440	1,194	1,245	Gore	25.7%	10.1%	41.4%	11.1%	11.6%
SEVIER	2,733	600	375	998	209	551	Gore	22.0%	13.7%	36.5%	7.6%	20.2%
SHARP	4,088	1,134	778	1,244	243	689	Gore	27.7%	19.0%	30.4%	5.9%	16.9%
STONE	3,681	761	591	1,364	258	707	Gore	20.7%	16.1%	37.1%	7.0%	19.2%
UNION	11,115	1,458	1,361	4,080	2,050	2,166	Gore	13.1%	12.2%	36.7%	18.4%	19.5%
VAN BUREN	5,564	1,103	807	2,310	326	1,018	Gore	19.8%	14.5%	41.5%	5.9%	18.3%
WASHINGTON	14,176	3,805	1,066	5,896	1,527	1,882	Gore	26.8%	7.5%	41.6%	10.8%	13.3%
WHITE	9,496	1,820	1,234	4,449	694	1,299	Gore	19.2%	13.0%	46.9%	7.3%	13.7%
WOODRUFF	1,878	253	203	705	502	215	Gore	13.5%	10.8%	37.5%	26.7%	11.4%
YELL	5,867	1,279	919	2,108	337	1,224	Gore	21.8%	15.7%	35.9%	5.7%	20.9%
TOTAL	497,544	94,103	59,711	185,758	85,003	72,969	Gore	18.9%	12.0%	37.3%	17.1%	14.7%

ARKANSAS REPUBLICAN

1988

County	Total Vote	Bush	Dole	Robertson	Other	Winner	Percentage of Total Vote Bush	Dole	Robertson	Other
ARKANSAS	99	40	26	23	10	Bush	40.4%	26.3%	23.2%	10.1%
ASHLEY	232	52	22	149	9	Robertson	22.4%	9.5%	64.2%	3.9%
BAXTER	3,137	1,647	757	375	358	Bush	52.5%	24.1%	12.0%	11.4%
BENTON	10,971	5,065	3,756	1,149	1,001	Bush	46.2%	34.2%	10.5%	9.1%
BOONE	1,555	741	362	302	150	Bush	47.7%	23.3%	19.4%	9.6%
BRADLEY	42	27	8	6	1	Bush	64.3%	19.0%	14.3%	2.4%
CALHOUN	18	1	3	12	2	Robertson	5.6%	16.7%	66.7%	11.1%
CARROLL	687	303	180	162	42	Bush	44.1%	26.2%	23.6%	6.1%
CHICOT	47	8	1	34	4	Robertson	17.0%	2.1%	72.3%	8.5%
CLARK	406	168	134	83	21	Bush	41.4%	33.0%	20.4%	5.2%
CLAY	63	24	18	21		Bush	38.1%	28.6%	33.3%	
CLEBURNE	288	156	59	49	24	Bush	54.2%	20.5%	17.0%	8.3%
CLEVELAND	21	15	3	1	2	Bush	71.4%	14.3%	4.8%	9.5%
COLUMBIA	322	161	42	76	43	Bush	50.0%	13.0%	23.6%	13.4%
CONWAY	62	37	10	6	9	Bush	59.7%	16.1%	9.7%	14.5%
CRAIGHEAD	865	215	138	450	62	Robertson	24.9%	16.0%	52.0%	7.2%
CRAWFORD	591	300	128	135	28	Bush	50.8%	21.7%	22.8%	4.7%
CRITTENDEN	136	67	11	42	16	Bush	49.3%	8.1%	30.9%	11.8%
CROSS	76	30	5	34	7	Robertson	39.5%	6.6%	44.7%	9.2%
DALLAS	28	6	4	17	1	Robertson	21.4%	14.3%	60.7%	3.6%
DESHA	94	27	10	53	4	Robertson	28.7%	10.6%	56.4%	4.3%
DREW	139	63	29	28	19	Bush	45.3%	20.9%	20.1%	13.7%
FAULKNER	1,543	683	360	323	177	Bush	44.3%	23.3%	20.9%	11.5%
FRANKLIN	268	140	43	65	20	Bush	52.2%	16.0%	24.3%	7.5%
FULTON	163	79	45	31	8	Bush	48.5%	27.6%	19.0%	4.9%
GARLAND	3,814	1,972	781	770	291	Bush	51.7%	20.5%	20.2%	7.6%
GRANT	120	58	18	34	10	Bush	48.3%	15.0%	28.3%	8.3%
GREENE	86	48	17	17	4	Bush	55.8%	19.8%	19.8%	4.7%
HEMPSTEAD	326	182	59	64	21	Bush	55.8%	18.1%	19.6%	6.4%
HOT SPRING	179	66	22	81	10	Robertson	36.9%	12.3%	45.3%	5.6%
HOWARD	72	37	16	12	7	Bush	51.4%	22.2%	16.7%	9.7%
INDEPENDENCE	403	160	67	155	21	Bush	39.7%	16.6%	38.5%	5.2%
IZARD	278	143	87	32	16	Bush	51.4%	31.3%	11.5%	5.8%
JACKSON	176	78	36	21	41	Bush	44.3%	20.5%	11.9%	23.3%
JEFFERSON	698	346	125	184	43	Bush	49.6%	17.9%	26.4%	6.2%
JOHNSON	310	156	62	79	13	Bush	50.3%	20.0%	25.5%	4.2%
LAFAYETTE	21	7	4	5	5	Bush	33.3%	19.0%	23.8%	23.8%
LAWRENCE	54	26	5	19	4	Bush	48.1%	9.3%	35.2%	7.4%
LEE	18	5	7	1	5	Dole	27.8%	38.9%	5.6%	27.8%
LINCOLN	18	7	2	9		Robertson	38.9%	11.1%	50.0%	
LITTLE RIVER	46	10	8	26	2	Robertson	21.7%	17.4%	56.5%	4.3%
LOGAN	297	110	51	122	14	Robertson	37.0%	17.2%	41.1%	4.7%
LONOKE	609	278	124	136	71	Bush	45.6%	20.4%	22.3%	11.7%
MADISON	552	265	205	54	28	Bush	48.0%	37.1%	9.8%	5.1%
MARION	453	231	97	68	57	Bush	51.0%	21.4%	15.0%	12.6%
MILLER	506	162	67	248	29	Robertson	32.0%	13.2%	49.0%	5.7%
MISSISSIPPI	404	207	70	88	39	Bush	51.2%	17.3%	21.8%	9.7%
MONROE	40	15	11	11	3	Bush	37.5%	27.5%	27.5%	7.5%
MONTGOMERY	30	15	5	9	1	Bush	50.0%	16.7%	30.0%	3.3%
NEVADA	37	21	11	3	2	Bush	56.8%	29.7%	8.1%	5.4%

ARKANSAS REPUBLICAN

1988

County	Total Vote	Bush	Dole	Robertson	Other	Winner	Percentage of Total Vote Bush	Dole	Robertson	Other
NEWTON	378	223	69	59	27	Bush	59.0%	18.3%	15.6%	7.1%
OUACHITA	501	157	102	192	50	Robertson	31.3%	20.4%	38.3%	10.0%
PERRY	79	35	23	19	2	Bush	44.3%	29.1%	24.1%	2.5%
PHILLIPS	52	13	10	29		Robertson	25.0%	19.2%	55.8%	
PIKE	38	11	12	9	6	Dole	28.9%	31.6%	23.7%	15.8%
POINSETT	57	14	13	29	1	Robertson	24.6%	22.8%	50.9%	1.8%
POLK	492	182	100	189	21	Robertson	37.0%	20.3%	38.4%	4.3%
POPE	805	326	156	279	44	Bush	40.5%	19.4%	34.7%	5.5%
PRAIRIE	68	19	34	13	2	Dole	27.9%	50.0%	19.1%	2.9%
PULASKI	13,833	6,656	3,276	2,785	1,116	Bush	48.1%	23.7%	20.1%	8.1%
RANDOLPH	78	38	7	30	3	Bush	48.7%	9.0%	38.5%	3.8%
ST. FRANCIS	61	21	8	29	3	Robertson	34.4%	13.1%	47.5%	4.9%
SALINE	1,608	849	292	349	118	Bush	52.8%	18.2%	21.7%	7.3%
SCOTT	82	33	17	29	3	Bush	40.2%	20.7%	35.4%	3.7%
SEARCY	1,164	601	340	100	123	Bush	51.6%	29.2%	8.6%	10.6%
SEBASTIAN	7,996	3,935	2,383	1,156	522	Bush	49.2%	29.8%	14.5%	6.5%
SEVIER	237	124	44	58	11	Bush	52.3%	18.6%	24.5%	4.6%
SHARP	523	252	124	127	20	Bush	48.2%	23.7%	24.3%	3.8%
STONE	76	24	14	35	3	Robertson	31.6%	18.4%	46.1%	3.9%
UNION	676	251	90	236	99	Bush	37.1%	13.3%	34.9%	14.6%
VAN BUREN	225	141	45	28	11	Bush	62.7%	20.0%	12.4%	4.9%
WASHINGTON	6,533	2,918	2,137	985	493	Bush	44.7%	32.7%	15.1%	7.5%
WHITE	1,250	603	239	241	167	Bush	48.2%	19.1%	19.3%	13.4%
WOODRUFF	28	8	11	8	1	Dole	28.6%	39.3%	28.6%	3.6%
YELL	65	20	10	30	5	Robertson	30.8%	15.4%	46.2%	7.7%
TOTAL	68,305	32,114	17,667	12,918	5,606	Bush	47.0%	25.9%	18.9%	8.2%

ARKANSAS DEMOCRATIC

1992

County	Total Vote	Brown	Cllinton	Uncommitted	LaRouche	Winner	Percentage of Total Vote Brown	Cllinton	Uncom.	LaRouche
ARKANSAS	5,752	696	3,733	1,222	101	Clinton	12.1%	64.9%	21.2%	1.8%
ASHLEY	6,412	520	4,511	1,192	189	Clinton	8.1%	70.4%	18.6%	2.9%
BAXTER	3,637	544	2,955		138	Clinton	15.0%	81.2%		3.8%
BENTON	6,627	364	5,372	804	87	Clinton	5.5%	81.1%	12.1%	1.3%
BOONE	3,370	405	2,268	618	79	Clinton	12.0%	67.3%	18.3%	2.3%
BRADLEY	4,131	406	2,728	899	98	Clinton	9.8%	66.0%	21.8%	2.4%
CALHOUN	1,833	361	1,386		86	Clinton	19.7%	75.6%		4.7%
CARROLL	3,015	337	1,795	782	101	Clinton	11.2%	59.5%	25.9%	3.3%
CHICOT	3,751	211	2,915	557	68	Clinton	5.6%	77.7%	14.8%	1.8%
CLARK	6,492	544	4,750	1,110	88	Clinton	8.4%	73.2%	17.1%	1.4%
CLAY	3,953	221	3,021	603	108	Clinton	5.6%	76.4%	15.3%	2.7%
CLEBURNE	6,865	965	3,918	1,835	147	Clinton	14.1%	57.1%	26.7%	2.1%
CLEVELAND	2,538	260	1,365	825	88	Clinton	10.2%	53.8%	32.5%	3.5%
COLUMBIA	5,425	935	4,001		489	Clinton	17.2%	73.8%		9.0%
CONWAY	6,648	962	4,246	1,192	248	Clinton	14.5%	63.9%	17.9%	3.7%
CRAIGHEAD	11,446	577	8,118	1,688	1,063	Clinton	5.0%	70.9%	14.7%	9.3%
CRAWFORD	8,194	953	4,580	2,438	223	Clinton	11.6%	55.9%	29.8%	2.7%
CRITTENDEN	9,006	850	6,884	1,042	230	Clinton	9.4%	76.4%	11.6%	2.6%
CROSS	4,629	336	3,250	902	141	Clinton	7.3%	70.2%	19.5%	3.0%
DALLAS	3,565	493	2,151	823	98	Clinton	13.8%	60.3%	23.1%	2.7%
DESHA	4,137	328	3,087	620	102	Clinton	7.9%	74.6%	15.0%	2.5%
DREW	4,401	408	2,927	954	112	Clinton	9.3%	66.5%	21.7%	2.5%
FAULKNER	12,456	2,184	8,233	1,610	429	Clinton	17.5%	66.1%	12.9%	3.4%
FRANKLIN	4,263	465	2,455	1,153	190	Clinton	10.9%	57.6%	27.0%	4.5%
FULTON	3,472	291	2,318	768	95	Clinton	8.4%	66.8%	22.1%	2.7%
GARLAND	16,240	1,768	11,636	2,587	249	Clinton	10.9%	71.7%	15.9%	1.5%
GRANT	3,704	559	2,107	900	138	Clinton	15.1%	56.9%	24.3%	3.7%
GREENE	8,709	557	6,162	1,736	254	Clinton	6.4%	70.8%	19.9%	2.9%
HEMPSTEAD	5,923	921	4,628		374	Clinton	15.5%	78.1%		6.3%
HOT SPRING	7,933	1,207	4,690	1,796	240	Clinton	15.2%	59.1%	22.6%	3.0%
HOWARD	3,484	201	2,324	890	69	Clinton	5.8%	66.7%	25.5%	2.0%
INDEPENDENCE	8,973	998	5,857	1,848	270	Clinton	11.1%	65.3%	20.6%	3.0%
IZARD	3,277	279	2,273	624	101	Clinton	8.5%	69.4%	19.0%	3.1%
JACKSON	4,594	351	3,329	809	105	Clinton	7.6%	72.5%	17.6%	2.3%
JEFFERSON	18,591	1,598	14,256	2,373	364	Clinton	8.6%	76.7%	12.8%	2.0%
JOHNSON	5,108	586	3,004	1,337	181	Clinton	11.5%	58.8%	26.2%	3.5%
LAFAYETTE	3,188	192	2,143	741	112	Clinton	6.0%	67.2%	23.2%	3.5%
LAWRENCE	3,838	341	2,671	707	119	Clinton	8.9%	69.6%	18.4%	3.1%
LEE	4,256	274	3,180	699	103	Clinton	6.4%	74.7%	16.4%	2.4%
LINCOLN	3,588	285	2,406	766	131	Clinton	7.9%	67.1%	21.3%	3.7%
LITTLE RIVER	3,968	203	2,768	921	76	Clinton	5.1%	69.8%	23.2%	1.9%
LOGAN	5,521	811	3,035	1,403	272	Clinton	14.7%	55.0%	25.4%	4.9%
LONOKE	9,759	1,128	5,849	2,537	245	Clinton	11.6%	59.9%	26.0%	2.5%
MADISON	1,694	141	1,297	212	44	Clinton	8.3%	76.6%	12.5%	2.6%
MARION	2,744	552	2,025		167	Clinton	20.1%	73.8%		6.1%
MILLER	8,389	322	5,683	2,295	89	Clinton	3.8%	67.7%	27.4%	1.1%
MISSISSIPPI	9,868	688	7,257	1,527	396	Clinton	7.0%	73.5%	15.5%	4.0%
MONROE	3,076	601	2,288		187	Clinton	19.5%	74.4%		6.1%
MONTGOMERY	3,060	360	1,680	914	106	Clinton	11.8%	54.9%	29.9%	3.5%
NEVADA	3,490	377	2,281	747	85	Clinton	10.8%	65.4%	21.4%	2.4%

ARKANSAS DEMOCRATIC

1992

County	Total Vote	Brown	Cllinton	Uncommitted	LaRouche	Winner	Percentage of Total Vote Brown	Cllinton	Uncom.	LaRouche
NEWTON	785.00	75	617	78	15	Clinton	9.6%	78.6%	9.9%	1.9%
OUACHITA	9,286	779	6,291	2,004	212	Clinton	8.4%	67.7%	21.6%	2.3%
PERRY	1,988	355	1,237	308	88	Clinton	17.9%	62.2%	15.5%	4.4%
PHILLIPS	6,104	529	4,483	926	166	Clinton	8.7%	73.4%	15.2%	2.7%
PIKE	3,324	372	2,032	828	92	Clinton	11.2%	61.1%	24.9%	2.8%
POINSETT	5,377	439	4,295	457	186	Clinton	8.2%	79.9%	8.5%	3.5%
POLK	4,677	449	2,493	1,591	144	Clinton	9.6%	53.3%	34.0%	3.1%
POPE	10,040	1,411	5,383	3,019	227	Clinton	14.1%	53.6%	30.1%	2.3%
PRAIRIE	2,939	298	1,884	686	71	Clinton	10.1%	64.1%	23.3%	2.4%
PULASKI	62,358	7,646	45,875	8,166	671	Clinton	12.3%	73.6%	13.1%	1.1%
RANDOLPH	4,687	448	3,225	886	128	Clinton	9.6%	68.8%	18.9%	2.7%
ST. FRANCIS	6,651	556	4,491	1,429	175	Clinton	8.4%	67.5%	21.5%	2.6%
SALINE	14,415	1,851	9,046	3,223	295	Clinton	12.8%	62.8%	22.4%	2.0%
SCOTT	3,077	399	1,601	969	108	Clinton	13.0%	52.0%	31.5%	3.5%
SEARCY	981.00	135	768	55	23	Clinton	13.8%	78.3%	5.6%	2.3%
SEBASTIAN	13,354	1,238	8,389	3,504	223	Clinton	9.3%	62.8%	26.2%	1.7%
SEVIER	3,617	230	2,395	932	60	Clinton	6.4%	66.2%	25.8%	1.7%
SHARP	4,775	492	3,019	1,105	159	Clinton	10.3%	63.2%	23.1%	3.3%
STONE	4,268	630	2,448	979	211	Clinton	14.8%	57.4%	22.9%	4.9%
UNION	11,898	1,702	7,146	2,467	583	Clinton	14.3%	60.1%	20.7%	4.9%
VAN BUREN	5,470	788	3,157	1,343	182	Clinton	14.4%	57.7%	24.6%	3.3%
WASHINGTON	13,518	1,105	10,341	1,845	227	Clinton	8.2%	76.5%	13.6%	1.7%
WHITE	11,330	2,479	7,994		857	Clinton	21.9%	70.6%		7.6%
WOODRUFF	2,786	172	2,179	365	70	Clinton	6.2%	78.2%	13.1%	2.5%
YELL	5,919	740	3,432	1,539	208	Clinton	12.5%	58.0%	26.0%	3.5%
TOTAL	502,617	55,234	342,017	90,710	14,656	Clinton	11.0%	68.0%	18.0%	2.9%

ARKANSAS REPUBLICAN

1992

County	Total Vote	Buchanan	Bush	Winner	Percentage of Total Vote Buchanan	Percentage of Total Vote Bush
ARKANSAS	59	6	53	Bush	10.2%	89.8%
ASHLEY	34	4	30	Bush	11.8%	88.2%
BAXTER	1,849	343	1,506	Bush	18.6%	81.4%
BENTON	9,758	957	8,801	Bush	9.8%	90.2%
BOONE	736	138	598	Bush	18.8%	81.3%
BRADLEY	19	4	15	Bush	21.1%	78.9%
CALHOUN	12	1	11	Bush	8.3%	91.7%
CARROLL	642	114	528	Bush	17.8%	82.2%
CHICOT	19		19	Bush		100.0%
CLARK	134	20	114	Bush	14.9%	85.1%
CLAY	20	2	18	Bush	10.0%	90.0%
CLEBURNE	213	24	189	Bush	11.3%	88.7%
CLEVELAND	21	3	18	Bush	14.3%	85.7%
COLUMBIA	385	32	353	Bush	8.3%	91.7%
CONWAY	23	3	20	Bush	13.0%	87.0%
CRAIGHEAD	609	95	514	Bush	15.6%	84.4%
CRAWFORD	998	154	844	Bush	15.4%	84.6%
CRITTENDEN	83	15	68	Bush	18.1%	81.9%
CROSS	42	1	41	Bush	2.4%	97.6%
DALLAS	4	2	2		50.0%	50.0%
DESHA	12	1	11	Bush	8.3%	91.7%
DREW	71	12	59	Bush	16.9%	83.1%
FAULKNER	1,159	142	1,017	Bush	12.3%	87.7%
FRANKLIN	215	37	178	Bush	17.2%	82.8%
FULTON	57	6	51	Bush	10.5%	89.5%
GARLAND	2,875	364	2,511	Bush	12.7%	87.3%
GRANT	68	19	49	Bush	27.9%	72.1%
GREENE	63	13	50	Bush	20.6%	79.4%
HEMPSTEAD	181	24	157	Bush	13.3%	86.7%
HOT SPRING	87	14	73	Bush	16.1%	83.9%
HOWARD	40	3	37	Bush	7.5%	92.5%
INDEPENDENCE	158	21	137	Bush	13.3%	86.7%
IZARD	163	30	133	Bush	18.4%	81.6%
JACKSON	68	7	61	Bush	10.3%	89.7%
JEFFERSON	836	93	743	Bush	11.1%	88.9%
JOHNSON	323	40	283	Bush	12.4%	87.6%
LAFAYETTE	29	7	22	Bush	24.1%	75.9%
LAWRENCE	62	14	48	Bush	22.6%	77.4%
LEE	1	1		Buchanan	100.0%	
LINCOLN	16	2	14	Bush	12.5%	87.5%
LITTLE RIVER	31	3	28	Bush	9.7%	90.3%
LOGAN	221	38	183	Bush	17.2%	82.8%
LONOKE	368	70	298	Bush	19.0%	81.0%
MADISON	511	52	459	Bush	10.2%	89.8%
MARION	327	55	272	Bush	16.8%	83.2%
MILLER	811	105	706	Bush	12.9%	87.1%
MISSISSIPPI	144	15	129	Bush	10.4%	89.6%
MONROE	31	6	25	Bush	19.4%	80.6%
MONTGOMERY	14	3	11	Bush	21.4%	78.6%
NEVADA	14		14	Bush		100.0%

ARKANSAS REPUBLICAN

1992

County	Total Vote	Buchanan	Bush	Winner	Percentage of Total Vote: Buchanan	Percentage of Total Vote: Bush
NEWTON	119	14	105	Bush	11.8%	88.2%
OUACHITA	159	37	122	Bush	23.3%	76.7%
PERRY	49	6	43	Bush	12.2%	87.8%
PHILLIPS	16		16	Bush		100.0%
PIKE	33	4	29	Bush	12.1%	87.9%
POINSETT	60	14	46	Bush	23.3%	76.7%
POLK	149	21	128	Bush	14.1%	85.9%
POPE	843	92	751	Bush	10.9%	89.1%
PRAIRIE	77	8	69	Bush	10.4%	89.6%
PULASKI	8,961	985	7,976	Bush	11.0%	89.0%
RANDOLPH	42	8	34	Bush	19.0%	81.0%
ST. FRANCIS	43	4	39	Bush	9.3%	90.7%
SALINE	1,552	182	1,370	Bush	11.7%	88.3%
SCOTT	64	12	52	Bush	18.8%	81.3%
SEARCY	647	86	561	Bush	13.3%	86.7%
SEBASTIAN	5,952	780	5,172	Bush	13.1%	86.9%
SEVIER	81	9	72	Bush	11.1%	88.9%
SHARP	323	44	279	Bush	13.6%	86.4%
STONE	40	10	30	Bush	25.0%	75.0%
UNION	178	49	129	Bush	27.5%	72.5%
VAN BUREN	167	16	151	Bush	9.6%	90.4%
WASHINGTON	7,148	927	6,221	Bush	13.0%	87.0%
WHITE	738	113	625	Bush	15.3%	84.7%
WOODRUFF	10	1	9	Bush	10.0%	90.0%
YELL	74	14	60	Bush	18.9%	81.1%
TOTAL	52,141	6,551	45,590	Bush	12.6%	87.4%

ARKANSAS DEMOCRATIC

1996

County	Total Vote	Clinton	Uncommitted	Other	Winner	Percentage of Total Vote Clinton	Uncom.	Other
ARKANSAS	2,123	1,984		139	Clinton	93.5%		6.5%
ASHLEY	4,508	3,658		850	Clinton	81.1%		18.9%
BAXTER	3,925	3,287		638	Clinton	83.7%		16.3%
BENTON	2,964	2,750		214	Clinton	92.8%		7.2%
BOONE	2,097	1,728		369	Clinton	82.4%		17.6%
BRADLEY	1,525	1,396		129	Clinton	91.5%		8.5%
CALHOUN	1,195	842	256	97	Clinton	70.5%	21.4%	8.1%
CARROLL	2,241	1,939		302	Clinton	86.5%		13.5%
CHICOT	2,648	2,014	528	106	Clinton	76.1%	19.9%	4.0%
CLARK	4,339	3,764		575	Clinton	86.7%		13.3%
CLAY	2,203	1,773	354	76	Clinton	80.5%	16.1%	3.4%
CLEBURNE	4,457	2,744	1,333	380	Clinton	61.6%	29.9%	8.5%
CLEVELAND	794	727		67	Clinton	91.6%		8.4%
COLUMBIA	4,640	3,624		1,016	Clinton	78.1%		21.9%
CONWAY	5,514	4,178		1,336	Clinton	75.8%		24.2%
CRAIGHEAD	9,221	7,771		1,450	Clinton	84.3%		15.7%
CRAWFORD	6,967	4,001	2,493	473	Clinton	57.4%	35.8%	6.8%
CRITTENDEN	3,036	2,710		326	Clinton	89.3%		10.7%
CROSS	2,585	2,376		209	Clinton	91.9%		8.1%
DALLAS	1,455	995	355	105	Clinton	68.4%	24.4%	7.2%
DESHA	2,413	2,178		235	Clinton	90.3%		9.7%
DREW	3,841	2,807	839	195	Clinton	73.1%	21.8%	5.1%
FAULKNER	8,340	6,476		1,844	Clinton	77.9%		22.1%
FRANKLIN	3,864	2,966		898	Clinton	76.8%		23.2%
FULTON	1,769	1,629		140	Clinton	92.1%		7.9%
GARLAND	9,070	6,878	1,468	724	Clinton	75.8%	16.2%	8.0%
GRANT	1,975	1,761		214	Clinton	89.2%		10.8%
GREENE	5,111	4,750		361	Clinton	92.8%		7.1%
HEMPSTEAD	5,455	4,067	1,159	229	Clinton	74.6%	21.2%	4.2%
HOT SPRING	5,949	3,941	1,593	415	Clinton	66.2%	26.8%	7.0%
HOWARD	3,854	2,537	1,117	200	Clinton	65.8%	29.0%	5.2%
INDEPENDENCE	4,041	3,610		431	Clinton	89.3%		10.7%
IZARD	2,948	2,069	661	218	Clinton	70.2%	22.4%	7.4%
JACKSON	2,915	2,733		182	Clinton	93.8%		6.2%
JEFFERSON	9,588	7,324	1,478	786	Clinton	76.4%	15.4%	8.2%
JOHNSON	3,954	2,452	1,178	324	Clinton	62.0%	29.8%	8.2%
LAFAYETTE	2,398	2,212		186	Clinton	92.2%		7.8%
LAWRENCE	3,414	2,515	725	174	Clinton	73.7%	21.2%	5.1%
LEE	3,727	2,903	719	105	Clinton	77.9%	19.3%	2.8%
LINCOLN	2,271	2,051		220	Clinton	90.3%		9.7%
LITTLE RIVER	2,721	2,517		204	Clinton	92.5%		7.5%
LOGAN	2,800	2,169		631	Clinton	77.5%		22.5%
LONOKE	5,750	4,405		1,345	Clinton	76.6%		23.4%
MADISON	872	826		46	Clinton	94.7%		5.3%
MARION	2,607	1,688	625	294	Clinton	64.7%	24.0%	11.3%
MILLER	4,605	3,599		1,006	Clinton	78.2%		21.8%
MISSISSIPPI	3,317	2,795		522	Clinton	84.3%		15.7%
MONROE	1,621	1,186	340	95	Clinton	73.2%	21.0%	5.9%
MONTGOMERY	2,017	1,244	613	160	Clinton	61.7%	30.4%	7.9%
NEVADA	3,060	2,083	798	179	Clinton	68.1%	26.1%	5.8%

ARKANSAS DEMOCRATIC

1996

County	Total Vote	Clinton	Uncommitted	Other	Winner	Percentage of Total Vote Clinton	Uncom.	Other
NEWTON	739	642		97	Clinton	86.9%		13.1%
OUACHITA	4,924	4,579		345	Clinton	93.0%		7.0%
PERRY	2,040	1,513		527	Clinton	74.2%		25.8%
PHILLIPS	4,818	3,921	708	189	Clinton	81.4%	14.7%	3.9%
PIKE	2,935	2,255		680	Clinton	76.8%		23.2%
POINSETT	2,997	2,814		183	Clinton	93.9%		6.1%
POLK	2,424	1,361	831	232	Clinton	56.1%	34.3%	9.6%
POPE	4,783	4,206		577	Clinton	87.9%		12.1%
PRAIRIE	1,607	1,465		142	Clinton	91.2%		8.8%
PULASKI	33,461	26,904	4,529	2,028	Clinton	80.4%	13.5%	6.1%
RANDOLPH	2,005	1,830		175	Clinton	91.3%		8.7%
ST. FRANCIS	1,545	1,420		125	Clinton	91.9%		8.1%
SALINE	10,708	7,430	2,427	851	Clinton	69.4%	22.7%	7.9%
SCOTT	1,263	1,082		181	Clinton	85.7%		14.3%
SEARCY	352	317		35	Clinton	90.1%		9.9%
SEBASTIAN	6,593	5,279		1,314	Clinton	80.1%		19.9%
SEVIER	1,595	1,128	361	106	Clinton	70.7%	22.6%	6.6%
SHARP	3,160	2,125	804	231	Clinton	67.2%	25.4%	7.3%
STONE	3,254	1,899	1,055	300	Clinton	58.4%	32.4%	9.2%
UNION	3,359	2,614		745	Clinton	77.8%		22.2%
VAN BUREN	4,254	3,197		1,057	Clinton	75.2%		24.8%
WASHINGTON	6,948	5,487	1,069	392	Clinton	79.0%	15.4%	5.6%
WHITE	4,934	4,448		486	Clinton	90.1%		9.9%
WOODRUFF	964	918		46	Clinton	95.2%		4.8%
YELL	4,023	3,061		962	Clinton	76.1%		23.9%
TOTAL	300,389	236,547	30,416	33,426	Clinton	78.7%	10.1%	11.1%

ARKANSAS REPUBLICAN

1996

County	Total Vote	Buchanan	Dole	Uncommitted	Winner	Percentage of Total Vote Buchanan	Dole	Uncom.
ARKANSAS	96	69	27		Buchanan	71.9%	28.1%	
ASHLEY	92	32	60		Dole	34.8%	65.2%	
BAXTER	2,078	482	1,596		Dole	23.2%	76.8%	
BENTON	9,211	2,254	6,957		Dole	24.5%	75.5%	
BOONE	1,382	349	1,033		Dole	25.3%	74.7%	
BRADLEY	41	27	14		Buchanan	65.9%	34.1%	
CALHOUN	33	8	25		Dole	24.2%	75.8%	
CARROLL	303	80	223		Dole	26.4%	73.6%	
CHICOT	8	2	6		Dole	25.0%	75.0%	
CLARK	157	31	126		Dole	19.7%	80.3%	
CLAY	66	23	43		Dole	34.8%	65.2%	
CLEBURNE	398	86	312		Dole	21.6%	78.4%	
CLEVELAND	54	20	34		Dole	37.0%	63.0%	
COLUMBIA	170	51	119		Dole	30.0%	70.0%	
CONWAY	102	28	74		Dole	27.5%	72.5%	
CRAIGHEAD	853	218	635		Dole	25.6%	74.4%	
CRAWFORD	405	90	315		Dole	22.2%	77.8%	
CRITTENDEN	333	75	258		Dole	22.5%	77.5%	
CROSS	35	10	25		Dole	28.6%	71.4%	
DALLAS	8	3	5		Dole	37.5%	62.5%	
DESHA	39	8	31		Dole	20.5%	79.5%	
DREW	83	17	66		Dole	20.5%	79.5%	
FAULKNER	1,258	341	917		Dole	27.1%	72.9%	
FRANKLIN	72	15	57		Dole	20.8%	79.2%	
FULTON	68	23	45		Dole	33.8%	66.2%	
GARLAND	1,765	422	1,343		Dole	23.9%	76.1%	
GRANT	123	34	89		Dole	27.6%	72.4%	
GREENE	60	10	50		Dole	16.7%	83.3%	
HEMPSTEAD	81	18	63		Dole	22.2%	77.8%	
HOT SPRING	100	33	67		Dole	33.0%	67.0%	
HOWARD	12	2	10		Dole	16.7%	83.3%	
INDEPENDENCE	187	45	142		Dole	24.1%	75.9%	
IZARD	136	43	93		Dole	31.6%	68.4%	
JACKSON	69	45	24		Buchanan	65.2%	34.8%	
JEFFERSON	501	135	323	43	Dole	26.9%	64.5%	8.6%
JOHNSON	146	31	115		Dole	21.2%	78.8%	
LAFAYETTE	23	4	19		Dole	17.4%	82.6%	
LAWRENCE	110	22	88		Dole	20.0%	80.0%	
LEE	10	3	7		Dole	30.0%	70.0%	
LINCOLN	18	2	16		Dole	11.1%	88.9%	
LITTLE RIVER	22	7	15		Dole	31.8%	68.2%	
LOGAN	213	70	143		Dole	32.9%	67.1%	
LONOKE	403	94	309		Dole	23.3%	76.7%	
MADISON	215	34	181		Dole	15.8%	84.2%	
MARION	132	29	103		Dole	22.0%	78.0%	
MILLER	131	25	106		Dole	19.1%	80.9%	
MISSISSIPPI	150	35	115		Dole	23.3%	76.7%	
MONROE	45	10	35		Dole	22.2%	77.8%	
MONTGOMERY	110	47	63		Dole	42.7%	57.3%	
NEVADA	12	9	3		Buchanan	75.0%	25.0%	

ARKANSAS REPUBLICAN

1996

County	Total Vote	Buchanan	Dole	Uncommitted	Winner	Percentage of Total Vote Buchanan	Dole	Uncom.
NEWTON	769	230	539		Dole	29.9%	70.1%	
OUACHITA	75	31	44		Dole	41.3%	58.7%	
PERRY	102	34	68		Dole	33.3%	66.7%	
PHILLIPS	43	3	40		Dole	7.0%	93.0%	
PIKE	32	6	26		Dole	18.8%	81.3%	
POINSETT	64	7	57		Dole	10.9%	89.1%	
POLK	200	59	141		Dole	29.5%	70.5%	
POPE	499	132	367		Dole	26.5%	73.5%	
PRAIRIE	44	14	30		Dole	31.8%	68.2%	
PULASKI	8,587	1,425	7,162		Dole	16.6%	83.4%	
RANDOLPH	111	42	69		Dole	37.8%	62.2%	
ST. FRANCIS	13	6	7		Dole	46.2%	53.8%	
SALINE	2,146	494	1,652		Dole	23.0%	77.0%	
SCOTT	54	9	45		Dole	16.7%	83.3%	
SEARCY	1,025	339	686		Dole	33.1%	66.9%	
SEBASTIAN	1,922	450	1,472		Dole	23.4%	76.6%	
SEVIER	60	6	54		Dole	10.0%	90.0%	
SHARP	185	45	140		Dole	24.3%	75.7%	
STONE	44	13	31		Dole	29.5%	70.5%	
UNION	283	70	213		Dole	24.7%	75.3%	
VAN BUREN	359	80	279		Dole	22.3%	77.7%	
WASHINGTON	2,675	726	1,949		Dole	27.1%	72.9%	
WHITE	1,256	278	978		Dole	22.1%	77.9%	
WOODRUFF	43	12	31		Dole	27.9%	72.1%	
YELL	104	22	82		Dole	21.2%	78.8%	
TOTAL	42,814	10,084	32,687	43	Dole	23.6%	76.3%	0.1%

CALIFORNIA

Hubert Humphrey once called California "the Super Bowl of the primaries." But during the last quarter century, the nation's most populous state has been anything but that. The proliferation of primaries that increased the clout of Iowa and New Hampshire at the beginning of the calendar reduced California's significance at the end.

A generation ago, California's late-inning position often lent drama to the proceedings in one party or the other. The state's 1964 primary was critical for the Republicans; the 1968 and 1972 events offered high drama for Democrats.

But since then, the California primary has receded to the status of epilogue. In 1976, it was a mere formality, thanks to the home-state candidacies of then-Gov. Jerry Brown and former Gov. Ronald Reagan. In the presidential contests since then, California has voted long after the nominees in both parties were all but certain, even in 1996 when the primary was moved up to late March. Hence, the March 7 date in 2000 as California seeks to recover its lost luster.

Over the years, the California primary has been hospitable to political outsiders willing to take on their national party establishment. Two of the Kennedy brothers—Robert and Edward—won the Democratic primary; so did George McGovern and Gary Hart. Barry Goldwater won the 1964 Republican primary, a pivotal triumph for him and for conservative insurgents attempting to take over the party.

California voters have also been willing to support the presidential ambitions of their governors, giving Democrat Brown and Republican Reagan one-sided primary victories (Brown in 1976; Reagan each time he was on the primary ballot since 1968). In national terms, both Brown and Reagan were also outsiders when they launched their presidential campaigns.

But voter interest in the presidential primary has declined as its stature diminished. More Republicans voted in the party's 1980 primary than the 1996 contest between Bob Dole and Pat Buchanan, even though the number of registered California Republicans had increased by more than 1.5 million in the meantime. Similarly, the number of ballots cast in each of the Democratic primaries in the 1990s was lower than any since 1964.

Recent California Primary Results

California held its first presidential primary in 1912.

	DEMOCRATS			REPUBLICANS		
Year	Turnout	Candidates	%	Turnout	Candidates	%
1996 (March 26)	2,523,062	BILL CLINTON*	93	2,452,312	BOB DOLE	66
					Pat Buchanan	18
1992 (June 2)	2,863,609	BILL CLINTON	47	2,156,464	GEORGE BUSH*	74
		Jerry Brown	40		Pat Buchanan	26
1988 (June 7)	3,138,734	MICHAEL DUKAKIS	61	2,240,387	GEORGE BUSH	83
		Jesse Jackson	35		Bob Dole	13
1984 (June 5)	2,970,903	GARY HART	39	1,874,975	RONALD REAGAN*	100
		Walter Mondale	35			
		Jesse Jackson	18			
1980 (June 3)	3,363,969	EDWARD KENNEDY	45	2,564,072	RONALD REAGAN	80
		Jimmy Carter*	38		John Anderson	14
		Unpledged	11			
1976 (June 8)	3,409,701	JERRY BROWN	59	2,450,511	RONALD REAGAN	65
		Jimmy Carter	20		Gerald Ford*	35
1972 (June 6)	3,564,518	GEORGE McGOVERN	44	2,283,922	RICHARD NIXON*	90
		Hubert Humphrey	39			
1968 (June 4)	3,181,753	ROBERT KENNEDY	46	1,525,091	RONALD REAGAN	100
		Eugene McCarthy	42			
		No Preference	12			

Note: All candidates are listed that drew at least 10 percent of their party's primary vote. The names of winning candidates are capitalized. An asterisk (*) indicates an incumbent president. There was no direct vote for candidates in the 1984 Democratic primary; results are based on the vote for delegates.

Historically, California elections often have pitted the state's north against its south. But that has become an unfair contest, with most of the population growth concentrated in the south. Roughly 40 percent of the vote in any California primary, Democratic or Republican, is cast in just three southern counties: Los Angeles, Orange and San Diego.

For more than a quarter century, Southern California's GOP has had a distinctly conservative cast. In the pivotal 1964 primary, Nelson Rockefeller swept the San Francisco Bay area and built up a big lead in the north. But Goldwater more than offset that in Southern California to win the primary, 52 to 48 percent.

The tenor of Southern California Republicanism had not changed that much by 1976, as Reagan swept Los Angeles, Orange and San Diego counties with at least two-thirds of the vote. President Gerald Ford carried just two counties, San Francisco and its affluent suburban neighbor, Marin.

Democratic primary results sometime follow the same north-south variation. Both McGovern in 1972 and Hart in 1984 fashioned their victories in Northern California, particularly in the Bay area, which includes the high-tech "Silicon Valley." Both lost Los Angeles County, the anchor of Southern California.

Yet in the 1988 Democratic primary between Michael Dukakis and Jesse Jackson, there was evidence of another faultline developing between the coastal counties and those inland. Jackson ran relatively well in many of the coastal counties where most liberal Democrats are found. But Dukakis dominated in the more conservative counties to the east across the coast range and swamped Jackson statewide.

Some of the same dynamics were present in the Democratic primary four years later. Brown carried many of the environmentally conscious coastal counties in the Bay area and north, the usual starting point for any liberal candidate running in California. But Brown fell short statewide, in part because he lost several counties in the Bay area, including Alameda (which includes Oakland, where Brown was subsequently elected mayor).

Yet even with turnout for the presidential primary at a low ebb, more than twice as many ballots were cast in California in 1996 than any other state, both in the Democratic and Republican primaries.

In much of the Sun Belt, population growth has been synonymous with Republican growth. But not in California, where the population has taken on a rainbow hue, with a large influx of Hispanics and Asians. Since the 1930s, Democrats have been able to maintain a wide voter registration edge.

CALIFORNIA DEMOCRATIC

1968

County	Total Vote	R. Kennedy	McCarthy	Uncommitted	Winner	Percentage of Total Vote R. Kennedy	McCarthy	Uncom.
ALAMEDA	211,069	104,759	84,364	21,946	R. Kennedy	49.6%	40.0%	10.4%
ALPINE	94	51	30	13	R. Kennedy	54.3%	31.9%	13.8%
AMADOR	2,994	1,232	1,415	347	McCarthy	41.1%	47.3%	11.6%
BUTTE	15,749	4,975	8,963	1,811	McCarthy	31.6%	56.9%	11.5%
CALAVERAS	2,762	941	1,445	376	McCarthy	34.1%	52.3%	13.6%
COLUSA	2,296	993	1,096	207	McCarthy	43.2%	47.7%	9.0%
CONTRA COSTA	100,633	44,225	44,329	12,079	McCarthy	43.9%	44.1%	12.0%
DEL NORTE	2,566	1,003	1,364	199	McCarthy	39.1%	53.2%	7.8%
EL DORADO	6,744	2,615	3,220	909	McCarthy	38.8%	47.7%	13.5%
FRESNO	68,995	32,608	29,182	7,205	R. Kennedy	47.3%	42.3%	10.4%
GLENN	3,269	1,326	1,617	326	McCarthy	40.6%	49.5%	10.0%
HUMBOLDT	17,605	7,459	8,517	1,629	McCarthy	42.4%	48.4%	9.3%
IMPERIAL	9,609	4,904	3,883	822	R. Kennedy	51.0%	40.4%	8.6%
INYO	2,891	962	1,433	496	McCarthy	33.3%	49.6%	17.2%
KERN	52,271	19,584	25,421	7,266	McCarthy	37.5%	48.6%	13.9%
KINGS	9,446	4,937	3,613	896	R. Kennedy	52.3%	38.2%	9.5%
LAKE	4,016	1,404	1,938	674	McCarthy	35.0%	48.3%	16.8%
LASSEN	3,394	1,350	1,561	483	McCarthy	39.8%	46.0%	14.2%
LOS ANGELES	1,178,884	586,619	463,928	128,337	R. Kennedy	49.8%	39.4%	10.9%
MADERA	7,387	3,768	2,893	726	R. Kennedy	51.0%	39.2%	9.8%
MARIN	31,465	11,305	16,560	3,600	McCarthy	35.9%	52.6%	11.4%
MARIPOSA	1,344	474	644	226	McCarthy	35.3%	47.9%	16.8%
MENDOCINO	8,985	3,586	4,372	1,027	McCarthy	39.9%	48.7%	11.4%
MERCED	15,120	7,792	5,776	1,552	R. Kennedy	51.5%	38.2%	10.3%
MODOC	1,696	655	864	177	McCarthy	38.6%	50.9%	10.4%
MONO	678	208	355	115	McCarthy	30.7%	52.4%	17.0%
MONTEREY	27,417	12,685	11,807	2,925	R. Kennedy	46.3%	43.1%	10.7%
NAPA	14,808	5,222	7,402	2,184	McCarthy	35.3%	50.0%	14.7%
NEVADA	4,983	1,918	2,392	673	McCarthy	38.5%	48.0%	13.5%
ORANGE	157,498	64,937	72,019	20,542	McCarthy	41.2%	45.7%	13.0%
PLACER	14,961	6,866	6,248	1,847	R. Kennedy	45.9%	41.8%	12.3%
PLUMAS	3,355	1,431	1,536	388	McCarthy	42.7%	45.8%	11.6%
RIVERSIDE	60,734	27,921	25,161	7,652	R. Kennedy	46.0%	41.4%	12.6%
SACRAMENTO	115,194	55,602	44,689	14,903	R. Kennedy	48.3%	38.8%	12.9%
SAN BENITO	3,224	1,845	1,151	228	R. Kennedy	57.2%	35.7%	7.1%
SAN BERNARDINO	90,165	36,732	39,829	13,604	McCarthy	40.7%	44.2%	15.1%
SAN DIEGO	166,093	66,881	72,918	26,294	McCarthy	40.3%	43.9%	15.8%
SAN FRANCISCO	165,352	78,942	64,991	21,419	R. Kennedy	47.7%	39.3%	13.0%
SAN JOAQUIN	45,832	21,512	18,994	5,326	R. Kennedy	46.9%	41.4%	11.6%
SAN LUIS OBISPO	15,352	5,699	7,620	2,033	McCarthy	37.1%	49.6%	13.2%
SAN MATEO	100,116	43,124	44,746	12,246	McCarthy	43.1%	44.7%	12.2%
SANTA BARBARA	36,143	15,031	16,302	4,810	McCarthy	41.6%	45.1%	13.3%
SANTA CLARA	156,051	71,121	64,431	20,499	R. Kennedy	45.6%	41.3%	13.1%
SANTA CRUZ	19,838	7,825	9,182	2,831	McCarthy	39.4%	46.3%	14.3%
SHASTA	14,982	6,297	7,214	1,471	McCarthy	42.0%	48.2%	9.8%
SIERRA	570	209	267	94	McCarthy	36.7%	46.8%	16.5%
SISKIYOU	7,293	3,219	3,270	804	McCarthy	44.1%	44.8%	11.0%
SOLANO	26,994	12,173	10,695	4,126	R. Kennedy	45.1%	39.6%	15.3%
SONOMA	33,053	13,057	15,729	4,267	McCarthy	39.5%	47.6%	12.9%
STANISLAUS	30,766	15,786	12,002	2,978	R. Kennedy	51.3%	39.0%	9.7%

CALIFORNIA DEMOCRATIC

1968

County	Total Vote	R. Kennedy	McCarthy	Uncommitted	Winner	Percentage of Total Vote R. Kennedy	McCarthy	Uncom.
SUTTER	5,957	2,223	3,151	583	McCarthy	37.3%	52.9%	9.8%
TEHAMA	5,490	2,126	2,759	605	McCarthy	38.7%	50.3%	11.0%
TRINITY	1,720	702	851	167	McCarthy	40.8%	49.5%	9.7%
TULARE	23,702	10,227	10,783	2,692	McCarthy	43.1%	45.5%	11.4%
TUOLUMNE	4,423	1,729	2,143	551	McCarthy	39.1%	48.5%	12.5%
VENTURA	47,855	20,932	20,917	6,006	R. Kennedy	43.7%	43.7%	12.6%
YOLO	14,638	6,224	6,850	1,564	McCarthy	42.5%	46.8%	10.7%
YUBA	5,232	2,233	2,469	530	McCarthy	42.7%	47.2%	10.1%
TOTAL	3,181,753	1,472,166	1,329,301	380,286	R. Kennedy	46.3%	41.8%	12.0%

CALIFORNIA DEMOCRATIC

1972

County	Total Vote	Humphrey	McGovern	Other	Winner	Percentage of Total Vote Humphrey	McGovern	Other
ALAMEDA	234,228	69,388	121,068	43,772	McGovern	29.6%	51.7%	18.7%
ALPINE	135	29	67	39	McGovern	21.5%	49.6%	28.9%
AMADOR	3,370	1,252	1,363	755	McGovern	37.2%	40.4%	22.4%
BUTTE	19,523	6,418	9,224	3,881	McGovern	32.9%	47.2%	19.9%
CALAVERAS	3,114	1,122	1,286	706	McGovern	36.0%	41.3%	22.7%
COLUSA	2,210	761	1,077	372	McGovern	34.4%	48.7%	16.8%
CONTRA COSTA	113,088	38,412	52,789	21,887	McGovern	34.0%	46.7%	19.4%
DEL NORTE	2,359	835	1,091	433	McGovern	35.4%	46.2%	18.4%
EL DORADO	8,163	2,801	3,668	1,694	McGovern	34.3%	44.9%	20.8%
FRESNO	77,537	25,669	38,737	13,131	McGovern	33.1%	50.0%	16.9%
GLENN	3,358	1,213	1,439	706	McGovern	36.1%	42.9%	21.0%
HUMBOLDT	20,405	6,653	10,011	3,741	McGovern	32.6%	49.1%	18.3%
IMPERIAL	9,197	2,928	3,855	2,414	McGovern	31.8%	41.9%	26.2%
INYO	2,876	1,195	881	800	Humphrey	41.6%	30.6%	27.8%
KERN	54,147	21,684	18,486	13,977	Humphrey	40.0%	34.1%	25.8%
KINGS	9,380	2,868	4,428	2,084	McGovern	30.6%	47.2%	22.2%
LAKE	5,272	2,103	2,004	1,165	Humphrey	39.9%	38.0%	22.1%
LASSEN	3,947	1,202	1,806	939	McGovern	30.5%	45.8%	23.8%
LOS ANGELES	1,266,081	567,355	486,358	212,368	Humphrey	44.8%	38.4%	16.8%
MADERA	7,555	2,369	3,538	1,648	McGovern	31.4%	46.8%	21.8%
MARIN	39,599	9,738	24,239	5,622	McGovern	24.6%	61.2%	14.2%
MARIPOSA	1,633	524	730	379	McGovern	32.1%	44.7%	23.2%
MENDOCINO	9,422	2,876	4,506	2,040	McGovern	30.5%	47.8%	21.7%
MERCED	15,715	5,405	7,838	2,472	McGovern	34.4%	49.9%	15.7%
MODOC	1,652	500	771	381	McGovern	30.3%	46.7%	23.1%

CALIFORNIA DEMOCRATIC

1972

County	Total Vote	Humphrey	McGovern	Other	Winner	Percentage of Total Vote Humphrey	McGovern	Other
MONO	1,068	305	464	299	McGovern	28.6%	43.4%	28.0%
MONTEREY	27,554	9,507	12,911	5,136	McGovern	34.5%	46.9%	18.6%
NAPA	16,594	5,766	7,522	3,306	McGovern	34.7%	45.3%	19.9%
NEVADA	6,021	2,029	2,800	1,192	McGovern	33.7%	46.5%	19.8%
ORANGE	203,685	86,979	73,375	43,331	Humphrey	42.7%	36.0%	21.3%
PLACER	16,994	6,273	7,713	3,008	McGovern	36.9%	45.4%	17.7%
PLUMAS	3,530	1,089	1,724	717	McGovern	30.8%	48.8%	20.3%
RIVERSIDE	74,504	27,296	31,402	15,806	McGovern	36.6%	42.1%	21.2%
SACRAMENTO	136,804	50,480	64,598	21,726	McGovern	36.9%	47.2%	15.9%
SAN BENITO	2,910	1,141	1,276	493	McGovern	39.2%	43.8%	16.9%
SAN BERNARDINO	100,708	42,774	35,240	22,694	Humphrey	42.5%	35.0%	22.5%
SAN DIEGO	210,796	76,037	91,563	43,196	McGovern	36.1%	43.4%	20.5%
SAN FRANCISCO	154,032	49,730	82,361	21,941	McGovern	32.3%	53.5%	14.2%
SAN JOAQUIN	50,253	17,241	22,173	10,839	McGovern	34.3%	44.1%	21.6%
SAN LUIS OBISPO	19,462	6,595	9,670	3,197	McGovern	33.9%	49.7%	16.4%
SAN MATEO	106,969	38,380	52,286	16,303	McGovern	35.9%	48.9%	15.2%
SANTA BARBARA	46,907	14,733	23,960	8,214	McGovern	31.4%	51.1%	17.5%
SANTA CLARA	181,667	61,164	95,728	24,775	McGovern	33.7%	52.7%	13.6%
SANTA CRUZ	26,855	8,074	14,440	4,341	McGovern	30.1%	53.8%	16.2%
SHASTA	17,710	6,576	7,986	3,148	McGovern	37.1%	45.1%	17.8%
SIERRA	716	198	382	136	McGovern	27.7%	53.4%	19.0%
SISKIYOU	7,570	2,332	3,742	1,496	McGovern	30.8%	49.4%	19.8%
SOLANO	30,134	12,526	11,833	5,775	Humphrey	41.6%	39.3%	19.2%
SONOMA	43,057	13,834	20,927	8,296	McGovern	32.1%	48.6%	19.3%
STANISLAUS	34,152	11,032	18,699	4,421	McGovern	32.3%	54.8%	12.9%
SUTTER	6,511	2,297	2,763	1,451	McGovern	35.3%	42.4%	22.3%
TEHAMA	5,931	1,961	2,704	1,266	McGovern	33.1%	45.6%	21.3%
TRINITY	1,940	613	870	457	McGovern	31.6%	44.8%	23.6%
TULARE	24,558	8,331	11,119	5,108	McGovern	33.9%	45.3%	20.8%
TUOLUMNE	5,237	1,797	2,514	926	McGovern	34.3%	48.0%	17.7%
VENTURA	58,485	24,851	19,880	13,754	Humphrey	42.5%	34.0%	23.5%
YOLO	21,213	5,699	12,426	3,088	McGovern	26.9%	58.6%	14.6%
YUBA	6,025	2,124	2,341	1,560	McGovern	35.3%	38.9%	25.9%
TOTAL	3,564,518	1,375,064	1,550,652	638,802	McGovern	38.6%	43.5%	17.9%

CALIFORNIA REPUBLICAN

1972

County	Total Vote	Nixon	Other	Winner	Percentage of Total Vote	
					Nixon	Other
ALAMEDA	95,665	86,014	9,651	Nixon	89.9%	10.1%
ALPINE	203	175	28	Nixon	86.2%	13.8%
AMADOR	1,886	1,683	203	Nixon	89.2%	10.8%
BUTTE	15,816	14,492	1,324	Nixon	91.6%	8.4%
CALAVERAS	2,336	2,129	207	Nixon	91.1%	8.9%
COLUSA	1,489	1,371	118	Nixon	92.1%	7.9%
CONTRA COSTA	70,828	64,698	6,130	Nixon	91.3%	8.7%
DEL NORTE	1,567	1,471	96	Nixon	93.9%	6.1%
EL DORADO	5,589	5,049	540	Nixon	90.3%	9.7%
FRESNO	37,108	34,045	3,063	Nixon	91.7%	8.3%
GLENN	2,423	2,201	222	Nixon	90.8%	9.2%
HUMBOLDT	11,416	10,306	1,110	Nixon	90.3%	9.7%
IMPERIAL	6,496	6,091	405	Nixon	93.8%	6.2%
INYO	2,474	2,309	165	Nixon	93.3%	6.7%
KERN	33,846	31,194	2,652	Nixon	92.2%	7.8%
KINGS	4,590	4,182	408	Nixon	91.1%	8.9%
LAKE	3,809	3,483	326	Nixon	91.4%	8.6%
LASSEN	1,687	1,515	172	Nixon	89.8%	10.2%
LOS ANGELES	744,967	671,337	73,630	Nixon	90.1%	9.9%
MADERA	3,964	3,689	275	Nixon	93.1%	6.9%
MARIN	31,172	27,523	3,649	Nixon	88.3%	11.7%
MARIPOSA	1,305	1,189	116	Nixon	91.1%	8.9%
MENDOCINO	5,958	5,297	661	Nixon	88.9%	11.1%
MERCED	7,233	6,764	469	Nixon	93.5%	6.5%
MODOC	1,176	1,065	111	Nixon	90.6%	9.4%
MONO	1,187	1,105	82	Nixon	93.1%	6.9%
MONTEREY	23,212	21,070	2,142	Nixon	90.8%	9.2%
NAPA	10,999	10,036	963	Nixon	91.2%	8.8%
NEVADA	4,990	4,275	715	Nixon	85.7%	14.3%
ORANGE	233,872	211,546	22,326	Nixon	90.5%	9.5%
PLACER	9,783	8,751	1,032	Nixon	89.5%	10.5%
PLUMAS	1,639	1,451	188	Nixon	88.5%	11.5%
RIVERSIDE	59,555	54,535	5,020	Nixon	91.6%	8.4%
SACRAMENTO	69,448	61,923	7,525	Nixon	89.2%	10.8%
SAN BENITO	1,897	1,732	165	Nixon	91.3%	8.7%
SAN BERNARDINO	69,505	63,510	5,995	Nixon	91.4%	8.6%
SAN DIEGO	190,296	169,443	20,853	Nixon	89.0%	11.0%
SAN FRANCISCO	54,773	49,488	5,285	Nixon	90.4%	9.6%
SAN JOAQUIN	30,949	28,279	2,670	Nixon	91.4%	8.6%
SAN LUIS OBISPO	15,463	14,047	1,416	Nixon	90.8%	9.2%
SAN MATEO	69,411	61,997	7,414	Nixon	89.3%	10.7%
SANTA BARBARA	35,636	31,854	3,782	Nixon	89.4%	10.6%
SANTA CLARA	122,149	108,317	13,832	Nixon	88.7%	11.3%
SANTA CRUZ	19,114	16,849	2,265	Nixon	88.2%	11.8%
SHASTA	8,507	7,440	1,067	Nixon	87.5%	12.5%
SIERRA	417	365	52	Nixon	87.5%	12.5%
SISKIYOU	3,979	3,620	359	Nixon	91.0%	9.0%
SOLANO	12,212	11,020	1,192	Nixon	90.2%	9.8%
SONOMA	30,087	26,849	3,238	Nixon	89.2%	10.8%
STANISLAUS	20,112	18,556	1,556	Nixon	92.3%	7.7%

CALIFORNIA REPUBLICAN

1972

County	Total Vote	Nixon	Other	Winner	Percentage of Total Vote Nixon	Other
SUTTER	5,907	5,379	528	Nixon	91.1%	8.9%
TEHAMA	3,668	3,271	397	Nixon	89.2%	10.8%
TRINITY	995	867	128	Nixon	87.1%	12.9%
TULARE	17,797	16,599	1,198	Nixon	93.3%	6.7%
TUOLUMNE	3,354	3,045	309	Nixon	90.8%	9.2%
VENTURA	45,216	41,004	4,212	Nixon	90.7%	9.3%
YOLO	9,470	8,380	1,090	Nixon	88.5%	11.5%
YUBA	3,257	2,950	307	Nixon	90.6%	9.4%
TOTAL	2,283,859	2,058,825	225,034	Nixon	90.1%	9.9%
Certified Totals	2,283,922	2,058,825	225,097	Nixon	90.1%	9.9%

CALIFORNIA DEMOCRATIC

1976

County	Total Vote	Brown	Carter	Other	Winner	Percentage of Total Vote Brown	Carter	Other
ALAMEDA	205,606	124,759	31,393	49,454	Brown	60.7%	15.3%	24.1%
ALPINE	193	123	31	39	Brown	63.7%	16.1%	20.2%
AMADOR	4,320	2,433	1,035	852	Brown	56.3%	24.0%	19.7%
BUTTE	20,493	10,825	4,971	4,697	Brown	52.8%	24.3%	22.9%
CALAVERAS	3,385	1,757	875	753	Brown	51.9%	25.8%	22.2%
COLUSA	2,312	1,121	654	537	Brown	48.5%	28.3%	23.2%
CONTRA COSTA	111,902	66,622	20,856	24,424	Brown	59.5%	18.6%	21.8%
DEL NORTE	2,348	852	699	797	Brown	36.3%	29.8%	33.9%
EL DORADO	11,006	6,029	2,644	2,333	Brown	54.8%	24.0%	21.2%
FRESNO	66,061	34,395	19,482	12,184	Brown	52.1%	29.5%	18.4%
GLENN	3,508	1,657	961	890	Brown	47.2%	27.4%	25.4%
HUMBOLDT	21,984	11,007	4,460	6,517	Brown	50.1%	20.3%	29.6%
IMPERIAL	8,936	4,480	2,911	1,545	Brown	50.1%	32.6%	17.3%
INYO	2,852	1,140	876	836	Brown	40.0%	30.7%	29.3%
KERN	49,684	23,886	16,130	9,668	Brown	48.1%	32.5%	19.5%
KINGS	7,936	4,106	2,470	1,360	Brown	51.7%	31.1%	17.1%
LAKE	5,873	3,071	1,569	1,233	Brown	52.3%	26.7%	21.0%
LASSEN	3,690	1,915	994	781	Brown	51.9%	26.9%	21.2%
LOS ANGELES	1,107,141	660,678	223,736	222,727	Brown	59.7%	20.2%	20.1%
MADERA	6,534	3,109	2,234	1,191	Brown	47.6%	34.2%	18.2%
MARIN	44,382	24,755	6,086	13,541	Brown	55.8%	13.7%	30.5%
MARIPOSA	1,873	985	482	406	Brown	52.6%	25.7%	21.7%
MENDOCINO	10,652	5,855	2,381	2,416	Brown	55.0%	22.4%	22.7%
MERCED	15,705	8,727	3,974	3,004	Brown	55.6%	25.3%	19.1%
MODOC	1,784	835	471	478	Brown	46.8%	26.4%	26.8%

CALIFORNIA DEMOCRATIC

1976

County	Total Vote	Brown	Carter	Other	Winner	Percentage of Total Vote Brown	Carter	Other
MONO	931	499	258	174	Brown	53.6%	27.7%	18.7%
MONTEREY	32,937	19,362	7,446	6,129	Brown	58.8%	22.6%	18.6%
NAPA	17,446	10,255	3,706	3,485	Brown	58.8%	21.2%	20.0%
NEVADA	7,236	3,864	1,828	1,544	Brown	53.4%	25.3%	21.3%
ORANGE	234,267	142,189	52,161	39,917	Brown	60.7%	22.3%	17.0%
PLACER	19,068	10,407	5,018	3,643	Brown	54.6%	26.3%	19.1%
PLUMAS	3,540	1,923	848	769	Brown	54.3%	24.0%	21.7%
RIVERSIDE	76,521	42,594	20,915	13,012	Brown	55.7%	27.3%	17.0%
SACRAMENTO	126,324	70,590	29,747	25,987	Brown	55.9%	23.5%	20.6%
SAN BENITO	3,197	1,885	706	606	Brown	59.0%	22.1%	19.0%
SAN BERNARDINO	90,021	53,124	21,774	15,123	Brown	59.0%	24.2%	16.8%
SAN DIEGO	230,442	138,852	45,559	46,031	Brown	60.3%	19.8%	20.0%
SAN FRANCISCO	137,363	84,430	16,664	36,269	Brown	61.5%	12.1%	26.4%
SAN JOAQUIN	44,750	25,684	11,250	7,816	Brown	57.4%	25.1%	17.5%
SAN LUIS OBISPO	22,998	13,221	5,871	3,906	Brown	57.5%	25.5%	17.0%
SAN MATEO	101,625	64,926	14,516	22,183	Brown	63.9%	14.3%	21.8%
SANTA BARBARA	51,559	30,664	9,368	11,527	Brown	59.5%	18.2%	22.4%
SANTA CLARA	185,154	120,082	28,864	36,208	Brown	64.9%	15.6%	19.6%
SANTA CRUZ	34,856	22,067	5,051	7,738	Brown	63.3%	14.5%	22.2%
SHASTA	18,011	10,140	3,685	4,186	Brown	56.3%	20.5%	23.2%
SIERRA	773	414	226	133	Brown	53.6%	29.2%	17.2%
SISKIYOU	7,501	3,985	1,829	1,687	Brown	53.1%	24.4%	22.5%
SOLANO	30,494	18,123	6,469	5,902	Brown	59.4%	21.2%	19.4%
SONOMA	47,548	29,330	7,901	10,317	Brown	61.7%	16.6%	21.7%
STANISLAUS	33,483	18,392	9,541	5,550	Brown	54.9%	28.5%	16.6%
SUTTER	6,556	3,056	2,039	1,461	Brown	46.6%	31.1%	22.3%
TEHAMA	6,444	3,492	1,509	1,443	Brown	54.2%	23.4%	22.4%
TRINITY	2,171	1,112	463	596	Brown	51.2%	21.3%	27.5%
TULARE	23,035	10,198	8,381	4,456	Brown	44.3%	36.4%	19.3%
TUOLUMNE	6,460	3,263	1,873	1,324	Brown	50.5%	29.0%	20.5%
VENTURA	57,835	34,714	13,212	9,909	Brown	60.0%	22.8%	17.1%
YOLO	23,169	12,430	4,372	6,367	Brown	53.6%	18.9%	27.5%
YUBA	5,561	2,821	1,667	1,073	Brown	50.7%	30.0%	19.3%
TOTAL	3,409,651	2,013,210	697,092	699,349	Brown	59.0%	20.4%	20.5%
Certified Totals	3,409,701	2,013,210	697,092	699,399	Brown	59.0%	20.4%	20.5%

Note: The statewide total for "Total Vote" and "Other" includes 215 scattered write-in votes that are not included in the county-by-county results.

CALIFORNIA REPUBLICAN

1976

County	Total Vote	Ford	Reagan	Winner	Percentage of Total Vote Ford	Reagan
ALAMEDA	88,246	36,093	52,153	Reagan	40.9%	59.1%
ALPINE	194	73	121	Reagan	37.6%	62.4%
AMADOR	2,438	737	1,701	Reagan	30.2%	69.8%
BUTTE	16,971	5,088	11,883	Reagan	30.0%	70.0%
CALAVERAS	2,546	757	1,789	Reagan	29.7%	70.3%
COLUSA	1,676	533	1,143	Reagan	31.8%	68.2%
CONTRA COSTA	155,530	66,798	88,732	Reagan	42.9%	57.1%
DEL NORTE	1,602	446	1,156	Reagan	27.8%	72.2%
EL DORADO	8,156	2,234	5,922	Reagan	27.4%	72.6%
FRESNO	39,040	13,947	25,093	Reagan	35.7%	64.3%
GLENN	2,552	823	1,729	Reagan	32.2%	67.8%
HUMBOLDT	11,776	4,456	7,320	Reagan	37.8%	62.2%
IMPERIAL	6,536	1,648	4,888	Reagan	25.2%	74.8%
INYO	2,566	728	1,838	Reagan	28.4%	71.6%
KERN	35,180	8,195	26,985	Reagan	23.3%	76.7%
KINGS	4,516	1,561	2,955	Reagan	34.6%	65.4%
LAKE	4,256	1,226	3,030	Reagan	28.8%	71.2%
LASSEN	1,786	515	1,271	Reagan	28.8%	71.2%
LOS ANGELES	702,521	216,999	485,522	Reagan	30.9%	69.1%
MADERA	4,109	1,354	2,755	Reagan	33.0%	67.0%
MARIN	32,910	16,597	16,313	Ford	50.4%	49.6%
MARIPOSA	1,515	500	1,015	Reagan	33.0%	67.0%
MENDOCINO	6,340	2,444	3,896	Reagan	38.5%	61.5%
MERCED	7,834	2,832	5,002	Reagan	36.2%	63.8%
MODOC	1,304	340	964	Reagan	26.1%	73.9%
MONO	1,048	303	745	Reagan	28.9%	71.1%
MONTEREY	25,491	10,425	15,066	Reagan	40.9%	59.1%
NAPA	12,532	4,976	7,556	Reagan	39.7%	60.3%
NEVADA	6,015	1,631	4,384	Reagan	27.1%	72.9%
ORANGE	277,275	83,941	193,334	Reagan	30.3%	69.7%
PLACER	11,578	3,530	8,048	Reagan	30.5%	69.5%
PLUMAS	1,855	615	1,240	Reagan	33.2%	66.8%
RIVERSIDE	65,194	19,007	46,187	Reagan	29.2%	70.8%
SACRAMENTO	69,041	25,770	43,271	Reagan	37.3%	62.7%
SAN BENITO	2,051	684	1,367	Reagan	33.3%	66.7%
SAN BERNARDINO	71,090	19,824	51,266	Reagan	27.9%	72.1%
SAN DIEGO	221,643	69,349	152,294	Reagan	31.3%	68.7%
SAN FRANCISCO	50,031	25,885	24,146	Ford	51.7%	48.3%
SAN JOAQUIN	30,713	10,303	20,410	Reagan	33.5%	66.5%
SAN LUIS OBISPO	18,544	6,230	12,314	Reagan	33.6%	66.4%
SAN MATEO	70,416	33,232	37,184	Reagan	47.2%	52.8%
SANTA BARBARA	40,248	13,931	26,317	Reagan	34.6%	65.4%
SANTA CLARA	129,987	57,389	72,598	Reagan	44.1%	55.9%
SANTA CRUZ	21,442	8,397	13,045	Reagan	39.2%	60.8%
SHASTA	9,906	3,556	6,350	Reagan	35.9%	64.1%
SIERRA	449	140	309	Reagan	31.2%	68.8%
SISKIYOU	4,383	1,395	2,988	Reagan	31.8%	68.2%
SOLANO	13,657	4,537	9,120	Reagan	33.2%	66.8%
SONOMA	32,467	12,965	19,502	Reagan	39.9%	60.1%
STANISLAUS	20,831	7,622	13,209	Reagan	36.6%	63.4%

CALIFORNIA REPUBLICAN

1976

County	Total Vote	Ford	Reagan	Winner	Percentage of Total Vote Ford	Reagan
SUTTER	6,017	1,663	4,354	Reagan	27.6%	72.4%
TEHAMA	4,143	1,266	2,877	Reagan	30.6%	69.4%
TRINITY	1,245	412	833	Reagan	33.1%	66.9%
TULARE	19,117	6,227	12,890	Reagan	32.6%	67.4%
TUOLUMNE	3,999	1,275	2,724	Reagan	31.9%	68.1%
VENTURA	51,959	16,458	35,501	Reagan	31.7%	68.3%
YOLO	10,876	4,986	5,890	Reagan	45.8%	54.2%
YUBA	3,148	807	2,341	Reagan	25.6%	74.4%
TOTAL	2,450,511	845,655	1,604,836	Reagan	34.5%	65.5%

Note: The statewide total for "Total Vote" includes 20 scattered write-in votes that are not included in the county-by-county results.

CALIFORNIA DEMOCRATIC

1980

County	Total Vote	Carter	E. Kennedy	Uncommitted	Other	Winner	Percentage of Total Vote Carter	E. Kennedy	Uncom.	Other
ALAMEDA	194,716	65,822	96,757	20,553	11,584	E. Kennedy	33.8%	49.7%	10.6%	5.9%
ALPINE	158	68	65	15	10	Carter	43.0%	41.1%	9.5%	6.3%
AMADOR	4,239	1,810	1,625	471	333	Carter	42.7%	38.3%	11.1%	7.9%
BUTTE	23,146	10,106	8,072	3,073	1,895	Carter	43.7%	34.9%	13.3%	8.2%
CALAVERAS	4,039	1,845	1,398	471	325	Carter	45.7%	34.6%	11.7%	8.0%
COLUSA	2,100	901	796	254	149	Carter	42.9%	37.9%	12.1%	7.1%
CONTRA COSTA	116,719	42,944	52,518	15,648	5,609	E. Kennedy	36.8%	45.0%	13.4%	4.8%
DEL NORTE	2,942	1,418	1,012	310	202	Carter	48.2%	34.4%	10.5%	6.9%
EL DORADO	13,695	5,558	5,175	1,932	1,030	Carter	40.6%	37.8%	14.1%	7.5%
FRESNO	66,305	33,327	23,108	6,335	3,535	Carter	50.3%	34.9%	9.6%	5.3%
GLENN	3,310	1,422	1,244	437	207	Carter	43.0%	37.6%	13.2%	6.3%
HUMBOLDT	21,897	8,296	8,280	3,188	2,133	Carter	37.9%	37.8%	14.6%	9.7%
IMPERIAL	8,961	3,513	4,148	636	664	E. Kennedy	39.2%	46.3%	7.1%	7.4%
INYO	2,804	1,261	878	444	221	Carter	45.0%	31.3%	15.8%	7.9%
KERN	48,080	23,113	17,518	4,302	3,147	Carter	48.1%	36.4%	8.9%	6.5%
KINGS	8,120	3,960	2,872	796	492	Carter	48.8%	35.4%	9.8%	6.1%
LAKE	7,323	3,105	2,851	861	506	Carter	42.4%	38.9%	11.8%	6.9%
LASSEN	3,586	1,628	1,193	545	220	Carter	45.4%	33.3%	15.2%	6.1%
LOS ANGELES	1,037,269	354,242	511,234	114,107	57,686	E. Kennedy	34.2%	49.3%	11.0%	5.6%
MADERA	8,245	4,047	2,567	1,157	474	Carter	49.1%	31.1%	14.0%	5.7%
MARIN	39,124	12,934	16,461	7,358	2,371	E. Kennedy	33.1%	42.1%	18.8%	6.1%
MARIPOSA	2,074	1,064	559	321	130	Carter	51.3%	27.0%	15.5%	6.3%
MENDOCINO	11,489	4,768	4,409	1,277	1,035	Carter	41.5%	38.4%	11.1%	9.0%
MERCED	15,932	7,444	5,922	1,635	931	Carter	46.7%	37.2%	10.3%	5.8%
MODOC	1,642	805	480	249	108	Carter	49.0%	29.2%	15.2%	6.6%

CALIFORNIA DEMOCRATIC

1980

County	Total Vote	Carter	E. Kennedy	Uncommitted	Other	Winner	Percentage of Total Vote: Carter	E. Kennedy	Uncom.	Other
MONO	1,055	469	336	148	102	Carter	44.5%	31.8%	14.0%	9.7%
MONTEREY	32,169	12,840	13,770	3,449	2,110	E. Kennedy	39.9%	42.8%	10.7%	6.6%
NAPA	17,828	7,583	6,978	2,069	1,198	Carter	42.5%	39.1%	11.6%	6.7%
NEVADA	9,112	3,820	3,222	1,305	765	Carter	41.9%	35.4%	14.3%	8.4%
ORANGE	217,555	81,231	93,631	25,775	16,918	E. Kennedy	37.3%	43.0%	11.8%	7.8%
PLACER	21,832	8,840	8,728	2,672	1,592	Carter	40.5%	40.0%	12.2%	7.3%
PLUMAS	3,616	1,522	1,310	545	239	Carter	42.1%	36.2%	15.1%	6.6%
RIVERSIDE	85,341	31,705	36,278	12,952	4,406	E. Kennedy	37.2%	42.5%	15.2%	5.2%
SACRAMENTO	145,101	55,858	63,173	17,693	8,377	E. Kennedy	38.5%	43.5%	12.2%	5.8%
SAN BENITO	3,190	1,300	1,528	193	169	E. Kennedy	40.8%	47.9%	6.1%	5.3%
SAN BERNARDINO	108,264	43,074	49,514	8,346	7,330	E. Kennedy	39.8%	45.7%	7.7%	6.8%
SAN DIEGO	224,447	92,814	84,930	32,095	14,608	Carter	41.4%	37.8%	14.3%	6.5%
SAN FRANCISCO	119,396	39,205	64,592	9,639	5,960	E. Kennedy	32.8%	54.1%	8.1%	5.0%
SAN JOAQUIN	50,002	20,768	23,029	2,821	3,384	E. Kennedy	41.5%	46.1%	5.6%	6.8%
SAN LUIS OBISPO	23,942	10,940	8,440	2,735	1,827	Carter	45.7%	35.3%	11.4%	7.6%
SAN MATEO	97,142	35,030	44,190	11,871	6,051	E. Kennedy	36.1%	45.5%	12.2%	6.2%
SANTA BARBARA	45,061	17,279	19,272	4,834	3,676	E. Kennedy	38.3%	42.8%	10.7%	8.2%
SANTA CLARA	181,192	71,904	77,893	19,140	12,255	E. Kennedy	39.7%	43.0%	10.6%	6.8%
SANTA CRUZ	36,083	12,994	15,988	3,897	3,204	E. Kennedy	36.0%	44.3%	10.8%	8.9%
SHASTA	19,800	8,695	6,840	2,988	1,277	Carter	43.9%	34.5%	15.1%	6.4%
SIERRA	756	378	256	68	54	Carter	50.0%	33.9%	9.0%	7.1%
SISKIYOU	7,098	3,219	2,641	792	446	Carter	45.4%	37.2%	11.2%	6.3%
SOLANO	35,937	13,510	16,172	4,323	1,932	E. Kennedy	37.6%	45.0%	12.0%	5.4%
SONOMA	50,984	18,605	20,939	7,603	3,837	E. Kennedy	36.5%	41.1%	14.9%	7.5%
STANISLAUS	35,824	15,979	14,329	3,797	1,719	Carter	44.6%	40.0%	10.6%	4.8%
SUTTER	6,901	3,055	2,411	937	498	Carter	44.3%	34.9%	13.6%	7.2%
TEHAMA	6,730	3,037	2,282	950	461	Carter	45.1%	33.9%	14.1%	6.8%
TRINITY	2,234	1,040	683	331	180	Carter	46.6%	30.6%	14.8%	8.1%
TULARE	25,759	13,596	8,663	1,913	1,587	Carter	52.8%	33.6%	7.4%	6.2%
TUOLUMNE	6,516	3,080	2,581	379	476	Carter	47.3%	39.6%	5.8%	7.3%
VENTURA	65,945	25,093	29,439	7,088	4,325	E. Kennedy	38.1%	44.6%	10.7%	6.6%
YOLO	22,890	9,578	9,748	2,263	1,301	E. Kennedy	41.8%	42.6%	9.9%	5.7%
YUBA	6,241	2,774	2,214	773	480	Carter	44.4%	35.5%	12.4%	7.7%
TOTAL	3,363,909	1,266,216	1,507,142	382,759	207,792	E. Kennedy	37.6%	44.8%	11.4%	6.2%
Certified Totals	3,363,969	1,266,276	1,507,142	382,759	207,792	E. Kennedy	37.6%	44.8%	11.4%	6.2%

Note: The statewide total for "Total Vote" and "Other" includes 51 scattered write-in votes that are not included in the county-by-county results.

CALIFORNIA REPUBLICAN

1980

County	Total Vote	Anderson	Reagan	Other	Winner	Percentage of Total Vote Anderson	Reagan	Other
ALAMEDA	93,081	19,604	65,822	7,655	Reagan	21.1%	70.7%	8.2%
ALPINE	182	26	144	12	Reagan	14.3%	79.1%	6.6%
AMADOR	3,034	320	2,548	166	Reagan	10.5%	84.0%	5.5%
BUTTE	22,367	2,504	18,757	1,106	Reagan	11.2%	83.9%	4.9%
CALAVERAS	3,566	347	3,031	188	Reagan	9.7%	85.0%	5.3%
COLUSA	1,678	156	1,437	85	Reagan	9.3%	85.6%	5.1%
CONTRA COSTA	87,949	16,802	63,985	7,162	Reagan	19.1%	72.8%	8.1%
DEL NORTE	2,225	209	1,870	146	Reagan	9.4%	84.0%	6.6%
EL DORADO	11,840	1,257	9,942	641	Reagan	10.6%	84.0%	5.4%
FRESNO	44,426	5,481	36,213	2,732	Reagan	12.3%	81.5%	6.1%
GLENN	2,899	261	2,484	154	Reagan	9.0%	85.7%	5.3%
HUMBOLDT	14,248	2,467	10,874	907	Reagan	17.3%	76.3%	6.4%
IMPERIAL	7,174	563	6,281	330	Reagan	7.8%	87.6%	4.6%
INYO	3,154	282	2,710	162	Reagan	8.9%	85.9%	5.1%
KERN	39,214	2,821	34,400	1,993	Reagan	7.2%	87.7%	5.1%
KINGS	5,383	459	4,627	297	Reagan	8.5%	86.0%	5.5%
LAKE	5,266	482	4,522	262	Reagan	9.2%	85.9%	5.0%
LASSEN	2,105	207	1,772	126	Reagan	9.8%	84.2%	6.0%
LOS ANGELES	677,932	81,341	558,735	37,856	Reagan	12.0%	82.4%	5.6%
MADERA	5,886	502	4,989	395	Reagan	8.5%	84.8%	6.7%
MARIN	33,678	8,493	22,061	3,124	Reagan	25.2%	65.5%	9.3%
MARIPOSA	1,835	209	1,517	109	Reagan	11.4%	82.7%	5.9%
MENDOCINO	7,702	1,273	5,865	564	Reagan	16.5%	76.1%	7.3%
MERCED	9,415	1,135	7,656	624	Reagan	12.1%	81.3%	6.6%
MODOC	1,417	98	1,257	62	Reagan	6.9%	88.7%	4.4%
MONO	1,347	121	1,158	68	Reagan	9.0%	86.0%	5.0%
MONTEREY	27,489	3,581	21,984	1,924	Reagan	13.0%	80.0%	7.0%
NAPA	14,224	2,144	11,089	991	Reagan	15.1%	78.0%	7.0%
NEVADA	9,046	1,000	7,567	479	Reagan	11.1%	83.7%	5.3%
ORANGE	293,377	29,535	249,582	14,260	Reagan	10.1%	85.1%	4.9%
PLACER	16,245	1,974	13,429	842	Reagan	12.2%	82.7%	5.2%
PLUMAS	2,442	314	1,975	153	Reagan	12.9%	80.9%	6.3%
RIVERSIDE	80,345	8,191	68,352	3,802	Reagan	10.2%	85.1%	4.7%
SACRAMENTO	85,832	13,641	66,528	5,663	Reagan	15.9%	77.5%	6.6%
SAN BENITO	2,465	243	2,073	149	Reagan	9.9%	84.1%	6.0%
SAN BERNARDINO	91,550	8,827	78,178	4,545	Reagan	9.6%	85.4%	5.0%
SAN DIEGO	237,759	26,962	198,335	12,462	Reagan	11.3%	83.4%	5.2%
SAN FRANCISCO	47,155	12,999	30,296	3,860	Reagan	27.6%	64.2%	8.2%
SAN JOAQUIN	35,671	3,814	29,799	2,058	Reagan	10.7%	83.5%	5.8%
SAN LUIS OBISPO	24,329	3,536	19,462	1,331	Reagan	14.5%	80.0%	5.5%
SAN MATEO	72,529	15,358	50,915	6,256	Reagan	21.2%	70.2%	8.6%
SANTA BARBARA	42,795	6,549	32,958	3,288	Reagan	15.3%	77.0%	7.7%
SANTA CLARA	143,010	28,604	102,156	12,250	Reagan	20.0%	71.4%	8.6%
SANTA CRUZ	24,627	4,213	18,881	1,533	Reagan	17.1%	76.7%	6.2%
SHASTA	13,483	1,455	11,050	978	Reagan	10.8%	82.0%	7.3%
SIERRA	536	43	448	45	Reagan	8.0%	83.6%	8.4%
SISKIYOU	5,136	509	4,294	333	Reagan	9.9%	83.6%	6.5%
SOLANO	18,354	2,462	14,662	1,230	Reagan	13.4%	79.9%	6.7%
SONOMA	38,269	7,028	28,480	2,761	Reagan	18.4%	74.4%	7.2%
STANISLAUS	24,661	3,372	19,780	1,509	Reagan	13.7%	80.2%	6.1%

CALIFORNIA REPUBLICAN

1980

County	Total Vote	Anderson	Reagan	Other	Winner	Percentage of Total Vote Anderson	Reagan	Other
SUTTER	6,765	467	6,027	271	Reagan	6.9%	89.1%	4.0%
TEHAMA	4,900	499	4,030	371	Reagan	10.2%	82.2%	7.6%
TRINITY	1,656	187	1,322	147	Reagan	11.3%	79.8%	8.9%
TULARE	23,225	1,829	20,153	1,243	Reagan	7.9%	86.8%	5.4%
TUOLUMNE	4,903	535	4,080	288	Reagan	10.9%	83.2%	5.9%
VENTURA	64,565	7,759	53,174	3,632	Reagan	12.0%	82.4%	5.6%
YOLO	13,891	3,952	8,899	1,040	Reagan	28.5%	64.1%	7.5%
YUBA	3,821	313	3,308	200	Reagan	8.2%	86.6%	5.2%
TOTAL	2,564,072	349,315	2,057,923	156,834	Reagan	13.6%	80.3%	6.1%

Note: The statewide total for "Total Vote" and "Other" includes 14 scattered write-in votes that are not included in the county-by-county results.

CALIFORNIA DEMOCRATIC

1984

County	Total Vote	Hart	J. Jackson	Mondale	Other	Winner	Percentage of Total Vote Hart	J. Jackson	Mondale	Other
ALAMEDA	198,590	66,742	61,688	58,533	11,627	Hart	33.6%	31.1%	29.5%	5.9%
ALPINE	159	72	27	40	20	Hart	45.3%	17.0%	25.2%	12.6%
AMADOR	4,371	1,989	285	1,479	618	Hart	45.5%	6.5%	33.8%	14.1%
BUTTE	20,896	9,975	2,274	6,824	1,823	Hart	47.7%	10.9%	32.7%	8.7%
CALAVERAS	4,606	2,244	339	1,734	289	Hart	48.7%	7.4%	37.6%	6.3%
COLUSA	1,721	775	278	496	172	Hart	45.0%	16.2%	28.8%	10.0%
CONTRA COSTA	103,603	43,903	19,784	34,103	5,813	Hart	42.4%	19.1%	32.9%	5.6%
DEL NORTE	2,276	1,164	198	727	187	Hart	51.1%	8.7%	31.9%	8.2%
EL DORADO	12,001	5,907	1,005	3,685	1,404	Hart	49.2%	8.4%	30.7%	11.7%
FRESNO	58,493	22,935	9,519	22,734	3,305	Hart	39.2%	16.3%	38.9%	5.7%
GLENN	2,792	1,422	195	923	252	Hart	50.9%	7.0%	33.1%	9.0%
HUMBOLDT	20,659	10,441	3,294	5,644	1,280	Hart	50.5%	15.9%	27.3%	6.2%
IMPERIAL	8,302	3,060	934	2,568	1,740	Hart	36.9%	11.3%	30.9%	21.0%
INYO	2,202	1,150	174	683	195	Hart	52.2%	7.9%	31.0%	8.9%
KERN	40,341	15,963	5,811	14,916	3,651	Hart	39.6%	14.4%	37.0%	9.1%
KINGS	6,404	2,444	688	2,727	545	Mondale	38.2%	10.7%	42.6%	8.5%
LAKE	7,646	3,660	640	2,766	580	Hart	47.9%	8.4%	36.2%	7.6%
LASSEN	3,312	1,729	211	1,148	224	Hart	52.2%	6.4%	34.7%	6.8%
LOS ANGELES	904,159	288,127	217,108	330,856	68,068	Mondale	31.9%	24.0%	36.6%	7.5%
MADERA	5,180	2,223	510	1,992	455	Hart	42.9%	9.8%	38.5%	8.8%
MARIN	37,862	19,060	6,099	11,219	1,484	Hart	50.3%	16.1%	29.6%	3.9%
MARIPOSA	2,086	1,073	202	629	182	Hart	51.4%	9.7%	30.2%	8.7%
MENDOCINO	11,570	5,947	1,735	2,984	904	Hart	51.4%	15.0%	25.8%	7.8%
MERCED	12,123	5,271	1,374	4,214	1,264	Hart	43.5%	11.3%	34.8%	10.4%
MODOC	1,403	735	93	446	129	Hart	52.4%	6.6%	31.8%	9.2%

CALIFORNIA DEMOCRATIC

1984

County	Total Vote	Hart	J. Jackson	Mondale	Other	Winner	Percentage of Total Vote Hart	J. Jackson	Mondale	Other
MONO	1,023	533	122	288	80	Hart	52.1%	11.9%	28.2%	7.8%
MONTEREY	34,438	14,840	4,340	13,385	1,873	Hart	43.1%	12.6%	38.9%	5.4%
NAPA	16,855	8,602	1,670	5,332	1,251	Hart	51.0%	9.9%	31.6%	7.4%
NEVADA	9,049	4,834	990	2,630	595	Hart	53.4%	10.9%	29.1%	6.6%
ORANGE	184,287	81,272	18,325	67,310	17,380	Hart	44.1%	9.9%	36.5%	9.4%
PLACER	18,397	8,807	1,513	6,354	1,723	Hart	47.9%	8.2%	34.5%	9.4%
PLUMAS	3,255	1,585	267	1,055	348	Hart	48.7%	8.2%	32.4%	10.7%
RIVERSIDE	79,054	29,008	8,969	33,841	7,236	Mondale	36.7%	11.3%	42.8%	9.2%
SACRAMENTO	123,118	51,020	18,877	44,167	9,054	Hart	41.4%	15.3%	35.9%	7.4%
SAN BENITO	2,652	781	267	1,373	231	Mondale	29.4%	10.1%	51.8%	8.7%
SAN BERNARDINO	85,554	31,210	10,631	35,061	8,652	Mondale	36.5%	12.4%	41.0%	10.1%
SAN DIEGO	183,867	76,771	28,114	64,970	14,012	Hart	41.8%	15.3%	35.3%	7.6%
SAN FRANCISCO	121,905	43,055	32,398	41,000	5,452	Hart	35.3%	26.6%	33.6%	4.5%
SAN JOAQUIN	40,209	16,460	4,295	15,050	4,404	Hart	40.9%	10.7%	37.4%	11.0%
SAN LUIS OBISPO	20,974	9,518	2,253	7,551	1,652	Hart	45.4%	10.7%	36.0%	7.9%
SAN MATEO	89,440	35,797	13,836	35,269	4,538	Hart	40.0%	15.5%	39.4%	5.1%
SANTA BARBARA	37,637	19,286	4,582	10,988	2,781	Hart	51.2%	12.2%	29.2%	7.4%
SANTA CLARA	155,397	69,789	21,414	54,370	9,824	Hart	44.9%	13.8%	35.0%	6.3%
SANTA CRUZ	38,283	17,697	8,619	9,861	2,106	Hart	46.2%	22.5%	25.8%	5.5%
SHASTA	17,255	7,922	1,514	6,597	1,222	Hart	45.9%	8.8%	38.2%	7.1%
SIERRA	763	420	71	230	42	Hart	55.0%	9.3%	30.1%	5.5%
SISKIYOU	6,674	3,281	622	2,332	439	Hart	49.2%	9.3%	34.9%	6.6%
SOLANO	34,231	15,118	6,205	10,702	2,206	Hart	44.2%	18.1%	31.3%	6.4%
SONOMA	50,257	24,911	7,407	14,864	3,075	Hart	49.6%	14.7%	29.6%	6.1%
STANISLAUS	26,851	11,347	2,099	9,585	3,820	Hart	42.3%	7.8%	35.7%	14.2%
SUTTER	4,791	1,974	693	1,575	549	Hart	41.2%	14.5%	32.9%	11.5%
TEHAMA	6,259	3,012	546	2,239	462	Hart	48.1%	8.7%	35.8%	7.4%
TRINITY	2,649	1,387	235	777	250	Hart	52.4%	8.9%	29.3%	9.4%
TULARE	19,228	8,508	2,040	7,139	1,541	Hart	44.2%	10.6%	37.1%	8.0%
TUOLUMNE	6,425	3,128	576	2,388	333	Hart	48.7%	9.0%	37.2%	5.2%
VENTURA	52,652	23,640	5,626	18,967	4,419	Hart	44.9%	10.7%	36.0%	8.4%
YOLO	19,312	9,634	2,489	6,091	1,098	Hart	49.9%	12.9%	31.5%	5.7%
YUBA	5,379	2,341	623	1,931	484	Hart	43.5%	11.6%	35.9%	9.0%
TOTAL	2,970,903	1,155,499	546,693	1,049,342	219,369	Hart	38.9%	18.4%	35.3%	7.4%

Note: California Democrats did not hold a presidential preference vote in 1984. The votes are for each candidate's highest delegate vote-getter in each of California's congressional districts. The statewide total for "Total Vote" and "Other" includes 26 scattered write-in votes that are not included in the county-by-county results.

CALIFORNIA DEMOCRATIC

1988

County	Total Vote	Dukakis	J. Jackson	Other	Winner	Percentage of Total Vote: Dukakis	J. Jackson	Other
ALAMEDA	200,719	96,573	98,051	6,095	J. Jackson	48.1%	48.8%	3.0%
ALPINE	185	97	79	9	Dukakis	52.4%	42.7%	4.9%
AMADOR	4,510	3,457	809	244	Dukakis	76.7%	17.9%	5.4%
BUTTE	21,574	14,603	5,979	992	Dukakis	67.7%	27.7%	4.6%
CALAVERAS	4,726	3,465	1,046	215	Dukakis	73.3%	22.1%	4.5%
COLUSA	1,739	1,367	268	104	Dukakis	78.6%	15.4%	6.0%
CONTRA COSTA	116,624	72,391	40,276	3,957	Dukakis	62.1%	34.5%	3.4%
DEL NORTE	2,930	2,110	665	155	Dukakis	72.0%	22.7%	5.3%
EL DORADO	14,989	10,871	3,264	854	Dukakis	72.5%	21.8%	5.7%
FRESNO	63,997	39,392	21,496	3,109	Dukakis	61.6%	33.6%	4.9%
GLENN	2,642	2,033	425	184	Dukakis	76.9%	16.1%	7.0%
HUMBOLDT	20,085	11,390	7,738	957	Dukakis	56.7%	38.5%	4.8%
IMPERIAL	9,088	5,955	2,629	504	Dukakis	65.5%	28.9%	5.5%
INYO	2,366	1,716	536	114	Dukakis	72.5%	22.7%	4.8%
KERN	42,685	27,858	12,877	1,950	Dukakis	65.3%	30.2%	4.6%
KINGS	6,539	4,562	1,662	315	Dukakis	69.8%	25.4%	4.8%
LAKE	7,809	5,904	1,624	281	Dukakis	75.6%	20.8%	3.6%
LASSEN	3,450	2,562	646	242	Dukakis	74.3%	18.7%	7.0%
LOS ANGELES	920,421	505,507	382,137	32,777	Dukakis	54.9%	41.5%	3.6%
MADERA	8,355	5,660	2,301	394	Dukakis	67.7%	27.5%	4.7%
MARIN	40,258	23,351	15,297	1,610	Dukakis	58.0%	38.0%	4.0%
MARIPOSA	2,333	1,615	596	122	Dukakis	69.2%	25.5%	5.2%
MENDOCINO	13,429	7,348	5,605	476	Dukakis	54.7%	41.7%	3.5%
MERCED	14,933	10,543	3,724	666	Dukakis	70.6%	24.9%	4.5%
MODOC	1,527	1,156	260	111	Dukakis	75.7%	17.0%	7.3%
MONO	1,143	758	339	46	Dukakis	66.3%	29.7%	4.0%
MONTEREY	31,809	18,443	12,289	1,077	Dukakis	58.0%	38.6%	3.4%
NAPA	16,433	11,945	3,856	632	Dukakis	72.7%	23.5%	3.8%
NEVADA	10,692	7,499	2,729	464	Dukakis	70.1%	25.5%	4.3%
ORANGE	177,894	126,625	42,048	9,221	Dukakis	71.2%	23.6%	5.2%
PLACER	21,052	15,644	4,285	1,123	Dukakis	74.3%	20.4%	5.3%
PLUMAS	3,823	2,821	838	164	Dukakis	73.8%	21.9%	4.3%
RIVERSIDE	83,619	59,480	21,166	2,973	Dukakis	71.1%	25.3%	3.6%
SACRAMENTO	146,656	98,601	40,714	7,341	Dukakis	67.2%	27.8%	5.0%
SAN BENITO	3,923	2,550	1,219	154	Dukakis	65.0%	31.1%	3.9%
SAN BERNARDINO	103,178	69,009	29,395	4,774	Dukakis	66.9%	28.5%	4.6%
SAN DIEGO	198,842	130,555	58,761	9,526	Dukakis	65.7%	29.6%	4.8%
SAN FRANCISCO	127,479	58,291	64,956	4,232	J. Jackson	45.7%	51.0%	3.3%
SAN JOAQUIN	44,692	30,819	12,162	1,711	Dukakis	69.0%	27.2%	3.8%
SAN LUIS OBISPO	24,131	15,924	7,181	1,026	Dukakis	66.0%	29.8%	4.3%
SAN MATEO	83,883	54,845	25,476	3,562	Dukakis	65.4%	30.4%	4.2%
SANTA BARBARA	41,669	24,901	15,118	1,650	Dukakis	59.8%	36.3%	4.0%
SANTA CLARA	171,404	111,459	53,141	6,804	Dukakis	65.0%	31.0%	4.0%
SANTA CRUZ	42,955	21,392	20,441	1,122	Dukakis	49.8%	47.6%	2.6%
SHASTA	17,680	13,200	3,425	1,055	Dukakis	74.7%	19.4%	6.0%
SIERRA	684	515	136	33	Dukakis	75.3%	19.9%	4.8%
SISKIYOU	7,032	5,071	1,609	352	Dukakis	72.1%	22.9%	5.0%
SOLANO	37,000	23,141	12,483	1,376	Dukakis	62.5%	33.7%	3.7%
SONOMA	58,043	35,803	20,462	1,778	Dukakis	61.7%	35.3%	3.1%
STANISLAUS	29,986	22,639	6,188	1,159	Dukakis	75.5%	20.6%	3.9%

CALIFORNIA DEMOCRATIC

1988

County	Total Vote	Dukakis	J. Jackson	Other	Winner	Percentage of Total Vote Dukakis	J. Jackson	Other
SUTTER	5,866	4,533	1,015	318	Dukakis	77.3%	17.3%	5.4%
TEHAMA	6,755	5,129	1,219	407	Dukakis	75.9%	18.0%	6.0%
TRINITY	2,337	1,651	529	157	Dukakis	70.6%	22.6%	6.7%
TULARE	22,597	15,595	5,735	1,267	Dukakis	69.0%	25.4%	5.6%
TUOLUMNE	6,824	4,954	1,573	297	Dukakis	72.6%	23.1%	4.4%
VENTURA	55,804	38,619	14,611	2,574	Dukakis	69.2%	26.2%	4.6%
YOLO	20,132	13,261	6,109	762	Dukakis	65.9%	30.3%	3.8%
YUBA	4,804	3,650	895	259	Dukakis	76.0%	18.6%	5.4%
TOTAL	3,138,734	1,910,808	1,102,093	125,833	Dukakis	60.9%	35.1%	4.0%

CALIFORNIA REPUBLICAN

1988

County	Total Vote	Bush	Dole	Robertson	Winner	Percentage of Total Vote Bush	Dole	Robertson
ALAMEDA	65,677	52,274	11,092	2,311	Bush	79.6%	16.9%	3.5%
ALPINE	199	147	37	15	Bush	73.9%	18.6%	7.5%
AMADOR	3,552	2,893	467	192	Bush	81.4%	13.1%	5.4%
BUTTE	20,499	16,887	2,488	1,124	Bush	82.4%	12.1%	5.5%
CALAVERAS	4,281	3,518	570	193	Bush	82.2%	13.3%	4.5%
COLUSA	1,551	1,266	221	64	Bush	81.6%	14.2%	4.1%
CONTRA COSTA	70,648	57,644	10,680	2,324	Bush	81.6%	15.1%	3.3%
DEL NORTE	1,978	1,526	332	120	Bush	77.1%	16.8%	6.1%
EL DORADO	14,406	12,141	1,660	605	Bush	84.3%	11.5%	4.2%
FRESNO	42,829	34,177	6,123	2,529	Bush	79.8%	14.3%	5.9%
GLENN	2,518	2,031	332	155	Bush	80.7%	13.2%	6.2%
HUMBOLDT	11,224	8,617	1,822	785	Bush	76.8%	16.2%	7.0%
IMPERIAL	7,102	6,015	800	287	Bush	84.7%	11.3%	4.0%
INYO	2,955	2,507	321	127	Bush	84.8%	10.9%	4.3%
KERN	42,395	35,057	4,770	2,568	Bush	82.7%	11.3%	6.1%
KINGS	4,718	3,862	567	289	Bush	81.9%	12.0%	6.1%
LAKE	5,266	4,205	776	285	Bush	79.9%	14.7%	5.4%
LASSEN	2,207	1,733	331	143	Bush	78.5%	15.0%	6.5%
LOS ANGELES	510,518	428,503	60,727	21,288	Bush	83.9%	11.9%	4.2%
MADERA	6,079	4,914	815	350	Bush	80.8%	13.4%	5.8%
MARIN	24,117	19,076	4,456	585	Bush	79.1%	18.5%	2.4%
MARIPOSA	2,123	1,644	351	128	Bush	77.4%	16.5%	6.0%
MENDOCINO	7,457	5,748	1,393	316	Bush	77.1%	18.7%	4.2%
MERCED	8,245	6,592	1,201	452	Bush	80.0%	14.6%	5.5%
MODOC	1,313	1,017	223	73	Bush	77.5%	17.0%	5.6%

CALIFORNIA REPUBLICAN

1988

County	Total Vote	Bush	Dole	Robertson	Winner	Percentage of Total Vote Bush	Dole	Robertson
MONO	1,385	1,139	171	75	Bush	82.2%	12.3%	5.4%
MONTEREY	23,110	19,005	3,307	798	Bush	82.2%	14.3%	3.5%
NAPA	12,426	10,155	1,895	376	Bush	81.7%	15.3%	3.0%
NEVADA	11,483	9,557	1,451	475	Bush	83.2%	12.6%	4.1%
ORANGE	280,094	241,265	27,631	11,198	Bush	86.1%	9.9%	4.0%
PLACER	18,780	15,438	2,421	921	Bush	82.2%	12.9%	4.9%
PLUMAS	2,758	2,216	403	139	Bush	80.3%	14.6%	5.0%
RIVERSIDE	84,525	71,593	9,054	3,878	Bush	84.7%	10.7%	4.6%
SACRAMENTO	95,932	79,557	12,075	4,300	Bush	82.9%	12.6%	4.5%
SAN BENITO	2,976	2,470	405	101	Bush	83.0%	13.6%	3.4%
SAN BERNARDINO	99,691	83,579	10,603	5,509	Bush	83.8%	10.6%	5.5%
SAN DIEGO	214,571	179,697	26,965	7,909	Bush	83.7%	12.6%	3.7%
SAN FRANCISCO	31,667	25,853	5,274	540	Bush	81.6%	16.7%	1.7%
SAN JOAQUIN	32,309	26,689	4,026	1,594	Bush	82.6%	12.5%	4.9%
SAN LUIS OBISPO	25,865	20,635	3,865	1,365	Bush	79.8%	14.9%	5.3%
SAN MATEO	49,410	40,141	8,092	1,177	Bush	81.2%	16.4%	2.4%
SANTA BARBARA	37,585	31,386	4,864	1,335	Bush	83.5%	12.9%	3.6%
SANTA CLARA	118,989	92,845	21,364	4,780	Bush	78.0%	18.0%	4.0%
SANTA CRUZ	21,799	17,177	3,607	1,015	Bush	78.8%	16.5%	4.7%
SHASTA	14,493	11,522	2,195	776	Bush	79.5%	15.1%	5.4%
SIERRA	495	394	83	18	Bush	79.6%	16.8%	3.6%
SISKIYOU	4,970	3,812	902	256	Bush	76.7%	18.1%	5.2%
SOLANO	19,051	15,505	2,775	771	Bush	81.4%	14.6%	4.0%
SONOMA	34,375	27,156	5,786	1,433	Bush	79.0%	16.8%	4.2%
STANISLAUS	22,155	18,076	2,983	1,096	Bush	81.6%	13.5%	4.9%
SUTTER	7,242	6,151	778	313	Bush	84.9%	10.7%	4.3%
TEHAMA	5,050	4,048	765	237	Bush	80.2%	15.1%	4.7%
TRINITY	1,770	1,390	248	132	Bush	78.5%	14.0%	7.5%
TULARE	21,727	17,520	2,685	1,522	Bush	80.6%	12.4%	7.0%
TUOLUMNE	5,360	4,459	662	239	Bush	83.2%	12.4%	4.5%
VENTURA	59,550	49,850	7,088	2,612	Bush	83.7%	11.9%	4.4%
YOLO	10,960	8,735	1,840	385	Bush	79.7%	16.8%	3.5%
YUBA	3,862	3,264	402	196	Bush	84.5%	10.4%	5.1%
TOTAL	2,240,387	1,856,273	289,220	94,779	Bush	82.9%	12.9%	4.2%

Note: the statewide total for "Total Vote" includes 115 scattered write-in votes that are not included in the county-by-county results.

CALIFORNIA DEMOCRATIC

1992

County	Total Vote	Brown	Clinton	Other	Winner	Percentage of Total Vote Brown	Clinton	Other
ALAMEDA	178,779	78,573	80,718	19,488	Clinton	43.9%	45.1%	10.9%
ALPINE	149	84	48	17	Brown	56.4%	32.2%	11.4%
AMADOR	4,267	1,582	2,107	578	Clinton	37.1%	49.4%	13.5%
BUTTE	19,041	7,019	9,143	2,879	Clinton	36.9%	48.0%	15.1%
CALAVERAS	4,248	1,759	1,848	641	Clinton	41.4%	43.5%	15.1%
COLUSA	1,623	503	849	271	Clinton	31.0%	52.3%	16.7%
CONTRA COSTA	102,217	41,133	49,470	11,614	Clinton	40.2%	48.4%	11.4%
DEL NORTE	2,743	909	1,471	363	Clinton	33.1%	53.6%	13.2%
EL DORADO	14,260	6,192	5,691	2,377	Brown	43.4%	39.9%	16.7%
FRESNO	49,905	15,247	27,642	7,016	Clinton	30.6%	55.4%	14.1%
GLENN	2,254	594	1,247	413	Clinton	26.4%	55.3%	18.3%
HUMBOLDT	18,461	8,156	7,334	2,971	Brown	44.2%	39.7%	16.1%
IMPERIAL	6,265	2,145	3,161	959	Clinton	34.2%	50.5%	15.3%
INYO	2,029	719	936	374	Clinton	35.4%	46.1%	18.4%
KERN	36,937	11,116	20,657	5,164	Clinton	30.1%	55.9%	14.0%
KINGS	5,782	1,737	3,317	728	Clinton	30.0%	57.4%	12.6%
LAKE	6,486	2,419	3,374	693	Clinton	37.3%	52.0%	10.7%
LASSEN	3,019	967	1,510	542	Clinton	32.0%	50.0%	18.0%
LOS ANGELES	834,756	317,751	426,646	90,359	Clinton	38.1%	51.1%	10.8%
MADERA	6,101	1,739	3,369	993	Clinton	28.5%	55.2%	16.3%
MARIN	43,744	22,989	15,993	4,762	Brown	52.6%	36.6%	10.9%
MARIPOSA	2,022	718	974	330	Clinton	35.5%	48.2%	16.3%
MENDOCINO	13,319	6,976	4,795	1,548	Brown	52.4%	36.0%	11.6%
MERCED	12,399	3,981	6,686	1,732	Clinton	32.1%	53.9%	14.0%
MODOC	1,440	378	791	271	Clinton	26.3%	54.9%	18.8%
MONO	847	452	278	117	Brown	53.4%	32.8%	13.8%
MONTEREY	26,018	10,871	11,605	3,542	Clinton	41.8%	44.6%	13.6%
NAPA	15,771	6,427	7,318	2,026	Clinton	40.8%	46.4%	12.8%
NEVADA	9,331	4,202	3,777	1,352	Brown	45.0%	40.5%	14.5%
ORANGE	151,999	59,439	69,620	22,940	Clinton	39.1%	45.8%	15.1%
PLACER	19,633	8,165	8,451	3,017	Clinton	41.6%	43.0%	15.4%
PLUMAS	3,144	1,141	1,481	522	Clinton	36.3%	47.1%	16.6%
RIVERSIDE	80,087	26,393	44,848	8,846	Clinton	33.0%	56.0%	11.0%
SACRAMENTO	130,221	52,067	58,069	20,085	Clinton	40.0%	44.6%	15.4%
SAN BENITO	3,196	1,234	1,484	478	Clinton	38.6%	46.4%	15.0%
SAN BERNARDINO	93,260	34,510	46,298	12,452	Clinton	37.0%	49.6%	13.4%
SAN DIEGO	193,451	75,130	91,587	26,734	Clinton	38.8%	47.3%	13.8%
SAN FRANCISCO	117,778	58,703	48,731	10,344	Brown	49.8%	41.4%	8.8%
SAN JOAQUIN	38,119	14,656	18,920	4,543	Clinton	38.4%	49.6%	11.9%
SAN LUIS OBISPO	23,042	11,056	8,714	3,272	Brown	48.0%	37.8%	14.2%
SAN MATEO	81,904	38,068	33,926	9,910	Brown	46.5%	41.4%	12.1%
SANTA BARBARA	36,469	15,868	15,341	5,260	Brown	43.5%	42.1%	14.4%
SANTA CLARA	169,535	71,806	74,717	23,012	Clinton	42.4%	44.1%	13.6%
SANTA CRUZ	35,521	19,211	12,208	4,102	Brown	54.1%	34.4%	11.5%
SHASTA	16,132	4,771	8,623	2,738	Clinton	29.6%	53.5%	17.0%
SIERRA	533	215	219	99	Clinton	40.3%	41.1%	18.6%
SISKIYOU	6,130	2,162	3,099	869	Clinton	35.3%	50.6%	14.2%
SOLANO	34,897	14,394	15,765	4,738	Clinton	41.2%	45.2%	13.6%
SONOMA	59,951	30,451	23,428	6,072	Brown	50.8%	39.1%	10.1%
STANISLAUS	29,217	9,895	15,676	3,646	Clinton	33.9%	53.7%	12.5%

CALIFORNIA DEMOCRATIC

1992

County	Total Vote	Brown	Clinton	Other	Winner	Percentage of Total Vote Brown	Clinton	Other
SUTTER	5,464	1,761	2,845	858	Clinton	32.2%	52.1%	15.7%
TEHAMA	5,746	1,682	3,251	813	Clinton	29.3%	56.6%	14.1%
TRINITY	1,894	695	901	298	Clinton	36.7%	47.6%	15.7%
TULARE	18,564	5,573	10,378	2,613	Clinton	30.0%	55.9%	14.1%
TUOLUMNE	6,558	2,839	2,800	919	Brown	43.3%	42.7%	14.0%
VENTURA	53,194	21,469	24,602	7,123	Clinton	40.4%	46.2%	13.4%
YOLO	19,470	8,359	8,331	2,780	Brown	42.9%	42.8%	14.3%
YUBA	4,097	1,409	2,044	644	Clinton	34.4%	49.9%	15.7%
TOTAL	2,863,609	1,150,460	1,359,112	354,037	Clinton	40.2%	47.5%	12.4%

CALIFORNIA REPUBLICAN

1992

County	Total Vote	Buchanan	Bush	Winner	Percentage of Total Vote Buchanan	Bush
ALAMEDA	61,319	14,242	47,077	Bush	23.2%	76.8%
ALPINE	200	42	158	Bush	21.0%	79.0%
AMADOR	3,926	903	3,023	Bush	23.0%	77.0%
BUTTE	19,958	4,974	14,984	Bush	24.9%	75.1%
CALAVERAS	4,105	1,048	3,057	Bush	25.5%	74.5%
COLUSA	1,812	370	1,442	Bush	20.4%	79.6%
CONTRA COSTA	66,093	13,096	52,997	Bush	19.8%	80.2%
DEL NORTE	2,175	567	1,608	Bush	26.1%	73.9%
EL DORADO	15,914	4,002	11,912	Bush	25.1%	74.9%
FRESNO	43,561	9,611	33,950	Bush	22.1%	77.9%
GLENN	2,388	631	1,757	Bush	26.4%	73.6%
HUMBOLDT	11,642	3,267	8,375	Bush	28.1%	71.9%
IMPERIAL	6,060	1,174	4,886	Bush	19.4%	80.6%
INYO	2,785	665	2,120	Bush	23.9%	76.1%
KERN	45,201	11,270	33,931	Bush	24.9%	75.1%
KINGS	4,919	897	4,022	Bush	18.2%	81.8%
LAKE	4,314	1,051	3,263	Bush	24.4%	75.6%
LASSEN	2,412	603	1,809	Bush	25.0%	75.0%
LOS ANGELES	472,335	141,835	330,500	Bush	30.0%	70.0%
MADERA	6,238	1,446	4,792	Bush	23.2%	76.8%
MARIN	21,926	4,795	17,131	Bush	21.9%	78.1%
MARIPOSA	2,044	485	1,559	Bush	23.7%	76.3%
MENDOCINO	7,003	1,941	5,062	Bush	27.7%	72.3%
MERCED	8,388	1,950	6,438	Bush	23.2%	76.8%
MODOC	1,413	348	1,065	Bush	24.6%	75.4%

CALIFORNIA REPUBLICAN

1992

County	Total Vote	Buchanan	Bush	Winner	Percentage of Total Vote Buchanan	Percentage of Total Vote Bush
MONO	1,046	208	838	Bush	19.9%	80.1%
MONTEREY	19,440	4,081	15,359	Bush	21.0%	79.0%
NAPA	11,202	2,482	8,720	Bush	22.2%	77.8%
NEVADA	12,006	3,043	8,963	Bush	25.3%	74.7%
ORANGE	236,699	65,249	171,450	Bush	27.6%	72.4%
PLACER	22,207	5,580	16,627	Bush	25.1%	74.9%
PLUMAS	2,625	602	2,023	Bush	22.9%	77.1%
RIVERSIDE	94,579	24,277	70,302	Bush	25.7%	74.3%
SACRAMENTO	95,270	25,470	69,800	Bush	26.7%	73.3%
SAN BENITO	2,590	546	2,044	Bush	21.1%	78.9%
SAN BERNARDINO	100,162	30,018	70,144	Bush	30.0%	70.0%
SAN DIEGO	228,414	66,331	162,083	Bush	29.0%	71.0%
SAN FRANCISCO	26,363	5,346	21,017	Bush	20.3%	79.7%
SAN JOAQUIN	31,770	6,319	25,451	Bush	19.9%	80.1%
SAN LUIS OBISPO	26,766	6,501	20,265	Bush	24.3%	75.7%
SAN MATEO	45,138	10,188	34,950	Bush	22.6%	77.4%
SANTA BARBARA	40,089	8,952	31,137	Bush	22.3%	77.7%
SANTA CLARA	111,878	26,195	85,683	Bush	23.4%	76.6%
SANTA CRUZ	16,078	3,798	12,280	Bush	23.6%	76.4%
SHASTA	17,146	4,729	12,417	Bush	27.6%	72.4%
SIERRA	483	99	384	Bush	20.5%	79.5%
SISKIYOU	4,703	1,166	3,537	Bush	24.8%	75.2%
SOLANO	19,757	4,911	14,846	Bush	24.9%	75.1%
SONOMA	31,691	7,423	24,268	Bush	23.4%	76.6%
STANISLAUS	23,718	5,027	18,691	Bush	21.2%	78.8%
SUTTER	8,254	1,767	6,487	Bush	21.4%	78.6%
TEHAMA	4,884	1,230	3,654	Bush	25.2%	74.8%
TRINITY	1,559	488	1,071	Bush	31.3%	68.7%
TULARE	21,727	4,120	17,607	Bush	19.0%	81.0%
TUOLUMNE	5,863	1,482	4,381	Bush	25.3%	74.7%
VENTURA	59,483	16,561	42,922	Bush	27.8%	72.2%
YOLO	10,585	2,541	8,044	Bush	24.0%	76.0%
YUBA	3,955	949	3,006	Bush	24.0%	76.0%
TOTAL	2,156,464	568,892	1,587,369	Bush	26.4%	73.6%

CALIFORNIA DEMOCRATIC

1996

County	Total Vote	Clinton	Other	Winner	Percentage of Total Vote Clinton	Other
ALAMEDA	155,330	147,298	8,032	Clinton	94.8%	5.2%
ALPINE	181	160	21	Clinton	88.4%	11.6%
AMADOR	4,331	3,958	373	Clinton	91.4%	8.6%
BUTTE	20,235	18,220	2,015	Clinton	90.0%	10.0%
CALAVERAS	5,360	4,803	557	Clinton	89.6%	10.4%
COLUSA	1,554	1,335	219	Clinton	85.9%	14.1%
CONTRA COSTA	101,138	95,609	5,529	Clinton	94.5%	5.5%
DEL NORTE	2,485	2,213	272	Clinton	89.1%	10.9%
EL DORADO	15,448	13,779	1,669	Clinton	89.2%	10.8%
FRESNO	54,847	49,396	5,451	Clinton	90.1%	9.9%
GLENN	2,142	1,780	362	Clinton	83.1%	16.9%
HUMBOLDT	16,562	14,928	1,634	Clinton	90.1%	9.9%
IMPERIAL	9,022	8,062	960	Clinton	89.4%	10.6%
INYO	1,886	1,642	244	Clinton	87.1%	12.9%
KERN	32,926	28,844	4,082	Clinton	87.6%	12.4%
KINGS	6,461	5,815	646	Clinton	90.0%	10.0%
LAKE	7,994	7,421	573	Clinton	92.8%	7.2%
LASSEN	2,681	2,220	461	Clinton	82.8%	17.2%
LOS ANGELES	641,257	599,271	41,986	Clinton	93.5%	6.5%
MADERA	7,088	6,230	858	Clinton	87.9%	12.1%
MARIN	37,890	36,015	1,875	Clinton	95.1%	4.9%
MARIPOSA	2,092	1,855	237	Clinton	88.7%	11.3%
MENDOCINO	11,473	10,437	1,036	Clinton	91.0%	9.0%
MERCED	12,129	11,046	1,083	Clinton	91.1%	8.9%
MODOC	1,367	1,145	222	Clinton	83.8%	16.2%
MONO	986	915	71	Clinton	92.8%	7.2%
MONTEREY	29,076	27,200	1,876	Clinton	93.5%	6.5%
NAPA	17,224	16,066	1,158	Clinton	93.3%	6.7%
NEVADA	10,062	9,344	718	Clinton	92.9%	7.1%
ORANGE	142,200	130,304	11,896	Clinton	91.6%	8.4%
PLACER	20,775	18,721	2,054	Clinton	90.1%	9.9%
PLUMAS	2,813	2,486	327	Clinton	88.4%	11.6%
RIVERSIDE	77,966	71,870	6,096	Clinton	92.2%	7.8%
SACRAMENTO	120,600	110,790	9,810	Clinton	91.9%	8.1%
SAN BENITO	3,907	3,604	303	Clinton	92.2%	7.8%
SAN BERNARDINO	83,809	75,316	8,493	Clinton	89.9%	10.1%
SAN DIEGO	149,099	137,933	11,166	Clinton	92.5%	7.5%
SAN FRANCISCO	106,730	103,454	3,276	Clinton	96.9%	3.1%
SAN JOAQUIN	39,444	36,237	3,207	Clinton	91.9%	8.1%
SAN LUIS OBISPO	23,100	21,460	1,640	Clinton	92.9%	7.1%
SAN MATEO	73,808	70,607	3,201	Clinton	95.7%	4.3%
SANTA BARBARA	35,307	32,873	2,434	Clinton	93.1%	6.9%
SANTA CLARA	140,586	131,255	9,331	Clinton	93.4%	6.6%
SANTA CRUZ	33,868	31,995	1,873	Clinton	94.5%	5.5%
SHASTA	14,272	12,244	2,028	Clinton	85.8%	14.2%
SIERRA	526	435	91	Clinton	82.7%	17.3%
SISKIYOU	5,913	5,239	674	Clinton	88.6%	11.4%
SOLANO	33,262	30,308	2,954	Clinton	91.1%	8.9%
SONOMA	59,668	56,245	3,423	Clinton	94.3%	5.7%
STANISLAUS	29,915	27,492	2,423	Clinton	91.9%	8.1%

CALIFORNIA DEMOCRATIC

1996

County	Total Vote	Clinton	Other	Winner	Percentage of Total Vote	
					Clinton	Other
SUTTER	5,064	4,403	661	Clinton	86.9%	13.1%
TEHAMA	5,631	4,765	866	Clinton	84.6%	15.4%
TRINITY	1,840	1,565	275	Clinton	85.1%	14.9%
TULARE	17,306	15,321	1,985	Clinton	88.5%	11.5%
TUOLUMNE	6,312	5,808	504	Clinton	92.0%	8.0%
VENTURA	55,262	51,497	3,765	Clinton	93.2%	6.8%
YOLO	18,592	17,279	1,313	Clinton	92.9%	7.1%
YUBA	4,260	3,672	588	Clinton	86.2%	13.8%
TOTAL	2,523,062	2,342,185	180,877	Clinton	92.8%	7.2%

CALIFORNIA REPUBLICAN

1996

County	Total Vote	Buchanan	Dole	Other	Winner	Percentage of Total Vote		
						Buchanan	Dole	Other
ALAMEDA	65,909	11,433	43,783	10,693	Dole	17.3%	66.4%	16.2%
ALPINE	258	43	163	52	Dole	16.7%	63.2%	20.2%
AMADOR	5,003	1,118	3,189	696	Dole	22.3%	63.7%	13.9%
BUTTE	26,803	6,421	16,674	3,708	Dole	24.0%	62.2%	13.8%
CALAVERAS	6,575	1,515	4,023	1,037	Dole	23.0%	61.2%	15.8%
COLUSA	2,058	353	1,426	279	Dole	17.2%	69.3%	13.6%
CONTRA COSTA	81,082	12,134	56,445	12,503	Dole	15.0%	69.6%	15.4%
DEL NORTE	2,559	600	1,493	466	Dole	23.4%	58.3%	18.2%
EL DORADO	22,905	3,890	15,252	3,763	Dole	17.0%	66.6%	16.4%
FRESNO	64,816	9,350	45,077	10,389	Dole	14.4%	69.5%	16.0%
GLENN	3,149	778	1,970	401	Dole	24.7%	62.6%	12.7%
HUMBOLDT	12,891	2,286	8,322	2,283	Dole	17.7%	64.6%	17.7%
IMPERIAL	7,700	1,414	5,335	951	Dole	18.4%	69.3%	12.4%
INYO	3,130	625	2,136	369	Dole	20.0%	68.2%	11.8%
KERN	58,373	11,795	38,094	8,484	Dole	20.2%	65.3%	14.5%
KINGS	7,638	1,330	5,331	977	Dole	17.4%	69.8%	12.8%
LAKE	6,360	1,175	4,276	909	Dole	18.5%	67.2%	14.3%
LASSEN	3,032	685	1,953	394	Dole	22.6%	64.4%	13.0%
LOS ANGELES	472,325	98,962	302,611	70,752	Dole	21.0%	64.1%	15.0%
MADERA	10,244	2,002	6,712	1,530	Dole	19.5%	65.5%	14.9%
MARIN	23,472	2,918	16,398	4,156	Dole	12.4%	69.9%	17.7%
MARIPOSA	2,833	650	1,703	480	Dole	22.9%	60.1%	16.9%
MENDOCINO	7,778	1,354	5,241	1,183	Dole	17.4%	67.4%	15.2%
MERCED	11,061	2,021	7,534	1,506	Dole	18.3%	68.1%	13.6%
MODOC	1,782	345	1,189	248	Dole	19.4%	66.7%	13.9%

CALIFORNIA REPUBLICAN

1996

County	Total Vote	Buchanan	Dole	Other	Winner	Percentage of Total Vote Buchanan	Dole	Other
MONO	1,618	300	1,059	259	Dole	18.5%	65.5%	16.0%
MONTEREY	25,605	3,238	17,975	4,392	Dole	12.6%	70.2%	17.2%
NAPA	14,429	2,537	9,884	2,008	Dole	17.6%	68.5%	13.9%
NEVADA	16,139	2,499	11,309	2,331	Dole	15.5%	70.1%	14.4%
ORANGE	286,757	50,989	185,634	50,134	Dole	17.8%	64.7%	17.5%
PLACER	31,963	5,394	21,437	5,132	Dole	16.9%	67.1%	16.1%
PLUMAS	3,360	655	2,177	528	Dole	19.5%	64.8%	15.7%
RIVERSIDE	117,347	23,854	77,269	16,224	Dole	20.3%	65.8%	13.8%
SACRAMENTO	108,838	17,684	74,349	16,805	Dole	16.2%	68.3%	15.4%
SAN BENITO	3,609	609	2,530	470	Dole	16.9%	70.1%	13.0%
SAN BERNARDINO	113,743	26,549	71,106	16,088	Dole	23.3%	62.5%	14.1%
SAN DIEGO	227,552	40,091	152,920	34,541	Dole	17.6%	67.2%	15.2%
SAN FRANCISCO	29,007	3,618	20,341	5,048	Dole	12.5%	70.1%	17.4%
SAN JOAQUIN	41,239	8,346	27,704	5,189	Dole	20.2%	67.2%	12.6%
SAN LUIS OBISPO	32,660	5,592	22,113	4,955	Dole	17.1%	67.7%	15.2%
SAN MATEO	48,391	6,788	34,142	7,461	Dole	14.0%	70.6%	15.4%
SANTA BARBARA	43,023	6,914	30,045	6,064	Dole	16.1%	69.8%	14.1%
SANTA CLARA	111,506	17,565	75,764	18,177	Dole	15.8%	67.9%	16.3%
SANTA CRUZ	19,508	2,567	12,601	4,340	Dole	13.2%	64.6%	22.2%
SHASTA	20,252	4,401	12,894	2,957	Dole	21.7%	63.7%	14.6%
SIERRA	628	138	382	108	Dole	22.0%	60.8%	17.2%
SISKIYOU	6,558	1,190	4,291	1,077	Dole	18.1%	65.4%	16.4%
SOLANO	24,029	4,471	15,972	3,586	Dole	18.6%	66.5%	14.9%
SONOMA	39,368	6,198	26,759	6,411	Dole	15.7%	68.0%	16.3%
STANISLAUS	31,044	6,423	19,430	5,191	Dole	20.7%	62.6%	16.7%
SUTTER	9,125	1,648	6,262	1,215	Dole	18.1%	68.6%	13.3%
TEHAMA	6,581	1,722	4,057	802	Dole	26.2%	61.6%	12.2%
TRINITY	1,914	470	1,139	305	Dole	24.6%	59.5%	15.9%
TULARE	27,068	5,420	18,108	3,540	Dole	20.0%	66.9%	13.1%
TUOLUMNE	7,397	1,407	4,909	1,081	Dole	19.0%	66.4%	14.6%
VENTURA	74,176	13,302	46,760	14,114	Dole	17.9%	63.0%	19.0%
YOLO	12,841	1,812	8,730	2,299	Dole	14.1%	68.0%	17.9%
YUBA	5,301	1,107	3,549	645	Dole	20.9%	66.9%	12.2%
TOTAL	2,452,312	450,695	1,619,931	381,686	Dole	18.4%	66.1%	15.6%

COLORADO

Colorado's decision to hold its first presidential primary in 1992 was due in no small part to the contentious caucus process that Democrats went through four years earlier.

The precinct caucuses in 1988 were held in early April, just as Jesse Jackson's candidacy was peaking. The critical Wisconsin primary was to be held the next day. When Colorado Democratic officials seemed slow in tallying the caucus results, Jackson cried foul. He accused the state party chairman, a supporter of Michael Dukakis, of delaying the count so that Colorado would not influence Wisconsin.

State party officials countered that they were tabulating the votes from the nearly 3,000 precinct caucuses more quickly than they usually did. But they were clearly caught off-guard by the clamor of both Jackson and the national media for quicker returns. When the results were finally in, Dukakis had won (as sample precincts had indicated from the beginning), but the whole episode helped fuel momentum for a state-operated presidential primary.

When the first primary was held four years later, Jackson and Dukakis were gone from the scene, but the race on the Democratic side was as closely contested as it had been in 1988. The early March date that Colorado voted was at a time when all of the candidates were looking for traction. And when the nearly quarter million votes were cast, less than 8,000 separated the top three finishers. Jerry Brown emerged the winner, one of only two primaries he was to win in 1992; the other was Connecticut.

Brown won with a pro-environment, anti-establishment appeal that swept Colorado's liberal "granola belt," which extends westward from Denver through the college town of Boulder and skiing communities on the Western Slope, such as Aspen (Pitkin County), Vail (Eagle) and Telluride (San Miguel). Denver and Boulder counties, in particular, have a disproportionate influence on Democratic primaries. In 1992, 20 percent of the ballots cast in the party's presidential primary came from Denver, 10 percent from Boulder County.

Bill Clinton finished a close second by winning the farm counties of the High Plains, ranching counties of the Western Slope, Hispanic counties of southern Colorado and blue-collar strongholds such as Pueblo and Adams counties (the latter in the Denver suburbs). Paul Tsongas ran a close third by carrying the more upscale suburban counties of Arapahoe and Douglas, as well as El Paso County (Colorado Springs).

None of the Republican presidential primaries have been nearly as compelling as the inaugural Democratic contest in 1992. Each GOP primary has given a boost to the front-runner.

President George Bush swept all 63 counties in winning the Republican primary in 1992. His lone challenger, Pat Buchanan, reached 40 percent only in tiny Gilpin County, high in the mountains west of Denver.

Bob Dole won Colorado's Republican primary in 1996 almost as convincingly. He garnered more votes than his two nearest rivals combined, Buchanan and Steve Forbes, and carried every county except small, predominantly Hispanic Costilla, along Colorado's southern border. It went for Forbes.

The bulk of both parties' voters, though, can be found in a strip less than 200 miles long along the Front Range of the Rocky Mountains. Democrats tend to be strongest at the two ends—Boulder, Adams and Denver counties on the north and Pueblo on the south. Republicans tend to be stronger in between: in the affluent suburbs of Arapahoe and Jefferson counties near Denver, and just to the south in El Paso County (Colorado Springs), with its large representation of military and Christian conservatives.

Recent Colorado Primary Results

Colorado held its first presidential primary in 1992.

	DEMOCRATS			REPUBLICANS		
Year	Turnout	Candidates	%	Turnout	Candidates	%
1996 (March 5)	54,527	BILL CLINTON*	89	247,930	BOB DOLE	44
		Lyndon LaRouche	11		Pat Buchanan	22
					Steve Forbes	21
1992 (March 3)	239,643	JERRY BROWN	29	195,690	GEORGE BUSH*	68
		Bill Clinton	27		Pat Buchanan	30
		Paul Tsongas	26			
		Bob Kerrey	12			

Note: All candidates are listed who drew at least 10 percent of their party's primary vote. The names of winning candidates are capitalized. An asterisk (*) indicates an incumbent president.

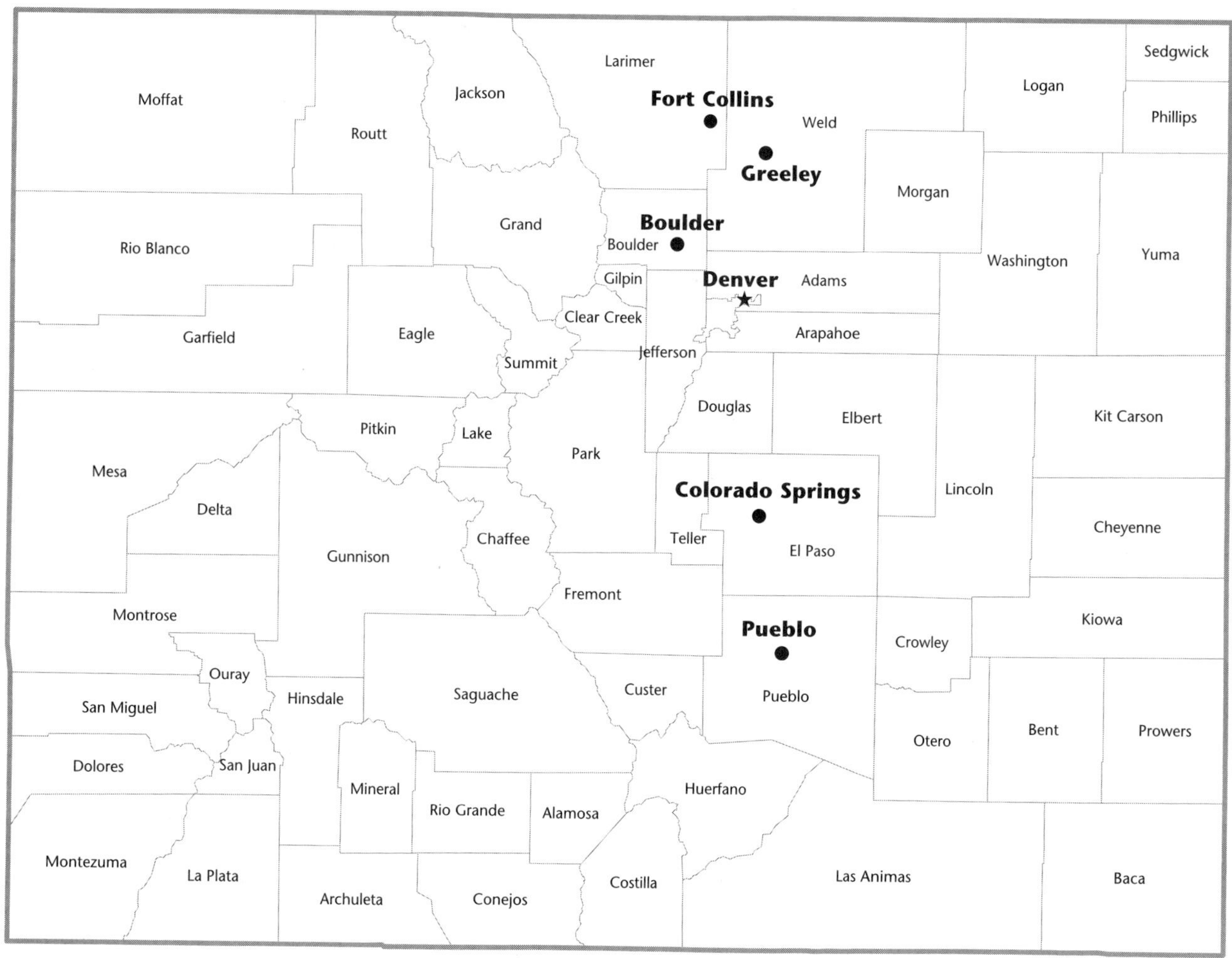

Moffat
Jackson
Larimer
Fort Collins
Weld
Logan
Sedgwick
Phillips
Routt
Greeley
Morgan
Rio Blanco
Grand
Boulder
Boulder
Washington
Yuma
Gilpin
Denver
Adams
Clear Creek
Garfield
Eagle
Arapahoe
Summit
Jefferson
Douglas
Elbert
Kit Carson
Pitkin
Lake
Mesa
Park
Colorado Springs
Lincoln
Delta
Cheyenne
Chaffee
Teller
El Paso
Gunnison
Fremont
Montrose
Pueblo
Kiowa
Crowley
Ouray
San Miguel
Hinsdale
Saguache
Custer
Pueblo
Bent
Prowers
Otero
Dolores
San Juan
Mineral
Huerfano
Rio Grande
Alamosa
Montezuma
La Plata
Costilla
Las Animas
Baca
Archuleta
Conejos

COLORADO DEMOCRATIC

1992

County	Total Vote	Brown	Clinton	Kerrey	Tsongas	Other	Winner	Percentage of Total Vote: Brown	Clinton	Kerrey	Tsongas	Other
ADAMS	15,229	3,862	5,094	2,123	3,169	981	Clinton	25.4%	33.4%	13.9%	20.8%	6.4%
ALAMOSA	752	139	257	101	198	57	Clinton	18.5%	34.2%	13.4%	26.3%	7.6%
ARAPAHOE	24,982	6,977	6,059	3,293	7,483	1,170	Tsongas	27.9%	24.3%	13.2%	30.0%	4.7%
ARCHULETA	241	59	69	33	62	18	Clinton	24.5%	28.6%	13.7%	25.7%	7.5%
BACA	563	96	221	61	102	83	Clinton	17.1%	39.3%	10.8%	18.1%	14.7%
BENT	442	80	173	52	54	83	Clinton	18.1%	39.1%	11.8%	12.2%	18.8%
BOULDER	24,170	10,334	3,631	2,446	6,578	1,181	Brown	42.8%	15.0%	10.1%	27.2%	4.9%
CHAFFEE	802	184	241	132	172	73	Clinton	22.9%	30.0%	16.5%	21.4%	9.1%
CHEYENNE	169	37	52	32	23	25	Clinton	21.9%	30.8%	18.9%	13.6%	14.8%
CLEAR CREEK	656	245	110	92	167	42	Brown	37.3%	16.8%	14.0%	25.5%	6.4%
CONEJOS	502	67	293	44	68	30	Clinton	13.3%	58.4%	8.8%	13.5%	6.0%
COSTILLA	561	56	403	28	47	27	Clinton	10.0%	71.8%	5.0%	8.4%	4.8%
CROWLEY	285	44	144	31	46	20	Clinton	15.4%	50.5%	10.9%	16.1%	7.0%
CUSTER	149	31	50	21	32	15	Clinton	20.8%	33.6%	14.1%	21.5%	10.1%
DELTA	1,564	387	498	244	290	145	Clinton	24.7%	31.8%	15.6%	18.5%	9.3%
DENVER	48,530	15,466	12,845	4,673	13,207	2,339	Brown	31.9%	26.5%	9.6%	27.2%	4.8%
DOLORES	174	26	78	30	31	9	Clinton	14.9%	44.8%	17.2%	17.8%	5.2%
DOUGLAS	2,819	854	561	412	861	131	Tsongas	30.3%	19.9%	14.6%	30.5%	4.6%
EAGLE	1,040	375	190	155	263	57	Brown	36.1%	18.3%	14.9%	25.3%	5.5%
ELBERT	502	145	129	69	126	33	Brown	28.9%	25.7%	13.7%	25.1%	6.6%
EL PASO	15,239	3,575	4,347	1,673	4,519	1,125	Tsongas	23.5%	28.5%	11.0%	29.7%	7.4%
FREMONT	2,076	362	887	283	418	126	Clinton	17.4%	42.7%	13.6%	20.1%	6.1%
GARFIELD	2,115	659	518	361	437	140	Brown	31.2%	24.5%	17.1%	20.7%	6.6%
GILPIN	261	109	39	26	74	13	Brown	41.8%	14.9%	10.0%	28.4%	5.0%
GRAND	448	123	105	71	122	27	Brown	27.5%	23.4%	15.8%	27.2%	6.0%
GUNNISON	905	423	145	121	166	50	Brown	46.7%	16.0%	13.4%	18.3%	5.5%
HINSDALE	55	19	6	9	20	1	Tsongas	34.5%	10.9%	16.4%	36.4%	1.8%
HUERFANO	951	215	423	114	136	63	Clinton	22.6%	44.5%	12.0%	14.3%	6.6%
JACKSON	85	14	29	12	17	13	Clinton	16.5%	34.1%	14.1%	20.0%	15.3%
JEFFERSON	33,416	10,119	7,514	4,233	9,606	1,944	Brown	30.3%	22.5%	12.7%	28.7%	5.8%
KIOWA	187	19	105	27	26	10	Clinton	10.2%	56.1%	14.4%	13.9%	5.3%
KIT CARSON	422	77	161	71	81	32	Clinton	18.2%	38.2%	16.8%	19.2%	7.6%
LAKE	680	191	193	94	150	52	Clinton	28.1%	28.4%	13.8%	22.1%	7.6%
LA PLATA	1,911	623	364	238	537	149	Brown	32.6%	19.0%	12.5%	28.1%	7.8%
LARIMER	12,019	3,662	2,442	1,773	3,379	763	Brown	30.5%	20.3%	14.8%	28.1%	6.3%
LAS ANIMAS	2,402	246	646	127	278	1,105	Clinton	10.2%	26.9%	5.3%	11.6%	46.0%
LINCOLN	366	51	156	57	62	40	Clinton	13.9%	42.6%	15.6%	16.9%	10.9%
LOGAN	1,076	193	326	264	226	67	Clinton	17.9%	30.3%	24.5%	21.0%	6.2%
MESA	7,239	1,825	1,970	1,347	1,531	566	Clinton	25.2%	27.2%	18.6%	21.1%	7.8%
MINERAL	129	22	46	14	32	15	Clinton	17.1%	35.7%	10.9%	24.8%	11.6%
MOFFAT	535	128	141	55	141	70		23.9%	26.4%	10.3%	26.4%	13.1%
MONTEZUMA	974	222	284	137	214	117	Clinton	22.8%	29.2%	14.1%	22.0%	12.0%
MONTROSE	1,664	408	458	332	306	160	Clinton	24.5%	27.5%	20.0%	18.4%	9.6%
MORGAN	851	151	342	134	166	58	Clinton	17.7%	40.2%	15.7%	19.5%	6.8%
OTERO	1,076	158	477	143	195	103	Clinton	14.7%	44.3%	13.3%	18.1%	9.6%
OURAY	150	50	28	23	36	13	Brown	33.3%	18.7%	15.3%	24.0%	8.7%
PARK	523	178	112	61	130	42	Brown	34.0%	21.4%	11.7%	24.9%	8.0%
PHILLIPS	275	46	79	79	56	15		16.7%	28.7%	28.7%	20.4%	5.5%
PITKIN	1,045	405	121	122	307	90	Brown	38.8%	11.6%	11.7%	29.4%	8.6%
PROWERS	582	94	236	98	107	47	Clinton	16.2%	40.5%	16.8%	18.4%	8.1%

COLORADO DEMOCRATIC

1992

County	Total Vote	Brown	Clinton	Kerrey	Tsongas	Other	Winner	Percentage of Total Vote Brown	Clinton	Kerrey	Tsongas	Other
PUEBLO	14,623	2,291	7,418	1,824	2,279	811	Clinton	15.7%	50.7%	12.5%	15.6%	5.5%
RIO BLANCO	309	47	97	60	56	49	Clinton	15.2%	31.4%	19.4%	18.1%	15.9%
RIO GRANDE	570	101	202	54	152	61	Clinton	17.7%	35.4%	9.5%	26.7%	10.7%
ROUTT	1,141	403	241	139	296	62	Brown	35.3%	21.1%	12.2%	25.9%	5.4%
SAGUACHE	344	113	104	33	62	32	Brown	32.8%	30.2%	9.6%	18.0%	9.3%
SAN JUAN	69	26	12	12	19		Brown	37.7%	17.4%	17.4%	27.5%	
SAN MIGUEL	408	157	70	41	115	25	Brown	38.5%	17.2%	10.0%	28.2%	6.1%
SEDGWICK	146	19	50	38	23	16	Clinton	13.0%	34.2%	26.0%	15.8%	11.0%
SUMMIT	789	275	103	117	245	49	Brown	34.9%	13.1%	14.8%	31.1%	6.2%
TELLER	695	217	173	88	163	54	Brown	31.2%	24.9%	12.7%	23.5%	7.8%
WASHINGTON	260	34	94	38	68	26	Clinton	13.1%	36.2%	14.6%	26.2%	10.0%
WELD	5,960	1,473	1,925	857	1,309	396	Clinton	24.7%	32.3%	14.4%	22.0%	6.6%
YUMA	540	86	183	100	119	52	Clinton	15.9%	33.9%	18.5%	22.0%	9.6%
TOTAL	239,643	69,073	64,470	29,572	61,360	15,168	Brown	28.8%	26.9%	12.3%	25.6%	6.3%

COLORADO REPUBLICAN

1992

County	Total Vote	Buchanan	Bush	Other	Winner	Percentage of Total Vote Buchanan	Bush	Other
ADAMS	7,917	2,467	5,222	228	Bush	31.2%	66.0%	2.9%
ALAMOSA	579	124	444	11	Bush	21.4%	76.7%	1.9%
ARAPAHOE	27,979	8,224	19,129	626	Bush	29.4%	68.4%	2.2%
ARCHULETA	417	128	285	4	Bush	30.7%	68.3%	1.0%
BACA	409	97	308	4	Bush	23.7%	75.3%	1.0%
BENT	222	68	151	3	Bush	30.6%	68.0%	1.4%
BOULDER	11,775	3,554	7,917	304	Bush	30.2%	67.2%	2.6%
CHAFFEE	811	246	524	41	Bush	30.3%	64.6%	5.1%
CHEYENNE	283	102	176	5	Bush	36.0%	62.2%	1.8%
CLEAR CREEK	509	182	311	16	Bush	35.8%	61.1%	3.1%
CONEJOS	419	121	286	12	Bush	28.9%	68.3%	2.9%
COSTILLA	55	18	34	3	Bush	32.7%	61.8%	5.5%
CROWLEY	295	50	235	10	Bush	16.9%	79.7%	3.4%
CUSTER	339	80	246	13	Bush	23.6%	72.6%	3.8%
DELTA	2,142	705	1,389	48	Bush	32.9%	64.8%	2.2%
DENVER	20,050	5,608	13,750	692	Bush	28.0%	68.6%	3.5%
DOLORES	86	33	50	3	Bush	38.4%	58.1%	3.5%
DOUGLAS	4,688	1,498	3,122	68	Bush	32.0%	66.6%	1.5%
EAGLE	900	288	585	27	Bush	32.0%	65.0%	3.0%
ELBERT	688	206	472	10	Bush	29.9%	68.6%	1.5%
EL PASO	25,122	8,010	16,706	406	Bush	31.9%	66.5%	1.6%
FREMONT	2,200	609	1,539	52	Bush	27.7%	70.0%	2.4%
GARFIELD	1,724	500	1,185	39	Bush	29.0%	68.7%	2.3%
GILPIN	166	67	91	8	Bush	40.4%	54.8%	4.8%
GRAND	1,140	386	721	33	Bush	33.9%	63.2%	2.9%

COLORADO REPUBLICAN

1992

County	Total Vote	Buchanan	Bush	Other	Winner	Percentage of Total Vote Buchanan	Bush	Other
GUNNISON	626	230	379	17	Bush	36.7%	60.5%	2.7%
HINSDALE	148	57	86	5	Bush	38.5%	58.1%	3.4%
HUERFANO	141	27	114		Bush	19.1%	80.9%	
JACKSON	208	48	158	2	Bush	23.1%	76.0%	1.0%
JEFFERSON	32,398	10,166	21,418	814	Bush	31.4%	66.1%	2.5%
KIOWA	176	42	133	1	Bush	23.9%	75.6%	0.6%
KIT CARSON	851	243	600	8	Bush	28.6%	70.5%	0.9%
LAKE	209	69	133	7	Bush	33.0%	63.6%	3.3%
LA PLATA	1,869	585	1,228	56	Bush	31.3%	65.7%	3.0%
LARIMER	13,053	3,809	8,852	392	Bush	29.2%	67.8%	3.0%
LAS ANIMAS	351	63	176	112	Bush	17.9%	50.1%	31.9%
LINCOLN	583	171	398	14	Bush	29.3%	68.3%	2.4%
LOGAN	1,216	332	858	26	Bush	27.3%	70.6%	2.1%
MESA	7,915	2,348	5,356	211	Bush	29.7%	67.7%	2.7%
MINERAL	45	14	29	2	Bush	31.1%	64.4%	4.4%
MOFFAT	883	306	547	30	Bush	34.7%	61.9%	3.4%
MONTEZUMA	1,027	337	657	33	Bush	32.8%	64.0%	3.2%
MONTROSE	1,930	624	1,269	37	Bush	32.3%	65.8%	1.9%
MORGAN	1,266	324	925	17	Bush	25.6%	73.1%	1.3%
OTERO	942	242	657	43	Bush	25.7%	69.7%	4.6%
OURAY	408	108	290	10	Bush	26.5%	71.1%	2.5%
PARK	549	202	333	14	Bush	36.8%	60.7%	2.6%
PHILLIPS	458	129	322	7	Bush	28.2%	70.3%	1.5%
PITKIN	579	164	398	17	Bush	28.3%	68.7%	2.9%
PROWERS	595	135	449	11	Bush	22.7%	75.5%	1.8%
PUEBLO	4,238	1,032	3,103	103	Bush	24.4%	73.2%	2.4%
RIO BLANCO	622	196	413	13	Bush	31.5%	66.4%	2.1%
RIO GRANDE	646	166	465	15	Bush	25.7%	72.0%	2.3%
ROUTT	729	248	466	15	Bush	34.0%	63.9%	2.1%
SAGUACHE	254	69	182	3	Bush	27.2%	71.7%	1.2%
SAN JUAN	48	19	29		Bush	39.6%	60.4%	
SAN MIGUEL	223	69	151	3	Bush	30.9%	67.7%	1.3%
SEDGWICK	288	89	195	4	Bush	30.9%	67.7%	1.4%
SUMMIT	664	199	457	8	Bush	30.0%	68.8%	1.2%
TELLER	952	288	648	16	Bush	30.3%	68.1%	1.7%
WASHINGTON	630	224	396	10	Bush	35.6%	62.9%	1.6%
WELD	6,323	1,829	4,406	88	Bush	28.9%	69.7%	1.4%
YUMA	732	179	546	7	Bush	24.5%	74.6%	1.0%
TOTAL	195,690	58,753	132,100	4,837	Bush	30.0%	67.5%	2.5%

COLORADO DEMOCRATIC

1996

County	Total Vote	Clinton	LaRouche	Gunderson	Winner	Percentage of Total Vote Clinton	LaRouche	Gunderson
ADAMS	3,146	2,803	336	7	Clinton	89.1%	10.7%	0.2%
ALAMOSA	222	187	24	11	Clinton	84.2%	10.8%	5.0%
ARAPAHOE	7,037	6,415	622		Clinton	91.2%	8.8%	
ARCHULETA	92	75	17		Clinton	81.5%	18.5%	
BACA	230	182	48		Clinton	79.1%	20.9%	
BENT	179	146	33		Clinton	81.6%	18.4%	
BOULDER	3,713	3,425	270	18	Clinton	92.2%	7.3%	0.5%
CHAFFEE	253	227	26		Clinton	89.7%	10.3%	
CHEYENNE	56	43	13		Clinton	76.8%	23.2%	
CLEAR CREEK	109	93	15	1	Clinton	85.3%	13.8%	0.9%
CONEJOS	275	250	25		Clinton	90.9%	9.1%	
COSTILLA	243	221	22		Clinton	90.9%	9.1%	
CROWLEY	116	103	13		Clinton	88.8%	11.2%	
CUSTER	59	45	12	2	Clinton	76.3%	20.3%	3.4%
DELTA	538	462	76		Clinton	85.9%	14.1%	
DENVER	9,906	9,179	725	2	Clinton	92.7%	7.3%	
DOLORES	98	68	30		Clinton	69.4%	30.6%	
DOUGLAS	799	693	106		Clinton	86.7%	13.3%	
EAGLE	156	126	17	13	Clinton	80.8%	10.9%	8.3%
ELBERT	121	102	19		Clinton	84.3%	15.7%	
EL PASO	4,597	3,900	687	10	Clinton	84.8%	14.9%	0.2%
FREMONT	402	350	52		Clinton	87.1%	12.9%	
GARFIELD	403	354	49		Clinton	87.8%	12.2%	
GILPIN	48	40	8		Clinton	83.3%	16.7%	
GRAND	112	109	3		Clinton	97.3%	2.7%	
GUNNISON	148	136	12		Clinton	91.9%	8.1%	
HINSDALE	28	24	4		Clinton	85.7%	14.3%	
HUERFANO	244	207	37		Clinton	84.8%	15.2%	
JACKSON	36	28	8		Clinton	77.8%	22.2%	
JEFFERSON	6,819	6,019	789	11	Clinton	88.3%	11.6%	0.2%
KIOWA	29	26	3		Clinton	89.7%	10.3%	
KIT CARSON	126	114	12		Clinton	90.5%	9.5%	
LAKE	274	245	29		Clinton	89.4%	10.6%	
LA PLATA	418	363	55		Clinton	86.8%	13.2%	
LARIMER	2,402	2,146	249	7	Clinton	89.3%	10.4%	0.3%
LAS ANIMAS	807	713	94		Clinton	88.4%	11.6%	
LINCOLN	150	124	26		Clinton	82.7%	17.3%	
LOGAN	373	327	46		Clinton	87.7%	12.3%	
MESA	2,469	2,065	403	1	Clinton	83.6%	16.3%	
MINERAL	58	44	14		Clinton	75.9%	24.1%	
MOFFAT	172	145	24	3	Clinton	84.3%	14.0%	1.7%
MONTEZUMA	305	249	56		Clinton	81.6%	18.4%	
MONTROSE	514	429	85		Clinton	83.5%	16.5%	
MORGAN	293	273	20		Clinton	93.2%	6.8%	
OTERO	301	271	30		Clinton	90.0%	10.0%	
OURAY	37	36	1		Clinton	97.3%	2.7%	
PARK	139	112	27		Clinton	80.6%	19.4%	
PHILLIPS	25	17	8		Clinton	68.0%	32.0%	
PITKIN	170	162	7	1	Clinton	95.3%	4.1%	0.6%
PROWERS	158	137	21		Clinton	86.7%	13.3%	

COLORADO DEMOCRATIC

1996

County	Total Vote	Clinton	LaRouche	Gunderson	Winner	Percentage of Total Vote Clinton	LaRouche	Gunderson
PUEBLO	2,285	1,983	300	2	Clinton	86.8%	13.1%	0.1%
RIO BLANCO	108	98	10		Clinton	90.7%	9.3%	
RIO GRANDE	306	277	29		Clinton	90.5%	9.5%	
ROUTT	245	224	21		Clinton	91.4%	8.6%	
SAGUACHE	93	72	20	1	Clinton	77.4%	21.5%	1.1%
SAN JUAN	17	17			Clinton	100.0%		
SAN MIGUEL	85	74	11		Clinton	87.1%	12.9%	
SEDGWICK	61	59	2		Clinton	96.7%	3.3%	
SUMMIT	106	95	11		Clinton	89.6%	10.4%	
TELLER	194	156	38		Clinton	80.4%	19.6%	
WASHINGTON	87	66	21		Clinton	75.9%	24.1%	
WELD	1,314	1,135	177	2	Clinton	86.4%	13.5%	0.2%
YUMA	221	188	33		Clinton	85.1%	14.9%	
TOTAL	54,527	48,454	5,981	92	Clinton	88.9%	11.0%	0.2%

COLORADO REPUBLICAN

1996

County	Total Vote	Buchanan	Dole	Forbes	Other	Winner	Percentage of Total Vote Buchanan	Dole	Forbes	Other
ADAMS	9,686	2,851	3,742	1,907	1,186	Dole	29.4%	38.6%	19.7%	12.2%
ALAMOSA	649	114	267	220	48	Dole	17.6%	41.1%	33.9%	7.4%
ARAPAHOE	36,322	6,973	16,953	7,908	4,488	Dole	19.2%	46.7%	21.8%	12.4%
ARCHULETA	704	234	286	126	58	Dole	33.2%	40.6%	17.9%	8.2%
BACA	540	146	278	46	70	Dole	27.0%	51.5%	8.5%	13.0%
BENT	303	58	136	70	39	Dole	19.1%	44.9%	23.1%	12.9%
BOULDER	14,083	2,745	6,129	3,017	2,192	Dole	19.5%	43.5%	21.4%	15.6%
CHAFFEE	1,085	262	495	186	142	Dole	24.1%	45.6%	17.1%	13.1%
CHEYENNE	332	92	148	46	46	Dole	27.7%	44.6%	13.9%	13.9%
CLEAR CREEK	643	112	279	157	95	Dole	17.4%	43.4%	24.4%	14.8%
CONEJOS	462	104	242	94	22	Dole	22.5%	52.4%	20.3%	4.8%
COSTILLA	96	12	23	55	6	Forbes	12.5%	24.0%	57.3%	6.3%
CROWLEY	323	91	140	52	40	Dole	28.2%	43.3%	16.1%	12.4%
CUSTER	425	93	176	81	75	Dole	21.9%	41.4%	19.1%	17.6%
DELTA	2,608	687	1,171	422	328	Dole	26.3%	44.9%	16.2%	12.6%
DENVER	20,509	3,304	10,112	4,431	2,662	Dole	16.1%	49.3%	21.6%	13.0%
DOLORES	110	36	50	17	7	Dole	32.7%	45.5%	15.5%	6.4%
DOUGLAS	10,206	2,016	4,325	2,533	1,332	Dole	19.8%	42.4%	24.8%	13.1%
EAGLE	965	166	411	253	135	Dole	17.2%	42.6%	26.2%	14.0%
ELBERT	1,247	369	469	227	182	Dole	29.6%	37.6%	18.2%	14.6%
EL PASO	40,526	9,228	14,798	9,041	7,459	Dole	22.8%	36.5%	22.3%	18.4%
FREMONT	2,332	627	976	449	280	Dole	26.9%	41.9%	19.3%	12.0%
GARFIELD	1,989	409	948	334	298	Dole	20.6%	47.7%	16.8%	15.0%
GILPIN	202	50	74	56	22	Dole	24.8%	36.6%	27.7%	10.9%
GRAND	910	179	384	209	138	Dole	19.7%	42.2%	23.0%	15.2%

COLORADO REPUBLICAN

1996

County	Total Vote	Buchanan	Dole	Forbes	Other	Winner	Percentage of Total Vote Buchanan	Dole	Forbes	Other
GUNNISON	596	118	290	93	95	Dole	19.8%	48.7%	15.6%	15.9%
HINSDALE	144	22	62	31	29	Dole	15.3%	43.1%	21.5%	20.1%
HUERFANO	192	37	93	46	16	Dole	19.3%	48.4%	24.0%	8.3%
JACKSON	187	31	109	31	16	Dole	16.6%	58.3%	16.6%	8.6%
JEFFERSON	37,247	8,144	16,434	7,929	4,740	Dole	21.9%	44.1%	21.3%	12.7%
KIOWA	187	34	97	26	30	Dole	18.2%	51.9%	13.9%	16.0%
KIT CARSON	793	216	395	92	90	Dole	27.2%	49.8%	11.6%	11.3%
LAKE	207	44	100	34	29	Dole	21.3%	48.3%	16.4%	14.0%
LA PLATA	2,301	600	1,060	426	215	Dole	26.1%	46.1%	18.5%	9.3%
LARIMER	16,358	3,822	6,846	3,109	2,581	Dole	23.4%	41.9%	19.0%	15.8%
LAS ANIMAS	445	96	205	94	50	Dole	21.6%	46.1%	21.1%	11.2%
LINCOLN	598	114	314	91	79	Dole	19.1%	52.5%	15.2%	13.2%
LOGAN	1,290	235	664	218	173	Dole	18.2%	51.5%	16.9%	13.4%
MESA	9,514	2,071	4,627	1,532	1,284	Dole	21.8%	48.6%	16.1%	13.5%
MINERAL	65	13	28	13	11	Dole	20.0%	43.1%	20.0%	16.9%
MOFFAT	933	293	399	122	119	Dole	31.4%	42.8%	13.1%	12.8%
MONTEZUMA	1,396	422	608	232	134	Dole	30.2%	43.6%	16.6%	9.6%
MONTROSE	2,685	611	1,171	537	366	Dole	22.8%	43.6%	20.0%	13.6%
MORGAN	1,510	356	729	221	204	Dole	23.6%	48.3%	14.6%	13.5%
OTERO	1,049	218	479	198	154	Dole	20.8%	45.7%	18.9%	14.7%
OURAY	503	99	225	124	55	Dole	19.7%	44.7%	24.7%	10.9%
PARK	930	253	302	248	127	Dole	27.2%	32.5%	26.7%	13.7%
PHILLIPS	507	95	301	46	65	Dole	18.7%	59.4%	9.1%	12.8%
PITKIN	507	66	236	128	77	Dole	13.0%	46.5%	25.2%	15.2%
PROWERS	660	130	356	81	93	Dole	19.7%	53.9%	12.3%	14.1%
PUEBLO	4,577	819	2,047	1,142	569	Dole	17.9%	44.7%	25.0%	12.4%
RIO BLANCO	849	201	399	136	113	Dole	23.7%	47.0%	16.0%	13.3%
RIO GRANDE	858	186	387	172	113	Dole	21.7%	45.1%	20.0%	13.2%
ROUTT	1,006	176	439	214	177	Dole	17.5%	43.6%	21.3%	17.6%
SAGUACHE	264	56	124	64	20	Dole	21.2%	47.0%	24.2%	7.6%
SAN JUAN	48	13	16	12	7	Dole	27.1%	33.3%	25.0%	14.6%
SAN MIGUEL	239	37	121	55	26	Dole	15.5%	50.6%	23.0%	10.9%
SEDGWICK	307	58	178	35	36	Dole	18.9%	58.0%	11.4%	11.7%
SUMMIT	933	121	409	264	139	Dole	13.0%	43.8%	28.3%	14.9%
TELLER	1,590	395	549	407	239	Dole	24.8%	34.5%	25.6%	15.0%
WASHINGTON	758	166	396	96	100	Dole	21.9%	52.2%	12.7%	13.2%
WELD	7,614	1,885	3,431	1,267	1,031	Dole	24.8%	45.1%	16.6%	13.5%
YUMA	826	165	485	89	87	Dole	20.0%	58.7%	10.8%	10.5%
TOTAL	247,930	53,376	108,123	51,592	34,839	Dole	21.5%	43.6%	20.8%	14.1%

CONNECTICUT

For years, Connecticut was the home base of the Bush family. George Bush was raised in Greenwich and educated at Yale University. His father, Prescott Bush, served the state in the U.S. Senate from 1952 to 1963.

But Connecticut is large and diverse enough that in the GOP's last hotly contested presidential primary, in 1980, Bush, Ronald Reagan and John Anderson were all able to find toeholds.

Bush fashioned his 39 percent to 34 percent victory over Reagan in Connecticut's traditional Republican strongholds, the upper-crust suburbs near New York City and the Yankee towns and villages on the north and east sides of the state.

Reagan nearly offset all that by combining the votes of conservative activists and blue-collar workers in industrial cities such as Bridgeport, Norwalk, Waterbury and New Britain. But to Bush's advantage, more Republican primary votes were cast in suburban Greenwich alone than in any of the state's larger urban centers. Meanwhile, Anderson took 22 percent of the primary vote by carrying communities with large academic institutions, such as New Haven (Yale) and Mansfield (the University of Connecticut).

Bush had a much easier time in 1988 and 1992. Dole withdrew from the race on the day of the Connecticut voting in late March 1988, while Pat Robertson could muster just 3 percent of the vote, his weakest showing of the primary season.

Pat Buchanan did better four years later by tapping into Connecticut's sudden economic discomfort. He took more than 35 percent of the vote in Waterbury, a figure that he almost matched in 1996. But in the latter year, Buchanan finished third in the statewide primary vote behind both Dole and Steve Forbes, who ran best in upscale suburbs such as Greenwich and New Canaan.

Connecticut's most competitive presidential primary of the 1990s took place on the Democratic side, where Jerry Brown slowed Bill Clinton's bandwagon in 1992 just as it had been picking up steam with a sweep of the Super Tuesday South and St. Patrick's Day voting in Illinois and Michigan. Brown won in Connecticut by fewer than 3,000 votes out of 170,000 cast. But the result, at least temporarily, reopened doubts about the strength of Clinton's candidacy.

Several factors worked to Brown's benefit in Connecticut: a one-on-one shot against Clinton (Paul Tsongas had withdrawn from the race less than a week earlier); a geographically compact electorate, much of which Brown could reach with a media blitz on Hartford television; and low turnout, particularly in the cities where Clinton had hoped to tap the sizable minority vote.

The Democratic base in Connecticut is more urban than the Republican. Still, no Connecticut city dominates the political landscape. The largest are Bridgeport, Hartford and New Haven, and none of the three has more than 5 percent of the

Recent Connecticut Primary Results

Connecticut held its first presidential primary in 1980.

	DEMOCRATS			REPUBLICANS		
Year	Turnout	Candidates	%	Turnout	Candidates	%
1996 (March 5)	—	NO PRIMARY		130,418	BOB DOLE	54
					Steve Forbes	20
					Pat Buchanan	15
1992 (March 24)	173,119	JERRY BROWN	37	99,473	GEORGE BUSH*	67
		Bill Clinton	36		Pat Buchanan	22
		Paul Tsongas	20			
1988 (March 29)	241,395	MICHAEL DUKAKIS	58	104,171	GEORGE BUSH	71
		Jesse Jackson	28		Bob Dole	20
1984 (March 27)	220,842	GARY HART	53	—	NO PRIMARY	
		Walter Mondale	29			
		Jesse Jackson	12			
1980 (March 25)	210,275	EDWARD KENNEDY	47	182,284	GEORGE BUSH	39
		Jimmy Carter*	41		Ronald Reagan	34
					John Anderson	22

Note: All candidates are listed that drew at least 10 percent of their party's primary vote. The names of winning candidates are capitalized. An asterisk (*) indicates an incumbent president.

state population.

Hartford, the state capital, is nearly 40 percent black. Jesse Jackson carried the city in 1984 and 1988, adding victories in Bridgeport and New Haven (both more than 25 percent black) in the latter campaign.

But Jackson was unable to make headway elsewhere in the state, where Gary Hart marched to victory in 1984 and Michael Dukakis did the same four years later. Dukakis benefited from Al Gore's decision to forgo the all-out effort in Connecticut that might have produced a more competitive three-way contest. (Gore took just 8 percent of the Democratic primary vote in 1988.)

CONNECTICUT DEMOCRATIC

1980

City/Town	Total Vote	Carter	E. Kennedy	Other	Winner	Percentage of Total Vote Carter	E. Kennedy	Other
BRIDGEPORT	8,934	3,722	4,266	946	E. Kennedy	41.7%	47.8%	10.6%
BRISTOL	4,826	1,753	2,711	362	E. Kennedy	36.3%	56.2%	7.5%
DANBURY	2,677	1,222	1,178	277	Carter	45.6%	44.0%	10.3%
DARIEN	598	297	212	89	Carter	49.7%	35.5%	14.9%
FAIRFIELD	3,364	1,454	1,486	424	E. Kennedy	43.2%	44.2%	12.6%
GREENWICH	2,685	1,315	1,052	318	Carter	49.0%	39.2%	11.8%
GROTON	1,078	504	438	136	Carter	46.8%	40.6%	12.6%
HAMDEN	2,459	1,029	1,162	268	E. Kennedy	41.8%	47.3%	10.9%
HARTFORD	13,098	5,670	6,184	1,244	E. Kennedy	43.3%	47.2%	9.5%
LITCHFIELD	379	169	139	71	Carter	44.6%	36.7%	18.7%
MANCHESTER	4,292	1,819	1,885	588	E. Kennedy	42.4%	43.9%	13.7%
MANSFIELD	1,170	415	569	186	E. Kennedy	35.5%	48.6%	15.9%
MERIDEN	3,117	1,292	1,537	288	E. Kennedy	41.5%	49.3%	9.2%
MIDDLETOWN	3,811	1,417	1,937	457	E. Kennedy	37.2%	50.8%	12.0%
NAUGATUCK	1,799	638	1,001	160	E. Kennedy	35.5%	55.6%	8.9%
NEW BRITAIN	10,221	3,937	5,334	950	E. Kennedy	38.5%	52.2%	9.3%
NEW CANAAN	786	353	279	154	Carter	44.9%	35.5%	19.6%
NEW HAVEN	11,896	4,709	5,860	1,327	E. Kennedy	39.6%	49.3%	11.2%
NEW LONDON	1,522	562	779	181	E. Kennedy	36.9%	51.2%	11.9%
NORWALK	3,524	1,483	1,629	412	E. Kennedy	42.1%	46.2%	11.7%
OLD LYME	406	192	161	53	Carter	47.3%	39.7%	13.1%
STAMFORD	7,049	3,136	3,188	725	E. Kennedy	44.5%	45.2%	10.3%
WATERBURY	10,536	3,769	5,750	1,017	E. Kennedy	35.8%	54.6%	9.7%
WEST HARTFORD	7,453	2,830	3,661	962	E. Kennedy	38.0%	49.1%	12.9%
WEST HAVEN	3,240	1,310	1,649	281	E. Kennedy	40.4%	50.9%	8.7%
STATE TOTAL	210,275	87,207	98,662	24,406	E. Kennedy	41.5%	46.9%	11.6%

Note: The presidential primary vote was not compiled by county in Connecticut until the 1990s. This table, and those through 1988, includes only the vote from major cities and towns with a 1996 population estimate of 50,000 or more, as well as a few selected others. The totals for these cities and towns do not add to the state total.

CONNECTICUT REPUBLICAN

1980

City/Town	Total Vote	Anderson	Bush	Reagan	Other	Winner	Percentage of Total Vote Anderson	Bush	Reagan	Other
BRIDGEPORT	3,323	490	766	1,793	274	Reagan	14.7%	23.1%	54.0%	8.2%
BRISTOL	1,858	442	656	642	118	Bush	23.8%	35.3%	34.6%	6.4%
DANBURY	1,989	292	600	982	115	Reagan	14.7%	30.2%	49.4%	5.8%
DARIEN	4,096	839	1,851	1,249	157	Bush	20.5%	45.2%	30.5%	3.8%
FAIRFIELD	5,221	1,021	1,792	2,178	230	Reagan	19.6%	34.3%	41.7%	4.4%
GREENWICH	9,463	1,715	4,844	2,525	379	Bush	18.1%	51.2%	26.7%	4.0%
GROTON	1,665	435	604	555	71	Bush	26.1%	36.3%	33.3%	4.3%
HAMDEN	2,090	383	937	678	92	Bush	18.3%	44.8%	32.4%	4.4%
HARTFORD	2,336	776	767	619	174	Anderson	33.2%	32.8%	26.5%	7.4%
LITCHFIELD	762	147	382	198	35	Bush	19.3%	50.1%	26.0%	4.6%
MANCHESTER	3,837	1,039	1,675	941	182	Bush	27.1%	43.7%	24.5%	4.7%
MANSFIELD	872	405	259	157	51	Anderson	46.4%	29.7%	18.0%	5.8%
MERIDEN	2,029	520	678	740	91	Reagan	25.6%	33.4%	36.5%	4.5%
MIDDLETOWN	1,516	645	397	390	84	Anderson	42.5%	26.2%	25.7%	5.5%
NAUGATUCK	690	82	297	266	45	Bush	11.9%	43.0%	38.6%	6.5%
NEW BRITAIN	3,058	827	881	1,073	277	Reagan	27.0%	28.8%	35.1%	9.1%
NEW CANAAN	3,384	784	1,428	1,047	125	Bush	23.2%	42.2%	30.9%	3.7%
NEW HAVEN	1,581	650	479	370	82	Anderson	41.1%	30.3%	23.4%	5.2%
NEW LONDON	643	160	231	208	44	Bush	24.9%	35.9%	32.3%	6.8%
NORWALK	3,602	573	842	1,972	215	Reagan	15.9%	23.4%	54.7%	6.0%
OLD LYME	861	183	430	208	40	Bush	21.3%	49.9%	24.2%	4.6%
STAMFORD	7,590	1,606	2,528	3,054	402	Reagan	21.2%	33.3%	40.2%	5.3%
WATERBURY	2,915	356	1,136	1,240	183	Reagan	12.2%	39.0%	42.5%	6.3%
WEST HARTFORD	7,303	2,037	3,334	1,571	361	Bush	27.9%	45.7%	21.5%	4.9%
WEST HAVEN	1,519	207	579	616	117	Reagan	13.6%	38.1%	40.6%	7.7%
STATE TOTAL	182,284	40,354	70,367	61,735	9,828	Bush	22.1%	38.6%	33.9%	5.4%

CONNECTICUT DEMOCRATIC

1984

City/Town	Total Vote	Hart	J. Jackson	Mondale	Other	Winner	Percentage of Total Vote Hart	J. Jackson	Mondale	Other
BRIDGEPORT	8,486	3,152	2,330	2,153	851	Hart	37.1%	27.5%	25.4%	10.0%
BRISTOL	4,654	2,527	187	1,670	270	Hart	54.3%	4.0%	35.9%	5.8%
DANBURY	2,898	1,541	347	839	171	Hart	53.2%	12.0%	29.0%	5.9%
DARIEN	754	473	36	202	43	Hart	62.7%	4.8%	26.8%	5.7%
FAIRFIELD	3,045	1,728	127	989	201	Hart	56.7%	4.2%	32.5%	6.6%
GREENWICH	2,639	1,431	160	894	154	Hart	54.2%	6.1%	33.9%	5.8%
GROTON	1,404	699	140	480	85	Hart	49.8%	10.0%	34.2%	6.1%
HAMDEN	3,559	1,962	351	993	253	Hart	55.1%	9.9%	27.9%	7.1%
HARTFORD	15,054	4,618	6,047	3,832	557	J. Jackson	30.7%	40.2%	25.5%	3.7%
LITCHFIELD	441	274	28	117	22	Hart	62.1%	6.3%	26.5%	5.0%
MANCHESTER	4,168	2,536	207	1,133	292	Hart	60.8%	5.0%	27.2%	7.0%
MANSFIELD	1,490	891	150	390	59	Hart	59.8%	10.1%	26.2%	4.0%
MERIDEN	2,961	1,699	156	846	260	Hart	57.4%	5.3%	28.6%	8.8%
MIDDLETOWN	3,713	1,933	542	1,123	115	Hart	52.1%	14.6%	30.2%	3.1%
NAUGATUCK	1,486	871	49	441	125	Hart	58.6%	3.3%	29.7%	8.4%
NEW BRITAIN	9,732	4,626	857	3,535	714	Hart	47.5%	8.8%	36.3%	7.3%
NEW CANAAN	684	404	39	197	44	Hart	59.1%	5.7%	28.8%	6.4%
NEW HAVEN	14,836	5,359	4,182	3,862	1,433	Hart	36.1%	28.2%	26.0%	9.7%
NEW LONDON	1,841	720	309	689	123	Hart	39.1%	16.8%	37.4%	6.7%
NORWALK	3,635	1,642	643	1,125	225	Hart	45.2%	17.7%	30.9%	6.2%
OLD LYME	414	263	33	94	24	Hart	63.5%	8.0%	22.7%	5.8%
STAMFORD	8,689	4,053	1,451	2,602	583	Hart	46.6%	16.7%	29.9%	6.7%
WATERBURY	9,402	4,711	1,012	3,015	664	Hart	50.1%	10.8%	32.1%	7.1%
WEST HARTFORD	7,726	4,394	320	2,810	202	Hart	56.9%	4.1%	36.4%	2.6%
WEST HAVEN	3,289	1,747	358	909	275	Hart	53.1%	10.9%	27.6%	8.4%
STATE TOTAL	220,842	116,286	26,395	64,230	13,931	Hart	52.7%	12.0%	29.1%	6.3%

CONNECTICUT DEMOCRATIC

1988

City/Town	Total Vote	Dukakis	J. Jackson	Other	Winner	Percentage of Total Vote Dukakis	J. Jackson	Other
BRIDGEPORT	9,746	3,907	4,851	988	J. Jackson	40.1%	49.8%	10.1%
BRISTOL	4,594	3,262	768	564	Dukakis	71.0%	16.7%	12.3%
DANBURY	2,881	1,780	807	294	Dukakis	61.8%	28.0%	10.2%
DARIEN	664	436	124	104	Dukakis	65.7%	18.7%	15.7%
FAIRFIELD	3,087	2,038	513	536	Dukakis	66.0%	16.6%	17.4%
GREENWICH	2,508	1,491	550	467	Dukakis	59.4%	21.9%	18.6%
GROTON	1,559	781	485	293	Dukakis	50.1%	31.1%	18.8%
HAMDEN	4,407	2,381	1,189	837	Dukakis	54.0%	27.0%	19.0%
HARTFORD	16,064	4,926	10,078	1,060	J. Jackson	30.7%	62.7%	6.6%
LITCHFIELD	487	267	145	75	Dukakis	54.8%	29.8%	15.4%
MANCHESTER	4,843	3,342	922	579	Dukakis	69.0%	19.0%	12.0%
MANSFIELD	1,663	890	546	227	Dukakis	53.5%	32.8%	13.7%
MERIDEN	3,028	1,985	589	454	Dukakis	65.6%	19.5%	15.0%
MIDDLETOWN	5,365	2,838	2,028	499	Dukakis	52.9%	37.8%	9.3%
NAUGATUCK	1,591	1,080	252	259	Dukakis	67.9%	15.8%	16.3%
NEW BRITAIN	9,269	6,309	1,731	1,229	Dukakis	68.1%	18.7%	13.3%
NEW CANAAN	732	413	179	140	Dukakis	56.4%	24.5%	19.1%
NEW HAVEN	16,979	6,465	8,395	2,119	J. Jackson	38.1%	49.4%	12.5%
NEW LONDON	1,752	778	709	265	Dukakis	44.4%	40.5%	15.1%
NORWALK	4,263	2,184	1,699	380	Dukakis	51.2%	39.9%	8.9%
OLD LYME	351	189	103	59	Dukakis	53.8%	29.3%	16.8%
STAMFORD	8,949	5,004	2,753	1,192	Dukakis	55.9%	30.8%	13.3%
WATERBURY	8,914	5,029	2,471	1,414	Dukakis	56.4%	27.7%	15.9%
WEST HARTFORD	8,300	5,767	1,231	1,302	Dukakis	69.5%	14.8%	15.7%
WEST HAVEN	5,077	2,855	1,392	830	Dukakis	56.2%	27.4%	16.3%
STATE TOTAL	241,395	140,291	68,372	32,732	Dukakis	58.1%	28.3%	13.6%

CONNECTICUT REPUBLICAN

1988

City/Town	Total Vote	Bush	Dole	Other	Winner	Percentage of Total Vote Bush	Dole	Other
BRIDGEPORT	1,630	1,139	290	201	Bush	69.9%	17.8%	12.3%
BRISTOL	1,256	867	273	116	Bush	69.0%	21.7%	9.2%
DANBURY	1,182	833	225	124	Bush	70.5%	19.0%	10.5%
DARIEN	1,890	1,439	307	144	Bush	76.1%	16.2%	7.6%
FAIRFIELD	2,660	1,947	485	228	Bush	73.2%	18.2%	8.6%
GREENWICH	4,685	3,683	727	275	Bush	78.6%	15.5%	5.9%
GROTON	953	665	213	75	Bush	69.8%	22.4%	7.9%
HAMDEN	1,961	1,288	453	220	Bush	65.7%	23.1%	11.2%
HARTFORD	1,135	694	243	198	Bush	61.1%	21.4%	17.4%
LITCHFIELD	552	387	109	56	Bush	70.1%	19.7%	10.1%
MANCHESTER	2,189	1,518	484	187	Bush	69.3%	22.1%	8.5%
MANSFIELD	537	312	162	63	Bush	58.1%	30.2%	11.7%
MERIDEN	1,054	681	260	113	Bush	64.6%	24.7%	10.7%
MIDDLETOWN	885	535	242	108	Bush	60.5%	27.3%	12.2%
NAUGATUCK	462	330	80	52	Bush	71.4%	17.3%	11.3%
NEW BRITAIN	1,648	1,121	365	162	Bush	68.0%	22.1%	9.8%
NEW CANAAN	1,478	1,136	232	110	Bush	76.9%	15.7%	7.4%
NEW HAVEN	918	562	232	124	Bush	61.2%	25.3%	13.5%
NEW LONDON	386	257	76	53	Bush	66.6%	19.7%	13.7%
NORWALK	1,967	1,520	275	172	Bush	77.3%	14.0%	8.7%
OLD LYME	453	325	99	29	Bush	71.7%	21.9%	6.4%
STAMFORD	3,699	2,617	760	322	Bush	70.7%	20.5%	8.7%
WATERBURY	1,913	1,375	365	173	Bush	71.9%	19.1%	9.0%
WEST HARTFORD	3,292	2,356	700	236	Bush	71.6%	21.3%	7.2%
WEST HAVEN	1,170	834	196	140	Bush	71.3%	16.8%	12.0%
STATE TOTAL	104,171	73,501	21,005	9,665	Bush	70.6%	20.2%	9.3%

CONNECTICUT DEMOCRATIC

1992

County	Total Vote	Brown	Clinton	Tsongas	Other	Winner	Percentage of Total Vote Brown	Clinton	Tsongas	Other
FAIRFIELD	35,328	14,411	12,256	5,905	2,756	Brown	40.8%	34.7%	16.7%	7.8%
HARTFORD	56,811	18,618	20,631	13,335	4,227	Clinton	32.8%	36.3%	23.5%	7.4%
LITCHFIELD	8,387	3,468	2,629	1,627	663	Brown	41.3%	31.3%	19.4%	7.9%
MIDDLESEX	8,290	3,180	2,901	1,721	488	Brown	38.4%	35.0%	20.8%	5.9%
NEW HAVEN	40,373	15,906	14,780	6,264	3,423	Brown	39.4%	36.6%	15.5%	8.5%
NEW LONDON	11,687	3,986	4,810	2,161	730	Clinton	34.1%	41.2%	18.5%	6.2%
TOLLAND	7,243	2,905	2,068	1,771	499	Brown	40.1%	28.6%	24.5%	6.9%
WINDHAM	5,000	1,998	1,623	1,027	352	Brown	40.0%	32.5%	20.5%	7.0%
TOTAL	173,119	64,472	61,698	33,811	13,138	Brown	37.2%	35.6%	19.5%	7.6%

City/Town	Total Vote	Brown	Clinton	Tsongas	Other	Winner	Brown	Clinton	Tsongas	Other
BRIDGEPORT	4,816	1,920	2,122	322	452	Clinton	39.9%	44.1%	6.7%	9.4%
BRISTOL	3,826	1,473	1,399	713	241	Brown	38.5%	36.6%	18.6%	6.3%
DANBURY	1,831	717	662	325	127	Brown	39.2%	36.2%	17.7%	6.9%
DARIEN	644	243	191	159	51	Brown	37.7%	29.7%	24.7%	7.9%
FAIRFIELD	2,665	1,237	770	487	171	Brown	46.4%	28.9%	18.3%	6.4%
GREENWICH	1,889	736	623	374	156	Brown	39.0%	33.0%	19.8%	8.3%
GROTON	1,305	423	566	234	82	Clinton	32.4%	43.4%	17.9%	6.3%
HAMDEN	2,735	1,061	973	516	185	Brown	38.8%	35.6%	18.9%	6.8%
HARTFORD	6,689	1,913	3,186	1,035	555	Clinton	28.6%	47.6%	15.5%	8.3%
LITCHFIELD	411	191	101	87	32	Brown	46.5%	24.6%	21.2%	7.8%
MANCHESTER	3,194	1,158	1,025	817	194	Brown	36.3%	32.1%	25.6%	6.1%
MANSFIELD	1,381	621	346	336	78	Brown	45.0%	25.1%	24.3%	5.6%
MERIDEN	3,080	1,209	1,159	451	261	Brown	39.3%	37.6%	14.6%	8.5%
MIDDLETOWN	2,681	941	1,064	506	170	Clinton	35.1%	39.7%	18.9%	6.3%
NAUGATUCK	1,387	597	519	171	100	Brown	43.0%	37.4%	12.3%	7.2%
NEW BRITAIN	5,886	1,871	2,523	909	583	Clinton	31.8%	42.9%	15.4%	9.9%
NEW CANAAN	644	242	180	179	43	Brown	37.6%	28.0%	27.8%	6.7%
NEW HAVEN	9,159	3,059	3,762	1,188	1,150	Clinton	33.4%	41.1%	13.0%	12.6%
NEW LONDON	1,208	438	561	147	62	Clinton	36.3%	46.4%	12.2%	5.1%
NORWALK	2,930	1,156	1,003	571	200	Brown	39.5%	34.2%	19.5%	6.8%
OLD LYME	355	138	116	84	17	Brown	38.9%	32.7%	23.7%	4.8%
STAMFORD	7,610	2,644	2,922	1,272	772	Clinton	34.7%	38.4%	16.7%	10.1%
WATERBURY	5,318	2,249	1,757	773	539	Brown	42.3%	33.0%	14.5%	10.1%
WEST HARTFORD	6,418	1,789	2,129	2,105	395	Clinton	27.9%	33.2%	32.8%	6.2%
WEST HAVEN	2,571	1,000	1,089	285	197	Clinton	38.9%	42.4%	11.1%	7.7%

CONNECTICUT REPUBLICAN

1992

County	Total Vote	Buchanan	Bush	Other	Winner	Percentage of Total Vote: Buchanan	Bush	Other
FAIRFIELD	30,111	6,043	21,152	2,916	Bush	20.1%	70.2%	9.7%
HARTFORD	25,984	5,605	17,029	3,350	Bush	21.6%	65.5%	12.9%
LITCHFIELD	7,004	1,523	4,607	874	Bush	21.7%	65.8%	12.5%
MIDDLESEX	5,192	1,172	3,344	676	Bush	22.6%	64.4%	13.0%
NEW HAVEN	18,269	4,226	12,298	1,745	Bush	23.1%	67.3%	9.6%
NEW LONDON	6,838	1,823	4,106	909	Bush	26.7%	60.0%	13.3%
TOLLAND	3,602	850	2,215	537	Bush	23.6%	61.5%	14.9%
WINDHAM	2,473	573	1,605	295	Bush	23.2%	64.9%	11.9%
TOTAL	99,473	21,815	66,356	11,302	Bush	21.9%	66.7%	11.4%

City/Town	Total Vote	Buchanan	Bush	Other	Winner	Buchanan %	Bush %	Other %
BRIDGEPORT	1,293	285	897	111	Bush	22.0%	69.4%	8.6%
BRISTOL	1,363	395	828	140	Bush	29.0%	60.7%	10.3%
DANBURY	920	223	633	64	Bush	24.2%	68.8%	7.0%
DARIEN	1,759	327	1,267	165	Bush	18.6%	72.0%	9.4%
FAIRFIELD	2,427	503	1,678	246	Bush	20.7%	69.1%	10.1%
GREENWICH	3,225	584	2,347	294	Bush	18.1%	72.8%	9.1%
GROTON	931	258	547	126	Bush	27.7%	58.8%	13.5%
HAMDEN	1,161	263	801	97	Bush	22.7%	69.0%	8.4%
HARTFORD	751	179	461	111	Bush	23.8%	61.4%	14.8%
LITCHFIELD	464	95	304	65	Bush	20.5%	65.5%	14.0%
MANCHESTER	1,811	390	1,194	227	Bush	21.5%	65.9%	12.5%
MANSFIELD	348	68	230	50	Bush	19.5%	66.1%	14.4%
MERIDEN	1,513	358	989	166	Bush	23.7%	65.4%	11.0%
MIDDLETOWN	798	214	481	103	Bush	26.8%	60.3%	12.9%
NAUGATUCK	545	142	361	42	Bush	26.1%	66.2%	7.7%
NEW BRITAIN	1,484	354	895	235	Bush	23.9%	60.3%	15.8%
NEW CANAAN	1,284	204	965	115	Bush	15.9%	75.2%	9.0%
NEW HAVEN	732	149	487	96	Bush	20.4%	66.5%	13.1%
NEW LONDON	370	98	222	50	Bush	26.5%	60.0%	13.5%
NORWALK	1,731	391	1,196	144	Bush	22.6%	69.1%	8.3%
OLD LYME	424	99	258	67	Bush	23.3%	60.8%	15.8%
STAMFORD	4,779	969	3,341	469	Bush	20.3%	69.9%	9.8%
WATERBURY	1,507	556	826	125	Bush	36.9%	54.8%	8.3%
WEST HARTFORD	2,961	535	2,072	354	Bush	18.1%	70.0%	12.0%
WEST HAVEN	775	142	543	90	Bush	18.3%	70.1%	11.6%

CONNECTICUT REPUBLICAN

1996

County	Total Vote	Buchanan	Dole	Forbes	Other	Winner	Percentage of Total Vote Buchanan	Dole	Forbes	Other
FAIRFIELD	40,000	5,107	22,336	8,733	3,824	Dole	12.8%	55.8%	21.8%	9.6%
HARTFORD	30,980	4,004	17,367	6,099	3,510	Dole	12.9%	56.1%	19.7%	11.3%
LITCHFIELD	9,399	1,497	4,726	2,140	1,036	Dole	15.9%	50.3%	22.8%	11.0%
MIDDLESEX	6,794	1,005	3,606	1,381	802	Dole	14.8%	53.1%	20.3%	11.8%
NEW HAVEN	26,210	5,331	13,698	4,730	2,451	Dole	20.3%	52.3%	18.0%	9.4%
NEW LONDON	8,726	1,273	4,868	1,666	919	Dole	14.6%	55.8%	19.1%	10.5%
TOLLAND	4,735	723	2,528	916	568	Dole	15.3%	53.4%	19.3%	12.0%
WINDHAM	3,574	724	1,869	588	393	Dole	20.3%	52.3%	16.5%	11.0%
TOTAL	130,418	19,664	70,998	26,253	13,503	Dole	15.1%	54.4%	20.1%	10.4%

City/Town	Total Vote	Buchanan	Dole	Forbes	Other	Winner	Buchanan %	Dole %	Forbes %	Other %
BRIDGEPORT	1,263	274	630	221	138	Dole	21.7%	49.9%	17.5%	10.9%
BRISTOL	1,620	314	873	259	174	Dole	19.4%	53.9%	16.0%	10.7%
DANBURY	1,408	291	712	274	131	Dole	20.7%	50.6%	19.5%	9.3%
DARIEN	2,339	145	1,459	517	218	Dole	6.2%	62.4%	22.1%	9.3%
FAIRFIELD	3,427	446	1,954	698	329	Dole	13.0%	57.0%	20.4%	9.6%
GREENWICH	4,775	422	2,665	1,256	432	Dole	8.8%	55.8%	26.3%	9.0%
GROTON	1,087	132	655	199	101	Dole	12.1%	60.3%	18.3%	9.3%
HAMDEN	1,949	385	1,094	295	175	Dole	19.8%	56.1%	15.1%	9.0%
HARTFORD	629	103	302	132	92	Dole	16.4%	48.0%	21.0%	14.6%
LITCHFIELD	579	73	304	136	66	Dole	12.6%	52.5%	23.5%	11.4%
MANCHESTER	1,858	236	1,047	344	231	Dole	12.7%	56.4%	18.5%	12.4%
MANSFIELD	405	47	236	68	54	Dole	11.6%	58.3%	16.8%	13.3%
MERIDEN	1,270	275	607	240	148	Dole	21.7%	47.8%	18.9%	11.7%
MIDDLETOWN	1,054	188	533	202	131	Dole	17.8%	50.6%	19.2%	12.4%
NAUGATUCK	826	203	374	181	68	Dole	24.6%	45.3%	21.9%	8.2%
NEW BRITAIN	1,479	291	748	285	155	Dole	19.7%	50.6%	19.3%	10.5%
NEW CANAAN	2,169	168	1,215	558	228	Dole	7.7%	56.0%	25.7%	10.5%
NEW HAVEN	798	170	406	128	94	Dole	21.3%	50.9%	16.0%	11.8%
NEW LONDON	428	74	230	72	52	Dole	17.3%	53.7%	16.8%	12.1%
NORWALK	2,279	285	1,273	508	213	Dole	12.5%	55.9%	22.3%	9.3%
OLD LYME	645	64	380	139	62	Dole	9.9%	58.9%	21.6%	9.6%
STAMFORD	4,214	550	2,415	856	393	Dole	13.1%	57.3%	20.3%	9.3%
WATERBURY	2,274	793	896	387	198	Dole	34.9%	39.4%	17.0%	8.7%
WEST HARTFORD	3,402	308	2,060	666	368	Dole	9.1%	60.6%	19.6%	10.8%
WEST HAVEN	1,354	280	742	193	139	Dole	20.7%	54.8%	14.3%	10.3%

DELAWARE

Delaware never held a presidential primary before 1996. But when it did, it aimed high, setting a date just four days after New Hampshire's first-in-the-nation primary.

That created conflict for Delaware on two fronts—with the national Democratic Party, which forbids states other than Iowa and New Hampshire from voting before March—and with New Hampshire, which has a state statute requiring a seven-day hiatus between its primary and any that follow.

New Hampshire's displeasure with Delaware's chutzpah had its effect. In deference to the Granite State and its political importance, most of the Republican candidates scaled back their Delaware campaigning. One who did not was Steve Forbes, who campaigned around the state by bus and ran his usual media blitz.

Forbes, though, did not have a clear track to victory. His main rivals were on the Delaware ballot. And Bob Dole had the backing of several big-name Delaware Republicans, including Sen. William V. Roth Jr., who endorsed Dole three days before the primary. But Dole did not come to the state to receive the endorsement. He accepted it by phone while travelling on his campaign plane.

Meanwhile, Forbes's assiduous personal attention to the state probably provided him with the margin of victory, as he defeated Dole by barely 5 percentage points.

President Bill Clinton easily won Delaware's initial Democratic presidential primary in 1996. But there was uncertainty about whether he would be on the ballot to begin with. At first, Clinton opted not to run and there was talking of fielding the state's venerable former governor, Elbert N. Carvel (1949–1953, 1961–1965), as a favorite son.

But Delaware officials took matters into their own hands by putting Clinton on the ballot, along with those major GOP presidential contenders who also did not file for fear of upsetting voters in New Hampshire. After talk among national Democratic officials of penalizing Delaware for its forwardness, the state's Democrats were allowed to keep all their delegates.

Neither primary, though, highlighted the political geography of the state. Delaware is divided into two parts by the Chesapeake and Delaware Canal, which slices across the northern quarter of the state. The portion north of the canal comprises the heart of populous New Castle County, with Wilmington and its suburbs. It is part of the busy Northeast Corridor. Below the canal, the state is rural and lightly settled; its values, attitude and voting behavior are similar to those of the border South.

Republican Pat Buchanan ran best in the southern portion of Delaware in the 1996 Republican primary, as did Lyndon LaRouche (Clinton's lone opponent) on the Democratic side. But elections in Delaware tend to be won and lost in New Castle County, which cast nearly two-thirds of the vote in both the Democratic and Republican presidential primaries in 1996.

Recent Delaware Primary Results

Delaware held its first presidential primary in 1996.

	DEMOCRATS			REPUBLICANS		
Year	Turnout	Candidates	%	Turnout	Candidates	%
1996 (Feb. 24)	10,740	BILL CLINTON*	90	32,773	STEVE FORBES	33
					Bob Dole	27
					Pat Buchanan	19

Note: All candidates are listed that drew at least 10 percent of their party's primary vote. The names of winning candidates are capitalized. An asterisk (*) indicates an incumbent president.

Wilmington
Newark
New Castle
Dover
Kent
Sussex

DELAWARE DEMOCRATIC

1996

County	Total Vote	Clinton	LaRouche	Winner	Percentage of Total Vote: Clinton	LaRouche
KENT	1,759	1,519	240	Clinton	86.4%	13.6%
NEW CASTLE	6,807	6,242	565	Clinton	91.7%	8.3%
SUSSEX	2,174	1,933	241	Clinton	88.9%	11.1%
TOTAL	10,740	9,694	1,046	Clinton	90.3%	9.7%

DELAWARE REPUBLICAN

1996

County	Total Vote	Alexander	Buchanan	Dole	Forbes	Other	Winner	Percentage of Total Vote: Alexander	Buchanan	Dole	Forbes	Other
KENT	4,865	453	983	1,297	1,703	429	Forbes	9.3%	20.2%	26.7%	35.0%	8.8%
NEW CASTLE	21,337	3,249	3,567	5,991	6,693	1,837	Forbes	15.2%	16.7%	28.1%	31.4%	8.6%
SUSSEX	6,571	673	1,568	1,621	2,313	396	Forbes	10.2%	23.9%	24.7%	35.2%	6.0%
TOTAL	32,773	4,375	6,118	8,909	10,709	2,662	Forbes	13.3%	18.7%	27.2%	32.7%	8.1%

FLORIDA

In the beginning, there was Florida. The state enacted the nation's first presidential primary law in 1901. But it was not until 1972, when Florida officials began scheduling the primary on the second Tuesday in March that the Sunshine State became an important stop for White House aspirants looking for something other than rest and recreation. In the years that followed, Florida was joined on its early March date by other Southern states that created a regional votefest known as "Super Tuesday." But as one of the most populous states in the country, Florida—along with Texas—has tended to dominate the event.

From 1976 through 1988, the candidates who won the first-in-the-nation primary in New Hampshire also won in Florida. But what had been a one-week interval between the two primaries in the early 1970s had grown to three weeks in the 1990s, a length of time in which the momentum from the New Hampshire primary could largely dissipate. In 1996, Granite State winner Pat Buchanan ran third in Florida's GOP primary with less than one-third the vote of the victorious Bob Dole. Four years earlier, New Hampshire winner Paul Tsongas was beaten by Bill Clinton in Democratic voting in Florida

Arkansas native Clinton was the latest in a line of Southern Democrats to run well in Florida's presidential primary. Sen. George A. Smathers won as a favorite-son candidate in 1968. Alabama's George Wallace capitalized on strong antibusing sentiment to overwhelm a large Democratic field in 1972. Georgia's Jimmy Carter scored critical primary victories in Florida in 1976 and 1980, beating Wallace and Edward Kennedy, respectively.

But Southerners do not always win Florida's Democratic primary. That was conspicuously the case in 1988, when

Recent Florida Primary Results

Florida held its first presidential primary in 1928.

	DEMOCRATS			REPUBLICANS		
Year	Turnout	Candidates	%	Turnout	Candidates	%
1996 (March 12)	—	NO PRIMARY		898,516	BOB DOLE	57
					Steve Forbes	20
					Pat Buchanan	18
1992 (March 10)	1,123,857	BILL CLINTON	51	893,463	GEORGE BUSH*	68
		Paul Tsongas	35		Pat Buchanan	32
		Jerry Brown	12			
1988 (March 8)	1,273,298	MICHAEL DUKAKIS	41	901,222	GEORGE BUSH	62
		Jesse Jackson	20		Bob Dole	21
		Richard Gephardt	14		Pat Robertson	11
		Al Gore	13			
1984 (March 13)	1,182,190	GARY HART	39	344,150	RONALD REAGAN*	100
		Walter Mondale	33			
		Jesse Jackson	12			
		John Glenn	11			
1980 (March 11)	1,098,003	JIMMY CARTER*	61	614,995	RONALD REAGAN	56
		Edward Kennedy	23		George Bush	30
1976 (March 9)	1,300,330	JIMMY CARTER	35	609,819	GERALD FORD*	53
		George Wallace	31		Ronald Reagan	47
		Henry Jackson	24			
1972 (March 14)	1,264,554	GEORGE WALLACE	42	414,207	RICHARD NIXON*	87
		Hubert Humphrey	19			
		Henry Jackson	13			
1968 (May 28)	512,357	GEORGE SMATHERS	46	51,509	UNCOMMITTED	100
		Eugene McCarthy	29			
		Uncommitted	25			

Note: All candidates are listed that drew at least 10 percent of their party's primary vote. The names of winning candidates are capitalized. An asterisk (*) indicates an incumbent president.

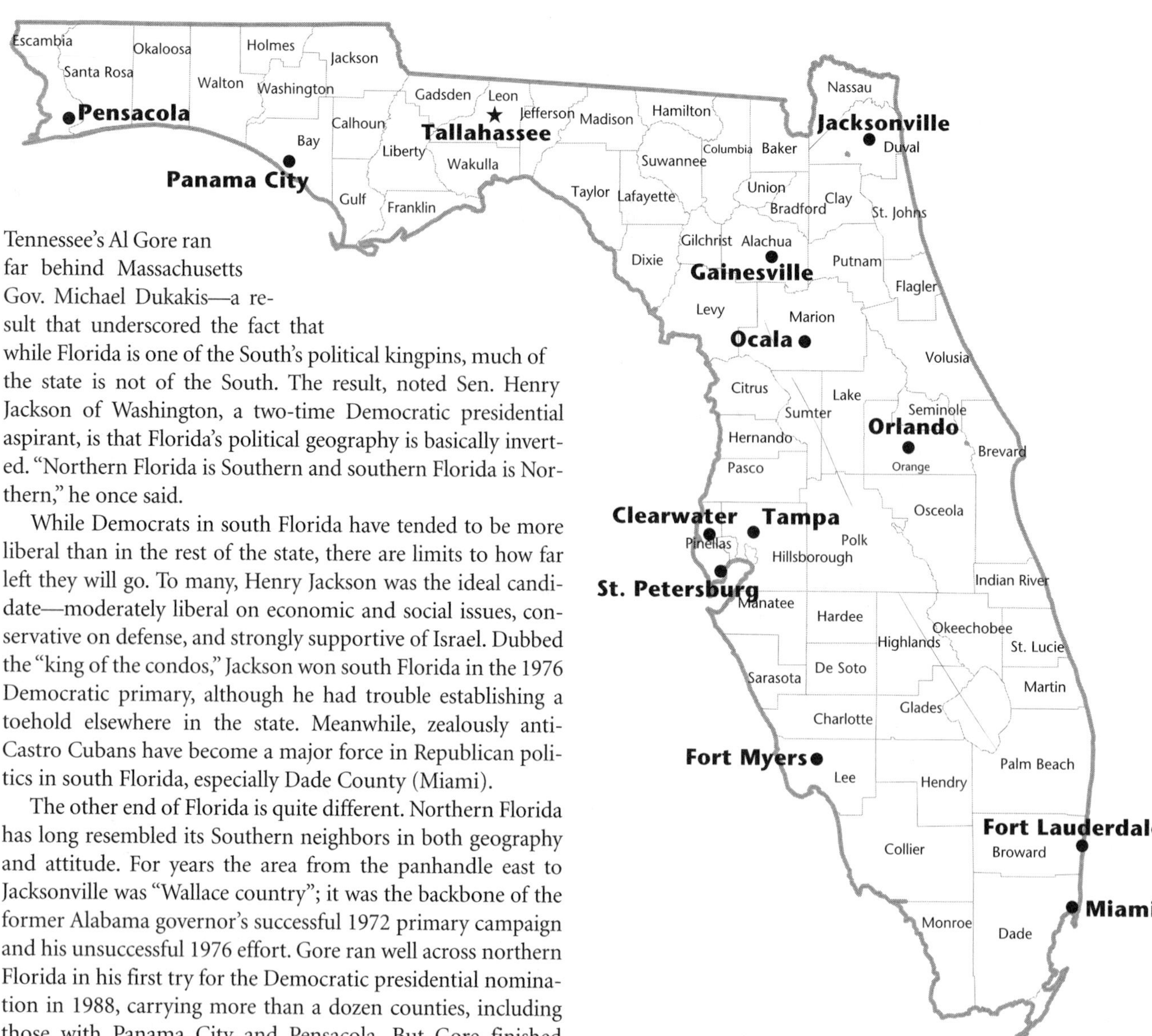

Tennessee's Al Gore ran far behind Massachusetts Gov. Michael Dukakis—a result that underscored the fact that while Florida is one of the South's political kingpins, much of the state is not of the South. The result, noted Sen. Henry Jackson of Washington, a two-time Democratic presidential aspirant, is that Florida's political geography is basically inverted. "Northern Florida is Southern and southern Florida is Northern," he once said.

While Democrats in south Florida have tended to be more liberal than in the rest of the state, there are limits to how far left they will go. To many, Henry Jackson was the ideal candidate—moderately liberal on economic and social issues, conservative on defense, and strongly supportive of Israel. Dubbed the "king of the condos," Jackson won south Florida in the 1976 Democratic primary, although he had trouble establishing a toehold elsewhere in the state. Meanwhile, zealously anti-Castro Cubans have become a major force in Republican politics in south Florida, especially Dade County (Miami).

The other end of Florida is quite different. Northern Florida has long resembled its Southern neighbors in both geography and attitude. For years the area from the panhandle east to Jacksonville was "Wallace country"; it was the backbone of the former Alabama governor's successful 1972 primary campaign and his unsuccessful 1976 effort. Gore ran well across northern Florida in his first try for the Democratic presidential nomination in 1988, carrying more than a dozen counties, including those with Panama City and Pensacola. But Gore finished fourth statewide because he ran poorly in the other, more populous portions of the state.

In between the two ends of the state is central Florida, which includes the GOP's historic base in the retirement communities along the Gulf Coast. It is in central Florida where many primary battles are decided. That includes the Ford-Reagan contest of 1976, which not only had ideological overtones but was by far the most competitive presidential primary that Florida Republicans have ever had. Reagan won north and south Florida, but still lost because of Ford's strength in central Florida and the Gulf Coast.

Although Florida Republicans are approaching parity with the long-dominant Democrats in voter registration, the burgeoning size of the GOP has not resulted in increased competition in the party's presidential primary. Only the Ford-Reagan contest was decided by a margin of less than 25 percentage points.

FLORIDA DEMOCRATIC

1968

County	Total Vote	McCarthy	Smathers	Uncommitted	Winner	Percentage of Total Vote McCarthy	Smathers	Uncom.
ALACHUA	10,863	4,196	4,863	1,804	Smathers	38.6%	44.8%	16.6%
BAKER	822	185	457	180	Smathers	22.5%	55.6%	21.9%
BAY	5,691	1,061	3,004	1,626	Smathers	18.6%	52.8%	28.6%
BRADFORD	1,621	315	986	320	Smathers	19.4%	60.8%	19.7%
BREVARD	13,274	4,080	6,042	3,152	Smathers	30.7%	45.5%	23.7%
BROWARD	29,093	10,636	13,130	5,327	Smathers	36.6%	45.1%	18.3%
CALHOUN	1,704	335	1,006	363	Smathers	19.7%	59.0%	21.3%
CHARLOTTE	2,098	476	1,185	437	Smathers	22.7%	56.5%	20.8%
CITRUS	2,536	621	1,338	577	Smathers	24.5%	52.8%	22.8%
CLAY	2,559	620	1,395	544	Smathers	24.2%	54.5%	21.3%
COLLIER	1,855	570	890	395	Smathers	30.7%	48.0%	21.3%
COLUMBIA	3,168	627	1,655	886	Smathers	19.8%	52.2%	28.0%
DADE	90,221	36,479	30,990	22,752	McCarthy	40.4%	34.3%	25.2%
DESOTO	1,594	341	826	427	Smathers	21.4%	51.8%	26.8%
DIXIE	964	118	538	308	Smathers	12.2%	55.8%	32.0%
DUVAL	36,292	9,310	19,076	7,906	Smathers	25.7%	52.6%	21.8%
ESCAMBIA	28,892	3,642	11,876	13,374	Uncommitted	12.6%	41.1%	46.3%
FLAGLER	720	139	291	290	Smathers	19.3%	40.4%	40.3%
FRANKLIN	1,224	215	582	427	Smathers	17.6%	47.5%	34.9%
GADSDEN	3,465	697	2,023	745	Smathers	20.1%	58.4%	21.5%
GILCHRIST	635	68	378	189	Smathers	10.7%	59.5%	29.8%
GLADES	424	100	195	129	Smathers	23.6%	46.0%	30.4%
GULF	1,959	282	833	844	Uncommitted	14.4%	42.5%	43.1%
HAMILTON	1,049	147	530	372	Smathers	14.0%	50.5%	35.5%
HARDEE	1,511	362	791	358	Smathers	24.0%	52.3%	23.7%
HENDRY	979	289	461	229	Smathers	29.5%	47.1%	23.4%
HERNANDO	1,519	358	832	329	Smathers	23.6%	54.8%	21.7%
HIGHLANDS	2,834	640	1,657	537	Smathers	22.6%	58.5%	18.9%
HILLSBOROUGH	47,806	12,658	23,437	11,711	Smathers	26.5%	49.0%	24.5%
HOLMES	2,912	314	1,826	772	Smathers	10.8%	62.7%	26.5%
INDIAN RIVER	2,353	859	1,079	415	Smathers	36.5%	45.9%	17.6%
JACKSON	2,751	829	939	983	Uncommitted	30.1%	34.1%	35.7%
JEFFERSON	1,103	257	598	248	Smathers	23.3%	54.2%	22.5%
LAFAYETTE	764	99	402	263	Smathers	13.0%	52.6%	34.4%
LAKE	4,771	1,113	2,908	750	Smathers	23.3%	61.0%	15.7%
LEE	8,081	2,081	4,222	1,778	Smathers	25.8%	52.2%	22.0%
LEON	10,616	3,638	5,321	1,657	Smathers	34.3%	50.1%	15.6%
LEVY	1,399	313	809	277	Smathers	22.4%	57.8%	19.8%
LIBERTY	776	122	497	157	Smathers	15.7%	64.0%	20.2%
MADISON	1,579	347	768	464	Smathers	22.0%	48.6%	29.4%
MANATEE	6,765	1,862	3,509	1,394	Smathers	27.5%	51.9%	20.6%
MARION	5,508	1,439	2,719	1,350	Smathers	26.1%	49.4%	24.5%
MARTIN	1,768	603	775	390	Smathers	34.1%	43.8%	22.1%
MONROE	4,363	1,163	2,448	752	Smathers	26.7%	56.1%	17.2%
NASSAU	2,780	648	1,401	731	Smathers	23.3%	50.4%	26.3%
OKALOOSA	7,070	1,067	3,393	2,610	Smathers	15.1%	48.0%	36.9%
OKEECHOBEE	898	230	433	235	Smathers	25.6%	48.2%	26.2%
ORANGE	21,395	6,551	10,846	3,998	Smathers	30.6%	50.7%	18.7%
OSCEOLA	2,022	478	1,251	293	Smathers	23.6%	61.9%	14.5%
PALM BEACH	15,058	4,718	6,821	3,519	Smathers	31.3%	45.3%	23.4%

FLORIDA DEMOCRATIC

1968

County	Total Vote	McCarthy	Smathers	Uncommitted	Winner	Percentage of Total Vote McCarthy	Smathers	Uncom.
PASCO	5,065	1,289	2,548	1,228	Smathers	25.4%	50.3%	24.2%
PINELLAS	29,579	8,823	14,551	6,205	Smathers	29.8%	49.2%	21.0%
POLK	22,743	5,562	11,083	6,098	Smathers	24.5%	48.7%	26.8%
PUTNAM	4,832	1,056	2,239	1,537	Smathers	21.9%	46.3%	31.8%
ST. JOHNS	2,768	792	1,313	663	Smathers	28.6%	47.4%	24.0%
ST. LUCIE	3,434	1,022	1,642	770	Smathers	29.8%	47.8%	22.4%
SANTA ROSA	4,448	468	1,786	2,194	Uncommitted	10.5%	40.2%	49.3%
SARASOTA	4,857	1,647	2,203	1,007	Smathers	33.9%	45.4%	20.7%
SEMINOLE	5,654	1,497	3,141	1,016	Smathers	26.5%	55.6%	18.0%
SUMTER	1,141	187	744	210	Smathers	16.4%	65.2%	18.4%
SUWANNEE	2,214	427	1,270	517	Smathers	19.3%	57.4%	23.4%
TAYLOR	2,014	438	1,086	490	Smathers	21.7%	53.9%	24.3%
UNION	590	88	377	125	Smathers	14.9%	63.9%	21.2%
VOLUSIA	15,490	4,642	6,016	4,832	Smathers	30.0%	38.8%	31.2%
WAKULLA	704	152	340	212	Smathers	21.6%	48.3%	30.1%
WALTON	2,896	453	1,079	1,364	Uncommitted	15.6%	37.3%	47.1%
WASHINGTON	1,824	375	592	857	Uncommitted	20.6%	32.5%	47.0%
TOTAL	512,357	147,216	236,242	128,899	Smathers	28.7%	46.1%	25.2%

FLORIDA DEMOCRATIC

1972

County	Total Vote	Humphrey	H. Jackson	McGovern	Wallace	Other	Winner	Percentage of Total Vote Humphrey	H. Jackson	McGovern	Wallace	Other
ALACHUA	23,626	3,532	1,848	5,386	7,326	5,534	Wallace	14.9%	7.8%	22.8%	31.0%	23.4%
BAKER	1,889	120	125	11	1,524	109	Wallace	6.4%	6.6%	0.6%	80.7%	5.8%
BAY	16,693	756	2,526	201	10,959	2,251	Wallace	4.5%	15.1%	1.2%	65.7%	13.5%
BRADFORD	3,537	460	312	65	2,295	405	Wallace	13.0%	8.8%	1.8%	64.9%	11.5%
BREVARD	34,686	10,852	6,545	1,088	12,402	3,799	Wallace	31.3%	18.9%	3.1%	35.8%	11.0%
BROWARD	94,321	19,041	11,984	8,359	31,847	23,090	Wallace	20.2%	12.7%	8.9%	33.8%	24.5%
CALHOUN	2,093	100	136	34	1,666	157	Wallace	4.8%	6.5%	1.6%	79.6%	7.5%
CHARLOTTE	4,879	921	1,038	133	1,768	1,019	Wallace	18.9%	21.3%	2.7%	36.2%	20.9%
CITRUS	4,796	729	632	121	2,569	745	Wallace	15.2%	13.2%	2.5%	53.6%	15.5%
CLAY	6,262	731	1,075	170	3,582	704	Wallace	11.7%	17.2%	2.7%	57.2%	11.2%
COLLIER	4,376	706	596	283	2,068	723	Wallace	16.1%	13.6%	6.5%	47.3%	16.5%
COLUMBIA	5,779	503	409	130	4,143	594	Wallace	8.7%	7.1%	2.2%	71.7%	10.3%
DADE	249,121	64,450	33,308	29,678	68,126	53,559	Wallace	25.9%	13.4%	11.9%	27.3%	21.5%
DESOTO	2,429	270	209	31	1,556	363	Wallace	11.1%	8.6%	1.3%	64.1%	14.9%
DIXIE	1,480	86	102	23	1,121	148	Wallace	5.8%	6.9%	1.6%	75.7%	10.0%
DUVAL	115,509	21,370	16,669	2,544	53,862	21,064	Wallace	18.5%	14.4%	2.2%	46.6%	18.2%
ESCAMBIA	49,283	6,172	9,971	1,201	24,921	7,018	Wallace	12.5%	20.2%	2.4%	50.6%	14.2%
FLAGLER	1,189	184	98	14	711	182	Wallace	15.5%	8.2%	1.2%	59.8%	15.3%
FRANKLIN	1,734	124	186	32	1,153	239	Wallace	7.2%	10.7%	1.8%	66.5%	13.8%
GADSDEN	8,118	1,030	563	87	3,804	2,634	Wallace	12.7%	6.9%	1.1%	46.9%	32.4%

FLORIDA DEMOCRATIC

1972

County	Total Vote	Humphrey	H. Jackson	McGovern	Wallace	Other	Winner	Percentage of Total Vote Humphrey	H. Jackson	McGovern	Wallace	Other
GILCHRIST	1,304	57	104	34	1,023	86	Wallace	4.4%	8.0%	2.6%	78.5%	6.6%
GLADES	870	85	80	12	611	82	Wallace	9.8%	9.2%	1.4%	70.2%	9.4%
GULF	2,656	160	306	20	1,934	236	Wallace	6.0%	11.5%	0.8%	72.8%	8.9%
HAMILTON	1,669	196	123	15	1,164	171	Wallace	11.7%	7.4%	0.9%	69.7%	10.2%
HARDEE	3,000	300	285	37	2,102	276	Wallace	10.0%	9.5%	1.2%	70.1%	9.2%
HENDRY	2,421	343	243	38	1,546	251	Wallace	14.2%	10.0%	1.6%	63.9%	10.4%
HERNANDO	3,834	630	543	101	1,938	622	Wallace	16.4%	14.2%	2.6%	50.5%	16.2%
HIGHLANDS	5,985	948	822	146	3,094	975	Wallace	15.8%	13.7%	2.4%	51.7%	16.3%
HILLSBOROUGH	91,790	13,721	15,194	3,529	35,328	24,018	Wallace	14.9%	16.6%	3.8%	38.5%	26.2%
HOLMES	3,064	56	187	28	2,648	145	Wallace	1.8%	6.1%	0.9%	86.4%	4.7%
INDIAN RIVER	6,018	1,153	551	275	2,937	1,102	Wallace	19.2%	9.2%	4.6%	48.8%	18.3%
JACKSON	8,992	503	429	95	6,626	1,339	Wallace	5.6%	4.8%	1.1%	73.7%	14.9%
JEFFERSON	2,290	253	141	31	1,334	531	Wallace	11.0%	6.2%	1.4%	58.3%	23.2%
LAFAYETTE	1,024	47	76	3	852	46	Wallace	4.6%	7.4%	0.3%	83.2%	4.5%
LAKE	10,986	1,479	1,327	279	6,633	1,268	Wallace	13.5%	12.1%	2.5%	60.4%	11.5%
LEE	17,851	2,581	3,065	561	8,864	2,780	Wallace	14.5%	17.2%	3.1%	49.7%	15.6%
LEON	25,520	2,689	2,769	2,938	10,907	6,217	Wallace	10.5%	10.9%	11.5%	42.7%	24.4%
LEVY	2,714	259	229	45	1,874	307	Wallace	9.5%	8.4%	1.7%	69.0%	11.3%
LIBERTY	1,135	48	63	11	918	95	Wallace	4.2%	5.6%	1.0%	80.9%	8.4%
MADISON	3,585	385	197	34	2,381	588	Wallace	10.7%	5.5%	0.9%	66.4%	16.4%
MANATEE	14,635	2,436	1,863	494	6,602	3,240	Wallace	16.6%	12.7%	3.4%	45.1%	22.1%
MARION	14,294	1,575	1,439	326	8,696	2,258	Wallace	11.0%	10.1%	2.3%	60.8%	15.8%
MARTIN	4,879	758	470	239	2,428	984	Wallace	15.5%	9.6%	4.9%	49.8%	20.2%
MONROE	8,729	893	922	513	4,620	1,781	Wallace	10.2%	10.6%	5.9%	52.9%	20.4%
NASSAU	4,012	532	461	73	2,419	527	Wallace	13.3%	11.5%	1.8%	60.3%	13.1%
OKALOOSA	13,968	696	3,066	333	8,578	1,295	Wallace	5.0%	22.0%	2.4%	61.4%	9.3%
OKEECHOBEE	1,968	201	117	33	1,429	188	Wallace	10.2%	5.9%	1.7%	72.6%	9.6%
ORANGE	48,446	9,389	7,382	2,269	21,770	7,636	Wallace	19.4%	15.2%	4.7%	44.9%	15.8%
OSCEOLA	4,574	760	661	16	2,562	575	Wallace	16.6%	14.5%	0.3%	56.0%	12.6%
PALM BEACH	59,258	10,751	6,560	4,606	22,484	14,857	Wallace	18.1%	11.1%	7.8%	37.9%	25.1%
PASCO	13,875	2,869	1,563	451	6,065	2,927	Wallace	20.7%	11.3%	3.3%	43.7%	21.1%
PINELLAS	86,137	20,115	9,753	6,154	23,420	26,695	Wallace	23.4%	11.3%	7.1%	27.2%	31.0%
POLK	46,853	5,908	7,301	981	25,128	7,535	Wallace	12.6%	15.6%	2.1%	53.6%	16.1%
PUTNAM	7,366	966	870	188	4,467	875	Wallace	13.1%	11.8%	2.6%	60.6%	11.9%
ST. JOHNS	6,449	783	851	134	3,757	924	Wallace	12.1%	13.2%	2.1%	58.3%	14.3%
ST. LUCIE	8,587	1,050	715	314	4,595	1,913	Wallace	12.2%	8.3%	3.7%	53.5%	22.3%
SANTA ROSA	8,201	418	1,576	183	5,421	603	Wallace	5.1%	19.2%	2.2%	66.1%	7.4%
SARASOTA	14,035	2,547	1,693	850	4,664	4,281	Wallace	18.1%	12.1%	6.1%	33.2%	30.5%
SEMINOLE	12,613	2,575	1,994	491	5,801	1,752	Wallace	20.4%	15.8%	3.9%	46.0%	13.9%
SUMTER	3,096	367	267	54	2,116	292	Wallace	11.9%	8.6%	1.7%	68.3%	9.4%
SUWANNEE	3,907	326	364	63	2,750	404	Wallace	8.3%	9.3%	1.6%	70.4%	10.3%
TAYLOR	3,213	251	223	41	2,344	354	Wallace	7.8%	6.9%	1.3%	73.0%	11.0%
UNION	1,250	90	68	33	978	81	Wallace	7.2%	5.4%	2.6%	78.2%	6.5%
VOLUSIA	35,657	9,854	3,981	1,471	13,723	6,628	Wallace	27.6%	11.2%	4.1%	38.5%	18.6%
WAKULLA	1,843	100	109	23	1,454	157	Wallace	5.4%	5.9%	1.2%	78.9%	8.5%
WALTON	4,817	288	568	46	3,549	366	Wallace	6.0%	11.8%	1.0%	73.7%	7.6%
WASHINGTON	3,384	130	253	30	2,714	257	Wallace	3.8%	7.5%	0.9%	80.2%	7.6%
TOTAL	1,264,554	234,658	170,156	78,232	526,651	254,857	Wallace	18.6%	13.5%	6.2%	41.6%	20.2%

FLORIDA REPUBLICAN

1972

County	Total Vote	Nixon	Other	Winner	Percentage of Total Vote Nixon	Other
ALACHUA	3,545	2,834	711	Nixon	79.9%	20.1%
BAKER	18	17	1	Nixon	94.4%	5.6%
BAY	1,153	1,048	105	Nixon	90.9%	9.1%
BRADFORD	123	105	18	Nixon	85.4%	14.6%
BREVARD	17,203	14,700	2,503	Nixon	85.5%	14.5%
BROWARD	63,663	55,455	8,208	Nixon	87.1%	12.9%
CALHOUN	42	36	6	Nixon	85.7%	14.3%
CHARLOTTE	3,902	3,500	402	Nixon	89.7%	10.3%
CITRUS	1,420	1,300	120	Nixon	91.5%	8.5%
CLAY	999	892	107	Nixon	89.3%	10.7%
COLLIER	3,711	3,292	419	Nixon	88.7%	11.3%
COLUMBIA	330	270	60	Nixon	81.8%	18.2%
DADE	45,027	38,133	6,894	Nixon	84.7%	15.3%
DESOTO	158	40	118	Ashbrook	25.3%	74.7%
DIXIE	1	1		Nixon	100.0%	
DUVAL	12,337	10,896	1,441	Nixon	88.3%	11.7%
ESCAMBIA	4,249	3,756	493	Nixon	88.4%	11.6%
FLAGLER	89	73	16	Nixon	82.0%	18.0%
FRANKLIN	87	81	6	Nixon	93.1%	6.9%
GADSDEN	173	143	30	Nixon	82.7%	17.3%
GILCHRIST	4	4		Nixon	100.0%	
GLADES	26	21	5	Nixon	80.8%	19.2%
GULF	22	16	6	Nixon	72.7%	27.3%
HAMILTON	11	11		Nixon	100.0%	
HARDEE	103	88	15	Nixon	85.4%	14.6%
HENDRY	120	103	17	Nixon	85.8%	14.2%
HERNANDO	1,049	937	112	Nixon	89.3%	10.7%
HIGHLANDS	1,692	1,525	167	Nixon	90.1%	9.9%
HILLSBOROUGH	14,603	12,913	1,690	Nixon	88.4%	11.6%
HOLMES	35	32	3	Nixon	91.4%	8.6%
INDIAN RIVER	3,296	2,852	444	Nixon	86.5%	13.5%
JACKSON	225	199	26	Nixon	88.4%	11.6%
JEFFERSON	82	65	17	Nixon	79.3%	20.7%
LAFAYETTE	15	13	2	Nixon	86.7%	13.3%
LAKE	5,411	4,972	439	Nixon	91.9%	8.1%
LEE	9,620	8,510	1,110	Nixon	88.5%	11.5%
LEON	3,744	3,045	699	Nixon	81.3%	18.7%
LEVY	143	124	19	Nixon	86.7%	13.3%
LIBERTY	18	15	3	Nixon	83.3%	16.7%
MADISON	83	68	15	Nixon	81.9%	18.1%
MANATEE	9,169	8,242	927	Nixon	89.9%	10.1%
MARION	2,431	2,168	263	Nixon	89.2%	10.8%
MARTIN	2,626	2,272	354	Nixon	86.5%	13.5%
MONROE	983	841	142	Nixon	85.6%	14.4%
NASSAU	162	142	20	Nixon	87.7%	12.3%
OKALOOSA	1,351	1,211	140	Nixon	89.6%	10.4%
OKEECHOBEE	175	162	13	Nixon	92.6%	7.4%
ORANGE	23,582	20,997	2,585	Nixon	89.0%	11.0%
OSCEOLA	2,084	1,943	141	Nixon	93.2%	6.8%
PALM BEACH	35,590	30,837	4,753	Nixon	86.6%	13.4%

FLORIDA REPUBLICAN

1972

County	Total Vote	Nixon	Other	Winner	Percentage of Total Vote Nixon	Other
PASCO	7,432	6,455	977	Nixon	86.9%	13.1%
PINELLAS	77,130	66,094	11,036	Nixon	85.7%	14.3%
POLK	8,637	7,716	921	Nixon	89.3%	10.7%
PUTNAM	726	650	76	Nixon	89.5%	10.5%
ST. JOHNS	966	847	119	Nixon	87.7%	12.3%
ST. LUCIE	2,899	2,638	261	Nixon	91.0%	9.0%
SANTA ROSA	611	518	93	Nixon	84.8%	15.2%
SARASOTA	19,392	17,057	2,335	Nixon	88.0%	12.0%
SEMINOLE	5,762	5,030	732	Nixon	87.3%	12.7%
SUMTER	207	184	23	Nixon	88.9%	11.1%
SUWANNEE	98	64	34	Nixon	65.3%	34.7%
TAYLOR	106	98	8	Nixon	92.5%	7.5%
UNION	11	8	3	Nixon	72.7%	27.3%
VOLUSIA	13,286	11,806	1,480	Nixon	88.9%	11.1%
WAKULLA	30	26	4	Nixon	86.7%	13.3%
WALTON	148	117	31	Nixon	79.1%	20.9%
WASHINGTON	81	70	11	Nixon	86.4%	13.6%
TOTAL	414,207	360,278	53,929	Nixon	87.0%	13.0%

FLORIDA DEMOCRATIC

1976

County	Total Vote	Carter	H. Jackson	Wallace	Other	Winner	Percentage of Total Vote Carter	H. Jackson	Wallace	Other
ALACHUA	21,785	9,901	2,575	5,847	3,462	Carter	45.4%	11.8%	26.8%	15.9%
BAKER	2,248	413	118	1,634	83	Wallace	18.4%	5.2%	72.7%	3.7%
BAY	13,236	2,638	1,676	8,088	834	Wallace	19.9%	12.7%	61.1%	6.3%
BRADFORD	3,465	1,086	344	1,839	196	Wallace	31.3%	9.9%	53.1%	5.7%
BREVARD	35,733	13,143	7,601	10,353	4,636	Carter	36.8%	21.3%	29.0%	13.0%
BROWARD	121,688	36,700	47,452	22,921	14,615	H. Jackson	30.2%	39.0%	18.8%	12.0%
CALHOUN	2,037	292	132	1,477	136	Wallace	14.3%	6.5%	72.5%	6.7%
CHARLOTTE	6,807	2,611	1,630	1,855	711	Carter	38.4%	23.9%	27.3%	10.4%
CITRUS	7,181	2,086	1,402	3,010	683	Wallace	29.0%	19.5%	41.9%	9.5%
CLAY	7,878	2,632	1,071	3,440	735	Wallace	33.4%	13.6%	43.7%	9.3%
COLLIER	6,009	2,320	1,127	1,790	772	Carter	38.6%	18.8%	29.8%	12.8%
COLUMBIA	5,395	1,457	424	3,154	360	Wallace	27.0%	7.9%	58.5%	6.7%
DADE	268,420	87,604	99,735	46,421	34,660	H. Jackson	32.6%	37.2%	17.3%	12.9%
DESOTO	2,591	846	296	1,256	193	Wallace	32.7%	11.4%	48.5%	7.4%
DIXIE	1,462	426	100	903	33	Wallace	29.1%	6.8%	61.8%	2.3%
DUVAL	89,423	33,920	13,414	34,426	7,663	Wallace	37.9%	15.0%	38.5%	8.6%
ESCAMBIA	42,716	8,918	7,082	23,110	3,606	Wallace	20.9%	16.6%	54.1%	8.4%
FLAGLER	1,512	695	232	422	163	Carter	46.0%	15.3%	27.9%	10.8%
FRANKLIN	1,487	367	163	840	117	Wallace	24.7%	11.0%	56.5%	7.9%
GADSDEN	6,302	2,478	550	2,521	753	Wallace	39.3%	8.7%	40.0%	11.9%

FLORIDA DEMOCRATIC

1976

County	Total Vote	Carter	H. Jackson	Wallace	Other	Winner	Percentage of Total Vote: Carter	H. Jackson	Wallace	Other
GILCHRIST	1,302	358	68	832	44	Wallace	27.5%	5.2%	63.9%	3.4%
GLADES	1,101	353	110	583	55	Wallace	32.1%	10.0%	53.0%	5.0%
GULF	2,117	336	239	1,402	140	Wallace	15.9%	11.3%	66.2%	6.6%
HAMILTON	1,473	350	123	823	177	Wallace	23.8%	8.4%	55.9%	12.0%
HARDEE	2,538	637	236	1,422	243	Wallace	25.1%	9.3%	56.0%	9.6%
HENDRY	2,615	864	235	1,349	167	Wallace	33.0%	9.0%	51.6%	6.4%
HERNANDO	6,290	2,204	1,061	2,273	752	Wallace	35.0%	16.9%	36.1%	12.0%
HIGHLANDS	6,129	1,906	1,010	2,598	615	Wallace	31.1%	16.5%	42.4%	10.0%
HILLSBOROUGH	79,200	27,696	17,280	25,276	8,948	Carter	35.0%	21.8%	31.9%	11.3%
HOLMES	3,037	268	188	2,460	121	Wallace	8.8%	6.2%	81.0%	4.0%
INDIAN RIVER	5,696	2,315	893	1,849	639	Carter	40.6%	15.7%	32.5%	11.2%
JACKSON	8,444	1,674	663	5,531	576	Wallace	19.8%	7.9%	65.5%	6.8%
JEFFERSON	2,197	846	190	1,026	135	Wallace	38.5%	8.6%	46.7%	6.1%
LAFAYETTE	884	193	55	620	16	Wallace	21.8%	6.2%	70.1%	1.8%
LAKE	10,815	3,803	1,590	4,393	1,029	Wallace	35.2%	14.7%	40.6%	9.5%
LEE	23,335	9,622	3,792	7,627	2,294	Carter	41.2%	16.3%	32.7%	9.8%
LEON	24,399	10,919	2,238	7,860	3,382	Carter	44.8%	9.2%	32.2%	13.9%
LEVY	3,130	869	313	1,762	186	Wallace	27.8%	10.0%	56.3%	5.9%
LIBERTY	1,011	136	62	738	75	Wallace	13.5%	6.1%	73.0%	7.4%
MADISON	3,164	1,074	269	1,667	154	Wallace	33.9%	8.5%	52.7%	4.9%
MANATEE	17,289	6,553	3,450	5,512	1,774	Carter	37.9%	20.0%	31.9%	10.3%
MARION	15,165	4,683	1,942	7,406	1,134	Wallace	30.9%	12.8%	48.8%	7.5%
MARTIN	5,813	2,622	979	1,603	609	Carter	45.1%	16.8%	27.6%	10.5%
MONROE	8,949	2,786	1,506	3,562	1,095	Wallace	31.1%	16.8%	39.8%	12.2%
NASSAU	4,088	1,170	379	2,276	263	Wallace	28.6%	9.3%	55.7%	6.4%
OKALOOSA	15,704	2,518	2,445	9,287	1,454	Wallace	16.0%	15.6%	59.1%	9.3%
OKEECHOBEE	2,074	763	172	1,031	108	Wallace	36.8%	8.3%	49.7%	5.2%
ORANGE	46,286	18,990	7,776	14,114	5,406	Carter	41.0%	16.8%	30.5%	11.7%
OSCEOLA	4,740	1,646	678	1,924	492	Wallace	34.7%	14.3%	40.6%	10.4%
PALM BEACH	69,774	27,709	20,023	13,646	8,396	Carter	39.7%	28.7%	19.6%	12.0%
PASCO	22,292	7,824	5,466	7,004	1,998	Carter	35.1%	24.5%	31.4%	9.0%
PINELLAS	90,994	39,105	22,798	18,459	10,632	Carter	43.0%	25.1%	20.3%	11.7%
POLK	40,075	12,930	5,856	17,567	3,722	Wallace	32.3%	14.6%	43.8%	9.3%
PUTNAM	8,060	2,552	1,105	3,786	617	Wallace	31.7%	13.7%	47.0%	7.7%
ST. JOHNS	6,868	2,178	878	3,145	667	Wallace	31.7%	12.8%	45.8%	9.7%
ST. LUCIE	8,454	3,290	1,378	2,859	927	Carter	38.9%	16.3%	33.8%	11.0%
SANTA ROSA	9,142	1,352	1,012	6,150	628	Wallace	14.8%	11.1%	67.3%	6.9%
SARASOTA	18,362	6,868	4,623	4,253	2,618	Carter	37.4%	25.2%	23.2%	14.3%
SEMINOLE	14,288	5,698	2,479	4,310	1,801	Carter	39.9%	17.4%	30.2%	12.6%
SUMTER	3,795	1,169	443	1,912	271	Wallace	30.8%	11.7%	50.4%	7.1%
SUWANNEE	4,004	1,159	330	2,344	171	Wallace	28.9%	8.2%	58.5%	4.3%
TAYLOR	2,604	656	138	1,669	141	Wallace	25.2%	5.3%	64.1%	5.4%
UNION	1,328	344	80	845	59	Wallace	25.9%	6.0%	63.6%	4.4%
VOLUSIA	34,311	15,782	6,379	8,062	4,088	Carter	46.0%	18.6%	23.5%	11.9%
WAKULLA	2,174	457	131	1,454	132	Wallace	21.0%	6.0%	66.9%	6.1%
WALTON	4,131	604	446	2,888	193	Wallace	14.6%	10.8%	69.9%	4.7%
WASHINGTON	3,314	480	313	2,354	167	Wallace	14.5%	9.4%	71.0%	5.0%
TOTAL	1,300,330	448,844	310,944	396,820	143,722	Carter	34.5%	23.9%	30.5%	11.1%

FLORIDA REPUBLICAN

1976

County	Total Vote	Ford	Reagan	Winner	Percentage of Total Vote	
					Ford	Reagan
ALACHUA	4,271	2,473	1,798	Ford	57.9%	42.1%
BAKER	24	9	15	Reagan	37.5%	62.5%
BAY	2,213	820	1,393	Reagan	37.1%	62.9%
BRADFORD	145	59	86	Reagan	40.7%	59.3%
BREVARD	22,792	11,385	11,407	Reagan	50.0%	50.0%
BROWARD	83,673	41,256	42,417	Reagan	49.3%	50.7%
CALHOUN	62	26	36	Reagan	41.9%	58.1%
CHARLOTTE	8,075	4,150	3,925	Ford	51.4%	48.6%
CITRUS	3,081	1,715	1,366	Ford	55.7%	44.3%
CLAY	2,357	1,088	1,269	Reagan	46.2%	53.8%
COLLIER	8,833	4,636	4,197	Ford	52.5%	47.5%
COLUMBIA	375	177	198	Reagan	47.2%	52.8%
DADE	64,689	27,565	37,124	Reagan	42.6%	57.4%
DESOTO	224	112	112		50.0%	50.0%
DIXIE	15	9	6	Ford	60.0%	40.0%
DUVAL	15,613	7,569	8,044	Reagan	48.5%	51.5%
ESCAMBIA	6,346	2,611	3,735	Reagan	41.1%	58.9%
FLAGLER	334	204	130	Ford	61.1%	38.9%
FRANKLIN	95	45	50	Reagan	47.4%	52.6%
GADSDEN	172	65	107	Reagan	37.8%	62.2%
GILCHRIST	11	6	5	Ford	54.5%	45.5%
GLADES	29	19	10	Ford	65.5%	34.5%
GULF	74	19	55	Reagan	25.7%	74.3%
HAMILTON	14	5	9	Reagan	35.7%	64.3%
HARDEE	103	48	55	Reagan	46.6%	53.4%
HENDRY	204	98	106	Reagan	48.0%	52.0%
HERNANDO	2,627	1,508	1,119	Ford	57.4%	42.6%
HIGHLANDS	2,695	1,582	1,113	Ford	58.7%	41.3%
HILLSBOROUGH	18,908	10,414	8,494	Ford	55.1%	44.9%
HOLMES	52	17	35	Reagan	32.7%	67.3%
INDIAN RIVER	4,995	2,830	2,165	Ford	56.7%	43.3%
JACKSON	265	104	161	Reagan	39.2%	60.8%
JEFFERSON	78	25	53	Reagan	32.1%	67.9%
LAFAYETTE	12	6	6		50.0%	50.0%
LAKE	9,081	5,400	3,681	Ford	59.5%	40.5%
LEE	20,785	11,106	9,679	Ford	53.4%	46.6%
LEON	4,791	2,092	2,699	Reagan	43.7%	56.3%
LEVY	263	134	129	Ford	51.0%	49.0%
LIBERTY	15	3	12	Reagan	20.0%	80.0%
MADISON	94	42	52	Reagan	44.7%	55.3%
MANATEE	15,686	9,504	6,182	Ford	60.6%	39.4%
MARION	4,324	2,117	2,207	Reagan	49.0%	51.0%
MARTIN	6,748	3,677	3,071	Ford	54.5%	45.5%
MONROE	1,531	755	776	Reagan	49.3%	50.7%
NASSAU	291	126	165	Reagan	43.3%	56.7%
OKALOOSA	4,066	1,250	2,816	Reagan	30.7%	69.3%
OKEECHOBEE	224	107	117	Reagan	47.8%	52.2%
ORANGE	30,348	15,777	14,571	Ford	52.0%	48.0%
OSCEOLA	3,145	1,758	1,387	Ford	55.9%	44.1%
PALM BEACH	52,099	29,436	22,663	Ford	56.5%	43.5%

FLORIDA REPUBLICAN

1976

County	Total Vote	Ford	Reagan	Winner	Percentage of Total Vote	
					Ford	Reagan
PASCO	16,471	8,792	7,679	Ford	53.4%	46.6%
PINELLAS	102,649	61,047	41,602	Ford	59.5%	40.5%
POLK	12,392	6,603	5,789	Ford	53.3%	46.7%
PUTNAM	1,183	615	568	Ford	52.0%	48.0%
ST. JOHNS	1,623	741	882	Reagan	45.7%	54.3%
ST. LUCIE	4,687	2,453	2,234	Ford	52.3%	47.7%
SANTA ROSA	1,264	506	758	Reagan	40.0%	60.0%
SARASOTA	32,940	19,317	13,623	Ford	58.6%	41.4%
SEMINOLE	10,565	5,126	5,439	Reagan	48.5%	51.5%
SUMTER	385	195	190	Ford	50.6%	49.4%
SUWANNEE	207	103	104	Reagan	49.8%	50.2%
TAYLOR	118	47	71	Reagan	39.8%	60.2%
UNION	15	6	9	Reagan	40.0%	60.0%
VOLUSIA	17,882	10,333	7,549	Ford	57.8%	42.2%
WAKULLA	74	20	54	Reagan	27.0%	73.0%
WALTON	278	94	184	Reagan	33.8%	66.2%
WASHINGTON	139	45	94	Reagan	32.4%	67.6%
TOTAL	609,819	321,982	287,837	Ford	52.8%	47.2%

FLORIDA DEMOCRATIC

1980

County	Total Vote	Carter	E. Kennedy	Other	Winner	Percentage of Total Vote		
						Carter	E. Kennedy	Other
ALACHUA	18,738	13,082	2,965	2,691	Carter	69.8%	15.8%	14.4%
BAKER	1,896	1,447	190	259	Carter	76.3%	10.0%	13.7%
BAY	13,638	9,284	1,451	2,903	Carter	68.1%	10.6%	21.3%
BRADFORD	3,041	2,228	343	470	Carter	73.3%	11.3%	15.5%
BREVARD	31,803	19,797	6,428	5,578	Carter	62.2%	20.2%	17.5%
BROWARD	117,252	49,767	49,648	17,837	Carter	42.4%	42.3%	15.2%
CALHOUN	2,126	1,633	194	299	Carter	76.8%	9.1%	14.1%
CHARLOTTE	7,757	4,992	1,562	1,203	Carter	64.4%	20.1%	15.5%
CITRUS	8,100	5,181	1,694	1,225	Carter	64.0%	20.9%	15.1%
CLAY	7,499	5,127	897	1,475	Carter	68.4%	12.0%	19.7%
COLLIER	5,628	3,537	1,148	943	Carter	62.8%	20.4%	16.8%
COLUMBIA	4,582	3,318	510	754	Carter	72.4%	11.1%	16.5%
DADE	162,188	80,285	55,116	26,787	Carter	49.5%	34.0%	16.5%
DESOTO	2,003	1,477	240	286	Carter	73.7%	12.0%	14.3%
DIXIE	1,264	1,058	107	99	Carter	83.7%	8.5%	7.8%
DUVAL	77,992	52,399	11,742	13,851	Carter	67.2%	15.1%	17.8%
ESCAMBIA	29,976	18,481	4,488	7,007	Carter	61.7%	15.0%	23.4%
FLAGLER	2,023	1,445	327	251	Carter	71.4%	16.2%	12.4%
FRANKLIN	1,410	1,033	168	209	Carter	73.3%	11.9%	14.8%
GADSDEN	5,282	3,775	816	691	Carter	71.5%	15.4%	13.1%

FLORIDA DEMOCRATIC

1980

County	Total Vote	Carter	E. Kennedy	Other	Winner	Percentage of Total Vote Carter	E. Kennedy	Other
GILCHRIST	1,305	999	155	151	Carter	76.6%	11.9%	11.6%
GLADES	978	674	149	155	Carter	68.9%	15.2%	15.8%
GULF	2,223	1,680	198	345	Carter	75.6%	8.9%	15.5%
HAMILTON	1,139	808	143	188	Carter	70.9%	12.6%	16.5%
HARDEE	2,152	1,675	205	272	Carter	77.8%	9.5%	12.6%
HENDRY	1,986	1,403	277	306	Carter	70.6%	13.9%	15.4%
HERNANDO	7,190	4,689	1,594	907	Carter	65.2%	22.2%	12.6%
HIGHLANDS	5,851	4,074	848	929	Carter	69.6%	14.5%	15.9%
HILLSBOROUGH	72,418	47,705	13,417	11,296	Carter	65.9%	18.5%	15.6%
HOLMES	2,824	2,128	252	444	Carter	75.4%	8.9%	15.7%
INDIAN RIVER	6,122	4,118	1,119	885	Carter	67.3%	18.3%	14.5%
JACKSON	6,015	4,503	682	830	Carter	74.9%	11.3%	13.8%
JEFFERSON	2,005	1,377	353	275	Carter	68.7%	17.6%	13.7%
LAFAYETTE	808	669	60	79	Carter	82.8%	7.4%	9.8%
LAKE	10,025	6,942	1,416	1,667	Carter	69.2%	14.1%	16.6%
LEE	22,750	14,255	4,476	4,019	Carter	62.7%	19.7%	17.7%
LEON	22,982	15,374	3,768	3,840	Carter	66.9%	16.4%	16.7%
LEVY	3,006	2,328	315	363	Carter	77.4%	10.5%	12.1%
LIBERTY	1,202	882	135	185	Carter	73.4%	11.2%	15.4%
MADISON	2,676	1,968	375	333	Carter	73.5%	14.0%	12.4%
MANATEE	15,118	10,411	2,475	2,232	Carter	68.9%	16.4%	14.8%
MARION	13,446	9,159	2,034	2,253	Carter	68.1%	15.1%	16.8%
MARTIN	5,401	3,507	1,052	842	Carter	64.9%	19.5%	15.6%
MONROE	8,771	5,249	1,764	1,758	Carter	59.8%	20.1%	20.0%
NASSAU	4,078	2,940	490	648	Carter	72.1%	12.0%	15.9%
OKALOOSA	15,210	9,458	1,558	4,194	Carter	62.2%	10.2%	27.6%
OKEECHOBEE	1,832	1,393	251	188	Carter	76.0%	13.7%	10.3%
ORANGE	34,616	22,621	6,018	5,977	Carter	65.3%	17.4%	17.3%
OSCEOLA	4,388	2,968	732	688	Carter	67.6%	16.7%	15.7%
PALM BEACH	71,630	36,643	23,310	11,677	Carter	51.2%	32.5%	16.3%
PASCO	24,962	15,231	6,528	3,203	Carter	61.0%	26.2%	12.8%
PINELLAS	73,985	48,817	16,289	8,879	Carter	66.0%	22.0%	12.0%
POLK	32,555	23,690	4,157	4,708	Carter	72.8%	12.8%	14.5%
PUTNAM	7,858	5,707	1,001	1,150	Carter	72.6%	12.7%	14.6%
ST. JOHNS	6,428	4,270	927	1,231	Carter	66.4%	14.4%	19.2%
ST. LUCIE	7,814	5,054	1,554	1,206	Carter	64.7%	19.9%	15.4%
SANTA ROSA	8,339	5,388	943	2,008	Carter	64.6%	11.3%	24.1%
SARASOTA	17,652	11,698	3,397	2,557	Carter	66.3%	19.2%	14.5%
SEMINOLE	12,220	7,778	2,301	2,141	Carter	63.6%	18.8%	17.5%
SUMTER	3,057	2,286	358	413	Carter	74.8%	11.7%	13.5%
SUWANNEE	3,671	2,808	310	553	Carter	76.5%	8.4%	15.1%
TAYLOR	2,165	1,623	215	327	Carter	75.0%	9.9%	15.1%
UNION	1,143	869	114	160	Carter	76.0%	10.0%	14.0%
VOLUSIA	33,686	23,388	6,016	4,282	Carter	69.4%	17.9%	12.7%
WAKULLA	1,707	1,245	184	278	Carter	72.9%	10.8%	16.3%
WALTON	3,389	2,370	393	626	Carter	69.9%	11.6%	18.5%
WASHINGTON	3,027	2,153	385	489	Carter	71.1%	12.7%	16.2%
TOTAL	1,098,003	666,321	254,727	176,955	Carter	60.7%	23.2%	16.1%

FLORIDA REPUBLICAN

1980

County	Total Vote	Bush	Reagan	Other	Winner	Percentage of Total Vote Bush	Reagan	Other
ALACHUA	4,674	1,870	1,750	1,054	Bush	40.0%	37.4%	22.6%
BAKER	28	3	22	3	Reagan	10.7%	78.6%	10.7%
BAY	2,475	370	1,747	358	Reagan	14.9%	70.6%	14.5%
BRADFORD	183	32	123	28	Reagan	17.5%	67.2%	15.3%
BREVARD	25,519	8,102	14,606	2,811	Reagan	31.7%	57.2%	11.0%
BROWARD	73,966	19,673	44,459	9,834	Reagan	26.6%	60.1%	13.3%
CALHOUN	40	7	29	4	Reagan	17.5%	72.5%	10.0%
CHARLOTTE	9,930	3,454	5,540	936	Reagan	34.8%	55.8%	9.4%
CITRUS	3,639	903	2,245	491	Reagan	24.8%	61.7%	13.5%
CLAY	2,715	761	1,586	368	Reagan	28.0%	58.4%	13.6%
COLLIER	10,859	3,713	5,772	1,374	Reagan	34.2%	53.2%	12.7%
COLUMBIA	443	82	300	61	Reagan	18.5%	67.7%	13.8%
DADE	54,734	12,704	36,108	5,922	Reagan	23.2%	66.0%	10.8%
DESOTO	278	72	178	28	Reagan	25.9%	64.0%	10.1%
DIXIE	19	9	8	2	Bush	47.4%	42.1%	10.5%
DUVAL	16,383	4,742	9,841	1,800	Reagan	28.9%	60.1%	11.0%
ESCAMBIA	6,119	1,414	3,923	782	Reagan	23.1%	64.1%	12.8%
FLAGLER	796	269	411	116	Reagan	33.8%	51.6%	14.6%
FRANKLIN	67	10	47	10	Reagan	14.9%	70.1%	14.9%
GADSDEN	129	18	84	27	Reagan	14.0%	65.1%	20.9%
GILCHRIST	15	3	6	6	Reagan	20.0%	40.0%	40.0%
GLADES	46	10	35	1	Reagan	21.7%	76.1%	2.2%
GULF	51	8	39	4	Reagan	15.7%	76.5%	7.8%
HAMILTON	27	4	19	4	Reagan	14.8%	70.4%	14.8%
HARDEE	126	42	75	9	Reagan	33.3%	59.5%	7.1%
HENDRY	238	67	139	32	Reagan	28.2%	58.4%	13.4%
HERNANDO	3,937	1,109	2,249	579	Reagan	28.2%	57.1%	14.7%
HIGHLANDS	3,315	941	1,984	390	Reagan	28.4%	59.8%	11.8%
HILLSBOROUGH	20,975	7,245	11,045	2,685	Reagan	34.5%	52.7%	12.8%
HOLMES	59	5	45	9	Reagan	8.5%	76.3%	15.3%
INDIAN RIVER	6,563	2,573	3,222	768	Reagan	39.2%	49.1%	11.7%
JACKSON	190	32	134	24	Reagan	16.8%	70.5%	12.6%
JEFFERSON	88	12	58	18	Reagan	13.6%	65.9%	20.5%
LAFAYETTE	16	4	8	4	Reagan	25.0%	50.0%	25.0%
LAKE	10,305	3,367	5,918	1,020	Reagan	32.7%	57.4%	9.9%
LEE	25,210	7,616	15,044	2,550	Reagan	30.2%	59.7%	10.1%
LEON	4,056	1,095	2,113	848	Reagan	27.0%	52.1%	20.9%
LEVY	338	71	227	40	Reagan	21.0%	67.2%	11.8%
LIBERTY	13	3	10		Reagan	23.1%	76.9%	
MADISON	100	7	76	17	Reagan	7.0%	76.0%	17.0%
MANATEE	16,325	5,457	9,224	1,644	Reagan	33.4%	56.5%	10.1%
MARION	5,228	1,237	3,559	432	Reagan	23.7%	68.1%	8.3%
MARTIN	8,154	2,718	4,262	1,174	Reagan	33.3%	52.3%	14.4%
MONROE	1,913	576	1,021	316	Reagan	30.1%	53.4%	16.5%
NASSAU	373	79	253	41	Reagan	21.2%	67.8%	11.0%
OKALOOSA	4,821	941	3,277	603	Reagan	19.5%	68.0%	12.5%
OKEECHOBEE	247	62	151	34	Reagan	25.1%	61.1%	13.8%
ORANGE	27,058	9,194	14,909	2,955	Reagan	34.0%	55.1%	10.9%
OSCEOLA	3,007	764	1,827	416	Reagan	25.4%	60.8%	13.8%
PALM BEACH	56,850	20,476	28,520	7,854	Reagan	36.0%	50.2%	13.8%

FLORIDA REPUBLICAN

1980

County	Total Vote	Bush	Reagan	Other	Winner	Percentage of Total Vote: Bush	Reagan	Other
PASCO	20,079	4,742	12,412	2,925	Reagan	23.6%	61.8%	14.6%
PINELLAS	90,765	26,379	44,951	19,435	Reagan	29.1%	49.5%	21.4%
POLK	13,580	3,983	7,853	1,744	Reagan	29.3%	57.8%	12.8%
PUTNAM	1,308	306	868	134	Reagan	23.4%	66.4%	10.2%
ST. JOHNS	2,262	728	1,272	262	Reagan	32.2%	56.2%	11.6%
ST. LUCIE	5,521	1,498	3,398	625	Reagan	27.1%	61.5%	11.3%
SANTA ROSA	1,430	279	958	193	Reagan	19.5%	67.0%	13.5%
SARASOTA	35,245	13,512	18,573	3,160	Reagan	38.3%	52.7%	9.0%
SEMINOLE	11,437	4,188	6,078	1,171	Reagan	36.6%	53.1%	10.2%
SUMTER	451	111	283	57	Reagan	24.6%	62.7%	12.6%
SUWANNEE	310	50	214	46	Reagan	16.1%	69.0%	14.8%
TAYLOR	108	21	72	15	Reagan	19.4%	66.7%	13.9%
UNION	21	11	10		Bush	52.4%	47.6%	
VOLUSIA	19,322	6,176	10,169	2,977	Reagan	32.0%	52.6%	15.4%
WAKULLA	89	18	46	25	Reagan	20.2%	51.7%	28.1%
WALTON	256	39	193	24	Reagan	15.2%	75.4%	9.4%
WASHINGTON	171	29	121	21	Reagan	17.0%	70.8%	12.3%
TOTAL	614,995	185,996	345,699	83,300	Reagan	30.2%	56.2%	13.5%

FLORIDA DEMOCRATIC

1984

County	Total Vote	Glenn	Hart	J. Jackson	Mondale	Other	Winner	Percentage of Total Vote: Glenn	Hart	J. Jackson	Mondale	Other
ALACHUA	20,216	2,375	9,198	2,561	4,765	1,317	Hart	11.7%	45.5%	12.7%	23.6%	6.5%
BAKER	1,304	166	438	206	430	64	Hart	12.7%	33.6%	15.8%	33.0%	4.9%
BAY	10,535	2,592	4,237	1,026	2,401	279	Hart	24.6%	40.2%	9.7%	22.8%	2.6%
BRADFORD	2,593	291	1,091	409	697	105	Hart	11.2%	42.1%	15.8%	26.9%	4.0%
BREVARD	35,013	6,102	14,868	3,067	9,304	1,672	Hart	17.4%	42.5%	8.8%	26.6%	4.8%
BROWARD	158,881	8,267	66,707	10,581	68,101	5,225	Mondale	5.2%	42.0%	6.7%	42.9%	3.3%
CALHOUN	1,929	454	759	150	501	65	Hart	23.5%	39.3%	7.8%	26.0%	3.4%
CHARLOTTE	8,930	713	4,601	237	2,878	501	Hart	8.0%	51.5%	2.7%	32.2%	5.6%
CITRUS	9,337	965	4,459	316	3,209	388	Hart	10.3%	47.8%	3.4%	34.4%	4.2%
CLAY	8,308	1,556	3,661	321	2,236	534	Hart	18.7%	44.1%	3.9%	26.9%	6.4%
COLLIER	6,876	736	3,549	290	1,826	475	Hart	10.7%	51.6%	4.2%	26.6%	6.9%
COLUMBIA	4,665	715	1,773	714	1,254	209	Hart	15.3%	38.0%	15.3%	26.9%	4.5%
DADE	167,492	10,272	54,823	29,535	65,873	6,989	Mondale	6.1%	32.7%	17.6%	39.3%	4.2%
DESOTO	2,100	222	941	285	528	124	Hart	10.6%	44.8%	13.6%	25.1%	5.9%
DIXIE	1,870	231	872	117	548	102	Hart	12.4%	46.6%	6.3%	29.3%	5.5%
DUVAL	70,266	7,852	19,402	16,099	23,863	3,050	Mondale	11.2%	27.6%	22.9%	34.0%	4.3%
ESCAMBIA	33,424	9,019	9,852	6,057	7,184	1,312	Hart	27.0%	29.5%	18.1%	21.5%	3.9%
FLAGLER	2,201	290	913	103	756	139	Hart	13.2%	41.5%	4.7%	34.3%	6.3%
FRANKLIN	1,392	235	515	263	323	56	Hart	16.9%	37.0%	18.9%	23.2%	4.0%
GADSDEN	6,170	616	1,342	2,478	1,406	328	J. Jackson	10.0%	21.8%	40.2%	22.8%	5.3%

FLORIDA DEMOCRATIC

1984

County	Total Vote	Glenn	Hart	J. Jackson	Mondale	Other	Winner	Percentage of Total Vote Glenn	Hart	J. Jackson	Mondale	Other
GILCHRIST	1,307	210	600	43	384	70	Hart	16.1%	45.9%	3.3%	29.4%	5.4%
GLADES	959	106	418	89	284	62	Hart	11.1%	43.6%	9.3%	29.6%	6.5%
GULF	2,815	560	1,046	553	569	87	Hart	19.9%	37.2%	19.6%	20.2%	3.1%
HAMILTON	1,195	121	303	319	294	158	J. Jackson	10.1%	25.4%	26.7%	24.6%	13.2%
HARDEE	1,893	263	772	264	436	158	Hart	13.9%	40.8%	13.9%	23.0%	8.3%
HENDRY	1,866	266	728	263	509	100	Hart	14.3%	39.0%	14.1%	27.3%	5.4%
HERNANDO	8,952	782	4,273	269	3,310	318	Hart	8.7%	47.7%	3.0%	37.0%	3.6%
HIGHLANDS	6,087	678	2,851	669	1,626	263	Hart	11.1%	46.8%	11.0%	26.7%	4.3%
HILLSBOROUGH	66,105	6,879	23,931	10,780	21,383	3,132	Hart	10.4%	36.2%	16.3%	32.3%	4.7%
HOLMES	2,137	667	796	100	481	93	Hart	31.2%	37.2%	4.7%	22.5%	4.4%
INDIAN RIVER	7,075	683	3,713	474	1,882	323	Hart	9.7%	52.5%	6.7%	26.6%	4.6%
JACKSON	7,529	1,636	2,375	1,658	1,583	277	Hart	21.7%	31.5%	22.0%	21.0%	3.7%
JEFFERSON	2,025	244	533	703	418	127	J. Jackson	12.0%	26.3%	34.7%	20.6%	6.3%
LAFAYETTE	749	106	350	28	224	41	Hart	14.2%	46.7%	3.7%	29.9%	5.5%
LAKE	10,913	1,592	4,764	983	3,050	524	Hart	14.6%	43.7%	9.0%	27.9%	4.8%
LEE	22,046	2,165	10,680	1,166	6,856	1,179	Hart	9.8%	48.4%	5.3%	31.1%	5.3%
LEON	25,997	3,080	9,376	7,368	4,771	1,402	Hart	11.8%	36.1%	28.3%	18.4%	5.4%
LEVY	3,241	438	1,499	218	962	124	Hart	13.5%	46.3%	6.7%	29.7%	3.8%
LIBERTY	776	183	288	74	194	37	Hart	23.6%	37.1%	9.5%	25.0%	4.8%
MADISON	2,540	277	755	768	636	104	J. Jackson	10.9%	29.7%	30.2%	25.0%	4.1%
MANATEE	14,994	1,446	7,063	1,353	4,470	662	Hart	9.6%	47.1%	9.0%	29.8%	4.4%
MARION	13,860	1,875	5,947	1,581	3,925	532	Hart	13.5%	42.9%	11.4%	28.3%	3.8%
MARTIN	5,887	535	2,941	457	1,714	240	Hart	9.1%	50.0%	7.8%	29.1%	4.1%
MONROE	8,492	892	4,368	462	2,295	475	Hart	10.5%	51.4%	5.4%	27.0%	5.6%
NASSAU	3,332	516	1,071	443	1,151	151	Mondale	15.5%	32.1%	13.3%	34.5%	4.5%
OKALOOSA	11,482	4,404	3,966	684	2,048	380	Glenn	38.4%	34.5%	6.0%	17.8%	3.3%
OKEECHOBEE	2,033	198	1,056	70	633	76	Hart	9.7%	51.9%	3.4%	31.1%	3.7%
ORANGE	39,254	6,614	13,231	6,815	10,792	1,802	Hart	16.8%	33.7%	17.4%	27.5%	4.6%
OSCEOLA	5,195	800	2,273	275	1,574	273	Hart	15.4%	43.8%	5.3%	30.3%	5.3%
PALM BEACH	88,420	6,076	37,630	7,557	33,939	3,218	Hart	6.9%	42.6%	8.5%	38.4%	3.6%
PASCO	26,790	1,944	12,180	524	11,115	1,027	Hart	7.3%	45.5%	2.0%	41.5%	3.8%
PINELLAS	77,593	5,776	35,100	7,365	26,185	3,167	Hart	7.4%	45.2%	9.5%	33.7%	4.1%
POLK	39,400	5,771	15,933	4,115	11,294	2,287	Hart	14.6%	40.4%	10.4%	28.7%	5.8%
PUTNAM	6,645	756	2,495	700	2,389	305	Hart	11.4%	37.5%	10.5%	36.0%	4.6%
ST. JOHNS	6,090	832	2,426	864	1,625	343	Hart	13.7%	39.8%	14.2%	26.7%	5.6%
ST. LUCIE	8,611	879	3,679	1,201	2,501	351	Hart	10.2%	42.7%	13.9%	29.0%	4.1%
SANTA ROSA	8,750	3,290	3,111	345	1,557	447	Glenn	37.6%	35.6%	3.9%	17.8%	5.1%
SARASOTA	17,874	1,493	9,004	821	5,819	737	Hart	8.4%	50.4%	4.6%	32.6%	4.1%
SEMINOLE	14,472	2,468	5,920	1,603	3,746	735	Hart	17.1%	40.9%	11.1%	25.9%	5.1%
SUMTER	2,889	317	1,195	301	906	170	Hart	11.0%	41.4%	10.4%	31.4%	5.9%
SUWANNEE	3,460	511	1,327	564	903	155	Hart	14.8%	38.4%	16.3%	26.1%	4.5%
TAYLOR	2,203	346	781	286	604	186	Hart	15.7%	35.5%	13.0%	27.4%	8.4%
UNION	724	101	299	59	244	21	Hart	14.0%	41.3%	8.1%	33.7%	2.9%
VOLUSIA	35,663	3,753	13,664	3,232	13,087	1,927	Hart	10.5%	38.3%	9.1%	36.7%	5.4%
WAKULLA	1,827	247	826	237	424	93	Hart	13.5%	45.2%	13.0%	23.2%	5.1%
WALTON	3,532	1,064	1,213	265	841	149	Hart	30.1%	34.3%	7.5%	23.8%	4.2%
WASHINGTON	2,669	645	910	446	563	105	Hart	24.2%	34.1%	16.7%	21.1%	3.9%
Absentees	340	55	138	34	71	42	Hart	16.2%	40.6%	10.0%	20.9%	12.4%
TOTAL	1,182,190	128,209	463,799	144,263	394,350	51,569	Hart	10.8%	39.2%	12.2%	33.4%	4.4%

FLORIDA DEMOCRATIC

1988

County	Total Vote	Dukakis	Gephardt	Gore	J. Jackson	Other	Winner	Percentage of Total Vote				
								Dukakis	Gephardt	Gore	J. Jackson	Other
ALACHUA	23,514	7,422	2,172	4,583	6,436	2,901	Dukakis	31.6%	9.2%	19.5%	27.4%	12.3%
BAKER	1,640	362	269	437	291	281	Gore	22.1%	16.4%	26.6%	17.7%	17.1%
BAY	16,396	3,472	2,673	4,276	2,286	3,689	Gore	21.2%	16.3%	26.1%	13.9%	22.5%
BRADFORD	2,915	718	427	707	658	405	Dukakis	24.6%	14.6%	24.3%	22.6%	13.9%
BREVARD	36,852	14,541	6,730	5,388	5,473	4,720	Dukakis	39.5%	18.3%	14.6%	14.9%	12.8%
BROWARD	144,736	82,131	20,632	7,325	20,504	14,144	Dukakis	56.7%	14.3%	5.1%	14.2%	9.8%
CALHOUN	1,670	241	395	474	310	250	Gore	14.4%	23.7%	28.4%	18.6%	15.0%
CHARLOTTE	9,000	4,796	1,625	823	870	886	Dukakis	53.3%	18.1%	9.1%	9.7%	9.8%
CITRUS	10,037	4,744	1,852	1,552	787	1,102	Dukakis	47.3%	18.5%	15.5%	7.8%	11.0%
CLAY	9,141	2,976	1,562	2,120	1,025	1,458	Dukakis	32.6%	17.1%	23.2%	11.2%	16.0%
COLLIER	6,645	3,070	825	755	797	1,198	Dukakis	46.2%	12.4%	11.4%	12.0%	18.0%
COLUMBIA	5,913	1,357	874	1,470	1,304	908	Gore	22.9%	14.8%	24.9%	22.1%	15.4%
DADE	157,943	64,256	18,825	8,115	49,699	17,048	Dukakis	40.7%	11.9%	5.1%	31.5%	10.8%
DESOTO	2,292	741	485	350	395	321	Dukakis	32.3%	21.2%	15.3%	17.2%	14.0%
DIXIE	1,431	329	256	407	173	266	Gore	23.0%	17.9%	28.4%	12.1%	18.6%
DUVAL	105,022	26,133	13,690	17,390	30,984	16,825	J. Jackson	24.9%	13.0%	16.6%	29.5%	16.0%
ESCAMBIA	37,229	6,567	4,009	11,845	9,282	5,526	Gore	17.6%	10.8%	31.8%	24.9%	14.8%
FLAGLER	2,885	1,301	516	322	365	381	Dukakis	45.1%	17.9%	11.2%	12.7%	13.2%
FRANKLIN	1,398	361	219	255	318	245	Dukakis	25.8%	15.7%	18.2%	22.7%	17.5%
GADSDEN	7,685	855	724	902	4,505	699	J. Jackson	11.1%	9.4%	11.7%	58.6%	9.1%
GILCHRIST	1,328	372	229	371	99	257	Dukakis	28.0%	17.2%	27.9%	7.5%	19.4%
GLADES	1,070	351	197	170	169	183	Dukakis	32.8%	18.4%	15.9%	15.8%	17.1%
GULF	2,157	316	422	589	464	366	Gore	14.6%	19.6%	27.3%	21.5%	17.0%
HAMILTON	1,412	188	195	302	417	310	J. Jackson	13.3%	13.8%	21.4%	29.5%	22.0%
HARDEE	2,453	569	571	652	263	398	Gore	23.2%	23.3%	26.6%	10.7%	16.2%
HENDRY	2,068	566	321	314	585	282	J. Jackson	27.4%	15.5%	15.2%	28.3%	13.6%
HERNANDO	11,372	6,197	1,841	1,231	947	1,156	Dukakis	54.5%	16.2%	10.8%	8.3%	10.2%
HIGHLANDS	8,469	3,255	1,793	1,139	938	1,344	Dukakis	38.4%	21.2%	13.4%	11.1%	15.9%
HILLSBOROUGH	69,200	26,948	9,849	8,940	15,776	7,687	Dukakis	38.9%	14.2%	12.9%	22.8%	11.1%
HOLMES	2,145	304	423	941	181	296	Gore	14.2%	19.7%	43.9%	8.4%	13.8%
INDIAN RIVER	7,188	3,272	1,297	650	1,041	928	Dukakis	45.5%	18.0%	9.0%	14.5%	12.9%
JACKSON	7,436	999	1,189	2,179	2,000	1,069	Gore	13.4%	16.0%	29.3%	26.9%	14.4%
JEFFERSON	2,794	435	363	447	1,125	424	J. Jackson	15.6%	13.0%	16.0%	40.3%	15.2%
LAFAYETTE	759	159	169	236	45	150	Gore	20.9%	22.3%	31.1%	5.9%	19.8%
LAKE	11,921	4,733	2,476	1,719	1,658	1,335	Dukakis	39.7%	20.8%	14.4%	13.9%	11.2%
LEE	26,634	12,355	3,671	3,621	3,587	3,400	Dukakis	46.4%	13.8%	13.6%	13.5%	12.8%
LEON	31,240	8,427	3,495	4,827	10,962	3,529	J. Jackson	27.0%	11.2%	15.5%	35.1%	11.3%
LEVY	3,252	944	486	923	416	483	Dukakis	29.0%	14.9%	28.4%	12.8%	14.9%
LIBERTY	774	123	165	218	128	140	Gore	15.9%	21.3%	28.2%	16.5%	18.1%
MADISON	2,501	356	400	516	949	280	J. Jackson	14.2%	16.0%	20.6%	37.9%	11.2%
MANATEE	20,178	9,636	3,269	1,961	2,731	2,581	Dukakis	47.8%	16.2%	9.7%	13.5%	12.8%
MARION	17,721	6,047	3,528	2,661	3,307	2,178	Dukakis	34.1%	19.9%	15.0%	18.7%	12.3%
MARTIN	6,926	3,282	1,270	608	1,024	742	Dukakis	47.4%	18.3%	8.8%	14.8%	10.7%
MONROE	8,742	3,558	1,484	667	1,351	1,682	Dukakis	40.7%	17.0%	7.6%	15.5%	19.2%
NASSAU	4,207	1,038	704	978	737	750	Dukakis	24.7%	16.7%	23.2%	17.5%	17.8%
OKALOOSA	11,440	2,489	1,443	4,222	1,338	1,948	Gore	21.8%	12.6%	36.9%	11.7%	17.0%
OKEECHOBEE	2,149	814	573	283	207	272	Dukakis	37.9%	26.7%	13.2%	9.6%	12.7%
ORANGE	41,797	14,299	6,224	5,908	11,039	4,327	Dukakis	34.2%	14.9%	14.1%	26.4%	10.4%
OSCEOLA	8,101	3,147	1,384	1,158	856	1,556	Dukakis	38.8%	17.1%	14.3%	10.6%	19.2%
PALM BEACH	98,351	57,591	12,852	6,216	12,584	9,108	Dukakis	58.6%	13.1%	6.3%	12.8%	9.3%

FLORIDA DEMOCRATIC

1988

County	Total Vote	Dukakis	Gephardt	Gore	J. Jackson	Other	Winner	Percentage of Total Vote Dukakis	Gephardt	Gore	J. Jackson	Other
PASCO	28,054	15,569	4,725	2,634	2,116	3,010	Dukakis	55.5%	16.8%	9.4%	7.5%	10.7%
PINELLAS	79,338	44,067	8,533	6,886	12,723	7,129	Dukakis	55.5%	10.8%	8.7%	16.0%	9.0%
POLK	34,265	12,563	6,098	5,985	5,662	3,957	Dukakis	36.7%	17.8%	17.5%	16.5%	11.5%
PUTNAM	8,360	2,320	1,675	1,609	1,414	1,342	Dukakis	27.8%	20.0%	19.2%	16.9%	16.1%
ST. JOHNS	9,614	3,021	1,357	1,807	1,514	1,915	Dukakis	31.4%	14.1%	18.8%	15.7%	19.9%
ST. LUCIE	12,770	5,588	2,134	947	2,423	1,678	Dukakis	43.8%	16.7%	7.4%	19.0%	13.1%
SANTA ROSA	9,093	1,710	1,310	3,881	744	1,448	Gore	18.8%	14.4%	42.7%	8.2%	15.9%
SARASOTA	22,356	11,132	4,045	1,851	2,928	2,400	Dukakis	49.8%	18.1%	8.3%	13.1%	10.7%
SEMINOLE	15,260	6,128	2,281	2,385	2,838	1,628	Dukakis	40.2%	14.9%	15.6%	18.6%	10.7%
SUMTER	3,271	1,111	757	503	501	399	Dukakis	34.0%	23.1%	15.4%	15.3%	12.2%
SUWANNEE	3,462	726	707	895	766	368	Gore	21.0%	20.4%	25.9%	22.1%	10.6%
TAYLOR	2,204	426	545	511	382	340	Gephardt	19.3%	24.7%	23.2%	17.3%	15.4%
UNION	1,002	220	174	274	122	212	Gore	22.0%	17.4%	27.3%	12.2%	21.2%
VOLUSIA	35,318	15,562	5,919	4,304	5,856	3,677	Dukakis	44.1%	16.8%	12.2%	16.6%	10.4%
WAKULLA	2,378	617	464	476	451	370	Dukakis	25.9%	19.5%	20.0%	19.0%	15.6%
WALTON	3,587	672	660	1,213	429	613	Gore	18.7%	18.4%	33.8%	12.0%	17.1%
WASHINGTON	2,580	386	404	851	601	338	Gore	15.0%	15.7%	33.0%	23.3%	13.1%
Absentees	257	80	30	10	56	81	Dukakis	31.1%	11.7%	3.9%	21.8%	31.5%
TOTAL	1,273,298	521,041	182,861	161,165	254,912	153,319	Dukakis	40.9%	14.4%	12.7%	20.0%	12.0%

FLORIDA REPUBLICAN

1988

County	Total Vote	Bush	Dole	Robertson	Other	Winner	Percentage of Total Vote Bush	Dole	Robertson	Other
ALACHUA	8,053	3,929	2,292	1,181	651	Bush	48.8%	28.5%	14.7%	8.1%
BAKER	102	38	17	39	8	Robertson	37.3%	16.7%	38.2%	7.8%
BAY	5,481	3,032	1,110	902	437	Bush	55.3%	20.3%	16.5%	8.0%
BRADFORD	402	224	82	69	27	Bush	55.7%	20.4%	17.2%	6.7%
BREVARD	38,492	23,631	7,600	4,913	2,348	Bush	61.4%	19.7%	12.8%	6.1%
BROWARD	79,251	50,191	17,038	7,050	4,972	Bush	63.3%	21.5%	8.9%	6.3%
CALHOUN	139	39	21	70	9	Robertson	28.1%	15.1%	50.4%	6.5%
CHARLOTTE	13,791	9,184	2,644	1,261	702	Bush	66.6%	19.2%	9.1%	5.1%
CITRUS	6,655	4,072	1,491	770	322	Bush	61.2%	22.4%	11.6%	4.8%
CLAY	6,346	3,548	1,413	920	465	Bush	55.9%	22.3%	14.5%	7.3%
COLLIER	20,034	13,182	4,311	1,270	1,271	Bush	65.8%	21.5%	6.3%	6.3%
COLUMBIA	1,081	520	220	263	78	Bush	48.1%	20.4%	24.3%	7.2%
DADE	90,275	67,854	12,718	5,729	3,974	Bush	75.2%	14.1%	6.3%	4.4%
DESOTO	637	376	122	99	40	Bush	59.0%	19.2%	15.5%	6.3%
DIXIE	140	69	18	50	3	Bush	49.3%	12.9%	35.7%	2.1%
DUVAL	36,309	20,414	8,559	4,806	2,530	Bush	56.2%	23.6%	13.2%	7.0%
ESCAMBIA	13,227	6,784	2,992	1,971	1,480	Bush	51.3%	22.6%	14.9%	11.2%
FLAGLER	2,223	1,413	547	139	124	Bush	63.6%	24.6%	6.3%	5.6%
FRANKLIN	138	68	23	36	11	Bush	49.3%	16.7%	26.1%	8.0%
GADSDEN	365	166	66	104	29	Bush	45.5%	18.1%	28.5%	7.9%

FLORIDA REPUBLICAN

1988

County	Total Vote	Bush	Dole	Robertson	Other	Winner	Percentage of Total Vote Bush	Dole	Robertson	Other
GILCHRIST	164	88	28	34	14	Bush	53.7%	17.1%	20.7%	8.5%
GLADES	204	153	30	12	9	Bush	75.0%	14.7%	5.9%	4.4%
GULF	148	62	19	46	21	Bush	41.9%	12.8%	31.1%	14.2%
HAMILTON	63	33	6	19	5	Bush	52.4%	9.5%	30.2%	7.9%
HARDEE	335	176	70	74	15	Bush	52.5%	20.9%	22.1%	4.5%
HENDRY	548	331	90	99	28	Bush	60.4%	16.4%	18.1%	5.1%
HERNANDO	9,682	5,865	2,353	939	525	Bush	60.6%	24.3%	9.7%	5.4%
HIGHLANDS	6,503	4,203	1,359	556	385	Bush	64.6%	20.9%	8.5%	5.9%
HILLSBOROUGH	38,318	22,971	8,237	4,949	2,161	Bush	59.9%	21.5%	12.9%	5.6%
HOLMES	111	67	20	16	8	Bush	60.4%	18.0%	14.4%	7.2%
INDIAN RIVER	11,735	7,404	2,533	1,182	616	Bush	63.1%	21.6%	10.1%	5.2%
JACKSON	560	286	68	179	27	Bush	51.1%	12.1%	32.0%	4.8%
JEFFERSON	183	92	45	28	18	Bush	50.3%	24.6%	15.3%	9.8%
LAFAYETTE	28	15	8	4	1	Bush	53.6%	28.6%	14.3%	3.6%
LAKE	15,120	9,166	2,956	2,135	863	Bush	60.6%	19.6%	14.1%	5.7%
LEE	38,367	24,440	8,121	3,642	2,164	Bush	63.7%	21.2%	9.5%	5.6%
LEON	7,941	3,463	2,316	1,429	733	Bush	43.6%	29.2%	18.0%	9.2%
LEVY	715	440	125	117	33	Bush	61.5%	17.5%	16.4%	4.6%
LIBERTY	31	14	5	9	3	Bush	45.2%	16.1%	29.0%	9.7%
MADISON	188	108	34	37	9	Bush	57.4%	18.1%	19.7%	4.8%
MANATEE	25,329	15,254	6,085	2,648	1,342	Bush	60.2%	24.0%	10.5%	5.3%
MARION	11,247	7,073	2,108	1,322	744	Bush	62.9%	18.7%	11.8%	6.6%
MARTIN	14,579	10,260	2,491	1,020	808	Bush	70.4%	17.1%	7.0%	5.5%
MONROE	5,000	3,177	1,053	430	340	Bush	63.5%	21.1%	8.6%	6.8%
NASSAU	963	500	236	154	73	Bush	51.9%	24.5%	16.0%	7.6%
OKALOOSA	9,028	4,649	1,957	1,724	698	Bush	51.5%	21.7%	19.1%	7.7%
OKEECHOBEE	698	388	142	129	39	Bush	55.6%	20.3%	18.5%	5.6%
ORANGE	43,034	23,888	8,523	7,852	2,771	Bush	55.5%	19.8%	18.2%	6.4%
OSCEOLA	6,674	4,022	1,183	1,092	377	Bush	60.3%	17.7%	16.4%	5.6%
PALM BEACH	73,929	50,299	13,813	5,075	4,742	Bush	68.0%	18.7%	6.9%	6.4%
PASCO	24,656	14,723	6,190	2,341	1,402	Bush	59.7%	25.1%	9.5%	5.7%
PINELLAS	89,859	51,297	25,464	7,652	5,446	Bush	57.1%	28.3%	8.5%	6.1%
POLK	21,513	11,555	4,912	3,937	1,109	Bush	53.7%	22.8%	18.3%	5.2%
PUTNAM	2,101	1,239	441	274	147	Bush	59.0%	21.0%	13.0%	7.0%
ST. JOHNS	5,642	3,388	1,266	550	438	Bush	60.0%	22.4%	9.7%	7.8%
ST. LUCIE	11,934	8,058	1,996	1,140	740	Bush	67.5%	16.7%	9.6%	6.2%
SANTA ROSA	3,380	1,790	785	431	374	Bush	53.0%	23.2%	12.8%	11.1%
SARASOTA	46,283	30,580	9,637	3,348	2,718	Bush	66.1%	20.8%	7.2%	5.9%
SEMINOLE	20,812	11,603	4,319	3,540	1,350	Bush	55.8%	20.8%	17.0%	6.5%
SUMTER	1,425	864	244	238	79	Bush	60.6%	17.1%	16.7%	5.5%
SUWANNEE	584	243	106	204	31	Bush	41.6%	18.2%	34.9%	5.3%
TAYLOR	335	106	59	154	16	Robertson	31.6%	17.6%	46.0%	4.8%
UNION	50	23	12	10	5	Bush	46.0%	24.0%	20.0%	10.0%
VOLUSIA	26,344	15,806	6,102	3,077	1,359	Bush	60.0%	23.2%	11.7%	5.2%
WAKULLA	216	102	63	40	11	Bush	47.2%	29.2%	18.5%	5.1%
WALTON	897	462	170	210	55	Bush	51.5%	19.0%	23.4%	6.1%
WASHINGTON	259	161	29	50	19	Bush	62.2%	11.2%	19.3%	7.3%
Absentees	366	200	103	36	27	Bush	54.6%	28.1%	9.8%	7.4%
TOTAL	901,222	559,821	191,196	95,826	54,379	Bush	62.1%	21.2%	10.6%	6.0%
Published Totals	901,222	559,820	191,197	95,826	54,379	Bush	62.1%	21.2%	10.6%	6.0%

FLORIDA DEMOCRATIC

1992

County	Total Vote	Brown	Clinton	Tsongas	Other	Winner	Percentage of Total Vote Brown	Clinton	Tsongas	Other
ALACHUA	23,428	3,898	9,363	9,380	787	Tsongas	16.6%	40.0%	40.0%	3.4%
BAKER	1,477	165	953	307	52	Clinton	11.2%	64.5%	20.8%	3.5%
BAY	8,272	1,069	4,223	2,632	348	Clinton	12.9%	51.1%	31.8%	4.2%
BRADFORD	2,156	215	1,296	565	80	Clinton	10.0%	60.1%	26.2%	3.7%
BREVARD	36,627	5,467	16,646	13,675	839	Clinton	14.9%	45.4%	37.3%	2.3%
BROWARD	140,205	14,435	75,205	48,451	2,114	Clinton	10.3%	53.6%	34.6%	1.5%
CALHOUN	1,022	135	645	202	40	Clinton	13.2%	63.1%	19.8%	3.9%
CHARLOTTE	9,965	1,262	5,456	3,003	244	Clinton	12.7%	54.8%	30.1%	2.4%
CITRUS	12,384	1,294	6,605	4,185	300	Clinton	10.4%	53.3%	33.8%	2.4%
CLAY	7,355	904	3,826	2,343	282	Clinton	12.3%	52.0%	31.9%	3.8%
COLLIER	8,838	1,316	3,954	3,262	306	Clinton	14.9%	44.7%	36.9%	3.5%
COLUMBIA	4,665	519	2,853	1,130	163	Clinton	11.1%	61.2%	24.2%	3.5%
DADE	120,029	11,705	64,777	41,053	2,494	Clinton	9.8%	54.0%	34.2%	2.1%
DESOTO	1,852	195	1,121	477	59	Clinton	10.5%	60.5%	25.8%	3.2%
DIXIE	1,572	164	1,050	306	52	Clinton	10.4%	66.8%	19.5%	3.3%
DUVAL	56,483	7,692	29,188	17,913	1,690	Clinton	13.6%	51.7%	31.7%	3.0%
ESCAMBIA	32,150	3,960	17,201	9,311	1,678	Clinton	12.3%	53.5%	29.0%	5.2%
FLAGLER	2,961	410	1,504	988	59	Clinton	13.8%	50.8%	33.4%	2.0%
FRANKLIN	917	147	508	226	36	Clinton	16.0%	55.4%	24.6%	3.9%
GADSDEN	3,797	759	2,346	568	124	Clinton	20.0%	61.8%	15.0%	3.3%
GILCHRIST	1,415	207	810	351	47	Clinton	14.6%	57.2%	24.8%	3.3%
GLADES	935	99	586	213	37	Clinton	10.6%	62.7%	22.8%	4.0%
GULF	1,348	159	782	332	75	Clinton	11.8%	58.0%	24.6%	5.6%
HAMILTON	777	58	581	120	18	Clinton	7.5%	74.8%	15.4%	2.3%
HARDEE	1,626	136	1,043	404	43	Clinton	8.4%	64.1%	24.8%	2.6%
HENDRY	1,825	216	1,076	447	86	Clinton	11.8%	59.0%	24.5%	4.7%
HERNANDO	14,077	1,358	8,049	4,426	244	Clinton	9.6%	57.2%	31.4%	1.7%
HIGHLANDS	8,198	968	4,699	2,335	196	Clinton	11.8%	57.3%	28.5%	2.4%
HILLSBOROUGH	61,960	7,701	30,378	22,621	1,260	Clinton	12.4%	49.0%	36.5%	2.0%
HOLMES	1,674	187	1,107	313	67	Clinton	11.2%	66.1%	18.7%	4.0%
INDIAN RIVER	6,498	784	2,835	2,727	152	Clinton	12.1%	43.6%	42.0%	2.3%
JACKSON	3,981	521	2,596	683	181	Clinton	13.1%	65.2%	17.2%	4.5%
JEFFERSON	1,795	217	1,207	320	51	Clinton	12.1%	67.2%	17.8%	2.8%
LAFAYETTE	703.00	55	512	108	28	Clinton	7.8%	72.8%	15.4%	4.0%
LAKE	14,520	2,312	7,500	4,450	258	Clinton	15.9%	51.7%	30.6%	1.8%
LEE	24,351	3,593	13,348	6,739	671	Clinton	14.8%	54.8%	27.7%	2.8%
LEON	27,479	5,750	13,236	7,882	611	Clinton	20.9%	48.2%	28.7%	2.2%
LEVY	3,022	375	1,715	849	83	Clinton	12.4%	56.8%	28.1%	2.7%
LIBERTY	565	76	383	82	24	Clinton	13.5%	67.8%	14.5%	4.2%
MADISON	1,622	202	1,082	304	34	Clinton	12.5%	66.7%	18.7%	2.1%
MANATEE	17,697	2,102	9,174	6,011	410	Clinton	11.9%	51.8%	34.0%	2.3%
MARION	17,827	2,015	9,573	5,784	455	Clinton	11.3%	53.7%	32.4%	2.6%
MARTIN	6,242	679	2,229	3,180	154	Tsongas	10.9%	35.7%	50.9%	2.5%
MONROE	6,787	1,284	2,683	2,604	216	Clinton	18.9%	39.5%	38.4%	3.2%
NASSAU	4,080	474	2,293	1,182	131	Clinton	11.6%	56.2%	29.0%	3.2%
OKALOOSA	10,201	1,230	5,119	3,347	505	Clinton	12.1%	50.2%	32.8%	5.0%
OKEECHOBEE	2,034	175	1,158	638	63	Clinton	8.6%	56.9%	31.4%	3.1%
ORANGE	38,550	8,444	15,809	13,677	620	Clinton	21.9%	41.0%	35.5%	1.6%
OSCEOLA	7,525	1,213	3,913	2,221	178	Clinton	16.1%	52.0%	29.5%	2.4%
PALM BEACH	92,388	8,667	40,635	41,605	1,481	Tsongas	9.4%	44.0%	45.0%	1.6%

FLORIDA DEMOCRATIC

1992

County	Total Vote	Brown	Clinton	Tsongas	Other	Winner	Percentage of Total Vote Brown	Clinton	Tsongas	Other
PASCO	31,778	3,240	17,991	9,939	608	Clinton	10.2%	56.6%	31.3%	1.9%
PINELLAS	78,681	8,927	38,270	30,037	1,447	Clinton	11.3%	48.6%	38.2%	1.8%
POLK	30,606	2,732	18,254	8,968	652	Clinton	8.9%	59.6%	29.3%	2.1%
PUTNAM	7,601	843	4,561	1,991	206	Clinton	11.1%	60.0%	26.2%	2.7%
ST. JOHNS	7,758	1,378	3,310	2,859	211	Clinton	17.8%	42.7%	36.9%	2.7%
ST. LUCIE	11,828	1,213	5,440	4,900	275	Clinton	10.3%	46.0%	41.4%	2.3%
SANTA ROSA	7,346	920	3,871	2,224	331	Clinton	12.5%	52.7%	30.3%	4.5%
SARASOTA	22,787	2,809	10,473	9,130	375	Clinton	12.3%	46.0%	40.1%	1.6%
SEMINOLE	16,815	3,662	6,405	6,490	258	Tsongas	21.8%	38.1%	38.6%	1.5%
SUMTER	3,306	366	2,064	799	77	Clinton	11.1%	62.4%	24.2%	2.3%
SUWANNEE	2,950	352	1,780	734	84	Clinton	11.9%	60.3%	24.9%	2.8%
TAYLOR	2,066	270	1,356	369	71	Clinton	13.1%	65.6%	17.9%	3.4%
UNION	761	75	501	167	18	Clinton	9.9%	65.8%	21.9%	2.4%
VOLUSIA	34,966	4,758	17,566	12,062	580	Clinton	13.6%	50.2%	34.5%	1.7%
WAKULLA	1,790	299	1,120	318	53	Clinton	16.7%	62.6%	17.8%	3.0%
WALTON	3,125	517	1,683	789	136	Clinton	16.5%	53.9%	25.2%	4.4%
WASHINGTON	1,836	240	1,090	416	90	Clinton	13.1%	59.4%	22.7%	4.9%
TOTAL	1,123,857	139,569	570,566	388,124	25,598	Clinton	12.4%	50.8%	34.5%	2.3%

FLORIDA REPUBLICAN

1992

County	Total Vote	Buchanan	Bush	Winner	Percentage of Total Vote Buchanan	Bush
ALACHUA	9,362	3,509	5,853	Bush	37.5%	62.5%
BAKER	114	43	71	Bush	37.7%	62.3%
BAY	4,102	1,467	2,635	Bush	35.8%	64.2%
BRADFORD	385	134	251	Bush	34.8%	65.2%
BREVARD	39,653	13,107	26,546	Bush	33.1%	66.9%
BROWARD	71,143	22,286	48,857	Bush	31.3%	68.7%
CALHOUN	88	31	57	Bush	35.2%	64.8%
CHARLOTTE	14,703	5,131	9,572	Bush	34.9%	65.1%
CITRUS	8,791	3,041	5,750	Bush	34.6%	65.4%
CLAY	7,495	2,198	5,297	Bush	29.3%	70.7%
COLLIER	25,815	8,143	17,672	Bush	31.5%	68.5%
COLUMBIA	1,218	442	776	Bush	36.3%	63.7%
DADE	77,622	14,133	63,489	Bush	18.2%	81.8%
DESOTO	613	194	419	Bush	31.6%	68.4%
DIXIE	137	45	92	Bush	32.8%	67.2%
DUVAL	26,472	7,948	18,524	Bush	30.0%	70.0%
ESCAMBIA	16,396	4,610	11,786	Bush	28.1%	71.9%
FLAGLER	2,675	991	1,684	Bush	37.0%	63.0%
FRANKLIN	128	41	87	Bush	32.0%	68.0%
GADSDEN	281	112	169	Bush	39.9%	60.1%

FLORIDA REPUBLICAN

1992

County	Total Vote	Buchanan	Bush	Winner	Percentage of Total Vote Buchanan	Bush
GILCHRIST	169	49	120	Bush	29.0%	71.0%
GLADES	227	70	157	Bush	30.8%	69.2%
GULF	179	44	135	Bush	24.6%	75.4%
HAMILTON	51	17	34	Bush	33.3%	66.7%
HARDEE	311	220	91	Buchanan	70.7%	29.3%
HENDRY	637	214	423	Bush	33.6%	66.4%
HERNANDO	13,653	5,094	8,559	Bush	37.3%	62.7%
HIGHLANDS	7,616	2,233	5,383	Bush	29.3%	70.7%
HILLSBOROUGH	38,582	12,375	26,207	Bush	32.1%	67.9%
HOLMES	114	37	77	Bush	32.5%	67.5%
INDIAN RIVER	12,725	4,139	8,586	Bush	32.5%	67.5%
JACKSON	541	181	360	Bush	33.5%	66.5%
JEFFERSON	217	88	129	Bush	40.6%	59.4%
LAFAYETTE	36	10	26	Bush	27.8%	72.2%
LAKE	19,215	6,474	12,741	Bush	33.7%	66.3%
LEE	38,070	13,236	24,834	Bush	34.8%	65.2%
LEON	8,850	3,021	5,829	Bush	34.1%	65.9%
LEVY	762	271	491	Bush	35.6%	64.4%
LIBERTY	32	6	26	Bush	18.8%	81.3%
MADISON	175	61	114	Bush	34.9%	65.1%
MANATEE	23,710	7,737	15,973	Bush	32.6%	67.4%
MARION	14,079	4,826	9,253	Bush	34.3%	65.7%
MARTIN	12,845	3,982	8,863	Bush	31.0%	69.0%
MONROE	5,225	1,749	3,476	Bush	33.5%	66.5%
NASSAU	1,545	519	1,026	Bush	33.6%	66.4%
OKALOOSA	11,825	3,790	8,035	Bush	32.1%	67.9%
OKEECHOBEE	632	205	427	Bush	32.4%	67.6%
ORANGE	40,432	13,109	27,323	Bush	32.4%	67.6%
OSCEOLA	6,535	2,152	4,383	Bush	32.9%	67.1%
PALM BEACH	69,238	20,348	48,890	Bush	29.4%	70.6%
PASCO	27,913	10,842	17,071	Bush	38.8%	61.2%
PINELLAS	87,386	32,399	54,987	Bush	37.1%	62.9%
POLK	21,414	6,873	14,541	Bush	32.1%	67.9%
PUTNAM	2,257	833	1,424	Bush	36.9%	63.1%
ST. JOHNS	6,598	2,406	4,192	Bush	36.5%	63.5%
ST. LUCIE	11,721	4,128	7,593	Bush	35.2%	64.8%
SANTA ROSA	4,327	1,444	2,883	Bush	33.4%	66.6%
SARASOTA	43,127	13,478	29,649	Bush	31.3%	68.7%
SEMINOLE	22,232	8,016	14,216	Bush	36.1%	63.9%
SUMTER	1,496	459	1,037	Bush	30.7%	69.3%
SUWANNEE	632	239	393	Bush	37.8%	62.2%
TAYLOR	209	57	152	Bush	27.3%	72.7%
UNION	44	19	25	Bush	43.2%	56.8%
VOLUSIA	26,982	9,713	17,269	Bush	36.0%	64.0%
WAKULLA	276	97	179	Bush	35.1%	64.9%
WALTON	1,169	436	733	Bush	37.3%	62.7%
WASHINGTON	259	84	175	Bush	32.4%	67.6%
TOTAL	893,463	285,386	608,077	Bush	31.9%	68.1%

FLORIDA REPUBLICAN

1996

County	Total Vote	Buchanan	Dole	Forbes	Other	Winner	Percentage of Total Vote Buchanan	Dole	Forbes	Other
ALACHUA	8,704	2,151	4,326	1,628	599	Dole	24.7%	49.7%	18.7%	6.9%
BAKER	257	73	146	28	10	Dole	28.4%	56.8%	10.9%	3.9%
BAY	6,252	1,816	3,218	886	332	Dole	29.0%	51.5%	14.2%	5.3%
BRADFORD	568	155	314	71	28	Dole	27.3%	55.3%	12.5%	4.9%
BREVARD	45,104	7,927	23,457	11,269	2,451	Dole	17.6%	52.0%	25.0%	5.4%
BROWARD	58,080	10,966	31,401	12,611	3,102	Dole	18.9%	54.1%	21.7%	5.3%
CALHOUN	107	41	53	6	7	Dole	38.3%	49.5%	5.6%	6.5%
CHARLOTTE	14,397	2,982	8,255	2,535	625	Dole	20.7%	57.3%	17.6%	4.3%
CITRUS	10,222	2,293	5,387	2,121	421	Dole	22.4%	52.7%	20.7%	4.1%
CLAY	11,166	2,351	6,699	1,671	445	Dole	21.1%	60.0%	15.0%	4.0%
COLLIER	21,065	2,722	12,918	4,516	909	Dole	12.9%	61.3%	21.4%	4.3%
COLUMBIA	2,007	657	980	271	99	Dole	32.7%	48.8%	13.5%	4.9%
DADE	79,608	6,349	63,110	6,994	3,155	Dole	8.0%	79.3%	8.8%	4.0%
DESOTO	793	189	436	136	32	Dole	23.8%	55.0%	17.2%	4.0%
DIXIE	153	55	68	25	5	Dole	35.9%	44.4%	16.3%	3.3%
DUVAL	35,607	7,051	21,796	5,295	1,465	Dole	19.8%	61.2%	14.9%	4.1%
ESCAMBIA	18,520	4,977	9,491	2,770	1,282	Dole	26.9%	51.2%	15.0%	6.9%
FLAGLER	3,564	629	2,131	690	114	Dole	17.6%	59.8%	19.4%	3.2%
FRANKLIN	175	32	79	59	5	Dole	18.3%	45.1%	33.7%	2.9%
GADSDEN	432	138	205	61	28	Dole	31.9%	47.5%	14.1%	6.5%
GILCHRIST	342	106	172	49	15	Dole	31.0%	50.3%	14.3%	4.4%
GLADES	258	58	159	32	9	Dole	22.5%	61.6%	12.4%	3.5%
GULF	300	105	142	38	15	Dole	35.0%	47.3%	12.7%	5.0%
HAMILTON	90	37	45	7	1	Dole	41.1%	50.0%	7.8%	1.1%
HARDEE	347	97	178	57	15	Dole	28.0%	51.3%	16.4%	4.3%
HENDRY	653	183	368	76	26	Dole	28.0%	56.4%	11.6%	4.0%
HERNANDO	13,532	2,645	7,247	3,059	581	Dole	19.5%	53.6%	22.6%	4.3%
HIGHLANDS	6,373	1,096	3,970	1,058	249	Dole	17.2%	62.3%	16.6%	3.9%
HILLSBOROUGH	42,685	7,267	22,898	10,461	2,059	Dole	17.0%	53.6%	24.5%	4.8%
HOLMES	171	62	84	16	9	Dole	36.3%	49.1%	9.4%	5.3%
INDIAN RIVER	12,348	1,797	7,182	2,874	495	Dole	14.6%	58.2%	23.3%	4.0%
JACKSON	1,009	390	494	89	36	Dole	38.7%	49.0%	8.8%	3.6%
JEFFERSON	294	99	137	42	16	Dole	33.7%	46.6%	14.3%	5.4%
LAFAYETTE	64	15	39	5	5	Dole	23.4%	60.9%	7.8%	7.8%
LAKE	17,274	3,531	9,279	3,670	794	Dole	20.4%	53.7%	21.2%	4.6%
LEE	40,332	7,359	23,899	7,029	2,045	Dole	18.2%	59.3%	17.4%	5.1%
LEON	9,268	2,222	4,931	1,469	646	Dole	24.0%	53.2%	15.9%	7.0%
LEVY	988	330	456	172	30	Dole	33.4%	46.2%	17.4%	3.0%
LIBERTY	40	18	17	1	4	Buchanan	45.0%	42.5%	2.5%	10.0%
MADISON	273	109	116	37	11	Dole	39.9%	42.5%	13.6%	4.0%
MANATEE	23,299	4,804	12,130	5,307	1,058	Dole	20.6%	52.1%	22.8%	4.5%
MARION	16,891	4,483	8,605	3,018	785	Dole	26.5%	50.9%	17.9%	4.6%
MARTIN	19,315	2,497	11,185	4,694	939	Dole	12.9%	57.9%	24.3%	4.9%
MONROE	5,509	862	2,938	1,377	332	Dole	15.6%	53.3%	25.0%	6.0%
NASSAU	2,774	628	1,571	469	106	Dole	22.6%	56.6%	16.9%	3.8%
OKALOOSA	16,307	4,147	8,695	2,297	1,168	Dole	25.4%	53.3%	14.1%	7.2%
OKEECHOBEE	685	149	400	112	24	Dole	21.8%	58.4%	16.4%	3.5%
ORANGE	37,125	7,203	19,556	8,386	1,980	Dole	19.4%	52.7%	22.6%	5.3%
OSCEOLA	6,424	1,499	3,251	1,365	309	Dole	23.3%	50.6%	21.2%	4.8%
PALM BEACH	57,597	8,788	33,195	12,886	2,728	Dole	15.3%	57.6%	22.4%	4.7%

FLORIDA REPUBLICAN

1996

County	Total Vote	Buchanan	Dole	Forbes	Other	Winner	Percentage of Total Vote Buchanan	Dole	Forbes	Other
PASCO	21,589	4,675	11,016	5,091	807	Dole	21.7%	51.0%	23.6%	3.7%
PINELLAS	77,954	12,116	41,196	21,078	3,564	Dole	15.5%	52.8%	27.0%	4.6%
POLK	23,864	5,157	13,714	4,056	937	Dole	21.6%	57.5%	17.0%	3.9%
PUTNAM	3,618	952	1,875	587	204	Dole	26.3%	51.8%	16.2%	5.6%
ST. JOHNS	9,548	1,885	5,486	1,850	327	Dole	19.7%	57.5%	19.4%	3.4%
ST. LUCIE	17,308	3,229	9,507	3,838	734	Dole	18.7%	54.9%	22.2%	4.2%
SANTA ROSA	8,236	2,536	4,093	1,178	429	Dole	30.8%	49.7%	14.3%	5.2%
SARASOTA	37,339	5,660	20,595	9,462	1,622	Dole	15.2%	55.2%	25.3%	4.3%
SEMINOLE	20,453	4,052	10,388	4,956	1,057	Dole	19.8%	50.8%	24.2%	5.2%
SUMTER	2,105	481	1,115	426	83	Dole	22.9%	53.0%	20.2%	3.9%
SUWANNEE	954	376	430	106	42	Dole	39.4%	45.1%	11.1%	4.4%
TAYLOR	312	99	151	37	25	Dole	31.7%	48.4%	11.9%	8.0%
UNION	118	45	57	10	6	Dole	38.1%	48.3%	8.5%	5.1%
VOLUSIA	22,786	4,441	12,479	4,916	950	Dole	19.5%	54.8%	21.6%	4.2%
WAKULLA	399	133	184	57	25	Dole	33.3%	46.1%	14.3%	6.3%
WALTON	1,702	546	823	235	98	Dole	32.1%	48.4%	13.8%	5.8%
WASHINGTON	437	190	190	30	27		43.5%	43.5%	6.9%	6.2%
Absentees	446	57	269	60	60	Dole	12.8%	60.3%	13.5%	13.5%
TOTAL	898,516	162,770	511,377	181,768	42,601	Dole	18.1%	56.9%	20.2%	4.7%

GEORGIA DEMOCRATIC

1976

County	Total Vote	Carter	Wallace	Other	Winner	Percentage of Total Vote: Carter	Wallace	Other
MITCHELL	1,885	1,447	415	23	Carter	76.8%	22.0%	1.2%
MONROE	1,510	1,287	169	54	Carter	85.2%	11.2%	3.6%
MONTGOMERY	595	439	128	28	Carter	73.8%	21.5%	4.7%
MORGAN	1,368	1,202	142	24	Carter	87.9%	10.4%	1.8%
MURRAY	1,212	1,033	132	47	Carter	85.2%	10.9%	3.9%
MUSCOGEE	13,987	10,851	2,661	475	Carter	77.6%	19.0%	3.4%
NEWTON	5,969	4,916	733	320	Carter	82.4%	12.3%	5.4%
OCONEE	1,258	1,036	181	41	Carter	82.4%	14.4%	3.3%
OGLETHORPE	924	695	218	11	Carter	75.2%	23.6%	1.2%
PAULDING	2,293	1,932	287	74	Carter	84.3%	12.5%	3.2%
PEACH	2,544	2,167	188	189	Carter	85.2%	7.4%	7.4%
PICKENS	830	761	54	15	Carter	91.7%	6.5%	1.8%
PIERCE	880	741	106	33	Carter	84.2%	12.0%	3.8%
PIKE	987	779	175	33	Carter	78.9%	17.7%	3.3%
POLK	2,763	2,255	405	103	Carter	81.6%	14.7%	3.7%
PULASKI	1,227	1,130	82	15	Carter	92.1%	6.7%	1.2%
PUTNAM	755	611	100	44	Carter	80.9%	13.2%	5.8%
QUITMAN	355	272	66	17	Carter	76.6%	18.6%	4.8%
RABUN	1,287	1,162	93	32	Carter	90.3%	7.2%	2.5%
RANDOLPH	1,180	819	337	24	Carter	69.4%	28.6%	2.0%
RICHMOND	14,975	11,358	2,140	1,477	Carter	75.8%	14.3%	9.9%
ROCKDALE	3,387	2,941	304	142	Carter	86.8%	9.0%	4.2%
SCHLEY	391	290	70	31	Carter	74.2%	17.9%	7.9%
SCREVEN	911	746	102	63	Carter	81.9%	11.2%	6.9%
SEMINOLE	805	561	234	10	Carter	69.7%	29.1%	1.2%
SPALDING	4,530	3,890	450	190	Carter	85.9%	9.9%	4.2%
STEPHENS	1,630	1,449	120	61	Carter	88.9%	7.4%	3.7%
STEWART	732	536	111	85	Carter	73.2%	15.2%	11.6%
SUMTER	3,955	3,187	539	229	Carter	80.6%	13.6%	5.8%
TALBOT	707	532	144	31	Carter	75.2%	20.4%	4.4%
TALIAFERRO	245	203	39	3	Carter	82.9%	15.9%	1.2%
TATTNALL	924	725	169	30	Carter	78.5%	18.3%	3.2%
TAYLOR	1,058	842	200	16	Carter	79.6%	18.9%	1.5%
TELFAIR	1,247	1,027	148	72	Carter	82.4%	11.9%	5.8%
TERRELL	1,437	1,201	222	14	Carter	83.6%	15.4%	1.0%
THOMAS	3,254	2,648	395	211	Carter	81.4%	12.1%	6.5%
TIFT	2,661	2,189	328	144	Carter	82.3%	12.3%	5.4%
TOOMBS	1,187	885	244	58	Carter	74.6%	20.6%	4.9%
TOWNS	607	558	25	24	Carter	91.9%	4.1%	4.0%
TREUTLEN	779	654	117	8	Carter	84.0%	15.0%	1.0%
TROUP	3,997	3,256	671	70	Carter	81.5%	16.8%	1.8%
TURNER	951	800	143	8	Carter	84.1%	15.0%	0.8%
TWIGGS	844	696	127	21	Carter	82.5%	15.0%	2.5%
UNION	1,087	1,007	70	10	Carter	92.6%	6.4%	0.9%
UPSON	2,191	1,567	567	57	Carter	71.5%	25.9%	2.6%
WALKER	2,814	2,106	622	86	Carter	74.8%	22.1%	3.1%
WALTON	2,533	2,202	250	81	Carter	86.9%	9.9%	3.2%
WARE	4,267	3,362	689	216	Carter	78.8%	16.1%	5.1%
WARREN	539	391	81	67	Carter	72.5%	15.0%	12.4%
WASHINGTON	2,848	2,126	471	251	Carter	74.6%	16.5%	8.8%

GEORGIA DEMOCRATIC

1976

County	Total Vote	Carter	Wallace	Other	Winner	Percentage of Total Vote Carter	Wallace	Other
WAYNE	1,525	1,262	220	43	Carter	82.8%	14.4%	2.8%
WEBSTER	346	267	59	20	Carter	77.2%	17.1%	5.8%
WHEELER	487	419	62	6	Carter	86.0%	12.7%	1.2%
WHITE	1,499	1,326	148	25	Carter	88.5%	9.9%	1.7%
WHITFIELD	5,913	4,989	623	301	Carter	84.4%	10.5%	5.1%
WILCOX	955	797	145	13	Carter	83.5%	15.2%	1.4%
WILKES	1,110	910	158	42	Carter	82.0%	14.2%	3.8%
WILKINSON	1,050	792	222	36	Carter	75.4%	21.1%	3.4%
WORTH	1,256	856	332	68	Carter	68.2%	26.4%	5.4%
TOTAL	502,471	419,272	57,594	25,605	Carter	83.4%	11.5%	5.1%

GEORGIA REPUBLICAN

1976

County	Total Vote	Ford	Reagan	Winner	Percentage of Total Vote Ford	Reagan
APPLING	222	38	184	Reagan	17.1%	82.9%
ATKINSON	91	21	70	Reagan	23.1%	76.9%
BACON	167	34	133	Reagan	20.4%	79.6%
BAKER	89	20	69	Reagan	22.5%	77.5%
BALDWIN	866	312	554	Reagan	36.0%	64.0%
BANKS	55	10	45	Reagan	18.2%	81.8%
BARROW	428	127	301	Reagan	29.7%	70.3%
BARTOW	457	140	317	Reagan	30.6%	69.4%
BEN HILL	192	36	156	Reagan	18.8%	81.3%
BERRIEN	192	21	171	Reagan	10.9%	89.1%
BIBB	6,362	2,025	4,337	Reagan	31.8%	68.2%
BLECKLEY	202	47	155	Reagan	23.3%	76.7%
BRANTLEY	105	23	82	Reagan	21.9%	78.1%
BROOKS	388	82	306	Reagan	21.1%	78.9%
BRYAN	221	48	173	Reagan	21.7%	78.3%
BULLOCH	704	183	521	Reagan	26.0%	74.0%
BURKE	411	94	317	Reagan	22.9%	77.1%
BUTTS	329	81	248	Reagan	24.6%	75.4%
CALHOUN	125	22	103	Reagan	17.6%	82.4%
CAMDEN	247	76	171	Reagan	30.8%	69.2%
CANDLER	129	36	93	Reagan	27.9%	72.1%
CARROLL	1,160	367	793	Reagan	31.6%	68.4%
CATOOSA	536	134	402	Reagan	25.0%	75.0%
CHARLTON	136	28	108	Reagan	20.6%	79.4%
CHATHAM	10,396	2,424	7,972	Reagan	23.3%	76.7%

GEORGIA REPUBLICAN

1976

County	Total Vote	Ford	Reagan	Winner	Percentage of Total Vote Ford	Percentage of Total Vote Reagan
CHATTAHOOCHEE	49	12	37	Reagan	24.5%	75.5%
CHATTOOGA	379	126	253	Reagan	33.2%	66.8%
CHEROKEE	937	271	666	Reagan	28.9%	71.1%
CLARKE	2,552	938	1,614	Reagan	36.8%	63.2%
CLAY	61	14	47	Reagan	23.0%	77.0%
CLAYTON	5,517	1,135	4,382	Reagan	20.6%	79.4%
CLINCH	120	39	81	Reagan	32.5%	67.5%
COBB	12,884	3,761	9,123	Reagan	29.2%	70.8%
COFFEE	649	143	506	Reagan	22.0%	78.0%
COLQUITT	918	200	718	Reagan	21.8%	78.2%
COLUMBIA	1,232	382	850	Reagan	31.0%	69.0%
COOK	238	44	194	Reagan	18.5%	81.5%
COWETA	1,116	267	849	Reagan	23.9%	76.1%
CRAWFORD	137	22	115	Reagan	16.1%	83.9%
CRISP	312	86	226	Reagan	27.6%	72.4%
DADE	168	58	110	Reagan	34.5%	65.5%
DAWSON	128	51	77	Reagan	39.8%	60.2%
DECATUR	542	145	397	Reagan	26.8%	73.2%
DE KALB	35,524	13,167	22,357	Reagan	37.1%	62.9%
DODGE	171	45	126	Reagan	26.3%	73.7%
DOOLY	172	45	127	Reagan	26.2%	73.8%
DOUGHERTY	5,037	1,029	4,008	Reagan	20.4%	79.6%
DOUGLAS	1,781	341	1,440	Reagan	19.1%	80.9%
EARLY	308	72	236	Reagan	23.4%	76.6%
ECHOLS	18	5	13	Reagan	27.8%	72.2%
EFFINGHAM	627	92	535	Reagan	14.7%	85.3%
ELBERT	229	72	157	Reagan	31.4%	68.6%
EMANUEL	409	72	337	Reagan	17.6%	82.4%
EVANS	193	36	157	Reagan	18.7%	81.3%
FANNIN	650	330	320	Ford	50.8%	49.2%
FAYETTE	1,311	334	977	Reagan	25.5%	74.5%
FLOYD	2,075	756	1,319	Reagan	36.4%	63.6%
FORSYTH	712	194	518	Reagan	27.2%	72.8%
FRANKLIN	123	36	87	Reagan	29.3%	70.7%
FULTON	25,516	9,984	15,532	Reagan	39.1%	60.9%
GILMER	336	131	205	Reagan	39.0%	61.0%
GLASCOCK	49	9	40	Reagan	18.4%	81.6%
GLYNN	2,730	1,274	1,456	Reagan	46.7%	53.3%
GORDON	412	153	259	Reagan	37.1%	62.9%
GRADY	402	107	295	Reagan	26.6%	73.4%
GREENE	170	43	127	Reagan	25.3%	74.7%
GWINNETT	6,240	1,843	4,397	Reagan	29.5%	70.5%
HABERSHAM	430	161	269	Reagan	37.4%	62.6%
HALL	1,853	585	1,268	Reagan	31.6%	68.4%
HANCOCK	103	20	83	Reagan	19.4%	80.6%
HARALSON	534	127	407	Reagan	23.8%	76.2%
HARRIS	529	182	347	Reagan	34.4%	65.6%
HART	127	47	80	Reagan	37.0%	63.0%
HEARD	108	45	63	Reagan	41.7%	58.3%
HENRY	1,163	221	942	Reagan	19.0%	81.0%

GEORGIA REPUBLICAN

1976

County	Total Vote	Ford	Reagan	Winner	Percentage of Total Vote Ford	Percentage of Total Vote Reagan
HOUSTON	2,320	544	1,776	Reagan	23.4%	76.6%
IRWIN	176	35	141	Reagan	19.9%	80.1%
JACKSON	358	88	270	Reagan	24.6%	75.4%
JASPER	186	61	125	Reagan	32.8%	67.2%
JEFF DAVIS	133	28	105	Reagan	21.1%	78.9%
JEFFERSON	364	92	272	Reagan	25.3%	74.7%
JENKINS	131	31	100	Reagan	23.7%	76.3%
JOHNSON	260	35	225	Reagan	13.5%	86.5%
JONES	345	85	260	Reagan	24.6%	75.4%
LAMAR	244	66	178	Reagan	27.0%	73.0%
LANIER	37	19	18	Ford	51.4%	48.6%
LAURENS	736	169	567	Reagan	23.0%	77.0%
LEE	394	45	349	Reagan	11.4%	88.6%
LIBERTY	250	74	176	Reagan	29.6%	70.4%
LINCOLN	153	47	106	Reagan	30.7%	69.3%
LONG	56	16	40	Reagan	28.6%	71.4%
LOWNDES	1,155	340	815	Reagan	29.4%	70.6%
LUMPKIN	194	66	128	Reagan	34.0%	66.0%
MCDUFFIE	461	126	335	Reagan	27.3%	72.7%
MCINTOSH	171	45	126	Reagan	26.3%	73.7%
MACON	194	62	132	Reagan	32.0%	68.0%
MADISON	325	54	271	Reagan	16.6%	83.4%
MARION	59	15	44	Reagan	25.4%	74.6%
MERIWETHER	554	156	398	Reagan	28.2%	71.8%
MILLER	98	8	90	Reagan	8.2%	91.8%
MITCHELL	417	65	352	Reagan	15.6%	84.4%
MONROE	362	88	274	Reagan	24.3%	75.7%
MONTGOMERY	175	35	140	Reagan	20.0%	80.0%
MORGAN	274	76	198	Reagan	27.7%	72.3%
MURRAY	143	53	90	Reagan	37.1%	62.9%
MUSCOGEE	5,457	2,019	3,438	Reagan	37.0%	63.0%
NEWTON	916	239	677	Reagan	26.1%	73.9%
OCONEE	416	98	318	Reagan	23.6%	76.4%
OGLETHORPE	275	60	215	Reagan	21.8%	78.2%
PAULDING	502	91	411	Reagan	18.1%	81.9%
PEACH	478	111	367	Reagan	23.2%	76.8%
PICKENS	228	89	139	Reagan	39.0%	61.0%
PIERCE	194	59	135	Reagan	30.4%	69.6%
PIKE	203	44	159	Reagan	21.7%	78.3%
POLK	588	181	407	Reagan	30.8%	69.2%
PULASKI	84	23	61	Reagan	27.4%	72.6%
PUTNAM	223	56	167	Reagan	25.1%	74.9%
QUITMAN	33	11	22	Reagan	33.3%	66.7%
RABUN	160	72	88	Reagan	45.0%	55.0%
RANDOLPH	218	56	162	Reagan	25.7%	74.3%
RICHMOND	9,609	3,534	6,075	Reagan	36.8%	63.2%
ROCKDALE	1,251	297	954	Reagan	23.7%	76.3%
SCHLEY	67	13	54	Reagan	19.4%	80.6%
SCREVEN	354	93	261	Reagan	26.3%	73.7%
SEMINOLE	166	40	126	Reagan	24.1%	75.9%

GEORGIA REPUBLICAN

1976

County	Total Vote	Ford	Reagan	Winner	Percentage of Total Vote Ford	Reagan
SPALDING	1,340	365	975	Reagan	27.2%	72.8%
STEPHENS	243	84	159	Reagan	34.6%	65.4%
STEWART	96	26	70	Reagan	27.1%	72.9%
SUMTER	427	101	326	Reagan	23.7%	76.3%
TALBOT	116	27	89	Reagan	23.3%	76.7%
TALIAFERRO	29	11	18	Reagan	37.9%	62.1%
TATTNALL	129	16	113	Reagan	12.4%	87.6%
TAYLOR	103	35	68	Reagan	34.0%	66.0%
TELFAIR	120	35	85	Reagan	29.2%	70.8%
TERRELL	374	63	311	Reagan	16.8%	83.2%
THOMAS	1,086	525	561	Reagan	48.3%	51.7%
TIFT	682	171	511	Reagan	25.1%	74.9%
TOOMBS	599	115	484	Reagan	19.2%	80.8%
TOWNS	160	68	92	Reagan	42.5%	57.5%
TREUTLEN	120	21	99	Reagan	17.5%	82.5%
TROUP	1,013	325	688	Reagan	32.1%	67.9%
TURNER	138	27	111	Reagan	19.6%	80.4%
TWIGGS	147	35	112	Reagan	23.8%	76.2%
UNION	254	80	174	Reagan	31.5%	68.5%
UPSON	771	209	562	Reagan	27.1%	72.9%
WALKER	775	287	488	Reagan	37.0%	63.0%
WALTON	552	161	391	Reagan	29.2%	70.8%
WARE	862	287	575	Reagan	33.3%	66.7%
WARREN	198	43	155	Reagan	21.7%	78.3%
WASHINGTON	634	188	446	Reagan	29.7%	70.3%
WAYNE	354	79	275	Reagan	22.3%	77.7%
WEBSTER	33	7	26	Reagan	21.2%	78.8%
WHEELER	71	12	59	Reagan	16.9%	83.1%
WHITE	242	83	159	Reagan	34.3%	65.7%
WHITFIELD	1,413	603	810	Reagan	42.7%	57.3%
WILCOX	84	14	70	Reagan	16.7%	83.3%
WILKES	283	81	202	Reagan	28.6%	71.4%
WILKINSON	227	47	180	Reagan	20.7%	79.3%
WORTH	459	79	380	Reagan	17.2%	82.8%
TOTAL	188,472	59,801	128,671	Reagan	31.7%	68.3%

GEORGIA DEMOCRATIC

1980

County	Total Vote	Carter	Other	Winner	Percentage of Total Vote Carter	Other
APPLING	2,395	2,148	247	Carter	89.7%	10.3%
ATKINSON	536	476	60	Carter	88.8%	11.2%
BACON	488	452	36	Carter	92.6%	7.4%
BAKER	290	249	41	Carter	85.9%	14.1%
BALDWIN	1,909	1,573	336	Carter	82.4%	17.6%
BANKS	881	818	63	Carter	92.8%	7.2%
BARROW	1,644	1,502	142	Carter	91.4%	8.6%
BARTOW	3,017	2,795	222	Carter	92.6%	7.4%
BEN HILL	1,092	1,020	72	Carter	93.4%	6.6%
BERRIEN	1,023	977	46	Carter	95.5%	4.5%
BIBB	12,395	11,157	1,238	Carter	90.0%	10.0%
BLECKLEY	941	859	82	Carter	91.3%	8.7%
BRANTLEY	838	782	56	Carter	93.3%	6.7%
BROOKS	1,014	910	104	Carter	89.7%	10.3%
BRYAN	684	620	64	Carter	90.6%	9.4%
BULLOCH	1,971	1,758	213	Carter	89.2%	10.8%
BURKE	1,159	941	218	Carter	81.2%	18.8%
BUTTS	1,160	1,020	140	Carter	87.9%	12.1%
CALHOUN	613	551	62	Carter	89.9%	10.1%
CAMDEN	1,163	1,019	144	Carter	87.6%	12.4%
CANDLER	563	513	50	Carter	91.1%	8.9%
CARROLL	6,067	5,449	618	Carter	89.8%	10.2%
CATOOSA	1,726	1,546	180	Carter	89.6%	10.4%
CHARLTON	602	512	90	Carter	85.0%	15.0%
CHATHAM	14,109	11,816	2,293	Carter	83.7%	16.3%
CHATTAHOOCHEE	193	156	37	Carter	80.8%	19.2%
CHATTOOGA	1,585	1,407	178	Carter	88.8%	11.2%
CHEROKEE	2,806	2,600	206	Carter	92.7%	7.3%
CLARKE	5,475	4,765	710	Carter	87.0%	13.0%
CLAY	346	287	59	Carter	82.9%	17.1%
CLAYTON	7,983	7,242	741	Carter	90.7%	9.3%
CLINCH	574	521	53	Carter	90.8%	9.2%
COBB	17,631	15,962	1,669	Carter	90.5%	9.5%
COFFEE	1,761	1,596	165	Carter	90.6%	9.4%
COLQUITT	2,966	2,783	183	Carter	93.8%	6.2%
COLUMBIA	1,571	1,351	220	Carter	86.0%	14.0%
COOK	882	811	71	Carter	92.0%	8.0%
COWETA	2,963	2,671	292	Carter	90.1%	9.9%
CRAWFORD	667	563	104	Carter	84.4%	15.6%
CRISP	925	842	83	Carter	91.0%	9.0%
DADE	491	449	42	Carter	91.4%	8.6%
DAWSON	423	387	36	Carter	91.5%	8.5%
DECATUR	1,534	1,288	246	Carter	84.0%	16.0%
DE KALB	32,555	28,291	4,264	Carter	86.9%	13.1%
DODGE	1,454	1,333	121	Carter	91.7%	8.3%
DOOLY	1,158	1,001	157	Carter	86.4%	13.6%
DOUGHERTY	6,563	5,668	895	Carter	86.4%	13.6%
DOUGLAS	4,576	4,074	502	Carter	89.0%	11.0%
EARLY	1,176	1,076	100	Carter	91.5%	8.5%
ECHOLS	183	173	10	Carter	94.5%	5.5%

GEORGIA DEMOCRATIC

1980

County	Total Vote	Carter	Other	Winner	Percentage of Total Vote Carter	Other
EFFINGHAM	1,470	1,312	158	Carter	89.3%	10.7%
ELBERT	1,360	1,255	105	Carter	92.3%	7.7%
EMANUEL	1,826	1,691	135	Carter	92.6%	7.4%
EVANS	486	446	40	Carter	91.8%	8.2%
FANNIN	788	723	65	Carter	91.8%	8.2%
FAYETTE	2,052	1,868	184	Carter	91.0%	9.0%
FLOYD	6,698	6,093	605	Carter	91.0%	9.0%
FORSYTH	1,988	1,865	123	Carter	93.8%	6.2%
FRANKLIN	1,041	968	73	Carter	93.0%	7.0%
FULTON	44,346	36,280	8,066	Carter	81.8%	18.2%
GILMER	649	604	45	Carter	93.1%	6.9%
GLASCOCK	176	166	10	Carter	94.3%	5.7%
GLYNN	3,402	3,027	375	Carter	89.0%	11.0%
GORDON	2,213	1,963	250	Carter	88.7%	11.3%
GRADY	1,340	1,201	139	Carter	89.6%	10.4%
GREENE	1,231	1,083	148	Carter	88.0%	12.0%
GWINNETT	11,489	10,474	1,015	Carter	91.2%	8.8%
HABERSHAM	1,999	1,840	159	Carter	92.0%	8.0%
HALL	5,841	5,329	512	Carter	91.2%	8.8%
HANCOCK	542	435	107	Carter	80.3%	19.7%
HARALSON	1,532	1,413	119	Carter	92.2%	7.8%
HARRIS	1,215	1,060	155	Carter	87.2%	12.8%
HART	1,011	922	89	Carter	91.2%	8.8%
HEARD	627	555	72	Carter	88.5%	11.5%
HENRY	2,962	2,663	299	Carter	89.9%	10.1%
HOUSTON	7,999	6,845	1,154	Carter	85.6%	14.4%
IRWIN	622	598	24	Carter	96.1%	3.9%
JACKSON	2,037	1,901	136	Carter	93.3%	6.7%
JASPER	813	667	146	Carter	82.0%	18.0%
JEFF DAVIS	691	620	71	Carter	89.7%	10.3%
JEFFERSON	1,674	1,341	333	Carter	80.1%	19.9%
JENKINS	652	577	75	Carter	88.5%	11.5%
JOHNSON	628	576	52	Carter	91.7%	8.3%
JONES	1,308	1,114	194	Carter	85.2%	14.8%
LAMAR	1,292	1,118	174	Carter	86.5%	13.5%
LANIER	330	302	28	Carter	91.5%	8.5%
LAURENS	3,270	2,827	443	Carter	86.5%	13.5%
LEE	824	710	114	Carter	86.2%	13.8%
LIBERTY	1,338	1,145	193	Carter	85.6%	14.4%
LINCOLN	517	452	65	Carter	87.4%	12.6%
LONG	493	437	56	Carter	88.6%	11.4%
LOWNDES	2,947	2,636	311	Carter	89.4%	10.6%
LUMPKIN	888	820	68	Carter	92.3%	7.7%
MCDUFFIE	902	760	142	Carter	84.3%	15.7%
MCINTOSH	688	590	98	Carter	85.8%	14.2%
MACON	1,224	1,031	193	Carter	84.2%	15.8%
MADISON	1,046	965	81	Carter	92.3%	7.7%
MARION	390	346	44	Carter	88.7%	11.3%
MERIWETHER	1,664	1,471	193	Carter	88.4%	11.6%
MILLER	387	356	31	Carter	92.0%	8.0%

GEORGIA DEMOCRATIC

1980

County	Total Vote	Carter	Other	Winner	Percentage of Total Vote Carter	Other
MITCHELL	1,817	1,602	215	Carter	88.2%	11.8%
MONROE	1,367	1,184	183	Carter	86.6%	13.4%
MONTGOMERY	493	448	45	Carter	90.9%	9.1%
MORGAN	1,123	961	162	Carter	85.6%	14.4%
MURRAY	1,062	945	117	Carter	89.0%	11.0%
MUSCOGEE	8,840	7,822	1,018	Carter	88.5%	11.5%
NEWTON	2,640	2,420	220	Carter	91.7%	8.3%
OCONEE	1,178	1,109	69	Carter	94.1%	5.9%
OGLETHORPE	865	767	98	Carter	88.7%	11.3%
PAULDING	1,967	1,789	178	Carter	91.0%	9.0%
PEACH	1,877	1,582	295	Carter	84.3%	15.7%
PICKENS	735	684	51	Carter	93.1%	6.9%
PIERCE	766	699	67	Carter	91.3%	8.7%
PIKE	785	702	83	Carter	89.4%	10.6%
POLK	2,671	2,381	290	Carter	89.1%	10.9%
PULASKI	739	658	81	Carter	89.0%	11.0%
PUTNAM	630	539	91	Carter	85.6%	14.4%
QUITMAN	287	237	50	Carter	82.6%	17.4%
RABUN	1,048	976	72	Carter	93.1%	6.9%
RANDOLPH	902	799	103	Carter	88.6%	11.4%
RICHMOND	8,431	7,184	1,247	Carter	85.2%	14.8%
ROCKDALE	2,270	2,056	214	Carter	90.6%	9.4%
SCHLEY	263	232	31	Carter	88.2%	11.8%
SCREVEN	881	781	100	Carter	88.6%	11.4%
SEMINOLE	736	673	63	Carter	91.4%	8.6%
SPALDING	3,619	3,232	387	Carter	89.3%	10.7%
STEPHENS	3,327	3,028	299	Carter	91.0%	9.0%
STEWART	583	466	117	Carter	79.9%	20.1%
SUMTER	2,505	2,203	302	Carter	87.9%	12.1%
TALBOT	665	555	110	Carter	83.5%	16.5%
TALIAFERRO	171	152	19	Carter	88.9%	11.1%
TATTNALL	996	886	110	Carter	89.0%	11.0%
TAYLOR	953	860	93	Carter	90.2%	9.8%
TELFAIR	1,041	885	156	Carter	85.0%	15.0%
TERRELL	1,062	962	100	Carter	90.6%	9.4%
THOMAS	2,592	2,242	350	Carter	86.5%	13.5%
TIFT	2,306	2,106	200	Carter	91.3%	8.7%
TOOMBS	1,241	1,050	191	Carter	84.6%	15.4%
TOWNS	521	485	36	Carter	93.1%	6.9%
TREUTLEN	532	477	55	Carter	89.7%	10.3%
TROUP	3,145	2,830	315	Carter	90.0%	10.0%
TURNER	803	755	48	Carter	94.0%	6.0%
TWIGGS	845	690	155	Carter	81.7%	18.3%
UNION	848	784	64	Carter	92.5%	7.5%
UPSON	2,619	2,355	264	Carter	89.9%	10.1%
WALKER	2,028	1,856	172	Carter	91.5%	8.5%
WALTON	2,113	1,946	167	Carter	92.1%	7.9%
WARE	2,838	2,585	253	Carter	91.1%	8.9%
WARREN	521	420	101	Carter	80.6%	19.4%
WASHINGTON	1,529	1,282	247	Carter	83.8%	16.2%

GEORGIA DEMOCRATIC

1980

County	Total Vote	Carter	Other	Winner	Percentage of Total Vote Carter	Other
WAYNE	2,205	2,002	203	Carter	90.8%	9.2%
WEBSTER	234	204	30	Carter	87.2%	12.8%
WHEELER	374	341	33	Carter	91.2%	8.8%
WHITE	922	880	42	Carter	95.4%	4.6%
WHITFIELD	3,635	3,339	296	Carter	91.9%	8.1%
WILCOX	771	715	56	Carter	92.7%	7.3%
WILKES	1,051	845	206	Carter	80.4%	19.6%
WILKINSON	854	723	131	Carter	84.7%	15.3%
WORTH	1,319	1,200	119	Carter	91.0%	9.0%
TOTAL	384,770	338,772	45,998	Carter	88.0%	12.0%
Certified Totals	384,780	338,772	46,008	Carter	88.0%	12.0%

GEORGIA REPUBLICAN

1980

County	Total Vote	Bush	Reagan	Other	Winner	Percentage of Total Vote Bush	Reagan	Other
APPLING	699	29	622	48	Reagan	4.1%	89.0%	6.9%
ATKINSON	132	9	117	6	Reagan	6.8%	88.6%	4.5%
BACON	205	9	184	12	Reagan	4.4%	89.8%	5.9%
BAKER	155	6	138	11	Reagan	3.9%	89.0%	7.1%
BALDWIN	902	127	637	138	Reagan	14.1%	70.6%	15.3%
BANKS	176	17	145	14	Reagan	9.7%	82.4%	8.0%
BARROW	637	35	542	60	Reagan	5.5%	85.1%	9.4%
BARTOW	710	66	577	67	Reagan	9.3%	81.3%	9.4%
BEN HILL	287	27	246	14	Reagan	9.4%	85.7%	4.9%
BERRIEN	306	12	287	7	Reagan	3.9%	93.8%	2.3%
BIBB	4,330	616	2,976	738	Reagan	14.2%	68.7%	17.0%
BLECKLEY	319	37	242	40	Reagan	11.6%	75.9%	12.5%
BRANTLEY	205	14	181	10	Reagan	6.8%	88.3%	4.9%
BROOKS	470	33	395	42	Reagan	7.0%	84.0%	8.9%
BRYAN	327	10	293	24	Reagan	3.1%	89.6%	7.3%
BULLOCH	878	83	639	156	Reagan	9.5%	72.8%	17.8%
BURKE	614	36	511	67	Reagan	5.9%	83.2%	10.9%
BUTTS	338	32	278	28	Reagan	9.5%	82.2%	8.3%
CALHOUN	147	11	127	9	Reagan	7.5%	86.4%	6.1%
CAMDEN	270	38	200	32	Reagan	14.1%	74.1%	11.9%
CANDLER	313	12	234	67	Reagan	3.8%	74.8%	21.4%
CARROLL	1,971	260	1,466	245	Reagan	13.2%	74.4%	12.4%
CATOOSA	896	75	751	70	Reagan	8.4%	83.8%	7.8%
CHARLTON	182	16	148	18	Reagan	8.8%	81.3%	9.9%
CHATHAM	10,650	888	8,729	1,033	Reagan	8.3%	82.0%	9.7%

GEORGIA REPUBLICAN

1980

County	Total Vote	Bush	Reagan	Other	Winner	Percentage of Total Vote Bush	Reagan	Other
CHATTAHOOCHEE	35	3	30	2	Reagan	8.6%	85.7%	5.7%
CHATTOOGA	389	42	318	29	Reagan	10.8%	81.7%	7.5%
CHEROKEE	1,248	122	968	158	Reagan	9.8%	77.6%	12.7%
CLARKE	3,460	531	1,985	944	Reagan	15.3%	57.4%	27.3%
CLAY	85	9	70	6	Reagan	10.6%	82.4%	7.1%
CLAYTON	6,017	513	4,703	801	Reagan	8.5%	78.2%	13.3%
CLINCH	117	7	104	6	Reagan	6.0%	88.9%	5.1%
COBB	15,551	2,126	10,941	2,484	Reagan	13.7%	70.4%	16.0%
COFFEE	555	34	481	40	Reagan	6.1%	86.7%	7.2%
COLQUITT	987	84	819	84	Reagan	8.5%	83.0%	8.5%
COLUMBIA	1,561	150	1,263	148	Reagan	9.6%	80.9%	9.5%
COOK	302	15	261	26	Reagan	5.0%	86.4%	8.6%
COWETA	1,226	127	978	121	Reagan	10.4%	79.8%	9.9%
CRAWFORD	155	8	133	14	Reagan	5.2%	85.8%	9.0%
CRISP	254	27	199	28	Reagan	10.6%	78.3%	11.0%
DADE	293	19	245	29	Reagan	6.5%	83.6%	9.9%
DAWSON	177	8	142	27	Reagan	4.5%	80.2%	15.3%
DECATUR	867	62	737	68	Reagan	7.2%	85.0%	7.8%
DE KALB	28,991	4,621	18,057	6,313	Reagan	15.9%	62.3%	21.8%
DODGE	284	14	242	28	Reagan	4.9%	85.2%	9.9%
DOOLY	263	23	210	30	Reagan	8.7%	79.8%	11.4%
DOUGHERTY	4,123	369	3,544	210	Reagan	8.9%	86.0%	5.1%
DOUGLAS	2,439	218	1,961	260	Reagan	8.9%	80.4%	10.7%
EARLY	499	24	461	14	Reagan	4.8%	92.4%	2.8%
ECHOLS	40	2	38		Reagan	5.0%	95.0%	
EFFINGHAM	919	43	826	50	Reagan	4.7%	89.9%	5.4%
ELBERT	424	27	372	25	Reagan	6.4%	87.7%	5.9%
EMANUEL	542	29	481	32	Reagan	5.4%	88.7%	5.9%
EVANS	275	9	259	7	Reagan	3.3%	94.2%	2.5%
FANNIN	696	47	559	90	Reagan	6.8%	80.3%	12.9%
FAYETTE	1,852	158	1,463	231	Reagan	8.5%	79.0%	12.5%
FLOYD	2,359	296	1,766	297	Reagan	12.5%	74.9%	12.6%
FORSYTH	1,041	107	813	121	Reagan	10.3%	78.1%	11.6%
FRANKLIN	343	34	281	28	Reagan	9.9%	81.9%	8.2%
FULTON	26,146	5,447	15,654	5,045	Reagan	20.8%	59.9%	19.3%
GILMER	438	14	396	28	Reagan	3.2%	90.4%	6.4%
GLASCOCK	111	1	106	4	Reagan	0.9%	95.5%	3.6%
GLYNN	2,199	534	1,376	289	Reagan	24.3%	62.6%	13.1%
GORDON	660	80	509	71	Reagan	12.1%	77.1%	10.8%
GRADY	439	34	361	44	Reagan	7.7%	82.2%	10.0%
GREENE	259	13	237	9	Reagan	5.0%	91.5%	3.5%
GWINNETT	8,095	1,105	5,762	1,228	Reagan	13.7%	71.2%	15.2%
HABERSHAM	582	62	454	66	Reagan	10.7%	78.0%	11.3%
HALL	1,992	278	1,437	277	Reagan	14.0%	72.1%	13.9%
HANCOCK	91		87	4	Reagan		95.6%	4.4%
HARALSON	574	47	496	31	Reagan	8.2%	86.4%	5.4%
HARRIS	530	83	380	67	Reagan	15.7%	71.7%	12.6%
HART	341	45	272	24	Reagan	13.2%	79.8%	7.0%
HEARD	199	15	167	17	Reagan	7.5%	83.9%	8.5%
HENRY	1,689	97	1,454	138	Reagan	5.7%	86.1%	8.2%

GEORGIA REPUBLICAN

1980

County	Total Vote	Bush	Reagan	Other	Winner	Percentage of Total Vote Bush	Reagan	Other
HOUSTON	3,000	453	2,048	499	Reagan	15.1%	68.3%	16.6%
IRWIN	255	15	234	6	Reagan	5.9%	91.8%	2.4%
JACKSON	631	30	555	46	Reagan	4.8%	88.0%	7.3%
JASPER	213	16	164	33	Reagan	7.5%	77.0%	15.5%
JEFF DAVIS	212	8	187	17	Reagan	3.8%	88.2%	8.0%
JEFFERSON	541	32	459	50	Reagan	5.9%	84.8%	9.2%
JENKINS	255	15	221	19	Reagan	5.9%	86.7%	7.5%
JOHNSON	274	6	253	15	Reagan	2.2%	92.3%	5.5%
JONES	344	37	264	43	Reagan	10.8%	76.7%	12.5%
LAMAR	338	36	267	35	Reagan	10.7%	79.0%	10.4%
LANIER	95	6	84	5	Reagan	6.3%	88.4%	5.3%
LAURENS	937	72	776	89	Reagan	7.7%	82.8%	9.5%
LEE	545	29	497	19	Reagan	5.3%	91.2%	3.5%
LIBERTY	373	24	304	45	Reagan	6.4%	81.5%	12.1%
LINCOLN	206	12	188	6	Reagan	5.8%	91.3%	2.9%
LONG	85	3	74	8	Reagan	3.5%	87.1%	9.4%
LOWNDES	1,468	185	1,146	137	Reagan	12.6%	78.1%	9.3%
LUMPKIN	261	16	204	41	Reagan	6.1%	78.2%	15.7%
MCDUFFIE	582	39	503	40	Reagan	6.7%	86.4%	6.9%
MCINTOSH	182	14	147	21	Reagan	7.7%	80.8%	11.5%
MACON	222	30	156	36	Reagan	13.5%	70.3%	16.2%
MADISON	684	38	601	45	Reagan	5.6%	87.9%	6.6%
MARION	109	8	98	3	Reagan	7.3%	89.9%	2.8%
MERIWETHER	517	41	399	77	Reagan	7.9%	77.2%	14.9%
MILLER	189	8	167	14	Reagan	4.2%	88.4%	7.4%
MITCHELL	600	38	535	27	Reagan	6.3%	89.2%	4.5%
MONROE	384	46	300	38	Reagan	12.0%	78.1%	9.9%
MONTGOMERY	253	10	234	9	Reagan	4.0%	92.5%	3.6%
MORGAN	258	19	224	15	Reagan	7.4%	86.8%	5.8%
MURRAY	189	18	152	19	Reagan	9.5%	80.4%	10.1%
MUSCOGEE	4,360	776	3,092	492	Reagan	17.8%	70.9%	11.3%
NEWTON	938	84	763	91	Reagan	9.0%	81.3%	9.7%
OCONEE	733	53	601	79	Reagan	7.2%	82.0%	10.8%
OGLETHORPE	562	23	507	32	Reagan	4.1%	90.2%	5.7%
PAULDING	599	33	514	52	Reagan	5.5%	85.8%	8.7%
PEACH	443	45	334	64	Reagan	10.2%	75.4%	14.4%
PICKENS	358	32	296	30	Reagan	8.9%	82.7%	8.4%
PIERCE	168	20	125	23	Reagan	11.9%	74.4%	13.7%
PIKE	392	33	324	35	Reagan	8.4%	82.7%	8.9%
POLK	709	59	580	70	Reagan	8.3%	81.8%	9.9%
PULASKI	244	29	186	29	Reagan	11.9%	76.2%	11.9%
PUTNAM	273	18	228	27	Reagan	6.6%	83.5%	9.9%
QUITMAN	16	1	12	3	Reagan	6.3%	75.0%	18.8%
RABUN	268	35	197	36	Reagan	13.1%	73.5%	13.4%
RANDOLPH	272	14	245	13	Reagan	5.1%	90.1%	4.8%
RICHMOND	7,206	716	5,685	805	Reagan	9.9%	78.9%	11.2%
ROCKDALE	1,461	154	1,093	214	Reagan	10.5%	74.8%	14.6%
SCHLEY	110	3	102	5	Reagan	2.7%	92.7%	4.5%
SCREVEN	509	20	449	40	Reagan	3.9%	88.2%	7.9%
SEMINOLE	300	15	270	15	Reagan	5.0%	90.0%	5.0%

GEORGIA REPUBLICAN

1980

County	Total Vote	Bush	Reagan	Other	Winner	Percentage of Total Vote Bush	Reagan	Other
SPALDING	1,429	134	1,129	166	Reagan	9.4%	79.0%	11.6%
STEPHENS	721	87	554	80	Reagan	12.1%	76.8%	11.1%
STEWART	154	13	127	14	Reagan	8.4%	82.5%	9.1%
SUMTER	687	49	568	70	Reagan	7.1%	82.7%	10.2%
TALBOT	136	9	115	12	Reagan	6.6%	84.6%	8.8%
TALIAFERRO	73	2	67	4	Reagan	2.7%	91.8%	5.5%
TATTNALL	440	13	397	30	Reagan	3.0%	90.2%	6.8%
TAYLOR	245	17	205	23	Reagan	6.9%	83.7%	9.4%
TELFAIR	176	9	138	29	Reagan	5.1%	78.4%	16.5%
TERRELL	440	19	405	16	Reagan	4.3%	92.0%	3.6%
THOMAS	1,358	176	1,002	180	Reagan	13.0%	73.8%	13.3%
TIFT	810	89	630	91	Reagan	11.0%	77.8%	11.2%
TOOMBS	821	42	716	63	Reagan	5.1%	87.2%	7.7%
TOWNS	171	19	127	25	Reagan	11.1%	74.3%	14.6%
TREUTLEN	147	5	138	4	Reagan	3.4%	93.9%	2.7%
TROUP	1,010	138	789	83	Reagan	13.7%	78.1%	8.2%
TURNER	170	4	157	9	Reagan	2.4%	92.4%	5.3%
TWIGGS	127	10	105	12	Reagan	7.9%	82.7%	9.4%
UNION	319	15	287	17	Reagan	4.7%	90.0%	5.3%
UPSON	771	47	673	51	Reagan	6.1%	87.3%	6.6%
WALKER	979	105	781	93	Reagan	10.7%	79.8%	9.5%
WALTON	730	64	582	84	Reagan	8.8%	79.7%	11.5%
WARE	793	93	620	80	Reagan	11.7%	78.2%	10.1%
WARREN	272	13	246	13	Reagan	4.8%	90.4%	4.8%
WASHINGTON	484	35	407	42	Reagan	7.2%	84.1%	8.7%
WAYNE	614	39	504	71	Reagan	6.4%	82.1%	11.6%
WEBSTER	78	5	67	6	Reagan	6.4%	85.9%	7.7%
WHEELER	116	3	104	9	Reagan	2.6%	89.7%	7.8%
WHITE	336	30	263	43	Reagan	8.9%	78.3%	12.8%
WHITFIELD	1,224	187	858	179	Reagan	15.3%	70.1%	14.6%
WILCOX	172	7	145	20	Reagan	4.1%	84.3%	11.6%
WILKES	414	25	330	59	Reagan	6.0%	79.7%	14.3%
WILKINSON	241	6	221	14	Reagan	2.5%	91.7%	5.8%
WORTH	557	56	476	25	Reagan	10.1%	85.5%	4.5%
TOTAL	200,171	25,293	146,500	28,378	Reagan	12.6%	73.2%	14.2%

GEORGIA DEMOCRATIC

1984

County	Total Vote	Glenn	Hart	J. Jackson	Mondale	Other	Winner	Percentage of Total Vote				
								Glenn	Hart	J. Jackson	Mondale	Other
APPLING	2,203	335	619	503	657	89	Mondale	15.2%	28.1%	22.8%	29.8%	4.0%
ATKINSON	1,251	291	310	156	391	103	Mondale	23.3%	24.8%	12.5%	31.3%	8.2%
BACON	689	124	228	33	276	28	Mondale	18.0%	33.1%	4.8%	40.1%	4.1%
BAKER	532	84	88	148	147	65	J. Jackson	15.8%	16.5%	27.8%	27.6%	12.2%
BALDWIN	4,277	1,012	1,002	1,256	836	171	J. Jackson	23.7%	23.4%	29.4%	19.5%	4.0%
BANKS	1,781	298	719	30	658	76	Hart	16.7%	40.4%	1.7%	36.9%	4.3%
BARROW	2,484	485	807	227	910	55	Mondale	19.5%	32.5%	9.1%	36.6%	2.2%
BARTOW	4,399	833	1,467	278	1,717	104	Mondale	18.9%	33.3%	6.3%	39.0%	2.4%
BEN HILL	1,477	286	348	217	603	23	Mondale	19.4%	23.6%	14.7%	40.8%	1.6%
BERRIEN	1,445	249	470	120	582	24	Mondale	17.2%	32.5%	8.3%	40.3%	1.7%
BIBB	26,900	3,844	5,849	8,017	8,817	373	Mondale	14.3%	21.7%	29.8%	32.8%	1.4%
BLECKLEY	1,671	324	529	150	583	85	Mondale	19.4%	31.7%	9.0%	34.9%	5.1%
BRANTLEY	1,173	146	430	56	474	67	Mondale	12.4%	36.7%	4.8%	40.4%	5.7%
BROOKS	1,464	184	370	266	501	143	Mondale	12.6%	25.3%	18.2%	34.2%	9.8%
BRYAN	1,370	188	369	366	345	102	Hart	13.7%	26.9%	26.7%	25.2%	7.4%
BULLOCH	3,164	609	948	675	864	68	Hart	19.2%	30.0%	21.3%	27.3%	2.1%
BURKE	2,918	300	526	1,355	546	191	J. Jackson	10.3%	18.0%	46.4%	18.7%	6.5%
BUTTS	1,801	329	523	331	559	59	Mondale	18.3%	29.0%	18.4%	31.0%	3.3%
CALHOUN	1,035	108	190	407	305	25	J. Jackson	10.4%	18.4%	39.3%	29.5%	2.4%
CAMDEN	1,859	130	365	807	509	48	J. Jackson	7.0%	19.6%	43.4%	27.4%	2.6%
CANDLER	885	142	264	197	247	35	Hart	16.0%	29.8%	22.3%	27.9%	4.0%
CARROLL	6,620	1,574	2,471	364	1,963	248	Hart	23.8%	37.3%	5.5%	29.7%	3.7%
CATOOSA	2,286	523	867	28	819	49	Hart	22.9%	37.9%	1.2%	35.8%	2.1%
CHARLTON	916	142	187	227	295	65	Mondale	15.5%	20.4%	24.8%	32.2%	7.1%
CHATHAM	34,880	3,964	7,396	14,391	8,359	770	J. Jackson	11.4%	21.2%	41.3%	24.0%	2.2%
CHATTAHOOCHEE	367	36	85	78	136	32	Mondale	9.8%	23.2%	21.3%	37.1%	8.7%
CHATTOOGA	2,078	339	849	117	707	66	Hart	16.3%	40.9%	5.6%	34.0%	3.2%
CHEROKEE	5,482	1,421	2,009	117	1,696	239	Hart	25.9%	36.6%	2.1%	30.9%	4.4%
CLARKE	9,416	1,923	2,767	1,997	2,267	462	Hart	20.4%	29.4%	21.2%	24.1%	4.9%
CLAY	542	55	103	219	154	11	J. Jackson	10.1%	19.0%	40.4%	28.4%	2.0%
CLAYTON	13,261	3,449	4,596	663	4,227	326	Hart	26.0%	34.7%	5.0%	31.9%	2.5%
CLINCH	544	60	154	62	228	40	Mondale	11.0%	28.3%	11.4%	41.9%	7.4%
COBB	30,841	8,567	11,038	1,377	8,938	921	Hart	27.8%	35.8%	4.5%	29.0%	3.0%
COFFEE	2,381	616	599	451	617	98	Mondale	25.9%	25.2%	18.9%	25.9%	4.1%
COLQUITT	3,622	762	1,174	302	1,238	146	Mondale	21.0%	32.4%	8.3%	34.2%	4.0%
COLUMBIA	3,636	865	1,388	420	889	74	Hart	23.8%	38.2%	11.6%	24.4%	2.0%
COOK	1,484	203	495	251	502	33	Mondale	13.7%	33.4%	16.9%	33.8%	2.2%
COWETA	3,885	792	1,307	445	1,222	119	Hart	20.4%	33.6%	11.5%	31.5%	3.1%
CRAWFORD	1,398	186	305	440	351	116	J. Jackson	13.3%	21.8%	31.5%	25.1%	8.3%
CRISP	1,627	359	331	311	533	93	Mondale	22.1%	20.3%	19.1%	32.8%	5.7%
DADE	1,232	240	534	18	384	56	Hart	19.5%	43.3%	1.5%	31.2%	4.5%
DAWSON	659	113	303	9	220	14	Hart	17.1%	46.0%	1.4%	33.4%	2.1%
DECATUR	2,751	367	553	702	775	354	Mondale	13.3%	20.1%	25.5%	28.2%	12.9%
DE KALB	62,475	12,674	17,245	12,563	17,917	2,076	Mondale	20.3%	27.6%	20.1%	28.7%	3.3%
DODGE	2,974	466	1,135	358	885	130	Hart	15.7%	38.2%	12.0%	29.8%	4.4%
DOOLY	1,819	232	396	537	481	173	J. Jackson	12.8%	21.8%	29.5%	26.4%	9.5%
DOUGHERTY	13,847	2,322	2,573	4,663	4,130	159	J. Jackson	16.8%	18.6%	33.7%	29.8%	1.1%
DOUGLAS	5,946	1,359	2,161	331	1,852	243	Hart	22.9%	36.3%	5.6%	31.1%	4.1%
EARLY	1,532	283	314	477	426	32	J. Jackson	18.5%	20.5%	31.1%	27.8%	2.1%
ECHOLS	241	28	78	30	92	13	Mondale	11.6%	32.4%	12.4%	38.2%	5.4%

GEORGIA DEMOCRATIC

1984

County	Total Vote	Glenn	Hart	J. Jackson	Mondale	Other	Winner	Percentage of Total Vote Glenn	Hart	J. Jackson	Mondale	Other
EFFINGHAM	2,151	414	674	339	617	107	Hart	19.2%	31.3%	15.8%	28.7%	5.0%
ELBERT	2,297	592	661	301	709	34	Mondale	25.8%	28.8%	13.1%	30.9%	1.5%
EMANUEL	2,131	311	711	466	594	49	Hart	14.6%	33.4%	21.9%	27.9%	2.3%
EVANS	1,169	294	240	318	271	46	J. Jackson	25.1%	20.5%	27.2%	23.2%	3.9%
FANNIN	1,075	117	438	15	459	46	Mondale	10.9%	40.7%	1.4%	42.7%	4.3%
FAYETTE	5,588	1,867	2,005	98	1,392	226	Hart	33.4%	35.9%	1.8%	24.9%	4.0%
FLOYD	11,758	2,818	3,733	649	4,140	418	Mondale	24.0%	31.7%	5.5%	35.2%	3.6%
FORSYTH	2,711	568	1,047	34	1,003	59	Hart	21.0%	38.6%	1.3%	37.0%	2.2%
FRANKLIN	1,599	244	561	66	692	36	Mondale	15.3%	35.1%	4.1%	43.3%	2.3%
FULTON	100,432	12,941	18,385	36,070	30,699	2,337	J. Jackson	12.9%	18.3%	35.9%	30.6%	2.3%
GILMER	1,067	163	463	19	402	20	Hart	15.3%	43.4%	1.8%	37.7%	1.9%
GLASCOCK	227	33	107	9	76	2	Hart	14.5%	47.1%	4.0%	33.5%	0.9%
GLYNN	6,378	962	1,670	1,373	2,219	154	Mondale	15.1%	26.2%	21.5%	34.8%	2.4%
GORDON	4,101	865	1,587	105	1,366	178	Hart	21.1%	38.7%	2.6%	33.3%	4.3%
GRADY	1,994	243	604	395	610	142	Mondale	12.2%	30.3%	19.8%	30.6%	7.1%
GREENE	1,826	235	398	476	675	42	Mondale	12.9%	21.8%	26.1%	37.0%	2.3%
GWINNETT	16,225	4,087	6,169	358	4,766	845	Hart	25.2%	38.0%	2.2%	29.4%	5.2%
HABERSHAM	3,321	652	1,462	42	999	166	Hart	19.6%	44.0%	1.3%	30.1%	5.0%
HALL	9,151	1,847	3,230	724	2,941	409	Hart	20.2%	35.3%	7.9%	32.1%	4.5%
HANCOCK	1,280	58	90	851	201	80	J. Jackson	4.5%	7.0%	66.5%	15.7%	6.3%
HARALSON	2,658	479	1,097	67	889	126	Hart	18.0%	41.3%	2.5%	33.4%	4.7%
HARRIS	2,542	449	685	477	808	123	Mondale	17.7%	26.9%	18.8%	31.8%	4.8%
HART	2,068	283	745	255	679	106	Hart	13.7%	36.0%	12.3%	32.8%	5.1%
HEARD	787	125	318	46	262	36	Hart	15.9%	40.4%	5.8%	33.3%	4.6%
HENRY	4,147	1,002	1,273	374	1,362	136	Mondale	24.2%	30.7%	9.0%	32.8%	3.3%
HOUSTON	11,359	2,895	3,440	1,714	2,861	449	Hart	25.5%	30.3%	15.1%	25.2%	4.0%
IRWIN	867	201	232	118	277	39	Mondale	23.2%	26.8%	13.6%	31.9%	4.5%
JACKSON	2,671	511	1,043	124	929	64	Hart	19.1%	39.0%	4.6%	34.8%	2.4%
JASPER	1,271	193	335	291	386	66	Mondale	15.2%	26.4%	22.9%	30.4%	5.2%
JEFF DAVIS	1,042	208	294	171	325	44	Mondale	20.0%	28.2%	16.4%	31.2%	4.2%
JEFFERSON	2,383	314	537	804	607	121	J. Jackson	13.2%	22.5%	33.7%	25.5%	5.1%
JENKINS	948	112	238	305	226	67	J. Jackson	11.8%	25.1%	32.2%	23.8%	7.1%
JOHNSON	1,018	131	317	231	313	26	Hart	12.9%	31.1%	22.7%	30.7%	2.6%
JONES	3,065	453	747	881	823	161	J. Jackson	14.8%	24.4%	28.7%	26.9%	5.3%
LAMAR	1,665	313	465	225	546	116	Mondale	18.8%	27.9%	13.5%	32.8%	7.0%
LANIER	436	56	115	88	140	37	Mondale	12.8%	26.4%	20.2%	32.1%	8.5%
LAURENS	4,622	759	1,240	1,262	1,251	110	J. Jackson	16.4%	26.8%	27.3%	27.1%	2.4%
LEE	1,421	255	383	339	422	22	Mondale	17.9%	27.0%	23.9%	29.7%	1.5%
LIBERTY	2,746	208	498	1,468	507	65	J. Jackson	7.6%	18.1%	53.5%	18.5%	2.4%
LINCOLN	880	97	305	184	270	24	Hart	11.0%	34.7%	20.9%	30.7%	2.7%
LONG	714	102	220	158	205	29	Hart	14.3%	30.8%	22.1%	28.7%	4.1%
LOWNDES	5,617	739	1,272	1,639	1,785	182	Mondale	13.2%	22.6%	29.2%	31.8%	3.2%
LUMPKIN	1,342	244	595	35	422	46	Hart	18.2%	44.3%	2.6%	31.4%	3.4%
MCDUFFIE	1,423	275	418	286	361	83	Hart	19.3%	29.4%	20.1%	25.4%	5.8%
MCINTOSH	1,754	154	340	734	416	110	J. Jackson	8.8%	19.4%	41.8%	23.7%	6.3%
MACON	2,704	438	377	1,031	622	236	J. Jackson	16.2%	13.9%	38.1%	23.0%	8.7%
MADISON	1,742	391	604	134	548	65	Hart	22.4%	34.7%	7.7%	31.5%	3.7%
MARION	834	89	187	208	308	42	Mondale	10.7%	22.4%	24.9%	36.9%	5.0%
MERIWETHER	2,770	479	800	426	997	68	Mondale	17.3%	28.9%	15.4%	36.0%	2.5%
MILLER	557	73	214	57	192	21	Hart	13.1%	38.4%	10.2%	34.5%	3.8%

GEORGIA DEMOCRATIC

1984

County	Total Vote	Glenn	Hart	J. Jackson	Mondale	Other	Winner	Percentage of Total Vote Glenn	Hart	J. Jackson	Mondale	Other
MITCHELL	2,900	520	675	833	836	36	Mondale	17.9%	23.3%	28.7%	28.8%	1.2%
MONROE	2,265	388	575	705	547	50	J. Jackson	17.1%	25.4%	31.1%	24.2%	2.2%
MONTGOMERY	773	162	188	210	189	24	J. Jackson	21.0%	24.3%	27.2%	24.5%	3.1%
MORGAN	2,119	471	622	316	637	73	Mondale	22.2%	29.4%	14.9%	30.1%	3.4%
MURRAY	1,307	211	472	17	545	62	Mondale	16.1%	36.1%	1.3%	41.7%	4.7%
MUSCOGEE	21,029	2,995	4,962	4,738	7,908	426	Mondale	14.2%	23.6%	22.5%	37.6%	2.0%
NEWTON	3,590	823	1,137	314	1,197	119	Mondale	22.9%	31.7%	8.7%	33.3%	3.3%
OCONEE	1,897	528	728	94	476	71	Hart	27.8%	38.4%	5.0%	25.1%	3.7%
OGLETHORPE	1,281	311	395	150	392	33	Hart	24.3%	30.8%	11.7%	30.6%	2.6%
PAULDING	2,713	525	1,054	75	949	110	Hart	19.4%	38.8%	2.8%	35.0%	4.1%
PEACH	3,724	491	817	1,352	834	230	J. Jackson	13.2%	21.9%	36.3%	22.4%	6.2%
PICKENS	1,009	195	403	13	368	30	Hart	19.3%	39.9%	1.3%	36.5%	3.0%
PIERCE	1,306	249	406	128	479	44	Mondale	19.1%	31.1%	9.8%	36.7%	3.4%
PIKE	1,354	287	440	194	397	36	Hart	21.2%	32.5%	14.3%	29.3%	2.7%
POLK	3,751	742	1,251	241	1,374	143	Mondale	19.8%	33.4%	6.4%	36.6%	3.8%
PULASKI	1,394	189	319	191	614	81	Mondale	13.6%	22.9%	13.7%	44.0%	5.8%
PUTNAM	1,289	217	369	328	318	57	Hart	16.8%	28.6%	25.4%	24.7%	4.4%
QUITMAN	400	42	90	156	93	19	J. Jackson	10.5%	22.5%	39.0%	23.3%	4.8%
RABUN	1,398	236	659	17	421	65	Hart	16.9%	47.1%	1.2%	30.1%	4.6%
RANDOLPH	1,530	195	239	557	504	35	J. Jackson	12.7%	15.6%	36.4%	32.9%	2.3%
RICHMOND	17,638	2,660	4,881	3,969	5,859	269	Mondale	15.1%	27.7%	22.5%	33.2%	1.5%
ROCKDALE	4,580	1,245	1,535	215	1,417	168	Hart	27.2%	33.5%	4.7%	30.9%	3.7%
SCHLEY	515	90	110	118	154	43	Mondale	17.5%	21.4%	22.9%	29.9%	8.3%
SCREVEN	1,828	221	407	716	372	112	J. Jackson	12.1%	22.3%	39.2%	20.4%	6.1%
SEMINOLE	978	109	253	173	413	30	Mondale	11.1%	25.9%	17.7%	42.2%	3.1%
SPALDING	5,476	1,190	1,725	676	1,684	201	Hart	21.7%	31.5%	12.3%	30.8%	3.7%
STEPHENS	1,994	362	684	130	741	77	Mondale	18.2%	34.3%	6.5%	37.2%	3.9%
STEWART	1,497	173	260	486	464	114	J. Jackson	11.6%	17.4%	32.5%	31.0%	7.6%
SUMTER	3,509	643	585	756	1,320	205	Mondale	18.3%	16.7%	21.5%	37.6%	5.8%
TALBOT	1,251	136	237	404	425	49	Mondale	10.9%	18.9%	32.3%	34.0%	3.9%
TALIAFERRO	400	32	75	162	122	9	J. Jackson	8.0%	18.8%	40.5%	30.5%	2.3%
TATTNALL	1,744	318	515	273	566	72	Mondale	18.2%	29.5%	15.7%	32.5%	4.1%
TAYLOR	1,385	154	332	370	481	48	Mondale	11.1%	24.0%	26.7%	34.7%	3.5%
TELFAIR	1,477	262	420	313	416	66	Hart	17.7%	28.4%	21.2%	28.2%	4.5%
TERRELL	1,426	237	220	455	362	152	J. Jackson	16.6%	15.4%	31.9%	25.4%	10.7%
THOMAS	4,689	547	1,145	1,258	1,536	203	Mondale	11.7%	24.4%	26.8%	32.8%	4.3%
TIFT	2,709	783	621	377	861	67	Mondale	28.9%	22.9%	13.9%	31.8%	2.5%
TOOMBS	1,875	413	570	330	495	67	Hart	22.0%	30.4%	17.6%	26.4%	3.6%
TOWNS	756	88	387	22	233	26	Hart	11.6%	51.2%	2.9%	30.8%	3.4%
TREUTLEN	808	97	232	170	280	29	Mondale	12.0%	28.7%	21.0%	34.7%	3.6%
TROUP	4,544	806	1,376	780	1,506	76	Mondale	17.7%	30.3%	17.2%	33.1%	1.7%
TURNER	1,312	223	384	281	401	23	Mondale	17.0%	29.3%	21.4%	30.6%	1.8%
TWIGGS	1,862	151	339	847	501	24	J. Jackson	8.1%	18.2%	45.5%	26.9%	1.3%
UNION	1,080	152	446	8	440	34	Hart	14.1%	41.3%	0.7%	40.7%	3.1%
UPSON	2,980	689	728	555	960	48	Mondale	23.1%	24.4%	18.6%	32.2%	1.6%
WALKER	3,626	888	1,367	146	1,151	74	Hart	24.5%	37.7%	4.0%	31.7%	2.0%
WALTON	2,931	561	1,010	261	1,002	97	Hart	19.1%	34.5%	8.9%	34.2%	3.3%
WARE	3,939	582	1,049	565	1,521	222	Mondale	14.8%	26.6%	14.3%	38.6%	5.6%
WARREN	909	114	235	282	203	75	J. Jackson	12.5%	25.9%	31.0%	22.3%	8.3%
WASHINGTON	3,115	323	631	1,218	631	312	J. Jackson	10.4%	20.3%	39.1%	20.3%	10.0%

GEORGIA DEMOCRATIC

1984

County	Total Vote	Glenn	Hart	J. Jackson	Mondale	Other	Winner	Percentage of Total Vote: Glenn	Hart	J. Jackson	Mondale	Other
WAYNE	2,568	583	784	268	869	64	Mondale	22.7%	30.5%	10.4%	33.8%	2.5%
WEBSTER	481	61	82	114	178	46	Mondale	12.7%	17.0%	23.7%	37.0%	9.6%
WHEELER	714	123	228	188	163	12	Hart	17.2%	31.9%	26.3%	22.8%	1.7%
WHITE	1,380	315	547	38	429	51	Hart	22.8%	39.6%	2.8%	31.1%	3.7%
WHITFIELD	4,186	886	1,354	221	1,613	112	Mondale	21.2%	32.3%	5.3%	38.5%	2.7%
WILCOX	1,166	194	326	189	426	31	Mondale	16.6%	28.0%	16.2%	36.5%	2.7%
WILKES	1,697	258	466	336	508	129	Mondale	15.2%	27.5%	19.8%	29.9%	7.6%
WILKINSON	2,205	236	494	709	700	66	J. Jackson	10.7%	22.4%	32.2%	31.7%	3.0%
WORTH	2,228	502	659	339	707	21	Mondale	22.5%	29.6%	15.2%	31.7%	0.9%
TOTAL	684,541	122,744	186,903	143,730	208,588	22,576	Mondale	17.9%	27.3%	21.0%	30.5%	3.3%

GEORGIA DEMOCRATIC

1988

County	Total Vote	Dukakis	Gore	J. Jackson	Other	Winner	Percentage of Total Vote: Dukakis	Gore	J. Jackson	Other
APPLING	1,398	121	518	470	289	Gore	8.7%	37.1%	33.6%	20.7%
ATKINSON	747	59	273	285	130	J. Jackson	7.9%	36.5%	38.2%	17.4%
BACON	456	61	202	77	116	Gore	13.4%	44.3%	16.9%	25.4%
BAKER	624	22	136	366	100	J. Jackson	3.5%	21.8%	58.7%	16.0%
BALDWIN	3,854	500	1,117	1,729	508	J. Jackson	13.0%	29.0%	44.9%	13.2%
BANKS	960	179	538	52	191	Gore	18.6%	56.0%	5.4%	19.9%
BARROW	2,129	317	1,087	396	329	Gore	14.9%	51.1%	18.6%	15.5%
BARTOW	3,543	534	1,798	675	536	Gore	15.1%	50.7%	19.1%	15.1%
BEN HILL	1,425	148	477	574	226	J. Jackson	10.4%	33.5%	40.3%	15.9%
BERRIEN	1,134	136	518	203	277	Gore	12.0%	45.7%	17.9%	24.4%
BIBB	23,274	2,576	7,104	11,276	2,318	J. Jackson	11.1%	30.5%	48.4%	10.0%
BLECKLEY	1,777	210	933	250	384	Gore	11.8%	52.5%	14.1%	21.6%
BRANTLEY	944	163	486	109	186	Gore	17.3%	51.5%	11.5%	19.7%
BROOKS	1,701	137	524	648	392	J. Jackson	8.1%	30.8%	38.1%	23.0%
BRYAN	1,367	212	335	504	316	J. Jackson	15.5%	24.5%	36.9%	23.1%
BULLOCH	3,076	384	1,032	1,101	559	J. Jackson	12.5%	33.6%	35.8%	18.2%
BURKE	2,232	125	368	1,484	255	J. Jackson	5.6%	16.5%	66.5%	11.4%
BUTTS	1,660	169	629	689	173	J. Jackson	10.2%	37.9%	41.5%	10.4%
CALHOUN	930	45	164	635	86	J. Jackson	4.8%	17.6%	68.3%	9.2%
CAMDEN	1,967	293	409	870	395	J. Jackson	14.9%	20.8%	44.2%	20.1%
CANDLER	895	112	232	324	227	J. Jackson	12.5%	25.9%	36.2%	25.4%
CARROLL	5,574	919	2,818	1,142	695	Gore	16.5%	50.6%	20.5%	12.5%
CATOOSA	2,522	292	1,832	129	269	Gore	11.6%	72.6%	5.1%	10.7%
CHARLTON	750	113	222	279	136	J. Jackson	15.1%	29.6%	37.2%	18.1%
CHATHAM	24,682	4,164	3,316	14,498	2,704	J. Jackson	16.9%	13.4%	58.7%	11.0%

GEORGIA DEMOCRATIC

1988

County	Total Vote	Dukakis	Gore	J. Jackson	Other	Winner	Percentage of Total Vote Dukakis	Gore	J. Jackson	Other
CHATTAHOOCHEE	323	35	81	151	56	J. Jackson	10.8%	25.1%	46.7%	17.3%
CHATTOOGA	1,792	236	1,091	218	247	Gore	13.2%	60.9%	12.2%	13.8%
CHEROKEE	4,082	909	2,180	370	623	Gore	22.3%	53.4%	9.1%	15.3%
CLARKE	8,326	2,216	2,189	2,814	1,107	J. Jackson	26.6%	26.3%	33.8%	13.3%
CLAY	594	19	121	415	39	J. Jackson	3.2%	20.4%	69.9%	6.6%
CLAYTON	13,623	2,866	5,921	2,874	1,962	Gore	21.0%	43.5%	21.1%	14.4%
CLINCH	458	63	174	124	97	Gore	13.8%	38.0%	27.1%	21.2%
COBB	27,992	7,160	12,890	4,443	3,499	Gore	25.6%	46.0%	15.9%	12.5%
COFFEE	2,312	220	819	943	330	J. Jackson	9.5%	35.4%	40.8%	14.3%
COLQUITT	4,091	317	2,049	916	809	Gore	7.7%	50.1%	22.4%	19.8%
COLUMBIA	3,958	664	1,674	870	750	Gore	16.8%	42.3%	22.0%	18.9%
COOK	1,155	77	412	420	246	J. Jackson	6.7%	35.7%	36.4%	21.3%
COWETA	4,094	716	1,733	1,106	539	Gore	17.5%	42.3%	27.0%	13.2%
CRAWFORD	1,350	101	475	571	203	J. Jackson	7.5%	35.2%	42.3%	15.0%
CRISP	1,573	122	627	569	255	Gore	7.8%	39.9%	36.2%	16.2%
DADE	702	78	477	49	98	Gore	11.1%	67.9%	7.0%	14.0%
DAWSON	634	95	383	37	119	Gore	15.0%	60.4%	5.8%	18.8%
DECATUR	2,306	189	508	1,211	398	J. Jackson	8.2%	22.0%	52.5%	17.3%
DE KALB	64,835	14,931	15,175	29,370	5,359	J. Jackson	23.0%	23.4%	45.3%	8.3%
DODGE	2,105	163	1,041	478	423	Gore	7.7%	49.5%	22.7%	20.1%
DOOLY	1,734	72	510	858	294	J. Jackson	4.2%	29.4%	49.5%	17.0%
DOUGHERTY	12,690	788	2,648	8,197	1,057	J. Jackson	6.2%	20.9%	64.6%	8.3%
DOUGLAS	4,655	931	2,184	820	720	Gore	20.0%	46.9%	17.6%	15.5%
EARLY	1,480	86	480	759	155	J. Jackson	5.8%	32.4%	51.3%	10.5%
ECHOLS	186	32	78	30	46	Gore	17.2%	41.9%	16.1%	24.7%
EFFINGHAM	1,757	268	471	572	446	J. Jackson	15.3%	26.8%	32.6%	25.4%
ELBERT	1,800	279	724	567	230	Gore	15.5%	40.2%	31.5%	12.8%
EMANUEL	1,865	177	717	750	221	J. Jackson	9.5%	38.4%	40.2%	11.8%
EVANS	917	97	287	332	201	J. Jackson	10.6%	31.3%	36.2%	21.9%
FANNIN	1,412	251	819	73	269	Gore	17.8%	58.0%	5.2%	19.1%
FAYETTE	4,119	985	2,058	457	619	Gore	23.9%	50.0%	11.1%	15.0%
FLOYD	10,093	1,506	5,334	1,867	1,386	Gore	14.9%	52.8%	18.5%	13.7%
FORSYTH	2,567	466	1,539	117	445	Gore	18.2%	60.0%	4.6%	17.3%
FRANKLIN	1,232	258	559	161	254	Gore	20.9%	45.4%	13.1%	20.6%
FULTON	90,939	13,563	13,244	59,413	4,719	J. Jackson	14.9%	14.6%	65.3%	5.2%
GILMER	1,393	220	830	93	250	Gore	15.8%	59.6%	6.7%	17.9%
GLASCOCK	182	31	85	20	46	Gore	17.0%	46.7%	11.0%	25.3%
GLYNN	5,722	1,161	1,116	2,782	663	J. Jackson	20.3%	19.5%	48.6%	11.6%
GORDON	2,458	390	1,479	263	326	Gore	15.9%	60.2%	10.7%	13.3%
GRADY	2,072	268	530	805	469	J. Jackson	12.9%	25.6%	38.9%	22.6%
GREENE	1,861	171	513	1,019	158	J. Jackson	9.2%	27.6%	54.8%	8.5%
GWINNETT	17,645	4,801	8,197	1,984	2,663	Gore	27.2%	46.5%	11.2%	15.1%
HABERSHAM	3,316	681	1,740	255	640	Gore	20.5%	52.5%	7.7%	19.3%
HALL	10,813	1,874	5,585	1,385	1,969	Gore	17.3%	51.7%	12.8%	18.2%
HANCOCK	1,676	29	136	1,336	175	J. Jackson	1.7%	8.1%	79.7%	10.4%
HARALSON	1,928	298	1,204	180	246	Gore	15.5%	62.4%	9.3%	12.8%
HARRIS	1,857	242	570	678	367	J. Jackson	13.0%	30.7%	36.5%	19.8%
HART	1,620	334	601	357	328	Gore	20.6%	37.1%	22.0%	20.2%
HEARD	795	108	402	161	124	Gore	13.6%	50.6%	20.3%	15.6%
HENRY	4,220	681	2,014	978	547	Gore	16.1%	47.7%	23.2%	13.0%

GEORGIA DEMOCRATIC

1988

County	Total Vote	Dukakis	Gore	J. Jackson	Other	Winner	Percentage of Total Vote: Dukakis	Gore	J. Jackson	Other
HOUSTON	10,670	1,657	4,689	2,803	1,521	Gore	15.5%	43.9%	26.3%	14.3%
IRWIN	884	68	343	270	203	Gore	7.7%	38.8%	30.5%	23.0%
JACKSON	2,399	410	1,243	373	373	Gore	17.1%	51.8%	15.5%	15.5%
JASPER	1,196	125	371	533	167	J. Jackson	10.5%	31.0%	44.6%	14.0%
JEFF DAVIS	894	108	314	277	195	Gore	12.1%	35.1%	31.0%	21.8%
JEFFERSON	2,259	132	483	1,258	386	J. Jackson	5.8%	21.4%	55.7%	17.1%
JENKINS	727	50	201	340	136	J. Jackson	6.9%	27.6%	46.8%	18.7%
JOHNSON	841	67	386	280	108	Gore	8.0%	45.9%	33.3%	12.8%
JONES	2,820	312	997	1,086	425	J. Jackson	11.1%	35.4%	38.5%	15.1%
LAMAR	2,309	299	817	856	337	J. Jackson	12.9%	35.4%	37.1%	14.6%
LANIER	503	35	194	176	98	Gore	7.0%	38.6%	35.0%	19.5%
LAURENS	4,270	376	1,567	1,850	477	J. Jackson	8.8%	36.7%	43.3%	11.2%
LEE	1,317	118	450	548	201	J. Jackson	9.0%	34.2%	41.6%	15.3%
LIBERTY	2,550	237	380	1,601	332	J. Jackson	9.3%	14.9%	62.8%	13.0%
LINCOLN	822	54	198	464	106	J. Jackson	6.6%	24.1%	56.4%	12.9%
LONG	576	69	155	198	154	J. Jackson	12.0%	26.9%	34.4%	26.7%
LOWNDES	4,917	635	1,520	2,147	615	J. Jackson	12.9%	30.9%	43.7%	12.5%
LUMPKIN	1,274	233	716	135	190	Gore	18.3%	56.2%	10.6%	14.9%
MCDUFFIE	1,424	141	397	667	219	J. Jackson	9.9%	27.9%	46.8%	15.4%
MCINTOSH	1,352	115	204	839	194	J. Jackson	8.5%	15.1%	62.1%	14.3%
MACON	2,147	115	435	1,327	270	J. Jackson	5.4%	20.3%	61.8%	12.6%
MADISON	1,404	266	658	245	235	Gore	18.9%	46.9%	17.5%	16.7%
MARION	944	89	210	505	140	J. Jackson	9.4%	22.2%	53.5%	14.8%
MERIWETHER	2,804	288	940	1,321	255	J. Jackson	10.3%	33.5%	47.1%	9.1%
MILLER	514	60	212	118	124	Gore	11.7%	41.2%	23.0%	24.1%
MITCHELL	2,766	140	751	1,516	359	J. Jackson	5.1%	27.2%	54.8%	13.0%
MONROE	2,235	232	831	907	265	J. Jackson	10.4%	37.2%	40.6%	11.9%
MONTGOMERY	675	60	276	247	92	Gore	8.9%	40.9%	36.6%	13.6%
MORGAN	1,648	180	681	652	135	Gore	10.9%	41.3%	39.6%	8.2%
MURRAY	1,367	183	954	59	171	Gore	13.4%	69.8%	4.3%	12.5%
MUSCOGEE	17,886	2,429	4,276	9,001	2,180	J. Jackson	13.6%	23.9%	50.3%	12.2%
NEWTON	3,182	525	1,424	837	396	Gore	16.5%	44.8%	26.3%	12.4%
OCONEE	1,684	382	818	231	253	Gore	22.7%	48.6%	13.7%	15.0%
OGLETHORPE	1,104	198	424	340	142	Gore	17.9%	38.4%	30.8%	12.9%
PAULDING	2,561	398	1,525	235	403	Gore	15.5%	59.5%	9.2%	15.7%
PEACH	3,306	229	876	1,784	417	J. Jackson	6.9%	26.5%	54.0%	12.6%
PICKENS	1,260	193	643	70	354	Gore	15.3%	51.0%	5.6%	28.1%
PIERCE	1,892	268	728	325	571	Gore	14.2%	38.5%	17.2%	30.2%
PIKE	1,188	145	466	429	148	Gore	12.2%	39.2%	36.1%	12.5%
POLK	2,945	415	1,662	514	354	Gore	14.1%	56.4%	17.5%	12.0%
PULASKI	1,606	150	699	486	271	Gore	9.3%	43.5%	30.3%	16.9%
PUTNAM	1,686	185	658	548	295	Gore	11.0%	39.0%	32.5%	17.5%
QUITMAN	426	22	74	283	47	J. Jackson	5.2%	17.4%	66.4%	11.0%
RABUN	1,100	271	491	85	253	Gore	24.6%	44.6%	7.7%	23.0%
RANDOLPH	1,266	40	245	861	120	J. Jackson	3.2%	19.4%	68.0%	9.5%
RICHMOND	15,301	1,542	3,333	8,999	1,427	J. Jackson	10.1%	21.8%	58.8%	9.3%
ROCKDALE	3,802	895	1,765	566	576	Gore	23.5%	46.4%	14.9%	15.1%
SCHLEY	452	51	118	217	66	J. Jackson	11.3%	26.1%	48.0%	14.6%
SCREVEN	1,394	136	316	676	266	J. Jackson	9.8%	22.7%	48.5%	19.1%
SEMINOLE	1,013	70	296	459	188	J. Jackson	6.9%	29.2%	45.3%	18.6%

GEORGIA DEMOCRATIC

1988

County	Total Vote	Dukakis	Gore	J. Jackson	Other	Winner	Percentage of Total Vote Dukakis	Gore	J. Jackson	Other
SPALDING	4,931	602	2,028	1,644	657	Gore	12.2%	41.1%	33.3%	13.3%
STEPHENS	1,675	350	663	285	377	Gore	20.9%	39.6%	17.0%	22.5%
STEWART	949	76	136	562	175	J. Jackson	8.0%	14.3%	59.2%	18.4%
SUMTER	3,920	565	980	1,836	539	J. Jackson	14.4%	25.0%	46.8%	13.8%
TALBOT	1,006	60	201	632	113	J. Jackson	6.0%	20.0%	62.8%	11.2%
TALIAFERRO	420	21	95	274	30	J. Jackson	5.0%	22.6%	65.2%	7.1%
TATTNALL	1,316	174	479	354	309	Gore	13.2%	36.4%	26.9%	23.5%
TAYLOR	1,250	85	335	668	162	J. Jackson	6.8%	26.8%	53.4%	13.0%
TELFAIR	1,436	87	605	542	202	Gore	6.1%	42.1%	37.7%	14.1%
TERRELL	1,441	51	268	900	222	J. Jackson	3.5%	18.6%	62.5%	15.4%
THOMAS	3,588	384	658	1,858	688	J. Jackson	10.7%	18.3%	51.8%	19.2%
TIFT	2,571	247	986	922	416	Gore	9.6%	38.4%	35.9%	16.2%
TOOMBS	1,476	186	590	447	253	Gore	12.6%	40.0%	30.3%	17.1%
TOWNS	658	140	371	36	111	Gore	21.3%	56.4%	5.5%	16.9%
TREUTLEN	736	90	246	268	132	J. Jackson	12.2%	33.4%	36.4%	17.9%
TROUP	4,389	655	1,703	1,523	508	Gore	14.9%	38.8%	34.7%	11.6%
TURNER	1,025	60	367	398	200	J. Jackson	5.9%	35.8%	38.8%	19.5%
TWIGGS	1,646	116	346	1,004	180	J. Jackson	7.0%	21.0%	61.0%	10.9%
UNION	1,065	187	651	60	167	Gore	17.6%	61.1%	5.6%	15.7%
UPSON	2,899	346	1,057	1,153	343	J. Jackson	11.9%	36.5%	39.8%	11.8%
WALKER	3,595	392	2,442	360	401	Gore	10.9%	67.9%	10.0%	11.2%
WALTON	2,906	497	1,365	589	455	Gore	17.1%	47.0%	20.3%	15.7%
WARE	3,273	411	1,316	1,118	428	Gore	12.6%	40.2%	34.2%	13.1%
WARREN	952	45	221	529	157	J. Jackson	4.7%	23.2%	55.6%	16.5%
WASHINGTON	2,238	134	617	1,119	368	J. Jackson	6.0%	27.6%	50.0%	16.4%
WAYNE	2,101	301	707	528	565	Gore	14.3%	33.7%	25.1%	26.9%
WEBSTER	420	23	91	233	73	J. Jackson	5.5%	21.7%	55.5%	17.4%
WHEELER	393	15	159	177	42	J. Jackson	3.8%	40.5%	45.0%	10.7%
WHITE	1,326	225	745	118	238	Gore	17.0%	56.2%	8.9%	17.9%
WHITFIELD	4,455	635	2,647	520	653	Gore	14.3%	59.4%	11.7%	14.7%
WILCOX	1,143	58	537	389	159	Gore	5.1%	47.0%	34.0%	13.9%
WILKES	1,392	120	376	685	211	J. Jackson	8.6%	27.0%	49.2%	15.2%
WILKINSON	1,739	115	495	921	208	J. Jackson	6.6%	28.5%	53.0%	12.0%
WORTH	1,930	112	855	652	311	Gore	5.8%	44.3%	33.8%	16.1%
TOTAL	622,752	97,179	201,490	247,831	76,252	J. Jackson	15.6%	32.4%	39.8%	12.2%

GEORGIA REPUBLICAN

1988

County	Total Vote	Bush	Dole	Robertson	Other	Winner	Percentage of Total Vote: Bush	Dole	Robertson	Other
APPLING	695	362	106	206	21	Bush	52.1%	15.3%	29.6%	3.0%
ATKINSON	205	103	47	51	4	Bush	50.2%	22.9%	24.9%	2.0%
BACON	356	148	62	130	16	Bush	41.6%	17.4%	36.5%	4.5%
BAKER	162	103	30	21	8	Bush	63.6%	18.5%	13.0%	4.9%
BALDWIN	1,938	1,093	515	253	77	Bush	56.4%	26.6%	13.1%	4.0%
BANKS	505	262	130	90	23	Bush	51.9%	25.7%	17.8%	4.6%
BARROW	1,516	759	325	348	84	Bush	50.1%	21.4%	23.0%	5.5%
BARTOW	2,158	1,029	438	578	113	Bush	47.7%	20.3%	26.8%	5.2%
BEN HILL	567	297	106	141	23	Bush	52.4%	18.7%	24.9%	4.1%
BERRIEN	496	246	139	92	19	Bush	49.6%	28.0%	18.5%	3.8%
BIBB	11,137	5,096	3,109	2,519	413	Bush	45.8%	27.9%	22.6%	3.7%
BLECKLEY	783	345	245	141	52	Bush	44.1%	31.3%	18.0%	6.6%
BRANTLEY	411	231	58	117	5	Bush	56.2%	14.1%	28.5%	1.2%
BROOKS	871	498	180	172	21	Bush	57.2%	20.7%	19.7%	2.4%
BRYAN	1,097	705	196	159	37	Bush	64.3%	17.9%	14.5%	3.4%
BULLOCH	2,142	1,144	522	354	122	Bush	53.4%	24.4%	16.5%	5.7%
BURKE	921	635	157	119	10	Bush	68.9%	17.0%	12.9%	1.1%
BUTTS	672	389	148	88	47	Bush	57.9%	22.0%	13.1%	7.0%
CALHOUN	187	117	30	32	8	Bush	62.6%	16.0%	17.1%	4.3%
CAMDEN	972	521	215	186	50	Bush	53.6%	22.1%	19.1%	5.1%
CANDLER	581	322	180	48	31	Bush	55.4%	31.0%	8.3%	5.3%
CARROLL	4,027	2,163	910	726	228	Bush	53.7%	22.6%	18.0%	5.7%
CATOOSA	2,003	947	408	497	151	Bush	47.3%	20.4%	24.8%	7.5%
CHARLTON	282	174	46	46	16	Bush	61.7%	16.3%	16.3%	5.7%
CHATHAM	17,164	11,123	3,331	1,893	817	Bush	64.8%	19.4%	11.0%	4.8%
CHATTAHOOCHEE	90	60	12	13	5	Bush	66.7%	13.3%	14.4%	5.6%
CHATTOOGA	824	416	206	167	35	Bush	50.5%	25.0%	20.3%	4.2%
CHEROKEE	4,692	2,406	1,068	856	362	Bush	51.3%	22.8%	18.2%	7.7%
CLARKE	4,617	2,076	1,454	717	370	Bush	45.0%	31.5%	15.5%	8.0%
CLAY	115	79	25	4	7	Bush	68.7%	21.7%	3.5%	6.1%
CLAYTON	11,511	5,916	2,595	2,049	951	Bush	51.4%	22.5%	17.8%	8.3%
CLINCH	213	98	42	62	11	Bush	46.0%	19.7%	29.1%	5.2%
COBB	38,337	19,774	10,262	5,259	3,042	Bush	51.6%	26.8%	13.7%	7.9%
COFFEE	843	471	210	125	37	Bush	55.9%	24.9%	14.8%	4.4%
COLQUITT	2,437	1,282	529	531	95	Bush	52.6%	21.7%	21.8%	3.9%
COLUMBIA	5,801	3,495	1,077	795	434	Bush	60.2%	18.6%	13.7%	7.5%
COOK	433	235	103	72	23	Bush	54.3%	23.8%	16.6%	5.3%
COWETA	3,352	1,803	762	526	261	Bush	53.8%	22.7%	15.7%	7.8%
CRAWFORD	350	185	94	62	9	Bush	52.9%	26.9%	17.7%	2.6%
CRISP	769	444	173	130	22	Bush	57.7%	22.5%	16.9%	2.9%
DADE	568	319	114	102	33	Bush	56.2%	20.1%	18.0%	5.8%
DAWSON	590	374	127	63	26	Bush	63.4%	21.5%	10.7%	4.4%
DECATUR	1,022	680	168	130	44	Bush	66.5%	16.4%	12.7%	4.3%
DE KALB	40,544	21,774	10,849	4,711	3,210	Bush	53.7%	26.8%	11.6%	7.9%
DODGE	543	260	159	101	23	Bush	47.9%	29.3%	18.6%	4.2%
DOOLY	394	191	107	54	42	Bush	48.5%	27.2%	13.7%	10.7%
DOUGHERTY	6,184	3,855	938	1,076	315	Bush	62.3%	15.2%	17.4%	5.1%
DOUGLAS	4,628	2,413	952	942	321	Bush	52.1%	20.6%	20.4%	6.9%
EARLY	593	364	131	70	28	Bush	61.4%	22.1%	11.8%	4.7%
ECHOLS	67	39	18	7	3	Bush	58.2%	26.9%	10.4%	4.5%

GEORGIA REPUBLICAN

1988

County	Total Vote	Bush	Dole	Robertson	Other	Winner	Percentage of Total Vote Bush	Dole	Robertson	Other
EFFINGHAM	1,330	807	266	201	56	Bush	60.7%	20.0%	15.1%	4.2%
ELBERT	787	383	190	143	71	Bush	48.7%	24.1%	18.2%	9.0%
EMANUEL	912	534	166	184	28	Bush	58.6%	18.2%	20.2%	3.1%
EVANS	493	309	123	36	25	Bush	62.7%	24.9%	7.3%	5.1%
FANNIN	1,993	1,341	430	181	41	Bush	67.3%	21.6%	9.1%	2.1%
FAYETTE	6,516	3,426	1,431	1,058	601	Bush	52.6%	22.0%	16.2%	9.2%
FLOYD	5,442	2,766	1,260	1,053	363	Bush	50.8%	23.2%	19.3%	6.7%
FORSYTH	2,666	1,415	621	468	162	Bush	53.1%	23.3%	17.6%	6.1%
FRANKLIN	858	371	168	284	35	Bush	43.2%	19.6%	33.1%	4.1%
FULTON	37,637	21,426	10,043	3,525	2,643	Bush	56.9%	26.7%	9.4%	7.0%
GILMER	1,360	738	345	213	64	Bush	54.3%	25.4%	15.7%	4.7%
GLASCOCK	155	123	23	6	3	Bush	79.4%	14.8%	3.9%	1.9%
GLYNN	5,342	2,774	1,151	1,180	237	Bush	51.9%	21.5%	22.1%	4.4%
GORDON	1,670	795	386	383	106	Bush	47.6%	23.1%	22.9%	6.3%
GRADY	881	484	194	170	33	Bush	54.9%	22.0%	19.3%	3.7%
GREENE	515	325	110	59	21	Bush	63.1%	21.4%	11.5%	4.1%
GWINNETT	26,217	12,812	7,223	4,048	2,134	Bush	48.9%	27.6%	15.4%	8.1%
HABERSHAM	1,824	1,005	435	283	101	Bush	55.1%	23.8%	15.5%	5.5%
HALL	7,345	4,095	1,838	1,017	395	Bush	55.8%	25.0%	13.8%	5.4%
HANCOCK	194	139	39	12	4	Bush	71.6%	20.1%	6.2%	2.1%
HARALSON	1,199	650	273	208	68	Bush	54.2%	22.8%	17.3%	5.7%
HARRIS	1,288	765	230	237	56	Bush	59.4%	17.9%	18.4%	4.3%
HART	1,143	515	294	266	68	Bush	45.1%	25.7%	23.3%	5.9%
HEARD	320	195	58	52	15	Bush	60.9%	18.1%	16.3%	4.7%
HENRY	3,743	1,830	818	816	279	Bush	48.9%	21.9%	21.8%	7.5%
HOUSTON	6,269	2,621	1,572	1,619	457	Bush	41.8%	25.1%	25.8%	7.3%
IRWIN	337	167	92	71	7	Bush	49.6%	27.3%	21.1%	2.1%
JACKSON	1,322	670	325	254	73	Bush	50.7%	24.6%	19.2%	5.5%
JASPER	542	332	131	54	25	Bush	61.3%	24.2%	10.0%	4.6%
JEFF DAVIS	423	158	97	150	18	Bush	37.4%	22.9%	35.5%	4.3%
JEFFERSON	777	519	127	70	61	Bush	66.8%	16.3%	9.0%	7.9%
JENKINS	262	155	63	38	6	Bush	59.2%	24.0%	14.5%	2.3%
JOHNSON	363	174	116	61	12	Bush	47.9%	32.0%	16.8%	3.3%
JONES	1,133	587	313	190	43	Bush	51.8%	27.6%	16.8%	3.8%
LAMAR	767	382	198	133	54	Bush	49.8%	25.8%	17.3%	7.0%
LANIER	148	105	25	14	4	Bush	70.9%	16.9%	9.5%	2.7%
LAURENS	2,049	908	697	349	95	Bush	44.3%	34.0%	17.0%	4.6%
LEE	1,042	634	176	177	55	Bush	60.8%	16.9%	17.0%	5.3%
LIBERTY	1,077	650	196	185	46	Bush	60.4%	18.2%	17.2%	4.3%
LINCOLN	394	270	48	63	13	Bush	68.5%	12.2%	16.0%	3.3%
LONG	179	112	44	19	4	Bush	62.6%	24.6%	10.6%	2.2%
LOWNDES	3,246	1,615	733	723	175	Bush	49.8%	22.6%	22.3%	5.4%
LUMPKIN	700	400	170	81	49	Bush	57.1%	24.3%	11.6%	7.0%
MCDUFFIE	1,004	675	152	122	55	Bush	67.2%	15.1%	12.2%	5.5%
MCINTOSH	493	259	77	146	11	Bush	52.5%	15.6%	29.6%	2.2%
MACON	410	230	116	49	15	Bush	56.1%	28.3%	12.0%	3.7%
MADISON	1,110	572	285	177	76	Bush	51.5%	25.7%	15.9%	6.8%
MARION	280	149	60	57	14	Bush	53.2%	21.4%	20.4%	5.0%
MERIWETHER	1,003	577	231	155	40	Bush	57.5%	23.0%	15.5%	4.0%
MILLER	271	171	55	34	11	Bush	63.1%	20.3%	12.5%	4.1%

GEORGIA REPUBLICAN

1988

County	Total Vote	Bush	Dole	Robertson	Other	Winner	Percentage of Total Vote Bush	Dole	Robertson	Other
MITCHELL	727	439	126	129	33	Bush	60.4%	17.3%	17.7%	4.5%
MONROE	891	461	200	160	70	Bush	51.7%	22.4%	18.0%	7.9%
MONTGOMERY	272	157	52	55	8	Bush	57.7%	19.1%	20.2%	2.9%
MORGAN	674	369	140	120	45	Bush	54.7%	20.8%	17.8%	6.7%
MURRAY	680	398	147	97	38	Bush	58.5%	21.6%	14.3%	5.6%
MUSCOGEE	11,037	6,210	2,090	2,285	452	Bush	56.3%	18.9%	20.7%	4.1%
NEWTON	2,149	1,099	482	480	88	Bush	51.1%	22.4%	22.3%	4.1%
OCONEE	1,554	746	421	303	84	Bush	48.0%	27.1%	19.5%	5.4%
OGLETHORPE	673	384	179	76	34	Bush	57.1%	26.6%	11.3%	5.1%
PAULDING	1,836	944	376	388	128	Bush	51.4%	20.5%	21.1%	7.0%
PEACH	1,054	444	222	333	55	Bush	42.1%	21.1%	31.6%	5.2%
PICKENS	1,078	629	241	159	49	Bush	58.3%	22.4%	14.7%	4.5%
PIERCE	711	328	142	219	22	Bush	46.1%	20.0%	30.8%	3.1%
PIKE	825	409	134	228	54	Bush	49.6%	16.2%	27.6%	6.5%
POLK	1,539	827	344	291	77	Bush	53.7%	22.4%	18.9%	5.0%
PULASKI	387	180	125	58	24	Bush	46.5%	32.3%	15.0%	6.2%
PUTNAM	876	447	260	144	25	Bush	51.0%	29.7%	16.4%	2.9%
QUITMAN	73	57	9	5	2	Bush	78.1%	12.3%	6.8%	2.7%
RABUN	680	392	138	86	64	Bush	57.6%	20.3%	12.6%	9.4%
RANDOLPH	274	155	76	36	7	Bush	56.6%	27.7%	13.1%	2.6%
RICHMOND	11,891	7,422	1,848	1,768	853	Bush	62.4%	15.5%	14.9%	7.2%
ROCKDALE	4,695	2,480	1,226	666	323	Bush	52.8%	26.1%	14.2%	6.9%
SCHLEY	247	120	59	65	3	Bush	48.6%	23.9%	26.3%	1.2%
SCREVEN	858	494	203	130	31	Bush	57.6%	23.7%	15.2%	3.6%
SEMINOLE	388	240	88	46	14	Bush	61.9%	22.7%	11.9%	3.6%
SPALDING	3,066	1,594	589	731	152	Bush	52.0%	19.2%	23.8%	5.0%
STEPHENS	1,282	514	282	392	94	Bush	40.1%	22.0%	30.6%	7.3%
STEWART	215	121	35	48	11	Bush	56.3%	16.3%	22.3%	5.1%
SUMTER	1,966	1,011	361	515	79	Bush	51.4%	18.4%	26.2%	4.0%
TALBOT	266	170	43	48	5	Bush	63.9%	16.2%	18.0%	1.9%
TALIAFERRO	42	31	8	2	1	Bush	73.8%	19.0%	4.8%	2.4%
TATTNALL	817	422	173	189	33	Bush	51.7%	21.2%	23.1%	4.0%
TAYLOR	416	177	119	109	11	Bush	42.5%	28.6%	26.2%	2.6%
TELFAIR	363	155	118	74	16	Bush	42.7%	32.5%	20.4%	4.4%
TERRELL	477	292	93	81	11	Bush	61.2%	19.5%	17.0%	2.3%
THOMAS	2,494	1,389	427	625	53	Bush	55.7%	17.1%	25.1%	2.1%
TIFT	1,453	742	328	303	80	Bush	51.1%	22.6%	20.9%	5.5%
TOOMBS	1,282	641	266	306	69	Bush	50.0%	20.7%	23.9%	5.4%
TOWNS	455	260	93	83	19	Bush	57.1%	20.4%	18.2%	4.2%
TREUTLEN	240	109	64	61	6	Bush	45.4%	26.7%	25.4%	2.5%
TROUP	3,212	1,729	610	685	188	Bush	53.8%	19.0%	21.3%	5.9%
TURNER	261	115	59	72	15	Bush	44.1%	22.6%	27.6%	5.7%
TWIGGS	322	154	82	76	10	Bush	47.8%	25.5%	23.6%	3.1%
UNION	605	350	130	88	37	Bush	57.9%	21.5%	14.5%	6.1%
UPSON	1,429	769	290	326	44	Bush	53.8%	20.3%	22.8%	3.1%
WALKER	2,652	1,303	562	599	188	Bush	49.1%	21.2%	22.6%	7.1%
WALTON	1,967	1,014	477	379	97	Bush	51.6%	24.3%	19.3%	4.9%
WARE	1,476	626	281	525	44	Bush	42.4%	19.0%	35.6%	3.0%
WARREN	291	181	52	40	18	Bush	62.2%	17.9%	13.7%	6.2%
WASHINGTON	809	463	184	125	37	Bush	57.2%	22.7%	15.5%	4.6%

GEORGIA REPUBLICAN

1988

County	Total Vote	Bush	Dole	Robertson	Other	Winner	Percentage of Total Vote Bush	Dole	Robertson	Other
WAYNE	1,238	565	174	438	61	Bush	45.6%	14.1%	35.4%	4.9%
WEBSTER	95	47	25	19	4	Bush	49.5%	26.3%	20.0%	4.2%
WHEELER	162	75	42	37	8	Bush	46.3%	25.9%	22.8%	4.9%
WHITE	820	483	179	110	48	Bush	58.9%	21.8%	13.4%	5.9%
WHITFIELD	3,832	2,058	813	719	242	Bush	53.7%	21.2%	18.8%	6.3%
WILCOX	228	112	54	53	9	Bush	49.1%	23.7%	23.2%	3.9%
WILKES	525	332	101	67	25	Bush	63.2%	19.2%	12.8%	4.8%
WILKINSON	472	246	139	58	29	Bush	52.1%	29.4%	12.3%	6.1%
WORTH	833	499	146	148	40	Bush	59.9%	17.5%	17.8%	4.8%
TOTAL	400,928	215,516	94,749	65,163	25,500	Bush	53.8%	23.6%	16.3%	6.4%

GEORGIA DEMOCRATIC

1992

County	Total Vote	Clinton	Tsongas	Other	Winner	Percentage of Total Vote Clinton	Tsongas	Other
APPLING	895	617	106	172	Clinton	68.9%	11.8%	19.2%
ATKINSON	504	391	44	69	Clinton	77.6%	8.7%	13.7%
BACON	460	326	73	61	Clinton	70.9%	15.9%	13.3%
BAKER	253	169	45	39	Clinton	66.8%	17.8%	15.4%
BALDWIN	2,575	1,574	466	535	Clinton	61.1%	18.1%	20.8%
BANKS	845	587	108	150	Clinton	69.5%	12.8%	17.8%
BARROW	1,933	1,231	348	354	Clinton	63.7%	18.0%	18.3%
BARTOW	4,017	2,557	715	745	Clinton	63.7%	17.8%	18.5%
BEN HILL	1,126	734	179	213	Clinton	65.2%	15.9%	18.9%
BERRIEN	818	583	115	120	Clinton	71.3%	14.1%	14.7%
BIBB	12,480	8,974	1,817	1,689	Clinton	71.9%	14.6%	13.5%
BLECKLEY	1,404	998	145	261	Clinton	71.1%	10.3%	18.6%
BRANTLEY	728	495	81	152	Clinton	68.0%	11.1%	20.9%
BROOKS	678	421	108	149	Clinton	62.1%	15.9%	22.0%
BRYAN	782	489	147	146	Clinton	62.5%	18.8%	18.7%
BULLOCH	1,786	1,070	385	331	Clinton	59.9%	21.6%	18.5%
BURKE	1,137	789	115	233	Clinton	69.4%	10.1%	20.5%
BUTTS	1,675	1,095	261	319	Clinton	65.4%	15.6%	19.0%
CALHOUN	501	363	65	73	Clinton	72.5%	13.0%	14.6%
CAMDEN	1,082	601	233	248	Clinton	55.5%	21.5%	22.9%
CANDLER	450	306	66	78	Clinton	68.0%	14.7%	17.3%
CARROLL	4,334	2,494	1,062	778	Clinton	57.5%	24.5%	18.0%
CATOOSA	2,195	1,428	402	365	Clinton	65.1%	18.3%	16.6%
CHARLTON	864	520	122	222	Clinton	60.2%	14.1%	25.7%
CHATHAM	12,366	7,289	2,754	2,323	Clinton	58.9%	22.3%	18.8%

GEORGIA DEMOCRATIC

1992

County	Total Vote	Clinton	Tsongas	Other	Winner	Percentage of Total Vote Clinton	Tsongas	Other
CHATTAHOOCHEE	235	153	25	57	Clinton	65.1%	10.6%	24.3%
CHATTOOGA	2,703	1,781	394	528	Clinton	65.9%	14.6%	19.5%
CHEROKEE	5,194	2,801	1,317	1,076	Clinton	53.9%	25.4%	20.7%
CLARKE	7,537	2,537	2,807	2,193	Tsongas	33.7%	37.2%	29.1%
CLAY	324	237	29	58	Clinton	73.1%	9.0%	17.9%
CLAYTON	11,398	6,659	2,570	2,169	Clinton	58.4%	22.5%	19.0%
CLINCH	280	176	45	59	Clinton	62.9%	16.1%	21.1%
COBB	28,350	12,460	9,901	5,989	Clinton	44.0%	34.9%	21.1%
COFFEE	1,468	947	273	248	Clinton	64.5%	18.6%	16.9%
COLQUITT	1,717	1,108	363	246	Clinton	64.5%	21.1%	14.3%
COLUMBIA	2,622	1,538	565	519	Clinton	58.7%	21.5%	19.8%
COOK	893	623	120	150	Clinton	69.8%	13.4%	16.8%
COWETA	3,308	1,937	734	637	Clinton	58.6%	22.2%	19.3%
CRAWFORD	818	583	76	159	Clinton	71.3%	9.3%	19.4%
CRISP	916	596	149	171	Clinton	65.1%	16.3%	18.7%
DADE	1,372	859	211	302	Clinton	62.6%	15.4%	22.0%
DAWSON	700	431	148	121	Clinton	61.6%	21.1%	17.3%
DECATUR	1,166	692	186	288	Clinton	59.3%	16.0%	24.7%
DE KALB	51,426	23,108	18,160	10,158	Clinton	44.9%	35.3%	19.8%
DODGE	1,247	969	88	190	Clinton	77.7%	7.1%	15.2%
DOOLY	891	636	98	157	Clinton	71.4%	11.0%	17.6%
DOUGHERTY	6,259	3,847	1,485	927	Clinton	61.5%	23.7%	14.8%
DOUGLAS	4,691	2,696	1,040	955	Clinton	57.5%	22.2%	20.4%
EARLY	853	570	150	133	Clinton	66.8%	17.6%	15.6%
ECHOLS	120	83	12	25	Clinton	69.2%	10.0%	20.8%
EFFINGHAM	1,206	792	184	230	Clinton	65.7%	15.3%	19.1%
ELBERT	1,956	1,317	250	389	Clinton	67.3%	12.8%	19.9%
EMANUEL	957	659	145	153	Clinton	68.9%	15.2%	16.0%
EVANS	489	345	52	92	Clinton	70.6%	10.6%	18.8%
FANNIN	974	674	145	155	Clinton	69.2%	14.9%	15.9%
FAYETTE	4,295	1,888	1,493	914	Clinton	44.0%	34.8%	21.3%
FLOYD	5,843	3,513	1,180	1,150	Clinton	60.1%	20.2%	19.7%
FORSYTH	3,819	2,118	850	851	Clinton	55.5%	22.3%	22.3%
FRANKLIN	2,147	1,445	255	447	Clinton	67.3%	11.9%	20.8%
FULTON	59,496	30,599	18,630	10,267	Clinton	51.4%	31.3%	17.3%
GILMER	898	592	159	147	Clinton	65.9%	17.7%	16.4%
GLASCOCK	97	65	10	22	Clinton	67.0%	10.3%	22.7%
GLYNN	3,551	1,889	941	721	Clinton	53.2%	26.5%	20.3%
GORDON	2,214	1,384	392	438	Clinton	62.5%	17.7%	19.8%
GRADY	1,219	790	188	241	Clinton	64.8%	15.4%	19.8%
GREENE	1,063	757	160	146	Clinton	71.2%	15.1%	13.7%
GWINNETT	19,712	8,590	6,903	4,219	Clinton	43.6%	35.0%	21.4%
HABERSHAM	1,997	1,197	387	413	Clinton	59.9%	19.4%	20.7%
HALL	6,456	3,440	1,446	1,570	Clinton	53.3%	22.4%	24.3%
HANCOCK	906	625	123	158	Clinton	69.0%	13.6%	17.4%
HARALSON	1,773	1,275	260	238	Clinton	71.9%	14.7%	13.4%
HARRIS	1,348	859	237	252	Clinton	63.7%	17.6%	18.7%
HART	1,296	814	221	261	Clinton	62.8%	17.1%	20.1%
HEARD	966	647	125	194	Clinton	67.0%	12.9%	20.1%
HENRY	3,847	2,239	855	753	Clinton	58.2%	22.2%	19.6%

GEORGIA DEMOCRATIC

1992

County	Total Vote	Clinton	Tsongas	Other	Winner	Percentage of Total Vote Clinton	Tsongas	Other
HOUSTON	7,232	4,736	1,181	1,315	Clinton	65.5%	16.3%	18.2%
IRWIN	479	309	93	77	Clinton	64.5%	19.4%	16.1%
JACKSON	2,240	1,513	372	355	Clinton	67.5%	16.6%	15.8%
JASPER	823	496	136	191	Clinton	60.3%	16.5%	23.2%
JEFF DAVIS	786	549	90	147	Clinton	69.8%	11.5%	18.7%
JEFFERSON	943	643	117	183	Clinton	68.2%	12.4%	19.4%
JENKINS	395	246	36	113	Clinton	62.3%	9.1%	28.6%
JOHNSON	651	510	48	93	Clinton	78.3%	7.4%	14.3%
JONES	1,699	1,217	216	266	Clinton	71.6%	12.7%	15.7%
LAMAR	1,094	693	197	204	Clinton	63.3%	18.0%	18.6%
LANIER	280	181	44	55	Clinton	64.6%	15.7%	19.6%
LAURENS	2,693	1,963	321	409	Clinton	72.9%	11.9%	15.2%
LEE	1,102	668	225	209	Clinton	60.6%	20.4%	19.0%
LIBERTY	1,357	867	225	265	Clinton	63.9%	16.6%	19.5%
LINCOLN	544	386	50	108	Clinton	71.0%	9.2%	19.9%
LONG	413	287	49	77	Clinton	69.5%	11.9%	18.6%
LOWNDES	2,759	1,595	613	551	Clinton	57.8%	22.2%	20.0%
LUMPKIN	1,586	862	361	363	Clinton	54.4%	22.8%	22.9%
MCDUFFIE	2,428	1,539	288	601	Clinton	63.4%	11.9%	24.8%
MCINTOSH	779	447	144	188	Clinton	57.4%	18.5%	24.1%
MACON	1,041	699	135	207	Clinton	67.1%	13.0%	19.9%
MADISON	1,322	789	241	292	Clinton	59.7%	18.2%	22.1%
MARION	525	362	72	91	Clinton	69.0%	13.7%	17.3%
MERIWETHER	1,829	1,300	251	278	Clinton	71.1%	13.7%	15.2%
MILLER	354	254	32	68	Clinton	71.8%	9.0%	19.2%
MITCHELL	1,352	933	223	196	Clinton	69.0%	16.5%	14.5%
MONROE	1,321	900	207	214	Clinton	68.1%	15.7%	16.2%
MONTGOMERY	507	344	48	115	Clinton	67.9%	9.5%	22.7%
MORGAN	1,503	897	288	318	Clinton	59.7%	19.2%	21.2%
MURRAY	1,368	874	239	255	Clinton	63.9%	17.5%	18.6%
MUSCOGEE	11,549	8,498	1,662	1,389	Clinton	73.6%	14.4%	12.0%
NEWTON	3,883	2,373	777	733	Clinton	61.1%	20.0%	18.9%
OCONEE	1,596	700	488	408	Clinton	43.9%	30.6%	25.6%
OGLETHORPE	835	476	195	164	Clinton	57.0%	23.4%	19.6%
PAULDING	2,720	1,736	537	447	Clinton	63.8%	19.7%	16.4%
PEACH	2,226	1,595	249	382	Clinton	71.7%	11.2%	17.2%
PICKENS	1,537	969	284	284	Clinton	63.0%	18.5%	18.5%
PIERCE	818	554	105	159	Clinton	67.7%	12.8%	19.4%
PIKE	846	568	124	154	Clinton	67.1%	14.7%	18.2%
POLK	2,653	1,874	392	387	Clinton	70.6%	14.8%	14.6%
PULASKI	793	595	93	105	Clinton	75.0%	11.7%	13.2%
PUTNAM	1,057	710	150	197	Clinton	67.2%	14.2%	18.6%
QUITMAN	158	110	15	33	Clinton	69.6%	9.5%	20.9%
RABUN	1,444	908	284	252	Clinton	62.9%	19.7%	17.5%
RANDOLPH	725	509	102	114	Clinton	70.2%	14.1%	15.7%
RICHMOND	7,856	5,272	1,297	1,287	Clinton	67.1%	16.5%	16.4%
ROCKDALE	4,104	2,013	1,162	929	Clinton	49.0%	28.3%	22.6%
SCHLEY	306	202	54	50	Clinton	66.0%	17.6%	16.3%
SCREVEN	801	533	109	159	Clinton	66.5%	13.6%	19.9%
SEMINOLE	570	409	78	83	Clinton	71.8%	13.7%	14.6%

GEORGIA DEMOCRATIC

1992

County	Total Vote	Clinton	Tsongas	Other	Winner	Percentage of Total Vote Clinton	Tsongas	Other
SPALDING	3,500	2,141	753	606	Clinton	61.2%	21.5%	17.3%
STEPHENS	2,336	1,411	383	542	Clinton	60.4%	16.4%	23.2%
STEWART	848	440	59	349	Clinton	51.9%	7.0%	41.2%
SUMTER	1,749	1,015	429	305	Clinton	58.0%	24.5%	17.4%
TALBOT	660	473	71	116	Clinton	71.7%	10.8%	17.6%
TALIAFERRO	166	126	17	23	Clinton	75.9%	10.2%	13.9%
TATTNALL	1,000	680	128	192	Clinton	68.0%	12.8%	19.2%
TAYLOR	661	483	69	109	Clinton	73.1%	10.4%	16.5%
TELFAIR	825	577	109	139	Clinton	69.9%	13.2%	16.8%
TERRELL	657	401	144	112	Clinton	61.0%	21.9%	17.0%
THOMAS	1,582	930	358	294	Clinton	58.8%	22.6%	18.6%
TIFT	1,858	1,206	341	311	Clinton	64.9%	18.4%	16.7%
TOOMBS	1,055	690	164	201	Clinton	65.4%	15.5%	19.1%
TOWNS	640	396	126	118	Clinton	61.9%	19.7%	18.4%
TREUTLEN	400	301	43	56	Clinton	75.3%	10.8%	14.0%
TROUP	2,626	1,624	602	400	Clinton	61.8%	22.9%	15.2%
TURNER	546	402	78	66	Clinton	73.6%	14.3%	12.1%
TWIGGS	896	666	82	148	Clinton	74.3%	9.2%	16.5%
UNION	1,202	738	223	241	Clinton	61.4%	18.6%	20.0%
UPSON	1,661	1,194	271	196	Clinton	71.9%	16.3%	11.8%
WALKER	2,815	1,840	516	459	Clinton	65.4%	18.3%	16.3%
WALTON	3,450	2,133	669	648	Clinton	61.8%	19.4%	18.8%
WARE	2,277	1,494	341	442	Clinton	65.6%	15.0%	19.4%
WARREN	506	324	55	127	Clinton	64.0%	10.9%	25.1%
WASHINGTON	1,691	1,187	197	307	Clinton	70.2%	11.6%	18.2%
WAYNE	1,469	996	198	275	Clinton	67.8%	13.5%	18.7%
WEBSTER	227	159	21	47	Clinton	70.0%	9.3%	20.7%
WHEELER	265	183	22	60	Clinton	69.1%	8.3%	22.6%
WHITE	1,446	786	282	378	Clinton	54.4%	19.5%	26.1%
WHITFIELD	3,029	1,821	738	470	Clinton	60.1%	24.4%	15.5%
WILCOX	643	483	53	107	Clinton	75.1%	8.2%	16.6%
WILKES	724	468	112	144	Clinton	64.6%	15.5%	19.9%
WILKINSON	1,253	975	109	169	Clinton	77.8%	8.7%	13.5%
WORTH	1,185	860	187	138	Clinton	72.6%	15.8%	11.6%
TOTAL	454,631	259,907	109,148	85,576	Clinton	57.2%	24.0%	18.8%

GEORGIA REPUBLICAN

1992

County	Total Vote	Buchanan	Bush	Winner	Percentage of Total Vote Buchanan	Bush
APPLING	820	355	465	Bush	43.3%	56.7%
ATKINSON	262	105	157	Bush	40.1%	59.9%
BACON	405	182	223	Bush	44.9%	55.1%
BAKER	153	68	85	Bush	44.4%	55.6%
BALDWIN	2,305	951	1,354	Bush	41.3%	58.7%
BANKS	561	203	358	Bush	36.2%	63.8%
BARROW	1,973	781	1,192	Bush	39.6%	60.4%
BARTOW	3,280	1,071	2,209	Bush	32.7%	67.3%
BEN HILL	849	435	414	Buchanan	51.2%	48.8%
BERRIEN	522	228	294	Bush	43.7%	56.3%
BIBB	10,139	4,518	5,621	Bush	44.6%	55.4%
BLECKLEY	1,160	574	586	Bush	49.5%	50.5%
BRANTLEY	433	198	235	Bush	45.7%	54.3%
BROOKS	563	222	341	Bush	39.4%	60.6%
BRYAN	1,067	365	702	Bush	34.2%	65.8%
BULLOCH	2,338	882	1,456	Bush	37.7%	62.3%
BURKE	1,092	492	600	Bush	45.1%	54.9%
BUTTS	1,112	338	774	Bush	30.4%	69.6%
CALHOUN	193	97	96	Buchanan	50.3%	49.7%
CAMDEN	1,062	434	628	Bush	40.9%	59.1%
CANDLER	459	190	269	Bush	41.4%	58.6%
CARROLL	4,672	1,617	3,055	Bush	34.6%	65.4%
CATOOSA	2,761	1,066	1,695	Bush	38.6%	61.4%
CHARLTON	522	190	332	Bush	36.4%	63.6%
CHATHAM	18,124	5,327	12,797	Bush	29.4%	70.6%
CHATTAHOOCHEE	134	70	64	Buchanan	52.2%	47.8%
CHATTOOGA	1,688	561	1,127	Bush	33.2%	66.8%
CHEROKEE	8,512	2,895	5,617	Bush	34.0%	66.0%
CLARKE	4,579	1,582	2,997	Bush	34.5%	65.5%
CLAY	108	54	54		50.0%	50.0%
CLAYTON	12,078	4,503	7,575	Bush	37.3%	62.7%
CLINCH	147	57	90	Bush	38.8%	61.2%
COBB	45,385	14,985	30,400	Bush	33.0%	67.0%
COFFEE	1,169	498	671	Bush	42.6%	57.4%
COLQUITT	1,522	558	964	Bush	36.7%	63.3%
COLUMBIA	6,648	3,102	3,546	Bush	46.7%	53.3%
COOK	496	175	321	Bush	35.3%	64.7%
COWETA	4,723	1,837	2,886	Bush	38.9%	61.1%
CRAWFORD	507	291	216	Buchanan	57.4%	42.6%
CRISP	798	337	461	Bush	42.2%	57.8%
DADE	1,387	452	935	Bush	32.6%	67.4%
DAWSON	721	278	443	Bush	38.6%	61.4%
DECATUR	1,069	369	700	Bush	34.5%	65.5%
DE KALB	37,850	11,545	26,305	Bush	30.5%	69.5%
DODGE	913	528	385	Buchanan	57.8%	42.2%
DOOLY	445	214	231	Bush	48.1%	51.9%
DOUGHERTY	5,859	1,864	3,995	Bush	31.8%	68.2%
DOUGLAS	6,090	2,265	3,825	Bush	37.2%	62.8%
EARLY	626	265	361	Bush	42.3%	57.7%
ECHOLS	56	16	40	Bush	28.6%	71.4%

GEORGIA REPUBLICAN

1992

County	Total Vote	Buchanan	Bush	Winner	Percentage of Total Vote Buchanan	Percentage of Total Vote Bush
EFFINGHAM	1,510	499	1,011	Bush	33.0%	67.0%
ELBERT	1,159	378	781	Bush	32.6%	67.4%
EMANUEL	931	418	513	Bush	44.9%	55.1%
EVANS	525	198	327	Bush	37.7%	62.3%
FANNIN	1,456	429	1,027	Bush	29.5%	70.5%
FAYETTE	9,022	3,054	5,968	Bush	33.9%	66.1%
FLOYD	5,515	1,854	3,661	Bush	33.6%	66.4%
FORSYTH	4,707	1,528	3,179	Bush	32.5%	67.5%
FRANKLIN	1,320	438	882	Bush	33.2%	66.8%
FULTON	38,799	10,796	28,003	Bush	27.8%	72.2%
GILMER	1,393	699	694	Buchanan	50.2%	49.8%
GLASCOCK	184	81	103	Bush	44.0%	56.0%
GLYNN	5,178	1,949	3,229	Bush	37.6%	62.4%
GORDON	2,064	736	1,328	Bush	35.7%	64.3%
GRADY	833	327	506	Bush	39.3%	60.7%
GREENE	547	174	373	Bush	31.8%	68.2%
GWINNETT	34,772	11,624	23,148	Bush	33.4%	66.6%
HABERSHAM	1,697	619	1,078	Bush	36.5%	63.5%
HALL	6,519	2,041	4,478	Bush	31.3%	68.7%
HANCOCK	201	82	119	Bush	40.8%	59.2%
HARALSON	1,388	573	815	Bush	41.3%	58.7%
HARRIS	1,488	528	960	Bush	35.5%	64.5%
HART	881	320	561	Bush	36.3%	63.7%
HEARD	642	264	378	Bush	41.1%	58.9%
HENRY	5,659	2,221	3,438	Bush	39.2%	60.8%
HOUSTON	7,629	3,943	3,686	Buchanan	51.7%	48.3%
IRWIN	373	187	186	Buchanan	50.1%	49.9%
JACKSON	1,768	636	1,132	Bush	36.0%	64.0%
JASPER	661	246	415	Bush	37.2%	62.8%
JEFF DAVIS	507	251	256	Bush	49.5%	50.5%
JEFFERSON	870	382	488	Bush	43.9%	56.1%
JENKINS	350	199	151	Buchanan	56.9%	43.1%
JOHNSON	550	259	291	Bush	47.1%	52.9%
JONES	1,389	677	712	Bush	48.7%	51.3%
LAMAR	972	409	563	Bush	42.1%	57.9%
LANIER	160	50	110	Bush	31.3%	68.8%
LAURENS	2,247	957	1,290	Bush	42.6%	57.4%
LEE	1,284	460	824	Bush	35.8%	64.2%
LIBERTY	1,233	404	829	Bush	32.8%	67.2%
LINCOLN	553	226	327	Bush	40.9%	59.1%
LONG	238	92	146	Bush	38.7%	61.3%
LOWNDES	3,328	1,326	2,002	Bush	39.8%	60.2%
LUMPKIN	1,092	370	722	Bush	33.9%	66.1%
MCDUFFIE	2,385	860	1,525	Bush	36.1%	63.9%
MCINTOSH	415	173	242	Bush	41.7%	58.3%
MACON	504	200	304	Bush	39.7%	60.3%
MADISON	1,303	469	834	Bush	36.0%	64.0%
MARION	299	118	181	Bush	39.5%	60.5%
MERIWETHER	1,221	434	787	Bush	35.5%	64.5%
MILLER	250	101	149	Bush	40.4%	59.6%

GEORGIA REPUBLICAN

1992

County	Total Vote	Buchanan	Bush	Winner	Percentage of Total Vote Buchanan	Percentage of Total Vote Bush
MITCHELL	678	267	411	Bush	39.4%	60.6%
MONROE	1,215	540	675	Bush	44.4%	55.6%
MONTGOMERY	381	174	207	Bush	45.7%	54.3%
MORGAN	1,096	336	760	Bush	30.7%	69.3%
MURRAY	1,098	423	675	Bush	38.5%	61.5%
MUSCOGEE	10,877	3,356	7,521	Bush	30.9%	69.1%
NEWTON	3,653	1,122	2,531	Bush	30.7%	69.3%
OCONEE	1,872	642	1,230	Bush	34.3%	65.7%
OGLETHORPE	781	239	542	Bush	30.6%	69.4%
PAULDING	2,743	1,025	1,718	Bush	37.4%	62.6%
PEACH	1,435	790	645	Buchanan	55.1%	44.9%
PICKENS	1,775	647	1,128	Bush	36.5%	63.5%
PIERCE	500	225	275	Bush	45.0%	55.0%
PIKE	944	385	559	Bush	40.8%	59.2%
POLK	1,895	685	1,210	Bush	36.1%	63.9%
PULASKI	516	289	227	Buchanan	56.0%	44.0%
PUTNAM	818	373	445	Bush	45.6%	54.4%
QUITMAN	94	24	70	Bush	25.5%	74.5%
RABUN	993	338	655	Bush	34.0%	66.0%
RANDOLPH	348	161	187	Bush	46.3%	53.7%
RICHMOND	11,187	5,382	5,805	Bush	48.1%	51.9%
ROCKDALE	6,348	2,115	4,233	Bush	33.3%	66.7%
SCHLEY	263	111	152	Bush	42.2%	57.8%
SCREVEN	809	306	503	Bush	37.8%	62.2%
SEMINOLE	314	112	202	Bush	35.7%	64.3%
SPALDING	3,693	1,378	2,315	Bush	37.3%	62.7%
STEPHENS	1,624	588	1,036	Bush	36.2%	63.8%
STEWART	267	100	167	Bush	37.5%	62.5%
SUMTER	1,478	699	779	Bush	47.3%	52.7%
TALBOT	299	107	192	Bush	35.8%	64.2%
TALIAFERRO	82	29	53	Bush	35.4%	64.6%
TATTNALL	838	310	528	Bush	37.0%	63.0%
TAYLOR	431	195	236	Bush	45.2%	54.8%
TELFAIR	518	268	250	Buchanan	51.7%	48.3%
TERRELL	510	214	296	Bush	42.0%	58.0%
THOMAS	1,744	612	1,132	Bush	35.1%	64.9%
TIFT	1,860	698	1,162	Bush	37.5%	62.5%
TOOMBS	1,357	580	777	Bush	42.7%	57.3%
TOWNS	506	145	361	Bush	28.7%	71.3%
TREUTLEN	325	141	184	Bush	43.4%	56.6%
TROUP	3,495	1,821	1,674	Buchanan	52.1%	47.9%
TURNER	281	142	139	Buchanan	50.5%	49.5%
TWIGGS	417	194	223	Bush	46.5%	53.5%
UNION	796	275	521	Bush	34.5%	65.5%
UPSON	1,729	732	997	Bush	42.3%	57.7%
WALKER	3,088	1,259	1,829	Bush	40.8%	59.2%
WALTON	3,153	1,107	2,046	Bush	35.1%	64.9%
WARE	1,781	677	1,104	Bush	38.0%	62.0%
WARREN	364	152	212	Bush	41.8%	58.2%
WASHINGTON	1,101	443	658	Bush	40.2%	59.8%

GEORGIA REPUBLICAN

1992

County	Total Vote	Buchanan	Bush	Winner	Percentage of Total Vote: Buchanan	Percentage of Total Vote: Bush
WAYNE	1,117	451	666	Bush	40.4%	59.6%
WEBSTER	124	60	64	Bush	48.4%	51.6%
WHEELER	177	85	92	Bush	48.0%	52.0%
WHITE	1,261	381	880	Bush	30.2%	69.8%
WHITFIELD	3,987	1,549	2,438	Bush	38.9%	61.1%
WILCOX	362	200	162	Buchanan	55.2%	44.8%
WILKES	561	209	352	Bush	37.3%	62.7%
WILKINSON	634	301	333	Bush	47.5%	52.5%
WORTH	1,089	467	622	Bush	42.9%	57.1%
TOTAL	453,990	162,085	291,905	Bush	35.7%	64.3%

GEORGIA REPUBLICAN

1996

County	Total Vote	Alexander	Buchanan	Dole	Forbes	Other	Winner	Percentage of Total Vote: Alexander	Buchanan	Dole	Forbes	Other
APPLING	1,097	105	502	388	79	23	Buchanan	9.6%	45.8%	35.4%	7.2%	2.1%
ATKINSON	255	11	110	113	15	6	Dole	4.3%	43.1%	44.3%	5.9%	2.4%
BACON	409	29	198	154	20	8	Buchanan	7.1%	48.4%	37.7%	4.9%	2.0%
BAKER	186	11	82	76	12	5	Buchanan	5.9%	44.1%	40.9%	6.5%	2.7%
BALDWIN	3,951	636	1,032	1,749	426	108	Dole	16.1%	26.1%	44.3%	10.8%	2.7%
BANKS	888	136	351	300	75	26	Buchanan	15.3%	39.5%	33.8%	8.4%	2.9%
BARROW	3,109	461	1,107	1,076	357	108	Buchanan	14.8%	35.6%	34.6%	11.5%	3.5%
BARTOW	4,047	537	1,542	1,213	571	184	Buchanan	13.3%	38.1%	30.0%	14.1%	4.5%
BEN HILL	566	58	244	222	32	10	Buchanan	10.2%	43.1%	39.2%	5.7%	1.8%
BERRIEN	660	51	291	261	46	11	Buchanan	7.7%	44.1%	39.5%	7.0%	1.7%
BIBB	10,248	1,556	3,011	4,464	968	249	Dole	15.2%	29.4%	43.6%	9.4%	2.4%
BLECKLEY	966	126	410	350	56	24	Buchanan	13.0%	42.4%	36.2%	5.8%	2.5%
BRANTLEY	573	41	276	170	64	22	Buchanan	7.2%	48.2%	29.7%	11.2%	3.8%
BROOKS	688	50	246	323	51	18	Dole	7.3%	35.8%	46.9%	7.4%	2.6%
BRYAN	1,419	170	399	605	195	50	Dole	12.0%	28.1%	42.6%	13.7%	3.5%
BULLOCH	2,439	298	771	1,001	273	96	Dole	12.2%	31.6%	41.0%	11.2%	3.9%
BURKE	1,253	82	492	476	149	54	Buchanan	6.5%	39.3%	38.0%	11.9%	4.3%
BUTTS	1,113	172	395	403	117	26	Dole	15.5%	35.5%	36.2%	10.5%	2.3%
CALHOUN	206	15	74	107	10		Dole	7.3%	35.9%	51.9%	4.9%	
CAMDEN	1,536	115	556	589	219	57	Dole	7.5%	36.2%	38.3%	14.3%	3.7%
CANDLER	495	49	184	209	44	9	Dole	9.9%	37.2%	42.2%	8.9%	1.8%
CARROLL	7,224	1,119	2,468	2,612	776	249	Dole	15.5%	34.2%	36.2%	10.7%	3.4%
CATOOSA	3,337	803	1,377	891	148	118	Buchanan	24.1%	41.3%	26.7%	4.4%	3.5%
CHARLTON	473	32	206	174	52	9	Buchanan	6.8%	43.6%	36.8%	11.0%	1.9%
CHATHAM	18,799	2,484	4,153	8,651	2,839	672	Dole	13.2%	22.1%	46.0%	15.1%	3.6%

GEORGIA REPUBLICAN

1996

County	Total Vote	Alexander	Buchanan	Dole	Forbes	Other	Winner	Percentage of Total Vote				
								Alexander	Buchanan	Dole	Forbes	Other
CHATTAHOOCHEE	155	17	56	60	18	4	Dole	11.0%	36.1%	38.7%	11.6%	2.6%
CHATTOOGA	1,281	244	576	355	73	33	Buchanan	19.0%	45.0%	27.7%	5.7%	2.6%
CHEROKEE	12,171	1,788	3,468	4,218	2,084	613	Dole	14.7%	28.5%	34.7%	17.1%	5.0%
CLARKE	5,780	972	1,207	2,638	654	309	Dole	16.8%	20.9%	45.6%	11.3%	5.3%
CLAY	209	21	68	90	23	7	Dole	10.0%	32.5%	43.1%	11.0%	3.3%
CLAYTON	11,324	1,560	3,546	4,190	1,497	531	Dole	13.8%	31.3%	37.0%	13.2%	4.7%
CLINCH	193	12	81	75	19	6	Buchanan	6.2%	42.0%	38.9%	9.8%	3.1%
COBB	62,488	9,628	14,979	25,096	10,030	2,755	Dole	15.4%	24.0%	40.2%	16.1%	4.4%
COFFEE	1,587	171	582	642	134	58	Dole	10.8%	36.7%	40.5%	8.4%	3.7%
COLQUITT	1,906	133	876	716	144	37	Buchanan	7.0%	46.0%	37.6%	7.6%	1.9%
COLUMBIA	10,245	615	3,743	4,323	1,232	332	Dole	6.0%	36.5%	42.2%	12.0%	3.2%
COOK	666	73	280	254	48	11	Buchanan	11.0%	42.0%	38.1%	7.2%	1.7%
COWETA	6,298	776	2,056	2,416	770	280	Dole	12.3%	32.6%	38.4%	12.2%	4.4%
CRAWFORD	613	104	244	195	53	17	Buchanan	17.0%	39.8%	31.8%	8.6%	2.8%
CRISP	800	78	256	403	49	14	Dole	9.8%	32.0%	50.4%	6.1%	1.8%
DADE	951	196	427	238	44	46	Buchanan	20.6%	44.9%	25.0%	4.6%	4.8%
DAWSON	1,196	165	406	423	186	16	Dole	13.8%	33.9%	35.4%	15.6%	1.3%
DECATUR	1,168	103	494	461	80	30	Buchanan	8.8%	42.3%	39.5%	6.8%	2.6%
DE KALB	45,199	7,064	7,512	20,634	6,774	3,215	Dole	15.6%	16.6%	45.7%	15.0%	7.1%
DODGE	1,091	123	547	328	66	27	Buchanan	11.3%	50.1%	30.1%	6.0%	2.5%
DOOLY	488	53	215	182	24	14	Buchanan	10.9%	44.1%	37.3%	4.9%	2.9%
DOUGHERTY	5,860	512	1,755	3,063	421	109	Dole	8.7%	29.9%	52.3%	7.2%	1.9%
DOUGLAS	7,251	1,002	2,564	2,384	1,023	278	Buchanan	13.8%	35.4%	32.9%	14.1%	3.8%
EARLY	619	23	261	266	32	37	Dole	3.7%	42.2%	43.0%	5.2%	6.0%
ECHOLS	71	8	37	17	6	3	Buchanan	11.3%	52.1%	23.9%	8.5%	4.2%
EFFINGHAM	1,827	197	674	711	186	59	Dole	10.8%	36.9%	38.9%	10.2%	3.2%
ELBERT	1,616	145	648	641	141	41	Buchanan	9.0%	40.1%	39.7%	8.7%	2.5%
EMANUEL	987	88	398	392	84	25	Buchanan	8.9%	40.3%	39.7%	8.5%	2.5%
EVANS	504	47	192	210	41	14	Dole	9.3%	38.1%	41.7%	8.1%	2.8%
FANNIN	1,719	359	584	625	125	26	Dole	20.9%	34.0%	36.4%	7.3%	1.5%
FAYETTE	10,970	1,440	2,809	4,653	1,554	514	Dole	13.1%	25.6%	42.4%	14.2%	4.7%
FLOYD	5,987	719	2,209	2,201	628	230	Buchanan	12.0%	36.9%	36.8%	10.5%	3.8%
FORSYTH	7,992	1,265	2,151	2,968	1,372	236	Dole	15.8%	26.9%	37.1%	17.2%	3.0%
FRANKLIN	1,028	97	436	380	93	22	Buchanan	9.4%	42.4%	37.0%	9.0%	2.1%
FULTON	46,664	7,026	6,733	22,104	8,292	2,509	Dole	15.1%	14.4%	47.4%	17.8%	5.4%
GILMER	1,673	221	761	516	131	44	Buchanan	13.2%	45.5%	30.8%	7.8%	2.6%
GLASCOCK	190	6	105	66	10	3	Buchanan	3.2%	55.3%	34.7%	5.3%	1.6%
GLYNN	5,560	470	1,468	2,553	873	196	Dole	8.5%	26.4%	45.9%	15.7%	3.5%
GORDON	2,322	430	851	711	248	82	Buchanan	18.5%	36.6%	30.6%	10.7%	3.5%
GRADY	1,720	152	706	678	144	40	Buchanan	8.8%	41.0%	39.4%	8.4%	2.3%
GREENE	854	118	214	385	123	14	Dole	13.8%	25.1%	45.1%	14.4%	1.6%
GWINNETT	48,357	7,937	11,874	18,941	7,400	2,205	Dole	16.4%	24.6%	39.2%	15.3%	4.6%
HABERSHAM	2,315	314	874	826	232	69	Buchanan	13.6%	37.8%	35.7%	10.0%	3.0%
HALL	9,703	1,486	2,878	3,981	1,077	281	Dole	15.3%	29.7%	41.0%	11.1%	2.9%
HANCOCK	351	42	120	153	30	6	Dole	12.0%	34.2%	43.6%	8.5%	1.7%
HARALSON	1,635	178	767	532	130	28	Buchanan	10.9%	46.9%	32.5%	8.0%	1.7%
HARRIS	2,103	181	790	887	174	71	Dole	8.6%	37.6%	42.2%	8.3%	3.4%
HART	1,365	118	560	543	115	29	Buchanan	8.6%	41.0%	39.8%	8.4%	2.1%
HEARD	677	72	344	192	56	13	Buchanan	10.6%	50.8%	28.4%	8.3%	1.9%
HENRY	8,099	1,061	2,864	2,905	939	330	Dole	13.1%	35.4%	35.9%	11.6%	4.1%

GEORGIA REPUBLICAN

1996

County	Total Vote	Alexander	Buchanan	Dole	Forbes	Other	Winner	Percentage of Total Vote Alexander	Buchanan	Dole	Forbes	Other
HOUSTON	8,115	988	2,989	3,224	700	214	Dole	12.2%	36.8%	39.7%	8.6%	2.6%
IRWIN	499	42	218	203	22	14	Buchanan	8.4%	43.7%	40.7%	4.4%	2.8%
JACKSON	2,355	352	837	856	224	86	Dole	14.9%	35.5%	36.3%	9.5%	3.7%
JASPER	736	110	231	289	87	19	Dole	14.9%	31.4%	39.3%	11.8%	2.6%
JEFF DAVIS	517	36	268	167	37	9	Buchanan	7.0%	51.8%	32.3%	7.2%	1.7%
JEFFERSON	833	38	318	362	97	18	Dole	4.6%	38.2%	43.5%	11.6%	2.2%
JENKINS	333	22	142	121	37	11	Buchanan	6.6%	42.6%	36.3%	11.1%	3.3%
JOHNSON	422	26	193	151	45	7	Buchanan	6.2%	45.7%	35.8%	10.7%	1.7%
JONES	1,534	200	548	597	153	36	Dole	13.0%	35.7%	38.9%	10.0%	2.3%
LAMAR	1,145	151	426	421	107	40	Buchanan	13.2%	37.2%	36.8%	9.3%	3.5%
LANIER	210	17	86	90	13	4	Dole	8.1%	41.0%	42.9%	6.2%	1.9%
LAURENS	2,110	246	838	836	127	63	Buchanan	11.7%	39.7%	39.6%	6.0%	3.0%
LEE	1,579	110	634	703	106	26	Dole	7.0%	40.2%	44.5%	6.7%	1.6%
LIBERTY	1,380	178	386	544	219	53	Dole	12.9%	28.0%	39.4%	15.9%	3.8%
LINCOLN	551	35	213	215	74	14	Dole	6.4%	38.7%	39.0%	13.4%	2.5%
LONG	307	33	117	119	32	6	Dole	10.7%	38.1%	38.8%	10.4%	2.0%
LOWNDES	4,066	345	1,671	1,601	332	117	Buchanan	8.5%	41.1%	39.4%	8.2%	2.9%
LUMPKIN	1,316	196	463	465	152	40	Dole	14.9%	35.2%	35.3%	11.6%	3.0%
MCDUFFIE	1,307	78	502	542	149	36	Dole	6.0%	38.4%	41.5%	11.4%	2.8%
MCINTOSH	586	46	173	267	92	8	Dole	7.8%	29.5%	45.6%	15.7%	1.4%
MACON	551	69	183	240	46	13	Dole	12.5%	33.2%	43.6%	8.3%	2.4%
MADISON	1,842	184	744	708	156	50	Buchanan	10.0%	40.4%	38.4%	8.5%	2.7%
MARION	323	23	158	126	12	4	Buchanan	7.1%	48.9%	39.0%	3.7%	1.2%
MERIWETHER	1,222	150	490	446	104	32	Buchanan	12.3%	40.1%	36.5%	8.5%	2.6%
MILLER	328	24	177	110	12	5	Buchanan	7.3%	54.0%	33.5%	3.7%	1.5%
MITCHELL	1,221	106	441	574	88	12	Dole	8.7%	36.1%	47.0%	7.2%	1.0%
MONROE	1,468	176	530	554	152	56	Dole	12.0%	36.1%	37.7%	10.4%	3.8%
MONTGOMERY	439	42	211	148	37	1	Buchanan	9.6%	48.1%	33.7%	8.4%	0.2%
MORGAN	1,174	163	387	461	123	40	Dole	13.9%	33.0%	39.3%	10.5%	3.4%
MURRAY	1,175	245	470	321	104	35	Buchanan	20.9%	40.0%	27.3%	8.9%	3.0%
MUSCOGEE	10,957	856	3,182	5,659	954	306	Dole	7.8%	29.0%	51.6%	8.7%	2.8%
NEWTON	4,832	786	1,585	1,801	501	159	Dole	16.3%	32.8%	37.3%	10.4%	3.3%
OCONEE	4,360	716	1,160	1,849	463	172	Dole	16.4%	26.6%	42.4%	10.6%	3.9%
OGLETHORPE	933	105	332	387	85	24	Dole	11.3%	35.6%	41.5%	9.1%	2.6%
PAULDING	4,957	629	2,001	1,487	677	163	Buchanan	12.7%	40.4%	30.0%	13.7%	3.3%
PEACH	1,434	191	545	535	119	44	Buchanan	13.3%	38.0%	37.3%	8.3%	3.1%
PICKENS	1,496	238	454	561	187	56	Dole	15.9%	30.3%	37.5%	12.5%	3.7%
PIERCE	805	51	377	287	74	16	Buchanan	6.3%	46.8%	35.7%	9.2%	2.0%
PIKE	1,189	135	505	404	104	41	Buchanan	11.4%	42.5%	34.0%	8.7%	3.4%
POLK	2,117	226	924	675	203	89	Buchanan	10.7%	43.6%	31.9%	9.6%	4.2%
PULASKI	560	75	222	188	62	13	Buchanan	13.4%	39.6%	33.6%	11.1%	2.3%
PUTNAM	939	153	278	405	92	11	Dole	16.3%	29.6%	43.1%	9.8%	1.2%
QUITMAN	79	3	30	40	4	2	Dole	3.8%	38.0%	50.6%	5.1%	2.5%
RABUN	1,061	110	380	382	139	50	Dole	10.4%	35.8%	36.0%	13.1%	4.7%
RANDOLPH	287	9	104	153	18	3	Dole	3.1%	36.2%	53.3%	6.3%	1.0%
RICHMOND	12,302	659	4,060	5,693	1,454	436	Dole	5.4%	33.0%	46.3%	11.8%	3.5%
ROCKDALE	8,345	1,490	2,239	3,224	1,083	309	Dole	17.9%	26.8%	38.6%	13.0%	3.7%
SCHLEY	235	20	94	106	9	6	Dole	8.5%	40.0%	45.1%	3.8%	2.6%
SCREVEN	743	67	260	340	62	14	Dole	9.0%	35.0%	45.8%	8.3%	1.9%
SEMINOLE	487	29	199	212	34	13	Dole	6.0%	40.9%	43.5%	7.0%	2.7%

GEORGIA REPUBLICAN

1996

County	Total Vote	Alexander	Buchanan	Dole	Forbes	Other	Winner	Percentage of Total Vote: Alexander	Buchanan	Dole	Forbes	Other
SPALDING	3,819	453	1,376	1,450	404	136	Dole	11.9%	36.0%	38.0%	10.6%	3.6%
STEPHENS	1,830	186	784	585	149	126	Buchanan	10.2%	42.8%	32.0%	8.1%	6.9%
STEWART	262	12	107	107	30	6		4.6%	40.8%	40.8%	11.5%	2.3%
SUMTER	1,584	118	568	555	104	239	Buchanan	7.4%	35.9%	35.0%	6.6%	15.1%
TALBOT	307	25	125	140	14	3	Dole	8.1%	40.7%	45.6%	4.6%	1.0%
TALIAFERRO	125	6	48	55	15	1	Dole	4.8%	38.4%	44.0%	12.0%	0.8%
TATTNALL	1,103	96	481	431	72	23	Buchanan	8.7%	43.6%	39.1%	6.5%	2.1%
TAYLOR	552	48	239	227	21	17	Buchanan	8.7%	43.3%	41.1%	3.8%	3.1%
TELFAIR	413	35	186	149	29	14	Buchanan	8.5%	45.0%	36.1%	7.0%	3.4%
TERRELL	543	33	225	241	33	11	Dole	6.1%	41.4%	44.4%	6.1%	2.0%
THOMAS	2,446	202	914	1,105	163	62	Dole	8.3%	37.4%	45.2%	6.7%	2.5%
TIFT	2,017	216	671	886	191	53	Dole	10.7%	33.3%	43.9%	9.5%	2.6%
TOOMBS	1,711	172	790	617	89	43	Buchanan	10.1%	46.2%	36.1%	5.2%	2.5%
TOWNS	709	92	200	327	69	21	Dole	13.0%	28.2%	46.1%	9.7%	3.0%
TREUTLEN	307	27	163	98	14	5	Buchanan	8.8%	53.1%	31.9%	4.6%	1.6%
TROUP	5,714	502	3,064	1,625	438	85	Buchanan	8.8%	53.6%	28.4%	7.7%	1.5%
TURNER	319	27	163	110	15	4	Buchanan	8.5%	51.1%	34.5%	4.7%	1.3%
TWIGGS	427	46	187	148	33	13	Buchanan	10.8%	43.8%	34.7%	7.7%	3.0%
UNION	1,068	121	371	459	103	14	Dole	11.3%	34.7%	43.0%	9.6%	1.3%
UPSON	1,798	178	699	720	170	31	Dole	9.9%	38.9%	40.0%	9.5%	1.7%
WALKER	3,875	902	1,621	980	189	183	Buchanan	23.3%	41.8%	25.3%	4.9%	4.7%
WALTON	4,044	572	1,437	1,489	437	109	Dole	14.1%	35.5%	36.8%	10.8%	2.7%
WARE	1,558	86	675	606	161	30	Buchanan	5.5%	43.3%	38.9%	10.3%	1.9%
WARREN	361	19	146	156	25	15	Dole	5.3%	40.4%	43.2%	6.9%	4.2%
WASHINGTON	928	126	322	388	67	25	Dole	13.6%	34.7%	41.8%	7.2%	2.7%
WAYNE	1,375	131	530	509	174	31	Buchanan	9.5%	38.5%	37.0%	12.7%	2.3%
WEBSTER	90	6	50	33	1		Buchanan	6.7%	55.6%	36.7%	1.1%	
WHEELER	218	23	106	70	14	5	Buchanan	10.6%	48.6%	32.1%	6.4%	2.3%
WHITE	1,714	284	482	704	209	35	Dole	16.6%	28.1%	41.1%	12.2%	2.0%
WHITFIELD	5,219	1,110	1,790	1,733	409	177	Buchanan	21.3%	34.3%	33.2%	7.8%	3.4%
WILCOX	342	31	186	110	9	6	Buchanan	9.1%	54.4%	32.2%	2.6%	1.8%
WILKES	616	48	207	285	66	10	Dole	7.8%	33.6%	46.3%	10.7%	1.6%
WILKINSON	613	94	268	200	39	12	Buchanan	15.3%	43.7%	32.6%	6.4%	2.0%
WORTH	1,533	92	748	587	81	25	Buchanan	6.0%	48.8%	38.3%	5.3%	1.6%
TOTAL	559,067	75,855	162,627	226,732	71,276	22,577	Dole	13.6%	29.1%	40.6%	12.7%	4.0%

HAWAII

If it were simply a matter of the candidates' personal preference, Hawaii most likely would be glutted with presidential aspirants canvassing its beaches for the state's late-winter caucuses. But the small size of the delegate harvest and the absence of a presidential primary to attract some media attention has kept Hawaii a distant sideshow in the presidential nominating process.

Hawaii Republicans sought to make a splash in 1988 by scheduling their precinct caucuses in late January—before even Iowa had spoken. And for much of 1987, Bob Dole looked like the best bet to win the early event. He was the choice of the moderate element dominant within the Hawaii GOP.

But in the month preceding the caucuses, the party was inundated with new registrants, most wanting to vote for evangelist Pat Robertson. The number of card-carrying Republicans swelled from barely 11,000 to more than 18,000. State GOP officials were stunned by the unexpected influx. First, they postponed the caucuses indefinitely. Then, with Robertson denouncing "banana republic" politics, the vote was rescheduled for a week after the original date.

When the caucuses were finally held in early February, an estimated 4,000 to 5,000 Republicans showed up and voted overwhelmingly for Robertson delegates to the June state convention. His candidacy had collapsed by the time the state convention was held, but his supporters pushed through a platform that emphasized the conservative "family values" that he had espoused in his campaign.

Robertson's control of the state GOP, though, proved temporary. Party regulars regained the upper hand in 1992 and the state party issued no platform at all.

For most of the state's history, Hawaii—with its rainbow-hued electorate—has not harbored any affection for ideological activism on either end of the political spectrum. Hawaii Republicans gave President Gerald Ford all but one of their delegates in 1976 and were slow to embrace Ronald Reagan in 1980. Even as opposition to Reagan was crumbling nationally in the spring of 1980, the state party selected a predominantly uncommitted delegation to send to the national convention in Detroit.

Democratic caucus voters in Hawaii have traditionally followed the wishes of the party leadership. Typical was the situation in 1988. The multiracial nature of Hawaii's political landscape seemed tailor-made for Jesse Jackson. But less than a week before the early March caucuses, then-Gov. John Waihee III endorsed his gubernatorial colleague, Michael Dukakis. A stream of endorsements for Dukakis followed from lesser Democratic elected officials on the islands. And when the caucuses were held, Dukakis won easily with 55 percent of the nearly 5,000 votes cast.

Four years later the result was similar. Waihee threw his support to another gubernatorial colleague, Bill Clinton, who also won a majority of the Democratic caucus vote.

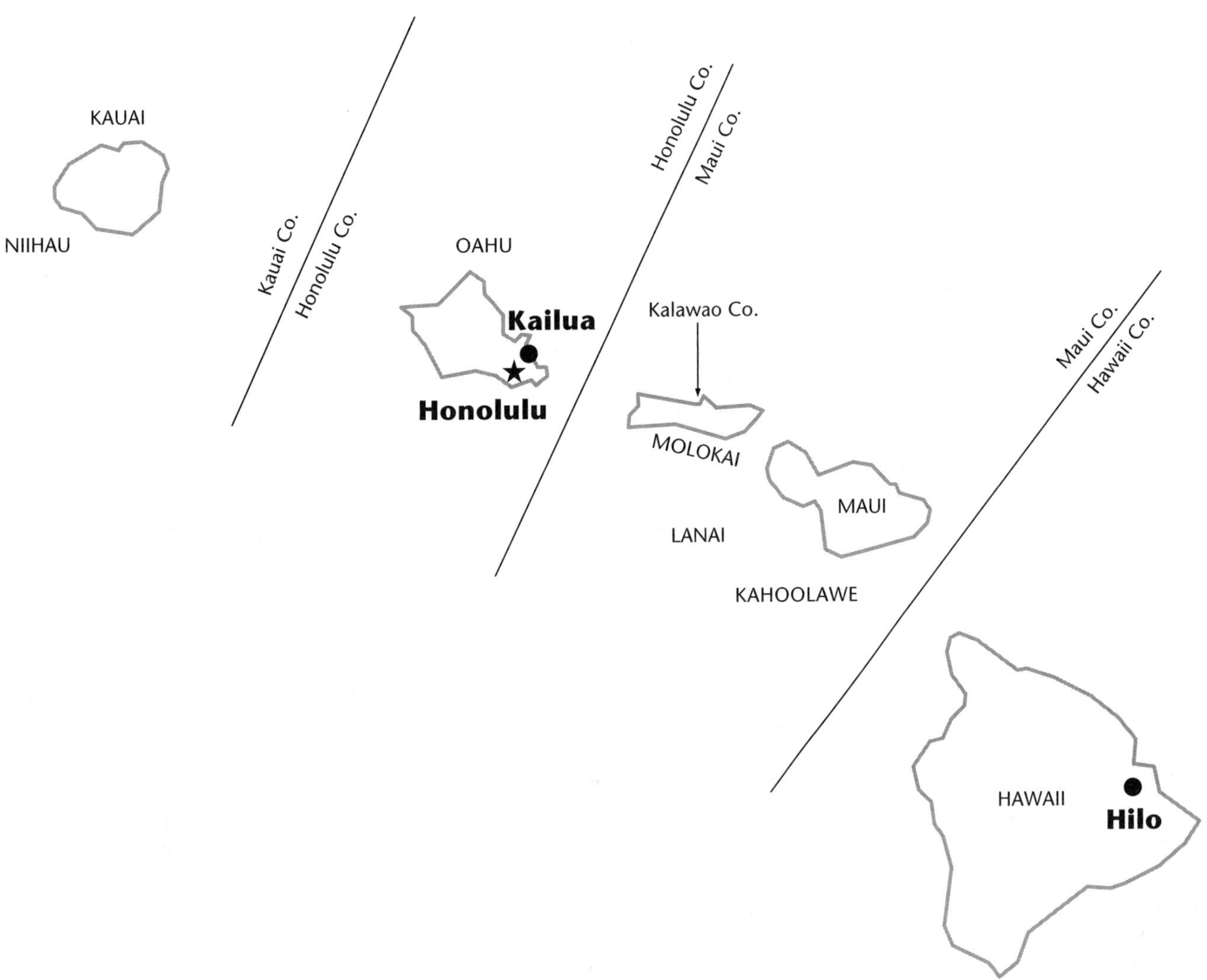
KAUAI
NIIHAU
Kauai Co.
Honolulu Co.
OAHU
Kailua
Honolulu
Honolulu Co.
Maui Co.
Kalawao Co.
MOLOKAI
MAUI
LANAI
KAHOOLAWE
Maui Co.
Hawaii Co.
HAWAII
Hilo

IDAHO

Idaho has held a presidential primary for the last quarter century, but never has it been competitive. None of the Democratic or Republican contests have been decided by less than 20 percentage points.

That is largely because Idaho votes late in the primary season, well after the field has been winnowed. But Idaho voters are far from a rubber stamp. Nearly 40 percent of those who participated in the 1992 and 1996 Republican primaries withheld their votes from the presumptive nominees, George Bush and Bob Dole, respectively.

Meanwhile, Bill Clinton won Idaho's Democratic primary in 1992 with less than a majority of the vote, and actually lost resort-oriented Blaine County (Sun Valley) to a line designated "None of the Names Shown."

Idaho Democrats in recent years have held both a primary and a caucus. The caucus process that begins in early March is to select delegates, while Democrats use the May primary as a "beauty contest" to reflect broader popular sentiment.

The low-turnout caucuses tend to be influenced by liberal elements within the Democratic Party. In 1992, for instance, Clinton ran a distant fourth in the caucus vote of roughly 3,000 Democrats. The winner was Sen. Tom Harkin of Iowa, who ran as an unapologetic New Deal liberal.

Idaho Republicans have stuck with the primary as their principal method of delegate selection. The backbone of GOP strength is the farm and ranch country of southeast Idaho, a heavily Mormon area that ranks among the most conservative in the country. In his 1976 primary victory over President Gerald Ford, Ronald Reagan carried a number of counties in the region with more than 80 percent of the vote.

Moderate Republicans are more apt to be found in the Boise area. In the 1980 GOP primary, John Anderson drew nearly one out of every five ballots in Ada County (Boise), even though he had already bolted the party to mount his independent presidential campaign. Reagan, though, still won handily in the Boise area, as he did statewide.

Recent Idaho Primary Results

Idaho held its first presidential primary in 1976.

	DEMOCRATS			REPUBLICANS		
Year	Turnout	Candidates	%	Turnout	Candidates	%
1996 (May 28)	40,228	BILL CLINTON*	88	118,715	BOB DOLE	62
		"None"	12		Pat Buchanan	22
					"None"	10
1992 (May 26)	55,124	BILL CLINTON	49	115,502	GEORGE BUSH*	63
		"None"	29		"None"	23
		Jerry Brown	17		Pat Buchanan	13
1988 (May 24)	51,370	MICHAEL DUKAKIS	73	68,275	GEORGE BUSH	81
		Jesse Jackson	16		"None"	10
1984 (May 22)	54,722	GARY HART	58	105,687	RONALD REAGAN*	92
		Walter Mondale	30			
1980 (May 27)	50,482	JIMMY CARTER*	62	134,879	RONALD REAGAN	83
		Edward Kennedy	22			
		"None"	12			
1976 (May 25)	74,405	FRANK CHURCH	79	89,793	RONALD REAGAN	74
		Jimmy Carter	12		Gerald Ford*	25

Note: All candidates are listed that drew at least 10 percent of their party's primary vote. The names of winning candidates are capitalized. An asterisk (*) indicates an incumbent president.

Boundary
Bonner
Coeur d'Alene
Kootenai
Benewah
Shoshone
Moscow
Latah
Clearwater
Nez Perce
Lewiston
Lewis
Idaho
Adams
Valley
Lemhi
Washington
Custer
Clark
Fremont
Payette
Boise
Gem
Jefferson
Madison
Teton
Butte
Canyon
Boise
Idaho Falls
Camas
Blaine
Elmore
Ada
Bingham
Bonneville
Gooding
Lincoln
Pocatello
Caribou
Jerome
Minidoka
Power
Owyhee
Bannock
Twin Falls
Cassia
Bear Lake
Oneida
Twin Falls
Franklin

IDAHO DEMOCRATIC

1976

County	Total Vote	Carter	Church	Other	Winner	Percentage of Total Vote		
						Carter	Church	Other
ADA	16,698	2,001	13,356	1,341	Church	12.0%	80.0%	8.0%
ADAMS	354	54	265	35	Church	15.3%	74.9%	9.9%
BANNOCK	5,882	493	4,983	406	Church	8.4%	84.7%	6.9%
BEAR LAKE	847	65	713	69	Church	7.7%	84.2%	8.1%
BENEWAH	725	138	423	164	Church	19.0%	58.3%	22.6%
BINGHAM	2,226	144	1,995	87	Church	6.5%	89.6%	3.9%
BLAINE	759	99	558	102	Church	13.0%	73.5%	13.4%
BOISE	355	34	304	17	Church	9.6%	85.6%	4.8%
BONNER	2,247	308	1,543	396	Church	13.7%	68.7%	17.6%
BONNEVILLE	4,333	400	3,583	350	Church	9.2%	82.7%	8.1%
BOUNDARY	690	105	451	134	Church	15.2%	65.4%	19.4%
BUTTE	386	25	336	25	Church	6.5%	87.0%	6.5%
CAMAS	110	12	90	8	Church	10.9%	81.8%	7.3%
CANYON	5,433	929	4,063	441	Church	17.1%	74.8%	8.1%
CARIBOU	578	66	452	60	Church	11.4%	78.2%	10.4%
CASSIA	789	98	588	103	Church	12.4%	74.5%	13.1%
CLARK	103	11	82	10	Church	10.7%	79.6%	9.7%
CLEARWATER	1,122	109	896	117	Church	9.7%	79.9%	10.4%
CUSTER	353	64	243	46	Church	18.1%	68.8%	13.0%
ELMORE	1,703	212	1,307	184	Church	12.4%	76.7%	10.8%
FRANKLIN	524	51	414	59	Church	9.7%	79.0%	11.3%
FREMONT	890	80	759	51	Church	9.0%	85.3%	5.7%
GEM	1,033	162	805	66	Church	15.7%	77.9%	6.4%
GOODING	875	130	678	67	Church	14.9%	77.5%	7.7%
IDAHO	1,493	208	1,091	194	Church	13.9%	73.1%	13.0%
JEFFERSON	958	73	825	60	Church	7.6%	86.1%	6.3%
JEROME	818	135	592	91	Church	16.5%	72.4%	11.1%
KOOTENAI	3,779	517	2,647	615	Church	13.7%	70.0%	16.3%
LATAH	2,684	249	2,114	321	Church	9.3%	78.8%	12.0%
LEMHI	564	79	421	64	Church	14.0%	74.6%	11.3%
LEWIS	571	52	458	61	Church	9.1%	80.2%	10.7%
LINCOLN	311	31	245	35	Church	10.0%	78.8%	11.3%
MADISON	801	62	692	47	Church	7.7%	86.4%	5.9%
MINIDOKA	1,332	176	1,055	101	Church	13.2%	79.2%	7.6%
NEZ PERCE	3,374	290	2,810	274	Church	8.6%	83.3%	8.1%
ONEIDA	352	20	311	21	Church	5.7%	88.4%	6.0%
OWYHEE	569	84	441	44	Church	14.8%	77.5%	7.7%
PAYETTE	1,070	137	857	76	Church	12.8%	80.1%	7.1%
POWER	507	32	452	23	Church	6.3%	89.2%	4.5%
SHOSHONE	1,707	179	1,277	251	Church	10.5%	74.8%	14.7%
TETON	226	4	210	12	Church	1.8%	92.9%	5.3%
TWIN FALLS	2,817	491	2,041	285	Church	17.4%	72.5%	10.1%
VALLEY	496	68	382	46	Church	13.7%	77.0%	9.3%
WASHINGTON	961	141	762	58	Church	14.7%	79.3%	6.0%
TOTAL	74,405	8,818	58,570	7,017	Church	11.9%	78.7%	9.4%

IDAHO REPUBLICAN

1976

County	Total Vote	Ford	Reagan	Uncommitted	Winner	Percentage of Total Vote Ford	Reagan	Uncom.
ADA	20,905	5,756	14,905	244	Reagan	27.5%	71.3%	1.2%
ADAMS	365	87	277	1	Reagan	23.8%	75.9%	0.3%
BANNOCK	4,782	1,200	3,548	34	Reagan	25.1%	74.2%	0.7%
BEAR LAKE	937	222	712	3	Reagan	23.7%	76.0%	0.3%
BENEWAH	472	153	314	5	Reagan	32.4%	66.5%	1.1%
BINGHAM	2,736	397	2,327	12	Reagan	14.5%	85.1%	0.4%
BLAINE	736	237	490	9	Reagan	32.2%	66.6%	1.2%
BOISE	298	73	225		Reagan	24.5%	75.5%	
BONNER	1,865	592	1,258	15	Reagan	31.7%	67.5%	0.8%
BONNEVILLE	7,358	1,255	6,066	37	Reagan	17.1%	82.4%	0.5%
BOUNDARY	587	155	422	10	Reagan	26.4%	71.9%	1.7%
BUTTE	405	78	323	4	Reagan	19.3%	79.8%	1.0%
CAMAS	145	44	101		Reagan	30.3%	69.7%	
CANYON	8,433	2,011	6,349	73	Reagan	23.8%	75.3%	0.9%
CARIBOU	895	160	731	4	Reagan	17.9%	81.7%	0.4%
CASSIA	2,019	512	1,487	20	Reagan	25.4%	73.7%	1.0%
CLARK	169	44	125		Reagan	26.0%	74.0%	
CLEARWATER	391	174	208	9	Reagan	44.5%	53.2%	2.3%
CUSTER	421	100	319	2	Reagan	23.8%	75.8%	0.5%
ELMORE	1,446	355	1,082	9	Reagan	24.6%	74.8%	0.6%
FRANKLIN	1,052	246	801	5	Reagan	23.4%	76.1%	0.5%
FREMONT	1,294	230	1,063	1	Reagan	17.8%	82.1%	0.1%
GEM	1,211	212	994	5	Reagan	17.5%	82.1%	0.4%
GOODING	1,397	332	1,059	6	Reagan	23.8%	75.8%	0.4%
IDAHO	1,216	308	902	6	Reagan	25.3%	74.2%	0.5%
JEFFERSON	2,161	229	1,932		Reagan	10.6%	89.4%	
JEROME	1,631	337	1,292	2	Reagan	20.7%	79.2%	0.1%
KOOTENAI	3,404	1,134	2,237	33	Reagan	33.3%	65.7%	1.0%
LATAH	1,647	739	882	26	Reagan	44.9%	53.6%	1.6%
LEMHI	913	158	754	1	Reagan	17.3%	82.6%	0.1%
LEWIS	280	94	184	2	Reagan	33.6%	65.7%	0.7%
LINCOLN	482	124	357	1	Reagan	25.7%	74.1%	0.2%
MADISON	1,802	310	1,484	8	Reagan	17.2%	82.4%	0.4%
MINIDOKA	2,056	472	1,559	25	Reagan	23.0%	75.8%	1.2%
NEZ PERCE	1,487	693	778	16	Reagan	46.6%	52.3%	1.1%
ONEIDA	402	116	282	4	Reagan	28.9%	70.1%	1.0%
OWYHEE	697	123	574		Reagan	17.6%	82.4%	
PAYETTE	1,510	380	1,125	5	Reagan	25.2%	74.5%	0.3%
POWER	540	136	402	2	Reagan	25.2%	74.4%	0.4%
SHOSHONE	1,110	405	691	14	Reagan	36.5%	62.3%	1.3%
TETON	417	75	337	5	Reagan	18.0%	80.8%	1.2%
TWIN FALLS	5,930	1,462	4,408	60	Reagan	24.7%	74.3%	1.0%
VALLEY	591	162	429		Reagan	27.4%	72.6%	
WASHINGTON	1,098	241	848	9	Reagan	21.9%	77.2%	0.8%
TOTAL	89,693	22,323	66,643	727	Reagan	24.9%	74.3%	0.8%
Certified Totals	89,793	22,323	66,743	727	Reagan	24.9%	74.3%	0.8%

IDAHO DEMOCRATIC

1980

County	Total Vote	Brown	Carter	E. Kennedy	Uncommitted	Winner	Percentage of Total Vote Brown	Carter	E. Kennedy	Uncom.
ADA	8,033	196	4,996	1,728	1,113	Carter	2.4%	62.2%	21.5%	13.9%
ADAMS	332	11	235	53	33	Carter	3.3%	70.8%	16.0%	9.9%
BANNOCK	3,846	182	2,272	880	512	Carter	4.7%	59.1%	22.9%	13.3%
BEAR LAKE	594	36	319	150	89	Carter	6.1%	53.7%	25.3%	15.0%
BENEWAH	974	71	562	221	120	Carter	7.3%	57.7%	22.7%	12.3%
BINGHAM	1,058	41	645	278	94	Carter	3.9%	61.0%	26.3%	8.9%
BLAINE	841	52	476	189	124	Carter	6.2%	56.6%	22.5%	14.7%
BOISE	221	11	151	49	10	Carter	5.0%	68.3%	22.2%	4.5%
BONNER	2,936	186	1,762	655	333	Carter	6.3%	60.0%	22.3%	11.3%
BONNEVILLE	1,604	67	980	380	177	Carter	4.2%	61.1%	23.7%	11.0%
BOUNDARY	1,056	97	654	180	125	Carter	9.2%	61.9%	17.0%	11.8%
BUTTE	199	8	118	50	23	Carter	4.0%	59.3%	25.1%	11.6%
CAMAS	43	1	37	4	1	Carter	2.3%	86.0%	9.3%	2.3%
CANYON	3,460	78	2,235	758	389	Carter	2.3%	64.6%	21.9%	11.2%
CARIBOU	275	11	138	115	11	Carter	4.0%	50.2%	41.8%	4.0%
CASSIA	368	17	240	91	20	Carter	4.6%	65.2%	24.7%	5.4%
CLARK	57		41	12	4	Carter		71.9%	21.1%	7.0%
CLEARWATER	979	41	606	181	151	Carter	4.2%	61.9%	18.5%	15.4%
CUSTER	212	52	117	33	10	Carter	24.5%	55.2%	15.6%	4.7%
ELMORE	1,335	47	827	295	166	Carter	3.5%	61.9%	22.1%	12.4%
FRANKLIN	164	10	95	45	14	Carter	6.1%	57.9%	27.4%	8.5%
FREMONT	692	23	388	193	88	Carter	3.3%	56.1%	27.9%	12.7%
GEM	726	15	492	163	56	Carter	2.1%	67.8%	22.5%	7.7%
GOODING	391	13	288	70	20	Carter	3.3%	73.7%	17.9%	5.1%
IDAHO	1,303	59	813	286	145	Carter	4.5%	62.4%	21.9%	11.1%
JEFFERSON	263	14	195	54		Carter	5.3%	74.1%	20.5%	
JEROME	427	15	308	82	22	Carter	3.5%	72.1%	19.2%	5.2%
KOOTENAI	4,015	160	2,441	917	497	Carter	4.0%	60.8%	22.8%	12.4%
LATAH	1,642	61	1,016	325	240	Carter	3.7%	61.9%	19.8%	14.6%
LEMHI	258	10	180	53	15	Carter	3.9%	69.8%	20.5%	5.8%
LEWIS	547	25	332	112	78	Carter	4.6%	60.7%	20.5%	14.3%
LINCOLN	113	7	74	25	7	Carter	6.2%	65.5%	22.1%	6.2%
MADISON	377	12	223	106	36	Carter	3.2%	59.2%	28.1%	9.5%
MINIDOKA	585	16	347	153	69	Carter	2.7%	59.3%	26.2%	11.8%
NEZ PERCE	3,763	138	2,262	755	608	Carter	3.7%	60.1%	20.1%	16.2%
ONEIDA	192	16	125	44	7	Carter	8.3%	65.1%	22.9%	3.6%
OWYHEE	349	12	259	78		Carter	3.4%	74.2%	22.3%	
PAYETTE	776	18	535	161	62	Carter	2.3%	68.9%	20.7%	8.0%
POWER	237		173	48	16	Carter		73.0%	20.3%	6.8%
SHOSHONE	2,805	173	1,690	610	332	Carter	6.2%	60.2%	21.7%	11.8%
TETON	206	16	127	52	11	Carter	7.8%	61.7%	25.2%	5.3%
TWIN FALLS	1,272	41	926	270	35	Carter	3.2%	72.8%	21.2%	2.8%
VALLEY	345	10	248	60	27	Carter	2.9%	71.9%	17.4%	7.8%
WASHINGTON	611	9	435	123	44	Carter	1.5%	71.2%	20.1%	7.2%
TOTAL	50,482	2,078	31,383	11,087	5,934	Carter	4.1%	62.2%	22.0%	11.8%

IDAHO REPUBLICAN

1980

County	Total Vote	Reagan	Other	Winner	Percentage of Total Vote Reagan	Other
ADA	26,507	19,409	7,098	Reagan	73.2%	26.8%
ADAMS	818	689	129	Reagan	84.2%	15.8%
BANNOCK	7,880	6,324	1,556	Reagan	80.3%	19.7%
BEAR LAKE	1,408	1,278	130	Reagan	90.8%	9.2%
BENEWAH	646	552	94	Reagan	85.4%	14.6%
BINGHAM	5,406	4,786	620	Reagan	88.5%	11.5%
BLAINE	961	716	245	Reagan	74.5%	25.5%
BOISE	667	515	152	Reagan	77.2%	22.8%
BONNER	2,290	1,990	300	Reagan	86.9%	13.1%
BONNEVILLE	10,375	8,867	1,508	Reagan	85.5%	14.5%
BOUNDARY	1,027	865	162	Reagan	84.2%	15.8%
BUTTE	757	673	84	Reagan	88.9%	11.1%
CAMAS	277	233	44	Reagan	84.1%	15.9%
CANYON	12,431	10,413	2,018	Reagan	83.8%	16.2%
CARIBOU	1,080	1,011	69	Reagan	93.6%	6.4%
CASSIA	3,004	2,735	269	Reagan	91.0%	9.0%
CLARK	225	201	24	Reagan	89.3%	10.7%
CLEARWATER	535	430	105	Reagan	80.4%	19.6%
CUSTER	829	731	98	Reagan	88.2%	11.8%
ELMORE	1,528	1,221	307	Reagan	79.9%	20.1%
FRANKLIN	1,996	1,835	161	Reagan	91.9%	8.1%
FREMONT	2,532	2,304	228	Reagan	91.0%	9.0%
GEM	1,752	1,473	279	Reagan	84.1%	15.9%
GOODING	3,480	2,897	583	Reagan	83.2%	16.8%
IDAHO	1,911	1,660	251	Reagan	86.9%	13.1%
JEFFERSON	3,704	3,435	269	Reagan	92.7%	7.3%
JEROME	2,884	2,547	337	Reagan	88.3%	11.7%
KOOTENAI	5,569	4,730	839	Reagan	84.9%	15.1%
LATAH	2,177	1,528	649	Reagan	70.2%	29.8%
LEMHI	1,262	1,093	169	Reagan	86.6%	13.4%
LEWIS	441	364	77	Reagan	82.5%	17.5%
LINCOLN	1,179	962	217	Reagan	81.6%	18.4%
MADISON	3,166	2,954	212	Reagan	93.3%	6.7%
MINIDOKA	2,589	2,281	308	Reagan	88.1%	11.9%
NEZ PERCE	1,706	1,356	350	Reagan	79.5%	20.5%
ONEIDA	586	544	42	Reagan	92.8%	7.2%
OWYHEE	1,093	953	140	Reagan	87.2%	12.8%
PAYETTE	2,901	2,413	488	Reagan	83.2%	16.8%
POWER	1,407	1,179	228	Reagan	83.8%	16.2%
SHOSHONE	1,101	919	182	Reagan	83.5%	16.5%
TETON	726	678	48	Reagan	93.4%	6.6%
TWIN FALLS	8,920	7,612	1,308	Reagan	85.3%	14.7%
VALLEY	1,236	952	284	Reagan	77.0%	23.0%
WASHINGTON	1,910	1,560	350	Reagan	81.7%	18.3%
TOTAL	134,879	111,868	23,011	Reagan	82.9%	17.1%

IDAHO DEMOCRATIC

1984

County	Total Vote	Hart	Mondale	Other	Winner	Percentage of Total Vote Hart	Mondale	Other
ADA	7,841	5,148	1,880	813	Hart	65.7%	24.0%	10.4%
ADAMS	490	338	93	59	Hart	69.0%	19.0%	12.0%
BANNOCK	3,943	2,015	1,410	518	Hart	51.1%	35.8%	13.1%
BEAR LAKE	301	190	89	22	Hart	63.1%	29.6%	7.3%
BENEWAH	1,121	711	259	151	Hart	63.4%	23.1%	13.5%
BINGHAM	1,548	772	572	204	Hart	49.9%	37.0%	13.2%
BLAINE	574	345	124	105	Hart	60.1%	21.6%	18.3%
BOISE	233	137	60	36	Hart	58.8%	25.8%	15.5%
BONNER	3,026	1,788	891	347	Hart	59.1%	29.4%	11.5%
BONNEVILLE	1,881	937	739	205	Hart	49.8%	39.3%	10.9%
BOUNDARY	1,096	637	347	112	Hart	58.1%	31.7%	10.2%
BUTTE	693	313	257	123	Hart	45.2%	37.1%	17.7%
CAMAS	154	112	25	17	Hart	72.7%	16.2%	11.0%
CANYON	3,042	1,774	967	301	Hart	58.3%	31.8%	9.9%
CARIBOU	251	155	85	11	Hart	61.8%	33.9%	4.4%
CASSIA	410	224	144	42	Hart	54.6%	35.1%	10.2%
CLARK	61	38	17	6	Hart	62.3%	27.9%	9.8%
CLEARWATER	729	426	243	60	Hart	58.4%	33.3%	8.2%
CUSTER	233	139	60	34	Hart	59.7%	25.8%	14.6%
ELMORE	1,564	972	409	183	Hart	62.1%	26.2%	11.7%
FRANKLIN	165	117	33	15	Hart	70.9%	20.0%	9.1%
FREMONT	540	321	166	53	Hart	59.4%	30.7%	9.8%
GEM	1,033	634	306	93	Hart	61.4%	29.6%	9.0%
GOODING	477	271	157	49	Hart	56.8%	32.9%	10.3%
IDAHO	1,815	1,115	488	212	Hart	61.4%	26.9%	11.7%
JEFFERSON	326	154	134	38	Hart	47.2%	41.1%	11.7%
JEROME	409	197	161	51	Hart	48.2%	39.4%	12.5%
KOOTENAI	3,024	1,696	994	334	Hart	56.1%	32.9%	11.0%
LATAH	2,837	1,647	761	429	Hart	58.1%	26.8%	15.1%
LEMHI	315	162	122	31	Hart	51.4%	38.7%	9.8%
LEWIS	468	271	138	59	Hart	57.9%	29.5%	12.6%
LINCOLN	206	138	36	32	Hart	67.0%	17.5%	15.5%
MADISON	514	297	149	68	Hart	57.8%	29.0%	13.2%
MINIDOKA	501	247	187	67	Hart	49.3%	37.3%	13.4%
NEZ PERCE	4,750	2,393	1,653	704	Hart	50.4%	34.8%	14.8%
ONEIDA	202	134	65	3	Hart	66.3%	32.2%	1.5%
OWYHEE	367	260	74	33	Hart	70.8%	20.2%	9.0%
PAYETTE	973	632	212	129	Hart	65.0%	21.8%	13.3%
POWER	317	171	110	36	Hart	53.9%	34.7%	11.4%
SHOSHONE	3,172	1,742	1,046	384	Hart	54.9%	33.0%	12.1%
TETON	106	69	29	8	Hart	65.1%	27.4%	7.5%
TWIN FALLS	1,436	842	426	168	Hart	58.6%	29.7%	11.7%
VALLEY	313	228	56	29	Hart	72.8%	17.9%	9.3%
WASHINGTON	1,265	828	286	151	Hart	65.5%	22.6%	11.9%
TOTAL	54,722	31,737	16,460	6,525	Hart	58.0%	30.1%	11.9%

IDAHO REPUBLICAN

1984

County	Total Vote	Reagan	Uncommitted	Winner	Percentage of Total Vote	
					Reagan	Uncom.
ADA	19,602	17,285	2,317	Reagan	88.2%	11.8%
ADAMS	812	742	70	Reagan	91.4%	8.6%
BANNOCK	5,035	4,489	546	Reagan	89.2%	10.8%
BEAR LAKE	1,558	1,513	45	Reagan	97.1%	2.9%
BENEWAH	363	351	12	Reagan	96.7%	3.3%
BINGHAM	6,047	5,616	431	Reagan	92.9%	7.1%
BLAINE	821	751	70	Reagan	91.5%	8.5%
BOISE	647	568	79	Reagan	87.8%	12.2%
BONNER	1,880	1,830	50	Reagan	97.3%	2.7%
BONNEVILLE	9,364	8,840	524	Reagan	94.4%	5.6%
BOUNDARY	1,033	998	35	Reagan	96.6%	3.4%
BUTTE	510	489	21	Reagan	95.9%	4.1%
CAMAS	170	161	9	Reagan	94.7%	5.3%
CANYON	11,848	10,660	1,188	Reagan	90.0%	10.0%
CARIBOU	1,463	1,385	78	Reagan	94.7%	5.3%
CASSIA	3,265	3,124	141	Reagan	95.7%	4.3%
CLARK	163	155	8	Reagan	95.1%	4.9%
CLEARWATER	238	230	8	Reagan	96.6%	3.4%
CUSTER	883	811	72	Reagan	91.8%	8.2%
ELMORE	1,411	1,357	54	Reagan	96.2%	3.8%
FRANKLIN	890	850	40	Reagan	95.5%	4.5%
FREMONT	1,591	1,569	22	Reagan	98.6%	1.4%
GEM	1,215	1,114	101	Reagan	91.7%	8.3%
GOODING	2,239	2,017	222	Reagan	90.1%	9.9%
IDAHO	1,630	1,545	85	Reagan	94.8%	5.2%
JEFFERSON	522	497	25	Reagan	95.2%	4.8%
JEROME	2,593	2,477	116	Reagan	95.5%	4.5%
KOOTENAI	4,674	4,165	509	Reagan	89.1%	10.9%
LATAH	1,167	1,051	116	Reagan	90.1%	9.9%
LEMHI	1,534	1,446	88	Reagan	94.3%	5.7%
LEWIS	167	160	7	Reagan	95.8%	4.2%
LINCOLN	654	593	61	Reagan	90.7%	9.3%
MADISON	2,449	2,397	52	Reagan	97.9%	2.1%
MINIDOKA	4,074	3,675	399	Reagan	90.2%	9.8%
NEZ PERCE	778	754	24	Reagan	96.9%	3.1%
ONEIDA	483	479	4	Reagan	99.2%	0.8%
OWYHEE	765	736	29	Reagan	96.2%	3.8%
PAYETTE	1,423	1,336	87	Reagan	93.9%	6.1%
POWER	1,044	949	95	Reagan	90.9%	9.1%
SHOSHONE	479	453	26	Reagan	94.6%	5.4%
TETON	688	676	12	Reagan	98.3%	1.7%
TWIN FALLS	5,838	5,550	288	Reagan	95.1%	4.9%
VALLEY	713	674	39	Reagan	94.5%	5.5%
WASHINGTON	964	932	32	Reagan	96.7%	3.3%
TOTAL	105,687	97,450	8,237	Reagan	92.2%	7.8%

IDAHO DEMOCRATIC

1988

County	Total Vote	Dukakis	J. Jackson	Other	Winner	Percentage of Total Vote Dukakis	J. Jackson	Other
ADA	4,566	3,341	877	348	Dukakis	73.2%	19.2%	7.6%
ADAMS	245	174	49	22	Dukakis	71.0%	20.0%	9.0%
BANNOCK	5,159	3,720	754	685	Dukakis	72.1%	14.6%	13.3%
BEAR LAKE	515	442	34	39	Dukakis	85.8%	6.6%	7.6%
BENEWAH	632	445	129	58	Dukakis	70.4%	20.4%	9.2%
BINGHAM	1,415	1,086	173	156	Dukakis	76.7%	12.2%	11.0%
BLAINE	843	554	204	85	Dukakis	65.7%	24.2%	10.1%
BOISE	231	189	32	10	Dukakis	81.8%	13.9%	4.3%
BONNER	3,287	2,295	617	375	Dukakis	69.8%	18.8%	11.4%
BONNEVILLE	1,083	840	146	97	Dukakis	77.6%	13.5%	9.0%
BOUNDARY	1,136	830	191	115	Dukakis	73.1%	16.8%	10.1%
BUTTE	243	196	26	21	Dukakis	80.7%	10.7%	8.6%
CAMAS	63	41	11	11	Dukakis	65.1%	17.5%	17.5%
CANYON	1,905	1,502	264	139	Dukakis	78.8%	13.9%	7.3%
CARIBOU	635	511	53	71	Dukakis	80.5%	8.3%	11.2%
CASSIA	504	387	68	49	Dukakis	76.8%	13.5%	9.7%
CLARK	48	43	1	4	Dukakis	89.6%	2.1%	8.3%
CLEARWATER	1,019	739	146	134	Dukakis	72.5%	14.3%	13.2%
CUSTER	157	116	29	12	Dukakis	73.9%	18.5%	7.6%
ELMORE	1,420	1,069	204	147	Dukakis	75.3%	14.4%	10.4%
FRANKLIN	223	186	13	24	Dukakis	83.4%	5.8%	10.8%
FREMONT	430	355	37	38	Dukakis	82.6%	8.6%	8.8%
GEM	739	609	68	62	Dukakis	82.4%	9.2%	8.4%
GOODING	432	340	66	26	Dukakis	78.7%	15.3%	6.0%
IDAHO	2,541	1,829	328	384	Dukakis	72.0%	12.9%	15.1%
JEFFERSON	306	241	27	38	Dukakis	78.8%	8.8%	12.4%
JEROME	410	314	76	20	Dukakis	76.6%	18.5%	4.9%
KOOTENAI	2,727	2,024	496	207	Dukakis	74.2%	18.2%	7.6%
LATAH	3,402	2,155	785	462	Dukakis	63.3%	23.1%	13.6%
LEMHI	430	326	68	36	Dukakis	75.8%	15.8%	8.4%
LEWIS	905	667	125	113	Dukakis	73.7%	13.8%	12.5%
LINCOLN	165	130	26	9	Dukakis	78.8%	15.8%	5.5%
MADISON	314	260	25	29	Dukakis	82.8%	8.0%	9.2%
MINIDOKA	635	524	67	44	Dukakis	82.5%	10.6%	6.9%
NEZ PERCE	6,219	4,457	924	838	Dukakis	71.7%	14.9%	13.5%
ONEIDA	225	179	17	29	Dukakis	79.6%	7.6%	12.9%
OWYHEE	306	231	52	23	Dukakis	75.5%	17.0%	7.5%
PAYETTE	454	356	65	33	Dukakis	78.4%	14.3%	7.3%
POWER	295	240	38	17	Dukakis	81.4%	12.9%	5.8%
SHOSHONE	2,786	1,956	406	424	Dukakis	70.2%	14.6%	15.2%
TETON	96	74	14	8	Dukakis	77.1%	14.6%	8.3%
TWIN FALLS	1,649	1,273	251	125	Dukakis	77.2%	15.2%	7.6%
VALLEY	206	159	35	12	Dukakis	77.2%	17.0%	5.8%
WASHINGTON	369	291	49	29	Dukakis	78.9%	13.3%	7.9%
TOTAL	51,370	37,696	8,066	5,608	Dukakis	73.4%	15.7%	10.9%

IDAHO REPUBLICAN

1988

County	Total Vote	Bush	Robertson	Uncommitted	Winner	Percentage of Total Vote Bush	Robertson	Uncom.
ADA	11,324	9,281	823	1,220	Bush	82.0%	7.3%	10.8%
ADAMS	839	621	93	125	Bush	74.0%	11.1%	14.9%
BANNOCK	1,721	1,471	133	117	Bush	85.5%	7.7%	6.8%
BEAR LAKE	1,098	954	97	47	Bush	86.9%	8.8%	4.3%
BENEWAH	245	176	51	18	Bush	71.8%	20.8%	7.3%
BINGHAM	2,842	2,428	154	260	Bush	85.4%	5.4%	9.1%
BLAINE	1,256	917	87	252	Bush	73.0%	6.9%	20.1%
BOISE	575	469	53	53	Bush	81.6%	9.2%	9.2%
BONNER	1,240	1,035	116	89	Bush	83.5%	9.4%	7.2%
BONNEVILLE	3,175	2,723	207	245	Bush	85.8%	6.5%	7.7%
BOUNDARY	461	374	50	37	Bush	81.1%	10.8%	8.0%
BUTTE	364	308	25	31	Bush	84.6%	6.9%	8.5%
CAMAS	212	158	13	41	Bush	74.5%	6.1%	19.3%
CANYON	7,020	5,605	592	823	Bush	79.8%	8.4%	11.7%
CARIBOU	1,099	943	76	80	Bush	85.8%	6.9%	7.3%
CASSIA	1,921	1,412	395	114	Bush	73.5%	20.6%	5.9%
CLARK	241	197	11	33	Bush	81.7%	4.6%	13.7%
CLEARWATER	166	137	23	6	Bush	82.5%	13.9%	3.6%
CUSTER	576	428	50	98	Bush	74.3%	8.7%	17.0%
ELMORE	741	648	63	30	Bush	87.4%	8.5%	4.0%
FRANKLIN	1,008	823	83	102	Bush	81.6%	8.2%	10.1%
FREMONT	754	697	34	23	Bush	92.4%	4.5%	3.1%
GEM	1,288	1,014	123	151	Bush	78.7%	9.5%	11.7%
GOODING	1,983	1,501	240	242	Bush	75.7%	12.1%	12.2%
IDAHO	667	554	87	26	Bush	83.1%	13.0%	3.9%
JEFFERSON	2,563	2,153	159	251	Bush	84.0%	6.2%	9.8%
JEROME	2,086	1,714	209	163	Bush	82.2%	10.0%	7.8%
KOOTENAI	3,107	2,470	343	294	Bush	79.5%	11.0%	9.5%
LATAH	795	666	84	45	Bush	83.8%	10.6%	5.7%
LEMHI	1,533	1,242	92	199	Bush	81.0%	6.0%	13.0%
LEWIS	106	90	12	4	Bush	84.9%	11.3%	3.8%
LINCOLN	596	432	73	91	Bush	72.5%	12.2%	15.3%
MADISON	1,489	1,298	87	104	Bush	87.2%	5.8%	7.0%
MINIDOKA	1,682	1,323	132	227	Bush	78.7%	7.8%	13.5%
NEZ PERCE	684	538	95	51	Bush	78.7%	13.9%	7.5%
ONEIDA	538	434	39	65	Bush	80.7%	7.2%	12.1%
OWYHEE	445	375	37	33	Bush	84.3%	8.3%	7.4%
PAYETTE	1,826	1,437	191	198	Bush	78.7%	10.5%	10.8%
POWER	376	329	30	17	Bush	87.5%	8.0%	4.5%
SHOSHONE	252	214	29	9	Bush	84.9%	11.5%	3.6%
TETON	402	349	22	31	Bush	86.8%	5.5%	7.7%
TWIN FALLS	4,060	3,339	342	379	Bush	82.2%	8.4%	9.3%
VALLEY	1,394	1,030	88	276	Bush	73.9%	6.3%	19.8%
WASHINGTON	1,525	1,157	133	235	Bush	75.9%	8.7%	15.4%
TOTAL	68,275	55,464	5,876	6,935	Bush	81.2%	8.6%	10.2%

IDAHO DEMOCRATIC

1992

County	Total Vote	Brown	Clinton	Uncommitted	Other	Winner	Percentage of Total Vote Brown	Clinton	Uncom.	Other
ADA	9,193	1,670	4,307	2,902	314	Clinton	18.2%	46.9%	31.6%	3.4%
ADAMS	193	34	105	35	19	Clinton	17.6%	54.4%	18.1%	9.8%
BANNOCK	3,794	826	2,116	595	257	Clinton	21.8%	55.8%	15.7%	6.8%
BEAR LAKE	225	41	150	18	16	Clinton	18.2%	66.7%	8.0%	7.1%
BENEWAH	671	125	396	109	41	Clinton	18.6%	59.0%	16.2%	6.1%
BINGHAM	1,472	213	660	494	105	Clinton	14.5%	44.8%	33.6%	7.1%
BLAINE	1,048	263	290	478	17	Uncommitted	25.1%	27.7%	45.6%	1.6%
BOISE	259	50	140	54	15	Clinton	19.3%	54.1%	20.8%	5.8%
BONNER	3,118	734	1,586	634	164	Clinton	23.5%	50.9%	20.3%	5.3%
BONNEVILLE	2,100	352	995	627	126	Clinton	16.8%	47.4%	29.9%	6.0%
BOUNDARY	448	69	260	94	25	Clinton	15.4%	58.0%	21.0%	5.6%
BUTTE	284	32	142	90	20	Clinton	11.3%	50.0%	31.7%	7.0%
CAMAS	68	12	34	17	5	Clinton	17.6%	50.0%	25.0%	7.4%
CANYON	2,549	425	1,406	550	168	Clinton	16.7%	55.2%	21.6%	6.6%
CARIBOU	344	75	183	50	36	Clinton	21.8%	53.2%	14.5%	10.5%
CASSIA	572	90	293	143	46	Clinton	15.7%	51.2%	25.0%	8.0%
CLARK	20	4	11	4	1	Clinton	20.0%	55.0%	20.0%	5.0%
CLEARWATER	1,057	147	514	343	53	Clinton	13.9%	48.6%	32.5%	5.0%
CUSTER	238	45	125	53	15	Clinton	18.9%	52.5%	22.3%	6.3%
ELMORE	1,366	172	699	442	53	Clinton	12.6%	51.2%	32.4%	3.9%
FRANKLIN	313	55	138	98	22	Clinton	17.6%	44.1%	31.3%	7.0%
FREMONT	477	66	206	154	51	Clinton	13.8%	43.2%	32.3%	10.7%
GEM	644	58	349	204	33	Clinton	9.0%	54.2%	31.7%	5.1%
GOODING	382	52	248	64	18	Clinton	13.6%	64.9%	16.8%	4.7%
IDAHO	1,357	188	711	376	82	Clinton	13.9%	52.4%	27.7%	6.0%
JEFFERSON	447	56	203	149	39	Clinton	12.5%	45.4%	33.3%	8.7%
JEROME	407	66	236	67	38	Clinton	16.2%	58.0%	16.5%	9.3%
KOOTENAI	4,782	883	2,113	1,633	153	Clinton	18.5%	44.2%	34.1%	3.2%
LATAH	2,463	456	1,107	644	256	Clinton	18.5%	44.9%	26.1%	10.4%
LEMHI	428	54	250	105	19	Clinton	12.6%	58.4%	24.5%	4.4%
LEWIS	809	84	378	309	38	Clinton	10.4%	46.7%	38.2%	4.7%
LINCOLN	137	29	85	15	8	Clinton	21.2%	62.0%	10.9%	5.8%
MADISON	346	42	185	84	35	Clinton	12.1%	53.5%	24.3%	10.1%
MINIDOKA	633	110	282	177	64	Clinton	17.4%	44.5%	28.0%	10.1%
NEZ PERCE	4,018	487	1,863	1,515	153	Clinton	12.1%	46.4%	37.7%	3.8%
ONEIDA	270	33	133	86	18	Clinton	12.2%	49.3%	31.9%	6.7%
OWYHEE	298	45	177	53	23	Clinton	15.1%	59.4%	17.8%	7.7%
PAYETTE	647	95	340	184	28	Clinton	14.7%	52.6%	28.4%	4.3%
POWER	366	54	211	81	20	Clinton	14.8%	57.7%	22.1%	5.5%
SHOSHONE	4,562	530	2,009	1,856	167	Clinton	11.6%	44.0%	40.7%	3.7%
TETON	193	32	109	41	11	Clinton	16.6%	56.5%	21.2%	5.7%
TWIN FALLS	1,388	247	831	242	68	Clinton	17.8%	59.9%	17.4%	4.9%
VALLEY	275	62	143	57	13	Clinton	22.5%	52.0%	20.7%	4.7%
WASHINGTON	463	49	285	103	26	Clinton	10.6%	61.6%	22.2%	5.6%
TOTAL	55,124	9,212	27,004	16,029	2,879	Clinton	16.7%	49.0%	29.1%	5.2%

IDAHO REPUBLICAN

1992

County	Total Vote	Buchanan	Bush	Uncommitted	Winner	Percentage of Total Vote Buchanan	Bush	Uncom.
ADA	28,357	2,792	17,932	7,633	Bush	9.8%	63.2%	26.9%
ADAMS	713	121	437	155	Bush	17.0%	61.3%	21.7%
BANNOCK	3,313	523	2,514	276	Bush	15.8%	75.9%	8.3%
BEAR LAKE	1,225	170	919	136	Bush	13.9%	75.0%	11.1%
BENEWAH	562	78	421	63	Bush	13.9%	74.9%	11.2%
BINGHAM	5,437	755	3,228	1,454	Bush	13.9%	59.4%	26.7%
BLAINE	808	69	472	267	Bush	8.5%	58.4%	33.0%
BOISE	641	91	454	96	Bush	14.2%	70.8%	15.0%
BONNER	1,804	183	1,428	193	Bush	10.1%	79.2%	10.7%
BONNEVILLE	12,021	1,879	7,183	2,959	Bush	15.6%	59.8%	24.6%
BOUNDARY	571	90	386	95	Bush	15.8%	67.6%	16.6%
BUTTE	349	42	230	77	Bush	12.0%	65.9%	22.1%
CAMAS	172	12	129	31	Bush	7.0%	75.0%	18.0%
CANYON	11,572	1,453	7,517	2,602	Bush	12.6%	65.0%	22.5%
CARIBOU	910	170	678	62	Bush	18.7%	74.5%	6.8%
CASSIA	2,047	226	1,357	464	Bush	11.0%	66.3%	22.7%
CLARK	251	48	139	64	Bush	19.1%	55.4%	25.5%
CLEARWATER	300	47	206	47	Bush	15.7%	68.7%	15.7%
CUSTER	852	120	484	248	Bush	14.1%	56.8%	29.1%
ELMORE	1,435	151	1,035	249	Bush	10.5%	72.1%	17.4%
FRANKLIN	858	83	622	153	Bush	9.7%	72.5%	17.8%
FREMONT	1,552	263	1,067	222	Bush	16.9%	68.8%	14.3%
GEM	1,295	164	787	344	Bush	12.7%	60.8%	26.6%
GOODING	2,068	354	1,167	547	Bush	17.1%	56.4%	26.5%
IDAHO	1,598	250	1,078	270	Bush	15.6%	67.5%	16.9%
JEFFERSON	2,966	465	1,631	870	Bush	15.7%	55.0%	29.3%
JEROME	2,262	375	1,425	462	Bush	16.6%	63.0%	20.4%
KOOTENAI	3,275	426	2,132	717	Bush	13.0%	65.1%	21.9%
LATAH	1,306	221	867	218	Bush	16.9%	66.4%	16.7%
LEMHI	1,514	194	849	471	Bush	12.8%	56.1%	31.1%
LEWIS	152	23	104	25	Bush	15.1%	68.4%	16.4%
LINCOLN	617	94	364	159	Bush	15.2%	59.0%	25.8%
MADISON	3,405	497	2,330	578	Bush	14.6%	68.4%	17.0%
MINIDOKA	3,387	590	1,637	1,160	Bush	17.4%	48.3%	34.2%
NEZ PERCE	1,345	146	954	245	Bush	10.9%	70.9%	18.2%
ONEIDA	790	130	503	157	Bush	16.5%	63.7%	19.9%
OWYHEE	879	149	591	139	Bush	17.0%	67.2%	15.8%
PAYETTE	1,773	216	1,098	459	Bush	12.2%	61.9%	25.9%
POWER	510	69	370	71	Bush	13.5%	72.5%	13.9%
SHOSHONE	236	30	154	52	Bush	12.7%	65.3%	22.0%
TETON	587	96	369	122	Bush	16.4%	62.9%	20.8%
TWIN FALLS	6,718	951	4,194	1,573	Bush	14.2%	62.4%	23.4%
VALLEY	1,740	194	1,013	533	Bush	11.1%	58.2%	30.6%
WASHINGTON	1,329	167	842	320	Bush	12.6%	63.4%	24.1%
TOTAL	115,502	15,167	73,297	27,038	Bush	13.1%	63.5%	23.4%

IDAHO DEMOCRATIC

1996

County	Total Vote	Clinton	Uncommitted	Winner	Percentage of Total Vote	
					Clinton	Uncom.
ADA	8,058	7,408	650	Clinton	91.9%	8.1%
ADAMS	107	101	6	Clinton	94.4%	5.6%
BANNOCK	4,080	3,340	740	Clinton	81.9%	18.1%
BEAR LAKE	242	231	11	Clinton	95.5%	4.5%
BENEWAH	719	617	102	Clinton	85.8%	14.2%
BINGHAM	804	701	103	Clinton	87.2%	12.8%
BLAINE	2,319	1,937	382	Clinton	83.5%	16.5%
BOISE	218	132	86	Clinton	60.6%	39.4%
BONNER	1,817	1,657	160	Clinton	91.2%	8.8%
BONNEVILLE	1,227	1,100	127	Clinton	89.6%	10.4%
BOUNDARY	316	295	21	Clinton	93.4%	6.6%
BUTTE	105	99	6	Clinton	94.3%	5.7%
CAMAS	11	10	1	Clinton	90.9%	9.1%
CANYON	1,635	1,454	181	Clinton	88.9%	11.1%
CARIBOU	200	188	12	Clinton	94.0%	6.0%
CASSIA	229	198	31	Clinton	86.5%	13.5%
CLARK	23	23		Clinton	100.0%	
CLEARWATER	825	661	164	Clinton	80.1%	19.9%
CUSTER	92	90	2	Clinton	97.8%	2.2%
ELMORE	681	619	62	Clinton	90.9%	9.1%
FRANKLIN	112	96	16	Clinton	85.7%	14.3%
FREMONT	441	293	148	Clinton	66.4%	33.6%
GEM	322	299	23	Clinton	92.9%	7.1%
GOODING	215	197	18	Clinton	91.6%	8.4%
IDAHO	1,053	930	123	Clinton	88.3%	11.7%
JEFFERSON	196	159	37	Clinton	81.1%	18.9%
JEROME	145	140	5	Clinton	96.6%	3.4%
KOOTENAI	1,891	1,777	114	Clinton	94.0%	6.0%
LATAH	1,797	1,613	184	Clinton	89.8%	10.2%
LEMHI	268	247	21	Clinton	92.2%	7.8%
LEWIS	334	304	30	Clinton	91.0%	9.0%
LINCOLN	171	150	21	Clinton	87.7%	12.3%
MADISON	132	119	13	Clinton	90.2%	9.8%
MINIDOKA	261	240	21	Clinton	92.0%	8.0%
NEZ PERCE	3,482	2,882	600	Clinton	82.8%	17.2%
ONEIDA	91	84	7	Clinton	92.3%	7.7%
OWYHEE	153	148	5	Clinton	96.7%	3.3%
PAYETTE	464	422	42	Clinton	90.9%	9.1%
POWER	309	276	33	Clinton	89.3%	10.7%
SHOSHONE	2,912	2,392	520	Clinton	82.1%	17.9%
TETON	373	355	18	Clinton	95.2%	4.8%
TWIN FALLS	801	753	48	Clinton	94.0%	6.0%
VALLEY	138	131	7	Clinton	94.9%	5.1%
WASHINGTON	459	409	50	Clinton	89.1%	10.9%
TOTAL	40,228	35,277	4,951	Clinton	87.7%	12.3%

IDAHO REPUBLICAN

1996

County	Total Vote	Buchanan	Dole	Keyes	Uncommitted	Winner	Percentage of Total Vote Buchanan	Dole	Keyes	Uncom.
ADA	23,302	4,223	14,816	1,699	2,564	Dole	18.1%	63.6%	7.3%	11.0%
ADAMS	1,247	359	639	50	199	Dole	28.8%	51.2%	4.0%	16.0%
BANNOCK	3,181	798	2,114	110	159	Dole	25.1%	66.5%	3.5%	5.0%
BEAR LAKE	1,929	385	1,235	48	261	Dole	20.0%	64.0%	2.5%	13.5%
BENEWAH	706	177	444	39	46	Dole	25.1%	62.9%	5.5%	6.5%
BINGHAM	6,354	1,540	3,823	173	818	Dole	24.2%	60.2%	2.7%	12.9%
BLAINE	1,498	162	1,076	60	200	Dole	10.8%	71.8%	4.0%	13.4%
BOISE	1,273	320	738	91	124	Dole	25.1%	58.0%	7.1%	9.7%
BONNER	4,242	747	2,629	235	631	Dole	17.6%	62.0%	5.5%	14.9%
BONNEVILLE	9,861	2,354	6,377	422	708	Dole	23.9%	64.7%	4.3%	7.2%
BOUNDARY	1,035	208	671	48	108	Dole	20.1%	64.8%	4.6%	10.4%
BUTTE	685	197	423	20	45	Dole	28.8%	61.8%	2.9%	6.6%
CAMAS	461	131	222	30	78	Dole	28.4%	48.2%	6.5%	16.9%
CANYON	8,995	2,147	5,465	492	891	Dole	23.9%	60.8%	5.5%	9.9%
CARIBOU	614	135	452	16	11	Dole	22.0%	73.6%	2.6%	1.8%
CASSIA	3,079	655	1,900	224	300	Dole	21.3%	61.7%	7.3%	9.7%
CLARK	240	68	156	8	8	Dole	28.3%	65.0%	3.3%	3.3%
CLEARWATER	619	161	363	29	66	Dole	26.0%	58.6%	4.7%	10.7%
CUSTER	1,169	271	754	50	94	Dole	23.2%	64.5%	4.3%	8.0%
ELMORE	1,734	389	1,087	81	177	Dole	22.4%	62.7%	4.7%	10.2%
FRANKLIN	582	102	393	16	71	Dole	17.5%	67.5%	2.7%	12.2%
FREMONT	2,023	521	1,306	52	144	Dole	25.8%	64.6%	2.6%	7.1%
GEM	2,310	593	1,308	139	270	Dole	25.7%	56.6%	6.0%	11.7%
GOODING	2,462	773	1,262	84	343	Dole	31.4%	51.3%	3.4%	13.9%
IDAHO	2,411	666	1,475	116	154	Dole	27.6%	61.2%	4.8%	6.4%
JEFFERSON	2,030	552	1,262	49	167	Dole	27.2%	62.2%	2.4%	8.2%
JEROME	2,658	774	1,488	95	301	Dole	29.1%	56.0%	3.6%	11.3%
KOOTENAI	7,002	1,315	4,470	342	875	Dole	18.8%	63.8%	4.9%	12.5%
LATAH	2,689	373	1,664	230	422	Dole	13.9%	61.9%	8.6%	15.7%
LEMHI	1,603	333	1,053	47	170	Dole	20.8%	65.7%	2.9%	10.6%
LEWIS	278	62	192	4	20	Dole	22.3%	69.1%	1.4%	7.2%
LINCOLN	603	209	344	22	28	Dole	34.7%	57.0%	3.6%	4.6%
MADISON	3,444	793	2,291	84	276	Dole	23.0%	66.5%	2.4%	8.0%
MINIDOKA	2,531	588	1,505	91	347	Dole	23.2%	59.5%	3.6%	13.7%
NEZ PERCE	2,148	310	1,481	103	254	Dole	14.4%	68.9%	4.8%	11.8%
ONEIDA	264	44	187	14	19	Dole	16.7%	70.8%	5.3%	7.2%
OWYHEE	1,630	457	1,059	60	54	Dole	28.0%	65.0%	3.7%	3.3%
PAYETTE	1,205	299	763	42	101	Dole	24.8%	63.3%	3.5%	8.4%
POWER	485	131	323	9	22	Dole	27.0%	66.6%	1.9%	4.5%
SHOSHONE	376	87	228	33	28	Dole	23.1%	60.6%	8.8%	7.4%
TETON	699	171	485	21	22	Dole	24.5%	69.4%	3.0%	3.1%
TWIN FALLS	3,312	1,122	1,879	124	187	Dole	33.9%	56.7%	3.7%	5.6%
VALLEY	2,280	403	1,282	136	459	Dole	17.7%	56.2%	6.0%	20.1%
WASHINGTON	1,466	356	927	66	117	Dole	24.3%	63.2%	4.5%	8.0%
TOTAL	118,715	26,461	74,011	5,904	12,339	Dole	22.3%	62.3%	5.0%	10.4%

ILLINOIS

For years, the Illinois primary stood alone as a gateway to the later primaries in the industrial Frost Belt. But no more. Once near the beginning of the presidential nominating process, Illinois' mid-March vote is, at best, somewhere near the middle.

Yet Illinois still offers a rich harvest of delegates plus the reputation it has earned as a harbinger of things to come. Every Republican presidential nominee since 1976 and five of the last six Democratic nominees have first won the Illinois preference primary.

When candidates come to Illinois, there is no guesswork as to where they go. Democrats head to Chicago—nearly 40 percent black, 20 percent Hispanic (in 1990)—and the source of roughly half the party's statewide primary vote.

Republicans go to the suburban "collar" counties that surround Chicago on the north, south and west, before campaigning in the small cities, towns and farm country downstate.

The collar counties, paced by Du Page and Lake, are among the most affluent in the country. Loaded with white-collar professionals, they tend to prefer more moderate Republican candidates than do GOP voters in rural Illinois. In 1980, native-son John Anderson won Cook (which includes Chicago) and Lake counties and ran virtually even with Ronald Reagan in Du Page.

Downstate, there is a more conservative brand of Republicanism that Reagan knew intimately. He was born in Tampico in the northwest part of the state and grew up in nearby Dixon.

Reagan's Illinois roots were not much help in his 1976 challenge to President Gerald Ford, as Ford easily swept the state. But in 1980, downstate Republicans found Reagan preferable to Anderson, which pushed Reagan to a comfortable victory statewide and Anderson toward an independent presidential bid.

Recent Illinois Primary Results

Illinois held its first presidential primary in 1912.

	DEMOCRATS			REPUBLICANS		
Year	Turnout	Candidates	%	Turnout	Candidates	%
1996 (March 19)	800,676	BILL CLINTON*	96	818,364	BOB DOLE	65
					Pat Buchanan	23
1992 (March 17)	1,504,130	BILL CLINTON	52	831,140	GEORGE BUSH*	76
		Paul Tsongas	26		Pat Buchanan	22
		Jerry Brown	15			
1988 (March 15)	1,500,930	PAUL SIMON	42	858,637	GEORGE BUSH	55
		Jesse Jackson	32		Bob Dole	36
		Michael Dukakis	16			
1984 (March 20)	1,659,425	WALTER MONDALE	40	595,078	RONALD REAGAN*	100
		Gary Hart	35			
		Jesse Jackson	21			
1980 (March 18)	1,201,067	JIMMY CARTER*	65	1,130,081	RONALD REAGAN	48
		Edward Kennedy	30		John Anderson	37
					George Bush	11
1976 (March 16)	1,311,914	JIMMY CARTER	48	775,893	GERALD FORD*	59
		George Wallace	28		Ronald Reagan	40
		Sargent Shriver	16			
1972 (March 21)	1,225,144	EDMUND MUSKIE	63	33,569	RICHARD NIXON* #	97
		Eugene McCarthy	36			
1968 (June 11)	12,038	EUGENE McCARTHY#	39	22,403	RICHARD NIXON#	78
		Edward Kennedy#	34			
		Hubert Humphrey#	17			

Note: All candidates are listed that drew at least 10 percent of their party's primary vote. The names of winning candidates are capitalized. An asterisk (*) indicates an incumbent president. A pound sign (#) indicates a write-in candidate.

In 1980, Illinois was still near the beginning of the primary calendar. Not so in 1988. Then, the Republican presidential contest essentially ended in Illinois. Bob Dole had considered dropping out of the race after winning zero states on Super Tuesday. But he chose instead to plunge on into Illinois the next week, hoping that support from farm areas would revive his candidacy and raise fresh doubts about George Bush.

It was not to be. Dole carried a few rural counties but did not come close to the breakthrough he needed in the mother lode: Chicago's Republican suburbs.

The Illinois Democratic primary has rarely produced much drama. For years, Democratic presidential politics in Illinois was neat and tidy. Chicago Mayor Richard J. Daley controlled the bulk of the delegation and took it to the national convention uncommitted. Since Daley's death in 1976, the party's Democratic nominating process within the state has been less orderly. But the Democratic primary has often provided a big win for the early front-runner at a critical point in the process.

President Jimmy Carter's 1980 demolition of Edward Kennedy (the margin was more than 2-to-1) essentially removed Kennedy as a realistic threat to Carter's renomination. In 1984, Walter Mondale's 5 percentage point victory over Gary Hart brought Mondale back from the verge of elimination and marked Hart's last chance to land a knockout blow. In 1992, Bill Clinton so thoroughly dominated the mid-March primaries in Illinois and Michigan that his major rival, Paul Tsongas, quit the race shortly thereafter.

ILLINOIS DEMOCRATIC

1972

County	Total Vote	McCarthy	Muskie	Other	Winner	Percentage of Total Vote McCarthy	Muskie	Other
ADAMS	4,982	1,672	3,197	113	Muskie	33.6%	64.2%	2.3%
ALEXANDER	1,376	276	974	126	Muskie	20.1%	70.8%	9.2%
BOND	1,419	425	984	10	Muskie	30.0%	69.3%	0.7%
BOONE	1,496	508	900	88	Muskie	34.0%	60.2%	5.9%
BROWN	1,162	404	742	16	Muskie	34.8%	63.9%	1.4%
BUREAU	2,744	878	1,866		Muskie	32.0%	68.0%	
CALHOUN	884	288	588	8	Muskie	32.6%	66.5%	0.9%
CARROLL	1,007	332	654	21	Muskie	33.0%	64.9%	2.1%
CASS	1,873	460	1,413		Muskie	24.6%	75.4%	
CHAMPAIGN	15,447	7,697	6,633	1,117	McCarthy	49.8%	42.9%	7.2%
CHRISTIAN	4,361	1,388	2,973		Muskie	31.8%	68.2%	
CLARK	1,634	442	1,174	18	Muskie	27.1%	71.8%	1.1%
CLAY	1,242	308	934		Muskie	24.8%	75.2%	
CLINTON	2,193	730	1,431	32	Muskie	33.3%	65.3%	1.5%
COLES	4,255	1,713	2,542		Muskie	40.3%	59.7%	
COOK	772,750	291,853	476,107	4,790	Muskie	37.8%	61.6%	0.6%
CRAWFORD	1,725	533	1,155	37	Muskie	30.9%	67.0%	2.1%
CUMBERLAND	1,743	602	1,122	19	Muskie	34.5%	64.4%	1.1%
DE KALB	6,012	3,019	2,774	219	McCarthy	50.2%	46.1%	3.6%
DE WITT	1,354	501	851	2	Muskie	37.0%	62.9%	0.1%
DOUGLAS	1,561	607	954		Muskie	38.9%	61.1%	
DU PAGE	34,173	15,642	18,531		Muskie	45.8%	54.2%	
EDGAR	2,444	791	1,615	38	Muskie	32.4%	66.1%	1.6%
EDWARDS	550	123	427		Muskie	22.4%	77.6%	
EFFINGHAM	2,760	786	1,933	41	Muskie	28.5%	70.0%	1.5%
FAYETTE	2,741	706	2,035		Muskie	25.8%	74.2%	
FORD	947	342	590	15	Muskie	36.1%	62.3%	1.6%
FRANKLIN	7,317	2,095	5,222		Muskie	28.6%	71.4%	
FULTON	5,119	1,381	3,738		Muskie	27.0%	73.0%	
GALLATIN	1,872	560	1,281	31	Muskie	29.9%	68.4%	1.7%
GREENE	1,706	448	1,258		Muskie	26.3%	73.7%	
GRUNDY	1,711	525	1,186		Muskie	30.7%	69.3%	
HAMILTON	1,899	533	1,366		Muskie	28.1%	71.9%	
HANCOCK	1,642	514	1,063	65	Muskie	31.3%	64.7%	4.0%
HARDIN	636	121	506	9	Muskie	19.0%	79.6%	1.4%
HENDERSON	810	205	590	15	Muskie	25.3%	72.8%	1.9%
HENRY	2,697	798	1,821	78	Muskie	29.6%	67.5%	2.9%
IROQUOIS	1,771	667	1,063	41	Muskie	37.7%	60.0%	2.3%
JACKSON	4,970	1,727	3,094	149	Muskie	34.7%	62.3%	3.0%
JASPER	1,242	370	841	31	Muskie	29.8%	67.7%	2.5%
JEFFERSON	4,094	1,038	2,933	123	Muskie	25.4%	71.6%	3.0%
JERSEY	1,851	510	1,307	34	Muskie	27.6%	70.6%	1.8%
JO DAVIESS	1,066	356	696	14	Muskie	33.4%	65.3%	1.3%
JOHNSON	890	175	715		Muskie	19.7%	80.3%	
KANE	11,777	4,834	6,943		Muskie	41.0%	59.0%	
KANKAKEE	3,653	1,152	2,428	73	Muskie	31.5%	66.5%	2.0%
KENDALL	1,159	498	661		Muskie	43.0%	57.0%	
KNOX	3,021	1,083	1,869	69	Muskie	35.8%	61.9%	2.3%
LAKE	22,095	8,915	12,388	792	Muskie	40.3%	56.1%	3.6%
LA SALLE	9,177	2,635	6,493	49	Muskie	28.7%	70.8%	0.5%

ILLINOIS DEMOCRATIC

1972

County	Total Vote	McCarthy	Muskie	Other	Winner	Percentage of Total Vote McCarthy	Muskie	Other
LAWRENCE	1,199	317	882		Muskie	26.4%	73.6%	
LEE	2,669	887	1,771	11	Muskie	33.2%	66.4%	0.4%
LIVINGSTON	2,280	618	1,662		Muskie	27.1%	72.9%	
LOGAN	2,266	664	1,602		Muskie	29.3%	70.7%	
MCDONOUGH	2,358	963	1,395		Muskie	40.8%	59.2%	
MCHENRY	6,168	2,464	3,521	183	Muskie	39.9%	57.1%	3.0%
MCLEAN	7,948	2,726	4,914	308	Muskie	34.3%	61.8%	3.9%
MACON	9,776	3,631	5,895	250	Muskie	37.1%	60.3%	2.6%
MACOUPIN	7,649	2,031	5,413	205	Muskie	26.6%	70.8%	2.7%
MADISON	24,180	7,491	16,689		Muskie	31.0%	69.0%	
MARION	4,172	1,205	2,903	64	Muskie	28.9%	69.6%	1.5%
MARSHALL	1,278	308	970		Muskie	24.1%	75.9%	
MASON	1,941	456	1,444	41	Muskie	23.5%	74.4%	2.1%
MASSAC	849	237	579	33	Muskie	27.9%	68.2%	3.9%
MENARD	888	189	681	18	Muskie	21.3%	76.7%	2.0%
MERCER	1,999	559	1,359	81	Muskie	28.0%	68.0%	4.1%
MONROE	1,152	442	682	28	Muskie	38.4%	59.2%	2.4%
MONTGOMERY	4,056	937	3,119		Muskie	23.1%	76.9%	
MORGAN	3,159	967	2,192		Muskie	30.6%	69.4%	
MOULTRIE	1,680	446	1,122	112	Muskie	26.5%	66.8%	6.7%
OGLE	2,251	896	1,355		Muskie	39.8%	60.2%	
PEORIA	18,089	4,855	11,598	1,636	Muskie	26.8%	64.1%	9.0%
PERRY	2,954	892	2,062		Muskie	30.2%	69.8%	
PIATT	1,339	485	854		Muskie	36.2%	63.8%	
PIKE	2,565	679	1,854	32	Muskie	26.5%	72.3%	1.2%
POPE	444	111	333		Muskie	25.0%	75.0%	
PULASKI	692	171	503	18	Muskie	24.7%	72.7%	2.6%
PUTNAM	560	153	407		Muskie	27.3%	72.7%	
RANDOLPH	3,563	701	2,832	30	Muskie	19.7%	79.5%	0.8%
RICHLAND	1,103	295	752	56	Muskie	26.7%	68.2%	5.1%
ROCK ISLAND	11,079	3,676	7,403		Muskie	33.2%	66.8%	
ST. CLAIR	23,578	8,603	14,975		Muskie	36.5%	63.5%	
SALINE	3,672	921	2,751		Muskie	25.1%	74.9%	
SANGAMON	18,594	4,929	13,411	254	Muskie	26.5%	72.1%	1.4%
SCHUYLER	836	213	605	18	Muskie	25.5%	72.4%	2.2%
SCOTT	777	204	573		Muskie	26.3%	73.7%	
SHELBY	2,703	1,009	1,694		Muskie	37.3%	62.7%	
STARK	562	175	373	14	Muskie	31.1%	66.4%	2.5%
STEPHENSON	3,326	1,093	2,233		Muskie	32.9%	67.1%	
TAZEWELL	9,380	2,796	6,584		Muskie	29.8%	70.2%	
UNION	2,634	554	1,699	381	Muskie	21.0%	64.5%	14.5%
VERMILION	6,748	2,426	4,049	273	Muskie	36.0%	60.0%	4.0%
WABASH	1,060	269	772	19	Muskie	25.4%	72.8%	1.8%
WARREN	1,369	395	909	65	Muskie	28.9%	66.4%	4.7%
WASHINGTON	1,329	284	1,010	35	Muskie	21.4%	76.0%	2.6%
WAYNE	1,473	340	1,133		Muskie	23.1%	76.9%	
WHITE	3,076	789	1,967	320	Muskie	25.7%	63.9%	10.4%
WHITESIDE	3,310	1,107	2,203		Muskie	33.4%	66.6%	
WILL	16,209	5,389	10,124	696	Muskie	33.2%	62.5%	4.3%
WILLIAMSON	4,120	961	3,075	84	Muskie	23.3%	74.6%	2.0%

ILLINOIS DEMOCRATIC

1972

County	Total Vote	McCarthy	Muskie	Other	Winner	Percentage of Total Vote McCarthy	Muskie	Other
WINNEBAGO	19,228	6,649	12,190	389	Muskie	34.6%	63.4%	2.0%
WOODFORD	1,844	536	1,275	33	Muskie	29.1%	69.1%	1.8%
TOTAL	1,225,144	444,260	766,914	13,970	Muskie	36.3%	62.6%	1.1%

ILLINOIS DEMOCRATIC

1976

County	Total Vote	Carter	Shriver	Wallace	Other	Winner	Percentage of Total Vote Carter	Shriver	Wallace	Other
ADAMS	7,541	2,899	561	3,555	526	Wallace	38.4%	7.4%	47.1%	7.0%
ALEXANDER	2,181	939	261	931	50	Carter	43.1%	12.0%	42.7%	2.3%
BOND	1,863	856	218	718	71	Carter	45.9%	11.7%	38.5%	3.8%
BOONE	2,021	1,039	158	720	104	Carter	51.4%	7.8%	35.6%	5.1%
BROWN	1,400	618	110	617	55	Carter	44.1%	7.9%	44.1%	3.9%
BUREAU	3,641	1,897	447	1,173	124	Carter	52.1%	12.3%	32.2%	3.4%
CALHOUN	750	380	76	264	30	Carter	50.7%	10.1%	35.2%	4.0%
CARROLL	1,456	812	175	399	70	Carter	55.8%	12.0%	27.4%	4.8%
CASS	2,025	1,049	215	677	84	Carter	51.8%	10.6%	33.4%	4.1%
CHAMPAIGN	13,554	7,369	1,398	1,908	2,879	Carter	54.4%	10.3%	14.1%	21.2%
CHRISTIAN	6,386	3,726	525	1,891	244	Carter	58.3%	8.2%	29.6%	3.8%
CLARK	2,499	1,196	159	948	196	Carter	47.9%	6.4%	37.9%	7.8%
CLAY	1,620	781	122	656	61	Carter	48.2%	7.5%	40.5%	3.8%
CLINTON	2,571	1,190	282	976	123	Carter	46.3%	11.0%	38.0%	4.8%
COLES	5,034	3,100	229	953	752	Carter	61.6%	4.5%	18.9%	14.9%
COOK	732,394	330,010	153,537	184,763	64,084	Carter	45.1%	21.0%	25.2%	8.7%
CRAWFORD	2,338	1,322	132	760	124	Carter	56.5%	5.6%	32.5%	5.3%
CUMBERLAND	2,093	1,166	120	697	110	Carter	55.7%	5.7%	33.3%	5.3%
DE KALB	6,230	3,332	672	1,275	951	Carter	53.5%	10.8%	20.5%	15.3%
DE WITT	1,592	1,007	110	411	64	Carter	63.3%	6.9%	25.8%	4.0%
DOUGLAS	1,863	1,315	95	392	61	Carter	70.6%	5.1%	21.0%	3.3%
DU PAGE	39,112	20,437	5,471	9,745	3,459	Carter	52.3%	14.0%	24.9%	8.8%
EDGAR	2,716	1,439	143	1,002	132	Carter	53.0%	5.3%	36.9%	4.9%
EDWARDS	878	540	50	250	38	Carter	61.5%	5.7%	28.5%	4.3%
EFFINGHAM	4,807	2,475	395	1,699	238	Carter	51.5%	8.2%	35.3%	5.0%
FAYETTE	2,870	1,506	255	965	144	Carter	52.5%	8.9%	33.6%	5.0%
FORD	1,171	737	143	243	48	Carter	62.9%	12.2%	20.8%	4.1%
FRANKLIN	8,588	4,854	535	2,758	441	Carter	56.5%	6.2%	32.1%	5.1%
FULTON	6,301	3,691	500	1,935	175	Carter	58.6%	7.9%	30.7%	2.8%
GALLATIN	2,356	1,293	173	812	78	Carter	54.9%	7.3%	34.5%	3.3%
GREENE	2,218	1,174	159	788	97	Carter	52.9%	7.2%	35.5%	4.4%
GRUNDY	2,701	1,345	344	875	137	Carter	49.8%	12.7%	32.4%	5.1%
HAMILTON	1,957	1,135	84	687	51	Carter	58.0%	4.3%	35.1%	2.6%
HANCOCK	2,079	998	172	762	147	Carter	48.0%	8.3%	36.7%	7.1%
HARDIN	1,103	600	83	383	37	Carter	54.4%	7.5%	34.7%	3.4%

ILLINOIS DEMOCRATIC

1976

County	Total Vote	Carter	Shriver	Wallace	Other	Winner	Percentage of Total Vote Carter	Shriver	Wallace	Other
HENDERSON	903	520	58	278	47	Carter	57.6%	6.4%	30.8%	5.2%
HENRY	3,434	1,755	353	1,101	225	Carter	51.1%	10.3%	32.1%	6.6%
IROQUOIS	2,229	1,244	222	694	69	Carter	55.8%	10.0%	31.1%	3.1%
JACKSON	5,944	2,914	355	1,431	1,244	Carter	49.0%	6.0%	24.1%	20.9%
JASPER	2,084	877	159	917	131	Wallace	42.1%	7.6%	44.0%	6.3%
JEFFERSON	6,725	3,611	284	2,642	188	Carter	53.7%	4.2%	39.3%	2.8%
JERSEY	2,287	1,071	201	912	103	Carter	46.8%	8.8%	39.9%	4.5%
JO DAVIESS	1,485	737	300	371	77	Carter	49.6%	20.2%	25.0%	5.2%
JOHNSON	1,129	641	28	430	30	Carter	56.8%	2.5%	38.1%	2.7%
KANE	15,468	7,798	2,363	4,263	1,044	Carter	50.4%	15.3%	27.6%	6.7%
KANKAKEE	6,222	3,008	979	1,934	301	Carter	48.3%	15.7%	31.1%	4.8%
KENDALL	1,832	906	197	642	87	Carter	49.5%	10.8%	35.0%	4.7%
KNOX	3,703	1,934	515	1,000	254	Carter	52.2%	13.9%	27.0%	6.9%
LAKE	31,520	15,934	4,478	7,119	3,989	Carter	50.6%	14.2%	22.6%	12.7%
LA SALLE	9,943	5,138	1,461	2,681	663	Carter	51.7%	14.7%	27.0%	6.7%
LAWRENCE	2,059	993	132	823	111	Carter	48.2%	6.4%	40.0%	5.4%
LEE	2,771	1,582	320	668	201	Carter	57.1%	11.5%	24.1%	7.3%
LIVINGSTON	2,692	1,537	358	604	193	Carter	57.1%	13.3%	22.4%	7.2%
LOGAN	2,589	1,626	193	693	77	Carter	62.8%	7.5%	26.8%	3.0%
MCDONOUGH	2,398	1,269	264	624	241	Carter	52.9%	11.0%	26.0%	10.1%
MCHENRY	8,722	4,335	1,346	2,469	572	Carter	49.7%	15.4%	28.3%	6.6%
MCLEAN	7,499	3,956	966	1,668	909	Carter	52.8%	12.9%	22.2%	12.1%
MACON	13,229	8,492	1,017	3,137	583	Carter	64.2%	7.7%	23.7%	4.4%
MACOUPIN	7,959	3,980	668	2,928	383	Carter	50.0%	8.4%	36.8%	4.8%
MADISON	34,115	14,103	3,101	14,764	2,147	Wallace	41.3%	9.1%	43.3%	6.3%
MARION	5,274	2,365	611	2,039	259	Carter	44.8%	11.6%	38.7%	4.9%
MARSHALL	1,402	802	153	410	37	Carter	57.2%	10.9%	29.2%	2.6%
MASON	2,174	1,267	195	642	70	Carter	58.3%	9.0%	29.5%	3.2%
MASSAC	1,708	875	55	707	71	Carter	51.2%	3.2%	41.4%	4.2%
MENARD	1,148	649	103	352	44	Carter	56.5%	9.0%	30.7%	3.8%
MERCER	2,087	1,021	215	745	106	Carter	48.9%	10.3%	35.7%	5.1%
MONROE	1,579	687	146	650	96	Carter	43.5%	9.2%	41.2%	6.1%
MONTGOMERY	4,990	2,638	436	1,629	287	Carter	52.9%	8.7%	32.6%	5.8%
MORGAN	4,326	2,320	510	1,283	213	Carter	53.6%	11.8%	29.7%	4.9%
MOULTRIE	1,840	1,238	106	447	49	Carter	67.3%	5.8%	24.3%	2.7%
OGLE	2,780	1,532	265	866	117	Carter	55.1%	9.5%	31.2%	4.2%
PEORIA	18,889	10,291	1,727	5,536	1,335	Carter	54.5%	9.1%	29.3%	7.1%
PERRY	2,761	1,369	210	1,058	124	Carter	49.6%	7.6%	38.3%	4.5%
PIATT	1,753	1,224	78	375	76	Carter	69.8%	4.4%	21.4%	4.3%
PIKE	2,966	1,471	194	1,191	110	Carter	49.6%	6.5%	40.2%	3.7%
POPE	610	318	19	249	24	Carter	52.1%	3.1%	40.8%	3.9%
PULASKI	1,091	581	51	442	17	Carter	53.3%	4.7%	40.5%	1.6%
PUTNAM	870	423	91	333	23	Carter	48.6%	10.5%	38.3%	2.6%
RANDOLPH	5,728	2,595	455	2,452	226	Carter	45.3%	7.9%	42.8%	3.9%
RICHLAND	1,979	894	102	885	98	Carter	45.2%	5.2%	44.7%	5.0%
ROCK ISLAND	17,107	9,106	2,118	4,357	1,526	Carter	53.2%	12.4%	25.5%	8.9%
ST. CLAIR	31,033	13,331	4,463	10,715	2,524	Carter	43.0%	14.4%	34.5%	8.1%
SALINE	4,205	2,473	264	1,266	202	Carter	58.8%	6.3%	30.1%	4.8%
SANGAMON	25,278	13,890	2,697	6,878	1,813	Carter	54.9%	10.7%	27.2%	7.2%
SCHUYLER	1,484	736	82	611	55	Carter	49.6%	5.5%	41.2%	3.7%

ILLINOIS DEMOCRATIC

1976

County	Total Vote	Carter	Shriver	Wallace	Other	Winner	Percentage of Total Vote Carter	Shriver	Wallace	Other
SCOTT	880	434	69	330	47	Carter	49.3%	7.8%	37.5%	5.3%
SHELBY	3,273	2,034	168	974	97	Carter	62.1%	5.1%	29.8%	3.0%
STARK	576	316	53	186	21	Carter	54.9%	9.2%	32.3%	3.6%
STEPHENSON	3,563	1,909	455	990	209	Carter	53.6%	12.8%	27.8%	5.9%
TAZEWELL	13,419	7,280	1,081	4,548	510	Carter	54.3%	8.1%	33.9%	3.8%
UNION	3,408	1,987	130	1,052	239	Carter	58.3%	3.8%	30.9%	7.0%
VERMILION	9,690	5,510	602	2,928	650	Carter	56.9%	6.2%	30.2%	6.7%
WABASH	2,069	1,173	143	650	103	Carter	56.7%	6.9%	31.4%	5.0%
WARREN	1,559	854	153	461	91	Carter	54.8%	9.8%	29.6%	5.8%
WASHINGTON	1,557	687	125	678	67	Carter	44.1%	8.0%	43.5%	4.3%
WAYNE	2,447	1,522	120	715	90	Carter	62.2%	4.9%	29.2%	3.7%
WHITE	3,708	2,457	257	902	92	Carter	66.3%	6.9%	24.3%	2.5%
WHITESIDE	3,571	2,340	283	777	171	Carter	65.5%	7.9%	21.8%	4.8%
WILL	24,531	11,300	3,859	8,074	1,298	Carter	46.1%	15.7%	32.9%	5.3%
WILLIAMSON	6,917	4,097	290	2,140	390	Carter	59.2%	4.2%	30.9%	5.6%
WINNEBAGO	24,338	13,494	2,278	7,154	1,412	Carter	55.4%	9.4%	29.4%	5.8%
WOODFORD	2,257	1,237	185	740	95	Carter	54.8%	8.2%	32.8%	4.2%
TOTAL	1,311,675	630,915	214,024	361,798	104,938	Carter	48.1%	16.3%	27.6%	8.0%
Certified Totals	1,311,914	630,915	214,024	361,798	105,177	Carter	48.1%	16.3%	27.6%	8.0%

ILLINOIS REPUBLICAN

1976

County	Total Vote	Ford	Reagan	Other	Winner	Percentage of Total Vote Ford	Reagan	Other
ADAMS	6,045	2,563	3,458	24	Reagan	42.4%	57.2%	0.4%
ALEXANDER	661	364	292	5	Ford	55.1%	44.2%	0.8%
BOND	1,573	941	629	3	Ford	59.8%	40.0%	0.2%
BOONE	3,398	2,067	1,318	13	Ford	60.8%	38.8%	0.4%
BROWN	537	224	310	3	Reagan	41.7%	57.7%	0.6%
BUREAU	5,393	2,788	2,587	18	Ford	51.7%	48.0%	0.3%
CALHOUN	396	265	131		Ford	66.9%	33.1%	
CARROLL	2,918	1,459	1,440	19	Ford	50.0%	49.3%	0.7%
CASS	1,142	790	349	3	Ford	69.2%	30.6%	0.3%
CHAMPAIGN	15,066	9,362	5,598	106	Ford	62.1%	37.2%	0.7%
CHRISTIAN	2,079	1,237	839	3	Ford	59.5%	40.4%	0.1%
CLARK	1,803	864	935	4	Reagan	47.9%	51.9%	0.2%
CLAY	1,442	761	675	6	Ford	52.8%	46.8%	0.4%
CLINTON	1,858	1,123	724	11	Ford	60.4%	39.0%	0.6%
COLES	4,086	2,086	1,987	13	Ford	51.1%	48.6%	0.3%
COOK	229,895	144,998	80,672	4,225	Ford	63.1%	35.1%	1.8%
CRAWFORD	3,458	1,751	1,693	14	Ford	50.6%	49.0%	0.4%
CUMBERLAND	1,016	503	510	3	Reagan	49.5%	50.2%	0.3%
DE KALB	7,539	4,787	2,682	70	Ford	63.5%	35.6%	0.9%
DE WITT	2,327	1,173	1,147	7	Ford	50.4%	49.3%	0.3%

ILLINOIS REPUBLICAN

1976

County	Total Vote	Ford	Reagan	Other	Winner	Percentage of Total Vote: Ford	Reagan	Other
DOUGLAS	2,954	1,576	1,371	7	Ford	53.4%	46.4%	0.2%
DU PAGE	67,556	41,737	25,281	538	Ford	61.8%	37.4%	0.8%
EDGAR	2,767	1,558	1,201	8	Ford	56.3%	43.4%	0.3%
EDWARDS	1,249	765	483	1	Ford	61.2%	38.7%	0.1%
EFFINGHAM	2,154	1,130	1,018	6	Ford	52.5%	47.3%	0.3%
FAYETTE	1,997	1,108	880	9	Ford	55.5%	44.1%	0.5%
FORD	2,866	1,543	1,316	7	Ford	53.8%	45.9%	0.2%
FRANKLIN	2,280	1,417	837	26	Ford	62.1%	36.7%	1.1%
FULTON	2,932	1,810	1,115	7	Ford	61.7%	38.0%	0.2%
GALLATIN	603	411	189	3	Ford	68.2%	31.3%	0.5%
GREENE	1,205	566	634	5	Reagan	47.0%	52.6%	0.4%
GRUNDY	4,021	2,234	1,768	19	Ford	55.6%	44.0%	0.5%
HAMILTON	1,118	618	496	4	Ford	55.3%	44.4%	0.4%
HANCOCK	3,449	1,451	1,991	7	Reagan	42.1%	57.7%	0.2%
HARDIN	776	491	279	6	Ford	63.3%	36.0%	0.8%
HENDERSON	1,755	759	991	5	Reagan	43.2%	56.5%	0.3%
HENRY	4,559	2,720	1,822	17	Ford	59.7%	40.0%	0.4%
IROQUOIS	6,476	2,819	3,618	39	Reagan	43.5%	55.9%	0.6%
JACKSON	2,790	1,928	828	34	Ford	69.1%	29.7%	1.2%
JASPER	1,014	391	620	3	Reagan	38.6%	61.1%	0.3%
JEFFERSON	2,640	1,551	1,084	5	Ford	58.8%	41.1%	0.2%
JERSEY	1,598	795	797	6	Reagan	49.7%	49.9%	0.4%
JO DAVIESS	2,393	1,457	924	12	Ford	60.9%	38.6%	0.5%
JOHNSON	2,358	1,275	1,068	15	Ford	54.1%	45.3%	0.6%
KANE	26,955	16,362	10,400	193	Ford	60.7%	38.6%	0.7%
KANKAKEE	7,803	4,143	3,533	127	Ford	53.1%	45.3%	1.6%
KENDALL	4,664	2,433	2,213	18	Ford	52.2%	47.4%	0.4%
KNOX	6,820	3,936	2,846	38	Ford	57.7%	41.7%	0.6%
LAKE	37,333	22,816	14,092	425	Ford	61.1%	37.7%	1.1%
LA SALLE	8,971	5,265	3,657	49	Ford	58.7%	40.8%	0.5%
LAWRENCE	1,727	1,061	659	7	Ford	61.4%	38.2%	0.4%
LEE	4,930	1,102	3,818	10	Reagan	22.4%	77.4%	0.2%
LIVINGSTON	4,693	2,789	1,893	11	Ford	59.4%	40.3%	0.2%
LOGAN	4,763	2,495	2,256	12	Ford	52.4%	47.4%	0.3%
MCDONOUGH	5,457	2,499	2,943	15	Reagan	45.8%	53.9%	0.3%
MCHENRY	13,294	7,940	5,232	122	Ford	59.7%	39.4%	0.9%
MCLEAN	13,758	7,915	5,754	89	Ford	57.5%	41.8%	0.6%
MACON	8,980	5,025	3,919	36	Ford	56.0%	43.6%	0.4%
MACOUPIN	2,602	1,434	1,135	33	Ford	55.1%	43.6%	1.3%
MADISON	8,571	4,461	3,958	152	Ford	52.0%	46.2%	1.8%
MARION	2,728	1,573	1,133	22	Ford	57.7%	41.5%	0.8%
MARSHALL	1,689	955	731	3	Ford	56.5%	43.3%	0.2%
MASON	1,197	658	538	1	Ford	55.0%	44.9%	0.1%
MASSAC	2,093	1,041	1,041	11		49.7%	49.7%	0.5%
MENARD	1,707	945	762		Ford	55.4%	44.6%	
MERCER	2,664	1,523	1,134	7	Ford	57.2%	42.6%	0.3%
MONROE	2,176	1,298	860	18	Ford	59.7%	39.5%	0.8%
MONTGOMERY	2,306	1,384	916	6	Ford	60.0%	39.7%	0.3%
MORGAN	4,173	2,601	1,561	11	Ford	62.3%	37.4%	0.3%
MOULTRIE	1,239	637	596	6	Ford	51.4%	48.1%	0.5%

ILLINOIS REPUBLICAN

1976

County	Total Vote	Ford	Reagan	Other	Winner	Percentage of Total Vote Ford	Reagan	Other
OGLE	6,123	2,982	3,115	26	Reagan	48.7%	50.9%	0.4%
PEORIA	20,482	12,447	7,861	174	Ford	60.8%	38.4%	0.8%
PERRY	1,954	1,172	775	7	Ford	60.0%	39.7%	0.4%
PIATT	2,463	1,422	1,038	3	Ford	57.7%	42.1%	0.1%
PIKE	1,905	1,068	833	4	Ford	56.1%	43.7%	0.2%
POPE	708	458	248	2	Ford	64.7%	35.0%	0.3%
PULASKI	852	585	261	6	Ford	68.7%	30.6%	0.7%
PUTNAM	569	328	237	4	Ford	57.6%	41.7%	0.7%
RANDOLPH	2,148	1,357	781	10	Ford	63.2%	36.4%	0.5%
RICHLAND	1,271	711	559	1	Ford	55.9%	44.0%	0.1%
ROCK ISLAND	9,245	5,381	3,846	18	Ford	58.2%	41.6%	0.2%
ST. CLAIR	9,670	5,278	4,179	213	Ford	54.6%	43.2%	2.2%
SALINE	2,179	1,429	748	2	Ford	65.6%	34.3%	0.1%
SANGAMON	17,119	11,136	5,908	75	Ford	65.1%	34.5%	0.4%
SCHUYLER	1,087	534	552	1	Reagan	49.1%	50.8%	0.1%
SCOTT	859	458	399	2	Ford	53.3%	46.4%	0.2%
SHELBY	1,891	885	1,002	4	Reagan	46.8%	53.0%	0.2%
STARK	1,072	615	452	5	Ford	57.4%	42.2%	0.5%
STEPHENSON	4,532	3,113	1,406	13	Ford	68.7%	31.0%	0.3%
TAZEWELL	10,866	6,203	4,583	80	Ford	57.1%	42.2%	0.7%
UNION	1,205	800	404	1	Ford	66.4%	33.5%	0.1%
VERMILION	8,234	4,255	3,938	41	Ford	51.7%	47.8%	0.5%
WABASH	1,543	970	564	9	Ford	62.9%	36.6%	0.6%
WARREN	3,747	1,809	1,932	6	Reagan	48.3%	51.6%	0.2%
WASHINGTON	2,203	1,344	844	15	Ford	61.0%	38.3%	0.7%
WAYNE	3,595	2,087	1,492	16	Ford	58.1%	41.5%	0.4%
WHITE	1,483	850	628	5	Ford	57.3%	42.3%	0.3%
WHITESIDE	7,840	2,719	5,105	16	Reagan	34.7%	65.1%	0.2%
WILL	19,022	9,851	8,976	195	Ford	51.8%	47.2%	1.0%
WILLIAMSON	3,911	2,335	1,568	8	Ford	59.7%	40.1%	0.2%
WINNEBAGO	22,514	13,625	8,773	116	Ford	60.5%	39.0%	0.5%
WOODFORD	4,166	2,036	2,121	9	Reagan	48.9%	50.9%	0.2%
TOTAL	775,893	456,750	311,295	7,848	Ford	58.9%	40.1%	1.0%

ILLINOIS DEMOCRATIC

1980

County	Total Vote	Carter	E. Kennedy	Other	Winner	Percentage of Total Vote Carter	E. Kennedy	Other
ADAMS	4,403	3,240	935	228	Carter	73.6%	21.2%	5.2%
ALEXANDER	1,830	1,332	438	60	Carter	72.8%	23.9%	3.3%
BOND	1,640	1,176	391	73	Carter	71.7%	23.8%	4.5%
BOONE	1,172	799	322	51	Carter	68.2%	27.5%	4.4%
BROWN	699	487	178	34	Carter	69.7%	25.5%	4.9%
BUREAU	2,142	1,305	741	96	Carter	60.9%	34.6%	4.5%
CALHOUN	1,057	605	381	71	Carter	57.2%	36.0%	6.7%
CARROLL	842	614	200	28	Carter	72.9%	23.8%	3.3%
CASS	1,539	1,043	425	71	Carter	67.8%	27.6%	4.6%
CHAMPAIGN	7,063	4,623	2,230	210	Carter	65.5%	31.6%	3.0%
CHRISTIAN	3,691	2,391	1,172	128	Carter	64.8%	31.8%	3.5%
CLARK	1,678	1,253	321	104	Carter	74.7%	19.1%	6.2%
CLAY	1,127	868	208	51	Carter	77.0%	18.5%	4.5%
CLINTON	2,304	1,488	691	125	Carter	64.6%	30.0%	5.4%
COLES	3,145	2,283	717	145	Carter	72.6%	22.8%	4.6%
COOK	797,855	505,419	248,157	44,279	Carter	63.3%	31.1%	5.5%
CRAWFORD	1,692	1,324	306	62	Carter	78.3%	18.1%	3.7%
CUMBERLAND	1,098	760	267	71	Carter	69.2%	24.3%	6.5%
DE KALB	3,296	2,224	945	127	Carter	67.5%	28.7%	3.9%
DE WITT	938	635	264	39	Carter	67.7%	28.1%	4.2%
DOUGLAS	1,132	833	264	35	Carter	73.6%	23.3%	3.1%
DU PAGE	23,908	17,087	6,035	786	Carter	71.5%	25.2%	3.3%
EDGAR	1,702	1,222	394	86	Carter	71.8%	23.1%	5.1%
EDWARDS	556	422	113	21	Carter	75.9%	20.3%	3.8%
EFFINGHAM	2,509	1,907	492	110	Carter	76.0%	19.6%	4.4%
FAYETTE	2,255	1,722	460	73	Carter	76.4%	20.4%	3.2%
FORD	619	431	179	9	Carter	69.6%	28.9%	1.5%
FRANKLIN	7,908	5,409	2,188	311	Carter	68.4%	27.7%	3.9%
FULTON	3,830	2,615	1,090	125	Carter	68.3%	28.5%	3.3%
GALLATIN	1,570	986	511	73	Carter	62.8%	32.5%	4.6%
GREENE	2,500	1,632	704	164	Carter	65.3%	28.2%	6.6%
GRUNDY	1,554	1,066	439	49	Carter	68.6%	28.2%	3.2%
HAMILTON	1,521	1,076	370	75	Carter	70.7%	24.3%	4.9%
HANCOCK	1,507	1,205	260	42	Carter	80.0%	17.3%	2.8%
HARDIN	677	479	183	15	Carter	70.8%	27.0%	2.2%
HENDERSON	623	498	110	15	Carter	79.9%	17.7%	2.4%
HENRY	2,145	1,458	621	66	Carter	68.0%	29.0%	3.1%
IROQUOIS	1,214	821	349	44	Carter	67.6%	28.7%	3.6%
JACKSON	4,903	3,666	996	241	Carter	74.8%	20.3%	4.9%
JASPER	1,496	1,046	358	92	Carter	69.9%	23.9%	6.1%
JEFFERSON	5,011	3,665	1,084	262	Carter	73.1%	21.6%	5.2%
JERSEY	1,735	1,104	540	91	Carter	63.6%	31.1%	5.2%
JO DAVIESS	1,105	691	365	49	Carter	62.5%	33.0%	4.4%
JOHNSON	763	626	119	18	Carter	82.0%	15.6%	2.4%
KANE	10,542	7,384	2,849	309	Carter	70.0%	27.0%	2.9%
KANKAKEE	3,137	2,098	939	100	Carter	66.9%	29.9%	3.2%
KENDALL	1,209	942	228	39	Carter	77.9%	18.9%	3.2%
KNOX	2,746	1,802	848	96	Carter	65.6%	30.9%	3.5%
LAKE	16,294	10,858	4,936	500	Carter	66.6%	30.3%	3.1%
LA SALLE	7,275	4,181	2,804	290	Carter	57.5%	38.5%	4.0%

ILLINOIS DEMOCRATIC

1980

County	Total Vote	Carter	E. Kennedy	Other	Winner	Percentage of Total Vote: Carter	E. Kennedy	Other
LAWRENCE	1,440	1,134	247	59	Carter	78.8%	17.2%	4.1%
LEE	1,466	956	458	52	Carter	65.2%	31.2%	3.5%
LIVINGSTON	1,516	1,045	433	38	Carter	68.9%	28.6%	2.5%
LOGAN	1,653	1,181	417	55	Carter	71.4%	25.2%	3.3%
MCDONOUGH	1,452	1,148	254	50	Carter	79.1%	17.5%	3.4%
MCHENRY	5,116	3,612	1,301	203	Carter	70.6%	25.4%	4.0%
MCLEAN	4,893	3,475	1,238	180	Carter	71.0%	25.3%	3.7%
MACON	9,410	6,487	2,685	238	Carter	68.9%	28.5%	2.5%
MACOUPIN	7,775	4,882	2,345	548	Carter	62.8%	30.2%	7.0%
MADISON	26,082	16,620	7,817	1,645	Carter	63.7%	30.0%	6.3%
MARION	5,651	4,002	1,321	328	Carter	70.8%	23.4%	5.8%
MARSHALL	815	584	189	42	Carter	71.7%	23.2%	5.2%
MASON	1,352	948	351	53	Carter	70.1%	26.0%	3.9%
MASSAC	1,196	952	212	32	Carter	79.6%	17.7%	2.7%
MENARD	781	586	170	25	Carter	75.0%	21.8%	3.2%
MERCER	2,314	1,685	550	79	Carter	72.8%	23.8%	3.4%
MONROE	880	623	217	40	Carter	70.8%	24.7%	4.5%
MONTGOMERY	3,486	2,182	1,135	169	Carter	62.6%	32.6%	4.8%
MORGAN	3,085	2,196	754	135	Carter	71.2%	24.4%	4.4%
MOULTRIE	1,230	912	267	51	Carter	74.1%	21.7%	4.1%
OGLE	1,452	1,075	350	27	Carter	74.0%	24.1%	1.9%
PEORIA	13,885	9,978	3,486	421	Carter	71.9%	25.1%	3.0%
PERRY	1,754	1,179	507	68	Carter	67.2%	28.9%	3.9%
PIATT	989	724	225	40	Carter	73.2%	22.8%	4.0%
PIKE	2,695	2,037	530	128	Carter	75.6%	19.7%	4.7%
POPE	512	349	142	21	Carter	68.2%	27.7%	4.1%
PULASKI	637	485	144	8	Carter	76.1%	22.6%	1.3%
PUTNAM	762	461	260	41	Carter	60.5%	34.1%	5.4%
RANDOLPH	2,888	2,095	688	105	Carter	72.5%	23.8%	3.6%
RICHLAND	1,358	1,076	220	62	Carter	79.2%	16.2%	4.6%
ROCK ISLAND	14,462	9,247	4,666	549	Carter	63.9%	32.3%	3.8%
ST. CLAIR	27,645	17,116	9,223	1,306	Carter	61.9%	33.4%	4.7%
SALINE	4,032	2,704	1,173	155	Carter	67.1%	29.1%	3.8%
SANGAMON	19,096	12,375	6,087	634	Carter	64.8%	31.9%	3.3%
SCHUYLER	798	634	137	27	Carter	79.4%	17.2%	3.4%
SCOTT	710	525	165	20	Carter	73.9%	23.2%	2.8%
SHELBY	2,332	1,709	520	103	Carter	73.3%	22.3%	4.4%
STARK	358	245	100	13	Carter	68.4%	27.9%	3.6%
STEPHENSON	2,282	1,554	658	70	Carter	68.1%	28.8%	3.1%
TAZEWELL	10,151	7,347	2,324	480	Carter	72.4%	22.9%	4.7%
UNION	3,321	2,513	669	139	Carter	75.7%	20.1%	4.2%
VERMILION	6,403	4,394	1,669	340	Carter	68.6%	26.1%	5.3%
WABASH	1,195	896	236	63	Carter	75.0%	19.7%	5.3%
WARREN	892	659	214	19	Carter	73.9%	24.0%	2.1%
WASHINGTON	1,250	823	377	50	Carter	65.8%	30.2%	4.0%
WAYNE	1,805	1,495	260	50	Carter	82.8%	14.4%	2.8%
WHITE	2,159	1,583	494	82	Carter	73.3%	22.9%	3.8%
WHITESIDE	2,475	1,709	683	83	Carter	69.1%	27.6%	3.4%
WILL	18,004	11,607	5,878	519	Carter	64.5%	32.6%	2.9%
WILLIAMSON	5,415	3,896	1,355	164	Carter	71.9%	25.0%	3.0%

ILLINOIS DEMOCRATIC

1980

County	Total Vote	Carter	E. Kennedy	Other	Winner	Percentage of Total Vote Carter	E. Kennedy	Other
WINNEBAGO	13,123	9,130	3,686	307	Carter	69.6%	28.1%	2.3%
WOODFORD	1,477	1,156	271	50	Carter	78.3%	18.3%	3.4%
TOTAL	1,201,067	780,787	359,875	60,405	Carter	65.0%	30.0%	5.0%

ILLINOIS REPUBLICAN

1980

County	Total Vote	Anderson	Bush	Reagan	Other	Winner	Percentage of Total Vote Anderson	Bush	Reagan	Other
ADAMS	9,199	2,281	789	5,801	328	Reagan	24.8%	8.6%	63.1%	3.6%
ALEXANDER	1,040	83	61	866	30	Reagan	8.0%	5.9%	83.3%	2.9%
BOND	1,966	337	213	1,298	118	Reagan	17.1%	10.8%	66.0%	6.0%
BOONE	5,424	2,508	364	2,426	126	Anderson	46.2%	6.7%	44.7%	2.3%
BROWN	606	99	53	429	25	Reagan	16.3%	8.7%	70.8%	4.1%
BUREAU	4,874	1,268	474	2,960	172	Reagan	26.0%	9.7%	60.7%	3.5%
CALHOUN	672	81	35	546	10	Reagan	12.1%	5.2%	81.3%	1.5%
CARROLL	2,878	915	149	1,753	61	Reagan	31.8%	5.2%	60.9%	2.1%
CASS	1,578	218	330	1,003	27	Reagan	13.8%	20.9%	63.6%	1.7%
CHAMPAIGN	22,957	9,888	3,384	9,228	457	Anderson	43.1%	14.7%	40.2%	2.0%
CHRISTIAN	2,649	389	332	1,845	83	Reagan	14.7%	12.5%	69.6%	3.1%
CLARK	2,204	278	161	1,649	116	Reagan	12.6%	7.3%	74.8%	5.3%
CLAY	1,601	212	125	1,181	83	Reagan	13.2%	7.8%	73.8%	5.2%
CLINTON	2,681	400	190	1,987	104	Reagan	14.9%	7.1%	74.1%	3.9%
COLES	5,875	1,398	595	3,651	231	Reagan	23.8%	10.1%	62.1%	3.9%
COOK	364,777	174,659	35,058	139,467	15,593	Anderson	47.9%	9.6%	38.2%	4.3%
CRAWFORD	2,997	670	275	1,886	166	Reagan	22.4%	9.2%	62.9%	5.5%
CUMBERLAND	1,245	189	101	897	58	Reagan	15.2%	8.1%	72.0%	4.7%
DE KALB	10,410	5,089	954	3,896	471	Anderson	48.9%	9.2%	37.4%	4.5%
DE WITT	2,687	476	363	1,744	104	Reagan	17.7%	13.5%	64.9%	3.9%
DOUGLAS	3,052	637	380	1,867	168	Reagan	20.9%	12.5%	61.2%	5.5%
DU PAGE	98,825	40,775	11,908	41,606	4,536	Reagan	41.3%	12.0%	42.1%	4.6%
EDGAR	3,308	681	320	2,013	294	Reagan	20.6%	9.7%	60.9%	8.9%
EDWARDS	1,348	218	90	911	129	Reagan	16.2%	6.7%	67.6%	9.6%
EFFINGHAM	2,813	420	344	1,843	206	Reagan	14.9%	12.2%	65.5%	7.3%
FAYETTE	2,744	300	187	2,153	104	Reagan	10.9%	6.8%	78.5%	3.8%
FORD	3,054	644	354	1,962	94	Reagan	21.1%	11.6%	64.2%	3.1%
FRANKLIN	3,229	520	209	2,369	131	Reagan	16.1%	6.5%	73.4%	4.1%
FULTON	4,184	885	606	2,580	113	Reagan	21.2%	14.5%	61.7%	2.7%
GALLATIN	632	91	59	451	31	Reagan	14.4%	9.3%	71.4%	4.9%
GREENE	1,604	182	104	1,273	45	Reagan	11.3%	6.5%	79.4%	2.8%
GRUNDY	3,701	866	459	2,137	239	Reagan	23.4%	12.4%	57.7%	6.5%
HAMILTON	1,609	210	95	1,259	45	Reagan	13.1%	5.9%	78.2%	2.8%
HANCOCK	3,377	715	278	2,270	114	Reagan	21.2%	8.2%	67.2%	3.4%
HARDIN	1,137	113	87	903	34	Reagan	9.9%	7.7%	79.4%	3.0%

ILLINOIS REPUBLICAN

1980

County	Total Vote	Anderson	Bush	Reagan	Other	Winner	Percentage of Total Vote Anderson	Bush	Reagan	Other
HENDERSON	1,372	263	148	907	54	Reagan	19.2%	10.8%	66.1%	3.9%
HENRY	5,816	1,486	1,131	3,040	159	Reagan	25.6%	19.4%	52.3%	2.7%
IROQUOIS	5,645	850	624	3,987	184	Reagan	15.1%	11.1%	70.6%	3.3%
JACKSON	4,380	1,564	458	2,253	105	Reagan	35.7%	10.5%	51.4%	2.4%
JASPER	1,468	207	104	1,077	80	Reagan	14.1%	7.1%	73.4%	5.4%
JEFFERSON	2,895	385	289	2,128	93	Reagan	13.3%	10.0%	73.5%	3.2%
JERSEY	1,995	365	127	1,435	68	Reagan	18.3%	6.4%	71.9%	3.4%
JO DAVIESS	2,941	1,321	178	1,363	79	Reagan	44.9%	6.1%	46.3%	2.7%
JOHNSON	2,803	338	193	2,190	82	Reagan	12.1%	6.9%	78.1%	2.9%
KANE	36,576	13,296	4,759	17,268	1,253	Reagan	36.4%	13.0%	47.2%	3.4%
KANKAKEE	10,086	2,324	1,319	6,120	323	Reagan	23.0%	13.1%	60.7%	3.2%
KENDALL	5,874	1,509	658	3,488	219	Reagan	25.7%	11.2%	59.4%	3.7%
KNOX	8,250	2,279	868	4,888	215	Reagan	27.6%	10.5%	59.2%	2.6%
LAKE	61,856	28,023	8,299	22,708	2,826	Anderson	45.3%	13.4%	36.7%	4.6%
LA SALLE	11,230	3,114	1,262	6,466	388	Reagan	27.7%	11.2%	57.6%	3.5%
LAWRENCE	1,931	363	183	1,268	117	Reagan	18.8%	9.5%	65.7%	6.1%
LEE	6,472	896	206	5,266	104	Reagan	13.8%	3.2%	81.4%	1.6%
LIVINGSTON	5,711	1,522	640	3,368	181	Reagan	26.7%	11.2%	59.0%	3.2%
LOGAN	5,726	1,189	815	3,478	244	Reagan	20.8%	14.2%	60.7%	4.3%
MCDONOUGH	6,289	1,771	851	3,488	179	Reagan	28.2%	13.5%	55.5%	2.8%
MCHENRY	23,887	9,605	2,988	10,576	718	Reagan	40.2%	12.5%	44.3%	3.0%
MCLEAN	18,494	5,329	3,218	9,529	418	Reagan	28.8%	17.4%	51.5%	2.3%
MACON	13,230	2,728	2,774	7,484	244	Reagan	20.6%	21.0%	56.6%	1.8%
MACOUPIN	3,794	634	284	2,757	119	Reagan	16.7%	7.5%	72.7%	3.1%
MADISON	14,738	2,896	1,177	10,257	408	Reagan	19.6%	8.0%	69.6%	2.8%
MARION	3,511	450	208	2,715	138	Reagan	12.8%	5.9%	77.3%	3.9%
MARSHALL	2,536	556	336	1,552	92	Reagan	21.9%	13.2%	61.2%	3.6%
MASON	1,401	241	202	913	45	Reagan	17.2%	14.4%	65.2%	3.2%
MASSAC	2,413	264	124	1,957	68	Reagan	10.9%	5.1%	81.1%	2.8%
MENARD	1,828	302	229	1,256	41	Reagan	16.5%	12.5%	68.7%	2.2%
MERCER	3,517	1,132	410	1,859	116	Reagan	32.2%	11.7%	52.9%	3.3%
MONROE	2,308	440	209	1,561	98	Reagan	19.1%	9.1%	67.6%	4.2%
MONTGOMERY	3,371	597	328	2,307	139	Reagan	17.7%	9.7%	68.4%	4.1%
MORGAN	5,664	1,174	565	3,749	176	Reagan	20.7%	10.0%	66.2%	3.1%
MOULTRIE	1,456	279	192	921	64	Reagan	19.2%	13.2%	63.3%	4.4%
OGLE	9,097	2,878	448	5,587	184	Reagan	31.6%	4.9%	61.4%	2.0%
PEORIA	29,963	7,953	4,839	15,564	1,607	Reagan	26.5%	16.1%	51.9%	5.4%
PERRY	1,756	274	179	1,218	85	Reagan	15.6%	10.2%	69.4%	4.8%
PIATT	2,760	621	468	1,543	128	Reagan	22.5%	17.0%	55.9%	4.6%
PIKE	2,311	460	223	1,530	98	Reagan	19.9%	9.6%	66.2%	4.2%
POPE	1,132	127	59	898	48	Reagan	11.2%	5.2%	79.3%	4.2%
PULASKI	1,790	272	129	1,312	77	Reagan	15.2%	7.2%	73.3%	4.3%
PUTNAM	1,163	334	165	635	29	Reagan	28.7%	14.2%	54.6%	2.5%
RANDOLPH	2,466	346	153	1,900	67	Reagan	14.0%	6.2%	77.0%	2.7%
RICHLAND	1,906	356	203	1,269	78	Reagan	18.7%	10.7%	66.6%	4.1%
ROCK ISLAND	14,122	4,592	2,552	6,640	338	Reagan	32.5%	18.1%	47.0%	2.4%
ST. CLAIR	14,317	2,576	1,498	9,520	723	Reagan	18.0%	10.5%	66.5%	5.0%
SALINE	2,968	481	287	2,021	179	Reagan	16.2%	9.7%	68.1%	6.0%
SANGAMON	25,664	5,850	4,915	14,152	747	Reagan	22.8%	19.2%	55.1%	2.9%
SCHUYLER	1,132	169	128	803	32	Reagan	14.9%	11.3%	70.9%	2.8%

ILLINOIS REPUBLICAN

1980

County	Total Vote	Anderson	Bush	Reagan	Other	Winner	Percentage of Total Vote Anderson	Bush	Reagan	Other
SCOTT	1,218	188	90	899	41	Reagan	15.4%	7.4%	73.8%	3.4%
SHELBY	2,223	271	283	1,571	98	Reagan	12.2%	12.7%	70.7%	4.4%
STARK	1,157	252	128	700	77	Reagan	21.8%	11.1%	60.5%	6.7%
STEPHENSON	7,481	3,941	387	2,976	177	Anderson	52.7%	5.2%	39.8%	2.4%
TAZEWELL	15,313	3,159	2,124	9,129	901	Reagan	20.6%	13.9%	59.6%	5.9%
UNION	1,594	300	233	1,002	59	Reagan	18.8%	14.6%	62.9%	3.7%
VERMILION	10,568	2,332	1,005	6,633	598	Reagan	22.1%	9.5%	62.8%	5.7%
WABASH	1,467	270	172	908	117	Reagan	18.4%	11.7%	61.9%	8.0%
WARREN	3,791	786	334	2,542	129	Reagan	20.7%	8.8%	67.1%	3.4%
WASHINGTON	2,628	318	220	2,027	63	Reagan	12.1%	8.4%	77.1%	2.4%
WAYNE	3,248	215	202	2,626	205	Reagan	6.6%	6.2%	80.8%	6.3%
WHITE	1,780	281	143	1,275	81	Reagan	15.8%	8.0%	71.6%	4.6%
WHITESIDE	7,946	1,413	712	5,662	159	Reagan	17.8%	9.0%	71.3%	2.0%
WILL	27,741	8,154	3,469	15,235	883	Reagan	29.4%	12.5%	54.9%	3.2%
WILLIAMSON	5,682	855	492	4,178	157	Reagan	15.0%	8.7%	73.5%	2.8%
WINNEBAGO	43,592	25,726	1,359	15,891	616	Anderson	59.0%	3.1%	36.5%	1.4%
WOODFORD	5,704	1,056	616	3,820	212	Reagan	18.5%	10.8%	67.0%	3.7%
TOTAL	1,130,081	415,193	124,057	547,355	43,476	Reagan	36.7%	11.0%	48.4%	3.8%

ILLINOIS DEMOCRATIC

1984

County	Total Vote	Hart	J. Jackson	Mondale	Other	Winner	Percentage of Total Vote Hart	J. Jackson	Mondale	Other
ADAMS	5,511	3,164	256	1,907	184	Hart	57.4%	4.6%	34.6%	3.3%
ALEXANDER	2,777	1,054	640	941	142	Hart	38.0%	23.0%	33.9%	5.1%
BOND	1,816	849	52	856	59	Mondale	46.8%	2.9%	47.1%	3.2%
BOONE	2,064	950	54	989	71	Mondale	46.0%	2.6%	47.9%	3.4%
BROWN	696	436	8	221	31	Hart	62.6%	1.1%	31.8%	4.5%
BUREAU	3,151	1,690	63	1,293	105	Hart	53.6%	2.0%	41.0%	3.3%
CALHOUN	1,406	767	27	522	90	Hart	54.6%	1.9%	37.1%	6.4%
CARROLL	1,103	678	30	344	51	Hart	61.5%	2.7%	31.2%	4.6%
CASS	1,728	868	29	765	66	Hart	50.2%	1.7%	44.3%	3.8%
CHAMPAIGN	17,034	8,973	2,018	5,352	691	Hart	52.7%	11.8%	31.4%	4.1%
CHRISTIAN	6,868	3,644	119	2,764	341	Hart	53.1%	1.7%	40.2%	5.0%
CLARK	1,957	1,153	26	709	69	Hart	58.9%	1.3%	36.2%	3.5%
CLAY	1,499	917	34	462	86	Hart	61.2%	2.3%	30.8%	5.7%
CLINTON	2,539	1,345	50	1,083	61	Hart	53.0%	2.0%	42.7%	2.4%
COLES	5,485	2,908	138	2,226	213	Hart	53.0%	2.5%	40.6%	3.9%
COOK	1,052,159	299,510	298,725	421,240	32,684	Mondale	28.5%	28.4%	40.0%	3.1%
CRAWFORD	2,034	1,214	27	710	83	Hart	59.7%	1.3%	34.9%	4.1%
CUMBERLAND	1,321	798	33	426	64	Hart	60.4%	2.5%	32.2%	4.8%
DE KALB	6,338	3,546	527	2,068	197	Hart	55.9%	8.3%	32.6%	3.1%
DE WITT	1,119	541	17	520	41	Hart	48.3%	1.5%	46.5%	3.7%

ILLINOIS DEMOCRATIC

1984

County	Total Vote	Hart	J. Jackson	Mondale	Other	Winner	Percentage of Total Vote Hart	J. Jackson	Mondale	Other
DOUGLAS	1,598	798	34	700	66	Hart	49.9%	2.1%	43.8%	4.1%
DU PAGE	42,078	21,365	2,335	17,031	1,347	Hart	50.8%	5.5%	40.5%	3.2%
EDGAR	2,011	1,234	34	666	77	Hart	61.4%	1.7%	33.1%	3.8%
EDWARDS	577	338	14	204	21	Hart	58.6%	2.4%	35.4%	3.6%
EFFINGHAM	2,709	1,616	44	921	128	Hart	59.7%	1.6%	34.0%	4.7%
FAYETTE	2,868	1,634	38	1,163	33	Hart	57.0%	1.3%	40.6%	1.2%
FORD	1,016	642	21	309	44	Hart	63.2%	2.1%	30.4%	4.3%
FRANKLIN	10,132	3,817	164	5,600	551	Mondale	37.7%	1.6%	55.3%	5.4%
FULTON	6,362	3,234	126	2,743	259	Hart	50.8%	2.0%	43.1%	4.1%
GALLATIN	2,686	1,302	68	1,121	195	Hart	48.5%	2.5%	41.7%	7.3%
GREENE	2,761	1,691	64	832	174	Hart	61.2%	2.3%	30.1%	6.3%
GRUNDY	3,399	1,775	69	1,395	160	Hart	52.2%	2.0%	41.0%	4.7%
HAMILTON	1,580	837	28	656	59	Hart	53.0%	1.8%	41.5%	3.7%
HANCOCK	1,725	1,093	34	537	61	Hart	63.4%	2.0%	31.1%	3.5%
HARDIN	748	319	12	383	34	Mondale	42.6%	1.6%	51.2%	4.5%
HENDERSON	920	527	15	341	37	Hart	57.3%	1.6%	37.1%	4.0%
HENRY	4,462	2,191	91	2,081	99	Hart	49.1%	2.0%	46.6%	2.2%
IROQUOIS	1,820	1,123	37	589	71	Hart	61.7%	2.0%	32.4%	3.9%
JACKSON	9,464	4,926	851	3,309	378	Hart	52.0%	9.0%	35.0%	4.0%
JASPER	1,679	1,081	25	472	101	Hart	64.4%	1.5%	28.1%	6.0%
JEFFERSON	6,012	2,994	238	2,530	250	Hart	49.8%	4.0%	42.1%	4.2%
JERSEY	2,018	1,056	38	841	83	Hart	52.3%	1.9%	41.7%	4.1%
JO DAVIESS	1,450	927	46	421	56	Hart	63.9%	3.2%	29.0%	3.9%
JOHNSON	1,196	554	15	575	52	Mondale	46.3%	1.3%	48.1%	4.3%
KANE	17,564	8,282	1,942	6,772	568	Hart	47.2%	11.1%	38.6%	3.2%
KANKAKEE	5,950	2,211	1,286	2,186	267	Hart	37.2%	21.6%	36.7%	4.5%
KENDALL	1,979	981	74	836	88	Hart	49.6%	3.7%	42.2%	4.4%
KNOX	5,107	2,737	206	2,070	94	Hart	53.6%	4.0%	40.5%	1.8%
LAKE	32,803	14,779	4,134	12,912	978	Hart	45.1%	12.6%	39.4%	3.0%
LA SALLE	10,179	4,673	213	4,946	347	Mondale	45.9%	2.1%	48.6%	3.4%
LAWRENCE	1,651	916	39	613	83	Hart	55.5%	2.4%	37.1%	5.0%
LEE	2,774	1,707	87	882	98	Hart	61.5%	3.1%	31.8%	3.5%
LIVINGSTON	2,469	1,433	54	895	87	Hart	58.0%	2.2%	36.2%	3.5%
LOGAN	2,467	1,288	75	1,017	87	Hart	52.2%	3.0%	41.2%	3.5%
MCDONOUGH	2,079	1,293	72	618	96	Hart	62.2%	3.5%	29.7%	4.6%
MCHENRY	8,596	4,596	384	3,311	305	Hart	53.5%	4.5%	38.5%	3.5%
MCLEAN	8,460	3,974	562	3,597	327	Hart	47.0%	6.6%	42.5%	3.9%
MACON	18,031	7,303	1,608	8,467	653	Mondale	40.5%	8.9%	47.0%	3.6%
MACOUPIN	8,456	4,513	172	3,404	367	Hart	53.4%	2.0%	40.3%	4.3%
MADISON	31,857	13,696	2,236	14,873	1,052	Mondale	43.0%	7.0%	46.7%	3.3%
MARION	6,289	2,982	378	2,754	175	Hart	47.4%	6.0%	43.8%	2.8%
MARSHALL	977	478	24	435	40	Hart	48.9%	2.5%	44.5%	4.1%
MASON	2,041	1,157	34	787	63	Hart	56.7%	1.7%	38.6%	3.1%
MASSAC	1,729	747	92	828	62	Mondale	43.2%	5.3%	47.9%	3.6%
MENARD	984	555	22	368	39	Hart	56.4%	2.2%	37.4%	4.0%
MERCER	1,988	1,111	23	794	60	Hart	55.9%	1.2%	39.9%	3.0%
MONROE	2,579	1,353	58	1,049	119	Hart	52.5%	2.2%	40.7%	4.6%
MONTGOMERY	4,655	2,526	94	1,812	223	Hart	54.3%	2.0%	38.9%	4.8%
MORGAN	3,124	1,799	132	1,077	116	Hart	57.6%	4.2%	34.5%	3.7%
MOULTRIE	1,536	855	34	564	83	Hart	55.7%	2.2%	36.7%	5.4%

ILLINOIS DEMOCRATIC

1984

County	Total Vote	Hart	J. Jackson	Mondale	Other	Winner	Percentage of Total Vote Hart	J. Jackson	Mondale	Other
OGLE	2,714	1,558	88	976	92	Hart	57.4%	3.2%	36.0%	3.4%
PEORIA	19,554	7,814	2,974	8,300	466	Mondale	40.0%	15.2%	42.4%	2.4%
PERRY	3,339	1,128	96	1,957	158	Mondale	33.8%	2.9%	58.6%	4.7%
PIATT	1,578	882	31	603	62	Hart	55.9%	2.0%	38.2%	3.9%
PIKE	3,366	2,055	54	1,113	144	Hart	61.1%	1.6%	33.1%	4.3%
POPE	583	257	27	278	21	Mondale	44.1%	4.6%	47.7%	3.6%
PULASKI	818	305	152	324	37	Mondale	37.3%	18.6%	39.6%	4.5%
PUTNAM	771	389	15	336	31	Hart	50.5%	1.9%	43.6%	4.0%
RANDOLPH	5,468	2,586	133	2,437	312	Hart	47.3%	2.4%	44.6%	5.7%
RICHLAND	2,138	1,317	77	645	99	Hart	61.6%	3.6%	30.2%	4.6%
ROCK ISLAND	19,478	8,438	920	9,387	733	Mondale	43.3%	4.7%	48.2%	3.8%
ST. CLAIR	37,802	10,813	9,832	15,943	1,214	Mondale	28.6%	26.0%	42.2%	3.2%
SALINE	5,289	2,268	190	2,584	247	Mondale	42.9%	3.6%	48.9%	4.7%
SANGAMON	21,931	9,973	2,720	8,315	923	Hart	45.5%	12.4%	37.9%	4.2%
SCHUYLER	841	589	13	205	34	Hart	70.0%	1.5%	24.4%	4.0%
SCOTT	610	397	7	176	30	Hart	65.1%	1.1%	28.9%	4.9%
SHELBY	3,423	1,915	44	1,299	165	Hart	55.9%	1.3%	37.9%	4.8%
STARK	355	238	10	101	6	Hart	67.0%	2.8%	28.5%	1.7%
STEPHENSON	3,121	1,695	278	1,045	103	Hart	54.3%	8.9%	33.5%	3.3%
TAZEWELL	13,209	6,397	289	6,064	459	Hart	48.4%	2.2%	45.9%	3.5%
UNION	3,685	2,016	61	1,438	170	Hart	54.7%	1.7%	39.0%	4.6%
VERMILION	8,879	3,709	891	3,984	295	Mondale	41.8%	10.0%	44.9%	3.3%
WABASH	1,112	589	26	454	43	Hart	53.0%	2.3%	40.8%	3.9%
WARREN	1,285	777	27	461	20	Hart	60.5%	2.1%	35.9%	1.6%
WASHINGTON	1,468	734	30	631	73	Hart	50.0%	2.0%	43.0%	5.0%
WAYNE	1,586	902	39	576	69	Hart	56.9%	2.5%	36.3%	4.4%
WHITE	2,688	1,511	50	997	130	Hart	56.2%	1.9%	37.1%	4.8%
WHITESIDE	5,873	2,903	122	2,620	228	Hart	49.4%	2.1%	44.6%	3.9%
WILL	27,541	10,917	4,361	11,356	907	Mondale	39.6%	15.8%	41.2%	3.3%
WILLIAMSON	9,582	3,701	307	5,071	503	Mondale	38.6%	3.2%	52.9%	5.2%
WINNEBAGO	31,182	14,751	3,589	11,767	1,075	Hart	47.3%	11.5%	37.7%	3.4%
WOODFORD	1,956	1,031	41	823	61	Hart	52.7%	2.1%	42.1%	3.1%
TOTAL	1,659,425	584,579	348,843	670,951	55,052	Mondale	35.2%	21.0%	40.4%	3.3%

ILLINOIS DEMOCRATIC

1988

County	Total Vote	Dukakis	J. Jackson	Simon	Other	Winner	Percentage of Total Vote Dukakis	J. Jackson	Simon	Other
ADAMS	7,543	1,330	716	3,990	1,507	Simon	17.6%	9.5%	52.9%	20.0%
ALEXANDER	2,778	92	951	1,506	229	Simon	3.3%	34.2%	54.2%	8.2%
BOND	2,518	311	224	1,611	372	Simon	12.4%	8.9%	64.0%	14.8%
BOONE	1,893	495	215	837	346	Simon	26.1%	11.4%	44.2%	18.3%
BROWN	942	158	58	528	198	Simon	16.8%	6.2%	56.1%	21.0%
BUREAU	2,795	499	194	1,782	320	Simon	17.9%	6.9%	63.8%	11.4%
CALHOUN	866	115	61	538	152	Simon	13.3%	7.0%	62.1%	17.6%
CARROLL	1,000	207	119	488	186	Simon	20.7%	11.9%	48.8%	18.6%
CASS	1,937	335	116	1,163	323	Simon	17.3%	6.0%	60.0%	16.7%
CHAMPAIGN	13,390	2,421	2,734	6,758	1,477	Simon	18.1%	20.4%	50.5%	11.0%
CHRISTIAN	5,111	974	321	2,905	911	Simon	19.1%	6.3%	56.8%	17.8%
CLARK	1,803	311	151	912	429	Simon	17.2%	8.4%	50.6%	23.8%
CLAY	1,349	198	166	743	242	Simon	14.7%	12.3%	55.1%	17.9%
CLINTON	3,115	411	169	1,939	596	Simon	13.2%	5.4%	62.2%	19.1%
COLES	3,856	533	343	2,418	562	Simon	13.8%	8.9%	62.7%	14.6%
COOK	927,211	149,985	400,921	315,888	60,417	J. Jackson	16.2%	43.2%	34.1%	6.5%
CRAWFORD	2,357	456	215	1,125	561	Simon	19.3%	9.1%	47.7%	23.8%
CUMBERLAND	1,497	238	131	715	413	Simon	15.9%	8.8%	47.8%	27.6%
DE KALB	4,860	912	646	2,727	575	Simon	18.8%	13.3%	56.1%	11.8%
DE WITT	1,025	165	83	588	189	Simon	16.1%	8.1%	57.4%	18.4%
DOUGLAS	1,543	282	127	823	311	Simon	18.3%	8.2%	53.3%	20.2%
DU PAGE	44,875	11,023	4,627	24,398	4,827	Simon	24.6%	10.3%	54.4%	10.8%
EDGAR	1,551	265	128	838	320	Simon	17.1%	8.3%	54.0%	20.6%
EDWARDS	561	75	38	342	106	Simon	13.4%	6.8%	61.0%	18.9%
EFFINGHAM	2,816	374	200	1,703	539	Simon	13.3%	7.1%	60.5%	19.1%
FAYETTE	2,664	347	148	1,795	374	Simon	13.0%	5.6%	67.4%	14.0%
FORD	547	83	38	332	94	Simon	15.2%	6.9%	60.7%	17.2%
FRANKLIN	9,782	440	375	8,153	814	Simon	4.5%	3.8%	83.3%	8.3%
FULTON	5,411	1,130	399	3,034	848	Simon	20.9%	7.4%	56.1%	15.7%
GALLATIN	2,501	107	100	2,068	226	Simon	4.3%	4.0%	82.7%	9.0%
GREENE	1,710	203	117	1,093	297	Simon	11.9%	6.8%	63.9%	17.4%
GRUNDY	2,564	508	118	1,574	364	Simon	19.8%	4.6%	61.4%	14.2%
HAMILTON	2,212	79	76	1,894	163	Simon	3.6%	3.4%	85.6%	7.4%
HANCOCK	1,871	385	209	919	358	Simon	20.6%	11.2%	49.1%	19.1%
HARDIN	1,130	53	31	968	78	Simon	4.7%	2.7%	85.7%	6.9%
HENDERSON	723	130	55	400	138	Simon	18.0%	7.6%	55.3%	19.1%
HENRY	4,616	970	461	2,399	786	Simon	21.0%	10.0%	52.0%	17.0%
IROQUOIS	1,436	339	115	764	218	Simon	23.6%	8.0%	53.2%	15.2%
JACKSON	7,429	308	1,007	5,785	329	Simon	4.1%	13.6%	77.9%	4.4%
JASPER	1,920	275	192	985	468	Simon	14.3%	10.0%	51.3%	24.4%
JEFFERSON	5,947	534	487	4,236	690	Simon	9.0%	8.2%	71.2%	11.6%
JERSEY	2,054	264	149	1,280	361	Simon	12.9%	7.3%	62.3%	17.6%
JO DAVIESS	1,410	297	143	655	315	Simon	21.1%	10.1%	46.5%	22.3%
JOHNSON	1,083	24	27	985	47	Simon	2.2%	2.5%	91.0%	4.3%
KANE	18,709	4,389	3,060	9,271	1,989	Simon	23.5%	16.4%	49.6%	10.6%
KANKAKEE	5,024	749	1,535	2,116	624	Simon	14.9%	30.6%	42.1%	12.4%
KENDALL	2,077	491	193	1,102	291	Simon	23.6%	9.3%	53.1%	14.0%
KNOX	4,876	1,188	648	2,453	587	Simon	24.4%	13.3%	50.3%	12.0%
LAKE	32,148	7,182	5,867	16,275	2,824	Simon	22.3%	18.2%	50.6%	8.8%
LA SALLE	8,966	1,546	599	5,785	1,036	Simon	17.2%	6.7%	64.5%	11.6%

ILLINOIS DEMOCRATIC

1988

County	Total Vote	Dukakis	J. Jackson	Simon	Other	Winner	Percentage of Total Vote: Dukakis	J. Jackson	Simon	Other
LAWRENCE	1,386	217	135	772	262	Simon	15.7%	9.7%	55.7%	18.9%
LEE	1,730	310	209	971	240	Simon	17.9%	12.1%	56.1%	13.9%
LIVINGSTON	1,869	334	124	1,167	244	Simon	17.9%	6.6%	62.4%	13.1%
LOGAN	1,632	245	117	1,072	198	Simon	15.0%	7.2%	65.7%	12.1%
MCDONOUGH	1,805	304	205	1,060	236	Simon	16.8%	11.4%	58.7%	13.1%
MCHENRY	7,248	1,705	658	4,090	795	Simon	23.5%	9.1%	56.4%	11.0%
MCLEAN	7,542	1,234	1,202	4,266	840	Simon	16.4%	15.9%	56.6%	11.1%
MACON	11,579	1,704	2,390	5,772	1,713	Simon	14.7%	20.6%	49.8%	14.8%
MACOUPIN	8,336	1,178	644	5,063	1,451	Simon	14.1%	7.7%	60.7%	17.4%
MADISON	40,400	4,508	4,933	24,756	6,203	Simon	11.2%	12.2%	61.3%	15.4%
MARION	6,216	757	541	3,801	1,117	Simon	12.2%	8.7%	61.1%	18.0%
MARSHALL	1,014	141	49	613	211	Simon	13.9%	4.8%	60.5%	20.8%
MASON	1,649	296	112	1,019	222	Simon	18.0%	6.8%	61.8%	13.5%
MASSAC	2,635	76	196	2,154	209	Simon	2.9%	7.4%	81.7%	7.9%
MENARD	785	100	41	530	114	Simon	12.7%	5.2%	67.5%	14.5%
MERCER	2,444	568	219	1,168	489	Simon	23.2%	9.0%	47.8%	20.0%
MONROE	1,783	163	85	1,279	256	Simon	9.1%	4.8%	71.7%	14.4%
MONTGOMERY	5,237	831	387	3,036	983	Simon	15.9%	7.4%	58.0%	18.8%
MORGAN	2,528	437	225	1,486	380	Simon	17.3%	8.9%	58.8%	15.0%
MOULTRIE	2,629	417	231	1,332	649	Simon	15.9%	8.8%	50.7%	24.7%
OGLE	2,247	461	268	1,046	472	Simon	20.5%	11.9%	46.6%	21.0%
PEORIA	16,098	2,695	3,193	8,604	1,606	Simon	16.7%	19.8%	53.4%	10.0%
PERRY	2,745	167	123	2,242	213	Simon	6.1%	4.5%	81.7%	7.8%
PIATT	1,097	195	72	594	236	Simon	17.8%	6.6%	54.1%	21.5%
PIKE	2,755	428	196	1,486	645	Simon	15.5%	7.1%	53.9%	23.4%
POPE	654	15	26	580	33	Simon	2.3%	4.0%	88.7%	5.0%
PULASKI	1,014	9	313	636	56	Simon	0.9%	30.9%	62.7%	5.5%
PUTNAM	614	114	38	384	78	Simon	18.6%	6.2%	62.5%	12.7%
RANDOLPH	5,667	443	264	4,381	579	Simon	7.8%	4.7%	77.3%	10.2%
RICHLAND	1,988	264	217	1,022	485	Simon	13.3%	10.9%	51.4%	24.4%
ROCK ISLAND	21,469	4,958	3,040	10,127	3,344	Simon	23.1%	14.2%	47.2%	15.6%
ST. CLAIR	40,160	3,824	14,456	16,096	5,784	Simon	9.5%	36.0%	40.1%	14.4%
SALINE	6,251	201	299	5,350	401	Simon	3.2%	4.8%	85.6%	6.4%
SANGAMON	18,254	2,624	3,426	10,539	1,665	Simon	14.4%	18.8%	57.7%	9.1%
SCHUYLER	746	91	76	448	131	Simon	12.2%	10.2%	60.1%	17.6%
SCOTT	533	82	19	363	69	Simon	15.4%	3.6%	68.1%	12.9%
SHELBY	2,660	350	203	1,543	564	Simon	13.2%	7.6%	58.0%	21.2%
STARK	627	114	42	389	82	Simon	18.2%	6.7%	62.0%	13.1%
STEPHENSON	2,576	431	617	1,098	430	Simon	16.7%	24.0%	42.6%	16.7%
TAZEWELL	12,763	2,679	844	7,263	1,977	Simon	21.0%	6.6%	56.9%	15.5%
UNION	3,634	133	124	3,157	220	Simon	3.7%	3.4%	86.9%	6.1%
VERMILION	6,751	1,242	1,310	3,035	1,164	Simon	18.4%	19.4%	45.0%	17.2%
WABASH	1,436	185	85	921	245	Simon	12.9%	5.9%	64.1%	17.1%
WARREN	1,166	213	113	617	223	Simon	18.3%	9.7%	52.9%	19.1%
WASHINGTON	1,354	155	68	935	196	Simon	11.4%	5.0%	69.1%	14.5%
WAYNE	1,946	292	133	1,173	348	Simon	15.0%	6.8%	60.3%	17.9%
WHITE	3,165	234	163	2,378	390	Simon	7.4%	5.2%	75.1%	12.3%
WHITESIDE	4,440	1,048	578	2,109	705	Simon	23.6%	13.0%	47.5%	15.9%
WILL	25,724	5,702	5,681	11,915	2,426	Simon	22.2%	22.1%	46.3%	9.4%
WILLIAMSON	8,643	363	453	7,289	538	Simon	4.2%	5.2%	84.3%	6.2%

ILLINOIS DEMOCRATIC

1988

County	Total Vote	Dukakis	J. Jackson	Simon	Other	Winner	Percentage of Total Vote Dukakis	J. Jackson	Simon	Other
WINNEBAGO	21,436	5,508	5,153	7,401	3,374	Simon	25.7%	24.0%	34.5%	15.7%
WOODFORD	1,868	358	134	1,105	271	Simon	19.2%	7.2%	59.2%	14.5%
TOTAL	1,500,930	245,289	484,233	635,219	136,189	Simon	16.3%	32.3%	42.3%	9.1%

ILLINOIS REPUBLICAN

1988

County	Total Vote	Bush	Dole	Other	Winner	Percentage of Total Vote Bush	Dole	Other
ADAMS	8,791	4,676	3,164	951	Bush	53.2%	36.0%	10.8%
ALEXANDER	470	302	95	73	Bush	64.3%	20.2%	15.5%
BOND	2,158	984	920	254	Bush	45.6%	42.6%	11.8%
BOONE	4,632	2,467	1,662	503	Bush	53.3%	35.9%	10.9%
BROWN	694	337	289	68	Bush	48.6%	41.6%	9.8%
BUREAU	3,395	1,649	1,381	365	Bush	48.6%	40.7%	10.8%
CALHOUN	580	259	295	26	Dole	44.7%	50.9%	4.5%
CARROLL	2,819	1,392	1,119	308	Bush	49.4%	39.7%	10.9%
CASS	1,095	551	459	85	Bush	50.3%	41.9%	7.8%
CHAMPAIGN	13,806	6,115	5,959	1,732	Bush	44.3%	43.2%	12.5%
CHRISTIAN	2,208	1,154	849	205	Bush	52.3%	38.5%	9.3%
CLARK	2,402	1,247	890	265	Bush	51.9%	37.1%	11.0%
CLAY	1,235	703	367	165	Bush	56.9%	29.7%	13.4%
CLINTON	2,496	1,490	801	205	Bush	59.7%	32.1%	8.2%
COLES	4,132	2,061	1,637	434	Bush	49.9%	39.6%	10.5%
COOK	233,158	141,268	76,082	15,808	Bush	60.6%	32.6%	6.8%
CRAWFORD	2,724	1,446	808	470	Bush	53.1%	29.7%	17.3%
CUMBERLAND	977	510	376	91	Bush	52.2%	38.5%	9.3%
DE KALB	9,084	4,141	4,212	731	Dole	45.6%	46.4%	8.0%
DE WITT	3,003	1,403	1,223	377	Bush	46.7%	40.7%	12.6%
DOUGLAS	2,752	1,249	1,215	288	Bush	45.4%	44.1%	10.5%
DU PAGE	89,779	48,280	35,857	5,642	Bush	53.8%	39.9%	6.3%
EDGAR	2,524	1,259	1,004	261	Bush	49.9%	39.8%	10.3%
EDWARDS	1,106	643	303	160	Bush	58.1%	27.4%	14.5%
EFFINGHAM	2,389	1,361	782	246	Bush	57.0%	32.7%	10.3%
FAYETTE	2,449	1,452	753	244	Bush	59.3%	30.7%	10.0%
FORD	3,637	1,603	1,656	378	Dole	44.1%	45.5%	10.4%
FRANKLIN	3,050	1,287	894	869	Bush	42.2%	29.3%	28.5%
FULTON	2,725	1,426	998	301	Bush	52.3%	36.6%	11.0%
GALLATIN	472	258	139	75	Bush	54.7%	29.4%	15.9%
GREENE	1,520	753	650	117	Bush	49.5%	42.8%	7.7%
GRUNDY	3,166	1,753	1,102	311	Bush	55.4%	34.8%	9.8%
HAMILTON	975	517	328	130	Bush	53.0%	33.6%	13.3%
HANCOCK	2,917	1,293	1,237	387	Bush	44.3%	42.4%	13.3%
HARDIN	753	456	196	101	Bush	60.6%	26.0%	13.4%

ILLINOIS REPUBLICAN

1988

County	Total Vote	Bush	Dole	Other	Winner	Percentage of Total Vote Bush	Dole	Other
HENDERSON	1,112	410	585	117	Dole	36.9%	52.6%	10.5%
HENRY	6,182	2,852	2,715	615	Bush	46.1%	43.9%	9.9%
IROQUOIS	4,466	2,383	1,745	338	Bush	53.4%	39.1%	7.6%
JACKSON	2,974	1,275	1,001	698	Bush	42.9%	33.7%	23.5%
JASPER	916	478	337	101	Bush	52.2%	36.8%	11.0%
JEFFERSON	2,427	1,375	663	389	Bush	56.7%	27.3%	16.0%
JERSEY	1,528	811	517	200	Bush	53.1%	33.8%	13.1%
JO DAVIESS	2,715	1,301	1,158	256	Bush	47.9%	42.7%	9.4%
JOHNSON	2,303	1,189	768	346	Bush	51.6%	33.3%	15.0%
KANE	33,367	18,639	12,177	2,551	Bush	55.9%	36.5%	7.6%
KANKAKEE	7,653	4,389	2,639	625	Bush	57.4%	34.5%	8.2%
KENDALL	5,084	2,786	1,830	468	Bush	54.8%	36.0%	9.2%
KNOX	7,697	3,241	3,659	797	Dole	42.1%	47.5%	10.4%
LAKE	44,416	24,404	16,839	3,173	Bush	54.9%	37.9%	7.1%
LA SALLE	7,341	3,805	2,862	674	Bush	51.8%	39.0%	9.2%
LAWRENCE	1,807	912	681	214	Bush	50.5%	37.7%	11.8%
LEE	5,392	3,071	1,759	562	Bush	57.0%	32.6%	10.4%
LIVINGSTON	4,986	2,339	2,240	407	Bush	46.9%	44.9%	8.2%
LOGAN	6,428	3,083	2,680	665	Bush	48.0%	41.7%	10.3%
MCDONOUGH	5,574	2,496	2,513	565	Dole	44.8%	45.1%	10.1%
MCHENRY	20,589	11,501	7,546	1,542	Bush	55.9%	36.7%	7.5%
MCLEAN	17,584	8,089	7,599	1,896	Bush	46.0%	43.2%	10.8%
MACON	8,126	3,970	3,237	919	Bush	48.9%	39.8%	11.3%
MACOUPIN	2,905	1,522	1,085	298	Bush	52.4%	37.3%	10.3%
MADISON	9,798	5,241	3,037	1,520	Bush	53.5%	31.0%	15.5%
MARION	2,747	1,544	783	420	Bush	56.2%	28.5%	15.3%
MARSHALL	2,316	1,063	1,055	198	Bush	45.9%	45.6%	8.5%
MASON	1,349	708	512	129	Bush	52.5%	38.0%	9.6%
MASSAC	1,678	923	569	186	Bush	55.0%	33.9%	11.1%
MENARD	2,736	1,449	1,104	183	Bush	53.0%	40.4%	6.7%
MERCER	1,638	643	778	217	Dole	39.3%	47.5%	13.2%
MONROE	1,557	828	563	166	Bush	53.2%	36.2%	10.7%
MONTGOMERY	3,004	1,605	1,085	314	Bush	53.4%	36.1%	10.5%
MORGAN	4,160	2,137	1,727	296	Bush	51.4%	41.5%	7.1%
MOULTRIE	1,478	726	602	150	Bush	49.1%	40.7%	10.1%
OGLE	6,394	3,424	2,050	920	Bush	53.6%	32.1%	14.4%
PEORIA	16,159	8,464	5,899	1,796	Bush	52.4%	36.5%	11.1%
PERRY	1,708	742	652	314	Bush	43.4%	38.2%	18.4%
PIATT	2,648	1,059	1,307	282	Dole	40.0%	49.4%	10.6%
PIKE	1,630	895	584	151	Bush	54.9%	35.8%	9.3%
POPE	883	547	238	98	Bush	61.9%	27.0%	11.1%
PULASKI	948	501	272	175	Bush	52.8%	28.7%	18.5%
PUTNAM	504	234	231	39	Bush	46.4%	45.8%	7.7%
RANDOLPH	2,338	1,291	778	269	Bush	55.2%	33.3%	11.5%
RICHLAND	1,840	995	489	356	Bush	54.1%	26.6%	19.3%
ROCK ISLAND	8,985	4,138	3,308	1,539	Bush	46.1%	36.8%	17.1%
ST. CLAIR	8,787	4,637	2,505	1,645	Bush	52.8%	28.5%	18.7%
SALINE	2,362	1,256	777	329	Bush	53.2%	32.9%	13.9%
SANGAMON	27,145	16,035	9,011	2,099	Bush	59.1%	33.2%	7.7%
SCHUYLER	955	469	395	91	Bush	49.1%	41.4%	9.5%

ILLINOIS REPUBLICAN

1988

County	Total Vote	Bush	Dole	Other	Winner	Percentage of Total Vote Bush	Dole	Other
SCOTT	810	364	350	96	Bush	44.9%	43.2%	11.9%
SHELBY	1,594	730	715	149	Bush	45.8%	44.9%	9.3%
STARK	1,331	545	686	100	Dole	40.9%	51.5%	7.5%
STEPHENSON	5,977	2,752	2,458	767	Bush	46.0%	41.1%	12.8%
TAZEWELL	13,308	6,370	4,932	2,006	Bush	47.9%	37.1%	15.1%
UNION	1,916	943	618	355	Bush	49.2%	32.3%	18.5%
VERMILION	7,360	3,914	2,735	711	Bush	53.2%	37.2%	9.7%
WABASH	1,344	775	366	203	Bush	57.7%	27.2%	15.1%
WARREN	3,325	1,380	1,577	368	Dole	41.5%	47.4%	11.1%
WASHINGTON	1,869	925	766	178	Bush	49.5%	41.0%	9.5%
WAYNE	2,971	1,691	901	379	Bush	56.9%	30.3%	12.8%
WHITE	1,440	845	416	179	Bush	58.7%	28.9%	12.4%
WHITESIDE	8,027	4,158	2,825	1,044	Bush	51.8%	35.2%	13.0%
WILL	30,565	18,432	9,462	2,671	Bush	60.3%	31.0%	8.7%
WILLIAMSON	4,221	1,837	1,187	1,197	Bush	43.5%	28.1%	28.4%
WINNEBAGO	28,315	15,510	8,376	4,429	Bush	54.8%	29.6%	15.6%
WOODFORD	4,872	2,360	2,035	477	Bush	48.4%	41.8%	9.8%
TOTAL	858,637	469,151	309,253	80,233	Bush	54.6%	36.0%	9.3%

ILLINOIS DEMOCRATIC

1992

County	Total Vote	Brown	Clinton	Tsongas	Other	Winner	Percentage of Total Vote Brown	Clinton	Tsongas	Other
ADAMS	6,180	777	3,672	1,212	519	Clinton	12.6%	59.4%	19.6%	8.4%
ALEXANDER	1,565	103	1,208	101	153	Clinton	6.6%	77.2%	6.5%	9.8%
BOND	1,676	188	1,184	181	123	Clinton	11.2%	70.6%	10.8%	7.3%
BOONE	2,326	391	1,343	466	126	Clinton	16.8%	57.7%	20.0%	5.4%
BROWN	563	53	385	81	44	Clinton	9.4%	68.4%	14.4%	7.8%
BUREAU	4,901	689	2,620	860	732	Clinton	14.1%	53.5%	17.5%	14.9%
CALHOUN	807	71	590	76	70	Clinton	8.8%	73.1%	9.4%	8.7%
CARROLL	954	153	485	229	87	Clinton	16.0%	50.8%	24.0%	9.1%
CASS	1,479	141	912	307	119	Clinton	9.5%	61.7%	20.8%	8.0%
CHAMPAIGN	16,562	3,063	6,012	6,343	1,144	Tsongas	18.5%	36.3%	38.3%	6.9%
CHRISTIAN	6,509	628	4,131	1,165	585	Clinton	9.6%	63.5%	17.9%	9.0%
CLARK	1,676	215	1,098	212	151	Clinton	12.8%	65.5%	12.6%	9.0%
CLAY	1,570	155	1,020	234	161	Clinton	9.9%	65.0%	14.9%	10.3%
CLINTON	2,523	289	1,735	329	170	Clinton	11.5%	68.8%	13.0%	6.7%
COLES	4,860	612	2,620	1,199	429	Clinton	12.6%	53.9%	24.7%	8.8%
COOK	867,003	126,551	435,599	236,101	68,752	Clinton	14.6%	50.2%	27.2%	7.9%
CRAWFORD	2,055	297	1,238	276	244	Clinton	14.5%	60.2%	13.4%	11.9%
CUMBERLAND	1,291	134	794	218	145	Clinton	10.4%	61.5%	16.9%	11.2%
DE KALB	5,730	1,209	2,444	1,770	307	Clinton	21.1%	42.7%	30.9%	5.4%
DE WITT	1,277	139	850	215	73	Clinton	10.9%	66.6%	16.8%	5.7%

ILLINOIS DEMOCRATIC

1992

County	Total Vote	Brown	Clinton	Tsongas	Other	Winner	Percentage of Total Vote Brown	Clinton	Tsongas	Other
DOUGLAS	1,617	166	1,022	326	103	Clinton	10.3%	63.2%	20.2%	6.4%
DU PAGE	61,563	12,272	20,515	26,130	2,646	Tsongas	19.9%	33.3%	42.4%	4.3%
EDGAR	1,649	183	1,097	245	124	Clinton	11.1%	66.5%	14.9%	7.5%
EDWARDS	768	83	485	113	87	Clinton	10.8%	63.2%	14.7%	11.3%
EFFINGHAM	3,737	540	1,940	904	353	Clinton	14.5%	51.9%	24.2%	9.4%
FAYETTE	1,920	190	1,288	280	162	Clinton	9.9%	67.1%	14.6%	8.4%
FORD	838	98	490	189	61	Clinton	11.7%	58.5%	22.6%	7.3%
FRANKLIN	11,114	875	8,024	1,121	1,094	Clinton	7.9%	72.2%	10.1%	9.8%
FULTON	6,573	741	4,189	926	717	Clinton	11.3%	63.7%	14.1%	10.9%
GALLATIN	2,293	127	1,737	202	227	Clinton	5.5%	75.8%	8.8%	9.9%
GREENE	1,945	167	1,344	250	184	Clinton	8.6%	69.1%	12.9%	9.5%
GRUNDY	2,763	484	1,464	657	158	Clinton	17.5%	53.0%	23.8%	5.7%
HAMILTON	2,486	174	1,805	261	246	Clinton	7.0%	72.6%	10.5%	9.9%
HANCOCK	1,601	214	918	323	146	Clinton	13.4%	57.3%	20.2%	9.1%
HARDIN	1,151	73	835	101	142	Clinton	6.3%	72.5%	8.8%	12.3%
HENDERSON	853	113	454	152	134	Clinton	13.2%	53.2%	17.8%	15.7%
HENRY	4,103	593	2,034	984	492	Clinton	14.5%	49.6%	24.0%	12.0%
IROQUOIS	1,721	283	948	398	92	Clinton	16.4%	55.1%	23.1%	5.3%
JACKSON	6,936	900	4,271	1,319	446	Clinton	13.0%	61.6%	19.0%	6.4%
JASPER	1,941	170	1,195	316	260	Clinton	8.8%	61.6%	16.3%	13.4%
JEFFERSON	6,689	594	4,363	983	749	Clinton	8.9%	65.2%	14.7%	11.2%
JERSEY	3,011	327	2,103	354	227	Clinton	10.9%	69.8%	11.8%	7.5%
JO DAVIESS	2,324	388	1,077	546	313	Clinton	16.7%	46.3%	23.5%	13.5%
JOHNSON	1,395	112	983	200	100	Clinton	8.0%	70.5%	14.3%	7.2%
KANE	20,402	4,010	8,927	6,431	1,034	Clinton	19.7%	43.8%	31.5%	5.1%
KANKAKEE	5,309	1,035	2,849	1,180	245	Clinton	19.5%	53.7%	22.2%	4.6%
KENDALL	2,415	475	1,138	697	105	Clinton	19.7%	47.1%	28.9%	4.3%
KNOX	4,578	713	2,392	913	560	Clinton	15.6%	52.2%	19.9%	12.2%
LAKE	43,965	7,266	16,393	17,940	2,366	Tsongas	16.5%	37.3%	40.8%	5.4%
LA SALLE	12,436	2,021	6,840	2,543	1,032	Clinton	16.3%	55.0%	20.4%	8.3%
LAWRENCE	2,086	239	1,290	273	284	Clinton	11.5%	61.8%	13.1%	13.6%
LEE	2,316	373	1,341	413	189	Clinton	16.1%	57.9%	17.8%	8.2%
LIVINGSTON	1,817	284	1,047	348	138	Clinton	15.6%	57.6%	19.2%	7.6%
LOGAN	1,574	185	983	291	115	Clinton	11.8%	62.5%	18.5%	7.3%
MCDONOUGH	2,051	272	1,098	529	152	Clinton	13.3%	53.5%	25.8%	7.4%
MCHENRY	11,907	2,671	4,700	3,936	600	Clinton	22.4%	39.5%	33.1%	5.0%
MCLEAN	9,395	1,709	4,346	2,684	656	Clinton	18.2%	46.3%	28.6%	7.0%
MACON	15,585	1,802	9,263	3,457	1,063	Clinton	11.6%	59.4%	22.2%	6.8%
MACOUPIN	7,971	984	5,100	1,141	746	Clinton	12.3%	64.0%	14.3%	9.4%
MADISON	37,007	5,052	23,295	5,631	3,029	Clinton	13.7%	62.9%	15.2%	8.2%
MARION	6,362	595	4,334	840	593	Clinton	9.4%	68.1%	13.2%	9.3%
MARSHALL	1,257	171	788	198	100	Clinton	13.6%	62.7%	15.8%	8.0%
MASON	2,029	192	1,366	280	191	Clinton	9.5%	67.3%	13.8%	9.4%
MASSAC	2,364	208	1,559	329	268	Clinton	8.8%	65.9%	13.9%	11.3%
MENARD	765	84	463	163	55	Clinton	11.0%	60.5%	21.3%	7.2%
MERCER	1,980	278	1,050	402	250	Clinton	14.0%	53.0%	20.3%	12.6%
MONROE	2,026	307	1,202	346	171	Clinton	15.2%	59.3%	17.1%	8.4%
MONTGOMERY	3,921	424	2,548	600	349	Clinton	10.8%	65.0%	15.3%	8.9%
MORGAN	2,366	259	1,335	610	162	Clinton	10.9%	56.4%	25.8%	6.8%
MOULTRIE	1,867	175	1,176	370	146	Clinton	9.4%	63.0%	19.8%	7.8%

ILLINOIS DEMOCRATIC

1992

County	Total Vote	Brown	Clinton	Tsongas	Other	Winner	Percentage of Total Vote Brown	Clinton	Tsongas	Other
OGLE	2,504	432	1,432	475	165	Clinton	17.3%	57.2%	19.0%	6.6%
PEORIA	15,963	2,520	8,982	3,274	1,187	Clinton	15.8%	56.3%	20.5%	7.4%
PERRY	2,837	236	2,168	231	202	Clinton	8.3%	76.4%	8.1%	7.1%
PIATT	1,640	221	938	379	102	Clinton	13.5%	57.2%	23.1%	6.2%
PIKE	2,409	200	1,621	280	308	Clinton	8.3%	67.3%	11.6%	12.8%
POPE	616	63	423	72	58	Clinton	10.2%	68.7%	11.7%	9.4%
PULASKI	929	37	774	54	64	Clinton	4.0%	83.3%	5.8%	6.9%
PUTNAM	1,400	179	769	220	232	Clinton	12.8%	54.9%	15.7%	16.6%
RANDOLPH	5,780	541	3,934	605	700	Clinton	9.4%	68.1%	10.5%	12.1%
RICHLAND	2,101	299	1,183	363	256	Clinton	14.2%	56.3%	17.3%	12.2%
ROCK ISLAND	20,781	3,209	8,903	5,684	2,985	Clinton	15.4%	42.8%	27.4%	14.4%
ST. CLAIR	37,402	4,446	23,033	5,480	4,443	Clinton	11.9%	61.6%	14.7%	11.9%
SALINE	6,227	525	4,401	711	590	Clinton	8.4%	70.7%	11.4%	9.5%
SANGAMON	17,077	1,908	9,235	4,665	1,269	Clinton	11.2%	54.1%	27.3%	7.4%
SCHUYLER	687	64	456	113	54	Clinton	9.3%	66.4%	16.4%	7.9%
SCOTT	440	42	286	72	40	Clinton	9.5%	65.0%	16.4%	9.1%
SHELBY	3,590	348	2,313	632	297	Clinton	9.7%	64.4%	17.6%	8.3%
STARK	646	82	391	112	61	Clinton	12.7%	60.5%	17.3%	9.4%
STEPHENSON	2,907	475	1,616	616	200	Clinton	16.3%	55.6%	21.2%	6.9%
TAZEWELL	11,238	1,663	6,686	1,895	994	Clinton	14.8%	59.5%	16.9%	8.8%
UNION	3,938	381	2,859	363	335	Clinton	9.7%	72.6%	9.2%	8.5%
VERMILION	8,395	1,374	4,959	1,483	579	Clinton	16.4%	59.1%	17.7%	6.9%
WABASH	1,688	264	973	271	180	Clinton	15.6%	57.6%	16.1%	10.7%
WARREN	1,178	153	606	296	123	Clinton	13.0%	51.4%	25.1%	10.4%
WASHINGTON	1,271	138	901	149	83	Clinton	10.9%	70.9%	11.7%	6.5%
WAYNE	1,843	145	1,287	230	181	Clinton	7.9%	69.8%	12.5%	9.8%
WHITE	3,856	369	2,546	501	440	Clinton	9.6%	66.0%	13.0%	11.4%
WHITESIDE	4,269	753	2,146	977	393	Clinton	17.6%	50.3%	22.9%	9.2%
WILL	34,080	6,309	16,601	8,948	2,222	Clinton	18.5%	48.7%	26.3%	6.5%
WILLIAMSON	11,422	1,118	7,840	1,485	979	Clinton	9.8%	68.6%	13.0%	8.6%
WINNEBAGO	24,842	4,028	14,160	5,442	1,212	Clinton	16.2%	57.0%	21.9%	4.9%
WOODFORD	1,925	315	1,063	413	134	Clinton	16.4%	55.2%	21.5%	7.0%
TOTAL	1,504,130	220,346	776,829	387,891	119,064	Clinton	14.6%	51.6%	25.8%	7.9%

ILLINOIS REPUBLICAN

1992

County	Total Vote	Buchanan	Bush	Horton	Winner	Percentage of Total Vote: Buchanan	Bush	Horton
ADAMS	5,632	1,054	4,506	72	Bush	18.7%	80.0%	1.3%
ALEXANDER	350	82	264	4	Bush	23.4%	75.4%	1.1%
BOND	1,281	228	1,041	12	Bush	17.8%	81.3%	0.9%
BOONE	4,370	1,114	3,193	63	Bush	25.5%	73.1%	1.4%
BROWN	577	123	447	7	Bush	21.3%	77.5%	1.2%
BUREAU	3,383	760	2,580	43	Bush	22.5%	76.3%	1.3%
CALHOUN	385	80	300	5	Bush	20.8%	77.9%	1.3%
CARROLL	2,071	490	1,564	17	Bush	23.7%	75.5%	0.8%
CASS	1,186	227	945	14	Bush	19.1%	79.7%	1.2%
CHAMPAIGN	12,515	3,087	9,314	114	Bush	24.7%	74.4%	0.9%
CHRISTIAN	2,851	648	2,170	33	Bush	22.7%	76.1%	1.2%
CLARK	1,553	402	1,135	16	Bush	25.9%	73.1%	1.0%
CLAY	1,131	275	840	16	Bush	24.3%	74.3%	1.4%
CLINTON	1,853	410	1,413	30	Bush	22.1%	76.3%	1.6%
COLES	5,497	1,421	3,988	88	Bush	25.9%	72.5%	1.6%
COOK	198,916	42,900	153,799	2,217	Bush	21.6%	77.3%	1.1%
CRAWFORD	2,146	528	1,587	31	Bush	24.6%	74.0%	1.4%
CUMBERLAND	924	248	665	11	Bush	26.8%	72.0%	1.2%
DE KALB	6,654	1,543	5,016	95	Bush	23.2%	75.4%	1.4%
DE WITT	2,531	698	1,808	25	Bush	27.6%	71.4%	1.0%
DOUGLAS	2,344	612	1,700	32	Bush	26.1%	72.5%	1.4%
DU PAGE	105,667	22,863	81,741	1,063	Bush	21.6%	77.4%	1.0%
EDGAR	2,589	655	1,906	28	Bush	25.3%	73.6%	1.1%
EDWARDS	945	227	712	6	Bush	24.0%	75.3%	0.6%
EFFINGHAM	2,430	617	1,787	26	Bush	25.4%	73.5%	1.1%
FAYETTE	1,871	349	1,495	27	Bush	18.7%	79.9%	1.4%
FORD	2,581	600	1,946	35	Bush	23.2%	75.4%	1.4%
FRANKLIN	1,806	416	1,373	17	Bush	23.0%	76.0%	0.9%
FULTON	2,417	460	1,927	30	Bush	19.0%	79.7%	1.2%
GALLATIN	352	66	283	3	Bush	18.8%	80.4%	0.9%
GREENE	1,409	301	1,097	11	Bush	21.4%	77.9%	0.8%
GRUNDY	3,442	715	2,685	42	Bush	20.8%	78.0%	1.2%
HAMILTON	884	222	648	14	Bush	25.1%	73.3%	1.6%
HANCOCK	1,827	444	1,351	32	Bush	24.3%	73.9%	1.8%
HARDIN	464	86	372	6	Bush	18.5%	80.2%	1.3%
HENDERSON	971	200	757	14	Bush	20.6%	78.0%	1.4%
HENRY	4,253	860	3,349	44	Bush	20.2%	78.7%	1.0%
IROQUOIS	3,781	919	2,789	73	Bush	24.3%	73.8%	1.9%
JACKSON	2,765	776	1,952	37	Bush	28.1%	70.6%	1.3%
JASPER	698	147	537	14	Bush	21.1%	76.9%	2.0%
JEFFERSON	2,030	380	1,622	28	Bush	18.7%	79.9%	1.4%
JERSEY	1,629	358	1,253	18	Bush	22.0%	76.9%	1.1%
JO DAVIESS	3,392	797	2,544	51	Bush	23.5%	75.0%	1.5%
JOHNSON	1,652	352	1,267	33	Bush	21.3%	76.7%	2.0%
KANE	39,551	9,311	29,729	511	Bush	23.5%	75.2%	1.3%
KANKAKEE	5,285	1,217	3,986	82	Bush	23.0%	75.4%	1.6%
KENDALL	6,003	1,469	4,460	74	Bush	24.5%	74.3%	1.2%
KNOX	5,517	1,341	4,101	75	Bush	24.3%	74.3%	1.4%
LAKE	58,072	12,393	44,950	729	Bush	21.3%	77.4%	1.3%
LA SALLE	8,750	1,945	6,684	121	Bush	22.2%	76.4%	1.4%

ILLINOIS REPUBLICAN

1992

County	Total Vote	Buchanan	Bush	Horton	Winner	Percentage of Total Vote Buchanan	Bush	Horton
LAWRENCE	2,417	581	1,787	49	Bush	24.0%	73.9%	2.0%
LEE	4,146	987	3,112	47	Bush	23.8%	75.1%	1.1%
LIVINGSTON	7,399	1,669	5,645	85	Bush	22.6%	76.3%	1.1%
LOGAN	5,593	1,318	4,212	63	Bush	23.6%	75.3%	1.1%
MCDONOUGH	4,435	1,044	3,320	71	Bush	23.5%	74.9%	1.6%
MCHENRY	29,370	7,103	21,877	390	Bush	24.2%	74.5%	1.3%
MCLEAN	19,705	4,409	15,113	183	Bush	22.4%	76.7%	0.9%
MACON	8,762	1,858	6,843	61	Bush	21.2%	78.1%	0.7%
MACOUPIN	2,300	438	1,833	29	Bush	19.0%	79.7%	1.3%
MADISON	8,598	2,036	6,451	111	Bush	23.7%	75.0%	1.3%
MARION	2,192	425	1,737	30	Bush	19.4%	79.2%	1.4%
MARSHALL	1,500	344	1,143	13	Bush	22.9%	76.2%	0.9%
MASON	1,536	298	1,229	9	Bush	19.4%	80.0%	0.6%
MASSAC	1,074	206	858	10	Bush	19.2%	79.9%	0.9%
MENARD	2,689	596	2,064	29	Bush	22.2%	76.8%	1.1%
MERCER	1,501	299	1,185	17	Bush	19.9%	78.9%	1.1%
MONROE	2,377	551	1,781	45	Bush	23.2%	74.9%	1.9%
MONTGOMERY	2,421	544	1,850	27	Bush	22.5%	76.4%	1.1%
MORGAN	3,389	767	2,576	46	Bush	22.6%	76.0%	1.4%
MOULTRIE	1,324	342	958	24	Bush	25.8%	72.4%	1.8%
OGLE	7,599	1,964	5,524	111	Bush	25.8%	72.7%	1.5%
PEORIA	14,266	2,911	11,242	113	Bush	20.4%	78.8%	0.8%
PERRY	1,382	397	955	30	Bush	28.7%	69.1%	2.2%
PIATT	1,750	430	1,299	21	Bush	24.6%	74.2%	1.2%
PIKE	1,391	240	1,134	17	Bush	17.3%	81.5%	1.2%
POPE	781	167	602	12	Bush	21.4%	77.1%	1.5%
PULASKI	1,096	284	795	17	Bush	25.9%	72.5%	1.6%
PUTNAM	362	51	307	4	Bush	14.1%	84.8%	1.1%
RANDOLPH	1,628	371	1,233	24	Bush	22.8%	75.7%	1.5%
RICHLAND	1,665	443	1,199	23	Bush	26.6%	72.0%	1.4%
ROCK ISLAND	8,072	1,589	6,402	81	Bush	19.7%	79.3%	1.0%
ST. CLAIR	9,316	2,175	6,974	167	Bush	23.3%	74.9%	1.8%
SALINE	1,687	347	1,313	27	Bush	20.6%	77.8%	1.6%
SANGAMON	27,272	5,885	21,111	276	Bush	21.6%	77.4%	1.0%
SCHUYLER	1,050	214	817	19	Bush	20.4%	77.8%	1.8%
SCOTT	842	222	612	8	Bush	26.4%	72.7%	1.0%
SHELBY	1,656	420	1,214	22	Bush	25.4%	73.3%	1.3%
STARK	1,180	263	894	23	Bush	22.3%	75.8%	1.9%
STEPHENSON	7,632	2,067	5,448	117	Bush	27.1%	71.4%	1.5%
TAZEWELL	10,117	2,323	7,716	78	Bush	23.0%	76.3%	0.8%
UNION	1,503	315	1,172	16	Bush	21.0%	78.0%	1.1%
VERMILION	6,097	1,646	4,352	99	Bush	27.0%	71.4%	1.6%
WABASH	1,731	419	1,298	14	Bush	24.2%	75.0%	0.8%
WARREN	2,628	582	2,013	33	Bush	22.1%	76.6%	1.3%
WASHINGTON	1,683	388	1,264	31	Bush	23.1%	75.1%	1.8%
WAYNE	3,553	1,030	2,467	56	Bush	29.0%	69.4%	1.6%
WHITE	1,082	177	894	11	Bush	16.4%	82.6%	1.0%
WHITESIDE	4,249	948	3,258	43	Bush	22.3%	76.7%	1.0%
WILL	31,551	7,656	23,566	329	Bush	24.3%	74.7%	1.0%
WILLIAMSON	2,638	561	2,052	25	Bush	21.3%	77.8%	0.9%

ILLINOIS REPUBLICAN

1992

County	Total Vote	Buchanan	Bush	Horton	Winner	Percentage of Total Vote Buchanan	Bush	Horton
WINNEBAGO	24,250	5,837	18,202	211	Bush	24.1%	75.1%	0.9%
WOODFORD	5,520	1,362	4,107	51	Bush	24.7%	74.4%	0.9%
TOTAL	831,140	186,915	634,588	9,637	Bush	22.5%	76.4%	1.2%

ILLINOIS DEMOCRATIC

1996

County	Total Vote	Clinton	Other	Winner	Percentage of Total Vote Clinton	Other
ADAMS	2,460	2,360	100	Clinton	95.9%	4.1%
ALEXANDER	1,344	1,265	79	Clinton	94.1%	5.9%
BOND	946	904	42	Clinton	95.6%	4.4%
BOONE	683	662	21	Clinton	96.9%	3.1%
BROWN	301	292	9	Clinton	97.0%	3.0%
BUREAU	2,307	2,206	101	Clinton	95.6%	4.4%
CALHOUN	937	901	36	Clinton	96.2%	3.8%
CARROLL	471	463	8	Clinton	98.3%	1.7%
CASS	673	654	19	Clinton	97.2%	2.8%
CHAMPAIGN	6,185	6,021	164	Clinton	97.3%	2.7%
CHRISTIAN	3,876	3,648	228	Clinton	94.1%	5.9%
CLARK	874	830	44	Clinton	95.0%	5.0%
CLAY	464	440	24	Clinton	94.8%	5.2%
CLINTON	1,192	1,148	44	Clinton	96.3%	3.7%
COLES	1,848	1,784	64	Clinton	96.5%	3.5%
COOK	498,738	480,251	18,487	Clinton	96.3%	3.7%
CRAWFORD	843	812	31	Clinton	96.3%	3.7%
CUMBERLAND	413	392	21	Clinton	94.9%	5.1%
DE KALB	2,079	2,001	78	Clinton	96.2%	3.8%
DE WITT	534	511	23	Clinton	95.7%	4.3%
DOUGLAS	568	548	20	Clinton	96.5%	3.5%
DU PAGE	25,034	24,244	790	Clinton	96.8%	3.2%
EDGAR	1,069	1,005	64	Clinton	94.0%	6.0%
EDWARDS	184	177	7	Clinton	96.2%	3.8%
EFFINGHAM	1,117	1,049	68	Clinton	93.9%	6.1%
FAYETTE	1,058	1,005	53	Clinton	95.0%	5.0%
FORD	347	335	12	Clinton	96.5%	3.5%
FRANKLIN	5,700	5,357	343	Clinton	94.0%	6.0%
FULTON	4,714	4,459	255	Clinton	94.6%	5.4%
GALLATIN	1,821	1,664	157	Clinton	91.4%	8.6%
GREENE	1,327	1,251	76	Clinton	94.3%	5.7%
GRUNDY	1,460	1,395	65	Clinton	95.5%	4.5%
HAMILTON	1,167	1,124	43	Clinton	96.3%	3.7%
HANCOCK	991	947	44	Clinton	95.6%	4.4%
HARDIN	328	317	11	Clinton	96.6%	3.4%

ILLINOIS DEMOCRATIC

1996

County	Total Vote	Clinton	Other	Winner	Percentage of Total Vote	
					Clinton	Other
HENDERSON	623	592	31	Clinton	95.0%	5.0%
HENRY	2,787	2,728	59	Clinton	97.9%	2.1%
IROQUOIS	718	680	38	Clinton	94.7%	5.3%
JACKSON	4,406	4,256	150	Clinton	96.6%	3.4%
JASPER	457	429	28	Clinton	93.9%	6.1%
JEFFERSON	3,176	2,968	208	Clinton	93.5%	6.5%
JERSEY	1,005	967	38	Clinton	96.2%	3.8%
JO DAVIESS	608	588	20	Clinton	96.7%	3.3%
JOHNSON	618	597	21	Clinton	96.6%	3.4%
KANE	7,464	7,226	238	Clinton	96.8%	3.2%
KANKAKEE	1,716	1,651	65	Clinton	96.2%	3.8%
KENDALL	1,001	969	32	Clinton	96.8%	3.2%
KNOX	2,065	1,999	66	Clinton	96.8%	3.2%
LAKE	16,209	15,757	452	Clinton	97.2%	2.8%
LA SALLE	5,958	5,709	249	Clinton	95.8%	4.2%
LAWRENCE	488	460	28	Clinton	94.3%	5.7%
LEE	1,174	1,131	43	Clinton	96.3%	3.7%
LIVINGSTON	772	742	30	Clinton	96.1%	3.9%
LOGAN	678	660	18	Clinton	97.3%	2.7%
MCDONOUGH	1,026	994	32	Clinton	96.9%	3.1%
MCHENRY	4,769	4,574	195	Clinton	95.9%	4.1%
MCLEAN	5,327	5,184	143	Clinton	97.3%	2.7%
MACON	6,329	6,168	161	Clinton	97.5%	2.5%
MACOUPIN	5,637	5,314	323	Clinton	94.3%	5.7%
MADISON	18,241	17,239	1,002	Clinton	94.5%	5.5%
MARION	2,395	2,289	106	Clinton	95.6%	4.4%
MARSHALL	417	401	16	Clinton	96.2%	3.8%
MASON	830	803	27	Clinton	96.7%	3.3%
MASSAC	540	526	14	Clinton	97.4%	2.6%
MENARD	493	484	9	Clinton	98.2%	1.8%
MERCER	913	886	27	Clinton	97.0%	3.0%
MONROE	642	613	29	Clinton	95.5%	4.5%
MONTGOMERY	2,811	2,694	117	Clinton	95.8%	4.2%
MORGAN	1,053	1,024	29	Clinton	97.2%	2.8%
MOULTRIE	723	689	34	Clinton	95.3%	4.7%
OGLE	1,135	1,105	30	Clinton	97.4%	2.6%
PEORIA	11,534	11,190	344	Clinton	97.0%	3.0%
PERRY	2,721	2,595	126	Clinton	95.4%	4.6%
PIATT	594	578	16	Clinton	97.3%	2.7%
PIKE	1,335	1,271	64	Clinton	95.2%	4.8%
POPE	190	185	5	Clinton	97.4%	2.6%
PULASKI	319	310	9	Clinton	97.2%	2.8%
PUTNAM	471	449	22	Clinton	95.3%	4.7%
RANDOLPH	3,259	3,116	143	Clinton	95.6%	4.4%
RICHLAND	434	417	17	Clinton	96.1%	3.9%
ROCK ISLAND	12,787	12,182	605	Clinton	95.3%	4.7%
ST. CLAIR	19,817	18,915	902	Clinton	95.4%	4.6%
SALINE	2,732	2,591	141	Clinton	94.8%	5.2%
SANGAMON	9,684	9,475	209	Clinton	97.8%	2.2%
SCHUYLER	420	402	18	Clinton	95.7%	4.3%

ILLINOIS DEMOCRATIC

1996

County	Total Vote	Clinton	Other	Winner	Percentage of Total Vote	
					Clinton	Other
SCOTT	237	229	8	Clinton	96.6%	3.4%
SHELBY	2,447	2,264	183	Clinton	92.5%	7.5%
STARK	228	218	10	Clinton	95.6%	4.4%
STEPHENSON	1,002	966	36	Clinton	96.4%	3.6%
TAZEWELL	7,430	7,179	251	Clinton	96.6%	3.4%
UNION	3,000	2,785	215	Clinton	92.8%	7.2%
VERMILION	3,775	3,616	159	Clinton	95.8%	4.2%
WABASH	367	339	28	Clinton	92.4%	7.6%
WARREN	507	496	11	Clinton	97.8%	2.2%
WASHINGTON	760	731	29	Clinton	96.2%	3.8%
WAYNE	664	626	38	Clinton	94.3%	5.7%
WHITE	1,803	1,654	149	Clinton	91.7%	8.3%
WHITESIDE	1,912	1,854	58	Clinton	97.0%	3.0%
WILL	15,114	14,597	517	Clinton	96.6%	3.4%
WILLIAMSON	5,325	5,008	317	Clinton	94.0%	6.0%
WINNEBAGO	9,689	9,404	285	Clinton	97.1%	2.9%
WOODFORD	862	841	21	Clinton	97.6%	2.4%
TOTAL	800,676	770,001	30,675	Clinton	96.2%	3.8%

ILLINOIS REPUBLICAN

1996

County	Total Vote	Buchanan	Dole	Other	Winner	Percentage of Total Vote		
						Buchanan	Dole	Other
ADAMS	5,640	1,182	3,727	731	Dole	21.0%	66.1%	13.0%
ALEXANDER	366	94	249	23	Dole	25.7%	68.0%	6.3%
BOND	1,319	293	911	115	Dole	22.2%	69.1%	8.7%
BOONE	4,072	1,009	2,457	606	Dole	24.8%	60.3%	14.9%
BROWN	692	130	503	59	Dole	18.8%	72.7%	8.5%
BUREAU	5,054	1,291	2,993	770	Dole	25.5%	59.2%	15.2%
CALHOUN	656	191	434	31	Dole	29.1%	66.2%	4.7%
CARROLL	2,132	487	1,285	360	Dole	22.8%	60.3%	16.9%
CASS	1,069	257	764	48	Dole	24.0%	71.5%	4.5%
CHAMPAIGN	13,251	2,378	8,994	1,879	Dole	17.9%	67.9%	14.2%
CHRISTIAN	2,157	543	1,443	171	Dole	25.2%	66.9%	7.9%
CLARK	1,771	435	1,105	231	Dole	24.6%	62.4%	13.0%
CLAY	1,405	403	860	142	Dole	28.7%	61.2%	10.1%
CLINTON	2,045	465	1,447	133	Dole	22.7%	70.8%	6.5%
COLES	3,838	874	2,537	427	Dole	22.8%	66.1%	11.1%
COOK	187,863	43,569	123,725	20,569	Dole	23.2%	65.9%	10.9%
CRAWFORD	1,481	406	918	157	Dole	27.4%	62.0%	10.6%
CUMBERLAND	808	242	492	74	Dole	30.0%	60.9%	9.2%
DE KALB	7,538	1,605	4,821	1,112	Dole	21.3%	64.0%	14.8%
DE WITT	2,780	718	1,731	331	Dole	25.8%	62.3%	11.9%

ILLINOIS REPUBLICAN

1996

County	Total Vote	Buchanan	Dole	Other	Winner	Percentage of Total Vote Buchanan	Dole	Other
DOUGLAS	2,638	611	1,695	332	Dole	23.2%	64.3%	12.6%
DU PAGE	109,699	21,367	73,173	15,159	Dole	12.5%	66.7%	13.8%
EDGAR	2,201	427	1,534	240	Dole	19.4%	69.7%	10.9%
EDWARDS	473	100	317	56	Dole	21.1%	67.0%	11.8%
EFFINGHAM	2,301	758	1,355	188	Dole	32.9%	58.9%	8.2%
FAYETTE	2,074	576	1,359	139	Dole	27.8%	65.5%	6.7%
FORD	1,821	383	1,209	229	Dole	21.0%	66.4%	12.6%
FRANKLIN	2,889	927	1,711	251	Dole	32.1%	59.2%	8.7%
FULTON	2,435	553	1,663	219	Dole	22.7%	68.3%	9.0%
GALLATIN	269	76	181	12	Dole	28.3%	67.3%	4.5%
GREENE	1,043	297	688	58	Dole	28.5%	66.0%	5.6%
GRUNDY	4,349	1,154	2,740	455	Dole	26.5%	63.0%	10.5%
HAMILTON	770	225	496	49	Dole	29.2%	64.4%	6.4%
HANCOCK	2,991	681	1,838	472	Dole	22.8%	61.5%	15.8%
HARDIN	406	100	279	27	Dole	24.6%	68.7%	6.7%
HENDERSON	1,165	257	688	220	Dole	22.1%	59.1%	18.9%
HENRY	5,053	1,161	3,093	799	Dole	23.0%	61.2%	15.8%
IROQUOIS	6,032	1,497	3,848	687	Dole	24.8%	63.8%	11.4%
JACKSON	2,937	840	1,859	238	Dole	28.6%	63.3%	8.1%
JASPER	630	180	397	53	Dole	28.6%	63.0%	8.4%
JEFFERSON	2,118	541	1,414	163	Dole	25.5%	66.8%	7.7%
JERSEY	1,441	472	863	106	Dole	32.8%	59.9%	7.4%
JO DAVIESS	2,339	599	1,364	376	Dole	25.6%	58.3%	16.1%
JOHNSON	1,962	557	1,270	135	Dole	28.4%	64.7%	6.9%
KANE	33,525	7,827	21,216	4,482	Dole	23.3%	63.3%	13.4%
KANKAKEE	5,861	1,487	3,563	811	Dole	25.4%	60.8%	13.8%
KENDALL	7,817	1,999	4,789	1,029	Dole	25.6%	61.3%	13.2%
KNOX	4,213	972	2,655	586	Dole	23.1%	63.0%	13.9%
LAKE	59,505	11,088	39,606	8,811	Dole	18.6%	66.6%	14.8%
LA SALLE	6,564	1,742	4,131	691	Dole	26.5%	62.9%	10.5%
LAWRENCE	816	206	503	107	Dole	25.2%	61.6%	13.1%
LEE	5,746	1,376	3,567	803	Dole	23.9%	62.1%	14.0%
LIVINGSTON	5,640	1,168	3,944	528	Dole	20.7%	69.9%	9.4%
LOGAN	5,968	1,386	3,968	614	Dole	23.2%	66.5%	10.3%
MCDONOUGH	2,981	617	2,016	348	Dole	20.7%	67.6%	11.7%
MCHENRY	28,957	7,061	17,682	4,214	Dole	24.4%	61.1%	14.6%
MCLEAN	21,502	3,929	14,523	3,050	Dole	18.3%	67.5%	14.2%
MACON	7,878	1,915	5,212	751	Dole	24.3%	66.2%	9.5%
MACOUPIN	2,562	700	1,705	157	Dole	27.3%	66.5%	6.1%
MADISON	11,404	3,591	6,731	1,082	Dole	31.5%	59.0%	9.5%
MARION	2,416	653	1,552	211	Dole	27.0%	64.2%	8.7%
MARSHALL	2,316	681	1,426	209	Dole	29.4%	61.6%	9.0%
MASON	1,336	290	966	80	Dole	21.7%	72.3%	6.0%
MASSAC	1,200	304	828	68	Dole	25.3%	69.0%	5.7%
MENARD	2,237	423	1,620	194	Dole	18.9%	72.4%	8.7%
MERCER	1,477	364	857	256	Dole	24.6%	58.0%	17.3%
MONROE	1,555	448	1,003	104	Dole	28.8%	64.5%	6.7%
MONTGOMERY	2,469	670	1,639	160	Dole	27.1%	66.4%	6.5%
MORGAN	3,068	733	2,096	239	Dole	23.9%	68.3%	7.8%
MOULTRIE	1,011	258	657	96	Dole	25.5%	65.0%	9.5%

ILLINOIS REPUBLICAN

1996

County	Total Vote	Buchanan	Dole	Other	Winner	Percentage of Total Vote Buchanan	Dole	Other
OGLE	5,744	1,292	3,665	787	Dole	22.5%	63.8%	13.7%
PEORIA	15,188	3,196	10,506	1,486	Dole	21.0%	69.2%	9.8%
PERRY	1,766	567	1,056	143	Dole	32.1%	59.8%	8.1%
PIATT	1,510	328	1,023	159	Dole	21.7%	67.7%	10.5%
PIKE	1,746	452	1,156	138	Dole	25.9%	66.2%	7.9%
POPE	601	155	400	46	Dole	25.8%	66.6%	7.7%
PULASKI	583	116	425	42	Dole	19.9%	72.9%	7.2%
PUTNAM	446	109	302	35	Dole	24.4%	67.7%	7.8%
RANDOLPH	1,913	604	1,195	114	Dole	31.6%	62.5%	6.0%
RICHLAND	1,142	416	624	102	Dole	36.4%	54.6%	8.9%
ROCK ISLAND	6,790	1,811	3,838	1,141	Dole	26.7%	56.5%	16.8%
ST. CLAIR	9,949	2,465	6,583	901	Dole	24.8%	66.2%	9.1%
SALINE	1,959	602	1,193	164	Dole	30.7%	60.9%	8.4%
SANGAMON	25,428	4,619	18,596	2,213	Dole	18.2%	73.1%	8.7%
SCHUYLER	1,028	243	681	104	Dole	23.6%	66.2%	10.1%
SCOTT	837	216	564	57	Dole	25.8%	67.4%	6.8%
SHELBY	1,545	520	898	127	Dole	33.7%	58.1%	8.2%
STARK	643	172	414	57	Dole	26.7%	64.4%	8.9%
STEPHENSON	4,025	813	2,634	578	Dole	20.2%	65.4%	14.4%
TAZEWELL	14,121	3,480	9,222	1,419	Dole	24.6%	65.3%	10.0%
UNION	1,487	417	951	119	Dole	28.0%	64.0%	8.0%
VERMILION	6,464	1,645	4,054	765	Dole	25.4%	62.7%	11.8%
WABASH	495	124	318	53	Dole	25.1%	64.2%	10.7%
WARREN	2,778	641	1,645	492	Dole	23.1%	59.2%	17.7%
WASHINGTON	1,883	451	1,309	123	Dole	24.0%	69.5%	6.5%
WAYNE	2,920	788	1,807	325	Dole	27.0%	61.9%	11.1%
WHITE	726	163	500	63	Dole	22.5%	68.9%	8.7%
WHITESIDE	3,401	792	2,040	569	Dole	23.3%	60.0%	16.7%
WILL	29,925	8,087	18,432	3,406	Dole	27.0%	61.6%	11.4%
WILLIAMSON	3,445	1,148	2,086	211	Dole	33.3%	60.6%	6.1%
WINNEBAGO	27,162	5,789	16,425	4,948	Dole	21.3%	60.5%	18.2%
WOODFORD	4,717	1,157	3,040	520	Dole	24.5%	64.4%	11.0%
TOTAL	818,364	186,177	532,467	99,720	Dole	22.7%	65.1%	12.2%

INDIANA

What the West Virginia primary did for John F. Kennedy in 1960, Indiana's did for his brother Robert eight years later, providing a high-profile victory on uncertain political terrain.

Indiana has a more conservative political milieu than many of its larger Midwestern neighbors, which made it a dramatic launching pad for Robert Kennedy's ill-fated, but memorable, presidential campaign. Kennedy crossed and crisscrossed the state, wooing minority voters in the inner cities (where he quoted Aeschylus on the night of the assassination of Martin Luther King) and white voters in the small towns that dot the state. For a time, Kennedy rode on a photogenic campaign train that followed the route of the old Wabash Cannonball.

And on primary day, he rolled to a clear-cut victory over both Eugene McCarthy and Roger Branigin, the state's governor and favorite-son presidential candidate. Kennedy swept most of the major population centers as well as much of rural Indiana, giving the first indication in 1968 of his broad-based voter appeal.

No Indiana primary since then has captured such national attention, although the Hoosier State has an unmistakable history of backing political outsiders that some of its larger Midwestern neighbors would not. George Wallace ran well in the Democratic primary in 1964 and 1972. Ronald Reagan won the 1976 GOP vote, his only primary victory over President Gerald Ford in a Frost Belt state east of the Great Plains. And in the 1984 Democratic contest, Gary Hart edged Walter Mondale, the favorite almost everywhere else in the industrial Frost Belt.

Coupled with his victory the same day in Ohio, Hart's win in Indiana revived his faltering campaign. But it was by the narrowest of margins, barely 6,000 votes out of more than 700,000 cast. Basically, Hart won rural Indiana while Mondale had the edge in the urban centers. Jesse Jackson, though, won Marion County (Indianapolis) and sliced away enough of the vote in other major population centers to enable Hart to prevail statewide.

The 1976 Republican contest was nearly as close. Ford carried the southwest and northeast portions of Indiana, includ-

Recent Indiana Primary Results

Indiana held its first presidential primary in 1916.

	DEMOCRATS			REPUBLICANS		
Year	Turnout	Candidates	%	Turnout	Candidates	%
1996 (May 7)	329,462	BILL CLINTON*	100	516,514	BOB DOLE	71
					Pat Buchanan	19
1992 (May 5)	476,849	BILL CLINTON	63	467,615	GEORGE BUSH*	80
		Jerry Brown	21		Pat Buchanan	20
		Paul Tsongas	12			
1988 (May 3)	645,708	MICHAEL DUKAKIS	70	437,655	GEORGE BUSH	80
		Jesse Jackson	22			
1984 (May 8)	716,955	GARY HART	42	428,559	RONALD REAGAN*	100
		Walter Mondale	41			
		Jesse Jackson	14			
1980 (May 6)	589,441	JIMMY CARTER*	68	568,313	RONALD REAGAN	74
		Edward Kennedy	32		George Bush	16
1976 (May 4)	614,389	JIMMY CARTER	68	631,292	RONALD REAGAN	51
		George Wallace	15		Gerald Ford*	49
		Henry Jackson	12			
1972 (May 2)	751,458	HUBERT HUMPHREY	47	417,069	RICHARD NIXON*	100
		George Wallace	41			
		Edmund Muskie	12			
1968 (May 7)	776,513	ROBERT KENNEDY	42	508,362	RICHARD NIXON	100
		Roger Branigin	31			
		Eugene McCarthy	27			

Note: All candidates are listed that drew at least 10 percent of their party's primary vote. The names of winning candidates are capitalized. An asterisk (*) indicates an incumbent president.

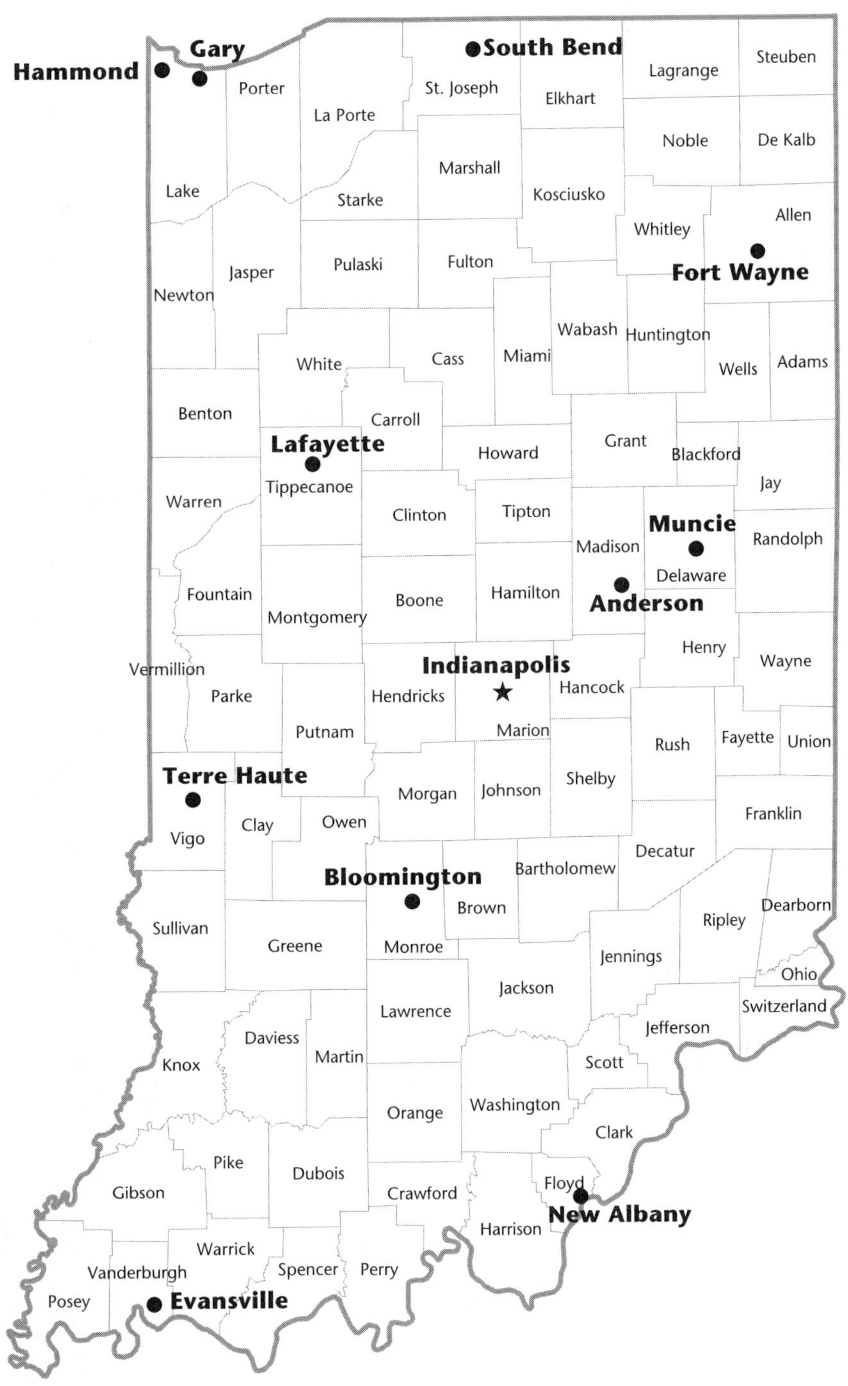

ing traditional industrial counties such as Allen (Fort Wayne) and St. Joseph (South Bend) near his home state of Michigan. Reagan drew much of his strength from vocal and influential conservatives concentrated in the Indianapolis area and several industrial centers nearby.

The Indiana GOP, though, has not been noted for pursuing ideological crusades. And when Pat Buchanan ran in 1992 and 1996, he could not break 20 percent either time.

Still, Indiana has been a reliably Republican state in the fall presidential voting, and Democrat Bill Clinton was unable to carry its electoral votes in either of his presidential victories in the 1990s. But in 1992, Indiana gave him his largest share of the primary vote (63 percent) in any non-Southern state except West Virginia. Clinton won decisively in every Indiana county but Monroe, home of Indiana University in Bloomington, where he edged Jerry Brown by just 2 percentage points.

INDIANA DEMOCRATIC

1968

County	Total Vote	Branigin	R. Kennedy	McCarthy	Winner	Percentage of Total Vote Branigin	R. Kennedy	McCarthy
ADAMS	5,079	1,721	1,635	1,723	McCarthy	33.9%	32.2%	33.9%
ALLEN	33,766	7,016	16,098	10,652	R. Kennedy	20.8%	47.7%	31.5%
BARTHOLOMEW	7,493	3,419	2,239	1,835	Branigin	45.6%	29.9%	24.5%
BENTON	1,529	527	701	301	R. Kennedy	34.5%	45.8%	19.7%
BLACKFORD	2,494	839	989	666	R. Kennedy	33.6%	39.7%	26.7%
BOONE	3,839	2,052	1,020	767	Branigin	53.5%	26.6%	20.0%
BROWN	1,853	836	561	456	Branigin	45.1%	30.3%	24.6%
CARROLL	2,360	1,086	811	463	Branigin	46.0%	34.4%	19.6%
CASS	6,271	2,516	2,374	1,381	Branigin	40.1%	37.9%	22.0%
CLARK	12,944	4,243	5,361	3,340	R. Kennedy	32.8%	41.4%	25.8%
CLAY	4,644	1,783	1,647	1,214	Branigin	38.4%	35.5%	26.1%
CLINTON	4,296	1,702	1,593	1,001	Branigin	39.6%	37.1%	23.3%
CRAWFORD	1,271	433	660	178	R. Kennedy	34.1%	51.9%	14.0%
DAVIESS	3,726	1,194	1,750	782	R. Kennedy	32.0%	47.0%	21.0%
DEARBORN	4,560	1,795	1,684	1,081	Branigin	39.4%	36.9%	23.7%
DECATUR	2,361	907	1,074	380	R. Kennedy	38.4%	45.5%	16.1%
DE KALB	3,677	1,103	1,499	1,075	R. Kennedy	30.0%	40.8%	29.2%
DELAWARE	16,465	5,310	6,464	4,691	R. Kennedy	32.3%	39.3%	28.5%
DUBOIS	7,832	1,425	4,731	1,676	R. Kennedy	18.2%	60.4%	21.4%
ELKHART	10,238	2,179	4,584	3,475	R. Kennedy	21.3%	44.8%	33.9%
FAYETTE	3,248	1,692	901	655	Branigin	52.1%	27.7%	20.2%
FLOYD	8,604	2,007	4,797	1,800	R. Kennedy	23.3%	55.8%	20.9%
FOUNTAIN	3,058	1,068	1,351	639	R. Kennedy	34.9%	44.2%	20.9%
FRANKLIN	2,456	815	1,049	592	R. Kennedy	33.2%	42.7%	24.1%
FULTON	2,332	933	826	573	Branigin	40.0%	35.4%	24.6%
GIBSON	5,920	2,383	2,018	1,519	Branigin	40.3%	34.1%	25.7%
GRANT	9,676	2,891	4,015	2,770	R. Kennedy	29.9%	41.5%	28.6%
GREENE	5,835	2,572	2,086	1,177	Branigin	44.1%	35.7%	20.2%
HAMILTON	4,309	1,912	1,267	1,130	Branigin	44.4%	29.4%	26.2%
HANCOCK	3,921	2,053	913	955	Branigin	52.4%	23.3%	24.4%
HARRISON	4,250	1,214	2,059	977	R. Kennedy	28.6%	48.4%	23.0%
HENDRICKS	4,583	2,620	1,043	920	Branigin	57.2%	22.8%	20.1%
HENRY	5,627	2,776	1,674	1,177	Branigin	49.3%	29.7%	20.9%
HOWARD	10,245	3,079	4,035	3,131	R. Kennedy	30.1%	39.4%	30.6%
HUNTINGTON	5,499	1,415	2,370	1,714	R. Kennedy	25.7%	43.1%	31.2%
JACKSON	6,937	2,329	2,682	1,926	R. Kennedy	33.6%	38.7%	27.8%
JASPER	1,805	613	638	554	R. Kennedy	34.0%	35.3%	30.7%
JAY	3,116	1,042	1,270	804	R. Kennedy	33.4%	40.8%	25.8%
JEFFERSON	3,665	833	1,966	866	R. Kennedy	22.7%	53.6%	23.6%
JENNINGS	2,757	991	1,106	660	R. Kennedy	35.9%	40.1%	23.9%
JOHNSON	5,999	3,394	1,345	1,260	Branigin	56.6%	22.4%	21.0%
KNOX	9,781	4,114	3,341	2,326	Branigin	42.1%	34.2%	23.8%
KOSCIUSKO	5,076	1,449	2,201	1,426	R. Kennedy	28.5%	43.4%	28.1%
LAGRANGE	1,349	382	542	425	R. Kennedy	28.3%	40.2%	31.5%
LAKE	124,428	23,330	58,259	42,839	R. Kennedy	18.7%	46.8%	34.4%
LA PORTE	12,773	2,871	6,065	3,837	R. Kennedy	22.5%	47.5%	30.0%
LAWRENCE	4,477	1,233	2,305	939	R. Kennedy	27.5%	51.5%	21.0%
MADISON	21,871	7,834	9,405	4,632	R. Kennedy	35.8%	43.0%	21.2%
MARION	103,833	34,447	49,633	19,753	R. Kennedy	33.2%	47.8%	19.0%
MARSHALL	4,087	1,355	1,552	1,180	R. Kennedy	33.2%	38.0%	28.9%

INDIANA DEMOCRATIC

1968

County	Total Vote	Branigin	R. Kennedy	McCarthy	Winner	Percentage of Total Vote Branigin	R. Kennedy	McCarthy
MARTIN	3,132	1,159	1,481	492	R. Kennedy	37.0%	47.3%	15.7%
MIAMI	4,561	1,578	1,859	1,124	R. Kennedy	34.6%	40.8%	24.6%
MONROE	12,607	2,495	4,482	5,630	McCarthy	19.8%	35.6%	44.7%
MONTGOMERY	4,179	1,609	1,308	1,262	Branigin	38.5%	31.3%	30.2%
MORGAN	4,037	2,019	1,175	843	Branigin	50.0%	29.1%	20.9%
NEWTON	1,356	470	547	339	R. Kennedy	34.7%	40.3%	25.0%
NOBLE	4,246	1,076	1,910	1,260	R. Kennedy	25.3%	45.0%	29.7%
OHIO	737	351	283	103	Branigin	47.6%	38.4%	14.0%
ORANGE	2,494	735	1,399	360	R. Kennedy	29.5%	56.1%	14.4%
OWEN	2,015	1,032	585	398	Branigin	51.2%	29.0%	19.8%
PARKE	2,482	928	1,011	543	R. Kennedy	37.4%	40.7%	21.9%
PERRY	4,051	989	2,136	926	R. Kennedy	24.4%	52.7%	22.9%
PIKE	3,167	1,546	976	645	Branigin	48.8%	30.8%	20.4%
PORTER	8,933	2,718	2,725	3,490	McCarthy	30.4%	30.5%	39.1%
POSEY	3,816	1,325	1,279	1,212	Branigin	34.7%	33.5%	31.8%
PULASKI	1,626	731	515	380	Branigin	45.0%	31.7%	23.4%
PUTNAM	5,336	2,831	1,358	1,147	Branigin	53.1%	25.4%	21.5%
RANDOLPH	3,173	1,173	1,142	858	Branigin	37.0%	36.0%	27.0%
RIPLEY	2,943	1,251	1,167	525	Branigin	42.5%	39.7%	17.8%
RUSH	2,059	1,156	530	373	Branigin	56.1%	25.7%	18.1%
ST. JOSEPH	43,421	8,628	20,767	14,026	R. Kennedy	19.9%	47.8%	32.3%
SCOTT	2,893	940	1,457	496	R. Kennedy	32.5%	50.4%	17.1%
SHELBY	6,786	3,463	1,808	1,515	Branigin	51.0%	26.6%	22.3%
SPENCER	3,130	902	1,590	638	R. Kennedy	28.8%	50.8%	20.4%
STARKE	2,251	797	902	552	R. Kennedy	35.4%	40.1%	24.5%
STEUBEN	1,629	520	592	517	R. Kennedy	31.9%	36.3%	31.7%
SULLIVAN	5,668	2,416	1,995	1,257	Branigin	42.6%	35.2%	22.2%
SWITZERLAND	1,894	713	751	430	R. Kennedy	37.6%	39.7%	22.7%
TIPPECANOE	13,464	3,857	5,309	4,298	R. Kennedy	28.6%	39.4%	31.9%
TIPTON	2,216	1,075	723	418	Branigin	48.5%	32.6%	18.9%
UNION	656	304	235	117	Branigin	46.3%	35.8%	17.8%
VANDERBURGH	31,634	11,647	10,773	9,214	Branigin	36.8%	34.1%	29.1%
VERMILLION	4,611	1,667	1,890	1,054	R. Kennedy	36.2%	41.0%	22.9%
VIGO	22,201	7,261	9,639	5,301	R. Kennedy	32.7%	43.4%	23.9%
WABASH	3,385	916	1,546	923	R. Kennedy	27.1%	45.7%	27.3%
WARREN	1,122	442	426	254	Branigin	39.4%	38.0%	22.6%
WARRICK	4,483	1,764	1,460	1,259	Branigin	39.3%	32.6%	28.1%
WASHINGTON	2,624	1,063	1,147	414	R. Kennedy	40.5%	43.7%	15.8%
WAYNE	6,723	2,064	3,223	1,436	R. Kennedy	30.7%	47.9%	21.4%
WELLS	4,406	1,384	1,468	1,554	McCarthy	31.4%	33.3%	35.3%
WHITE	2,722	986	1,095	641	R. Kennedy	36.2%	40.2%	23.5%
WHITLEY	3,429	986	1,265	1,178	R. Kennedy	28.8%	36.9%	34.4%
TOTAL	776,513	238,700	328,118	209,695	R. Kennedy	30.7%	42.3%	27.0%

INDIANA DEMOCRATIC

1972

County	Total Vote	Humphrey	Muskie	Wallace	Winner	Percentage of Total Vote Humphrey	Muskie	Wallace
ADAMS	5,397	2,807	793	1,797	Humphrey	52.0%	14.7%	33.3%
ALLEN	31,988	15,590	4,194	12,204	Humphrey	48.7%	13.1%	38.2%
BARTHOLOMEW	7,868	4,013	779	3,076	Humphrey	51.0%	9.9%	39.1%
BENTON	1,100	560	183	357	Humphrey	50.9%	16.6%	32.5%
BLACKFORD	2,786	1,510	341	935	Humphrey	54.2%	12.2%	33.6%
BOONE	3,497	1,721	275	1,501	Humphrey	49.2%	7.9%	42.9%
BROWN	2,227	988	217	1,022	Wallace	44.4%	9.7%	45.9%
CARROLL	2,501	1,201	356	944	Humphrey	48.0%	14.2%	37.7%
CASS	6,643	3,639	680	2,324	Humphrey	54.8%	10.2%	35.0%
CLARK	16,027	7,151	2,035	6,841	Humphrey	44.6%	12.7%	42.7%
CLAY	5,554	2,101	460	2,993	Wallace	37.8%	8.3%	53.9%
CLINTON	3,615	2,016	404	1,195	Humphrey	55.8%	11.2%	33.1%
CRAWFORD	1,605	747	191	667	Humphrey	46.5%	11.9%	41.6%
DAVIESS	3,737	1,682	381	1,674	Humphrey	45.0%	10.2%	44.8%
DEARBORN	4,409	2,253	785	1,371	Humphrey	51.1%	17.8%	31.1%
DECATUR	2,320	1,340	231	749	Humphrey	57.8%	10.0%	32.3%
DE KALB	3,104	1,634	375	1,095	Humphrey	52.6%	12.1%	35.3%
DELAWARE	17,239	9,192	1,625	6,422	Humphrey	53.3%	9.4%	37.3%
DUBOIS	6,336	2,800	1,163	2,373	Humphrey	44.2%	18.4%	37.5%
ELKHART	9,354	4,066	1,362	3,926	Humphrey	43.5%	14.6%	42.0%
FAYETTE	2,639	1,444	304	891	Humphrey	54.7%	11.5%	33.8%
FLOYD	8,353	4,154	1,146	3,053	Humphrey	49.7%	13.7%	36.5%
FOUNTAIN	2,909	1,286	317	1,306	Wallace	44.2%	10.9%	44.9%
FRANKLIN	2,763	1,237	503	1,023	Humphrey	44.8%	18.2%	37.0%
FULTON	2,587	1,092	287	1,208	Wallace	42.2%	11.1%	46.7%
GIBSON	5,800	2,408	704	2,688	Wallace	41.5%	12.1%	46.3%
GRANT	9,474	4,555	814	4,105	Humphrey	48.1%	8.6%	43.3%
GREENE	5,617	2,529	425	2,663	Wallace	45.0%	7.6%	47.4%
HAMILTON	4,775	1,971	365	2,439	Wallace	41.3%	7.6%	51.1%
HANCOCK	4,608	1,884	374	2,350	Wallace	40.9%	8.1%	51.0%
HARRISON	4,691	2,073	687	1,931	Humphrey	44.2%	14.6%	41.2%
HENDRICKS	6,556	2,350	412	3,794	Wallace	35.8%	6.3%	57.9%
HENRY	6,211	3,046	486	2,679	Humphrey	49.0%	7.8%	43.1%
HOWARD	11,148	5,280	1,089	4,779	Humphrey	47.4%	9.8%	42.9%
HUNTINGTON	4,207	2,101	538	1,568	Humphrey	49.9%	12.8%	37.3%
JACKSON	6,270	2,841	656	2,773	Humphrey	45.3%	10.5%	44.2%
JASPER	1,623	627	219	777	Wallace	38.6%	13.5%	47.9%
JAY	2,764	1,626	297	841	Humphrey	58.8%	10.7%	30.4%
JEFFERSON	3,960	2,001	483	1,476	Humphrey	50.5%	12.2%	37.3%
JENNINGS	2,351	1,099	209	1,043	Humphrey	46.7%	8.9%	44.4%
JOHNSON	6,471	2,583	463	3,425	Wallace	39.9%	7.2%	52.9%
KNOX	9,529	3,940	896	4,693	Wallace	41.3%	9.4%	49.2%
KOSCIUSKO	4,576	2,131	477	1,968	Humphrey	46.6%	10.4%	43.0%
LAGRANGE	1,405	598	215	592	Humphrey	42.6%	15.3%	42.1%
LAKE	118,039	52,634	14,936	50,469	Humphrey	44.6%	12.7%	42.8%
LA PORTE	11,067	4,384	1,907	4,776	Wallace	39.6%	17.2%	43.2%
LAWRENCE	4,055	1,698	260	2,097	Wallace	41.9%	6.4%	51.7%
MADISON	24,192	11,998	1,906	10,288	Humphrey	49.6%	7.9%	42.5%
MARION	95,002	56,078	7,951	30,973	Humphrey	59.0%	8.4%	32.6%
MARSHALL	3,566	1,476	392	1,698	Wallace	41.4%	11.0%	47.6%

INDIANA DEMOCRATIC

1972

County	Total Vote	Humphrey	Muskie	Wallace	Winner	Percentage of Total Vote Humphrey	Muskie	Wallace
MARTIN	2,890	1,363	331	1,196	Humphrey	47.2%	11.5%	41.4%
MIAMI	4,264	2,271	435	1,558	Humphrey	53.3%	10.2%	36.5%
MONROE	11,319	5,402	3,059	2,858	Humphrey	47.7%	27.0%	25.2%
MONTGOMERY	3,463	1,788	399	1,276	Humphrey	51.6%	11.5%	36.8%
MORGAN	4,750	1,761	243	2,746	Wallace	37.1%	5.1%	57.8%
NEWTON	1,260	478	205	577	Wallace	37.9%	16.3%	45.8%
NOBLE	3,481	1,746	439	1,296	Humphrey	50.2%	12.6%	37.2%
OHIO	638	358	94	186	Humphrey	56.1%	14.7%	29.2%
ORANGE	2,005	1,038	185	782	Humphrey	51.8%	9.2%	39.0%
OWEN	2,225	961	199	1,065	Wallace	43.2%	8.9%	47.9%
PARKE	2,658	1,064	229	1,365	Wallace	40.0%	8.6%	51.4%
PERRY	3,132	1,533	533	1,066	Humphrey	48.9%	17.0%	34.0%
PIKE	3,164	1,418	325	1,421	Wallace	44.8%	10.3%	44.9%
PORTER	10,208	3,046	1,342	5,820	Wallace	29.8%	13.1%	57.0%
POSEY	5,108	1,517	1,528	2,063	Wallace	29.7%	29.9%	40.4%
PULASKI	1,652	611	200	841	Wallace	37.0%	12.1%	50.9%
PUTNAM	4,156	1,916	418	1,822	Humphrey	46.1%	10.1%	43.8%
RANDOLPH	3,551	1,592	440	1,519	Humphrey	44.8%	12.4%	42.8%
RIPLEY	3,251	1,559	505	1,187	Humphrey	48.0%	15.5%	36.5%
RUSH	1,541	729	168	644	Humphrey	47.3%	10.9%	41.8%
ST. JOSEPH	44,404	18,075	6,400	19,929	Wallace	40.7%	14.4%	44.9%
SCOTT	2,760	1,446	261	1,053	Humphrey	52.4%	9.5%	38.2%
SHELBY	5,394	2,589	441	2,364	Humphrey	48.0%	8.2%	43.8%
SPENCER	2,906	1,099	474	1,333	Wallace	37.8%	16.3%	45.9%
STARKE	2,833	1,102	323	1,408	Wallace	38.9%	11.4%	49.7%
STEUBEN	1,631	784	175	672	Humphrey	48.1%	10.7%	41.2%
SULLIVAN	6,191	2,749	476	2,966	Wallace	44.4%	7.7%	47.9%
SWITZERLAND	1,928	896	285	747	Humphrey	46.5%	14.8%	38.7%
TIPPECANOE	9,987	5,362	2,229	2,396	Humphrey	53.7%	22.3%	24.0%
TIPTON	2,141	1,074	203	864	Humphrey	50.2%	9.5%	40.4%
UNION	552	257	66	229	Humphrey	46.6%	12.0%	41.5%
VANDERBURGH	22,995	9,564	2,495	10,936	Wallace	41.6%	10.9%	47.6%
VERMILLION	4,788	2,158	395	2,235	Wallace	45.1%	8.2%	46.7%
VIGO	26,733	11,876	2,264	12,593	Wallace	44.4%	8.5%	47.1%
WABASH	3,508	1,868	524	1,116	Humphrey	53.2%	14.9%	31.8%
WARREN	1,002	429	129	444	Wallace	42.8%	12.9%	44.3%
WARRICK	4,758	1,800	565	2,393	Wallace	37.8%	11.9%	50.3%
WASHINGTON	2,737	1,341	291	1,105	Humphrey	49.0%	10.6%	40.4%
WAYNE	5,805	3,068	728	2,009	Humphrey	52.9%	12.5%	34.6%
WELLS	3,541	1,768	416	1,357	Humphrey	49.9%	11.7%	38.3%
WHITE	2,465	1,200	304	961	Humphrey	48.7%	12.3%	39.0%
WHITLEY	3,176	1,461	450	1,265	Humphrey	46.0%	14.2%	39.8%
TOTAL	751,466	354,252	87,719	309,495	Humphrey	47.1%	11.7%	41.2%
Certified Totals	751,458	354,244	87,719	309,495	Humphrey	47.1%	11.7%	41.2%

INDIANA DEMOCRATIC

1976

County	Total Vote	Carter	H. Jackson	McCormack	Wallace	Winner	Percentage of Total Vote Carter	H. Jackson	McCormack	Wallace
ADAMS	4,607	3,207	529	321	550	Carter	69.6%	11.5%	7.0%	11.9%
ALLEN	21,203	14,116	3,041	1,900	2,146	Carter	66.6%	14.3%	9.0%	10.1%
BARTHOLOMEW	7,022	5,074	759	181	1,008	Carter	72.3%	10.8%	2.6%	14.4%
BENTON	952	644	87	111	110	Carter	67.6%	9.1%	11.7%	11.6%
BLACKFORD	1,963	1,381	238	86	258	Carter	70.4%	12.1%	4.4%	13.1%
BOONE	2,675	1,988	262	66	359	Carter	74.3%	9.8%	2.5%	13.4%
BROWN	1,750	1,203	173	40	334	Carter	68.7%	9.9%	2.3%	19.1%
CARROLL	2,384	1,622	264	94	404	Carter	68.0%	11.1%	3.9%	16.9%
CASS	4,504	3,025	562	206	711	Carter	67.2%	12.5%	4.6%	15.8%
CLARK	13,406	8,871	1,139	580	2,816	Carter	66.2%	8.5%	4.3%	21.0%
CLAY	5,089	3,312	512	100	1,165	Carter	65.1%	10.1%	2.0%	22.9%
CLINTON	2,994	2,179	387	102	326	Carter	72.8%	12.9%	3.4%	10.9%
CRAWFORD	1,771	1,331	99	29	312	Carter	75.2%	5.6%	1.6%	17.6%
DAVIESS	3,075	2,131	270	208	466	Carter	69.3%	8.8%	6.8%	15.2%
DEARBORN	3,501	2,294	465	229	513	Carter	65.5%	13.3%	6.5%	14.7%
DECATUR	2,007	1,429	225	102	251	Carter	71.2%	11.2%	5.1%	12.5%
DE KALB	2,944	2,102	401	142	299	Carter	71.4%	13.6%	4.8%	10.2%
DELAWARE	14,032	9,398	2,035	423	2,176	Carter	67.0%	14.5%	3.0%	15.5%
DUBOIS	6,440	4,393	728	424	895	Carter	68.2%	11.3%	6.6%	13.9%
ELKHART	7,457	5,202	942	355	958	Carter	69.8%	12.6%	4.8%	12.8%
FAYETTE	2,687	1,850	355	71	411	Carter	68.9%	13.2%	2.6%	15.3%
FLOYD	7,168	4,841	700	361	1,266	Carter	67.5%	9.8%	5.0%	17.7%
FOUNTAIN	2,229	1,605	207	45	372	Carter	72.0%	9.3%	2.0%	16.7%
FRANKLIN	2,578	1,649	281	171	477	Carter	64.0%	10.9%	6.6%	18.5%
FULTON	1,635	1,131	169	73	262	Carter	69.2%	10.3%	4.5%	16.0%
GIBSON	5,883	3,977	649	370	887	Carter	67.6%	11.0%	6.3%	15.1%
GRANT	7,320	4,970	909	242	1,199	Carter	67.9%	12.4%	3.3%	16.4%
GREENE	4,877	3,409	448	82	938	Carter	69.9%	9.2%	1.7%	19.2%
HAMILTON	3,491	2,530	351	139	471	Carter	72.5%	10.1%	4.0%	13.5%
HANCOCK	3,688	2,552	427	89	620	Carter	69.2%	11.6%	2.4%	16.8%
HARRISON	4,473	2,969	356	207	941	Carter	66.4%	8.0%	4.6%	21.0%
HENDRICKS	4,477	3,046	490	137	804	Carter	68.0%	10.9%	3.1%	18.0%
HENRY	4,335	3,129	452	105	649	Carter	72.2%	10.4%	2.4%	15.0%
HOWARD	7,578	5,647	913	394	624	Carter	74.5%	12.0%	5.2%	8.2%
HUNTINGTON	3,322	2,174	434	358	356	Carter	65.4%	13.1%	10.8%	10.7%
JACKSON	5,963	4,171	619	114	1,059	Carter	69.9%	10.4%	1.9%	17.8%
JASPER	1,743	1,181	143	116	303	Carter	67.8%	8.2%	6.7%	17.4%
JAY	2,346	1,647	270	86	343	Carter	70.2%	11.5%	3.7%	14.6%
JEFFERSON	3,564	2,555	312	167	530	Carter	71.7%	8.8%	4.7%	14.9%
JENNINGS	2,523	1,818	170	130	405	Carter	72.1%	6.7%	5.2%	16.1%
JOHNSON	5,235	3,677	510	134	914	Carter	70.2%	9.7%	2.6%	17.5%
KNOX	8,641	5,777	741	362	1,761	Carter	66.9%	8.6%	4.2%	20.4%
KOSCIUSKO	3,256	2,306	422	138	390	Carter	70.8%	13.0%	4.2%	12.0%
LAGRANGE	1,375	1,018	133	43	181	Carter	74.0%	9.7%	3.1%	13.2%
LAKE	103,283	64,657	12,090	7,778	18,758	Carter	62.6%	11.7%	7.5%	18.2%
LA PORTE	10,408	7,125	1,141	507	1,635	Carter	68.5%	11.0%	4.9%	15.7%
LAWRENCE	3,638	2,486	314	143	695	Carter	68.3%	8.6%	3.9%	19.1%
MADISON	20,558	14,376	2,492	795	2,895	Carter	69.9%	12.1%	3.9%	14.1%
MARION	69,165	50,979	8,372	3,207	6,607	Carter	73.7%	12.1%	4.6%	9.6%
MARSHALL	3,082	2,080	395	195	412	Carter	67.5%	12.8%	6.3%	13.4%

INDIANA DEMOCRATIC

1976

County	Total Vote	Carter	H. Jackson	McCormack	Wallace	Winner	Percentage of Total Vote: Carter	H. Jackson	McCormack	Wallace
MARTIN	3,254	1,606	938	210	500	Carter	49.4%	28.8%	6.5%	15.4%
MIAMI	3,488	2,430	419	169	470	Carter	69.7%	12.0%	4.8%	13.5%
MONROE	7,987	5,777	1,268	265	677	Carter	72.3%	15.9%	3.3%	8.5%
MONTGOMERY	2,529	1,855	287	82	305	Carter	73.3%	11.3%	3.2%	12.1%
MORGAN	3,499	2,309	402	69	719	Carter	66.0%	11.5%	2.0%	20.5%
NEWTON	1,058	729	94	59	176	Carter	68.9%	8.9%	5.6%	16.6%
NOBLE	2,981	2,098	389	206	288	Carter	70.4%	13.0%	6.9%	9.7%
OHIO	506	382	67	6	51	Carter	75.5%	13.2%	1.2%	10.1%
ORANGE	1,708	1,311	136	36	225	Carter	76.8%	8.0%	2.1%	13.2%
OWEN	2,068	1,482	162	43	381	Carter	71.7%	7.8%	2.1%	18.4%
PARKE	2,019	1,414	158	51	396	Carter	70.0%	7.8%	2.5%	19.6%
PERRY	3,618	2,736	336	135	411	Carter	75.6%	9.3%	3.7%	11.4%
PIKE	2,515	1,766	279	50	420	Carter	70.2%	11.1%	2.0%	16.7%
PORTER	8,808	5,367	1,032	506	1,903	Carter	60.9%	11.7%	5.7%	21.6%
POSEY	3,478	2,622	334	124	398	Carter	75.4%	9.6%	3.6%	11.4%
PULASKI	2,140	1,516	142	87	395	Carter	70.8%	6.6%	4.1%	18.5%
PUTNAM	2,787	2,009	312	52	414	Carter	72.1%	11.2%	1.9%	14.9%
RANDOLPH	2,475	1,720	297	69	389	Carter	69.5%	12.0%	2.8%	15.7%
RIPLEY	2,348	1,640	255	94	359	Carter	69.8%	10.9%	4.0%	15.3%
RUSH	1,326	930	164	32	200	Carter	70.1%	12.4%	2.4%	15.1%
ST. JOSEPH	35,234	22,131	4,544	2,757	5,802	Carter	62.8%	12.9%	7.8%	16.5%
SCOTT	2,605	1,985	177	38	405	Carter	76.2%	6.8%	1.5%	15.5%
SHELBY	4,469	3,101	523	113	732	Carter	69.4%	11.7%	2.5%	16.4%
SPENCER	2,274	1,617	232	126	299	Carter	71.1%	10.2%	5.5%	13.1%
STARKE	2,758	1,921	249	84	504	Carter	69.7%	9.0%	3.0%	18.3%
STEUBEN	1,339	1,000	148	45	146	Carter	74.7%	11.1%	3.4%	10.9%
SULLIVAN	4,034	2,747	387	72	828	Carter	68.1%	9.6%	1.8%	20.5%
SWITZERLAND	1,656	1,254	132	26	244	Carter	75.7%	8.0%	1.6%	14.7%
TIPPECANOE	7,476	4,850	1,181	655	790	Carter	64.9%	15.8%	8.8%	10.6%
TIPTON	2,145	1,489	220	103	333	Carter	69.4%	10.3%	4.8%	15.5%
UNION	497	323	62	12	100	Carter	65.0%	12.5%	2.4%	20.1%
VANDERBURGH	20,108	14,434	2,469	887	2,318	Carter	71.8%	12.3%	4.4%	11.5%
VERMILLION	4,012	2,629	417	133	833	Carter	65.5%	10.4%	3.3%	20.8%
VIGO	24,279	15,494	3,252	1,107	4,426	Carter	63.8%	13.4%	4.6%	18.2%
WABASH	2,482	1,832	299	99	252	Carter	73.8%	12.0%	4.0%	10.2%
WARREN	863	634	54	28	147	Carter	73.5%	6.3%	3.2%	17.0%
WARRICK	4,128	2,944	422	132	630	Carter	71.3%	10.2%	3.2%	15.3%
WASHINGTON	2,190	1,549	164	56	421	Carter	70.7%	7.5%	2.6%	19.2%
WAYNE	4,192	2,922	486	154	630	Carter	69.7%	11.6%	3.7%	15.0%
WELLS	2,333	1,668	283	65	317	Carter	71.5%	12.1%	2.8%	13.6%
WHITE	1,824	1,253	191	81	299	Carter	68.7%	10.5%	4.4%	16.4%
WHITLEY	2,602	1,770	334	132	366	Carter	68.0%	12.8%	5.1%	14.1%
TOTAL	614,389	417,480	72,080	31,708	93,121	Carter	68.0%	11.7%	5.2%	15.2%

INDIANA REPUBLICAN

1976

County	Total Vote	Ford	Reagan	Winner	Percentage of Total Vote	
					Ford	Reagan
ADAMS	2,262	1,385	877	Ford	61.2%	38.8%
ALLEN	39,312	21,468	17,844	Ford	54.6%	45.4%
BARTHOLOMEW	8,533	4,228	4,305	Reagan	49.5%	50.5%
BENTON	2,789	1,236	1,553	Reagan	44.3%	55.7%
BLACKFORD	1,522	789	733	Ford	51.8%	48.2%
BOONE	5,366	2,394	2,972	Reagan	44.6%	55.4%
BROWN	1,432	598	834	Reagan	41.8%	58.2%
CARROLL	3,100	1,531	1,569	Reagan	49.4%	50.6%
CASS	4,957	2,573	2,384	Ford	51.9%	48.1%
CLARK	3,554	1,251	2,303	Reagan	35.2%	64.8%
CLAY	3,949	1,647	2,302	Reagan	41.7%	58.3%
CLINTON	5,863	2,745	3,118	Reagan	46.8%	53.2%
CRAWFORD	1,590	614	976	Reagan	38.6%	61.4%
DAVIESS	5,172	2,679	2,493	Ford	51.8%	48.2%
DEARBORN	2,144	1,212	932	Ford	56.5%	43.5%
DECATUR	3,153	1,535	1,618	Reagan	48.7%	51.3%
DE KALB	5,267	2,923	2,344	Ford	55.5%	44.5%
DELAWARE	15,170	7,211	7,959	Reagan	47.5%	52.5%
DUBOIS	1,679	1,002	677	Ford	59.7%	40.3%
ELKHART	15,202	8,683	6,519	Ford	57.1%	42.9%
FAYETTE	2,329	1,120	1,209	Reagan	48.1%	51.9%
FLOYD	4,170	1,806	2,364	Reagan	43.3%	56.7%
FOUNTAIN	3,487	1,584	1,903	Reagan	45.4%	54.6%
FRANKLIN	1,184	579	605	Reagan	48.9%	51.1%
FULTON	3,064	1,618	1,446	Ford	52.8%	47.2%
GIBSON	3,134	1,844	1,290	Ford	58.8%	41.2%
GRANT	9,126	4,265	4,861	Reagan	46.7%	53.3%
GREENE	3,575	1,538	2,037	Reagan	43.0%	57.0%
HAMILTON	15,158	6,895	8,263	Reagan	45.5%	54.5%
HANCOCK	5,441	2,281	3,160	Reagan	41.9%	58.1%
HARRISON	2,196	973	1,223	Reagan	44.3%	55.7%
HENDRICKS	11,011	4,278	6,733	Reagan	38.9%	61.1%
HENRY	6,395	2,965	3,430	Reagan	46.4%	53.6%
HOWARD	10,206	5,086	5,120	Reagan	49.8%	50.2%
HUNTINGTON	5,066	2,534	2,532	Ford	50.0%	50.0%
JACKSON	4,222	1,870	2,352	Reagan	44.3%	55.7%
JASPER	3,999	1,840	2,159	Reagan	46.0%	54.0%
JAY	2,758	1,494	1,264	Ford	54.2%	45.8%
JEFFERSON	2,851	1,349	1,502	Reagan	47.3%	52.7%
JENNINGS	2,341	1,056	1,285	Reagan	45.1%	54.9%
JOHNSON	10,088	4,110	5,978	Reagan	40.7%	59.3%
KNOX	3,592	1,636	1,956	Reagan	45.5%	54.5%
KOSCIUSKO	9,853	5,432	4,421	Ford	55.1%	44.9%
LAGRANGE	2,742	1,600	1,142	Ford	58.4%	41.6%
LAKE	26,136	10,650	15,486	Reagan	40.7%	59.3%
LA PORTE	10,734	5,307	5,427	Reagan	49.4%	50.6%
LAWRENCE	5,062	2,279	2,783	Reagan	45.0%	55.0%
MADISON	17,483	7,264	10,219	Reagan	41.5%	58.5%
MARION	104,775	48,653	56,122	Reagan	46.4%	53.6%
MARSHALL	5,072	2,791	2,281	Ford	55.0%	45.0%

INDIANA REPUBLICAN

1976

County	Total Vote	Ford	Reagan	Winner	Percentage of Total Vote Ford	Percentage of Total Vote Reagan
MARTIN	1,347	601	746	Reagan	44.6%	55.4%
MIAMI	4,186	1,971	2,215	Reagan	47.1%	52.9%
MONROE	9,373	5,586	3,787	Ford	59.6%	40.4%
MONTGOMERY	6,366	2,828	3,538	Reagan	44.4%	55.6%
MORGAN	7,864	2,442	5,422	Reagan	31.1%	68.9%
NEWTON	2,190	1,025	1,165	Reagan	46.8%	53.2%
NOBLE	3,963	2,237	1,726	Ford	56.4%	43.6%
OHIO	320	157	163	Reagan	49.1%	50.9%
ORANGE	3,258	1,438	1,820	Reagan	44.1%	55.9%
OWEN	1,963	792	1,171	Reagan	40.3%	59.7%
PARKE	2,646	1,128	1,518	Reagan	42.6%	57.4%
PERRY	1,635	970	665	Ford	59.3%	40.7%
PIKE	1,949	1,184	765	Ford	60.7%	39.3%
PORTER	14,282	6,821	7,461	Reagan	47.8%	52.2%
POSEY	2,208	1,377	831	Ford	62.4%	37.6%
PULASKI	2,538	1,224	1,314	Reagan	48.2%	51.8%
PUTNAM	3,371	1,395	1,976	Reagan	41.4%	58.6%
RANDOLPH	5,210	2,226	2,984	Reagan	42.7%	57.3%
RIPLEY	2,565	1,385	1,180	Ford	54.0%	46.0%
RUSH	3,427	1,518	1,909	Reagan	44.3%	55.7%
ST. JOSEPH	20,158	11,362	8,796	Ford	56.4%	43.6%
SCOTT	962	449	513	Reagan	46.7%	53.3%
SHELBY	4,715	1,902	2,813	Reagan	40.3%	59.7%
SPENCER	2,643	1,600	1,043	Ford	60.5%	39.5%
STARKE	2,094	1,036	1,058	Reagan	49.5%	50.5%
STEUBEN	3,735	1,894	1,841	Ford	50.7%	49.3%
SULLIVAN	1,824	754	1,070	Reagan	41.3%	58.7%
SWITZERLAND	528	288	240	Ford	54.5%	45.5%
TIPPECANOE	16,775	8,611	8,164	Ford	51.3%	48.7%
TIPTON	2,780	1,331	1,449	Reagan	47.9%	52.1%
UNION	915	430	485	Reagan	47.0%	53.0%
VANDERBURGH	18,132	12,222	5,910	Ford	67.4%	32.6%
VERMILLION	1,810	801	1,009	Reagan	44.3%	55.7%
VIGO	10,030	4,980	5,050	Reagan	49.7%	50.3%
WABASH	5,727	3,140	2,587	Ford	54.8%	45.2%
WARREN	1,525	692	833	Reagan	45.4%	54.6%
WARRICK	3,379	2,110	1,269	Ford	62.4%	37.6%
WASHINGTON	1,833	756	1,077	Reagan	41.2%	58.8%
WAYNE	11,380	5,085	6,295	Reagan	44.7%	55.3%
WELLS	2,647	1,475	1,172	Ford	55.7%	44.3%
WHITE	4,105	1,973	2,132	Reagan	48.1%	51.9%
WHITLEY	3,668	1,916	1,752	Ford	52.2%	47.8%
TOTAL	631,292	307,513	323,779	Reagan	48.7%	51.3%

INDIANA DEMOCRATIC

1980

County	Total Vote	Carter	E. Kennedy	Winner	Percentage of Total Vote Carter	E. Kennedy
ADAMS	4,723	3,439	1,284	Carter	72.8%	27.2%
ALLEN	22,276	14,348	7,928	Carter	64.4%	35.6%
BARTHOLOMEW	6,580	4,994	1,586	Carter	75.9%	24.1%
BENTON	951	670	281	Carter	70.5%	29.5%
BLACKFORD	2,310	1,550	760	Carter	67.1%	32.9%
BOONE	2,841	2,264	577	Carter	79.7%	20.3%
BROWN	1,722	1,323	399	Carter	76.8%	23.2%
CARROLL	2,229	1,674	555	Carter	75.1%	24.9%
CASS	4,282	2,908	1,374	Carter	67.9%	32.1%
CLARK	13,046	9,524	3,522	Carter	73.0%	27.0%
CLAY	4,503	3,501	1,002	Carter	77.7%	22.3%
CLINTON	3,122	2,428	694	Carter	77.8%	22.2%
CRAWFORD	1,651	1,224	427	Carter	74.1%	25.9%
DAVIESS	2,812	1,917	895	Carter	68.2%	31.8%
DEARBORN	4,234	3,005	1,229	Carter	71.0%	29.0%
DECATUR	1,911	1,422	489	Carter	74.4%	25.6%
DE KALB	2,985	2,055	930	Carter	68.8%	31.2%
DELAWARE	14,417	9,679	4,738	Carter	67.1%	32.9%
DUBOIS	6,145	4,143	2,002	Carter	67.4%	32.6%
ELKHART	7,877	5,116	2,761	Carter	64.9%	35.1%
FAYETTE	2,917	2,150	767	Carter	73.7%	26.3%
FLOYD	7,122	5,283	1,839	Carter	74.2%	25.8%
FOUNTAIN	1,684	1,240	444	Carter	73.6%	26.4%
FRANKLIN	3,153	2,107	1,046	Carter	66.8%	33.2%
FULTON	1,873	1,329	544	Carter	71.0%	29.0%
GIBSON	5,568	4,025	1,543	Carter	72.3%	27.7%
GRANT	8,475	5,631	2,844	Carter	66.4%	33.6%
GREENE	4,508	3,502	1,006	Carter	77.7%	22.3%
HAMILTON	3,760	2,789	971	Carter	74.2%	25.8%
HANCOCK	3,418	2,638	780	Carter	77.2%	22.8%
HARRISON	4,155	3,053	1,102	Carter	73.5%	26.5%
HENDRICKS	4,480	3,537	943	Carter	79.0%	21.0%
HENRY	4,988	3,372	1,616	Carter	67.6%	32.4%
HOWARD	9,289	6,458	2,831	Carter	69.5%	30.5%
HUNTINGTON	3,261	2,315	946	Carter	71.0%	29.0%
JACKSON	5,456	4,333	1,123	Carter	79.4%	20.6%
JASPER	1,424	1,030	394	Carter	72.3%	27.7%
JAY	2,663	1,788	875	Carter	67.1%	32.9%
JEFFERSON	4,082	3,044	1,038	Carter	74.6%	25.4%
JENNINGS	2,419	1,795	624	Carter	74.2%	25.8%
JOHNSON	5,407	4,197	1,210	Carter	77.6%	22.4%
KNOX	8,217	6,020	2,197	Carter	73.3%	26.7%
KOSCIUSKO	3,435	2,420	1,015	Carter	70.5%	29.5%
LAGRANGE	1,325	897	428	Carter	67.7%	32.3%
LAKE	92,512	53,797	38,715	Carter	58.2%	41.8%
LA PORTE	9,743	6,205	3,538	Carter	63.7%	36.3%
LAWRENCE	2,972	2,167	805	Carter	72.9%	27.1%
MADISON	18,982	11,625	7,357	Carter	61.2%	38.8%
MARION	65,395	43,754	21,641	Carter	66.9%	33.1%
MARSHALL	3,173	2,237	936	Carter	70.5%	29.5%

INDIANA DEMOCRATIC

1980

County	Total Vote	Carter	E. Kennedy	Winner	Percentage of Total Vote Carter	Percentage of Total Vote E. Kennedy
MARTIN	2,681	1,898	783	Carter	70.8%	29.2%
MIAMI	3,577	2,521	1,056	Carter	70.5%	29.5%
MONROE	7,340	4,755	2,585	Carter	64.8%	35.2%
MONTGOMERY	2,646	2,038	608	Carter	77.0%	23.0%
MORGAN	3,128	2,462	666	Carter	78.7%	21.3%
NEWTON	1,006	704	302	Carter	70.0%	30.0%
NOBLE	3,139	2,111	1,028	Carter	67.3%	32.7%
OHIO	647	494	153	Carter	76.4%	23.6%
ORANGE	1,446	1,084	362	Carter	75.0%	25.0%
OWEN	1,884	1,452	432	Carter	77.1%	22.9%
PARKE	1,923	1,546	377	Carter	80.4%	19.6%
PERRY	3,633	2,311	1,322	Carter	63.6%	36.4%
PIKE	2,466	1,820	646	Carter	73.8%	26.2%
PORTER	8,531	5,718	2,813	Carter	67.0%	33.0%
POSEY	3,601	2,432	1,169	Carter	67.5%	32.5%
PULASKI	1,545	1,099	446	Carter	71.1%	28.9%
PUTNAM	2,636	2,139	497	Carter	81.1%	18.9%
RANDOLPH	2,461	1,725	736	Carter	70.1%	29.9%
RIPLEY	3,271	2,383	888	Carter	72.9%	27.1%
RUSH	1,350	1,084	266	Carter	80.3%	19.7%
ST. JOSEPH	33,175	19,875	13,300	Carter	59.9%	40.1%
SCOTT	2,910	2,166	744	Carter	74.4%	25.6%
SHELBY	4,632	3,509	1,123	Carter	75.8%	24.2%
SPENCER	2,296	1,605	691	Carter	69.9%	30.1%
STARKE	2,946	1,914	1,032	Carter	65.0%	35.0%
STEUBEN	1,297	842	455	Carter	64.9%	35.1%
SULLIVAN	4,277	3,219	1,058	Carter	75.3%	24.7%
SWITZERLAND	1,720	1,294	426	Carter	75.2%	24.8%
TIPPECANOE	7,328	5,072	2,256	Carter	69.2%	30.8%
TIPTON	1,835	1,369	466	Carter	74.6%	25.4%
UNION	487	382	105	Carter	78.4%	21.6%
VANDERBURGH	17,628	12,487	5,141	Carter	70.8%	29.2%
VERMILLION	2,598	2,532	66	Carter	97.5%	2.5%
VIGO	18,584	12,928	5,656	Carter	69.6%	30.4%
WABASH	2,432	1,611	821	Carter	66.2%	33.8%
WARREN	670	502	168	Carter	74.9%	25.1%
WARRICK	4,645	3,327	1,318	Carter	71.6%	28.4%
WASHINGTON	2,465	1,927	538	Carter	78.2%	21.8%
WAYNE	4,467	3,192	1,275	Carter	71.5%	28.5%
WELLS	2,880	2,169	711	Carter	75.3%	24.7%
WHITE	2,082	1,505	577	Carter	72.3%	27.7%
WHITLEY	2,703	1,824	879	Carter	67.5%	32.5%
TOTAL	589,441	398,949	190,492	Carter	67.7%	32.3%

INDIANA REPUBLICAN

1980

County	Total Vote	Anderson	Bush	Reagan	Winner	Percentage of Total Vote Anderson	Bush	Reagan
ADAMS	2,315	233	438	1,644	Reagan	10.1%	18.9%	71.0%
ALLEN	34,375	4,369	6,455	23,551	Reagan	12.7%	18.8%	68.5%
BARTHOLOMEW	7,825	916	1,313	5,596	Reagan	11.7%	16.8%	71.5%
BENTON	1,997	155	235	1,607	Reagan	7.8%	11.8%	80.5%
BLACKFORD	1,439	111	222	1,106	Reagan	7.7%	15.4%	76.9%
BOONE	4,989	444	712	3,833	Reagan	8.9%	14.3%	76.8%
BROWN	1,371	113	153	1,105	Reagan	8.2%	11.2%	80.6%
CARROLL	3,085	255	350	2,480	Reagan	8.3%	11.3%	80.4%
CASS	5,185	464	731	3,990	Reagan	8.9%	14.1%	77.0%
CLARK	3,411	287	483	2,641	Reagan	8.4%	14.2%	77.4%
CLAY	3,451	249	373	2,829	Reagan	7.2%	10.8%	82.0%
CLINTON	5,002	347	735	3,920	Reagan	6.9%	14.7%	78.4%
CRAWFORD	1,452	72	163	1,217	Reagan	5.0%	11.2%	83.8%
DAVIESS	4,311	336	654	3,321	Reagan	7.8%	15.2%	77.0%
DEARBORN	1,936	185	241	1,510	Reagan	9.6%	12.4%	78.0%
DECATUR	2,083	165	248	1,670	Reagan	7.9%	11.9%	80.2%
DE KALB	4,563	584	952	3,027	Reagan	12.8%	20.9%	66.3%
DELAWARE	14,076	1,299	2,190	10,587	Reagan	9.2%	15.6%	75.2%
DUBOIS	1,476	150	244	1,082	Reagan	10.2%	16.5%	73.3%
ELKHART	14,440	1,750	3,319	9,371	Reagan	12.1%	23.0%	64.9%
FAYETTE	2,170	159	284	1,727	Reagan	7.3%	13.1%	79.6%
FLOYD	3,634	427	663	2,544	Reagan	11.8%	18.2%	70.0%
FOUNTAIN	3,027	200	440	2,387	Reagan	6.6%	14.5%	78.9%
FRANKLIN	1,287	70	146	1,071	Reagan	5.4%	11.3%	83.2%
FULTON	3,417	416	684	2,317	Reagan	12.2%	20.0%	67.8%
GIBSON	2,391	224	410	1,757	Reagan	9.4%	17.1%	73.5%
GRANT	8,519	645	1,123	6,751	Reagan	7.6%	13.2%	79.2%
GREENE	3,181	228	376	2,577	Reagan	7.2%	11.8%	81.0%
HAMILTON	15,320	1,325	2,650	11,345	Reagan	8.6%	17.3%	74.1%
HANCOCK	5,333	325	734	4,274	Reagan	6.1%	13.8%	80.1%
HARRISON	1,849	138	235	1,476	Reagan	7.5%	12.7%	79.8%
HENDRICKS	11,128	822	1,461	8,845	Reagan	7.4%	13.1%	79.5%
HENRY	6,434	443	869	5,122	Reagan	6.9%	13.5%	79.6%
HOWARD	9,598	700	1,252	7,646	Reagan	7.3%	13.0%	79.7%
HUNTINGTON	4,753	496	734	3,523	Reagan	10.4%	15.4%	74.1%
JACKSON	3,265	214	369	2,682	Reagan	6.6%	11.3%	82.1%
JASPER	3,726	285	748	2,693	Reagan	7.6%	20.1%	72.3%
JAY	2,544	226	436	1,882	Reagan	8.9%	17.1%	74.0%
JEFFERSON	2,865	278	378	2,209	Reagan	9.7%	13.2%	77.1%
JENNINGS	2,332	192	245	1,895	Reagan	8.2%	10.5%	81.3%
JOHNSON	11,705	912	1,579	9,214	Reagan	7.8%	13.5%	78.7%
KNOX	3,127	262	409	2,456	Reagan	8.4%	13.1%	78.5%
KOSCIUSKO	9,365	1,045	1,849	6,471	Reagan	11.2%	19.7%	69.1%
LAGRANGE	2,628	320	618	1,690	Reagan	12.2%	23.5%	64.3%
LAKE	24,274	2,790	4,394	17,090	Reagan	11.5%	18.1%	70.4%
LA PORTE	10,106	1,033	2,180	6,893	Reagan	10.2%	21.6%	68.2%
LAWRENCE	5,183	357	582	4,244	Reagan	6.9%	11.2%	81.9%
MADISON	16,106	1,196	2,168	12,742	Reagan	7.4%	13.5%	79.1%
MARION	87,422	9,241	13,443	64,738	Reagan	10.6%	15.4%	74.1%
MARSHALL	4,788	614	1,002	3,172	Reagan	12.8%	20.9%	66.2%

INDIANA REPUBLICAN

1980

County	Total Vote	Anderson	Bush	Reagan	Winner	Percentage of Total Vote: Anderson	Bush	Reagan
MARTIN	1,678	90	192	1,396	Reagan	5.4%	11.4%	83.2%
MIAMI	3,780	356	510	2,914	Reagan	9.4%	13.5%	77.1%
MONROE	9,186	1,364	1,408	6,414	Reagan	14.8%	15.3%	69.8%
MONTGOMERY	5,863	352	724	4,787	Reagan	6.0%	12.3%	81.6%
MORGAN	7,284	416	632	6,236	Reagan	5.7%	8.7%	85.6%
NEWTON	2,163	178	401	1,584	Reagan	8.2%	18.5%	73.2%
NOBLE	3,536	368	782	2,386	Reagan	10.4%	22.1%	67.5%
OHIO	265	17	24	224	Reagan	6.4%	9.1%	84.5%
ORANGE	2,098	114	224	1,760	Reagan	5.4%	10.7%	83.9%
OWEN	1,932	120	218	1,594	Reagan	6.2%	11.3%	82.5%
PARKE	2,633	172	381	2,080	Reagan	6.5%	14.5%	79.0%
PERRY	1,220	108	199	913	Reagan	8.9%	16.3%	74.8%
PIKE	1,526	126	243	1,157	Reagan	8.3%	15.9%	75.8%
PORTER	14,451	1,854	3,620	8,977	Reagan	12.8%	25.1%	62.1%
POSEY	1,876	220	383	1,273	Reagan	11.7%	20.4%	67.9%
PULASKI	1,903	135	317	1,451	Reagan	7.1%	16.7%	76.2%
PUTNAM	3,246	228	478	2,540	Reagan	7.0%	14.7%	78.3%
RANDOLPH	4,942	334	614	3,994	Reagan	6.8%	12.4%	80.8%
RIPLEY	1,666	155	180	1,331	Reagan	9.3%	10.8%	79.9%
RUSH	3,087	223	362	2,502	Reagan	7.2%	11.7%	81.0%
ST. JOSEPH	18,923	2,567	5,055	11,301	Reagan	13.6%	26.7%	59.7%
SCOTT	913	68	147	698	Reagan	7.4%	16.1%	76.5%
SHELBY	5,197	380	519	4,298	Reagan	7.3%	10.0%	82.7%
SPENCER	1,662	128	297	1,237	Reagan	7.7%	17.9%	74.4%
STARKE	1,878	192	361	1,325	Reagan	10.2%	19.2%	70.6%
STEUBEN	3,345	466	706	2,173	Reagan	13.9%	21.1%	65.0%
SULLIVAN	1,411	99	168	1,144	Reagan	7.0%	11.9%	81.1%
SWITZERLAND	462	31	53	378	Reagan	6.7%	11.5%	81.8%
TIPPECANOE	15,063	1,858	2,188	11,017	Reagan	12.3%	14.5%	73.1%
TIPTON	2,486	168	284	2,034	Reagan	6.8%	11.4%	81.8%
UNION	1,426	130	245	1,051	Reagan	9.1%	17.2%	73.7%
VANDERBURGH	11,482	1,481	2,240	7,761	Reagan	12.9%	19.5%	67.6%
VERMILLION	1,276	83	159	1,034	Reagan	6.5%	12.5%	81.0%
VIGO	8,329	730	1,194	6,405	Reagan	8.8%	14.3%	76.9%
WABASH	5,259	658	873	3,728	Reagan	12.5%	16.6%	70.9%
WARREN	1,279	69	116	1,094	Reagan	5.4%	9.1%	85.5%
WARRICK	2,873	332	592	1,949	Reagan	11.6%	20.6%	67.8%
WASHINGTON	1,927	141	223	1,563	Reagan	7.3%	11.6%	81.1%
WAYNE	9,196	766	1,434	6,996	Reagan	8.3%	15.6%	76.1%
WELLS	2,189	257	416	1,516	Reagan	11.7%	19.0%	69.3%
WHITE	3,986	371	578	3,037	Reagan	9.3%	14.5%	76.2%
WHITLEY	3,157	370	543	2,244	Reagan	11.7%	17.2%	71.1%
TOTAL	568,313	56,342	92,955	419,016	Reagan	9.9%	16.4%	73.7%

INDIANA DEMOCRATIC

1984

County	Total Vote	Hart	J. Jackson	Mondale	Other	Winner	Percentage of Total Vote Hart	J. Jackson	Mondale	Other
ADAMS	4,720	2,457	160	1,908	195	Hart	52.1%	3.4%	40.4%	4.1%
ALLEN	23,760	9,830	3,947	9,483	500	Hart	41.4%	16.6%	39.9%	2.1%
BARTHOLOMEW	7,015	3,575	475	2,622	343	Hart	51.0%	6.8%	37.4%	4.9%
BENTON	953	529	32	371	21	Hart	55.5%	3.4%	38.9%	2.2%
BLACKFORD	2,420	1,202	73	1,052	93	Hart	49.7%	3.0%	43.5%	3.8%
BOONE	2,832	1,485	145	1,037	165	Hart	52.4%	5.1%	36.6%	5.8%
BROWN	2,089	1,067	139	788	95	Hart	51.1%	6.7%	37.7%	4.5%
CARROLL	2,032	1,003	75	914	40	Hart	49.4%	3.7%	45.0%	2.0%
CASS	4,691	2,111	285	2,149	146	Mondale	45.0%	6.1%	45.8%	3.1%
CLARK	16,180	8,303	1,122	6,150	605	Hart	51.3%	6.9%	38.0%	3.7%
CLAY	4,979	2,682	211	1,911	175	Hart	53.9%	4.2%	38.4%	3.5%
CLINTON	3,138	1,483	101	1,384	170	Hart	47.3%	3.2%	44.1%	5.4%
CRAWFORD	1,847	790	78	925	54	Mondale	42.8%	4.2%	50.1%	2.9%
DAVIESS	2,877	1,516	103	1,179	79	Hart	52.7%	3.6%	41.0%	2.7%
DEARBORN	4,561	2,299	179	1,863	220	Hart	50.4%	3.9%	40.8%	4.8%
DECATUR	1,821	977	75	713	56	Hart	53.7%	4.1%	39.2%	3.1%
DE KALB	2,742	1,344	86	1,233	79	Hart	49.0%	3.1%	45.0%	2.9%
DELAWARE	20,077	8,345	2,196	8,972	564	Mondale	41.6%	10.9%	44.7%	2.8%
DUBOIS	7,774	3,915	285	3,270	304	Hart	50.4%	3.7%	42.1%	3.9%
ELKHART	8,196	3,636	1,097	3,269	194	Hart	44.4%	13.4%	39.9%	2.4%
FAYETTE	3,606	1,573	163	1,716	154	Mondale	43.6%	4.5%	47.6%	4.3%
FLOYD	8,517	4,023	539	3,586	369	Hart	47.2%	6.3%	42.1%	4.3%
FOUNTAIN	1,902	1,055	64	735	48	Hart	55.5%	3.4%	38.6%	2.5%
FRANKLIN	2,722	1,476	120	1,013	113	Hart	54.2%	4.4%	37.2%	4.2%
FULTON	1,729	865	91	715	58	Hart	50.0%	5.3%	41.4%	3.4%
GIBSON	6,872	3,035	235	3,432	170	Mondale	44.2%	3.4%	49.9%	2.5%
GRANT	9,818	4,000	1,305	4,131	382	Mondale	40.7%	13.3%	42.1%	3.9%
GREENE	5,212	2,601	158	2,282	171	Hart	49.9%	3.0%	43.8%	3.3%
HAMILTON	4,325	2,288	241	1,608	188	Hart	52.9%	5.6%	37.2%	4.3%
HANCOCK	3,627	2,055	123	1,377	72	Hart	56.7%	3.4%	38.0%	2.0%
HARRISON	5,177	2,686	198	2,089	204	Hart	51.9%	3.8%	40.4%	3.9%
HENDRICKS	4,518	2,141	154	2,023	200	Hart	47.4%	3.4%	44.8%	4.4%
HENRY	6,063	2,443	234	3,219	167	Mondale	40.3%	3.9%	53.1%	2.8%
HOWARD	8,581	3,164	921	4,214	282	Mondale	36.9%	10.7%	49.1%	3.3%
HUNTINGTON	3,380	1,710	117	1,380	173	Hart	50.6%	3.5%	40.8%	5.1%
JACKSON	5,794	3,041	193	2,357	203	Hart	52.5%	3.3%	40.7%	3.5%
JASPER	1,862	825	62	908	67	Mondale	44.3%	3.3%	48.8%	3.6%
JAY	2,732	1,393	94	1,144	101	Hart	51.0%	3.4%	41.9%	3.7%
JEFFERSON	4,407	2,292	288	1,626	201	Hart	52.0%	6.5%	36.9%	4.6%
JENNINGS	2,957	1,438	141	1,241	137	Hart	48.6%	4.8%	42.0%	4.6%
JOHNSON	5,959	3,035	240	2,520	164	Hart	50.9%	4.0%	42.3%	2.8%
KNOX	8,567	4,582	321	3,321	343	Hart	53.5%	3.7%	38.8%	4.0%
KOSCIUSKO	3,210	1,607	159	1,339	105	Hart	50.1%	5.0%	41.7%	3.3%
LAGRANGE	1,287	671	58	524	34	Hart	52.1%	4.5%	40.7%	2.6%
LAKE	124,701	39,566	28,547	51,628	4,960	Mondale	31.7%	22.9%	41.4%	4.0%
LA PORTE	13,236	5,559	1,202	6,064	411	Mondale	42.0%	9.1%	45.8%	3.1%
LAWRENCE	3,183	1,335	104	1,613	131	Mondale	41.9%	3.3%	50.7%	4.1%
MADISON	22,217	9,162	2,474	9,923	658	Mondale	41.2%	11.1%	44.7%	3.0%
MARION	92,510	27,425	32,577	28,080	4,428	J. Jackson	29.6%	35.2%	30.4%	4.8%
MARSHALL	3,415	1,595	144	1,536	140	Hart	46.7%	4.2%	45.0%	4.1%

INDIANA DEMOCRATIC

1984

County	Total Vote	Hart	J. Jackson	Mondale	Other	Winner	Percentage of Total Vote Hart	J. Jackson	Mondale	Other
MARTIN	2,849	1,460	93	1,175	121	Hart	51.2%	3.3%	41.2%	4.2%
MIAMI	3,454	1,638	142	1,464	210	Hart	47.4%	4.1%	42.4%	6.1%
MONROE	9,257	4,697	1,170	3,142	248	Hart	50.7%	12.6%	33.9%	2.7%
MONTGOMERY	3,253	1,793	171	1,193	96	Hart	55.1%	5.3%	36.7%	3.0%
MORGAN	3,558	1,648	117	1,554	239	Hart	46.3%	3.3%	43.7%	6.7%
NEWTON	1,236	593	36	568	39	Hart	48.0%	2.9%	46.0%	3.2%
NOBLE	2,932	1,469	115	1,244	104	Hart	50.1%	3.9%	42.4%	3.5%
OHIO	625	281	30	299	15	Mondale	45.0%	4.8%	47.8%	2.4%
ORANGE	1,970	1,012	60	843	55	Hart	51.4%	3.0%	42.8%	2.8%
OWEN	2,211	1,157	77	896	81	Hart	52.3%	3.5%	40.5%	3.7%
PARKE	2,077	1,190	72	761	54	Hart	57.3%	3.5%	36.6%	2.6%
PERRY	4,615	2,105	124	2,246	140	Mondale	45.6%	2.7%	48.7%	3.0%
PIKE	2,953	1,206	83	1,554	110	Mondale	40.8%	2.8%	52.6%	3.7%
PORTER	13,767	6,223	383	6,779	382	Mondale	45.2%	2.8%	49.2%	2.8%
POSEY	3,988	2,014	148	1,730	96	Hart	50.5%	3.7%	43.4%	2.4%
PULASKI	1,638	798	48	707	85	Hart	48.7%	2.9%	43.2%	5.2%
PUTNAM	3,087	1,666	130	1,202	89	Hart	54.0%	4.2%	38.9%	2.9%
RANDOLPH	3,014	1,376	134	1,412	92	Mondale	45.7%	4.4%	46.8%	3.1%
RIPLEY	3,617	2,002	162	1,244	209	Hart	55.3%	4.5%	34.4%	5.8%
RUSH	1,586	889	63	594	40	Hart	56.1%	4.0%	37.5%	2.5%
ST. JOSEPH	42,526	16,874	5,518	18,974	1,160	Mondale	39.7%	13.0%	44.6%	2.7%
SCOTT	3,457	1,613	145	1,579	120	Hart	46.7%	4.2%	45.7%	3.5%
SHELBY	1,828	863	80	794	91	Hart	47.2%	4.4%	43.4%	5.0%
SPENCER	2,811	1,353	72	1,324	62	Hart	48.1%	2.6%	47.1%	2.2%
STARKE	3,609	1,634	91	1,742	142	Mondale	45.3%	2.5%	48.3%	3.9%
STEUBEN	1,214	548	55	563	48	Mondale	45.1%	4.5%	46.4%	4.0%
SULLIVAN	5,380	2,746	157	2,292	185	Hart	51.0%	2.9%	42.6%	3.4%
SWITZERLAND	2,013	1,017	82	823	91	Hart	50.5%	4.1%	40.9%	4.5%
TIPPECANOE	9,191	4,258	972	3,769	192	Hart	46.3%	10.6%	41.0%	2.1%
TIPTON	1,992	961	72	873	86	Hart	48.2%	3.6%	43.8%	4.3%
UNION	578	285	25	251	17	Hart	49.3%	4.3%	43.4%	2.9%
VANDERBURGH	20,281	8,172	2,029	9,658	422	Mondale	40.3%	10.0%	47.6%	2.1%
VERMILLION	4,800	2,495	150	1,958	197	Hart	52.0%	3.1%	40.8%	4.1%
VIGO	21,360	11,124	1,548	7,966	722	Hart	52.1%	7.2%	37.3%	3.4%
WABASH	2,845	1,366	161	1,154	164	Hart	48.0%	5.7%	40.6%	5.8%
WARREN	707	397	29	257	24	Hart	56.2%	4.1%	36.4%	3.4%
WARRICK	7,034	3,186	211	3,456	181	Mondale	45.3%	3.0%	49.1%	2.6%
WASHINGTON	2,429	1,249	70	1,002	108	Hart	51.4%	2.9%	41.3%	4.4%
WAYNE	6,468	2,653	925	2,712	178	Mondale	41.0%	14.3%	41.9%	2.8%
WELLS	2,950	1,619	86	1,153	92	Hart	54.9%	2.9%	39.1%	3.1%
WHITE	2,563	1,377	119	985	82	Hart	53.7%	4.6%	38.4%	3.2%
WHITLEY	2,442	1,294	104	984	60	Hart	53.0%	4.3%	40.3%	2.5%
TOTAL	716,955	299,491	98,190	293,413	25,861	Hart	41.8%	13.7%	40.9%	3.6%

INDIANA DEMOCRATIC

1988

County	Total Vote	Dukakis	J. Jackson	Other	Winner	Percentage of Total Vote Dukakis	J. Jackson	Other
ADAMS	4,296	3,293	592	411	Dukakis	76.7%	13.8%	9.6%
ALLEN	21,453	13,490	6,835	1,128	Dukakis	62.9%	31.9%	5.3%
BARTHOLOMEW	7,046	5,541	967	538	Dukakis	78.6%	13.7%	7.6%
BENTON	816	659	81	76	Dukakis	80.8%	9.9%	9.3%
BLACKFORD	1,962	1,540	226	196	Dukakis	78.5%	11.5%	10.0%
BOONE	2,544	2,035	318	191	Dukakis	80.0%	12.5%	7.5%
BROWN	2,128	1,589	330	209	Dukakis	74.7%	15.5%	9.8%
CARROLL	2,005	1,529	255	221	Dukakis	76.3%	12.7%	11.0%
CASS	4,854	3,902	499	453	Dukakis	80.4%	10.3%	9.3%
CLARK	15,483	11,523	2,008	1,952	Dukakis	74.4%	13.0%	12.6%
CLAY	4,169	3,322	398	449	Dukakis	79.7%	9.5%	10.8%
CLINTON	2,674	2,122	308	244	Dukakis	79.4%	11.5%	9.1%
CRAWFORD	1,774	1,266	220	288	Dukakis	71.4%	12.4%	16.2%
DAVIESS	2,622	1,980	323	319	Dukakis	75.5%	12.3%	12.2%
DEARBORN	4,055	3,303	464	288	Dukakis	81.5%	11.4%	7.1%
DECATUR	1,813	1,496	218	99	Dukakis	82.5%	12.0%	5.5%
DE KALB	2,936	2,346	427	163	Dukakis	79.9%	14.5%	5.6%
DELAWARE	18,414	13,309	3,446	1,659	Dukakis	72.3%	18.7%	9.0%
DUBOIS	6,163	4,856	557	750	Dukakis	78.8%	9.0%	12.2%
ELKHART	7,422	5,062	1,878	482	Dukakis	68.2%	25.3%	6.5%
FAYETTE	3,290	2,643	372	275	Dukakis	80.3%	11.3%	8.4%
FLOYD	8,637	6,525	1,147	965	Dukakis	75.5%	13.3%	11.2%
FOUNTAIN	2,271	1,790	235	246	Dukakis	78.8%	10.3%	10.8%
FRANKLIN	2,348	1,891	292	165	Dukakis	80.5%	12.4%	7.0%
FULTON	1,874	1,442	270	162	Dukakis	76.9%	14.4%	8.6%
GIBSON	6,934	5,327	770	837	Dukakis	76.8%	11.1%	12.1%
GRANT	8,111	6,018	1,586	507	Dukakis	74.2%	19.6%	6.3%
GREENE	5,193	4,213	533	447	Dukakis	81.1%	10.3%	8.6%
HAMILTON	4,199	3,270	675	254	Dukakis	77.9%	16.1%	6.0%
HANCOCK	3,536	2,906	374	256	Dukakis	82.2%	10.6%	7.2%
HARRISON	5,309	3,906	521	882	Dukakis	73.6%	9.8%	16.6%
HENDRICKS	4,232	3,482	435	315	Dukakis	82.3%	10.3%	7.4%
HENRY	5,631	4,556	622	453	Dukakis	80.9%	11.0%	8.0%
HOWARD	9,899	7,123	1,909	867	Dukakis	72.0%	19.3%	8.8%
HUNTINGTON	2,943	2,402	360	181	Dukakis	81.6%	12.2%	6.2%
JACKSON	5,614	4,389	566	659	Dukakis	78.2%	10.1%	11.7%
JASPER	1,702	1,460	106	136	Dukakis	85.8%	6.2%	8.0%
JAY	2,416	1,922	294	200	Dukakis	79.6%	12.2%	8.3%
JEFFERSON	4,140	3,164	641	335	Dukakis	76.4%	15.5%	8.1%
JENNINGS	2,718	2,124	302	292	Dukakis	78.1%	11.1%	10.7%
JOHNSON	5,966	4,801	719	446	Dukakis	80.5%	12.1%	7.5%
KNOX	7,357	5,668	840	849	Dukakis	77.0%	11.4%	11.5%
KOSCIUSKO	3,278	2,444	552	282	Dukakis	74.6%	16.8%	8.6%
LAGRANGE	1,150	872	188	90	Dukakis	75.8%	16.3%	7.8%
LAKE	100,868	57,684	37,483	5,701	Dukakis	57.2%	37.2%	5.7%
LA PORTE	13,224	10,289	1,962	973	Dukakis	77.8%	14.8%	7.4%
LAWRENCE	2,952	2,376	353	223	Dukakis	80.5%	12.0%	7.6%
MADISON	20,806	15,556	3,609	1,641	Dukakis	74.8%	17.3%	7.9%
MARION	77,845	40,775	33,868	3,202	Dukakis	52.4%	43.5%	4.1%
MARSHALL	2,724	2,102	382	240	Dukakis	77.2%	14.0%	8.8%

INDIANA DEMOCRATIC

1988

County	Total Vote	Dukakis	J. Jackson	Other	Winner	Percentage of Total Vote Dukakis	J. Jackson	Other
MARTIN	2,782	2,085	265	432	Dukakis	74.9%	9.5%	15.5%
MIAMI	3,344	2,686	378	280	Dukakis	80.3%	11.3%	8.4%
MONROE	9,032	5,680	2,782	570	Dukakis	62.9%	30.8%	6.3%
MONTGOMERY	2,574	1,969	392	213	Dukakis	76.5%	15.2%	8.3%
MORGAN	3,135	2,551	300	284	Dukakis	81.4%	9.6%	9.1%
NEWTON	1,189	1,009	80	100	Dukakis	84.9%	6.7%	8.4%
NOBLE	2,780	2,158	422	200	Dukakis	77.6%	15.2%	7.2%
OHIO	658	520	97	41	Dukakis	79.0%	14.7%	6.2%
ORANGE	1,847	1,391	236	220	Dukakis	75.3%	12.8%	11.9%
OWEN	2,217	1,757	227	233	Dukakis	79.3%	10.2%	10.5%
PARKE	1,930	1,559	192	179	Dukakis	80.8%	9.9%	9.3%
PERRY	4,674	3,610	407	657	Dukakis	77.2%	8.7%	14.1%
PIKE	2,703	2,069	287	347	Dukakis	76.5%	10.6%	12.8%
PORTER	13,159	11,201	956	1,002	Dukakis	85.1%	7.3%	7.6%
POSEY	3,193	2,495	301	397	Dukakis	78.1%	9.4%	12.4%
PULASKI	1,537	1,293	124	120	Dukakis	84.1%	8.1%	7.8%
PUTNAM	2,920	2,242	428	250	Dukakis	76.8%	14.7%	8.6%
RANDOLPH	2,444	1,880	390	174	Dukakis	76.9%	16.0%	7.1%
RIPLEY	2,605	2,020	392	193	Dukakis	77.5%	15.0%	7.4%
RUSH	1,552	1,247	188	117	Dukakis	80.3%	12.1%	7.5%
ST. JOSEPH	35,837	24,899	8,124	2,814	Dukakis	69.5%	22.7%	7.9%
SCOTT	3,028	2,333	289	406	Dukakis	77.0%	9.5%	13.4%
SHELBY	4,087	3,457	376	254	Dukakis	84.6%	9.2%	6.2%
SPENCER	2,373	1,869	185	319	Dukakis	78.8%	7.8%	13.4%
STARKE	2,845	2,362	236	247	Dukakis	83.0%	8.3%	8.7%
STEUBEN	1,382	1,055	238	89	Dukakis	76.3%	17.2%	6.4%
SULLIVAN	4,481	3,622	412	447	Dukakis	80.8%	9.2%	10.0%
SWITZERLAND	1,761	1,393	193	175	Dukakis	79.1%	11.0%	9.9%
TIPPECANOE	8,693	5,988	2,026	679	Dukakis	68.9%	23.3%	7.8%
TIPTON	1,779	1,462	199	118	Dukakis	82.2%	11.2%	6.6%
UNION	523	395	86	42	Dukakis	75.5%	16.4%	8.0%
VANDERBURGH	21,450	14,806	4,229	2,415	Dukakis	69.0%	19.7%	11.3%
VERMILLION	4,572	3,617	416	539	Dukakis	79.1%	9.1%	11.8%
VIGO	20,438	15,523	2,822	2,093	Dukakis	76.0%	13.8%	10.2%
WABASH	2,612	1,887	581	144	Dukakis	72.2%	22.2%	5.5%
WARREN	805	625	110	70	Dukakis	77.6%	13.7%	8.7%
WARRICK	6,281	4,728	651	902	Dukakis	75.3%	10.4%	14.4%
WASHINGTON	2,347	1,794	258	295	Dukakis	76.4%	11.0%	12.6%
WAYNE	5,463	3,638	1,462	363	Dukakis	66.6%	26.8%	6.6%
WELLS	2,414	1,939	317	158	Dukakis	80.3%	13.1%	6.5%
WHITE	2,194	1,731	249	214	Dukakis	78.9%	11.3%	9.8%
WHITLEY	2,543	1,937	403	203	Dukakis	76.2%	15.8%	8.0%
TOTAL	645,979	449,765	145,022	51,192	Dukakis	69.6%	22.4%	7.9%
Certified Totals	645,708	449,495	145,021	51,192	Dukakis	69.6%	22.5%	7.9%

INDIANA REPUBLICAN

1988

County	Total Vote	Bush	Other	Winner	Percentage of Total Vote Bush	Other
ADAMS	1,854	1,408	446	Bush	75.9%	24.1%
ALLEN	21,641	16,899	4,742	Bush	78.1%	21.9%
BARTHOLOMEW	7,371	6,123	1,248	Bush	83.1%	16.9%
BENTON	1,549	1,156	393	Bush	74.6%	25.4%
BLACKFORD	864	701	163	Bush	81.1%	18.9%
BOONE	4,865	3,980	885	Bush	81.8%	18.2%
BROWN	1,240	993	247	Bush	80.1%	19.9%
CARROLL	1,997	1,547	450	Bush	77.5%	22.5%
CASS	4,655	3,681	974	Bush	79.1%	20.9%
CLARK	2,466	1,997	469	Bush	81.0%	19.0%
CLAY	1,954	1,537	417	Bush	78.7%	21.3%
CLINTON	3,407	2,809	598	Bush	82.4%	17.6%
CRAWFORD	1,147	927	220	Bush	80.8%	19.2%
DAVIESS	4,296	3,523	773	Bush	82.0%	18.0%
DEARBORN	2,052	1,758	294	Bush	85.7%	14.3%
DECATUR	2,477	1,968	509	Bush	79.5%	20.5%
DE KALB	3,997	3,093	904	Bush	77.4%	22.6%
DELAWARE	9,422	7,549	1,873	Bush	80.1%	19.9%
DUBOIS	1,642	1,393	249	Bush	84.8%	15.2%
ELKHART	12,479	9,704	2,775	Bush	77.8%	22.2%
FAYETTE	2,075	1,751	324	Bush	84.4%	15.6%
FLOYD	2,436	1,992	444	Bush	81.8%	18.2%
FOUNTAIN	2,252	1,831	421	Bush	81.3%	18.7%
FRANKLIN	1,226	1,029	197	Bush	83.9%	16.1%
FULTON	2,164	1,702	462	Bush	78.7%	21.3%
GIBSON	1,671	1,257	414	Bush	75.2%	24.8%
GRANT	7,210	5,634	1,576	Bush	78.1%	21.9%
GREENE	3,206	2,679	527	Bush	83.6%	16.4%
HAMILTON	14,169	11,509	2,660	Bush	81.2%	18.8%
HANCOCK	4,101	3,212	889	Bush	78.3%	21.7%
HARRISON	1,649	1,319	330	Bush	80.0%	20.0%
HENDRICKS	10,544	8,344	2,200	Bush	79.1%	20.9%
HENRY	4,328	3,494	834	Bush	80.7%	19.3%
HOWARD	6,766	5,281	1,485	Bush	78.1%	21.9%
HUNTINGTON	2,935	2,484	451	Bush	84.6%	15.4%
JACKSON	3,134	2,465	669	Bush	78.7%	21.3%
JASPER	3,969	3,098	871	Bush	78.1%	21.9%
JAY	2,553	1,966	587	Bush	77.0%	23.0%
JEFFERSON	1,929	1,535	394	Bush	79.6%	20.4%
JENNINGS	2,324	1,901	423	Bush	81.8%	18.2%
JOHNSON	11,371	9,063	2,308	Bush	79.7%	20.3%
KNOX	2,881	2,376	505	Bush	82.5%	17.5%
KOSCIUSKO	8,394	6,532	1,862	Bush	77.8%	22.2%
LAGRANGE	2,212	1,702	510	Bush	76.9%	23.1%
LAKE	15,671	13,152	2,519	Bush	83.9%	16.1%
LA PORTE	6,351	5,150	1,201	Bush	81.1%	18.9%
LAWRENCE	4,281	3,466	815	Bush	81.0%	19.0%
MADISON	11,692	9,418	2,274	Bush	80.6%	19.4%
MARION	64,985	54,236	10,749	Bush	83.5%	16.5%
MARSHALL	4,505	3,562	943	Bush	79.1%	20.9%

INDIANA REPUBLICAN

1988

County	Total Vote	Bush	Other	Winner	Percentage of Total Vote Bush	Other
MARTIN	1,064	881	183	Bush	82.8%	17.2%
MIAMI	2,928	2,412	516	Bush	82.4%	17.6%
MONROE	6,893	5,619	1,274	Bush	81.5%	18.5%
MONTGOMERY	4,527	3,634	893	Bush	80.3%	19.7%
MORGAN	6,624	5,338	1,286	Bush	80.6%	19.4%
NEWTON	1,841	1,454	387	Bush	79.0%	21.0%
NOBLE	2,791	2,204	587	Bush	79.0%	21.0%
OHIO	270	222	48	Bush	82.2%	17.8%
ORANGE	2,547	2,120	427	Bush	83.2%	16.8%
OWEN	1,816	1,452	364	Bush	80.0%	20.0%
PARKE	1,933	1,562	371	Bush	80.8%	19.2%
PERRY	647	545	102	Bush	84.2%	15.8%
PIKE	1,206	958	248	Bush	79.4%	20.6%
PORTER	12,650	9,930	2,720	Bush	78.5%	21.5%
POSEY	1,328	1,095	233	Bush	82.5%	17.5%
PULASKI	1,800	1,494	306	Bush	83.0%	17.0%
PUTNAM	2,628	2,133	495	Bush	81.2%	18.8%
RANDOLPH	3,924	3,015	909	Bush	76.8%	23.2%
RIPLEY	2,655	2,227	428	Bush	83.9%	16.1%
RUSH	2,957	2,330	627	Bush	78.8%	21.2%
ST. JOSEPH	11,871	9,643	2,228	Bush	81.2%	18.8%
SCOTT	702	571	131	Bush	81.3%	18.7%
SHELBY	3,649	2,996	653	Bush	82.1%	17.9%
SPENCER	2,196	1,774	422	Bush	80.8%	19.2%
STARKE	1,327	1,088	239	Bush	82.0%	18.0%
STEUBEN	3,240	2,524	716	Bush	77.9%	22.1%
SULLIVAN	1,029	843	186	Bush	81.9%	18.1%
SWITZERLAND	397	341	56	Bush	85.9%	14.1%
TIPPECANOE	9,642	7,437	2,205	Bush	77.1%	22.9%
TIPTON	1,776	1,456	320	Bush	82.0%	18.0%
UNION	826	683	143	Bush	82.7%	17.3%
VANDERBURGH	9,137	7,740	1,397	Bush	84.7%	15.3%
VERMILLION	728	578	150	Bush	79.4%	20.6%
VIGO	5,518	4,409	1,109	Bush	79.9%	20.1%
WABASH	4,412	3,431	981	Bush	77.8%	22.2%
WARREN	1,112	855	257	Bush	76.9%	23.1%
WARRICK	2,683	2,194	489	Bush	81.8%	18.2%
WASHINGTON	1,603	1,317	286	Bush	82.2%	17.8%
WAYNE	7,715	6,229	1,486	Bush	80.7%	19.3%
WELLS	1,632	1,257	375	Bush	77.0%	23.0%
WHITE	2,789	2,185	604	Bush	78.3%	21.7%
WHITLEY	2,283	1,767	516	Bush	77.4%	22.6%
TOTAL	443,655	357,829	85,826	Bush	80.7%	19.3%
Certified Totals	437,655	351,829	85,826	Bush	80.4%	19.6%

INDIANA DEMOCRATIC

1992

County	Total Vote	Brown	Clinton	Kerrey	Tsongas	Winner	Percentage of Total Vote Brown	Clinton	Kerrey	Tsongas
ADAMS	3,249	727	1,963	131	428	Clinton	22.4%	60.4%	4.0%	13.2%
ALLEN	17,220	5,436	9,397	431	1,956	Clinton	31.6%	54.6%	2.5%	11.4%
BARTHOLOMEW	4,153	779	2,684	130	560	Clinton	18.8%	64.6%	3.1%	13.5%
BENTON	544	92	355	22	75	Clinton	16.9%	65.3%	4.0%	13.8%
BLACKFORD	1,662	328	1,061	39	234	Clinton	19.7%	63.8%	2.3%	14.1%
BOONE	1,553	322	936	54	241	Clinton	20.7%	60.3%	3.5%	15.5%
BROWN	1,583	401	900	41	241	Clinton	25.3%	56.9%	2.6%	15.2%
CARROLL	1,416	210	994	58	154	Clinton	14.8%	70.2%	4.1%	10.9%
CASS	3,114	728	1,912	130	344	Clinton	23.4%	61.4%	4.2%	11.0%
CLARK	13,798	2,182	9,970	260	1,386	Clinton	15.8%	72.3%	1.9%	10.0%
CLAY	2,664	451	1,777	100	336	Clinton	16.9%	66.7%	3.8%	12.6%
CLINTON	1,800	288	1,229	62	221	Clinton	16.0%	68.3%	3.4%	12.3%
CRAWFORD	1,953	241	1,456	78	178	Clinton	12.3%	74.6%	4.0%	9.1%
DAVIESS	1,917	395	1,242	48	232	Clinton	20.6%	64.8%	2.5%	12.1%
DEARBORN	2,643	440	1,761	94	348	Clinton	16.6%	66.6%	3.6%	13.2%
DECATUR	1,269	240	795	52	182	Clinton	18.9%	62.6%	4.1%	14.3%
DE KALB	2,519	588	1,591	73	267	Clinton	23.3%	63.2%	2.9%	10.6%
DELAWARE	13,828	2,644	9,077	504	1,603	Clinton	19.1%	65.6%	3.6%	11.6%
DUBOIS	5,348	1,146	3,298	159	745	Clinton	21.4%	61.7%	3.0%	13.9%
ELKHART	5,799	1,325	3,525	153	796	Clinton	22.8%	60.8%	2.6%	13.7%
FAYETTE	2,439	454	1,640	56	289	Clinton	18.6%	67.2%	2.3%	11.8%
FLOYD	7,100	1,237	4,871	158	834	Clinton	17.4%	68.6%	2.2%	11.7%
FOUNTAIN	1,375	198	960	39	178	Clinton	14.4%	69.8%	2.8%	12.9%
FRANKLIN	1,977	269	1,338	88	282	Clinton	13.6%	67.7%	4.5%	14.3%
FULTON	1,326	219	875	47	185	Clinton	16.5%	66.0%	3.5%	14.0%
GIBSON	4,329	701	2,885	187	556	Clinton	16.2%	66.6%	4.3%	12.8%
GRANT	4,485	901	2,940	132	512	Clinton	20.1%	65.6%	2.9%	11.4%
GREENE	3,864	600	2,695	147	422	Clinton	15.5%	69.7%	3.8%	10.9%
HAMILTON	3,460	784	1,982	86	608	Clinton	22.7%	57.3%	2.5%	17.6%
HANCOCK	2,247	393	1,395	161	298	Clinton	17.5%	62.1%	7.2%	13.3%
HARRISON	4,900	778	3,310	177	635	Clinton	15.9%	67.6%	3.6%	13.0%
HENDRICKS	2,847	625	1,699	90	433	Clinton	22.0%	59.7%	3.2%	15.2%
HENRY	4,273	763	2,858	125	527	Clinton	17.9%	66.9%	2.9%	12.3%
HOWARD	6,444	1,265	4,157	234	788	Clinton	19.6%	64.5%	3.6%	12.2%
HUNTINGTON	2,080	465	1,355	66	194	Clinton	22.4%	65.1%	3.2%	9.3%
JACKSON	3,810	686	2,552	97	475	Clinton	18.0%	67.0%	2.5%	12.5%
JASPER	1,433	230	1,021	38	144	Clinton	16.1%	71.2%	2.7%	10.0%
JAY	2,001	308	1,405	63	225	Clinton	15.4%	70.2%	3.1%	11.2%
JEFFERSON	3,734	608	2,594	81	451	Clinton	16.3%	69.5%	2.2%	12.1%
JENNINGS	2,605	456	1,725	93	331	Clinton	17.5%	66.2%	3.6%	12.7%
JOHNSON	3,877	918	2,311	136	512	Clinton	23.7%	59.6%	3.5%	13.2%
KNOX	5,727	1,046	3,644	235	802	Clinton	18.3%	63.6%	4.1%	14.0%
KOSCIUSKO	2,197	450	1,372	81	294	Clinton	20.5%	62.4%	3.7%	13.4%
LAGRANGE	1,061	200	684	43	134	Clinton	18.9%	64.5%	4.1%	12.6%
LAKE	72,374	14,797	47,819	1,961	7,797	Clinton	20.4%	66.1%	2.7%	10.8%
LA PORTE	12,023	2,420	7,674	329	1,600	Clinton	20.1%	63.8%	2.7%	13.3%
LAWRENCE	2,460	451	1,683	60	266	Clinton	18.3%	68.4%	2.4%	10.8%
MADISON	14,168	2,578	9,488	422	1,680	Clinton	18.2%	67.0%	3.0%	11.9%
MARION	52,049	16,521	28,998	1,024	5,506	Clinton	31.7%	55.7%	2.0%	10.6%
MARSHALL	2,057	440	1,306	68	243	Clinton	21.4%	63.5%	3.3%	11.8%

INDIANA DEMOCRATIC

1992

County	Total Vote	Brown	Clinton	Kerrey	Tsongas	Winner	Percentage of Total Vote Brown	Clinton	Kerrey	Tsongas
MARTIN	2,387	377	1,611	101	298	Clinton	15.8%	67.5%	4.2%	12.5%
MIAMI	2,179	484	1,392	63	240	Clinton	22.2%	63.9%	2.9%	11.0%
MONROE	8,063	3,197	3,395	154	1,317	Clinton	39.7%	42.1%	1.9%	16.3%
MONTGOMERY	1,548	289	993	53	213	Clinton	18.7%	64.1%	3.4%	13.8%
MORGAN	2,088	453	1,307	83	245	Clinton	21.7%	62.6%	4.0%	11.7%
NEWTON	906	137	635	29	105	Clinton	15.1%	70.1%	3.2%	11.6%
NOBLE	2,368	554	1,485	68	261	Clinton	23.4%	62.7%	2.9%	11.0%
OHIO	454	51	343	15	45	Clinton	11.2%	75.6%	3.3%	9.9%
ORANGE	1,450	206	1,048	47	149	Clinton	14.2%	72.3%	3.2%	10.3%
OWEN	1,810	334	1,171	63	242	Clinton	18.5%	64.7%	3.5%	13.4%
PARKE	1,706	254	1,169	64	219	Clinton	14.9%	68.5%	3.8%	12.8%
PERRY	4,887	796	3,310	173	608	Clinton	16.3%	67.7%	3.5%	12.4%
PIKE	2,261	367	1,505	86	303	Clinton	16.2%	66.6%	3.8%	13.4%
PORTER	11,056	2,594	6,493	354	1,615	Clinton	23.5%	58.7%	3.2%	14.6%
POSEY	2,515	378	1,636	108	393	Clinton	15.0%	65.0%	4.3%	15.6%
PULASKI	1,132	212	778	29	113	Clinton	18.7%	68.7%	2.6%	10.0%
PUTNAM	2,041	339	1,363	78	261	Clinton	16.6%	66.8%	3.8%	12.8%
RANDOLPH	1,632	243	1,190	44	155	Clinton	14.9%	72.9%	2.7%	9.5%
RIPLEY	1,578	267	1,035	63	213	Clinton	16.9%	65.6%	4.0%	13.5%
RUSH	1,004	167	686	26	125	Clinton	16.6%	68.3%	2.6%	12.5%
ST. JOSEPH	25,021	5,782	14,773	928	3,538	Clinton	23.1%	59.0%	3.7%	14.1%
SCOTT	3,379	507	2,466	93	313	Clinton	15.0%	73.0%	2.8%	9.3%
SHELBY	2,588	482	1,722	82	302	Clinton	18.6%	66.5%	3.2%	11.7%
SPENCER	2,507	360	1,739	102	306	Clinton	14.4%	69.4%	4.1%	12.2%
STARKE	3,011	555	2,160	87	209	Clinton	18.4%	71.7%	2.9%	6.9%
STEUBEN	1,406	359	860	33	154	Clinton	25.5%	61.2%	2.3%	11.0%
SULLIVAN	3,729	585	2,518	131	495	Clinton	15.7%	67.5%	3.5%	13.3%
SWITZERLAND	1,404	177	1,022	40	165	Clinton	12.6%	72.8%	2.8%	11.8%
TIPPECANOE	6,834	1,575	3,889	197	1,173	Clinton	23.0%	56.9%	2.9%	17.2%
TIPTON	1,329	225	893	46	165	Clinton	16.9%	67.2%	3.5%	12.4%
UNION	365	53	255	8	49	Clinton	14.5%	69.9%	2.2%	13.4%
VANDERBURGH	10,436	2,046	6,751	319	1,320	Clinton	19.6%	64.7%	3.1%	12.6%
VERMILLION	3,732	627	2,490	138	477	Clinton	16.8%	66.7%	3.7%	12.8%
VIGO	14,829	2,559	9,428	644	2,198	Clinton	17.3%	63.6%	4.3%	14.8%
WABASH	3,095	747	1,960	45	343	Clinton	24.1%	63.3%	1.5%	11.1%
WARREN	637	77	468	20	72	Clinton	12.1%	73.5%	3.1%	11.3%
WARRICK	5,293	1,014	3,319	222	738	Clinton	19.2%	62.7%	4.2%	13.9%
WASHINGTON	2,422	372	1,700	78	272	Clinton	15.4%	70.2%	3.2%	11.2%
WAYNE	3,236	622	2,123	103	388	Clinton	19.2%	65.6%	3.2%	12.0%
WELLS	2,000	454	1,256	64	226	Clinton	22.7%	62.8%	3.2%	11.3%
WHITE	1,591	293	1,036	52	210	Clinton	18.4%	65.1%	3.3%	13.2%
WHITLEY	2,186	485	1,373	74	254	Clinton	22.2%	62.8%	3.4%	11.6%
TOTAL	476,849	102,379	301,905	14,350	58,215	Clinton	21.5%	63.3%	3.0%	12.2%

INDIANA REPUBLICAN

1992

County	Total Vote	Buchanan	Bush	Winner	Percentage of Total Vote Buchanan	Bush
ADAMS	1,832	417	1,415	Bush	22.8%	77.2%
ALLEN	21,528	6,133	15,395	Bush	28.5%	71.5%
BARTHOLOMEW	6,373	1,121	5,252	Bush	17.6%	82.4%
BENTON	1,413	316	1,097	Bush	22.4%	77.6%
BLACKFORD	851	40	811	Bush	4.7%	95.3%
BOONE	5,569	1,018	4,551	Bush	18.3%	81.7%
BROWN	1,177	217	960	Bush	18.4%	81.6%
CARROLL	2,315	450	1,865	Bush	19.4%	80.6%
CASS	4,265	874	3,391	Bush	20.5%	79.5%
CLARK	3,486	555	2,931	Bush	15.9%	84.1%
CLAY	2,017	348	1,669	Bush	17.3%	82.7%
CLINTON	4,157	657	3,500	Bush	15.8%	84.2%
CRAWFORD	743	105	638	Bush	14.1%	85.9%
DAVIESS	3,815	617	3,198	Bush	16.2%	83.8%
DEARBORN	2,086	327	1,759	Bush	15.7%	84.3%
DECATUR	2,180	338	1,842	Bush	15.5%	84.5%
DE KALB	4,623	1,117	3,506	Bush	24.2%	75.8%
DELAWARE	9,872	1,503	8,369	Bush	15.2%	84.8%
DUBOIS	1,555	243	1,312	Bush	15.6%	84.4%
ELKHART	12,314	2,408	9,906	Bush	19.6%	80.4%
FAYETTE	1,840	254	1,586	Bush	13.8%	86.2%
FLOYD	3,064	494	2,570	Bush	16.1%	83.9%
FOUNTAIN	1,817	390	1,427	Bush	21.5%	78.5%
FRANKLIN	1,500	247	1,253	Bush	16.5%	83.5%
FULTON	2,314	442	1,872	Bush	19.1%	80.9%
GIBSON	1,277	247	1,030	Bush	19.3%	80.7%
GRANT	6,490	1,091	5,399	Bush	16.8%	83.2%
GREENE	2,741	498	2,243	Bush	18.2%	81.8%
HAMILTON	21,148	3,915	17,233	Bush	18.5%	81.5%
HANCOCK	5,713	1,198	4,515	Bush	21.0%	79.0%
HARRISON	2,110	359	1,751	Bush	17.0%	83.0%
HENDRICKS	10,768	2,233	8,535	Bush	20.7%	79.3%
HENRY	5,014	791	4,223	Bush	15.8%	84.2%
HOWARD	7,409	1,407	6,002	Bush	19.0%	81.0%
HUNTINGTON	3,885	659	3,226	Bush	17.0%	83.0%
JACKSON	2,626	450	2,176	Bush	17.1%	82.9%
JASPER	3,913	848	3,065	Bush	21.7%	78.3%
JAY	2,339	450	1,889	Bush	19.2%	80.8%
JEFFERSON	2,234	331	1,903	Bush	14.8%	85.2%
JENNINGS	2,553	451	2,102	Bush	17.7%	82.3%
JOHNSON	11,297	2,352	8,945	Bush	20.8%	79.2%
KNOX	2,961	484	2,477	Bush	16.3%	83.7%
KOSCIUSKO	7,032	1,436	5,596	Bush	20.4%	79.6%
LAGRANGE	2,456	472	1,984	Bush	19.2%	80.8%
LAKE	15,138	2,919	12,219	Bush	19.3%	80.7%
LA PORTE	7,525	1,532	5,993	Bush	20.4%	79.6%
LAWRENCE	5,238	1,141	4,097	Bush	21.8%	78.2%
MADISON	11,749	2,055	9,694	Bush	17.5%	82.5%
MARION	70,143	14,524	55,619	Bush	20.7%	79.3%
MARSHALL	3,899	708	3,191	Bush	18.2%	81.8%

INDIANA REPUBLICAN

1992

County	Total Vote	Buchanan	Bush	Winner	Percentage of Total Vote Buchanan	Percentage of Total Vote Bush
MARTIN	1,083	167	916	Bush	15.4%	84.6%
MIAMI	3,566	748	2,818	Bush	21.0%	79.0%
MONROE	6,635	1,197	5,438	Bush	18.0%	82.0%
MONTGOMERY	5,672	1,168	4,504	Bush	20.6%	79.4%
MORGAN	7,197	1,602	5,595	Bush	22.3%	77.7%
NEWTON	2,301	578	1,723	Bush	25.1%	74.9%
NOBLE	3,135	749	2,386	Bush	23.9%	76.1%
OHIO	270	25	245	Bush	9.3%	90.7%
ORANGE	2,943	557	2,386	Bush	18.9%	81.1%
OWEN	1,581	305	1,276	Bush	19.3%	80.7%
PARKE	1,998	359	1,639	Bush	18.0%	82.0%
PERRY	604	88	516	Bush	14.6%	85.4%
PIKE	925	179	746	Bush	19.4%	80.6%
PORTER	12,742	3,216	9,526	Bush	25.2%	74.8%
POSEY	984	181	803	Bush	18.4%	81.6%
PULASKI	1,798	343	1,455	Bush	19.1%	80.9%
PUTNAM	3,219	669	2,550	Bush	20.8%	79.2%
RANDOLPH	3,574	755	2,819	Bush	21.1%	78.9%
RIPLEY	1,765	288	1,477	Bush	16.3%	83.7%
RUSH	2,907	521	2,386	Bush	17.9%	82.1%
ST. JOSEPH	13,582	2,668	10,914	Bush	19.6%	80.4%
SCOTT	724	137	587	Bush	18.9%	81.1%
SHELBY	3,286	580	2,706	Bush	17.7%	82.3%
SPENCER	2,037	287	1,750	Bush	14.1%	85.9%
STARKE	1,268	247	1,021	Bush	19.5%	80.5%
STEUBEN	3,595	783	2,812	Bush	21.8%	78.2%
SULLIVAN	1,011	207	804	Bush	20.5%	79.5%
SWITZERLAND	408	54	354	Bush	13.2%	86.8%
TIPPECANOE	12,798	2,688	10,110	Bush	21.0%	79.0%
TIPTON	2,388	381	2,007	Bush	16.0%	84.0%
UNION	1,241	247	994	Bush	19.9%	80.1%
VANDERBURGH	7,097	1,222	5,875	Bush	17.2%	82.8%
VERMILLION	532	119	413	Bush	22.4%	77.6%
VIGO	4,886	1,099	3,787	Bush	22.5%	77.5%
WABASH	6,359	1,178	5,181	Bush	18.5%	81.5%
WARREN	915	216	699	Bush	23.6%	76.4%
WARRICK	2,356	439	1,917	Bush	18.6%	81.4%
WASHINGTON	2,471	429	2,042	Bush	17.4%	82.6%
WAYNE	7,355	1,306	6,049	Bush	17.8%	82.2%
WELLS	2,373	522	1,851	Bush	22.0%	78.0%
WHITE	2,608	492	2,116	Bush	18.9%	81.1%
WHITLEY	3,062	771	2,291	Bush	25.2%	74.8%
TOTAL	467,615	92,949	374,666	Bush	19.9%	80.1%

INDIANA REPUBLICAN

1996

County	Total Vote	Buchanan	Dole	Forbes	Winner	Percentage of Total Vote Buchanan	Dole	Forbes
ADAMS	2,604	641	1,769	194	Dole	24.6%	67.9%	7.5%
ALLEN	26,117	5,036	18,477	2,604	Dole	19.3%	70.7%	10.0%
BARTHOLOMEW	6,826	1,093	5,005	728	Dole	16.0%	73.3%	10.7%
BENTON	2,083	423	1,411	249	Dole	20.3%	67.7%	12.0%
BLACKFORD	1,169	229	807	133	Dole	19.6%	69.0%	11.4%
BOONE	7,425	1,230	5,509	686	Dole	16.6%	74.2%	9.2%
BROWN	1,493	321	1,050	122	Dole	21.5%	70.3%	8.2%
CARROLL	2,692	553	1,866	273	Dole	20.5%	69.3%	10.1%
CASS	3,954	791	2,840	323	Dole	20.0%	71.8%	8.2%
CLARK	2,728	539	1,989	200	Dole	19.8%	72.9%	7.3%
CLAY	3,323	775	2,308	240	Dole	23.3%	69.5%	7.2%
CLINTON	3,055	555	2,206	294	Dole	18.2%	72.2%	9.6%
CRAWFORD	942	208	681	53	Dole	22.1%	72.3%	5.6%
DAVIESS	3,860	774	2,794	292	Dole	20.1%	72.4%	7.6%
DEARBORN	3,123	583	2,241	299	Dole	18.7%	71.8%	9.6%
DECATUR	3,411	685	2,400	326	Dole	20.1%	70.4%	9.6%
DE KALB	4,133	1,008	2,712	413	Dole	24.4%	65.6%	10.0%
DELAWARE	9,893	1,817	7,174	902	Dole	18.4%	72.5%	9.1%
DUBOIS	1,711	262	1,307	142	Dole	15.3%	76.4%	8.3%
ELKHART	14,799	2,760	10,515	1,524	Dole	18.6%	71.1%	10.3%
FAYETTE	1,885	350	1,386	149	Dole	18.6%	73.5%	7.9%
FLOYD	2,611	521	1,917	173	Dole	20.0%	73.4%	6.6%
FOUNTAIN	2,244	484	1,561	199	Dole	21.6%	69.6%	8.9%
FRANKLIN	1,429	273	1,031	125	Dole	19.1%	72.1%	8.7%
FULTON	2,659	543	1,834	282	Dole	20.4%	69.0%	10.6%
GIBSON	1,739	379	1,222	138	Dole	21.8%	70.3%	7.9%
GRANT	7,634	1,486	5,458	690	Dole	19.5%	71.5%	9.0%
GREENE	3,180	650	2,289	241	Dole	20.4%	72.0%	7.6%
HAMILTON	23,770	3,413	17,855	2,502	Dole	14.4%	75.1%	10.5%
HANCOCK	7,872	1,497	5,618	757	Dole	19.0%	71.4%	9.6%
HARRISON	1,835	360	1,357	118	Dole	19.6%	74.0%	6.4%
HENDRICKS	14,421	2,858	10,169	1,394	Dole	19.8%	70.5%	9.7%
HENRY	6,201	1,158	4,535	508	Dole	18.7%	73.1%	8.2%
HOWARD	8,466	1,821	5,850	795	Dole	21.5%	69.1%	9.4%
HUNTINGTON	4,649	837	3,375	437	Dole	18.0%	72.6%	9.4%
JACKSON	2,645	504	1,935	206	Dole	19.1%	73.2%	7.8%
JASPER	4,361	960	2,949	452	Dole	22.0%	67.6%	10.4%
JAY	2,713	576	1,857	280	Dole	21.2%	68.4%	10.3%
JEFFERSON	1,630	291	1,217	122	Dole	17.9%	74.7%	7.5%
JENNINGS	2,226	461	1,589	176	Dole	20.7%	71.4%	7.9%
JOHNSON	15,252	2,955	10,765	1,532	Dole	19.4%	70.6%	10.0%
KNOX	3,390	579	2,506	305	Dole	17.1%	73.9%	9.0%
KOSCIUSKO	9,420	1,962	6,472	986	Dole	20.8%	68.7%	10.5%
LAGRANGE	2,947	544	2,107	296	Dole	18.5%	71.5%	10.0%
LAKE	14,230	3,257	9,610	1,363	Dole	22.9%	67.5%	9.6%
LA PORTE	7,038	1,285	4,917	836	Dole	18.3%	69.9%	11.9%
LAWRENCE	5,059	1,206	3,412	441	Dole	23.8%	67.4%	8.7%
MADISON	12,526	2,245	9,213	1,068	Dole	17.9%	73.6%	8.5%
MARION	65,797	12,444	46,063	7,290	Dole	18.9%	70.0%	11.1%
MARSHALL	3,745	715	2,673	357	Dole	19.1%	71.4%	9.5%

INDIANA REPUBLICAN

1996

County	Total Vote	Buchanan	Dole	Forbes	Winner	Percentage of Total Vote Buchanan	Dole	Forbes
MARTIN	1,127	210	846	71	Dole	18.6%	75.1%	6.3%
MIAMI	3,637	817	2,538	282	Dole	22.5%	69.8%	7.8%
MONROE	7,711	1,148	5,676	887	Dole	14.9%	73.6%	11.5%
MONTGOMERY	5,995	1,390	4,605		Dole	23.2%	76.8%	
MORGAN	9,138	2,227	6,004	907	Dole	24.4%	65.7%	9.9%
NEWTON	1,594	351	1,035	208	Dole	22.0%	64.9%	13.0%
NOBLE	3,772	781	2,636	355	Dole	20.7%	69.9%	9.4%
OHIO	332	59	253	20	Dole	17.8%	76.2%	6.0%
ORANGE	2,426	476	1,721	229	Dole	19.6%	70.9%	9.4%
OWEN	1,918	420	1,342	156	Dole	21.9%	70.0%	8.1%
PARKE	2,419	483	1,714	222	Dole	20.0%	70.9%	9.2%
PERRY	801	138	596	67	Dole	17.2%	74.4%	8.4%
PIKE	1,251	265	878	108	Dole	21.2%	70.2%	8.6%
PORTER	10,916	2,311	7,214	1,391	Dole	21.2%	66.1%	12.7%
POSEY	1,401	268	1,017	116	Dole	19.1%	72.6%	8.3%
PULASKI	1,581	306	1,157	118	Dole	19.4%	73.2%	7.5%
PUTNAM	3,634	776	2,520	338	Dole	21.4%	69.3%	9.3%
RANDOLPH	3,407	732	2,346	329	Dole	21.5%	68.9%	9.7%
RIPLEY	2,524	545	1,785	194	Dole	21.6%	70.7%	7.7%
RUSH	3,506	771	2,403	332	Dole	22.0%	68.5%	9.5%
ST. JOSEPH	13,351	2,485	9,672	1,194	Dole	18.6%	72.4%	8.9%
SCOTT	793	220	527	46	Dole	27.7%	66.5%	5.8%
SHELBY	4,968	978	3,534	456	Dole	19.7%	71.1%	9.2%
SPENCER	1,946	398	1,361	187	Dole	20.5%	69.9%	9.6%
STARKE	1,463	324	1,036	103	Dole	22.1%	70.8%	7.0%
STEUBEN	3,737	699	2,510	528	Dole	18.7%	67.2%	14.1%
SULLIVAN	1,363	379	897	87	Dole	27.8%	65.8%	6.4%
SWITZERLAND	460	91	338	31	Dole	19.8%	73.5%	6.7%
TIPPECANOE	15,671	2,611	10,971	2,089	Dole	16.7%	70.0%	13.3%
TIPTON	3,103	613	2,191	299	Dole	19.8%	70.6%	9.6%
UNION	857	148	619	90	Dole	17.3%	72.2%	10.5%
VANDERBURGH	12,309	2,144	8,774	1,391	Dole	17.4%	71.3%	11.3%
VERMILLION	874	184	608	82	Dole	21.1%	69.6%	9.4%
VIGO	6,449	1,298	4,578	573	Dole	20.1%	71.0%	8.9%
WABASH	4,771	902	3,427	442	Dole	18.9%	71.8%	9.3%
WARREN	1,095	227	747	121	Dole	20.7%	68.2%	11.1%
WARRICK	4,403	846	3,058	499	Dole	19.2%	69.5%	11.3%
WASHINGTON	2,503	548	1,753	202	Dole	21.9%	70.0%	8.1%
WAYNE	8,539	1,451	6,144	944	Dole	17.0%	72.0%	11.1%
WELLS	2,301	537	1,764		Dole	23.3%	76.7%	
WHITE	4,369	934	2,879	556	Dole	21.4%	65.9%	12.7%
WHITLEY	3,184	778	2,091	315	Dole	24.4%	65.7%	9.9%
TOTAL	516,514	100,166	365,568	50,780	Dole	19.4%	70.8%	9.8%

IOWA

For all its importance, Iowa is a relative newcomer to the national spotlight. It stepped into the nation's political consciousness on a snowy January night in 1972, when George McGovern ran unexpectedly close to Edmund Muskie in the Democratic precinct caucus voting. While the results drew only a smidgen of attention in the next day's newspapers, it was enough to lend credibility to McGovern's dark-horse candidacy.

McGovern spent only a day and a half campaigning in Iowa before he made his breakthrough in 1972. Now it is routine for every candidate to spend at least several weeks in the state, and for little-known dark-horse contenders to devote even more time than that.

Candidates, though, who have tried to win Iowa by making only an occasional stop in the state do so at their peril. Ronald Reagan essentially bypassed the state in 1980 and lost the caucuses to George Bush, and then had to work overtime in New Hampshire to regain his position as the Republican front-runner.

Yet the thinking of Reagan's strategists was understandable. Front-runners, by and large, have little to gain in Iowa. At best, they survive.

That ability to flummox the experts has helped make the Iowa caucuses one of the most successful political inventions of recent times. And results are often not measured by who won and who lost, but who exceeded expectations and who did not. Sometimes, it has been the runner-up who enjoyed the big "Iowa bounce" and landed at the center of the national imagination.

McGovern was the first beneficiary of this momentum in

Recent Iowa Caucus Results

Iowa held its only presidential primary in 1916. Since 1972, its precinct caucuses have been a notable part of the political scene.

	DEMOCRATS			REPUBLICANS		
Year	Estimated Turnout	Candidates	%	Turnout	Candidates	%
1996 (Feb. 12)	50,000	BILL CLINTON*	100	96,451	BOB DOLE	26
					Pat Buchanan	23
					Lamar Alexander	18
					Steve Forbes	10
1992 (Feb. 10)	30,000	TOM HARKIN	76	—	NO CAUCUS VOTE	
		Uncommitted	12			
1988 (Feb. 8)	126,000	RICHARD GEPHARDT	31	108,838	BOB DOLE	37
		Paul Simon	27		Pat Robertson	25
		Michael Dukakis	22		George Bush	19
					Jack Kemp	11
1984 (Feb. 20)	75,000	WALTER MONDALE	49	—	NO CAUCUS VOTE	
		Gary Hart	16			
		George McGovern	10			
1980 (Jan. 21)	100,000	JIMMY CARTER*	59	106,051	GEORGE BUSH	32
		Edward Kennedy	31		Ronald Reagan	30
					Howard Baker	15
1976 (Jan. 19)	38,500	UNCOMMITTED	38	20,000	GERALD FORD*	45
		Jimmy Carter	29		Ronald Reagan	42
		Birch Bayh	11			
1972 (Jan. 24)	20,000	UNCOMMITTED	36	—	NO CAUCUS VOTE	
		Edmund Muskie	36			
		George McGovern	23			

Note: Democratic turnouts are estimates. Republican results are from the straw vote held in conjunction with the precinct caucuses. Percentages for Democratic candidates are based on a weighted measurement compiled by the Iowa Democratic Party. The 1976 GOP results are based on returns from a sampling of precincts. All candidates are listed that drew at least 10 percent of their party's vote. The names of winning candidates are capitalized. An asterisk (*) indicates an incumbent president.

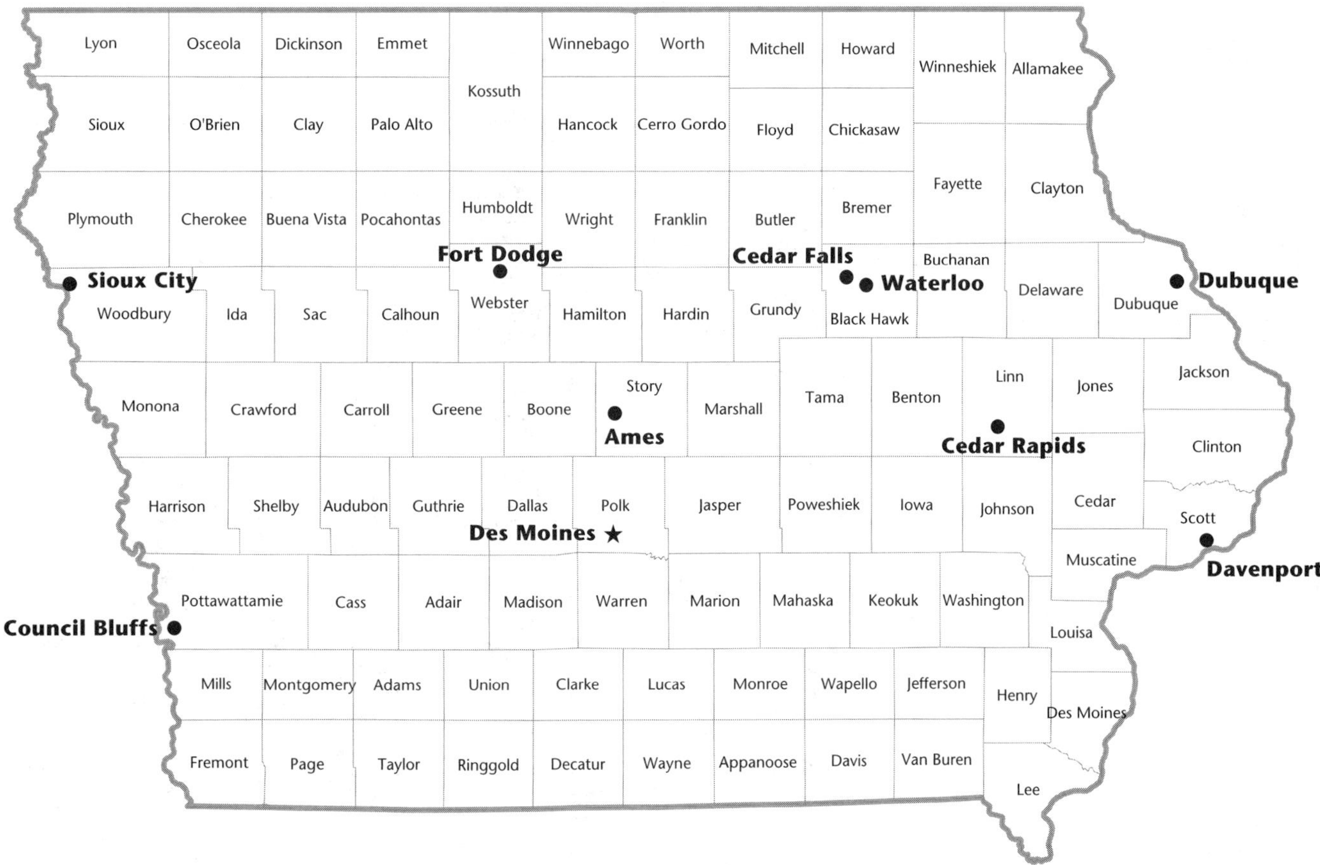

1972. Four years later, Iowa helped create the phenomenon of Jimmy Carter. Perhaps the quintessential Iowa bounce, though, was the one that surprised even its beneficiary, Gary Hart.

Walter Mondale came down from Minnesota to claim about half the 1984 Democratic caucus vote. But Hart got half the momentum with just 16 percent of the vote because he exceeded the modest expectations of the media (and because John Glenn and Alan Cranston fell miserably short by the same standard). A week later, Hart won New Hampshire.

In recent years, Iowa has been more successful at winnowing the field than serving as a harbinger of things to come. In 1988, the eventual nominees—Michael Dukakis and George Bush—both placed third in Iowa, while the two Iowa winners—Richard Gephardt and Bob Dole—were both out of the race by the end of March.

In 1992, Iowa Democrats rallied around their home-state senator, Tom Harkin, who was unable to gain traction elsewhere and also quit the race in March.

In 1996, Pat Buchanan got the Iowa bounce with a close second-place finish to Dole, but was unable to make the momentum extend beyond victory in New Hampshire.

Dole's winning vote share in Iowa fell by more than 10 percentage points from eight years earlier to 26 percent. Meanwhile, Buchanan nearly matched the 25 percent share that runner-up Pat Robertson had garnered in 1988.

But Buchanan's showing was not simply a reprise of Robertson's. Robertson carried 14 Iowa counties, mostly in the industrialized eastern half of the state and many in Democratic areas where the Republican caucuses offered a vacuum to be filled.

Buchanan carried 24 counties, mostly in rural southwest Iowa, where concern about the encroachment of big agricultural interests melded with social-issue conservatism. (Exit polling showed that religious conservatives cast about one-third of the statewide GOP caucus vote in 1996.)

Dole, though, enjoyed broad-based success in 1996 that belied his modest winning percentage. Of Iowa's 99 counties, he carried 70. As in 1988, Dole ran best in the small towns and farm country of rural Iowa. He was weaker in the larger population centers, carrying Polk County (Des Moines) by just seven votes over Lamar Alexander, and Linn County (Cedar Rapids) by just three votes over Alan Keyes.

Still, Dole was able to make his victory go further than he had eight years earlier, when his failures in the rest of the country led to joking references to him as "the president of Iowa."

IOWA REPUBLICAN CAUCUSES

1980

County	Total Vote	Baker	Bush	Reagan	Other	Winner	Percentage of Total Vote Baker	Bush	Reagan	Other
ADAIR	566	66	139	263	98	Reagan	11.7%	24.6%	46.5%	17.3%
ADAMS	252	35	35	104	78	Reagan	13.9%	13.9%	41.3%	31.0%
ALLAMAKEE	715	101	182	310	122	Reagan	14.1%	25.5%	43.4%	17.1%
APPANOOSE	393	41	67	227	58	Reagan	10.4%	17.0%	57.8%	14.8%
AUDUBON	348	26	99	110	113	Reagan	7.5%	28.4%	31.6%	32.5%
BENTON	920	117	268	214	321	Bush	12.7%	29.1%	23.3%	34.9%
BLACK HAWK	4,554	635	1,375	1,282	1,262	Bush	13.9%	30.2%	28.2%	27.7%
BOONE	969	117	320	304	228	Bush	12.1%	33.0%	31.4%	23.5%
BREMER	1,025	123	258	280	364	Reagan	12.0%	25.2%	27.3%	35.5%
BUCHANAN	604	70	160	189	185	Reagan	11.6%	26.5%	31.3%	30.6%
BUENA VISTA	764	200	248	194	122	Bush	26.2%	32.5%	25.4%	16.0%
BUTLER	736	97	181	328	130	Reagan	13.2%	24.6%	44.6%	17.7%
CALHOUN	290	44	80	103	63	Reagan	15.2%	27.6%	35.5%	21.7%
CARROLL	547	61	184	136	166	Bush	11.2%	33.6%	24.9%	30.3%
CASS	861	66	186	462	147	Reagan	7.7%	21.6%	53.7%	17.1%
CEDAR	599	67	228	125	179	Bush	11.2%	38.1%	20.9%	29.9%
CERRO GORDO	1,692	416	511	527	238	Reagan	24.6%	30.2%	31.1%	14.1%
CHEROKEE	385	65	184	92	44	Bush	16.9%	47.8%	23.9%	11.4%
CHICKASAW	438	64	97	142	135	Reagan	14.6%	22.1%	32.4%	30.8%
CLARKE	221	24	72	85	40	Reagan	10.9%	32.6%	38.5%	18.1%
CLAY	769	107	328	179	155	Bush	13.9%	42.7%	23.3%	20.2%
CLAYTON	594	112	176	142	164	Bush	18.9%	29.6%	23.9%	27.6%
CLINTON	1,527	303	582	412	230	Bush	19.8%	38.1%	27.0%	15.1%
CRAWFORD	671	72	262	190	147	Bush	10.7%	39.0%	28.3%	21.9%
DALLAS	1,175	198	423	326	228	Bush	16.9%	36.0%	27.7%	19.4%
DAVIS	236	28	26	145	37	Reagan	11.9%	11.0%	61.4%	15.7%
DECATUR	377	70	50	176	81	Reagan	18.6%	13.3%	46.7%	21.5%
DELAWARE	526	79	170	123	154	Bush	15.0%	32.3%	23.4%	29.3%
DES MOINES	1,108	154	456	303	195	Bush	13.9%	41.2%	27.3%	17.6%
DICKINSON	572	166	177	133	96	Bush	29.0%	30.9%	23.3%	16.8%
DUBUQUE	1,834	232	714	309	579	Bush	12.6%	38.9%	16.8%	31.6%
EMMET	466	102	118	141	105	Reagan	21.9%	25.3%	30.3%	22.5%
FAYETTE	1,086	98	279	402	307	Reagan	9.0%	25.7%	37.0%	28.3%
FLOYD	601	102	125	172	202	Reagan	17.0%	20.8%	28.6%	33.6%
FRANKLIN	729	132	239	214	144	Bush	18.1%	32.8%	29.4%	19.8%
FREMONT	287	30	72	139	46	Reagan	10.5%	25.1%	48.4%	16.0%
GREENE	554	90	193	137	134	Bush	16.2%	34.8%	24.7%	24.2%
GRUNDY	653	91	118	250	194	Reagan	13.9%	18.1%	38.3%	29.7%
GUTHRIE	530	55	141	239	95	Reagan	10.4%	26.6%	45.1%	17.9%
HAMILTON	904	108	126	548	122	Reagan	11.9%	13.9%	60.6%	13.5%
HANCOCK	565	77	128	266	94	Reagan	13.6%	22.7%	47.1%	16.6%
HARDIN	976	159	193	318	306	Reagan	16.3%	19.8%	32.6%	31.4%
HARRISON	638	40	177	245	176	Reagan	6.3%	27.7%	38.4%	27.6%
HENRY	704	181	183	197	143	Reagan	25.7%	26.0%	28.0%	20.3%
HOWARD	311	72	96	110	33	Reagan	23.2%	30.9%	35.4%	10.6%
HUMBOLDT	418	63	77	188	90	Reagan	15.1%	18.4%	45.0%	21.5%
IDA	324	52	100	120	52	Reagan	16.0%	30.9%	37.0%	16.0%
IOWA	603	72	198	134	199	Bush	11.9%	32.8%	22.2%	33.0%
JACKSON	466	88	156	125	97	Bush	18.9%	33.5%	26.8%	20.8%
JASPER	1,594	271	404	448	471	Reagan	17.0%	25.3%	28.1%	29.5%

IOWA REPUBLICAN CAUCUSES

1980

County	Total Vote	Baker	Bush	Reagan	Other	Winner	Percentage of Total Vote Baker	Bush	Reagan	Other
JEFFERSON	320	37	78	122	83	Reagan	11.6%	24.4%	38.1%	25.9%
JOHNSON	3,619	436	1,494	417	1,272	Bush	12.0%	41.3%	11.5%	35.1%
JONES	606	75	202	102	227	Bush	12.4%	33.3%	16.8%	37.5%
KEOKUK	404	61	97	142	104	Reagan	15.1%	24.0%	35.1%	25.7%
KOSSUTH	542	159	116	165	102	Reagan	29.3%	21.4%	30.4%	18.8%
LEE	688	70	242	197	179	Bush	10.2%	35.2%	28.6%	26.0%
LINN	5,591	713	2,259	805	1,814	Bush	12.8%	40.4%	14.4%	32.4%
LOUISA	438	80	113	119	126	Reagan	18.3%	25.8%	27.2%	28.8%
LUCAS	358	78	62	129	89	Reagan	21.8%	17.3%	36.0%	24.9%
LYON	389	47	101	179	62	Reagan	12.1%	26.0%	46.0%	15.9%
MADISON	1,040	191	254	395	200	Reagan	18.4%	24.4%	38.0%	19.2%
MAHASKA	906	188	177	397	144	Reagan	20.8%	19.5%	43.8%	15.9%
MARION	971	210	315	269	177	Bush	21.6%	32.4%	27.7%	18.2%
MARSHALL	2,387	311	772	831	473	Reagan	13.0%	32.3%	34.8%	19.8%
MILLS	452	27	121	235	69	Reagan	6.0%	26.8%	52.0%	15.3%
MITCHELL	535	99	178	159	99	Bush	18.5%	33.3%	29.7%	18.5%
MONONA	256	33	74	84	65	Reagan	12.9%	28.9%	32.8%	25.4%
MONROE	248	49	70	100	29	Reagan	19.8%	28.2%	40.3%	11.7%
MONTGOMERY	649	81	171	208	189	Reagan	12.5%	26.3%	32.0%	29.1%
MUSCATINE	1,172	141	577	247	207	Bush	12.0%	49.2%	21.1%	17.7%
O'BRIEN	620	98	144	217	161	Reagan	15.8%	23.2%	35.0%	26.0%
OSCEOLA	228	60	50	77	41	Reagan	26.3%	21.9%	33.8%	18.0%
PAGE	795	182	189	282	142	Reagan	22.9%	23.8%	35.5%	17.9%
PALO ALTO	287	25	127	88	47	Bush	8.7%	44.3%	30.7%	16.4%
PLYMOUTH	816	179	247	269	121	Reagan	21.9%	30.3%	33.0%	14.8%
POCAHONTAS	322	46	107	99	70	Bush	14.3%	33.2%	30.7%	21.7%
POLK	14,945	2,951	4,985	3,245	3,764	Bush	19.7%	33.4%	21.7%	25.2%
POTTAWATTAMIE	2,236	261	556	1,094	325	Reagan	11.7%	24.9%	48.9%	14.5%
POWESHIEK	752	151	229	187	185	Bush	20.1%	30.5%	24.9%	24.6%
RINGGOLD	403	77	96	171	59	Reagan	19.1%	23.8%	42.4%	14.6%
SAC	497	115	175	110	97	Bush	23.1%	35.2%	22.1%	19.5%
SCOTT	5,121	513	2,061	1,703	844	Bush	10.0%	40.2%	33.3%	16.5%
SHELBY	693	47	151	378	117	Reagan	6.8%	21.8%	54.5%	16.9%
SIOUX	1,231	177	376	397	281	Reagan	16.4%	30.5%	32.3%	22.8%
STORY	3,888	546	1,431	820	1,091	Bush	14.0%	36.8%	21.1%	28.1%
TAMA	868	69	205	361	233	Reagan	7.9%	23.6%	41.6%	26.8%
TAYLOR	326	41	75	142	68	Reagan	12.6%	23.0%	43.6%	20.9%
UNION	426	56	106	167	97	Reagan	13.1%	24.9%	39.2%	22.8%
VAN BUREN	512	56	123	244	89	Reagan	10.9%	24.0%	47.7%	17.4%
WAPELLO	1,041	158	363	371	149	Reagan	15.2%	34.9%	35.6%	14.3%
WARREN	1,584	234	503	420	427	Bush	14.8%	31.8%	26.5%	27.0%
WASHINGTON	562	103	163	137	159	Bush	18.3%	29.0%	24.4%	28.3%
WAYNE	391	43	61	198	89	Reagan	11.0%	15.6%	50.6%	22.8%
WEBSTER	1,362	184	406	576	196	Reagan	13.5%	29.8%	42.3%	14.4%
WINNEBAGO	605	81	210	238	76	Reagan	13.4%	34.7%	39.3%	12.6%
WINNESHIEK	782	196	219	112	255	Bush	25.1%	28.0%	14.3%	32.6%
WOODBURY	3,554	426	1,138	1,139	851	Reagan	12.0%	32.0%	32.0%	23.9%
WORTH	178	51	36	73	18	Reagan	28.7%	20.2%	41.0%	10.1%
WRIGHT	814	164	154	318	178	Reagan	20.1%	18.9%	39.1%	21.9%
TOTAL	106,087	16,215	33,520	31,243	25,109	Bush	15.3%	31.6%	29.5%	23.7%
Published Totals	106,051	16,216	33,530	31,348	24,957	Bush	15.3%	31.6%	29.6%	23.5%

IOWA REPUBLICAN CAUCUSES

1988

County	Total Vote	Bush	Dole	Kemp	Robertson	Other	Winner	Percentage of Total Vote Bush	Dole	Kemp	Robertson	Other
ADAIR	441	64	218	30	95	34	Dole	14.5%	49.4%	6.8%	21.5%	7.7%
ADAMS	268	34	163	33	30	8	Dole	12.7%	60.8%	12.3%	11.2%	3.0%
ALLAMAKEE	611	143	158	49	217	44	Robertson	23.4%	25.9%	8.0%	35.5%	7.2%
APPANOOSE	474	92	236	22	101	23	Dole	19.4%	49.8%	4.6%	21.3%	4.9%
AUDUBON	260	31	146	24	47	12	Dole	11.9%	56.2%	9.2%	18.1%	4.6%
BENTON	721	100	319	66	173	63	Dole	13.9%	44.2%	9.2%	24.0%	8.7%
BLACK HAWK	3,447	718	1,291	530	673	235	Dole	20.8%	37.5%	15.4%	19.5%	6.8%
BOONE	1,056	161	409	116	316	54	Dole	15.2%	38.7%	11.0%	29.9%	5.1%
BREMER	903	133	498	83	118	71	Dole	14.7%	55.1%	9.2%	13.1%	7.9%
BUCHANAN	749	92	267	167	189	34	Dole	12.3%	35.6%	22.3%	25.2%	4.5%
BUENA VISTA	979	154	388	82	253	102	Dole	15.7%	39.6%	8.4%	25.8%	10.4%
BUTLER	595	106	312	51	92	34	Dole	17.8%	52.4%	8.6%	15.5%	5.7%
CALHOUN	445	83	199	24	127	12	Dole	18.7%	44.7%	5.4%	28.5%	2.7%
CARROLL	438	72	219	47	69	31	Dole	16.4%	50.0%	10.7%	15.8%	7.1%
CASS	1,042	143	452	70	289	88	Dole	13.7%	43.4%	6.7%	27.7%	8.4%
CEDAR	586	101	244	81	128	32	Dole	17.2%	41.6%	13.8%	21.8%	5.5%
CERRO GORDO	1,857	242	669	207	548	191	Dole	13.0%	36.0%	11.1%	29.5%	10.3%
CHEROKEE	883	231	382	61	177	32	Dole	26.2%	43.3%	6.9%	20.0%	3.6%
CHICKASAW	299	67	166	22	30	14	Dole	22.4%	55.5%	7.4%	10.0%	4.7%
CLARKE	273	45	122	37	54	15	Dole	16.5%	44.7%	13.6%	19.8%	5.5%
CLAY	741	177	291	48	194	31	Dole	23.9%	39.3%	6.5%	26.2%	4.2%
CLAYTON	561	83	246	49	124	59	Dole	14.8%	43.9%	8.7%	22.1%	10.5%
CLINTON	1,860	436	514	104	555	251	Robertson	23.4%	27.6%	5.6%	29.8%	13.5%
CRAWFORD	464	71	207	36	131	19	Dole	15.3%	44.6%	7.8%	28.2%	4.1%
DALLAS	1,408	286	515	120	380	107	Dole	20.3%	36.6%	8.5%	27.0%	7.6%
DAVIS	306	41	107	17	130	11	Robertson	13.4%	35.0%	5.6%	42.5%	3.6%
DECATUR	378	60	159	26	86	47	Dole	15.9%	42.1%	6.9%	22.8%	12.4%
DELAWARE	495	96	188	79	108	24	Dole	19.4%	38.0%	16.0%	21.8%	4.8%
DES MOINES	1,673	382	452	118	604	117	Robertson	22.8%	27.0%	7.1%	36.1%	7.0%
DICKINSON	582	118	233	38	172	21	Dole	20.3%	40.0%	6.5%	29.6%	3.6%
DUBUQUE	1,716	284	518	237	573	104	Robertson	16.6%	30.2%	13.8%	33.4%	6.1%
EMMET	350	68	145	30	96	11	Dole	19.4%	41.4%	8.6%	27.4%	3.1%
FAYETTE	807	159	320	50	207	71	Dole	19.7%	39.7%	6.2%	25.7%	8.8%
FLOYD	578	64	263	49	128	74	Dole	11.1%	45.5%	8.5%	22.1%	12.8%
FRANKLIN	559	79	294	50	102	34	Dole	14.1%	52.6%	8.9%	18.2%	6.1%
FREMONT	344	101	130	22	73	18	Dole	29.4%	37.8%	6.4%	21.2%	5.2%
GREENE	622	72	272	34	212	32	Dole	11.6%	43.7%	5.5%	34.1%	5.1%
GRUNDY	633	99	306	72	114	42	Dole	15.6%	48.3%	11.4%	18.0%	6.6%
GUTHRIE	422	61	195	34	98	34	Dole	14.5%	46.2%	8.1%	23.2%	8.1%
HAMILTON	846	99	337	77	291	42	Dole	11.7%	39.8%	9.1%	34.4%	5.0%
HANCOCK	627	50	204	80	238	55	Robertson	8.0%	32.5%	12.8%	38.0%	8.8%
HARDIN	903	98	404	91	255	55	Dole	10.9%	44.7%	10.1%	28.2%	6.1%
HARRISON	448	57	185	49	133	24	Dole	12.7%	41.3%	10.9%	29.7%	5.4%
HENRY	917	171	332	48	327	39	Dole	18.6%	36.2%	5.2%	35.7%	4.3%
HOWARD	329	72	113	21	81	42	Dole	21.9%	34.3%	6.4%	24.6%	12.8%
HUMBOLDT	387	62	191	49	66	19	Dole	16.0%	49.4%	12.7%	17.1%	4.9%
IDA	428	73	157	30	156	12	Dole	17.1%	36.7%	7.0%	36.4%	2.8%
IOWA	465	80	217	51	86	31	Dole	17.2%	46.7%	11.0%	18.5%	6.7%
JACKSON	623	78	214	19	227	85	Robertson	12.5%	34.3%	3.0%	36.4%	13.6%
JASPER	1,467	282	506	199	334	146	Dole	19.2%	34.5%	13.6%	22.8%	10.0%

IOWA REPUBLICAN CAUCUSES

1988

County	Total Vote	Bush	Dole	Kemp	Robertson	Other	Winner	Percentage of Total Vote				
								Bush	Dole	Kemp	Robertson	Other
JEFFERSON	785	170	243	31	297	44	Robertson	21.7%	31.0%	3.9%	37.8%	5.6%
JOHNSON	3,443	721	1,410	405	595	312	Dole	20.9%	41.0%	11.8%	17.3%	9.1%
JONES	659	104	328	35	158	34	Dole	15.8%	49.8%	5.3%	24.0%	5.2%
KEOKUK	475	83	198	24	146	24	Dole	17.5%	41.7%	5.1%	30.7%	5.1%
KOSSUTH	656	71	259	73	207	46	Dole	10.8%	39.5%	11.1%	31.6%	7.0%
LEE	928	198	264	80	297	89	Robertson	21.3%	28.4%	8.6%	32.0%	9.6%
LINN	6,449	1,105	1,999	726	1,911	708	Dole	17.1%	31.0%	11.3%	29.6%	11.0%
LOUISA	470	64	272	31	86	17	Dole	13.6%	57.9%	6.6%	18.3%	3.6%
LUCAS	305	61	123	44	63	14	Dole	20.0%	40.3%	14.4%	20.7%	4.6%
LYON	519	92	243	75	92	17	Dole	17.7%	46.8%	14.5%	17.7%	3.3%
MADISON	553	99	219	68	122	45	Dole	17.9%	39.6%	12.3%	22.1%	8.1%
MAHASKA	1,083	129	368	57	474	55	Robertson	11.9%	34.0%	5.3%	43.8%	5.1%
MARION	1,255	156	377	298	321	103	Dole	12.4%	30.0%	23.7%	25.6%	8.2%
MARSHALL	1,963	489	691	165	497	121	Dole	24.9%	35.2%	8.4%	25.3%	6.2%
MILLS	404	83	183	36	74	28	Dole	20.5%	45.3%	8.9%	18.3%	6.9%
MITCHELL	416	101	207	34	56	18	Dole	24.3%	49.8%	8.2%	13.5%	4.3%
MONONA	382	67	178	25	104	8	Dole	17.5%	46.6%	6.5%	27.2%	2.1%
MONROE	252	35	138	26	44	9	Dole	13.9%	54.8%	10.3%	17.5%	3.6%
MONTGOMERY	621	121	322	41	86	51	Dole	19.5%	51.9%	6.6%	13.8%	8.2%
MUSCATINE	1,235	357	410	93	224	151	Dole	28.9%	33.2%	7.5%	18.1%	12.2%
O'BRIEN	785	131	320	150	132	52	Dole	16.7%	40.8%	19.1%	16.8%	6.6%
OSCEOLA	421	35	178	111	40	57	Dole	8.3%	42.3%	26.4%	9.5%	13.5%
PAGE	906	183	292	55	295	81	Robertson	20.2%	32.2%	6.1%	32.6%	8.9%
PALO ALTO	300	60	131	30	63	16	Dole	20.0%	43.7%	10.0%	21.0%	5.3%
PLYMOUTH	989	166	345	151	212	115	Dole	16.8%	34.9%	15.3%	21.4%	11.6%
POCAHONTAS	286	54	109	32	83	8	Dole	18.9%	38.1%	11.2%	29.0%	2.8%
POLK	15,795	3,443	5,757	1,801	3,043	1,751	Dole	21.8%	36.4%	11.4%	19.3%	11.1%
POTTAWATTAMIE	2,481	461	826	318	610	266	Dole	18.6%	33.3%	12.8%	24.6%	10.7%
POWESHIEK	668	165	282	95	65	61	Dole	24.7%	42.2%	14.2%	9.7%	9.1%
RINGGOLD	315	57	146	38	56	18	Dole	18.1%	46.3%	12.1%	17.8%	5.7%
SAC	517	74	256	37	101	49	Dole	14.3%	49.5%	7.2%	19.5%	9.5%
SCOTT	5,428	1,309	1,559	537	1,489	534	Dole	24.1%	28.7%	9.9%	27.4%	9.8%
SHELBY	738	79	233	109	237	80	Robertson	10.7%	31.6%	14.8%	32.1%	10.8%
SIOUX	1,981	273	626	585	441	56	Dole	16.4%	31.6%	29.5%	22.3%	2.8%
STORY	4,047	675	1,795	541	677	359	Dole	16.7%	44.4%	13.4%	16.7%	8.9%
TAMA	608	83	241	49	210	25	Dole	13.7%	39.6%	8.1%	34.5%	4.1%
TAYLOR	495	96	245	53	85	16	Dole	19.4%	49.5%	10.7%	17.2%	3.2%
UNION	472	109	136	55	152	20	Robertson	23.1%	28.8%	11.7%	32.2%	4.2%
VAN BUREN	443	116	209	41	60	17	Dole	26.2%	47.2%	9.3%	13.5%	3.8%
WAPELLO	1,008	158	212	117	485	36	Robertson	15.7%	21.0%	11.6%	48.1%	3.6%
WARREN	1,575	260	563	182	425	145	Dole	16.5%	35.7%	11.6%	27.0%	9.2%
WASHINGTON	783	118	290	71	248	56	Dole	15.1%	37.0%	9.1%	31.7%	7.2%
WAYNE	246	41	85	41	69	10	Dole	16.7%	34.6%	16.7%	28.0%	4.1%
WEBSTER	1,173	192	485	108	287	101	Dole	16.4%	41.3%	9.2%	24.5%	8.6%
WINNEBAGO	577	114	243	39	166	15	Dole	19.8%	42.1%	6.8%	28.8%	2.6%
WINNESHIEK	671	103	284	40	106	138	Dole	15.4%	42.3%	6.0%	15.8%	20.6%
WOODBURY	3,234	584	869	536	868	377	Dole	18.1%	26.9%	16.6%	26.8%	11.7%
WORTH	180	30	111	6	22	11	Dole	16.7%	61.7%	3.3%	12.2%	6.1%
WRIGHT	597	72	296	54	141	34	Dole	12.1%	49.6%	9.0%	23.6%	5.7%
TOTAL	108,838	20,218	40,629	12,078	26,729	9,184	Dole	18.6%	37.3%	11.1%	24.6%	8.4%

Note: Results were tabulated by the News Election Service (NES) and distributed by the Iowa Republican Party.

IOWA REPUBLICAN CAUCUSES

1996

County	Total Vote	Alexander	Buchanan	Dole	Forbes	Other	Winner	Percentage of Total Vote: Alexander	Buchanan	Dole	Forbes	Other
ADAIR	343	92	40	128	16	67	Dole	26.8%	11.7%	37.3%	4.7%	19.5%
ADAMS	214	30	56	68	20	40	Dole	14.0%	26.2%	31.8%	9.3%	18.7%
ALLAMAKEE	518	81	177	140	41	79	Buchanan	15.6%	34.2%	27.0%	7.9%	15.3%
APPANOOSE	425	52	70	151	49	103	Dole	12.2%	16.5%	35.5%	11.5%	24.2%
AUDUBON	154	38	25	68	10	13	Dole	24.7%	16.2%	44.2%	6.5%	8.4%
BENTON	687	57	172	201	55	202	Dole	8.3%	25.0%	29.3%	8.0%	29.4%
BLACK HAWK	3,486	475	724	1,055	333	899	Dole	13.6%	20.8%	30.3%	9.6%	25.8%
BOONE	874	178	242	203	73	178	Buchanan	20.4%	27.7%	23.2%	8.4%	20.4%
BREMER	820	128	137	300	86	169	Dole	15.6%	16.7%	36.6%	10.5%	20.6%
BUCHANAN	653	81	149	214	65	144	Dole	12.4%	22.8%	32.8%	10.0%	22.1%
BUENA VISTA	957	165	296	231	74	191	Buchanan	17.2%	30.9%	24.1%	7.7%	20.0%
BUTLER	586	116	119	197	51	103	Dole	19.8%	20.3%	33.6%	8.7%	17.6%
CALHOUN	328	49	105	92	23	59	Buchanan	14.9%	32.0%	28.0%	7.0%	18.0%
CARROLL	387	68	144	75	26	74	Buchanan	17.6%	37.2%	19.4%	6.7%	19.1%
CASS	734	149	110	263	71	141	Dole	20.3%	15.0%	35.8%	9.7%	19.2%
CEDAR	550	56	128	188	49	129	Dole	10.2%	23.3%	34.2%	8.9%	23.5%
CERRO GORDO	1,481	112	376	434	231	328	Dole	7.6%	25.4%	29.3%	15.6%	22.1%
CHEROKEE	492	100	120	150	42	80	Dole	20.3%	24.4%	30.5%	8.5%	16.3%
CHICKASAW	411	47	94	134	32	104	Dole	11.4%	22.9%	32.6%	7.8%	25.3%
CLARKE	257	56	54	72	23	52	Dole	21.8%	21.0%	28.0%	8.9%	20.2%
CLAY	811	221	110	273	86	121	Dole	27.3%	13.6%	33.7%	10.6%	14.9%
CLAYTON	435	63	100	141	44	87	Dole	14.5%	23.0%	32.4%	10.1%	20.0%
CLINTON	1,313	328	269	280	132	304	Alexander	25.0%	20.5%	21.3%	10.1%	23.2%
CRAWFORD	278	24	88	92	24	50	Dole	8.6%	31.7%	33.1%	8.6%	18.0%
DALLAS	1,617	378	324	401	219	295	Dole	23.4%	20.0%	24.8%	13.5%	18.2%
DAVIS	463	42	91	126	49	155	Dole	9.1%	19.7%	27.2%	10.6%	33.5%
DECATUR	255	55	64	87	13	36	Dole	21.6%	25.1%	34.1%	5.1%	14.1%
DELAWARE	470	64	105	127	47	127	Dole	13.6%	22.3%	27.0%	10.0%	27.0%
DES MOINES	1,109	197	318	269	129	196	Buchanan	17.8%	28.7%	24.3%	11.6%	17.7%
DICKINSON	486	65	73	152	67	129	Dole	13.4%	15.0%	31.3%	13.8%	26.5%
DUBUQUE	1,926	135	757	327	132	575	Buchanan	7.0%	39.3%	17.0%	6.9%	29.9%
EMMET	241	42	44	89	8	58	Dole	17.4%	18.3%	36.9%	3.3%	24.1%
FAYETTE	795	95	139	250	56	255	Dole	11.9%	17.5%	31.4%	7.0%	32.1%
FLOYD	433	83	108	125	39	78	Dole	19.2%	24.9%	28.9%	9.0%	18.0%
FRANKLIN	500	77	93	191	39	100	Dole	15.4%	18.6%	38.2%	7.8%	20.0%
FREMONT	247	10	27	112	21	77	Dole	4.0%	10.9%	45.3%	8.5%	31.2%
GREENE	451	113	104	115	24	95	Dole	25.1%	23.1%	25.5%	5.3%	21.1%
GRUNDY	464	120	92	147	27	78	Dole	25.9%	19.8%	31.7%	5.8%	16.8%
GUTHRIE	489	110	119	129	36	95	Dole	22.5%	24.3%	26.4%	7.4%	19.4%
HAMILTON	636	120	201	192	45	78	Buchanan	18.9%	31.6%	30.2%	7.1%	12.3%
HANCOCK	473	68	161	151	20	73	Buchanan	14.4%	34.0%	31.9%	4.2%	15.4%
HARDIN	732	120	152	166	82	212	Dole	16.4%	20.8%	22.7%	11.2%	29.0%
HARRISON	493	90	144	173	48	38	Dole	18.3%	29.2%	35.1%	9.7%	7.7%
HENRY	572	119	141	146	51	115	Dole	20.8%	24.7%	25.5%	8.9%	20.1%
HOWARD	281	41	95	91	20	34	Buchanan	14.6%	33.8%	32.4%	7.1%	12.1%
HUMBOLDT	370	48	92	110	33	87	Dole	13.0%	24.9%	29.7%	8.9%	23.5%
IDA	318	45	145	78	22	28	Buchanan	14.2%	45.6%	24.5%	6.9%	8.8%
IOWA	643	157	109	128	30	219	Alexander	24.4%	17.0%	19.9%	4.7%	34.1%
JACKSON	447	49	130	154	48	66	Dole	11.0%	29.1%	34.5%	10.7%	14.8%
JASPER	1,284	278	279	349	97	281	Dole	21.7%	21.7%	27.2%	7.6%	21.9%

IOWA REPUBLICAN CAUCUSES

1996

County	Total Vote	Alexander	Buchanan	Dole	Forbes	Other	Winner	Percentage of Total Vote Alexander	Buchanan	Dole	Forbes	Other
JEFFERSON	587	51	111	156	85	184	Dole	8.7%	18.9%	26.6%	14.5%	31.3%
JOHNSON	2,579	496	360	638	331	754	Dole	19.2%	14.0%	24.7%	12.8%	29.2%
JONES	642	106	156	181	56	143	Dole	16.5%	24.3%	28.2%	8.7%	22.3%
KEOKUK	327	38	88	109	27	65	Dole	11.6%	26.9%	33.3%	8.3%	19.9%
KOSSUTH	556	62	173	209	24	88	Dole	11.2%	31.1%	37.6%	4.3%	15.8%
LEE	694	85	158	180	84	187	Dole	12.2%	22.8%	25.9%	12.1%	26.9%
LINN	6,359	1,103	1,179	1,372	610	2,095	Dole	17.3%	18.5%	21.6%	9.6%	32.9%
LOUISA	368	56	83	129	46	54	Dole	15.2%	22.6%	35.1%	12.5%	14.7%
LUCAS	275	70	68	63	17	57	Alexander	25.5%	24.7%	22.9%	6.2%	20.7%
LYON	427	96	143	111	19	58	Buchanan	22.5%	33.5%	26.0%	4.4%	13.6%
MADISON	527	112	125	135	57	98	Dole	21.3%	23.7%	25.6%	10.8%	18.6%
MAHASKA	938	152	255	252	49	230	Buchanan	16.2%	27.2%	26.9%	5.2%	24.5%
MARION	1,094	203	274	230	78	309	Buchanan	18.6%	25.0%	21.0%	7.1%	28.2%
MARSHALL	1,452	392	364	355	148	193	Alexander	27.0%	25.1%	24.4%	10.2%	13.3%
MILLS	446	13	73	159	30	171	Dole	2.9%	16.4%	35.7%	6.7%	38.3%
MITCHELL	582	59	120	273	51	79	Dole	10.1%	20.6%	46.9%	8.8%	13.6%
MONONA	264	18	127	82	15	22	Buchanan	6.8%	48.1%	31.1%	5.7%	8.3%
MONROE	148	19	36	58	13	22	Dole	12.8%	24.3%	39.2%	8.8%	14.9%
MONTGOMERY	354	49	69	146	33	57	Dole	13.8%	19.5%	41.2%	9.3%	16.1%
MUSCATINE	1,148	240	160	265	123	360	Dole	20.9%	13.9%	23.1%	10.7%	31.4%
O'BRIEN	705	133	234	181	47	110	Buchanan	18.9%	33.2%	25.7%	6.7%	15.6%
OSCEOLA	174	16	68	54	12	24	Buchanan	9.2%	39.1%	31.0%	6.9%	13.8%
PAGE	468	66	71	215	33	83	Dole	14.1%	15.2%	45.9%	7.1%	17.7%
PALO ALTO	215	51	47	65	6	46	Dole	23.7%	21.9%	30.2%	2.8%	21.4%
PLYMOUTH	945	122	293	259	80	191	Buchanan	12.9%	31.0%	27.4%	8.5%	20.2%
POCAHONTAS	272	35	72	69	19	77	Buchanan	12.9%	26.5%	25.4%	7.0%	28.3%
POLK	15,951	3,542	3,157	3,549	2,287	3,416	Dole	22.2%	19.8%	22.2%	14.3%	21.4%
POTTAWATTAMIE	2,098	249	602	636	199	412	Dole	11.9%	28.7%	30.3%	9.5%	19.6%
POWESHIEK	626	173	122	167	49	115	Alexander	27.6%	19.5%	26.7%	7.8%	18.4%
RINGGOLD	175	39	32	69	18	17	Dole	22.3%	18.3%	39.4%	10.3%	9.7%
SAC	447	97	124	140	29	57	Dole	21.7%	27.7%	31.3%	6.5%	12.8%
SCOTT	4,813	932	902	1,096	556	1,327	Dole	19.4%	18.7%	22.8%	11.6%	27.6%
SHELBY	432	39	139	114	20	120	Buchanan	9.0%	32.2%	26.4%	4.6%	27.8%
SIOUX	2,180	357	845	420	68	490	Buchanan	16.4%	38.8%	19.3%	3.1%	22.5%
STORY	3,400	628	586	906	329	951	Dole	18.5%	17.2%	26.6%	9.7%	28.0%
TAMA	229	32	49	75	28	45	Dole	14.0%	21.4%	32.8%	12.2%	19.7%
TAYLOR	155	20	34	77	3	21	Dole	12.9%	21.9%	49.7%	1.9%	13.5%
UNION	408	63	102	138	37	68	Dole	15.4%	25.0%	33.8%	9.1%	16.7%
VAN BUREN	282	27	79	70	43	63	Buchanan	9.6%	28.0%	24.8%	15.2%	22.3%
WAPELLO	734	53	171	227	68	215	Dole	7.2%	23.3%	30.9%	9.3%	29.3%
WARREN	1,533	333	374	399	214	213	Dole	21.7%	24.4%	26.0%	14.0%	13.9%
WASHINGTON	676	119	166	214	48	129	Dole	17.6%	24.6%	31.7%	7.1%	19.1%
WAYNE	224	50	67	74	15	18	Dole	22.3%	29.9%	33.0%	6.7%	8.0%
WEBSTER	1,134	157	370	217	150	240	Buchanan	13.8%	32.6%	19.1%	13.2%	21.2%
WINNEBAGO	419	48	96	164	21	90	Dole	11.5%	22.9%	39.1%	5.0%	21.5%
WINNESHIEK	590	112	116	188	67	107	Dole	19.0%	19.7%	31.9%	11.4%	18.1%
WOODBURY	3,152	452	1,291	663	358	388	Buchanan	14.3%	41.0%	21.0%	11.4%	12.3%
WORTH	197	27	41	86	13	30	Dole	13.7%	20.8%	43.7%	6.6%	15.2%
WRIGHT	661	124	128	208	45	156	Dole	18.8%	19.4%	31.5%	6.8%	23.6%
TOTAL	96,451	17,003	22,512	25,378	9,816	21,742	Dole	17.6%	23.3%	26.3%	10.2%	22.5%

KANSAS

Kansas was the birthplace of several candidates who sought the White House in the late twentieth century. Gary Hart grew up in Ottawa in the eastern part of the state. Arlen Specter (who briefly pursued the 1996 Republican nomination) was born in Wichita.

But none made their mark in Kansas politics like Bob Dole, who was born, raised and sunk roots in the small town of Russell. And for nearly two decades, Kansas tried hard to boost Dole's presidential ambitions, although the results were not always as planned.

On Dole's first try for the White House in 1980, Kansas created its first-ever presidential primary. But his candidacy collapsed quickly, and he did not even enter his home-state primary that spring.

On Dole's second presidential run in 1988, Kansas Republicans got their licks in early with a pre–Super Tuesday caucus that Dole dominated. Pat Robertson tried to rally religious conservatives in parts of Kansas but failed to win a single delegate. Yet ultimately, Dole abandoned his candidacy before the convention, and all the Kansas delegates ended up voting for nominee George Bush.

In 1996, Kansas first scheduled a presidential primary, then canceled it, although the change did not threaten Dole's control of the delegation.

Not only were Kansas Republicans loyal to their longtime senator, but they sometimes looked askance at his presidential rivals, even when Dole was not on the ballot. President Bush won a comparatively modest 62 percent of the Kansas GOP primary vote in 1992, his second-lowest share of the primary season behind New Hampshire.

Republicans dominate the political scene in Kansas but they are not all of a like mind. Voters in small-town Kansas—the party's traditional backbone—do not always vote the same as those in the more affluent suburbs outside Kansas City.

The disparity between the two was noticeable in the 1980 GOP primary. Ronald Reagan won easily, but while he rolled up more than 70 percent of the vote in many rural counties, he was held to a bare majority in suburban Johnson County, where both George Bush and John Anderson established toeholds.

The two Democratic presidential primaries in Kansas have been won by Southerners who were able to appeal to the state's rural nature. President Jimmy Carter trounced Edward Kennedy by 25 percentage points in 1980. Twelve years later, Bill Clinton won a majority of the vote against a crowded Democratic field.

Yet Clinton did not win everywhere in Kansas. Rawlins County, in the far northwest corner of the state, opted for its local entry, Dean Beamgard, a longtime community activist and retired postmaster. The vote in Rawlins County: Beamgard, 174; Clinton, 89.

Recent Kansas Primary Results

Kansas held its first presidential primary in 1980.

	DEMOCRATS			REPUBLICANS		
Year	Turnout	Candidates	%	Turnout	Candidates	%
1996	—	NO PRIMARY		—	NO PRIMARY	
1992 (April 7)	160,251	BILL CLINTON	51	213,196	GEORGE BUSH*	62
		Paul Tsongas	15		Uncommitted	17
		Uncommitted	14		Pat Buchanan	15
		Jerry Brown	13			
1988	—	NO PRIMARY		—	NO PRIMARY	
1984	—	NO PRIMARY		—	NO PRIMARY	
1980 (April 1)	193,918	JIMMY CARTER*	57	285,398	RONALD REAGAN	63
		Edward Kennedy	32		John Anderson	18
					George Bush	13

Note: All candidates are listed that drew at least 10 percent of their party's primary vote. The names of winning candidates are capitalized. An asterisk (*) indicates an incumbent president.

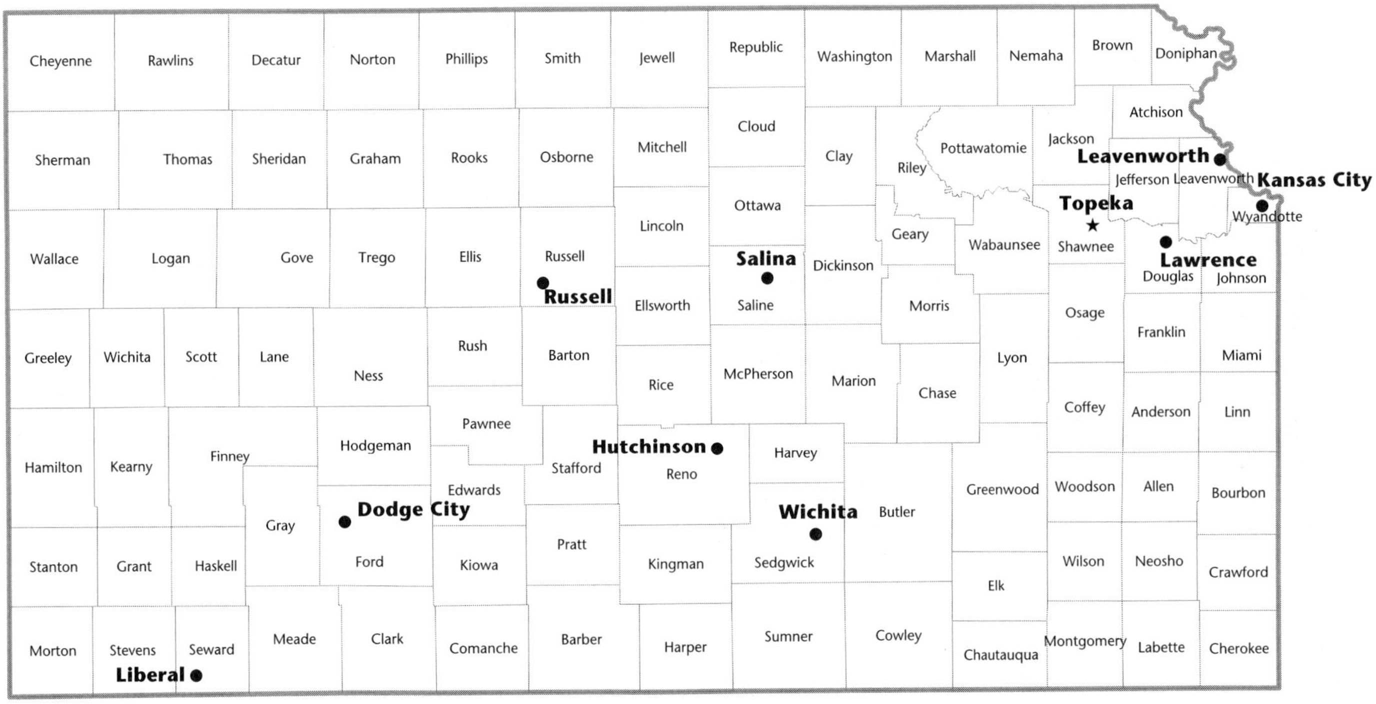

Cheyenne
Rawlins
Decatur
Norton
Phillips
Smith
Jewell
Republic
Washington
Marshall
Nemaha
Brown
Doniphan
Sherman
Thomas
Sheridan
Graham
Rooks
Osborne
Mitchell
Cloud
Clay
Riley
Pottawatomie
Jackson
Atchison
Leavenworth
Jefferson
Leavenworth
Kansas City
Wallace
Logan
Gove
Trego
Ellis
Russell
Lincoln
Ottawa
Geary
Wabaunsee
Topeka
Shawnee
Wyandotte
Salina
Dickinson
Lawrence
Douglas
Johnson
Russell
Ellsworth
Saline
Morris
Osage
Greeley
Wichita
Scott
Lane
Ness
Rush
Barton
Franklin
Miami
Rice
McPherson
Marion
Chase
Lyon
Coffey
Anderson
Linn
Pawnee
Hamilton
Kearny
Finney
Hodgeman
Stafford
Hutchinson
Reno
Harvey
Edwards
Greenwood
Woodson
Allen
Bourbon
Gray
Dodge City
Wichita
Butler
Stanton
Grant
Haskell
Ford
Kiowa
Pratt
Kingman
Sedgwick
Wilson
Neosho
Crawford
Elk
Morton
Stevens
Seward
Liberal
Meade
Clark
Comanche
Barber
Harper
Sumner
Cowley
Chautauqua
Montgomery
Labette
Cherokee

KANSAS DEMOCRATIC

1980

County	Total Vote	Carter	E. Kennedy	Other	Winner	Percentage of Total Vote Carter	E. Kennedy	Other
ALLEN	1,406	837	374	195	Carter	59.5%	26.6%	13.9%
ANDERSON	807	451	227	129	Carter	55.9%	28.1%	16.0%
ATCHISON	1,899	1,045	553	301	Carter	55.0%	29.1%	15.9%
BARBER	591	363	162	66	Carter	61.4%	27.4%	11.2%
BARTON	2,584	1,310	927	347	Carter	50.7%	35.9%	13.4%
BOURBON	1,471	967	363	141	Carter	65.7%	24.7%	9.6%
BROWN	780	440	232	108	Carter	56.4%	29.7%	13.8%
BUTLER	4,198	2,584	1,167	447	Carter	61.6%	27.8%	10.6%
CHASE	264	164	63	37	Carter	62.1%	23.9%	14.0%
CHAUTAUQUA	280	178	66	36	Carter	63.6%	23.6%	12.9%
CHEROKEE	3,090	1,941	824	325	Carter	62.8%	26.7%	10.5%
CHEYENNE	219	111	68	40	Carter	50.7%	31.1%	18.3%
CLARK	243	142	58	43	Carter	58.4%	23.9%	17.7%
CLAY	541	308	156	77	Carter	56.9%	28.8%	14.2%
CLOUD	1,035	593	286	156	Carter	57.3%	27.6%	15.1%
COFFEY	567	344	135	88	Carter	60.7%	23.8%	15.5%
COMANCHE	308	203	74	31	Carter	65.9%	24.0%	10.1%
COWLEY	3,483	2,220	844	419	Carter	63.7%	24.2%	12.0%
CRAWFORD	4,975	2,686	1,826	463	Carter	54.0%	36.7%	9.3%
DECATUR	328	176	91	61	Carter	53.7%	27.7%	18.6%
DICKINSON	1,485	836	456	193	Carter	56.3%	30.7%	13.0%
DONIPHAN	465	269	143	53	Carter	57.8%	30.8%	11.4%
DOUGLAS	4,293	2,249	1,505	539	Carter	52.4%	35.1%	12.6%
EDWARDS	523	265	167	91	Carter	50.7%	31.9%	17.4%
ELK	358	242	80	36	Carter	67.6%	22.3%	10.1%
ELLIS	3,231	1,180	1,752	299	E. Kennedy	36.5%	54.2%	9.3%
ELLSWORTH	662	348	234	80	Carter	52.6%	35.3%	12.1%
FINNEY	1,304	641	432	231	Carter	49.2%	33.1%	17.7%
FORD	2,535	1,376	773	386	Carter	54.3%	30.5%	15.2%
FRANKLIN	1,659	1,063	379	217	Carter	64.1%	22.8%	13.1%
GEARY	1,676	961	534	181	Carter	57.3%	31.9%	10.8%
GOVE	325	113	159	53	E. Kennedy	34.8%	48.9%	16.3%
GRAHAM	206	109	67	30	Carter	52.9%	32.5%	14.6%
GRANT	475	282	118	75	Carter	59.4%	24.8%	15.8%
GRAY	517	234	178	105	Carter	45.3%	34.4%	20.3%
GREELEY	98	54	23	21	Carter	55.1%	23.5%	21.4%
GREENWOOD	936	590	234	112	Carter	63.0%	25.0%	12.0%
HAMILTON	357	197	88	72	Carter	55.2%	24.6%	20.2%
HARPER	650	394	190	66	Carter	60.6%	29.2%	10.2%
HARVEY	2,196	1,319	615	262	Carter	60.1%	28.0%	11.9%
HASKELL	384	194	122	68	Carter	50.5%	31.8%	17.7%
HODGEMAN	308	150	88	70	Carter	48.7%	28.6%	22.7%
JACKSON	733	407	212	114	Carter	55.5%	28.9%	15.6%
JEFFERSON	873	526	243	104	Carter	60.3%	27.8%	11.9%
JEWELL	360	180	120	60	Carter	50.0%	33.3%	16.7%
JOHNSON	12,819	7,056	4,221	1,542	Carter	55.0%	32.9%	12.0%
KEARNY	233	122	73	38	Carter	52.4%	31.3%	16.3%
KINGMAN	723	336	278	109	Carter	46.5%	38.5%	15.1%
KIOWA	373	223	98	52	Carter	59.8%	26.3%	13.9%
LABETTE	2,526	1,606	700	220	Carter	63.6%	27.7%	8.7%

KANSAS DEMOCRATIC

1980

County	Total Vote	Carter	E. Kennedy	Other	Winner	Percentage of Total Vote Carter	E. Kennedy	Other
LANE	220	83	85	52	E. Kennedy	37.7%	38.6%	23.6%
LEAVENWORTH	3,362	1,878	1,181	303	Carter	55.9%	35.1%	9.0%
LINCOLN	350	209	94	47	Carter	59.7%	26.9%	13.4%
LINN	531	331	150	50	Carter	62.3%	28.2%	9.4%
LOGAN	314	143	85	86	Carter	45.5%	27.1%	27.4%
LYON	2,065	1,273	553	239	Carter	61.6%	26.8%	11.6%
MCPHERSON	1,874	1,152	507	215	Carter	61.5%	27.1%	11.5%
MARION	969	525	311	133	Carter	54.2%	32.1%	13.7%
MARSHALL	1,178	591	436	151	Carter	50.2%	37.0%	12.8%
MEADE	355	175	129	51	Carter	49.3%	36.3%	14.4%
MIAMI	1,858	1,096	572	190	Carter	59.0%	30.8%	10.2%
MITCHELL	777	346	300	131	Carter	44.5%	38.6%	16.9%
MONTGOMERY	3,556	2,392	831	333	Carter	67.3%	23.4%	9.4%
MORRIS	498	311	136	51	Carter	62.4%	27.3%	10.2%
MORTON	429	178	155	96	Carter	41.5%	36.1%	22.4%
NEMAHA	1,204	552	481	171	Carter	45.8%	40.0%	14.2%
NEOSHO	1,497	904	412	181	Carter	60.4%	27.5%	12.1%
NESS	300	145	112	43	Carter	48.3%	37.3%	14.3%
NORTON	539	268	175	96	Carter	49.7%	32.5%	17.8%
OSAGE	1,070	641	302	127	Carter	59.9%	28.2%	11.9%
OSBORNE	440	224	142	74	Carter	50.9%	32.3%	16.8%
OTTAWA	458	263	124	71	Carter	57.4%	27.1%	15.5%
PAWNEE	776	394	239	143	Carter	50.8%	30.8%	18.4%
PHILLIPS	489	294	109	86	Carter	60.1%	22.3%	17.6%
POTTAWATOMIE	961	546	287	128	Carter	56.8%	29.9%	13.3%
PRATT	1,141	676	312	153	Carter	59.2%	27.3%	13.4%
RAWLINS	213	114	67	32	Carter	53.5%	31.5%	15.0%
RENO	6,104	3,806	1,534	764	Carter	62.4%	25.1%	12.5%
REPUBLIC	556	318	156	82	Carter	57.2%	28.1%	14.7%
RICE	1,211	760	328	123	Carter	62.8%	27.1%	10.2%
RILEY	2,275	1,320	661	294	Carter	58.0%	29.1%	12.9%
ROOKS	562	273	214	75	Carter	48.6%	38.1%	13.3%
RUSH	576	183	294	99	E. Kennedy	31.8%	51.0%	17.2%
RUSSELL	711	344	266	101	Carter	48.4%	37.4%	14.2%
SALINE	4,692	2,783	1,247	662	Carter	59.3%	26.6%	14.1%
SCOTT	283	143	77	63	Carter	50.5%	27.2%	22.3%
SEDGWICK	33,685	19,843	10,950	2,892	Carter	58.9%	32.5%	8.6%
SEWARD	1,790	1,071	419	300	Carter	59.8%	23.4%	16.8%
SHAWNEE	11,308	6,597	3,433	1,278	Carter	58.3%	30.4%	11.3%
SHERIDAN	469	172	183	114	E. Kennedy	36.7%	39.0%	24.3%
SHERMAN	604	302	226	76	Carter	50.0%	37.4%	12.6%
SMITH	390	223	102	65	Carter	57.2%	26.2%	16.7%
STAFFORD	717	418	199	100	Carter	58.3%	27.8%	13.9%
STANTON	166	77	53	36	Carter	46.4%	31.9%	21.7%
STEVENS	380	218	82	80	Carter	57.4%	21.6%	21.1%
SUMNER	2,934	1,743	807	384	Carter	59.4%	27.5%	13.1%
THOMAS	1,126	526	368	232	Carter	46.7%	32.7%	20.6%
TREGO	304	155	89	60	Carter	51.0%	29.3%	19.7%
WABAUNSEE	453	268	127	58	Carter	59.2%	28.0%	12.8%
WALLACE	66	26	23	17	Carter	39.4%	34.8%	25.8%

KANSAS DEMOCRATIC

1980

County	Total Vote	Carter	E. Kennedy	Other	Winner	Percentage of Total Vote Carter	E. Kennedy	Other
WASHINGTON	435	234	138	63	Carter	53.8%	31.7%	14.5%
WICHITA	174	73	68	33	Carter	42.0%	39.1%	19.0%
WILSON	787	493	191	103	Carter	62.6%	24.3%	13.1%
WOODSON	428	281	108	39	Carter	65.7%	25.2%	9.1%
WYANDOTTE	20,956	10,868	7,910	2,178	Carter	51.9%	37.7%	10.4%
TOTAL	193,918	109,807	61,318	22,793	Carter	56.6%	31.6%	11.8%

KANSAS REPUBLICAN

1980

County	Total Vote	Anderson	Bush	Reagan	Other	Winner	Percentage of Total Vote Anderson	Bush	Reagan	Other
ALLEN	2,542	594	196	1,506	246	Reagan	23.4%	7.7%	59.2%	9.7%
ANDERSON	1,292	166	115	929	82	Reagan	12.8%	8.9%	71.9%	6.3%
ATCHISON	2,145	228	223	1,519	175	Reagan	10.6%	10.4%	70.8%	8.2%
BARBER	914	152	79	635	48	Reagan	16.6%	8.6%	69.5%	5.3%
BARTON	4,019	575	326	2,914	204	Reagan	14.3%	8.1%	72.5%	5.1%
BOURBON	1,627	194	172	1,170	91	Reagan	11.9%	10.6%	71.9%	5.6%
BROWN	2,425	282	257	1,703	183	Reagan	11.6%	10.6%	70.2%	7.5%
BUTLER	4,899	788	697	3,072	342	Reagan	16.1%	14.2%	62.7%	7.0%
CHASE	614	74	60	438	42	Reagan	12.1%	9.8%	71.3%	6.8%
CHAUTAUQUA	853	63	54	707	29	Reagan	7.4%	6.3%	82.9%	3.4%
CHEROKEE	2,293	200	163	1,753	177	Reagan	8.7%	7.1%	76.5%	7.7%
CHEYENNE	507	53	52	363	39	Reagan	10.5%	10.3%	71.6%	7.7%
CLARK	488	93	40	313	42	Reagan	19.1%	8.2%	64.1%	8.6%
CLAY	2,278	260	261	1,612	145	Reagan	11.4%	11.5%	70.8%	6.4%
CLOUD	1,837	272	180	1,235	150	Reagan	14.8%	9.8%	67.2%	8.2%
COFFEY	1,196	125	127	849	95	Reagan	10.5%	10.6%	71.0%	7.9%
COMANCHE	464	88	51	296	29	Reagan	19.0%	11.0%	63.8%	6.3%
COWLEY	4,561	690	555	3,002	314	Reagan	15.1%	12.2%	65.8%	6.9%
CRAWFORD	4,528	785	460	2,922	361	Reagan	17.3%	10.2%	64.5%	8.0%
DECATUR	586	65	31	445	45	Reagan	11.1%	5.3%	75.9%	7.7%
DICKINSON	3,623	482	317	2,580	244	Reagan	13.3%	8.7%	71.2%	6.7%
DONIPHAN	1,899	178	174	1,384	163	Reagan	9.4%	9.2%	72.9%	8.6%
DOUGLAS	9,083	3,273	1,083	4,316	411	Reagan	36.0%	11.9%	47.5%	4.5%
EDWARDS	855	182	56	552	65	Reagan	21.3%	6.5%	64.6%	7.6%
ELK	711	31	55	613	12	Reagan	4.4%	7.7%	86.2%	1.7%
ELLIS	1,838	567	223	929	119	Reagan	30.8%	12.1%	50.5%	6.5%
ELLSWORTH	905	114	97	638	56	Reagan	12.6%	10.7%	70.5%	6.2%
FINNEY	2,109	461	198	1,283	167	Reagan	21.9%	9.4%	60.8%	7.9%
FORD	2,910	565	333	1,777	235	Reagan	19.4%	11.4%	61.1%	8.1%
FRANKLIN	3,028	418	354	2,099	157	Reagan	13.8%	11.7%	69.3%	5.2%

KANSAS REPUBLICAN

1980

County	Total Vote	Anderson	Bush	Reagan	Other	Winner	Percentage of Total Vote Anderson	Bush	Reagan	Other
GEARY	2,193	300	253	1,519	121	Reagan	13.7%	11.5%	69.3%	5.5%
GOVE	512	77	27	369	39	Reagan	15.0%	5.3%	72.1%	7.6%
GRAHAM	788	99	67	562	60	Reagan	12.6%	8.5%	71.3%	7.6%
GRANT	896	133	76	605	82	Reagan	14.8%	8.5%	67.5%	9.2%
GRAY	569	95	45	373	56	Reagan	16.7%	7.9%	65.6%	9.8%
GREELEY	295	91	32	138	34	Reagan	30.8%	10.8%	46.8%	11.5%
GREENWOOD	1,606	176	144	1,192	94	Reagan	11.0%	9.0%	74.2%	5.9%
HAMILTON	475	60	35	345	35	Reagan	12.6%	7.4%	72.6%	7.4%
HARPER	1,326	209	157	880	80	Reagan	15.8%	11.8%	66.4%	6.0%
HARVEY	4,167	1,155	494	2,279	239	Reagan	27.7%	11.9%	54.7%	5.7%
HASKELL	737	101	54	534	48	Reagan	13.7%	7.3%	72.5%	6.5%
HODGEMAN	498	110	39	316	33	Reagan	22.1%	7.8%	63.5%	6.6%
JACKSON	1,579	164	184	1,132	99	Reagan	10.4%	11.7%	71.7%	6.3%
JEFFERSON	1,767	230	191	1,240	106	Reagan	13.0%	10.8%	70.2%	6.0%
JEWELL	1,203	116	102	868	117	Reagan	9.6%	8.5%	72.2%	9.7%
JOHNSON	33,973	7,255	6,818	17,853	2,047	Reagan	21.4%	20.1%	52.6%	6.0%
KEARNY	537	82	58	343	54	Reagan	15.3%	10.8%	63.9%	10.1%
KINGMAN	1,301	241	138	836	86	Reagan	18.5%	10.6%	64.3%	6.6%
KIOWA	784	123	86	533	42	Reagan	15.7%	11.0%	68.0%	5.4%
LABETTE	2,724	513	235	1,811	165	Reagan	18.8%	8.6%	66.5%	6.1%
LANE	415	94	36	249	36	Reagan	22.7%	8.7%	60.0%	8.7%
LEAVENWORTH	3,893	623	455	2,617	198	Reagan	16.0%	11.7%	67.2%	5.1%
LINCOLN	899	116	55	668	60	Reagan	12.9%	6.1%	74.3%	6.7%
LINN	1,018	92	76	797	53	Reagan	9.0%	7.5%	78.3%	5.2%
LOGAN	620	74	38	446	62	Reagan	11.9%	6.1%	71.9%	10.0%
LYON	3,633	789	444	2,144	256	Reagan	21.7%	12.2%	59.0%	7.0%
MCPHERSON	4,060	1,075	389	2,392	204	Reagan	26.5%	9.6%	58.9%	5.0%
MARION	2,585	572	247	1,590	176	Reagan	22.1%	9.6%	61.5%	6.8%
MARSHALL	2,080	221	132	1,643	84	Reagan	10.6%	6.3%	79.0%	4.0%
MEADE	743	112	58	528	45	Reagan	15.1%	7.8%	71.1%	6.1%
MIAMI	1,908	253	272	1,271	112	Reagan	13.3%	14.3%	66.6%	5.9%
MITCHELL	1,471	200	124	1,046	101	Reagan	13.6%	8.4%	71.1%	6.9%
MONTGOMERY	5,387	375	429	4,365	218	Reagan	7.0%	8.0%	81.0%	4.0%
MORRIS	1,127	132	81	845	69	Reagan	11.7%	7.2%	75.0%	6.1%
MORTON	444	43	31	342	28	Reagan	9.7%	7.0%	77.0%	6.3%
NEMAHA	1,490	171	152	1,078	89	Reagan	11.5%	10.2%	72.3%	6.0%
NEOSHO	2,311	390	176	1,527	218	Reagan	16.9%	7.6%	66.1%	9.4%
NESS	598	141	50	372	35	Reagan	23.6%	8.4%	62.2%	5.9%
NORTON	1,658	95	54	1,194	315	Reagan	5.7%	3.3%	72.0%	19.0%
OSAGE	1,630	218	150	1,189	73	Reagan	13.4%	9.2%	72.9%	4.5%
OSBORNE	1,013	126	81	754	52	Reagan	12.4%	8.0%	74.4%	5.1%
OTTAWA	1,109	125	94	818	72	Reagan	11.3%	8.5%	73.8%	6.5%
PAWNEE	1,013	209	67	655	82	Reagan	20.6%	6.6%	64.7%	8.1%
PHILLIPS	1,525	180	96	1,106	143	Reagan	11.8%	6.3%	72.5%	9.4%
POTTAWATOMIE	2,328	364	215	1,534	215	Reagan	15.6%	9.2%	65.9%	9.2%
PRATT	1,671	367	218	981	105	Reagan	22.0%	13.0%	58.7%	6.3%
RAWLINS	428	33	28	341	26	Reagan	7.7%	6.5%	79.7%	6.1%
RENO	7,917	2,235	668	4,514	500	Reagan	28.2%	8.4%	57.0%	6.3%
REPUBLIC	1,366	117	95	1,111	43	Reagan	8.6%	7.0%	81.3%	3.1%
RICE	1,967	518	230	1,088	131	Reagan	26.3%	11.7%	55.3%	6.7%

KANSAS REPUBLICAN

1980

County	Total Vote	Anderson	Bush	Reagan	Other	Winner	Percentage of Total Vote Anderson	Bush	Reagan	Other
RILEY	5,431	1,859	699	2,562	311	Reagan	34.2%	12.9%	47.2%	5.7%
ROOKS	1,170	182	71	839	78	Reagan	15.6%	6.1%	71.7%	6.7%
RUSH	872	131	65	618	58	Reagan	15.0%	7.5%	70.9%	6.7%
RUSSELL	1,569	229	126	1,088	126	Reagan	14.6%	8.0%	69.3%	8.0%
SALINE	8,010	1,416	906	5,120	568	Reagan	17.7%	11.3%	63.9%	7.1%
SCOTT	859	135	53	619	52	Reagan	15.7%	6.2%	72.1%	6.1%
SEDGWICK	37,470	7,290	6,669	21,844	1,667	Reagan	19.5%	17.8%	58.3%	4.4%
SEWARD	2,572	312	303	1,798	159	Reagan	12.1%	11.8%	69.9%	6.2%
SHAWNEE	18,550	3,525	2,902	10,887	1,236	Reagan	19.0%	15.6%	58.7%	6.7%
SHERIDAN	525	66	39	385	35	Reagan	12.6%	7.4%	73.3%	6.7%
SHERMAN	918	105	85	671	57	Reagan	11.4%	9.3%	73.1%	6.2%
SMITH	920	97	64	703	56	Reagan	10.5%	7.0%	76.4%	6.1%
STAFFORD	1,142	235	83	747	77	Reagan	20.6%	7.3%	65.4%	6.7%
STANTON	343	35	18	256	34	Reagan	10.2%	5.2%	74.6%	9.9%
STEVENS	733	82	79	531	41	Reagan	11.2%	10.8%	72.4%	5.6%
SUMNER	3,198	417	475	2,112	194	Reagan	13.0%	14.9%	66.0%	6.1%
THOMAS	1,816	300	183	1,176	157	Reagan	16.5%	10.1%	64.8%	8.6%
TREGO	399	67	33	282	17	Reagan	16.8%	8.3%	70.7%	4.3%
WABAUNSEE	1,226	126	116	889	95	Reagan	10.3%	9.5%	72.5%	7.7%
WALLACE	265	28	20	201	16	Reagan	10.6%	7.5%	75.8%	6.0%
WASHINGTON	1,687	157	123	1,332	75	Reagan	9.3%	7.3%	79.0%	4.4%
WICHITA	353	54	19	255	25	Reagan	15.3%	5.4%	72.2%	7.1%
WILSON	1,968	197	131	1,532	108	Reagan	10.0%	6.7%	77.8%	5.5%
WOODSON	929	109	70	698	52	Reagan	11.7%	7.5%	75.1%	5.6%
WYANDOTTE	9,207	1,362	1,041	6,107	697	Reagan	14.8%	11.3%	66.3%	7.6%
TOTAL	285,398	51,924	35,838	179,739	17,897	Reagan	18.2%	12.6%	63.0%	6.3%

KANSAS DEMOCRATIC

1992

County	Total Vote	Brown	Clinton	Tsongas	Uncommitted	Other	Winner	Percentage of Total Vote Brown	Clinton	Tsongas	Uncom.	Other
ALLEN	1,132	95	657	125	172	83	Clinton	8.4%	58.0%	11.0%	15.2%	7.3%
ANDERSON	446	39	271	55	52	29	Clinton	8.7%	60.8%	12.3%	11.7%	6.5%
ATCHISON	840	103	401	154	115	67	Clinton	12.3%	47.7%	18.3%	13.7%	8.0%
BARBER	498	40	261	64	102	31	Clinton	8.0%	52.4%	12.9%	20.5%	6.2%
BARTON	1,578	203	767	218	284	106	Clinton	12.9%	48.6%	13.8%	18.0%	6.7%
BOURBON	893	83	488	120	139	63	Clinton	9.3%	54.6%	13.4%	15.6%	7.1%
BROWN	510	46	271	66	83	44	Clinton	9.0%	53.1%	12.9%	16.3%	8.6%
BUTLER	3,578	365	1,919	505	596	193	Clinton	10.2%	53.6%	14.1%	16.7%	5.4%
CHASE	167	15	91	16	32	13	Clinton	9.0%	54.5%	9.6%	19.2%	7.8%
CHAUTAUQUA	227	15	146	31	24	11	Clinton	6.6%	64.3%	13.7%	10.6%	4.8%

KANSAS DEMOCRATIC

1992

County	Total Vote	Brown	Clinton	Tsongas	Uncommitted	Other	Winner	Percentage of Total Vote Brown	Clinton	Tsongas	Uncom.	Other
CHEROKEE	2,005	114	1,418	156	236	81	Clinton	5.7%	70.7%	7.8%	11.8%	4.0%
CHEYENNE	193	8	89	30	19	47	Clinton	4.1%	46.1%	15.5%	9.8%	24.4%
CLARK	155	10	78	20	36	11	Clinton	6.5%	50.3%	12.9%	23.2%	7.1%
CLAY	267	27	131	34	46	29	Clinton	10.1%	49.1%	12.7%	17.2%	10.9%
CLOUD	960	115	481	103	121	140	Clinton	12.0%	50.1%	10.7%	12.6%	14.6%
COFFEY	365	33	198	39	62	33	Clinton	9.0%	54.2%	10.7%	17.0%	9.0%
COMANCHE	162	11	86	27	28	10	Clinton	6.8%	53.1%	16.7%	17.3%	6.2%
COWLEY	2,289	226	1,315	310	321	117	Clinton	9.9%	57.4%	13.5%	14.0%	5.1%
CRAWFORD	2,776	254	1,782	245	360	135	Clinton	9.1%	64.2%	8.8%	13.0%	4.9%
DECATUR	311	10	169	24	46	62	Clinton	3.2%	54.3%	7.7%	14.8%	19.9%
DICKINSON	867	79	497	96	118	77	Clinton	9.1%	57.3%	11.1%	13.6%	8.9%
DONIPHAN	214	12	132	23	28	19	Clinton	5.6%	61.7%	10.7%	13.1%	8.9%
DOUGLAS	4,839	1,133	1,809	1,145	545	207	Clinton	23.4%	37.4%	23.7%	11.3%	4.3%
EDWARDS	340	21	154	48	96	21	Clinton	6.2%	45.3%	14.1%	28.2%	6.2%
ELK	253	18	140	33	36	26	Clinton	7.1%	55.3%	13.0%	14.2%	10.3%
ELLIS	3,403	503	1,705	409	475	311	Clinton	14.8%	50.1%	12.0%	14.0%	9.1%
ELLSWORTH	941	107	455	96	194	89	Clinton	11.4%	48.4%	10.2%	20.6%	9.5%
FINNEY	1,133	160	483	201	219	70	Clinton	14.1%	42.6%	17.7%	19.3%	6.2%
FORD	2,064	175	967	249	531	142	Clinton	8.5%	46.9%	12.1%	25.7%	6.9%
FRANKLIN	1,091	107	580	176	149	79	Clinton	9.8%	53.2%	16.1%	13.7%	7.2%
GEARY	894	126	471	145	108	44	Clinton	14.1%	52.7%	16.2%	12.1%	4.9%
GOVE	203	23	83	20	34	43	Clinton	11.3%	40.9%	9.9%	16.7%	21.2%
GRAHAM	173	31	78	20	16	28	Clinton	17.9%	45.1%	11.6%	9.2%	16.2%
GRANT	327	16	166	52	70	23	Clinton	4.9%	50.8%	15.9%	21.4%	7.0%
GRAY	298	37	130	40	69	22	Clinton	12.4%	43.6%	13.4%	23.2%	7.4%
GREELEY	67	2	31	5	21	8	Clinton	3.0%	46.3%	7.5%	31.3%	11.9%
GREENWOOD	785	41	482	80	149	33	Clinton	5.2%	61.4%	10.2%	19.0%	4.2%
HAMILTON	162	11	78	21	34	18	Clinton	6.8%	48.1%	13.0%	21.0%	11.1%
HARPER	470	37	269	60	78	26	Clinton	7.9%	57.2%	12.8%	16.6%	5.5%
HARVEY	2,537	326	1,202	454	425	130	Clinton	12.8%	47.4%	17.9%	16.8%	5.1%
HASKELL	189	10	105	18	40	16	Clinton	5.3%	55.6%	9.5%	21.2%	8.5%
HODGEMAN	120	8	51	11	33	17	Clinton	6.7%	42.5%	9.2%	27.5%	14.2%
JACKSON	726	75	373	104	121	53	Clinton	10.3%	51.4%	14.3%	16.7%	7.3%
JEFFERSON	858	116	403	134	144	61	Clinton	13.5%	47.0%	15.6%	16.8%	7.1%
JEWELL	142	13	68	18	25	18	Clinton	9.2%	47.9%	12.7%	17.6%	12.7%
JOHNSON	16,698	2,501	7,367	3,675	2,292	863	Clinton	15.0%	44.1%	22.0%	13.7%	5.2%
KEARNY	213	21	96	32	49	15	Clinton	9.9%	45.1%	15.0%	23.0%	7.0%
KINGMAN	573	43	279	81	124	46	Clinton	7.5%	48.7%	14.1%	21.6%	8.0%
KIOWA	242	18	119	27	65	13	Clinton	7.4%	49.2%	11.2%	26.9%	5.4%
LABETTE	1,564	148	1,047	157	133	79	Clinton	9.5%	66.9%	10.0%	8.5%	5.1%
LANE	112	9	43	19	30	11	Clinton	8.0%	38.4%	17.0%	26.8%	9.8%
LEAVENWORTH	2,485	337	1,246	435	337	130	Clinton	13.6%	50.1%	17.5%	13.6%	5.2%
LINCOLN	202	19	113	21	25	24	Clinton	9.4%	55.9%	10.4%	12.4%	11.9%
LINN	434	34	285	47	38	30	Clinton	7.8%	65.7%	10.8%	8.8%	6.9%
LOGAN	177	10	104	15	22	26	Clinton	5.6%	58.8%	8.5%	12.4%	14.7%
LYON	1,706	233	799	281	266	127	Clinton	13.7%	46.8%	16.5%	15.6%	7.4%
MCPHERSON	1,428	169	652	227	288	92	Clinton	11.8%	45.7%	15.9%	20.2%	6.4%
MARION	694	62	372	97	107	56	Clinton	8.9%	53.6%	14.0%	15.4%	8.1%
MARSHALL	783	86	408	74	126	89	Clinton	11.0%	52.1%	9.5%	16.1%	11.4%
MEADE	271	18	116	31	82	24	Clinton	6.6%	42.8%	11.4%	30.3%	8.9%

KANSAS DEMOCRATIC

1992

County	Total Vote	Brown	Clinton	Tsongas	Uncommitted	Other	Winner	Percentage of Total Vote Brown	Clinton	Tsongas	Uncom.	Other
MIAMI	2,182	184	1,185	303	379	131	Clinton	8.4%	54.3%	13.9%	17.4%	6.0%
MITCHELL	458	31	198	30	59	140	Clinton	6.8%	43.2%	6.6%	12.9%	30.6%
MONTGOMERY	2,235	112	1,430	225	312	156	Clinton	5.0%	64.0%	10.1%	14.0%	7.0%
MORRIS	409	46	213	41	83	26	Clinton	11.2%	52.1%	10.0%	20.3%	6.4%
MORTON	346	33	158	55	79	21	Clinton	9.5%	45.7%	15.9%	22.8%	6.1%
NEMAHA	642	88	300	65	116	73	Clinton	13.7%	46.7%	10.1%	18.1%	11.4%
NEOSHO	1,018	66	640	124	118	70	Clinton	6.5%	62.9%	12.2%	11.6%	6.9%
NESS	260	21	145	25	49	20	Clinton	8.1%	55.8%	9.6%	18.8%	7.7%
NORTON	327	23	168	40	43	53	Clinton	7.0%	51.4%	12.2%	13.1%	16.2%
OSAGE	956	113	533	100	159	51	Clinton	11.8%	55.8%	10.5%	16.6%	5.3%
OSBORNE	294	21	143	42	47	41	Clinton	7.1%	48.6%	14.3%	16.0%	13.9%
OTTAWA	314	30	158	29	45	52	Clinton	9.6%	50.3%	9.2%	14.3%	16.6%
PAWNEE	454	37	198	83	107	29	Clinton	8.1%	43.6%	18.3%	23.6%	6.4%
PHILLIPS	268	30	125	27	41	45	Clinton	11.2%	46.6%	10.1%	15.3%	16.8%
POTTAWATOMIE	1,091	150	480	136	246	79	Clinton	13.7%	44.0%	12.5%	22.5%	7.2%
PRATT	790	72	415	99	161	43	Clinton	9.1%	52.5%	12.5%	20.4%	5.4%
RAWLINS	339	22	89	19	19	190	Beamgard	6.5%	26.3%	5.6%	5.6%	56.0%
RENO	4,052	421	1,971	477	969	214	Clinton	10.4%	48.6%	11.8%	23.9%	5.3%
REPUBLIC	372	34	152	39	63	84	Clinton	9.1%	40.9%	10.5%	16.9%	22.6%
RICE	747	75	340	108	175	49	Clinton	10.0%	45.5%	14.5%	23.4%	6.6%
RILEY	2,453	419	1,028	568	301	137	Clinton	17.1%	41.9%	23.2%	12.3%	5.6%
ROOKS	403	41	199	36	71	56	Clinton	10.2%	49.4%	8.9%	17.6%	13.9%
RUSH	343	31	172	51	55	34	Clinton	9.0%	50.1%	14.9%	16.0%	9.9%
RUSSELL	604	76	318	59	102	49	Clinton	12.6%	52.6%	9.8%	16.9%	8.1%
SALINE	2,832	310	1,385	339	381	417	Clinton	10.9%	48.9%	12.0%	13.5%	14.7%
SCOTT	219	19	95	44	41	20	Clinton	8.7%	43.4%	20.1%	18.7%	9.1%
SEDGWICK	35,186	5,542	18,623	6,179	3,113	1,729	Clinton	15.8%	52.9%	17.6%	8.8%	4.9%
SEWARD	927	78	476	133	178	62	Clinton	8.4%	51.3%	14.3%	19.2%	6.7%
SHAWNEE	11,850	2,012	5,722	1,725	1,637	754	Clinton	17.0%	48.3%	14.6%	13.8%	6.4%
SHERIDAN	202	22	77	31	32	40	Clinton	10.9%	38.1%	15.3%	15.8%	19.8%
SHERMAN	772	79	353	81	123	136	Clinton	10.2%	45.7%	10.5%	15.9%	17.6%
SMITH	219	14	112	25	33	35	Clinton	6.4%	51.1%	11.4%	15.1%	16.0%
STAFFORD	388	28	177	40	110	33	Clinton	7.2%	45.6%	10.3%	28.4%	8.5%
STANTON	144	11	64	23	35	11	Clinton	7.6%	44.4%	16.0%	24.3%	7.6%
STEVENS	454	32	220	58	109	35	Clinton	7.0%	48.5%	12.8%	24.0%	7.7%
SUMNER	2,396	219	1,332	314	390	141	Clinton	9.1%	55.6%	13.1%	16.3%	5.9%
THOMAS	640	51	292	69	85	143	Clinton	8.0%	45.6%	10.8%	13.3%	22.3%
TREGO	266	21	139	24	40	42	Clinton	7.9%	52.3%	9.0%	15.0%	15.8%
WABAUNSEE	438	54	206	45	86	47	Clinton	12.3%	47.0%	10.3%	19.6%	10.7%
WALLACE	73	6	38	7	9	13	Clinton	8.2%	52.1%	9.6%	12.3%	17.8%
WASHINGTON	266	32	138	28	24	44	Clinton	12.0%	51.9%	10.5%	9.0%	16.5%
WICHITA	121	3	57	18	36	7	Clinton	2.5%	47.1%	14.9%	29.8%	5.8%
WILSON	501	37	328	46	57	33	Clinton	7.4%	65.5%	9.2%	11.4%	6.6%
WOODSON	257	27	161	18	28	23	Clinton	10.5%	62.6%	7.0%	10.9%	8.9%
WYANDOTTE	10,713	1,331	6,415	1,166	1,197	604	Clinton	12.4%	59.9%	10.9%	11.2%	5.6%
TOTAL	160,251	20,811	82,145	24,413	22,159	10,723	Clinton	13.0%	51.3%	15.2%	13.8%	6.7%

Note: The winner in Rawlins County with 174 votes was Dean Beamgard, a local entry.

KANSAS REPUBLICAN

1992

County	Total Vote	Buchanan	Bush	Uncommitted	Other	Winner	Percentage of Total Vote Buchanan	Bush	Uncom.	Other
ALLEN	1,803	231	1,116	324	132	Bush	12.8%	61.9%	18.0%	7.3%
ANDERSON	493	69	298	80	46	Bush	14.0%	60.4%	16.2%	9.3%
ATCHISON	677	100	432	85	60	Bush	14.8%	63.8%	12.6%	8.9%
BARBER	918	156	501	180	81	Bush	17.0%	54.6%	19.6%	8.8%
BARTON	2,274	323	1,313	484	154	Bush	14.2%	57.7%	21.3%	6.8%
BOURBON	829	98	549	141	41	Bush	11.8%	66.2%	17.0%	4.9%
BROWN	1,542	182	929	309	122	Bush	11.8%	60.2%	20.0%	7.9%
BUTLER	3,992	645	2,486	598	263	Bush	16.2%	62.3%	15.0%	6.6%
CHASE	359	55	191	77	36	Bush	15.3%	53.2%	21.4%	10.0%
CHAUTAUQUA	563	82	335	99	47	Bush	14.6%	59.5%	17.6%	8.3%
CHEROKEE	1,265	154	902	154	55	Bush	12.2%	71.3%	12.2%	4.3%
CHEYENNE	352	46	239	43	24	Bush	13.1%	67.9%	12.2%	6.8%
CLARK	309	30	190	68	21	Bush	9.7%	61.5%	22.0%	6.8%
CLAY	1,137	116	689	248	84	Bush	10.2%	60.6%	21.8%	7.4%
CLOUD	1,598	244	946	292	116	Bush	15.3%	59.2%	18.3%	7.3%
COFFEY	759	105	442	150	62	Bush	13.8%	58.2%	19.8%	8.2%
COMANCHE	351	46	214	70	21	Bush	13.1%	61.0%	19.9%	6.0%
COWLEY	2,699	410	1,673	450	166	Bush	15.2%	62.0%	16.7%	6.2%
CRAWFORD	1,671	209	1,074	271	117	Bush	12.5%	64.3%	16.2%	7.0%
DECATUR	425	66	267	58	34	Bush	15.5%	62.8%	13.6%	8.0%
DICKINSON	1,842	301	1,045	340	156	Bush	16.3%	56.7%	18.5%	8.5%
DONIPHAN	562	108	309	91	54	Bush	19.2%	55.0%	16.2%	9.6%
DOUGLAS	4,282	617	2,498	896	271	Bush	14.4%	58.3%	20.9%	6.3%
EDWARDS	544	64	272	160	48	Bush	11.8%	50.0%	29.4%	8.8%
ELK	437	59	296	50	32	Bush	13.5%	67.7%	11.4%	7.3%
ELLIS	2,121	314	1,356	321	130	Bush	14.8%	63.9%	15.1%	6.1%
ELLSWORTH	1,177	154	726	205	92	Bush	13.1%	61.7%	17.4%	7.8%
FINNEY	1,730	217	1,157	256	100	Bush	12.5%	66.9%	14.8%	5.8%
FORD	2,687	266	1,720	557	144	Bush	9.9%	64.0%	20.7%	5.4%
FRANKLIN	1,469	248	797	288	136	Bush	16.9%	54.3%	19.6%	9.3%
GEARY	957	116	626	161	54	Bush	12.1%	65.4%	16.8%	5.6%
GOVE	319	40	184	67	28	Bush	12.5%	57.7%	21.0%	8.8%
GRAHAM	572	87	324	101	60	Bush	15.2%	56.6%	17.7%	10.5%
GRANT	741	85	480	141	35	Bush	11.5%	64.8%	19.0%	4.7%
GRAY	318	51	186	58	23	Bush	16.0%	58.5%	18.2%	7.2%
GREELEY	227	21	122	70	14	Bush	9.3%	53.7%	30.8%	6.2%
GREENWOOD	1,155	184	704	186	81	Bush	15.9%	61.0%	16.1%	7.0%
HAMILTON	233	25	161	33	14	Bush	10.7%	69.1%	14.2%	6.0%
HARPER	747	90	472	131	54	Bush	12.0%	63.2%	17.5%	7.2%
HARVEY	4,098	633	2,547	687	231	Bush	15.4%	62.2%	16.8%	5.6%
HASKELL	518	62	343	86	27	Bush	12.0%	66.2%	16.6%	5.2%
HODGEMAN	275	35	157	52	31	Bush	12.7%	57.1%	18.9%	11.3%
JACKSON	1,130	144	644	264	78	Bush	12.7%	57.0%	23.4%	6.9%
JEFFERSON	1,137	180	603	242	112	Bush	15.8%	53.0%	21.3%	9.9%
JEWELL	480	79	297	79	25	Bush	16.5%	61.9%	16.5%	5.2%
JOHNSON	33,041	4,935	20,699	5,526	1,881	Bush	14.9%	62.6%	16.7%	5.7%
KEARNY	524	54	357	88	25	Bush	10.3%	68.1%	16.8%	4.8%
KINGMAN	975	162	498	244	71	Bush	16.6%	51.1%	25.0%	7.3%
KIOWA	698	85	426	147	40	Bush	12.2%	61.0%	21.1%	5.7%
LABETTE	1,384	188	881	223	92	Bush	13.6%	63.7%	16.1%	6.6%

KANSAS REPUBLICAN

1992

County	Total Vote	Buchanan	Bush	Uncommitted	Other	Winner	Percentage of Total Vote: Buchanan	Bush	Uncom.	Other
LANE	292	25	200	52	15	Bush	8.6%	68.5%	17.8%	5.1%
LEAVENWORTH	2,195	376	1,321	367	131	Bush	17.1%	60.2%	16.7%	6.0%
LINCOLN	389	53	220	93	23	Bush	13.6%	56.6%	23.9%	5.9%
LINN	606	99	362	96	49	Bush	16.3%	59.7%	15.8%	8.1%
LOGAN	291	48	172	45	26	Bush	16.5%	59.1%	15.5%	8.9%
LYON	2,260	365	1,212	466	217	Bush	16.2%	53.6%	20.6%	9.6%
MCPHERSON	2,801	370	1,645	602	184	Bush	13.2%	58.7%	21.5%	6.6%
MARION	1,716	221	1,124	280	91	Bush	12.9%	65.5%	16.3%	5.3%
MARSHALL	1,049	173	555	231	90	Bush	16.5%	52.9%	22.0%	8.6%
MEADE	626	93	379	127	27	Bush	14.9%	60.5%	20.3%	4.3%
MIAMI	1,994	286	1,170	400	138	Bush	14.3%	58.7%	20.1%	6.9%
MITCHELL	858	114	505	156	83	Bush	13.3%	58.9%	18.2%	9.7%
MONTGOMERY	3,251	431	2,126	445	249	Bush	13.3%	65.4%	13.7%	7.7%
MORRIS	592	85	304	132	71	Bush	14.4%	51.4%	22.3%	12.0%
MORTON	444	81	264	59	40	Bush	18.2%	59.5%	13.3%	9.0%
NEMAHA	773	108	491	122	52	Bush	14.0%	63.5%	15.8%	6.7%
NEOSHO	1,304	205	812	198	89	Bush	15.7%	62.3%	15.2%	6.8%
NESS	385	41	218	96	30	Bush	10.6%	56.6%	24.9%	7.8%
NORTON	838	113	513	141	71	Bush	13.5%	61.2%	16.8%	8.5%
OSAGE	1,074	184	547	242	101	Bush	17.1%	50.9%	22.5%	9.4%
OSBORNE	528	76	322	90	40	Bush	14.4%	61.0%	17.0%	7.6%
OTTAWA	684	103	403	126	52	Bush	15.1%	58.9%	18.4%	7.6%
PAWNEE	646	62	375	171	38	Bush	9.6%	58.0%	26.5%	5.9%
PHILLIPS	805	107	502	126	70	Bush	13.3%	62.4%	15.7%	8.7%
POTTAWATOMIE	2,544	462	1,370	518	194	Bush	18.2%	53.9%	20.4%	7.6%
PRATT	1,261	177	749	247	88	Bush	14.0%	59.4%	19.6%	7.0%
RAWLINS	854	96	584	111	63	Bush	11.2%	68.4%	13.0%	7.4%
RENO	4,478	583	2,365	1,247	283	Bush	13.0%	52.8%	27.8%	6.3%
REPUBLIC	878	107	575	130	66	Bush	12.2%	65.5%	14.8%	7.5%
RICE	1,044	132	597	254	61	Bush	12.6%	57.2%	24.3%	5.8%
RILEY	3,869	524	2,423	688	234	Bush	13.5%	62.6%	17.8%	6.0%
ROOKS	883	122	508	160	93	Bush	13.8%	57.5%	18.1%	10.5%
RUSH	563	70	310	134	49	Bush	12.4%	55.1%	23.8%	8.7%
RUSSELL	1,190	190	624	276	100	Bush	16.0%	52.4%	23.2%	8.4%
SALINE	3,944	580	2,276	814	274	Bush	14.7%	57.7%	20.6%	6.9%
SCOTT	665	75	456	84	50	Bush	11.3%	68.6%	12.6%	7.5%
SEDGWICK	42,896	6,995	29,235	4,389	2,277	Bush	16.3%	68.2%	10.2%	5.3%
SEWARD	1,997	220	1,327	328	122	Bush	11.0%	66.4%	16.4%	6.1%
SHAWNEE	14,327	2,202	8,416	2,640	1,069	Bush	15.4%	58.7%	18.4%	7.5%
SHERIDAN	278	32	163	58	25	Bush	11.5%	58.6%	20.9%	9.0%
SHERMAN	1,379	183	885	187	124	Bush	13.3%	64.2%	13.6%	9.0%
SMITH	470	53	303	80	34	Bush	11.3%	64.5%	17.0%	7.2%
STAFFORD	518	57	270	151	40	Bush	11.0%	52.1%	29.2%	7.7%
STANTON	271	33	176	43	19	Bush	12.2%	64.9%	15.9%	7.0%
STEVENS	1,024	116	628	190	90	Bush	11.3%	61.3%	18.6%	8.8%
SUMNER	2,547	439	1,474	437	197	Bush	17.2%	57.9%	17.2%	7.7%
THOMAS	1,044	151	662	147	84	Bush	14.5%	63.4%	14.1%	8.0%
TREGO	293	45	168	55	25	Bush	15.4%	57.3%	18.8%	8.5%
WABAUNSEE	967	132	476	269	90	Bush	13.7%	49.2%	27.8%	9.3%
WALLACE	260	39	158	36	27	Bush	15.0%	60.8%	13.8%	10.4%

KANSAS REPUBLICAN

1992

County	Total Vote	Buchanan	Bush	Uncommitted	Other	Winner	Percentage of Total Vote Buchanan	Bush	Uncom.	Other
WASHINGTON	853	149	475	166	63	Bush	17.5%	55.7%	19.5%	7.4%
WICHITA	207	29	125	43	10	Bush	14.0%	60.4%	20.8%	4.8%
WILSON	1,106	141	720	163	82	Bush	12.7%	65.1%	14.7%	7.4%
WOODSON	492	76	298	67	51	Bush	15.4%	60.6%	13.6%	10.4%
WYANDOTTE	3,297	494	1,920	544	339	Bush	15.0%	58.2%	16.5%	10.3%
TOTAL	213,196	31,494	132,131	35,450	14,121	Bush	14.8%	62.0%	16.6%	6.6%

KENTUCKY

Basketball and politics are two of the leading spectator sports in Kentucky, but the state's presidential primary has never drawn more than a collective yawn. That has been due in no small part to the fact that it has generally been held in late May, a time when recent nominating contests have been in the mop-up stage.

Since Kentucky held its first presidential primary in 1976, its only vote of significance came in the GOP contest that year between President Gerald Ford and Ronald Reagan. Out of nearly 135,000 votes cast, Ford won by barely 5,000—a narrow victory, but an important one in slowing the momentum that Reagan had built up earlier that month with a series of primary victories.

Reagan carried one stronghold of Kentucky Republicanism—the relatively affluent Louisville suburbs. Ford carried the other—the state's mountainous southeastern corner. Many of the mountaineers are "New Deal Republicans"—joined in poverty with Democrats in nearby hills and hollows but separated from them politically by partisan divisions dating to the Civil War.

The Democratic eastern end of Kentucky is similar to neighboring West Virginia. The region has a long union tradition and the voters have looked favorably on New Deal-style Democrats. It was the only part of Kentucky where Edward Kennedy ran reasonably close to President Jimmy Carter in Kennedy's landslide 1980 primary loss.

Across the state in the western panhandle is a different breed of Democrat. That area resembles the Deep South in its voting habits and contains the only Kentucky counties that supported George Wallace's 1968 third-party presidential bid.

The winner of the Democratic primary has often been the candidate that the Democratic governor supported. (Kentucky has not elected a Republican governor since 1967.)

In 1988, Gov. Wallace G. Wilkinson backed Al Gore, who won easily. In 1992, Gov. Brereton Jones backed Bill Clinton, who carried the Kentucky primary by an even larger vote.

As it was, Gore's winning 46 percent share in Kentucky was his highest percentage in any 1988 primary outside his home state of Tennessee. Gore had trouble shaking his two closest rivals, Michael Dukakis and Jesse Jackson, in Kentucky's two leading population centers, Jefferson (Louisville) and Fayette (Lexington) counties.

But moving south across the state toward the Tennessee border, Gore's vote share increased dramatically. In Monroe County, which lies about 30 miles north of his hometown of Carthage, Tenn., Gore won 95 percent of the votes cast.

As in much of the rest of the South, George Bush's victory

Recent Kentucky Primary Results

Kentucky held its first presidential primary in 1976.

	DEMOCRATS			REPUBLICANS		
Year	Turnout	Candidates	%	Turnout	Candidates	%
1996 (May 28)	276,019	BILL CLINTON* Uncommitted	77 16	103,839	BOB DOLE	74
1992 (May 26)	370,578	BILL CLINTON Uncommitted	56 28	101,119	GEORGE BUSH* Uncommitted	75 25
1988 (March 8)	318,721	AL GORE Michael Dukakis Jesse Jackson	46 19 16	121,402	GEORGE BUSH Bob Dole Pat Robertson	59 23 11
1984	—	NO PRIMARY		—	NO PRIMARY	
1980 (May 27)	240,331	JIMMY CARTER* Edward Kennedy	67 23	94,795	RONALD REAGAN	82
1976 (May 25)	306,006	JIMMY CARTER George Wallace Morris Udall	59 17 11	133,528	GERALD FORD* Ronald Reagan	51 47

Note: All candidates are listed that drew at least 10 percent of their party's primary vote. The names of winning candidates are capitalized. An asterisk (*) indicates an incumbent president.

in the 1988 Republican primary in Kentucky was notable for its completeness. He lost only one county, Ballard, a rural Democratic enclave bordering Illinois and Missouri that was carried by Bob Dole.

In 1992 and 1996, neither of the Republican primary winners, Bush and Dole, respectively, lost a single county.

KENTUCKY DEMOCRATIC

1976

County	Total Vote	Carter	Udall	Wallace	Other	Winner	Percentage of Total Vote Carter	Udall	Wallace	Other
ADAIR	755	518	36	179	22	Carter	68.6%	4.8%	23.7%	2.9%
ALLEN	574	425	25	88	36	Carter	74.0%	4.4%	15.3%	6.3%
ANDERSON	1,232	741	144	186	161	Carter	60.1%	11.7%	15.1%	13.1%
BALLARD	1,599	1,204	43	280	72	Carter	75.3%	2.7%	17.5%	4.5%
BARREN	3,003	1,989	143	577	294	Carter	66.2%	4.8%	19.2%	9.8%
BATH	877	641	44	117	75	Carter	73.1%	5.0%	13.3%	8.6%
BELL	1,567	1,195	133	162	77	Carter	76.3%	8.5%	10.3%	4.9%
BOONE	3,064	1,660	265	440	699	Carter	54.2%	8.6%	14.4%	22.8%
BOURBON	1,665	1,063	198	260	144	Carter	63.8%	11.9%	15.6%	8.6%
BOYD	4,644	3,035	570	494	545	Carter	65.4%	12.3%	10.6%	11.7%
BOYLE	2,071	1,239	265	366	201	Carter	59.8%	12.8%	17.7%	9.7%
BRACKEN	788	515	45	96	132	Carter	65.4%	5.7%	12.2%	16.8%
BREATHITT	1,922	1,673	28	162	59	Carter	87.0%	1.5%	8.4%	3.1%
BRECKINRIDGE	1,165	706	107	199	153	Carter	60.6%	9.2%	17.1%	13.1%
BULLITT	3,241	1,499	286	1,110	346	Carter	46.3%	8.8%	34.2%	10.7%
BUTLER	504	370	16	85	33	Carter	73.4%	3.2%	16.9%	6.5%
CALDWELL	2,157	1,551	88	351	167	Carter	71.9%	4.1%	16.3%	7.7%
CALLOWAY	3,127	2,324	208	400	195	Carter	74.3%	6.7%	12.8%	6.2%
CAMPBELL	7,702	2,975	824	841	3,062	Carter	38.6%	10.7%	10.9%	39.8%
CARLISLE	994	696	25	228	45	Carter	70.0%	2.5%	22.9%	4.5%
CARROLL	974	655	112	122	85	Carter	67.2%	11.5%	12.5%	8.7%
CARTER	1,269	1,003	86	109	71	Carter	79.0%	6.8%	8.6%	5.6%
CASEY	463	327	37	67	32	Carter	70.6%	8.0%	14.5%	6.9%
CHRISTIAN	3,852	2,798	183	641	230	Carter	72.6%	4.8%	16.6%	6.0%
CLARK	3,312	2,272	285	515	240	Carter	68.6%	8.6%	15.5%	7.2%
CLAY	601	488	24	76	13	Carter	81.2%	4.0%	12.6%	2.2%
CLINTON	350	309	6	23	12	Carter	88.3%	1.7%	6.6%	3.4%
CRITTENDEN	670	549	23	67	31	Carter	81.9%	3.4%	10.0%	4.6%
CUMBERLAND	282	219	15	40	8	Carter	77.7%	5.3%	14.2%	2.8%
DAVIESS	7,669	3,961	787	1,007	1,914	Carter	51.6%	10.3%	13.1%	25.0%
EDMONSON	710	435	34	174	67	Carter	61.3%	4.8%	24.5%	9.4%
ELLIOTT	1,832	1,448	54	186	144	Carter	79.0%	2.9%	10.2%	7.9%
ESTILL	702	558	45	60	39	Carter	79.5%	6.4%	8.5%	5.6%
FAYETTE	16,664	9,189	3,858	2,083	1,534	Carter	55.1%	23.2%	12.5%	9.2%
FLEMING	1,097	726	64	235	72	Carter	66.2%	5.8%	21.4%	6.6%
FLOYD	4,519	3,216	252	764	287	Carter	71.2%	5.6%	16.9%	6.4%
FRANKLIN	7,897	4,782	1,022	1,155	938	Carter	60.6%	12.9%	14.6%	11.9%
FULTON	1,271	716	26	402	127	Carter	56.3%	2.0%	31.6%	10.0%
GALLATIN	520	365	37	69	49	Carter	70.2%	7.1%	13.3%	9.4%
GARRARD	598	474	40	68	16	Carter	79.3%	6.7%	11.4%	2.7%
GRANT	1,043	706	67	182	88	Carter	67.7%	6.4%	17.4%	8.4%
GRAVES	4,098	2,711	107	1,098	182	Carter	66.2%	2.6%	26.8%	4.4%
GRAYSON	1,097	689	73	191	144	Carter	62.8%	6.7%	17.4%	13.1%
GREEN	483	353	33	79	18	Carter	73.1%	6.8%	16.4%	3.7%
GREENUP	2,459	1,683	241	284	251	Carter	68.4%	9.8%	11.5%	10.2%
HANCOCK	503	342	48	57	56	Carter	68.0%	9.5%	11.3%	11.1%
HARDIN	4,863	2,694	462	988	719	Carter	55.4%	9.5%	20.3%	14.8%
HARLAN	2,421	1,694	193	379	155	Carter	70.0%	8.0%	15.7%	6.4%
HARRISON	1,451	985	135	201	130	Carter	67.9%	9.3%	13.9%	9.0%
HART	1,022	735	60	159	68	Carter	71.9%	5.9%	15.6%	6.7%

KENTUCKY DEMOCRATIC

1976

County	Total Vote	Carter	Udall	Wallace	Other	Winner	Percentage of Total Vote: Carter	Udall	Wallace	Other
HENDERSON	4,153	3,150	231	413	359	Carter	75.8%	5.6%	9.9%	8.6%
HENRY	1,823	1,245	121	339	118	Carter	68.3%	6.6%	18.6%	6.5%
HICKMAN	1,191	753	25	369	44	Carter	63.2%	2.1%	31.0%	3.7%
HOPKINS	3,750	2,608	183	728	231	Carter	69.5%	4.9%	19.4%	6.2%
JACKSON	162	126	10	16	10	Carter	77.8%	6.2%	9.9%	6.2%
JEFFERSON	68,112	29,797	12,846	14,519	10,950	Carter	43.7%	18.9%	21.3%	16.1%
JESSAMINE	1,488	913	185	296	94	Carter	61.4%	12.4%	19.9%	6.3%
JOHNSON	1,840	1,367	96	202	175	Carter	74.3%	5.2%	11.0%	9.5%
KENTON	12,386	4,624	1,287	1,502	4,973	Carter	37.3%	10.4%	12.1%	40.2%
KNOTT	1,729	1,403	75	158	93	Carter	81.1%	4.3%	9.1%	5.4%
KNOX	866	626	70	100	70	Carter	72.3%	8.1%	11.5%	8.1%
LARUE	1,032	606	94	228	104	Carter	58.7%	9.1%	22.1%	10.1%
LAUREL	1,038	778	67	120	73	Carter	75.0%	6.5%	11.6%	7.0%
LAWRENCE	806	609	33	108	56	Carter	75.6%	4.1%	13.4%	6.9%
LEE	398	283	35	60	20	Carter	71.1%	8.8%	15.1%	5.0%
LESLIE	477	413	25	28	11	Carter	86.6%	5.2%	5.9%	2.3%
LETCHER	1,576	1,186	73	259	58	Carter	75.3%	4.6%	16.4%	3.7%
LEWIS	472	398	20	31	23	Carter	84.3%	4.2%	6.6%	4.9%
LINCOLN	1,137	836	57	195	49	Carter	73.5%	5.0%	17.2%	4.3%
LIVINGSTON	1,357	985	41	268	63	Carter	72.6%	3.0%	19.7%	4.6%
LOGAN	2,183	1,694	85	291	113	Carter	77.6%	3.9%	13.3%	5.2%
LYON	1,161	883	31	185	62	Carter	76.1%	2.7%	15.9%	5.3%
MCCRACKEN	9,280	6,344	588	1,707	641	Carter	68.4%	6.3%	18.4%	6.9%
MCCREARY	317	262	26	17	12	Carter	82.6%	8.2%	5.4%	3.8%
MCLEAN	845	594	51	121	79	Carter	70.3%	6.0%	14.3%	9.3%
MADISON	3,398	2,231	516	479	172	Carter	65.7%	15.2%	14.1%	5.1%
MAGOFFIN	805	587	112	82	24	Carter	72.9%	13.9%	10.2%	3.0%
MARION	1,690	572	111	205	802	McCormack	33.8%	6.6%	12.1%	47.5%
MARSHALL	5,830	4,029	211	1,254	336	Carter	69.1%	3.6%	21.5%	5.8%
MARTIN	190	138	25	16	11	Carter	72.6%	13.2%	8.4%	5.8%
MASON	1,787	1,203	138	230	216	Carter	67.3%	7.7%	12.9%	12.1%
MEADE	1,680	806	164	406	304	Carter	48.0%	9.8%	24.2%	18.1%
MENIFEE	367	283	11	61	12	Carter	77.1%	3.0%	16.6%	3.3%
MERCER	1,556	1,083	126	259	88	Carter	69.6%	8.1%	16.6%	5.7%
METCALFE	593	459	28	75	31	Carter	77.4%	4.7%	12.6%	5.2%
MONROE	312	265	8	32	7	Carter	84.9%	2.6%	10.3%	2.2%
MONTGOMERY	1,356	966	99	192	99	Carter	71.2%	7.3%	14.2%	7.3%
MORGAN	1,079	882	34	105	58	Carter	81.7%	3.2%	9.7%	5.4%
MUHLENBERG	2,081	1,516	99	324	142	Carter	72.8%	4.8%	15.6%	6.8%
NELSON	2,889	1,356	267	413	853	Carter	46.9%	9.2%	14.3%	29.5%
NICHOLAS	583	403	49	86	45	Carter	69.1%	8.4%	14.8%	7.7%
OHIO	981	721	66	128	66	Carter	73.5%	6.7%	13.0%	6.7%
OLDHAM	1,696	850	214	414	218	Carter	50.1%	12.6%	24.4%	12.9%
OWEN	1,213	805	84	218	106	Carter	66.4%	6.9%	18.0%	8.7%
OWSLEY	112	86	3	15	8	Carter	76.8%	2.7%	13.4%	7.1%
PENDLETON	867	637	30	116	84	Carter	73.5%	3.5%	13.4%	9.7%
PERRY	2,646	1,929	131	464	122	Carter	72.9%	5.0%	17.5%	4.6%
PIKE	5,067	3,825	305	547	390	Carter	75.5%	6.0%	10.8%	7.7%
POWELL	702	578	19	92	13	Carter	82.3%	2.7%	13.1%	1.9%
PULASKI	2,217	1,692	144	244	137	Carter	76.3%	6.5%	11.0%	6.2%

KENTUCKY DEMOCRATIC

1976

County	Total Vote	Carter	Udall	Wallace	Other	Winner	Percentage of Total Vote Carter	Udall	Wallace	Other
ROBERTSON	252	190	6	49	7	Carter	75.4%	2.4%	19.4%	2.8%
ROCKCASTLE	525	410	36	58	21	Carter	78.1%	6.9%	11.0%	4.0%
ROWAN	1,331	961	151	120	99	Carter	72.2%	11.3%	9.0%	7.4%
RUSSELL	716	534	43	106	33	Carter	74.6%	6.0%	14.8%	4.6%
SCOTT	1,715	1,119	160	315	121	Carter	65.2%	9.3%	18.4%	7.1%
SHELBY	2,317	1,394	215	472	236	Carter	60.2%	9.3%	20.4%	10.2%
SIMPSON	1,098	764	43	161	130	Carter	69.6%	3.9%	14.7%	11.8%
SPENCER	1,017	546	90	285	96	Carter	53.7%	8.8%	28.0%	9.4%
TAYLOR	981	670	65	192	54	Carter	68.3%	6.6%	19.6%	5.5%
TODD	1,254	924	37	237	56	Carter	73.7%	3.0%	18.9%	4.5%
TRIGG	1,881	1,367	56	341	117	Carter	72.7%	3.0%	18.1%	6.2%
TRIMBLE	674	430	63	105	76	Carter	63.8%	9.3%	15.6%	11.3%
UNION	1,429	1,007	99	178	145	Carter	70.5%	6.9%	12.5%	10.1%
WARREN	5,103	2,957	456	1,168	522	Carter	57.9%	8.9%	22.9%	10.2%
WASHINGTON	953	525	60	124	244	Carter	55.1%	6.3%	13.0%	25.6%
WAYNE	826	626	61	109	30	Carter	75.8%	7.4%	13.2%	3.6%
WEBSTER	1,750	1,308	69	230	143	Carter	74.7%	3.9%	13.1%	8.2%
WHITLEY	901	680	52	104	65	Carter	75.5%	5.8%	11.5%	7.2%
WOLFE	637	510	23	69	35	Carter	80.1%	3.6%	10.8%	5.5%
WOODFORD	2,027	1,282	226	298	221	Carter	63.2%	11.1%	14.7%	10.9%
TOTAL	306,006	181,690	33,262	51,540	39,514	Carter	59.4%	10.9%	16.8%	12.9%

KENTUCKY REPUBLICAN

1976

County	Total Vote	Ford	Reagan	Other	Winner	Percentage of Total Vote Ford	Reagan	Other
ADAIR	1,080	558	502	20	Ford	51.7%	46.5%	1.9%
ALLEN	701	324	363	14	Reagan	46.2%	51.8%	2.0%
ANDERSON	219	108	111		Reagan	49.3%	50.7%	
BALLARD	78	39	36	3	Ford	50.0%	46.2%	3.8%
BARREN	1,217	423	767	27	Reagan	34.8%	63.0%	2.2%
BATH	112	70	38	4	Ford	62.5%	33.9%	3.6%
BELL	1,777	1,175	532	70	Ford	66.1%	29.9%	3.9%
BOONE	858	421	405	32	Ford	49.1%	47.2%	3.7%
BOURBON	255	145	104	6	Ford	56.9%	40.8%	2.4%
BOYD	3,488	2,066	1,320	102	Ford	59.2%	37.8%	2.9%
BOYLE	419	209	204	6	Ford	49.9%	48.7%	1.4%
BRACKEN	114	65	46	3	Ford	57.0%	40.4%	2.6%
BREATHITT	131	72	53	6	Ford	55.0%	40.5%	4.6%
BRECKINRIDGE	718	294	407	17	Reagan	40.9%	56.7%	2.4%
BULLITT	287	82	202	3	Reagan	28.6%	70.4%	1.0%
BUTLER	777	354	404	19	Reagan	45.6%	52.0%	2.4%
CALDWELL	454	237	207	10	Ford	52.2%	45.6%	2.2%
CALLOWAY	207	99	106	2	Reagan	47.8%	51.2%	1.0%
CAMPBELL	4,447	2,229	2,058	160	Ford	50.1%	46.3%	3.6%
CARLISLE	25	17	8		Ford	68.0%	32.0%	

KENTUCKY REPUBLICAN

1976

County	Total Vote	Ford	Reagan	Other	Winner	Percentage of Total Vote Ford	Reagan	Other
CARROLL	77	41	36		Ford	53.2%	46.8%	
CARTER	1,059	554	487	18	Ford	52.3%	46.0%	1.7%
CASEY	1,317	668	635	14	Ford	50.7%	48.2%	1.1%
CHRISTIAN	593	251	323	19	Reagan	42.3%	54.5%	3.2%
CLARK	400	196	187	17	Ford	49.0%	46.8%	4.3%
CLAY	1,297	894	373	30	Ford	68.9%	28.8%	2.3%
CLINTON	860	488	350	22	Ford	56.7%	40.7%	2.6%
CRITTENDEN	536	268	259	9	Ford	50.0%	48.3%	1.7%
CUMBERLAND	631	383	220	28	Ford	60.7%	34.9%	4.4%
DAVIESS	1,858	926	871	61	Ford	49.8%	46.9%	3.3%
EDMONSON	1,534	578	917	39	Reagan	37.7%	59.8%	2.5%
ELLIOTT	43	30	12	1	Ford	69.8%	27.9%	2.3%
ESTILL	927	558	355	14	Ford	60.2%	38.3%	1.5%
FAYETTE	8,105	4,373	3,634	98	Ford	54.0%	44.8%	1.2%
FLEMING	281	165	111	5	Ford	58.7%	39.5%	1.8%
FLOYD	516	303	192	21	Ford	58.7%	37.2%	4.1%
FRANKLIN	501	231	249	21	Reagan	46.1%	49.7%	4.2%
FULTON	82	33	43	6	Reagan	40.2%	52.4%	7.3%
GALLATIN	54	25	28	1	Reagan	46.3%	51.9%	1.9%
GARRARD	517	210	293	14	Reagan	40.6%	56.7%	2.7%
GRANT	145	89	54	2	Ford	61.4%	37.2%	1.4%
GRAVES	177	50	117	10	Reagan	28.2%	66.1%	5.6%
GRAYSON	1,267	609	633	25	Reagan	48.1%	50.0%	2.0%
GREEN	643	281	340	22	Reagan	43.7%	52.9%	3.4%
GREENUP	1,287	681	583	23	Ford	52.9%	45.3%	1.8%
HANCOCK	291	172	109	10	Ford	59.1%	37.5%	3.4%
HARDIN	1,238	545	671	22	Reagan	44.0%	54.2%	1.8%
HARLAN	1,811	1,068	696	47	Ford	59.0%	38.4%	2.6%
HARRISON	196	138	51	7	Ford	70.4%	26.0%	3.6%
HART	509	177	312	20	Reagan	34.8%	61.3%	3.9%
HENDERSON	329	184	127	18	Ford	55.9%	38.6%	5.5%
HENRY	130	59	69	2	Reagan	45.4%	53.1%	1.5%
HICKMAN	48	12	36		Reagan	25.0%	75.0%	
HOPKINS	471	270	196	5	Ford	57.3%	41.6%	1.1%
JACKSON	809	527	262	20	Ford	65.1%	32.4%	2.5%
JEFFERSON	38,189	15,064	22,562	563	Reagan	39.4%	59.1%	1.5%
JESSAMINE	364	168	190	6	Reagan	46.2%	52.2%	1.6%
JOHNSON	2,770	1,655	1,039	76	Ford	59.7%	37.5%	2.7%
KENTON	3,585	1,779	1,680	126	Ford	49.6%	46.9%	3.5%
KNOTT	79	55	18	6	Ford	69.6%	22.8%	7.6%
KNOX	1,404	952	398	54	Ford	67.8%	28.3%	3.8%
LARUE	191	72	114	5	Reagan	37.7%	59.7%	2.6%
LAUREL	2,771	1,563	1,131	77	Ford	56.4%	40.8%	2.8%
LAWRENCE	521	297	213	11	Ford	57.0%	40.9%	2.1%
LEE	517	336	168	13	Ford	65.0%	32.5%	2.5%
LESLIE	1,160	864	263	33	Ford	74.5%	22.7%	2.8%
LETCHER	748	499	226	23	Ford	66.7%	30.2%	3.1%
LEWIS	914	456	439	19	Ford	49.9%	48.0%	2.1%
LINCOLN	754	384	355	15	Ford	50.9%	47.1%	2.0%
LIVINGSTON	102	56	46		Ford	54.9%	45.1%	

KENTUCKY REPUBLICAN

1976

County	Total Vote	Ford	Reagan	Other	Winner	Percentage of Total Vote Ford	Reagan	Other
LOGAN	235	118	111	6	Ford	50.2%	47.2%	2.6%
LYON	74	39	33	2	Ford	52.7%	44.6%	2.7%
MCCRACKEN	869	411	448	10	Reagan	47.3%	51.6%	1.2%
MCCREARY	1,247	844	372	31	Ford	67.7%	29.8%	2.5%
MCLEAN	204	97	101	6	Reagan	47.5%	49.5%	2.9%
MADISON	1,339	785	524	30	Ford	58.6%	39.1%	2.2%
MAGOFFIN	332	213	115	4	Ford	64.2%	34.6%	1.2%
MARION	97	38	56	3	Reagan	39.2%	57.7%	3.1%
MARSHALL	334	186	140	8	Ford	55.7%	41.9%	2.4%
MARTIN	784	567	198	19	Ford	72.3%	25.3%	2.4%
MASON	479	276	194	9	Ford	57.6%	40.5%	1.9%
MEADE	164	66	93	5	Reagan	40.2%	56.7%	3.0%
MENIFEE	55	23	31	1	Reagan	41.8%	56.4%	1.8%
MERCER	395	156	236	3	Reagan	39.5%	59.7%	0.8%
METCALFE	493	228	251	14	Reagan	46.2%	50.9%	2.8%
MONROE	2,268	1,673	563	32	Ford	73.8%	24.8%	1.4%
MONTGOMERY	213	118	90	5	Ford	55.4%	42.3%	2.3%
MORGAN	103	80	23		Ford	77.7%	22.3%	
MUHLENBERG	960	537	407	16	Ford	55.9%	42.4%	1.7%
NELSON	266	124	133	9	Reagan	46.6%	50.0%	3.4%
NICHOLAS	65	34	31		Ford	52.3%	47.7%	
OHIO	1,470	737	705	28	Ford	50.1%	48.0%	1.9%
OLDHAM	649	279	356	14	Reagan	43.0%	54.9%	2.2%
OWEN	67	32	33	2	Reagan	47.8%	49.3%	3.0%
OWSLEY	322	201	115	6	Ford	62.4%	35.7%	1.9%
PENDLETON	189	97	89	3	Ford	51.3%	47.1%	1.6%
PERRY	1,203	889	291	23	Ford	73.9%	24.2%	1.9%
PIKE	1,986	1,446	513	27	Ford	72.8%	25.8%	1.4%
POWELL	244	154	89	1	Ford	63.1%	36.5%	0.4%
PULASKI	4,216	2,834	1,293	89	Ford	67.2%	30.7%	2.1%
ROBERTSON	45	23	22		Ford	51.1%	48.9%	
ROCKCASTLE	1,104	578	490	36	Ford	52.4%	44.4%	3.3%
ROWAN	517	278	227	12	Ford	53.8%	43.9%	2.3%
RUSSELL	1,116	546	541	29	Ford	48.9%	48.5%	2.6%
SCOTT	182	86	92	4	Reagan	47.3%	50.5%	2.2%
SHELBY	293	145	142	6	Ford	49.5%	48.5%	2.0%
SIMPSON	161	80	76	5	Ford	49.7%	47.2%	3.1%
SPENCER	127	35	86	6	Reagan	27.6%	67.7%	4.7%
TAYLOR	906	462	429	15	Ford	51.0%	47.4%	1.7%
TODD	55	29	23	3	Ford	52.7%	41.8%	5.5%
TRIGG	92	67	23	2	Ford	72.8%	25.0%	2.2%
TRIMBLE	57	26	30	1	Reagan	45.6%	52.6%	1.8%
UNION	108	58	48	2	Ford	53.7%	44.4%	1.9%
WARREN	1,103	483	593	27	Reagan	43.8%	53.8%	2.4%
WASHINGTON	350	146	194	10	Reagan	41.7%	55.4%	2.9%
WAYNE	1,258	858	370	30	Ford	68.2%	29.4%	2.4%
WEBSTER	122	80	39	3	Ford	65.6%	32.0%	2.5%
WHITLEY	2,202	1,290	849	63	Ford	58.6%	38.6%	2.9%
WOLFE	99	53	45	1	Ford	53.5%	45.5%	1.0%
WOODFORD	337	147	184	6	Reagan	43.6%	54.6%	1.8%
TOTAL	133,528	67,976	62,683	2,869	Ford	50.9%	46.9%	2.1%

KENTUCKY DEMOCRATIC

1980

County	Total Vote	Carter	E. Kennedy	Other	Winner	Percentage of Total Vote Carter	E. Kennedy	Other
ADAIR	749	596	107	46	Carter	79.6%	14.3%	6.1%
ALLEN	427	329	68	30	Carter	77.0%	15.9%	7.0%
ANDERSON	1,213	925	172	116	Carter	76.3%	14.2%	9.6%
BALLARD	1,221	1,022	121	78	Carter	83.7%	9.9%	6.4%
BARREN	1,498	1,070	277	151	Carter	71.4%	18.5%	10.1%
BATH	860	607	166	87	Carter	70.6%	19.3%	10.1%
BELL	1,287	759	423	105	Carter	59.0%	32.9%	8.2%
BOONE	2,591	1,654	577	360	Carter	63.8%	22.3%	13.9%
BOURBON	1,501	1,038	286	177	Carter	69.2%	19.1%	11.8%
BOYD	3,258	2,245	700	313	Carter	68.9%	21.5%	9.6%
BOYLE	2,011	1,364	373	274	Carter	67.8%	18.5%	13.6%
BRACKEN	654	483	115	56	Carter	73.9%	17.6%	8.6%
BREATHITT	2,883	1,944	746	193	Carter	67.4%	25.9%	6.7%
BRECKINRIDGE	941	685	196	60	Carter	72.8%	20.8%	6.4%
BULLITT	2,440	1,705	537	198	Carter	69.9%	22.0%	8.1%
BUTLER	411	296	84	31	Carter	72.0%	20.4%	7.5%
CALDWELL	1,318	977	232	109	Carter	74.1%	17.6%	8.3%
CALLOWAY	2,922	2,168	397	357	Carter	74.2%	13.6%	12.2%
CAMPBELL	5,807	3,304	1,670	833	Carter	56.9%	28.8%	14.3%
CARLISLE	912	694	140	78	Carter	76.1%	15.4%	8.6%
CARROLL	944	712	176	56	Carter	75.4%	18.6%	5.9%
CARTER	991	651	247	93	Carter	65.7%	24.9%	9.4%
CASEY	425	299	99	27	Carter	70.4%	23.3%	6.4%
CHRISTIAN	3,637	2,376	675	586	Carter	65.3%	18.6%	16.1%
CLARK	2,208	1,466	484	258	Carter	66.4%	21.9%	11.7%
CLAY	508	298	178	32	Carter	58.7%	35.0%	6.3%
CLINTON	238	175	51	12	Carter	73.5%	21.4%	5.0%
CRITTENDEN	609	421	130	58	Carter	69.1%	21.3%	9.5%
CUMBERLAND	269	225	30	14	Carter	83.6%	11.2%	5.2%
DAVIESS	5,995	3,972	1,210	813	Carter	66.3%	20.2%	13.6%
EDMONSON	285	218	49	18	Carter	76.5%	17.2%	6.3%
ELLIOTT	549	392	123	34	Carter	71.4%	22.4%	6.2%
ESTILL	607	459	101	47	Carter	75.6%	16.6%	7.7%
FAYETTE	14,388	8,722	3,586	2,080	Carter	60.6%	24.9%	14.5%
FLEMING	851	627	153	71	Carter	73.7%	18.0%	8.3%
FLOYD	4,667	2,600	1,708	359	Carter	55.7%	36.6%	7.7%
FRANKLIN	9,917	6,993	1,871	1,053	Carter	70.5%	18.9%	10.6%
FULTON	957	709	98	150	Carter	74.1%	10.2%	15.7%
GALLATIN	414	285	82	47	Carter	68.8%	19.8%	11.4%
GARRARD	609	487	83	39	Carter	80.0%	13.6%	6.4%
GRANT	1,026	762	181	83	Carter	74.3%	17.6%	8.1%
GRAVES	3,942	2,740	775	427	Carter	69.5%	19.7%	10.8%
GRAYSON	850	611	177	62	Carter	71.9%	20.8%	7.3%
GREEN	435	357	62	16	Carter	82.1%	14.3%	3.7%
GREENUP	2,232	1,579	497	156	Carter	70.7%	22.3%	7.0%
HANCOCK	395	278	87	30	Carter	70.4%	22.0%	7.6%
HARDIN	4,108	2,573	1,005	530	Carter	62.6%	24.5%	12.9%
HARLAN	1,979	1,087	757	135	Carter	54.9%	38.3%	6.8%
HARRISON	1,978	1,427	311	240	Carter	72.1%	15.7%	12.1%
HART	817	617	151	49	Carter	75.5%	18.5%	6.0%

KENTUCKY DEMOCRATIC

1980

County	Total Vote	Carter	E. Kennedy	Other	Winner	Percentage of Total Vote Carter	E. Kennedy	Other
HENDERSON	2,821	1,898	585	338	Carter	67.3%	20.7%	12.0%
HENRY	1,808	1,367	248	193	Carter	75.6%	13.7%	10.7%
HICKMAN	1,013	752	162	99	Carter	74.2%	16.0%	9.8%
HOPKINS	3,931	2,804	674	453	Carter	71.3%	17.1%	11.5%
JACKSON	152	98	36	18	Carter	64.5%	23.7%	11.8%
JEFFERSON	41,520	26,045	11,717	3,758	Carter	62.7%	28.2%	9.1%
JESSAMINE	1,732	1,107	405	220	Carter	63.9%	23.4%	12.7%
JOHNSON	815	538	208	69	Carter	66.0%	25.5%	8.5%
KENTON	9,021	5,225	2,590	1,206	Carter	57.9%	28.7%	13.4%
KNOTT	1,996	1,191	672	133	Carter	59.7%	33.7%	6.7%
KNOX	888	578	256	54	Carter	65.1%	28.8%	6.1%
LARUE	873	635	149	89	Carter	72.7%	17.1%	10.2%
LAUREL	1,069	755	237	77	Carter	70.6%	22.2%	7.2%
LAWRENCE	744	520	175	49	Carter	69.9%	23.5%	6.6%
LEE	481	325	115	41	Carter	67.6%	23.9%	8.5%
LESLIE	249	155	65	29	Carter	62.2%	26.1%	11.6%
LETCHER	1,304	674	511	119	Carter	51.7%	39.2%	9.1%
LEWIS	377	288	61	28	Carter	76.4%	16.2%	7.4%
LINCOLN	989	780	153	56	Carter	78.9%	15.5%	5.7%
LIVINGSTON	1,075	820	167	88	Carter	76.3%	15.5%	8.2%
LOGAN	1,574	1,185	263	126	Carter	75.3%	16.7%	8.0%
LYON	701	495	154	52	Carter	70.6%	22.0%	7.4%
MCCRACKEN	5,470	4,163	873	434	Carter	76.1%	16.0%	7.9%
MCCREARY	333	196	110	27	Carter	58.9%	33.0%	8.1%
MCLEAN	896	678	129	89	Carter	75.7%	14.4%	9.9%
MADISON	3,172	2,204	660	308	Carter	69.5%	20.8%	9.7%
MAGOFFIN	895	558	304	33	Carter	62.3%	34.0%	3.7%
MARION	1,139	707	315	117	Carter	62.1%	27.7%	10.3%
MARSHALL	2,505	1,879	352	274	Carter	75.0%	14.1%	10.9%
MARTIN	270	181	64	25	Carter	67.0%	23.7%	9.3%
MASON	1,213	806	277	130	Carter	66.4%	22.8%	10.7%
MEADE	1,334	875	343	116	Carter	65.6%	25.7%	8.7%
MENIFEE	352	252	82	18	Carter	71.6%	23.3%	5.1%
MERCER	1,504	1,083	320	101	Carter	72.0%	21.3%	6.7%
METCALFE	615	439	126	50	Carter	71.4%	20.5%	8.1%
MONROE	265	182	65	18	Carter	68.7%	24.5%	6.8%
MONTGOMERY	2,007	1,324	421	262	Carter	66.0%	21.0%	13.1%
MORGAN	841	611	166	64	Carter	72.7%	19.7%	7.6%
MUHLENBERG	1,780	1,287	343	150	Carter	72.3%	19.3%	8.4%
NELSON	2,050	1,455	440	155	Carter	71.0%	21.5%	7.6%
NICHOLAS	508	375	93	40	Carter	73.8%	18.3%	7.9%
OHIO	968	722	186	60	Carter	74.6%	19.2%	6.2%
OLDHAM	1,211	835	234	142	Carter	69.0%	19.3%	11.7%
OWEN	1,400	1,080	173	147	Carter	77.1%	12.4%	10.5%
OWSLEY	126	91	26	9	Carter	72.2%	20.6%	7.1%
PENDLETON	981	698	169	114	Carter	71.2%	17.2%	11.6%
PERRY	1,464	914	456	94	Carter	62.4%	31.1%	6.4%
PIKE	4,432	2,550	1,647	235	Carter	57.5%	37.2%	5.3%
POWELL	679	478	162	39	Carter	70.4%	23.9%	5.7%
PULASKI	2,158	1,589	377	192	Carter	73.6%	17.5%	8.9%

KENTUCKY DEMOCRATIC

1980

County	Total Vote	Carter	E. Kennedy	Other	Winner	Percentage of Total Vote Carter	E. Kennedy	Other
ROBERTSON	237	142	57	38	Carter	59.9%	24.1%	16.0%
ROCKCASTLE	501	385	88	28	Carter	76.8%	17.6%	5.6%
ROWAN	1,114	732	271	111	Carter	65.7%	24.3%	10.0%
RUSSELL	634	455	126	53	Carter	71.8%	19.9%	8.4%
SCOTT	1,740	1,300	283	157	Carter	74.7%	16.3%	9.0%
SHELBY	2,127	1,558	332	237	Carter	73.2%	15.6%	11.1%
SIMPSON	675	492	106	77	Carter	72.9%	15.7%	11.4%
SPENCER	497	407	55	35	Carter	81.9%	11.1%	7.0%
TAYLOR	870	680	160	30	Carter	78.2%	18.4%	3.4%
TODD	895	659	143	93	Carter	73.6%	16.0%	10.4%
TRIGG	1,190	826	218	146	Carter	69.4%	18.3%	12.3%
TRIMBLE	602	458	86	58	Carter	76.1%	14.3%	9.6%
UNION	1,656	1,140	336	180	Carter	68.8%	20.3%	10.9%
WARREN	3,568	2,514	621	433	Carter	70.5%	17.4%	12.1%
WASHINGTON	773	600	132	41	Carter	77.6%	17.1%	5.3%
WAYNE	851	630	160	61	Carter	74.0%	18.8%	7.2%
WEBSTER	1,473	998	289	186	Carter	67.8%	19.6%	12.6%
WHITLEY	915	640	215	60	Carter	69.9%	23.5%	6.6%
WOLFE	622	469	120	33	Carter	75.4%	19.3%	5.3%
WOODFORD	1,956	1,304	329	323	Carter	66.7%	16.8%	16.5%
TOTAL	240,331	160,819	55,167	24,345	Carter	66.9%	23.0%	10.1%

KENTUCKY REPUBLICAN

1980

County	Total Vote	Reagan	Other	Winner	Percentage of Total Vote Reagan	Other
ADAIR	1,652	1,488	164	Reagan	90.1%	9.9%
ALLEN	435	369	66	Reagan	84.8%	15.2%
ANDERSON	136	108	28	Reagan	79.4%	20.6%
BALLARD	38	32	6	Reagan	84.2%	15.8%
BARREN	555	487	68	Reagan	87.7%	12.3%
BATH	66	62	4	Reagan	93.9%	6.1%
BELL	2,324	1,861	463	Reagan	80.1%	19.9%
BOONE	586	481	105	Reagan	82.1%	17.9%
BOURBON	116	88	28	Reagan	75.9%	24.1%
BOYD	1,586	1,199	387	Reagan	75.6%	24.4%
BOYLE	282	198	84	Reagan	70.2%	29.8%
BRACKEN	73	58	15	Reagan	79.5%	20.5%
BREATHITT	121	102	19	Reagan	84.3%	15.7%
BRECKINRIDGE	301	258	43	Reagan	85.7%	14.3%
BULLITT	251	210	41	Reagan	83.7%	16.3%
BUTLER	493	446	47	Reagan	90.5%	9.5%
CALDWELL	216	181	35	Reagan	83.8%	16.2%
CALLOWAY	132	100	32	Reagan	75.8%	24.2%
CAMPBELL	2,300	1,742	558	Reagan	75.7%	24.3%
CARLISLE	24	18	6	Reagan	75.0%	25.0%

KENTUCKY REPUBLICAN

1980

County	Total Vote	Reagan	Other	Winner	Percentage of Total Vote	
					Reagan	Other
CARROLL	50	39	11	Reagan	78.0%	22.0%
CARTER	540	467	73	Reagan	86.5%	13.5%
CASEY	2,254	2,033	221	Reagan	90.2%	9.8%
CHRISTIAN	397	352	45	Reagan	88.7%	11.3%
CLARK	240	195	45	Reagan	81.3%	18.8%
CLAY	2,304	2,032	272	Reagan	88.2%	11.8%
CLINTON	1,606	1,457	149	Reagan	90.7%	9.3%
CRITTENDEN	355	312	43	Reagan	87.9%	12.1%
CUMBERLAND	1,021	899	122	Reagan	88.1%	11.9%
DAVIESS	952	729	223	Reagan	76.6%	23.4%
EDMONSON	452	414	38	Reagan	91.6%	8.4%
ELLIOTT	13	9	4	Reagan	69.2%	30.8%
ESTILL	965	818	147	Reagan	84.8%	15.2%
FAYETTE	3,682	2,285	1,397	Reagan	62.1%	37.9%
FLEMING	208	187	21	Reagan	89.9%	10.1%
FLOYD	353	291	62	Reagan	82.4%	17.6%
FRANKLIN	355	264	91	Reagan	74.4%	25.6%
FULTON	43	37	6	Reagan	86.0%	14.0%
GALLATIN	38	33	5	Reagan	86.8%	13.2%
GARRARD	1,040	886	154	Reagan	85.2%	14.8%
GRANT	93	76	17	Reagan	81.7%	18.3%
GRAVES	123	105	18	Reagan	85.4%	14.6%
GRAYSON	860	768	92	Reagan	89.3%	10.7%
GREEN	872	744	128	Reagan	85.3%	14.7%
GREENUP	731	589	142	Reagan	80.6%	19.4%
HANCOCK	159	130	29	Reagan	81.8%	18.2%
HARDIN	848	694	154	Reagan	81.8%	18.2%
HARLAN	1,950	1,524	426	Reagan	78.2%	21.8%
HARRISON	94	75	19	Reagan	79.8%	20.2%
HART	268	237	31	Reagan	88.4%	11.6%
HENDERSON	165	129	36	Reagan	78.2%	21.8%
HENRY	66	54	12	Reagan	81.8%	18.2%
HICKMAN	36	32	4	Reagan	88.9%	11.1%
HOPKINS	325	248	77	Reagan	76.3%	23.7%
JACKSON	1,288	1,150	138	Reagan	89.3%	10.7%
JEFFERSON	14,753	11,339	3,414	Reagan	76.9%	23.1%
JESSAMINE	393	285	108	Reagan	72.5%	27.5%
JOHNSON	747	632	115	Reagan	84.6%	15.4%
KENTON	1,915	1,546	369	Reagan	80.7%	19.3%
KNOTT	38	29	9	Reagan	76.3%	23.7%
KNOX	2,054	1,623	431	Reagan	79.0%	21.0%
LARUE	133	108	25	Reagan	81.2%	18.8%
LAUREL	3,634	3,103	531	Reagan	85.4%	14.6%
LAWRENCE	428	358	70	Reagan	83.6%	16.4%
LEE	738	620	118	Reagan	84.0%	16.0%
LESLIE	1,305	1,142	163	Reagan	87.5%	12.5%
LETCHER	431	367	64	Reagan	85.2%	14.8%
LEWIS	558	484	74	Reagan	86.7%	13.3%
LINCOLN	863	733	130	Reagan	84.9%	15.1%
LIVINGSTON	85	75	10	Reagan	88.2%	11.8%

KENTUCKY REPUBLICAN

1980

County	Total Vote	Reagan	Other	Winner	Percentage of Total Vote: Reagan	Percentage of Total Vote: Other
LOGAN	149	124	25	Reagan	83.2%	16.8%
LYON	52	42	10	Reagan	80.8%	19.2%
MCCRACKEN	398	338	60	Reagan	84.9%	15.1%
MCCREARY	1,373	1,197	176	Reagan	87.2%	12.8%
MCLEAN	133	108	25	Reagan	81.2%	18.8%
MADISON	1,326	1,041	285	Reagan	78.5%	21.5%
MAGOFFIN	299	277	22	Reagan	92.6%	7.4%
MARION	67	56	11	Reagan	83.6%	16.4%
MARSHALL	132	110	22	Reagan	83.3%	16.7%
MARTIN	810	667	143	Reagan	82.3%	17.7%
MASON	247	206	41	Reagan	83.4%	16.6%
MEADE	99	85	14	Reagan	85.9%	14.1%
MENIFEE	53	47	6	Reagan	88.7%	11.3%
MERCER	285	251	34	Reagan	88.1%	11.9%
METCALFE	963	850	113	Reagan	88.3%	11.7%
MONROE	2,351	2,116	235	Reagan	90.0%	10.0%
MONTGOMERY	147	116	31	Reagan	78.9%	21.1%
MORGAN	63	59	4	Reagan	93.7%	6.3%
MUHLENBERG	384	327	57	Reagan	85.2%	14.8%
NELSON	133	94	39	Reagan	70.7%	29.3%
NICHOLAS	46	37	9	Reagan	80.4%	19.6%
OHIO	1,012	861	151	Reagan	85.1%	14.9%
OLDHAM	372	296	76	Reagan	79.6%	20.4%
OWEN	54	46	8	Reagan	85.2%	14.8%
OWSLEY	444	375	69	Reagan	84.5%	15.5%
PENDLETON	121	100	21	Reagan	82.6%	17.4%
PERRY	579	485	94	Reagan	83.8%	16.2%
PIKE	1,180	1,035	145	Reagan	87.7%	12.3%
POWELL	174	147	27	Reagan	84.5%	15.5%
PULASKI	5,826	4,990	836	Reagan	85.7%	14.3%
ROBERTSON	36	30	6	Reagan	83.3%	16.7%
ROCKCASTLE	1,416	1,215	201	Reagan	85.8%	14.2%
ROWAN	308	257	51	Reagan	83.4%	16.6%
RUSSELL	1,613	1,465	148	Reagan	90.8%	9.2%
SCOTT	139	104	35	Reagan	74.8%	25.2%
SHELBY	124	99	25	Reagan	79.8%	20.2%
SIMPSON	72	55	17	Reagan	76.4%	23.6%
SPENCER	58	46	12	Reagan	79.3%	20.7%
TAYLOR	1,131	1,014	117	Reagan	89.7%	10.3%
TODD	20	19	1	Reagan	95.0%	5.0%
TRIGG	64	50	14	Reagan	78.1%	21.9%
TRIMBLE	43	39	4	Reagan	90.7%	9.3%
UNION	77	61	16	Reagan	79.2%	20.8%
WARREN	603	501	102	Reagan	83.1%	16.9%
WASHINGTON	165	146	19	Reagan	88.5%	11.5%
WAYNE	1,981	1,746	235	Reagan	88.1%	11.9%
WEBSTER	85	71	14	Reagan	83.5%	16.5%
WHITLEY	3,362	2,792	570	Reagan	83.0%	17.0%
WOLFE	71	64	7	Reagan	90.1%	9.9%
WOODFORD	184	118	66	Reagan	64.1%	35.9%
TOTAL	95,332	78,601	16,731	Reagan	82.4%	17.6%
Certified Totals	94,795	78,072	16,723	Reagan	82.4%	17.6%

KENTUCKY DEMOCRATIC

1988

County	Total Vote	Dukakis	Gore	J. Jackson	Other	Winner	Percentage of Total Vote Dukakis	Gore	J. Jackson	Other
ALLEN	1,001	32	890	34	45	Gore	3.2%	88.9%	3.4%	4.5%
ANDERSON	1,774	379	956	129	310	Gore	21.4%	53.9%	7.3%	17.5%
BALLARD	1,336	122	628	51	535	Gore	9.1%	47.0%	3.8%	40.0%
BARREN	3,162	186	2,513	203	260	Gore	5.9%	79.5%	6.4%	8.2%
BATH	962	118	585	99	160	Gore	12.3%	60.8%	10.3%	16.6%
BELL	1,728	246	1,077	158	247	Gore	14.2%	62.3%	9.1%	14.3%
BOONE	2,824	631	864	320	1,009	Gore	22.3%	30.6%	11.3%	35.7%
BOURBON	1,992	377	912	346	357	Gore	18.9%	45.8%	17.4%	17.9%
BOYD	3,370	902	1,149	246	1,073	Gore	26.8%	34.1%	7.3%	31.8%
BOYLE	2,196	540	1,030	301	325	Gore	24.6%	46.9%	13.7%	14.8%
BRACKEN	672	119	272	43	238	Gore	17.7%	40.5%	6.4%	35.4%
BREATHITT	1,165	180	721	86	178	Gore	15.5%	61.9%	7.4%	15.3%
BRECKINRIDGE	1,489	206	922	101	260	Gore	13.8%	61.9%	6.8%	17.5%
BULLITT	3,796	783	1,773	263	977	Gore	20.6%	46.7%	6.9%	25.7%
BUTLER	542	24	444	21	53	Gore	4.4%	81.9%	3.9%	9.8%
CALDWELL	1,617	197	836	123	461	Gore	12.2%	51.7%	7.6%	28.5%
CALLOWAY	3,212	334	1,904	243	731	Gore	10.4%	59.3%	7.6%	22.8%
CAMPBELL	4,976	1,441	1,217	580	1,738	Dukakis	29.0%	24.5%	11.7%	34.9%
CARLISLE	807	61	356	47	343	Gore	7.6%	44.1%	5.8%	42.5%
CARROLL	920	182	404	73	261	Gore	19.8%	43.9%	7.9%	28.4%
CARTER	1,261	254	481	113	413	Gore	20.1%	38.1%	9.0%	32.8%
CASEY	581	63	404	37	77	Gore	10.8%	69.5%	6.4%	13.3%
CHRISTIAN	6,186	313	3,987	1,338	548	Gore	5.1%	64.5%	21.6%	8.9%
CLARK	2,812	596	1,293	375	548	Gore	21.2%	46.0%	13.3%	19.5%
CLAY	586	64	441	31	50	Gore	10.9%	75.3%	5.3%	8.5%
CLINTON	406	13	333	20	40	Gore	3.2%	82.0%	4.9%	9.9%
CRITTENDEN	651	90	247	28	286	Gore	13.8%	37.9%	4.3%	43.9%
CUMBERLAND	324	23	250	31	20	Gore	7.1%	77.2%	9.6%	6.2%
DAVIESS	9,901	1,446	5,451	772	2,232	Gore	14.6%	55.1%	7.8%	22.5%
EDMONSON	438	37	330	18	53	Gore	8.4%	75.3%	4.1%	12.1%
ELLIOTT	586	70	251	54	211	Gore	11.9%	42.8%	9.2%	36.0%
ESTILL	670	117	425	40	88	Gore	17.5%	63.4%	6.0%	13.1%
FAYETTE	20,639	5,510	6,596	5,442	3,091	Gore	26.7%	32.0%	26.4%	15.0%
FLEMING	1,103	154	647	85	217	Gore	14.0%	58.7%	7.7%	19.7%
FLOYD	3,891	582	2,088	408	813	Gore	15.0%	53.7%	10.5%	20.9%
FRANKLIN	10,333	2,288	4,985	1,265	1,795	Gore	22.1%	48.2%	12.2%	17.4%
FULTON	1,103	105	563	135	300	Gore	9.5%	51.0%	12.2%	27.2%
GALLATIN	434	79	149	62	144	Gore	18.2%	34.3%	14.3%	33.2%
GARRARD	623	117	384	30	92	Gore	18.8%	61.6%	4.8%	14.8%
GRANT	1,151	228	478	93	352	Gore	19.8%	41.5%	8.1%	30.6%
GRAVES	3,522	300	1,867	230	1,125	Gore	8.5%	53.0%	6.5%	31.9%
GRAYSON	1,166	153	717	92	204	Gore	13.1%	61.5%	7.9%	17.5%
GREEN	737	78	520	45	94	Gore	10.6%	70.6%	6.1%	12.8%
GREENUP	2,558	594	723	175	1,066	Gephardt	23.2%	28.3%	6.8%	41.7%
HANCOCK	734	97	439	50	148	Gore	13.2%	59.8%	6.8%	20.2%
HARDIN	5,911	1,116	3,010	672	1,113	Gore	18.9%	50.9%	11.4%	18.8%
HARLAN	2,269	360	1,275	302	332	Gore	15.9%	56.2%	13.3%	14.6%
HARRISON	1,699	306	861	154	378	Gore	18.0%	50.7%	9.1%	22.2%
HART	1,359	139	875	136	209	Gore	10.2%	64.4%	10.0%	15.4%
HENDERSON	3,895	720	1,563	451	1,161	Gore	18.5%	40.1%	11.6%	29.8%

KENTUCKY DEMOCRATIC

1988

County	Total Vote	Dukakis	Gore	J. Jackson	Other	Winner	Percentage of Total Vote Dukakis	Gore	J. Jackson	Other
HENRY	1,795	292	848	158	497	Gore	16.3%	47.2%	8.8%	27.7%
HICKMAN	938	79	502	96	261	Gore	8.4%	53.5%	10.2%	27.8%
HOPKINS	3,790	512	2,080	390	808	Gore	13.5%	54.9%	10.3%	21.3%
JACKSON	168	20	111	21	16	Gore	11.9%	66.1%	12.5%	9.5%
JEFFERSON	72,384	17,470	21,633	21,009	12,272	Gore	24.1%	29.9%	29.0%	17.0%
JESSAMINE	2,335	450	1,103	274	508	Gore	19.3%	47.2%	11.7%	21.8%
JOHNSON	929	140	516	61	212	Gore	15.1%	55.5%	6.6%	22.8%
KENTON	8,264	2,289	2,100	1,169	2,706	Dukakis	27.7%	25.4%	14.1%	32.7%
KNOTT	1,519	228	872	156	263	Gore	15.0%	57.4%	10.3%	17.3%
KNOX	997	178	537	120	162	Gore	17.9%	53.9%	12.0%	16.2%
LARUE	1,204	165	731	90	218	Gore	13.7%	60.7%	7.5%	18.1%
LAUREL	1,293	224	765	126	178	Gore	17.3%	59.2%	9.7%	13.8%
LAWRENCE	761	164	294	69	234	Gore	21.6%	38.6%	9.1%	30.7%
LEE	466	88	283	38	57	Gore	18.9%	60.7%	8.2%	12.2%
LESLIE	258	26	184	20	28	Gore	10.1%	71.3%	7.8%	10.9%
LETCHER	1,814	256	904	296	358	Gore	14.1%	49.8%	16.3%	19.7%
LEWIS	407	93	161	26	127	Gore	22.9%	39.6%	6.4%	31.2%
LINCOLN	1,144	190	716	72	166	Gore	16.6%	62.6%	6.3%	14.5%
LIVINGSTON	1,118	107	467	74	470	Gore	9.6%	41.8%	6.6%	42.0%
LOGAN	3,152	99	2,626	194	233	Gore	3.1%	83.3%	6.2%	7.4%
LYON	789	78	446	33	232	Gore	9.9%	56.5%	4.2%	29.4%
MCCRACKEN	7,143	915	2,779	1,183	2,266	Gore	12.8%	38.9%	16.6%	31.7%
MCCREARY	467	46	318	40	63	Gore	9.9%	68.1%	8.6%	13.5%
MCLEAN	1,142	121	701	44	276	Gore	10.6%	61.4%	3.9%	24.2%
MADISON	4,496	1,008	2,112	650	726	Gore	22.4%	47.0%	14.5%	16.1%
MAGOFFIN	634	84	451	26	73	Gore	13.2%	71.1%	4.1%	11.5%
MARION	1,586	310	862	132	282	Gore	19.5%	54.4%	8.3%	17.8%
MARSHALL	2,719	319	1,291	131	978	Gore	11.7%	47.5%	4.8%	36.0%
MARTIN	207	43	100	11	53	Gore	20.8%	48.3%	5.3%	25.6%
MASON	1,377	281	563	177	356	Gore	20.4%	40.9%	12.9%	25.9%
MEADE	2,179	368	1,197	183	431	Gore	16.9%	54.9%	8.4%	19.8%
MENIFEE	409	82	236	26	65	Gore	20.0%	57.7%	6.4%	15.9%
MERCER	1,944	354	1,051	181	358	Gore	18.2%	54.1%	9.3%	18.4%
METCALFE	802	42	589	52	119	Gore	5.2%	73.4%	6.5%	14.8%
MONROE	398	9	377	6	6	Gore	2.3%	94.7%	1.5%	1.5%
MONTGOMERY	1,886	313	1,010	243	320	Gore	16.6%	53.6%	12.9%	17.0%
MORGAN	704	108	429	46	121	Gore	15.3%	60.9%	6.5%	17.2%
MUHLENBERG	3,028	311	2,036	201	480	Gore	10.3%	67.2%	6.6%	15.9%
NELSON	3,196	676	1,603	283	634	Gore	21.2%	50.2%	8.9%	19.8%
NICHOLAS	707	107	371	59	170	Gore	15.1%	52.5%	8.3%	24.0%
OHIO	1,385	168	848	79	290	Gore	12.1%	61.2%	5.7%	20.9%
OLDHAM	2,715	622	1,083	335	675	Gore	22.9%	39.9%	12.3%	24.9%
OWEN	1,247	189	585	107	366	Gore	15.2%	46.9%	8.6%	29.4%
OWSLEY	174	15	126	9	24	Gore	8.6%	72.4%	5.2%	13.8%
PENDLETON	809	133	300	63	313	Gore	16.4%	37.1%	7.8%	38.7%
PERRY	1,708	298	887	275	248	Gore	17.4%	51.9%	16.1%	14.5%
PIKE	5,641	998	3,226	400	1,017	Gore	17.7%	57.2%	7.1%	18.0%
POWELL	941	152	564	51	174	Gore	16.2%	59.9%	5.4%	18.5%
PULASKI	2,289	391	1,431	153	314	Gore	17.1%	62.5%	6.7%	13.7%
ROBERTSON	277	47	143	25	62	Gore	17.0%	51.6%	9.0%	22.4%

KENTUCKY DEMOCRATIC

1988

County	Total Vote	Dukakis	Gore	J. Jackson	Other	Winner	Percentage of Total Vote Dukakis	Gore	J. Jackson	Other
ROCKCASTLE	445	89	287	25	44	Gore	20.0%	64.5%	5.6%	9.9%
ROWAN	1,421	311	642	149	319	Gore	21.9%	45.2%	10.5%	22.4%
RUSSELL	718	97	470	43	108	Gore	13.5%	65.5%	6.0%	15.0%
SCOTT	2,106	426	934	360	386	Gore	20.2%	44.3%	17.1%	18.3%
SHELBY	2,914	593	1,333	433	555	Gore	20.4%	45.7%	14.9%	19.0%
SIMPSON	2,252	64	1,683	357	148	Gore	2.8%	74.7%	15.9%	6.6%
SPENCER	802	177	390	60	175	Gore	22.1%	48.6%	7.5%	21.8%
TAYLOR	1,878	238	1,132	249	259	Gore	12.7%	60.3%	13.3%	13.8%
TODD	1,755	64	1,401	135	155	Gore	3.6%	79.8%	7.7%	8.8%
TRIGG	1,896	123	1,313	186	274	Gore	6.5%	69.3%	9.8%	14.5%
TRIMBLE	760	136	387	44	193	Gore	17.9%	50.9%	5.8%	25.4%
UNION	1,478	217	634	139	488	Gore	14.7%	42.9%	9.4%	33.0%
WARREN	6,736	670	4,414	745	907	Gore	9.9%	65.5%	11.1%	13.5%
WASHINGTON	1,158	221	630	108	199	Gore	19.1%	54.4%	9.3%	17.2%
WAYNE	887	101	622	43	121	Gore	11.4%	70.1%	4.8%	13.6%
WEBSTER	1,766	233	879	179	475	Gore	13.2%	49.8%	10.1%	26.9%
WHITLEY	980	163	624	67	126	Gore	16.6%	63.7%	6.8%	12.9%
WOLFE	571	101	329	51	90	Gore	17.7%	57.6%	8.9%	15.8%
WOODFORD	2,458	569	1,012	434	443	Gore	23.1%	41.2%	17.7%	18.0%
TOTAL	318,721	59,433	145,988	49,667	63,633	Gore	18.6%	45.8%	15.6%	20.0%

KENTUCKY REPUBLICAN

1988

County	Total Vote	Bush	Dole	Robertson	Other	Winner	Percentage of Total Vote Bush	Dole	Robertson	Other
ADAIR	1,358	1,000	216	90	52	Bush	73.6%	15.9%	6.6%	3.8%
ALLEN	702	452	143	48	59	Bush	64.4%	20.4%	6.8%	8.4%
ANDERSON	278	159	51	43	25	Bush	57.2%	18.3%	15.5%	9.0%
BALLARD	67	27	28	10	2	Dole	40.3%	41.8%	14.9%	3.0%
BARREN	924	558	220	91	55	Bush	60.4%	23.8%	9.8%	6.0%
BATH	78	46	24	4	4	Bush	59.0%	30.8%	5.1%	5.1%
BELL	1,811	1,146	325	243	97	Bush	63.3%	17.9%	13.4%	5.4%
BOONE	1,231	626	286	204	115	Bush	50.9%	23.2%	16.6%	9.3%
BOURBON	221	132	63	7	19	Bush	59.7%	28.5%	3.2%	8.6%
BOYD	1,927	1,028	531	199	169	Bush	53.3%	27.6%	10.3%	8.8%
BOYLE	524	292	147	43	42	Bush	55.7%	28.1%	8.2%	8.0%
BRACKEN	89	54	26	4	5	Bush	60.7%	29.2%	4.5%	5.6%
BREATHITT	106	67	18	15	6	Bush	63.2%	17.0%	14.2%	5.7%
BRECKINRIDGE	783	437	196	111	39	Bush	55.8%	25.0%	14.2%	5.0%
BULLITT	804	345	162	247	50	Bush	42.9%	20.1%	30.7%	6.2%
BUTLER	798	503	171	64	60	Bush	63.0%	21.4%	8.0%	7.5%
CALDWELL	340	209	67	39	25	Bush	61.5%	19.7%	11.5%	7.4%
CALLOWAY	328	150	86	44	48	Bush	45.7%	26.2%	13.4%	14.6%
CAMPBELL	3,310	2,083	704	209	314	Bush	62.9%	21.3%	6.3%	9.5%
CARLISLE	27	16	9		2	Bush	59.3%	33.3%		7.4%

KENTUCKY REPUBLICAN

1988

County	Total Vote	Bush	Dole	Robertson	Other	Winner	Percentage of Total Vote Bush	Dole	Robertson	Other
CARROLL	57	23	15	15	4	Bush	40.4%	26.3%	26.3%	7.0%
CARTER	784	467	170	94	53	Bush	59.6%	21.7%	12.0%	6.8%
CASEY	925	674	175	44	32	Bush	72.9%	18.9%	4.8%	3.5%
CHRISTIAN	754	399	134	165	56	Bush	52.9%	17.8%	21.9%	7.4%
CLARK	516	262	139	73	42	Bush	50.8%	26.9%	14.1%	8.1%
CLAY	1,185	858	192	100	35	Bush	72.4%	16.2%	8.4%	3.0%
CLINTON	958	668	207	55	28	Bush	69.7%	21.6%	5.7%	2.9%
CRITTENDEN	502	295	127	46	34	Bush	58.8%	25.3%	9.2%	6.8%
CUMBERLAND	667	519	86	34	28	Bush	77.8%	12.9%	5.1%	4.2%
DAVIESS	2,179	1,084	520	377	198	Bush	49.7%	23.9%	17.3%	9.1%
EDMONSON	702	440	211	22	29	Bush	62.7%	30.1%	3.1%	4.1%
ELLIOTT	16	10	4		2	Bush	62.5%	25.0%		12.5%
ESTILL	763	576	119	41	27	Bush	75.5%	15.6%	5.4%	3.5%
FAYETTE	9,021	4,690	2,607	1,018	706	Bush	52.0%	28.9%	11.3%	7.8%
FLEMING	314	191	80	19	24	Bush	60.8%	25.5%	6.1%	7.6%
FLOYD	365	196	79	61	29	Bush	53.7%	21.6%	16.7%	7.9%
FRANKLIN	660	316	189	103	52	Bush	47.9%	28.6%	15.6%	7.9%
FULTON	144	77	44	12	11	Bush	53.5%	30.6%	8.3%	7.6%
GALLATIN	54	42	9	1	2	Bush	77.8%	16.7%	1.9%	3.7%
GARRARD	608	401	129	42	36	Bush	66.0%	21.2%	6.9%	5.9%
GRANT	202	121	41	23	17	Bush	59.9%	20.3%	11.4%	8.4%
GRAVES	227	94	65	50	18	Bush	41.4%	28.6%	22.0%	7.9%
GRAYSON	1,226	773	331	67	55	Bush	63.1%	27.0%	5.5%	4.5%
GREEN	934	588	253	55	38	Bush	63.0%	27.1%	5.9%	4.1%
GREENUP	1,123	596	286	142	99	Bush	53.1%	25.5%	12.6%	8.8%
HANCOCK	287	162	84	21	20	Bush	56.4%	29.3%	7.3%	7.0%
HARDIN	1,640	991	350	189	110	Bush	60.4%	21.3%	11.5%	6.7%
HARLAN	1,147	688	177	234	48	Bush	60.0%	15.4%	20.4%	4.2%
HARRISON	136	77	40	12	7	Bush	56.6%	29.4%	8.8%	5.1%
HART	463	327	86	30	20	Bush	70.6%	18.6%	6.5%	4.3%
HENDERSON	398	173	101	80	44	Bush	43.5%	25.4%	20.1%	11.1%
HENRY	77	38	22	11	6	Bush	49.4%	28.6%	14.3%	7.8%
HICKMAN	37	12	10	8	7	Bush	32.4%	27.0%	21.6%	18.9%
HOPKINS	621	296	136	142	47	Bush	47.7%	21.9%	22.9%	7.6%
JACKSON	755	580	110	44	21	Bush	76.8%	14.6%	5.8%	2.8%
JEFFERSON	31,414	18,044	7,428	4,052	1,890	Bush	57.4%	23.6%	12.9%	6.0%
JESSAMINE	953	361	235	301	56	Bush	37.9%	24.7%	31.6%	5.9%
JOHNSON	1,048	624	286	68	70	Bush	59.5%	27.3%	6.5%	6.7%
KENTON	3,299	1,937	742	268	352	Bush	58.7%	22.5%	8.1%	10.7%
KNOTT	46	22	12	6	6	Bush	47.8%	26.1%	13.0%	13.0%
KNOX	1,394	885	291	134	84	Bush	63.5%	20.9%	9.6%	6.0%
LARUE	198	109	57	22	10	Bush	55.1%	28.8%	11.1%	5.1%
LAUREL	2,847	1,949	504	290	104	Bush	68.5%	17.7%	10.2%	3.7%
LAWRENCE	522	340	95	57	30	Bush	65.1%	18.2%	10.9%	5.7%
LEE	413	288	72	37	16	Bush	69.7%	17.4%	9.0%	3.9%
LESLIE	850	572	175	58	45	Bush	67.3%	20.6%	6.8%	5.3%
LETCHER	595	350	132	70	43	Bush	58.8%	22.2%	11.8%	7.2%
LEWIS	750	477	168	51	54	Bush	63.6%	22.4%	6.8%	7.2%
LINCOLN	615	376	157	34	48	Bush	61.1%	25.5%	5.5%	7.8%
LIVINGSTON	100	56	27	12	5	Bush	56.0%	27.0%	12.0%	5.0%

KENTUCKY REPUBLICAN

1988

County	Total Vote	Bush	Dole	Robertson	Other	Winner	Percentage of Total Vote Bush	Dole	Robertson	Other
LOGAN	402	237	101	44	20	Bush	59.0%	25.1%	10.9%	5.0%
LYON	89	43	29	9	8	Bush	48.3%	32.6%	10.1%	9.0%
MCCRACKEN	930	496	220	136	78	Bush	53.3%	23.7%	14.6%	8.4%
MCCREARY	1,021	696	162	103	60	Bush	68.2%	15.9%	10.1%	5.9%
MCLEAN	200	107	43	28	22	Bush	53.5%	21.5%	14.0%	11.0%
MADISON	1,534	882	380	149	123	Bush	57.5%	24.8%	9.7%	8.0%
MAGOFFIN	326	234	72	8	12	Bush	71.8%	22.1%	2.5%	3.7%
MARION	84	44	16	16	8	Bush	52.4%	19.0%	19.0%	9.5%
MARSHALL	267	125	47	76	19	Bush	46.8%	17.6%	28.5%	7.1%
MARTIN	651	384	102	93	72	Bush	59.0%	15.7%	14.3%	11.1%
MASON	323	201	71	26	25	Bush	62.2%	22.0%	8.0%	7.7%
MEADE	252	145	41	49	17	Bush	57.5%	16.3%	19.4%	6.7%
MENIFEE	63	33	14	9	7	Bush	52.4%	22.2%	14.3%	11.1%
MERCER	375	200	99	45	31	Bush	53.3%	26.4%	12.0%	8.3%
METCALFE	359	241	74	17	27	Bush	67.1%	20.6%	4.7%	7.5%
MONROE	953	583	252	56	62	Bush	61.2%	26.4%	5.9%	6.5%
MONTGOMERY	234	133	51	25	25	Bush	56.8%	21.8%	10.7%	10.7%
MORGAN	46	27	15	3	1	Bush	58.7%	32.6%	6.5%	2.2%
MUHLENBERG	604	381	138	57	28	Bush	63.1%	22.8%	9.4%	4.6%
NELSON	312	161	64	51	36	Bush	51.6%	20.5%	16.3%	11.5%
NICHOLAS	54	35	16	2	1	Bush	64.8%	29.6%	3.7%	1.9%
OHIO	1,249	695	345	96	113	Bush	55.6%	27.6%	7.7%	9.0%
OLDHAM	1,507	818	367	209	113	Bush	54.3%	24.4%	13.9%	7.5%
OWEN	80	36	25	13	6	Bush	45.0%	31.3%	16.3%	7.5%
OWSLEY	332	242	40	38	12	Bush	72.9%	12.0%	11.4%	3.6%
PENDLETON	157	87	49	10	11	Bush	55.4%	31.2%	6.4%	7.0%
PERRY	870	625	116	81	48	Bush	71.8%	13.3%	9.3%	5.5%
PIKE	1,710	1,135	340	151	84	Bush	66.4%	19.9%	8.8%	4.9%
POWELL	242	166	46	20	10	Bush	68.6%	19.0%	8.3%	4.1%
PULASKI	4,226	2,500	1,053	332	341	Bush	59.2%	24.9%	7.9%	8.1%
ROBERTSON	49	35	10	2	2	Bush	71.4%	20.4%	4.1%	4.1%
ROCKCASTLE	1,063	741	229	31	62	Bush	69.7%	21.5%	2.9%	5.8%
ROWAN	495	256	148	50	41	Bush	51.7%	29.9%	10.1%	8.3%
RUSSELL	1,276	1,002	181	59	34	Bush	78.5%	14.2%	4.6%	2.7%
SCOTT	261	149	76	23	13	Bush	57.1%	29.1%	8.8%	5.0%
SHELBY	373	192	84	85	12	Bush	51.5%	22.5%	22.8%	3.2%
SIMPSON	153	83	42	17	11	Bush	54.2%	27.5%	11.1%	7.2%
SPENCER	70	37	11	16	6	Bush	52.9%	15.7%	22.9%	8.6%
TAYLOR	1,300	832	314	114	40	Bush	64.0%	24.2%	8.8%	3.1%
TODD	45	26	3	10	6	Bush	57.8%	6.7%	22.2%	13.3%
TRIGG	122	73	30	12	7	Bush	59.8%	24.6%	9.8%	5.7%
TRIMBLE	66	36	12	16	2	Bush	54.5%	18.2%	24.2%	3.0%
UNION	69	32	17	11	9	Bush	46.4%	24.6%	15.9%	13.0%
WARREN	1,389	817	284	161	127	Bush	58.8%	20.4%	11.6%	9.1%
WASHINGTON	315	229	50	23	13	Bush	72.7%	15.9%	7.3%	4.1%
WAYNE	1,007	754	168	48	37	Bush	74.9%	16.7%	4.8%	3.7%
WEBSTER	111	65	27	17	2	Bush	58.6%	24.3%	15.3%	1.8%
WHITLEY	2,035	1,262	451	206	116	Bush	62.0%	22.2%	10.1%	5.7%
WOLFE	72	53	8	6	5	Bush	73.6%	11.1%	8.3%	6.9%
WOODFORD	482	230	153	62	37	Bush	47.7%	31.7%	12.9%	7.7%
TOTAL	121,402	72,020	27,868	13,526	7,988	Bush	59.3%	23.0%	11.1%	6.6%

KENTUCKY DEMOCRATIC

1992

County	Total Vote	Clinton	Uncommitted	Other	Winner	Percentage of Total Vote Clinton	Uncom.	Other
ADAIR	655	471	107	77	Clinton	71.9%	16.3%	11.8%
ALLEN	492	368	76	48	Clinton	74.8%	15.4%	9.8%
ANDERSON	1,829	866	677	286	Clinton	47.3%	37.0%	15.6%
BALLARD	1,967	1,217	582	168	Clinton	61.9%	29.6%	8.5%
BARREN	3,334	2,100	815	419	Clinton	63.0%	24.4%	12.6%
BATH	935	609	227	99	Clinton	65.1%	24.3%	10.6%
BELL	1,405	984	225	196	Clinton	70.0%	16.0%	14.0%
BOONE	4,980	1,922	2,264	794	Uncommitted	38.6%	45.5%	15.9%
BOURBON	1,448	737	462	249	Clinton	50.9%	31.9%	17.2%
BOYD	4,789	2,851	1,227	711	Clinton	59.5%	25.6%	14.8%
BOYLE	3,411	1,675	1,264	472	Clinton	49.1%	37.1%	13.8%
BRACKEN	495	268	154	73	Clinton	54.1%	31.1%	14.7%
BREATHITT	3,216	2,283	591	342	Clinton	71.0%	18.4%	10.6%
BRECKINRIDGE	2,087	1,344	467	276	Clinton	64.4%	22.4%	13.2%
BULLITT	4,510	2,462	1,126	922	Clinton	54.6%	25.0%	20.4%
BUTLER	496	382	72	42	Clinton	77.0%	14.5%	8.5%
CALDWELL	2,048	1,178	631	239	Clinton	57.5%	30.8%	11.7%
CALLOWAY	3,866	2,043	1,361	462	Clinton	52.8%	35.2%	12.0%
CAMPBELL	4,307	1,902	1,471	934	Clinton	44.2%	34.2%	21.7%
CARLISLE	1,192	723	343	126	Clinton	60.7%	28.8%	10.6%
CARROLL	757	449	214	94	Clinton	59.3%	28.3%	12.4%
CARTER	1,727	1,206	277	244	Clinton	69.8%	16.0%	14.1%
CASEY	533	343	123	67	Clinton	64.4%	23.1%	12.6%
CHRISTIAN	6,049	2,902	2,211	936	Clinton	48.0%	36.6%	15.5%
CLARK	4,328	2,143	1,626	559	Clinton	49.5%	37.6%	12.9%
CLAY	651	440	117	94	Clinton	67.6%	18.0%	14.4%
CLINTON	243	197	19	27	Clinton	81.1%	7.8%	11.1%
CRITTENDEN	1,028	729	213	86	Clinton	70.9%	20.7%	8.4%
CUMBERLAND	211	154	32	25	Clinton	73.0%	15.2%	11.8%
DAVIESS	7,275	3,584	2,462	1,229	Clinton	49.3%	33.8%	16.9%
EDMONSON	378	281	57	40	Clinton	74.3%	15.1%	10.6%
ELLIOTT	592	444	80	68	Clinton	75.0%	13.5%	11.5%
ESTILL	653	457	116	80	Clinton	70.0%	17.8%	12.3%
FAYETTE	19,189	8,192	7,038	3,959	Clinton	42.7%	36.7%	20.6%
FLEMING	893	597	164	132	Clinton	66.9%	18.4%	14.8%
FLOYD	10,322	7,543	1,692	1,087	Clinton	73.1%	16.4%	10.5%
FRANKLIN	10,050	3,794	4,748	1,508	Uncommitted	37.8%	47.2%	15.0%
FULTON	1,789	1,075	553	161	Clinton	60.1%	30.9%	9.0%
GALLATIN	1,017	527	357	133	Clinton	51.8%	35.1%	13.1%
GARRARD	627	396	166	65	Clinton	63.2%	26.5%	10.4%
GRANT	929	466	326	137	Clinton	50.2%	35.1%	14.7%
GRAVES	7,179	4,141	2,297	741	Clinton	57.7%	32.0%	10.3%
GRAYSON	1,497	979	336	182	Clinton	65.4%	22.4%	12.2%
GREEN	468	336	68	64	Clinton	71.8%	14.5%	13.7%
GREENUP	3,304	2,245	661	398	Clinton	67.9%	20.0%	12.0%
HANCOCK	645	400	159	86	Clinton	62.0%	24.7%	13.3%
HARDIN	9,369	4,497	3,267	1,605	Clinton	48.0%	34.9%	17.1%
HARLAN	5,912	3,788	1,349	775	Clinton	64.1%	22.8%	13.1%
HARRISON	1,551	839	491	221	Clinton	54.1%	31.7%	14.2%
HART	1,560	1,079	266	215	Clinton	69.2%	17.1%	13.8%

KENTUCKY DEMOCRATIC

1992

County	Total Vote	Clinton	Uncommitted	Other	Winner	Percentage of Total Vote: Clinton	Uncom.	Other
HENDERSON	7,601	3,360	3,325	916	Clinton	44.2%	43.7%	12.1%
HENRY	1,538	866	416	256	Clinton	56.3%	27.0%	16.6%
HICKMAN	1,218	719	396	103	Clinton	59.0%	32.5%	8.5%
HOPKINS	4,609	2,580	1,427	602	Clinton	56.0%	31.0%	13.1%
JACKSON	146	90	33	23	Clinton	61.6%	22.6%	15.8%
JEFFERSON	73,874	40,301	17,293	16,280	Clinton	54.6%	23.4%	22.0%
JESSAMINE	2,624	1,204	971	449	Clinton	45.9%	37.0%	17.1%
JOHNSON	1,454	993	288	173	Clinton	68.3%	19.8%	11.9%
KENTON	6,340	2,556	2,419	1,365	Clinton	40.3%	38.2%	21.5%
KNOTT	3,777	2,739	586	452	Clinton	72.5%	15.5%	12.0%
KNOX	1,215	857	207	151	Clinton	70.5%	17.0%	12.4%
LARUE	1,636	908	437	291	Clinton	55.5%	26.7%	17.8%
LAUREL	1,529	1,031	304	194	Clinton	67.4%	19.9%	12.7%
LAWRENCE	1,080	797	155	128	Clinton	73.8%	14.4%	11.9%
LEE	599	391	114	94	Clinton	65.3%	19.0%	15.7%
LESLIE	363	278	41	44	Clinton	76.6%	11.3%	12.1%
LETCHER	3,949	2,769	711	469	Clinton	70.1%	18.0%	11.9%
LEWIS	339	245	54	40	Clinton	72.3%	15.9%	11.8%
LINCOLN	1,207	786	282	139	Clinton	65.1%	23.4%	11.5%
LIVINGSTON	1,645	1,068	416	161	Clinton	64.9%	25.3%	9.8%
LOGAN	2,802	1,630	799	373	Clinton	58.2%	28.5%	13.3%
LYON	1,198	661	398	139	Clinton	55.2%	33.2%	11.6%
MCCRACKEN	11,162	5,930	3,945	1,287	Clinton	53.1%	35.3%	11.5%
MCCREARY	585	373	110	102	Clinton	63.8%	18.8%	17.4%
MCLEAN	1,088	623	346	119	Clinton	57.3%	31.8%	10.9%
MADISON	3,592	1,928	1,093	571	Clinton	53.7%	30.4%	15.9%
MAGOFFIN	1,319	1,048	144	127	Clinton	79.5%	10.9%	9.6%
MARION	1,273	757	333	183	Clinton	59.5%	26.2%	14.4%
MARSHALL	4,935	2,649	1,687	599	Clinton	53.7%	34.2%	12.1%
MARTIN	431	323	53	55	Clinton	74.9%	12.3%	12.8%
MASON	902	502	243	157	Clinton	55.7%	26.9%	17.4%
MEADE	3,145	1,705	894	546	Clinton	54.2%	28.4%	17.4%
MENIFEE	690	506	107	77	Clinton	73.3%	15.5%	11.2%
MERCER	2,923	1,526	926	471	Clinton	52.2%	31.7%	16.1%
METCALFE	664	482	89	93	Clinton	72.6%	13.4%	14.0%
MONROE	230	172	25	33	Clinton	74.8%	10.9%	14.3%
MONTGOMERY	1,792	1,039	503	250	Clinton	58.0%	28.1%	14.0%
MORGAN	1,935	1,330	383	222	Clinton	68.7%	19.8%	11.5%
MUHLENBERG	3,854	2,580	837	437	Clinton	66.9%	21.7%	11.3%
NELSON	2,363	1,203	658	502	Clinton	50.9%	27.8%	21.2%
NICHOLAS	589	380	111	98	Clinton	64.5%	18.8%	16.6%
OHIO	1,526	1,002	313	211	Clinton	65.7%	20.5%	13.8%
OLDHAM	2,312	1,031	696	585	Clinton	44.6%	30.1%	25.3%
OWEN	1,050	601	287	162	Clinton	57.2%	27.3%	15.4%
OWSLEY	368	271	37	60	Clinton	73.6%	10.1%	16.3%
PENDLETON	769	390	257	122	Clinton	50.7%	33.4%	15.9%
PERRY	4,482	2,941	857	684	Clinton	65.6%	19.1%	15.3%
PIKE	13,269	9,903	1,929	1,437	Clinton	74.6%	14.5%	10.8%
POWELL	1,358	855	312	191	Clinton	63.0%	23.0%	14.1%
PULASKI	2,069	1,194	588	287	Clinton	57.7%	28.4%	13.9%

KENTUCKY DEMOCRATIC

1992

County	Total Vote	Clinton	Uncommitted	Other	Winner	Percentage of Total Vote Clinton	Uncom.	Other
ROBERTSON	207	109	62	36	Clinton	52.7%	30.0%	17.4%
ROCKCASTLE	321	245	32	44	Clinton	76.3%	10.0%	13.7%
ROWAN	2,460	1,334	717	409	Clinton	54.2%	29.1%	16.6%
RUSSELL	937	628	202	107	Clinton	67.0%	21.6%	11.4%
SCOTT	2,034	1,008	683	343	Clinton	49.6%	33.6%	16.9%
SHELBY	2,604	1,327	713	564	Clinton	51.0%	27.4%	21.7%
SIMPSON	787	441	224	122	Clinton	56.0%	28.5%	15.5%
SPENCER	719	389	182	148	Clinton	54.1%	25.3%	20.6%
TAYLOR	972	690	165	117	Clinton	71.0%	17.0%	12.0%
TODD	1,760	971	533	256	Clinton	55.2%	30.3%	14.5%
TRIGG	1,635	948	476	211	Clinton	58.0%	29.1%	12.9%
TRIMBLE	553	324	156	73	Clinton	58.6%	28.2%	13.2%
UNION	2,584	1,272	1,007	305	Clinton	49.2%	39.0%	11.8%
WARREN	4,179	2,180	1,320	679	Clinton	52.2%	31.6%	16.2%
WASHINGTON	827	495	193	139	Clinton	59.9%	23.3%	16.8%
WAYNE	683	497	114	72	Clinton	72.8%	16.7%	10.5%
WEBSTER	2,185	1,224	695	266	Clinton	56.0%	31.8%	12.2%
WHITLEY	1,038	687	220	131	Clinton	66.2%	21.2%	12.6%
WOLFE	1,840	1,308	259	273	Clinton	71.1%	14.1%	14.8%
WOODFORD	2,647	1,046	1,175	426	Uncommitted	39.5%	44.4%	16.1%
TOTAL	370,578	207,804	103,590	59,184	Clinton	56.1%	28.0%	16.0%

KENTUCKY REPUBLICAN

1992

County	Total Vote	Bush	Uncommitted	Winner	Percentage of Total Vote Bush	Uncom.
ADAIR	689	577	112	Bush	83.7%	16.3%
ALLEN	440	366	74	Bush	83.2%	16.8%
ANDERSON	187	148	39	Bush	79.1%	20.9%
BALLARD	40	28	12	Bush	70.0%	30.0%
BARREN	541	426	115	Bush	78.7%	21.3%
BATH	53	38	15	Bush	71.7%	28.3%
BELL	903	700	203	Bush	77.5%	22.5%
BOONE	1,358	976	382	Bush	71.9%	28.1%
BOURBON	149	99	50	Bush	66.4%	33.6%
BOYD	1,716	1,239	477	Bush	72.2%	27.8%
BOYLE	392	298	94	Bush	76.0%	24.0%
BRACKEN	71	57	14	Bush	80.3%	19.7%
BREATHITT	92	75	17	Bush	81.5%	18.5%
BRECKINRIDGE	549	430	119	Bush	78.3%	21.7%
BULLITT	743	549	194	Bush	73.9%	26.1%
BUTLER	1,086	835	251	Bush	76.9%	23.1%
CALDWELL	215	162	53	Bush	75.3%	24.7%
CALLOWAY	227	131	96	Bush	57.7%	42.3%
CAMPBELL	1,726	1,249	477	Bush	72.4%	27.6%
CARLISLE	33	25	8	Bush	75.8%	24.2%

KENTUCKY REPUBLICAN

1992

County	Total Vote	Bush	Uncommitted	Winner	Percentage of Total Vote	
					Bush	Uncom.
CARROLL	41	29	12	Bush	70.7%	29.3%
CARTER	678	539	139	Bush	79.5%	20.5%
CASEY	984	821	163	Bush	83.4%	16.6%
CHRISTIAN	433	309	124	Bush	71.4%	28.6%
CLARK	495	314	181	Bush	63.4%	36.6%
CLAY	2,599	2,048	551	Bush	78.8%	21.2%
CLINTON	521	429	92	Bush	82.3%	17.7%
CRITTENDEN	313	229	84	Bush	73.2%	26.8%
CUMBERLAND	659	565	94	Bush	85.7%	14.3%
DAVIESS	1,042	734	308	Bush	70.4%	29.6%
EDMONSON	425	334	91	Bush	78.6%	21.4%
ELLIOTT	18	16	2	Bush	88.9%	11.1%
ESTILL	799	636	163	Bush	79.6%	20.4%
FAYETTE	6,851	4,653	2,198	Bush	67.9%	32.1%
FLEMING	162	143	19	Bush	88.3%	11.7%
FLOYD	495	368	127	Bush	74.3%	25.7%
FRANKLIN	613	397	216	Bush	64.8%	35.2%
FULTON	117	96	21	Bush	82.1%	17.9%
GALLATIN	46	38	8	Bush	82.6%	17.4%
GARRARD	453	355	98	Bush	78.4%	21.6%
GRANT	113	81	32	Bush	71.7%	28.3%
GRAVES	184	139	45	Bush	75.5%	24.5%
GRAYSON	972	794	178	Bush	81.7%	18.3%
GREEN	424	387	37	Bush	91.3%	8.7%
GREENUP	871	657	214	Bush	75.4%	24.6%
HANCOCK	186	145	41	Bush	78.0%	22.0%
HARDIN	1,653	1,216	437	Bush	73.6%	26.4%
HARLAN	1,028	762	266	Bush	74.1%	25.9%
HARRISON	127	93	34	Bush	73.2%	26.8%
HART	241	215	26	Bush	89.2%	10.8%
HENDERSON	502	324	178	Bush	64.5%	35.5%
HENRY	63	51	12	Bush	81.0%	19.0%
HICKMAN	25	21	4	Bush	84.0%	16.0%
HOPKINS	336	235	101	Bush	69.9%	30.1%
JACKSON	921	785	136	Bush	85.2%	14.8%
JEFFERSON	24,122	17,634	6,488	Bush	73.1%	26.9%
JESSAMINE	563	429	134	Bush	76.2%	23.8%
JOHNSON	1,588	1,165	423	Bush	73.4%	26.6%
KENTON	2,179	1,573	606	Bush	72.2%	27.8%
KNOTT	44	36	8	Bush	81.8%	18.2%
KNOX	1,835	1,402	433	Bush	76.4%	23.6%
LARUE	125	93	32	Bush	74.4%	25.6%
LAUREL	3,396	2,428	968	Bush	71.5%	28.5%
LAWRENCE	583	493	90	Bush	84.6%	15.4%
LEE	634	519	115	Bush	81.9%	18.1%
LESLIE	1,004	784	220	Bush	78.1%	21.9%
LETCHER	869	671	198	Bush	77.2%	22.8%
LEWIS	550	449	101	Bush	81.6%	18.4%
LINCOLN	412	330	82	Bush	80.1%	19.9%
LIVINGSTON	72	54	18	Bush	75.0%	25.0%

KENTUCKY REPUBLICAN

1992

County	Total Vote	Bush	Uncommitted	Winner	Percentage of Total Vote Bush	Uncom.
LOGAN	195	147	48	Bush	75.4%	24.6%
LYON	57	38	19	Bush	66.7%	33.3%
MCCRACKEN	737	500	237	Bush	67.8%	32.2%
MCCREARY	1,936	1,514	422	Bush	78.2%	21.8%
MCLEAN	101	71	30	Bush	70.3%	29.7%
MADISON	847	631	216	Bush	74.5%	25.5%
MAGOFFIN	377	334	43	Bush	88.6%	11.4%
MARION	51	34	17	Bush	66.7%	33.3%
MARSHALL	247	168	79	Bush	68.0%	32.0%
MARTIN	918	657	261	Bush	71.6%	28.4%
MASON	175	134	41	Bush	76.6%	23.4%
MEADE	251	192	59	Bush	76.5%	23.5%
MENIFEE	41	28	13	Bush	68.3%	31.7%
MERCER	284	217	67	Bush	76.4%	23.6%
METCALFE	219	197	22	Bush	90.0%	10.0%
MONROE	486	382	104	Bush	78.6%	21.4%
MONTGOMERY	151	108	43	Bush	71.5%	28.5%
MORGAN	74	61	13	Bush	82.4%	17.6%
MUHLENBERG	399	296	103	Bush	74.2%	25.8%
NELSON	201	142	59	Bush	70.6%	29.4%
NICHOLAS	35	27	8	Bush	77.1%	22.9%
OHIO	1,067	727	340	Bush	68.1%	31.9%
OLDHAM	1,003	717	286	Bush	71.5%	28.5%
OWEN	68	41	27	Bush	60.3%	39.7%
OWSLEY	672	540	132	Bush	80.4%	19.6%
PENDLETON	99	74	25	Bush	74.7%	25.3%
PERRY	934	724	210	Bush	77.5%	22.5%
PIKE	1,538	1,271	267	Bush	82.6%	17.4%
POWELL	242	198	44	Bush	81.8%	18.2%
PULASKI	3,476	2,580	896	Bush	74.2%	25.8%
ROBERTSON	26	23	3	Bush	88.5%	11.5%
ROCKCASTLE	607	502	105	Bush	82.7%	17.3%
ROWAN	581	435	146	Bush	74.9%	25.1%
RUSSELL	1,195	1,000	195	Bush	83.7%	16.3%
SCOTT	225	149	76	Bush	66.2%	33.8%
SHELBY	253	191	62	Bush	75.5%	24.5%
SIMPSON	66	53	13	Bush	80.3%	19.7%
SPENCER	62	48	14	Bush	77.4%	22.6%
TAYLOR	652	534	118	Bush	81.9%	18.1%
TODD	41	25	16	Bush	61.0%	39.0%
TRIGG	77	47	30	Bush	61.0%	39.0%
TRIMBLE	28	24	4	Bush	85.7%	14.3%
UNION	58	29	29		50.0%	50.0%
WARREN	918	682	236	Bush	74.3%	25.7%
WASHINGTON	136	112	24	Bush	82.4%	17.6%
WAYNE	697	607	90	Bush	87.1%	12.9%
WEBSTER	78	56	22	Bush	71.8%	28.2%
WHITLEY	3,516	2,358	1,158	Bush	67.1%	32.9%
WOLFE	77	70	7	Bush	90.9%	9.1%
WOODFORD	369	250	119	Bush	67.8%	32.2%
TOTAL	101,119	75,371	25,748	Bush	74.5%	25.5%

KENTUCKY DEMOCRATIC

1996

County	Total Vote	Clinton	LaRouche	Uncommitted	Winner	Percentage of Total Vote Clinton	LaRouche	Uncom.
ADAIR	769	627	66	76	Clinton	81.5%	8.6%	9.9%
ALLEN	395	334	21	40	Clinton	84.6%	5.3%	10.1%
ANDERSON	1,525	1,125	171	229	Clinton	73.8%	11.2%	15.0%
BALLARD	1,555	1,240	59	256	Clinton	79.7%	3.8%	16.5%
BARREN	1,163	930	84	149	Clinton	80.0%	7.2%	12.8%
BATH	684	544	59	81	Clinton	79.5%	8.6%	11.8%
BELL	1,431	1,146	171	114	Clinton	80.1%	11.9%	8.0%
BOONE	2,035	1,310	237	488	Clinton	64.4%	11.6%	24.0%
BOURBON	1,515	1,138	134	243	Clinton	75.1%	8.8%	16.0%
BOYD	2,652	2,141	150	361	Clinton	80.7%	5.7%	13.6%
BOYLE	1,793	1,364	147	282	Clinton	76.1%	8.2%	15.7%
BRACKEN	606	398	84	124	Clinton	65.7%	13.9%	20.5%
BREATHITT	834	670	57	107	Clinton	80.3%	6.8%	12.8%
BRECKINRIDGE	1,051	833	105	113	Clinton	79.3%	10.0%	10.8%
BULLITT	3,966	2,736	414	816	Clinton	69.0%	10.4%	20.6%
BUTLER	290	248	16	26	Clinton	85.5%	5.5%	9.0%
CALDWELL	1,267	939	77	251	Clinton	74.1%	6.1%	19.8%
CALLOWAY	1,904	1,394	129	381	Clinton	73.2%	6.8%	20.0%
CAMPBELL	3,395	2,378	335	682	Clinton	70.0%	9.9%	20.1%
CARLISLE	831	618	50	163	Clinton	74.4%	6.0%	19.6%
CARROLL	500	368	47	85	Clinton	73.6%	9.4%	17.0%
CARTER	1,124	901	97	126	Clinton	80.2%	8.6%	11.2%
CASEY	311	230	36	45	Clinton	74.0%	11.6%	14.5%
CHRISTIAN	4,686	2,959	508	1,219	Clinton	63.1%	10.8%	26.0%
CLARK	2,650	1,951	224	475	Clinton	73.6%	8.5%	17.9%
CLAY	252	209	28	15	Clinton	82.9%	11.1%	6.0%
CLINTON	212	182	16	14	Clinton	85.8%	7.5%	6.6%
CRITTENDEN	484	397	32	55	Clinton	82.0%	6.6%	11.4%
CUMBERLAND	129	103	13	13	Clinton	79.8%	10.1%	10.1%
DAVIESS	6,361	4,480	633	1,248	Clinton	70.4%	10.0%	19.6%
EDMONSON	241	215	11	15	Clinton	89.2%	4.6%	6.2%
ELLIOTT	350	279	28	43	Clinton	79.7%	8.0%	12.3%
ESTILL	465	402	33	30	Clinton	86.5%	7.1%	6.5%
FAYETTE	17,129	13,126	1,143	2,860	Clinton	76.6%	6.7%	16.7%
FLEMING	848	649	99	100	Clinton	76.5%	11.7%	11.8%
FLOYD	3,159	2,598	232	329	Clinton	82.2%	7.3%	10.4%
FRANKLIN	12,518	9,266	793	2,459	Clinton	74.0%	6.3%	19.6%
FULTON	714	516	41	157	Clinton	72.3%	5.7%	22.0%
GALLATIN	1,283	934	88	261	Clinton	72.8%	6.9%	20.3%
GARRARD	394	313	32	49	Clinton	79.4%	8.1%	12.4%
GRANT	1,865	1,353	150	362	Clinton	72.5%	8.0%	19.4%
GRAVES	3,878	2,871	263	744	Clinton	74.0%	6.8%	19.2%
GRAYSON	629	515	60	54	Clinton	81.9%	9.5%	8.6%
GREEN	358	278	43	37	Clinton	77.7%	12.0%	10.3%
GREENUP	4,796	3,810	277	709	Clinton	79.4%	5.8%	14.8%
HANCOCK	427	337	39	51	Clinton	78.9%	9.1%	11.9%
HARDIN	4,354	3,106	463	785	Clinton	71.3%	10.6%	18.0%
HARLAN	5,353	4,169	459	725	Clinton	77.9%	8.6%	13.5%
HARRISON	1,989	1,490	160	339	Clinton	74.9%	8.0%	17.0%
HART	780	620	84	76	Clinton	79.5%	10.8%	9.7%

KENTUCKY DEMOCRATIC

1996

County	Total Vote	Clinton	LaRouche	Uncommitted	Winner	Percentage of Total Vote Clinton	LaRouche	Uncom.
HENDERSON	4,702	3,495	244	963	Clinton	74.3%	5.2%	20.5%
HENRY	1,160	813	87	260	Clinton	70.1%	7.5%	22.4%
HICKMAN	733	512	45	176	Clinton	69.8%	6.1%	24.0%
HOPKINS	3,362	2,530	255	577	Clinton	75.3%	7.6%	17.2%
JACKSON	98	79	9	10	Clinton	80.6%	9.2%	10.2%
JEFFERSON	57,796	47,272	2,725	7,799	Clinton	81.8%	4.7%	13.5%
JESSAMINE	1,561	1,047	190	324	Clinton	67.1%	12.2%	20.8%
JOHNSON	708	588	56	64	Clinton	83.1%	7.9%	9.0%
KENTON	5,987	4,043	564	1,380	Clinton	67.5%	9.4%	23.0%
KNOTT	3,672	3,056	214	402	Clinton	83.2%	5.8%	10.9%
KNOX	722	611	60	51	Clinton	84.6%	8.3%	7.1%
LARUE	676	483	80	113	Clinton	71.4%	11.8%	16.7%
LAUREL	809	669	69	71	Clinton	82.7%	8.5%	8.8%
LAWRENCE	646	538	59	49	Clinton	83.3%	9.1%	7.6%
LEE	323	255	28	40	Clinton	78.9%	8.7%	12.4%
LESLIE	161	138	10	13	Clinton	85.7%	6.2%	8.1%
LETCHER	2,235	1,833	143	259	Clinton	82.0%	6.4%	11.6%
LEWIS	264	206	22	36	Clinton	78.0%	8.3%	13.6%
LINCOLN	651	532	59	60	Clinton	81.7%	9.1%	9.2%
LIVINGSTON	965	742	67	156	Clinton	76.9%	6.9%	16.2%
LOGAN	2,594	1,823	255	516	Clinton	70.3%	9.8%	19.9%
LYON	753	597	44	112	Clinton	79.3%	5.8%	14.9%
MCCRACKEN	5,437	4,055	341	1,041	Clinton	74.6%	6.3%	19.1%
MCCREARY	309	225	37	47	Clinton	72.8%	12.0%	15.2%
MCLEAN	742	546	52	144	Clinton	73.6%	7.0%	19.4%
MADISON	3,513	2,680	312	521	Clinton	76.3%	8.9%	14.8%
MAGOFFIN	1,451	1,230	100	121	Clinton	84.8%	6.9%	8.3%
MARION	1,382	1,023	135	224	Clinton	74.0%	9.8%	16.2%
MARSHALL	2,877	2,182	182	513	Clinton	75.8%	6.3%	17.8%
MARTIN	213	179	19	15	Clinton	84.0%	8.9%	7.0%
MASON	1,375	1,021	113	241	Clinton	74.3%	8.2%	17.5%
MEADE	1,916	1,416	163	337	Clinton	73.9%	8.5%	17.6%
MENIFEE	274	209	35	30	Clinton	76.3%	12.8%	10.9%
MERCER	1,068	787	120	161	Clinton	73.7%	11.2%	15.1%
METCALFE	819	615	118	86	Clinton	75.1%	14.4%	10.5%
MONROE	194	158	14	22	Clinton	81.4%	7.2%	11.3%
MONTGOMERY	1,060	790	84	186	Clinton	74.5%	7.9%	17.5%
MORGAN	628	441	75	112	Clinton	70.2%	11.9%	17.8%
MUHLENBERG	3,978	3,187	222	569	Clinton	80.1%	5.6%	14.3%
NELSON	3,288	2,427	287	574	Clinton	73.8%	8.7%	17.5%
NICHOLAS	329	243	45	41	Clinton	73.9%	13.7%	12.5%
OHIO	975	795	83	97	Clinton	81.5%	8.5%	9.9%
OLDHAM	1,646	1,137	116	393	Clinton	69.1%	7.0%	23.9%
OWEN	842	609	93	140	Clinton	72.3%	11.0%	16.6%
OWSLEY	122	92	14	16	Clinton	75.4%	11.5%	13.1%
PENDLETON	1,325	901	152	272	Clinton	68.0%	11.5%	20.5%
PERRY	4,220	3,432	326	462	Clinton	81.3%	7.7%	10.9%
PIKE	11,078	9,147	691	1,240	Clinton	82.6%	6.2%	11.2%
POWELL	620	512	52	56	Clinton	82.6%	8.4%	9.0%
PULASKI	1,271	1,011	129	131	Clinton	79.5%	10.1%	10.3%

KENTUCKY DEMOCRATIC

1996

County	Total Vote	Clinton	LaRouche	Uncommitted	Winner	Percentage of Total Vote Clinton	LaRouche	Uncom.
ROBERTSON	249	172	30	47	Clinton	69.1%	12.0%	18.9%
ROCKCASTLE	234	196	18	20	Clinton	83.8%	7.7%	8.5%
ROWAN	927	759	53	115	Clinton	81.9%	5.7%	12.4%
RUSSELL	611	458	61	92	Clinton	75.0%	10.0%	15.1%
SCOTT	3,080	2,210	244	626	Clinton	71.8%	7.9%	20.3%
SHELBY	2,013	1,415	232	366	Clinton	70.3%	11.5%	18.2%
SIMPSON	486	348	44	94	Clinton	71.6%	9.1%	19.3%
SPENCER	580	412	68	100	Clinton	71.0%	11.7%	17.2%
TAYLOR	1,349	1,072	120	157	Clinton	79.5%	8.9%	11.6%
TODD	843	526	97	220	Clinton	62.4%	11.5%	26.1%
TRIGG	1,287	895	118	274	Clinton	69.5%	9.2%	21.3%
TRIMBLE	422	314	45	63	Clinton	74.4%	10.7%	14.9%
UNION	933	711	69	153	Clinton	76.2%	7.4%	16.4%
WARREN	4,592	3,264	411	917	Clinton	71.1%	9.0%	20.0%
WASHINGTON	630	464	73	93	Clinton	73.7%	11.6%	14.8%
WAYNE	581	496	54	31	Clinton	85.4%	9.3%	5.3%
WEBSTER	1,485	1,110	146	229	Clinton	74.7%	9.8%	15.4%
WHITLEY	514	440	34	40	Clinton	85.6%	6.6%	7.8%
WOLFE	927	714	82	131	Clinton	77.0%	8.8%	14.1%
WOODFORD	2,846	2,039	232	575	Clinton	71.6%	8.2%	20.2%
TOTAL	276,019	211,667	20,324	44,028	Clinton	76.7%	7.4%	16.0%

KENTUCKY REPUBLICAN

1996

County	Total Vote	Dole	Other	Winner	Percentage of Total Vote Dole	Other
ADAIR	1,320	1,032	288	Dole	78.2%	21.8%
ALLEN	422	326	96	Dole	77.3%	22.7%
ANDERSON	288	223	65	Dole	77.4%	22.6%
BALLARD	65	41	24	Dole	63.1%	36.9%
BARREN	331	253	78	Dole	76.4%	23.6%
BATH	100	77	23	Dole	77.0%	23.0%
BELL	1,448	962	486	Dole	66.4%	33.6%
BOONE	1,429	1,034	395	Dole	72.4%	27.6%
BOURBON	243	180	63	Dole	74.1%	25.9%
BOYD	1,680	1,217	463	Dole	72.4%	27.6%
BOYLE	536	396	140	Dole	73.9%	26.1%
BRACKEN	88	65	23	Dole	73.9%	26.1%
BREATHITT	76	56	20	Dole	73.7%	26.3%
BRECKINRIDGE	487	369	118	Dole	75.8%	24.2%
BULLITT	753	509	244	Dole	67.6%	32.4%
BUTLER	458	333	125	Dole	72.7%	27.3%
CALDWELL	200	159	41	Dole	79.5%	20.5%
CALLOWAY	265	179	86	Dole	67.5%	32.5%
CAMPBELL	2,250	1,673	577	Dole	74.4%	25.6%
CARLISLE	24	20	4	Dole	83.3%	16.7%

KENTUCKY REPUBLICAN

1996

County	Total Vote	Dole	Other	Winner	Percentage of Total Vote Dole	Other
CARROLL	49	35	14	Dole	71.4%	28.6%
CARTER	1,355	1,000	355	Dole	73.8%	26.2%
CASEY	1,148	924	224	Dole	80.5%	19.5%
CHRISTIAN	522	383	139	Dole	73.4%	26.6%
CLARK	572	415	157	Dole	72.6%	27.4%
CLAY	694	524	170	Dole	75.5%	24.5%
CLINTON	888	649	239	Dole	73.1%	26.9%
CRITTENDEN	203	147	56	Dole	72.4%	27.6%
CUMBERLAND	634	442	192	Dole	69.7%	30.3%
DAVIESS	1,845	1,248	597	Dole	67.6%	32.4%
EDMONSON	401	343	58	Dole	85.5%	14.5%
ELLIOTT	16	11	5	Dole	68.8%	31.3%
ESTILL	1,118	862	256	Dole	77.1%	22.9%
FAYETTE	9,730	7,342	2,388	Dole	75.5%	24.5%
FLEMING	246	203	43	Dole	82.5%	17.5%
FLOYD	305	243	62	Dole	79.7%	20.3%
FRANKLIN	870	629	241	Dole	72.3%	27.7%
FULTON	34	30	4	Dole	88.2%	11.8%
GALLATIN	62	51	11	Dole	82.3%	17.7%
GARRARD	1,249	983	266	Dole	78.7%	21.3%
GRANT	219	161	58	Dole	73.5%	26.5%
GRAVES	193	129	64	Dole	66.8%	33.2%
GRAYSON	640	462	178	Dole	72.2%	27.8%
GREEN	605	486	119	Dole	80.3%	19.7%
GREENUP	2,057	1,492	565	Dole	72.5%	27.5%
HANCOCK	191	135	56	Dole	70.7%	29.3%
HARDIN	1,454	1,069	385	Dole	73.5%	26.5%
HARLAN	1,197	834	363	Dole	69.7%	30.3%
HARRISON	192	138	54	Dole	71.9%	28.1%
HART	272	207	65	Dole	76.1%	23.9%
HENDERSON	490	307	183	Dole	62.7%	37.3%
HENRY	83	60	23	Dole	72.3%	27.7%
HICKMAN	25	18	7	Dole	72.0%	28.0%
HOPKINS	341	218	123	Dole	63.9%	36.1%
JACKSON	484	381	103	Dole	78.7%	21.3%
JEFFERSON	18,794	13,712	5,082	Dole	73.0%	27.0%
JESSAMINE	1,025	785	240	Dole	76.6%	23.4%
JOHNSON	719	547	172	Dole	76.1%	23.9%
KENTON	3,765	2,735	1,030	Dole	72.6%	27.4%
KNOTT	51	35	16	Dole	68.6%	31.4%
KNOX	2,429	1,630	799	Dole	67.1%	32.9%
LARUE	122	95	27	Dole	77.9%	22.1%
LAUREL	2,727	2,079	648	Dole	76.2%	23.8%
LAWRENCE	434	328	106	Dole	75.6%	24.4%
LEE	290	242	48	Dole	83.4%	16.6%
LESLIE	487	346	141	Dole	71.0%	29.0%
LETCHER	396	291	105	Dole	73.5%	26.5%
LEWIS	879	680	199	Dole	77.4%	22.6%
LINCOLN	596	484	112	Dole	81.2%	18.8%
LIVINGSTON	65	45	20	Dole	69.2%	30.8%

KENTUCKY REPUBLICAN

1996

County	Total Vote	Dole	Other	Winner	Percentage of Total Vote Dole	Other
LOGAN	432	313	119	Dole	72.5%	27.5%
LYON	75	61	14	Dole	81.3%	18.7%
MCCRACKEN	539	378	161	Dole	70.1%	29.9%
MCCREARY	941	660	281	Dole	70.1%	29.9%
MCLEAN	130	79	51	Dole	60.8%	39.2%
MADISON	1,672	1,303	369	Dole	77.9%	22.1%
MAGOFFIN	267	212	55	Dole	79.4%	20.6%
MARION	64	45	19	Dole	70.3%	29.7%
MARSHALL	200	147	53	Dole	73.5%	26.5%
MARTIN	482	329	153	Dole	68.3%	31.7%
MASON	340	264	76	Dole	77.6%	22.4%
MEADE	280	189	91	Dole	67.5%	32.5%
MENIFEE	51	32	19	Dole	62.7%	37.3%
MERCER	346	253	93	Dole	73.1%	26.9%
METCALFE	337	257	80	Dole	76.3%	23.7%
MONROE	963	670	293	Dole	69.6%	30.4%
MONTGOMERY	231	177	54	Dole	76.6%	23.4%
MORGAN	64	57	7	Dole	89.1%	10.9%
MUHLENBERG	634	426	208	Dole	67.2%	32.8%
NELSON	486	308	178	Dole	63.4%	36.6%
NICHOLAS	30	20	10	Dole	66.7%	33.3%
OHIO	785	533	252	Dole	67.9%	32.1%
OLDHAM	1,391	1,069	322	Dole	76.9%	23.1%
OWEN	96	67	29	Dole	69.8%	30.2%
OWSLEY	190	135	55	Dole	71.1%	28.9%
PENDLETON	164	123	41	Dole	75.0%	25.0%
PERRY	836	637	199	Dole	76.2%	23.8%
PIKE	1,563	1,216	347	Dole	77.8%	22.2%
POWELL	229	182	47	Dole	79.5%	20.5%
PULASKI	4,071	3,125	946	Dole	76.8%	23.2%
ROBERTSON	27	21	6	Dole	77.8%	22.2%
ROCKCASTLE	611	454	157	Dole	74.3%	25.7%
ROWAN	267	211	56	Dole	79.0%	21.0%
RUSSELL	2,315	1,764	551	Dole	76.2%	23.8%
SCOTT	461	337	124	Dole	73.1%	26.9%
SHELBY	326	253	73	Dole	77.6%	22.4%
SIMPSON	53	39	14	Dole	73.6%	26.4%
SPENCER	108	84	24	Dole	77.8%	22.2%
TAYLOR	1,534	1,184	350	Dole	77.2%	22.8%
TODD	64	49	15	Dole	76.6%	23.4%
TRIGG	124	84	40	Dole	67.7%	32.3%
TRIMBLE	41	32	9	Dole	78.0%	22.0%
UNION	46	31	15	Dole	67.4%	32.6%
WARREN	1,281	931	350	Dole	72.7%	27.3%
WASHINGTON	168	138	30	Dole	82.1%	17.9%
WAYNE	952	763	189	Dole	80.1%	19.9%
WEBSTER	51	38	13	Dole	74.5%	25.5%
WHITLEY	1,216	760	456	Dole	62.5%	37.5%
WOLFE	70	60	10	Dole	85.7%	14.3%
WOODFORD	609	470	139	Dole	77.2%	22.8%
TOTAL	103,839	76,669	27,170	Dole	73.8%	26.2%

LOUISIANA

Louisiana Republicans have been the most ambitious of the players challenging Iowa for the lead-off position on the presidential nominating calendar. They held delegate-selection caucuses in early February 1996, a week before the Iowa caucuses and had planned a similar event in 2000 before abandoning it.

But Louisiana's caucuses in 1996 were sparsely attended (less than 25,000 of the roughly 500,000 registered Republicans) and virtually ignored by most of the contenders. Bob Dole led a lobbying effort on Iowa's behalf, and most of the Republican candidates signed a letter urging Louisiana to stick with its Super Tuesday primary.

Ultimately, only Phil Gramm, Pat Buchanan and Alan Keyes competed in Louisiana. Yet while the early event did not make the Bayou State a kingmaker, it did establish which candidate would anchor the right side of the GOP field.

The caucuses severely wounded Gramm, who had appeared to be a prohibitive favorite to win them. But Buchanan closed fast, and won 13 of the 21 delegates at stake in the district caucuses. Dole won the remaining Louisiana delegates that were at stake in the Super Tuesday primary.

All and all, the experience was not out of character for Louisiana. While state and local politics are often colorful and absorbing, Louisiana voters have seemed less than enchanted with presidential politics.

Cost-conscious state officials tried to kill the presidential primary in 1984, just four years after it was instituted. When a federal court intervened, then-Gov. Edwin Edwards encouraged voters to stay away from the polls. Many white Democrats took his advice, which helped Jesse Jackson score his only primary win that year outside the District of Columbia.

In 1988, Louisiana Democrats joined the Super Tuesday lineup and doubled their primary turnout to more than 600,000. But the result was the same: Jackson won again. In predominantly black New Orleans, Jackson took nearly two-thirds of the vote. Elsewhere, he and runner-up Al Gore ran about even. Jackson won the large population centers—including Caddo (Shreveport), East Baton Rouge (Baton Rouge) and Calcasieu (Lake Charles) parishes—as well as the largely black parishes on the Mississippi River.

Gore carried Winn Parish, birthplace of the legendary Huey Long, and much of the rest of Protestant northern Louisiana. And he won Lafayette Parish, the heart of Cajun country. But Gore had to share his base. Michael Dukakis carried New Orleans' major suburban parishes—Jefferson, St. Bernard and St. Tammany.

The Republican primary in 1988 was not so close. George Bush outpolled runner-up Pat Robertson by a margin of more than 3-to-1. Dole ran second to Bush in the New

Recent Louisiana Primary Results

Louisiana held its first presidential primary in 1980.

	DEMOCRATS			REPUBLICANS		
Year	Turnout	Candidates	%	Turnout	Candidates	%
1996 (March 12)	154,701	BILL CLINTON*	81	77,789	BOB DOLE	48
		Lyndon LaRouche	12		Pat Buchanan	33
					Steve Forbes	13
1992 (March 10)	384,397	BILL CLINTON	69	135,109	GEORGE BUSH*	62
		Paul Tsongas	11		Pat Buchanan	27
1988 (March 8)	624,450	JESSE JACKSON	35	144,781	GEORGE BUSH	58
		Al Gore	28		Pat Robertson	18
		Michael Dukakis	15		Bob Dole	18
		Richard Gephardt	11			
1984 (May 5)	318,810	JESSE JACKSON	43	16,687	RONALD REAGAN*	90
		Gary Hart	25		Uncommitted	10
		Walter Mondale	22			
1980 (April 5)	358,741	JIMMY CARTER*	56	41,683	RONALD REAGAN	75
		Edward Kennedy	23		George Bush	19
		Uncommitted	12			

Note: All candidates are listed that drew at least 10 percent of their party's primary vote. The names of winning candidates are capitalized. An asterisk (*) indicates an incumbent president.

Orleans area, but Robertson won three small parishes in southwestern Louisiana and finished second most everywhere else.

Bush was an easy winner again four years later. But the big story was the collapse of David Duke as a credible political force. The former Ku Klux Klan leader had frightened Louisiana's political establishment with unexpectedly strong runs for the Senate in 1990 and governor in 1991. But Duke's share in the 1992 GOP presidential primary was just 9 percent.

Pat Buchanan finished a distant second in the 1992 Republican primary, but he did better in 1996. His 33 percent share was his best in any Sun Belt primary that year. Buchanan carried more than two dozen parishes, about evenly divided between Protestant northern Louisiana and the Catholic Cajun country to the south.

LOUISIANA DEMOCRATIC

1980

Parish	Total Vote	Carter	E. Kennedy	Uncommitted	Other	Winner	Percentage of Total Vote Carter	E. Kennedy	Uncom.	Other
ACADIA	2,135	1,088	602	254	191	Carter	51.0%	28.2%	11.9%	8.9%
ALLEN	2,556	1,416	796	174	170	Carter	55.4%	31.1%	6.8%	6.7%
ASCENSION	7,698	4,482	1,835	812	569	Carter	58.2%	23.8%	10.5%	7.4%
ASSUMPTION	2,605	1,064	830	471	240	Carter	40.8%	31.9%	18.1%	9.2%
AVOYELLES	3,397	1,632	1,207	250	308	Carter	48.0%	35.5%	7.4%	9.1%
BEAUREGARD	3,331	2,312	429	393	197	Carter	69.4%	12.9%	11.8%	5.9%
BIENVILLE	1,907	1,295	309	94	209	Carter	67.9%	16.2%	4.9%	11.0%
BOSSIER	5,978	4,024	745	699	510	Carter	67.3%	12.5%	11.7%	8.5%
CADDO	17,278	11,861	2,268	1,845	1,304	Carter	68.6%	13.1%	10.7%	7.5%
CALCASIEU	14,558	8,695	3,071	1,825	967	Carter	59.7%	21.1%	12.5%	6.6%
CALDWELL	1,203	715	208	102	178	Carter	59.4%	17.3%	8.5%	14.8%
CAMERON	1,840	1,012	582	132	114	Carter	55.0%	31.6%	7.2%	6.2%
CATAHOULA	1,056	711	161	87	97	Carter	67.3%	15.2%	8.2%	9.2%
CLAIBORNE	1,284	935	132	62	155	Carter	72.8%	10.3%	4.8%	12.1%
CONCORDIA	3,915	2,236	817	395	467	Carter	57.1%	20.9%	10.1%	11.9%
DE SOTO	3,011	2,083	497	147	284	Carter	69.2%	16.5%	4.9%	9.4%
EAST BATON ROUGE	16,388	9,383	3,805	1,994	1,206	Carter	57.3%	23.2%	12.2%	7.4%
EAST CARROLL	845	523	169	84	69	Carter	61.9%	20.0%	9.9%	8.2%
EAST FELICIANA	2,378	1,170	775	253	180	Carter	49.2%	32.6%	10.6%	7.6%
EVANGELINE	3,795	1,988	925	399	483	Carter	52.4%	24.4%	10.5%	12.7%
FRANKLIN	4,320	2,539	552	541	688	Carter	58.8%	12.8%	12.5%	15.9%
GRANT	2,449	1,592	388	238	231	Carter	65.0%	15.8%	9.7%	9.4%
IBERIA	8,127	3,981	2,239	1,042	865	Carter	49.0%	27.6%	12.8%	10.6%
IBERVILLE	3,767	1,964	1,183	335	285	Carter	52.1%	31.4%	8.9%	7.6%
JACKSON	2,214	1,453	383	189	189	Carter	65.6%	17.3%	8.5%	8.5%
JEFFERSON	27,700	13,284	6,078	4,034	4,304	Carter	48.0%	21.9%	14.6%	15.5%
JEFFERSON DAVIS	1,598	954	322	216	106	Carter	59.7%	20.2%	13.5%	6.6%
LAFAYETTE	20,388	10,885	4,554	2,798	2,151	Carter	53.4%	22.3%	13.7%	10.6%
LAFOURCHE	8,115	3,900	2,435	953	827	Carter	48.1%	30.0%	11.7%	10.2%
LA SALLE	2,880	1,923	360	234	363	Carter	66.8%	12.5%	8.1%	12.6%
LINCOLN	3,752	2,767	460	254	271	Carter	73.7%	12.3%	6.8%	7.2%
LIVINGSTON	3,968	2,587	648	493	240	Carter	65.2%	16.3%	12.4%	6.0%
MADISON	1,306	869	285	71	81	Carter	66.5%	21.8%	5.4%	6.2%
MOREHOUSE	3,533	2,222	577	391	343	Carter	62.9%	16.3%	11.1%	9.7%
NATCHITOCHES	4,685	2,901	1,097	302	385	Carter	61.9%	23.4%	6.4%	8.2%
ORLEANS	44,660	21,545	13,018	4,746	5,351	Carter	48.2%	29.1%	10.6%	12.0%
OUACHITA	18,011	11,052	2,829	2,251	1,879	Carter	61.4%	15.7%	12.5%	10.4%
PLAQUEMINES	1,213	559	243	223	188	Carter	46.1%	20.0%	18.4%	15.5%
POINTE COUPEE	1,858	877	624	197	160	Carter	47.2%	33.6%	10.6%	8.6%
RAPIDES	13,896	8,227	2,462	1,691	1,516	Carter	59.2%	17.7%	12.2%	10.9%
RED RIVER	1,641	1,080	235	121	205	Carter	65.8%	14.3%	7.4%	12.5%
RICHLAND	2,605	1,638	360	319	288	Carter	62.9%	13.8%	12.2%	11.1%
SABINE	2,106	1,541	346	103	116	Carter	73.2%	16.4%	4.9%	5.5%
ST. BERNARD	2,720	1,398	590	310	422	Carter	51.4%	21.7%	11.4%	15.5%
ST. CHARLES	4,552	2,351	1,247	492	462	Carter	51.6%	27.4%	10.8%	10.1%
ST. HELENA	988	577	228	110	73	Carter	58.4%	23.1%	11.1%	7.4%
ST. JAMES	2,249	1,048	774	221	206	Carter	46.6%	34.4%	9.8%	9.2%
ST. JOHN THE BAPTIST	8,070	3,331	3,143	830	766	Carter	41.3%	38.9%	10.3%	9.5%
ST. LANDRY	3,957	1,919	1,255	445	338	Carter	48.5%	31.7%	11.2%	8.5%
ST. MARTIN	3,926	1,890	1,155	560	321	Carter	48.1%	29.4%	14.3%	8.2%

LOUISIANA DEMOCRATIC

1980

Parish	Total Vote	Carter	E. Kennedy	Uncommitted	Other	Winner	Percentage of Total Vote Carter	E. Kennedy	Uncom.	Other
ST. MARY	6,078	3,117	1,217	1,187	557	Carter	51.3%	20.0%	19.5%	9.2%
ST. TAMMANY	6,413	3,489	1,158	947	819	Carter	54.4%	18.1%	14.8%	12.8%
TANGIPAHOA	5,381	2,979	1,242	643	517	Carter	55.4%	23.1%	11.9%	9.6%
TENSAS	1,409	861	361	90	97	Carter	61.1%	25.6%	6.4%	6.9%
TERREBONNE	7,257	3,486	1,649	1,274	848	Carter	48.0%	22.7%	17.6%	11.7%
UNION	2,202	1,463	342	230	167	Carter	66.4%	15.5%	10.4%	7.6%
VERMILION	5,408	2,808	1,460	700	440	Carter	51.9%	27.0%	12.9%	8.1%
VERNON	2,908	1,922	549	192	245	Carter	66.1%	18.9%	6.6%	8.4%
WASHINGTON	2,471	1,559	451	243	218	Carter	63.1%	18.3%	9.8%	8.8%
WEBSTER	3,564	2,699	429	154	282	Carter	75.7%	12.0%	4.3%	7.9%
WEST BATON ROUGE	3,427	1,843	978	384	222	Carter	53.8%	28.5%	11.2%	6.5%
WEST CARROLL	1,106	693	118	100	195	Carter	62.7%	10.7%	9.0%	17.6%
WEST FELICIANA	1,227	538	408	181	100	Carter	43.8%	33.3%	14.8%	8.1%
WINN	1,478	1,020	202	107	149	Carter	69.0%	13.7%	7.2%	10.1%
TOTAL	358,741	199,956	80,797	41,614	36,374	Carter	55.7%	22.5%	11.6%	10.1%

LOUISIANA REPUBLICAN

1980

Parish	Total Vote	Bush	Reagan	Other	Winner	Percentage of Total Vote Bush	Reagan	Other
ACADIA	179	14	155	10	Reagan	7.8%	86.6%	5.6%
ALLEN	80	6	72	2	Reagan	7.5%	90.0%	2.5%
ASCENSION	168	30	117	21	Reagan	17.9%	69.6%	12.5%
ASSUMPTION	101	7	55	39	Reagan	6.9%	54.5%	38.6%
AVOYELLES	146	11	132	3	Reagan	7.5%	90.4%	2.1%
BEAUREGARD	164	21	134	9	Reagan	12.8%	81.7%	5.5%
BIENVILLE	60	4	49	7	Reagan	6.7%	81.7%	11.7%
BOSSIER	1,206	142	994	70	Reagan	11.8%	82.4%	5.8%
CADDO	4,283	490	3,533	260	Reagan	11.4%	82.5%	6.1%
CALCASIEU	1,461	252	1,094	115	Reagan	17.2%	74.9%	7.9%
CALDWELL	99	3	91	5	Reagan	3.0%	91.9%	5.1%
CAMERON	27	3	22	2	Reagan	11.1%	81.5%	7.4%
CATAHOULA	72	8	58	6	Reagan	11.1%	80.6%	8.3%
CLAIBORNE	152	6	140	6	Reagan	3.9%	92.1%	3.9%
CONCORDIA	137	9	117	11	Reagan	6.6%	85.4%	8.0%
DE SOTO	144	17	120	7	Reagan	11.8%	83.3%	4.9%
EAST BATON ROUGE	4,305	1,123	2,870	312	Reagan	26.1%	66.7%	7.2%
EAST CARROLL	53	4	49		Reagan	7.5%	92.5%	
EAST FELICIANA	123	19	96	8	Reagan	15.4%	78.0%	6.5%
EVANGELINE	54	2	45	7	Reagan	3.7%	83.3%	13.0%

LOUISIANA REPUBLICAN

1980

Parish	Total Vote	Bush	Reagan	Other	Winner	Percentage of Total Vote Bush	Reagan	Other
FRANKLIN	175	7	158	10	Reagan	4.0%	90.3%	5.7%
GRANT	83	8	70	5	Reagan	9.6%	84.3%	6.0%
IBERIA	676	69	569	38	Reagan	10.2%	84.2%	5.6%
IBERVILLE	83	9	62	12	Reagan	10.8%	74.7%	14.5%
JACKSON	101	11	86	4	Reagan	10.9%	85.1%	4.0%
JEFFERSON	5,000	1,134	3,571	295	Reagan	22.7%	71.4%	5.9%
JEFFERSON DAVIS	162	20	119	23	Reagan	12.3%	73.5%	14.2%
LAFAYETTE	2,643	463	2,025	155	Reagan	17.5%	76.6%	5.9%
LAFOURCHE	524	90	381	53	Reagan	17.2%	72.7%	10.1%
LA SALLE	183	18	158	7	Reagan	9.8%	86.3%	3.8%
LINCOLN	535	54	439	42	Reagan	10.1%	82.1%	7.9%
LIVINGSTON	214	17	183	14	Reagan	7.9%	85.5%	6.5%
MADISON	277	8	264	5	Reagan	2.9%	95.3%	1.8%
MOREHOUSE	526	29	481	16	Reagan	5.5%	91.4%	3.0%
NATCHITOCHES	257	30	209	18	Reagan	11.7%	81.3%	7.0%
ORLEANS	5,655	1,918	3,404	333	Reagan	33.9%	60.2%	5.9%
OUACHITA	2,509	231	2,201	77	Reagan	9.2%	87.7%	3.1%
PLAQUEMINES	85	6	68	11	Reagan	7.1%	80.0%	12.9%
POINTE COUPEE	71	9	55	7	Reagan	12.7%	77.5%	9.9%
RAPIDES	1,111	130	885	96	Reagan	11.7%	79.7%	8.6%
RED RIVER	47	5	41	1	Reagan	10.6%	87.2%	2.1%
RICHLAND	227	17	204	6	Reagan	7.5%	89.9%	2.6%
SABINE	149	11	130	8	Reagan	7.4%	87.2%	5.4%
ST. BERNARD	405	61	333	11	Reagan	15.1%	82.2%	2.7%
ST. CHARLES	313	58	225	30	Reagan	18.5%	71.9%	9.6%
ST. HELENA	53	5	45	3	Reagan	9.4%	84.9%	5.7%
ST. JAMES	59	5	46	8	Reagan	8.5%	78.0%	13.6%
ST. JOHN THE BAPTIST	260	44	199	17	Reagan	16.9%	76.5%	6.5%
ST. LANDRY	304	37	248	19	Reagan	12.2%	81.6%	6.3%
ST. MARTIN	120	14	97	9	Reagan	11.7%	80.8%	7.5%
ST. MARY	590	131	379	80	Reagan	22.2%	64.2%	13.6%
ST. TAMMANY	2,588	659	1,782	147	Reagan	25.5%	68.9%	5.7%
TANGIPAHOA	446	70	336	40	Reagan	15.7%	75.3%	9.0%
TENSAS	69	5	57	7	Reagan	7.2%	82.6%	10.1%
TERREBONNE	801	104	648	49	Reagan	13.0%	80.9%	6.1%
UNION	144	6	134	4	Reagan	4.2%	93.1%	2.8%
VERMILION	215	32	161	22	Reagan	14.9%	74.9%	10.2%
VERNON	96	14	81	1	Reagan	14.6%	84.4%	1.0%
WASHINGTON	223	28	173	22	Reagan	12.6%	77.6%	9.9%
WEBSTER	303	23	261	19	Reagan	7.6%	86.1%	6.3%
WEST BATON ROUGE	83	29	36	18	Reagan	34.9%	43.4%	21.7%
WEST CARROLL	152	4	145	3	Reagan	2.6%	95.4%	2.0%
WEST FELICIANA	65	13	47	5	Reagan	20.0%	72.3%	7.7%
WINN	87	11	73	3	Reagan	12.6%	83.9%	3.4%
TOTAL	41,683	7,818	31,212	2,653	Reagan	18.8%	74.9%	6.4%

LOUISIANA DEMOCRATIC

1984

Parish	Total Vote	Hart	J. Jackson	Mondale	Other	Winner	Percentage of Total Vote Hart	J. Jackson	Mondale	Other
ACADIA	2,918	1,035	757	854	272	Hart	35.5%	25.9%	29.3%	9.3%
ALLEN	1,657	414	682	432	129	J. Jackson	25.0%	41.2%	26.1%	7.8%
ASCENSION	5,631	1,379	2,377	1,465	410	J. Jackson	24.5%	42.2%	26.0%	7.3%
ASSUMPTION	3,121	854	1,362	666	239	J. Jackson	27.4%	43.6%	21.3%	7.7%
AVOYELLES	7,913	3,118	1,784	2,099	912	Hart	39.4%	22.5%	26.5%	11.5%
BEAUREGARD	3,954	1,413	612	1,171	758	Hart	35.7%	15.5%	29.6%	19.2%
BIENVILLE	1,831	466	786	333	246	J. Jackson	25.5%	42.9%	18.2%	13.4%
BOSSIER	4,688	1,642	919	1,348	779	Hart	35.0%	19.6%	28.8%	16.6%
CADDO	16,750	2,931	8,989	3,320	1,510	J. Jackson	17.5%	53.7%	19.8%	9.0%
CALCASIEU	9,326	2,432	2,793	3,123	978	Mondale	26.1%	29.9%	33.5%	10.5%
CALDWELL	1,010	326	326	247	111		32.3%	32.3%	24.5%	11.0%
CAMERON	569	237	46	196	90	Hart	41.7%	8.1%	34.4%	15.8%
CATAHOULA	922	278	362	175	107	J. Jackson	30.2%	39.3%	19.0%	11.6%
CLAIBORNE	1,066	347	398	187	134	J. Jackson	32.6%	37.3%	17.5%	12.6%
CONCORDIA	3,029	831	1,151	641	406	J. Jackson	27.4%	38.0%	21.2%	13.4%
DE SOTO	1,446	324	616	291	215	J. Jackson	22.4%	42.6%	20.1%	14.9%
EAST BATON ROUGE	22,672	4,335	12,516	4,507	1,314	J. Jackson	19.1%	55.2%	19.9%	5.8%
EAST CARROLL	1,499	321	713	288	177	J. Jackson	21.4%	47.6%	19.2%	11.8%
EAST FELICIANA	2,087	423	1,031	446	187	J. Jackson	20.3%	49.4%	21.4%	9.0%
EVANGELINE	3,887	991	1,931	676	289	J. Jackson	25.5%	49.7%	17.4%	7.4%
FRANKLIN	2,413	680	986	456	291	J. Jackson	28.2%	40.9%	18.9%	12.1%
GRANT	2,217	904	357	630	326	Hart	40.8%	16.1%	28.4%	14.7%
IBERIA	3,321	991	1,280	711	339	J. Jackson	29.8%	38.5%	21.4%	10.2%
IBERVILLE	4,201	632	2,691	658	220	J. Jackson	15.0%	64.1%	15.7%	5.2%
JACKSON	2,204	582	826	534	262	J. Jackson	26.4%	37.5%	24.2%	11.9%
JEFFERSON	21,652	7,377	5,289	6,224	2,762	Hart	34.1%	24.4%	28.7%	12.8%
JEFFERSON DAVIS	1,704	467	705	385	147	J. Jackson	27.4%	41.4%	22.6%	8.6%
LAFAYETTE	6,150	2,184	1,675	1,655	636	Hart	35.5%	27.2%	26.9%	10.3%
LAFOURCHE	5,340	2,059	1,077	1,575	629	Hart	38.6%	20.2%	29.5%	11.8%
LA SALLE	1,700	734	168	487	311	Hart	43.2%	9.9%	28.6%	18.3%
LINCOLN	2,443	447	1,453	373	170	J. Jackson	18.3%	59.5%	15.3%	7.0%
LIVINGSTON	2,754	904	361	1,188	301	Mondale	32.8%	13.1%	43.1%	10.9%
MADISON	1,263	139	831	191	102	J. Jackson	11.0%	65.8%	15.1%	8.1%
MOREHOUSE	2,579	455	1,325	495	304	J. Jackson	17.6%	51.4%	19.2%	11.8%
NATCHITOCHES	3,887	795	1,878	731	483	J. Jackson	20.5%	48.3%	18.8%	12.4%
ORLEANS	56,950	7,437	38,142	8,386	2,985	J. Jackson	13.1%	67.0%	14.7%	5.2%
OUACHITA	8,856	1,841	4,417	1,748	850	J. Jackson	20.8%	49.9%	19.7%	9.6%
PLAQUEMINES	1,550	386	673	316	175	J. Jackson	24.9%	43.4%	20.4%	11.3%
POINTE COUPEE	1,847	302	997	437	111	J. Jackson	16.4%	54.0%	23.7%	6.0%
RAPIDES	7,219	1,940	3,108	1,563	608	J. Jackson	26.9%	43.1%	21.7%	8.4%
RED RIVER	812	221	322	168	101	J. Jackson	27.2%	39.7%	20.7%	12.4%
RICHLAND	1,704	485	690	319	210	J. Jackson	28.5%	40.5%	18.7%	12.3%
SABINE	3,195	1,132	412	1,021	630	Hart	35.4%	12.9%	32.0%	19.7%
ST. BERNARD	2,991	1,125	347	1,156	363	Mondale	37.6%	11.6%	38.6%	12.1%
ST. CHARLES	5,386	1,748	1,677	1,250	711	Hart	32.5%	31.1%	23.2%	13.2%
ST. HELENA	1,326	272	705	222	127	J. Jackson	20.5%	53.2%	16.7%	9.6%
ST. JAMES	2,461	339	1,693	330	99	J. Jackson	13.8%	68.8%	13.4%	4.0%
ST. JOHN THE BAPTIST	5,077	1,347	2,246	920	564	J. Jackson	26.5%	44.2%	18.1%	11.1%
ST. LANDRY	12,219	3,217	5,133	2,607	1,262	J. Jackson	26.3%	42.0%	21.3%	10.3%
ST. MARTIN	2,129	537	980	447	165	J. Jackson	25.2%	46.0%	21.0%	7.8%

LOUISIANA DEMOCRATIC

1984

Parish	Total Vote	Hart	J. Jackson	Mondale	Other	Winner	Percentage of Total Vote Hart	J. Jackson	Mondale	Other
ST. MARY	4,820	1,145	2,241	1,029	405	J. Jackson	23.8%	46.5%	21.3%	8.4%
ST. TAMMANY	6,143	2,312	895	1,744	1,192	Hart	37.6%	14.6%	28.4%	19.4%
TANGIPAHOA	4,602	1,246	1,817	1,096	443	J. Jackson	27.1%	39.5%	23.8%	9.6%
TENSAS	871	138	503	158	72	J. Jackson	15.8%	57.7%	18.1%	8.3%
TERREBONNE	4,048	1,167	1,631	870	380	J. Jackson	28.8%	40.3%	21.5%	9.4%
UNION	1,895	518	778	386	213	J. Jackson	27.3%	41.1%	20.4%	11.2%
VERMILION	2,552	995	499	760	298	Hart	39.0%	19.6%	29.8%	11.7%
VERNON	4,365	1,718	429	1,399	819	Hart	39.4%	9.8%	32.1%	18.8%
WASHINGTON	3,119	784	1,149	840	346	J. Jackson	25.1%	36.8%	26.9%	11.1%
WEBSTER	4,964	1,727	1,123	1,233	881	Hart	34.8%	22.6%	24.8%	17.7%
WEST BATON ROUGE	4,325	1,013	1,792	1,177	343	J. Jackson	23.4%	41.4%	27.2%	7.9%
WEST CARROLL	1,054	415	220	282	137	Hart	39.4%	20.9%	26.8%	13.0%
WEST FELICIANA	1,252	263	606	242	141	J. Jackson	21.0%	48.4%	19.3%	11.3%
WINN	1,274	376	429	298	171	J. Jackson	29.5%	33.7%	23.4%	13.4%
TOTAL	318,810	79,593	136,707	71,162	31,348	J. Jackson	25.0%	42.9%	22.3%	9.8%

LOUISIANA REPUBLICAN

1984

Parish	Total Vote	Reagan	Uncommitted	Winner	Percentage of Total Vote Reagan	Uncom.
ACADIA	104	94	10	Reagan	90.4%	9.6%
ALLEN	42	35	7	Reagan	83.3%	16.7%
ASCENSION	206	192	14	Reagan	93.2%	6.8%
ASSUMPTION	85	77	8	Reagan	90.6%	9.4%
AVOYELLES	187	168	19	Reagan	89.8%	10.2%
BEAUREGARD	243	232	11	Reagan	95.5%	4.5%
BIENVILLE	53	43	10	Reagan	81.1%	18.9%
BOSSIER	629	591	38	Reagan	94.0%	6.0%
CADDO	1,260	1,133	127	Reagan	89.9%	10.1%
CALCASIEU	534	496	38	Reagan	92.9%	7.1%
CALDWELL	66	59	7	Reagan	89.4%	10.6%
CAMERON	9	8	1	Reagan	88.9%	11.1%
CATAHOULA	34	26	8	Reagan	76.5%	23.5%
CLAIBORNE	72	65	7	Reagan	90.3%	9.7%
CONCORDIA	112	105	7	Reagan	93.8%	6.3%
DE SOTO	37	34	3	Reagan	91.9%	8.1%
EAST BATON ROUGE	1,377	1,234	143	Reagan	89.6%	10.4%
EAST CARROLL	102	95	7	Reagan	93.1%	6.9%
EAST FELICIANA	90	80	10	Reagan	88.9%	11.1%
EVANGELINE	54	49	5	Reagan	90.7%	9.3%

LOUISIANA REPUBLICAN

1984

Parish	Total Vote	Reagan	Uncommitted	Winner	Percentage of Total Vote	
					Reagan	Uncom.
FRANKLIN	82	79	3	Reagan	96.3%	3.7%
GRANT	91	80	11	Reagan	87.9%	12.1%
IBERIA	236	211	25	Reagan	89.4%	10.6%
IBERVILLE	53	39	14	Reagan	73.6%	26.4%
JACKSON	83	80	3	Reagan	96.4%	3.6%
JEFFERSON	1,402	1,255	147	Reagan	89.5%	10.5%
JEFFERSON DAVIS	58	55	3	Reagan	94.8%	5.2%
LAFAYETTE	581	532	49	Reagan	91.6%	8.4%
LAFOURCHE	234	216	18	Reagan	92.3%	7.7%
LA SALLE	117	113	4	Reagan	96.6%	3.4%
LINCOLN	158	147	11	Reagan	93.0%	7.0%
LIVINGSTON	147	141	6	Reagan	95.9%	4.1%
MADISON	119	104	15	Reagan	87.4%	12.6%
MOREHOUSE	181	168	13	Reagan	92.8%	7.2%
NATCHITOCHES	123	118	5	Reagan	95.9%	4.1%
ORLEANS	1,744	1,307	437	Reagan	74.9%	25.1%
OUACHITA	650	619	31	Reagan	95.2%	4.8%
PLAQUEMINES	58	47	11	Reagan	81.0%	19.0%
POINTE COUPEE	26	24	2	Reagan	92.3%	7.7%
RAPIDES	355	318	37	Reagan	89.6%	10.4%
RED RIVER	28	26	2	Reagan	92.9%	7.1%
RICHLAND	93	86	7	Reagan	92.5%	7.5%
SABINE	190	182	8	Reagan	95.8%	4.2%
ST. BERNARD	115	103	12	Reagan	89.6%	10.4%
ST. CHARLES	412	375	37	Reagan	91.0%	9.0%
ST. HELENA	44	42	2	Reagan	95.5%	4.5%
ST. JAMES	38	34	4	Reagan	89.5%	10.5%
ST. JOHN THE BAPTIST	228	214	14	Reagan	93.9%	6.1%
ST. LANDRY	435	385	50	Reagan	88.5%	11.5%
ST. MARTIN	62	55	7	Reagan	88.7%	11.3%
ST. MARY	212	196	16	Reagan	92.5%	7.5%
ST. TAMMANY	1,558	1,442	116	Reagan	92.6%	7.4%
TANGIPAHOA	209	192	17	Reagan	91.9%	8.1%
TENSAS	39	36	3	Reagan	92.3%	7.7%
TERREBONNE	211	177	34	Reagan	83.9%	16.1%
UNION	77	72	5	Reagan	93.5%	6.5%
VERMILION	99	86	13	Reagan	86.9%	13.1%
VERNON	155	145	10	Reagan	93.5%	6.5%
WASHINGTON	96	90	6	Reagan	93.8%	6.3%
WEBSTER	329	312	17	Reagan	94.8%	5.2%
WEST BATON ROUGE	89	81	8	Reagan	91.0%	9.0%
WEST CARROLL	88	82	6	Reagan	93.2%	6.8%
WEST FELICIANA	37	35	2	Reagan	94.6%	5.4%
WINN	49	47	2	Reagan	95.9%	4.1%
TOTAL	16,687	14,964	1,723	Reagan	89.7%	10.3%

LOUISIANA DEMOCRATIC

1988

Parish	Total Vote	Dukakis	Gephardt	Gore	J. Jackson	Other	Winner	Percentage of Total Vote Dukakis	Gephardt	Gore	J. Jackson	Other
ACADIA	7,985	933	1,745	2,558	1,682	1,067	Gore	11.7%	21.9%	32.0%	21.1%	13.4%
ALLEN	3,630	501	945	798	951	435	J. Jackson	13.8%	26.0%	22.0%	26.2%	12.0%
ASCENSION	11,902	1,477	1,167	4,875	2,862	1,521	Gore	12.4%	9.8%	41.0%	24.0%	12.8%
ASSUMPTION	4,671	565	484	1,460	1,484	678	J. Jackson	12.1%	10.4%	31.3%	31.8%	14.5%
AVOYELLES	4,009	638	655	1,140	1,062	514	Gore	15.9%	16.3%	28.4%	26.5%	12.8%
BEAUREGARD	3,944	587	1,027	1,343	609	378	Gore	14.9%	26.0%	34.1%	15.4%	9.6%
BIENVILLE	4,241	373	313	1,258	1,600	697	J. Jackson	8.8%	7.4%	29.7%	37.7%	16.4%
BOSSIER	12,998	1,994	1,346	6,064	2,266	1,328	Gore	15.3%	10.4%	46.7%	17.4%	10.2%
CADDO	44,528	6,110	3,448	15,776	16,435	2,759	J. Jackson	13.7%	7.7%	35.4%	36.9%	6.2%
CALCASIEU	21,168	3,378	4,410	5,825	6,301	1,254	J. Jackson	16.0%	20.8%	27.5%	29.8%	5.9%
CALDWELL	2,193	125	323	1,027	493	225	Gore	5.7%	14.7%	46.8%	22.5%	10.3%
CAMERON	1,499	297	394	476	142	190	Gore	19.8%	26.3%	31.8%	9.5%	12.7%
CATAHOULA	1,847	90	185	835	613	124	Gore	4.9%	10.0%	45.2%	33.2%	6.7%
CLAIBORNE	3,853	303	290	1,431	1,260	569	Gore	7.9%	7.5%	37.1%	32.7%	14.8%
CONCORDIA	5,215	344	501	1,847	2,118	405	J. Jackson	6.6%	9.6%	35.4%	40.6%	7.8%
DE SOTO	6,266	641	545	2,014	2,229	837	J. Jackson	10.2%	8.7%	32.1%	35.6%	13.4%
EAST BATON ROUGE	46,542	5,371	2,925	15,871	19,195	3,180	J. Jackson	11.5%	6.3%	34.1%	41.2%	6.8%
EAST CARROLL	1,702	69	138	416	979	100	J. Jackson	4.1%	8.1%	24.4%	57.5%	5.9%
EAST FELICIANA	3,560	268	216	1,129	1,452	495	J. Jackson	7.5%	6.1%	31.7%	40.8%	13.9%
EVANGELINE	4,604	426	619	1,392	1,445	722	J. Jackson	9.3%	13.4%	30.2%	31.4%	15.7%
FRANKLIN	3,675	135	437	1,506	1,356	241	Gore	3.7%	11.9%	41.0%	36.9%	6.6%
GRANT	2,360	308	504	892	433	223	Gore	13.1%	21.4%	37.8%	18.3%	9.4%
IBERIA	9,622	1,201	954	3,099	3,608	760	J. Jackson	12.5%	9.9%	32.2%	37.5%	7.9%
IBERVILLE	8,184	692	510	1,963	4,192	827	J. Jackson	8.5%	6.2%	24.0%	51.2%	10.1%
JACKSON	2,968	182	280	1,153	1,162	191	J. Jackson	6.1%	9.4%	38.8%	39.2%	6.4%
JEFFERSON	44,061	13,366	5,026	8,865	9,642	7,162	Dukakis	30.3%	11.4%	20.1%	21.9%	16.3%
JEFFERSON DAVIS	3,475	484	153	1,284	1,086	468	Gore	13.9%	4.4%	36.9%	31.3%	13.5%
LAFAYETTE	25,685	3,876	4,454	7,783	6,983	2,589	Gore	15.1%	17.3%	30.3%	27.2%	10.1%
LAFOURCHE	8,879	2,476	1,260	2,462	1,259	1,422	Dukakis	27.9%	14.2%	27.7%	14.2%	16.0%
LA SALLE	2,132	193	366	1,145	240	188	Gore	9.1%	17.2%	53.7%	11.3%	8.8%
LINCOLN	5,788	401	362	2,009	2,738	278	J. Jackson	6.9%	6.3%	34.7%	47.3%	4.8%
LIVINGSTON	10,542	1,444	1,147	5,470	1,071	1,410	Gore	13.7%	10.9%	51.9%	10.2%	13.4%
MADISON	1,721	59	142	349	1,060	111	J. Jackson	3.4%	8.3%	20.3%	61.6%	6.4%
MOREHOUSE	4,308	240	593	1,127	2,131	217	J. Jackson	5.6%	13.8%	26.2%	49.5%	5.0%
NATCHITOCHES	7,913	880	815	2,457	3,089	672	J. Jackson	11.1%	10.3%	31.1%	39.0%	8.5%
ORLEANS	81,026	12,717	3,186	7,123	52,036	5,964	J. Jackson	15.7%	3.9%	8.8%	64.2%	7.4%
OUACHITA	18,386	1,415	2,304	6,240	7,279	1,148	J. Jackson	7.7%	12.5%	33.9%	39.6%	6.2%
PLAQUEMINES	3,473	732	265	511	1,364	601	J. Jackson	21.1%	7.6%	14.7%	39.3%	17.3%
POINTE COUPEE	4,526	337	524	1,185	2,105	375	J. Jackson	7.4%	11.6%	26.2%	46.5%	8.3%
RAPIDES	11,963	1,975	2,006	3,842	3,130	1,010	Gore	16.5%	16.8%	32.1%	26.2%	8.4%
RED RIVER	2,708	310	284	967	816	331	Gore	11.4%	10.5%	35.7%	30.1%	12.2%
RICHLAND	3,185	131	491	1,257	1,089	217	Gore	4.1%	15.4%	39.5%	34.2%	6.8%
SABINE	4,500	730	620	1,846	791	513	Gore	16.2%	13.8%	41.0%	17.6%	11.4%
ST. BERNARD	13,651	4,753	1,782	2,817	859	3,440	Dukakis	34.8%	13.1%	20.6%	6.3%	25.2%
ST. CHARLES	6,264	1,448	572	1,118	2,220	906	J. Jackson	23.1%	9.1%	17.8%	35.4%	14.5%
ST. HELENA	2,965	174	197	759	1,504	331	J. Jackson	5.9%	6.6%	25.6%	50.7%	11.2%
ST. JAMES	4,294	472	204	674	2,525	419	J. Jackson	11.0%	4.8%	15.7%	58.8%	9.8%
ST. JOHN THE BAPTIST	9,065	1,512	734	1,232	4,112	1,475	J. Jackson	16.7%	8.1%	13.6%	45.4%	16.3%
ST. LANDRY	14,618	1,492	1,633	3,305	6,864	1,324	J. Jackson	10.2%	11.2%	22.6%	47.0%	9.1%
ST. MARTIN	6,137	777	762	1,901	2,073	624	J. Jackson	12.7%	12.4%	31.0%	33.8%	10.2%

LOUISIANA DEMOCRATIC

1988

Parish	Total Vote	Dukakis	Gephardt	Gore	J. Jackson	Other	Winner	Percentage of Total Vote: Dukakis	Gephardt	Gore	J. Jackson	Other
ST. MARY	12,303	1,798	1,180	3,274	4,486	1,565	J. Jackson	14.6%	9.6%	26.6%	36.5%	12.7%
ST. TAMMANY	12,440	3,298	1,514	3,255	2,404	1,969	Dukakis	26.5%	12.2%	26.2%	19.3%	15.8%
TANGIPAHOA	15,655	2,553	1,462	4,686	4,594	2,360	Gore	16.3%	9.3%	29.9%	29.3%	15.1%
TENSAS	1,659	73	106	417	972	91	J. Jackson	4.4%	6.4%	25.1%	58.6%	5.5%
TERREBONNE	13,648	3,300	1,892	3,215	3,114	2,127	Dukakis	24.2%	13.9%	23.6%	22.8%	15.6%
UNION	3,566	184	347	1,555	1,227	253	Gore	5.2%	9.7%	43.6%	34.4%	7.1%
VERMILION	7,214	904	1,552	2,727	1,316	715	Gore	12.5%	21.5%	37.8%	18.2%	9.9%
VERNON	6,203	1,045	1,497	2,086	882	693	Gore	16.8%	24.1%	33.6%	14.2%	11.2%
WASHINGTON	6,124	946	564	1,723	2,174	717	J. Jackson	15.4%	9.2%	28.1%	35.5%	11.7%
WEBSTER	10,237	1,251	985	3,969	2,671	1,361	Gore	12.2%	9.6%	38.8%	26.1%	13.3%
WEST BATON ROUGE	4,437	513	351	1,588	1,527	458	Gore	11.6%	7.9%	35.8%	34.4%	10.3%
WEST CARROLL	2,401	126	416	1,110	442	307	Gore	5.2%	17.3%	46.2%	18.4%	12.8%
WEST FELICIANA	1,670	104	64	383	986	133	J. Jackson	6.2%	3.8%	22.9%	59.0%	8.0%
WINN	2,462	170	261	1,110	742	179	Gore	6.9%	10.6%	45.1%	30.1%	7.3%
TOTAL	624,450	95,667	66,434	174,974	221,532	65,843	J. Jackson	15.3%	10.6%	28.0%	35.5%	10.5%

LOUISIANA REPUBLICAN

1988

Parish	Total Vote	Bush	Dole	Robertson	Other	Winner	Percentage of Total Vote: Bush	Dole	Robertson	Other
ACADIA	1,160	473	150	474	63	Robertson	40.8%	12.9%	40.9%	5.4%
ALLEN	340	148	52	119	21	Bush	43.5%	15.3%	35.0%	6.2%
ASCENSION	1,281	488	276	421	96	Bush	38.1%	21.5%	32.9%	7.5%
ASSUMPTION	309	144	65	86	14	Bush	46.6%	21.0%	27.8%	4.5%
AVOYELLES	454	211	113	116	14	Bush	46.5%	24.9%	25.6%	3.1%
BEAUREGARD	745	378	121	187	59	Bush	50.7%	16.2%	25.1%	7.9%
BIENVILLE	354	230	67	40	17	Bush	65.0%	18.9%	11.3%	4.8%
BOSSIER	4,432	2,801	781	644	206	Bush	63.2%	17.6%	14.5%	4.6%
CADDO	15,342	9,393	2,603	2,563	783	Bush	61.2%	17.0%	16.7%	5.1%
CALCASIEU	4,689	2,132	630	1,673	254	Bush	45.5%	13.4%	35.7%	5.4%
CALDWELL	311	180	48	51	32	Bush	57.9%	15.4%	16.4%	10.3%
CAMERON	99	36	12	43	8	Robertson	36.4%	12.1%	43.4%	8.1%
CATAHOULA	199	90	37	61	11	Bush	45.2%	18.6%	30.7%	5.5%
CLAIBORNE	508	335	93	53	27	Bush	65.9%	18.3%	10.4%	5.3%
CONCORDIA	600	328	96	142	34	Bush	54.7%	16.0%	23.7%	5.7%
DE SOTO	638	363	119	119	37	Bush	56.9%	18.7%	18.7%	5.8%
EAST BATON ROUGE	15,863	8,885	3,260	2,262	1,456	Bush	56.0%	20.6%	14.3%	9.2%
EAST CARROLL	272	124	36	98	14	Bush	45.6%	13.2%	36.0%	5.1%
EAST FELICIANA	406	210	61	97	38	Bush	51.7%	15.0%	23.9%	9.4%
EVANGELINE	418	166	75	157	20	Bush	39.7%	17.9%	37.6%	4.8%

LOUISIANA REPUBLICAN

1988

Parish	Total Vote	Bush	Dole	Robertson	Other	Winner	Percentage of Total Vote Bush	Dole	Robertson	Other
FRANKLIN	493	228	74	168	23	Bush	46.2%	15.0%	34.1%	4.7%
GRANT	325	163	52	97	13	Bush	50.2%	16.0%	29.8%	4.0%
IBERIA	2,102	915	353	717	117	Bush	43.5%	16.8%	34.1%	5.6%
IBERVILLE	396	171	77	121	27	Bush	43.2%	19.4%	30.6%	6.8%
JACKSON	368	206	58	92	12	Bush	56.0%	15.8%	25.0%	3.3%
JEFFERSON	20,209	13,413	3,536	2,142	1,118	Bush	66.4%	17.5%	10.6%	5.5%
JEFFERSON DAVIS	659	268	86	254	51	Bush	40.7%	13.1%	38.5%	7.7%
LAFAYETTE	8,111	4,022	1,682	1,814	593	Bush	49.6%	20.7%	22.4%	7.3%
LAFOURCHE	1,308	618	230	388	72	Bush	47.2%	17.6%	29.7%	5.5%
LA SALLE	316	174	43	73	26	Bush	55.1%	13.6%	23.1%	8.2%
LINCOLN	1,656	970	310	258	118	Bush	58.6%	18.7%	15.6%	7.1%
LIVINGSTON	1,422	773	296	239	114	Bush	54.4%	20.8%	16.8%	8.0%
MADISON	595	371	101	98	25	Bush	62.4%	17.0%	16.5%	4.2%
MOREHOUSE	927	500	140	239	48	Bush	53.9%	15.1%	25.8%	5.2%
NATCHITOCHES	1,101	615	223	183	80	Bush	55.9%	20.3%	16.6%	7.3%
ORLEANS	15,039	10,175	2,763	1,030	1,071	Bush	67.7%	18.4%	6.8%	7.1%
OUACHITA	7,077	3,893	690	2,153	341	Bush	55.0%	9.7%	30.4%	4.8%
PLAQUEMINES	482	278	74	92	38	Bush	57.7%	15.4%	19.1%	7.9%
POINTE COUPEE	347	145	56	126	20	Bush	41.8%	16.1%	36.3%	5.8%
RAPIDES	3,851	2,154	802	701	194	Bush	55.9%	20.8%	18.2%	5.0%
RED RIVER	192	115	34	30	13	Bush	59.9%	17.7%	15.6%	6.8%
RICHLAND	690	322	64	271	33	Bush	46.7%	9.3%	39.3%	4.8%
SABINE	505	310	97	68	30	Bush	61.4%	19.2%	13.5%	5.9%
ST. BERNARD	1,762	956	288	384	134	Bush	54.3%	16.3%	21.8%	7.6%
ST. CHARLES	1,317	796	277	168	76	Bush	60.4%	21.0%	12.8%	5.8%
ST. HELENA	229	99	63	43	24	Bush	43.2%	27.5%	18.8%	10.5%
ST. JAMES	176	74	37	47	18	Bush	42.0%	21.0%	26.7%	10.2%
ST. JOHN THE BAPTIST	1,200	589	210	321	80	Bush	49.1%	17.5%	26.8%	6.7%
ST. LANDRY	1,433	654	311	391	77	Bush	45.6%	21.7%	27.3%	5.4%
ST. MARTIN	594	263	106	189	36	Bush	44.3%	17.8%	31.8%	6.1%
ST. MARY	2,310	1,163	437	605	105	Bush	50.3%	18.9%	26.2%	4.5%
ST. TAMMANY	8,311	5,274	1,467	948	622	Bush	63.5%	17.7%	11.4%	7.5%
TANGIPAHOA	2,287	1,319	434	368	166	Bush	57.7%	19.0%	16.1%	7.3%
TENSAS	284	184	33	59	8	Bush	64.8%	11.6%	20.8%	2.8%
TERREBONNE	2,967	1,443	499	885	140	Bush	48.6%	16.8%	29.8%	4.7%
UNION	649	378	80	166	25	Bush	58.2%	12.3%	25.6%	3.9%
VERMILION	859	324	148	334	53	Robertson	37.7%	17.2%	38.9%	6.2%
VERNON	682	375	143	127	37	Bush	55.0%	21.0%	18.6%	5.4%
WASHINGTON	562	385	93	50	34	Bush	68.5%	16.5%	8.9%	6.0%
WEBSTER	1,358	805	256	211	86	Bush	59.3%	18.9%	15.5%	6.3%
WEST BATON ROUGE	296	166	62	43	25	Bush	56.1%	20.9%	14.5%	8.4%
WEST CARROLL	406	232	57	104	13	Bush	57.1%	14.0%	25.6%	3.2%
WEST FELICIANA	191	109	30	33	19	Bush	57.1%	15.7%	17.3%	9.9%
WINN	317	185	59	59	14	Bush	58.4%	18.6%	18.6%	4.4%
TOTAL	144,781	83,687	25,626	26,295	9,173	Bush	57.8%	17.7%	18.2%	6.3%

LOUISIANA DEMOCRATIC

1992

Parish	Total Vote	Clinton	Tsongas	Other	Winner	Percentage of Total Vote Clinton	Tsongas	Other
ACADIA	3,509	2,505	323	681	Clinton	71.4%	9.2%	19.4%
ALLEN	3,582	2,574	280	728	Clinton	71.9%	7.8%	20.3%
ASCENSION	4,261	3,143	370	748	Clinton	73.8%	8.7%	17.6%
ASSUMPTION	6,141	3,744	361	2,036	Clinton	61.0%	5.9%	33.2%
AVOYELLES	9,817	6,031	731	3,055	Clinton	61.4%	7.4%	31.1%
BEAUREGARD	1,847	1,259	196	392	Clinton	68.2%	10.6%	21.2%
BIENVILLE	1,876	1,360	72	444	Clinton	72.5%	3.8%	23.7%
BOSSIER	4,558	3,438	349	771	Clinton	75.4%	7.7%	16.9%
CADDO	14,978	12,028	1,387	1,563	Clinton	80.3%	9.3%	10.4%
CALCASIEU	13,931	9,530	1,600	2,801	Clinton	68.4%	11.5%	20.1%
CALDWELL	1,489	1,083	79	327	Clinton	72.7%	5.3%	22.0%
CAMERON	686	489	45	152	Clinton	71.3%	6.6%	22.2%
CATAHOULA	3,601	2,388	162	1,051	Clinton	66.3%	4.5%	29.2%
CLAIBORNE	1,648	1,206	121	321	Clinton	73.2%	7.3%	19.5%
CONCORDIA	3,668	2,502	203	963	Clinton	68.2%	5.5%	26.3%
DE SOTO	2,603	1,967	114	522	Clinton	75.6%	4.4%	20.1%
EAST BATON ROUGE	25,000	17,957	3,387	3,656	Clinton	71.8%	13.5%	14.6%
EAST CARROLL	878	633	39	206	Clinton	72.1%	4.4%	23.5%
EAST FELICIANA	3,614	2,850	192	572	Clinton	78.9%	5.3%	15.8%
EVANGELINE	2,874	2,094	130	650	Clinton	72.9%	4.5%	22.6%
FRANKLIN	3,641	2,766	148	727	Clinton	76.0%	4.1%	20.0%
GRANT	2,197	1,569	172	456	Clinton	71.4%	7.8%	20.8%
IBERIA	4,178	2,394	528	1,256	Clinton	57.3%	12.6%	30.1%
IBERVILLE	3,274	2,425	257	592	Clinton	74.1%	7.8%	18.1%
JACKSON	1,692	1,264	84	344	Clinton	74.7%	5.0%	20.3%
JEFFERSON	30,254	19,387	5,817	5,050	Clinton	64.1%	19.2%	16.7%
JEFFERSON DAVIS	2,303	1,718	176	409	Clinton	74.6%	7.6%	17.8%
LAFAYETTE	20,655	12,482	3,028	5,145	Clinton	60.4%	14.7%	24.9%
LAFOURCHE	6,148	4,038	665	1,445	Clinton	65.7%	10.8%	23.5%
LA SALLE	1,321	960	75	286	Clinton	72.7%	5.7%	21.7%
LINCOLN	2,517	1,752	218	547	Clinton	69.6%	8.7%	21.7%
LIVINGSTON	8,520	6,072	742	1,706	Clinton	71.3%	8.7%	20.0%
MADISON	1,017	732	40	245	Clinton	72.0%	3.9%	24.1%
MOREHOUSE	3,399	2,493	209	697	Clinton	73.3%	6.1%	20.5%
NATCHITOCHES	3,951	2,531	323	1,097	Clinton	64.1%	8.2%	27.8%
ORLEANS	59,717	43,316	8,266	8,135	Clinton	72.5%	13.8%	13.6%
OUACHITA	13,984	10,017	969	2,998	Clinton	71.6%	6.9%	21.4%
PLAQUEMINES	1,848	1,336	220	292	Clinton	72.3%	11.9%	15.8%
POINTE COUPEE	1,888	1,419	135	334	Clinton	75.2%	7.2%	17.7%
RAPIDES	8,008	5,225	910	1,873	Clinton	65.2%	11.4%	23.4%
RED RIVER	1,065	837	33	195	Clinton	78.6%	3.1%	18.3%
RICHLAND	1,424	1,018	63	343	Clinton	71.5%	4.4%	24.1%
SABINE	1,877	1,297	106	474	Clinton	69.1%	5.6%	25.3%
ST. BERNARD	6,621	4,436	990	1,195	Clinton	67.0%	15.0%	18.0%
ST. CHARLES	3,155	2,210	437	508	Clinton	70.0%	13.9%	16.1%
ST. HELENA	1,341	1,013	40	288	Clinton	75.5%	3.0%	21.5%
ST. JAMES	1,739	1,354	117	268	Clinton	77.9%	6.7%	15.4%
ST. JOHN THE BAPTIST	2,521	1,854	273	394	Clinton	73.5%	10.8%	15.6%
ST. LANDRY	5,009	3,639	406	964	Clinton	72.6%	8.1%	19.2%
ST. MARTIN	8,951	5,145	720	3,086	Clinton	57.5%	8.0%	34.5%

LOUISIANA DEMOCRATIC

1992

Parish	Total Vote	Clinton	Tsongas	Other	Winner	Percentage of Total Vote Clinton	Tsongas	Other
ST. MARY	3,719	2,522	367	830	Clinton	67.8%	9.9%	22.3%
ST. TAMMANY	15,192	10,103	2,577	2,512	Clinton	66.5%	17.0%	16.5%
TANGIPAHOA	6,960	4,936	674	1,350	Clinton	70.9%	9.7%	19.4%
TENSAS	1,272	908	55	309	Clinton	71.4%	4.3%	24.3%
TERREBONNE	5,522	3,823	665	1,034	Clinton	69.2%	12.0%	18.7%
UNION	3,499	2,521	179	799	Clinton	72.0%	5.1%	22.8%
VERMILION	4,194	2,685	336	1,173	Clinton	64.0%	8.0%	28.0%
VERNON	2,553	1,713	220	620	Clinton	67.1%	8.6%	24.3%
WASHINGTON	8,479	6,171	617	1,691	Clinton	72.8%	7.3%	19.9%
WEBSTER	3,151	2,432	162	557	Clinton	77.2%	5.1%	17.7%
WEST BATON ROUGE	1,745	1,325	138	282	Clinton	75.9%	7.9%	16.2%
WEST CARROLL	964	719	47	198	Clinton	74.6%	4.9%	20.5%
WEST FELICIANA	943	723	70	150	Clinton	76.7%	7.4%	15.9%
WINN	1,428	941	93	394	Clinton	65.9%	6.5%	27.6%
TOTAL	384,397	267,002	42,508	74,887	Clinton	69.5%	11.1%	19.5%

LOUISIANA REPUBLICAN

1992

Parish	Total Vote	Buchanan	Bush	Other	Winner	Percentage of Total Vote Buchanan	Bush	Other
ACADIA	695	241	393	61	Bush	34.7%	56.5%	8.8%
ALLEN	386	66	268	52	Bush	17.1%	69.4%	13.5%
ASCENSION	988	344	549	95	Bush	34.8%	55.6%	9.6%
ASSUMPTION	498	110	269	119	Bush	22.1%	54.0%	23.9%
AVOYELLES	1,058	246	533	279	Bush	23.3%	50.4%	26.4%
BEAUREGARD	575	111	372	92	Bush	19.3%	64.7%	16.0%
BIENVILLE	271	56	170	45	Bush	20.7%	62.7%	16.6%
BOSSIER	2,834	574	1,860	400	Bush	20.3%	65.6%	14.1%
CADDO	8,701	1,694	6,331	676	Bush	19.5%	72.8%	7.8%
CALCASIEU	3,870	877	2,673	320	Bush	22.7%	69.1%	8.3%
CALDWELL	318	72	153	93	Bush	22.6%	48.1%	29.2%
CAMERON	71	27	38	6	Bush	38.0%	53.5%	8.5%
CATAHOULA	485	89	245	151	Bush	18.4%	50.5%	31.1%
CLAIBORNE	413	61	280	72	Bush	14.8%	67.8%	17.4%
CONCORDIA	717	164	403	150	Bush	22.9%	56.2%	20.9%
DE SOTO	430	82	261	87	Bush	19.1%	60.7%	20.2%
EAST BATON ROUGE	15,538	4,287	10,353	898	Bush	27.6%	66.6%	5.8%
EAST CARROLL	210	33	125	52	Bush	15.7%	59.5%	24.8%
EAST FELICIANA	587	178	315	94	Bush	30.3%	53.7%	16.0%
EVANGELINE	360	116	157	87	Bush	32.2%	43.6%	24.2%

LOUISIANA REPUBLICAN

1992

Parish	Total Vote	Buchanan	Bush	Other	Winner	Percentage of Total Vote Buchanan	Bush	Other
FRANKLIN	782	165	359	258	Bush	21.1%	45.9%	33.0%
GRANT	474	81	287	106	Bush	17.1%	60.5%	22.4%
IBERIA	1,445	435	774	236	Bush	30.1%	53.6%	16.3%
IBERVILLE	385	88	252	45	Bush	22.9%	65.5%	11.7%
JACKSON	332	79	185	68	Bush	23.8%	55.7%	20.5%
JEFFERSON	20,954	6,546	12,143	2,265	Bush	31.2%	58.0%	10.8%
JEFFERSON DAVIS	394	83	262	49	Bush	21.1%	66.5%	12.4%
LAFAYETTE	9,248	2,896	5,742	610	Bush	31.3%	62.1%	6.6%
LAFOURCHE	1,343	399	745	199	Bush	29.7%	55.5%	14.8%
LA SALLE	273	50	166	57	Bush	18.3%	60.8%	20.9%
LINCOLN	1,339	271	877	191	Bush	20.2%	65.5%	14.3%
LIVINGSTON	1,940	557	1,111	272	Bush	28.7%	57.3%	14.0%
MADISON	424	89	236	99	Bush	21.0%	55.7%	23.3%
MOREHOUSE	936	204	560	172	Bush	21.8%	59.8%	18.4%
NATCHITOCHES	853	172	498	183	Bush	20.2%	58.4%	21.5%
ORLEANS	14,165	3,718	9,303	1,144	Bush	26.2%	65.7%	8.1%
OUACHITA	6,881	1,414	4,691	776	Bush	20.5%	68.2%	11.3%
PLAQUEMINES	465	165	246	54	Bush	35.5%	52.9%	11.6%
POINTE COUPEE	298	94	166	38	Bush	31.5%	55.7%	12.8%
RAPIDES	3,167	746	2,053	368	Bush	23.6%	64.8%	11.6%
RED RIVER	137	25	80	32	Bush	18.2%	58.4%	23.4%
RICHLAND	483	109	266	108	Bush	22.6%	55.1%	22.4%
SABINE	419	90	239	90	Bush	21.5%	57.0%	21.5%
ST. BERNARD	1,584	540	806	238	Bush	34.1%	50.9%	15.0%
ST. CHARLES	1,391	404	872	115	Bush	29.0%	62.7%	8.3%
ST. HELENA	252	53	118	81	Bush	21.0%	46.8%	32.1%
ST. JAMES	162	63	78	21	Bush	38.9%	48.1%	13.0%
ST. JOHN THE BAPTIST	876	300	495	81	Bush	34.2%	56.5%	9.2%
ST. LANDRY	1,018	394	502	122	Bush	38.7%	49.3%	12.0%
ST. MARTIN	885	267	443	175	Bush	30.2%	50.1%	19.8%
ST. MARY	1,259	343	762	154	Bush	27.2%	60.5%	12.2%
ST. TAMMANY	11,455	3,430	7,124	901	Bush	29.9%	62.2%	7.9%
TANGIPAHOA	2,034	640	1,120	274	Bush	31.5%	55.1%	13.5%
TENSAS	326	69	203	54	Bush	21.2%	62.3%	16.6%
TERREBONNE	2,384	859	1,300	225	Bush	36.0%	54.5%	9.4%
UNION	884	145	529	210	Bush	16.4%	59.8%	23.8%
VERMILION	602	198	310	94	Bush	32.9%	51.5%	15.6%
VERNON	535	106	318	111	Bush	19.8%	59.4%	20.7%
WASHINGTON	1,259	316	648	295	Bush	25.1%	51.5%	23.4%
WEBSTER	919	166	538	215	Bush	18.1%	58.5%	23.4%
WEST BATON ROUGE	312	102	166	44	Bush	32.7%	53.2%	14.1%
WEST CARROLL	339	90	153	96	Bush	26.5%	45.1%	28.3%
WEST FELICIANA	212	79	105	28	Bush	37.3%	49.5%	13.2%
WINN	279	57	165	57	Bush	20.4%	59.1%	20.4%
TOTAL	135,109	36,525	83,744	14,840	Bush	27.0%	62.0%	11.0%

LOUISIANA DEMOCRATIC

1996

Parish	Total Vote	Clinton	LaRouche	Lloyd-Duffie	Winner	Percentage of Total Vote Clinton	LaRouche	Lloyd-Duffie
ACADIA	1,571	1,327	141	103	Clinton	84.5%	9.0%	6.6%
ALLEN	912	723	134	55	Clinton	79.3%	14.7%	6.0%
ASCENSION	3,299	2,824	288	187	Clinton	85.6%	8.7%	5.7%
ASSUMPTION	649	551	62	36	Clinton	84.9%	9.6%	5.5%
AVOYELLES	1,084	896	113	75	Clinton	82.7%	10.4%	6.9%
BEAUREGARD	564	408	96	60	Clinton	72.3%	17.0%	10.6%
BIENVILLE	1,068	851	138	79	Clinton	79.7%	12.9%	7.4%
BOSSIER	5,762	4,672	706	384	Clinton	81.1%	12.3%	6.7%
CADDO	5,064	4,235	532	297	Clinton	83.6%	10.5%	5.9%
CALCASIEU	2,311	1,853	262	196	Clinton	80.2%	11.3%	8.5%
CALDWELL	1,045	735	203	107	Clinton	70.3%	19.4%	10.2%
CAMERON	275	205	34	36	Clinton	74.5%	12.4%	13.1%
CATAHOULA	2,286	1,646	365	275	Clinton	72.0%	16.0%	12.0%
CLAIBORNE	1,433	1,160	163	110	Clinton	80.9%	11.4%	7.7%
CONCORDIA	3,774	2,869	613	292	Clinton	76.0%	16.2%	7.7%
DE SOTO	684	556	78	50	Clinton	81.3%	11.4%	7.3%
EAST BATON ROUGE	7,501	6,412	708	381	Clinton	85.5%	9.4%	5.1%
EAST CARROLL	1,032	908	74	50	Clinton	88.0%	7.2%	4.8%
EAST FELICIANA	1,364	1,109	155	100	Clinton	81.3%	11.4%	7.3%
EVANGELINE	4,939	3,830	633	476	Clinton	77.5%	12.8%	9.6%
FRANKLIN	2,392	1,727	410	255	Clinton	72.2%	17.1%	10.7%
GRANT	701	514	91	96	Clinton	73.3%	13.0%	13.7%
IBERIA	971	762	104	105	Clinton	78.5%	10.7%	10.8%
IBERVILLE	2,153	1,812	221	120	Clinton	84.2%	10.3%	5.6%
JACKSON	1,417	1,066	233	118	Clinton	75.2%	16.4%	8.3%
JEFFERSON	9,817	7,647	1,332	838	Clinton	77.9%	13.6%	8.5%
JEFFERSON DAVIS	817	660	83	74	Clinton	80.8%	10.2%	9.1%
LAFAYETTE	4,035	3,368	378	289	Clinton	83.5%	9.4%	7.2%
LAFOURCHE	3,131	2,518	376	237	Clinton	80.4%	12.0%	7.6%
LA SALLE	807	514	166	127	Clinton	63.7%	20.6%	15.7%
LINCOLN	2,431	1,863	344	224	Clinton	76.6%	14.2%	9.2%
LIVINGSTON	2,532	1,787	447	298	Clinton	70.6%	17.7%	11.8%
MADISON	773	657	74	42	Clinton	85.0%	9.6%	5.4%
MOREHOUSE	1,417	1,080	204	133	Clinton	76.2%	14.4%	9.4%
NATCHITOCHES	4,129	3,257	490	382	Clinton	78.9%	11.9%	9.3%
ORLEANS	12,295	11,437	505	353	Clinton	93.0%	4.1%	2.9%
OUACHITA	12,413	10,082	1,469	862	Clinton	81.2%	11.8%	6.9%
PLAQUEMINES	485	384	51	50	Clinton	79.2%	10.5%	10.3%
POINTE COUPEE	1,045	897	90	58	Clinton	85.8%	8.6%	5.6%
RAPIDES	8,212	6,491	989	732	Clinton	79.0%	12.0%	8.9%
RED RIVER	534	476	33	25	Clinton	89.1%	6.2%	4.7%
RICHLAND	1,585	1,083	317	185	Clinton	68.3%	20.0%	11.7%
SABINE	687	479	120	88	Clinton	69.7%	17.5%	12.8%
ST. BERNARD	889	657	130	102	Clinton	73.9%	14.6%	11.5%
ST. CHARLES	593	462	72	59	Clinton	77.9%	12.1%	9.9%
ST. HELENA	783	642	96	45	Clinton	82.0%	12.3%	5.7%
ST. JAMES	707	630	54	23	Clinton	89.1%	7.6%	3.3%
ST. JOHN THE BAPTIST	591	509	41	41	Clinton	86.1%	6.9%	6.9%
ST. LANDRY	2,760	2,355	270	135	Clinton	85.3%	9.8%	4.9%
ST. MARTIN	2,911	2,432	290	189	Clinton	83.5%	10.0%	6.5%

LOUISIANA DEMOCRATIC

1996

Parish	Total Vote	Clinton	LaRouche	Lloyd-Duffie	Winner	Percentage of Total Vote Clinton	LaRouche	Lloyd-Duffie
ST. MARY	1,165	981	102	82	Clinton	84.2%	8.8%	7.0%
ST. TAMMANY	3,220	2,478	430	312	Clinton	77.0%	13.4%	9.7%
TANGIPAHOA	5,453	4,257	751	445	Clinton	78.1%	13.8%	8.2%
TENSAS	893	763	87	43	Clinton	85.4%	9.7%	4.8%
TERREBONNE	1,547	1,284	137	126	Clinton	83.0%	8.9%	8.1%
UNION	1,837	1,307	339	191	Clinton	71.1%	18.5%	10.4%
VERMILION	1,337	1,117	120	100	Clinton	83.5%	9.0%	7.5%
VERNON	1,706	1,308	229	169	Clinton	76.7%	13.4%	9.9%
WASHINGTON	1,546	1,247	170	129	Clinton	80.7%	11.0%	8.3%
WEBSTER	2,877	2,234	462	181	Clinton	77.7%	16.1%	6.3%
WEST BATON ROUGE	370	298	47	25	Clinton	80.5%	12.7%	6.8%
WEST CARROLL	605	387	136	82	Clinton	64.0%	22.5%	13.6%
WEST FELICIANA	569	481	49	39	Clinton	84.5%	8.6%	6.9%
WINN	946	771	113	62	Clinton	81.5%	11.9%	6.6%
TOTAL	154,701	124,931	18,150	11,620	Clinton	80.8%	11.7%	7.5%

LOUISIANA REPUBLICAN

1996

Parish	Total Vote	Buchanan	Dole	Forbes	Other	Winner	Percentage of Total Vote Buchanan	Dole	Forbes	Other
ACADIA	459	191	190	45	33	Buchanan	41.6%	41.4%	9.8%	7.2%
ALLEN	161	89	50	13	9	Buchanan	55.3%	31.1%	8.1%	5.6%
ASCENSION	641	248	252	90	51	Dole	38.7%	39.3%	14.0%	8.0%
ASSUMPTION	114	38	59	14	3	Dole	33.3%	51.8%	12.3%	2.6%
AVOYELLES	261	114	120	15	12	Dole	43.7%	46.0%	5.7%	4.6%
BEAUREGARD	311	157	115	22	17	Buchanan	50.5%	37.0%	7.1%	5.5%
BIENVILLE	194	88	63	21	22	Buchanan	45.4%	32.5%	10.8%	11.3%
BOSSIER	3,776	1,074	2,012	459	231	Dole	28.4%	53.3%	12.2%	6.1%
CADDO	4,258	1,155	2,455	493	155	Dole	27.1%	57.7%	11.6%	3.6%
CALCASIEU	1,856	897	718	153	88	Buchanan	48.3%	38.7%	8.2%	4.7%
CALDWELL	395	177	153	40	25	Buchanan	44.8%	38.7%	10.1%	6.3%
CAMERON	50	31	14	3	2	Buchanan	62.0%	28.0%	6.0%	4.0%
CATAHOULA	407	185	159	36	27	Buchanan	45.5%	39.1%	8.8%	6.6%
CLAIBORNE	398	134	183	52	29	Dole	33.7%	46.0%	13.1%	7.3%
CONCORDIA	829	375	333	78	43	Buchanan	45.2%	40.2%	9.4%	5.2%
DE SOTO	213	90	83	27	13	Buchanan	42.3%	39.0%	12.7%	6.1%
EAST BATON ROUGE	6,856	1,964	3,477	1,003	412	Dole	28.6%	50.7%	14.6%	6.0%
EAST CARROLL	212	105	81	17	9	Buchanan	49.5%	38.2%	8.0%	4.2%
EAST FELICIANA	412	204	145	45	18	Buchanan	49.5%	35.2%	10.9%	4.4%
EVANGELINE	592	301	215	47	29	Buchanan	50.8%	36.3%	7.9%	4.9%

LOUISIANA REPUBLICAN

1996

Parish	Total Vote	Buchanan	Dole	Forbes	Other	Winner	Percentage of Total Vote Buchanan	Dole	Forbes	Other
FRANKLIN	771	387	276	71	37	Buchanan	50.2%	35.8%	9.2%	4.8%
GRANT	250	105	120	18	7	Dole	42.0%	48.0%	7.2%	2.8%
IBERIA	680	272	291	78	39	Dole	40.0%	42.8%	11.5%	5.7%
IBERVILLE	318	63	68	26	161	Taylor	19.8%	21.4%	8.2%	50.6%
JACKSON	411	206	129	33	43	Buchanan	50.1%	31.4%	8.0%	10.5%
JEFFERSON	10,268	2,831	5,198	1,756	483	Dole	27.6%	50.6%	17.1%	4.7%
JEFFERSON DAVIS	276	123	114	23	16	Buchanan	44.6%	41.3%	8.3%	5.8%
LAFAYETTE	3,665	1,048	1,858	505	254	Dole	28.6%	50.7%	13.8%	6.9%
LAFOURCHE	905	268	448	130	59	Dole	29.6%	49.5%	14.4%	6.5%
LA SALLE	254	106	104	24	20	Buchanan	41.7%	40.9%	9.4%	7.9%
LINCOLN	1,706	624	769	208	105	Dole	36.6%	45.1%	12.2%	6.2%
LIVINGSTON	1,280	569	489	160	62	Buchanan	44.5%	38.2%	12.5%	4.8%
MADISON	387	190	140	44	13	Buchanan	49.1%	36.2%	11.4%	3.4%
MOREHOUSE	859	347	389	88	35	Dole	40.4%	45.3%	10.2%	4.1%
NATCHITOCHES	1,124	353	584	105	82	Dole	31.4%	52.0%	9.3%	7.3%
ORLEANS	4,033	837	2,192	714	290	Dole	20.8%	54.4%	17.7%	7.2%
OUACHITA	7,673	2,665	3,626	954	428	Dole	34.7%	47.3%	12.4%	5.6%
PLAQUEMINES	234	91	106	22	15	Dole	38.9%	45.3%	9.4%	6.4%
POINTE COUPEE	189	74	85	18	12	Dole	39.2%	45.0%	9.5%	6.3%
RAPIDES	3,241	1,163	1,575	318	185	Dole	35.9%	48.6%	9.8%	5.7%
RED RIVER	119	48	52	8	11	Dole	40.3%	43.7%	6.7%	9.2%
RICHLAND	726	378	263	57	28	Buchanan	52.1%	36.2%	7.9%	3.9%
SABINE	313	125	146	31	11	Dole	39.9%	46.6%	9.9%	3.5%
ST. BERNARD	668	301	244	96	27	Buchanan	45.1%	36.5%	14.4%	4.0%
ST. CHARLES	625	170	297	117	41	Dole	27.2%	47.5%	18.7%	6.6%
ST. HELENA	212	103	73	16	20	Buchanan	48.6%	34.4%	7.5%	9.4%
ST. JAMES	82	34	33	6	9	Buchanan	41.5%	40.2%	7.3%	11.0%
ST. JOHN THE BAPTIST	235	95	96	35	9	Dole	40.4%	40.9%	14.9%	3.8%
ST. LANDRY	733	318	308	61	46	Buchanan	43.4%	42.0%	8.3%	6.3%
ST. MARTIN	419	159	174	46	40	Dole	37.9%	41.5%	11.0%	9.5%
ST. MARY	582	230	252	71	29	Dole	39.5%	43.3%	12.2%	5.0%
ST. TAMMANY	5,429	1,292	2,827	978	332	Dole	23.8%	52.1%	18.0%	6.1%
TANGIPAHOA	1,840	651	805	261	123	Dole	35.4%	43.8%	14.2%	6.7%
TENSAS	208	93	86	15	14	Buchanan	44.7%	41.3%	7.2%	6.7%
TERREBONNE	1,039	321	514	152	52	Dole	30.9%	49.5%	14.6%	5.0%
UNION	705	338	276	58	33	Buchanan	47.9%	39.1%	8.2%	4.7%
VERMILION	362	136	168	37	21	Dole	37.6%	46.4%	10.2%	5.8%
VERNON	403	171	168	36	28	Buchanan	42.4%	41.7%	8.9%	6.9%
WASHINGTON	495	184	224	66	21	Dole	37.2%	45.3%	13.3%	4.2%
WEBSTER	800	289	349	70	92	Dole	36.1%	43.6%	8.8%	11.5%
WEST BATON ROUGE	136	64	47	20	5	Buchanan	47.1%	34.6%	14.7%	3.7%
WEST CARROLL	339	182	129	18	10	Buchanan	53.7%	38.1%	5.3%	2.9%
WEST FELICIANA	172	51	87	23	11	Dole	29.7%	50.6%	13.4%	6.4%
WINN	228	85	114	19	10	Dole	37.3%	50.0%	8.3%	4.4%
TOTAL	77,789	25,757	37,170	10,265	4,597	Dole	33.1%	47.8%	13.2%	5.9%

Note: Maurice "Morry" Taylor was certified as the winner in Iberville Parish with 76 votes, even though he received less than 1 percent of the statewide primary vote.

MAINE

Maine held its first presidential primary in early March 1996 as part of a New England regional event. But neither the regional primary, in general, or the Maine primary, in particular, proved to be very compelling.

In Maine and the rest of New England, Bob Dole easily beat back his challengers on the Republican side while President Bill Clinton faced only nominal opposition on the Democratic side. Primary turnout in Maine for both parties was less than 100,000 voters, barely half the number that turned out later in the year for the state's U.S. Senate primaries.

The predictable outcome of the presidential primary belied Maine's image in the 1990s as a place where political contrariness and individualism flourish. In the presidential elections of 1992 and 1996, Maine gave Ross Perot a higher percentage of the vote than any other state. In 1994 and 1998, Maine was the only state to elect an independent governor (Angus King). And in the Democratic caucuses in 1992, Maine gave Jerry Brown his first victory of the year, a narrow 1 percentage point victory over the New Hampshire primary winner and regional favorite son, Paul Tsongas.

Brown's victory broke a trend evident throughout the 1980s—that the winner in New Hampshire would also win the Maine vote several days later. In 1980, the double winner was President Jimmy Carter, whose New Hampshire and Maine victories put an early chill on Edward Kennedy in his New England backyard. In 1984, Gary Hart's stunning breakthrough win in New Hampshire yanked him from down-in-the-weeds status in Maine to a victorious 50-percent share of the caucus vote. In 1988, Michael Dukakis swept out of New Hampshire to win Maine's caucuses handily 12 days later.

Meanwhile, on the Republican side, Maine was long the personal preserve of George Bush. From his youth, he had vacationed at his family's seaside compound in Kennebunkport, establishing a personal relationship with Maine voters that helped launch him onto the presidential stage with an upset victory in a party-sponsored straw poll in late 1979. The following spring he swept virtually all of Maine's delegates, even as his first bid for the White House was crumbling nationally.

Maine was also in Bush's corner when he successfully pursued the GOP presidential nomination in 1988 and 1992. Dole won the state's Republican presidential primary in 1996, although he drew a majority of the vote in only two counties. One of them, though, was Cumberland (Portland), the state's most populous. The primary runner-up, Pat Buchanan, could dent the 30 percent-mark in only two counties, the largest of which was historically blue-collar and heavily Democratic Androscoggin (Lewiston).

Maine Primary Results

Maine held its first presidential primary in 1996.

	DEMOCRATS			REPUBLICANS		
Year	Turnout	Candidates	%	Turnout	Candidates	%
1996 (March 5)	27,027	BILL CLINTON*	88	67,280	BOB DOLE	46
					Pat Buchanan	24
					Steve Forbes	15

Note: All candidates are listed who drew at least 10 percent of their party's primary vote. The names of winning candidates are capitalized. An asterisk (*) indicates an incumbent president.

Aroostook
Piscataquis
Somerset
Penobscot
Washington
Franklin
Bangor
Hancock
Oxford
Kennebec
Waldo
Augusta
Androscoggin
Lewiston
Lincoln
Knox
Sagadahoc
Cumberland
Portland
York

MAINE DEMOCRATIC

1996

County	Total Vote	Clinton	Other	Winner	Percentage of Total Vote Clinton	Other
ANDROSCOGGIN	2,785	2,390	395	Clinton	85.8%	14.2%
AROOSTOOK	1,428	1,270	158	Clinton	88.9%	11.1%
CUMBERLAND	5,551	5,007	544	Clinton	90.2%	9.8%
FRANKLIN	492	443	49	Clinton	90.0%	10.0%
HANCOCK	1,517	1,375	142	Clinton	90.6%	9.4%
KENNEBEC	1,966	1,747	219	Clinton	88.9%	11.1%
KNOX	797	732	65	Clinton	91.8%	8.2%
LINCOLN	648	573	75	Clinton	88.4%	11.6%
OXFORD	1,228	1,115	113	Clinton	90.8%	9.2%
PENOBSCOT	3,264	2,856	408	Clinton	87.5%	12.5%
PISCATAQUIS	427	359	68	Clinton	84.1%	15.9%
SAGADAHOC	813	726	87	Clinton	89.3%	10.7%
SOMERSET	1,088	936	152	Clinton	86.0%	14.0%
WALDO	807	689	118	Clinton	85.4%	14.6%
WASHINGTON	868	721	147	Clinton	83.1%	16.9%
YORK	3,348	2,940	408	Clinton	87.8%	12.2%
TOTAL	27,027	23,879	3,148	Clinton	88.4%	11.6%

MAINE REPUBLICAN

1996

County	Total Vote	Buchanan	Dole	Forbes	Other	Winner	Percentage of Total Vote Buchanan	Dole	Forbes	Other
ANDROSCOGGIN	4,188	1,301	1,706	642	539	Dole	31.1%	40.7%	15.3%	12.9%
AROOSTOOK	3,150	888	1,474	338	450	Dole	28.2%	46.8%	10.7%	14.3%
CUMBERLAND	14,036	2,609	7,365	2,172	1,890	Dole	18.6%	52.5%	15.5%	13.5%
FRANKLIN	1,698	459	711	251	277	Dole	27.0%	41.9%	14.8%	16.3%
HANCOCK	4,020	749	1,932	719	620	Dole	18.6%	48.1%	17.9%	15.4%
KENNEBEC	5,190	1,371	2,383	735	701	Dole	26.4%	45.9%	14.2%	13.5%
KNOX	2,757	652	1,239	427	439	Dole	23.6%	44.9%	15.5%	15.9%
LINCOLN	2,591	525	1,260	444	362	Dole	20.3%	48.6%	17.1%	14.0%
OXFORD	2,845	744	1,228	465	408	Dole	26.2%	43.2%	16.3%	14.3%
PENOBSCOT	8,000	2,185	3,588	993	1,234	Dole	27.3%	44.9%	12.4%	15.4%
PISCATAQUIS	1,184	302	520	192	170	Dole	25.5%	43.9%	16.2%	14.4%
SAGADAHOC	2,005	381	1,004	295	325	Dole	19.0%	50.1%	14.7%	16.2%
SOMERSET	2,493	737	986	365	405	Dole	29.6%	39.6%	14.6%	16.2%
WALDO	2,325	665	958	333	369	Dole	28.6%	41.2%	14.3%	15.9%
WASHINGTON	1,885	576	803	244	262	Dole	30.6%	42.6%	12.9%	13.9%
YORK	8,913	2,334	3,990	1,376	1,213	Dole	26.2%	44.8%	15.4%	13.6%
TOTAL	67,280	16,478	31,147	9,991	9,664	Dole	24.5%	46.3%	14.8%	14.4%

MARYLAND

When H.L. Mencken was penning his bitingly incisive political essays early in the twentieth century, his hometown of Baltimore dominated the state. But that is no longer the case. Fast-growing suburbs have grown to define Maryland politically.

Yet while large tracts of suburbia give Republicans a strong base in many states, that has not been the case in Maryland, where a large complement of federal workers and minority voters, and a heritage closely linked to the South, has long given Democrats the upper hand and meant the Democratic primary is often where the action takes place.

Sometimes, the vote in the Democratic presidential primary has reflected the Southern character of this border state. In 1964, George Wallace collected a surprising 43 percent of the vote against the state's favorite-son candidate, Sen. Daniel Brewster. Embarrassed by that outcome, state officials scrubbed the primary in 1968. But when it was reinstituted in 1972, Wallace was back to win it easily, one day after an assassination attempt in Laurel left him paralyzed from the waist down.

Wallace swept not only the conservative counties of Maryland's Eastern Shore, which have a cultural affinity to Dixie, but most of the suburban counties as well. Among the venues he carried that year was Prince George's County outside Washington, then a predominantly white, blue-collar constituency that has since become primarily black.

Yet since then, with the exception of Jimmy Carter's victory in 1980 over Edward Kennedy, the result of the Democratic primary in Maryland has tended to accent the state's ties to the northern side of the Mason-Dixon line. Al Gore drew only 9 percent of the vote in Maryland during his 1988 presidential run. Bill Clinton did better four years later, but he lost to Paul Tsongas (who scored his lone primary victory outside his native New England).

Tsongas built up his margin of victory among "Volvo Democrats" in the suburban corridor from Baltimore to Washington, swamping Clinton in Montgomery and Howard counties by margins of more than 2-to-1. Clinton won rural Maryland—the mountainous western panhandle that is part of Appalachia, as well as southern Maryland and the Eastern Shore. And Clinton won the city of Baltimore and Prince George's County, both with black majorities, which had

Recent Maryland Primary Results

Maryland held its first presidential primary in 1912.

	DEMOCRATS			REPUBLICANS		
Year	Turnout	Candidates	%	Turnout	Candidates	%
1996 (March 5)	293,829	BILL CLINTON* Uncommitted	84 11	254,246	BOB DOLE Pat Buchanan Steve Forbes	53 21 13
1992 (March 3)	567,243	PAUL TSONGAS Bill Clinton	41 33	240,021	GEORGE BUSH* Pat Buchanan	70 30
1988 (March 8)	531,335	MICHAEL DUKAKIS Jesse Jackson	46 29	200,754	GEORGE BUSH Bob Dole	53 32
1984 (May 8)	506,886	WALTER MONDALE Jesse Jackson Gary Hart	42 26 24	73,663	RONALD REAGAN*	100
1980 (May 13)	477,090	JIMMY CARTER* Edward Kennedy	47 38	167,303	RONALD REAGAN George Bush	48 41
1976 (May 18)	591,746	JERRY BROWN Jimmy Carter	48 37	165,971	GERALD FORD* Ronald Reagan	58 42
1972 (May 16)	568,131	GEORGE WALLACE Hubert Humphrey George McGovern	39 27 22	115,249	RICHARD NIXON*	86
1968	—	NO PRIMARY		—	NO PRIMARY	

Note: All candidates are listed who drew at least 10 percent of their party's primary vote. The names of winning candidates are capitalized. An asterisk (*) indicates an incumbent president.

boosted Jesse Jackson to second-place primary finishes in both 1984 and 1988.

None of the Democratic primary winners from 1972 through 1992 was able to attract a majority of the Maryland vote. Winners on the Republican side, though, have often won by lopsided margins, and moderates have fared well. President Gerald Ford easily won Maryland's GOP primary in 1976 by beating Ronald Reagan in Baltimore and all the major suburban counties. Reagan triumphed in May 1980 at a time his campaign was moving into overdrive. Yet George Bush still carried Baltimore and much of the suburban corridor, and might have beaten Reagan if John Anderson had not drained away nearly 10 percent of the primary vote.

Bush dominated the Maryland primary in 1988 and 1992, carrying every county each time. Pat Robertson's 6 percent showing in Maryland in 1988 was his weakest in any state south of the Mason-Dixon line. Four years later, Bush defeated Pat Buchanan, a native of nearby Washington, D.C., who lived for a time in the Maryland suburb of Chevy Chase.

In 1996, Buchanan was joined on the ballot by another conservative Marylander, Alan Keyes. But Buchanan (21 percent) and Keyes (5 percent) combined to draw only half the vote of the victorious Bob Dole. Dole won every county, piling up his highest vote share (61 percent) in affluent Montgomery, the prime source of both Republican and Democratic primary votes in the 1990s.

MARYLAND DEMOCRATIC

1972

County	Total Vote	Humphrey	McGovern	Wallace	Other	Winner	Percentage of Total Vote Humphrey	McGovern	Wallace	Other
ALLEGANY	8,476	3,553	1,521	2,833	569	Humphrey	41.9%	17.9%	33.4%	6.7%
ANNE ARUNDEL	42,319	7,725	7,573	21,661	5,360	Wallace	18.3%	17.9%	51.2%	12.7%
BALTIMORE CITY	151,611	58,474	21,748	42,909	28,480	Humphrey	38.6%	14.3%	28.3%	18.8%
BALTIMORE COUNTY	110,016	24,857	25,107	48,104	11,948	Wallace	22.6%	22.8%	43.7%	10.9%
CALVERT	2,310	402	266	1,505	137	Wallace	17.4%	11.5%	65.2%	5.9%
CAROLINE	2,166	279	207	1,536	144	Wallace	12.9%	9.6%	70.9%	6.6%
CARROLL	5,953	994	1,050	3,154	755	Wallace	16.7%	17.6%	53.0%	12.7%
CECIL	5,280	1,030	695	3,260	295	Wallace	19.5%	13.2%	61.7%	5.6%
CHARLES	4,534	733	619	2,872	310	Wallace	16.2%	13.7%	63.3%	6.8%
DORCHESTER	4,436	495	218	3,230	493	Wallace	11.2%	4.9%	72.8%	11.1%
FREDERICK	9,398	1,760	2,145	4,578	915	Wallace	18.7%	22.8%	48.7%	9.7%
GARRETT	1,594	491	212	770	121	Wallace	30.8%	13.3%	48.3%	7.6%
HARFORD	13,838	3,136	2,390	7,172	1,140	Wallace	22.7%	17.3%	51.8%	8.2%
HOWARD	10,818	2,046	3,951	3,830	991	McGovern	18.9%	36.5%	35.4%	9.2%
KENT	2,371	346	313	1,589	123	Wallace	14.6%	13.2%	67.0%	5.2%
MONTGOMERY	82,954	21,700	34,938	18,025	8,291	McGovern	26.2%	42.1%	21.7%	10.0%
PRINCE GEORGE'S	72,049	15,949	19,322	30,020	6,758	Wallace	22.1%	26.8%	41.7%	9.4%
QUEEN ANNE'S	2,860	406	277	2,042	135	Wallace	14.2%	9.7%	71.4%	4.7%
ST. MARY'S	7,171	1,231	993	4,405	542	Wallace	17.2%	13.8%	61.4%	7.6%
SOMERSET	2,727	479	112	2,013	123	Wallace	17.6%	4.1%	73.8%	4.5%
TALBOT	2,785	402	406	1,804	173	Wallace	14.4%	14.6%	64.8%	6.2%
WASHINGTON	12,844	3,944	1,955	5,892	1,053	Wallace	30.7%	15.2%	45.9%	8.2%
WICOMICO	6,397	1,104	739	4,134	420	Wallace	17.3%	11.6%	64.6%	6.6%
WORCESTER	3,224	445	221	2,349	209	Wallace	13.8%	6.9%	72.9%	6.5%
TOTAL	568,131	151,981	126,978	219,687	69,485	Wallace	26.8%	22.4%	38.7%	12.2%

MARYLAND REPUBLICAN

1972

County	Total Vote	Nixon	Other	Winner	Percentage of Total Vote	
					Nixon	Other
ALLEGANY	5,485	4,861	624	Nixon	88.6%	11.4%
ANNE ARUNDEL	9,611	8,333	1,278	Nixon	86.7%	13.3%
BALTIMORE CITY	10,801	7,991	2,810	Nixon	74.0%	26.0%
BALTIMORE COUNTY	16,051	14,149	1,902	Nixon	88.2%	11.8%
CALVERT	499	404	95	Nixon	81.0%	19.0%
CAROLINE	555	503	52	Nixon	90.6%	9.4%
CARROLL	2,508	2,259	249	Nixon	90.1%	9.9%
CECIL	1,581	1,432	149	Nixon	90.6%	9.4%
CHARLES	1,663	1,422	241	Nixon	85.5%	14.5%
DORCHESTER	852	744	108	Nixon	87.3%	12.7%
FREDERICK	3,653	3,199	454	Nixon	87.6%	12.4%
GARRETT	1,762	1,609	153	Nixon	91.3%	8.7%
HARFORD	2,878	2,592	286	Nixon	90.1%	9.9%
HOWARD	2,734	2,334	400	Nixon	85.4%	14.6%
KENT	429	375	54	Nixon	87.4%	12.6%
MONTGOMERY	24,470	21,021	3,449	Nixon	85.9%	14.1%
PRINCE GEORGE'S	16,698	14,222	2,476	Nixon	85.2%	14.8%
QUEEN ANNE'S	502	421	81	Nixon	83.9%	16.1%
ST. MARY'S	1,188	1,073	115	Nixon	90.3%	9.7%
SOMERSET	603	521	82	Nixon	86.4%	13.6%
TALBOT	1,262	1,142	120	Nixon	90.5%	9.5%
WASHINGTON	7,305	6,767	538	Nixon	92.6%	7.4%
WICOMICO	1,651	1,480	171	Nixon	89.6%	10.4%
WORCESTER	508	454	54	Nixon	89.4%	10.6%
TOTAL	115,249	99,308	15,941	Nixon	86.2%	13.8%

MARYLAND DEMOCRATIC

1976

County	Total Vote	Brown	Carter	Other	Winner	Percentage of Total Vote Brown	Carter	Other
ALLEGANY	9,317	4,198	4,181	938	Brown	45.1%	44.9%	10.1%
ANNE ARUNDEL	43,043	19,325	17,757	5,961	Brown	44.9%	41.3%	13.8%
BALTIMORE CITY	136,517	69,457	52,290	14,770	Brown	50.9%	38.3%	10.8%
BALTIMORE COUNTY	124,796	67,292	43,395	14,109	Brown	53.9%	34.8%	11.3%
CALVERT	2,425	889	1,175	361	Carter	36.7%	48.5%	14.9%
CAROLINE	1,960	717	1,057	186	Carter	36.6%	53.9%	9.5%
CARROLL	7,009	3,094	2,867	1,048	Brown	44.1%	40.9%	15.0%
CECIL	5,129	1,805	2,610	714	Carter	35.2%	50.9%	13.9%
CHARLES	5,012	1,915	2,333	764	Carter	38.2%	46.5%	15.2%
DORCHESTER	3,460	1,096	1,797	567	Carter	31.7%	51.9%	16.4%
FREDERICK	10,576	4,348	4,515	1,713	Carter	41.1%	42.7%	16.2%
GARRETT	1,890	482	1,074	334	Carter	25.5%	56.8%	17.7%
HARFORD	18,640	9,158	7,650	1,832	Brown	49.1%	41.0%	9.8%
HOWARD	16,810	7,892	6,142	2,776	Brown	46.9%	36.5%	16.5%
KENT	2,301	921	1,120	260	Carter	40.0%	48.7%	11.3%
MONTGOMERY	98,904	49,815	25,434	23,655	Brown	50.4%	25.7%	23.9%
PRINCE GEORGE'S	68,166	30,651	25,906	11,609	Brown	45.0%	38.0%	17.0%
QUEEN ANNE'S	2,712	980	1,403	329	Carter	36.1%	51.7%	12.1%
ST. MARY'S	5,514	2,165	2,536	813	Carter	39.3%	46.0%	14.7%
SOMERSET	1,992	531	1,250	211	Carter	26.7%	62.8%	10.6%
TALBOT	2,917	1,171	1,413	333	Carter	40.1%	48.4%	11.4%
WASHINGTON	12,493	5,112	5,867	1,514	Carter	40.9%	47.0%	12.1%
WICOMICO	7,075	2,493	3,972	610	Carter	35.2%	56.1%	8.6%
WORCESTER	3,088	1,165	1,660	263	Carter	37.7%	53.8%	8.5%
TOTAL	591,746	286,672	219,404	85,670	Brown	48.4%	37.1%	14.5%

MARYLAND REPUBLICAN

1976

County	Total Vote	Ford	Reagan	Winner	Percentage of Total Vote	
					Ford	Reagan
ALLEGANY	7,032	3,565	3,467	Ford	50.7%	49.3%
ANNE ARUNDEL	14,620	8,077	6,543	Ford	55.2%	44.8%
BALTIMORE CITY	13,244	8,606	4,638	Ford	65.0%	35.0%
BALTIMORE COUNTY	26,351	15,331	11,020	Ford	58.2%	41.8%
CALVERT	792	474	318	Ford	59.8%	40.2%
CAROLINE	550	245	305	Reagan	44.5%	55.5%
CARROLL	4,198	2,388	1,810	Ford	56.9%	43.1%
CECIL	1,967	922	1,045	Reagan	46.9%	53.1%
CHARLES	2,053	1,087	966	Ford	52.9%	47.1%
DORCHESTER	992	541	451	Ford	54.5%	45.5%
FREDERICK	5,651	3,301	2,350	Ford	58.4%	41.6%
GARRETT	2,542	1,431	1,111	Ford	56.3%	43.7%
HARFORD	5,550	3,041	2,509	Ford	54.8%	45.2%
HOWARD	5,229	3,018	2,211	Ford	57.7%	42.3%
KENT	666	377	289	Ford	56.6%	43.4%
MONTGOMERY	38,979	24,654	14,325	Ford	63.2%	36.8%
PRINCE GEORGE'S	21,085	11,604	9,481	Ford	55.0%	45.0%
QUEEN ANNE'S	656	381	275	Ford	58.1%	41.9%
ST. MARY'S	1,056	551	505	Ford	52.2%	47.8%
SOMERSET	723	414	309	Ford	57.3%	42.7%
TALBOT	1,651	1,048	603	Ford	63.5%	36.5%
WASHINGTON	7,057	3,420	3,637	Reagan	48.5%	51.5%
WICOMICO	2,579	1,387	1,192	Ford	53.8%	46.2%
WORCESTER	748	428	320	Ford	57.2%	42.8%
TOTAL	165,971	96,291	69,680	Ford	58.0%	42.0%

MARYLAND DEMOCRATIC

1980

County	Total Vote	Carter	E. Kennedy	Other	Winner	Percentage of Total Vote Carter	E. Kennedy	Other
ALLEGANY	7,149	3,433	2,694	1,022	Carter	48.0%	37.7%	14.3%
ANNE ARUNDEL	35,438	19,019	10,695	5,724	Carter	53.7%	30.2%	16.2%
BALTIMORE CITY	112,607	54,554	46,451	11,602	Carter	48.4%	41.3%	10.3%
BALTIMORE COUNTY	95,331	51,766	30,819	12,746	Carter	54.3%	32.3%	13.4%
CALVERT	2,473	1,320	830	323	Carter	53.4%	33.6%	13.1%
CAROLINE	1,573	967	338	268	Carter	61.5%	21.5%	17.0%
CARROLL	7,680	4,548	1,930	1,202	Carter	59.2%	25.1%	15.7%
CECIL	5,628	3,289	1,411	928	Carter	58.4%	25.1%	16.5%
CHARLES	5,656	2,721	2,033	902	Carter	48.1%	35.9%	15.9%
DORCHESTER	2,555	1,523	631	401	Carter	59.6%	24.7%	15.7%
FREDERICK	9,012	4,351	3,002	1,659	Carter	48.3%	33.3%	18.4%
GARRETT	2,299	1,417	538	344	Carter	61.6%	23.4%	15.0%
HARFORD	14,146	7,962	3,851	2,333	Carter	56.3%	27.2%	16.5%
HOWARD	13,939	6,236	5,497	2,206	Carter	44.7%	39.4%	15.8%
KENT	2,208	1,383	402	423	Carter	62.6%	18.2%	19.2%
MONTGOMERY	75,380	23,981	36,366	15,033	E. Kennedy	31.8%	48.2%	19.9%
PRINCE GEORGE'S	54,301	21,177	25,461	7,663	E. Kennedy	39.0%	46.9%	14.1%
QUEEN ANNE'S	2,568	1,588	546	434	Carter	61.8%	21.3%	16.9%
ST. MARY'S	4,286	2,014	1,562	710	Carter	47.0%	36.4%	16.6%
SOMERSET	1,970	1,222	456	292	Carter	62.0%	23.1%	14.8%
TALBOT	2,378	1,497	464	417	Carter	63.0%	19.5%	17.5%
WASHINGTON	9,818	5,286	3,053	1,479	Carter	53.8%	31.1%	15.1%
WICOMICO	5,134	3,152	1,238	744	Carter	61.4%	24.1%	14.5%
WORCESTER	3,561	2,122	823	616	Carter	59.6%	23.1%	17.3%
TOTAL	477,090	226,528	181,091	69,471	Carter	47.5%	38.0%	14.6%

MARYLAND REPUBLICAN

1980

County	Total Vote	Bush	Reagan	Other	Winner	Percentage of Total Vote Bush	Reagan	Other
ALLEGANY	6,836	1,893	4,469	474	Reagan	27.7%	65.4%	6.9%
ANNE ARUNDEL	15,542	7,517	6,556	1,469	Bush	48.4%	42.2%	9.5%
BALTIMORE CITY	11,351	5,457	3,813	2,081	Bush	48.1%	33.6%	18.3%
BALTIMORE COUNTY	24,061	10,765	10,690	2,606	Bush	44.7%	44.4%	10.8%
CALVERT	889	289	500	100	Reagan	32.5%	56.2%	11.2%
CAROLINE	567	172	337	58	Reagan	30.3%	59.4%	10.2%
CARROLL	5,286	1,861	2,950	475	Reagan	35.2%	55.8%	9.0%
CECIL	2,583	805	1,451	327	Reagan	31.2%	56.2%	12.7%
CHARLES	2,933	825	1,768	340	Reagan	28.1%	60.3%	11.6%
DORCHESTER	814	238	493	83	Reagan	29.2%	60.6%	10.2%
FREDERICK	6,168	1,998	3,468	702	Reagan	32.4%	56.2%	11.4%
GARRETT	3,671	897	2,567	207	Reagan	24.4%	69.9%	5.6%
HARFORD	5,581	2,359	2,645	577	Reagan	42.3%	47.4%	10.3%
HOWARD	5,367	2,113	2,554	700	Reagan	39.4%	47.6%	13.0%
KENT	848	338	391	119	Reagan	39.9%	46.1%	14.0%
MONTGOMERY	41,024	18,506	17,973	4,545	Bush	45.1%	43.8%	11.1%
PRINCE GEORGE'S	18,942	7,359	9,604	1,979	Reagan	38.9%	50.7%	10.4%
QUEEN ANNE'S	866	336	428	102	Reagan	38.8%	49.4%	11.8%
ST. MARY'S	1,120	404	592	124	Reagan	36.1%	52.9%	11.1%
SOMERSET	819	234	501	84	Reagan	28.6%	61.2%	10.3%
TALBOT	1,730	805	723	202	Bush	46.5%	41.8%	11.7%
WASHINGTON	6,847	1,973	4,254	620	Reagan	28.8%	62.1%	9.1%
WICOMICO	2,349	902	1,200	247	Reagan	38.4%	51.1%	10.5%
WORCESTER	1,109	343	630	136	Reagan	30.9%	56.8%	12.3%
TOTAL	167,303	68,389	80,557	18,357	Reagan	40.9%	48.2%	11.0%

MARYLAND DEMOCRATIC

1984

County	Total Vote	Hart	J. Jackson	Mondale	Other	Winner	Percentage of Total Vote Hart	J. Jackson	Mondale	Other
ALLEGANY	7,048	2,411	280	3,687	670	Mondale	34.2%	4.0%	52.3%	9.5%
ANNE ARUNDEL	35,185	11,399	4,762	15,732	3,292	Mondale	32.4%	13.5%	44.7%	9.4%
BALTIMORE CITY	132,796	14,293	56,286	52,856	9,361	J. Jackson	10.8%	42.4%	39.8%	7.0%
BALTIMORE COUNTY	82,569	23,431	8,508	43,339	7,291	Mondale	28.4%	10.3%	52.5%	8.8%
CALVERT	3,162	997	647	1,301	217	Mondale	31.5%	20.5%	41.1%	6.9%
CAROLINE	1,451	505	130	651	165	Mondale	34.8%	9.0%	44.9%	11.4%
CARROLL	6,220	2,491	426	2,810	493	Mondale	40.0%	6.8%	45.2%	7.9%
CECIL	3,959	1,272	247	2,054	386	Mondale	32.1%	6.2%	51.9%	9.7%
CHARLES	5,546	1,842	935	2,365	404	Mondale	33.2%	16.9%	42.6%	7.3%
DORCHESTER	2,134	695	331	770	338	Mondale	32.6%	15.5%	36.1%	15.8%
FREDERICK	8,603	3,392	954	3,529	728	Mondale	39.4%	11.1%	41.0%	8.5%
GARRETT	1,589	655	58	736	140	Mondale	41.2%	3.7%	46.3%	8.8%
HARFORD	15,702	5,469	1,692	6,714	1,827	Mondale	34.8%	10.8%	42.8%	11.6%
HOWARD	14,384	4,483	3,397	5,479	1,025	Mondale	31.2%	23.6%	38.1%	7.1%
KENT	1,944	731	223	759	231	Mondale	37.6%	11.5%	39.0%	11.9%
MONTGOMERY	75,747	22,918	11,824	36,039	4,966	Mondale	30.3%	15.6%	47.6%	6.6%
PRINCE GEORGE'S	79,775	15,481	34,687	24,823	4,784	J. Jackson	19.4%	43.5%	31.1%	6.0%
QUEEN ANNE'S	2,468	876	247	1,044	301	Mondale	35.5%	10.0%	42.3%	12.2%
ST. MARY'S	4,722	1,618	853	1,885	366	Mondale	34.3%	18.1%	39.9%	7.8%
SOMERSET	2,022	674	430	684	234	Mondale	33.3%	21.3%	33.8%	11.6%
TALBOT	2,065	851	263	735	216	Hart	41.2%	12.7%	35.6%	10.5%
WASHINGTON	9,420	3,876	495	4,288	761	Mondale	41.1%	5.3%	45.5%	8.1%
WICOMICO	5,476	1,871	1,177	1,985	443	Mondale	34.2%	21.5%	36.2%	8.1%
WORCESTER	2,899	1,134	535	957	273	Hart	39.1%	18.5%	33.0%	9.4%
TOTAL	506,886	123,365	129,387	215,222	38,912	Mondale	24.3%	25.5%	42.5%	7.7%

MARYLAND DEMOCRATIC

1988

County	Total Vote	Dukakis	J. Jackson	Other	Winner	Percentage of Total Vote Dukakis	J. Jackson	Other
ALLEGANY	6,862	3,677	508	2,677	Dukakis	53.6%	7.4%	39.0%
ANNE ARUNDEL	41,679	22,099	6,493	13,087	Dukakis	53.0%	15.6%	31.4%
BALTIMORE CITY	110,206	38,182	58,547	13,477	J. Jackson	34.6%	53.1%	12.2%
BALTIMORE COUNTY	91,256	56,214	11,810	23,232	Dukakis	61.6%	12.9%	25.5%
CALVERT	4,295	1,622	1,046	1,627	Dukakis	37.8%	24.4%	37.9%
CAROLINE	1,764	1,105	176	483	Dukakis	62.6%	10.0%	27.4%
CARROLL	8,856	5,117	815	2,924	Dukakis	57.8%	9.2%	33.0%
CECIL	4,655	2,390	383	1,882	Dukakis	51.3%	8.2%	40.4%
CHARLES	6,318	2,485	1,260	2,573	Dukakis	39.3%	19.9%	40.7%
DORCHESTER	2,897	1,342	588	967	Dukakis	46.3%	20.3%	33.4%
FREDERICK	10,316	4,662	1,412	4,242	Dukakis	45.2%	13.7%	41.1%
GARRETT	1,536	723	157	656	Dukakis	47.1%	10.2%	42.7%
HARFORD	15,858	9,488	2,022	4,348	Dukakis	59.8%	12.8%	27.4%
HOWARD	20,777	9,980	5,098	5,699	Dukakis	48.0%	24.5%	27.4%
KENT	2,952	1,610	472	870	Dukakis	54.5%	16.0%	29.5%
MONTGOMERY	90,883	45,925	17,536	27,422	Dukakis	50.5%	19.3%	30.2%
PRINCE GEORGE'S	76,323	20,672	39,025	16,626	J. Jackson	27.1%	51.1%	21.8%
QUEEN ANNE'S	3,169	1,783	359	1,027	Dukakis	56.3%	11.3%	32.4%
ST. MARY'S	5,771	2,342	1,217	2,212	Dukakis	40.6%	21.1%	38.3%
SOMERSET	2,123	770	514	839	Dukakis	36.3%	24.2%	39.5%
TALBOT	2,852	1,579	449	824	Dukakis	55.4%	15.7%	28.9%
WASHINGTON	9,713	4,174	775	4,764	Dukakis	43.0%	8.0%	49.0%
WICOMICO	6,849	2,958	1,360	2,531	Dukakis	43.2%	19.9%	37.0%
WORCESTER	3,425	1,580	620	1,225	Dukakis	46.1%	18.1%	35.8%
TOTAL	531,335	242,479	152,642	136,214	Dukakis	45.6%	28.7%	25.6%

MARYLAND REPUBLICAN

1988

County	Total Vote	Bush	Dole	Other	Winner	Percentage of Total Vote Bush	Dole	Other
ALLEGANY	7,179	4,030	1,896	1,253	Bush	56.1%	26.4%	17.5%
ANNE ARUNDEL	21,895	12,203	6,883	2,809	Bush	55.7%	31.4%	12.8%
BALTIMORE CITY	8,596	4,319	2,985	1,292	Bush	50.2%	34.7%	15.0%
BALTIMORE COUNTY	27,784	14,341	9,400	4,043	Bush	51.6%	33.8%	14.6%
CALVERT	2,184	1,204	608	372	Bush	55.1%	27.8%	17.0%
CAROLINE	794	472	171	151	Bush	59.4%	21.5%	19.0%
CARROLL	7,248	3,776	2,378	1,094	Bush	52.1%	32.8%	15.1%
CECIL	2,439	1,343	638	458	Bush	55.1%	26.2%	18.8%
CHARLES	3,805	2,148	1,045	612	Bush	56.5%	27.5%	16.1%
DORCHESTER	1,139	709	280	150	Bush	62.2%	24.6%	13.2%
FREDERICK	8,042	4,263	2,455	1,324	Bush	53.0%	30.5%	16.5%
GARRETT	2,760	1,733	582	445	Bush	62.8%	21.1%	16.1%
HARFORD	7,726	3,830	2,808	1,088	Bush	49.6%	36.3%	14.1%
HOWARD	10,578	5,065	4,070	1,443	Bush	47.9%	38.5%	13.6%
KENT	1,262	726	355	181	Bush	57.5%	28.1%	14.3%
MONTGOMERY	46,692	24,670	16,217	5,805	Bush	52.8%	34.7%	12.4%
PRINCE GEORGE'S	21,181	11,363	6,667	3,151	Bush	53.6%	31.5%	14.9%
QUEEN ANNE'S	1,476	857	382	237	Bush	58.1%	25.9%	16.1%
ST. MARY'S	1,961	1,113	529	319	Bush	56.8%	27.0%	16.3%
SOMERSET	1,003	515	286	202	Bush	51.3%	28.5%	20.1%
TALBOT	2,113	1,351	528	234	Bush	63.9%	25.0%	11.1%
WASHINGTON	7,565	4,229	2,221	1,115	Bush	55.9%	29.4%	14.7%
WICOMICO	3,671	1,865	1,151	655	Bush	50.8%	31.4%	17.8%
WORCESTER	1,661	901	452	308	Bush	54.2%	27.2%	18.5%
TOTAL	200,754	107,026	64,987	28,741	Bush	53.3%	32.4%	14.3%

MARYLAND DEMOCRATIC

1992

County	Total Vote	Clinton	Tsongas	Other	Winner	Percentage of Total Vote: Clinton	Tsongas	Other
ALLEGANY	7,374	2,581	2,482	2,311	Clinton	35.0%	33.7%	31.3%
ANNE ARUNDEL	47,911	14,205	19,745	13,961	Tsongas	29.6%	41.2%	29.1%
BALTIMORE CITY	96,011	42,803	32,466	20,742	Clinton	44.6%	33.8%	21.6%
BALTIMORE COUNTY	101,473	30,203	44,355	26,915	Tsongas	29.8%	43.7%	26.5%
CALVERT	5,256	2,060	1,862	1,334	Clinton	39.2%	35.4%	25.4%
CAROLINE	2,072	916	618	538	Clinton	44.2%	29.8%	26.0%
CARROLL	11,639	3,197	5,236	3,206	Tsongas	27.5%	45.0%	27.5%
CECIL	6,087	2,618	1,896	1,573	Clinton	43.0%	31.1%	25.8%
CHARLES	7,342	2,796	2,601	1,945	Clinton	38.1%	35.4%	26.5%
DORCHESTER	3,014	1,289	838	887	Clinton	42.8%	27.8%	29.4%
FREDERICK	13,950	4,317	5,397	4,236	Tsongas	30.9%	38.7%	30.4%
GARRETT	1,721	642	529	550	Clinton	37.3%	30.7%	32.0%
HARFORD	20,083	6,237	8,233	5,613	Tsongas	31.1%	41.0%	27.9%
HOWARD	24,127	5,674	12,540	5,913	Tsongas	23.5%	52.0%	24.5%
KENT	2,256	845	828	583	Clinton	37.5%	36.7%	25.8%
MONTGOMERY	103,109	24,277	51,880	26,952	Tsongas	23.5%	50.3%	26.1%
PRINCE GEORGE'S	76,021	31,275	26,179	18,567	Clinton	41.1%	34.4%	24.4%
QUEEN ANNES	3,666	1,405	1,336	925	Clinton	38.3%	36.4%	25.2%
ST. MARYS	6,720	2,504	2,500	1,716	Clinton	37.3%	37.2%	25.5%
SOMERSET	2,141	980	559	602	Clinton	45.8%	26.1%	28.1%
TALBOT	2,864	992	1,176	696	Tsongas	34.6%	41.1%	24.3%
WASHINGTON	10,911	3,914	3,630	3,367	Clinton	35.9%	33.3%	30.9%
WICOMICO	7,353	2,677	2,315	2,361	Clinton	36.4%	31.5%	32.1%
WORCESTER	4,142	1,498	1,289	1,355	Clinton	36.2%	31.1%	32.7%
TOTAL	567,243	189,905	230,490	146,848	Tsongas	33.5%	40.6%	25.9%

MARYLAND REPUBLICAN

1992

County	Total Vote	Buchanan	Bush	Winner	Percentage of Total Vote	
					Buchanan	Bush
ALLEGANY	7,281	2,264	5,017	Bush	31.1%	68.9%
ANNE ARUNDEL	29,512	8,720	20,792	Bush	29.5%	70.5%
BALTIMORE CITY	8,503	2,795	5,708	Bush	32.9%	67.1%
BALTIMORE COUNTY	33,825	9,353	24,472	Bush	27.7%	72.3%
CALVERT	3,554	1,162	2,392	Bush	32.7%	67.3%
CAROLINE	1,268	375	893	Bush	29.6%	70.4%
CARROLL	10,750	3,196	7,554	Bush	29.7%	70.3%
CECIL	3,368	953	2,415	Bush	28.3%	71.7%
CHARLES	4,992	1,664	3,328	Bush	33.3%	66.7%
DORCHESTER	1,512	396	1,116	Bush	26.2%	73.8%
FREDERICK	11,912	3,498	8,414	Bush	29.4%	70.6%
GARRETT	3,065	864	2,201	Bush	28.2%	71.8%
HARFORD	11,836	3,325	8,511	Bush	28.1%	71.9%
HOWARD	12,988	3,905	9,083	Bush	30.1%	69.9%
KENT	1,349	339	1,010	Bush	25.1%	74.9%
MONTGOMERY	49,262	14,974	34,288	Bush	30.4%	69.6%
PRINCE GEORGE'S	20,271	6,558	13,713	Bush	32.4%	67.6%
QUEEN ANNES	2,326	673	1,653	Bush	28.9%	71.1%
ST. MARYS	2,951	942	2,009	Bush	31.9%	68.1%
SOMERSET	1,185	356	829	Bush	30.0%	70.0%
TALBOT	2,838	730	2,108	Bush	25.7%	74.3%
WASHINGTON	8,149	2,398	5,751	Bush	29.4%	70.6%
WICOMICO	4,948	1,469	3,479	Bush	29.7%	70.3%
WORCESTER	2,376	738	1,638	Bush	31.1%	68.9%
TOTAL	240,021	71,647	168,374	Bush	29.9%	70.1%

MARYLAND DEMOCRATIC

1996

County	Total Vote	Clinton	LaRouche	Uncommitted	Winner	Percentage of Total Vote Clinton	LaRouche	Uncom.
ALLEGANY	5,357	4,416	225	716	Clinton	82.4%	4.2%	13.4%
ANNE ARUNDEL	29,195	22,170	1,899	5,126	Clinton	75.9%	6.5%	17.6%
BALTIMORE CITY	54,848	50,839	1,579	2,430	Clinton	92.7%	2.9%	4.4%
BALTIMORE COUNTY	46,782	37,637	3,364	5,781	Clinton	80.5%	7.2%	12.4%
CALVERT	3,183	2,637	143	403	Clinton	82.8%	4.5%	12.7%
CAROLINE	1,162	903	113	146	Clinton	77.7%	9.7%	12.6%
CARROLL	4,694	3,454	476	764	Clinton	73.6%	10.1%	16.3%
CECIL	2,686	2,088	205	393	Clinton	77.7%	7.6%	14.6%
CHARLES	4,545	3,682	181	682	Clinton	81.0%	4.0%	15.0%
DORCHESTER	1,728	1,286	111	331	Clinton	74.4%	6.4%	19.2%
FREDERICK	6,313	5,233	308	772	Clinton	82.9%	4.9%	12.2%
GARRETT	1,377	1,058	107	212	Clinton	76.8%	7.8%	15.4%
HARFORD	9,965	7,309	878	1,778	Clinton	73.3%	8.8%	17.8%
HOWARD	18,074	14,907	610	2,557	Clinton	82.5%	3.4%	14.1%
KENT	1,095	859	72	164	Clinton	78.4%	6.6%	15.0%
MONTGOMERY	56,807	49,765	821	6,221	Clinton	87.6%	1.4%	11.0%
PRINCE GEORGE'S	26,984	24,167	735	2,082	Clinton	89.6%	2.7%	7.7%
QUEEN ANNES	2,194	1,668	189	337	Clinton	76.0%	8.6%	15.4%
ST. MARYS	3,566	2,809	203	554	Clinton	78.8%	5.7%	15.5%
SOMERSET	999	784	76	139	Clinton	78.5%	7.6%	13.9%
TALBOT	1,531	1,236	85	210	Clinton	80.7%	5.6%	13.7%
WASHINGTON	5,903	4,672	292	939	Clinton	79.1%	4.9%	15.9%
WICOMICO	2,936	2,333	151	452	Clinton	79.5%	5.1%	15.4%
WORCESTER	1,905	1,580	97	228	Clinton	82.9%	5.1%	12.0%
TOTAL	293,829	247,492	12,920	33,417	Clinton	84.2%	4.4%	11.4%

MARYLAND REPUBLICAN

1996

County	Total Vote	Buchanan	Dole	Forbes	Other	Winner	Percentage of Total Vote: Buchanan	Dole	Forbes	Other
ALLEGANY	7,284	2,134	3,666	678	806	Dole	29.3%	50.3%	9.3%	11.1%
ANNE ARUNDEL	33,721	7,187	17,502	4,428	4,604	Dole	21.3%	51.9%	13.1%	13.7%
BALTIMORE CITY	7,446	1,603	3,254	1,032	1,557	Dole	21.5%	43.7%	13.9%	20.9%
BALTIMORE COUNTY	33,752	7,704	17,323	4,942	3,783	Dole	22.8%	51.3%	14.6%	11.2%
CALVERT	4,442	1,052	2,346	430	614	Dole	23.7%	52.8%	9.7%	13.8%
CAROLINE	1,484	424	605	272	183	Dole	28.6%	40.8%	18.3%	12.3%
CARROLL	11,436	3,389	5,451	1,298	1,298	Dole	29.6%	47.7%	11.4%	11.4%
CECIL	3,400	830	1,560	627	383	Dole	24.4%	45.9%	18.4%	11.3%
CHARLES	6,189	1,520	3,365	578	726	Dole	24.6%	54.4%	9.3%	11.7%
DORCHESTER	1,553	332	695	337	189	Dole	21.4%	44.8%	21.7%	12.2%
FREDERICK	13,104	2,940	7,256	1,330	1,578	Dole	22.4%	55.4%	10.1%	12.0%
GARRETT	3,426	1,065	1,599	346	416	Dole	31.1%	46.7%	10.1%	12.1%
HARFORD	13,091	3,426	6,166	2,052	1,447	Dole	26.2%	47.1%	15.7%	11.1%
HOWARD	17,312	3,095	9,381	2,370	2,466	Dole	17.9%	54.2%	13.7%	14.2%
KENT	1,226	206	701	211	108	Dole	16.8%	57.2%	17.2%	8.8%
MONTGOMERY	51,802	7,575	31,556	5,485	7,186	Dole	14.6%	60.9%	10.6%	13.9%
PRINCE GEORGE'S	16,454	3,343	9,037	1,584	2,490	Dole	20.3%	54.9%	9.6%	15.1%
QUEEN ANNES	2,812	711	1,344	432	325	Dole	25.3%	47.8%	15.4%	11.6%
ST. MARYS	3,787	885	1,984	416	502	Dole	23.4%	52.4%	11.0%	13.3%
SOMERSET	1,152	302	475	255	120	Dole	26.2%	41.2%	22.1%	10.4%
TALBOT	3,035	432	1,726	557	320	Dole	14.2%	56.9%	18.4%	10.5%
WASHINGTON	8,841	2,004	5,046	762	1,029	Dole	22.7%	57.1%	8.6%	11.6%
WICOMICO	4,734	881	2,172	1,164	517	Dole	18.6%	45.9%	24.6%	10.9%
WORCESTER	2,763	545	1,312	621	285	Dole	19.7%	47.5%	22.5%	10.3%
TOTAL	254,246	53,585	135,522	32,207	32,932	Dole	21.1%	53.3%	12.7%	13.0%

MASSACHUSETTS

Ever since George McGovern went one for 50 in the presidential election of 1972—carrying Massachusetts but no other—the Bay State has been widely regarded as the premier bastion of Democratic liberalism in the United States. That perception may not be untrue, but it is not as simple as that either. Massachusetts has several faces.

There is Yankee Massachusetts that gave President William Howard Taft his only victory over insurgent Teddy Roosevelt in the 1912 Republican primaries.

There is blue-collar Massachusetts, which gave Henry Jackson his biggest win of the 1976 Democratic primaries.

And there is the liberal Massachusetts of suburbia and academe, which has given long-shot challengers such as George McGovern and John Anderson a base to build from in the state's presidential primary.

Much of the Democratic electorate lives within 25 miles of Boston; roughly 10 percent lives within the city itself. Boston contains two key elements of the Democratic Party statewide—ethnic neighborhoods and academic institutions—but it adds a third element not found in large numbers elsewhere in Massachusetts—minorities.

The combustible mixture can produce unexpected results. When the Democratic primary occurred during the height of a school busing crisis in 1976, George Wallace carried the city.

The Democrats used to be the party of the cities, but as Massachusetts has made the transformation from a declining manufacturing-based economy to the bustling world of high technology, the party has taken root in the growing suburbs.

That has not left much room for the Republicans. The dominant party in Massachusetts for nearly a century after the Civil War, the GOP was the choice of less than one of every seven registered voters in Massachusetts by the late 1990s.

Yet while the Republican Party is small, it is not static. For years, the Massachusetts GOP was dominated by moderate

Recent Massachusetts Primary Results

Massachusetts held its first presidential primary in 1912.

	DEMOCRATS			REPUBLICANS		
Year	Turnout	Candidates	%	Turnout	Candidates	%
1996 (March 5)	155,470	BILL CLINTON*	87	284,833	BOB DOLE Pat Buchanan Steve Forbes	48 25 14
1992 (March 10)	792,885	PAUL TSONGAS Jerry Brown Bill Clinton	66 15 11	269,701	GEORGE BUSH* Pat Buchanan	66 28
1988 (March 8)	713,447	MICHAEL DUKAKIS Jesse Jackson Richard Gephardt	59 19 10	241,181	GEORGE BUSH Bob Dole	59 26
1984 (March 13)	630,962	GARY HART Walter Mondale George McGovern	39 25 21	65,937	RONALD REAGAN*	89
1980 (March 4)	907,323	EDWARD KENNEDY Jimmy Carter*	65 29	400,826	GEORGE BUSH John Anderson Ronald Reagan	31 31 29
1976 (March 2)	735,821	HENRY JACKSON Morris Udall George Wallace Jimmy Carter	22 18 17 14	188,449	GERALD FORD* Ronald Reagan	61 34
1972 (April 25)	618,516	GEORGE McGOVERN Edmund Muskie	53 21	122,139	RICHARD NIXON* Paul McCloskey	81 13
1968 (April 30)	248,903	EUGENE McCARTHY Robert Kennedy# Hubert Humphrey#	49 28 18	106,521	NELSON ROCKEFELLER# John Volpe Richard Nixon#	30 30 26

Note: All candidates are listed that drew at least 10 percent of their party's primary vote. The names of winning candidates are capitalized. An asterisk (*) indicates an incumbent president. A pound sign (#) indicates a write-in candidate.

Yankees. President Gerald Ford easily won the Republican primary over Ronald Reagan in 1976; George Bush was a narrow winner four years later.

Bush, who was born in Milton and educated at the Phillips Academy in Andover, ran well in old-line Yankee Republican communities, barely offsetting Anderson's appeal in liberal suburbs and academic centers. Reagan finished a close third by carrying many of the working-class mill towns.

Bush won the Republican primaries again in 1988 and 1992, but his victories were not nail-biters like 1980. He swept virtually every community in Massachusetts each time.

But there is a conservative element within the state GOP, often of the ethnic, lunch-bucket variety, that Pat Buchanan was able to tap in the 1990s with his message of economic protest. Buchanan made his most conspicuous inroads in the 1996 primary by carrying old industrial cities like Lawrence, Lowell and Lynn. Bob Dole, though, still easily won the statewide GOP vote.

A big variable in the Republican equation is turnout, which can vary widely from one primary to another. Unenrolled voters (the Massachusetts parlance for independents) account for nearly half the electorate and have been allowed to vote in either party's primary. They often get swallowed up in large-turnout Democratic contests but can shape the outcome in lower-turnout Republican affairs.

Meanwhile, Massachusetts Democrats have had their largest turnouts when one of their own has been on the presidential primary ballot. There have been three home-state entries in recent years—Sen. Edward Kennedy in 1980, Gov. Michael S. Dukakis in 1988 and former Sen. Paul Tsongas in 1992. All were easy winners. But somewhat surprisingly, the one that ran best, Tsongas, was the only one who was not an incumbent officeholder at the time.

MASSACHUSETTS DEMOCRATIC

1968

District	Total Vote	Humphrey	R. Kennedy	McCarthy	Other	Winner	Percentage of Total Vote Humphrey	R. Kennedy	McCarthy	Other
DISTRICT 1	13,663	2,143	3,052	7,891	577	McCarthy	15.7%	22.3%	57.8%	4.2%
DISTRICT 2	10,918	1,820	2,526	6,056	516	McCarthy	16.7%	23.1%	55.5%	4.7%
DISTRICT 3	23,116	3,460	5,565	13,203	888	McCarthy	15.0%	24.1%	57.1%	3.8%
DISTRICT 4	16,940	2,816	5,520	7,849	755	McCarthy	16.6%	32.6%	46.3%	4.5%
DISTRICT 5	25,854	4,271	8,091	12,272	1,220	McCarthy	16.5%	31.3%	47.5%	4.7%
DISTRICT 6	19,522	3,810	6,028	8,568	1,116	McCarthy	19.5%	30.9%	43.9%	5.7%
DISTRICT 7	29,735	5,806	8,975	13,064	1,890	McCarthy	19.5%	30.2%	43.9%	6.4%
DISTRICT 8	31,053	4,959	6,655	17,796	1,643	McCarthy	16.0%	21.4%	57.3%	5.3%
DISTRICT 9	18,940	3,893	4,390	9,130	1,527	McCarthy	20.6%	23.2%	48.2%	8.1%
DISTRICT 10	16,340	2,377	4,573	8,802	588	McCarthy	14.5%	28.0%	53.9%	3.6%
DISTRICT 11	26,599	6,018	7,748	10,992	1,841	McCarthy	22.6%	29.1%	41.3%	6.9%
DISTRICT 12	16,223	2,783	5,481	7,074	885	McCarthy	17.2%	33.8%	43.6%	5.5%
TOTAL	248,903	44,156	68,604	122,697	13,446	McCarthy	17.7%	27.6%	49.3%	5.4%

Note: The official results from the 1968 Democratic primary were available only on a congressional district basis. The districts are as they existed in 1968. McCarthy was the only candidate listed on the Democratic primary ballot. All other votes cast were write-ins.

MASSACHUSETTS REPUBLICAN

1968

District	Total Vote	Nixon	Rockefeller	Volpe	Other	Winner	Percentage of Total Vote: Nixon	Rockefeller	Volpe	Other
DISTRICT 1	6,131	1,332	1,849	2,311	639	Volpe	21.7%	30.2%	37.7%	10.4%
DISTRICT 2	4,624	1,100	1,087	1,884	553	Volpe	23.8%	23.5%	40.7%	12.0%
DISTRICT 3	11,575	2,852	4,000	2,973	1,750	Rockefeller	24.6%	34.6%	25.7%	15.1%
DISTRICT 4	8,052	2,110	2,666	2,119	1,157	Rockefeller	26.2%	33.1%	26.3%	14.4%
DISTRICT 5	9,803	2,562	2,681	3,083	1,477	Volpe	26.1%	27.3%	31.4%	15.1%
DISTRICT 6	12,161	3,476	3,599	2,988	2,098	Rockefeller	28.6%	29.6%	24.6%	17.3%
DISTRICT 7	10,562	2,562	2,754	3,718	1,528	Volpe	24.3%	26.1%	35.2%	14.5%
DISTRICT 8	6,158	1,060	2,183	1,837	1,078	Rockefeller	17.2%	35.4%	29.8%	17.5%
DISTRICT 9	2,377	438	474	1,198	267	Volpe	18.4%	19.9%	50.4%	11.2%
DISTRICT 10	12,218	3,398	4,296	2,664	1,860	Rockefeller	27.8%	35.2%	21.8%	15.2%
DISTRICT 11	8,979	2,397	2,520	2,748	1,314	Volpe	26.7%	28.1%	30.6%	14.6%
DISTRICT 12	13,881	4,160	3,855	3,942	1,924	Nixon	30.0%	27.8%	28.4%	13.9%
TOTAL	106,521	27,447	31,964	31,465	15,645	Rockefeller	25.8%	30.0%	29.5%	14.7%

Note: The official results from the 1968 Republican primary were available only on a congressional district basis. The districts are as they existed in 1968. The only candidate listed on the Republican primary ballot was John A. Volpe, the state's Republican governor and a favorite-son candidate. All other votes cast were write-ins.

MASSACHUSETTS DEMOCRATIC

1972

City/Town	Total Vote	McGovern	Muskie	Other	Winner	Percentage of Total Vote McGovern	Muskie	Other
AMHERST	3,441	2,731	257	453	McGovern	79.4%	7.5%	13.2%
BOSTON	83,324	39,188	15,298	28,838	McGovern	47.0%	18.4%	34.6%
BROCKTON	9,513	5,089	1,583	2,841	McGovern	53.5%	16.6%	29.9%
BROOKLINE	10,532	6,958	1,106	2,468	McGovern	66.1%	10.5%	23.4%
CAMBRIDGE	19,813	11,397	3,123	5,293	McGovern	57.5%	15.8%	26.7%
CHICOPEE	7,406	2,483	3,434	1,489	Muskie	33.5%	46.4%	20.1%
FALL RIVER	9,375	4,543	2,600	2,232	McGovern	48.5%	27.7%	23.8%
FRAMINGHAM	7,719	4,595	1,289	1,835	McGovern	59.5%	16.7%	23.8%
HAVERHILL	5,044	2,475	1,329	1,240	McGovern	49.1%	26.3%	24.6%
LAWRENCE	10,643	4,771	3,064	2,808	McGovern	44.8%	28.8%	26.4%
LENOX	483	277	85	121	McGovern	57.3%	17.6%	25.1%
LOWELL	12,834	6,005	3,594	3,235	McGovern	46.8%	28.0%	25.2%
LYNN	13,271	6,103	3,187	3,981	McGovern	46.0%	24.0%	30.0%
MALDEN	7,956	2,901	1,223	3,832	McGovern	36.5%	15.4%	48.2%
MEDFORD	9,836	4,867	1,972	2,997	McGovern	49.5%	20.0%	30.5%
NEW BEDFORD	10,596	4,711	2,369	3,516	McGovern	44.5%	22.4%	33.2%
NEWTON	14,521	10,211	1,755	2,555	McGovern	70.3%	12.1%	17.6%
PROVINCETOWN	498	332	29	137	McGovern	66.7%	5.8%	27.5%
QUINCY	12,474	6,118	2,841	3,515	McGovern	49.0%	22.8%	28.2%
SOMERVILLE	10,982	5,977	2,067	2,938	McGovern	54.4%	18.8%	26.8%
SPRINGFIELD	13,282	5,941	3,814	3,527	McGovern	44.7%	28.7%	26.6%
TAUNTON	3,268	1,701	752	815	McGovern	52.1%	23.0%	24.9%
WALTHAM	5,518	3,210	1,109	1,199	McGovern	58.2%	20.1%	21.7%
WELLESLEY	2,858	1,947	399	512	McGovern	68.1%	14.0%	17.9%
WEYMOUTH	6,619	3,687	1,295	1,637	McGovern	55.7%	19.6%	24.7%
WORCESTER	19,236	8,491	6,078	4,667	McGovern	44.1%	31.6%	24.3%
STATE TOTAL	618,516	325,673	131,709	161,134	McGovern	52.7%	21.3%	26.1%

Note: The presidential primary vote is not officially compiled by county in Massachusetts. This table, and those through 1988, includes only the vote from major cities and towns with a 1996 population estimate of 50,000 or more, as well as selected others. The state total is the aggregate vote from all communities in Massachusetts.

MASSACHUSETTS REPUBLICAN

1972

City/Town	Total Vote	McCloskey	Nixon	Other	Winner	Percentage of Total Vote McCloskey	Nixon	Other
AMHERST	410	63	310	37	Nixon	15.4%	75.6%	9.0%
BOSTON	4,691	824	3,458	409	Nixon	17.6%	73.7%	8.7%
BROCKTON	1,295	161	1,065	69	Nixon	12.4%	82.2%	5.3%
BROOKLINE	1,552	306	1,137	109	Nixon	19.7%	73.3%	7.0%
CAMBRIDGE	1,366	285	985	96	Nixon	20.9%	72.1%	7.0%
CHICOPEE	398	83	293	22	Nixon	20.9%	73.6%	5.5%
FALL RIVER	617	94	490	33	Nixon	15.2%	79.4%	5.3%
FRAMINGHAM	1,189	195	963	31	Nixon	16.4%	81.0%	2.6%
HAVERHILL	1,381	182	1,127	72	Nixon	13.2%	81.6%	5.2%
LAWRENCE	877	148	685	44	Nixon	16.9%	78.1%	5.0%
LENOX	135	11	115	9	Nixon	8.1%	85.2%	6.7%
LOWELL	1,322	218	1,020	84	Nixon	16.5%	77.2%	6.4%
LYNN	1,551	258	1,229	64	Nixon	16.6%	79.2%	4.1%
MALDEN	867	163	660	44	Nixon	18.8%	76.1%	5.1%
MEDFORD	960	122	779	59	Nixon	12.7%	81.1%	6.1%
NEW BEDFORD	1,715	210	1,378	127	Nixon	12.2%	80.3%	7.4%
NEWTON	2,636	526	1,943	167	Nixon	20.0%	73.7%	6.3%
PROVINCETOWN	57	7	49	1	Nixon	12.3%	86.0%	1.8%
QUINCY	2,302	321	1,921	60	Nixon	13.9%	83.4%	2.6%
SOMERVILLE	590	62	498	30	Nixon	10.5%	84.4%	5.1%
SPRINGFIELD	1,501	146	1,213	142	Nixon	9.7%	80.8%	9.5%
TAUNTON	470	70	390	10	Nixon	14.9%	83.0%	2.1%
WALTHAM	761	80	613	68	Nixon	10.5%	80.6%	8.9%
WELLESLEY	1,750	290	1,310	150	Nixon	16.6%	74.9%	8.6%
WEYMOUTH	1,494	178	1,259	57	Nixon	11.9%	84.3%	3.8%
WORCESTER	3,058	326	2,606	126	Nixon	10.7%	85.2%	4.1%
STATE TOTAL	122,139	16,435	99,150	6,554	Nixon	13.5%	81.2%	5.4%

MASSACHUSETTS DEMOCRATIC

1976

City/Town	Total Vote	Carter	H. Jackson	Udall	Wallace	Other	Winner	Percentage of Total Vote Carter	H. Jackson	Udall	Wallace	Other
AMHERST	4,184	315	269	1,648	142	1,810	Udall	7.5%	6.4%	39.4%	3.4%	43.3%
BOSTON	82,419	9,419	17,044	10,600	23,661	21,695	Wallace	11.4%	20.7%	12.9%	28.7%	26.3%
BROCKTON	11,604	2,119	3,089	1,273	2,244	2,879	H. Jackson	18.3%	26.6%	11.0%	19.3%	24.8%
BROOKLINE	11,018	552	3,820	3,232	587	2,827	H. Jackson	5.0%	34.7%	29.3%	5.3%	25.7%
CAMBRIDGE	18,466	1,692	1,913	5,771	2,059	7,031	Udall	9.2%	10.4%	31.3%	11.2%	38.1%
CHICOPEE	9,661	1,477	2,224	905	3,011	2,044	Wallace	15.3%	23.0%	9.4%	31.2%	21.2%
FALL RIVER	12,736	1,723	4,342	799	1,858	4,014	H. Jackson	13.5%	34.1%	6.3%	14.6%	31.5%
FRAMINGHAM	8,900	887	2,555	1,949	803	2,706	H. Jackson	10.0%	28.7%	21.9%	9.0%	30.4%
HAVERHILL	3,257	573	583	574	357	1,170	H. Jackson	17.6%	17.9%	17.6%	11.0%	35.9%
LAWRENCE	9,783	1,553	2,130	1,279	1,578	3,243	H. Jackson	15.9%	21.8%	13.1%	16.1%	33.1%
LENOX	721	94	106	155	94	272	Udall	13.0%	14.7%	21.5%	13.0%	37.7%
LOWELL	12,058	1,842	3,162	1,795	1,643	3,616	H. Jackson	15.3%	26.2%	14.9%	13.6%	30.0%
LYNN	11,657	1,505	2,991	1,236	2,079	3,846	H. Jackson	12.9%	25.7%	10.6%	17.8%	33.0%
MALDEN	8,159	1,090	2,202	1,101	1,194	2,572	H. Jackson	13.4%	27.0%	13.5%	14.6%	31.5%
MEDFORD	10,002	1,296	2,200	1,403	1,822	3,281	H. Jackson	13.0%	22.0%	14.0%	18.2%	32.8%
NEW BEDFORD	12,653	1,890	3,391	938	2,576	3,858	H. Jackson	14.9%	26.8%	7.4%	20.4%	30.5%
NEWTON	15,954	1,000	3,778	5,939	873	4,364	Udall	6.3%	23.7%	37.2%	5.5%	27.4%
PROVINCETOWN	572	103	49	177	37	206	Udall	18.0%	8.6%	30.9%	6.5%	36.0%
QUINCY	15,819	1,784	3,934	1,994	3,446	4,661	H. Jackson	11.3%	24.9%	12.6%	21.8%	29.5%
SOMERVILLE	12,309	1,526	2,389	1,803	2,393	4,198	Wallace	12.4%	19.4%	14.6%	19.4%	34.1%
SPRINGFIELD	18,769	2,767	5,707	2,706	3,932	3,657	H. Jackson	14.7%	30.4%	14.4%	20.9%	19.5%
TAUNTON	3,689	699	780	385	707	1,118	H. Jackson	18.9%	21.1%	10.4%	19.2%	30.3%
WALTHAM	5,762	719	1,417	1,235	767	1,624	H. Jackson	12.5%	24.6%	21.4%	13.3%	28.2%
WELLESLEY	3,367	385	429	1,398	161	994	Udall	11.4%	12.7%	41.5%	4.8%	29.5%
WEYMOUTH	8,457	979	1,885	1,459	1,521	2,613	H. Jackson	11.6%	22.3%	17.3%	18.0%	30.9%
WORCESTER	21,540	2,592	6,817	3,155	2,733	6,243	H. Jackson	12.0%	31.6%	14.6%	12.7%	29.0%
STATE TOTAL	735,821	101,948	164,393	130,440	123,112	215,928	H. Jackson	13.9%	22.3%	17.7%	16.7%	29.3%

MASSACHUSETTS REPUBLICAN

1976

City/Town	Total Vote	Ford	Reagan	Other	Winner	Percentage of Total Vote Ford	Reagan	Other
AMHERST	553	359	151	43	Ford	64.9%	27.3%	7.8%
BOSTON	5,882	3,571	1,915	396	Ford	60.7%	32.6%	6.7%
BROCKTON	1,771	919	761	91	Ford	51.9%	43.0%	5.1%
BROOKLINE	2,151	1,519	539	93	Ford	70.6%	25.1%	4.3%
CAMBRIDGE	1,523	1,100	336	87	Ford	72.2%	22.1%	5.7%
CHICOPEE	984	519	396	69	Ford	52.7%	40.2%	7.0%
FALL RIVER	1,152	675	405	72	Ford	58.6%	35.2%	6.3%
FRAMINGHAM	2,003	1,286	664	53	Ford	64.2%	33.2%	2.6%
HAVERHILL	975	551	362	62	Ford	56.5%	37.1%	6.4%
LAWRENCE	731	356	317	58	Ford	48.7%	43.4%	7.9%
LENOX	245	160	71	14	Ford	65.3%	29.0%	5.7%
LOWELL	1,545	842	641	62	Ford	54.5%	41.5%	4.0%
LYNN	1,591	931	530	130	Ford	58.5%	33.3%	8.2%
MALDEN	1,184	753	359	72	Ford	63.6%	30.3%	6.1%
MEDFORD	1,391	826	490	75	Ford	59.4%	35.2%	5.4%
NEW BEDFORD	2,195	1,049	952	194	Ford	47.8%	43.4%	8.8%
NEWTON	3,300	2,288	877	135	Ford	69.3%	26.6%	4.1%
PROVINCETOWN	83	35	42	6	Reagan	42.2%	50.6%	7.2%
QUINCY	3,034	1,883	994	157	Ford	62.1%	32.8%	5.2%
SOMERVILLE	949	567	336	46	Ford	59.7%	35.4%	4.8%
SPRINGFIELD	2,878	1,824	912	142	Ford	63.4%	31.7%	4.9%
TAUNTON	823	475	309	39	Ford	57.7%	37.5%	4.7%
WALTHAM	1,166	690	439	37	Ford	59.2%	37.7%	3.2%
WELLESLEY	3,071	2,071	862	138	Ford	67.4%	28.1%	4.5%
WEYMOUTH	2,050	1,176	721	153	Ford	57.4%	35.2%	7.5%
WORCESTER	4,108	2,716	1,219	173	Ford	66.1%	29.7%	4.2%
STATE TOTAL	188,449	115,375	63,555	9,519	Ford	61.2%	33.7%	5.1%

MASSACHUSETTS DEMOCRATIC

1980

City/Town	Total Vote	Carter	E. Kennedy	Other	Winner	Percentage of Total Vote Carter	E. Kennedy	Other
AMHERST	3,524	1,139	1,979	406	E. Kennedy	32.3%	56.2%	11.5%
BOSTON	89,714	30,067	53,528	6,119	E. Kennedy	33.5%	59.7%	6.8%
BROCKTON	13,582	3,304	9,314	964	E. Kennedy	24.3%	68.6%	7.1%
BROOKLINE	10,370	2,443	7,307	620	E. Kennedy	23.6%	70.5%	6.0%
CAMBRIDGE	18,879	4,823	12,233	1,823	E. Kennedy	25.5%	64.8%	9.7%
CHICOPEE	9,348	3,655	5,127	566	E. Kennedy	39.1%	54.8%	6.1%
FALL RIVER	16,297	2,998	12,533	766	E. Kennedy	18.4%	76.9%	4.7%
FRAMINGHAM	10,674	3,226	6,883	565	E. Kennedy	30.2%	64.5%	5.3%
HAVERHILL	7,159	1,765	5,009	385	E. Kennedy	24.7%	70.0%	5.4%
LAWRENCE	12,973	3,299	8,857	817	E. Kennedy	25.4%	68.3%	6.3%
LENOX	666	271	319	76	E. Kennedy	40.7%	47.9%	11.4%
LOWELL	15,479	3,677	10,981	821	E. Kennedy	23.8%	70.9%	5.3%
LYNN	15,415	3,743	10,863	809	E. Kennedy	24.3%	70.5%	5.2%
MALDEN	11,552	2,716	7,839	997	E. Kennedy	23.5%	67.9%	8.6%
MEDFORD	13,758	3,182	9,919	657	E. Kennedy	23.1%	72.1%	4.8%
NEW BEDFORD	15,783	2,466	12,516	801	E. Kennedy	15.6%	79.3%	5.1%
NEWTON	16,363	3,831	11,616	916	E. Kennedy	23.4%	71.0%	5.6%
PROVINCETOWN	652	106	492	54	E. Kennedy	16.3%	75.5%	8.3%
QUINCY	19,510	5,534	12,575	1,401	E. Kennedy	28.4%	64.5%	7.2%
SOMERVILLE	16,490	3,811	11,708	971	E. Kennedy	23.1%	71.0%	5.9%
SPRINGFIELD	18,830	7,078	10,780	972	E. Kennedy	37.6%	57.2%	5.2%
TAUNTON	5,177	1,128	3,769	280	E. Kennedy	21.8%	72.8%	5.4%
WALTHAM	8,372	2,004	5,998	370	E. Kennedy	23.9%	71.6%	4.4%
WELLESLEY	3,607	1,285	2,045	277	E. Kennedy	35.6%	56.7%	7.7%
WEYMOUTH	10,798	3,117	6,771	910	E. Kennedy	28.9%	62.7%	8.4%
WORCESTER	27,051	6,984	18,911	1,156	E. Kennedy	25.8%	69.9%	4.3%
STATE TOTAL	907,323	260,401	590,393	56,529	E. Kennedy	28.7%	65.1%	6.2%

MASSACHUSETTS REPUBLICAN

1980

City/Town	Total Vote	Anderson	Bush	Reagan	Other	Winner	Percentage of Total Vote Anderson	Bush	Reagan	Other
AMHERST	2,417	1,507	543	262	105	Anderson	62.4%	22.5%	10.8%	4.3%
BOSTON	18,000	7,205	4,313	4,995	1,487	Anderson	40.0%	24.0%	27.8%	8.3%
BROCKTON	3,437	836	921	1,370	310	Reagan	24.3%	26.8%	39.9%	9.0%
BROOKLINE	5,353	2,653	1,463	954	283	Anderson	49.6%	27.3%	17.8%	5.3%
CAMBRIDGE	5,705	3,697	1,037	585	386	Anderson	64.8%	18.2%	10.3%	6.8%
CHICOPEE	1,491	330	521	511	129	Bush	22.1%	34.9%	34.3%	8.7%
FALL RIVER	1,826	391	416	786	233	Reagan	21.4%	22.8%	43.0%	12.8%
FRAMINGHAM	4,890	1,772	1,368	1,206	544	Anderson	36.2%	28.0%	24.7%	11.1%
HAVERHILL	2,924	572	921	1,018	413	Reagan	19.6%	31.5%	34.8%	14.1%
LAWRENCE	1,547	271	403	702	171	Reagan	17.5%	26.1%	45.4%	11.1%
LENOX	472	159	151	123	39	Anderson	33.7%	32.0%	26.1%	8.3%
LOWELL	3,532	676	1,104	1,367	385	Reagan	19.1%	31.3%	38.7%	10.9%
LYNN	3,141	695	951	1,244	251	Reagan	22.1%	30.3%	39.6%	8.0%
MALDEN	2,449	638	704	733	374	Reagan	26.1%	28.7%	29.9%	15.3%
MEDFORD	2,972	858	901	958	255	Reagan	28.9%	30.3%	32.2%	8.6%
NEW BEDFORD	3,193	643	917	1,299	334	Reagan	20.1%	28.7%	40.7%	10.5%
NEWTON	8,432	3,816	2,476	1,597	543	Anderson	45.3%	29.4%	18.9%	6.4%
PROVINCETOWN	196	91	40	52	13	Anderson	46.4%	20.4%	26.5%	6.6%
QUINCY	5,632	1,194	1,572	2,291	575	Reagan	21.2%	27.9%	40.7%	10.2%
SOMERVILLE	2,486	1,013	501	784	188	Anderson	40.7%	20.2%	31.5%	7.6%
SPRINGFIELD	4,299	1,286	1,521	1,170	322	Bush	29.9%	35.4%	27.2%	7.5%
TAUNTON	1,559	304	412	681	162	Reagan	19.5%	26.4%	43.7%	10.4%
WALTHAM	3,045	971	795	995	284	Reagan	31.9%	26.1%	32.7%	9.3%
WELLESLEY	5,633	1,678	2,360	1,106	489	Bush	29.8%	41.9%	19.6%	8.7%
WEYMOUTH	3,836	983	1,141	1,416	296	Reagan	25.6%	29.7%	36.9%	7.7%
WORCESTER	7,481	2,467	2,053	2,244	717	Anderson	33.0%	27.4%	30.0%	9.6%
STATE TOTAL	400,826	122,987	124,365	115,334	38,140	Bush	30.7%	31.0%	28.8%	9.5%

MASSACHUSETTS DEMOCRATIC

1984

City/Town	Total Vote	Hart	McGovern	Mondale	Other	Winner	Percentage of Total Vote Hart	McGovern	Mondale	Other
AMHERST	5,203	1,736	1,353	931	1,183	Hart	33.4%	26.0%	17.9%	22.7%
BOSTON	72,253	19,878	16,101	18,971	17,303	Hart	27.5%	22.3%	26.3%	23.9%
BROCKTON	9,217	3,924	1,618	2,197	1,478	Hart	42.6%	17.6%	23.8%	16.0%
BROOKLINE	9,096	2,781	2,741	2,867	707	Mondale	30.6%	30.1%	31.5%	7.8%
CAMBRIDGE	18,398	5,471	6,009	4,387	2,531	McGovern	29.7%	32.7%	23.8%	13.8%
CHICOPEE	4,768	1,956	551	1,830	431	Hart	41.0%	11.6%	38.4%	9.0%
FALL RIVER	8,299	3,459	595	3,507	738	Mondale	41.7%	7.2%	42.3%	8.9%
FRAMINGHAM	8,507	3,629	1,897	1,928	1,053	Hart	42.7%	22.3%	22.7%	12.4%
HAVERHILL	4,833	2,206	844	1,237	546	Hart	45.6%	17.5%	25.6%	11.3%
LAWRENCE	7,195	2,962	1,178	2,173	882	Hart	41.2%	16.4%	30.2%	12.3%
LENOX	473	245	66	92	70	Hart	51.8%	14.0%	19.5%	14.8%
LOWELL	8,622	3,607	1,432	2,401	1,182	Hart	41.8%	16.6%	27.8%	13.7%
LYNN	8,576	2,973	1,681	2,741	1,181	Hart	34.7%	19.6%	32.0%	13.8%
MALDEN	6,647	2,333	1,471	1,898	945	Hart	35.1%	22.1%	28.6%	14.2%
MEDFORD	7,655	2,497	1,664	2,386	1,108	Hart	32.6%	21.7%	31.2%	14.5%
NEW BEDFORD	9,735	3,512	797	4,021	1,405	Mondale	36.1%	8.2%	41.3%	14.4%
NEWTON	14,351	4,765	4,275	4,082	1,229	Hart	33.2%	29.8%	28.4%	8.6%
PROVINCETOWN	614	292	145	99	78	Hart	47.6%	23.6%	16.1%	12.7%
QUINCY	10,961	3,863	2,339	3,187	1,572	Hart	35.2%	21.3%	29.1%	14.3%
SOMERVILLE	10,308	3,469	2,907	2,738	1,194	Hart	33.7%	28.2%	26.6%	11.6%
SPRINGFIELD	11,315	3,480	1,212	3,291	3,332	Hart	30.8%	10.7%	29.1%	29.4%
TAUNTON	3,149	1,417	423	953	356	Hart	45.0%	13.4%	30.3%	11.3%
WALTHAM	5,232	2,138	1,200	1,306	588	Hart	40.9%	22.9%	25.0%	11.2%
WELLESLEY	3,443	1,298	1,007	786	352	Hart	37.7%	29.2%	22.8%	10.2%
WEYMOUTH	6,496	2,537	1,405	1,658	896	Hart	39.1%	21.6%	25.5%	13.8%
WORCESTER	14,946	6,048	2,323	4,649	1,926	Hart	40.5%	15.5%	31.1%	12.9%
STATE TOTAL	630,962	245,943	134,341	160,893	89,785	Hart	39.0%	21.3%	25.5%	14.2%

MASSACHUSETTS REPUBLICAN

1984

City/Town	Total Vote	Reagan	Other	Winner	Percentage of Total Vote: Reagan	Percentage of Total Vote: Other
AMHERST	188	154	34	Reagan	81.9%	18.1%
BOSTON	2,361	2,067	294	Reagan	87.5%	12.5%
BROCKTON	556	501	55	Reagan	90.1%	9.9%
BROOKLINE	688	626	62	Reagan	91.0%	9.0%
CAMBRIDGE	572	426	146	Reagan	74.5%	25.5%
CHICOPEE	289	265	24	Reagan	91.7%	8.3%
FALL RIVER	347	295	52	Reagan	85.0%	15.0%
FRAMINGHAM	899	855	44	Reagan	95.1%	4.9%
HAVERHILL	522	449	73	Reagan	86.0%	14.0%
LAWRENCE	470	412	58	Reagan	87.7%	12.3%
LENOX	235	230	5	Reagan	97.9%	2.1%
LOWELL	566	500	66	Reagan	88.3%	11.7%
LYNN	480	435	45	Reagan	90.6%	9.4%
MALDEN	324	288	36	Reagan	88.9%	11.1%
MEDFORD	437	377	60	Reagan	86.3%	13.7%
NEW BEDFORD	707	570	137	Reagan	80.6%	19.4%
NEWTON	1,115	987	128	Reagan	88.5%	11.5%
PROVINCETOWN	62	53	9	Reagan	85.5%	14.5%
QUINCY	1,057	935	122	Reagan	88.5%	11.5%
SOMERVILLE	302	256	46	Reagan	84.8%	15.2%
SPRINGFIELD	400	329	71	Reagan	82.3%	17.8%
TAUNTON	356	313	43	Reagan	87.9%	12.1%
WALTHAM	398	371	27	Reagan	93.2%	6.8%
WELLESLEY	1,009	881	128	Reagan	87.3%	12.7%
WEYMOUTH	559	488	71	Reagan	87.3%	12.7%
WORCESTER	1,047	895	152	Reagan	85.5%	14.5%
STATE TOTAL	66,476	59,500	6,976	Reagan	89.5%	10.5%
Published Totals	65,937	58,996	6,941	Reagan	89.5%	10.5%

MASSACHUSETTS DEMOCRATIC

1988

City/Town	Total Vote	Dukakis	Gephardt	J. Jackson	Other	Winner	Percentage of Total Vote Dukakis	Gephardt	J. Jackson	Other
AMHERST	4,398	1,443	118	2,155	682	J. Jackson	32.8%	2.7%	49.0%	15.5%
BOSTON	73,552	34,846	7,256	23,323	8,127	Dukakis	47.4%	9.9%	31.7%	11.0%
BROCKTON	9,335	4,858	1,503	1,465	1,509	Dukakis	52.0%	16.1%	15.7%	16.2%
BROOKLINE	9,744	6,588	421	1,615	1,120	Dukakis	67.6%	4.3%	16.6%	11.5%
CAMBRIDGE	19,260	9,087	1,016	6,776	2,381	Dukakis	47.2%	5.3%	35.2%	12.4%
CHICOPEE	6,665	5,244	431	409	581	Dukakis	78.7%	6.5%	6.1%	8.7%
FALL RIVER	10,206	8,158	573	647	828	Dukakis	79.9%	5.6%	6.3%	8.1%
FRAMINGHAM	8,031	4,715	897	1,303	1,116	Dukakis	58.7%	11.2%	16.2%	13.9%
HAVERHILL	6,296	3,948	662	859	827	Dukakis	62.7%	10.5%	13.6%	13.1%
LAWRENCE	7,139	3,331	1,441	1,064	1,303	Dukakis	46.7%	20.2%	14.9%	18.3%
LENOX	440	320	22	60	38	Dukakis	72.7%	5.0%	13.6%	8.6%
LOWELL	11,087	6,827	1,490	1,286	1,484	Dukakis	61.6%	13.4%	11.6%	13.4%
LYNN	10,727	6,818	1,217	1,498	1,194	Dukakis	63.6%	11.3%	14.0%	11.1%
MALDEN	7,306	4,514	841	1,053	898	Dukakis	61.8%	11.5%	14.4%	12.3%
MEDFORD	10,193	5,755	1,299	1,719	1,420	Dukakis	56.5%	12.7%	16.9%	13.9%
NEW BEDFORD	11,514	8,727	655	1,327	805	Dukakis	75.8%	5.7%	11.5%	7.0%
NEWTON	14,273	9,168	878	2,333	1,894	Dukakis	64.2%	6.2%	16.3%	13.3%
PROVINCETOWN	625	312	18	251	44	Dukakis	49.9%	2.9%	40.2%	7.0%
QUINCY	12,681	7,019	1,875	1,765	2,022	Dukakis	55.4%	14.8%	13.9%	15.9%
SOMERVILLE	11,865	6,319	1,248	2,780	1,518	Dukakis	53.3%	10.5%	23.4%	12.8%
SPRINGFIELD	11,727	7,473	737	2,602	915	Dukakis	63.7%	6.3%	22.2%	7.8%
TAUNTON	4,421	3,098	428	460	435	Dukakis	70.1%	9.7%	10.4%	9.8%
WALTHAM	6,061	3,483	744	1,017	817	Dukakis	57.5%	12.3%	16.8%	13.5%
WELLESLEY	3,316	1,980	245	587	504	Dukakis	59.7%	7.4%	17.7%	15.2%
WEYMOUTH	7,707	4,199	1,163	1,199	1,146	Dukakis	54.5%	15.1%	15.6%	14.9%
WORCESTER	18,050	11,432	1,909	2,522	2,187	Dukakis	63.3%	10.6%	14.0%	12.1%
STATE TOTAL	713,553	418,256	72,944	133,141	89,212	Dukakis	58.6%	10.2%	18.7%	12.5%
Published Totals	713,447	418,256	72,944	133,141	89,106	Dukakis	58.6%	10.2%	18.7%	12.5%

MASSACHUSETTS REPUBLICAN

1988

City/Town	Total Vote	Bush	Dole	Other	Winner	Percentage of Total Vote Bush	Dole	Other
AMHERST	834	376	322	136	Bush	45.1%	38.6%	16.3%
BOSTON	8,776	4,724	2,431	1,621	Bush	53.8%	27.7%	18.5%
BROCKTON	2,128	1,310	406	412	Bush	61.6%	19.1%	19.4%
BROOKLINE	1,985	1,044	726	215	Bush	52.6%	36.6%	10.8%
CAMBRIDGE	1,899	849	767	283	Bush	44.7%	40.4%	14.9%
CHICOPEE	1,043	680	228	135	Bush	65.2%	21.9%	12.9%
FALL RIVER	1,108	629	268	211	Bush	56.8%	24.2%	19.0%
FRAMINGHAM	2,712	1,455	803	454	Bush	53.7%	29.6%	16.7%
HAVERHILL	2,166	1,327	472	367	Bush	61.3%	21.8%	16.9%
LAWRENCE	1,110	717	182	211	Bush	64.6%	16.4%	19.0%
LENOX	229	103	81	45	Bush	45.0%	35.4%	19.7%
LOWELL	2,412	1,483	523	406	Bush	61.5%	21.7%	16.8%
LYNN	1,889	1,165	356	368	Bush	61.7%	18.8%	19.5%
MALDEN	1,435	811	329	295	Bush	56.5%	22.9%	20.6%
MEDFORD	1,756	1,064	409	283	Bush	60.6%	23.3%	16.1%
NEW BEDFORD	1,544	885	312	347	Bush	57.3%	20.2%	22.5%
NEWTON	3,225	1,738	1,098	389	Bush	53.9%	34.0%	12.1%
PROVINCETOWN	122	67	41	14	Bush	54.9%	33.6%	11.5%
QUINCY	3,408	2,080	730	598	Bush	61.0%	21.4%	17.5%
SOMERVILLE	1,009	544	286	179	Bush	53.9%	28.3%	17.7%
SPRINGFIELD	2,058	1,241	472	345	Bush	60.3%	22.9%	16.8%
TAUNTON	1,071	600	281	190	Bush	56.0%	26.2%	17.7%
WALTHAM	1,691	984	462	245	Bush	58.2%	27.3%	14.5%
WELLESLEY	3,125	1,843	930	352	Bush	59.0%	29.8%	11.3%
WEYMOUTH	2,317	1,411	514	392	Bush	60.9%	22.2%	16.9%
WORCESTER	4,375	2,618	1,134	623	Bush	59.8%	25.9%	14.2%
STATE TOTAL	241,181	141,113	63,392	36,676	Bush	58.5%	26.3%	15.2%

MASSACHUSETTS DEMOCRATIC

1992

County	Total Vote	Brown	Clinton	Tsongas	Other	Winner	Percentage of Total Vote Brown	Clinton	Tsongas	Other
BARNSTABLE	25,238	4,323	2,623	16,604	1,688	Tsongas	17.1%	10.4%	65.8%	6.7%
BERKSHIRE	13,438	1,905	1,675	8,185	1,673	Tsongas	14.2%	12.5%	60.9%	12.4%
BRISTOL	51,328	6,496	8,922	31,382	4,528	Tsongas	12.7%	17.4%	61.1%	8.8%
DUKES	2,746	594	334	1,570	248	Tsongas	21.6%	12.2%	57.2%	9.0%
ESSEX	95,445	13,864	9,184	64,653	7,744	Tsongas	14.5%	9.6%	67.7%	8.1%
FRANKLIN	8,228	1,969	747	4,694	818	Tsongas	23.9%	9.1%	57.0%	9.9%
HAMPDEN	39,720	3,679	4,311	27,437	4,293	Tsongas	9.3%	10.9%	69.1%	10.8%
HAMPSHIRE	17,925	3,860	1,710	10,397	1,958	Tsongas	21.5%	9.5%	58.0%	10.9%
MIDDLESEX	231,139	32,771	20,479	161,879	16,010	Tsongas	14.2%	8.9%	70.0%	6.9%
NANTUCKET	929	192	111	570	56	Tsongas	20.7%	11.9%	61.4%	6.0%
NORFOLK	99,681	14,663	9,551	67,616	7,851	Tsongas	14.7%	9.6%	67.8%	7.9%
PLYMOUTH	49,513	8,501	5,252	31,765	3,995	Tsongas	17.2%	10.6%	64.2%	8.1%
SUFFOLK	77,564	13,519	10,858	46,322	6,865	Tsongas	17.4%	14.0%	59.7%	8.9%
WORCESTER	79,991	9,410	11,060	53,223	6,298	Tsongas	11.8%	13.8%	66.5%	7.9%
TOTAL	792,885	115,746	86,817	526,297	64,025	Tsongas	14.6%	10.9%	66.4%	8.1%
Certified Totals	794,115	115,746	86,817	526,297	65,255	Tsongas	14.6%	10.9%	66.3%	8.2%

City/Town	Total Vote	Brown	Clinton	Tsongas	Other	Winner	Brown	Clinton	Tsongas	Other
AMHERST	3,787	1,044	404	1,911	428	Tsongas	27.6%	10.7%	50.5%	11.3%
BOSTON	64,666	11,805	9,170	38,095	5,596	Tsongas	18.3%	14.2%	58.9%	8.7%
BROCKTON	9,366	1,423	1,283	5,737	923	Tsongas	15.2%	13.7%	61.3%	9.9%
BROOKLINE	10,206	1,790	1,170	6,619	627	Tsongas	17.5%	11.5%	64.9%	6.1%
CAMBRIDGE	16,790	3,821	2,015	9,480	1,474	Tsongas	22.8%	12.0%	56.5%	8.8%
CHICOPEE	6,270	478	702	4,354	736	Tsongas	7.6%	11.2%	69.4%	11.7%
FALL RIVER	8,774	744	1,558	5,464	1,008	Tsongas	8.5%	17.8%	62.3%	11.5%
FRAMINGHAM	9,508	1,204	908	6,740	656	Tsongas	12.7%	9.5%	70.9%	6.9%
HAVERHILL	7,174	980	881	4,807	506	Tsongas	13.7%	12.3%	67.0%	7.1%
LAWRENCE	6,444	643	779	4,287	735	Tsongas	10.0%	12.1%	66.5%	11.4%
LENOX	685	103	68	420	94	Tsongas	15.0%	9.9%	61.3%	13.7%
LOWELL	14,110	1,018	921	11,420	751	Tsongas	7.2%	6.5%	80.9%	5.3%
LYNN	10,078	1,266	1,054	6,886	872	Tsongas	12.6%	10.5%	68.3%	8.7%
MALDEN	8,035	1,063	922	5,150	900	Tsongas	13.2%	11.5%	64.1%	11.2%
MEDFORD	10,236	1,453	1,130	6,820	833	Tsongas	14.2%	11.0%	66.6%	8.1%
NEW BEDFORD	11,293	1,417	2,506	6,299	1,071	Tsongas	12.5%	22.2%	55.8%	9.5%
NEWTON	17,071	2,327	1,645	12,210	889	Tsongas	13.6%	9.6%	71.5%	5.2%
PROVINCETOWN	722	192	94	386	50	Tsongas	26.6%	13.0%	53.5%	6.9%
QUINCY	12,900	2,004	1,339	8,206	1,351	Tsongas	15.5%	10.4%	63.6%	10.5%
SOMERVILLE	12,064	2,281	1,450	7,152	1,181	Tsongas	18.9%	12.0%	59.3%	9.8%
SPRINGFIELD	11,706	1,052	1,536	7,836	1,282	Tsongas	9.0%	13.1%	66.9%	11.0%
TAUNTON	4,173	594	826	2,421	332	Tsongas	14.2%	19.8%	58.0%	8.0%
WALTHAM	6,693	1,011	710	4,502	470	Tsongas	15.1%	10.6%	67.3%	7.0%
WELLESLEY	4,020	542	345	2,940	193	Tsongas	13.5%	8.6%	73.1%	4.8%
WEYMOUTH	8,379	1,274	768	5,583	754	Tsongas	15.2%	9.2%	66.6%	9.0%
WORCESTER	17,335	1,992	2,305	11,583	1,455	Tsongas	11.5%	13.3%	66.8%	8.4%

Note: Following publication of the 1992 primary returns, Massachusetts election officials made small corrections in the "Other" vote for both parties. The results in both the 1992 Democratic and Republican tables reflect the initial returns.

MASSACHUSETTS REPUBLICAN

1992

County	Total Vote	Buchanan	Bush	Other	Winner	Percentage of Total Vote Buchanan	Bush	Other
BARNSTABLE	15,623	3,727	10,923	973	Bush	23.9%	69.9%	6.2%
BERKSHIRE	4,755	1,376	2,906	473	Bush	28.9%	61.1%	9.9%
BRISTOL	16,110	5,141	9,855	1,114	Bush	31.9%	61.2%	6.9%
DUKES	1,342	332	902	108	Bush	24.7%	67.2%	8.0%
ESSEX	36,712	9,803	24,510	2,399	Bush	26.7%	66.8%	6.5%
FRANKLIN	3,235	813	2,213	209	Bush	25.1%	68.4%	6.5%
HAMPDEN	14,309	3,741	9,548	1,020	Bush	26.1%	66.7%	7.1%
HAMPSHIRE	4,687	1,287	3,082	318	Bush	27.5%	65.8%	6.8%
MIDDLESEX	66,735	18,880	43,278	4,577	Bush	28.3%	64.9%	6.9%
NANTUCKET	469	118	316	35	Bush	25.2%	67.4%	7.5%
NORFOLK	36,533	10,208	23,952	2,373	Bush	27.9%	65.6%	6.5%
PLYMOUTH	23,968	6,764	15,610	1,594	Bush	28.2%	65.1%	6.7%
SUFFOLK	11,940	3,960	6,969	1,011	Bush	33.2%	58.4%	8.5%
WORCESTER	33,283	8,647	22,804	1,832	Bush	26.0%	68.5%	5.5%
TOTAL	269,701	74,797	176,868	18,036	Bush	27.7%	65.6%	6.7%
Certified Totals	269,702	74,797	176,868	18,037	Bush	27.7%	65.6%	6.7%

City/Town	Total Vote	Buchanan	Bush	Other	Winner	Buchanan	Bush	Other
AMHERST	541	121	376	44	Bush	22.4%	69.5%	8.1%
BOSTON	9,602	3,203	5,591	808	Bush	33.4%	58.2%	8.4%
BROCKTON	2,550	703	1,616	231	Bush	27.6%	63.4%	9.1%
BROOKLINE	1,852	384	1,290	178	Bush	20.7%	69.7%	9.6%
CAMBRIDGE	1,534	432	928	174	Bush	28.2%	60.5%	11.3%
CHICOPEE	1,291	421	802	68	Bush	32.6%	62.1%	5.3%
FALL RIVER	1,098	390	617	91	Bush	35.5%	56.2%	8.3%
FRAMINGHAM	3,027	818	1,998	211	Bush	27.0%	66.0%	7.0%
HAVERHILL	2,652	802	1,654	196	Bush	30.2%	62.4%	7.4%
LAWRENCE	1,343	403	858	82	Bush	30.0%	63.9%	6.1%
LENOX	296	72	204	20	Bush	24.3%	68.9%	6.8%
LOWELL	2,468	771	1,466	231	Bush	31.2%	59.4%	9.4%
LYNN	2,053	575	1,323	155	Bush	28.0%	64.4%	7.5%
MALDEN	1,652	549	1,000	103	Bush	33.2%	60.5%	6.2%
MEDFORD	2,124	695	1,286	143	Bush	32.7%	60.5%	6.7%
NEW BEDFORD	1,708	616	943	149	Bush	36.1%	55.2%	8.7%
NEWTON	3,519	835	2,400	284	Bush	23.7%	68.2%	8.1%
PROVINCETOWN	98	27	61	10	Bush	27.6%	62.2%	10.2%
QUINCY	3,457	1,114	2,101	242	Bush	32.2%	60.8%	7.0%
SOMERVILLE	1,337	442	757	138	Bush	33.1%	56.6%	10.3%
SPRINGFIELD	2,573	668	1,691	214	Bush	26.0%	65.7%	8.3%
TAUNTON	1,311	390	835	86	Bush	29.7%	63.7%	6.6%
WALTHAM	2,043	575	1,350	118	Bush	28.1%	66.1%	5.8%
WELLESLEY	2,552	568	1,843	141	Bush	22.3%	72.2%	5.5%
WEYMOUTH	2,895	941	1,792	162	Bush	32.5%	61.9%	5.6%
WORCESTER	4,485	1,177	3,014	294	Bush	26.2%	67.2%	6.6%

MASSACHUSETTS DEMOCRATIC

1996

County	Total Vote	Clinton	Other	Winner	Percentage of Total Vote Clinton	Percentage of Total Vote Other
BARNSTABLE	6,212	5,689	523	Clinton	91.6%	8.4%
BERKSHIRE	2,932	2,649	283	Clinton	90.3%	9.7%
BRISTOL	11,244	10,109	1,135	Clinton	89.9%	10.1%
DUKES	641	617	24	Clinton	96.3%	3.7%
ESSEX	19,926	17,213	2,713	Clinton	86.4%	13.6%
FRANKLIN	1,232	1,127	105	Clinton	91.5%	8.5%
HAMPDEN	6,276	5,302	974	Clinton	84.5%	15.5%
HAMPSHIRE	2,355	2,115	240	Clinton	89.8%	10.2%
MIDDLESEX	40,550	35,645	4,905	Clinton	87.9%	12.1%
NANTUCKET	261	245	16	Clinton	93.9%	6.1%
NORFOLK	21,676	18,426	3,250	Clinton	85.0%	15.0%
PLYMOUTH	10,405	8,969	1,436	Clinton	86.2%	13.8%
SUFFOLK	19,054	16,083	2,971	Clinton	84.4%	15.6%
WORCESTER	12,706	11,171	1,535	Clinton	87.9%	12.1%
TOTAL	155,470	135,360	20,110	Clinton	87.1%	12.9%

City/Town	Total Vote	Clinton	Other	Winner	Percentage of Total Vote Clinton	Percentage of Total Vote Other
AMHERST	505	464	41	Clinton	91.9%	8.1%
BOSTON	15,895	13,410	2,485	Clinton	84.4%	15.6%
BROCKTON	1,613	1,296	317	Clinton	80.3%	19.7%
BROOKLINE	1,737	1,639	98	Clinton	94.4%	5.6%
CAMBRIDGE	3,036	2,710	326	Clinton	89.3%	10.7%
CHICOPEE	1,103	903	200	Clinton	81.9%	18.1%
FALL RIVER	2,467	2,243	224	Clinton	90.9%	9.1%
FRAMINGHAM	3,055	2,716	339	Clinton	88.9%	11.1%
HAVERHILL	4,545	3,977	568	Clinton	87.5%	12.5%
LAWRENCE	1,604	1,324	280	Clinton	82.5%	17.5%
LENOX	145	135	10	Clinton	93.1%	6.9%
LOWELL	1,772	1,477	295	Clinton	83.4%	16.6%
LYNN	1,909	1,580	329	Clinton	82.8%	17.2%
MALDEN	1,663	1,462	201	Clinton	87.9%	12.1%
MEDFORD	1,714	1,489	225	Clinton	86.9%	13.1%
NEW BEDFORD	2,687	2,480	207	Clinton	92.3%	7.7%
NEWTON	2,184	2,009	175	Clinton	92.0%	8.0%
PROVINCETOWN	274	261	13	Clinton	95.3%	4.7%
QUINCY	3,135	2,467	668	Clinton	78.7%	21.3%
SOMERVILLE	2,599	2,212	387	Clinton	85.1%	14.9%
SPRINGFIELD	1,770	1,516	254	Clinton	85.6%	14.4%
TAUNTON	759	669	90	Clinton	88.1%	11.9%
WALTHAM	1,023	885	138	Clinton	86.5%	13.5%
WELLESLEY	692	630	62	Clinton	91.0%	9.0%
WEYMOUTH	2,141	1,817	324	Clinton	84.9%	15.1%
WORCESTER	2,773	2,416	357	Clinton	87.1%	12.9%

MASSACHUSETTS REPUBLICAN

1996

County	Total Vote	Buchanan	Dole	Forbes	Other	Winner	Percentage of Total Vote Buchanan	Dole	Forbes	Other
BARNSTABLE	18,551	3,618	9,597	2,984	2,352	Dole	19.5%	51.7%	16.1%	12.7%
BERKSHIRE	4,420	910	2,146	741	623	Dole	20.6%	48.6%	16.8%	14.1%
BRISTOL	15,905	4,510	7,191	2,175	2,029	Dole	28.4%	45.2%	13.7%	12.8%
DUKES	1,024	175	489	156	204	Dole	17.1%	47.8%	15.2%	19.9%
ESSEX	39,720	9,891	18,267	6,255	5,307	Dole	24.9%	46.0%	15.7%	13.4%
FRANKLIN	2,974	633	1,409	398	534	Dole	21.3%	47.4%	13.4%	18.0%
HAMPDEN	12,942	2,813	6,804	1,913	1,412	Dole	21.7%	52.6%	14.8%	10.9%
HAMPSHIRE	4,248	975	2,066	648	559	Dole	23.0%	48.6%	15.3%	13.2%
MIDDLESEX	72,777	18,080	34,658	9,923	10,116	Dole	24.8%	47.6%	13.6%	13.9%
NANTUCKET	519	80	236	117	86	Dole	15.4%	45.5%	22.5%	16.6%
NORFOLK	40,923	10,373	20,384	5,015	5,151	Dole	25.3%	49.8%	12.3%	12.6%
PLYMOUTH	27,144	7,629	12,617	3,534	3,364	Dole	28.1%	46.5%	13.0%	12.4%
SUFFOLK	12,084	4,158	4,889	1,479	1,558	Dole	34.4%	40.5%	12.2%	12.9%
WORCESTER	31,602	7,843	15,193	4,267	4,299	Dole	24.8%	48.1%	13.5%	13.6%
TOTAL	284,833	71,688	135,946	39,605	37,594	Dole	25.2%	47.7%	13.9%	13.2%

City/Town	Total Vote	Buchanan	Dole	Forbes	Other	Winner	Buchanan %	Dole %	Forbes %	Other %
AMHERST	509	77	281	52	99	Dole	15.1%	55.2%	10.2%	19.4%
BOSTON	9,846	3,318	3,999	1,219	1,310	Dole	33.7%	40.6%	12.4%	13.3%
BROCKTON	2,252	772	979	249	252	Dole	34.3%	43.5%	11.1%	11.2%
BROOKLINE	2,289	265	1,300	384	340	Dole	11.6%	56.8%	16.8%	14.9%
CAMBRIDGE	1,667	338	732	268	329	Dole	20.3%	43.9%	16.1%	19.7%
CHICOPEE	1,189	354	529	180	126	Dole	29.8%	44.5%	15.1%	10.6%
FALL RIVER	982	351	408	113	110	Dole	35.7%	41.5%	11.5%	11.2%
FRAMINGHAM	3,624	680	1,883	547	514	Dole	18.8%	52.0%	15.1%	14.2%
HAVERHILL	3,958	1,160	1,508	643	647	Dole	29.3%	38.1%	16.2%	16.3%
LAWRENCE	959	386	310	147	116	Buchanan	40.3%	32.3%	15.3%	12.1%
LENOX	254	46	142	32	34	Dole	18.1%	55.9%	12.6%	13.4%
LOWELL	1,968	827	659	241	241	Buchanan	42.0%	33.5%	12.2%	12.2%
LYNN	2,008	775	750	232	251	Buchanan	38.6%	37.4%	11.6%	12.5%
MALDEN	1,598	585	608	177	228	Dole	36.6%	38.0%	11.1%	14.3%
MEDFORD	1,973	804	796	176	197	Buchanan	40.8%	40.3%	8.9%	10.0%
NEW BEDFORD	1,361	480	521	195	165	Dole	35.3%	38.3%	14.3%	12.1%
NEWTON	3,747	558	2,089	615	485	Dole	14.9%	55.8%	16.4%	12.9%
PROVINCETOWN	113	13	23	41	36	Forbes	11.5%	20.4%	36.3%	31.9%
QUINCY	3,128	1,145	1,341	294	348	Dole	36.6%	42.9%	9.4%	11.1%
SOMERVILLE	1,197	430	437	150	180	Dole	35.9%	36.5%	12.5%	15.0%
SPRINGFIELD	1,950	480	998	259	213	Dole	24.6%	51.2%	13.3%	10.9%
TAUNTON	1,311	428	518	176	189	Dole	32.6%	39.5%	13.4%	14.4%
WALTHAM	2,177	592	1,114	236	235	Dole	27.2%	51.2%	10.8%	10.8%
WELLESLEY	3,017	348	1,826	427	416	Dole	11.5%	60.5%	14.2%	13.8%
WEYMOUTH	2,867	1,088	1,158	338	283	Dole	37.9%	40.4%	11.8%	9.9%
WORCESTER	3,876	998	1,968	442	468	Dole	25.7%	50.8%	11.4%	12.1%

MICHIGAN

Michigan has had an on-again, off-again relationship with its presidential primary. It was on through the 1970s, off through much of the 1980s, and on again in the 1990s. In 2000, Michigan plans to split the difference, with Republicans holding a February primary and Democrats scheduling a caucus vote in March.

Basically, when Michigan has not had a primary, it has been because of a conflict with national Democratic rules. In the 1980s, the crossover feature of Michigan's primary led to its demise. National Democratic rules require voters to identify themselves publicly as Democrats, a feature the Michigan primary lacked.

Troubling to Democratic leaders was the uncontrollable nature of the state's "open" primary. A flood of independents and Republicans entered the Democratic contest in 1972 to vote for George Wallace, who won easily despite the opposition of Democratic leaders.

The 1970s, though, was an era of mass participation in the state's primary. The Democratic primary in 1972 drew nearly 1.6 million voters. The Republican primary in 1976 attracted more than 1 million voters, who helped give Michigan's own Gerald Ford a decisive victory over Ronald Reagan.

In contrast, the decade of the 1980s gave party leaders tighter control over the process at the expense of light turnouts and controversy. In 1980, the Democratic statewide caucuses attracted only 16,000 voters. Strict rules on caucus participation that reduced turnout in 1980 were relaxed in 1984 so voters did not have to go through a pre-enrollment process. Still, the Democratic turnout barely reached 130,000.

Labor support for Walter Mondale provided him with a big win in the 1984 caucuses. But critics complained that the administration of the event was stacked in Mondale's favor. It was estimated that roughly 10 percent of the voting places were union halls. And separate ballot boxes were set up for each of the candidates, publicly discouraging any union member from casting their vote for anyone but Mondale.

In 1988, it was the Republicans who were the center of controversy. In a bid to be first on the calendar, the GOP held caucuses that were called the "Beirut of American politics." The caucuses revealed the organizational muscle of George Bush's campaign and the potency of Pat Robertson's "invisible army." But the convoluted and often rancorous nature of the process led many party leaders to favor the primary format in 1992, a move that Democratic leaders were ready to join.

Pat Buchanan targeted Michigan and its large blue-collar constituency in both 1992 and 1996. His first time out Buchanan was thrown on the defensive, as the Bush campaign pounded away at the nationalistic-sounding Buchanan for dri-

Recent Michigan Primary Results

Michigan held its first presidential primary in 1916, although no primary was held between 1928 and 1972.

	DEMOCRATS			REPUBLICANS		
Year	Turnout	Candidates	%	Turnout	Candidates	%
1996 (March 19)	142,750	UNCOMMITTED	87	524,161	BOB DOLE	51
					Pat Buchanan	34
1992 (March 17)	585,972	BILL CLINTON	51	449,133	GEORGE BUSH*	67
		Jerry Brown	26		Pat Buchanan	25
		Paul Tsongas	17			
1988	—	NO PRIMARY		—	NO PRIMARY	
1984	—	NO PRIMARY		—	NO PRIMARY	
1980 (May 20)	78,424	UNCOMMITTED	46	595,176	GEORGE BUSH	57
		Jerry Brown	29		Ronald Reagan	32
		Lyndon LaRouche	13			
1976 (May 18)	708,666	JIMMY CARTER	43	1,062,814	GERALD FORD*	65
		Morris Udall	43		Ronald Reagan	34
1972 (May 16)	1,588,073	GEORGE WALLACE	51	336,743	RICHARD NIXON*	96
		George McGovern	27			
		Hubert Humphrey	16			

Note: All candidates are listed that drew at least 10 percent of their party's primary vote. The names of winning candidates are capitalized. An asterisk (*) indicates an incumbent president.

ving a Merecedes-Benz and for referring to two Cadillacs he had bought as "lemons." It helped Bush win the Michigan primary for the second time. He had won the last Republican primary in 1980 over Ronald Reagan, and beat Buchanan even more convincingly in 1992.

Jerry Brown made his own effort on the Democratic side to harness the economic discontent of the working class. He regaled union members in his white turtleneck and a blue UAW (United Auto Workers) windbreaker. He managed to win the support of several union locals, and he even drew kind words from filmmaker Michael Moore, who chronicled the decline of Flint in the documentary *Roger and Me.*

But Brown was more successful attracting publicity than votes in the 1992 primary. Going from union hall to union hall, he stirred the passions of the assembled members, but he failed to expand his base beyond them. Clinton beat Brown by a margin of nearly 2-to-1.

Brown was gone by 1996, but Buchanan was back on the GOP side and ran better in Michigan than he had the first time. He carried seven counties and came within 5 percentage points of winning Macomb County, the quintessential suburban blue-collar constituency. Dole easily won the primary vote statewide, but Buchanan's 34 percent vote share was the highest he would receive in the 1996 primaries.

MICHIGAN DEMOCRATIC

1972

County	Total Vote	Humphrey	McGovern	Wallace	Other	Winner	Percentage of Total Vote Humphrey	McGovern	Wallace	Other
ALCONA	1,425	215	282	882	46	Wallace	15.1%	19.8%	61.9%	3.2%
ALGER	1,678	456	281	872	69	Wallace	27.2%	16.7%	52.0%	4.1%
ALLEGAN	8,248	1,021	1,902	4,845	480	Wallace	12.4%	23.1%	58.7%	5.8%
ALPENA	6,324	909	2,091	2,820	504	Wallace	14.4%	33.1%	44.6%	8.0%
ANTRIM	2,116	273	368	1,357	118	Wallace	12.9%	17.4%	64.1%	5.6%
ARENAC	1,584	205	387	927	65	Wallace	12.9%	24.4%	58.5%	4.1%
BARAGA	1,345	295	227	776	47	Wallace	21.9%	16.9%	57.7%	3.5%
BARRY	5,227	598	1,439	2,922	268	Wallace	11.4%	27.5%	55.9%	5.1%
BAY	17,883	2,448	6,956	7,350	1,129	Wallace	13.7%	38.9%	41.1%	6.3%
BENZIE	1,373	235	284	792	62	Wallace	17.1%	20.7%	57.7%	4.5%
BERRIEN	19,174	2,686	3,820	11,578	1,090	Wallace	14.0%	19.9%	60.4%	5.7%
BRANCH	4,282	607	1,238	2,151	286	Wallace	14.2%	28.9%	50.2%	6.7%
CALHOUN	18,041	2,663	5,113	9,223	1,042	Wallace	14.8%	28.3%	51.1%	5.8%
CASS	4,655	828	688	2,865	274	Wallace	17.8%	14.8%	61.5%	5.9%
CHARLEVOIX	2,787	334	766	1,536	151	Wallace	12.0%	27.5%	55.1%	5.4%
CHEBOYGAN	2,877	412	662	1,668	135	Wallace	14.3%	23.0%	58.0%	4.7%
CHIPPEWA	4,476	524	1,538	2,211	203	Wallace	11.7%	34.4%	49.4%	4.5%
CLARE	2,899	410	595	1,766	128	Wallace	14.1%	20.5%	60.9%	4.4%
CLINTON	7,734	871	2,014	4,566	283	Wallace	11.3%	26.0%	59.0%	3.7%
CRAWFORD	1,383	193	317	808	65	Wallace	14.0%	22.9%	58.4%	4.7%
DELTA	5,231	1,011	1,311	2,610	299	Wallace	19.3%	25.1%	49.9%	5.7%
DICKINSON	3,885	841	1,002	1,830	212	Wallace	21.6%	25.8%	47.1%	5.5%
EATON	11,322	1,366	3,097	6,459	400	Wallace	12.1%	27.4%	57.0%	3.5%
EMMET	2,918	381	857	1,504	176	Wallace	13.1%	29.4%	51.5%	6.0%
GENESEE	73,877	9,927	21,220	38,501	4,229	Wallace	13.4%	28.7%	52.1%	5.7%
GLADWIN	2,273	356	474	1,348	95	Wallace	15.7%	20.9%	59.3%	4.2%
GOGEBIC	3,587	995	770	1,591	231	Wallace	27.7%	21.5%	44.4%	6.4%
GRAND TRAVERSE	5,566	581	1,711	2,965	309	Wallace	10.4%	30.7%	53.3%	5.6%
GRATIOT	3,969	495	1,201	2,127	146	Wallace	12.5%	30.3%	53.6%	3.7%
HILLSDALE	4,148	574	1,036	2,331	207	Wallace	13.8%	25.0%	56.2%	5.0%
HOUGHTON	5,587	1,130	1,639	2,531	287	Wallace	20.2%	29.3%	45.3%	5.1%
HURON	4,343	421	1,023	2,651	248	Wallace	9.7%	23.6%	61.0%	5.7%
INGHAM	59,026	6,291	28,333	22,036	2,366	McGovern	10.7%	48.0%	37.3%	4.0%
IONIA	5,736	853	1,592	3,017	274	Wallace	14.9%	27.8%	52.6%	4.8%
IOSCO	3,055	495	759	1,661	140	Wallace	16.2%	24.8%	54.4%	4.6%
IRON	2,910	725	437	1,570	178	Wallace	24.9%	15.0%	54.0%	6.1%
ISABELLA	6,000	622	2,824	2,184	370	McGovern	10.4%	47.1%	36.4%	6.2%
JACKSON	19,062	2,230	4,901	10,963	968	Wallace	11.7%	25.7%	57.5%	5.1%
KALAMAZOO	29,275	2,851	10,866	13,491	2,067	Wallace	9.7%	37.1%	46.1%	7.1%
KALKASKA	1,127	146	141	781	59	Wallace	13.0%	12.5%	69.3%	5.2%
KENT	69,376	11,000	22,907	31,305	4,164	Wallace	15.9%	33.0%	45.1%	6.0%
KEWEENAW	537	134	97	277	29	Wallace	25.0%	18.1%	51.6%	5.4%
LAKE	1,305	356	193	646	110	Wallace	27.3%	14.8%	49.5%	8.4%
LAPEER	6,914	729	1,415	4,517	253	Wallace	10.5%	20.5%	65.3%	3.7%
LEELANAU	2,120	182	487	1,248	203	Wallace	8.6%	23.0%	58.9%	9.6%
LENAWEE	9,722	1,324	3,445	4,422	531	Wallace	13.6%	35.4%	45.5%	5.5%
LIVINGSTON	9,911	981	2,293	6,175	462	Wallace	9.9%	23.1%	62.3%	4.7%
LUCE	806	92	202	485	27	Wallace	11.4%	25.1%	60.2%	3.3%
MACKINAC	1,662	228	373	983	78	Wallace	13.7%	22.4%	59.1%	4.7%
MACOMB	135,854	13,734	25,410	90,473	6,237	Wallace	10.1%	18.7%	66.6%	4.6%

MICHIGAN DEMOCRATIC

1972

County	Total Vote	Humphrey	McGovern	Wallace	Other	Winner	Percentage of Total Vote: Humphrey	McGovern	Wallace	Other
MANISTEE	3,284	464	605	2,022	193	Wallace	14.1%	18.4%	61.6%	5.9%
MARQUETTE	11,026	2,600	3,192	4,711	523	Wallace	23.6%	28.9%	42.7%	4.7%
MASON	3,492	580	604	2,126	182	Wallace	16.6%	17.3%	60.9%	5.2%
MECOSTA	3,822	399	1,176	2,034	213	Wallace	10.4%	30.8%	53.2%	5.6%
MENOMINEE	4,408	928	1,152	1,959	369	Wallace	21.1%	26.1%	44.4%	8.4%
MIDLAND	10,570	1,184	4,003	4,614	769	Wallace	11.2%	37.9%	43.7%	7.3%
MISSAUKEE	1,315	141	131	1,009	34	Wallace	10.7%	10.0%	76.7%	2.6%
MONROE	14,011	2,180	3,730	7,348	753	Wallace	15.6%	26.6%	52.4%	5.4%
MONTCALM	4,867	659	1,285	2,646	277	Wallace	13.5%	26.4%	54.4%	5.7%
MONTMORENCY	1,277	186	174	854	63	Wallace	14.6%	13.6%	66.9%	4.9%
MUSKEGON	23,121	3,765	4,904	13,177	1,275	Wallace	16.3%	21.2%	57.0%	5.5%
NEWAYGO	4,241	609	876	2,548	208	Wallace	14.4%	20.7%	60.1%	4.9%
OAKLAND	186,586	21,869	54,951	100,809	8,957	Wallace	11.7%	29.5%	54.0%	4.8%
OCEANA	2,684	285	510	1,772	117	Wallace	10.6%	19.0%	66.0%	4.4%
OGEMAW	1,997	330	447	1,139	81	Wallace	16.5%	22.4%	57.0%	4.1%
ONTONAGON	2,106	519	429	1,023	135	Wallace	24.6%	20.4%	48.6%	6.4%
OSCEOLA	2,314	240	346	1,635	93	Wallace	10.4%	15.0%	70.7%	4.0%
OSCODA	786	98	128	515	45	Wallace	12.5%	16.3%	65.5%	5.7%
OTSEGO	1,705	206	402	977	120	Wallace	12.1%	23.6%	57.3%	7.0%
OTTAWA	16,363	2,070	4,885	8,647	761	Wallace	12.7%	29.9%	52.8%	4.7%
PRESQUE ISLE	2,630	331	390	1,673	236	Wallace	12.6%	14.8%	63.6%	9.0%
ROSCOMMON	2,544	361	439	1,518	226	Wallace	14.2%	17.3%	59.7%	8.9%
SAGINAW	28,049	3,684	6,231	16,561	1,573	Wallace	13.1%	22.2%	59.0%	5.6%
ST. CLAIR	19,739	2,205	4,345	12,271	918	Wallace	11.2%	22.0%	62.2%	4.7%
ST. JOSEPH	4,779	716	1,109	2,736	218	Wallace	15.0%	23.2%	57.3%	4.6%
SANILAC	5,427	454	824	3,964	185	Wallace	8.4%	15.2%	73.0%	3.4%
SCHOOLCRAFT	1,234	295	194	686	59	Wallace	23.9%	15.7%	55.6%	4.8%
SHIAWASSEE	9,483	1,192	2,837	5,092	362	Wallace	12.6%	29.9%	53.7%	3.8%
TUSCOLA	5,823	557	1,295	3,720	251	Wallace	9.6%	22.2%	63.9%	4.3%
VAN BUREN	7,212	1,012	1,430	4,388	382	Wallace	14.0%	19.8%	60.8%	5.3%
WASHTENAW	49,073	4,050	26,493	14,559	3,971	McGovern	8.3%	54.0%	29.7%	8.1%
WAYNE	542,037	117,989	122,483	253,706	47,859	Wallace	21.8%	22.6%	46.8%	8.8%
WEXFORD	3,453	406	710	2,203	134	Wallace	11.8%	20.6%	63.8%	3.9%
TOTAL	1,588,073	249,798	425,694	809,239	103,342	Wallace	15.7%	26.8%	51.0%	6.5%

MICHIGAN REPUBLICAN

1972

County	Total Vote	Nixon	Other	Winner	Percentage of Total Vote Nixon	Other
ALCONA	608	593	15	Nixon	97.5%	2.5%
ALGER	311	300	11	Nixon	96.5%	3.5%
ALLEGAN	4,177	3,956	221	Nixon	94.7%	5.3%
ALPENA	2,238	2,130	108	Nixon	95.2%	4.8%
ANTRIM	980	924	56	Nixon	94.3%	5.7%
ARENAC	548	527	21	Nixon	96.2%	3.8%
BARAGA	291	277	14	Nixon	95.2%	4.8%
BARRY	1,894	1,750	144	Nixon	92.4%	7.6%
BAY	3,313	3,129	184	Nixon	94.4%	5.6%
BENZIE	618	590	28	Nixon	95.5%	4.5%
BERRIEN	7,129	6,765	364	Nixon	94.9%	5.1%
BRANCH	1,765	1,654	111	Nixon	93.7%	6.3%
CALHOUN	5,035	4,684	351	Nixon	93.0%	7.0%
CASS	1,408	1,308	100	Nixon	92.9%	7.1%
CHARLEVOIX	1,053	977	76	Nixon	92.8%	7.2%
CHEBOYGAN	744	712	32	Nixon	95.7%	4.3%
CHIPPEWA	1,543	1,467	76	Nixon	95.1%	4.9%
CLARE	936	894	42	Nixon	95.5%	4.5%
CLINTON	2,374	2,250	124	Nixon	94.8%	5.2%
CRAWFORD	411	383	28	Nixon	93.2%	6.8%
DELTA	1,138	1,050	88	Nixon	92.3%	7.7%
DICKINSON	943	893	50	Nixon	94.7%	5.3%
EATON	3,446	3,276	170	Nixon	95.1%	4.9%
EMMET	1,268	1,175	93	Nixon	92.7%	7.3%
GENESEE	13,697	13,257	440	Nixon	96.8%	3.2%
GLADWIN	644	611	33	Nixon	94.9%	5.1%
GOGEBIC	791	749	42	Nixon	94.7%	5.3%
GRAND TRAVERSE	1,922	1,835	87	Nixon	95.5%	4.5%
GRATIOT	1,841	1,758	83	Nixon	95.5%	4.5%
HILLSDALE	2,035	1,904	131	Nixon	93.6%	6.4%
HOUGHTON	1,547	1,484	63	Nixon	95.9%	4.1%
HURON	2,063	1,924	139	Nixon	93.3%	6.7%
INGHAM	12,312	11,969	343	Nixon	97.2%	2.8%
IONIA	2,094	1,980	114	Nixon	94.6%	5.4%
IOSCO	1,291	1,245	46	Nixon	96.4%	3.6%
IRON	780	748	32	Nixon	95.9%	4.1%
ISABELLA	1,890	1,779	111	Nixon	94.1%	5.9%
JACKSON	6,105	5,832	273	Nixon	95.5%	4.5%
KALAMAZOO	7,902	7,476	426	Nixon	94.6%	5.4%
KALKASKA	322	300	22	Nixon	93.2%	6.8%
KENT	23,716	22,875	841	Nixon	96.5%	3.5%
KEWEENAW	200	195	5	Nixon	97.5%	2.5%
LAKE	310	287	23	Nixon	92.6%	7.4%
LAPEER	2,303	2,204	99	Nixon	95.7%	4.3%
LEELANAU	821	775	46	Nixon	94.4%	5.6%
LENAWEE	3,811	3,588	223	Nixon	94.1%	5.9%
LIVINGSTON	2,848	2,695	153	Nixon	94.6%	5.4%
LUCE	279	255	24	Nixon	91.4%	8.6%
MACKINAC	567	533	34	Nixon	94.0%	6.0%
MACOMB	15,335	14,704	631	Nixon	95.9%	4.1%

MICHIGAN REPUBLICAN

1972

County	Total Vote	Nixon	Other	Winner	Percentage of Total Vote Nixon	Other
MANISTEE	1,057	1,013	44	Nixon	95.8%	4.2%
MARQUETTE	2,377	2,246	131	Nixon	94.5%	5.5%
MASON	1,320	1,290	30	Nixon	97.7%	2.3%
MECOSTA	1,328	1,246	82	Nixon	93.8%	6.2%
MENOMINEE	1,555	1,477	78	Nixon	95.0%	5.0%
MIDLAND	4,133	3,982	151	Nixon	96.3%	3.7%
MISSAUKEE	645	627	18	Nixon	97.2%	2.8%
MONROE	2,874	2,731	143	Nixon	95.0%	5.0%
MONTCALM	1,894	1,766	128	Nixon	93.2%	6.8%
MONTMORENCY	353	337	16	Nixon	95.5%	4.5%
MUSKEGON	5,860	5,669	191	Nixon	96.7%	3.3%
NEWAYGO	1,902	1,802	100	Nixon	94.7%	5.3%
OAKLAND	42,367	40,485	1,882	Nixon	95.6%	4.4%
OCEANA	864	812	52	Nixon	94.0%	6.0%
OGEMAW	654	631	23	Nixon	96.5%	3.5%
ONTONAGON	657	634	23	Nixon	96.5%	3.5%
OSCEOLA	969	914	55	Nixon	94.3%	5.7%
OSCODA	361	330	31	Nixon	91.4%	8.6%
OTSEGO	464	431	33	Nixon	92.9%	7.1%
OTTAWA	8,870	8,559	311	Nixon	96.5%	3.5%
PRESQUE ISLE	735	713	22	Nixon	97.0%	3.0%
ROSCOMMON	933	885	48	Nixon	94.9%	5.1%
SAGINAW	6,846	6,621	225	Nixon	96.7%	3.3%
ST. CLAIR	5,677	5,416	261	Nixon	95.4%	4.6%
ST. JOSEPH	2,146	1,975	171	Nixon	92.0%	8.0%
SANILAC	2,556	2,501	55	Nixon	97.8%	2.2%
SCHOOLCRAFT	384	361	23	Nixon	94.0%	6.0%
SHIAWASSEE	3,127	3,007	120	Nixon	96.2%	3.8%
TUSCOLA	2,178	2,061	117	Nixon	94.6%	5.4%
VAN BUREN	2,534	2,394	140	Nixon	94.5%	5.5%
WASHTENAW	9,706	9,061	645	Nixon	93.4%	6.6%
WAYNE	66,727	64,019	2,708	Nixon	95.9%	4.1%
WEXFORD	1,093	1,030	63	Nixon	94.2%	5.8%
TOTAL	336,743	321,652	15,091	Nixon	95.5%	4.5%

MICHIGAN DEMOCRATIC

1976

County	Total Vote	Carter	Udall	Other	Winner	Percentage of Total Vote: Carter	Udall	Other
ALCONA	728	460	140	128	Carter	63.2%	19.2%	17.6%
ALGER	884	377	374	133	Carter	42.6%	42.3%	15.0%
ALLEGAN	3,339	1,848	924	567	Carter	55.3%	27.7%	17.0%
ALPENA	2,106	1,063	805	238	Carter	50.5%	38.2%	11.3%
ANTRIM	1,164	681	314	169	Carter	58.5%	27.0%	14.5%
ARENAC	805	537	156	112	Carter	66.7%	19.4%	13.9%
BARAGA	944	385	393	166	Udall	40.8%	41.6%	17.6%
BARRY	2,243	1,139	742	362	Carter	50.8%	33.1%	16.1%
BAY	9,316	5,126	2,985	1,205	Carter	55.0%	32.0%	12.9%
BENZIE	734	429	207	98	Carter	58.4%	28.2%	13.4%
BERRIEN	6,946	4,084	1,230	1,632	Carter	58.8%	17.7%	23.5%
BRANCH	1,822	998	483	341	Carter	54.8%	26.5%	18.7%
CALHOUN	7,721	4,341	2,408	972	Carter	56.2%	31.2%	12.6%
CASS	2,202	1,318	406	478	Carter	59.9%	18.4%	21.7%
CHARLEVOIX	1,374	772	376	226	Carter	56.2%	27.4%	16.4%
CHEBOYGAN	1,407	903	308	196	Carter	64.2%	21.9%	13.9%
CHIPPEWA	2,326	1,180	832	314	Carter	50.7%	35.8%	13.5%
CLARE	1,505	975	352	178	Carter	64.8%	23.4%	11.8%
CLINTON	2,792	1,327	998	467	Carter	47.5%	35.7%	16.7%
CRAWFORD	763	531	125	107	Carter	69.6%	16.4%	14.0%
DELTA	3,141	1,351	1,476	314	Udall	43.0%	47.0%	10.0%
DICKINSON	3,117	1,626	1,040	451	Carter	52.2%	33.4%	14.5%
EATON	4,678	2,268	1,783	627	Carter	48.5%	38.1%	13.4%
EMMET	1,310	677	433	200	Carter	51.7%	33.1%	15.3%
GENESEE	32,926	17,902	10,789	4,235	Carter	54.4%	32.8%	12.9%
GLADWIN	1,263	804	282	177	Carter	63.7%	22.3%	14.0%
GOGEBIC	2,663	1,254	894	515	Carter	47.1%	33.6%	19.3%
GRAND TRAVERSE	2,439	1,052	1,056	331	Udall	43.1%	43.3%	13.6%
GRATIOT	1,772	1,053	489	230	Carter	59.4%	27.6%	13.0%
HILLSDALE	1,660	893	492	275	Carter	53.8%	29.6%	16.6%
HOUGHTON	3,086	1,300	1,312	474	Udall	42.1%	42.5%	15.4%
HURON	1,945	1,285	337	323	Carter	66.1%	17.3%	16.6%
INGHAM	25,016	7,562	14,954	2,500	Udall	30.2%	59.8%	10.0%
IONIA	2,472	1,410	701	361	Carter	57.0%	28.4%	14.6%
IOSCO	1,627	1,011	416	200	Carter	62.1%	25.6%	12.3%
IRON	2,636	1,270	954	412	Carter	48.2%	36.2%	15.6%
ISABELLA	2,332	1,078	965	289	Carter	46.2%	41.4%	12.4%
JACKSON	8,640	4,059	3,365	1,216	Carter	47.0%	38.9%	14.1%
KALAMAZOO	11,556	4,417	5,615	1,524	Udall	38.2%	48.6%	13.2%
KALKASKA	804	483	201	120	Carter	60.1%	25.0%	14.9%
KENT	23,994	11,598	9,302	3,094	Carter	48.3%	38.8%	12.9%
KEWEENAW	299	141	104	54	Carter	47.2%	34.8%	18.1%
LAKE	738	460	158	120	Carter	62.3%	21.4%	16.3%
LAPEER	3,529	1,893	1,143	493	Carter	53.6%	32.4%	14.0%
LEELANAU	904	500	262	142	Carter	55.3%	29.0%	15.7%
LENAWEE	4,598	2,351	1,501	746	Carter	51.1%	32.6%	16.2%
LIVINGSTON	5,038	2,122	2,185	731	Udall	42.1%	43.4%	14.5%
LUCE	451	253	126	72	Carter	56.1%	27.9%	16.0%
MACKINAC	825	476	214	135	Carter	57.7%	25.9%	16.4%
MACOMB	59,893	20,941	28,997	9,955	Udall	35.0%	48.4%	16.6%

MICHIGAN DEMOCRATIC

1976

County	Total Vote	Carter	Udall	Other	Winner	Percentage of Total Vote Carter	Udall	Other
MANISTEE	1,300	736	350	214	Carter	56.6%	26.9%	16.5%
MARQUETTE	5,830	2,051	3,116	663	Udall	35.2%	53.4%	11.4%
MASON	1,480	822	419	239	Carter	55.5%	28.3%	16.1%
MECOSTA	1,466	803	445	218	Carter	54.8%	30.4%	14.9%
MENOMINEE	1,763	1,000	461	302	Carter	56.7%	26.1%	17.1%
MIDLAND	4,465	2,176	1,673	616	Carter	48.7%	37.5%	13.8%
MISSAUKEE	576	365	98	113	Carter	63.4%	17.0%	19.6%
MONROE	8,439	3,926	2,950	1,563	Carter	46.5%	35.0%	18.5%
MONTCALM	2,137	1,228	615	294	Carter	57.5%	28.8%	13.8%
MONTMORENCY	606	408	87	111	Carter	67.3%	14.4%	18.3%
MUSKEGON	11,559	5,476	3,869	2,214	Carter	47.4%	33.5%	19.2%
NEWAYGO	1,785	939	539	307	Carter	52.6%	30.2%	17.2%
OAKLAND	84,930	25,148	49,959	9,823	Udall	29.6%	58.8%	11.6%
OCEANA	1,024	534	291	199	Carter	52.1%	28.4%	19.4%
OGEMAW	1,064	697	228	139	Carter	65.5%	21.4%	13.1%
ONTONAGON	1,449	794	353	302	Carter	54.8%	24.4%	20.8%
OSCEOLA	1,023	596	242	185	Carter	58.3%	23.7%	18.1%
OSCODA	352	218	69	65	Carter	61.9%	19.6%	18.5%
OTSEGO	988	643	217	128	Carter	65.1%	22.0%	13.0%
OTTAWA	6,101	3,170	2,035	896	Carter	52.0%	33.4%	14.7%
PRESQUE ISLE	1,135	686	250	199	Carter	60.4%	22.0%	17.5%
ROSCOMMON	1,609	1,033	321	255	Carter	64.2%	20.0%	15.8%
SAGINAW	11,697	6,972	3,119	1,606	Carter	59.6%	26.7%	13.7%
ST. CLAIR	8,330	3,526	3,481	1,323	Carter	42.3%	41.8%	15.9%
ST. JOSEPH	1,857	1,074	433	350	Carter	57.8%	23.3%	18.8%
SANILAC	2,305	1,363	603	339	Carter	59.1%	26.2%	14.7%
SCHOOLCRAFT	672	327	244	101	Carter	48.7%	36.3%	15.0%
SHIAWASSEE	4,618	2,378	1,466	774	Carter	51.5%	31.7%	16.8%
TUSCOLA	2,796	1,762	629	405	Carter	63.0%	22.5%	14.5%
VAN BUREN	2,940	1,710	687	543	Carter	58.2%	23.4%	18.5%
WASHTENAW	24,678	5,955	16,978	1,745	Udall	24.1%	68.8%	7.1%
WAYNE	239,778	106,256	102,367	31,155	Carter	44.3%	42.7%	13.0%
WEXFORD	1,469	853	436	180	Carter	58.1%	29.7%	12.3%
TOTAL	708,694	307,589	305,134	95,971	Carter	43.4%	43.1%	13.5%
Certified Totals	708,666	307,559	305,134	95,973	Carter	43.4%	43.1%	13.5%

MICHIGAN REPUBLICAN

1976

County	Total Vote	Ford	Reagan	Other	Winner	Percentage of Total Vote Ford	Reagan	Other
ALCONA	1,500	846	632	22	Ford	56.4%	42.1%	1.5%
ALGER	972	568	397	7	Ford	58.4%	40.8%	0.7%
ALLEGAN	11,699	8,638	2,982	79	Ford	73.8%	25.5%	0.7%
ALPENA	3,780	2,327	1,414	39	Ford	61.6%	37.4%	1.0%
ANTRIM	2,923	1,806	1,073	44	Ford	61.8%	36.7%	1.5%
ARENAC	1,720	1,012	699	9	Ford	58.8%	40.6%	0.5%
BARAGA	1,129	742	372	15	Ford	65.7%	32.9%	1.3%
BARRY	6,122	4,213	1,870	39	Ford	68.8%	30.5%	0.6%
BAY	14,047	8,489	5,445	113	Ford	60.4%	38.8%	0.8%
BENZIE	1,809	1,231	564	14	Ford	68.0%	31.2%	0.8%
BERRIEN	23,369	14,904	8,273	192	Ford	63.8%	35.4%	0.8%
BRANCH	4,539	2,704	1,787	48	Ford	59.6%	39.4%	1.1%
CALHOUN	16,587	10,819	5,685	83	Ford	65.2%	34.3%	0.5%
CASS	5,599	3,409	2,125	65	Ford	60.9%	38.0%	1.2%
CHARLEVOIX	2,933	1,864	1,024	45	Ford	63.6%	34.9%	1.5%
CHEBOYGAN	2,757	1,658	1,075	24	Ford	60.1%	39.0%	0.9%
CHIPPEWA	4,352	2,381	1,900	71	Ford	54.7%	43.7%	1.6%
CLARE	2,950	1,711	1,224	15	Ford	58.0%	41.5%	0.5%
CLINTON	7,385	4,685	2,659	41	Ford	63.4%	36.0%	0.6%
CRAWFORD	1,230	799	421	10	Ford	65.0%	34.2%	0.8%
DELTA	3,994	2,199	1,775	20	Ford	55.1%	44.4%	0.5%
DICKINSON	4,047	2,445	1,575	27	Ford	60.4%	38.9%	0.7%
EATON	11,925	8,089	3,762	74	Ford	67.8%	31.5%	0.6%
EMMET	3,024	2,017	981	26	Ford	66.7%	32.4%	0.9%
GENESEE	45,764	27,813	17,669	282	Ford	60.8%	38.6%	0.6%
GLADWIN	2,328	1,284	1,019	25	Ford	55.2%	43.8%	1.1%
GOGEBIC	2,933	1,300	1,598	35	Reagan	44.3%	54.5%	1.2%
GRAND TRAVERSE	7,153	4,748	2,365	40	Ford	66.4%	33.1%	0.6%
GRATIOT	5,481	3,732	1,701	48	Ford	68.1%	31.0%	0.9%
HILLSDALE	5,111	2,796	2,266	49	Ford	54.7%	44.3%	1.0%
HOUGHTON	4,527	2,752	1,734	41	Ford	60.8%	38.3%	0.9%
HURON	5,954	3,864	2,054	36	Ford	64.9%	34.5%	0.6%
INGHAM	37,833	27,457	10,108	268	Ford	72.6%	26.7%	0.7%
IONIA	7,156	5,207	1,904	45	Ford	72.8%	26.6%	0.6%
IOSCO	3,656	2,002	1,595	59	Ford	54.8%	43.6%	1.6%
IRON	2,785	1,539	1,209	37	Ford	55.3%	43.4%	1.3%
ISABELLA	5,083	3,309	1,751	23	Ford	65.1%	34.4%	0.5%
JACKSON	18,012	11,429	6,460	123	Ford	63.5%	35.9%	0.7%
KALAMAZOO	27,559	19,293	8,095	171	Ford	70.0%	29.4%	0.6%
KALKASKA	1,492	852	624	16	Ford	57.1%	41.8%	1.1%
KENT	80,480	68,077	12,018	385	Ford	84.6%	14.9%	0.5%
KEWEENAW	417	250	161	6	Ford	60.0%	38.6%	1.4%
LAKE	1,193	738	444	11	Ford	61.9%	37.2%	0.9%
LAPEER	6,934	4,086	2,776	72	Ford	58.9%	40.0%	1.0%
LEELANAU	2,556	1,729	815	12	Ford	67.6%	31.9%	0.5%
LENAWEE	9,453	5,779	3,616	58	Ford	61.1%	38.3%	0.6%
LIVINGSTON	10,619	6,119	4,391	109	Ford	57.6%	41.4%	1.0%
LUCE	1,033	625	387	21	Ford	60.5%	37.5%	2.0%
MACKINAC	1,778	1,101	650	27	Ford	61.9%	36.6%	1.5%
MACOMB	66,893	35,800	30,685	408	Ford	53.5%	45.9%	0.6%

MICHIGAN REPUBLICAN

1976

County	Total Vote	Ford	Reagan	Other	Winner	Percentage of Total Vote Ford	Reagan	Other
MANISTEE	3,088	2,017	1,051	20	Ford	65.3%	34.0%	0.6%
MARQUETTE	6,137	4,054	2,031	52	Ford	66.1%	33.1%	0.8%
MASON	4,238	2,612	1,594	32	Ford	61.6%	37.6%	0.8%
MECOSTA	3,691	2,372	1,291	28	Ford	64.3%	35.0%	0.8%
MENOMINEE	3,003	1,702	1,276	25	Ford	56.7%	42.5%	0.8%
MIDLAND	11,445	7,482	3,804	159	Ford	65.4%	33.2%	1.4%
MISSAUKEE	1,683	1,133	542	8	Ford	67.3%	32.2%	0.5%
MONROE	10,103	5,571	4,395	137	Ford	55.1%	43.5%	1.4%
MONTCALM	5,769	4,202	1,529	38	Ford	72.8%	26.5%	0.7%
MONTMORENCY	1,345	731	594	20	Ford	54.3%	44.2%	1.5%
MUSKEGON	23,511	15,086	8,197	228	Ford	64.2%	34.9%	1.0%
NEWAYGO	5,282	3,469	1,765	48	Ford	65.7%	33.4%	0.9%
OAKLAND	127,628	84,185	42,362	1,081	Ford	66.0%	33.2%	0.8%
OCEANA	2,912	1,904	978	30	Ford	65.4%	33.6%	1.0%
OGEMAW	2,211	1,199	987	25	Ford	54.2%	44.6%	1.1%
ONTONAGON	1,824	953	830	41	Ford	52.2%	45.5%	2.2%
OSCEOLA	2,676	1,710	943	23	Ford	63.9%	35.2%	0.9%
OSCODA	805	513	285	7	Ford	63.7%	35.4%	0.9%
OTSEGO	1,874	1,171	682	21	Ford	62.5%	36.4%	1.1%
OTTAWA	29,402	24,970	4,335	97	Ford	84.9%	14.7%	0.3%
PRESQUE ISLE	2,140	1,255	868	17	Ford	58.6%	40.6%	0.8%
ROSCOMMON	3,088	1,980	1,070	38	Ford	64.1%	34.7%	1.2%
SAGINAW	26,332	17,730	8,410	192	Ford	67.3%	31.9%	0.7%
ST. CLAIR	16,809	9,499	7,183	127	Ford	56.5%	42.7%	0.8%
ST. JOSEPH	6,594	3,959	2,563	72	Ford	60.0%	38.9%	1.1%
SANILAC	6,726	4,001	2,680	45	Ford	59.5%	39.8%	0.7%
SCHOOLCRAFT	1,119	614	494	11	Ford	54.9%	44.1%	1.0%
SHIAWASSEE	9,693	5,791	3,839	63	Ford	59.7%	39.6%	0.6%
TUSCOLA	6,727	4,357	2,310	60	Ford	64.8%	34.3%	0.9%
VAN BUREN	7,890	4,944	2,888	58	Ford	62.7%	36.6%	0.7%
WASHTENAW	29,474	20,723	8,570	181	Ford	70.3%	29.1%	0.6%
WAYNE	189,766	113,063	74,661	2,042	Ford	59.6%	39.3%	1.1%
WEXFORD	3,266	1,998	1,236	32	Ford	61.2%	37.8%	1.0%
TOTAL	1,062,826	690,187	364,052	8,587	Ford	64.9%	34.3%	0.8%
Certified Totals	1,062,814	690,180	364,052	8,582	Ford	64.9%	34.3%	0.8%

MICHIGAN REPUBLICAN

1980

County	Total Vote	Bush	Reagan	Other	Winner	Percentage of Total Vote Bush	Reagan	Other
ALCONA	915	475	336	104	Bush	51.9%	36.7%	11.4%
ALGER	533	263	188	82	Bush	49.3%	35.3%	15.4%
ALLEGAN	4,683	2,168	2,035	480	Bush	46.3%	43.5%	10.2%
ALPENA	1,881	1,164	502	215	Bush	61.9%	26.7%	11.4%
ANTRIM	1,860	1,004	591	265	Bush	54.0%	31.8%	14.2%
ARENAC	987	525	382	80	Bush	53.2%	38.7%	8.1%
BARAGA	478	265	166	47	Bush	55.4%	34.7%	9.8%
BARRY	2,071	1,121	714	236	Bush	54.1%	34.5%	11.4%
BAY	5,859	3,488	1,755	616	Bush	59.5%	30.0%	10.5%
BENZIE	958	506	328	124	Bush	52.8%	34.2%	12.9%
BERRIEN	8,269	3,173	4,032	1,064	Reagan	38.4%	48.8%	12.9%
BRANCH	1,913	847	818	248	Bush	44.3%	42.8%	13.0%
CALHOUN	6,405	3,774	1,881	750	Bush	58.9%	29.4%	11.7%
CASS	2,034	794	983	257	Reagan	39.0%	48.3%	12.6%
CHARLEVOIX	1,293	693	382	218	Bush	53.6%	29.5%	16.9%
CHEBOYGAN	1,450	749	500	201	Bush	51.7%	34.5%	13.9%
CHIPPEWA	1,842	1,054	616	172	Bush	57.2%	33.4%	9.3%
CLARE	1,562	755	631	176	Bush	48.3%	40.4%	11.3%
CLINTON	5,380	3,022	1,737	621	Bush	56.2%	32.3%	11.5%
CRAWFORD	627	357	216	54	Bush	56.9%	34.4%	8.6%
DELTA	1,481	888	465	128	Bush	60.0%	31.4%	8.6%
DICKINSON	1,360	752	476	132	Bush	55.3%	35.0%	9.7%
EATON	6,210	3,694	1,750	766	Bush	59.5%	28.2%	12.3%
EMMET	1,621	931	464	226	Bush	57.4%	28.6%	13.9%
GENESEE	41,455	23,978	12,813	4,664	Bush	57.8%	30.9%	11.3%
GLADWIN	1,361	723	519	119	Bush	53.1%	38.1%	8.7%
GOGEBIC	1,006	356	511	139	Reagan	35.4%	50.8%	13.8%
GRAND TRAVERSE	3,323	2,050	940	333	Bush	61.7%	28.3%	10.0%
GRATIOT	2,228	1,170	739	319	Bush	52.5%	33.2%	14.3%
HILLSDALE	2,701	1,290	1,157	254	Bush	47.8%	42.8%	9.4%
HOUGHTON	1,969	1,260	505	204	Bush	64.0%	25.6%	10.4%
HURON	2,938	1,533	1,113	292	Bush	52.2%	37.9%	9.9%
INGHAM	19,494	12,038	4,442	3,014	Bush	61.8%	22.8%	15.5%
IONIA	2,637	1,567	783	287	Bush	59.4%	29.7%	10.9%
IOSCO	1,785	928	703	154	Bush	52.0%	39.4%	8.6%
IRON	871	440	319	112	Bush	50.5%	36.6%	12.9%
ISABELLA	3,304	1,655	1,212	437	Bush	50.1%	36.7%	13.2%
JACKSON	8,389	5,177	2,578	634	Bush	61.7%	30.7%	7.6%
KALAMAZOO	9,440	5,162	2,858	1,420	Bush	54.7%	30.3%	15.0%
KALKASKA	723	345	304	74	Bush	47.7%	42.0%	10.2%
KENT	26,328	16,222	6,668	3,438	Bush	61.6%	25.3%	13.1%
KEWEENAW	265	157	86	22	Bush	59.2%	32.5%	8.3%
LAKE	628	329	220	79	Bush	52.4%	35.0%	12.6%
LAPEER	3,848	2,270	1,293	285	Bush	59.0%	33.6%	7.4%
LEELANAU	1,916	1,100	567	249	Bush	57.4%	29.6%	13.0%
LENAWEE	4,975	2,764	1,747	464	Bush	55.6%	35.1%	9.3%
LIVINGSTON	6,825	3,966	2,298	561	Bush	58.1%	33.7%	8.2%
LUCE	410	216	130	64	Bush	52.7%	31.7%	15.6%
MACKINAC	1,015	534	346	135	Bush	52.6%	34.1%	13.3%
MACOMB	44,171	25,080	15,353	3,738	Bush	56.8%	34.8%	8.5%

MICHIGAN REPUBLICAN

1980

County	Total Vote	Bush	Reagan	Other	Winner	Percentage of Total Vote Bush	Reagan	Other
MANISTEE	1,401	718	485	198	Bush	51.2%	34.6%	14.1%
MARQUETTE	5,214	3,117	1,407	690	Bush	59.8%	27.0%	13.2%
MASON	1,860	930	708	222	Bush	50.0%	38.1%	11.9%
MECOSTA	1,617	901	558	158	Bush	55.7%	34.5%	9.8%
MENOMINEE	1,345	562	623	160	Reagan	41.8%	46.3%	11.9%
MIDLAND	10,340	5,969	2,797	1,574	Bush	57.7%	27.1%	15.2%
MISSAUKEE	786	384	304	98	Bush	48.9%	38.7%	12.5%
MONROE	7,364	3,908	2,602	854	Bush	53.1%	35.3%	11.6%
MONTCALM	2,489	1,372	809	308	Bush	55.1%	32.5%	12.4%
MONTMORENCY	1,224	601	460	163	Bush	49.1%	37.6%	13.3%
MUSKEGON	7,993	4,194	2,943	856	Bush	52.5%	36.8%	10.7%
NEWAYGO	2,200	1,159	804	237	Bush	52.7%	36.5%	10.8%
OAKLAND	87,755	54,564	24,970	8,221	Bush	62.2%	28.5%	9.4%
OCEANA	1,420	728	526	166	Bush	51.3%	37.0%	11.7%
OGEMAW	1,050	563	367	120	Bush	53.6%	35.0%	11.4%
ONTONAGON	721	305	322	94	Reagan	42.3%	44.7%	13.0%
OSCEOLA	1,371	727	469	175	Bush	53.0%	34.2%	12.8%
OSCODA	586	269	267	50	Bush	45.9%	45.6%	8.5%
OTSEGO	978	555	306	117	Bush	56.7%	31.3%	12.0%
OTTAWA	11,731	6,560	4,135	1,036	Bush	55.9%	35.2%	8.8%
PRESQUE ISLE	978	500	358	120	Bush	51.1%	36.6%	12.3%
ROSCOMMON	1,640	827	646	167	Bush	50.4%	39.4%	10.2%
SAGINAW	10,384	6,214	3,167	1,003	Bush	59.8%	30.5%	9.7%
ST. CLAIR	10,144	5,743	3,496	905	Bush	56.6%	34.5%	8.9%
ST. JOSEPH	2,117	914	913	290	Bush	43.2%	43.1%	13.7%
SANILAC	4,033	2,084	1,692	257	Bush	51.7%	42.0%	6.4%
SCHOOLCRAFT	379	197	140	42	Bush	52.0%	36.9%	11.1%
SHIAWASSEE	4,611	2,691	1,441	479	Bush	58.4%	31.3%	10.4%
TUSCOLA	3,028	1,665	1,084	279	Bush	55.0%	35.8%	9.2%
VAN BUREN	3,269	1,493	1,355	421	Bush	45.7%	41.4%	12.9%
WASHTENAW	18,038	11,969	3,815	2,254	Bush	66.4%	21.1%	12.5%
WAYNE	129,267	73,701	42,347	13,219	Bush	57.0%	32.8%	10.2%
WEXFORD	2,166	1,142	716	308	Bush	52.7%	33.1%	14.2%
TOTAL	595,176	341,998	189,184	63,994	Bush	57.5%	31.8%	10.8%

MICHIGAN DEMOCRATIC

1992

County	Total Vote	Brown	Clinton	Tsongas	Other	Winner	Percentage of Total Vote Brown	Clinton	Tsongas	Other
ALCONA	533	130	307	68	28	Clinton	24.4%	57.6%	12.8%	5.3%
ALGER	511	215	189	78	29	Brown	42.1%	37.0%	15.3%	5.7%
ALLEGAN	2,667	853	1,147	538	129	Clinton	32.0%	43.0%	20.2%	4.8%
ALPENA	1,664	493	791	220	160	Clinton	29.6%	47.5%	13.2%	9.6%
ANTRIM	753	262	285	157	49	Clinton	34.8%	37.8%	20.8%	6.5%
ARENAC	769	196	450	87	36	Clinton	25.5%	58.5%	11.3%	4.7%
BARAGA	438	132	223	54	29	Clinton	30.1%	50.9%	12.3%	6.6%
BARRY	1,785	518	798	338	131	Clinton	29.0%	44.7%	18.9%	7.3%
BAY	7,820	2,084	3,537	1,399	800	Clinton	26.6%	45.2%	17.9%	10.2%
BENZIE	644	186	261	138	59	Clinton	28.9%	40.5%	21.4%	9.2%
BERRIEN	5,838	1,312	2,993	1,197	336	Clinton	22.5%	51.3%	20.5%	5.8%
BRANCH	1,273	240	706	217	110	Clinton	18.9%	55.5%	17.0%	8.6%
CALHOUN	4,843	1,095	2,601	908	239	Clinton	22.6%	53.7%	18.7%	4.9%
CASS	1,680	445	862	274	99	Clinton	26.5%	51.3%	16.3%	5.9%
CHARLEVOIX	887	321	318	197	51	Brown	36.2%	35.9%	22.2%	5.7%
CHEBOYGAN	929	221	470	170	68	Clinton	23.8%	50.6%	18.3%	7.3%
CHIPPEWA	1,711	443	831	313	124	Clinton	25.9%	48.6%	18.3%	7.2%
CLARE	1,246	303	737	138	68	Clinton	24.3%	59.1%	11.1%	5.5%
CLINTON	2,444	659	1,132	488	165	Clinton	27.0%	46.3%	20.0%	6.8%
CRAWFORD	413	128	185	71	29	Clinton	31.0%	44.8%	17.2%	7.0%
DELTA	1,834	575	812	330	117	Clinton	31.4%	44.3%	18.0%	6.4%
DICKINSON	1,513	491	690	243	89	Clinton	32.5%	45.6%	16.1%	5.9%
EATON	4,005	898	1,844	988	275	Clinton	22.4%	46.0%	24.7%	6.9%
EMMET	891	366	261	216	48	Brown	41.1%	29.3%	24.2%	5.4%
GENESEE	32,721	9,036	18,404	3,174	2,107	Clinton	27.6%	56.2%	9.7%	6.4%
GLADWIN	1,107	274	616	148	69	Clinton	24.8%	55.6%	13.4%	6.2%
GOGEBIC	702	191	328	130	53	Clinton	27.2%	46.7%	18.5%	7.5%
GRAND TRAVERSE	2,100	743	621	635	101	Brown	35.4%	29.6%	30.2%	4.8%
GRATIOT	1,101	265	573	187	76	Clinton	24.1%	52.0%	17.0%	6.9%
HILLSDALE	1,208	293	598	224	93	Clinton	24.3%	49.5%	18.5%	7.7%
HOUGHTON	1,759	585	666	410	98	Clinton	33.3%	37.9%	23.3%	5.6%
HURON	1,466	342	826	209	89	Clinton	23.3%	56.3%	14.3%	6.1%
INGHAM	19,494	5,145	8,215	5,121	1,013	Clinton	26.4%	42.1%	26.3%	5.2%
IONIA	1,581	396	793	286	106	Clinton	25.0%	50.2%	18.1%	6.7%
IOSCO	1,382	340	744	218	80	Clinton	24.6%	53.8%	15.8%	5.8%
IRON	1,092	363	483	183	63	Clinton	33.2%	44.2%	16.8%	5.8%
ISABELLA	1,967	670	681	430	186	Clinton	34.1%	34.6%	21.9%	9.5%
JACKSON	4,933	1,213	2,480	945	295	Clinton	24.6%	50.3%	19.2%	6.0%
KALAMAZOO	10,408	3,387	3,361	3,012	648	Brown	32.5%	32.3%	28.9%	6.2%
KALKASKA	427	114	207	74	32	Clinton	26.7%	48.5%	17.3%	7.5%
KENT	22,177	5,978	9,506	5,133	1,560	Clinton	27.0%	42.9%	23.1%	7.0%
KEWEENAW	195	64	77	41	13	Clinton	32.8%	39.5%	21.0%	6.7%
LAKE	650	129	411	66	44	Clinton	19.8%	63.2%	10.2%	6.8%
LAPEER	3,369	1,229	1,472	423	245	Clinton	36.5%	43.7%	12.6%	7.3%
LEELANAU	926	337	267	271	51	Brown	36.4%	28.8%	29.3%	5.5%
LENAWEE	3,703	1,255	1,759	541	148	Clinton	33.9%	47.5%	14.6%	4.0%
LIVINGSTON	5,258	1,861	1,958	1,146	293	Clinton	35.4%	37.2%	21.8%	5.6%
LUCE	344	69	162	47	66	Clinton	20.1%	47.1%	13.7%	19.2%
MACKINAC	580	153	254	124	49	Clinton	26.4%	43.8%	21.4%	8.4%
MACOMB	44,203	12,952	20,658	7,019	3,574	Clinton	29.3%	46.7%	15.9%	8.1%

MICHIGAN DEMOCRATIC

1992

County	Total Vote	Brown	Clinton	Tsongas	Other	Winner	Percentage of Total Vote Brown	Clinton	Tsongas	Other
MANISTEE	1,028	296	465	201	66	Clinton	28.8%	45.2%	19.6%	6.4%
MARQUETTE	3,598	1,540	1,156	654	248	Brown	42.8%	32.1%	18.2%	6.9%
MASON	1,329	342	668	248	71	Clinton	25.7%	50.3%	18.7%	5.3%
MECOSTA	1,146	321	527	229	69	Clinton	28.0%	46.0%	20.0%	6.0%
MENOMINEE	1,100	298	505	217	80	Clinton	27.1%	45.9%	19.7%	7.3%
MIDLAND	3,678	938	1,418	1,094	228	Clinton	25.5%	38.6%	29.7%	6.2%
MISSAUKEE	436	122	232	56	26	Clinton	28.0%	53.2%	12.8%	6.0%
MONROE	7,113	2,401	3,124	1,028	560	Clinton	33.8%	43.9%	14.5%	7.9%
MONTCALM	1,600	432	865	215	88	Clinton	27.0%	54.1%	13.4%	5.5%
MONTMORENCY	441	102	241	66	32	Clinton	23.1%	54.6%	15.0%	7.3%
MUSKEGON	8,007	1,684	4,585	1,154	584	Clinton	21.0%	57.3%	14.4%	7.3%
NEWAYGO	1,506	360	865	184	97	Clinton	23.9%	57.4%	12.2%	6.4%
OAKLAND	70,367	18,110	31,152	16,245	4,860	Clinton	25.7%	44.3%	23.1%	6.9%
OCEANA	873	233	470	126	44	Clinton	26.7%	53.8%	14.4%	5.0%
OGEMAW	1,059	238	627	135	59	Clinton	22.5%	59.2%	12.7%	5.6%
ONTONAGON	630	163	325	85	57	Clinton	25.9%	51.6%	13.5%	9.0%
OSCEOLA	797	229	434	80	54	Clinton	28.7%	54.5%	10.0%	6.8%
OSCODA	330	96	180	37	17	Clinton	29.1%	54.5%	11.2%	5.2%
OTSEGO	664	225	264	132	43	Clinton	33.9%	39.8%	19.9%	6.5%
OTTAWA	5,066	1,483	1,930	1,328	325	Clinton	29.3%	38.1%	26.2%	6.4%
PRESQUE ISLE	693	150	398	99	46	Clinton	21.6%	57.4%	14.3%	6.6%
ROSCOMMON	1,118	335	589	131	63	Clinton	30.0%	52.7%	11.7%	5.6%
SAGINAW	10,545	2,566	5,924	1,415	640	Clinton	24.3%	56.2%	13.4%	6.1%
ST. CLAIR	6,579	2,089	3,069	974	447	Clinton	31.8%	46.6%	14.8%	6.8%
ST. JOSEPH	1,537	407	735	292	103	Clinton	26.5%	47.8%	19.0%	6.7%
SANILAC	1,523	413	813	191	106	Clinton	27.1%	53.4%	12.5%	7.0%
SCHOOLCRAFT	453	127	229	71	26	Clinton	28.0%	50.6%	15.7%	5.7%
SHIAWASSEE	3,365	1,029	1,663	452	221	Clinton	30.6%	49.4%	13.4%	6.6%
TUSCOLA	2,435	738	1,218	316	163	Clinton	30.3%	50.0%	13.0%	6.7%
VAN BUREN	2,638	725	1,260	495	158	Clinton	27.5%	47.8%	18.8%	6.0%
WASHTENAW	29,527	10,502	8,872	8,892	1,261	Brown	35.6%	30.0%	30.1%	4.3%
WAYNE	201,738	42,478	123,350	20,966	14,944	Clinton	21.1%	61.1%	10.4%	7.4%
WEXFORD	1,109	278	577	185	69	Clinton	25.1%	52.0%	16.7%	6.2%
TOTAL	585,972	151,400	297,280	97,017	40,275	Clinton	25.8%	50.7%	16.6%	6.9%

MICHIGAN REPUBLICAN

1992

County	Total Vote	Buchanan	Bush	Other	Winner	Percentage of Total Vote Buchanan	Bush	Other
ALCONA	725	232	430	63	Bush	32.0%	59.3%	8.7%
ALGER	289	80	197	12	Bush	27.7%	68.2%	4.2%
ALLEGAN	5,734	1,360	4,006	368	Bush	23.7%	69.9%	6.4%
ALPENA	1,452	473	871	108	Bush	32.6%	60.0%	7.4%
ANTRIM	1,193	329	790	74	Bush	27.6%	66.2%	6.2%
ARENAC	550	122	389	39	Bush	22.2%	70.7%	7.1%
BARAGA	226	78	129	19	Bush	34.5%	57.1%	8.4%
BARRY	2,558	606	1,750	202	Bush	23.7%	68.4%	7.9%
BAY	4,904	1,668	2,829	407	Bush	34.0%	57.7%	8.3%
BENZIE	810	223	534	53	Bush	27.5%	65.9%	6.5%
BERRIEN	9,430	2,119	6,739	572	Bush	22.5%	71.5%	6.1%
BRANCH	1,948	428	1,369	151	Bush	22.0%	70.3%	7.8%
CALHOUN	5,031	1,140	3,542	349	Bush	22.7%	70.4%	6.9%
CASS	2,009	560	1,282	167	Bush	27.9%	63.8%	8.3%
CHARLEVOIX	1,099	352	660	87	Bush	32.0%	60.1%	7.9%
CHEBOYGAN	1,008	323	611	74	Bush	32.0%	60.6%	7.3%
CHIPPEWA	1,975	524	1,276	175	Bush	26.5%	64.6%	8.9%
CLARE	1,322	338	875	109	Bush	25.6%	66.2%	8.2%
CLINTON	3,509	1,012	2,283	214	Bush	28.8%	65.1%	6.1%
CRAWFORD	621	201	386	34	Bush	32.4%	62.2%	5.5%
DELTA	1,013	274	658	81	Bush	27.0%	65.0%	8.0%
DICKINSON	770	221	495	54	Bush	28.7%	64.3%	7.0%
EATON	5,611	1,391	3,823	397	Bush	24.8%	68.1%	7.1%
EMMET	1,211	306	830	75	Bush	25.3%	68.5%	6.2%
GENESEE	12,449	3,263	7,921	1,265	Bush	26.2%	63.6%	10.2%
GLADWIN	834	180	589	65	Bush	21.6%	70.6%	7.8%
GOGEBIC	337	113	200	24	Bush	33.5%	59.3%	7.1%
GRAND TRAVERSE	3,440	1,056	2,204	180	Bush	30.7%	64.1%	5.2%
GRATIOT	1,598	385	1,078	135	Bush	24.1%	67.5%	8.4%
HILLSDALE	2,227	478	1,579	170	Bush	21.5%	70.9%	7.6%
HOUGHTON	1,106	361	665	80	Bush	32.6%	60.1%	7.2%
HURON	1,951	495	1,295	161	Bush	25.4%	66.4%	8.3%
INGHAM	14,310	3,346	9,932	1,032	Bush	23.4%	69.4%	7.2%
IONIA	2,220	585	1,485	150	Bush	26.4%	66.9%	6.8%
IOSCO	1,586	419	1,041	126	Bush	26.4%	65.6%	7.9%
IRON	486	132	302	52	Bush	27.2%	62.1%	10.7%
ISABELLA	1,976	628	1,196	152	Bush	31.8%	60.5%	7.7%
JACKSON	6,516	1,373	4,716	427	Bush	21.1%	72.4%	6.6%
KALAMAZOO	10,761	2,437	7,601	723	Bush	22.6%	70.6%	6.7%
KALKASKA	564	159	378	27	Bush	28.2%	67.0%	4.8%
KENT	37,075	7,543	27,246	2,286	Bush	20.3%	73.5%	6.2%
KEWEENAW	133	36	91	6	Bush	27.1%	68.4%	4.5%
LAKE	490	114	327	49	Bush	23.3%	66.7%	10.0%
LAPEER	3,538	1,061	2,150	327	Bush	30.0%	60.8%	9.2%
LEELANAU	1,269	356	836	77	Bush	28.1%	65.9%	6.1%
LENAWEE	3,866	931	2,616	319	Bush	24.1%	67.7%	8.3%
LIVINGSTON	7,141	1,997	4,563	581	Bush	28.0%	63.9%	8.1%
LUCE	610	138	386	86	Bush	22.6%	63.3%	14.1%
MACKINAC	863	184	601	78	Bush	21.3%	69.6%	9.0%
MACOMB	35,975	10,538	22,300	3,137	Bush	29.3%	62.0%	8.7%

MICHIGAN REPUBLICAN

1992

County	Total Vote	Buchanan	Bush	Other	Winner	Percentage of Total Vote Buchanan	Bush	Other
MANISTEE	1,125	341	695	89	Bush	30.3%	61.8%	7.9%
MARQUETTE	1,551	445	979	127	Bush	28.7%	63.1%	8.2%
MASON	1,861	414	1,328	119	Bush	22.2%	71.4%	6.4%
MECOSTA	1,736	444	1,160	132	Bush	25.6%	66.8%	7.6%
MENOMINEE	953	219	661	73	Bush	23.0%	69.4%	7.7%
MIDLAND	5,685	1,352	3,945	388	Bush	23.8%	69.4%	6.8%
MISSAUKEE	957	211	657	89	Bush	22.0%	68.7%	9.3%
MONROE	4,638	1,298	2,963	377	Bush	28.0%	63.9%	8.1%
MONTCALM	2,317	500	1,603	214	Bush	21.6%	69.2%	9.2%
MONTMORENCY	553	153	353	47	Bush	27.7%	63.8%	8.5%
MUSKEGON	6,563	1,649	4,450	464	Bush	25.1%	67.8%	7.1%
NEWAYGO	2,142	462	1,504	176	Bush	21.6%	70.2%	8.2%
OAKLAND	72,973	18,258	48,725	5,990	Bush	25.0%	66.8%	8.2%
OCEANA	1,328	300	922	106	Bush	22.6%	69.4%	8.0%
OGEMAW	784	214	499	71	Bush	27.3%	63.6%	9.1%
ONTONAGON	347	110	216	21	Bush	31.7%	62.2%	6.1%
OSCEOLA	1,329	351	895	83	Bush	26.4%	67.3%	6.2%
OSCODA	429	139	268	22	Bush	32.4%	62.5%	5.1%
OTSEGO	879	299	512	68	Bush	34.0%	58.2%	7.7%
OTTAWA	16,380	2,927	12,676	777	Bush	17.9%	77.4%	4.7%
PRESQUE ISLE	666	214	400	52	Bush	32.1%	60.1%	7.8%
ROSCOMMON	1,276	374	817	85	Bush	29.3%	64.0%	6.7%
SAGINAW	7,544	2,008	5,044	492	Bush	26.6%	66.9%	6.5%
ST. CLAIR	7,068	1,760	4,765	543	Bush	24.9%	67.4%	7.7%
ST. JOSEPH	2,401	561	1,674	166	Bush	23.4%	69.7%	6.9%
SANILAC	2,612	580	1,821	211	Bush	22.2%	69.7%	8.1%
SCHOOLCRAFT	236	63	156	17	Bush	26.7%	66.1%	7.2%
SHIAWASSEE	2,876	746	1,892	238	Bush	25.9%	65.8%	8.3%
TUSCOLA	2,281	687	1,404	190	Bush	30.1%	61.6%	8.3%
VAN BUREN	3,162	807	2,136	219	Bush	25.5%	67.6%	6.9%
WASHTENAW	13,234	3,012	9,185	1,037	Bush	22.8%	69.4%	7.8%
WAYNE	71,401	18,165	46,546	6,690	Bush	25.4%	65.2%	9.4%
WEXFORD	1,527	391	1,045	91	Bush	25.6%	68.4%	6.0%
TOTAL	449,133	112,122	301,948	35,063	Bush	25.0%	67.2%	7.8%

MICHIGAN REPUBLICAN

1996

County	Total Vote	Buchanan	Dole	Other	Winner	Percentage of Total Vote Buchanan	Dole	Other
ALCONA	737	233	379	125	Dole	31.6%	51.4%	17.0%
ALGER	513	176	250	87	Dole	34.3%	48.7%	17.0%
ALLEGAN	5,580	1,847	3,003	730	Dole	33.1%	53.8%	13.1%
ALPENA	1,364	485	702	177	Dole	35.6%	51.5%	13.0%
ANTRIM	1,869	484	1,040	345	Dole	25.9%	55.6%	18.5%
ARENAC	744	291	384	69	Dole	39.1%	51.6%	9.3%
BARAGA	409	199	170	40	Buchanan	48.7%	41.6%	9.8%
BARRY	3,152	1,007	1,716	429	Dole	31.9%	54.4%	13.6%
BAY	6,535	2,830	2,738	967	Buchanan	43.3%	41.9%	14.8%
BENZIE	933	227	593	113	Dole	24.3%	63.6%	12.1%
BERRIEN	7,400	1,940	4,542	918	Dole	26.2%	61.4%	12.4%
BRANCH	1,864	606	1,007	251	Dole	32.5%	54.0%	13.5%
CALHOUN	5,994	1,724	3,630	640	Dole	28.8%	60.6%	10.7%
CASS	2,030	682	1,092	256	Dole	33.6%	53.8%	12.6%
CHARLEVOIX	1,273	441	656	176	Dole	34.6%	51.5%	13.8%
CHEBOYGAN	1,224	475	602	147	Dole	38.8%	49.2%	12.0%
CHIPPEWA	1,578	471	880	227	Dole	29.8%	55.8%	14.4%
CLARE	1,243	478	611	154	Dole	38.5%	49.2%	12.4%
CLINTON	3,460	1,156	1,875	429	Dole	33.4%	54.2%	12.4%
CRAWFORD	726	268	340	118	Dole	36.9%	46.8%	16.3%
DELTA	1,112	357	548	207	Dole	32.1%	49.3%	18.6%
DICKINSON	1,006	410	477	119	Dole	40.8%	47.4%	11.8%
EATON	6,250	1,812	3,461	977	Dole	29.0%	55.4%	15.6%
EMMET	1,501	585	722	194	Dole	39.0%	48.1%	12.9%
GENESEE	13,024	5,829	6,074	1,121	Dole	44.8%	46.6%	8.6%
GLADWIN	1,095	455	539	101	Dole	41.6%	49.2%	9.2%
GOGEBIC	757	291	382	84	Dole	38.4%	50.5%	11.1%
GRAND TRAVERSE	4,090	972	2,564	554	Dole	23.8%	62.7%	13.5%
GRATIOT	1,699	523	1,009	167	Dole	30.8%	59.4%	9.8%
HILLSDALE	3,823	1,280	1,935	608	Dole	33.5%	50.6%	15.9%
HOUGHTON	1,339	616	552	171	Buchanan	46.0%	41.2%	12.8%
HURON	2,292	934	1,109	249	Dole	40.8%	48.4%	10.9%
INGHAM	14,376	3,694	8,449	2,233	Dole	25.7%	58.8%	15.5%
IONIA	2,578	847	1,364	367	Dole	32.9%	52.9%	14.2%
IOSCO	1,918	620	993	305	Dole	32.3%	51.8%	15.9%
IRON	787	331	369	87	Dole	42.1%	46.9%	11.1%
ISABELLA	3,158	906	1,732	520	Dole	28.7%	54.8%	16.5%
JACKSON	8,091	2,889	4,138	1,064	Dole	35.7%	51.1%	13.2%
KALAMAZOO	11,095	3,164	6,562	1,369	Dole	28.5%	59.1%	12.3%
KALKASKA	710	259	371	80	Dole	36.5%	52.3%	11.3%
KENT	35,419	9,542	20,676	5,201	Dole	26.9%	58.4%	14.7%
KEWEENAW	231	68	119	44	Dole	29.4%	51.5%	19.0%
LAKE	781	252	402	127	Dole	32.3%	51.5%	16.3%
LAPEER	4,644	2,285	1,888	471	Buchanan	49.2%	40.7%	10.1%
LEELANAU	1,643	306	1,069	268	Dole	18.6%	65.1%	16.3%
LENAWEE	5,548	1,895	2,823	830	Dole	34.2%	50.9%	15.0%
LIVINGSTON	8,582	3,053	4,433	1,096	Dole	35.6%	51.7%	12.8%
LUCE	714	223	344	147	Dole	31.2%	48.2%	20.6%
MACKINAC	803	239	435	129	Dole	29.8%	54.2%	16.1%
MACOMB	47,184	19,344	21,233	6,607	Dole	41.0%	45.0%	14.0%

MICHIGAN REPUBLICAN

1996

County	Total Vote	Buchanan	Dole	Other	Winner	Percentage of Total Vote Buchanan	Dole	Other
MANISTEE	1,231	388	695	148	Dole	31.5%	56.5%	12.0%
MARQUETTE	2,194	793	1,136	265	Dole	36.1%	51.8%	12.1%
MASON	4,109	1,239	2,213	657	Dole	30.2%	53.9%	16.0%
MECOSTA	1,555	521	867	167	Dole	33.5%	55.8%	10.7%
MENOMINEE	1,075	330	593	152	Dole	30.7%	55.2%	14.1%
MIDLAND	4,845	1,396	2,898	551	Dole	28.8%	59.8%	11.4%
MISSAUKEE	856	274	473	109	Dole	32.0%	55.3%	12.7%
MONROE	7,561	2,748	3,605	1,208	Dole	36.3%	47.7%	16.0%
MONTCALM	2,605	873	1,381	351	Dole	33.5%	53.0%	13.5%
MONTMORENCY	636	215	344	77	Dole	33.8%	54.1%	12.1%
MUSKEGON	7,059	2,359	3,710	990	Dole	33.4%	52.6%	14.0%
NEWAYGO	4,233	1,508	2,088	637	Dole	35.6%	49.3%	15.0%
OAKLAND	82,512	24,358	43,811	14,343	Dole	29.5%	53.1%	17.4%
OCEANA	1,456	529	754	173	Dole	36.3%	51.8%	11.9%
OGEMAW	895	379	421	95	Dole	42.3%	47.0%	10.6%
ONTONAGON	677	256	337	84	Dole	37.8%	49.8%	12.4%
OSCEOLA	1,275	423	697	155	Dole	33.2%	54.7%	12.2%
OSCODA	1,094	414	493	187	Dole	37.8%	45.1%	17.1%
OTSEGO	998	469	408	121	Buchanan	47.0%	40.9%	12.1%
OTTAWA	15,839	4,678	9,139	2,022	Dole	29.5%	57.7%	12.8%
PRESQUE ISLE	757	294	361	102	Dole	38.8%	47.7%	13.5%
ROSCOMMON	1,397	496	746	155	Dole	35.5%	53.4%	11.1%
SAGINAW	8,244	3,197	4,335	712	Dole	38.8%	52.6%	8.6%
ST. CLAIR	8,481	3,734	3,662	1,085	Buchanan	44.0%	43.2%	12.8%
ST. JOSEPH	2,128	708	1,159	261	Dole	33.3%	54.5%	12.3%
SANILAC	3,250	1,275	1,649	326	Dole	39.2%	50.7%	10.0%
SCHOOLCRAFT	392	130	214	48	Dole	33.2%	54.6%	12.2%
SHIAWASSEE	3,287	1,342	1,571	374	Dole	40.8%	47.8%	11.4%
TUSCOLA	3,080	1,544	1,259	277	Buchanan	50.1%	40.9%	9.0%
VAN BUREN	3,725	1,304	1,934	487	Dole	35.0%	51.9%	13.1%
WASHTENAW	11,743	3,506	6,433	1,804	Dole	29.9%	54.8%	15.4%
WAYNE	98,560	35,398	42,243	20,919	Dole	35.9%	42.9%	21.2%
WEXFORD	1,534	483	814	237	Dole	31.5%	53.1%	15.4%
TOTAL	524,161	177,562	265,425	81,174	Dole	33.9%	50.6%	15.5%

MINNESOTA

Every generation or so, a presidential primary appears in Minnesota like Brigadoon. There was one in 1916, a pair in the 1950s, and another in 1992. The rest of the time the residents of Minnesota have been content to elect their delegates through caucuses.

The state's presidential primary, though occasional, has often been memorable. In 1952, Dwight D. Eisenhower showed his vote-getting appeal by generating over 100,000 write-in votes in the Republican primary.

In 1956, Theodore H. White laid the groundwork for his series of *Making of the President* books by chronicling for *Collier's* magazine Estes Kefauver's upset victory over Adlai Stevenson in the state's Democratic balloting.

And Bill Clinton's narrow victory over Jerry Brown in the 1992 Democratic primary was the closest of any presidential primary that year.

Yet the caucus system reigns supreme in Minnesota, in part because it heightens the role of activists in both parties. In the Republican camp, many of those activists are evangelical Christians energized by social issues such as abortion.

The Democrats, too, have an ardent anti-abortion element that sent more than a dozen delegates to the 1984 Democratic convention. On the whole, however, the state party that nursed the presidential aspirations of Hubert Humphrey and Walter Mondale remains one of the most liberal in the country.

That was evident during the party's nonbinding presidential primary in April 1992. Although Clinton's campaign was rolling into high gear nationally, he prevailed over Brown in Minnesota by a margin of barely 1,000 votes out of more than 200,000 cast. Clinton offset Brown's edge in the Twin Cities area (Minneapolis and St. Paul) with a stronger showing in rural parts of the state.

On the Republican side, George Bush was a big winner. He swept every county and nearly two-thirds of the 130,000 ballots cast. Former Minnesota Gov. Harold Stassen, who had beaten back Eisenhower's write-in campaign to win the state's Republican presidential primary in 1952, drew only 3 percent of the primary vote in 1992 but qualified for a delegate. Stassen wanted to cast his one vote for himself at the national convention, but the state convention refused to elect him as a delegate.

Sandwiched around Bush's primary victory in 1992 were two caucus triumphs by Bob Dole. His successful effort in 1988 capitalized on his farm-state ties and the momentum from his win in Iowa barely two weeks earlier. In 1996, Dole had the backing of Minnesota's moderate Republican governor, Arne Carlson.

But with the strong conservative presence among GOP activists, neither of Dole's caucus victories was a landslide. In 1988, he defeated Pat Robertson, 43 to 28 percent, with Robertson running best in the Twin Cities' suburbs and the hard-scrabble Iron Range, a Democratic stronghold in northeast Minnesota.

In 1996, Dole defeated Pat Buchanan, 41 to 33 percent—about a 10 percentage point improvement for Buchanan over his primary showing in 1992.

Recent Minnesota Primary Results

Minnesota held its first presidential primary in 1916, but only three times since then—1952, 1956 and 1992.

	DEMOCRATS			REPUBLICANS		
Year	Turnout	Candidates	%	Turnout	Candidates	%
1996	—	NO PRIMARY		—	NO PRIMARY	
1992 (April 7)	204,170	BILL CLINTON	31	132,756	GEORGE BUSH*	64
		Jerry Brown	31		Pat Buchanan	24
		Paul Tsongas	21			

Note: All candidates are listed that drew at least 10 percent of their party's primary vote. The names of winning candidates are capitalized. An asterisk (*) indicates an incumbent president.

Kittson
Roseau
Lake of the Woods
Marshall
Koochiching
Pennington
Beltrami
Red Lake
Cook
Polk
Lake
St. Louis
Clearwater
Itasca
Norman
Mahnomen
Hubbard
Cass
Clay
Becker
Duluth
Wadena
Aitkin
Carlton
Wilkin
Crow Wing
Otter Tail
Pine
Todd
Mille Lacs
Morrison
Grant
Douglas
Kanabec
Traverse
Stearns
Benton
Stevens
Pope
St. Cloud
Isanti
Big Stone
Chisago
Sherburne
Swift
Anoka
Kandiyohi
Meeker
Wright
Washington
Hennepin
Chippewa
Minneapolis
St. Paul
Lac Qui Parle
McLeod
Carver
Yellow Medicine
Renville
Dakota
Scott
Sibley
Lincoln
Lyon
Goodhue
Redwood
Nicollet
Le Sueur
Rice
Wabasha
Brown
Dodge
Pipestone
Murray
Cottonwood
Blue Earth
Waseca
Steele
Rochester
Watonwan
Olmsted
Winona
Rock
Nobles
Jackson
Martin
Faribault
Freeborn
Mower
Fillmore
Houston

MINNESOTA DEMOCRATIC

1992

County	Total Vote	Brown	Clinton	Tsongas	Other	Winner	Percentage of Total Vote: Brown	Clinton	Tsongas	Other
AITKIN	1,008	286	377	160	185	Clinton	28.4%	37.4%	15.9%	18.4%
ANOKA	10,208	3,241	3,035	2,130	1,802	Brown	31.7%	29.7%	20.9%	17.7%
BECKER	833	217	342	122	152	Clinton	26.1%	41.1%	14.6%	18.2%
BELTRAMI	1,315	433	470	189	223	Clinton	32.9%	35.7%	14.4%	17.0%
BENTON	846	332	239	120	155	Brown	39.2%	28.3%	14.2%	18.3%
BIG STONE	369	91	188	42	48	Clinton	24.7%	50.9%	11.4%	13.0%
BLUE EARTH	1,593	482	466	287	358	Brown	30.3%	29.3%	18.0%	22.5%
BROWN	665	220	203	130	112	Brown	33.1%	30.5%	19.5%	16.8%
CARLTON	1,877	701	627	289	260	Brown	37.3%	33.4%	15.4%	13.9%
CARVER	1,290	452	341	297	200	Brown	35.0%	26.4%	23.0%	15.5%
CASS	1,238	361	493	166	218	Clinton	29.2%	39.8%	13.4%	17.6%
CHIPPEWA	421	115	178	62	66	Clinton	27.3%	42.3%	14.7%	15.7%
CHISAGO	1,511	474	506	278	253	Clinton	31.4%	33.5%	18.4%	16.7%
CLAY	908	170	383	208	147	Clinton	18.7%	42.2%	22.9%	16.2%
CLEARWATER	352	64	185	56	47	Clinton	18.2%	52.6%	15.9%	13.4%
COOK	319	106	74	72	67	Brown	33.2%	23.2%	22.6%	21.0%
COTTONWOOD	397	93	158	57	89	Clinton	23.4%	39.8%	14.4%	22.4%
CROW WING	1,821	569	674	320	258	Clinton	31.2%	37.0%	17.6%	14.2%
DAKOTA	10,854	3,264	3,034	2,737	1,819	Brown	30.1%	28.0%	25.2%	16.8%
DODGE	417	102	160	56	99	Clinton	24.5%	38.4%	13.4%	23.7%
DOUGLAS	1,023	291	387	175	170	Clinton	28.4%	37.8%	17.1%	16.6%
FARIBAULT	587	124	251	84	128	Clinton	21.1%	42.8%	14.3%	21.8%
FILLMORE	680	139	284	114	143	Clinton	20.4%	41.8%	16.8%	21.0%
FREEBORN	833	234	332	118	149	Clinton	28.1%	39.9%	14.2%	17.9%
GOODHUE	1,675	463	538	392	282	Clinton	27.6%	32.1%	23.4%	16.8%
GRANT	313	51	141	68	53	Clinton	16.3%	45.0%	21.7%	16.9%
HENNEPIN	59,149	18,468	16,438	14,660	9,583	Brown	31.2%	27.8%	24.8%	16.2%
HOUSTON	747	207	263	150	127	Clinton	27.7%	35.2%	20.1%	17.0%
HUBBARD	1,472	397	563	201	311	Clinton	27.0%	38.2%	13.7%	21.1%
ISANTI	1,212	365	419	207	221	Clinton	30.1%	34.6%	17.1%	18.2%
ITASCA	2,848	869	1,024	404	551	Clinton	30.5%	36.0%	14.2%	19.3%
JACKSON	335	78	163	34	60	Clinton	23.3%	48.7%	10.1%	17.9%
KANABEC	612	190	226	91	105	Clinton	31.0%	36.9%	14.9%	17.2%
KANDIYOHI	1,175	303	454	243	175	Clinton	25.8%	38.6%	20.7%	14.9%
KITTSON	212	50	110	30	22	Clinton	23.6%	51.9%	14.2%	10.4%
KOOCHICHING	1,138	418	399	119	202	Brown	36.7%	35.1%	10.5%	17.8%
LAC QUI PARLE	508	113	232	75	88	Clinton	22.2%	45.7%	14.8%	17.3%
LAKE	1,032	345	348	181	158	Clinton	33.4%	33.7%	17.5%	15.3%
LAKE OF THE WOODS	160	41	69	24	26	Clinton	25.6%	43.1%	15.0%	16.3%
LE SUEUR	775	244	245	133	153	Clinton	31.5%	31.6%	17.2%	19.7%
LINCOLN	275	53	130	32	60	Clinton	19.3%	47.3%	11.6%	21.8%
LYON	697	224	259	106	108	Clinton	32.1%	37.2%	15.2%	15.5%
MCLEOD	569	171	201	111	86	Clinton	30.1%	35.3%	19.5%	15.1%
MAHNOMEN	194	29	96	22	47	Clinton	14.9%	49.5%	11.3%	24.2%
MARSHALL	405	73	197	79	56	Clinton	18.0%	48.6%	19.5%	13.8%
MARTIN	389	86	168	61	74	Clinton	22.1%	43.2%	15.7%	19.0%
MEEKER	640	188	226	99	127	Clinton	29.4%	35.3%	15.5%	19.8%
MILLE LACS	733	223	288	102	120	Clinton	30.4%	39.3%	13.9%	16.4%
MORRISON	1,081	323	417	147	194	Clinton	29.9%	38.6%	13.6%	17.9%
MOWER	1,417	347	593	201	276	Clinton	24.5%	41.8%	14.2%	19.5%

MINNESOTA DEMOCRATIC

1992

County	Total Vote	Brown	Clinton	Tsongas	Other	Winner	Percentage of Total Vote Brown	Clinton	Tsongas	Other
MURRAY	394	80	173	67	74	Clinton	20.3%	43.9%	17.0%	18.8%
NICOLLET	876	262	279	165	170	Clinton	29.9%	31.8%	18.8%	19.4%
NOBLES	481	103	215	65	98	Clinton	21.4%	44.7%	13.5%	20.4%
NORMAN	292	40	156	44	52	Clinton	13.7%	53.4%	15.1%	17.8%
OLMSTED	3,796	1,045	1,046	1,009	696	Clinton	27.5%	27.6%	26.6%	18.3%
OTTER TAIL	1,583	430	606	263	284	Clinton	27.2%	38.3%	16.6%	17.9%
PENNINGTON	487	102	201	81	103	Clinton	20.9%	41.3%	16.6%	21.1%
PINE	1,334	429	465	200	240	Clinton	32.2%	34.9%	15.0%	18.0%
PIPESTONE	660	114	324	81	141	Clinton	17.3%	49.1%	12.3%	21.4%
POLK	1,234	234	515	253	232	Clinton	19.0%	41.7%	20.5%	18.8%
POPE	508	132	227	66	83	Clinton	26.0%	44.7%	13.0%	16.3%
RAMSEY	29,064	8,041	8,399	7,632	4,992	Clinton	27.7%	28.9%	26.3%	17.2%
RED LAKE	165	25	70	34	36	Clinton	15.2%	42.4%	20.6%	21.8%
REDWOOD	519	126	192	92	109	Clinton	24.3%	37.0%	17.7%	21.0%
RENVILLE	539	123	223	85	108	Clinton	22.8%	41.4%	15.8%	20.0%
RICE	1,903	555	603	440	305	Clinton	29.2%	31.7%	23.1%	16.0%
ROCK	232	33	124	27	48	Clinton	14.2%	53.4%	11.6%	20.7%
ROSEAU	324	77	135	53	59	Clinton	23.8%	41.7%	16.4%	18.2%
ST. LOUIS	16,769	6,622	5,081	2,365	2,701	Brown	39.5%	30.3%	14.1%	16.1%
SCOTT	1,810	646	560	333	271	Brown	35.7%	30.9%	18.4%	15.0%
SHERBURNE	1,297	422	394	251	230	Brown	32.5%	30.4%	19.4%	17.7%
SIBLEY	429	127	146	71	85	Clinton	29.6%	34.0%	16.6%	19.8%
STEARNS	3,028	1,166	897	505	460	Brown	38.5%	29.6%	16.7%	15.2%
STEELE	779	239	258	140	142	Clinton	30.7%	33.1%	18.0%	18.2%
STEVENS	334	80	111	88	55	Clinton	24.0%	33.2%	26.3%	16.5%
SWIFT	371	81	197	41	52	Clinton	21.8%	53.1%	11.1%	14.0%
TODD	874	245	382	137	110	Clinton	28.0%	43.7%	15.7%	12.6%
TRAVERSE	192	40	95	26	31	Clinton	20.8%	49.5%	13.5%	16.1%
WABASHA	597	200	182	103	112	Brown	33.5%	30.5%	17.3%	18.8%
WADENA	450	139	199	63	49	Clinton	30.9%	44.2%	14.0%	10.9%
WASECA	475	153	174	77	71	Clinton	32.2%	36.6%	16.2%	14.9%
WASHINGTON	6,431	2,007	1,706	1,669	1,049	Brown	31.2%	26.5%	26.0%	16.3%
WATONWAN	374	104	153	48	69	Clinton	27.8%	40.9%	12.8%	18.4%
WILKIN	114	14	49	26	25	Clinton	12.3%	43.0%	22.8%	21.9%
WINONA	1,588	512	499	268	309	Brown	32.2%	31.4%	16.9%	19.5%
WRIGHT	2,210	731	710	396	373	Brown	33.1%	32.1%	17.9%	16.9%
YELLOW MEDICINE	529	115	244	83	87	Clinton	21.7%	46.1%	15.7%	16.4%
TOTAL	204,170	62,474	63,584	43,588	34,524	Clinton	30.6%	31.1%	21.3%	16.9%

MINNESOTA REPUBLICAN

1992

County	Total Vote	Buchanan	Bush	Other	Winner	Percentage of Total Vote Buchanan	Bush	Other
AITKIN	512	118	325	69	Bush	23.0%	63.5%	13.5%
ANOKA	6,331	1,968	3,682	681	Bush	31.1%	58.2%	10.8%
BECKER	688	102	522	64	Bush	14.8%	75.9%	9.3%
BELTRAMI	792	183	478	131	Bush	23.1%	60.4%	16.5%
BENTON	569	158	353	58	Bush	27.8%	62.0%	10.2%
BIG STONE	182	26	137	19	Bush	14.3%	75.3%	10.4%
BLUE EARTH	1,265	276	821	168	Bush	21.8%	64.9%	13.3%
BROWN	788	183	523	82	Bush	23.2%	66.4%	10.4%
CARLTON	690	222	382	86	Bush	32.2%	55.4%	12.5%
CARVER	1,508	379	935	194	Bush	25.1%	62.0%	12.9%
CASS	965	153	695	117	Bush	15.9%	72.0%	12.1%
CHIPPEWA	348	52	263	33	Bush	14.9%	75.6%	9.5%
CHISAGO	960	288	563	109	Bush	30.0%	58.6%	11.4%
CLAY	719	99	563	57	Bush	13.8%	78.3%	7.9%
CLEARWATER	194	32	139	23	Bush	16.5%	71.6%	11.9%
COOK	204	31	141	32	Bush	15.2%	69.1%	15.7%
COTTONWOOD	440	88	317	35	Bush	20.0%	72.0%	8.0%
CROW WING	1,517	257	1,104	156	Bush	16.9%	72.8%	10.3%
DAKOTA	8,575	2,288	5,123	1,164	Bush	26.7%	59.7%	13.6%
DODGE	516	110	356	50	Bush	21.3%	69.0%	9.7%
DOUGLAS	1,007	194	701	112	Bush	19.3%	69.6%	11.1%
FARIBAULT	514	110	351	53	Bush	21.4%	68.3%	10.3%
FILLMORE	703	119	500	84	Bush	16.9%	71.1%	11.9%
FREEBORN	679	173	448	58	Bush	25.5%	66.0%	8.5%
GOODHUE	1,607	291	1,120	196	Bush	18.1%	69.7%	12.2%
GRANT	204	27	165	12	Bush	13.2%	80.9%	5.9%
HENNEPIN	36,756	8,593	22,925	5,238	Bush	23.4%	62.4%	14.3%
HOUSTON	645	135	442	68	Bush	20.9%	68.5%	10.5%
HUBBARD	1,367	213	1,008	146	Bush	15.6%	73.7%	10.7%
ISANTI	888	204	587	97	Bush	23.0%	66.1%	10.9%
ITASCA	1,240	289	798	153	Bush	23.3%	64.4%	12.3%
JACKSON	235	34	180	21	Bush	14.5%	76.6%	8.9%
KANABEC	403	88	279	36	Bush	21.8%	69.2%	8.9%
KANDIYOHI	896	201	629	66	Bush	22.4%	70.2%	7.4%
KITTSON	115	25	83	7	Bush	21.7%	72.2%	6.1%
KOOCHICHING	461	79	344	38	Bush	17.1%	74.6%	8.2%
LAC QUI PARLE	350	92	220	38	Bush	26.3%	62.9%	10.9%
LAKE	328	99	197	32	Bush	30.2%	60.1%	9.8%
LAKE OF THE WOODS	116	21	85	10	Bush	18.1%	73.3%	8.6%
LE SUEUR	632	156	419	57	Bush	24.7%	66.3%	9.0%
LINCOLN	231	61	142	28	Bush	26.4%	61.5%	12.1%
LYON	710	154	492	64	Bush	21.7%	69.3%	9.0%
MCLEOD	702	171	473	58	Bush	24.4%	67.4%	8.3%
MAHNOMEN	94	20	63	11	Bush	21.3%	67.0%	11.7%
MARSHALL	283	59	204	20	Bush	20.8%	72.1%	7.1%
MARTIN	621	144	427	50	Bush	23.2%	68.8%	8.1%
MEEKER	672	129	470	73	Bush	19.2%	69.9%	10.9%
MILLE LACS	472	96	326	50	Bush	20.3%	69.1%	10.6%
MORRISON	721	171	489	61	Bush	23.7%	67.8%	8.5%
MOWER	973	241	653	79	Bush	24.8%	67.1%	8.1%

MINNESOTA REPUBLICAN

1992

County	Total Vote	Buchanan	Bush	Other	Winner	Percentage of Total Vote Buchanan	Bush	Other
MURRAY	252	59	170	23	Bush	23.4%	67.5%	9.1%
NICOLLET	724	180	456	88	Bush	24.9%	63.0%	12.2%
NOBLES	418	78	303	37	Bush	18.7%	72.5%	8.9%
NORMAN	240	30	201	9	Bush	12.5%	83.8%	3.8%
OLMSTED	4,920	1,024	3,465	431	Bush	20.8%	70.4%	8.8%
OTTER TAIL	1,667	299	1,201	167	Bush	17.9%	72.0%	10.0%
PENNINGTON	248	49	182	17	Bush	19.8%	73.4%	6.9%
PINE	730	208	457	65	Bush	28.5%	62.6%	8.9%
PIPESTONE	584	100	443	41	Bush	17.1%	75.9%	7.0%
POLK	880	122	665	93	Bush	13.9%	75.6%	10.6%
POPE	391	66	286	39	Bush	16.9%	73.1%	10.0%
RAMSEY	14,297	3,939	8,419	1,939	Bush	27.6%	58.9%	13.6%
RED LAKE	90	31	53	6	Bush	34.4%	58.9%	6.7%
REDWOOD	709	177	477	55	Bush	25.0%	67.3%	7.8%
RENVILLE	555	123	383	49	Bush	22.2%	69.0%	8.8%
RICE	1,133	231	778	124	Bush	20.4%	68.7%	10.9%
ROCK	344	27	287	30	Bush	7.8%	83.4%	8.7%
ROSEAU	295	64	220	11	Bush	21.7%	74.6%	3.7%
ST. LOUIS	4,886	1,533	2,874	479	Bush	31.4%	58.8%	9.8%
SCOTT	1,382	425	803	154	Bush	30.8%	58.1%	11.1%
SHERBURNE	931	263	581	87	Bush	28.2%	62.4%	9.3%
SIBLEY	455	134	288	33	Bush	29.5%	63.3%	7.3%
STEARNS	2,152	628	1,366	158	Bush	29.2%	63.5%	7.3%
STEELE	929	186	645	98	Bush	20.0%	69.4%	10.5%
STEVENS	265	60	181	24	Bush	22.6%	68.3%	9.1%
SWIFT	207	64	129	14	Bush	30.9%	62.3%	6.8%
TODD	627	153	429	45	Bush	24.4%	68.4%	7.2%
TRAVERSE	154	34	109	11	Bush	22.1%	70.8%	7.1%
WABASHA	539	120	375	44	Bush	22.3%	69.6%	8.2%
WADENA	412	86	292	34	Bush	20.9%	70.9%	8.3%
WASECA	443	101	296	46	Bush	22.8%	66.8%	10.4%
WASHINGTON	4,546	1,227	2,726	593	Bush	27.0%	60.0%	13.0%
WATONWAN	349	74	238	37	Bush	21.2%	68.2%	10.6%
WILKIN	139	9	114	16	Bush	6.5%	82.0%	11.5%
WINONA	1,228	241	882	105	Bush	19.6%	71.8%	8.6%
WRIGHT	1,841	441	1,158	242	Bush	24.0%	62.9%	13.1%
YELLOW MEDICINE	406	106	267	33	Bush	26.1%	65.8%	8.1%
TOTAL	132,756	32,094	84,841	15,821	Bush	24.2%	63.9%	11.9%

MISSISSIPPI

Mississippi's presidential primary has been distinguished more by who has not done well in it than who has.

Mississippi is in the midst of the Bible Belt and would seem to have been favorable terrain for religious broadcaster Pat Robertson. But Robertson drew only 13 percent of the vote in the 1988 GOP primary.

Mississippi has a reputation for rock-ribbed conservatism. Yet Pat Buchanan never reached 30 percent of the vote there in two tries for the Republican presidential nomination.

Rather, voters in the Mississippi primary have seemed comfortable casting a pragmatic vote for the presidential front-runner, especially in Republican balloting.

In 1988, Mississippi provided George Bush with his highest percentage of the vote in any Southern primary—66 percent, with Robertson and Bob Dole dividing most of the other ballots.

Bush won an even larger share in the 1992 primary, even though Buchanan bought TV ads and paid a well-publicized visit to a Confederate cemetery. Buchanan netted only 17 percent of the vote and had to share the anti-Bush element of the primary electorate with David Duke, who reached his only double-digit percentage of the primary season in Mississippi.

The Magnolia State's only close presidential primary was on the Democratic side four years earlier, when Jesse Jackson defeated Al Gore, 45 to 33 percent. Blacks make up 36 percent of Mississippi's population (the highest percentage of any state), and exit polls showed nearly half the Democratic ballots were cast by blacks. By all indications, they voted almost unanimously for Jackson. He won in most parts of the state, including virtually all the major population centers.

Gore swept most of the predominantly white Hill Country of northeast Mississippi (which borders Gore's home state of Tennessee), the high-growth suburbs of Jackson and Memphis, Tennessee, and a scattering of majority-white counties in other parts of the state.

Several of those counties that Gore carried were longtime symbols of the white South. Lafayette County (Oxford) includes "Ole Miss," the University of Mississippi, as well as the home of novelist William Faulkner. Lee County (Tupelo) was the birthplace of Elvis Presley. And Neshoba County has been best known for its annual county fair that draws politicians from across the state, although Neshoba acquired a more infamous reputation in 1964 when three civil rights workers were slain near the county seat of Philadelphia.

In those days, the state Democratic Party was bitterly divided. The conservative "regular" faction held control of the party machinery at the state and local level, while a "loyalist" faction of blacks and liberal whites controlled the presidential delegate-selection process.

The two factions merged before the 1976 election. And since then, the state party has been in the mainstream of Southern Democratic politics. That biracial spirit was evident in the party's presidential primary in 1992, when Bill Clinton swept all parts of Mississippi and nearly three-fourths of the vote.

Recent Mississippi Primary Results

Mississippi Republicans held a presidential primary to select delegates in 1980. Both parties held their first primary with a direct vote for candidates in 1988.

	DEMOCRATS			REPUBLICANS		
Year	Turnout	Candidates	%	Turnout	Candidates	%
1996 (March 12)	93,788	BILL CLINTON*	92	151,925	BOB DOLE	60
					Pat Buchanan	26
1992 (March 10)	191,357	BILL CLINTON	73	154,708	GEORGE BUSH*	72
					Pat Buchanan	17
					David Duke	11
1988 (March 8)	359,417	JESSE JACKSON	45	158,526	GEORGE BUSH	66
		Al Gore	33		Bob Dole	17
					Pat Robertson	13
1984	—	NO PRIMARY		—	NO PRIMARY	
1980 (June 3)	—	NO PRIMARY		25,751	RONALD REAGAN	89

Note: All candidates are listed that drew at least 10 percent of their party's primary vote. The names of winning candidates are capitalized. An asterisk (*) indicates an incumbent president. There was no direct vote for candidates in the 1980 Republican primary; results are based on the vote for delegates.

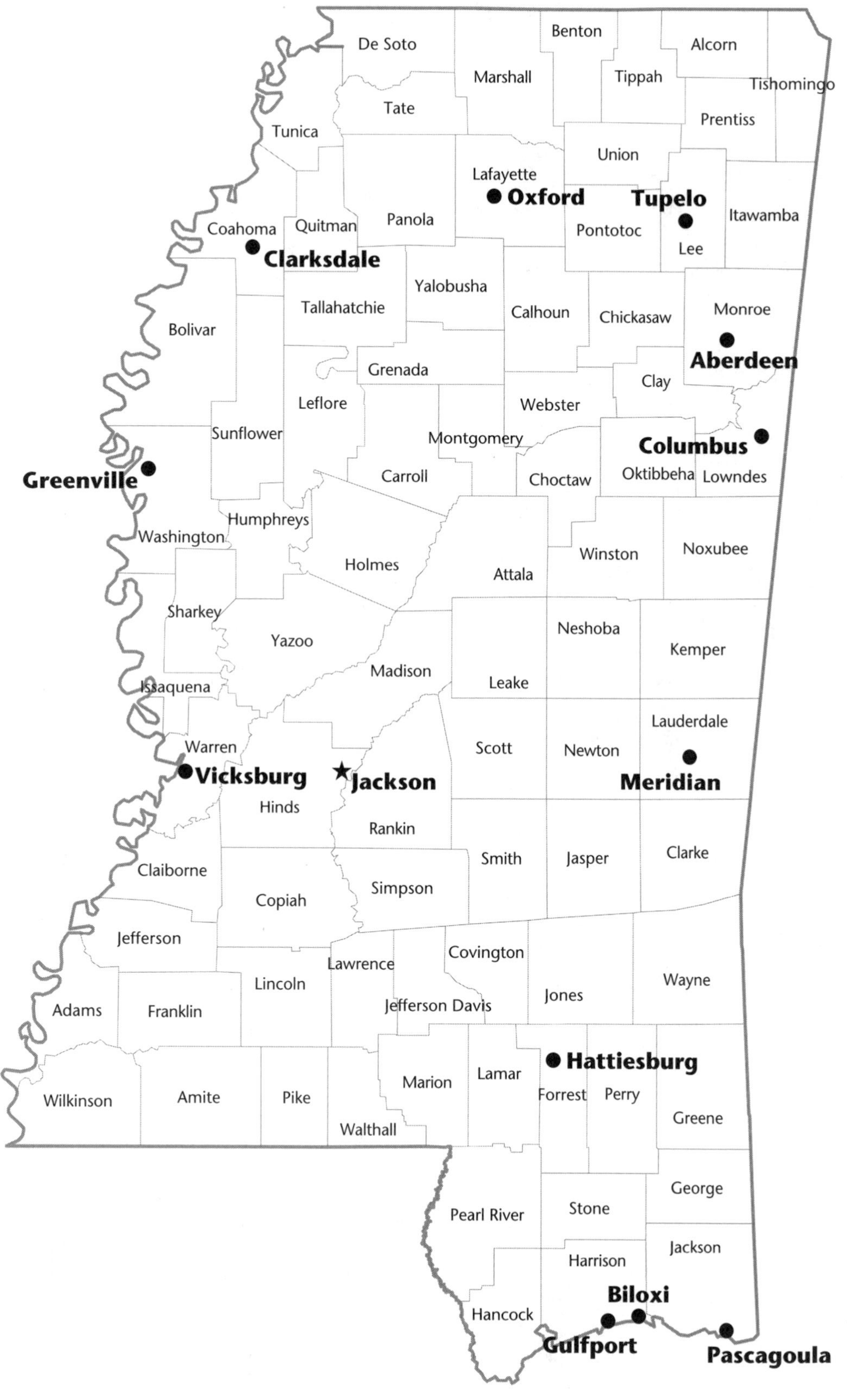
De Soto
Benton
Alcorn
Marshall
Tippah
Tishomingo
Tate
Prentiss
Tunica
Union
Lafayette
Oxford
Tupelo
Itawamba
Coahoma
Quitman
Panola
Pontotoc
Lee
Clarksdale
Yalobusha
Tallahatchie
Calhoun
Chickasaw
Monroe
Bolivar
Aberdeen
Grenada
Clay
Leflore
Webster
Sunflower
Montgomery
Columbus
Greenville
Carroll
Choctaw
Oktibbeha
Lowndes
Humphreys
Washington
Holmes
Winston
Noxubee
Attala
Sharkey
Yazoo
Neshoba
Kemper
Madison
Leake
Issaquena
Lauderdale
Warren
Scott
Newton
Vicksburg
Jackson
Meridian
Hinds
Rankin
Smith
Jasper
Clarke
Claiborne
Simpson
Copiah
Jefferson
Covington
Lawrence
Lincoln
Wayne
Adams
Franklin
Jefferson Davis
Jones
Hattiesburg
Marion
Lamar
Forrest
Perry
Wilkinson
Amite
Pike
Greene
Walthall
George
Pearl River
Stone
Jackson
Harrison
Biloxi
Hancock
Gulfport
Pascagoula

MISSISSIPPI REPUBLICAN

1980

County	Total Vote	Reagan	Other	Winner	Percentage of Total Vote Reagan	Percentage of Total Vote Other
ADAMS	516	375	141	Reagan	72.7%	27.3%
ALCORN	85	70	15	Reagan	82.4%	17.6%
AMITE	269	250	19	Reagan	92.9%	7.1%
ATTALA	290	274	16	Reagan	94.5%	5.5%
BENTON	23	23		Reagan	100.0%	
BOLIVAR	330	282	48	Reagan	85.5%	14.5%
CALHOUN	202	180	22	Reagan	89.1%	10.9%
CARROLL	206	182	24	Reagan	88.3%	11.7%
CHICKASAW	151	138	13	Reagan	91.4%	8.6%
CHOCTAW	186	176	10	Reagan	94.6%	5.4%
CLAIBORNE	108	103	5	Reagan	95.4%	4.6%
CLARKE	73	57	16	Reagan	78.1%	21.9%
CLAY	119	106	13	Reagan	89.1%	10.9%
COAHOMA	332	286	46	Reagan	86.1%	13.9%
COPIAH	157	139	18	Reagan	88.5%	11.5%
COVINGTON	145	145		Reagan	100.0%	
DE SOTO	818	655	163	Reagan	80.1%	19.9%
FORREST	486	466	20	Reagan	95.9%	4.1%
FRANKLIN	140	138	2	Reagan	98.6%	1.4%
GEORGE	159	145	14	Reagan	91.2%	8.8%
GREENE	66	64	2	Reagan	97.0%	3.0%
GRENADA	176	161	15	Reagan	91.5%	8.5%
HANCOCK	271	264	7	Reagan	97.4%	2.6%
HARRISON	1,454	1,307	147	Reagan	89.9%	10.1%
HINDS	3,181	2,880	301	Reagan	90.5%	9.5%
HOLMES	209	190	19	Reagan	90.9%	9.1%
HUMPHREYS	36	30	6	Reagan	83.3%	16.7%
ISSAQUENA	12	12		Reagan	100.0%	
ITAWAMBA	26	25	1	Reagan	96.2%	3.8%
JACKSON	1,001	917	84	Reagan	91.6%	8.4%
JASPER	170	161	9	Reagan	94.7%	5.3%
JEFFERSON	140	138	2	Reagan	98.6%	1.4%
JEFFERSON DAVIS	42	42		Reagan	100.0%	
JONES	535	519	16	Reagan	97.0%	3.0%
KEMPER	230	205	25	Reagan	89.1%	10.9%
LAFAYETTE	239	199	40	Reagan	83.3%	16.7%
LAMAR	271	265	6	Reagan	97.8%	2.2%
LAUDERDALE	1,415	1,066	349	Reagan	75.3%	24.7%
LAWRENCE	228	211	17	Reagan	92.5%	7.5%
LEAKE	213	205	8	Reagan	96.2%	3.8%
LEE	235	191	44	Reagan	81.3%	18.7%
LEFLORE	286	254	32	Reagan	88.8%	11.2%
LINCOLN	762	706	56	Reagan	92.7%	7.3%
LOWNDES	497	436	61	Reagan	87.7%	12.3%
MADISON	319	229	90	Reagan	71.8%	28.2%
MARION	205	199	6	Reagan	97.1%	2.9%
MARSHALL	40	35	5	Reagan	87.5%	12.5%
MONROE	150	126	24	Reagan	84.0%	16.0%
MONTGOMERY	213	195	18	Reagan	91.5%	8.5%
NESHOBA	350	292	58	Reagan	83.4%	16.6%

MISSISSIPPI REPUBLICAN

1980

County	Total Vote	Reagan	Other	Winner	Percentage of Total Vote Reagan	Other
NEWTON	239	223	16	Reagan	93.3%	6.7%
NOXUBEE	105	103	2	Reagan	98.1%	1.9%
OKTIBBEHA	405	362	43	Reagan	89.4%	10.6%
PANOLA	270	256	14	Reagan	94.8%	5.2%
PEARL RIVER	360	337	23	Reagan	93.6%	6.4%
PERRY	70	67	3	Reagan	95.7%	4.3%
PIKE	645	574	71	Reagan	89.0%	11.0%
PONTOTOC	182	166	16	Reagan	91.2%	8.8%
PRENTISS	64	62	2	Reagan	96.9%	3.1%
QUITMAN	123	117	6	Reagan	95.1%	4.9%
RANKIN	827	719	108	Reagan	86.9%	13.1%
SCOTT	188	165	23	Reagan	87.8%	12.2%
SHARKEY	24	24		Reagan	100.0%	
SIMPSON	616	579	37	Reagan	94.0%	6.0%
SMITH	175	171	4	Reagan	97.7%	2.3%
STONE	38	36	2	Reagan	94.7%	5.3%
SUNFLOWER	203	191	12	Reagan	94.1%	5.9%
TALLAHATCHIE	150	147	3	Reagan	98.0%	2.0%
TATE	91	85	6	Reagan	93.4%	6.6%
TIPPAH	35	35		Reagan	100.0%	
TISHOMINGO	97	90	7	Reagan	92.8%	7.2%
TUNICA	18	18		Reagan	100.0%	
UNION	36	32	4	Reagan	88.9%	11.1%
WALTHALL	270	257	13	Reagan	95.2%	4.8%
WARREN	699	605	94	Reagan	86.6%	13.4%
WASHINGTON	432	350	82	Reagan	81.0%	19.0%
WAYNE	282	273	9	Reagan	96.8%	3.2%
WEBSTER	217	207	10	Reagan	95.4%	4.6%
WILKINSON	77	71	6	Reagan	92.2%	7.8%
WINSTON	440	414	26	Reagan	94.1%	5.9%
YALOBUSHA	167	161	6	Reagan	96.4%	3.6%
YAZOO	338	308	30	Reagan	91.1%	8.9%
TOTAL	25,650	22,919	2,731	Reagan	89.4%	10.6%
Published Totals	25,751	23,028	2,723	Reagan	89.4%	10.6%

Note: There was no direct vote for president. Totals reflect the vote for each candidate's highest delegate vote-getter in each of Mississippi's five congressional districts.

MISSISSIPPI DEMOCRATIC

1988

County	Total Vote	Dukakis	Gore	J. Jackson	Other	Winner	Percentage of Total Vote: Dukakis	Gore	J. Jackson	Other
ADAMS	6,560	715	1,693	3,360	792	J. Jackson	10.9%	25.8%	51.2%	12.1%
ALCORN	4,159	238	2,726	629	566	Gore	5.7%	65.5%	15.1%	13.6%
AMITE	3,486	232	1,049	1,697	508	J. Jackson	6.7%	30.1%	48.7%	14.6%
ATTALA	3,002	187	1,119	1,336	360	J. Jackson	6.2%	37.3%	44.5%	12.0%
BENTON	1,449	43	663	644	99	Gore	3.0%	45.8%	44.4%	6.8%
BOLIVAR	5,607	307	874	3,914	512	J. Jackson	5.5%	15.6%	69.8%	9.1%
CALHOUN	2,504	144	1,548	543	269	Gore	5.8%	61.8%	21.7%	10.7%
CARROLL	1,722	126	542	837	217	J. Jackson	7.3%	31.5%	48.6%	12.6%
CHICKASAW	2,761	146	1,247	1,145	223	Gore	5.3%	45.2%	41.5%	8.1%
CHOCTAW	1,638	146	723	529	240	Gore	8.9%	44.1%	32.3%	14.7%
CLAIBORNE	2,171	75	234	1,728	134	J. Jackson	3.5%	10.8%	79.6%	6.2%
CLARKE	2,909	206	1,084	1,266	353	J. Jackson	7.1%	37.3%	43.5%	12.1%
CLAY	3,846	216	1,073	2,239	318	J. Jackson	5.6%	27.9%	58.2%	8.3%
COAHOMA	4,859	201	896	3,370	392	J. Jackson	4.1%	18.4%	69.4%	8.1%
COPIAH	5,440	348	1,580	2,694	818	J. Jackson	6.4%	29.0%	49.5%	15.0%
COVINGTON	2,689	243	877	1,126	443	J. Jackson	9.0%	32.6%	41.9%	16.5%
DE SOTO	5,043	335	2,910	1,386	412	Gore	6.6%	57.7%	27.5%	8.2%
FORREST	7,421	1,017	1,948	3,318	1,138	J. Jackson	13.7%	26.2%	44.7%	15.3%
FRANKLIN	2,564	222	1,084	740	518	Gore	8.7%	42.3%	28.9%	20.2%
GEORGE	2,263	224	1,080	386	573	Gore	9.9%	47.7%	17.1%	25.3%
GREENE	1,230	106	407	426	291	J. Jackson	8.6%	33.1%	34.6%	23.7%
GRENADA	3,269	169	843	1,992	265	J. Jackson	5.2%	25.8%	60.9%	8.1%
HANCOCK	3,712	1,154	976	578	1,004	Dukakis	31.1%	26.3%	15.6%	27.0%
HARRISON	13,255	2,615	3,714	4,465	2,461	J. Jackson	19.7%	28.0%	33.7%	18.6%
HINDS	39,169	2,558	8,544	24,531	3,536	J. Jackson	6.5%	21.8%	62.6%	9.0%
HOLMES	4,432	145	532	3,473	282	J. Jackson	3.3%	12.0%	78.4%	6.4%
HUMPHREYS	2,310	104	428	1,556	222	J. Jackson	4.5%	18.5%	67.4%	9.6%
ISSAQUENA	561	21	89	282	169	J. Jackson	3.7%	15.9%	50.3%	30.1%
ITAWAMBA	2,926	238	1,978	274	436	Gore	8.1%	67.6%	9.4%	14.9%
JACKSON	10,997	1,485	3,418	3,766	2,328	J. Jackson	13.5%	31.1%	34.2%	21.2%
JASPER	2,478	187	151	1,746	394	J. Jackson	7.5%	6.1%	70.5%	15.9%
JEFFERSON	1,967	58	231	1,587	91	J. Jackson	2.9%	11.7%	80.7%	4.6%
JEFFERSON DAVIS	3,123	183	775	1,787	378	J. Jackson	5.9%	24.8%	57.2%	12.1%
JONES	8,043	971	3,085	2,358	1,629	Gore	12.1%	38.4%	29.3%	20.3%
KEMPER	2,326	91	761	1,265	209	J. Jackson	3.9%	32.7%	54.4%	9.0%
LAFAYETTE	3,893	377	1,790	1,319	407	Gore	9.7%	46.0%	33.9%	10.5%
LAMAR	2,931	444	1,106	742	639	Gore	15.1%	37.7%	25.3%	21.8%
LAUDERDALE	7,588	802	2,857	2,875	1,054	J. Jackson	10.6%	37.7%	37.9%	13.9%
LAWRENCE	3,344	275	1,268	1,229	572	Gore	8.2%	37.9%	36.8%	17.1%
LEAKE	2,596	158	991	1,173	274	J. Jackson	6.1%	38.2%	45.2%	10.6%
LEE	6,900	437	4,076	1,678	709	Gore	6.3%	59.1%	24.3%	10.3%
LEFLORE	5,144	460	983	3,348	353	J. Jackson	8.9%	19.1%	65.1%	6.9%
LINCOLN	8,294	678	3,656	2,301	1,659	Gore	8.2%	44.1%	27.7%	20.0%
LOWNDES	5,371	531	1,541	2,666	633	J. Jackson	9.9%	28.7%	49.6%	11.8%
MADISON	6,870	366	1,353	4,491	660	J. Jackson	5.3%	19.7%	65.4%	9.6%
MARION	4,622	424	1,572	1,933	693	J. Jackson	9.2%	34.0%	41.8%	15.0%
MARSHALL	5,165	203	1,424	3,219	319	J. Jackson	3.9%	27.6%	62.3%	6.2%
MONROE	4,357	340	2,137	1,396	484	Gore	7.8%	49.0%	32.0%	11.1%
MONTGOMERY	2,029	127	746	935	221	J. Jackson	6.3%	36.8%	46.1%	10.9%
NESHOBA	4,894	408	2,696	1,035	755	Gore	8.3%	55.1%	21.1%	15.4%

MISSISSIPPI DEMOCRATIC

1988

County	Total Vote	Dukakis	Gore	J. Jackson	Other	Winner	Percentage of Total Vote Dukakis	Gore	J. Jackson	Other
NEWTON	3,244	208	1,614	992	430	Gore	6.4%	49.8%	30.6%	13.3%
NOXUBEE	2,338	73	380	1,661	224	J. Jackson	3.1%	16.3%	71.0%	9.6%
OKTIBBEHA	5,496	408	1,288	2,720	1,080	J. Jackson	7.4%	23.4%	49.5%	19.7%
PANOLA	4,771	191	1,439	2,876	265	J. Jackson	4.0%	30.2%	60.3%	5.6%
PEARL RIVER	2,756	554	680	854	668	J. Jackson	20.1%	24.7%	31.0%	24.2%
PERRY	1,367	175	377	528	287	J. Jackson	12.8%	27.6%	38.6%	21.0%
PIKE	8,659	758	2,689	3,728	1,484	J. Jackson	8.8%	31.1%	43.1%	17.1%
PONTOTOC	3,053	190	2,050	488	325	Gore	6.2%	67.1%	16.0%	10.6%
PRENTISS	2,735	182	2,027	230	296	Gore	6.7%	74.1%	8.4%	10.8%
QUITMAN	2,449	70	578	1,613	188	J. Jackson	2.9%	23.6%	65.9%	7.7%
RANKIN	8,736	926	3,858	2,503	1,449	Gore	10.6%	44.2%	28.7%	16.6%
SCOTT	3,927	238	1,598	1,622	469	J. Jackson	6.1%	40.7%	41.3%	11.9%
SHARKEY	1,447	58	273	735	381	J. Jackson	4.0%	18.9%	50.8%	26.3%
SIMPSON	4,002	251	1,593	1,549	609	Gore	6.3%	39.8%	38.7%	15.2%
SMITH	2,241	202	1,155	519	365	Gore	9.0%	51.5%	23.2%	16.3%
STONE	1,422	213	477	402	330	Gore	15.0%	33.5%	28.3%	23.2%
SUNFLOWER	3,550	208	736	2,214	392	J. Jackson	5.9%	20.7%	62.4%	11.0%
TALLAHATCHIE	3,087	169	1,012	1,527	379	J. Jackson	5.5%	32.8%	49.5%	12.3%
TATE	3,127	159	1,407	1,351	210	Gore	5.1%	45.0%	43.2%	6.7%
TIPPAH	3,180	179	2,214	499	288	Gore	5.6%	69.6%	15.7%	9.1%
TISHOMINGO	2,735	284	1,852	201	398	Gore	10.4%	67.7%	7.3%	14.6%
TUNICA	1,281	46	206	962	67	J. Jackson	3.6%	16.1%	75.1%	5.2%
UNION	3,651	212	2,498	556	385	Gore	5.8%	68.4%	15.2%	10.5%
WALTHALL	2,725	211	907	1,088	519	J. Jackson	7.7%	33.3%	39.9%	19.0%
WARREN	6,539	587	1,838	3,190	924	J. Jackson	9.0%	28.1%	48.8%	14.1%
WASHINGTON	7,792	562	1,074	4,325	1,831	J. Jackson	7.2%	13.8%	55.5%	23.5%
WAYNE	2,674	246	788	1,206	434	J. Jackson	9.2%	29.5%	45.1%	16.2%
WEBSTER	2,165	173	1,175	428	389	Gore	8.0%	54.3%	19.8%	18.0%
WILKINSON	2,412	102	364	1,641	305	J. Jackson	4.2%	15.1%	68.0%	12.6%
WINSTON	3,893	218	1,422	1,817	436	J. Jackson	5.6%	36.5%	46.7%	11.2%
YALOBUSHA	2,254	147	895	973	239	J. Jackson	6.5%	39.7%	43.2%	10.6%
YAZOO	3,820	255	822	2,340	403	J. Jackson	6.7%	21.5%	61.3%	10.5%
TOTAL	359,417	29,941	120,364	160,651	48,461	J. Jackson	8.3%	33.5%	44.7%	13.5%

MISSISSIPPI REPUBLICAN

1988

County	Total Vote	Bush	Dole	Kemp	Robertson	Winner	Percentage of Total Vote Bush	Dole	Kemp	Robertson
ADAMS	1,966	1,171	372	57	366	Bush	59.6%	18.9%	2.9%	18.6%
ALCORN	508	306	78	30	94	Bush	60.2%	15.4%	5.9%	18.5%
AMITE	398	268	66	13	51	Bush	67.3%	16.6%	3.3%	12.8%
ATTALA	1,012	633	131	19	229	Bush	62.5%	12.9%	1.9%	22.6%
BENTON	238	170	36	5	27	Bush	71.4%	15.1%	2.1%	11.3%
BOLIVAR	1,297	719	312	47	219	Bush	55.4%	24.1%	3.6%	16.9%
CALHOUN	591	353	96	22	120	Bush	59.7%	16.2%	3.7%	20.3%
CARROLL	590	409	72	17	92	Bush	69.3%	12.2%	2.9%	15.6%
CHICKASAW	567	364	104	37	62	Bush	64.2%	18.3%	6.5%	10.9%
CHOCTAW	506	313	106	15	72	Bush	61.9%	20.9%	3.0%	14.2%
CLAIBORNE	329	214	46	8	61	Bush	65.0%	14.0%	2.4%	18.5%
CLARKE	1,107	791	185	20	111	Bush	71.5%	16.7%	1.8%	10.0%
CLAY	794	494	119	10	171	Bush	62.2%	15.0%	1.3%	21.5%
COAHOMA	1,073	695	168	30	180	Bush	64.8%	15.7%	2.8%	16.8%
COPIAH	1,278	846	217	33	182	Bush	66.2%	17.0%	2.6%	14.2%
COVINGTON	996	747	132	29	88	Bush	75.0%	13.3%	2.9%	8.8%
DE SOTO	3,158	2,010	431	114	603	Bush	63.6%	13.6%	3.6%	19.1%
FORREST	6,092	4,042	1,008	261	781	Bush	66.3%	16.5%	4.3%	12.8%
FRANKLIN	271	171	38	8	54	Bush	63.1%	14.0%	3.0%	19.9%
GEORGE	1,410	1,003	213	56	138	Bush	71.1%	15.1%	4.0%	9.8%
GREENE	745	550	105	18	72	Bush	73.8%	14.1%	2.4%	9.7%
GRENADA	1,180	789	182	40	169	Bush	66.9%	15.4%	3.4%	14.3%
HANCOCK	2,301	1,614	369	95	223	Bush	70.1%	16.0%	4.1%	9.7%
HARRISON	17,446	12,031	3,131	654	1,630	Bush	69.0%	17.9%	3.7%	9.3%
HINDS	19,869	12,357	3,750	867	2,895	Bush	62.2%	18.9%	4.4%	14.6%
HOLMES	754	462	117	44	131	Bush	61.3%	15.5%	5.8%	17.4%
HUMPHREYS	235	142	47	3	43	Bush	60.4%	20.0%	1.3%	18.3%
ISSAQUENA	34	18	3	13		Bush	52.9%	8.8%	38.2%	
ITAWAMBA	546	359	109	16	62	Bush	65.8%	20.0%	2.9%	11.4%
JACKSON	14,344	10,458	1,985	553	1,348	Bush	72.9%	13.8%	3.9%	9.4%
JASPER	700	503	105	25	67	Bush	71.9%	15.0%	3.6%	9.6%
JEFFERSON	99	61	14	2	22	Bush	61.6%	14.1%	2.0%	22.2%
JEFFERSON DAVIS	622	465	86	10	61	Bush	74.8%	13.8%	1.6%	9.8%
JONES	5,102	3,511	700	179	712	Bush	68.8%	13.7%	3.5%	14.0%
KEMPER	527	354	94	18	61	Bush	67.2%	17.8%	3.4%	11.6%
LAFAYETTE	1,265	855	226	43	141	Bush	67.6%	17.9%	3.4%	11.1%
LAMAR	3,355	2,242	537	163	413	Bush	66.8%	16.0%	4.9%	12.3%
LAUDERDALE	4,494	3,151	727	69	547	Bush	70.1%	16.2%	1.5%	12.2%
LAWRENCE	511	386	93	15	17	Bush	75.5%	18.2%	2.9%	3.3%
LEAKE	863	612	125	41	85	Bush	70.9%	14.5%	4.8%	9.8%
LEE	2,535	1,609	385	82	459	Bush	63.5%	15.2%	3.2%	18.1%
LEFLORE	1,403	975	278	40	110	Bush	69.5%	19.8%	2.9%	7.8%
LINCOLN	1,061	710	133	26	192	Bush	66.9%	12.5%	2.5%	18.1%
LOWNDES	3,684	1,958	842	91	793	Bush	53.1%	22.9%	2.5%	21.5%
MADISON	2,782	1,708	560	100	414	Bush	61.4%	20.1%	3.6%	14.9%
MARION	1,824	1,275	259	50	240	Bush	69.9%	14.2%	2.7%	13.2%
MARSHALL	919	598	143	29	149	Bush	65.1%	15.6%	3.2%	16.2%
MONROE	1,104	721	191	21	171	Bush	65.3%	17.3%	1.9%	15.5%
MONTGOMERY	625	435	110	31	49	Bush	69.6%	17.6%	5.0%	7.8%
NESHOBA	896	609	124	28	135	Bush	68.0%	13.8%	3.1%	15.1%

MISSISSIPPI REPUBLICAN

1988

County	Total Vote	Bush	Dole	Kemp	Robertson	Winner	Percentage of Total Vote: Bush	Dole	Kemp	Robertson
NEWTON	1,244	829	278	32	105	Bush	66.6%	22.3%	2.6%	8.4%
NOXUBEE	451	235	148	8	60	Bush	52.1%	32.8%	1.8%	13.3%
OKTIBBEHA	2,409	1,321	579	85	424	Bush	54.8%	24.0%	3.5%	17.6%
PANOLA	1,309	906	200	55	148	Bush	69.2%	15.3%	4.2%	11.3%
PEARL RIVER	3,904	2,615	591	132	566	Bush	67.0%	15.1%	3.4%	14.5%
PERRY	1,004	742	154	28	80	Bush	73.9%	15.3%	2.8%	8.0%
PIKE	1,063	684	186	26	167	Bush	64.3%	17.5%	2.4%	15.7%
PONTOTOC	702	457	103	16	126	Bush	65.1%	14.7%	2.3%	17.9%
PRENTISS	471	314	86	10	61	Bush	66.7%	18.3%	2.1%	13.0%
QUITMAN	444	299	71	8	66	Bush	67.3%	16.0%	1.8%	14.9%
RANKIN	6,238	3,783	1,098	234	1,123	Bush	60.6%	17.6%	3.8%	18.0%
SCOTT	1,184	746	155	22	261	Bush	63.0%	13.1%	1.9%	22.0%
SHARKEY	320	252	35	8	25	Bush	78.8%	10.9%	2.5%	7.8%
SIMPSON	1,781	1,127	285	27	342	Bush	63.3%	16.0%	1.5%	19.2%
SMITH	818	551	130	15	122	Bush	67.4%	15.9%	1.8%	14.9%
STONE	1,145	782	216	33	114	Bush	68.3%	18.9%	2.9%	10.0%
SUNFLOWER	902	567	171	19	145	Bush	62.9%	19.0%	2.1%	16.1%
TALLAHATCHIE	273	159	56	2	56	Bush	58.2%	20.5%	0.7%	20.5%
TATE	804	537	119	35	113	Bush	66.8%	14.8%	4.4%	14.1%
TIPPAH	423	271	87	25	40	Bush	64.1%	20.6%	5.9%	9.5%
TISHOMINGO	342	224	70	8	40	Bush	65.5%	20.5%	2.3%	11.7%
TUNICA	280	195	44	9	32	Bush	69.6%	15.7%	3.2%	11.4%
UNION	828	543	140	28	117	Bush	65.6%	16.9%	3.4%	14.1%
WALTHALL	556	321	114	16	105	Bush	57.7%	20.5%	2.9%	18.9%
WARREN	3,193	1,989	578	107	519	Bush	62.3%	18.1%	3.4%	16.3%
WASHINGTON	5,519	3,601	968	182	768	Bush	65.2%	17.5%	3.3%	13.9%
WAYNE	1,507	1,052	233	33	189	Bush	69.8%	15.5%	2.2%	12.5%
WEBSTER	597	392	93	21	91	Bush	65.7%	15.6%	3.5%	15.2%
WILKINSON	202	148	31	12	11	Bush	73.3%	15.3%	5.9%	5.4%
WINSTON	1,016	657	186	36	137	Bush	64.7%	18.3%	3.5%	13.5%
YALOBUSHA	395	267	65	6	57	Bush	67.6%	16.5%	1.5%	14.4%
YAZOO	1,499	1,011	274	51	163	Bush	67.4%	18.3%	3.4%	10.9%
TOTAL	158,829	104,814	27,004	5,526	21,485	Bush	66.0%	17.0%	3.5%	13.5%
Certified Totals	158,526	104,814	26,855	5,479	21,378	Bush	66.1%	16.9%	3.5%	13.5%

MISSISSIPPI DEMOCRATIC

1992

County	Total Vote	Clinton	Other	Winner	Percentage of Total Vote: Clinton	Percentage of Total Vote: Other
ADAMS	3,107	2,492	615	Clinton	80.2%	19.8%
ALCORN	2,481	1,969	512	Clinton	79.4%	20.6%
AMITE	1,133	940	193	Clinton	83.0%	17.0%
ATTALA	1,867	1,352	515	Clinton	72.4%	27.6%
BENTON	1,051	937	114	Clinton	89.2%	10.8%
BOLIVAR	2,879	2,466	413	Clinton	85.7%	14.3%
CALHOUN	1,562	1,219	343	Clinton	78.0%	22.0%
CARROLL	895	715	180	Clinton	79.9%	20.1%
CHICKASAW	1,631	1,144	487	Clinton	70.1%	29.9%
CHOCTAW	875	606	269	Clinton	69.3%	30.7%
CLAIBORNE	1,188	903	285	Clinton	76.0%	24.0%
CLARKE	1,493	1,041	452	Clinton	69.7%	30.3%
CLAY	2,295	1,613	682	Clinton	70.3%	29.7%
COAHOMA	2,608	1,997	611	Clinton	76.6%	23.4%
COPIAH	2,021	1,467	554	Clinton	72.6%	27.4%
COVINGTON	1,001	755	246	Clinton	75.4%	24.6%
DE SOTO	4,139	3,427	712	Clinton	82.8%	17.2%
FORREST	3,142	2,139	1,003	Clinton	68.1%	31.9%
FRANKLIN	770	613	157	Clinton	79.6%	20.4%
GEORGE	1,144	809	335	Clinton	70.7%	29.3%
GREENE	711	570	141	Clinton	80.2%	19.8%
GRENADA	1,358	1,066	292	Clinton	78.5%	21.5%
HANCOCK	2,169	1,419	750	Clinton	65.4%	34.6%
HARRISON	15,977	10,741	5,236	Clinton	67.2%	32.8%
HINDS	19,047	13,362	5,685	Clinton	70.2%	29.8%
HOLMES	2,680	2,162	518	Clinton	80.7%	19.3%
HUMPHREYS	1,032	748	284	Clinton	72.5%	27.5%
ISSAQUENA	309	210	99	Clinton	68.0%	32.0%
ITAWAMBA	1,833	1,418	415	Clinton	77.4%	22.6%
JACKSON	8,192	5,113	3,079	Clinton	62.4%	37.6%
JASPER	1,398	990	408	Clinton	70.8%	29.2%
JEFFERSON	990	750	240	Clinton	75.8%	24.2%
JEFFERSON DAVIS	1,361	978	383	Clinton	71.9%	28.1%
JONES	3,179	2,328	851	Clinton	73.2%	26.8%
KEMPER	992	746	246	Clinton	75.2%	24.8%
LAFAYETTE	3,035	2,148	887	Clinton	70.8%	29.2%
LAMAR	1,235	795	440	Clinton	64.4%	35.6%
LAUDERDALE	3,267	1,992	1,275	Clinton	61.0%	39.0%
LAWRENCE	1,223	943	280	Clinton	77.1%	22.9%
LEAKE	1,337	1,042	295	Clinton	77.9%	22.1%
LEE	4,606	3,149	1,457	Clinton	68.4%	31.6%
LEFLORE	4,606	2,064	450	Clinton	68.4%	31.6%
LINCOLN	2,514	1,584	520	Clinton	82.1%	17.9%
LOWNDES	2,104	1,614	991	Clinton	75.3%	24.7%
MADISON	2,605	3,857	1,426	Clinton	62.0%	38.0%
MARION	5,283	1,396	395	Clinton	73.0%	27.0%
MARSHALL	1,791	2,156	432	Clinton	77.9%	22.1%
MONROE	2,588	1,890	844	Clinton	83.3%	16.7%
MONTGOMERY	2,734	836	295	Clinton	69.1%	30.9%
NESHOBA	1,131	1,331	665	Clinton	73.9%	26.1%

MISSISSIPPI DEMOCRATIC

1992

County	Total Vote	Clinton	Other	Winner	Percentage of Total Vote Clinton	Other
NEWTON	1,996	926	398	Clinton	66.7%	33.3%
NOXUBEE	1,324	499	255	Clinton	69.9%	30.1%
OKTIBBEHA	754	1,694	842	Clinton	66.2%	33.8%
PANOLA	2,536	2,543	578	Clinton	66.8%	33.2%
PEARL RIVER	3,121	1,342	424	Clinton	81.5%	18.5%
PERRY	1,766	440	150	Clinton	76.0%	24.0%
PIKE	590	1,855	548	Clinton	74.6%	25.4%
PONTOTOC	2,403	2,177	896	Clinton	77.2%	22.8%
PRENTISS	3,073	1,383	438	Clinton	70.8%	29.2%
QUITMAN	1,821	1,063	198	Clinton	75.9%	24.1%
RANKIN	1,261	2,372	941	Clinton	84.3%	15.7%
SCOTT	3,313	1,287	544	Clinton	71.6%	28.4%
SHARKEY	1,831	295	170	Clinton	70.3%	29.7%
SIMPSON	465	1,119	462	Clinton	63.4%	36.6%
SMITH	1,581	713	241	Clinton	70.8%	29.2%
STONE	954	573	234	Clinton	74.7%	25.3%
SUNFLOWER	807	1,253	255	Clinton	71.0%	29.0%
TALLAHATCHIE	1,508	1,743	624	Clinton	83.1%	16.9%
TATE	2,367	1,756	307	Clinton	73.6%	26.4%
TIPPAH	2,063	1,462	315	Clinton	85.1%	14.9%
TISHOMINGO	1,777	1,305	391	Clinton	82.3%	17.7%
TUNICA	1,696	395	52	Clinton	76.9%	23.1%
UNION	447	1,860	450	Clinton	88.4%	11.6%
WALTHALL	2,310	776	277	Clinton	80.5%	19.5%
WARREN	1,053	2,172	835	Clinton	73.7%	26.3%
WASHINGTON	3,007	1,934	837	Clinton	72.2%	27.8%
WAYNE	2,771	916	326	Clinton	69.8%	30.2%
WEBSTER	1,242	894	330	Clinton	73.8%	26.2%
WILKINSON	1,224	1,155	169	Clinton	73.0%	27.0%
WINSTON	1,324	1,301	286	Clinton	87.2%	12.8%
YALOBUSHA	1,587	1,307	328	Clinton	82.0%	18.0%
YAZOO	1,635	1,381	406	Clinton	79.9%	20.1%
TOTAL	191,357	139,893	51,464	Clinton	73.1%	26.9%

MISSISSIPPI REPUBLICAN

1992

County	Total Vote	Buchanan	Bush	Duke	Other	Winner	Percentage of Total Vote Buchanan	Bush	Duke	Other
ADAMS	1,323	303	891	128	1	Bush	22.9%	67.3%	9.7%	0.1%
ALCORN	619	149	421	48	1	Bush	24.1%	68.0%	7.8%	0.2%
AMITE	609	122	350	137		Bush	20.0%	57.5%	22.5%	
ATTALA	1,011	133	741	132	5	Bush	13.2%	73.3%	13.1%	0.5%
BENTON	218	47	159	11	1	Bush	21.6%	72.9%	5.0%	0.5%
BOLIVAR	1,163	147	901	114	1	Bush	12.6%	77.5%	9.8%	0.1%
CALHOUN	652	107	468	76	1	Bush	16.4%	71.8%	11.7%	0.2%
CARROLL	408	40	280	88		Bush	9.8%	68.6%	21.6%	
CHICKASAW	366	76	252	35	3	Bush	20.8%	68.9%	9.6%	0.8%
CHOCTAW	477	89	311	74	3	Bush	18.7%	65.2%	15.5%	0.6%
CLAIBORNE	379	33	287	58	1	Bush	8.7%	75.7%	15.3%	0.3%
CLARKE	1,078	92	882	102	2	Bush	8.5%	81.8%	9.5%	0.2%
CLAY	455	71	302	82		Bush	15.6%	66.4%	18.0%	
COAHOMA	480	64	372	44		Bush	13.3%	77.5%	9.2%	
COPIAH	1,774	173	1,389	210	2	Bush	9.8%	78.3%	11.8%	0.1%
COVINGTON	1,008	128	717	156	7	Bush	12.7%	71.1%	15.5%	0.7%
DE SOTO	3,270	831	2,240	195	4	Bush	25.4%	68.5%	6.0%	0.1%
FORREST	4,615	678	3,412	505	20	Bush	14.7%	73.9%	10.9%	0.4%
FRANKLIN	536	48	409	78	1	Bush	9.0%	76.3%	14.6%	0.2%
GEORGE	1,080	145	796	136	3	Bush	13.4%	73.7%	12.6%	0.3%
GREENE	613	59	478	74	2	Bush	9.6%	78.0%	12.1%	0.3%
GRENADA	942	139	702	99	2	Bush	14.8%	74.5%	10.5%	0.2%
HANCOCK	2,324	638	1,332	350	4	Bush	27.5%	57.3%	15.1%	0.2%
HARRISON	24,012	5,256	16,331	2,260	165	Bush	21.9%	68.0%	9.4%	0.7%
HINDS	20,695	3,292	15,649	1,712	42	Bush	15.9%	75.6%	8.3%	0.2%
HOLMES	734	67	564	99	4	Bush	9.1%	76.8%	13.5%	0.5%
HUMPHREYS	323	22	242	59		Bush	6.8%	74.9%	18.3%	
ISSAQUENA	51	1	38	11	1	Bush	2.0%	74.5%	21.6%	2.0%
ITAWAMBA	438	84	312	42		Bush	19.2%	71.2%	9.6%	
JACKSON	10,881	2,257	7,733	854	37	Bush	20.7%	71.1%	7.8%	0.3%
JASPER	659	68	484	97	10	Bush	10.3%	73.4%	14.7%	1.5%
JEFFERSON	146	13	116	16	1	Bush	8.9%	79.5%	11.0%	0.7%
JEFFERSON DAVIS	751	75	546	127	3	Bush	10.0%	72.7%	16.9%	0.4%
JONES	3,521	422	2,703	394	2	Bush	12.0%	76.8%	11.2%	0.1%
KEMPER	636	51	491	93	1	Bush	8.0%	77.2%	14.6%	0.2%
LAFAYETTE	859	187	613	59		Bush	21.8%	71.4%	6.9%	
LAMAR	2,633	374	1,918	338	3	Bush	14.2%	72.8%	12.8%	0.1%
LAUDERDALE	4,247	472	3,340	408	27	Bush	11.1%	78.6%	9.6%	0.6%
LAWRENCE	830	77	596	155	2	Bush	9.3%	71.8%	18.7%	0.2%
LEAKE	1,054	67	851	134	2	Bush	6.4%	80.7%	12.7%	0.2%
LEE	1,876	531	1,202	140	3	Bush	28.3%	64.1%	7.5%	0.2%
LEFLORE	1,262	249	827	156	30	Bush	19.7%	65.5%	12.4%	2.4%
LINCOLN	2,008	208	1,495	302	3	Bush	10.4%	74.5%	15.0%	0.1%
LOWNDES	1,994	492	1,264	236	2	Bush	24.7%	63.4%	11.8%	0.1%
MADISON	4,967	800	3,796	360	11	Bush	16.1%	76.4%	7.2%	0.2%
MARION	1,490	192	1,016	278	4	Bush	12.9%	68.2%	18.7%	0.3%
MARSHALL	511	102	374	33	2	Bush	20.0%	73.2%	6.5%	0.4%
MONROE	687	109	483	93	2	Bush	15.9%	70.3%	13.5%	0.3%
MONTGOMERY	469	61	352	56		Bush	13.0%	75.1%	11.9%	
NESHOBA	1,241	72	1,046	121	2	Bush	5.8%	84.3%	9.8%	0.2%

MISSISSIPPI REPUBLICAN

1992

County	Total Vote	Buchanan	Bush	Duke	Other	Winner	Percentage of Total Vote Buchanan	Bush	Duke	Other
NEWTON	1,446	130	1,160	150	6	Bush	9.0%	80.2%	10.4%	0.4%
NOXUBEE	347	70	236	41		Bush	20.2%	68.0%	11.8%	
OKTIBBEHA	1,605	306	1,145	148	6	Bush	19.1%	71.3%	9.2%	0.4%
PANOLA	760	98	593	64	5	Bush	12.9%	78.0%	8.4%	0.7%
PEARL RIVER	2,292	521	1,387	373	11	Bush	22.7%	60.5%	16.3%	0.5%
PERRY	671	76	488	102	5	Bush	11.3%	72.7%	15.2%	0.7%
PIKE	1,620	259	1,165	193	3	Bush	16.0%	71.9%	11.9%	0.2%
PONTOTOC	333	98	199	36		Bush	29.4%	59.8%	10.8%	
PRENTISS	365	75	220	70		Bush	20.5%	60.3%	19.2%	
QUITMAN	293	32	239	21	1	Bush	10.9%	81.6%	7.2%	0.3%
RANKIN	9,940	1,529	7,338	1,053	20	Bush	15.4%	73.8%	10.6%	0.2%
SCOTT	1,383	130	1,108	145		Bush	9.4%	80.1%	10.5%	
SHARKEY	342	54	236	44	8	Bush	15.8%	69.0%	12.9%	2.3%
SIMPSON	1,814	167	1,405	235	7	Bush	9.2%	77.5%	13.0%	0.4%
SMITH	971	98	679	182	12	Bush	10.1%	69.9%	18.7%	1.2%
STONE	863	120	622	116	5	Bush	13.9%	72.1%	13.4%	0.6%
SUNFLOWER	961	123	698	139	1	Bush	12.8%	72.6%	14.5%	0.1%
TALLAHATCHIE	180	20	134	26		Bush	11.1%	74.4%	14.4%	
TATE	648	134	478	28	8	Bush	20.7%	73.8%	4.3%	1.2%
TIPPAH	445	86	308	50	1	Bush	19.3%	69.2%	11.2%	0.2%
TISHOMINGO	311	50	236	23	2	Bush	16.1%	75.9%	7.4%	0.6%
TUNICA	129	18	102	9		Bush	14.0%	79.1%	7.0%	
UNION	660	139	469	51	1	Bush	21.1%	71.1%	7.7%	0.2%
WALTHALL	623	89	375	121	38	Bush	14.3%	60.2%	19.4%	6.1%
WARREN	3,568	459	2,655	450	4	Bush	12.9%	74.4%	12.6%	0.1%
WASHINGTON	2,631	441	1,871	299	20	Bush	16.8%	71.1%	11.4%	0.8%
WAYNE	1,094	156	793	140	5	Bush	14.3%	72.5%	12.8%	1.8%
WEBSTER	613	77	415	121		Bush	12.6%	67.7%	19.7%	0.8%
WILKINSON	312	57	210	45		Bush	18.3%	67.3%	14.4%	
WINSTON	833	110	584	138	1	Bush	13.2%	70.1%	16.6%	
YALOBUSHA	380	53	291	35	1	Bush	13.9%	76.6%	9.2%	0.3%
YAZOO	1,900	203	1,481	213	3	Bush	10.7%	77.9%	11.2%	0.1%
TOTAL	154,708	25,891	111,794	16,426	597	Bush	16.7%	72.3%	10.6%	0.4%

MISSISSIPPI DEMOCRATIC

1996

County	Total Vote	Clinton	LaRouche	Winner	Percentage of Total Vote Clinton	Percentage of Total Vote LaRouche
ADAMS	2,633	2,521	112	Clinton	95.7%	4.3%
ALCORN	481	433	48	Clinton	90.0%	10.0%
AMITE	877	792	85	Clinton	90.3%	9.7%
ATTALA	1,049	982	67	Clinton	93.6%	6.4%
BENTON	582	548	34	Clinton	94.2%	5.8%
BOLIVAR	1,186	1,158	28	Clinton	97.6%	2.4%
CALHOUN	724	652	72	Clinton	90.1%	9.9%
CARROLL	234	219	15	Clinton	93.6%	6.4%
CHICKASAW	650	621	29	Clinton	95.5%	4.5%
CHOCTAW	453	410	43	Clinton	90.5%	9.5%
CLAIBORNE	939	905	34	Clinton	96.4%	3.6%
CLARKE	1,011	930	81	Clinton	92.0%	8.0%
CLAY	1,995	1,849	146	Clinton	92.7%	7.3%
COAHOMA	1,628	1,372	256	Clinton	84.3%	15.7%
COPIAH	1,233	1,164	69	Clinton	94.4%	5.6%
COVINGTON	820	751	69	Clinton	91.6%	8.4%
DE SOTO	572	531	41	Clinton	92.8%	7.2%
FORREST	1,522	1,460	62	Clinton	95.9%	4.1%
FRANKLIN	617	571	46	Clinton	92.5%	7.5%
GEORGE	753	633	120	Clinton	84.1%	15.9%
GREENE	415	358	57	Clinton	86.3%	13.7%
GRENADA	411	389	22	Clinton	94.6%	5.4%
HANCOCK	1,257	1,088	169	Clinton	86.6%	13.4%
HARRISON	4,354	3,965	389	Clinton	91.1%	8.9%
HINDS	8,904	8,598	306	Clinton	96.6%	3.4%
HOLMES	1,163	1,110	53	Clinton	95.4%	4.6%
HUMPHREYS	376	353	23	Clinton	93.9%	6.1%
ISSAQUENA	182	170	12	Clinton	93.4%	6.6%
ITAWAMBA	647	578	69	Clinton	89.3%	10.7%
JACKSON	2,856	2,659	197	Clinton	93.1%	6.9%
JASPER	1,229	1,138	91	Clinton	92.6%	7.4%
JEFFERSON	731	708	23	Clinton	96.9%	3.1%
JEFFERSON DAVIS	1,010	899	111	Clinton	89.0%	11.0%
JONES	2,232	1,955	277	Clinton	87.6%	12.4%
KEMPER	1,006	950	56	Clinton	94.4%	5.6%
LAFAYETTE	634	600	34	Clinton	94.6%	5.4%
LAMAR	577	517	60	Clinton	89.6%	10.4%
LAUDERDALE	2,848	2,661	187	Clinton	93.4%	6.6%
LAWRENCE	848	767	81	Clinton	90.4%	9.6%
LEAKE	915	831	84	Clinton	90.8%	9.2%
LEE	1,342	1,257	85	Clinton	93.7%	6.3%
LEFLORE	1,102	1,003	99	Clinton	91.0%	9.0%
LINCOLN	833	751	82	Clinton	90.2%	9.8%
LOWNDES	1,701	1,605	96	Clinton	94.4%	5.6%
MADISON	1,417	1,348	69	Clinton	95.1%	4.9%
MARION	1,346	1,255	91	Clinton	93.2%	6.8%
MARSHALL	1,498	1,445	53	Clinton	96.5%	3.5%
MONROE	1,248	1,150	98	Clinton	92.1%	7.9%
MONTGOMERY	542	512	30	Clinton	94.5%	5.5%
NESHOBA	1,222	1,049	173	Clinton	85.8%	14.2%

MISSISSIPPI DEMOCRATIC

1996

County	Total Vote	Clinton	LaRouche	Winner	Percentage of Total Vote Clinton	LaRouche
NEWTON	942	838	104	Clinton	89.0%	11.0%
NOXUBEE	860	800	60	Clinton	93.0%	7.0%
OKTIBBEHA	1,807	1,693	114	Clinton	93.7%	6.3%
PANOLA	1,283	1,243	40	Clinton	96.9%	3.1%
PEARL RIVER	1,066	893	173	Clinton	83.8%	16.2%
PERRY	381	324	57	Clinton	85.0%	15.0%
PIKE	1,802	1,702	100	Clinton	94.5%	5.5%
PONTOTOC	671	615	56	Clinton	91.7%	8.3%
PRENTISS	481	440	41	Clinton	91.5%	8.5%
QUITMAN	871	725	146	Clinton	83.2%	16.8%
RANKIN	1,982	1,853	129	Clinton	93.5%	6.5%
SCOTT	1,190	1,081	109	Clinton	90.8%	9.2%
SHARKEY	224	208	16	Clinton	92.9%	7.1%
SIMPSON	821	767	54	Clinton	93.4%	6.6%
SMITH	675	593	82	Clinton	87.9%	12.1%
STONE	555	480	75	Clinton	86.5%	13.5%
SUNFLOWER	885	797	88	Clinton	90.1%	9.9%
TALLAHATCHIE	830	777	53	Clinton	93.6%	6.4%
TATE	458	441	17	Clinton	96.3%	3.7%
TIPPAH	581	536	45	Clinton	92.3%	7.7%
TISHOMINGO	602	540	62	Clinton	89.7%	10.3%
TUNICA	831	685	146	Clinton	82.4%	17.6%
UNION	1,105	977	128	Clinton	88.4%	11.6%
WALTHALL	698	631	67	Clinton	90.4%	9.6%
WARREN	1,192	1,156	36	Clinton	97.0%	3.0%
WASHINGTON	898	861	37	Clinton	95.9%	4.1%
WAYNE	789	670	119	Clinton	84.9%	15.1%
WEBSTER	505	467	38	Clinton	92.5%	7.5%
WILKINSON	1,105	1,055	50	Clinton	95.5%	4.5%
WINSTON	1,688	1,547	141	Clinton	91.6%	8.4%
YALOBUSHA	505	478	27	Clinton	94.7%	5.3%
YAZOO	700	672	28	Clinton	96.0%	4.0%
TOTAL	93,788	86,716	7,072	Clinton	92.5%	7.5%

MISSISSIPPI REPUBLICAN

1996

County	Total Vote	Buchanan	Dole	Other	Winner	Percentage of Total Vote Buchanan	Dole	Other
ADAMS	1,333	412	772	149	Dole	30.9%	57.9%	11.2%
ALCORN	796	377	326	93	Buchanan	47.4%	41.0%	11.7%
AMITE	569	250	260	59	Dole	43.9%	45.7%	10.4%
ATTALA	1,293	369	805	119	Dole	28.5%	62.3%	9.2%
BENTON	322	107	190	25	Dole	33.2%	59.0%	7.8%
BOLIVAR	1,475	211	730	534	Dole	14.3%	49.5%	36.2%
CALHOUN	684	210	421	53	Dole	30.7%	61.5%	7.7%
CARROLL	575	176	354	45	Dole	30.6%	61.6%	7.8%
CHICKASAW	717	202	446	69	Dole	28.2%	62.2%	9.6%
CHOCTAW	647	223	371	53	Dole	34.5%	57.3%	8.2%
CLAIBORNE	257	60	178	19	Dole	23.3%	69.3%	7.4%
CLARKE	2,339	676	1,412	251	Dole	28.9%	60.4%	10.7%
CLAY	1,229	326	760	143	Dole	26.5%	61.8%	11.6%
COAHOMA	496	123	309	64	Dole	24.8%	62.3%	12.9%
COPIAH	1,415	298	978	139	Dole	21.1%	69.1%	9.8%
COVINGTON	986	304	601	81	Dole	30.8%	61.0%	8.2%
DE SOTO	4,121	1,858	1,851	412	Buchanan	45.1%	44.9%	10.0%
FORREST	3,385	840	2,133	412	Dole	24.8%	63.0%	12.2%
FRANKLIN	554	152	347	55	Dole	27.4%	62.6%	9.9%
GEORGE	909	255	553	101	Dole	28.1%	60.8%	11.1%
GREENE	347	96	226	25	Dole	27.7%	65.1%	7.2%
GRENADA	1,004	240	661	103	Dole	23.9%	65.8%	10.3%
HANCOCK	1,747	380	995	372	Dole	21.8%	57.0%	21.3%
HARRISON	8,446	1,510	5,460	1,476	Dole	17.9%	64.6%	17.5%
HINDS	13,680	2,742	8,946	1,992	Dole	20.0%	65.4%	14.6%
HOLMES	371	91	252	28	Dole	24.5%	67.9%	7.5%
HUMPHREYS	297	64	210	23	Dole	21.5%	70.7%	7.7%
ISSAQUENA	71	15	51	5	Dole	21.1%	71.8%	7.0%
ITAWAMBA	716	255	388	73	Dole	35.6%	54.2%	10.2%
JACKSON	7,798	1,779	4,820	1,199	Dole	22.8%	61.8%	15.4%
JASPER	918	6	788	124	Dole	0.7%	85.8%	13.5%
JEFFERSON	99	16	70	13	Dole	16.2%	70.7%	13.1%
JEFFERSON DAVIS	583	185	366	32	Dole	31.7%	62.8%	5.5%
JONES	4,633	1,678	2,580	375	Dole	36.2%	55.7%	8.1%
KEMPER	1,180	301	758	121	Dole	25.5%	64.2%	10.3%
LAFAYETTE	1,198	350	671	177	Dole	29.2%	56.0%	14.8%
LAMAR	2,153	576	1,324	253	Dole	26.8%	61.5%	11.8%
LAUDERDALE	10,937	2,478	6,765	1,694	Dole	22.7%	61.9%	15.5%
LAWRENCE	648	190	406	52	Dole	29.3%	62.7%	8.0%
LEAKE	1,440	404	939	97	Dole	28.1%	65.2%	6.7%
LEE	3,022	1,070	1,562	390	Dole	35.4%	51.7%	12.9%
LEFLORE	1,347	346	853	148	Dole	25.7%	63.3%	11.0%
LINCOLN	1,383	352	879	152	Dole	25.5%	63.6%	11.0%
LOWNDES	4,355	1,199	2,597	559	Dole	27.5%	59.6%	12.8%
MADISON	5,519	1,027	3,531	961	Dole	18.6%	64.0%	17.4%
MARION	1,143	316	722	105	Dole	27.6%	63.2%	9.2%
MARSHALL	867	332	464	71	Dole	38.3%	53.5%	8.2%
MONROE	1,415	464	787	164	Dole	32.8%	55.6%	11.6%
MONTGOMERY	539	129	369	41	Dole	23.9%	68.5%	7.6%
NESHOBA	2,834	763	1,726	345	Dole	26.9%	60.9%	12.2%

MISSISSIPPI REPUBLICAN

1996

County	Total Vote	Buchanan	Dole	Other	Winner	Percentage of Total Vote: Buchanan	Dole	Other
NEWTON	2,530	642	1,607	281	Dole	25.4%	63.5%	11.1%
NOXUBEE	943	280	573	90	Dole	29.7%	60.8%	9.5%
OKTIBBEHA	2,896	604	1,843	449	Dole	20.9%	63.6%	15.5%
PANOLA	1,096	344	648	104	Dole	31.4%	59.1%	9.5%
PEARL RIVER	2,181	614	1,188	379	Dole	28.2%	54.5%	17.4%
PERRY	350	87	234	29	Dole	24.9%	66.9%	8.3%
PIKE	1,309	398	767	144	Dole	30.4%	58.6%	11.0%
PONTOTOC	1,188	485	586	117	Dole	40.8%	49.3%	9.8%
PRENTISS	728	278	389	61	Dole	38.2%	53.4%	8.4%
QUITMAN	211	60	136	15	Dole	28.4%	64.5%	7.1%
RANKIN	12,464	2,890	7,747	1,827	Dole	23.2%	62.2%	14.7%
SCOTT	1,886	461	1,255	170	Dole	24.4%	66.5%	9.0%
SHARKEY	258	48	159	51	Dole	18.6%	61.6%	19.8%
SIMPSON	1,523	401	1,007	115	Dole	26.3%	66.1%	7.6%
SMITH	1,376	379	901	96	Dole	27.5%	65.5%	7.0%
STONE	586	148	354	84	Dole	25.3%	60.4%	14.3%
SUNFLOWER	728	155	515	58	Dole	21.3%	70.7%	8.0%
TALLAHATCHIE	549	155	346	48	Dole	28.2%	63.0%	8.7%
TATE	880	323	473	84	Dole	36.7%	53.8%	9.5%
TIPPAH	899	355	438	106	Dole	39.5%	48.7%	11.8%
TISHOMINGO	570	184	306	80	Dole	32.3%	53.7%	14.0%
TUNICA	53	8	34	11	Dole	15.1%	64.2%	20.8%
UNION	1,272	452	687	133	Dole	35.5%	54.0%	10.5%
WALTHALL	526	122	329	75	Dole	23.2%	62.5%	14.3%
WARREN	2,919	867	1,657	395	Dole	29.7%	56.8%	13.5%
WASHINGTON	1,815	363	17	1,435	Dornan[1]	20.0%	0.9%	79.1%
WAYNE	873	251	547	75	Dole	28.8%	62.7%	8.6%
WEBSTER	791	202	522	67	Dole	25.5%	66.0%	8.5%
WILKINSON	256	90	142	24	Dole	35.2%	55.5%	9.4%
WINSTON	1,610	463	988	159	Dole	28.8%	61.4%	9.9%
YALOBUSHA	474	124	297	53	Dole	26.2%	62.7%	11.2%
YAZOO	1,393	308	984	101	Dole	22.1%	70.6%	7.3%
TOTAL	151,925	39,324	91,639	20,962	Dole	25.9%	60.3%	13.8%

[1]Votes are listed as certified by Mississippi state party officials. Unofficial news sources reported Washington County went for Dole.

MISSOURI

Situated at the juncture of the industrial Frost Belt, the agrarian Midwest and the rural South, Missouri likes to present itself as one of the nation's foremost political bellwethers. In all but two presidential elections this century, it has voted for the winning candidate.

But Missouri has not had much chance to prove its perspicacity in presidential primaries. It has held just one—in 1988—and that was skewed toward the home-state candidacy of Rep. Richard Gephardt.

The primary itself had been created largely to aid Gephardt, as state party officials thought such an event would do their native son more good than the traditional caucuses the state had held previously.

None of the other Democratic presidential hopefuls seriously challenged Gephardt in Missouri. He rolled up nearly 60 percent of the vote, easily his best showing of the primary season.

There was some embarrassment for Gephardt, though, in the returns. He narrowly lost his home base, the city of St. Louis, to Jesse Jackson. Jackson won handily in the heavily black precincts in the northern part of the city. Gephardt, though, did swamp Jackson in that southern portion of St. Louis that was part of his congressional district. Meanwhile, Al Gore had trouble finding a toehold anywhere in Missouri and drew only 3 percent of the vote statewide.

What the Democrats lacked in competition in 1988, the Republicans had in abundance. Bob Dole, who did not win any Super Tuesday primary, came closest in Missouri. For much of the night it appeared that he might defeat George Bush in the Show Me State, and in the end he lost by less than 5,000 votes out of 400,000 cast.

Dole's basic asset was the proximity of western Missouri to his home state of Kansas. Dole swept most of western Missouri, including the Kansas City area. Bush won most of the eastern half, including St. Louis and its suburbs.

In its caucus days, Democrats in Harry Truman's home state showed a clear preference for traditional "New Deal" Democrats, such as Hubert Humphrey, Henry Jackson and Walter Mondale. Bill Clinton won Missouri's first-round caucuses in 1992, although the turnout of about 25,000 was less than 5 percent of the number that participated in the Democratic primary four years earlier.

Meanwhile, if Missouri Republicans needed an excuse to reinstitute the presidential primary, their 1996 caucus process gave them one. Tapping into strong anti-abortion sentiment in suburban St. Louis County, Pat Buchanan won the first-round caucuses over Dole by 8 percentage points, with 9 percent going to Alan Keyes. But to the chagrin of the Buchanan legions, Keyes's supporters aligned with the Dole forces at the state convention to give Dole a majority of the Missouri delegates.

Recent Missouri Primary Results

Missouri held its first presidential primary in 1988.

	DEMOCRATS			REPUBLICANS		
Year	Turnout	Candidates	%	Turnout	Candidates	%
1996	—	NO PRIMARY		—	NO PRIMARY	
1992	—	NO PRIMARY		—	NO PRIMARY	
1988	527,805	RICHARD GEPHARDT	58	400,300	GEORGE BUSH	42
(March 8)		Jesse Jackson	20		Bob Dole	41
		Michael Dukakis	12		Pat Robertson	11

Note: All candidates are listed that drew at least 10 percent of their party's primary vote. The names of winning candidates are capitalized.

Atchison
Nodaway
Worth
Harrison
Mercer
Putnam
Schuyler
Scotland
Clark
Holt
Gentry
Grundy
Sullivan
Adair
Knox
Lewis
Andrew
De Kalb
Daviess
Linn
Macon
Shelby
Marion
St. Joseph
Livingston
Caldwell
Buchanan
Clinton
Chariton
Monroe
Ralls
Platte
Carroll
Randolph
Clay
Ray
Pike
Audrain
Saline
Howard
Boone
Kansas City
Independence
Lafayette
Lincoln
Montgomery
Jackson
Columbia
Cooper
St. Charles
Warren
Callaway
Johnson
Pettis
St. Louis
Cass
Moniteau
Gasconade
Jefferson City
Morgan
Cole
Osage
Henry
Franklin
Jefferson
Bates
Benton
Miller
Maries
St. Clair
Camden
Hickory
Washington
Vernon
Ste. Genevieve
Phelps
Crawford
Pulaski
Cedar
Dallas
Laclede
St. Francois
Perry
Polk
Dent
Barton
Iron
Dade
Reynolds
Madison
Cape Girardeau
Greene
Bollinger
Texas
Webster
Wright
Jasper
Springfield
Cape Girardeau
Lawrence
Shannon
Wayne
Joplin
Christian
Scott
Douglas
Carter
Newton
Stoddard
Mississippi
Howell
Stone
Butler
Oregon
Taney
Ozark
Ripley
McDonald
Barry
New Madrid
Pemiscot
Dunklin

MISSOURI DEMOCRATIC

1988

County	Total Vote	Dukakis	Gephardt	J. Jackson	Other	Winner	Percentage of Total Vote Dukakis	Gephardt	J. Jackson	Other
ADAIR	1,604	153	1,107	188	156	Gephardt	9.5%	69.0%	11.7%	9.7%
ANDREW	1,082	108	785	94	95	Gephardt	10.0%	72.6%	8.7%	8.8%
ATCHISON	636	47	501	31	57	Gephardt	7.4%	78.8%	4.9%	9.0%
AUDRAIN	2,816	330	1,975	245	266	Gephardt	11.7%	70.1%	8.7%	9.4%
BARRY	2,200	381	1,383	154	282	Gephardt	17.3%	62.9%	7.0%	12.8%
BARTON	747	126	488	52	81	Gephardt	16.9%	65.3%	7.0%	10.8%
BATES	1,611	199	1,167	94	151	Gephardt	12.4%	72.4%	5.8%	9.4%
BENTON	1,227	160	858	79	130	Gephardt	13.0%	69.9%	6.4%	10.6%
BOLLINGER	671	36	420	46	169	Gephardt	5.4%	62.6%	6.9%	25.2%
BOONE	11,345	2,149	5,286	2,445	1,465	Gephardt	18.9%	46.6%	21.6%	12.9%
BUCHANAN	7,669	958	5,111	804	796	Gephardt	12.5%	66.6%	10.5%	10.4%
BUTLER	2,035	215	1,280	160	380	Gephardt	10.6%	62.9%	7.9%	18.7%
CALDWELL	593	61	402	73	57	Gephardt	10.3%	67.8%	12.3%	9.6%
CALLAWAY	2,807	313	1,911	316	267	Gephardt	11.2%	68.1%	11.3%	9.5%
CAMDEN	2,034	337	1,287	157	253	Gephardt	16.6%	63.3%	7.7%	12.4%
CAPE GIRARDEAU	3,252	408	1,688	314	842	Gephardt	12.5%	51.9%	9.7%	25.9%
CARROLL	936	113	672	59	92	Gephardt	12.1%	71.8%	6.3%	9.8%
CARTER	698	77	448	36	137	Gephardt	11.0%	64.2%	5.2%	19.6%
CASS	5,083	813	3,282	376	612	Gephardt	16.0%	64.6%	7.4%	12.0%
CEDAR	808	123	508	86	91	Gephardt	15.2%	62.9%	10.6%	11.3%
CHARITON	1,230	126	914	81	109	Gephardt	10.2%	74.3%	6.6%	8.9%
CHRISTIAN	2,004	267	1,291	209	237	Gephardt	13.3%	64.4%	10.4%	11.8%
CLARK	801	104	574	41	82	Gephardt	13.0%	71.7%	5.1%	10.2%
CLAY	14,073	2,473	8,321	1,444	1,835	Gephardt	17.6%	59.1%	10.3%	13.0%
CLINTON	1,537	183	1,078	151	125	Gephardt	11.9%	70.1%	9.8%	8.1%
COLE	5,306	638	3,504	584	580	Gephardt	12.0%	66.0%	11.0%	10.9%
COOPER	1,171	125	785	172	89	Gephardt	10.7%	67.0%	14.7%	7.6%
CRAWFORD	1,338	111	1,021	88	118	Gephardt	8.3%	76.3%	6.6%	8.8%
DADE	538	63	362	42	71	Gephardt	11.7%	67.3%	7.8%	13.2%
DALLAS	941	116	625	75	125	Gephardt	12.3%	66.4%	8.0%	13.3%
DAVIESS	801	85	542	77	97	Gephardt	10.6%	67.7%	9.6%	12.1%
DE KALB	791	64	592	61	74	Gephardt	8.1%	74.8%	7.7%	9.4%
DENT	1,253	118	949	70	116	Gephardt	9.4%	75.7%	5.6%	9.3%
DOUGLAS	792	101	480	116	95	Gephardt	12.8%	60.6%	14.6%	12.0%
DUNKLIN	2,013	236	1,171	174	432	Gephardt	11.7%	58.2%	8.6%	21.5%
FRANKLIN	6,352	567	5,056	287	442	Gephardt	8.9%	79.6%	4.5%	7.0%
GASCONADE	776	71	575	63	67	Gephardt	9.1%	74.1%	8.1%	8.6%
GENTRY	773	58	589	50	76	Gephardt	7.5%	76.2%	6.5%	9.8%
GREENE	16,749	2,656	10,130	2,049	1,914	Gephardt	15.9%	60.5%	12.2%	11.4%
GRUNDY	718	83	474	88	73	Gephardt	11.6%	66.0%	12.3%	10.2%
HARRISON	677	61	481	63	72	Gephardt	9.0%	71.0%	9.3%	10.6%
HENRY	2,186	261	1,597	98	230	Gephardt	11.9%	73.1%	4.5%	10.5%
HICKORY	802	117	544	51	90	Gephardt	14.6%	67.8%	6.4%	11.2%
HOLT	427	44	309	26	48	Gephardt	10.3%	72.4%	6.1%	11.2%
HOWARD	1,269	150	857	146	116	Gephardt	11.8%	67.5%	11.5%	9.1%
HOWELL	2,260	288	1,489	206	277	Gephardt	12.7%	65.9%	9.1%	12.3%
IRON	1,173	134	836	50	153	Gephardt	11.4%	71.3%	4.3%	13.0%
JACKSON	84,105	12,254	37,468	26,100	8,283	Gephardt	14.6%	44.5%	31.0%	9.8%
JASPER	3,428	676	1,946	388	418	Gephardt	19.7%	56.8%	11.3%	12.2%
JEFFERSON	16,887	1,565	12,963	789	1,570	Gephardt	9.3%	76.8%	4.7%	9.3%

MISSOURI DEMOCRATIC

1988

County	Total Vote	Dukakis	Gephardt	J. Jackson	Other	Winner	Percentage of Total Vote Dukakis	Gephardt	J. Jackson	Other
JOHNSON	2,451	381	1,504	257	309	Gephardt	15.5%	61.4%	10.5%	12.6%
KNOX	528	37	429	33	29	Gephardt	7.0%	81.3%	6.3%	5.5%
LACLEDE	1,396	197	872	136	191	Gephardt	14.1%	62.5%	9.7%	13.7%
LAFAYETTE	2,458	316	1,721	186	235	Gephardt	12.9%	70.0%	7.6%	9.6%
LAWRENCE	2,110	273	1,472	136	229	Gephardt	12.9%	69.8%	6.4%	10.9%
LEWIS	1,145	76	918	31	120	Gephardt	6.6%	80.2%	2.7%	10.5%
LINCOLN	2,444	252	1,832	137	223	Gephardt	10.3%	75.0%	5.6%	9.1%
LINN	1,654	156	1,221	141	136	Gephardt	9.4%	73.8%	8.5%	8.2%
LIVINGSTON	1,411	163	947	167	134	Gephardt	11.6%	67.1%	11.8%	9.5%
MCDONALD	963	168	553	95	147	Gephardt	17.4%	57.4%	9.9%	15.3%
MACON	1,605	108	1,349	73	75	Gephardt	6.7%	84.0%	4.5%	4.7%
MADISON	998	101	699	44	154	Gephardt	10.1%	70.0%	4.4%	15.4%
MARIES	985	68	788	49	80	Gephardt	6.9%	80.0%	5.0%	8.1%
MARION	2,314	181	1,730	161	242	Gephardt	7.8%	74.8%	7.0%	10.5%
MERCER	286	20	208	32	26	Gephardt	7.0%	72.7%	11.2%	9.1%
MILLER	1,082	120	776	91	95	Gephardt	11.1%	71.7%	8.4%	8.8%
MISSISSIPPI	1,268	101	686	239	242	Gephardt	8.0%	54.1%	18.8%	19.1%
MONITEAU	1,037	73	743	107	114	Gephardt	7.0%	71.6%	10.3%	11.0%
MONROE	1,419	97	1,104	76	142	Gephardt	6.8%	77.8%	5.4%	10.0%
MONTGOMERY	932	108	663	83	78	Gephardt	11.6%	71.1%	8.9%	8.4%
MORGAN	1,448	186	1,004	81	177	Gephardt	12.8%	69.3%	5.6%	12.2%
NEW MADRID	1,614	108	1,001	188	317	Gephardt	6.7%	62.0%	11.6%	19.6%
NEWTON	2,200	410	1,296	216	278	Gephardt	18.6%	58.9%	9.8%	12.6%
NODAWAY	1,746	206	1,205	123	212	Gephardt	11.8%	69.0%	7.0%	12.1%
OREGON	1,148	135	803	57	153	Gephardt	11.8%	69.9%	5.0%	13.3%
OSAGE	1,124	102	898	54	70	Gephardt	9.1%	79.9%	4.8%	6.2%
OZARK	635	86	386	77	86	Gephardt	13.5%	60.8%	12.1%	13.5%
PEMISCOT	1,479	114	653	356	356	Gephardt	7.7%	44.2%	24.1%	24.1%
PERRY	778	96	512	48	122	Gephardt	12.3%	65.8%	6.2%	15.7%
PETTIS	2,833	348	1,954	240	291	Gephardt	12.3%	69.0%	8.5%	10.3%
PHELPS	3,471	356	2,483	274	358	Gephardt	10.3%	71.5%	7.9%	10.3%
PIKE	1,962	173	1,472	118	199	Gephardt	8.8%	75.0%	6.0%	10.1%
PLATTE	4,728	839	2,695	578	616	Gephardt	17.7%	57.0%	12.2%	13.0%
POLK	1,638	183	1,128	134	193	Gephardt	11.2%	68.9%	8.2%	11.8%
PULASKI	2,019	208	1,405	126	280	Gephardt	10.3%	69.6%	6.2%	13.9%
PUTNAM	298	31	222	18	27	Gephardt	10.4%	74.5%	6.0%	9.1%
RALLS	879	68	703	35	73	Gephardt	7.7%	80.0%	4.0%	8.3%
RANDOLPH	3,100	291	2,325	231	253	Gephardt	9.4%	75.0%	7.5%	8.2%
RAY	2,143	243	1,517	189	194	Gephardt	11.3%	70.8%	8.8%	9.1%
REYNOLDS	993	89	715	44	145	Gephardt	9.0%	72.0%	4.4%	14.6%
RIPLEY	806	135	447	46	178	Gephardt	16.7%	55.5%	5.7%	22.1%
ST. CHARLES	14,168	1,558	10,122	1,056	1,432	Gephardt	11.0%	71.4%	7.5%	10.1%
ST. CLAIR	1,021	133	723	64	101	Gephardt	13.0%	70.8%	6.3%	9.9%
ST. FRANCOIS	3,238	329	2,477	163	269	Gephardt	10.2%	76.5%	5.0%	8.3%
ST. LOUIS COUNTY	118,361	13,323	67,992	24,534	12,512	Gephardt	11.3%	57.4%	20.7%	10.6%
ST. LOUIS CITY	74,736	4,478	31,896	33,328	5,034	J. Jackson	6.0%	42.7%	44.6%	6.7%
STE. GENEVIEVE	1,542	149	1,191	58	144	Gephardt	9.7%	77.2%	3.8%	9.3%
SALINE	2,462	268	1,688	221	285	Gephardt	10.9%	68.6%	9.0%	11.6%
SCHUYLER	485	24	380	45	36	Gephardt	4.9%	78.4%	9.3%	7.4%
SCOTLAND	611	53	426	45	87	Gephardt	8.7%	69.7%	7.4%	14.2%

MISSOURI DEMOCRATIC

1988

County	Total Vote	Dukakis	Gephardt	J. Jackson	Other	Winner	Percentage of Total Vote Dukakis	Gephardt	J. Jackson	Other
SCOTT	3,070	320	1,777	366	607	Gephardt	10.4%	57.9%	11.9%	19.8%
SHANNON	1,069	89	793	53	134	Gephardt	8.3%	74.2%	5.0%	12.5%
SHELBY	993	71	794	33	95	Gephardt	7.2%	80.0%	3.3%	9.6%
STODDARD	2,006	163	1,372	111	360	Gephardt	8.1%	68.4%	5.5%	17.9%
STONE	1,562	277	965	141	179	Gephardt	17.7%	61.8%	9.0%	11.5%
SULLIVAN	663	68	490	55	50	Gephardt	10.3%	73.9%	8.3%	7.5%
TANEY	1,947	371	1,119	219	238	Gephardt	19.1%	57.5%	11.2%	12.2%
TEXAS	2,359	284	1,631	162	282	Gephardt	12.0%	69.1%	6.9%	12.0%
VERNON	1,861	316	1,154	114	277	Gephardt	17.0%	62.0%	6.1%	14.9%
WARREN	1,289	128	958	89	114	Gephardt	9.9%	74.3%	6.9%	8.8%
WASHINGTON	1,689	109	1,385	71	124	Gephardt	6.5%	82.0%	4.2%	7.3%
WAYNE	1,078	126	716	50	186	Gephardt	11.7%	66.4%	4.6%	17.3%
WEBSTER	1,780	227	1,240	143	170	Gephardt	12.8%	69.7%	8.0%	9.6%
WORTH	336	22	247	33	34	Gephardt	6.5%	73.5%	9.8%	10.1%
WRIGHT	926	112	630	77	107	Gephardt	12.1%	68.0%	8.3%	11.6%
TOTAL	527,805	61,303	305,287	106,386	54,829	Gephardt	11.6%	57.8%	20.2%	10.4%

MISSOURI REPUBLICAN

1988

County	Total Vote	Bush	Dole	Robertson	Other	Winner	Percentage of Total Vote Bush	Dole	Robertson	Other
ADAIR	1,646	730	628	220	68	Bush	44.3%	38.2%	13.4%	4.1%
ANDREW	1,333	391	697	200	45	Dole	29.3%	52.3%	15.0%	3.4%
ATCHISON	450	159	208	50	33	Dole	35.3%	46.2%	11.1%	7.3%
AUDRAIN	1,976	838	723	345	70	Bush	42.4%	36.6%	17.5%	3.5%
BARRY	3,426	1,678	1,299	308	141	Bush	49.0%	37.9%	9.0%	4.1%
BARTON	1,302	329	639	301	33	Dole	25.3%	49.1%	23.1%	2.5%
BATES	1,154	389	569	149	47	Dole	33.7%	49.3%	12.9%	4.1%
BENTON	1,330	581	604	93	52	Dole	43.7%	45.4%	7.0%	3.9%
BOLLINGER	645	225	287	96	37	Dole	34.9%	44.5%	14.9%	5.7%
BOONE	9,464	3,644	4,123	1,202	495	Dole	38.5%	43.6%	12.7%	5.2%
BUCHANAN	5,323	1,638	2,614	887	184	Dole	30.8%	49.1%	16.7%	3.5%
BUTLER	1,910	658	792	387	73	Dole	34.5%	41.5%	20.3%	3.8%
CALDWELL	721	222	336	128	35	Dole	30.8%	46.6%	17.8%	4.9%
CALLAWAY	2,031	859	828	256	88	Bush	42.3%	40.8%	12.6%	4.3%
CAMDEN	3,247	1,595	1,096	396	160	Bush	49.1%	33.8%	12.2%	4.9%
CAPE GIRARDEAU	4,548	1,527	2,190	632	199	Dole	33.6%	48.2%	13.9%	4.4%
CARROLL	1,027	396	499	97	35	Dole	38.6%	48.6%	9.4%	3.4%
CARTER	487	205	199	59	24	Bush	42.1%	40.9%	12.1%	4.9%
CASS	4,508	1,266	2,144	876	222	Dole	28.1%	47.6%	19.4%	4.9%
CEDAR	1,293	513	599	127	54	Dole	39.7%	46.3%	9.8%	4.2%

MISSOURI REPUBLICAN

1988

County	Total Vote	Bush	Dole	Robertson	Other	Winner	Percentage of Total Vote Bush	Dole	Robertson	Other
CHARITON	627	264	292	53	18	Dole	42.1%	46.6%	8.5%	2.9%
CHRISTIAN	3,010	1,245	1,247	380	138	Dole	41.4%	41.4%	12.6%	4.6%
CLARK	432	177	181	47	27	Dole	41.0%	41.9%	10.9%	6.3%
CLAY	13,664	4,239	6,808	1,786	831	Dole	31.0%	49.8%	13.1%	6.1%
CLINTON	1,047	260	498	248	41	Dole	24.8%	47.6%	23.7%	3.9%
COLE	5,611	2,704	2,242	323	342	Bush	48.2%	40.0%	5.8%	6.1%
COOPER	1,291	607	567	73	44	Bush	47.0%	43.9%	5.7%	3.4%
CRAWFORD	1,249	596	427	176	50	Bush	47.7%	34.2%	14.1%	4.0%
DADE	1,003	374	499	97	33	Dole	37.3%	49.8%	9.7%	3.3%
DALLAS	1,133	479	511	81	62	Dole	42.3%	45.1%	7.1%	5.5%
DAVIESS	646	239	281	103	23	Dole	37.0%	43.5%	15.9%	3.6%
DE KALB	680	194	312	150	24	Dole	28.5%	45.9%	22.1%	3.5%
DENT	832	391	256	136	49	Bush	47.0%	30.8%	16.3%	5.9%
DOUGLAS	1,256	618	464	122	52	Bush	49.2%	36.9%	9.7%	4.1%
DUNKLIN	911	347	371	146	47	Dole	38.1%	40.7%	16.0%	5.2%
FRANKLIN	5,423	2,522	1,921	660	320	Bush	46.5%	35.4%	12.2%	5.9%
GASCONADE	1,517	710	602	130	75	Bush	46.8%	39.7%	8.6%	4.9%
GENTRY	486	169	229	66	22	Dole	34.8%	47.1%	13.6%	4.5%
GREENE	23,449	9,907	9,584	2,927	1,031	Bush	42.2%	40.9%	12.5%	4.4%
GRUNDY	885	310	385	153	37	Dole	35.0%	43.5%	17.3%	4.2%
HARRISON	960	311	453	140	56	Dole	32.4%	47.2%	14.6%	5.8%
HENRY	1,070	411	505	119	35	Dole	38.4%	47.2%	11.1%	3.3%
HICKORY	912	379	385	95	53	Dole	41.6%	42.2%	10.4%	5.8%
HOLT	584	168	279	122	15	Dole	28.8%	47.8%	20.9%	2.6%
HOWARD	542	216	251	54	21	Dole	39.9%	46.3%	10.0%	3.9%
HOWELL	2,889	1,321	1,004	396	168	Bush	45.7%	34.8%	13.7%	5.8%
IRON	513	216	188	73	36	Bush	42.1%	36.6%	14.2%	7.0%
JACKSON	56,066	18,230	28,096	6,564	3,176	Dole	32.5%	50.1%	11.7%	5.7%
JASPER	7,250	3,074	2,941	885	350	Bush	42.4%	40.6%	12.2%	4.8%
JEFFERSON	8,484	3,807	2,709	1,421	547	Bush	44.9%	31.9%	16.7%	6.4%
JOHNSON	2,625	884	1,263	341	137	Dole	33.7%	48.1%	13.0%	5.2%
KNOX	262	94	122	34	12	Dole	35.9%	46.6%	13.0%	4.6%
LACLEDE	2,112	948	847	216	101	Bush	44.9%	40.1%	10.2%	4.8%
LAFAYETTE	2,285	862	1,115	233	75	Dole	37.7%	48.8%	10.2%	3.3%
LAWRENCE	3,339	1,383	1,334	500	122	Bush	41.4%	40.0%	15.0%	3.7%
LEWIS	426	170	188	38	30	Dole	39.9%	44.1%	8.9%	7.0%
LINCOLN	1,246	457	509	220	60	Dole	36.7%	40.9%	17.7%	4.8%
LINN	1,089	379	465	204	41	Dole	34.8%	42.7%	18.7%	3.8%
LIVINGSTON	1,284	387	586	270	41	Dole	30.1%	45.6%	21.0%	3.2%
MCDONALD	1,292	579	491	154	68	Bush	44.8%	38.0%	11.9%	5.3%
MACON	760	305	320	109	26	Dole	40.1%	42.1%	14.3%	3.4%
MADISON	707	301	277	96	33	Bush	42.6%	39.2%	13.6%	4.7%
MARIES	563	269	212	61	21	Bush	47.8%	37.7%	10.8%	3.7%
MARION	1,189	459	439	228	63	Bush	38.6%	36.9%	19.2%	5.3%
MERCER	356	90	199	56	11	Dole	25.3%	55.9%	15.7%	3.1%
MILLER	1,906	898	758	167	83	Bush	47.1%	39.8%	8.8%	4.4%
MISSISSIPPI	558	169	273	101	15	Dole	30.3%	48.9%	18.1%	2.7%
MONITEAU	1,338	592	568	106	72	Bush	44.2%	42.5%	7.9%	5.4%
MONROE	359	134	156	42	27	Dole	37.3%	43.5%	11.7%	7.5%
MONTGOMERY	952	411	421	79	41	Dole	43.2%	44.2%	8.3%	4.3%

MISSOURI REPUBLICAN

1988

County	Total Vote	Bush	Dole	Robertson	Other	Winner	Percentage of Total Vote: Bush	Dole	Robertson	Other
MORGAN	1,643	770	583	192	98	Bush	46.9%	35.5%	11.7%	6.0%
NEW MADRID	631	190	307	114	20	Dole	30.1%	48.7%	18.1%	3.2%
NEWTON	3,796	1,580	1,483	560	173	Bush	41.6%	39.1%	14.8%	4.6%
NODAWAY	1,207	353	666	148	40	Dole	29.2%	55.2%	12.3%	3.3%
OREGON	478	233	159	56	30	Bush	48.7%	33.3%	11.7%	6.3%
OSAGE	1,212	571	517	50	74	Bush	47.1%	42.7%	4.1%	6.1%
OZARK	1,060	549	382	81	48	Bush	51.8%	36.0%	7.6%	4.5%
PEMISCOT	517	264	151	81	21	Bush	51.1%	29.2%	15.7%	4.1%
PERRY	1,098	403	564	88	43	Dole	36.7%	51.4%	8.0%	3.9%
PETTIS	3,216	1,190	1,330	538	158	Dole	37.0%	41.4%	16.7%	4.9%
PHELPS	2,807	1,149	1,091	420	147	Bush	40.9%	38.9%	15.0%	5.2%
PIKE	856	339	320	154	43	Bush	39.6%	37.4%	18.0%	5.0%
PLATTE	4,880	1,515	2,465	593	307	Dole	31.0%	50.5%	12.2%	6.3%
POLK	2,142	916	948	197	81	Dole	42.8%	44.3%	9.2%	3.8%
PULASKI	1,362	686	509	118	49	Bush	50.4%	37.4%	8.7%	3.6%
PUTNAM	428	145	220	37	26	Dole	33.9%	51.4%	8.6%	6.1%
RALLS	277	127	93	36	21	Bush	45.8%	33.6%	13.0%	7.6%
RANDOLPH	1,389	571	530	215	73	Bush	41.1%	38.2%	15.5%	5.3%
RAY	1,094	283	505	263	43	Dole	25.9%	46.2%	24.0%	3.9%
REYNOLDS	244	94	108	32	10	Dole	38.5%	44.3%	13.1%	4.1%
RIPLEY	609	255	203	120	31	Bush	41.9%	33.3%	19.7%	5.1%
ST. CHARLES	14,557	6,501	5,344	1,703	1,009	Bush	44.7%	36.7%	11.7%	6.9%
ST. CLAIR	974	351	488	98	37	Dole	36.0%	50.1%	10.1%	3.8%
ST. FRANCOIS	1,998	960	684	253	101	Bush	48.0%	34.2%	12.7%	5.1%
ST. LOUIS COUNTY	97,211	49,173	34,221	7,155	6,662	Bush	50.6%	35.2%	7.4%	6.9%
ST. LOUIS CITY	14,654	7,796	4,835	1,030	993	Bush	53.2%	33.0%	7.0%	6.8%
STE. GENEVIEVE	546	260	201	48	37	Bush	47.6%	36.8%	8.8%	6.8%
SALINE	1,408	540	675	149	44	Dole	38.4%	47.9%	10.6%	3.1%
SCHUYLER	238	120	82	20	16	Bush	50.4%	34.5%	8.4%	6.7%
SCOTLAND	294	119	130	29	16	Dole	40.5%	44.2%	9.9%	5.4%
SCOTT	2,135	652	1,004	401	78	Dole	30.5%	47.0%	18.8%	3.7%
SHANNON	343	166	148	19	10	Bush	48.4%	43.1%	5.5%	2.9%
SHELBY	355	137	163	32	23	Dole	38.6%	45.9%	9.0%	6.5%
STODDARD	1,225	402	553	217	53	Dole	32.8%	45.1%	17.7%	4.3%
STONE	2,699	1,356	1,017	178	148	Bush	50.2%	37.7%	6.6%	5.5%
SULLIVAN	543	222	256	46	19	Dole	40.9%	47.1%	8.5%	3.5%
TANEY	3,213	1,521	1,245	258	189	Bush	47.3%	38.7%	8.0%	5.9%
TEXAS	1,586	647	595	242	102	Bush	40.8%	37.5%	15.3%	6.4%
VERNON	1,573	538	704	252	79	Dole	34.2%	44.8%	16.0%	5.0%
WARREN	1,521	681	586	168	86	Bush	44.8%	38.5%	11.0%	5.7%
WASHINGTON	755	399	250	68	38	Bush	52.8%	33.1%	9.0%	5.0%
WAYNE	708	273	297	113	25	Dole	38.6%	41.9%	16.0%	3.5%
WEBSTER	2,102	823	992	193	94	Dole	39.2%	47.2%	9.2%	4.5%
WORTH	219	91	98	18	12	Dole	41.6%	44.7%	8.2%	5.5%
WRIGHT	1,606	802	587	132	85	Bush	49.9%	36.6%	8.2%	5.3%
TOTAL	400,300	168,812	164,394	44,705	22,389	Bush	42.2%	41.1%	11.2%	5.6%

MONTANA

Since its inception, Montana's presidential primary has been an afterthought to an afterthought. It has often been the least populous state to vote on the last big day of the primary season.

The only presidential candidate in recent times to make a significant effort in Montana was Frank Church of neighboring Idaho. His 10 visits in 1976 earned him nearly 60 percent of the Democratic primary vote and victory over Jimmy Carter. Carter followed the norm of most candidates: he did not visit the state at all.

The last time a Republican presidential contest seriously involved Montana was that same year, when Ronald Reagan and President Gerald Ford were nearing the end of their long-running battle for the nomination. Reagan won the Montana primary with 63 percent of the vote, then swept all the delegates (traditionally chosen separately at the GOP state convention).

Generally, a libertarian rather than moralistic strain of Republicanism is dominant in Montana. President George Bush won the primary easily in 1992, with Pat Buchanan running a distant third behind the "no preference" line. Buchanan managed to beat the "no preference" line in 1996, but still trailed Bob Dole by a wide margin.

The last Democratic presidential primary in Montana with much significance came in 1980, when President Carter defeated Edward Kennedy, 51 to 37 percent. While Carter carried most of the state, including its leading population centers, Kennedy took the Native American counties of Big Horn and Glacier and a number of politically volatile wheat-growing counties in northeast Montana, where farmers were unhappy with the Carter administration's grain embargo.

Conspicuously, though, Kennedy failed to win in the Democratic counties of western Montana, such as Deer Lodge (Anaconda) and Silver Bow (Butte), where there is a large ethnic population and a strong union tradition built around the copper mines. Silver Bow is among the largest source of votes in a Democratic primary, even though it is not one of Montana's more populous counties.

Bill Clinton scored a lackluster win in Democratic voting in 1992, the party's last presidential primary that was even vaguely competitive. Even though Clinton was already the apparent nominee, he drew less than a majority of the primary vote. He was ambushed by the "no preference" forces in rural Treasure County, which is in the vicinity of the Little Bighorn battlefield.

Recent Montana Primary Results

Montana held its first presidential primary in 1916, but only one between 1924 and 1976, that in 1956.

	DEMOCRATS			REPUBLICANS		
Year	Turnout	Candidates	%	Turnout	Candidates	%
1996 (June 4)	91,725	BILL CLINTON*	90	117,746	BOB DOLE	61
		No Preference	10		Pat Buchanan	24
1992 (June 2)	117,471	BILL CLINTON	47	90,975	GEORGE BUSH*	72
		No Preference	24		No Preference	17
		Jerry Brown	18		Pat Buchanan	12
		Paul Tsongas	11			
1988 (June 7)	121,871	MICHAEL DUKAKIS	69	86,380	GEORGE BUSH	73
		Jesse Jackson	22		Bob Dole	19
1984 (June 5)	34,214	NO PREFERENCE	83	71,887	RONALD REAGAN*	92
1980 (June 3)	130,059	JIMMY CARTER*	51	79,423	RONALD REAGAN	87
		Edward Kennedy	37			
		No Preference	12			
1976 (June 1)	106,841	FRANK CHURCH	59	89,779	RONALD REAGAN	63
		Jimmy Carter	25		Gerald Ford*	35

Note: All candidates are listed that drew at least 10 percent of their party's primary vote. The names of winning candidates are capitalized. An asterisk (*) indicates an incumbent president.

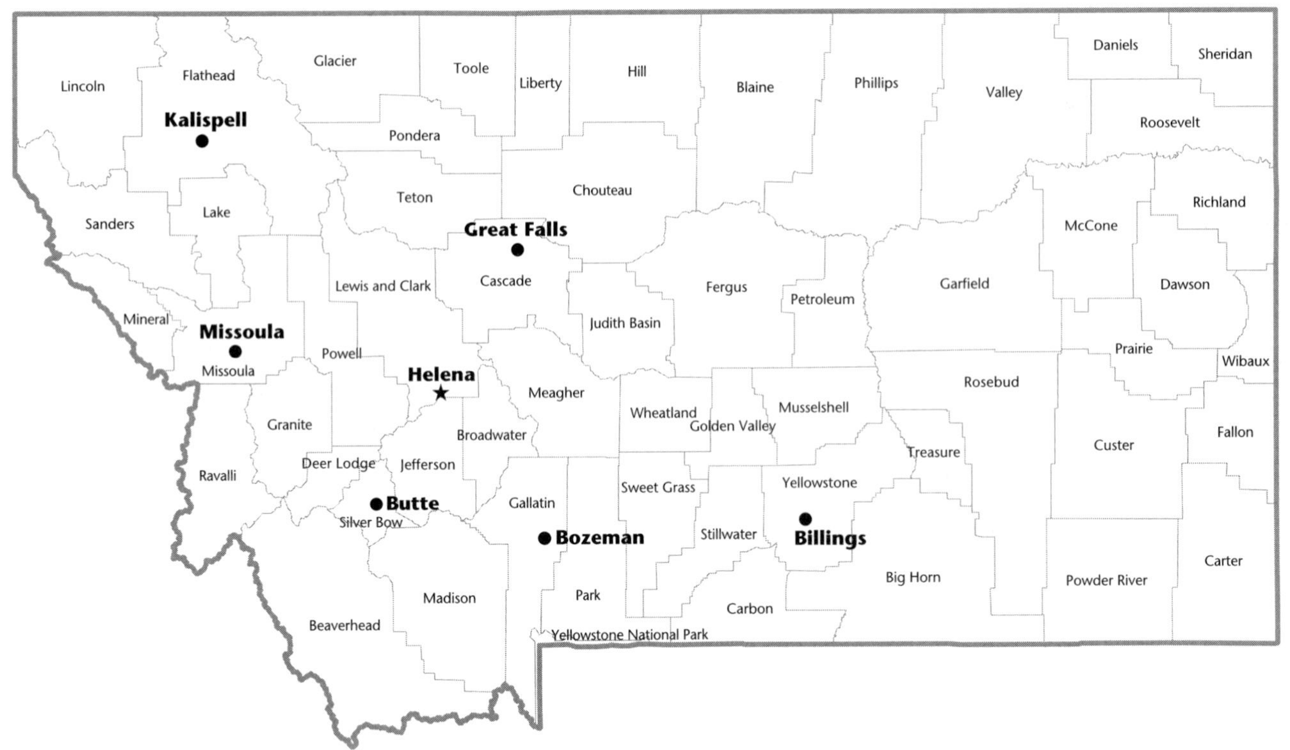
Lincoln
Flathead
Glacier
Toole
Liberty
Hill
Blaine
Phillips
Valley
Daniels
Sheridan
Roosevelt
Kalispell
Pondera
Teton
Chouteau
Lake
Sanders
Great Falls
Cascade
Lewis and Clark
Richland
McCone
Dawson
Garfield
Fergus
Petroleum
Judith Basin
Mineral
Missoula
Missoula
Powell
Helena
Meagher
Prairie
Wibaux
Rosebud
Wheatland
Golden Valley
Musselshell
Granite
Broadwater
Deer Lodge
Jefferson
Ravalli
Treasure
Custer
Fallon
Sweet Grass
Yellowstone
Butte
Silver Bow
Gallatin
Bozeman
Stillwater
Billings
Big Horn
Powder River
Carter
Madison
Park
Carbon
Beaverhead
Yellowstone National Park

MONTANA DEMOCRATIC

1976

County	Total Vote	Carter	Church	Other	Winner	Percentage of Total Vote Carter	Church	Other
BEAVERHEAD	930	268	515	147	Church	28.8%	55.4%	15.8%
BIG HORN	1,178	336	551	291	Church	28.5%	46.8%	24.7%
BLAINE	948	261	535	152	Church	27.5%	56.4%	16.0%
BROADWATER	380	109	216	55	Church	28.7%	56.8%	14.5%
CARBON	1,361	320	851	190	Church	23.5%	62.5%	14.0%
CARTER	248	106	90	52	Carter	42.7%	36.3%	21.0%
CASCADE	10,678	2,493	6,490	1,695	Church	23.3%	60.8%	15.9%
CHOUTEAU	1,164	303	702	159	Church	26.0%	60.3%	13.7%
CUSTER	1,605	453	944	208	Church	28.2%	58.8%	13.0%
DANIELS	414	170	181	63	Church	41.1%	43.7%	15.2%
DAWSON	1,436	480	746	210	Church	33.4%	51.9%	14.6%
DEER LODGE	3,735	696	2,529	510	Church	18.6%	67.7%	13.7%
FALLON	515	158	283	74	Church	30.7%	55.0%	14.4%
FERGUS	1,756	545	910	301	Church	31.0%	51.8%	17.1%
FLATHEAD	4,881	1,089	3,016	776	Church	22.3%	61.8%	15.9%
GALLATIN	4,082	932	2,488	662	Church	22.8%	61.0%	16.2%
GARFIELD	201	63	88	50	Church	31.3%	43.8%	24.9%
GLACIER	1,309	418	576	315	Church	31.9%	44.0%	24.1%
GOLDEN VALLEY	213	63	122	28	Church	29.6%	57.3%	13.1%
GRANITE	397	85	259	53	Church	21.4%	65.2%	13.4%
HILL	2,700	721	1,522	457	Church	26.7%	56.4%	16.9%
JEFFERSON	972	208	607	157	Church	21.4%	62.4%	16.2%
JUDITH BASIN	519	103	346	70	Church	19.8%	66.7%	13.5%
LAKE	1,861	494	1,133	234	Church	26.5%	60.9%	12.6%
LEWIS AND CLARK	5,916	1,380	3,613	923	Church	23.3%	61.1%	15.6%
LIBERTY	386	110	217	59	Church	28.5%	56.2%	15.3%
LINCOLN	2,476	703	1,264	509	Church	28.4%	51.1%	20.6%
MCCONE	580	218	296	66	Church	37.6%	51.0%	11.4%
MADISON	595	146	368	81	Church	24.5%	61.8%	13.6%
MEAGHER	227	52	131	44	Church	22.9%	57.7%	19.4%
MINERAL	776	180	488	108	Church	23.2%	62.9%	13.9%
MISSOULA	11,028	2,119	7,043	1,866	Church	19.2%	63.9%	16.9%
MUSSELSHELL	726	185	400	141	Church	25.5%	55.1%	19.4%
PARK	1,466	417	771	278	Church	28.4%	52.6%	19.0%
PETROLEUM	98	30	49	19	Church	30.6%	50.0%	19.4%
PHILLIPS	678	214	352	112	Church	31.6%	51.9%	16.5%
PONDERA	1,027	261	628	138	Church	25.4%	61.1%	13.4%
POWDER RIVER	292	115	116	61	Church	39.4%	39.7%	20.9%
POWELL	1,047	278	626	143	Church	26.6%	59.8%	13.7%
PRAIRIE	255	73	144	38	Church	28.6%	56.5%	14.9%
RAVALLI	2,919	713	1,743	463	Church	24.4%	59.7%	15.9%
RICHLAND	1,212	550	498	164	Carter	45.4%	41.1%	13.5%
ROOSEVELT	1,068	431	469	168	Church	40.4%	43.9%	15.7%
ROSEBUD	969	281	477	211	Church	29.0%	49.2%	21.8%
SANDERS	1,107	293	648	166	Church	26.5%	58.5%	15.0%
SHERIDAN	867	363	371	133	Church	41.9%	42.8%	15.3%
SILVER BOW	10,899	2,006	7,398	1,495	Church	18.4%	67.9%	13.7%
STILLWATER	745	189	435	121	Church	25.4%	58.4%	16.2%
SWEET GRASS	341	100	177	64	Church	29.3%	51.9%	18.8%
TETON	1,146	235	779	132	Church	20.5%	68.0%	11.5%

MONTANA DEMOCRATIC

1976

County	Total Vote	Carter	Church	Other	Winner	Percentage of Total Vote Carter	Church	Other
TOOLE	708	179	389	140	Church	25.3%	54.9%	19.8%
TREASURE	221	53	120	48	Church	24.0%	54.3%	21.7%
VALLEY	1,645	575	737	333	Church	35.0%	44.8%	20.2%
WHEATLAND	448	79	286	83	Church	17.6%	63.8%	18.5%
WIBAUX	236	91	107	38	Church	38.6%	45.3%	16.1%
YELLOWSTONE	11,254	2,836	6,608	1,810	Church	25.2%	58.7%	16.1%
TOTAL	106,841	26,329	63,448	17,064	Church	24.6%	59.4%	16.0%

MONTANA REPUBLICAN

1976

County	Total Vote	Ford	Reagan	Uncommitted	Winner	Percentage of Total Vote Ford	Reagan	Uncom.
BEAVERHEAD	1,828	570	1,215	43	Reagan	31.2%	66.5%	2.4%
BIG HORN	843	298	525	20	Reagan	35.3%	62.3%	2.4%
BLAINE	830	207	620	3	Reagan	24.9%	74.7%	0.4%
BROADWATER	582	160	411	11	Reagan	27.5%	70.6%	1.9%
CARBON	1,188	461	714	13	Reagan	38.8%	60.1%	1.1%
CARTER	421	82	331	8	Reagan	19.5%	78.6%	1.9%
CASCADE	6,961	2,499	4,286	176	Reagan	35.9%	61.6%	2.5%
CHOUTEAU	1,236	206	1,013	17	Reagan	16.7%	82.0%	1.4%
CUSTER	1,582	615	945	22	Reagan	38.9%	59.7%	1.4%
DANIELS	574	206	351	17	Reagan	35.9%	61.1%	3.0%
DAWSON	1,295	493	767	35	Reagan	38.1%	59.2%	2.7%
DEER LODGE	790	369	408	13	Reagan	46.7%	51.6%	1.6%
FALLON	511	140	363	8	Reagan	27.4%	71.0%	1.6%
FERGUS	2,379	721	1,607	51	Reagan	30.3%	67.5%	2.1%
FLATHEAD	4,608	1,418	3,092	98	Reagan	30.8%	67.1%	2.1%
GALLATIN	5,373	1,784	3,506	83	Reagan	33.2%	65.3%	1.5%
GARFIELD	441	118	318	5	Reagan	26.8%	72.1%	1.1%
GLACIER	955	216	725	14	Reagan	22.6%	75.9%	1.5%
GOLDEN VALLEY	198	55	140	3	Reagan	27.8%	70.7%	1.5%
GRANITE	443	159	281	3	Reagan	35.9%	63.4%	0.7%
HILL	1,614	419	1,159	36	Reagan	26.0%	71.8%	2.2%
JEFFERSON	718	201	498	19	Reagan	28.0%	69.4%	2.6%
JUDITH BASIN	754	177	553	24	Reagan	23.5%	73.3%	3.2%
LAKE	2,510	722	1,746	42	Reagan	28.8%	69.6%	1.7%
LEWIS AND CLARK	5,753	1,993	3,604	156	Reagan	34.6%	62.6%	2.7%
LIBERTY	425	64	356	5	Reagan	15.1%	83.8%	1.2%
LINCOLN	1,195	461	705	29	Reagan	38.6%	59.0%	2.4%
MCCONE	487	114	361	12	Reagan	23.4%	74.1%	2.5%
MADISON	1,329	403	886	40	Reagan	30.3%	66.7%	3.0%
MEAGHER	440	124	300	16	Reagan	28.2%	68.2%	3.6%

MONTANA REPUBLICAN

1976

County	Total Vote	Ford	Reagan	Uncommitted	Winner	Percentage of Total Vote Ford	Reagan	Uncom.
MINERAL	303	127	164	12	Reagan	41.9%	54.1%	4.0%
MISSOULA	8,133	3,450	4,442	241	Reagan	42.4%	54.6%	3.0%
MUSSELSHELL	536	190	336	10	Reagan	35.4%	62.7%	1.9%
PARK	1,771	594	1,141	36	Reagan	33.5%	64.4%	2.0%
PETROLEUM	124	43	77	4	Reagan	34.7%	62.1%	3.2%
PHILLIPS	794	247	528	19	Reagan	31.1%	66.5%	2.4%
PONDERA	1,018	240	766	12	Reagan	23.6%	75.2%	1.2%
POWDER RIVER	480	108	356	16	Reagan	22.5%	74.2%	3.3%
POWELL	1,015	395	601	19	Reagan	38.9%	59.2%	1.9%
PRAIRIE	406	115	282	9	Reagan	28.3%	69.5%	2.2%
RAVALLI	2,688	806	1,834	48	Reagan	30.0%	68.2%	1.8%
RICHLAND	1,368	436	891	41	Reagan	31.9%	65.1%	3.0%
ROOSEVELT	979	308	650	21	Reagan	31.5%	66.4%	2.1%
ROSEBUD	622	237	367	18	Reagan	38.1%	59.0%	2.9%
SANDERS	917	328	582	7	Reagan	35.8%	63.5%	0.8%
SHERIDAN	707	257	425	25	Reagan	36.4%	60.1%	3.5%
SILVER BOW	2,102	985	1,037	80	Reagan	46.9%	49.3%	3.8%
STILLWATER	983	315	650	18	Reagan	32.0%	66.1%	1.8%
SWEET GRASS	772	295	457	20	Reagan	38.2%	59.2%	2.6%
TETON	1,126	244	863	19	Reagan	21.7%	76.6%	1.7%
TOOLE	913	207	692	14	Reagan	22.7%	75.8%	1.5%
TREASURE	199	76	117	6	Reagan	38.2%	58.8%	3.0%
VALLEY	1,263	370	869	24	Reagan	29.3%	68.8%	1.9%
WHEATLAND	474	171	286	17	Reagan	36.1%	60.3%	3.6%
WIBAUX	193	44	146	3	Reagan	22.8%	75.6%	1.6%
YELLOWSTONE	11,630	5,057	6,338	235	Reagan	43.5%	54.5%	2.0%
TOTAL	89,779	31,100	56,683	1,996	Reagan	34.6%	63.1%	2.2%

MONTANA DEMOCRATIC

1980

County	Total Vote	Carter	E. Kennedy	Other	Winner	Percentage of Total Vote Carter	E. Kennedy	Other
BEAVERHEAD	1,563	824	400	339	Carter	52.7%	25.6%	21.7%
BIG HORN	1,234	560	567	107	E. Kennedy	45.4%	45.9%	8.7%
BLAINE	1,200	596	455	149	Carter	49.7%	37.9%	12.4%
BROADWATER	638	351	191	96	Carter	55.0%	29.9%	15.0%
CARBON	1,779	884	755	140	Carter	49.7%	42.4%	7.9%
CARTER	234	142	64	28	Carter	60.7%	27.4%	12.0%
CASCADE	12,534	6,334	4,669	1,531	Carter	50.5%	37.3%	12.2%
CHOUTEAU	1,776	819	608	349	Carter	46.1%	34.2%	19.7%
CUSTER	1,730	934	613	183	Carter	54.0%	35.4%	10.6%
DANIELS	570	233	250	87	E. Kennedy	40.9%	43.9%	15.3%
DAWSON	1,626	806	550	270	Carter	49.6%	33.8%	16.6%
DEER LODGE	4,064	1,942	1,795	327	Carter	47.8%	44.2%	8.0%
FALLON	674	308	281	85	Carter	45.7%	41.7%	12.6%
FERGUS	2,028	1,080	630	318	Carter	53.3%	31.1%	15.7%
FLATHEAD	6,294	3,557	1,768	969	Carter	56.5%	28.1%	15.4%
GALLATIN	5,301	3,025	1,624	652	Carter	57.1%	30.6%	12.3%
GARFIELD	249	123	81	45	Carter	49.4%	32.5%	18.1%
GLACIER	1,826	675	906	245	E. Kennedy	37.0%	49.6%	13.4%
GOLDEN VALLEY	175	86	62	27	Carter	49.1%	35.4%	15.4%
GRANITE	513	282	179	52	Carter	55.0%	34.9%	10.1%
HILL	3,326	1,589	1,194	543	Carter	47.8%	35.9%	16.3%
JEFFERSON	1,273	728	483	62	Carter	57.2%	37.9%	4.9%
JUDITH BASIN	662	316	227	119	Carter	47.7%	34.3%	18.0%
LAKE	2,651	1,628	803	220	Carter	61.4%	30.3%	8.3%
LEWIS AND CLARK	8,866	4,766	3,390	710	Carter	53.8%	38.2%	8.0%
LIBERTY	452	234	143	75	Carter	51.8%	31.6%	16.6%
LINCOLN	3,259	1,849	851	559	Carter	56.7%	26.1%	17.2%
MCCONE	532	219	239	74	E. Kennedy	41.2%	44.9%	13.9%
MADISON	679	424	167	88	Carter	62.4%	24.6%	13.0%
MEAGHER	279	180	68	31	Carter	64.5%	24.4%	11.1%
MINERAL	784	395	269	120	Carter	50.4%	34.3%	15.3%
MISSOULA	12,163	6,322	4,012	1,829	Carter	52.0%	33.0%	15.0%
MUSSELSHELL	754	410	269	75	Carter	54.4%	35.7%	9.9%
PARK	1,702	906	595	201	Carter	53.2%	35.0%	11.8%
PETROLEUM	114	68	29	17	Carter	59.6%	25.4%	14.9%
PHILLIPS	728	397	252	79	Carter	54.5%	34.6%	10.9%
PONDERA	1,400	696	480	224	Carter	49.7%	34.3%	16.0%
POWDER RIVER	257	147	84	26	Carter	57.2%	32.7%	10.1%
POWELL	1,237	657	400	180	Carter	53.1%	32.3%	14.6%
PRAIRIE	286	170	94	22	Carter	59.4%	32.9%	7.7%
RAVALLI	3,436	2,008	935	493	Carter	58.4%	27.2%	14.3%
RICHLAND	1,348	601	511	236	Carter	44.6%	37.9%	17.5%
ROOSEVELT	1,680	652	812	216	E. Kennedy	38.8%	48.3%	12.9%
ROSEBUD	923	507	291	125	Carter	54.9%	31.5%	13.5%
SANDERS	1,286	778	354	154	Carter	60.5%	27.5%	12.0%
SHERIDAN	898	379	387	132	E. Kennedy	42.2%	43.1%	14.7%
SILVER BOW	14,483	6,750	6,454	1,279	Carter	46.6%	44.6%	8.8%
STILLWATER	1,023	556	347	120	Carter	54.3%	33.9%	11.7%
SWEET GRASS	348	240	81	27	Carter	69.0%	23.3%	7.8%
TETON	1,442	695	531	216	Carter	48.2%	36.8%	15.0%

MONTANA DEMOCRATIC

1980

County	Total Vote	Carter	E. Kennedy	Other	Winner	Percentage of Total Vote Carter	E. Kennedy	Other
TOOLE	946	455	368	123	Carter	48.1%	38.9%	13.0%
TREASURE	208	114	72	22	Carter	54.8%	34.6%	10.6%
VALLEY	1,744	824	752	168	Carter	47.2%	43.1%	9.6%
WHEATLAND	493	226	217	50	Carter	45.8%	44.0%	10.1%
WIBAUX	309	121	156	32	E. Kennedy	39.2%	50.5%	10.4%
YELLOWSTONE	12,080	6,354	4,906	820	Carter	52.6%	40.6%	6.8%
TOTAL	130,059	66,922	47,671	15,466	Carter	51.5%	36.7%	11.9%

MONTANA REPUBLICAN

1980

County	Total Vote	Reagan	Other	Winner	Percentage of Total Vote Reagan	Other
BEAVERHEAD	1,016	923	93	Reagan	90.8%	9.2%
BIG HORN	748	636	112	Reagan	85.0%	15.0%
BLAINE	620	586	34	Reagan	94.5%	5.5%
BROADWATER	356	324	32	Reagan	91.0%	9.0%
CARBON	837	731	106	Reagan	87.3%	12.7%
CARTER	338	316	22	Reagan	93.5%	6.5%
CASCADE	4,575	3,931	644	Reagan	85.9%	14.1%
CHOUTEAU	809	743	66	Reagan	91.8%	8.2%
CUSTER	1,498	1,274	224	Reagan	85.0%	15.0%
DANIELS	436	390	46	Reagan	89.4%	10.6%
DAWSON	1,259	1,101	158	Reagan	87.5%	12.5%
DEER LODGE	366	316	50	Reagan	86.3%	13.7%
FALLON	542	493	49	Reagan	91.0%	9.0%
FERGUS	2,154	1,897	257	Reagan	88.1%	11.9%
FLATHEAD	5,963	5,353	610	Reagan	89.8%	10.2%
GALLATIN	5,497	4,739	758	Reagan	86.2%	13.8%
GARFIELD	329	302	27	Reagan	91.8%	8.2%
GLACIER	668	625	43	Reagan	93.6%	6.4%
GOLDEN VALLEY	169	144	25	Reagan	85.2%	14.8%
GRANITE	436	382	54	Reagan	87.6%	12.4%
HILL	1,106	993	113	Reagan	89.8%	10.2%
JEFFERSON	596	544	52	Reagan	91.3%	8.7%
JUDITH BASIN	452	383	69	Reagan	84.7%	15.3%
LAKE	2,420	2,207	213	Reagan	91.2%	8.8%
LEWIS AND CLARK	4,003	3,099	904	Reagan	77.4%	22.6%
LIBERTY	356	329	27	Reagan	92.4%	7.6%
LINCOLN	1,011	907	104	Reagan	89.7%	10.3%
MCCONE	371	343	28	Reagan	92.5%	7.5%
MADISON	1,523	1,313	210	Reagan	86.2%	13.8%
MEAGHER	343	301	42	Reagan	87.8%	12.2%

MONTANA REPUBLICAN

1980

County	Total Vote	Reagan	Other	Winner	Percentage of Total Vote Reagan	Other
MINERAL	225	188	37	Reagan	83.6%	16.4%
MISSOULA	5,707	4,785	922	Reagan	83.8%	16.2%
MUSSELSHELL	643	531	112	Reagan	82.6%	17.4%
PARK	2,121	1,827	294	Reagan	86.1%	13.9%
PETROLEUM	111	92	19	Reagan	82.9%	17.1%
PHILLIPS	773	688	85	Reagan	89.0%	11.0%
PONDERA	922	873	49	Reagan	94.7%	5.3%
POWDER RIVER	717	625	92	Reagan	87.2%	12.8%
POWELL	730	648	82	Reagan	88.8%	11.2%
PRAIRIE	392	355	37	Reagan	90.6%	9.4%
RAVALLI	3,136	2,809	327	Reagan	89.6%	10.4%
RICHLAND	1,009	925	84	Reagan	91.7%	8.3%
ROOSEVELT	723	666	57	Reagan	92.1%	7.9%
ROSEBUD	795	673	122	Reagan	84.7%	15.3%
SANDERS	1,220	1,004	216	Reagan	82.3%	17.7%
SHERIDAN	643	565	78	Reagan	87.9%	12.1%
SILVER BOW	674	575	99	Reagan	85.3%	14.7%
STILLWATER	838	717	121	Reagan	85.6%	14.4%
SWEET GRASS	815	681	134	Reagan	83.6%	16.4%
TETON	1,053	954	99	Reagan	90.6%	9.4%
TOOLE	819	769	50	Reagan	93.9%	6.1%
TREASURE	152	113	39	Reagan	74.3%	25.7%
VALLEY	1,136	1,067	69	Reagan	93.9%	6.1%
WHEATLAND	389	318	71	Reagan	81.7%	18.3%
WIBAUX	133	123	10	Reagan	92.5%	7.5%
YELLOWSTONE	12,750	10,548	2,202	Reagan	82.7%	17.3%
TOTAL	79,423	68,744	10,679	Reagan	86.6%	13.4%

MONTANA REPUBLICAN

1984

County	Total Vote	Reagan	Uncommitted	Winner	Percentage of Total Vote Reagan	Uncom.
BEAVERHEAD	1,825	1,702	123	Reagan	93.3%	6.7%
BIG HORN	710	627	83	Reagan	88.3%	11.7%
BLAINE	385	366	19	Reagan	95.1%	4.9%
BROADWATER	647	580	67	Reagan	89.6%	10.4%
CARBON	1,021	932	89	Reagan	91.3%	8.7%
CARTER	295	278	17	Reagan	94.2%	5.8%
CASCADE	4,411	4,203	208	Reagan	95.3%	4.7%
CHOUTEAU	1,391	1,293	98	Reagan	93.0%	7.0%
CUSTER	1,203	1,109	94	Reagan	92.2%	7.8%
DANIELS	406	375	31	Reagan	92.4%	7.6%
DAWSON	1,192	1,091	101	Reagan	91.5%	8.5%
DEER LODGE	291	272	19	Reagan	93.5%	6.5%
FALLON	327	317	10	Reagan	96.9%	3.1%
FERGUS	1,568	1,502	66	Reagan	95.8%	4.2%
FLATHEAD	5,111	4,793	318	Reagan	93.8%	6.2%
GALLATIN	3,229	3,047	182	Reagan	94.4%	5.6%
GARFIELD	373	358	15	Reagan	96.0%	4.0%
GLACIER	828	783	45	Reagan	94.6%	5.4%
GOLDEN VALLEY	157	147	10	Reagan	93.6%	6.4%
GRANITE	342	308	34	Reagan	90.1%	9.9%
HILL	904	806	98	Reagan	89.2%	10.8%
JEFFERSON	629	590	39	Reagan	93.8%	6.2%
JUDITH BASIN	384	374	10	Reagan	97.4%	2.6%
LAKE	3,006	2,667	339	Reagan	88.7%	11.3%
LEWIS AND CLARK	3,564	3,328	236	Reagan	93.4%	6.6%
LIBERTY	632	551	81	Reagan	87.2%	12.8%
LINCOLN	1,264	1,008	256	Reagan	79.7%	20.3%
MCCONE	317	308	9	Reagan	97.2%	2.8%
MADISON	1,248	1,162	86	Reagan	93.1%	6.9%
MEAGHER	320	302	18	Reagan	94.4%	5.6%
MINERAL	92	84	8	Reagan	91.3%	8.7%
MISSOULA	3,996	3,709	287	Reagan	92.8%	7.2%
MUSSELSHELL	672	608	64	Reagan	90.5%	9.5%
PARK	2,035	1,782	253	Reagan	87.6%	12.4%
PETROLEUM	89	86	3	Reagan	96.6%	3.4%
PHILLIPS	620	581	39	Reagan	93.7%	6.3%
PONDERA	938	878	60	Reagan	93.6%	6.4%
POWDER RIVER	785	693	92	Reagan	88.3%	11.7%
POWELL	704	695	9	Reagan	98.7%	1.3%
PRAIRIE	414	385	29	Reagan	93.0%	7.0%
RAVALLI	2,808	2,654	154	Reagan	94.5%	5.5%
RICHLAND	1,027	959	68	Reagan	93.4%	6.6%
ROOSEVELT	516	491	25	Reagan	95.2%	4.8%
ROSEBUD	589	535	54	Reagan	90.8%	9.2%
SANDERS	943	845	98	Reagan	89.6%	10.4%
SHERIDAN	672	630	42	Reagan	93.8%	6.3%
SILVER BOW	809	745	64	Reagan	92.1%	7.9%
STILLWATER	755	721	34	Reagan	95.5%	4.5%
SWEET GRASS	803	734	69	Reagan	91.4%	8.6%
TETON	898	873	25	Reagan	97.2%	2.8%

MONTANA REPUBLICAN

1984

County	Total Vote	Reagan	Uncommitted	Winner	Percentage of Total Vote: Reagan	Uncom.
TOOLE	936	859	77	Reagan	91.8%	8.2%
TREASURE	128	116	12	Reagan	90.6%	9.4%
VALLEY	934	906	28	Reagan	97.0%	3.0%
WHEATLAND	323	306	17	Reagan	94.7%	5.3%
WIBAUX	178	158	20	Reagan	88.8%	11.2%
YELLOWSTONE	11,166	10,220	946	Reagan	91.5%	8.5%
TOTAL	71,810	66,432	5,378	Reagan	92.5%	7.5%

Note: The 1984 edition of *America Votes* lists 77 scattered write-in votes in the Republican primary, which were not readily available on a county-by-county basis.

MONTANA DEMOCRATIC

1988

County	Total Vote	Dukakis	J. Jackson	Other	Winner	Percentage of Total Vote: Dukakis	J. Jackson	Other
BEAVERHEAD	869	634	170	65	Dukakis	73.0%	19.6%	7.5%
BIG HORN	1,440	686	633	121	Dukakis	47.6%	44.0%	8.4%
BLAINE	984	629	260	95	Dukakis	63.9%	26.4%	9.7%
BROADWATER	548	353	100	95	Dukakis	64.4%	18.2%	17.3%
CARBON	2,206	1,632	274	300	Dukakis	74.0%	12.4%	13.6%
CARTER	176	120	26	30	Dukakis	68.2%	14.8%	17.0%
CASCADE	11,605	8,599	2,032	974	Dukakis	74.1%	17.5%	8.4%
CHOUTEAU	1,277	954	160	163	Dukakis	74.7%	12.5%	12.8%
CUSTER	1,910	1,450	274	186	Dukakis	75.9%	14.3%	9.7%
DANIELS	344	268	43	33	Dukakis	77.9%	12.5%	9.6%
DAWSON	1,910	1,380	268	262	Dukakis	72.3%	14.0%	13.7%
DEER LODGE	3,170	2,377	542	251	Dukakis	75.0%	17.1%	7.9%
FALLON	367	283	46	38	Dukakis	77.1%	12.5%	10.4%
FERGUS	1,755	1,322	227	206	Dukakis	75.3%	12.9%	11.7%
FLATHEAD	7,440	5,057	1,567	816	Dukakis	68.0%	21.1%	11.0%
GALLATIN	5,431	2,944	2,068	419	Dukakis	54.2%	38.1%	7.7%
GARFIELD	279	169	19	91	Dukakis	60.6%	6.8%	32.6%
GLACIER	2,633	1,379	913	341	Dukakis	52.4%	34.7%	13.0%
GOLDEN VALLEY	149	117	19	13	Dukakis	78.5%	12.8%	8.7%
GRANITE	377	270	65	42	Dukakis	71.6%	17.2%	11.1%
HILL	2,862	1,972	634	256	Dukakis	68.9%	22.2%	8.9%
JEFFERSON	1,722	1,158	394	170	Dukakis	67.2%	22.9%	9.9%
JUDITH BASIN	604	446	96	62	Dukakis	73.8%	15.9%	10.3%
LAKE	2,845	1,724	910	211	Dukakis	60.6%	32.0%	7.4%
LEWIS AND CLARK	9,714	6,373	2,453	888	Dukakis	65.6%	25.3%	9.1%
LIBERTY	344	265	41	38	Dukakis	77.0%	11.9%	11.0%
LINCOLN	3,050	2,086	577	387	Dukakis	68.4%	18.9%	12.7%
MCCONE	440	295	88	57	Dukakis	67.0%	20.0%	13.0%
MADISON	639	420	146	73	Dukakis	65.7%	22.8%	11.4%
MEAGHER	284	226	34	24	Dukakis	79.6%	12.0%	8.5%

MONTANA DEMOCRATIC

1988

County	Total Vote	Dukakis	J. Jackson	Other	Winner	Percentage of Total Vote Dukakis	J. Jackson	Other
MINERAL	796	542	165	89	Dukakis	68.1%	20.7%	11.2%
MISSOULA	11,443	6,768	3,858	817	Dukakis	59.1%	33.7%	7.1%
MUSSELSHELL	627	494	85	48	Dukakis	78.8%	13.6%	7.7%
PARK	1,715	1,255	319	141	Dukakis	73.2%	18.6%	8.2%
PETROLEUM	97	67	19	11	Dukakis	69.1%	19.6%	11.3%
PHILLIPS	526	381	82	63	Dukakis	72.4%	15.6%	12.0%
PONDERA	996	697	205	94	Dukakis	70.0%	20.6%	9.4%
POWDER RIVER	255	186	42	27	Dukakis	72.9%	16.5%	10.6%
POWELL	1,018	743	172	103	Dukakis	73.0%	16.9%	10.1%
PRAIRIE	257	193	36	28	Dukakis	75.1%	14.0%	10.9%
RAVALLI	3,404	2,366	747	291	Dukakis	69.5%	21.9%	8.5%
RICHLAND	1,047	752	163	132	Dukakis	71.8%	15.6%	12.6%
ROOSEVELT	979	638	224	117	Dukakis	65.2%	22.9%	12.0%
ROSEBUD	1,106	773	238	95	Dukakis	69.9%	21.5%	8.6%
SANDERS	1,338	908	291	139	Dukakis	67.9%	21.7%	10.4%
SHERIDAN	848	671	85	92	Dukakis	79.1%	10.0%	10.8%
SILVER BOW	10,557	7,657	2,136	764	Dukakis	72.5%	20.2%	7.2%
STILLWATER	1,170	899	166	105	Dukakis	76.8%	14.2%	9.0%
SWEET GRASS	317	232	59	26	Dukakis	73.2%	18.6%	8.2%
TETON	1,263	935	171	157	Dukakis	74.0%	13.5%	12.4%
TOOLE	808	599	108	101	Dukakis	74.1%	13.4%	12.5%
TREASURE	159	116	21	22	Dukakis	73.0%	13.2%	13.8%
VALLEY	1,668	1,235	226	207	Dukakis	74.0%	13.5%	12.4%
WHEATLAND	404	318	43	43	Dukakis	78.7%	10.6%	10.6%
WIBAUX	310	202	46	62	Dukakis	65.2%	14.8%	20.0%
YELLOWSTONE	11,389	8,469	2,122	798	Dukakis	74.4%	18.6%	7.0%
TOTAL	121,871	83,684	26,908	11,279	Dukakis	68.7%	22.1%	9.3%

MONTANA REPUBLICAN

1988

County	Total Vote	Bush	Dole	Uncommitted	Winner	Percentage of Total Vote Bush	Dole	Uncom.
BEAVERHEAD	1,896	1,364	360	172	Bush	71.9%	19.0%	9.1%
BIG HORN	711	508	138	65	Bush	71.4%	19.4%	9.1%
BLAINE	688	514	133	41	Bush	74.7%	19.3%	6.0%
BROADWATER	569	411	122	36	Bush	72.2%	21.4%	6.3%
CARBON	782	593	152	37	Bush	75.8%	19.4%	4.7%
CARTER	378	259	80	39	Bush	68.5%	21.2%	10.3%
CASCADE	5,937	4,550	1,045	342	Bush	76.6%	17.6%	5.8%
CHOUTEAU	1,082	783	224	75	Bush	72.4%	20.7%	6.9%
CUSTER	1,525	1,181	230	114	Bush	77.4%	15.1%	7.5%
DANIELS	528	326	143	59	Bush	61.7%	27.1%	11.2%
DAWSON	1,157	831	232	94	Bush	71.8%	20.1%	8.1%
DEER LODGE	369	277	62	30	Bush	75.1%	16.8%	8.1%
FALLON	713	476	151	86	Bush	66.8%	21.2%	12.1%
FERGUS	1,907	1,383	380	144	Bush	72.5%	19.9%	7.6%
FLATHEAD	6,798	4,960	1,268	570	Bush	73.0%	18.7%	8.4%
GALLATIN	5,319	3,740	1,237	342	Bush	70.3%	23.3%	6.4%
GARFIELD	271	208	57	6	Bush	76.8%	21.0%	2.2%
GLACIER	515	400	96	19	Bush	77.7%	18.6%	3.7%
GOLDEN VALLEY	213	142	54	17	Bush	66.7%	25.4%	8.0%
GRANITE	430	297	98	35	Bush	69.1%	22.8%	8.1%
HILL	2,131	1,491	437	203	Bush	70.0%	20.5%	9.5%
JEFFERSON	823	592	178	53	Bush	71.9%	21.6%	6.4%
JUDITH BASIN	464	357	87	20	Bush	76.9%	18.8%	4.3%
LAKE	3,058	2,221	560	277	Bush	72.6%	18.3%	9.1%
LEWIS AND CLARK	5,484	3,729	1,238	517	Bush	68.0%	22.6%	9.4%
LIBERTY	516	350	119	47	Bush	67.8%	23.1%	9.1%
LINCOLN	1,369	1,009	260	100	Bush	73.7%	19.0%	7.3%
MCCONE	429	325	78	26	Bush	75.8%	18.2%	6.1%
MADISON	1,366	945	263	158	Bush	69.2%	19.3%	11.6%
MEAGHER	396	296	75	25	Bush	74.7%	18.9%	6.3%
MINERAL	171	117	35	19	Bush	68.4%	20.5%	11.1%
MISSOULA	5,718	4,366	1,043	309	Bush	76.4%	18.2%	5.4%
MUSSELSHELL	589	450	104	35	Bush	76.4%	17.7%	5.9%
PARK	1,869	1,434	305	130	Bush	76.7%	16.3%	7.0%
PETROLEUM	87	61	20	6	Bush	70.1%	23.0%	6.9%
PHILLIPS	695	502	132	61	Bush	72.2%	19.0%	8.8%
PONDERA	1,075	751	240	84	Bush	69.9%	22.3%	7.8%
POWDER RIVER	618	405	147	66	Bush	65.5%	23.8%	10.7%
POWELL	783	588	145	50	Bush	75.1%	18.5%	6.4%
PRAIRIE	344	253	71	20	Bush	73.5%	20.6%	5.8%
RAVALLI	3,392	2,568	568	256	Bush	75.7%	16.7%	7.5%
RICHLAND	891	604	224	63	Bush	67.8%	25.1%	7.1%
ROOSEVELT	627	459	128	40	Bush	73.2%	20.4%	6.4%
ROSEBUD	700	473	154	73	Bush	67.6%	22.0%	10.4%
SANDERS	1,001	678	227	96	Bush	67.7%	22.7%	9.6%
SHERIDAN	710	535	126	49	Bush	75.4%	17.7%	6.9%
SILVER BOW	1,326	1,011	227	88	Bush	76.2%	17.1%	6.6%
STILLWATER	1,179	861	248	70	Bush	73.0%	21.0%	5.9%
SWEET GRASS	796	610	136	50	Bush	76.6%	17.1%	6.3%
TETON	918	687	176	55	Bush	74.8%	19.2%	6.0%

MONTANA REPUBLICAN

1988

County	Total Vote	Bush	Dole	Uncommitted	Winner	Percentage of Total Vote Bush	Dole	Uncom.
TOOLE	945	643	234	68	Bush	68.0%	24.8%	7.2%
TREASURE	204	119	51	34	Bush	58.3%	25.0%	16.7%
VALLEY	1,563	1,039	360	164	Bush	66.5%	23.0%	10.5%
WHEATLAND	359	269	72	18	Bush	74.9%	20.1%	5.0%
WIBAUX	107	69	32	6	Bush	64.5%	29.9%	5.6%
YELLOWSTONE	11,889	9,028	2,000	861	Bush	75.9%	16.8%	7.2%
TOTAL	86,380	63,098	16,762	6,520	Bush	73.0%	19.4%	7.5%

MONTANA DEMOCRATIC

1992

County	Total Vote	Brown	Clinton	Tsongas	Uncommitted	Winner	Percentage of Total Vote Brown	Clinton	Tsongas	Uncom.
BEAVERHEAD	502	104	313	85		Clinton	20.7%	62.4%	16.9%	
BIG HORN	1,246	246	629	158	213	Clinton	19.7%	50.5%	12.7%	17.1%
BLAINE	1,192	183	626	123	260	Clinton	15.4%	52.5%	10.3%	21.8%
BROADWATER	381	69	221	83	8	Clinton	18.1%	58.0%	21.8%	2.1%
CARBON	1,245	263	559	138	285	Clinton	21.1%	44.9%	11.1%	22.9%
CARTER	98	19	58	8	13	Clinton	19.4%	59.2%	8.2%	13.3%
CASCADE	11,287	1,994	5,522	1,082	2,689	Clinton	17.7%	48.9%	9.6%	23.8%
CHOUTEAU	929	137	454	106	232	Clinton	14.7%	48.9%	11.4%	25.0%
CUSTER	1,462	331	895	236		Clinton	22.6%	61.2%	16.1%	
DANIELS	265	37	156	29	43	Clinton	14.0%	58.9%	10.9%	16.2%
DAWSON	1,331	239	903	189		Clinton	18.0%	67.8%	14.2%	
DEER LODGE	2,626	493	1,384	221	528	Clinton	18.8%	52.7%	8.4%	20.1%
FALLON	379	42	179	37	121	Clinton	11.1%	47.2%	9.8%	31.9%
FERGUS	1,606	251	741	180	434	Clinton	15.6%	46.1%	11.2%	27.0%
FLATHEAD	7,691	1,421	3,105	811	2,354	Clinton	18.5%	40.4%	10.5%	30.6%
GALLATIN	6,682	1,445	2,394	814	2,029	Clinton	21.6%	35.8%	12.2%	30.4%
GARFIELD	131	14	72	17	28	Clinton	10.7%	55.0%	13.0%	21.4%
GLACIER	1,967	335	880	191	561	Clinton	17.0%	44.7%	9.7%	28.5%
GOLDEN VALLEY	114	21	64	11	18	Clinton	18.4%	56.1%	9.6%	15.8%
GRANITE	300	45	138	30	87	Clinton	15.0%	46.0%	10.0%	29.0%
HILL	3,712	600	1,748	320	1,044	Clinton	16.2%	47.1%	8.6%	28.1%
JEFFERSON	1,488	262	647	191	388	Clinton	17.6%	43.5%	12.8%	26.1%
JUDITH BASIN	383	71	252	60		Clinton	18.5%	65.8%	15.7%	
LAKE	2,318	375	1,076	216	651	Clinton	16.2%	46.4%	9.3%	28.1%
LEWIS AND CLARK	9,513	1,987	4,431	1,140	1,955	Clinton	20.9%	46.6%	12.0%	20.6%
LIBERTY	378	49	195	44	90	Clinton	13.0%	51.6%	11.6%	23.8%
LINCOLN	3,136	405	1,298	354	1,079	Clinton	12.9%	41.4%	11.3%	34.4%
MCCONE	338	60	197	28	53	Clinton	17.8%	58.3%	8.3%	15.7%
MADISON	601	110	247	51	193	Clinton	18.3%	41.1%	8.5%	32.1%
MEAGHER	198	47	121	30		Clinton	23.7%	61.1%	15.2%	

MONTANA DEMOCRATIC

1992

County	Total Vote	Brown	Clinton	Tsongas	Uncommitted	Winner	Percentage of Total Vote Brown	Clinton	Tsongas	Uncom.
MINERAL	792	104	341	86	261	Clinton	13.1%	43.1%	10.9%	33.0%
MISSOULA	12,320	2,777	5,549	1,269	2,725	Clinton	22.5%	45.0%	10.3%	22.1%
MUSSELSHELL	490	72	253	54	111	Clinton	14.7%	51.6%	11.0%	22.7%
PARK	1,565	321	677	169	398	Clinton	20.5%	43.3%	10.8%	25.4%
PETROLEUM	63	17	25	5	16	Clinton	27.0%	39.7%	7.9%	25.4%
PHILLIPS	314	38	198	26	52	Clinton	12.1%	63.1%	8.3%	16.6%
PONDERA	1,398	221	661	127	389	Clinton	15.8%	47.3%	9.1%	27.8%
POWDER RIVER	88	12	56	11	9	Clinton	13.6%	63.6%	12.5%	10.2%
POWELL	770	125	375	79	191	Clinton	16.2%	48.7%	10.3%	24.8%
PRAIRIE	190	21	118	14	37	Clinton	11.1%	62.1%	7.4%	19.5%
RAVALLI	3,149	548	1,362	309	930	Clinton	17.4%	43.3%	9.8%	29.5%
RICHLAND	1,012	122	526	122	242	Clinton	12.1%	52.0%	12.1%	23.9%
ROOSEVELT	1,559	253	697	139	470	Clinton	16.2%	44.7%	8.9%	30.1%
ROSEBUD	1,087	180	528	127	252	Clinton	16.6%	48.6%	11.7%	23.2%
SANDERS	1,360	272	830	187	71	Clinton	20.0%	61.0%	13.8%	5.2%
SHERIDAN	1,138	146	600	120	272	Clinton	12.8%	52.7%	10.5%	23.9%
SILVER BOW	10,410	1,826	4,543	892	3,149	Clinton	17.5%	43.6%	8.6%	30.2%
STILLWATER	876	115	453	95	213	Clinton	13.1%	51.7%	10.8%	24.3%
SWEET GRASS	249	53	125	23	48	Clinton	21.3%	50.2%	9.2%	19.3%
TETON	1,194	175	588	116	315	Clinton	14.7%	49.2%	9.7%	26.4%
TOOLE	695	92	351	71	181	Clinton	13.2%	50.5%	10.2%	26.0%
TREASURE	270	44	95	34	97	Uncommitted	16.3%	35.2%	12.6%	35.9%
VALLEY	1,257	197	747	128	185	Clinton	15.7%	59.4%	10.2%	14.7%
WHEATLAND	243	64	174		5	Clinton	26.3%	71.6%		2.1%
WIBAUX	167	30	87	18	32	Clinton	18.0%	52.1%	10.8%	19.2%
YELLOWSTONE	11,316	2,224	5,525	1,410	2,157	Clinton	19.7%	48.8%	12.5%	19.1%
TOTAL	117,471	21,704	54,989	12,614	28,164	Clinton	18.5%	46.8%	10.7%	24.0%

MONTANA REPUBLICAN

1992

County	Total Vote	Buchanan	Bush	Uncommitted	Winner	Percentage of Total Vote Buchanan	Bush	Uncom.
BEAVERHEAD	1,526	280	1,246		Bush	18.3%	81.7%	
BIG HORN	693	67	558	68	Bush	9.7%	80.5%	9.8%
BLAINE	549	50	425	74	Bush	9.1%	77.4%	13.5%
BROADWATER	705	147	550	8	Bush	20.9%	78.0%	1.1%
CARBON	1,388	164	965	259	Bush	11.8%	69.5%	18.7%
CARTER	454	58	321	75	Bush	12.8%	70.7%	16.5%
CASCADE	6,915	643	5,212	1,060	Bush	9.3%	75.4%	15.3%
CHOUTEAU	1,032	97	774	161	Bush	9.4%	75.0%	15.6%
CUSTER	1,412	205	1,207		Bush	14.5%	85.5%	
DANIELS	523	94	323	106	Bush	18.0%	61.8%	20.3%
DAWSON	1,248	240	1,008		Bush	19.2%	80.8%	
DEER LODGE	442	63	318	61	Bush	14.3%	71.9%	13.8%
FALLON	528	60	386	82	Bush	11.4%	73.1%	15.5%
FERGUS	2,007	271	1,412	324	Bush	13.5%	70.4%	16.1%
FLATHEAD	8,181	1,129	4,911	2,141	Bush	13.8%	60.0%	26.2%
GALLATIN	5,906	641	4,046	1,219	Bush	10.9%	68.5%	20.6%
GARFIELD	344	55	220	69	Bush	16.0%	64.0%	20.1%
GLACIER	669	94	434	141	Bush	14.1%	64.9%	21.1%
GOLDEN VALLEY	161	28	106	27	Bush	17.4%	65.8%	16.8%
GRANITE	457	48	306	103	Bush	10.5%	67.0%	22.5%
HILL	1,357	148	958	251	Bush	10.9%	70.6%	18.5%
JEFFERSON	1,007	118	736	153	Bush	11.7%	73.1%	15.2%
JUDITH BASIN	408	64	344		Bush	15.7%	84.3%	
LAKE	2,406	289	1,627	490	Bush	12.0%	67.6%	20.4%
LEWIS AND CLARK	6,263	531	4,962	770	Bush	8.5%	79.2%	12.3%
LIBERTY	387	38	291	58	Bush	9.8%	75.2%	15.0%
LINCOLN	1,447	183	880	384	Bush	12.6%	60.8%	26.5%
MCCONE	355	42	276	37	Bush	11.8%	77.7%	10.4%
MADISON	1,451	177	891	383	Bush	12.2%	61.4%	26.4%
MEAGHER	400	81	319		Bush	20.3%	79.8%	
MINERAL	176	19	117	40	Bush	10.8%	66.5%	22.7%
MISSOULA	6,659	607	4,828	1,224	Bush	9.1%	72.5%	18.4%
MUSSELSHELL	609	92	447	70	Bush	15.1%	73.4%	11.5%
PARK	1,858	358	1,188	312	Bush	19.3%	63.9%	16.8%
PETROLEUM	105	11	78	16	Bush	10.5%	74.3%	15.2%
PHILLIPS	1,197	173	738	286	Bush	14.5%	61.7%	23.9%
PONDERA	879	106	618	155	Bush	12.1%	70.3%	17.6%
POWDER RIVER	591	84	400	107	Bush	14.2%	67.7%	18.1%
POWELL	953	107	633	213	Bush	11.2%	66.4%	22.4%
PRAIRIE	338	44	249	45	Bush	13.0%	73.7%	13.3%
RAVALLI	3,185	316	2,062	807	Bush	9.9%	64.7%	25.3%
RICHLAND	1,050	162	726	162	Bush	15.4%	69.1%	15.4%
ROOSEVELT	662	80	473	109	Bush	12.1%	71.5%	16.5%
ROSEBUD	665	80	491	94	Bush	12.0%	73.8%	14.1%
SANDERS	745	138	586	21	Bush	18.5%	78.7%	2.8%
SHERIDAN	517	56	397	64	Bush	10.8%	76.8%	12.4%
SILVER BOW	2,101	213	1,451	437	Bush	10.1%	69.1%	20.8%
STILLWATER	1,161	120	855	186	Bush	10.3%	73.6%	16.0%
SWEET GRASS	804	88	609	107	Bush	10.9%	75.7%	13.3%
TETON	1,031	117	726	188	Bush	11.3%	70.4%	18.2%

MONTANA REPUBLICAN

1992

County	Total Vote	Buchanan	Bush	Uncommitted	Winner	Percentage of Total Vote Buchanan	Bush	Uncom.
TOOLE	1,066	153	629	284	Bush	14.4%	59.0%	26.6%
TREASURE	95	13	71	11	Bush	13.7%	74.7%	11.6%
VALLEY	1,324	192	871	261	Bush	14.5%	65.8%	19.7%
WHEATLAND	346	59	278	9	Bush	17.1%	80.3%	2.6%
WIBAUX	146	15	109	22	Bush	10.3%	74.7%	15.1%
YELLOWSTONE	12,091	1,193	9,534	1,364	Bush	9.9%	78.9%	11.3%
TOTAL	90,975	10,701	65,176	15,098	Bush	11.8%	71.6%	16.6%

MONTANA DEMOCRATIC

1996

County	Total Vote	Clinton	Uncommitted	Winner	Percentage of Total Vote Clinton	Uncom.
BEAVERHEAD	522	486	36	Clinton	93.1%	6.9%
BIG HORN	1,410	1,269	141	Clinton	90.0%	10.0%
BLAINE	1,098	934	164	Clinton	85.1%	14.9%
BROADWATER	470	360	110	Clinton	76.6%	23.4%
CARBON	1,106	956	150	Clinton	86.4%	13.6%
CARTER	82	71	11	Clinton	86.6%	13.4%
CASCADE	8,560	7,885	675	Clinton	92.1%	7.9%
CHOUTEAU	517	479	38	Clinton	92.6%	7.4%
CUSTER	1,006	922	84	Clinton	91.7%	8.3%
DANIELS	286	266	20	Clinton	93.0%	7.0%
DAWSON	1,720	1,543	177	Clinton	89.7%	10.3%
DEER LODGE	3,098	2,843	255	Clinton	91.8%	8.2%
FALLON	325	249	76	Clinton	76.6%	23.4%
FERGUS	907	777	130	Clinton	85.7%	14.3%
FLATHEAD	5,122	4,473	649	Clinton	87.3%	12.7%
GALLATIN	3,893	3,563	330	Clinton	91.5%	8.5%
GARFIELD	74	57	17	Clinton	77.0%	23.0%
GLACIER	1,792	1,446	346	Clinton	80.7%	19.3%
GOLDEN VALLEY	106	95	11	Clinton	89.6%	10.4%
GRANITE	243	215	28	Clinton	88.5%	11.5%
HILL	2,882	2,404	478	Clinton	83.4%	16.6%
JEFFERSON	1,120	962	158	Clinton	85.9%	14.1%
JUDITH BASIN	234	217	17	Clinton	92.7%	7.3%
LAKE	1,812	1,709	103	Clinton	94.3%	5.7%
LEWIS AND CLARK	7,046	6,383	663	Clinton	90.6%	9.4%
LIBERTY	237	206	31	Clinton	86.9%	13.1%
LINCOLN	1,805	1,505	300	Clinton	83.4%	16.6%
MCCONE	254	237	17	Clinton	93.3%	6.7%
MADISON	354	318	36	Clinton	89.8%	10.2%
MEAGHER	96	89	7	Clinton	92.7%	7.3%

MONTANA DEMOCRATIC

1996

County	Total Vote	Clinton	Uncommitted	Winner	Percentage of Total Vote Clinton	Percentage of Total Vote Uncom.
MINERAL	579	469	110	Clinton	81.0%	19.0%
MISSOULA	8,556	7,935	621	Clinton	92.7%	7.3%
MUSSELSHELL	389	357	32	Clinton	91.8%	8.2%
PARK	1,191	1,090	101	Clinton	91.5%	8.5%
PETROLEUM	37	37		Clinton	100.0%	
PHILLIPS	401	352	49	Clinton	87.8%	12.2%
PONDERA	667	609	58	Clinton	91.3%	8.7%
POWDER RIVER	80	69	11	Clinton	86.3%	13.8%
POWELL	606	539	67	Clinton	88.9%	11.1%
PRAIRIE	186	174	12	Clinton	93.5%	6.5%
RAVALLI	2,331	2,151	180	Clinton	92.3%	7.7%
RICHLAND	880	746	134	Clinton	84.8%	15.2%
ROOSEVELT	1,285	1,166	119	Clinton	90.7%	9.3%
ROSEBUD	1,038	887	151	Clinton	85.5%	14.5%
SANDERS	1,379	1,042	337	Clinton	75.6%	24.4%
SHERIDAN	906	816	90	Clinton	90.1%	9.9%
SILVER BOW	9,514	8,792	722	Clinton	92.4%	7.6%
STILLWATER	723	666	57	Clinton	92.1%	7.9%
SWEET GRASS	194	181	13	Clinton	93.3%	6.7%
TETON	657	600	57	Clinton	91.3%	8.7%
TOOLE	994	734	260	Clinton	73.8%	26.2%
TREASURE	119	103	16	Clinton	86.6%	13.4%
VALLEY	832	740	92	Clinton	88.9%	11.1%
WHEATLAND	211	200	11	Clinton	94.8%	5.2%
WIBAUX	152	122	30	Clinton	80.3%	19.7%
YELLOWSTONE	9,641	9,053	588	Clinton	93.9%	6.1%
TOTAL	91,725	82,549	9,176	Clinton	90.0%	10.0%

MONTANA REPUBLICAN

1996

County	Total Vote	Buchanan	Dole	Other	Winner	Percentage of Total Vote		
						Buchanan	Dole	Other
BEAVERHEAD	1,785	321	1,217	247	Dole	18.0%	68.2%	13.8%
BIG HORN	782	195	495	92	Dole	24.9%	63.3%	11.8%
BLAINE	539	110	370	59	Dole	20.4%	68.6%	10.9%
BROADWATER	645	197	384	64	Dole	30.5%	59.5%	9.9%
CARBON	1,502	481	832	189	Dole	32.0%	55.4%	12.6%
CARTER	404	69	279	56	Dole	17.1%	69.1%	13.9%
CASCADE	9,623	2,139	5,997	1,487	Dole	22.2%	62.3%	15.5%
CHOUTEAU	1,509	408	906	195	Dole	27.0%	60.0%	12.9%
CUSTER	1,463	334	943	186	Dole	22.8%	64.5%	12.7%
DANIELS	478	108	317	53	Dole	22.6%	66.3%	11.1%
DAWSON	1,818	420	1,117	281	Dole	23.1%	61.4%	15.5%
DEER LODGE	719	206	384	129	Dole	28.7%	53.4%	17.9%
FALLON	497	113	309	75	Dole	22.7%	62.2%	15.1%
FERGUS	2,716	644	1,692	380	Dole	23.7%	62.3%	14.0%
FLATHEAD	11,630	2,866	6,889	1,875	Dole	24.6%	59.2%	16.1%
GALLATIN	7,214	1,668	4,640	906	Dole	23.1%	64.3%	12.6%
GARFIELD	421	143	248	30	Dole	34.0%	58.9%	7.1%
GLACIER	567	133	359	75	Dole	23.5%	63.3%	13.2%
GOLDEN VALLEY	226	81	123	22	Dole	35.8%	54.4%	9.7%
GRANITE	538	119	342	77	Dole	22.1%	63.6%	14.3%
HILL	1,457	309	979	169	Dole	21.2%	67.2%	11.6%
JEFFERSON	1,479	380	881	218	Dole	25.7%	59.6%	14.7%
JUDITH BASIN	590	156	367	67	Dole	26.4%	62.2%	11.4%
LAKE	4,088	986	2,419	683	Dole	24.1%	59.2%	16.7%
LEWIS AND CLARK	7,143	1,371	4,861	911	Dole	19.2%	68.1%	12.8%
LIBERTY	584	139	380	65	Dole	23.8%	65.1%	11.1%
LINCOLN	2,697	615	1,494	588	Dole	22.8%	55.4%	21.8%
MCCONE	447	125	278	44	Dole	28.0%	62.2%	9.8%
MADISON	1,898	461	1,071	366	Dole	24.3%	56.4%	19.3%
MEAGHER	494	122	302	70	Dole	24.7%	61.1%	14.2%
MINERAL	339	84	190	65	Dole	24.8%	56.0%	19.2%
MISSOULA	8,654	2,040	5,382	1,232	Dole	23.6%	62.2%	14.2%
MUSSELSHELL	780	230	482	68	Dole	29.5%	61.8%	8.7%
PARK	2,091	567	1,299	225	Dole	27.1%	62.1%	10.8%
PETROLEUM	164	58	84	22	Dole	35.4%	51.2%	13.4%
PHILLIPS	1,265	352	756	157	Dole	27.8%	59.8%	12.4%
PONDERA	1,320	337	779	204	Dole	25.5%	59.0%	15.5%
POWDER RIVER	544	174	284	86	Dole	32.0%	52.2%	15.8%
POWELL	978	277	564	137	Dole	28.3%	57.7%	14.0%
PRAIRIE	301	74	195	32	Dole	24.6%	64.8%	10.6%
RAVALLI	5,848	1,555	3,460	833	Dole	26.6%	59.2%	14.2%
RICHLAND	1,202	232	773	197	Dole	19.3%	64.3%	16.4%
ROOSEVELT	639	141	417	81	Dole	22.1%	65.3%	12.7%
ROSEBUD	847	243	483	121	Dole	28.7%	57.0%	14.3%
SANDERS	1,134	298	695	141	Dole	26.3%	61.3%	12.4%
SHERIDAN	660	84	433	143	Dole	12.7%	65.6%	21.7%
SILVER BOW	3,095	670	1,799	626	Dole	21.6%	58.1%	20.2%
STILLWATER	1,549	489	830	230	Dole	31.6%	53.6%	14.8%
SWEET GRASS	800	167	496	137	Dole	20.9%	62.0%	17.1%
TETON	1,452	367	917	168	Dole	25.3%	63.2%	11.6%

MONTANA REPUBLICAN

1996

County	Total Vote	Buchanan	Dole	Other	Winner	Percentage of Total Vote Buchanan	Dole	Other
TOOLE	691	187	405	99	Dole	27.1%	58.6%	14.3%
TREASURE	196	73	94	29	Dole	37.2%	48.0%	14.8%
VALLEY	1,243	375	712	156	Dole	30.2%	57.3%	12.6%
WHEATLAND	428	119	267	42	Dole	27.8%	62.4%	9.8%
WIBAUX	278	65	146	67	Dole	23.4%	52.5%	24.1%
YELLOWSTONE	15,295	3,904	9,359	2,032	Dole	25.5%	61.2%	13.3%
TOTAL	117,746	28,581	72,176	16,989	Dole	24.3%	61.3%	14.4%

NEBRASKA

Nebraska's presidential primary is not nearly as important as it once was. A generation ago, when there were only a handful of primaries, Nebraska served as a connecting rod between the opening round of contests in states such as New Hampshire and Wisconsin with the climactic round of voting in Oregon and California.

That was true as late as 1968, when Robert Kennedy scored a notable victory over Eugene McCarthy in Nebraska. But as primaries have become more important since then, Nebraska's became less so. The proliferation of such events, coupled with Nebraska's late date and small delegate yield, robbed the event of much of its significance.

From time to time, though, Nebraska voters still use their primary to send a message. Disenchanted with President Jimmy Carter in 1980 for imposing a grain embargo on the Soviet Union (and canceling the state's grain sales), farmers in many of the crop-growing counties in eastern Nebraska cast their primary ballots for Edward Kennedy.

In 1976, Republican primary voters turned their back on President Gerald Ford, who was born in Omaha under the name Leslie King Jr. Ford carried Douglas (Omaha) and Lancaster (Lincoln) counties, but was crushed by Ronald Reagan in the state's vast rural sector.

Reagan's victory was in line with the previous voting behavior of Nebraska Republicans, who had tended to prefer the most doctrinaire conservative in the primary field. They chose Robert A. Taft over Dwight Eisenhower in 1952, and Barry Goldwater over several more moderate alternatives in 1964.

Nebraska Democrats have a quite different tradition that goes back to the prairie populism of the state's most famous Democrat, William Jennings Bryan. Given a choice, Democratic voters have preferred "new ideas" Democrats over more traditional "New Dealers." In 1972, George McGovern defeated Hubert Humphrey. Twelve years later, McGovern's former campaign manager, Gary Hart, beat Humphrey's protégé, Walter Mondale.

The McGovern-Humphrey race was fairly close; the Hart-Mondale race was not. While Humphrey carried the Omaha area and a sprinkling of counties elsewhere, Mondale lost all 93 counties. Hart ran particularly well in the western part of the

Recent Nebraska Primary Results

Nebraska held its first presidential primary in 1912.

	DEMOCRATS			REPUBLICANS		
Year	Turnout	Candidates	%	Turnout	Candidates	%
1996 (May 14)	94,176	BILL CLINTON* Lyndon LaRouche	87 11	170,591	BOB DOLE Pat Buchanan	76 10
1992 (May 12)	150,587	BILL CLINTON Jerry Brown Uncommitted	46 21 16	192,098	GEORGE BUSH* Pat Buchanan	81 13
1988 (May 10)	169,008	MICHAEL DUKAKIS Jesse Jackson	63 26	204,049	GEORGE BUSH Bob Dole	68 22
1984 (May 15)	148,855	GARY HART Walter Mondale	58 27	146,648	RONALD REAGAN*	99
1980 (May 13)	153,881	JIMMY CARTER* Edward Kennedy	47 38	205,203	RONALD REAGAN George Bush	76 15
1976 (May 11)	175,013	FRANK CHURCH Jimmy Carter	38 38	208,414	RONALD REAGAN Gerald Ford*	54 45
1972 (May 9)	192,137	GEORGE McGOVERN Hubert Humphrey George Wallace	41 34 12	194,272	RICHARD NIXON*	92
1968 (May 14)	162,611	ROBERT KENNEDY Eugene McCarthy	52 31	200,476	RICHARD NIXON Ronald Reagan	70 21

Note: All candidates are listed that drew at least 10 percent of their party's primary vote. The names of winning candidates are capitalized. An asterisk (*) indicates an incumbent president.

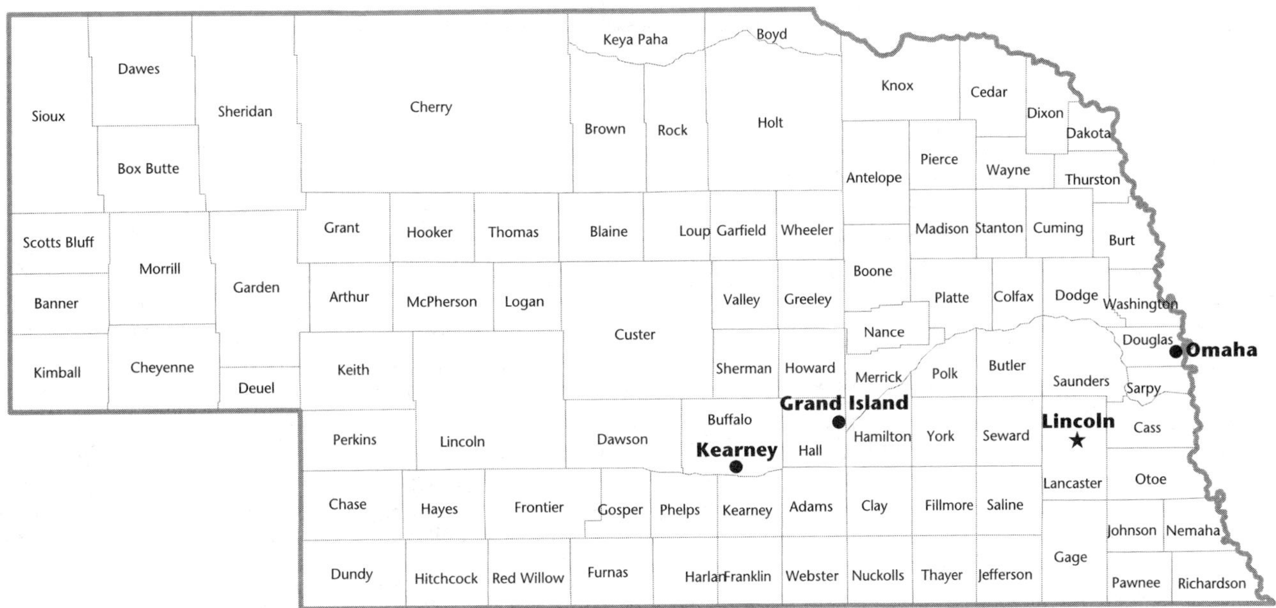

state, where the Corn Belt gives way to wheat growing and ranching.

Democratic candidates from the South, even those with campaigns that arrived in Nebraska in overdrive, have had only mixed success in the state's primary. In 1976, peanut farmer Carter lost narrowly to Frank Church. In 1980, Carter won the Nebraska primary but with less than a majority of the vote. In 1992, Bill Clinton also won the Democratic primary with less than 50 percent. Part of the antipathy to Clinton, no doubt was due to his rivalry with the state's popular senator, Bob Kerrey, who had been forced from the Democratic presidential race long before his home state voted.

NEBRASKA DEMOCRATIC

1968

County	Total Vote	R. Kennedy	McCarthy	Other	Winner	Percentage of Total Vote R. Kennedy	McCarthy	Other
ADAMS	3,097	1,717	942	438	R. Kennedy	55.4%	30.4%	14.1%
ANTELOPE	1,067	662	289	116	R. Kennedy	62.0%	27.1%	10.9%
ARTHUR	60	39	16	5	R. Kennedy	65.0%	26.7%	8.3%
BANNER	121	55	57	9	McCarthy	45.5%	47.1%	7.4%
BLAINE	101	34	42	25	McCarthy	33.7%	41.6%	24.8%
BOONE	993	580	306	107	R. Kennedy	58.4%	30.8%	10.8%
BOX BUTTE	929	485	374	70	R. Kennedy	52.2%	40.3%	7.5%
BOYD	658	399	175	84	R. Kennedy	60.6%	26.6%	12.8%
BROWN	321	152	91	78	R. Kennedy	47.4%	28.3%	24.3%
BUFFALO	3,140	1,633	935	572	R. Kennedy	52.0%	29.8%	18.2%
BURT	792	360	274	158	R. Kennedy	45.5%	34.6%	19.9%
BUTLER	1,758	1,272	405	81	R. Kennedy	72.4%	23.0%	4.6%
CASS	1,507	731	496	280	R. Kennedy	48.5%	32.9%	18.6%
CEDAR	1,781	1,461	230	90	R. Kennedy	82.0%	12.9%	5.1%
CHASE	392	234	118	40	R. Kennedy	59.7%	30.1%	10.2%
CHERRY	605	287	213	105	R. Kennedy	47.4%	35.2%	17.4%
CHEYENNE	1,115	636	356	123	R. Kennedy	57.0%	31.9%	11.0%
CLAY	881	442	306	133	R. Kennedy	50.2%	34.7%	15.1%
COLFAX	1,196	785	288	123	R. Kennedy	65.6%	24.1%	10.3%
CUMING	952	606	303	43	R. Kennedy	63.7%	31.8%	4.5%
CUSTER	1,330	658	446	226	R. Kennedy	49.5%	33.5%	17.0%
DAKOTA	1,143	627	357	159	R. Kennedy	54.9%	31.2%	13.9%
DAWES	757	428	218	111	R. Kennedy	56.5%	28.8%	14.7%
DAWSON	1,628	929	524	175	R. Kennedy	57.1%	32.2%	10.7%
DEUEL	184	105	65	14	R. Kennedy	57.1%	35.3%	7.6%
DIXON	806	435	202	169	R. Kennedy	54.0%	25.1%	21.0%
DODGE	3,385	1,761	1,092	532	R. Kennedy	52.0%	32.3%	15.7%
DOUGLAS	50,028	23,994	13,866	12,168	R. Kennedy	48.0%	27.7%	24.3%
DUNDY	207	102	74	31	R. Kennedy	49.3%	35.7%	15.0%
FILLMORE	1,160	708	321	131	R. Kennedy	61.0%	27.7%	11.3%
FRANKLIN	617	337	189	91	R. Kennedy	54.6%	30.6%	14.7%
FRONTIER	430	205	178	47	R. Kennedy	47.7%	41.4%	10.9%
FURNAS	783	391	278	114	R. Kennedy	49.9%	35.5%	14.6%
GAGE	2,558	1,415	805	338	R. Kennedy	55.3%	31.5%	13.2%
GARDEN	313	161	127	25	R. Kennedy	51.4%	40.6%	8.0%
GARFIELD	165	109	51	5	R. Kennedy	66.1%	30.9%	3.0%
GOSPER	305	166	99	40	R. Kennedy	54.4%	32.5%	13.1%
GRANT	101	53	28	20	R. Kennedy	52.5%	27.7%	19.8%
GREELEY	937	567	277	93	R. Kennedy	60.5%	29.6%	9.9%
HALL	4,012	1,884	1,444	684	R. Kennedy	47.0%	36.0%	17.0%
HAMILTON	739	428	245	66	R. Kennedy	57.9%	33.2%	8.9%
HARLAN	655	330	206	119	R. Kennedy	50.4%	31.5%	18.2%
HAYES	159	80	67	12	R. Kennedy	50.3%	42.1%	7.5%
HITCHCOCK	438	254	122	62	R. Kennedy	58.0%	27.9%	14.2%
HOLT	1,360	946	353	61	R. Kennedy	69.6%	26.0%	4.5%
HOOKER	37	17	12	8	R. Kennedy	45.9%	32.4%	21.6%
HOWARD	916	527	344	45	R. Kennedy	57.5%	37.6%	4.9%
JEFFERSON	1,243	696	359	188	R. Kennedy	56.0%	28.9%	15.1%
JOHNSON	781	438	255	88	R. Kennedy	56.1%	32.7%	11.3%
KEARNEY	941	423	346	172	R. Kennedy	45.0%	36.8%	18.3%

NEBRASKA DEMOCRATIC

1968

County	Total Vote	R. Kennedy	McCarthy	Other	Winner	Percentage of Total Vote R. Kennedy	McCarthy	Other
KEITH	842	569	205	68	R. Kennedy	67.6%	24.3%	8.1%
KEYA PAHA	118	47	53	18	McCarthy	39.8%	44.9%	15.3%
KIMBALL	528	332	118	78	R. Kennedy	62.9%	22.3%	14.8%
KNOX	1,216	779	303	134	R. Kennedy	64.1%	24.9%	11.0%
LANCASTER	18,867	7,536	7,554	3,777	McCarthy	39.9%	40.0%	20.0%
LINCOLN	2,752	1,453	1,121	178	R. Kennedy	52.8%	40.7%	6.5%
LOGAN	126	53	53	20		42.1%	42.1%	15.9%
LOUP	84	34	33	17	R. Kennedy	40.5%	39.3%	20.2%
MCPHERSON	69	36	26	7	R. Kennedy	52.2%	37.7%	10.1%
MADISON	2,042	1,314	637	91	R. Kennedy	64.3%	31.2%	4.5%
MERRICK	810	323	361	126	McCarthy	39.9%	44.6%	15.6%
MORRILL	498	298	177	23	R. Kennedy	59.8%	35.5%	4.6%
NANCE	770	475	216	79	R. Kennedy	61.7%	28.1%	10.3%
NEMAHA	1,034	586	272	176	R. Kennedy	56.7%	26.3%	17.0%
NUCKOLLS	992	536	287	169	R. Kennedy	54.0%	28.9%	17.0%
OTOE	1,540	796	535	209	R. Kennedy	51.7%	34.7%	13.6%
PAWNEE	489	258	157	74	R. Kennedy	52.8%	32.1%	15.1%
PERKINS	372	208	120	44	R. Kennedy	55.9%	32.3%	11.8%
PHELPS	944	416	362	166	R. Kennedy	44.1%	38.3%	17.6%
PIERCE	772	460	255	57	R. Kennedy	59.6%	33.0%	7.4%
PLATTE	3,421	2,097	955	369	R. Kennedy	61.3%	27.9%	10.8%
POLK	745	317	307	121	R. Kennedy	42.6%	41.2%	16.2%
RED WILLOW	1,250	683	355	212	R. Kennedy	54.6%	28.4%	17.0%
RICHARDSON	1,509	837	414	258	R. Kennedy	55.5%	27.4%	17.1%
ROCK	166	62	52	52	R. Kennedy	37.3%	31.3%	31.3%
SALINE	2,334	1,550	560	224	R. Kennedy	66.4%	24.0%	9.6%
SARPY	3,430	1,512	1,247	671	R. Kennedy	44.1%	36.4%	19.6%
SAUNDERS	2,229	1,341	653	235	R. Kennedy	60.2%	29.3%	10.5%
SCOTTS BLUFF	2,821	1,736	844	241	R. Kennedy	61.5%	29.9%	8.5%
SEWARD	1,444	801	446	197	R. Kennedy	55.5%	30.9%	13.6%
SHERIDAN	550	344	181	25	R. Kennedy	62.5%	32.9%	4.5%
SHERMAN	770	529	213	28	R. Kennedy	68.7%	27.7%	3.6%
SIOUX	154	99	42	13	R. Kennedy	64.3%	27.3%	8.4%
STANTON	518	307	150	61	R. Kennedy	59.3%	29.0%	11.8%
THAYER	913	487	296	130	R. Kennedy	53.3%	32.4%	14.2%
THOMAS	83	54	24	5	R. Kennedy	65.1%	28.9%	6.0%
THURSTON	817	439	279	99	R. Kennedy	53.7%	34.1%	12.1%
VALLEY	792	478	237	77	R. Kennedy	60.4%	29.9%	9.7%
WASHINGTON	1,272	468	551	253	McCarthy	36.8%	43.3%	19.9%
WAYNE	859	555	200	104	R. Kennedy	64.6%	23.3%	12.1%
WEBSTER	844	489	239	116	R. Kennedy	57.9%	28.3%	13.7%
WHEELER	168	87	75	6	R. Kennedy	51.8%	44.6%	3.6%
YORK	1,073	577	324	172	R. Kennedy	53.8%	30.2%	16.0%
TOTAL	162,611	84,102	50,655	27,854	R. Kennedy	51.7%	31.2%	17.1%

NEBRASKA REPUBLICAN

1968

County	Total Vote	Nixon	Reagan	Other	Winner	Percentage of Total Vote Nixon	Reagan	Other
ADAMS	4,822	3,677	705	440	Nixon	76.3%	14.6%	9.1%
ANTELOPE	1,840	1,334	406	100	Nixon	72.5%	22.1%	5.4%
ARTHUR	173	124	45	4	Nixon	71.7%	26.0%	2.3%
BANNER	258	139	108	11	Nixon	53.9%	41.9%	4.3%
BLAINE	243	182	50	11	Nixon	74.9%	20.6%	4.5%
BOONE	1,404	1,104	238	62	Nixon	78.6%	17.0%	4.4%
BOX BUTTE	1,817	1,234	471	112	Nixon	67.9%	25.9%	6.2%
BOYD	689	503	117	69	Nixon	73.0%	17.0%	10.0%
BROWN	748	599	96	53	Nixon	80.1%	12.8%	7.1%
BUFFALO	4,699	3,288	1,035	376	Nixon	70.0%	22.0%	8.0%
BURT	1,554	1,141	319	94	Nixon	73.4%	20.5%	6.0%
BUTLER	872	694	136	42	Nixon	79.6%	15.6%	4.8%
CASS	1,941	1,353	456	132	Nixon	69.7%	23.5%	6.8%
CEDAR	1,495	1,176	195	124	Nixon	78.7%	13.0%	8.3%
CHASE	759	471	242	46	Nixon	62.1%	31.9%	6.1%
CHERRY	1,412	1,056	260	96	Nixon	74.8%	18.4%	6.8%
CHEYENNE	1,596	1,272	241	83	Nixon	79.7%	15.1%	5.2%
CLAY	1,398	1,110	219	69	Nixon	79.4%	15.7%	4.9%
COLFAX	1,235	886	253	96	Nixon	71.7%	20.5%	7.8%
CUMING	1,814	1,466	305	43	Nixon	80.8%	16.8%	2.4%
CUSTER	2,828	2,065	611	152	Nixon	73.0%	21.6%	5.4%
DAKOTA	1,351	1,049	188	114	Nixon	77.6%	13.9%	8.4%
DAWES	1,984	1,266	575	143	Nixon	63.8%	29.0%	7.2%
DAWSON	3,142	2,474	628	40	Nixon	78.7%	20.0%	1.3%
DEUEL	550	468	76	6	Nixon	85.1%	13.8%	1.1%
DIXON	1,088	856	171	61	Nixon	78.7%	15.7%	5.6%
DODGE	4,983	3,378	1,235	370	Nixon	67.8%	24.8%	7.4%
DOUGLAS	42,385	26,834	10,874	4,677	Nixon	63.3%	25.7%	11.0%
DUNDY	493	365	98	30	Nixon	74.0%	19.9%	6.1%
FILLMORE	1,422	1,080	232	110	Nixon	75.9%	16.3%	7.7%
FRANKLIN	846	678	131	37	Nixon	80.1%	15.5%	4.4%
FRONTIER	815	556	206	53	Nixon	68.2%	25.3%	6.5%
FURNAS	1,424	1,057	312	55	Nixon	74.2%	21.9%	3.9%
GAGE	3,488	2,360	768	360	Nixon	67.7%	22.0%	10.3%
GARDEN	839	619	176	44	Nixon	73.8%	21.0%	5.2%
GARFIELD	584	455	104	25	Nixon	77.9%	17.8%	4.3%
GOSPER	458	341	95	22	Nixon	74.5%	20.7%	4.8%
GRANT	220	168	38	14	Nixon	76.4%	17.3%	6.4%
GREELEY	483	349	91	43	Nixon	72.3%	18.8%	8.9%
HALL	5,089	3,795	991	303	Nixon	74.6%	19.5%	6.0%
HAMILTON	1,545	1,277	244	24	Nixon	82.7%	15.8%	1.6%
HARLAN	1,022	729	230	63	Nixon	71.3%	22.5%	6.2%
HAYES	349	245	95	9	Nixon	70.2%	27.2%	2.6%
HITCHCOCK	713	418	261	34	Nixon	58.6%	36.6%	4.8%
HOLT	1,820	1,389	382	49	Nixon	76.3%	21.0%	2.7%
HOOKER	228	177	40	11	Nixon	77.6%	17.5%	4.8%
HOWARD	705	535	137	33	Nixon	75.9%	19.4%	4.7%
JEFFERSON	1,822	1,370	278	174	Nixon	75.2%	15.3%	9.5%
JOHNSON	1,040	728	203	109	Nixon	70.0%	19.5%	10.5%
KEARNEY	1,136	868	201	67	Nixon	76.4%	17.7%	5.9%

NEBRASKA REPUBLICAN

1968

County	Total Vote	Nixon	Reagan	Other	Winner	Percentage of Total Vote Nixon	Reagan	Other
KEITH	1,398	897	426	75	Nixon	64.2%	30.5%	5.4%
KEYA PAHA	307	234	46	27	Nixon	76.2%	15.0%	8.8%
KIMBALL	912	670	167	75	Nixon	73.5%	18.3%	8.2%
KNOX	1,595	1,299	180	116	Nixon	81.4%	11.3%	7.3%
LANCASTER	23,616	15,410	3,647	4,559	Nixon	65.3%	15.4%	19.3%
LINCOLN	3,651	2,496	1,052	103	Nixon	68.4%	28.8%	2.8%
LOGAN	277	172	86	19	Nixon	62.1%	31.0%	6.9%
LOUP	243	194	38	11	Nixon	79.8%	15.6%	4.5%
MCPHERSON	156	79	58	19	Nixon	50.6%	37.2%	12.2%
MADISON	4,100	3,232	806	62	Nixon	78.8%	19.7%	1.5%
MERRICK	1,222	898	224	100	Nixon	73.5%	18.3%	8.2%
MORRILL	1,037	748	269	20	Nixon	72.1%	25.9%	1.9%
NANCE	877	661	162	54	Nixon	75.4%	18.5%	6.2%
NEMAHA	1,512	1,049	380	83	Nixon	69.4%	25.1%	5.5%
NUCKOLLS	1,002	791	144	67	Nixon	78.9%	14.4%	6.7%
OTOE	2,332	1,667	500	165	Nixon	71.5%	21.4%	7.1%
PAWNEE	796	580	157	59	Nixon	72.9%	19.7%	7.4%
PERKINS	656	422	203	31	Nixon	64.3%	30.9%	4.7%
PHELPS	2,050	1,619	317	114	Nixon	79.0%	15.5%	5.6%
PIERCE	1,238	978	192	68	Nixon	79.0%	15.5%	5.5%
PLATTE	3,217	2,295	651	271	Nixon	71.3%	20.2%	8.4%
POLK	1,163	901	200	62	Nixon	77.5%	17.2%	5.3%
RED WILLOW	1,896	1,213	554	129	Nixon	64.0%	29.2%	6.8%
RICHARDSON	1,969	1,438	384	147	Nixon	73.0%	19.5%	7.5%
ROCK	570	430	113	27	Nixon	75.4%	19.8%	4.7%
SALINE	1,566	1,101	226	239	Nixon	70.3%	14.4%	15.3%
SARPY	3,126	2,117	833	176	Nixon	67.7%	26.6%	5.6%
SAUNDERS	2,034	1,489	395	150	Nixon	73.2%	19.4%	7.4%
SCOTTS BLUFF	4,553	2,995	1,318	240	Nixon	65.8%	28.9%	5.3%
SEWARD	1,709	1,152	279	278	Nixon	67.4%	16.3%	16.3%
SHERIDAN	1,472	845	599	28	Nixon	57.4%	40.7%	1.9%
SHERMAN	514	399	102	13	Nixon	77.6%	19.8%	2.5%
SIOUX	407	230	159	18	Nixon	56.5%	39.1%	4.4%
STANTON	844	636	162	46	Nixon	75.4%	19.2%	5.5%
THAYER	1,346	1,028	219	99	Nixon	76.4%	16.3%	7.4%
THOMAS	218	165	46	7	Nixon	75.7%	21.1%	3.2%
THURSTON	825	572	206	47	Nixon	69.3%	25.0%	5.7%
VALLEY	1,222	930	213	79	Nixon	76.1%	17.4%	6.5%
WASHINGTON	1,877	1,278	450	149	Nixon	68.1%	24.0%	7.9%
WAYNE	1,701	1,324	293	84	Nixon	77.8%	17.2%	4.9%
WEBSTER	1,117	834	216	67	Nixon	74.7%	19.3%	6.0%
WHEELER	219	149	55	15	Nixon	68.0%	25.1%	6.8%
YORK	2,284	1,701	408	175	Nixon	74.5%	17.9%	7.7%
TOTAL	200,447	140,076	42,703	17,668	Nixon	69.9%	21.3%	8.8%
Published Totals	200,476	140,336	42,703	17,437	Nixon	70.0%	21.3%	8.7%

Note: Results published immediately after the 1968 Republican primary gave Nixon 140,336 votes, but his vote in the official state canvass was listed as 140,076.

NEBRASKA DEMOCRATIC

1972

County	Total Vote	Humphrey	McGovern	Wallace	Other	Winner	Percentage of Total Vote Humphrey	McGovern	Wallace	Other
ADAMS	4,454	1,252	2,389	443	370	McGovern	28.1%	53.6%	9.9%	8.3%
ANTELOPE	1,038	377	425	121	115	McGovern	36.3%	40.9%	11.7%	11.1%
ARTHUR	54	12	30	2	10	McGovern	22.2%	55.6%	3.7%	18.5%
BANNER	143	37	61	32	13	McGovern	25.9%	42.7%	22.4%	9.1%
BLAINE	78	24	21	18	15	Humphrey	30.8%	26.9%	23.1%	19.2%
BOONE	1,147	392	514	124	117	McGovern	34.2%	44.8%	10.8%	10.2%
BOX BUTTE	1,344	476	597	135	136	McGovern	35.4%	44.4%	10.0%	10.1%
BOYD	633	224	175	148	86	Humphrey	35.4%	27.6%	23.4%	13.6%
BROWN	490	176	173	70	71	Humphrey	35.9%	35.3%	14.3%	14.5%
BUFFALO	3,927	1,102	2,022	404	399	McGovern	28.1%	51.5%	10.3%	10.2%
BURT	885	300	392	80	113	McGovern	33.9%	44.3%	9.0%	12.8%
BUTLER	2,143	615	1,111	198	219	McGovern	28.7%	51.8%	9.2%	10.2%
CASS	2,256	832	833	344	247	McGovern	36.9%	36.9%	15.2%	10.9%
CEDAR	1,627	445	762	180	240	McGovern	27.4%	46.8%	11.1%	14.8%
CHASE	386	114	144	66	62	McGovern	29.5%	37.3%	17.1%	16.1%
CHERRY	832	353	213	161	105	Humphrey	42.4%	25.6%	19.4%	12.6%
CHEYENNE	1,132	430	399	163	140	Humphrey	38.0%	35.2%	14.4%	12.4%
CLAY	1,098	388	510	89	111	McGovern	35.3%	46.4%	8.1%	10.1%
COLFAX	1,504	394	739	170	201	McGovern	26.2%	49.1%	11.3%	13.4%
CUMING	1,238	339	616	120	163	McGovern	27.4%	49.8%	9.7%	13.2%
CUSTER	1,382	481	567	157	177	McGovern	34.8%	41.0%	11.4%	12.8%
DAKOTA	1,440	505	685	129	121	McGovern	35.1%	47.6%	9.0%	8.4%
DAWES	709	266	216	131	96	Humphrey	37.5%	30.5%	18.5%	13.5%
DAWSON	1,976	657	926	189	204	McGovern	33.2%	46.9%	9.6%	10.3%
DEUEL	236	96	83	26	31	Humphrey	40.7%	35.2%	11.0%	13.1%
DIXON	961	379	361	102	119	Humphrey	39.4%	37.6%	10.6%	12.4%
DODGE	4,236	1,307	2,092	371	466	McGovern	30.9%	49.4%	8.8%	11.0%
DOUGLAS	58,969	23,341	17,948	9,792	7,888	Humphrey	39.6%	30.4%	16.6%	13.4%
DUNDY	273	81	115	39	38	McGovern	29.7%	42.1%	14.3%	13.9%
FILLMORE	1,360	500	688	97	75	McGovern	36.8%	50.6%	7.1%	5.5%
FRANKLIN	712	252	306	71	83	McGovern	35.4%	43.0%	10.0%	11.7%
FRONTIER	407	118	199	48	42	McGovern	29.0%	48.9%	11.8%	10.3%
FURNAS	831	301	336	99	95	McGovern	36.2%	40.4%	11.9%	11.4%
GAGE	2,999	1,065	1,408	231	295	McGovern	35.5%	46.9%	7.7%	9.8%
GARDEN	267	78	107	49	33	McGovern	29.2%	40.1%	18.4%	12.4%
GARFIELD	243	64	122	21	36	McGovern	26.3%	50.2%	8.6%	14.8%
GOSPER	234	94	92	23	25	Humphrey	40.2%	39.3%	9.8%	10.7%
GRANT	123	50	35	17	21	Humphrey	40.7%	28.5%	13.8%	17.1%
GREELEY	1,074	325	525	95	129	McGovern	30.3%	48.9%	8.8%	12.0%
HALL	4,991	1,693	2,148	520	630	McGovern	33.9%	43.0%	10.4%	12.6%
HAMILTON	1,065	332	555	73	105	McGovern	31.2%	52.1%	6.9%	9.9%
HARLAN	682	237	288	84	73	McGovern	34.8%	42.2%	12.3%	10.7%
HAYES	116	27	65	11	13	McGovern	23.3%	56.0%	9.5%	11.2%
HITCHCOCK	431	129	154	88	60	McGovern	29.9%	35.7%	20.4%	13.9%
HOLT	1,425	619	390	196	220	Humphrey	43.4%	27.4%	13.8%	15.4%
HOOKER	84	25	26	22	11	McGovern	29.8%	31.0%	26.2%	13.1%
HOWARD	1,306	450	602	102	152	McGovern	34.5%	46.1%	7.8%	11.6%
JEFFERSON	1,315	560	558	100	97	Humphrey	42.6%	42.4%	7.6%	7.4%
JOHNSON	913	271	466	68	108	McGovern	29.7%	51.0%	7.4%	11.8%
KEARNEY	1,078	406	478	92	102	McGovern	37.7%	44.3%	8.5%	9.5%

NEBRASKA DEMOCRATIC

1972

County	Total Vote	Humphrey	McGovern	Wallace	Other	Winner	Percentage of Total Vote: Humphrey	McGovern	Wallace	Other
KEITH	710	203	332	71	104	McGovern	28.6%	46.8%	10.0%	14.6%
KEYA PAHA	142	45	54	18	25	McGovern	31.7%	38.0%	12.7%	17.6%
KIMBALL	504	146	223	80	55	McGovern	29.0%	44.2%	15.9%	10.9%
KNOX	1,243	439	459	142	203	McGovern	35.3%	36.9%	11.4%	16.3%
LANCASTER	22,671	6,189	12,791	1,483	2,208	McGovern	27.3%	56.4%	6.5%	9.7%
LINCOLN	3,407	1,077	1,535	379	416	McGovern	31.6%	45.1%	11.1%	12.2%
LOGAN	100	28	39	11	22	McGovern	28.0%	39.0%	11.0%	22.0%
LOUP	120	24	45	35	16	McGovern	20.0%	37.5%	29.2%	13.3%
MCPHERSON	70	20	31	5	14	McGovern	28.6%	44.3%	7.1%	20.0%
MADISON	2,518	891	1,050	224	353	McGovern	35.4%	41.7%	8.9%	14.0%
MERRICK	926	306	422	88	110	McGovern	33.0%	45.6%	9.5%	11.9%
MORRILL	501	177	167	98	59	Humphrey	35.3%	33.3%	19.6%	11.8%
NANCE	775	272	307	60	136	McGovern	35.1%	39.6%	7.7%	17.5%
NEMAHA	1,065	325	458	129	153	McGovern	30.5%	43.0%	12.1%	14.4%
NUCKOLLS	1,185	445	516	105	119	McGovern	37.6%	43.5%	8.9%	10.0%
OTOE	1,976	533	936	268	239	McGovern	27.0%	47.4%	13.6%	12.1%
PAWNEE	554	185	242	65	62	McGovern	33.4%	43.7%	11.7%	11.2%
PERKINS	387	144	165	38	40	McGovern	37.2%	42.6%	9.8%	10.3%
PHELPS	1,068	405	377	135	151	Humphrey	37.9%	35.3%	12.6%	14.1%
PIERCE	882	310	361	114	97	McGovern	35.1%	40.9%	12.9%	11.0%
PLATTE	3,870	1,251	1,476	447	696	McGovern	32.3%	38.1%	11.6%	18.0%
POLK	891	301	387	111	92	McGovern	33.8%	43.4%	12.5%	10.3%
RED WILLOW	1,207	374	522	157	154	McGovern	31.0%	43.2%	13.0%	12.8%
RICHARDSON	1,666	561	647	242	216	McGovern	33.7%	38.8%	14.5%	13.0%
ROCK	183	75	53	37	18	Humphrey	41.0%	29.0%	20.2%	9.8%
SALINE	2,528	783	1,402	148	195	McGovern	31.0%	55.5%	5.9%	7.7%
SARPY	5,715	2,128	1,591	1,275	721	Humphrey	37.2%	27.8%	22.3%	12.6%
SAUNDERS	2,710	660	1,483	302	265	McGovern	24.4%	54.7%	11.1%	9.8%
SCOTTS BLUFF	2,757	962	1,197	348	250	McGovern	34.9%	43.4%	12.6%	9.1%
SEWARD	1,970	583	1,140	112	135	McGovern	29.6%	57.9%	5.7%	6.9%
SHERIDAN	491	163	187	70	71	McGovern	33.2%	38.1%	14.3%	14.5%
SHERMAN	1,002	316	423	87	176	McGovern	31.5%	42.2%	8.7%	17.6%
SIOUX	134	43	70	10	11	McGovern	32.1%	52.2%	7.5%	8.2%
STANTON	474	171	196	58	49	McGovern	36.1%	41.4%	12.2%	10.3%
THAYER	1,021	331	477	98	115	McGovern	32.4%	46.7%	9.6%	11.3%
THOMAS	109	31	56	13	9	McGovern	28.4%	51.4%	11.9%	8.3%
THURSTON	820	289	350	99	82	McGovern	35.2%	42.7%	12.1%	10.0%
VALLEY	906	354	333	117	102	Humphrey	39.1%	36.8%	12.9%	11.3%
WASHINGTON	1,565	484	672	237	172	McGovern	30.9%	42.9%	15.1%	11.0%
WAYNE	809	238	386	84	101	McGovern	29.4%	47.7%	10.4%	12.5%
WEBSTER	750	233	383	59	75	McGovern	31.1%	51.1%	7.9%	10.0%
WHEELER	167	46	79	13	29	McGovern	27.5%	47.3%	7.8%	17.4%
YORK	1,341	436	622	129	154	McGovern	32.5%	46.4%	9.6%	11.5%
TOTAL	192,137	65,968	79,309	23,912	22,948	McGovern	34.3%	41.3%	12.4%	11.9%

NEBRASKA REPUBLICAN

1972

County	Total Vote	Nixon	Other	Winner	Percentage of Total Vote Nixon	Other
ADAMS	5,199	4,749	450	Nixon	91.3%	8.7%
ANTELOPE	1,583	1,501	82	Nixon	94.8%	5.2%
ARTHUR	145	139	6	Nixon	95.9%	4.1%
BANNER	206	197	9	Nixon	95.6%	4.4%
BLAINE	167	157	10	Nixon	94.0%	6.0%
BOONE	1,200	1,117	83	Nixon	93.1%	6.9%
BOX BUTTE	2,023	1,892	131	Nixon	93.5%	6.5%
BOYD	760	713	47	Nixon	93.8%	6.2%
BROWN	916	855	61	Nixon	93.3%	6.7%
BUFFALO	4,914	4,567	347	Nixon	92.9%	7.1%
BURT	1,368	1,283	85	Nixon	93.8%	6.2%
BUTLER	912	832	80	Nixon	91.2%	8.8%
CASS	2,155	1,975	180	Nixon	91.6%	8.4%
CEDAR	1,407	1,332	75	Nixon	94.7%	5.3%
CHASE	621	576	45	Nixon	92.8%	7.2%
CHERRY	1,773	1,706	67	Nixon	96.2%	3.8%
CHEYENNE	1,584	1,502	82	Nixon	94.8%	5.2%
CLAY	1,538	1,417	121	Nixon	92.1%	7.9%
COLFAX	1,323	1,198	125	Nixon	90.6%	9.4%
CUMING	1,977	1,876	101	Nixon	94.9%	5.1%
CUSTER	2,511	2,370	141	Nixon	94.4%	5.6%
DAKOTA	1,466	1,346	120	Nixon	91.8%	8.2%
DAWES	1,785	1,665	120	Nixon	93.3%	6.7%
DAWSON	3,244	3,078	166	Nixon	94.9%	5.1%
DEUEL	595	559	36	Nixon	93.9%	6.1%
DIXON	1,191	1,116	75	Nixon	93.7%	6.3%
DODGE	4,881	4,486	395	Nixon	91.9%	8.1%
DOUGLAS	37,783	34,729	3,054	Nixon	91.9%	8.1%
DUNDY	556	521	35	Nixon	93.7%	6.3%
FILLMORE	1,420	1,304	116	Nixon	91.8%	8.2%
FRANKLIN	884	824	60	Nixon	93.2%	6.8%
FRONTIER	684	645	39	Nixon	94.3%	5.7%
FURNAS	1,284	1,209	75	Nixon	94.2%	5.8%
GAGE	3,485	3,099	386	Nixon	88.9%	11.1%
GARDEN	650	623	27	Nixon	95.8%	4.2%
GARFIELD	686	644	42	Nixon	93.9%	6.1%
GOSPER	342	322	20	Nixon	94.2%	5.8%
GRANT	266	256	10	Nixon	96.2%	3.8%
GREELEY	504	462	42	Nixon	91.7%	8.3%
HALL	5,353	4,982	371	Nixon	93.1%	6.9%
HAMILTON	1,819	1,685	134	Nixon	92.6%	7.4%
HARLAN	913	855	58	Nixon	93.6%	6.4%
HAYES	202	189	13	Nixon	93.6%	6.4%
HITCHCOCK	573	531	42	Nixon	92.7%	7.3%
HOLT	2,079	1,964	115	Nixon	94.5%	5.5%
HOOKER	285	274	11	Nixon	96.1%	3.9%
HOWARD	811	750	61	Nixon	92.5%	7.5%
JEFFERSON	1,861	1,677	184	Nixon	90.1%	9.9%
JOHNSON	964	879	85	Nixon	91.2%	8.8%
KEARNEY	1,184	1,133	51	Nixon	95.7%	4.3%

NEBRASKA REPUBLICAN

1972

County	Total Vote	Nixon	Other	Winner	Percentage of Total Vote Nixon	Other
KEITH	1,250	1,198	52	Nixon	95.8%	4.2%
KEYA PAHA	416	378	38	Nixon	90.9%	9.1%
KIMBALL	937	875	62	Nixon	93.4%	6.6%
KNOX	1,575	1,489	86	Nixon	94.5%	5.5%
LANCASTER	20,532	18,294	2,238	Nixon	89.1%	10.9%
LINCOLN	3,522	3,233	289	Nixon	91.8%	8.2%
LOGAN	191	173	18	Nixon	90.6%	9.4%
LOUP	288	270	18	Nixon	93.8%	6.3%
MCPHERSON	162	156	6	Nixon	96.3%	3.7%
MADISON	4,548	4,302	246	Nixon	94.6%	5.4%
MERRICK	1,210	1,120	90	Nixon	92.6%	7.4%
MORRILL	906	848	58	Nixon	93.6%	6.4%
NANCE	774	718	56	Nixon	92.8%	7.2%
NEMAHA	1,441	1,333	108	Nixon	92.5%	7.5%
NUCKOLLS	1,052	1,001	51	Nixon	95.2%	4.8%
OTOE	2,807	2,594	213	Nixon	92.4%	7.6%
PAWNEE	688	622	66	Nixon	90.4%	9.6%
PERKINS	584	528	56	Nixon	90.4%	9.6%
PHELPS	1,833	1,740	93	Nixon	94.9%	5.1%
PIERCE	1,200	1,141	59	Nixon	95.1%	4.9%
PLATTE	3,277	3,062	215	Nixon	93.4%	6.6%
POLK	1,019	949	70	Nixon	93.1%	6.9%
RED WILLOW	1,768	1,651	117	Nixon	93.4%	6.6%
RICHARDSON	2,067	1,919	148	Nixon	92.8%	7.2%
ROCK	520	506	14	Nixon	97.3%	2.7%
SALINE	1,495	1,330	165	Nixon	89.0%	11.0%
SARPY	3,860	3,606	254	Nixon	93.4%	6.6%
SAUNDERS	2,166	1,980	186	Nixon	91.4%	8.6%
SCOTTS BLUFF	3,896	3,619	277	Nixon	92.9%	7.1%
SEWARD	2,168	1,977	191	Nixon	91.2%	8.8%
SHERIDAN	1,152	1,099	53	Nixon	95.4%	4.6%
SHERMAN	553	517	36	Nixon	93.5%	6.5%
SIOUX	317	298	19	Nixon	94.0%	6.0%
STANTON	850	790	60	Nixon	92.9%	7.1%
THAYER	1,300	1,219	81	Nixon	93.8%	6.2%
THOMAS	309	297	12	Nixon	96.1%	3.9%
THURSTON	734	677	57	Nixon	92.2%	7.8%
VALLEY	1,315	1,203	112	Nixon	91.5%	8.5%
WASHINGTON	2,028	1,882	146	Nixon	92.8%	7.2%
WAYNE	1,467	1,369	98	Nixon	93.3%	6.7%
WEBSTER	860	787	73	Nixon	91.5%	8.5%
WHEELER	198	179	19	Nixon	90.4%	9.6%
YORK	3,005	2,774	231	Nixon	92.3%	7.7%
TOTAL	194,272	179,464	14,808	Nixon	92.4%	7.6%

NEBRASKA DEMOCRATIC

1976

County	Total Vote	Carter	Church	Other	Winner	Percentage of Total Vote Carter	Church	Other
ADAMS	4,014	1,501	1,783	730	Church	37.4%	44.4%	18.2%
ANTELOPE	1,008	424	296	288	Carter	42.1%	29.4%	28.6%
ARTHUR	55	27	21	7	Carter	49.1%	38.2%	12.7%
BANNER	159	93	45	21	Carter	58.5%	28.3%	13.2%
BLAINE	82	32	29	21	Carter	39.0%	35.4%	25.6%
BOONE	1,076	540	340	196	Carter	50.2%	31.6%	18.2%
BOX BUTTE	1,045	471	279	295	Carter	45.1%	26.7%	28.2%
BOYD	544	241	113	190	Carter	44.3%	20.8%	34.9%
BROWN	429	184	163	82	Carter	42.9%	38.0%	19.1%
BUFFALO	3,458	1,478	1,296	684	Carter	42.7%	37.5%	19.8%
BURT	920	488	265	167	Carter	53.0%	28.8%	18.2%
BUTLER	1,935	678	841	416	Church	35.0%	43.5%	21.5%
CASS	2,360	909	914	537	Church	38.5%	38.7%	22.8%
CEDAR	1,467	591	260	616	Carter	40.3%	17.7%	42.0%
CHASE	531	269	162	100	Carter	50.7%	30.5%	18.8%
CHERRY	793	309	230	254	Carter	39.0%	29.0%	32.0%
CHEYENNE	859	330	314	215	Carter	38.4%	36.6%	25.0%
CLAY	966	405	403	158	Carter	41.9%	41.7%	16.4%
COLFAX	1,524	531	712	281	Church	34.8%	46.7%	18.4%
CUMING	1,024	454	346	224	Carter	44.3%	33.8%	21.9%
CUSTER	1,302	522	502	278	Carter	40.1%	38.6%	21.4%
DAKOTA	1,029	414	190	425	Carter	40.2%	18.5%	41.3%
DAWES	724	365	183	176	Carter	50.4%	25.3%	24.3%
DAWSON	1,685	799	554	332	Carter	47.4%	32.9%	19.7%
DEUEL	180	82	77	21	Carter	45.6%	42.8%	11.7%
DIXON	843	371	164	308	Carter	44.0%	19.5%	36.5%
DODGE	4,047	1,607	1,579	861	Carter	39.7%	39.0%	21.3%
DOUGLAS	50,175	15,979	19,566	14,630	Church	31.8%	39.0%	29.2%
DUNDY	231	143	55	33	Carter	61.9%	23.8%	14.3%
FILLMORE	1,136	390	523	223	Church	34.3%	46.0%	19.6%
FRANKLIN	574	273	195	106	Carter	47.6%	34.0%	18.5%
FRONTIER	413	196	152	65	Carter	47.5%	36.8%	15.7%
FURNAS	811	410	281	120	Carter	50.6%	34.6%	14.8%
GAGE	2,491	1,000	1,067	424	Church	40.1%	42.8%	17.0%
GARDEN	280	129	84	67	Carter	46.1%	30.0%	23.9%
GARFIELD	232	132	66	34	Carter	56.9%	28.4%	14.7%
GOSPER	256	107	116	33	Church	41.8%	45.3%	12.9%
GRANT	92	54	20	18	Carter	58.7%	21.7%	19.6%
GREELEY	899	389	333	177	Carter	43.3%	37.0%	19.7%
HALL	4,280	1,918	1,642	720	Carter	44.8%	38.4%	16.8%
HAMILTON	981	383	462	136	Church	39.0%	47.1%	13.9%
HARLAN	610	279	211	120	Carter	45.7%	34.6%	19.7%
HAYES	151	90	32	29	Carter	59.6%	21.2%	19.2%
HITCHCOCK	488	257	126	105	Carter	52.7%	25.8%	21.5%
HOLT	1,512	816	348	348	Carter	54.0%	23.0%	23.0%
HOOKER	86	26	42	18	Church	30.2%	48.8%	20.9%
HOWARD	1,081	473	391	217	Carter	43.8%	36.2%	20.1%
JEFFERSON	1,312	497	565	250	Church	37.9%	43.1%	19.1%
JOHNSON	743	317	270	156	Carter	42.7%	36.3%	21.0%
KEARNEY	1,034	441	408	185	Carter	42.6%	39.5%	17.9%

NEBRASKA DEMOCRATIC

1976

County	Total Vote	Carter	Church	Other	Winner	Percentage of Total Vote Carter	Church	Other
KEITH	1,004	395	401	208	Church	39.3%	39.9%	20.7%
KEYA PAHA	127	57	49	21	Carter	44.9%	38.6%	16.5%
KIMBALL	448	175	195	78	Church	39.1%	43.5%	17.4%
KNOX	1,272	606	220	446	Carter	47.6%	17.3%	35.1%
LANCASTER	20,730	6,198	10,239	4,293	Church	29.9%	49.4%	20.7%
LINCOLN	3,549	1,317	1,534	698	Church	37.1%	43.2%	19.7%
LOGAN	94	37	38	19	Church	39.4%	40.4%	20.2%
LOUP	96	42	39	15	Carter	43.8%	40.6%	15.6%
MCPHERSON	65	23	25	17	Church	35.4%	38.5%	26.2%
MADISON	2,215	1,052	589	574	Carter	47.5%	26.6%	25.9%
MERRICK	1,042	419	451	172	Church	40.2%	43.3%	16.5%
MORRILL	587	324	118	145	Carter	55.2%	20.1%	24.7%
NANCE	673	264	274	135	Church	39.2%	40.7%	20.1%
NEMAHA	951	425	360	166	Carter	44.7%	37.9%	17.5%
NUCKOLLS	948	452	329	167	Carter	47.7%	34.7%	17.6%
OTOE	1,898	837	719	342	Carter	44.1%	37.9%	18.0%
PAWNEE	532	212	209	111	Carter	39.8%	39.3%	20.9%
PERKINS	417	181	163	73	Carter	43.4%	39.1%	17.5%
PHELPS	1,018	453	372	193	Carter	44.5%	36.5%	19.0%
PIERCE	715	324	181	210	Carter	45.3%	25.3%	29.4%
PLATTE	3,813	1,406	1,293	1,114	Carter	36.9%	33.9%	29.2%
POLK	906	427	327	152	Carter	47.1%	36.1%	16.8%
RED WILLOW	1,142	529	304	309	Carter	46.3%	26.6%	27.1%
RICHARDSON	1,779	836	504	439	Carter	47.0%	28.3%	24.7%
ROCK	317	155	77	85	Carter	48.9%	24.3%	26.8%
SALINE	2,316	944	1,021	351	Church	40.8%	44.1%	15.2%
SARPY	6,420	2,276	2,253	1,891	Carter	35.5%	35.1%	29.5%
SAUNDERS	2,504	873	1,115	516	Church	34.9%	44.5%	20.6%
SCOTTS BLUFF	2,808	1,316	844	648	Carter	46.9%	30.1%	23.1%
SEWARD	1,867	692	835	340	Church	37.1%	44.7%	18.2%
SHERIDAN	509	269	115	125	Carter	52.8%	22.6%	24.6%
SHERMAN	987	406	405	176	Carter	41.1%	41.0%	17.8%
SIOUX	156	87	43	26	Carter	55.8%	27.6%	16.7%
STANTON	466	227	149	90	Carter	48.7%	32.0%	19.3%
THAYER	887	374	333	180	Carter	42.2%	37.5%	20.3%
THOMAS	86	41	28	17	Carter	47.7%	32.6%	19.8%
THURSTON	773	345	170	258	Carter	44.6%	22.0%	33.4%
VALLEY	749	312	297	140	Carter	41.7%	39.7%	18.7%
WASHINGTON	1,600	655	616	329	Carter	40.9%	38.5%	20.6%
WAYNE	702	341	187	174	Carter	48.6%	26.6%	24.8%
WEBSTER	727	294	322	111	Church	40.4%	44.3%	15.3%
WHEELER	106	50	32	24	Carter	47.2%	30.2%	22.6%
YORK	1,085	371	506	208	Church	34.2%	46.6%	19.2%
TOTAL	175,013	65,833	67,297	41,883	Church	37.6%	38.5%	23.9%

NEBRASKA REPUBLICAN

1976

County	Total Vote	Ford	Reagan	Write-in	Winner	Percentage of Total Vote Ford	Reagan	Write-in
ADAMS	5,263	2,605	2,642	16	Reagan	49.5%	50.2%	0.3%
ANTELOPE	1,759	704	1,055		Reagan	40.0%	60.0%	
ARTHUR	160	57	103		Reagan	35.6%	64.4%	
BANNER	256	47	209		Reagan	18.4%	81.6%	
BLAINE	254	103	151		Reagan	40.6%	59.4%	
BOONE	1,371	595	776		Reagan	43.4%	56.6%	
BOX BUTTE	1,971	757	1,214		Reagan	38.4%	61.6%	
BOYD	787	308	479		Reagan	39.1%	60.9%	
BROWN	878	432	445	1	Reagan	49.2%	50.7%	0.1%
BUFFALO	5,231	2,241	2,977	13	Reagan	42.8%	56.9%	0.2%
BURT	1,679	691	986	2	Reagan	41.2%	58.7%	0.1%
BUTLER	911	395	515	1	Reagan	43.4%	56.5%	0.1%
CASS	2,496	1,058	1,438		Reagan	42.4%	57.6%	
CEDAR	1,514	702	812		Reagan	46.4%	53.6%	
CHASE	848	255	593		Reagan	30.1%	69.9%	
CHERRY	1,870	628	1,242		Reagan	33.6%	66.4%	
CHEYENNE	1,475	448	1,027		Reagan	30.4%	69.6%	
CLAY	1,501	686	815		Reagan	45.7%	54.3%	
COLFAX	1,450	547	903		Reagan	37.7%	62.3%	
CUMING	1,918	786	1,130	2	Reagan	41.0%	58.9%	0.1%
CUSTER	2,590	1,025	1,565		Reagan	39.6%	60.4%	
DAKOTA	1,150	549	601		Reagan	47.7%	52.3%	
DAWES	1,720	491	1,227	2	Reagan	28.5%	71.3%	0.1%
DAWSON	3,312	1,560	1,752		Reagan	47.1%	52.9%	
DEUEL	542	244	298		Reagan	45.0%	55.0%	
DIXON	1,230	576	654		Reagan	46.8%	53.2%	
DODGE	5,334	2,523	2,803	8	Reagan	47.3%	52.5%	0.1%
DOUGLAS	42,375	21,237	20,976	162	Ford	50.1%	49.5%	0.4%
DUNDY	531	151	380		Reagan	28.4%	71.6%	
FILLMORE	1,334	653	681		Reagan	49.0%	51.0%	
FRANKLIN	893	347	546		Reagan	38.9%	61.1%	
FRONTIER	809	277	528	4	Reagan	34.2%	65.3%	0.5%
FURNAS	1,388	503	885		Reagan	36.2%	63.8%	
GAGE	3,228	1,561	1,667		Reagan	48.4%	51.6%	
GARDEN	715	214	501		Reagan	29.9%	70.1%	
GARFIELD	636	278	356	2	Reagan	43.7%	56.0%	0.3%
GOSPER	434	201	233		Reagan	46.3%	53.7%	
GRANT	259	99	159	1	Reagan	38.2%	61.4%	0.4%
GREELEY	447	159	288		Reagan	35.6%	64.4%	
HALL	5,197	2,499	2,698		Reagan	48.1%	51.9%	
HAMILTON	1,797	907	890		Ford	50.5%	49.5%	
HARLAN	972	398	574		Reagan	40.9%	59.1%	
HAYES	359	82	274	3	Reagan	22.8%	76.3%	0.8%
HITCHCOCK	809	183	626		Reagan	22.6%	77.4%	
HOLT	2,409	1,012	1,397		Reagan	42.0%	58.0%	
HOOKER	266	121	145		Reagan	45.5%	54.5%	
HOWARD	757	299	456	2	Reagan	39.5%	60.2%	0.3%
JEFFERSON	1,800	821	973	6	Reagan	45.6%	54.1%	0.3%
JOHNSON	957	430	526	1	Reagan	44.9%	55.0%	0.1%
KEARNEY	1,236	527	709		Reagan	42.6%	57.4%	

NEBRASKA REPUBLICAN

1976

County	Total Vote	Ford	Reagan	Write-in	Winner	Percentage of Total Vote Ford	Reagan	Write-in
KEITH	1,775	610	1,165		Reagan	34.4%	65.6%	
KEYA PAHA	417	178	239		Reagan	42.7%	57.3%	
KIMBALL	946	251	695		Reagan	26.5%	73.5%	
KNOX	1,700	820	880		Reagan	48.2%	51.8%	
LANCASTER	22,229	13,478	8,667	84	Ford	60.6%	39.0%	0.4%
LINCOLN	4,188	1,610	2,571	7	Reagan	38.4%	61.4%	0.2%
LOGAN	221	72	149		Reagan	32.6%	67.4%	
LOUP	237	82	155		Reagan	34.6%	65.4%	
MCPHERSON	178	33	142	3	Reagan	18.5%	79.8%	1.7%
MADISON	4,564	1,876	2,688		Reagan	41.1%	58.9%	
MERRICK	1,616	624	992		Reagan	38.6%	61.4%	
MORRILL	1,025	328	697		Reagan	32.0%	68.0%	
NANCE	705	299	406		Reagan	42.4%	57.6%	
NEMAHA	1,353	576	777		Reagan	42.6%	57.4%	
NUCKOLLS	1,020	489	531		Reagan	47.9%	52.1%	
OTOE	2,773	1,161	1,608	4	Reagan	41.9%	58.0%	0.1%
PAWNEE	694	280	414		Reagan	40.3%	59.7%	
PERKINS	699	227	472		Reagan	32.5%	67.5%	
PHELPS	2,127	840	1,284	3	Reagan	39.5%	60.4%	0.1%
PIERCE	1,128	432	696		Reagan	38.3%	61.7%	
PLATTE	3,703	1,618	2,072	13	Reagan	43.7%	56.0%	0.4%
POLK	1,182	559	621	2	Reagan	47.3%	52.5%	0.2%
RED WILLOW	2,136	459	1,674	3	Reagan	21.5%	78.4%	0.1%
RICHARDSON	2,227	960	1,267		Reagan	43.1%	56.9%	
ROCK	489	240	249		Reagan	49.1%	50.9%	
SALINE	1,389	739	650		Ford	53.2%	46.8%	
SARPY	5,122	2,200	2,898	24	Reagan	43.0%	56.6%	0.5%
SAUNDERS	2,310	960	1,350		Reagan	41.6%	58.4%	
SCOTTS BLUFF	4,595	1,639	2,954	2	Reagan	35.7%	64.3%	
SEWARD	2,080	1,143	937		Ford	55.0%	45.0%	
SHERIDAN	1,511	371	1,140		Reagan	24.6%	75.4%	
SHERMAN	546	225	321		Reagan	41.2%	58.8%	
SIOUX	452	112	340		Reagan	24.8%	75.2%	
STANTON	945	309	636		Reagan	32.7%	67.3%	
THAYER	1,234	577	657		Reagan	46.8%	53.2%	
THOMAS	329	129	200		Reagan	39.2%	60.8%	
THURSTON	798	311	486	1	Reagan	39.0%	60.9%	0.1%
VALLEY	1,148	463	685		Reagan	40.3%	59.7%	
WASHINGTON	2,275	985	1,289	1	Reagan	43.3%	56.7%	
WAYNE	1,437	618	819		Reagan	43.0%	57.0%	
WEBSTER	1,044	393	651		Reagan	37.6%	62.4%	
WHEELER	199	62	136	1	Reagan	31.2%	68.3%	0.5%
YORK	2,590	1,232	1,353	5	Reagan	47.6%	52.2%	0.2%
TOTAL	208,414	94,542	113,493	379	Reagan	45.4%	54.5%	0.2%

NEBRASKA DEMOCRATIC

1980

County	Total Vote	Carter	E. Kennedy	Uncommitted	Other	Winner	Percentage of Total Vote Carter	E. Kennedy	Uncom.	Other
ADAMS	3,179	1,581	1,163	297	138	Carter	49.7%	36.6%	9.3%	4.3%
ANTELOPE	815	331	346	87	51	E. Kennedy	40.6%	42.5%	10.7%	6.3%
ARTHUR	63	32	26	2	3	Carter	50.8%	41.3%	3.2%	4.8%
BANNER	109	30	42	24	13	E. Kennedy	27.5%	38.5%	22.0%	11.9%
BLAINE	74	36	26	4	8	Carter	48.6%	35.1%	5.4%	10.8%
BOONE	910	343	431	89	47	E. Kennedy	37.7%	47.4%	9.8%	5.2%
BOX BUTTE	1,130	493	400	155	82	Carter	43.6%	35.4%	13.7%	7.3%
BOYD	555	259	211	43	42	Carter	46.7%	38.0%	7.7%	7.6%
BROWN	340	159	119	34	28	Carter	46.8%	35.0%	10.0%	8.2%
BUFFALO	2,990	1,361	1,167	282	180	Carter	45.5%	39.0%	9.4%	6.0%
BURT	672	354	231	64	23	Carter	52.7%	34.4%	9.5%	3.4%
BUTLER	1,504	488	813	138	65	E. Kennedy	32.4%	54.1%	9.2%	4.3%
CASS	2,208	1,010	857	245	96	Carter	45.7%	38.8%	11.1%	4.3%
CEDAR	1,249	481	598	104	66	E. Kennedy	38.5%	47.9%	8.3%	5.3%
CHASE	442	166	183	65	28	E. Kennedy	37.6%	41.4%	14.7%	6.3%
CHERRY	445	230	141	44	30	Carter	51.7%	31.7%	9.9%	6.7%
CHEYENNE	895	365	328	138	64	Carter	40.8%	36.6%	15.4%	7.2%
CLAY	850	385	330	96	39	Carter	45.3%	38.8%	11.3%	4.6%
COLFAX	1,512	579	741	117	75	E. Kennedy	38.3%	49.0%	7.7%	5.0%
CUMING	841	388	310	87	56	Carter	46.1%	36.9%	10.3%	6.7%
CUSTER	1,192	569	449	128	46	Carter	47.7%	37.7%	10.7%	3.9%
DAKOTA	1,167	542	467	115	43	Carter	46.4%	40.0%	9.9%	3.7%
DAWES	670	354	181	93	42	Carter	52.8%	27.0%	13.9%	6.3%
DAWSON	1,520	758	529	164	69	Carter	49.9%	34.8%	10.8%	4.5%
DEUEL	121	61	37	15	8	Carter	50.4%	30.6%	12.4%	6.6%
DIXON	913	419	353	86	55	Carter	45.9%	38.7%	9.4%	6.0%
DODGE	3,155	1,591	1,076	342	146	Carter	50.4%	34.1%	10.8%	4.6%
DOUGLAS	45,748	23,086	15,509	4,826	2,327	Carter	50.5%	33.9%	10.5%	5.1%
DUNDY	336	123	127	55	31	E. Kennedy	36.6%	37.8%	16.4%	9.2%
FILLMORE	1,027	421	482	80	44	E. Kennedy	41.0%	46.9%	7.8%	4.3%
FRANKLIN	493	201	214	51	27	E. Kennedy	40.8%	43.4%	10.3%	5.5%
FRONTIER	314	119	137	46	12	E. Kennedy	37.9%	43.6%	14.6%	3.8%
FURNAS	665	288	264	69	44	Carter	43.3%	39.7%	10.4%	6.6%
GAGE	2,018	810	917	188	103	E. Kennedy	40.1%	45.4%	9.3%	5.1%
GARDEN	276	129	82	39	26	Carter	46.7%	29.7%	14.1%	9.4%
GARFIELD	192	65	87	27	13	E. Kennedy	33.9%	45.3%	14.1%	6.8%
GOSPER	241	100	94	37	10	Carter	41.5%	39.0%	15.4%	4.1%
GRANT	77	41	25	8	3	Carter	53.2%	32.5%	10.4%	3.9%
GREELEY	787	279	412	62	34	E. Kennedy	35.5%	52.4%	7.9%	4.3%
HALL	4,064	1,870	1,530	458	206	Carter	46.0%	37.6%	11.3%	5.1%
HAMILTON	712	311	298	78	25	Carter	43.7%	41.9%	11.0%	3.5%
HARLAN	537	241	217	51	28	Carter	44.9%	40.4%	9.5%	5.2%
HAYES	103	33	42	19	9	E. Kennedy	32.0%	40.8%	18.4%	8.7%
HITCHCOCK	403	182	143	53	25	Carter	45.2%	35.5%	13.2%	6.2%
HOLT	1,118	472	462	113	71	Carter	42.2%	41.3%	10.1%	6.4%
HOOKER	85	41	22	11	11	Carter	48.2%	25.9%	12.9%	12.9%
HOWARD	843	344	375	71	53	E. Kennedy	40.8%	44.5%	8.4%	6.3%
JEFFERSON	986	462	406	77	41	Carter	46.9%	41.2%	7.8%	4.2%
JOHNSON	719	261	349	67	42	E. Kennedy	36.3%	48.5%	9.3%	5.8%
KEARNEY	884	349	370	116	49	E. Kennedy	39.5%	41.9%	13.1%	5.5%

NEBRASKA DEMOCRATIC

1980

County	Total Vote	Carter	E. Kennedy	Uncommitted	Other	Winner	Percentage of Total Vote: Carter	E. Kennedy	Uncom.	Other
KEITH	846	370	315	112	49	Carter	43.7%	37.2%	13.2%	5.8%
KEYA PAHA	106	58	29	9	10	Carter	54.7%	27.4%	8.5%	9.4%
KIMBALL	365	167	116	54	28	Carter	45.8%	31.8%	14.8%	7.7%
KNOX	1,094	485	425	98	86	Carter	44.3%	38.8%	9.0%	7.9%
LANCASTER	16,791	8,201	6,500	1,552	538	Carter	48.8%	38.7%	9.2%	3.2%
LINCOLN	3,658	1,813	1,144	461	240	Carter	49.6%	31.3%	12.6%	6.6%
LOGAN	73	36	22	10	5	Carter	49.3%	30.1%	13.7%	6.8%
LOUP	82	36	31	10	5	Carter	43.9%	37.8%	12.2%	6.1%
MCPHERSON	64	28	18	5	13	Carter	43.8%	28.1%	7.8%	20.3%
MADISON	1,977	964	678	234	101	Carter	48.8%	34.3%	11.8%	5.1%
MERRICK	760	343	304	64	49	Carter	45.1%	40.0%	8.4%	6.4%
MORRILL	500	226	168	67	39	Carter	45.2%	33.6%	13.4%	7.8%
NANCE	636	241	298	63	34	E. Kennedy	37.9%	46.9%	9.9%	5.3%
NEMAHA	972	460	389	82	41	Carter	47.3%	40.0%	8.4%	4.2%
NUCKOLLS	791	368	303	82	38	Carter	46.5%	38.3%	10.4%	4.8%
OTOE	1,680	763	690	167	60	Carter	45.4%	41.1%	9.9%	3.6%
PAWNEE	517	206	232	52	27	E. Kennedy	39.8%	44.9%	10.1%	5.2%
PERKINS	376	134	166	47	29	E. Kennedy	35.6%	44.1%	12.5%	7.7%
PHELPS	723	344	246	90	43	Carter	47.6%	34.0%	12.4%	5.9%
PIERCE	714	307	262	82	63	Carter	43.0%	36.7%	11.5%	8.8%
PLATTE	3,234	1,435	1,222	337	240	Carter	44.4%	37.8%	10.4%	7.4%
POLK	601	243	269	58	31	E. Kennedy	40.4%	44.8%	9.7%	5.2%
RED WILLOW	1,042	522	328	121	71	Carter	50.1%	31.5%	11.6%	6.8%
RICHARDSON	1,651	753	632	173	93	Carter	45.6%	38.3%	10.5%	5.6%
ROCK	155	84	47	17	7	Carter	54.2%	30.3%	11.0%	4.5%
SALINE	1,969	800	934	159	76	E. Kennedy	40.6%	47.4%	8.1%	3.9%
SARPY	5,724	2,721	1,992	674	337	Carter	47.5%	34.8%	11.8%	5.9%
SAUNDERS	2,711	1,065	1,187	308	151	E. Kennedy	39.3%	43.8%	11.4%	5.6%
SCOTTS BLUFF	2,412	1,142	790	322	158	Carter	47.3%	32.8%	13.3%	6.6%
SEWARD	1,594	654	759	132	49	E. Kennedy	41.0%	47.6%	8.3%	3.1%
SHERIDAN	343	160	102	51	30	Carter	46.6%	29.7%	14.9%	8.7%
SHERMAN	846	291	452	71	32	E. Kennedy	34.4%	53.4%	8.4%	3.8%
SIOUX	118	52	49	11	6	Carter	44.1%	41.5%	9.3%	5.1%
STANTON	443	189	190	38	26	E. Kennedy	42.7%	42.9%	8.6%	5.9%
THAYER	962	478	364	77	43	Carter	49.7%	37.8%	8.0%	4.5%
THOMAS	60	32	20	6	2	Carter	53.3%	33.3%	10.0%	3.3%
THURSTON	674	273	311	55	35	E. Kennedy	40.5%	46.1%	8.2%	5.2%
VALLEY	762	305	360	67	30	E. Kennedy	40.0%	47.2%	8.8%	3.9%
WASHINGTON	1,356	699	444	151	62	Carter	51.5%	32.7%	11.1%	4.6%
WAYNE	687	364	213	66	44	Carter	53.0%	31.0%	9.6%	6.4%
WEBSTER	611	258	279	40	34	E. Kennedy	42.2%	45.7%	6.5%	5.6%
WHEELER	104	39	48	9	8	E. Kennedy	37.5%	46.2%	8.7%	7.7%
YORK	948	418	379	97	54	Carter	44.1%	40.0%	10.2%	5.7%
TOTAL	153,881	72,120	57,826	16,041	7,894	Carter	46.9%	37.6%	10.4%	5.1%

NEBRASKA REPUBLICAN

1980

County	Total Vote	Bush	Reagan	Other	Winner	Percentage of Total Vote: Bush	Reagan	Other
ADAMS	4,807	707	3,654	446	Reagan	14.7%	76.0%	9.3%
ANTELOPE	1,688	131	1,483	74	Reagan	7.8%	87.9%	4.4%
ARTHUR	189	18	163	8	Reagan	9.5%	86.2%	4.2%
BANNER	270	13	244	13	Reagan	4.8%	90.4%	4.8%
BLAINE	228	18	198	12	Reagan	7.9%	86.8%	5.3%
BOONE	1,422	136	1,220	66	Reagan	9.6%	85.8%	4.6%
BOX BUTTE	2,211	210	1,821	180	Reagan	9.5%	82.4%	8.1%
BOYD	672	40	587	45	Reagan	6.0%	87.4%	6.7%
BROWN	876	99	717	60	Reagan	11.3%	81.8%	6.8%
BUFFALO	4,809	599	3,745	465	Reagan	12.5%	77.9%	9.7%
BURT	1,429	189	1,156	84	Reagan	13.2%	80.9%	5.9%
BUTLER	815	124	647	44	Reagan	15.2%	79.4%	5.4%
CASS	2,523	400	1,915	208	Reagan	15.9%	75.9%	8.2%
CEDAR	1,315	173	1,049	93	Reagan	13.2%	79.8%	7.1%
CHASE	840	72	716	52	Reagan	8.6%	85.2%	6.2%
CHERRY	1,362	92	1,196	74	Reagan	6.8%	87.8%	5.4%
CHEYENNE	1,507	130	1,298	79	Reagan	8.6%	86.1%	5.2%
CLAY	1,647	178	1,322	147	Reagan	10.8%	80.3%	8.9%
COLFAX	1,622	209	1,331	82	Reagan	12.9%	82.1%	5.1%
CUMING	1,900	201	1,610	89	Reagan	10.6%	84.7%	4.7%
CUSTER	2,521	233	2,150	138	Reagan	9.2%	85.3%	5.5%
DAKOTA	1,327	241	964	122	Reagan	18.2%	72.6%	9.2%
DAWES	1,966	163	1,680	123	Reagan	8.3%	85.5%	6.3%
DAWSON	3,293	343	2,731	219	Reagan	10.4%	82.9%	6.7%
DEUEL	561	94	430	37	Reagan	16.8%	76.6%	6.6%
DIXON	1,376	210	1,077	89	Reagan	15.3%	78.3%	6.5%
DODGE	4,727	796	3,565	366	Reagan	16.8%	75.4%	7.7%
DOUGLAS	43,274	8,972	29,952	4,350	Reagan	20.7%	69.2%	10.1%
DUNDY	780	49	698	33	Reagan	6.3%	89.5%	4.2%
FILLMORE	1,274	213	949	112	Reagan	16.7%	74.5%	8.8%
FRANKLIN	838	79	695	64	Reagan	9.4%	82.9%	7.6%
FRONTIER	721	58	621	42	Reagan	8.0%	86.1%	5.8%
FURNAS	1,387	93	1,228	66	Reagan	6.7%	88.5%	4.8%
GAGE	2,858	523	2,085	250	Reagan	18.3%	73.0%	8.7%
GARDEN	656	35	590	31	Reagan	5.3%	89.9%	4.7%
GARFIELD	541	69	436	36	Reagan	12.8%	80.6%	6.7%
GOSPER	449	50	369	30	Reagan	11.1%	82.2%	6.7%
GRANT	253	25	217	11	Reagan	9.9%	85.8%	4.3%
GREELEY	412	36	347	29	Reagan	8.7%	84.2%	7.0%
HALL	5,589	733	4,447	409	Reagan	13.1%	79.6%	7.3%
HAMILTON	1,673	207	1,321	145	Reagan	12.4%	79.0%	8.7%
HARLAN	898	91	740	67	Reagan	10.1%	82.4%	7.5%
HAYES	280	13	259	8	Reagan	4.6%	92.5%	2.9%
HITCHCOCK	833	53	727	53	Reagan	6.4%	87.3%	6.4%
HOLT	2,263	212	1,962	89	Reagan	9.4%	86.7%	3.9%
HOOKER	307	27	260	20	Reagan	8.8%	84.7%	6.5%
HOWARD	762	75	642	45	Reagan	9.8%	84.3%	5.9%
JEFFERSON	1,547	246	1,161	140	Reagan	15.9%	75.0%	9.0%
JOHNSON	990	137	759	94	Reagan	13.8%	76.7%	9.5%
KEARNEY	1,247	133	1,005	109	Reagan	10.7%	80.6%	8.7%

NEBRASKA REPUBLICAN

1980

County	Total Vote	Bush	Reagan	Other	Winner	Percentage of Total Vote Bush	Reagan	Other
KEITH	1,811	161	1,520	130	Reagan	8.9%	83.9%	7.2%
KEYA PAHA	335	36	280	19	Reagan	10.7%	83.6%	5.7%
KIMBALL	924	60	821	43	Reagan	6.5%	88.9%	4.7%
KNOX	1,539	175	1,246	118	Reagan	11.4%	81.0%	7.7%
LANCASTER	20,003	5,042	11,801	3,160	Reagan	25.2%	59.0%	15.8%
LINCOLN	4,466	512	3,583	371	Reagan	11.5%	80.2%	8.3%
LOGAN	300	32	256	12	Reagan	10.7%	85.3%	4.0%
LOUP	280	36	220	24	Reagan	12.9%	78.6%	8.6%
MCPHERSON	170	9	156	5	Reagan	5.3%	91.8%	2.9%
MADISON	5,202	510	4,449	243	Reagan	9.8%	85.5%	4.7%
MERRICK	1,383	148	1,152	83	Reagan	10.7%	83.3%	6.0%
MORRILL	1,048	79	903	66	Reagan	7.5%	86.2%	6.3%
NANCE	726	70	604	52	Reagan	9.6%	83.2%	7.2%
NEMAHA	1,556	227	1,238	91	Reagan	14.6%	79.6%	5.8%
NUCKOLLS	932	104	755	73	Reagan	11.2%	81.0%	7.8%
OTOE	2,428	324	1,912	192	Reagan	13.3%	78.7%	7.9%
PAWNEE	801	108	637	56	Reagan	13.5%	79.5%	7.0%
PERKINS	670	51	575	44	Reagan	7.6%	85.8%	6.6%
PHELPS	1,673	162	1,424	87	Reagan	9.7%	85.1%	5.2%
PIERCE	1,342	122	1,166	54	Reagan	9.1%	86.9%	4.0%
PLATTE	3,548	408	2,870	270	Reagan	11.5%	80.9%	7.6%
POLK	967	121	774	72	Reagan	12.5%	80.0%	7.4%
RED WILLOW	2,048	131	1,805	112	Reagan	6.4%	88.1%	5.5%
RICHARDSON	2,293	256	1,848	189	Reagan	11.2%	80.6%	8.2%
ROCK	520	48	449	23	Reagan	9.2%	86.3%	4.4%
SALINE	1,335	299	897	139	Reagan	22.4%	67.2%	10.4%
SARPY	5,633	1,150	3,935	548	Reagan	20.4%	69.9%	9.7%
SAUNDERS	2,452	371	1,891	190	Reagan	15.1%	77.1%	7.7%
SCOTTS BLUFF	4,515	460	3,631	424	Reagan	10.2%	80.4%	9.4%
SEWARD	1,851	486	1,104	261	Reagan	26.3%	59.6%	14.1%
SHERIDAN	1,276	67	1,159	50	Reagan	5.3%	90.8%	3.9%
SHERMAN	428	44	362	22	Reagan	10.3%	84.6%	5.1%
SIOUX	366	30	327	9	Reagan	8.2%	89.3%	2.5%
STANTON	953	71	839	43	Reagan	7.5%	88.0%	4.5%
THAYER	1,393	150	1,105	138	Reagan	10.8%	79.3%	9.9%
THOMAS	294	26	258	10	Reagan	8.8%	87.8%	3.4%
THURSTON	774	85	612	77	Reagan	11.0%	79.1%	9.9%
VALLEY	1,191	144	965	82	Reagan	12.1%	81.0%	6.9%
WASHINGTON	2,204	333	1,704	167	Reagan	15.1%	77.3%	7.6%
WAYNE	1,753	231	1,398	124	Reagan	13.2%	79.7%	7.1%
WEBSTER	898	87	759	52	Reagan	9.7%	84.5%	5.8%
WHEELER	187	16	163	8	Reagan	8.6%	87.2%	4.3%
YORK	3,000	450	2,303	247	Reagan	15.0%	76.8%	8.2%
TOTAL	205,203	31,380	155,995	17,828	Reagan	15.3%	76.0%	8.7%

NEBRASKA DEMOCRATIC

1984

County	Total Vote	Hart	Mondale	Other	Winner	Percentage of Total Vote Hart	Mondale	Other
ADAMS	2,746	1,808	645	293	Hart	65.8%	23.5%	10.7%
ANTELOPE	841	565	187	89	Hart	67.2%	22.2%	10.6%
ARTHUR	51	42	3	6	Hart	82.4%	5.9%	11.8%
BANNER	85	60	10	15	Hart	70.6%	11.8%	17.6%
BLAINE	76	52	11	13	Hart	68.4%	14.5%	17.1%
BOONE	804	504	203	97	Hart	62.7%	25.2%	12.1%
BOX BUTTE	1,102	679	260	163	Hart	61.6%	23.6%	14.8%
BOYD	386	227	112	47	Hart	58.8%	29.0%	12.2%
BROWN	273	163	74	36	Hart	59.7%	27.1%	13.2%
BUFFALO	2,216	1,489	498	229	Hart	67.2%	22.5%	10.3%
BURT	721	495	169	57	Hart	68.7%	23.4%	7.9%
BUTLER	1,583	1,081	311	191	Hart	68.3%	19.6%	12.1%
CASS	2,064	1,141	665	258	Hart	55.3%	32.2%	12.5%
CEDAR	1,111	774	234	103	Hart	69.7%	21.1%	9.3%
CHASE	405	274	77	54	Hart	67.7%	19.0%	13.3%
CHERRY	502	305	131	66	Hart	60.8%	26.1%	13.1%
CHEYENNE	885	604	181	100	Hart	68.2%	20.5%	11.3%
CLAY	1,093	774	200	119	Hart	70.8%	18.3%	10.9%
COLFAX	1,184	782	259	143	Hart	66.0%	21.9%	12.1%
CUMING	732	454	181	97	Hart	62.0%	24.7%	13.3%
CUSTER	1,049	721	223	105	Hart	68.7%	21.3%	10.0%
DAKOTA	1,101	583	432	86	Hart	53.0%	39.2%	7.8%
DAWES	861	565	187	109	Hart	65.6%	21.7%	12.7%
DAWSON	1,154	793	246	115	Hart	68.7%	21.3%	10.0%
DEUEL	119	84	20	15	Hart	70.6%	16.8%	12.6%
DIXON	697	455	187	55	Hart	65.3%	26.8%	7.9%
DODGE	2,948	1,720	907	321	Hart	58.3%	30.8%	10.9%
DOUGLAS	41,698	18,378	13,165	10,155	Hart	44.1%	31.6%	24.4%
DUNDY	223	157	46	20	Hart	70.4%	20.6%	9.0%
FILLMORE	967	688	208	71	Hart	71.1%	21.5%	7.3%
FRANKLIN	434	326	76	32	Hart	75.1%	17.5%	7.4%
FRONTIER	308	232	41	35	Hart	75.3%	13.3%	11.4%
FURNAS	627	432	152	43	Hart	68.9%	24.2%	6.9%
GAGE	1,927	1,299	457	171	Hart	67.4%	23.7%	8.9%
GARDEN	233	165	53	15	Hart	70.8%	22.7%	6.4%
GARFIELD	186	131	38	17	Hart	70.4%	20.4%	9.1%
GOSPER	188	145	30	13	Hart	77.1%	16.0%	6.9%
GRANT	69	48	13	8	Hart	69.6%	18.8%	11.6%
GREELEY	588	404	136	48	Hart	68.7%	23.1%	8.2%
HALL	4,496	2,736	1,131	629	Hart	60.9%	25.2%	14.0%
HAMILTON	777	557	144	76	Hart	71.7%	18.5%	9.8%
HARLAN	489	370	79	40	Hart	75.7%	16.2%	8.2%
HAYES	112	84	18	10	Hart	75.0%	16.1%	8.9%
HITCHCOCK	389	274	70	45	Hart	70.4%	18.0%	11.6%
HOLT	1,054	678	249	127	Hart	64.3%	23.6%	12.0%
HOOKER	55	44	9	2	Hart	80.0%	16.4%	3.6%
HOWARD	892	610	211	71	Hart	68.4%	23.7%	8.0%
JEFFERSON	1,138	725	310	103	Hart	63.7%	27.2%	9.1%
JOHNSON	769	533	162	74	Hart	69.3%	21.1%	9.6%
KEARNEY	703	499	139	65	Hart	71.0%	19.8%	9.2%

NEBRASKA DEMOCRATIC

1984

County	Total Vote	Hart	Mondale	Other	Winner	Percentage of Total Vote Hart	Mondale	Other
KEITH	696	507	136	53	Hart	72.8%	19.5%	7.6%
KEYA PAHA	72	44	11	17	Hart	61.1%	15.3%	23.6%
KIMBALL	353	238	65	50	Hart	67.4%	18.4%	14.2%
KNOX	1,139	740	270	129	Hart	65.0%	23.7%	11.3%
LANCASTER	19,651	11,558	5,451	2,642	Hart	58.8%	27.7%	13.4%
LINCOLN	4,236	2,899	1,016	321	Hart	68.4%	24.0%	7.6%
LOGAN	81	61	14	6	Hart	75.3%	17.3%	7.4%
LOUP	90	58	20	12	Hart	64.4%	22.2%	13.3%
MCPHERSON	75	62	10	3	Hart	82.7%	13.3%	4.0%
MADISON	1,688	1,123	353	212	Hart	66.5%	20.9%	12.6%
MERRICK	670	429	173	68	Hart	64.0%	25.8%	10.1%
MORRILL	440	291	96	53	Hart	66.1%	21.8%	12.0%
NANCE	480	333	97	50	Hart	69.4%	20.2%	10.4%
NEMAHA	834	534	210	90	Hart	64.0%	25.2%	10.8%
NUCKOLLS	784	512	205	67	Hart	65.3%	26.1%	8.5%
OTOE	1,868	1,289	389	190	Hart	69.0%	20.8%	10.2%
PAWNEE	446	312	82	52	Hart	70.0%	18.4%	11.7%
PERKINS	430	297	78	55	Hart	69.1%	18.1%	12.8%
PHELPS	770	525	162	83	Hart	68.2%	21.0%	10.8%
PIERCE	540	345	130	65	Hart	63.9%	24.1%	12.0%
PLATTE	2,976	1,899	679	398	Hart	63.8%	22.8%	13.4%
POLK	684	511	97	76	Hart	74.7%	14.2%	11.1%
RED WILLOW	1,173	668	342	163	Hart	56.9%	29.2%	13.9%
RICHARDSON	1,701	1,000	529	172	Hart	58.8%	31.1%	10.1%
ROCK	150	97	29	24	Hart	64.7%	19.3%	16.0%
SALINE	1,909	1,337	409	163	Hart	70.0%	21.4%	8.5%
SARPY	5,818	3,003	1,754	1,061	Hart	51.6%	30.1%	18.2%
SAUNDERS	2,498	1,568	654	276	Hart	62.8%	26.2%	11.0%
SCOTTS BLUFF	2,381	1,662	481	238	Hart	69.8%	20.2%	10.0%
SEWARD	1,572	1,038	389	145	Hart	66.0%	24.7%	9.2%
SHERIDAN	436	284	87	65	Hart	65.1%	20.0%	14.9%
SHERMAN	774	515	196	63	Hart	66.5%	25.3%	8.1%
SIOUX	109	87	12	10	Hart	79.8%	11.0%	9.2%
STANTON	390	268	69	53	Hart	68.7%	17.7%	13.6%
THAYER	910	616	210	84	Hart	67.7%	23.1%	9.2%
THOMAS	64	47	13	4	Hart	73.4%	20.3%	6.3%
THURSTON	701	364	217	120	Hart	51.9%	31.0%	17.1%
VALLEY	660	442	153	65	Hart	67.0%	23.2%	9.8%
WASHINGTON	1,095	664	304	127	Hart	60.6%	27.8%	11.6%
WAYNE	708	460	173	75	Hart	65.0%	24.4%	10.6%
WEBSTER	792	572	139	81	Hart	72.2%	17.6%	10.2%
WHEELER	104	75	19	10	Hart	72.1%	18.3%	9.6%
YORK	796	539	162	95	Hart	67.7%	20.4%	11.9%
TOTAL	148,855	86,582	39,635	22,638	Hart	58.2%	26.6%	15.2%

NEBRASKA DEMOCRATIC

1988

County	Total Vote	Dukakis	J. Jackson	Other	Winner	Percentage of Total Vote Dukakis	J. Jackson	Other
ADAMS	2,883	1,926	618	339	Dukakis	66.8%	21.4%	11.8%
ANTELOPE	801	555	136	110	Dukakis	69.3%	17.0%	13.7%
ARTHUR	45	34	5	6	Dukakis	75.6%	11.1%	13.3%
BANNER	65	44	11	10	Dukakis	67.7%	16.9%	15.4%
BLAINE	62	42	9	11	Dukakis	67.7%	14.5%	17.7%
BOONE	832	567	146	119	Dukakis	68.1%	17.5%	14.3%
BOX BUTTE	1,169	851	179	139	Dukakis	72.8%	15.3%	11.9%
BOYD	341	220	60	61	Dukakis	64.5%	17.6%	17.9%
BROWN	319	207	69	43	Dukakis	64.9%	21.6%	13.5%
BUFFALO	3,356	1,866	1,140	350	Dukakis	55.6%	34.0%	10.4%
BURT	933	587	209	137	Dukakis	62.9%	22.4%	14.7%
BUTLER	1,420	905	289	226	Dukakis	63.7%	20.4%	15.9%
CASS	2,359	1,514	538	307	Dukakis	64.2%	22.8%	13.0%
CEDAR	1,174	803	183	188	Dukakis	68.4%	15.6%	16.0%
CHASE	477	335	66	76	Dukakis	70.2%	13.8%	15.9%
CHERRY	457	324	56	77	Dukakis	70.9%	12.3%	16.8%
CHEYENNE	893	650	107	136	Dukakis	72.8%	12.0%	15.2%
CLAY	778	498	192	88	Dukakis	64.0%	24.7%	11.3%
COLFAX	1,181	767	256	158	Dukakis	64.9%	21.7%	13.4%
CUMING	761	508	147	106	Dukakis	66.8%	19.3%	13.9%
CUSTER	1,068	703	245	120	Dukakis	65.8%	22.9%	11.2%
DAKOTA	1,228	869	188	171	Dukakis	70.8%	15.3%	13.9%
DAWES	588	389	112	87	Dukakis	66.2%	19.0%	14.8%
DAWSON	1,419	914	310	195	Dukakis	64.4%	21.8%	13.7%
DEUEL	114	82	9	23	Dukakis	71.9%	7.9%	20.2%
DIXON	808	573	112	123	Dukakis	70.9%	13.9%	15.2%
DODGE	3,616	2,473	689	454	Dukakis	68.4%	19.1%	12.6%
DOUGLAS	53,347	32,076	15,768	5,503	Dukakis	60.1%	29.6%	10.3%
DUNDY	178	121	26	31	Dukakis	68.0%	14.6%	17.4%
FILLMORE	1,012	666	241	105	Dukakis	65.8%	23.8%	10.4%
FRANKLIN	522	340	122	60	Dukakis	65.1%	23.4%	11.5%
FRONTIER	271	173	54	44	Dukakis	63.8%	19.9%	16.2%
FURNAS	597	438	90	69	Dukakis	73.4%	15.1%	11.6%
GAGE	2,097	1,356	546	195	Dukakis	64.7%	26.0%	9.3%
GARDEN	285	216	33	36	Dukakis	75.8%	11.6%	12.6%
GARFIELD	168	124	29	15	Dukakis	73.8%	17.3%	8.9%
GOSPER	234	168	42	24	Dukakis	71.8%	17.9%	10.3%
GRANT	51	37	9	5	Dukakis	72.5%	17.6%	9.8%
GREELEY	575	363	121	91	Dukakis	63.1%	21.0%	15.8%
HALL	4,279	2,857	992	430	Dukakis	66.8%	23.2%	10.0%
HAMILTON	846	542	203	101	Dukakis	64.1%	24.0%	11.9%
HARLAN	541	382	96	63	Dukakis	70.6%	17.7%	11.6%
HAYES	137	97	26	14	Dukakis	70.8%	19.0%	10.2%
HITCHCOCK	363	250	61	52	Dukakis	68.9%	16.8%	14.3%
HOLT	1,080	792	157	131	Dukakis	73.3%	14.5%	12.1%
HOOKER	46	34	10	2	Dukakis	73.9%	21.7%	4.3%
HOWARD	915	589	221	105	Dukakis	64.4%	24.2%	11.5%
JEFFERSON	1,040	672	288	80	Dukakis	64.6%	27.7%	7.7%
JOHNSON	665	396	165	104	Dukakis	59.5%	24.8%	15.6%
KEARNEY	832	523	199	110	Dukakis	62.9%	23.9%	13.2%

NEBRASKA DEMOCRATIC

1988

County	Total Vote	Dukakis	J. Jackson	Other	Winner	Percentage of Total Vote Dukakis	J. Jackson	Other
KEITH	737	520	109	108	Dukakis	70.6%	14.8%	14.7%
KEYA PAHA	132	88	16	28	Dukakis	66.7%	12.1%	21.2%
KIMBALL	258	179	31	48	Dukakis	69.4%	12.0%	18.6%
KNOX	868	578	153	137	Dukakis	66.6%	17.6%	15.8%
LANCASTER	23,739	13,764	8,147	1,828	Dukakis	58.0%	34.3%	7.7%
LINCOLN	4,392	2,876	990	526	Dukakis	65.5%	22.5%	12.0%
LOGAN	48	31	7	10	Dukakis	64.6%	14.6%	20.8%
LOUP	73	45	16	12	Dukakis	61.6%	21.9%	16.4%
MCPHERSON	59	42	13	4	Dukakis	71.2%	22.0%	6.8%
MADISON	1,757	1,250	290	217	Dukakis	71.1%	16.5%	12.4%
MERRICK	756	476	188	92	Dukakis	63.0%	24.9%	12.2%
MORRILL	381	257	69	55	Dukakis	67.5%	18.1%	14.4%
NANCE	663	433	161	69	Dukakis	65.3%	24.3%	10.4%
NEMAHA	1,030	621	233	176	Dukakis	60.3%	22.6%	17.1%
NUCKOLLS	775	567	130	78	Dukakis	73.2%	16.8%	10.1%
OTOE	1,844	1,158	386	300	Dukakis	62.8%	20.9%	16.3%
PAWNEE	476	292	124	60	Dukakis	61.3%	26.1%	12.6%
PERKINS	394	284	59	51	Dukakis	72.1%	15.0%	12.9%
PHELPS	821	533	181	107	Dukakis	64.9%	22.0%	13.0%
PIERCE	653	448	96	109	Dukakis	68.6%	14.7%	16.7%
PLATTE	2,964	1,886	546	532	Dukakis	63.6%	18.4%	17.9%
POLK	600	384	147	69	Dukakis	64.0%	24.5%	11.5%
RED WILLOW	1,036	731	161	144	Dukakis	70.6%	15.5%	13.9%
RICHARDSON	1,364	895	251	218	Dukakis	65.6%	18.4%	16.0%
ROCK	150	98	34	18	Dukakis	65.3%	22.7%	12.0%
SALINE	2,210	1,334	603	273	Dukakis	60.4%	27.3%	12.4%
SARPY	7,439	4,971	1,560	908	Dukakis	66.8%	21.0%	12.2%
SAUNDERS	2,574	1,681	555	338	Dukakis	65.3%	21.6%	13.1%
SCOTTS BLUFF	2,366	1,645	388	333	Dukakis	69.5%	16.4%	14.1%
SEWARD	1,600	1,006	406	188	Dukakis	62.9%	25.4%	11.8%
SHERIDAN	377	262	55	60	Dukakis	69.5%	14.6%	15.9%
SHERMAN	687	463	141	83	Dukakis	67.4%	20.5%	12.1%
SIOUX	110	78	13	19	Dukakis	70.9%	11.8%	17.3%
STANTON	405	257	88	60	Dukakis	63.5%	21.7%	14.8%
THAYER	938	630	224	84	Dukakis	67.2%	23.9%	9.0%
THOMAS	54	35	11	8	Dukakis	64.8%	20.4%	14.8%
THURSTON	667	326	266	75	Dukakis	48.9%	39.9%	11.2%
VALLEY	616	409	143	64	Dukakis	66.4%	23.2%	10.4%
WASHINGTON	1,498	935	296	267	Dukakis	62.4%	19.8%	17.8%
WAYNE	566	371	108	87	Dukakis	65.5%	19.1%	15.4%
WEBSTER	623	404	133	86	Dukakis	64.8%	21.3%	13.8%
WHEELER	116	82	14	20	Dukakis	70.7%	12.1%	17.2%
YORK	964	591	258	115	Dukakis	61.3%	26.8%	11.9%
TOTAL	169,008	106,334	43,380	19,294	Dukakis	62.9%	25.7%	11.4%

NEBRASKA REPUBLICAN

1988

County	Total Vote	Bush	Dole	Other	Winner	Percentage of Total Vote Bush	Dole	Other
ADAMS	4,595	3,079	1,124	392	Bush	67.0%	24.5%	8.5%
ANTELOPE	1,441	997	320	124	Bush	69.2%	22.2%	8.6%
ARTHUR	148	118	25	5	Bush	79.7%	16.9%	3.4%
BANNER	269	148	92	29	Bush	55.0%	34.2%	10.8%
BLAINE	191	124	53	14	Bush	64.9%	27.7%	7.3%
BOONE	1,142	711	296	135	Bush	62.3%	25.9%	11.8%
BOX BUTTE	1,858	1,237	449	172	Bush	66.6%	24.2%	9.3%
BOYD	545	340	148	57	Bush	62.4%	27.2%	10.5%
BROWN	888	585	190	113	Bush	65.9%	21.4%	12.7%
BUFFALO	5,149	3,395	1,313	441	Bush	65.9%	25.5%	8.6%
BURT	1,435	952	355	128	Bush	66.3%	24.7%	8.9%
BUTLER	796	565	177	54	Bush	71.0%	22.2%	6.8%
CASS	2,457	1,666	523	268	Bush	67.8%	21.3%	10.9%
CEDAR	966	596	261	109	Bush	61.7%	27.0%	11.3%
CHASE	792	456	268	68	Bush	57.6%	33.8%	8.6%
CHERRY	1,445	966	326	153	Bush	66.9%	22.6%	10.6%
CHEYENNE	1,542	1,054	345	143	Bush	68.4%	22.4%	9.3%
CLAY	1,353	852	380	121	Bush	63.0%	28.1%	8.9%
COLFAX	1,245	835	305	105	Bush	67.1%	24.5%	8.4%
CUMING	1,472	1,002	373	97	Bush	68.1%	25.3%	6.6%
CUSTER	2,301	1,617	485	199	Bush	70.3%	21.1%	8.6%
DAKOTA	1,238	815	250	173	Bush	65.8%	20.2%	14.0%
DAWES	1,528	1,005	340	183	Bush	65.8%	22.3%	12.0%
DAWSON	2,993	2,124	650	219	Bush	71.0%	21.7%	7.3%
DEUEL	444	294	118	32	Bush	66.2%	26.6%	7.2%
DIXON	1,095	712	249	134	Bush	65.0%	22.7%	12.2%
DODGE	4,851	3,347	1,103	401	Bush	69.0%	22.7%	8.3%
DOUGLAS	46,328	33,849	7,889	4,590	Bush	73.1%	17.0%	9.9%
DUNDY	382	212	124	46	Bush	55.5%	32.5%	12.0%
FILLMORE	1,218	761	373	84	Bush	62.5%	30.6%	6.9%
FRANKLIN	812	509	241	62	Bush	62.7%	29.7%	7.6%
FRONTIER	616	385	186	45	Bush	62.5%	30.2%	7.3%
FURNAS	1,046	648	335	63	Bush	62.0%	32.0%	6.0%
GAGE	2,648	1,746	702	200	Bush	65.9%	26.5%	7.6%
GARDEN	669	480	152	37	Bush	71.7%	22.7%	5.5%
GARFIELD	565	367	142	56	Bush	65.0%	25.1%	9.9%
GOSPER	493	289	170	34	Bush	58.6%	34.5%	6.9%
GRANT	206	141	57	8	Bush	68.4%	27.7%	3.9%
GREELEY	320	212	68	40	Bush	66.3%	21.3%	12.5%
HALL	5,772	4,009	1,176	587	Bush	69.5%	20.4%	10.2%
HAMILTON	1,792	1,180	452	160	Bush	65.8%	25.2%	8.9%
HARLAN	883	526	279	78	Bush	59.6%	31.6%	8.8%
HAYES	321	197	97	27	Bush	61.4%	30.2%	8.4%
HITCHCOCK	661	383	217	61	Bush	57.9%	32.8%	9.2%
HOLT	2,166	1,438	438	290	Bush	66.4%	20.2%	13.4%
HOOKER	285	199	54	32	Bush	69.8%	18.9%	11.2%
HOWARD	751	482	196	73	Bush	64.2%	26.1%	9.7%
JEFFERSON	1,383	829	413	141	Bush	59.9%	29.9%	10.2%
JOHNSON	803	459	268	76	Bush	57.2%	33.4%	9.5%
KEARNEY	1,255	809	356	90	Bush	64.5%	28.4%	7.2%

NEBRASKA REPUBLICAN

1988

County	Total Vote	Bush	Dole	Other	Winner	Percentage of Total Vote Bush	Dole	Other
KEITH	1,662	1,183	391	88	Bush	71.2%	23.5%	5.3%
KEYA PAHA	376	218	116	42	Bush	58.0%	30.9%	11.2%
KIMBALL	644	411	190	43	Bush	63.8%	29.5%	6.7%
KNOX	1,196	841	258	97	Bush	70.3%	21.6%	8.1%
LANCASTER	22,596	15,077	5,350	2,169	Bush	66.7%	23.7%	9.6%
LINCOLN	5,147	3,497	1,062	588	Bush	67.9%	20.6%	11.4%
LOGAN	303	201	70	32	Bush	66.3%	23.1%	10.6%
LOUP	198	111	50	37	Bush	56.1%	25.3%	18.7%
MCPHERSON	180	118	37	25	Bush	65.6%	20.6%	13.9%
MADISON	4,274	3,126	743	405	Bush	73.1%	17.4%	9.5%
MERRICK	1,259	869	273	117	Bush	69.0%	21.7%	9.3%
MORRILL	946	600	233	113	Bush	63.4%	24.6%	11.9%
NANCE	536	354	138	44	Bush	66.0%	25.7%	8.2%
NEMAHA	1,350	851	364	135	Bush	63.0%	27.0%	10.0%
NUCKOLLS	816	534	213	69	Bush	65.4%	26.1%	8.5%
OTOE	2,479	1,661	606	212	Bush	67.0%	24.4%	8.6%
PAWNEE	555	296	208	51	Bush	53.3%	37.5%	9.2%
PERKINS	599	405	144	50	Bush	67.6%	24.0%	8.3%
PHELPS	1,798	1,177	478	143	Bush	65.5%	26.6%	8.0%
PIERCE	1,208	870	254	84	Bush	72.0%	21.0%	7.0%
PLATTE	3,593	2,446	789	358	Bush	68.1%	22.0%	10.0%
POLK	937	574	239	124	Bush	61.3%	25.5%	13.2%
RED WILLOW	1,839	1,112	542	185	Bush	60.5%	29.5%	10.1%
RICHARDSON	1,657	1,016	469	172	Bush	61.3%	28.3%	10.4%
ROCK	483	315	120	48	Bush	65.2%	24.8%	9.9%
SALINE	1,263	779	360	124	Bush	61.7%	28.5%	9.8%
SARPY	8,051	5,838	1,405	808	Bush	72.5%	17.5%	10.0%
SAUNDERS	2,188	1,433	534	221	Bush	65.5%	24.4%	10.1%
SCOTTS BLUFF	4,424	2,892	954	578	Bush	65.4%	21.6%	13.1%
SEWARD	1,893	1,155	527	211	Bush	61.0%	27.8%	11.1%
SHERIDAN	1,272	870	296	106	Bush	68.4%	23.3%	8.3%
SHERMAN	405	250	104	51	Bush	61.7%	25.7%	12.6%
SIOUX	353	217	94	42	Bush	61.5%	26.6%	11.9%
STANTON	784	528	183	73	Bush	67.3%	23.3%	9.3%
THAYER	1,333	808	434	91	Bush	60.6%	32.6%	6.8%
THOMAS	295	186	72	37	Bush	63.1%	24.4%	12.5%
THURSTON	696	427	178	91	Bush	61.4%	25.6%	13.1%
VALLEY	957	613	246	98	Bush	64.1%	25.7%	10.2%
WASHINGTON	2,637	1,795	568	274	Bush	68.1%	21.5%	10.4%
WAYNE	1,321	873	317	131	Bush	66.1%	24.0%	9.9%
WEBSTER	784	499	220	65	Bush	63.6%	28.1%	8.3%
WHEELER	152	106	31	15	Bush	69.7%	20.4%	9.9%
YORK	3,056	1,950	809	297	Bush	63.8%	26.5%	9.7%
TOTAL	204,049	138,784	45,572	19,693	Bush	68.0%	22.3%	9.7%

NEBRASKA DEMOCRATIC

1992

County	Total Vote	Brown	Clinton	Uncommitted	Other	Winner	Percentage of Total Vote			
							Brown	Clinton	Uncom.	Other
ADAMS	2,258	388	1,121	419	330	Clinton	17.2%	49.6%	18.6%	14.6%
ANTELOPE	758	108	397	116	137	Clinton	14.2%	52.4%	15.3%	18.1%
ARTHUR	31	4	10	8	9	Clinton	12.9%	32.3%	25.8%	29.0%
BANNER	39	6	19	9	5	Clinton	15.4%	48.7%	23.1%	12.8%
BLAINE	71	10	34	6	21	Clinton	14.1%	47.9%	8.5%	29.6%
BOONE	712	139	343	113	117	Clinton	19.5%	48.2%	15.9%	16.4%
BOX BUTTE	1,186	206	673	138	169	Clinton	17.4%	56.7%	11.6%	14.2%
BOYD	321	50	189	27	55	Clinton	15.6%	58.9%	8.4%	17.1%
BROWN	270	37	141	61	31	Clinton	13.7%	52.2%	22.6%	11.5%
BUFFALO	2,609	595	1,077	544	393	Clinton	22.8%	41.3%	20.9%	15.1%
BURT	843	146	465	115	117	Clinton	17.3%	55.2%	13.6%	13.9%
BUTLER	1,500	364	662	226	248	Clinton	24.3%	44.1%	15.1%	16.5%
CASS	2,064	401	946	369	348	Clinton	19.4%	45.8%	17.9%	16.9%
CEDAR	1,380	159	668	206	347	Clinton	11.5%	48.4%	14.9%	25.1%
CHASE	431	42	222	97	70	Clinton	9.7%	51.5%	22.5%	16.2%
CHERRY	436	53	236	93	54	Clinton	12.2%	54.1%	21.3%	12.4%
CHEYENNE	702	95	376	145	86	Clinton	13.5%	53.6%	20.7%	12.3%
CLAY	659	112	345	97	105	Clinton	17.0%	52.4%	14.7%	15.9%
COLFAX	1,143	226	555	145	217	Clinton	19.8%	48.6%	12.7%	19.0%
CUMING	718	146	316	117	139	Clinton	20.3%	44.0%	16.3%	19.4%
CUSTER	997	189	626		182	Clinton	19.0%	62.8%		18.3%
DAKOTA	958	67	551	149	191	Clinton	7.0%	57.5%	15.6%	19.9%
DAWES	596	98	299	92	107	Clinton	16.4%	50.2%	15.4%	18.0%
DAWSON	1,349	203	660	264	222	Clinton	15.0%	48.9%	19.6%	16.5%
DEUEL	96	7	48	18	23	Clinton	7.3%	50.0%	18.8%	24.0%
DIXON	701	39	412	107	143	Clinton	5.6%	58.8%	15.3%	20.4%
DODGE	3,924	800	1,748	682	694	Clinton	20.4%	44.5%	17.4%	17.7%
DOUGLAS	40,431	10,194	16,481	6,726	7,030	Clinton	25.2%	40.8%	16.6%	17.4%
DUNDY	250	22	153	35	40	Clinton	8.8%	61.2%	14.0%	16.0%
FILLMORE	912	149	459	146	158	Clinton	16.3%	50.3%	16.0%	17.3%
FRANKLIN	420	71	228	58	63	Clinton	16.9%	54.3%	13.8%	15.0%
FRONTIER	335	45	167	66	57	Clinton	13.4%	49.9%	19.7%	17.0%
FURNAS	493	50	308	72	63	Clinton	10.1%	62.5%	14.6%	12.8%
GAGE	1,894	407	966	339	182	Clinton	21.5%	51.0%	17.9%	9.6%
GARDEN	225	30	103	46	46	Clinton	13.3%	45.8%	20.4%	20.4%
GARFIELD	180	28	99	23	30	Clinton	15.6%	55.0%	12.8%	16.7%
GOSPER	196	36	108	23	29	Clinton	18.4%	55.1%	11.7%	14.8%
GRANT	59	6	31	10	12	Clinton	10.2%	52.5%	16.9%	20.3%
GREELEY	559	91	282	105	81	Clinton	16.3%	50.4%	18.8%	14.5%
HALL	4,163	700	1,914	877	672	Clinton	16.8%	46.0%	21.1%	16.1%
HAMILTON	717	107	364	145	101	Clinton	14.9%	50.8%	20.2%	14.1%
HARLAN	534	76	277	104	77	Clinton	14.2%	51.9%	19.5%	14.4%
HAYES	129	8	65	30	26	Clinton	6.2%	50.4%	23.3%	20.2%
HITCHCOCK	397	40	210	83	64	Clinton	10.1%	52.9%	20.9%	16.1%
HOLT	994	159	489	187	159	Clinton	16.0%	49.2%	18.8%	16.0%
HOOKER	51	10	26	8	7	Clinton	19.6%	51.0%	15.7%	13.7%
HOWARD	726	121	360	128	117	Clinton	16.7%	49.6%	17.6%	16.1%
JEFFERSON	1,120	186	634	128	172	Clinton	16.6%	56.6%	11.4%	15.4%
JOHNSON	592	128	276	87	101	Clinton	21.6%	46.6%	14.7%	17.1%
KEARNEY	657	104	329	112	112	Clinton	15.8%	50.1%	17.0%	17.0%

NEBRASKA DEMOCRATIC

1992

County	Total Vote	Brown	Clinton	Uncommitted	Other	Winner	Percentage of Total Vote Brown	Clinton	Uncom.	Other
KEITH	553	82	298	81	92	Clinton	14.8%	53.9%	14.6%	16.6%
KEYA PAHA	164	18	82	31	33	Clinton	11.0%	50.0%	18.9%	20.1%
KIMBALL	290	39	157	42	52	Clinton	13.4%	54.1%	14.5%	17.9%
KNOX	947	110	466	169	202	Clinton	11.6%	49.2%	17.8%	21.3%
LANCASTER	24,094	6,013	10,202	3,525	4,354	Clinton	25.0%	42.3%	14.6%	18.1%
LINCOLN	4,754	969	2,326	766	693	Clinton	20.4%	48.9%	16.1%	14.6%
LOGAN	47	8	29	5	5	Clinton	17.0%	61.7%	10.6%	10.6%
LOUP	62	14	26	8	14	Clinton	22.6%	41.9%	12.9%	22.6%
MCPHERSON	56	8	31	5	12	Clinton	14.3%	55.4%	8.9%	21.4%
MADISON	1,659	271	769	316	303	Clinton	16.3%	46.4%	19.0%	18.3%
MERRICK	603	110	307	107	79	Clinton	18.2%	50.9%	17.7%	13.1%
MORRILL	384	68	203	51	62	Clinton	17.7%	52.9%	13.3%	16.1%
NANCE	564	96	298	83	87	Clinton	17.0%	52.8%	14.7%	15.4%
NEMAHA	777	163	360	93	161	Clinton	21.0%	46.3%	12.0%	20.7%
NUCKOLLS	689	93	398	96	102	Clinton	13.5%	57.8%	13.9%	14.8%
OTOE	1,701	312	853	277	259	Clinton	18.3%	50.1%	16.3%	15.2%
PAWNEE	447	77	219	76	75	Clinton	17.2%	49.0%	17.0%	16.8%
PERKINS	331	56	150	65	60	Clinton	16.9%	45.3%	19.6%	18.1%
PHELPS	736	123	402	118	93	Clinton	16.7%	54.6%	16.0%	12.6%
PIERCE	676	88	329	120	139	Clinton	13.0%	48.7%	17.8%	20.6%
PLATTE	2,557	559	1,041	459	498	Clinton	21.9%	40.7%	18.0%	19.5%
POLK	624	145	269	103	107	Clinton	23.2%	43.1%	16.5%	17.1%
RED WILLOW	1,095	117	597	205	176	Clinton	10.7%	54.5%	18.7%	16.1%
RICHARDSON	1,269	170	724	135	240	Clinton	13.4%	57.1%	10.6%	18.9%
ROCK	145	25	64	23	33	Clinton	17.2%	44.1%	15.9%	22.8%
SALINE	1,856	375	1,014	231	236	Clinton	20.2%	54.6%	12.4%	12.7%
SARPY	6,935	1,560	2,796	1,419	1,160	Clinton	22.5%	40.3%	20.5%	16.7%
SAUNDERS	2,874	625	1,306	443	500	Clinton	21.7%	45.4%	15.4%	17.4%
SCOTTS BLUFF	2,640	474	1,331	401	434	Clinton	18.0%	50.4%	15.2%	16.4%
SEWARD	1,540	339	712	226	263	Clinton	22.0%	46.2%	14.7%	17.1%
SHERIDAN	394	49	207	53	85	Clinton	12.4%	52.5%	13.5%	21.6%
SHERMAN	575	106	281	87	101	Clinton	18.4%	48.9%	15.1%	17.6%
SIOUX	109	11	60	20	18	Clinton	10.1%	55.0%	18.3%	16.5%
STANTON	372	57	182	59	74	Clinton	15.3%	48.9%	15.9%	19.9%
THAYER	797	107	430	145	115	Clinton	13.4%	54.0%	18.2%	14.4%
THOMAS	47	3	29	4	11	Clinton	6.4%	61.7%	8.5%	23.4%
THURSTON	623	68	312	110	133	Clinton	10.9%	50.1%	17.7%	21.3%
VALLEY	541	103	297	69	72	Clinton	19.0%	54.9%	12.8%	13.3%
WASHINGTON	1,325	277	589	239	220	Clinton	20.9%	44.5%	18.0%	16.6%
WAYNE	534	84	244	87	119	Clinton	15.7%	45.7%	16.3%	22.3%
WEBSTER	482	72	244	93	73	Clinton	14.9%	50.6%	19.3%	15.1%
WHEELER	91	22	41	12	16	Clinton	24.2%	45.1%	13.2%	17.6%
YORK	842	149	419	156	118	Clinton	17.7%	49.8%	18.5%	14.0%
TOTAL	150,587	31,673	68,562	24,714	25,638	Clinton	21.0%	45.5%	16.4%	17.0%

NEBRASKA REPUBLICAN

1992

County	Total Vote	Buchanan	Bush	Other	Winner	Percentage of Total Vote Buchanan	Bush	Other
ADAMS	3,658	456	3,052	150	Bush	12.5%	83.4%	4.1%
ANTELOPE	1,540	201	1,276	63	Bush	13.1%	82.9%	4.1%
ARTHUR	149	14	126	9	Bush	9.4%	84.6%	6.0%
BANNER	228	42	181	5	Bush	18.4%	79.4%	2.2%
BLAINE	253	32	204	17	Bush	12.6%	80.6%	6.7%
BOONE	944	142	764	38	Bush	15.0%	80.9%	4.0%
BOX BUTTE	1,592	336	1,200	56	Bush	21.1%	75.4%	3.5%
BOYD	756	201	490	65	Bush	26.6%	64.8%	8.6%
BROWN	944	104	807	33	Bush	11.0%	85.5%	3.5%
BUFFALO	4,617	586	3,889	142	Bush	12.7%	84.2%	3.1%
BURT	1,278	169	1,045	64	Bush	13.2%	81.8%	5.0%
BUTLER	876	107	726	43	Bush	12.2%	82.9%	4.9%
CASS	2,215	353	1,729	133	Bush	15.9%	78.1%	6.0%
CEDAR	1,161	177	944	40	Bush	15.2%	81.3%	3.4%
CHASE	732	115	585	32	Bush	15.7%	79.9%	4.4%
CHERRY	1,426	157	1,229	40	Bush	11.0%	86.2%	2.8%
CHEYENNE	1,311	199	1,070	42	Bush	15.2%	81.6%	3.2%
CLAY	1,402	190	1,146	66	Bush	13.6%	81.7%	4.7%
COLFAX	1,185	173	951	61	Bush	14.6%	80.3%	5.1%
CUMING	1,616	185	1,343	88	Bush	11.4%	83.1%	5.4%
CUSTER	2,483	279	2,133	71	Bush	11.2%	85.9%	2.9%
DAKOTA	1,132	168	907	57	Bush	14.8%	80.1%	5.0%
DAWES	1,559	263	1,202	94	Bush	16.9%	77.1%	6.0%
DAWSON	2,793	283	2,395	115	Bush	10.1%	85.8%	4.1%
DEUEL	467	64	371	32	Bush	13.7%	79.4%	6.9%
DIXON	1,026	107	857	62	Bush	10.4%	83.5%	6.0%
DODGE	5,097	671	4,181	245	Bush	13.2%	82.0%	4.8%
DOUGLAS	37,855	4,427	31,063	2,365	Bush	11.7%	82.1%	6.2%
DUNDY	606	87	478	41	Bush	14.4%	78.9%	6.8%
FILLMORE	1,195	166	983	46	Bush	13.9%	82.3%	3.8%
FRANKLIN	739	101	586	52	Bush	13.7%	79.3%	7.0%
FRONTIER	729	100	599	30	Bush	13.7%	82.2%	4.1%
FURNAS	928	135	760	33	Bush	14.5%	81.9%	3.6%
GAGE	2,505	448	1,974	83	Bush	17.9%	78.8%	3.3%
GARDEN	599	71	495	33	Bush	11.9%	82.6%	5.5%
GARFIELD	588	92	471	25	Bush	15.6%	80.1%	4.3%
GOSPER	372	41	305	26	Bush	11.0%	82.0%	7.0%
GRANT	230	28	188	14	Bush	12.2%	81.7%	6.1%
GREELEY	328	41	272	15	Bush	12.5%	82.9%	4.6%
HALL	5,962	705	4,970	287	Bush	11.8%	83.4%	4.8%
HAMILTON	1,650	172	1,415	63	Bush	10.4%	85.8%	3.8%
HARLAN	761	111	598	52	Bush	14.6%	78.6%	6.8%
HAYES	324	41	259	24	Bush	12.7%	79.9%	7.4%
HITCHCOCK	670	91	546	33	Bush	13.6%	81.5%	4.9%
HOLT	2,162	343	1,724	95	Bush	15.9%	79.7%	4.4%
HOOKER	251	27	207	17	Bush	10.8%	82.5%	6.8%
HOWARD	729	90	600	39	Bush	12.3%	82.3%	5.3%
JEFFERSON	1,681	270	1,310	101	Bush	16.1%	77.9%	6.0%
JOHNSON	729	143	558	28	Bush	19.6%	76.5%	3.8%
KEARNEY	1,076	134	879	63	Bush	12.5%	81.7%	5.9%

NEBRASKA REPUBLICAN

1992

County	Total Vote	Buchanan	Bush	Other	Winner	Percentage of Total Vote Buchanan	Bush	Other
KEITH	1,298	175	1,062	61	Bush	13.5%	81.8%	4.7%
KEYA PAHA	308	37	263	8	Bush	12.0%	85.4%	2.6%
KIMBALL	811	117	631	63	Bush	14.4%	77.8%	7.8%
KNOX	1,372	181	1,124	67	Bush	13.2%	81.9%	4.9%
LANCASTER	22,478	3,367	17,782	1,329	Bush	15.0%	79.1%	5.9%
LINCOLN	5,476	724	4,434	318	Bush	13.2%	81.0%	5.8%
LOGAN	249	47	193	9	Bush	18.9%	77.5%	3.6%
LOUP	205	21	175	9	Bush	10.2%	85.4%	4.4%
MCPHERSON	206	19	177	10	Bush	9.2%	85.9%	4.9%
MADISON	4,292	523	3,648	121	Bush	12.2%	85.0%	2.8%
MERRICK	1,194	157	991	46	Bush	13.1%	83.0%	3.9%
MORRILL	887	194	623	70	Bush	21.9%	70.2%	7.9%
NANCE	443	45	376	22	Bush	10.2%	84.9%	5.0%
NEMAHA	1,121	172	891	58	Bush	15.3%	79.5%	5.2%
NUCKOLLS	740	108	597	35	Bush	14.6%	80.7%	4.7%
OTOE	2,320	331	1,914	75	Bush	14.3%	82.5%	3.2%
PAWNEE	592	123	418	51	Bush	20.8%	70.6%	8.6%
PERKINS	613	87	501	25	Bush	14.2%	81.7%	4.1%
PHELPS	1,746	205	1,508	33	Bush	11.7%	86.4%	1.9%
PIERCE	1,327	182	1,098	47	Bush	13.7%	82.7%	3.5%
PLATTE	3,466	420	2,891	155	Bush	12.1%	83.4%	4.5%
POLK	989	144	797	48	Bush	14.6%	80.6%	4.9%
RED WILLOW	1,882	267	1,485	130	Bush	14.2%	78.9%	6.9%
RICHARDSON	1,566	246	1,218	102	Bush	15.7%	77.8%	6.5%
ROCK	534	61	450	23	Bush	11.4%	84.3%	4.3%
SALINE	1,018	181	760	77	Bush	17.8%	74.7%	7.6%
SARPY	8,117	990	6,769	358	Bush	12.2%	83.4%	4.4%
SAUNDERS	2,356	325	1,918	113	Bush	13.8%	81.4%	4.8%
SCOTTS BLUFF	4,370	650	3,427	293	Bush	14.9%	78.4%	6.7%
SEWARD	1,833	266	1,469	98	Bush	14.5%	80.1%	5.3%
SHERIDAN	1,225	161	996	68	Bush	13.1%	81.3%	5.6%
SHERMAN	322	45	257	20	Bush	14.0%	79.8%	6.2%
SIOUX	368	54	300	14	Bush	14.7%	81.5%	3.8%
STANTON	856	120	679	57	Bush	14.0%	79.3%	6.7%
THAYER	1,167	182	943	42	Bush	15.6%	80.8%	3.6%
THOMAS	264	26	222	16	Bush	9.8%	84.1%	6.1%
THURSTON	583	89	462	32	Bush	15.3%	79.2%	5.5%
VALLEY	917	148	742	27	Bush	16.1%	80.9%	2.9%
WASHINGTON	2,461	344	2,009	108	Bush	14.0%	81.6%	4.4%
WAYNE	1,421	167	1,197	57	Bush	11.8%	84.2%	4.0%
WEBSTER	707	100	565	42	Bush	14.1%	79.9%	5.9%
WHEELER	175	17	137	21	Bush	9.7%	78.3%	12.0%
YORK	2,714	391	2,204	119	Bush	14.4%	81.2%	4.4%
TOTAL	192,098	25,847	156,346	9,905	Bush	13.5%	81.4%	5.2%

NEBRASKA DEMOCRATIC

1996

County	Total Vote	Clinton	LaRouche	Other	Winner	Percentage of Total Vote Clinton	LaRouche	Other
ADAMS	1,266	1,085	149	32	Clinton	85.7%	11.8%	2.5%
ANTELOPE	460	393	67		Clinton	85.4%	14.6%	
ARTHUR	30	19	11		Clinton	63.3%	36.7%	
BANNER	16	14	2		Clinton	87.5%	12.5%	
BLAINE	36	27	8	1	Clinton	75.0%	22.2%	2.8%
BOONE	385	324	61		Clinton	84.2%	15.8%	
BOX BUTTE	505	434	60	11	Clinton	85.9%	11.9%	2.2%
BOYD	179	145	34		Clinton	81.0%	19.0%	
BROWN	311	263	48		Clinton	84.6%	15.4%	
BUFFALO	1,826	1,542	226	58	Clinton	84.4%	12.4%	3.2%
BURT	485	445	32	8	Clinton	91.8%	6.6%	1.6%
BUTLER	698	532	166		Clinton	76.2%	23.8%	
CASS	1,326	1,132	165	29	Clinton	85.4%	12.4%	2.2%
CEDAR	571	462	100	9	Clinton	80.9%	17.5%	1.6%
CHASE	217	184	30	3	Clinton	84.8%	13.8%	1.4%
CHERRY	321	273	40	8	Clinton	85.0%	12.5%	2.5%
CHEYENNE	375	311	64		Clinton	82.9%	17.1%	
CLAY	432	369	57	6	Clinton	85.4%	13.2%	1.4%
COLFAX	700	565	130	5	Clinton	80.7%	18.6%	0.7%
CUMING	412	348	55	9	Clinton	84.5%	13.3%	2.2%
CUSTER	572	499	68	5	Clinton	87.2%	11.9%	0.9%
DAKOTA	452	408	33	11	Clinton	90.3%	7.3%	2.4%
DAWES	362	329	32	1	Clinton	90.9%	8.8%	0.3%
DAWSON	758	653	91	14	Clinton	86.1%	12.0%	1.8%
DEUEL	78	69	9		Clinton	88.5%	11.5%	
DIXON	363	326	34	3	Clinton	89.8%	9.4%	0.8%
DODGE	2,005	1,731	237	37	Clinton	86.3%	11.8%	1.8%
DOUGLAS	26,996	23,599	2,530	867	Clinton	87.4%	9.4%	3.2%
DUNDY	135	105	30		Clinton	77.8%	22.2%	
FILLMORE	566	522	44		Clinton	92.2%	7.8%	
FRANKLIN	257	221	34	2	Clinton	86.0%	13.2%	0.8%
FRONTIER	143	126	15	2	Clinton	88.1%	10.5%	1.4%
FURNAS	309	264	45		Clinton	85.4%	14.6%	
GAGE	2,765	2,470	263	32	Clinton	89.3%	9.5%	1.2%
GARDEN	187	160	27		Clinton	85.6%	14.4%	
GARFIELD	129	111	16	2	Clinton	86.0%	12.4%	1.6%
GOSPER	146	126	17	3	Clinton	86.3%	11.6%	2.1%
GRANT	48	42	6		Clinton	87.5%	12.5%	
GREELEY	426	374	45	7	Clinton	87.8%	10.6%	1.6%
HALL	3,058	2,721	287	50	Clinton	89.0%	9.4%	1.6%
HAMILTON	418	369	42	7	Clinton	88.3%	10.0%	1.7%
HARLAN	339	281	53	5	Clinton	82.9%	15.6%	1.5%
HAYES	62	47	14	1	Clinton	75.8%	22.6%	1.6%
HITCHCOCK	230	189	41		Clinton	82.2%	17.8%	
HOLT	741	608	130	3	Clinton	82.1%	17.5%	0.4%
HOOKER	33	30	3		Clinton	90.9%	9.1%	
HOWARD	413	357	53	3	Clinton	86.4%	12.8%	0.7%
JEFFERSON	579	529	48	2	Clinton	91.4%	8.3%	0.3%
JOHNSON	411	361	48	2	Clinton	87.8%	11.7%	0.5%
KEARNEY	409	361	45	3	Clinton	88.3%	11.0%	0.7%

NEBRASKA DEMOCRATIC

1996

County	Total Vote	Clinton	LaRouche	Other	Winner	Percentage of Total Vote: Clinton	LaRouche	Other
KEITH	297	254	36	7	Clinton	85.5%	12.1%	2.4%
KEYA PAHA	69	55	14		Clinton	79.7%	20.3%	
KIMBALL	183	167	16		Clinton	91.3%	8.7%	
KNOX	511	433	73	5	Clinton	84.7%	14.3%	1.0%
LANCASTER	12,638	11,462	890	286	Clinton	90.7%	7.0%	2.3%
LINCOLN	3,022	2,627	321	74	Clinton	86.9%	10.6%	2.4%
LOGAN	36	27	7	2	Clinton	75.0%	19.4%	5.6%
LOUP	34	29	4	1	Clinton	85.3%	11.8%	2.9%
MCPHERSON	54	47	7		Clinton	87.0%	13.0%	
MADISON	969	837	108	24	Clinton	86.4%	11.1%	2.5%
MERRICK	868	745	105	18	Clinton	85.8%	12.1%	2.1%
MORRILL	257	220	31	6	Clinton	85.6%	12.1%	2.3%
NANCE	472	418	54		Clinton	88.6%	11.4%	
NEMAHA	554	486	57	11	Clinton	87.7%	10.3%	2.0%
NUCKOLLS	313	253	56	4	Clinton	80.8%	17.9%	1.3%
OTOE	1,329	1,148	157	24	Clinton	86.4%	11.8%	1.8%
PAWNEE	324	274	50		Clinton	84.6%	15.4%	
PERKINS	220	184	34	2	Clinton	83.6%	15.5%	0.9%
PHELPS	609	524	78	7	Clinton	86.0%	12.8%	1.1%
PIERCE	321	253	66	2	Clinton	78.8%	20.6%	0.6%
PLATTE	1,436	1,076	312	48	Clinton	74.9%	21.7%	3.3%
POLK	302	257	41	4	Clinton	85.1%	13.6%	1.3%
RED WILLOW	601	494	100	7	Clinton	82.2%	16.6%	1.2%
RICHARDSON	847	726	108	13	Clinton	85.7%	12.8%	1.5%
ROCK	97	84	13		Clinton	86.6%	13.4%	
SALINE	1,250	1,105	123	22	Clinton	88.4%	9.8%	1.8%
SARPY	4,218	3,578	474	166	Clinton	84.8%	11.2%	3.9%
SAUNDERS	1,637	1,293	302	42	Clinton	79.0%	18.4%	2.6%
SCOTTS BLUFF	1,644	1,441	176	27	Clinton	87.7%	10.7%	1.6%
SEWARD	840	753	79	8	Clinton	89.6%	9.4%	1.0%
SHERIDAN	256	224	32		Clinton	87.5%	12.5%	
SHERMAN	362	305	57		Clinton	84.3%	15.7%	
SIOUX	96	77	19		Clinton	80.2%	19.8%	
STANTON	206	166	37	3	Clinton	80.6%	18.0%	1.5%
THAYER	509	459	50		Clinton	90.2%	9.8%	
THOMAS	35	27	8		Clinton	77.1%	22.9%	
THURSTON	309	273	31	5	Clinton	88.3%	10.0%	1.6%
VALLEY	377	345	29	3	Clinton	91.5%	7.7%	0.8%
WASHINGTON	688	591	81	16	Clinton	85.9%	11.8%	2.3%
WAYNE	550	501	44	5	Clinton	91.1%	8.0%	0.9%
WEBSTER	299	258	41		Clinton	86.3%	13.7%	
WHEELER	75	62	13		Clinton	82.7%	17.3%	
YORK	521	461	49	11	Clinton	88.5%	9.4%	2.1%
TOTAL	94,176	81,854	10,228	2,094	Clinton	86.9%	10.9%	2.2%

NEBRASKA REPUBLICAN

1996

County	Total Vote	Buchanan	Dole	Other	Winner	Percentage of Total Vote Buchanan	Dole	Other
ADAMS	3,018	401	2,233	384	Dole	13.3%	74.0%	12.7%
ANTELOPE	1,040	136	786	118	Dole	13.1%	75.6%	11.3%
ARTHUR	125	12	102	11	Dole	9.6%	81.6%	8.8%
BANNER	171	35	115	21	Dole	20.5%	67.3%	12.3%
BLAINE	152	15	121	16	Dole	9.9%	79.6%	10.5%
BOONE	857	79	675	103	Dole	9.2%	78.8%	12.0%
BOX BUTTE	1,089	157	751	181	Dole	14.4%	69.0%	16.6%
BOYD	339	71	221	47	Dole	20.9%	65.2%	13.9%
BROWN	1,147	151	847	149	Dole	13.2%	73.8%	13.0%
BUFFALO	4,761	365	3,796	600	Dole	7.7%	79.7%	12.6%
BURT	1,043	122	793	128	Dole	11.7%	76.0%	12.3%
BUTLER	656	102	477	77	Dole	15.5%	72.7%	11.7%
CASS	2,171	245	1,607	319	Dole	11.3%	74.0%	14.7%
CEDAR	737	127	508	102	Dole	17.2%	68.9%	13.8%
CHASE	537	49	437	51	Dole	9.1%	81.4%	9.5%
CHERRY	1,323	151	1,001	171	Dole	11.4%	75.7%	12.9%
CHEYENNE	1,061	105	798	158	Dole	9.9%	75.2%	14.9%
CLAY	1,152	137	893	122	Dole	11.9%	77.5%	10.6%
COLFAX	879	89	676	114	Dole	10.1%	76.9%	13.0%
CUMING	1,295	143	992	160	Dole	11.0%	76.6%	12.4%
CUSTER	1,841	173	1,494	174	Dole	9.4%	81.2%	9.5%
DAKOTA	718	146	445	127	Dole	20.3%	62.0%	17.7%
DAWES	330	143	19	168	Buchanan	43.3%	5.8%	50.9%
DAWSON	2,240	256	1,762	222	Dole	11.4%	78.7%	9.9%
DEUEL	428	35	324	69	Dole	8.2%	75.7%	16.1%
DIXON	699	118	466	115	Dole	16.9%	66.7%	16.5%
DODGE	3,895	337	2,952	606	Dole	8.7%	75.8%	15.6%
DOUGLAS	37,876	3,424	28,945	5,507	Dole	9.0%	76.4%	14.5%
DUNDY	433	45	338	50	Dole	10.4%	78.1%	11.5%
FILLMORE	941	70	784	87	Dole	7.4%	83.3%	9.2%
FRANKLIN	560	47	465	48	Dole	8.4%	83.0%	8.6%
FRONTIER	511	44	422	45	Dole	8.6%	82.6%	8.8%
FURNAS	804	71	648	85	Dole	8.8%	80.6%	10.6%
GAGE	3,881	464	2,859	558	Dole	12.0%	73.7%	14.4%
GARDEN	615	46	502	67	Dole	7.5%	81.6%	10.9%
GARFIELD	515	82	369	64	Dole	15.9%	71.7%	12.4%
GOSPER	394	31	323	40	Dole	7.9%	82.0%	10.2%
GRANT	221	19	177	25	Dole	8.6%	80.1%	11.3%
GREELEY	275	23	233	19	Dole	8.4%	84.7%	6.9%
HALL	5,367	466	4,193	708	Dole	8.7%	78.1%	13.2%
HAMILTON	1,340	138	1,035	167	Dole	10.3%	77.2%	12.5%
HARLAN	593	54	470	69	Dole	9.1%	79.3%	11.6%
HAYES	278	36	204	38	Dole	12.9%	73.4%	13.7%
HITCHCOCK	533	53	433	47	Dole	9.9%	81.2%	8.8%
HOLT	1,966	339	1,374	253	Dole	17.2%	69.9%	12.9%
HOOKER	180	24	137	19	Dole	13.3%	76.1%	10.6%
HOWARD	603	50	485	68	Dole	8.3%	80.4%	11.3%
JEFFERSON	1,122	123	862	137	Dole	11.0%	76.8%	12.2%
JOHNSON	663	93	470	100	Dole	14.0%	70.9%	15.1%
KEARNEY	940	88	747	105	Dole	9.4%	79.5%	11.2%

NEBRASKA REPUBLICAN

1996

County	Total Vote	Buchanan	Dole	Other	Winner	Percentage of Total Vote Buchanan	Dole	Other
KEITH	1,044	93	848	103	Dole	8.9%	81.2%	9.9%
KEYA PAHA	215	43	151	21	Dole	20.0%	70.2%	9.8%
KIMBALL	645	76	491	78	Dole	11.8%	76.1%	12.1%
KNOX	1,018	127	739	152	Dole	12.5%	72.6%	14.9%
LANCASTER	19,729	1,775	14,581	3,373	Dole	9.0%	73.9%	17.1%
LINCOLN	4,514	493	3,463	558	Dole	10.9%	76.7%	12.4%
LOGAN	242	37	177	28	Dole	15.3%	73.1%	11.6%
LOUP	166	11	145	10	Dole	6.6%	87.3%	6.0%
MCPHERSON	146	22	102	22	Dole	15.1%	69.9%	15.1%
MADISON	3,550	384	2,590	576	Dole	10.8%	73.0%	16.2%
MERRICK	1,753	194	1,333	226	Dole	11.1%	76.0%	12.9%
MORRILL	617	100	413	104	Dole	16.2%	66.9%	16.9%
NANCE	442	33	366	43	Dole	7.5%	82.8%	9.7%
NEMAHA	966	89	723	154	Dole	9.2%	74.8%	15.9%
NUCKOLLS	554	60	435	59	Dole	10.8%	78.5%	10.6%
OTOE	2,178	204	1,667	307	Dole	9.4%	76.5%	14.1%
PAWNEE	509	64	374	71	Dole	12.6%	73.5%	13.9%
PERKINS	498	47	403	48	Dole	9.4%	80.9%	9.6%
PHELPS	1,760	161	1,415	184	Dole	9.1%	80.4%	10.5%
PIERCE	729	86	534	109	Dole	11.8%	73.3%	15.0%
PLATTE	3,218	321	2,516	381	Dole	10.0%	78.2%	11.8%
POLK	784	87	583	114	Dole	11.1%	74.4%	14.5%
RED WILLOW	1,457	157	1,134	166	Dole	10.8%	77.8%	11.4%
RICHARDSON	1,296	177	923	196	Dole	13.7%	71.2%	15.1%
ROCK	450	74	340	36	Dole	16.4%	75.6%	8.0%
SALINE	925	129	683	113	Dole	13.9%	73.8%	12.2%
SARPY	8,346	767	6,392	1,187	Dole	9.2%	76.6%	14.2%
SAUNDERS	2,002	241	1,481	280	Dole	12.0%	74.0%	14.0%
SCOTTS BLUFF	3,720	517	2,680	523	Dole	13.9%	72.0%	14.1%
SEWARD	1,502	168	1,123	211	Dole	11.2%	74.8%	14.0%
SHERIDAN	1,007	117	749	141	Dole	11.6%	74.4%	14.0%
SHERMAN	315	40	232	43	Dole	12.7%	73.7%	13.7%
SIOUX	352	56	258	38	Dole	15.9%	73.3%	10.8%
STANTON	766	90	550	126	Dole	11.7%	71.8%	16.4%
THAYER	980	88	811	81	Dole	9.0%	82.8%	8.3%
THOMAS	203	12	173	18	Dole	5.9%	85.2%	8.9%
THURSTON	347	56	235	56	Dole	16.1%	67.7%	16.1%
VALLEY	845	116	617	112	Dole	13.7%	73.0%	13.3%
WASHINGTON	1,986	178	1,523	285	Dole	9.0%	76.7%	14.4%
WAYNE	1,514	186	1,066	262	Dole	12.3%	70.4%	17.3%
WEBSTER	534	62	426	46	Dole	11.6%	79.8%	8.6%
WHEELER	175	26	130	19	Dole	14.9%	74.3%	10.9%
YORK	2,277	247	1,790	240	Dole	10.8%	78.6%	10.5%
TOTAL	170,591	17,741	129,131	23,719	Dole	10.4%	75.7%	13.9%

Note: The vote in Dawes County is anomaly, but is listed as reported by the state.

NEVADA

The mention of Nevada often conjures up images of garish gambling palaces, quickie marriages and speedy divorces. And when it comes to presidential nominating politics, there is an open climate as well.

Nevada has been willing to bet its chips on candidates that face long odds at the national level, or to vote "no" on all the candidates when dissatisfied with the choices. It has even turned thumbs down on its presidential primary, holding ones in 1976 and 1980, then taking an hiatus until 1996.

Nevada's free-wheeling behavior was evident from the start. In 1976, its primary voters opted for two Californians, Jerry Brown and Ronald Reagan, neither of whom was to win his party's nomination that year. Faced with a choice in 1980 between Jimmy Carter and Edward Kennedy, one-third of Nevada primary voters cast ballots for the line marked "None of These Candidates."

In 1988, Nevada Democrats gave a first-round caucus victory to Al Gore, one of only two caucus states that Gore was to win on his first try for the White House. (Wyoming was the other.) Gore had help from his Senate colleague, Harry Reid, and won the state by combining support in Reid's home base of Clark County (Las Vegas) with a strong showing in many of the more conservative, lightly populated "Cow Counties" to the north.

But the real action that year was on the Republican side, where well-organized and procedure-savvy supporters of Pat Robertson not only took over the caucus process but stayed to contend for control of the state GOP apparatus. In the end, Robertson's followers won a majority of the Nevada delegation.

In 1992, Nevada Democrats were back in Brown's corner, giving him a first-round caucus victory over Bill Clinton. While campaigning in Nevada, Brown took an unusual step to cultivate labor support, grabbing a picket sign and joining striking culinary workers outside a Las Vegas hotel. The Culinary Union, a major factor in a state dependent on the tourist industry, returned the favor with a caucus-eve endorsement of Brown.

In 1996, the presidential primary was back, but only for the Republicans, and only with balloting by mail. Bob Dole won the late March event easily, a vote that also served to underscore the booming population growth of the state in general and the Republican Party in particular. Roughly 140,000 GOP primary ballots were cast, nearly double the number in any previous presidential primary in Nevada, Democrat or Republican. Slightly more than half the ballots were cast in Clark County and one-quarter in Washoe County (Reno).

Recent Nevada Primary Results

Nevada held its first presidential primary in 1976.

	DEMOCRATS			REPUBLICANS		
Year	Turnout	Candidates	%	Turnout	Candidates	%
1996 (March 26)	—	NO PRIMARY		140,637	BOB DOLE	52
					Steve Forbes	19
					Pat Buchanan	15
1992	—	NO PRIMARY		—	NO PRIMARY	
1988	—	NO PRIMARY		—	NO PRIMARY	
1984	—	NO PRIMARY		—	NO PRIMARY	
1980 (May 27)	66,948	JIMMY CARTER*	38	47,395	RONALD REAGAN	83
		"None"	34		"None"	10
		Edward Kennedy	29			
1976 (May 25)	75,242	JERRY BROWN	53	47,749	RONALD REAGAN	66
		Jimmy Carter	23		Gerald Ford*	29

Note: All candidates are listed that drew at least 10 percent of their party's primary vote. The names of winning candidates are capitalized. An asterisk (*) indicates an incumbent president.

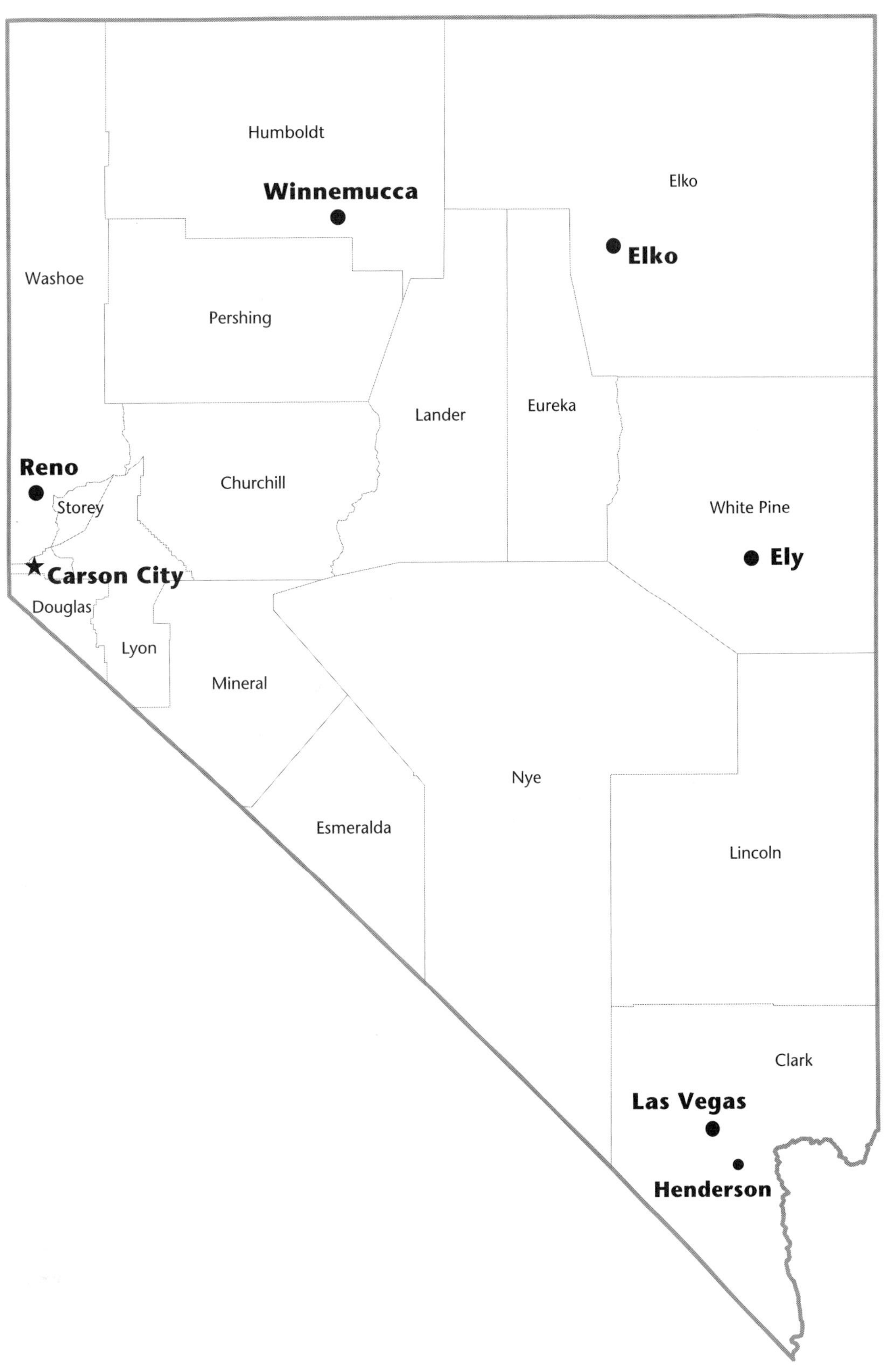
Humboldt
Winnemucca
Elko
Elko
Washoe
Pershing
Lander
Eureka
Reno
Churchill
Storey
White Pine
Ely
Carson City
Douglas
Lyon
Mineral
Nye
Esmeralda
Lincoln
Clark
Las Vegas
Henderson

NEVADA DEMOCRATIC

1976

County	Total Vote	Brown	Carter	Other	Winner	Percentage of Total Vote Brown	Carter	Other
CARSON CITY	3,451	1,670	859	922	Brown	48.4%	24.9%	26.7%
CHURCHILL	1,498	620	505	373	Brown	41.4%	33.7%	24.9%
CLARK	38,491	21,482	7,863	9,146	Brown	55.8%	20.4%	23.8%
DOUGLAS	1,293	633	355	305	Brown	49.0%	27.5%	23.6%
ELKO	1,905	850	448	607	Brown	44.6%	23.5%	31.9%
ESMERALDA	218	55	80	83	Carter	25.2%	36.7%	38.1%
EUREKA	159	57	65	37	Carter	35.8%	40.9%	23.3%
HUMBOLDT	886	341	269	276	Brown	38.5%	30.4%	31.2%
LANDER	371	94	155	122	Carter	25.3%	41.8%	32.9%
LINCOLN	671	278	186	207	Brown	41.4%	27.7%	30.8%
LYON	1,552	632	538	382	Brown	40.7%	34.7%	24.6%
MINERAL	1,414	550	478	386	Brown	38.9%	33.8%	27.3%
NYE	1,297	523	366	408	Brown	40.3%	28.2%	31.5%
PERSHING	524	240	163	121	Brown	45.8%	31.1%	23.1%
STOREY	258	133	74	51	Brown	51.6%	28.7%	19.8%
WASHOE	19,314	10,460	4,763	4,091	Brown	54.2%	24.7%	21.2%
WHITE PINE	1,920	1,053	380	487	Brown	54.8%	19.8%	25.4%
TOTAL	75,222	39,671	17,547	18,004	Brown	52.7%	23.3%	23.9%
Certified Totals	75,242	39,671	17,567	18,004	Brown	52.7%	23.3%	23.9%

NEVADA REPUBLICAN

1976

County	Total Vote	Ford	Reagan	"None"	Winner	Percentage of Total Vote Ford	Reagan	"None"
CARSON CITY	3,342	851	2,327	164	Reagan	25.5%	69.6%	4.9%
CHURCHILL	1,221	194	995	32	Reagan	15.9%	81.5%	2.6%
CLARK	17,982	6,260	10,696	1,026	Reagan	34.8%	59.5%	5.7%
DOUGLAS	2,273	537	1,624	112	Reagan	23.6%	71.4%	4.9%
ELKO	1,448	311	1,118	19	Reagan	21.5%	77.2%	1.3%
ESMERALDA	79	13	62	4	Reagan	16.5%	78.5%	5.1%
EUREKA	126	27	98	1	Reagan	21.4%	77.8%	0.8%
HUMBOLDT	664	91	553	20	Reagan	13.7%	83.3%	3.0%
LANDER	288	53	226	9	Reagan	18.4%	78.5%	3.1%
LINCOLN	174	32	137	5	Reagan	18.4%	78.7%	2.9%
LYON	1,195	228	904	63	Reagan	19.1%	75.6%	5.3%
MINERAL	456	88	349	19	Reagan	19.3%	76.5%	4.2%
NYE	453	109	330	14	Reagan	24.1%	72.8%	3.1%
PERSHING	336	67	257	12	Reagan	19.9%	76.5%	3.6%
STOREY	191	36	144	11	Reagan	18.8%	75.4%	5.8%
WASHOE	16,930	4,704	11,403	823	Reagan	27.8%	67.4%	4.9%
WHITE PINE	591	146	414	31	Reagan	24.7%	70.1%	5.2%
TOTAL	47,749	13,747	31,637	2,365	Reagan	28.8%	66.3%	5.0%

NEVADA DEMOCRATIC

1980

County	Total Vote	Carter	E. Kennedy	"None"	Winner	Percentage of Total Vote Carter	E. Kennedy	"None"
CARSON CITY	2,446	899	670	877	Carter	36.8%	27.4%	35.9%
CHURCHILL	1,019	445	190	384	Carter	43.7%	18.6%	37.7%
CLARK	34,931	12,462	11,117	11,352	Carter	35.7%	31.8%	32.5%
DOUGLAS	1,118	399	301	418	"None"	35.7%	26.9%	37.4%
ELKO	1,808	882	313	613	Carter	48.8%	17.3%	33.9%
ESMERALDA	175	75	24	76	"None"	42.9%	13.7%	43.4%
EUREKA	118	42	23	53	"None"	35.6%	19.5%	44.9%
HUMBOLDT	841	358	203	280	Carter	42.6%	24.1%	33.3%
LANDER	430	168	106	156	Carter	39.1%	24.7%	36.3%
LINCOLN	555	254	101	200	Carter	45.8%	18.2%	36.0%
LYON	1,358	601	296	461	Carter	44.3%	21.8%	33.9%
MINERAL	1,254	477	268	509	"None"	38.0%	21.4%	40.6%
NYE	1,494	631	299	564	Carter	42.2%	20.0%	37.8%
PERSHING	348	154	93	101	Carter	44.3%	26.7%	29.0%
STOREY	211	86	65	60	Carter	40.8%	30.8%	28.4%
WASHOE	17,942	6,802	5,008	6,132	Carter	37.9%	27.9%	34.2%
WHITE PINE	900	424	219	257	Carter	47.1%	24.3%	28.6%
TOTAL	66,948	25,159	19,296	22,493	Carter	37.6%	28.8%	33.6%

NEVADA REPUBLICAN

1980

County	Total Vote	Bush	Reagan	"None"	Winner	Percentage of Total Vote Bush	Reagan	"None"
CARSON CITY	2,577	135	2,208	234	Reagan	5.2%	85.7%	9.1%
CHURCHILL	1,097	31	991	75	Reagan	2.8%	90.3%	6.8%
CLARK	18,955	1,296	15,515	2,144	Reagan	6.8%	81.9%	11.3%
DOUGLAS	1,746	91	1,517	138	Reagan	5.2%	86.9%	7.9%
ELKO	1,529	68	1,392	69	Reagan	4.4%	91.0%	4.5%
ESMERALDA	73		66	7	Reagan		90.4%	9.6%
EUREKA	136	8	124	4	Reagan	5.9%	91.2%	2.9%
HUMBOLDT	670	30	605	35	Reagan	4.5%	90.3%	5.2%
LANDER	372	19	310	43	Reagan	5.1%	83.3%	11.6%
LINCOLN	195	6	170	19	Reagan	3.1%	87.2%	9.7%
LYON	1,040	43	931	66	Reagan	4.1%	89.5%	6.3%
MINERAL	465	25	408	32	Reagan	5.4%	87.7%	6.9%
NYE	681	35	593	53	Reagan	5.1%	87.1%	7.8%
PERSHING	270	12	241	17	Reagan	4.4%	89.3%	6.3%
STOREY	134	6	116	12	Reagan	4.5%	86.6%	9.0%
WASHOE	17,145	1,248	13,898	1,999	Reagan	7.3%	81.1%	11.7%
WHITE PINE	310	25	267	18	Reagan	8.1%	86.1%	5.8%
TOTAL	47,395	3,078	39,352	4,965	Reagan	6.5%	83.0%	10.5%

NEVADA REPUBLICAN

1996

County	Total Vote	Buchanan	Dole	Forbes	Other	Winner	Percentage of Total Vote: Buchanan	Dole	Forbes	Other
CARSON CITY	7,090	1,034	3,718	1,337	1,001	Dole	14.6%	52.4%	18.9%	14.1%
CHURCHILL	3,176	433	1,861	457	425	Dole	13.6%	58.6%	14.4%	13.4%
CLARK	73,692	11,656	36,209	15,245	10,582	Dole	15.8%	49.1%	20.7%	14.4%
DOUGLAS	6,212	837	3,494	1,093	788	Dole	13.5%	56.2%	17.6%	12.7%
ELKO	3,826	616	1,969	807	434	Dole	16.1%	51.5%	21.1%	11.3%
ESMERALDA	156	38	64	35	19	Dole	24.4%	41.0%	22.4%	12.2%
EUREKA	292	68	144	53	27	Dole	23.3%	49.3%	18.2%	9.2%
HUMBOLDT	1,651	257	902	270	222	Dole	15.6%	54.6%	16.4%	13.4%
LANDER	826	160	414	133	119	Dole	19.4%	50.1%	16.1%	14.4%
LINCOLN	442	80	249	62	51	Dole	18.1%	56.3%	14.0%	11.5%
LYON	3,324	617	1,631	571	505	Dole	18.6%	49.1%	17.2%	15.2%
MINERAL	457	84	198	102	73	Dole	18.4%	43.3%	22.3%	16.0%
NYE	2,509	517	1,390	276	326	Dole	20.6%	55.4%	11.0%	13.0%
PERSHING	518	86	264	103	65	Dole	16.6%	51.0%	19.9%	12.5%
STOREY	477	94	243	78	62	Dole	19.7%	50.9%	16.4%	13.0%
WASHOE	35,205	4,605	19,767	6,304	4,529	Dole	13.1%	56.1%	17.9%	12.9%
WHITE PINE	784	139	415	137	93	Dole	17.7%	52.9%	17.5%	11.9%
TOTAL	140,637	21,321	72,932	27,063	19,321	Dole	15.2%	51.9%	19.2%	13.7%

NEW HAMPSHIRE

Like the New York Yankees, the New Hampshire presidential primary has never been willing to settle for anything less than first.

A state, of course, has means beyond a baseball team: New Hampshire has decreed that its primary be held before that of any other state as a matter of law. Despite all the frowning and frustration in other states, New Hampshire has attracted candidates to its first-in-the-nation presidential primary since it became a major part of the political landscape in 1952.

The primary lost a bit of its luster in the 1990s. In 1992 Bill Clinton became the first candidate since 1952 to be elected president without first winning the New Hampshire primary; he was second in the state's Democratic voting. In 1996 Pat Buchanan won the Republican balloting in New Hampshire but no other primary that followed, throwing into question the whole idea that momentum accrues to a Granite State winner.

Yet New Hampshire has remained a rite of passage for anyone who seriously covets the White House, and for long shots it is a place where hope springs eternal. In a state whose motto is "Live Free or Die," voters have never been reluctant to deliver a blow against the politically high and mighty.

Two presidents—Harry Truman and Lyndon Johnson—decided not to seek reelection after poor showings in New Hampshire. Truman was upset in the 1952 Democratic primary by Sen. Estes Kefauver of Tennessee. A write-in campaign for Johnson in the 1968 Democratic balloting could muster only 49.6 percent of the vote against the lightly regarded anti–Vietnam War candidacy of Eugene McCarthy.

Since then, Presidents Gerald Ford (in 1976), Jimmy Carter (in 1980), and George Bush (in 1992) have also been chastened

Recent New Hampshire Primary Results

New Hampshire held its first presidential primary in 1916.

	DEMOCRATS			REPUBLICANS		
Year	Turnout	Candidates	%	Turnout	Candidates	%
1996 (Feb. 20)	91,562	BILL CLINTON*	84	208,938	PAT BUCHANAN	27
					Bob Dole	26
					Lamar Alexander	23
					Steve Forbes	12
1992 (Feb. 18)	167,819	PAUL TSONGAS	33	174,165	GEORGE BUSH*	53
		Bill Clinton	25		Pat Buchanan	37
		Bob Kerrey	11			
		Tom Harkin	10			
1988 (Feb. 16)	123,512	MICHAEL DUKAKIS	36	157,644	GEORGE BUSH	38
		Richard Gephardt	20		Bob Dole	28
		Paul Simon	17		Jack Kemp	13
					Pierre du Pont	10
1984 (Feb. 28)	101,131	GARY HART	37	75,570	RONALD REAGAN*	86
		Walter Mondale	28			
		John Glenn	12			
1980 (Feb. 26)	111,930	JIMMY CARTER*	47	147,157	RONALD REAGAN	50
		Edward Kennedy	37		George Bush	23
					Howard Baker	13
1976 (Feb. 24)	82,381	JIMMY CARTER	28	111,674	GERALD FORD*	49
		Morris Udall	23		Ronald Reagan	48
		Birch Bayh	15			
		Fred Harris	11			
1972 (March 7)	88,854	EDMUND MUSKIE	46	117,208	RICHARD NIXON*	68
		George McGovern	37		Paul McCloskey	20
1968 (March 12)	55,464	LYNDON JOHNSON*#	50	103,938	RICHARD NIXON	78
		Eugene McCarthy	42		Nelson Rockefeller#	11

Note: All candidates are listed that drew at least 10 percent of their party's primary vote. The names of winning candidates are capitalized. An asterisk (*) indicates an incumbent president. A pound sign (#) indicates a write-in candidate.

by New Hampshire primary voters. They won, but with less than 55 percent of the vote, and all three lost the general election that followed.

New Hampshire is a great leveler. It is small enough that any candidate with time, energy and a knack for grass-roots organization has a good chance of winning. As Kefauver and McCarthy came to national prominence in New Hampshire, so did George McGovern in 1972 and Gary Hart in 1984.

McGovern did not beat the Democratic front-runner, Sen. Edmund Muskie of Maine, but he ran so far above expectations that Muskie's campaign lost respect and soon slid into political oblivion. Hart defeated Walter Mondale in the 1984 Democratic contest, sending the erstwhile front-runner into a tailspin from which he barely recovered.

For all its traditionalism, New Hampshire lacks strong party structures and the politically potent interest groups that all but rule in other states. But the state's primary places great pressure on dark-horse hopefuls. For those who do not make a breakthrough in Iowa, a caucus state, New Hampshire can be their last chance. It certainly is the final opportunity for candidates to extensively woo voters personally before the whirl of subsequent primaries forces surviving candidates to focus on media advertising campaigns.

New Hampshire's Republican electorate has a conservative hue, but in presidential primaries it has not always supported the champion of the GOP right. Robert Taft lost to Dwight Eisenhower in 1952; Barry Goldwater ran far behind the 1964 write-in winner, Henry Cabot Lodge; and in 1976 Ronald Reagan lost narrowly to President Ford.

Voices on the right are amplified by the unabashedly conservative Manchester *Union Leader,* which plays a role in shaping political debate within the state. In 1992 and 1996, the *Union Leader* backed the insurgent candidacy of Pat Buchanan, who staggered President Bush by taking 37 percent of the vote in the 1992 GOP primary and won the event over a crowded Republican field four years later.

For conservative candidates from Taft to Buchanan, the city of Manchester has been a most reliable source of votes. The state's largest urban center, it was the only New Hampshire city to back Taft in 1952 and Goldwater in the 1964 GOP contest. It also went overwhelmingly for Reagan in both 1976 and 1980, as well as Buchanan in 1996.

That year, Buchanan also won old mill towns around the state, much of the conservative mountainous North Country, communities near Manchester that were loyal readers of the *Union Leader,* and communities where Ross Perot ran particularly well as an independent presidential candidate in 1992.

Generally, the strongholds of moderate Republicanism mirror the hotbeds of liberal Democrats—the seacoast area of southeast New Hampshire, the major academic communities of Hanover (Dartmouth College) and Durham (University of New Hampshire), and the state capital of Concord and its environs. Bob Dole won many of these communities in the 1996 GOP primary, but not all. Lamar Alexander carried Bow (near Concord) and almost beat Dole in several others.

In the last competitive Democratic primary, in 1992, the victorious Paul Tsongas carried the most affluent as well as the most liberal communities in the state. Tsongas had less appeal in blue-collar mill towns such as Berlin and Claremont, where he was beaten decisively by Bill Clinton, who also carried many smaller urban centers such as Concord and Keene.

To that extent, Clinton followed the script of the last successful southern Democrat in New Hampshire, Jimmy Carter. But Clinton lacked one piece of the centrist coalition that Carter put together when he first won the primary in 1976. That was the bedroom communities of southern New Hampshire (including the cities of Manchester and Nashua). There, Tsongas prevailed.

A month or so before the 1992 New Hampshire primary, it looked like Clinton was well positioned to win. But in short order, he suffered two big blows: a tabloid tale of womanizing and hints of draft evasion during the Vietnam War. Yet by finishing a clear second in New Hampshire, Clinton survived, and he could leave New Hampshire boasting that he was the "Comeback Kid."

NEW HAMPSHIRE DEMOCRATIC

1968

County	Total Vote	Johnson	McCarthy	Other	Winner	Percentage of Total Vote Johnson	McCarthy	Other
BELKNAP	2,020	949	858	213	Johnson	47.0%	42.5%	10.5%
CARROLL	663	292	303	68	McCarthy	44.0%	45.7%	10.3%
CHESHIRE	2,657	1,220	1,210	227	Johnson	45.9%	45.5%	8.5%
COOS	4,889	2,231	2,373	285	McCarthy	45.6%	48.5%	5.8%
GRAFTON	2,998	1,093	1,639	266	McCarthy	36.5%	54.7%	8.9%
HILLSBOROUGH	22,532	12,791	7,684	2,057	Johnson	56.8%	34.1%	9.1%
MERRIMACK	5,231	2,503	2,242	486	Johnson	47.8%	42.9%	9.3%
ROCKINGHAM	7,692	3,155	3,866	671	McCarthy	41.0%	50.3%	8.7%
STRAFFORD	4,575	2,076	2,235	264	McCarthy	45.4%	48.9%	5.8%
SULLIVAN	2,211	1,210	859	142	Johnson	54.7%	38.9%	6.4%
TOTAL	55,468	27,520	23,269	4,679	Johnson	49.6%	42.0%	8.4%
Certified Totals	55,464	27,520	23,263	4,681	Johnson	49.6%	41.9%	8.4%

City/Town	Total Vote	Johnson	McCarthy	Other	Winner	Johnson	McCarthy	Other
AMHERST	153	61	87	5	McCarthy	39.9%	56.9%	3.3%
ATKINSON	153	54	82	17	McCarthy	35.3%	53.6%	11.1%
BARRINGTON	81	30	42	9	McCarthy	37.0%	51.9%	11.1%
BEDFORD	398	185	171	42	Johnson	46.5%	43.0%	10.6%
BELMONT	210	82	93	35	McCarthy	39.0%	44.3%	16.7%
BERLIN	3,282	1,524	1,636	122	McCarthy	46.4%	49.8%	3.7%
BOW	67	28	39		McCarthy	41.8%	58.2%	
CLAREMONT	1,131	673	411	47	Johnson	59.5%	36.3%	4.2%
CONCORD	1,396	606	707	83	McCarthy	43.4%	50.6%	5.9%
CONWAY	137	54	65	18	McCarthy	39.4%	47.4%	13.1%
DERRY	545	256	232	57	Johnson	47.0%	42.6%	10.5%
DOVER	1,352	676	625	51	Johnson	50.0%	46.2%	3.8%
DURHAM	363	54	298	11	McCarthy	14.9%	82.1%	3.0%
EPPING	151	96	54	1	Johnson	63.6%	35.8%	0.7%
EXETER	430	172	232	26	McCarthy	40.0%	54.0%	6.0%
FARMINGTON	177	70	91	16	McCarthy	39.5%	51.4%	9.0%
FRANKLIN	567	302	213	52	Johnson	53.3%	37.6%	9.2%
GILFORD	148	49	78	21	McCarthy	33.1%	52.7%	14.2%
GOFFSTOWN	843	452	318	73	Johnson	53.6%	37.7%	8.7%
HAMPSTEAD	108	60	41	7	Johnson	55.6%	38.0%	6.5%
HAMPTON	477	183	252	42	McCarthy	38.4%	52.8%	8.8%
HANOVER	596	86	485	25	McCarthy	14.4%	81.4%	4.2%
HOLLIS	89	29	56	4	McCarthy	32.6%	62.9%	4.5%
HOOKSETT	543	275	189	79	Johnson	50.6%	34.8%	14.5%
HUDSON	1,028	524	412	92	Johnson	51.0%	40.1%	8.9%
JAFFREY	254	119	114	21	Johnson	46.9%	44.9%	8.3%
KEENE	975	470	411	94	Johnson	48.2%	42.2%	9.6%
KINGSTON	134	67	59	8	Johnson	50.0%	44.0%	6.0%
LACONIA	966	527	344	95	Johnson	54.6%	35.6%	9.8%
LEBANON	509	250	237	22	Johnson	49.1%	46.6%	4.3%
LITCHFIELD	103	44	45	14	McCarthy	42.7%	43.7%	13.6%
LITTLETON	236	129	87	20	Johnson	54.7%	36.9%	8.5%
LONDONDERRY	322	139	129	54	Johnson	43.2%	40.1%	16.8%
MANCHESTER	12,367	7,591	3,412	1,364	Johnson	61.4%	27.6%	11.0%
MERRIMACK TOWN	398	195	172	31	Johnson	49.0%	43.2%	7.8%

NEW HAMPSHIRE DEMOCRATIC

1968

City/Town	Total Vote	Johnson	McCarthy	Other	Winner	Percentage of Total Vote Johnson	McCarthy	Other
MILFORD	436	245	150	41	Johnson	56.2%	34.4%	9.4%
NASHUA	4,529	2,585	1,776	168	Johnson	57.1%	39.2%	3.7%
NEWMARKET	536	308	209	19	Johnson	57.5%	39.0%	3.5%
NEWPORT	480	260	174	46	Johnson	54.2%	36.3%	9.6%
PELHAM	480	183	252	45	McCarthy	38.1%	52.5%	9.4%
PEMBROKE	698	359	267	72	Johnson	51.4%	38.3%	10.3%
PETERBOROUGH	247	93	127	27	McCarthy	37.7%	51.4%	10.9%
PLAISTOW	198	69	105	24	McCarthy	34.8%	53.0%	12.1%
PLYMOUTH	117	31	65	21	McCarthy	26.5%	55.6%	17.9%
PORTSMOUTH	924	268	599	57	McCarthy	29.0%	64.8%	6.2%
RAYMOND	206	97	82	27	Johnson	47.1%	39.8%	13.1%
ROCHESTER	870	394	410	66	McCarthy	45.3%	47.1%	7.6%
SALEM	1,520	597	776	147	McCarthy	39.3%	51.1%	9.7%
SEABROOK	179	58	99	22	McCarthy	32.4%	55.3%	12.3%
SOMERSWORTH	1,103	600	444	59	Johnson	54.4%	40.3%	5.3%
SWANZEY	158	78	65	15	Johnson	49.4%	41.1%	9.5%
WEARE	90	45	25	20	Johnson	50.0%	27.8%	22.2%
WINDHAM	215	89	109	17	McCarthy	41.4%	50.7%	7.9%

Note: The votes cast for Johnson were write-ins. McCarthy was listed on the ballot. The principal source for New Hampshire primary results in this table and those that follow is the New Hampshire Manual for the General Court, which is published by the New Hampshire secretary of state after each election. The cities and towns in this and other New Hampshire tables include those with a 1990 population in excess of 5,000.

NEW HAMPSHIRE REPUBLICAN

1968

County	Total Vote	Nixon	Rockefeller	Other	Winner	Percentage of Total Vote Nixon	Rockefeller	Other
BELKNAP	5,967	4,794	526	647	Nixon	80.3%	8.8%	10.8%
CARROLL	4,982	4,176	459	347	Nixon	83.8%	9.2%	7.0%
CHESHIRE	7,151	5,383	952	816	Nixon	75.3%	13.3%	11.4%
COOS	4,807	3,854	330	623	Nixon	80.2%	6.9%	13.0%
GRAFTON	9,228	7,063	1,134	1,031	Nixon	76.5%	12.3%	11.2%
HILLSBOROUGH	24,919	19,740	2,328	2,851	Nixon	79.2%	9.3%	11.4%
MERRIMACK	13,775	10,325	1,672	1,778	Nixon	75.0%	12.1%	12.9%
ROCKINGHAM	21,679	16,643	2,536	2,500	Nixon	76.8%	11.7%	11.5%
STRAFFORD	7,113	5,447	860	806	Nixon	76.6%	12.1%	11.3%
SULLIVAN	4,317	3,241	444	632	Nixon	75.1%	10.3%	14.6%
TOTAL	103,938	80,666	11,241	12,031	Nixon	77.6%	10.8%	11.6%

City/Town								
AMHERST	917	642	141	134	Nixon	70.0%	15.4%	14.6%
ATKINSON	401	319	61	21	Nixon	79.6%	15.2%	5.2%
BARRINGTON	294	236	31	27	Nixon	80.3%	10.5%	9.2%
BEDFORD	1,161	962	77	122	Nixon	82.9%	6.6%	10.5%
BELMONT	425	358	28	39	Nixon	84.2%	6.6%	9.2%

NEW HAMPSHIRE REPUBLICAN

1968

City/Town	Total Vote	Nixon	Rockefeller	Other	Winner	Percentage of Total Vote Nixon	Rockefeller	Other
BERLIN	1,649	1,168	139	342	Nixon	70.8%	8.4%	20.7%
BOW	401	393		8	Nixon	98.0%		2.0%
CLAREMONT	1,475	1,115	146	214	Nixon	75.6%	9.9%	14.5%
CONCORD	5,518	3,670	897	951	Nixon	66.5%	16.3%	17.2%
CONWAY	1,226	1,012	116	98	Nixon	82.5%	9.5%	8.0%
DERRY	1,839	1,455	143	241	Nixon	79.1%	7.8%	13.1%
DOVER	2,044	1,560	245	239	Nixon	76.3%	12.0%	11.7%
DURHAM	961	520	249	192	Nixon	54.1%	25.9%	20.0%
EPPING	206	195		11	Nixon	94.7%		5.3%
EXETER	2,209	1,467	279	463	Nixon	66.4%	12.6%	21.0%
FARMINGTON	534	465	33	36	Nixon	87.1%	6.2%	6.7%
FRANKLIN	677	540	64	73	Nixon	79.8%	9.5%	10.8%
GILFORD	718	515	95	108	Nixon	71.7%	13.2%	15.0%
GOFFSTOWN	1,322	1,136	55	131	Nixon	85.9%	4.2%	9.9%
HAMPSTEAD	578	463	71	44	Nixon	80.1%	12.3%	7.6%
HAMPTON	1,419	1,028	196	195	Nixon	72.4%	13.8%	13.7%
HANOVER	1,062	388	406	268	Rockefeller	36.5%	38.2%	25.2%
HOLLIS	625	453	105	67	Nixon	72.5%	16.8%	10.7%
HOOKSETT	745	646	26	73	Nixon	86.7%	3.5%	9.8%
HUDSON	982	714	105	163	Nixon	72.7%	10.7%	16.6%
JAFFREY	511	395	47	69	Nixon	77.3%	9.2%	13.5%
KEENE	2,611	1,902	365	344	Nixon	72.8%	14.0%	13.2%
KINGSTON	631	510	69	52	Nixon	80.8%	10.9%	8.2%
LACONIA	2,220	1,796	197	227	Nixon	80.9%	8.9%	10.2%
LEBANON	1,069	729	177	163	Nixon	68.2%	16.6%	15.2%
LITCHFIELD	175	136	14	25	Nixon	77.7%	8.0%	14.3%
LITTLETON	1,127	962	68	97	Nixon	85.4%	6.0%	8.6%
LONDONDERRY	792	685	36	71	Nixon	86.5%	4.5%	9.0%
MANCHESTER	8,206	6,793	522	891	Nixon	82.8%	6.4%	10.9%
MERRIMACK TOWN	814	647	78	89	Nixon	79.5%	9.6%	10.9%
MILFORD	1,133	954	82	97	Nixon	84.2%	7.2%	8.6%
NASHUA	3,897	2,784	561	552	Nixon	71.4%	14.4%	14.2%
NEWMARKET	172	146	24	2	Nixon	84.9%	14.0%	1.2%
NEWPORT	786	579	92	115	Nixon	73.7%	11.7%	14.6%
PELHAM	597	416	109	72	Nixon	69.7%	18.3%	12.1%
PEMBROKE	670	546	66	58	Nixon	81.5%	9.9%	8.7%
PETERBOROUGH	1,046	780	133	133	Nixon	74.6%	12.7%	12.7%
PLAISTOW	707	534	114	59	Nixon	75.5%	16.1%	8.3%
PLYMOUTH	734	617	50	67	Nixon	84.1%	6.8%	9.1%
PORTSMOUTH	1,759	1,292	219	248	Nixon	73.5%	12.5%	14.1%
RAYMOND	499	454	23	22	Nixon	91.0%	4.6%	4.4%
ROCHESTER	1,611	1,340	135	136	Nixon	83.2%	8.4%	8.4%
SALEM	2,430	1,784	396	250	Nixon	73.4%	16.3%	10.3%
SEABROOK	666	581	53	32	Nixon	87.2%	8.0%	4.8%
SOMERSWORTH	380	303	33	44	Nixon	79.7%	8.7%	11.6%
SWANZEY	501	376	61	64	Nixon	75.0%	12.2%	12.8%
WEARE	378	332	17	29	Nixon	87.8%	4.5%	7.7%
WINDHAM	512	403	65	44	Nixon	78.7%	12.7%	8.6%

Note: The votes cast for Rockefeller were write-ins. Nixon was listed on the ballot.

NEW HAMPSHIRE DEMOCRATIC

1972

County	Total Vote	McGovern	Muskie	Other	Winner	Percentage of Total Vote McGovern	Muskie	Other
BELKNAP	3,317	1,339	1,582	396	Muskie	40.4%	47.7%	11.9%
CARROLL	1,150	512	482	156	McGovern	44.5%	41.9%	13.6%
CHESHIRE	5,595	2,433	2,681	481	Muskie	43.5%	47.9%	8.6%
COOS	5,814	1,619	3,386	809	Muskie	27.8%	58.2%	13.9%
GRAFTON	5,403	2,537	2,063	803	McGovern	47.0%	38.2%	14.9%
HILLSBOROUGH	33,475	11,760	13,848	7,867	Muskie	35.1%	41.4%	23.5%
MERRIMACK	7,759	3,328	3,185	1,246	McGovern	42.9%	41.0%	16.1%
ROCKINGHAM	14,222	5,580	7,174	1,468	Muskie	39.2%	50.4%	10.3%
STRAFFORD	8,252	2,765	4,606	881	Muskie	33.5%	55.8%	10.7%
SULLIVAN	3,867	1,134	2,228	505	Muskie	29.3%	57.6%	13.1%
TOTAL	88,854	33,007	41,235	14,612	Muskie	37.1%	46.4%	16.4%

City/Town	Total Vote	McGovern	Muskie	Other	Winner	McGovern	Muskie	Other
AMHERST	408	197	143	68	McGovern	48.3%	35.0%	16.7%
ATKINSON	239	99	108	32	Muskie	41.4%	45.2%	13.4%
BARRINGTON	164	78	58	28	McGovern	47.6%	35.4%	17.1%
BEDFORD	616	247	226	143	McGovern	40.1%	36.7%	23.2%
BELMONT	334	139	146	49	Muskie	41.6%	43.7%	14.7%
BERLIN	3,533	855	2,240	438	Muskie	24.2%	63.4%	12.4%
BOW	162	84	68	10	McGovern	51.9%	42.0%	6.2%
CLAREMONT	1,831	464	1,144	223	Muskie	25.3%	62.5%	12.2%
CONCORD	1,996	907	875	214	McGovern	45.4%	43.8%	10.7%
CONWAY	242	97	86	59	McGovern	40.1%	35.5%	24.4%
DERRY	1,049	507	378	164	McGovern	48.3%	36.0%	15.6%
DOVER	2,239	808	1,228	203	Muskie	36.1%	54.8%	9.1%
DURHAM	656	443	172	41	McGovern	67.5%	26.2%	6.3%
EPPING	395	161	178	56	Muskie	40.8%	45.1%	14.2%
EXETER	456	229	198	29	McGovern	50.2%	43.4%	6.4%
FARMINGTON	385	101	214	70	Muskie	26.2%	55.6%	18.2%
FRANKLIN	951	344	479	128	Muskie	36.2%	50.4%	13.5%
GILFORD	305	156	120	29	McGovern	51.1%	39.3%	9.5%
GOFFSTOWN	1,320	566	438	316	McGovern	42.9%	33.2%	23.9%
HAMPSTEAD	219	100	110	9	Muskie	45.7%	50.2%	4.1%
HAMPTON	798	313	444	41	Muskie	39.2%	55.6%	5.1%
HANOVER	1,099	836	215	48	McGovern	76.1%	19.6%	4.4%
HOLLIS	238	139	77	22	McGovern	58.4%	32.4%	9.2%
HOOKSETT	872	404	250	218	McGovern	46.3%	28.7%	25.0%
HUDSON	1,548	522	812	214	Muskie	33.7%	52.5%	13.8%
JAFFREY	507	197	236	74	Muskie	38.9%	46.5%	14.6%
KEENE	2,001	869	959	173	Muskie	43.4%	47.9%	8.6%
KINGSTON	320	119	151	50	Muskie	37.2%	47.2%	15.6%
LACONIA	1,463	506	831	126	Muskie	34.6%	56.8%	8.6%
LEBANON	958	452	445	61	McGovern	47.2%	46.5%	6.4%
LITCHFIELD	184	67	83	34	Muskie	36.4%	45.1%	18.5%
LITTLETON	476	118	269	89	Muskie	24.8%	56.5%	18.7%
LONDONDERRY	462	216	170	76	McGovern	46.8%	36.8%	16.5%
MANCHESTER	17,293	5,694	6,204	5,395	Muskie	32.9%	35.9%	31.2%
MERRIMACK TOWN	891	347	356	188	Muskie	38.9%	40.0%	21.1%

NEW HAMPSHIRE DEMOCRATIC

1972

City/Town	Total Vote	McGovern	Muskie	Other	Winner	Percentage of Total Vote McGovern	Muskie	Other
MILFORD	727	217	270	240	Muskie	29.8%	37.1%	33.0%
NASHUA	6,534	2,256	3,737	541	Muskie	34.5%	57.2%	8.3%
NEWMARKET	878	420	414	44	McGovern	47.8%	47.2%	5.0%
NEWPORT	810	223	476	111	Muskie	27.5%	58.8%	13.7%
PELHAM	1,013	341	573	99	Muskie	33.7%	56.6%	9.8%
PEMBROKE	725	233	318	174	Muskie	32.1%	43.9%	24.0%
PETERBOROUGH	412	263	98	51	McGovern	63.8%	23.8%	12.4%
PLAISTOW	468	160	283	25	Muskie	34.2%	60.5%	5.3%
PLYMOUTH	236	131	62	43	McGovern	55.5%	26.3%	18.2%
PORTSMOUTH	1,853	589	1,154	110	Muskie	31.8%	62.3%	5.9%
RAYMOND	409	148	142	119	McGovern	36.2%	34.7%	29.1%
ROCHESTER	1,886	517	1,100	269	Muskie	27.4%	58.3%	14.3%
SALEM	2,878	1,065	1,594	219	Muskie	37.0%	55.4%	7.6%
SEABROOK	294	86	171	37	Muskie	29.3%	58.2%	12.6%
SOMERSWORTH	1,875	430	1,268	177	Muskie	22.9%	67.6%	9.4%
SWANZEY	340	164	164	12		48.2%	48.2%	3.5%
WEARE	183	98	44	41	McGovern	53.6%	24.0%	22.4%
WINDHAM	464	189	256	19	Muskie	40.7%	55.2%	4.1%

NEW HAMPSHIRE REPUBLICAN

1972

County	Total Vote	McCloskey	Nixon	Other	Winner	Percentage of Total Vote McCloskey	Nixon	Other
BELKNAP	6,726	1,028	4,604	1,094	Nixon	15.3%	68.5%	16.3%
CARROLL	5,561	894	4,022	645	Nixon	16.1%	72.3%	11.6%
CHESHIRE	8,300	1,693	5,543	1,064	Nixon	20.4%	66.8%	12.8%
COOS	4,557	607	3,292	658	Nixon	13.3%	72.2%	14.4%
GRAFTON	11,070	2,349	7,238	1,483	Nixon	21.2%	65.4%	13.4%
HILLSBOROUGH	27,496	4,173	19,302	4,021	Nixon	15.2%	70.2%	14.6%
MERRIMACK	15,875	3,663	10,425	1,787	Nixon	23.1%	65.7%	11.3%
ROCKINGHAM	24,350	5,497	16,365	2,488	Nixon	22.6%	67.2%	10.2%
STRAFFORD	8,246	2,042	5,370	834	Nixon	24.8%	65.1%	10.1%
SULLIVAN	5,027	1,244	3,078	705	Nixon	24.7%	61.2%	14.0%
TOTAL	117,208	23,190	79,239	14,779	Nixon	19.8%	67.6%	12.6%

City/Town								
AMHERST	1,315	263	874	178	Nixon	20.0%	66.5%	13.5%
ATKINSON	463	111	323	29	Nixon	24.0%	69.8%	6.3%
BARRINGTON	313	77	204	32	Nixon	24.6%	65.2%	10.2%
BEDFORD	1,320	130	992	198	Nixon	9.8%	75.2%	15.0%
BELMONT	511	79	373	59	Nixon	15.5%	73.0%	11.5%

NEW HAMPSHIRE REPUBLICAN

1972

City/Town	Total Vote	McCloskey	Nixon	Other	Winner	Percentage of Total Vote McCloskey	Nixon	Other
BERLIN	1,289	227	877	185	Nixon	17.6%	68.0%	14.4%
BOW	829	193	566	70	Nixon	23.3%	68.3%	8.4%
CLAREMONT	1,598	455	979	164	Nixon	28.5%	61.3%	10.3%
CONCORD	5,657	1,656	3,531	470	Nixon	29.3%	62.4%	8.3%
CONWAY	1,238	260	780	198	Nixon	21.0%	63.0%	16.0%
DERRY	2,064	398	1,332	334	Nixon	19.3%	64.5%	16.2%
DOVER	2,428	666	1,544	218	Nixon	27.4%	63.6%	9.0%
DURHAM	1,085	397	606	82	Nixon	36.6%	55.9%	7.6%
EPPING	393	58	290	45	Nixon	14.8%	73.8%	11.5%
EXETER	1,482	464	892	126	Nixon	31.3%	60.2%	8.5%
FARMINGTON	645	89	483	73	Nixon	13.8%	74.9%	11.3%
FRANKLIN	757	221	457	79	Nixon	29.2%	60.4%	10.4%
GILFORD	825	185	575	65	Nixon	22.4%	69.7%	7.9%
GOFFSTOWN	1,432	126	1,063	243	Nixon	8.8%	74.2%	17.0%
HAMPSTEAD	671	119	490	62	Nixon	17.7%	73.0%	9.2%
HAMPTON	1,819	498	1,182	139	Nixon	27.4%	65.0%	7.6%
HANOVER	1,375	707	595	73	McCloskey	51.4%	43.3%	5.3%
HOLLIS	724	109	527	88	Nixon	15.1%	72.8%	12.2%
HOOKSETT	820	79	606	135	Nixon	9.6%	73.9%	16.5%
HUDSON	1,146	237	764	145	Nixon	20.7%	66.7%	12.7%
JAFFREY	611	98	409	104	Nixon	16.0%	66.9%	17.0%
KEENE	2,855	711	1,823	321	Nixon	24.9%	63.9%	11.2%
KINGSTON	731	122	530	79	Nixon	16.7%	72.5%	10.8%
LACONIA	2,131	335	1,589	207	Nixon	15.7%	74.6%	9.7%
LEBANON	1,231	379	740	112	Nixon	30.8%	60.1%	9.1%
LITCHFIELD	233	29	181	23	Nixon	12.4%	77.7%	9.9%
LITTLETON	1,211	146	853	212	Nixon	12.1%	70.4%	17.5%
LONDONDERRY	803	108	569	126	Nixon	13.4%	70.9%	15.7%
MANCHESTER	8,381	1,043	5,902	1,436	Nixon	12.4%	70.4%	17.1%
MERRIMACK TOWN	1,111	157	772	182	Nixon	14.1%	69.5%	16.4%
MILFORD	1,266	196	903	167	Nixon	15.5%	71.3%	13.2%
NASHUA	3,843	800	2,631	412	Nixon	20.8%	68.5%	10.7%
NEWMARKET	269	81	172	16	Nixon	30.1%	63.9%	5.9%
NEWPORT	863	204	544	115	Nixon	23.6%	63.0%	13.3%
PELHAM	720	114	502	104	Nixon	15.8%	69.7%	14.4%
PEMBROKE	710	111	529	70	Nixon	15.6%	74.5%	9.9%
PETERBOROUGH	1,180	210	852	118	Nixon	17.8%	72.2%	10.0%
PLAISTOW	892	174	657	61	Nixon	19.5%	73.7%	6.8%
PLYMOUTH	790	133	535	122	Nixon	16.8%	67.7%	15.4%
PORTSMOUTH	2,110	695	1,268	147	Nixon	32.9%	60.1%	7.0%
RAYMOND	593	75	401	117	Nixon	12.6%	67.6%	19.7%
ROCHESTER	1,940	394	1,371	175	Nixon	20.3%	70.7%	9.0%
SALEM	2,871	686	1,962	223	Nixon	23.9%	68.3%	7.8%
SEABROOK	717	151	490	76	Nixon	21.1%	68.3%	10.6%
SOMERSWORTH	444	114	288	42	Nixon	25.7%	64.9%	9.5%
SWANZEY	542	132	364	46	Nixon	24.4%	67.2%	8.5%
WEARE	492	54	341	97	Nixon	11.0%	69.3%	19.7%
WINDHAM	618	118	438	62	Nixon	19.1%	70.9%	10.0%

NEW HAMPSHIRE DEMOCRATIC

1976

County	Total Vote	Bayh	Carter	Harris	Udall	Other	Winner	Percentage of Total Vote Bayh	Carter	Harris	Udall	Other
BELKNAP	3,423	659	1,079	235	724	726	Carter	19.3%	31.5%	6.9%	21.2%	21.2%
CARROLL	1,511	179	349	232	486	265	Udall	11.8%	23.1%	15.4%	32.2%	17.5%
CHESHIRE	5,621	973	1,102	840	1,381	1,325	Udall	17.3%	19.6%	14.9%	24.6%	23.6%
COOS	5,753	1,017	2,449	520	673	1,094	Carter	17.7%	42.6%	9.0%	11.7%	19.0%
GRAFTON	4,699	583	1,111	556	1,538	911	Udall	12.4%	23.6%	11.8%	32.7%	19.4%
HILLSBOROUGH	26,296	4,334	7,173	2,484	5,362	6,943	Carter	16.5%	27.3%	9.4%	20.4%	26.4%
MERRIMACK	7,465	1,157	1,957	945	1,841	1,565	Carter	15.5%	26.2%	12.7%	24.7%	21.0%
ROCKINGHAM	14,979	1,875	4,224	1,567	3,739	3,574	Carter	12.5%	28.2%	10.5%	25.0%	23.9%
STRAFFORD	8,885	1,034	2,709	1,029	2,296	1,817	Carter	11.6%	30.5%	11.6%	25.8%	20.5%
SULLIVAN	3,704	699	1,220	455	670	660	Carter	18.9%	32.9%	12.3%	18.1%	17.8%
TOTAL	82,336	12,510	23,373	8,863	18,710	18,880	Carter	15.2%	28.4%	10.8%	22.7%	22.9%
Certified Totals	82,381	12,510	23,373	8,863	18,710	18,925	Carter	15.2%	28.4%	10.8%	22.7%	23.0%

City/Town	Total Vote	Bayh	Carter	Harris	Udall	Other	Winner	Bayh	Carter	Harris	Udall	Other
AMHERST	479	62	112	38	160	107	Udall	12.9%	23.4%	7.9%	33.4%	22.3%
ATKINSON	244	25	64	26	49	80	Carter	10.2%	26.2%	10.7%	20.1%	32.8%
BARRINGTON	289	39	75	54	101	20	Udall	13.5%	26.0%	18.7%	34.9%	6.9%
BEDFORD	768	111	193	63	158	243	Carter	14.5%	25.1%	8.2%	20.6%	31.6%
BELMONT	306	43	101	25	47	90	Carter	14.1%	33.0%	8.2%	15.4%	29.4%
BERLIN	3,902	745	1,795	317	411	634	Carter	19.1%	46.0%	8.1%	10.5%	16.2%
BOW	262	44	88	17	61	52	Carter	16.8%	33.6%	6.5%	23.3%	19.8%
CLAREMONT	1,732	384	549	248	256	295	Carter	22.2%	31.7%	14.3%	14.8%	17.0%
CONCORD	2,494	462	602	298	658	474	Udall	18.5%	24.1%	11.9%	26.4%	19.0%
CONWAY	327	49	72	60	84	62	Udall	15.0%	22.0%	18.3%	25.7%	19.0%
DERRY	1,158	156	334	132	228	308	Carter	13.5%	28.8%	11.4%	19.7%	26.6%
DOVER	2,723	342	875	264	659	583	Carter	12.6%	32.1%	9.7%	24.2%	21.4%
DURHAM	938	91	142	196	430	79	Udall	9.7%	15.1%	20.9%	45.8%	8.4%
EPPING	339	49	156	21	32	81	Carter	14.5%	46.0%	6.2%	9.4%	23.9%
EXETER	613	79	138	65	234	97	Udall	12.9%	22.5%	10.6%	38.2%	15.8%
FARMINGTON	254	26	105	25	22	76	Carter	10.2%	41.3%	9.8%	8.7%	29.9%
FRANKLIN	810	90	232	97	180	211	Carter	11.1%	28.6%	12.0%	22.2%	26.0%
GILFORD	329	43	113	17	93	63	Carter	13.1%	34.3%	5.2%	28.3%	19.1%
GOFFSTOWN	1,284	136	345	125	240	438	Carter	10.6%	26.9%	9.7%	18.7%	34.1%
HAMPSTEAD	272	27	65	21	105	54	Udall	9.9%	23.9%	7.7%	38.6%	19.9%
HAMPTON	941	95	238	87	268	253	Udall	10.1%	25.3%	9.2%	28.5%	26.9%
HANOVER	1,096	122	126	142	592	114	Udall	11.1%	11.5%	13.0%	54.0%	10.4%
HOLLIS	317	17	69	18	172	41	Udall	5.4%	21.8%	5.7%	54.3%	12.9%
HOOKSETT	607	141	196	51	109	110	Carter	23.2%	32.3%	8.4%	18.0%	18.1%
HUDSON	1,552	132	526	83	335	476	Carter	8.5%	33.9%	5.3%	21.6%	30.7%
JAFFREY	376	55	97	35	114	75	Udall	14.6%	25.8%	9.3%	30.3%	19.9%
KEENE	2,132	468	392	384	533	355	Udall	22.0%	18.4%	18.0%	25.0%	16.7%
KINGSTON	273	27	74	21	62	89	Carter	9.9%	27.1%	7.7%	22.7%	32.6%
LACONIA	1,631	394	539	75	309	314	Carter	24.2%	33.0%	4.6%	18.9%	19.3%
LEBANON	897	132	190	104	310	161	Udall	14.7%	21.2%	11.6%	34.6%	17.9%
LITCHFIELD	213	33	64	21	35	60	Carter	15.5%	30.0%	9.9%	16.4%	28.2%
LITTLETON	429	52	171	50	57	99	Carter	12.1%	39.9%	11.7%	13.3%	23.1%
LONDONDERRY	722	91	227	83	137	184	Carter	12.6%	31.4%	11.5%	19.0%	25.5%
MANCHESTER	12,210	2,577	3,260	1,196	1,880	3,297	Carter	21.1%	26.7%	9.8%	15.4%	27.0%
MERRIMACK TOWN	1,270	193	422	98	222	335	Carter	15.2%	33.2%	7.7%	17.5%	26.4%

NEW HAMPSHIRE DEMOCRATIC

1976

City/Town	Total Vote	Bayh	Carter	Harris	Udall	Other	Winner	Percentage of Total Vote Bayh	Carter	Harris	Udall	Other
MILFORD	733	191	162	75	161	144	Bayh	26.1%	22.1%	10.2%	22.0%	19.6%
NASHUA	4,048	594	1,120	379	983	972	Carter	14.7%	27.7%	9.4%	24.3%	24.0%
NEWMARKET	796	121	186	85	199	205	Udall	15.2%	23.4%	10.7%	25.0%	25.8%
NEWPORT	718	131	300	49	92	146	Carter	18.2%	41.8%	6.8%	12.8%	20.3%
PELHAM	911	67	228	58	260	298	Udall	7.4%	25.0%	6.4%	28.5%	32.7%
PEMBROKE	352	35	130	45	88	54	Carter	9.9%	36.9%	12.8%	25.0%	15.3%
PETERBOROUGH	397	33	86	51	160	67	Udall	8.3%	21.7%	12.8%	40.3%	16.9%
PLAISTOW	372	33	102	34	99	104	Carter	8.9%	27.4%	9.1%	26.6%	28.0%
PLYMOUTH	203	35	53	20	50	45	Carter	17.2%	26.1%	9.9%	24.6%	22.2%
PORTSMOUTH	1,839	321	526	188	507	297	Carter	17.5%	28.6%	10.2%	27.6%	16.2%
RAYMOND	391	48	127	62	56	98	Carter	12.3%	32.5%	15.9%	14.3%	25.1%
ROCHESTER	2,119	232	667	214	452	554	Carter	10.9%	31.5%	10.1%	21.3%	26.1%
SALEM	2,908	331	849	269	726	733	Carter	11.4%	29.2%	9.3%	25.0%	25.2%
SEABROOK	389	36	91	41	72	149	Carter	9.3%	23.4%	10.5%	18.5%	38.3%
SOMERSWORTH	1,558	178	508	127	404	341	Carter	11.4%	32.6%	8.2%	25.9%	21.9%
SWANZEY	437	115	90	62	76	94	Bayh	26.3%	20.6%	14.2%	17.4%	21.5%
WEARE	219	21	60	31	43	64	Carter	9.6%	27.4%	14.2%	19.6%	29.2%
WINDHAM	436	57	128	56	129	66	Udall	13.1%	29.4%	12.8%	29.6%	15.1%

Note: Returns in the 1976 New Hampshire tables, both for the Democrats and Republicans, were compiled with reference to "The New Hampshire Primary Guide" by Charles Brereton and CBS News' "Campaign '76: A Reference of Official Vote Returns."

NEW HAMPSHIRE REPUBLICAN

1976

County	Total Vote	Ford	Reagan	Other	Winner	Percentage of Total Vote Ford	Reagan	Otherx
BELKNAP	6,621	3,001	3,442	178	Reagan	45.3%	52.0%	2.7%
CARROLL	5,947	2,834	3,031	82	Reagan	47.7%	51.0%	1.4%
CHESHIRE	8,368	5,017	3,095	256	Ford	60.0%	37.0%	3.1%
COOS	4,294	1,745	2,448	101	Reagan	40.6%	57.0%	2.4%
GRAFTON	9,734	4,910	4,591	233	Ford	50.4%	47.2%	2.4%
HILLSBOROUGH	26,171	11,379	14,114	678	Reagan	43.5%	53.9%	2.6%
MERRIMACK	15,373	8,111	6,884	378	Ford	52.8%	44.8%	2.5%
ROCKINGHAM	22,550	11,314	10,604	632	Ford	50.2%	47.0%	2.8%
STRAFFORD	8,312	4,628	3,436	248	Ford	55.7%	41.3%	3.0%
SULLIVAN	4,304	2,217	1,924	163	Ford	51.5%	44.7%	3.8%
TOTAL	111,674	55,156	53,569	2,949	Ford	49.4%	48.0%	2.6%

City/Town	Total Vote	Ford	Reagan	Other	Winner	Ford	Reagan	Otherx
AMHERST	1,581	840	678	63	Ford	53.1%	42.9%	4.0%
ATKINSON	541	265	235	41	Ford	49.0%	43.4%	7.6%
BARRINGTON	436	253	183		Ford	58.0%	42.0%	
BEDFORD	1,636	582	1,038	16	Reagan	35.6%	63.4%	1.0%
BELMONT	454	177	244	33	Reagan	39.0%	53.7%	7.3%

NEW HAMPSHIRE REPUBLICAN

1976

City/Town	Total Vote	Ford	Reagan	Other	Winner	Percentage of Total Vote Ford	Reagan	Otherx
BERLIN	1,384	556	778	50	Reagan	40.2%	56.2%	3.6%
BOW	870	462	389	19	Ford	53.1%	44.7%	2.2%
CLAREMONT	1,329	735	545	49	Ford	55.3%	41.0%	3.7%
CONCORD	5,231	3,234	1,849	148	Ford	61.8%	35.3%	2.8%
CONWAY	1,144	486	630	28	Reagan	42.5%	55.1%	2.4%
DERRY	2,147	724	1,359	64	Reagan	33.7%	63.3%	3.0%
DOVER	2,319	1,391	881	47	Ford	60.0%	38.0%	2.0%
DURHAM	1,065	748	256	61	Ford	70.2%	24.0%	5.7%
EPPING	354	136	204	14	Reagan	38.4%	57.6%	4.0%
EXETER	1,573	968	592	13	Ford	61.5%	37.6%	0.8%
FARMINGTON	484	203	281		Reagan	41.9%	58.1%	
FRANKLIN	765	309	422	34	Reagan	40.4%	55.2%	4.4%
GILFORD	988	483	482	23	Ford	48.9%	48.8%	2.3%
GOFFSTOWN	1,631	490	1,056	85	Reagan	30.0%	64.7%	5.2%
HAMPSTEAD	663	344	300	19	Ford	51.9%	45.2%	2.9%
HAMPTON	1,549	1,017	470	62	Ford	65.7%	30.3%	4.0%
HANOVER	980	797	183		Ford	81.3%	18.7%	
HOLLIS	748	461	287		Ford	61.6%	38.4%	
HOOKSETT	956	232	724		Reagan	24.3%	75.7%	
HUDSON	1,082	523	513	46	Ford	48.3%	47.4%	4.3%
JAFFREY	562	266	296		Reagan	47.3%	52.7%	
KEENE	2,951	1,985	888	78	Ford	67.3%	30.1%	2.6%
KINGSTON	613	283	306	24	Reagan	46.2%	49.9%	3.9%
LACONIA	2,020	939	1,047	34	Reagan	46.5%	51.8%	1.7%
LEBANON	1,113	689	369	55	Ford	61.9%	33.2%	4.9%
LITCHFIELD	198	79	109	10	Reagan	39.9%	55.1%	5.1%
LITTLETON	1,014	430	556	28	Reagan	42.4%	54.8%	2.8%
LONDONDERRY	1,115	373	716	26	Reagan	33.5%	64.2%	2.3%
MANCHESTER	6,628	2,170	4,342	116	Reagan	32.7%	65.5%	1.8%
MERRIMACK TOWN	1,455	663	728	64	Reagan	45.6%	50.0%	4.4%
MILFORD	1,249	544	662	43	Reagan	43.6%	53.0%	3.4%
NASHUA	3,453	1,931	1,452	70	Ford	55.9%	42.1%	2.0%
NEWMARKET	260	132	111	17	Ford	50.8%	42.7%	6.5%
NEWPORT	695	331	350	14	Reagan	47.6%	50.4%	2.0%
PELHAM	644	291	329	24	Reagan	45.2%	51.1%	3.7%
PEMBROKE	656	348	308		Ford	53.0%	47.0%	
PETERBOROUGH	1,173	724	419	30	Ford	61.7%	35.7%	2.6%
PLAISTOW	677	295	357	25	Reagan	43.6%	52.7%	3.7%
PLYMOUTH	688	306	370	12	Reagan	44.5%	53.8%	1.7%
PORTSMOUTH	1,667	1,258	392	17	Ford	75.5%	23.5%	1.0%
RAYMOND	580	162	408	10	Reagan	27.9%	70.3%	1.7%
ROCHESTER	2,153	1,051	1,021	81	Ford	48.8%	47.4%	3.8%
SALEM	2,197	1,006	1,129	62	Reagan	45.8%	51.4%	2.8%
SEABROOK	504	224	263	17	Reagan	44.4%	52.2%	3.4%
SOMERSWORTH	449	244	196	9	Ford	54.3%	43.7%	2.0%
SWANZEY	732	436	258	38	Ford	59.6%	35.2%	5.2%
WEARE	514	157	342	15	Reagan	30.5%	66.5%	2.9%
WINDHAM	593	260	333		Reagan	43.8%	56.2%	

NEW HAMPSHIRE DEMOCRATIC

1980

County	Total Vote	Carter	E. Kennedy	Other	Winner	Percentage of Total Vote Carter	E. Kennedy	Other
BELKNAP	4,032	2,058	1,303	671	Carter	51.0%	32.3%	16.6%
CARROLL	2,020	1,021	671	328	Carter	50.5%	33.2%	16.2%
CHESHIRE	6,755	3,214	2,312	1,229	Carter	47.6%	34.2%	18.2%
COOS	5,905	2,930	2,307	668	Carter	49.6%	39.1%	11.3%
GRAFTON	5,837	3,051	1,688	1,098	Carter	52.3%	28.9%	18.8%
HILLSBOROUGH	39,180	19,035	14,280	5,865	Carter	48.6%	36.4%	15.0%
MERRIMACK	9,986	5,174	3,011	1,801	Carter	51.8%	30.2%	18.0%
ROCKINGHAM	22,295	8,792	10,237	3,266	E. Kennedy	39.4%	45.9%	14.6%
STRAFFORD	11,619	5,140	4,597	1,882	Carter	44.2%	39.6%	16.2%
SULLIVAN	4,180	2,233	1,281	666	Carter	53.4%	30.6%	15.9%
TOTAL	111,809	52,648	41,687	17,474	Carter	47.1%	37.3%	15.6%
Published Totals	111,930	52,692	41,745	17,493	Carter	47.1%	37.3%	15.6%

City/Town	Total Vote	Carter	E. Kennedy	Other	Winner	Carter	E. Kennedy	Other
AMHERST	623	319	215	89	Carter	51.2%	34.5%	14.3%
ATKINSON	522	217	258	47	E. Kennedy	41.6%	49.4%	9.0%
BARRINGTON	494	237	139	118	Carter	48.0%	28.1%	23.9%
BEDFORD	985	522	372	91	Carter	53.0%	37.8%	9.2%
BELMONT	350	188	113	49	Carter	53.7%	32.3%	14.0%
BERLIN	3,522	1,729	1,529	264	Carter	49.1%	43.4%	7.5%
BOW	317	181	97	39	Carter	57.1%	30.6%	12.3%
CLAREMONT	1,861	975	693	193	Carter	52.4%	37.2%	10.4%
CONCORD	3,003	1,516	1,042	445	Carter	50.5%	34.7%	14.8%
CONWAY	479	246	175	58	Carter	51.4%	36.5%	12.1%
DERRY	1,616	743	702	171	Carter	46.0%	43.4%	10.6%
DOVER	3,422	1,408	1,593	421	E. Kennedy	41.1%	46.6%	12.3%
DURHAM	1,034	433	388	213	Carter	41.9%	37.5%	20.6%
EPPING	519	230	210	79	Carter	44.3%	40.5%	15.2%
EXETER	1,092	452	460	180	E. Kennedy	41.4%	42.1%	16.5%
FARMINGTON	371	214	103	54	Carter	57.7%	27.8%	14.6%
FRANKLIN	999	554	326	119	Carter	55.5%	32.6%	11.9%
GILFORD	411	199	154	58	Carter	48.4%	37.5%	14.1%
GOFFSTOWN	1,339	744	389	206	Carter	55.6%	29.1%	15.4%
HAMPSTEAD	415	176	211	28	E. Kennedy	42.4%	50.8%	6.7%
HAMPTON	1,489	518	773	198	E. Kennedy	34.8%	51.9%	13.3%
HANOVER	952	499	312	141	Carter	52.4%	32.8%	14.8%
HOLLIS	393	224	124	45	Carter	57.0%	31.6%	11.5%
HOOKSETT	786	451	256	79	Carter	57.4%	32.6%	10.1%
HUDSON	1,957	997	745	215	Carter	50.9%	38.1%	11.0%
JAFFREY	489	248	194	47	Carter	50.7%	39.7%	9.6%
KEENE	2,477	1,206	942	329	Carter	48.7%	38.0%	13.3%
KINGSTON	399	163	161	75	Carter	40.9%	40.4%	18.8%
LACONIA	1,693	878	637	178	Carter	51.9%	37.6%	10.5%
LEBANON	1,052	552	378	122	Carter	52.5%	35.9%	11.6%
LITCHFIELD	448	196	191	61	Carter	43.8%	42.6%	13.6%
LITTLETON	555	377	133	45	Carter	67.9%	24.0%	8.1%
LONDONDERRY	1,188	533	548	107	E. Kennedy	44.9%	46.1%	9.0%
MANCHESTER	15,969	8,095	5,901	1,973	Carter	50.7%	37.0%	12.4%
MERRIMACK TOWN	1,450	730	573	147	Carter	50.3%	39.5%	10.1%

NEW HAMPSHIRE DEMOCRATIC

1980

City/Town	Total Vote	Carter	E. Kennedy	Other	Winner	Percentage of Total Vote Carter	E. Kennedy	Other
MILFORD	850	377	348	125	Carter	44.4%	40.9%	14.7%
NASHUA	9,508	4,743	3,906	859	Carter	49.9%	41.1%	9.0%
NEWMARKET	950	418	392	140	Carter	44.0%	41.3%	14.7%
NEWPORT	765	469	210	86	Carter	61.3%	27.5%	11.2%
PELHAM	1,305	570	605	130	E. Kennedy	43.7%	46.4%	10.0%
PEMBROKE	588	343	160	85	Carter	58.3%	27.2%	14.5%
PETERBOROUGH	429	204	145	80	Carter	47.6%	33.8%	18.6%
PLAISTOW	503	203	258	42	E. Kennedy	40.4%	51.3%	8.3%
PLYMOUTH	250	115	93	42	Carter	46.0%	37.2%	16.8%
PORTSMOUTH	3,131	1,188	1,528	415	E. Kennedy	37.9%	48.8%	13.3%
RAYMOND	506	203	220	83	E. Kennedy	40.1%	43.5%	16.4%
ROCHESTER	2,706	1,331	1,038	337	Carter	49.2%	38.4%	12.5%
SALEM	3,611	1,236	2,115	260	E. Kennedy	34.2%	58.6%	7.2%
SEABROOK	589	202	315	72	E. Kennedy	34.3%	53.5%	12.2%
SOMERSWORTH	1,919	847	889	183	E. Kennedy	44.1%	46.3%	9.5%
SWANZEY	475	233	181	61	Carter	49.1%	38.1%	12.8%
WEARE	238	127	60	51	Carter	53.4%	25.2%	21.4%
WINDHAM	611	288	269	54	Carter	47.1%	44.0%	8.8%

Note: The 1980 Democratic and Republican county tables also include scattered write-in votes that were not included in the New Hampshire Manual for the General Court, but were tallied and distributed by state election officials immediately after the primary. City and town results are as they appeared in the Manual, without write-in votes.

NEW HAMPSHIRE REPUBLICAN

1980

County	Total Vote	Baker	Bush	Reagan	Other	Winner	Percentage of Total Vote Baker	Bush	Reagan	Other
BELKNAP	8,451	973	1,753	4,783	942	Reagan	11.5%	20.7%	56.6%	11.1%
CARROLL	7,855	867	2,227	3,948	813	Reagan	11.0%	28.4%	50.3%	10.4%
CHESHIRE	10,170	1,383	2,447	4,211	2,129	Reagan	13.6%	24.1%	41.4%	20.9%
COOS	4,872	594	832	3,066	380	Reagan	12.2%	17.1%	62.9%	7.8%
GRAFTON	12,039	1,466	2,993	5,629	1,951	Reagan	12.2%	24.9%	46.8%	16.2%
HILLSBOROUGH	38,421	4,151	7,341	21,969	4,960	Reagan	10.8%	19.1%	57.2%	12.9%
MERRIMACK	19,112	2,883	4,075	9,026	3,128	Reagan	15.1%	21.3%	47.2%	16.4%
ROCKINGHAM	30,401	4,041	7,529	14,174	4,657	Reagan	13.3%	24.8%	46.6%	15.3%
STRAFFORD	10,513	1,705	2,785	3,908	2,115	Reagan	16.2%	26.5%	37.2%	20.1%
SULLIVAN	5,323	880	1,461	2,269	713	Reagan	16.5%	27.4%	42.6%	13.4%
TOTAL	147,157	18,943	33,443	72,983	21,788	Reagan	12.9%	22.7%	49.6%	14.8%

City/Town	Total Vote	Baker	Bush	Reagan	Other	Winner	Baker	Bush	Reagan	Other
AMHERST	2,199	303	634	858	404	Reagan	13.8%	28.8%	39.0%	18.4%
ATKINSON	765	101	247	307	110	Reagan	13.2%	32.3%	40.1%	14.4%
BARRINGTON	604	134	130	234	106	Reagan	22.2%	21.5%	38.7%	17.5%
BEDFORD	2,361	217	337	1,597	210	Reagan	9.2%	14.3%	67.6%	8.9%
BELMONT	576	64	112	346	54	Reagan	11.1%	19.4%	60.1%	9.4%

NEW HAMPSHIRE REPUBLICAN

1980

City/Town	Total Vote	Baker	Bush	Reagan	Other	Winner	Percentage of Total Vote: Baker	Bush	Reagan	Other
BERLIN	1,294	135	268	802	89	Reagan	10.4%	20.7%	62.0%	6.9%
BOW	1,063	194	223	493	153	Reagan	18.3%	21.0%	46.4%	14.4%
CLAREMONT	1,533	358	383	642	150	Reagan	23.4%	25.0%	41.9%	9.8%
CONCORD	5,606	937	1,323	2,144	1,202	Reagan	16.7%	23.6%	38.2%	21.4%
CONWAY	1,526	172	402	813	139	Reagan	11.3%	26.3%	53.3%	9.1%
DERRY	2,644	291	397	1,702	254	Reagan	11.0%	15.0%	64.4%	9.6%
DOVER	2,917	466	847	1,018	586	Reagan	16.0%	29.0%	34.9%	20.1%
DURHAM	1,450	205	476	271	498	Bush	14.1%	32.8%	18.7%	34.3%
EPPING	498	40	99	278	81	Reagan	8.0%	19.9%	55.8%	16.3%
EXETER	2,316	379	676	920	341	Reagan	16.4%	29.2%	39.7%	14.7%
FARMINGTON	588	98	95	337	58	Reagan	16.7%	16.2%	57.3%	9.9%
FRANKLIN	1,094	190	213	612	79	Reagan	17.4%	19.5%	55.9%	7.2%
GILFORD	1,333	139	340	718	136	Reagan	10.4%	25.5%	53.9%	10.2%
GOFFSTOWN	1,837	133	134	1,426	144	Reagan	7.2%	7.3%	77.6%	7.8%
HAMPSTEAD	886	115	251	421	99	Reagan	13.0%	28.3%	47.5%	11.2%
HAMPTON	2,062	338	602	679	443	Reagan	16.4%	29.2%	32.9%	21.5%
HANOVER	1,347	116	590	98	543	Bush	8.6%	43.8%	7.3%	40.3%
HOLLIS	1,129	146	400	403	180	Reagan	12.9%	35.4%	35.7%	15.9%
HOOKSETT	1,259	110	88	985	76	Reagan	8.7%	7.0%	78.2%	6.0%
HUDSON	1,619	226	366	816	211	Reagan	14.0%	22.6%	50.4%	13.0%
JAFFREY	769	71	163	449	86	Reagan	9.2%	21.2%	58.4%	11.2%
KEENE	3,418	496	907	1,285	730	Reagan	14.5%	26.5%	37.6%	21.4%
KINGSTON	767	108	190	345	124	Reagan	14.1%	24.8%	45.0%	16.2%
LACONIA	2,462	277	542	1,375	268	Reagan	11.3%	22.0%	55.8%	10.9%
LEBANON	1,430	231	486	381	332	Bush	16.2%	34.0%	26.6%	23.2%
LITCHFIELD	477	52	92	274	59	Reagan	10.9%	19.3%	57.4%	12.4%
LITTLETON	1,131	98	211	751	71	Reagan	8.7%	18.7%	66.4%	6.3%
LONDONDERRY	1,901	226	281	1,186	208	Reagan	11.9%	14.8%	62.4%	10.9%
MANCHESTER	9,751	743	913	7,297	798	Reagan	7.6%	9.4%	74.8%	8.2%
MERRIMACK TOWN	1,990	331	320	1,113	226	Reagan	16.6%	16.1%	55.9%	11.4%
MILFORD	1,587	164	293	938	192	Reagan	10.3%	18.5%	59.1%	12.1%
NASHUA	6,915	928	2,022	3,004	961	Reagan	13.4%	29.2%	43.4%	13.9%
NEWMARKET	399	55	86	145	113	Reagan	13.8%	21.6%	36.3%	28.3%
NEWPORT	751	111	162	407	71	Reagan	14.8%	21.6%	54.2%	9.5%
PELHAM	799	101	251	362	85	Reagan	12.6%	31.4%	45.3%	10.6%
PEMBROKE	821	126	127	482	86	Reagan	15.3%	15.5%	58.7%	10.5%
PETERBOROUGH	1,411	236	362	523	290	Reagan	16.7%	25.7%	37.1%	20.6%
PLAISTOW	794	78	267	333	116	Reagan	9.8%	33.6%	41.9%	14.6%
PLYMOUTH	804	97	136	496	75	Reagan	12.1%	16.9%	61.7%	9.3%
PORTSMOUTH	2,593	458	814	762	559	Bush	17.7%	31.4%	29.4%	21.6%
RAYMOND	850	68	84	618	80	Reagan	8.0%	9.9%	72.7%	9.4%
ROCHESTER	2,433	426	606	1,103	298	Reagan	17.5%	24.9%	45.3%	12.2%
SALEM	2,638	307	787	1,205	339	Reagan	11.6%	29.8%	45.7%	12.9%
SEABROOK	655	72	190	338	55	Reagan	11.0%	29.0%	51.6%	8.4%
SOMERSWORTH	615	113	190	226	86	Reagan	18.4%	30.9%	36.7%	14.0%
SWANZEY	771	110	167	378	116	Reagan	14.3%	21.7%	49.0%	15.0%
WEARE	674	55	55	496	68	Reagan	8.2%	8.2%	73.6%	10.1%
WINDHAM	899	84	221	468	126	Reagan	9.3%	24.6%	52.1%	14.0%

NEW HAMPSHIRE DEMOCRATIC

1984

County	Total Vote	Glenn	Hart	Mondale	Other	Winner	Percentage of Total Vote Glenn	Hart	Mondale	Other
BELKNAP	3,611	363	1,655	852	741	Hart	10.1%	45.8%	23.6%	20.5%
CARROLL	1,921	229	758	426	508	Hart	11.9%	39.5%	22.2%	26.4%
CHESHIRE	6,326	536	2,333	1,755	1,702	Hart	8.5%	36.9%	27.7%	26.9%
COOS	4,660	318	1,453	1,820	1,069	Mondale	6.8%	31.2%	39.1%	22.9%
GRAFTON	6,412	486	2,437	1,528	1,961	Hart	7.6%	38.0%	23.8%	30.6%
HILLSBOROUGH	34,431	4,949	11,742	10,257	7,483	Hart	14.4%	34.1%	29.8%	21.7%
MERRIMACK	9,681	912	4,227	2,215	2,327	Hart	9.4%	43.7%	22.9%	24.0%
ROCKINGHAM	19,410	2,704	7,478	4,938	4,290	Hart	13.9%	38.5%	25.4%	22.1%
STRAFFORD	10,388	1,293	3,786	3,155	2,154	Hart	12.4%	36.4%	30.4%	20.7%
SULLIVAN	4,291	298	1,833	1,227	933	Hart	6.9%	42.7%	28.6%	21.7%
TOTAL	101,131	12,088	37,702	28,173	23,168	Hart	12.0%	37.3%	27.9%	22.9%

City/Town	Total Vote	Glenn	Hart	Mondale	Other	Winner	Glenn	Hart	Mondale	Other
AMHERST	683	95	303	126	159	Hart	13.9%	44.4%	18.4%	23.3%
ATKINSON	371	57	168	90	56	Hart	15.4%	45.3%	24.3%	15.1%
BARRINGTON	516	71	175	133	137	Hart	13.8%	33.9%	25.8%	26.6%
BEDFORD	986	142	348	227	269	Hart	14.4%	35.3%	23.0%	27.3%
BELMONT	303	15	160	64	64	Hart	5.0%	52.8%	21.1%	21.1%
BERLIN	2,771	181	821	1,177	592	Mondale	6.5%	29.6%	42.5%	21.4%
BOW	301	22	166	57	56	Hart	7.3%	55.1%	18.9%	18.6%
CLAREMONT	1,924	119	785	668	352	Hart	6.2%	40.8%	34.7%	18.3%
CONCORD	3,378	333	1,499	797	749	Hart	9.9%	44.4%	23.6%	22.2%
CONWAY	417	42	143	121	111	Hart	10.1%	34.3%	29.0%	26.6%
DERRY	1,340	207	537	293	303	Hart	15.4%	40.1%	21.9%	22.6%
DOVER	3,039	348	1,115	947	629	Hart	11.5%	36.7%	31.2%	20.7%
DURHAM	1,238	98	452	227	461	Hart	7.9%	36.5%	18.3%	37.2%
EPPING	431	43	144	97	147	Hart	10.0%	33.4%	22.5%	34.1%
EXETER	1,125	119	409	315	282	Hart	10.6%	36.4%	28.0%	25.1%
FARMINGTON	317	50	103	118	46	Mondale	15.8%	32.5%	37.2%	14.5%
FRANKLIN	819	77	357	201	184	Hart	9.4%	43.6%	24.5%	22.5%
GILFORD	379	30	197	69	83	Hart	7.9%	52.0%	18.2%	21.9%
GOFFSTOWN	1,633	196	536	424	477	Hart	12.0%	32.8%	26.0%	29.2%
HAMPSTEAD	334	58	141	77	58	Hart	17.4%	42.2%	23.1%	17.4%
HAMPTON	1,306	169	557	339	241	Hart	12.9%	42.6%	26.0%	18.5%
HANOVER	1,380	107	519	333	421	Hart	7.8%	37.6%	24.1%	30.5%
HOLLIS	476	69	182	159	66	Hart	14.5%	38.2%	33.4%	13.9%
HOOKSETT	645	74	258	142	171	Hart	11.5%	40.0%	22.0%	26.5%
HUDSON	1,515	239	544	511	221	Hart	15.8%	35.9%	33.7%	14.6%
JAFFREY	423	51	137	124	111	Hart	12.1%	32.4%	29.3%	26.2%
KEENE	2,626	223	996	734	673	Hart	8.5%	37.9%	28.0%	25.6%
KINGSTON	352	60	142	77	73	Hart	17.0%	40.3%	21.9%	20.7%
LACONIA	1,436	161	638	396	241	Hart	11.2%	44.4%	27.6%	16.8%
LEBANON	1,377	126	527	346	378	Hart	9.2%	38.3%	25.1%	27.5%
LITCHFIELD	407	69	173	108	57	Hart	17.0%	42.5%	26.5%	14.0%
LITTLETON	478	23	180	122	153	Hart	4.8%	37.7%	25.5%	32.0%
LONDONDERRY	1,181	215	483	204	279	Hart	18.2%	40.9%	17.3%	23.6%
MANCHESTER	13,631	2,128	4,397	4,083	3,023	Hart	15.6%	32.3%	30.0%	22.2%
MERRIMACK TOWN	1,298	178	494	328	298	Hart	13.7%	38.1%	25.3%	23.0%

NEW HAMPSHIRE DEMOCRATIC

1984

City/Town	Total Vote	Glenn	Hart	Mondale	Other	Winner	Percentage of Total Vote Glenn	Hart	Mondale	Other
MILFORD	728	75	303	152	198	Hart	10.3%	41.6%	20.9%	27.2%
NASHUA	9,095	1,281	2,838	3,255	1,721	Mondale	14.1%	31.2%	35.8%	18.9%
NEWMARKET	819	97	330	202	190	Hart	11.8%	40.3%	24.7%	23.2%
NEWPORT	625	53	274	165	133	Hart	8.5%	43.8%	26.4%	21.3%
PELHAM	916	158	350	253	155	Hart	17.2%	38.2%	27.6%	16.9%
PEMBROKE	532	47	187	163	135	Hart	8.8%	35.2%	30.6%	25.4%
PETERBOROUGH	437	36	165	95	141	Hart	8.2%	37.8%	21.7%	32.3%
PLAISTOW	452	72	163	148	69	Hart	15.9%	36.1%	32.7%	15.3%
PLYMOUTH	303	16	132	57	98	Hart	5.3%	43.6%	18.8%	32.3%
PORTSMOUTH	2,981	324	900	908	849	Mondale	10.9%	30.2%	30.5%	28.5%
RAYMOND	434	64	160	129	81	Hart	14.7%	36.9%	29.7%	18.7%
ROCHESTER	2,527	420	881	840	386	Hart	16.6%	34.9%	33.2%	15.3%
SALEM	2,736	472	1,064	744	456	Hart	17.3%	38.9%	27.2%	16.7%
SEABROOK	510	66	196	168	80	Hart	12.9%	38.4%	32.9%	15.7%
SOMERSWORTH	1,420	138	550	528	204	Hart	9.7%	38.7%	37.2%	14.4%
SWANZEY	498	38	180	149	131	Hart	7.6%	36.1%	29.9%	26.3%
WEARE	260	22	113	58	67	Hart	8.5%	43.5%	22.3%	25.8%
WINDHAM	599	132	248	115	104	Hart	22.0%	41.4%	19.2%	17.4%

Note: The 1984 Democratic and Republican county tables also include scattered write-in votes that were not included in the New Hampshire Manual for the General Court, but were tallied and distributed by state election officials immediately after the primary. City and town results are as they appeared in the Manual, without scattered write-in votes.

NEW HAMPSHIRE REPUBLICAN

1984

County	Total Vote	Reagan	Other	Winner	Percentage of Total Vote Reagan	Other
BELKNAP	4,219	3,674	545	Reagan	87.1%	12.9%
CARROLL	4,083	3,653	430	Reagan	89.5%	10.5%
CHESHIRE	4,606	3,898	708	Reagan	84.6%	15.4%
COOS	2,934	2,600	334	Reagan	88.6%	11.4%
GRAFTON	6,632	5,632	1,000	Reagan	84.9%	15.1%
HILLSBOROUGH	19,768	17,674	2,094	Reagan	89.4%	10.6%
MERRIMACK	10,064	8,182	1,882	Reagan	81.3%	18.7%
ROCKINGHAM	15,074	13,065	2,009	Reagan	86.7%	13.3%
STRAFFORD	5,130	4,143	987	Reagan	80.8%	19.2%
SULLIVAN	3,060	2,512	548	Reagan	82.1%	17.9%
TOTAL	75,570	65,033	10,537	Reagan	86.1%	13.9%

City/Town	Total Vote	Reagan	Other	Winner	Reagan	Other
AMHERST	1,007	861	146	Reagan	85.5%	14.5%
ATKINSON	300	262	38	Reagan	87.3%	12.7%
BARRINGTON	284	233	51	Reagan	82.0%	18.0%
BEDFORD	1,342	1,206	136	Reagan	89.9%	10.1%
BELMONT	318	283	35	Reagan	89.0%	11.0%

NEW HAMPSHIRE REPUBLICAN

1984

City/Town	Total Vote	Reagan	Other	Winner	Percentage of Total Vote Reagan	Other
BERLIN	834	736	98	Reagan	88.2%	11.8%
BOW	621	505	116	Reagan	81.3%	18.7%
CLAREMONT	919	741	178	Reagan	80.6%	19.4%
CONCORD	2,839	2,150	689	Reagan	75.7%	24.3%
CONWAY	647	565	82	Reagan	87.3%	12.7%
DERRY	1,218	1,063	155	Reagan	87.3%	12.7%
DOVER	1,396	1,137	259	Reagan	81.4%	18.6%
DURHAM	701	492	209	Reagan	70.2%	29.8%
EPPING	229	227	2	Reagan	99.1%	0.9%
EXETER	1,008	871	137	Reagan	86.4%	13.6%
FARMINGTON	288	249	39	Reagan	86.5%	13.5%
FRANKLIN	553	474	79	Reagan	85.7%	14.3%
GILFORD	531	447	84	Reagan	84.2%	15.8%
GOFFSTOWN	1,182	1,085	97	Reagan	91.8%	8.2%
HAMPSTEAD	400	353	47	Reagan	88.3%	11.8%
HAMPTON	949	795	154	Reagan	83.8%	16.2%
HANOVER	582	451	131	Reagan	77.5%	22.5%
HOLLIS	577	504	73	Reagan	87.3%	12.7%
HOOKSETT	682	618	64	Reagan	90.6%	9.4%
HUDSON	773	706	67	Reagan	91.3%	8.7%
JAFFREY	416	368	48	Reagan	88.5%	11.5%
KEENE	1,615	1,360	255	Reagan	84.2%	15.8%
KINGSTON	457	380	77	Reagan	83.2%	16.8%
LACONIA	1,242	1,081	161	Reagan	87.0%	13.0%
LEBANON	829	635	194	Reagan	76.6%	23.4%
LITCHFIELD	231	201	30	Reagan	87.0%	13.0%
LITTLETON	643	596	47	Reagan	92.7%	7.3%
LONDONDERRY	899	824	75	Reagan	91.7%	8.3%
MANCHESTER	5,427	4,994	433	Reagan	92.0%	8.0%
MERRIMACK TOWN	959	848	111	Reagan	88.4%	11.6%
MILFORD	777	700	77	Reagan	90.1%	9.9%
NASHUA	3,093	2,813	280	Reagan	90.9%	9.1%
NEWMARKET	228	194	34	Reagan	85.1%	14.9%
NEWPORT	431	383	48	Reagan	88.9%	11.1%
PELHAM	458	392	66	Reagan	85.6%	14.4%
PEMBROKE	398	358	40	Reagan	89.9%	10.1%
PETERBOROUGH	680	549	131	Reagan	80.7%	19.3%
PLAISTOW	339	281	58	Reagan	82.9%	17.1%
PLYMOUTH	455	383	72	Reagan	84.2%	15.8%
PORTSMOUTH	1,272	1,093	179	Reagan	85.9%	14.1%
RAYMOND	475	417	58	Reagan	87.8%	12.2%
ROCHESTER	1,207	1,038	169	Reagan	86.0%	14.0%
SALEM	1,376	1,207	169	Reagan	87.7%	12.3%
SEABROOK	331	297	34	Reagan	89.7%	10.3%
SOMERSWORTH	293	247	46	Reagan	84.3%	15.7%
SWANZEY	383	314	69	Reagan	82.0%	18.0%
WEARE	348	305	43	Reagan	87.6%	12.4%
WINDHAM	353	300	53	Reagan	85.0%	15.0%

NEW HAMPSHIRE DEMOCRATIC

1988

County	Total Vote	Dukakis	Gephardt	Simon	Other	Winner	Percentage of Total Vote Dukakis	Gephardt	Simon	Other
BELKNAP	4,469	1,763	828	655	1,223	Dukakis	39.4%	18.5%	14.7%	27.4%
CARROLL	2,762	1,075	438	476	773	Dukakis	38.9%	15.9%	17.2%	28.0%
CHESHIRE	8,066	3,192	1,161	1,319	2,394	Dukakis	39.6%	14.4%	16.4%	29.7%
COOS	4,390	1,400	1,129	362	1,499	Dukakis	31.9%	25.7%	8.2%	34.1%
GRAFTON	6,917	2,700	743	1,176	2,298	Dukakis	39.0%	10.7%	17.0%	33.2%
HILLSBOROUGH	41,114	13,456	9,669	6,916	11,073	Dukakis	32.7%	23.5%	16.8%	26.9%
MERRIMACK	12,736	4,404	1,882	2,120	4,330	Dukakis	34.6%	14.8%	16.6%	34.0%
ROCKINGHAM	26,365	9,782	5,401	4,998	6,184	Dukakis	37.1%	20.5%	19.0%	23.5%
STRAFFORD	12,265	4,480	2,535	2,430	2,820	Dukakis	36.5%	20.7%	19.8%	23.0%
SULLIVAN	4,428	1,860	727	642	1,199	Dukakis	42.0%	16.4%	14.5%	27.1%
TOTAL	123,512	44,112	24,513	21,094	33,793	Dukakis	35.7%	19.8%	17.1%	27.4%

City/Town	Total Vote	Dukakis	Gephardt	Simon	Other	Winner	Dukakis	Gephardt	Simon	Other
AMHERST	894	281	123	236	254	Dukakis	31.4%	13.8%	26.4%	28.4%
ATKINSON	494	192	102	106	94	Dukakis	38.9%	20.6%	21.5%	19.0%
BARRINGTON	706	268	114	159	165	Dukakis	38.0%	16.1%	22.5%	23.4%
BEDFORD	1,421	374	291	271	485	Dukakis	26.3%	20.5%	19.1%	34.1%
BELMONT	428	171	105	44	108	Dukakis	40.0%	24.5%	10.3%	25.2%
BERLIN	2,411	777	641	156	837	Dukakis	32.2%	26.6%	6.5%	34.7%
BOW	533	154	86	115	178	Dukakis	28.9%	16.1%	21.6%	33.4%
CLAREMONT	1,787	770	349	229	439	Dukakis	43.1%	19.5%	12.8%	24.6%
CONCORD	4,391	1,439	469	777	1,706	Dukakis	32.8%	10.7%	17.7%	38.9%
CONWAY	529	216	75	85	153	Dukakis	40.8%	14.2%	16.1%	28.9%
DERRY	2,069	693	390	477	509	Dukakis	33.5%	18.8%	23.1%	24.6%
DOVER	3,430	1,299	688	702	741	Dukakis	37.9%	20.1%	20.5%	21.6%
DURHAM	1,257	372	112	368	405	Dukakis	29.6%	8.9%	29.3%	32.2%
EPPING	538	144	126	111	157	Dukakis	26.8%	23.4%	20.6%	29.2%
EXETER	1,475	548	235	337	355	Dukakis	37.2%	15.9%	22.8%	24.1%
FARMINGTON	435	158	121	61	95	Dukakis	36.3%	27.8%	14.0%	21.8%
FRANKLIN	837	342	165	90	240	Dukakis	40.9%	19.7%	10.8%	28.7%
GILFORD	534	229	85	97	123	Dukakis	42.9%	15.9%	18.2%	23.0%
GOFFSTOWN	1,609	407	425	276	501	Gephardt	25.3%	26.4%	17.2%	31.1%
HAMPSTEAD	677	239	139	157	142	Dukakis	35.3%	20.5%	23.2%	21.0%
HAMPTON	1,817	840	348	244	385	Dukakis	46.2%	19.2%	13.4%	21.2%
HANOVER	1,383	583	48	285	467	Dukakis	42.2%	3.5%	20.6%	33.8%
HOLLIS	696	263	109	171	153	Dukakis	37.8%	15.7%	24.6%	22.0%
HOOKSETT	899	269	243	135	252	Dukakis	29.9%	27.0%	15.0%	28.0%
HUDSON	1,903	673	495	330	405	Dukakis	35.4%	26.0%	17.3%	21.3%
JAFFREY	527	210	104	88	125	Dukakis	39.8%	19.7%	16.7%	23.7%
KEENE	3,253	1,261	486	546	960	Dukakis	38.8%	14.9%	16.8%	29.5%
KINGSTON	447	178	93	98	78	Dukakis	39.8%	20.8%	21.9%	17.4%
LACONIA	1,595	689	301	253	352	Dukakis	43.2%	18.9%	15.9%	22.1%
LEBANON	1,369	623	116	212	418	Dukakis	45.5%	8.5%	15.5%	30.5%
LITCHFIELD	513	210	110	72	121	Dukakis	40.9%	21.4%	14.0%	23.6%
LITTLETON	372	105	72	64	131	Dukakis	28.2%	19.4%	17.2%	35.2%
LONDONDERRY	1,580	500	360	350	370	Dukakis	31.6%	22.8%	22.2%	23.4%
MANCHESTER	15,119	4,101	4,259	2,407	4,352	Gephardt	27.1%	28.2%	15.9%	28.8%
MERRIMACK TOWN	1,956	671	472	331	482	Dukakis	34.3%	24.1%	16.9%	24.6%

NEW HAMPSHIRE DEMOCRATIC

1988

City/Town	Total Vote	Dukakis	Gephardt	Simon	Other	Winner	Percentage of Total Vote: Dukakis	Gephardt	Simon	Other
MILFORD	1,039	326	183	226	304	Dukakis	31.4%	17.6%	21.8%	29.3%
NASHUA	10,114	4,129	2,220	1,596	2,169	Dukakis	40.8%	21.9%	15.8%	21.4%
NEWMARKET	1,014	359	205	204	246	Dukakis	35.4%	20.2%	20.1%	24.3%
NEWPORT	618	242	134	101	141	Dukakis	39.2%	21.7%	16.3%	22.8%
PELHAM	1,189	381	341	187	280	Dukakis	32.0%	28.7%	15.7%	23.5%
PEMBROKE	680	206	125	127	222	Dukakis	30.3%	18.4%	18.7%	32.6%
PETERBOROUGH	584	187	56	124	217	Dukakis	32.0%	9.6%	21.2%	37.2%
PLAISTOW	597	259	123	106	109	Dukakis	43.4%	20.6%	17.8%	18.3%
PLYMOUTH	359	113	25	78	143	Dukakis	31.5%	7.0%	21.7%	39.8%
PORTSMOUTH	3,561	1,424	604	559	974	Dukakis	40.0%	17.0%	15.7%	27.4%
RAYMOND	663	259	136	91	177	Dukakis	39.1%	20.5%	13.7%	26.7%
ROCHESTER	2,881	1,099	729	467	586	Dukakis	38.1%	25.3%	16.2%	20.3%
SALEM	3,428	1,102	950	721	655	Dukakis	32.1%	27.7%	21.0%	19.1%
SEABROOK	705	306	209	79	111	Dukakis	43.4%	29.6%	11.2%	15.7%
SOMERSWORTH	1,615	614	422	251	328	Dukakis	38.0%	26.1%	15.5%	20.3%
SWANZEY	581	245	95	90	151	Dukakis	42.2%	16.4%	15.5%	26.0%
WEARE	464	158	70	75	161	Dukakis	34.1%	15.1%	16.2%	34.7%
WINDHAM	888	293	179	226	190	Dukakis	33.0%	20.2%	25.5%	21.4%

Note: The 1988 Democratic and Republican county tables also include scattered write-in votes that were not included in the New Hampshire Manual for the General Court, but were tallied and distributed by state election officials immediately after the primary. City and town results are as they appeared in the Manual, without scattered write-in votes.

NEW HAMPSHIRE REPUBLICAN

1988

County	Total Vote	Bush	Dole	du Pont	Kemp	Other	Winner	Percentage of Total Vote: Bush	Dole	du Pont	Kemp	Other
BELKNAP	8,610	3,379	2,129	918	1,244	940	Bush	39.2%	24.7%	10.7%	14.4%	10.9%
CARROLL	8,478	3,742	2,322	872	825	717	Bush	44.1%	27.4%	10.3%	9.7%	8.5%
CHESHIRE	9,532	3,057	3,358	646	1,327	1,144	Dole	32.1%	35.2%	6.8%	13.9%	12.0%
COOS	4,306	1,836	937	515	387	631	Bush	42.6%	21.8%	12.0%	9.0%	14.7%
GRAFTON	11,403	4,433	3,206	1,158	1,053	1,553	Bush	38.9%	28.1%	10.2%	9.2%	13.6%
HILLSBOROUGH	45,083	15,985	12,503	5,376	6,201	5,018	Bush	35.5%	27.7%	11.9%	13.8%	11.1%
MERRIMACK	19,410	6,776	5,652	2,130	3,126	1,726	Bush	34.9%	29.1%	11.0%	16.1%	8.9%
ROCKINGHAM	34,750	13,900	10,046	2,948	4,257	3,599	Bush	40.0%	28.9%	8.5%	12.3%	10.4%
STRAFFORD	10,634	4,321	3,123	740	1,125	1,325	Bush	40.6%	29.4%	7.0%	10.6%	12.5%
SULLIVAN	5,438	1,861	1,521	582	569	905	Bush	34.2%	28.0%	10.7%	10.5%	16.6%
TOTAL	157,644	59,290	44,797	15,885	20,114	17,558	Bush	37.6%	28.4%	10.1%	12.8%	11.1%

City/Town	Total Vote	Bush	Dole	du Pont	Kemp	Other	Winner	Bush	Dole	du Pont	Kemp	Other
AMHERST	2,398	938	799	225	254	182	Bush	39.1%	33.3%	9.4%	10.6%	7.6%
ATKINSON	931	396	281	65	117	72	Bush	42.5%	30.2%	7.0%	12.6%	7.7%
BARRINGTON	732	280	193	47	97	115	Bush	38.3%	26.4%	6.4%	13.3%	15.7%
BEDFORD	3,276	1,100	907	542	472	255	Bush	33.6%	27.7%	16.5%	14.4%	7.8%
BELMONT	695	250	163	74	126	82	Bush	36.0%	23.5%	10.6%	18.1%	11.8%

NEW HAMPSHIRE REPUBLICAN

1988

City/Town	Total Vote	Bush	Dole	du Pont	Kemp	Other	Winner	Percentage of Total Vote Bush	Dole	du Pont	Kemp	Other
BERLIN	1,007	469	237	117	73	111	Bush	46.6%	23.5%	11.6%	7.2%	11.0%
BOW	1,363	431	425	188	226	93	Bush	31.6%	31.2%	13.8%	16.6%	6.8%
CLAREMONT	1,477	471	369	193	137	307	Bush	31.9%	25.0%	13.1%	9.3%	20.8%
CONCORD	5,420	1,895	1,792	423	804	506	Bush	35.0%	33.1%	7.8%	14.8%	9.3%
CONWAY	1,422	606	404	124	120	168	Bush	42.6%	28.4%	8.7%	8.4%	11.8%
DERRY	3,044	1,068	826	305	441	404	Bush	35.1%	27.1%	10.0%	14.5%	13.3%
DOVER	2,885	1,261	854	175	273	322	Bush	43.7%	29.6%	6.1%	9.5%	11.2%
DURHAM	1,086	433	439	74	74	66	Dole	39.9%	40.4%	6.8%	6.8%	6.1%
EPPING	574	213	145	53	62	101	Bush	37.1%	25.3%	9.2%	10.8%	17.6%
EXETER	2,435	994	763	190	296	192	Bush	40.8%	31.3%	7.8%	12.2%	7.9%
FARMINGTON	611	245	176	40	66	84	Bush	40.1%	28.8%	6.5%	10.8%	13.7%
FRANKLIN	1,014	345	205	151	211	102	Bush	34.0%	20.2%	14.9%	20.8%	10.1%
GILFORD	1,302	527	343	139	203	90	Bush	40.5%	26.3%	10.7%	15.6%	6.9%
GOFFSTOWN	2,188	693	511	379	332	273	Bush	31.7%	23.4%	17.3%	15.2%	12.5%
HAMPSTEAD	1,108	508	311	81	124	84	Bush	45.8%	28.1%	7.3%	11.2%	7.6%
HAMPTON	2,035	817	644	164	214	196	Bush	40.1%	31.6%	8.1%	10.5%	9.6%
HANOVER	1,105	416	469	112	55	53	Dole	37.6%	42.4%	10.1%	5.0%	4.8%
HOLLIS	1,275	513	457	86	126	93	Bush	40.2%	35.8%	6.7%	9.9%	7.3%
HOOKSETT	1,329	407	337	228	241	116	Bush	30.6%	25.4%	17.2%	18.1%	8.7%
HUDSON	2,084	880	589	143	259	213	Bush	42.2%	28.3%	6.9%	12.4%	10.2%
JAFFREY	719	247	196	75	100	101	Bush	34.4%	27.3%	10.4%	13.9%	14.0%
KEENE	3,068	1,044	1,149	189	419	267	Dole	34.0%	37.5%	6.2%	13.7%	8.7%
KINGSTON	870	339	258	82	114	77	Bush	39.0%	29.7%	9.4%	13.1%	8.9%
LACONIA	2,387	933	611	231	312	300	Bush	39.1%	25.6%	9.7%	13.1%	12.6%
LEBANON	1,309	509	397	95	118	190	Bush	38.9%	30.3%	7.3%	9.0%	14.5%
LITCHFIELD	598	216	163	56	90	73	Bush	36.1%	27.3%	9.4%	15.1%	12.2%
LITTLETON	895	357	240	94	98	106	Bush	39.9%	26.8%	10.5%	10.9%	11.8%
LONDONDERRY	2,739	950	801	330	387	271	Bush	34.7%	29.2%	12.0%	14.1%	9.9%
MANCHESTER	10,272	3,292	2,341	1,864	1,585	1,190	Bush	32.0%	22.8%	18.1%	15.4%	11.6%
MERRIMACK TOWN	2,790	976	812	307	403	292	Bush	35.0%	29.1%	11.0%	14.4%	10.5%
MILFORD	1,947	664	490	193	286	314	Bush	34.1%	25.2%	9.9%	14.7%	16.1%
NASHUA	9,114	3,406	3,012	640	1,107	949	Bush	37.4%	33.0%	7.0%	12.1%	10.4%
NEWMARKET	603	226	198	44	68	67	Bush	37.5%	32.8%	7.3%	11.3%	11.1%
NEWPORT	789	267	255	78	92	97	Bush	33.8%	32.3%	9.9%	11.7%	12.3%
PELHAM	1,035	472	272	47	136	108	Bush	45.6%	26.3%	4.5%	13.1%	10.4%
PEMBROKE	886	315	278	77	132	84	Bush	35.6%	31.4%	8.7%	14.9%	9.5%
PETERBOROUGH	1,205	409	440	136	121	99	Dole	33.9%	36.5%	11.3%	10.0%	8.2%
PLAISTOW	810	353	238	39	117	63	Bush	43.6%	29.4%	4.8%	14.4%	7.8%
PLYMOUTH	754	264	191	97	73	129	Bush	35.0%	25.3%	12.9%	9.7%	17.1%
PORTSMOUTH	2,505	1,032	802	140	294	237	Bush	41.2%	32.0%	5.6%	11.7%	9.5%
RAYMOND	1,073	325	278	156	164	150	Bush	30.3%	25.9%	14.5%	15.3%	14.0%
ROCHESTER	2,536	1,044	626	189	309	368	Bush	41.2%	24.7%	7.5%	12.2%	14.5%
SALEM	3,128	1,451	835	167	390	285	Bush	46.4%	26.7%	5.3%	12.5%	9.1%
SEABROOK	779	386	172	26	97	98	Bush	49.6%	22.1%	3.3%	12.5%	12.6%
SOMERSWORTH	707	287	188	49	64	119	Bush	40.6%	26.6%	6.9%	9.1%	16.8%
SWANZEY	802	256	261	64	129	92	Dole	31.9%	32.5%	8.0%	16.1%	11.5%
WEARE	808	252	198	118	138	102	Bush	31.2%	24.5%	14.6%	17.1%	12.6%
WINDHAM	1,340	607	407	91	119	116	Bush	45.3%	30.4%	6.8%	8.9%	8.7%

NEW HAMPSHIRE DEMOCRATIC

1992

County	Total Vote	Clinton	Harkin	Kerrey	Tsongas	Other	Winner	Percentage of Total Vote Clinton	Harkin	Kerrey	Tsongas	Other
BELKNAP	6,362	1,626	606	845	1,842	1,443	Tsongas	25.6%	9.5%	13.3%	29.0%	22.7%
CARROLL	3,997	794	264	366	1,454	1,119	Tsongas	19.9%	6.6%	9.2%	36.4%	28.0%
CHESHIRE	10,432	2,811	871	1,149	2,806	2,795	Clinton	26.9%	8.3%	11.0%	26.9%	26.8%
COOS	4,948	1,494	912	611	922	1,009	Clinton	30.2%	18.4%	12.3%	18.6%	20.4%
GRAFTON	9,481	2,326	812	943	3,292	2,108	Tsongas	24.5%	8.6%	9.9%	34.7%	22.2%
HILLSBOROUGH	53,946	13,114	4,938	5,862	19,521	10,511	Tsongas	24.3%	9.2%	10.9%	36.2%	19.5%
MERRIMACK	18,673	5,099	2,408	2,026	5,177	3,963	Tsongas	27.3%	12.9%	10.8%	27.7%	21.2%
ROCKINGHAM	37,083	8,071	3,494	3,790	14,403	7,325	Tsongas	21.8%	9.4%	10.2%	38.8%	19.8%
STRAFFORD	17,056	4,358	1,993	2,266	4,901	3,538	Tsongas	25.6%	11.7%	13.3%	28.7%	20.7%
SULLIVAN	5,841	1,829	759	717	1,320	1,216	Clinton	31.3%	13.0%	12.3%	22.6%	20.8%
TOTAL	167,819	41,522	17,057	18,575	55,638	35,027	Tsongas	24.7%	10.2%	11.1%	33.2%	20.9%

City/Town	Total Vote	Clinton	Harkin	Kerrey	Tsongas	Other	Winner	Clinton	Harkin	Kerrey	Tsongas	Other
AMHERST	1,249	224	63	134	605	223	Tsongas	17.9%	5.0%	10.7%	48.4%	17.9%
ATKINSON	740	127	41	77	397	98	Tsongas	17.2%	5.5%	10.4%	53.6%	13.2%
BARRINGTON	951	185	101	130	284	251	Tsongas	19.5%	10.6%	13.7%	29.9%	26.4%
BEDFORD	1,998	397	168	207	838	388	Tsongas	19.9%	8.4%	10.4%	41.9%	19.4%
BELMONT	640	141	67	93	192	147	Tsongas	22.0%	10.5%	14.5%	30.0%	23.0%
BERLIN	2,409	738	535	271	396	469	Clinton	30.6%	22.2%	11.2%	16.4%	19.5%
BOW	654	191	67	62	239	95	Tsongas	29.2%	10.2%	9.5%	36.5%	14.5%
CLAREMONT	2,228	857	356	309	337	369	Clinton	38.5%	16.0%	13.9%	15.1%	16.6%
CONCORD	6,275	1,837	864	636	1,747	1,191	Clinton	29.3%	13.8%	10.1%	27.8%	19.0%
CONWAY	773	135	52	83	262	241	Tsongas	17.5%	6.7%	10.7%	33.9%	31.2%
DERRY	3,355	655	323	227	1,474	676	Tsongas	19.5%	9.6%	6.8%	43.9%	20.1%
DOVER	4,232	1,082	516	496	1,304	834	Tsongas	25.6%	12.2%	11.7%	30.8%	19.7%
DURHAM	2,444	507	288	223	954	472	Tsongas	20.7%	11.8%	9.1%	39.0%	19.3%
EPPING	859	224	107	95	270	163	Tsongas	26.1%	12.5%	11.1%	31.4%	19.0%
EXETER	1,839	405	169	204	593	468	Tsongas	22.0%	9.2%	11.1%	32.2%	25.4%
FARMINGTON	719	169	129	142	125	154	Clinton	23.5%	17.9%	19.7%	17.4%	21.4%
FRANKLIN	1,099	363	150	129	208	249	Clinton	33.0%	13.6%	11.7%	18.9%	22.7%
GILFORD	788	172	76	107	254	179	Tsongas	21.8%	9.6%	13.6%	32.2%	22.7%
GOFFSTOWN	2,156	569	255	243	696	228	Tsongas	28.6%	12.8%	12.2%	35.0%	11.5%
HAMPSTEAD	1,021	173	73	103	481	393	Tsongas	26.4%	11.8%	11.3%	32.3%	18.2%
HAMPTON	2,495	564	265	249	969	448	Tsongas	22.6%	10.6%	10.0%	38.8%	18.0%
HANOVER	2,155	475	158	107	1,042	373	Tsongas	22.0%	7.3%	5.0%	48.4%	17.3%
HOLLIS	870	152	52	88	439	139	Tsongas	17.5%	6.0%	10.1%	50.5%	16.0%
HOOKSETT	1,293	263	177	170	412	271	Tsongas	20.3%	13.7%	13.1%	31.9%	21.0%
HUDSON	2,923	595	182	317	1,292	537	Tsongas	20.4%	6.2%	10.8%	44.2%	18.4%
JAFFREY	699	199	53	72	244	131	Tsongas	28.5%	7.6%	10.3%	34.9%	18.7%
KEENE	3,841	1,099	317	376	940	1,109	Clinton	28.6%	8.3%	9.8%	24.5%	28.9%
KINGSTON	701	153	59	77	284	128	Tsongas	21.8%	8.4%	11.0%	40.5%	18.3%
LACONIA	1,957	500	217	308	554	378	Tsongas	25.5%	11.1%	15.7%	28.3%	19.3%
LEBANON	1,457	446	133	146	444	288	Clinton	30.6%	9.1%	10.0%	30.5%	19.8%
LITCHFIELD	733	175	51	90	310	107	Tsongas	23.9%	7.0%	12.3%	42.3%	14.6%
LITTLETON	510	124	40	63	151	132	Tsongas	24.3%	7.8%	12.4%	29.6%	25.9%
LONDONDERRY	2,644	533	224	326	1,171	390	Tsongas	20.2%	8.5%	12.3%	44.3%	14.8%
MANCHESTER	17,602	4,647	2,360	2,321	4,776	3,498	Tsongas	26.4%	13.4%	13.2%	27.1%	19.9%
MERRIMACK TOWN	3,210	839	225	289	1,242	615	Tsongas	26.1%	7.0%	9.0%	38.7%	19.2%

NEW HAMPSHIRE DEMOCRATIC

1992

City/Town	Total Vote	Clinton	Harkin	Kerrey	Tsongas	Other	Winner	Percentage of Total Vote Clinton	Harkin	Kerrey	Tsongas	Other
MILFORD	1,607	285	122	190	582	428	Tsongas	17.7%	7.6%	11.8%	36.2%	26.6%
NASHUA	13,425	3,757	867	1,261	5,368	2,172	Tsongas	28.0%	6.5%	9.4%	40.0%	16.2%
NEWMARKET	1,474	334	184	133	488	335	Tsongas	22.7%	12.5%	9.0%	33.1%	22.7%
NEWPORT	803	287	95	101	172	148	Clinton	35.7%	11.8%	12.6%	21.4%	18.4%
PELHAM	1,585	213	86	113	924	249	Tsongas	13.4%	5.4%	7.1%	58.3%	15.7%
PEMBROKE	1,109	320	116	135	280	258	Clinton	28.9%	10.5%	12.2%	25.2%	23.3%
PETERBOROUGH	828	146	52	44	341	245	Tsongas	17.6%	6.3%	5.3%	41.2%	29.6%
PLAISTOW	938	188	67	84	415	184	Tsongas	20.0%	7.1%	9.0%	44.2%	19.6%
PLYMOUTH	619	138	88	78	171	144	Tsongas	22.3%	14.2%	12.6%	27.6%	23.3%
PORTSMOUTH	4,747	1,312	509	508	1,446	972	Tsongas	27.6%	10.7%	10.7%	30.5%	20.5%
RAYMOND	960	212	105	117	336	190	Tsongas	22.1%	10.9%	12.2%	35.0%	19.8%
ROCHESTER	3,962	1,127	415	585	981	854	Clinton	28.4%	10.5%	14.8%	24.8%	21.6%
SALEM	4,185	925	347	490	1,782	641	Tsongas	22.1%	8.3%	11.7%	42.6%	15.3%
SEABROOK	966	243	83	119	341	180	Tsongas	25.2%	8.6%	12.3%	35.3%	18.6%
SOMERSWORTH	1,984	648	247	324	418	347	Clinton	32.7%	12.4%	16.3%	21.1%	17.5%
SWANZEY	856	298	63	115	177	203	Clinton	34.8%	7.4%	13.4%	20.7%	23.7%
WEARE	749	195	64	77	220	193	Tsongas	26.0%	8.5%	10.3%	29.4%	25.8%
WINDHAM	1,176	165	66	99	666	180	Tsongas	14.0%	5.6%	8.4%	56.6%	15.3%

Note: The Democratic and Republican county tables were based on returns distributed by state election officials immediately after the primary and includes scattered write-in votes. City and town results are as they appeared in the New Hampshire Manual for the General Court, without scattered write-in votes.

NEW HAMPSHIRE REPUBLICAN

1992

County	Total Vote	Buchanan	Bush	Other	Winner	Percentage of Total Vote Buchanan	Bush	Other
BELKNAP	9,725	3,571	5,098	1,056	Bush	36.7%	52.4%	10.9%
CARROLL	8,732	3,278	4,739	715	Bush	37.5%	54.3%	8.2%
CHESHIRE	10,202	3,426	5,295	1,481	Bush	33.6%	51.9%	14.5%
COOS	4,506	2,059	2,100	347	Bush	45.7%	46.6%	7.7%
GRAFTON	12,227	4,729	6,333	1,165	Bush	38.7%	51.8%	9.5%
HILLSBOROUGH	49,797	19,350	25,833	4,614	Bush	38.9%	51.9%	9.3%
MERRIMACK	21,510	7,252	11,353	2,905	Bush	33.7%	52.8%	13.5%
ROCKINGHAM	39,298	14,801	21,606	2,891	Bush	37.7%	55.0%	7.4%
STRAFFORD	12,532	4,240	7,175	1,117	Bush	33.8%	57.3%	8.9%
SULLIVAN	5,636	2,381	2,701	554	Bush	42.2%	47.9%	9.8%
TOTAL	174,165	65,087	92,233	16,845	Bush	37.4%	53.0%	9.7%

City/Town								
AMHERST	2,290	838	1,218	234	Bush	36.6%	53.2%	10.2%
ATKINSON	962	366	561	35	Bush	38.0%	58.3%	3.6%
BARRINGTON	820	312	420	88	Bush	38.0%	51.2%	10.7%
BEDFORD	3,547	1,437	1,868	242	Bush	40.5%	52.7%	6.8%
BELMONT	831	318	424	89	Bush	38.3%	51.0%	10.7%

NEW HAMPSHIRE REPUBLICAN

1992

City/Town	Total Vote	Buchanan	Bush	Other	Winner	Percentage of Total Vote Buchanan	Bush	Other
BERLIN	1,019	471	450	98	Buchanan	46.2%	44.2%	9.6%
BOW	1,509	501	831	177	Bush	33.2%	55.1%	11.7%
CLAREMONT	1,512	653	709	150	Bush	43.2%	46.9%	9.9%
CONCORD	5,618	1,727	2,996	895	Bush	30.7%	53.3%	15.9%
CONWAY	1,354	550	703	101	Bush	40.6%	51.9%	7.5%
DERRY	3,834	1,527	2,172	135	Bush	39.8%	56.7%	3.5%
DOVER	3,161	1,068	1,827	266	Bush	33.8%	57.8%	8.4%
DURHAM	1,343	338	883	122	Bush	25.2%	65.7%	9.1%
EPPING	679	293	336	50	Bush	43.2%	49.5%	7.4%
EXETER	2,247	820	1,231	196	Bush	36.5%	54.8%	8.7%
FARMINGTON	665	226	381	58	Bush	34.0%	57.3%	8.7%
FRANKLIN	989	373	509	107	Bush	37.7%	51.5%	10.8%
GILFORD	1,438	493	792	153	Bush	34.3%	55.1%	10.6%
GOFFSTOWN	2,519	1,024	1,325	170	Bush	40.7%	52.6%	6.7%
HAMPSTEAD	1,373	481	791	101	Bush	35.0%	57.6%	7.4%
HAMPTON	2,160	785	1,234	141	Bush	36.3%	57.1%	6.5%
HANOVER	1,305	361	810	134	Bush	27.7%	62.1%	10.3%
HOLLIS	1,467	461	854	152	Bush	31.4%	58.2%	10.4%
HOOKSETT	1,676	726	816	134	Bush	43.3%	48.7%	8.0%
HUDSON	2,483	909	1,385	189	Bush	36.6%	55.8%	7.6%
JAFFREY	840	327	416	97	Bush	38.9%	49.5%	11.5%
KEENE	3,162	954	1,715	493	Bush	30.2%	54.2%	15.6%
KINGSTON	1,106	425	602	79	Bush	38.4%	54.4%	7.1%
LACONIA	2,609	1,007	1,377	225	Bush	38.6%	52.8%	8.6%
LEBANON	1,343	429	788	126	Bush	31.9%	58.7%	9.4%
LITCHFIELD	777	328	376	73	Bush	42.2%	48.4%	9.4%
LITTLETON	945	438	447	60	Bush	46.3%	47.3%	6.3%
LONDONDERRY	3,239	1,381	1,645	213	Bush	42.6%	50.8%	6.6%
MANCHESTER	11,459	5,090	5,285	1,084	Bush	44.4%	46.1%	9.5%
MERRIMACK TOWN	3,374	1,339	1,766	269	Bush	39.7%	52.3%	8.0%
MILFORD	1,885	672	1,043	170	Bush	35.6%	55.3%	9.0%
NASHUA	9,902	3,573	5,595	734	Bush	36.1%	56.5%	7.4%
NEWMARKET	748	265	428	55	Bush	35.4%	57.2%	7.4%
NEWPORT	804	376	361	67	Buchanan	46.8%	44.9%	8.3%
PELHAM	1,187	422	675	90	Bush	35.6%	56.9%	7.6%
PEMBROKE	1,092	398	577	117	Bush	36.4%	52.8%	10.7%
PETERBOROUGH	1,125	321	608	196	Bush	28.5%	54.0%	17.4%
PLAISTOW	893	316	497	80	Bush	35.4%	55.7%	9.0%
PLYMOUTH	731	279	357	95	Bush	38.2%	48.8%	13.0%
PORTSMOUTH	2,552	796	1,558	198	Bush	31.2%	61.1%	7.8%
RAYMOND	1,131	522	548	61	Bush	46.2%	48.5%	5.4%
ROCHESTER	3,082	1,127	1,702	253	Bush	36.6%	55.2%	8.2%
SALEM	3,413	1,233	1,945	235	Bush	36.1%	57.0%	6.9%
SEABROOK	903	320	516	67	Bush	35.4%	57.1%	7.4%
SOMERSWORTH	879	284	533	62	Bush	32.3%	60.6%	7.1%
SWANZEY	949	298	513	138	Bush	31.4%	54.1%	14.5%
WEARE	1,073	431	532	110	Bush	40.2%	49.6%	10.3%
WINDHAM	1,563	566	937	60	Bush	36.2%	59.9%	3.8%

NEW HAMPSHIRE DEMOCRATIC

1996

County	Total Vote	Clinton	Other	Winner	Percentage of Total Vote: Clinton	Percentage of Total Vote: Other
BELKNAP	3,635	2,976	659	Clinton	81.9%	18.1%
CARROLL	2,117	1,926	191	Clinton	91.0%	9.0%
CHESHIRE	6,507	5,969	538	Clinton	91.7%	8.3%
COOS	2,974	2,329	645	Clinton	78.3%	21.7%
GRAFTON	5,499	4,855	644	Clinton	88.3%	11.7%
HILLSBOROUGH	29,213	23,562	5,651	Clinton	80.7%	19.3%
MERRIMACK	11,052	9,526	1,526	Clinton	86.2%	13.8%
ROCKINGHAM	18,464	15,337	3,127	Clinton	83.1%	16.9%
STRAFFORD	8,794	7,579	1,215	Clinton	86.2%	13.8%
SULLIVAN	3,307	2,738	569	Clinton	82.8%	17.2%
TOTAL	91,562	76,797	14,765	Clinton	83.9%	16.1%

City/Town	Total Vote	Clinton	Other	Winner	Percentage of Total Vote: Clinton	Percentage of Total Vote: Other
AMHERST	668	557	111	Clinton	83.4%	16.6%
ATKINSON	362	258	104	Clinton	71.3%	28.7%
BARRINGTON	541	426	115	Clinton	78.7%	21.3%
BEDFORD	1,140	945	195	Clinton	82.9%	17.1%
BELMONT	326	251	75	Clinton	77.0%	23.0%
BERLIN	1,587	1,217	370	Clinton	76.7%	23.3%
BOW	535	519	16	Clinton	97.0%	3.0%
CLAREMONT	1,272	1,083	189	Clinton	85.1%	14.9%
CONCORD	4,198	3,515	683	Clinton	83.7%	16.3%
CONWAY	379	342	37	Clinton	90.2%	9.8%
DERRY	1,443	1,207	236	Clinton	83.6%	16.4%
DOVER	2,222	1,946	276	Clinton	87.6%	12.4%
DURHAM	893	812	81	Clinton	90.9%	9.1%
EPPING	317	275	42	Clinton	86.8%	13.2%
EXETER	1,107	963	144	Clinton	87.0%	13.0%
FARMINGTON	392	311	81	Clinton	79.3%	20.7%
FRANKLIN	518	430	88	Clinton	83.0%	17.0%
GILFORD	409	343	66	Clinton	83.9%	16.1%
GOFFSTOWN	1,254	980	274	Clinton	78.1%	21.9%
HAMPSTEAD	431	344	87	Clinton	79.8%	20.2%
HAMPTON	1,289	1,118	171	Clinton	86.7%	13.3%
HANOVER	1,110	1,066	44	Clinton	96.0%	4.0%
HOLLIS	478	421	57	Clinton	88.1%	11.9%
HOOKSETT	684	573	111	Clinton	83.8%	16.2%
HUDSON	1,375	1,062	313	Clinton	77.2%	22.8%
JAFFREY	455	418	37	Clinton	91.9%	8.1%
KEENE	2,601	2,401	200	Clinton	92.3%	7.7%
KINGSTON	350	278	72	Clinton	79.4%	20.6%
LACONIA	1,235	1,031	204	Clinton	83.5%	16.5%
LEBANON	966	880	86	Clinton	91.1%	8.9%
LITCHFIELD	497	420	77	Clinton	84.5%	15.5%
LITTLETON	277	195	82	Clinton	70.4%	29.6%
LONDONDERRY	1,144	917	227	Clinton	80.2%	19.8%
MANCHESTER	10,161	7,786	2375	Clinton	76.6%	23.4%
MERRIMACK TOWN	1,823	1,440	383	Clinton	79.0%	21.0%

NEW HAMPSHIRE DEMOCRATIC

1996

City/Town	Total Vote	Clinton	Other	Winner	Percentage of Total Vote Clinton	Percentage of Total Vote Other
MILFORD	790	652	138	Clinton	82.5%	17.5%
NASHUA	6,437	5,570	867	Clinton	86.5%	13.5%
NEWMARKET	690	606	84	Clinton	87.8%	12.2%
NEWPORT	440	380	60	Clinton	86.4%	13.6%
PELHAM	831	490	341	Clinton	59.0%	41.0%
PEMBROKE	508	447	61	Clinton	88.0%	12.0%
PETERBOROUGH	545	499	46	Clinton	91.6%	8.4%
PLAISTOW	325	237	88	Clinton	72.9%	27.1%
PLYMOUTH	428	386	42	Clinton	90.2%	9.8%
PORTSMOUTH	2,387	2,203	184	Clinton	92.3%	7.7%
RAYMOND	584	426	158	Clinton	72.9%	27.1%
ROCHESTER	2,145	1,815	330	Clinton	84.6%	15.4%
SALEM	2,167	1,814	353	Clinton	83.7%	16.3%
SEABROOK	459	375	84	Clinton	81.7%	18.3%
SOMERSWORTH	1,029	921	108	Clinton	89.5%	10.5%
SWANZEY	520	465	55	Clinton	89.4%	10.6%
WEARE	428	346	82	Clinton	80.8%	19.2%
WINDHAM	718	438	280	Clinton	61.0%	39.0%

Note: Results in the Democratic and Republican tables include scattered write-in votes, which are not part of the returns published in the New Hampshire Manual for the General Court.

NEW HAMPSHIRE REPUBLICAN

1996

County	Total Vote	Alexander	Buchanan	Dole	Forbes	Other	Winner	Percentage of Total Vote Alexander	Buchanan	Dole	Forbes	Other
BELKNAP	10,856	2,603	2,757	2,861	1,322	1,313	Dole	24.0%	25.4%	26.4%	12.2%	12.1%
CARROLL	9,567	2,357	2,268	2,695	1,156	1,091	Dole	24.6%	23.7%	28.2%	12.1%	11.4%
CHESHIRE	11,291	2,703	2,548	3,018	1,349	1,673	Dole	23.9%	22.6%	26.7%	11.9%	14.8%
COOS	4,981	793	2,059	1,059	573	497	Buchanan	15.9%	41.3%	21.3%	11.5%	10.0%
GRAFTON	14,261	3,129	3,440	4,058	1,841	1,793	Dole	21.9%	24.1%	28.5%	12.9%	12.6%
HILLSBOROUGH	61,767	13,713	18,920	15,436	7,052	6,646	Buchanan	22.2%	30.6%	25.0%	11.4%	10.8%
MERRIMACK	26,580	6,611	6,121	6,494	3,281	4,073	Alexander	24.9%	23.0%	24.4%	12.3%	15.3%
ROCKINGHAM	48,060	10,644	13,269	13,097	6,217	4,833	Buchanan	22.1%	27.6%	27.3%	12.9%	10.1%
STRAFFORD	14,727	3,390	3,602	4,134	1,638	1,963	Dole	23.0%	24.5%	28.1%	11.1%	13.3%
SULLIVAN	6,848	1,205	1,890	1,886	1,076	791	Buchanan	17.6%	27.6%	27.5%	15.7%	11.6%
TOTAL	208,938	47,148	56,874	54,738	25,505	24,673	Buchanan	22.6%	27.2%	26.2%	12.2%	11.8%
City/Town												
AMHERST	2,788	651	528	909	403	297	Dole	23.4%	18.9%	32.6%	14.5%	10.7%
ATKINSON	1,306	222	342	456	192	94	Dole	17.0%	26.2%	34.9%	14.7%	7.2%
BARRINGTON	1,124	263	280	270	120	191	Buchanan	23.4%	24.9%	24.0%	10.7%	17.0%
BEDFORD	4,583	1,180	1,194	1,214	598	397	Dole	25.7%	26.1%	26.5%	13.0%	8.7%
BELMONT	936	241	263	204	106	122	Buchanan	25.7%	28.1%	21.8%	11.3%	13.0%

NEW HAMPSHIRE REPUBLICAN

1996

City/Town	Total Vote	Alexander	Buchanan	Dole	Forbes	Other	Winner	Percentage of Total Vote: Alexander	Buchanan	Dole	Forbes	Other
BERLIN	1,122	136	534	221	114	117	Buchanan	12.1%	47.6%	19.7%	10.2%	10.4%
BOW	1,921	564	370	531	213	243	Alexander	29.4%	19.3%	27.6%	11.1%	12.6%
CLAREMONT	1,710	245	539	424	275	227	Buchanan	14.3%	31.5%	24.8%	16.1%	13.3%
CONCORD	7,031	1,716	1,248	1,817	796	1,454	Dole	24.4%	17.7%	25.8%	11.3%	20.7%
CONWAY	1,420	298	406	361	185	170	Buchanan	21.0%	28.6%	25.4%	13.0%	12.0%
DERRY	4,886	1,055	1,574	1,168	560	529	Buchanan	21.6%	32.2%	23.9%	11.5%	10.8%
DOVER	3,546	808	710	1,136	414	478	Dole	22.8%	20.0%	32.0%	11.7%	13.5%
DURHAM	1,344	405	177	410	141	211	Dole	30.1%	13.2%	30.5%	10.5%	15.7%
EPPING	874	203	312	151	110	98	Buchanan	23.2%	35.7%	17.3%	12.6%	11.2%
EXETER	2,974	669	782	916	305	302	Dole	22.5%	26.3%	30.8%	10.3%	10.2%
FARMINGTON	641	144	219	158	54	66	Buchanan	22.5%	34.2%	24.6%	8.4%	10.3%
FRANKLIN	1,147	290	350	255	102	150	Buchanan	25.3%	30.5%	22.2%	8.9%	13.1%
GILFORD	1,598	409	332	468	205	184	Dole	25.6%	20.8%	29.3%	12.8%	11.5%
GOFFSTOWN	3,101	678	1,175	626	338	284	Buchanan	21.9%	37.9%	20.2%	10.9%	9.2%
HAMPSTEAD	1,530	353	403	430	208	136	Dole	23.1%	26.3%	28.1%	13.6%	8.9%
HAMPTON	2,791	648	555	914	396	278	Dole	23.2%	19.9%	32.7%	14.2%	10.0%
HANOVER	1,678	431	118	654	234	241	Dole	25.7%	7.0%	39.0%	13.9%	14.4%
HOLLIS	1,811	423	308	629	222	229	Dole	23.4%	17.0%	34.7%	12.3%	12.6%
HOOKSETT	2,241	618	780	418	239	186	Buchanan	27.6%	34.8%	18.7%	10.7%	8.3%
HUDSON	2,788	345	920	789	381	353	Buchanan	12.4%	33.0%	28.3%	13.7%	12.7%
JAFFREY	884	186	241	236	108	113	Buchanan	21.0%	27.3%	26.7%	12.2%	12.8%
KEENE	3,320	820	545	978	411	566	Dole	24.7%	16.4%	29.5%	12.4%	17.0%
KINGSTON	1,216	274	351	316	147	128	Buchanan	22.5%	28.9%	26.0%	12.1%	10.5%
LACONIA	2,830	616	702	816	344	352	Dole	21.8%	24.8%	28.8%	12.2%	12.4%
LEBANON	1,743	380	295	585	205	278	Dole	21.8%	16.9%	33.6%	11.8%	15.9%
LITCHFIELD	1,245	276	431	245	160	133	Buchanan	22.2%	34.6%	19.7%	12.9%	10.7%
LITTLETON	1,047	214	345	255	163	70	Buchanan	20.4%	33.0%	24.4%	15.6%	6.7%
LONDONDERRY	4,156	968	1,360	1,081	405	342	Buchanan	23.3%	32.7%	26.0%	9.7%	8.2%
MANCHESTER	14,552	3,035	5,735	2,976	1,452	1,354	Buchanan	20.9%	39.4%	20.5%	10.0%	9.3%
MERRIMACK TOWN	4,776	1,171	1,368	1,209	516	512	Buchanan	24.5%	28.6%	25.3%	10.8%	10.7%
MILFORD	2,538	685	715	670	208	260	Buchanan	27.0%	28.2%	26.4%	8.2%	10.2%
NASHUA	11,129	2,449	2,929	3,181	1,343	1,227	Dole	22.0%	26.3%	28.6%	12.1%	11.0%
NEWMARKET	1,103	259	270	245	163	166	Buchanan	23.5%	24.5%	22.2%	14.8%	15.0%
NEWPORT	949	164	285	283	132	85	Buchanan	17.3%	30.0%	29.8%	13.9%	9.0%
PELHAM	1,479	261	491	436	175	116	Buchanan	17.6%	33.2%	29.5%	11.8%	7.8%
PEMBROKE	1,330	337	367	317	155	154	Buchanan	25.3%	27.6%	23.8%	11.7%	11.6%
PETERBOROUGH	1,288	330	233	392	152	181	Dole	25.6%	18.1%	30.4%	11.8%	14.1%
PLAISTOW	1,180	220	348	349	168	95	Dole	18.6%	29.5%	29.6%	14.2%	8.1%
PLYMOUTH	938	250	231	239	100	118	Alexander	26.7%	24.6%	25.5%	10.7%	12.6%
PORTSMOUTH	2,911	679	520	951	420	341	Dole	23.3%	17.9%	32.7%	14.4%	11.7%
RAYMOND	1,511	351	602	197	187	174	Buchanan	23.2%	39.8%	13.0%	12.4%	11.5%
ROCHESTER	3,731	736	1,180	977	402	436	Buchanan	19.7%	31.6%	26.2%	10.8%	11.7%
SALEM	3,727	611	1,078	1,077	639	322	Buchanan	16.4%	28.9%	28.9%	17.1%	8.6%
SEABROOK	975	164	354	292	89	76	Buchanan	16.8%	36.3%	29.9%	9.1%	7.8%
SOMERSWORTH	1,189	264	311	327	142	145	Dole	22.2%	26.2%	27.5%	11.9%	12.2%
SWANZEY	1,039	242	218	273	126	180	Dole	23.3%	21.0%	26.3%	12.1%	17.3%
WEARE	1,463	358	438	307	154	206	Buchanan	24.5%	29.9%	21.0%	10.5%	14.1%
WINDHAM	2,106	446	500	662	351	147	Dole	21.2%	23.7%	31.4%	16.7%	7.0%

NEW JERSEY

For decades, New Jersey joined with California to provide bicoastal bookends for the final big day of the primary season. But starting in 1996, New Jersey has been the only megastate voting in early June, as California has moved its primary to March in a bid to become a major player in the nominating process.

Occasionally, New Jersey's role has been noteworthy even on its late date. In 1984, Walter Mondale essentially nailed down the Democratic nomination with a victory in the Garden State over Gary Hart. And in 1980, Edward Kennedy scored a last hurrah of sorts with Democratic primary wins over the front-running Jimmy Carter in both New Jersey and California.

More typically, the exercise has been a yawn, as primary voters often were asked merely to ratify delegate slates put together by their parties' leadership. New Jersey Republicans have not had a competitive primary since 1952, when Dwight Eisenhower swamped Robert Taft by a margin of nearly 2-to-1. And the moderate tone of the state GOP has not seemed to change a lot since then.

Ronald Reagan did not even enter the 1976 preference primary, and President Gerald Ford took all but four of the state's delegates. In 1980, Reagan entered the primary, but his competition evaporated before the June vote. It has been a similar story since then; the eventual nominees have been acceptable to the state party establishment and have won the New Jersey primary with little or no opposition.

Democratic contests in recent years have been a bit closer and a bit more consequential. In 1980, Kennedy swept New Jersey by a margin of 3-to-2, helping keep alive his challenge for the Democratic nomination—at least in spirit.

In 1984, New Jersey gave Mondale a desperately needed win that offset a loss the same day to Gary Hart in California. Mondale beat Hart by a decisive 15 percentage points in New Jersey, winning virtually all the major suburban counties of northern New Jersey, as well as Camden and Mercer (Trenton) to the south. Mondale's New Jersey win ensured that he would have enough delegates at the convention to secure a first-ballot nomination.

Winning margins in the Democratic primary have grown wider since then, with New Jersey giving Bill Clinton one of his

Recent New Jersey Primary Results

New Jersey held its first presidential primary in 1912.

	DEMOCRATS			REPUBLICANS		
Year	Turnout	Candidates	%	Turnout	Candidates	%
1996 (June 4)	266,740	BILL CLINTON*	95	218,812	BOB DOLE	82
					Pat Buchanan	11
1992 (June 2)	392,626	BILL CLINTON	62	310,270	GEORGE BUSH*	78
		Jerry Brown	20		Pat Buchanan	15
		Paul Tsongas	12			
1988 (June 7)	654,302	MICHAEL DUKAKIS	63	241,033	GEORGE BUSH	100
		Jesse Jackson	33			
1984 (June 5)	676,561	WALTER MONDALE	45	240,054	RONALD REAGAN*	100
		Gary Hart	30			
		Jesse Jackson	24			
1980 (June 3)	560,908	EDWARD KENNEDY	56	277,977	RONALD REAGAN	81
		Jimmy Carter*	38		George Bush	17
1976 (June 8)	360,839	JIMMY CARTER	58	242,122	GERALD FORD*	100
		Frank Church	14			
1972 (June 6)	76,834	SHIRLEY CHISHOLM	67	215,719	UNPLEDGED	100
		Terry Sanford	33			
1968 (June 4)	27,446	EUGENE McCARTHY#	36	88,592	RICHARD NIXON#	81
		Robert Kennedy#	31		Nelson Rockefeller#	13
		Hubert Humphrey#	20			

Note: All candidates are listed that drew at least 10 percent of their party's primary vote. The names of winning candidates are capitalized. An asterisk (*) indicates an incumbent president. A pound sign (#) indicates a write-in candidate.

more convincing primary victories in 1992 outside the South. Clinton won more than 60 percent of the vote, running best in Essex County (Newark) with its large minority population; Jesse Jackson had carried the county in Democratic primary voting in 1984 and 1988.

Now that it is the last major stop on the campaign trail, New Jersey may find it hard to match the glitz and glitter that California once offered at the end of the primary season. But at least New Jersey will be spared the comparisons between the two. (Hart got himself in trouble in 1984 with a joke about the state's reputation for toxic-waste dumps.)

And occasionally, New Jersey is able to offer some glamour of its own. Among its Democratic delegates in 1988 was Academy Award-winning actress Olympia Dukakis, a cousin of the New Jersey primary winner that year and the party's eventual nominee, Michael Dukakis.

NEW JERSEY REPUBLICAN

1968

County	Total Vote	Nixon	Rockefeller	Other	Winner	Percentage of Total Vote Nixon	Rockefeller	Other
ATLANTIC	1,801	1,497	232	72	Nixon	83.1%	12.9%	4.0%
BERGEN	12,934	10,173	1,535	1,226	Nixon	78.7%	11.9%	9.5%
BURLINGTON	3,186	2,289	490	407	Nixon	71.8%	15.4%	12.8%
CAMDEN	2,774	2,261	358	155	Nixon	81.5%	12.9%	5.6%
CAPE MAY	No Vote							
CUMBERLAND	3,188	2,452	461	275	Nixon	76.9%	14.5%	8.6%
ESSEX	10,076	8,299	1,520	257	Nixon	82.4%	15.1%	2.6%
GLOUCESTER	5,421	4,120	807	494	Nixon	76.0%	14.9%	9.1%
HUDSON	961	852	76	33	Nixon	88.7%	7.9%	3.4%
HUNTERDON	2,433	2,017	326	90	Nixon	82.9%	13.4%	3.7%
MERCER	2,160	1,417	691	52	Nixon	65.6%	32.0%	2.4%
MIDDLESEX	3,135	2,703	320	112	Nixon	86.2%	10.2%	3.6%
MONMOUTH	4,681	3,926	570	185	Nixon	83.9%	12.2%	4.0%
MORRIS	10,143	7,881	1,294	968	Nixon	77.7%	12.8%	9.5%
OCEAN	3,147	2,725	325	97	Nixon	86.6%	10.3%	3.1%
PASSAIC	3,548	3,186	239	123	Nixon	89.8%	6.7%	3.5%
SALEM	1,085	1,030		55	Nixon	94.9%		5.1%
SOMERSET	3,745	3,032	465	248	Nixon	81.0%	12.4%	6.6%
SUSSEX	2,963	2,540	342	81	Nixon	85.7%	11.5%	2.7%
UNION	9,018	7,539	1,233	246	Nixon	83.6%	13.7%	2.7%
WARREN	2,193	1,870	246	77	Nixon	85.3%	11.2%	3.5%
TOTAL	88,592	71,809	11,530	5,253	Nixon	81.1%	13.0%	5.9%

Note: All votes cast were write-ins.

NEW JERSEY DEMOCRATIC

1976

County	Total Vote	Carter	Church	Other	Winner	Percentage of Total Vote Carter	Church	Other
ATLANTIC	5,746	3,104	994	1,648	Carter	54.0%	17.3%	28.7%
BERGEN	36,703	22,504	5,794	8,405	Carter	61.3%	15.8%	22.9%
BURLINGTON	16,111	10,155	2,794	3,162	Carter	63.0%	17.3%	19.6%
CAMDEN	29,941	17,094	5,091	7,756	Carter	57.1%	17.0%	25.9%
CAPE MAY	2,761	1,874	343	544	Carter	67.9%	12.4%	19.7%
CUMBERLAND	6,947	5,161	610	1,176	Carter	74.3%	8.8%	16.9%
ESSEX	55,252	29,723	7,404	18,125	Carter	53.8%	13.4%	32.8%
GLOUCESTER	9,442	6,628	1,190	1,624	Carter	70.2%	12.6%	17.2%
HUDSON	33,554	18,070	4,203	11,281	Carter	53.9%	12.5%	33.6%
HUNTERDON	3,127	2,015	508	604	Carter	64.4%	16.2%	19.3%
MERCER	18,475	11,200	2,465	4,810	Carter	60.6%	13.3%	26.0%
MIDDLESEX	32,507	19,065	3,696	9,746	Carter	58.6%	11.4%	30.0%
MONMOUTH	19,377	11,905	2,533	4,939	Carter	61.4%	13.1%	25.5%
MORRIS	17,481	9,238	2,386	5,857	Carter	52.8%	13.6%	33.5%
OCEAN	13,990	7,027	1,277	5,686	Carter	50.2%	9.1%	40.6%
PASSAIC	13,780	9,071	1,537	3,172	Carter	65.8%	11.2%	23.0%
SALEM	2,475	1,735	346	394	Carter	70.1%	14.0%	15.9%
SOMERSET	8,303	4,805	1,918	1,580	Carter	57.9%	23.1%	19.0%
SUSSEX	3,394	2,192	463	739	Carter	64.6%	13.6%	21.8%
UNION	27,440	15,594	2,879	8,967	Carter	56.8%	10.5%	32.7%
WARREN	4,033	2,495	603	935	Carter	61.9%	15.0%	23.2%
TOTAL	360,839	210,655	49,034	101,150	Carter	58.4%	13.6%	28.0%

NEW JERSEY DEMOCRATIC

1980

County	Total Vote	Carter	E. Kennedy	Other	Winner	Percentage of Total Vote: Carter	E. Kennedy	Other
ATLANTIC	9,620	3,648	5,783	189	E. Kennedy	37.9%	60.1%	2.0%
BERGEN	55,340	17,484	34,613	3,243	E. Kennedy	31.6%	62.5%	5.9%
BURLINGTON	24,588	8,521	14,000	2,067	E. Kennedy	34.7%	56.9%	8.4%
CAMDEN	42,141	13,426	25,335	3,380	E. Kennedy	31.9%	60.1%	8.0%
CAPE MAY	4,176	1,959	1,952	265	Carter	46.9%	46.7%	6.3%
CUMBERLAND	6,703	2,600	3,839	264	E. Kennedy	38.8%	57.3%	3.9%
ESSEX	74,207	24,801	45,761	3,645	E. Kennedy	33.4%	61.7%	4.9%
GLOUCESTER	13,954	5,714	7,707	533	E. Kennedy	40.9%	55.2%	3.8%
HUDSON	74,576	34,178	35,803	4,595	E. Kennedy	45.8%	48.0%	6.2%
HUNTERDON	3,759	1,718	1,810	231	E. Kennedy	45.7%	48.2%	6.1%
MERCER	26,073	9,357	15,567	1,149	E. Kennedy	35.9%	59.7%	4.4%
MIDDLESEX	57,998	23,849	30,281	3,868	E. Kennedy	41.1%	52.2%	6.7%
MONMOUTH	31,374	12,367	18,223	784	E. Kennedy	39.4%	58.1%	2.5%
MORRIS	20,123	7,506	10,563	2,054	E. Kennedy	37.3%	52.5%	10.2%
OCEAN	19,771	7,729	10,910	1,132	E. Kennedy	39.1%	55.2%	5.7%
PASSAIC	26,801	9,499	15,944	1,358	E. Kennedy	35.4%	59.5%	5.1%
SALEM	3,332	1,707	1,509	116	Carter	51.2%	45.3%	3.5%
SOMERSET	10,170	4,116	5,187	867	E. Kennedy	40.5%	51.0%	8.5%
SUSSEX	4,828	2,168	2,384	276	E. Kennedy	44.9%	49.4%	5.7%
UNION	45,765	17,534	25,193	3,038	E. Kennedy	38.3%	55.0%	6.6%
WARREN	5,609	2,506	2,745	358	E. Kennedy	44.7%	48.9%	6.4%
TOTAL	560,908	212,387	315,109	33,412	E. Kennedy	37.9%	56.2%	6.0%

NEW JERSEY REPUBLICAN

1980

County	Total Vote	Bush	Reagan	Stassen	Winner	Percentage of Total Vote Bush	Reagan	Stassen
ATLANTIC	10,471	1,646	8,716	109	Reagan	15.7%	83.2%	1.0%
BERGEN	35,090	5,725	28,885	480	Reagan	16.3%	82.3%	1.4%
BURLINGTON	15,387	3,325	11,844	218	Reagan	21.6%	77.0%	1.4%
CAMDEN	13,131	2,945	9,812	374	Reagan	22.4%	74.7%	2.8%
CAPE MAY	9,248	1,225	7,832	191	Reagan	13.2%	84.7%	2.1%
CUMBERLAND	3,865	512	3,307	46	Reagan	13.2%	85.6%	1.2%
ESSEX	20,557	3,410	16,670	477	Reagan	16.6%	81.1%	2.3%
GLOUCESTER	7,933	1,776	6,040	117	Reagan	22.4%	76.1%	1.5%
HUDSON	6,510	599	5,798	113	Reagan	9.2%	89.1%	1.7%
HUNTERDON	4,946	1,142	3,744	60	Reagan	23.1%	75.7%	1.2%
MERCER	8,589	2,272	6,174	143	Reagan	26.5%	71.9%	1.7%
MIDDLESEX	13,388	1,663	11,511	214	Reagan	12.4%	86.0%	1.6%
MONMOUTH	19,145	2,503	16,440	202	Reagan	13.1%	85.9%	1.1%
MORRIS	26,940	4,789	21,592	559	Reagan	17.8%	80.1%	2.1%
OCEAN	23,796	2,856	20,671	269	Reagan	12.0%	86.9%	1.1%
PASSAIC	11,695	1,389	10,136	170	Reagan	11.9%	86.7%	1.5%
SALEM	1,891	416	1,452	23	Reagan	22.0%	76.8%	1.2%
SOMERSET	13,244	3,419	9,625	200	Reagan	25.8%	72.7%	1.5%
SUSSEX	6,752	1,127	5,490	135	Reagan	16.7%	81.3%	2.0%
UNION	21,420	3,852	17,160	408	Reagan	18.0%	80.1%	1.9%
WARREN	3,979	856	3,060	63	Reagan	21.5%	76.9%	1.6%
TOTAL	277,977	47,447	225,959	4,571	Reagan	17.1%	81.3%	1.6%

NEW JERSEY DEMOCRATIC

1984

County	Total Vote	Hart	J. Jackson	LaRouche	Mondale	Winner	Percentage of Total Vote			
							Hart	J. Jackson	LaRouche	Mondale
ATLANTIC	11,832	3,003	3,881	127	4,821	Mondale	25.4%	32.8%	1.1%	40.7%
BERGEN	66,574	23,733	8,663	568	33,610	Mondale	35.6%	13.0%	0.9%	50.5%
BURLINGTON	27,974	9,692	5,451	290	12,541	Mondale	34.6%	19.5%	1.0%	44.8%
CAMDEN	49,726	14,590	11,381	1,017	22,738	Mondale	29.3%	22.9%	2.0%	45.7%
CAPE MAY	4,506	1,826	390	151	2,139	Mondale	40.5%	8.7%	3.4%	47.5%
CUMBERLAND	10,814	3,494	2,160	90	5,070	Mondale	32.3%	20.0%	0.8%	46.9%
ESSEX	105,757	15,954	52,109	1,316	36,378	J. Jackson	15.1%	49.3%	1.2%	34.4%
GLOUCESTER	19,981	7,738	2,883	296	9,064	Mondale	38.7%	14.4%	1.5%	45.4%
HUDSON	87,098	26,898	19,383	1,485	39,332	Mondale	30.9%	22.3%	1.7%	45.2%
HUNTERDON	4,867	2,196	454	78	2,139	Hart	45.1%	9.3%	1.6%	43.9%
MERCER	35,944	10,106	9,087	824	15,927	Mondale	28.1%	25.3%	2.3%	44.3%
MIDDLESEX	58,941	19,832	7,786	679	30,644	Mondale	33.6%	13.2%	1.2%	52.0%
MONMOUTH	34,104	11,571	5,617	409	16,507	Mondale	33.9%	16.5%	1.2%	48.4%
MORRIS	23,025	9,271	2,904	255	10,595	Mondale	40.3%	12.6%	1.1%	46.0%
OCEAN	23,611	7,831	1,933	526	13,321	Mondale	33.2%	8.2%	2.2%	56.4%
PASSAIC	33,690	9,015	8,925	477	15,273	Mondale	26.8%	26.5%	1.4%	45.3%
SALEM	3,480	1,222	621	48	1,589	Mondale	35.1%	17.8%	1.4%	45.7%
SOMERSET	12,784	4,467	2,135	175	6,007	Mondale	34.9%	16.7%	1.4%	47.0%
SUSSEX	5,138	2,538	357	96	2,147	Hart	49.4%	6.9%	1.9%	41.8%
UNION	51,267	13,677	13,310	1,334	22,946	Mondale	26.7%	26.0%	2.6%	44.8%
WARREN	5,448	2,294	358	68	2,728	Mondale	42.1%	6.6%	1.2%	50.1%
TOTAL	676,561	200,948	159,788	10,309	305,516	Mondale	29.7%	23.6%	1.5%	45.2%

NEW JERSEY DEMOCRATIC

1988

County	Total Vote	Dukakis	J. Jackson	Other	Winner	Percentage of Total Vote Dukakis	J. Jackson	Other
ATLANTIC	10,827	4,855	4,479	1,493	Dukakis	44.8%	41.4%	13.8%
BERGEN	59,358	45,993	11,563	1,802	Dukakis	77.5%	19.5%	3.0%
BURLINGTON	28,363	17,345	9,856	1,162	Dukakis	61.2%	34.7%	4.1%
CAMDEN	47,575	30,783	14,920	1,872	Dukakis	64.7%	31.4%	3.9%
CAPE MAY	4,949	3,719	969	261	Dukakis	75.1%	19.6%	5.3%
CUMBERLAND	9,327	6,065	2,882	380	Dukakis	65.0%	30.9%	4.1%
ESSEX	109,134	39,019	66,826	3,289	J. Jackson	35.8%	61.2%	3.0%
GLOUCESTER	18,554	13,940	4,038	576	Dukakis	75.1%	21.8%	3.1%
HUDSON	72,198	49,523	18,920	3,755	Dukakis	68.6%	26.2%	5.2%
HUNTERDON	4,392	3,371	817	204	Dukakis	76.8%	18.6%	4.6%
MERCER	32,855	19,109	12,606	1,140	Dukakis	58.2%	38.4%	3.5%
MIDDLESEX	58,514	45,053	10,976	2,485	Dukakis	77.0%	18.8%	4.2%
MONMOUTH	38,051	25,969	10,302	1,780	Dukakis	68.2%	27.1%	4.7%
MORRIS	20,112	15,715	3,638	759	Dukakis	78.1%	18.1%	3.8%
OCEAN	24,313	21,240	2,637	436	Dukakis	87.4%	10.8%	1.8%
PASSAIC	32,424	18,783	11,734	1,907	Dukakis	57.9%	36.2%	5.9%
SALEM	3,936	2,418	1,396	122	Dukakis	61.4%	35.5%	3.1%
SOMERSET	12,687	8,766	3,476	445	Dukakis	69.1%	27.4%	3.5%
SUSSEX	4,748	3,842	614	292	Dukakis	80.9%	12.9%	6.1%
UNION	57,184	35,281	20,458	1,445	Dukakis	61.7%	35.8%	2.5%
WARREN	4,801	4,040	598	163	Dukakis	84.1%	12.5%	3.4%
TOTAL	654,302	414,829	213,705	25,768	Dukakis	63.4%	32.7%	3.9%

NEW JERSEY DEMOCRATIC

1992

County	Total Vote	Brown	Clinton	Tsongas	Other	Winner	Percentage of Total Vote Brown	Clinton	Tsongas	Other
ATLANTIC	8,349	1,719	5,312	1,089	229	Clinton	20.6%	63.6%	13.0%	2.7%
BERGEN	37,839	6,002	23,517	5,071	3,249	Clinton	15.9%	62.2%	13.4%	8.6%
BURLINGTON	21,896	5,186	12,110	1,861	2,739	Clinton	23.7%	55.3%	8.5%	12.5%
CAMDEN	26,595	6,658	15,595	2,691	1,651	Clinton	25.0%	58.6%	10.1%	6.2%
CAPE MAY	3,844	825	2,158	492	369	Clinton	21.5%	56.1%	12.8%	9.6%
CUMBERLAND	4,978	807	3,176	583	412	Clinton	16.2%	63.8%	11.7%	8.3%
ESSEX	50,951	7,555	36,949	5,222	1,225	Clinton	14.8%	72.5%	10.2%	2.4%
GLOUCESTER	12,794	2,801	8,283	1,317	393	Clinton	21.9%	64.7%	10.3%	3.1%
HUDSON	46,917	10,538	30,640	4,556	1,183	Clinton	22.5%	65.3%	9.7%	2.5%
HUNTERDON	3,328	828	1,625	562	313	Clinton	24.9%	48.8%	16.9%	9.4%
MERCER	15,428	2,677	9,003	2,164	1,584	Clinton	17.4%	58.4%	14.0%	10.3%
MIDDLESEX	38,016	10,037	22,772	3,013	2,194	Clinton	26.4%	59.9%	7.9%	5.8%
MONMOUTH	26,281	6,170	14,677	4,165	1,269	Clinton	23.5%	55.8%	15.8%	4.8%
MORRIS	14,016	3,152	7,145	2,519	1,200	Clinton	22.5%	51.0%	18.0%	8.6%
OCEAN	17,518	2,597	11,891	1,109	1,921	Clinton	14.8%	67.9%	6.3%	11.0%
PASSAIC	18,278	3,359	11,111	2,439	1,369	Clinton	18.4%	60.8%	13.3%	7.5%
SALEM	2,090	288	1,297	270	235	Clinton	13.8%	62.1%	12.9%	11.2%
SOMERSET	8,213	1,664	4,925	1,183	441	Clinton	20.3%	60.0%	14.4%	5.4%
SUSSEX	2,810	918	1,294	512	86	Clinton	32.7%	46.0%	18.2%	3.1%
UNION	29,379	5,272	18,461	3,978	1,668	Clinton	17.9%	62.8%	13.5%	5.7%
WARREN	3,106	824	1,800	395	87	Clinton	26.5%	58.0%	12.7%	2.8%
TOTAL	392,626	79,877	243,741	45,191	23,817	Clinton	20.3%	62.1%	11.5%	6.1%

NEW JERSEY REPUBLICAN

1992

County	Total Vote	Buchanan	Bush	Perot	Winner	Percentage of Total Vote Buchanan	Bush	Perot
ATLANTIC	8,128	1,715	6,413		Bush	21.1%	78.9%	
BERGEN	34,973	5,443	26,737	2,793	Bush	15.6%	76.5%	8.0%
BURLINGTON	21,533	3,583	15,495	2,455	Bush	16.6%	72.0%	11.4%
CAMDEN	11,057	1,849	8,574	634	Bush	16.7%	77.5%	5.7%
CAPE MAY	8,550	1,642	6,610	298	Bush	19.2%	77.3%	3.5%
CUMBERLAND	4,359	670	3,327	362	Bush	15.4%	76.3%	8.3%
ESSEX	19,416	2,417	15,620	1,379	Bush	12.4%	80.4%	7.1%
GLOUCESTER	9,045	1,172	5,899	1,974	Bush	13.0%	65.2%	21.8%
HUDSON	9,747	1,744	8,003		Bush	17.9%	82.1%	
HUNTERDON	9,562	1,222	7,180	1,160	Bush	12.8%	75.1%	12.1%
MERCER	7,339	990	5,733	616	Bush	13.5%	78.1%	8.4%
MIDDLESEX	15,831	2,275	12,430	1,126	Bush	14.4%	78.5%	7.1%
MONMOUTH	22,565	2,799	17,833	1,933	Bush	12.4%	79.0%	8.6%
MORRIS	37,173	6,262	28,935	1,976	Bush	16.8%	77.8%	5.3%
OCEAN	25,685	3,578	20,062	2,045	Bush	13.9%	78.1%	8.0%
PASSAIC	16,231	2,631	13,329	271	Bush	16.2%	82.1%	1.7%
SALEM	1,851	307	1,418	126	Bush	16.6%	76.6%	6.8%
SOMERSET	11,859	1,627	9,898	334	Bush	13.7%	83.5%	2.8%
SUSSEX	12,219	1,453	8,626	2,140	Bush	11.9%	70.6%	17.5%
UNION	15,906	2,089	13,538	279	Bush	13.1%	85.1%	1.8%
WARREN	7,241	964	4,875	1,402	Bush	13.3%	67.3%	19.4%
TOTAL	310,270	46,432	240,535	23,303	Bush	15.0%	77.5%	7.5%

NEW JERSEY DEMOCRATIC

1996

County	Total Vote	Clinton	LaRouche	Winner	Percentage of Total Vote: Clinton	Percentage of Total Vote: LaRouche
ATLANTIC	4,734	4,524	210	Clinton	95.6%	4.4%
BERGEN	21,754	20,972	782	Clinton	96.4%	3.6%
BURLINGTON	13,547	12,898	649	Clinton	95.2%	4.8%
CAMDEN	16,431	15,629	802	Clinton	95.1%	4.9%
CAPE MAY	2,764	2,583	181	Clinton	93.5%	6.5%
CUMBERLAND	3,570	3,349	221	Clinton	93.8%	6.2%
ESSEX	42,647	40,287	2,360	Clinton	94.5%	5.5%
GLOUCESTER	10,277	9,435	842	Clinton	91.8%	8.2%
HUDSON	38,251	36,579	1,672	Clinton	95.6%	4.4%
HUNTERDON	2,346	2,232	114	Clinton	95.1%	4.9%
MERCER	13,718	13,217	501	Clinton	96.3%	3.7%
MIDDLESEX	19,677	18,776	901	Clinton	95.4%	4.6%
MONMOUTH	13,241	12,506	735	Clinton	94.4%	5.6%
MORRIS	7,265	6,886	379	Clinton	94.8%	5.2%
OCEAN	10,588	10,193	395	Clinton	96.3%	3.7%
PASSAIC	11,057	10,533	524	Clinton	95.3%	4.7%
SALEM	1,923	1,765	158	Clinton	91.8%	8.2%
SOMERSET	3,995	3,830	165	Clinton	95.9%	4.1%
SUSSEX	1,557	1,432	125	Clinton	92.0%	8.0%
UNION	25,536	24,655	881	Clinton	96.5%	3.5%
WARREN	1,862	1,723	139	Clinton	92.5%	7.5%
TOTAL	266,740	254,004	12,736	Clinton	95.2%	4.8%

NEW JERSEY REPUBLICAN

1996

County	Total Vote	Buchanan	Dole	Keyes	Winner	Percentage of Total Vote Buchanan	Dole	Keyes
ATLANTIC	7,906	1,145	6,308	453	Dole	14.5%	79.8%	5.7%
BERGEN	20,708	2,195	17,405	1,108	Dole	10.6%	84.0%	5.4%
BURLINGTON	14,927	1,427	12,658	842	Dole	9.6%	84.8%	5.6%
CAMDEN	6,766	954	5,150	662	Dole	14.1%	76.1%	9.8%
CAPE MAY	8,047	909	6,766	372	Dole	11.3%	84.1%	4.6%
CUMBERLAND	3,670	507	2,948	215	Dole	13.8%	80.3%	5.9%
ESSEX	11,070	1,035	9,487	548	Dole	9.3%	85.7%	5.0%
GLOUCESTER	7,869	1,405	5,708	756	Dole	17.9%	72.5%	9.6%
HUDSON	7,375	1,097	5,235	1,043	Dole	14.9%	71.0%	14.1%
HUNTERDON	7,983	708	6,679	596	Dole	8.9%	83.7%	7.5%
MERCER	7,135	672	5,917	546	Dole	9.4%	82.9%	7.7%
MIDDLESEX	9,721	1,219	7,845	657	Dole	12.5%	80.7%	6.8%
MONMOUTH	18,217	1,715	15,344	1,158	Dole	9.4%	84.2%	6.4%
MORRIS	24,026	1,920	20,444	1,662	Dole	8.0%	85.1%	6.9%
OCEAN	17,762	1,945	15,161	656	Dole	11.0%	85.4%	3.7%
PASSAIC	9,893	909	8,372	612	Dole	9.2%	84.6%	6.2%
SALEM	1,632	223	1,280	129	Dole	13.7%	78.4%	7.9%
SOMERSET	9,179	862	7,502	815	Dole	9.4%	81.7%	8.9%
SUSSEX	8,000	1,235	6,133	632	Dole	15.4%	76.7%	7.9%
UNION	11,685	991	9,952	742	Dole	8.5%	85.2%	6.4%
WARREN	5,241	716	4,118	407	Dole	13.7%	78.6%	7.8%
TOTAL	218,812	23,789	180,412	14,611	Dole	10.9%	82.5%	6.7%

NEW MEXICO

New Mexico is different than other states in the Mountain West in the degree to which minorities affect its demographics. The state is nearly 40 percent Hispanic and almost 10 percent Native American, so that anyone who wants to win comfortably, especially in the Democratic primary, must be able to bridge the gap between non-Hispanic whites and minorities.

Clinton was able to do so in 1992, carrying every county, from those of Hispanic northern New Mexico to conservative, overwhelmingly non-Hispanic "Little Texas" in the southeast part of the state. New Mexico was the only Western state where he captured a majority of the primary vote.

Michael Dukakis also ran well in both parts of New Mexico in the 1988 Democratic primary. Jesse Jackson carried McKinley County (Gallup), the lone Native American-majority county in New Mexico, but Jackson's limited appeal to the Hispanic vote was apparent in his failure to win any of the Hispanic-majority counties. Jackson came fairly close in a few, such as Taos County, which has a large artists' colony and a more liberal bent. But in others, he was beaten soundly by Dukakis, whose ability to speak fluent Spanish was widely publicized.

But in some of the earlier Democratic primaries, there were racial fault lines. In the state's first presidential primary in 1972, "Little Texas" went for George Wallace, enabling him to finish within 5 percentage points of statewide winner George McGovern. In 1980, the region voted virtually en masse for President Jimmy Carter, as he nearly offset the large lead that Edward Kennedy built up in Bernalillo County (Albuquerque), Santa Fe and heavily Catholic Hispanic counties to the north.

New Mexico Republicans have not had much luck with their presidential primary. It was created just in time to elect the only delegate to vote against the renomination of President Richard Nixon. (The delegate went to GOP Rep. Paul McCloskey of California, who mounted a quixotic antiwar challenge to Nixon in the 1972 primaries.)

The primary was abandoned in 1976, just in time to miss the party's hottest nominating battle of the last quarter century. Since its revival in 1980, the state has seen a succession of GOP contests that were decided long before New Mexico voted in June.

When New Mexico Republicans have put together their delegation through the caucus process, it has tended to mirror the conservatism of their GOP counterparts in other Rocky Mountain states. The delegation voted as a bloc for Barry Goldwater in 1964 and Ronald Reagan in 1976.

Recent New Mexico Primary Results

New Mexico held its first presidential primary in 1972.

	DEMOCRATS			REPUBLICANS		
Year	Turnout	Candidates	%	Turnout	Candidates	%
1996 (June 4)	121,362	BILL CLINTON*	90	70,464	BOB DOLE	76
1992 (June 2)	181,443	BILL CLINTON	53	86,967	GEORGE BUSH*	64
		Uncommitted	19		Uncommitted	27
		Jerry Brown	17			
1988 (June 7)	188,610	MICHAEL DUKAKIS	61	88,744	GEORGE BUSH	78
		Jesse Jackson	28		Bob Dole	10
1984 (June 5)	187,403	GARY HART	47	42,994	RONALD REAGAN*	95
		Walter Mondale	36			
		Jesse Jackson	12			
1980 (June 3)	159,364	EDWARD KENNEDY	46	59,546	RONALD REAGAN	64
		Jimmy Carter*	42		John Anderson	12
1976	—	NO PRIMARY		—	NO PRIMARY	
1972 (June 6)	153,293	GEORGE McGOVERN	33	55,469	RICHARD NIXON*	88
		George Wallace	29			
		Hubert Humphrey	26			

Note: All candidates are listed that drew at least 10 percent of their party's primary vote. The names of winning candidates are capitalized. An asterisk (*) indicates an incumbent president.

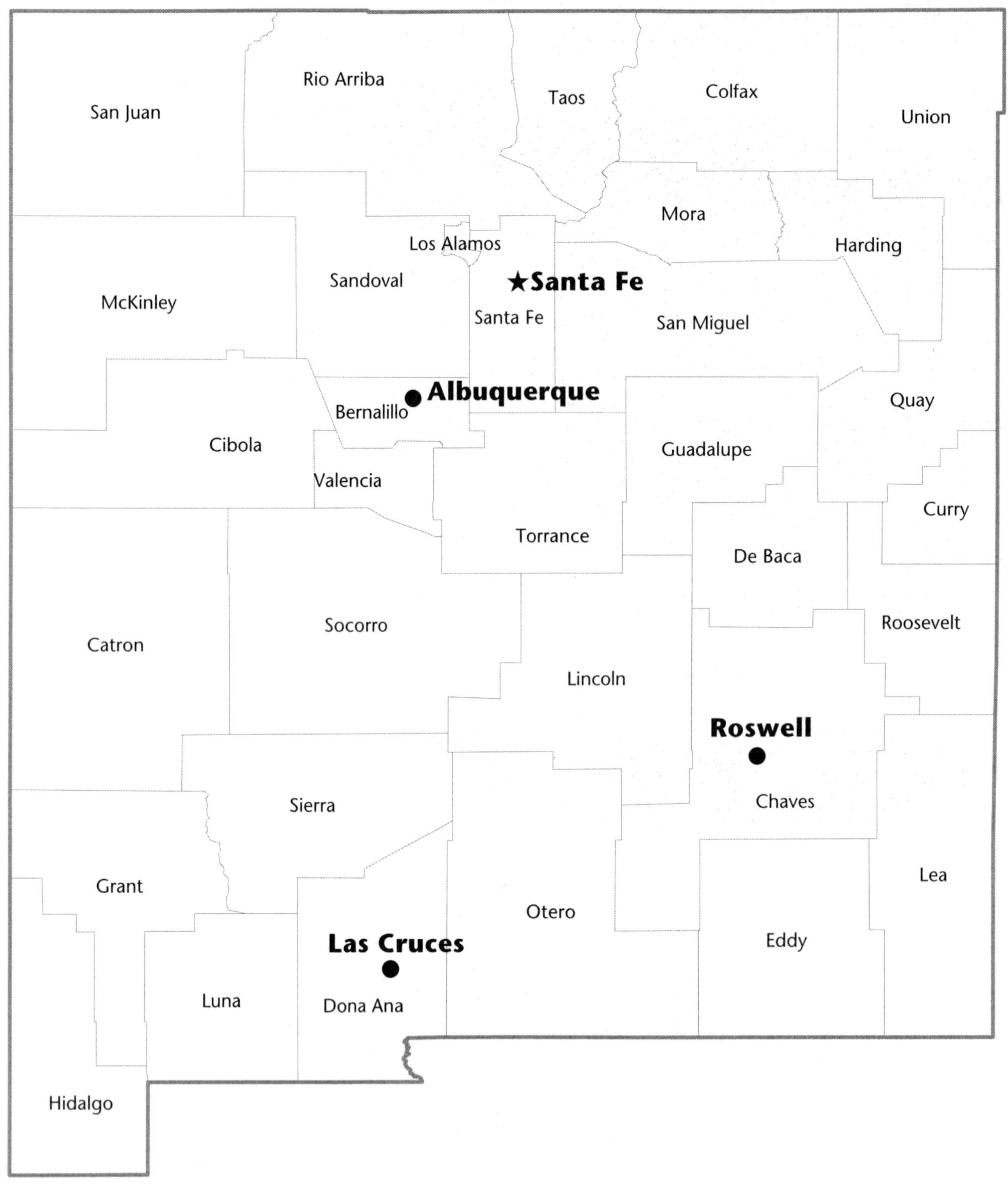
San Juan
Rio Arriba
Taos
Colfax
Union
Mora
Harding
Los Alamos
Sandoval
McKinley
★Santa Fe
Santa Fe
San Miguel
Albuquerque
Bernalillo
Cibola
Quay
Guadalupe
Valencia
Curry
Torrance
De Baca
Socorro
Roosevelt
Catron
Lincoln
Roswell
Chaves
Sierra
Lea
Grant
Otero
Eddy
Las Cruces
Dona Ana
Luna
Hidalgo

NEW MEXICO DEMOCRATIC

1972

County	Total Vote	Humphrey	McGovern	Wallace	Other	Winner	Percentage of Total Vote Humphrey	McGovern	Wallace	Other
BERNALILLO	42,729	11,269	17,855	8,957	4,648	McGovern	26.4%	41.8%	21.0%	10.9%
CATRON	373	83	60	175	55	Wallace	22.3%	16.1%	46.9%	14.7%
CHAVES	4,388	965	864	1,882	677	Wallace	22.0%	19.7%	42.9%	15.4%
COLFAX	2,113	627	700	551	235	McGovern	29.7%	33.1%	26.1%	11.1%
CURRY	5,249	923	791	2,876	659	Wallace	17.6%	15.1%	54.8%	12.6%
DE BACA	647	127	114	279	127	Wallace	19.6%	17.6%	43.1%	19.6%
DONA ANA	8,991	2,266	3,536	2,191	998	McGovern	25.2%	39.3%	24.4%	11.1%
EDDY	7,026	2,244	1,087	2,663	1,032	Wallace	31.9%	15.5%	37.9%	14.7%
GRANT	5,695	1,690	1,570	1,709	726	Wallace	29.7%	27.6%	30.0%	12.7%
GUADALUPE	1,372	342	713	191	126	McGovern	24.9%	52.0%	13.9%	9.2%
HARDING	236	48	56	82	50	Wallace	20.3%	23.7%	34.7%	21.2%
HIDALGO	1,181	382	185	489	125	Wallace	32.3%	15.7%	41.4%	10.6%
LEA	9,186	1,733	1,120	4,851	1,482	Wallace	18.9%	12.2%	52.8%	16.1%
LINCOLN	1,060	191	244	495	130	Wallace	18.0%	23.0%	46.7%	12.3%
LOS ALAMOS	2,949	811	1,053	660	425	McGovern	27.5%	35.7%	22.4%	14.4%
LUNA	2,124	493	456	900	275	Wallace	23.2%	21.5%	42.4%	12.9%
MCKINLEY	4,883	1,306	1,341	1,670	566	Wallace	26.7%	27.5%	34.2%	11.6%
MORA	811	312	404	68	27	McGovern	38.5%	49.8%	8.4%	3.3%
OTERO	4,518	1,316	807	1,786	609	Wallace	29.1%	17.9%	39.5%	13.5%
QUAY	2,679	509	411	1,407	352	Wallace	19.0%	15.3%	52.5%	13.1%
RIO ARRIBA	5,835	2,147	2,628	721	339	McGovern	36.8%	45.0%	12.4%	5.8%
ROOSEVELT	3,169	419	519	1,849	382	Wallace	13.2%	16.4%	58.3%	12.1%
SANDOVAL	3,157	903	1,411	579	264	McGovern	28.6%	44.7%	18.3%	8.4%
SAN JUAN	3,872	912	764	1,749	447	Wallace	23.6%	19.7%	45.2%	11.5%
SAN MIGUEL	3,760	1,044	2,017	462	237	McGovern	27.8%	53.6%	12.3%	6.3%
SANTA FE	10,791	2,691	5,207	1,454	1,439	McGovern	24.9%	48.3%	13.5%	13.3%
SIERRA	1,039	240	236	470	93	Wallace	23.1%	22.7%	45.2%	9.0%
SOCORRO	1,607	500	615	384	108	McGovern	31.1%	38.3%	23.9%	6.7%
TAOS	3,361	1,040	1,667	379	275	McGovern	30.9%	49.6%	11.3%	8.2%
TORRANCE	1,083	274	287	429	93	Wallace	25.3%	26.5%	39.6%	8.6%
UNION	999	235	161	432	171	Wallace	23.5%	16.1%	43.2%	17.1%
VALENCIA	6,410	1,726	2,132	2,053	499	McGovern	26.9%	33.3%	32.0%	7.8%
TOTAL	153,293	39,768	51,011	44,843	17,671	McGovern	25.9%	33.3%	29.3%	11.5%

NEW MEXICO REPUBLICAN

1972

County	Total Vote	Nixon	Other	Winner	Percentage of Total Vote Nixon	Other
BERNALILLO	24,071	21,419	2,652	Nixon	89.0%	11.0%
CATRON	267	229	38	Nixon	85.8%	14.2%
CHAVES	2,114	1,926	188	Nixon	91.1%	8.9%
COLFAX	582	509	73	Nixon	87.5%	12.5%
CURRY	1,010	906	104	Nixon	89.7%	10.3%
DE BACA	69	61	8	Nixon	88.4%	11.6%
DONA ANA	2,641	2,357	284	Nixon	89.2%	10.8%
EDDY	1,058	968	90	Nixon	91.5%	8.5%
GRANT	752	675	77	Nixon	89.8%	10.2%
GUADALUPE	302	275	27	Nixon	91.1%	8.9%
HARDING	119	111	8	Nixon	93.3%	6.7%
HIDALGO	133	121	12	Nixon	91.0%	9.0%
LEA	1,556	1,448	108	Nixon	93.1%	6.9%
LINCOLN	758	659	99	Nixon	86.9%	13.1%
LOS ALAMOS	1,804	1,570	234	Nixon	87.0%	13.0%
LUNA	605	548	57	Nixon	90.6%	9.4%
MCKINLEY	1,180	924	256	Nixon	78.3%	21.7%
MORA	451	413	38	Nixon	91.6%	8.4%
OTERO	1,079	916	163	Nixon	84.9%	15.1%
QUAY	536	492	44	Nixon	91.8%	8.2%
RIO ARRIBA	1,077	925	152	Nixon	85.9%	14.1%
ROOSEVELT	488	428	60	Nixon	87.7%	12.3%
SANDOVAL	773	692	81	Nixon	89.5%	10.5%
SAN JUAN	2,950	2,511	439	Nixon	85.1%	14.9%
SAN MIGUEL	987	829	158	Nixon	84.0%	16.0%
SANTA FE	3,033	2,656	377	Nixon	87.6%	12.4%
SIERRA	483	427	56	Nixon	88.4%	11.6%
SOCORRO	676	567	109	Nixon	83.9%	16.1%
TAOS	1,190	1,060	130	Nixon	89.1%	10.9%
TORRANCE	516	470	46	Nixon	91.1%	8.9%
UNION	244	211	33	Nixon	86.5%	13.5%
VALENCIA	1,965	1,764	201	Nixon	89.8%	10.2%
TOTAL	55,469	49,067	6,402	Nixon	88.5%	11.5%

NEW MEXICO DEMOCRATIC

1980

County	Total Vote	Carter	E. Kennedy	Other	Winner	Percentage of Total Vote Carter	E. Kennedy	Other
BERNALILLO	41,277	15,330	21,197	4,750	E. Kennedy	37.1%	51.4%	11.5%
CATRON	598	339	183	76	Carter	56.7%	30.6%	12.7%
CHAVES	4,757	2,558	1,422	777	Carter	53.8%	29.9%	16.3%
COLFAX	2,402	1,125	990	287	Carter	46.8%	41.2%	11.9%
CURRY	4,474	2,661	1,091	722	Carter	59.5%	24.4%	16.1%
DE BACA	629	381	166	82	Carter	60.6%	26.4%	13.0%
DONA ANA	10,762	4,708	4,690	1,364	Carter	43.7%	43.6%	12.7%
EDDY	7,894	4,526	2,323	1,045	Carter	57.3%	29.4%	13.2%
GRANT	5,349	2,418	2,466	465	E. Kennedy	45.2%	46.1%	8.7%
GUADALUPE	1,385	367	898	120	E. Kennedy	26.5%	64.8%	8.7%
HARDING	199	99	76	24	Carter	49.7%	38.2%	12.1%
HIDALGO	1,410	726	559	125	Carter	51.5%	39.6%	8.9%
LEA	5,545	3,651	999	895	Carter	65.8%	18.0%	16.1%
LINCOLN	1,117	639	340	138	Carter	57.2%	30.4%	12.4%
LOS ALAMOS	2,336	1,199	720	417	Carter	51.3%	30.8%	17.9%
LUNA	2,722	1,422	957	343	Carter	52.2%	35.2%	12.6%
MCKINLEY	5,537	1,821	3,121	595	E. Kennedy	32.9%	56.4%	10.7%
MORA	1,282	351	808	123	E. Kennedy	27.4%	63.0%	9.6%
OTERO	4,324	2,181	1,517	626	Carter	50.4%	35.1%	14.5%
QUAY	1,465	832	455	178	Carter	56.8%	31.1%	12.2%
RIO ARRIBA	6,300	1,157	4,592	551	E. Kennedy	18.4%	72.9%	8.7%
ROOSEVELT	2,635	1,718	591	326	Carter	65.2%	22.4%	12.4%
SANDOVAL	5,290	1,726	3,000	564	E. Kennedy	32.6%	56.7%	10.7%
SAN JUAN	5,324	2,738	1,846	740	Carter	51.4%	34.7%	13.9%
SAN MIGUEL	4,650	1,175	2,967	508	E. Kennedy	25.3%	63.8%	10.9%
SANTA FE	12,776	4,292	7,100	1,384	E. Kennedy	33.6%	55.6%	10.8%
SIERRA	1,158	657	377	124	Carter	56.7%	32.6%	10.7%
SOCORRO	1,997	730	1,055	212	E. Kennedy	36.6%	52.8%	10.6%
TAOS	4,935	1,410	3,067	458	E. Kennedy	28.6%	62.1%	9.3%
TORRANCE	1,527	755	606	166	Carter	49.4%	39.7%	10.9%
UNION	678	401	181	96	Carter	59.1%	26.7%	14.2%
VALENCIA	6,630	2,528	3,361	741	E. Kennedy	38.1%	50.7%	11.2%
TOTAL	159,364	66,621	73,721	19,022	E. Kennedy	41.8%	46.3%	11.9%

NEW MEXICO REPUBLICAN

1980

County	Total Vote	Anderson	Reagan	Other	Winner	Percentage of Total Vote Anderson	Reagan	Other
BERNALILLO	23,373	3,679	14,241	5,453	Reagan	15.7%	60.9%	23.3%
CATRON	283	15	220	48	Reagan	5.3%	77.7%	17.0%
CHAVES	3,421	227	2,708	486	Reagan	6.6%	79.2%	14.2%
COLFAX	554	38	352	164	Reagan	6.9%	63.5%	29.6%
CURRY	1,347	70	981	296	Reagan	5.2%	72.8%	22.0%
DE BACA	62	2	49	11	Reagan	3.2%	79.0%	17.7%
DONA ANA	3,287	397	2,106	784	Reagan	12.1%	64.1%	23.9%
EDDY	1,130	63	901	166	Reagan	5.6%	79.7%	14.7%
GRANT	916	106	613	197	Reagan	11.6%	66.9%	21.5%
GUADALUPE	233	10	144	79	Reagan	4.3%	61.8%	33.9%
HARDING	150	9	87	54	Reagan	6.0%	58.0%	36.0%
HIDALGO	134	10	97	27	Reagan	7.5%	72.4%	20.1%
LEA	1,599	57	1,280	262	Reagan	3.6%	80.1%	16.4%
LINCOLN	968	59	691	218	Reagan	6.1%	71.4%	22.5%
LOS ALAMOS	1,745	344	972	429	Reagan	19.7%	55.7%	24.6%
LUNA	853	47	651	155	Reagan	5.5%	76.3%	18.2%
MCKINLEY	1,509	171	823	515	Reagan	11.3%	54.5%	34.1%
MORA	348	21	200	127	Reagan	6.0%	57.5%	36.5%
OTERO	1,098	92	660	346	Reagan	8.4%	60.1%	31.5%
QUAY	263	10	188	65	Reagan	3.8%	71.5%	24.7%
RIO ARRIBA	739	53	394	292	Reagan	7.2%	53.3%	39.5%
ROOSEVELT	694	47	483	164	Reagan	6.8%	69.6%	23.6%
SANDOVAL	1,928	230	1,248	450	Reagan	11.9%	64.7%	23.3%
SAN JUAN	3,147	232	2,040	875	Reagan	7.4%	64.8%	27.8%
SAN MIGUEL	725	65	412	248	Reagan	9.0%	56.8%	34.2%
SANTA FE	3,048	554	1,716	778	Reagan	18.2%	56.3%	25.5%
SIERRA	633	55	453	125	Reagan	8.7%	71.6%	19.7%
SOCORRO	862	116	454	292	Reagan	13.5%	52.7%	33.9%
TAOS	1,152	120	656	376	Reagan	10.4%	56.9%	32.6%
TORRANCE	619	36	448	135	Reagan	5.8%	72.4%	21.8%
UNION	248	8	167	73	Reagan	3.2%	67.3%	29.4%
VALENCIA	2,478	228	1,547	703	Reagan	9.2%	62.4%	28.4%
TOTAL	59,546	7,171	37,982	14,393	Reagan	12.0%	63.8%	24.2%

NEW MEXICO DEMOCRATIC

1984

County	Total Vote	Hart	J. Jackson	Mondale	Other	Winner	Percentage of Total Vote Hart	J. Jackson	Mondale	Other
BERNALILLO	48,199	22,444	6,741	16,870	2,144	Hart	46.6%	14.0%	35.0%	4.4%
CATRON	737	428	65	201	43	Hart	58.1%	8.8%	27.3%	5.8%
CHAVES	3,965	1,784	426	1,459	296	Hart	45.0%	10.7%	36.8%	7.5%
CIBOLA	3,272	1,365	303	1,410	194	Mondale	41.7%	9.3%	43.1%	5.9%
COLFAX	3,126	1,677	209	1,102	138	Hart	53.6%	6.7%	35.3%	4.4%
CURRY	5,462	2,893	399	1,791	379	Hart	53.0%	7.3%	32.8%	6.9%
DE BACA	718	425	37	218	38	Hart	59.2%	5.2%	30.4%	5.3%
DONA ANA	11,898	5,883	970	4,357	688	Hart	49.4%	8.2%	36.6%	5.8%
EDDY	8,878	3,574	845	3,862	597	Mondale	40.3%	9.5%	43.5%	6.7%
GRANT	5,947	2,529	513	2,591	314	Mondale	42.5%	8.6%	43.6%	5.3%
GUADALUPE	1,456	658	143	579	76	Hart	45.2%	9.8%	39.8%	5.2%
HARDING	228	109	14	89	16	Hart	47.8%	6.1%	39.0%	7.0%
HIDALGO	1,531	745	124	584	78	Hart	48.7%	8.1%	38.1%	5.1%
LEA	6,877	3,431	1,050	1,928	468	Hart	49.9%	15.3%	28.0%	6.8%
LINCOLN	1,379	790	107	384	98	Hart	57.3%	7.8%	27.8%	7.1%
LOS ALAMOS	2,599	1,410	259	773	157	Hart	54.3%	10.0%	29.7%	6.0%
LUNA	2,754	1,330	196	1,005	223	Hart	48.3%	7.1%	36.5%	8.1%
MCKINLEY	6,756	2,902	1,008	2,413	433	Hart	43.0%	14.9%	35.7%	6.4%
MORA	1,439	734	113	545	47	Hart	51.0%	7.9%	37.9%	3.3%
OTERO	4,943	2,646	375	1,630	292	Hart	53.5%	7.6%	33.0%	5.9%
QUAY	1,859	993	120	604	142	Hart	53.4%	6.5%	32.5%	7.6%
RIO ARRIBA	6,795	2,091	842	3,660	202	Mondale	30.8%	12.4%	53.9%	3.0%
ROOSEVELT	2,305	1,285	125	736	159	Hart	55.7%	5.4%	31.9%	6.9%
SANDOVAL	6,341	2,761	895	2,367	318	Hart	43.5%	14.1%	37.3%	5.0%
SAN JUAN	6,743	2,975	925	2,346	497	Hart	44.1%	13.7%	34.8%	7.4%
SAN MIGUEL	5,793	2,717	563	2,268	245	Hart	46.9%	9.7%	39.2%	4.2%
SANTA FE	17,380	8,511	2,943	5,239	687	Hart	49.0%	16.9%	30.1%	4.0%
SIERRA	1,477	778	93	504	102	Hart	52.7%	6.3%	34.1%	6.9%
SOCORRO	2,460	1,040	313	961	146	Hart	42.3%	12.7%	39.1%	5.9%
TAOS	5,118	2,413	674	1,845	186	Hart	47.1%	13.2%	36.0%	3.6%
TORRANCE	1,654	837	142	566	109	Hart	50.6%	8.6%	34.2%	6.6%
UNION	952	554	46	279	73	Hart	58.2%	4.8%	29.3%	7.7%
VALENCIA	6,362	2,898	590	2,509	365	Hart	45.6%	9.3%	39.4%	5.7%
TOTAL	187,403	87,610	22,168	67,675	9,950	Hart	46.7%	11.8%	36.1%	5.3%

NEW MEXICO REPUBLICAN

1984

County	Total Vote	Reagan	Uncommitted	Winner	Percentage of Total Vote	
					Reagan	Uncom.
BERNALILLO	14,670	13,917	753	Reagan	94.9%	5.1%
CATRON	176	168	8	Reagan	95.5%	4.5%
CHAVES	1,726	1,680	46	Reagan	97.3%	2.7%
CIBOLA	588	541	47	Reagan	92.0%	8.0%
COLFAX	489	470	19	Reagan	96.1%	3.9%
CURRY	1,328	1,298	30	Reagan	97.7%	2.3%
DE BACA	56	56		Reagan	100.0%	
DONA ANA	2,442	2,269	173	Reagan	92.9%	7.1%
EDDY	1,216	1,181	35	Reagan	97.1%	2.9%
GRANT	552	519	33	Reagan	94.0%	6.0%
GUADALUPE	116	110	6	Reagan	94.8%	5.2%
HARDING	126	123	3	Reagan	97.6%	2.4%
HIDALGO	155	148	7	Reagan	95.5%	4.5%
LEA	1,277	1,237	40	Reagan	96.9%	3.1%
LINCOLN	898	869	29	Reagan	96.8%	3.2%
LOS ALAMOS	1,031	969	62	Reagan	94.0%	6.0%
LUNA	705	676	29	Reagan	95.9%	4.1%
MCKINLEY	969	882	87	Reagan	91.0%	9.0%
MORA	209	186	23	Reagan	89.0%	11.0%
OTERO	1,213	1,170	43	Reagan	96.5%	3.5%
QUAY	284	278	6	Reagan	97.9%	2.1%
RIO ARRIBA	615	575	40	Reagan	93.5%	6.5%
ROOSEVELT	502	482	20	Reagan	96.0%	4.0%
SANDOVAL	1,684	1,592	92	Reagan	94.5%	5.5%
SAN JUAN	3,373	3,211	162	Reagan	95.2%	4.8%
SAN MIGUEL	606	561	45	Reagan	92.6%	7.4%
SANTA FE	1,863	1,736	127	Reagan	93.2%	6.8%
SIERRA	552	526	26	Reagan	95.3%	4.7%
SOCORRO	832	776	56	Reagan	93.3%	6.7%
TAOS	701	655	46	Reagan	93.4%	6.6%
TORRANCE	554	535	19	Reagan	96.6%	3.4%
UNION	172	166	6	Reagan	96.5%	3.5%
VALENCIA	1,314	1,243	71	Reagan	94.6%	5.4%
TOTAL	42,994	40,805	2,189	Reagan	94.9%	5.1%

NEW MEXICO DEMOCRATIC

1988

County	Total Vote	Dukakis	J. Jackson	Other	Winner	Percentage of Total Vote: Dukakis	J. Jackson	Other
BERNALILLO	52,951	32,891	16,382	3,678	Dukakis	62.1%	30.9%	6.9%
CATRON	681	410	114	157	Dukakis	60.2%	16.7%	23.1%
CHAVES	4,398	2,891	871	636	Dukakis	65.7%	19.8%	14.5%
CIBOLA	3,229	1,869	1,002	358	Dukakis	57.9%	31.0%	11.1%
COLFAX	2,760	1,894	544	322	Dukakis	68.6%	19.7%	11.7%
CURRY	4,459	3,123	590	746	Dukakis	70.0%	13.2%	16.7%
DE BACA	856	509	141	206	Dukakis	59.5%	16.5%	24.1%
DONA ANA	11,377	7,467	2,436	1,474	Dukakis	65.6%	21.4%	13.0%
EDDY	8,010	5,452	1,467	1,091	Dukakis	68.1%	18.3%	13.6%
GRANT	5,237	3,573	1,138	526	Dukakis	68.2%	21.7%	10.0%
GUADALUPE	1,371	745	377	249	Dukakis	54.3%	27.5%	18.2%
HARDING	286	204	46	36	Dukakis	71.3%	16.1%	12.6%
HIDALGO	1,187	705	229	253	Dukakis	59.4%	19.3%	21.3%
LEA	5,599	3,808	1,017	774	Dukakis	68.0%	18.2%	13.8%
LINCOLN	1,495	1,028	185	282	Dukakis	68.8%	12.4%	18.9%
LOS ALAMOS	2,399	1,646	464	289	Dukakis	68.6%	19.3%	12.0%
LUNA	2,566	1,780	479	307	Dukakis	69.4%	18.7%	12.0%
MCKINLEY	7,837	3,192	3,332	1,313	J. Jackson	40.7%	42.5%	16.8%
MORA	1,366	749	450	167	Dukakis	54.8%	32.9%	12.2%
OTERO	5,116	3,278	1,032	806	Dukakis	64.1%	20.2%	15.8%
QUAY	2,565	1,804	400	361	Dukakis	70.3%	15.6%	14.1%
RIO ARRIBA	6,517	4,002	1,875	640	Dukakis	61.4%	28.8%	9.8%
ROOSEVELT	1,931	1,314	295	322	Dukakis	68.0%	15.3%	16.7%
SANDOVAL	6,836	3,790	2,407	639	Dukakis	55.4%	35.2%	9.3%
SAN JUAN	6,463	3,770	1,798	895	Dukakis	58.3%	27.8%	13.8%
SAN MIGUEL	5,935	2,928	2,371	636	Dukakis	49.3%	39.9%	10.7%
SANTA FE	17,670	9,536	6,799	1,335	Dukakis	54.0%	38.5%	7.6%
SIERRA	1,455	1,058	177	220	Dukakis	72.7%	12.2%	15.1%
SOCORRO	2,252	1,341	611	300	Dukakis	59.5%	27.1%	13.3%
TAOS	5,411	2,623	2,098	690	Dukakis	48.5%	38.8%	12.8%
TORRANCE	1,609	1,065	352	192	Dukakis	66.2%	21.9%	11.9%
UNION	884	663	103	118	Dukakis	75.0%	11.7%	13.3%
VALENCIA	5,902	3,860	1,406	636	Dukakis	65.4%	23.8%	10.8%
TOTAL	188,610	114,968	52,988	20,654	Dukakis	61.0%	28.1%	11.0%

NEW MEXICO REPUBLICAN

1988

County	Total Vote	Bush	Dole	Other	Winner	Percentage of Total Vote Bush	Dole	Other
BERNALILLO	35,938	28,907	3,712	3,319	Bush	80.4%	10.3%	9.2%
CATRON	506	376	55	75	Bush	74.3%	10.9%	14.8%
CHAVES	4,456	3,567	414	475	Bush	80.0%	9.3%	10.7%
CIBOLA	828	674	68	86	Bush	81.4%	8.2%	10.4%
COLFAX	656	462	74	120	Bush	70.4%	11.3%	18.3%
CURRY	1,723	1,377	123	223	Bush	79.9%	7.1%	12.9%
DE BACA	117	96	10	11	Bush	82.1%	8.5%	9.4%
DONA ANA	5,502	4,234	592	676	Bush	77.0%	10.8%	12.3%
EDDY	1,954	1,505	167	282	Bush	77.0%	8.5%	14.4%
GRANT	982	762	139	81	Bush	77.6%	14.2%	8.2%
GUADALUPE	275	223	31	21	Bush	81.1%	11.3%	7.6%
HARDING	221	174	24	23	Bush	78.7%	10.9%	10.4%
HIDALGO	240	188	27	25	Bush	78.3%	11.3%	10.4%
LEA	2,857	2,331	303	223	Bush	81.6%	10.6%	7.8%
LINCOLN	1,667	1,321	139	207	Bush	79.2%	8.3%	12.4%
LOS ALAMOS	2,174	1,656	306	212	Bush	76.2%	14.1%	9.8%
LUNA	1,109	832	121	156	Bush	75.0%	10.9%	14.1%
MCKINLEY	1,666	1,083	213	370	Bush	65.0%	12.8%	22.2%
MORA	489	325	59	105	Bush	66.5%	12.1%	21.5%
OTERO	2,658	1,942	284	432	Bush	73.1%	10.7%	16.3%
QUAY	490	353	52	85	Bush	72.0%	10.6%	17.3%
RIO ARRIBA	782	542	79	161	Bush	69.3%	10.1%	20.6%
ROOSEVELT	708	550	72	86	Bush	77.7%	10.2%	12.1%
SANDOVAL	3,192	2,541	305	346	Bush	79.6%	9.6%	10.8%
SAN JUAN	5,671	4,450	570	651	Bush	78.5%	10.1%	11.5%
SAN MIGUEL	814	576	105	133	Bush	70.8%	12.9%	16.3%
SANTA FE	3,997	3,064	496	437	Bush	76.7%	12.4%	10.9%
SIERRA	955	731	89	135	Bush	76.5%	9.3%	14.1%
SOCORRO	1,078	819	109	150	Bush	76.0%	10.1%	13.9%
TAOS	1,061	756	159	146	Bush	71.3%	15.0%	13.8%
TORRANCE	921	722	91	108	Bush	78.4%	9.9%	11.7%
UNION	301	231	26	44	Bush	76.7%	8.6%	14.6%
VALENCIA	2,756	1,989	291	476	Bush	72.2%	10.6%	17.3%
TOTAL	88,744	69,359	9,305	10,080	Bush	78.2%	10.5%	11.4%

NEW MEXICO DEMOCRATIC

1992

County	Total Vote	Brown	Clinton	Uncommitted	Other	Winner	Percentage of Total Vote: Brown	Clinton	Uncom.	Other
BERNALILLO	50,477	10,348	23,949	11,726	4,454	Clinton	20.5%	47.4%	23.2%	8.8%
CATRON	484	72	246	66	100	Clinton	14.9%	50.8%	13.6%	20.7%
CHAVES	3,931	438	1,989	914	590	Clinton	11.1%	50.6%	23.3%	15.0%
CIBOLA	3,079	420	1,891	380	388	Clinton	13.6%	61.4%	12.3%	12.6%
COLFAX	2,497	449	1,399	359	290	Clinton	18.0%	56.0%	14.4%	11.6%
CURRY	3,418	296	2,070	710	342	Clinton	8.7%	60.6%	20.8%	10.0%
DE BACA	768	70	439	161	98	Clinton	9.1%	57.2%	21.0%	12.8%
DONA ANA	12,555	1,786	6,925	2,306	1,538	Clinton	14.2%	55.2%	18.4%	12.3%
EDDY	6,452	580	3,342	1,473	1,057	Clinton	9.0%	51.8%	22.8%	16.4%
GRANT	4,649	544	2,762	933	410	Clinton	11.7%	59.4%	20.1%	8.8%
GUADALUPE	1,582	250	1,121	86	125	Clinton	15.8%	70.9%	5.4%	7.9%
HARDING	247	28	166	26	27	Clinton	11.3%	67.2%	10.5%	10.9%
HIDALGO	1,344	128	780	229	207	Clinton	9.5%	58.0%	17.0%	15.4%
LEA	3,984	337	2,292	864	491	Clinton	8.5%	57.5%	21.7%	12.3%
LINCOLN	1,311	197	632	343	139	Clinton	15.0%	48.2%	26.2%	10.6%
LOS ALAMOS	2,315	337	829	701	448	Clinton	14.6%	35.8%	30.3%	19.4%
LUNA	1,952	271	871	594	216	Clinton	13.9%	44.6%	30.4%	11.1%
MCKINLEY	7,777	1,010	4,830	695	1,242	Clinton	13.0%	62.1%	8.9%	16.0%
MORA	1,550	230	1,122	71	127	Clinton	14.8%	72.4%	4.6%	8.2%
OTERO	4,866	416	2,532	1,396	522	Clinton	8.5%	52.0%	28.7%	10.7%
QUAY	2,428	230	1,397	483	318	Clinton	9.5%	57.5%	19.9%	13.1%
RIO ARRIBA	7,715	1,171	5,069	755	720	Clinton	15.2%	65.7%	9.8%	9.3%
ROOSEVELT	1,526	143	888	362	133	Clinton	9.4%	58.2%	23.7%	8.7%
SANDOVAL	7,440	1,453	3,840	1,440	707	Clinton	19.5%	51.6%	19.4%	9.5%
SAN JUAN	7,570	868	4,160	1,499	1,043	Clinton	11.5%	55.0%	19.8%	13.8%
SAN MIGUEL	6,111	985	4,025	612	489	Clinton	16.1%	65.9%	10.0%	8.0%
SANTA FE	16,186	4,474	7,352	3,148	1,212	Clinton	27.6%	45.4%	19.4%	7.5%
SIERRA	1,323	157	742	322	102	Clinton	11.9%	56.1%	24.3%	7.7%
SOCORRO	1,975	311	1,059	271	334	Clinton	15.7%	53.6%	13.7%	16.9%
TAOS	5,407	1,326	2,795	512	774	Clinton	24.5%	51.7%	9.5%	14.3%
TORRANCE	1,609	272	909	321	107	Clinton	16.9%	56.5%	20.0%	6.7%
UNION	781	97	415	140	129	Clinton	12.4%	53.1%	17.9%	16.5%
VALENCIA	6,228	1,011	3,095	1,371	751	Clinton	16.2%	49.7%	22.0%	12.1%
TOTAL	181,443	30,705	95,933	35,269	19,536	Clinton	16.9%	52.9%	19.4%	10.8%

NEW MEXICO REPUBLICAN

1992

County	Total Vote	Buchanan	Bush	Uncommitted	Winner	Percentage of Total Vote Buchanan	Bush	Uncom.
BERNALILLO	34,609	2,692	22,118	9,799	Bush	7.8%	63.9%	28.3%
CATRON	413	54	246	113	Bush	13.1%	59.6%	27.4%
CHAVES	4,852	417	3,005	1,430	Bush	8.6%	61.9%	29.5%
CIBOLA	815	96	566	153	Bush	11.8%	69.4%	18.8%
COLFAX	682	89	451	142	Bush	13.0%	66.1%	20.8%
CURRY	1,446	183	1,057	206	Bush	12.7%	73.1%	14.2%
DE BACA	103	3	76	24	Bush	2.9%	73.8%	23.3%
DONA ANA	5,801	585	3,518	1,698	Bush	10.1%	60.6%	29.3%
EDDY	1,903	145	1,172	586	Bush	7.6%	61.6%	30.8%
GRANT	1,077	89	605	383	Bush	8.3%	56.2%	35.6%
GUADALUPE	291	36	229	26	Bush	12.4%	78.7%	8.9%
HARDING	224	34	161	29	Bush	15.2%	71.9%	12.9%
HIDALGO	263	20	186	57	Bush	7.6%	70.7%	21.7%
LEA	2,058	184	1,400	474	Bush	8.9%	68.0%	23.0%
LINCOLN	1,888	199	1,224	465	Bush	10.5%	64.8%	24.6%
LOS ALAMOS	1,995	144	1,128	723	Bush	7.2%	56.5%	36.2%
LUNA	882	89	471	322	Bush	10.1%	53.4%	36.5%
MCKINLEY	1,720	223	1,268	229	Bush	13.0%	73.7%	13.3%
MORA	463	59	363	41	Bush	12.7%	78.4%	8.9%
OTERO	3,166	229	1,922	1,015	Bush	7.2%	60.7%	32.1%
QUAY	475	37	329	109	Bush	7.8%	69.3%	22.9%
RIO ARRIBA	719	91	523	105	Bush	12.7%	72.7%	14.6%
ROOSEVELT	875	90	623	162	Bush	10.3%	71.2%	18.5%
SANDOVAL	3,441	392	2,096	953	Bush	11.4%	60.9%	27.7%
SAN JUAN	5,452	629	3,669	1,154	Bush	11.5%	67.3%	21.2%
SAN MIGUEL	855	108	634	113	Bush	12.6%	74.2%	13.2%
SANTA FE	3,510	257	1,959	1,294	Bush	7.3%	55.8%	36.9%
SIERRA	990	103	591	296	Bush	10.4%	59.7%	29.9%
SOCORRO	1,152	119	771	262	Bush	10.3%	66.9%	22.7%
TAOS	1,017	142	682	193	Bush	14.0%	67.1%	19.0%
TORRANCE	996	88	688	220	Bush	8.8%	69.1%	22.1%
UNION	224	17	163	44	Bush	7.6%	72.8%	19.6%
VALENCIA	2,610	228	1,628	754	Bush	8.7%	62.4%	28.9%
TOTAL	86,967	7,871	55,522	23,574	Bush	9.1%	63.8%	27.1%

NEW MEXICO DEMOCRATIC

1996

County	Total Vote	Clinton	Uncommitted	Winner	Percentage of Total Vote Clinton	Uncom.
BERNALILLO	29,566	27,545	2,021	Clinton	93.2%	6.8%
CATRON	209	131	78	Clinton	62.7%	37.3%
CHAVES	1,441	1,264	177	Clinton	87.7%	12.3%
CIBOLA	2,043	1,874	169	Clinton	91.7%	8.3%
COLFAX	1,693	1,577	116	Clinton	93.1%	6.9%
CURRY	1,954	1,457	497	Clinton	74.6%	25.4%
DE BACA	456	363	93	Clinton	79.6%	20.4%
DONA ANA	7,915	7,047	868	Clinton	89.0%	11.0%
EDDY	6,107	4,950	1,157	Clinton	81.1%	18.9%
GRANT	4,962	4,226	736	Clinton	85.2%	14.8%
GUADALUPE	1,238	1,146	92	Clinton	92.6%	7.4%
HARDING	163	144	19	Clinton	88.3%	11.7%
HIDALGO	618	491	127	Clinton	79.4%	20.6%
LEA	1,336	1,152	184	Clinton	86.2%	13.8%
LINCOLN	710	622	88	Clinton	87.6%	12.4%
LOS ALAMOS	1,547	1,291	256	Clinton	83.5%	16.5%
LUNA	1,550	1,304	246	Clinton	84.1%	15.9%
MCKINLEY	5,205	4,577	628	Clinton	87.9%	12.1%
MORA	1,265	1,221	44	Clinton	96.5%	3.5%
OTERO	2,123	1,759	364	Clinton	82.9%	17.1%
QUAY	1,537	1,214	323	Clinton	79.0%	21.0%
RIO ARRIBA	6,563	6,162	401	Clinton	93.9%	6.1%
ROOSEVELT	599	473	126	Clinton	79.0%	21.0%
SANDOVAL	5,321	4,950	371	Clinton	93.0%	7.0%
SAN JUAN	5,284	4,647	637	Clinton	87.9%	12.1%
SAN MIGUEL	5,307	5,133	174	Clinton	96.7%	3.3%
SANTA FE	13,491	12,533	958	Clinton	92.9%	7.1%
SIERRA	820	710	110	Clinton	86.6%	13.4%
SOCORRO	1,152	1,047	105	Clinton	90.9%	9.1%
TAOS	4,388	4,246	142	Clinton	96.8%	3.2%
TORRANCE	1,101	982	119	Clinton	89.2%	10.8%
UNION	341	269	72	Clinton	78.9%	21.1%
VALENCIA	3,357	3,088	269	Clinton	92.0%	8.0%
TOTAL	121,362	109,595	11,767	Clinton	90.3%	9.7%

NEW MEXICO REPUBLICAN

1996

County	Total Vote	Dole	Other	Winner	Percentage of Total Vote Dole	Other
BERNALILLO	24,478	18,861	5,617	Dole	77.1%	22.9%
CATRON	438	300	138	Dole	68.5%	31.5%
CHAVES	2,700	2,142	558	Dole	79.3%	20.7%
CIBOLA	718	498	220	Dole	69.4%	30.6%
COLFAX	553	402	151	Dole	72.7%	27.3%
CURRY	1,295	1,072	223	Dole	82.8%	17.2%
DE BACA	92	73	19	Dole	79.3%	20.7%
DONA ANA	4,993	3,829	1,164	Dole	76.7%	23.3%
EDDY	2,362	1,871	491	Dole	79.2%	20.8%
GRANT	1,409	1,018	391	Dole	72.2%	27.8%
GUADALUPE	137	101	36	Dole	73.7%	26.3%
HARDING	141	121	20	Dole	85.8%	14.2%
HIDALGO	235	166	69	Dole	70.6%	29.4%
LEA	1,362	1,000	362	Dole	73.4%	26.6%
LINCOLN	2,038	1,524	514	Dole	74.8%	25.2%
LOS ALAMOS	1,541	1,134	407	Dole	73.6%	26.4%
LUNA	878	679	199	Dole	77.3%	22.7%
MCKINLEY	1,130	720	410	Dole	63.7%	36.3%
MORA	217	157	60	Dole	72.4%	27.6%
OTERO	3,384	2,655	729	Dole	78.5%	21.5%
QUAY	416	328	88	Dole	78.8%	21.2%
RIO ARRIBA	508	376	132	Dole	74.0%	26.0%
ROOSEVELT	456	344	112	Dole	75.4%	24.6%
SANDOVAL	3,099	2,280	819	Dole	73.6%	26.4%
SAN JUAN	6,553	4,745	1,808	Dole	72.4%	27.6%
SAN MIGUEL	614	440	174	Dole	71.7%	28.3%
SANTA FE	2,623	1,914	709	Dole	73.0%	27.0%
SIERRA	934	734	200	Dole	78.6%	21.4%
SOCORRO	925	683	242	Dole	73.8%	26.2%
TAOS	796	560	236	Dole	70.4%	29.6%
TORRANCE	873	645	228	Dole	73.9%	26.1%
UNION	164	128	36	Dole	78.0%	22.0%
VALENCIA	2,402	1,800	602	Dole	74.9%	25.1%
TOTAL	70,464	53,300	17,164	Dole	75.6%	24.4%

NEW YORK

For much of the twentieth century, New York's political leaders chose control of their state's nominating process over widespread voter participation. The Empire State held a presidential primary, but it was often a late spring event devoted solely to the election of delegates on a district-by-district basis; it produced a delegation that was readily transferable to the preferred candidate of the party's kingpins. That ballot access was difficult and voter interest often minimal was just fine with party leaders.

It was not until 1980 that New York Democrats held their first presidential primary with voters able to ballot directly for the candidates. But New York GOP leaders have been slow to jettison the old system, and in 1996 lined up early behind Bob Dole.

Members of Congress, state lawmakers and prominent local party leaders across the Empire State ran as Dole delegates. Steve Forbes and Pat Buchanan had to go to court just to get delegates on the primary ballot. And though Forbes mounted a late drive, with a saturation media campaign and a last-minute endorsement from former New York Rep. Jack Kemp, Forbes was unable to stir much voter interest or stem the Dole bandwagon. With estimated turnout of about 400,000, or barely 10 percent of the state's registered Republicans, Dole swept all 93 delegates at stake.

Compared with the Republicans, New York's Democratic presidential primary has been open and showy, and in recent years, hotly contested.

The state's ethnically variegated Democratic electorate has been comfortable with traditional New Deal-style politicians. Henry M. Jackson won more delegates than anyone else in New York in 1976; Edward Kennedy won easily in 1980, as did Walter Mondale in 1984 and Michael Dukakis in 1988.

Bill Clinton won the primary in 1992 by piecing together a biracial coalition in New York City and holding his own in the rest of the state. But like many of Clinton's other primary triumphs in 1992, his New York victory was not overwhelming. He took barely 40 percent of the vote against Jerry Brown and Paul Tsongas, who had suspended his campaign more than two weeks before the April balloting, but still placed second. Only in one county, the Bronx, did Clinton win a majority of the vote.

None of the candidates seemed to excite the voters. Turnout for the Democratic primary in 1992 was barely 1 million, the lowest since 1980, and Clinton's winning total was almost 400,000 votes less than Dukakis' four years earlier.

Clinton's winning coalition was also different. In 1988, Dukakis narrowly lost New York City to Jesse Jackson, but swamped Jackson in the more conservative suburbs and upstate. In contrast, Clinton built up a big lead in New York City but barely beat Tsongas in the suburbs and was caught in

Recent New York Primary Results

New York Democrats instituted a presidential primary with a direct vote for candidates in 1980. New York Republicans have cast their primary ballots for delegates without a direct vote for presidential candidates.

	DEMOCRATS			REPUBLICANS
Year	Turnout	Candidates	%	
1996	—	NO PRIMARY		NO PRIMARY
1992 (April 7)	1,007,726	BILL CLINTON	41	NO PRIMARY
		Paul Tsongas	29	
		Jerry Brown	26	
1988 (April 19)	1,575,186	MICHAEL DUKAKIS	51	NO PRIMARY
		Jesse Jackson	37	
		Al Gore	10	
1984 (April 3)	1,387,950	WALTER MONDALE	45	NO PRIMARY
		Gary Hart	27	
		Jesse Jackson	26	
1980 (March 25)	989,062	EDWARD KENNEDY	59	NO PRIMARY
		Jimmy Carter*	41	

Note: All candidates are listed that drew at least 10 percent of their party's primary vote. The names of winning candidates are capitalized. An asterisk (*) indicates an incumbent president.

a close battle with Brown and Tsongas in the small cities and towns of upstate New York. Clinton was strong in the western end of the state, which faces the Midwest. Tsongas and Brown dominated voting in the Hudson River Valley, which is adjacent to New England.

But the prime battleground was New York City, where more than half the Democratic primary ballots are cast, and there Clinton readily prevailed with a significant edge among the city's large component of Jewish and black voters. It enabled him to become the first Southern Democrat to win the New York primary.

Jimmy Carter had lost it twice, denouncing the primary in 1976 as boss-dominated. Al Gore finished a weak third in New York in 1988—despite heavy emphasis on the event—and shortly thereafter suspended his campaign. Gore drew less than 10 percent of the primary vote in the city, less than 15 percent in the suburbs, and could crack 20 percent in only two small upstate counties.

NEW YORK DEMOCRATIC

1980

County	Total Vote	Carter	E. Kennedy	Winner	Percentage of Total Vote Carter	E. Kennedy
ALBANY	23,654	12,700	10,954	Carter	53.7%	46.3%
ALLEGANY	1,203	763	440	Carter	63.4%	36.6%
BRONX	95,668	36,325	59,343	E. Kennedy	38.0%	62.0%
BROOME	8,099	4,096	4,003	Carter	50.6%	49.4%
CATTARAUGUS	2,973	1,741	1,232	Carter	58.6%	41.4%
CAYUGA	3,207	1,520	1,687	E. Kennedy	47.4%	52.6%
CHAUTAUQUA	4,741	2,417	2,324	Carter	51.0%	49.0%
CHEMUNG	3,762	2,090	1,672	Carter	55.6%	44.4%
CHENANGO	1,264	761	503	Carter	60.2%	39.8%
CLINTON	2,030	1,038	992	Carter	51.1%	48.9%
COLUMBIA	1,789	869	920	E. Kennedy	48.6%	51.4%
CORTLAND	1,542	881	661	Carter	57.1%	42.9%
DELAWARE	1,310	866	444	Carter	66.1%	33.9%
DUTCHESS	6,188	2,828	3,360	E. Kennedy	45.7%	54.3%
ERIE	61,729	31,549	30,180	Carter	51.1%	48.9%
ESSEX	1,156	655	501	Carter	56.7%	43.3%
FRANKLIN	1,122	643	479	Carter	57.3%	42.7%
FULTON	1,588	848	740	Carter	53.4%	46.6%
GENESEE	1,586	888	698	Carter	56.0%	44.0%
GREENE	1,104	582	522	Carter	52.7%	47.3%
HAMILTON	263	178	85	Carter	67.7%	32.3%
HERKIMER	2,409	1,263	1,146	Carter	52.4%	47.6%
JEFFERSON	2,836	1,744	1,092	Carter	61.5%	38.5%
KINGS	167,533	60,328	107,205	E. Kennedy	36.0%	64.0%
LEWIS	620	402	218	Carter	64.8%	35.2%
LIVINGSTON	1,442	839	603	Carter	58.2%	41.8%
MADISON	1,464	774	690	Carter	52.9%	47.1%
MONROE	27,906	15,259	12,647	Carter	54.7%	45.3%
MONTGOMERY	2,751	1,152	1,599	E. Kennedy	41.9%	58.1%
NASSAU	64,771	21,190	43,581	E. Kennedy	32.7%	67.3%
NEW YORK	142,675	50,698	91,977	E. Kennedy	35.5%	64.5%
NIAGARA	12,761	6,411	6,350	Carter	50.2%	49.8%
ONEIDA	11,091	6,167	4,924	Carter	55.6%	44.4%
ONONDAGA	12,292	6,152	6,140	Carter	50.0%	50.0%
ONTARIO	2,253	1,173	1,080	Carter	52.1%	47.9%
ORANGE	7,422	3,436	3,986	E. Kennedy	46.3%	53.7%
ORLEANS	1,036	541	495	Carter	52.2%	47.8%
OSWEGO	2,784	1,435	1,349	Carter	51.5%	48.5%
OTSEGO	1,742	971	771	Carter	55.7%	44.3%
PUTNAM	2,032	973	1,059	E. Kennedy	47.9%	52.1%
QUEENS	144,747	55,585	89,162	E. Kennedy	38.4%	61.6%
RENSSELAER	4,879	2,038	2,841	E. Kennedy	41.8%	58.2%
RICHMOND	18,209	8,767	9,442	E. Kennedy	48.1%	51.9%
ROCKLAND	16,626	5,920	10,706	E. Kennedy	35.6%	64.4%
ST. LAWRENCE	3,299	1,810	1,489	Carter	54.9%	45.1%
SARATOGA	3,836	1,865	1,971	E. Kennedy	48.6%	51.4%
SCHENECTADY	6,299	3,114	3,185	E. Kennedy	49.4%	50.6%
SCHOHARIE	751	482	269	Carter	64.2%	35.8%
SCHUYLER	445	263	182	Carter	59.1%	40.9%
SENECA	994	462	532	E. Kennedy	46.5%	53.5%

NEW YORK DEMOCRATIC

1980

County	Total Vote	Carter	E. Kennedy	Winner	Percentage of Total Vote: Carter	E. Kennedy
STEUBEN	2,456	1,441	1,015	Carter	58.7%	41.3%
SUFFOLK	32,135	13,819	18,316	E. Kennedy	43.0%	57.0%
SULLIVAN	2,659	1,067	1,592	E. Kennedy	40.1%	59.9%
TIOGA	1,420	877	543	Carter	61.8%	38.2%
TOMPKINS	2,841	1,441	1,400	Carter	50.7%	49.3%
ULSTER	4,384	2,084	2,300	E. Kennedy	47.5%	52.5%
WARREN	1,800	947	853	Carter	52.6%	47.4%
WASHINGTON	1,226	588	638	E. Kennedy	48.0%	52.0%
WAYNE	1,740	1,080	660	Carter	62.1%	37.9%
WESTCHESTER	43,106	16,704	26,402	E. Kennedy	38.8%	61.2%
WYOMING	854	488	366	Carter	57.1%	42.9%
YATES	558	317	241	Carter	56.8%	43.2%
TOTAL	989,062	406,305	582,757	E. Kennedy	41.1%	58.9%

Note: The vote in New York City was Kennedy 357,129 (62.8 percent); Carter 211,703 (37.2 percent). A total of 568,832 votes were cast.

NEW YORK DEMOCRATIC

1984

County	Total Vote	Hart	J. Jackson	Mondale	Other	Winner	Percentage of Total Vote: Hart	J. Jackson	Mondale	Other
ALBANY	35,291	12,424	4,776	17,350	741	Mondale	35.2%	13.5%	49.2%	2.1%
ALLEGANY	1,873	1,003	130	708	32	Hart	53.6%	6.9%	37.8%	1.7%
BRONX	128,657	18,509	50,447	56,267	3,434	Mondale	14.4%	39.2%	43.7%	2.7%
BROOME	12,569	6,616	1,075	4,637	241	Hart	52.6%	8.6%	36.9%	1.9%
CATTARAUGUS	4,495	2,241	204	1,889	161	Hart	49.9%	4.5%	42.0%	3.6%
CAYUGA	4,060	2,142	286	1,551	81	Hart	52.8%	7.0%	38.2%	2.0%
CHAUTAUQUA	6,969	3,283	396	3,173	117	Hart	47.1%	5.7%	45.5%	1.7%
CHEMUNG	4,962	2,267	598	2,016	81	Hart	45.7%	12.1%	40.6%	1.6%
CHENANGO	1,974	1,196	142	603	33	Hart	60.6%	7.2%	30.5%	1.7%
CLINTON	2,882	1,615	184	1,006	77	Hart	56.0%	6.4%	34.9%	2.7%
COLUMBIA	2,608	1,255	252	1,033	68	Hart	48.1%	9.7%	39.6%	2.6%
CORTLAND	2,064	1,127	236	665	36	Hart	54.6%	11.4%	32.2%	1.7%
DELAWARE	1,963	1,115	175	643	30	Hart	56.8%	8.9%	32.8%	1.5%
DUTCHESS	9,843	4,014	1,955	3,648	226	Hart	40.8%	19.9%	37.1%	2.3%
ERIE	103,592	29,036	20,569	51,050	2,937	Mondale	28.0%	19.9%	49.3%	2.8%
ESSEX	1,535	916	120	470	29	Hart	59.7%	7.8%	30.6%	1.9%
FRANKLIN	2,089	1,171	99	767	52	Hart	56.1%	4.7%	36.7%	2.5%
FULTON	2,285	1,084	119	1,042	40	Hart	47.4%	5.2%	45.6%	1.8%
GENESEE	2,242	949	141	1,055	97	Mondale	42.3%	6.3%	47.1%	4.3%
GREENE	1,441	707	107	585	42	Hart	49.1%	7.4%	40.6%	2.9%

NEW YORK DEMOCRATIC

1984

County	Total Vote	Hart	J. Jackson	Mondale	Other	Winner	Percentage of Total Vote Hart	J. Jackson	Mondale	Other
HAMILTON	394	242	23	118	11	Hart	61.4%	5.8%	29.9%	2.8%
HERKIMER	3,423	1,779	155	1,404	85	Hart	52.0%	4.5%	41.0%	2.5%
JEFFERSON	3,974	2,103	190	1,616	65	Hart	52.9%	4.8%	40.7%	1.6%
KINGS	233,646	36,142	87,968	104,107	5,429	Mondale	15.5%	37.7%	44.6%	2.3%
LEWIS	925	588	58	265	14	Hart	63.6%	6.3%	28.6%	1.5%
LIVINGSTON	1,915	989	156	719	51	Hart	51.6%	8.1%	37.5%	2.7%
MADISON	2,223	1,188	177	809	49	Hart	53.4%	8.0%	36.4%	2.2%
MONROE	37,193	13,887	8,083	14,445	778	Mondale	37.3%	21.7%	38.8%	2.1%
MONTGOMERY	3,747	1,824	129	1,642	152	Hart	48.7%	3.4%	43.8%	4.1%
NASSAU	77,776	25,222	10,465	39,752	2,337	Mondale	32.4%	13.5%	51.1%	3.0%
NEW YORK	204,781	50,256	63,863	86,982	3,680	Mondale	24.5%	31.2%	42.5%	1.8%
NIAGARA	16,984	5,917	1,771	8,953	343	Mondale	34.8%	10.4%	52.7%	2.0%
ONEIDA	14,007	5,608	1,657	6,459	283	Mondale	40.0%	11.8%	46.1%	2.0%
ONONDAGA	20,892	8,401	3,317	8,831	343	Mondale	40.2%	15.9%	42.3%	1.6%
ONTARIO	3,409	1,927	310	1,122	50	Hart	56.5%	9.1%	32.9%	1.5%
ORANGE	11,013	4,251	1,904	4,596	262	Mondale	38.6%	17.3%	41.7%	2.4%
ORLEANS	1,474	629	92	714	39	Mondale	42.7%	6.2%	48.4%	2.6%
OSWEGO	4,024	2,268	229	1,431	96	Hart	56.4%	5.7%	35.6%	2.4%
OTSEGO	2,814	1,605	238	921	50	Hart	57.0%	8.5%	32.7%	1.8%
PUTNAM	2,730	1,162	253	1,247	68	Mondale	42.6%	9.3%	45.7%	2.5%
QUEENS	193,489	41,588	58,526	90,241	3,134	Mondale	21.5%	30.2%	46.6%	1.6%
RENSSELAER	7,542	2,668	557	4,158	159	Mondale	35.4%	7.4%	55.1%	2.1%
RICHMOND	23,325	6,922	3,848	12,073	482	Mondale	29.7%	16.5%	51.8%	2.1%
ROCKLAND	21,227	7,644	2,639	10,467	477	Mondale	36.0%	12.4%	49.3%	2.2%
ST. LAWRENCE	5,186	2,770	291	2,024	101	Hart	53.4%	5.6%	39.0%	1.9%
SARATOGA	6,105	3,003	516	2,500	86	Hart	49.2%	8.5%	41.0%	1.4%
SCHENECTADY	9,613	3,929	1,026	4,432	226	Mondale	40.9%	10.7%	46.1%	2.4%
SCHOHARIE	1,259	625	127	465	42	Hart	49.6%	10.1%	36.9%	3.3%
SCHUYLER	775	415	76	270	14	Hart	53.5%	9.8%	34.8%	1.8%
SENECA	1,658	866	110	620	62	Hart	52.2%	6.6%	37.4%	3.7%
STEUBEN	3,755	2,037	301	1,323	94	Hart	54.2%	8.0%	35.2%	2.5%
SUFFOLK	43,522	15,497	7,060	20,077	888	Mondale	35.6%	16.2%	46.1%	2.0%
SULLIVAN	3,752	1,503	397	1,754	98	Mondale	40.1%	10.6%	46.7%	2.6%
TIOGA	1,967	1,178	158	582	49	Hart	59.9%	8.0%	29.6%	2.5%
TOMPKINS	6,495	3,032	1,595	1,756	112	Hart	46.7%	24.6%	27.0%	1.7%
ULSTER	6,543	2,863	945	2,547	188	Hart	43.8%	14.4%	38.9%	2.9%
WARREN	2,124	1,082	164	835	43	Hart	50.9%	7.7%	39.3%	2.0%
WASHINGTON	1,747	953	95	662	37	Hart	54.6%	5.4%	37.9%	2.1%
WAYNE	2,485	1,331	210	861	83	Hart	53.6%	8.5%	34.6%	3.3%
WESTCHESTER	62,590	20,905	13,718	26,893	1,074	Mondale	33.4%	21.9%	43.0%	1.7%
WYOMING	1,258	621	58	517	62	Hart	49.4%	4.6%	41.1%	4.9%
YATES	795	474	75	233	13	Hart	59.6%	9.4%	29.3%	1.6%
TOTAL	1,387,950	380,564	355,541	621,581	30,264	Mondale	27.4%	25.6%	44.8%	2.2%

Note: The vote in New York City was Mondale 349,670 (44.6 percent); J. Jackson 264,652 (33.8 percent); Hart 153,417 (19.6 percent); other 16,159 (2.1 percent). A total of 783,898 votes were cast.

NEW YORK DEMOCRATIC

1988

County	Total Vote	Dukakis	Gore	J. Jackson	Other	Winner	Percentage of Total Vote Dukakis	Gore	J. Jackson	Other
ALBANY	34,868	21,119	4,127	8,092	1,530	Dukakis	60.6%	11.8%	23.2%	4.4%
ALLEGANY	1,353	837	190	256	70	Dukakis	61.9%	14.0%	18.9%	5.2%
BRONX	152,317	56,444	9,503	85,494	876	J. Jackson	37.1%	6.2%	56.1%	0.6%
BROOME	13,979	9,011	1,571	2,970	427	Dukakis	64.5%	11.2%	21.2%	3.1%
CATTARAUGUS	3,711	2,336	566	574	235	Dukakis	62.9%	15.3%	15.5%	6.3%
CAYUGA	4,208	2,576	504	867	261	Dukakis	61.2%	12.0%	20.6%	6.2%
CHAUTAUQUA	7,106	5,025	813	1,062	206	Dukakis	70.7%	11.4%	14.9%	2.9%
CHEMUNG	5,017	2,531	1,175	1,189	122	Dukakis	50.4%	23.4%	23.7%	2.4%
CHENANGO	1,754	1,024	230	452	48	Dukakis	58.4%	13.1%	25.8%	2.7%
CLINTON	2,593	1,613	266	564	150	Dukakis	62.2%	10.3%	21.8%	5.8%
COLUMBIA	3,065	1,749	493	670	153	Dukakis	57.1%	16.1%	21.9%	5.0%
CORTLAND	2,089	1,135	268	610	76	Dukakis	54.3%	12.8%	29.2%	3.6%
DELAWARE	2,021	1,243	241	458	79	Dukakis	61.5%	11.9%	22.7%	3.9%
DUTCHESS	10,655	5,975	1,151	3,289	240	Dukakis	56.1%	10.8%	30.9%	2.3%
ERIE	102,782	58,312	7,746	33,379	3,345	Dukakis	56.7%	7.5%	32.5%	3.3%
ESSEX	1,386	833	186	287	80	Dukakis	60.1%	13.4%	20.7%	5.8%
FRANKLIN	1,936	1,261	215	320	140	Dukakis	65.1%	11.1%	16.5%	7.2%
FULTON	2,126	1,402	256	327	141	Dukakis	65.9%	12.0%	15.4%	6.6%
GENESEE	2,213	1,380	337	357	139	Dukakis	62.4%	15.2%	16.1%	6.3%
GREENE	1,455	925	177	263	90	Dukakis	63.6%	12.2%	18.1%	6.2%
HAMILTON	340	215	40	63	22	Dukakis	63.2%	11.8%	18.5%	6.5%
HERKIMER	2,686	1,681	308	514	183	Dukakis	62.6%	11.5%	19.1%	6.8%
JEFFERSON	3,498	2,201	496	488	313	Dukakis	62.9%	14.2%	14.0%	8.9%
KINGS	276,458	113,861	26,743	133,567	2,287	J. Jackson	41.2%	9.7%	48.3%	0.8%
LEWIS	733	415	112	160	46	Dukakis	56.6%	15.3%	21.8%	6.3%
LIVINGSTON	2,048	1,215	327	422	84	Dukakis	59.3%	16.0%	20.6%	4.1%
MADISON	2,134	1,218	297	531	88	Dukakis	57.1%	13.9%	24.9%	4.1%
MONROE	45,048	24,564	4,474	14,893	1,117	Dukakis	54.5%	9.9%	33.1%	2.5%
MONTGOMERY	3,966	2,693	523	463	287	Dukakis	67.9%	13.2%	11.7%	7.2%
NASSAU	95,209	62,006	12,303	18,208	2,692	Dukakis	65.1%	12.9%	19.1%	2.8%
NEW YORK	221,355	97,977	19,742	101,515	2,121	J. Jackson	44.3%	8.9%	45.9%	1.0%
NIAGARA	15,310	10,150	1,482	3,152	526	Dukakis	66.3%	9.7%	20.6%	3.4%
ONEIDA	13,092	8,414	1,340	2,825	513	Dukakis	64.3%	10.2%	21.6%	3.9%
ONONDAGA	23,940	11,638	2,814	7,571	1,917	Dukakis	48.6%	11.8%	31.6%	8.0%
ONTARIO	3,723	2,297	379	919	128	Dukakis	61.7%	10.2%	24.7%	3.4%
ORANGE	12,738	7,616	1,732	3,026	364	Dukakis	59.8%	13.6%	23.8%	2.9%
ORLEANS	1,297	857	158	242	40	Dukakis	66.1%	12.2%	18.7%	3.1%
OSWEGO	3,723	2,267	471	773	212	Dukakis	60.9%	12.7%	20.8%	5.7%
OTSEGO	2,652	1,639	256	681	76	Dukakis	61.8%	9.7%	25.7%	2.9%
PUTNAM	3,356	2,187	481	496	192	Dukakis	65.2%	14.3%	14.8%	5.7%
QUEENS	231,610	118,784	22,102	89,006	1,718	Dukakis	51.3%	9.5%	38.4%	0.7%
RENSSELAER	7,074	4,338	831	1,465	440	Dukakis	61.3%	11.7%	20.7%	6.2%
RICHMOND	31,967	21,042	4,346	6,334	245	Dukakis	65.8%	13.6%	19.8%	0.8%
ROCKLAND	26,621	17,443	3,965	4,628	585	Dukakis	65.5%	14.9%	17.4%	2.2%
ST. LAWRENCE	4,327	2,423	549	818	537	Dukakis	56.0%	12.7%	18.9%	12.4%
SARATOGA	5,897	3,552	639	1,171	535	Dukakis	60.2%	10.8%	19.9%	9.1%
SCHENECTADY	9,477	6,108	983	2,088	298	Dukakis	64.5%	10.4%	22.0%	3.1%
SCHOHARIE	1,243	767	112	297	67	Dukakis	61.7%	9.0%	23.9%	5.4%
SCHUYLER	743	385	154	169	35	Dukakis	51.8%	20.7%	22.7%	4.7%
SENECA	1,442	895	130	335	82	Dukakis	62.1%	9.0%	23.2%	5.7%

NEW YORK DEMOCRATIC

1988

County	Total Vote	Dukakis	Gore	J. Jackson	Other	Winner	Percentage of Total Vote Dukakis	Gore	J. Jackson	Other
STEUBEN	3,182	1,945	559	547	131	Dukakis	61.1%	17.6%	17.2%	4.1%
SUFFOLK	54,462	31,810	7,286	14,149	1,217	Dukakis	58.4%	13.4%	26.0%	2.2%
SULLIVAN	4,506	2,751	657	911	187	Dukakis	61.1%	14.6%	20.2%	4.2%
TIOGA	2,067	1,226	259	498	84	Dukakis	59.3%	12.5%	24.1%	4.1%
TOMPKINS	7,043	3,567	419	2,819	238	Dukakis	50.6%	5.9%	40.0%	3.4%
ULSTER	8,455	4,899	894	2,302	360	Dukakis	57.9%	10.6%	27.2%	4.3%
WARREN	1,833	1,183	218	345	87	Dukakis	64.5%	11.9%	18.8%	4.7%
WASHINGTON	1,627	1,035	143	329	120	Dukakis	63.6%	8.8%	20.2%	7.4%
WAYNE	2,397	1,462	283	540	112	Dukakis	61.0%	11.8%	22.5%	4.7%
WESTCHESTER	77,431	42,853	8,288	23,979	2,311	Dukakis	55.3%	10.7%	31.0%	3.0%
WYOMING	1,109	704	167	177	61	Dukakis	63.5%	15.1%	16.0%	5.5%
YATES	733	443	82	180	28	Dukakis	60.4%	11.2%	24.6%	3.8%
TOTAL	1,575,186	801,457	157,559	585,076	31,094	Dukakis	50.9%	10.0%	37.1%	2.0%

Note: The vote in New York City was J. Jackson 415,916 (45.5 percent); Dukakis 408,108 (44.7 percent); Gore 82,436 (9.0 percent); Other 7,247 (0.8 percent). A total of 913,707 votes were cast.

NEW YORK DEMOCRATIC

1992

County	Total Vote	Brown	Clinton	Tsongas	Other	Winner	Percentage of Total Vote Brown	Clinton	Tsongas	Other
ALBANY	26,587	8,799	6,901	9,565	1,322	Tsongas	33.1%	26.0%	36.0%	5.0%
ALLEGANY	1,132	329	397	346	60	Clinton	29.1%	35.1%	30.6%	5.3%
BRONX	71,235	18,540	36,274	12,219	4,202	Clinton	26.0%	50.9%	17.2%	5.9%
BROOME	9,091	2,557	3,048	3,154	332	Tsongas	28.1%	33.5%	34.7%	3.7%
CATTARAUGUS	2,689	781	991	760	157	Clinton	29.0%	36.9%	28.3%	5.8%
CAYUGA	3,279	990	1,317	860	112	Clinton	30.2%	40.2%	26.2%	3.4%
CHAUTAUQUA	5,426	1,706	1,958	1,539	223	Clinton	31.4%	36.1%	28.4%	4.1%
CHEMUNG	3,127	681	1,148	1,172	126	Tsongas	21.8%	36.7%	37.5%	4.0%
CHENANGO	1,454	456	487	452	59	Clinton	31.4%	33.5%	31.1%	4.1%
CLINTON	2,174	512	793	766	103	Clinton	23.6%	36.5%	35.2%	4.7%
COLUMBIA	2,629	959	755	805	110	Brown	36.5%	28.7%	30.6%	4.2%
CORTLAND	1,710	621	559	474	56	Brown	36.3%	32.7%	27.7%	3.3%
DELAWARE	1,624	491	544	498	91	Clinton	30.2%	33.5%	30.7%	5.6%
DUTCHESS	9,920	3,155	2,708	3,746	311	Tsongas	31.8%	27.3%	37.8%	3.1%
ERIE	65,297	19,139	25,366	16,159	4,633	Clinton	29.3%	38.8%	24.7%	7.1%
ESSEX	1,269	309	407	488	65	Tsongas	24.3%	32.1%	38.5%	5.1%
FRANKLIN	1,531	350	585	511	85	Clinton	22.9%	38.2%	33.4%	5.6%
FULTON	1,855	642	673	483	57	Clinton	34.6%	36.3%	26.0%	3.1%
GENESEE	1,756	563	578	510	105	Clinton	32.1%	32.9%	29.0%	6.0%
GREENE	1,305	478	378	394	55	Brown	36.6%	29.0%	30.2%	4.2%

NEW YORK DEMOCRATIC

1992

County	Total Vote	Brown	Clinton	Tsongas	Other	Winner	Percentage of Total Vote: Brown	Clinton	Tsongas	Other
HAMILTON	307	105	99	84	19	Brown	34.2%	32.2%	27.4%	6.2%
HERKIMER	2,165	621	724	738	82	Tsongas	28.7%	33.4%	34.1%	3.8%
JEFFERSON	2,863	989	1,069	688	117	Clinton	34.5%	37.3%	24.0%	4.1%
KINGS	140,965	33,350	70,198	31,296	6,121	Clinton	23.7%	49.8%	22.2%	4.3%
LEWIS	678	260	243	144	31	Brown	38.3%	35.8%	21.2%	4.6%
LIVINGSTON	1,696	422	634	568	72	Clinton	24.9%	37.4%	33.5%	4.2%
MADISON	2,131	599	758	699	75	Clinton	28.1%	35.6%	32.8%	3.5%
MONROE	31,790	7,995	11,565	11,132	1,098	Clinton	25.1%	36.4%	35.0%	3.5%
MONTGOMERY	2,750	944	908	799	99	Brown	34.3%	33.0%	29.1%	3.6%
NASSAU	62,662	11,629	24,530	24,413	2,090	Clinton	18.6%	39.1%	39.0%	3.3%
NEW YORK	165,295	47,703	70,669	40,947	5,976	Clinton	28.9%	42.8%	24.8%	3.6%
NIAGARA	10,740	3,683	3,895	2,454	708	Clinton	34.3%	36.3%	22.8%	6.6%
ONEIDA	8,242	2,184	2,944	2,741	373	Clinton	26.5%	35.7%	33.3%	4.5%
ONONDAGA	18,039	5,369	6,381	5,709	580	Clinton	29.8%	35.4%	31.6%	3.2%
ONTARIO	2,914	792	966	1,059	97	Tsongas	27.2%	33.2%	36.3%	3.3%
ORANGE	10,468	3,287	3,638	3,132	411	Clinton	31.4%	34.8%	29.9%	3.9%
ORLEANS	899	225	375	268	31	Clinton	25.0%	41.7%	29.8%	3.4%
OSWEGO	2,972	902	1,075	876	119	Clinton	30.3%	36.2%	29.5%	4.0%
OTSEGO	2,284	761	648	798	77	Tsongas	33.3%	28.4%	34.9%	3.4%
PUTNAM	2,963	941	882	1,050	90	Tsongas	31.8%	29.8%	35.4%	3.0%
QUEENS	129,477	28,115	58,098	38,408	4,856	Clinton	21.7%	44.9%	29.7%	3.8%
RENSSELAER	6,223	2,060	1,565	2,323	275	Tsongas	33.1%	25.1%	37.3%	4.4%
RICHMOND	18,485	5,093	6,570	6,100	722	Clinton	27.6%	35.5%	33.0%	3.9%
ROCKLAND	19,420	4,092	7,529	7,160	639	Clinton	21.1%	38.8%	36.9%	3.3%
ST. LAWRENCE	3,240	968	1,081	902	289	Clinton	29.9%	33.4%	27.8%	8.9%
SARATOGA	6,121	2,130	1,497	2,269	225	Tsongas	34.8%	24.5%	37.1%	3.7%
SCHENECTADY	7,706	2,596	2,086	2,754	270	Tsongas	33.7%	27.1%	35.7%	3.5%
SCHOHARIE	1,066	328	350	351	37	Tsongas	30.8%	32.8%	32.9%	3.5%
SCHUYLER	654	213	194	214	33	Tsongas	32.6%	29.7%	32.7%	5.0%
SENECA	1,164	308	441	367	48	Clinton	26.5%	37.9%	31.5%	4.1%
STEUBEN	2,795	723	1,117	845	110	Clinton	25.9%	40.0%	30.2%	3.9%
SUFFOLK	39,385	11,330	12,557	13,850	1,648	Tsongas	28.8%	31.9%	35.2%	4.2%
SULLIVAN	3,191	833	1,353	883	122	Clinton	26.1%	42.4%	27.7%	3.8%
TIOGA	1,825	494	565	685	81	Tsongas	27.1%	31.0%	37.5%	4.4%
TOMPKINS	7,900	2,798	2,153	2,574	375	Brown	35.4%	27.3%	32.6%	4.7%
ULSTER	8,218	3,621	2,213	2,066	318	Brown	44.1%	26.9%	25.1%	3.9%
WARREN	2,058	644	564	754	96	Tsongas	31.3%	27.4%	36.6%	4.7%
WASHINGTON	1,510	487	446	508	69	Tsongas	32.3%	29.5%	33.6%	4.6%
WAYNE	1,813	464	681	599	69	Clinton	25.6%	37.6%	33.0%	3.8%
WESTCHESTER	56,020	11,743	22,651	19,737	1,889	Clinton	21.0%	40.4%	35.2%	3.4%
WYOMING	872	252	330	248	42	Clinton	28.9%	37.8%	28.4%	4.8%
YATES	670	167	240	237	26	Clinton	24.9%	35.8%	35.4%	3.9%
TOTAL	1,007,726	264,278	412,349	288,330	42,769	Clinton	26.2%	40.9%	28.6%	4.2%

Note: The vote in New York City was Clinton 241,809 (46.0 percent); Brown 132,801 (25.3 percent); Tsongas 128,970 (24.5 percent); other 21,877 (4.2 percent). A total of 525,457 votes were cast.

NEW YORK REPUBLICAN

1996

Congressional District	Total Vote	Buchanan	Dole	Forbes	Winner	Percentage of Total Vote Buchanan	Dole	Forbes
1	50,587	8,145	30,673	11,769	Dole	16.1%	60.6%	23.3%
2	34,227		23,130	11,097	Dole		67.6%	32.4%
3	57,785	9,753	34,906	13,126	Dole	16.9%	60.4%	22.7%
4	59,185	9,210	38,040	11,935	Dole	15.6%	64.3%	20.2%
5	29,318		18,410	10,908	Dole		62.8%	37.2%
6	5,343		3,360	1,983	Dole		62.9%	37.1%
7	12,785	2,301	7,806	2,678	Dole	18.0%	61.1%	20.9%
8	12,165		7,114	5,051	Dole		58.5%	41.5%
9	15,171		10,087	5,084	Dole		66.5%	33.5%
10	3,877		2,362	1,515	Dole		60.9%	39.1%
11	2,844	309	1,673	862	Dole	10.9%	58.8%	30.3%
12	3,125		2,092	1,033	Dole		66.9%	33.1%
13	24,816	4,584	15,644	4,588	Dole	18.5%	63.0%	18.5%
14	26,196	2,268	15,273	8,655	Dole	8.7%	58.3%	33.0%
15	3,450	407	2,081	962	Dole	11.8%	60.3%	27.9%
16	1,462		1,041	421	Dole		71.2%	28.8%
17	5,875	904	3,364	1,607	Dole	15.4%	57.3%	27.4%
18	31,310	4,374	19,066	7,870	Dole	14.0%	60.9%	25.1%
19	37,867	5,577	22,006	10,284	Dole	14.7%	58.1%	27.2%
20	35,018	5,346	21,226	8,446	Dole	15.3%	60.6%	24.1%
21	42,831	7,817	22,507	12,507	Dole	18.3%	52.5%	29.2%
22	70,313	12,572	36,974	20,767	Dole	17.9%	52.6%	29.5%
23	59,265	10,654	29,913	18,698	Dole	18.0%	50.5%	31.5%
24	58,981	10,196	30,462	18,323	Dole	17.3%	51.6%	31.1%
25	53,781	7,900	25,528	20,353	Dole	14.7%	47.5%	37.8%
26	46,114	8,564	23,472	14,078	Dole	18.6%	50.9%	30.5%
27	76,990	11,109	39,339	26,542	Dole	14.4%	51.1%	34.5%
28	62,155	8,608	32,794	20,753	Dole	13.8%	52.8%	33.4%
29	57,776	11,239	25,751	20,786	Dole	19.5%	44.6%	36.0%
30	40,207	7,956	17,713	14,538	Dole	19.8%	44.1%	36.2%
31	67,505	13,572	35,941	17,992	Dole	20.1%	53.2%	26.7%
Total	1,088,324	163,365	599,748	325,211	Dole	15.0%	55.1%	29.9%

Note: Vote was for delegates only, with three elected per district. Totals reflect vote for all delegates, so the turnout was roughly one-third of the total votes listed above, or probably no more than 400,000. Dole and Forbes ran delegates in all 31 districts. Buchanan did not. There was no direct vote for candidates.

NORTH CAROLINA

The best known of North Carolina's presidential primaries remains the 1976 duel between Ronald Reagan and President Gerald Ford. Had Reagan not won, his political career probably would have ended there.

Reagan had lost the first five primaries of 1976. But with backing from Sen. Jesse Helms and his potent political organization, Reagan edged Ford in the Tarheel State by about 12,500 votes out of nearly 200,000 cast. It proved a pivotal victory for Reagan that revived his 1976 campaign and helped position him to win the nomination and the White House in 1980.

In besting Ford, Reagan ran well in parts of the state where Helms had demonstrated strength—in the blue-collar, textile-producing centers of the Piedmont, in Helms's home base in the Raleigh area, and in tobacco-growing eastern North Carolina. Ford held his own in populous Mecklenburg County (Charlotte) and beat Reagan in the western mountains, the historic cornerstone of the North Carolina GOP since the Civil War.

At the same time that North Carolina Republicans were resurrecting Reagan's presidential ambitions, the state's Democratic voters were sounding the death knell for those of George Wallace. In the 1972 primary, Wallace had swamped the favorite-son candidacy of former North Carolina Gov. Terry Sanford by putting together much the same coalition on the Democratic side that Reagan did on the Republican.

But when North Carolina voted in 1976, Wallace was a fading force, both nationally and in the South. Jimmy Carter had gone head-to-head with him in Florida in early March and won by 4 percentage points. Two weeks later in North Carolina, Carter's margin expanded to nearly 20 points, and Wallace was done as a serious presidential contender.

The only other time that the North Carolina primary had a make-or-break quality was in 1988, when Bob Dole suffered a critical loss that enabled George Bush to sweep the Super Tuesday South and essentially wrap up the Republican nomination. North Carolina was one of Dole's best chances for a Super Tuesday victory that year, due in no small part to his wife, Elizabeth, who was born in the textile-producing town of Salisbury and graduated from Duke University in Durham. Dole carried several urban counties, including Mecklenburg and Wake (Raleigh). But Bush won most of the rest of the state, and prevailed narrowly.

It was a considerably better showing for Bush than his first presidential run against Reagan in 1980. Then, he could carry

Recent North Carolina Primary Results

North Carolina held its first presidential primary in 1920, but did not hold another until 1972.

	DEMOCRATS			REPUBLICANS		
Year	Turnout	Candidates	%	Turnout	Candidates	%
1996 (May 7)	572,160	BILL CLINTON* Uncommitted	81 12	284,212	BOB DOLE Pat Buchanan	71 13
1992 (May 5)	691,875	BILL CLINTON Uncommitted Jerry Brown	64 15 10	283,571	GEORGE BUSH* Pat Buchanan	71 20
1988 (March 8)	679,958	AL GORE Jesse Jackson Michael Dukakis	35 33 20	273,801	GEORGE BUSH Bob Dole	45 39
1984 (May 8)	960,857	WALTER MONDALE Gary Hart Jesse Jackson	36 30 25		NO PRIMARY	
1980 (May 6)	737,262	JIMMY CARTER* Edward Kennedy	70 18	168,391	RONALD REAGAN George Bush	68 22
1976 (March 23)	604,832	JIMMY CARTER George Wallace	54 35	193,727	RONALD REAGAN Gerald Ford*	52 46
1972 (May 6)	821,410	GEORGE WALLACE Terry Sanford	50 37	167,899	RICHARD NIXON*	95

Note: All candidates are listed that drew at least 10 percent of their party's primary vote. The names of winning candidates are capitalized. An asterisk (*) indicates an incumbent president.

only the most liberal of North Carolina's 100 counties—Orange, home of the University of North Carolina at Chapel Hill and a cornerstone of the state's Research Triangle.

Pat Buchanan tried to emulate Reagan's success in his 1992 challenge to Bush, highlighting themes tailored to conservative Republicans—from criticism of the Voting Rights Act to putting the Confederate stars and bars on his North Carolina bumper stickers. But Buchanan could not come close to carrying a single county, either in 1992 against Bush or in 1996 against Dole.

Over the course of much of the twentieth century, North Carolina was a model for peace and prosperity in the South. And from 1972 through 1996, every Democratic primary winner except one (Walter Mondale in 1984) was a son of the South. Wallace, Carter (twice), Al Gore, and Bill Clinton (twice) all won North Carolina's Democratic primary.

Gore's 2-percentage point victory over Jesse Jackson in 1988 was the closest of the recent Democratic contests. Gore swept most of the western half of the state, which is adjacent to Tennessee; Jackson won most of the eastern half, which includes the state's largest concentration of black voters. The party's eventual nominee, Michael Dukakis, carried Orange County.

NORTH CAROLINA DEMOCRATIC

1972

County	Total Vote	Sanford	Wallace	Other	Winner	Percentage of Total Vote: Sanford	Wallace	Other
ALAMANCE	15,995	5,966	8,808	1,221	Wallace	37.3%	55.1%	7.6%
ALEXANDER	2,137	830	1,180	127	Wallace	38.8%	55.2%	5.9%
ALLEGHANY	1,976	688	1,155	133	Wallace	34.8%	58.5%	6.7%
ANSON	5,188	1,676	2,791	721	Wallace	32.3%	53.8%	13.9%
ASHE	2,906	1,591	1,092	223	Sanford	54.7%	37.6%	7.7%
AVERY	703	339	312	52	Sanford	48.2%	44.4%	7.4%
BEAUFORT	6,702	1,991	3,992	719	Wallace	29.7%	59.6%	10.7%
BERTIE	4,151	951	2,050	1,150	Wallace	22.9%	49.4%	27.7%
BLADEN	5,563	1,592	3,393	578	Wallace	28.6%	61.0%	10.4%
BRUNSWICK	5,629	1,573	3,436	620	Wallace	27.9%	61.0%	11.0%
BUNCOMBE	19,794	7,628	9,306	2,860	Wallace	38.5%	47.0%	14.4%
BURKE	6,864	3,337	2,944	583	Sanford	48.6%	42.9%	8.5%
CABARRUS	10,345	3,666	5,785	894	Wallace	35.4%	55.9%	8.6%
CALDWELL	5,172	2,167	2,485	520	Wallace	41.9%	48.0%	10.1%
CAMDEN	1,403	353	917	133	Wallace	25.2%	65.4%	9.5%
CARTERET	5,932	2,684	2,665	583	Sanford	45.2%	44.9%	9.8%
CASWELL	3,887	1,350	2,061	476	Wallace	34.7%	53.0%	12.2%
CATAWBA	9,942	4,243	4,716	983	Wallace	42.7%	47.4%	9.9%
CHATHAM	5,814	2,285	2,949	580	Wallace	39.3%	50.7%	10.0%
CHEROKEE	2,086	772	1,028	286	Wallace	37.0%	49.3%	13.7%
CHOWAN	2,171	823	1,096	252	Wallace	37.9%	50.5%	11.6%
CLAY	657	278	305	74	Wallace	42.3%	46.4%	11.3%
CLEVELAND	12,176	3,844	7,146	1,186	Wallace	31.6%	58.7%	9.7%
COLUMBUS	10,536	2,693	6,974	869	Wallace	25.6%	66.2%	8.2%
CRAVEN	8,964	2,594	5,304	1,066	Wallace	28.9%	59.2%	11.9%
CUMBERLAND	23,095	9,062	11,258	2,775	Wallace	39.2%	48.7%	12.0%
CURRITUCK	1,973	522	1,287	164	Wallace	26.5%	65.2%	8.3%
DARE	1,835	780	931	124	Wallace	42.5%	50.7%	6.8%
DAVIDSON	11,007	3,960	5,986	1,061	Wallace	36.0%	54.4%	9.6%
DAVIE	2,112	795	1,122	195	Wallace	37.6%	53.1%	9.2%
DUPLIN	7,457	2,184	4,684	589	Wallace	29.3%	62.8%	7.9%
DURHAM	26,199	10,458	10,637	5,104	Wallace	39.9%	40.6%	19.5%
EDGECOMBE	11,693	4,415	5,397	1,881	Wallace	37.8%	46.2%	16.1%
FORSYTH	31,352	12,110	14,345	4,897	Wallace	38.6%	45.8%	15.6%
FRANKLIN	7,267	2,452	4,240	575	Wallace	33.7%	58.3%	7.9%
GASTON	15,129	4,667	9,002	1,460	Wallace	30.8%	59.5%	9.7%
GATES	2,340	1,039	997	304	Sanford	44.4%	42.6%	13.0%
GRAHAM	998	491	398	109	Sanford	49.2%	39.9%	10.9%
GRANVILLE	8,809	2,858	4,583	1,368	Wallace	32.4%	52.0%	15.5%
GREENE	2,897	720	2,033	144	Wallace	24.9%	70.2%	5.0%
GUILFORD	44,845	16,041	21,729	7,075	Wallace	35.8%	48.5%	15.8%
HALIFAX	11,484	3,244	5,963	2,277	Wallace	28.2%	51.9%	19.8%
HARNETT	8,128	2,427	5,124	577	Wallace	29.9%	63.0%	7.1%
HAYWOOD	6,926	2,696	3,401	829	Wallace	38.9%	49.1%	12.0%
HENDERSON	3,978	1,511	2,050	417	Wallace	38.0%	51.5%	10.5%
HERTFORD	3,591	1,204	1,579	808	Wallace	33.5%	44.0%	22.5%
HOKE	3,012	1,451	1,339	222	Sanford	48.2%	44.5%	7.4%
HYDE	1,392	491	779	122	Wallace	35.3%	56.0%	8.8%
IREDELL	10,787	2,955	6,957	875	Wallace	27.4%	64.5%	8.1%
JACKSON	3,070	1,381	1,179	510	Sanford	45.0%	38.4%	16.6%

NORTH CAROLINA DEMOCRATIC

1972

County	Total Vote	Sanford	Wallace	Other	Winner	Percentage of Total Vote: Sanford	Wallace	Other
JOHNSTON	10,180	3,203	6,239	738	Wallace	31.5%	61.3%	7.2%
JONES	2,661	653	1,433	575	Wallace	24.5%	53.9%	21.6%
LEE	5,834	2,148	3,343	343	Wallace	36.8%	57.3%	5.9%
LENOIR	10,813	2,510	6,923	1,380	Wallace	23.2%	64.0%	12.8%
LINCOLN	5,942	2,697	2,738	507	Wallace	45.4%	46.1%	8.5%
MCDOWELL	4,237	1,242	2,555	440	Wallace	29.3%	60.3%	10.4%
MACON	2,373	1,059	1,088	226	Wallace	44.6%	45.8%	9.5%
MADISON	2,066	677	1,053	336	Wallace	32.8%	51.0%	16.3%
MARTIN	5,305	1,964	2,731	610	Wallace	37.0%	51.5%	11.5%
MECKLENBURG	51,935	21,360	21,786	8,789	Wallace	41.1%	41.9%	16.9%
MITCHELL	728	326	329	73	Wallace	44.8%	45.2%	10.0%
MONTGOMERY	3,775	1,550	1,805	420	Wallace	41.1%	47.8%	11.1%
MOORE	6,767	2,921	3,255	591	Wallace	43.2%	48.1%	8.7%
NASH	13,673	4,526	7,523	1,624	Wallace	33.1%	55.0%	11.9%
NEW HANOVER	13,807	4,128	7,809	1,870	Wallace	29.9%	56.6%	13.5%
NORTHAMPTON	6,725	3,235	2,614	876	Sanford	48.1%	38.9%	13.0%
ONSLOW	9,149	2,503	5,649	997	Wallace	27.4%	61.7%	10.9%
ORANGE	15,376	9,517	3,759	2,100	Sanford	61.9%	24.4%	13.7%
PAMLICO	1,942	619	1,030	293	Wallace	31.9%	53.0%	15.1%
PASQUOTANK	4,207	1,899	1,884	424	Sanford	45.1%	44.8%	10.1%
PENDER	3,401	965	2,146	290	Wallace	28.4%	63.1%	8.5%
PERQUIMANS	1,543	619	789	135	Wallace	40.1%	51.1%	8.7%
PERSON	6,554	1,978	3,434	1,142	Wallace	30.2%	52.4%	17.4%
PITT	13,678	4,341	7,538	1,799	Wallace	31.7%	55.1%	13.2%
POLK	1,907	663	1,094	150	Wallace	34.8%	57.4%	7.9%
RANDOLPH	8,207	3,234	4,210	763	Wallace	39.4%	51.3%	9.3%
RICHMOND	7,613	2,650	4,064	899	Wallace	34.8%	53.4%	11.8%
ROBESON	17,880	7,533	8,061	2,286	Wallace	42.1%	45.1%	12.8%
ROCKINGHAM	12,112	3,537	7,305	1,270	Wallace	29.2%	60.3%	10.5%
ROWAN	11,390	4,263	6,053	1,074	Wallace	37.4%	53.1%	9.4%
RUTHERFORD	6,881	2,554	3,814	513	Wallace	37.1%	55.4%	7.5%
SAMPSON	5,778	2,389	2,709	680	Wallace	41.3%	46.9%	11.8%
SCOTLAND	4,207	1,819	1,721	667	Sanford	43.2%	40.9%	15.9%
STANLY	7,165	2,955	3,503	707	Wallace	41.2%	48.9%	9.9%
STOKES	4,883	1,482	3,027	374	Wallace	30.4%	62.0%	7.7%
SURRY	6,792	3,187	3,143	462	Sanford	46.9%	46.3%	6.8%
SWAIN	1,357	488	680	189	Wallace	36.0%	50.1%	13.9%
TRANSYLVANIA	3,017	1,110	1,486	421	Wallace	36.8%	49.3%	14.0%
TYRRELL	1,205	495	575	135	Wallace	41.1%	47.7%	11.2%
UNION	8,887	2,810	5,129	948	Wallace	31.6%	57.7%	10.7%
VANCE	7,669	2,413	4,142	1,114	Wallace	31.5%	54.0%	14.5%
WAKE	49,801	23,633	20,502	5,666	Sanford	47.5%	41.2%	11.4%
WARREN	3,944	1,126	1,853	965	Wallace	28.5%	47.0%	24.5%
WASHINGTON	3,265	1,587	1,459	219	Sanford	48.6%	44.7%	6.7%
WATAUGA	2,732	1,692	836	204	Sanford	61.9%	30.6%	7.5%
WAYNE	12,645	3,641	7,134	1,870	Wallace	28.8%	56.4%	14.8%
WILKES	4,353	2,304	1,767	282	Sanford	52.9%	40.6%	6.5%
WILSON	12,924	3,927	7,179	1,818	Wallace	30.4%	55.5%	14.1%
YADKIN	2,160	908	1,143	109	Wallace	42.0%	52.9%	5.0%
YANCEY	1,896	1,146	586	164	Sanford	60.4%	30.9%	8.6%
TOTAL	821,410	306,014	413,518	101,878	Wallace	37.3%	50.3%	12.4%

NORTH CAROLINA REPUBLICAN

1972

County	Total Vote	McCloskey	Nixon	Winner	Percentage of Total Vote McCloskey	Percentage of Total Vote Nixon
ALAMANCE	2,871	153	2,718	Nixon	5.3%	94.7%
ALEXANDER	1,131	36	1,095	Nixon	3.2%	96.8%
ALLEGHANY	595	14	581	Nixon	2.4%	97.6%
ANSON	140	9	131	Nixon	6.4%	93.6%
ASHE	1,783	30	1,753	Nixon	1.7%	98.3%
AVERY	2,443	136	2,307	Nixon	5.6%	94.4%
BEAUFORT	482	24	458	Nixon	5.0%	95.0%
BERTIE	48	4	44	Nixon	8.3%	91.7%
BLADEN	167	14	153	Nixon	8.4%	91.6%
BRUNSWICK	819	45	774	Nixon	5.5%	94.5%
BUNCOMBE	4,166	229	3,937	Nixon	5.5%	94.5%
BURKE	3,118	117	3,001	Nixon	3.8%	96.2%
CABARRUS	2,796	151	2,645	Nixon	5.4%	94.6%
CALDWELL	2,385	94	2,291	Nixon	3.9%	96.1%
CAMDEN	29	2	27	Nixon	6.9%	93.1%
CARTERET	1,779	71	1,708	Nixon	4.0%	96.0%
CASWELL	150	15	135	Nixon	10.0%	90.0%
CATAWBA	4,451	173	4,278	Nixon	3.9%	96.1%
CHATHAM	1,176	43	1,133	Nixon	3.7%	96.3%
CHEROKEE	909	16	893	Nixon	1.8%	98.2%
CHOWAN	93	7	86	Nixon	7.5%	92.5%
CLAY	585	14	571	Nixon	2.4%	97.6%
CLEVELAND	923	71	852	Nixon	7.7%	92.3%
COLUMBUS	489	23	466	Nixon	4.7%	95.3%
CRAVEN	754	42	712	Nixon	5.6%	94.4%
CUMBERLAND	2,626	163	2,463	Nixon	6.2%	93.8%
CURRITUCK	23	1	22	Nixon	4.3%	95.7%
DARE	260	8	252	Nixon	3.1%	96.9%
DAVIDSON	4,213	202	4,011	Nixon	4.8%	95.2%
DAVIE	2,018	119	1,899	Nixon	5.9%	94.1%
DUPLIN	552	26	526	Nixon	4.7%	95.3%
DURHAM	3,155	221	2,934	Nixon	7.0%	93.0%
EDGECOMBE	749	74	675	Nixon	9.9%	90.1%
FORSYTH	7,175	553	6,622	Nixon	7.7%	92.3%
FRANKLIN	316	31	285	Nixon	9.8%	90.2%
GASTON	2,828	127	2,701	Nixon	4.5%	95.5%
GATES	29	1	28	Nixon	3.4%	96.6%
GRAHAM	927	22	905	Nixon	2.4%	97.6%
GRANVILLE	234	25	209	Nixon	10.7%	89.3%
GREENE	242	14	228	Nixon	5.8%	94.2%
GUILFORD	9,921	610	9,311	Nixon	6.1%	93.9%
HALIFAX	266	23	243	Nixon	8.6%	91.4%
HARNETT	1,194	39	1,155	Nixon	3.3%	96.7%
HAYWOOD	1,030	36	994	Nixon	3.5%	96.5%
HENDERSON	3,052	151	2,901	Nixon	4.9%	95.1%
HERTFORD	98	11	87	Nixon	11.2%	88.8%
HOKE	96	6	90	Nixon	6.3%	93.8%
HYDE	98	9	89	Nixon	9.2%	90.8%
IREDELL	2,633	134	2,499	Nixon	5.1%	94.9%
JACKSON	750	15	735	Nixon	2.0%	98.0%

NORTH CAROLINA REPUBLICAN

1972

County	Total Vote	McCloskey	Nixon	Winner	Percentage of Total Vote McCloskey	Nixon
JOHNSTON	1,468	50	1,418	Nixon	3.4%	96.6%
JONES	66	2	64	Nixon	3.0%	97.0%
LEE	550	26	524	Nixon	4.7%	95.3%
LENOIR	1,165	62	1,103	Nixon	5.3%	94.7%
LINCOLN	1,555	36	1,519	Nixon	2.3%	97.7%
MCDOWELL	644	24	620	Nixon	3.7%	96.3%
MACON	556	15	541	Nixon	2.7%	97.3%
MADISON	568	17	551	Nixon	3.0%	97.0%
MARTIN	187	13	174	Nixon	7.0%	93.0%
MECKLENBURG	16,537	1,001	15,536	Nixon	6.1%	93.9%
MITCHELL	3,165	166	2,999	Nixon	5.2%	94.8%
MONTGOMERY	923	26	897	Nixon	2.8%	97.2%
MOORE	2,604	111	2,493	Nixon	4.3%	95.7%
NASH	1,767	134	1,633	Nixon	7.6%	92.4%
NEW HANOVER	2,937	168	2,769	Nixon	5.7%	94.3%
NORTHAMPTON	25	2	23	Nixon	8.0%	92.0%
ONSLOW	1,001	72	929	Nixon	7.2%	92.8%
ORANGE	1,779	183	1,596	Nixon	10.3%	89.7%
PAMLICO	145	4	141	Nixon	2.8%	97.2%
PASQUOTANK	170	11	159	Nixon	6.5%	93.5%
PENDER	181	10	171	Nixon	5.5%	94.5%
PERQUIMANS	42	1	41	Nixon	2.4%	97.6%
PERSON	378	28	350	Nixon	7.4%	92.6%
PITT	1,548	107	1,441	Nixon	6.9%	93.1%
POLK	597	23	574	Nixon	3.9%	96.1%
RANDOLPH	5,360	163	5,197	Nixon	3.0%	97.0%
RICHMOND	197	6	191	Nixon	3.0%	97.0%
ROBESON	409	46	363	Nixon	11.2%	88.8%
ROCKINGHAM	1,505	78	1,427	Nixon	5.2%	94.8%
ROWAN	5,067	262	4,805	Nixon	5.2%	94.8%
RUTHERFORD	1,300	43	1,257	Nixon	3.3%	96.7%
SAMPSON	2,857	75	2,782	Nixon	2.6%	97.4%
SCOTLAND	183	14	169	Nixon	7.7%	92.3%
STANLY	2,642	127	2,515	Nixon	4.8%	95.2%
STOKES	2,143	90	2,053	Nixon	4.2%	95.8%
SURRY	1,560	72	1,488	Nixon	4.6%	95.4%
SWAIN	399	14	385	Nixon	3.5%	96.5%
TRANSYLVANIA	901	50	851	Nixon	5.5%	94.5%
TYRRELL	35	2	33	Nixon	5.7%	94.3%
UNION	903	40	863	Nixon	4.4%	95.6%
VANCE	365	22	343	Nixon	6.0%	94.0%
WAKE	8,534	512	8,022	Nixon	6.0%	94.0%
WARREN	177	58	119	Nixon	32.8%	67.2%
WASHINGTON	146	9	137	Nixon	6.2%	93.8%
WATAUGA	1,832	55	1,777	Nixon	3.0%	97.0%
WAYNE	1,501	73	1,428	Nixon	4.9%	95.1%
WILKES	5,752	232	5,520	Nixon	4.0%	96.0%
WILSON	1,337	111	1,226	Nixon	8.3%	91.7%
YADKIN	2,860	123	2,737	Nixon	4.3%	95.7%
YANCEY	609	9	600	Nixon	1.5%	98.5%
TOTAL	167,899	8,732	159,167	Nixon	5.2%	94.8%

NORTH CAROLINA DEMOCRATIC

1976

County	Total Vote	Carter	Wallace	Other	Winner	Percentage of Total Vote Carter	Wallace	Other
ALAMANCE	11,273	5,535	4,602	1,136	Carter	49.1%	40.8%	10.1%
ALEXANDER	2,285	1,404	760	121	Carter	61.4%	33.3%	5.3%
ALLEGHANY	1,309	707	453	149	Carter	54.0%	34.6%	11.4%
ANSON	3,370	1,390	1,702	278	Wallace	41.2%	50.5%	8.2%
ASHE	2,334	1,625	502	207	Carter	69.6%	21.5%	8.9%
AVERY	965	527	292	146	Carter	54.6%	30.3%	15.1%
BEAUFORT	4,610	2,088	2,087	435	Carter	45.3%	45.3%	9.4%
BERTIE	2,022	1,093	765	164	Carter	54.1%	37.8%	8.1%
BLADEN	3,844	2,016	1,589	239	Carter	52.4%	41.3%	6.2%
BRUNSWICK	4,367	2,437	1,599	331	Carter	55.8%	36.6%	7.6%
BUNCOMBE	18,375	9,785	5,612	2,978	Carter	53.3%	30.5%	16.2%
BURKE	7,395	4,955	1,831	609	Carter	67.0%	24.8%	8.2%
CABARRUS	8,438	4,611	3,134	693	Carter	54.6%	37.1%	8.2%
CALDWELL	5,370	3,239	1,632	499	Carter	60.3%	30.4%	9.3%
CAMDEN	774	318	376	80	Wallace	41.1%	48.6%	10.3%
CARTERET	4,449	2,583	1,344	522	Carter	58.1%	30.2%	11.7%
CASWELL	2,562	1,161	1,216	185	Wallace	45.3%	47.5%	7.2%
CATAWBA	9,501	5,881	2,796	824	Carter	61.9%	29.4%	8.7%
CHATHAM	4,069	2,189	1,355	525	Carter	53.8%	33.3%	12.9%
CHEROKEE	1,635	1,176	310	149	Carter	71.9%	19.0%	9.1%
CHOWAN	917	438	347	132	Carter	47.8%	37.8%	14.4%
CLAY	634	474	95	65	Carter	74.8%	15.0%	10.3%
CLEVELAND	8,123	4,134	3,386	603	Carter	50.9%	41.7%	7.4%
COLUMBUS	6,251	3,472	2,460	319	Carter	55.5%	39.4%	5.1%
CRAVEN	6,833	3,453	2,860	520	Carter	50.5%	41.9%	7.6%
CUMBERLAND	17,718	9,741	6,054	1,923	Carter	55.0%	34.2%	10.9%
CURRITUCK	1,071	443	502	126	Wallace	41.4%	46.9%	11.8%
DARE	1,294	655	410	229	Carter	50.6%	31.7%	17.7%
DAVIDSON	9,260	4,941	3,161	1,158	Carter	53.4%	34.1%	12.5%
DAVIE	1,665	936	591	138	Carter	56.2%	35.5%	8.3%
DUPLIN	5,139	2,477	2,396	266	Carter	48.2%	46.6%	5.2%
DURHAM	18,601	9,623	5,651	3,327	Carter	51.7%	30.4%	17.9%
EDGECOMBE	6,106	3,232	2,418	456	Carter	52.9%	39.6%	7.5%
FORSYTH	23,980	13,288	7,154	3,538	Carter	55.4%	29.8%	14.8%
FRANKLIN	4,058	1,784	2,006	268	Wallace	44.0%	49.4%	6.6%
GASTON	12,763	5,915	5,730	1,118	Carter	46.3%	44.9%	8.8%
GATES	1,156	698	339	119	Carter	60.4%	29.3%	10.3%
GRAHAM	671	449	141	81	Carter	66.9%	21.0%	12.1%
GRANVILLE	4,281	1,869	1,964	448	Wallace	43.7%	45.9%	10.5%
GREENE	2,082	831	1,166	85	Wallace	39.9%	56.0%	4.1%
GUILFORD	33,168	17,916	9,819	5,433	Carter	54.0%	29.6%	16.4%
HALIFAX	6,184	2,955	2,561	668	Carter	47.8%	41.4%	10.8%
HARNETT	6,307	3,080	2,651	576	Carter	48.8%	42.0%	9.1%
HAYWOOD	6,759	3,565	2,170	1,024	Carter	52.7%	32.1%	15.2%
HENDERSON	4,200	2,288	1,336	576	Carter	54.5%	31.8%	13.7%
HERTFORD	1,979	1,108	645	226	Carter	56.0%	32.6%	11.4%
HOKE	2,027	1,231	635	161	Carter	60.7%	31.3%	7.9%
HYDE	948	443	458	47	Wallace	46.7%	48.3%	5.0%
IREDELL	8,921	4,642	3,598	681	Carter	52.0%	40.3%	7.6%
JACKSON	3,214	2,144	576	494	Carter	66.7%	17.9%	15.4%

NORTH CAROLINA DEMOCRATIC

1976

County	Total Vote	Carter	Wallace	Other	Winner	Percentage of Total Vote Carter	Wallace	Other
JOHNSTON	7,275	3,290	3,430	555	Wallace	45.2%	47.1%	7.6%
JONES	1,940	892	955	93	Wallace	46.0%	49.2%	4.8%
LEE	3,803	1,757	1,635	411	Carter	46.2%	43.0%	10.8%
LENOIR	7,408	2,564	4,316	528	Wallace	34.6%	58.3%	7.1%
LINCOLN	4,601	2,987	1,320	294	Carter	64.9%	28.7%	6.4%
MCDOWELL	3,283	1,743	1,217	323	Carter	53.1%	37.1%	9.8%
MACON	2,681	1,603	743	335	Carter	59.8%	27.7%	12.5%
MADISON	1,484	835	494	155	Carter	56.3%	33.3%	10.4%
MARTIN	2,878	1,432	1,234	212	Carter	49.8%	42.9%	7.4%
MECKLENBURG	40,311	23,960	10,652	5,699	Carter	59.4%	26.4%	14.1%
MITCHELL	765	429	240	96	Carter	56.1%	31.4%	12.5%
MONTGOMERY	2,602	1,476	918	208	Carter	56.7%	35.3%	8.0%
MOORE	5,261	2,889	1,764	608	Carter	54.9%	33.5%	11.6%
NASH	7,766	3,596	3,656	514	Wallace	46.3%	47.1%	6.6%
NEW HANOVER	9,840	5,393	3,299	1,148	Carter	54.8%	33.5%	11.7%
NORTHAMPTON	3,501	2,238	983	280	Carter	63.9%	28.1%	8.0%
ONSLOW	6,302	2,286	3,300	716	Wallace	36.3%	52.4%	11.4%
ORANGE	12,797	6,242	2,396	4,159	Carter	48.8%	18.7%	32.5%
PAMLICO	1,685	1,036	549	100	Carter	61.5%	32.6%	5.9%
PASQUOTANK	3,175	1,663	1,113	399	Carter	52.4%	35.1%	12.6%
PENDER	2,831	1,566	1,046	219	Carter	55.3%	36.9%	7.7%
PERQUIMANS	1,097	556	421	120	Carter	50.7%	38.4%	10.9%
PERSON	2,699	1,121	1,313	265	Wallace	41.5%	48.6%	9.8%
PITT	9,280	4,297	3,946	1,037	Carter	46.3%	42.5%	11.2%
POLK	1,546	777	640	129	Carter	50.3%	41.4%	8.3%
RANDOLPH	6,128	3,320	2,183	625	Carter	54.2%	35.6%	10.2%
RICHMOND	7,382	3,802	2,878	702	Carter	51.5%	39.0%	9.5%
ROBESON	10,022	5,762	3,428	832	Carter	57.5%	34.2%	8.3%
ROCKINGHAM	8,320	3,935	3,382	1,003	Carter	47.3%	40.6%	12.1%
ROWAN	9,711	5,356	3,359	996	Carter	55.2%	34.6%	10.3%
RUTHERFORD	5,781	3,152	2,070	559	Carter	54.5%	35.8%	9.7%
SAMPSON	4,339	2,459	1,490	390	Carter	56.7%	34.3%	9.0%
SCOTLAND	2,761	1,528	973	260	Carter	55.3%	35.2%	9.4%
STANLY	5,509	3,473	1,691	345	Carter	63.0%	30.7%	6.3%
STOKES	3,150	1,479	1,443	228	Carter	47.0%	45.8%	7.2%
SURRY	5,100	3,391	1,216	493	Carter	66.5%	23.8%	9.7%
SWAIN	1,092	683	291	118	Carter	62.5%	26.6%	10.8%
TRANSYLVANIA	2,562	1,457	715	390	Carter	56.9%	27.9%	15.2%
TYRRELL	624	357	221	46	Carter	57.2%	35.4%	7.4%
UNION	6,626	3,540	2,594	492	Carter	53.4%	39.1%	7.4%
VANCE	4,124	1,881	1,888	355	Wallace	45.6%	45.8%	8.6%
WAKE	38,772	22,382	10,529	5,861	Carter	57.7%	27.2%	15.1%
WARREN	2,508	1,278	1,022	208	Carter	51.0%	40.7%	8.3%
WASHINGTON	1,891	1,069	657	165	Carter	56.5%	34.7%	8.7%
WATAUGA	2,685	1,705	443	537	Carter	63.5%	16.5%	20.0%
WAYNE	8,584	4,157	3,754	673	Carter	48.4%	43.7%	7.8%
WILKES	4,156	2,822	939	395	Carter	67.9%	22.6%	9.5%
WILSON	7,333	3,448	3,203	682	Carter	47.0%	43.7%	9.3%
YADKIN	1,958	1,227	623	108	Carter	62.7%	31.8%	5.5%
YANCEY	1,656	1,201	357	98	Carter	72.5%	21.6%	5.9%
TOTAL	604,842	324,437	210,166	70,239	Carter	53.6%	34.7%	11.6%
Certified Totals	604,832	324,437	210,166	70,229	Carter	53.6%	34.7%	11.6%

NORTH CAROLINA REPUBLICAN

1976

County	Total Vote	Ford	Reagan	Uncommitted	Winner	Percentage of Total Vote Ford	Reagan	Uncom.
ALAMANCE	2,885	1,174	1,666	45	Reagan	40.7%	57.7%	1.6%
ALEXANDER	1,522	640	872	10	Reagan	42.0%	57.3%	0.7%
ALLEGHANY	373	197	170	6	Ford	52.8%	45.6%	1.6%
ANSON	204	95	105	4	Reagan	46.6%	51.5%	2.0%
ASHE	1,553	1,017	512	24	Ford	65.5%	33.0%	1.5%
AVERY	2,671	1,695	835	141	Ford	63.5%	31.3%	5.3%
BEAUFORT	654	187	448	19	Reagan	28.6%	68.5%	2.9%
BERTIE	70	27	41	2	Reagan	38.6%	58.6%	2.9%
BLADEN	197	69	123	5	Reagan	35.0%	62.4%	2.5%
BRUNSWICK	1,279	634	614	31	Ford	49.6%	48.0%	2.4%
BUNCOMBE	6,312	3,461	2,744	107	Ford	54.8%	43.5%	1.7%
BURKE	3,707	1,802	1,850	55	Reagan	48.6%	49.9%	1.5%
CABARRUS	3,200	1,114	2,025	61	Reagan	34.8%	63.3%	1.9%
CALDWELL	3,561	1,516	1,999	46	Reagan	42.6%	56.1%	1.3%
CAMDEN	30	13	16	1	Reagan	43.3%	53.3%	3.3%
CARTERET	2,003	696	1,292	15	Reagan	34.7%	64.5%	0.7%
CASWELL	151	55	90	6	Reagan	36.4%	59.6%	4.0%
CATAWBA	6,298	3,037	3,208	53	Reagan	48.2%	50.9%	0.8%
CHATHAM	1,123	554	554	15		49.3%	49.3%	1.3%
CHEROKEE	941	701	235	5	Ford	74.5%	25.0%	0.5%
CHOWAN	123	54	68	1	Reagan	43.9%	55.3%	0.8%
CLAY	460	326	124	10	Ford	70.9%	27.0%	2.2%
CLEVELAND	1,210	583	591	36	Reagan	48.2%	48.8%	3.0%
COLUMBUS	618	257	340	21	Reagan	41.6%	55.0%	3.4%
CRAVEN	1,121	319	794	8	Reagan	28.5%	70.8%	0.7%
CUMBERLAND	3,255	1,225	1,963	67	Reagan	37.6%	60.3%	2.1%
CURRITUCK	34	12	20	2	Reagan	35.3%	58.8%	5.9%
DARE	300	181	113	6	Ford	60.3%	37.7%	2.0%
DAVIDSON	5,350	1,988	3,273	89	Reagan	37.2%	61.2%	1.7%
DAVIE	1,827	826	977	24	Reagan	45.2%	53.5%	1.3%
DUPLIN	620	148	459	13	Reagan	23.9%	74.0%	2.1%
DURHAM	3,485	1,646	1,773	66	Reagan	47.2%	50.9%	1.9%
EDGECOMBE	678	152	522	4	Reagan	22.4%	77.0%	0.6%
FORSYTH	9,148	4,056	4,921	171	Reagan	44.3%	53.8%	1.9%
FRANKLIN	335	63	264	8	Reagan	18.8%	78.8%	2.4%
GASTON	4,852	1,766	3,030	56	Reagan	36.4%	62.4%	1.2%
GATES	24	14	9	1	Ford	58.3%	37.5%	4.2%
GRAHAM	557	380	171	6	Ford	68.2%	30.7%	1.1%
GRANVILLE	255	103	143	9	Reagan	40.4%	56.1%	3.5%
GREENE	208	29	178	1	Reagan	13.9%	85.6%	0.5%
GUILFORD	11,929	5,636	6,054	239	Reagan	47.2%	50.8%	2.0%
HALIFAX	355	116	234	5	Reagan	32.7%	65.9%	1.4%
HARNETT	1,350	508	822	20	Reagan	37.6%	60.9%	1.5%
HAYWOOD	1,568	907	621	40	Ford	57.8%	39.6%	2.6%
HENDERSON	4,174	2,067	2,062	45	Ford	49.5%	49.4%	1.1%
HERTFORD	92	37	51	4	Reagan	40.2%	55.4%	4.3%
HOKE	121	43	76	2	Reagan	35.5%	62.8%	1.7%
HYDE	98	18	75	5	Reagan	18.4%	76.5%	5.1%
IREDELL	2,715	1,124	1,539	52	Reagan	41.4%	56.7%	1.9%
JACKSON	1,253	767	476	10	Ford	61.2%	38.0%	0.8%

NORTH CAROLINA REPUBLICAN

1976

County	Total Vote	Ford	Reagan	Uncommitted	Winner	Percentage of Total Vote Ford	Reagan	Uncom.
JOHNSTON	1,444	525	907	12	Reagan	36.4%	62.8%	0.8%
JONES	115	22	91	2	Reagan	19.1%	79.1%	1.7%
LEE	668	306	351	11	Reagan	45.8%	52.5%	1.6%
LENOIR	1,389	243	1,137	9	Reagan	17.5%	81.9%	0.6%
LINCOLN	2,040	1,009	1,003	28	Ford	49.5%	49.2%	1.4%
MCDOWELL	995	593	384	18	Ford	59.6%	38.6%	1.8%
MACON	1,183	713	451	19	Ford	60.3%	38.1%	1.6%
MADISON	576	365	203	8	Ford	63.4%	35.2%	1.4%
MARTIN	223	66	149	8	Reagan	29.6%	66.8%	3.6%
MECKLENBURG	18,372	8,773	9,224	375	Reagan	47.8%	50.2%	2.0%
MITCHELL	1,653	1,088	540	25	Ford	65.8%	32.7%	1.5%
MONTGOMERY	895	423	456	16	Reagan	47.3%	50.9%	1.8%
MOORE	2,920	1,587	1,286	47	Ford	54.3%	44.0%	1.6%
NASH	1,612	377	1,215	20	Reagan	23.4%	75.4%	1.2%
NEW HANOVER	4,080	1,424	2,603	53	Reagan	34.9%	63.8%	1.3%
NORTHAMPTON	45	15	30		Reagan	33.3%	66.7%	
ONSLOW	976	319	640	17	Reagan	32.7%	65.6%	1.7%
ORANGE	2,253	1,283	896	74	Ford	56.9%	39.8%	3.3%
PAMLICO	199	84	111	4	Reagan	42.2%	55.8%	2.0%
PASQUOTANK	278	114	160	4	Reagan	41.0%	57.6%	1.4%
PENDER	379	168	197	14	Reagan	44.3%	52.0%	3.7%
PERQUIMANS	62	25	36	1	Reagan	40.3%	58.1%	1.6%
PERSON	280	90	186	4	Reagan	32.1%	66.4%	1.4%
PITT	1,750	614	1,106	30	Reagan	35.1%	63.2%	1.7%
POLK	854	464	386	4	Ford	54.3%	45.2%	0.5%
RANDOLPH	5,127	2,326	2,710	91	Reagan	45.4%	52.9%	1.8%
RICHMOND	425	204	201	20	Ford	48.0%	47.3%	4.7%
ROBESON	515	255	242	18	Ford	49.5%	47.0%	3.5%
ROCKINGHAM	1,677	775	850	52	Reagan	46.2%	50.7%	3.1%
ROWAN	5,070	1,797	3,179	94	Reagan	35.4%	62.7%	1.9%
RUTHERFORD	1,766	1,112	633	21	Ford	63.0%	35.8%	1.2%
SAMPSON	2,576	1,211	1,328	37	Reagan	47.0%	51.6%	1.4%
SCOTLAND	198	105	88	5	Ford	53.0%	44.4%	2.5%
STANLY	2,742	1,392	1,308	42	Ford	50.8%	47.7%	1.5%
STOKES	1,700	960	705	35	Ford	56.5%	41.5%	2.1%
SURRY	1,732	1,026	678	28	Ford	59.2%	39.1%	1.6%
SWAIN	399	246	151	2	Ford	61.7%	37.8%	0.5%
TRANSYLVANIA	1,287	718	552	17	Ford	55.8%	42.9%	1.3%
TYRRELL	37	14	23		Reagan	37.8%	62.2%	
UNION	1,100	503	576	21	Reagan	45.7%	52.4%	1.9%
VANCE	412	109	296	7	Reagan	26.5%	71.8%	1.7%
WAKE	11,186	4,632	6,367	187	Reagan	41.4%	56.9%	1.7%
WARREN	148	83	53	12	Ford	56.1%	35.8%	8.1%
WASHINGTON	145	35	96	14	Reagan	24.1%	66.2%	9.7%
WATAUGA	2,020	1,217	760	43	Ford	60.2%	37.6%	2.1%
WAYNE	1,484	388	1,075	21	Reagan	26.1%	72.4%	1.4%
WILKES	5,379	3,071	2,241	67	Ford	57.1%	41.7%	1.2%
WILSON	1,245	319	913	13	Reagan	25.6%	73.3%	1.0%
YADKIN	2,551	1,281	1,238	32	Ford	50.2%	48.5%	1.3%
YANCEY	716	393	315	8	Ford	54.9%	44.0%	1.1%
TOTAL	193,727	88,897	101,468	3,362	Reagan	45.9%	52.4%	1.7%

NORTH CAROLINA DEMOCRATIC

1980

County	Total Vote	Carter	E. Kennedy	Other	Winner	Percentage of Total Vote Carter	E. Kennedy	Other
ALAMANCE	13,656	10,030	1,950	1,676	Carter	73.4%	14.3%	12.3%
ALEXANDER	2,179	1,841	202	136	Carter	84.5%	9.3%	6.2%
ALLEGHANY	1,986	1,505	312	169	Carter	75.8%	15.7%	8.5%
ANSON	5,315	3,685	1,054	576	Carter	69.3%	19.8%	10.8%
ASHE	2,683	2,171	353	159	Carter	80.9%	13.2%	5.9%
AVERY	841	678	95	68	Carter	80.6%	11.3%	8.1%
BEAUFORT	6,471	4,627	905	939	Carter	71.5%	14.0%	14.5%
BERTIE	3,622	2,448	879	295	Carter	67.6%	24.3%	8.1%
BLADEN	5,204	3,797	1,013	394	Carter	73.0%	19.5%	7.6%
BRUNSWICK	6,180	4,067	1,466	647	Carter	65.8%	23.7%	10.5%
BUNCOMBE	18,585	13,820	2,601	2,164	Carter	74.4%	14.0%	11.6%
BURKE	8,930	6,431	1,435	1,064	Carter	72.0%	16.1%	11.9%
CABARRUS	8,699	6,002	1,206	1,491	Carter	69.0%	13.9%	17.1%
CALDWELL	5,369	3,790	850	729	Carter	70.6%	15.8%	13.6%
CAMDEN	1,594	954	389	251	Carter	59.8%	24.4%	15.7%
CARTERET	6,140	4,668	897	575	Carter	76.0%	14.6%	9.4%
CASWELL	2,780	1,695	673	412	Carter	61.0%	24.2%	14.8%
CATAWBA	8,971	6,469	1,240	1,262	Carter	72.1%	13.8%	14.1%
CHATHAM	6,093	4,175	1,328	590	Carter	68.5%	21.8%	9.7%
CHEROKEE	1,596	1,369	158	69	Carter	85.8%	9.9%	4.3%
CHOWAN	2,114	1,546	341	227	Carter	73.1%	16.1%	10.7%
CLAY	858	659	154	45	Carter	76.8%	17.9%	5.2%
CLEVELAND	10,162	7,675	1,105	1,382	Carter	75.5%	10.9%	13.6%
COLUMBUS	10,210	7,663	1,640	907	Carter	75.1%	16.1%	8.9%
CRAVEN	8,865	6,169	1,393	1,303	Carter	69.6%	15.7%	14.7%
CUMBERLAND	23,856	14,606	5,681	3,569	Carter	61.2%	23.8%	15.0%
CURRITUCK	2,438	1,521	433	484	Carter	62.4%	17.8%	19.9%
DARE	2,819	1,985	345	489	Carter	70.4%	12.2%	17.3%
DAVIDSON	12,041	8,592	2,180	1,269	Carter	71.4%	18.1%	10.5%
DAVIE	2,221	1,652	335	234	Carter	74.4%	15.1%	10.5%
DUPLIN	7,416	5,403	1,188	825	Carter	72.9%	16.0%	11.1%
DURHAM	22,683	12,540	7,220	2,923	Carter	55.3%	31.8%	12.9%
EDGECOMBE	7,527	5,296	1,313	918	Carter	70.4%	17.4%	12.2%
FORSYTH	16,978	11,099	3,959	1,920	Carter	65.4%	23.3%	11.3%
FRANKLIN	6,053	3,987	1,420	646	Carter	65.9%	23.5%	10.7%
GASTON	15,325	11,310	1,773	2,242	Carter	73.8%	11.6%	14.6%
GATES	2,437	1,398	681	358	Carter	57.4%	27.9%	14.7%
GRAHAM	1,101	860	170	71	Carter	78.1%	15.4%	6.4%
GRANVILLE	6,006	3,801	1,553	652	Carter	63.3%	25.9%	10.9%
GREENE	2,828	2,022	379	427	Carter	71.5%	13.4%	15.1%
GUILFORD	34,136	23,717	5,884	4,535	Carter	69.5%	17.2%	13.3%
HALIFAX	9,639	5,864	2,378	1,397	Carter	60.8%	24.7%	14.5%
HARNETT	9,338	6,934	1,507	897	Carter	74.3%	16.1%	9.6%
HAYWOOD	6,754	5,307	833	614	Carter	78.6%	12.3%	9.1%
HENDERSON	4,432	3,443	526	463	Carter	77.7%	11.9%	10.4%
HERTFORD	3,324	2,252	732	340	Carter	67.7%	22.0%	10.2%
HOKE	3,067	2,081	739	247	Carter	67.9%	24.1%	8.1%
HYDE	1,309	962	190	157	Carter	73.5%	14.5%	12.0%
IREDELL	9,402	7,436	953	1,013	Carter	79.1%	10.1%	10.8%
JACKSON	3,751	3,019	431	301	Carter	80.5%	11.5%	8.0%

NORTH CAROLINA DEMOCRATIC

1980

County	Total Vote	Carter	E. Kennedy	Other	Winner	Percentage of Total Vote: Carter	E. Kennedy	Other
JOHNSTON	11,126	8,438	1,434	1,254	Carter	75.8%	12.9%	11.3%
JONES	2,544	1,726	496	322	Carter	67.8%	19.5%	12.7%
LEE	6,205	4,637	926	642	Carter	74.7%	14.9%	10.3%
LENOIR	8,897	6,333	1,286	1,278	Carter	71.2%	14.5%	14.4%
LINCOLN	5,853	4,484	758	611	Carter	76.6%	13.0%	10.4%
MCDOWELL	3,602	2,666	544	392	Carter	74.0%	15.1%	10.9%
MACON	2,443	2,020	218	205	Carter	82.7%	8.9%	8.4%
MADISON	2,159	1,711	319	129	Carter	79.2%	14.8%	6.0%
MARTIN	3,895	3,092	518	285	Carter	79.4%	13.3%	7.3%
MECKLENBURG	45,037	29,312	8,646	7,079	Carter	65.1%	19.2%	15.7%
MITCHELL	933	762	106	65	Carter	81.7%	11.4%	7.0%
MONTGOMERY	3,931	2,767	853	311	Carter	70.4%	21.7%	7.9%
MOORE	6,537	4,996	827	714	Carter	76.4%	12.7%	10.9%
NASH	8,437	6,165	1,076	1,196	Carter	73.1%	12.8%	14.2%
NEW HANOVER	12,807	8,872	2,150	1,785	Carter	69.3%	16.8%	13.9%
NORTHAMPTON	4,032	2,378	1,152	502	Carter	59.0%	28.6%	12.5%
ONSLOW	9,700	6,705	1,640	1,355	Carter	69.1%	16.9%	14.0%
ORANGE	14,008	8,614	3,295	2,099	Carter	61.5%	23.5%	15.0%
PAMLICO	2,680	1,907	510	263	Carter	71.2%	19.0%	9.8%
PASQUOTANK	4,182	2,606	920	656	Carter	62.3%	22.0%	15.7%
PENDER	3,859	2,631	859	369	Carter	68.2%	22.3%	9.6%
PERQUIMANS	1,703	1,024	333	346	Carter	60.1%	19.6%	20.3%
PERSON	4,462	3,027	977	458	Carter	67.8%	21.9%	10.3%
PITT	12,985	9,196	1,678	2,111	Carter	70.8%	12.9%	16.3%
POLK	1,857	1,433	261	163	Carter	77.2%	14.1%	8.8%
RANDOLPH	6,266	4,975	754	537	Carter	79.4%	12.0%	8.6%
RICHMOND	7,017	4,696	1,426	895	Carter	66.9%	20.3%	12.8%
ROBESON	17,358	11,419	4,178	1,761	Carter	65.8%	24.1%	10.1%
ROCKINGHAM	9,320	6,368	1,789	1,163	Carter	68.3%	19.2%	12.5%
ROWAN	8,966	6,105	1,508	1,353	Carter	68.1%	16.8%	15.1%
RUTHERFORD	6,688	5,172	794	722	Carter	77.3%	11.9%	10.8%
SAMPSON	6,563	4,678	1,430	455	Carter	71.3%	21.8%	6.9%
SCOTLAND	3,698	2,654	643	401	Carter	71.8%	17.4%	10.8%
STANLY	6,027	4,694	710	623	Carter	77.9%	11.8%	10.3%
STOKES	3,527	2,678	555	294	Carter	75.9%	15.7%	8.3%
SURRY	5,222	4,102	739	381	Carter	78.6%	14.2%	7.3%
SWAIN	1,554	1,261	213	80	Carter	81.1%	13.7%	5.1%
TRANSYLVANIA	2,796	2,152	367	277	Carter	77.0%	13.1%	9.9%
TYRRELL	852	593	153	106	Carter	69.6%	18.0%	12.4%
UNION	8,740	6,453	974	1,313	Carter	73.8%	11.1%	15.0%
VANCE	6,326	4,036	1,497	793	Carter	63.8%	23.7%	12.5%
WAKE	47,821	34,328	7,932	5,561	Carter	71.8%	16.6%	11.6%
WARREN	4,656	2,519	1,704	433	Carter	54.1%	36.6%	9.3%
WASHINGTON	2,930	2,171	418	341	Carter	74.1%	14.3%	11.6%
WATAUGA	3,015	2,330	391	294	Carter	77.3%	13.0%	9.8%
WAYNE	10,347	7,069	1,878	1,400	Carter	68.3%	18.2%	13.5%
WILKES	4,511	3,600	599	312	Carter	79.8%	13.3%	6.9%
WILSON	8,673	6,611	1,190	872	Carter	76.2%	13.7%	10.1%
YADKIN	2,153	1,701	269	183	Carter	79.0%	12.5%	8.5%
YANCEY	2,378	1,890	349	139	Carter	79.5%	14.7%	5.8%
TOTAL	737,262	516,778	130,684	89,800	Carter	70.1%	17.7%	12.2%

NORTH CAROLINA REPUBLICAN

1980

County	Total Vote	Bush	Reagan	Other	Winner	Percentage of Total Vote Bush	Reagan	Other
ALAMANCE	2,489	494	1,727	268	Reagan	19.8%	69.4%	10.8%
ALEXANDER	1,050	141	831	78	Reagan	13.4%	79.1%	7.4%
ALLEGHANY	246	32	204	10	Reagan	13.0%	82.9%	4.1%
ANSON	201	38	145	18	Reagan	18.9%	72.1%	9.0%
ASHE	1,363	168	1,129	66	Reagan	12.3%	82.8%	4.8%
AVERY	2,694	406	1,943	345	Reagan	15.1%	72.1%	12.8%
BEAUFORT	666	92	530	44	Reagan	13.8%	79.6%	6.6%
BERTIE	105	16	78	11	Reagan	15.2%	74.3%	10.5%
BLADEN	149	25	106	18	Reagan	16.8%	71.1%	12.1%
BRUNSWICK	1,087	158	840	89	Reagan	14.5%	77.3%	8.2%
BUNCOMBE	5,641	1,906	3,212	523	Reagan	33.8%	56.9%	9.3%
BURKE	3,535	877	2,395	263	Reagan	24.8%	67.8%	7.4%
CABARRUS	2,493	413	1,826	254	Reagan	16.6%	73.2%	10.2%
CALDWELL	3,226	628	2,349	249	Reagan	19.5%	72.8%	7.7%
CAMDEN	110	3	19	88	Uncommitted	2.7%	17.3%	80.0%
CARTERET	1,646	265	1,244	137	Reagan	16.1%	75.6%	8.3%
CASWELL	118	15	86	17	Reagan	12.7%	72.9%	14.4%
CATAWBA	5,491	1,326	3,627	538	Reagan	24.1%	66.1%	9.8%
CHATHAM	861	155	603	103	Reagan	18.0%	70.0%	12.0%
CHEROKEE	595	55	503	37	Reagan	9.2%	84.5%	6.2%
CHOWAN	132	26	89	17	Reagan	19.7%	67.4%	12.9%
CLAY	715	56	645	14	Reagan	7.8%	90.2%	2.0%
CLEVELAND	1,167	291	744	132	Reagan	24.9%	63.8%	11.3%
COLUMBUS	644	73	509	62	Reagan	11.3%	79.0%	9.6%
CRAVEN	1,136	165	844	127	Reagan	14.5%	74.3%	11.2%
CUMBERLAND	3,359	695	2,262	402	Reagan	20.7%	67.3%	12.0%
CURRITUCK	90	8	75	7	Reagan	8.9%	83.3%	7.8%
DARE	305	83	178	44	Reagan	27.2%	58.4%	14.4%
DAVIDSON	5,370	933	3,858	579	Reagan	17.4%	71.8%	10.8%
DAVIE	2,567	469	1,847	251	Reagan	18.3%	72.0%	9.8%
DUPLIN	513	48	440	25	Reagan	9.4%	85.8%	4.9%
DURHAM	2,994	825	1,656	513	Reagan	27.6%	55.3%	17.1%
EDGECOMBE	604	71	488	45	Reagan	11.8%	80.8%	7.5%
FORSYTH	3,377	953	2,008	416	Reagan	28.2%	59.5%	12.3%
FRANKLIN	302	38	240	24	Reagan	12.6%	79.5%	7.9%
GASTON	3,455	615	2,512	328	Reagan	17.8%	72.7%	9.5%
GATES	22	3	15	4	Reagan	13.6%	68.2%	18.2%
GRAHAM	532	39	466	27	Reagan	7.3%	87.6%	5.1%
GRANVILLE	255	53	153	49	Reagan	20.8%	60.0%	19.2%
GREENE	136	5	119	12	Reagan	3.7%	87.5%	8.8%
GUILFORD	9,328	2,281	5,711	1,336	Reagan	24.5%	61.2%	14.3%
HALIFAX	408	74	293	41	Reagan	18.1%	71.8%	10.0%
HARNETT	981	151	756	74	Reagan	15.4%	77.1%	7.5%
HAYWOOD	1,073	249	735	89	Reagan	23.2%	68.5%	8.3%
HENDERSON	4,715	1,023	3,268	424	Reagan	21.7%	69.3%	9.0%
HERTFORD	150	27	96	27	Reagan	18.0%	64.0%	18.0%
HOKE	106	19	72	15	Reagan	17.9%	67.9%	14.2%
HYDE	82	8	67	7	Reagan	9.8%	81.7%	8.5%
IREDELL	2,294	448	1,615	231	Reagan	19.5%	70.4%	10.1%
JACKSON	749	154	538	57	Reagan	20.6%	71.8%	7.6%

NORTH CAROLINA REPUBLICAN

1980

County	Total Vote	Bush	Reagan	Other	Winner	Percentage of Total Vote Bush	Reagan	Other
JOHNSTON	1,085	145	856	84	Reagan	13.4%	78.9%	7.7%
JONES	63	2	54	7	Reagan	3.2%	85.7%	11.1%
LEE	614	185	366	63	Reagan	30.1%	59.6%	10.3%
LENOIR	1,091	94	922	75	Reagan	8.6%	84.5%	6.9%
LINCOLN	1,513	290	1,123	100	Reagan	19.2%	74.2%	6.6%
MCDOWELL	613	134	437	42	Reagan	21.9%	71.3%	6.9%
MACON	967	179	709	79	Reagan	18.5%	73.3%	8.2%
MADISON	390	89	275	26	Reagan	22.8%	70.5%	6.7%
MARTIN	208	24	168	16	Reagan	11.5%	80.8%	7.7%
MECKLENBURG	14,613	4,832	7,422	2,359	Reagan	33.1%	50.8%	16.1%
MITCHELL	3,288	586	2,414	288	Reagan	17.8%	73.4%	8.8%
MONTGOMERY	657	111	513	33	Reagan	16.9%	78.1%	5.0%
MOORE	3,949	1,230	2,286	433	Reagan	31.1%	57.9%	11.0%
NASH	1,363	177	1,095	91	Reagan	13.0%	80.3%	6.7%
NEW HANOVER	3,406	539	2,494	373	Reagan	15.8%	73.2%	11.0%
NORTHAMPTON	43	10	26	7	Reagan	23.3%	60.5%	16.3%
ONSLOW	926	149	670	107	Reagan	16.1%	72.4%	11.6%
ORANGE	2,138	810	798	530	Bush	37.9%	37.3%	24.8%
PAMLICO	185	35	136	14	Reagan	18.9%	73.5%	7.6%
PASQUOTANK	262	48	187	27	Reagan	18.3%	71.4%	10.3%
PENDER	465	61	346	58	Reagan	13.1%	74.4%	12.5%
PERQUIMANS	54	8	41	5	Reagan	14.8%	75.9%	9.3%
PERSON	263	54	176	33	Reagan	20.5%	66.9%	12.5%
PITT	1,893	354	1,327	212	Reagan	18.7%	70.1%	11.2%
POLK	1,123	271	776	76	Reagan	24.1%	69.1%	6.8%
RANDOLPH	4,516	772	3,397	347	Reagan	17.1%	75.2%	7.7%
RICHMOND	266	53	178	35	Reagan	19.9%	66.9%	13.2%
ROBESON	396	88	255	53	Reagan	22.2%	64.4%	13.4%
ROCKINGHAM	999	212	666	121	Reagan	21.2%	66.7%	12.1%
ROWAN	4,077	664	3,066	347	Reagan	16.3%	75.2%	8.5%
RUTHERFORD	1,162	213	887	62	Reagan	18.3%	76.3%	5.3%
SAMPSON	2,800	421	2,156	223	Reagan	15.0%	77.0%	8.0%
SCOTLAND	278	84	149	45	Reagan	30.2%	53.6%	16.2%
STANLY	2,272	495	1,585	192	Reagan	21.8%	69.8%	8.5%
STOKES	2,021	331	1,567	123	Reagan	16.4%	77.5%	6.1%
SURRY	1,446	274	1,073	99	Reagan	18.9%	74.2%	6.8%
SWAIN	321	44	259	18	Reagan	13.7%	80.7%	5.6%
TRANSYLVANIA	1,447	348	957	142	Reagan	24.0%	66.1%	9.8%
TYRRELL	44	6	34	4	Reagan	13.6%	77.3%	9.1%
UNION	1,173	272	748	153	Reagan	23.2%	63.8%	13.0%
VANCE	277	45	217	15	Reagan	16.2%	78.3%	5.4%
WAKE	8,997	2,461	5,274	1,262	Reagan	27.4%	58.6%	14.0%
WARREN	147	39	63	45	Reagan	26.5%	42.9%	30.6%
WASHINGTON	99	10	81	8	Reagan	10.1%	81.8%	8.1%
WATAUGA	2,143	485	1,457	201	Reagan	22.6%	68.0%	9.4%
WAYNE	1,149	168	887	94	Reagan	14.6%	77.2%	8.2%
WILKES	5,352	801	4,216	335	Reagan	15.0%	78.8%	6.3%
WILSON	873	123	658	92	Reagan	14.1%	75.4%	10.5%
YADKIN	2,790	584	2,030	176	Reagan	20.9%	72.8%	6.3%
YANCEY	847	125	681	41	Reagan	14.8%	80.4%	4.8%
TOTAL	168,391	36,631	113,854	17,906	Reagan	21.8%	67.6%	10.6%

NORTH CAROLINA DEMOCRATIC

1984

County	Total Vote	Hart	J. Jackson	Mondale	Other	Winner	Percentage of Total Vote Hart	J. Jackson	Mondale	Other
ALAMANCE	15,653	5,233	3,591	5,280	1,549	Mondale	33.4%	22.9%	33.7%	9.9%
ALEXANDER	2,535	1,005	215	1,174	141	Mondale	39.6%	8.5%	46.3%	5.6%
ALLEGHANY	2,276	1,044	81	999	152	Hart	45.9%	3.6%	43.9%	6.7%
ANSON	6,572	1,605	2,614	1,953	400	J. Jackson	24.4%	39.8%	29.7%	6.1%
ASHE	3,556	1,259	99	2,015	183	Mondale	35.4%	2.8%	56.7%	5.1%
AVERY	926	291	66	465	104	Mondale	31.4%	7.1%	50.2%	11.2%
BEAUFORT	8,171	2,577	1,620	2,875	1,099	Mondale	31.5%	19.8%	35.2%	13.5%
BERTIE	5,637	1,323	2,393	1,218	703	J. Jackson	23.5%	42.5%	21.6%	12.5%
BLADEN	6,838	1,840	2,046	2,299	653	Mondale	26.9%	29.9%	33.6%	9.5%
BRUNSWICK	8,087	2,568	2,181	2,721	617	Mondale	31.8%	27.0%	33.6%	7.6%
BUNCOMBE	23,092	7,691	2,880	10,581	1,940	Mondale	33.3%	12.5%	45.8%	8.4%
BURKE	10,346	4,211	1,072	4,471	592	Mondale	40.7%	10.4%	43.2%	5.7%
CABARRUS	11,728	4,158	2,058	4,391	1,121	Mondale	35.5%	17.5%	37.4%	9.6%
CALDWELL	6,477	2,548	597	2,904	428	Mondale	39.3%	9.2%	44.8%	6.6%
CAMDEN	1,846	623	399	609	215	Hart	33.7%	21.6%	33.0%	11.6%
CARTERET	7,236	2,630	681	3,267	658	Mondale	36.3%	9.4%	45.1%	9.1%
CASWELL	6,233	1,497	2,538	1,690	508	J. Jackson	24.0%	40.7%	27.1%	8.2%
CATAWBA	10,980	4,137	1,362	4,734	747	Mondale	37.7%	12.4%	43.1%	6.8%
CHATHAM	9,634	2,853	2,894	3,030	857	Mondale	29.6%	30.0%	31.5%	8.9%
CHEROKEE	1,890	636	60	1,087	107	Mondale	33.7%	3.2%	57.5%	5.7%
CHOWAN	2,139	607	750	655	127	J. Jackson	28.4%	35.1%	30.6%	5.9%
CLAY	720	264	17	406	33	Mondale	36.7%	2.4%	56.4%	4.6%
CLEVELAND	13,474	4,665	1,859	5,536	1,414	Mondale	34.6%	13.8%	41.1%	10.5%
COLUMBUS	12,730	3,482	3,400	4,690	1,158	Mondale	27.4%	26.7%	36.8%	9.1%
CRAVEN	9,695	2,972	2,284	3,197	1,242	Mondale	30.7%	23.6%	33.0%	12.8%
CUMBERLAND	29,053	7,386	9,210	9,746	2,711	Mondale	25.4%	31.7%	33.5%	9.3%
CURRITUCK	2,716	974	566	824	352	Hart	35.9%	20.8%	30.3%	13.0%
DARE	2,999	1,180	268	1,047	504	Hart	39.3%	8.9%	34.9%	16.8%
DAVIDSON	10,866	4,072	1,499	4,453	842	Mondale	37.5%	13.8%	41.0%	7.7%
DAVIE	2,671	861	480	1,138	192	Mondale	32.2%	18.0%	42.6%	7.2%
DUPLIN	8,344	2,351	2,187	3,062	744	Mondale	28.2%	26.2%	36.7%	8.9%
DURHAM	34,687	7,741	16,311	8,516	2,119	J. Jackson	22.3%	47.0%	24.6%	6.1%
EDGECOMBE	15,463	3,425	6,715	4,158	1,165	J. Jackson	22.1%	43.4%	26.9%	7.5%
FORSYTH	34,753	8,246	13,033	11,286	2,188	J. Jackson	23.7%	37.5%	32.5%	6.3%
FRANKLIN	7,369	1,974	2,293	2,468	634	Mondale	26.8%	31.1%	33.5%	8.6%
GASTON	17,807	6,668	2,188	6,941	2,010	Mondale	37.4%	12.3%	39.0%	11.3%
GATES	3,378	802	1,302	955	319	J. Jackson	23.7%	38.5%	28.3%	9.4%
GRAHAM	1,265	337	45	800	83	Mondale	26.6%	3.6%	63.2%	6.6%
GRANVILLE	8,915	2,252	3,533	2,475	655	J. Jackson	25.3%	39.6%	27.8%	7.3%
GREENE	4,501	1,185	1,195	1,610	511	Mondale	26.3%	26.5%	35.8%	11.4%
GUILFORD	43,836	12,104	15,141	13,156	3,435	J. Jackson	27.6%	34.5%	30.0%	7.8%
HALIFAX	13,664	3,502	5,103	3,908	1,151	J. Jackson	25.6%	37.3%	28.6%	8.4%
HARNETT	10,483	2,712	1,796	4,916	1,059	Mondale	25.9%	17.1%	46.9%	10.1%
HAYWOOD	7,713	2,515	266	4,373	559	Mondale	32.6%	3.4%	56.7%	7.2%
HENDERSON	5,706	2,305	416	2,532	453	Mondale	40.4%	7.3%	44.4%	7.9%
HERTFORD	6,041	1,136	2,680	1,423	802	J. Jackson	18.8%	44.4%	23.6%	13.3%
HOKE	4,094	898	1,556	1,318	322	J. Jackson	21.9%	38.0%	32.2%	7.9%
HYDE	1,643	526	334	588	195	Mondale	32.0%	20.3%	35.8%	11.9%
IREDELL	12,705	4,848	2,178	4,475	1,204	Hart	38.2%	17.1%	35.2%	9.5%
JACKSON	3,681	1,192	192	2,112	185	Mondale	32.4%	5.2%	57.4%	5.0%

NORTH CAROLINA DEMOCRATIC

1984

County	Total Vote	Hart	J. Jackson	Mondale	Other	Winner	Percentage of Total Vote Hart	J. Jackson	Mondale	Other
JOHNSTON	12,346	4,273	1,869	4,782	1,422	Mondale	34.6%	15.1%	38.7%	11.5%
JONES	2,958	743	1,136	799	280	J. Jackson	25.1%	38.4%	27.0%	9.5%
LEE	7,418	2,692	1,386	2,736	604	Mondale	36.3%	18.7%	36.9%	8.1%
LENOIR	12,651	3,477	3,848	3,768	1,558	J. Jackson	27.5%	30.4%	29.8%	12.3%
LINCOLN	6,567	2,428	508	3,112	519	Mondale	37.0%	7.7%	47.4%	7.9%
MCDOWELL	4,193	1,547	309	1,966	371	Mondale	36.9%	7.4%	46.9%	8.8%
MACON	3,687	1,353	120	1,883	331	Mondale	36.7%	3.3%	51.1%	9.0%
MADISON	2,823	862	93	1,733	135	Mondale	30.5%	3.3%	61.4%	4.8%
MARTIN	5,079	1,409	1,528	1,832	310	Mondale	27.7%	30.1%	36.1%	6.1%
MECKLENBURG	59,676	17,582	17,027	20,247	4,820	Mondale	29.5%	28.5%	33.9%	8.1%
MITCHELL	955	326	34	533	62	Mondale	34.1%	3.6%	55.8%	6.5%
MONTGOMERY	4,335	1,282	988	1,719	346	Mondale	29.6%	22.8%	39.7%	8.0%
MOORE	7,254	2,268	1,459	2,831	696	Mondale	31.3%	20.1%	39.0%	9.6%
NASH	15,657	4,610	4,307	5,004	1,736	Mondale	29.4%	27.5%	32.0%	11.1%
NEW HANOVER	15,565	5,840	3,627	4,595	1,503	Hart	37.5%	23.3%	29.5%	9.7%
NORTHAMPTON	6,801	1,490	2,802	1,888	621	J. Jackson	21.9%	41.2%	27.8%	9.1%
ONSLOW	9,682	3,162	1,875	3,205	1,440	Mondale	32.7%	19.4%	33.1%	14.9%
ORANGE	17,769	5,794	5,311	5,374	1,290	Hart	32.6%	29.9%	30.2%	7.3%
PAMLICO	3,275	877	942	1,028	428	Mondale	26.8%	28.8%	31.4%	13.1%
PASQUOTANK	5,077	1,343	1,773	1,311	650	J. Jackson	26.5%	34.9%	25.8%	12.8%
PENDER	5,262	1,625	1,510	1,703	424	Mondale	30.9%	28.7%	32.4%	8.1%
PERQUIMANS	2,280	721	593	719	247	Hart	31.6%	26.0%	31.5%	10.8%
PERSON	6,322	1,862	2,195	1,803	462	J. Jackson	29.5%	34.7%	28.5%	7.3%
PITT	17,048	5,047	4,398	5,721	1,882	Mondale	29.6%	25.8%	33.6%	11.0%
POLK	2,313	835	283	1,019	176	Mondale	36.1%	12.2%	44.1%	7.6%
RANDOLPH	6,968	2,561	717	3,184	506	Mondale	36.8%	10.3%	45.7%	7.3%
RICHMOND	9,315	2,421	2,278	3,675	941	Mondale	26.0%	24.5%	39.5%	10.1%
ROBESON	19,990	4,894	5,928	7,367	1,801	Mondale	24.5%	29.7%	36.9%	9.0%
ROCKINGHAM	13,158	3,865	2,952	4,888	1,453	Mondale	29.4%	22.4%	37.1%	11.0%
ROWAN	11,013	3,936	1,788	4,440	849	Mondale	35.7%	16.2%	40.3%	7.7%
RUTHERFORD	7,497	2,590	914	3,312	681	Mondale	34.5%	12.2%	44.2%	9.1%
SAMPSON	9,166	1,996	2,797	3,818	555	Mondale	21.8%	30.5%	41.7%	6.1%
SCOTLAND	5,323	1,635	1,370	1,826	492	Mondale	30.7%	25.7%	34.3%	9.2%
STANLY	6,506	2,210	901	2,934	461	Mondale	34.0%	13.8%	45.1%	7.1%
STOKES	4,584	1,386	592	2,330	276	Mondale	30.2%	12.9%	50.8%	6.0%
SURRY	6,925	2,636	581	3,359	349	Mondale	38.1%	8.4%	48.5%	5.0%
SWAIN	1,466	511	42	843	70	Mondale	34.9%	2.9%	57.5%	4.8%
TRANSYLVANIA	2,867	985	255	1,391	236	Mondale	34.4%	8.9%	48.5%	8.2%
TYRRELL	1,218	314	362	391	151	Mondale	25.8%	29.7%	32.1%	12.4%
UNION	9,931	3,529	1,515	3,887	1,000	Mondale	35.5%	15.3%	39.1%	10.1%
VANCE	9,987	2,585	3,835	2,742	825	J. Jackson	25.9%	38.4%	27.5%	8.3%
WAKE	62,088	20,218	14,930	21,002	5,938	Mondale	32.6%	24.0%	33.8%	9.6%
WARREN	5,659	1,137	2,877	1,238	407	J. Jackson	20.1%	50.8%	21.9%	7.2%
WASHINGTON	4,184	934	1,902	1,080	268	J. Jackson	22.3%	45.5%	25.8%	6.4%
WATAUGA	4,173	1,675	347	1,864	287	Mondale	40.1%	8.3%	44.7%	6.9%
WAYNE	14,784	3,990	4,377	4,584	1,833	Mondale	27.0%	29.6%	31.0%	12.4%
WILKES	5,265	1,865	357	2,717	326	Mondale	35.4%	6.8%	51.6%	6.2%
WILSON	12,852	3,589	3,844	4,184	1,235	Mondale	27.9%	29.9%	32.6%	9.6%
YADKIN	2,552	963	167	1,278	144	Mondale	37.7%	6.5%	50.1%	5.6%
YANCEY	3,569	1,093	152	2,152	172	Mondale	30.6%	4.3%	60.3%	4.8%
TOTAL	960,857	289,877	243,945	342,324	84,711	Mondale	30.2%	25.4%	35.6%	8.8%

NORTH CAROLINA DEMOCRATIC

1988

County	Total Vote	Dukakis	Gore	J. Jackson	Other	Winner	Percentage of Total Vote Dukakis	Gore	J. Jackson	Other
ALAMANCE	11,506	2,296	4,767	3,160	1,283	Gore	20.0%	41.4%	27.5%	11.2%
ALEXANDER	2,051	417	1,213	224	197	Gore	20.3%	59.1%	10.9%	9.6%
ALLEGHANY	1,201	192	783	74	152	Gore	16.0%	65.2%	6.2%	12.7%
ANSON	3,281	583	963	1,369	366	J. Jackson	17.8%	29.4%	41.7%	11.2%
ASHE	4,247	878	2,388	198	783	Gore	20.7%	56.2%	4.7%	18.4%
AVERY	492	162	254	41	35	Gore	32.9%	51.6%	8.3%	7.1%
BEAUFORT	7,259	875	3,048	1,701	1,635	Gore	12.1%	42.0%	23.4%	22.5%
BERTIE	3,749	178	1,047	2,249	275	J. Jackson	4.7%	27.9%	60.0%	7.3%
BLADEN	5,616	666	1,746	2,397	807	J. Jackson	11.9%	31.1%	42.7%	14.4%
BRUNSWICK	4,998	1,120	1,507	1,663	708	J. Jackson	22.4%	30.2%	33.3%	14.2%
BUNCOMBE	15,712	4,636	5,565	3,297	2,214	Gore	29.5%	35.4%	21.0%	14.1%
BURKE	6,030	1,876	2,657	821	676	Gore	31.1%	44.1%	13.6%	11.2%
CABARRUS	10,919	3,056	3,719	2,144	2,000	Gore	28.0%	34.1%	19.6%	18.3%
CALDWELL	3,748	801	2,036	526	385	Gore	21.4%	54.3%	14.0%	10.3%
CAMDEN	1,017	109	409	405	94	Gore	10.7%	40.2%	39.8%	9.2%
CARTERET	5,325	1,373	2,231	907	814	Gore	25.8%	41.9%	17.0%	15.3%
CASWELL	2,979	262	1,077	1,409	231	J. Jackson	8.8%	36.2%	47.3%	7.8%
CATAWBA	6,834	1,924	2,782	1,264	864	Gore	28.2%	40.7%	18.5%	12.6%
CHATHAM	5,691	1,054	1,917	2,183	537	J. Jackson	18.5%	33.7%	38.4%	9.4%
CHEROKEE	1,558	372	878	86	222	Gore	23.9%	56.4%	5.5%	14.2%
CHOWAN	1,553	179	458	736	180	J. Jackson	11.5%	29.5%	47.4%	11.6%
CLAY	713	128	471	34	80	Gore	18.0%	66.1%	4.8%	11.2%
CLEVELAND	9,545	2,499	3,400	2,067	1,579	Gore	26.2%	35.6%	21.7%	16.5%
COLUMBUS	6,319	846	2,259	2,457	757	J. Jackson	13.4%	35.7%	38.9%	12.0%
CRAVEN	7,460	949	2,972	2,580	959	Gore	12.7%	39.8%	34.6%	12.9%
CUMBERLAND	19,446	3,837	5,987	7,870	1,752	J. Jackson	19.7%	30.8%	40.5%	9.0%
CURRITUCK	1,594	255	654	420	265	Gore	16.0%	41.0%	26.3%	16.6%
DARE	2,304	501	811	301	691	Gore	21.7%	35.2%	13.1%	30.0%
DAVIDSON	8,260	2,631	3,498	1,329	802	Gore	31.9%	42.3%	16.1%	9.7%
DAVIE	2,146	363	1,085	443	255	Gore	16.9%	50.6%	20.6%	11.9%
DUPLIN	5,391	648	2,060	1,958	725	Gore	12.0%	38.2%	36.3%	13.4%
DURHAM	24,549	4,868	5,223	12,392	2,066	J. Jackson	19.8%	21.3%	50.5%	8.4%
EDGECOMBE	8,881	749	2,289	5,204	639	J. Jackson	8.4%	25.8%	58.6%	7.2%
FORSYTH	30,499	5,809	9,715	12,155	2,820	J. Jackson	19.0%	31.9%	39.9%	9.2%
FRANKLIN	4,969	636	1,770	2,160	403	J. Jackson	12.8%	35.6%	43.5%	8.1%
GASTON	10,150	2,442	3,923	2,371	1,414	Gore	24.1%	38.7%	23.4%	13.9%
GATES	1,808	125	540	981	162	J. Jackson	6.9%	29.9%	54.3%	9.0%
GRAHAM	678	117	419	43	99	Gore	17.3%	61.8%	6.3%	14.6%
GRANVILLE	5,278	679	1,741	2,418	440	J. Jackson	12.9%	33.0%	45.8%	8.3%
GREENE	2,614	131	1,170	1,027	286	Gore	5.0%	44.8%	39.3%	10.9%
GUILFORD	40,098	8,586	12,625	14,363	4,524	J. Jackson	21.4%	31.5%	35.8%	11.3%
HALIFAX	10,398	1,388	3,310	4,215	1,485	J. Jackson	13.3%	31.8%	40.5%	14.3%
HARNETT	6,208	1,067	3,156	1,332	653	Gore	17.2%	50.8%	21.5%	10.5%
HAYWOOD	5,291	1,610	2,305	451	925	Gore	30.4%	43.6%	8.5%	17.5%
HENDERSON	4,569	1,469	1,662	643	795	Gore	32.2%	36.4%	14.1%	17.4%
HERTFORD	4,218	265	1,071	2,480	402	J. Jackson	6.3%	25.4%	58.8%	9.5%
HOKE	2,558	255	833	1,239	231	J. Jackson	10.0%	32.6%	48.4%	9.0%
HYDE	1,125	108	415	423	179	J. Jackson	9.6%	36.9%	37.6%	15.9%
IREDELL	7,908	1,740	3,452	1,921	795	Gore	22.0%	43.7%	24.3%	10.1%
JACKSON	2,868	824	1,292	276	476	Gore	28.7%	45.0%	9.6%	16.6%

NORTH CAROLINA DEMOCRATIC

1988

County	Total Vote	Dukakis	Gore	J. Jackson	Other	Winner	Percentage of Total Vote Dukakis	Gore	J. Jackson	Other
JOHNSTON	8,244	1,324	4,049	1,784	1,087	Gore	16.1%	49.1%	21.6%	13.2%
JONES	1,999	131	645	1,012	211	J. Jackson	6.6%	32.3%	50.6%	10.6%
LEE	4,099	835	1,854	940	470	Gore	20.4%	45.2%	22.9%	11.5%
LENOIR	8,887	862	3,396	3,502	1,127	J. Jackson	9.7%	38.2%	39.4%	12.7%
LINCOLN	3,594	1,039	1,698	350	507	Gore	28.9%	47.2%	9.7%	14.1%
MCDOWELL	2,562	755	1,180	265	362	Gore	29.5%	46.1%	10.3%	14.1%
MACON	2,492	800	1,106	165	421	Gore	32.1%	44.4%	6.6%	16.9%
MADISON	1,404	266	838	129	171	Gore	18.9%	59.7%	9.2%	12.2%
MARTIN	3,596	292	1,377	1,491	436	J. Jackson	8.1%	38.3%	41.5%	12.1%
MECKLENBURG	46,694	11,885	9,710	20,345	4,754	J. Jackson	25.5%	20.8%	43.6%	10.2%
MITCHELL	387	103	200	40	44	Gore	26.6%	51.7%	10.3%	11.4%
MONTGOMERY	2,811	409	1,301	787	314	Gore	14.5%	46.3%	28.0%	11.2%
MOORE	5,364	1,303	2,102	1,375	584	Gore	24.3%	39.2%	25.6%	10.9%
NASH	9,575	1,420	3,536	3,533	1,086	Gore	14.8%	36.9%	36.9%	11.3%
NEW HANOVER	11,386	3,596	2,730	3,664	1,396	J. Jackson	31.6%	24.0%	32.2%	12.3%
NORTHAMPTON	4,333	326	1,069	2,389	549	J. Jackson	7.5%	24.7%	55.1%	12.7%
ONSLOW	8,967	1,691	3,323	2,313	1,640	Gore	18.9%	37.1%	25.8%	18.3%
ORANGE	13,439	4,537	3,176	4,277	1,449	Dukakis	33.8%	23.6%	31.8%	10.8%
PAMLICO	2,092	229	744	885	234	J. Jackson	10.9%	35.6%	42.3%	11.2%
PASQUOTANK	3,549	397	1,004	1,792	356	J. Jackson	11.2%	28.3%	50.5%	10.0%
PENDER	3,624	709	878	1,561	476	J. Jackson	19.6%	24.2%	43.1%	13.1%
PERQUIMANS	1,448	172	508	580	188	J. Jackson	11.9%	35.1%	40.1%	13.0%
PERSON	3,484	489	1,420	1,204	371	Gore	14.0%	40.8%	34.6%	10.6%
PITT	12,740	1,677	4,841	4,716	1,506	Gore	13.2%	38.0%	37.0%	11.8%
POLK	1,246	325	443	255	223	Gore	26.1%	35.6%	20.5%	17.9%
RANDOLPH	5,641	1,191	2,840	1,007	603	Gore	21.1%	50.3%	17.9%	10.7%
RICHMOND	4,143	962	1,428	1,257	496	Gore	23.2%	34.5%	30.3%	12.0%
ROBESON	20,119	2,912	4,828	8,536	3,843	J. Jackson	14.5%	24.0%	42.4%	19.1%
ROCKINGHAM	8,666	1,612	3,493	2,594	967	Gore	18.6%	40.3%	29.9%	11.2%
ROWAN	8,302	2,050	2,962	2,123	1,167	Gore	24.7%	35.7%	25.6%	14.1%
RUTHERFORD	3,967	1,055	1,787	469	656	Gore	26.6%	45.0%	11.8%	16.5%
SAMPSON	4,760	587	1,729	2,065	379	J. Jackson	12.3%	36.3%	43.4%	8.0%
SCOTLAND	2,697	417	891	1,084	305	J. Jackson	15.5%	33.0%	40.2%	11.3%
STANLY	4,610	1,302	1,821	803	684	Gore	28.2%	39.5%	17.4%	14.8%
STOKES	3,162	504	1,674	583	401	Gore	15.9%	52.9%	18.4%	12.7%
SURRY	4,719	809	2,748	586	576	Gore	17.1%	58.2%	12.4%	12.2%
SWAIN	947	315	349	80	203	Gore	33.3%	36.9%	8.4%	21.4%
TRANSYLVANIA	2,266	632	898	308	428	Gore	27.9%	39.6%	13.6%	18.9%
TYRRELL	786	84	262	320	120	J. Jackson	10.7%	33.3%	40.7%	15.3%
UNION	8,022	2,213	3,157	1,399	1,253	Gore	27.6%	39.4%	17.4%	15.6%
VANCE	5,640	708	1,664	2,795	473	J. Jackson	12.6%	29.5%	49.6%	8.4%
WAKE	46,436	11,726	15,653	14,030	5,027	Gore	25.3%	33.7%	30.2%	10.8%
WARREN	3,810	345	851	2,346	268	J. Jackson	9.1%	22.3%	61.6%	7.0%
WASHINGTON	2,622	207	802	1,335	278	J. Jackson	7.9%	30.6%	50.9%	10.6%
WATAUGA	2,562	720	1,148	397	297	Gore	28.1%	44.8%	15.5%	11.6%
WAYNE	9,486	1,162	3,296	3,944	1,084	J. Jackson	12.2%	34.7%	41.6%	11.4%
WILKES	3,126	698	1,654	363	411	Gore	22.3%	52.9%	11.6%	13.1%
WILSON	8,549	1,082	3,089	3,640	738	J. Jackson	12.7%	36.1%	42.6%	8.6%
YADKIN	1,760	252	1,150	190	168	Gore	14.3%	65.3%	10.8%	9.5%
YANCEY	1,533	342	814	162	215	Gore	22.3%	53.1%	10.6%	14.0%
TOTAL	679,958	137,993	235,669	224,177	82,119	Gore	20.3%	34.7%	33.0%	12.1%

NORTH CAROLINA REPUBLICAN

1988

County	Total Vote	Bush	Dole	Other	Winner	Percentage of Total Vote Bush	Dole	Other
ALAMANCE	4,556	2,078	1,835	643	Bush	45.6%	40.3%	14.1%
ALEXANDER	1,780	760	777	243	Dole	42.7%	43.7%	13.7%
ALLEGHANY	354	151	165	38	Dole	42.7%	46.6%	10.7%
ANSON	272	143	85	44	Bush	52.6%	31.3%	16.2%
ASHE	3,964	2,288	1,379	297	Bush	57.7%	34.8%	7.5%
AVERY	1,495	767	492	236	Bush	51.3%	32.9%	15.8%
BEAUFORT	1,862	1,012	439	411	Bush	54.4%	23.6%	22.1%
BERTIE	133	65	40	28	Bush	48.9%	30.1%	21.1%
BLADEN	381	198	119	64	Bush	52.0%	31.2%	16.8%
BRUNSWICK	2,543	1,326	714	503	Bush	52.1%	28.1%	19.8%
BUNCOMBE	8,082	4,134	2,588	1,360	Bush	51.2%	32.0%	16.8%
BURKE	3,393	1,628	1,342	423	Bush	48.0%	39.6%	12.5%
CABARRUS	6,479	2,658	2,730	1,091	Dole	41.0%	42.1%	16.8%
CALDWELL	3,165	1,386	1,415	364	Dole	43.8%	44.7%	11.5%
CAMDEN	42	26	10	6	Bush	61.9%	23.8%	14.3%
CARTERET	3,278	1,684	857	737	Bush	51.4%	26.1%	22.5%
CASWELL	202	106	59	37	Bush	52.5%	29.2%	18.3%
CATAWBA	4,162	3,141	329	692	Bush	75.5%	7.9%	16.6%
CHATHAM	1,527	685	668	174	Bush	44.9%	43.7%	11.4%
CHEROKEE	1,174	723	292	159	Bush	61.6%	24.9%	13.5%
CHOWAN	259	123	78	58	Bush	47.5%	30.1%	22.4%
CLAY	681	386	179	116	Bush	56.7%	26.3%	17.0%
CLEVELAND	2,483	1,156	858	469	Bush	46.6%	34.6%	18.9%
COLUMBUS	683	338	203	142	Bush	49.5%	29.7%	20.8%
CRAVEN	2,702	1,387	742	573	Bush	51.3%	27.5%	21.2%
CUMBERLAND	4,647	2,002	1,657	988	Bush	43.1%	35.7%	21.3%
CURRITUCK	236	106	52	78	Bush	44.9%	22.0%	33.1%
DARE	1,113	506	265	342	Bush	45.5%	23.8%	30.7%
DAVIDSON	6,174	2,716	2,780	678	Dole	44.0%	45.0%	11.0%
DAVIE	2,548	1,132	1,140	276	Dole	44.4%	44.7%	10.8%
DUPLIN	654	352	210	92	Bush	53.8%	32.1%	14.1%
DURHAM	5,146	1,709	2,545	892	Dole	33.2%	49.5%	17.3%
EDGECOMBE	890	363	336	191	Bush	40.8%	37.8%	21.5%
FORSYTH	14,618	6,312	6,379	1,927	Dole	43.2%	43.6%	13.2%
FRANKLIN	692	294	272	126	Bush	42.5%	39.3%	18.2%
GASTON	6,180	2,925	2,141	1,114	Bush	47.3%	34.6%	18.0%
GATES	55	27	19	9	Bush	49.1%	34.5%	16.4%
GRAHAM	694	444	173	77	Bush	64.0%	24.9%	11.1%
GRANVILLE	376	146	167	63	Dole	38.8%	44.4%	16.8%
GREENE	169	70	67	32	Bush	41.4%	39.6%	18.9%
GUILFORD	19,491	8,829	7,961	2,701	Bush	45.3%	40.8%	13.9%
HALIFAX	874	396	299	179	Bush	45.3%	34.2%	20.5%
HARNETT	1,392	608	526	258	Bush	43.7%	37.8%	18.5%
HAYWOOD	1,535	782	468	285	Bush	50.9%	30.5%	18.6%
HENDERSON	6,439	3,720	1,849	870	Bush	57.8%	28.7%	13.5%
HERTFORD	279	106	101	72	Bush	38.0%	36.2%	25.8%
HOKE	188	89	68	31	Bush	47.3%	36.2%	16.5%
HYDE	105	54	24	27	Bush	51.4%	22.9%	25.7%
IREDELL	4,072	1,688	1,648	736	Bush	41.5%	40.5%	18.1%
JACKSON	1,102	594	360	148	Bush	53.9%	32.7%	13.4%

NORTH CAROLINA REPUBLICAN

1988

County	Total Vote	Bush	Dole	Other	Winner	Percentage of Total Vote Bush	Dole	Other
JOHNSTON	2,041	857	880	304	Dole	42.0%	43.1%	14.9%
JONES	102	63	16	23	Bush	61.8%	15.7%	22.5%
LEE	1,031	464	428	139	Bush	45.0%	41.5%	13.5%
LENOIR	1,404	689	416	299	Bush	49.1%	29.6%	21.3%
LINCOLN	2,669	1,209	1,072	388	Bush	45.3%	40.2%	14.5%
MCDOWELL	1,026	482	374	170	Bush	47.0%	36.5%	16.6%
MACON	1,745	1,053	429	263	Bush	60.3%	24.6%	15.1%
MADISON	572	351	170	51	Bush	61.4%	29.7%	8.9%
MARTIN	318	137	119	62	Bush	43.1%	37.4%	19.5%
MECKLENBURG	30,797	12,159	13,935	4,703	Dole	39.5%	45.2%	15.3%
MITCHELL	1,366	755	464	147	Bush	55.3%	34.0%	10.8%
MONTGOMERY	900	491	328	81	Bush	54.6%	36.4%	9.0%
MOORE	5,480	3,037	1,915	528	Bush	55.4%	34.9%	9.6%
NASH	2,554	1,129	870	555	Bush	44.2%	34.1%	21.7%
NEW HANOVER	6,105	2,994	1,822	1,289	Bush	49.0%	29.8%	21.1%
NORTHAMPTON	103	55	25	23	Bush	53.4%	24.3%	22.3%
ONSLOW	2,370	1,295	650	425	Bush	54.6%	27.4%	17.9%
ORANGE	3,243	1,118	1,638	487	Dole	34.5%	50.5%	15.0%
PAMLICO	373	226	90	57	Bush	60.6%	24.1%	15.3%
PASQUOTANK	533	243	151	139	Bush	45.6%	28.3%	26.1%
PENDER	850	455	244	151	Bush	53.5%	28.7%	17.8%
PERQUIMANS	151	76	31	44	Bush	50.3%	20.5%	29.1%
PERSON	410	179	177	54	Bush	43.7%	43.2%	13.2%
PITT	3,058	1,246	1,081	731	Bush	40.7%	35.3%	23.9%
POLK	1,322	831	330	161	Bush	62.9%	25.0%	12.2%
RANDOLPH	6,300	2,879	2,608	813	Bush	45.7%	41.4%	12.9%
RICHMOND	505	212	197	96	Bush	42.0%	39.0%	19.0%
ROBESON	1,734	758	677	299	Bush	43.7%	39.0%	17.2%
ROCKINGHAM	2,292	1,069	918	305	Bush	46.6%	40.1%	13.3%
ROWAN	7,041	1,765	4,503	773	Dole	25.1%	64.0%	11.0%
RUTHERFORD	1,681	853	535	293	Bush	50.7%	31.8%	17.4%
SAMPSON	1,824	851	807	166	Bush	46.7%	44.2%	9.1%
SCOTLAND	397	165	160	72	Bush	41.6%	40.3%	18.1%
STANLY	2,771	1,275	1,178	318	Bush	46.0%	42.5%	11.5%
STOKES	1,861	927	760	174	Bush	49.8%	40.8%	9.3%
SURRY	1,964	1,056	692	216	Bush	53.8%	35.2%	11.0%
SWAIN	399	230	109	60	Bush	57.6%	27.3%	15.0%
TRANSYLVANIA	2,088	1,121	587	380	Bush	53.7%	28.1%	18.2%
TYRRELL	41	21	10	10	Bush	51.2%	24.4%	24.4%
UNION	3,839	1,566	1,585	688	Dole	40.8%	41.3%	17.9%
VANCE	337	131	147	59	Dole	38.9%	43.6%	17.5%
WAKE	19,585	7,157	8,848	3,580	Dole	36.5%	45.2%	18.3%
WARREN	147	54	60	33	Dole	36.7%	40.8%	22.4%
WASHINGTON	163	77	47	39	Bush	47.2%	28.8%	23.9%
WATAUGA	2,114	903	932	279	Dole	42.7%	44.1%	13.2%
WAYNE	2,209	928	818	463	Bush	42.0%	37.0%	21.0%
WILKES	3,905	2,030	1,539	336	Bush	52.0%	39.4%	8.6%
WILSON	1,634	711	585	338	Bush	43.5%	35.8%	20.7%
YADKIN	2,291	1,127	950	214	Bush	49.2%	41.5%	9.3%
YANCEY	835	481	223	131	Bush	57.6%	26.7%	15.7%
TOTAL	273,801	124,260	107,032	42,509	Bush	45.4%	39.1%	15.5%

NORTH CAROLINA DEMOCRATIC

1992

County	Total Vote	Brown	Clinton	Uncommitted	Other	Winner	Percentage of Total Vote Brown	Clinton	Uncom.	Other
ALAMANCE	11,639	1,508	6,522	2,081	1,528	Clinton	13.0%	56.0%	17.9%	13.1%
ALEXANDER	1,801	125	1,401	155	120	Clinton	6.9%	77.8%	8.6%	6.7%
ALLEGHANY	1,774	132	1,290	206	146	Clinton	7.4%	72.7%	11.6%	8.2%
ANSON	3,591	262	2,498	533	298	Clinton	7.3%	69.6%	14.8%	8.3%
ASHE	2,297	137	1,713	302	145	Clinton	6.0%	74.6%	13.1%	6.3%
AVERY	531	58	381	59	33	Clinton	10.9%	71.8%	11.1%	6.2%
BEAUFORT	7,309	861	4,085	1,707	656	Clinton	11.8%	55.9%	23.4%	9.0%
BERTIE	3,444	336	2,543	384	181	Clinton	9.8%	73.8%	11.1%	5.3%
BLADEN	5,623	419	4,084	682	438	Clinton	7.5%	72.6%	12.1%	7.8%
BRUNSWICK	7,046	545	4,981	919	601	Clinton	7.7%	70.7%	13.0%	8.5%
BUNCOMBE	18,768	2,102	11,521	2,817	2,328	Clinton	11.2%	61.4%	15.0%	12.4%
BURKE	5,383	554	3,683	674	472	Clinton	10.3%	68.4%	12.5%	8.8%
CABARRUS	7,798	901	4,701	1,335	861	Clinton	11.6%	60.3%	17.1%	11.0%
CALDWELL	3,537	326	2,506	438	267	Clinton	9.2%	70.9%	12.4%	7.5%
CAMDEN	1,320	105	737	368	110	Clinton	8.0%	55.8%	27.9%	8.3%
CARTERET	5,451	567	3,408	812	664	Clinton	10.4%	62.5%	14.9%	12.2%
CASWELL	4,298	365	2,641	943	349	Clinton	8.5%	61.4%	21.9%	8.1%
CATAWBA	6,359	667	4,199	856	637	Clinton	10.5%	66.0%	13.5%	10.0%
CHATHAM	5,587	707	3,630	675	575	Clinton	12.7%	65.0%	12.1%	10.3%
CHEROKEE	1,824	147	1,423	136	118	Clinton	8.1%	78.0%	7.5%	6.5%
CHOWAN	1,857	141	1,252	324	140	Clinton	7.6%	67.4%	17.4%	7.5%
CLAY	714	48	560	62	44	Clinton	6.7%	78.4%	8.7%	6.2%
CLEVELAND	8,814	784	5,365	1,855	810	Clinton	8.9%	60.9%	21.0%	9.2%
COLUMBUS	10,627	804	7,945	1,195	683	Clinton	7.6%	74.8%	11.2%	6.4%
CRAVEN	7,538	920	4,643	1,189	786	Clinton	12.2%	61.6%	15.8%	10.4%
CUMBERLAND	21,859	2,077	13,612	4,195	1,975	Clinton	9.5%	62.3%	19.2%	9.0%
CURRITUCK	2,143	229	1,137	566	211	Clinton	10.7%	53.1%	26.4%	9.8%
DARE	3,480	470	1,739	876	395	Clinton	13.5%	50.0%	25.2%	11.4%
DAVIDSON	8,339	712	5,334	1,418	875	Clinton	8.5%	64.0%	17.0%	10.5%
DAVIE	1,724	135	1,148	285	156	Clinton	7.8%	66.6%	16.5%	9.0%
DUPLIN	5,947	518	4,095	857	477	Clinton	8.7%	68.9%	14.4%	8.0%
DURHAM	30,642	3,587	19,230	4,603	3,222	Clinton	11.7%	62.8%	15.0%	10.5%
EDGECOMBE	9,775	1,015	6,685	1,350	725	Clinton	10.4%	68.4%	13.8%	7.4%
FORSYTH	22,571	2,566	13,475	3,574	2,956	Clinton	11.4%	59.7%	15.8%	13.1%
FRANKLIN	5,265	552	3,757	529	427	Clinton	10.5%	71.4%	10.0%	8.1%
GASTON	14,114	1,410	8,309	2,890	1,505	Clinton	10.0%	58.9%	20.5%	10.7%
GATES	1,978	151	1,239	442	146	Clinton	7.6%	62.6%	22.3%	7.4%
GRAHAM	891	44	726	83	38	Clinton	4.9%	81.5%	9.3%	4.3%
GRANVILLE	6,501	681	4,045	1,276	499	Clinton	10.5%	62.2%	19.6%	7.7%
GREENE	3,251	267	2,012	705	267	Clinton	8.2%	61.9%	21.7%	8.2%
GUILFORD	31,598	3,364	20,134	4,270	3,830	Clinton	10.6%	63.7%	13.5%	12.1%
HALIFAX	8,083	877	5,186	1,368	652	Clinton	10.8%	64.2%	16.9%	8.1%
HARNETT	8,074	783	5,164	1,443	684	Clinton	9.7%	64.0%	17.9%	8.5%
HAYWOOD	7,884	643	5,555	1,010	676	Clinton	8.2%	70.5%	12.8%	8.6%
HENDERSON	4,352	454	2,787	567	544	Clinton	10.4%	64.0%	13.0%	12.5%
HERTFORD	2,997	349	2,086	370	192	Clinton	11.6%	69.6%	12.3%	6.4%
HOKE	3,326	245	2,161	659	261	Clinton	7.4%	65.0%	19.8%	7.8%
HYDE	1,445	116	885	325	119	Clinton	8.0%	61.2%	22.5%	8.2%
IREDELL	9,053	926	5,367	1,906	854	Clinton	10.2%	59.3%	21.1%	9.4%
JACKSON	3,838	331	2,820	347	340	Clinton	8.6%	73.5%	9.0%	8.9%

NORTH CAROLINA DEMOCRATIC

1992

County	Total Vote	Brown	Clinton	Uncommitted	Other	Winner	Percentage of Total Vote: Brown	Clinton	Uncom.	Other
JOHNSTON	10,237	1,000	6,157	2,140	940	Clinton	9.8%	60.1%	20.9%	9.2%
JONES	1,804	124	1,289	268	123	Clinton	6.9%	71.5%	14.9%	6.8%
LEE	5,548	512	3,187	1,284	565	Clinton	9.2%	57.4%	23.1%	10.2%
LENOIR	7,842	813	5,077	1,202	750	Clinton	10.4%	64.7%	15.3%	9.6%
LINCOLN	4,014	315	2,856	489	354	Clinton	7.8%	71.2%	12.2%	8.8%
MCDOWELL	3,734	337	2,411	687	299	Clinton	9.0%	64.6%	18.4%	8.0%
MACON	2,968	237	2,173	306	252	Clinton	8.0%	73.2%	10.3%	8.5%
MADISON	1,935	136	1,644	60	95	Clinton	7.0%	85.0%	3.1%	4.9%
MARTIN	3,946	354	2,793	521	278	Clinton	9.0%	70.8%	13.2%	7.0%
MECKLENBURG	41,157	4,717	27,389	4,653	4,398	Clinton	11.5%	66.5%	11.3%	10.7%
MITCHELL	463	37	322	52	52	Clinton	8.0%	69.5%	11.2%	11.2%
MONTGOMERY	3,019	192	2,136	485	206	Clinton	6.4%	70.8%	16.1%	6.8%
MOORE	4,749	484	3,259	580	426	Clinton	10.2%	68.6%	12.2%	9.0%
NASH	8,299	948	5,111	1,342	898	Clinton	11.4%	61.6%	16.2%	10.8%
NEW HANOVER	12,821	1,284	7,585	2,334	1,618	Clinton	10.0%	59.2%	18.2%	12.6%
NORTHAMPTON	4,210	445	2,880	684	201	Clinton	10.6%	68.4%	16.2%	4.8%
ONSLOW	7,205	847	4,042	1,554	762	Clinton	11.8%	56.1%	21.6%	10.6%
ORANGE	13,262	2,261	7,380	1,651	1,970	Clinton	17.0%	55.6%	12.4%	14.9%
PAMLICO	1,941	239	1,130	383	189	Clinton	12.3%	58.2%	19.7%	9.7%
PASQUOTANK	3,708	369	2,538	566	235	Clinton	10.0%	68.4%	15.3%	6.3%
PENDER	4,968	483	3,328	729	428	Clinton	9.7%	67.0%	14.7%	8.6%
PERQUIMANS	1,723	123	1,030	420	150	Clinton	7.1%	59.8%	24.4%	8.7%
PERSON	4,050	407	2,673	641	329	Clinton	10.0%	66.0%	15.8%	8.1%
PITT	14,043	1,516	8,995	2,094	1,438	Clinton	10.8%	64.1%	14.9%	10.2%
POLK	1,719	98	1,305	174	142	Clinton	5.7%	75.9%	10.1%	8.3%
RANDOLPH	4,417	381	2,982	671	383	Clinton	8.6%	67.5%	15.2%	8.7%
RICHMOND	5,889	542	3,949	940	458	Clinton	9.2%	67.1%	16.0%	7.8%
ROBESON	17,367	1,551	12,122	2,497	1,197	Clinton	8.9%	69.8%	14.4%	6.9%
ROCKINGHAM	7,953	732	5,004	1,445	772	Clinton	9.2%	62.9%	18.2%	9.7%
ROWAN	8,209	1,022	4,900	1,479	808	Clinton	12.4%	59.7%	18.0%	9.8%
RUTHERFORD	4,705	387	3,130	828	360	Clinton	8.2%	66.5%	17.6%	7.7%
SAMPSON	4,701	334	3,656	436	275	Clinton	7.1%	77.8%	9.3%	5.8%
SCOTLAND	3,752	268	2,516	680	288	Clinton	7.1%	67.1%	18.1%	7.7%
STANLY	3,965	365	2,697	531	372	Clinton	9.2%	68.0%	13.4%	9.4%
STOKES	3,245	258	2,455	330	202	Clinton	8.0%	75.7%	10.2%	6.2%
SURRY	4,260	350	3,086	464	360	Clinton	8.2%	72.4%	10.9%	8.5%
SWAIN	1,085	60	867	105	53	Clinton	5.5%	79.9%	9.7%	4.9%
TRANSYLVANIA	2,640	227	1,768	367	278	Clinton	8.6%	67.0%	13.9%	10.5%
TYRRELL	1,086	105	678	211	92	Clinton	9.7%	62.4%	19.4%	8.5%
UNION	6,345	611	4,004	1,075	655	Clinton	9.6%	63.1%	16.9%	10.3%
VANCE	6,046	664	3,634	1,251	497	Clinton	11.0%	60.1%	20.7%	8.2%
WAKE	48,676	6,266	28,041	6,884	7,485	Clinton	12.9%	57.6%	14.1%	15.4%
WARREN	4,048	344	2,883	571	250	Clinton	8.5%	71.2%	14.1%	6.2%
WASHINGTON	2,301	174	1,665	265	197	Clinton	7.6%	72.4%	11.5%	8.6%
WATAUGA	2,849	380	1,795	378	296	Clinton	13.3%	63.0%	13.3%	10.4%
WAYNE	9,286	1,179	5,784	1,213	1,110	Clinton	12.7%	62.3%	13.1%	12.0%
WILKES	3,736	300	2,678	470	288	Clinton	8.0%	71.7%	12.6%	7.7%
WILSON	7,594	868	4,926	1,181	619	Clinton	11.4%	64.9%	15.6%	8.2%
YADKIN	1,969	132	1,413	289	135	Clinton	6.7%	71.8%	14.7%	6.9%
YANCEY	2,326	183	1,775	216	152	Clinton	7.9%	76.3%	9.3%	6.5%
TOTAL	691,875	71,984	443,498	106,697	69,696	Clinton	10.4%	64.1%	15.4%	10.1%

NORTH CAROLINA REPUBLICAN

1992

County	Total Vote	Buchanan	Bush	Uncommitted	Winner	Percentage of Total Vote Buchanan	Bush	Uncom.
ALAMANCE	5,277	1,126	3,696	455	Bush	21.3%	70.0%	8.6%
ALEXANDER	1,263	230	963	70	Bush	18.2%	76.2%	5.5%
ALLEGHANY	297	43	234	20	Bush	14.5%	78.8%	6.7%
ANSON	245	35	198	12	Bush	14.3%	80.8%	4.9%
ASHE	1,572	190	1,269	113	Bush	12.1%	80.7%	7.2%
AVERY	3,106	477	2,135	494	Bush	15.4%	68.7%	15.9%
BEAUFORT	1,482	290	1,076	116	Bush	19.6%	72.6%	7.8%
BERTIE	185	44	124	17	Bush	23.8%	67.0%	9.2%
BLADEN	372	65	271	36	Bush	17.5%	72.8%	9.7%
BRUNSWICK	2,797	468	1,946	383	Bush	16.7%	69.6%	13.7%
BUNCOMBE	7,528	1,209	5,494	825	Bush	16.1%	73.0%	11.0%
BURKE	2,729	508	2,009	212	Bush	18.6%	73.6%	7.8%
CABARRUS	4,723	1,011	3,284	428	Bush	21.4%	69.5%	9.1%
CALDWELL	3,511	689	2,497	325	Bush	19.6%	71.1%	9.3%
CAMDEN	101	23	72	6	Bush	22.8%	71.3%	5.9%
CARTERET	3,389	555	2,501	333	Bush	16.4%	73.8%	9.8%
CASWELL	239	47	163	29	Bush	19.7%	68.2%	12.1%
CATAWBA	6,842	1,255	4,963	624	Bush	18.3%	72.5%	9.1%
CHATHAM	1,387	255	991	141	Bush	18.4%	71.4%	10.2%
CHEROKEE	1,053	117	828	108	Bush	11.1%	78.6%	10.3%
CHOWAN	467	68	337	62	Bush	14.6%	72.2%	13.3%
CLAY	623	60	520	43	Bush	9.6%	83.5%	6.9%
CLEVELAND	1,826	342	1,288	196	Bush	18.7%	70.5%	10.7%
COLUMBUS	1,169	211	852	106	Bush	18.0%	72.9%	9.1%
CRAVEN	3,001	602	2,092	307	Bush	20.1%	69.7%	10.2%
CUMBERLAND	6,109	1,067	4,423	619	Bush	17.5%	72.4%	10.1%
CURRITUCK	239	45	172	22	Bush	18.8%	72.0%	9.2%
DARE	1,463	222	1,041	200	Bush	15.2%	71.2%	13.7%
DAVIDSON	6,250	1,276	4,438	536	Bush	20.4%	71.0%	8.6%
DAVIE	3,385	575	2,541	269	Bush	17.0%	75.1%	7.9%
DUPLIN	1,138	191	885	62	Bush	16.8%	77.8%	5.4%
DURHAM	7,941	1,444	5,586	911	Bush	18.2%	70.3%	11.5%
EDGECOMBE	859	186	588	85	Bush	21.7%	68.5%	9.9%
FORSYTH	13,368	3,528	8,619	1,221	Bush	26.4%	64.5%	9.1%
FRANKLIN	912	271	592	49	Bush	29.7%	64.9%	5.4%
GASTON	8,271	1,553	6,057	661	Bush	18.8%	73.2%	8.0%
GATES	72	9	56	7	Bush	12.5%	77.8%	9.7%
GRAHAM	733	48	639	46	Bush	6.5%	87.2%	6.3%
GRANVILLE	480	101	330	49	Bush	21.0%	68.8%	10.2%
GREENE	213	39	162	12	Bush	18.3%	76.1%	5.6%
GUILFORD	16,533	3,531	11,318	1,684	Bush	21.4%	68.5%	10.2%
HALIFAX	539	114	363	62	Bush	21.2%	67.3%	11.5%
HARNETT	1,834	399	1,339	96	Bush	21.8%	73.0%	5.2%
HAYWOOD	1,558	244	1,178	136	Bush	15.7%	75.6%	8.7%
HENDERSON	5,481	825	3,986	670	Bush	15.1%	72.7%	12.2%
HERTFORD	251	45	186	20	Bush	17.9%	74.1%	8.0%
HOKE	313	44	244	25	Bush	14.1%	78.0%	8.0%
HYDE	86	16	62	8	Bush	18.6%	72.1%	9.3%
IREDELL	5,087	968	3,634	485	Bush	19.0%	71.4%	9.5%
JACKSON	1,199	157	937	105	Bush	13.1%	78.1%	8.8%

NORTH CAROLINA REPUBLICAN

1992

County	Total Vote	Buchanan	Bush	Uncommitted	Winner	Percentage of Total Vote Buchanan	Bush	Uncom.
JOHNSTON	2,694	614	1,902	178	Bush	22.8%	70.6%	6.6%
JONES	110	23	79	8	Bush	20.9%	71.8%	7.3%
LEE	1,293	207	983	103	Bush	16.0%	76.0%	8.0%
LENOIR	969	202	705	62	Bush	20.8%	72.8%	6.4%
LINCOLN	2,215	391	1,663	161	Bush	17.7%	75.1%	7.3%
MCDOWELL	1,018	154	793	71	Bush	15.1%	77.9%	7.0%
MACON	1,678	254	1,275	149	Bush	15.1%	76.0%	8.9%
MADISON	414	50	338	26	Bush	12.1%	81.6%	6.3%
MARTIN	545	97	403	45	Bush	17.8%	73.9%	8.3%
MECKLENBURG	27,086	5,914	17,664	3,508	Bush	21.8%	65.2%	13.0%
MITCHELL	3,438	467	2,502	469	Bush	13.6%	72.8%	13.6%
MONTGOMERY	823	122	658	43	Bush	14.8%	80.0%	5.2%
MOORE	6,841	896	5,199	746	Bush	13.1%	76.0%	10.9%
NASH	2,564	745	1,654	165	Bush	29.1%	64.5%	6.4%
NEW HANOVER	6,201	1,139	4,295	767	Bush	18.4%	69.3%	12.4%
NORTHAMPTON	114	28	67	19	Bush	24.6%	58.8%	16.7%
ONSLOW	2,251	427	1,568	256	Bush	19.0%	69.7%	11.4%
ORANGE	2,738	610	1,715	413	Bush	22.3%	62.6%	15.1%
PAMLICO	404	73	297	34	Bush	18.1%	73.5%	8.4%
PASQUOTANK	615	115	421	79	Bush	18.7%	68.5%	12.8%
PENDER	1,204	239	819	146	Bush	19.9%	68.0%	12.1%
PERQUIMANS	205	40	135	30	Bush	19.5%	65.9%	14.6%
PERSON	530	83	388	59	Bush	15.7%	73.2%	11.1%
PITT	3,360	673	2,403	284	Bush	20.0%	71.5%	8.5%
POLK	1,402	190	1,041	171	Bush	13.6%	74.3%	12.2%
RANDOLPH	6,683	1,258	4,862	563	Bush	18.8%	72.8%	8.4%
RICHMOND	626	112	446	68	Bush	17.9%	71.2%	10.9%
ROBESON	964	188	688	88	Bush	19.5%	71.4%	9.1%
ROCKINGHAM	2,092	468	1,435	189	Bush	22.4%	68.6%	9.0%
ROWAN	6,770	1,435	4,725	610	Bush	21.2%	69.8%	9.0%
RUTHERFORD	1,390	214	1,045	131	Bush	15.4%	75.2%	9.4%
SAMPSON	2,415	278	2,031	106	Bush	11.5%	84.1%	4.4%
SCOTLAND	500	70	351	79	Bush	14.0%	70.2%	15.8%
STANLY	2,085	317	1,653	115	Bush	15.2%	79.3%	5.5%
STOKES	1,978	341	1,539	98	Bush	17.2%	77.8%	5.0%
SURRY	1,518	297	1,118	103	Bush	19.6%	73.6%	6.8%
SWAIN	316	34	258	24	Bush	10.8%	81.6%	7.6%
TRANSYLVANIA	1,588	243	1,165	180	Bush	15.3%	73.4%	11.3%
TYRRELL	57	8	48	1	Bush	14.0%	84.2%	1.8%
UNION	3,668	811	2,539	318	Bush	22.1%	69.2%	8.7%
VANCE	411	76	308	27	Bush	18.5%	74.9%	6.6%
WAKE	22,653	5,853	14,616	2,184	Bush	25.8%	64.5%	9.6%
WARREN	222	32	166	24	Bush	14.4%	74.8%	10.8%
WASHINGTON	187	43	133	11	Bush	23.0%	71.1%	5.9%
WATAUGA	2,144	335	1,586	223	Bush	15.6%	74.0%	10.4%
WAYNE	1,980	439	1,436	105	Bush	22.2%	72.5%	5.3%
WILKES	6,592	891	5,172	529	Bush	13.5%	78.5%	8.0%
WILSON	1,766	420	1,223	123	Bush	23.8%	69.3%	7.0%
YADKIN	3,423	570	2,592	261	Bush	16.7%	75.7%	7.6%
YANCEY	1,333	116	1,106	111	Bush	8.7%	83.0%	8.3%
TOTAL	283,571	55,420	200,387	27,764	Bush	19.5%	70.7%	9.8%

NORTH CAROLINA DEMOCRATIC

1996

County	Total Vote	Clinton	LaRouche	Uncommitted	Winner	Percentage of Total Vote: Clinton	LaRouche	Uncom.
ALAMANCE	7,942	6,137	739	1,066	Clinton	77.3%	9.3%	13.4%
ALEXANDER	1,036	889	68	79	Clinton	85.8%	6.6%	7.6%
ALLEGHANY	1,454	1,129	111	214	Clinton	77.6%	7.6%	14.7%
ANSON	3,793	3,072	254	467	Clinton	81.0%	6.7%	12.3%
ASHE	1,639	1,429	80	130	Clinton	87.2%	4.9%	7.9%
AVERY	381	324	12	45	Clinton	85.0%	3.1%	11.8%
BEAUFORT	4,609	3,166	580	863	Clinton	68.7%	12.6%	18.7%
BERTIE	3,019	2,596	158	265	Clinton	86.0%	5.2%	8.8%
BLADEN	4,461	3,440	406	615	Clinton	77.1%	9.1%	13.8%
BRUNSWICK	6,022	4,996	395	631	Clinton	83.0%	6.6%	10.5%
BUNCOMBE	13,194	11,312	719	1,163	Clinton	85.7%	5.4%	8.8%
BURKE	4,734	3,878	342	514	Clinton	81.9%	7.2%	10.9%
CABARRUS	9,473	7,022	914	1,537	Clinton	74.1%	9.6%	16.2%
CALDWELL	2,563	2,158	175	230	Clinton	84.2%	6.8%	9.0%
CAMDEN	1,280	860	117	303	Clinton	67.2%	9.1%	23.7%
CARTERET	4,574	3,532	405	637	Clinton	77.2%	8.9%	13.9%
CASWELL	3,444	2,582	289	573	Clinton	75.0%	8.4%	16.6%
CATAWBA	3,770	3,174	260	336	Clinton	84.2%	6.9%	8.9%
CHATHAM	6,413	5,340	415	658	Clinton	83.3%	6.5%	10.3%
CHEROKEE	626	561	21	44	Clinton	89.6%	3.4%	7.0%
CHOWAN	1,132	945	63	124	Clinton	83.5%	5.6%	11.0%
CLAY	342	311	11	20	Clinton	90.9%	3.2%	5.8%
CLEVELAND	8,209	6,214	644	1,351	Clinton	75.7%	7.8%	16.5%
COLUMBUS	7,672	6,071	525	1,076	Clinton	79.1%	6.8%	14.0%
CRAVEN	5,429	4,333	485	611	Clinton	79.8%	8.9%	11.3%
CUMBERLAND	21,092	16,593	1,704	2,795	Clinton	78.7%	8.1%	13.3%
CURRITUCK	1,756	1,173	173	410	Clinton	66.8%	9.9%	23.3%
DARE	3,408	2,536	237	635	Clinton	74.4%	7.0%	18.6%
DAVIDSON	5,110	4,161	422	527	Clinton	81.4%	8.3%	10.3%
DAVIE	1,520	1,218	96	206	Clinton	80.1%	6.3%	13.6%
DUPLIN	3,942	3,137	325	480	Clinton	79.6%	8.2%	12.2%
DURHAM	25,783	21,996	1,209	2,578	Clinton	85.3%	4.7%	10.0%
EDGECOMBE	9,462	7,399	652	1,411	Clinton	78.2%	6.9%	14.9%
FORSYTH	18,839	15,788	1,190	1,861	Clinton	83.8%	6.3%	9.9%
FRANKLIN	4,929	3,794	439	696	Clinton	77.0%	8.9%	14.1%
GASTON	7,472	5,725	684	1,063	Clinton	76.6%	9.2%	14.2%
GATES	1,153	981	58	114	Clinton	85.1%	5.0%	9.9%
GRAHAM	456	400	17	39	Clinton	87.7%	3.7%	8.6%
GRANVILLE	5,917	4,474	485	958	Clinton	75.6%	8.2%	16.2%
GREENE	2,779	1,808	308	663	Clinton	65.1%	11.1%	23.9%
GUILFORD	29,023	24,947	1,807	2,269	Clinton	86.0%	6.2%	7.8%
HALIFAX	7,678	5,962	557	1,159	Clinton	77.7%	7.3%	15.1%
HARNETT	6,679	4,733	727	1,219	Clinton	70.9%	10.9%	18.3%
HAYWOOD	3,464	3,001	168	295	Clinton	86.6%	4.8%	8.5%
HENDERSON	2,898	2,493	159	246	Clinton	86.0%	5.5%	8.5%
HERTFORD	2,800	2,375	121	304	Clinton	84.8%	4.3%	10.9%
HOKE	2,792	2,258	190	344	Clinton	80.9%	6.8%	12.3%
HYDE	1,073	756	107	210	Clinton	70.5%	10.0%	19.6%
IREDELL	7,726	5,610	823	1,293	Clinton	72.6%	10.7%	16.7%
JACKSON	1,489	1,330	58	101	Clinton	89.3%	3.9%	6.8%

NORTH CAROLINA DEMOCRATIC

1996

County	Total Vote	Clinton	LaRouche	Uncommitted	Winner	Percentage of Total Vote Clinton	LaRouche	Uncom.
JOHNSTON	6,555	4,864	715	976	Clinton	74.2%	10.9%	14.9%
JONES	2,077	1,473	218	386	Clinton	70.9%	10.5%	18.6%
LEE	4,962	3,553	396	1,013	Clinton	71.6%	8.0%	20.4%
LENOIR	6,418	4,723	625	1,070	Clinton	73.6%	9.7%	16.7%
LINCOLN	3,432	2,825	240	367	Clinton	82.3%	7.0%	10.7%
MCDOWELL	1,795	1,416	161	218	Clinton	78.9%	9.0%	12.1%
MACON	1,791	1,547	114	130	Clinton	86.4%	6.4%	7.3%
MADISON	1,666	1,428	101	137	Clinton	85.7%	6.1%	8.2%
MARTIN	3,515	2,535	267	713	Clinton	72.1%	7.6%	20.3%
MECKLENBURG	34,088	30,435	1,389	2,264	Clinton	89.3%	4.1%	6.6%
MITCHELL	284	260	10	14	Clinton	91.5%	3.5%	4.9%
MONTGOMERY	1,769	1,480	154	135	Clinton	83.7%	8.7%	7.6%
MOORE	3,668	3,232	184	252	Clinton	88.1%	5.0%	6.9%
NASH	7,548	5,653	777	1,118	Clinton	74.9%	10.3%	14.8%
NEW HANOVER	11,402	9,492	717	1,193	Clinton	83.2%	6.3%	10.5%
NORTHAMPTON	4,372	3,561	195	616	Clinton	81.5%	4.5%	14.1%
ONSLOW	7,142	4,778	890	1,474	Clinton	66.9%	12.5%	20.6%
ORANGE	14,456	12,798	631	1,027	Clinton	88.5%	4.4%	7.1%
PAMLICO	1,666	1,281	144	241	Clinton	76.9%	8.6%	14.5%
PASQUOTANK	3,525	2,785	228	512	Clinton	79.0%	6.5%	14.5%
PENDER	3,941	3,120	324	497	Clinton	79.2%	8.2%	12.6%
PERQUIMANS	1,765	1,299	114	352	Clinton	73.6%	6.5%	19.9%
PERSON	3,163	2,328	262	573	Clinton	73.6%	8.3%	18.1%
PITT	11,793	8,952	979	1,862	Clinton	75.9%	8.3%	15.8%
POLK	1,239	1,104	53	82	Clinton	89.1%	4.3%	6.6%
RANDOLPH	3,168	2,684	194	290	Clinton	84.7%	6.1%	9.2%
RICHMOND	6,227	4,715	467	1,045	Clinton	75.7%	7.5%	16.8%
ROBESON	17,467	13,201	1,391	2,875	Clinton	75.6%	8.0%	16.5%
ROCKINGHAM	6,869	5,220	595	1,054	Clinton	76.0%	8.7%	15.3%
ROWAN	5,634	4,331	520	783	Clinton	76.9%	9.2%	13.9%
RUTHERFORD	3,433	2,583	322	528	Clinton	75.2%	9.4%	15.4%
SAMPSON	3,824	3,264	210	350	Clinton	85.4%	5.5%	9.2%
SCOTLAND	3,262	2,776	146	340	Clinton	85.1%	4.5%	10.4%
STANLY	2,973	2,390	231	352	Clinton	80.4%	7.8%	11.8%
STOKES	2,270	1,893	147	230	Clinton	83.4%	6.5%	10.1%
SURRY	2,785	2,356	186	243	Clinton	84.6%	6.7%	8.7%
SWAIN	622	554	30	38	Clinton	89.1%	4.8%	6.1%
TRANSYLVANIA	2,020	1,670	141	209	Clinton	82.7%	7.0%	10.3%
TYRRELL	888	684	58	146	Clinton	77.0%	6.5%	16.4%
UNION	4,421	3,484	365	572	Clinton	78.8%	8.3%	12.9%
VANCE	4,392	3,394	322	676	Clinton	77.3%	7.3%	15.4%
WAKE	43,924	37,291	2,804	3,829	Clinton	84.9%	6.4%	8.7%
WARREN	4,453	3,573	335	545	Clinton	80.2%	7.5%	12.2%
WASHINGTON	1,913	1,549	126	238	Clinton	81.0%	6.6%	12.4%
WATAUGA	1,934	1,686	109	139	Clinton	87.2%	5.6%	7.2%
WAYNE	7,233	5,132	698	1,403	Clinton	71.0%	9.7%	19.4%
WILKES	3,286	2,794	170	322	Clinton	85.0%	5.2%	9.8%
WILSON	5,616	4,622	370	624	Clinton	82.3%	6.6%	11.1%
YADKIN	1,167	932	107	128	Clinton	79.9%	9.2%	11.0%
YANCEY	1,896	1,615	100	181	Clinton	85.2%	5.3%	9.5%
TOTAL	572,160	461,434	40,936	69,790	Clinton	80.6%	7.2%	12.2%

NORTH CAROLINA REPUBLICAN

1996

County	Total Vote	Buchanan	Dole	Other	Winner	Percentage of Total Vote Buchanan	Dole	Other
ALAMANCE	4,276	800	2,848	628	Dole	18.7%	66.6%	14.7%
ALEXANDER	951	135	729	87	Dole	14.2%	76.7%	9.1%
ALLEGHANY	399	36	328	35	Dole	9.0%	82.2%	8.8%
ANSON	237	40	168	29	Dole	16.9%	70.9%	12.2%
ASHE	2,265	218	1,764	283	Dole	9.6%	77.9%	12.5%
AVERY	3,203	551	1,930	722	Dole	17.2%	60.3%	22.5%
BEAUFORT	1,830	266	1,323	241	Dole	14.5%	72.3%	13.2%
BERTIE	136	18	94	24	Dole	13.2%	69.1%	17.6%
BLADEN	356	59	255	42	Dole	16.6%	71.6%	11.8%
BRUNSWICK	2,401	276	1,663	462	Dole	11.5%	69.3%	19.2%
BUNCOMBE	6,089	735	3,913	1441	Dole	12.1%	64.3%	23.7%
BURKE	3,210	621	2,170	419	Dole	19.3%	67.6%	13.1%
CABARRUS	9,449	1,441	6,509	1499	Dole	15.3%	68.9%	15.9%
CALDWELL	3,001	532	2,134	335	Dole	17.7%	71.1%	11.2%
CAMDEN	165	24	107	34	Dole	14.5%	64.8%	20.6%
CARTERET	3,314	361	2,493	460	Dole	10.9%	75.2%	13.9%
CASWELL	281	58	180	43	Dole	20.6%	64.1%	15.3%
CATAWBA	5,889	807	4,313	769	Dole	13.7%	73.2%	13.1%
CHATHAM	1,810	210	1,324	276	Dole	11.6%	73.1%	15.2%
CHEROKEE	426	81	286	59	Dole	19.0%	67.1%	13.8%
CHOWAN	239	26	176	37	Dole	10.9%	73.6%	15.5%
CLAY	382	43	287	52	Dole	11.3%	75.1%	13.6%
CLEVELAND	2,418	417	1,617	384	Dole	17.2%	66.9%	15.9%
COLUMBUS	708	96	514	98	Dole	13.6%	72.6%	13.8%
CRAVEN	2,488	299	1,788	401	Dole	12.0%	71.9%	16.1%
CUMBERLAND	6,816	849	5,086	881	Dole	12.5%	74.6%	12.9%
CURRITUCK	256	46	163	47	Dole	18.0%	63.7%	18.4%
DARE	1,332	141	950	241	Dole	10.6%	71.3%	18.1%
DAVIDSON	6,250	856	4,765	629	Dole	13.7%	76.2%	10.1%
DAVIE	3,273	319	2,584	370	Dole	9.7%	78.9%	11.3%
DUPLIN	724	106	552	66	Dole	14.6%	76.2%	9.1%
DURHAM	6,048	667	4,130	1251	Dole	11.0%	68.3%	20.7%
EDGECOMBE	767	144	523	100	Dole	18.8%	68.2%	13.0%
FORSYTH	13,098	1,374	9,641	2083	Dole	10.5%	73.6%	15.9%
FRANKLIN	1,123	209	757	157	Dole	18.6%	67.4%	14.0%
GASTON	5,902	1,074	4,021	807	Dole	18.2%	68.1%	13.7%
GATES	52	4	37	11	Dole	7.7%	71.2%	21.2%
GRAHAM	571	64	419	88	Dole	11.2%	73.4%	15.4%
GRANVILLE	610	104	416	90	Dole	17.0%	68.2%	14.8%
GREENE	197	32	149	16	Dole	16.2%	75.6%	8.1%
GUILFORD	17,092	1,970	12,300	2822	Dole	11.5%	72.0%	16.5%
HALIFAX	621	118	399	104	Dole	19.0%	64.3%	16.7%
HARNETT	2,073	325	1,532	216	Dole	15.7%	73.9%	10.4%
HAYWOOD	1,015	226	611	178	Dole	22.3%	60.2%	17.5%
HENDERSON	6,159	664	4,338	1157	Dole	10.8%	70.4%	18.8%
HERTFORD	257	32	187	38	Dole	12.5%	72.8%	14.8%
HOKE	245	33	173	39	Dole	13.5%	70.6%	15.9%
HYDE	100	7	80	13	Dole	7.0%	80.0%	13.0%
IREDELL	6,883	942	4,939	1002	Dole	13.7%	71.8%	14.6%
JACKSON	619	92	422	105	Dole	14.9%	68.2%	17.0%

NORTH CAROLINA REPUBLICAN

1996

County	Total Vote	Buchanan	Dole	Other	Winner	Percentage of Total Vote Buchanan	Dole	Other
JOHNSTON	2,653	389	1,952	312	Dole	14.7%	73.6%	11.8%
JONES	134	22	91	21	Dole	16.4%	67.9%	15.7%
LEE	1,632	168	1,193	271	Dole	10.3%	73.1%	16.6%
LENOIR	914	102	705	107	Dole	11.2%	77.1%	11.7%
LINCOLN	3,053	493	2,184	376	Dole	16.1%	71.5%	12.3%
MCDOWELL	1,011	190	663	158	Dole	18.8%	65.6%	15.6%
MACON	1,325	232	845	248	Dole	17.5%	63.8%	18.7%
MADISON	746	89	539	118	Dole	11.9%	72.3%	15.8%
MARTIN	408	52	294	62	Dole	12.7%	72.1%	15.2%
MECKLENBURG	29,384	3,349	20,790	5245	Dole	11.4%	70.8%	17.8%
MITCHELL	2,726	469	1,678	579	Dole	17.2%	61.6%	21.2%
MONTGOMERY	545	78	410	57	Dole	14.3%	75.2%	10.5%
MOORE	5,095	480	3,918	697	Dole	9.4%	76.9%	13.7%
NASH	2,581	477	1,796	308	Dole	18.5%	69.6%	11.9%
NEW HANOVER	9,095	1,049	6,451	1595	Dole	11.5%	70.9%	17.5%
NORTHAMPTON	102	21	66	15	Dole	20.6%	64.7%	14.7%
ONSLOW	3,457	471	2,439	547	Dole	13.6%	70.6%	15.8%
ORANGE	2,760	328	1,848	584	Dole	11.9%	67.0%	21.2%
PAMLICO	446	37	336	73	Dole	8.3%	75.3%	16.4%
PASQUOTANK	568	106	354	108	Dole	18.7%	62.3%	19.0%
PENDER	1,441	159	1,052	230	Dole	11.0%	73.0%	16.0%
PERQUIMANS	229	33	149	47	Dole	14.4%	65.1%	20.5%
PERSON	495	73	356	66	Dole	14.7%	71.9%	13.3%
PITT	2,902	385	2,033	484	Dole	13.3%	70.1%	16.7%
POLK	1,054	98	790	166	Dole	9.3%	75.0%	15.7%
RANDOLPH	4,842	767	3,483	592	Dole	15.8%	71.9%	12.2%
RICHMOND	623	110	418	95	Dole	17.7%	67.1%	15.2%
ROBESON	993	143	675	175	Dole	14.4%	68.0%	17.6%
ROCKINGHAM	2,241	319	1,638	284	Dole	14.2%	73.1%	12.7%
ROWAN	6,322	855	4,791	676	Dole	13.5%	75.8%	10.7%
RUTHERFORD	1,795	263	1,242	290	Dole	14.7%	69.2%	16.2%
SAMPSON	1,990	206	1,610	174	Dole	10.4%	80.9%	8.7%
SCOTLAND	528	51	374	103	Dole	9.7%	70.8%	19.5%
STANLY	2,664	374	2,005	285	Dole	14.0%	75.3%	10.7%
STOKES	1,962	205	1,550	207	Dole	10.4%	79.0%	10.6%
SURRY	1,296	141	998	157	Dole	10.9%	77.0%	12.1%
SWAIN	211	33	143	35	Dole	15.6%	67.8%	16.6%
TRANSYLVANIA	1,990	236	1,359	395	Dole	11.9%	68.3%	19.8%
TYRRELL	74	11	56	7	Dole	14.9%	75.7%	9.5%
UNION	4,596	667	3,109	820	Dole	14.5%	67.6%	17.8%
VANCE	291	34	214	43	Dole	11.7%	73.5%	14.8%
WAKE	22,500	2,699	15,836	3,965	Dole	12.0%	70.4%	17.6%
WARREN	239	32	166	41	Dole	13.4%	69.5%	17.2%
WASHINGTON	158	21	117	20	Dole	13.3%	74.1%	12.7%
WATAUGA	1,652	213	1,124	315	Dole	12.9%	68.0%	19.1%
WAYNE	2,444	341	1,831	272	Dole	14.0%	74.9%	11.1%
WILKES	6,002	748	4,464	790	Dole	12.5%	74.4%	13.2%
WILSON	1,217	231	851	135	Dole	19.0%	69.9%	11.1%
YADKIN	3,641	364	2,933	344	Dole	10.0%	80.6%	9.4%
YANCEY	1,179	164	857	158	Dole	13.9%	72.7%	13.4%
TOTAL	284,212	37,126	202,863	44,223	Dole	13.1%	71.4%	15.6%

NORTH DAKOTA

North Dakota has a long populist tradition characterized by a suspicion of concentrated business interests—such as railroads, banks and grain companies. When the new innovation of the presidential primary blossomed across the country in 1912, it was North Dakota that was first in line to vote.

But the idea of a late-winter primary on the frigid upper Plains did not last long, and by the mid-1930s North Dakota had switched to a caucus process to select its delegates. The presidential primary was resurrected in the 1980s. But again it failed to take root, as candidates relegated it to the ranks of states whose scant prize was appraised as less precious than the time needed to win it.

George Bush's lone opponent in the Republican primary in 1988 was Mary Jane Rachner, a retired teacher from Minnesota who sought to buy billboard space to read: "Stamp Out Homosexuality." Bush won with 94 percent of the vote. The primary ballot in 1992 included Lyndon LaRouche and two comedians. Bush won the GOP primary again; Ross Perot won the Democratic primary on write-ins.

From 1984 through 1992, North Dakota held its presidential primary in June after all the other states had balloted. In 1996, it moved to the front end of the calendar, joining South Dakota on a date in late February. Bob Dole carried both Dakotas to win his first primaries of the year. With his farm-state roots, Dole garnered more votes in North Dakota's Republican primary than runner-up Steve Forbes and third-place finisher Pat Buchanan combined.

Buchanan had the benefit of momentum from his victory the previous week in New Hampshire. But he failed to connect in North Dakota. On one hand, he had to deal with the "ghost" of Phil Gramm in bidding for votes on the right side of the Republican spectrum. By the time of the North Dakota primary, Gramm was out of the race. But with North Dakota allowing votes to be cast by mail beginning in January (when Gramm was still an active candidate), the Texas senator drew nearly 10 percent.

Nor was Buchanan, a native of Washington, D.C., helped by his urban roots. "Buchanan is a city kid," read an editorial in North Dakota's largest newspaper, the *Forum* of Fargo. "If he knows the difference between production agriculture and 'Green Acres,' he's yet to articulate it."

The early primary date in 1996, though, was unable to make the event a rousing hit at the ballot box. Turnout on the Republican side was barely half the number that voted in the GOP primary in 1924, which was won by President Calvin Coolidge. Barely 1,500 North Dakotans voted in the Democratic primary in 1996, which President Bill Clinton skipped.

Recent North Dakota Primary Results

North Dakota held its first presidential primary in 1912, but none were held between 1932 and 1984.

	DEMOCRATS			REPUBLICANS		
Year	Turnout	Candidates	%	Turnout	Candidates	%
1996 (Feb. 27)	1,584	ROLAND RIEMERS	41	63,734	BOB DOLE	42
		Lyndon LaRouche	35		Steve Forbes	20
		Vernon Clemenson	24		Pat Buchanan	18
1992 (June 9)	32,786	ROSS PEROT#	29	47,808	GEORGE BUSH*	83
		Lyndon LaRouche	21			
		Charles Woods	20			
		Tom Shiekman	15			
		Bill Clinton#	15			
1988 (June 14)	3,405	MICHAEL DUKAKIS#	85	39,434	GEORGE BUSH	94
		Jesse Jackson#	15			
1984 (June 12)	33,555	GARY HART	85	44,109	RONALD REAGAN*	100
		Lyndon LaRouche	12			

Note: All candidates are listed that drew at least 10 percent of their party's primary vote. The names of winning candidates are capitalized. An asterisk (*) indicates an incumbent president. A pound sign (#) indicates candidate received votes as a write-in.

Divide
Burke
Renville
Bottineau
Rolette
Towner
Cavalier
Pembina
Williams
Williston
Mountrail
Minot
Ward
McHenry
Pierce
Ramsey
Walsh
Benson
Grand Forks
Nelson
Grand Forks
McKenzie
McLean
Sheridan
Wells
Eddy
Foster
Griggs
Steele
Traill
Dunn
Mercer
Oliver
Burleigh
Billings
Kidder
Jamestown
Barnes
Cass
Golden Valley
Dickinson
Stark
Bismarck
Stutsman
Fargo
Morton
Slope
Hettinger
Grant
Logan
La Moure
Ransom
Emmons
Richland
Bowman
Adams
Sioux
McIntosh
Dickey
Sargent

NORTH DAKOTA DEMOCRATIC

1984

County	Total Vote	Hart	LaRouche	Mondale	Winner	Percentage of Total Vote Hart	LaRouche	Mondale
ADAMS	273	227	30	16	Hart	83.2%	11.0%	5.9%
BARNES	784	698	86		Hart	89.0%	11.0%	
BENSON	540	424	65	51	Hart	78.5%	12.0%	9.4%
BILLINGS	87	74	13		Hart	85.1%	14.9%	
BOTTINEAU	556	496	60		Hart	89.2%	10.8%	
BOWMAN	327	292	35		Hart	89.3%	10.7%	
BURKE	420	359	35	26	Hart	85.5%	8.3%	6.2%
BURLEIGH	2,228	1,918	310		Hart	86.1%	13.9%	
CASS	2,749	2,414	335		Hart	87.8%	12.2%	
CAVALIER	610	527	83		Hart	86.4%	13.6%	
DICKEY	420	326	51	43	Hart	77.6%	12.1%	10.2%
DIVIDE	457	380	56	21	Hart	83.2%	12.3%	4.6%
DUNN	363	299	42	22	Hart	82.4%	11.6%	6.1%
EDDY	320	242	41	37	Hart	75.6%	12.8%	11.6%
EMMONS	278	244	34		Hart	87.8%	12.2%	
FOSTER	430	375	55		Hart	87.2%	12.8%	
GOLDEN VALLEY	201	159	27	15	Hart	79.1%	13.4%	7.5%
GRAND FORKS	1,742	1,553	189		Hart	89.2%	10.8%	
GRANT	397	342	55		Hart	86.1%	13.9%	
GRIGGS	400	323	50	27	Hart	80.8%	12.5%	6.8%
HETTINGER	340	286	54		Hart	84.1%	15.9%	
KIDDER	328	277	39	12	Hart	84.5%	11.9%	3.7%
LA MOURE	391	342	48	1	Hart	87.5%	12.3%	0.3%
LOGAN	251	206	34	11	Hart	82.1%	13.5%	4.4%
MCHENRY	731	640	91		Hart	87.6%	12.4%	
MCINTOSH	189	147	35	7	Hart	77.8%	18.5%	3.7%
MCKENZIE	457	413	44		Hart	90.4%	9.6%	
MCLEAN	883	762	121		Hart	86.3%	13.7%	
MERCER	350	289	61		Hart	82.6%	17.4%	
MORTON	1,319	1,157	162		Hart	87.7%	12.3%	
MOUNTRAIL	1,139	954	101	84	Hart	83.8%	8.9%	7.4%
NELSON	172	150	22		Hart	87.2%	12.8%	
OLIVER	185	141	22	22	Hart	76.2%	11.9%	11.9%
PEMBINA	231	189	42		Hart	81.8%	18.2%	
PIERCE	394	310	77	7	Hart	78.7%	19.5%	1.8%
RAMSEY	579	507	72		Hart	87.6%	12.4%	
RANSOM	350	311	39		Hart	88.9%	11.1%	
RENVILLE	360	325	35		Hart	90.3%	9.7%	
RICHLAND	784	688	96		Hart	87.8%	12.2%	
ROLETTE	532	448	84		Hart	84.2%	15.8%	
SARGENT	327	285	42		Hart	87.2%	12.8%	
SHERIDAN	239	209	30		Hart	87.4%	12.6%	
SIOUX	142	108	19	15	Hart	76.1%	13.4%	10.6%
SLOPE	131	112	12	7	Hart	85.5%	9.2%	5.3%
STARK	889	795	94		Hart	89.4%	10.6%	
STEELE	395	305	47	43	Hart	77.2%	11.9%	10.9%
STUTSMAN	1,003	901	92	10	Hart	89.8%	9.2%	1.0%
TOWNER	236	205	31		Hart	86.9%	13.1%	
TRAILL	423	355	60	8	Hart	83.9%	14.2%	1.9%
WALSH	546	465	78	3	Hart	85.2%	14.3%	0.5%

NORTH DAKOTA DEMOCRATIC

1984

County	Total Vote	Hart	LaRouche	Mondale	Winner	Percentage of Total Vote Hart	LaRouche	Mondale
WARD	3,700	2,874	380	446	Hart	77.7%	10.3%	12.1%
WELLS	641	559	82		Hart	87.2%	12.8%	
WILLIAMS	1,336	1,216	120		Hart	91.0%	9.0%	
TOTAL	33,555	28,603	4,018	934	Hart	85.2%	12.0%	2.8%

Note: The votes for Mondale were write-ins.

NORTH DAKOTA REPUBLICAN

1988

County	Total Vote	Bush	Rachner	Winner	Percentage of Total Vote Bush	Rachner
ADAMS	388	363	25	Bush	93.6%	6.4%
BARNES	876	836	40	Bush	95.4%	4.6%
BENSON	461	431	30	Bush	93.5%	6.5%
BILLINGS	161	151	10	Bush	93.8%	6.2%
BOTTINEAU	766	732	34	Bush	95.6%	4.4%
BOWMAN	384	341	43	Bush	88.8%	11.2%
BURKE	363	343	20	Bush	94.5%	5.5%
BURLEIGH	3,989	3,771	218	Bush	94.5%	5.5%
CASS	4,655	4,433	222	Bush	95.2%	4.8%
CAVALIER	734	678	56	Bush	92.4%	7.6%
DICKEY	497	466	31	Bush	93.8%	6.2%
DIVIDE	297	278	19	Bush	93.6%	6.4%
DUNN	743	691	52	Bush	93.0%	7.0%
EDDY	268	247	21	Bush	92.2%	7.8%
EMMONS	586	545	41	Bush	93.0%	7.0%
FOSTER	318	298	20	Bush	93.7%	6.3%
GOLDEN VALLEY	381	358	23	Bush	94.0%	6.0%
GRAND FORKS	2,117	1,996	121	Bush	94.3%	5.7%
GRANT	560	528	32	Bush	94.3%	5.7%
GRIGGS	323	297	26	Bush	92.0%	8.0%
HETTINGER	471	444	27	Bush	94.3%	5.7%
KIDDER	422	379	43	Bush	89.8%	10.2%
LA MOURE	539	514	25	Bush	95.4%	4.6%
LOGAN	519	475	44	Bush	91.5%	8.5%
MCHENRY	641	595	46	Bush	92.8%	7.2%
MCINTOSH	587	544	43	Bush	92.7%	7.3%
MCKENZIE	554	528	26	Bush	95.3%	4.7%
MCLEAN	890	842	48	Bush	94.6%	5.4%
MERCER	1,086	1,031	55	Bush	94.9%	5.1%
MORTON	1,006	950	56	Bush	94.4%	5.6%

NORTH DAKOTA REPUBLICAN

1988

County	Total Vote	Bush	Rachner	Winner	Percentage of Total Vote: Bush	Rachner
MOUNTRAIL	479	432	47	Bush	90.2%	9.8%
NELSON	254	230	24	Bush	90.6%	9.4%
OLIVER	226	205	21	Bush	90.7%	9.3%
PEMBINA	575	544	31	Bush	94.6%	5.4%
PIERCE	284	267	17	Bush	94.0%	6.0%
RAMSEY	649	606	43	Bush	93.4%	6.6%
RANSOM	339	313	26	Bush	92.3%	7.7%
RENVILLE	294	270	24	Bush	91.8%	8.2%
RICHLAND	995	930	65	Bush	93.5%	6.5%
ROLETTE	180	170	10	Bush	94.4%	5.6%
SARGENT	307	290	17	Bush	94.5%	5.5%
SHERIDAN	430	405	25	Bush	94.2%	5.8%
SIOUX	87	77	10	Bush	88.5%	11.5%
SLOPE	108	95	13	Bush	88.0%	12.0%
STARK	1,036	977	59	Bush	94.3%	5.7%
STEELE	286	263	23	Bush	92.0%	8.0%
STUTSMAN	1,467	1,370	97	Bush	93.4%	6.6%
TOWNER	245	229	16	Bush	93.5%	6.5%
TRAILL	582	554	28	Bush	95.2%	4.8%
WALSH	620	588	32	Bush	94.8%	5.2%
WARD	2,570	2,428	142	Bush	94.5%	5.5%
WELLS	785	745	40	Bush	94.9%	5.1%
WILLIAMS	1,054	989	65	Bush	93.8%	6.2%
TOTAL	39,434	37,062	2,372	Bush	94.0%	6.0%

NORTH DAKOTA DEMOCRATIC

1992

County	Total Vote	Clinton	LaRouche	Perot	Shiekman	Woods	Winner	Percentage of Total Vote: Clinton	LaRouche	Perot	Shiekman	Woods
ADAMS	268	40	67	81	37	43	Perot	14.9%	25.0%	30.2%	13.8%	16.0%
BARNES	648	25	162	207	109	145	Perot	3.9%	25.0%	31.9%	16.8%	22.4%
BENSON	465	66	114	134	61	90	Perot	14.2%	24.5%	28.8%	13.1%	19.4%
BILLINGS	149	15	19	91	12	12	Perot	10.1%	12.8%	61.1%	8.1%	8.1%
BOTTINEAU	417	65	83	126	65	78	Perot	15.6%	19.9%	30.2%	15.6%	18.7%
BOWMAN	289	31	63	103	45	47	Perot	10.7%	21.8%	35.6%	15.6%	16.3%
BURKE	251	41	34	111	26	39	Perot	16.3%	13.5%	44.2%	10.4%	15.5%
BURLEIGH	2,779	119	876		698	1,086	Woods	4.3%	31.5%		25.1%	39.1%
CASS	5,327	1,512	683	2,090	426	616	Perot	28.4%	12.8%	39.2%	8.0%	11.6%
CAVALIER	518	34	137	98	101	148	Woods	6.6%	26.4%	18.9%	19.5%	28.6%

NORTH DAKOTA DEMOCRATIC

1992

County	Total Vote	Clinton	LaRouche	Perot	Shiekman	Woods	Winner	Percentage of Total Vote Clinton	LaRouche	Perot	Shiekman	Woods
DICKEY	440	44	103	167	64	62	Perot	10.0%	23.4%	38.0%	14.5%	14.1%
DIVIDE	196		48	104	19	25	Perot		24.5%	53.1%	9.7%	12.8%
DUNN	353	53	65	161	33	41	Perot	15.0%	18.4%	45.6%	9.3%	11.6%
EDDY	258	42	47	83	33	53	Perot	16.3%	18.2%	32.2%	12.8%	20.5%
EMMONS	383	19	106	143	51	64	Perot	5.0%	27.7%	37.3%	13.3%	16.7%
FOSTER	313	49	48	149	31	36	Perot	15.7%	15.3%	47.6%	9.9%	11.5%
GOLDEN VALLEY	136	23	26	54	12	21	Perot	16.9%	19.1%	39.7%	8.8%	15.4%
GRAND FORKS	2,684	594	351	845	476	418	Perot	22.1%	13.1%	31.5%	17.7%	15.6%
GRANT	314	30	65	122	48	49	Perot	9.6%	20.7%	38.9%	15.3%	15.6%
GRIGGS	232	39	45	96	24	28	Perot	16.8%	19.4%	41.4%	10.3%	12.1%
HETTINGER	307	26	80	121	36	44	Perot	8.5%	26.1%	39.4%	11.7%	14.3%
KIDDER	215	19	49	84	23	40	Perot	8.8%	22.8%	39.1%	10.7%	18.6%
LA MOURE	375	51	58	157	55	54	Perot	13.6%	15.5%	41.9%	14.7%	14.4%
LOGAN	169		53	52	30	34	LaRouche		31.4%	30.8%	17.8%	20.1%
MCHENRY	480	94	118	144	51	73	Perot	19.6%	24.6%	30.0%	10.6%	15.2%
MCINTOSH	167	19	50	48	18	32	LaRouche	11.4%	29.9%	28.7%	10.8%	19.2%
MCKENZIE	358	62	64	150	38	44	Perot	17.3%	17.9%	41.9%	10.6%	12.3%
MCLEAN	578	6	214	52	126	180	LaRouche	1.0%	37.0%	9.0%	21.8%	31.1%
MERCER	678	103	126	284	66	99	Perot	15.2%	18.6%	41.9%	9.7%	14.6%
MORTON	1,109	21	363	128	232	365	Woods	1.9%	32.7%	11.5%	20.9%	32.9%
MOUNTRAIL	575	106	115	216	66	72	Perot	18.4%	20.0%	37.6%	11.5%	12.5%
NELSON	248	12	71	39	61	65	LaRouche	4.8%	28.6%	15.7%	24.6%	26.2%
OLIVER	174		45	86	17	26	Perot		25.9%	49.4%	9.8%	14.9%
PEMBINA	319	9	94	8	85	123	Woods	2.8%	29.5%	2.5%	26.6%	38.6%
PIERCE	203	22	64	55	24	38	LaRouche	10.8%	31.5%	27.1%	11.8%	18.7%
RAMSEY	638	82	133	209	96	118	Perot	12.9%	20.8%	32.8%	15.0%	18.5%
RANSOM	429	88	74	147	58	62	Perot	20.5%	17.2%	34.3%	13.5%	14.5%
RENVILLE	229	34	48	79	27	41	Perot	14.8%	21.0%	34.5%	11.8%	17.9%
RICHLAND	596	21	203	19	133	220	Woods	3.5%	34.1%	3.2%	22.3%	36.9%
ROLETTE	482	7	196	10	127	142	LaRouche	1.5%	40.7%	2.1%	26.3%	29.5%
SARGENT	216	20	62	21	45	68	Woods	9.3%	28.7%	9.7%	20.8%	31.5%
SHERIDAN	178	34	52	50	18	24	LaRouche	19.1%	29.2%	28.1%	10.1%	13.5%
SIOUX	259	10	89	72	39	49	LaRouche	3.9%	34.4%	27.8%	15.1%	18.9%
SLOPE	94	15	11	39	14	15	Perot	16.0%	11.7%	41.5%	14.9%	16.0%
STARK	1,111	228	171	450	121	141	Perot	20.5%	15.4%	40.5%	10.9%	12.7%
STEELE	240	47	38	105	17	33	Perot	19.6%	15.8%	43.8%	7.1%	13.8%
STUTSMAN	1,007	56	250	234	191	276	Woods	5.6%	24.8%	23.2%	19.0%	27.4%
TOWNER	277	41	45	97	37	57	Perot	14.8%	16.2%	35.0%	13.4%	20.6%
TRAILL	582	106	74	233	68	101	Perot	18.2%	12.7%	40.0%	11.7%	17.4%
WALSH	538	11	178	23	144	182	Woods	2.0%	33.1%	4.3%	26.8%	33.8%
WARD	2,626	508	443	910	285	480	Perot	19.3%	16.9%	34.7%	10.9%	18.3%
WELLS	406	61	77	165	42	61	Perot	15.0%	19.0%	40.6%	10.3%	15.0%
WILLIAMS	503		153	64	105	181	Woods		30.4%	12.7%	20.9%	36.0%
TOTAL	32,786	4,760	7,003	9,516	4,866	6,641	Perot	14.5%	21.4%	29.0%	14.8%	20.3%

Note: Votes cast for Clinton and Perot were write-ins.

NORTH DAKOTA REPUBLICAN

1992

County	Total Vote	Bush	Other	Winner	Percentage of Total Vote	
					Bush	Other
ADAMS	515	380	135	Bush	73.8%	26.2%
BARNES	920	794	126	Bush	86.3%	13.7%
BENSON	389	303	86	Bush	77.9%	22.1%
BILLINGS	166	93	73	Bush	56.0%	44.0%
BOTTINEAU	790	679	111	Bush	85.9%	14.1%
BOWMAN	625	470	155	Bush	75.2%	24.8%
BURKE	285	218	67	Bush	76.5%	23.5%
BURLEIGH	4,474	4,035	439	Bush	90.2%	9.8%
CASS	6,627	5,484	1,143	Bush	82.8%	17.2%
CAVALIER	445	385	60	Bush	86.5%	13.5%
DICKEY	572	468	104	Bush	81.8%	18.2%
DIVIDE	288	248	40	Bush	86.1%	13.9%
DUNN	436	317	119	Bush	72.7%	27.3%
EDDY	285	205	80	Bush	71.9%	28.1%
EMMONS	773	583	190	Bush	75.4%	24.6%
FOSTER	315	241	74	Bush	76.5%	23.5%
GOLDEN VALLEY	276	214	62	Bush	77.5%	22.5%
GRAND FORKS	4,115	3,468	647	Bush	84.3%	15.7%
GRANT	520	398	122	Bush	76.5%	23.5%
GRIGGS	424	350	74	Bush	82.5%	17.5%
HETTINGER	400	305	95	Bush	76.3%	23.8%
KIDDER	510	375	135	Bush	73.5%	26.5%
LA MOURE	520	435	85	Bush	83.7%	16.3%
LOGAN	607	440	167	Bush	72.5%	27.5%
MCHENRY	634	517	117	Bush	81.5%	18.5%
MCINTOSH	809	681	128	Bush	84.2%	15.8%
MCKENZIE	620	497	123	Bush	80.2%	19.8%
MCLEAN	835	735	100	Bush	88.0%	12.0%
MERCER	827	652	175	Bush	78.8%	21.2%
MORTON	1,484	1,263	221	Bush	85.1%	14.9%
MOUNTRAIL	476	343	133	Bush	72.1%	27.9%
NELSON	307	270	37	Bush	87.9%	12.1%
OLIVER	213	155	58	Bush	72.8%	27.2%
PEMBINA	588	534	54	Bush	90.8%	9.2%
PIERCE	379	322	57	Bush	85.0%	15.0%
RAMSEY	769	658	111	Bush	85.6%	14.4%
RANSOM	439	352	87	Bush	80.2%	19.8%
RENVILLE	269	229	40	Bush	85.1%	14.9%
RICHLAND	1,126	1,031	95	Bush	91.6%	8.4%
ROLETTE	271	236	35	Bush	87.1%	12.9%
SARGENT	312	280	32	Bush	89.7%	10.3%
SHERIDAN	455	353	102	Bush	77.6%	22.4%
SIOUX	136	99	37	Bush	72.8%	27.2%
SLOPE	119	75	44	Bush	63.0%	37.0%
STARK	1,558	1,212	346	Bush	77.8%	22.2%
STEELE	215	173	42	Bush	80.5%	19.5%
STUTSMAN	1,657	1,413	244	Bush	85.3%	14.7%
TOWNER	225	172	53	Bush	76.4%	23.6%
TRAILL	658	566	92	Bush	86.0%	14.0%
WALSH	836	765	71	Bush	91.5%	8.5%

NORTH DAKOTA REPUBLICAN

1992

County	Total Vote	Bush	Other	Winner	Percentage of Total Vote	
					Bush	Other
WARD	4,206	3,584	622	Bush	85.2%	14.8%
WELLS	886	680	206	Bush	76.7%	23.3%
WILLIAMS	1,222	1,128	94	Bush	92.3%	7.7%
TOTAL	47,808	39,863	7,945	Bush	83.4%	16.6%

NORTH DAKOTA REPUBLICAN

1996

County	Total Vote	Buchanan	Dole	Forbes	Other	Winner	Percentage of Total Vote			
							Buchanan	Dole	Forbes	Other
ADAMS	666	162	255	126	123	Dole	24.3%	38.3%	18.9%	18.5%
BARNES	988	168	439	172	209	Dole	17.0%	44.4%	17.4%	21.2%
BENSON	549	94	286	73	96	Dole	17.1%	52.1%	13.3%	17.5%
BILLINGS	216	50	87	47	32	Dole	23.1%	40.3%	21.8%	14.8%
BOTTINEAU	1,015	193	442	183	197	Dole	19.0%	43.5%	18.0%	19.4%
BOWMAN	408	111	131	78	88	Dole	27.2%	32.1%	19.1%	21.6%
BURKE	364	76	145	66	77	Dole	20.9%	39.8%	18.1%	21.2%
BURLEIGH	7,741	1,626	3,191	1,417	1,507	Dole	21.0%	41.2%	18.3%	19.5%
CASS	9,552	1,238	4,271	2,057	1,986	Dole	13.0%	44.7%	21.5%	20.8%
CAVALIER	675	124	348	106	97	Dole	18.4%	51.6%	15.7%	14.4%
DICKEY	611	108	259	101	143	Dole	17.7%	42.4%	16.5%	23.4%
DIVIDE	400	68	172	87	73	Dole	17.0%	43.0%	21.8%	18.3%
DUNN	564	115	252	95	102	Dole	20.4%	44.7%	16.8%	18.1%
EDDY	341	64	155	56	66	Dole	18.8%	45.5%	16.4%	19.4%
EMMONS	619	146	256	116	101	Dole	23.6%	41.4%	18.7%	16.3%
FOSTER	509	76	245	106	82	Dole	14.9%	48.1%	20.8%	16.1%
GOLDEN VALLEY	341	87	142	55	57	Dole	25.5%	41.6%	16.1%	16.7%
GRAND FORKS	4,339	581	1,877	863	1,018	Dole	13.4%	43.3%	19.9%	23.5%
GRANT	534	149	211	70	104	Dole	27.9%	39.5%	13.1%	19.5%
GRIGGS	379	65	186	66	62	Dole	17.2%	49.1%	17.4%	16.4%
HETTINGER	504	134	208	59	103	Dole	26.6%	41.3%	11.7%	20.4%
KIDDER	539	170	198	89	82	Dole	31.5%	36.7%	16.5%	15.2%
LA MOURE	624	134	262	102	126	Dole	21.5%	42.0%	16.3%	20.2%
LOGAN	402	103	168	67	64	Dole	25.6%	41.8%	16.7%	15.9%
MCHENRY	818	153	360	138	167	Dole	18.7%	44.0%	16.9%	20.4%
MCINTOSH	623	115	300	121	87	Dole	18.5%	48.2%	19.4%	14.0%
MCKENZIE	825	181	356	152	136	Dole	21.9%	43.2%	18.4%	16.5%
MCLEAN	1,337	259	544	277	257	Dole	19.4%	40.7%	20.7%	19.2%
MERCER	1,233	254	478	225	276	Dole	20.6%	38.8%	18.2%	22.4%
MORTON	2,588	600	939	543	506	Dole	23.2%	36.3%	21.0%	19.6%

NORTH DAKOTA REPUBLICAN

1996

County	Total Vote	Buchanan	Dole	Forbes	Other	Winner	Percentage of Total Vote Buchanan	Dole	Forbes	Other
MOUNTRAIL	661	129	276	120	136	Dole	19.5%	41.8%	18.2%	20.6%
NELSON	448	68	192	93	95	Dole	15.2%	42.9%	20.8%	21.2%
OLIVER	351	103	121	65	62	Dole	29.3%	34.5%	18.5%	17.7%
PEMBINA	1,046	187	498	176	185	Dole	17.9%	47.6%	16.8%	17.7%
PIERCE	639	164	282	102	91	Dole	25.7%	44.1%	16.0%	14.2%
RAMSEY	965	182	422	147	214	Dole	18.9%	43.7%	15.2%	22.2%
RANSOM	511	79	223	96	113	Dole	15.5%	43.6%	18.8%	22.1%
RENVILLE	531	115	210	103	103	Dole	21.7%	39.5%	19.4%	19.4%
RICHLAND	1,409	245	604	268	292	Dole	17.4%	42.9%	19.0%	20.7%
ROLETTE	514	101	209	95	109	Dole	19.6%	40.7%	18.5%	21.2%
SARGENT	529	65	249	106	109	Dole	12.3%	47.1%	20.0%	20.6%
SHERIDAN	418	112	160	56	90	Dole	26.8%	38.3%	13.4%	21.5%
SIOUX	147	40	47	40	20	Dole	27.2%	32.0%	27.2%	13.6%
SLOPE	168	36	69	22	41	Dole	21.4%	41.1%	13.1%	24.4%
STARK	2,422	498	983	458	483	Dole	20.6%	40.6%	18.9%	19.9%
STEELE	289	54	129	50	56	Dole	18.7%	44.6%	17.3%	19.4%
STUTSMAN	2,099	343	783	559	414	Dole	16.3%	37.3%	26.6%	19.7%
TOWNER	396	66	171	76	83	Dole	16.7%	43.2%	19.2%	21.0%
TRAILL	701	85	330	159	127	Dole	12.1%	47.1%	22.7%	18.1%
WALSH	1,346	222	566	245	313	Dole	16.5%	42.1%	18.2%	23.3%
WARD	4,563	772	1,903	984	904	Dole	16.9%	41.7%	21.6%	19.8%
WELLS	869	154	392	146	177	Dole	17.7%	45.1%	16.8%	20.4%
WILLIAMS	2,408	429	850	576	553	Dole	17.8%	35.3%	23.9%	23.0%
TOTAL	63,734	11,653	26,832	12,455	12,794	Dole	18.3%	42.1%	19.5%	20.1%

OHIO

Ohio likes to portray itself as a bellwether, a microcosm of the national mood. In the 25 presidential elections held in the twentieth century, Ohio voted for the winner 23 times, a success rate exceeded by no other state and matched by just one, Missouri.

For its part, Ohio's presidential primary has been as much a harbinger as a bellwether, particularly on the Democratic side. Nominees who have struggled in the primary have rarely had much success in winning the pivotal Buckeye State in the general election. Hubert Humphrey edged George McGovern in the 1972 Democratic primary, giving the party an early warning of McGovern's lackluster appeal among blue-collar Democrats. Jimmy Carter scored a big win in Ohio on the final day of the primary season in 1976, offsetting a loss the same day in California and taking the air out of an incipient stop-Carter movement.

As president, Carter won the Ohio primary again in 1980. But with much of the state in the economic doldrums, the vote was much closer. Edward Kennedy had strong labor backing and ran tough television ads. ("Carter equals Hoover equals Depression," said one.) Kennedy carried much of the state's industrial northern tier from Toledo to Youngstown, traditionally the source of about half the Democratic primary vote. But Kennedy did not have enough strength elsewhere in the state to win the primary.

Four years later, Gary Hart appropriated a similar message, tying Walter Mondale to the Carter administration's economic record. Hart ended up running virtually even with Mondale in northern Ohio's industrial belt. And with his edge in rural Ohio, Hart scored a narrow victory that revitalized his struggling campaign for the final wave of primaries.

The Democratic primaries since then have been more one-sided. Michael Dukakis lost Franklin (Columbus) and Hamilton (Cincinnati) counties to Jesse Jackson in 1988, but still rolled up more than 60 percent of the vote statewide. Bill Clinton also surpassed 60 percent in 1992, with his "weakest" showing in Cuyahoga County (Cleveland), where he was held to 53 percent.

The Republican side of the presidential primary ballot in Ohio has not tended to be very competitive. Since Ray Bliss

Recent Ohio Primary Results

Ohio held its first presidential primary in 1912.

	DEMOCRATS			REPUBLICANS		
Year	Turnout	Candidates	%	Turnout	Candidates	%
1996 (March 19)	776,530	BILL CLINTON*	92	963,422	BOB DOLE Pat Buchanan	67 22
1992 (June 2)	1,042,335	BILL CLINTON Jerry Brown Paul Tsongas	61 19 11	860,453	GEORGE BUSH* Pat Buchanan	83 17
1988 (May 3)	1,383,572	MICHAEL DUKAKIS Jesse Jackson	63 27	794,904	GEORGE BUSH Bob Dole	81 12
1984 (May 8)	1,447,236	GARY HART Walter Mondale Jesse Jackson	42 40 16	658,169	RONALD REAGAN*	100
1980 (June 3)	1,186,410	JIMMY CARTER* Edward Kennedy	51 44	856,773	RONALD REAGAN George Bush	81 19
1976 (June 8)	1,134,374	JIMMY CARTER Morris Udall Frank Church	52 21 14	935,757	GERALD FORD* Ronald Reagan	55 45
1972 (May 2)	1,212,330	HUBERT HUMPHREY George McGovern	41 40	692,828	RICHARD NIXON*	100
1968 (May 7)	549,140	STEPHEN YOUNG	100	614,492	JAMES RHODES	100

Note: All candidates are listed that drew at least 10 percent of their party's primary vote. The names of winning candidates are capitalized. An asterisk (*) indicates an incumbent president.

chaired the Ohio GOP in the 1950s and early 1960s, the party has emphasized nuts-and-bolts organization and political pragmatism. It gave President Gerald Ford an early endorsement that discouraged Ronald Reagan from mounting a full-scale effort in Ohio in 1976. Although Ford won the primary with a modest 55 percent of the vote, his tally was remarkably consistent around the state and gave him the delegates he needed to stake his claim to a first-ballot nomination.

For all practical purposes, 1976 was the last year that Ohio Republicans had a say in their party's nominating process, because over the next two decades the GOP contest was usually over before the state voted. Ronald Reagan in 1980 and 1984, and George Bush in 1988 and 1992, each took more than 80 percent of the Ohio GOP primary vote. Dole won almost as easily in 1996.

Pat Buchanan was a distant second in both the 1992 and 1996 primaries, and failed to carry even one of Ohio's 88 counties. The best Buchanan could do was to take slightly more than one-third of the vote in 1996 in a trio of counties in the industrial Youngstown area.

OHIO DEMOCRATIC

1972

County	Total Vote	Humphrey	McGovern	Other	Winner	Percentage of Total Vote Humphrey	McGovern	Other
ADAMS	1,823	993	406	424	Humphrey	54.5%	22.3%	23.3%
ALLEN	10,278	3,835	4,407	2,036	McGovern	37.3%	42.9%	19.8%
ASHLAND	4,109	1,510	1,878	721	McGovern	36.7%	45.7%	17.5%
ASHTABULA	10,289	4,485	3,594	2,210	Humphrey	43.6%	34.9%	21.5%
ATHENS	5,714	1,712	3,242	760	McGovern	30.0%	56.7%	13.3%
AUGLAIZE	2,884	1,107	1,117	660	McGovern	38.4%	38.7%	22.9%
BELMONT	12,880	6,626	4,211	2,043	Humphrey	51.4%	32.7%	15.9%
BROWN	2,900	1,213	900	787	Humphrey	41.8%	31.0%	27.1%
BUTLER	17,718	6,261	7,562	3,895	McGovern	35.3%	42.7%	22.0%
CARROLL	1,527	708	546	273	Humphrey	46.4%	35.8%	17.9%
CHAMPAIGN	1,955	690	877	388	McGovern	35.3%	44.9%	19.8%
CLARK	14,521	5,981	5,844	2,696	Humphrey	41.2%	40.2%	18.6%
CLERMONT	6,852	2,908	2,219	1,725	Humphrey	42.4%	32.4%	25.2%
CLINTON	2,032	809	817	406	McGovern	39.8%	40.2%	20.0%
COLUMBIANA	8,833	4,196	3,177	1,460	Humphrey	47.5%	36.0%	16.5%
COSHOCTON	2,784	1,233	1,100	451	Humphrey	44.3%	39.5%	16.2%
CRAWFORD	4,313	1,566	1,910	837	McGovern	36.3%	44.3%	19.4%
CUYAHOGA	247,782	104,994	99,225	43,563	Humphrey	42.4%	40.0%	17.6%
DARKE	5,162	1,928	2,164	1,070	McGovern	37.3%	41.9%	20.7%
DEFIANCE	3,190	1,156	1,386	648	McGovern	36.2%	43.4%	20.3%
DELAWARE	3,882	1,342	1,589	951	McGovern	34.6%	40.9%	24.5%
ERIE	6,772	2,421	3,248	1,103	McGovern	35.8%	48.0%	16.3%
FAIRFIELD	9,438	3,535	3,923	1,980	McGovern	37.5%	41.6%	21.0%
FAYETTE	1,572	723	471	378	Humphrey	46.0%	30.0%	24.0%
FRANKLIN	88,365	37,149	34,981	16,235	Humphrey	42.0%	39.6%	18.4%
FULTON	1,820	641	795	384	McGovern	35.2%	43.7%	21.1%
GALLIA	1,866	886	619	361	Humphrey	47.5%	33.2%	19.3%
GEAUGA	5,423	1,723	2,592	1,108	McGovern	31.8%	47.8%	20.4%
GREENE	10,731	3,666	4,656	2,409	McGovern	34.2%	43.4%	22.4%
GUERNSEY	3,473	1,611	1,235	627	Humphrey	46.4%	35.6%	18.1%
HAMILTON	78,516	31,973	32,265	14,278	McGovern	40.7%	41.1%	18.2%
HANCOCK	4,605	1,670	2,158	777	McGovern	36.3%	46.9%	16.9%
HARDIN	2,328	998	770	560	Humphrey	42.9%	33.1%	24.1%
HARRISON	1,720	886	502	332	Humphrey	51.5%	29.2%	19.3%
HENRY	1,719	645	751	323	McGovern	37.5%	43.7%	18.8%
HIGHLAND	2,174	1,013	609	552	Humphrey	46.6%	28.0%	25.4%
HOCKING	2,426	1,078	802	546	Humphrey	44.4%	33.1%	22.5%
HOLMES	1,534	605	648	281	McGovern	39.4%	42.2%	18.3%
HURON	3,130	1,221	1,329	580	McGovern	39.0%	42.5%	18.5%
JACKSON	1,923	913	549	461	Humphrey	47.5%	28.5%	24.0%
JEFFERSON	23,642	13,221	6,333	4,088	Humphrey	55.9%	26.8%	17.3%
KNOX	3,398	1,498	1,289	611	Humphrey	44.1%	37.9%	18.0%
LAKE	19,968	7,144	8,837	3,987	McGovern	35.8%	44.3%	20.0%
LAWRENCE	5,614	3,098	1,522	994	Humphrey	55.2%	27.1%	17.7%
LICKING	12,211	5,536	4,156	2,519	Humphrey	45.3%	34.0%	20.6%
LOGAN	2,337	952	855	530	Humphrey	40.7%	36.6%	22.7%
LORAIN	28,437	10,462	12,729	5,246	McGovern	36.8%	44.8%	18.4%
LUCAS	51,049	21,422	20,238	9,389	Humphrey	42.0%	39.6%	18.4%
MADISON	1,893	806	636	451	Humphrey	42.6%	33.6%	23.8%
MAHONING	67,592	29,376	22,258	15,958	Humphrey	43.5%	32.9%	23.6%

OHIO DEMOCRATIC

1972

County	Total Vote	Humphrey	McGovern	Other	Winner	Percentage of Total Vote Humphrey	McGovern	Other
MARION	7,971	2,951	3,228	1,792	McGovern	37.0%	40.5%	22.5%
MEDINA	7,329	2,467	3,446	1,416	McGovern	33.7%	47.0%	19.3%
MEIGS	1,457	688	435	334	Humphrey	47.2%	29.9%	22.9%
MERCER	4,206	1,512	1,788	906	McGovern	35.9%	42.5%	21.5%
MIAMI	7,206	2,768	2,968	1,470	McGovern	38.4%	41.2%	20.4%
MONROE	3,486	1,589	1,043	854	Humphrey	45.6%	29.9%	24.5%
MONTGOMERY	53,646	21,818	21,221	10,607	Humphrey	40.7%	39.6%	19.8%
MORGAN	847	400	303	144	Humphrey	47.2%	35.8%	17.0%
MORROW	2,301	984	745	572	Humphrey	42.8%	32.4%	24.9%
MUSKINGUM	8,289	3,284	3,652	1,353	McGovern	39.6%	44.1%	16.3%
NOBLE	846	445	253	148	Humphrey	52.6%	29.9%	17.5%
OTTAWA	4,605	1,924	1,836	845	Humphrey	41.8%	39.9%	18.3%
PAULDING	1,565	741	439	385	Humphrey	47.3%	28.1%	24.6%
PERRY	2,213	1,089	748	376	Humphrey	49.2%	33.8%	17.0%
PICKAWAY	3,369	1,422	1,088	859	Humphrey	42.2%	32.3%	25.5%
PIKE	2,856	1,690	518	648	Humphrey	59.2%	18.1%	22.7%
PORTAGE	16,221	5,157	8,655	2,409	McGovern	31.8%	53.4%	14.9%
PREBLE	2,936	1,236	1,025	675	Humphrey	42.1%	34.9%	23.0%
PUTNAM	5,571	1,757	2,388	1,426	McGovern	31.5%	42.9%	25.6%
RICHLAND	11,435	4,129	5,446	1,860	McGovern	36.1%	47.6%	16.3%
ROSS	5,365	2,085	1,536	1,744	Humphrey	38.9%	28.6%	32.5%
SANDUSKY	6,314	2,482	2,777	1,055	McGovern	39.3%	44.0%	16.7%
SCIOTO	9,087	4,912	2,204	1,971	Humphrey	54.1%	24.3%	21.7%
SENECA	6,201	1,964	3,123	1,114	McGovern	31.7%	50.4%	18.0%
SHELBY	4,325	1,618	1,644	1,063	McGovern	37.4%	38.0%	24.6%
STARK	44,612	19,679	16,701	8,232	Humphrey	44.1%	37.4%	18.5%
SUMMIT	78,760	29,812	36,388	12,560	McGovern	37.9%	46.2%	15.9%
TRUMBULL	36,205	15,529	13,222	7,454	Humphrey	42.9%	36.5%	20.6%
TUSCARAWAS	13,060	4,909	5,345	2,806	McGovern	37.6%	40.9%	21.5%
UNION	2,045	940	683	422	Humphrey	46.0%	33.4%	20.6%
VAN WERT	2,507	1,155	780	572	Humphrey	46.1%	31.1%	22.8%
VINTON	1,074	485	305	284	Humphrey	45.2%	28.4%	26.4%
WARREN	5,193	2,130	1,797	1,266	Humphrey	41.0%	34.6%	24.4%
WASHINGTON	3,907	1,791	1,175	941	Humphrey	45.8%	30.1%	24.1%
WAYNE	8,269	3,074	3,823	1,372	McGovern	37.2%	46.2%	16.6%
WILLIAMS	1,815	865	655	295	Humphrey	47.7%	36.1%	16.3%
WOOD	9,150	3,239	4,376	1,535	McGovern	35.4%	47.8%	16.8%
WYANDOT	1,846	693	748	405	McGovern	37.5%	40.5%	21.9%
TOTAL	1,205,194	497,538	478,434	229,222	Humphrey	41.3%	39.7%	19.0%
Certified Totals	1,212,330	499,680	480,320	232,330	Humphrey	41.2%	39.6%	19.2%

Note: The certified totals are based on each candidate's highest vote-getting at-large delegate, whose vote was not readily available on a county-by-county basis.

OHIO DEMOCRATIC

1976

County	Total Vote	Carter	Church	Udall	Other	Winner	Percentage of Total Vote Carter	Church	Udall	Other
ADAMS	2,299	1,810	132	100	257	Carter	78.7%	5.7%	4.3%	11.2%
ALLEN	8,895	5,208	951	1,548	1,188	Carter	58.5%	10.7%	17.4%	13.4%
ASHLAND	3,312	1,782	478	562	490	Carter	53.8%	14.4%	17.0%	14.8%
ASHTABULA	10,701	5,110	1,444	2,809	1,338	Carter	47.8%	13.5%	26.2%	12.5%
ATHENS	5,237	2,255	645	1,940	397	Carter	43.1%	12.3%	37.0%	7.6%
AUGLAIZE	2,987	1,656	501	417	413	Carter	55.4%	16.8%	14.0%	13.8%
BELMONT	16,204	9,482	1,736	2,417	2,569	Carter	58.5%	10.7%	14.9%	15.9%
BROWN	3,570	2,621	268	214	467	Carter	73.4%	7.5%	6.0%	13.1%
BUTLER	14,535	8,706	1,830	2,452	1,547	Carter	59.9%	12.6%	16.9%	10.6%
CARROLL	2,084	1,234	265	310	275	Carter	59.2%	12.7%	14.9%	13.2%
CHAMPAIGN	2,125	1,257	281	297	290	Carter	59.2%	13.2%	14.0%	13.6%
CLARK	15,012	8,016	2,375	2,175	2,446	Carter	53.4%	15.8%	14.5%	16.3%
CLERMONT	7,165	4,911	653	713	888	Carter	68.5%	9.1%	10.0%	12.4%
CLINTON	2,041	1,367	255	192	227	Carter	67.0%	12.5%	9.4%	11.1%
COLUMBIANA	10,301	5,788	1,445	1,619	1,449	Carter	56.2%	14.0%	15.7%	14.1%
COSHOCTON	2,798	1,544	397	357	500	Carter	55.2%	14.2%	12.8%	17.9%
CRAWFORD	5,119	2,586	939	831	763	Carter	50.5%	18.3%	16.2%	14.9%
CUYAHOGA	190,993	78,910	26,285	59,131	26,667	Carter	41.3%	13.8%	31.0%	14.0%
DARKE	3,987	2,260	774	500	453	Carter	56.7%	19.4%	12.5%	11.4%
DEFIANCE	3,148	1,313	675	730	430	Carter	41.7%	21.4%	23.2%	13.7%
DELAWARE	4,206	2,243	477	844	642	Carter	53.3%	11.3%	20.1%	15.3%
ERIE	6,144	2,696	1,012	1,371	1,065	Carter	43.9%	16.5%	22.3%	17.3%
FAIRFIELD	11,674	6,559	1,432	1,676	2,007	Carter	56.2%	12.3%	14.4%	17.2%
FAYETTE	1,629	1,054	165	150	260	Carter	64.7%	10.1%	9.2%	16.0%
FRANKLIN	86,627	45,822	9,865	17,036	13,904	Carter	52.9%	11.4%	19.7%	16.1%
FULTON	2,161	1,063	349	521	228	Carter	49.2%	16.1%	24.1%	10.6%
GALLIA	2,773	1,957	206	278	332	Carter	70.6%	7.4%	10.0%	12.0%
GEAUGA	5,619	2,745	898	1,367	609	Carter	48.9%	16.0%	24.3%	10.8%
GREENE	11,646	6,387	1,882	2,173	1,204	Carter	54.8%	16.2%	18.7%	10.3%
GUERNSEY	3,572	2,172	433	426	541	Carter	60.8%	12.1%	11.9%	15.1%
HAMILTON	62,076	36,359	7,823	11,811	6,083	Carter	58.6%	12.6%	19.0%	9.8%
HANCOCK	3,852	1,786	707	947	412	Carter	46.4%	18.4%	24.6%	10.7%
HARDIN	2,113	1,083	334	311	385	Carter	51.3%	15.8%	14.7%	18.2%
HARRISON	2,011	1,221	209	233	348	Carter	60.7%	10.4%	11.6%	17.3%
HENRY	2,102	1,123	333	406	240	Carter	53.4%	15.8%	19.3%	11.4%
HIGHLAND	2,985	2,206	241	189	349	Carter	73.9%	8.1%	6.3%	11.7%
HOCKING	2,571	1,628	239	330	374	Carter	63.3%	9.3%	12.8%	14.5%
HOLMES	2,034	1,155	295	284	300	Carter	56.8%	14.5%	14.0%	14.7%
HURON	3,552	1,717	711	673	451	Carter	48.3%	20.0%	18.9%	12.7%
JACKSON	1,980	1,383	144	181	272	Carter	69.8%	7.3%	9.1%	13.7%
JEFFERSON	19,665	11,942	2,093	2,507	3,123	Carter	60.7%	10.6%	12.7%	15.9%
KNOX	3,691	1,680	548	765	698	Carter	45.5%	14.8%	20.7%	18.9%
LAKE	21,603	10,209	3,001	5,754	2,639	Carter	47.3%	13.9%	26.6%	12.2%
LAWRENCE	5,768	3,678	584	677	829	Carter	63.8%	10.1%	11.7%	14.4%
LICKING	11,503	6,475	1,367	2,246	1,415	Carter	56.3%	11.9%	19.5%	12.3%
LOGAN	2,305	1,340	306	275	384	Carter	58.1%	13.3%	11.9%	16.7%
LORAIN	28,948	14,281	4,126	7,302	3,239	Carter	49.3%	14.3%	25.2%	11.2%
LUCAS	56,261	24,610	10,839	16,026	4,786	Carter	43.7%	19.3%	28.5%	8.5%
MADISON	2,160	1,375	194	255	336	Carter	63.7%	9.0%	11.8%	15.6%
MAHONING	52,856	31,690	7,663	7,170	6,333	Carter	60.0%	14.5%	13.6%	12.0%

OHIO DEMOCRATIC

1976

County	Total Vote	Carter	Church	Udall	Other	Winner	Percentage of Total Vote Carter	Church	Udall	Other
MARION	7,581	4,162	1,022	1,214	1,183	Carter	54.9%	13.5%	16.0%	15.6%
MEDINA	9,205	4,544	1,336	2,417	908	Carter	49.4%	14.5%	26.3%	9.9%
MEIGS	1,632	1,021	163	204	244	Carter	62.6%	10.0%	12.5%	15.0%
MERCER	3,233	1,598	683	417	535	Carter	49.4%	21.1%	12.9%	16.5%
MIAMI	7,553	4,462	1,199	1,134	758	Carter	59.1%	15.9%	15.0%	10.0%
MONROE	4,240	2,904	361	427	548	Carter	68.5%	8.5%	10.1%	12.9%
MONTGOMERY	56,796	32,274	8,990	9,149	6,383	Carter	56.8%	15.8%	16.1%	11.2%
MORGAN	911	601	87	106	117	Carter	66.0%	9.5%	11.6%	12.8%
MORROW	2,268	1,422	208	275	363	Carter	62.7%	9.2%	12.1%	16.0%
MUSKINGUM	6,328	4,286	661	749	632	Carter	67.7%	10.4%	11.8%	10.0%
NOBLE	1,192	755	101	112	224	Carter	63.3%	8.5%	9.4%	18.8%
OTTAWA	4,459	2,105	723	1,057	574	Carter	47.2%	16.2%	23.7%	12.9%
PAULDING	1,652	894	275	194	289	Carter	54.1%	16.6%	11.7%	17.5%
PERRY	2,544	1,570	304	335	335	Carter	61.7%	11.9%	13.2%	13.2%
PICKAWAY	3,940	2,212	410	449	869	Carter	56.1%	10.4%	11.4%	22.1%
PIKE	2,933	2,042	188	284	419	Carter	69.6%	6.4%	9.7%	14.3%
PORTAGE	15,260	6,521	2,532	4,629	1,578	Carter	42.7%	16.6%	30.3%	10.3%
PREBLE	2,996	1,869	379	339	409	Carter	62.4%	12.7%	11.3%	13.7%
PUTNAM	4,517	2,496	542	815	664	Carter	55.3%	12.0%	18.0%	14.7%
RICHLAND	12,418	6,832	2,186	1,867	1,533	Carter	55.0%	17.6%	15.0%	12.3%
ROSS	5,033	3,247	530	500	756	Carter	64.5%	10.5%	9.9%	15.0%
SANDUSKY	5,666	2,648	916	1,507	595	Carter	46.7%	16.2%	26.6%	10.5%
SCIOTO	9,018	5,955	832	922	1,309	Carter	66.0%	9.2%	10.2%	14.5%
SENECA	6,187	2,654	997	1,768	768	Carter	42.9%	16.1%	28.6%	12.4%
SHELBY	4,643	2,694	803	486	660	Carter	58.0%	17.3%	10.5%	14.2%
STARK	49,671	28,060	7,328	8,402	5,881	Carter	56.5%	14.8%	16.9%	11.8%
SUMMIT	82,116	42,379	11,108	21,502	7,127	Carter	51.6%	13.5%	26.2%	8.7%
TRUMBULL	37,169	20,091	5,662	6,989	4,427	Carter	54.1%	15.2%	18.8%	11.9%
TUSCARAWAS	8,899	4,003	1,420	1,504	1,972	Carter	45.0%	16.0%	16.9%	22.2%
UNION	1,761	1,077	240	230	214	Carter	61.2%	13.6%	13.1%	12.2%
VAN WERT	2,370	1,311	412	327	320	Carter	55.3%	17.4%	13.8%	13.5%
VINTON	1,250	884	94	88	184	Carter	70.7%	7.5%	7.0%	14.7%
WARREN	5,860	3,956	626	582	696	Carter	67.5%	10.7%	9.9%	11.9%
WASHINGTON	3,916	2,206	406	584	720	Carter	56.3%	10.4%	14.9%	18.4%
WAYNE	7,462	3,982	1,093	1,699	688	Carter	53.4%	14.6%	22.8%	9.2%
WILLIAMS	2,313	1,108	479	411	315	Carter	47.9%	20.7%	17.8%	13.6%
WOOD	9,176	3,963	1,540	2,916	757	Carter	43.2%	16.8%	31.8%	8.2%
WYANDOT	1,606	887	243	254	222	Carter	55.2%	15.1%	15.8%	13.8%
TOTAL	1,134,374	593,130	157,884	240,342	143,018	Carter	52.3%	13.9%	21.2%	12.6%

OHIO REPUBLICAN

1976

County	Total Vote	Ford	Reagan	Winner	Percentage of Total Vote Ford	Reagan
ADAMS	3,204	1,669	1,535	Ford	52.1%	47.9%
ALLEN	16,343	8,213	8,130	Ford	50.3%	49.7%
ASHLAND	4,539	2,118	2,421	Reagan	46.7%	53.3%
ASHTABULA	9,558	4,924	4,634	Ford	51.5%	48.5%
ATHENS	4,342	2,582	1,760	Ford	59.5%	40.5%
AUGLAIZE	4,017	1,882	2,135	Reagan	46.9%	53.1%
BELMONT	4,274	2,761	1,513	Ford	64.6%	35.4%
BROWN	1,982	1,033	949	Ford	52.1%	47.9%
BUTLER	23,105	11,721	11,384	Ford	50.7%	49.3%
CARROLL	2,688	1,462	1,226	Ford	54.4%	45.6%
CHAMPAIGN	4,024	2,368	1,656	Ford	58.8%	41.2%
CLARK	16,249	9,840	6,409	Ford	60.6%	39.4%
CLERMONT	8,448	4,117	4,331	Reagan	48.7%	51.3%
CLINTON	4,827	2,596	2,231	Ford	53.8%	46.2%
COLUMBIANA	9,512	5,439	4,073	Ford	57.2%	42.8%
COSHOCTON	2,934	1,351	1,583	Reagan	46.0%	54.0%
CRAWFORD	5,151	2,400	2,751	Reagan	46.6%	53.4%
CUYAHOGA	79,729	43,016	36,713	Ford	54.0%	46.0%
DARKE	3,989	2,148	1,841	Ford	53.8%	46.2%
DEFIANCE	3,757	2,260	1,497	Ford	60.2%	39.8%
DELAWARE	8,413	4,072	4,341	Reagan	48.4%	51.6%
ERIE	6,857	3,750	3,107	Ford	54.7%	45.3%
FAIRFIELD	10,725	5,128	5,597	Reagan	47.8%	52.2%
FAYETTE	3,175	1,521	1,654	Reagan	47.9%	52.1%
FRANKLIN	90,398	49,109	41,289	Ford	54.3%	45.7%
FULTON	4,907	3,218	1,689	Ford	65.6%	34.4%
GALLIA	5,381	2,742	2,639	Ford	51.0%	49.0%
GEAUGA	6,232	3,376	2,856	Ford	54.2%	45.8%
GREENE	13,378	7,232	6,146	Ford	54.1%	45.9%
GUERNSEY	4,781	2,648	2,133	Ford	55.4%	44.6%
HAMILTON	86,217	49,701	36,516	Ford	57.6%	42.4%
HANCOCK	9,003	5,486	3,517	Ford	60.9%	39.1%
HARDIN	3,595	1,794	1,801	Reagan	49.9%	50.1%
HARRISON	1,560	940	620	Ford	60.3%	39.7%
HENRY	3,768	2,208	1,560	Ford	58.6%	41.4%
HIGHLAND	3,939	2,038	1,901	Ford	51.7%	48.3%
HOCKING	2,022	983	1,039	Reagan	48.6%	51.4%
HOLMES	1,154	688	466	Ford	59.6%	40.4%
HURON	4,864	2,538	2,326	Ford	52.2%	47.8%
JACKSON	4,673	2,268	2,405	Reagan	48.5%	51.5%
JEFFERSON	6,088	3,838	2,250	Ford	63.0%	37.0%
KNOX	5,442	2,733	2,709	Ford	50.2%	49.8%
LAKE	14,442	7,412	7,030	Ford	51.3%	48.7%
LAWRENCE	7,800	3,915	3,885	Ford	50.2%	49.8%
LICKING	11,843	5,895	5,948	Reagan	49.8%	50.2%
LOGAN	5,167	2,719	2,448	Ford	52.6%	47.4%
LORAIN	13,968	7,077	6,891	Ford	50.7%	49.3%
LUCAS	36,028	24,512	11,516	Ford	68.0%	32.0%
MADISON	3,873	1,906	1,967	Reagan	49.2%	50.8%
MAHONING	18,648	11,557	7,091	Ford	62.0%	38.0%

OHIO REPUBLICAN

1976

County	Total Vote	Ford	Reagan	Winner	Percentage of Total Vote	
					Ford	Reagan
MARION	7,354	3,991	3,363	Ford	54.3%	45.7%
MEDINA	10,116	5,504	4,612	Ford	54.4%	45.6%
MEIGS	5,132	2,609	2,523	Ford	50.8%	49.2%
MERCER	2,126	1,003	1,123	Reagan	47.2%	52.8%
MIAMI	11,744	6,617	5,127	Ford	56.3%	43.7%
MONROE	653	425	228	Ford	65.1%	34.9%
MONTGOMERY	45,737	26,503	19,234	Ford	57.9%	42.1%
MORGAN	3,113	1,529	1,584	Reagan	49.1%	50.9%
MORROW	3,718	1,706	2,012	Reagan	45.9%	54.1%
MUSKINGUM	8,916	4,569	4,347	Ford	51.2%	48.8%
NOBLE	1,943	1,058	885	Ford	54.5%	45.5%
OTTAWA	2,959	1,826	1,133	Ford	61.7%	38.3%
PAULDING	1,948	1,092	856	Ford	56.1%	43.9%
PERRY	2,726	1,497	1,229	Ford	54.9%	45.1%
PICKAWAY	3,584	1,571	2,013	Reagan	43.8%	56.2%
PIKE	1,656	923	733	Ford	55.7%	44.3%
PORTAGE	7,726	4,241	3,485	Ford	54.9%	45.1%
PREBLE	4,009	2,017	1,992	Ford	50.3%	49.7%
PUTNAM	2,974	1,502	1,472	Ford	50.5%	49.5%
RICHLAND	10,865	5,176	5,689	Reagan	47.6%	52.4%
ROSS	6,150	2,861	3,289	Reagan	46.5%	53.5%
SANDUSKY	7,862	4,670	3,192	Ford	59.4%	40.6%
SCIOTO	7,694	3,182	4,512	Reagan	41.4%	58.6%
SENECA	6,718	3,592	3,126	Ford	53.5%	46.5%
SHELBY	3,416	1,885	1,531	Ford	55.2%	44.8%
STARK	43,499	22,976	20,523	Ford	52.8%	47.2%
SUMMIT	38,178	23,450	14,728	Ford	61.4%	38.6%
TRUMBULL	16,259	9,104	7,155	Ford	56.0%	44.0%
TUSCARAWAS	4,202	2,273	1,929	Ford	54.1%	45.9%
UNION	4,191	2,040	2,151	Reagan	48.7%	51.3%
VAN WERT	4,341	2,575	1,766	Ford	59.3%	40.7%
VINTON	1,532	847	685	Ford	55.3%	44.7%
WARREN	8,431	4,299	4,132	Ford	51.0%	49.0%
WASHINGTON	6,590	3,096	3,494	Reagan	47.0%	53.0%
WAYNE	7,832	5,022	2,810	Ford	64.1%	35.9%
WILLIAMS	4,947	3,131	1,816	Ford	63.3%	36.7%
WOOD	11,430	7,532	3,898	Ford	65.9%	34.1%
WYANDOT	2,473	1,313	1,160	Ford	53.1%	46.9%
TOTAL	935,757	516,111	419,646	Ford	55.2%	44.8%

OHIO DEMOCRATIC

1980

County	Total Vote	Carter	E. Kennedy	Other	Winner	Percentage of Total Vote Carter	E. Kennedy	Other
ADAMS	2,748	1,869	771	108	Carter	68.0%	28.1%	3.9%
ALLEN	9,007	5,589	2,877	541	Carter	62.1%	31.9%	6.0%
ASHLAND	3,723	1,986	1,414	323	Carter	53.3%	38.0%	8.7%
ASHTABULA	11,659	4,983	6,113	563	E. Kennedy	42.7%	52.4%	4.8%
ATHENS	5,221	3,276	1,790	155	Carter	62.7%	34.3%	3.0%
AUGLAIZE	3,584	2,296	1,073	215	Carter	64.1%	29.9%	6.0%
BELMONT	14,991	7,647	6,495	849	Carter	51.0%	43.3%	5.7%
BROWN	4,231	2,755	1,235	241	Carter	65.1%	29.2%	5.7%
BUTLER	16,289	10,215	5,414	660	Carter	62.7%	33.2%	4.1%
CARROLL	2,580	1,550	875	155	Carter	60.1%	33.9%	6.0%
CHAMPAIGN	2,266	1,541	623	102	Carter	68.0%	27.5%	4.5%
CLARK	13,401	7,713	5,190	498	Carter	57.6%	38.7%	3.7%
CLERMONT	8,021	5,020	2,510	491	Carter	62.6%	31.3%	6.1%
CLINTON	1,959	1,262	619	78	Carter	64.4%	31.6%	4.0%
COLUMBIANA	12,222	6,878	4,699	645	Carter	56.3%	38.4%	5.3%
COSHOCTON	2,787	1,784	802	201	Carter	64.0%	28.8%	7.2%
CRAWFORD	4,983	2,834	1,822	327	Carter	56.9%	36.6%	6.6%
CUYAHOGA	212,949	87,007	114,979	10,963	E. Kennedy	40.9%	54.0%	5.1%
DARKE	4,963	3,095	1,628	240	Carter	62.4%	32.8%	4.8%
DEFIANCE	3,514	1,796	1,550	168	Carter	51.1%	44.1%	4.8%
DELAWARE	3,783	2,470	1,103	210	Carter	65.3%	29.2%	5.6%
ERIE	9,015	4,254	4,418	343	E. Kennedy	47.2%	49.0%	3.8%
FAIRFIELD	11,605	7,649	2,989	967	Carter	65.9%	25.8%	8.3%
FAYETTE	1,665	1,071	514	80	Carter	64.3%	30.9%	4.8%
FRANKLIN	81,567	46,605	29,992	4,970	Carter	57.1%	36.8%	6.1%
FULTON	2,445	1,151	1,182	112	E. Kennedy	47.1%	48.3%	4.6%
GALLIA	3,010	1,971	919	120	Carter	65.5%	30.5%	4.0%
GEAUGA	6,580	3,161	2,800	619	Carter	48.0%	42.6%	9.4%
GREENE	10,137	6,291	3,437	409	Carter	62.1%	33.9%	4.0%
GUERNSEY	4,174	2,446	1,528	200	Carter	58.6%	36.6%	4.8%
HAMILTON	62,059	36,830	23,598	1,631	Carter	59.3%	38.0%	2.6%
HANCOCK	3,914	2,223	1,319	372	Carter	56.8%	33.7%	9.5%
HARDIN	2,332	1,469	624	239	Carter	63.0%	26.8%	10.2%
HARRISON	2,132	1,167	864	101	Carter	54.7%	40.5%	4.7%
HENRY	1,899	1,148	658	93	Carter	60.5%	34.6%	4.9%
HIGHLAND	2,501	1,656	720	125	Carter	66.2%	28.8%	5.0%
HOCKING	2,784	1,892	779	113	Carter	68.0%	28.0%	4.1%
HOLMES	1,806	1,120	591	95	Carter	62.0%	32.7%	5.3%
HURON	3,895	1,800	1,907	188	E. Kennedy	46.2%	49.0%	4.8%
JACKSON	1,740	1,194	488	58	Carter	68.6%	28.0%	3.3%
JEFFERSON	18,108	9,195	7,936	977	Carter	50.8%	43.8%	5.4%
KNOX	3,033	1,848	936	249	Carter	60.9%	30.9%	8.2%
LAKE	24,430	11,421	11,604	1,405	E. Kennedy	46.7%	47.5%	5.8%
LAWRENCE	5,360	3,046	2,128	186	Carter	56.8%	39.7%	3.5%
LICKING	12,873	8,118	4,020	735	Carter	63.1%	31.2%	5.7%
LOGAN	2,053	1,328	621	104	Carter	64.7%	30.2%	5.1%
LORAIN	36,929	14,436	20,940	1,553	E. Kennedy	39.1%	56.7%	4.2%
LUCAS	51,671	23,372	26,995	1,304	E. Kennedy	45.2%	52.2%	2.5%
MADISON	1,957	1,295	559	103	Carter	66.2%	28.6%	5.3%
MAHONING	62,374	25,377	34,582	2,415	E. Kennedy	40.7%	55.4%	3.9%

OHIO DEMOCRATIC

1980

County	Total Vote	Carter	E. Kennedy	Other	Winner	Percentage of Total Vote Carter	E. Kennedy	Other
MARION	7,716	4,442	2,852	422	Carter	57.6%	37.0%	5.5%
MEDINA	10,331	4,974	4,873	484	Carter	48.1%	47.2%	4.7%
MEIGS	1,586	1,115	414	57	Carter	70.3%	26.1%	3.6%
MERCER	4,508	2,818	1,456	234	Carter	62.5%	32.3%	5.2%
MIAMI	6,682	4,377	1,987	318	Carter	65.5%	29.7%	4.8%
MONROE	4,035	2,564	1,226	245	Carter	63.5%	30.4%	6.1%
MONTGOMERY	53,104	31,391	20,073	1,640	Carter	59.1%	37.8%	3.1%
MORGAN	961	699	228	34	Carter	72.7%	23.7%	3.5%
MORROW	2,198	1,450	608	140	Carter	66.0%	27.7%	6.4%
MUSKINGUM	7,054	4,485	2,185	384	Carter	63.6%	31.0%	5.4%
NOBLE	1,510	901	542	67	Carter	59.7%	35.9%	4.4%
OTTAWA	5,477	2,844	2,379	254	Carter	51.9%	43.4%	4.6%
PAULDING	2,070	1,114	837	119	Carter	53.8%	40.4%	5.7%
PERRY	2,713	1,637	928	148	Carter	60.3%	34.2%	5.5%
PICKAWAY	4,426	2,787	1,227	412	Carter	63.0%	27.7%	9.3%
PIKE	3,807	2,705	981	121	Carter	71.1%	25.8%	3.2%
PORTAGE	16,340	7,295	8,261	784	E. Kennedy	44.6%	50.6%	4.8%
PREBLE	2,916	1,958	833	125	Carter	67.1%	28.6%	4.3%
PUTNAM	5,571	3,196	1,995	380	Carter	57.4%	35.8%	6.8%
RICHLAND	14,106	7,450	5,926	730	Carter	52.8%	42.0%	5.2%
ROSS	4,472	2,917	1,199	356	Carter	65.2%	26.8%	8.0%
SANDUSKY	5,420	2,773	2,398	249	Carter	51.2%	44.2%	4.6%
SCIOTO	9,046	6,057	2,674	315	Carter	67.0%	29.6%	3.5%
SENECA	5,546	2,707	2,534	305	Carter	48.8%	45.7%	5.5%
SHELBY	5,051	3,225	1,555	271	Carter	63.8%	30.8%	5.4%
STARK	48,119	24,150	21,178	2,791	Carter	50.2%	44.0%	5.8%
SUMMIT	81,409	38,157	39,700	3,552	E. Kennedy	46.9%	48.8%	4.4%
TRUMBULL	40,691	18,208	20,662	1,821	E. Kennedy	44.7%	50.8%	4.5%
TUSCARAWAS	11,262	5,973	4,607	682	Carter	53.0%	40.9%	6.1%
UNION	1,886	1,311	488	87	Carter	69.5%	25.9%	4.6%
VAN WERT	2,788	1,706	957	125	Carter	61.2%	34.3%	4.5%
VINTON	1,519	1,037	428	54	Carter	68.3%	28.2%	3.6%
WARREN	6,096	3,955	1,858	283	Carter	64.9%	30.5%	4.6%
WASHINGTON	5,203	3,453	1,585	165	Carter	66.4%	30.5%	3.2%
WAYNE	8,316	4,728	3,177	411	Carter	56.9%	38.2%	4.9%
WILLIAMS	2,171	1,246	828	97	Carter	57.4%	38.1%	4.5%
WOOD	9,666	4,783	4,489	394	Carter	49.5%	46.4%	4.1%
WYANDOT	1,709	1,056	516	137	Carter	61.8%	30.2%	8.0%
TOTAL	1,186,410	605,744	523,874	56,792	Carter	51.1%	44.2%	4.8%

OHIO REPUBLICAN

1980

County	Total Vote	Bush	Reagan	Winner	Percentage of Total Vote Bush	Percentage of Total Vote Reagan
ADAMS	3,023	304	2,719	Reagan	10.1%	89.9%
ALLEN	14,974	2,040	12,934	Reagan	13.6%	86.4%
ASHLAND	5,763	849	4,914	Reagan	14.7%	85.3%
ASHTABULA	8,628	1,721	6,907	Reagan	19.9%	80.1%
ATHENS	3,812	619	3,193	Reagan	16.2%	83.8%
AUGLAIZE	4,841	716	4,125	Reagan	14.8%	85.2%
BELMONT	3,703	708	2,995	Reagan	19.1%	80.9%
BROWN	2,052	257	1,795	Reagan	12.5%	87.5%
BUTLER	19,657	3,271	16,386	Reagan	16.6%	83.4%
CARROLL	3,226	502	2,724	Reagan	15.6%	84.4%
CHAMPAIGN	4,174	900	3,274	Reagan	21.6%	78.4%
CLARK	12,341	3,070	9,271	Reagan	24.9%	75.1%
CLERMONT	9,700	1,474	8,226	Reagan	15.2%	84.8%
CLINTON	4,805	843	3,962	Reagan	17.5%	82.5%
COLUMBIANA	9,953	2,238	7,715	Reagan	22.5%	77.5%
COSHOCTON	4,057	516	3,541	Reagan	12.7%	87.3%
CRAWFORD	4,665	731	3,934	Reagan	15.7%	84.3%
CUYAHOGA	73,588	14,548	59,040	Reagan	19.8%	80.2%
DARKE	4,102	853	3,249	Reagan	20.8%	79.2%
DEFIANCE	3,842	742	3,100	Reagan	19.3%	80.7%
DELAWARE	7,337	1,198	6,139	Reagan	16.3%	83.7%
ERIE	5,324	1,073	4,251	Reagan	20.2%	79.8%
FAIRFIELD	11,374	1,697	9,677	Reagan	14.9%	85.1%
FAYETTE	3,049	368	2,681	Reagan	12.1%	87.9%
FRANKLIN	83,744	13,381	70,363	Reagan	16.0%	84.0%
FULTON	4,947	1,142	3,805	Reagan	23.1%	76.9%
GALLIA	3,996	593	3,403	Reagan	14.8%	85.2%
GEAUGA	6,555	1,274	5,281	Reagan	19.4%	80.6%
GREENE	10,568	2,944	7,624	Reagan	27.9%	72.1%
GUERNSEY	5,198	816	4,382	Reagan	15.7%	84.3%
HAMILTON	70,258	10,391	59,867	Reagan	14.8%	85.2%
HANCOCK	10,594	1,814	8,780	Reagan	17.1%	82.9%
HARDIN	3,275	548	2,727	Reagan	16.7%	83.3%
HARRISON	1,679	244	1,435	Reagan	14.5%	85.5%
HENRY	3,199	514	2,685	Reagan	16.1%	83.9%
HIGHLAND	3,805	464	3,341	Reagan	12.2%	87.8%
HOCKING	2,045	241	1,804	Reagan	11.8%	88.2%
HOLMES	1,590	282	1,308	Reagan	17.7%	82.3%
HURON	4,466	796	3,670	Reagan	17.8%	82.2%
JACKSON	3,558	446	3,112	Reagan	12.5%	87.5%
JEFFERSON	4,894	1,085	3,809	Reagan	22.2%	77.8%
KNOX	4,475	808	3,667	Reagan	18.1%	81.9%
LAKE	13,188	2,329	10,859	Reagan	17.7%	82.3%
LAWRENCE	8,055	1,137	6,918	Reagan	14.1%	85.9%
LICKING	12,867	2,109	10,758	Reagan	16.4%	83.6%
LOGAN	5,129	826	4,303	Reagan	16.1%	83.9%
LORAIN	14,804	2,566	12,238	Reagan	17.3%	82.7%
LUCAS	27,434	5,821	21,613	Reagan	21.2%	78.8%
MADISON	4,139	640	3,499	Reagan	15.5%	84.5%
MAHONING	14,384	2,892	11,492	Reagan	20.1%	79.9%

OHIO REPUBLICAN

1980

County	Total Vote	Bush	Reagan	Winner	Percentage of Total Vote Bush	Reagan
MARION	6,012	963	5,049	Reagan	16.0%	84.0%
MEDINA	9,468	2,302	7,166	Reagan	24.3%	75.7%
MEIGS	3,606	548	3,058	Reagan	15.2%	84.8%
MERCER	2,138	406	1,732	Reagan	19.0%	81.0%
MIAMI	11,115	2,967	8,148	Reagan	26.7%	73.3%
MONROE	693	102	591	Reagan	14.7%	85.3%
MONTGOMERY	34,998	11,773	23,225	Reagan	33.6%	66.4%
MORGAN	2,731	365	2,366	Reagan	13.4%	86.6%
MORROW	2,980	379	2,601	Reagan	12.7%	87.3%
MUSKINGUM	11,018	1,817	9,201	Reagan	16.5%	83.5%
NOBLE	1,942	243	1,699	Reagan	12.5%	87.5%
OTTAWA	3,102	573	2,529	Reagan	18.5%	81.5%
PAULDING	2,165	339	1,826	Reagan	15.7%	84.3%
PERRY	2,659	400	2,259	Reagan	15.0%	85.0%
PICKAWAY	3,588	386	3,202	Reagan	10.8%	89.2%
PIKE	1,603	170	1,433	Reagan	10.6%	89.4%
PORTAGE	6,918	1,790	5,128	Reagan	25.9%	74.1%
PREBLE	4,040	808	3,232	Reagan	20.0%	80.0%
PUTNAM	2,917	367	2,550	Reagan	12.6%	87.4%
RICHLAND	12,503	2,359	10,144	Reagan	18.9%	81.1%
ROSS	5,877	854	5,023	Reagan	14.5%	85.5%
SANDUSKY	7,424	1,666	5,758	Reagan	22.4%	77.6%
SCIOTO	7,891	801	7,090	Reagan	10.2%	89.8%
SENECA	5,861	963	4,898	Reagan	16.4%	83.6%
SHELBY	2,929	709	2,220	Reagan	24.2%	75.8%
STARK	38,387	6,965	31,422	Reagan	18.1%	81.9%
SUMMIT	34,312	12,811	21,501	Reagan	37.3%	62.7%
TRUMBULL	13,575	2,694	10,881	Reagan	19.8%	80.2%
TUSCARAWAS	4,241	666	3,575	Reagan	15.7%	84.3%
UNION	3,945	594	3,351	Reagan	15.1%	84.9%
VAN WERT	4,588	824	3,764	Reagan	18.0%	82.0%
VINTON	1,573	171	1,402	Reagan	10.9%	89.1%
WARREN	8,425	1,367	7,058	Reagan	16.2%	83.8%
WASHINGTON	7,628	994	6,634	Reagan	13.0%	87.0%
WAYNE	10,055	2,524	7,531	Reagan	25.1%	74.9%
WILLIAMS	4,184	819	3,365	Reagan	19.6%	80.4%
WOOD	10,591	2,330	8,261	Reagan	22.0%	78.0%
WYANDOT	2,255	335	1,920	Reagan	14.9%	85.1%
TOTAL	856,773	164,485	692,288	Reagan	19.2%	80.8%

OHIO DEMOCRATIC

1984

County	Total Vote	Hart	J. Jackson	Mondale	Other	Winner	Percentage of Total Vote Hart	J. Jackson	Mondale	Other
ADAMS	2,772	1,329		1,443		Mondale	47.9%		52.1%	
ALLEN	9,969	4,247	1,798	3,924		Hart	42.6%	18.0%	39.4%	
ASHLAND	3,709	1,952	155	1,530	72	Hart	52.6%	4.2%	41.3%	1.9%
ASHTABULA	16,174	7,539	1,082	7,153	400	Hart	46.6%	6.7%	44.2%	2.5%
ATHENS	6,904	3,208	865	2,686	145	Hart	46.5%	12.5%	38.9%	2.1%
AUGLAIZE	3,668	2,087	163	1,418		Hart	56.9%	4.4%	38.7%	
BELMONT	18,965	7,426	743	10,586	210	Mondale	39.2%	3.9%	55.8%	1.1%
BROWN	4,960	2,835	234	1,891		Hart	57.2%	4.7%	38.1%	
BUTLER	17,019	7,096	2,192	7,157	574	Mondale	41.7%	12.9%	42.1%	3.4%
CARROLL	3,184	1,548	171	1,402	63	Hart	48.6%	5.4%	44.0%	2.0%
CHAMPAIGN	2,781	1,567	214	944	56	Hart	56.3%	7.7%	33.9%	2.0%
CLARK	17,088	7,554	3,027	6,139	368	Hart	44.2%	17.7%	35.9%	2.2%
CLERMONT	8,808	4,368	493	3,947		Hart	49.6%	5.6%	44.8%	
CLINTON	2,181	1,380		801		Hart	63.3%		36.7%	
COLUMBIANA	13,901	6,781	805	6,185	130	Hart	48.8%	5.8%	44.5%	0.9%
COSHOCTON	3,455	1,805	187	1,433	30	Hart	52.2%	5.4%	41.5%	0.9%
CRAWFORD	5,571	3,229	296	2,046		Hart	58.0%	5.3%	36.7%	
CUYAHOGA	318,058	113,586	72,781	128,150	3,541	Mondale	35.7%	22.9%	40.3%	1.1%
DARKE	5,346	3,100	253	1,819	174	Hart	58.0%	4.7%	34.0%	3.3%
DEFIANCE	4,002	2,072	186	1,744		Hart	51.8%	4.6%	43.6%	
DELAWARE	4,505	2,353	482	1,559	111	Hart	52.2%	10.7%	34.6%	2.5%
ERIE	10,480	4,742	1,375	4,363		Hart	45.2%	13.1%	41.6%	
FAIRFIELD	11,184	6,074	550	4,267	293	Hart	54.3%	4.9%	38.2%	2.6%
FAYETTE	1,664	937	55	660	12	Hart	56.3%	3.3%	39.7%	0.7%
FRANKLIN	90,170	32,649	28,265	28,728	528	Hart	36.2%	31.3%	31.9%	0.6%
FULTON	2,431	1,265	116	1,002	48	Hart	52.0%	4.8%	41.2%	2.0%
GALLIA	3,951	1,597	188	2,054	112	Mondale	40.4%	4.8%	52.0%	2.8%
GEAUGA	7,438	3,831	537	2,765	305	Hart	51.5%	7.2%	37.2%	4.1%
GREENE	12,875	6,054	2,353	4,251	217	Hart	47.0%	18.3%	33.0%	1.7%
GUERNSEY	4,681	2,369	226	2,031	55	Hart	50.6%	4.8%	43.4%	1.2%
HAMILTON	77,788	23,726	27,299	26,388	375	J. Jackson	30.5%	35.1%	33.9%	0.5%
HANCOCK	3,570	1,918	248	1,404		Hart	53.7%	6.9%	39.3%	
HARDIN	2,984	1,625	148	1,211		Hart	54.5%	5.0%	40.6%	
HARRISON	3,159	1,374	170	1,586	29	Mondale	43.5%	5.4%	50.2%	0.9%
HENRY	2,232	1,260	90	882		Hart	56.5%	4.0%	39.5%	
HIGHLAND	2,730	1,595		1,135		Hart	58.4%		41.6%	
HOCKING	3,604	1,972		1,632		Hart	54.7%		45.3%	
HOLMES	2,350	1,355	133	789	73	Hart	57.7%	5.7%	33.6%	3.1%
HURON	4,742	2,536	251	1,878	77	Hart	53.5%	5.3%	39.6%	1.6%
JACKSON	2,867	1,144		1,723		Mondale	39.9%		60.1%	
JEFFERSON	23,004	8,959	1,874	11,891	280	Mondale	38.9%	8.1%	51.7%	1.2%
KNOX	4,303	2,341	251	1,711		Hart	54.4%	5.8%	39.8%	
LAKE	28,689	13,984	1,294	12,842	569	Hart	48.7%	4.5%	44.8%	2.0%
LAWRENCE	7,970	2,618	370	4,763	219	Mondale	32.8%	4.6%	59.8%	2.7%
LICKING	13,424	6,591	910	5,534	389	Hart	49.1%	6.8%	41.2%	2.9%
LOGAN	2,574	1,412	139	965	58	Hart	54.9%	5.4%	37.5%	2.3%
LORAIN	45,209	19,222	4,929	20,338	720	Mondale	42.5%	10.9%	45.0%	1.6%
LUCAS	61,315	20,686	12,149	27,155	1,325	Mondale	33.7%	19.8%	44.3%	2.2%
MADISON	2,466	1,304	134	1,020	8	Hart	52.9%	5.4%	41.4%	0.3%
MAHONING	71,328	31,258	13,801	25,717	552	Hart	43.8%	19.3%	36.1%	0.8%

OHIO DEMOCRATIC

1984

County	Total Vote	Hart	J. Jackson	Mondale	Other	Winner	Percentage of Total Vote Hart	J. Jackson	Mondale	Other
MARION	8,955	4,236	656	3,852	211	Hart	47.3%	7.3%	43.0%	2.4%
MEDINA	11,483	6,076	585	4,630	192	Hart	52.9%	5.1%	40.3%	1.7%
MEIGS	2,427	951	113	1,309	54	Mondale	39.2%	4.7%	53.9%	2.2%
MERCER	6,484	3,668	292	2,290	234	Hart	56.6%	4.5%	35.3%	3.6%
MIAMI	7,187	3,821	522	2,653	191	Hart	53.2%	7.3%	36.9%	2.7%
MONROE	4,580	2,193	177	2,170	40	Hart	47.9%	3.9%	47.4%	0.9%
MONTGOMERY	65,376	24,882	18,375	21,693	426	Hart	38.1%	28.1%	33.2%	0.7%
MORGAN	1,314	577	64	633	40	Mondale	43.9%	4.9%	48.2%	3.0%
MORROW	2,571	1,394	125	994	58	Hart	54.2%	4.9%	38.7%	2.3%
MUSKINGUM	7,080	3,554	451	2,902	173	Hart	50.2%	6.4%	41.0%	2.4%
NOBLE	1,854	877	85	874	18	Hart	47.3%	4.6%	47.1%	1.0%
OTTAWA	6,586	3,484	258	2,844		Hart	52.9%	3.9%	43.2%	
PAULDING	2,879	1,519	128	1,232		Hart	52.8%	4.4%	42.8%	
PERRY	3,289	1,541	139	1,525	84	Hart	46.9%	4.2%	46.4%	2.6%
PICKAWAY	4,934	2,877	210	1,746	101	Hart	58.3%	4.3%	35.4%	2.0%
PIKE	3,083	1,187		1,896		Mondale	38.5%		61.5%	
PORTAGE	19,603	9,999	1,616	7,538	450	Hart	51.0%	8.2%	38.5%	2.3%
PREBLE	3,457	1,963	141	1,222	131	Hart	56.8%	4.1%	35.3%	3.8%
PUTNAM	6,549	3,807	292	2,450		Hart	58.1%	4.5%	37.4%	
RICHLAND	11,925	5,599	1,376	4,914	36	Hart	47.0%	11.5%	41.2%	0.3%
ROSS	6,720	3,524		3,196		Hart	52.4%		47.6%	
SANDUSKY	5,845	3,039	430	2,376		Hart	52.0%	7.4%	40.7%	
SCIOTO	13,250	5,242		8,008		Mondale	39.6%		60.4%	
SENECA	6,252	3,606	346	2,300		Hart	57.7%	5.5%	36.8%	
SHELBY	6,221	3,735	326	2,160		Hart	60.0%	5.2%	34.7%	
STARK	55,798	25,054	5,447	23,899	1,398	Hart	44.9%	9.8%	42.8%	2.5%
SUMMIT	79,538	35,839	12,530	30,475	694	Hart	45.1%	15.8%	38.3%	0.9%
TRUMBULL	51,727	22,175	5,784	23,215	553	Mondale	42.9%	11.2%	44.9%	1.1%
TUSCARAWAS	13,345	6,677	624	5,841	203	Hart	50.0%	4.7%	43.8%	1.5%
UNION	2,040	1,075	152	768	45	Hart	52.7%	7.5%	37.6%	2.2%
VAN WERT	2,537	1,364	101	993	79	Hart	53.8%	4.0%	39.1%	3.1%
VINTON	2,003	908		1,095		Mondale	45.3%		54.7%	
WARREN	6,458	3,516		2,942		Hart	54.4%		45.6%	
WASHINGTON	6,251	2,796	295	3,041	119	Mondale	44.7%	4.7%	48.6%	1.9%
WAYNE	9,958	5,443	631	3,630	254	Hart	54.7%	6.3%	36.5%	2.6%
WILLIAMS	1,958	1,090	97	771		Hart	55.7%	5.0%	39.4%	
WOOD	9,580	4,610	698	4,194	78	Hart	48.1%	7.3%	43.8%	0.8%
WYANDOT	1,937	1,170	85	682		Hart	60.4%	4.4%	35.2%	
TOTAL	1,447,236	608,528	237,133	583,595	17,980	Hart	42.0%	16.4%	40.3%	1.2%

Note: The statewide vote in the Ohio Democratic primary is traditionally a compilation of votes cast for district delegates. Not every candidate ran delegates in every district; hence, the absence of votes for some candidates in various counties.

OHIO DEMOCRATIC

1988

County	Total Vote	Dukakis	J. Jackson	Other	Winner	Percentage of Total Vote Dukakis	J. Jackson	Other
ADAMS	2,317	1,792	359	166	Dukakis	77.3%	15.5%	7.2%
ALLEN	9,842	6,338	2,867	637	Dukakis	64.4%	29.1%	6.5%
ASHLAND	3,110	2,535		575	Dukakis	81.5%		18.5%
ASHTABULA	12,360	8,940	2,474	946	Dukakis	72.3%	20.0%	7.7%
ATHENS	6,081	4,083	241	1,757	Dukakis	67.1%	4.0%	28.9%
AUGLAIZE	2,835	2,189	435	211	Dukakis	77.2%	15.3%	7.4%
BELMONT	17,740	8,332	2,130	7,278	Dukakis	47.0%	12.0%	41.0%
BROWN	4,593	3,688	566	339	Dukakis	80.3%	12.3%	7.4%
BUTLER	20,837	14,545	5,172	1,120	Dukakis	69.8%	24.8%	5.4%
CARROLL	3,029	1,730	467	832	Dukakis	57.1%	15.4%	27.5%
CHAMPAIGN	2,395	1,720	497	178	Dukakis	71.8%	20.8%	7.4%
CLARK	17,218	11,299	4,822	1,097	Dukakis	65.6%	28.0%	6.4%
CLERMONT	11,134	8,648	1,878	608	Dukakis	77.7%	16.9%	5.5%
CLINTON	2,003	1,442	465	96	Dukakis	72.0%	23.2%	4.8%
COLUMBIANA	15,500	8,772	2,118	4,610	Dukakis	56.6%	13.7%	29.7%
COSHOCTON	3,984	2,476	657	851	Dukakis	62.1%	16.5%	21.4%
CRAWFORD	5,270	3,930	866	474	Dukakis	74.6%	16.4%	9.0%
CUYAHOGA	277,088	155,499	112,243	9,346	Dukakis	56.1%	40.5%	3.4%
DARKE	4,190	3,168	725	297	Dukakis	75.6%	17.3%	7.1%
DEFIANCE	2,902	2,554		348	Dukakis	88.0%		12.0%
DELAWARE	4,781	3,261	1,340	180	Dukakis	68.2%	28.0%	3.8%
ERIE	8,507	7,687		820	Dukakis	90.4%		9.6%
FAIRFIELD	9,452	8,036		1,416	Dukakis	85.0%		15.0%
FAYETTE	1,790	1,365	328	97	Dukakis	76.3%	18.3%	5.4%
FRANKLIN	96,785	46,119	47,092	3,574	J. Jackson	47.7%	48.7%	3.7%
FULTON	2,700	2,140	381	179	Dukakis	79.3%	14.1%	6.6%
GALLIA	3,190	2,534		656	Dukakis	79.4%		20.6%
GEAUGA	7,577	5,407	1,528	642	Dukakis	71.4%	20.2%	8.5%
GREENE	11,778	7,566	3,605	607	Dukakis	64.2%	30.6%	5.2%
GUERNSEY	3,600	1,923	577	1,100	Dukakis	53.4%	16.0%	30.6%
HAMILTON	78,669	36,598	39,703	2,368	J. Jackson	46.5%	50.5%	3.0%
HANCOCK	4,176	2,938	871	367	Dukakis	70.4%	20.9%	8.8%
HARDIN	2,348	1,610	457	281	Dukakis	68.6%	19.5%	12.0%
HARRISON	3,080	1,146	428	1,506	Applegate	37.2%	13.9%	48.9%
HENRY	1,933	1,729		204	Dukakis	89.4%		10.6%
HIGHLAND	3,087	2,363	538	186	Dukakis	76.5%	17.4%	6.0%
HOCKING	3,193	2,429	582	182	Dukakis	76.1%	18.2%	5.7%
HOLMES	1,938	1,345	411	182	Dukakis	69.4%	21.2%	9.4%
HURON	3,563	2,898		665	Dukakis	81.3%		18.7%
JACKSON	2,319	1,786	406	127	Dukakis	77.0%	17.5%	5.5%
JEFFERSON	22,087	9,708	3,097	9,282	Dukakis	44.0%	14.0%	42.0%
KNOX	4,105	2,826	996	283	Dukakis	68.8%	24.3%	6.9%
LAKE	32,102	25,057	4,752	2,293	Dukakis	78.1%	14.8%	7.1%
LAWRENCE	5,336	4,423		913	Dukakis	82.9%		17.1%
LICKING	13,929	11,246	1,105	1,578	Dukakis	80.7%	7.9%	11.3%
LOGAN	2,592	1,872	536	184	Dukakis	72.2%	20.7%	7.1%
LORAIN	42,241	32,127	91	10,023	Dukakis	76.1%	0.2%	23.7%
LUCAS	62,053	38,371	21,416	2,266	Dukakis	61.8%	34.5%	3.7%
MADISON	2,273	1,720	454	99	Dukakis	75.7%	20.0%	4.4%
MAHONING	68,225	39,698	14,224	14,303	Dukakis	58.2%	20.8%	21.0%

OHIO DEMOCRATIC

1988

County	Total Vote	Dukakis	J. Jackson	Other	Winner	Percentage of Total Vote Dukakis	J. Jackson	Other
MARION	7,725	5,424	1,719	582	Dukakis	70.2%	22.3%	7.5%
MEDINA	12,002	9,991		2,011	Dukakis	83.2%		16.8%
MEIGS	1,732	1,411		321	Dukakis	81.5%		18.5%
MERCER	4,636	3,502	703	431	Dukakis	75.5%	15.2%	9.3%
MIAMI	7,029	5,193	1,400	436	Dukakis	73.9%	19.9%	6.2%
MONROE	4,876	2,050	585	2,241	Dukakis	42.0%	12.0%	46.0%
MONTGOMERY	69,455	38,370	28,590	2,495	Dukakis	55.2%	41.2%	3.6%
MORGAN	1,291	1,020		271	Dukakis	79.0%		21.0%
MORROW	2,576	1,930	477	169	Dukakis	74.9%	18.5%	6.6%
MUSKINGUM	7,423	6,006		1,417	Dukakis	80.9%		19.1%
NOBLE	1,431	720	194	517	Dukakis	50.3%	13.6%	36.1%
OTTAWA	5,039	4,501		538	Dukakis	89.3%		10.7%
PAULDING	2,100	1,865		235	Dukakis	88.8%		11.2%
PERRY	3,781	3,161		620	Dukakis	83.6%		16.4%
PICKAWAY	4,659	3,531	766	362	Dukakis	75.8%	16.4%	7.8%
PIKE	3,820	2,915	523	382	Dukakis	76.3%	13.7%	10.0%
PORTAGE	20,797	14,357	4,567	1,873	Dukakis	69.0%	22.0%	9.0%
PREBLE	3,089	2,403	480	206	Dukakis	77.8%	15.5%	6.7%
PUTNAM	4,976	4,273		703	Dukakis	85.9%		14.1%
RICHLAND	13,689	9,673	2,333	1,683	Dukakis	70.7%	17.0%	12.3%
ROSS	6,487	4,789	1,101	597	Dukakis	73.8%	17.0%	9.2%
SANDUSKY	4,747	4,212		535	Dukakis	88.7%		11.3%
SCIOTO	10,220	7,981	1,475	764	Dukakis	78.1%	14.4%	7.5%
SENECA	5,802	5,119		683	Dukakis	88.2%		11.8%
SHELBY	4,928	3,748	683	497	Dukakis	76.1%	13.9%	10.1%
STARK	52,810	37,711	11,519	3,580	Dukakis	71.4%	21.8%	6.8%
SUMMIT	80,262	52,626	23,196	4,440	Dukakis	65.6%	28.9%	5.5%
TRUMBULL	48,810	30,197	7,445	11,168	Dukakis	61.9%	15.3%	22.9%
TUSCARAWAS	13,429	8,329	1,812	3,288	Dukakis	62.0%	13.5%	24.5%
UNION	2,041	1,402	487	152	Dukakis	68.7%	23.9%	7.4%
VAN WERT	2,547	1,914	404	229	Dukakis	75.1%	15.9%	9.0%
VINTON	1,514	1,087	301	126	Dukakis	71.8%	19.9%	8.3%
WARREN	6,900	5,345	1,221	334	Dukakis	77.5%	17.7%	4.8%
WASHINGTON	5,607	4,640	128	839	Dukakis	82.8%	2.3%	15.0%
WAYNE	8,815	6,111	2,074	630	Dukakis	69.3%	23.5%	7.1%
WILLIAMS	1,882	1,703		179	Dukakis	90.5%		9.5%
WOOD	8,758	7,474	416	868	Dukakis	85.3%	4.7%	9.9%
WYANDOT	2,050	1,500	367	183	Dukakis	73.2%	17.9%	8.9%
TOTAL	1,383,572	869,792	378,866	134,914	Dukakis	62.9%	27.4%	9.8%

Note: The totals are a compilation of votes cast for slates of district delegates. Not ever candidate ran slates in every district; hence, there is no vote for some candidates in various counties. The winner in Harrison County was Rep. Douglas Applegate.

OHIO REPUBLICAN

1988

County	Total Vote	Bush	Dole	Robertson	Winner	Percentage of Total Vote Bush	Dole	Robertson
ADAMS	3,281	2,675	380	226	Bush	81.5%	11.6%	6.9%
ALLEN	11,269	9,333	1,011	925	Bush	82.8%	9.0%	8.2%
ASHLAND	4,976	3,982	604	390	Bush	80.0%	12.1%	7.8%
ASHTABULA	6,037	4,598	852	587	Bush	76.2%	14.1%	9.7%
ATHENS	3,355	2,712	440	203	Bush	80.8%	13.1%	6.1%
AUGLAIZE	3,106	2,530	293	283	Bush	81.5%	9.4%	9.1%
BELMONT	3,383	2,642	435	306	Bush	78.1%	12.9%	9.0%
BROWN	2,073	1,716	237	120	Bush	82.8%	11.4%	5.8%
BUTLER	19,860	16,939	1,753	1,168	Bush	85.3%	8.8%	5.9%
CARROLL	2,909	2,208	389	312	Bush	75.9%	13.4%	10.7%
CHAMPAIGN	3,971	3,015	615	341	Bush	75.9%	15.5%	8.6%
CLARK	13,590	10,930	1,594	1,066	Bush	80.4%	11.7%	7.8%
CLERMONT	13,892	11,470	1,478	944	Bush	82.6%	10.6%	6.8%
CLINTON	4,894	3,815	752	327	Bush	78.0%	15.4%	6.7%
COLUMBIANA	9,607	7,248	1,438	921	Bush	75.4%	15.0%	9.6%
COSHOCTON	3,932	3,005	494	433	Bush	76.4%	12.6%	11.0%
CRAWFORD	4,625	3,631	623	371	Bush	78.5%	13.5%	8.0%
CUYAHOGA	57,526	48,676	6,265	2,585	Bush	84.6%	10.9%	4.5%
DARKE	3,412	2,535	466	411	Bush	74.3%	13.7%	12.0%
DEFIANCE	4,795	3,620	788	387	Bush	75.5%	16.4%	8.1%
DELAWARE	8,395	6,913	1,102	380	Bush	82.3%	13.1%	4.5%
ERIE	6,257	5,064	728	465	Bush	80.9%	11.6%	7.4%
FAIRFIELD	11,436	9,175	1,355	906	Bush	80.2%	11.8%	7.9%
FAYETTE	3,123	2,529	385	209	Bush	81.0%	12.3%	6.7%
FRANKLIN	63,848	54,535	5,532	3,781	Bush	85.4%	8.7%	5.9%
FULTON	5,518	4,268	860	390	Bush	77.3%	15.6%	7.1%
GALLIA	4,600	3,498	738	364	Bush	76.0%	16.0%	7.9%
GEAUGA	5,946	4,990	599	357	Bush	83.9%	10.1%	6.0%
GREENE	13,641	11,063	1,630	948	Bush	81.1%	11.9%	6.9%
GUERNSEY	3,991	3,003	549	439	Bush	75.2%	13.8%	11.0%
HAMILTON	45,336	39,998	3,518	1,820	Bush	88.2%	7.8%	4.0%
HANCOCK	9,104	7,265	1,119	720	Bush	79.8%	12.3%	7.9%
HARDIN	3,441	2,815	419	207	Bush	81.8%	12.2%	6.0%
HARRISON	1,657	1,252	224	181	Bush	75.6%	13.5%	10.9%
HENRY	4,866	3,763	752	351	Bush	77.3%	15.5%	7.2%
HIGHLAND	4,253	3,437	577	239	Bush	80.8%	13.6%	5.6%
HOCKING	2,124	1,732	233	159	Bush	81.5%	11.0%	7.5%
HOLMES	2,142	1,558	287	297	Bush	72.7%	13.4%	13.9%
HURON	3,972	3,043	562	367	Bush	76.6%	14.1%	9.2%
JACKSON	4,542	3,515	666	361	Bush	77.4%	14.7%	7.9%
JEFFERSON	4,334	3,333	542	459	Bush	76.9%	12.5%	10.6%
KNOX	5,483	4,256	795	432	Bush	77.6%	14.5%	7.9%
LAKE	13,563	11,672	1,143	748	Bush	86.1%	8.4%	5.5%
LAWRENCE	6,234	5,015	810	409	Bush	80.4%	13.0%	6.6%
LICKING	13,705	10,924	1,664	1,117	Bush	79.7%	12.1%	8.2%
LOGAN	6,446	4,913	1,025	508	Bush	76.2%	15.9%	7.9%
LORAIN	13,502	10,246	2,099	1,157	Bush	75.9%	15.5%	8.6%
LUCAS	23,899	20,328	2,219	1,352	Bush	85.1%	9.3%	5.7%
MADISON	3,761	3,024	511	226	Bush	80.4%	13.6%	6.0%
MAHONING	14,269	11,436	1,778	1,055	Bush	80.1%	12.5%	7.4%

OHIO REPUBLICAN

1988

County	Total Vote	Bush	Dole	Robertson	Winner	Percentage of Total Vote Bush	Dole	Robertson
MARION	6,201	4,889	950	362	Bush	78.8%	15.3%	5.8%
MEDINA	8,691	6,913	1,195	583	Bush	79.5%	13.7%	6.7%
MEIGS	4,645	3,481	735	429	Bush	74.9%	15.8%	9.2%
MERCER	2,728	2,086	355	287	Bush	76.5%	13.0%	10.5%
MIAMI	9,624	7,517	1,344	763	Bush	78.1%	14.0%	7.9%
MONROE	688	496	124	68	Bush	72.1%	18.0%	9.9%
MONTGOMERY	39,201	33,017	3,808	2,376	Bush	84.2%	9.7%	6.1%
MORGAN	2,850	2,220	448	182	Bush	77.9%	15.7%	6.4%
MORROW	3,306	2,570	471	265	Bush	77.7%	14.2%	8.0%
MUSKINGUM	10,318	7,982	1,530	806	Bush	77.4%	14.8%	7.8%
NOBLE	1,704	1,342	221	141	Bush	78.8%	13.0%	8.3%
OTTAWA	3,253	2,570	466	217	Bush	79.0%	14.3%	6.7%
PAULDING	3,053	2,160	562	331	Bush	70.8%	18.4%	10.8%
PERRY	3,826	2,859	597	370	Bush	74.7%	15.6%	9.7%
PICKAWAY	3,715	3,064	460	191	Bush	82.5%	12.4%	5.1%
PIKE	1,836	1,570	144	122	Bush	85.5%	7.8%	6.6%
PORTAGE	6,924	5,355	965	604	Bush	77.3%	13.9%	8.7%
PREBLE	3,787	2,969	505	313	Bush	78.4%	13.3%	8.3%
PUTNAM	3,740	2,896	461	383	Bush	77.4%	12.3%	10.2%
RICHLAND	9,629	7,452	1,341	836	Bush	77.4%	13.9%	8.7%
ROSS	5,715	4,812	548	355	Bush	84.2%	9.6%	6.2%
SANDUSKY	6,335	4,907	973	455	Bush	77.5%	15.4%	7.2%
SCIOTO	6,519	5,356	712	451	Bush	82.2%	10.9%	6.9%
SENECA	7,457	5,561	1,345	551	Bush	74.6%	18.0%	7.4%
SHELBY	2,865	2,291	325	249	Bush	80.0%	11.3%	8.7%
STARK	37,913	30,478	4,302	3,133	Bush	80.4%	11.3%	8.3%
SUMMIT	27,506	21,573	3,818	2,115	Bush	78.4%	13.9%	7.7%
TRUMBULL	11,927	8,879	1,657	1,391	Bush	74.4%	13.9%	11.7%
TUSCARAWAS	4,968	3,940	495	533	Bush	79.3%	10.0%	10.7%
UNION	4,368	3,492	603	273	Bush	79.9%	13.8%	6.3%
VAN WERT	6,069	4,533	941	595	Bush	74.7%	15.5%	9.8%
VINTON	1,662	1,367	210	85	Bush	82.3%	12.6%	5.1%
WARREN	10,647	8,869	1,124	654	Bush	83.3%	10.6%	6.1%
WASHINGTON	6,058	5,071	607	380	Bush	83.7%	10.0%	6.3%
WAYNE	9,588	7,068	1,526	994	Bush	73.7%	15.9%	10.4%
WILLIAMS	6,417	4,654	1,128	635	Bush	72.5%	17.6%	9.9%
WOOD	12,142	9,357	1,888	897	Bush	77.1%	15.5%	7.4%
WYANDOT	3,148	2,448	438	262	Bush	77.8%	13.9%	8.3%
TOTAL	794,904	643,907	94,650	56,347	Bush	81.0%	11.9%	7.1%

OHIO DEMOCRATIC

1992

County	Total Vote	Brown	Clinton	Tsongas	Other	Winner	Percentage of Total Vote Brown	Clinton	Tsongas	Other
ADAMS	1,794	246	1,330	134	84	Clinton	13.7%	74.1%	7.5%	4.7%
ALLEN	7,740	1,263	4,879	974	624	Clinton	16.3%	63.0%	12.6%	8.1%
ASHLAND	2,906	496	1,973	263	174	Clinton	17.1%	67.9%	9.1%	6.0%
ASHTABULA	11,387	2,273	7,194	1,170	750	Clinton	20.0%	63.2%	10.3%	6.6%
ATHENS	6,984	1,622	4,302	697	363	Clinton	23.2%	61.6%	10.0%	5.2%
AUGLAIZE	2,613	555	1,634	240	184	Clinton	21.2%	62.5%	9.2%	7.0%
BELMONT	16,328	2,937	10,577	1,671	1,143	Clinton	18.0%	64.8%	10.2%	7.0%
BROWN	3,149	549	2,146	255	199	Clinton	17.4%	68.1%	8.1%	6.3%
BUTLER	12,902	2,379	8,453	1,354	716	Clinton	18.4%	65.5%	10.5%	5.5%
CARROLL	2,755	485	1,810	264	196	Clinton	17.6%	65.7%	9.6%	7.1%
CHAMPAIGN	2,293	349	1,615	183	146	Clinton	15.2%	70.4%	8.0%	6.4%
CLARK	12,759	1,989	8,672	1,261	837	Clinton	15.6%	68.0%	9.9%	6.6%
CLERMONT	6,485	1,270	4,140	652	423	Clinton	19.6%	63.8%	10.1%	6.5%
CLINTON	5,389	1,039	3,131	920	299	Clinton	19.3%	58.1%	17.1%	5.5%
COLUMBIANA	12,182	2,640	7,663	1,158	721	Clinton	21.7%	62.9%	9.5%	5.9%
COSHOCTON	3,107	447	1,943	402	315	Clinton	14.4%	62.5%	12.9%	10.1%
CRAWFORD	3,822	817	2,347	423	235	Clinton	21.4%	61.4%	11.1%	6.1%
CUYAHOGA	220,143	39,147	117,753	22,188	41,055	Clinton	17.8%	53.5%	10.1%	18.6%
DARKE	3,113	601	1,985	307	220	Clinton	19.3%	63.8%	9.9%	7.1%
DEFIANCE	2,589		1,765	523	301	Clinton		68.2%	20.2%	11.6%
DELAWARE	3,371	752	1,933	479	207	Clinton	22.3%	57.3%	14.2%	6.1%
ERIE	6,301		4,691	1,020	590	Clinton		74.4%	16.2%	9.4%
FAIRFIELD	7,492	1,478	4,705	788	521	Clinton	19.7%	62.8%	10.5%	7.0%
FAYETTE	1,419	236	985	119	79	Clinton	16.6%	69.4%	8.4%	5.6%
FRANKLIN	54,005	10,872	32,773	6,194	4,166	Clinton	20.1%	60.7%	11.5%	7.7%
FULTON	1,818	238	1,232	221	127	Clinton	13.1%	67.8%	12.2%	7.0%
GALLIA	3,692	596	2,616	259	221	Clinton	16.1%	70.9%	7.0%	6.0%
GEAUGA	7,401	1,593	4,167	1,031	610	Clinton	21.5%	56.3%	13.9%	8.2%
GREENE	8,829	1,737	5,718	906	468	Clinton	19.7%	64.8%	10.3%	5.3%
GUERNSEY	4,463	1,042	2,714	396	311	Clinton	23.3%	60.8%	8.9%	7.0%
HAMILTON	32,155	7,229	19,615	3,654	1,657	Clinton	22.5%	61.0%	11.4%	5.2%
HANCOCK	2,693	477	1,578	369	269	Clinton	17.7%	58.6%	13.7%	10.0%
HARDIN	1,977	302	1,213	233	229	Clinton	15.3%	61.4%	11.8%	11.6%
HARRISON	3,128	611	2,033	275	209	Clinton	19.5%	65.0%	8.8%	6.7%
HENRY	1,740		1,215	326	199	Clinton		69.8%	18.7%	11.4%
HIGHLAND	1,968	313	1,394	168	93	Clinton	15.9%	70.8%	8.5%	4.7%
HOCKING	2,931	538	1,986	299	108	Clinton	18.4%	67.8%	10.2%	3.7%
HOLMES	1,877	378	1,160	189	150	Clinton	20.1%	61.8%	10.1%	8.0%
HURON	3,993	641	2,589	471	292	Clinton	16.1%	64.8%	11.8%	7.3%
JACKSON	2,211	341	1,596	155	119	Clinton	15.4%	72.2%	7.0%	5.4%
JEFFERSON	19,539	3,923	12,213	2,066	1,337	Clinton	20.1%	62.5%	10.6%	6.8%
KNOX	2,688	525	1,741	267	155	Clinton	19.5%	64.8%	9.9%	5.8%
LAKE	23,888	4,863	14,585	2,486	1,954	Clinton	20.4%	61.1%	10.4%	8.2%
LAWRENCE	4,422	740	3,245	261	176	Clinton	16.7%	73.4%	5.9%	4.0%
LICKING	9,510	1,966	5,794	1,050	700	Clinton	20.7%	60.9%	11.0%	7.4%
LOGAN	2,001	354	1,315	194	138	Clinton	17.7%	65.7%	9.7%	6.9%
LORAIN	35,495	7,408	22,560	3,214	2,313	Clinton	20.9%	63.6%	9.1%	6.5%
LUCAS	27,324	5,093	16,819	2,940	2,472	Clinton	18.6%	61.6%	10.8%	9.0%
MADISON	1,415	243	979	117	76	Clinton	17.2%	69.2%	8.3%	5.4%
MAHONING	51,171	13,188	30,552	4,606	2,825	Clinton	25.8%	59.7%	9.0%	5.5%

OHIO DEMOCRATIC

1992

County	Total Vote	Brown	Clinton	Tsongas	Other	Winner	Percentage of Total Vote Brown	Clinton	Tsongas	Other
MARION	6,167	1,035	4,113	593	426	Clinton	16.8%	66.7%	9.6%	6.9%
MEDINA	12,274	2,527	7,669	1,348	730	Clinton	20.6%	62.5%	11.0%	5.9%
MEIGS	1,804	286	1,303	130	85	Clinton	15.9%	72.2%	7.2%	4.7%
MERCER	3,953	831	2,334	453	335	Clinton	21.0%	59.0%	11.5%	8.5%
MIAMI	5,296	1,023	3,408	540	325	Clinton	19.3%	64.4%	10.2%	6.1%
MONROE	3,677	589	2,573	269	246	Clinton	16.0%	70.0%	7.3%	6.7%
MONTGOMERY	55,323	9,765	36,524	6,221	2,813	Clinton	17.7%	66.0%	11.2%	5.1%
MORGAN	1,072	182	748	78	64	Clinton	17.0%	69.8%	7.3%	6.0%
MORROW	2,373	441	1,519	193	220	Clinton	18.6%	64.0%	8.1%	9.3%
MUSKINGUM	4,985	908	3,239	496	342	Clinton	18.2%	65.0%	9.9%	6.9%
NOBLE	1,668	335	1,079	136	118	Clinton	20.1%	64.7%	8.2%	7.1%
OTTAWA	4,241		2,952	884	405	Clinton		69.6%	20.8%	9.5%
PAULDING	2,088		1,547	325	216	Clinton		74.1%	15.6%	10.3%
PERRY	3,382	653	2,218	278	233	Clinton	19.3%	65.6%	8.2%	6.9%
PICKAWAY	3,078	534	2,056	293	195	Clinton	17.3%	66.8%	9.5%	6.3%
PIKE	2,720	359	2,015	231	115	Clinton	13.2%	74.1%	8.5%	4.2%
PORTAGE	17,667	4,079	10,207	2,106	1,275	Clinton	23.1%	57.8%	11.9%	7.2%
PREBLE	2,391	383	1,676	176	156	Clinton	16.0%	70.1%	7.4%	6.5%
PUTNAM	4,355		2,775	1,002	578	Clinton		63.7%	23.0%	13.3%
RICHLAND	13,850	2,964	8,691	1,326	869	Clinton	21.4%	62.8%	9.6%	6.3%
ROSS	4,545	741	3,194	424	186	Clinton	16.3%	70.3%	9.3%	4.1%
SANDUSKY	4,164		3,041	716	407	Clinton		73.0%	17.2%	9.8%
SCIOTO	7,304	1,171	5,203	546	384	Clinton	16.0%	71.2%	7.5%	5.3%
SENECA	4,838		3,498	813	527	Clinton		72.3%	16.8%	10.9%
SHELBY	4,117	902	2,480	415	320	Clinton	21.9%	60.2%	10.1%	7.8%
STARK	44,412	8,849	28,198	4,560	2,805	Clinton	19.9%	63.5%	10.3%	6.3%
SUMMIT	59,487	11,885	37,425	6,549	3,628	Clinton	20.0%	62.9%	11.0%	6.1%
TRUMBULL	42,894	10,625	25,095	4,367	2,807	Clinton	24.8%	58.5%	10.2%	6.5%
TUSCARAWAS	12,143	2,543	7,334	1,388	878	Clinton	20.9%	60.4%	11.4%	7.2%
UNION	1,555	301	1,012	144	98	Clinton	19.4%	65.1%	9.3%	6.3%
VAN WERT	1,829	388	1,147	176	118	Clinton	21.2%	62.7%	9.6%	6.5%
VINTON	1,638	251	1,193	108	86	Clinton	15.3%	72.8%	6.6%	5.3%
WARREN	5,488	943	3,664	566	315	Clinton	17.2%	66.8%	10.3%	5.7%
WASHINGTON	5,473	890	3,861	457	265	Clinton	16.3%	70.5%	8.4%	4.8%
WAYNE	7,091	1,376	4,495	748	472	Clinton	19.4%	63.4%	10.5%	6.7%
WILLIAMS	2,201		1,566	420	215	Clinton		71.1%	19.1%	9.8%
WOOD	7,905	574	5,343	1,349	639	Clinton	7.3%	67.6%	17.1%	8.1%
WYANDOT	1,530	335	924	157	114	Clinton	21.9%	60.4%	10.3%	7.5%
TOTAL	1,042,335	197,449	638,347	110,773	95,766	Clinton	18.9%	61.2%	10.6%	9.2%

OHIO REPUBLICAN

1992

County	Total Vote	Buchanan	Bush	Winner	Percentage of Total Vote Buchanan	Bush
ADAMS	3,331	523	2,808	Bush	15.7%	84.3%
ALLEN	17,613	3,451	14,162	Bush	19.6%	80.4%
ASHLAND	5,029	774	4,255	Bush	15.4%	84.6%
ASHTABULA	6,840	1,230	5,610	Bush	18.0%	82.0%
ATHENS	3,706	561	3,145	Bush	15.1%	84.9%
AUGLAIZE	4,461	656	3,805	Bush	14.7%	85.3%
BELMONT	3,221	526	2,695	Bush	16.3%	83.7%
BROWN	2,055	305	1,750	Bush	14.8%	85.2%
BUTLER	24,870	3,798	21,072	Bush	15.3%	84.7%
CARROLL	4,130	1,011	3,119	Bush	24.5%	75.5%
CHAMPAIGN	4,438	651	3,787	Bush	14.7%	85.3%
CLARK	13,788	2,303	11,485	Bush	16.7%	83.3%
CLERMONT	12,759	2,297	10,462	Bush	18.0%	82.0%
CLINTON	5,931	964	4,967	Bush	16.3%	83.7%
COLUMBIANA	8,029	1,508	6,521	Bush	18.8%	81.2%
COSHOCTON	3,326	581	2,745	Bush	17.5%	82.5%
CRAWFORD	4,502	776	3,726	Bush	17.2%	82.8%
CUYAHOGA	81,614	12,959	68,655	Bush	15.9%	84.1%
DARKE	7,061	1,414	5,647	Bush	20.0%	80.0%
DEFIANCE	4,055	839	3,216	Bush	20.7%	79.3%
DELAWARE	10,024	1,617	8,407	Bush	16.1%	83.9%
ERIE	6,210	1,033	5,177	Bush	16.6%	83.4%
FAIRFIELD	12,967	2,176	10,791	Bush	16.8%	83.2%
FAYETTE	3,947	608	3,339	Bush	15.4%	84.6%
FRANKLIN	62,212	8,762	53,450	Bush	14.1%	85.9%
FULTON	5,125	891	4,234	Bush	17.4%	82.6%
GALLIA	4,919	811	4,108	Bush	16.5%	83.5%
GEAUGA	10,673	1,483	9,190	Bush	13.9%	86.1%
GREENE	13,595	2,009	11,586	Bush	14.8%	85.2%
GUERNSEY	4,635	901	3,734	Bush	19.4%	80.6%
HAMILTON	54,075	9,212	44,863	Bush	17.0%	83.0%
HANCOCK	10,382	2,131	8,251	Bush	20.5%	79.5%
HARDIN	3,903	657	3,246	Bush	16.8%	83.2%
HARRISON	1,480	251	1,229	Bush	17.0%	83.0%
HENRY	4,224	705	3,519	Bush	16.7%	83.3%
HIGHLAND	3,165	445	2,720	Bush	14.1%	85.9%
HOCKING	1,901	277	1,624	Bush	14.6%	85.4%
HOLMES	2,565	398	2,167	Bush	15.5%	84.5%
HURON	4,464	794	3,670	Bush	17.8%	82.2%
JACKSON	5,228	1,046	4,182	Bush	20.0%	80.0%
JEFFERSON	4,273	688	3,585	Bush	16.1%	83.9%
KNOX	5,948	1,201	4,747	Bush	20.2%	79.8%
LAKE	19,984	3,604	16,380	Bush	18.0%	82.0%
LAWRENCE	5,141	947	4,194	Bush	18.4%	81.6%
LICKING	12,060	1,860	10,200	Bush	15.4%	84.6%
LOGAN	5,662	820	4,842	Bush	14.5%	85.5%
LORAIN	18,115	3,131	14,984	Bush	17.3%	82.7%
LUCAS	17,776	2,595	15,181	Bush	14.6%	85.4%
MADISON	3,318	477	2,841	Bush	14.4%	85.6%
MAHONING	11,567	1,806	9,761	Bush	15.6%	84.4%

OHIO REPUBLICAN

1992

County	Total Vote	Buchanan	Bush	Winner	Percentage of Total Vote Buchanan	Bush
MARION	7,461	1,163	6,298	Bush	15.6%	84.4%
MEDINA	14,250	2,294	11,956	Bush	16.1%	83.9%
MEIGS	3,885	872	3,013	Bush	22.4%	77.6%
MERCER	2,622	431	2,191	Bush	16.4%	83.6%
MIAMI	10,611	1,699	8,912	Bush	16.0%	84.0%
MONROE	644	108	536	Bush	16.8%	83.2%
MONTGOMERY	39,737	5,795	33,942	Bush	14.6%	85.4%
MORGAN	2,504	518	1,986	Bush	20.7%	79.3%
MORROW	3,627	619	3,008	Bush	17.1%	82.9%
MUSKINGUM	7,833	1,412	6,421	Bush	18.0%	82.0%
NOBLE	2,017	385	1,632	Bush	19.1%	80.9%
OTTAWA	2,337	348	1,989	Bush	14.9%	85.1%
PAULDING	2,207	498	1,709	Bush	22.6%	77.4%
PERRY	4,257	887	3,370	Bush	20.8%	79.2%
PICKAWAY	3,971	494	3,477	Bush	12.4%	87.6%
PIKE	1,700	203	1,497	Bush	11.9%	88.1%
PORTAGE	8,358	1,447	6,911	Bush	17.3%	82.7%
PREBLE	5,550	1,007	4,543	Bush	18.1%	81.9%
PUTNAM	3,688	560	3,128	Bush	15.2%	84.8%
RICHLAND	14,773	2,692	12,081	Bush	18.2%	81.8%
ROSS	4,749	721	4,028	Bush	15.2%	84.8%
SANDUSKY	5,813	1,146	4,667	Bush	19.7%	80.3%
SCIOTO	5,665	862	4,803	Bush	15.2%	84.8%
SENECA	5,690	1,128	4,562	Bush	19.8%	80.2%
SHELBY	3,647	484	3,163	Bush	13.3%	86.7%
STARK	36,483	6,820	29,663	Bush	18.7%	81.3%
SUMMIT	30,496	5,718	24,778	Bush	18.8%	81.3%
TRUMBULL	12,332	2,312	10,020	Bush	18.7%	81.3%
TUSCARAWAS	4,540	735	3,805	Bush	16.2%	83.8%
UNION	4,107	567	3,540	Bush	13.8%	86.2%
VAN WERT	4,497	840	3,657	Bush	18.7%	81.3%
VINTON	1,632	278	1,354	Bush	17.0%	83.0%
WARREN	14,227	2,290	11,937	Bush	16.1%	83.9%
WASHINGTON	7,270	1,023	6,247	Bush	14.1%	85.9%
WAYNE	9,774	1,830	7,944	Bush	18.7%	81.3%
WILLIAMS	5,232	944	4,288	Bush	18.0%	82.0%
WOOD	9,317	1,620	7,697	Bush	17.4%	82.6%
WYANDOT	2,653	474	2,179	Bush	17.9%	82.1%
TOTAL	860,453	143,687	716,766	Bush	16.7%	83.3%

OHIO DEMOCRATIC

1996

County	Total Vote	Clinton	LaRouche	Winner	Percentage of Total Vote Clinton	LaRouche
ADAMS	1,151	1,049	102	Clinton	91.1%	8.9%
ALLEN	4,965	4,447	518	Clinton	89.6%	10.4%
ASHLAND	2,031	1,837	194	Clinton	90.4%	9.6%
ASHTABULA	10,981	9,780	1,201	Clinton	89.1%	10.9%
ATHENS	7,097	6,349	748	Clinton	89.5%	10.5%
AUGLAIZE	2,638	2,383	255	Clinton	90.3%	9.7%
BELMONT	15,804	13,777	2,027	Clinton	87.2%	12.8%
BROWN	3,649	3,191	458	Clinton	87.4%	12.6%
BUTLER	8,121	7,510	611	Clinton	92.5%	7.5%
CARROLL	2,637	2,348	289	Clinton	89.0%	11.0%
CHAMPAIGN	1,841	1,690	151	Clinton	91.8%	8.2%
CLARK	11,335	10,586	749	Clinton	93.4%	6.6%
CLERMONT	5,308	4,864	444	Clinton	91.6%	8.4%
CLINTON	1,208	1,132	76	Clinton	93.7%	6.3%
COLUMBIANA	9,052	8,157	895	Clinton	90.1%	9.9%
COSHOCTON	2,111	1,904	207	Clinton	90.2%	9.8%
CRAWFORD	3,400	3,019	381	Clinton	88.8%	11.2%
CUYAHOGA	125,424	117,577	7,847	Clinton	93.7%	6.3%
DARKE	3,084	2,827	257	Clinton	91.7%	8.3%
DEFIANCE	2,747	2,504	243	Clinton	91.2%	8.8%
DELAWARE	4,075	3,843	232	Clinton	94.3%	5.7%
ERIE	7,973	7,372	601	Clinton	92.5%	7.5%
FAIRFIELD	7,903	7,192	711	Clinton	91.0%	9.0%
FAYETTE	865	786	79	Clinton	90.9%	9.1%
FRANKLIN	28,826	27,458	1,368	Clinton	95.3%	4.7%
FULTON	1,004	945	59	Clinton	94.1%	5.9%
GALLIA	2,160	1,937	223	Clinton	89.7%	10.3%
GEAUGA	4,199	3,879	320	Clinton	92.4%	7.6%
GREENE	7,041	6,598	443	Clinton	93.7%	6.3%
GUERNSEY	3,161	2,815	346	Clinton	89.1%	10.9%
HAMILTON	57,623	54,847	2,776	Clinton	95.2%	4.8%
HANCOCK	1,775	1,669	106	Clinton	94.0%	6.0%
HARDIN	1,139	1,043	96	Clinton	91.6%	8.4%
HARRISON	3,392	2,946	446	Clinton	86.9%	13.1%
HENRY	1,578	1,469	109	Clinton	93.1%	6.9%
HIGHLAND	1,303	1,214	89	Clinton	93.2%	6.8%
HOCKING	2,850	2,502	348	Clinton	87.8%	12.2%
HOLMES	1,182	1,031	151	Clinton	87.2%	12.8%
HURON	3,068	2,804	264	Clinton	91.4%	8.6%
JACKSON	1,548	1,436	112	Clinton	92.8%	7.2%
JEFFERSON	16,599	14,795	1,804	Clinton	89.1%	10.9%
KNOX	2,856	2,677	179	Clinton	93.7%	6.3%
LAKE	16,871	15,679	1,192	Clinton	92.9%	7.1%
LAWRENCE	3,533	3,197	336	Clinton	90.5%	9.5%
LICKING	9,844	8,921	923	Clinton	90.6%	9.4%
LOGAN	1,329	1,197	132	Clinton	90.1%	9.9%
LORAIN	22,605	20,707	1,898	Clinton	91.6%	8.4%
LUCAS	19,750	18,532	1,218	Clinton	93.8%	6.2%
MADISON	1,680	1,553	127	Clinton	92.4%	7.6%
MAHONING	52,583	47,695	4,888	Clinton	90.7%	9.3%

OHIO DEMOCRATIC

1996

County	Total Vote	Clinton	LaRouche	Winner	Percentage of Total Vote Clinton	LaRouche
MARION	5,342	4,780	562	Clinton	89.5%	10.5%
MEDINA	8,099	7,385	714	Clinton	91.2%	8.8%
MEIGS	2,005	1,798	207	Clinton	89.7%	10.3%
MERCER	3,752	3,128	624	Clinton	83.4%	16.6%
MIAMI	3,874	3,609	265	Clinton	93.2%	6.8%
MONROE	3,643	3,132	511	Clinton	86.0%	14.0%
MONTGOMERY	22,663	21,451	1,212	Clinton	94.7%	5.3%
MORGAN	891	803	88	Clinton	90.1%	9.9%
MORROW	2,140	1,884	256	Clinton	88.0%	12.0%
MUSKINGUM	2,501	2,240	261	Clinton	89.6%	10.4%
NOBLE	1,108	960	148	Clinton	86.6%	13.4%
OTTAWA	2,567	2,341	226	Clinton	91.2%	8.8%
PAULDING	1,804	1,576	228	Clinton	87.4%	12.6%
PERRY	2,023	1,845	178	Clinton	91.2%	8.8%
PICKAWAY	2,491	2,289	202	Clinton	91.9%	8.1%
PIKE	2,395	2,199	196	Clinton	91.8%	8.2%
PORTAGE	14,254	12,801	1,453	Clinton	89.8%	10.2%
PREBLE	1,289	1,160	129	Clinton	90.0%	10.0%
PUTNAM	3,469	2,805	664	Clinton	80.9%	19.1%
RICHLAND	9,777	8,820	957	Clinton	90.2%	9.8%
ROSS	4,591	4,327	264	Clinton	94.2%	5.8%
SANDUSKY	3,754	3,439	315	Clinton	91.6%	8.4%
SCIOTO	7,915	7,000	915	Clinton	88.4%	11.6%
SENECA	2,772	2,504	268	Clinton	90.3%	9.7%
SHELBY	2,881	2,517	364	Clinton	87.4%	12.6%
STARK	40,937	37,055	3,882	Clinton	90.5%	9.5%
SUMMIT	32,307	30,126	2,181	Clinton	93.2%	6.8%
TRUMBULL	32,316	29,131	3,185	Clinton	90.1%	9.9%
TUSCARAWAS	12,364	10,697	1,667	Clinton	86.5%	13.5%
UNION	1,631	1,474	157	Clinton	90.4%	9.6%
VAN WERT	1,657	1,484	173	Clinton	89.6%	10.4%
VINTON	1,314	1,190	124	Clinton	90.6%	9.4%
WARREN	3,272	3,021	251	Clinton	92.3%	7.7%
WASHINGTON	3,436	3,093	343	Clinton	90.0%	10.0%
WAYNE	4,938	4,527	411	Clinton	91.7%	8.3%
WILLIAMS	1,095	1,007	88	Clinton	92.0%	8.0%
WOOD	7,034	6,686	348	Clinton	95.1%	4.9%
WYANDOT	1,330	1,199	131	Clinton	90.2%	9.8%
TOTAL	776,530	713,153	63,377	Clinton	91.8%	8.2%

OHIO REPUBLICAN

1996

County	Total Vote	Buchanan	Dole	Other	Winner	Percentage of Total Vote Buchanan	Dole	Other
ADAMS	4,755	1,084	3,106	565	Dole	22.8%	65.3%	11.9%
ALLEN	14,535	3,047	9,895	1,593	Dole	21.0%	68.1%	11.0%
ASHLAND	5,102	1,170	3,312	620	Dole	22.9%	64.9%	12.2%
ASHTABULA	7,398	1,958	4,597	843	Dole	26.5%	62.1%	11.4%
ATHENS	3,530	734	2,277	519	Dole	20.8%	64.5%	14.7%
AUGLAIZE	6,007	1,364	4,007	636	Dole	22.7%	66.7%	10.6%
BELMONT	3,612	815	2,382	415	Dole	22.6%	65.9%	11.5%
BROWN	2,870	681	1,944	245	Dole	23.7%	67.7%	8.5%
BUTLER	31,471	5,359	22,502	3,610	Dole	17.0%	71.5%	11.5%
CARROLL	3,967	1,262	2,289	416	Dole	31.8%	57.7%	10.5%
CHAMPAIGN	5,676	1,196	3,717	763	Dole	21.1%	65.5%	13.4%
CLARK	14,642	3,092	9,616	1,934	Dole	21.1%	65.7%	13.2%
CLERMONT	17,734	3,234	12,584	1,916	Dole	18.2%	71.0%	10.8%
CLINTON	5,303	1,013	3,662	628	Dole	19.1%	69.1%	11.8%
COLUMBIANA	9,002	3,212	4,836	954	Dole	35.7%	53.7%	10.6%
COSHOCTON	3,771	958	2,391	422	Dole	25.4%	63.4%	11.2%
CRAWFORD	5,199	1,291	3,238	670	Dole	24.8%	62.3%	12.9%
CUYAHOGA	65,678	15,857	42,904	6,917	Dole	24.1%	65.3%	10.5%
DARKE	6,004	1,351	3,909	744	Dole	22.5%	65.1%	12.4%
DEFIANCE	4,620	1,031	2,983	606	Dole	22.3%	64.6%	13.1%
DELAWARE	14,827	2,680	10,178	1,969	Dole	18.1%	68.6%	13.3%
ERIE	6,461	1,636	4,136	689	Dole	25.3%	64.0%	10.7%
FAIRFIELD	16,672	3,280	11,476	1,916	Dole	19.7%	68.8%	11.5%
FAYETTE	3,903	659	2,767	477	Dole	16.9%	70.9%	12.2%
FRANKLIN	65,367	10,300	46,791	8,276	Dole	15.8%	71.6%	12.7%
FULTON	4,158	990	2,732	436	Dole	23.8%	65.7%	10.5%
GALLIA	3,795	943	2,510	342	Dole	24.8%	66.1%	9.0%
GEAUGA	9,229	2,036	6,037	1,156	Dole	22.1%	65.4%	12.5%
GREENE	16,722	3,251	11,392	2,079	Dole	19.4%	68.1%	12.4%
GUERNSEY	4,436	1,074	2,937	425	Dole	24.2%	66.2%	9.6%
HAMILTON	110,583	14,357	83,704	12,522	Dole	13.0%	75.7%	11.3%
HANCOCK	11,697	2,403	7,077	2,217	Dole	20.5%	60.5%	19.0%
HARDIN	3,518	706	2,253	559	Dole	20.1%	64.0%	15.9%
HARRISON	1,499	331	990	178	Dole	22.1%	66.0%	11.9%
HENRY	4,739	956	3,247	536	Dole	20.2%	68.5%	11.3%
HIGHLAND	4,400	837	3,104	459	Dole	19.0%	70.5%	10.4%
HOCKING	1,950	489	1,245	216	Dole	25.1%	63.8%	11.1%
HOLMES	2,655	738	1,638	279	Dole	27.8%	61.7%	10.5%
HURON	4,790	1,304	2,918	568	Dole	27.2%	60.9%	11.9%
JACKSON	5,742	1,399	3,719	624	Dole	24.4%	64.8%	10.9%
JEFFERSON	5,062	1,336	3,026	700	Dole	26.4%	59.8%	13.8%
KNOX	7,002	1,500	4,609	893	Dole	21.4%	65.8%	12.8%
LAKE	19,696	4,739	12,648	2,309	Dole	24.1%	64.2%	11.7%
LAWRENCE	5,305	1,512	3,253	540	Dole	28.5%	61.3%	10.2%
LICKING	18,151	3,718	12,256	2,177	Dole	20.5%	67.5%	12.0%
LOGAN	6,102	1,171	4,151	780	Dole	19.2%	68.0%	12.8%
LORAIN	16,544	4,335	10,436	1,773	Dole	26.2%	63.1%	10.7%
LUCAS	23,295	5,562	14,974	2,759	Dole	23.9%	64.3%	11.8%
MADISON	4,907	888	3,468	551	Dole	18.1%	70.7%	11.2%
MAHONING	14,797	5,044	8,290	1,463	Dole	34.1%	56.0%	9.9%

OHIO REPUBLICAN

1996

County	Total Vote	Buchanan	Dole	Other	Winner	Percentage of Total Vote Buchanan	Dole	Other
MARION	7,513	1,515	5,048	950	Dole	20.2%	67.2%	12.6%
MEDINA	14,720	3,824	9,124	1,772	Dole	26.0%	62.0%	12.0%
MEIGS	4,290	1,066	2,733	491	Dole	24.8%	63.7%	11.4%
MERCER	2,953	634	1,968	351	Dole	21.5%	66.6%	11.9%
MIAMI	12,612	2,514	8,366	1,732	Dole	19.9%	66.3%	13.7%
MONROE	968	303	556	109	Dole	31.3%	57.4%	11.3%
MONTGOMERY	35,214	7,443	23,778	3,993	Dole	21.1%	67.5%	11.3%
MORGAN	3,160	1,014	1,772	374	Dole	32.1%	56.1%	11.8%
MORROW	4,141	990	2,680	471	Dole	23.9%	64.7%	11.4%
MUSKINGUM	6,441	1,787	4,021	633	Dole	27.7%	62.4%	9.8%
NOBLE	1,470	390	946	134	Dole	26.5%	64.4%	9.1%
OTTAWA	2,803	628	1,839	336	Dole	22.4%	65.6%	12.0%
PAULDING	2,525	687	1,469	369	Dole	27.2%	58.2%	14.6%
PERRY	3,046	868	1,918	260	Dole	28.5%	63.0%	8.5%
PICKAWAY	4,175	789	2,769	617	Dole	18.9%	66.3%	14.8%
PIKE	2,075	377	1,492	206	Dole	18.2%	71.9%	9.9%
PORTAGE	9,702	2,723	5,688	1,291	Dole	28.1%	58.6%	13.3%
PREBLE	3,870	914	2,466	490	Dole	23.6%	63.7%	12.7%
PUTNAM	4,277	956	2,854	467	Dole	22.4%	66.7%	10.9%
RICHLAND	13,185	3,154	8,412	1,619	Dole	23.9%	63.8%	12.3%
ROSS	5,729	1,056	4,110	563	Dole	18.4%	71.7%	9.8%
SANDUSKY	6,407	1,715	3,946	746	Dole	26.8%	61.6%	11.6%
SCIOTO	6,100	1,579	3,994	527	Dole	25.9%	65.5%	8.6%
SENECA	5,296	1,287	3,349	660	Dole	24.3%	63.2%	12.5%
SHELBY	3,962	917	2,540	505	Dole	23.1%	64.1%	12.7%
STARK	42,422	11,316	25,780	5,326	Dole	26.7%	60.8%	12.6%
SUMMIT	29,720	7,154	18,402	4,164	Dole	24.1%	61.9%	14.0%
TRUMBULL	12,171	4,523	6,401	1,247	Dole	37.2%	52.6%	10.2%
TUSCARAWAS	6,067	1,613	3,783	671	Dole	26.6%	62.4%	11.1%
UNION	6,773	1,237	4,659	877	Dole	18.3%	68.8%	12.9%
VAN WERT	4,739	932	3,019	788	Dole	19.7%	63.7%	16.6%
VINTON	1,259	261	875	123	Dole	20.7%	69.5%	9.8%
WARREN	15,155	2,970	10,478	1,707	Dole	19.6%	69.1%	11.3%
WASHINGTON	7,886	1,893	5,205	788	Dole	24.0%	66.0%	10.0%
WAYNE	11,475	2,675	7,196	1,604	Dole	23.3%	62.7%	14.0%
WILLIAMS	4,936	1,223	2,985	728	Dole	24.8%	60.5%	14.7%
WOOD	12,581	2,565	8,435	1,581	Dole	20.4%	67.0%	12.6%
WYANDOT	2,724	637	1,785	302	Dole	24.8%	60.5%	14.7%
TOTAL	963,422	208,012	640,954	114,456	Dole	21.6%	66.5%	11.9%

OKLAHOMA

Oklahoma's first presidential primary was in 1988, as the Sooner State helped anchor the western flank of that year's huge, Southern-oriented primary dubbed Super Tuesday. While other Southern states have dropped out of Super Tuesday since then, Oklahoma has remained, although none of its primaries were as compelling as the first one.

Oklahoma Republicans staged one of the closest and most evenly contested votes of the truncated GOP primary season. George Bush beat Bob Dole, as he did in every primary on Super Tuesday. But in Oklahoma, as almost nowhere else, the outcome was in doubt until the next day.

It was a border war—Bush from Texas, Dole from Kansas. And in the end, Bush won Oklahoma by barely 5,000 votes out of more than 200,000 cast, with his winning 37 percent vote share by far his lowest in the vast array of primaries held on Super Tuesday that year.

Dole swept much of the Republican-oriented farm and ranch country in the northern part of the state that abuts Kansas. But Bush capitalized on the urban orientation of the Oklahoma GOP to narrowly prevail. More than half the vote was cast in Oklahoma (Oklahoma City), Tulsa and Cleveland (Norman) counties, and Bush won all three.

Evangelist Pat Robertson ran a strong third in Oklahoma with 21 percent of the vote, his best showing in any 1988 primary. Robertson ran particularly well in the rural counties of southern Oklahoma, carrying nine and finishing second in roughly a dozen more.

Oklahoma's Republican presidential primaries in the 1990s were less competitive. Bush won big in 1992; so did Dole in 1996. Pat Buchanan was a distant runner-up both times, carrying none of Oklahoma's 77 counties in 1992, and only one (McCurtain) in 1996.

Oklahoma's Democratic primary has given a boost to the ambitions of candidates from Dixie—Al Gore in 1988, Bill Clinton in the 1990s. Gore won with his Southern roots, his relatively conservative image and his support from an array of big-name Oklahoma Democrats, featuring Sen. David L. Boren.

Gore rolled up his highest percentages in the rural counties of south-central Oklahoma, including historically Democratic "Little Dixie." But like Bush in the Republican primary voting, Gore also carried Oklahoma's major population centers. The only three counties not carried by Gore were won by Richard Gephardt, the most populous being Ottawa in the northeast corner of the state adjacent to Gephardt's native Missouri.

Clinton easily won Oklahoma's Democratic primary in the 1990s. His 70 percent share was one of his highest of the 1992 primary season; but his 76 percent share in 1996 was his lowest of the year. That fall, Republicans carried Oklahoma's electoral votes for the eighth straight election.

Recent Oklahoma Primary Results

Oklahoma held its first presidential primary in 1988.

	DEMOCRATS			REPUBLICANS		
Year	Turnout	Candidates	%	Turnout	Candidates	%
1996 (March 12)	366,604	BILL CLINTON*	76	264,542	BOB DOLE	59
		Lyndon LaRouche	13		Pat Buchanan	22
		Elvena Lloyd-Duffie	11		Steve Forbes	14
1992 (March 10)	416,129	BILL CLINTON	70	217,721	GEORGE BUSH*	70
		Jerry Brown	17		Pat Buchanan	27
1988 (March 8)	392,727	AL GORE	41	208,938	GEORGE BUSH	37
		Richard Gephardt	21		Bob Dole	35
		Michael Dukakis	17		Pat Robertson	21
		Jesse Jackson	13			

Note: All candidates are listed that drew at least 10 percent of their party's primary vote. The names of winning candidates are capitalized. An asterisk (*) indicates an incumbent president.

Cimarron
Texas
Beaver
Harper
Woods
Alfalfa
Grant
Kay
Osage
Washington
Nowata
Craig
Ottawa
Woodward
Enid
Major
Garfield
Noble
Pawnee
Rogers
Mayes
Delaware
Ellis
Tulsa
Payne
Stillwater
Tulsa
Wagoner
Cherokee
Adair
Dewey
Blaine
Kingfisher
Logan
Creek
Muskogee
Roger Mills
Custer
Oklahoma
Lincoln
Okmulgee
Muskogee
Oklahoma City
Canadian
Okfuskee
Sequoyah
McIntosh
Beckham
Washita
Caddo
Grady
Pottawatomie
Cleveland
Seminole
Haskell
Hughes
Pittsburg
Greer
Kiowa
McClain
Latimer
Le Flore
Harmon
Lawton
Garvin
Pontotoc
Jackson
Comanche
Coal
Stephens
Murray
Tillman
Atoka
Pushmataha
Cotton
Johnston
Carter
Jefferson
Marshall
McCurtain
Love
Choctaw
Bryan

OKLAHOMA DEMOCRATIC

1988

County	Total Vote	Dukakis	Gephardt	Gore	J. Jackson	Other	Winner	Percentage of Total Vote Dukakis	Gephardt	Gore	J. Jackson	Other
ADAIR	1,693	237	352	866	108	130	Gore	14.0%	20.8%	51.2%	6.4%	7.7%
ALFALFA	833	104	246	354	54	75	Gore	12.5%	29.5%	42.5%	6.5%	9.0%
ATOKA	1,894	234	501	857	163	139	Gore	12.4%	26.5%	45.2%	8.6%	7.3%
BEAVER	742	145	274	182	41	100	Gephardt	19.5%	36.9%	24.5%	5.5%	13.5%
BECKHAM	2,972	483	668	1,416	200	205	Gore	16.3%	22.5%	47.6%	6.7%	6.9%
BLAINE	1,578	174	408	704	172	120	Gore	11.0%	25.9%	44.6%	10.9%	7.6%
BRYAN	4,556	788	1,174	1,926	304	364	Gore	17.3%	25.8%	42.3%	6.7%	8.0%
CADDO	4,487	520	1,067	2,187	377	336	Gore	11.6%	23.8%	48.7%	8.4%	7.5%
CANADIAN	8,394	1,310	1,837	3,864	714	669	Gore	15.6%	21.9%	46.0%	8.5%	8.0%
CARTER	6,438	777	1,325	3,134	770	432	Gore	12.1%	20.6%	48.7%	12.0%	6.7%
CHEROKEE	4,010	713	811	1,805	366	315	Gore	17.8%	20.2%	45.0%	9.1%	7.9%
CHOCTAW	2,319	378	519	793	371	258	Gore	16.3%	22.4%	34.2%	16.0%	11.1%
CIMARRON	608	101	187	207	28	85	Gore	16.6%	30.8%	34.0%	4.6%	14.0%
CLEVELAND	16,708	3,168	3,556	6,408	2,290	1,286	Gore	19.0%	21.3%	38.4%	13.7%	7.7%
COAL	960	116	202	498	57	87	Gore	12.1%	21.0%	51.9%	5.9%	9.1%
COMANCHE	10,057	1,865	2,097	3,645	1,595	855	Gore	18.5%	20.9%	36.2%	15.9%	8.5%
COTTON	1,227	201	334	489	72	131	Gore	16.4%	27.2%	39.9%	5.9%	10.7%
CRAIG	2,541	380	765	991	203	202	Gore	15.0%	30.1%	39.0%	8.0%	7.9%
CREEK	7,032	1,323	1,725	2,852	650	482	Gore	18.8%	24.5%	40.6%	9.2%	6.9%
CUSTER	3,642	497	867	1,641	359	278	Gore	13.6%	23.8%	45.1%	9.9%	7.6%
DELAWARE	3,787	827	1,058	1,328	221	353	Gore	21.8%	27.9%	35.1%	5.8%	9.3%
DEWEY	1,015	116	220	521	47	111	Gore	11.4%	21.7%	51.3%	4.6%	10.9%
ELLIS	728	90	194	320	40	84	Gore	12.4%	26.6%	44.0%	5.5%	11.5%
GARFIELD	5,892	1,075	1,260	2,418	670	469	Gore	18.2%	21.4%	41.0%	11.4%	8.0%
GARVIN	4,872	543	1,104	2,558	321	346	Gore	11.1%	22.7%	52.5%	6.6%	7.1%
GRADY	5,836	729	1,229	2,897	559	422	Gore	12.5%	21.1%	49.6%	9.6%	7.2%
GRANT	1,073	142	311	455	78	87	Gore	13.2%	29.0%	42.4%	7.3%	8.1%
GREER	1,333	157	304	668	68	136	Gore	11.8%	22.8%	50.1%	5.1%	10.2%
HARMON	787	96	250	354	36	51	Gore	12.2%	31.8%	45.0%	4.6%	6.5%
HARPER	702	109	163	305	40	85	Gore	15.5%	23.2%	43.4%	5.7%	12.1%
HASKELL	1,781	277	395	911	75	123	Gore	15.6%	22.2%	51.2%	4.2%	6.9%
HUGHES	2,765	302	481	1,630	188	164	Gore	10.9%	17.4%	59.0%	6.8%	5.9%
JACKSON	3,316	445	650	1,703	285	233	Gore	13.4%	19.6%	51.4%	8.6%	7.0%
JEFFERSON	1,646	244	530	581	100	191	Gore	14.8%	32.2%	35.3%	6.1%	11.6%
JOHNSTON	1,539	185	471	675	86	122	Gore	12.0%	30.6%	43.9%	5.6%	7.9%
KAY	5,854	1,284	1,336	2,159	581	494	Gore	21.9%	22.8%	36.9%	9.9%	8.4%
KINGFISHER	1,723	219	424	794	152	134	Gore	12.7%	24.6%	46.1%	8.8%	7.8%
KIOWA	1,948	244	508	899	129	168	Gore	12.5%	26.1%	46.1%	6.6%	8.6%
LATIMER	2,566	403	519	1,206	141	297	Gore	15.7%	20.2%	47.0%	5.5%	11.6%
LE FLORE	5,857	1,066	858	3,083	456	394	Gore	18.2%	14.6%	52.6%	7.8%	6.7%
LINCOLN	3,754	428	819	1,959	274	274	Gore	11.4%	21.8%	52.2%	7.3%	7.3%
LOGAN	3,714	440	727	1,459	830	258	Gore	11.8%	19.6%	39.3%	22.3%	6.9%
LOVE	1,795	202	391	966	108	128	Gore	11.3%	21.8%	53.8%	6.0%	7.1%
MCCLAIN	3,601	454	799	1,858	230	260	Gore	12.6%	22.2%	51.6%	6.4%	7.2%
MCCURTAIN	3,823	672	859	1,290	579	423	Gore	17.6%	22.5%	33.7%	15.1%	11.1%
MCINTOSH	3,050	445	693	1,398	306	208	Gore	14.6%	22.7%	45.8%	10.0%	6.8%
MAJOR	788	117	218	342	47	64	Gore	14.8%	27.7%	43.4%	6.0%	8.1%
MARSHALL	3,407	459	779	1,685	190	294	Gore	13.5%	22.9%	49.5%	5.6%	8.6%
MAYES	4,668	850	1,185	2,031	288	314	Gore	18.2%	25.4%	43.5%	6.2%	6.7%
MURRAY	2,247	210	536	1,151	122	228	Gore	9.3%	23.9%	51.2%	5.4%	10.1%

OKLAHOMA DEMOCRATIC

1988

County	Total Vote	Dukakis	Gephardt	Gore	J. Jackson	Other	Winner	Percentage of Total Vote Dukakis	Gephardt	Gore	J. Jackson	Other
MUSKOGEE	9,897	1,340	1,901	4,566	1,580	510	Gore	13.5%	19.2%	46.1%	16.0%	5.2%
NOBLE	1,883	298	456	833	148	148	Gore	15.8%	24.2%	44.2%	7.9%	7.9%
NOWATA	1,542	277	388	643	104	130	Gore	18.0%	25.2%	41.7%	6.7%	8.4%
OKFUSKEE	1,871	195	377	789	375	135	Gore	10.4%	20.1%	42.2%	20.0%	7.2%
OKLAHOMA	64,262	10,314	10,619	23,227	15,989	4,113	Gore	16.0%	16.5%	36.1%	24.9%	6.4%
OKMULGEE	5,535	873	1,138	2,263	916	345	Gore	15.8%	20.6%	40.9%	16.5%	6.2%
OSAGE	5,813	987	1,225	2,251	977	373	Gore	17.0%	21.1%	38.7%	16.8%	6.4%
OTTAWA	3,986	960	1,524	818	368	316	Gephardt	24.1%	38.2%	20.5%	9.2%	7.9%
PAWNEE	2,162	367	550	939	161	145	Gore	17.0%	25.4%	43.4%	7.4%	6.7%
PAYNE	7,311	1,693	1,478	2,816	773	551	Gore	23.2%	20.2%	38.5%	10.6%	7.5%
PITTSBURG	9,744	1,709	1,720	4,610	670	1,035	Gore	17.5%	17.7%	47.3%	6.9%	10.6%
PONTOTOC	5,273	700	1,059	2,759	408	347	Gore	13.3%	20.1%	52.3%	7.7%	6.6%
POTTAWATOMIE	8,696	828	1,173	5,640	615	440	Gore	9.5%	13.5%	64.9%	7.1%	5.1%
PUSHMATAHA	1,920	289	483	833	133	182	Gore	15.1%	25.2%	43.4%	6.9%	9.5%
ROGER MILLS	874	103	232	428	49	62	Gore	11.8%	26.5%	49.0%	5.6%	7.1%
ROGERS	6,862	1,322	1,783	2,879	454	424	Gore	19.3%	26.0%	42.0%	6.6%	6.2%
SEMINOLE	4,234	439	713	2,333	467	282	Gore	10.4%	16.8%	55.1%	11.0%	6.7%
SEQUOYAH	4,062	520	521	2,612	218	191	Gore	12.8%	12.8%	64.3%	5.4%	4.7%
STEPHENS	6,421	944	1,740	2,815	437	485	Gore	14.7%	27.1%	43.8%	6.8%	7.6%
TEXAS	1,807	395	531	516	105	260	Gephardt	21.9%	29.4%	28.6%	5.8%	14.4%
TILLMAN	2,301	338	792	797	168	206	Gore	14.7%	34.4%	34.6%	7.3%	9.0%
TULSA	50,058	11,882	9,808	15,278	9,661	3,429	Gore	23.7%	19.6%	30.5%	19.3%	6.9%
WAGONER	6,667	1,221	1,569	2,732	665	480	Gore	18.3%	23.5%	41.0%	10.0%	7.2%
WASHINGTON	5,027	1,076	1,218	1,983	444	306	Gore	21.4%	24.2%	39.4%	8.8%	6.1%
WASHITA	2,241	295	511	1,169	101	165	Gore	13.2%	22.8%	52.2%	4.5%	7.4%
WOODS	1,423	214	329	646	111	123	Gore	15.0%	23.1%	45.4%	7.8%	8.6%
WOODWARD	2,297	355	572	986	179	205	Gore	15.5%	24.9%	42.9%	7.8%	8.9%
TOTAL	392,727	66,278	82,596	162,584	52,417	28,852	Gore	16.9%	21.0%	41.4%	13.3%	7.3%

OKLAHOMA REPUBLICAN

1988

County	Total Vote	Bush	Dole	Robertson	Other	Winner	Percentage of Total Vote Bush	Dole	Robertson	Other
ADAIR	778	338	277	121	42	Bush	43.4%	35.6%	15.6%	5.4%
ALFALFA	1,001	237	578	140	46	Dole	23.7%	57.7%	14.0%	4.6%
ATOKA	199	59	24	112	4	Robertson	29.6%	12.1%	56.3%	2.0%
BEAVER	724	219	322	126	57	Dole	30.2%	44.5%	17.4%	7.9%
BECKHAM	666	175	172	286	33	Robertson	26.3%	25.8%	42.9%	5.0%
BLAINE	1,286	317	589	299	81	Dole	24.7%	45.8%	23.3%	6.3%
BRYAN	492	184	95	188	25	Robertson	37.4%	19.3%	38.2%	5.1%
CADDO	795	226	277	243	49	Dole	28.4%	34.8%	30.6%	6.2%
CANADIAN	5,597	2,015	1,820	1,322	440	Bush	36.0%	32.5%	23.6%	7.9%
CARTER	1,539	641	388	380	130	Bush	41.7%	25.2%	24.7%	8.4%
CHEROKEE	1,234	512	433	217	72	Bush	41.5%	35.1%	17.6%	5.8%
CHOCTAW	109	44	26	34	5	Bush	40.4%	23.9%	31.2%	4.6%
CIMARRON	285	104	99	48	34	Bush	36.5%	34.7%	16.8%	11.9%
CLEVELAND	10,429	3,520	3,518	2,585	806	Bush	33.8%	33.7%	24.8%	7.7%
COAL	77	30	17	27	3	Bush	39.0%	22.1%	35.1%	3.9%
COMANCHE	3,307	1,561	739	786	221	Bush	47.2%	22.3%	23.8%	6.7%
COTTON	79	42	19	16	2	Bush	53.2%	24.1%	20.3%	2.5%
CRAIG	554	226	192	103	33	Bush	40.8%	34.7%	18.6%	6.0%
CREEK	3,247	1,273	1,096	685	193	Bush	39.2%	33.8%	21.1%	5.9%
CUSTER	1,503	418	549	451	85	Dole	27.8%	36.5%	30.0%	5.7%
DELAWARE	1,647	696	629	251	71	Bush	42.3%	38.2%	15.2%	4.3%
DEWEY	388	114	160	85	29	Dole	29.4%	41.2%	21.9%	7.5%
ELLIS	598	175	320	73	30	Dole	29.3%	53.5%	12.2%	5.0%
GARFIELD	7,792	2,273	3,737	1,387	395	Dole	29.2%	48.0%	17.8%	5.1%
GARVIN	782	281	214	233	54	Bush	35.9%	27.4%	29.8%	6.9%
GRADY	1,728	568	553	493	114	Bush	32.9%	32.0%	28.5%	6.6%
GRANT	746	208	393	92	53	Dole	27.9%	52.7%	12.3%	7.1%
GREER	136	61	38	31	6	Bush	44.9%	27.9%	22.8%	4.4%
HARMON	18	6	4	5	3	Bush	33.3%	22.2%	27.8%	16.7%
HARPER	483	144	198	106	35	Dole	29.8%	41.0%	21.9%	7.2%
HASKELL	143	61	54	22	6	Bush	42.7%	37.8%	15.4%	4.2%
HUGHES	185	84	61	33	7	Bush	45.4%	33.0%	17.8%	3.8%
JACKSON	576	232	148	155	41	Bush	40.3%	25.7%	26.9%	7.1%
JEFFERSON	44	25	6	6	7	Bush	56.8%	13.6%	13.6%	15.9%
JOHNSTON	110	24	22	57	7	Robertson	21.8%	20.0%	51.8%	6.4%
KAY	5,633	1,863	2,671	766	333	Dole	33.1%	47.4%	13.6%	5.9%
KINGFISHER	1,782	507	928	259	88	Dole	28.5%	52.1%	14.5%	4.9%
KIOWA	254	86	80	76	12	Bush	33.9%	31.5%	29.9%	4.7%
LATIMER	166	67	61	28	10	Bush	40.4%	36.7%	16.9%	6.0%
LE FLORE	670	328	195	116	31	Bush	49.0%	29.1%	17.3%	4.6%
LINCOLN	1,720	671	581	372	96	Bush	39.0%	33.8%	21.6%	5.6%
LOGAN	2,582	851	949	603	179	Dole	33.0%	36.8%	23.4%	6.9%
LOVE	129	54	40	18	17	Bush	41.9%	31.0%	14.0%	13.2%
MCCLAIN	802	254	235	259	54	Robertson	31.7%	29.3%	32.3%	6.7%
MCCURTAIN	271	83	37	133	18	Robertson	30.6%	13.7%	49.1%	6.6%
MCINTOSH	352	115	96	129	12	Robertson	32.7%	27.3%	36.6%	3.4%
MAJOR	1,416	311	709	316	80	Dole	22.0%	50.1%	22.3%	5.6%
MARSHALL	329	126	99	69	35	Bush	38.3%	30.1%	21.0%	10.6%
MAYES	1,593	612	549	317	115	Bush	38.4%	34.5%	19.9%	7.2%
MURRAY	168	68	45	41	14	Bush	40.5%	26.8%	24.4%	8.3%

OKLAHOMA REPUBLICAN

1988

County	Total Vote	Bush	Dole	Robertson	Other	Winner	Percentage of Total Vote Bush	Dole	Robertson	Other
MUSKOGEE	2,266	800	784	552	130	Bush	35.3%	34.6%	24.4%	5.7%
NOBLE	1,217	486	485	185	61	Bush	39.9%	39.9%	15.2%	5.0%
NOWATA	702	233	308	115	46	Dole	33.2%	43.9%	16.4%	6.6%
OKFUSKEE	183	87	54	30	12	Bush	47.5%	29.5%	16.4%	6.6%
OKLAHOMA	46,336	17,689	15,372	9,591	3,684	Bush	38.2%	33.2%	20.7%	8.0%
OKMULGEE	1,171	482	341	289	59	Bush	41.2%	29.1%	24.7%	5.0%
OSAGE	2,014	755	749	378	132	Bush	37.5%	37.2%	18.8%	6.6%
OTTAWA	1,225	470	522	168	65	Dole	38.4%	42.6%	13.7%	5.3%
PAWNEE	1,227	507	481	160	79	Bush	41.3%	39.2%	13.0%	6.4%
PAYNE	5,158	1,712	2,209	935	302	Dole	33.2%	42.8%	18.1%	5.9%
PITTSBURG	899	342	291	206	60	Bush	38.0%	32.4%	22.9%	6.7%
PONTOTOC	1,078	416	284	312	66	Bush	38.6%	26.3%	28.9%	6.1%
POTTAWATOMIE	2,399	825	715	685	174	Bush	34.4%	29.8%	28.6%	7.3%
PUSHMATAHA	108	49	22	28	9	Bush	45.4%	20.4%	25.9%	8.3%
ROGER MILLS	122	35	39	46	2	Robertson	28.7%	32.0%	37.7%	1.6%
ROGERS	3,510	1,320	1,117	853	220	Bush	37.6%	31.8%	24.3%	6.3%
SEMINOLE	670	245	213	166	46	Bush	36.6%	31.8%	24.8%	6.9%
SEQUOYAH	737	320	215	161	41	Bush	43.4%	29.2%	21.8%	5.6%
STEPHENS	1,540	563	430	420	127	Bush	36.6%	27.9%	27.3%	8.2%
TEXAS	1,181	449	445	203	84	Bush	38.0%	37.7%	17.2%	7.1%
TILLMAN	142	55	33	38	16	Bush	38.7%	23.2%	26.8%	11.3%
TULSA	54,256	22,440	17,505	11,283	3,028	Bush	41.4%	32.3%	20.8%	5.6%
WAGONER	3,355	1,170	1,131	845	209	Bush	34.9%	33.7%	25.2%	6.2%
WASHINGTON	6,588	2,610	2,678	832	468	Dole	39.6%	40.6%	12.6%	7.1%
WASHITA	366	76	102	166	22	Robertson	20.8%	27.9%	45.4%	6.0%
WOODS	1,278	373	648	163	94	Dole	29.2%	50.7%	12.8%	7.4%
WOODWARD	2,066	626	801	557	82	Dole	30.3%	38.8%	27.0%	4.0%
TOTAL	208,938	78,224	73,016	44,067	13,631	Bush	37.4%	34.9%	21.1%	6.5%

OKLAHOMA DEMOCRATIC

1992

County	Total Vote	Brown	Clinton	Other	Winner	Percentage of Total Vote: Brown	Clinton	Other
ADAIR	2,071	231	1,677	163	Clinton	11.2%	81.0%	7.9%
ALFALFA	889	122	653	114	Clinton	13.7%	73.5%	12.8%
ATOKA	2,569	238	1,752	579	Clinton	9.3%	68.2%	22.5%
BEAVER	785	115	531	139	Clinton	14.6%	67.6%	17.7%
BECKHAM	3,095	399	2,352	344	Clinton	12.9%	76.0%	11.1%
BLAINE	1,571	212	1,173	186	Clinton	13.5%	74.7%	11.8%
BRYAN	5,269	520	3,929	820	Clinton	9.9%	74.6%	15.6%
CADDO	5,136	676	3,802	658	Clinton	13.2%	74.0%	12.8%
CANADIAN	8,779	1,716	5,599	1,464	Clinton	19.5%	63.8%	16.7%
CARTER	6,792	747	4,833	1,212	Clinton	11.0%	71.2%	17.8%
CHEROKEE	5,175	806	3,904	465	Clinton	15.6%	75.4%	9.0%
CHOCTAW	2,698	215	2,028	455	Clinton	8.0%	75.2%	16.9%
CIMARRON	585	72	428	85	Clinton	12.3%	73.2%	14.5%
CLEVELAND	21,296	5,016	13,103	3,177	Clinton	23.6%	61.5%	14.9%
COAL	1,274	127	894	253	Clinton	10.0%	70.2%	19.9%
COMANCHE	12,178	1,989	8,572	1,617	Clinton	16.3%	70.4%	13.3%
COTTON	1,417	140	1,104	173	Clinton	9.9%	77.9%	12.2%
CRAIG	2,511	276	2,008	227	Clinton	11.0%	80.0%	9.0%
CREEK	7,712	1,184	5,746	782	Clinton	15.4%	74.5%	10.1%
CUSTER	4,070	536	3,006	528	Clinton	13.2%	73.9%	13.0%
DELAWARE	3,552	482	2,702	368	Clinton	13.6%	76.1%	10.4%
DEWEY	1,269	188	868	213	Clinton	14.8%	68.4%	16.8%
ELLIS	837	123	589	125	Clinton	14.7%	70.4%	14.9%
GARFIELD	6,336	1,168	4,342	826	Clinton	18.4%	68.5%	13.0%
GARVIN	5,461	700	3,951	810	Clinton	12.8%	72.3%	14.8%
GRADY	7,120	1,054	4,949	1,117	Clinton	14.8%	69.5%	15.7%
GRANT	1,107	190	762	155	Clinton	17.2%	68.8%	14.0%
GREER	1,365	178	1,026	161	Clinton	13.0%	75.2%	11.8%
HARMON	747	85	583	79	Clinton	11.4%	78.0%	10.6%
HARPER	782	141	524	117	Clinton	18.0%	67.0%	15.0%
HASKELL	2,245	197	1,871	177	Clinton	8.8%	83.3%	7.9%
HUGHES	2,819	327	2,175	317	Clinton	11.6%	77.2%	11.2%
JACKSON	3,948	523	2,864	561	Clinton	13.2%	72.5%	14.2%
JEFFERSON	1,377	112	1,033	232	Clinton	8.1%	75.0%	16.8%
JOHNSTON	2,407	198	1,702	507	Clinton	8.2%	70.7%	21.1%
KAY	5,790	1,070	3,999	721	Clinton	18.5%	69.1%	12.5%
KINGFISHER	1,815	313	1,184	318	Clinton	17.2%	65.2%	17.5%
KIOWA	2,211	271	1,651	289	Clinton	12.3%	74.7%	13.1%
LATIMER	2,317	193	1,916	208	Clinton	8.3%	82.7%	9.0%
LE FLORE	6,255	818	4,621	816	Clinton	13.1%	73.9%	13.0%
LINCOLN	4,397	682	3,055	660	Clinton	15.5%	69.5%	15.0%
LOGAN	3,940	690	2,703	547	Clinton	17.5%	68.6%	13.9%
LOVE	1,465	111	1,069	285	Clinton	7.6%	73.0%	19.5%
MCCLAIN	4,301	694	2,900	707	Clinton	16.1%	67.4%	16.4%
MCCURTAIN	4,479	400	3,532	547	Clinton	8.9%	78.9%	12.2%
MCINTOSH	3,942	460	3,134	348	Clinton	11.7%	79.5%	8.8%
MAJOR	838	127	597	114	Clinton	15.2%	71.2%	13.6%
MARSHALL	2,382	199	1,728	455	Clinton	8.4%	72.5%	19.1%
MAYES	5,408	674	4,206	528	Clinton	12.5%	77.8%	9.8%
MURRAY	2,595	297	1,910	388	Clinton	11.4%	73.6%	15.0%

OKLAHOMA DEMOCRATIC

1992

County	Total Vote	Brown	Clinton	Other	Winner	Percentage of Total Vote Brown	Clinton	Other
MUSKOGEE	10,398	1,328	8,203	867	Clinton	12.8%	78.9%	8.3%
NOBLE	1,784	316	1,214	254	Clinton	17.7%	68.0%	14.2%
NOWATA	1,530	195	1,183	152	Clinton	12.7%	77.3%	9.9%
OKFUSKEE	2,163	286	1,591	286	Clinton	13.2%	73.6%	13.2%
OKLAHOMA	62,629	13,750	39,804	9,075	Clinton	22.0%	63.6%	14.5%
OKMULGEE	6,140	905	4,628	607	Clinton	14.7%	75.4%	9.9%
OSAGE	6,183	954	4,588	641	Clinton	15.4%	74.2%	10.4%
OTTAWA	4,203	564	3,380	259	Clinton	13.4%	80.4%	6.2%
PAWNEE	2,463	389	1,830	244	Clinton	15.8%	74.3%	9.9%
PAYNE	7,259	1,527	4,885	847	Clinton	21.0%	67.3%	11.7%
PITTSBURG	8,244	1,103	6,269	872	Clinton	13.4%	76.0%	10.6%
PONTOTOC	6,556	1,090	4,646	820	Clinton	16.6%	70.9%	12.5%
POTTAWATOMIE	9,905	1,779	6,917	1,209	Clinton	18.0%	69.8%	12.2%
PUSHMATAHA	2,257	188	1,705	364	Clinton	8.3%	75.5%	16.1%
ROGER MILLS	1,061	129	790	142	Clinton	12.2%	74.5%	13.4%
ROGERS	8,034	1,494	5,662	878	Clinton	18.6%	70.5%	10.9%
SEMINOLE	4,564	707	3,309	548	Clinton	15.5%	72.5%	12.0%
SEQUOYAH	4,894	729	3,665	500	Clinton	14.9%	74.9%	10.2%
STEPHENS	8,264	861	6,374	1,029	Clinton	10.4%	77.1%	12.5%
TEXAS	2,404	291	1,646	467	Clinton	12.1%	68.5%	19.4%
TILLMAN	1,872	176	1,440	256	Clinton	9.4%	76.9%	13.7%
TULSA	45,572	9,914	30,921	4,737	Clinton	21.8%	67.9%	10.4%
WAGONER	6,079	897	4,609	573	Clinton	14.8%	75.8%	9.4%
WASHINGTON	5,599	1,020	4,003	576	Clinton	18.2%	71.5%	10.3%
WASHITA	2,608	392	1,874	342	Clinton	15.0%	71.9%	13.1%
WOODS	1,604	241	1,110	253	Clinton	15.0%	69.2%	15.8%
WOODWARD	2,481	397	1,780	304	Clinton	16.0%	71.7%	12.3%
TOTAL	416,129	69,624	293,266	53,239	Clinton	16.7%	70.5%	12.8%

OKLAHOMA REPUBLICAN

1992

County	Total Vote	Buchanan	Bush	Other	Winner	Percentage of Total Vote Buchanan	Bush	Other
ADAIR	811	156	625	30	Bush	19.2%	77.1%	3.7%
ALFALFA	1,055	273	738	44	Bush	25.9%	70.0%	4.2%
ATOKA	163	34	122	7	Bush	20.9%	74.8%	4.3%
BEAVER	795	199	576	20	Bush	25.0%	72.5%	2.5%
BECKHAM	649	207	417	25	Bush	31.9%	64.3%	3.9%
BLAINE	1,248	356	843	49	Bush	28.5%	67.5%	3.9%
BRYAN	390	102	274	14	Bush	26.2%	70.3%	3.6%
CADDO	815	200	581	34	Bush	24.5%	71.3%	4.2%
CANADIAN	6,799	1,772	4,769	258	Bush	26.1%	70.1%	3.8%
CARTER	1,329	343	948	38	Bush	25.8%	71.3%	2.9%
CHEROKEE	1,306	280	975	51	Bush	21.4%	74.7%	3.9%
CHOCTAW	99	24	72	3	Bush	24.2%	72.7%	3.0%
CIMARRON	280	98	177	5	Bush	35.0%	63.2%	1.8%
CLEVELAND	13,569	3,766	9,272	531	Bush	27.8%	68.3%	3.9%
COAL	69	15	51	3	Bush	21.7%	73.9%	4.3%
COMANCHE	3,949	909	2,898	142	Bush	23.0%	73.4%	3.6%
COTTON	96	32	62	2	Bush	33.3%	64.6%	2.1%
CRAIG	505	129	360	16	Bush	25.5%	71.3%	3.2%
CREEK	3,488	921	2,396	171	Bush	26.4%	68.7%	4.9%
CUSTER	1,503	354	1,099	50	Bush	23.6%	73.1%	3.3%
DELAWARE	1,433	325	1,058	50	Bush	22.7%	73.8%	3.5%
DEWEY	468	109	334	25	Bush	23.3%	71.4%	5.3%
ELLIS	637	180	431	26	Bush	28.3%	67.7%	4.1%
GARFIELD	7,634	2,005	5,352	277	Bush	26.3%	70.1%	3.6%
GARVIN	786	234	514	38	Bush	29.8%	65.4%	4.8%
GRADY	2,137	570	1,477	90	Bush	26.7%	69.1%	4.2%
GRANT	774	241	504	29	Bush	31.1%	65.1%	3.7%
GREER	122	26	94	2	Bush	21.3%	77.0%	1.6%
HARMON	35	6	28	1	Bush	17.1%	80.0%	2.9%
HARPER	501	149	328	24	Bush	29.7%	65.5%	4.8%
HASKELL	121	28	84	9	Bush	23.1%	69.4%	7.4%
HUGHES	166	42	117	7	Bush	25.3%	70.5%	4.2%
JACKSON	697	177	501	19	Bush	25.4%	71.9%	2.7%
JEFFERSON	49	10	38	1	Bush	20.4%	77.6%	2.0%
JOHNSTON	92	11	76	5	Bush	12.0%	82.6%	5.4%
KAY	5,447	1,575	3,703	169	Bush	28.9%	68.0%	3.1%
KINGFISHER	1,928	501	1,360	67	Bush	26.0%	70.5%	3.5%
KIOWA	273	65	188	20	Bush	23.8%	68.9%	7.3%
LATIMER	139	36	95	8	Bush	25.9%	68.3%	5.8%
LE FLORE	635	155	459	21	Bush	24.4%	72.3%	3.3%
LINCOLN	2,042	476	1,467	99	Bush	23.3%	71.8%	4.8%
LOGAN	3,087	815	2,134	138	Bush	26.4%	69.1%	4.5%
LOVE	137	36	98	3	Bush	26.3%	71.5%	2.2%
MCCLAIN	1,026	298	695	33	Bush	29.0%	67.7%	3.2%
MCCURTAIN	192	45	133	14	Bush	23.4%	69.3%	7.3%
MCINTOSH	301	69	217	15	Bush	22.9%	72.1%	5.0%
MAJOR	1,454	421	975	58	Bush	29.0%	67.1%	4.0%
MARSHALL	221	54	161	6	Bush	24.4%	72.9%	2.7%
MAYES	1,595	438	1,112	45	Bush	27.5%	69.7%	2.8%
MURRAY	201	51	141	9	Bush	25.4%	70.1%	4.5%

OKLAHOMA REPUBLICAN

1992

County	Total Vote	Buchanan	Bush	Other	Winner	Percentage of Total Vote: Buchanan	Bush	Other
MUSKOGEE	2,040	539	1,416	85	Bush	26.4%	69.4%	4.2%
NOBLE	1,158	252	854	52	Bush	21.8%	73.7%	4.5%
NOWATA	686	207	440	39	Bush	30.2%	64.1%	5.7%
OKFUSKEE	181	44	125	12	Bush	24.3%	69.1%	6.6%
OKLAHOMA	53,627	13,835	37,868	1,924	Bush	25.8%	70.6%	3.6%
OKMULGEE	1,035	287	685	63	Bush	27.7%	66.2%	6.1%
OSAGE	2,084	589	1,389	106	Bush	28.3%	66.7%	5.1%
OTTAWA	1,066	270	759	37	Bush	25.3%	71.2%	3.5%
PAWNEE	1,217	302	864	51	Bush	24.8%	71.0%	4.2%
PAYNE	4,990	1,176	3,623	191	Bush	23.6%	72.6%	3.8%
PITTSBURG	735	178	523	34	Bush	24.2%	71.2%	4.6%
PONTOTOC	1,021	266	714	41	Bush	26.1%	69.9%	4.0%
POTTAWATOMIE	2,789	719	1,943	127	Bush	25.8%	69.7%	4.6%
PUSHMATAHA	84	22	58	4	Bush	26.2%	69.0%	4.8%
ROGER MILLS	115	33	78	4	Bush	28.7%	67.8%	3.5%
ROGERS	3,630	1,032	2,439	159	Bush	28.4%	67.2%	4.4%
SEMINOLE	742	190	532	20	Bush	25.6%	71.7%	2.7%
SEQUOYAH	677	153	498	26	Bush	22.6%	73.6%	3.8%
STEPHENS	1,555	478	1,021	56	Bush	30.7%	65.7%	3.6%
TEXAS	1,500	421	1,037	42	Bush	28.1%	69.1%	2.8%
TILLMAN	133	38	90	5	Bush	28.6%	67.7%	3.8%
TULSA	49,436	13,949	33,729	1,758	Bush	28.2%	68.2%	3.6%
WAGONER	2,982	886	1,948	148	Bush	29.7%	65.3%	5.0%
WASHINGTON	6,990	1,662	5,100	228	Bush	23.8%	73.0%	3.3%
WASHITA	373	104	257	12	Bush	27.9%	68.9%	3.2%
WOODS	1,542	398	1,066	78	Bush	25.8%	69.1%	5.1%
WOODWARD	2,085	585	1,427	73	Bush	28.1%	68.4%	3.5%
TOTAL	217,721	57,933	151,612	8,176	Bush	26.6%	69.6%	3.8%

OKLAHOMA DEMOCRATIC

1996

County	Total Vote	Clinton	LaRouche	Lloyd-Duffie	Winner	Percentage of Total Vote: Clinton	LaRouche	Lloyd-Duffie
ADAIR	1,786	1,320	259	207	Clinton	73.9%	14.5%	11.6%
ALFALFA	819	626	111	82	Clinton	76.4%	13.6%	10.0%
ATOKA	2,070	1,488	317	265	Clinton	71.9%	15.3%	12.8%
BEAVER	633	377	138	118	Clinton	59.6%	21.8%	18.6%
BECKHAM	2,421	1,817	335	269	Clinton	75.1%	13.8%	11.1%
BLAINE	1,329	1,044	157	128	Clinton	78.6%	11.8%	9.6%
BRYAN	4,196	3,328	427	441	Clinton	79.3%	10.2%	10.5%
CADDO	4,186	3,232	508	446	Clinton	77.2%	12.1%	10.7%
CANADIAN	7,680	5,395	1,220	1,065	Clinton	70.2%	15.9%	13.9%
CARTER	5,393	3,923	774	696	Clinton	72.7%	14.4%	12.9%
CHEROKEE	4,877	3,913	512	452	Clinton	80.2%	10.5%	9.3%
CHOCTAW	1,874	1,442	232	200	Clinton	76.9%	12.4%	10.7%
CIMARRON	496	274	118	104	Clinton	55.2%	23.8%	21.0%
CLEVELAND	17,665	13,671	2,063	1,931	Clinton	77.4%	11.7%	10.9%
COAL	987	694	165	128	Clinton	70.3%	16.7%	13.0%
COMANCHE	9,335	6,813	1,340	1,182	Clinton	73.0%	14.4%	12.7%
COTTON	1,198	882	158	158	Clinton	73.6%	13.2%	13.2%
CRAIG	2,415	1,860	311	244	Clinton	77.0%	12.9%	10.1%
CREEK	7,810	6,090	952	768	Clinton	78.0%	12.2%	9.8%
CUSTER	3,695	2,749	525	421	Clinton	74.4%	14.2%	11.4%
DELAWARE	3,518	2,634	462	422	Clinton	74.9%	13.1%	12.0%
DEWEY	998	675	194	129	Clinton	67.6%	19.4%	12.9%
ELLIS	672	498	93	81	Clinton	74.1%	13.8%	12.1%
GARFIELD	5,324	4,349	520	455	Clinton	81.7%	9.8%	8.5%
GARVIN	3,928	2,919	554	455	Clinton	74.3%	14.1%	11.6%
GRADY	5,660	4,099	904	657	Clinton	72.4%	16.0%	11.6%
GRANT	882	670	125	87	Clinton	76.0%	14.2%	9.9%
GREER	1,176	882	158	136	Clinton	75.0%	13.4%	11.6%
HARMON	630	516	63	51	Clinton	81.9%	10.0%	8.1%
HARPER	678	462	107	109	Clinton	68.1%	15.8%	16.1%
HASKELL	2,002	1,546	244	212	Clinton	77.2%	12.2%	10.6%
HUGHES	2,366	1,829	301	236	Clinton	77.3%	12.7%	10.0%
JACKSON	2,925	1,981	480	464	Clinton	67.7%	16.4%	15.9%
JEFFERSON	1,087	867	103	117	Clinton	79.8%	9.5%	10.8%
JOHNSTON	1,685	1,249	199	237	Clinton	74.1%	11.8%	14.1%
KAY	5,069	3,921	633	515	Clinton	77.4%	12.5%	10.2%
KINGFISHER	1,653	1,172	258	223	Clinton	70.9%	15.6%	13.5%
KIOWA	1,800	1,298	298	204	Clinton	72.1%	16.6%	11.3%
LATIMER	1,804	1,329	281	194	Clinton	73.7%	15.6%	10.8%
LE FLORE	5,276	3,640	936	700	Clinton	69.0%	17.7%	13.3%
LINCOLN	3,899	2,887	594	418	Clinton	74.0%	15.2%	10.7%
LOGAN	3,109	2,335	417	357	Clinton	75.1%	13.4%	11.5%
LOVE	1,274	982	164	128	Clinton	77.1%	12.9%	10.0%
MCCLAIN	3,340	2,343	549	448	Clinton	70.1%	16.4%	13.4%
MCCURTAIN	3,420	2,096	739	585	Clinton	61.3%	21.6%	17.1%
MCINTOSH	3,555	2,740	440	375	Clinton	77.1%	12.4%	10.5%
MAJOR	760	568	111	81	Clinton	74.7%	14.6%	10.7%
MARSHALL	1,886	1,401	274	211	Clinton	74.3%	14.5%	11.2%
MAYES	5,615	4,473	568	574	Clinton	79.7%	10.1%	10.2%
MURRAY	2,238	1,715	290	233	Clinton	76.6%	13.0%	10.4%

OKLAHOMA DEMOCRATIC

1996

County	Total Vote	Clinton	LaRouche	Lloyd-Duffie	Winner	Percentage of Total Vote Clinton	LaRouche	Lloyd-Duffie
MUSKOGEE	9,336	7,352	1,116	868	Clinton	78.7%	12.0%	9.3%
NOBLE	1,542	1,113	231	198	Clinton	72.2%	15.0%	12.8%
NOWATA	1,350	1,065	151	134	Clinton	78.9%	11.2%	9.9%
OKFUSKEE	1,946	1,418	311	217	Clinton	72.9%	16.0%	11.2%
OKLAHOMA	52,423	39,840	6,875	5,708	Clinton	76.0%	13.1%	10.9%
OKMULGEE	5,727	4,656	539	532	Clinton	81.3%	9.4%	9.3%
OSAGE	5,807	4,591	593	623	Clinton	79.1%	10.2%	10.7%
OTTAWA	3,778	3,010	379	389	Clinton	79.7%	10.0%	10.3%
PAWNEE	2,211	1,765	236	210	Clinton	79.8%	10.7%	9.5%
PAYNE	7,752	6,338	688	726	Clinton	81.8%	8.9%	9.4%
PITTSBURG	7,087	5,106	1,003	978	Clinton	72.0%	14.2%	13.8%
PONTOTOC	5,262	3,880	726	656	Clinton	73.7%	13.8%	12.5%
POTTAWATOMIE	8,181	5,942	1,200	1,039	Clinton	72.6%	14.7%	12.7%
PUSHMATAHA	1,752	1,265	259	228	Clinton	72.2%	14.8%	13.0%
ROGER MILLS	797	551	131	115	Clinton	69.1%	16.4%	14.4%
ROGERS	8,751	6,395	1,219	1,137	Clinton	73.1%	13.9%	13.0%
SEMINOLE	3,554	2,701	450	403	Clinton	76.0%	12.7%	11.3%
SEQUOYAH	4,207	2,907	733	567	Clinton	69.1%	17.4%	13.5%
STEPHENS	6,148	4,459	912	777	Clinton	72.5%	14.8%	12.6%
TEXAS	1,802	1,051	382	369	Clinton	58.3%	21.2%	20.5%
TILLMAN	1,504	1,091	243	170	Clinton	72.5%	16.2%	11.3%
TULSA	50,809	41,715	4,449	4,645	Clinton	82.1%	8.8%	9.1%
WAGONER	5,720	4,456	660	604	Clinton	77.9%	11.5%	10.6%
WASHINGTON	4,697	3,813	469	415	Clinton	81.2%	10.0%	8.8%
WASHITA	2,035	1,436	313	286	Clinton	70.6%	15.4%	14.1%
WOODS	1,263	996	149	118	Clinton	78.9%	11.8%	9.3%
WOODWARD	2,069	1,528	294	247	Clinton	73.9%	14.2%	11.9%
TOTAL	366,604	279,454	46,392	40,758	Clinton	76.2%	12.7%	11.1%

OKLAHOMA REPUBLICAN

1996

County	Total Vote	Buchanan	Dole	Forbes	Other	Winner	Percentage of Total Vote Buchanan	Dole	Forbes	Other
ADAIR	933	186	633	80	34	Dole	19.9%	67.8%	8.6%	3.6%
ALFALFA	1,128	196	748	132	52	Dole	17.4%	66.3%	11.7%	4.6%
ATOKA	199	69	97	15	18	Dole	34.7%	48.7%	7.5%	9.0%
BEAVER	856	166	563	85	42	Dole	19.4%	65.8%	9.9%	4.9%
BECKHAM	737	199	418	88	32	Dole	27.0%	56.7%	11.9%	4.3%
BLAINE	1,244	288	765	130	61	Dole	23.2%	61.5%	10.5%	4.9%
BRYAN	535	146	263	81	45	Dole	27.3%	49.2%	15.1%	8.4%
CADDO	972	258	574	85	55	Dole	26.5%	59.1%	8.7%	5.7%
CANADIAN	8,448	2,242	4,778	1,081	347	Dole	26.5%	56.6%	12.8%	4.1%
CARTER	1,644	448	876	230	90	Dole	27.3%	53.3%	14.0%	5.5%
CHEROKEE	1,634	349	1,013	163	109	Dole	21.4%	62.0%	10.0%	6.7%
CHOCTAW	148	45	78	19	6	Dole	30.4%	52.7%	12.8%	4.1%
CIMARRON	366	96	191	35	44	Dole	26.2%	52.2%	9.6%	12.0%
CLEVELAND	16,086	3,938	9,028	2,286	834	Dole	24.5%	56.1%	14.2%	5.2%
COAL	110	38	55	13	4	Dole	34.5%	50.0%	11.8%	3.6%
COMANCHE	4,137	721	2,582	609	225	Dole	17.4%	62.4%	14.7%	5.4%
COTTON	120	27	63	21	9	Dole	22.5%	52.5%	17.5%	7.5%
CRAIG	635	134	402	69	30	Dole	21.1%	63.3%	10.9%	4.7%
CREEK	4,744	1,115	2,771	609	249	Dole	23.5%	58.4%	12.8%	5.2%
CUSTER	1,811	429	1,061	206	115	Dole	23.7%	58.6%	11.4%	6.4%
DELAWARE	1,914	391	1,124	288	111	Dole	20.4%	58.7%	15.0%	5.8%
DEWEY	535	126	320	55	34	Dole	23.6%	59.8%	10.3%	6.4%
ELLIS	692	101	458	80	53	Dole	14.6%	66.2%	11.6%	7.7%
GARFIELD	8,153	1,337	5,199	1,158	459	Dole	16.4%	63.8%	14.2%	5.6%
GARVIN	839	235	463	91	50	Dole	28.0%	55.2%	10.8%	6.0%
GRADY	2,627	810	1,379	304	134	Dole	30.8%	52.5%	11.6%	5.1%
GRANT	808	181	498	92	37	Dole	22.4%	61.6%	11.4%	4.6%
GREER	115	31	59	20	5	Dole	27.0%	51.3%	17.4%	4.3%
HARMON	46	15	18	10	3	Dole	32.6%	39.1%	21.7%	6.5%
HARPER	559	119	348	63	29	Dole	21.3%	62.3%	11.3%	5.2%
HASKELL	164	30	105	17	12	Dole	18.3%	64.0%	10.4%	7.3%
HUGHES	247	74	127	27	19	Dole	30.0%	51.4%	10.9%	7.7%
JACKSON	903	163	597	100	43	Dole	18.1%	66.1%	11.1%	4.8%
JEFFERSON	87	32	40	11	4	Dole	36.8%	46.0%	12.6%	4.6%
JOHNSTON	141	46	75	12	8	Dole	32.6%	53.2%	8.5%	5.7%
KAY	5,786	1,322	3,402	727	335	Dole	22.8%	58.8%	12.6%	5.8%
KINGFISHER	2,168	476	1,367	257	68	Dole	22.0%	63.1%	11.9%	3.1%
KIOWA	329	83	199	39	8	Dole	25.2%	60.5%	11.9%	2.4%
LATIMER	119	31	58	17	13	Dole	26.1%	48.7%	14.3%	10.9%
LE FLORE	875	309	435	84	47	Dole	35.3%	49.7%	9.6%	5.4%
LINCOLN	2,425	595	1,421	305	104	Dole	24.5%	58.6%	12.6%	4.3%
LOGAN	3,302	902	1,793	427	180	Dole	27.3%	54.3%	12.9%	5.5%
LOVE	196	48	111	29	8	Dole	24.5%	56.6%	14.8%	4.1%
MCCLAIN	1,298	388	700	149	61	Dole	29.9%	53.9%	11.5%	4.7%
MCCURTAIN	285	129	116	24	16	Buchanan	45.3%	40.7%	8.4%	5.6%
MCINTOSH	523	138	311	61	13	Dole	26.4%	59.5%	11.7%	2.5%
MAJOR	1,649	390	1,003	177	79	Dole	23.7%	60.8%	10.7%	4.8%
MARSHALL	237	66	131	34	6	Dole	27.8%	55.3%	14.3%	2.5%
MAYES	2,167	536	1,256	284	91	Dole	24.7%	58.0%	13.1%	4.2%
MURRAY	298	77	166	33	22	Dole	25.8%	55.7%	11.1%	7.4%

OKLAHOMA REPUBLICAN

1996

County	Total Vote	Buchanan	Dole	Forbes	Other	Winner	Percentage of Total Vote: Buchanan	Dole	Forbes	Other
MUSKOGEE	2,422	585	1,426	296	115	Dole	24.2%	58.9%	12.2%	4.7%
NOBLE	1,321	252	822	188	59	Dole	19.1%	62.2%	14.2%	4.5%
NOWATA	769	168	441	114	46	Dole	21.8%	57.3%	14.8%	6.0%
OKFUSKEE	270	86	140	31	13	Dole	31.9%	51.9%	11.5%	4.8%
OKLAHOMA	59,718	12,764	35,730	8,331	2,893	Dole	21.4%	59.8%	14.0%	4.8%
OKMULGEE	1,366	349	760	195	62	Dole	25.5%	55.6%	14.3%	4.5%
OSAGE	2,508	573	1,414	387	134	Dole	22.8%	56.4%	15.4%	5.3%
OTTAWA	1,225	275	741	122	87	Dole	22.4%	60.5%	10.0%	7.1%
PAWNEE	1,372	313	779	218	62	Dole	22.8%	56.8%	15.9%	4.5%
PAYNE	6,476	1,134	3,895	985	462	Dole	17.5%	60.1%	15.2%	7.1%
PITTSBURG	917	250	498	121	48	Dole	27.3%	54.3%	13.2%	5.2%
PONTOTOC	1,181	322	666	132	61	Dole	27.3%	56.4%	11.2%	5.2%
POTTAWATOMIE	3,295	870	1,799	444	182	Dole	26.4%	54.6%	13.5%	5.5%
PUSHMATAHA	114	31	54	25	4	Dole	27.2%	47.4%	21.9%	3.5%
ROGER MILLS	237	57	144	25	11	Dole	24.1%	60.8%	10.5%	4.6%
ROGERS	5,718	1,498	3,144	801	275	Dole	26.2%	55.0%	14.0%	4.8%
SEMINOLE	823	208	482	108	25	Dole	25.3%	58.6%	13.1%	3.0%
SEQUOYAH	920	270	497	122	31	Dole	29.3%	54.0%	13.3%	3.4%
STEPHENS	2,207	596	1,212	283	116	Dole	27.0%	54.9%	12.8%	5.3%
TEXAS	1,572	309	1,010	164	89	Dole	19.7%	64.2%	10.4%	5.7%
TILLMAN	179	67	88	19	5	Dole	37.4%	49.2%	10.6%	2.8%
TULSA	67,663	12,641	40,781	10,769	3,472	Dole	18.7%	60.3%	15.9%	5.1%
WAGONER	4,304	1,086	2,432	611	175	Dole	25.2%	56.5%	14.2%	4.1%
WASHINGTON	7,760	1,176	5,008	1,116	460	Dole	15.2%	64.5%	14.4%	5.9%
WASHITA	436	124	246	41	25	Dole	28.4%	56.4%	9.4%	5.7%
WOODS	1,507	241	997	181	88	Dole	16.0%	66.2%	12.0%	5.8%
WOODWARD	2,288	433	1,385	372	98	Dole	18.9%	60.5%	16.3%	4.3%
TOTAL	264,542	56,949	156,829	37,213	13,551	Dole	21.5%	59.3%	14.1%	5.1%

OREGON

Oregon made history in 1996 by being the first state to hold its presidential primary by mail. It was hoped that the innovation would decrease election costs and increase voter participation, and the experiment proved successful enough to make balloting by mail a permanent fixture on the Oregon political scene.

That Oregon would be the first to try a ballot-by-mail primary (beating Nevada to that distinction, as it turns out, by two weeks) is not surprising. Oregon has been in the forefront of creative election procedures, from the establishment of one of the first presidential primaries early this century to widespread use of absentee ballots in recent years.

Oregon's primary voters have often supported the presidential candidate who "cares enough to come" to this part of the Pacific Northwest. Nelson Rockefeller used that slogan in upsetting Barry Goldwater in the 1964 Republican primary. Four years later, Eugene McCarthy gave the Kennedy family its first electoral defeat in a quarter century, defeating Robert Kennedy in the Democratic balloting.

On the whole, Oregon voters have tended to support moderate Republicans and fairly liberal Democrats in its presidential primary. Twice before he won the Republican nomination in 1980, Ronald Reagan was on the Oregon GOP primary ballot—in 1968 and 1976—and lost both times. Democratic primary winners have included George McGovern, Frank Church and Gary Hart. In 1988, Jesse Jackson drew 38 percent of the Democratic vote, his best showing that year in any of the 16 primary states that voted after Super Tuesday—including New York, Illinois and California.

Jackson's performance was built around victories in the two academic-oriented counties, Lane (Eugene) and Benton (Corvallis), the homes of the University of Oregon and Oregon State, respectively, as well as a decent showing in the trio of counties that make up metropolitan Portland. About 40 percent of both parties' primary vote comes from the Portland area.

The Oregon GOP has grown more conservative of late. But in

Recent Oregon Primary Results

Oregon held its first presidential primary in 1912.

	DEMOCRATS			REPUBLICANS		
Year	Turnout	Candidates	%	Turnout	Candidates	%
1996 (March 12)	369,178	BILL CLINTON*	95	407,514	BOB DOLE	51
					Pat Buchanan	21
					Steve Forbes	13
1992 (May 19)	354,332	BILL CLINTON	45	304,159	GEORGE BUSH*	67
		Jerry Brown	31		Pat Buchanan	19
		Paul Tsongas	10			
1988 (May 17)	388,932	MICHAEL DUKAKIS	57	274,486	GEORGE BUSH	73
		Jesse Jackson	38		Bob Dole	18
1984 (May 15)	399,679	GARY HART	58	243,346	RONALD REAGAN*	98
		Walter Mondale	28			
1980 (May 20)	368,322	JIMMY CARTER*	57	315,366	RONALD REAGAN	54
		Edward Kennedy	31		George Bush	35
					John Anderson	10
1976 (May 25)	432,632	FRANK CHURCH	34	298,535	GERALD FORD*	50
		Jimmy Carter	27		Ronald Reagan	46
		Jerry Brown#	25			
1972 (May 23)	408,644	GEORGE McGOVERN	50	282,010	RICHARD NIXON*	82
		George Wallace	20		Paul McCloskey	10
		Hubert Humphrey	13			
1968 (May 28)	373,070	EUGENE McCARTHY	44	312,159	RICHARD NIXON	65
		Robert Kennedy	38		Ronald Reagan	20
		Lyndon Johnson*	12		Nelson Rockefeller#	12

Note: All candidates are listed that drew at least 10 percent of their party's primary vote. The names of winning candidates are capitalized. An asterisk (*) indicates an incumbent president. A pound sign (#) indicates a write-in candidate.

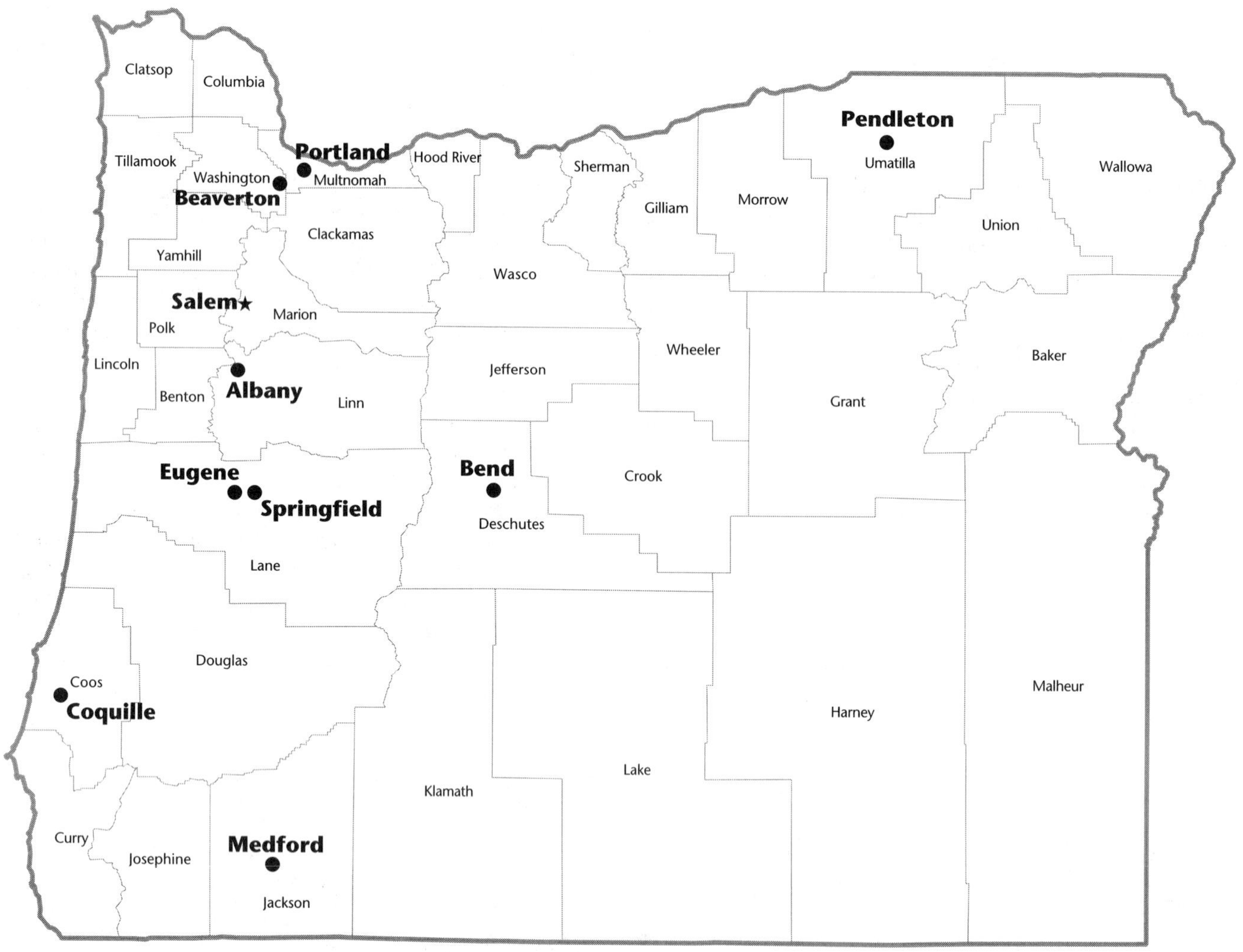

the most memorable of the state's Republican primaries, the more moderate entries ran quite well. A dozen years after Rockefeller's victory, President Gerald Ford narrowly beat Reagan in Oregon, Reagan's only loss that year in a primary west of the Mississippi. In 1980, George Bush and John Anderson together collected nearly half the primary vote, even as Reagan was moving at full gallop toward the Republican nomination.

A generation ago, Oregon held the penultimate primary, with its May contest setting up the make-or-break vote in early June in California. But none of the recent contests have drawn much attention.

Oregon moved its primary to the second Tuesday in March in 1996 in an attempt to return the state to the front ranks of presidential primaries. With both the ease and novelty of balloting by mail, combined turnout in the Democratic and Republican presidential primaries was up by more than 100,000 from 1992. But the vote was still held too late to have much impact on the nominating contest.

OREGON DEMOCRATIC

1968

County	Total Vote	Johnson	R. Kennedy	McCarthy	Other	Winner	Percentage of Total Vote Johnson	R. Kennedy	McCarthy	Other
BAKER	3,165	336	1,223	1,329	277	McCarthy	10.6%	38.6%	42.0%	8.8%
BENTON	7,379	595	2,425	3,635	724	McCarthy	8.1%	32.9%	49.3%	9.8%
CLACKAMAS	28,669	3,502	10,904	13,385	878	McCarthy	12.2%	38.0%	46.7%	3.1%
CLATSOP	5,753	746	2,277	2,362	368	McCarthy	13.0%	39.6%	41.1%	6.4%
COLUMBIA	6,161	795	2,537	2,438	391	R. Kennedy	12.9%	41.2%	39.6%	6.3%
COOS	11,503	1,542	4,822	4,696	443	R. Kennedy	13.4%	41.9%	40.8%	3.9%
CROOK	1,655	235	553	671	196	McCarthy	14.2%	33.4%	40.5%	11.8%
CURRY	2,153	261	762	953	177	McCarthy	12.1%	35.4%	44.3%	8.2%
DESCHUTES	5,196	516	1,770	2,486	424	McCarthy	9.9%	34.1%	47.8%	8.2%
DOUGLAS	11,944	1,263	4,533	4,875	1,273	McCarthy	10.6%	38.0%	40.8%	10.7%
GILLIAM	483	43	198	189	53	R. Kennedy	8.9%	41.0%	39.1%	11.0%
GRANT	1,100	116	370	536	78	McCarthy	10.5%	33.6%	48.7%	7.1%
HARNEY	1,291	150	438	531	172	McCarthy	11.6%	33.9%	41.1%	13.3%
HOOD RIVER	2,380	329	772	1,084	195	McCarthy	13.8%	32.4%	45.5%	8.2%
JACKSON	13,944	1,362	5,215	6,280	1,087	McCarthy	9.8%	37.4%	45.0%	7.8%
JEFFERSON	1,358	139	525	563	131	McCarthy	10.2%	38.7%	41.5%	9.6%
JOSEPHINE	5,865	511	2,127	2,586	641	McCarthy	8.7%	36.3%	44.1%	10.9%
KLAMATH	7,005	958	2,495	3,524	28	McCarthy	13.7%	35.6%	50.3%	0.4%
LAKE	1,095	119	358	518	100	McCarthy	10.9%	32.7%	47.3%	9.1%
LANE	35,957	4,129	13,157	16,401	2,270	McCarthy	11.5%	36.6%	45.6%	6.3%
LINCOLN	5,041	710	1,947	2,117	267	McCarthy	14.1%	38.6%	42.0%	5.3%
LINN	10,974	1,326	4,665	4,248	735	R. Kennedy	12.1%	42.5%	38.7%	6.7%
MALHEUR	2,862	207	1,184	1,209	262	McCarthy	7.2%	41.4%	42.2%	9.2%
MARION	21,295	2,567	8,700	8,503	1,525	R. Kennedy	12.1%	40.9%	39.9%	7.2%
MORROW	826	127	250	386	63	McCarthy	15.4%	30.3%	46.7%	7.6%
MULTNOMAH	125,237	16,046	47,740	55,295	6,156	McCarthy	12.8%	38.1%	44.2%	4.9%
POLK	5,045	618	1,899	2,074	454	McCarthy	12.2%	37.6%	41.1%	9.0%
SHERMAN	461	59	156	220	26	McCarthy	12.8%	33.8%	47.7%	5.6%
TILLAMOOK	3,705	462	1,485	1,466	292	R. Kennedy	12.5%	40.1%	39.6%	7.9%
UMATILLA	6,687	1,059	2,324	2,805	499	McCarthy	15.8%	34.8%	41.9%	7.5%
UNION	3,846	531	1,530	1,511	274	R. Kennedy	13.8%	39.8%	39.3%	7.1%
WALLOWA	1,319	152	381	651	135	McCarthy	11.5%	28.9%	49.4%	10.2%
WASCO	3,941	486	1,917	1,274	264	R. Kennedy	12.3%	48.6%	32.3%	6.7%
WASHINGTON	22,083	2,454	7,702	10,842	1,085	McCarthy	11.1%	34.9%	49.1%	4.9%
WHEELER	320	43	149	128		R. Kennedy	13.4%	46.6%	40.0%	
YAMHILL	5,372	680	2,141	2,219	332	McCarthy	12.7%	39.9%	41.3%	6.2%
TOTAL	373,070	45,174	141,631	163,990	22,275	McCarthy	12.1%	38.0%	44.0%	6.0%

OREGON REPUBLICAN

1968

County	Total Vote	Nixon	Reagan	Rockefeller	Other	Winner	Percentage of Total Vote Nixon	Reagan	Rockefeller	Other
BAKER	2,053	1,273	526	208	46	Nixon	62.0%	25.6%	10.1%	2.2%
BENTON	8,881	5,994	1,450	1,255	182	Nixon	67.5%	16.3%	14.1%	2.0%
CLACKAMAS	23,888	16,285	4,979	2,007	617	Nixon	68.2%	20.8%	8.4%	2.6%
CLATSOP	4,781	3,171	792	655	163	Nixon	66.3%	16.6%	13.7%	3.4%
COLUMBIA	3,109	1,920	742	351	96	Nixon	61.8%	23.9%	11.3%	3.1%
COOS	6,278	3,498	1,689	1,043	48	Nixon	55.7%	26.9%	16.6%	0.8%
CROOK	1,137	758	239	134	6	Nixon	66.7%	21.0%	11.8%	0.5%
CURRY	1,750	1,074	413	207	56	Nixon	61.4%	23.6%	11.8%	3.2%
DESCHUTES	4,126	2,351	1,019	551	205	Nixon	57.0%	24.7%	13.4%	5.0%
DOUGLAS	9,632	6,279	2,395	830	128	Nixon	65.2%	24.9%	8.6%	1.3%
GILLIAM	468	350	68	36	14	Nixon	74.8%	14.5%	7.7%	3.0%
GRANT	1,225	771	305	116	33	Nixon	62.9%	24.9%	9.5%	2.7%
HARNEY	965	674	210	45	36	Nixon	69.8%	21.8%	4.7%	3.7%
HOOD RIVER	1,993	1,366	384	201	42	Nixon	68.5%	19.3%	10.1%	2.1%
JACKSON	13,713	8,339	3,845	1,113	416	Nixon	60.8%	28.0%	8.1%	3.0%
JEFFERSON	1,248	820	291	105	32	Nixon	65.7%	23.3%	8.4%	2.6%
JOSEPHINE	6,211	3,898	1,793	375	145	Nixon	62.8%	28.9%	6.0%	2.3%
KLAMATH	6,122	4,184	1,561	237	140	Nixon	68.3%	25.5%	3.9%	2.3%
LAKE	1,176	717	358	77	24	Nixon	61.0%	30.4%	6.5%	2.0%
LANE	30,031	17,644	5,971	5,833	583	Nixon	58.8%	19.9%	19.4%	1.9%
LINCOLN	3,868	2,507	848	416	97	Nixon	64.8%	21.9%	10.8%	2.5%
LINN	9,054	6,180	1,928	711	235	Nixon	68.3%	21.3%	7.9%	2.6%
MALHEUR	3,640	2,220	1,203	173	44	Nixon	61.0%	33.0%	4.8%	1.2%
MARION	24,508	16,538	4,797	2,555	618	Nixon	67.5%	19.6%	10.4%	2.5%
MORROW	863	547	216	87	13	Nixon	63.4%	25.0%	10.1%	1.5%
MULTNOMAH	87,159	56,961	15,238	11,519	3,441	Nixon	65.4%	17.5%	13.2%	3.9%
POLK	5,911	4,068	1,000	705	138	Nixon	68.8%	16.9%	11.9%	2.3%
SHERMAN	483	350	92	41		Nixon	72.5%	19.0%	8.5%	
TILLAMOOK	2,796	1,743	588	372	93	Nixon	62.3%	21.0%	13.3%	3.3%
UMATILLA	6,248	4,457	1,090	566	135	Nixon	71.3%	17.4%	9.1%	2.2%
UNION	2,602	1,579	715	238	70	Nixon	60.7%	27.5%	9.1%	2.7%
WALLOWA	1,019	751	158	72	38	Nixon	73.7%	15.5%	7.1%	3.7%
WASCO	3,176	2,160	570	349	97	Nixon	68.0%	17.9%	11.0%	3.1%
WASHINGTON	25,874	17,254	4,975	2,697	948	Nixon	66.7%	19.2%	10.4%	3.7%
WHEELER	328	250	55	23		Nixon	76.2%	16.8%	7.0%	
YAMHILL	5,843	4,106	1,204	402	131	Nixon	70.3%	20.6%	6.9%	2.2%
TOTAL	312,159	203,037	63,707	36,305	9,110	Nixon	65.0%	20.4%	11.6%	2.9%

Note: The votes for Rockefeller were write-ins.

OREGON DEMOCRATIC

1972

County	Total Vote	Humphrey	McGovern	Wallace	Other	Winner	Percentage of Total Vote Humphrey	McGovern	Wallace	Other
BAKER	2,995	361	1,264	699	671	McGovern	12.1%	42.2%	23.3%	22.4%
BENTON	8,767	569	5,636	1,191	1,371	McGovern	6.5%	64.3%	13.6%	15.6%
CLACKAMAS	32,868	4,018	16,741	6,295	5,814	McGovern	12.2%	50.9%	19.2%	17.7%
CLATSOP	5,582	693	2,827	921	1,141	McGovern	12.4%	50.6%	16.5%	20.4%
COLUMBIA	7,011	944	3,086	1,589	1,392	McGovern	13.5%	44.0%	22.7%	19.9%
COOS	12,461	1,465	6,278	2,882	1,836	McGovern	11.8%	50.4%	23.1%	14.7%
CROOK	1,941	281	854	486	320	McGovern	14.5%	44.0%	25.0%	16.5%
CURRY	2,286	355	918	545	468	McGovern	15.5%	40.2%	23.8%	20.5%
DESCHUTES	6,087	806	3,149	1,241	891	McGovern	13.2%	51.7%	20.4%	14.6%
DOUGLAS	11,436	1,116	4,540	3,921	1,859	McGovern	9.8%	39.7%	34.3%	16.3%
GILLIAM	457	56	169	80	152	McGovern	12.3%	37.0%	17.5%	33.3%
GRANT	1,202	182	464	286	270	McGovern	15.1%	38.6%	23.8%	22.5%
HARNEY	1,399	248	486	352	313	McGovern	17.7%	34.7%	25.2%	22.4%
HOOD RIVER	2,589	355	1,263	503	468	McGovern	13.7%	48.8%	19.4%	18.1%
JACKSON	14,069	1,492	6,623	3,463	2,491	McGovern	10.6%	47.1%	24.6%	17.7%
JEFFERSON	1,403	176	548	347	332	McGovern	12.5%	39.1%	24.7%	23.7%
JOSEPHINE	5,861	690	2,184	2,181	806	McGovern	11.8%	37.3%	37.2%	13.8%
KLAMATH	7,986	943	3,020	2,513	1,510	McGovern	11.8%	37.8%	31.5%	18.9%
LAKE	1,232	136	444	411	241	McGovern	11.0%	36.0%	33.4%	19.6%
LANE	44,351	4,324	24,046	9,670	6,311	McGovern	9.7%	54.2%	21.8%	14.2%
LINCOLN	5,138	689	2,370	1,200	879	McGovern	13.4%	46.1%	23.4%	17.1%
LINN	11,433	1,409	5,200	2,931	1,893	McGovern	12.3%	45.5%	25.6%	16.6%
MALHEUR	2,696	328	901	791	676	McGovern	12.2%	33.4%	29.3%	25.1%
MARION	23,950	2,979	11,679	4,966	4,326	McGovern	12.4%	48.8%	20.7%	18.1%
MORROW	830	130	340	171	189	McGovern	15.7%	41.0%	20.6%	22.8%
MULTNOMAH	131,388	18,797	70,350	20,734	21,507	McGovern	14.3%	53.5%	15.8%	16.4%
POLK	5,712	686	2,809	1,221	996	McGovern	12.0%	49.2%	21.4%	17.4%
SHERMAN	452	49	192	85	126	McGovern	10.8%	42.5%	18.8%	27.9%
TILLAMOOK	3,978	552	1,902	756	768	McGovern	13.9%	47.8%	19.0%	19.3%
UMATILLA	7,688	997	3,241	1,460	1,990	McGovern	13.0%	42.2%	19.0%	25.9%
UNION	4,144	527	2,000	874	743	McGovern	12.7%	48.3%	21.1%	17.9%
WALLOWA	1,628	199	675	337	417	McGovern	12.2%	41.5%	20.7%	25.6%
WASCO	4,205	601	2,079	758	767	McGovern	14.3%	49.4%	18.0%	18.2%
WASHINGTON	26,885	3,116	14,162	4,453	5,154	McGovern	11.6%	52.7%	16.6%	19.2%
WHEELER	354	51	128	94	81	McGovern	14.4%	36.2%	26.6%	22.9%
YAMHILL	6,180	843	2,760	1,461	1,116	McGovern	13.6%	44.7%	23.6%	18.1%
TOTAL	408,644	51,163	205,328	81,868	70,285	McGovern	12.5%	50.2%	20.0%	17.2%

OREGON REPUBLICAN

1972

County	Total Vote	McCloskey	Nixon	Other	Winner	Percentage of Total Vote McCloskey	Nixon	Other
BAKER	1,711	133	1,427	151	Nixon	7.8%	83.4%	8.8%
BENTON	8,289	1,077	6,813	399	Nixon	13.0%	82.2%	4.8%
CLACKAMAS	23,479	2,632	19,062	1,785	Nixon	11.2%	81.2%	7.6%
CLATSOP	3,670	486	2,750	434	Nixon	13.2%	74.9%	11.8%
COLUMBIA	2,891	331	2,247	313	Nixon	11.4%	77.7%	10.8%
COOS	5,520	565	4,494	461	Nixon	10.2%	81.4%	8.4%
CROOK	1,092	92	876	124	Nixon	8.4%	80.2%	11.4%
CURRY	1,630	148	1,327	155	Nixon	9.1%	81.4%	9.5%
DESCHUTES	4,244	416	3,359	469	Nixon	9.8%	79.1%	11.1%
DOUGLAS	8,233	561	6,901	771	Nixon	6.8%	83.8%	9.4%
GILLIAM	421	31	359	31	Nixon	7.4%	85.3%	7.4%
GRANT	1,102	79	887	136	Nixon	7.2%	80.5%	12.3%
HARNEY	981	64	769	148	Nixon	6.5%	78.4%	15.1%
HOOD RIVER	1,790	163	1,494	133	Nixon	9.1%	83.5%	7.4%
JACKSON	12,532	1,097	10,513	922	Nixon	8.8%	83.9%	7.4%
JEFFERSON	1,102	106	879	117	Nixon	9.6%	79.8%	10.6%
JOSEPHINE	5,414	427	4,429	558	Nixon	7.9%	81.8%	10.3%
KLAMATH	5,589	397	4,569	623	Nixon	7.1%	81.7%	11.1%
LAKE	972	66	792	114	Nixon	6.8%	81.5%	11.7%
LANE	26,485	3,328	21,657	1,500	Nixon	12.6%	81.8%	5.7%
LINCOLN	3,569	397	2,888	284	Nixon	11.1%	80.9%	8.0%
LINN	8,248	855	6,693	700	Nixon	10.4%	81.1%	8.5%
MALHEUR	3,250	178	2,765	307	Nixon	5.5%	85.1%	9.4%
MARION	22,062	2,315	17,964	1,783	Nixon	10.5%	81.4%	8.1%
MORROW	645	65	463	117	Nixon	10.1%	71.8%	18.1%
MULTNOMAH	73,863	8,154	60,741	4,968	Nixon	11.0%	82.2%	6.7%
POLK	5,862	563	4,895	404	Nixon	9.6%	83.5%	6.9%
SHERMAN	407	24	350	33	Nixon	5.9%	86.0%	8.1%
TILLAMOOK	2,572	260	2,074	238	Nixon	10.1%	80.6%	9.3%
UMATILLA	5,850	437	4,888	525	Nixon	7.5%	83.6%	9.0%
UNION	2,569	199	2,110	260	Nixon	7.7%	82.1%	10.1%
WALLOWA	1,127	45	907	175	Nixon	4.0%	80.5%	15.5%
WASCO	2,832	234	2,299	299	Nixon	8.3%	81.2%	10.6%
WASHINGTON	26,008	2,842	21,516	1,650	Nixon	10.9%	82.7%	6.3%
WHEELER	277	21	232	24	Nixon	7.6%	83.8%	8.7%
YAMHILL	5,722	577	4,762	383	Nixon	10.1%	83.2%	6.7%
TOTAL	282,010	29,365	231,151	21,494	Nixon	10.4%	82.0%	7.6%

OREGON DEMOCRATIC

1976

County	Total Vote	Brown	Carter	Church	Other	Winner	Percentage of Total Vote: Brown	Carter	Church	Other
BAKER	3,609	444	1,096	1,591	478	Church	12.3%	30.4%	44.1%	13.2%
BENTON	9,772	3,593	2,213	2,689	1,277	Brown	36.8%	22.6%	27.5%	13.1%
CLACKAMAS	38,448	8,580	9,486	14,891	5,491	Church	22.3%	24.7%	38.7%	14.3%
CLATSOP	5,549	1,056	1,330	2,066	1,097	Church	19.0%	24.0%	37.2%	19.8%
COLUMBIA	7,493	1,346	1,974	2,751	1,422	Church	18.0%	26.3%	36.7%	19.0%
COOS	12,432	3,302	3,606	4,014	1,510	Church	26.6%	29.0%	32.3%	12.1%
CROOK	2,160	343	793	766	258	Carter	15.9%	36.7%	35.5%	11.9%
CURRY	2,591	541	717	856	477	Church	20.9%	27.7%	33.0%	18.4%
DESCHUTES	7,808	1,856	2,700	2,325	927	Carter	23.8%	34.6%	29.8%	11.9%
DOUGLAS	13,558	3,572	4,439	3,359	2,188	Carter	26.3%	32.7%	24.8%	16.1%
GILLIAM	481	83	125	179	94	Church	17.3%	26.0%	37.2%	19.5%
GRANT	1,287	143	349	622	173	Church	11.1%	27.1%	48.3%	13.4%
HARNEY	1,552	222	415	654	261	Church	14.3%	26.7%	42.1%	16.8%
HOOD RIVER	2,470	398	882	842	348	Carter	16.1%	35.7%	34.1%	14.1%
JACKSON	17,472	6,353	4,584	4,197	2,338	Brown	36.4%	26.2%	24.0%	13.4%
JEFFERSON	1,406	183	515	518	190	Church	13.0%	36.6%	36.8%	13.5%
JOSEPHINE	7,519	2,259	2,399	1,468	1,393	Carter	30.0%	31.9%	19.5%	18.5%
KLAMATH	9,445	3,075	2,960	1,827	1,583	Brown	32.6%	31.3%	19.3%	16.8%
LAKE	1,542	346	504	439	253	Carter	22.4%	32.7%	28.5%	16.4%
LANE	47,785	15,697	11,952	13,955	6,181	Brown	32.8%	25.0%	29.2%	12.9%
LINCOLN	5,913	1,065	1,784	2,181	883	Church	18.0%	30.2%	36.9%	14.9%
LINN	12,467	2,374	4,370	3,943	1,780	Carter	19.0%	35.1%	31.6%	14.3%
MALHEUR	3,741	368	967	1,805	601	Church	9.8%	25.8%	48.2%	16.1%
MARION	27,126	6,881	8,863	7,702	3,680	Carter	25.4%	32.7%	28.4%	13.6%
MORROW	949	114	304	337	194	Church	12.0%	32.0%	35.5%	20.4%
MULTNOMAH	122,121	29,316	27,408	45,766	19,631	Church	24.0%	22.4%	37.5%	16.1%
POLK	6,260	1,453	2,194	1,850	763	Carter	23.2%	35.0%	29.6%	12.2%
SHERMAN	453	61	133	179	80	Church	13.5%	29.4%	39.5%	17.7%
TILLAMOOK	4,242	872	1,303	1,418	649	Church	20.6%	30.7%	33.4%	15.3%
UMATILLA	6,506	562	2,277	2,319	1,348	Church	8.6%	35.0%	35.6%	20.7%
UNION	4,253	686	1,129	1,699	739	Church	16.1%	26.5%	39.9%	17.4%
WALLOWA	1,281	170	339	428	344	Church	13.3%	26.5%	33.4%	26.9%
WASCO	3,938	603	1,229	1,448	658	Church	15.3%	31.2%	36.8%	16.7%
WASHINGTON	31,532	7,452	7,665	11,735	4,680	Church	23.6%	24.3%	37.2%	14.8%
WHEELER	357	38	116	141	62	Church	10.6%	32.5%	39.5%	17.4%
YAMHILL	7,114	1,405	2,190	2,434	1,085	Church	19.7%	30.8%	34.2%	15.3%
TOTAL	432,632	106,812	115,310	145,394	65,116	Church	24.7%	26.7%	33.6%	15.1%

Note: The votes for Brown were write-ins.

OREGON REPUBLICAN

1976

County	Total Vote	Ford	Reagan	Other	Winner	Percentage of Total Vote: Ford	Reagan	Other
BAKER	2,080	776	1,265	39	Reagan	37.3%	60.8%	1.9%
BENTON	8,582	4,735	3,546	301	Ford	55.2%	41.3%	3.5%
CLACKAMAS	27,805	15,194	11,745	866	Ford	54.6%	42.2%	3.1%
CLATSOP	3,638	2,073	1,347	218	Ford	57.0%	37.0%	6.0%
COLUMBIA	2,959	1,488	1,348	123	Ford	50.3%	45.6%	4.2%
COOS	5,542	2,555	2,754	233	Reagan	46.1%	49.7%	4.2%
CROOK	1,284	575	640	69	Reagan	44.8%	49.8%	5.4%
CURRY	1,912	764	1,095	53	Reagan	40.0%	57.3%	2.8%
DESCHUTES	5,677	2,343	3,004	330	Reagan	41.3%	52.9%	5.8%
DOUGLAS	9,716	3,535	5,885	296	Reagan	36.4%	60.6%	3.0%
GILLIAM	394	195	189	10	Ford	49.5%	48.0%	2.5%
GRANT	1,090	419	648	23	Reagan	38.4%	59.4%	2.1%
HARNEY	1,054	338	626	90	Reagan	32.1%	59.4%	8.5%
HOOD RIVER	1,768	920	813	35	Ford	52.0%	46.0%	2.0%
JACKSON	15,053	5,554	8,803	696	Reagan	36.9%	58.5%	4.6%
JEFFERSON	1,321	505	771	45	Reagan	38.2%	58.4%	3.4%
JOSEPHINE	7,150	1,910	5,009	231	Reagan	26.7%	70.1%	3.2%
KLAMATH	6,493	2,116	3,907	470	Reagan	32.6%	60.2%	7.2%
LAKE	1,056	347	653	56	Reagan	32.9%	61.8%	5.3%
LANE	27,572	14,279	12,170	1,123	Ford	51.8%	44.1%	4.1%
LINCOLN	3,924	1,956	1,755	213	Ford	49.8%	44.7%	5.4%
LINN	8,425	3,832	4,307	286	Reagan	45.5%	51.1%	3.4%
MALHEUR	4,254	1,212	3,002	40	Reagan	28.5%	70.6%	0.9%
MARION	24,356	12,569	10,651	1,136	Ford	51.6%	43.7%	4.7%
MORROW	746	281	411	54	Reagan	37.7%	55.1%	7.2%
MULTNOMAH	66,756	38,844	25,035	2,877	Ford	58.2%	37.5%	4.3%
POLK	5,982	3,173	2,573	236	Ford	53.0%	43.0%	3.9%
SHERMAN	387	167	215	5	Reagan	43.2%	55.6%	1.3%
TILLAMOOK	2,455	1,312	1,127	16	Ford	53.4%	45.9%	0.7%
UMATILLA	5,570	2,495	3,002	73	Reagan	44.8%	53.9%	1.3%
UNION	2,839	1,182	1,561	96	Reagan	41.6%	55.0%	3.4%
WALLOWA	1,061	419	607	35	Reagan	39.5%	57.2%	3.3%
WASCO	2,699	1,391	1,202	106	Ford	51.5%	44.5%	3.9%
WASHINGTON	30,474	17,417	12,087	970	Ford	57.2%	39.7%	3.2%
WHEELER	288	145	138	5	Ford	50.3%	47.9%	1.7%
YAMHILL	6,173	3,165	2,800	208	Ford	51.3%	45.4%	3.4%
TOTAL	298,535	150,181	136,691	11,663	Ford	50.3%	45.8%	3.9%

OREGON DEMOCRATIC

1980

County	Total Vote	Carter	E. Kennedy	Other	Winner	Percentage of Total Vote Carter	E. Kennedy	Other
BAKER	3,011	1,697	724	590	Carter	56.4%	24.0%	19.6%
BENTON	7,796	4,612	2,015	1,169	Carter	59.2%	25.8%	15.0%
CLACKAMAS	33,343	19,439	10,373	3,531	Carter	58.3%	31.1%	10.6%
CLATSOP	5,025	2,753	1,638	634	Carter	54.8%	32.6%	12.6%
COLUMBIA	6,693	3,795	2,040	858	Carter	56.7%	30.5%	12.8%
COOS	11,014	5,878	3,735	1,401	Carter	53.4%	33.9%	12.7%
CROOK	1,910	1,199	475	236	Carter	62.8%	24.9%	12.4%
CURRY	2,815	1,539	851	425	Carter	54.7%	30.2%	15.1%
DESCHUTES	8,404	4,989	2,237	1,178	Carter	59.4%	26.6%	14.0%
DOUGLAS	12,173	6,979	3,403	1,791	Carter	57.3%	28.0%	14.7%
GILLIAM	405	238	112	55	Carter	58.8%	27.7%	13.6%
GRANT	1,494	906	311	277	Carter	60.6%	20.8%	18.5%
HARNEY	1,551	828	392	331	Carter	53.4%	25.3%	21.3%
HOOD RIVER	2,117	1,370	524	223	Carter	64.7%	24.8%	10.5%
JACKSON	14,543	8,003	4,360	2,180	Carter	55.0%	30.0%	15.0%
JEFFERSON	1,482	875	391	216	Carter	59.0%	26.4%	14.6%
JOSEPHINE	7,541	4,218	2,009	1,314	Carter	55.9%	26.6%	17.4%
KLAMATH	7,672	4,122	2,321	1,229	Carter	53.7%	30.3%	16.0%
LAKE	1,522	844	416	262	Carter	55.5%	27.3%	17.2%
LANE	40,742	21,759	13,876	5,107	Carter	53.4%	34.1%	12.5%
LINCOLN	5,522	3,202	1,589	731	Carter	58.0%	28.8%	13.2%
LINN	10,953	6,634	3,050	1,269	Carter	60.6%	27.8%	11.6%
MALHEUR	2,619	1,509	723	387	Carter	57.6%	27.6%	14.8%
MARION	23,734	13,968	6,344	3,422	Carter	58.9%	26.7%	14.4%
MORROW	1,055	621	260	174	Carter	58.9%	24.6%	16.5%
MULTNOMAH	95,940	53,350	33,506	9,084	Carter	55.6%	34.9%	9.5%
POLK	5,558	3,338	1,386	834	Carter	60.1%	24.9%	15.0%
SHERMAN	382	219	86	77	Carter	57.3%	22.5%	20.2%
TILLAMOOK	4,146	2,466	1,172	508	Carter	59.5%	28.3%	12.3%
UMATILLA	5,655	3,012	1,991	652	Carter	53.3%	35.2%	11.5%
UNION	3,120	1,707	788	625	Carter	54.7%	25.3%	20.0%
WALLOWA	1,063	592	258	213	Carter	55.7%	24.3%	20.0%
WASCO	2,887	1,731	850	306	Carter	60.0%	29.4%	10.6%
WASHINGTON	27,771	16,342	8,567	2,862	Carter	58.8%	30.8%	10.3%
WHEELER	263	166	75	22	Carter	63.1%	28.5%	8.4%
YAMHILL	6,401	3,793	1,803	805	Carter	59.3%	28.2%	12.6%
TOTAL	368,322	208,693	114,651	44,978	Carter	56.7%	31.1%	12.2%

OREGON REPUBLICAN

1980

County	Total Vote	Anderson	Bush	Reagan	Other	Winner	Percentage of Total Vote Anderson	Bush	Reagan	Other
BAKER	2,244	168	465	1,576	35	Reagan	7.5%	20.7%	70.2%	1.6%
BENTON	9,033	1,446	3,387	4,116	84	Reagan	16.0%	37.5%	45.6%	0.9%
CLACKAMAS	30,529	2,974	12,220	15,017	318	Reagan	9.7%	40.0%	49.2%	1.0%
CLATSOP	3,660	500	1,436	1,653	71	Reagan	13.7%	39.2%	45.2%	1.9%
COLUMBIA	3,207	290	1,148	1,699	70	Reagan	9.0%	35.8%	53.0%	2.2%
COOS	6,003	504	1,814	3,615	70	Reagan	8.4%	30.2%	60.2%	1.2%
CROOK	1,415	99	469	827	20	Reagan	7.0%	33.1%	58.4%	1.4%
CURRY	2,292	141	455	1,668	28	Reagan	6.2%	19.9%	72.8%	1.2%
DESCHUTES	7,324	673	2,405	4,137	109	Reagan	9.2%	32.8%	56.5%	1.5%
DOUGLAS	10,813	609	2,642	7,463	99	Reagan	5.6%	24.4%	69.0%	0.9%
GILLIAM	393	41	102	244	6	Reagan	10.4%	26.0%	62.1%	1.5%
GRANT	1,245	81	221	919	24	Reagan	6.5%	17.8%	73.8%	1.9%
HARNEY	1,115	79	242	761	33	Reagan	7.1%	21.7%	68.3%	3.0%
HOOD RIVER	1,816	148	586	1,058	24	Reagan	8.1%	32.3%	58.3%	1.3%
JACKSON	15,706	1,155	3,228	11,203	120	Reagan	7.4%	20.6%	71.3%	0.8%
JEFFERSON	1,419	109	449	839	22	Reagan	7.7%	31.6%	59.1%	1.6%
JOSEPHINE	8,375	354	1,299	6,656	66	Reagan	4.2%	15.5%	79.5%	0.8%
KLAMATH	5,310	326	1,334	3,544	106	Reagan	6.1%	25.1%	66.7%	2.0%
LAKE	1,195	48	276	861	10	Reagan	4.0%	23.1%	72.1%	0.8%
LANE	30,383	3,728	11,321	15,043	291	Reagan	12.3%	37.3%	49.5%	1.0%
LINCOLN	4,204	461	1,442	2,236	65	Reagan	11.0%	34.3%	53.2%	1.5%
LINN	9,085	643	3,198	5,166	78	Reagan	7.1%	35.2%	56.9%	0.9%
MALHEUR	3,880	236	487	3,110	47	Reagan	6.1%	12.6%	80.2%	1.2%
MARION	25,997	3,203	9,386	13,059	349	Reagan	12.3%	36.1%	50.2%	1.3%
MORROW	973	87	206	669	11	Reagan	8.9%	21.2%	68.8%	1.1%
MULTNOMAH	64,937	7,654	25,930	30,608	745	Reagan	11.8%	39.9%	47.1%	1.1%
POLK	6,224	797	2,211	3,135	81	Reagan	12.8%	35.5%	50.4%	1.3%
SHERMAN	427	31	138	254	4	Reagan	7.3%	32.3%	59.5%	0.9%
TILLAMOOK	2,797	241	1,166	1,354	36	Reagan	8.6%	41.7%	48.4%	1.3%
UMATILLA	5,895	625	979	4,201	90	Reagan	10.6%	16.6%	71.3%	1.5%
UNION	2,783	249	459	2,048	27	Reagan	8.9%	16.5%	73.6%	1.0%
WALLOWA	1,083	68	144	847	24	Reagan	6.3%	13.3%	78.2%	2.2%
WASCO	2,392	231	796	1,350	15	Reagan	9.7%	33.3%	56.4%	0.6%
WASHINGTON	34,129	3,424	14,723	15,671	311	Reagan	10.0%	43.1%	45.9%	0.9%
WHEELER	261	20	69	163	9	Reagan	7.7%	26.4%	62.5%	3.4%
YAMHILL	6,822	675	2,377	3,679	91	Reagan	9.9%	34.8%	53.9%	1.3%
TOTAL	315,366	32,118	109,210	170,449	3,589	Reagan	10.2%	34.6%	54.0%	1.1%

OREGON DEMOCRATIC

1984

County	Total Vote	Hart	Mondale	Other	Winner	Percentage of Total Vote Hart	Mondale	Other
BAKER	2,952	1,878	689	385	Hart	63.6%	23.3%	13.0%
BENTON	9,667	5,731	2,188	1,748	Hart	59.3%	22.6%	18.1%
CLACKAMAS	35,540	21,846	9,375	4,319	Hart	61.5%	26.4%	12.2%
CLATSOP	5,286	3,171	1,533	582	Hart	60.0%	29.0%	11.0%
COLUMBIA	7,394	4,451	2,229	714	Hart	60.2%	30.1%	9.7%
COOS	11,553	6,891	3,383	1,279	Hart	59.6%	29.3%	11.1%
CROOK	2,110	1,312	599	199	Hart	62.2%	28.4%	9.4%
CURRY	3,662	2,154	1,072	436	Hart	58.8%	29.3%	11.9%
DESCHUTES	8,800	5,784	2,170	846	Hart	65.7%	24.7%	9.6%
DOUGLAS	12,676	7,680	3,578	1,418	Hart	60.6%	28.2%	11.2%
GILLIAM	379	256	88	35	Hart	67.5%	23.2%	9.2%
GRANT	1,578	946	436	196	Hart	59.9%	27.6%	12.4%
HARNEY	1,372	856	355	161	Hart	62.4%	25.9%	11.7%
HOOD RIVER	2,707	1,713	707	287	Hart	63.3%	26.1%	10.6%
JACKSON	16,908	9,712	4,812	2,384	Hart	57.4%	28.5%	14.1%
JEFFERSON	1,633	1,036	391	206	Hart	63.4%	23.9%	12.6%
JOSEPHINE	7,889	4,618	2,138	1,133	Hart	58.5%	27.1%	14.4%
KLAMATH	7,922	4,436	2,319	1,167	Hart	56.0%	29.3%	14.7%
LAKE	1,542	904	451	187	Hart	58.6%	29.2%	12.1%
LANE	41,333	23,704	11,450	6,179	Hart	57.3%	27.7%	14.9%
LINCOLN	6,697	4,129	1,726	842	Hart	61.7%	25.8%	12.6%
LINN	12,449	7,285	3,766	1,398	Hart	58.5%	30.3%	11.2%
MALHEUR	2,417	1,580	539	298	Hart	65.4%	22.3%	12.3%
MARION	26,208	15,250	7,804	3,154	Hart	58.2%	29.8%	12.0%
MORROW	1,154	717	329	108	Hart	62.1%	28.5%	9.4%
MULTNOMAH	103,702	56,338	29,684	17,680	Hart	54.3%	28.6%	17.0%
POLK	6,221	3,505	1,875	841	Hart	56.3%	30.1%	13.5%
SHERMAN	458	276	127	55	Hart	60.3%	27.7%	12.0%
TILLAMOOK	4,538	2,837	1,224	477	Hart	62.5%	27.0%	10.5%
UMATILLA	6,021	3,676	1,781	564	Hart	61.1%	29.6%	9.4%
UNION	3,406	2,033	725	648	Hart	59.7%	21.3%	19.0%
WALLOWA	1,780	1,013	475	292	Hart	56.9%	26.7%	16.4%
WASCO	4,208	2,382	1,083	743	Hart	56.6%	25.7%	17.7%
WASHINGTON	30,245	19,160	7,285	3,800	Hart	63.3%	24.1%	12.6%
WHEELER	221	138	62	21	Hart	62.4%	28.1%	9.5%
YAMHILL	7,050	4,240	1,926	884	Hart	60.1%	27.3%	12.5%
TOTAL	399,678	233,638	110,374	55,666	Hart	58.5%	27.6%	13.9%
Certified Totals	399,679	233,638	110,374	55,667	Hart	58.5%	27.6%	13.9%

OREGON DEMOCRATIC

1988

County	Total Vote	Dukakis	J. Jackson	Other	Winner	Percentage of Total Vote Dukakis	J. Jackson	Other
BAKER	2,683	1,964	482	237	Dukakis	73.2%	18.0%	8.8%
BENTON	9,382	3,941	5,150	291	J. Jackson	42.0%	54.9%	3.1%
CLACKAMAS	33,262	19,847	11,801	1,614	Dukakis	59.7%	35.5%	4.9%
CLATSOP	5,193	3,128	1,787	278	Dukakis	60.2%	34.4%	5.4%
COLUMBIA	6,656	4,365	1,888	403	Dukakis	65.6%	28.4%	6.1%
COOS	10,314	5,817	3,961	536	Dukakis	56.4%	38.4%	5.2%
CROOK	2,001	1,297	561	143	Dukakis	64.8%	28.0%	7.1%
CURRY	2,864	1,808	824	232	Dukakis	63.1%	28.8%	8.1%
DESCHUTES	9,571	5,167	3,967	437	Dukakis	54.0%	41.4%	4.6%
DOUGLAS	11,961	7,859	3,294	808	Dukakis	65.7%	27.5%	6.8%
GILLIAM	314	217	73	24	Dukakis	69.1%	23.2%	7.6%
GRANT	1,460	1,077	220	163	Dukakis	73.8%	15.1%	11.2%
HARNEY	1,215	873	223	119	Dukakis	71.9%	18.4%	9.8%
HOOD RIVER	2,133	1,315	681	137	Dukakis	61.7%	31.9%	6.4%
JACKSON	17,397	9,123	7,405	869	Dukakis	52.4%	42.6%	5.0%
JEFFERSON	1,797	1,087	605	105	Dukakis	60.5%	33.7%	5.8%
JOSEPHINE	8,181	4,745	2,916	520	Dukakis	58.0%	35.6%	6.4%
KLAMATH	7,054	4,463	2,065	526	Dukakis	63.3%	29.3%	7.5%
LAKE	1,349	966	289	94	Dukakis	71.6%	21.4%	7.0%
LANE	42,442	20,234	20,671	1,537	J. Jackson	47.7%	48.7%	3.6%
LINCOLN	6,201	3,610	2,251	340	Dukakis	58.2%	36.3%	5.5%
LINN	11,536	6,783	4,095	658	Dukakis	58.8%	35.5%	5.7%
MALHEUR	2,438	1,775	417	246	Dukakis	72.8%	17.1%	10.1%
MARION	24,069	14,083	8,776	1,210	Dukakis	58.5%	36.5%	5.0%
MORROW	979	685	188	106	Dukakis	70.0%	19.2%	10.8%
MULTNOMAH	103,159	56,061	42,812	4,286	Dukakis	54.3%	41.5%	4.2%
POLK	5,743	3,167	2,297	279	Dukakis	55.1%	40.0%	4.9%
SHERMAN	366	256	75	35	Dukakis	69.9%	20.5%	9.6%
TILLAMOOK	4,100	2,621	1,265	214	Dukakis	63.9%	30.9%	5.2%
UMATILLA	5,067	3,355	1,076	636	Dukakis	66.2%	21.2%	12.6%
UNION	3,609	2,510	833	266	Dukakis	69.5%	23.1%	7.4%
WALLOWA	1,403	999	250	154	Dukakis	71.2%	17.8%	11.0%
WASCO	3,635	2,438	952	245	Dukakis	67.1%	26.2%	6.7%
WASHINGTON	32,137	18,905	11,737	1,495	Dukakis	58.8%	36.5%	4.7%
WHEELER	223	158	46	19	Dukakis	70.9%	20.6%	8.5%
YAMHILL	7,038	4,349	2,274	415	Dukakis	61.8%	32.3%	5.9%
TOTAL	388,932	221,048	148,207	19,677	Dukakis	56.8%	38.1%	5.1%

OREGON REPUBLICAN

1988

County	Total Vote	Bush	Dole	Other	Winner	Percentage of Total Vote Bush	Dole	Other
BAKER	2,176	1,564	357	255	Bush	71.9%	16.4%	11.7%
BENTON	6,442	4,414	1,428	600	Bush	68.5%	22.2%	9.3%
CLACKAMAS	24,750	18,417	4,379	1,954	Bush	74.4%	17.7%	7.9%
CLATSOP	3,225	2,442	565	218	Bush	75.7%	17.5%	6.8%
COLUMBIA	2,802	1,894	526	382	Bush	67.6%	18.8%	13.6%
COOS	4,960	3,380	916	664	Bush	68.1%	18.5%	13.4%
CROOK	1,475	1,052	270	153	Bush	71.3%	18.3%	10.4%
CURRY	2,606	1,945	431	230	Bush	74.6%	16.5%	8.8%
DESCHUTES	7,951	5,754	1,444	753	Bush	72.4%	18.2%	9.5%
DOUGLAS	9,666	7,058	1,584	1,024	Bush	73.0%	16.4%	10.6%
GILLIAM	269	183	75	11	Bush	68.0%	27.9%	4.1%
GRANT	1,302	950	194	158	Bush	73.0%	14.9%	12.1%
HARNEY	1,062	810	146	106	Bush	76.3%	13.7%	10.0%
HOOD RIVER	1,734	1,194	377	163	Bush	68.9%	21.7%	9.4%
JACKSON	15,843	12,312	2,357	1,174	Bush	77.7%	14.9%	7.4%
JEFFERSON	1,663	1,198	297	168	Bush	72.0%	17.9%	10.1%
JOSEPHINE	9,611	7,721	1,201	689	Bush	80.3%	12.5%	7.2%
KLAMATH	6,229	4,379	1,075	775	Bush	70.3%	17.3%	12.4%
LAKE	1,168	853	221	94	Bush	73.0%	18.9%	8.0%
LANE	23,189	15,843	4,788	2,558	Bush	68.3%	20.6%	11.0%
LINCOLN	3,889	2,759	774	356	Bush	70.9%	19.9%	9.2%
LINN	8,213	5,904	1,462	847	Bush	71.9%	17.8%	10.3%
MALHEUR	3,440	2,710	523	207	Bush	78.8%	15.2%	6.0%
MARION	21,555	15,286	3,740	2,529	Bush	70.9%	17.4%	11.7%
MORROW	801	547	163	91	Bush	68.3%	20.3%	11.4%
MULTNOMAH	51,243	37,356	9,269	4,618	Bush	72.9%	18.1%	9.0%
POLK	5,389	3,826	1,028	535	Bush	71.0%	19.1%	9.9%
SHERMAN	351	258	76	17	Bush	73.5%	21.7%	4.8%
TILLAMOOK	2,496	1,842	395	259	Bush	73.8%	15.8%	10.4%
UMATILLA	4,489	3,201	983	305	Bush	71.3%	21.9%	6.8%
UNION	3,176	2,357	516	303	Bush	74.2%	16.2%	9.5%
WALLOWA	1,160	833	148	179	Bush	71.8%	12.8%	15.4%
WASCO	2,537	1,709	541	287	Bush	67.4%	21.3%	11.3%
WASHINGTON	30,946	23,108	5,731	2,107	Bush	74.7%	18.5%	6.8%
WHEELER	220	159	43	18	Bush	72.3%	19.5%	8.2%
YAMHILL	6,458	4,720	1,105	633	Bush	73.1%	17.1%	9.8%
TOTAL	274,486	199,938	49,128	25,420	Bush	72.8%	17.9%	9.3%

OREGON DEMOCRATIC

1992

County	Total Vote	Brown	Clinton	Tsongas	Other	Winner	Percentage of Total Vote Brown	Clinton	Tsongas	Other
BAKER	1,914	344	956	210	404	Clinton	18.0%	49.9%	11.0%	21.1%
BENTON	9,832	4,078	3,762	1,365	627	Brown	41.5%	38.3%	13.9%	6.4%
CLACKAMAS	31,678	10,159	14,221	4,029	3,269	Clinton	32.1%	44.9%	12.7%	10.3%
CLATSOP	4,675	1,406	2,222	540	507	Clinton	30.1%	47.5%	11.6%	10.8%
COLUMBIA	6,014	1,276	2,775	579	1,384	Clinton	21.2%	46.1%	9.6%	23.0%
COOS	8,965	2,187	3,986	668	2,124	Clinton	24.4%	44.5%	7.5%	23.7%
CROOK	1,772	323	840	161	448	Clinton	18.2%	47.4%	9.1%	25.3%
CURRY	2,727	634	1,187	207	699	Clinton	23.2%	43.5%	7.6%	25.6%
DESCHUTES	9,990	3,128	3,741	986	2,135	Clinton	31.3%	37.4%	9.9%	21.4%
DOUGLAS	9,805	2,705	4,938	1,067	1,095	Clinton	27.6%	50.4%	10.9%	11.2%
GILLIAM	262	59	135	32	36	Clinton	22.5%	51.5%	12.2%	13.7%
GRANT	1,114	190	563	123	238	Clinton	17.1%	50.5%	11.0%	21.4%
HARNEY	806	149	407	72	178	Clinton	18.5%	50.5%	8.9%	22.1%
HOOD RIVER	2,219	656	1,120	259	184	Clinton	29.6%	50.5%	11.7%	8.3%
JACKSON	14,828	5,637	6,763	1,268	1,160	Clinton	38.0%	45.6%	8.6%	7.8%
JEFFERSON	1,477	343	650	149	335	Clinton	23.2%	44.0%	10.1%	22.7%
JOSEPHINE	7,237	2,302	3,074	620	1,241	Clinton	31.8%	42.5%	8.6%	17.1%
KLAMATH	6,858	1,668	3,290	613	1,287	Clinton	24.3%	48.0%	8.9%	18.8%
LAKE	1,110	222	615	112	161	Clinton	20.0%	55.4%	10.1%	14.5%
LANE	41,647	15,076	19,413	3,391	3,767	Clinton	36.2%	46.6%	8.1%	9.0%
LINCOLN	5,913	1,795	2,694	590	834	Clinton	30.4%	45.6%	10.0%	14.1%
LINN	10,459	2,785	5,449	1,141	1,084	Clinton	26.6%	52.1%	10.9%	10.4%
MALHEUR	1,989	321	898	242	528	Clinton	16.1%	45.1%	12.2%	26.5%
MARION	22,791	6,501	10,072	2,305	3,913	Clinton	28.5%	44.2%	10.1%	17.2%
MORROW	805	141	396	113	155	Clinton	17.5%	49.2%	14.0%	19.3%
MULTNOMAH	88,369	29,519	38,716	9,033	11,101	Clinton	33.4%	43.8%	10.2%	12.6%
POLK	5,118	1,645	2,356	645	472	Clinton	32.1%	46.0%	12.6%	9.2%
SHERMAN	355	62	161	47	85	Clinton	17.5%	45.4%	13.2%	23.9%
TILLAMOOK	4,016	858	1,900	341	917	Clinton	21.4%	47.3%	8.5%	22.8%
UMATILLA	4,624	879	2,448	528	769	Clinton	19.0%	52.9%	11.4%	16.6%
UNION	2,931	687	1,229	285	730	Clinton	23.4%	41.9%	9.7%	24.9%
WALLOWA	1,175	184	541	121	329	Clinton	15.7%	46.0%	10.3%	28.0%
WASCO	2,890	754	1,471	322	343	Clinton	26.1%	50.9%	11.1%	11.9%
WASHINGTON	30,918	10,113	13,703	4,280	2,822	Clinton	32.7%	44.3%	13.8%	9.1%
WHEELER	236	39	114	22	61	Clinton	16.5%	48.3%	9.3%	25.8%
YAMHILL	6,813	1,669	2,996	673	1,475	Clinton	24.5%	44.0%	9.9%	21.6%
TOTAL	354,332	110,494	159,802	37,139	46,897	Clinton	31.2%	45.1%	10.5%	13.2%

OREGON REPUBLICAN

1992

County	Total Vote	Buchanan	Bush	Other	Winner	Percentage of Total Vote Buchanan	Bush	Other
BAKER	1,937	335	1,221	381	Bush	17.3%	63.0%	19.7%
BENTON	8,722	1,884	6,322	516	Bush	21.6%	72.5%	5.9%
CLACKAMAS	30,208	6,151	21,206	2,851	Bush	20.4%	70.2%	9.4%
CLATSOP	3,207	704	2,200	303	Bush	22.0%	68.6%	9.4%
COLUMBIA	3,226	570	1,945	711	Bush	17.7%	60.3%	22.0%
COOS	5,941	931	3,444	1,566	Bush	15.7%	58.0%	26.4%
CROOK	1,812	230	1,207	375	Bush	12.7%	66.6%	20.7%
CURRY	3,136	549	1,706	881	Bush	17.5%	54.4%	28.1%
DESCHUTES	10,866	1,508	6,750	2,608	Bush	13.9%	62.1%	24.0%
DOUGLAS	10,325	2,230	7,265	830	Bush	21.6%	70.4%	8.0%
GILLIAM	291	50	207	34	Bush	17.2%	71.1%	11.7%
GRANT	1,260	227	838	195	Bush	18.0%	66.5%	15.5%
HARNEY	977	128	599	250	Bush	13.1%	61.3%	25.6%
HOOD RIVER	2,142	397	1,542	203	Bush	18.5%	72.0%	9.5%
JACKSON	15,000	3,653	10,092	1,255	Bush	24.4%	67.3%	8.4%
JEFFERSON	1,552	215	1,028	309	Bush	13.9%	66.2%	19.9%
JOSEPHINE	10,461	2,263	6,226	1,972	Bush	21.6%	59.5%	18.9%
KLAMATH	7,944	1,342	5,353	1,249	Bush	16.9%	67.4%	15.7%
LAKE	1,338	231	928	179	Bush	17.3%	69.4%	13.4%
LANE	27,437	5,228	19,401	2,808	Bush	19.1%	70.7%	10.2%
LINCOLN	4,315	985	2,637	693	Bush	22.8%	61.1%	16.1%
LINN	9,562	2,036	6,749	777	Bush	21.3%	70.6%	8.1%
MALHEUR	3,463	490	2,419	554	Bush	14.1%	69.9%	16.0%
MARION	25,613	3,850	17,297	4,466	Bush	15.0%	67.5%	17.4%
MORROW	760	130	488	142	Bush	17.1%	64.2%	18.7%
MULTNOMAH	50,548	9,968	31,916	8,664	Bush	19.7%	63.1%	17.1%
POLK	5,765	1,089	4,235	441	Bush	18.9%	73.5%	7.6%
SHERMAN	444	69	295	80	Bush	15.5%	66.4%	18.0%
TILLAMOOK	2,806	498	1,647	661	Bush	17.7%	58.7%	23.6%
UMATILLA	4,668	787	3,270	611	Bush	16.9%	70.1%	13.1%
UNION	2,890	465	1,701	724	Bush	16.1%	58.9%	25.1%
WALLOWA	1,296	187	843	266	Bush	14.4%	65.0%	20.5%
WASCO	2,460	494	1,739	227	Bush	20.1%	70.7%	9.2%
WASHINGTON	33,611	6,520	24,043	3,048	Bush	19.4%	71.5%	9.1%
WHEELER	331	69	213	49	Bush	20.8%	64.4%	14.8%
YAMHILL	7,845	1,267	4,985	1,593	Bush	16.2%	63.5%	20.3%
TOTAL	304,159	57,730	203,957	42,472	Bush	19.0%	67.1%	14.0%

OREGON DEMOCRATIC

1996

County	Total Vote	Clinton	Other	Winner	Percentage of Total Vote	
					Clinton	Other
BAKER	2,038	1,770	268	Clinton	86.8%	13.2%
BENTON	6,894	6,512	382	Clinton	94.5%	5.5%
CLACKAMAS	34,789	34,174	615	Clinton	98.2%	1.8%
CLATSOP	4,916	4,612	304	Clinton	93.8%	6.2%
COLUMBIA	6,156	5,626	530	Clinton	91.4%	8.6%
COOS	9,801	8,535	1,266	Clinton	87.1%	12.9%
CROOK	1,914	1,736	178	Clinton	90.7%	9.3%
CURRY	3,125	2,766	359	Clinton	88.5%	11.5%
DESCHUTES	9,489	8,816	673	Clinton	92.9%	7.1%
DOUGLAS	10,493	9,222	1,271	Clinton	87.9%	12.1%
GILLIAM	300	277	23	Clinton	92.3%	7.7%
GRANT	954	740	214	Clinton	77.6%	22.4%
HARNEY	817	651	166	Clinton	79.7%	20.3%
HOOD RIVER	2,034	1,932	102	Clinton	95.0%	5.0%
JACKSON	15,624	15,130	494	Clinton	96.8%	3.2%
JEFFERSON	1,862	1,698	164	Clinton	91.2%	8.8%
JOSEPHINE	7,276	6,459	817	Clinton	88.8%	11.2%
KLAMATH	5,601	5,028	573	Clinton	89.8%	10.2%
LAKE	705	630	75	Clinton	89.4%	10.6%
LANE	41,092	40,130	962	Clinton	97.7%	2.3%
LINCOLN	6,879	6,390	489	Clinton	92.9%	7.1%
LINN	9,671	9,418	253	Clinton	97.4%	2.6%
MALHEUR	2,061	1,792	269	Clinton	86.9%	13.1%
MARION	28,144	25,875	2,269	Clinton	91.9%	8.1%
MORROW	1,026	929	97	Clinton	90.5%	9.5%
MULTNOMAH	88,094	83,871	4,223	Clinton	95.2%	4.8%
POLK	5,526	5,412	114	Clinton	97.9%	2.1%
SHERMAN	304	282	22	Clinton	92.8%	7.2%
TILLAMOOK	4,142	3,873	269	Clinton	93.5%	6.5%
UMATILLA	4,893	4,893		Clinton	100.0%	
UNION	3,207	2,986	221	Clinton	93.1%	6.9%
WALLOWA	1,134	908	226	Clinton	80.1%	19.9%
WASCO	2,962	2,788	174	Clinton	94.1%	5.9%
WASHINGTON	37,156	36,609	547	Clinton	98.5%	1.5%
WHEELER	201	176	25	Clinton	87.6%	12.4%
YAMHILL	7,898	7,225	673	Clinton	91.5%	8.5%
TOTAL	369,178	349,871	19,307	Clinton	94.8%	5.2%

OREGON REPUBLICAN

1996

County	Total Vote	Buchanan	Dole	Forbes	Other	Winner	Percentage of Total Vote Buchanan	Dole	Forbes	Other
BAKER	2,720	884	1,199	278	359	Dole	32.5%	44.1%	10.2%	13.2%
BENTON	9,122	1,337	4,997	1,398	1,390	Dole	14.7%	54.8%	15.3%	15.2%
CLACKAMAS	43,910	7,970	23,054	6,734	6,152	Dole	18.2%	52.5%	15.3%	14.0%
CLATSOP	4,310	896	2,038	632	744	Dole	20.8%	47.3%	14.7%	17.3%
COLUMBIA	4,306	1,169	1,959	542	636	Dole	27.1%	45.5%	12.6%	14.8%
COOS	7,893	2,224	3,297	1,275	1,097	Dole	28.2%	41.8%	16.2%	13.9%
CROOK	2,379	624	1,204	247	304	Dole	26.2%	50.6%	10.4%	12.8%
CURRY	4,157	1,244	1,807	537	569	Dole	29.9%	43.5%	12.9%	13.7%
DESCHUTES	15,113	3,224	7,254	2,322	2,313	Dole	21.3%	48.0%	15.4%	15.3%
DOUGLAS	14,929	4,288	6,982	1,671	1,988	Dole	28.7%	46.8%	11.2%	13.3%
GILLIAM	343	81	196	29	37	Dole	23.6%	57.1%	8.5%	10.8%
GRANT	1,390	418	643	126	203	Dole	30.1%	46.3%	9.1%	14.6%
HARNEY	1,244	353	602	116	173	Dole	28.4%	48.4%	9.3%	13.9%
HOOD RIVER	2,223	446	1,189	268	320	Dole	20.1%	53.5%	12.1%	14.4%
JACKSON	24,724	6,336	12,429	2,994	2,965	Dole	25.6%	50.3%	12.1%	12.0%
JEFFERSON	2,353	559	1,162	276	356	Dole	23.8%	49.4%	11.7%	15.1%
JOSEPHINE	12,736	3,696	5,951	1,545	1,544	Dole	29.0%	46.7%	12.1%	12.1%
KLAMATH	9,247	2,584	4,452	1,295	916	Dole	27.9%	48.1%	14.0%	9.9%
LAKE	1,327	379	675	135	138	Dole	28.6%	50.9%	10.2%	10.4%
LANE	36,507	8,602	17,890	4,430	5,585	Dole	23.6%	49.0%	12.1%	15.3%
LINCOLN	5,871	1,158	2,735	965	1,013	Dole	19.7%	46.6%	16.4%	17.3%
LINN	12,207	3,127	6,068	1,288	1,724	Dole	25.6%	49.7%	10.6%	14.1%
MALHEUR	4,288	980	2,372	382	554	Dole	22.9%	55.3%	8.9%	12.9%
MARION	36,580	7,070	19,334	4,598	5,578	Dole	19.3%	52.9%	12.6%	15.2%
MORROW	1,071	267	534	128	142	Dole	24.9%	49.9%	12.0%	13.3%
MULTNOMAH	56,961	10,503	29,088	7,703	9,667	Dole	18.4%	51.1%	13.5%	17.0%
POLK	8,574	1,702	4,650	893	1,329	Dole	19.9%	54.2%	10.4%	15.5%
SHERMAN	407	63	241	46	57	Dole	15.5%	59.2%	11.3%	14.0%
TILLAMOOK	3,343	749	1,611	463	520	Dole	22.4%	48.2%	13.8%	15.6%
UMATILLA	6,821	1,510	3,634	879	798	Dole	22.1%	53.3%	12.9%	11.7%
UNION	4,040	905	2,005	514	616	Dole	22.4%	49.6%	12.7%	15.2%
WALLOWA	1,730	433	845	232	220	Dole	25.0%	48.8%	13.4%	12.7%
WASCO	2,929	639	1,473	372	445	Dole	21.8%	50.3%	12.7%	15.2%
WASHINGTON	50,898	8,234	27,885	7,323	7,456	Dole	16.2%	54.8%	14.4%	14.6%
WHEELER	306	89	152	36	29	Dole	29.1%	49.7%	11.8%	9.5%
YAMHILL	10,555	2,244	5,331	1,449	1,531	Dole	21.3%	50.5%	13.7%	14.5%
TOTAL	407,514	86,987	206,938	54,121	59,468	Dole	21.3%	50.8%	13.3%	14.6%

PENNSYLVANIA

Pennsylvania held its first presidential primary on April 13, 1912—just hours before the Titanic encountered the iceberg. But the heyday of the Keystone State primary came more than a half century later, when candidates who fashioned themselves as champions of the lunch-bucket crowd first had to prove themselves in Pennsylvania.

Hubert Humphrey in 1972, Edward Kennedy in 1980 and Walter Mondale in 1984 all scored key victories in Democratic primary voting in Pennsylvania that advanced their candidacies. Henry Jackson lost the Pennsylvania primary decisively to Jimmy Carter in 1976, and folded his campaign shortly thereafter.

The state's electorate is less trendy and liberal than some of its Eastern neighbors. Rather, it has earned a reputation as the quintessential Frost Belt industrial state. Long dependent on coal and steel, it has a strong union tradition, a rich variety of ethnic groups, and fairly potent party organizations in the major population centers.

Pennsylvania's blue-collar Democrats have looked with suspicion on some of the party's more liberal presidential aspirants. George McGovern in 1972 and Morris Udall in 1976 both ran a poor third in the primary. Gary Hart fared little better in 1984, running nearly 200,000 votes behind Mondale. Of Pennsylvania's 67 counties, the only one to vote for McGovern, Udall and Hart was Centre County (which includes Penn State University).

Candidates, though, do not spend much time around Penn State in bucolic central Pennsylvania. The greatest concentration of votes is at opposite ends of the state, which frequently leads to intense regional competition. The Philadelphia area is an integral part of the Eastern megalopolis that spreads from Washington, D.C., to Boston. Western Pennsylvania, anchored by Allegheny County (Pittsburgh), faces the industrial Midwest. It tends to vote more like the adjacent "smokestack" region of Ohio than more cosmopolitan Philadelphia 300 miles away.

Recent Pennsylvania Primary Results

Pennsylvania held its first presidential primary in 1912.

	DEMOCRATS			REPUBLICANS		
Year	Turnout	Candidates	%	Turnout	Candidates	%
1996	724,069	BILL CLINTON*	92	684,204	BOB DOLE	64
(April 23)					Pat Buchanan	18
1992	1,265,495	BILL CLINTON	57	1,008,777	GEORGE BUSH*	77
(April 28)		Jerry Brown	26		Pat Buchanan	23
		Paul Tsongas	13			
1988	1,507,690	MICHAEL DUKAKIS	66	870,549	GEORGE BUSH	79
(April 26)		Jesse Jackson	27		Bob Dole	12
1984	1,656,294	WALTER MONDALE	45	621,206	RONALD REAGAN*	99
(April 10)		Gary Hart	33			
		Jesse Jackson	16			
1980	1,613,551	EDWARD KENNEDY	46	1,241,411	GEORGE BUSH	50
(April 22)		Jimmy Carter*	45		Ronald Reagan	43
1976	1,385,042	JIMMY CARTER	37	796,660	GERALD FORD*	92
(April 27)		Henry Jackson	25			
		Morris Udall	19			
		George Wallace	11			
1972	1,374,839	HUBERT HUMPHREY	35	184,801	RICHARD NIXON*#	83
(April 25)		George Wallace	21		George Wallace#	11
		George McGovern	20			
		Edmund Muskie	20			
1968	597,089	EUGENE McCARTHY	72	287,573	RICHARD NIXON#	60
(April 23)		Robert Kennedy#	11		Nelson Rockefeller#	18

Note: All candidates are listed that drew at least 10 percent of their party's primary vote. The names of winning candidates are capitalized. An asterisk (*) indicates an incumbent president. A pound sign (#) indicates a write-in candidate.

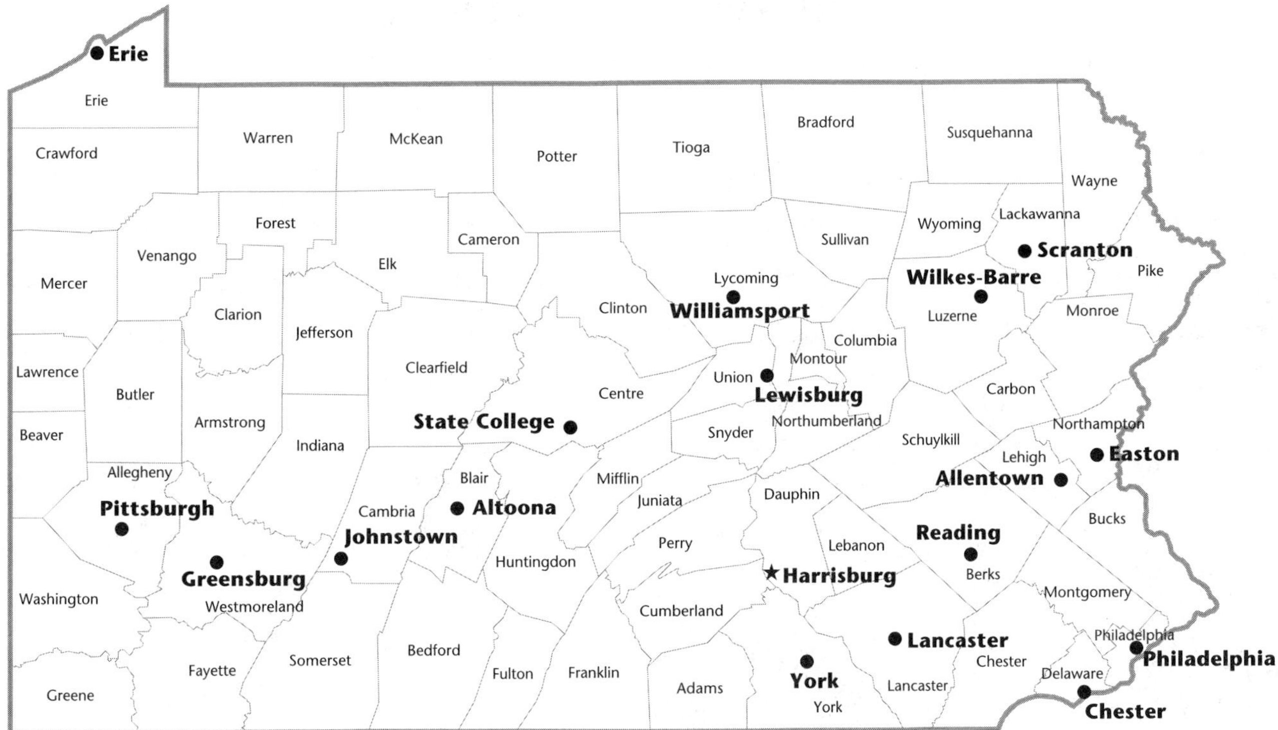

The regional rivalry can be quite sharp in Democratic contests. When Kennedy beat President Carter in 1980 by barely 4,000 votes, Kennedy won decisively in the Philadelphia area and carried several other industrial counties in eastern Pennsylvania. But west of the Susquehanna River, Kennedy could carry just one county.

The Democratic primary was not close at all in 1984, since Mondale was able to win both ends of the state. And it has not been particularly relevant since then, with the April voting coming too late to affect the nominating contests. Jesse Jackson could carry little more than Philadelphia in 1988 against Michael Dukakis. Four years later against Bill Clinton, Jerry Brown won only Luzerne (Wilkes-Barre) and Lacakawanna (Scranton) counties, the home base of the state's anti-abortion Democratic governor, Robert P. Casey.

Republican strength in Pennsylvania is concentrated in two areas—the Philadelphia suburbs and a part of the state known as the Republican "T." The latter is the predominantly rural central portion of the state that extends northward from the Pennsylvania Dutch country through the Susquehanna River Valley to the forested northern tier of counties along the New York border.

In defeating Ronald Reagan in the 1980 GOP primary, George Bush built up a lead in the Philadelphia suburbs and western Pennsylvania that Reagan could not overcome in the Republican "T" and Philadelphia, where Reagan had the backing of the city's GOP leadership.

Bush's victory in Pennsylvania in 1980, though, came too late to slow Reagan's bid for the GOP nomination. But it did embellish Bush's credentials as a potential running mate for Reagan, an eventuality that came to pass several months later.

PENNSYLVANIA DEMOCRATIC

1968

County	Total Vote	McCarthy	R. Kennedy	Other	Winner	Percentage of Total Vote McCarthy	R. Kennedy	Other
ADAMS	1,942	1,494	3	445	McCarthy	76.9%	0.2%	22.9%
ALLEGHENY	135,041	93,975	13,168	27,898	McCarthy	69.6%	9.8%	20.7%
ARMSTRONG	4,047	2,200	714	1,133	McCarthy	54.4%	17.6%	28.0%
BEAVER	16,107	9,402	2,665	4,040	McCarthy	58.4%	16.5%	25.1%
BEDFORD	1,821	1,028	322	471	McCarthy	56.5%	17.7%	25.9%
BERKS	18,776	16,561	787	1,428	McCarthy	88.2%	4.2%	7.6%
BLAIR	6,988	4,172	1,141	1,675	McCarthy	59.7%	16.3%	24.0%
BRADFORD	1,670	1,200	222	248	McCarthy	71.9%	13.3%	14.9%
BUCKS	16,188	12,637	1,274	2,277	McCarthy	78.1%	7.9%	14.1%
BUTLER	5,127	3,675	554	898	McCarthy	71.7%	10.8%	17.5%
CAMBRIA	17,740	9,061	2,892	5,787	McCarthy	51.1%	16.3%	32.6%
CAMERON	369	231	61	77	McCarthy	62.6%	16.5%	20.9%
CARBON	2,247	1,998	129	120	McCarthy	88.9%	5.7%	5.3%
CENTRE	3,868	2,374	555	939	McCarthy	61.4%	14.3%	24.3%
CHESTER	8,341	4,336	1,582	2,423	McCarthy	52.0%	19.0%	29.0%
CLARION	2,274	1,520	331	423	McCarthy	66.8%	14.6%	18.6%
CLEARFIELD	5,812	4,106	750	956	McCarthy	70.6%	12.9%	16.4%
CLINTON	1,530	793	273	464	McCarthy	51.8%	17.8%	30.3%
COLUMBIA	3,309	2,018	549	742	McCarthy	61.0%	16.6%	22.4%
CRAWFORD	2,371	1,755	241	375	McCarthy	74.0%	10.2%	15.8%
CUMBERLAND	4,274	3,613	268	393	McCarthy	84.5%	6.3%	9.2%
DAUPHIN	4,915	4,293	310	312	McCarthy	87.3%	6.3%	6.3%
DELAWARE	6,547	4,325	850	1,372	McCarthy	66.1%	13.0%	21.0%
ELK	2,260	1,520	397	343	McCarthy	67.3%	17.6%	15.2%
ERIE	10,543	9,320	629	594	McCarthy	88.4%	6.0%	5.6%
FAYETTE	10,119	9,442	259	418	McCarthy	93.3%	2.6%	4.1%
FOREST	221	116	43	62	McCarthy	52.5%	19.5%	28.1%
FRANKLIN	4,190	2,596	659	935	McCarthy	62.0%	15.7%	22.3%
FULTON	363	225	46	92	McCarthy	62.0%	12.7%	25.3%
GREENE	4,072	2,517	613	942	McCarthy	61.8%	15.1%	23.1%
HUNTINGDON	1,618	864	314	440	McCarthy	53.4%	19.4%	27.2%
INDIANA	3,979	2,143	752	1,084	McCarthy	53.9%	18.9%	27.2%
JEFFERSON	2,524	1,432	540	552	McCarthy	56.7%	21.4%	21.9%
JUNIATA	902	529	185	188	McCarthy	58.6%	20.5%	20.8%
LACKAWANNA	14,078	12,652	714	712	McCarthy	89.9%	5.1%	5.1%
LANCASTER	6,504	4,504	860	1,140	McCarthy	69.2%	13.2%	17.5%
LAWRENCE	5,836	3,583	1,190	1,063	McCarthy	61.4%	20.4%	18.2%
LEBANON	1,655	1,430	88	137	McCarthy	86.4%	5.3%	8.3%
LEHIGH	8,020	6,676	510	834	McCarthy	83.2%	6.4%	10.4%
LUZERNE	13,059	11,143	1,161	755	McCarthy	85.3%	8.9%	5.8%
LYCOMING	4,799	2,748	901	1,150	McCarthy	57.3%	18.8%	24.0%
MCKEAN	1,128	953	96	79	McCarthy	84.5%	8.5%	7.0%
MERCER	4,664	3,991	320	353	McCarthy	85.6%	6.9%	7.6%
MIFFLIN	1,403	1,197	97	109	McCarthy	85.3%	6.9%	7.8%
MONROE	1,922	1,651	83	188	McCarthy	85.9%	4.3%	9.8%
MONTGOMERY	17,185	13,284	1,401	2,500	McCarthy	77.3%	8.2%	14.5%
MONTOUR	864	474	206	184	McCarthy	54.9%	23.8%	21.3%
NORTHAMPTON	10,050	8,607	603	840	McCarthy	85.6%	6.0%	8.4%
NORTHUMBERLAND	5,422	3,080	1,506	836	McCarthy	56.8%	27.8%	15.4%
PERRY	1,191	875	143	173	McCarthy	73.5%	12.0%	14.5%

PENNSYLVANIA DEMOCRATIC

1968

County	Total Vote	McCarthy	R. Kennedy	Other	Winner	Percentage of Total Vote McCarthy	R. Kennedy	Other
PHILADELPHIA	102,909	82,684	8,889	11,336	McCarthy	80.3%	8.6%	11.0%
PIKE	363	288	14	61	McCarthy	79.3%	3.9%	16.8%
POTTER	768	478	141	149	McCarthy	62.2%	18.4%	19.4%
SCHUYLKILL	7,092	3,654	1,514	1,924	McCarthy	51.5%	21.3%	27.1%
SNYDER	925	501	225	199	McCarthy	54.2%	24.3%	21.5%
SOMERSET	5,514	3,587	707	1,220	McCarthy	65.1%	12.8%	22.1%
SULLIVAN	437	277	103	57	McCarthy	63.4%	23.6%	13.0%
SUSQUEHANNA	1,395	894	266	235	McCarthy	64.1%	19.1%	16.8%
TIOGA	1,104	598	223	283	McCarthy	54.2%	20.2%	25.6%
UNION	896	516	186	194	McCarthy	57.6%	20.8%	21.7%
VENANGO	2,005	1,150	321	534	McCarthy	57.4%	16.0%	26.6%
WARREN	1,077	882	108	87	McCarthy	81.9%	10.0%	8.1%
WASHINGTON	22,667	12,775	3,936	5,956	McCarthy	56.4%	17.4%	26.3%
WAYNE	845	690	72	83	McCarthy	81.7%	8.5%	9.8%
WESTMORELAND	33,094	20,816	4,261	8,017	McCarthy	62.9%	12.9%	24.2%
WYOMING	755	428	108	219	McCarthy	56.7%	14.3%	29.0%
YORK	9,050	7,722	399	929	McCarthy	85.3%	4.4%	10.3%
TOTAL	601,986	432,259	65,430	104,297	McCarthy	71.8%	10.9%	17.3%
Published Totals	597,089	428,259	65,430	103,400	McCarthy	71.7%	11.0%	17.3%

Note: McCarthy was the only candidate listed on the ballot. All other votes cast, including those for R. Kennedy, were write-ins. The "Total Vote" and "Other" vote totals include 1,215 scattered write-ins that were not readily available on a county-by-county basis.

PENNSYLVANIA REPUBLICAN

1968

County	Total Vote	Nixon	Rockefeller	Other	Winner	Percentage of Total Vote Nixon	Rockefeller	Other
ADAMS	3,219	2,372	447	400	Nixon	73.7%	13.9%	12.4%
ALLEGHENY	37,750	19,436	8,130	10,184	Nixon	51.5%	21.5%	27.0%
ARMSTRONG	4,837	3,103	742	992	Nixon	64.2%	15.3%	20.5%
BEAVER	5,166	4,139		1,027	Nixon	80.1%		19.9%
BEDFORD	3,339	2,642	331	366	Nixon	79.1%	9.9%	11.0%
BERKS	2,454	1,378	535	541	Nixon	56.2%	21.8%	22.0%
BLAIR	11,589	8,674	949	1,966	Nixon	74.8%	8.2%	17.0%
BRADFORD	4,329	3,226	447	656	Nixon	74.5%	10.3%	15.2%
BUCKS	4,578	1,961	1,422	1,195	Nixon	42.8%	31.1%	26.1%
BUTLER	3,315	2,192	482	641	Nixon	66.1%	14.5%	19.3%
CAMBRIA	10,948	7,403	1,450	2,095	Nixon	67.6%	13.2%	19.1%
CAMERON	598	477	35	86	Nixon	79.8%	5.9%	14.4%
CARBON	261	170	55	36	Nixon	65.1%	21.1%	13.8%
CENTRE	5,389	3,272	1,047	1,070	Nixon	60.7%	19.4%	19.9%
CHESTER	19,381	10,133	3,877	5,371	Nixon	52.3%	20.0%	27.7%
CLARION	2,515	1,812	266	437	Nixon	72.0%	10.6%	17.4%
CLEARFIELD	3,588	2,690	339	559	Nixon	75.0%	9.4%	15.6%
CLINTON	1,938	1,148	436	354	Nixon	59.2%	22.5%	18.3%
COLUMBIA	2,662	1,881	332	449	Nixon	70.7%	12.5%	16.9%
CRAWFORD	1,801	1,214	289	298	Nixon	67.4%	16.0%	16.5%

PENNSYLVANIA REPUBLICAN

1968

County	Total Vote	Nixon	Rockefeller	Other	Winner	Percentage of Total Vote Nixon	Rockefeller	Other
CUMBERLAND	1,632	887	435	310	Nixon	54.4%	26.7%	19.0%
DAUPHIN	1,270	779	332	159	Nixon	61.3%	26.1%	12.5%
DELAWARE	5,760	2,374	1,376	2,010	Nixon	41.2%	23.9%	34.9%
ELK	1,407	924	212	271	Nixon	65.7%	15.1%	19.3%
ERIE	1,404	766	393	245	Nixon	54.6%	28.0%	17.5%
FAYETTE	391	299	63	29	Nixon	76.5%	16.1%	7.4%
FOREST	440	311	54	75	Nixon	70.7%	12.3%	17.0%
FRANKLIN	5,296	3,388	1,056	852	Nixon	64.0%	19.9%	16.1%
FULTON	451	360	35	56	Nixon	79.8%	7.8%	12.4%
GREENE	980	775	126	79	Nixon	79.1%	12.9%	8.1%
HUNTINGDON	3,338	2,477	312	549	Nixon	74.2%	9.3%	16.4%
INDIANA	6,369	4,196	847	1,326	Nixon	65.9%	13.3%	20.8%
JEFFERSON	3,791	2,710	476	605	Nixon	71.5%	12.6%	16.0%
JUNIATA	1,104	923	156	25	Nixon	83.6%	14.1%	2.3%
LACKAWANNA	692	436	256		Nixon	63.0%	37.0%	
LANCASTER	7,586	5,059	1,227	1,300	Nixon	66.7%	16.2%	17.1%
LAWRENCE	4,115	2,615	721	779	Nixon	63.5%	17.5%	18.9%
LEBANON	943	605	161	177	Nixon	64.2%	17.1%	18.8%
LEHIGH	1,945	1,002	570	373	Nixon	51.5%	29.3%	19.2%
LUZERNE	1,562	940	387	235	Nixon	60.2%	24.8%	15.0%
LYCOMING	6,090	3,982	1,389	719	Nixon	65.4%	22.8%	11.8%
MCKEAN	545	396	70	79	Nixon	72.7%	12.8%	14.5%
MERCER	1,385	925	197	263	Nixon	66.8%	14.2%	19.0%
MIFFLIN	395	269	66	60	Nixon	68.1%	16.7%	15.2%
MONROE	450	257	103	90	Nixon	57.1%	22.9%	20.0%
MONTGOMERY	15,304	5,081	4,821	5,402	Nixon	33.2%	31.5%	35.3%
MONTOUR	962	695	137	130	Nixon	72.2%	14.2%	13.5%
NORTHAMPTON	1,811	837	466	508	Nixon	46.2%	25.7%	28.1%
NORTHUMBERLAND	5,629	4,181	850	598	Nixon	74.3%	15.1%	10.6%
PERRY	1,342	996	172	174	Nixon	74.2%	12.8%	13.0%
PHILADELPHIA	14,852	5,584	5,712	3,556	Rockefeller	37.6%	38.5%	23.9%
PIKE	420	303	64	53	Nixon	72.1%	15.2%	12.6%
POTTER	1,440	1,080	174	186	Nixon	75.0%	12.1%	12.9%
SCHUYLKILL	9,198	5,095	1,596	2,507	Nixon	55.4%	17.4%	27.3%
SNYDER	2,529	2,000	144	385	Nixon	79.1%	5.7%	15.2%
SOMERSET	5,639	4,462	647	530	Nixon	79.1%	11.5%	9.4%
SULLIVAN	513	357	84	72	Nixon	69.6%	16.4%	14.0%
SUSQUEHANNA	2,561	1,763	361	437	Nixon	68.8%	14.1%	17.1%
TIOGA	3,161	2,225	334	602	Nixon	70.4%	10.6%	19.0%
UNION	2,270	1,617	295	358	Nixon	71.2%	13.0%	15.8%
VENANGO	4,489	3,174	514	801	Nixon	70.7%	11.5%	17.8%
WARREN	622	402	110	110	Nixon	64.6%	17.7%	17.7%
WASHINGTON	6,918	5,225	1,268	425	Nixon	75.5%	18.3%	6.1%
WAYNE	1,064	785	135	144	Nixon	73.8%	12.7%	13.5%
WESTMORELAND	10,989	6,773	1,791	2,425	Nixon	61.6%	16.3%	22.1%
WYOMING	1,539	1,084	229	226	Nixon	70.4%	14.9%	14.7%
YORK	1,836	1,118	380	338	Nixon	60.9%	20.7%	18.4%
TOTAL	286,649	171,815	52,915	61,919	Nixon	59.9%	18.5%	21.6%
Published Totals	287,573	171,815	52,915	62,843	Nixon	59.7%	18.4%	21.9%

Note: All votes cast were write-ins. The "Total Vote" and "Other" vote totals include 2,563 scattered write-ins that were not readily available on a county-by-county basis.

PENNSYLVANIA DEMOCRATIC

1972

County	Total Vote	Humphrey	McGovern	Muskie	Wallace	Other	Winner	Percentage of Total Vote Humphrey	McGovern	Muskie	Wallace	Other
ADAMS	3,933	1,183	865	813	945	127	Humphrey	30.1%	22.0%	20.7%	24.0%	3.2%
ALLEGHENY	274,394	87,487	54,379	41,714	84,693	6,121	Humphrey	31.9%	19.8%	15.2%	30.9%	2.2%
ARMSTRONG	7,586	3,831	980	1,190	1,467	118	Humphrey	50.5%	12.9%	15.7%	19.3%	1.6%
BEAVER	32,991	14,424	3,829	4,572	9,640	526	Humphrey	43.7%	11.6%	13.9%	29.2%	1.6%
BEDFORD	3,503	1,197	446	780	971	109	Humphrey	34.2%	12.7%	22.3%	27.7%	3.1%
BERKS	37,407	14,045	7,993	6,552	7,458	1,359	Humphrey	37.5%	21.4%	17.5%	19.9%	3.6%
BLAIR	10,005	4,209	1,454	1,688	2,324	330	Humphrey	42.1%	14.5%	16.9%	23.2%	3.3%
BRADFORD	3,791	1,399	734	857	702	99	Humphrey	36.9%	19.4%	22.6%	18.5%	2.6%
BUCKS	35,566	8,931	12,216	6,570	6,679	1,170	McGovern	25.1%	34.3%	18.5%	18.8%	3.3%
BUTLER	12,310	5,721	2,075	1,666	2,641	207	Humphrey	46.5%	16.9%	13.5%	21.5%	1.7%
CAMBRIA	29,653	14,145	2,966	5,241	6,460	841	Humphrey	47.7%	10.0%	17.7%	21.8%	2.8%
CAMERON	726	298	83	181	146	18	Humphrey	41.0%	11.4%	24.9%	20.1%	2.5%
CARBON	5,629	1,845	762	2,006	855	161	Muskie	32.8%	13.5%	35.6%	15.2%	2.9%
CENTRE	7,813	2,215	2,820	1,617	959	202	McGovern	28.4%	36.1%	20.7%	12.3%	2.6%
CHESTER	16,680	4,982	5,053	2,817	3,379	449	McGovern	29.9%	30.3%	16.9%	20.3%	2.7%
CLARION	4,022	1,627	718	580	1,010	87	Humphrey	40.5%	17.9%	14.4%	25.1%	2.2%
CLEARFIELD	9,309	3,960	1,086	2,157	1,826	280	Humphrey	42.5%	11.7%	23.2%	19.6%	3.0%
CLINTON	4,085	1,645	920	822	601	97	Humphrey	40.3%	22.5%	20.1%	14.7%	2.4%
COLUMBIA	6,402	1,677	1,525	1,216	1,805	179	Wallace	26.2%	23.8%	19.0%	28.2%	2.8%
CRAWFORD	5,868	1,987	1,337	1,099	1,205	240	Humphrey	33.9%	22.8%	18.7%	20.5%	4.1%
CUMBERLAND	10,368	3,052	2,666	1,873	2,397	380	Humphrey	29.4%	25.7%	18.1%	23.1%	3.7%
DAUPHIN	15,231	4,662	3,146	3,241	3,344	838	Humphrey	30.6%	20.7%	21.3%	22.0%	5.5%
DELAWARE	36,217	9,449	13,784	6,730	5,098	1,156	McGovern	26.1%	38.1%	18.6%	14.1%	3.2%
ELK	4,062	1,569	656	795	933	109	Humphrey	38.6%	16.1%	19.6%	23.0%	2.7%
ERIE	36,533	10,233	8,369	10,218	7,073	640	Humphrey	28.0%	22.9%	28.0%	19.4%	1.8%
FAYETTE	30,487	12,861	2,594	4,332	10,000	700	Humphrey	42.2%	8.5%	14.2%	32.8%	2.3%
FOREST	469	181	53	91	125	19	Humphrey	38.6%	11.3%	19.4%	26.7%	4.1%
FRANKLIN	7,128	3,233	1,061	823	1,726	285	Humphrey	45.4%	14.9%	11.5%	24.2%	4.0%
FULTON	1,091	411	101	187	358	34	Humphrey	37.7%	9.3%	17.1%	32.8%	3.1%
GREENE	8,211	3,480	954	1,210	2,378	189	Humphrey	42.4%	11.6%	14.7%	29.0%	2.3%
HUNTINGDON	2,910	1,147	397	676	626	64	Humphrey	39.4%	13.6%	23.2%	21.5%	2.2%
INDIANA	7,969	3,209	1,468	1,652	1,508	132	Humphrey	40.3%	18.4%	20.7%	18.9%	1.7%
JEFFERSON	3,986	1,580	527	989	781	109	Humphrey	39.6%	13.2%	24.8%	19.6%	2.7%
JUNIATA	1,744	752	268	309	366	49	Humphrey	43.1%	15.4%	17.7%	21.0%	2.8%
LACKAWANNA	43,799	12,779	7,851	18,092	4,288	789	Muskie	29.2%	17.9%	41.3%	9.8%	1.8%
LANCASTER	11,285	3,346	3,612	1,736	2,223	368	McGovern	29.6%	32.0%	15.4%	19.7%	3.3%
LAWRENCE	13,892	6,187	1,670	2,935	2,750	350	Humphrey	44.5%	12.0%	21.1%	19.8%	2.5%
LEBANON	3,777	1,223	863	554	934	203	Humphrey	32.4%	22.8%	14.7%	24.7%	5.4%
LEHIGH	21,420	9,062	4,119	4,423	3,093	723	Humphrey	42.3%	19.2%	20.6%	14.4%	3.4%
LUZERNE	41,036	7,943	6,486	19,115	6,596	896	Muskie	19.4%	15.8%	46.6%	16.1%	2.2%
LYCOMING	9,831	3,653	2,243	1,656	2,074	205	Humphrey	37.2%	22.8%	16.8%	21.1%	2.1%
MCKEAN	2,911	1,304	506	529	451	121	Humphrey	44.8%	17.4%	18.2%	15.5%	4.2%
MERCER	12,828	4,813	2,812	2,330	2,334	539	Humphrey	37.5%	21.9%	18.2%	18.2%	4.2%
MIFFLIN	2,898	1,287	580	383	525	123	Humphrey	44.4%	20.0%	13.2%	18.1%	4.2%
MONROE	4,989	1,646	1,092	808	1,276	167	Humphrey	33.0%	21.9%	16.2%	25.6%	3.3%
MONTGOMERY	37,938	10,017	16,151	6,382	4,130	1,258	McGovern	26.4%	42.6%	16.8%	10.9%	3.3%
MONTOUR	1,755	574	306	389	437	49	Humphrey	32.7%	17.4%	22.2%	24.9%	2.8%
NORTHAMPTON	24,052	9,981	4,946	4,827	3,655	643	Humphrey	41.5%	20.6%	20.1%	15.2%	2.7%
NORTHUMBERLAND	11,981	2,548	1,596	5,474	2,157	206	Muskie	21.3%	13.3%	45.7%	18.0%	1.7%
PERRY	2,460	790	375	464	769	62	Humphrey	32.1%	15.2%	18.9%	31.3%	2.5%

PENNSYLVANIA DEMOCRATIC

1972

County	Total Vote	Humphrey	McGovern	Muskie	Wallace	Other	Winner	Percentage of Total Vote Humphrey	McGovern	Muskie	Wallace	Other
PHILADELPHIA	276,613	112,787	59,708	55,388	37,306	11,424	Humphrey	40.8%	21.6%	20.0%	13.5%	4.1%
PIKE	902	290	177	173	229	33	Humphrey	32.2%	19.6%	19.2%	25.4%	3.7%
POTTER	1,680	682	258	330	373	37	Humphrey	40.6%	15.4%	19.6%	22.2%	2.2%
SCHUYLKILL	18,510	4,657	1,940	8,780	2,774	359	Muskie	25.2%	10.5%	47.4%	15.0%	1.9%
SNYDER	1,418	438	319	253	374	34	Humphrey	30.9%	22.5%	17.8%	26.4%	2.4%
SOMERSET	8,059	3,963	634	1,314	1,981	167	Humphrey	49.2%	7.9%	16.3%	24.6%	2.1%
SULLIVAN	978	381	120	266	189	22	Humphrey	39.0%	12.3%	27.2%	19.3%	2.2%
SUSQUEHANNA	3,303	849	681	1,142	585	46	Muskie	25.7%	20.6%	34.6%	17.7%	1.4%
TIOGA	2,858	965	600	673	567	53	Humphrey	33.8%	21.0%	23.5%	19.8%	1.9%
UNION	1,526	414	550	232	301	29	McGovern	27.1%	36.0%	15.2%	19.7%	1.9%
VENANGO	3,843	1,728	646	727	677	65	Humphrey	45.0%	16.8%	18.9%	17.6%	1.7%
WARREN	2,756	1,060	610	588	418	80	Humphrey	38.5%	22.1%	21.3%	15.2%	2.9%
WASHINGTON	39,367	14,036	4,926	7,298	12,428	679	Humphrey	35.7%	12.5%	18.5%	31.6%	1.7%
WAYNE	1,967	461	423	684	349	50	Muskie	23.4%	21.5%	34.8%	17.7%	2.5%
WESTMORELAND	61,795	21,736	10,397	10,722	17,637	1,303	Humphrey	35.2%	16.8%	17.4%	28.5%	2.1%
WYOMING	2,066	658	557	446	371	34	Humphrey	31.8%	27.0%	21.6%	18.0%	1.6%
YORK	21,619	7,015	4,822	3,606	5,407	769	Humphrey	32.4%	22.3%	16.7%	25.0%	3.6%
TOTAL	1,374,539	481,900	280,861	279,983	292,137	39,658	Humphrey	35.1%	20.4%	20.4%	21.3%	2.9%
Certified Totals	1,374,839	481,900	280,861	279,983	292,437	39,658	Humphrey	35.1%	20.4%	20.4%	21.3%	2.9%

Note: The "Total Vote" and "Other" vote totals include 348 scattered write-ins that were not readily available on a county-by-county basis.

PENNSYLVANIA REPUBLICAN

1972

County	Total Vote	Nixon	Wallace	Other	Winner	Percentage of Total Vote Nixon	Wallace	Other
ADAMS	3,482	3,105	240	137	Nixon	89.2%	6.9%	3.9%
ALLEGHENY	5,201	1,529	2,679	993	Wallace	29.4%	51.5%	19.1%
ARMSTRONG	5,022	3,807	632	583	Nixon	75.8%	12.6%	11.6%
BEAVER	8,004	5,968	1,601	435	Nixon	74.6%	20.0%	5.4%
BEDFORD	4,180	3,799	334	47	Nixon	90.9%	8.0%	1.1%
BERKS	702	199	53	450	Humphrey	28.3%	7.5%	64.1%
BLAIR	12,400	11,271	1,129		Nixon	90.9%	9.1%	
BRADFORD	4,944	4,187	377	380	Nixon	84.7%	7.6%	7.7%
BUCKS	307	182	75	50	Nixon	59.3%	24.4%	16.3%
BUTLER	3,217	2,440	550	227	Nixon	75.8%	17.1%	7.1%
CAMBRIA	11,680	10,088	1,184	408	Nixon	86.4%	10.1%	3.5%
CAMERON	655	566	64	25	Nixon	86.4%	9.8%	3.8%
CARBON	101	87	14		Nixon	86.1%	13.9%	
CENTRE	5,147	4,367	332	448	Nixon	84.8%	6.5%	8.7%
CHESTER	8,444	7,590	854		Nixon	89.9%	10.1%	
CLARION	2,695	2,284	273	138	Nixon	84.7%	10.1%	5.1%
CLEARFIELD	3,315	2,845	286	184	Nixon	85.8%	8.6%	5.6%
CLINTON	2,994	2,455	241	298	Nixon	82.0%	8.0%	10.0%
COLUMBIA	2,601	2,144	353	104	Nixon	82.4%	13.6%	4.0%
CRAWFORD	1,322	1,153	116	53	Nixon	87.2%	8.8%	4.0%

PENNSYLVANIA REPUBLICAN

1972

County	Total Vote	Nixon	Wallace	Other	Winner	Percentage of Total Vote Nixon	Wallace	Other
CUMBERLAND	222	150	59	13	Nixon	67.6%	26.6%	5.9%
DAUPHIN	260	195	54	11	Nixon	75.0%	20.8%	4.2%
DELAWARE	125	88	37		Nixon	70.4%	29.6%	
ELK	1,634	1,449	154	31	Nixon	88.7%	9.4%	1.9%
ERIE	375	270	81	24	Nixon	72.0%	21.6%	6.4%
FAYETTE	43	37	6		Nixon	86.0%	14.0%	
FOREST	425	373	31	21	Nixon	87.8%	7.3%	4.9%
FRANKLIN	3,468	2,979	314	175	Nixon	85.9%	9.1%	5.0%
FULTON	499	466	23	10	Nixon	93.4%	4.6%	2.0%
GREENE	1,197	983	178	36	Nixon	82.1%	14.9%	3.0%
HUNTINGDON	2,538	2,538			Nixon	100.0%		
INDIANA	5,570	4,767	639	164	Nixon	85.6%	11.5%	2.9%
JEFFERSON	3,811	3,309	301	201	Nixon	86.8%	7.9%	5.3%
JUNIATA	1,449	1,348	81	20	Nixon	93.0%	5.6%	1.4%
LACKAWANNA	404	391	13		Nixon	96.8%	3.2%	
LANCASTER	5,539	5,125	312	102	Nixon	92.5%	5.6%	1.8%
LAWRENCE	5,138	3,753	770	615	Nixon	73.0%	15.0%	12.0%
LEBANON	170	142	19	9	Nixon	83.5%	11.2%	5.3%
LEHIGH	646	596	50		Nixon	92.3%	7.7%	
LUZERNE	412	332	80		Nixon	80.6%	19.4%	
LYCOMING	6,456	6,456			Nixon	100.0%		
MCKEAN	383	318	38	27	Nixon	83.0%	9.9%	7.0%
MERCER	622	541	58	23	Nixon	87.0%	9.3%	3.7%
MIFFLIN	213	182	18	13	Nixon	85.4%	8.5%	6.1%
MONROE	238	87	127	24	Wallace	36.6%	53.4%	10.1%
MONTGOMERY	797	440	209	148	Nixon	55.2%	26.2%	18.6%
MONTOUR	994	806	137	51	Nixon	81.1%	13.8%	5.1%
NORTHAMPTON	125	99	26		Nixon	79.2%	20.8%	
NORTHUMBERLAND	8,587	7,574	773	240	Nixon	88.2%	9.0%	2.8%
PERRY	1,275	1,126	149		Nixon	88.3%	11.7%	
PHILADELPHIA	446	369	77		Nixon	82.7%	17.3%	
PIKE	166	131	33	2	Nixon	78.9%	19.9%	1.2%
POTTER	1,313	1,137	109	67	Nixon	86.6%	8.3%	5.1%
SCHUYLKILL	8,240	6,641	854	745	Nixon	80.6%	10.4%	9.0%
SNYDER	2,741	2,323	304	114	Nixon	84.8%	11.1%	4.2%
SOMERSET	6,636	5,867	544	225	Nixon	88.4%	8.2%	3.4%
SULLIVAN	676	603	60	13	Nixon	89.2%	8.9%	1.9%
SUSQUEHANNA	2,260	2,260			Nixon	100.0%		
TIOGA	3,558	3,558			Nixon	100.0%		
UNION	2,221	1,879	231	111	Nixon	84.6%	10.4%	5.0%
VENANGO	4,059	3,145	478	436	Nixon	77.5%	11.8%	10.7%
WARREN	505	414	54	37	Nixon	82.0%	10.7%	7.3%
WASHINGTON	8,197	6,417	1,211	569	Nixon	78.3%	14.8%	6.9%
WAYNE	790	666	82	42	Nixon	84.3%	10.4%	5.3%
WESTMORELAND	774	435	257	82	Nixon	56.2%	33.2%	10.6%
WYOMING	1,854	1,582	152	120	Nixon	85.3%	8.2%	6.5%
YORK	324	279	39	6	Nixon	86.1%	12.0%	1.9%
TOTAL	185,795	154,692	20,609	10,494	Nixon	83.3%	11.1%	5.6%
Certified Totals	184,801	153,886	20,472	10,443	Nixon	83.3%	11.1%	5.7%

Note: All votes cast were write-ins. Wallace and Humphrey were Democrats. The "Total Vote" and "Other" vote totals include 1,007 scattered write-ins that were not readily available on a county-by-county basis.

PENNSYLVANIA DEMOCRATIC

1976

County	Total Vote	Carter	H. Jackson	Udall	Wallace	Other	Winner	Percentage of Total Vote Carter	H. Jackson	Udall	Wallace	Other
ADAMS	4,304	2,095	591	806	539	273	Carter	48.7%	13.7%	18.7%	12.5%	6.3%
ALLEGHENY	251,117	91,430	52,234	47,711	35,339	24,403	Carter	36.4%	20.8%	19.0%	14.1%	9.7%
ARMSTRONG	8,224	3,727	1,654	1,053	904	886	Carter	45.3%	20.1%	12.8%	11.0%	10.8%
BEAVER	34,278	14,084	7,058	3,974	4,913	4,249	Carter	41.1%	20.6%	11.6%	14.3%	12.4%
BEDFORD	3,931	2,073	731	324	533	270	Carter	52.7%	18.6%	8.2%	13.6%	6.9%
BERKS	35,250	13,058	7,525	7,681	4,346	2,640	Carter	37.0%	21.3%	21.8%	12.3%	7.5%
BLAIR	10,846	5,212	2,146	1,096	1,181	1,211	Carter	48.1%	19.8%	10.1%	10.9%	11.2%
BRADFORD	4,249	1,826	893	592	481	457	Carter	43.0%	21.0%	13.9%	11.3%	10.8%
BUCKS	35,878	11,568	7,672	9,898	3,943	2,797	Carter	32.2%	21.4%	27.6%	11.0%	7.8%
BUTLER	13,594	6,698	1,942	2,355	1,694	905	Carter	49.3%	14.3%	17.3%	12.5%	6.7%
CAMBRIA	26,991	9,246	7,955	3,734	2,859	3,197	Carter	34.3%	29.5%	13.8%	10.6%	11.8%
CAMERON	879	508	135	60	93	83	Carter	57.8%	15.4%	6.8%	10.6%	9.4%
CARBON	5,128	2,040	1,240	820	523	505	Carter	39.8%	24.2%	16.0%	10.2%	9.8%
CENTRE	10,549	3,725	1,353	3,815	705	951	Udall	35.3%	12.8%	36.2%	6.7%	9.0%
CHESTER	14,828	6,042	2,362	4,379	1,162	883	Carter	40.7%	15.9%	29.5%	7.8%	6.0%
CLARION	4,133	2,129	631	611	559	203	Carter	51.5%	15.3%	14.8%	13.5%	4.9%
CLEARFIELD	8,478	3,768	1,981	1,190	970	569	Carter	44.4%	23.4%	14.0%	11.4%	6.7%
CLINTON	3,053	1,469	490	558	259	277	Carter	48.1%	16.0%	18.3%	8.5%	9.1%
COLUMBIA	8,786	4,108	1,437	1,694	919	628	Carter	46.8%	16.4%	19.3%	10.5%	7.1%
CRAWFORD	7,628	3,309	1,592	1,321	970	436	Carter	43.4%	20.9%	17.3%	12.7%	5.7%
CUMBERLAND	14,134	5,734	2,351	3,046	1,383	1,620	Carter	40.6%	16.6%	21.6%	9.8%	11.5%
DAUPHIN	18,771	6,903	3,462	4,056	2,120	2,230	Carter	36.8%	18.4%	21.6%	11.3%	11.9%
DELAWARE	34,233	10,753	7,699	10,115	2,490	3,176	Carter	31.4%	22.5%	29.5%	7.3%	9.3%
ELK	4,390	1,968	834	491	553	544	Carter	44.8%	19.0%	11.2%	12.6%	12.4%
ERIE	41,040	16,440	8,668	7,424	5,219	3,289	Carter	40.1%	21.1%	18.1%	12.7%	8.0%
FAYETTE	29,992	10,818	8,703	3,355	5,614	1,502	Carter	36.1%	29.0%	11.2%	18.7%	5.0%
FOREST	562	265	109	82	73	33	Carter	47.2%	19.4%	14.6%	13.0%	5.9%
FRANKLIN	7,104	2,725	1,160	1,204	1,017	998	Carter	38.4%	16.3%	16.9%	14.3%	14.0%
FULTON	1,413	725	182	95	347	64	Carter	51.3%	12.9%	6.7%	24.6%	4.5%
GREENE	8,818	3,898	1,387	1,007	1,591	935	Carter	44.2%	15.7%	11.4%	18.0%	10.6%
HUNTINGDON	3,160	1,484	547	346	441	342	Carter	47.0%	17.3%	10.9%	14.0%	10.8%
INDIANA	8,264	3,160	2,260	1,410	931	503	Carter	38.2%	27.3%	17.1%	11.3%	6.1%
JEFFERSON	4,580	2,192	895	532	483	478	Carter	47.9%	19.5%	11.6%	10.5%	10.4%
JUNIATA	2,048	1,056	350	178	245	219	Carter	51.6%	17.1%	8.7%	12.0%	10.7%
LACKAWANNA	34,227	15,929	7,951	4,571	3,382	2,394	Carter	46.5%	23.2%	13.4%	9.9%	7.0%
LANCASTER	15,151	6,477	1,811	3,939	1,378	1,546	Carter	42.7%	12.0%	26.0%	9.1%	10.2%
LAWRENCE	14,216	5,807	2,906	2,208	2,029	1,266	Carter	40.8%	20.4%	15.5%	14.3%	8.9%
LEBANON	4,991	2,006	978	913	751	343	Carter	40.2%	19.6%	18.3%	15.0%	6.9%
LEHIGH	21,611	8,138	4,961	4,719	1,741	2,052	Carter	37.7%	23.0%	21.8%	8.1%	9.5%
LUZERNE	47,336	16,633	15,444	6,032	4,928	4,299	Carter	35.1%	32.6%	12.7%	10.4%	9.1%
LYCOMING	10,831	5,947	1,657	1,454	1,034	739	Carter	54.9%	15.3%	13.4%	9.5%	6.8%
MCKEAN	2,940	1,099	551	494	411	385	Carter	37.4%	18.7%	16.8%	14.0%	13.1%
MERCER	14,154	5,286	3,529	2,563	1,791	985	Carter	37.3%	24.9%	18.1%	12.7%	7.0%
MIFFLIN	3,580	1,700	742	538	330	270	Carter	47.5%	20.7%	15.0%	9.2%	7.5%
MONROE	5,245	2,087	1,039	1,002	624	493	Carter	39.8%	19.8%	19.1%	11.9%	9.4%
MONTGOMERY	40,373	12,336	9,766	13,433	2,012	2,826	Udall	30.6%	24.2%	33.3%	5.0%	7.0%
MONTOUR	2,084	1,144	334	265	224	117	Carter	54.9%	16.0%	12.7%	10.7%	5.6%
NORTHAMPTON	27,567	11,353	6,604	5,369	2,338	1,903	Carter	41.2%	24.0%	19.5%	8.5%	6.9%
NORTHUMBERLAND	12,304	5,348	2,468	2,199	1,402	887	Carter	43.5%	20.1%	17.9%	11.4%	7.2%
PERRY	2,806	1,266	411	396	426	307	Carter	45.1%	14.6%	14.1%	15.2%	10.9%

PENNSYLVANIA DEMOCRATIC

1976

County	Total Vote	Carter	H. Jackson	Udall	Wallace	Other	Winner	Percentage of Total Vote Carter	H. Jackson	Udall	Wallace	Other
PHILADELPHIA	285,320	80,941	104,347	57,725	23,307	19,000	H. Jackson	28.4%	36.6%	20.2%	8.2%	6.7%
PIKE	1,055	350	236	163	195	111	Carter	33.2%	22.4%	15.5%	18.5%	10.5%
POTTER	2,336	817	395	310	395	419	Carter	35.0%	16.9%	13.3%	16.9%	17.9%
SCHUYLKILL	13,498	5,331	3,639	1,444	1,326	1,758	Carter	39.5%	27.0%	10.7%	9.8%	13.0%
SNYDER	1,753	919	229	233	247	125	Carter	52.4%	13.1%	13.3%	14.1%	7.1%
SOMERSET	7,728	3,114	2,320	923	903	468	Carter	40.3%	30.0%	11.9%	11.7%	6.1%
SULLIVAN	1,022	476	196	65	131	154	Carter	46.6%	19.2%	6.4%	12.8%	15.1%
SUSQUEHANNA	3,107	1,332	676	489	358	252	Carter	42.9%	21.8%	15.7%	11.5%	8.1%
TIOGA	3,106	1,443	529	483	381	270	Carter	46.5%	17.0%	15.6%	12.3%	8.7%
UNION	1,944	1,012	183	388	207	154	Carter	52.1%	9.4%	20.0%	10.6%	7.9%
VENANGO	4,212	1,836	740	713	475	448	Carter	43.6%	17.6%	16.9%	11.3%	10.6%
WARREN	3,058	1,246	553	574	341	344	Carter	40.7%	18.1%	18.8%	11.2%	11.2%
WASHINGTON	42,997	17,224	9,233	5,685	6,607	4,248	Carter	40.1%	21.5%	13.2%	15.4%	9.9%
WAYNE	2,412	1,037	441	372	290	272	Carter	43.0%	18.3%	15.4%	12.0%	11.3%
WESTMORELAND	56,764	24,208	10,520	8,495	8,352	5,189	Carter	42.6%	18.5%	15.0%	14.7%	9.1%
WYOMING	1,773	898	289	240	229	117	Carter	50.6%	16.3%	13.5%	12.9%	6.6%
YORK	23,077	10,929	4,403	3,756	1,958	2,031	Carter	47.4%	19.1%	16.3%	8.5%	8.8%
TOTAL	1,385,211	511,905	340,310	259,166	155,902	117,928	Carter	37.0%	24.6%	18.7%	11.3%	8.5%
Certified Totals	1,385,042	511,905	340,340	259,166	155,902	117,729	Carter	37.0%	24.6%	18.7%	11.3%	8.5%

PENNSYLVANIA REPUBLICAN

1976

County	Total Vote	Ford	Reagan	Other	Winner	Percentage of Total Vote Ford	Reagan	Other
ADAMS	4,369	4,369			Ford	100.0%		
ALLEGHENY	96,596	87,030	6,060	3,506	Ford	90.1%	6.3%	3.6%
ARMSTRONG	6,985	5,726		1,259	Ford	82.0%		18.0%
BEAVER	14,108	11,216		2,892	Ford	79.5%		20.5%
BEDFORD	4,467	3,796	610	61	Ford	85.0%	13.7%	1.4%
BERKS	14,002	13,085	859	58	Ford	93.5%	6.1%	0.4%
BLAIR	15,017	11,987	3,030		Ford	79.8%	20.2%	
BRADFORD	7,025	5,765	1,127	133	Ford	82.1%	16.0%	1.9%
BUCKS	26,006	26,006			Ford	100.0%		
BUTLER	10,473	10,473			Ford	100.0%		
CAMBRIA	11,139	11,139			Ford	100.0%		
CAMERON	795	795			Ford	100.0%		
CARBON	3,348	3,348			Ford	100.0%		
CENTRE	9,715	8,278	1,437		Ford	85.2%	14.8%	
CHESTER	26,329	26,329			Ford	100.0%		
CLARION	3,736	3,284	452		Ford	87.9%	12.1%	
CLEARFIELD	5,489	5,489			Ford	100.0%		
CLINTON	3,121	2,819	253	49	Ford	90.3%	8.1%	1.6%
COLUMBIA	5,895	4,600	1,054	241	Ford	78.0%	17.9%	4.1%
CRAWFORD	6,465	6,465			Ford	100.0%		

PENNSYLVANIA REPUBLICAN

1976

County	Total Vote	Ford	Reagan	Other	Winner	Percentage of Total Vote		
						Ford	Reagan	Other
CUMBERLAND	16,151	15,342	773	36	Ford	95.0%	4.8%	0.2%
DAUPHIN	21,810	21,208	602		Ford	97.2%	2.8%	
DELAWARE	49,842	48,795	1,047		Ford	97.9%	2.1%	
ELK	1,183	1,183			Ford	100.0%		
ERIE	18,064	18,064			Ford	100.0%		
FAYETTE	5,333	5,076	170	87	Ford	95.2%	3.2%	1.6%
FOREST	580	580			Ford	100.0%		
FRANKLIN	6,574	5,252	1,088	234	Ford	79.9%	16.6%	3.6%
FULTON	724	618	106		Ford	85.4%	14.6%	
GREENE	1,826	1,585	241		Ford	86.8%	13.2%	
HUNTINGDON	4,338	3,681	558	99	Ford	84.9%	12.9%	2.3%
INDIANA	6,158	6,158			Ford	100.0%		
JEFFERSON	3,728	3,728			Ford	100.0%		
JUNIATA	1,904	1,667	209	28	Ford	87.6%	11.0%	1.5%
LACKAWANNA	10,073	10,073			Ford	100.0%		
LANCASTER	34,482	31,207	2,878	397	Ford	90.5%	8.3%	1.2%
LAWRENCE	8,728	7,490	875	363	Ford	85.8%	10.0%	4.2%
LEBANON	9,623	9,623			Ford	100.0%		
LEHIGH	12,376	11,793	516	67	Ford	95.3%	4.2%	0.5%
LUZERNE	19,749	19,131	618		Ford	96.9%	3.1%	
LYCOMING	9,981	8,757	1,023	201	Ford	87.7%	10.2%	2.0%
MCKEAN	5,179	4,970	209		Ford	96.0%	4.0%	
MERCER	9,348	9,348			Ford	100.0%		
MIFFLIN	3,016	2,885	112	19	Ford	95.7%	3.7%	0.6%
MONROE	3,408	3,255	153		Ford	95.5%	4.5%	
MONTGOMERY	61,028	57,809	3,219		Ford	94.7%	5.3%	
MONTOUR	1,196	1,196			Ford	100.0%		
NORTHAMPTON	10,222	9,954	268		Ford	97.4%	2.6%	
NORTHUMBERLAND	9,071	8,528	543		Ford	94.0%	6.0%	
PERRY	3,492	3,061	367	64	Ford	87.7%	10.5%	1.8%
PHILADELPHIA	57,337	56,536	397	404	Ford	98.6%	0.7%	0.7%
PIKE	1,164	1,065	55	44	Ford	91.5%	4.7%	3.8%
POTTER	2,037	1,747	241	49	Ford	85.8%	11.8%	2.4%
SCHUYLKILL	14,619	12,747	1,872		Ford	87.2%	12.8%	
SNYDER	3,728	2,964	677	87	Ford	79.5%	18.2%	2.3%
SOMERSET	8,022	6,920	1,102		Ford	86.3%	13.7%	
SULLIVAN	802	695	107		Ford	86.7%	13.3%	
SUSQUEHANNA	3,969	3,969			Ford	100.0%		
TIOGA	4,015	4,015			Ford	100.0%		
UNION	3,646	2,812	659	175	Ford	77.1%	18.1%	4.8%
VENANGO	6,837	5,955	882		Ford	87.1%	12.9%	
WARREN	3,999	3,781	218		Ford	94.5%	5.5%	
WASHINGTON	12,213	10,059	1,583	571	Ford	82.4%	13.0%	4.7%
WAYNE	3,183	3,110	57	16	Ford	97.7%	1.8%	0.5%
WESTMORELAND	17,654	16,661	868	125	Ford	94.4%	4.9%	0.7%
WYOMING	3,054	2,517	537		Ford	82.4%	17.6%	
YORK	14,778	13,903	802	73	Ford	94.1%	5.4%	0.5%
TOTAL	785,324	733,472	40,514	11,338	Ford	93.4%	5.2%	1.4%
Certified Totals	796,660	733,472	40,510	22,678	Ford	92.1%	5.1%	2.8%

Note: Ford was the only candidate listed on the ballot. All other votes cast were write-ins.

PENNSYLVANIA DEMOCRATIC

1980

County	Total Vote	Carter	E. Kennedy	Other	Winner	Percentage of Total Vote: Carter	E. Kennedy	Other
ADAMS	4,905	3,060	1,422	423	Carter	62.4%	29.0%	8.6%
ALLEGHENY	288,770	143,687	115,311	29,772	Carter	49.8%	39.9%	10.3%
ARMSTRONG	8,723	4,826	3,074	823	Carter	55.3%	35.2%	9.4%
BEAVER	38,345	18,897	16,100	3,348	Carter	49.3%	42.0%	8.7%
BEDFORD	4,036	2,724	987	325	Carter	67.5%	24.5%	8.1%
BERKS	39,435	21,025	14,160	4,250	Carter	53.3%	35.9%	10.8%
BLAIR	11,557	6,725	3,522	1,310	Carter	58.2%	30.5%	11.3%
BRADFORD	3,694	2,034	1,372	288	Carter	55.1%	37.1%	7.8%
BUCKS	46,371	17,794	24,545	4,032	E. Kennedy	38.4%	52.9%	8.7%
BUTLER	14,482	7,501	5,430	1,551	Carter	51.8%	37.5%	10.7%
CAMBRIA	34,260	18,391	12,836	3,033	Carter	53.7%	37.5%	8.9%
CAMERON	863	512	275	76	Carter	59.3%	31.9%	8.8%
CARBON	7,154	2,877	3,791	486	E. Kennedy	40.2%	53.0%	6.8%
CENTRE	10,198	6,019	3,424	755	Carter	59.0%	33.6%	7.4%
CHESTER	16,963	7,902	7,630	1,431	Carter	46.6%	45.0%	8.4%
CLARION	4,547	2,775	1,248	524	Carter	61.0%	27.4%	11.5%
CLEARFIELD	9,755	5,577	3,396	782	Carter	57.2%	34.8%	8.0%
CLINTON	3,344	1,783	1,285	276	Carter	53.3%	38.4%	8.3%
COLUMBIA	8,654	4,743	3,274	637	Carter	54.8%	37.8%	7.4%
CRAWFORD	7,849	4,759	2,526	564	Carter	60.6%	32.2%	7.2%
CUMBERLAND	13,929	8,654	4,007	1,268	Carter	62.1%	28.8%	9.1%
DAUPHIN	17,845	9,643	6,747	1,455	Carter	54.0%	37.8%	8.2%
DELAWARE	38,294	14,623	20,214	3,457	E. Kennedy	38.2%	52.8%	9.0%
ELK	5,949	3,238	1,998	713	Carter	54.4%	33.6%	12.0%
ERIE	40,282	20,687	16,852	2,743	Carter	51.4%	41.8%	6.8%
FAYETTE	28,094	13,922	12,029	2,143	Carter	49.6%	42.8%	7.6%
FOREST	620	375	185	60	Carter	60.5%	29.8%	9.7%
FRANKLIN	7,598	4,988	2,238	372	Carter	65.6%	29.5%	4.9%
FULTON	1,271	882	263	126	Carter	69.4%	20.7%	9.9%
GREENE	8,583	4,976	3,010	597	Carter	58.0%	35.1%	7.0%
HUNTINGDON	3,339	2,076	988	275	Carter	62.2%	29.6%	8.2%
INDIANA	8,909	4,889	3,683	337	Carter	54.9%	41.3%	3.8%
JEFFERSON	4,932	2,739	1,709	484	Carter	55.5%	34.7%	9.8%
JUNIATA	1,957	1,359	467	131	Carter	69.4%	23.9%	6.7%
LACKAWANNA	43,269	16,866	23,800	2,603	E. Kennedy	39.0%	55.0%	6.0%
LANCASTER	15,002	9,137	4,738	1,127	Carter	60.9%	31.6%	7.5%
LAWRENCE	14,933	6,578	7,160	1,195	E. Kennedy	44.1%	47.9%	8.0%
LEBANON	5,408	3,122	1,736	550	Carter	57.7%	32.1%	10.2%
LEHIGH	29,239	15,017	11,516	2,706	Carter	51.4%	39.4%	9.3%
LUZERNE	66,993	21,351	41,900	3,742	E. Kennedy	31.9%	62.5%	5.6%
LYCOMING	10,068	6,162	3,091	815	Carter	61.2%	30.7%	8.1%
MCKEAN	2,933	1,680	997	256	Carter	57.3%	34.0%	8.7%
MERCER	14,315	7,701	5,596	1,018	Carter	53.8%	39.1%	7.1%
MIFFLIN	3,570	2,259	1,076	235	Carter	63.3%	30.1%	6.6%
MONROE	6,808	3,620	2,519	669	Carter	53.2%	37.0%	9.8%
MONTGOMERY	46,385	16,577	26,020	3,788	E. Kennedy	35.7%	56.1%	8.2%
MONTOUR	1,948	1,116	686	146	Carter	57.3%	35.2%	7.5%
NORTHAMPTON	31,818	15,468	13,650	2,700	Carter	48.6%	42.9%	8.5%
NORTHUMBERLAND	10,615	5,149	4,678	788	Carter	48.5%	44.1%	7.4%
PERRY	2,734	1,826	650	258	Carter	66.8%	23.8%	9.4%

PENNSYLVANIA DEMOCRATIC

1980

County	Total Vote	Carter	E. Kennedy	Other	Winner	Percentage of Total Vote Carter	E. Kennedy	Other
PHILADELPHIA	358,237	122,570	214,033	21,634	E. Kennedy	34.2%	59.7%	6.0%
PIKE	1,308	680	497	131	Carter	52.0%	38.0%	10.0%
POTTER	1,640	1,063	442	135	Carter	64.8%	27.0%	8.2%
SCHUYLKILL	17,872	6,068	10,579	1,225	E. Kennedy	34.0%	59.2%	6.9%
SNYDER	1,672	1,045	469	158	Carter	62.5%	28.1%	9.4%
SOMERSET	9,133	5,365	3,073	695	Carter	58.7%	33.6%	7.6%
SULLIVAN	938	510	342	86	Carter	54.4%	36.5%	9.2%
SUSQUEHANNA	3,343	1,641	1,399	303	Carter	49.1%	41.8%	9.1%
TIOGA	2,461	1,388	831	242	Carter	56.4%	33.8%	9.8%
UNION	1,769	1,083	543	143	Carter	61.2%	30.7%	8.1%
VENANGO	4,551	2,795	1,366	390	Carter	61.4%	30.0%	8.6%
WARREN	3,631	2,133	1,153	345	Carter	58.7%	31.8%	9.5%
WASHINGTON	44,307	21,892	18,306	4,109	Carter	49.4%	41.3%	9.3%
WAYNE	2,346	1,261	856	229	Carter	53.8%	36.5%	9.8%
WESTMORELAND	68,184	34,824	25,288	8,072	Carter	51.1%	37.1%	11.8%
WYOMING	1,929	990	772	167	Carter	51.3%	40.0%	8.7%
YORK	25,954	16,733	7,194	2,027	Carter	64.5%	27.7%	7.8%
TOTAL	1,600,820	732,332	736,954	131,534	E. Kennedy	45.7%	46.0%	8.2%
Published Totals	1,613,551	732,332	736,854	144,365	E. Kennedy	45.4%	45.7%	8.9%

Note: Published returns include 12,831 scattered write-in votes that were not readily available on a county-by-county basis.

PENNSYLVANIA REPUBLICAN

1980

County	Total Vote	Bush	Reagan	Other	Winner	Percentage of Total Vote Bush	Reagan	Other
ADAMS	6,847	2,905	3,726	216	Reagan	42.4%	54.4%	3.2%
ALLEGHENY	122,543	76,412	41,133	4,998	Bush	62.4%	33.6%	4.1%
ARMSTRONG	8,790	4,804	3,680	306	Bush	54.7%	41.9%	3.5%
BEAVER	16,298	8,867	6,801	630	Bush	54.4%	41.7%	3.9%
BEDFORD	6,336	2,018	4,069	249	Reagan	31.8%	64.2%	3.9%
BERKS	23,644	12,141	10,126	1,377	Bush	51.3%	42.8%	5.8%
BLAIR	18,994	6,993	11,281	720	Reagan	36.8%	59.4%	3.8%
BRADFORD	8,112	3,195	4,500	417	Reagan	39.4%	55.5%	5.1%
BUCKS	50,446	27,891	20,649	1,906	Bush	55.3%	40.9%	3.8%
BUTLER	15,655	8,233	6,632	790	Bush	52.6%	42.4%	5.0%
CAMBRIA	17,951	9,216	8,106	629	Bush	51.3%	45.2%	3.5%
CAMERON	1,021	359	621	41	Reagan	35.2%	60.8%	4.0%
CARBON	5,725	2,354	3,072	299	Reagan	41.1%	53.7%	5.2%
CENTRE	11,913	6,334	5,217	362	Bush	53.2%	43.8%	3.0%
CHESTER	45,607	27,748	15,921	1,938	Bush	60.8%	34.9%	4.2%
CLARION	5,008	2,596	2,238	174	Bush	51.8%	44.7%	3.5%
CLEARFIELD	8,750	3,930	4,472	348	Reagan	44.9%	51.1%	4.0%
CLINTON	3,955	2,027	1,733	195	Bush	51.3%	43.8%	4.9%
COLUMBIA	6,532	2,706	3,625	201	Reagan	41.4%	55.5%	3.1%
CRAWFORD	10,967	5,058	5,156	753	Reagan	46.1%	47.0%	6.9%

PENNSYLVANIA REPUBLICAN

1980

County	Total Vote	Bush	Reagan	Other	Winner	Percentage of Total Vote: Bush	Reagan	Other
CUMBERLAND	23,981	12,669	10,373	939	Bush	52.8%	43.3%	3.9%
DAUPHIN	29,943	15,216	13,302	1,425	Bush	50.8%	44.4%	4.8%
DELAWARE	103,904	55,361	42,276	6,267	Bush	53.3%	40.7%	6.0%
ELK	3,099	1,413	1,577	109	Reagan	45.6%	50.9%	3.5%
ERIE	24,848	14,876	8,809	1,163	Bush	59.9%	35.5%	4.7%
FAYETTE	7,413	3,593	3,472	348	Bush	48.5%	46.8%	4.7%
FOREST	806	374	400	32	Reagan	46.4%	49.6%	4.0%
FRANKLIN	10,490	3,512	6,505	473	Reagan	33.5%	62.0%	4.5%
FULTON	1,131	306	789	36	Reagan	27.1%	69.8%	3.2%
GREENE	2,163	1,088	1,014	61	Bush	50.3%	46.9%	2.8%
HUNTINGDON	5,562	2,224	3,122	216	Reagan	40.0%	56.1%	3.9%
INDIANA	10,414	5,304	4,762	348	Bush	50.9%	45.7%	3.3%
JEFFERSON	6,021	2,721	3,107	193	Reagan	45.2%	51.6%	3.2%
JUNIATA	2,454	995	1,357	102	Reagan	40.5%	55.3%	4.2%
LACKAWANNA	18,247	8,841	8,410	996	Bush	48.5%	46.1%	5.5%
LANCASTER	43,622	24,941	17,603	1,078	Bush	57.2%	40.4%	2.5%
LAWRENCE	11,130	4,725	5,808	597	Reagan	42.5%	52.2%	5.4%
LEBANON	13,198	5,438	7,203	557	Reagan	41.2%	54.6%	4.2%
LEHIGH	25,288	14,625	9,901	762	Bush	57.8%	39.2%	3.0%
LUZERNE	37,970	15,359	20,839	1,772	Reagan	40.5%	54.9%	4.7%
LYCOMING	13,379	6,094	6,782	503	Reagan	45.5%	50.7%	3.8%
MCKEAN	5,919	2,124	3,417	378	Reagan	35.9%	57.7%	6.4%
MERCER	12,530	5,612	6,011	907	Reagan	44.8%	48.0%	7.2%
MIFFLIN	4,367	2,025	2,100	242	Reagan	46.4%	48.1%	5.5%
MONROE	6,236	2,557	3,260	419	Reagan	41.0%	52.3%	6.7%
MONTGOMERY	102,149	60,577	36,300	5,272	Bush	59.3%	35.5%	5.2%
MONTOUR	2,057	920	1,060	77	Reagan	44.7%	51.5%	3.7%
NORTHAMPTON	14,276	7,879	5,759	638	Bush	55.2%	40.3%	4.5%
NORTHUMBERLAND	12,461	5,202	6,700	559	Reagan	41.7%	53.8%	4.5%
PERRY	5,011	2,176	2,607	228	Reagan	43.4%	52.0%	4.5%
PHILADELPHIA	97,669	45,369	46,364	5,936	Reagan	46.5%	47.5%	6.1%
PIKE	2,300	584	1,553	163	Reagan	25.4%	67.5%	7.1%
POTTER	2,360	656	1,567	137	Reagan	27.8%	66.4%	5.8%
SCHUYLKILL	25,059	10,857	13,336	866	Reagan	43.3%	53.2%	3.5%
SNYDER	5,181	1,821	3,216	144	Reagan	35.1%	62.1%	2.8%
SOMERSET	11,639	4,991	6,333	315	Reagan	42.9%	54.4%	2.7%
SULLIVAN	1,080	413	634	33	Reagan	38.2%	58.7%	3.1%
SUSQUEHANNA	5,837	2,548	2,952	337	Reagan	43.7%	50.6%	5.8%
TIOGA	5,880	1,908	3,659	313	Reagan	32.4%	62.2%	5.3%
UNION	4,581	2,207	2,269	105	Reagan	48.2%	49.5%	2.3%
VENANGO	8,079	3,921	3,862	296	Bush	48.5%	47.8%	3.7%
WARREN	5,630	2,885	2,454	291	Bush	51.2%	43.6%	5.2%
WASHINGTON	15,173	8,729	5,908	536	Bush	57.5%	38.9%	3.5%
WAYNE	5,066	1,815	2,904	347	Reagan	35.8%	57.3%	6.8%
WESTMORELAND	27,570	16,542	10,160	868	Bush	60.0%	36.9%	3.1%
WYOMING	4,110	1,904	2,060	146	Reagan	46.3%	50.1%	3.6%
YORK	27,445	15,075	11,302	1,068	Bush	54.9%	41.2%	3.9%
TOTAL	1,209,822	626,759	527,916	55,147	Bush	51.8%	43.6%	4.6%
Published Totals	1,241,411	626,759	527,916	86,736	Bush	50.5%	42.5%	7.0%

Note: Published returns include 26,890 write-in votes for Anderson and 4,699 scattered write-ins, which were not readily available on a county-by-county basis.

PENNSYLVANIA DEMOCRATIC

1984

County	Total Vote	Hart	J. Jackson	Mondale	Other	Winner	Percentage of Total Vote: Hart	J. Jackson	Mondale	Other
ADAMS	5,314	2,743	258	2,141	172	Hart	51.6%	4.9%	40.3%	3.2%
ALLEGHENY	303,897	90,711	47,390	139,050	26,746	Mondale	29.8%	15.6%	45.8%	8.8%
ARMSTRONG	9,065	3,228	366	5,191	280	Mondale	35.6%	4.0%	57.3%	3.1%
BEAVER	43,937	14,207	3,525	24,858	1,347	Mondale	32.3%	8.0%	56.6%	3.1%
BEDFORD	4,571	2,178	140	1,937	316	Hart	47.6%	3.1%	42.4%	6.9%
BERKS	33,287	14,199	1,804	14,410	2,874	Mondale	42.7%	5.4%	43.3%	8.6%
BLAIR	10,120	4,243	429	4,998	450	Mondale	41.9%	4.2%	49.4%	4.4%
BRADFORD	3,773	1,985	161	1,513	114	Hart	52.6%	4.3%	40.1%	3.0%
BUCKS	43,017	20,026	3,000	17,952	2,039	Hart	46.6%	7.0%	41.7%	4.7%
BUTLER	16,104	6,864	941	7,333	966	Mondale	42.6%	5.8%	45.5%	6.0%
CAMBRIA	33,113	11,681	913	19,749	770	Mondale	35.3%	2.8%	59.6%	2.3%
CAMERON	851	415	28	391	17	Hart	48.8%	3.3%	45.9%	2.0%
CARBON	6,181	2,126	182	3,398	475	Mondale	34.4%	2.9%	55.0%	7.7%
CENTRE	9,582	4,791	724	3,787	280	Hart	50.0%	7.6%	39.5%	2.9%
CHESTER	16,366	7,319	2,149	6,468	430	Hart	44.7%	13.1%	39.5%	2.6%
CLARION	4,699	2,337	217	1,986	159	Hart	49.7%	4.6%	42.3%	3.4%
CLEARFIELD	10,233	4,337	382	5,127	387	Mondale	42.4%	3.7%	50.1%	3.8%
CLINTON	3,119	1,409	121	1,442	147	Mondale	45.2%	3.9%	46.2%	4.7%
COLUMBIA	7,826	3,676	226	3,571	353	Hart	47.0%	2.9%	45.6%	4.5%
CRAWFORD	8,060	3,664	415	3,562	419	Hart	45.5%	5.1%	44.2%	5.2%
CUMBERLAND	13,153	6,282	774	5,614	483	Hart	47.8%	5.9%	42.7%	3.7%
DAUPHIN	18,941	6,761	3,857	7,358	965	Mondale	35.7%	20.4%	38.8%	5.1%
DELAWARE	35,982	14,260	4,500	14,922	2,300	Mondale	39.6%	12.5%	41.5%	6.4%
ELK	6,323	3,154	256	2,659	254	Hart	49.9%	4.0%	42.1%	4.0%
ERIE	41,638	15,085	3,834	20,872	1,847	Mondale	36.2%	9.2%	50.1%	4.4%
FAYETTE	29,465	8,078	1,529	18,378	1,480	Mondale	27.4%	5.2%	62.4%	5.0%
FOREST	648	319	32	281	16	Hart	49.2%	4.9%	43.4%	2.5%
FRANKLIN	7,770	3,746	334	3,470	220	Hart	48.2%	4.3%	44.7%	2.8%
FULTON	1,223	625	65	483	50	Hart	51.1%	5.3%	39.5%	4.1%
GREENE	10,188	3,218	413	6,194	363	Mondale	31.6%	4.1%	60.8%	3.6%
HUNTINGDON	3,352	1,491	195	1,553	113	Mondale	44.5%	5.8%	46.3%	3.4%
INDIANA	9,848	3,461	392	5,761	234	Mondale	35.1%	4.0%	58.5%	2.4%
JEFFERSON	4,742	2,223	195	2,162	162	Hart	46.9%	4.1%	45.6%	3.4%
JUNIATA	1,994	1,022	40	876	56	Hart	51.3%	2.0%	43.9%	2.8%
LACKAWANNA	41,733	17,111	1,015	21,441	2,166	Mondale	41.0%	2.4%	51.4%	5.2%
LANCASTER	14,842	6,586	1,340	5,760	1,156	Hart	44.4%	9.0%	38.8%	7.8%
LAWRENCE	15,862	5,679	1,154	8,583	446	Mondale	35.8%	7.3%	54.1%	2.8%
LEBANON	5,610	2,486	268	2,519	337	Mondale	44.3%	4.8%	44.9%	6.0%
LEHIGH	27,545	10,282	1,384	14,109	1,770	Mondale	37.3%	5.0%	51.2%	6.4%
LUZERNE	53,181	21,621	1,268	25,453	4,839	Mondale	40.7%	2.4%	47.9%	9.1%
LYCOMING	10,070	4,998	412	4,216	444	Hart	49.6%	4.1%	41.9%	4.4%
MCKEAN	2,970	1,207	127	1,506	130	Mondale	40.6%	4.3%	50.7%	4.4%
MERCER	15,883	5,774	1,804	7,543	762	Mondale	36.4%	11.4%	47.5%	4.8%
MIFFLIN	3,321	1,346	99	1,693	183	Mondale	40.5%	3.0%	51.0%	5.5%
MONROE	5,468	2,525	274	2,247	422	Hart	46.2%	5.0%	41.1%	7.7%
MONTGOMERY	43,634	18,203	4,377	19,244	1,810	Mondale	41.7%	10.0%	44.1%	4.1%
MONTOUR	1,706	851	37	760	58	Hart	49.9%	2.2%	44.5%	3.4%
NORTHAMPTON	28,862	10,868	1,477	15,152	1,365	Mondale	37.7%	5.1%	52.5%	4.7%
NORTHUMBERLAND	10,216	4,472	307	5,027	410	Mondale	43.8%	3.0%	49.2%	4.0%
PERRY	2,434	1,149	114	1,077	94	Hart	47.2%	4.7%	44.2%	3.9%

PENNSYLVANIA DEMOCRATIC

1984

County	Total Vote	Hart	J. Jackson	Mondale	Other	Winner	Percentage of Total Vote Hart	J. Jackson	Mondale	Other
PHILADELPHIA	422,057	92,873	160,399	148,389	20,396	J. Jackson	22.0%	38.0%	35.2%	4.8%
PIKE	1,450	602	74	602	172		41.5%	5.1%	41.5%	11.9%
POTTER	1,742	835	76	777	54	Hart	47.9%	4.4%	44.6%	3.1%
SCHUYLKILL	15,359	6,395	402	8,056	506	Mondale	41.6%	2.6%	52.5%	3.3%
SNYDER	1,634	856	85	628	65	Hart	52.4%	5.2%	38.4%	4.0%
SOMERSET	10,115	3,597	228	6,020	270	Mondale	35.6%	2.3%	59.5%	2.7%
SULLIVAN	887	422	37	388	40	Hart	47.6%	4.2%	43.7%	4.5%
SUSQUEHANNA	3,040	1,483	137	1,251	169	Hart	48.8%	4.5%	41.2%	5.6%
TIOGA	2,805	1,391	179	1,182	53	Hart	49.6%	6.4%	42.1%	1.9%
UNION	1,740	899	123	656	62	Hart	51.7%	7.1%	37.7%	3.6%
VENANGO	5,538	2,568	225	2,573	172	Mondale	46.4%	4.1%	46.5%	3.1%
WARREN	3,936	1,967	186	1,625	158	Hart	50.0%	4.7%	41.3%	4.0%
WASHINGTON	43,243	12,475	2,350	27,070	1,348	Mondale	28.8%	5.4%	62.6%	3.1%
WAYNE	2,309	1,130	101	889	189	Hart	48.9%	4.4%	38.5%	8.2%
WESTMORELAND	69,866	24,143	3,225	40,310	2,188	Mondale	34.6%	4.6%	57.7%	3.1%
WYOMING	1,860	913	69	797	81	Hart	49.1%	3.7%	42.8%	4.4%
YORK	25,651	11,764	1,323	10,277	2,287	Hart	45.9%	5.2%	40.1%	8.9%
TOTAL	1,654,951	551,335	264,463	747,267	91,886	Mondale	33.3%	16.0%	45.2%	5.6%
Published Totals	1,656,294	551,335	264,463	747,267	93,229	Mondale	33.3%	16.0%	45.1%	5.6%

Note: Published returns include 1,343 scattered write-in votes that were not readily available on a county-by-county basis.

PENNSYLVANIA DEMOCRATIC

1988

County	Total Vote	Dukakis	J. Jackson	Other	Winner	Percentage of Total Vote Dukakis	J. Jackson	Other
ADAMS	4,949	3,800	763	386	Dukakis	76.8%	15.4%	7.8%
ALLEGHENY	283,507	198,948	64,058	20,501	Dukakis	70.2%	22.6%	7.2%
ARMSTRONG	9,136	7,185	1,407	544	Dukakis	78.6%	15.4%	6.0%
BEAVER	39,981	31,752	6,550	1,679	Dukakis	79.4%	16.4%	4.2%
BEDFORD	3,655	2,842	487	326	Dukakis	77.8%	13.3%	8.9%
BERKS	33,548	25,643	4,892	3,013	Dukakis	76.4%	14.6%	9.0%
BLAIR	9,289	7,368	1,357	564	Dukakis	79.3%	14.6%	6.1%
BRADFORD	3,102	2,235	576	291	Dukakis	72.1%	18.6%	9.4%
BUCKS	42,388	33,836	6,160	2,392	Dukakis	79.8%	14.5%	5.6%
BUTLER	13,560	10,411	2,233	916	Dukakis	76.8%	16.5%	6.8%
CAMBRIA	28,803	22,020	4,193	2,590	Dukakis	76.5%	14.6%	9.0%
CAMERON	653	486	84	83	Dukakis	74.4%	12.9%	12.7%
CARBON	5,607	4,445	665	497	Dukakis	79.3%	11.9%	8.9%
CENTRE	9,386	6,460	2,411	515	Dukakis	68.8%	25.7%	5.5%
CHESTER	17,905	12,460	4,667	778	Dukakis	69.6%	26.1%	4.3%
CLARION	4,237	2,920	684	633	Dukakis	68.9%	16.1%	14.9%
CLEARFIELD	8,490	6,706	1,189	595	Dukakis	79.0%	14.0%	7.0%
CLINTON	3,757	2,075	1,405	277	Dukakis	55.2%	37.4%	7.4%
COLUMBIA	6,869	5,446	915	508	Dukakis	79.3%	13.3%	7.4%
CRAWFORD	7,319	5,096	1,603	620	Dukakis	69.6%	21.9%	8.5%

PENNSYLVANIA DEMOCRATIC

1988

County	Total Vote	Dukakis	J. Jackson	Other	Winner	Percentage of Total Vote Dukakis	J. Jackson	Other
CUMBERLAND	13,415	10,306	2,084	1,025	Dukakis	76.8%	15.5%	7.6%
DAUPHIN	18,714	11,710	6,132	872	Dukakis	62.6%	32.8%	4.7%
DELAWARE	36,474	25,919	8,349	2,206	Dukakis	71.1%	22.9%	6.0%
ELK	5,134	3,991	712	431	Dukakis	77.7%	13.9%	8.4%
ERIE	41,333	30,119	8,368	2,846	Dukakis	72.9%	20.2%	6.9%
FAYETTE	27,492	22,133	3,259	2,100	Dukakis	80.5%	11.9%	7.6%
FOREST	576	427	94	55	Dukakis	74.1%	16.3%	9.5%
FRANKLIN	7,217	5,590	960	667	Dukakis	77.5%	13.3%	9.2%
FULTON	1,177	818	186	173	Dukakis	69.5%	15.8%	14.7%
GREENE	7,908	6,235	1,080	593	Dukakis	78.8%	13.7%	7.5%
HUNTINGDON	2,919	2,237	458	224	Dukakis	76.6%	15.7%	7.7%
INDIANA	9,262	7,279	1,507	476	Dukakis	78.6%	16.3%	5.1%
JEFFERSON	4,422	3,415	644	363	Dukakis	77.2%	14.6%	8.2%
JUNIATA	1,943	1,493	263	187	Dukakis	76.8%	13.5%	9.6%
LACKAWANNA	33,412	26,727	3,490	3,195	Dukakis	80.0%	10.4%	9.6%
LANCASTER	13,274	8,475	3,870	929	Dukakis	63.8%	29.2%	7.0%
LAWRENCE	4,467	1,526	2,226	715	J. Jackson	34.2%	49.8%	16.0%
LEBANON	5,012	3,563	948	501	Dukakis	71.1%	18.9%	10.0%
LEHIGH	25,790	20,989	3,095	1,706	Dukakis	81.4%	12.0%	6.6%
LUZERNE	41,212	31,704	4,796	4,712	Dukakis	76.9%	11.6%	11.4%
LYCOMING	9,205	6,540	1,909	756	Dukakis	71.0%	20.7%	8.2%
MCKEAN	2,466	1,798	423	245	Dukakis	72.9%	17.2%	9.9%
MERCER	13,212	9,599	2,531	1,082	Dukakis	72.7%	19.2%	8.2%
MIFFLIN	3,239	2,528	406	305	Dukakis	78.0%	12.5%	9.4%
MONROE	6,396	4,775	978	643	Dukakis	74.7%	15.3%	10.1%
MONTGOMERY	45,932	35,521	8,500	1,911	Dukakis	77.3%	18.5%	4.2%
MONTOUR	1,455	1,132	211	112	Dukakis	77.8%	14.5%	7.7%
NORTHAMPTON	27,439	21,842	3,433	2,164	Dukakis	79.6%	12.5%	7.9%
NORTHUMBERLAND	10,752	8,699	1,162	891	Dukakis	80.9%	10.8%	8.3%
PERRY	2,304	1,768	314	222	Dukakis	76.7%	13.6%	9.6%
PHILADELPHIA	370,974	150,834	209,302	10,838	J. Jackson	40.7%	56.4%	2.9%
PIKE	1,397	1,049	194	154	Dukakis	75.1%	13.9%	11.0%
POTTER	1,455	1,097	202	156	Dukakis	75.4%	13.9%	10.7%
SCHUYLKILL	13,845	11,846	1,256	743	Dukakis	85.6%	9.1%	5.4%
SNYDER	1,856	1,403	315	138	Dukakis	75.6%	17.0%	7.4%
SOMERSET	8,165	6,352	1,177	636	Dukakis	77.8%	14.4%	7.8%
SULLIVAN	901	670	130	101	Dukakis	74.4%	14.4%	11.2%
SUSQUEHANNA	3,428	2,621	533	274	Dukakis	76.5%	15.5%	8.0%
TIOGA	2,412	1,746	394	272	Dukakis	72.4%	16.3%	11.3%
UNION	1,941	1,350	428	163	Dukakis	69.6%	22.1%	8.4%
VENANGO	4,741	3,353	926	462	Dukakis	70.7%	19.5%	9.7%
WARREN	3,775	2,882	573	320	Dukakis	76.3%	15.2%	8.5%
WASHINGTON	40,725	33,160	5,403	2,162	Dukakis	81.4%	13.3%	5.3%
WAYNE	2,297	1,690	344	263	Dukakis	73.6%	15.0%	11.4%
WESTMORELAND	65,093	52,530	7,537	5,026	Dukakis	80.7%	11.6%	7.7%
WYOMING	1,806	1,380	269	157	Dukakis	76.4%	14.9%	8.7%
YORK	23,185	17,525	3,590	2,070	Dukakis	75.6%	15.5%	8.9%
TOTAL	1,507,690	1,002,480	411,260	93,950	Dukakis	66.5%	27.3%	6.2%

Note: The returns from Lawrence County are suspect. Dukakis vote appears low but was certified as such.

PENNSYLVANIA REPUBLICAN

1988

County	Total Vote	Bush	Dole	Robertson	Winner	Percentage of Total Vote		
						Bush	Dole	Robertson
ADAMS	7,053	5,743	844	466	Bush	81.4%	12.0%	6.6%
ALLEGHENY	79,188	58,925	10,733	9,530	Bush	74.4%	13.6%	12.0%
ARMSTRONG	6,155	4,450	1,096	609	Bush	72.3%	17.8%	9.9%
BEAVER	10,821	7,594	1,678	1,549	Bush	70.2%	15.5%	14.3%
BEDFORD	4,922	3,917	559	446	Bush	79.6%	11.4%	9.1%
BERKS	17,499	14,067	1,819	1,613	Bush	80.4%	10.4%	9.2%
BLAIR	11,834	9,127	1,565	1,142	Bush	77.1%	13.2%	9.7%
BRADFORD	6,340	4,829	1,043	468	Bush	76.2%	16.5%	7.4%
BUCKS	35,878	28,528	3,697	3,653	Bush	79.5%	10.3%	10.2%
BUTLER	11,784	8,611	1,932	1,241	Bush	73.1%	16.4%	10.5%
CAMBRIA	10,406	8,015	1,453	938	Bush	77.0%	14.0%	9.0%
CAMERON	828	690	90	48	Bush	83.3%	10.9%	5.8%
CARBON	3,230	2,512	457	261	Bush	77.8%	14.1%	8.1%
CENTRE	9,007	6,932	1,359	716	Bush	77.0%	15.1%	7.9%
CHESTER	34,397	28,025	4,323	2,049	Bush	81.5%	12.6%	6.0%
CLARION	3,674	2,788	509	377	Bush	75.9%	13.9%	10.3%
CLEARFIELD	6,674	5,073	779	822	Bush	76.0%	11.7%	12.3%
CLINTON	2,786	2,090	466	230	Bush	75.0%	16.7%	8.3%
COLUMBIA	3,901	3,200	465	236	Bush	82.0%	11.9%	6.0%
CRAWFORD	8,513	6,566	1,145	802	Bush	77.1%	13.5%	9.4%
CUMBERLAND	19,838	15,676	2,819	1,343	Bush	79.0%	14.2%	6.8%
DAUPHIN	26,062	20,557	3,408	2,097	Bush	78.9%	13.1%	8.0%
DELAWARE	77,316	64,556	7,297	5,463	Bush	83.5%	9.4%	7.1%
ELK	2,597	2,007	281	309	Bush	77.3%	10.8%	11.9%
ERIE	19,727	15,277	2,708	1,742	Bush	77.4%	13.7%	8.8%
FAYETTE	4,965	3,825	558	582	Bush	77.0%	11.2%	11.7%
FOREST	649	499	104	46	Bush	76.9%	16.0%	7.1%
FRANKLIN	12,805	10,279	1,657	869	Bush	80.3%	12.9%	6.8%
FULTON	1,196	974	141	81	Bush	81.4%	11.8%	6.8%
GREENE	1,606	1,161	239	206	Bush	72.3%	14.9%	12.8%
HUNTINGDON	4,316	3,382	496	438	Bush	78.4%	11.5%	10.1%
INDIANA	7,303	5,366	1,146	791	Bush	73.5%	15.7%	10.8%
JEFFERSON	4,767	3,647	576	544	Bush	76.5%	12.1%	11.4%
JUNIATA	2,880	2,301	386	193	Bush	79.9%	13.4%	6.7%
LACKAWANNA	9,652	7,950	968	734	Bush	82.4%	10.0%	7.6%
LANCASTER	36,776	29,294	3,556	3,926	Bush	79.7%	9.7%	10.7%
LAWRENCE	7,433	5,426	1,229	778	Bush	73.0%	16.5%	10.5%
LEBANON	10,941	8,142	1,420	1,379	Bush	74.4%	13.0%	12.6%
LEHIGH	16,109	12,736	1,921	1,452	Bush	79.1%	11.9%	9.0%
LUZERNE	21,335	17,430	2,424	1,481	Bush	81.7%	11.4%	6.9%
LYCOMING	10,502	8,615	1,169	718	Bush	82.0%	11.1%	6.8%
MCKEAN	4,527	3,417	585	525	Bush	75.5%	12.9%	11.6%
MERCER	8,319	6,125	1,186	1,008	Bush	73.6%	14.3%	12.1%
MIFFLIN	3,684	2,940	478	266	Bush	79.8%	13.0%	7.2%
MONROE	4,862	3,859	576	427	Bush	79.4%	11.8%	8.8%
MONTGOMERY	66,075	52,559	7,867	5,649	Bush	79.5%	11.9%	8.5%
MONTOUR	1,241	987	187	67	Bush	79.5%	15.1%	5.4%
NORTHAMPTON	11,028	8,781	1,342	905	Bush	79.6%	12.2%	8.2%
NORTHUMBERLAND	7,677	6,291	819	567	Bush	81.9%	10.7%	7.4%
PERRY	5,137	3,896	778	463	Bush	75.8%	15.1%	9.0%

PENNSYLVANIA REPUBLICAN

1988

County	Total Vote	Bush	Dole	Robertson	Winner	Percentage of Total Vote		
						Bush	Dole	Robertson
PHILADELPHIA	65,654	53,921	6,287	5,446	Bush	82.1%	9.6%	8.3%
PIKE	1,808	1,440	226	142	Bush	79.6%	12.5%	7.9%
POTTER	2,123	1,604	311	208	Bush	75.6%	14.6%	9.8%
SCHUYLKILL	13,880	12,516	202	1,162	Bush	90.2%	1.5%	8.4%
SNYDER	4,341	3,554	510	277	Bush	81.9%	11.7%	6.4%
SOMERSET	7,491	5,867	840	784	Bush	78.3%	11.2%	10.5%
SULLIVAN	1,193	980	163	50	Bush	82.1%	13.7%	4.2%
SUSQUEHANNA	5,839	4,658	852	329	Bush	79.8%	14.6%	5.6%
TIOGA	5,264	3,926	812	526	Bush	74.6%	15.4%	10.0%
UNION	3,693	3,022	430	241	Bush	81.8%	11.6%	6.5%
VENANGO	6,105	4,360	1,023	722	Bush	71.4%	16.8%	11.8%
WARREN	4,690	3,563	608	519	Bush	76.0%	13.0%	11.1%
WASHINGTON	10,785	8,040	1,575	1,170	Bush	74.5%	14.6%	10.8%
WAYNE	4,512	3,591	540	381	Bush	79.6%	12.0%	8.4%
WESTMORELAND	20,185	15,055	2,392	2,738	Bush	74.6%	11.9%	13.6%
WYOMING	4,644	3,843	524	277	Bush	82.8%	11.3%	6.0%
YORK	22,127	17,746	2,135	2,246	Bush	80.2%	9.6%	10.2%
TOTAL	870,549	687,323	103,763	79,463	Bush	79.0%	11.9%	9.1%

PENNSYLVANIA DEMOCRATIC

1992

County	Total Vote	Brown	Clinton	Tsongas	Other	Winner	Percentage of Total Vote			
							Brown	Clinton	Tsongas	Other
ADAMS	4,453	975	2,439	850	189	Clinton	21.9%	54.8%	19.1%	4.2%
ALLEGHENY	229,900	55,134	129,145	30,016	15,605	Clinton	24.0%	56.2%	13.1%	6.8%
ARMSTRONG	8,258	1,815	5,433	671	339	Clinton	22.0%	65.8%	8.1%	4.1%
BEAVER	35,899	8,427	23,644	2,652	1,176	Clinton	23.5%	65.9%	7.4%	3.3%
BEDFORD	3,393	538	2,416	317	122	Clinton	15.9%	71.2%	9.3%	3.6%
BERKS	33,146	8,627	17,797	5,114	1,608	Clinton	26.0%	53.7%	15.4%	4.9%
BLAIR	7,995	2,293	4,154	1,038	510	Clinton	28.7%	52.0%	13.0%	6.4%
BRADFORD	2,648	604	1,543	395	106	Clinton	22.8%	58.3%	14.9%	4.0%
BUCKS	41,085	11,729	20,064	7,382	1,910	Clinton	28.5%	48.8%	18.0%	4.6%
BUTLER	14,372	3,794	8,210	1,711	657	Clinton	26.4%	57.1%	11.9%	4.6%
CAMBRIA	27,170	5,360	16,734	3,564	1,512	Clinton	19.7%	61.6%	13.1%	5.6%
CAMERON	541	110	339	68	24	Clinton	20.3%	62.7%	12.6%	4.4%
CARBON	5,263	1,612	2,767	610	274	Clinton	30.6%	52.6%	11.6%	5.2%
CENTRE	10,408	3,068	5,252	1,716	372	Clinton	29.5%	50.5%	16.5%	3.6%
CHESTER	19,712	6,239	9,514	3,469	490	Clinton	31.7%	48.3%	17.6%	2.5%
CLARION	4,388	868	2,875	482	163	Clinton	19.8%	65.5%	11.0%	3.7%
CLEARFIELD	8,102	1,704	5,265	837	296	Clinton	21.0%	65.0%	10.3%	3.7%
CLINTON	3,002	638	1,889	322	153	Clinton	21.3%	62.9%	10.7%	5.1%
COLUMBIA	6,551	1,961	3,401	786	403	Clinton	29.9%	51.9%	12.0%	6.2%
CRAWFORD	7,065	2,068	3,683	922	392	Clinton	29.3%	52.1%	13.1%	5.5%

PENNSYLVANIA DEMOCRATIC

1992

County	Total Vote	Brown	Clinton	Tsongas	Other	Winner	Percentage of Total Vote Brown	Clinton	Tsongas	Other
CUMBERLAND	12,984	2,813	6,653	2,830	688	Clinton	21.7%	51.2%	21.8%	5.3%
DAUPHIN	17,196	3,741	9,504	3,243	708	Clinton	21.8%	55.3%	18.9%	4.1%
DELAWARE	33,318	9,959	15,746	5,818	1,795	Clinton	29.9%	47.3%	17.5%	5.4%
ELK	4,150	1,070	2,386	505	189	Clinton	25.8%	57.5%	12.2%	4.6%
ERIE	37,188	12,575	16,271	6,209	2,133	Clinton	33.8%	43.8%	16.7%	5.7%
FAYETTE	26,563	4,526	18,865	2,279	893	Clinton	17.0%	71.0%	8.6%	3.4%
FOREST	525	89	361	48	27	Clinton	17.0%	68.8%	9.1%	5.1%
FRANKLIN	5,590	912	3,511	958	209	Clinton	16.3%	62.8%	17.1%	3.7%
FULTON	964	122	669	130	43	Clinton	12.7%	69.4%	13.5%	4.5%
GREENE	7,299	1,083	5,357	592	267	Clinton	14.8%	73.4%	8.1%	3.7%
HUNTINGDON	2,959	616	1,848	340	155	Clinton	20.8%	62.5%	11.5%	5.2%
INDIANA	8,196	1,834	5,353	699	310	Clinton	22.4%	65.3%	8.5%	3.8%
JEFFERSON	3,705	819	2,401	356	129	Clinton	22.1%	64.8%	9.6%	3.5%
JUNIATA	1,572	239	1,054	204	75	Clinton	15.2%	67.0%	13.0%	4.8%
LACKAWANNA	31,271	13,923	13,058	2,953	1,337	Brown	44.5%	41.8%	9.4%	4.3%
LANCASTER	16,847	4,670	8,017	3,138	1,022	Clinton	27.7%	47.6%	18.6%	6.1%
LAWRENCE	13,986	3,269	8,968	1,183	566	Clinton	23.4%	64.1%	8.5%	4.0%
LEBANON	5,699	1,299	2,880	1,158	362	Clinton	22.8%	50.5%	20.3%	6.4%
LEHIGH	24,854	8,407	11,543	3,779	1,125	Clinton	33.8%	46.4%	15.2%	4.5%
LUZERNE	36,380	16,488	14,863	3,517	1,512	Brown	45.3%	40.9%	9.7%	4.2%
LYCOMING	7,624	2,178	4,036	1,056	354	Clinton	28.6%	52.9%	13.9%	4.6%
MCKEAN	2,374	595	1,328	373	78	Clinton	25.1%	55.9%	15.7%	3.3%
MERCER	11,946	2,768	7,058	1,482	638	Clinton	23.2%	59.1%	12.4%	5.3%
MIFFLIN	2,891	573	1,718	433	167	Clinton	19.8%	59.4%	15.0%	5.8%
MONROE	6,131	1,923	2,830	991	387	Clinton	31.4%	46.2%	16.2%	6.3%
MONTGOMERY	47,247	12,484	25,303	8,363	1,097	Clinton	26.4%	53.6%	17.7%	2.3%
MONTOUR	1,343	372	673	219	79	Clinton	27.7%	50.1%	16.3%	5.9%
NORTHAMPTON	25,043	8,694	11,746	3,289	1,314	Clinton	34.7%	46.9%	13.1%	5.2%
NORTHUMBERLAND	8,204	2,165	4,390	1,226	423	Clinton	26.4%	53.5%	14.9%	5.2%
PERRY	2,356	470	1,354	402	130	Clinton	19.9%	57.5%	17.1%	5.5%
PHILADELPHIA	217,497	48,287	137,129	21,006	11,075	Clinton	22.2%	63.0%	9.7%	5.1%
PIKE	1,367	382	586	319	80	Clinton	27.9%	42.9%	23.3%	5.9%
POTTER	1,202	253	738	158	53	Clinton	21.0%	61.4%	13.1%	4.4%
SCHUYLKILL	13,226	3,470	7,889	1,330	537	Clinton	26.2%	59.6%	10.1%	4.1%
SNYDER	1,293	252	801	186	54	Clinton	19.5%	61.9%	14.4%	4.2%
SOMERSET	8,355	1,349	5,736	974	296	Clinton	16.1%	68.7%	11.7%	3.5%
SULLIVAN	629	148	390	63	28	Clinton	23.5%	62.0%	10.0%	4.5%
SUSQUEHANNA	2,534	694	1,456	279	105	Clinton	27.4%	57.5%	11.0%	4.1%
TIOGA	2,462	408	1,542	386	126	Clinton	16.6%	62.6%	15.7%	5.1%
UNION	1,604	431	778	331	64	Clinton	26.9%	48.5%	20.6%	4.0%
VENANGO	4,917	1,153	2,908	575	281	Clinton	23.4%	59.1%	11.7%	5.7%
WARREN	3,123	772	1,691	447	213	Clinton	24.7%	54.1%	14.3%	6.8%
WASHINGTON	36,218	7,168	24,598	3,139	1,313	Clinton	19.8%	67.9%	8.7%	3.6%
WAYNE	2,203	786	1,018	288	111	Clinton	35.7%	46.2%	13.1%	5.0%
WESTMORELAND	62,883	15,612	37,518	6,782	2,971	Clinton	24.8%	59.7%	10.8%	4.7%
WYOMING	1,508	542	752	150	64	Clinton	35.9%	49.9%	9.9%	4.2%
YORK	24,718	5,596	13,193	4,464	1,465	Clinton	22.6%	53.4%	18.1%	5.9%
TOTAL	1,265,495	325,543	715,031	161,572	63,349	Clinton	25.7%	56.5%	12.8%	5.0%

PENNSYLVANIA REPUBLICAN

1992

County	Total Vote	Buchanan	Bush	Winner	Percentage of Total Vote	
					Buchanan	Bush
ADAMS	6,819	1,139	5,680	Bush	16.7%	83.3%
ALLEGHENY	82,617	18,947	63,670	Bush	22.9%	77.1%
ARMSTRONG	6,181	1,945	4,236	Bush	31.5%	68.5%
BEAVER	11,545	3,073	8,472	Bush	26.6%	73.4%
BEDFORD	4,970	892	4,078	Bush	17.9%	82.1%
BERKS	26,703	5,642	21,061	Bush	21.1%	78.9%
BLAIR	14,991	3,136	11,855	Bush	20.9%	79.1%
BRADFORD	7,127	1,448	5,679	Bush	20.3%	79.7%
BUCKS	48,602	12,554	36,048	Bush	25.8%	74.2%
BUTLER	14,455	4,122	10,333	Bush	28.5%	71.5%
CAMBRIA	11,289	3,052	8,237	Bush	27.0%	73.0%
CAMERON	736	132	604	Bush	17.9%	82.1%
CARBON	3,718	906	2,812	Bush	24.4%	75.6%
CENTRE	11,451	2,396	9,055	Bush	20.9%	79.1%
CHESTER	47,519	10,421	37,098	Bush	21.9%	78.1%
CLARION	4,639	1,124	3,515	Bush	24.2%	75.8%
CLEARFIELD	7,042	1,680	5,362	Bush	23.9%	76.1%
CLINTON	3,063	693	2,370	Bush	22.6%	77.4%
COLUMBIA	5,646	1,023	4,623	Bush	18.1%	81.9%
CRAWFORD	8,741	2,042	6,699	Bush	23.4%	76.6%
CUMBERLAND	26,403	4,652	21,751	Bush	17.6%	82.4%
DAUPHIN	27,658	5,069	22,589	Bush	18.3%	81.7%
DELAWARE	88,004	23,750	64,254	Bush	27.0%	73.0%
ELK	2,751	687	2,064	Bush	25.0%	75.0%
ERIE	22,618	5,238	17,380	Bush	23.2%	76.8%
FAYETTE	5,571	1,391	4,180	Bush	25.0%	75.0%
FOREST	666	147	519	Bush	22.1%	77.9%
FRANKLIN	10,226	1,711	8,515	Bush	16.7%	83.3%
FULTON	1,116	200	916	Bush	17.9%	82.1%
GREENE	1,551	318	1,233	Bush	20.5%	79.5%
HUNTINGDON	5,342	1,042	4,300	Bush	19.5%	80.5%
INDIANA	7,061	1,792	5,269	Bush	25.4%	74.6%
JEFFERSON	4,732	1,118	3,614	Bush	23.6%	76.4%
JUNIATA	2,141	347	1,794	Bush	16.2%	83.8%
LACKAWANNA	11,510	2,489	9,021	Bush	21.6%	78.4%
LANCASTER	49,280	9,121	40,159	Bush	18.5%	81.5%
LAWRENCE	7,779	2,029	5,750	Bush	26.1%	73.9%
LEBANON	13,297	2,701	10,596	Bush	20.3%	79.7%
LEHIGH	19,927	4,836	15,091	Bush	24.3%	75.7%
LUZERNE	21,249	4,951	16,298	Bush	23.3%	76.7%
LYCOMING	10,577	2,198	8,379	Bush	20.8%	79.2%
MCKEAN	4,844	1,038	3,806	Bush	21.4%	78.6%
MERCER	10,125	2,295	7,830	Bush	22.7%	77.3%
MIFFLIN	3,678	737	2,941	Bush	20.0%	80.0%
MONROE	5,782	1,271	4,511	Bush	22.0%	78.0%
MONTGOMERY	85,495	21,069	64,426	Bush	24.6%	75.4%
MONTOUR	1,477	281	1,196	Bush	19.0%	81.0%
NORTHAMPTON	12,989	3,003	9,986	Bush	23.1%	76.9%
NORTHUMBERLAND	8,055	1,905	6,150	Bush	23.6%	76.4%
PERRY	6,246	1,196	5,050	Bush	19.1%	80.9%

PENNSYLVANIA REPUBLICAN

1992

County	Total Vote	Buchanan	Bush	Winner	Percentage of Total Vote Buchanan	Percentage of Total Vote Bush
PHILADELPHIA	67,199	18,790	48,409	Bush	28.0%	72.0%
PIKE	2,276	487	1,789	Bush	21.4%	78.6%
POTTER	2,509	474	2,035	Bush	18.9%	81.1%
SCHUYLKILL	16,834	4,085	12,749	Bush	24.3%	75.7%
SNYDER	3,912	611	3,301	Bush	15.6%	84.4%
SOMERSET	7,858	1,570	6,288	Bush	20.0%	80.0%
SULLIVAN	863	144	719	Bush	16.7%	83.3%
SUSQUEHANNA	4,495	917	3,578	Bush	20.4%	79.6%
TIOGA	7,558	1,471	6,087	Bush	19.5%	80.5%
UNION	3,572	629	2,943	Bush	17.6%	82.4%
VENANGO	7,655	2,117	5,538	Bush	27.7%	72.3%
WARREN	4,387	964	3,423	Bush	22.0%	78.0%
WASHINGTON	10,729	2,690	8,039	Bush	25.1%	74.9%
WAYNE	5,121	1,101	4,020	Bush	21.5%	78.5%
WESTMORELAND	21,854	5,589	16,265	Bush	25.6%	74.4%
WYOMING	3,485	655	2,830	Bush	18.8%	81.2%
YORK	32,466	6,669	25,797	Bush	20.5%	79.5%
TOTAL	1,008,777	233,912	774,865	Bush	23.2%	76.8%

PENNSYLVANIA DEMOCRATIC

1996

County	Total Vote	Clinton	LaRouche	Winner	Percentage of Total Vote Clinton	Percentage of Total Vote LaRouche
ADAMS	2,360	2,157	203	Clinton	91.4%	8.6%
ALLEGHENY	145,165	132,281	12,884	Clinton	91.1%	8.9%
ARMSTRONG	4,408	3,865	543	Clinton	87.7%	12.3%
BEAVER	16,684	15,214	1,470	Clinton	91.2%	8.8%
BEDFORD	1,893	1,717	176	Clinton	90.7%	9.3%
BERKS	12,425	10,863	1,562	Clinton	87.4%	12.6%
BLAIR	4,082	3,671	411	Clinton	89.9%	10.1%
BRADFORD	1,420	1,297	123	Clinton	91.3%	8.7%
BUCKS	14,801	13,760	1,041	Clinton	93.0%	7.0%
BUTLER	9,013	7,759	1,254	Clinton	86.1%	13.9%
CAMBRIA	21,064	19,348	1,716	Clinton	91.9%	8.1%
CAMERON	404	338	66	Clinton	83.7%	16.3%
CARBON	4,437	3,982	455	Clinton	89.7%	10.3%
CENTRE	5,330	4,926	404	Clinton	92.4%	7.6%
CHESTER	7,505	7,148	357	Clinton	95.2%	4.8%
CLARION	3,139	2,754	385	Clinton	87.7%	12.3%
CLEARFIELD	6,041	5,411	630	Clinton	89.6%	10.4%
CLINTON	1,928	1,730	198	Clinton	89.7%	10.3%
COLUMBIA	3,266	2,944	322	Clinton	90.1%	9.9%
CRAWFORD	3,785	3,442	343	Clinton	90.9%	9.1%

PENNSYLVANIA DEMOCRATIC

1996

County	Total Vote	Clinton	LaRouche	Winner	Percentage of Total Vote	
					Clinton	LaRouche
CUMBERLAND	5,958	5,584	374	Clinton	93.7%	6.3%
DAUPHIN	9,099	8,583	516	Clinton	94.3%	5.7%
DELAWARE	17,429	16,633	796	Clinton	95.4%	4.6%
ELK	3,319	2,904	415	Clinton	87.5%	12.5%
ERIE	19,788	18,215	1,573	Clinton	92.1%	7.9%
FAYETTE	13,767	12,335	1,432	Clinton	89.6%	10.4%
FOREST	413	376	37	Clinton	91.0%	9.0%
FRANKLIN	2,469	2,283	186	Clinton	92.5%	7.5%
FULTON	505	448	57	Clinton	88.7%	11.3%
GREENE	4,113	3,722	391	Clinton	90.5%	9.5%
HUNTINGDON	1,566	1,416	150	Clinton	90.4%	9.6%
INDIANA	5,187	4,777	410	Clinton	92.1%	7.9%
JEFFERSON	3,245	2,845	400	Clinton	87.7%	12.3%
JUNIATA	861	793	68	Clinton	92.1%	7.9%
LACKAWANNA	17,059	15,903	1,156	Clinton	93.2%	6.8%
LANCASTER	6,990	6,464	526	Clinton	92.5%	7.5%
LAWRENCE	11,250	10,433	817	Clinton	92.7%	7.3%
LEBANON	2,267	2,061	206	Clinton	90.9%	9.1%
LEHIGH	13,877	12,705	1,172	Clinton	91.6%	8.4%
LUZERNE	22,896	20,499	2,397	Clinton	89.5%	10.5%
LYCOMING	3,298	2,933	365	Clinton	88.9%	11.1%
MCKEAN	1,531	1,380	151	Clinton	90.1%	9.9%
MERCER	6,657	6,174	483	Clinton	92.7%	7.3%
MIFFLIN	1,383	1,277	106	Clinton	92.3%	7.7%
MONROE	2,793	2,519	274	Clinton	90.2%	9.8%
MONTGOMERY	17,416	16,784	632	Clinton	96.4%	3.6%
MONTOUR	669	607	62	Clinton	90.7%	9.3%
NORTHAMPTON	13,492	12,193	1,299	Clinton	90.4%	9.6%
NORTHUMBERLAND	4,946	4,426	520	Clinton	89.5%	10.5%
PERRY	1,142	1,060	82	Clinton	92.8%	7.2%
PHILADELPHIA	139,705	134,508	5,197	Clinton	96.3%	3.7%
PIKE	579	534	45	Clinton	92.2%	7.8%
POTTER	691	611	80	Clinton	88.4%	11.6%
SCHUYLKILL	7,814	7,181	633	Clinton	91.9%	8.1%
SNYDER	742	683	59	Clinton	92.0%	8.0%
SOMERSET	5,676	5,218	458	Clinton	91.9%	8.1%
SULLIVAN	403	366	37	Clinton	90.8%	9.2%
SUSQUEHANNA	1,576	1,444	132	Clinton	91.6%	8.4%
TIOGA	1,332	1,220	112	Clinton	91.6%	8.4%
UNION	963	883	80	Clinton	91.7%	8.3%
VENANGO	2,826	2,573	253	Clinton	91.0%	9.0%
WARREN	2,205	2,012	193	Clinton	91.2%	8.8%
WASHINGTON	20,143	18,165	1,978	Clinton	90.2%	9.8%
WAYNE	1,197	1,087	110	Clinton	90.8%	9.2%
WESTMORELAND	41,303	35,892	5,411	Clinton	86.9%	13.1%
WYOMING	943	883	60	Clinton	93.6%	6.4%
YORK	11,436	10,287	1,149	Clinton	90.0%	10.0%
TOTAL	724,069	666,486	57,583	Clinton	92.0%	8.0%

PENNSYLVANIA REPUBLICAN

1996

County	Total Vote	Buchanan	Dole	Other	Winner	Percentage of Total Vote Buchanan	Dole	Other
ADAMS	5,637	840	4,010	787	Dole	14.9%	71.1%	14.0%
ALLEGHENY	58,513	7,833	37,850	12,830	Dole	13.4%	64.7%	21.9%
ARMSTRONG	4,567	1,105	2,628	834	Dole	24.2%	57.5%	18.3%
BEAVER	7,697	1,701	4,537	1,459	Dole	22.1%	58.9%	19.0%
BEDFORD	3,664	648	2,586	430	Dole	17.7%	70.6%	11.7%
BERKS	16,156	2,217	10,942	2,997	Dole	13.7%	67.7%	18.6%
BLAIR	8,702	1,606	5,731	1,365	Dole	18.5%	65.9%	15.7%
BRADFORD	4,959	1,105	3,023	831	Dole	22.3%	61.0%	16.8%
BUCKS	27,622	5,339	16,543	5,740	Dole	19.3%	59.9%	20.8%
BUTLER	13,721	2,779	8,201	2,741	Dole	20.3%	59.8%	20.0%
CAMBRIA	9,156	2,106	5,774	1,276	Dole	23.0%	63.1%	13.9%
CAMERON	686	179	425	82	Dole	26.1%	62.0%	12.0%
CARBON	2,702	478	1,787	437	Dole	17.7%	66.1%	16.2%
CENTRE	11,461	1,505	7,913	2,043	Dole	13.1%	69.0%	17.8%
CHESTER	32,907	4,530	21,016	7,361	Dole	13.8%	63.9%	22.4%
CLARION	4,621	1,050	2,876	695	Dole	22.7%	62.2%	15.0%
CLEARFIELD	6,554	1,543	4,054	957	Dole	23.5%	61.9%	14.6%
CLINTON	2,441	479	1,575	387	Dole	19.6%	64.5%	15.9%
COLUMBIA	3,101	591	2,081	429	Dole	19.1%	67.1%	13.8%
CRAWFORD	7,330	1,575	4,679	1,076	Dole	21.5%	63.8%	14.7%
CUMBERLAND	16,586	2,061	12,186	2,339	Dole	12.4%	73.5%	14.1%
DAUPHIN	18,992	2,694	13,375	2,923	Dole	14.2%	70.4%	15.4%
DELAWARE	57,936	11,853	31,961	14,122	Dole	20.5%	55.2%	24.4%
ELK	2,757	695	1,681	381	Dole	25.2%	61.0%	13.8%
ERIE	16,429	3,548	10,322	2,559	Dole	21.6%	62.8%	15.6%
FAYETTE	3,621	873	2,178	570	Dole	24.1%	60.1%	15.7%
FOREST	716	132	475	109	Dole	18.4%	66.3%	15.2%
FRANKLIN	6,121	1,075	4,297	749	Dole	17.6%	70.2%	12.2%
FULTON	727	155	488	84	Dole	21.3%	67.1%	11.6%
GREENE	1,208	269	730	209	Dole	22.3%	60.4%	17.3%
HUNTINGDON	3,291	654	2,184	453	Dole	19.9%	66.4%	13.8%
INDIANA	6,246	1,293	3,981	972	Dole	20.7%	63.7%	15.6%
JEFFERSON	5,445	1,238	3,441	766	Dole	22.7%	63.2%	14.1%
JUNIATA	1,453	230	1,024	199	Dole	15.8%	70.5%	13.7%
LACKAWANNA	6,930	1,088	4,616	1,226	Dole	15.7%	66.6%	17.7%
LANCASTER	40,887	6,073	28,897	5,917	Dole	14.9%	70.7%	14.5%
LAWRENCE	6,566	1,401	4,122	1,043	Dole	21.3%	62.8%	15.9%
LEBANON	7,870	1,476	5,075	1,319	Dole	18.8%	64.5%	16.8%
LEHIGH	16,227	2,459	11,103	2,665	Dole	15.2%	68.4%	16.4%
LUZERNE	13,384	2,780	8,382	2,222	Dole	20.8%	62.6%	16.6%
LYCOMING	6,949	1,123	4,690	1,136	Dole	16.2%	67.5%	16.3%
MCKEAN	4,539	864	2,898	777	Dole	19.0%	63.8%	17.1%
MERCER	7,848	1,687	4,870	1,291	Dole	21.5%	62.1%	16.5%
MIFFLIN	2,329	361	1,592	376	Dole	15.5%	68.4%	16.1%
MONROE	4,087	691	2,708	688	Dole	16.9%	66.3%	16.8%
MONTGOMERY	43,244	7,121	26,107	10,016	Dole	16.5%	60.4%	23.2%
MONTOUR	868	143	585	140	Dole	16.5%	67.4%	16.1%
NORTHAMPTON	11,642	1,604	8,163	1,875	Dole	13.8%	70.1%	16.1%
NORTHUMBERLAND	5,149	1,279	3,105	765	Dole	24.8%	60.3%	14.9%
PERRY	3,322	609	2,288	425	Dole	18.3%	68.9%	12.8%

PENNSYLVANIA REPUBLICAN

1996

County	Total Vote	Buchanan	Dole	Other	Winner	Percentage of Total Vote Buchanan	Dole	Other
PHILADELPHIA	25,320	5,780	13,480	6,060	Dole	22.8%	53.2%	23.9%
PIKE	1,499	270	980	249	Dole	18.0%	65.4%	16.6%
POTTER	2,019	384	1,336	299	Dole	19.0%	66.2%	14.8%
SCHUYLKILL	11,336	2,342	7,454	1,540	Dole	20.7%	65.8%	13.6%
SNYDER	2,565	546	1,689	330	Dole	21.3%	65.8%	12.9%
SOMERSET	6,627	1,393	4,391	843	Dole	21.0%	66.3%	12.7%
SULLIVAN	633	79	463	91	Dole	12.5%	73.1%	14.4%
SUSQUEHANNA	3,759	683	2,446	630	Dole	18.2%	65.1%	16.8%
TIOGA	4,790	1,062	2,988	740	Dole	22.2%	62.4%	15.4%
UNION	3,259	613	2,125	521	Dole	18.8%	65.2%	16.0%
VENANGO	6,212	1,157	3,987	1,068	Dole	18.6%	64.2%	17.2%
WARREN	4,612	861	2,750	1,001	Dole	18.7%	59.6%	21.7%
WASHINGTON	7,262	1,368	4,372	1,522	Dole	18.8%	60.2%	21.0%
WAYNE	3,904	748	2,523	633	Dole	19.2%	64.6%	16.2%
WESTMORELAND	18,434	4,465	10,385	3,584	Dole	24.2%	56.3%	19.4%
WYOMING	2,521	436	1,703	382	Dole	17.3%	67.6%	15.2%
YORK	23,886	4,086	16,204	3,596	Dole	17.1%	67.8%	15.1%
TOTAL	684,204	123,011	435,031	126,162	Dole	18.0%	63.6%	18.4%

RHODE ISLAND

Rhode Island is heavily Catholic, urban and ethnic, and one of the most Democratic states in the country. But Rhode Island Democrats have often used their presidential primary to rebuke their party's eventual nominee. An uncommitted slate adopted by Jerry Brown beat Jimmy Carter in 1976; Edward Kennedy routed Carter in 1980; Gary Hart defeated Walter Mondale in 1984; and Paul Tsongas overwhelmed Bill Clinton in 1992.

These anomalous results were partly attributable to low turnout, which allowed relatively small numbers of voters to tip the results. Even though Rhode Island independents are permitted to vote in either the Democratic or Republican primary, as they are in much of New England, that allure has failed to produce high turnouts. Since the state's first presidential primary was held in 1972, no more than 75,000 of its roughly half-million voters have gone to the polls in any year.

With such a limited turnout, liberal activists have tended to have the upper hand in Democratic primary voting in spite of Rhode Island's heritage as a heavily unionized state with conservative social values.

But geography also has driven the vote in a number of Democratic primaries. In 1992, Tsongas continued Rhode Island's tradition of supporting candidates from neighboring Massachusetts.

Both Kennedy in 1980 and Michael Dukakis in 1988 took more than two-thirds of the primary ballots in Rhode Island, besting their showings in their home state. Tsongas won Rhode Island easily in 1992 with 53 percent of the vote, his best showing in a primary outside Massachusetts. Clinton finished a distant second statewide.

While Democratic interest in the presidential primary has never been high, the GOP turnout has been downright minuscule, never reaching 20,000. Most Rhode Islanders who cast Republican primary ballots seem satisfied with moderates of the Gerald Ford–George Bush stripe.

Conservative Republicans, even well-known ones, have had trouble reaching one-third of the vote in competitive GOP primaries in Rhode Island. Ronald Reagan drew only 31 percent against Ford in 1976. Pat Buchanan garnered only 32 percent against Bush in 1992. (Buchanan was not on the Rhode Island ballot in 1996.)

The Narragansett Bay provided a divide of sorts in the 1992 primary. Bush ran better on the eastern side of the bay, with its affluent communities by the water. Buchanan topped 40 percent in a number of towns on the western side.

Recent Rhode Island Primary Results

Rhode Island held its first presidential primary in 1972.

	DEMOCRATS			REPUBLICANS		
Year	Turnout	Candidates	%	Turnout	Candidates	%
1996 (March 5)	8,780	BILL CLINTON*	89	15,009	BOB DOLE	64
					Lamar Alexander	19
1992 (March 10)	50,709	PAUL TSONGAS	53	15,636	GEORGE BUSH*	63
		Bill Clinton	21		Pat Buchanan	32
		Jerry Brown	19			
1988 (March 8)	49,029	MICHAEL DUKAKIS	70	16,035	GEORGE BUSH	65
		Jesse Jackson	15		Bob Dole	23
1984 (March 13)	44,511	GARY HART	45	2,235	RONALD REAGAN*	91
		Walter Mondale	34			
1980 (June 3)	38,327	EDWARD KENNEDY	68	5,335	RONALD REAGAN	72
		Jimmy Carter*	26		George Bush	19
1976 (June 1)	60,348	UNCOMMITTED	32	14,352	GERALD FORD*	65
		Jimmy Carter	30		Ronald Reagan	31
		Frank Church	27			
1972 (May 23)	37,864	GEORGE McGOVERN	41	5,611	RICHARD NIXON*	88
		Edmund Muskie	21			
		Hubert Humphrey	20			
		George Wallace	15			

Note: All candidates are listed that drew at least 10 percent of their party's primary vote. The names of winning candidates are capitalized. An asterisk (*) indicates an incumbent president.

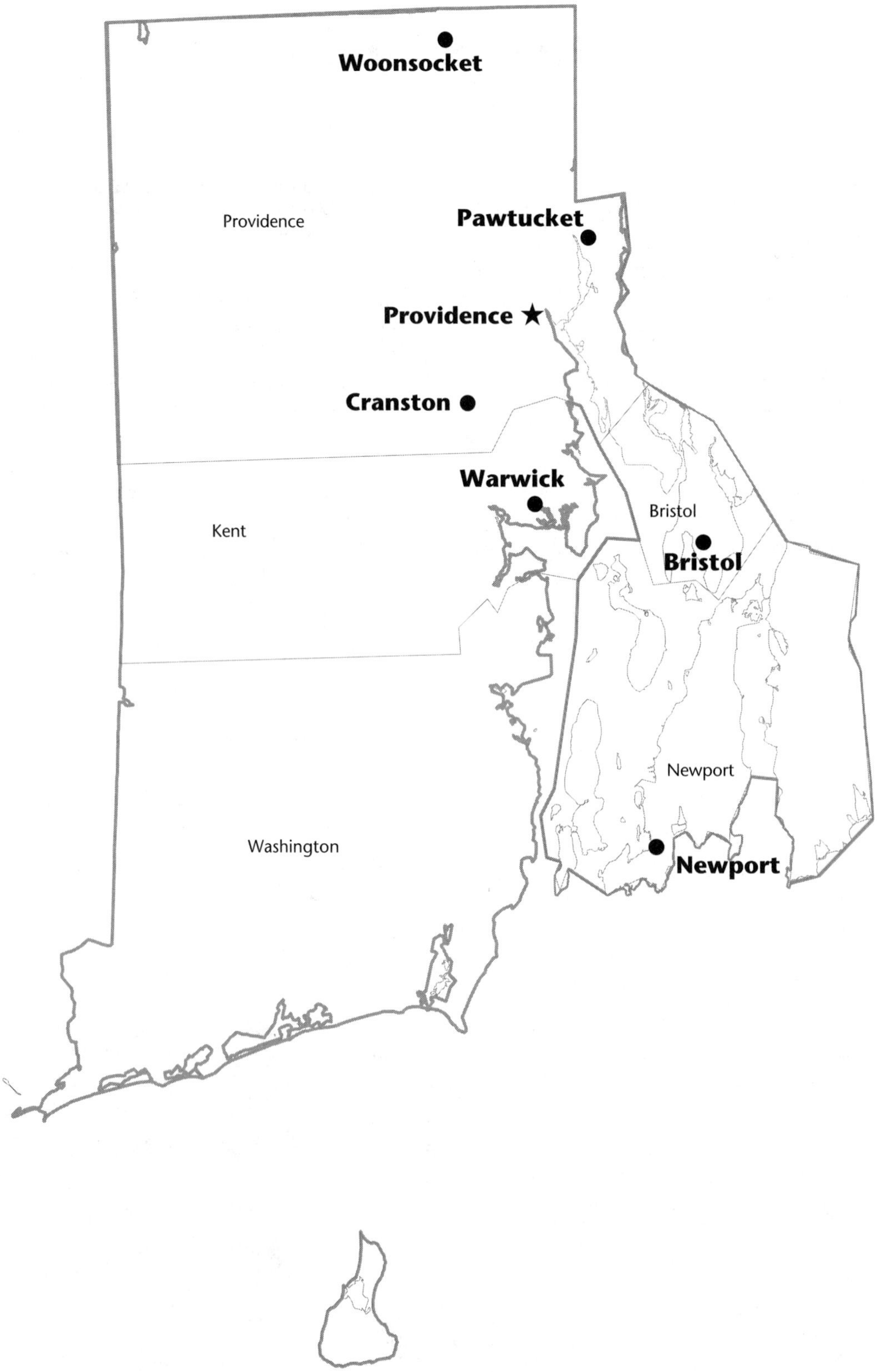

Woonsocket

Providence

Pawtucket

Providence ★

Cranston

Warwick

Kent

Bristol

Bristol

Newport

Washington

Newport

RHODE ISLAND DEMOCRATIC

1972

County	Total Vote	Humphrey	McGovern	Muskie	Wallace	Other	Winner	Percentage of Total Vote Humphrey	McGovern	Muskie	Wallace	Other
BRISTOL	1,574	247	1,020	154	131	22	McGovern	15.7%	64.8%	9.8%	8.3%	1.4%
KENT	4,895	875	2,020	1,132	756	112	McGovern	17.9%	41.3%	23.1%	15.4%	2.3%
NEWPORT	2,313	601	1,008	276	356	72	McGovern	26.0%	43.6%	11.9%	15.4%	3.1%
PROVIDENCE	26,318	5,636	9,828	6,055	4,207	592	McGovern	21.4%	37.3%	23.0%	16.0%	2.2%
WASHINGTON	2,704	342	1,727	221	352	62	McGovern	12.6%	63.9%	8.2%	13.0%	2.3%
TOTAL	37,804	7,701	15,603	7,838	5,802	860	McGovern	20.4%	41.3%	20.7%	15.3%	2.3%
Published Totals	37,864	7,701	15,603	7,838	5,802	920	McGovern	20.3%	41.2%	20.7%	15.3%	2.4%

RHODE ISLAND REPUBLICAN

1972

County	Total Vote	Nixon	Other	Winner	Percentage of Total Vote Nixon	Other
BRISTOL	471	410	61	Nixon	87.0%	13.0%
KENT	794	712	82	Nixon	89.7%	10.3%
NEWPORT	596	526	70	Nixon	88.3%	11.7%
PROVIDENCE	3,066	2,720	346	Nixon	88.7%	11.3%
WASHINGTON	644	555	89	Nixon	86.2%	13.8%
TOTAL	5,571	4,923	648	Nixon	88.4%	11.6%
Published Totals	5,611	4,953	658	Nixon	88.3%	11.7%

RHODE ISLAND DEMOCRATIC

1976

County	Total Vote	Carter	Church	Uncommitted	Other	Winner	Percentage of Total Vote Carter	Church	Uncom.	Other
BRISTOL	2,695	920	547	792	436	Carter	34.1%	20.3%	29.4%	16.2%
KENT	9,091	2,644	2,429	3,196	822	Uncommitted	29.1%	26.7%	35.2%	9.0%
NEWPORT	4,964	1,445	945	1,868	706	Uncommitted	29.1%	19.0%	37.6%	14.2%
PROVIDENCE	39,164	12,125	11,265	11,613	4,161	Carter	31.0%	28.8%	29.7%	10.6%
WASHINGTON	4,434	1,103	1,237	1,566	528	Uncommitted	24.9%	27.9%	35.3%	11.9%
TOTAL	60,348	18,237	16,423	19,035	6,653	Uncommitted	30.2%	27.2%	31.5%	11.0%

RHODE ISLAND REPUBLICAN

1976

County	Total Vote	Ford	Reagan	Uncommitted	Winner	Percentage of Total Vote Ford	Reagan	Uncom.
BRISTOL	1,321	957	330	34	Ford	72.4%	25.0%	2.6%
KENT	2,343	1,466	786	91	Ford	62.6%	33.5%	3.9%
NEWPORT	1,801	1,168	571	62	Ford	64.9%	31.7%	3.4%
PROVIDENCE	6,973	4,546	2,177	250	Ford	65.2%	31.2%	3.6%
WASHINGTON	1,914	1,228	616	70	Ford	64.2%	32.2%	3.7%
TOTAL	14,352	9,365	4,480	507	Ford	65.3%	31.2%	3.5%

RHODE ISLAND DEMOCRATIC

1980

County	Total Vote	Carter	E. Kennedy	Other	Winner	Percentage of Total Vote Carter	E. Kennedy	Other
BRISTOL	1,471	383	992	96	E. Kennedy	26.0%	67.4%	6.5%
KENT	4,760	1,178	3,333	249	E. Kennedy	24.7%	70.0%	5.2%
NEWPORT	2,631	719	1,739	173	E. Kennedy	27.3%	66.1%	6.6%
PROVIDENCE	27,195	6,878	18,738	1,579	E. Kennedy	25.3%	68.9%	5.8%
WASHINGTON	2,270	749	1,377	144	E. Kennedy	33.0%	60.7%	6.3%
TOTAL	38,327	9,907	26,179	2,241	E. Kennedy	25.8%	68.3%	5.8%

RHODE ISLAND REPUBLICAN

1980

County	Total Vote	Bush	Reagan	Other	Winner	Percentage of Total Vote Bush	Reagan	Other
BRISTOL	552	153	352	47	Reagan	27.7%	63.8%	8.5%
KENT	610	84	485	41	Reagan	13.8%	79.5%	6.7%
NEWPORT	801	167	556	78	Reagan	20.8%	69.4%	9.7%
PROVIDENCE	2,736	479	1,973	284	Reagan	17.5%	72.1%	10.4%
WASHINGTON	636	110	473	53	Reagan	17.3%	74.4%	8.3%
TOTAL	5,335	993	3,839	503	Reagan	18.6%	72.0%	9.4%

RHODE ISLAND DEMOCRATIC

1984

County	Total Vote	Hart	Mondale	Other	Winner	Percentage of Total Vote Hart	Mondale	Other
BRISTOL	1,572	762	595	215	Hart	48.5%	37.8%	13.7%
KENT	6,087	3,141	1,986	960	Hart	51.6%	32.6%	15.8%
NEWPORT	3,772	1,903	1,058	811	Hart	50.5%	28.0%	21.5%
PROVIDENCE	29,532	12,258	10,869	6,405	Hart	41.5%	36.8%	21.7%
WASHINGTON	3,548	1,947	830	771	Hart	54.9%	23.4%	21.7%
TOTAL	44,511	20,011	15,338	9,162	Hart	45.0%	34.5%	20.6%

RHODE ISLAND REPUBLICAN

1984

County	Total Vote	Reagan	Uncommitted	Winner	Percentage of Total Vote Reagan	Uncom.
BRISTOL	170	149	21	Reagan	87.6%	12.4%
KENT	316	295	21	Reagan	93.4%	6.6%
NEWPORT	426	391	35	Reagan	91.8%	8.2%
PROVIDENCE	1,083	975	108	Reagan	90.0%	10.0%
WASHINGTON	240	218	22	Reagan	90.8%	9.2%
TOTAL	2,235	2,028	207	Reagan	90.7%	9.3%

RHODE ISLAND DEMOCRATIC

1988

County	Total Vote	Dukakis	J. Jackson	Other	Winner	Percentage of Total Vote: Dukakis	J. Jackson	Other
BRISTOL	1,978	1,436	262	280	Dukakis	72.6%	13.2%	14.2%
KENT	6,719	4,891	816	1,012	Dukakis	72.8%	12.1%	15.1%
NEWPORT	4,134	2,905	673	556	Dukakis	70.3%	16.3%	13.4%
PROVIDENCE	32,477	22,792	4,856	4,829	Dukakis	70.2%	15.0%	14.9%
WASHINGTON	3,651	2,187	838	626	Dukakis	59.9%	23.0%	17.1%
TOTAL	48,959	34,211	7,445	7,303	Dukakis	69.9%	15.2%	14.9%
Certified Totals	49,029	34,211	7,445	7,373	Dukakis	69.8%	15.2%	15.0%

RHODE ISLAND REPUBLICAN

1988

County	Total Vote	Bush	Dole	Other	Winner	Percentage of Total Vote: Bush	Dole	Other
BRISTOL	1,529	1,026	378	125	Bush	67.1%	24.7%	8.2%
KENT	2,706	1,605	707	394	Bush	59.3%	26.1%	14.6%
NEWPORT	2,260	1,493	492	275	Bush	66.1%	21.8%	12.2%
PROVIDENCE	7,314	4,835	1,486	993	Bush	66.1%	20.3%	13.6%
WASHINGTON	2,236	1,442	565	229	Bush	64.5%	25.3%	10.2%
TOTAL	16,045	10,401	3,628	2,016	Bush	64.8%	22.6%	12.6%
Certified Totals	16,035	10,401	3,628	2,006	Bush	64.9%	22.6%	12.5%

RHODE ISLAND DEMOCRATIC

1992

County	Total Vote	Brown	Clinton	Tsongas	Other	Winner	Percentage of Total Vote: Brown	Clinton	Tsongas	Other
BRISTOL	2,630	379	567	1,559	125	Tsongas	14.4%	21.6%	59.3%	4.8%
KENT	8,086	1,461	1,857	4,264	504	Tsongas	18.1%	23.0%	52.7%	6.2%
NEWPORT	4,528	836	813	2,577	302	Tsongas	18.5%	18.0%	56.9%	6.7%
PROVIDENCE	30,371	5,738	6,655	15,871	2,107	Tsongas	18.9%	21.9%	52.3%	6.9%
WASHINGTON	4,787	1,127	870	2,554	236	Tsongas	23.5%	18.2%	53.4%	4.9%
TOTAL	50,709	9,541	10,762	26,825	3,581	Tsongas	18.8%	21.2%	52.9%	7.1%

RHODE ISLAND REPUBLICAN

1992

County	Total Vote	Buchanan	Bush	Other	Winner	Percentage of Total Vote: Buchanan	Bush	Other
BRISTOL	1,490	387	1,043	60	Bush	26.0%	70.0%	4.0%
KENT	2,827	1,016	1,699	112	Bush	35.9%	60.1%	4.0%
NEWPORT	2,161	578	1,444	139	Bush	26.7%	66.8%	6.4%
PROVIDENCE	6,722	2,282	4,122	318	Bush	33.9%	61.3%	4.7%
WASHINGTON	2,390	704	1,545	141	Bush	29.5%	64.6%	5.9%
TOTAL	15,636	4,967	9,853	816	Bush	31.8%	63.0%	5.2%

RHODE ISLAND DEMOCRATIC

1996

County	Total Vote	Clinton	Other	Winner	Percentage of Total Vote: Clinton	Other
BRISTOL	464	431	33	Clinton	92.9%	7.1%
KENT	1,109	963	146	Clinton	86.8%	13.2%
NEWPORT	947	868	79	Clinton	91.7%	8.3%
PROVIDENCE	5,463	4,873	590	Clinton	89.2%	10.8%
WASHINGTON	769	690	79	Clinton	89.7%	10.3%
TOTAL	8,780	7,825	955	Clinton	89.1%	10.9%

Note: The "Total Vote" and "Other" vote totals include 28 scattered write-ins that were not readily available on a county-by-county basis.

RHODE ISLAND REPUBLICAN

1996

County	Total Vote	Alexander	Dole	Other	Winner	Percentage of Total Vote: Alexander	Dole	Other
BRISTOL	1,303	216	947	140	Dole	16.6%	72.7%	10.7%
KENT	2,527	515	1,683	329	Dole	20.4%	66.6%	13.0%
NEWPORT	2,303	444	1,538	321	Dole	19.3%	66.8%	13.9%
PROVIDENCE	5,959	1,228	3,898	833	Dole	20.6%	65.4%	14.0%
WASHINGTON	2,335	456	1,598	281	Dole	19.5%	68.4%	12.0%
TOTAL	15,009	2,859	9,664	2,486	Dole	19.0%	64.4%	16.6%

Note: The "Total Vote" and "Other" vote totals include 582 write-ins that were not readily available on a county-by-county basis. Of these write-ins, 387 were for Buchanan, 128 for Forbes and 31 for Keyes.

SOUTH CAROLINA

In Republican nominating politics, South Carolina has become the gateway to the South—a New Hampshire below the Mason-Dixon line. It first emerged in that role in the 1980s, launching Ronald Reagan and then George Bush to sweeping Super Tuesday victories across the region. And it maintained its critical role in 1996 by handing Bob Dole a pivotal victory that separated him from the rest of the Republican field.

GOP candidates that have succeeded in South Carolina have arrived in the state with some momentum, either from a victory in New Hampshire (as was the case for Reagan and Bush) or from a triumph somewhere else (as was the case for Dole after primary wins in the Dakotas).

But for those Republican candidates without momentum, South Carolina has mainly offered a place to make a last stand. John Connally essentially opened and closed his 1980 presidential campaign in the state. Pat Robertson and Jack Kemp were relegated to also-ran status in 1988 after big efforts in South Carolina failed badly. David Duke's tepid third-place finish in the 1992 primary marked the end of the road for him as a national happening. And in 1996, both Lamar Alexander and Steve Forbes were gone from the race within two weeks of their high-stakes losses in South Carolina.

The state's presidential primary is a legacy of Lee Atwater. A native South Carolinian, Atwater worked the state for Reagan and Bush and encouraged holding the primary at least a few days before Super Tuesday to dominate the news leading up to the Dixie event.

It has proved an effective party-building tool for South Carolina Republicans. Before its creation, turnout for statewide GOP primaries rarely exceeded the 35,000 voters that turned out for the party's gubernatorial contest in 1974, when the featured candidate was former Gen. William C. Westmoreland.

But the party's first presidential primary in 1980 drew nearly 150,000 voters. The second in 1988 attracted almost 200,000, and turnout for the GOP presidential primary in 1996 surpassed 275,000. In the process, the South Carolina GOP has expanded beyond white-collar professionals and well-heeled retirees to include Christian conservatives and converts from the Democratic Party.

While the state's presidential primary has often been crucial, it has never been close. In 1980, Reagan beat runner-up Connally by a margin of nearly 2-to-1. Connally carried only a handful of counties, including Beaufort (with the coastal resort of Hilton Head).

Bush made a belated effort in the 1980 primary but finished a distant third. His leading backer in the state, former Nixon White House aide Harry Dent, sought to win votes for Bush by promoting him as "a good ol' Southern boy from Texas."

As a sitting vice president, Bush did better in 1988, sweeping every county in the state and winning almost as many votes

Recent South Carolina Primary Results

South Carolina Republicans held their first presidential primary in 1980; South Carolina Democrats in 1992.

	DEMOCRATS			REPUBLICANS		
Year	Turnout	Candidates	%	Turnout	Candidates	%
1996 (March 2)	—	NO PRIMARY		276,741	BOB DOLE	45
					Pat Buchanan	29
					Steve Forbes	13
					Lamar Alexander	10
1992 (March 7)	116,414	BILL CLINTON	63	148,840	GEORGE BUSH*	67
		Paul Tsongas	18		Pat Buchanan	26
1988 (March 5)	—	NO PRIMARY		195,292	GEORGE BUSH	49
					Bob Dole	21
					Pat Robertson	19
					Jack Kemp	11
1984	—	NO PRIMARY		—	NO PRIMARY	
1980 (March 8)	—	NO PRIMARY		145,501	RONALD REAGAN	55
					John Connally	30
					George Bush	15

Note: All candidates are listed that drew at least 10 percent of their party's primary vote. The names of winning candidates are capitalized. An asterisk (*) indicates an incumbent president.

as his rivals combined. Robertson had hoped to tap the state's large cadre of fundamentalist voters. According to exit polls, one-third of the Republican primary voters in South Carolina were born-again Christians. But Bush did nearly as well among these voters as Robertson.

In 1996, it was Dole who harnessed the momentum from victory in South Carolina, with a decisive triumph that covered all but three small counties in the northwest part of the state. Dole had lost three of the first five presidential primaries before the South Carolina primary in early March. After South Carolina, he was not to lose again.

As for the Democrats, they held their one and only presidential primary in 1992. It was a little-noticed event, won easily by the region's native son, Bill Clinton.

SOUTH CAROLINA REPUBLICAN

1980

County	Total Vote	Bush	Connally	Reagan	Other	Winner	Percentage of Total Vote: Bush	Connally	Reagan	Other
ABBEVILLE	502	59	163	276	4	Reagan	11.8%	32.5%	55.0%	0.8%
AIKEN	6,453	740	2,127	3,524	62	Reagan	11.5%	33.0%	54.6%	1.0%
ALLENDALE	290	30	94	161	5	Reagan	10.3%	32.4%	55.5%	1.7%
ANDERSON	5,322	693	1,556	3,018	55	Reagan	13.0%	29.2%	56.7%	1.0%
BAMBERG	588	52	134	395	7	Reagan	8.8%	22.8%	67.2%	1.2%
BARNWELL	767	74	236	451	6	Reagan	9.6%	30.8%	58.8%	0.8%
BEAUFORT	4,086	1,041	1,552	1,448	45	Connally	25.5%	38.0%	35.4%	1.1%
BERKELEY	2,901	292	1,005	1,595	9	Reagan	10.1%	34.6%	55.0%	0.3%
CALHOUN	518	67	71	379	1	Reagan	12.9%	13.7%	73.2%	0.2%
CHARLESTON	16,424	2,009	6,508	7,811	96	Reagan	12.2%	39.6%	47.6%	0.6%
CHEROKEE	950	120	373	451	6	Reagan	12.6%	39.3%	47.5%	0.6%
CHESTER	436	46	167	220	3	Reagan	10.6%	38.3%	50.5%	0.7%
CHESTERFIELD	523	62	209	250	2	Reagan	11.9%	40.0%	47.8%	0.4%
CLARENDON	978	64	298	613	3	Reagan	6.5%	30.5%	62.7%	0.3%
COLLETON	1,454	113	624	713	4	Reagan	7.8%	42.9%	49.0%	0.3%
DARLINGTON	2,080	242	935	890	13	Connally	11.6%	45.0%	42.8%	0.6%
DILLON	815	87	413	311	4	Connally	10.7%	50.7%	38.2%	0.5%
DORCHESTER	2,772	293	1,238	1,228	13	Connally	10.6%	44.7%	44.3%	0.5%
EDGEFIELD	660	49	248	361	2	Reagan	7.4%	37.6%	54.7%	0.3%
FAIRFIELD	465	52	95	312	6	Reagan	11.2%	20.4%	67.1%	1.3%
FLORENCE	5,297	761	2,228	2,266	42	Reagan	14.4%	42.1%	42.8%	0.8%
GEORGETOWN	1,768	226	819	711	12	Connally	12.8%	46.3%	40.2%	0.7%
GREENVILLE	19,741	3,329	4,429	11,790	193	Reagan	16.9%	22.4%	59.7%	1.0%
GREENWOOD	1,992	324	513	1,136	19	Reagan	16.3%	25.8%	57.0%	1.0%
HAMPTON	307	25	113	165	4	Reagan	8.1%	36.8%	53.7%	1.3%
HORRY	4,055	792	1,535	1,698	30	Reagan	19.5%	37.9%	41.9%	0.7%
JASPER	250	13	69	164	4	Reagan	5.2%	27.6%	65.6%	1.6%
KERSHAW	2,448	279	420	1,733	16	Reagan	11.4%	17.2%	70.8%	0.7%
LANCASTER	850	119	190	528	13	Reagan	14.0%	22.4%	62.1%	1.5%
LAURENS	1,682	264	474	932	12	Reagan	15.7%	28.2%	55.4%	0.7%
LEE	800	57	229	510	4	Reagan	7.1%	28.6%	63.8%	0.5%
LEXINGTON	10,122	1,446	1,908	6,677	91	Reagan	14.3%	18.9%	66.0%	0.9%
MCCORMICK	170	27	32	110	1	Reagan	15.9%	18.8%	64.7%	0.6%
MARION	947	104	550	281	12	Connally	11.0%	58.1%	29.7%	1.3%
MARLBORO	615	90	268	243	14	Connally	14.6%	43.6%	39.5%	2.3%
NEWBERRY	1,315	145	426	737	7	Reagan	11.0%	32.4%	56.0%	0.5%
OCONEE	1,236	233	392	596	15	Reagan	18.9%	31.7%	48.2%	1.2%
ORANGEBURG	3,667	376	808	2,465	18	Reagan	10.3%	22.0%	67.2%	0.5%
PICKENS	3,208	623	930	1,609	46	Reagan	19.4%	29.0%	50.2%	1.4%
RICHLAND	15,844	2,937	3,679	9,050	178	Reagan	18.5%	23.2%	57.1%	1.1%
SALUDA	462	49	103	308	2	Reagan	10.6%	22.3%	66.7%	0.4%
SPARTANBURG	10,663	1,971	2,642	5,922	128	Reagan	18.5%	24.8%	55.5%	1.2%
SUMTER	4,314	341	898	3,054	21	Reagan	7.9%	20.8%	70.8%	0.5%
UNION	851	92	325	432	2	Reagan	10.8%	38.2%	50.8%	0.2%
WILLIAMSBURG	1,175	96	464	612	3	Reagan	8.2%	39.5%	52.1%	0.3%
YORK	2,738	665	623	1,413	37	Reagan	24.3%	22.8%	51.6%	1.4%
TOTAL	145,501	21,569	43,113	79,549	1,270	Reagan	14.8%	29.6%	54.7%	0.9%

SOUTH CAROLINA REPUBLICAN

1988

County	Total Vote	Bush	Dole	Kemp	Robertson	Other	Winner	Percentage of Total Vote: Bush	Dole	Kemp	Robertson	Other
ABBEVILLE	854	302	173	102	276	1	Bush	35.4%	20.3%	11.9%	32.3%	0.1%
AIKEN	8,783	4,532	1,691	955	1,564	41	Bush	51.6%	19.3%	10.9%	17.8%	0.5%
ALLENDALE	198	99	70	6	23		Bush	50.0%	35.4%	3.0%	11.6%	
ANDERSON	6,974	3,024	1,332	733	1,872	13	Bush	43.4%	19.1%	10.5%	26.8%	0.2%
BAMBERG	529	268	105	40	116		Bush	50.7%	19.8%	7.6%	21.9%	
BARNWELL	1,070	500	213	70	286	1	Bush	46.7%	19.9%	6.5%	26.7%	0.1%
BEAUFORT	6,199	3,400	1,335	681	754	29	Bush	54.8%	21.5%	11.0%	12.2%	0.5%
BERKELEY	5,107	2,265	633	774	1,413	22	Bush	44.4%	12.4%	15.2%	27.7%	0.4%
CALHOUN	673	389	130	82	71	1	Bush	57.8%	19.3%	12.2%	10.5%	0.1%
CHARLESTON	18,689	10,098	2,218	3,336	2,911	126	Bush	54.0%	11.9%	17.9%	15.6%	0.7%
CHEROKEE	1,616	788	313	87	426	2	Bush	48.8%	19.4%	5.4%	26.4%	0.1%
CHESTER	840	325	284	49	180	2	Bush	38.7%	33.8%	5.8%	21.4%	0.2%
CHESTERFIELD	948	366	257	48	276	1	Bush	38.6%	27.1%	5.1%	29.1%	0.1%
CLARENDON	802	464	146	83	106	3	Bush	57.9%	18.2%	10.3%	13.2%	0.4%
COLLETON	1,113	517	143	192	259	2	Bush	46.5%	12.8%	17.3%	23.3%	0.2%
DARLINGTON	2,199	1,075	468	176	473	7	Bush	48.9%	21.3%	8.0%	21.5%	0.3%
DILLON	1,025	424	298	66	235	2	Bush	41.4%	29.1%	6.4%	22.9%	0.2%
DORCHESTER	4,458	2,099	764	766	807	22	Bush	47.1%	17.1%	17.2%	18.1%	0.5%
EDGEFIELD	1,394	700	376	103	209	6	Bush	50.2%	27.0%	7.4%	15.0%	0.4%
FAIRFIELD	834	398	151	79	201	5	Bush	47.7%	18.1%	9.5%	24.1%	0.6%
FLORENCE	6,034	3,124	1,400	421	1,072	17	Bush	51.8%	23.2%	7.0%	17.8%	0.3%
GEORGETOWN	2,072	906	402	198	561	5	Bush	43.7%	19.4%	9.6%	27.1%	0.2%
GREENVILLE	26,803	12,044	5,152	4,262	5,286	59	Bush	44.9%	19.2%	15.9%	19.7%	0.2%
GREENWOOD	2,870	1,131	678	341	717	3	Bush	39.4%	23.6%	11.9%	25.0%	0.1%
HAMPTON	670	302	121	44	201	2	Bush	45.1%	18.1%	6.6%	30.0%	0.3%
HORRY	7,604	3,531	2,462	423	1,168	20	Bush	46.4%	32.4%	5.6%	15.4%	0.3%
JASPER	539	256	68	14	198	3	Bush	47.5%	12.6%	2.6%	36.7%	0.6%
KERSHAW	3,225	1,862	569	259	526	9	Bush	57.7%	17.6%	8.0%	16.3%	0.3%
LANCASTER	1,565	692	424	72	374	3	Bush	44.2%	27.1%	4.6%	23.9%	0.2%
LAURENS	2,278	1,055	407	217	592	7	Bush	46.3%	17.9%	9.5%	26.0%	0.3%
LEE	547	294	123	27	103		Bush	53.7%	22.5%	4.9%	18.8%	
LEXINGTON	13,613	6,788	2,862	1,801	2,133	29	Bush	49.9%	21.0%	13.2%	15.7%	0.2%
MCCORMICK	157	71	46	19	20	1	Bush	45.2%	29.3%	12.1%	12.7%	0.6%
MARION	908	537	203	37	130	1	Bush	59.1%	22.4%	4.1%	14.3%	0.1%
MARLBORO	457	203	122	24	107	1	Bush	44.4%	26.7%	5.3%	23.4%	0.2%
NEWBERRY	1,786	993	320	176	288	9	Bush	55.6%	17.9%	9.9%	16.1%	0.5%
OCONEE	3,006	1,378	624	304	692	8	Bush	45.8%	20.8%	10.1%	23.0%	0.3%
ORANGEBURG	4,531	2,429	949	590	557	6	Bush	53.6%	20.9%	13.0%	12.3%	0.1%
PICKENS	5,390	2,515	1,346	638	881	10	Bush	46.7%	25.0%	11.8%	16.3%	0.2%
RICHLAND	18,043	9,293	4,277	2,117	2,316	40	Bush	51.5%	23.7%	11.7%	12.8%	0.2%
SALUDA	702	323	168	76	131	4	Bush	46.0%	23.9%	10.8%	18.7%	0.6%
SPARTANBURG	14,598	6,534	3,256	1,217	3,547	44	Bush	44.8%	22.3%	8.3%	24.3%	0.3%
SUMTER	4,747	2,871	880	326	662	8	Bush	60.5%	18.5%	6.9%	13.9%	0.2%
UNION	1,342	551	273	73	442	3	Bush	41.1%	20.3%	5.4%	32.9%	0.2%
WILLIAMSBURG	895	480	209	60	143	3	Bush	53.6%	23.4%	6.7%	16.0%	0.3%
YORK	6,605	2,542	1,824	267	1,956	16	Bush	38.5%	27.6%	4.0%	29.6%	0.2%
TOTAL	195,292	94,738	40,265	22,431	37,261	597	Bush	48.5%	20.6%	11.5%	19.1%	0.3%

SOUTH CAROLINA DEMOCRATIC

1992

County	Total Vote	Clinton	Tsongas	Other	Winner	Percentage of Total Vote Clinton	Tsongas	Other
ABBEVILLE	1,013	729	131	153	Clinton	72.0%	12.9%	15.1%
AIKEN	2,821	1,861	539	421	Clinton	66.0%	19.1%	14.9%
ALLENDALE	508	370	35	103	Clinton	72.8%	6.9%	20.3%
ANDERSON	4,125	2,631	885	609	Clinton	63.8%	21.5%	14.8%
BAMBERG	688	515	55	118	Clinton	74.9%	8.0%	17.2%
BARNWELL	582	383	65	134	Clinton	65.8%	11.2%	23.0%
BEAUFORT	2,190	1,028	804	358	Clinton	46.9%	36.7%	16.3%
BERKELEY	5,702	3,725	579	1,398	Clinton	65.3%	10.2%	24.5%
CALHOUN	584	447	58	79	Clinton	76.5%	9.9%	13.5%
CHARLESTON	9,074	4,897	2,419	1,758	Clinton	54.0%	26.7%	19.4%
CHEROKEE	1,366	985	149	232	Clinton	72.1%	10.9%	17.0%
CHESTER	1,209	889	125	195	Clinton	73.5%	10.3%	16.1%
CHESTERFIELD	1,336	964	134	238	Clinton	72.2%	10.0%	17.8%
CLARENDON	1,697	1,189	91	417	Clinton	70.1%	5.4%	24.6%
COLLETON	1,579	1,180	122	277	Clinton	74.7%	7.7%	17.5%
DARLINGTON	1,899	1,276	224	399	Clinton	67.2%	11.8%	21.0%
DILLON	954	683	83	188	Clinton	71.6%	8.7%	19.7%
DORCHESTER	1,831	1,095	392	344	Clinton	59.8%	21.4%	18.8%
EDGEFIELD	774	631	50	93	Clinton	81.5%	6.5%	12.0%
FAIRFIELD	1,696	1,128	108	460	Clinton	66.5%	6.4%	27.1%
FLORENCE	3,220	2,124	430	666	Clinton	66.0%	13.4%	20.7%
GEORGETOWN	1,925	1,043	266	616	Clinton	54.2%	13.8%	32.0%
GREENVILLE	8,349	4,396	2,653	1,300	Clinton	52.7%	31.8%	15.6%
GREENWOOD	1,403	919	287	197	Clinton	65.5%	20.5%	14.0%
HAMPTON	892	564	116	212	Clinton	63.2%	13.0%	23.8%
HORRY	3,583	2,152	731	700	Clinton	60.1%	20.4%	19.5%
JASPER	767	637	26	104	Clinton	83.1%	3.4%	13.6%
KERSHAW	2,333	1,731	307	295	Clinton	74.2%	13.2%	12.6%
LANCASTER	1,701	1,157	220	324	Clinton	68.0%	12.9%	19.0%
LAURENS	1,561	965	320	276	Clinton	61.8%	20.5%	17.7%
LEE	1,125	862	44	219	Clinton	76.6%	3.9%	19.5%
LEXINGTON	4,925	2,777	1,263	885	Clinton	56.4%	25.6%	18.0%
MCCORMICK	468	339	36	93	Clinton	72.4%	7.7%	19.9%
MARION	930	423	55	452	Clinton	45.5%	5.9%	48.6%
MARLBORO	962	744	55	163	Clinton	77.3%	5.7%	16.9%
NEWBERRY	1,231	896	161	174	Clinton	72.8%	13.1%	14.1%
OCONEE	2,298	1,341	541	416	Clinton	58.4%	23.5%	18.1%
ORANGEBURG	4,006	3,072	314	620	Clinton	76.7%	7.8%	15.5%
PICKENS	2,101	1,027	691	383	Clinton	48.9%	32.9%	18.2%
RICHLAND	15,861	9,366	3,492	3,003	Clinton	59.1%	22.0%	18.9%
SALUDA	694	502	58	134	Clinton	72.3%	8.4%	19.3%
SPARTANBURG	5,117	3,458	921	738	Clinton	67.6%	18.0%	14.4%
SUMTER	3,388	2,249	381	758	Clinton	66.4%	11.2%	22.4%
UNION	1,162	947	86	129	Clinton	81.5%	7.4%	11.1%
WILLIAMSBURG	1,680	1,242	68	370	Clinton	73.9%	4.0%	22.0%
YORK	3,104	1,682	768	654	Clinton	54.2%	24.7%	21.1%
TOTAL	116,414	73,221	21,338	21,855	Clinton	62.9%	18.3%	18.8%

SOUTH CAROLINA REPUBLICAN

1992

County	Total Vote	Buchanan	Bush	Other	Winner	Percentage of Total Vote: Buchanan	Bush	Other
ABBEVILLE	576	132	379	65	Bush	22.9%	65.8%	11.3%
AIKEN	7,045	2,076	4,371	598	Bush	29.5%	62.0%	8.5%
ALLENDALE	190	33	140	17	Bush	17.4%	73.7%	8.9%
ANDERSON	5,864	1,576	3,618	670	Bush	26.9%	61.7%	11.4%
BAMBERG	550	87	435	28	Bush	15.8%	79.1%	5.1%
BARNWELL	862	218	581	63	Bush	25.3%	67.4%	7.3%
BEAUFORT	5,510	1,307	4,032	171	Bush	23.7%	73.2%	3.1%
BERKELEY	4,596	1,257	2,722	617	Bush	27.3%	59.2%	13.4%
CALHOUN	625	105	472	48	Bush	16.8%	75.5%	7.7%
CHARLESTON	12,910	3,067	8,717	1,126	Bush	23.8%	67.5%	8.7%
CHEROKEE	876	252	497	127	Bush	28.8%	56.7%	14.5%
CHESTER	766	144	526	96	Bush	18.8%	68.7%	12.5%
CHESTERFIELD	595	135	407	53	Bush	22.7%	68.4%	8.9%
CLARENDON	856	145	620	91	Bush	16.9%	72.4%	10.6%
COLLETON	877	212	525	140	Bush	24.2%	59.9%	16.0%
DARLINGTON	1,456	294	1,015	147	Bush	20.2%	69.7%	10.1%
DILLON	494	122	320	52	Bush	24.7%	64.8%	10.5%
DORCHESTER	3,695	858	2,455	382	Bush	23.2%	66.4%	10.3%
EDGEFIELD	915	300	547	68	Bush	32.8%	59.8%	7.4%
FAIRFIELD	929	154	697	78	Bush	16.6%	75.0%	8.4%
FLORENCE	3,551	862	2,372	317	Bush	24.3%	66.8%	8.9%
GEORGETOWN	1,291	314	866	111	Bush	24.3%	67.1%	8.6%
GREENVILLE	18,385	5,717	11,746	922	Bush	31.1%	63.9%	5.0%
GREENWOOD	2,024	404	1,476	144	Bush	20.0%	72.9%	7.1%
HAMPTON	328	61	237	30	Bush	18.6%	72.3%	9.1%
HORRY	6,161	1,728	3,979	454	Bush	28.0%	64.6%	7.4%
JASPER	303	49	241	13	Bush	16.2%	79.5%	4.3%
KERSHAW	2,823	596	2,046	181	Bush	21.1%	72.5%	6.4%
LANCASTER	999	247	649	103	Bush	24.7%	65.0%	10.3%
LAURENS	1,270	285	863	122	Bush	22.4%	68.0%	9.6%
LEE	395	67	279	49	Bush	17.0%	70.6%	12.4%
LEXINGTON	12,877	3,393	8,840	644	Bush	26.3%	68.6%	5.0%
MCCORMICK	138	36	82	20	Bush	26.1%	59.4%	14.5%
MARION	491	34	411	46	Bush	6.9%	83.7%	9.4%
MARLBORO	275	118	140	17	Bush	42.9%	50.9%	6.2%
NEWBERRY	1,713	300	1,261	152	Bush	17.5%	73.6%	8.9%
OCONEE	2,740	619	1,904	217	Bush	22.6%	69.5%	7.9%
ORANGEBURG	3,420	650	2,476	294	Bush	19.0%	72.4%	8.6%
PICKENS	3,990	1,027	2,660	303	Bush	25.7%	66.7%	7.6%
RICHLAND	15,296	3,835	10,794	667	Bush	25.1%	70.6%	4.4%
SALUDA	625	130	403	92	Bush	20.8%	64.5%	14.7%
SPARTANBURG	10,072	3,238	6,090	744	Bush	32.1%	60.5%	7.4%
SUMTER	3,747	706	2,817	224	Bush	18.8%	75.2%	6.0%
UNION	720	203	449	68	Bush	28.2%	62.4%	9.4%
WILLIAMSBURG	857	106	611	140	Bush	12.4%	71.3%	16.3%
YORK	4,162	1,048	2,790	324	Bush	25.2%	67.0%	7.8%
TOTAL	148,840	38,247	99,558	11,035	Bush	25.7%	66.9%	7.4%

SOUTH CAROLINA REPUBLICAN

1996

County	Total Vote	Alexander	Buchanan	Dole	Forbes	Other	Winner	Percentage of Total Vote: Alexander	Buchanan	Dole	Forbes	Other
ABBEVILLE	1,162	93	490	465	97	17	Buchanan	8.0%	42.2%	40.0%	8.3%	1.5%
AIKEN	14,472	1,229	4,850	6,245	1,636	512	Dole	8.5%	33.5%	43.2%	11.3%	3.5%
ALLENDALE	297	23	92	136	40	6	Dole	7.7%	31.0%	45.8%	13.5%	2.0%
ANDERSON	11,444	982	4,787	4,217	1,185	273	Buchanan	8.6%	41.8%	36.8%	10.4%	2.4%
BAMBERG	614	55	164	326	58	11	Dole	9.0%	26.7%	53.1%	9.4%	1.8%
BARNWELL	1,422	107	430	741	123	21	Dole	7.5%	30.2%	52.1%	8.6%	1.5%
BEAUFORT	10,030	1,340	1,632	4,739	1,911	408	Dole	13.4%	16.3%	47.2%	19.1%	4.1%
BERKELEY	8,673	761	2,680	3,693	1,420	119	Dole	8.8%	30.9%	42.6%	16.4%	1.4%
CALHOUN	1,069	117	327	495	114	16	Dole	10.9%	30.6%	46.3%	10.7%	1.5%
CHARLESTON	25,169	2,337	5,424	12,252	4,776	380	Dole	9.3%	21.6%	48.7%	19.0%	1.5%
CHEROKEE	2,230	164	938	898	195	35	Buchanan	7.4%	42.1%	40.3%	8.7%	1.6%
CHESTER	1,024	79	384	424	123	14	Dole	7.7%	37.5%	41.4%	12.0%	1.4%
CHESTERFIELD	1,001	58	365	457	100	21	Dole	5.8%	36.5%	45.7%	10.0%	2.1%
CLARENDON	1,337	122	346	697	142	30	Dole	9.1%	25.9%	52.1%	10.6%	2.2%
COLLETON	1,793	130	512	869	266	16	Dole	7.3%	28.6%	48.5%	14.8%	0.9%
DARLINGTON	2,893	210	773	1,535	321	54	Dole	7.3%	26.7%	53.1%	11.1%	1.9%
DILLON	922	30	256	545	76	15	Dole	3.3%	27.8%	59.1%	8.2%	1.6%
DORCHESTER	8,001	800	2,076	3,607	1,371	147	Dole	10.0%	25.9%	45.1%	17.1%	1.8%
EDGEFIELD	1,519	103	517	688	169	42	Dole	6.8%	34.0%	45.3%	11.1%	2.8%
FAIRFIELD	1,144	121	335	543	117	28	Dole	10.6%	29.3%	47.5%	10.2%	2.4%
FLORENCE	7,715	378	2,312	3,929	944	152	Dole	4.9%	30.0%	50.9%	12.2%	2.0%
GEORGETOWN	3,020	331	697	1,405	533	54	Dole	11.0%	23.1%	46.5%	17.6%	1.8%
GREENVILLE	37,467	3,493	12,605	15,617	4,467	1,285	Dole	9.3%	33.6%	41.7%	11.9%	3.4%
GREENWOOD	3,573	328	1,043	1,775	357	70	Dole	9.2%	29.2%	49.7%	10.0%	2.0%
HAMPTON	533	38	164	259	62	10	Dole	7.1%	30.8%	48.6%	11.6%	1.9%
HORRY	12,125	1,287	3,125	5,153	2,363	197	Dole	10.6%	25.8%	42.5%	19.5%	1.6%
JASPER	362	30	120	187	22	3	Dole	8.3%	33.1%	51.7%	6.1%	0.8%
KERSHAW	4,624	502	1,399	2,195	440	88	Dole	10.9%	30.3%	47.5%	9.5%	1.9%
LANCASTER	1,865	130	699	825	169	42	Dole	7.0%	37.5%	44.2%	9.1%	2.3%
LAURENS	3,184	222	1,185	1,438	279	60	Dole	7.0%	37.2%	45.2%	8.8%	1.9%
LEE	640	43	219	324	49	5	Dole	6.7%	34.2%	50.6%	7.7%	0.8%
LEXINGTON	23,326	3,806	5,835	10,422	2,536	727	Dole	16.3%	25.0%	44.7%	10.9%	3.1%
MCCORMICK	376	21	95	178	73	9	Dole	5.6%	25.3%	47.3%	19.4%	2.4%
MARION	953	46	245	539	110	13	Dole	4.8%	25.7%	56.6%	11.5%	1.4%
MARLBORO	498	20	158	252	67	1	Dole	4.0%	31.7%	50.6%	13.5%	0.2%
NEWBERRY	2,375	266	590	1,251	220	48	Dole	11.2%	24.8%	52.7%	9.3%	2.0%
OCONEE	5,268	630	1,576	2,211	711	140	Dole	12.0%	29.9%	42.0%	13.5%	2.7%
ORANGEBURG	4,420	375	1,285	2,211	486	63	Dole	8.5%	29.1%	50.0%	11.0%	1.4%
PICKENS	8,252	767	2,925	3,478	828	254	Dole	9.3%	35.4%	42.1%	10.0%	3.1%
RICHLAND	24,492	3,883	4,952	11,865	2,698	1,094	Dole	15.9%	20.2%	48.4%	11.0%	4.5%
SALUDA	1,162	156	354	542	97	13	Dole	13.4%	30.5%	46.6%	8.3%	1.1%
SPARTANBURG	18,069	1,739	7,035	7,259	1,680	356	Dole	9.6%	38.9%	40.2%	9.3%	2.0%
SUMTER	5,910	472	1,582	3,210	538	108	Dole	8.0%	26.8%	54.3%	9.1%	1.8%
UNION	1,010	50	417	455	75	13	Dole	5.0%	41.3%	45.0%	7.4%	1.3%
WILLIAMSBURG	876	50	272	495	54	5	Dole	5.7%	31.1%	56.5%	6.2%	0.6%
YORK	8,430	723	2,557	3,857	941	352	Dole	8.6%	30.3%	45.8%	11.2%	4.2%
TOTAL	276,741	28,647	80,824	124,904	35,039	7,327	Dole	10.4%	29.2%	45.1%	12.7%	2.6%

SOUTH DAKOTA

South Dakota is a small state, with a long presidential primary tradition that dates back to 1912. But unlike New Hampshire, it has struggled to find a niche on the primary calendar—bouncing back and forth in recent years between dates in February and June.

Candidates that have made it to South Dakota find a state that straddles two regions. On the east side of the Missouri River is the relatively sedate farm land of the agrarian Midwest; on the other side is the wide-open ranch land of the West.

Most voters live in the eastern half, which adjoins the Corn Belt territory of Iowa and Minnesota. Democrats have a registration advantage in more than one-third of the counties in eastern South Dakota.

The western side of the state is strongly Republican, with plenty of frontier individualists eager for government to let them alone. The Democratic presence west of the Missouri does not extend much beyond the scattered Native American reservations.

The east-west variation was illustrated in the 1976 Republican primary between President Gerald Ford and Ronald Reagan. Ford carried seven of the eight counties on the eastern border, including the state's leading population and trade center, Minnehaha County (Sioux Falls). Reagan swept all six counties on the western border, including South Dakota's second-most populous county, Pennington (Rapid City). Reagan won the primary by also carrying nearly all the counties between Rapid City and Sioux Falls.

The effects of geography can sometimes be felt in the Democratic primary as well. South Dakota provided a farm-state showdown in 1992 between Sens. Bob Kerrey of Nebraska and Tom Harkin of Iowa. Harkin won nearly a dozen counties in the eastern part of the state. But Kerrey won the primary handily by sweeping the western half, rolling up some of his largest margins in the state's two most heavily Indian counties, Shannon and Todd, where Kerrey was the only one of the major Democratic candidates to spend much time campaigning.

Recent South Dakota Primary Results

South Dakota held its first presidential primary in 1912.

	DEMOCRATS			REPUBLICANS		
Year	Turnout	Candidates	%	Turnout	Candidates	%
1996 (Feb. 27)	—	NO PRIMARY		69,170	BOB DOLE Pat Buchanan Steve Forbes	45 29 13
1992 (Feb. 25)	59,503	BOB KERREY Tom Harkin Bill Clinton	40 25 19	44,671	GEORGE BUSH* Uncommitted	69 31
1988 (Feb. 23)	71,606	RICHARD GEPHARDT Michael Dukakis	44 31	93,405	BOB DOLE Pat Robertson George Bush	55 20 19
1984 (June 5)	52,561	GARY HART Walter Mondale	51 39	—	NO PRIMARY	
1980 (June 3)	68,763	EDWARD KENNEDY Jimmy Carter*	49 45	82,905	RONALD REAGAN	82
1976 (June 1)	58,671	JIMMY CARTER Morris Udall "None"	41 33 13	84,077	RONALD REAGAN Gerald Ford*	51 44
1972 (June 6)	28,017	GEORGE McGOVERN	100	52,820	RICHARD NIXON*	100
1968 (June 4)	64,287	ROBERT KENNEDY Lyndon Johnson* Eugene McCarthy	50 30 20	68,113	RICHARD NIXON	100

Note: All candidates are listed that drew at least 10 percent of their party's primary vote. The names of winning candidates are capitalized. An asterisk (*) indicates an incumbent president.

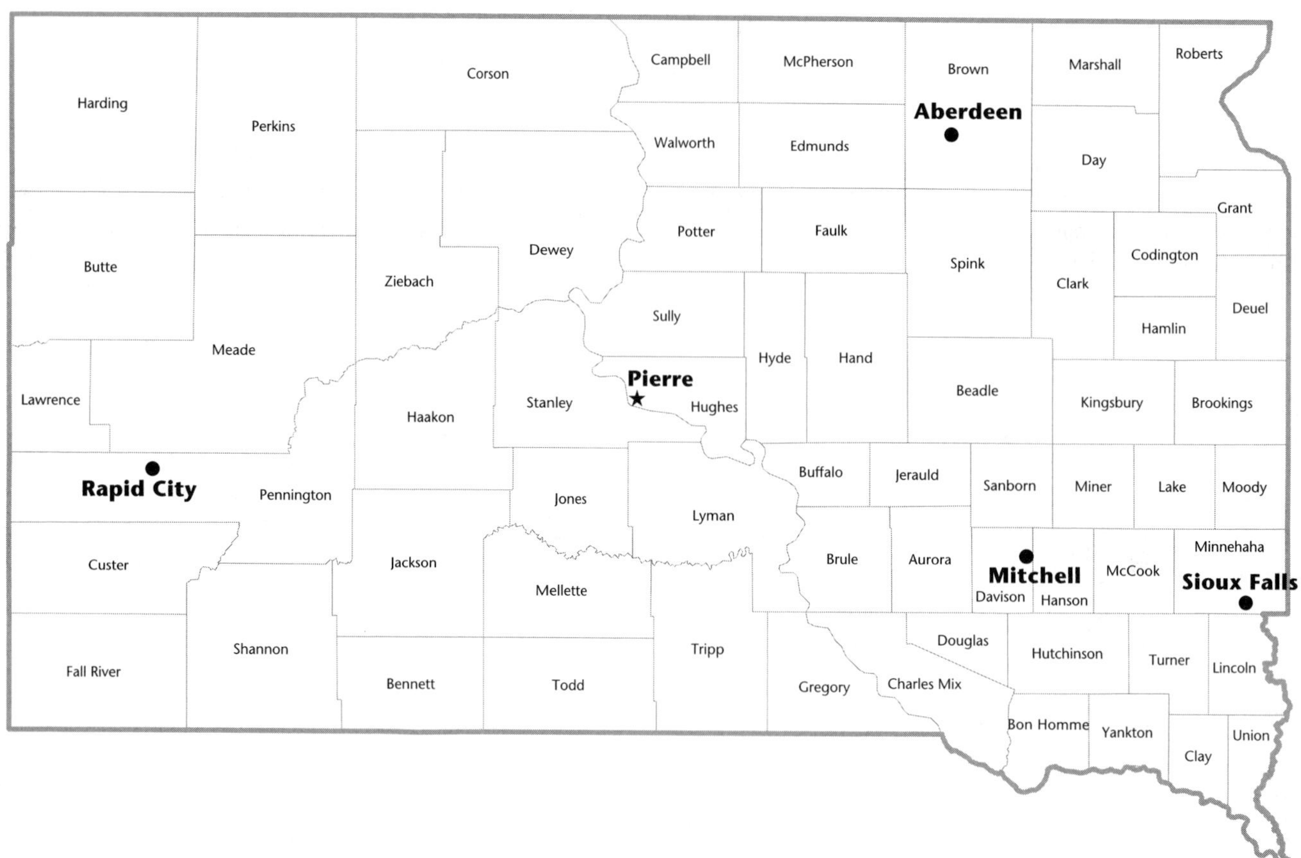

Good times or bad, there has always been a strong strain of agrarian populism among South Dakota Democrats. They cast their primary ballots for Robert Kennedy in 1968 and for his brother, Edward, in 1980. But the party's presidential primary has rarely been very predictive. It was last won by the eventual Democratic nominee in 1976, when Jimmy Carter defeated Morris Udall.

Nor has the primary always been that predictive on the Republican side. In 1988, it was only primary that George Bush lost (or for that matter, Bob Dole won). South Dakota had never seemed to offer much of a payday for Bush, who as vice president was at a disadvantage defending the Reagan administration's farm policy. After his loss in neighboring Iowa, Bush pulled out of South Dakota to focus on New Hampshire and other, more promising, terrain.

Dole won the South Dakota primary again in 1996, in a contest that was closer but far more helpful to his nomination chances than eight years earlier. His winning percentage was down 10 points from 1988, and after sweeping every county his first try, he lost four counties to Pat Buchanan in 1996. But Dole's South Dakota victory, along with one the same late February day in North Dakota, stabilized his campaign after a rough start and set the stage for a whirlwind of primary victories in March.

SOUTH DAKOTA DEMOCRATIC

1968

County	Total Vote	R. Kennedy	Johnson	McCarthy	Winner	Percentage of Total Vote R. Kennedy	Johnson	McCarthy
AURORA	845	439	242	164	R. Kennedy	52.0%	28.6%	19.4%
BEADLE	2,958	853	1,780	325	Johnson	28.8%	60.2%	11.0%
BENNETT	381	241	59	81	R. Kennedy	63.3%	15.5%	21.3%
BON HOMME	972	548	220	204	R. Kennedy	56.4%	22.6%	21.0%
BROOKINGS	1,271	618	387	266	R. Kennedy	48.6%	30.4%	20.9%
BROWN	4,495	2,111	1,524	860	R. Kennedy	47.0%	33.9%	19.1%
BRULE	1,192	541	368	283	R. Kennedy	45.4%	30.9%	23.7%
BUFFALO	229	151	41	37	R. Kennedy	65.9%	17.9%	16.2%
BUTTE	507	248	105	154	R. Kennedy	48.9%	20.7%	30.4%
CAMPBELL	83	40	24	19	R. Kennedy	48.2%	28.9%	22.9%
CHARLES MIX	1,735	993	424	318	R. Kennedy	57.2%	24.4%	18.3%
CLARK	662	226	361	75	Johnson	34.1%	54.5%	11.3%
CLAY	820	353	197	270	R. Kennedy	43.0%	24.0%	32.9%
CODINGTON	1,885	789	802	294	Johnson	41.9%	42.5%	15.6%
CORSON	649	423	89	137	R. Kennedy	65.2%	13.7%	21.1%
CUSTER	475	212	132	131	R. Kennedy	44.6%	27.8%	27.6%
DAVISON	2,151	1,164	570	417	R. Kennedy	54.1%	26.5%	19.4%
DAY	1,486	646	560	280	R. Kennedy	43.5%	37.7%	18.8%
DEUEL	456	261	136	59	R. Kennedy	57.2%	29.8%	12.9%
DEWEY	572	393	75	104	R. Kennedy	68.7%	13.1%	18.2%
DOUGLAS	342	190	79	73	R. Kennedy	55.6%	23.1%	21.3%
EDMUNDS	897	560	162	175	R. Kennedy	62.4%	18.1%	19.5%
FALL RIVER	562	258	136	168	R. Kennedy	45.9%	24.2%	29.9%
FAULK	647	344	170	133	R. Kennedy	53.2%	26.3%	20.6%
GRANT	725	408	198	119	R. Kennedy	56.3%	27.3%	16.4%
GREGORY	904	503	199	202	R. Kennedy	55.6%	22.0%	22.3%
HAAKON	250	97	75	78	R. Kennedy	38.8%	30.0%	31.2%
HAMLIN	512	252	192	68	R. Kennedy	49.2%	37.5%	13.3%
HAND	750	394	251	105	R. Kennedy	52.5%	33.5%	14.0%
HANSON	578	388	87	103	R. Kennedy	67.1%	15.1%	17.8%
HARDING	153	86	27	40	R. Kennedy	56.2%	17.6%	26.1%
HUGHES	895	435	256	204	R. Kennedy	48.6%	28.6%	22.8%
HUTCHINSON	649	401	125	123	R. Kennedy	61.8%	19.3%	19.0%
HYDE	422	245	96	81	R. Kennedy	58.1%	22.7%	19.2%
JACKSON	196	83	50	63	R. Kennedy	42.3%	25.5%	32.1%
JERAULD	442	211	159	72	R. Kennedy	47.7%	36.0%	16.3%
JONES	292	163	63	66	R. Kennedy	55.8%	21.6%	22.6%
KINGSBURY	592	228	264	100	Johnson	38.5%	44.6%	16.9%
LAKE	1,084	474	384	226	R. Kennedy	43.7%	35.4%	20.8%
LAWRENCE	1,191	647	258	286	R. Kennedy	54.3%	21.7%	24.0%
LINCOLN	780	356	261	163	R. Kennedy	45.6%	33.5%	20.9%
LYMAN	436	249	105	82	R. Kennedy	57.1%	24.1%	18.8%
MCCOOK	750	440	207	103	R. Kennedy	58.7%	27.6%	13.7%
MCPHERSON	231	116	54	61	R. Kennedy	50.2%	23.4%	26.4%
MARSHALL	896	344	339	213	R. Kennedy	38.4%	37.8%	23.8%
MEADE	1,050	517	201	332	R. Kennedy	49.2%	19.1%	31.6%
MELLETTE	257	152	53	52	R. Kennedy	59.1%	20.6%	20.2%
MINER	811	364	305	142	R. Kennedy	44.9%	37.6%	17.5%
MINNEHAHA	6,836	2,996	2,194	1,646	R. Kennedy	43.8%	32.1%	24.1%
MOODY	886	382	287	217	R. Kennedy	43.1%	32.4%	24.5%

SOUTH DAKOTA DEMOCRATIC

1968

County	Total Vote	R. Kennedy	Johnson	McCarthy	Winner	Percentage of Total Vote R. Kennedy	Johnson	McCarthy
PENNINGTON	3,476	1,805	862	809	R. Kennedy	51.9%	24.8%	23.3%
PERKINS	608	226	92	290	McCarthy	37.2%	15.1%	47.7%
POTTER	458	234	106	118	R. Kennedy	51.1%	23.1%	25.8%
ROBERTS	1,706	773	554	379	R. Kennedy	45.3%	32.5%	22.2%
SANBORN	486	285	155	46	R. Kennedy	58.6%	31.9%	9.5%
SHANNON	1,018	936	32	50	R. Kennedy	91.9%	3.1%	4.9%
SPINK	1,622	505	931	186	Johnson	31.1%	57.4%	11.5%
STANLEY	311	141	74	96	R. Kennedy	45.3%	23.8%	30.9%
SULLY	249	114	52	83	R. Kennedy	45.8%	20.9%	33.3%
TODD	680	512	96	72	R. Kennedy	75.3%	14.1%	10.6%
TRIPP	971	522	229	220	R. Kennedy	53.8%	23.6%	22.7%
TURNER	585	311	135	139	R. Kennedy	53.2%	23.1%	23.8%
UNION	769	402	180	187	R. Kennedy	52.3%	23.4%	24.3%
WALWORTH	672	354	187	131	R. Kennedy	52.7%	27.8%	19.5%
WASHABAUGH	169	119	17	33	R. Kennedy	70.4%	10.1%	19.5%
YANKTON	1,414	884	242	288	R. Kennedy	62.5%	17.1%	20.4%
ZIEBACH	253	170	39	44	R. Kennedy	67.2%	15.4%	17.4%
TOTAL	64,287	31,826	19,316	13,145	R. Kennedy	49.5%	30.0%	20.4%

Note: Shannon, Todd and Washabaugh were unorganized counties in 1968.

SOUTH DAKOTA DEMOCRATIC

1976

County	Total Vote	Carter	Udall	Uncommitted	Other	Winner	Percentage of Total Vote Carter	Udall	Uncom.	Other
AURORA	894	415	262	115	102	Carter	46.4%	29.3%	12.9%	11.4%
BEADLE	2,519	689	447	1,156	227	Uncommitted	27.4%	17.7%	45.9%	9.0%
BENNETT	246	142	44	33	27	Carter	57.7%	17.9%	13.4%	11.0%
BON HOMME	773	311	276	114	72	Carter	40.2%	35.7%	14.7%	9.3%
BROOKINGS	1,429	453	607	138	231	Udall	31.7%	42.5%	9.7%	16.2%
BROWN	4,635	1,932	1,687	520	496	Carter	41.7%	36.4%	11.2%	10.7%
BRULE	948	348	282	111	207	Carter	36.7%	29.7%	11.7%	21.8%
BUFFALO	108	41	37	18	12	Carter	38.0%	34.3%	16.7%	11.1%
BUTTE	481	274	124	47	36	Carter	57.0%	25.8%	9.8%	7.5%
CAMPBELL	119	63	41	7	8	Carter	52.9%	34.5%	5.9%	6.7%
CHARLES MIX	1,730	714	439	283	294	Carter	41.3%	25.4%	16.4%	17.0%
CLARK	609	246	217	98	48	Carter	40.4%	35.6%	16.1%	7.9%
CLAY	893	320	422	66	85	Udall	35.8%	47.3%	7.4%	9.5%
CODINGTON	1,386	537	421	239	189	Carter	38.7%	30.4%	17.2%	13.6%
CORSON	476	226	111	47	92	Carter	47.5%	23.3%	9.9%	19.3%
CUSTER	469	201	166	60	42	Carter	42.9%	35.4%	12.8%	9.0%
DAVISON	1,602	607	673	178	144	Udall	37.9%	42.0%	11.1%	9.0%
DAY	1,100	501	321	135	143	Carter	45.5%	29.2%	12.3%	13.0%
DEUEL	516	214	176	77	49	Carter	41.5%	34.1%	14.9%	9.5%
DEWEY	360	152	81	59	68	Carter	42.2%	22.5%	16.4%	18.9%

SOUTH DAKOTA DEMOCRATIC

1976

County	Total Vote	Carter	Udall	Uncommitted	Other	Winner	Percentage of Total Vote Carter	Udall	Uncom.	Other
DOUGLAS	302	153	97	25	27	Carter	50.7%	32.1%	8.3%	8.9%
EDMUNDS	691	359	166	79	87	Carter	52.0%	24.0%	11.4%	12.6%
FALL RIVER	663	313	195	82	73	Carter	47.2%	29.4%	12.4%	11.0%
FAULK	662	287	154	128	93	Carter	43.4%	23.3%	19.3%	14.0%
GRANT	578	257	151	56	114	Carter	44.5%	26.1%	9.7%	19.7%
GREGORY	817	349	262	89	117	Carter	42.7%	32.1%	10.9%	14.3%
HAAKON	279	115	62	37	65	Carter	41.2%	22.2%	13.3%	23.3%
HAMLIN	491	225	146	75	45	Carter	45.8%	29.7%	15.3%	9.2%
HAND	646	269	178	118	81	Carter	41.6%	27.6%	18.3%	12.5%
HANSON	381	133	136	46	66	Udall	34.9%	35.7%	12.1%	17.3%
HARDING	167	72	52	17	26	Carter	43.1%	31.1%	10.2%	15.6%
HUGHES	1,028	443	306	174	105	Carter	43.1%	29.8%	16.9%	10.2%
HUTCHINSON	576	240	206	54	76	Carter	41.7%	35.8%	9.4%	13.2%
HYDE	342	103	120	62	57	Udall	30.1%	35.1%	18.1%	16.7%
JACKSON	143	59	49	13	22	Carter	41.3%	34.3%	9.1%	15.4%
JERAULD	372	150	123	69	30	Carter	40.3%	33.1%	18.5%	8.1%
JONES	197	96	54	21	26	Carter	48.7%	27.4%	10.7%	13.2%
KINGSBURY	616	206	205	158	47	Carter	33.4%	33.3%	25.6%	7.6%
LAKE	971	366	403	128	74	Udall	37.7%	41.5%	13.2%	7.6%
LAWRENCE	1,221	557	404	136	124	Carter	45.6%	33.1%	11.1%	10.2%
LINCOLN	914	386	378	89	61	Carter	42.2%	41.4%	9.7%	6.7%
LYMAN	365	158	91	31	85	Carter	43.3%	24.9%	8.5%	23.3%
MCCOOK	684	269	226	71	118	Carter	39.3%	33.0%	10.4%	17.3%
MCPHERSON	228	119	46	19	44	Carter	52.2%	20.2%	8.3%	19.3%
MARSHALL	767	392	177	111	87	Carter	51.1%	23.1%	14.5%	11.3%
MEADE	1,057	507	281	72	197	Carter	48.0%	26.6%	6.8%	18.6%
MELLETTE	222	102	56	35	29	Carter	45.9%	25.2%	15.8%	13.1%
MINER	625	228	212	96	89	Carter	36.5%	33.9%	15.4%	14.2%
MINNEHAHA	6,788	2,610	3,066	512	600	Udall	38.5%	45.2%	7.5%	8.8%
MOODY	714	260	266	65	123	Udall	36.4%	37.3%	9.1%	17.2%
PENNINGTON	3,927	1,772	1,425	304	426	Carter	45.1%	36.3%	7.7%	10.8%
PERKINS	516	233	162	67	54	Carter	45.2%	31.4%	13.0%	10.5%
POTTER	411	176	128	45	62	Carter	42.8%	31.1%	10.9%	15.1%
ROBERTS	1,282	579	350	170	183	Carter	45.2%	27.3%	13.3%	14.3%
SANBORN	457	146	134	76	101	Carter	31.9%	29.3%	16.6%	22.1%
SHANNON	233	138	61	11	23	Carter	59.2%	26.2%	4.7%	9.9%
SPINK	1,305	522	367	317	99	Carter	40.0%	28.1%	24.3%	7.6%
STANLEY	248	111	56	34	47	Carter	44.8%	22.6%	13.7%	19.0%
SULLY	239	124	64	23	28	Carter	51.9%	26.8%	9.6%	11.7%
TODD	397	174	106	49	68	Carter	43.8%	26.7%	12.3%	17.1%
TRIPP	935	424	325	95	91	Carter	45.3%	34.8%	10.2%	9.7%
TURNER	606	268	237	60	41	Carter	44.2%	39.1%	9.9%	6.8%
UNION	790	325	241	125	99	Carter	41.1%	30.5%	15.8%	12.5%
WALWORTH	604	253	202	93	56	Carter	41.9%	33.4%	15.4%	9.3%
WASHABAUGH	84	42	15	10	17	Carter	50.0%	17.9%	11.9%	20.2%
YANKTON	1,690	670	497	203	320	Carter	39.6%	29.4%	12.0%	18.9%
ZIEBACH	147	60	38	20	29	Carter	40.8%	25.9%	13.6%	19.7%
TOTAL	58,671	24,186	19,510	7,871	7,104	Carter	41.2%	33.3%	13.4%	12.1%

Note: Shannon, Todd and Washabaugh were unorganized counties in 1976.

SOUTH DAKOTA REPUBLICAN

1976

County	Total Vote	Ford	Reagan	Uncommitted	Winner	Percentage of Total Vote Ford	Reagan	Uncom.
AURORA	500	225	246	29	Reagan	45.0%	49.2%	5.8%
BEADLE	2,007	804	1,064	139	Reagan	40.1%	53.0%	6.9%
BENNETT	352	94	241	17	Reagan	26.7%	68.5%	4.8%
BON HOMME	1,016	410	554	52	Reagan	40.4%	54.5%	5.1%
BROOKINGS	2,389	1,456	813	120	Ford	60.9%	34.0%	5.0%
BROWN	3,625	1,692	1,811	122	Reagan	46.7%	50.0%	3.4%
BRULE	457	212	226	19	Reagan	46.4%	49.5%	4.2%
BUFFALO	95	40	55		Reagan	42.1%	57.9%	
BUTTE	1,579	518	920	141	Reagan	32.8%	58.3%	8.9%
CAMPBELL	803	338	429	36	Reagan	42.1%	53.4%	4.5%
CHARLES MIX	795	371	384	40	Reagan	46.7%	48.3%	5.0%
CLARK	974	431	511	32	Reagan	44.3%	52.5%	3.3%
CLAY	1,000	549	414	37	Ford	54.9%	41.4%	3.7%
CODINGTON	1,599	893	641	65	Ford	55.8%	40.1%	4.1%
CORSON	573	217	324	32	Reagan	37.9%	56.5%	5.6%
CUSTER	758	235	476	47	Reagan	31.0%	62.8%	6.2%
DAVISON	1,466	776	615	75	Ford	52.9%	42.0%	5.1%
DAY	1,065	430	599	36	Reagan	40.4%	56.2%	3.4%
DEUEL	773	402	320	51	Ford	52.0%	41.4%	6.6%
DEWEY	580	191	367	22	Reagan	32.9%	63.3%	3.8%
DOUGLAS	897	407	456	34	Reagan	45.4%	50.8%	3.8%
EDMUNDS	783	313	451	19	Reagan	40.0%	57.6%	2.4%
FALL RIVER	1,344	397	879	68	Reagan	29.5%	65.4%	5.1%
FAULK	669	250	381	38	Reagan	37.4%	57.0%	5.7%
GRANT	1,002	527	399	76	Ford	52.6%	39.8%	7.6%
GREGORY	923	315	564	44	Reagan	34.1%	61.1%	4.8%
HAAKON	595	152	416	27	Reagan	25.5%	69.9%	4.5%
HAMLIN	997	500	444	53	Ford	50.2%	44.5%	5.3%
HAND	828	328	470	30	Reagan	39.6%	56.8%	3.6%
HANSON	364	183	171	10	Ford	50.3%	47.0%	2.7%
HARDING	443	94	330	19	Reagan	21.2%	74.5%	4.3%
HUGHES	2,170	1,120	958	92	Ford	51.6%	44.1%	4.2%
HUTCHINSON	2,039	876	1,035	128	Reagan	43.0%	50.8%	6.3%
HYDE	478	166	289	23	Reagan	34.7%	60.5%	4.8%
JACKSON	415	118	271	26	Reagan	28.4%	65.3%	6.3%
JERAULD	489	237	226	26	Ford	48.5%	46.2%	5.3%
JONES	364	132	216	16	Reagan	36.3%	59.3%	4.4%
KINGSBURY	1,340	636	626	78	Ford	47.5%	46.7%	5.8%
LAKE	1,512	840	602	70	Ford	55.6%	39.8%	4.6%
LAWRENCE	3,202	1,231	1,734	237	Reagan	38.4%	54.2%	7.4%
LINCOLN	1,785	869	836	80	Ford	48.7%	46.8%	4.5%
LYMAN	686	209	449	28	Reagan	30.5%	65.5%	4.1%
MCCOOK	873	402	420	51	Reagan	46.0%	48.1%	5.8%
MCPHERSON	1,417	604	751	62	Reagan	42.6%	53.0%	4.4%
MARSHALL	697	339	325	33	Ford	48.6%	46.6%	4.7%
MEADE	1,792	425	1,307	60	Reagan	23.7%	72.9%	3.3%
MELLETTE	326	85	228	13	Reagan	26.1%	69.9%	4.0%
MINER	447	211	213	23	Reagan	47.2%	47.7%	5.1%
MINNEHAHA	12,134	6,441	5,138	555	Ford	53.1%	42.3%	4.6%
MOODY	684	333	323	28	Ford	48.7%	47.2%	4.1%

SOUTH DAKOTA REPUBLICAN

1976

County	Total Vote	Ford	Reagan	Uncommitted	Winner	Percentage of Total Vote Ford	Reagan	Uncom.
PENNINGTON	6,564	2,417	3,924	223	Reagan	36.8%	59.8%	3.4%
PERKINS	1,092	294	745	53	Reagan	26.9%	68.2%	4.9%
POTTER	700	253	423	24	Reagan	36.1%	60.4%	3.4%
ROBERTS	882	410	419	53	Reagan	46.5%	47.5%	6.0%
SANBORN	619	256	325	38	Reagan	41.4%	52.5%	6.1%
SHANNON	111	31	77	3	Reagan	27.9%	69.4%	2.7%
SPINK	1,176	521	571	84	Reagan	44.3%	48.6%	7.1%
STANLEY	333	123	193	17	Reagan	36.9%	58.0%	5.1%
SULLY	427	166	250	11	Reagan	38.9%	58.5%	2.6%
TODD	280	113	154	13	Reagan	40.4%	55.0%	4.6%
TRIPP	1,032	350	652	30	Reagan	33.9%	63.2%	2.9%
TURNER	1,607	759	786	62	Reagan	47.2%	48.9%	3.9%
UNION	937	498	408	31	Ford	53.1%	43.5%	3.3%
WALWORTH	1,566	644	832	90	Reagan	41.1%	53.1%	5.7%
WASHABAUGH	164	28	128	8	Reagan	17.1%	78.0%	4.9%
YANKTON	2,304	1,037	1,137	130	Reagan	45.0%	49.3%	5.6%
ZIEBACH	182	52	126	4	Reagan	28.6%	69.2%	2.2%
TOTAL	84,077	36,976	43,068	4,033	Reagan	44.0%	51.2%	4.8%

Note: Shannon, Todd and Washabaugh were unorganized counties in 1976.

SOUTH DAKOTA DEMOCRATIC

1980

County	Total Vote	Carter	E. Kennedy	Uncommitted	Winner	Percentage of Total Vote Carter	E. Kennedy	Uncom.
AURORA	1,108	304	804		E. Kennedy	27.4%	72.6%	
BEADLE	2,775	1,501	1,274		Carter	54.1%	45.9%	
BENNETT	508	274	234		Carter	53.9%	46.1%	
BON HOMME	1,049	392	657		E. Kennedy	37.4%	62.6%	
BROOKINGS	1,536	666	669	201	E. Kennedy	43.4%	43.6%	13.1%
BROWN	4,484	1,960	1,937	587	Carter	43.7%	43.2%	13.1%
BRULE	1,011	471	540		E. Kennedy	46.6%	53.4%	
BUFFALO	124	39	85		E. Kennedy	31.5%	68.5%	
BUTTE	528	326	202		Carter	61.7%	38.3%	
CAMPBELL	124	42	82		E. Kennedy	33.9%	66.1%	
CHARLES MIX	1,947	909	1,038		E. Kennedy	46.7%	53.3%	
CLARK	678	272	324	82	E. Kennedy	40.1%	47.8%	12.1%
CLAY	978	386	387	205	E. Kennedy	39.5%	39.6%	21.0%
CODINGTON	2,448	1,039	1,050	359	E. Kennedy	42.4%	42.9%	14.7%
CORSON	451	170	281		E. Kennedy	37.7%	62.3%	
CUSTER	553	327	226		Carter	59.1%	40.9%	
DAVISON	1,858	847	1,011		E. Kennedy	45.6%	54.4%	
DAY	1,341	460	712	169	E. Kennedy	34.3%	53.1%	12.6%
DEUEL	575	254	254	67		44.2%	44.2%	11.7%
DEWEY	363	162	201		E. Kennedy	44.6%	55.4%	

SOUTH DAKOTA DEMOCRATIC

1980

County	Total Vote	Carter	E. Kennedy	Uncommitted	Winner	Percentage of Total Vote Carter	E. Kennedy	Uncom.
DOUGLAS	417	240	177		Carter	57.6%	42.4%	
EDMUNDS	856	317	539		E. Kennedy	37.0%	63.0%	
FALL RIVER	738	438	300		Carter	59.3%	40.7%	
FAULK	638	276	362		E. Kennedy	43.3%	56.7%	
GRANT	797	376	304	117	Carter	47.2%	38.1%	14.7%
GREGORY	885	377	508		E. Kennedy	42.6%	57.4%	
HAAKON	331	204	127		Carter	61.6%	38.4%	
HAMLIN	669	289	302	78	E. Kennedy	43.2%	45.1%	11.7%
HAND	796	412	384		Carter	51.8%	48.2%	
HANSON	423	139	284		E. Kennedy	32.9%	67.1%	
HARDING	179	102	77		Carter	57.0%	43.0%	
HUGHES	1,183	630	553		Carter	53.3%	46.7%	
HUTCHINSON	594	219	309	66	E. Kennedy	36.9%	52.0%	11.1%
HYDE	341	165	176		E. Kennedy	48.4%	51.6%	
JACKSON	237	132	105		Carter	55.7%	44.3%	
JERAULD	472	254	218		Carter	53.8%	46.2%	
JONES	253	156	97		Carter	61.7%	38.3%	
KINGSBURY	661	268	312	81	E. Kennedy	40.5%	47.2%	12.3%
LAKE	1,134	517	504	113	Carter	45.6%	44.4%	10.0%
LAWRENCE	1,366	700	666		Carter	51.2%	48.8%	
LINCOLN	1,223	503	577	143	E. Kennedy	41.1%	47.2%	11.7%
LYMAN	406	196	210		E. Kennedy	48.3%	51.7%	
MCCOOK	1,033	360	551	122	E. Kennedy	34.8%	53.3%	11.8%
MCPHERSON	241	112	129		E. Kennedy	46.5%	53.5%	
MARSHALL	903	387	426	90	E. Kennedy	42.9%	47.2%	10.0%
MEADE	1,481	827	654		Carter	55.8%	44.2%	
MELLETTE	220	109	111		E. Kennedy	49.5%	50.5%	
MINER	663	334	329		Carter	50.4%	49.6%	
MINNEHAHA	8,169	3,544	3,780	845	E. Kennedy	43.4%	46.3%	10.3%
MOODY	889	374	408	107	E. Kennedy	42.1%	45.9%	12.0%
PENNINGTON	5,166	2,689	2,477		Carter	52.1%	47.9%	
PERKINS	603	262	341		E. Kennedy	43.4%	56.6%	
POTTER	511	223	288		E. Kennedy	43.6%	56.4%	
ROBERTS	1,502	607	669	226	E. Kennedy	40.4%	44.5%	15.0%
SANBORN	560	238	322		E. Kennedy	42.5%	57.5%	
SHANNON	440	84	356		E. Kennedy	19.1%	80.9%	
SPINK	1,380	671	709		E. Kennedy	48.6%	51.4%	
STANLEY	285	165	120		Carter	57.9%	42.1%	
SULLY	236	109	127		E. Kennedy	46.2%	53.8%	
TODD	555	174	381		E. Kennedy	31.4%	68.6%	
TRIPP	798	401	397		Carter	50.3%	49.7%	
TURNER	773	371	345	57	Carter	48.0%	44.6%	7.4%
UNION	1,046	450	425	171	Carter	43.0%	40.6%	16.3%
WALWORTH	576	290	286		Carter	50.3%	49.7%	
YANKTON	1,492	666	618	208	Carter	44.6%	41.4%	13.9%
ZIEBACH	203	93	110		E. Kennedy	45.8%	54.2%	
TOTAL	68,763	31,251	33,418	4,094	E. Kennedy	45.4%	48.6%	6.0%

Note: Shannon and Todd were unorganized counties in 1980. The "Uncommitted" line was only an option in counties in the 1st Congressional District.

SOUTH DAKOTA REPUBLICAN

1980

County	Total Vote	Reagan	Other	Winner	Percentage of Total Vote	
					Reagan	Other
AURORA	512	460	52	Reagan	89.8%	10.2%
BEADLE	2,375	2,131	244	Reagan	89.7%	10.3%
BENNETT	563	531	32	Reagan	94.3%	5.7%
BON HOMME	1,332	1,173	159	Reagan	88.1%	11.9%
BROOKINGS	1,954	1,583	371	Reagan	81.0%	19.0%
BROWN	3,552	2,997	555	Reagan	84.4%	15.6%
BRULE	599	537	62	Reagan	89.6%	10.4%
BUFFALO	130	120	10	Reagan	92.3%	7.7%
BUTTE	1,717	1,570	147	Reagan	91.4%	8.6%
CAMPBELL	847	778	69	Reagan	91.9%	8.1%
CHARLES MIX	972	881	91	Reagan	90.6%	9.4%
CLARK	1,053	972	81	Reagan	92.3%	7.7%
CLAY	870	694	176	Reagan	79.8%	20.2%
CODINGTON	1,812	1,584	228	Reagan	87.4%	12.6%
CORSON	466	423	43	Reagan	90.8%	9.2%
CUSTER	832	760	72	Reagan	91.3%	8.7%
DAVISON	1,508	1,287	221	Reagan	85.3%	14.7%
DAY	1,106	1,008	98	Reagan	91.1%	8.9%
DEUEL	648	609	39	Reagan	94.0%	6.0%
DEWEY	416	379	37	Reagan	91.1%	8.9%
DOUGLAS	1,202	1,061	141	Reagan	88.3%	11.7%
EDMUNDS	750	701	49	Reagan	93.5%	6.5%
FALL RIVER	1,301	1,188	113	Reagan	91.3%	8.7%
FAULK	576	527	49	Reagan	91.5%	8.5%
GRANT	906	780	126	Reagan	86.1%	13.9%
GREGORY	942	868	74	Reagan	92.1%	7.9%
HAAKON	672	618	54	Reagan	92.0%	8.0%
HAMLIN	1,151	1,000	151	Reagan	86.9%	13.1%
HAND	991	904	87	Reagan	91.2%	8.8%
HANSON	355	320	35	Reagan	90.1%	9.9%
HARDING	503	461	42	Reagan	91.7%	8.3%
HUGHES	2,408	1,875	533	Reagan	77.9%	22.1%
HUTCHINSON	1,856	1,701	155	Reagan	91.6%	8.4%
HYDE	383	346	37	Reagan	90.3%	9.7%
JACKSON	595	540	55	Reagan	90.8%	9.2%
JERAULD	510	453	57	Reagan	88.8%	11.2%
JONES	397	368	29	Reagan	92.7%	7.3%
KINGSBURY	1,526	1,308	218	Reagan	85.7%	14.3%
LAKE	1,421	1,234	187	Reagan	86.8%	13.2%
LAWRENCE	2,984	2,567	417	Reagan	86.0%	14.0%
LINCOLN	1,568	1,330	238	Reagan	84.8%	15.2%
LYMAN	743	662	81	Reagan	89.1%	10.9%
MCCOOK	1,015	874	141	Reagan	86.1%	13.9%
MCPHERSON	1,332	1,283	49	Reagan	96.3%	3.7%
MARSHALL	746	694	52	Reagan	93.0%	7.0%
MEADE	2,510	2,326	184	Reagan	92.7%	7.3%
MELLETTE	308	275	33	Reagan	89.3%	10.7%
MINER	428	351	77	Reagan	82.0%	18.0%
MINNEHAHA	8,609	6,972	1,637	Reagan	81.0%	19.0%
MOODY	637	563	74	Reagan	88.4%	11.6%

SOUTH DAKOTA REPUBLICAN

1980

County	Total Vote	Reagan	Other	Winner	Percentage of Total Vote Reagan	Other
PENNINGTON	7,748	6,953	795	Reagan	89.7%	10.3%
PERKINS	960	888	72	Reagan	92.5%	7.5%
POTTER	868	785	83	Reagan	90.4%	9.6%
ROBERTS	892	821	71	Reagan	92.0%	8.0%
SANBORN	439	393	46	Reagan	89.5%	10.5%
SHANNON	125	104	21	Reagan	83.2%	16.8%
SPINK	1,195	1,071	124	Reagan	89.6%	10.4%
STANLEY	347	269	78	Reagan	77.5%	22.5%
SULLY	424	396	28	Reagan	93.4%	6.6%
TODD	264	234	30	Reagan	88.6%	11.4%
TRIPP	1,204	1,123	81	Reagan	93.3%	6.7%
TURNER	1,477	1,334	143	Reagan	90.3%	9.7%
UNION	764	648	116	Reagan	84.8%	15.2%
WALWORTH	1,265	1,175	90	Reagan	92.9%	7.1%
YANKTON	2,129	1,843	286	Reagan	86.6%	13.4%
ZIEBACH	215	197	18	Reagan	91.6%	8.4%
TOTAL	82,905	72,861	10,044	Reagan	87.9%	12.1%

Note: Shannon and Todd were unorganized counties in 1980.

SOUTH DAKOTA DEMOCRATIC

1984

County	Total Vote	Hart	Mondale	Other	Winner	Percentage of Total Vote Hart	Mondale	Other
AURORA	859	527	248	84	Hart	61.4%	28.9%	9.8%
BEADLE	1,984	891	896	197	Mondale	44.9%	45.2%	9.9%
BENNETT	283	163	91	29	Hart	57.6%	32.2%	10.2%
BON HOMME	613	340	225	48	Hart	55.5%	36.7%	7.8%
BROOKINGS	1,174	556	453	165	Hart	47.4%	38.6%	14.1%
BROWN	3,745	1,792	1,648	305	Hart	47.9%	44.0%	8.1%
BRULE	1,017	571	288	158	Hart	56.1%	28.3%	15.5%
BUFFALO	171	89	53	29	Hart	52.0%	31.0%	17.0%
BUTTE	396	238	131	27	Hart	60.1%	33.1%	6.8%
CAMPBELL	73	49	19	5	Hart	67.1%	26.0%	6.8%
CHARLES MIX	1,801	1,016	619	166	Hart	56.4%	34.4%	9.2%
CLARK	421	186	209	26	Mondale	44.2%	49.6%	6.2%
CLAY	1,373	767	417	189	Hart	55.9%	30.4%	13.8%
CODINGTON	1,171	524	528	119	Mondale	44.7%	45.1%	10.2%
CORSON	365	157	171	37	Mondale	43.0%	46.8%	10.1%
CUSTER	415	242	132	41	Hart	58.3%	31.8%	9.9%
DAVISON	1,568	831	624	113	Hart	53.0%	39.8%	7.2%
DAY	890	353	476	61	Mondale	39.7%	53.5%	6.9%
DEUEL	372	145	190	37	Mondale	39.0%	51.1%	9.9%
DEWEY	326	193	91	42	Hart	59.2%	27.9%	12.9%

SOUTH DAKOTA DEMOCRATIC

1984

County	Total Vote	Hart	Mondale	Other	Winner	Percentage of Total Vote Hart	Mondale	Other
DOUGLAS	279	145	110	24	Hart	52.0%	39.4%	8.6%
EDMUNDS	545	265	240	40	Hart	48.6%	44.0%	7.3%
FALL RIVER	971	552	323	96	Hart	56.8%	33.3%	9.9%
FAULK	483	277	161	45	Hart	57.3%	33.3%	9.3%
GRANT	515	212	249	54	Mondale	41.2%	48.3%	10.5%
GREGORY	822	437	268	117	Hart	53.2%	32.6%	14.2%
HAAKON	199	113	69	17	Hart	56.8%	34.7%	8.5%
HAMLIN	471	213	208	50	Hart	45.2%	44.2%	10.6%
HAND	608	330	216	62	Hart	54.3%	35.5%	10.2%
HANSON	259	142	91	26	Hart	54.8%	35.1%	10.0%
HARDING	114	69	35	10	Hart	60.5%	30.7%	8.8%
HUGHES	759	394	266	99	Hart	51.9%	35.0%	13.0%
HUTCHINSON	513	250	216	47	Hart	48.7%	42.1%	9.2%
HYDE	382	204	132	46	Hart	53.4%	34.6%	12.0%
JACKSON	197	119	53	25	Hart	60.4%	26.9%	12.7%
JERAULD	275	167	87	21	Hart	60.7%	31.6%	7.6%
JONES	141	86	41	14	Hart	61.0%	29.1%	9.9%
KINGSBURY	420	213	166	41	Hart	50.7%	39.5%	9.8%
LAKE	1,107	540	479	88	Hart	48.8%	43.3%	7.9%
LAWRENCE	956	581	286	89	Hart	60.8%	29.9%	9.3%
LINCOLN	837	413	350	74	Hart	49.3%	41.8%	8.8%
LYMAN	268	134	95	39	Hart	50.0%	35.4%	14.6%
MCCOOK	588	327	222	39	Hart	55.6%	37.8%	6.6%
MCPHERSON	216	111	87	18	Hart	51.4%	40.3%	8.3%
MARSHALL	716	308	366	42	Mondale	43.0%	51.1%	5.9%
MEADE	1,212	749	334	129	Hart	61.8%	27.6%	10.6%
MELLETTE	213	115	64	34	Hart	54.0%	30.0%	16.0%
MINER	877	438	359	80	Hart	49.9%	40.9%	9.1%
MINNEHAHA	6,877	2,921	3,180	776	Mondale	42.5%	46.2%	11.3%
MOODY	582	282	254	46	Hart	48.5%	43.6%	7.9%
PENNINGTON	3,206	1,846	1,016	344	Hart	57.6%	31.7%	10.7%
PERKINS	479	284	149	46	Hart	59.3%	31.1%	9.6%
POTTER	293	149	116	28	Hart	50.9%	39.6%	9.6%
ROBERTS	1,214	494	585	135	Mondale	40.7%	48.2%	11.1%
SANBORN	269	131	105	33	Hart	48.7%	39.0%	12.3%
SHANNON	519	268	140	111	Hart	51.6%	27.0%	21.4%
SPINK	889	436	374	79	Hart	49.0%	42.1%	8.9%
STANLEY	275	165	88	22	Hart	60.0%	32.0%	8.0%
SULLY	162	90	49	23	Hart	55.6%	30.2%	14.2%
TODD	542	284	147	111	Hart	52.4%	27.1%	20.5%
TRIPP	517	280	205	32	Hart	54.2%	39.7%	6.2%
TURNER	592	298	255	39	Hart	50.3%	43.1%	6.6%
UNION	677	353	264	60	Hart	52.1%	39.0%	8.9%
WALWORTH	379	206	146	27	Hart	54.4%	38.5%	7.1%
YANKTON	900	514	283	103	Hart	57.1%	31.4%	11.4%
ZIEBACH	229	106	57	66	Hart	46.3%	24.9%	28.8%
TOTAL	52,561	26,641	20,495	5,425	Hart	50.7%	39.0%	10.3%

SOUTH DAKOTA DEMOCRATIC

1988

County	Total Vote	Dukakis	Gephardt	Other	Winner	Percentage of Total Vote Dukakis	Gephardt	Other
AURORA	579	136	294	149	Gephardt	23.5%	50.8%	25.7%
BEADLE	2,707	598	1,394	715	Gephardt	22.1%	51.5%	26.4%
BENNETT	363	49	176	138	Gephardt	13.5%	48.5%	38.0%
BON HOMME	806	193	423	190	Gephardt	23.9%	52.5%	23.6%
BROOKINGS	1,748	519	667	562	Gephardt	29.7%	38.2%	32.2%
BROWN	4,731	1,488	2,132	1,111	Gephardt	31.5%	45.1%	23.5%
BRULE	740	206	379	155	Gephardt	27.8%	51.2%	20.9%
BUFFALO	141	34	58	49	Gephardt	24.1%	41.1%	34.8%
BUTTE	505	94	296	115	Gephardt	18.6%	58.6%	22.8%
CAMPBELL	89	25	37	27	Gephardt	28.1%	41.6%	30.3%
CHARLES MIX	1,513	650	554	309	Dukakis	43.0%	36.6%	20.4%
CLARK	598	130	341	127	Gephardt	21.7%	57.0%	21.2%
CLAY	1,269	401	422	446	Gephardt	31.6%	33.3%	35.1%
CODINGTON	2,201	655	1,126	420	Gephardt	29.8%	51.2%	19.1%
CORSON	376	86	147	143	Gephardt	22.9%	39.1%	38.0%
CUSTER	594	159	277	158	Gephardt	26.8%	46.6%	26.6%
DAVISON	2,012	918	705	389	Dukakis	45.6%	35.0%	19.3%
DAY	1,333	361	728	244	Gephardt	27.1%	54.6%	18.3%
DEUEL	558	94	363	101	Gephardt	16.8%	65.1%	18.1%
DEWEY	425	111	140	174	Gephardt	26.1%	32.9%	40.9%
DOUGLAS	312	85	164	63	Gephardt	27.2%	52.6%	20.2%
EDMUNDS	755	138	437	180	Gephardt	18.3%	57.9%	23.8%
FALL RIVER	753	241	321	191	Gephardt	32.0%	42.6%	25.4%
FAULK	502	87	280	135	Gephardt	17.3%	55.8%	26.9%
GRANT	794	214	407	173	Gephardt	27.0%	51.3%	21.8%
GREGORY	740	154	401	185	Gephardt	20.8%	54.2%	25.0%
HAAKON	250	65	126	59	Gephardt	26.0%	50.4%	23.6%
HAMLIN	551	105	320	126	Gephardt	19.1%	58.1%	22.9%
HAND	691	134	303	254	Gephardt	19.4%	43.8%	36.8%
HANSON	380	123	187	70	Gephardt	32.4%	49.2%	18.4%
HARDING	153	22	68	63	Gephardt	14.4%	44.4%	41.2%
HUGHES	1,448	568	438	442	Dukakis	39.2%	30.2%	30.5%
HUTCHINSON	617	144	349	124	Gephardt	23.3%	56.6%	20.1%
HYDE	260	48	153	59	Gephardt	18.5%	58.8%	22.7%
JACKSON	242	61	85	96	Gephardt	25.2%	35.1%	39.7%
JERAULD	381	71	212	98	Gephardt	18.6%	55.6%	25.7%
JONES	220	68	92	60	Gephardt	30.9%	41.8%	27.3%
KINGSBURY	636	114	368	154	Gephardt	17.9%	57.9%	24.2%
LAKE	1,335	409	565	361	Gephardt	30.6%	42.3%	27.0%
LAWRENCE	1,641	458	704	479	Gephardt	27.9%	42.9%	29.2%
LINCOLN	1,339	427	605	307	Gephardt	31.9%	45.2%	22.9%
LYMAN	294	82	146	66	Gephardt	27.9%	49.7%	22.4%
MCCOOK	686	181	366	139	Gephardt	26.4%	53.4%	20.3%
MCPHERSON	221	38	130	53	Gephardt	17.2%	58.8%	24.0%
MARSHALL	778	157	454	167	Gephardt	20.2%	58.4%	21.5%
MEADE	1,682	407	814	461	Gephardt	24.2%	48.4%	27.4%
MELLETTE	212	56	84	72	Gephardt	26.4%	39.6%	34.0%
MINER	547	127	285	135	Gephardt	23.2%	52.1%	24.7%
MINNEHAHA	12,467	5,688	4,040	2,739	Dukakis	45.6%	32.4%	22.0%
MOODY	899	265	459	175	Gephardt	29.5%	51.1%	19.5%

SOUTH DAKOTA DEMOCRATIC

1988

County	Total Vote	Dukakis	Gephardt	Other	Winner	Percentage of Total Vote Dukakis	Gephardt	Other
PENNINGTON	6,116	1,998	2,466	1,652	Gephardt	32.7%	40.3%	27.0%
PERKINS	500	91	279	130	Gephardt	18.2%	55.8%	26.0%
POTTER	307	79	169	59	Gephardt	25.7%	55.0%	19.2%
ROBERTS	1,301	324	684	293	Gephardt	24.9%	52.6%	22.5%
SANBORN	463	103	242	118	Gephardt	22.2%	52.3%	25.5%
SHANNON	750	133	87	530	J. Jackson	17.7%	11.6%	70.7%
SPINK	1,252	271	702	279	Gephardt	21.6%	56.1%	22.3%
STANLEY	283	84	109	90	Gephardt	29.7%	38.5%	31.8%
SULLY	232	61	126	45	Gephardt	26.3%	54.3%	19.4%
TODD	581	111	154	316	Gephardt	19.1%	26.5%	54.4%
TRIPP	727	143	406	178	Gephardt	19.7%	55.8%	24.5%
TURNER	758	239	346	173	Gephardt	31.5%	45.6%	22.8%
UNION	1,000	325	458	217	Gephardt	32.5%	45.8%	21.7%
WALWORTH	504	115	250	139	Gephardt	22.8%	49.6%	27.6%
YANKTON	1,564	585	605	374	Gephardt	37.4%	38.7%	23.9%
ZIEBACH	194	43	79	72	Gephardt	22.2%	40.7%	37.1%
TOTAL	71,606	22,349	31,184	18,073	Gephardt	31.2%	43.5%	25.2%

SOUTH DAKOTA REPUBLICAN

1988

County	Total Vote	Bush	Dole	Robertson	Other	Winner	Percentage of Total Vote Bush	Dole	Robertson	Other
AURORA	452	65	256	106	25	Dole	14.4%	56.6%	23.5%	5.5%
BEADLE	2,269	420	1,082	461	306	Dole	18.5%	47.7%	20.3%	13.5%
BENNETT	378	64	221	57	36	Dole	16.9%	58.5%	15.1%	9.5%
BON HOMME	1,143	140	723	228	52	Dole	12.2%	63.3%	19.9%	4.5%
BROOKINGS	3,072	412	1,888	586	186	Dole	13.4%	61.5%	19.1%	6.1%
BROWN	3,921	804	2,299	639	179	Dole	20.5%	58.6%	16.3%	4.6%
BRULE	557	98	346	83	30	Dole	17.6%	62.1%	14.9%	5.4%
BUFFALO	93	12	47	29	5	Dole	12.9%	50.5%	31.2%	5.4%
BUTTE	1,699	337	719	502	141	Dole	19.8%	42.3%	29.5%	8.3%
CAMPBELL	658	109	389	147	13	Dole	16.6%	59.1%	22.3%	2.0%
CHARLES MIX	982	141	598	201	42	Dole	14.4%	60.9%	20.5%	4.3%
CLARK	908	148	591	112	57	Dole	16.3%	65.1%	12.3%	6.3%
CLAY	1,161	215	717	144	85	Dole	18.5%	61.8%	12.4%	7.3%
CODINGTON	2,363	501	1,146	509	207	Dole	21.2%	48.5%	21.5%	8.8%
CORSON	413	69	240	91	13	Dole	16.7%	58.1%	22.0%	3.1%
CUSTER	1,185	248	578	276	83	Dole	20.9%	48.8%	23.3%	7.0%
DAVISON	1,915	481	962	390	82	Dole	25.1%	50.2%	20.4%	4.3%
DAY	1,021	149	625	190	57	Dole	14.6%	61.2%	18.6%	5.6%
DEUEL	709	93	451	110	55	Dole	13.1%	63.6%	15.5%	7.8%
DEWEY	468	91	273	82	22	Dole	19.4%	58.3%	17.5%	4.7%

SOUTH DAKOTA REPUBLICAN

1988

County	Total Vote	Bush	Dole	Robertson	Other	Winner	Percentage of Total Vote Bush	Dole	Robertson	Other
DOUGLAS	1,003	114	622	219	48	Dole	11.4%	62.0%	21.8%	4.8%
EDMUNDS	808	181	452	160	15	Dole	22.4%	55.9%	19.8%	1.9%
FALL RIVER	1,330	209	636	374	111	Dole	15.7%	47.8%	28.1%	8.3%
FAULK	558	95	352	88	23	Dole	17.0%	63.1%	15.8%	4.1%
GRANT	1,125	175	678	212	60	Dole	15.6%	60.3%	18.8%	5.3%
GREGORY	772	133	424	152	63	Dole	17.2%	54.9%	19.7%	8.2%
HAAKON	671	88	366	158	59	Dole	13.1%	54.5%	23.5%	8.8%
HAMLIN	997	150	596	200	51	Dole	15.0%	59.8%	20.1%	5.1%
HAND	874	136	509	182	47	Dole	15.6%	58.2%	20.8%	5.4%
HANSON	379	69	223	75	12	Dole	18.2%	58.8%	19.8%	3.2%
HARDING	435	77	187	128	43	Dole	17.7%	43.0%	29.4%	9.9%
HUGHES	3,057	746	1,693	447	171	Dole	24.4%	55.4%	14.6%	5.6%
HUTCHINSON	2,136	392	1,381	274	89	Dole	18.4%	64.7%	12.8%	4.2%
HYDE	366	63	211	69	23	Dole	17.2%	57.7%	18.9%	6.3%
JACKSON	546	55	309	122	60	Dole	10.1%	56.6%	22.3%	11.0%
JERAULD	464	83	265	91	25	Dole	17.9%	57.1%	19.6%	5.4%
JONES	409	47	272	58	32	Dole	11.5%	66.5%	14.2%	7.8%
KINGSBURY	1,316	173	820	246	77	Dole	13.1%	62.3%	18.7%	5.9%
LAKE	1,691	270	1,080	237	104	Dole	16.0%	63.9%	14.0%	6.2%
LAWRENCE	3,331	696	1,484	895	256	Dole	20.9%	44.6%	26.9%	7.7%
LINCOLN	1,844	375	984	395	90	Dole	20.3%	53.4%	21.4%	4.9%
LYMAN	596	69	392	99	36	Dole	11.6%	65.8%	16.6%	6.0%
MCCOOK	883	144	531	179	29	Dole	16.3%	60.1%	20.3%	3.3%
MCPHERSON	943	207	564	151	21	Dole	22.0%	59.8%	16.0%	2.2%
MARSHALL	657	118	449	64	26	Dole	18.0%	68.3%	9.7%	4.0%
MEADE	2,928	569	1,234	837	288	Dole	19.4%	42.1%	28.6%	9.8%
MELLETTE	282	48	174	42	18	Dole	17.0%	61.7%	14.9%	6.4%
MINER	381	72	218	69	22	Dole	18.9%	57.2%	18.1%	5.8%
MINNEHAHA	13,381	2,863	7,289	2,445	784	Dole	21.4%	54.5%	18.3%	5.9%
MOODY	758	141	427	134	56	Dole	18.6%	56.3%	17.7%	7.4%
PENNINGTON	10,445	2,092	4,950	2,360	1,043	Dole	20.0%	47.4%	22.6%	10.0%
PERKINS	893	119	474	229	71	Dole	13.3%	53.1%	25.6%	8.0%
POTTER	785	101	530	118	36	Dole	12.9%	67.5%	15.0%	4.6%
ROBERTS	908	170	525	176	37	Dole	18.7%	57.8%	19.4%	4.1%
SANBORN	518	101	322	70	25	Dole	19.5%	62.2%	13.5%	4.8%
SHANNON	158	26	90	27	15	Dole	16.5%	57.0%	17.1%	9.5%
SPINK	1,142	193	754	152	43	Dole	16.9%	66.0%	13.3%	3.8%
STANLEY	412	82	251	57	22	Dole	19.9%	60.9%	13.8%	5.3%
SULLY	412	62	224	110	16	Dole	15.0%	54.4%	26.7%	3.9%
TODD	265	47	160	40	18	Dole	17.7%	60.4%	15.1%	6.8%
TRIPP	1,033	231	597	166	39	Dole	22.4%	57.8%	16.1%	3.8%
TURNER	1,655	320	966	308	61	Dole	19.3%	58.4%	18.6%	3.7%
UNION	782	135	449	144	54	Dole	17.3%	57.4%	18.4%	6.9%
WALWORTH	1,220	213	709	263	35	Dole	17.5%	58.1%	21.6%	2.9%
YANKTON	2,297	314	1,519	312	152	Dole	13.7%	66.1%	13.6%	6.6%
ZIEBACH	192	43	106	33	10	Dole	22.4%	55.2%	17.2%	5.2%
TOTAL	93,405	17,404	51,599	18,310	6,092	Dole	18.6%	55.2%	19.6%	6.5%

SOUTH DAKOTA DEMOCRATIC

1992

County	Total Vote	Clinton	Harkin	Kerrey	Other	Winner	Percentage of Total Vote Clinton	Harkin	Kerrey	Other
AURORA	485	69	147	168	101	Kerrey	14.2%	30.3%	34.6%	20.8%
BEADLE	2,293	508	833	689	263	Harkin	22.2%	36.3%	30.0%	11.5%
BENNETT	309	50	45	176	38	Kerrey	16.2%	14.6%	57.0%	12.3%
BONHOMME	605	88	183	264	70	Kerrey	14.5%	30.2%	43.6%	11.6%
BROOKINGS	1,579	294	414	497	374	Kerrey	18.6%	26.2%	31.5%	23.7%
BROWN	4,071	785	1,254	1,400	632	Kerrey	19.3%	30.8%	34.4%	15.5%
BRULE	680	114	207	249	110	Kerrey	16.8%	30.4%	36.6%	16.2%
BUFFALO	123	22	36	44	21	Kerrey	17.9%	29.3%	35.8%	17.1%
BUTTE	417	70	63	241	43	Kerrey	16.8%	15.1%	57.8%	10.3%
CAMPBELL	85	30	17	26	12	Clinton	35.3%	20.0%	30.6%	14.1%
CHARLES MIX	1,184	114	258	717	95	Kerrey	9.6%	21.8%	60.6%	8.0%
CLARK	473	89	147	190	47	Kerrey	18.8%	31.1%	40.2%	9.9%
CLAY	1,058	218	223	378	239	Kerrey	20.6%	21.1%	35.7%	22.6%
CODINGTON	1,643	378	546	467	252	Harkin	23.0%	33.2%	28.4%	15.3%
CORSON	244	41	55	83	65	Kerrey	16.8%	22.5%	34.0%	26.6%
CUSTER	488	79	65	274	70	Kerrey	16.2%	13.3%	56.1%	14.3%
DAVISON	1,509	327	344	581	257	Kerrey	21.7%	22.8%	38.5%	17.0%
DAY	964	192	344	307	121	Harkin	19.9%	35.7%	31.8%	12.6%
DEUEL	505	101	179	170	55	Harkin	20.0%	35.4%	33.7%	10.9%
DEWEY	404	58	61	177	108	Kerrey	14.4%	15.1%	43.8%	26.7%
DOUGLAS	230	35	63	90	42	Kerrey	15.2%	27.4%	39.1%	18.3%
EDMUNDS	597	110	181	242	64	Kerrey	18.4%	30.3%	40.5%	10.7%
FALL RIVER	706	130	86	409	81	Kerrey	18.4%	12.2%	57.9%	11.5%
FAULK	370	75	83	157	55	Kerrey	20.3%	22.4%	42.4%	14.9%
GRANT	663	121	241	198	103	Harkin	18.3%	36.3%	29.9%	15.5%
GREGORY	661	129	176	251	105	Kerrey	19.5%	26.6%	38.0%	15.9%
HAAKON	184	19	42	95	28	Kerrey	10.3%	22.8%	51.6%	15.2%
HAMLIN	477	98	164	136	79	Harkin	20.5%	34.4%	28.5%	16.6%
HAND	490	100	174	141	75	Harkin	20.4%	35.5%	28.8%	15.3%
HANSON	318	61	114	107	36	Harkin	19.2%	35.8%	33.6%	11.3%
HARDING	113	18	18	55	22	Kerrey	15.9%	15.9%	48.7%	19.5%
HUGHES	1,106	263	223	404	216	Kerrey	23.8%	20.2%	36.5%	19.5%
HUTCHINSON	444	62	156	174	52	Kerrey	14.0%	35.1%	39.2%	11.7%
HYDE	218	41	68	83	26	Kerrey	18.8%	31.2%	38.1%	11.9%
JACKSON	211	30	43	112	26	Kerrey	14.2%	20.4%	53.1%	12.3%
JERAULD	297	53	118	100	26	Harkin	17.8%	39.7%	33.7%	8.8%
JONES	110	22	26	52	10	Kerrey	20.0%	23.6%	47.3%	9.1%
KINGSBURY	516	83	219	158	56	Harkin	16.1%	42.4%	30.6%	10.9%
LAKE	943	241	231	319	152	Kerrey	25.6%	24.5%	33.8%	16.1%
LAWRENCE	1,361	234	324	592	211	Kerrey	17.2%	23.8%	43.5%	15.5%
LINCOLN	1,142	232	291	486	133	Kerrey	20.3%	25.5%	42.6%	11.6%
LYMAN	257	50	59	97	51	Kerrey	19.5%	23.0%	37.7%	19.8%
MCCOOK	586	112	157	232	85	Kerrey	19.1%	26.8%	39.6%	14.5%
MCPHERSON	365	27	38	272	28	Kerrey	7.4%	10.4%	74.5%	7.7%
MARSHALL	461	177	148	64	72	Clinton	38.4%	32.1%	13.9%	15.6%
MEADE	1,428	243	208	805	172	Kerrey	17.0%	14.6%	56.4%	12.0%
MELLETTE	171	23	48	85	15	Kerrey	13.5%	28.1%	49.7%	8.8%
MINER	400	65	140	139	56	Harkin	16.3%	35.0%	34.8%	14.0%
MINNEHAHA	11,011	2,422	2,640	4,027	1,922	Kerrey	22.0%	24.0%	36.6%	17.5%
MOODY	654	116	204	257	77	Kerrey	17.7%	31.2%	39.3%	11.8%

SOUTH DAKOTA DEMOCRATIC

1992

County	Total Vote	Clinton	Harkin	Kerrey	Other	Winner	Percentage of Total Vote Clinton	Harkin	Kerrey	Other
PENNINGTON	5,090	804	648	2,799	839	Kerrey	15.8%	12.7%	55.0%	16.5%
PERKINS	354	61	65	193	35	Kerrey	17.2%	18.4%	54.5%	9.9%
POTTER	282	52	84	114	32	Kerrey	18.4%	29.8%	40.4%	11.3%
ROBERTS	1,045	317	280	283	165	Clinton	30.3%	26.8%	27.1%	15.8%
SANBORN	346	72	115	118	41	Kerrey	20.8%	33.2%	34.1%	11.8%
SHANNON	539	50	37	356	96	Kerrey	9.3%	6.9%	66.0%	17.8%
SPINK	954	171	274	379	130	Kerrey	17.9%	28.7%	39.7%	13.6%
STANLEY	242	69	53	77	43	Kerrey	28.5%	21.9%	31.8%	17.8%
SULLY	216	47	65	69	35	Kerrey	21.8%	30.1%	31.9%	16.2%
TODD	513	61	46	307	99	Kerrey	11.9%	9.0%	59.8%	19.3%
TRIPP	642	87	216	264	75	Kerrey	13.6%	33.6%	41.1%	11.7%
TURNER	643	140	140	282	81	Kerrey	21.8%	21.8%	43.9%	12.6%
UNION	861	115	242	368	136	Kerrey	13.4%	28.1%	42.7%	15.8%
WALWORTH	404	72	108	153	71	Kerrey	17.8%	26.7%	37.9%	17.6%
YANKTON	1,605	208	529	619	249	Kerrey	13.0%	33.0%	38.6%	15.5%
ZIEBACH	158	30	17	74	37	Kerrey	19.0%	10.8%	46.8%	23.4%
TOTAL	59,503	11,375	15,023	23,892	9,213	Kerrey	19.1%	25.2%	40.2%	15.5%

SOUTH DAKOTA REPUBLICAN

1992

County	Total Vote	Bush	Uncommitted	Winner	Percentage of Total Vote Bush	Uncom.
AURORA	190	127	63	Bush	66.8%	33.2%
BEADLE	1,050	816	234	Bush	77.7%	22.3%
BENNETT	181	135	46	Bush	74.6%	25.4%
BONHOMME	465	338	127	Bush	72.7%	27.3%
BROOKINGS	1,374	913	461	Bush	66.4%	33.6%
BROWN	2,240	1,593	647	Bush	71.1%	28.9%
BRULE	258	168	90	Bush	65.1%	34.9%
BUFFALO	61	48	13	Bush	78.7%	21.3%
BUTTE	797	525	272	Bush	65.9%	34.1%
CAMPBELL	315	165	150	Bush	52.4%	47.6%
CHARLES MIX	415	311	104	Bush	74.9%	25.1%
CLARK	469	301	168	Bush	64.2%	35.8%
CLAY	521	345	176	Bush	66.2%	33.8%
CODINGTON	1,148	807	341	Bush	70.3%	29.7%
CORSON	219	159	60	Bush	72.6%	27.4%
CUSTER	543	341	202	Bush	62.8%	37.2%
DAVISON	805	588	217	Bush	73.0%	27.0%
DAY	460	290	170	Bush	63.0%	37.0%
DEUEL	365	218	147	Bush	59.7%	40.3%
DEWEY	243	173	70	Bush	71.2%	28.8%

SOUTH DAKOTA REPUBLICAN

1992

County	Total Vote	Bush	Uncommitted	Winner	Percentage of Total Vote Bush	Uncom.
DOUGLAS	451	317	134	Bush	70.3%	29.7%
EDMUNDS	392	280	112	Bush	71.4%	28.6%
FALL RIVER	702	469	233	Bush	66.8%	33.2%
FAULK	305	183	122	Bush	60.0%	40.0%
GRANT	600	401	199	Bush	66.8%	33.2%
GREGORY	383	261	122	Bush	68.1%	31.9%
HAAKON	306	213	93	Bush	69.6%	30.4%
HAMLIN	581	358	223	Bush	61.6%	38.4%
HAND	475	344	131	Bush	72.4%	27.6%
HANSON	142	116	26	Bush	81.7%	18.3%
HARDING	229	169	60	Bush	73.8%	26.2%
HUGHES	1,510	1,126	384	Bush	74.6%	25.4%
HUTCHINSON	835	579	256	Bush	69.3%	30.7%
HYDE	197	140	57	Bush	71.1%	28.9%
JACKSON	256	198	58	Bush	77.3%	22.7%
JERAULD	153	116	37	Bush	75.8%	24.2%
JONES	174	122	52	Bush	70.1%	29.9%
KINGSBURY	722	431	291	Bush	59.7%	40.3%
LAKE	633	421	212	Bush	66.5%	33.5%
LAWRENCE	1,534	1,068	466	Bush	69.6%	30.4%
LINCOLN	766	540	226	Bush	70.5%	29.5%
LYMAN	242	159	83	Bush	65.7%	34.3%
MCCOOK	368	268	100	Bush	72.8%	27.2%
MCPHERSON	491	349	142	Bush	71.1%	28.9%
MARSHALL	339	259	80	Bush	76.4%	23.6%
MEADE	1,546	1,010	536	Bush	65.3%	34.7%
MELLETTE	140	100	40	Bush	71.4%	28.6%
MINER	164	108	56	Bush	65.9%	34.1%
MINNEHAHA	6,651	4,731	1,920	Bush	71.1%	28.9%
MOODY	226	163	63	Bush	72.1%	27.9%
PENNINGTON	5,072	3,548	1,524	Bush	70.0%	30.0%
PERKINS	393	283	110	Bush	72.0%	28.0%
POTTER	411	238	173	Bush	57.9%	42.1%
ROBERTS	488	329	159	Bush	67.4%	32.6%
SANBORN	223	152	71	Bush	68.2%	31.8%
SHANNON	83	50	33	Bush	60.2%	39.8%
SPINK	498	341	157	Bush	68.5%	31.5%
STANLEY	179	144	35	Bush	80.4%	19.6%
SULLY	177	125	52	Bush	70.6%	29.4%
TODD	143	103	40	Bush	72.0%	28.0%
TRIPP	519	365	154	Bush	70.3%	29.7%
TURNER	652	467	185	Bush	71.6%	28.4%
UNION	361	241	120	Bush	66.8%	33.2%
WALWORTH	618	385	233	Bush	62.3%	37.7%
YANKTON	1,113	746	367	Bush	67.0%	33.0%
ZIEBACH	109	87	22	Bush	79.8%	20.2%
TOTAL	44,671	30,964	13,707	Bush	69.3%	30.7%

SOUTH DAKOTA REPUBLICAN

1996

County	Total Vote	Buchanan	Dole	Forbes	Other	Winner	Percentage of Total Vote Buchanan	Dole	Forbes	Other
AURORA	320	117	140	29	34	Dole	36.6%	43.8%	9.1%	10.6%
BEADLE	1,438	368	744	190	136	Dole	25.6%	51.7%	13.2%	9.5%
BENNETT	260	69	141	28	22	Dole	26.5%	54.2%	10.8%	8.5%
BONHOMME	799	250	364	81	104	Dole	31.3%	45.6%	10.1%	13.0%
BROOKINGS	2,282	591	1,117	199	375	Dole	25.9%	48.9%	8.7%	16.4%
BROWN	2,279	555	1,161	257	306	Dole	24.4%	50.9%	11.3%	13.4%
BRULE	416	133	187	44	52	Dole	32.0%	45.0%	10.6%	12.5%
BUFFALO	75	26	32	3	14	Dole	34.7%	42.7%	4.0%	18.7%
BUTTE	1,139	349	414	200	176	Dole	30.6%	36.3%	17.6%	15.5%
CAMPBELL	305	135	112	30	28	Buchanan	44.3%	36.7%	9.8%	9.2%
CHARLES MIX	754	257	333	52	112	Dole	34.1%	44.2%	6.9%	14.9%
CLARK	586	187	271	64	64	Dole	31.9%	46.2%	10.9%	10.9%
CLAY	870	202	382	90	196	Dole	23.2%	43.9%	10.3%	22.5%
CODINGTON	1,476	475	675	148	178	Dole	32.2%	45.7%	10.0%	12.1%
CORSON	270	124	100	14	32	Buchanan	45.9%	37.0%	5.2%	11.9%
CUSTER	1,274	352	422	315	185	Dole	27.6%	33.1%	24.7%	14.5%
DAVISON	1,298	341	638	124	195	Dole	26.3%	49.2%	9.6%	15.0%
DAY	541	175	240	56	70	Dole	32.3%	44.4%	10.4%	12.9%
DEUEL	615	225	221	81	88	Buchanan	36.6%	35.9%	13.2%	14.3%
DEWEY	294	95	142	29	28	Dole	32.3%	48.3%	9.9%	9.5%
DOUGLAS	719	328	293	44	54	Buchanan	45.6%	40.8%	6.1%	7.5%
EDMUNDS	467	139	227	56	45	Dole	29.8%	48.6%	12.0%	9.6%
FALL RIVER	1,050	346	363	187	154	Dole	33.0%	34.6%	17.8%	14.7%
FAULK	391	117	182	51	41	Dole	29.9%	46.5%	13.0%	10.5%
GRANT	693	237	298	79	79	Dole	34.2%	43.0%	11.4%	11.4%
GREGORY	522	196	217	55	54	Dole	37.5%	41.6%	10.5%	10.3%
HAAKON	475	149	196	68	62	Dole	31.4%	41.3%	14.3%	13.1%
HAMLIN	674	216	304	69	85	Dole	32.0%	45.1%	10.2%	12.6%
HAND	400	78	188	61	73	Dole	19.5%	47.0%	15.3%	18.3%
HANSON	264	82	133	22	27	Dole	31.1%	50.4%	8.3%	10.2%
HARDING	361	125	156	46	34	Dole	34.6%	43.2%	12.7%	9.4%
HUGHES	2,585	467	1,331	334	453	Dole	18.1%	51.5%	12.9%	17.5%
HUTCHINSON	1,331	444	644	75	168	Dole	33.4%	48.4%	5.6%	12.6%
HYDE	240	69	123	23	25	Dole	28.8%	51.3%	9.6%	10.4%
JACKSON	418	141	174	61	42	Dole	33.7%	41.6%	14.6%	10.0%
JERAULD	294	69	146	39	40	Dole	23.5%	49.7%	13.3%	13.6%
JONES	310	108	144	24	34	Dole	34.8%	46.5%	7.7%	11.0%
KINGSBURY	869	253	378	97	141	Dole	29.1%	43.5%	11.2%	16.2%
LAKE	1,001	277	441	94	189	Dole	27.7%	44.1%	9.4%	18.9%
LAWRENCE	2,201	523	880	473	325	Dole	23.8%	40.0%	21.5%	14.8%
LINCOLN	1,901	539	818	215	329	Dole	28.4%	43.0%	11.3%	17.3%
LYMAN	420	122	205	44	49	Dole	29.0%	48.8%	10.5%	11.7%
MCCOOK	582	220	263	42	57	Dole	37.8%	45.2%	7.2%	9.8%
MCPHERSON	533	197	234	50	52	Dole	37.0%	43.9%	9.4%	9.8%
MARSHALL	383	81	202	35	65	Dole	21.1%	52.7%	9.1%	17.0%
MEADE	2,285	695	847	471	272	Dole	30.4%	37.1%	20.6%	11.9%
MELLETTE	223	74	101	27	21	Dole	33.2%	45.3%	12.1%	9.4%
MINER	226	58	104	27	37	Dole	25.7%	46.0%	11.9%	16.4%
MINNEHAHA	12,256	3,372	5,686	1,323	1,875	Dole	27.5%	46.4%	10.8%	15.3%
MOODY	481	148	225	49	59	Dole	30.8%	46.8%	10.2%	12.3%

SOUTH DAKOTA REPUBLICAN

1996

County	Total Vote	Buchanan	Dole	Forbes	Other	Winner	Percentage of Total Vote Buchanan	Dole	Forbes	Other
PENNINGTON	8,468	2,121	3,465	1,720	1,162	Dole	25.0%	40.9%	20.3%	13.7%
PERKINS	499	191	221	29	58	Dole	38.3%	44.3%	5.8%	11.6%
POTTER	546	141	246	69	90	Dole	25.8%	45.1%	12.6%	16.5%
ROBERTS	488	158	257	32	41	Dole	32.4%	52.7%	6.6%	8.4%
SANBORN	303	106	144	25	28	Dole	35.0%	47.5%	8.3%	9.2%
SHANNON	80	27	35	8	10	Dole	33.8%	43.8%	10.0%	12.5%
SPINK	681	153	363	74	91	Dole	22.5%	53.3%	10.9%	13.4%
STANLEY	352	94	160	53	45	Dole	26.7%	45.5%	15.1%	12.8%
SULLY	238	86	105	25	22	Dole	36.1%	44.1%	10.5%	9.2%
TODD	166	63	68	19	16	Dole	38.0%	41.0%	11.4%	9.6%
TRIPP	830	272	401	71	86	Dole	32.8%	48.3%	8.6%	10.4%
TURNER	1,140	370	528	86	156	Dole	32.5%	46.3%	7.5%	13.7%
UNION	787	279	301	70	137	Dole	35.5%	38.2%	8.9%	17.4%
WALWORTH	791	302	338	68	83	Dole	38.2%	42.7%	8.6%	10.5%
YANKTON	1,800	461	881	194	264	Dole	25.6%	48.9%	10.8%	14.7%
ZIEBACH	155	60	66	13	16	Dole	38.7%	42.6%	8.4%	10.3%
TOTAL	69,170	19,780	30,918	8,831	9,641	Dole	28.6%	44.7%	12.8%	13.9%

TENNESSEE

Tennessee has fielded a number of presidential candidates over the last half century—Republicans Howard Baker and Lamar Alexander on one side, Democrats Estes Kefauver and Al Gore on the other. But Gore was the only one to make it to Tennessee's presidential primary as an active candidate.

The state did not have a primary when Kefauver ran for president in the 1950s, and Baker (in 1980) and Alexander (in 1996) both had withdrawn from the race before the Volunteer State voted.

But Gore showed what Tennessee would do for a popular native son, taking 72 percent of the 1988 Democratic primary vote—a higher percentage than any of the other major contenders won in their home states that year.

Despite Gore's dominance, Jesse Jackson was able to establish a toehold in southwest Tennessee. Jackson carried three counties, including vote-rich Shelby (Memphis), which has a population nearly 50 percent black. But Jackson had done better than that in the 1984 primary, when he ran against Walter Mondale and Gary Hart. In that earlier race, Jackson was also able to win populous Davidson (Nashville) and Hamilton (Chattanooga) counties. Running against Gore, Jackson was trampled everywhere outside the Memphis area.

One reason was that Gore's presence on the 1988 ballot nearly doubled the Democratic primary turnout. Fewer than 325,000 voted in 1984, while more than 575,000 did so in 1988. It was a record high for a Democratic or Republican presidential primary in Tennessee.

With the active support of then-Gov. Ned McWherter, a skilled political operator with strong links to the rural courthouse crowd, Gore outpolled Jackson by a margin of at least 10-to-1 in many counties. In a few rural ones around Gore's home base of Carthage in middle Tennessee, the margins approached 100-to-1.

Bill Clinton swept Tennessee's Democratic primary in 1992 with two-thirds of the vote. He boasted endorsements from much of the state party leadership, but not Gore, who was never especially close to Clinton before being tapped as his running mate in July 1992. As Arkansas governor, Clinton had made no secret of his preference for Dukakis over Gore in the 1988 primaries.

The classic Republican presidential primary in Tennessee took place in 1976 between President Gerald Ford and Ronald Reagan, which pitted the two major power centers of Tennessee Republicanism against each other. Reagan swept the western half

Recent Tennessee Primary Results

Tennessee held its first presidential primary in 1972.

	DEMOCRATS			REPUBLICANS		
Year	Turnout	Candidates	%	Turnout	Candidates	%
1996 (March 12)	137,797	BILL CLINTON* Uncommitted	89 11	289,386	BOB DOLE Pat Buchanan Lamar Alexander	51 25 11
1992 (March 10)	318,482	BILL CLINTON Paul Tsongas	67 19	245,653	GEORGE BUSH* Pat Buchanan	73 22
1988 (March 8)	576,314	AL GORE Jesse Jackson	72 21	254,252	GEORGE BUSH Bob Dole Pat Robertson	60 22 13
1984 (May 1)	322,063	WALTER MONDALE Gary Hart Jesse Jackson	41 29 25	82,921	RONALD REAGAN*	91
1980 (May 6)	294,680	JIMMY CARTER* Edward Kennedy	75 18	195,210	RONALD REAGAN George Bush	74 18
1976 (May 25)	334,078	JIMMY CARTER George Wallace	78 11	242,535	GERALD FORD* Ronald Reagan	50 49
1972 (May 4)	492,721	GEORGE WALLACE Hubert Humphrey	68 16	114,489	RICHARD NIXON*	96

Note: All candidates are listed that drew at least 10 percent of their party's primary vote. The names of winning candidates are capitalized. An asterisk (*) indicates an incumbent president.

of the state, anchored by the burgeoning conservative suburbs around Memphis. Ford swept nearly all of the eastern half of the state, anchored by mountain counties that had been a bastion of racially moderate Republicanism since the Civil War. Nearly a quarter-million votes were cast and Ford won by less than 2,000.

GOP contests since then have been much more one-sided. Reagan beat George Bush in all of Tennessee's 95 counties in 1980. Bush came back to win all 95 in 1988. Bush's dominance was a bit surprising in that former Sen. William Brock, originally from the Chattanooga area, was the national chairman of Bob Dole's campaign.

Bush easily won the Tennessee primary again in 1992, even though Pat Buchanan sought to identify with the local economy by campaigning in a Saturn, a Tennessee-built car. Buchanan did not peak in Tennessee until his second try, when he took 25 percent of the GOP primary vote. But that was still less than half of the winning share in 1996 for Dole, who also ran better in Tennessee on his second try.

TENNESSEE DEMOCRATIC

1972

County	Total Vote	Humphrey	McGovern	Wallace	Other	Winner	Percentage of Total Vote Humphrey	McGovern	Wallace	Other
ANDERSON	6,734	1,470	1,392	3,185	687	Wallace	21.8%	20.7%	47.3%	10.2%
BEDFORD	3,307	408	166	2,569	164	Wallace	12.3%	5.0%	77.7%	5.0%
BENTON	2,307	279	74	1,870	84	Wallace	12.1%	3.2%	81.1%	3.6%
BLEDSOE	706	162	46	471	27	Wallace	22.9%	6.5%	66.7%	3.8%
BLOUNT	4,680	1,358	599	2,322	401	Wallace	29.0%	12.8%	49.6%	8.6%
BRADLEY	1,933	314	193	1,240	186	Wallace	16.2%	10.0%	64.1%	9.6%
CAMPBELL	827	217	48	514	48	Wallace	26.2%	5.8%	62.2%	5.8%
CANNON	1,045	137	48	808	52	Wallace	13.1%	4.6%	77.3%	5.0%
CARROLL	2,419	296	105	1,875	143	Wallace	12.2%	4.3%	77.5%	5.9%
CARTER	1,958	267	181	1,420	90	Wallace	13.6%	9.2%	72.5%	4.6%
CHEATHAM	1,755	115	51	1,498	91	Wallace	6.6%	2.9%	85.4%	5.2%
CHESTER	1,546	135	25	1,337	49	Wallace	8.7%	1.6%	86.5%	3.2%
CLAIBORNE	763	162	46	519	36	Wallace	21.2%	6.0%	68.0%	4.7%
CLAY	548	116	11	382	39	Wallace	21.2%	2.0%	69.7%	7.1%
COCKE	941	130	48	694	69	Wallace	13.8%	5.1%	73.8%	7.3%
COFFEE	6,551	955	386	4,343	867	Wallace	14.6%	5.9%	66.3%	13.2%
CROCKETT	2,295	240	30	1,984	41	Wallace	10.5%	1.3%	86.4%	1.8%
CUMBERLAND	2,751	513	176	1,829	233	Wallace	18.6%	6.4%	66.5%	8.5%
DAVIDSON	67,230	9,265	6,330	47,564	4,071	Wallace	13.8%	9.4%	70.7%	6.1%
DECATUR	1,470	185	62	1,168	55	Wallace	12.6%	4.2%	79.5%	3.7%
DE KALB	2,793	348	109	2,165	171	Wallace	12.5%	3.9%	77.5%	6.1%
DICKSON	3,187	335	140	2,547	165	Wallace	10.5%	4.4%	79.9%	5.2%
DYER	3,110	159	88	2,655	208	Wallace	5.1%	2.8%	85.4%	6.7%
FAYETTE	2,781	589	69	1,917	206	Wallace	21.2%	2.5%	68.9%	7.4%
FENTRESS	369	61	33	249	26	Wallace	16.5%	8.9%	67.5%	7.0%
FRANKLIN	3,693	422	362	2,715	194	Wallace	11.4%	9.8%	73.5%	5.3%
GIBSON	7,849	865	271	6,199	514	Wallace	11.0%	3.5%	79.0%	6.5%
GILES	1,801	178	95	1,368	160	Wallace	9.9%	5.3%	76.0%	8.9%
GRAINGER	476	114	32	273	57	Wallace	23.9%	6.7%	57.4%	12.0%
GREENE	2,907	657	253	1,645	352	Wallace	22.6%	8.7%	56.6%	12.1%
GRUNDY	2,583	552	113	1,750	168	Wallace	21.4%	4.4%	67.8%	6.5%
HAMBLEN	2,777	470	282	1,804	221	Wallace	16.9%	10.2%	65.0%	8.0%
HAMILTON	28,216	4,163	2,745	19,665	1,643	Wallace	14.8%	9.7%	69.7%	5.8%
HANCOCK	211	77	9	104	21	Wallace	36.5%	4.3%	49.3%	10.0%
HARDEMAN	4,764	594	100	2,804	1,266	Wallace	12.5%	2.1%	58.9%	26.6%
HARDIN	1,799	181	73	1,395	150	Wallace	10.1%	4.1%	77.5%	8.3%
HAWKINS	1,737	455	145	983	154	Wallace	26.2%	8.3%	56.6%	8.9%
HAYWOOD	5,516	1,743	99	3,347	327	Wallace	31.6%	1.8%	60.7%	5.9%
HENDERSON	1,524	186	42	1,249	47	Wallace	12.2%	2.8%	82.0%	3.1%
HENRY	3,973	502	167	3,039	265	Wallace	12.6%	4.2%	76.5%	6.7%
HICKMAN	1,524	159	54	1,240	71	Wallace	10.4%	3.5%	81.4%	4.7%
HOUSTON	801	117	51	576	57	Wallace	14.6%	6.4%	71.9%	7.1%
HUMPHREYS	2,140	256	89	1,691	104	Wallace	12.0%	4.2%	79.0%	4.9%
JACKSON	786	135	28	589	34	Wallace	17.2%	3.6%	74.9%	4.3%
JEFFERSON	1,105	226	93	706	80	Wallace	20.5%	8.4%	63.9%	7.2%
JOHNSON	463	74	39	313	37	Wallace	16.0%	8.4%	67.6%	8.0%
KNOX	32,922	6,840	6,276	17,340	2,466	Wallace	20.8%	19.1%	52.7%	7.5%
LAKE	839	91	28	669	51	Wallace	10.8%	3.3%	79.7%	6.1%
LAUDERDALE	3,006	348	48	2,454	156	Wallace	11.6%	1.6%	81.6%	5.2%
LAWRENCE	2,624	351	138	1,938	197	Wallace	13.4%	5.3%	73.9%	7.5%

TENNESSEE DEMOCRATIC

1972

County	Total Vote	Humphrey	McGovern	Wallace	Other	Winner	Percentage of Total Vote Humphrey	McGovern	Wallace	Other
LEWIS	1,292	208	62	977	45	Wallace	16.1%	4.8%	75.6%	3.5%
LINCOLN	2,065	221	117	1,579	148	Wallace	10.7%	5.7%	76.5%	7.2%
LOUDON	1,488	281	100	1,016	91	Wallace	18.9%	6.7%	68.3%	6.1%
MCMINN	3,166	680	246	1,989	251	Wallace	21.5%	7.8%	62.8%	7.9%
MCNAIRY	1,909	165	58	1,558	128	Wallace	8.6%	3.0%	81.6%	6.7%
MACON	191	13	5	171	2	Wallace	6.8%	2.6%	89.5%	1.0%
MADISON	14,290	2,171	571	10,503	1,045	Wallace	15.2%	4.0%	73.5%	7.3%
MARION	2,510	367	147	1,834	162	Wallace	14.6%	5.9%	73.1%	6.5%
MARSHALL	2,344	208	84	1,961	91	Wallace	8.9%	3.6%	83.7%	3.9%
MAURY	4,661	358	207	3,919	177	Wallace	7.7%	4.4%	84.1%	3.8%
MEIGS	565	134	30	276	125	Wallace	23.7%	5.3%	48.8%	22.1%
MONROE	1,319	416	87	659	157	Wallace	31.5%	6.6%	50.0%	11.9%
MONTGOMERY	5,423	1,109	551	3,386	377	Wallace	20.4%	10.2%	62.4%	7.0%
MOORE	570	51	30	456	33	Wallace	8.9%	5.3%	80.0%	5.8%
MORGAN	1,316	255	71	882	108	Wallace	19.4%	5.4%	67.0%	8.2%
OBION	2,750	203	106	2,298	143	Wallace	7.4%	3.9%	83.6%	5.2%
OVERTON	3,592	630	27	2,293	642	Wallace	17.5%	0.8%	63.8%	17.9%
PERRY	1,295	242	62	908	83	Wallace	18.7%	4.8%	70.1%	6.4%
PICKETT	201	65	13	113	10	Wallace	32.3%	6.5%	56.2%	5.0%
POLK	2,219	543	125	1,332	219	Wallace	24.5%	5.6%	60.0%	9.9%
PUTNAM	7,200	1,232	560	4,756	652	Wallace	17.1%	7.8%	66.1%	9.1%
RHEA	1,810	227	79	1,346	158	Wallace	12.5%	4.4%	74.4%	8.7%
ROANE	3,491	731	313	2,252	195	Wallace	20.9%	9.0%	64.5%	5.6%
ROBERTSON	3,646	431	144	2,939	132	Wallace	11.8%	3.9%	80.6%	3.6%
RUTHERFORD	9,880	1,256	727	7,042	855	Wallace	12.7%	7.4%	71.3%	8.7%
SCOTT	798	208	37	512	41	Wallace	26.1%	4.6%	64.2%	5.1%
SEQUATCHIE	797	84	22	645	46	Wallace	10.5%	2.8%	80.9%	5.8%
SEVIER	1,333	149	101	1,004	79	Wallace	11.2%	7.6%	75.3%	5.9%
SHELBY	120,654	21,116	5,396	77,559	16,583	Wallace	17.5%	4.5%	64.3%	13.7%
SMITH	1,625	226	41	1,224	134	Wallace	13.9%	2.5%	75.3%	8.2%
STEWART	1,172	235	75	793	69	Wallace	20.1%	6.4%	67.7%	5.9%
SULLIVAN	9,361	1,958	1,083	5,589	731	Wallace	20.9%	11.6%	59.7%	7.8%
SUMNER	5,647	529	276	4,548	294	Wallace	9.4%	4.9%	80.5%	5.2%
TIPTON	4,503	338	69	3,825	271	Wallace	7.5%	1.5%	84.9%	6.0%
TROUSDALE	608	95	15	473	25	Wallace	15.6%	2.5%	77.8%	4.1%
UNICOI	922	192	93	596	41	Wallace	20.8%	10.1%	64.6%	4.4%
UNION	318	69	24	195	30	Wallace	21.7%	7.5%	61.3%	9.4%
VAN BUREN	436	40	11	373	12	Wallace	9.2%	2.5%	85.6%	2.8%
WARREN	2,457	296	124	1,834	203	Wallace	12.0%	5.0%	74.6%	8.3%
WASHINGTON	4,070	661	692	2,449	268	Wallace	16.2%	17.0%	60.2%	6.6%
WAYNE	924	97	47	707	73	Wallace	10.5%	5.1%	76.5%	7.9%
WEAKLEY	6,071	726	244	4,761	340	Wallace	12.0%	4.0%	78.4%	5.6%
WHITE	3,636	551	188	2,618	279	Wallace	15.2%	5.2%	72.0%	7.7%
WILLIAMSON	3,850	253	198	3,225	174	Wallace	6.6%	5.1%	83.8%	4.5%
WILSON	4,304	358	205	3,502	239	Wallace	8.3%	4.8%	81.4%	5.6%
TOTAL	492,721	78,350	35,551	335,858	42,962	Wallace	15.9%	7.2%	68.2%	8.7%

TENNESSEE REPUBLICAN

1972

County	Total Vote	Nixon	Other	Winner	Percentage of Total Vote Nixon	Other
ANDERSON	1,788	1,691	97	Nixon	94.6%	5.4%
BEDFORD	265	258	7	Nixon	97.4%	2.6%
BENTON	249	244	5	Nixon	98.0%	2.0%
BLEDSOE	553	543	10	Nixon	98.2%	1.8%
BLOUNT	5,805	5,559	246	Nixon	95.8%	4.2%
BRADLEY	4,118	3,799	319	Nixon	92.3%	7.7%
CAMPBELL	1,808	1,715	93	Nixon	94.9%	5.1%
CANNON	97	97		Nixon	100.0%	
CARROLL	686	664	22	Nixon	96.8%	3.2%
CARTER	1,254	1,226	28	Nixon	97.8%	2.2%
CHEATHAM	114	105	9	Nixon	92.1%	7.9%
CHESTER	344	335	9	Nixon	97.4%	2.6%
CLAIBORNE	536	518	18	Nixon	96.6%	3.4%
CLAY	97	95	2	Nixon	97.9%	2.1%
COCKE	1,378	1,322	56	Nixon	95.9%	4.1%
COFFEE	258	241	17	Nixon	93.4%	6.6%
CROCKETT	108	107	1	Nixon	99.1%	0.9%
CUMBERLAND	1,712	1,632	80	Nixon	95.3%	4.7%
DAVIDSON	4,457	4,274	183	Nixon	95.9%	4.1%
DECATUR	338	329	9	Nixon	97.3%	2.7%
DE KALB	54	54		Nixon	100.0%	
DICKSON	372	357	15	Nixon	96.0%	4.0%
DYER	241	233	8	Nixon	96.7%	3.3%
FAYETTE	120	108	12	Nixon	90.0%	10.0%
FENTRESS	869	819	50	Nixon	94.2%	5.8%
FRANKLIN	229	213	16	Nixon	93.0%	7.0%
GIBSON	852	826	26	Nixon	96.9%	3.1%
GILES	194	182	12	Nixon	93.8%	6.2%
GRAINGER	1,477	1,408	69	Nixon	95.3%	4.7%
GREENE	4,034	3,823	211	Nixon	94.8%	5.2%
GRUNDY	178	172	6	Nixon	96.6%	3.4%
HAMBLEN	1,774	1,736	38	Nixon	97.9%	2.1%
HAMILTON	4,320	4,146	174	Nixon	96.0%	4.0%
HANCOCK	207	195	12	Nixon	94.2%	5.8%
HARDEMAN	416	393	23	Nixon	94.5%	5.5%
HARDIN	564	550	14	Nixon	97.5%	2.5%
HAWKINS	1,906	1,838	68	Nixon	96.4%	3.6%
HAYWOOD	48	48		Nixon	100.0%	
HENDERSON	1,139	1,124	15	Nixon	98.7%	1.3%
HENRY	426	418	8	Nixon	98.1%	1.9%
HICKMAN	183	179	4	Nixon	97.8%	2.2%
HOUSTON	96	90	6	Nixon	93.8%	6.3%
HUMPHREYS	242	230	12	Nixon	95.0%	5.0%
JACKSON	117	113	4	Nixon	96.6%	3.4%
JEFFERSON	1,231	1,185	46	Nixon	96.3%	3.7%
JOHNSON	657	641	16	Nixon	97.6%	2.4%
KNOX	18,989	18,261	728	Nixon	96.2%	3.8%
LAKE	67	62	5	Nixon	92.5%	7.5%
LAUDERDALE	137	131	6	Nixon	95.6%	4.4%
LAWRENCE	732	721	11	Nixon	98.5%	1.5%

TENNESSEE REPUBLICAN

1972

County	Total Vote	Nixon	Other	Winner	Percentage of Total Vote	
					Nixon	Other
LEWIS	89	89		Nixon	100.0%	
LINCOLN	198	195	3	Nixon	98.5%	1.5%
LOUDON	2,062	1,900	162	Nixon	92.1%	7.9%
MCMINN	1,261	1,218	43	Nixon	96.6%	3.4%
MCNAIRY	607	589	18	Nixon	97.0%	3.0%
MACON	2,069	1,817	252	Nixon	87.8%	12.2%
MADISON	500	488	12	Nixon	97.6%	2.4%
MARION	736	699	37	Nixon	95.0%	5.0%
MARSHALL	266	258	8	Nixon	97.0%	3.0%
MAURY	344	330	14	Nixon	95.9%	4.1%
MEIGS	550	487	63	Nixon	88.5%	11.5%
MONROE	2,713	2,609	104	Nixon	96.2%	3.8%
MONTGOMERY	538	524	14	Nixon	97.4%	2.6%
MOORE	32	31	1	Nixon	96.9%	3.1%
MORGAN	607	590	17	Nixon	97.2%	2.8%
OBION	236	229	7	Nixon	97.0%	3.0%
OVERTON	19	18	1	Nixon	94.7%	5.3%
PERRY	189	183	6	Nixon	96.8%	3.2%
PICKETT	829	799	30	Nixon	96.4%	3.6%
POLK	94	83	11	Nixon	88.3%	11.7%
PUTNAM	357	330	27	Nixon	92.4%	7.6%
RHEA	1,361	1,291	70	Nixon	94.9%	5.1%
ROANE	1,240	1,176	64	Nixon	94.8%	5.2%
ROBERTSON	233	229	4	Nixon	98.3%	1.7%
RUTHERFORD	784	757	27	Nixon	96.6%	3.4%
SCOTT	538	514	24	Nixon	95.5%	4.5%
SEQUATCHIE	114	109	5	Nixon	95.6%	4.4%
SEVIER	1,311	1,279	32	Nixon	97.6%	2.4%
SHELBY	14,352	13,912	440	Nixon	96.9%	3.1%
SMITH	245	240	5	Nixon	98.0%	2.0%
STEWART	110	105	5	Nixon	95.5%	4.5%
SULLIVAN	3,555	3,439	116	Nixon	96.7%	3.3%
SUMNER	584	563	21	Nixon	96.4%	3.6%
TIPTON	285	277	8	Nixon	97.2%	2.8%
TROUSDALE	36	36		Nixon	100.0%	
UNICOI	907	883	24	Nixon	97.4%	2.6%
UNION	305	298	7	Nixon	97.7%	2.3%
VAN BUREN	57	54	3	Nixon	94.7%	5.3%
WARREN	276	264	12	Nixon	95.7%	4.3%
WASHINGTON	3,957	3,731	226	Nixon	94.3%	5.7%
WAYNE	825	799	26	Nixon	96.8%	3.2%
WEAKLEY	270	268	2	Nixon	99.3%	0.7%
WHITE	68	68		Nixon	100.0%	
WILLIAMSON	533	524	9	Nixon	98.3%	1.7%
WILSON	411	404	7	Nixon	98.3%	1.7%
TOTAL	114,489	109,696	4,793	Nixon	95.8%	4.2%

TENNESSEE DEMOCRATIC

1976

County	Total Vote	Carter	Wallace	Other	Winner	Percentage of Total Vote Carter	Wallace	Other
ANDERSON	7,377	5,617	467	1,293	Carter	76.1%	6.3%	17.5%
BEDFORD	5,850	4,475	876	499	Carter	76.5%	15.0%	8.5%
BENTON	4,018	3,166	638	214	Carter	78.8%	15.9%	5.3%
BLEDSOE	636	558	43	35	Carter	87.7%	6.8%	5.5%
BLOUNT	3,030	2,492	170	368	Carter	82.2%	5.6%	12.1%
BRADLEY	3,048	2,478	359	211	Carter	81.3%	11.8%	6.9%
CAMPBELL	1,486	1,231	108	147	Carter	82.8%	7.3%	9.9%
CANNON	713	598	75	40	Carter	83.9%	10.5%	5.6%
CARROLL	2,131	1,718	269	144	Carter	80.6%	12.6%	6.8%
CARTER	1,832	1,590	97	145	Carter	86.8%	5.3%	7.9%
CHEATHAM	1,551	1,185	256	110	Carter	76.4%	16.5%	7.1%
CHESTER	1,178	760	287	131	Carter	64.5%	24.4%	11.1%
CLAIBORNE	610	514	56	40	Carter	84.3%	9.2%	6.6%
CLAY	583	491	58	34	Carter	84.2%	9.9%	5.8%
COCKE	365	297	21	47	Carter	81.4%	5.8%	12.9%
COFFEE	6,301	4,680	890	731	Carter	74.3%	14.1%	11.6%
CROCKETT	1,937	1,118	684	135	Carter	57.7%	35.3%	7.0%
CUMBERLAND	2,975	2,385	337	253	Carter	80.2%	11.3%	8.5%
DAVIDSON	41,024	30,237	4,760	6,027	Carter	73.7%	11.6%	14.7%
DECATUR	763	639	87	37	Carter	83.7%	11.4%	4.8%
DE KALB	2,542	2,128	268	146	Carter	83.7%	10.5%	5.7%
DICKSON	2,232	1,861	221	150	Carter	83.4%	9.9%	6.7%
DYER	1,807	1,251	392	164	Carter	69.2%	21.7%	9.1%
FAYETTE	1,187	1,088	22	77	Carter	91.7%	1.9%	6.5%
FENTRESS	421	360	32	29	Carter	85.5%	7.6%	6.9%
FRANKLIN	2,156	1,618	267	271	Carter	75.0%	12.4%	12.6%
GIBSON	6,282	4,566	1,295	421	Carter	72.7%	20.6%	6.7%
GILES	1,490	1,156	218	116	Carter	77.6%	14.6%	7.8%
GRAINGER	401	333	33	35	Carter	83.0%	8.2%	8.7%
GREENE	2,653	2,175	198	280	Carter	82.0%	7.5%	10.6%
GRUNDY	2,359	1,910	286	163	Carter	81.0%	12.1%	6.9%
HAMBLEN	2,193	1,826	166	201	Carter	83.3%	7.6%	9.2%
HAMILTON	21,945	15,892	3,105	2,948	Carter	72.4%	14.1%	13.4%
HANCOCK	122	99	13	10	Carter	81.1%	10.7%	8.2%
HARDEMAN	3,122	2,141	654	327	Carter	68.6%	20.9%	10.5%
HARDIN	938	787	99	52	Carter	83.9%	10.6%	5.5%
HAWKINS	1,852	1,530	133	189	Carter	82.6%	7.2%	10.2%
HAYWOOD	1,672	1,272	291	109	Carter	76.1%	17.4%	6.5%
HENDERSON	421	335	53	33	Carter	79.6%	12.6%	7.8%
HENRY	5,581	4,455	724	402	Carter	79.8%	13.0%	7.2%
HICKMAN	1,046	844	153	49	Carter	80.7%	14.6%	4.7%
HOUSTON	602	494	65	43	Carter	82.1%	10.8%	7.1%
HUMPHREYS	1,372	1,174	120	78	Carter	85.6%	8.7%	5.7%
JACKSON	917	802	74	41	Carter	87.5%	8.1%	4.5%
JEFFERSON	661	549	43	69	Carter	83.1%	6.5%	10.4%
JOHNSON	454	394	19	41	Carter	86.8%	4.2%	9.0%
KNOX	20,330	16,190	1,073	3,067	Carter	79.6%	5.3%	15.1%
LAKE	612	484	98	30	Carter	79.1%	16.0%	4.9%
LAUDERDALE	2,370	1,694	457	219	Carter	71.5%	19.3%	9.2%
LAWRENCE	2,215	1,895	168	152	Carter	85.6%	7.6%	6.9%

TENNESSEE DEMOCRATIC

1976

County	Total Vote	Carter	Wallace	Other	Winner	Percentage of Total Vote Carter	Wallace	Other
LEWIS	952	575	86	291	Carter	60.4%	9.0%	30.6%
LINCOLN	1,763	1,472	201	90	Carter	83.5%	11.4%	5.1%
LOUDON	1,301	1,100	87	114	Carter	84.6%	6.7%	8.8%
MCMINN	3,033	2,624	189	220	Carter	86.5%	6.2%	7.3%
MCNAIRY	1,213	999	138	76	Carter	82.4%	11.4%	6.3%
MACON	1,071	868	163	40	Carter	81.0%	15.2%	3.7%
MADISON	5,496	3,906	1,067	523	Carter	71.1%	19.4%	9.5%
MARION	3,815	3,091	481	243	Carter	81.0%	12.6%	6.4%
MARSHALL	1,529	1,237	210	82	Carter	80.9%	13.7%	5.4%
MAURY	3,400	2,612	539	249	Carter	76.8%	15.9%	7.3%
MEIGS	495	428	34	33	Carter	86.5%	6.9%	6.7%
MONROE	1,474	1,297	62	115	Carter	88.0%	4.2%	7.8%
MONTGOMERY	7,263	5,637	669	957	Carter	77.6%	9.2%	13.2%
MOORE	348	262	20	66	Carter	75.3%	5.7%	19.0%
MORGAN	1,029	847	75	107	Carter	82.3%	7.3%	10.4%
OBION	3,206	2,848	68	290	Carter	88.8%	2.1%	9.0%
OVERTON	2,093	1,756	202	135	Carter	83.9%	9.7%	6.5%
PERRY	1,527	1,294	155	78	Carter	84.7%	10.2%	5.1%
PICKETT	232	215	12	5	Carter	92.7%	5.2%	2.2%
POLK	1,891	1,730	82	79	Carter	91.5%	4.3%	4.2%
PUTNAM	4,027	3,281	375	371	Carter	81.5%	9.3%	9.2%
RHEA	2,496	1,993	275	228	Carter	79.8%	11.0%	9.1%
ROANE	3,406	2,824	186	396	Carter	82.9%	5.5%	11.6%
ROBERTSON	2,333	1,918	279	136	Carter	82.2%	12.0%	5.8%
RUTHERFORD	9,340	6,874	1,470	996	Carter	73.6%	15.7%	10.7%
SCOTT	563	497	31	35	Carter	88.3%	5.5%	6.2%
SEQUATCHIE	490	422	53	15	Carter	86.1%	10.8%	3.1%
SEVIER	1,265	1,049	90	126	Carter	82.9%	7.1%	10.0%
SHELBY	52,548	40,009	4,026	8,513	Carter	76.1%	7.7%	16.2%
SMITH	961	755	149	57	Carter	78.6%	15.5%	5.9%
STEWART	587	497	38	52	Carter	84.7%	6.5%	8.9%
SULLIVAN	7,337	5,831	557	949	Carter	79.5%	7.6%	12.9%
SUMNER	5,333	4,181	669	483	Carter	78.4%	12.5%	9.1%
TIPTON	1,622	1,058	441	123	Carter	65.2%	27.2%	7.6%
TROUSDALE	473	403	48	22	Carter	85.2%	10.1%	4.7%
UNICOI	564	495	12	57	Carter	87.8%	2.1%	10.1%
UNION	347	314	16	17	Carter	90.5%	4.6%	4.9%
VAN BUREN	356	291	59	6	Carter	81.7%	16.6%	1.7%
WARREN	2,287	1,941	222	124	Carter	84.9%	9.7%	5.4%
WASHINGTON	3,868	3,155	235	478	Carter	81.6%	6.1%	12.4%
WAYNE	468	420	35	13	Carter	89.7%	7.5%	2.8%
WEAKLEY	3,183	2,558	492	133	Carter	80.4%	15.5%	4.2%
WHITE	1,842	1,522	157	163	Carter	82.6%	8.5%	8.8%
WILLIAMSON	2,531	1,885	371	275	Carter	74.5%	14.7%	10.9%
WILSON	3,357	2,740	391	226	Carter	81.6%	11.6%	6.7%
TOTAL	334,078	259,243	36,495	38,340	Carter	77.6%	10.9%	11.5%

TENNESSEE REPUBLICAN

1976

County	Total Vote	Ford	Reagan	Other	Winner	Percentage of Total Vote Ford	Reagan	Other
ANDERSON	2,826	1,630	1,175	21	Ford	57.7%	41.6%	0.7%
BEDFORD	236	107	128	1	Reagan	45.3%	54.2%	0.4%
BENTON	966	477	472	17	Ford	49.4%	48.9%	1.8%
BLEDSOE	549	320	224	5	Ford	58.3%	40.8%	0.9%
BLOUNT	8,373	4,812	3,561		Ford	57.5%	42.5%	
BRADLEY	5,348	2,659	2,498	191	Ford	49.7%	46.7%	3.6%
CAMPBELL	1,923	1,062	807	54	Ford	55.2%	42.0%	2.8%
CANNON	187	85	102		Reagan	45.5%	54.5%	
CARROLL	1,532	755	755	22		49.3%	49.3%	1.4%
CARTER	2,813	1,693	1,095	25	Ford	60.2%	38.9%	0.9%
CHEATHAM	434	159	274	1	Reagan	36.6%	63.1%	0.2%
CHESTER	595	253	340	2	Reagan	42.5%	57.1%	0.3%
CLAIBORNE	733	446	287		Ford	60.8%	39.2%	
CLAY	183	109	72	2	Ford	59.6%	39.3%	1.1%
COCKE	4,861	2,447	2,213	201	Ford	50.3%	45.5%	4.1%
COFFEE	1,014	390	599	25	Reagan	38.5%	59.1%	2.5%
CROCKETT	189	58	130	1	Reagan	30.7%	68.8%	0.5%
CUMBERLAND	1,884	1,092	766	26	Ford	58.0%	40.7%	1.4%
DAVIDSON	19,913	8,461	11,336	116	Reagan	42.5%	56.9%	0.6%
DECATUR	318	160	157	1	Ford	50.3%	49.4%	0.3%
DE KALB	323	195	125	3	Ford	60.4%	38.7%	0.9%
DICKSON	623	232	387	4	Reagan	37.2%	62.1%	0.6%
DYER	1,133	426	707		Reagan	37.6%	62.4%	
FAYETTE	653	218	431	4	Reagan	33.4%	66.0%	0.6%
FENTRESS	660	342	307	11	Ford	51.8%	46.5%	1.7%
FRANKLIN	707	299	406	2	Reagan	42.3%	57.4%	0.3%
GIBSON	1,242	531	702	9	Reagan	42.8%	56.5%	0.7%
GILES	441	172	265	4	Reagan	39.0%	60.1%	0.9%
GRAINGER	2,009	1,240	711	58	Ford	61.7%	35.4%	2.9%
GREENE	5,218	2,605	2,499	114	Ford	49.9%	47.9%	2.2%
GRUNDY	109	67	42		Ford	61.5%	38.5%	
HAMBLEN	2,384	1,284	1,085	15	Ford	53.9%	45.5%	0.6%
HAMILTON	12,975	4,664	8,216	95	Reagan	35.9%	63.3%	0.7%
HANCOCK	1,044	622	387	35	Ford	59.6%	37.1%	3.4%
HARDEMAN	389	185	204		Reagan	47.6%	52.4%	
HARDIN	828	441	383	4	Ford	53.3%	46.3%	0.5%
HAWKINS	3,710	2,123	1,587		Ford	57.2%	42.8%	
HAYWOOD	695	319	373	3	Reagan	45.9%	53.7%	0.4%
HENDERSON	3,517	1,559	1,847	111	Reagan	44.3%	52.5%	3.2%
HENRY	1,115	464	638	13	Reagan	41.6%	57.2%	1.2%
HICKMAN	295	138	157		Reagan	46.8%	53.2%	
HOUSTON	153	39	112	2	Reagan	25.5%	73.2%	1.3%
HUMPHREYS	384	133	249	2	Reagan	34.6%	64.8%	0.5%
JACKSON	186	88	95	3	Reagan	47.3%	51.1%	1.6%
JEFFERSON	5,527	3,016	2,255	256	Ford	54.6%	40.8%	4.6%
JOHNSON	738	523	208	7	Ford	70.9%	28.2%	0.9%
KNOX	25,473	14,819	10,402	252	Ford	58.2%	40.8%	1.0%
LAKE	238	60	177	1	Reagan	25.2%	74.4%	0.4%
LAUDERDALE	804	307	482	15	Reagan	38.2%	60.0%	1.9%
LAWRENCE	1,142	611	528	3	Ford	53.5%	46.2%	0.3%

TENNESSEE REPUBLICAN

1976

County	Total Vote	Ford	Reagan	Other	Winner	Percentage of Total Vote Ford	Reagan	Other
LEWIS	192	55	136	1	Reagan	28.6%	70.8%	0.5%
LINCOLN	487	141	343	3	Reagan	29.0%	70.4%	0.6%
LOUDON	3,024	1,472	1,505	47	Reagan	48.7%	49.8%	1.6%
MCMINN	3,941	2,273	1,597	71	Ford	57.7%	40.5%	1.8%
MCNAIRY	905	467	430	8	Ford	51.6%	47.5%	0.9%
MACON	1,673	895	778		Ford	53.5%	46.5%	
MADISON	3,291	1,192	2,077	22	Reagan	36.2%	63.1%	0.7%
MARION	748	458	278	12	Ford	61.2%	37.2%	1.6%
MARSHALL	401	148	251	2	Reagan	36.9%	62.6%	0.5%
MAURY	1,745	714	1,020	11	Reagan	40.9%	58.5%	0.6%
MEIGS	710	358	328	24	Ford	50.4%	46.2%	3.4%
MONROE	2,333	1,431	885	17	Ford	61.3%	37.9%	0.7%
MONTGOMERY	1,426	664	749	13	Reagan	46.6%	52.5%	0.9%
MOORE	58	17	41		Reagan	29.3%	70.7%	
MORGAN	595	309	284	2	Ford	51.9%	47.7%	0.3%
OBION	498	153	261	84	Reagan	30.7%	52.4%	16.9%
OVERTON	285	143	136	6	Ford	50.2%	47.7%	2.1%
PERRY	40	24	16		Ford	60.0%	40.0%	
PICKETT	964	493	459	12	Ford	51.1%	47.6%	1.2%
POLK	383	275	108		Ford	71.8%	28.2%	
PUTNAM	1,124	583	529	12	Ford	51.9%	47.1%	1.1%
RHEA	1,618	786	805	27	Reagan	48.6%	49.8%	1.7%
ROANE	2,119	1,185	914	20	Ford	55.9%	43.1%	0.9%
ROBERTSON	782	302	477	3	Reagan	38.6%	61.0%	0.4%
RUTHERFORD	1,579	562	1,003	14	Reagan	35.6%	63.5%	0.9%
SCOTT	924	452	465	7	Reagan	48.9%	50.3%	0.8%
SEQUATCHIE	208	97	111		Reagan	46.6%	53.4%	
SEVIER	2,462	1,279	1,153	30	Ford	51.9%	46.8%	1.2%
SHELBY	50,995	24,270	26,396	329	Reagan	47.6%	51.8%	0.6%
SMITH	276	118	155	3	Reagan	42.8%	56.2%	1.1%
STEWART	139	69	70		Reagan	49.6%	50.4%	
SULLIVAN	7,422	4,653	2,724	45	Ford	62.7%	36.7%	0.6%
SUMNER	2,823	1,058	1,746	19	Reagan	37.5%	61.8%	0.7%
TIPTON	993	307	676	10	Reagan	30.9%	68.1%	1.0%
TROUSDALE	65	35	30		Ford	53.8%	46.2%	
UNICOI	945	611	324	10	Ford	64.7%	34.3%	1.1%
UNION	440	222	214	4	Ford	50.5%	48.6%	0.9%
VAN BUREN	46	32	13	1	Ford	69.6%	28.3%	2.2%
WARREN	774	301	468	5	Reagan	38.9%	60.5%	0.6%
WASHINGTON	8,141	4,928	2,991	222	Ford	60.5%	36.7%	2.7%
WAYNE	554	351	200	3	Ford	63.4%	36.1%	0.5%
WEAKLEY	806	276	530		Reagan	34.2%	65.8%	
WHITE	266	130	136		Reagan	48.9%	51.1%	
WILLIAMSON	2,518	1,045	1,462	11	Reagan	41.5%	58.1%	0.4%
WILSON	1,225	454	765	6	Reagan	37.1%	62.4%	0.5%
TOTAL	242,535	120,685	118,997	2,853	Ford	49.8%	49.1%	1.2%

TENNESSEE DEMOCRATIC

1980

County	Total Vote	Carter	E. Kennedy	Other	Winner	Percentage of Total Vote Carter	E. Kennedy	Other
ANDERSON	6,450	4,333	1,449	668	Carter	67.2%	22.5%	10.4%
BEDFORD	4,220	3,244	549	427	Carter	76.9%	13.0%	10.1%
BENTON	3,032	2,328	498	206	Carter	76.8%	16.4%	6.8%
BLEDSOE	450	392	51	7	Carter	87.1%	11.3%	1.6%
BLOUNT	2,396	1,888	382	126	Carter	78.8%	15.9%	5.3%
BRADLEY	4,793	3,823	682	288	Carter	79.8%	14.2%	6.0%
CAMPBELL	1,381	953	335	93	Carter	69.0%	24.3%	6.7%
CANNON	562	484	65	13	Carter	86.1%	11.6%	2.3%
CARROLL	2,208	1,816	297	95	Carter	82.2%	13.5%	4.3%
CARTER	1,289	1,026	227	36	Carter	79.6%	17.6%	2.8%
CHEATHAM	1,364	1,175	146	43	Carter	86.1%	10.7%	3.2%
CHESTER	667	549	87	31	Carter	82.3%	13.0%	4.6%
CLAIBORNE	726	582	113	31	Carter	80.2%	15.6%	4.3%
CLAY	379	278	86	15	Carter	73.4%	22.7%	4.0%
COCKE	369	259	83	27	Carter	70.2%	22.5%	7.3%
COFFEE	5,609	4,354	677	578	Carter	77.6%	12.1%	10.3%
CROCKETT	648	563	64	21	Carter	86.9%	9.9%	3.2%
CUMBERLAND	1,716	1,274	317	125	Carter	74.2%	18.5%	7.3%
DAVIDSON	65,461	45,401	13,000	7,060	Carter	69.4%	19.9%	10.8%
DECATUR	644	526	106	12	Carter	81.7%	16.5%	1.9%
DE KALB	1,164	1,016	119	29	Carter	87.3%	10.2%	2.5%
DICKSON	3,958	3,215	507	236	Carter	81.2%	12.8%	6.0%
DYER	2,137	1,705	328	104	Carter	79.8%	15.3%	4.9%
FAYETTE	1,190	795	363	32	Carter	66.8%	30.5%	2.7%
FENTRESS	429	332	68	29	Carter	77.4%	15.9%	6.8%
FRANKLIN	2,201	1,820	278	103	Carter	82.7%	12.6%	4.7%
GIBSON	6,235	5,084	691	460	Carter	81.5%	11.1%	7.4%
GILES	1,337	1,129	155	53	Carter	84.4%	11.6%	4.0%
GRAINGER	384	286	85	13	Carter	74.5%	22.1%	3.4%
GREENE	2,055	1,678	285	92	Carter	81.7%	13.9%	4.5%
GRUNDY	2,052	1,724	238	90	Carter	84.0%	11.6%	4.4%
HAMBLEN	1,541	1,197	288	56	Carter	77.7%	18.7%	3.6%
HAMILTON	14,354	11,608	1,952	794	Carter	80.9%	13.6%	5.5%
HANCOCK	164	120	39	5	Carter	73.2%	23.8%	3.0%
HARDEMAN	1,326	976	265	85	Carter	73.6%	20.0%	6.4%
HARDIN	796	666	97	33	Carter	83.7%	12.2%	4.1%
HAWKINS	1,540	1,187	288	65	Carter	77.1%	18.7%	4.2%
HAYWOOD	689	511	153	25	Carter	74.2%	22.2%	3.6%
HENDERSON	511	370	108	33	Carter	72.4%	21.1%	6.5%
HENRY	4,541	3,623	551	367	Carter	79.8%	12.1%	8.1%
HICKMAN	1,040	863	139	38	Carter	83.0%	13.4%	3.7%
HOUSTON	529	449	60	20	Carter	84.9%	11.3%	3.8%
HUMPHREYS	1,362	1,177	135	50	Carter	86.4%	9.9%	3.7%
JACKSON	967	733	197	37	Carter	75.8%	20.4%	3.8%
JEFFERSON	504	392	90	22	Carter	77.8%	17.9%	4.4%
JOHNSON	357	294	51	12	Carter	82.4%	14.3%	3.4%
KNOX	13,647	9,592	3,105	950	Carter	70.3%	22.8%	7.0%
LAKE	314	245	51	18	Carter	78.0%	16.2%	5.7%
LAUDERDALE	999	802	167	30	Carter	80.3%	16.7%	3.0%
LAWRENCE	2,066	1,747	252	67	Carter	84.6%	12.2%	3.2%

TENNESSEE DEMOCRATIC

1980

County	Total Vote	Carter	E. Kennedy	Other	Winner	Percentage of Total Vote Carter	E. Kennedy	Other
LEWIS	602	506	66	30	Carter	84.1%	11.0%	5.0%
LINCOLN	1,758	1,470	225	63	Carter	83.6%	12.8%	3.6%
LOUDON	1,121	830	225	66	Carter	74.0%	20.1%	5.9%
MCMINN	2,430	2,068	259	103	Carter	85.1%	10.7%	4.2%
MCNAIRY	1,120	944	136	40	Carter	84.3%	12.1%	3.6%
MACON	80	69	8	3	Carter	86.3%	10.0%	3.8%
MADISON	3,359	2,736	481	142	Carter	81.5%	14.3%	4.2%
MARION	3,519	2,849	437	233	Carter	81.0%	12.4%	6.6%
MARSHALL	1,395	1,200	145	50	Carter	86.0%	10.4%	3.6%
MAURY	2,397	2,027	285	85	Carter	84.6%	11.9%	3.5%
MEIGS	409	354	37	18	Carter	86.6%	9.0%	4.4%
MONROE	1,505	1,237	234	34	Carter	82.2%	15.5%	2.3%
MONTGOMERY	3,441	2,664	659	118	Carter	77.4%	19.2%	3.4%
MOORE	410	318	58	34	Carter	77.6%	14.1%	8.3%
MORGAN	1,035	772	211	52	Carter	74.6%	20.4%	5.0%
OBION	4,516	3,456	630	430	Carter	76.5%	14.0%	9.5%
OVERTON	2,773	2,015	603	155	Carter	72.7%	21.7%	5.6%
PERRY	902	672	189	41	Carter	74.5%	21.0%	4.5%
PICKETT	204	171	28	5	Carter	83.8%	13.7%	2.5%
POLK	1,556	1,232	258	66	Carter	79.2%	16.6%	4.2%
PUTNAM	4,693	3,608	696	389	Carter	76.9%	14.8%	8.3%
RHEA	1,380	1,180	135	65	Carter	85.5%	9.8%	4.7%
ROANE	2,303	1,671	504	128	Carter	72.6%	21.9%	5.6%
ROBERTSON	2,126	1,814	246	66	Carter	85.3%	11.6%	3.1%
RUTHERFORD	6,753	5,332	921	500	Carter	79.0%	13.6%	7.4%
SCOTT	376	262	102	12	Carter	69.7%	27.1%	3.2%
SEQUATCHIE	509	452	46	11	Carter	88.8%	9.0%	2.2%
SEVIER	897	661	187	49	Carter	73.7%	20.8%	5.5%
SHELBY	31,114	19,375	10,552	1,187	Carter	62.3%	33.9%	3.8%
SMITH	1,042	883	124	35	Carter	84.7%	11.9%	3.4%
STEWART	624	518	87	19	Carter	83.0%	13.9%	3.0%
SULLIVAN	5,994	5,130	692	172	Carter	85.6%	11.5%	2.9%
SUMNER	5,831	4,882	681	268	Carter	83.7%	11.7%	4.6%
TIPTON	1,445	1,186	208	51	Carter	82.1%	14.4%	3.5%
TROUSDALE	471	408	44	19	Carter	86.6%	9.3%	4.0%
UNICOI	520	424	75	21	Carter	81.5%	14.4%	4.0%
UNION	329	258	55	16	Carter	78.4%	16.7%	4.9%
VAN BUREN	258	223	29	6	Carter	86.4%	11.2%	2.3%
WARREN	1,398	1,190	148	60	Carter	85.1%	10.6%	4.3%
WASHINGTON	2,965	2,378	457	130	Carter	80.2%	15.4%	4.4%
WAYNE	416	326	77	13	Carter	78.4%	18.5%	3.1%
WEAKLEY	3,538	2,869	371	298	Carter	81.1%	10.5%	8.4%
WHITE	2,674	2,157	320	197	Carter	80.7%	12.0%	7.4%
WILLIAMSON	3,651	2,940	492	219	Carter	80.5%	13.5%	6.0%
WILSON	4,088	3,357	516	215	Carter	82.1%	12.6%	5.3%
TOTAL	294,680	221,658	53,258	19,764	Carter	75.2%	18.1%	6.7%

TENNESSEE REPUBLICAN

1980

County	Total Vote	Bush	Reagan	Other	Winner	Percentage of Total Vote Bush	Reagan	Other
ANDERSON	4,089	1,003	2,611	475	Reagan	24.5%	63.9%	11.6%
BEDFORD	262	28	204	30	Reagan	10.7%	77.9%	11.5%
BENTON	170	15	144	11	Reagan	8.8%	84.7%	6.5%
BLEDSOE	412	30	370	12	Reagan	7.3%	89.8%	2.9%
BLOUNT	5,435	1,043	3,983	409	Reagan	19.2%	73.3%	7.5%
BRADLEY	4,758	790	3,627	341	Reagan	16.6%	76.2%	7.2%
CAMPBELL	1,287	157	1,071	59	Reagan	12.2%	83.2%	4.6%
CANNON	173	19	140	14	Reagan	11.0%	80.9%	8.1%
CARROLL	1,380	121	1,183	76	Reagan	8.8%	85.7%	5.5%
CARTER	5,755	1,093	4,122	540	Reagan	19.0%	71.6%	9.4%
CHEATHAM	487	74	361	52	Reagan	15.2%	74.1%	10.7%
CHESTER	381	34	328	19	Reagan	8.9%	86.1%	5.0%
CLAIBORNE	878	122	713	43	Reagan	13.9%	81.2%	4.9%
CLAY	250	15	224	11	Reagan	6.0%	89.6%	4.4%
COCKE	4,295	719	3,176	400	Reagan	16.7%	73.9%	9.3%
COFFEE	655	95	516	44	Reagan	14.5%	78.8%	6.7%
CROCKETT	221	23	188	10	Reagan	10.4%	85.1%	4.5%
CUMBERLAND	1,685	268	1,286	131	Reagan	15.9%	76.3%	7.8%
DAVIDSON	11,106	2,233	7,670	1,203	Reagan	20.1%	69.1%	10.8%
DECATUR	300	28	265	7	Reagan	9.3%	88.3%	2.3%
DE KALB	619	44	534	41	Reagan	7.1%	86.3%	6.6%
DICKSON	1,006	104	836	66	Reagan	10.3%	83.1%	6.6%
DYER	1,194	192	935	67	Reagan	16.1%	78.3%	5.6%
FAYETTE	419	42	360	17	Reagan	10.0%	85.9%	4.1%
FENTRESS	499	37	444	18	Reagan	7.4%	89.0%	3.6%
FRANKLIN	676	111	497	68	Reagan	16.4%	73.5%	10.1%
GIBSON	553	85	420	48	Reagan	15.4%	75.9%	8.7%
GILES	386	52	315	19	Reagan	13.5%	81.6%	4.9%
GRAINGER	1,279	131	1,093	55	Reagan	10.2%	85.5%	4.3%
GREENE	6,096	1,096	4,517	483	Reagan	18.0%	74.1%	7.9%
GRUNDY	206	9	185	12	Reagan	4.4%	89.8%	5.8%
HAMBLEN	1,901	337	1,452	112	Reagan	17.7%	76.4%	5.9%
HAMILTON	13,956	1,933	11,405	618	Reagan	13.9%	81.7%	4.4%
HANCOCK	590	54	524	12	Reagan	9.2%	88.8%	2.0%
HARDEMAN	452	58	366	28	Reagan	12.8%	81.0%	6.2%
HARDIN	469	41	412	16	Reagan	8.7%	87.8%	3.4%
HAWKINS	4,395	777	3,136	482	Reagan	17.7%	71.4%	11.0%
HAYWOOD	324	61	258	5	Reagan	18.8%	79.6%	1.5%
HENDERSON	2,546	326	2,051	169	Reagan	12.8%	80.6%	6.6%
HENRY	311	49	243	19	Reagan	15.8%	78.1%	6.1%
HICKMAN	323	32	281	10	Reagan	9.9%	87.0%	3.1%
HOUSTON	160	17	133	10	Reagan	10.6%	83.1%	6.3%
HUMPHREYS	325	42	259	24	Reagan	12.9%	79.7%	7.4%
JACKSON	238	17	208	13	Reagan	7.1%	87.4%	5.5%
JEFFERSON	4,946	1,049	3,291	606	Reagan	21.2%	66.5%	12.3%
JOHNSON	737	67	625	45	Reagan	9.1%	84.8%	6.1%
KNOX	24,776	6,463	15,507	2,806	Reagan	26.1%	62.6%	11.3%
LAKE	141	13	125	3	Reagan	9.2%	88.7%	2.1%
LAUDERDALE	402	46	341	15	Reagan	11.4%	84.8%	3.7%
LAWRENCE	969	86	859	24	Reagan	8.9%	88.6%	2.5%

TENNESSEE REPUBLICAN

1980

County	Total Vote	Bush	Reagan	Other	Winner	Percentage of Total Vote Bush	Reagan	Other
LEWIS	180	16	152	12	Reagan	8.9%	84.4%	6.7%
LINCOLN	483	56	412	15	Reagan	11.6%	85.3%	3.1%
LOUDON	1,865	279	1,489	97	Reagan	15.0%	79.8%	5.2%
MCMINN	5,160	774	3,916	470	Reagan	15.0%	75.9%	9.1%
MCNAIRY	776	78	677	21	Reagan	10.1%	87.2%	2.7%
MACON	2,305	241	1,829	235	Reagan	10.5%	79.3%	10.2%
MADISON	1,842	362	1,383	97	Reagan	19.7%	75.1%	5.3%
MARION	1,342	133	1,122	87	Reagan	9.9%	83.6%	6.5%
MARSHALL	424	58	345	21	Reagan	13.7%	81.4%	5.0%
MAURY	1,166	165	935	66	Reagan	14.2%	80.2%	5.7%
MEIGS	330	32	291	7	Reagan	9.7%	88.2%	2.1%
MONROE	2,040	161	1,816	63	Reagan	7.9%	89.0%	3.1%
MONTGOMERY	1,566	325	1,101	140	Reagan	20.8%	70.3%	8.9%
MOORE	91	7	80	4	Reagan	7.7%	87.9%	4.4%
MORGAN	780	89	648	43	Reagan	11.4%	83.1%	5.5%
OBION	514	72	419	23	Reagan	14.0%	81.5%	4.5%
OVERTON	98	11	86	1	Reagan	11.2%	87.8%	1.0%
PERRY	208	17	181	10	Reagan	8.2%	87.0%	4.8%
PICKETT	872	57	778	37	Reagan	6.5%	89.2%	4.2%
POLK	285	36	241	8	Reagan	12.6%	84.6%	2.8%
PUTNAM	852	105	658	89	Reagan	12.3%	77.2%	10.4%
RHEA	1,464	162	1,229	73	Reagan	11.1%	83.9%	5.0%
ROANE	2,437	515	1,785	137	Reagan	21.1%	73.2%	5.6%
ROBERTSON	677	95	540	42	Reagan	14.0%	79.8%	6.2%
RUTHERFORD	1,998	340	1,454	204	Reagan	17.0%	72.8%	10.2%
SCOTT	685	60	596	29	Reagan	8.8%	87.0%	4.2%
SEQUATCHIE	277	11	258	8	Reagan	4.0%	93.1%	2.9%
SEVIER	3,099	481	2,342	276	Reagan	15.5%	75.6%	8.9%
SHELBY	24,169	4,680	17,791	1,698	Reagan	19.4%	73.6%	7.0%
SMITH	225	14	199	12	Reagan	6.2%	88.4%	5.3%
STEWART	170	23	135	12	Reagan	13.5%	79.4%	7.1%
SULLIVAN	5,080	1,599	3,196	285	Reagan	31.5%	62.9%	5.6%
SUMNER	3,010	468	2,310	232	Reagan	15.5%	76.7%	7.7%
TIPTON	736	99	605	32	Reagan	13.5%	82.2%	4.3%
TROUSDALE	74	12	61	1	Reagan	16.2%	82.4%	1.4%
UNICOI	803	142	630	31	Reagan	17.7%	78.5%	3.9%
UNION	434	44	368	22	Reagan	10.1%	84.8%	5.1%
VAN BUREN	57	9	43	5	Reagan	15.8%	75.4%	8.8%
WARREN	423	47	337	39	Reagan	11.1%	79.7%	9.2%
WASHINGTON	5,562	1,155	3,974	433	Reagan	20.8%	71.4%	7.8%
WAYNE	509	31	460	18	Reagan	6.1%	90.4%	3.5%
WEAKLEY	803	95	673	35	Reagan	11.8%	83.8%	4.4%
WHITE	183	15	157	11	Reagan	8.2%	85.8%	6.0%
WILLIAMSON	2,901	592	2,086	223	Reagan	20.4%	71.9%	7.7%
WILSON	1,382	230	1,043	109	Reagan	16.6%	75.5%	7.9%
TOTAL	195,210	35,274	144,625	15,311	Reagan	18.1%	74.1%	7.8%

TENNESSEE DEMOCRATIC

1984

County	Total Vote	Hart	J. Jackson	Mondale	Other	Winner	Percentage of Total Vote Hart	J. Jackson	Mondale	Other
ANDERSON	6,460	2,184	615	3,120	541	Mondale	33.8%	9.5%	48.3%	8.4%
BEDFORD	3,438	1,398	269	1,504	267	Mondale	40.7%	7.8%	43.7%	7.8%
BENTON	3,691	1,552	96	1,889	154	Mondale	42.0%	2.6%	51.2%	4.2%
BLEDSOE	561	166	12	358	25	Mondale	29.6%	2.1%	63.8%	4.5%
BLOUNT	3,289	847	409	1,909	124	Mondale	25.8%	12.4%	58.0%	3.8%
BRADLEY	2,608	842	268	1,363	135	Mondale	32.3%	10.3%	52.3%	5.2%
CAMPBELL	1,997	478	53	1,370	96	Mondale	23.9%	2.7%	68.6%	4.8%
CANNON	716	256	40	392	28	Mondale	35.8%	5.6%	54.7%	3.9%
CARROLL	2,140	725	319	1,034	62	Mondale	33.9%	14.9%	48.3%	2.9%
CARTER	1,067	328	64	637	38	Mondale	30.7%	6.0%	59.7%	3.6%
CHEATHAM	1,343	500	68	718	57	Mondale	37.2%	5.1%	53.5%	4.2%
CHESTER	794	225	92	449	28	Mondale	28.3%	11.6%	56.5%	3.5%
CLAIBORNE	728	202	29	468	29	Mondale	27.7%	4.0%	64.3%	4.0%
CLAY	503	178	31	284	10	Mondale	35.4%	6.2%	56.5%	2.0%
COCKE	368	115	29	185	39	Mondale	31.3%	7.9%	50.3%	10.6%
COFFEE	2,781	1,026	159	1,479	117	Mondale	36.9%	5.7%	53.2%	4.2%
CROCKETT	1,903	849	209	683	162	Hart	44.6%	11.0%	35.9%	8.5%
CUMBERLAND	2,487	929	110	1,297	151	Mondale	37.4%	4.4%	52.2%	6.1%
DAVIDSON	49,024	14,518	16,880	16,151	1,475	J. Jackson	29.6%	34.4%	32.9%	3.0%
DECATUR	1,083	380	38	586	79	Mondale	35.1%	3.5%	54.1%	7.3%
DE KALB	2,343	837	110	1,239	157	Mondale	35.7%	4.7%	52.9%	6.7%
DICKSON	2,622	881	182	1,468	91	Mondale	33.6%	6.9%	56.0%	3.5%
DYER	1,854	754	191	760	149	Mondale	40.7%	10.3%	41.0%	8.0%
FAYETTE	2,628	621	896	823	288	J. Jackson	23.6%	34.1%	31.3%	11.0%
FENTRESS	537	195	18	305	19	Mondale	36.3%	3.4%	56.8%	3.5%
FRANKLIN	2,347	731	176	1,328	112	Mondale	31.1%	7.5%	56.6%	4.8%
GIBSON	4,045	1,370	834	1,635	206	Mondale	33.9%	20.6%	40.4%	5.1%
GILES	1,196	459	128	578	31	Mondale	38.4%	10.7%	48.3%	2.6%
GRAINGER	510	149	14	334	13	Mondale	29.2%	2.7%	65.5%	2.5%
GREENE	2,082	732	162	1,071	117	Mondale	35.2%	7.8%	51.4%	5.6%
GRUNDY	1,789	398	51	1,208	132	Mondale	22.2%	2.9%	67.5%	7.4%
HAMBLEN	1,577	579	156	800	42	Mondale	36.7%	9.9%	50.7%	2.7%
HAMILTON	19,564	3,564	8,657	6,663	680	J. Jackson	18.2%	44.2%	34.1%	3.5%
HANCOCK	95	34	4	52	5	Mondale	35.8%	4.2%	54.7%	5.3%
HARDEMAN	1,787	375	666	687	59	Mondale	21.0%	37.3%	38.4%	3.3%
HARDIN	1,199	394	115	649	41	Mondale	32.9%	9.6%	54.1%	3.4%
HAWKINS	1,573	544	85	876	68	Mondale	34.6%	5.4%	55.7%	4.3%
HAYWOOD	1,423	198	858	334	33	J. Jackson	13.9%	60.3%	23.5%	2.3%
HENDERSON	697	195	126	353	23	Mondale	28.0%	18.1%	50.6%	3.3%
HENRY	4,236	1,552	372	2,015	297	Mondale	36.6%	8.8%	47.6%	7.0%
HICKMAN	1,139	366	70	649	54	Mondale	32.1%	6.1%	57.0%	4.7%
HOUSTON	751	193	39	491	28	Mondale	25.7%	5.2%	65.4%	3.7%
HUMPHREYS	1,454	456	50	902	46	Mondale	31.4%	3.4%	62.0%	3.2%
JACKSON	963	367	28	535	33	Mondale	38.1%	2.9%	55.6%	3.4%
JEFFERSON	868	250	66	511	41	Mondale	28.8%	7.6%	58.9%	4.7%
JOHNSON	300	145	11	137	7	Hart	48.3%	3.7%	45.7%	2.3%
KNOX	17,113	5,474	3,403	7,528	708	Mondale	32.0%	19.9%	44.0%	4.1%
LAKE	418	106	47	236	29	Mondale	25.4%	11.2%	56.5%	6.9%
LAUDERDALE	1,451	385	373	634	59	Mondale	26.5%	25.7%	43.7%	4.1%
LAWRENCE	1,907	712	59	1,081	55	Mondale	37.3%	3.1%	56.7%	2.9%

TENNESSEE DEMOCRATIC

1984

County	Total Vote	Hart	J. Jackson	Mondale	Other	Winner	Percentage of Total Vote Hart	J. Jackson	Mondale	Other
LEWIS	860	371	82	376	31	Mondale	43.1%	9.5%	43.7%	3.6%
LINCOLN	1,492	406	120	890	76	Mondale	27.2%	8.0%	59.7%	5.1%
LOUDON	1,154	356	69	682	47	Mondale	30.8%	6.0%	59.1%	4.1%
MCMINN	1,760	551	117	1,034	58	Mondale	31.3%	6.6%	58.8%	3.3%
MCNAIRY	1,216	423	81	678	34	Mondale	34.8%	6.7%	55.8%	2.8%
MACON	317	114	14	180	9	Mondale	36.0%	4.4%	56.8%	2.8%
MADISON	10,506	3,266	3,404	2,885	951	J. Jackson	31.1%	32.4%	27.5%	9.1%
MARION	3,549	1,021	247	1,955	326	Mondale	28.8%	7.0%	55.1%	9.2%
MARSHALL	1,197	479	90	581	47	Mondale	40.0%	7.5%	48.5%	3.9%
MAURY	3,021	1,139	448	1,325	109	Mondale	37.7%	14.8%	43.9%	3.6%
MEIGS	833	332	33	431	37	Mondale	39.9%	4.0%	51.7%	4.4%
MONROE	1,313	305	68	902	38	Mondale	23.2%	5.2%	68.7%	2.9%
MONTGOMERY	4,602	1,351	1,145	1,971	135	Mondale	29.4%	24.9%	42.8%	2.9%
MOORE	414	185	34	170	25	Hart	44.7%	8.2%	41.1%	6.0%
MORGAN	946	269	35	586	56	Mondale	28.4%	3.7%	61.9%	5.9%
OBION	2,326	805	184	1,096	241	Mondale	34.6%	7.9%	47.1%	10.4%
OVERTON	1,467	510	41	846	70	Mondale	34.8%	2.8%	57.7%	4.8%
PERRY	1,618	726	33	750	109	Mondale	44.9%	2.0%	46.4%	6.7%
PICKETT	223	76	9	138		Mondale	34.1%	4.0%	61.9%	
POLK	1,882	652	62	996	172	Mondale	34.6%	3.3%	52.9%	9.1%
PUTNAM	5,683	2,209	259	2,824	391	Mondale	38.9%	4.6%	49.7%	6.9%
RHEA	1,504	493	62	867	82	Mondale	32.8%	4.1%	57.6%	5.5%
ROANE	2,769	862	180	1,606	121	Mondale	31.1%	6.5%	58.0%	4.4%
ROBERTSON	2,564	936	364	1,184	80	Mondale	36.5%	14.2%	46.2%	3.1%
RUTHERFORD	7,470	2,841	1,175	3,018	436	Mondale	38.0%	15.7%	40.4%	5.8%
SCOTT	606	175	26	381	24	Mondale	28.9%	4.3%	62.9%	4.0%
SEQUATCHIE	459	148	14	270	27	Mondale	32.2%	3.1%	58.8%	5.9%
SEVIER	994	408	56	465	65	Mondale	41.0%	5.6%	46.8%	6.5%
SHELBY	53,671	6,891	31,927	13,517	1,336	J. Jackson	12.8%	59.5%	25.2%	2.5%
SMITH	1,281	442	76	732	31	Mondale	34.5%	5.9%	57.1%	2.4%
STEWART	926	310	23	551	42	Mondale	33.5%	2.5%	59.5%	4.5%
SULLIVAN	8,243	3,097	450	4,030	666	Mondale	37.6%	5.5%	48.9%	8.1%
SUMNER	5,348	2,160	508	2,523	157	Mondale	40.4%	9.5%	47.2%	2.9%
TIPTON	1,520	475	384	605	56	Mondale	31.3%	25.3%	39.8%	3.7%
TROUSDALE	572	203	90	257	22	Mondale	35.5%	15.7%	44.9%	3.8%
UNICOI	266	87	10	161	8	Mondale	32.7%	3.8%	60.5%	3.0%
UNION	452	168	15	262	7	Mondale	37.2%	3.3%	58.0%	1.5%
VAN BUREN	293	93	4	188	8	Mondale	31.7%	1.4%	64.2%	2.7%
WARREN	1,824	692	73	1,005	54	Mondale	37.9%	4.0%	55.1%	3.0%
WASHINGTON	2,571	965	250	1,213	143	Mondale	37.5%	9.7%	47.2%	5.6%
WAYNE	573	233	23	308	9	Mondale	40.7%	4.0%	53.8%	1.6%
WEAKLEY	4,832	1,944	261	1,950	677	Mondale	40.2%	5.4%	40.4%	14.0%
WHITE	2,791	1,103	117	1,315	256	Mondale	39.5%	4.2%	47.1%	9.2%
WILLIAMSON	2,940	1,338	464	1,046	92	Hart	45.5%	15.8%	35.6%	3.1%
WILSON	3,766	1,386	554	1,693	133	Mondale	36.8%	14.7%	45.0%	3.5%
TOTAL	322,063	93,710	81,418	132,201	14,734	Mondale	29.1%	25.3%	41.0%	4.6%

TENNESSEE REPUBLICAN

1984

County	Total Vote	Reagan	Other	Winner	Percentage of Total Vote: Reagan	Percentage of Total Vote: Other
ANDERSON	807	777	30	Reagan	96.3%	3.7%
BEDFORD	93	92	1	Reagan	98.9%	1.1%
BENTON	16	16		Reagan	100.0%	
BLEDSOE	135	130	5	Reagan	96.3%	3.7%
BLOUNT	4,473	3,988	485	Reagan	89.2%	10.8%
BRADLEY	1,330	1,259	71	Reagan	94.7%	5.3%
CAMPBELL	2,176	1,933	243	Reagan	88.8%	11.2%
CANNON	136	123	13	Reagan	90.4%	9.6%
CARROLL	369	361	8	Reagan	97.8%	2.2%
CARTER	2,774	2,377	397	Reagan	85.7%	14.3%
CHEATHAM	98	95	3	Reagan	96.9%	3.1%
CHESTER	133	129	4	Reagan	97.0%	3.0%
CLAIBORNE	204	201	3	Reagan	98.5%	1.5%
CLAY	70	67	3	Reagan	95.7%	4.3%
COCKE	3,640	3,072	568	Reagan	84.4%	15.6%
COFFEE	243	236	7	Reagan	97.1%	2.9%
CROCKETT	16	16		Reagan	100.0%	
CUMBERLAND	1,943	1,772	171	Reagan	91.2%	8.8%
DAVIDSON	3,433	3,339	94	Reagan	97.3%	2.7%
DECATUR	278	260	18	Reagan	93.5%	6.5%
DE KALB	103	97	6	Reagan	94.2%	5.8%
DICKSON	168	165	3	Reagan	98.2%	1.8%
DYER	176	169	7	Reagan	96.0%	4.0%
FAYETTE	70	70		Reagan	100.0%	
FENTRESS	116	114	2	Reagan	98.3%	1.7%
FRANKLIN	137	132	5	Reagan	96.4%	3.6%
GIBSON	227	220	7	Reagan	96.9%	3.1%
GILES	68	62	6	Reagan	91.2%	8.8%
GRAINGER	1,241	1,170	71	Reagan	94.3%	5.7%
GREENE	4,234	3,881	353	Reagan	91.7%	8.3%
GRUNDY	36	33	3	Reagan	91.7%	8.3%
HAMBLEN	382	382		Reagan	100.0%	
HAMILTON	2,926	2,383	543	Reagan	81.4%	18.6%
HANCOCK	757	714	43	Reagan	94.3%	5.7%
HARDEMAN	122	117	5	Reagan	95.9%	4.1%
HARDIN	213	213		Reagan	100.0%	
HAWKINS	2,765	2,429	336	Reagan	87.8%	12.2%
HAYWOOD	100	99	1	Reagan	99.0%	1.0%
HENDERSON	1,284	1,175	109	Reagan	91.5%	8.5%
HENRY	58	57	1	Reagan	98.3%	1.7%
HICKMAN	79	77	2	Reagan	97.5%	2.5%
HOUSTON	53	45	8	Reagan	84.9%	15.1%
HUMPHREYS	89	83	6	Reagan	93.3%	6.7%
JACKSON	70	66	4	Reagan	94.3%	5.7%
JEFFERSON	2,840	2,307	533	Reagan	81.2%	18.8%
JOHNSON	215	200	15	Reagan	93.0%	7.0%
KNOX	5,987	5,604	383	Reagan	93.6%	6.4%
LAKE	53	51	2	Reagan	96.2%	3.8%
LAUDERDALE	94	93	1	Reagan	98.9%	1.1%
LAWRENCE	212	209	3	Reagan	98.6%	1.4%

TENNESSEE REPUBLICAN

1984

County	Total Vote	Reagan	Other	Winner	Percentage of Total Vote	
					Reagan	Other
LEWIS	74	74		Reagan	100.0%	
LINCOLN	146	144	2	Reagan	98.6%	1.4%
LOUDON	330	325	5	Reagan	98.5%	1.5%
MCMINN	1,835	1,660	175	Reagan	90.5%	9.5%
MCNAIRY	364	353	11	Reagan	97.0%	3.0%
MACON	1,463	1,141	322	Reagan	78.0%	22.0%
MADISON	580	563	17	Reagan	97.1%	2.9%
MARION	1,071	962	109	Reagan	89.8%	10.2%
MARSHALL	118	115	3	Reagan	97.5%	2.5%
MAURY	250	245	5	Reagan	98.0%	2.0%
MEIGS	599	556	43	Reagan	92.8%	7.2%
MONROE	295	291	4	Reagan	98.6%	1.4%
MONTGOMERY	555	532	23	Reagan	95.9%	4.1%
MOORE	43	39	4	Reagan	90.7%	9.3%
MORGAN	134	132	2	Reagan	98.5%	1.5%
OBION	43	41	2	Reagan	95.3%	4.7%
OVERTON	74	72	2	Reagan	97.3%	2.7%
PERRY	10	9	1	Reagan	90.0%	10.0%
PICKETT	660	618	42	Reagan	93.6%	6.4%
POLK	409	392	17	Reagan	95.8%	4.2%
PUTNAM	213	193	20	Reagan	90.6%	9.4%
RHEA	754	721	33	Reagan	95.6%	4.4%
ROANE	515	495	20	Reagan	96.1%	3.9%
ROBERTSON	152	150	2	Reagan	98.7%	1.3%
RUTHERFORD	503	474	29	Reagan	94.2%	5.8%
SCOTT	183	175	8	Reagan	95.6%	4.4%
SEQUATCHIE	99	98	1	Reagan	99.0%	1.0%
SEVIER	4,402	3,849	553	Reagan	87.4%	12.6%
SHELBY	5,939	5,725	214	Reagan	96.4%	3.6%
SMITH	78	75	3	Reagan	96.2%	3.8%
STEWART	62	60	2	Reagan	96.8%	3.2%
SULLIVAN	2,465	2,369	96	Reagan	96.1%	3.9%
SUMNER	386	376	10	Reagan	97.4%	2.6%
TIPTON	203	193	10	Reagan	95.1%	4.9%
TROUSDALE	24	21	3	Reagan	87.5%	12.5%
UNICOI	1,893	1,629	264	Reagan	86.1%	13.9%
UNION	101	99	2	Reagan	98.0%	2.0%
VAN BUREN	20	18	2	Reagan	90.0%	10.0%
WARREN	111	109	2	Reagan	98.2%	1.8%
WASHINGTON	6,308	5,425	883	Reagan	86.0%	14.0%
WAYNE	208	204	4	Reagan	98.1%	1.9%
WEAKLEY	104	103	1	Reagan	99.0%	1.0%
WHITE	48	47	1	Reagan	97.9%	2.1%
WILLIAMSON	629	615	14	Reagan	97.8%	2.2%
WILSON	326	320	6	Reagan	98.2%	1.8%
TOTAL	82,021	74,467	7,554	Reagan	90.8%	9.2%
Certified Totals	82,921	75,367	7,554	Reagan	90.9%	9.1%

TENNESSEE DEMOCRATIC

1988

County	Total Vote	Dukakis	Gore	J. Jackson	Other	Winner	Percentage of Total Vote Dukakis	Gore	J. Jackson	Other
ANDERSON	8,496	371	7,111	648	366	Gore	4.4%	83.7%	7.6%	4.3%
BEDFORD	6,691	118	5,856	403	314	Gore	1.8%	87.5%	6.0%	4.7%
BENTON	4,171	109	3,787	117	158	Gore	2.6%	90.8%	2.8%	3.8%
BLEDSOE	909	21	839	19	30	Gore	2.3%	92.3%	2.1%	3.3%
BLOUNT	7,166	300	5,865	663	338	Gore	4.2%	81.8%	9.3%	4.7%
BRADLEY	4,596	364	3,467	429	336	Gore	7.9%	75.4%	9.3%	7.3%
CAMPBELL	2,952	104	2,628	86	134	Gore	3.5%	89.0%	2.9%	4.5%
CANNON	1,897	20	1,785	47	45	Gore	1.1%	94.1%	2.5%	2.4%
CARROLL	3,874	83	3,279	389	123	Gore	2.1%	84.6%	10.0%	3.2%
CARTER	1,867	122	1,518	129	98	Gore	6.5%	81.3%	6.9%	5.2%
CHEATHAM	2,879	42	2,637	126	74	Gore	1.5%	91.6%	4.4%	2.6%
CHESTER	1,605	10	1,441	116	38	Gore	0.6%	89.8%	7.2%	2.4%
CLAIBORNE	2,857	79	2,551	95	132	Gore	2.8%	89.3%	3.3%	4.6%
CLAY	1,262	4	1,201	35	22	Gore	0.3%	95.2%	2.8%	1.7%
COCKE	843	22	696	70	55	Gore	2.6%	82.6%	8.3%	6.5%
COFFEE	8,718	209	7,821	312	376	Gore	2.4%	89.7%	3.6%	4.3%
CROCKETT	1,889	29	1,541	247	72	Gore	1.5%	81.6%	13.1%	3.8%
CUMBERLAND	3,616	144	3,172	160	140	Gore	4.0%	87.7%	4.4%	3.9%
DAVIDSON	88,739	2,584	63,144	20,312	2,699	Gore	2.9%	71.2%	22.9%	3.0%
DECATUR	2,047	31	1,874	68	74	Gore	1.5%	91.5%	3.3%	3.6%
DE KALB	3,264	26	3,100	73	65	Gore	0.8%	95.0%	2.2%	2.0%
DICKSON	4,818	79	4,378	243	118	Gore	1.6%	90.9%	5.0%	2.4%
DYER	3,736	110	3,023	418	185	Gore	2.9%	80.9%	11.2%	5.0%
FAYETTE	2,701	53	1,138	1,413	97	J. Jackson	2.0%	42.1%	52.3%	3.6%
FENTRESS	1,422	13	1,364	28	17	Gore	0.9%	95.9%	2.0%	1.2%
FRANKLIN	8,075	268	6,919	510	378	Gore	3.3%	85.7%	6.3%	4.7%
GIBSON	8,806	234	6,531	1,523	518	Gore	2.7%	74.2%	17.3%	5.9%
GILES	4,975	95	4,251	444	185	Gore	1.9%	85.4%	8.9%	3.7%
GRAINGER	873	13	805	31	24	Gore	1.5%	92.2%	3.6%	2.7%
GREENE	2,950	105	2,511	186	148	Gore	3.6%	85.1%	6.3%	5.0%
GRUNDY	2,173	59	1,976	36	102	Gore	2.7%	90.9%	1.7%	4.7%
HAMBLEN	4,538	183	3,780	339	236	Gore	4.0%	83.3%	7.5%	5.2%
HAMILTON	25,371	1,478	13,851	8,838	1,204	Gore	5.8%	54.6%	34.8%	4.7%
HANCOCK	196	6	180	1	9	Gore	3.1%	91.8%	0.5%	4.6%
HARDEMAN	3,263	77	1,762	1,242	182	Gore	2.4%	54.0%	38.1%	5.6%
HARDIN	2,216	43	1,969	146	58	Gore	1.9%	88.9%	6.6%	2.6%
HAWKINS	2,753	89	2,337	168	159	Gore	3.2%	84.9%	6.1%	5.8%
HAYWOOD	2,650	55	1,176	1,336	83	J. Jackson	2.1%	44.4%	50.4%	3.1%
HENDERSON	1,665	17	1,439	143	66	Gore	1.0%	86.4%	8.6%	4.0%
HENRY	5,113	114	4,385	421	193	Gore	2.2%	85.8%	8.2%	3.8%
HICKMAN	2,839	47	2,571	146	75	Gore	1.7%	90.6%	5.1%	2.6%
HOUSTON	1,234	20	1,132	48	34	Gore	1.6%	91.7%	3.9%	2.8%
HUMPHREYS	3,065	49	2,857	91	68	Gore	1.6%	93.2%	3.0%	2.2%
JACKSON	2,265	20	2,207	22	16	Gore	0.9%	97.4%	1.0%	0.7%
JEFFERSON	1,761	64	1,475	149	73	Gore	3.6%	83.8%	8.5%	4.1%
JOHNSON	658	19	574	37	28	Gore	2.9%	87.2%	5.6%	4.3%
KNOX	28,891	1,589	21,559	4,674	1,069	Gore	5.5%	74.6%	16.2%	3.7%
LAKE	624	19	504	67	34	Gore	3.0%	80.8%	10.7%	5.4%
LAUDERDALE	2,668	61	1,764	737	106	Gore	2.3%	66.1%	27.6%	4.0%
LAWRENCE	4,483	77	4,175	115	116	Gore	1.7%	93.1%	2.6%	2.6%

TENNESSEE DEMOCRATIC

1988

County	Total Vote	Dukakis	Gore	J. Jackson	Other	Winner	Percentage of Total Vote Dukakis	Gore	J. Jackson	Other
LEWIS	1,602	19	1,443	92	48	Gore	1.2%	90.1%	5.7%	3.0%
LINCOLN	3,677	51	3,312	213	101	Gore	1.4%	90.1%	5.8%	2.7%
LOUDON	2,718	95	2,366	139	118	Gore	3.5%	87.0%	5.1%	4.3%
MCMINN	2,933	109	2,508	204	112	Gore	3.7%	85.5%	7.0%	3.8%
MCNAIRY	2,568	71	2,207	204	86	Gore	2.8%	85.9%	7.9%	3.3%
MACON	2,338	14	2,245	38	41	Gore	0.6%	96.0%	1.6%	1.8%
MADISON	10,047	309	6,892	2,502	344	Gore	3.1%	68.6%	24.9%	3.4%
MARION	3,814	215	3,140	234	225	Gore	5.6%	82.3%	6.1%	5.9%
MARSHALL	2,922	28	2,669	170	55	Gore	1.0%	91.3%	5.8%	1.9%
MAURY	6,644	121	5,477	900	146	Gore	1.8%	82.4%	13.5%	2.2%
MEIGS	668	20	601	25	22	Gore	3.0%	90.0%	3.7%	3.3%
MONROE	2,663	50	2,324	176	113	Gore	1.9%	87.3%	6.6%	4.2%
MONTGOMERY	7,921	304	5,995	1,375	247	Gore	3.8%	75.7%	17.4%	3.1%
MOORE	869	23	795	42	9	Gore	2.6%	91.5%	4.8%	1.0%
MORGAN	1,679	61	1,514	47	57	Gore	3.6%	90.2%	2.8%	3.4%
OBION	5,938	293	4,368	473	804	Gore	4.9%	73.6%	8.0%	13.5%
OVERTON	2,838	22	2,737	24	55	Gore	0.8%	96.4%	0.8%	1.9%
PERRY	1,844	40	1,683	50	71	Gore	2.2%	91.3%	2.7%	3.9%
PICKETT	530	3	515	2	10	Gore	0.6%	97.2%	0.4%	1.9%
POLK	2,154	136	1,815	49	154	Gore	6.3%	84.3%	2.3%	7.1%
PUTNAM	8,407	142	7,811	207	247	Gore	1.7%	92.9%	2.5%	2.9%
RHEA	2,536	167	2,078	117	174	Gore	6.6%	81.9%	4.6%	6.9%
ROANE	7,068	279	6,066	419	304	Gore	3.9%	85.8%	5.9%	4.3%
ROBERTSON	6,095	72	5,385	513	125	Gore	1.2%	88.4%	8.4%	2.1%
RUTHERFORD	14,045	295	12,012	1,334	404	Gore	2.1%	85.5%	9.5%	2.9%
SCOTT	1,093	24	977	45	47	Gore	2.2%	89.4%	4.1%	4.3%
SEQUATCHIE	794	33	721	11	29	Gore	4.2%	90.8%	1.4%	3.7%
SEVIER	1,652	91	1,372	107	82	Gore	5.5%	83.1%	6.5%	5.0%
SHELBY	94,437	4,167	30,815	56,661	2,794	J. Jackson	4.4%	32.6%	60.0%	3.0%
SMITH	4,924	14	4,816	55	39	Gore	0.3%	97.8%	1.1%	0.8%
STEWART	1,508	40	1,391	39	38	Gore	2.7%	92.2%	2.6%	2.5%
SULLIVAN	10,836	758	8,885	573	620	Gore	7.0%	82.0%	5.3%	5.7%
SUMNER	13,147	221	11,865	783	278	Gore	1.7%	90.2%	6.0%	2.1%
TIPTON	3,715	87	2,642	840	146	Gore	2.3%	71.1%	22.6%	3.9%
TROUSDALE	1,228	7	1,089	115	17	Gore	0.6%	88.7%	9.4%	1.4%
UNICOI	797	43	696	22	36	Gore	5.4%	87.3%	2.8%	4.5%
UNION	879	19	805	19	36	Gore	2.2%	91.6%	2.2%	4.1%
VAN BUREN	787	6	761	8	12	Gore	0.8%	96.7%	1.0%	1.5%
WARREN	5,116	70	4,790	138	118	Gore	1.4%	93.6%	2.7%	2.3%
WASHINGTON	4,980	307	3,858	525	290	Gore	6.2%	77.5%	10.5%	5.8%
WAYNE	1,121	23	1,021	28	49	Gore	2.1%	91.1%	2.5%	4.4%
WEAKLEY	4,162	164	3,461	210	327	Gore	3.9%	83.2%	5.0%	7.9%
WHITE	3,688	55	3,441	79	113	Gore	1.5%	93.3%	2.1%	3.1%
WILLIAMSON	8,818	269	7,641	698	210	Gore	3.1%	86.7%	7.9%	2.4%
WILSON	10,994	163	9,950	647	234	Gore	1.5%	90.5%	5.9%	2.1%
TOTAL	576,314	19,348	416,861	119,248	20,857	Gore	3.4%	72.3%	20.7%	3.6%

TENNESSEE REPUBLICAN

1988

County	Total Vote	Bush	Dole	Robertson	Other	Winner	Percentage of Total Vote Bush	Dole	Robertson	Other
ANDERSON	3,672	1,997	984	519	172	Bush	54.4%	26.8%	14.1%	4.7%
BEDFORD	344	221	50	60	13	Bush	64.2%	14.5%	17.4%	3.8%
BENTON	209	140	27	27	15	Bush	67.0%	12.9%	12.9%	7.2%
BLEDSOE	460	307	84	49	20	Bush	66.7%	18.3%	10.7%	4.3%
BLOUNT	10,205	6,412	2,270	1,119	404	Bush	62.8%	22.2%	11.0%	4.0%
BRADLEY	7,292	3,402	1,741	1,726	423	Bush	46.7%	23.9%	23.7%	5.8%
CAMPBELL	1,026	666	194	136	30	Bush	64.9%	18.9%	13.3%	2.9%
CANNON	176	111	41	12	12	Bush	63.1%	23.3%	6.8%	6.8%
CARROLL	1,131	797	180	114	40	Bush	70.5%	15.9%	10.1%	3.5%
CARTER	7,096	4,248	1,539	974	335	Bush	59.9%	21.7%	13.7%	4.7%
CHEATHAM	431	243	64	105	19	Bush	56.4%	14.8%	24.4%	4.4%
CHESTER	525	382	81	47	15	Bush	72.8%	15.4%	9.0%	2.9%
CLAIBORNE	1,866	1,254	462	121	29	Bush	67.2%	24.8%	6.5%	1.6%
CLAY	124	94	15	11	4	Bush	75.8%	12.1%	8.9%	3.2%
COCKE	3,383	2,219	762	264	138	Bush	65.6%	22.5%	7.8%	4.1%
COFFEE	1,249	737	252	176	84	Bush	59.0%	20.2%	14.1%	6.7%
CROCKETT	456	254	64	122	16	Bush	55.7%	14.0%	26.8%	3.5%
CUMBERLAND	2,557	1,753	480	231	93	Bush	68.6%	18.8%	9.0%	3.6%
DAVIDSON	17,439	10,437	3,555	2,045	1,402	Bush	59.8%	20.4%	11.7%	8.0%
DECATUR	602	418	90	69	25	Bush	69.4%	15.0%	11.5%	4.2%
DE KALB	236	156	43	24	13	Bush	66.1%	18.2%	10.2%	5.5%
DICKSON	706	464	116	86	40	Bush	65.7%	16.4%	12.2%	5.7%
DYER	1,397	862	253	223	59	Bush	61.7%	18.1%	16.0%	4.2%
FAYETTE	723	472	98	123	30	Bush	65.3%	13.6%	17.0%	4.1%
FENTRESS	497	325	116	46	10	Bush	65.4%	23.3%	9.3%	2.0%
FRANKLIN	464	257	86	97	24	Bush	55.4%	18.5%	20.9%	5.2%
GIBSON	1,127	635	204	240	48	Bush	56.3%	18.1%	21.3%	4.3%
GILES	741	498	130	83	30	Bush	67.2%	17.5%	11.2%	4.0%
GRAINGER	932	662	212	40	18	Bush	71.0%	22.7%	4.3%	1.9%
GREENE	6,638	4,392	1,507	532	207	Bush	66.2%	22.7%	8.0%	3.1%
GRUNDY	203	121	44	30	8	Bush	59.6%	21.7%	14.8%	3.9%
HAMBLEN	4,830	3,049	1,026	592	163	Bush	63.1%	21.2%	12.3%	3.4%
HAMILTON	19,325	10,046	4,758	3,146	1,375	Bush	52.0%	24.6%	16.3%	7.1%
HANCOCK	1,119	776	269	37	37	Bush	69.3%	24.0%	3.3%	3.3%
HARDEMAN	507	308	77	93	29	Bush	60.7%	15.2%	18.3%	5.7%
HARDIN	826	545	127	135	19	Bush	66.0%	15.4%	16.3%	2.3%
HAWKINS	3,257	2,253	647	267	90	Bush	69.2%	19.9%	8.2%	2.8%
HAYWOOD	621	419	100	83	19	Bush	67.5%	16.1%	13.4%	3.1%
HENDERSON	1,100	778	168	106	48	Bush	70.7%	15.3%	9.6%	4.4%
HENRY	539	293	106	104	36	Bush	54.4%	19.7%	19.3%	6.7%
HICKMAN	404	282	74	24	24	Bush	69.8%	18.3%	5.9%	5.9%
HOUSTON	109	69	12	21	7	Bush	63.3%	11.0%	19.3%	6.4%
HUMPHREYS	342	188	82	38	34	Bush	55.0%	24.0%	11.1%	9.9%
JACKSON	115	76	21	12	6	Bush	66.1%	18.3%	10.4%	5.2%
JEFFERSON	3,617	2,283	868	302	164	Bush	63.1%	24.0%	8.3%	4.5%
JOHNSON	851	619	151	68	13	Bush	72.7%	17.7%	8.0%	1.5%
KNOX	23,316	12,901	6,264	2,571	1,580	Bush	55.3%	26.9%	11.0%	6.8%
LAKE	119	57	26	29	7	Bush	47.9%	21.8%	24.4%	5.9%
LAUDERDALE	550	312	103	113	22	Bush	56.7%	18.7%	20.5%	4.0%
LAWRENCE	1,284	878	264	89	53	Bush	68.4%	20.6%	6.9%	4.1%

TENNESSEE REPUBLICAN

1988

County	Total Vote	Bush	Dole	Robertson	Other	Winner	Percentage of Total Vote Bush	Dole	Robertson	Other
LEWIS	137	93	21	17	6	Bush	67.9%	15.3%	12.4%	4.4%
LINCOLN	698	404	143	121	30	Bush	57.9%	20.5%	17.3%	4.3%
LOUDON	2,491	1,362	513	467	149	Bush	54.7%	20.6%	18.7%	6.0%
MCMINN	3,045	1,805	679	404	157	Bush	59.3%	22.3%	13.3%	5.2%
MCNAIRY	1,036	741	162	112	21	Bush	71.5%	15.6%	10.8%	2.0%
MACON	405	285	76	34	10	Bush	70.4%	18.8%	8.4%	2.5%
MADISON	3,106	1,697	490	779	140	Bush	54.6%	15.8%	25.1%	4.5%
MARION	1,513	955	358	120	80	Bush	63.1%	23.7%	7.9%	5.3%
MARSHALL	380	251	60	43	26	Bush	66.1%	15.8%	11.3%	6.8%
MAURY	1,069	706	184	117	62	Bush	66.0%	17.2%	10.9%	5.8%
MEIGS	457	268	129	44	16	Bush	58.6%	28.2%	9.6%	3.5%
MONROE	3,659	2,529	771	246	113	Bush	69.1%	21.1%	6.7%	3.1%
MONTGOMERY	2,080	1,226	445	303	106	Bush	58.9%	21.4%	14.6%	5.1%
MOORE	106	70	16	17	3	Bush	66.0%	15.1%	16.0%	2.8%
MORGAN	536	367	81	69	19	Bush	68.5%	15.1%	12.9%	3.5%
OBION	603	254	135	173	41	Bush	42.1%	22.4%	28.7%	6.8%
OVERTON	184	113	33	28	10	Bush	61.4%	17.9%	15.2%	5.4%
PERRY	58	34	8	11	5	Bush	58.6%	13.8%	19.0%	8.6%
PICKETT	586	400	146	25	15	Bush	68.3%	24.9%	4.3%	2.6%
POLK	736	499	143	62	32	Bush	67.8%	19.4%	8.4%	4.3%
PUTNAM	1,078	574	192	259	53	Bush	53.2%	17.8%	24.0%	4.9%
RHEA	2,007	1,195	416	295	101	Bush	59.5%	20.7%	14.7%	5.0%
ROANE	3,737	2,248	917	406	166	Bush	60.2%	24.5%	10.9%	4.4%
ROBERTSON	678	382	122	128	46	Bush	56.3%	18.0%	18.9%	6.8%
RUTHERFORD	2,878	1,611	530	409	328	Bush	56.0%	18.4%	14.2%	11.4%
SCOTT	593	399	108	70	16	Bush	67.3%	18.2%	11.8%	2.7%
SEQUATCHIE	296	163	79	38	16	Bush	55.1%	26.7%	12.8%	5.4%
SEVIER	6,744	4,200	1,587	658	299	Bush	62.3%	23.5%	9.8%	4.4%
SHELBY	43,530	27,063	8,354	4,445	3,668	Bush	62.2%	19.2%	10.2%	8.4%
SMITH	126	67	19	34	6	Bush	53.2%	15.1%	27.0%	4.8%
STEWART	221	148	54	12	7	Bush	67.0%	24.4%	5.4%	3.2%
SULLIVAN	7,816	4,945	1,398	1,260	213	Bush	63.3%	17.9%	16.1%	2.7%
SUMNER	2,488	1,475	458	425	130	Bush	59.3%	18.4%	17.1%	5.2%
TIPTON	1,166	659	182	256	69	Bush	56.5%	15.6%	22.0%	5.9%
TROUSDALE	50	42	5	3		Bush	84.0%	10.0%	6.0%	
UNICOI	1,983	1,257	484	169	73	Bush	63.4%	24.4%	8.5%	3.7%
UNION	516	370	103	30	13	Bush	71.7%	20.0%	5.8%	2.5%
VAN BUREN	46	36		7	3	Bush	78.3%		15.2%	6.5%
WARREN	584	348	99	108	29	Bush	59.6%	17.0%	18.5%	5.0%
WASHINGTON	9,999	5,393	2,846	1,407	353	Bush	53.9%	28.5%	14.1%	3.5%
WAYNE	642	461	122	42	17	Bush	71.8%	19.0%	6.5%	2.6%
WEAKLEY	791	423	161	154	53	Bush	53.5%	20.4%	19.5%	6.7%
WHITE	280	163	49	56	12	Bush	58.2%	17.5%	20.0%	4.3%
WILLIAMSON	4,608	2,729	951	532	396	Bush	59.2%	20.6%	11.5%	8.6%
WILSON	1,772	1,037	311	339	85	Bush	58.5%	17.6%	19.1%	4.8%
TOTAL	254,252	152,515	55,027	32,015	14,695	Bush	60.0%	21.6%	12.6%	5.8%

TENNESSEE DEMOCRATIC

1992

County	Total Vote	Clinton	Tsongas	Other	Winner	Percentage of Total Vote Clinton	Tsongas	Other
ANDERSON	6,060	3,148	2,257	655	Clinton	51.9%	37.2%	10.8%
BEDFORD	4,842	2,841	875	1,126	Clinton	58.7%	18.1%	23.3%
BENTON	1,601	1,267	197	137	Clinton	79.1%	12.3%	8.6%
BLEDSOE	1,385	1,033	142	210	Clinton	74.6%	10.3%	15.2%
BLOUNT	4,150	2,489	1,099	562	Clinton	60.0%	26.5%	13.5%
BRADLEY	4,111	2,704	732	675	Clinton	65.8%	17.8%	16.4%
CAMPBELL	2,507	1,853	349	305	Clinton	73.9%	13.9%	12.2%
CANNON	1,828	1,203	306	319	Clinton	65.8%	16.7%	17.5%
CARROLL	1,617	1,302	185	130	Clinton	80.5%	11.4%	8.0%
CARTER	1,398	967	253	178	Clinton	69.2%	18.1%	12.7%
CHEATHAM	1,467	980	293	194	Clinton	66.8%	20.0%	13.2%
CHESTER	758	669	48	41	Clinton	88.3%	6.3%	5.4%
CLAIBORNE	1,139	867	174	98	Clinton	76.1%	15.3%	8.6%
CLAY	433	360	36	37	Clinton	83.1%	8.3%	8.5%
COCKE	695	513	105	77	Clinton	73.8%	15.1%	11.1%
COFFEE	2,923	1,885	666	372	Clinton	64.5%	22.8%	12.7%
CROCKETT	794	711	44	39	Clinton	89.5%	5.5%	4.9%
CUMBERLAND	4,051	2,507	794	750	Clinton	61.9%	19.6%	18.5%
DAVIDSON	37,186	19,248	12,349	5,589	Clinton	51.8%	33.2%	15.0%
DECATUR	1,026	858	85	83	Clinton	83.6%	8.3%	8.1%
DE KALB	2,347	1,660	320	367	Clinton	70.7%	13.6%	15.6%
DICKSON	2,402	1,760	401	241	Clinton	73.3%	16.7%	10.0%
DYER	1,667	1,405	153	109	Clinton	84.3%	9.2%	6.5%
FAYETTE	3,138	2,379	254	505	Clinton	75.8%	8.1%	16.1%
FENTRESS	628	485	86	57	Clinton	77.2%	13.7%	9.1%
FRANKLIN	6,136	3,514	1,216	1,406	Clinton	57.3%	19.8%	22.9%
GIBSON	3,402	2,923	228	251	Clinton	85.9%	6.7%	7.4%
GILES	1,392	1,051	212	129	Clinton	75.5%	15.2%	9.3%
GRAINGER	540	423	65	52	Clinton	78.3%	12.0%	9.6%
GREENE	2,624	1,791	415	418	Clinton	68.3%	15.8%	15.9%
GRUNDY	2,255	1,724	190	341	Clinton	76.5%	8.4%	15.1%
HAMBLEN	1,993	1,274	447	272	Clinton	63.9%	22.4%	13.6%
HAMILTON	16,359	11,147	3,099	2,113	Clinton	68.1%	18.9%	12.9%
HANCOCK	106	84	9	13	Clinton	79.2%	8.5%	12.3%
HARDEMAN	2,512	2,004	190	318	Clinton	79.8%	7.6%	12.7%
HARDIN	1,275	1,098	90	87	Clinton	86.1%	7.1%	6.8%
HAWKINS	2,270	1,577	313	380	Clinton	69.5%	13.8%	16.7%
HAYWOOD	943	831	63	49	Clinton	88.1%	6.7%	5.2%
HENDERSON	770	658	60	52	Clinton	85.5%	7.8%	6.8%
HENRY	4,638	3,115	688	835	Clinton	67.2%	14.8%	18.0%
HICKMAN	1,085	801	182	102	Clinton	73.8%	16.8%	9.4%
HOUSTON	577	443	75	59	Clinton	76.8%	13.0%	10.2%
HUMPHREYS	1,269	1,002	166	101	Clinton	79.0%	13.1%	8.0%
JACKSON	883	727	86	70	Clinton	82.3%	9.7%	7.9%
JEFFERSON	1,001	681	208	112	Clinton	68.0%	20.8%	11.2%
JOHNSON	407	304	63	40	Clinton	74.7%	15.5%	9.8%
KNOX	20,133	10,156	7,113	2,864	Clinton	50.4%	35.3%	14.2%
LAKE	327	283	21	23	Clinton	86.5%	6.4%	7.0%
LAUDERDALE	1,250	1,122	63	65	Clinton	89.8%	5.0%	5.2%
LAWRENCE	1,984	1,618	206	160	Clinton	81.6%	10.4%	8.1%

TENNESSEE DEMOCRATIC

1992

County	Total Vote	Clinton	Tsongas	Other	Winner	Percentage of Total Vote Clinton	Tsongas	Other
LEWIS	1,384	1,023	143	218	Clinton	73.9%	10.3%	15.8%
LINCOLN	2,667	1,861	404	402	Clinton	69.8%	15.1%	15.1%
LOUDON	1,540	998	389	153	Clinton	64.8%	25.3%	9.9%
MCMINN	1,923	1,460	259	204	Clinton	75.9%	13.5%	10.6%
MCNAIRY	1,402	1,262	75	65	Clinton	90.0%	5.3%	4.6%
MACON	439	355	50	34	Clinton	80.9%	11.4%	7.7%
MADISON	4,053	3,297	446	310	Clinton	81.3%	11.0%	7.6%
MARION	3,386	2,640	273	473	Clinton	78.0%	8.1%	14.0%
MARSHALL	1,244	899	212	133	Clinton	72.3%	17.0%	10.7%
MAURY	2,852	1,855	696	301	Clinton	65.0%	24.4%	10.6%
MEIGS	505	408	41	56	Clinton	80.8%	8.1%	11.1%
MONROE	1,372	1,044	211	117	Clinton	76.1%	15.4%	8.5%
MONTGOMERY	3,957	2,636	880	441	Clinton	66.6%	22.2%	11.1%
MOORE	300	219	55	26	Clinton	73.0%	18.3%	8.7%
MORGAN	1,005	782	142	81	Clinton	77.8%	14.1%	8.1%
OBION	3,012	2,196	295	521	Clinton	72.9%	9.8%	17.3%
OVERTON	2,253	1,680	269	304	Clinton	74.6%	11.9%	13.5%
PERRY	1,802	1,236	211	355	Clinton	68.6%	11.7%	19.7%
PICKETT	184	155	14	15	Clinton	84.2%	7.6%	8.2%
POLK	2,551	1,946	287	318	Clinton	76.3%	11.3%	12.5%
PUTNAM	7,549	4,396	1,474	1,679	Clinton	58.2%	19.5%	22.2%
RHEA	1,243	984	134	125	Clinton	79.2%	10.8%	10.1%
ROANE	3,940	2,541	970	429	Clinton	64.5%	24.6%	10.9%
ROBERTSON	2,378	1,621	474	283	Clinton	68.2%	19.9%	11.9%
RUTHERFORD	9,722	5,699	2,324	1,699	Clinton	58.6%	23.9%	17.5%
SCOTT	795	585	119	91	Clinton	73.6%	15.0%	11.4%
SEQUATCHIE	546	443	66	37	Clinton	81.1%	12.1%	6.8%
SEVIER	1,350	775	356	219	Clinton	57.4%	26.4%	16.2%
SHELBY	41,524	34,114	3,966	3,444	Clinton	82.2%	9.6%	8.3%
SMITH	997	770	129	98	Clinton	77.2%	12.9%	9.8%
STEWART	803	610	111	82	Clinton	76.0%	13.8%	10.2%
SULLIVAN	8,549	5,310	1,910	1,329	Clinton	62.1%	22.3%	15.5%
SUMNER	5,890	3,841	1,350	699	Clinton	65.2%	22.9%	11.9%
TIPTON	2,140	1,887	130	123	Clinton	88.2%	6.1%	5.7%
TROUSDALE	523	428	47	48	Clinton	81.8%	9.0%	9.2%
UNICOI	440	268	79	93	Clinton	60.9%	18.0%	21.1%
UNION	656	523	76	57	Clinton	79.7%	11.6%	8.7%
VAN BUREN	759	621	83	55	Clinton	81.8%	10.9%	7.2%
WARREN	3,084	2,181	506	397	Clinton	70.7%	16.4%	12.9%
WASHINGTON	3,247	1,881	778	588	Clinton	57.9%	24.0%	18.1%
WAYNE	468	371	46	51	Clinton	79.3%	9.8%	10.9%
WEAKLEY	3,373	2,294	372	707	Clinton	68.0%	11.0%	21.0%
WHITE	3,411	2,262	441	708	Clinton	66.3%	12.9%	20.8%
WILLIAMSON	2,935	1,439	1,069	427	Clinton	49.0%	36.4%	14.5%
WILSON	8,045	5,244	1,684	1,117	Clinton	65.2%	20.9%	13.9%
TOTAL	318,482	214,485	61,717	42,280	Clinton	67.3%	19.4%	13.3%

TENNESSEE REPUBLICAN

1992

County	Total Vote	Buchanan	Bush	Other	Winner	Percentage of Total Vote Buchanan	Bush	Other
ANDERSON	3,441	654	2,621	166	Bush	19.0%	76.2%	4.8%
BEDFORD	336	82	229	25	Bush	24.4%	68.2%	7.4%
BENTON	332	88	218	26	Bush	26.5%	65.7%	7.8%
BLEDSOE	806	108	662	36	Bush	13.4%	82.1%	4.5%
BLOUNT	7,991	1,673	5,947	371	Bush	20.9%	74.4%	4.6%
BRADLEY	6,071	1,346	4,323	402	Bush	22.2%	71.2%	6.6%
CAMPBELL	2,701	606	1,863	232	Bush	22.4%	69.0%	8.6%
CANNON	149	35	98	16	Bush	23.5%	65.8%	10.7%
CARROLL	1,026	180	750	96	Bush	17.5%	73.1%	9.4%
CARTER	3,258	859	2,185	214	Bush	26.4%	67.1%	6.6%
CHEATHAM	826	237	529	60	Bush	28.7%	64.0%	7.3%
CHESTER	536	108	380	48	Bush	20.1%	70.9%	9.0%
CLAIBORNE	859	165	660	34	Bush	19.2%	76.8%	4.0%
CLAY	157	27	124	6	Bush	17.2%	79.0%	3.8%
COCKE	1,997	300	1,574	123	Bush	15.0%	78.8%	6.2%
COFFEE	1,410	339	997	74	Bush	24.0%	70.7%	5.2%
CROCKETT	317	38	249	30	Bush	12.0%	78.5%	9.5%
CUMBERLAND	3,219	608	2,449	162	Bush	18.9%	76.1%	5.0%
DAVIDSON	19,742	4,928	14,037	777	Bush	25.0%	71.1%	3.9%
DECATUR	482	71	373	38	Bush	14.7%	77.4%	7.9%
DE KALB	255	51	189	15	Bush	20.0%	74.1%	5.9%
DICKSON	1,010	246	698	66	Bush	24.4%	69.1%	6.5%
DYER	848	161	636	51	Bush	19.0%	75.0%	6.0%
FAYETTE	594	122	438	34	Bush	20.5%	73.7%	5.7%
FENTRESS	439	81	331	27	Bush	18.5%	75.4%	6.2%
FRANKLIN	455	113	318	24	Bush	24.8%	69.9%	5.3%
GIBSON	1,230	245	873	112	Bush	19.9%	71.0%	9.1%
GILES	458	141	280	37	Bush	30.8%	61.1%	8.1%
GRAINGER	845	138	665	42	Bush	16.3%	78.7%	5.0%
GREENE	5,920	1,250	4,260	410	Bush	21.1%	72.0%	6.9%
GRUNDY	116	36	72	8	Bush	31.0%	62.1%	6.9%
HAMBLEN	2,316	440	1,788	88	Bush	19.0%	77.2%	3.8%
HAMILTON	18,046	5,073	12,037	936	Bush	28.1%	66.7%	5.2%
HANCOCK	1,406	276	1,009	121	Bush	19.6%	71.8%	8.6%
HARDEMAN	427	116	277	34	Bush	27.2%	64.9%	8.0%
HARDIN	773	172	564	37	Bush	22.3%	73.0%	4.8%
HAWKINS	4,265	775	3,261	229	Bush	18.2%	76.5%	5.4%
HAYWOOD	495	72	396	27	Bush	14.5%	80.0%	5.5%
HENDERSON	909	121	720	68	Bush	13.3%	79.2%	7.5%
HENRY	425	67	336	22	Bush	15.8%	79.1%	5.2%
HICKMAN	434	102	299	33	Bush	23.5%	68.9%	7.6%
HOUSTON	179	62	98	19	Bush	34.6%	54.7%	10.6%
HUMPHREYS	384	119	239	26	Bush	31.0%	62.2%	6.8%
JACKSON	189	46	124	19	Bush	24.3%	65.6%	10.1%
JEFFERSON	4,257	888	2,993	376	Bush	20.9%	70.3%	8.8%
JOHNSON	717	110	558	49	Bush	15.3%	77.8%	6.8%
KNOX	21,640	4,648	16,253	739	Bush	21.5%	75.1%	3.4%
LAKE	126	29	88	9	Bush	23.0%	69.8%	7.1%
LAUDERDALE	452	104	315	33	Bush	23.0%	69.7%	7.3%
LAWRENCE	1,024	184	801	39	Bush	18.0%	78.2%	3.8%

TENNESSEE REPUBLICAN

1992

County	Total Vote	Buchanan	Bush	Other	Winner	Percentage of Total Vote Buchanan	Bush	Other
LEWIS	390	65	298	27	Bush	16.7%	76.4%	6.9%
LINCOLN	1,374	309	986	79	Bush	22.5%	71.8%	5.7%
LOUDON	2,156	398	1,647	111	Bush	18.5%	76.4%	5.1%
MCMINN	3,501	723	2,546	232	Bush	20.7%	72.7%	6.6%
MCNAIRY	881	201	621	59	Bush	22.8%	70.5%	6.7%
MACON	506	116	357	33	Bush	22.9%	70.6%	6.5%
MADISON	2,929	741	2,007	181	Bush	25.3%	68.5%	6.2%
MARION	1,440	367	971	102	Bush	25.5%	67.4%	7.1%
MARSHALL	576	135	402	39	Bush	23.4%	69.8%	6.8%
MAURY	1,592	398	1,111	83	Bush	25.0%	69.8%	5.2%
MEIGS	888	233	547	108	Bush	26.2%	61.6%	12.2%
MONROE	2,399	327	1,934	138	Bush	13.6%	80.6%	5.8%
MONTGOMERY	2,413	609	1,681	123	Bush	25.2%	69.7%	5.1%
MOORE	159	35	104	20	Bush	22.0%	65.4%	12.6%
MORGAN	519	107	387	25	Bush	20.6%	74.6%	4.8%
OBION	469	121	303	45	Bush	25.8%	64.6%	9.6%
OVERTON	191	48	130	13	Bush	25.1%	68.1%	6.8%
PERRY	103	12	80	11	Bush	11.7%	77.7%	10.7%
PICKETT	326	44	268	14	Bush	13.5%	82.2%	4.3%
POLK	562	87	441	34	Bush	15.5%	78.5%	6.0%
PUTNAM	857	202	602	53	Bush	23.6%	70.2%	6.2%
RHEA	3,089	776	2,032	281	Bush	25.1%	65.8%	9.1%
ROANE	2,841	537	2,178	126	Bush	18.9%	76.7%	4.4%
ROBERTSON	1,110	304	736	70	Bush	27.4%	66.3%	6.3%
RUTHERFORD	4,054	1,007	2,853	194	Bush	24.8%	70.4%	4.8%
SCOTT	775	155	582	38	Bush	20.0%	75.1%	4.9%
SEQUATCHIE	339	100	209	30	Bush	29.5%	61.7%	8.8%
SEVIER	8,080	1,745	5,730	605	Bush	21.6%	70.9%	7.5%
SHELBY	34,050	6,886	26,019	1,145	Bush	20.2%	76.4%	3.4%
SMITH	310	72	219	19	Bush	23.2%	70.6%	6.1%
STEWART	301	59	211	31	Bush	19.6%	70.1%	10.3%
SULLIVAN	8,651	1,672	6,699	280	Bush	19.3%	77.4%	3.2%
SUMNER	3,988	1,069	2,757	162	Bush	26.8%	69.1%	4.1%
TIPTON	1,409	292	1,038	79	Bush	20.7%	73.7%	5.6%
TROUSDALE	138	36	92	10	Bush	26.1%	66.7%	7.2%
UNICOI	2,272	564	1,509	199	Bush	24.8%	66.4%	8.8%
UNION	528	93	398	37	Bush	17.6%	75.4%	7.0%
VAN BUREN	216	33	160	23	Bush	15.3%	74.1%	10.6%
WARREN	656	166	431	59	Bush	25.3%	65.7%	9.0%
WASHINGTON	4,916	1,230	3,433	253	Bush	25.0%	69.8%	5.1%
WAYNE	446	73	355	18	Bush	16.4%	79.6%	4.0%
WEAKLEY	537	115	391	31	Bush	21.4%	72.8%	5.8%
WHITE	170	51	111	8	Bush	30.0%	65.3%	4.7%
WILLIAMSON	10,713	2,703	7,345	665	Bush	25.2%	68.6%	6.2%
WILSON	5,543	1,129	4,124	290	Bush	20.4%	74.4%	5.2%
TOTAL	245,653	54,585	178,219	12,849	Bush	22.2%	72.5%	5.2%

TENNESSEE DEMOCRATIC

1996

County	Total Vote	Clinton	Uncommitted	Write-in	Winner	Percentage of Total Vote Clinton	Uncom.	Write-in
ANDERSON	3,273	2,786	486	1	Clinton	85.1%	14.8%	
BEDFORD	3,877	2,911	966		Clinton	75.1%	24.9%	
BENTON	527	497	30		Clinton	94.3%	5.7%	
BLEDSOE	273	252	21		Clinton	92.3%	7.7%	
BLOUNT	995	938	57		Clinton	94.3%	5.7%	
BRADLEY	799	734	65		Clinton	91.9%	8.1%	
CAMPBELL	2,784	2,280	504		Clinton	81.9%	18.1%	
CANNON	1,453	1,167	286		Clinton	80.3%	19.7%	
CARROLL	498	475	23		Clinton	95.4%	4.6%	
CARTER	474	439	35		Clinton	92.6%	7.4%	
CHEATHAM	498	477	20	1	Clinton	95.8%	4.0%	0.2%
CHESTER	209	204	5		Clinton	97.6%	2.4%	
CLAIBORNE	287	265	21	1	Clinton	92.3%	7.3%	0.3%
CLAY	210	203	7		Clinton	96.7%	3.3%	
COCKE	686	622	64		Clinton	90.7%	9.3%	
COFFEE	2,769	2,276	493		Clinton	82.2%	17.8%	
CROCKETT	492	445	47		Clinton	90.4%	9.6%	
CUMBERLAND	2,340	1,999	341		Clinton	85.4%	14.6%	
DAVIDSON	19,754	18,152	1,591	11	Clinton	91.9%	8.1%	0.1%
DECATUR	483	451	30	2	Clinton	93.4%	6.2%	0.4%
DE KALB	1,265	1,106	158	1	Clinton	87.4%	12.5%	0.1%
DICKSON	812	786	26		Clinton	96.8%	3.2%	
DYER	516	461	55		Clinton	89.3%	10.7%	
FAYETTE	520	504	16		Clinton	96.9%	3.1%	
FENTRESS	156	152	4		Clinton	97.4%	2.6%	
FRANKLIN	946	839	107		Clinton	88.7%	11.3%	
GIBSON	1,235	1,181	54		Clinton	95.6%	4.4%	
GILES	1,917	1,784	133		Clinton	93.1%	6.9%	
GRAINGER	130	117	13		Clinton	90.0%	10.0%	
GREENE	2,002	1,812	187	3	Clinton	90.5%	9.3%	0.1%
GRUNDY	2,829	2,084	692	53	Clinton	73.7%	24.5%	1.9%
HAMBLEN	672	631	41		Clinton	93.9%	6.1%	
HAMILTON	6,481	6,054	427		Clinton	93.4%	6.6%	
HANCOCK	59	57	2		Clinton	96.6%	3.4%	
HARDEMAN	640	609	31		Clinton	95.2%	4.8%	
HARDIN	315	302	11	2	Clinton	95.9%	3.5%	0.6%
HAWKINS	708	638	70		Clinton	90.1%	9.9%	
HAYWOOD	604	597	7		Clinton	98.8%	1.2%	
HENDERSON	51	48	3		Clinton	94.1%	5.9%	
HENRY	1,958	1,673	283	2	Clinton	85.4%	14.5%	0.1%
HICKMAN	1,705	1,493	211	1	Clinton	87.6%	12.4%	0.1%
HOUSTON	250	239	11		Clinton	95.6%	4.4%	
HUMPHREYS	501	474	27		Clinton	94.6%	5.4%	
JACKSON	343	335	7	1	Clinton	97.7%	2.0%	0.3%
JEFFERSON	293	279	14		Clinton	95.2%	4.8%	
JOHNSON	190	176	14		Clinton	92.6%	7.4%	
KNOX	4,550	4,346	198	6	Clinton	95.5%	4.4%	0.1%
LAKE	173	168	5		Clinton	97.1%	2.9%	
LAUDERDALE	504	485	19		Clinton	96.2%	3.8%	
LAWRENCE	649	621	28		Clinton	95.7%	4.3%	

TENNESSEE DEMOCRATIC

1996

County	Total Vote	Clinton	Uncommitted	Write-in	Winner	Percentage of Total Vote Clinton	Uncom.	Write-in
LEWIS	356	340	16		Clinton	95.5%	4.5%	
LINCOLN	415	388	25	2	Clinton	93.5%	6.0%	0.5%
LOUDON	548	510	38		Clinton	93.1%	6.9%	
MCMINN	938	857	81		Clinton	91.4%	8.6%	
MCNAIRY	401	385	16		Clinton	96.0%	4.0%	
MACON	185	176	9		Clinton	95.1%	4.9%	
MADISON	765	726	39		Clinton	94.9%	5.1%	
MARION	3,184	2,500	684		Clinton	78.5%	21.5%	
MARSHALL	430	416	13	1	Clinton	96.7%	3.0%	0.2%
MAURY	892	865	25	2	Clinton	97.0%	2.8%	0.2%
MEIGS	203	186	17		Clinton	91.6%	8.4%	
MONROE	297	282	15		Clinton	94.9%	5.1%	
MONTGOMERY	1,592	1,513	77	2	Clinton	95.0%	4.8%	0.1%
MOORE	74	70	4		Clinton	94.6%	5.4%	
MORGAN	323	306	17		Clinton	94.7%	5.3%	
OBION	667	594	73		Clinton	89.1%	10.9%	
OVERTON	2,383	2,045	338		Clinton	85.8%	14.2%	
PERRY	1,004	854	150		Clinton	85.1%	14.9%	
PICKETT	62	60	2		Clinton	96.8%	3.2%	
POLK	2,142	1,684	458		Clinton	78.6%	21.4%	
PUTNAM	5,634	4,688	945	1	Clinton	83.2%	16.8%	
RHEA	1,692	1,383	302	7	Clinton	81.7%	17.8%	0.4%
ROANE	834	780	53	1	Clinton	93.5%	6.4%	0.1%
ROBERTSON	820	771	47	2	Clinton	94.0%	5.7%	0.2%
RUTHERFORD	5,616	4,851	764	1	Clinton	86.4%	13.6%	
SCOTT	137	132	5		Clinton	96.4%	3.6%	
SEQUATCHIE	117	114	3		Clinton	97.4%	2.6%	
SEVIER	468	443	24	1	Clinton	94.7%	5.1%	0.2%
SHELBY	12,394	12,015	379		Clinton	96.9%	3.1%	
SMITH	752	734	17	1	Clinton	97.6%	2.3%	0.1%
STEWART	419	390	29		Clinton	93.1%	6.9%	
SULLIVAN	2,769	2,389	380		Clinton	86.3%	13.7%	
SUMNER	1,730	1,646	80	4	Clinton	95.1%	4.6%	0.2%
TIPTON	1,307	1,201	106		Clinton	91.9%	8.1%	
TROUSDALE	234	229	5		Clinton	97.9%	2.1%	
UNICOI	77	74	3		Clinton	96.1%	3.9%	
UNION	553	515	37	1	Clinton	93.1%	6.7%	0.2%
VAN BUREN	112	110	2		Clinton	98.2%	1.8%	
WARREN	957	891	66		Clinton	93.1%	6.9%	
WASHINGTON	916	859	57		Clinton	93.8%	6.2%	
WAYNE	154	152	2		Clinton	98.7%	1.3%	
WEAKLEY	3,866	2,560	1,304	2	Clinton	66.2%	33.7%	0.1%
WHITE	1,530	1,155	375		Clinton	75.5%	24.5%	
WILLIAMSON	739	701	38		Clinton	94.9%	5.1%	
WILSON	1,454	1,374	78	2	Clinton	94.5%	5.4%	0.1%
TOTAL	137,797	122,538	15,144	115	Clinton	88.9%	11.0%	0.1%

TENNESSEE REPUBLICAN

1996

County	Total Vote	Alexander	Buchanan	Dole	Other	Winner	Percentage of Total Vote Alexander	Buchanan	Dole	Other
ANDERSON	3,968	397	1,021	2,065	485	Dole	10.0%	25.7%	52.0%	12.2%
BEDFORD	1,110	122	323	507	158	Dole	11.0%	29.1%	45.7%	14.2%
BENTON	492	51	179	218	44	Dole	10.4%	36.4%	44.3%	8.9%
BLEDSOE	635	29	187	366	53	Dole	4.6%	29.4%	57.6%	8.3%
BLOUNT	10,092	1,559	2,281	5,250	1,002	Dole	15.4%	22.6%	52.0%	9.9%
BRADLEY	4,766	523	1,419	2,290	534	Dole	11.0%	29.8%	48.0%	11.2%
CAMPBELL	850	78	232	454	86	Dole	9.2%	27.3%	53.4%	10.1%
CANNON	202	25	79	73	25	Buchanan	12.4%	39.1%	36.1%	12.4%
CARROLL	1,101	173	327	514	87	Dole	15.7%	29.7%	46.7%	7.9%
CARTER	5,391	927	1,191	2,632	641	Dole	17.2%	22.1%	48.8%	11.9%
CHEATHAM	1,123	119	345	492	167	Dole	10.6%	30.7%	43.8%	14.9%
CHESTER	574	69	175	283	47	Dole	12.0%	30.5%	49.3%	8.2%
CLAIBORNE	1,233	121	347	682	83	Dole	9.8%	28.1%	55.3%	6.7%
CLAY	234	44	57	116	17	Dole	18.8%	24.4%	49.6%	7.3%
COCKE	3,255	413	753	1,752	337	Dole	12.7%	23.1%	53.8%	10.4%
COFFEE	1,891	232	524	872	263	Dole	12.3%	27.7%	46.1%	13.9%
CROCKETT	627	69	182	327	49	Dole	11.0%	29.0%	52.2%	7.8%
CUMBERLAND	4,914	761	1,055	2,507	591	Dole	15.5%	21.5%	51.0%	12.0%
DAVIDSON	22,643	2,863	4,723	11,242	3,815	Dole	12.6%	20.9%	49.6%	16.8%
DECATUR	545	59	190	262	34	Dole	10.8%	34.9%	48.1%	6.2%
DE KALB	388	46	102	192	48	Dole	11.9%	26.3%	49.5%	12.4%
DICKSON	1,267	116	385	579	187	Dole	9.2%	30.4%	45.7%	14.8%
DYER	1,243	173	317	653	100	Dole	13.9%	25.5%	52.5%	8.0%
FAYETTE	1,212	71	462	574	105	Dole	5.9%	38.1%	47.4%	8.7%
FENTRESS	468	36	153	243	36	Dole	7.7%	32.7%	51.9%	7.7%
FRANKLIN	1,050	96	312	482	160	Dole	9.1%	29.7%	45.9%	15.2%
GIBSON	1,557	109	566	754	128	Dole	7.0%	36.4%	48.4%	8.2%
GILES	1,386	164	433	625	164	Dole	11.8%	31.2%	45.1%	11.8%
GRAINGER	967	108	219	578	62	Dole	11.2%	22.6%	59.8%	6.4%
GREENE	5,753	708	1,122	3,291	632	Dole	12.3%	19.5%	57.2%	11.0%
GRUNDY	210	20	79	90	21	Dole	9.5%	37.6%	42.9%	10.0%
HAMBLEN	3,011	391	718	1,620	282	Dole	13.0%	23.8%	53.8%	9.4%
HAMILTON	23,306	2,024	6,189	11,653	3,440	Dole	8.7%	26.6%	50.0%	14.8%
HANCOCK	376	50	77	222	27	Dole	13.3%	20.5%	59.0%	7.2%
HARDEMAN	727	85	257	335	50	Dole	11.7%	35.4%	46.1%	6.9%
HARDIN	885	40	303	456	86	Dole	4.5%	34.2%	51.5%	9.7%
HAWKINS	4,729	711	933	2,568	517	Dole	15.0%	19.7%	54.3%	10.9%
HAYWOOD	555	102	156	257	40	Dole	18.4%	28.1%	46.3%	7.2%
HENDERSON	3,584	706	908	1,609	361	Dole	19.7%	25.3%	44.9%	10.1%
HENRY	674	67	211	326	70	Dole	9.9%	31.3%	48.4%	10.4%
HICKMAN	419	62	108	178	71	Dole	14.8%	25.8%	42.5%	16.9%
HOUSTON	221	38	85	75	23	Buchanan	17.2%	38.5%	33.9%	10.4%
HUMPHREYS	494	80	143	224	47	Dole	16.2%	28.9%	45.3%	9.5%
JACKSON	220	31	73	96	20	Dole	14.1%	33.2%	43.6%	9.1%
JEFFERSON	2,531	227	652	1,412	240	Dole	9.0%	25.8%	55.8%	9.5%
JOHNSON	885	93	194	526	72	Dole	10.5%	21.9%	59.4%	8.1%
KNOX	22,241	2,350	5,551	11,415	2,925	Dole	10.6%	25.0%	51.3%	13.2%
LAKE	170	20	53	81	16	Dole	11.8%	31.2%	47.6%	9.4%
LAUDERDALE	691	63	253	330	45	Dole	9.1%	36.6%	47.8%	6.5%
LAWRENCE	1,142	131	360	533	118	Dole	11.5%	31.5%	46.7%	10.3%

TENNESSEE REPUBLICAN

1996

County	Total Vote	Alexander	Buchanan	Dole	Other	Winner	Percentage of Total Vote: Alexander	Buchanan	Dole	Other
LEWIS	381	41	151	155	34	Dole	10.8%	39.6%	40.7%	8.9%
LINCOLN	995	82	317	455	141	Dole	8.2%	31.9%	45.7%	14.2%
LOUDON	2,319	267	575	1,214	263	Dole	11.5%	24.8%	52.4%	11.3%
MCMINN	4,020	522	892	2,206	400	Dole	13.0%	22.2%	54.9%	10.0%
MCNAIRY	906	79	358	417	52	Dole	8.7%	39.5%	46.0%	5.7%
MACON	744	66	230	393	55	Dole	8.9%	30.9%	52.8%	7.4%
MADISON	3,078	283	1,178	1,298	319	Dole	9.2%	38.3%	42.2%	10.4%
MARION	895	67	292	427	109	Dole	7.5%	32.6%	47.7%	12.2%
MARSHALL	653	75	175	309	94	Dole	11.5%	26.8%	47.3%	14.4%
MAURY	1,972	255	500	952	265	Dole	12.9%	25.4%	48.3%	13.4%
MEIGS	594	85	127	321	61	Dole	14.3%	21.4%	54.0%	10.3%
MONROE	2,326	225	491	1,426	184	Dole	9.7%	21.1%	61.3%	7.9%
MONTGOMERY	3,298	446	677	1,701	474	Dole	13.5%	20.5%	51.6%	14.4%
MOORE	216	14	54	116	32	Dole	6.5%	25.0%	53.7%	14.8%
MORGAN	569	46	193	286	44	Dole	8.1%	33.9%	50.3%	7.7%
OBION	817	63	257	414	83	Dole	7.7%	31.5%	50.7%	10.2%
OVERTON	420	35	147	182	56	Dole	8.3%	35.0%	43.3%	13.3%
PERRY	137	58	22	46	11	Alexander	42.3%	16.1%	33.6%	8.0%
PICKETT	765	131	168	409	57	Dole	17.1%	22.0%	53.5%	7.5%
POLK	619	56	137	388	38	Dole	9.0%	22.1%	62.7%	6.1%
PUTNAM	3,395	478	773	1,610	534	Dole	14.1%	22.8%	47.4%	15.7%
RHEA	3,177	438	748	1,630	361	Dole	13.8%	23.5%	51.3%	11.4%
ROANE	3,103	365	843	1,575	320	Dole	11.8%	27.2%	50.8%	10.3%
ROBERTSON	1,544	124	462	744	214	Dole	8.0%	29.9%	48.2%	13.9%
RUTHERFORD	7,988	963	2,195	3,579	1,251	Dole	12.1%	27.5%	44.8%	15.7%
SCOTT	677	52	241	331	53	Dole	7.7%	35.6%	48.9%	7.8%
SEQUATCHIE	341	20	116	164	41	Dole	5.9%	34.0%	48.1%	12.0%
SEVIER	7,648	1,124	1,748	3,966	810	Dole	14.7%	22.9%	51.9%	10.6%
SHELBY	44,747	3,244	12,212	24,650	4,641	Dole	7.2%	27.3%	55.1%	10.4%
SMITH	430	63	122	196	49	Dole	14.7%	28.4%	45.6%	11.4%
STEWART	384	71	105	167	41	Dole	18.5%	27.3%	43.5%	10.7%
SULLIVAN	8,901	970	1,868	4,763	1,300	Dole	10.9%	21.0%	53.5%	14.6%
SUMNER	4,900	434	1,279	2,445	742	Dole	8.9%	26.1%	49.9%	15.1%
TIPTON	2,674	304	864	1,284	222	Dole	11.4%	32.3%	48.0%	8.3%
TROUSDALE	178	29	49	84	16	Dole	16.3%	27.5%	47.2%	9.0%
UNICOI	3,094	822	575	1,341	356	Dole	26.6%	18.6%	43.3%	11.5%
UNION	1,148	92	363	612	81	Dole	8.0%	31.6%	53.3%	7.1%
VAN BUREN	138	12	56	58	12	Dole	8.7%	40.6%	42.0%	8.7%
WARREN	875	95	235	409	136	Dole	10.9%	26.9%	46.7%	15.5%
WASHINGTON	6,256	924	1,171	3,349	812	Dole	14.8%	18.7%	53.5%	13.0%
WAYNE	508	44	181	247	36	Dole	8.7%	35.6%	48.6%	7.1%
WEAKLEY	826	88	289	369	80	Dole	10.7%	35.0%	44.7%	9.7%
WHITE	551	57	202	225	67	Dole	10.3%	36.7%	40.8%	12.2%
WILLIAMSON	8,699	1,143	1,411	4,599	1,546	Dole	13.1%	16.2%	52.9%	17.8%
WILSON	3,472	338	915	1,670	549	Dole	9.7%	26.4%	48.1%	15.8%
TOTAL	289,386	32,742	72,928	148,063	35,653	Dole	11.3%	25.2%	51.2%	12.3%

TEXAS

Texas is the most populous state in the South, the second-most populous in the nation, and has been the anchor of Super Tuesday voting since 1988.

Befitting a state so large, Texas has a variety of racial and ideological divisions. But these are most apparent among the once-dominant Democrats. Within the fast-growing Republican Party, there is little evidence of a moderate wing; rather, there are gradations of conservatism.

That has been plainly visible since the Texas GOP's first presidential primary in 1964 produced 104,137 votes for Barry Goldwater and 6,207 for Nelson Rockefeller. Faced with a choice in 1976 between Ronald Reagan and President Gerald Ford, Texas Republicans spurned Ford and elected their entire complement of 100 delegates for Reagan.

Reagan won again in 1980, but his margin over George Bush in the primary was less than 20,000 votes out of more than 500,000 cast. Reagan swept most of the state, but Bush ran close by winning his home base of Harris County (Houston) with 63 percent of the vote.

In 1988 and 1992, Texas formed the cornerstone of a Bush sweep of the Super Tuesday South. It was not the "kinder, gentler" Bush that dominated the Texas primary both years, but the Bush with the ten-gallon hat and the oilman's swagger.

Both times Bush won his adopted home state with roughly two-thirds of the vote. That left little room for Bob Dole, who finished a poor third in Texas in 1988 behind Pat Robertson. Dole ran a distant second in most of the urban areas, but Robertson ran better in rural Texas, where he won a handful of counties.

Pat Buchanan did not find a much better toehold in the 1992 primary. He taunted the New England-born Bush as an "inauthentic" Texan and conservative. But Buchanan spent little time in the state and carried only two west Texas counties where the total vote was in the dozens. Buchanan carried a few more small counties in 1996, but he ran only slightly closer to Dole in the statewide tally than he had to Bush four years earlier.

The bigger story in 1996 was the turnout in the GOP presidential primary; it exceeded the Democrats for the first time ever. And it was more than just the absence of competition on the Democratic side that produced it, since the ballots of both parties also featured contests for the Senate and House. But the Republican electorate is still mainly in Texas's metropolitan areas. The Democratic constituency is more disparate—a coalition of south Texas Hispanics, east Texas "Bubbas," urban blacks and Austin liberals.

The Democratic mosaic was vividly on display in the party's 1988 presidential primary, which Michael Dukakis won with just one-third of the vote. Dukakis, who could speak fluent

Recent Texas Primary Results

Texas Republicans held a presidential primary in 1964. The first year both parties held a presidential primary with a direct vote for candidates was in 1980.

	DEMOCRATS			REPUBLICANS		
Year	Turnout	Candidates	%	Turnout	Candidates	%
1996 (March 12)	921,256	BILL CLINTON*	86	1,019,803	BOB DOLE	56
					Pat Buchanan	21
					Steve Forbes	13
1992 (March 10)	1,482,975	BILL CLINTON	66	797,146	GEORGE BUSH*	70
		Paul Tsongas	19		Pat Buchanan	24
1988 (March 8)	1,767,045	MICHAEL DUKAKIS	33	1,014,956	GEORGE BUSH	64
		Jesse Jackson	25		Pat Robertson	15
		Al Gore	20		Bob Dole	14
		Richard Gephardt	14			
1984 (May 5)	—	NO PRIMARY		319,839	RONALD REAGAN*	97
1980 (May 3)	1,377,354	JIMMY CARTER*	56	526,769	RONALD REAGAN	51
		Edward Kennedy	23		George Bush	47
		Uncommitted	19			

Note: All candidates are listed that drew at least 10 percent of their party's primary vote. The names of winning candidates are capitalized. An asterisk (*) indicates an incumbent president.

Spanish, won south Texas and the western panhandle, Bexar (San Antonio) and Travis (Austin) counties, and many of the suburbs around the major population centers.

Jesse Jackson won most of the other big population centers—Harris, Dallas and Tarrant (Fort Worth) counties—all with significant minority populations. Al Gore and Richard Gephardt split much of the heavily white eastern, central and northern portions of the state.

In the 1992 Democratic primary, Bill Clinton swept everything, but the turnout was down nearly 300,000 from 1988. It was one of many recent signs that the broad base of "yellow dog" Democrats across Texas (those who would vote Democratic even if it meant voting for a yellow dog) was eroding.

TEXAS DEMOCRATIC

1980

County	Total Vote	Brown	Carter	E. Kennedy	Uncommitted	Winner	Percentage of Total Vote Brown	Carter	E. Kennedy	Uncom.
ANDERSON	7,482	178	4,693	795	1,816	Carter	2.4%	62.7%	10.6%	24.3%
ANDREWS	2,135	69	1,235	201	630	Carter	3.2%	57.8%	9.4%	29.5%
ANGELINA	12,317	455	8,392	1,278	2,192	Carter	3.7%	68.1%	10.4%	17.8%
ARANSAS	2,734	96	1,400	498	740	Carter	3.5%	51.2%	18.2%	27.1%
ARCHER	1,877	52	1,193	191	441	Carter	2.8%	63.6%	10.2%	23.5%
ARMSTRONG	679	25	352	66	236	Carter	3.7%	51.8%	9.7%	34.8%
ATASCOSA	5,273	148	2,242	1,716	1,167	Carter	2.8%	42.5%	32.5%	22.1%
AUSTIN	1,931	71	1,012	321	527	Carter	3.7%	52.4%	16.6%	27.3%
BAILEY	1,368	50	647	179	492	Carter	3.7%	47.3%	13.1%	36.0%
BANDERA	1,692	67	877	192	556	Carter	4.0%	51.8%	11.3%	32.9%
BASTROP	5,271	175	3,031	868	1,197	Carter	3.3%	57.5%	16.5%	22.7%
BAYLOR	1,412	36	912	154	310	Carter	2.5%	64.6%	10.9%	22.0%
BEE	4,161	119	1,675	1,478	889	Carter	2.9%	40.3%	35.5%	21.4%
BELL	12,712	348	7,885	1,885	2,594	Carter	2.7%	62.0%	14.8%	20.4%
BEXAR	77,958	1,964	36,049	31,688	8,257	Carter	2.5%	46.2%	40.6%	10.6%
BLANCO	337	4	260	31	42	Carter	1.2%	77.2%	9.2%	12.5%
BORDEN	245	6	145	17	77	Carter	2.4%	59.2%	6.9%	31.4%
BOSQUE	3,027	59	1,879	253	836	Carter	1.9%	62.1%	8.4%	27.6%
BOWIE	12,361	383	7,724	1,609	2,645	Carter	3.1%	62.5%	13.0%	21.4%
BRAZORIA	18,937	705	11,225	2,472	4,535	Carter	3.7%	59.3%	13.1%	23.9%
BRAZOS	11,552	372	6,859	1,590	2,731	Carter	3.2%	59.4%	13.8%	23.6%
BREWSTER	1,865	58	849	500	458	Carter	3.1%	45.5%	26.8%	24.6%
BRISCOE	643	22	380	77	164	Carter	3.4%	59.1%	12.0%	25.5%
BROOKS	3,187	30	841	2,063	253	E. Kennedy	0.9%	26.4%	64.7%	7.9%
BROWN	6,606	175	4,293	626	1,512	Carter	2.6%	65.0%	9.5%	22.9%
BURLESON	3,123	79	1,844	659	541	Carter	2.5%	59.0%	21.1%	17.3%
BURNET	4,093	73	2,845	322	853	Carter	1.8%	69.5%	7.9%	20.8%
CALDWELL	2,619	46	1,462	713	398	Carter	1.8%	55.8%	27.2%	15.2%
CALHOUN	4,009	119	2,044	884	962	Carter	3.0%	51.0%	22.1%	24.0%
CALLAHAN	2,152	33	1,526	160	433	Carter	1.5%	70.9%	7.4%	20.1%
CAMERON	22,186	597	7,743	11,658	2,188	E. Kennedy	2.7%	34.9%	52.5%	9.9%
CAMP	2,323	65	1,495	312	451	Carter	2.8%	64.4%	13.4%	19.4%
CARSON	1,290	39	729	175	347	Carter	3.0%	56.5%	13.6%	26.9%
CASS	6,642	111	4,398	663	1,470	Carter	1.7%	66.2%	10.0%	22.1%
CASTRO	1,994	44	793	454	703	Carter	2.2%	39.8%	22.8%	35.3%
CHAMBERS	3,664	106	1,912	667	979	Carter	2.9%	52.2%	18.2%	26.7%
CHEROKEE	7,116	178	4,540	835	1,563	Carter	2.5%	63.8%	11.7%	22.0%
CHILDRESS	No Vote									
CLAY	2,273	54	1,600	191	428	Carter	2.4%	70.4%	8.4%	18.8%
COCHRAN	919	23	405	131	360	Carter	2.5%	44.1%	14.3%	39.2%
COKE	930	22	677	55	176	Carter	2.4%	72.8%	5.9%	18.9%
COLEMAN	1,633	40	1,095	111	387	Carter	2.4%	67.1%	6.8%	23.7%
COLLIN	6,426	175	4,611	737	903	Carter	2.7%	71.8%	11.5%	14.1%
COLLINGSWORTH	1,494	45	822	134	493	Carter	3.0%	55.0%	9.0%	33.0%
COLORADO	2,954	84	1,589	585	696	Carter	2.8%	53.8%	19.8%	23.6%
COMAL	2,890	86	1,751	552	501	Carter	3.0%	60.6%	19.1%	17.3%
COMANCHE	2,083	55	1,570	148	310	Carter	2.6%	75.4%	7.1%	14.9%
CONCHO	723	18	414	136	155	Carter	2.5%	57.3%	18.8%	21.4%
COOKE	6,377	193	3,551	591	2,042	Carter	3.0%	55.7%	9.3%	32.0%
CORYELL	3,913	83	2,424	473	933	Carter	2.1%	61.9%	12.1%	23.8%

TEXAS DEMOCRATIC

1980

County	Total Vote	Brown	Carter	E. Kennedy	Uncommitted	Winner	Percentage of Total Vote Brown	Carter	E. Kennedy	Uncom.
COTTLE	828	29	459	113	227	Carter	3.5%	55.4%	13.6%	27.4%
CRANE	1,486	37	768	200	481	Carter	2.5%	51.7%	13.5%	32.4%
CROCKETT	830	30	304	233	263	Carter	3.6%	36.6%	28.1%	31.7%
CROSBY	1,912	31	946	447	488	Carter	1.6%	49.5%	23.4%	25.5%
CULBERSON	757	17	292	297	151	E. Kennedy	2.2%	38.6%	39.2%	19.9%
DALLAM	1,021	42	447	152	380	Carter	4.1%	43.8%	14.9%	37.2%
DALLAS	59,298	1,273	39,337	13,514	5,174	Carter	2.1%	66.3%	22.8%	8.7%
DAWSON	2,499	65	1,206	353	875	Carter	2.6%	48.3%	14.1%	35.0%
DEAF SMITH	2,486	105	1,093	440	848	Carter	4.2%	44.0%	17.7%	34.1%
DELTA	1,588	50	985	212	341	Carter	3.1%	62.0%	13.4%	21.5%
DENTON	7,295	176	4,946	947	1,226	Carter	2.4%	67.8%	13.0%	16.8%
DE WITT	2,029	57	1,061	321	590	Carter	2.8%	52.3%	15.8%	29.1%
DICKENS	1,052	21	652	115	264	Carter	2.0%	62.0%	10.9%	25.1%
DIMMIT	2,730	55	815	1,481	379	E. Kennedy	2.0%	29.9%	54.2%	13.9%
DONLEY	1,274	45	700	110	419	Carter	3.5%	54.9%	8.6%	32.9%
DUVAL	4,423	56	1,065	3,001	301	E. Kennedy	1.3%	24.1%	67.8%	6.8%
EASTLAND	4,100	111	2,703	404	882	Carter	2.7%	65.9%	9.9%	21.5%
ECTOR	11,696	426	6,245	1,660	3,365	Carter	3.6%	53.4%	14.2%	28.8%
EDWARDS	706	17	304	158	227	Carter	2.4%	43.1%	22.4%	32.2%
ELLIS	7,135	141	4,585	868	1,541	Carter	2.0%	64.3%	12.2%	21.6%
EL PASO	28,354	689	12,497	10,463	4,705	Carter	2.4%	44.1%	36.9%	16.6%
ERATH	3,939	94	2,833	245	767	Carter	2.4%	71.9%	6.2%	19.5%
FALLS	4,022	117	2,214	707	984	Carter	2.9%	55.0%	17.6%	24.5%
FANNIN	4,300	116	3,007	424	753	Carter	2.7%	69.9%	9.9%	17.5%
FAYETTE	4,640	206	2,195	1,047	1,192	Carter	4.4%	47.3%	22.6%	25.7%
FISHER	1,469	25	947	198	299	Carter	1.7%	64.5%	13.5%	20.4%
FLOYD	1,051	28	612	105	306	Carter	2.7%	58.2%	10.0%	29.1%
FOARD	639	18	391	99	131	Carter	2.8%	61.2%	15.5%	20.5%
FORT BEND	7,464	260	3,788	1,748	1,668	Carter	3.5%	50.8%	23.4%	22.3%
FRANKLIN	1,464	31	1,068	121	244	Carter	2.1%	73.0%	8.3%	16.7%
FREESTONE	3,791	83	2,240	735	733	Carter	2.2%	59.1%	19.4%	19.3%
FRIO	3,240	52	1,014	1,534	640	E. Kennedy	1.6%	31.3%	47.3%	19.8%
GAINES	2,134	65	1,098	295	676	Carter	3.0%	51.5%	13.8%	31.7%
GALVESTON	18,257	809	10,605	4,088	2,755	Carter	4.4%	58.1%	22.4%	15.1%
GARZA	1,037	45	505	181	306	Carter	4.3%	48.7%	17.5%	29.5%
GILLESPIE	525	15	372	66	72	Carter	2.9%	70.9%	12.6%	13.7%
GLASSCOCK	123	3	58	13	49	Carter	2.4%	47.2%	10.6%	39.8%
GOLIAD	1,567	49	634	447	437	Carter	3.1%	40.5%	28.5%	27.9%
GONZALES	3,597	114	1,880	648	955	Carter	3.2%	52.3%	18.0%	26.5%
GRAY	2,508	76	1,676	194	562	Carter	3.0%	66.8%	7.7%	22.4%
GRAYSON	12,541	392	8,285	1,290	2,574	Carter	3.1%	66.1%	10.3%	20.5%
GREGG	10,121	333	6,570	1,327	1,891	Carter	3.3%	64.9%	13.1%	18.7%
GRIMES	2,132	36	1,371	335	390	Carter	1.7%	64.3%	15.7%	18.3%
GUADALUPE	5,600	239	2,737	1,205	1,419	Carter	4.3%	48.9%	21.5%	25.3%
HALE	3,467	86	2,015	457	909	Carter	2.5%	58.1%	13.2%	26.2%
HALL	1,608	40	820	178	570	Carter	2.5%	51.0%	11.1%	35.4%
HAMILTON	1,778	40	1,190	128	420	Carter	2.2%	66.9%	7.2%	23.6%
HANSFORD	1,474	80	732	189	473	Carter	5.4%	49.7%	12.8%	32.1%
HARDEMAN	1,684	39	1,054	195	396	Carter	2.3%	62.6%	11.6%	23.5%
HARDIN	9,591	253	6,013	1,169	2,156	Carter	2.6%	62.7%	12.2%	22.5%

TEXAS DEMOCRATIC

1980

County	Total Vote	Brown	Carter	E. Kennedy	Uncommitted	Winner	Percentage of Total Vote			
							Brown	Carter	E. Kennedy	Uncom.
HARRIS	90,702	1,901	53,444	25,079	10,278	Carter	2.1%	58.9%	27.6%	11.3%
HARRISON	6,577	190	4,443	849	1,095	Carter	2.9%	67.6%	12.9%	16.6%
HARTLEY	757	33	338	117	269	Carter	4.4%	44.6%	15.5%	35.5%
HASKELL	2,419	51	1,559	210	599	Carter	2.1%	64.4%	8.7%	24.8%
HAYS	6,050	178	3,109	1,482	1,281	Carter	2.9%	51.4%	24.5%	21.2%
HEMPHILL	761	29	441	57	234	Carter	3.8%	58.0%	7.5%	30.7%
HENDERSON	9,141	252	5,856	1,004	2,029	Carter	2.8%	64.1%	11.0%	22.2%
HIDALGO	33,224	642	9,965	19,787	2,830	E. Kennedy	1.9%	30.0%	59.6%	8.5%
HILL	5,265	104	3,264	621	1,276	Carter	2.0%	62.0%	11.8%	24.2%
HOCKLEY	3,143	110	1,639	387	1,007	Carter	3.5%	52.1%	12.3%	32.0%
HOOD	3,212	70	2,074	276	792	Carter	2.2%	64.6%	8.6%	24.7%
HOPKINS	3,820	86	2,640	440	654	Carter	2.3%	69.1%	11.5%	17.1%
HOUSTON	5,538	126	3,509	824	1,079	Carter	2.3%	63.4%	14.9%	19.5%
HOWARD	5,038	119	2,797	779	1,343	Carter	2.4%	55.5%	15.5%	26.7%
HUDSPETH	873	17	420	261	175	Carter	1.9%	48.1%	29.9%	20.0%
HUNT	7,154	169	4,783	718	1,484	Carter	2.4%	66.9%	10.0%	20.7%
HUTCHINSON	3,073	96	1,870	203	904	Carter	3.1%	60.9%	6.6%	29.4%
IRION	244	7	150	20	67	Carter	2.9%	61.5%	8.2%	27.5%
JACK	2,028	49	1,255	157	567	Carter	2.4%	61.9%	7.7%	28.0%
JACKSON	2,614	64	1,474	413	663	Carter	2.4%	56.4%	15.8%	25.4%
JASPER	5,222	124	3,482	655	961	Carter	2.4%	66.7%	12.5%	18.4%
JEFF DAVIS	591	22	245	156	168	Carter	3.7%	41.5%	26.4%	28.4%
JEFFERSON	26,414	657	15,546	5,371	4,840	Carter	2.5%	58.9%	20.3%	18.3%
JIM HOGG	2,319	30	662	1,388	239	E. Kennedy	1.3%	28.5%	59.9%	10.3%
JIM WELLS	9,593	140	2,870	5,084	1,499	E. Kennedy	1.5%	29.9%	53.0%	15.6%
JOHNSON	6,684	169	4,691	546	1,278	Carter	2.5%	70.2%	8.2%	19.1%
JONES	2,805	50	1,955	250	550	Carter	1.8%	69.7%	8.9%	19.6%
KARNES	3,617	117	1,504	1,037	959	Carter	3.2%	41.6%	28.7%	26.5%
KAUFMAN	5,244	118	3,468	604	1,054	Carter	2.3%	66.1%	11.5%	20.1%
KENDALL	568	13	257	43	255	Carter	2.3%	45.2%	7.6%	44.9%
KENEDY	149	2	55	82	10	E. Kennedy	1.3%	36.9%	55.0%	6.7%
KENT	570	12	345	51	162	Carter	2.1%	60.5%	8.9%	28.4%
KERR	1,935	32	1,318	280	305	Carter	1.7%	68.1%	14.5%	15.8%
KIMBLE	1,111	36	633	122	320	Carter	3.2%	57.0%	11.0%	28.8%
KING	206	9	68	27	102	Uncommitted	4.4%	33.0%	13.1%	49.5%
KINNEY	922	34	416	254	218	Carter	3.7%	45.1%	27.5%	23.6%
KLEBERG	5,621	165	2,206	2,430	820	E. Kennedy	2.9%	39.2%	43.2%	14.6%
KNOX	773	9	578	47	139	Carter	1.2%	74.8%	6.1%	18.0%
LAMAR	6,725	222	4,437	628	1,438	Carter	3.3%	66.0%	9.3%	21.4%
LAMB	1,841	47	998	265	531	Carter	2.6%	54.2%	14.4%	28.8%
LAMPASAS	1,480	21	1,008	135	316	Carter	1.4%	68.1%	9.1%	21.4%
LA SALLE	2,099	36	575	1,127	361	E. Kennedy	1.7%	27.4%	53.7%	17.2%
LAVACA	3,383	117	1,864	689	713	Carter	3.5%	55.1%	20.4%	21.1%
LEE	1,604	50	1,009	205	340	Carter	3.1%	62.9%	12.8%	21.2%
LEON	2,448	36	1,689	251	472	Carter	1.5%	69.0%	10.3%	19.3%
LIBERTY	5,791	155	3,600	867	1,169	Carter	2.7%	62.2%	15.0%	20.2%
LIMESTONE	4,195	115	2,502	508	1,070	Carter	2.7%	59.6%	12.1%	25.5%
LIPSCOMB	1,126	73	538	138	377	Carter	6.5%	47.8%	12.3%	33.5%
LIVE OAK	2,217	136	1,320	675	86	Carter	6.1%	59.5%	30.4%	3.9%
LLANO	2,067	38	1,500	158	371	Carter	1.8%	72.6%	7.6%	17.9%

TEXAS DEMOCRATIC

1980

County	Total Vote	Brown	Carter	E. Kennedy	Uncommitted	Winner	Percentage of Total Vote Brown	Carter	E. Kennedy	Uncom.
LOVING	39	4	16	6	13	Carter	10.3%	41.0%	15.4%	33.3%
LUBBOCK	12,860	336	7,122	2,476	2,926	Carter	2.6%	55.4%	19.3%	22.8%
LYNN	1,860	65	960	277	558	Carter	3.5%	51.6%	14.9%	30.0%
MCCULLOCH	2,160	53	1,396	249	462	Carter	2.5%	64.6%	11.5%	21.4%
MCLENNAN	20,868	367	12,609	2,953	4,939	Carter	1.8%	60.4%	14.2%	23.7%
MCMULLEN	194	7	95	22	70	Carter	3.6%	49.0%	11.3%	36.1%
MADISON	2,039	31	1,445	235	328	Carter	1.5%	70.9%	11.5%	16.1%
MARION	1,979	37	1,131	360	451	Carter	1.9%	57.2%	18.2%	22.8%
MARTIN	1,157	23	618	181	335	Carter	2.0%	53.4%	15.6%	29.0%
MASON	358	4	287	31	36	Carter	1.1%	80.2%	8.7%	10.1%
MATAGORDA	4,867	145	2,585	921	1,216	Carter	3.0%	53.1%	18.9%	25.0%
MAVERICK	3,361	51	1,166	1,772	372	E. Kennedy	1.5%	34.7%	52.7%	11.1%
MEDINA	3,420	111	1,635	835	839	Carter	3.2%	47.8%	24.4%	24.5%
MENARD	429	3	267	48	111	Carter	0.7%	62.2%	11.2%	25.9%
MIDLAND	3,653	94	2,420	517	622	Carter	2.6%	66.2%	14.2%	17.0%
MILAM	3,689	83	2,206	630	770	Carter	2.2%	59.8%	17.1%	20.9%
MILLS	1,537	37	993	117	390	Carter	2.4%	64.6%	7.6%	25.4%
MITCHELL	2,116	52	1,353	224	487	Carter	2.5%	63.9%	10.6%	23.0%
MONTAGUE	2,745	2	2,203	279	261	Carter	0.1%	80.3%	10.2%	9.5%
MONTGOMERY	14,055	408	8,249	1,867	3,531	Carter	2.9%	58.7%	13.3%	25.1%
MOORE	3,734	160	1,845	417	1,312	Carter	4.3%	49.4%	11.2%	35.1%
MORRIS	3,412	63	2,275	380	694	Carter	1.8%	66.7%	11.1%	20.3%
MOTLEY	625	19	303	63	240	Carter	3.0%	48.5%	10.1%	38.4%
NACOGDOCHES	6,647	238	4,325	759	1,325	Carter	3.6%	65.1%	11.4%	19.9%
NAVARRO	6,399	144	4,336	673	1,246	Carter	2.3%	67.8%	10.5%	19.5%
NEWTON	3,176	68	1,979	540	589	Carter	2.1%	62.3%	17.0%	18.5%
NOLAN	3,092	63	2,001	352	676	Carter	2.0%	64.7%	11.4%	21.9%
NUECES	44,099	1,130	17,176	18,730	7,063	E. Kennedy	2.6%	38.9%	42.5%	16.0%
OCHILTREE	1,505	76	675	126	628	Carter	5.0%	44.9%	8.4%	41.7%
OLDHAM	461	13	268	34	146	Carter	2.8%	58.1%	7.4%	31.7%
ORANGE	10,362	265	6,700	1,272	2,125	Carter	2.6%	64.7%	12.3%	20.5%
PALO PINTO	3,665	92	2,324	386	863	Carter	2.5%	63.4%	10.5%	23.5%
PANOLA	4,713	113	2,939	393	1,268	Carter	2.4%	62.4%	8.3%	26.9%
PARKER	6,089	118	4,276	510	1,185	Carter	1.9%	70.2%	8.4%	19.5%
PARMER	1,315	49	554	131	581	Uncommitted	3.7%	42.1%	10.0%	44.2%
PECOS	2,885	84	1,337	787	677	Carter	2.9%	46.3%	27.3%	23.5%
POLK	4,735	117	2,952	613	1,053	Carter	2.5%	62.3%	12.9%	22.2%
POTTER	9,935	348	5,736	1,420	2,431	Carter	3.5%	57.7%	14.3%	24.5%
PRESIDIO	1,746	57	717	654	318	Carter	3.3%	41.1%	37.5%	18.2%
RAINS	1,315	28	925	145	217	Carter	2.1%	70.3%	11.0%	16.5%
RANDALL	5,561	149	3,525	588	1,299	Carter	2.7%	63.4%	10.6%	23.4%
REAGAN	971	27	469	129	346	Carter	2.8%	48.3%	13.3%	35.6%
REAL	911	32	486	154	239	Carter	3.5%	53.3%	16.9%	26.2%
RED RIVER	3,704	69	2,439	436	760	Carter	1.9%	65.8%	11.8%	20.5%
REEVES	3,702	80	1,451	1,450	721	Carter	2.2%	39.2%	39.2%	19.5%
REFUGIO	3,026	55	1,425	846	700	Carter	1.8%	47.1%	28.0%	23.1%
ROBERTS	424	15	198	41	170	Carter	3.5%	46.7%	9.7%	40.1%
ROBERTSON	3,964	67	2,520	709	668	Carter	1.7%	63.6%	17.9%	16.9%
ROCKWALL	No Vote									
RUNNELS	2,227	47	1,235	260	685	Carter	2.1%	55.5%	11.7%	30.8%

TEXAS DEMOCRATIC

1980

County	Total Vote	Brown	Carter	E. Kennedy	Uncommitted	Winner	Percentage of Total Vote Brown	Carter	E. Kennedy	Uncom.
RUSK	5,962	234	3,909	648	1,171	Carter	3.9%	65.6%	10.9%	19.6%
SABINE	2,137	49	1,380	357	351	Carter	2.3%	64.6%	16.7%	16.4%
SAN AUGUSTINE	2,244	53	1,368	343	480	Carter	2.4%	61.0%	15.3%	21.4%
SAN JACINTO	3,125	84	1,848	582	611	Carter	2.7%	59.1%	18.6%	19.6%
SAN PATRICIO	9,752	263	3,950	4,018	1,521	E. Kennedy	2.7%	40.5%	41.2%	15.6%
SAN SABA	1,437	31	1,044	129	233	Carter	2.2%	72.7%	9.0%	16.2%
SCHLEICHER	681	18	401	56	206	Carter	2.6%	58.9%	8.2%	30.2%
SCURRY	3,269	139	1,974	251	905	Carter	4.3%	60.4%	7.7%	27.7%
SHACKELFORD	820	20	487	85	228	Carter	2.4%	59.4%	10.4%	27.8%
SHELBY	6,540	190	3,877	766	1,707	Carter	2.9%	59.3%	11.7%	26.1%
SHERMAN	290	8	136	26	120	Carter	2.8%	46.9%	9.0%	41.4%
SMITH	9,881	201	6,940	1,306	1,434	Carter	2.0%	70.2%	13.2%	14.5%
SOMERVELL	1,202	27	772	145	258	Carter	2.2%	64.2%	12.1%	21.5%
STARR	5,440	65	1,320	3,895	160	E. Kennedy	1.2%	24.3%	71.6%	2.9%
STEPHENS	2,127	25	1,246	236	620	Carter	1.2%	58.6%	11.1%	29.1%
STERLING	456		276	41	139	Carter		60.5%	9.0%	30.5%
STONEWALL	818	25	570	104	119	Carter	3.1%	69.7%	12.7%	14.5%
SUTTON	500	14	232	83	171	Carter	2.8%	46.4%	16.6%	34.2%
SWISHER	1,480	28	915	205	332	Carter	1.9%	61.8%	13.9%	22.4%
TARRANT	43,044	964	29,370	7,234	5,476	Carter	2.2%	68.2%	16.8%	12.7%
TAYLOR	11,062	251	7,446	943	2,422	Carter	2.3%	67.3%	8.5%	21.9%
TERRELL	318	7	151	57	103	Carter	2.2%	47.5%	17.9%	32.4%
TERRY	2,669	68	1,285	390	926	Carter	2.5%	48.1%	14.6%	34.7%
THROCKMORTON	307	2	228	22	55	Carter	0.7%	74.3%	7.2%	17.9%
TITUS	3,493	95	2,453	367	578	Carter	2.7%	70.2%	10.5%	16.5%
TOM GREEN	7,720	235	4,584	1,029	1,872	Carter	3.0%	59.4%	13.3%	24.2%
TRAVIS	51,412	1,644	28,365	11,115	10,288	Carter	3.2%	55.2%	21.6%	20.0%
TRINITY	3,191	58	1,961	535	637	Carter	1.8%	61.5%	16.8%	20.0%
TYLER	4,753	92	3,356	507	798	Carter	1.9%	70.6%	10.7%	16.8%
UPSHUR	5,494	94	3,666	581	1,153	Carter	1.7%	66.7%	10.6%	21.0%
UPTON	1,361	39	614	230	478	Carter	2.9%	45.1%	16.9%	35.1%
UVALDE	2,435	64	1,220	592	559	Carter	2.6%	50.1%	24.3%	23.0%
VAL VERDE	5,175	129	1,816	1,817	1,413	E. Kennedy	2.5%	35.1%	35.1%	27.3%
VAN ZANDT	4,904	120	3,541	412	831	Carter	2.4%	72.2%	8.4%	16.9%
VICTORIA	6,470	198	3,217	1,361	1,694	Carter	3.1%	49.7%	21.0%	26.2%
WALKER	5,991	163	3,370	1,064	1,394	Carter	2.7%	56.3%	17.8%	23.3%
WALLER	3,055	101	1,657	613	684	Carter	3.3%	54.2%	20.1%	22.4%
WARD	3,187	114	1,571	503	999	Carter	3.6%	49.3%	15.8%	31.3%
WASHINGTON	3,956	131	1,962	590	1,273	Carter	3.3%	49.6%	14.9%	32.2%
WEBB	12,810	206	4,516	7,242	846	E. Kennedy	1.6%	35.3%	56.5%	6.6%
WHARTON	7,655	219	3,783	1,444	2,209	Carter	2.9%	49.4%	18.9%	28.9%
WHEELER	1,045	26	703	80	236	Carter	2.5%	67.3%	7.7%	22.6%
WICHITA	12,521	283	8,281	1,365	2,592	Carter	2.3%	66.1%	10.9%	20.7%
WILBARGER	2,420	42	1,555	221	602	Carter	1.7%	64.3%	9.1%	24.9%
WILLACY	4,633	107	1,545	2,487	494	E. Kennedy	2.3%	33.3%	53.7%	10.7%
WILLIAMSON	6,248	144	3,995	1,010	1,099	Carter	2.3%	63.9%	16.2%	17.6%
WILSON	4,286	129	1,938	1,307	912	Carter	3.0%	45.2%	30.5%	21.3%
WINKLER	2,165	48	1,208	244	665	Carter	2.2%	55.8%	11.3%	30.7%
WISE	4,503	97	3,144	420	842	Carter	2.2%	69.8%	9.3%	18.7%
WOOD	2,223	37	1,725	198	263	Carter	1.7%	77.6%	8.9%	11.8%

TEXAS DEMOCRATIC

1980

County	Total Vote	Brown	Carter	E. Kennedy	Uncommitted	Winner	Percentage of Total Vote Brown	Carter	E. Kennedy	Uncom.
YOAKUM	1,660	56	734	165	705	Carter	3.4%	44.2%	9.9%	42.5%
YOUNG	3,095	70	1,894	261	870	Carter	2.3%	61.2%	8.4%	28.1%
ZAPATA	2,125	33	663	1,173	256	E. Kennedy	1.6%	31.2%	55.2%	12.0%
ZAVALA	2,220	16	488	1,568	148	E. Kennedy	0.7%	22.0%	70.6%	6.7%
TOTAL	1,377,356	35,585	770,390	314,129	257,252	Carter	2.6%	55.9%	22.8%	18.7%
Published Totals	1,377,354	35,585	770,390	314,129	257,250	Carter	2.6%	55.9%	22.8%	18.7%

TEXAS REPUBLICAN

1980

County	Total Vote	Bush	Reagan	Uncommitted	Winner	Percentage of Total Vote Bush	Reagan	Uncom.
ANDERSON	218	79	135	4	Reagan	36.2%	61.9%	1.8%
ANDREWS	173	33	138	2	Reagan	19.1%	79.8%	1.2%
ANGELINA	599	236	351	12	Reagan	39.4%	58.6%	2.0%
ARANSAS	537	167	352	18	Reagan	31.1%	65.5%	3.4%
ARCHER	73	25	47	1	Reagan	34.2%	64.4%	1.4%
ARMSTRONG	49	14	35		Reagan	28.6%	71.4%	
ATASCOSA	174	50	122	2	Reagan	28.7%	70.1%	1.1%
AUSTIN	447	209	238		Reagan	46.8%	53.2%	
BAILEY	167	11	154	2	Reagan	6.6%	92.2%	1.2%
BANDERA	278	65	210	3	Reagan	23.4%	75.5%	1.1%
BASTROP	269	125	139	5	Reagan	46.5%	51.7%	1.9%
BAYLOR	No Vote							
BEE	290	84	206		Reagan	29.0%	71.0%	
BELL	2,304	914	1,334	56	Reagan	39.7%	57.9%	2.4%
BEXAR	40,013	16,587	22,909	517	Reagan	41.5%	57.3%	1.3%
BLANCO	165	46	116	3	Reagan	27.9%	70.3%	1.8%
BORDEN	14	2	12		Reagan	14.3%	85.7%	
BOSQUE	286	55	227	4	Reagan	19.2%	79.4%	1.4%
BOWIE	1,475	174	1,284	17	Reagan	11.8%	87.1%	1.2%
BRAZORIA	4,254	2,281	1,914	59	Bush	53.6%	45.0%	1.4%
BRAZOS	2,073	1,228	795	50	Bush	59.2%	38.4%	2.4%
BREWSTER	149	56	91	2	Reagan	37.6%	61.1%	1.3%
BRISCOE	28	1	27		Reagan	3.6%	96.4%	
BROOKS	No Vote							
BROWN	274	69	204	1	Reagan	25.2%	74.5%	0.4%
BURLESON	71	19	51	1	Reagan	26.8%	71.8%	1.4%
BURNET	555	248	296	11	Reagan	44.7%	53.3%	2.0%
CALDWELL	334	119	213	2	Reagan	35.6%	63.8%	0.6%
CALHOUN	239	142	85	12	Bush	59.4%	35.6%	5.0%
CALLAHAN	138	31	106	1	Reagan	22.5%	76.8%	0.7%

TEXAS REPUBLICAN

1980

County	Total Vote	Bush	Reagan	Uncommitted	Winner	Percentage of Total Vote Bush	Reagan	Uncom.
CAMERON	2,834	707	2,092	35	Reagan	24.9%	73.8%	1.2%
CAMP	46	8	38		Reagan	17.4%	82.6%	
CARSON	242	27	213	2	Reagan	11.2%	88.0%	0.8%
CASS	247	32	206	9	Reagan	13.0%	83.4%	3.6%
CASTRO	192	16	175	1	Reagan	8.3%	91.1%	0.5%
CHAMBERS	155	62	90	3	Reagan	40.0%	58.1%	1.9%
CHEROKEE	314	95	187	32	Reagan	30.3%	59.6%	10.2%
CHILDRESS	64	9	55		Reagan	14.1%	85.9%	
CLAY	72	17	54	1	Reagan	23.6%	75.0%	1.4%
COCHRAN	17	3	14		Reagan	17.6%	82.4%	
COKE	71	8	62	1	Reagan	11.3%	87.3%	1.4%
COLEMAN	170	28	142		Reagan	16.5%	83.5%	
COLLIN	9,431	4,520	4,733	178	Reagan	47.9%	50.2%	1.9%
COLLINGSWORTH	23	1	22		Reagan	4.3%	95.7%	
COLORADO	365	181	184		Reagan	49.6%	50.4%	
COMAL	2,666	1,027	1,610	29	Reagan	38.5%	60.4%	1.1%
COMANCHE	125	41	84		Reagan	32.8%	67.2%	
CONCHO	126	15	102	9	Reagan	11.9%	81.0%	7.1%
COOKE	273	95	178		Reagan	34.8%	65.2%	
CORYELL	739	316	418	5	Reagan	42.8%	56.6%	0.7%
COTTLE	No Vote							
CRANE	44	7	37		Reagan	15.9%	84.1%	
CROCKETT	37	5	21	11	Reagan	13.5%	56.8%	29.7%
CROSBY	36	11	25		Reagan	30.6%	69.4%	
CULBERSON	43	16	23	4	Reagan	37.2%	53.5%	9.3%
DALLAM	133	10	122	1	Reagan	7.5%	91.7%	0.8%
DALLAS	111,316	53,802	55,209	2,305	Reagan	48.3%	49.6%	2.1%
DAWSON	199	52	146	1	Reagan	26.1%	73.4%	0.5%
DEAF SMITH	342	34	308		Reagan	9.9%	90.1%	
DELTA	25	8	17		Reagan	32.0%	68.0%	
DENTON	6,489	2,842	3,516	131	Reagan	43.8%	54.2%	2.0%
DE WITT	384	147	232	5	Reagan	38.3%	60.4%	1.3%
DICKENS	14	6	8		Reagan	42.9%	57.1%	
DIMMIT	59	13	46		Reagan	22.0%	78.0%	
DONLEY	47	8	36	3	Reagan	17.0%	76.6%	6.4%
DUVAL	No Vote							
EASTLAND	214	47	167		Reagan	22.0%	78.0%	
ECTOR	6,158	1,119	4,870	169	Reagan	18.2%	79.1%	2.7%
EDWARDS	5	2	3		Reagan	40.0%	60.0%	
ELLIS	1,011	353	646	12	Reagan	34.9%	63.9%	1.2%
EL PASO	9,806	3,567	5,996	243	Reagan	36.4%	61.1%	2.5%
ERATH	395	130	263	2	Reagan	32.9%	66.6%	0.5%
FALLS	79	14	63	2	Reagan	17.7%	79.7%	2.5%
FANNIN	232	58	171	3	Reagan	25.0%	73.7%	1.3%
FAYETTE	255	105	146	4	Reagan	41.2%	57.3%	1.6%
FISHER	No Vote							
FLOYD	161	34	126	1	Reagan	21.1%	78.3%	0.6%
FOARD	24	6	17	1	Reagan	25.0%	70.8%	4.2%
FORT BEND	5,958	3,604	2,305	49	Bush	60.5%	38.7%	0.8%
FRANKLIN	69	15	54		Reagan	21.7%	78.3%	

TEXAS REPUBLICAN

1980

County	Total Vote	Bush	Reagan	Uncommitted	Winner	Percentage of Total Vote Bush	Reagan	Uncom.
FREESTONE	110	22	88		Reagan	20.0%	80.0%	
FRIO	68	19	47	2	Reagan	27.9%	69.1%	2.9%
GAINES	82	15	64	3	Reagan	18.3%	78.0%	3.7%
GALVESTON	5,474	2,892	2,508	74	Bush	52.8%	45.8%	1.4%
GARZA	28	11	16	1	Reagan	39.3%	57.1%	3.6%
GILLESPIE	1,268	441	801	26	Reagan	34.8%	63.2%	2.1%
GLASSCOCK	105	9	96		Reagan	8.6%	91.4%	
GOLIAD	No Vote							
GONZALES	111	38	73		Reagan	34.2%	65.8%	
GRAY	1,159	148	997	14	Reagan	12.8%	86.0%	1.2%
GRAYSON	1,442	512	899	31	Reagan	35.5%	62.3%	2.1%
GREGG	4,612	994	3,525	93	Reagan	21.6%	76.4%	2.0%
GRIMES	227	121	104	2	Bush	53.3%	45.8%	0.9%
GUADALUPE	1,279	500	750	29	Reagan	39.1%	58.6%	2.3%
HALE	1,027	214	796	17	Reagan	20.8%	77.5%	1.7%
HALL	No Vote							
HAMILTON	114	38	75	1	Reagan	33.3%	65.8%	0.9%
HANSFORD	126	10	113	3	Reagan	7.9%	89.7%	2.4%
HARDEMAN	28	10	17	1	Reagan	35.7%	60.7%	3.6%
HARDIN	238	61	176	1	Reagan	25.6%	73.9%	0.4%
HARRIS	131,488	82,480	47,703	1,305	Bush	62.7%	36.3%	1.0%
HARRISON	527	111	410	6	Reagan	21.1%	77.8%	1.1%
HARTLEY	155	22	125	8	Reagan	14.2%	80.6%	5.2%
HASKELL	No Vote							
HAYS	929	483	424	22	Bush	52.0%	45.6%	2.4%
HEMPHILL	120	27	92	1	Reagan	22.5%	76.7%	0.8%
HENDERSON	806	257	535	14	Reagan	31.9%	66.4%	1.7%
HIDALGO	3,708	890	2,813	5	Reagan	24.0%	75.9%	0.1%
HILL	248	79	169		Reagan	31.9%	68.1%	
HOCKLEY	159	23	136		Reagan	14.5%	85.5%	
HOOD	624	252	364	8	Reagan	40.4%	58.3%	1.3%
HOPKINS	255	79	174	2	Reagan	31.0%	68.2%	0.8%
HOUSTON	99	42	55	2	Reagan	42.4%	55.6%	2.0%
HOWARD	626	108	507	11	Reagan	17.3%	81.0%	1.8%
HUDSPETH	27	4	23		Reagan	14.8%	85.2%	
HUNT	1,028	385	625	18	Reagan	37.5%	60.8%	1.8%
HUTCHINSON	917	110	792	15	Reagan	12.0%	86.4%	1.6%
IRION	69	26	43		Reagan	37.7%	62.3%	
JACK	39	12	27		Reagan	30.8%	69.2%	
JACKSON	117	43	73	1	Reagan	36.8%	62.4%	0.9%
JASPER	224	84	140		Reagan	37.5%	62.5%	
JEFF DAVIS	No Vote							
JEFFERSON	3,402	1,215	2,137	50	Reagan	35.7%	62.8%	1.5%
JIM HOGG	8	3	5		Reagan	37.5%	62.5%	
JIM WELLS	237	63	170	4	Reagan	26.6%	71.7%	1.7%
JOHNSON	1,787	616	1,147	24	Reagan	34.5%	64.2%	1.3%
JONES	208	44	161	3	Reagan	21.2%	77.4%	1.4%
KARNES	82	38	44		Reagan	46.3%	53.7%	
KAUFMAN	592	218	365	9	Reagan	36.8%	61.7%	1.5%
KENDALL	1,313	411	865	37	Reagan	31.3%	65.9%	2.8%

TEXAS REPUBLICAN

1980

County	Total Vote	Bush	Reagan	Uncommitted	Winner	Percentage of Total Vote Bush	Reagan	Uncom.
KENEDY	9	5	4		Bush	55.6%	44.4%	
KENT	No Vote							
KERR	4,082	1,362	2,599	121	Reagan	33.4%	63.7%	3.0%
KIMBLE	No Vote							
KING	No Vote							
KINNEY	No Vote							
KLEBERG	366	141	218	7	Reagan	38.5%	59.6%	1.9%
KNOX	56	13	43		Reagan	23.2%	76.8%	
LAMAR	463	181	276	6	Reagan	39.1%	59.6%	1.3%
LAMB	309	45	261	3	Reagan	14.6%	84.5%	1.0%
LAMPASAS	217	74	139	4	Reagan	34.1%	64.1%	1.8%
LA SALLE	1		1		Reagan		100.0%	
LAVACA	207	60	146	1	Reagan	29.0%	70.5%	0.5%
LEE	121	59	60	2	Reagan	48.8%	49.6%	1.7%
LEON	18	4	14		Reagan	22.2%	77.8%	
LIBERTY	581	267	310	4	Reagan	46.0%	53.4%	0.7%
LIMESTONE	136	37	98	1	Reagan	27.2%	72.1%	0.7%
LIPSCOMB	22	2	17	3	Reagan	9.1%	77.3%	13.6%
LIVE OAK	94	24	69	1	Reagan	25.5%	73.4%	1.1%
LLANO	683	326	348	9	Reagan	47.7%	51.0%	1.3%
LOVING	8	1	6	1	Reagan	12.5%	75.0%	12.5%
LUBBOCK	7,301	2,249	4,935	117	Reagan	30.8%	67.6%	1.6%
LYNN	28	9	19		Reagan	32.1%	67.9%	
MCCULLOCH	126	38	87	1	Reagan	30.2%	69.0%	0.8%
MCLENNAN	4,918	1,695	3,136	87	Reagan	34.5%	63.8%	1.8%
MCMULLEN	26	11	14	1	Reagan	42.3%	53.8%	3.8%
MADISON	81	25	56		Reagan	30.9%	69.1%	
MARION	72	10	61	1	Reagan	13.9%	84.7%	1.4%
MARTIN	68	12	54	2	Reagan	17.6%	79.4%	2.9%
MASON	308	89	218	1	Reagan	28.9%	70.8%	0.3%
MATAGORDA	559	240	315	4	Reagan	42.9%	56.4%	0.7%
MAVERICK	19	2	16	1	Reagan	10.5%	84.2%	5.3%
MEDINA	291	50	241		Reagan	17.2%	82.8%	
MENARD	80	38	41	1	Reagan	47.5%	51.3%	1.3%
MIDLAND	8,009	3,173	4,753	83	Reagan	39.6%	59.3%	1.0%
MILAM	159	61	97	1	Reagan	38.4%	61.0%	0.6%
MILLS	No Vote							
MITCHELL	44	17	26	1	Reagan	38.6%	59.1%	2.3%
MONTAGUE	105	44	61		Reagan	41.9%	58.1%	
MONTGOMERY	4,890	2,437	2,381	72	Bush	49.8%	48.7%	1.5%
MOORE	187	36	145	6	Reagan	19.3%	77.5%	3.2%
MORRIS	113	22	86	5	Reagan	19.5%	76.1%	4.4%
MOTLEY	24	1	23		Reagan	4.2%	95.8%	
NACOGDOCHES	781	269	495	17	Reagan	34.4%	63.4%	2.2%
NAVARRO	1,009	809	192	8	Bush	80.2%	19.0%	0.8%
NEWTON	No Vote							
NOLAN	203	75	125	3	Reagan	36.9%	61.6%	1.5%
NUECES	5,551	1,831	3,549	171	Reagan	33.0%	63.9%	3.1%
OCHILTREE	214	15	196	3	Reagan	7.0%	91.6%	1.4%
OLDHAM	15	1	14		Reagan	6.7%	93.3%	

TEXAS REPUBLICAN

1980

County	Total Vote	Bush	Reagan	Uncommitted	Winner	Percentage of Total Vote Bush	Reagan	Uncom.
ORANGE	805	318	476	11	Reagan	39.5%	59.1%	1.4%
PALO PINTO	443	186	247	10	Reagan	42.0%	55.8%	2.3%
PANOLA	126	13	111	2	Reagan	10.3%	88.1%	1.6%
PARKER	1,332	471	850	11	Reagan	35.4%	63.8%	0.8%
PARMER	326	16	308	2	Reagan	4.9%	94.5%	0.6%
PECOS	170	38	128	4	Reagan	22.4%	75.3%	2.4%
POLK	248	91	152	5	Reagan	36.7%	61.3%	2.0%
POTTER	2,323	399	1,861	63	Reagan	17.2%	80.1%	2.7%
PRESIDIO	18		18		Reagan		100.0%	
RAINS	33	18	15		Bush	54.5%	45.5%	
RANDALL	4,665	890	3,687	88	Reagan	19.1%	79.0%	1.9%
REAGAN	No Vote							
REAL	33	8	23	2	Reagan	24.2%	69.7%	6.1%
RED RIVER	50	19	31		Reagan	38.0%	62.0%	
REEVES	89	14	73	2	Reagan	15.7%	82.0%	2.2%
REFUGIO	74	35	38	1	Reagan	47.3%	51.4%	1.4%
ROBERTS	42	5	37		Reagan	11.9%	88.1%	
ROBERTSON	28	6	22		Reagan	21.4%	78.6%	
ROCKWALL	801	312	474	15	Reagan	39.0%	59.2%	1.9%
RUNNELS	159	42	116	1	Reagan	26.4%	73.0%	0.6%
RUSK	798	157	627	14	Reagan	19.7%	78.6%	1.8%
SABINE	60	19	41		Reagan	31.7%	68.3%	
SAN AUGUSTINE	No Vote							
SAN JACINTO	77	30	47		Reagan	39.0%	61.0%	
SAN PATRICIO	770	249	506	15	Reagan	32.3%	65.7%	1.9%
SAN SABA	48	28	20		Bush	58.3%	41.7%	
SCHLEICHER	No Vote							
SCURRY	183	51	127	5	Reagan	27.9%	69.4%	2.7%
SHACKELFORD	73	27	46		Reagan	37.0%	63.0%	
SHELBY	No Vote							
SHERMAN	95	7	84	4	Reagan	7.4%	88.4%	4.2%
SMITH	6,730	1,612	5,063	55	Reagan	24.0%	75.2%	0.8%
SOMERVELL	33	14	18	1	Reagan	42.4%	54.5%	3.0%
STARR	34	11	23		Reagan	32.4%	67.6%	
STEPHENS	104	32	71	1	Reagan	30.8%	68.3%	1.0%
STERLING	25	4	19	2	Reagan	16.0%	76.0%	8.0%
STONEWALL	No Vote							
SUTTON	64	27	36	1	Reagan	42.2%	56.3%	1.6%
SWISHER	139	17	120	2	Reagan	12.2%	86.3%	1.4%
TARRANT	41,768	19,745	21,547	476	Reagan	47.3%	51.6%	1.1%
TAYLOR	2,108	895	1,161	52	Reagan	42.5%	55.1%	2.5%
TERRELL	13	2	11		Reagan	15.4%	84.6%	
TERRY	194	49	141	4	Reagan	25.3%	72.7%	2.1%
THROCKMORTON	35	15	20		Reagan	42.9%	57.1%	
TITUS	192	67	122	3	Reagan	34.9%	63.5%	1.6%
TOM GREEN	3,177	1,219	1,868	90	Reagan	38.4%	58.8%	2.8%
TRAVIS	17,252	11,135	5,837	280	Bush	64.5%	33.8%	1.6%
TRINITY	47	23	22	2	Bush	48.9%	46.8%	4.3%
TYLER	89	31	58		Reagan	34.8%	65.2%	
UPSHUR	220	31	187	2	Reagan	14.1%	85.0%	0.9%

TEXAS REPUBLICAN

1980

County	Total Vote	Bush	Reagan	Uncommitted	Winner	Percentage of Total Vote		
						Bush	Reagan	Uncom.
UPTON	No Vote							
UVALDE	361	101	257	3	Reagan	28.0%	71.2%	0.8%
VAL VERDE	345	99	228	18	Reagan	28.7%	66.1%	5.2%
VAN ZANDT	715	184	524	7	Reagan	25.7%	73.3%	1.0%
VICTORIA	1,512	665	828	19	Reagan	44.0%	54.8%	1.3%
WALKER	529	289	231	9	Bush	54.6%	43.7%	1.7%
WALLER	370	167	195	8	Reagan	45.1%	52.7%	2.2%
WARD	233	27	199	7	Reagan	11.6%	85.4%	3.0%
WASHINGTON	346	193	151	2	Bush	55.8%	43.6%	0.6%
WEBB	289	119	164	6	Reagan	41.2%	56.7%	2.1%
WHARTON	437	186	247	4	Reagan	42.6%	56.5%	0.9%
WHEELER	129	10	119		Reagan	7.8%	92.2%	
WICHITA	3,024	1,237	1,690	97	Reagan	40.9%	55.9%	3.2%
WILBARGER	301	104	187	10	Reagan	34.6%	62.1%	3.3%
WILLACY	41	8	33		Reagan	19.5%	80.5%	
WILLIAMSON	2,660	1,573	1,046	41	Bush	59.1%	39.3%	1.5%
WILSON	265	57	206	2	Reagan	21.5%	77.7%	0.8%
WINKLER	151	17	130	4	Reagan	11.3%	86.1%	2.6%
WISE	353	128	222	3	Reagan	36.3%	62.9%	0.8%
WOOD	735	181	543	11	Reagan	24.6%	73.9%	1.5%
YOAKUM	No Vote							
YOUNG	388	155	227	6	Reagan	39.9%	58.5%	1.5%
ZAPATA	No Vote							
ZAVALA	24	8	16		Reagan	33.3%	66.7%	
TOTAL	526,500	250,219	268,169	8,112	Reagan	47.5%	50.9%	1.5%
Published Totals	526,769	249,819	268,798	8,152	Reagan	47.4%	51.0%	1.5%

TEXAS REPUBLICAN

1984

County	Total Vote	Reagan	Uncommitted	Winner	Percentage of Total Vote	
					Reagan	Uncom.
ANDERSON	391	378	13	Reagan	96.7%	3.3%
ANDREWS	85	84	1	Reagan	98.8%	1.2%
ANGELINA	548	548		Reagan	100.0%	
ARANSAS	592	566	26	Reagan	95.6%	4.4%
ARCHER	63	61	2	Reagan	96.8%	3.2%
ARMSTRONG	14	14		Reagan	100.0%	
ATASCOSA	283	278	5	Reagan	98.2%	1.8%
AUSTIN	312	306	6	Reagan	98.1%	1.9%
BAILEY	35	34	1	Reagan	97.1%	2.9%
BANDERA	430	422	8	Reagan	98.1%	1.9%

TEXAS REPUBLICAN

1984

County	Total Vote	Reagan	Uncommitted	Winner	Percentage of Total Vote: Reagan	Percentage of Total Vote: Uncom.
BASTROP	295	284	11	Reagan	96.3%	3.7%
BAYLOR	18	18		Reagan	100.0%	
BEE	227	227		Reagan	100.0%	
BELL	2,272	2,225	47	Reagan	97.9%	2.1%
BEXAR	21,500	20,978	522	Reagan	97.6%	2.4%
BLANCO	179	179		Reagan	100.0%	
BORDEN	12	11	1	Reagan	91.7%	8.3%
BOSQUE	193	189	4	Reagan	97.9%	2.1%
BOWIE	512	512		Reagan	100.0%	
BRAZORIA	5,257	4,975	282	Reagan	94.6%	5.4%
BRAZOS	4,103	3,952	151	Reagan	96.3%	3.7%
BREWSTER	168	157	11	Reagan	93.5%	6.5%
BRISCOE	21	21		Reagan	100.0%	
BROOKS	3	3		Reagan	100.0%	
BROWN	232	232		Reagan	100.0%	
BURLESON	33	33		Reagan	100.0%	
BURNET	484	474	10	Reagan	97.9%	2.1%
CALDWELL	174	166	8	Reagan	95.4%	4.6%
CALHOUN	209	201	8	Reagan	96.2%	3.8%
CALLAHAN	No Vote					
CAMERON	1,661	1,652	9	Reagan	99.5%	0.5%
CAMP	28	28		Reagan	100.0%	
CARSON	175	163	12	Reagan	93.1%	6.9%
CASS	137	134	3	Reagan	97.8%	2.2%
CASTRO	105	101	4	Reagan	96.2%	3.8%
CHAMBERS	94	91	3	Reagan	96.8%	3.2%
CHEROKEE	141	139	2	Reagan	98.6%	1.4%
CHILDRESS	33	32	1	Reagan	97.0%	3.0%
CLAY	42	40	2	Reagan	95.2%	4.8%
COCHRAN	2	2		Reagan	100.0%	
COKE	42	41	1	Reagan	97.6%	2.4%
COLEMAN	103	99	4	Reagan	96.1%	3.9%
COLLIN	9,591	8,978	613	Reagan	93.6%	6.4%
COLLINGSWORTH	No Vote					
COLORADO	164	164		Reagan	100.0%	
COMAL	2,633	2,517	116	Reagan	95.6%	4.4%
COMANCHE	49	48	1	Reagan	98.0%	2.0%
CONCHO	42	42		Reagan	100.0%	
COOKE	214	212	2	Reagan	99.1%	0.9%
CORYELL	599	588	11	Reagan	98.2%	1.8%
COTTLE	No Vote					
CRANE	31	30	1	Reagan	96.8%	3.2%
CROCKETT	10	10		Reagan	100.0%	
CROSBY	40	39	1	Reagan	97.5%	2.5%
CULBERSON	17	17		Reagan	100.0%	
DALLAM	51	47	4	Reagan	92.2%	7.8%
DALLAS	59,767	57,914	1,853	Reagan	96.9%	3.1%
DAWSON	97	93	4	Reagan	95.9%	4.1%
DEAF SMITH	175	174	1	Reagan	99.4%	0.6%
DELTA	10	10		Reagan	100.0%	

TEXAS REPUBLICAN

1984

County	Total Vote	Reagan	Uncommitted	Winner	Percentage of Total Vote: Reagan	Uncom.
DENTON	5,017	4,803	214	Reagan	95.7%	4.3%
DE WITT	406	399	7	Reagan	98.3%	1.7%
DICKENS	No Vote					
DIMMIT	8	8		Reagan	100.0%	
DONLEY	No Vote					
DUVAL	No Vote					
EASTLAND	88	88		Reagan	100.0%	
ECTOR	3,533	3,438	95	Reagan	97.3%	2.7%
EDWARDS	14	14		Reagan	100.0%	
ELLIS	1,688	1,688		Reagan	100.0%	
EL PASO	7,296	7,296		Reagan	100.0%	
ERATH	137	135	2	Reagan	98.5%	1.5%
FALLS	92	92		Reagan	100.0%	
FANNIN	146	146		Reagan	100.0%	
FAYETTE	256	249	7	Reagan	97.3%	2.7%
FISHER	No Vote					
FLOYD	84	82	2	Reagan	97.6%	2.4%
FOARD	16	15	1	Reagan	93.8%	6.3%
FORT BEND	6,641	6,300	341	Reagan	94.9%	5.1%
FRANKLIN	56	56		Reagan	100.0%	
FREESTONE	192	190	2	Reagan	99.0%	1.0%
FRIO	19	19		Reagan	100.0%	
GAINES	46	44	2	Reagan	95.7%	4.3%
GALVESTON	3,269	3,129	140	Reagan	95.7%	4.3%
GARZA	29	28	1	Reagan	96.6%	3.4%
GILLESPIE	1,319	1,254	65	Reagan	95.1%	4.9%
GLASSCOCK	13	13		Reagan	100.0%	
GOLIAD	21	21		Reagan	100.0%	
GONZALES	71	71		Reagan	100.0%	
GRAY	675	662	13	Reagan	98.1%	1.9%
GRAYSON	1,261	1,219	42	Reagan	96.7%	3.3%
GREGG	1,894	1,846	48	Reagan	97.5%	2.5%
GRIMES	382	371	11	Reagan	97.1%	2.9%
GUADALUPE	1,526	1,491	35	Reagan	97.7%	2.3%
HALE	567	541	26	Reagan	95.4%	4.6%
HALL	No Vote					
HAMILTON	143	142	1	Reagan	99.3%	0.7%
HANSFORD	155	146	9	Reagan	94.2%	5.8%
HARDEMAN	No Vote					
HARDIN	93	93		Reagan	100.0%	
HARRIS	63,527	60,951	2,576	Reagan	95.9%	4.1%
HARRISON	260	255	5	Reagan	98.1%	1.9%
HARTLEY	61	59	2	Reagan	96.7%	3.3%
HASKELL	No Vote					
HAYS	909	847	62	Reagan	93.2%	6.8%
HEMPHILL	101	100	1	Reagan	99.0%	1.0%
HENDERSON	800	788	12	Reagan	98.5%	1.5%
HIDALGO	2,747	2,690	57	Reagan	97.9%	2.1%
HILL	319	318	1	Reagan	99.7%	0.3%
HOCKLEY	84	84		Reagan	100.0%	

TEXAS REPUBLICAN

1984

County	Total Vote	Reagan	Uncommitted	Winner	Percentage of Total Vote Reagan	Uncom.
HOOD	757	741	16	Reagan	97.9%	2.1%
HOPKINS	168	163	5	Reagan	97.0%	3.0%
HOUSTON	51	51		Reagan	100.0%	
HOWARD	476	456	20	Reagan	95.8%	4.2%
HUDSPETH	19	18	1	Reagan	94.7%	5.3%
HUNT	844	825	19	Reagan	97.7%	2.3%
HUTCHINSON	872	830	42	Reagan	95.2%	4.8%
IRION	13	13		Reagan	100.0%	
JACK	88	88		Reagan	100.0%	
JACKSON	57	57		Reagan	100.0%	
JASPER	203	200	3	Reagan	98.5%	1.5%
JEFF DAVIS	No Vote					
JEFFERSON	2,480	2,372	108	Reagan	95.6%	4.4%
JIM HOGG	6	6		Reagan	100.0%	
JIM WELLS	115	113	2	Reagan	98.3%	1.7%
JOHNSON	1,560	1,522	38	Reagan	97.6%	2.4%
JONES	62	62		Reagan	100.0%	
KARNES	19	19		Reagan	100.0%	
KAUFMAN	409	406	3	Reagan	99.3%	0.7%
KENDALL	1,041	985	56	Reagan	94.6%	5.4%
KENEDY	7	7		Reagan	100.0%	
KENT	No Vote					
KERR	5,058	4,665	393	Reagan	92.2%	7.8%
KIMBLE	56	55	1	Reagan	98.2%	1.8%
KING	No Vote					
KINNEY	No Vote					
KLEBERG	411	411		Reagan	100.0%	
KNOX	13	11	2	Reagan	84.6%	15.4%
LAMAR	253	252	1	Reagan	99.6%	0.4%
LAMB	138	134	4	Reagan	97.1%	2.9%
LAMPASAS	241	235	6	Reagan	97.5%	2.5%
LA SALLE	No Vote					
LAVACA	166	162	4	Reagan	97.6%	2.4%
LEE	51	50	1	Reagan	98.0%	2.0%
LEON	223	220	3	Reagan	98.7%	1.3%
LIBERTY	527	512	15	Reagan	97.2%	2.8%
LIMESTONE	279	272	7	Reagan	97.5%	2.5%
LIPSCOMB	15	15		Reagan	100.0%	
LIVE OAK	63	63		Reagan	100.0%	
LLANO	543	529	14	Reagan	97.4%	2.6%
LOVING	No Vote					
LUBBOCK	6,609	6,443	166	Reagan	97.5%	2.5%
LYNN	24	24		Reagan	100.0%	
MCCULLOCH	78	77	1	Reagan	98.7%	1.3%
MCLENNAN	4,408	4,323	85	Reagan	98.1%	1.9%
MCMULLEN	No Vote					
MADISON	80	80		Reagan	100.0%	
MARION	25	24	1	Reagan	96.0%	4.0%
MARTIN	40	39	1	Reagan	97.5%	2.5%
MASON	110	110		Reagan	100.0%	

TEXAS REPUBLICAN

1984

County	Total Vote	Reagan	Uncommitted	Winner	Percentage of Total Vote Reagan	Uncom.
MATAGORDA	372	354	18	Reagan	95.2%	4.8%
MAVERICK	20	20		Reagan	100.0%	
MEDINA	248	247	1	Reagan	99.6%	0.4%
MENARD	23	23		Reagan	100.0%	
MIDLAND	8,966	8,665	301	Reagan	96.6%	3.4%
MILAM	181	181		Reagan	100.0%	
MILLS	No Vote					
MITCHELL	37	37		Reagan	100.0%	
MONTAGUE	41	41		Reagan	100.0%	
MONTGOMERY	5,990	5,660	330	Reagan	94.5%	5.5%
MOORE	180	175	5	Reagan	97.2%	2.8%
MORRIS	53	50	3	Reagan	94.3%	5.7%
MOTLEY	10	10		Reagan	100.0%	
NACOGDOCHES	338	329	9	Reagan	97.3%	2.7%
NAVARRO	582	570	12	Reagan	97.9%	2.1%
NEWTON	27	27		Reagan	100.0%	
NOLAN	129	126	3	Reagan	97.7%	2.3%
NUECES	3,871	3,768	103	Reagan	97.3%	2.7%
OCHILTREE	110	110		Reagan	100.0%	
OLDHAM	No Vote					
ORANGE	255	246	9	Reagan	96.5%	3.5%
PALO PINTO	319	319		Reagan	100.0%	
PANOLA	29	29		Reagan	100.0%	
PARKER	851	831	20	Reagan	97.6%	2.4%
PARMER	101	96	5	Reagan	95.0%	5.0%
PECOS	102	98	4	Reagan	96.1%	3.9%
POLK	67	65	2	Reagan	97.0%	3.0%
POTTER	2,332	2,282	50	Reagan	97.9%	2.1%
PRESIDIO	No Vote					
RAINS	59	58	1	Reagan	98.3%	1.7%
RANDALL	4,411	4,292	119	Reagan	97.3%	2.7%
REAGAN	No Vote					
REAL	33	33		Reagan	100.0%	
RED RIVER	46	45	1	Reagan	97.8%	2.2%
REEVES	22	21	1	Reagan	95.5%	4.5%
REFUGIO	36	36		Reagan	100.0%	
ROBERTS	27	27		Reagan	100.0%	
ROBERTSON	65	65		Reagan	100.0%	
ROCKWALL	977	942	35	Reagan	96.4%	3.6%
RUNNELS	92	89	3	Reagan	96.7%	3.3%
RUSK	5	2	3	Uncommitted	40.0%	60.0%
SABINE	34	33	1	Reagan	97.1%	2.9%
SAN AUGUSTINE	No Vote					
SAN JACINTO	50	49	1	Reagan	98.0%	2.0%
SAN PATRICIO	805	774	31	Reagan	96.1%	3.9%
SAN SABA	34	34		Reagan	100.0%	
SCHLEICHER	No Vote					
SCURRY	173	172	1	Reagan	99.4%	0.6%
SHACKELFORD	43	43		Reagan	100.0%	
SHELBY	38	37	1	Reagan	97.4%	2.6%

TEXAS REPUBLICAN

1984

County	Total Vote	Reagan	Uncommitted	Winner	Percentage of Total Vote Reagan	Uncom.
SHERMAN	36	36		Reagan	100.0%	
SMITH	4,113	4,044	69	Reagan	98.3%	1.7%
SOMERVELL	58	58		Reagan	100.0%	
STARR	10	10		Reagan	100.0%	
STEPHENS	41	41		Reagan	100.0%	
STERLING	17	17		Reagan	100.0%	
STONEWALL	No Vote					
SUTTON	55	55		Reagan	100.0%	
SWISHER	34	34		Reagan	100.0%	
TARRANT	23,703	23,059	644	Reagan	97.3%	2.7%
TAYLOR	1,722	1,722		Reagan	100.0%	
TERRELL	1	1		Reagan	100.0%	
TERRY	186	182	4	Reagan	97.8%	2.2%
THROCKMORTON	No Vote					
TITUS	244	235	9	Reagan	96.3%	3.7%
TOM GREEN	2,395	2,322	73	Reagan	97.0%	3.0%
TRAVIS	9,861	9,558	303	Reagan	96.9%	3.1%
TRINITY	49	47	2	Reagan	95.9%	4.1%
TYLER	50	48	2	Reagan	96.0%	4.0%
UPSHUR	180	177	3	Reagan	98.3%	1.7%
UPTON	9	9		Reagan	100.0%	
UVALDE	243	239	4	Reagan	98.4%	1.6%
VAL VERDE	361	353	8	Reagan	97.8%	2.2%
VAN ZANDT	421	421		Reagan	100.0%	
VICTORIA	2,228	2,194	34	Reagan	98.5%	1.5%
WALKER	616	592	24	Reagan	96.1%	3.9%
WALLER	170	169	1	Reagan	99.4%	0.6%
WARD	59	56	3	Reagan	94.9%	5.1%
WASHINGTON	306	302	4	Reagan	98.7%	1.3%
WEBB	134	126	8	Reagan	94.0%	6.0%
WHARTON	354	339	15	Reagan	95.8%	4.2%
WHEELER	92	89	3	Reagan	96.7%	3.3%
WICHITA	1,763	1,686	77	Reagan	95.6%	4.4%
WILBARGER	120	119	1	Reagan	99.2%	0.8%
WILLACY	19	19		Reagan	100.0%	
WILLIAMSON	2,251	2,177	74	Reagan	96.7%	3.3%
WILSON	198	189	9	Reagan	95.5%	4.5%
WINKLER	95	93	2	Reagan	97.9%	2.1%
WISE	255	251	4	Reagan	98.4%	1.6%
WOOD	292	285	7	Reagan	97.6%	2.4%
YOAKUM	65	64	1	Reagan	98.5%	1.5%
YOUNG	187	180	7	Reagan	96.3%	3.7%
ZAPATA	33	33		Reagan	100.0%	
ZAVALA	No Vote					
TOTAL	334,527	323,496	11,031	Reagan	96.7%	3.3%
Published Totals	319,839	308,713	11,126	Reagan	96.5%	3.5%

TEXAS DEMOCRATIC

1988

County	Total Vote	Dukakis	Gephardt	Gore	J. Jackson	Other	Winner	Percentage of Total Vote Dukakis	Gephardt	Gore	J. Jackson	Other
ANDERSON	7,822	2,328	1,316	1,979	1,387	812	Dukakis	29.8%	16.8%	25.3%	17.7%	10.4%
ANDREWS	1,891	356	722	348	186	279	Gephardt	18.8%	38.2%	18.4%	9.8%	14.8%
ANGELINA	12,159	3,279	3,397	2,396	1,828	1,259	Gephardt	27.0%	27.9%	19.7%	15.0%	10.4%
ARANSAS	1,394	579	223	338	161	93	Dukakis	41.5%	16.0%	24.2%	11.5%	6.7%
ARCHER	1,920	341	622	621	97	239	Gephardt	17.8%	32.4%	32.3%	5.1%	12.4%
ARMSTRONG	679	125	179	246	31	98	Gore	18.4%	26.4%	36.2%	4.6%	14.4%
ATASCOSA	5,297	2,080	861	873	828	655	Dukakis	39.3%	16.3%	16.5%	15.6%	12.4%
AUSTIN	3,691	1,403	625	796	387	480	Dukakis	38.0%	16.9%	21.6%	10.5%	13.0%
BAILEY	1,081	293	268	322	95	103	Gore	27.1%	24.8%	29.8%	8.8%	9.5%
BANDERA	1,590	638	285	398	125	144	Dukakis	40.1%	17.9%	25.0%	7.9%	9.1%
BASTROP	8,251	3,350	926	1,421	1,752	802	Dukakis	40.6%	11.2%	17.2%	21.2%	9.7%
BAYLOR	1,678	370	554	369	101	284	Gephardt	22.1%	33.0%	22.0%	6.0%	16.9%
BEE	3,241	1,693	321	518	406	303	Dukakis	52.2%	9.9%	16.0%	12.5%	9.3%
BELL	13,145	3,584	3,711	2,029	2,580	1,241	Gephardt	27.3%	28.2%	15.4%	19.6%	9.4%
BEXAR	98,181	49,144	8,483	9,733	24,306	6,515	Dukakis	50.1%	8.6%	9.9%	24.8%	6.6%
BLANCO	548	195	102	121	83	47	Dukakis	35.6%	18.6%	22.1%	15.1%	8.6%
BORDEN	352	96	77	116	20	43	Gore	27.3%	21.9%	33.0%	5.7%	12.2%
BOSQUE	3,164	977	830	929	167	261	Dukakis	30.9%	26.2%	29.4%	5.3%	8.2%
BOWIE	14,130	2,988	2,769	4,053	3,267	1,053	Gore	21.1%	19.6%	28.7%	23.1%	7.5%
BRAZORIA	14,000	5,808	1,808	2,759	2,458	1,167	Dukakis	41.5%	12.9%	19.7%	17.6%	8.3%
BRAZOS	7,752	2,757	675	1,367	2,247	706	Dukakis	35.6%	8.7%	17.6%	29.0%	9.1%
BREWSTER	1,362	441	224	165	320	212	Dukakis	32.4%	16.4%	12.1%	23.5%	15.6%
BRISCOE	800	146	216	258	62	118	Gore	18.3%	27.0%	32.3%	7.8%	14.8%
BROOKS	3,481	1,834	168	486	579	414	Dukakis	52.7%	4.8%	14.0%	16.6%	11.9%
BROWN	5,034	1,423	1,471	1,447	351	342	Gephardt	28.3%	29.2%	28.7%	7.0%	6.8%
BURLESON	3,611	1,361	463	631	690	466	Dukakis	37.7%	12.8%	17.5%	19.1%	12.9%
BURNET	4,673	1,873	811	1,195	407	387	Dukakis	40.1%	17.4%	25.6%	8.7%	8.3%
CALDWELL	4,315	1,628	654	828	828	377	Dukakis	37.7%	15.2%	19.2%	19.2%	8.7%
CALHOUN	3,735	1,345	494	740	596	560	Dukakis	36.0%	13.2%	19.8%	16.0%	15.0%
CALLAHAN	3,041	895	755	984	127	280	Gore	29.4%	24.8%	32.4%	4.2%	9.2%
CAMERON	25,949	12,265	1,965	3,373	5,207	3,139	Dukakis	47.3%	7.6%	13.0%	20.1%	12.1%
CAMP	2,213	509	329	591	635	149	J. Jackson	23.0%	14.9%	26.7%	28.7%	6.7%
CARSON	1,426	303	396	467	69	191	Gore	21.2%	27.8%	32.7%	4.8%	13.4%
CASS	6,636	1,580	1,084	2,140	1,278	554	Gore	23.8%	16.3%	32.2%	19.3%	8.3%
CASTRO	1,173	220	424	315	114	100	Gephardt	18.8%	36.1%	26.9%	9.7%	8.5%
CHAMBERS	4,051	1,211	559	981	607	693	Dukakis	29.9%	13.8%	24.2%	15.0%	17.1%
CHEROKEE	7,499	2,709	1,252	1,622	1,149	767	Dukakis	36.1%	16.7%	21.6%	15.3%	10.2%
CHILDRESS	1,222	276	303	410	76	157	Gore	22.6%	24.8%	33.6%	6.2%	12.8%
CLAY	2,912	576	988	821	160	367	Gephardt	19.8%	33.9%	28.2%	5.5%	12.6%
COCHRAN	1,068	231	316	288	115	118	Gephardt	21.6%	29.6%	27.0%	10.8%	11.0%
COKE	942	266	240	269	46	121	Gore	28.2%	25.5%	28.6%	4.9%	12.8%
COLEMAN	2,897	730	770	840	142	415	Gore	25.2%	26.6%	29.0%	4.9%	14.3%
COLLIN	10,696	3,724	1,373	2,709	2,176	714	Dukakis	34.8%	12.8%	25.3%	20.3%	6.7%
COLLINGSWORTH	1,412	175	411	448	104	274	Gore	12.4%	29.1%	31.7%	7.4%	19.4%
COLORADO	3,701	1,301	534	773	609	484	Dukakis	35.2%	14.4%	20.9%	16.5%	13.1%
COMAL	2,449	1,151	335	364	377	222	Dukakis	47.0%	13.7%	14.9%	15.4%	9.1%
COMANCHE	3,396	812	635	1,434	235	280	Gore	23.9%	18.7%	42.2%	6.9%	8.2%
CONCHO	800	204	181	210	81	124	Gore	25.5%	22.6%	26.3%	10.1%	15.5%
COOKE	5,567	1,574	1,158	1,923	449	463	Gore	28.3%	20.8%	34.5%	8.1%	8.3%
CORYELL	3,568	850	1,415	676	373	254	Gephardt	23.8%	39.7%	18.9%	10.5%	7.1%

TEXAS DEMOCRATIC

1988

County	Total Vote	Dukakis	Gephardt	Gore	J. Jackson	Other	Winner	Percentage of Total Vote Dukakis	Gephardt	Gore	J. Jackson	Other
COTTLE	811	165	242	190	104	110	Gephardt	20.3%	29.8%	23.4%	12.8%	13.6%
CRANE	1,343	286	373	231	221	232	Gephardt	21.3%	27.8%	17.2%	16.5%	17.3%
CROCKETT	1,222	333	249	199	207	234	Dukakis	27.3%	20.4%	16.3%	16.9%	19.1%
CROSBY	1,587	423	290	501	199	174	Gore	26.7%	18.3%	31.6%	12.5%	11.0%
CULBERSON	298	96	49	44	66	43	Dukakis	32.2%	16.4%	14.8%	22.1%	14.4%
DALLAM	898	182	273	278	53	112	Gore	20.3%	30.4%	31.0%	5.9%	12.5%
DALLAS	128,984	33,112	10,673	19,982	59,687	5,530	J. Jackson	25.7%	8.3%	15.5%	46.3%	4.3%
DAWSON	3,261	910	541	868	514	428	Dukakis	27.9%	16.6%	26.6%	15.8%	13.1%
DEAF SMITH	1,943	430	487	482	257	287	Gephardt	22.1%	25.1%	24.8%	13.2%	14.8%
DELTA	1,514	364	284	610	114	142	Gore	24.0%	18.8%	40.3%	7.5%	9.4%
DENTON	12,469	4,115	1,554	2,842	3,000	958	Dukakis	33.0%	12.5%	22.8%	24.1%	7.7%
DE WITT	2,435	969	313	436	493	224	Dukakis	39.8%	12.9%	17.9%	20.2%	9.2%
DICKENS	966	213	148	438	68	99	Gore	22.0%	15.3%	45.3%	7.0%	10.2%
DIMMIT	2,430	879	207	698	392	254	Dukakis	36.2%	8.5%	28.7%	16.1%	10.5%
DONLEY	817	236	191	268	24	98	Gore	28.9%	23.4%	32.8%	2.9%	12.0%
DUVAL	4,124	1,683	268	919	396	858	Dukakis	40.8%	6.5%	22.3%	9.6%	20.8%
EASTLAND	3,821	1,221	789	1,270	222	319	Gore	32.0%	20.6%	33.2%	5.8%	8.3%
ECTOR	6,682	1,623	1,590	1,121	1,796	552	J. Jackson	24.3%	23.8%	16.8%	26.9%	8.3%
EDWARDS	353	133	41	65	58	56	Dukakis	37.7%	11.6%	18.4%	16.4%	15.9%
ELLIS	9,046	2,814	1,174	2,732	1,661	665	Dukakis	31.1%	13.0%	30.2%	18.4%	7.4%
EL PASO	43,420	21,945	4,716	2,957	9,222	4,580	Dukakis	50.5%	10.9%	6.8%	21.2%	10.5%
ERATH	4,659	1,320	947	1,696	314	382	Gore	28.3%	20.3%	36.4%	6.7%	8.2%
FALLS	3,318	645	1,242	423	758	250	Gephardt	19.4%	37.4%	12.7%	22.8%	7.5%
FANNIN	5,686	1,442	924	2,341	408	571	Gore	25.4%	16.3%	41.2%	7.2%	10.0%
FAYETTE	4,741	1,850	669	1,243	433	546	Dukakis	39.0%	14.1%	26.2%	9.1%	11.5%
FISHER	1,791	504	514	427	204	142	Gephardt	28.1%	28.7%	23.8%	11.4%	7.9%
FLOYD	1,693	500	314	536	172	171	Gore	29.5%	18.5%	31.7%	10.2%	10.1%
FOARD	615	190	178	132	39	76	Dukakis	30.9%	28.9%	21.5%	6.3%	12.4%
FORT BEND	13,730	3,715	1,202	1,716	6,133	964	J. Jackson	27.1%	8.8%	12.5%	44.7%	7.0%
FRANKLIN	1,501	520	271	442	114	154	Dukakis	34.6%	18.1%	29.4%	7.6%	10.3%
FREESTONE	3,838	880	605	1,150	926	277	Gore	22.9%	15.8%	30.0%	24.1%	7.2%
FRIO	3,522	1,671	349	483	620	399	Dukakis	47.4%	9.9%	13.7%	17.6%	11.3%
GAINES	2,358	571	603	547	240	397	Gephardt	24.2%	25.6%	23.2%	10.2%	16.8%
GALVESTON	26,087	9,509	2,633	3,533	8,154	2,258	Dukakis	36.5%	10.1%	13.5%	31.3%	8.7%
GARZA	1,352	383	201	455	149	164	Gore	28.3%	14.9%	33.7%	11.0%	12.1%
GILLESPIE	585	244	100	135	81	25	Dukakis	41.7%	17.1%	23.1%	13.8%	4.3%
GLASSCOCK	147	30	55	29	8	25	Gephardt	20.4%	37.4%	19.7%	5.4%	17.0%
GOLIAD	1,623	642	192	270	308	211	Dukakis	39.6%	11.8%	16.6%	19.0%	13.0%
GONZALES	3,978	1,372	694	850	604	458	Dukakis	34.5%	17.4%	21.4%	15.2%	11.5%
GRAY	2,592	576	707	767	175	367	Gore	22.2%	27.3%	29.6%	6.8%	14.2%
GRAYSON	13,483	3,251	2,093	5,817	1,418	904	Gore	24.1%	15.5%	43.1%	10.5%	6.7%
GREGG	10,738	2,732	1,577	2,076	3,090	1,263	J. Jackson	25.4%	14.7%	19.3%	28.8%	11.8%
GRIMES	3,081	928	387	687	631	448	Dukakis	30.1%	12.6%	22.3%	20.5%	14.5%
GUADALUPE	4,728	1,960	796	760	847	365	Dukakis	41.5%	16.8%	16.1%	17.9%	7.7%
HALE	3,087	849	516	1,096	422	204	Gore	27.5%	16.7%	35.5%	13.7%	6.6%
HALL	1,299	302	330	369	107	191	Gore	23.2%	25.4%	28.4%	8.2%	14.7%
HAMILTON	2,081	523	694	529	120	215	Gephardt	25.1%	33.3%	25.4%	5.8%	10.3%
HANSFORD	589	111	177	208	21	72	Gore	18.8%	30.1%	35.3%	3.6%	12.2%
HARDEMAN	1,232	268	293	351	87	233	Gore	21.8%	23.8%	28.5%	7.1%	18.9%
HARDIN	9,573	2,859	1,143	3,911	882	778	Gore	29.9%	11.9%	40.9%	9.2%	8.1%

TEXAS DEMOCRATIC

1988

County	Total Vote	Dukakis	Gephardt	Gore	J. Jackson	Other	Winner	Dukakis %	Gephardt %	Gore %	J. Jackson %	Other %
								Percentage of Total Vote				
HARRIS	171,291	48,095	12,992	18,965	81,174	10,065	J. Jackson	28.1%	7.6%	11.1%	47.4%	5.9%
HARRISON	10,127	2,007	1,633	2,726	2,587	1,174	Gore	19.8%	16.1%	26.9%	25.5%	11.6%
HARTLEY	858	178	262	289	36	93	Gore	20.7%	30.5%	33.7%	4.2%	10.8%
HASKELL	1,987	553	351	814	99	170	Gore	27.8%	17.7%	41.0%	5.0%	8.6%
HAYS	8,693	3,199	1,012	1,638	2,020	824	Dukakis	36.8%	11.6%	18.8%	23.2%	9.5%
HEMPHILL	527	128	193	123	36	47	Gephardt	24.3%	36.6%	23.3%	6.8%	8.9%
HENDERSON	10,427	3,278	1,682	3,134	1,433	900	Dukakis	31.4%	16.1%	30.1%	13.7%	8.6%
HIDALGO	38,282	17,419	3,039	3,250	9,789	4,785	Dukakis	45.5%	7.9%	8.5%	25.6%	12.5%
HILL	4,855	1,352	1,003	1,693	427	380	Gore	27.8%	20.7%	34.9%	8.8%	7.8%
HOCKLEY	4,014	1,105	674	1,314	455	466	Gore	27.5%	16.8%	32.7%	11.3%	11.6%
HOOD	2,628	923	357	1,007	163	178	Gore	35.1%	13.6%	38.3%	6.2%	6.8%
HOPKINS	5,092	1,168	1,571	1,444	630	279	Gephardt	22.9%	30.9%	28.4%	12.4%	5.5%
HOUSTON	4,351	1,065	641	1,166	1,106	373	Gore	24.5%	14.7%	26.8%	25.4%	8.6%
HOWARD	4,220	1,318	1,034	766	625	477	Dukakis	31.2%	24.5%	18.2%	14.8%	11.3%
HUDSPETH	655	225	110	40	125	155	Dukakis	34.4%	16.8%	6.1%	19.1%	23.7%
HUNT	6,889	2,150	947	2,275	1,046	471	Gore	31.2%	13.7%	33.0%	15.2%	6.8%
HUTCHINSON	3,294	777	828	1,109	199	381	Gore	23.6%	25.1%	33.7%	6.0%	11.6%
IRION	670	191	147	168	56	108	Dukakis	28.5%	21.9%	25.1%	8.4%	16.1%
JACK	2,246	579	524	708	143	292	Gore	25.8%	23.3%	31.5%	6.4%	13.0%
JACKSON	3,257	1,268	449	740	432	368	Dukakis	38.9%	13.8%	22.7%	13.3%	11.3%
JASPER	7,367	2,178	984	2,616	1,095	494	Gore	29.6%	13.4%	35.5%	14.9%	6.7%
JEFF DAVIS	448	120	82	84	83	79	Dukakis	26.8%	18.3%	18.8%	18.5%	17.6%
JEFFERSON	50,147	14,071	5,026	11,689	16,408	2,953	J. Jackson	28.1%	10.0%	23.3%	32.7%	5.9%
JIM HOGG	2,141	952	122	350	410	307	Dukakis	44.5%	5.7%	16.3%	19.1%	14.3%
JIM WELLS	9,867	5,204	723	1,268	1,499	1,173	Dukakis	52.7%	7.3%	12.9%	15.2%	11.9%
JOHNSON	10,206	3,338	1,646	3,450	952	820	Gore	32.7%	16.1%	33.8%	9.3%	8.0%
JONES	3,300	1,114	636	1,058	237	255	Dukakis	33.8%	19.3%	32.1%	7.2%	7.7%
KARNES	3,617	1,700	631	516	396	374	Dukakis	47.0%	17.4%	14.3%	10.9%	10.3%
KAUFMAN	6,293	1,433	742	2,063	1,599	456	Gore	22.8%	11.8%	32.8%	25.4%	7.2%
KENDALL	629	302	115	80	92	40	Dukakis	48.0%	18.3%	12.7%	14.6%	6.4%
KENEDY	122	49	9	27	30	7	Dukakis	40.2%	7.4%	22.1%	24.6%	5.7%
KENT	525	102	95	228	20	80	Gore	19.4%	18.1%	43.4%	3.8%	15.2%
KERR	1,324	606	184	202	226	106	Dukakis	45.8%	13.9%	15.3%	17.1%	8.0%
KIMBLE	725	194	161	196	68	106	Gore	26.8%	22.2%	27.0%	9.4%	14.6%
KING	183	40	62	40	10	31	Gephardt	21.9%	33.9%	21.9%	5.5%	16.9%
KINNEY	681	260	81	126	118	96	Dukakis	38.2%	11.9%	18.5%	17.3%	14.1%
KLEBERG	6,269	2,861	615	762	1,097	934	Dukakis	45.6%	9.8%	12.2%	17.5%	14.9%
KNOX	1,116	300	333	290	53	140	Gephardt	26.9%	29.8%	26.0%	4.7%	12.5%
LAMAR	9,799	2,823	1,618	2,962	1,430	966	Gore	28.8%	16.5%	30.2%	14.6%	9.9%
LAMB	2,043	544	441	698	204	156	Gore	26.6%	21.6%	34.2%	10.0%	7.6%
LAMPASAS	2,476	750	808	491	180	247	Gephardt	30.3%	32.6%	19.8%	7.3%	10.0%
LA SALLE	2,036	522	146	961	201	206	Gore	25.6%	7.2%	47.2%	9.9%	10.1%
LAVACA	4,451	1,841	709	949	346	606	Dukakis	41.4%	15.9%	21.3%	7.8%	13.6%
LEE	3,331	1,203	593	647	499	389	Dukakis	36.1%	17.8%	19.4%	15.0%	11.7%
LEON	2,185	609	410	566	374	226	Dukakis	27.9%	18.8%	25.9%	17.1%	10.3%
LIBERTY	9,661	2,459	1,310	3,396	1,684	812	Gore	25.5%	13.6%	35.2%	17.4%	8.4%
LIMESTONE	4,577	1,000	888	1,503	746	440	Gore	21.8%	19.4%	32.8%	16.3%	9.6%
LIPSCOMB	499	98	150	167	19	65	Gore	19.6%	30.1%	33.5%	3.8%	13.0%
LIVE OAK	2,028	810	338	487	162	231	Dukakis	39.9%	16.7%	24.0%	8.0%	11.4%
LLANO	2,331	998	422	560	187	164	Dukakis	42.8%	18.1%	24.0%	8.0%	7.0%

TEXAS DEMOCRATIC

1988

County	Total Vote	Dukakis	Gephardt	Gore	J. Jackson	Other	Winner	Percentage of Total Vote: Dukakis	Gephardt	Gore	J. Jackson	Other
LOVING	66	17	13	12	9	15	Dukakis	25.8%	19.7%	18.2%	13.6%	22.7%
LUBBOCK	16,350	5,621	1,696	4,134	3,950	949	Dukakis	34.4%	10.4%	25.3%	24.2%	5.8%
LYNN	1,725	449	276	658	152	190	Gore	26.0%	16.0%	38.1%	8.8%	11.0%
MCCULLOCH	1,956	559	427	534	177	259	Dukakis	28.6%	21.8%	27.3%	9.0%	13.2%
MCLENNAN	21,624	5,386	7,120	3,808	3,954	1,356	Gephardt	24.9%	32.9%	17.6%	18.3%	6.3%
MCMULLEN	155	39	22	58	17	19	Gore	25.2%	14.2%	37.4%	11.0%	12.3%
MADISON	2,486	735	424	491	463	373	Dukakis	29.6%	17.1%	19.8%	18.6%	15.0%
MARION	2,784	590	353	671	899	271	J. Jackson	21.2%	12.7%	24.1%	32.3%	9.7%
MARTIN	439	93	147	116	46	37	Gephardt	21.2%	33.5%	26.4%	10.5%	8.4%
MASON	1,050	337	204	268	96	145	Dukakis	32.1%	19.4%	25.5%	9.1%	13.8%
MATAGORDA	7,020	2,420	964	1,161	1,653	822	Dukakis	34.5%	13.7%	16.5%	23.5%	11.7%
MAVERICK	3,372	1,486	213	495	700	478	Dukakis	44.1%	6.3%	14.7%	20.8%	14.2%
MEDINA	5,371	1,951	866	1,072	1,052	430	Dukakis	36.3%	16.1%	20.0%	19.6%	8.0%
MENARD	749	223	168	179	57	122	Dukakis	29.8%	22.4%	23.9%	7.6%	16.3%
MIDLAND	4,380	1,085	863	542	1,599	291	J. Jackson	24.8%	19.7%	12.4%	36.5%	6.6%
MILAM	4,732	1,383	1,363	1,034	553	399	Dukakis	29.2%	28.8%	21.9%	11.7%	8.4%
MILLS	1,446	345	553	352	65	131	Gephardt	23.9%	38.2%	24.3%	4.5%	9.1%
MITCHELL	1,845	534	318	577	177	239	Gore	28.9%	17.2%	31.3%	9.6%	13.0%
MONTAGUE	4,048	803	947	1,667	245	386	Gore	19.8%	23.4%	41.2%	6.1%	9.5%
MONTGOMERY	12,094	4,375	1,961	2,367	2,036	1,355	Dukakis	36.2%	16.2%	19.6%	16.8%	11.2%
MOORE	2,645	612	729	704	179	421	Gephardt	23.1%	27.6%	26.6%	6.8%	15.9%
MORRIS	3,928	980	713	1,037	776	422	Gore	24.9%	18.2%	26.4%	19.8%	10.7%
MOTLEY	364	87	58	164	19	36	Gore	23.9%	15.9%	45.1%	5.2%	9.9%
NACOGDOCHES	8,294	2,559	1,377	1,980	1,346	1,032	Dukakis	30.9%	16.6%	23.9%	16.2%	12.4%
NAVARRO	6,525	1,632	833	2,006	1,481	573	Gore	25.0%	12.8%	30.7%	22.7%	8.8%
NEWTON	4,167	1,031	533	1,375	835	393	Gore	24.7%	12.8%	33.0%	20.0%	9.4%
NOLAN	4,279	1,305	962	1,106	372	534	Dukakis	30.5%	22.5%	25.8%	8.7%	12.5%
NUECES	34,539	14,488	3,699	6,572	6,222	3,558	Dukakis	41.9%	10.7%	19.0%	18.0%	10.3%
OCHILTREE	1,139	207	306	396	75	155	Gore	18.2%	26.9%	34.8%	6.6%	13.6%
OLDHAM	567	117	144	195	26	85	Gore	20.6%	25.4%	34.4%	4.6%	15.0%
ORANGE	19,193	6,004	2,932	6,449	2,263	1,545	Gore	31.3%	15.3%	33.6%	11.8%	8.0%
PALO PINTO	4,933	1,361	652	2,044	454	422	Gore	27.6%	13.2%	41.4%	9.2%	8.6%
PANOLA	6,317	1,312	1,086	2,066	1,140	713	Gore	20.8%	17.2%	32.7%	18.0%	11.3%
PARKER	8,492	2,709	1,346	3,052	643	742	Gore	31.9%	15.9%	35.9%	7.6%	8.7%
PARMER	1,486	298	472	480	67	169	Gore	20.1%	31.8%	32.3%	4.5%	11.4%
PECOS	2,699	660	546	418	488	587	Dukakis	24.5%	20.2%	15.5%	18.1%	21.7%
POLK	6,079	1,698	988	1,528	807	1,058	Dukakis	27.9%	16.3%	25.1%	13.3%	17.4%
POTTER	7,355	1,976	1,361	1,847	1,400	771	Dukakis	26.9%	18.5%	25.1%	19.0%	10.5%
PRESIDIO	1,377	488	181	124	289	295	Dukakis	35.4%	13.1%	9.0%	21.0%	21.4%
RAINS	1,716	432	309	582	199	194	Gore	25.2%	18.0%	33.9%	11.6%	11.3%
RANDALL	6,032	1,918	1,463	1,534	508	609	Dukakis	31.8%	24.3%	25.4%	8.4%	10.1%
REAGAN	857	166	256	178	115	142	Gephardt	19.4%	29.9%	20.8%	13.4%	16.6%
REAL	613	230	110	137	57	79	Dukakis	37.5%	17.9%	22.3%	9.3%	12.9%
RED RIVER	3,678	1,117	573	1,011	574	403	Dukakis	30.4%	15.6%	27.5%	15.6%	11.0%
REEVES	3,892	1,146	505	451	1,004	786	Dukakis	29.4%	13.0%	11.6%	25.8%	20.2%
REFUGIO	2,632	1,141	339	426	403	323	Dukakis	43.4%	12.9%	16.2%	15.3%	12.3%
ROBERTS	257	43	67	105	12	30	Gore	16.7%	26.1%	40.9%	4.7%	11.7%
ROBERTSON	4,447	1,127	905	785	1,196	434	J. Jackson	25.3%	20.4%	17.7%	26.9%	9.8%
ROCKWALL	1,844	549	243	650	244	158	Gore	29.8%	13.2%	35.2%	13.2%	8.6%
RUNNELS	2,734	791	783	677	175	308	Dukakis	28.9%	28.6%	24.8%	6.4%	11.3%

TEXAS DEMOCRATIC

1988

County	Total Vote	Dukakis	Gephardt	Gore	J. Jackson	Other	Winner	Percentage of Total Vote Dukakis	Gephardt	Gore	J. Jackson	Other
RUSK	8,244	2,183	1,546	1,890	1,545	1,080	Dukakis	26.5%	18.8%	22.9%	18.7%	13.1%
SABINE	4,150	1,922	632	792	388	416	Dukakis	46.3%	15.2%	19.1%	9.3%	10.0%
SAN AUGUSTINE	3,060	882	461	600	707	410	Dukakis	28.8%	15.1%	19.6%	23.1%	13.4%
SAN JACINTO	3,816	1,277	532	689	878	440	Dukakis	33.5%	13.9%	18.1%	23.0%	11.5%
SAN PATRICIO	8,890	3,816	1,033	1,752	1,145	1,144	Dukakis	42.9%	11.6%	19.7%	12.9%	12.9%
SAN SABA	1,733	514	565	334	116	204	Gephardt	29.7%	32.6%	19.3%	6.7%	11.8%
SCHLEICHER	1,018	248	241	212	138	179	Dukakis	24.4%	23.7%	20.8%	13.6%	17.6%
SCURRY	2,991	760	618	1,075	217	321	Gore	25.4%	20.7%	35.9%	7.3%	10.7%
SHACKELFORD	1,081	374	222	325	62	98	Dukakis	34.6%	20.5%	30.1%	5.7%	9.1%
SHELBY	7,176	1,544	1,129	2,405	1,097	1,001	Gore	21.5%	15.7%	33.5%	15.3%	13.9%
SHERMAN	837	175	228	270	34	130	Gore	20.9%	27.2%	32.3%	4.1%	15.5%
SMITH	12,448	3,269	1,670	2,144	4,653	712	J. Jackson	26.3%	13.4%	17.2%	37.4%	5.7%
SOMERVELL	1,537	386	278	571	88	214	Gore	25.1%	18.1%	37.2%	5.7%	13.9%
STARR	5,292	2,184	326	865	1,078	839	Dukakis	41.3%	6.2%	16.3%	20.4%	15.9%
STEPHENS	2,683	773	485	944	195	286	Gore	28.8%	18.1%	35.2%	7.3%	10.7%
STERLING	217	51	62	50	16	38	Gephardt	23.5%	28.6%	23.0%	7.4%	17.5%
STONEWALL	1,018	292	259	267	66	134	Dukakis	28.7%	25.4%	26.2%	6.5%	13.2%
SUTTON	921	243	202	178	137	161	Dukakis	26.4%	21.9%	19.3%	14.9%	17.5%
SWISHER	2,279	456	697	748	141	237	Gore	20.0%	30.6%	32.8%	6.2%	10.4%
TARRANT	81,648	24,801	9,012	17,950	25,094	4,791	J. Jackson	30.4%	11.0%	22.0%	30.7%	5.9%
TAYLOR	13,576	4,523	2,425	4,139	1,369	1,120	Dukakis	33.3%	17.9%	30.5%	10.1%	8.2%
TERRELL	527	187	77	60	57	146	Dukakis	35.5%	14.6%	11.4%	10.8%	27.7%
TERRY	3,189	783	547	1,063	385	411	Gore	24.6%	17.2%	33.3%	12.1%	12.9%
THROCKMORTON	804	174	278	199	47	106	Gephardt	21.6%	34.6%	24.8%	5.8%	13.2%
TITUS	5,513	1,159	777	2,360	819	398	Gore	21.0%	14.1%	42.8%	14.9%	7.2%
TOM GREEN	7,727	2,594	1,498	1,383	1,382	870	Dukakis	33.6%	19.4%	17.9%	17.9%	11.3%
TRAVIS	83,401	30,683	7,168	11,206	27,966	6,378	Dukakis	36.8%	8.6%	13.4%	33.5%	7.6%
TRINITY	4,203	1,231	817	746	718	691	Dukakis	29.3%	19.4%	17.7%	17.1%	16.4%
TYLER	5,549	1,411	784	2,203	640	511	Gore	25.4%	14.1%	39.7%	11.5%	9.2%
UPSHUR	7,182	2,321	1,527	1,453	1,224	657	Dukakis	32.3%	21.3%	20.2%	17.0%	9.1%
UPTON	1,347	247	340	219	233	308	Gephardt	18.3%	25.2%	16.3%	17.3%	22.9%
UVALDE	4,199	1,479	568	1,034	604	514	Dukakis	35.2%	13.5%	24.6%	14.4%	12.2%
VAL VERDE	1,815	878	213	222	314	188	Dukakis	48.4%	11.7%	12.2%	17.3%	10.4%
VAN ZANDT	6,874	2,152	1,039	2,335	521	827	Gore	31.3%	15.1%	34.0%	7.6%	12.0%
VICTORIA	8,492	3,090	851	1,632	1,669	1,250	Dukakis	36.4%	10.0%	19.2%	19.7%	14.7%
WALKER	6,162	1,920	888	1,297	1,359	698	Dukakis	31.2%	14.4%	21.0%	22.1%	11.3%
WALLER	4,576	983	585	658	1,966	384	J. Jackson	21.5%	12.8%	14.4%	43.0%	8.4%
WARD	3,522	707	911	493	652	759	Gephardt	20.1%	25.9%	14.0%	18.5%	21.6%
WASHINGTON	2,505	826	351	622	501	205	Dukakis	33.0%	14.0%	24.8%	20.0%	8.2%
WEBB	16,078	6,915	423	3,880	2,767	2,093	Dukakis	43.0%	2.6%	24.1%	17.2%	13.0%
WHARTON	5,497	2,080	706	1,023	1,122	566	Dukakis	37.8%	12.8%	18.6%	20.4%	10.3%
WHEELER	1,899	396	532	576	88	307	Gore	20.9%	28.0%	30.3%	4.6%	16.2%
WICHITA	11,103	2,505	2,901	2,830	1,682	1,185	Gephardt	22.6%	26.1%	25.5%	15.1%	10.7%
WILBARGER	2,448	530	739	649	188	342	Gephardt	21.7%	30.2%	26.5%	7.7%	14.0%
WILLACY	3,535	1,373	284	403	966	509	Dukakis	38.8%	8.0%	11.4%	27.3%	14.4%
WILLIAMSON	11,597	4,693	1,475	2,287	2,156	986	Dukakis	40.5%	12.7%	19.7%	18.6%	8.5%
WILSON	4,914	2,171	793	799	557	594	Dukakis	44.2%	16.1%	16.3%	11.3%	12.1%
WINKLER	1,550	310	463	368	192	217	Gephardt	20.0%	29.9%	23.7%	12.4%	14.0%
WISE	5,485	1,516	899	2,189	346	535	Gore	27.6%	16.4%	39.9%	6.3%	9.8%
WOOD	5,420	1,802	1,039	1,496	703	380	Dukakis	33.2%	19.2%	27.6%	13.0%	7.0%

TEXAS DEMOCRATIC

1988

County	Total Vote	Dukakis	Gephardt	Gore	J. Jackson	Other	Winner	Percentage of Total Vote: Dukakis	Gephardt	Gore	J. Jackson	Other
YOAKUM	888	258	195	263	60	112	Gore	29.1%	22.0%	29.6%	6.8%	12.6%
YOUNG	4,175	1,031	1,195	1,208	258	483	Gore	24.7%	28.6%	28.9%	6.2%	11.6%
ZAPATA	2,183	858	122	670	283	250	Dukakis	39.3%	5.6%	30.7%	13.0%	11.5%
ZAVALA	2,833	1,227	116	432	778	280	Dukakis	43.3%	4.1%	15.2%	27.5%	9.9%
TOTAL	1,767,045	579,713	240,158	357,764	433,335	156,075	Dukakis	32.8%	13.6%	20.2%	24.5%	8.8%

TEXAS REPUBLICAN

1988

County	Total Vote	Bush	Dole	Robertson	Other	Winner	Percentage of Total Vote: Bush	Dole	Robertson	Other
ANDERSON	1,524	946	176	324	78	Bush	62.1%	11.5%	21.3%	5.1%
ANDREWS	679	446	58	157	18	Bush	65.7%	8.5%	23.1%	2.7%
ANGELINA	1,719	1,098	168	362	91	Bush	63.9%	9.8%	21.1%	5.3%
ARANSAS	1,977	1,339	306	204	128	Bush	67.7%	15.5%	10.3%	6.5%
ARCHER	284	154	49	62	19	Bush	54.2%	17.3%	21.8%	6.7%
ARMSTRONG	117	63	8	31	15	Bush	53.8%	6.8%	26.5%	12.8%
ATASCOSA	775	543	80	116	36	Bush	70.1%	10.3%	15.0%	4.6%
AUSTIN	687	482	72	101	32	Bush	70.2%	10.5%	14.7%	4.7%
BAILEY	260	139	36	48	37	Bush	53.5%	13.8%	18.5%	14.2%
BANDERA	1,381	972	182	106	121	Bush	70.4%	13.2%	7.7%	8.8%
BASTROP	1,128	662	176	216	74	Bush	58.7%	15.6%	19.1%	6.6%
BAYLOR	57	31	5	17	4	Bush	54.4%	8.8%	29.8%	7.0%
BEE	1,103	822	92	130	59	Bush	74.5%	8.3%	11.8%	5.3%
BELL	7,259	4,477	958	1,366	458	Bush	61.7%	13.2%	18.8%	6.3%
BEXAR	70,166	45,157	11,711	7,956	5,342	Bush	64.4%	16.7%	11.3%	7.6%
BLANCO	454	289	73	59	33	Bush	63.7%	16.1%	13.0%	7.3%
BORDEN	16	8	1	5	2	Bush	50.0%	6.3%	31.3%	12.5%
BOSQUE	609	444	57	69	39	Bush	72.9%	9.4%	11.3%	6.4%
BOWIE	2,779	1,472	371	782	154	Bush	53.0%	13.4%	28.1%	5.5%
BRAZORIA	10,653	6,927	1,208	1,911	607	Bush	65.0%	11.3%	17.9%	5.7%
BRAZOS	11,522	7,142	2,088	1,297	995	Bush	62.0%	18.1%	11.3%	8.6%
BREWSTER	831	528	148	75	80	Bush	63.5%	17.8%	9.0%	9.6%
BRISCOE	27	12	2	6	7	Bush	44.4%	7.4%	22.2%	25.9%
BROOKS	No Vote									
BROWN	1,080	673	87	270	50	Bush	62.3%	8.1%	25.0%	4.6%
BURLESON	130	81	14	25	10	Bush	62.3%	10.8%	19.2%	7.7%
BURNET	1,489	1,040	217	154	78	Bush	69.8%	14.6%	10.3%	5.2%
CALDWELL	621	388	71	113	49	Bush	62.5%	11.4%	18.2%	7.9%
CALHOUN	592	343	45	172	32	Bush	57.9%	7.6%	29.1%	5.4%
CALLAHAN	311	185	16	95	15	Bush	59.5%	5.1%	30.5%	4.8%
CAMERON	5,510	3,430	609	1,137	334	Bush	62.3%	11.1%	20.6%	6.1%
CAMP	161	89	32	26	14	Bush	55.3%	19.9%	16.1%	8.7%
CARSON	499	350	56	63	30	Bush	70.1%	11.2%	12.6%	6.0%
CASS	606	319	58	197	32	Bush	52.6%	9.6%	32.5%	5.3%
CASTRO	439	239	78	85	37	Bush	54.4%	17.8%	19.4%	8.4%

TEXAS REPUBLICAN

1988

County	Total Vote	Bush	Dole	Robertson	Other	Winner	Percentage of Total Vote: Bush	Dole	Robertson	Other
CHAMBERS	399	224	21	131	23	Bush	56.1%	5.3%	32.8%	5.8%
CHEROKEE	899	540	118	208	33	Bush	60.1%	13.1%	23.1%	3.7%
CHILDRESS	188	123	21	29	15	Bush	65.4%	11.2%	15.4%	8.0%
CLAY	181	100	22	44	15	Bush	55.2%	12.2%	24.3%	8.3%
COCHRAN	78	33	11	28	6	Bush	42.3%	14.1%	35.9%	7.7%
COKE	81	50	8	17	6	Bush	61.7%	9.9%	21.0%	7.4%
COLEMAN	259	168	20	59	12	Bush	64.9%	7.7%	22.8%	4.6%
COLLIN	27,715	15,789	5,237	4,098	2,591	Bush	57.0%	18.9%	14.8%	9.3%
COLLINGSWORTH	No Vote									
COLORADO	436	301	52	71	12	Bush	69.0%	11.9%	16.3%	2.8%
COMAL	8,568	5,683	1,360	701	824	Bush	66.3%	15.9%	8.2%	9.6%
COMANCHE	168	106	10	43	9	Bush	63.1%	6.0%	25.6%	5.4%
CONCHO	60	44	10	3	3	Bush	73.3%	16.7%	5.0%	5.0%
COOKE	1,122	593	127	316	86	Bush	52.9%	11.3%	28.2%	7.7%
CORYELL	1,805	1,107	276	306	116	Bush	61.3%	15.3%	17.0%	6.4%
COTTLE	No Vote									
CRANE	No Vote									
CROCKETT	No Vote									
CROSBY	242	143	34	49	16	Bush	59.1%	14.0%	20.2%	6.6%
CULBERSON	No Vote									
DALLAM	233	120	46	40	27	Bush	51.5%	19.7%	17.2%	11.6%
DALLAS	158,499	97,324	24,136	24,107	12,932	Bush	61.4%	15.2%	15.2%	8.2%
DAWSON	305	193	26	75	11	Bush	63.3%	8.5%	24.6%	3.6%
DEAF SMITH	1,126	429	165	446	86	Robertson	38.1%	14.7%	39.6%	7.6%
DELTA	64	33	3	23	5	Bush	51.6%	4.7%	35.9%	7.8%
DENTON	24,439	13,034	4,254	4,672	2,479	Bush	53.3%	17.4%	19.1%	10.1%
DE WITT	1,081	803	79	143	56	Bush	74.3%	7.3%	13.2%	5.2%
DICKENS	No Vote									
DIMMIT	74	49	6	13	6	Bush	66.2%	8.1%	17.6%	8.1%
DONLEY	212	154	22	26	10	Bush	72.6%	10.4%	12.3%	4.7%
DUVAL	No Vote									
EASTLAND	833	434	53	312	34	Bush	52.1%	6.4%	37.5%	4.1%
ECTOR	12,182	8,463	1,067	2,044	608	Bush	69.5%	8.8%	16.8%	5.0%
EDWARDS	130	91	16	21	2	Bush	70.0%	12.3%	16.2%	1.5%
ELLIS	6,337	3,655	672	1,553	457	Bush	57.7%	10.6%	24.5%	7.2%
EL PASO	19,191	11,622	3,074	3,234	1,261	Bush	60.6%	16.0%	16.9%	6.6%
ERATH	839	488	93	194	64	Bush	58.2%	11.1%	23.1%	7.6%
FALLS	237	173	23	36	5	Bush	73.0%	9.7%	15.2%	2.1%
FANNIN	530	283	63	144	40	Bush	53.4%	11.9%	27.2%	7.5%
FAYETTE	836	586	124	78	48	Bush	70.1%	14.8%	9.3%	5.7%
FISHER	12	8		4		Bush	66.7%		33.3%	
FLOYD	231	162	25	27	17	Bush	70.1%	10.8%	11.7%	7.4%
FOARD	29	8	3	15	3	Robertson	27.6%	10.3%	51.7%	10.3%
FORT BEND	13,688	9,766	1,825	1,470	627	Bush	71.3%	13.3%	10.7%	4.6%
FRANKLIN	234	128	18	69	19	Bush	54.7%	7.7%	29.5%	8.1%
FREESTONE	560	319	55	154	32	Bush	57.0%	9.8%	27.5%	5.7%
FRIO	55	22	3	23	7	Robertson	40.0%	5.5%	41.8%	12.7%
GAINES	150	72	15	51	12	Bush	48.0%	10.0%	34.0%	8.0%
GALVESTON	9,309	6,519	1,081	1,227	482	Bush	70.0%	11.6%	13.2%	5.2%
GARZA	217	131	28	46	12	Bush	60.4%	12.9%	21.2%	5.5%

TEXAS REPUBLICAN

1988

County	Total Vote	Bush	Dole	Robertson	Other	Winner	Percentage of Total Vote: Bush	Dole	Robertson	Other
GILLESPIE	4,425	3,108	672	258	387	Bush	70.2%	15.2%	5.8%	8.7%
GLASSCOCK	126	66	14	38	8	Bush	52.4%	11.1%	30.2%	6.3%
GOLIAD	104	70	6	26	2	Bush	67.3%	5.8%	25.0%	1.9%
GONZALES	293	193	21	70	9	Bush	65.9%	7.2%	23.9%	3.1%
GRAY	2,916	1,846	345	555	170	Bush	63.3%	11.8%	19.0%	5.8%
GRAYSON	3,875	2,161	546	917	251	Bush	55.8%	14.1%	23.7%	6.5%
GREGG	9,433	5,859	1,100	1,887	587	Bush	62.1%	11.7%	20.0%	6.2%
GRIMES	557	398	62	70	27	Bush	71.5%	11.1%	12.6%	4.8%
GUADALUPE	4,997	3,465	712	544	276	Bush	69.3%	14.2%	10.9%	5.5%
HALE	1,922	1,116	211	499	96	Bush	58.1%	11.0%	26.0%	5.0%
HALL	82	54	11	13	4	Bush	65.9%	13.4%	15.9%	4.9%
HAMILTON	193	134	20	23	16	Bush	69.4%	10.4%	11.9%	8.3%
HANSFORD	794	480	144	110	60	Bush	60.5%	18.1%	13.9%	7.6%
HARDEMAN	68	39	10	11	8	Bush	57.4%	14.7%	16.2%	11.8%
HARDIN	609	319	55	200	35	Bush	52.4%	9.0%	32.8%	5.7%
HARRIS	168,961	124,700	19,924	16,066	8,271	Bush	73.8%	11.8%	9.5%	4.9%
HARRISON	1,988	1,097	165	627	99	Bush	55.2%	8.3%	31.5%	5.0%
HARTLEY	313	171	75	49	18	Bush	54.6%	24.0%	15.7%	5.8%
HASKELL	No Vote									
HAYS	3,148	1,858	591	397	302	Bush	59.0%	18.8%	12.6%	9.6%
HEMPHILL	515	350	51	84	30	Bush	68.0%	9.9%	16.3%	5.8%
HENDERSON	3,451	2,223	384	678	166	Bush	64.4%	11.1%	19.6%	4.8%
HIDALGO	7,054	4,074	839	1,700	441	Bush	57.8%	11.9%	24.1%	6.3%
HILL	923	526	90	254	53	Bush	57.0%	9.8%	27.5%	5.7%
HOCKLEY	566	346	44	148	28	Bush	61.1%	7.8%	26.1%	4.9%
HOOD	2,570	1,601	301	489	179	Bush	62.3%	11.7%	19.0%	7.0%
HOPKINS	1,036	545	127	275	89	Bush	52.6%	12.3%	26.5%	8.6%
HOUSTON	408	254	42	106	6	Bush	62.3%	10.3%	26.0%	1.5%
HOWARD	1,291	663	134	455	39	Bush	51.4%	10.4%	35.2%	3.0%
HUDSPETH	No Vote									
HUNT	3,664	2,132	444	865	223	Bush	58.2%	12.1%	23.6%	6.1%
HUTCHINSON	3,289	2,027	429	604	229	Bush	61.6%	13.0%	18.4%	7.0%
IRION	36	21	5	9	1	Bush	58.3%	13.9%	25.0%	2.8%
JACK	148	97	18	26	7	Bush	65.5%	12.2%	17.6%	4.7%
JACKSON	207	135	9	56	7	Bush	65.2%	4.3%	27.1%	3.4%
JASPER	541	356	47	105	33	Bush	65.8%	8.7%	19.4%	6.1%
JEFF DAVIS	117	54	14	42	7	Bush	46.2%	12.0%	35.9%	6.0%
JEFFERSON	6,283	3,804	822	1,278	379	Bush	60.5%	13.1%	20.3%	6.0%
JIM HOGG	32	29	1	2		Bush	90.6%	3.1%	6.3%	
JIM WELLS	467	317	48	75	27	Bush	67.9%	10.3%	16.1%	5.8%
JOHNSON	5,500	3,126	629	1,357	388	Bush	56.8%	11.4%	24.7%	7.1%
JONES	350	211	31	93	15	Bush	60.3%	8.9%	26.6%	4.3%
KARNES	120	75	7	32	6	Bush	62.5%	5.8%	26.7%	5.0%
KAUFMAN	2,446	1,391	289	576	190	Bush	56.9%	11.8%	23.5%	7.8%
KENDALL	2,597	1,847	301	205	244	Bush	71.1%	11.6%	7.9%	9.4%
KENEDY	11	11				Bush	100.0%			
KENT	No Vote									
KERR	8,368	5,245	1,262	875	986	Bush	62.7%	15.1%	10.5%	11.8%
KIMBLE	182	109	25	42	6	Bush	59.9%	13.7%	23.1%	3.3%
KING	No Vote									

TEXAS REPUBLICAN

1988

County	Total Vote	Bush	Dole	Robertson	Other	Winner	Percentage of Total Vote Bush	Dole	Robertson	Other
KINNEY	169	123	16	19	11	Bush	72.8%	9.5%	11.2%	6.5%
KLEBERG	638	367	78	133	60	Bush	57.5%	12.2%	20.8%	9.4%
KNOX	107	52	9	40	6	Bush	48.6%	8.4%	37.4%	5.6%
LAMAR	1,227	559	150	480	38	Bush	45.6%	12.2%	39.1%	3.1%
LAMB	436	267	47	97	25	Bush	61.2%	10.8%	22.2%	5.7%
LAMPASAS	536	357	71	55	53	Bush	66.6%	13.2%	10.3%	9.9%
LA SALLE	No Vote									
LAVACA	471	335	35	78	23	Bush	71.1%	7.4%	16.6%	4.9%
LEE	270	192	35	35	8	Bush	71.1%	13.0%	13.0%	3.0%
LEON	596	436	56	76	28	Bush	73.2%	9.4%	12.8%	4.7%
LIBERTY	1,160	665	78	341	76	Bush	57.3%	6.7%	29.4%	6.6%
LIMESTONE	465	269	38	114	44	Bush	57.8%	8.2%	24.5%	9.5%
LIPSCOMB	430	247	64	80	39	Bush	57.4%	14.9%	18.6%	9.1%
LIVE OAK	255	156	28		71	Bush	61.2%	11.0%		27.8%
LLANO	2,003	1,430	314	124	135	Bush	71.4%	15.7%	6.2%	6.7%
LOVING	No Vote									
LUBBOCK	22,736	15,676	2,285	3,225	1,550	Bush	68.9%	10.1%	14.2%	6.8%
LYNN	69	47	7	11	4	Bush	68.1%	10.1%	15.9%	5.8%
MCCULLOCH	275	198	37	26	14	Bush	72.0%	13.5%	9.5%	5.1%
MCLENNAN	8,773	5,448	1,077	1,642	606	Bush	62.1%	12.3%	18.7%	6.9%
MCMULLEN	No Vote									
MADISON	210	138	24	45	3	Bush	65.7%	11.4%	21.4%	1.4%
MARION	180	135	20	21	4	Bush	75.0%	11.1%	11.7%	2.2%
MARTIN	164	99	17	39	9	Bush	60.4%	10.4%	23.8%	5.5%
MASON	159	85	24	41	9	Bush	53.5%	15.1%	25.8%	5.7%
MATAGORDA	869	466	92	269	42	Bush	53.6%	10.6%	31.0%	4.8%
MAVERICK	393	300	36	37	20	Bush	76.3%	9.2%	9.4%	5.1%
MEDINA	1,154	766	129	175	84	Bush	66.4%	11.2%	15.2%	7.3%
MENARD	85	60	9	9	7	Bush	70.6%	10.6%	10.6%	8.2%
MIDLAND	18,507	12,579	2,518	2,262	1,148	Bush	68.0%	13.6%	12.2%	6.2%
MILAM	648	362	88	149	49	Bush	55.9%	13.6%	23.0%	7.6%
MILLS	No Vote									
MITCHELL	231	117	13	95	6	Bush	50.6%	5.6%	41.1%	2.6%
MONTAGUE	324	190	37	76	21	Bush	58.6%	11.4%	23.5%	6.5%
MONTGOMERY	17,736	11,651	2,322	2,480	1,283	Bush	65.7%	13.1%	14.0%	7.2%
MOORE	744	409	122	162	51	Bush	55.0%	16.4%	21.8%	6.9%
MORRIS	201	95	25	63	18	Bush	47.3%	12.4%	31.3%	9.0%
MOTLEY	97	62	14	14	7	Bush	63.9%	14.4%	14.4%	7.2%
NACOGDOCHES	1,745	1,136	248	243	118	Bush	65.1%	14.2%	13.9%	6.8%
NAVARRO	1,686	960	189	447	90	Bush	56.9%	11.2%	26.5%	5.3%
NEWTON	141	86	8	32	15	Bush	61.0%	5.7%	22.7%	10.6%
NOLAN	200	109	33	55	3	Bush	54.5%	16.5%	27.5%	1.5%
NUECES	12,061	7,634	1,726	2,027	674	Bush	63.3%	14.3%	16.8%	5.6%
OCHILTREE	900	492	118	218	72	Bush	54.7%	13.1%	24.2%	8.0%
OLDHAM	No Vote									
ORANGE	1,156	590	132	346	88	Bush	51.0%	11.4%	29.9%	7.6%
PALO PINTO	737	472	73	150	42	Bush	64.0%	9.9%	20.4%	5.7%
PANOLA	316	143	31	126	16	Bush	45.3%	9.8%	39.9%	5.1%
PARKER	4,320	2,549	406	1,140	225	Bush	59.0%	9.4%	26.4%	5.2%
PARMER	283	121	40	102	20	Bush	42.8%	14.1%	36.0%	7.1%

TEXAS REPUBLICAN

1988

County	Total Vote	Bush	Dole	Robertson	Other	Winner	Percentage of Total Vote: Bush	Dole	Robertson	Other
PECOS	270	184	21	48	17	Bush	68.1%	7.8%	17.8%	6.3%
POLK	810	525	74	154	57	Bush	64.8%	9.1%	19.0%	7.0%
POTTER	7,630	4,703	835	1,419	673	Bush	61.6%	10.9%	18.6%	8.8%
PRESIDIO	23	10	7	3	3	Bush	43.5%	30.4%	13.0%	13.0%
RAINS	126	92	9	18	7	Bush	73.0%	7.1%	14.3%	5.6%
RANDALL	14,472	8,991	1,943	2,250	1,288	Bush	62.1%	13.4%	15.5%	8.9%
REAGAN	57	26	6	25		Bush	45.6%	10.5%	43.9%	
REAL	222	127	24	61	10	Bush	57.2%	10.8%	27.5%	4.5%
RED RIVER	125	57	19	41	8	Bush	45.6%	15.2%	32.8%	6.4%
REEVES	No Vote									
REFUGIO	82	62	3	12	5	Bush	75.6%	3.7%	14.6%	6.1%
ROBERTS	130	78	15	25	12	Bush	60.0%	11.5%	19.2%	9.2%
ROBERTSON	304	190	47	48	19	Bush	62.5%	15.5%	15.8%	6.3%
ROCKWALL	3,313	1,752	437	775	349	Bush	52.9%	13.2%	23.4%	10.5%
RUNNELS	157	92	19	36	10	Bush	58.6%	12.1%	22.9%	6.4%
RUSK	1,496	927	129	360	80	Bush	62.0%	8.6%	24.1%	5.3%
SABINE	146	94	18	28	6	Bush	64.4%	12.3%	19.2%	4.1%
SAN AUGUSTINE	57	42	6	7	2	Bush	73.7%	10.5%	12.3%	3.5%
SAN JACINTO	208	127	15	48	18	Bush	61.1%	7.2%	23.1%	8.7%
SAN PATRICIO	1,915	1,109	244	434	128	Bush	57.9%	12.7%	22.7%	6.7%
SAN SABA	60	34	9	13	4	Bush	56.7%	15.0%	21.7%	6.7%
SCHLEICHER	No Vote									
SCURRY	502	293	57	134	18	Bush	58.4%	11.4%	26.7%	3.6%
SHACKELFORD	111	54	1	51	5	Bush	48.6%	0.9%	45.9%	4.5%
SHELBY	95	63	4	20	8	Bush	66.3%	4.2%	21.1%	8.4%
SHERMAN	180	100	40	29	11	Bush	55.6%	22.2%	16.1%	6.1%
SMITH	15,394	9,798	1,615	3,082	899	Bush	63.6%	10.5%	20.0%	5.8%
SOMERVELL	180	90	17	61	12	Bush	50.0%	9.4%	33.9%	6.7%
STARR	47	26	5	14	2	Bush	55.3%	10.6%	29.8%	4.3%
STEPHENS	188	98	13	69	8	Bush	52.1%	6.9%	36.7%	4.3%
STERLING	104	74	10	11	9	Bush	71.2%	9.6%	10.6%	8.7%
STONEWALL	20	9	1	9	1		45.0%	5.0%	45.0%	5.0%
SUTTON	228	165	26	20	17	Bush	72.4%	11.4%	8.8%	7.5%
SWISHER	110	49	18	33	10	Bush	44.5%	16.4%	30.0%	9.1%
TARRANT	91,373	54,241	12,318	18,052	6,762	Bush	59.4%	13.5%	19.8%	7.4%
TAYLOR	8,540	5,557	990	1,428	565	Bush	65.1%	11.6%	16.7%	6.6%
TERRELL	No Vote									
TERRY	321	195	50	53	23	Bush	60.7%	15.6%	16.5%	7.2%
THROCKMORTON	No Vote									
TITUS	594	355	72	143	24	Bush	59.8%	12.1%	24.1%	4.0%
TOM GREEN	7,176	4,322	1,281	1,137	436	Bush	60.2%	17.9%	15.8%	6.1%
TRAVIS	36,555	22,065	7,643	3,925	2,922	Bush	60.4%	20.9%	10.7%	8.0%
TRINITY	No Vote									
TYLER	106	86	4	14	2	Bush	81.1%	3.8%	13.2%	1.9%
UPSHUR	759	449	79	184	47	Bush	59.2%	10.4%	24.2%	6.2%
UPTON	No Vote									
UVALDE	817	417	93	250	57	Bush	51.0%	11.4%	30.6%	7.0%
VAL VERDE	1,140	681	199	176	84	Bush	59.7%	17.5%	15.4%	7.4%
VAN ZANDT	1,685	984	121	493	87	Bush	58.4%	7.2%	29.3%	5.2%
VICTORIA	4,292	2,794	308	926	264	Bush	65.1%	7.2%	21.6%	6.2%

TEXAS REPUBLICAN

1988

County	Total Vote	Bush	Dole	Robertson	Other	Winner	Percentage of Total Vote: Bush	Dole	Robertson	Other
WALKER	2,121	1,467	280	230	144	Bush	69.2%	13.2%	10.8%	6.8%
WALLER	553	384	57	68	44	Bush	69.4%	10.3%	12.3%	8.0%
WARD	251	109	23	112	7	Robertson	43.4%	9.2%	44.6%	2.8%
WASHINGTON	1,400	1,060	126	150	64	Bush	75.7%	9.0%	10.7%	4.6%
WEBB	885	601	82	149	53	Bush	67.9%	9.3%	16.8%	6.0%
WHARTON	1,660	1,157	182	251	70	Bush	69.7%	11.0%	15.1%	4.2%
WHEELER	328	162	44	102	20	Bush	49.4%	13.4%	31.1%	6.1%
WICHITA	7,071	4,084	1,121	1,252	614	Bush	57.8%	15.9%	17.7%	8.7%
WILBARGER	334	188	66	52	28	Bush	56.3%	19.8%	15.6%	8.4%
WILLACY	105	67	6	26	6	Bush	63.8%	5.7%	24.8%	5.7%
WILLIAMSON	9,272	5,299	1,914	1,310	749	Bush	57.2%	20.6%	14.1%	8.1%
WILSON	749	514	89	97	49	Bush	68.6%	11.9%	13.0%	6.5%
WINKLER	279	136	7	122	14	Bush	48.7%	2.5%	43.7%	5.0%
WISE	1,231	602	126	458	45	Bush	48.9%	10.2%	37.2%	3.7%
WOOD	1,473	947	121	334	71	Bush	64.3%	8.2%	22.7%	4.8%
YOAKUM	290	186	33	54	17	Bush	64.1%	11.4%	18.6%	5.9%
YOUNG	557	232	42	264	19	Robertson	41.7%	7.5%	47.4%	3.4%
ZAPATA	159	100	25	22	12	Bush	62.9%	15.7%	13.8%	7.5%
ZAVALA	No Vote									
TOTAL	1,014,956	648,178	140,795	155,449	70,534	Bush	63.9%	13.9%	15.3%	6.9%

TEXAS DEMOCRATIC

1992

County	Total Vote	Clinton	Tsongas	Other	Winner	Percentage of Total Vote: Clinton	Tsongas	Other
ANDERSON	7,819	5,532	1,381	906	Clinton	70.8%	17.7%	11.6%
ANDREWS	1,971	1,138	416	417	Clinton	57.7%	21.1%	21.2%
ANGELINA	11,248	8,438	1,558	1,252	Clinton	75.0%	13.9%	11.1%
ARANSAS	1,201	786	225	190	Clinton	65.4%	18.7%	15.8%
ARCHER	1,673	1,224	198	251	Clinton	73.2%	11.8%	15.0%
ARMSTRONG	497	334	67	96	Clinton	67.2%	13.5%	19.3%
ATASCOSA	3,739	2,233	823	683	Clinton	59.7%	22.0%	18.3%
AUSTIN	2,052	1,430	362	260	Clinton	69.7%	17.6%	12.7%
BAILEY	864	576	134	154	Clinton	66.7%	15.5%	17.8%
BANDERA	618	387	135	96	Clinton	62.6%	21.8%	15.5%
BASTROP	6,817	4,329	1,187	1,301	Clinton	63.5%	17.4%	19.1%
BAYLOR	1,484	1,032	208	244	Clinton	69.5%	14.0%	16.4%
BEE	3,165	2,089	565	511	Clinton	66.0%	17.9%	16.1%
BELL	8,733	5,952	1,675	1,106	Clinton	68.2%	19.2%	12.7%
BEXAR	68,568	37,490	18,550	12,528	Clinton	54.7%	27.1%	18.3%

TEXAS DEMOCRATIC

1992

County	Total Vote	Clinton	Tsongas	Other	Winner	Percentage of Total Vote		
						Clinton	Tsongas	Other
BLANCO	421	261	74	86	Clinton	62.0%	17.6%	20.4%
BORDEN	210	143	35	32	Clinton	68.1%	16.7%	15.2%
BOSQUE	2,598	1,871	412	315	Clinton	72.0%	15.9%	12.1%
BOWIE	15,194	12,075	1,543	1,576	Clinton	79.5%	10.2%	10.4%
BRAZORIA	10,768	7,138	2,075	1,555	Clinton	66.3%	19.3%	14.4%
BRAZOS	5,835	3,294	1,724	817	Clinton	56.5%	29.5%	14.0%
BREWSTER	986	554	212	220	Clinton	56.2%	21.5%	22.3%
BRISCOE	572	436	68	68	Clinton	76.2%	11.9%	11.9%
BROOKS	3,221	2,403	343	475	Clinton	74.6%	10.6%	14.7%
BROWN	6,397	4,226	1,210	961	Clinton	66.1%	18.9%	15.0%
BURLESON	3,455	2,514	480	461	Clinton	72.8%	13.9%	13.3%
BURNET	4,632	3,076	796	760	Clinton	66.4%	17.2%	16.4%
CALDWELL	3,168	2,104	547	517	Clinton	66.4%	17.3%	16.3%
CALHOUN	2,362	1,599	465	298	Clinton	67.7%	19.7%	12.6%
CALLAHAN	3,043	2,165	471	407	Clinton	71.1%	15.5%	13.4%
CAMERON	21,699	13,887	3,986	3,826	Clinton	64.0%	18.4%	17.6%
CAMP	2,097	1,614	224	259	Clinton	77.0%	10.7%	12.4%
CARSON	1,098	736	180	182	Clinton	67.0%	16.4%	16.6%
CASS	5,263	4,356	392	515	Clinton	82.8%	7.4%	9.8%
CASTRO	1,568	1,110	212	246	Clinton	70.8%	13.5%	15.7%
CHAMBERS	3,943	2,618	661	664	Clinton	66.4%	16.8%	16.8%
CHEROKEE	7,253	5,156	1,205	892	Clinton	71.1%	16.6%	12.3%
CHILDRESS	1,336	942	216	178	Clinton	70.5%	16.2%	13.3%
CLAY	2,966	2,109	395	462	Clinton	71.1%	13.3%	15.6%
COCHRAN	1,004	686	103	215	Clinton	68.3%	10.3%	21.4%
COKE	741	535	103	103	Clinton	72.2%	13.9%	13.9%
COLEMAN	2,232	1,647	287	298	Clinton	73.8%	12.9%	13.4%
COLLIN	10,380	5,175	3,506	1,699	Clinton	49.9%	33.8%	16.4%
COLLINGSWORTH	1,130	782	154	194	Clinton	69.2%	13.6%	17.2%
COLORADO	3,776	2,495	794	487	Clinton	66.1%	21.0%	12.9%
COMAL	2,847	1,631	724	492	Clinton	57.3%	25.4%	17.3%
COMANCHE	3,377	2,321	551	505	Clinton	68.7%	16.3%	15.0%
CONCHO	838	596	112	130	Clinton	71.1%	13.4%	15.5%
COOKE	6,531	3,865	1,502	1,164	Clinton	59.2%	23.0%	17.8%
CORYELL	4,393	3,016	801	576	Clinton	68.7%	18.2%	13.1%
COTTLE	627	489	61	77	Clinton	78.0%	9.7%	12.3%
CRANE	1,294	709	254	331	Clinton	54.8%	19.6%	25.6%
CROCKETT	1,027	646	174	207	Clinton	62.9%	16.9%	20.2%
CROSBY	813	566	115	132	Clinton	69.6%	14.1%	16.2%
CULBERSON	653	361	146	146	Clinton	55.3%	22.4%	22.4%
DALLAM	415	292	73	50	Clinton	70.4%	17.6%	12.0%
DALLAS	108,681	69,688	24,577	14,416	Clinton	64.1%	22.6%	13.3%
DAWSON	2,257	1,466	384	407	Clinton	65.0%	17.0%	18.0%
DEAF SMITH	1,976	1,185	394	397	Clinton	60.0%	19.9%	20.1%
DELTA	1,135	855	142	138	Clinton	75.3%	12.5%	12.2%
DENTON	10,423	5,516	3,068	1,839	Clinton	52.9%	29.4%	17.6%
DE WITT	2,782	1,840	577	365	Clinton	66.1%	20.7%	13.1%
DICKENS	820	580	92	148	Clinton	70.7%	11.2%	18.0%
DIMMIT	2,767	1,954	311	502	Clinton	70.6%	11.2%	18.1%
DONLEY	656	498	70	88	Clinton	75.9%	10.7%	13.4%

TEXAS DEMOCRATIC

1992

County	Total Vote	Clinton	Tsongas	Other	Winner	Percentage of Total Vote Clinton	Tsongas	Other
DUVAL	4,287	2,793	545	949	Clinton	65.2%	12.7%	22.1%
EASTLAND	3,156	2,254	478	424	Clinton	71.4%	15.1%	13.4%
ECTOR	5,049	3,708	717	624	Clinton	73.4%	14.2%	12.4%
EDWARDS	323	192	67	64	Clinton	59.4%	20.7%	19.8%
ELLIS	5,273	3,772	864	637	Clinton	71.5%	16.4%	12.1%
EL PASO	42,655	21,821	11,398	9,436	Clinton	51.2%	26.7%	22.1%
ERATH	4,166	2,640	892	634	Clinton	63.4%	21.4%	15.2%
FALLS	3,351	2,460	427	464	Clinton	73.4%	12.7%	13.8%
FANNIN	5,149	3,763	682	704	Clinton	73.1%	13.2%	13.7%
FAYETTE	3,732	2,685	578	469	Clinton	71.9%	15.5%	12.6%
FISHER	1,275	930	212	133	Clinton	72.9%	16.6%	10.4%
FLOYD	1,228	837	159	232	Clinton	68.2%	12.9%	18.9%
FOARD	546	379	71	96	Clinton	69.4%	13.0%	17.6%
FORT BEND	11,736	8,078	2,323	1,335	Clinton	68.8%	19.8%	11.4%
FRANKLIN	1,868	1,451	208	209	Clinton	77.7%	11.1%	11.2%
FREESTONE	2,998	2,179	514	305	Clinton	72.7%	17.1%	10.2%
FRIO	3,193	2,219	458	516	Clinton	69.5%	14.3%	16.2%
GAINES	1,665	1,065	246	354	Clinton	64.0%	14.8%	21.3%
GALVESTON	18,473	12,512	3,801	2,160	Clinton	67.7%	20.6%	11.7%
GARZA	1,245	771	191	283	Clinton	61.9%	15.3%	22.7%
GILLESPIE	614	389	130	95	Clinton	63.4%	21.2%	15.5%
GLASSCOCK	167	101	28	38	Clinton	60.5%	16.8%	22.8%
GOLIAD	1,153	740	236	177	Clinton	64.2%	20.5%	15.4%
GONZALES	2,597	1,646	570	381	Clinton	63.4%	21.9%	14.7%
GRAY	2,360	1,649	343	368	Clinton	69.9%	14.5%	15.6%
GRAYSON	10,654	7,243	2,010	1,401	Clinton	68.0%	18.9%	13.1%
GREGG	6,638	5,132	905	601	Clinton	77.3%	13.6%	9.1%
GRIMES	2,846	2,196	413	237	Clinton	77.2%	14.5%	8.3%
GUADALUPE	3,541	2,035	898	608	Clinton	57.5%	25.4%	17.2%
HALE	4,130	2,461	793	876	Clinton	59.6%	19.2%	21.2%
HALL	1,064	779	151	134	Clinton	73.2%	14.2%	12.6%
HAMILTON	1,506	1,099	242	165	Clinton	73.0%	16.1%	11.0%
HANSFORD	514	337	80	97	Clinton	65.6%	15.6%	18.9%
HARDEMAN	1,372	1,008	172	192	Clinton	73.5%	12.5%	14.0%
HARDIN	7,930	5,724	1,139	1,067	Clinton	72.2%	14.4%	13.5%
HARRIS	139,481	90,260	32,030	17,191	Clinton	64.7%	23.0%	12.3%
HARRISON	8,753	7,291	805	657	Clinton	83.3%	9.2%	7.5%
HARTLEY	762	500	124	138	Clinton	65.6%	16.3%	18.1%
HASKELL	1,859	1,443	225	191	Clinton	77.6%	12.1%	10.3%
HAYS	6,577	3,621	1,453	1,503	Clinton	55.1%	22.1%	22.9%
HEMPHILL	534	373	75	86	Clinton	69.9%	14.0%	16.1%
HENDERSON	8,456	6,387	1,187	882	Clinton	75.5%	14.0%	10.4%
HIDALGO	35,631	25,951	4,543	5,137	Clinton	72.8%	12.8%	14.4%
HILL	5,160	3,689	789	682	Clinton	71.5%	15.3%	13.2%
HOCKLEY	3,043	1,794	567	682	Clinton	59.0%	18.6%	22.4%
HOOD	3,785	2,585	743	457	Clinton	68.3%	19.6%	12.1%
HOPKINS	5,509	4,109	813	587	Clinton	74.6%	14.8%	10.7%
HOUSTON	4,543	3,462	614	467	Clinton	76.2%	13.5%	10.3%
HOWARD	4,043	2,774	686	583	Clinton	68.6%	17.0%	14.4%
HUDSPETH	686	434	117	135	Clinton	63.3%	17.1%	19.7%

TEXAS DEMOCRATIC

1992

County	Total Vote	Clinton	Tsongas	Other	Winner	Percentage of Total Vote Clinton	Tsongas	Other
HUNT	7,102	5,005	1,294	803	Clinton	70.5%	18.2%	11.3%
HUTCHINSON	1,977	1,418	318	241	Clinton	71.7%	16.1%	12.2%
IRION	408	282	74	52	Clinton	69.1%	18.1%	12.7%
JACK	2,169	1,543	282	344	Clinton	71.1%	13.0%	15.9%
JACKSON	2,767	1,831	545	391	Clinton	66.2%	19.7%	14.1%
JASPER	7,180	5,401	882	897	Clinton	75.2%	12.3%	12.5%
JEFF DAVIS	462	215	130	117	Clinton	46.5%	28.1%	25.3%
JEFFERSON	29,207	21,003	4,433	3,771	Clinton	71.9%	15.2%	12.9%
JIM HOGG	1,953	1,431	253	269	Clinton	73.3%	13.0%	13.8%
JIM WELLS	6,820	4,803	869	1,148	Clinton	70.4%	12.7%	16.8%
JOHNSON	10,008	6,733	1,969	1,306	Clinton	67.3%	19.7%	13.0%
JONES	2,275	1,687	307	281	Clinton	74.2%	13.5%	12.4%
KARNES	3,106	1,999	557	550	Clinton	64.4%	17.9%	17.7%
KAUFMAN	5,670	4,080	879	711	Clinton	72.0%	15.5%	12.5%
KENDALL	395	208	116	71	Clinton	52.7%	29.4%	18.0%
KENEDY	130	73	23	34	Clinton	56.2%	17.7%	26.2%
KENT	521	334	73	114	Clinton	64.1%	14.0%	21.9%
KERR	1,441	878	339	224	Clinton	60.9%	23.5%	15.5%
KIMBLE	537	361	73	103	Clinton	67.2%	13.6%	19.2%
KING	131	96	16	19	Clinton	73.3%	12.2%	14.5%
KINNEY	752	474	119	159	Clinton	63.0%	15.8%	21.1%
KLEBERG	5,008	3,104	936	968	Clinton	62.0%	18.7%	19.3%
KNOX	1,128	867	145	116	Clinton	76.9%	12.9%	10.3%
LAMAR	7,676	5,282	1,201	1,193	Clinton	68.8%	15.6%	15.5%
LAMB	2,657	1,748	405	504	Clinton	65.8%	15.2%	19.0%
LAMPASAS	1,743	1,180	292	271	Clinton	67.7%	16.8%	15.5%
LA SALLE	1,654	1,244	186	224	Clinton	75.2%	11.2%	13.5%
LAVACA	3,883	2,681	680	522	Clinton	69.0%	17.5%	13.4%
LEE	2,919	2,076	393	450	Clinton	71.1%	13.5%	15.4%
LEON	2,622	2,093	286	243	Clinton	79.8%	10.9%	9.3%
LIBERTY	7,314	5,375	1,103	836	Clinton	73.5%	15.1%	11.4%
LIMESTONE	3,119	2,385	369	365	Clinton	76.5%	11.8%	11.7%
LIPSCOMB	446	316	62	68	Clinton	70.9%	13.9%	15.2%
LIVE OAK	1,439	895	293	251	Clinton	62.2%	20.4%	17.4%
LLANO	2,971	2,101	506	364	Clinton	70.7%	17.0%	12.3%
LOVING	73	32	22	19	Clinton	43.8%	30.1%	26.0%
LUBBOCK	10,114	6,164	2,076	1,874	Clinton	60.9%	20.5%	18.5%
LYNN	1,541	1,027	208	306	Clinton	66.6%	13.5%	19.9%
MCCULLOCH	2,155	1,464	347	344	Clinton	67.9%	16.1%	16.0%
MCLENNAN	19,934	13,705	3,832	2,397	Clinton	68.8%	19.2%	12.0%
MCMULLEN	307	163	67	77	Clinton	53.1%	21.8%	25.1%
MADISON	1,940	1,511	227	202	Clinton	77.9%	11.7%	10.4%
MARION	2,446	1,935	236	275	Clinton	79.1%	9.6%	11.2%
MARTIN	1,038	671	175	192	Clinton	64.6%	16.9%	18.5%
MASON	597	402	132	63	Clinton	67.3%	22.1%	10.6%
MATAGORDA	7,550	4,913	1,563	1,074	Clinton	65.1%	20.7%	14.2%
MAVERICK	3,731	2,340	647	744	Clinton	62.7%	17.3%	19.9%
MEDINA	3,426	2,055	793	578	Clinton	60.0%	23.1%	16.9%
MENARD	695	465	101	129	Clinton	66.9%	14.5%	18.6%
MIDLAND	2,815	1,779	576	460	Clinton	63.2%	20.5%	16.3%

TEXAS DEMOCRATIC

1992

County	Total Vote	Clinton	Tsongas	Other	Winner	Percentage of Total Vote Clinton	Tsongas	Other
MILAM	4,256	3,077	672	507	Clinton	72.3%	15.8%	11.9%
MILLS	1,362	960	213	189	Clinton	70.5%	15.6%	13.9%
MITCHELL	1,992	1,397	326	269	Clinton	70.1%	16.4%	13.5%
MONTAGUE	3,578	2,515	513	550	Clinton	70.3%	14.3%	15.4%
MONTGOMERY	7,790	5,427	1,394	969	Clinton	69.7%	17.9%	12.4%
MOORE	1,453	937	260	256	Clinton	64.5%	17.9%	17.6%
MORRIS	3,721	2,991	342	388	Clinton	80.4%	9.2%	10.4%
MOTLEY	473	304	66	103	Clinton	64.3%	14.0%	21.8%
NACOGDOCHES	6,128	4,339	1,053	736	Clinton	70.8%	17.2%	12.0%
NAVARRO	5,132	3,738	838	556	Clinton	72.8%	16.3%	10.8%
NEWTON	2,456	1,907	260	289	Clinton	77.6%	10.6%	11.8%
NOLAN	3,692	2,399	721	572	Clinton	65.0%	19.5%	15.5%
NUECES	35,107	20,812	7,119	7,176	Clinton	59.3%	20.3%	20.4%
OCHILTREE	1,019	635	203	181	Clinton	62.3%	19.9%	17.8%
OLDHAM	603	350	118	135	Clinton	58.0%	19.6%	22.4%
ORANGE	14,119	10,129	2,173	1,817	Clinton	71.7%	15.4%	12.9%
PALO PINTO	3,721	2,520	660	541	Clinton	67.7%	17.7%	14.5%
PANOLA	4,982	3,866	486	630	Clinton	77.6%	9.8%	12.6%
PARKER	7,674	5,219	1,375	1,080	Clinton	68.0%	17.9%	14.1%
PARMER	953	627	209	117	Clinton	65.8%	21.9%	12.3%
PECOS	2,152	1,208	489	455	Clinton	56.1%	22.7%	21.1%
POLK	6,215	4,536	978	701	Clinton	73.0%	15.7%	11.3%
POTTER	5,739	3,881	989	869	Clinton	67.6%	17.2%	15.1%
PRESIDIO	1,152	726	186	240	Clinton	63.0%	16.1%	20.8%
RAINS	1,483	1,120	215	148	Clinton	75.5%	14.5%	10.0%
RANDALL	4,412	2,854	916	642	Clinton	64.7%	20.8%	14.6%
REAGAN	673	442	93	138	Clinton	65.7%	13.8%	20.5%
REAL	536	338	106	92	Clinton	63.1%	19.8%	17.2%
RED RIVER	3,656	2,838	454	364	Clinton	77.6%	12.4%	10.0%
REEVES	3,094	1,819	535	740	Clinton	58.8%	17.3%	23.9%
REFUGIO	1,256	823	209	224	Clinton	65.5%	16.6%	17.8%
ROBERTS	379	258	54	67	Clinton	68.1%	14.2%	17.7%
ROBERTSON	2,475	2,023	277	175	Clinton	81.7%	11.2%	7.1%
ROCKWALL	1,645	1,015	375	255	Clinton	61.7%	22.8%	15.5%
RUNNELS	2,584	1,732	437	415	Clinton	67.0%	16.9%	16.1%
RUSK	6,334	4,375	849	1,110	Clinton	69.1%	13.4%	17.5%
SABINE	3,676	2,878	359	439	Clinton	78.3%	9.8%	11.9%
SAN AUGUSTINE	2,888	2,168	281	439	Clinton	75.1%	9.7%	15.2%
SAN JACINTO	3,404	2,564	443	397	Clinton	75.3%	13.0%	11.7%
SAN PATRICIO	6,731	3,996	1,035	1,700	Clinton	59.4%	15.4%	25.3%
SAN SABA	1,469	1,034	241	194	Clinton	70.4%	16.4%	13.2%
SCHLEICHER	743	487	107	149	Clinton	65.5%	14.4%	20.1%
SCURRY	1,988	1,320	361	307	Clinton	66.4%	18.2%	15.4%
SHACKELFORD	1,035	735	170	130	Clinton	71.0%	16.4%	12.6%
SHELBY	6,516	5,024	582	910	Clinton	77.1%	8.9%	14.0%
SHERMAN	372	231	71	70	Clinton	62.1%	19.1%	18.8%
SMITH	8,219	6,370	1,037	812	Clinton	77.5%	12.6%	9.9%
SOMERVELL	1,362	906	244	212	Clinton	66.5%	17.9%	15.6%
STARR	4,483	3,209	623	651	Clinton	71.6%	13.9%	14.5%
STEPHENS	2,310	1,517	412	381	Clinton	65.7%	17.8%	16.5%

TEXAS DEMOCRATIC

1992

County	Total Vote	Clinton	Tsongas	Other	Winner	Percentage of Total Vote Clinton	Tsongas	Other
STERLING	197	134	35	28	Clinton	68.0%	17.8%	14.2%
STONEWALL	743	574	87	82	Clinton	77.3%	11.7%	11.0%
SUTTON	554	368	101	85	Clinton	66.4%	18.2%	15.3%
SWISHER	1,473	1,083	219	171	Clinton	73.5%	14.9%	11.6%
TARRANT	67,710	43,466	14,952	9,292	Clinton	64.2%	22.1%	13.7%
TAYLOR	10,320	6,789	2,248	1,283	Clinton	65.8%	21.8%	12.4%
TERRELL	412	258	88	66	Clinton	62.6%	21.4%	16.0%
TERRY	2,276	1,476	340	460	Clinton	64.9%	14.9%	20.2%
THROCKMORTON	767	524	91	152	Clinton	68.3%	11.9%	19.8%
TITUS	5,189	4,041	664	484	Clinton	77.9%	12.8%	9.3%
TOM GREEN	10,881	7,019	2,227	1,635	Clinton	64.5%	20.5%	15.0%
TRAVIS	70,784	33,959	17,800	19,025	Clinton	48.0%	25.1%	26.9%
TRINITY	3,360	2,582	333	445	Clinton	76.8%	9.9%	13.2%
TYLER	4,046	3,000	508	538	Clinton	74.1%	12.6%	13.3%
UPSHUR	4,986	3,963	468	555	Clinton	79.5%	9.4%	11.1%
UPTON	1,178	717	208	253	Clinton	60.9%	17.7%	21.5%
UVALDE	4,660	2,657	1,044	959	Clinton	57.0%	22.4%	20.6%
VAL VERDE	3,265	1,851	805	609	Clinton	56.7%	24.7%	18.7%
VAN ZANDT	6,757	5,052	978	727	Clinton	74.8%	14.5%	10.8%
VICTORIA	5,414	3,413	1,087	914	Clinton	63.0%	20.1%	16.9%
WALKER	3,926	2,714	694	518	Clinton	69.1%	17.7%	13.2%
WALLER	3,649	2,636	519	494	Clinton	72.2%	14.2%	13.5%
WARD	2,602	1,569	448	585	Clinton	60.3%	17.2%	22.5%
WASHINGTON	3,385	2,329	617	439	Clinton	68.8%	18.2%	13.0%
WEBB	15,214	10,414	2,273	2,527	Clinton	68.5%	14.9%	16.6%
WHARTON	6,533	4,426	1,218	889	Clinton	67.7%	18.6%	13.6%
WHEELER	1,659	1,174	229	256	Clinton	70.8%	13.8%	15.4%
WICHITA	10,924	7,563	1,850	1,511	Clinton	69.2%	16.9%	13.8%
WILBARGER	2,660	1,750	452	458	Clinton	65.8%	17.0%	17.2%
WILLACY	3,280	2,351	439	490	Clinton	71.7%	13.4%	14.9%
WILLIAMSON	11,074	6,486	2,463	2,125	Clinton	58.6%	22.2%	19.2%
WILSON	3,993	2,530	782	681	Clinton	63.4%	19.6%	17.1%
WINKLER	1,392	803	256	333	Clinton	57.7%	18.4%	23.9%
WISE	5,552	3,774	1,026	752	Clinton	68.0%	18.5%	13.5%
WOOD	4,444	3,404	574	466	Clinton	76.6%	12.9%	10.5%
YOAKUM	891	544	162	185	Clinton	61.1%	18.2%	20.8%
YOUNG	4,168	2,754	733	681	Clinton	66.1%	17.6%	16.3%
ZAPATA	1,811	1,357	189	265	Clinton	74.9%	10.4%	14.6%
ZAVALA	2,317	1,771	248	298	Clinton	76.4%	10.7%	12.9%
TOTAL	1,482,975	972,151	285,191	225,633	Clinton	65.6%	19.2%	15.2%

TEXAS REPUBLICAN

1992

County	Total Vote	Buchanan	Bush	Other	Winner	Percentage of Total Vote Buchanan	Bush	Other
ANDERSON	639	159	430	50	Bush	24.9%	67.3%	7.8%
ANDREWS	250	65	170	15	Bush	26.0%	68.0%	6.0%
ANGELINA	1,755	419	1,161	175	Bush	23.9%	66.2%	10.0%
ARANSAS	2,022	482	1,327	213	Bush	23.8%	65.6%	10.5%
ARCHER	126	44	75	7	Bush	34.9%	59.5%	5.6%
ARMSTRONG	70	32	37	1	Bush	45.7%	52.9%	1.4%
ATASCOSA	543	124	393	26	Bush	22.8%	72.4%	4.8%
AUSTIN	779	185	546	48	Bush	23.7%	70.1%	6.2%
BAILEY	146	45	97	4	Bush	30.8%	66.4%	2.7%
BANDERA	1,939	453	1,262	224	Bush	23.4%	65.1%	11.6%
BASTROP	868	264	564	40	Bush	30.4%	65.0%	4.6%
BAYLOR	30	3	27		Bush	10.0%	90.0%	
BEE	907	168	701	38	Bush	18.5%	77.3%	4.2%
BELL	6,341	1,529	4,376	436	Bush	24.1%	69.0%	6.9%
BEXAR	56,333	12,720	40,671	2,942	Bush	22.6%	72.2%	5.2%
BLANCO	361	89	259	13	Bush	24.7%	71.7%	3.6%
BORDEN	13	8	5		Buchanan	61.5%	38.5%	
BOSQUE	442	71	346	25	Bush	16.1%	78.3%	5.7%
BOWIE	1,284	262	925	97	Bush	20.4%	72.0%	7.6%
BRAZORIA	8,661	1,930	6,060	671	Bush	22.3%	70.0%	7.7%
BRAZOS	7,206	1,560	5,223	423	Bush	21.6%	72.5%	5.9%
BREWSTER	325	104	198	23	Bush	32.0%	60.9%	7.1%
BRISCOE	21	2	18	1	Bush	9.5%	85.7%	4.8%
BROOKS	No Vote							
BROWN	697	176	506	15	Bush	25.3%	72.6%	2.2%
BURLESON	100	21	73	6	Bush	21.0%	73.0%	6.0%
BURNET	1,116	228	848	40	Bush	20.4%	76.0%	3.6%
CALDWELL	501	151	327	23	Bush	30.1%	65.3%	4.6%
CALHOUN	392	75	287	30	Bush	19.1%	73.2%	7.7%
CALLAHAN	174	43	120	11	Bush	24.7%	69.0%	6.3%
CAMERON	4,150	1,434	2,546	170	Bush	34.6%	61.3%	4.1%
CAMP	No Vote							
CARSON	394	106	268	20	Bush	26.9%	68.0%	5.1%
CASS	448	70	345	33	Bush	15.6%	77.0%	7.4%
CASTRO	182	51	123	8	Bush	28.0%	67.6%	4.4%
CHAMBERS	276	69	185	22	Bush	25.0%	67.0%	8.0%
CHEROKEE	596	126	454	16	Bush	21.1%	76.2%	2.7%
CHILDRESS	97	16	80	1	Bush	16.5%	82.5%	1.0%
CLAY	90	15	71	4	Bush	16.7%	78.9%	4.4%
COCHRAN	68	18	47	3	Bush	26.5%	69.1%	4.4%
COKE	No Vote							
COLEMAN	152	32	110	10	Bush	21.1%	72.4%	6.6%
COLLIN	25,489	6,432	17,084	1,973	Bush	25.2%	67.0%	7.7%
COLLINGSWORTH	No Vote							
COLORADO	353	57	268	28	Bush	16.1%	75.9%	7.9%
COMAL	6,557	1,562	4,611	384	Bush	23.8%	70.3%	5.9%
COMANCHE	No Vote							
CONCHO	15		13	2	Bush		86.7%	13.3%
COOKE	615	132	464	19	Bush	21.5%	75.4%	3.1%
CORYELL	1,095	289	743	63	Bush	26.4%	67.9%	5.8%

TEXAS REPUBLICAN

1992

County	Total Vote	Buchanan	Bush	Other	Winner	Percentage of Total Vote Buchanan	Bush	Other
COTTLE	No Vote							
CRANE	28	19	9		Buchanan	67.9%	32.1%	
CROCKETT	No Vote							
CROSBY	101	27	70	4	Bush	26.7%	69.3%	4.0%
CULBERSON	No Vote							
DALLAM	267	90	164	13	Bush	33.7%	61.4%	4.9%
DALLAS	106,867	26,710	73,855	6,302	Bush	25.0%	69.1%	5.9%
DAWSON	223	31	183	9	Bush	13.9%	82.1%	4.0%
DEAF SMITH	449	135	302	12	Bush	30.1%	67.3%	2.7%
DELTA	47	8	36	3	Bush	17.0%	76.6%	6.4%
DENTON	17,615	5,402	10,821	1,392	Bush	30.7%	61.4%	7.9%
DE WITT	524	90	395	39	Bush	17.2%	75.4%	7.4%
DICKENS	No Vote							
DIMMIT	16	4	12		Bush	25.0%	75.0%	
DONLEY	158	35	119	4	Bush	22.2%	75.3%	2.5%
DUVAL	No Vote							
EASTLAND	410	143	252	15	Bush	34.9%	61.5%	3.7%
ECTOR	10,111	2,312	6,980	819	Bush	22.9%	69.0%	8.1%
EDWARDS	117	32	81	4	Bush	27.4%	69.2%	3.4%
ELLIS	4,517	1,183	3,041	293	Bush	26.2%	67.3%	6.5%
EL PASO	15,842	3,127	11,788	927	Bush	19.7%	74.4%	5.9%
ERATH	569	119	415	35	Bush	20.9%	72.9%	6.2%
FALLS	114	32	75	7	Bush	28.1%	65.8%	6.1%
FANNIN	262	84	164	14	Bush	32.1%	62.6%	5.3%
FAYETTE	1,014	203	732	79	Bush	20.0%	72.2%	7.8%
FISHER	12	5	7		Bush	41.7%	58.3%	
FLOYD	143	43	93	7	Bush	30.1%	65.0%	4.9%
FOARD	No Vote							
FORT BEND	13,181	2,791	9,533	857	Bush	21.2%	72.3%	6.5%
FRANKLIN	163	30	122	11	Bush	18.4%	74.8%	6.7%
FREESTONE	348	76	256	16	Bush	21.8%	73.6%	4.6%
FRIO	29	12	16	1	Bush	41.4%	55.2%	3.4%
GAINES	189	45	135	9	Bush	23.8%	71.4%	4.8%
GALVESTON	6,936	1,491	4,832	613	Bush	21.5%	69.7%	8.8%
GARZA	36	12	23	1	Bush	33.3%	63.9%	2.8%
GILLESPIE	3,283	733	2,350	200	Bush	22.3%	71.6%	6.1%
GLASSCOCK	131	50	75	6	Bush	38.2%	57.3%	4.6%
GOLIAD	63	13	47	3	Bush	20.6%	74.6%	4.8%
GONZALES	202	54	130	18	Bush	26.7%	64.4%	8.9%
GRAY	3,573	870	2,481	222	Bush	24.3%	69.4%	6.2%
GRAYSON	2,552	608	1,797	147	Bush	23.8%	70.4%	5.8%
GREGG	6,404	1,300	4,663	441	Bush	20.3%	72.8%	6.9%
GRIMES	470	79	357	34	Bush	16.8%	76.0%	7.2%
GUADALUPE	3,862	894	2,749	219	Bush	23.1%	71.2%	5.7%
HALE	780	227	540	13	Bush	29.1%	69.2%	1.7%
HALL	34	10	24		Bush	29.4%	70.6%	
HAMILTON	162	42	111	9	Bush	25.9%	68.5%	5.6%
HANSFORD	660	156	465	39	Bush	23.6%	70.5%	5.9%
HARDEMAN	31	7	20	4	Bush	22.6%	64.5%	12.9%
HARDIN	492	165	301	26	Bush	33.5%	61.2%	5.3%

TEXAS REPUBLICAN

1992

County	Total Vote	Buchanan	Bush	Other	Winner	Percentage of Total Vote Buchanan	Bush	Other
HARRIS	135,145	27,562	99,394	8,189	Bush	20.4%	73.5%	6.1%
HARRISON	1,362	272	1,008	82	Bush	20.0%	74.0%	6.0%
HARTLEY	230	54	167	9	Bush	23.5%	72.6%	3.9%
HASKELL	No Vote							
HAYS	2,898	753	1,961	184	Bush	26.0%	67.7%	6.3%
HEMPHILL	417	124	258	35	Bush	29.7%	61.9%	8.4%
HENDERSON	2,421	556	1,709	156	Bush	23.0%	70.6%	6.4%
HIDALGO	3,549	1,027	2,424	98	Bush	28.9%	68.3%	2.8%
HILL	557	111	410	36	Bush	19.9%	73.6%	6.5%
HOCKLEY	324	79	231	14	Bush	24.4%	71.3%	4.3%
HOOD	2,069	445	1,488	136	Bush	21.5%	71.9%	6.6%
HOPKINS	507	120	363	24	Bush	23.7%	71.6%	4.7%
HOUSTON	358	89	246	23	Bush	24.9%	68.7%	6.4%
HOWARD	650	192	444	14	Bush	29.5%	68.3%	2.2%
HUDSPETH	4		3	1	Bush		75.0%	25.0%
HUNT	3,046	733	2,153	160	Bush	24.1%	70.7%	5.3%
HUTCHINSON	3,393	829	2,339	225	Bush	24.4%	68.9%	6.6%
IRION	25	5	20		Bush	20.0%	80.0%	
JACK	69	14	46	9	Bush	20.3%	66.7%	13.0%
JACKSON	171	36	128	7	Bush	21.1%	74.9%	4.1%
JASPER	345	69	264	12	Bush	20.0%	76.5%	3.5%
JEFF DAVIS	No Vote							
JEFFERSON	6,306	1,674	4,338	294	Bush	26.5%	68.8%	4.7%
JIM HOGG	32	5	27		Bush	15.6%	84.4%	
JIM WELLS	283	56	212	15	Bush	19.8%	74.9%	5.3%
JOHNSON	3,690	1,078	2,367	245	Bush	29.2%	64.1%	6.6%
JONES	310	82	195	33	Bush	26.5%	62.9%	10.6%
KARNES	No Vote							
KAUFMAN	1,676	505	1,055	116	Bush	30.1%	62.9%	6.9%
KENDALL	2,997	630	2,108	259	Bush	21.0%	70.3%	8.6%
KENEDY	4		4		Bush		100.0%	
KENT	2		2		Bush		100.0%	
KERR	6,703	1,604	4,477	622	Bush	23.9%	66.8%	9.3%
KIMBLE	134	32	96	6	Bush	23.9%	71.6%	4.5%
KING	No Vote							
KINNEY	93	28	61	4	Bush	30.1%	65.6%	4.3%
KLEBERG	489	99	374	16	Bush	20.2%	76.5%	3.3%
KNOX	45	11	33	1	Bush	24.4%	73.3%	2.2%
LAMAR	684	144	509	31	Bush	21.1%	74.4%	4.5%
LAMB	106	22	82	2	Bush	20.8%	77.4%	1.9%
LAMPASAS	406	99	280	27	Bush	24.4%	69.0%	6.7%
LA SALLE	No Vote							
LAVACA	389	87	275	27	Bush	22.4%	70.7%	6.9%
LEE	234	33	187	14	Bush	14.1%	79.9%	6.0%
LEON	377	51	305	21	Bush	13.5%	80.9%	5.6%
LIBERTY	1,003	234	691	78	Bush	23.3%	68.9%	7.8%
LIMESTONE	361	65	273	23	Bush	18.0%	75.6%	6.4%
LIPSCOMB	359	98	233	28	Bush	27.3%	64.9%	7.8%
LIVE OAK	159	44	107	8	Bush	27.7%	67.3%	5.0%
LLANO	1,705	304	1,296	105	Bush	17.8%	76.0%	6.2%

TEXAS REPUBLICAN

1992

County	Total Vote	Buchanan	Bush	Other	Winner	Percentage of Total Vote Buchanan	Bush	Other
LOVING	No Vote							
LUBBOCK	20,480	4,432	14,867	1,181	Bush	21.6%	72.6%	5.8%
LYNN	39	13	26		Bush	33.3%	66.7%	
MCCULLOCH	70	11	54	5	Bush	15.7%	77.1%	7.1%
MCLENNAN	7,303	1,698	5,271	334	Bush	23.3%	72.2%	4.6%
MCMULLEN	No Vote							
MADISON	217	38	161	18	Bush	17.5%	74.2%	8.3%
MARION	61	9	44	8	Bush	14.8%	72.1%	13.1%
MARTIN	60	25	32	3	Bush	41.7%	53.3%	5.0%
MASON	188	59	127	2	Bush	31.4%	67.6%	1.1%
MATAGORDA	438	83	312	43	Bush	18.9%	71.2%	9.8%
MAVERICK	120	18	95	7	Bush	15.0%	79.2%	5.8%
MEDINA	809	177	594	38	Bush	21.9%	73.4%	4.7%
MENARD	26	4	22		Bush	15.4%	84.6%	
MIDLAND	19,334	6,089	11,613	1,632	Bush	31.5%	60.1%	8.4%
MILAM	452	97	330	25	Bush	21.5%	73.0%	5.5%
MILLS	29	6	22	1	Bush	20.7%	75.9%	3.4%
MITCHELL	76	14	61	1	Bush	18.4%	80.3%	1.3%
MONTAGUE	107	30	73	4	Bush	28.0%	68.2%	3.7%
MONTGOMERY	18,966	4,399	12,808	1,759	Bush	23.2%	67.5%	9.3%
MOORE	964	235	677	52	Bush	24.4%	70.2%	5.4%
MORRIS	103	20	65	18	Bush	19.4%	63.1%	17.5%
MOTLEY	23	5	18		Bush	21.7%	78.3%	
NACOGDOCHES	1,669	407	1,187	75	Bush	24.4%	71.1%	4.5%
NAVARRO	1,265	366	830	69	Bush	28.9%	65.6%	5.5%
NEWTON	156	43	98	15	Bush	27.6%	62.8%	9.6%
NOLAN	135	33	100	2	Bush	24.4%	74.1%	1.5%
NUECES	9,297	2,341	6,495	461	Bush	25.2%	69.9%	5.0%
OCHILTREE	938	268	635	35	Bush	28.6%	67.7%	3.7%
OLDHAM	No Vote							
ORANGE	992	326	620	46	Bush	32.9%	62.5%	4.6%
PALO PINTO	500	124	343	33	Bush	24.8%	68.6%	6.6%
PANOLA	114	43	68	3	Bush	37.7%	59.6%	2.6%
PARKER	3,166	916	2,033	217	Bush	28.9%	64.2%	6.9%
PARMER	236	95	139	2	Bush	40.3%	58.9%	0.8%
PECOS	163	36	120	7	Bush	22.1%	73.6%	4.3%
POLK	900	180	649	71	Bush	20.0%	72.1%	7.9%
POTTER	5,835	1,483	3,969	383	Bush	25.4%	68.0%	6.6%
PRESIDIO	64	17	34	13	Bush	26.6%	53.1%	20.3%
RAINS	102	22	71	9	Bush	21.6%	69.6%	8.8%
RANDALL	10,030	2,718	6,780	532	Bush	27.1%	67.6%	5.3%
REAGAN	61	12	47	2	Bush	19.7%	77.0%	3.3%
REAL	135	34	97	4	Bush	25.2%	71.9%	3.0%
RED RIVER	80	22	54	4	Bush	27.5%	67.5%	5.0%
REEVES	No Vote							
REFUGIO	103	19	80	4	Bush	18.4%	77.7%	3.9%
ROBERTS	38	13	24	1	Bush	34.2%	63.2%	2.6%
ROBERTSON	258	54	193	11	Bush	20.9%	74.8%	4.3%
ROCKWALL	3,497	965	2,250	282	Bush	27.6%	64.3%	8.1%
RUNNELS	95	20	71	4	Bush	21.1%	74.7%	4.2%

TEXAS REPUBLICAN

1992

County	Total Vote	Buchanan	Bush	Other	Winner	Percentage of Total Vote Buchanan	Bush	Other
RUSK	1,017	191	762	64	Bush	18.8%	74.9%	6.3%
SABINE	70	9	55	6	Bush	12.9%	78.6%	8.6%
SAN AUGUSTINE	34	7	24	3	Bush	20.6%	70.6%	8.8%
SAN JACINTO	257	67	179	11	Bush	26.1%	69.6%	4.3%
SAN PATRICIO	1,150	298	807	45	Bush	25.9%	70.2%	3.9%
SAN SABA	42	13	29		Bush	31.0%	69.0%	
SCHLEICHER	61	15	44	2	Bush	24.6%	72.1%	3.3%
SCURRY	365	77	273	15	Bush	21.1%	74.8%	4.1%
SHACKELFORD	45	16	27	2	Bush	35.6%	60.0%	4.4%
SHELBY	75	10	62	3	Bush	13.3%	82.7%	4.0%
SHERMAN	169	53	113	3	Bush	31.4%	66.9%	1.8%
SMITH	14,325	3,534	9,803	988	Bush	24.7%	68.4%	6.9%
SOMERVELL	116	23	78	15	Bush	19.8%	67.2%	12.9%
STARR	14	4	10		Bush	28.6%	71.4%	
STEPHENS	64	7	57		Bush	10.9%	89.1%	
STERLING	53	15	37	1	Bush	28.3%	69.8%	1.9%
STONEWALL	14	2	12		Bush	14.3%	85.7%	
SUTTON	96	25	66	5	Bush	26.0%	68.8%	5.2%
SWISHER	54	21	33		Bush	38.9%	61.1%	
TARRANT	70,527	19,430	45,965	5,132	Bush	27.5%	65.2%	7.3%
TAYLOR	9,191	1,922	6,738	531	Bush	20.9%	73.3%	5.8%
TERRELL	No Vote							
TERRY	181	41	136	4	Bush	22.7%	75.1%	2.2%
THROCKMORTON	No Vote							
TITUS	210	31	169	10	Bush	14.8%	80.5%	4.8%
TOM GREEN	4,833	1,181	3,360	292	Bush	24.4%	69.5%	6.0%
TRAVIS	32,371	7,713	23,237	1,421	Bush	23.8%	71.8%	4.4%
TRINITY	269	40	211	18	Bush	14.9%	78.4%	6.7%
TYLER	155	38	112	5	Bush	24.5%	72.3%	3.2%
UPSHUR	505	122	354	29	Bush	24.2%	70.1%	5.7%
UPTON	42	14	24	4	Bush	33.3%	57.1%	9.5%
UVALDE	296	91	190	15	Bush	30.7%	64.2%	5.1%
VAL VERDE	787	173	564	50	Bush	22.0%	71.7%	6.4%
VAN ZANDT	1,123	280	762	81	Bush	24.9%	67.9%	7.2%
VICTORIA	2,991	496	2,350	145	Bush	16.6%	78.6%	4.8%
WALKER	1,660	300	1,243	117	Bush	18.1%	74.9%	7.0%
WALLER	456	86	340	30	Bush	18.9%	74.6%	6.6%
WARD	162	51	100	11	Bush	31.5%	61.7%	6.8%
WASHINGTON	1,180	205	901	74	Bush	17.4%	76.4%	6.3%
WEBB	368	45	307	16	Bush	12.2%	83.4%	4.3%
WHARTON	650	115	500	35	Bush	17.7%	76.9%	5.4%
WHEELER	176	49	118	9	Bush	27.8%	67.0%	5.1%
WICHITA	4,557	1,018	3,289	250	Bush	22.3%	72.2%	5.5%
WILBARGER	187	38	134	15	Bush	20.3%	71.7%	8.0%
WILLACY	50	20	30		Bush	40.0%	60.0%	
WILLIAMSON	9,152	2,347	6,298	507	Bush	25.6%	68.8%	5.5%
WILSON	538	119	396	23	Bush	22.1%	73.6%	4.3%
WINKLER	124	41	71	12	Bush	33.1%	57.3%	9.7%
WISE	686	202	421	63	Bush	29.4%	61.4%	9.2%
WOOD	1,650	410	1,069	171	Bush	24.8%	64.8%	10.4%

TEXAS REPUBLICAN

1992

County	Total Vote	Buchanan	Bush	Other	Winner	Percentage of Total Vote: Buchanan	Bush	Other
YOAKUM	138	31	102	5	Bush	22.5%	73.9%	3.6%
YOUNG	180	61	110	9	Bush	33.9%	61.1%	5.0%
ZAPATA	344	81	241	22	Bush	23.5%	70.1%	6.4%
ZAVALA	No Vote							
TOTAL	797,146	190,572	556,280	50,294	Bush	23.9%	69.8%	6.3%

TEXAS DEMOCRATIC

1996

County	Total Vote	Clinton	Other	Winner	Percentage of Total Vote: Clinton	Other
ANDERSON	4,610	3,577	1,033	Clinton	77.6%	22.4%
ANDREWS	1,323	847	476	Clinton	64.0%	36.0%
ANGELINA	7,559	5,902	1,657	Clinton	78.1%	21.9%
ARANSAS	1,588	1,416	172	Clinton	89.2%	10.8%
ARCHER	909	752	157	Clinton	82.7%	17.3%
ARMSTRONG	81	63	18	Clinton	77.8%	22.2%
ATASCOSA	2,001	1,613	388	Clinton	80.6%	19.4%
AUSTIN	890	753	137	Clinton	84.6%	15.4%
BAILEY	349	260	89	Clinton	74.5%	25.5%
BANDERA	252	232	20	Clinton	92.1%	7.9%
BASTROP	3,785	3,188	597	Clinton	84.2%	15.8%
BAYLOR	1,064	869	195	Clinton	81.7%	18.3%
BEE	2,296	1,988	308	Clinton	86.6%	13.4%
BELL	5,033	4,604	429	Clinton	91.5%	8.5%
BEXAR	38,090	36,204	1,886	Clinton	95.0%	5.0%
BLANCO	224	195	29	Clinton	87.1%	12.9%
BORDEN	67	44	23	Clinton	65.7%	34.3%
BOSQUE	2,225	1,820	405	Clinton	81.8%	18.2%
BOWIE	9,423	8,389	1,034	Clinton	89.0%	11.0%
BRAZORIA	4,295	3,846	449	Clinton	89.5%	10.5%
BRAZOS	2,870	2,696	174	Clinton	93.9%	6.1%
BREWSTER	1,176	942	234	Clinton	80.1%	19.9%
BRISCOE	461	365	96	Clinton	79.2%	20.8%
BROOKS	3,120	2,701	419	Clinton	86.6%	13.4%
BROWN	2,202	1,781	421	Clinton	80.9%	19.1%
BURLESON	941	782	159	Clinton	83.1%	16.9%
BURNET	3,330	2,603	727	Clinton	78.2%	21.8%
CALDWELL	1,767	1,491	276	Clinton	84.4%	15.6%
CALHOUN	2,301	1,891	410	Clinton	82.2%	17.8%
CALLAHAN	1,239	950	289	Clinton	76.7%	23.3%
CAMERON	18,329	15,465	2,864	Clinton	84.4%	15.6%
CAMP	1,482	1,244	238	Clinton	83.9%	16.1%
CARSON	447	347	100	Clinton	77.6%	22.4%
CASS	4,973	4,030	943	Clinton	81.0%	19.0%
CASTRO	521	420	101	Clinton	80.6%	19.4%

TEXAS DEMOCRATIC

1996

County	Total Vote	Clinton	Other	Winner	Percentage of Total Vote Clinton	Other
CHAMBERS	2,541	1,831	710	Clinton	72.1%	27.9%
CHEROKEE	3,376	2,578	798	Clinton	76.4%	23.6%
CHILDRESS	902	686	216	Clinton	76.1%	23.9%
CLAY	1,060	893	167	Clinton	84.2%	15.8%
COCHRAN	655	484	171	Clinton	73.9%	26.1%
COKE	737	557	180	Clinton	75.6%	24.4%
COLEMAN	1,261	977	284	Clinton	77.5%	22.5%
COLLIN	2,935	2,749	186	Clinton	93.7%	6.3%
COLLINGSWORTH	766	553	213	Clinton	72.2%	27.8%
COLORADO	2,855	2,265	590	Clinton	79.3%	20.7%
COMAL	1,057	987	70	Clinton	93.4%	6.6%
COMANCHE	1,603	1,314	289	Clinton	82.0%	18.0%
CONCHO	523	407	116	Clinton	77.8%	22.2%
COOKE	1,258	1,095	163	Clinton	87.0%	13.0%
CORYELL	2,612	2,069	543	Clinton	79.2%	20.8%
COTTLE	375	311	64	Clinton	82.9%	17.1%
CRANE	1,132	730	402	Clinton	64.5%	35.5%
CROCKETT	965	741	224	Clinton	76.8%	23.2%
CROSBY	1,231	961	270	Clinton	78.1%	21.9%
CULBERSON	763	607	156	Clinton	79.6%	20.4%
DALLAM	139	111	28	Clinton	79.9%	20.1%
DALLAS	43,407	41,577	1,830	Clinton	95.8%	4.2%
DAWSON	860	612	248	Clinton	71.2%	28.8%
DEAF SMITH	743	534	209	Clinton	71.9%	28.1%
DELTA	1,096	903	193	Clinton	82.4%	17.6%
DENTON	3,128	2,975	153	Clinton	95.1%	4.9%
DE WITT	1,453	1,105	348	Clinton	76.0%	24.0%
DICKENS	679	521	158	Clinton	76.7%	23.3%
DIMMIT	3,214	2,805	409	Clinton	87.3%	12.7%
DONLEY	431	329	102	Clinton	76.3%	23.7%
DUVAL	4,690	4,423	267	Clinton	94.3%	5.7%
EASTLAND	1,844	1,464	380	Clinton	79.4%	20.6%
ECTOR	2,863	2,618	245	Clinton	91.4%	8.6%
EDWARDS	352	276	76	Clinton	78.4%	21.6%
ELLIS	2,447	2,284	163	Clinton	93.3%	6.7%
EL PASO	48,134	42,157	5,977	Clinton	87.6%	12.4%
ERATH	1,022	911	111	Clinton	89.1%	10.9%
FALLS	2,937	2,341	596	Clinton	79.7%	20.3%
FANNIN	2,778	2,337	441	Clinton	84.1%	15.9%
FAYETTE	2,236	1,910	326	Clinton	85.4%	14.6%
FISHER	828	747	81	Clinton	90.2%	9.8%
FLOYD	441	345	96	Clinton	78.2%	21.8%
FOARD	366	319	47	Clinton	87.2%	12.8%
FORT BEND	6,901	6,523	378	Clinton	94.5%	5.5%
FRANKLIN	1,491	1,211	280	Clinton	81.2%	18.8%
FREESTONE	3,079	2,351	728	Clinton	76.4%	23.6%
FRIO	3,261	2,756	505	Clinton	84.5%	15.5%
GAINES	280	226	54	Clinton	80.7%	19.3%
GALVESTON	13,305	12,151	1,154	Clinton	91.3%	8.7%
GARZA	743	553	190	Clinton	74.4%	25.6%

TEXAS DEMOCRATIC

1996

County	Total Vote	Clinton	Other	Winner	Percentage of Total Vote	
					Clinton	Other
GILLESPIE	254	244	10	Clinton	96.1%	3.9%
GLASSCOCK	36	26	10	Clinton	72.2%	27.8%
GOLIAD	755	629	126	Clinton	83.3%	16.7%
GONZALES	1,952	1,529	423	Clinton	78.3%	21.7%
GRAY	551	490	61	Clinton	88.9%	11.1%
GRAYSON	5,706	4,860	846	Clinton	85.2%	14.8%
GREGG	3,449	3,297	152	Clinton	95.6%	4.4%
GRIMES	2,190	1,795	395	Clinton	82.0%	18.0%
GUADALUPE	1,412	1,319	93	Clinton	93.4%	6.6%
HALE	3,505	2,381	1,124	Clinton	67.9%	32.1%
HALL	944	718	226	Clinton	76.1%	23.9%
HAMILTON	627	559	68	Clinton	89.2%	10.8%
HANSFORD	67	49	18	Clinton	73.1%	26.9%
HARDEMAN	467	407	60	Clinton	87.2%	12.8%
HARDIN	6,674	4,974	1,700	Clinton	74.5%	25.5%
HARRIS	75,600	71,185	4,415	Clinton	94.2%	5.8%
HARRISON	8,602	7,102	1,500	Clinton	82.6%	17.4%
HARTLEY	157	137	20	Clinton	87.3%	12.7%
HASKELL	1,487	1,263	224	Clinton	84.9%	15.1%
HAYS	3,907	3,494	413	Clinton	89.4%	10.6%
HEMPHILL	117	98	19	Clinton	83.8%	16.2%
HENDERSON	7,240	5,907	1,333	Clinton	81.6%	18.4%
HIDALGO	34,370	26,436	7,934	Clinton	76.9%	23.1%
HILL	2,282	1,959	323	Clinton	85.8%	14.2%
HOCKLEY	869	649	220	Clinton	74.7%	25.3%
HOOD	1,284	1,201	83	Clinton	93.5%	6.5%
HOPKINS	4,912	3,966	946	Clinton	80.7%	19.3%
HOUSTON	2,914	2,259	655	Clinton	77.5%	22.5%
HOWARD	1,958	1,654	304	Clinton	84.5%	15.5%
HUDSPETH	537	390	147	Clinton	72.6%	27.4%
HUNT	4,423	3,862	561	Clinton	87.3%	12.7%
HUTCHINSON	969	823	146	Clinton	84.9%	15.1%
IRION	399	282	117	Clinton	70.7%	29.3%
JACK	1,103	876	227	Clinton	79.4%	20.6%
JACKSON	2,226	1,704	522	Clinton	76.5%	23.5%
JASPER	5,015	3,808	1,207	Clinton	75.9%	24.1%
JEFF DAVIS	295	209	86	Clinton	70.8%	29.2%
JEFFERSON	26,239	22,708	3,531	Clinton	86.5%	13.5%
JIM HOGG	1,383	1,251	132	Clinton	90.5%	9.5%
JIM WELLS	6,685	5,673	1,012	Clinton	84.9%	15.1%
JOHNSON	2,579	2,350	229	Clinton	91.1%	8.9%
JONES	2,072	1,621	451	Clinton	78.2%	21.8%
KARNES	2,550	1,940	610	Clinton	76.1%	23.9%
KAUFMAN	4,489	3,702	787	Clinton	82.5%	17.5%
KENDALL	236	224	12	Clinton	94.9%	5.1%
KENEDY	179	155	24	Clinton	86.6%	13.4%
KENT	400	326	74	Clinton	81.5%	18.5%
KERR	755	723	32	Clinton	95.8%	4.2%
KIMBLE	621	466	155	Clinton	75.0%	25.0%
KING	109	73	36	Clinton	67.0%	33.0%

TEXAS DEMOCRATIC

1996

County	Total Vote	Clinton	Other	Winner	Percentage of Total Vote: Clinton	Other
KINNEY	512	382	130	Clinton	74.6%	25.4%
KLEBERG	4,689	4,158	531	Clinton	88.7%	11.3%
KNOX	672	579	93	Clinton	86.2%	13.8%
LAMAR	6,438	5,089	1,349	Clinton	79.0%	21.0%
LAMB	971	748	223	Clinton	77.0%	23.0%
LAMPASAS	653	583	70	Clinton	89.3%	10.7%
LA SALLE	1,393	1,242	151	Clinton	89.2%	10.8%
LAVACA	2,866	2,228	638	Clinton	77.7%	22.3%
LEE	1,698	1,304	394	Clinton	76.8%	23.2%
LEON	2,144	1,705	439	Clinton	79.5%	20.5%
LIBERTY	4,236	3,286	950	Clinton	77.6%	22.4%
LIMESTONE	3,555	2,819	736	Clinton	79.3%	20.7%
LIPSCOMB	452	296	156	Clinton	65.5%	34.5%
LIVE OAK	1,228	930	298	Clinton	75.7%	24.3%
LLANO	1,531	1,372	159	Clinton	89.6%	10.4%
LOVING	55	30	25	Clinton	54.5%	45.5%
LUBBOCK	4,236	3,940	296	Clinton	93.0%	7.0%
LYNN	640	566	74	Clinton	88.4%	11.6%
MCCULLOCH	1,550	1,201	349	Clinton	77.5%	22.5%
MCLENNAN	11,136	9,972	1,164	Clinton	89.5%	10.5%
MCMULLEN	180	96	84	Clinton	53.3%	46.7%
MADISON	1,454	1,171	283	Clinton	80.5%	19.5%
MARION	2,330	1,915	415	Clinton	82.2%	17.8%
MARTIN	450	306	144	Clinton	68.0%	32.0%
MASON	1,024	708	316	Clinton	69.1%	30.9%
MATAGORDA	4,811	3,710	1,101	Clinton	77.1%	22.9%
MAVERICK	4,979	4,467	512	Clinton	89.7%	10.3%
MEDINA	1,116	901	215	Clinton	80.7%	19.3%
MENARD	444	367	77	Clinton	82.7%	17.3%
MIDLAND	1,614	1,502	112	Clinton	93.1%	6.9%
MILAM	3,653	3,095	558	Clinton	84.7%	15.3%
MILLS	514	447	67	Clinton	87.0%	13.0%
MITCHELL	1,379	1,150	229	Clinton	83.4%	16.6%
MONTAGUE	2,149	1,755	394	Clinton	81.7%	18.3%
MONTGOMERY	2,928	2,752	176	Clinton	94.0%	6.0%
MOORE	565	414	151	Clinton	73.3%	26.7%
MORRIS	2,774	2,158	616	Clinton	77.8%	22.2%
MOTLEY	117	84	33	Clinton	71.8%	28.2%
NACOGDOCHES	5,211	3,942	1,269	Clinton	75.6%	24.4%
NAVARRO	3,801	3,223	578	Clinton	84.8%	15.2%
NEWTON	2,967	2,332	635	Clinton	78.6%	21.4%
NOLAN	2,707	2,130	577	Clinton	78.7%	21.3%
NUECES	26,563	23,510	3,053	Clinton	88.5%	11.5%
OCHILTREE	112	89	23	Clinton	79.5%	20.5%
OLDHAM	390	259	131	Clinton	66.4%	33.6%
ORANGE	8,979	7,273	1,706	Clinton	81.0%	19.0%
PALO PINTO	2,862	2,292	570	Clinton	80.1%	19.9%
PANOLA	4,047	2,876	1,171	Clinton	71.1%	28.9%
PARKER	3,140	2,802	338	Clinton	89.2%	10.8%
PARMER	305	218	87	Clinton	71.5%	28.5%

TEXAS DEMOCRATIC

1996

County	Total Vote	Clinton	Other	Winner	Percentage of Total Vote	
					Clinton	Other
PECOS	2,032	1,598	434	Clinton	78.6%	21.4%
POLK	3,256	2,744	512	Clinton	84.3%	15.7%
POTTER	2,033	1,893	140	Clinton	93.1%	6.9%
PRESIDIO	1,245	1,089	156	Clinton	87.5%	12.5%
RAINS	1,315	1,070	245	Clinton	81.4%	18.6%
RANDALL	1,421	1,342	79	Clinton	94.4%	5.6%
REAGAN	152	125	27	Clinton	82.2%	17.8%
REAL	121	107	14	Clinton	88.4%	11.6%
RED RIVER	2,030	1,696	334	Clinton	83.5%	16.5%
REEVES	2,692	2,353	339	Clinton	87.4%	12.6%
REFUGIO	799	681	118	Clinton	85.2%	14.8%
ROBERTS	48	36	12	Clinton	75.0%	25.0%
ROBERTSON	3,182	2,674	508	Clinton	84.0%	16.0%
ROCKWALL	506	476	30	Clinton	94.1%	5.9%
RUNNELS	1,122	853	269	Clinton	76.0%	24.0%
RUSK	4,243	3,258	985	Clinton	76.8%	23.2%
SABINE	2,739	2,046	693	Clinton	74.7%	25.3%
SAN AUGUSTINE	2,240	1,510	730	Clinton	67.4%	32.6%
SAN JACINTO	3,359	2,637	722	Clinton	78.5%	21.5%
SAN PATRICIO	5,203	4,457	746	Clinton	85.7%	14.3%
SAN SABA	882	692	190	Clinton	78.5%	21.5%
SCHLEICHER	689	530	159	Clinton	76.9%	23.1%
SCURRY	1,286	1,062	224	Clinton	82.6%	17.4%
SHACKELFORD	391	306	85	Clinton	78.3%	21.7%
SHELBY	5,498	3,161	2,337	Clinton	57.5%	42.5%
SHERMAN	105	71	34	Clinton	67.6%	32.4%
SMITH	3,322	3,139	183	Clinton	94.5%	5.5%
SOMERVELL	1,147	932	215	Clinton	81.3%	18.7%
STARR	7,871	7,342	529	Clinton	93.3%	6.7%
STEPHENS	1,565	1,116	449	Clinton	71.3%	28.7%
STERLING	62	50	12	Clinton	80.6%	19.4%
STONEWALL	468	398	70	Clinton	85.0%	15.0%
SUTTON	393	285	108	Clinton	72.5%	27.5%
SWISHER	889	710	179	Clinton	79.9%	20.1%
TARRANT	29,914	28,837	1,077	Clinton	96.4%	3.6%
TAYLOR	2,574	2,458	116	Clinton	95.5%	4.5%
TERRELL	163	122	41	Clinton	74.8%	25.2%
TERRY	474	363	111	Clinton	76.6%	23.4%
THROCKMORTON	507	393	114	Clinton	77.5%	22.5%
TITUS	3,950	3,179	771	Clinton	80.5%	19.5%
TOM GREEN	3,943	3,526	417	Clinton	89.4%	10.6%
TRAVIS	38,253	36,203	2,050	Clinton	94.6%	5.4%
TRINITY	3,195	2,465	730	Clinton	77.2%	22.8%
TYLER	2,815	2,316	499	Clinton	82.3%	17.7%
UPSHUR	4,116	3,248	868	Clinton	78.9%	21.1%
UPTON	513	351	162	Clinton	68.4%	31.6%
UVALDE	2,074	1,629	445	Clinton	78.5%	21.5%
VAL VERDE	1,645	1,453	192	Clinton	88.3%	11.7%
VAN ZANDT	3,274	2,577	697	Clinton	78.7%	21.3%
VICTORIA	2,938	2,488	450	Clinton	84.7%	15.3%

TEXAS DEMOCRATIC

1996

County	Total Vote	Clinton	Other	Winner	Percentage of Total Vote: Clinton	Percentage of Total Vote: Other
WALKER	4,229	3,365	864	Clinton	79.6%	20.4%
WALLER	2,270	1,991	279	Clinton	87.7%	12.3%
WARD	1,977	1,477	500	Clinton	74.7%	25.3%
WASHINGTON	982	866	116	Clinton	88.2%	11.8%
WEBB	16,996	15,296	1,700	Clinton	90.0%	10.0%
WHARTON	3,285	2,742	543	Clinton	83.5%	16.5%
WHEELER	911	709	202	Clinton	77.8%	22.2%
WICHITA	5,836	5,166	670	Clinton	88.5%	11.5%
WILBARGER	1,204	949	255	Clinton	78.8%	21.2%
WILLACY	3,053	2,521	532	Clinton	82.6%	17.4%
WILLIAMSON	3,705	3,461	244	Clinton	93.4%	6.6%
WILSON	1,997	1,717	280	Clinton	86.0%	14.0%
WINKLER	1,052	801	251	Clinton	76.1%	23.9%
WISE	2,795	2,258	537	Clinton	80.8%	19.2%
WOOD	1,546	1,358	188	Clinton	87.8%	12.2%
YOAKUM	590	393	197	Clinton	66.6%	33.4%
YOUNG	2,513	1,947	566	Clinton	77.5%	22.5%
ZAPATA	2,248	2,001	247	Clinton	89.0%	11.0%
ZAVALA	2,663	2,409	254	Clinton	90.5%	9.5%
TOTAL	921,256	796,041	125,215	Clinton	86.4%	13.6%

TEXAS REPUBLICAN

1996

County	Total Vote	Buchanan	Dole	Forbes	Other	Winner	Percentage of Total Vote: Buchanan	Percentage of Total Vote: Dole	Percentage of Total Vote: Forbes	Percentage of Total Vote: Other
ANDERSON	1,737	633	830	146	128	Dole	36.4%	47.8%	8.4%	7.4%
ANDREWS	474	186	195	50	43	Dole	39.2%	41.1%	10.5%	9.1%
ANGELINA	3,587	1,338	1,771	234	244	Dole	37.3%	49.4%	6.5%	6.8%
ARANSAS	2,131	344	1,239	306	242	Dole	16.1%	58.1%	14.4%	11.4%
ARCHER	327	105	149	57	16	Dole	32.1%	45.6%	17.4%	4.9%
ARMSTRONG	496	114	224	53	105	Dole	23.0%	45.2%	10.7%	21.2%
ATASCOSA	1,062	263	598	129	72	Dole	24.8%	56.3%	12.1%	6.8%
AUSTIN	2,452	580	1,362	248	262	Dole	23.7%	55.5%	10.1%	10.7%
BAILEY	190	43	111	27	9	Dole	22.6%	58.4%	14.2%	4.7%
BANDERA	2,218	463	1,197	324	234	Dole	20.9%	54.0%	14.6%	10.6%
BASTROP	2,204	510	1,174	292	228	Dole	23.1%	53.3%	13.2%	10.3%
BAYLOR	41	11	24	2	4	Dole	26.8%	58.5%	4.9%	9.8%
BEE	1,273	287	696	149	141	Dole	22.5%	54.7%	11.7%	11.1%
BELL	10,989	1,987	6,329	1,427	1,246	Dole	18.1%	57.6%	13.0%	11.3%
BEXAR	66,324	10,771	39,480	9,337	6,736	Dole	16.2%	59.5%	14.1%	10.2%

TEXAS REPUBLICAN

1996

County	Total Vote	Buchanan	Dole	Forbes	Other	Winner	Percentage of Total Vote Buchanan	Dole	Forbes	Other
BLANCO	751	182	405	117	47	Dole	24.2%	53.9%	15.6%	6.3%
BORDEN	47	9	27	10	1	Dole	19.1%	57.4%	21.3%	2.1%
BOSQUE	700	182	405	68	45	Dole	26.0%	57.9%	9.7%	6.4%
BOWIE	2,408	655	1,207	285	261	Dole	27.2%	50.1%	11.8%	10.8%
BRAZORIA	15,760	4,665	7,743	1,807	1,545	Dole	29.6%	49.1%	11.5%	9.8%
BRAZOS	10,154	1,680	5,558	1,250	1,666	Dole	16.5%	54.7%	12.3%	16.4%
BREWSTER	646	173	285	82	106	Dole	26.8%	44.1%	12.7%	16.4%
BRISCOE	63	8	45	4	6	Dole	12.7%	71.4%	6.3%	9.5%
BROOKS	19	6	12	1		Dole	31.6%	63.2%	5.3%	
BROWN	2,101	505	1,248	208	140	Dole	24.0%	59.4%	9.9%	6.7%
BURLESON	499	116	280	64	39	Dole	23.2%	56.1%	12.8%	7.8%
BURNET	1,811	297	1,181	214	119	Dole	16.4%	65.2%	11.8%	6.6%
CALDWELL	918	139	517	155	107	Dole	15.1%	56.3%	16.9%	11.7%
CALHOUN	753	192	400	88	73	Dole	25.5%	53.1%	11.7%	9.7%
CALLAHAN	435	127	231	43	34	Dole	29.2%	53.1%	9.9%	7.8%
CAMERON	5,032	943	2,806	834	449	Dole	18.7%	55.8%	16.6%	8.9%
CAMP	373	84	201	51	37	Dole	22.5%	53.9%	13.7%	9.9%
CARSON	491	99	305	55	32	Dole	20.2%	62.1%	11.2%	6.5%
CASS	575	150	337	57	31	Dole	26.1%	58.6%	9.9%	5.4%
CASTRO	325	88	173	24	40	Dole	27.1%	53.2%	7.4%	12.3%
CHAMBERS	711	279	309	73	50	Dole	39.2%	43.5%	10.3%	7.0%
CHEROKEE	1,383	472	702	114	95	Dole	34.1%	50.8%	8.2%	6.9%
CHILDRESS	115	17	86	4	8	Dole	14.8%	74.8%	3.5%	7.0%
CLAY	235	49	137	25	24	Dole	20.9%	58.3%	10.6%	10.2%
COCHRAN	88	25	44	4	15	Dole	28.4%	50.0%	4.5%	17.0%
COKE	73	31	31	5	6		42.5%	42.5%	6.8%	8.2%
COLEMAN	284	81	156	28	19	Dole	28.5%	54.9%	9.9%	6.7%
COLLIN	26,896	5,246	14,432	3,897	3,321	Dole	19.5%	53.7%	14.5%	12.3%
COLLINGSWORTH	53	16	28	2	7	Dole	30.2%	52.8%	3.8%	13.2%
COLORADO	895	183	561	84	67	Dole	20.4%	62.7%	9.4%	7.5%
COMAL	9,378	1,669	5,130	1,344	1,235	Dole	17.8%	54.7%	14.3%	13.2%
COMANCHE	419	119	217	49	34	Dole	28.4%	51.8%	11.7%	8.1%
CONCHO	33	5	20	3	5	Dole	15.2%	60.6%	9.1%	15.2%
COOKE	4,731	1,025	2,603	511	592	Dole	21.7%	55.0%	10.8%	12.5%
CORYELL	2,026	419	1,191	235	181	Dole	20.7%	58.8%	11.6%	8.9%
COTTLE	45	23	17		5	Buchanan	51.1%	37.8%		11.1%
CRANE	100	49	34	7	10	Buchanan	49.0%	34.0%	7.0%	10.0%
CROCKETT	9	2	3	3	1		22.2%	33.3%	33.3%	11.1%
CROSBY	105	32	55	8	10	Dole	30.5%	52.4%	7.6%	9.5%
CULBERSON	10	2	5		3	Dole	20.0%	50.0%		30.0%
DALLAM	235	63	118	19	35	Dole	26.8%	50.2%	8.1%	14.9%
DALLAS	101,254	20,264	58,001	13,317	9,672	Dole	20.0%	57.3%	13.2%	9.6%
DAWSON	518	97	343	39	39	Dole	18.7%	66.2%	7.5%	7.5%
DEAF SMITH	670	167	386	72	45	Dole	24.9%	57.6%	10.7%	6.7%
DELTA	59	23	29	3	4	Dole	39.0%	49.2%	5.1%	6.8%
DENTON	21,884	4,847	10,696	3,051	3,290	Dole	22.1%	48.9%	13.9%	15.0%
DE WITT	1,010	248	629	73	60	Dole	24.6%	62.3%	7.2%	5.9%
DICKENS	17	3	12		2	Dole	17.6%	70.6%		11.8%
DIMMIT	32	7	22	3		Dole	21.9%	68.8%	9.4%	
DONLEY	211	43	128	23	17	Dole	20.4%	60.7%	10.9%	8.1%

TEXAS REPUBLICAN

1996

County	Total Vote	Buchanan	Dole	Forbes	Other	Winner	Percentage of Total Vote Buchanan	Dole	Forbes	Other
DUVAL	39	4	27	8		Dole	10.3%	69.2%	20.5%	
EASTLAND	848	256	450	75	67	Dole	30.2%	53.1%	8.8%	7.9%
ECTOR	10,374	2,975	5,277	1,039	1,083	Dole	28.7%	50.9%	10.0%	10.4%
EDWARDS	223	51	111	17	44	Dole	22.9%	49.8%	7.6%	19.7%
ELLIS	8,106	2,091	4,260	798	957	Dole	25.8%	52.6%	9.8%	11.8%
EL PASO	15,103	2,492	9,139	1,840	1,632	Dole	16.5%	60.5%	12.2%	10.8%
ERATH	1,314	313	752	133	116	Dole	23.8%	57.2%	10.1%	8.8%
FALLS	223	49	136	24	14	Dole	22.0%	61.0%	10.8%	6.3%
FANNIN	737	254	354	69	60	Dole	34.5%	48.0%	9.4%	8.1%
FAYETTE	1,668	320	1,044	189	115	Dole	19.2%	62.6%	11.3%	6.9%
FISHER	36	17	15	1	3	Buchanan	47.2%	41.7%	2.8%	8.3%
FLOYD	283	73	152	27	31	Dole	25.8%	53.7%	9.5%	11.0%
FOARD	31	8	21	2		Dole	25.8%	67.7%	6.5%	
FORT BEND	21,787	4,214	12,246	3,066	2,261	Dole	19.3%	56.2%	14.1%	10.4%
FRANKLIN	282	64	175	26	17	Dole	22.7%	62.1%	9.2%	6.0%
FREESTONE	541	213	256	39	33	Dole	39.4%	47.3%	7.2%	6.1%
FRIO	100	38	39	13	10	Dole	38.0%	39.0%	13.0%	10.0%
GAINES	316	116	147	27	26	Dole	36.7%	46.5%	8.5%	8.2%
GALVESTON	11,200	2,692	5,972	1,572	964	Dole	24.0%	53.3%	14.0%	8.6%
GARZA	85	24	40	13	8	Dole	28.2%	47.1%	15.3%	9.4%
GILLESPIE	4,043	681	2,416	541	405	Dole	16.8%	59.8%	13.4%	10.0%
GLASSCOCK	137	35	81	15	6	Dole	25.5%	59.1%	10.9%	4.4%
GOLIAD	490	101	275	61	53	Dole	20.6%	56.1%	12.4%	10.8%
GONZALES	633	199	335	62	37	Dole	31.4%	52.9%	9.8%	5.8%
GRAY	3,908	859	2,158	472	419	Dole	22.0%	55.2%	12.1%	10.7%
GRAYSON	4,558	1,117	2,544	537	360	Dole	24.5%	55.8%	11.8%	7.9%
GREGG	11,483	2,328	6,691	1,094	1,370	Dole	20.3%	58.3%	9.5%	11.9%
GRIMES	808	213	423	94	78	Dole	26.4%	52.4%	11.6%	9.7%
GUADALUPE	7,438	1,344	4,202	1,028	864	Dole	18.1%	56.5%	13.8%	11.6%
HALE	1,153	268	630	142	113	Dole	23.2%	54.6%	12.3%	9.8%
HALL	21	4	11	6		Dole	19.0%	52.4%	28.6%	
HAMILTON	476	119	252	57	48	Dole	25.0%	52.9%	12.0%	10.1%
HANSFORD	822	122	523	71	106	Dole	14.8%	63.6%	8.6%	12.9%
HARDEMAN	97	34	52	6	5	Dole	35.1%	53.6%	6.2%	5.2%
HARDIN	2,027	814	909	156	148	Dole	40.2%	44.8%	7.7%	7.3%
HARRIS	157,169	33,501	88,465	22,872	12,331	Dole	21.3%	56.3%	14.6%	7.8%
HARRISON	2,284	633	1,223	172	256	Dole	27.7%	53.5%	7.5%	11.2%
HARTLEY	310	66	188	30	26	Dole	21.3%	60.6%	9.7%	8.4%
HASKELL	77	15	41	13	8	Dole	19.5%	53.2%	16.9%	10.4%
HAYS	5,128	985	2,823	802	518	Dole	19.2%	55.1%	15.6%	10.1%
HEMPHILL	478	132	237	56	53	Dole	27.6%	49.6%	11.7%	11.1%
HENDERSON	1,998	516	1,104	226	152	Dole	25.8%	55.3%	11.3%	7.6%
HIDALGO	5,733	1,148	3,214	790	581	Dole	20.0%	56.1%	13.8%	10.1%
HILL	1,247	314	677	150	106	Dole	25.2%	54.3%	12.0%	8.5%
HOCKLEY	915	232	512	97	74	Dole	25.4%	56.0%	10.6%	8.1%
HOOD	3,393	680	1,925	404	384	Dole	20.0%	56.7%	11.9%	11.3%
HOPKINS	733	197	415	58	63	Dole	26.9%	56.6%	7.9%	8.6%
HOUSTON	1,035	367	528	73	67	Dole	35.5%	51.0%	7.1%	6.5%
HOWARD	3,338	849	1,710	386	393	Dole	25.4%	51.2%	11.6%	11.8%
HUDSPETH	24	9	9	5	1		37.5%	37.5%	20.8%	4.2%

TEXAS REPUBLICAN

1996

County	Total Vote	Buchanan	Dole	Forbes	Other	Winner	Percentage of Total Vote Buchanan	Dole	Forbes	Other
HUNT	4,940	1,279	2,532	475	654	Dole	25.9%	51.3%	9.6%	13.2%
HUTCHINSON	4,811	873	3,005	424	509	Dole	18.1%	62.5%	8.8%	10.6%
IRION	20	5	13	2		Dole	25.0%	65.0%	10.0%	
JACK	174	57	86	18	13	Dole	32.8%	49.4%	10.3%	7.5%
JACKSON	302	89	152	48	13	Dole	29.5%	50.3%	15.9%	4.3%
JASPER	784	310	363	51	60	Dole	39.5%	46.3%	6.5%	7.7%
JEFF DAVIS	201	48	51	25	77	Dole	23.9%	25.4%	12.4%	38.3%
JEFFERSON	8,078	2,581	4,068	771	658	Dole	32.0%	50.4%	9.5%	8.1%
JIM HOGG	37	6	25	1	5	Dole	16.2%	67.6%	2.7%	13.5%
JIM WELLS	381	90	243	24	24	Dole	23.6%	63.8%	6.3%	6.3%
JOHNSON	5,448	1,494	2,817	581	556	Dole	27.4%	51.7%	10.7%	10.2%
JONES	343	92	187	35	29	Dole	26.8%	54.5%	10.2%	8.5%
KARNES	194	56	107	15	16	Dole	28.9%	55.2%	7.7%	8.2%
KAUFMAN	2,741	903	1,332	251	255	Dole	32.9%	48.6%	9.2%	9.3%
KENDALL	3,909	674	2,145	529	561	Dole	17.2%	54.9%	13.5%	14.4%
KENEDY	4	2	2				50.0%	50.0%		
KENT	1		1			Dole		100.0%		
KERR	9,920	1,570	5,575	1,424	1,351	Dole	15.8%	56.2%	14.4%	13.6%
KIMBLE	201	60	97	29	15	Dole	29.9%	48.3%	14.4%	7.5%
KING	6	1	3		2	Dole	16.7%	50.0%		33.3%
KINNEY	133	30	70	21	12	Dole	22.6%	52.6%	15.8%	9.0%
KLEBERG	540	112	328	60	40	Dole	20.7%	60.7%	11.1%	7.4%
KNOX	77	19	42	10	6	Dole	24.7%	54.5%	13.0%	7.8%
LAMAR	1,105	322	570	110	103	Dole	29.1%	51.6%	10.0%	9.3%
LAMB	420	104	241	31	44	Dole	24.8%	57.4%	7.4%	10.5%
LAMPASAS	1,117	271	663	118	65	Dole	24.3%	59.4%	10.6%	5.8%
LA SALLE	116	25	60	12	19	Dole	21.6%	51.7%	10.3%	16.4%
LAVACA	837	219	483	71	64	Dole	26.2%	57.7%	8.5%	7.6%
LEE	544	110	322	72	40	Dole	20.2%	59.2%	13.2%	7.4%
LEON	809	211	470	80	48	Dole	26.1%	58.1%	9.9%	5.9%
LIBERTY	1,939	743	897	154	145	Dole	38.3%	46.3%	7.9%	7.5%
LIMESTONE	430	126	226	35	43	Dole	29.3%	52.6%	8.1%	10.0%
LIPSCOMB	199	37	128	15	19	Dole	18.6%	64.3%	7.5%	9.5%
LIVE OAK	465	128	268	45	24	Dole	27.5%	57.6%	9.7%	5.2%
LLANO	2,625	370	1,629	369	257	Dole	14.1%	62.1%	14.1%	9.8%
LOVING	1		1			Dole		100.0%		
LUBBOCK	22,042	4,587	12,925	2,430	2,100	Dole	20.8%	58.6%	11.0%	9.5%
LYNN	86	25	53	5	3	Dole	29.1%	61.6%	5.8%	3.5%
MCCULLOCH	212	45	125	27	15	Dole	21.2%	59.0%	12.7%	7.1%
MCLENNAN	11,979	2,388	7,141	1,375	1,075	Dole	19.9%	59.6%	11.5%	9.0%
MCMULLEN	21	3	13	4	1	Dole	14.3%	61.9%	19.0%	4.8%
MADISON	481	135	248	41	57	Dole	28.1%	51.6%	8.5%	11.9%
MARION	113	29	70	7	7	Dole	25.7%	61.9%	6.2%	6.2%
MARTIN	127	53	54	13	7	Dole	41.7%	42.5%	10.2%	5.5%
MASON	170	60	78	13	19	Dole	35.3%	45.9%	7.6%	11.2%
MATAGORDA	1,267	318	709	129	111	Dole	25.1%	56.0%	10.2%	8.8%
MAVERICK	97	18	44	23	12	Dole	18.6%	45.4%	23.7%	12.4%
MEDINA	2,061	447	1,197	231	186	Dole	21.7%	58.1%	11.2%	9.0%
MENARD	85	14	52	9	10	Dole	16.5%	61.2%	10.6%	11.8%
MIDLAND	16,709	3,928	8,169	2,180	2,432	Dole	23.5%	48.9%	13.0%	14.6%

TEXAS REPUBLICAN

1996

County	Total Vote	Buchanan	Dole	Forbes	Other	Winner	Percentage of Total Vote: Buchanan	Dole	Forbes	Other
MILAM	569	174	295	59	41	Dole	30.6%	51.8%	10.4%	7.2%
MILLS	229	46	127	33	23	Dole	20.1%	55.5%	14.4%	10.0%
MITCHELL	98	29	52	11	6	Dole	29.6%	53.1%	11.2%	6.1%
MONTAGUE	497	127	265	62	43	Dole	25.6%	53.3%	12.5%	8.7%
MONTGOMERY	29,402	6,739	14,403	3,876	4,384	Dole	22.9%	49.0%	13.2%	14.9%
MOORE	888	199	542	84	63	Dole	22.4%	61.0%	9.5%	7.1%
MORRIS	214	58	119	25	12	Dole	27.1%	55.6%	11.7%	5.6%
MOTLEY	60	15	41	2	2	Dole	25.0%	68.3%	3.3%	3.3%
NACOGDOCHES	2,672	898	1,380	217	177	Dole	33.6%	51.6%	8.1%	6.6%
NAVARRO	1,580	521	775	163	121	Dole	33.0%	49.1%	10.3%	7.7%
NEWTON	313	121	134	19	39	Dole	38.7%	42.8%	6.1%	12.5%
NOLAN	206	68	97	23	18	Dole	33.0%	47.1%	11.2%	8.7%
NUECES	12,272	2,326	7,375	1,502	1,069	Dole	19.0%	60.1%	12.2%	8.7%
OCHILTREE	1,754	330	1,047	175	202	Dole	18.8%	59.7%	10.0%	11.5%
OLDHAM	80	30	36	8	6	Dole	37.5%	45.0%	10.0%	7.5%
ORANGE	3,192	1,364	1,340	257	231	Buchanan	42.7%	42.0%	8.1%	7.2%
PALO PINTO	667	169	366	74	58	Dole	25.3%	54.9%	11.1%	8.7%
PANOLA	634	236	286	64	48	Dole	37.2%	45.1%	10.1%	7.6%
PARKER	6,561	1,708	3,332	791	730	Dole	26.0%	50.8%	12.1%	11.1%
PARMER	543	129	310	53	51	Dole	23.8%	57.1%	9.8%	9.4%
PECOS	268	67	130	39	32	Dole	25.0%	48.5%	14.6%	11.9%
POLK	1,956	583	958	214	201	Dole	29.8%	49.0%	10.9%	10.3%
POTTER	7,069	1,511	3,964	870	724	Dole	21.4%	56.1%	12.3%	10.2%
PRESIDIO	28	5	16	5	2	Dole	17.9%	57.1%	17.9%	7.1%
RAINS	216	61	121	16	18	Dole	28.2%	56.0%	7.4%	8.3%
RANDALL	10,452	2,266	6,101	1,174	911	Dole	21.7%	58.4%	11.2%	8.7%
REAGAN	557	77	238	56	186	Dole	13.8%	42.7%	10.1%	33.4%
REAL	259	84	126	34	15	Dole	32.4%	48.6%	13.1%	5.8%
RED RIVER	168	55	80	22	11	Dole	32.7%	47.6%	13.1%	6.5%
REEVES	55	20	19	5	11	Buchanan	36.4%	34.5%	9.1%	20.0%
REFUGIO	316	54	215	29	18	Dole	17.1%	68.0%	9.2%	5.7%
ROBERTS	202	44	111	36	11	Dole	21.8%	55.0%	17.8%	5.4%
ROBERTSON	331	85	186	30	30	Dole	25.7%	56.2%	9.1%	9.1%
ROCKWALL	4,942	1,167	2,500	593	682	Dole	23.6%	50.6%	12.0%	13.8%
RUNNELS	253	66	124	32	31	Dole	26.1%	49.0%	12.6%	12.3%
RUSK	2,560	755	1,384	193	228	Dole	29.5%	54.1%	7.5%	8.9%
SABINE	205	72	99	12	22	Dole	35.1%	48.3%	5.9%	10.7%
SAN AUGUSTINE	55	18	24	5	8	Dole	32.7%	43.6%	9.1%	14.5%
SAN JACINTO	671	234	316	79	42	Dole	34.9%	47.1%	11.8%	6.3%
SAN PATRICIO	2,088	490	1,199	238	161	Dole	23.5%	57.4%	11.4%	7.7%
SAN SABA	224	49	138	26	11	Dole	21.9%	61.6%	11.6%	4.9%
SCHLEICHER	54	14	30	4	6	Dole	25.9%	55.6%	7.4%	11.1%
SCURRY	977	284	482	80	131	Dole	29.1%	49.3%	8.2%	13.4%
SHACKELFORD	137	34	80	12	11	Dole	24.8%	58.4%	8.8%	8.0%
SHELBY	399	177	147	30	45	Buchanan	44.4%	36.8%	7.5%	11.3%
SHERMAN	198	56	111	18	13	Dole	28.3%	56.1%	9.1%	6.6%
SMITH	13,952	3,353	7,499	1,506	1,594	Dole	24.0%	53.7%	10.8%	11.4%
SOMERVELL	245	69	107	27	42	Dole	28.2%	43.7%	11.0%	17.1%
STARR	138	11	49	2	76	Dole	8.0%	35.5%	1.4%	55.1%
STEPHENS	197	53	113	19	12	Dole	26.9%	57.4%	9.6%	6.1%

TEXAS REPUBLICAN

1996

County	Total Vote	Buchanan	Dole	Forbes	Other	Winner	Percentage of Total Vote Buchanan	Dole	Forbes	Other
STERLING	218	40	117	25	36	Dole	18.3%	53.7%	11.5%	16.5%
STONEWALL	105	20	62	14	9	Dole	19.0%	59.0%	13.3%	8.6%
SUTTON	126	25	59	25	17	Dole	19.8%	46.8%	19.8%	13.5%
SWISHER	106	34	52	11	9	Dole	32.1%	49.1%	10.4%	8.5%
TARRANT	79,582	16,857	44,406	9,846	8,473	Dole	21.2%	55.8%	12.4%	10.6%
TAYLOR	9,551	1,879	5,633	964	1,075	Dole	19.7%	59.0%	10.1%	11.3%
TERRELL	23	5	11	4	3	Dole	21.7%	47.8%	17.4%	13.0%
TERRY	403	102	229	29	43	Dole	25.3%	56.8%	7.2%	10.7%
THROCKMORTON	23	2	12	3	6	Dole	8.7%	52.2%	13.0%	26.1%
TITUS	603	202	290	71	40	Dole	33.5%	48.1%	11.8%	6.6%
TOM GREEN	7,384	1,382	4,166	1,110	726	Dole	18.7%	56.4%	15.0%	9.8%
TRAVIS	42,631	6,316	25,086	7,005	4,224	Dole	14.8%	58.8%	16.4%	9.9%
TRINITY	455	114	269	35	37	Dole	25.1%	59.1%	7.7%	8.1%
TYLER	733	234	387	51	61	Dole	31.9%	52.8%	7.0%	8.3%
UPSHUR	1,203	355	628	132	88	Dole	29.5%	52.2%	11.0%	7.3%
UPTON	83	42	24	7	10	Buchanan	50.6%	28.9%	8.4%	12.0%
UVALDE	857	247	459	87	64	Dole	28.8%	53.6%	10.2%	7.5%
VAL VERDE	1,486	300	818	210	158	Dole	20.2%	55.0%	14.1%	10.6%
VAN ZANDT	2,142	739	1,055	186	162	Dole	34.5%	49.3%	8.7%	7.6%
VICTORIA	5,571	1,339	2,994	525	713	Dole	24.0%	53.7%	9.4%	12.8%
WALKER	2,534	575	1,427	288	244	Dole	22.7%	56.3%	11.4%	9.6%
WALLER	1,095	291	573	145	86	Dole	26.6%	52.3%	13.2%	7.9%
WARD	151	58	70	8	15	Dole	38.4%	46.4%	5.3%	9.9%
WASHINGTON	2,260	413	1,379	269	199	Dole	18.3%	61.0%	11.9%	8.8%
WEBB	795	141	429	113	112	Dole	17.7%	54.0%	14.2%	14.1%
WHARTON	2,087	479	1,219	192	197	Dole	23.0%	58.4%	9.2%	9.4%
WHEELER	230	89	106	23	12	Dole	38.7%	46.1%	10.0%	5.2%
WICHITA	6,521	1,308	3,860	718	635	Dole	20.1%	59.2%	11.0%	9.7%
WILBARGER	553	102	330	65	56	Dole	18.4%	59.7%	11.8%	10.1%
WILLACY	117	23	65	19	10	Dole	19.7%	55.6%	16.2%	8.5%
WILLIAMSON	15,094	2,785	8,616	2,144	1,549	Dole	18.5%	57.1%	14.2%	10.3%
WILSON	1,446	326	824	182	114	Dole	22.5%	57.0%	12.6%	7.9%
WINKLER	164	61	64	19	20	Dole	37.2%	39.0%	11.6%	12.2%
WISE	1,453	478	701	141	133	Dole	32.9%	48.2%	9.7%	9.2%
WOOD	2,051	572	1,150	212	117	Dole	27.9%	56.1%	10.3%	5.7%
YOAKUM	285	94	127	31	33	Dole	33.0%	44.6%	10.9%	11.6%
YOUNG	514	160	247	61	46	Dole	31.1%	48.1%	11.9%	8.9%
ZAPATA	136	25	83	16	12	Dole	18.4%	61.0%	11.8%	8.8%
ZAVALA	30	5	12	7	6	Dole	16.7%	40.0%	23.3%	20.0%
TOTAL	1,019,803	217,974	567,164	130,938	103,727	Dole	21.4%	55.6%	12.8%	10.2%

UTAH

Throughout the twentieth century, Utah was content to play a bit part in the presidential nominating process. But with the start of a new century, Utah is seeking a bigger role. In 2000, it will be holding its first-ever presidential primary that could feature the state's senior senator, Orrin G. Hatch, on the Republican ballot. Hatch jumped into the GOP presidential race in June 1999.

While Utah has never held a presidential primary before, two things about the new event are fairly certain.

First, most of the votes will be cast in a four-county strip from Weber (Ogden) on the north to Utah (Provo) on the south. More than three-fourths of the state's population lives in this strip along the front of the Wasatch Range, with more than 40 percent living in Salt Lake County (Salt Lake City) alone.

Second, most of the primary action is likely to be on the GOP side of the ballot. While Utah has seen a gradual increase in recent years in its minority population (especially Hispanics), the state is still overwhelmingly white, Mormon and Republican.

Democrats have not elected a governor in Utah since 1980, a U.S. senator since 1970, or carried the state in a presidential election since 1964. In five of the last six presidential elections (including 1996), Utah has given the Republican presidential nominee a higher share of the vote than any other state.

Despite its large membership, the Utah Republican Party has often been of one mind when selecting a presidential nominee. In the party's great moderate-conservative nominating contests of the last half century, Utah consistently cast its vote for the conservative—from Robert A. Taft in 1952 to Barry Goldwater in 1964 to Ronald Reagan in 1976.

Utah's smaller cadre of Democrats have been more eclectic in their tastes. In 1984, the party's caucus attendees favored Gary Hart of neighboring Colorado. But in 1988 and 1992, Utah Democrats went for two Massachusetts natives, Michael Dukakis and Paul Tsongas, respectively. In 1992, Tsongas swept the populous four-county "Front Range" and took 33 percent of the 31,638 caucus votes cast statewide to defeat Jerry Brown (28 percent) and Bill Clinton (18 percent) in the early March balloting.

Yet over the years, Utah has rarely been more than a blip on the radar screen during the nominating season. In 1988, Utah's GOP caucuses were conducted so late in the process that the party ended up holding a straw vote to gauge preferences for vice president rather than for president. In 1996, Utah Republicans did not bother to hold a straw vote at all, either for president or vice president.

Box Elder
Cache
Rich
Great Salt Lake
Weber
Ogden
Davis
Morgan
Summit
Daggett
Salt Lake City
Salt Lake
Tooele
Wasatch
Duchesne
Uintah
Provo
Utah
Juab
Carbon
Sanpete
Emery
Grand
Millard
Sevier
Beaver
Piute
Wayne
Iron
Garfield
San Juan
Washington
Kane

VERMONT

Vermont has undergone a metamorphosis in recent years. Long associated with the flinty Yankee Republicanism of Calvin Coolidge, it is now as apt to be identified in the public mind with its socially conscious ice cream makers, Ben & Jerry.

But voting in the wake of neighboring New Hampshire, its presidential primary has been strongly affected by geography and momentum. Ever since Vermont reinstituted its primary in 1976 after a half-century hiatus, its winners have been the same as in the Granite State. That is, with one exception. In 1996, Pat Buchanan won New Hampshire; Bob Dole won Vermont, as the momentum in the Republican race shifted sharply in the two-week interval between the two contests.

By and large, moderate Republicans tend to run better in Vermont than New Hampshire. In 1980, John Anderson barely got on the radar screen in New Hampshire, but nearly won the GOP primary in Vermont. In 1996, Richard Lugar pulled barely 5 percent of the primary vote in New Hampshire, but rose to 14 percent in Vermont, where he chose to make his last stand.

On the other hand, conservative Republicans have not run that well in Vermont's presidential primary. Ronald Reagan won it in 1980 with only 30 percent of the vote. Buchanan drew less than 20 percent in 1996, just two weeks removed from his New Hampshire triumph.

For both parties, the more conservative voters are generally found in the northern part of the state, where there is a large concentration of French Canadians and rural Republicans. Both Reagan and Buchanan ran best in northern Vermont, each posting his highest percentage in Essex County in the farthest reaches of the sparsely populated and long-isolated "Northeast Kingdom."

To the south and west, voters generally tend to be more moderate. Anderson carried four counties in his 1980 primary run, including Vermont's most populous, Chittenden, which features several colleges and some high-tech industry around Burlington. Just to the south is Addison County, the home of Middlebury College, where Lugar made his best showing in 1996 (20 percent of the vote). Anderson also carried Addison, as did Dole in his 1988 primary challenge to George Bush. It was the only Vermont county that Dole won that year.

Meanwhile, Bennington County, in Vermont's southwest corner, was the only county to back Bush in the closely fought 1980 primary. It is an area of settled wealth where Republicans have been described as "moderate but not daring."

Recent Vermont Primary Results

Vermont held its first presidential primary in 1916, but none between 1920 and 1976.

	DEMOCRATS			REPUBLICANS		
Year	Turnout	Candidates	%	Turnout	Candidates	%
1996 (March 5)	30,838	BILL CLINTON*	97	58,113	BOB DOLE	40
					Pat Buchanan	17
					Steve Forbes	16
					Richard Lugar	14
					Lamar Alexander	11
1992	—	NO PRIMARY		—	NO PRIMARY	
1988 (March 1)	50,791	MICHAEL DUKAKIS	56	47,832	GEORGE BUSH	49
		Jesse Jackson	26		Bob Dole	39
1984 (March 6)	74,059	GARY HART	70	33,643	RONALD REAGAN*	99
		Walter Mondale	20			
1980 (March 4)	39,703	JIMMY CARTER*	73	65,611	RONALD REAGAN	30
		Edward Kennedy	26		John Anderson	29
					George Bush	22
					Howard Baker	12
1976 (March 2)	38,714	JIMMY CARTER	42	32,157	GERALD FORD*	84
		Sargent Shriver	28		Ronald Reagan#	15
		Fred Harris	13			

Note: All candidates are listed that drew at least 10 percent of their party's primary vote. The names of winning candidates are capitalized. An asterisk (*) indicates an incumbent president. A pound sign (#) indicates a write-in candidate.

The liberal nature of Vermont's activist Democrats has been less evident in the primary than the separate caucus process, which until 1996 elected the national convention delegates independent of the primary vote. For years, the two systems produced different winners, with the comparatively small cadre of caucus voters (around 6,000 in recent years) regularly opting for the more liberal alternative.

In 1980, for instance, President Jimmy Carter easily won the primary, but Edward Kennedy prevailed in the Democratic caucuses. In 1988, Michael Dukakis was the primary winner, while Jesse Jackson won the caucuses. In 1992, Jerry Brown won his highest share of the vote—primary or caucus—in Vermont. By winning nearly half of the state convention delegates, he finished a solid first in the first-round Democratic caucus voting, with uncommitted next. Bill Clinton ran third, even though Clinton boasted an endorsement from Democratic Gov. Howard Dean. Vermont did not hold a presidential primary in 1992.

VERMONT DEMOCRATIC

1976

County	Total Vote	Carter	Harris	Shriver	Other	Winner	Percentage of Total Vote: Carter	Harris	Shriver	Other
ADDISON	2,113	896	223	570	424	Carter	42.4%	10.6%	27.0%	20.1%
BENNINGTON	2,863	1,341	295	801	426	Carter	46.8%	10.3%	28.0%	14.9%
CALEDONIA	1,424	733	137	344	210	Carter	51.5%	9.6%	24.2%	14.7%
CHITTENDEN	8,452	2,877	935	2,976	1,664	Shriver	34.0%	11.1%	35.2%	19.7%
ESSEX	496	320	32	78	66	Carter	64.5%	6.5%	15.7%	13.3%
FRANKLIN	2,816	1,536	116	749	415	Carter	54.5%	4.1%	26.6%	14.7%
GRAND ISLE	596	293	31	179	93	Carter	49.2%	5.2%	30.0%	15.6%
LAMOILLE	854	370	106	182	196	Carter	43.3%	12.4%	21.3%	23.0%
ORANGE	1,300	614	198	224	264	Carter	47.2%	15.2%	17.2%	20.3%
ORLEANS	1,391	806	62	211	312	Carter	57.9%	4.5%	15.2%	22.4%
RUTLAND	4,569	1,871	448	1,431	819	Carter	40.9%	9.8%	31.3%	17.9%
WASHINGTON	4,268	1,535	709	1,478	546	Carter	36.0%	16.6%	34.6%	12.8%
WINDHAM	3,485	1,159	1,054	720	552	Carter	33.3%	30.2%	20.7%	15.8%
WINDSOR	4,086	1,984	547	756	799	Carter	48.6%	13.4%	18.5%	19.6%
TOTAL	38,713	16,335	4,893	10,699	6,786	Carter	42.2%	12.6%	27.6%	17.5%
Published Totals	38,714	16,335	4,893	10,699	6,787	Carter	42.2%	12.6%	27.6%	17.5%

VERMONT REPUBLICAN

1976

County	Total Vote	Ford	Reagan	Write-in	Winner	Percentage of Total Vote: Ford	Reagan	Write-in
ADDISON	2,062	1,661	388	13	Ford	80.6%	18.8%	0.6%
BENNINGTON	2,523	2,135	371	17	Ford	84.6%	14.7%	0.7%
CALEDONIA	1,547	1,187	355	5	Ford	76.7%	22.9%	0.3%
CHITTENDEN	4,967	4,356	588	23	Ford	87.7%	11.8%	0.5%
ESSEX	512	376	132	4	Ford	73.4%	25.8%	0.8%
FRANKLIN	2,104	1,789	292	23	Ford	85.0%	13.9%	1.1%
GRAND ISLE	441	373	64	4	Ford	84.6%	14.5%	0.9%
LAMOILLE	1,035	831	199	5	Ford	80.3%	19.2%	0.5%
ORANGE	1,478	1,215	215	48	Ford	82.2%	14.5%	3.2%
ORLEANS	1,376	940	419	17	Ford	68.3%	30.5%	1.2%
RUTLAND	3,967	3,431	508	28	Ford	86.5%	12.8%	0.7%
WASHINGTON	3,737	3,210	510	17	Ford	85.9%	13.6%	0.5%
WINDHAM	2,782	2,355	403	24	Ford	84.7%	14.5%	0.9%
WINDSOR	3,627	3,155	448	24	Ford	87.0%	12.4%	0.7%
TOTAL	32,158	27,014	4,892	252	Ford	84.0%	15.2%	0.8%
Published Totals	32,157	27,014	4,892	251	Ford	84.0%	15.2%	0.8%

Note: Ford was the only candidate listed on the ballot. All other votes cast were write-ins.

VERMONT DEMOCRATIC

1980

County	Total Vote	Carter	E. Kennedy	Write-in	Winner	Percentage of Total Vote: Carter	E. Kennedy	Write-in
ADDISON	1,963	1,603	332	28	Carter	81.7%	16.9%	1.4%
BENNINGTON	2,985	1,985	985	15	Carter	66.5%	33.0%	0.5%
CALEDONIA	1,283	939	322	22	Carter	73.2%	25.1%	1.7%
CHITTENDEN	9,239	7,057	2,082	100	Carter	76.4%	22.5%	1.1%
ESSEX	484	335	138	11	Carter	69.2%	28.5%	2.3%
FRANKLIN	3,046	2,233	795	18	Carter	73.3%	26.1%	0.6%
GRAND ISLE	658	497	152	9	Carter	75.5%	23.1%	1.4%
LAMOILLE	671	514	137	20	Carter	76.6%	20.4%	3.0%
ORANGE	1,253	907	303	43	Carter	72.4%	24.2%	3.4%
ORLEANS	1,455	1,054	383	18	Carter	72.4%	26.3%	1.2%
RUTLAND	5,701	4,264	1,398	39	Carter	74.8%	24.5%	0.7%
WASHINGTON	4,095	2,842	1,188	65	Carter	69.4%	29.0%	1.6%
WINDHAM	2,791	1,858	864	69	Carter	66.6%	31.0%	2.5%
WINDSOR	4,079	2,927	1,056	96	Carter	71.8%	25.9%	2.4%
TOTAL	39,703	29,015	10,135	553	Carter	73.1%	25.5%	1.4%

VERMONT REPUBLICAN

1980

County	Total Vote	Anderson	Baker	Bush	Reagan	Other	Winner	Percentage of Total Vote: Anderson	Baker	Bush	Reagan	Other
ADDISON	3,741	1,270	395	637	1,119	320	Anderson	33.9%	10.6%	17.0%	29.9%	8.6%
BENNINGTON	4,216	991	397	1,338	1,178	312	Bush	23.5%	9.4%	31.7%	27.9%	7.4%
CALEDONIA	3,114	514	414	427	1,613	146	Reagan	16.5%	13.3%	13.7%	51.8%	4.7%
CHITTENDEN	13,882	5,377	1,894	2,409	3,186	1,016	Anderson	38.7%	13.6%	17.4%	23.0%	7.3%
ESSEX	765	94	84	105	429	53	Reagan	12.3%	11.0%	13.7%	56.1%	6.9%
FRANKLIN	3,378	672	421	509	1,543	233	Reagan	19.9%	12.5%	15.1%	45.7%	6.9%
GRAND ISLE	692	149	91	157	222	73	Reagan	21.5%	13.2%	22.7%	32.1%	10.5%
LAMOILLE	1,936	581	226	348	623	158	Reagan	30.0%	11.7%	18.0%	32.2%	8.2%
ORANGE	2,816	804	373	529	899	211	Reagan	28.6%	13.2%	18.8%	31.9%	7.5%
ORLEANS	2,497	488	308	411	1,111	179	Reagan	19.5%	12.3%	16.5%	44.5%	7.2%
RUTLAND	7,887	1,666	852	2,384	2,424	561	Reagan	21.1%	10.8%	30.2%	30.7%	7.1%
WASHINGTON	7,255	2,239	777	1,539	2,268	432	Reagan	30.9%	10.7%	21.2%	31.3%	6.0%
WINDHAM	5,784	2,017	800	1,536	1,118	313	Anderson	34.9%	13.8%	26.6%	19.3%	5.4%
WINDSOR	7,648	2,168	1,023	1,897	1,987	573	Anderson	28.3%	13.4%	24.8%	26.0%	7.5%
TOTAL	65,611	19,030	8,055	14,226	19,720	4,580	Reagan	29.0%	12.3%	21.7%	30.1%	7.0%

VERMONT DEMOCRATIC

1984

County	Total Vote	Hart	Mondale	Other	Winner	Percentage of Total Vote Hart	Mondale	Other
ADDISON	4,555	3,235	851	469	Hart	71.0%	18.7%	10.3%
BENNINGTON	4,481	3,289	910	282	Hart	73.4%	20.3%	6.3%
CALEDONIA	2,540	1,882	397	261	Hart	74.1%	15.6%	10.3%
CHITTENDEN	18,134	12,066	4,311	1,757	Hart	66.5%	23.8%	9.7%
ESSEX	745	531	176	38	Hart	71.3%	23.6%	5.1%
FRANKLIN	4,889	3,271	1,292	326	Hart	66.9%	26.4%	6.7%
GRAND ISLE	894	606	235	53	Hart	67.8%	26.3%	5.9%
LAMOILLE	1,760	1,324	241	195	Hart	75.2%	13.7%	11.1%
ORANGE	2,730	1,862	436	432	Hart	68.2%	16.0%	15.8%
ORLEANS	2,542	1,824	528	190	Hart	71.8%	20.8%	7.5%
RUTLAND	9,292	6,823	1,850	619	Hart	73.4%	19.9%	6.7%
WASHINGTON	7,683	5,102	1,484	1,097	Hart	66.4%	19.3%	14.3%
WINDHAM	5,605	3,864	867	874	Hart	68.9%	15.5%	15.6%
WINDSOR	8,209	6,194	1,256	759	Hart	75.5%	15.3%	9.2%
TOTAL	74,059	51,873	14,834	7,352	Hart	70.0%	20.0%	9.9%

VERMONT DEMOCRATIC

1988

County	Total Vote	Dukakis	J. Jackson	Other	Winner	Percentage of Total Vote Dukakis	J. Jackson	Other
ADDISON	3,445	1,816	968	661	Dukakis	52.7%	28.1%	19.2%
BENNINGTON	3,383	2,184	530	669	Dukakis	64.6%	15.7%	19.8%
CALEDONIA	1,903	1,052	447	404	Dukakis	55.3%	23.5%	21.2%
CHITTENDEN	11,532	6,049	3,623	1,860	Dukakis	52.5%	31.4%	16.1%
ESSEX	435	235	65	135	Dukakis	54.0%	14.9%	31.0%
FRANKLIN	2,629	1,569	519	541	Dukakis	59.7%	19.7%	20.6%
GRAND ISLE	707	412	149	146	Dukakis	58.3%	21.1%	20.7%
LAMOILLE	982	500	305	177	Dukakis	50.9%	31.1%	18.0%
ORANGE	1,950	955	624	371	Dukakis	49.0%	32.0%	19.0%
ORLEANS	1,586	951	318	317	Dukakis	60.0%	20.1%	20.0%
RUTLAND	6,417	3,706	1,438	1,273	Dukakis	57.8%	22.4%	19.8%
WASHINGTON	5,528	2,894	1,747	887	Dukakis	52.4%	31.6%	16.0%
WINDHAM	4,417	2,616	1,005	796	Dukakis	59.2%	22.8%	18.0%
WINDSOR	5,877	3,414	1,306	1,157	Dukakis	58.1%	22.2%	19.7%
TOTAL	50,791	28,353	13,044	9,394	Dukakis	55.8%	25.7%	18.5%

VERMONT REPUBLICAN

1988

County	Total Vote	Bush	Dole	Other	Winner	Percentage of Total Vote Bush	Dole	Other
ADDISON	3,424	1,534	1,544	346	Dole	44.8%	45.1%	10.1%
BENNINGTON	3,623	1,911	1,214	498	Bush	52.7%	33.5%	13.7%
CALEDONIA	2,559	1,206	1,023	330	Bush	47.1%	40.0%	12.9%
CHITTENDEN	8,726	3,961	3,843	922	Bush	45.4%	44.0%	10.6%
ESSEX	608	349	191	68	Bush	57.4%	31.4%	11.2%
FRANKLIN	2,321	1,117	1,010	194	Bush	48.1%	43.5%	8.4%
GRAND ISLE	706	340	299	67	Bush	48.2%	42.4%	9.5%
LAMOILLE	1,346	667	534	145	Bush	49.6%	39.7%	10.8%
ORANGE	2,007	972	761	274	Bush	48.4%	37.9%	13.7%
ORLEANS	1,706	868	692	146	Bush	50.9%	40.6%	8.6%
RUTLAND	6,966	3,621	2,600	745	Bush	52.0%	37.3%	10.7%
WASHINGTON	5,240	2,620	2,055	565	Bush	50.0%	39.2%	10.8%
WINDHAM	3,270	1,741	1,033	496	Bush	53.2%	31.6%	15.2%
WINDSOR	5,330	2,658	1,856	816	Bush	49.9%	34.8%	15.3%
TOTAL	47,832	23,565	18,655	5,612	Bush	49.3%	39.0%	11.7%

VERMONT DEMOCRATIC

1996

County	Total Vote	Clinton	Other	Winner	Percentage of Total Vote Clinton	Othe
ADDISON	2,200	2,138	62	Clinton	97.2%	2.8%
BENNINGTON	1,602	1,538	64	Clinton	96.0%	4.0%
CALEDONIA	984	945	39	Clinton	96.0%	4.0%
CHITTENDEN	7,565	7,343	222	Clinton	97.1%	2.9%
ESSEX	365	348	17	Clinton	95.3%	4.7%
FRANKLIN	2,023	1,918	105	Clinton	94.8%	5.2%
GRAND ISLE	516	489	27	Clinton	94.8%	5.2%
LAMOILLE	846	823	23	Clinton	97.3%	2.7%
ORANGE	1,368	1,298	70	Clinton	94.9%	5.1%
ORLEANS	976	935	41	Clinton	95.8%	4.2%
RUTLAND	2,763	2,646	117	Clinton	95.8%	4.2%
WASHINGTON	3,365	3,252	113	Clinton	96.6%	3.4%
WINDHAM	2,650	2,567	83	Clinton	96.9%	3.1%
WINDSOR	3,615	3,523	92	Clinton	97.5%	2.5%
TOTAL	30,838	29,763	1,075	Clinton	96.5%	3.5%

VERMONT REPUBLICAN

1996

County	Total Vote	Alexander	Buchanan	Dole	Forbes	Lugar	Other	Winner	Percentage of Total Vote: Alexander	Buchanan	Dole	Forbes	Lugar	Other
ADDISON	3,943	422	564	1,526	500	798	133	Dole	10.7%	14.3%	38.7%	12.7%	20.2%	3.4%
BENNINGTON	3,479	299	550	1,576	682	295	77	Dole	8.6%	15.8%	45.3%	19.6%	8.5%	2.2%
CALEDONIA	2,671	286	497	905	603	282	98	Dole	10.7%	18.6%	33.9%	22.6%	10.6%	3.7%
CHITTENDEN	11,957	1,302	1,771	4,816	1,639	2,018	411	Dole	10.9%	14.8%	40.3%	13.7%	16.9%	3.4%
ESSEX	931	91	262	299	197	66	16	Dole	9.8%	28.1%	32.1%	21.2%	7.1%	1.7%
FRANKLIN	3,404	345	730	1,204	415	620	90	Dole	10.1%	21.4%	35.4%	12.2%	18.2%	2.6%
GRAND ISLE	840	92	113	364	94	147	30	Dole	11.0%	13.5%	43.3%	11.2%	17.5%	3.6%
LAMOILLE	2,116	215	273	890	350	293	95	Dole	10.2%	12.9%	42.1%	16.5%	13.8%	4.5%
ORANGE	2,923	289	517	1,149	506	351	111	Dole	9.9%	17.7%	39.3%	17.3%	12.0%	3.8%
ORLEANS	2,290	230	466	812	348	360	74	Dole	10.0%	20.3%	35.5%	15.2%	15.7%	3.2%
RUTLAND	7,108	745	1,223	3,199	1,079	684	178	Dole	10.5%	17.2%	45.0%	15.2%	9.6%	2.5%
WASHINGTON	6,171	738	922	2,477	829	979	226	Dole	12.0%	14.9%	40.1%	13.4%	15.9%	3.7%
WINDHAM	3,932	464	723	1,582	673	362	128	Dole	11.8%	18.4%	40.2%	17.1%	9.2%	3.3%
WINDSOR	6,348	627	1,119	2,620	1,151	626	205	Dole	9.9%	17.6%	41.3%	18.1%	9.9%	3.2%
TOTAL	58,113	6,145	9,730	23,419	9,066	7,881	1,872	Dole	10.6%	16.7%	40.3%	15.6%	13.6%	3.2%

VIRGINIA

Primaries are not a regular part of the political scene in Virginia. They have only been employed once at the presidential level—in 1988. But Republicans are trying again in 2000, hoping their late February primary will finally put the state on the map during the nominating season. For their part, Virginia Democrats are content to stay in the shadows. The party's traditional low-turnout caucus process will not begin until mid-April.

That Virginia held a presidential primary at all in the twentieth century is in large part a tribute to Democratic Sen. Charles S. Robb. He was instrumental in the creation of the Democratic Leadership Council in the 1980s as a counterweight to party liberals, and he pushed the Southern regional primary in 1988 (commonly known as Super Tuesday) as a means toward nominating a Southern-oriented candidate for president. The event, though, proved to be a disappointment for its sponsors, both in Virginia and across the region.

Michael Dukakis and Jesse Jackson both won chunks of the South away from Al Gore, the favorite of many Democratic leaders across the region. And in Virginia, Jackson was an easy winner.

The Democratic vote, though, did highlight the demographic diversity of the state. Dukakis won the northern Virginia suburbs outside Washington, D.C. (the southern fringe of the megalopolis that extends from Boston to Washington). Gore won the rural white counties west of the Blue Ridge Mountains, rolling up his best numbers in Virginia's mountainous western panhandle, which borders Gore's home state of Tennessee. Jackson won almost everywhere else, from the old plantation country of the Piedmont to the bustling cities of the Tidewater, where a heavy military presence mingles with a large black population.

Jackson carried some of the prime symbols of the old Confederacy in 1988, including Richmond, which has a black majority, and Lexington, a small college town in the Shenandoah Valley that is the burial place of Robert E. Lee. Virginia handed Jackson the highest vote share he received in any primary in 1988, even though it had the smallest black population of any primary state that he carried.

On the Republican side, the 1988 presidential primary spurred limited interest because it was a "beauty contest" that bound no delegates. George Bush dominated both the primary and the later caucuses that actually chose the delegates.

Probably the chief casualty of Bush's easy win was religious broadcaster Pat Robertson. The son of a Virginia senator, Robertson had based his nationwide television ministry in Virginia Beach. But Bush swept all of the state's 95 counties and 41 independent cities; Robertson could run no better than third, even in Virginia Beach. In the separate caucuses, Robertson controlled only the one held in Virginia Beach.

Bob Dole was not much more successful than Robertson in the 1988 GOP primary, running best in the northern Virginia suburbs and academic centers such as Charlottesville (home of the University of Virginia).

Turnout for the Democratic primary was disproportionately large in urban centers from Arlington and Alexandria in northern Virginia to cities of the Tidewater such as Norfolk and Portsmouth. Turnout for the Republican primary tended to be disproportionately skewed to suburban jurisdictions, led by the most populous jurisdiction in the state, northern Virginia's Fairfax County.

Yet the turnout for both the Republican and Democratic primaries in 1988 was comparatively light. Neither came close to matching the nearly half million voters that turned out for

Recent Virginia Primary Results

Virginia held its first presidential primary in 1988.

	DEMOCRATS			REPUBLICANS		
Year	Turnout	Candidates	%	Turnout	Candidates	%
1996	—	NO PRIMARY		—	NO PRIMARY	
1992	—	NO PRIMARY		—	NO PRIMARY	
1988 (March 8)	364,899	JESSE JACKSON Al Gore Michael Dukakis	45 22 22	234,142	GEORGE BUSH Bob Dole Pat Robertson	53 26 14

Note: All candidates are listed who drew at least 10 percent of their party's primary vote. The names of winning candidates are capitalized.

Virginia's last statewide primary in 1996—a challenge within the GOP to Sen. John W. Warner.

Jackson's primary victory, though, proved to be a harbinger of sorts. A year later, Democrat L. Douglas Wilder won the gubernatorial election in Virginia and became the nation's first elected black governor. Meanwhile, Republicans had their appetites whetted to try again—but with a presidential primary on an earlier date.

VIRGINIA DEMOCRATIC

1988

County	Total Vote	Dukakis	Gore	J. Jackson	Other	Winner	Percentage of Total Vote Dukakis	Gore	J. Jackson	Other
ACCOMACK	1,752	340	417	816	179	J. Jackson	19.4%	23.8%	46.6%	10.2%
ALBEMARLE	3,552	1,145	727	1,315	365	J. Jackson	32.2%	20.5%	37.0%	10.3%
ALLEGHANY	794	183	396	95	120	Gore	23.0%	49.9%	12.0%	15.1%
AMELIA	604	51	108	392	53	J. Jackson	8.4%	17.9%	64.9%	8.8%
AMHERST	1,175	168	327	577	103	J. Jackson	14.3%	27.8%	49.1%	8.8%
APPOMATTOX	721	67	322	252	80	Gore	9.3%	44.7%	35.0%	11.1%
ARLINGTON	16,442	6,864	2,343	4,219	3,016	Dukakis	41.7%	14.3%	25.7%	18.3%
AUGUSTA	1,312	328	516	266	202	Gore	25.0%	39.3%	20.3%	15.4%
BATH	315	83	128	50	54	Gore	26.3%	40.6%	15.9%	17.1%
BEDFORD COUNTY	1,576	335	761	308	172	Gore	21.3%	48.3%	19.5%	10.9%
BLAND	334	98	132	39	65	Gore	29.3%	39.5%	11.7%	19.5%
BOTETOURT	1,301	232	767	161	141	Gore	17.8%	59.0%	12.4%	10.8%
BRUNSWICK	1,808	55	149	1,473	131	J. Jackson	3.0%	8.2%	81.5%	7.2%
BUCHANAN	1,621	269	854	113	385	Gore	16.6%	52.7%	7.0%	23.8%
BUCKINGHAM	1,011	91	228	588	104	J. Jackson	9.0%	22.6%	58.2%	10.3%
CAMPBELL	1,840	225	642	825	148	J. Jackson	12.2%	34.9%	44.8%	8.0%
CAROLINE	1,372	138	153	976	105	J. Jackson	10.1%	11.2%	71.1%	7.7%
CARROLL	1,186	246	692	75	173	Gore	20.7%	58.3%	6.3%	14.6%
CHARLES CITY	667	23	33	571	40	J. Jackson	3.4%	4.9%	85.6%	6.0%
CHARLOTTE	841	73	241	472	55	J. Jackson	8.7%	28.7%	56.1%	6.5%
CHESTERFIELD	7,230	1,697	1,951	2,814	768	J. Jackson	23.5%	27.0%	38.9%	10.6%
CLARKE	414	124	95	135	60	J. Jackson	30.0%	22.9%	32.6%	14.5%
CRAIG	340	55	209	36	40	Gore	16.2%	61.5%	10.6%	11.8%
CULPEPER	1,014	235	236	418	125	J. Jackson	23.2%	23.3%	41.2%	12.3%
CUMBERLAND	669	50	91	497	31	J. Jackson	7.5%	13.6%	74.3%	4.6%
DICKENSON	928	205	531	47	145	Gore	22.1%	57.2%	5.1%	15.6%
DINWIDDIE	1,502	119	219	1,071	93	J. Jackson	7.9%	14.6%	71.3%	6.2%
ESSEX	356	55	64	201	36	J. Jackson	15.4%	18.0%	56.5%	10.1%
FAIRFAX COUNTY	47,319	21,017	7,726	11,032	7,544	Dukakis	44.4%	16.3%	23.3%	15.9%
FAUQUIER	1,853	534	389	653	277	J. Jackson	28.8%	21.0%	35.2%	14.9%
FLOYD	511	94	222	143	52	Gore	18.4%	43.4%	28.0%	10.2%
FLUVANNA	472	72	104	247	49	J. Jackson	15.3%	22.0%	52.3%	10.4%
FRANKLIN COUNTY	1,991	293	1,032	455	211	Gore	14.7%	51.8%	22.9%	10.6%
FREDERICK	805	283	267	140	115	Dukakis	35.2%	33.2%	17.4%	14.3%
GILES	892	177	504	109	102	Gore	19.8%	56.5%	12.2%	11.4%
GLOUCESTER	1,589	261	435	741	152	J. Jackson	16.4%	27.4%	46.6%	9.6%
GOOCHLAND	762	67	124	484	87	J. Jackson	8.8%	16.3%	63.5%	11.4%
GRAYSON	798	166	476	61	95	Gore	20.8%	59.6%	7.6%	11.9%
GREENE	256	58	74	80	44	J. Jackson	22.7%	28.9%	31.3%	17.2%
GREENSVILLE	1,225	56	113	886	170	J. Jackson	4.6%	9.2%	72.3%	13.9%
HALIFAX	1,946	107	360	1,361	118	J. Jackson	5.5%	18.5%	69.9%	6.1%
HANOVER	2,368	414	762	902	290	J. Jackson	17.5%	32.2%	38.1%	12.2%
HENRICO	10,534	2,233	2,404	4,992	905	J. Jackson	21.2%	22.8%	47.4%	8.6%
HENRY	2,826	301	1,381	884	260	Gore	10.7%	48.9%	31.3%	9.2%
HIGHLAND	195	32	87	22	54	Gore	16.4%	44.6%	11.3%	27.7%
ISLE OF WIGHT	2,666	172	393	1,896	205	J. Jackson	6.5%	14.7%	71.1%	7.7%
JAMES CITY	2,588	572	579	1,214	223	J. Jackson	22.1%	22.4%	46.9%	8.6%
KING AND QUEEN	512	22	54	394	42	J. Jackson	4.3%	10.5%	77.0%	8.2%
KING GEORGE	587	133	92	292	70	J. Jackson	22.7%	15.7%	49.7%	11.9%
KING WILLIAM	728	57	89	542	40	J. Jackson	7.8%	12.2%	74.5%	5.5%

VIRGINIA DEMOCRATIC

1988

County	Total Vote	Dukakis	Gore	J. Jackson	Other	Winner	Percentage of Total Vote Dukakis	Gore	J. Jackson	Other
LANCASTER	634	91	169	335	39	J. Jackson	14.4%	26.7%	52.8%	6.2%
LEE	1,320	129	948	76	167	Gore	9.8%	71.8%	5.8%	12.7%
LOUDOUN	3,793	1,265	616	1,137	775	Dukakis	33.4%	16.2%	30.0%	20.4%
LOUISA	907	127	202	502	76	J. Jackson	14.0%	22.3%	55.3%	8.4%
LUNENBURG	795	64	179	474	78	J. Jackson	8.1%	22.5%	59.6%	9.8%
MADISON	559	139	132	223	65	J. Jackson	24.9%	23.6%	39.9%	11.6%
MATHEWS	651	120	162	299	70	J. Jackson	18.4%	24.9%	45.9%	10.8%
MECKLENBURG	1,505	107	276	988	134	J. Jackson	7.1%	18.3%	65.6%	8.9%
MIDDLESEX	715	97	131	427	60	J. Jackson	13.6%	18.3%	59.7%	8.4%
MONTGOMERY	3,097	971	1,063	683	380	Gore	31.4%	34.3%	22.1%	12.3%
NELSON	854	160	250	346	98	J. Jackson	18.7%	29.3%	40.5%	11.5%
NEW KENT	710	85	124	451	50	J. Jackson	12.0%	17.5%	63.5%	7.0%
NORTHAMPTON	1,136	101	213	740	82	J. Jackson	8.9%	18.8%	65.1%	7.2%
NORTHUMBERLAND	736	105	129	436	66	J. Jackson	14.3%	17.5%	59.2%	9.0%
NOTTOWAY	953	67	190	629	67	J. Jackson	7.0%	19.9%	66.0%	7.0%
ORANGE	766	180	213	258	115	J. Jackson	23.5%	27.8%	33.7%	15.0%
PAGE	591	194	189	86	122	Dukakis	32.8%	32.0%	14.6%	20.6%
PATRICK	970	166	582	114	108	Gore	17.1%	60.0%	11.8%	11.1%
PITTSYLVANIA	2,911	237	604	1,863	207	J. Jackson	8.1%	20.7%	64.0%	7.1%
POWHATAN	487	69	101	264	53	J. Jackson	14.2%	20.7%	54.2%	10.9%
PRINCE EDWARD	1,202	108	176	838	80	J. Jackson	9.0%	14.6%	69.7%	6.7%
PRINCE GEORGE	1,127	141	213	691	82	J. Jackson	12.5%	18.9%	61.3%	7.3%
PRINCE WILLIAM	5,778	2,060	977	1,803	938	Dukakis	35.7%	16.9%	31.2%	16.2%
PULASKI	1,505	298	787	274	146	Gore	19.8%	52.3%	18.2%	9.7%
RAPPAHANNOCK	391	132	81	129	49	Dukakis	33.8%	20.7%	33.0%	12.5%
RICHMOND COUNTY	371	43	94	189	45	J. Jackson	11.6%	25.3%	50.9%	12.1%
ROANOKE COUNTY	4,621	1,089	2,463	607	462	Gore	23.6%	53.3%	13.1%	10.0%
ROCKBRIDGE	1,064	232	423	253	156	Gore	21.8%	39.8%	23.8%	14.7%
ROCKINGHAM	1,072	248	393	255	176	Gore	23.1%	36.7%	23.8%	16.4%
RUSSELL	1,553	203	982	105	263	Gore	13.1%	63.2%	6.8%	16.9%
SCOTT	891	103	654	53	81	Gore	11.6%	73.4%	5.9%	9.1%
SHENANDOAH	742	236	289	84	133	Gore	31.8%	38.9%	11.3%	17.9%
SMYTH	1,249	204	748	120	177	Gore	16.3%	59.9%	9.6%	14.2%
SOUTHAMPTON	1,633	116	294	1,078	145	J. Jackson	7.1%	18.0%	66.0%	8.9%
SPOTSYLVANIA	1,670	439	498	478	255	Gore	26.3%	29.8%	28.6%	15.3%
STAFFORD	1,734	587	435	368	344	Dukakis	33.9%	25.1%	21.2%	19.8%
SURRY	1,017	41	79	832	65	J. Jackson	4.0%	7.8%	81.8%	6.4%
SUSSEX	1,405	54	122	1,158	71	J. Jackson	3.8%	8.7%	82.4%	5.1%
TAZEWELL	1,938	458	814	223	443	Gore	23.6%	42.0%	11.5%	22.9%
WARREN	919	244	303	208	164	Gore	26.6%	33.0%	22.6%	17.8%
WASHINGTON	1,780	309	1,003	192	276	Gore	17.4%	56.3%	10.8%	15.5%
WESTMORELAND	951	174	118	569	90	J. Jackson	18.3%	12.4%	59.8%	9.5%
WISE	2,144	255	1,443	204	242	Gore	11.9%	67.3%	9.5%	11.3%
WYTHE	941	175	564	106	96	Gore	18.6%	59.9%	11.3%	10.2%
YORK	2,700	550	662	1,208	280	J. Jackson	20.4%	24.5%	44.7%	10.4%

VIRGINIA DEMOCRATIC

1988

City	Total Vote	Dukakis	Gore	J. Jackson	Other	Winner	Percentage of Total Vote: Dukakis	Gore	J. Jackson	Other
ALEXANDRIA	9,925	3,949	1,335	3,328	1,313	Dukakis	39.8%	13.5%	33.5%	13.2%
BEDFORD CITY	353	56	148	113	36	Gore	15.9%	41.9%	32.0%	10.2%
BRISTOL	1,066	183	660	110	113	Gore	17.2%	61.9%	10.3%	10.6%
BUENA VISTA	327	63	163	42	59	Gore	19.3%	49.8%	12.8%	18.0%
CHARLOTTESVILLE	3,073	907	514	1,358	294	J. Jackson	29.5%	16.7%	44.2%	9.6%
CHESAPEAKE	11,318	1,081	2,209	7,414	614	J. Jackson	9.6%	19.5%	65.5%	5.4%
CLIFTON FORGE	328	70	107	104	47	Gore	21.3%	32.6%	31.7%	14.3%
COLONIAL HEIGHTS	691	257	297	47	90	Gore	37.2%	43.0%	6.8%	13.0%
COVINGTON	577	102	228	179	68	Gore	17.7%	39.5%	31.0%	11.8%
DANVILLE	2,722	270	407	1,917	128	J. Jackson	9.9%	15.0%	70.4%	4.7%
EMPORIA	410	40	75	246	49	J. Jackson	9.8%	18.3%	60.0%	12.0%
FAIRFAX CITY	1,261	535	232	284	210	Dukakis	42.4%	18.4%	22.5%	16.7%
FALLS CHURCH	1,081	513	148	227	193	Dukakis	47.5%	13.7%	21.0%	17.9%
FRANKLIN CITY	967	55	120	720	72	J. Jackson	5.7%	12.4%	74.5%	7.4%
FREDERICKSBURG	975	239	182	396	158	J. Jackson	24.5%	18.7%	40.6%	16.2%
GALAX	294	57	169	38	30	Gore	19.4%	57.5%	12.9%	10.2%
HAMPTON	12,077	1,340	1,694	8,391	652	J. Jackson	11.1%	14.0%	69.5%	5.4%
HARRISONBURG	802	220	185	292	105	J. Jackson	27.4%	23.1%	36.4%	13.1%
HOPEWELL	996	200	243	470	83	J. Jackson	20.1%	24.4%	47.2%	8.3%
LEXINGTON	504	135	119	182	68	J. Jackson	26.8%	23.6%	36.1%	13.5%
LYNCHBURG	4,086	513	794	2,489	290	J. Jackson	12.6%	19.4%	60.9%	7.1%
MANASSAS	776	289	142	221	124	Dukakis	37.2%	18.3%	28.5%	16.0%
MANASSAS PARK	122	38	22	28	34	Dukakis	31.1%	18.0%	23.0%	27.9%
MARTINSVILLE	1,268	163	378	637	90	J. Jackson	12.9%	29.8%	50.2%	7.1%
NEWPORT NEWS	13,176	1,762	2,006	8,555	853	J. Jackson	13.4%	15.2%	64.9%	6.5%
NORFOLK	22,207	2,857	3,129	15,164	1,057	J. Jackson	12.9%	14.1%	68.3%	4.8%
NORTON	287	46	183	29	29	Gore	16.0%	63.8%	10.1%	10.1%
PETERSBURG	4,457	291	243	3,747	176	J. Jackson	6.5%	5.5%	84.1%	3.9%
POQUOSON	390	115	169	37	69	Gore	29.5%	43.3%	9.5%	17.7%
PORTSMOUTH	13,659	1,087	2,112	9,680	780	J. Jackson	8.0%	15.5%	70.9%	5.7%
RADFORD	616	121	310	130	55	Gore	19.6%	50.3%	21.1%	8.9%
RICHMOND CITY	21,377	2,220	1,968	15,619	1,570	J. Jackson	10.4%	9.2%	73.1%	7.3%
ROANOKE CITY	6,058	1,175	2,141	2,252	490	J. Jackson	19.4%	35.3%	37.2%	8.1%
SALEM	1,289	318	643	195	133	Gore	24.7%	49.9%	15.1%	10.3%
SOUTH BOSTON	384	33	82	248	21	J. Jackson	8.6%	21.4%	64.6%	5.5%
STAUNTON	869	240	214	319	96	J. Jackson	27.6%	24.6%	36.7%	11.0%
SUFFOLK	5,386	307	684	4,031	364	J. Jackson	5.7%	12.7%	74.8%	6.8%
VIRGINIA BEACH	15,894	4,021	4,270	6,069	1,534	J. Jackson	25.3%	26.9%	38.2%	9.7%
WAYNESBORO	817	220	261	237	99	Gore	26.9%	31.9%	29.0%	12.1%
WILLIAMSBURG	847	234	179	346	88	J. Jackson	27.6%	21.1%	40.9%	10.4%
WINCHESTER	599	213	167	130	89	Dukakis	35.6%	27.9%	21.7%	14.9%
TOTAL	364,899	80,183	81,419	164,709	38,588	J. Jackson	22.0%	22.3%	45.1%	10.6%

VIRGINIA REPUBLICAN

1988

County	Total Vote	Bush	Dole	Robertson	Other	Winner	Percentage of Total Vote Bush	Dole	Robertson	Other
ACCOMACK	1,631	877	407	230	117	Bush	53.8%	25.0%	14.1%	7.2%
ALBEMARLE	2,559	1,218	826	282	233	Bush	47.6%	32.3%	11.0%	9.1%
ALLEGHANY	454	232	120	76	26	Bush	51.1%	26.4%	16.7%	5.7%
AMELIA	274	147	46	58	23	Bush	53.6%	16.8%	21.2%	8.4%
AMHERST	595	298	160	85	52	Bush	50.1%	26.9%	14.3%	8.7%
APPOMATTOX	330	164	73	60	33	Bush	49.7%	22.1%	18.2%	10.0%
ARLINGTON	8,201	4,103	2,810	480	808	Bush	50.0%	34.3%	5.9%	9.9%
AUGUSTA	1,567	775	326	342	124	Bush	49.5%	20.8%	21.8%	7.9%
BATH	250	120	43	76	11	Bush	48.0%	17.2%	30.4%	4.4%
BEDFORD COUNTY	1,436	797	388	129	122	Bush	55.5%	27.0%	9.0%	8.5%
BLAND	195	124	47	18	6	Bush	63.6%	24.1%	9.2%	3.1%
BOTETOURT	704	364	206	87	47	Bush	51.7%	29.3%	12.4%	6.7%
BRUNSWICK	343	207	86	31	19	Bush	60.3%	25.1%	9.0%	5.5%
BUCHANAN	515	309	107	67	32	Bush	60.0%	20.8%	13.0%	6.2%
BUCKINGHAM	298	188	47	46	17	Bush	63.1%	15.8%	15.4%	5.7%
CAMPBELL	1,547	799	421	191	136	Bush	51.6%	27.2%	12.3%	8.8%
CAROLINE	393	259	71	38	25	Bush	65.9%	18.1%	9.7%	6.4%
CARROLL	1,516	956	428	76	56	Bush	63.1%	28.2%	5.0%	3.7%
CHARLES CITY	80	47	9	21	3	Bush	58.8%	11.3%	26.3%	3.8%
CHARLOTTE	321	192	80	36	13	Bush	59.8%	24.9%	11.2%	4.0%
CHESTERFIELD	8,841	4,811	1,961	1,373	696	Bush	54.4%	22.2%	15.5%	7.9%
CLARKE	280	181	53	15	31	Bush	64.6%	18.9%	5.4%	11.1%
CRAIG	160	75	49	23	13	Bush	46.9%	30.6%	14.4%	8.1%
CULPEPER	1,075	540	295	160	80	Bush	50.2%	27.4%	14.9%	7.4%
CUMBERLAND	226	125	38	44	19	Bush	55.3%	16.8%	19.5%	8.4%
DICKENSON	402	232	88	58	24	Bush	57.7%	21.9%	14.4%	6.0%
DINWIDDIE	449	247	76	95	31	Bush	55.0%	16.9%	21.2%	6.9%
ESSEX	268	168	62	19	19	Bush	62.7%	23.1%	7.1%	7.1%
FAIRFAX COUNTY	45,244	24,164	14,117	3,343	3,620	Bush	53.4%	31.2%	7.4%	8.0%
FAUQUIER	2,181	1,203	514	307	157	Bush	55.2%	23.6%	14.1%	7.2%
FLOYD	476	249	162	42	23	Bush	52.3%	34.0%	8.8%	4.8%
FLUVANNA	329	186	80	34	29	Bush	56.5%	24.3%	10.3%	8.8%
FRANKLIN COUNTY	910	454	267	121	68	Bush	49.9%	29.3%	13.3%	7.5%
FREDERICK	882	504	202	102	74	Bush	57.1%	22.9%	11.6%	8.4%
GILES	429	221	126	67	15	Bush	51.5%	29.4%	15.6%	3.5%
GLOUCESTER	1,210	624	298	232	56	Bush	51.6%	24.6%	19.2%	4.6%
GOOCHLAND	497	316	82	65	34	Bush	63.6%	16.5%	13.1%	6.8%
GRAYSON	565	338	167	37	23	Bush	59.8%	29.6%	6.5%	4.1%
GREENE	228	132	44	32	20	Bush	57.9%	19.3%	14.0%	8.8%
GREENSVILLE	254	147	50	36	21	Bush	57.9%	19.7%	14.2%	8.3%
HALIFAX	526	287	165	43	31	Bush	54.6%	31.4%	8.2%	5.9%
HANOVER	2,663	1,559	528	352	224	Bush	58.5%	19.8%	13.2%	8.4%
HENRICO	9,700	5,899	1,957	1,184	660	Bush	60.8%	20.2%	12.2%	6.8%
HENRY	1,298	693	363	172	70	Bush	53.4%	28.0%	13.3%	5.4%
HIGHLAND	123	58	32	28	5	Bush	47.2%	26.0%	22.8%	4.1%
ISLE OF WIGHT	1,050	506	255	240	49	Bush	48.2%	24.3%	22.9%	4.7%
JAMES CITY	1,955	1,062	499	274	120	Bush	54.3%	25.5%	14.0%	6.1%
KING AND QUEEN	164	82	44	26	12	Bush	50.0%	26.8%	15.9%	7.3%
KING GEORGE	394	195	120	42	37	Bush	49.5%	30.5%	10.7%	9.4%
KING WILLIAM	376	246	73	44	13	Bush	65.4%	19.4%	11.7%	3.5%

VIRGINIA REPUBLICAN

1988

County	Total Vote	Bush	Dole	Robertson	Other	Winner	Percentage of Total Vote Bush	Dole	Robertson	Other
LANCASTER	674	462	121	52	39	Bush	68.5%	18.0%	7.7%	5.8%
LEE	562	383	97	70	12	Bush	68.1%	17.3%	12.5%	2.1%
LOUDOUN	3,673	1,883	1,046	439	305	Bush	51.3%	28.5%	12.0%	8.3%
LOUISA	459	258	98	77	26	Bush	56.2%	21.4%	16.8%	5.7%
LUNENBURG	304	189	59	37	19	Bush	62.2%	19.4%	12.2%	6.3%
MADISON	284	155	83	18	28	Bush	54.6%	29.2%	6.3%	9.9%
MATHEWS	452	238	92	99	23	Bush	52.7%	20.4%	21.9%	5.1%
MECKLENBURG	873	448	256	104	65	Bush	51.3%	29.3%	11.9%	7.4%
MIDDLESEX	528	316	102	81	29	Bush	59.8%	19.3%	15.3%	5.5%
MONTGOMERY	1,853	759	678	290	126	Bush	41.0%	36.6%	15.7%	6.8%
NELSON	291	159	72	40	20	Bush	54.6%	24.7%	13.7%	6.9%
NEW KENT	382	226	84	41	31	Bush	59.2%	22.0%	10.7%	8.1%
NORTHAMPTON	453	277	96	50	30	Bush	61.1%	21.2%	11.0%	6.6%
NORTHUMBERLAND	582	380	108	50	44	Bush	65.3%	18.6%	8.6%	7.6%
NOTTOWAY	298	188	46	50	14	Bush	63.1%	15.4%	16.8%	4.7%
ORANGE	649	362	171	74	42	Bush	55.8%	26.3%	11.4%	6.5%
PAGE	510	288	112	85	25	Bush	56.5%	22.0%	16.7%	4.9%
PATRICK	618	350	206	38	24	Bush	56.6%	33.3%	6.1%	3.9%
PITTSYLVANIA	1,219	710	288	169	52	Bush	58.2%	23.6%	13.9%	4.3%
POWHATAN	422	233	80	65	44	Bush	55.2%	19.0%	15.4%	10.4%
PRINCE EDWARD	489	328	87	46	28	Bush	67.1%	17.8%	9.4%	5.7%
PRINCE GEORGE	665	406	109	109	41	Bush	61.1%	16.4%	16.4%	6.2%
PRINCE WILLIAM	6,483	3,267	1,771	900	545	Bush	50.4%	27.3%	13.9%	8.4%
PULASKI	734	349	245	92	48	Bush	47.5%	33.4%	12.5%	6.5%
RAPPAHANNOCK	300	150	64	54	32	Bush	50.0%	21.3%	18.0%	10.7%
RICHMOND COUNTY	257	170	49	29	9	Bush	66.1%	19.1%	11.3%	3.5%
ROANOKE COUNTY	3,912	1,963	1,216	487	246	Bush	50.2%	31.1%	12.4%	6.3%
ROCKBRIDGE	625	334	158	91	42	Bush	53.4%	25.3%	14.6%	6.7%
ROCKINGHAM	1,226	490	313	368	55	Bush	40.0%	25.5%	30.0%	4.5%
RUSSELL	496	273	129	68	26	Bush	55.0%	26.0%	13.7%	5.2%
SCOTT	868	596	171	84	17	Bush	68.7%	19.7%	9.7%	2.0%
SHENANDOAH	1,027	633	243	95	56	Bush	61.6%	23.7%	9.3%	5.5%
SMYTH	888	523	153	174	38	Bush	58.9%	17.2%	19.6%	4.3%
SOUTHAMPTON	597	297	130	124	46	Bush	49.7%	21.8%	20.8%	7.7%
SPOTSYLVANIA	1,541	792	429	216	104	Bush	51.4%	27.8%	14.0%	6.7%
STAFFORD	1,960	1,007	544	252	157	Bush	51.4%	27.8%	12.9%	8.0%
SURRY	226	117	42	49	18	Bush	51.8%	18.6%	21.7%	8.0%
SUSSEX	244	130	62	33	19	Bush	53.3%	25.4%	13.5%	7.8%
TAZEWELL	1,014	582	254	111	67	Bush	57.4%	25.0%	10.9%	6.6%
WARREN	695	380	151	112	52	Bush	54.7%	21.7%	16.1%	7.5%
WASHINGTON	1,202	692	275	167	68	Bush	57.6%	22.9%	13.9%	5.7%
WESTMORELAND	481	303	108	44	26	Bush	63.0%	22.5%	9.1%	5.4%
WISE	827	435	152	211	29	Bush	52.6%	18.4%	25.5%	3.5%
WYTHE	605	319	140	116	30	Bush	52.7%	23.1%	19.2%	5.0%
YORK	2,419	1,237	623	412	147	Bush	51.1%	25.8%	17.0%	6.1%

VIRGINIA REPUBLICAN

1988

City	Total Vote	Bush	Dole	Robertson	Other	Winner	Percentage of Total Vote Bush	Dole	Robertson	Other
ALEXANDRIA	5,237	2,720	1,775	246	496	Bush	51.9%	33.9%	4.7%	9.5%
BEDFORD CITY	181	100	50	13	18	Bush	55.2%	27.6%	7.2%	9.9%
BRISTOL	796	460	172	134	30	Bush	57.8%	21.6%	16.8%	3.8%
BUENA VISTA	138	52	31	41	14	Bush	37.7%	22.5%	29.7%	10.1%
CHARLOTTESVILLE	1,061	491	347	108	115	Bush	46.3%	32.7%	10.2%	10.8%
CHESAPEAKE	5,389	2,446	1,114	1,542	287	Bush	45.4%	20.7%	28.6%	5.3%
CLIFTON FORGE	136	53	43	26	14	Bush	39.0%	31.6%	19.1%	10.3%
COLONIAL HEIGHTS	993	562	183	193	55	Bush	56.6%	18.4%	19.4%	5.5%
COVINGTON	213	109	52	29	23	Bush	51.2%	24.4%	13.6%	10.8%
DANVILLE	1,342	790	313	181	58	Bush	58.9%	23.3%	13.5%	4.3%
EMPORIA	190	131	24	24	11	Bush	68.9%	12.6%	12.6%	5.8%
FAIRFAX CITY	1,380	680	389	179	132	Bush	49.3%	28.2%	13.0%	9.6%
FALLS CHURCH	776	425	230	45	76	Bush	54.8%	29.6%	5.8%	9.8%
FRANKLIN CITY	354	191	81	62	20	Bush	54.0%	22.9%	17.5%	5.6%
FREDERICKSBURG	614	346	164	57	47	Bush	56.4%	26.7%	9.3%	7.7%
GALAX	222	138	59	12	13	Bush	62.2%	26.6%	5.4%	5.9%
HAMPTON	5,062	2,615	1,135	1,087	225	Bush	51.7%	22.4%	21.5%	4.4%
HARRISONBURG	649	263	173	161	52	Bush	40.5%	26.7%	24.8%	8.0%
HOPEWELL	659	327	138	162	32	Bush	49.6%	20.9%	24.6%	4.9%
LEXINGTON	289	125	93	44	27	Bush	43.3%	32.2%	15.2%	9.3%
LYNCHBURG	2,614	1,462	597	317	238	Bush	55.9%	22.8%	12.1%	9.1%
MANASSAS	1,016	498	260	176	82	Bush	49.0%	25.6%	17.3%	8.1%
MANASSAS PARK	150	72	26	38	14	Bush	48.0%	17.3%	25.3%	9.3%
MARTINSVILLE	672	343	210	76	43	Bush	51.0%	31.3%	11.3%	6.4%
NEWPORT NEWS	7,686	3,958	1,729	1,613	386	Bush	51.5%	22.5%	21.0%	5.0%
NORFOLK	7,231	3,784	1,619	1,435	393	Bush	52.3%	22.4%	19.8%	5.4%
NORTON	75	31	28	14	2	Bush	41.3%	37.3%	18.7%	2.7%
PETERSBURG	852	553	125	127	47	Bush	64.9%	14.7%	14.9%	5.5%
POQUOSON	756	419	176	117	44	Bush	55.4%	23.3%	15.5%	5.8%
PORTSMOUTH	3,471	1,832	690	757	192	Bush	52.8%	19.9%	21.8%	5.5%
RADFORD	318	153	91	51	23	Bush	48.1%	28.6%	16.0%	7.2%
RICHMOND CITY	6,411	4,001	1,256	656	498	Bush	62.4%	19.6%	10.2%	7.8%
ROANOKE CITY	2,787	1,389	820	400	178	Bush	49.8%	29.4%	14.4%	6.4%
SALEM	911	451	280	124	56	Bush	49.5%	30.7%	13.6%	6.1%
SOUTH BOSTON	186	98	48	27	13	Bush	52.7%	25.8%	14.5%	7.0%
STAUNTON	863	437	157	196	73	Bush	50.6%	18.2%	22.7%	8.5%
SUFFOLK	1,908	1,076	368	382	82	Bush	56.4%	19.3%	20.0%	4.3%
VIRGINIA BEACH	17,464	8,401	4,380	3,721	962	Bush	48.1%	25.1%	21.3%	5.5%
WAYNESBORO	901	476	268	104	53	Bush	52.8%	29.7%	11.5%	5.9%
WILLIAMSBURG	444	251	122	43	28	Bush	56.5%	27.5%	9.7%	6.3%
WINCHESTER	514	312	124	41	37	Bush	60.7%	24.1%	8.0%	7.2%
TOTAL	234,142	124,738	60,921	32,173	16,310	Bush	53.3%	26.0%	13.7%	7.0%

WASHINGTON

One of the legacies of Pat Robertson's 1988 presidential candidacy is Washington's presidential primary, which was initiated in 1992.

To the surprise of the state party establishment, Robertson won the Washington GOP precinct caucuses on Super Tuesday 1988, providing George Bush with his lone defeat in a day of one-sided primary victories. It was not long afterward that the call for a presidential primary gained momentum. But it did not take long for the new primary to also veer into the realm of unpredictability, as it was Washington that gave the first direct evidence of Ross Perot's vote-getting appeal in 1992.

Before the May primary, the Perot phenomenon was plainly visible in the polls. In Washington Perot's clout began to be felt at the ballot box, as he drew nearly 20 percent of the vote in both the Democratic and Republican primaries on the basis of write-in votes. In both primaries, he carried San Juan County, a cluster of islands near the Canadian border. The strong vote for Perot overshadowed primary victories by Bush and Bill Clinton.

In 1996, the Washington primary went more to form. Dole was the easy winner on the Republican side; Clinton was virtually unopposed on the Democratic. But two-thirds of the primary voters cast a third ballot that listed both Democratic and Republican candidates. The results of this unique balloting had nothing to do with the delegate-selection process but did prove prescient. Clinton won the all-party primary with 51 percent of the vote. In the general election, his winning share in Washington was 50 percent.

Turnout for the Democratic presidential primary in 1996 was not much different than for recent caucuses in the state. An estimated 100,000 voters turned out for the Democratic caucuses in 1988 and gave Michael Dukakis a clear-cut victory over Jesse Jackson. Al Gore drew nearly 20 percent in the central Washington congressional district that included the Hanford Atomic Works. But Gore was not a factor statewide.

Conservative Republicans long enjoyed the upper hand in the state's GOP caucus process. Barry Goldwater swept nearly all the Washington delegates in his successful 1964 insurgency. So did Ronald Reagan in his 1976 challenge to President Gerald Ford.

But neither was as traumatic as Robertson's dominance in 1988, which was based in part on his ability to organize many precincts that had been neglected by party regulars in the past. Robertson took about 40 percent of the vote in a statewide straw vote held in conjunction with the March caucuses, and his supporters filled most of the delegation, even though Robertson's candidacy had collapsed nationally long before it was chosen.

Religious conservatives remained a visible presence in Washington's GOP delegate-selection process through the 1990s. In 1996, they were the backbone of Pat Buchanan's support within the delegation, which produced nine votes for Buchanan at the San Diego convention. That was more than he received from any other states except Missouri and Louisiana.

Recent Washington Primary Results

Washington held its first presidential primary in 1992.

	DEMOCRATS			REPUBLICANS		
Year	Turnout	Candidates	%	Turnout	Candidates	%
1996 (March 26)	98,946	BILL CLINTON*	99	120,684	BOB DOLE	63
					Pat Buchanan	21
1992 (May 19)	147,981	BILL CLINTON	42	129,655	GEORGE BUSH*	67
		Jerry Brown	23		Ross Perot#	20
		Ross Perot#	19		Pat Buchanan	10
		Paul Tsongas	13			

Note: All candidates are listed that drew at least 10 percent of their party's primary vote. The names of winning candidates are capitalized. An asterisk (*) indicates an incumbent president. A pound sign (#) indicates a write-in candidate. In 1996, there was also an unaffiliated ballot that listed candidates from both parties. A total of 444,619 votes were cast in this all-party primary, led by Democrat Bill Clinton with 51 percent and Republican Bob Dole with 28 percent.

Whatcom
Bellingham
San Juan
Skagit
Okanogan
Ferry
Stevens
Pend Oreille
Island
Snohomish
Clallam
Everett
Chelan
Douglas
Lincoln
Jefferson
Seattle
Spokane
Kitsap
King
Spokane
Mason
Tacoma
Grant
Grays Harbor
Kittitas
Pierce
Olympia
Adams
Whitman
Thurston
Yakima
Pacific
Lewis
Franklin
Garfield
Wahkiakum
Yakima
Benton
Columbia
Cowlitz
Richland
Walla Walla
Asotin
Skamania
Klickitat
Clark
Vancouver

WASHINGTON DEMOCRATIC

1992

County	Total Vote	Brown	Clinton	Perot	Tsongas	Other	Winner	Percentage of Total Vote Brown	Clinton	Perot	Tsongas	Other
ADAMS	360	50	208	37	47	18	Clinton	13.9%	57.8%	10.3%	13.1%	5.0%
ASOTIN	359	49	211	57	32	10	Clinton	13.6%	58.8%	15.9%	8.9%	2.8%
BENTON	2,536	432	1,313	138	529	124	Clinton	17.0%	51.8%	5.4%	20.9%	4.9%
CHELAN	1,265	222	641	183	184	35	Clinton	17.5%	50.7%	14.5%	14.5%	2.8%
CLALLAM	2,121	400	843	550	262	66	Clinton	18.9%	39.7%	25.9%	12.4%	3.1%
CLARK	7,684	2,218	3,431	1,038	797	200	Clinton	28.9%	44.7%	13.5%	10.4%	2.6%
COLUMBIA	126	14	63	30	11	8	Clinton	11.1%	50.0%	23.8%	8.7%	6.3%
COWLITZ	4,322	767	2,090	1,038	290	137	Clinton	17.7%	48.4%	24.0%	6.7%	3.2%
DOUGLAS	907	164	489	106	99	49	Clinton	18.1%	53.9%	11.7%	10.9%	5.4%
FERRY	347	66	148	83	39	11	Clinton	19.0%	42.7%	23.9%	11.2%	3.2%
FRANKLIN	785	101	498	96	66	24	Clinton	12.9%	63.4%	12.2%	8.4%	3.1%
GARFIELD	63	9	37	7	5	5	Clinton	14.3%	58.7%	11.1%	7.9%	7.9%
GRANT	1,885	326	946	368	182	63	Clinton	17.3%	50.2%	19.5%	9.7%	3.3%
GRAYS HARBOR	2,296	426	1,009	568	208	85	Clinton	18.6%	43.9%	24.7%	9.1%	3.7%
ISLAND	1,763	439	700	329	240	55	Clinton	24.9%	39.7%	18.7%	13.6%	3.1%
JEFFERSON	2,412	606	742	699	301	64	Clinton	25.1%	30.8%	29.0%	12.5%	2.7%
KING	46,790	12,410	17,617	8,212	7,317	1,234	Clinton	26.5%	37.7%	17.6%	15.6%	2.6%
KITSAP	5,084	1,212	1,947	990	750	185	Clinton	23.8%	38.3%	19.5%	14.8%	3.6%
KITTITAS	919	170	443	173	113	20	Clinton	18.5%	48.2%	18.8%	12.3%	2.2%
KLICKITAT	894	165	462	183	64	20	Clinton	18.5%	51.7%	20.5%	7.2%	2.2%
LEWIS	1,652	425	808	136	217	66	Clinton	25.7%	48.9%	8.2%	13.1%	4.0%
LINCOLN	448	72	269	29	52	26	Clinton	16.1%	60.0%	6.5%	11.6%	5.8%
MASON	1,561	347	630	365	178	41	Clinton	22.2%	40.4%	23.4%	11.4%	2.6%
OKANOGAN	946	190	444	170	92	50	Clinton	20.1%	46.9%	18.0%	9.7%	5.3%
PACIFIC	1,247	245	640	186	128	48	Clinton	19.6%	51.3%	14.9%	10.3%	3.8%
PEND OREILLE	767	156	360	158	72	21	Clinton	20.3%	46.9%	20.6%	9.4%	2.7%
PIERCE	14,226	2,771	6,049	3,588	1,503	315	Clinton	19.5%	42.5%	25.2%	10.6%	2.2%
SAN JUAN	744	179	181	267	106	11	Perot	24.1%	24.3%	35.9%	14.2%	1.5%
SKAGIT	1,970	459	750	464	233	64	Clinton	23.3%	38.1%	23.6%	11.8%	3.2%
SKAMANIA	485	131	171	125	40	18	Clinton	27.0%	35.3%	25.8%	8.2%	3.7%
SNOHOMISH	11,778	2,730	4,562	2,649	1,471	366	Clinton	23.2%	38.7%	22.5%	12.5%	3.1%
SPOKANE	8,814	1,374	3,949	2,489	753	249	Clinton	15.6%	44.8%	28.2%	8.5%	2.8%
STEVENS	1,501	286	710	283	169	53	Clinton	19.1%	47.3%	18.9%	11.3%	3.5%
THURSTON	7,238	2,233	2,511	1,241	1,013	240	Clinton	30.9%	34.7%	17.1%	14.0%	3.3%
WAHKIAKUM	483	85	170	158	56	14	Clinton	17.6%	35.2%	32.7%	11.6%	2.9%
WALLA WALLA	1,869	363	975	260	206	65	Clinton	19.4%	52.2%	13.9%	11.0%	3.5%
WHATCOM	2,915	770	1,266	416	355	108	Clinton	26.4%	43.4%	14.3%	12.2%	3.7%
WHITMAN	683	145	323	89	108	18	Clinton	21.2%	47.3%	13.0%	15.8%	2.6%
YAKIMA	5,736	904	3,565	353	693	221	Clinton	15.8%	62.2%	6.2%	12.1%	3.9%
TOTAL	147,981	34,111	62,171	28,311	18,981	4,407	Clinton	23.1%	42.0%	19.1%	12.8%	3.0%

Note: The votes cast for Perot were write-ins.

WASHINGTON REPUBLICAN

1992

County	Total Vote	Buchanan	Bush	Perot	Other	Winner	Percentage of Total Vote Buchanan	Bush	Perot	Other
ADAMS	557	78	427	38	14	Bush	14.0%	76.7%	6.8%	2.5%
ASOTIN	245	44	160	33	8	Bush	18.0%	65.3%	13.5%	3.3%
BENTON	4,456	426	3,775	158	97	Bush	9.6%	84.7%	3.5%	2.2%
CHELAN	1,968	219	1,529	190	30	Bush	11.1%	77.7%	9.7%	1.5%
CLALLAM	2,150	240	1,211	639	60	Bush	11.2%	56.3%	29.7%	2.8%
CLARK	5,683	767	3,979	799	138	Bush	13.5%	70.0%	14.1%	2.4%
COLUMBIA	168	22	105	36	5	Bush	13.1%	62.5%	21.4%	3.0%
COWLITZ	2,463	216	1,621	575	51	Bush	8.8%	65.8%	23.3%	2.1%
DOUGLAS	1,431	125	1,158	124	24	Bush	8.7%	80.9%	8.7%	1.7%
FERRY	235	24	136	64	11	Bush	10.2%	57.9%	27.2%	4.7%
FRANKLIN	734	70	565	78	21	Bush	9.5%	77.0%	10.6%	2.9%
GARFIELD	99	11	77	11		Bush	11.1%	77.8%	11.1%	
GRANT	2,187	267	1,602	286	32	Bush	12.2%	73.3%	13.1%	1.5%
GRAYS HARBOR	1,158	123	716	292	27	Bush	10.6%	61.8%	25.2%	2.3%
ISLAND	2,690	222	2,000	413	55	Bush	8.3%	74.3%	15.4%	2.0%
JEFFERSON	2,037	151	1,162	691	33	Bush	7.4%	57.0%	33.9%	1.6%
KING	35,769	3,593	22,384	7,924	1,868	Bush	10.0%	62.6%	22.2%	5.2%
KITSAP	4,556	470	2,902	1,058	126	Bush	10.3%	63.7%	23.2%	2.8%
KITTITAS	728	66	465	182	15	Bush	9.1%	63.9%	25.0%	2.1%
KLICKITAT	630	55	395	171	9	Bush	8.7%	62.7%	27.1%	1.4%
LEWIS	2,188	311	1,697	122	58	Bush	14.2%	77.6%	5.6%	2.7%
LINCOLN	494	74	383	18	19	Bush	15.0%	77.5%	3.6%	3.8%
MASON	1,253	125	826	280	22	Bush	10.0%	65.9%	22.3%	1.8%
OKANOGAN	818	102	556	145	15	Bush	12.5%	68.0%	17.7%	1.8%
PACIFIC	554	66	385	83	20	Bush	11.9%	69.5%	15.0%	3.6%
PEND OREILLE	581	68	396	99	18	Bush	11.7%	68.2%	17.0%	3.1%
PIERCE	11,543	921	7,228	3,164	230	Bush	8.0%	62.6%	27.4%	2.0%
SAN JUAN	868	37	370	446	15	Perot	4.3%	42.6%	51.4%	1.7%
SKAGIT	2,046	228	1,298	473	47	Bush	11.1%	63.4%	23.1%	2.3%
SKAMANIA	340	39	211	83	7	Bush	11.5%	62.1%	24.4%	2.1%
SNOHOMISH	9,889	1,098	6,291	2,238	262	Bush	11.1%	63.6%	22.6%	2.6%
SPOKANE	7,998	884	5,205	1,734	175	Bush	11.1%	65.1%	21.7%	2.2%
STEVENS	1,676	255	1,125	250	46	Bush	15.2%	67.1%	14.9%	2.7%
THURSTON	5,778	472	3,854	1,216	236	Bush	8.2%	66.7%	21.0%	4.1%
WAHKIAKUM	256	16	149	84	7	Bush	6.3%	58.2%	32.8%	2.7%
WALLA WALLA	2,277	179	1,723	327	48	Bush	7.9%	75.7%	14.4%	2.1%
WHATCOM	2,506	294	1,801	333	78	Bush	11.7%	71.9%	13.3%	3.1%
WHITMAN	741	121	499	99	22	Bush	16.3%	67.3%	13.4%	3.0%
YAKIMA	7,905	794	6,473	467	171	Bush	10.0%	81.9%	5.9%	2.2%
TOTAL	129,655	13,273	86,839	25,423	4,120	Bush	10.2%	67.0%	19.6%	3.2%

Note: The votes cast for Perot were write-ins.

WASHINGTON DEMOCRATIC

1996

County	Total Vote	Clinton	LaRouche	Winner	Percentage of Total Vote Clinton	Percentage of Total Vote LaRouche
ADAMS	97	94	3	Clinton	96.9%	3.1%
ASOTIN	135	134	1	Clinton	99.3%	0.7%
BENTON	1,092	1,041	51	Clinton	95.3%	4.7%
CHELAN	396	385	11	Clinton	97.2%	2.8%
CLALLAM	1,055	1,027	28	Clinton	97.3%	2.7%
CLARK	3,902	3,822	80	Clinton	97.9%	2.1%
COLUMBIA	138	131	7	Clinton	94.9%	5.1%
COWLITZ	2,227	2,189	38	Clinton	98.3%	1.7%
DOUGLAS	210	201	9	Clinton	95.7%	4.3%
FERRY	144	138	6	Clinton	95.8%	4.2%
FRANKLIN	420	409	11	Clinton	97.4%	2.6%
GARFIELD	52	51	1	Clinton	98.1%	1.9%
GRANT	373	364	9	Clinton	97.6%	2.4%
GRAYS HARBOR	823	799	24	Clinton	97.1%	2.9%
ISLAND	730	711	19	Clinton	97.4%	2.6%
JEFFERSON	424	411	13	Clinton	96.9%	3.1%
KING	52,826	52,315	511	Clinton	99.0%	1.0%
KITSAP	2,463	2,420	43	Clinton	98.3%	1.7%
KITTITAS	219	215	4	Clinton	98.2%	1.8%
KLICKITAT	105	101	4	Clinton	96.2%	3.8%
LEWIS	635	605	30	Clinton	95.3%	4.7%
LINCOLN	210	200	10	Clinton	95.2%	4.8%
MASON	641	622	19	Clinton	97.0%	3.0%
OKANOGAN	215	205	10	Clinton	95.3%	4.7%
PACIFIC	430	428	2	Clinton	99.5%	0.5%
PEND OREILLE	248	246	2	Clinton	99.2%	0.8%
PIERCE	9,822	9,682	140	Clinton	98.6%	1.4%
SAN JUAN	172	172		Clinton	100.0%	
SKAGIT	1,085	1,062	23	Clinton	97.9%	2.1%
SKAMANIA	171	166	5	Clinton	97.1%	2.9%
SNOHOMISH	7,023	6,902	121	Clinton	98.3%	1.7%
SPOKANE	3,376	3,298	78	Clinton	97.7%	2.3%
STEVENS	514	485	29	Clinton	94.4%	5.6%
THURSTON	2,993	2,959	34	Clinton	98.9%	1.1%
WAHKIAKUM	158	158		Clinton	100.0%	
WALLA WALLA	713	692	21	Clinton	97.1%	2.9%
WHATCOM	1,185	1,170	15	Clinton	98.7%	1.3%
WHITMAN	276	269	7	Clinton	97.5%	2.5%
YAKIMA	1,248	1,216	32	Clinton	97.4%	2.6%
TOTAL	98,946	97,495	1,451	Clinton	98.5%	1.5%

WASHINGTON REPUBLICAN

1996

County	Total Vote	Buchanan	Dole	Other	Winner	Percentage of Total Vote: Buchanan	Dole	Other
ADAMS	365	55	253	57	Dole	15.1%	69.3%	15.6%
ASOTIN	180	43	117	20	Dole	23.9%	65.0%	11.1%
BENTON	3,266	713	2,154	399	Dole	21.8%	66.0%	12.2%
CHELAN	1,551	277	1,088	186	Dole	17.9%	70.1%	12.0%
CLALLAM	2,207	394	1,477	336	Dole	17.9%	66.9%	15.2%
CLARK	6,513	1,400	4,224	889	Dole	21.5%	64.9%	13.6%
COLUMBIA	233	40	171	22	Dole	17.2%	73.4%	9.4%
COWLITZ	1,871	345	1,185	341	Dole	18.4%	63.3%	18.2%
DOUGLAS	594	119	347	128	Dole	20.0%	58.4%	21.5%
FERRY	202	67	114	21	Dole	33.2%	56.4%	10.4%
FRANKLIN	825	186	544	95	Dole	22.5%	65.9%	11.5%
GARFIELD	128	23	94	11	Dole	18.0%	73.4%	8.6%
GRANT	1,137	279	710	148	Dole	24.5%	62.4%	13.0%
GRAYS HARBOR	761	218	428	115	Dole	28.6%	56.2%	15.1%
ISLAND	2,399	390	1,623	386	Dole	16.3%	67.7%	16.1%
JEFFERSON	939	131	654	154	Dole	14.0%	69.6%	16.4%
KING	39,910	7,221	25,404	7,285	Dole	18.1%	63.7%	18.3%
KITSAP	4,859	1,006	2,937	916	Dole	20.7%	60.4%	18.9%
KITTITAS	383	75	262	46	Dole	19.6%	68.4%	12.0%
KLICKITAT	110	19	80	11	Dole	17.3%	72.7%	10.0%
LEWIS	1,865	377	1,265	223	Dole	20.2%	67.8%	12.0%
LINCOLN	484	121	298	65	Dole	25.0%	61.6%	13.4%
MASON	972	193	662	117	Dole	19.9%	68.1%	12.0%
OKANOGAN	574	196	325	53	Dole	34.1%	56.6%	9.2%
PACIFIC	341	65	239	37	Dole	19.1%	70.1%	10.9%
PEND OREILLE	362	134	183	45	Dole	37.0%	50.6%	12.4%
PIERCE	12,049	2,617	7,495	1,937	Dole	21.7%	62.2%	16.1%
SAN JUAN	355	42	243	70	Dole	11.8%	68.5%	19.7%
SKAGIT	2,435	526	1,554	355	Dole	21.6%	63.8%	14.6%
SKAMANIA	241	77	127	37	Dole	32.0%	52.7%	15.4%
SNOHOMISH	11,950	2,764	7,098	2,088	Dole	23.1%	59.4%	17.5%
SPOKANE	7,365	2,222	4,354	789	Dole	30.2%	59.1%	10.7%
STEVENS	1,464	566	714	184	Dole	38.7%	48.8%	12.6%
THURSTON	3,435	673	2,151	611	Dole	19.6%	62.6%	17.8%
WAHKIAKUM	141	26	92	23	Dole	18.4%	65.2%	16.3%
WALLA WALLA	1,361	199	1,040	122	Dole	14.6%	76.4%	9.0%
WHATCOM	2,520	603	1,489	428	Dole	23.9%	59.1%	17.0%
WHITMAN	765	108	556	101	Dole	14.1%	72.7%	13.2%
YAKIMA	3,572	737	2,404	431	Dole	20.6%	67.3%	12.1%
TOTAL	120,684	25,247	76,155	19,282	Dole	20.9%	63.1%	16.0%

WASHINGTON ALL PARTY

1996

County	Total Vote	Clinton (D)	Dole (R)	Other	Winner	Percentage of Total Vote Clinton (D)	Dole (R)	Other
ADAMS	854	286	358	210	Dole	33.5%	41.9%	24.6%
ASOTIN	379	132	124	123	Clinton	34.8%	32.7%	32.5%
BENTON	4,481	1,567	1,651	1,263	Dole	35.0%	36.8%	28.2%
CHELAN	2,852	1,077	1,163	612	Dole	37.8%	40.8%	21.5%
CLALLAM	3,758	1,675	1,143	940	Clinton	44.6%	30.4%	25.0%
CLARK	25,660	12,822	7,924	4,914	Clinton	50.0%	30.9%	19.2%
COLUMBIA	630	241	237	152	Clinton	38.3%	37.6%	24.1%
COWLITZ	20,273	11,005	5,026	4,242	Clinton	54.3%	24.8%	20.9%
DOUGLAS	5,633	2,133	1,990	1,510	Clinton	37.9%	35.3%	26.8%
FERRY	1,621	673	457	491	Clinton	41.5%	28.2%	30.3%
FRANKLIN	2,081	787	749	545	Clinton	37.8%	36.0%	26.2%
GARFIELD	589	225	249	115	Dole	38.2%	42.3%	19.5%
GRANT	3,700	1,324	1,366	1,010	Dole	35.8%	36.9%	27.3%
GRAYS HARBOR	3,060	1,721	696	643	Clinton	56.2%	22.7%	21.0%
ISLAND	2,509	1,187	795	527	Clinton	47.3%	31.7%	21.0%
JEFFERSON	2,609	1,267	733	609	Clinton	48.6%	28.1%	23.3%
KING	128,695	70,700	32,684	25,311	Clinton	54.9%	25.4%	19.7%
KITSAP	18,848	8,896	5,472	4,480	Clinton	47.2%	29.0%	23.8%
KITTITAS	967	385	308	274	Clinton	39.8%	31.9%	28.3%
KLICKITAT	460	229	112	119	Clinton	49.8%	24.3%	25.9%
LEWIS	3,842	1,443	1,404	995	Clinton	37.6%	36.5%	25.9%
LINCOLN	1,594	621	583	390	Clinton	39.0%	36.6%	24.5%
MASON	3,308	1,624	930	754	Clinton	49.1%	28.1%	22.8%
OKANOGAN	2,616	953	814	849	Clinton	36.4%	31.1%	32.5%
PACIFIC	1,364	765	340	259	Clinton	56.1%	24.9%	19.0%
PEND OREILLE	2,781	1,257	708	816	Clinton	45.2%	25.5%	29.3%
PIERCE	79,400	42,571	22,256	14,573	Clinton	53.6%	28.0%	18.4%
SAN JUAN	1,074	515	307	252	Clinton	48.0%	28.6%	23.5%
SKAGIT	4,117	1,852	1,331	934	Clinton	45.0%	32.3%	22.7%
SKAMANIA	420	174	115	131	Clinton	41.4%	27.4%	31.2%
SNOHOMISH	35,082	17,943	9,368	7,771	Clinton	51.1%	26.7%	22.2%
SPOKANE	10,493	4,726	3,430	2,337	Clinton	45.0%	32.7%	22.3%
STEVENS	2,044	782	592	670	Clinton	38.3%	29.0%	32.8%
THURSTON	42,147	23,005	11,309	7,833	Clinton	54.6%	26.8%	18.6%
WAHKIAKUM	1,101	559	316	226	Clinton	50.8%	28.7%	20.5%
WALLA WALLA	3,685	1,538	1,378	769	Clinton	41.7%	37.4%	20.9%
WHATCOM	9,539	4,230	2,872	2,437	Clinton	44.3%	30.1%	25.5%
WHITMAN	1,995	787	781	427	Clinton	39.4%	39.1%	21.4%
YAKIMA	8,358	3,443	3,083	1,832	Clinton	41.2%	36.9%	21.9%
TOTAL	444,619	227,120	125,154	92,345	Clinton	51.1%	28.1%	20.8%

WEST VIRGINIA

West Virginia's presidential primary assured itself a place in American political lore in 1960, when John F. Kennedy chose it as the place to test whether an urban Catholic could win in a rural Protestant environment. After an expensive and closely watched campaign that has become a part of "Camelot" lore, Kennedy defeated Hubert Humphrey, 61 to 39 percent, knocking Humphrey from the race and moving Kennedy's own candidacy a big step closer to the Democratic nomination.

No presidential primary before or since in West Virginia has had such an impact on the nominating process. In many years, it takes second billing on the May primary ballot to party gubernatorial contests that are decided at the same time.

Presidential candidates that do come to West Virginia find a state that is poor and viscerally Democratic. The backdrop has long made West Virginia fertile ground for Democratic candidates willing to embrace New Deal-style programs that are out of vogue in much of the rest of the country. Humphrey avenged his loss to Kennedy by swamping George Wallace by a margin of better than 2-to-1 in the 1972 primary. Twelve years later, Humphrey's protégé, Walter Mondale, took a majority of the Democratic vote. West Virginia was the only primary state that Mondale carried in 1984 with more than 50 percent.

Edward Kennedy sought to duplicate his brother's success in West Virginia in 1980, but fell short. Forced to choose between nostalgia and loyalty, West Virginia Democrats chose to be loyal. The United Mine Workers and much of the state party hierarchy lined up behind President Jimmy Carter, who carried all but one county.

Bill Clinton was an easy winner in the West Virginia primary the two times he ran, although in 1996 he lost 13 percent of the vote to Lyndon LaRouche. It was the largest share of the vote that LaRouche won that year in any primary where he went head-to-head with Clinton.

No recent Republican primaries have been very compelling. The closest was in 1976 between President Gerald Ford and Ronald Reagan. But with the backing of the state's most powerful Republican at the time, Gov. Arch Moore, Ford swept all but three of West Virginia's 55 counties. Wood County (Parkersburg) was the largest that voted for Reagan.

Recent West Virginia Primary Results

West Virginia held its first presidential primary in 1916.

	DEMOCRATS			REPUBLICANS		
Year	Turnout	Candidates	%	Turnout	Candidates	%
1996 (May 14)	297,121	BILL CLINTON*	87	127,454	BOB DOLE	69
		Lyndon LaRouche	13		Pat Buchanan	16
1992 (May 12)	306,866	BILL CLINTON	74	124,157	GEORGE BUSH*	81
		Jerry Brown	12		Pat Buchanan	15
1988 (May 10)	340,097	MICHAEL DUKAKIS	75	143,140	GEORGE BUSH	77
		Jesse Jackson	13		Bob Dole	11
1984 (June 5)	369,245	WALTER MONDALE	54	136,996	RONALD REAGAN*	92
		Gary Hart	37			
1980 (June 3)	317,934	JIMMY CARTER*	62	138,016	RONALD REAGAN	84
		Edward Kennedy	38		George Bush	14
1976 (May 11)	372,577	ROBERT BYRD	89	155,692	GERALD FORD*	57
		George Wallace	11		Ronald Reagan	43
1972 (May 9)	368,484	HUBERT HUMPHREY	67	95,813	UNPLEDGED	100
		George Wallace	33			
1968 (May 14)	149,282	UNPLEDGED	100	81,039	UNPLEDGED	100

Note: All candidates are listed that drew at least 10 percent of their party's primary vote. The names of winning candidates are capitalized. An asterisk (*) indicates an incumbent president.

Hancock
Brooke
Ohio
Wheeling
Marshall
Wetzel
Monongalia
Morgantown
Preston
Marion
Tyler
Pleasants
Parkersburg
Harrison
Taylor
Doddridge
Clarksburg
Ritchie
Wood
Mineral
Morgan
Berkeley
Martinsburg
Hampshire
Jefferson
Tucker
Grant
Barbour
Hardy
Wirt
Lewis
Gilmer
Upshur
Elkins
Randolph
Calhoun
Jackson
Mason
Roane
Pendleton
Braxton
Putnam
Webster
Cabell
Charleston
Clay
Huntington
Kanawha
Nicholas
Pocahontas
Wayne
Lincoln
Boone
Fayette
Greenbrier
Logan
Beckley
Raleigh
Summers
Mingo
Wyoming
Monroe
Mercer
McDowell
Bluefield

WEST VIRGINIA DEMOCRATIC

1972

County	Total Vote	Humphrey	Wallace	Winner	Percentage of Total Vote Humphrey	Wallace
BARBOUR	2,540	1,740	800	Humphrey	68.5%	31.5%
BERKELEY	5,654	2,672	2,982	Wallace	47.3%	52.7%
BOONE	7,665	5,045	2,620	Humphrey	65.8%	34.2%
BRAXTON	3,489	2,368	1,121	Humphrey	67.9%	32.1%
BROOKE	7,392	4,567	2,825	Humphrey	61.8%	38.2%
CABELL	18,783	13,445	5,338	Humphrey	71.6%	28.4%
CALHOUN	1,627	1,075	552	Humphrey	66.1%	33.9%
CLAY	2,040	1,407	633	Humphrey	69.0%	31.0%
DODDRIDGE	702	474	228	Humphrey	67.5%	32.5%
FAYETTE	15,624	11,014	4,610	Humphrey	70.5%	29.5%
GILMER	1,869	1,242	627	Humphrey	66.5%	33.5%
GRANT	569	324	245	Humphrey	56.9%	43.1%
GREENBRIER	7,216	4,495	2,721	Humphrey	62.3%	37.7%
HAMPSHIRE	2,636	1,197	1,439	Wallace	45.4%	54.6%
HANCOCK	10,747	6,187	4,560	Humphrey	57.6%	42.4%
HARDY	2,044	1,039	1,005	Humphrey	50.8%	49.2%
HARRISON	18,482	13,623	4,859	Humphrey	73.7%	26.3%
JACKSON	3,667	2,667	1,000	Humphrey	72.7%	27.3%
JEFFERSON	4,224	2,161	2,063	Humphrey	51.2%	48.8%
KANAWHA	44,542	32,439	12,103	Humphrey	72.8%	27.2%
LEWIS	2,893	1,819	1,074	Humphrey	62.9%	37.1%
LINCOLN	3,958	2,762	1,196	Humphrey	69.8%	30.2%
LOGAN	12,018	8,844	3,174	Humphrey	73.6%	26.4%
MCDOWELL	10,748	6,730	4,018	Humphrey	62.6%	37.4%
MARION	14,587	10,466	4,121	Humphrey	71.7%	28.3%
MARSHALL	6,589	4,682	1,907	Humphrey	71.1%	28.9%
MASON	4,716	3,606	1,110	Humphrey	76.5%	23.5%
MERCER	14,771	8,142	6,629	Humphrey	55.1%	44.9%
MINERAL	3,436	2,154	1,282	Humphrey	62.7%	37.3%
MINGO	8,283	5,241	3,042	Humphrey	63.3%	36.7%
MONONGALIA	12,350	8,400	3,950	Humphrey	68.0%	32.0%
MONROE	2,478	1,539	939	Humphrey	62.1%	37.9%
MORGAN	1,248	624	624		50.0%	50.0%
NICHOLAS	4,710	3,147	1,563	Humphrey	66.8%	33.2%
OHIO	12,175	8,881	3,294	Humphrey	72.9%	27.1%
PENDLETON	1,610	1,005	605	Humphrey	62.4%	37.6%
PLEASANTS	1,248	936	312	Humphrey	75.0%	25.0%
POCAHONTAS	1,747	1,116	631	Humphrey	63.9%	36.1%
PRESTON	3,536	2,357	1,179	Humphrey	66.7%	33.3%
PUTNAM	5,491	3,863	1,628	Humphrey	70.4%	29.6%
RALEIGH	17,530	11,401	6,129	Humphrey	65.0%	35.0%
RANDOLPH	5,891	3,610	2,281	Humphrey	61.3%	38.7%
RITCHIE	1,049	697	352	Humphrey	66.4%	33.6%
ROANE	2,057	1,520	537	Humphrey	73.9%	26.1%
SUMMERS	4,523	2,757	1,766	Humphrey	61.0%	39.0%
TAYLOR	2,369	1,545	824	Humphrey	65.2%	34.8%
TUCKER	1,734	1,107	627	Humphrey	63.8%	36.2%
TYLER	1,138	719	419	Humphrey	63.2%	36.8%
UPSHUR	2,110	1,387	723	Humphrey	65.7%	34.3%
WAYNE	9,232	6,566	2,666	Humphrey	71.1%	28.9%

WEST VIRGINIA DEMOCRATIC

1972

County	Total Vote	Humphrey	Wallace	Winner	Percentage of Total Vote Humphrey	Percentage of Total Vote Wallace
WEBSTER	2,869	2,002	867	Humphrey	69.8%	30.2%
WETZEL	4,548	2,953	1,595	Humphrey	64.9%	35.1%
WIRT	783	551	232	Humphrey	70.4%	29.6%
WOOD	14,379	9,111	5,268	Humphrey	63.4%	36.6%
WYOMING	8,168	5,175	2,993	Humphrey	63.4%	36.6%
TOTAL	368,484	246,596	121,888	Humphrey	66.9%	33.1%

WEST VIRGINIA DEMOCRATIC

1976

County	Total Vote	Byrd	Wallace	Winner	Percentage of Total Vote Byrd	Percentage of Total Vote Wallace
BARBOUR	2,938	2,708	230	Byrd	92.2%	7.8%
BERKELEY	6,894	5,761	1,133	Byrd	83.6%	16.4%
BOONE	8,513	7,731	782	Byrd	90.8%	9.2%
BRAXTON	3,682	3,331	351	Byrd	90.5%	9.5%
BROOKE	7,666	6,220	1,446	Byrd	81.1%	18.9%
CABELL	17,187	15,203	1,984	Byrd	88.5%	11.5%
CALHOUN	1,831	1,620	211	Byrd	88.5%	11.5%
CLAY	2,202	2,045	157	Byrd	92.9%	7.1%
DODDRIDGE	837	759	78	Byrd	90.7%	9.3%
FAYETTE	14,018	12,786	1,232	Byrd	91.2%	8.8%
GILMER	2,262	2,003	259	Byrd	88.5%	11.5%
GRANT	625	538	87	Byrd	86.1%	13.9%
GREENBRIER	7,828	7,035	793	Byrd	89.9%	10.1%
HAMPSHIRE	3,055	2,614	441	Byrd	85.6%	14.4%
HANCOCK	10,087	7,842	2,245	Byrd	77.7%	22.3%
HARDY	2,527	2,209	318	Byrd	87.4%	12.6%
HARRISON	19,388	17,488	1,900	Byrd	90.2%	9.8%
JACKSON	3,986	3,510	476	Byrd	88.1%	11.9%
JEFFERSON	5,149	4,382	767	Byrd	85.1%	14.9%
KANAWHA	44,965	41,193	3,772	Byrd	91.6%	8.4%
LEWIS	3,293	2,883	410	Byrd	87.5%	12.5%
LINCOLN	4,249	3,935	314	Byrd	92.6%	7.4%
LOGAN	12,494	11,529	965	Byrd	92.3%	7.7%
MCDOWELL	9,237	8,128	1,109	Byrd	88.0%	12.0%
MARION	14,410	12,790	1,620	Byrd	88.8%	11.2%
MARSHALL	6,642	6,020	622	Byrd	90.6%	9.4%
MASON	4,975	4,389	586	Byrd	88.2%	11.8%
MERCER	13,506	11,763	1,743	Byrd	87.1%	12.9%
MINERAL	3,514	3,056	458	Byrd	87.0%	13.0%
MINGO	6,556	5,813	743	Byrd	88.7%	11.3%

WEST VIRGINIA DEMOCRATIC

1976

County	Total Vote	Byrd	Wallace	Winner	Percentage of Total Vote Byrd	Percentage of Total Vote Wallace
MONONGALIA	11,971	10,255	1,716	Byrd	85.7%	14.3%
MONROE	2,807	2,536	271	Byrd	90.3%	9.7%
MORGAN	1,224	1,051	173	Byrd	85.9%	14.1%
NICHOLAS	5,352	4,868	484	Byrd	91.0%	9.0%
OHIO	9,724	8,908	816	Byrd	91.6%	8.4%
PENDLETON	1,808	1,620	188	Byrd	89.6%	10.4%
PLEASANTS	1,483	1,335	148	Byrd	90.0%	10.0%
POCAHONTAS	2,067	1,871	196	Byrd	90.5%	9.5%
PRESTON	4,414	3,801	613	Byrd	86.1%	13.9%
PUTNAM	6,488	5,865	623	Byrd	90.4%	9.6%
RALEIGH	17,657	16,126	1,531	Byrd	91.3%	8.7%
RANDOLPH	7,234	6,592	642	Byrd	91.1%	8.9%
RITCHIE	1,270	1,121	149	Byrd	88.3%	11.7%
ROANE	2,462	2,208	254	Byrd	89.7%	10.3%
SUMMERS	4,525	4,160	365	Byrd	91.9%	8.1%
TAYLOR	2,671	2,406	265	Byrd	90.1%	9.9%
TUCKER	2,020	1,720	300	Byrd	85.1%	14.9%
TYLER	1,263	1,104	159	Byrd	87.4%	12.6%
UPSHUR	2,357	2,103	254	Byrd	89.2%	10.8%
WAYNE	9,091	7,992	1,099	Byrd	87.9%	12.1%
WEBSTER	2,678	2,419	259	Byrd	90.3%	9.7%
WETZEL	4,658	4,182	476	Byrd	89.8%	10.2%
WIRT	1,024	918	106	Byrd	89.6%	10.4%
WOOD	13,580	11,763	1,817	Byrd	86.6%	13.4%
WYOMING	8,233	7,431	802	Byrd	90.3%	9.7%
TOTAL	372,577	331,639	40,938	Byrd	89.0%	11.0%

WEST VIRGINIA REPUBLICAN

1976

County	Total Vote	Ford	Reagan	Winner	Percentage of Total Vote Ford	Percentage of Total Vote Reagan
BARBOUR	1,839	1,235	604	Ford	67.2%	32.8%
BERKELEY	3,765	1,942	1,823	Ford	51.6%	48.4%
BOONE	1,088	659	429	Ford	60.6%	39.4%
BRAXTON	849	549	300	Ford	64.7%	35.3%
BROOKE	2,241	1,157	1,084	Ford	51.6%	48.4%
CABELL	9,027	5,036	3,991	Ford	55.8%	44.2%
CALHOUN	585	319	266	Ford	54.5%	45.5%
CLAY	640	349	291	Ford	54.5%	45.5%
DODDRIDGE	1,459	887	572	Ford	60.8%	39.2%
FAYETTE	2,078	1,336	742	Ford	64.3%	35.7%

WEST VIRGINIA REPUBLICAN

1976

County	Total Vote	Ford	Reagan	Winner	Percentage of Total Vote Ford	Reagan
GILMER	635	373	262	Ford	58.7%	41.3%
GRANT	2,706	1,608	1,098	Ford	59.4%	40.6%
GREENBRIER	2,298	1,385	913	Ford	60.3%	39.7%
HAMPSHIRE	690	399	291	Ford	57.8%	42.2%
HANCOCK	3,096	1,678	1,418	Ford	54.2%	45.8%
HARDY	536	324	212	Ford	60.4%	39.6%
HARRISON	7,950	4,688	3,262	Ford	59.0%	41.0%
JACKSON	3,865	1,951	1,914	Ford	50.5%	49.5%
JEFFERSON	1,350	800	550	Ford	59.3%	40.7%
KANAWHA	18,017	10,361	7,656	Ford	57.5%	42.5%
LEWIS	2,650	1,546	1,104	Ford	58.3%	41.7%
LINCOLN	1,458	892	566	Ford	61.2%	38.8%
LOGAN	1,473	878	595	Ford	59.6%	40.4%
MCDOWELL	1,015	635	380	Ford	62.6%	37.4%
MARION	4,421	2,786	1,635	Ford	63.0%	37.0%
MARSHALL	4,042	2,096	1,946	Ford	51.9%	48.1%
MASON	3,376	1,774	1,602	Ford	52.5%	47.5%
MERCER	3,628	1,941	1,687	Ford	53.5%	46.5%
MINERAL	2,977	1,623	1,354	Ford	54.5%	45.5%
MINGO	951	555	396	Ford	58.4%	41.6%
MONONGALIA	5,242	3,100	2,142	Ford	59.1%	40.9%
MONROE	1,745	1,118	627	Ford	64.1%	35.9%
MORGAN	1,612	797	815	Reagan	49.4%	50.6%
NICHOLAS	1,587	1,015	572	Ford	64.0%	36.0%
OHIO	6,715	3,544	3,171	Ford	52.8%	47.2%
PENDLETON	821	529	292	Ford	64.4%	35.6%
PLEASANTS	954	515	439	Ford	54.0%	46.0%
POCAHONTAS	1,011	652	359	Ford	64.5%	35.5%
PRESTON	5,286	2,950	2,336	Ford	55.8%	44.2%
PUTNAM	3,536	1,886	1,650	Ford	53.3%	46.7%
RALEIGH	4,036	2,451	1,585	Ford	60.7%	39.3%
RANDOLPH	1,762	1,182	580	Ford	67.1%	32.9%
RITCHIE	2,242	1,225	1,017	Ford	54.6%	45.4%
ROANE	2,210	1,227	983	Ford	55.5%	44.5%
SUMMERS	792	494	298	Ford	62.4%	37.6%
TAYLOR	1,603	888	715	Ford	55.4%	44.6%
TUCKER	910	511	399	Ford	56.2%	43.8%
TYLER	2,036	1,053	983	Ford	51.7%	48.3%
UPSHUR	3,265	2,039	1,226	Ford	62.5%	37.5%
WAYNE	3,000	1,698	1,302	Ford	56.6%	43.4%
WEBSTER	368	243	125	Ford	66.0%	34.0%
WETZEL	1,736	935	801	Ford	53.9%	46.1%
WIRT	705	340	365	Reagan	48.2%	51.8%
WOOD	10,012	4,985	5,027	Reagan	49.8%	50.2%
WYOMING	1,801	1,247	554	Ford	69.2%	30.8%
TOTAL	155,692	88,386	67,306	Ford	56.8%	43.2%

WEST VIRGINIA DEMOCRATIC

1980

County	Total Vote	Carter	E. Kennedy	Winner	Percentage of Total Vote Carter	E. Kennedy
BARBOUR	3,123	1,992	1,131	Carter	63.8%	36.2%
BERKELEY	5,334	3,228	2,106	Carter	60.5%	39.5%
BOONE	7,780	4,554	3,226	Carter	58.5%	41.5%
BRAXTON	4,074	2,727	1,347	Carter	66.9%	33.1%
BROOKE	5,764	3,348	2,416	Carter	58.1%	41.9%
CABELL	15,276	10,186	5,090	Carter	66.7%	33.3%
CALHOUN	1,677	999	678	Carter	59.6%	40.4%
CLAY	2,167	1,412	755	Carter	65.2%	34.8%
DODDRIDGE	691	464	227	Carter	67.1%	32.9%
FAYETTE	12,728	7,868	4,860	Carter	61.8%	38.2%
GILMER	2,273	1,502	771	Carter	66.1%	33.9%
GRANT	561	394	167	Carter	70.2%	29.8%
GREENBRIER	6,015	4,160	1,855	Carter	69.2%	30.8%
HAMPSHIRE	2,899	1,889	1,010	Carter	65.2%	34.8%
HANCOCK	9,996	5,652	4,344	Carter	56.5%	43.5%
HARDY	2,486	1,649	837	Carter	66.3%	33.7%
HARRISON	16,457	9,196	7,261	Carter	55.9%	44.1%
JACKSON	3,482	2,489	993	Carter	71.5%	28.5%
JEFFERSON	3,797	2,316	1,481	Carter	61.0%	39.0%
KANAWHA	33,339	21,437	11,902	Carter	64.3%	35.7%
LEWIS	3,218	2,025	1,193	Carter	62.9%	37.1%
LINCOLN	4,374	2,590	1,784	Carter	59.2%	40.8%
LOGAN	10,112	5,924	4,188	Carter	58.6%	41.4%
MCDOWELL	8,498	5,016	3,482	Carter	59.0%	41.0%
MARION	13,000	6,246	6,754	E. Kennedy	48.0%	52.0%
MARSHALL	6,137	3,539	2,598	Carter	57.7%	42.3%
MASON	4,523	3,188	1,335	Carter	70.5%	29.5%
MERCER	9,720	6,771	2,949	Carter	69.7%	30.3%
MINERAL	3,600	2,222	1,378	Carter	61.7%	38.3%
MINGO	7,365	4,279	3,086	Carter	58.1%	41.9%
MONONGALIA	11,591	6,062	5,529	Carter	52.3%	47.7%
MONROE	2,453	1,697	756	Carter	69.2%	30.8%
MORGAN	1,238	747	491	Carter	60.3%	39.7%
NICHOLAS	4,079	2,676	1,403	Carter	65.6%	34.4%
OHIO	7,602	4,261	3,341	Carter	56.1%	43.9%
PENDLETON	1,713	1,161	552	Carter	67.8%	32.2%
PLEASANTS	1,463	1,069	394	Carter	73.1%	26.9%
POCAHONTAS	2,036	1,339	697	Carter	65.8%	34.2%
PRESTON	3,543	2,031	1,512	Carter	57.3%	42.7%
PUTNAM	5,622	3,828	1,794	Carter	68.1%	31.9%
RALEIGH	13,670	8,495	5,175	Carter	62.1%	37.9%
RANDOLPH	5,586	4,021	1,565	Carter	72.0%	28.0%
RITCHIE	1,217	818	399	Carter	67.2%	32.8%
ROANE	2,065	1,364	701	Carter	66.1%	33.9%
SUMMERS	3,134	1,956	1,178	Carter	62.4%	37.6%
TAYLOR	2,531	1,639	892	Carter	64.8%	35.2%
TUCKER	1,895	1,228	667	Carter	64.8%	35.2%
TYLER	1,066	734	332	Carter	68.9%	31.1%
UPSHUR	1,900	1,360	540	Carter	71.6%	28.4%
WAYNE	7,919	5,394	2,525	Carter	68.1%	31.9%

WEST VIRGINIA DEMOCRATIC

1980

County	Total Vote	Carter	E. Kennedy	Winner	Percentage of Total Vote Carter	E. Kennedy
WEBSTER	2,682	1,735	947	Carter	64.7%	35.3%
WETZEL	3,800	2,630	1,170	Carter	69.2%	30.8%
WIRT	881	686	195	Carter	77.9%	22.1%
WOOD	11,060	7,711	3,349	Carter	69.7%	30.3%
WYOMING	6,722	3,783	2,939	Carter	56.3%	43.7%
TOTAL	317,934	197,687	120,247	Carter	62.2%	37.8%

WEST VIRGINIA REPUBLICAN

1980

County	Total Vote	Bush	Reagan	Stassen	Winner	Percentage of Total Vote Bush	Reagan	Stassen
BARBOUR	2,147	306	1,791	50	Reagan	14.3%	83.4%	2.3%
BERKELEY	3,512	342	3,122	48	Reagan	9.7%	88.9%	1.4%
BOONE	1,311	135	1,137	39	Reagan	10.3%	86.7%	3.0%
BRAXTON	997	88	870	39	Reagan	8.8%	87.3%	3.9%
BROOKE	1,484	349	1,103	32	Reagan	23.5%	74.3%	2.2%
CABELL	8,452	1,136	7,166	150	Reagan	13.4%	84.8%	1.8%
CALHOUN	589	42	534	13	Reagan	7.1%	90.7%	2.2%
CLAY	618	68	535	15	Reagan	11.0%	86.6%	2.4%
DODDRIDGE	1,505	166	1,298	41	Reagan	11.0%	86.2%	2.7%
FAYETTE	1,758	324	1,374	60	Reagan	18.4%	78.2%	3.4%
GILMER	525	60	454	11	Reagan	11.4%	86.5%	2.1%
GRANT	1,747	306	1,361	80	Reagan	17.5%	77.9%	4.6%
GREENBRIER	1,963	304	1,609	50	Reagan	15.5%	82.0%	2.5%
HAMPSHIRE	662	63	590	9	Reagan	9.5%	89.1%	1.4%
HANCOCK	2,402	570	1,775	57	Reagan	23.7%	73.9%	2.4%
HARDY	551	65	476	10	Reagan	11.8%	86.4%	1.8%
HARRISON	6,585	1,154	5,267	164	Reagan	17.5%	80.0%	2.5%
JACKSON	3,946	410	3,463	73	Reagan	10.4%	87.8%	1.8%
JEFFERSON	1,136	235	880	21	Reagan	20.7%	77.5%	1.8%
KANAWHA	15,879	2,497	12,957	425	Reagan	15.7%	81.6%	2.7%
LEWIS	2,373	310	2,063		Reagan	13.1%	86.9%	
LINCOLN	1,511	145	1,342	24	Reagan	9.6%	88.8%	1.6%
LOGAN	1,081	107	946	28	Reagan	9.9%	87.5%	2.6%
MCDOWELL	857	77	757	23	Reagan	9.0%	88.3%	2.7%
MARION	4,051	671	3,268	112	Reagan	16.6%	80.7%	2.8%
MARSHALL	3,402	655	2,657	90	Reagan	19.3%	78.1%	2.6%
MASON	3,585	349	3,138	98	Reagan	9.7%	87.5%	2.7%
MERCER	2,861	251	2,580	30	Reagan	8.8%	90.2%	1.0%
MINERAL	2,848	346	2,450	52	Reagan	12.1%	86.0%	1.8%
MINGO	859	74	769	16	Reagan	8.6%	89.5%	1.9%

WEST VIRGINIA REPUBLICAN

1980

County	Total Vote	Bush	Reagan	Stassen	Winner	Percentage of Total Vote Bush	Reagan	Stassen
MONONGALIA	5,133	880	4,122	131	Reagan	17.1%	80.3%	2.6%
MONROE	1,360	110	1,231	19	Reagan	8.1%	90.5%	1.4%
MORGAN	1,683	174	1,480	29	Reagan	10.3%	87.9%	1.7%
NICHOLAS	1,254	200	1,026	28	Reagan	15.9%	81.8%	2.2%
OHIO	5,561	1,129	4,296	136	Reagan	20.3%	77.3%	2.4%
PENDLETON	688	67	603	18	Reagan	9.7%	87.6%	2.6%
PLEASANTS	843	93	734	16	Reagan	11.0%	87.1%	1.9%
POCAHONTAS	236	120	95	21	Bush	50.8%	40.3%	8.9%
PRESTON	4,319	535	3,692	92	Reagan	12.4%	85.5%	2.1%
PUTNAM	3,259	376	2,808	75	Reagan	11.5%	86.2%	2.3%
RALEIGH	2,691	377	2,254	60	Reagan	14.0%	83.8%	2.2%
RANDOLPH	1,315	220	1,064	31	Reagan	16.7%	80.9%	2.4%
RITCHIE	2,299	200	2,059	40	Reagan	8.7%	89.6%	1.7%
ROANE	2,008	221	1,749	38	Reagan	11.0%	87.1%	1.9%
SUMMERS	580	56	511	13	Reagan	9.7%	88.1%	2.2%
TAYLOR	1,627	230	1,349	48	Reagan	14.1%	82.9%	3.0%
TUCKER	896	79	785	32	Reagan	8.8%	87.6%	3.6%
TYLER	1,740	218	1,489	33	Reagan	12.5%	85.6%	1.9%
UPSHUR	3,259	499	2,692	68	Reagan	15.3%	82.6%	2.1%
WAYNE	2,672	259	2,381	32	Reagan	9.7%	89.1%	1.2%
WEBSTER	458	52	390	16	Reagan	11.4%	85.2%	3.5%
WETZEL	1,244	207	1,010	27	Reagan	16.6%	81.2%	2.2%
WIRT	680	38	620	22	Reagan	5.6%	91.2%	3.2%
WOOD	9,583	1,400	7,995	188	Reagan	14.6%	83.4%	2.0%
WYOMING	1,431	164	1,240	27	Reagan	11.5%	86.7%	1.9%
TOTAL	138,016	19,509	115,407	3,100	Reagan	14.1%	83.6%	2.2%

Note: Results are listed as certified, although the Pocahontas County vote is extremely low and may not have been reported correctly.

WEST VIRGINIA DEMOCRATIC

1984

County	Total Vote	Hart	Mondale	Other	Winner	Percentage of Total Vote Hart	Mondale	Other
BARBOUR	3,119	1,193	1,702	224	Mondale	38.2%	54.6%	7.2%
BERKELEY	7,516	3,488	3,380	648	Hart	46.4%	45.0%	8.6%
BOONE	7,964	2,284	5,238	442	Mondale	28.7%	65.8%	5.5%
BRAXTON	4,323	1,744	2,311	268	Mondale	40.3%	53.5%	6.2%
BROOKE	6,604	2,605	3,611	388	Mondale	39.4%	54.7%	5.9%
CABELL	17,802	6,560	9,223	2,019	Mondale	36.8%	51.8%	11.3%
CALHOUN	1,794	780	865	149	Mondale	43.5%	48.2%	8.3%
CLAY	2,473	798	1,518	157	Mondale	32.3%	61.4%	6.3%
DODDRIDGE	857	405	390	62	Hart	47.3%	45.5%	7.2%
FAYETTE	13,564	3,905	8,157	1,502	Mondale	28.8%	60.1%	11.1%

WEST VIRGINIA DEMOCRATIC

1984

County	Total Vote	Hart	Mondale	Other	Winner	Percentage of Total Vote Hart	Mondale	Other
GILMER	2,510	1,182	1,123	205	Hart	47.1%	44.7%	8.2%
GRANT	599	267	292	40	Mondale	44.6%	48.7%	6.7%
GREENBRIER	6,702	2,876	3,169	657	Mondale	42.9%	47.3%	9.8%
HAMPSHIRE	3,146	1,621	1,319	206	Hart	51.5%	41.9%	6.5%
HANCOCK	9,159	3,925	4,433	801	Mondale	42.9%	48.4%	8.7%
HARDY	2,432	1,191	1,094	147	Hart	49.0%	45.0%	6.0%
HARRISON	19,679	7,931	10,063	1,685	Mondale	40.3%	51.1%	8.6%
JACKSON	4,190	1,642	2,270	278	Mondale	39.2%	54.2%	6.6%
JEFFERSON	4,618	2,126	1,924	568	Hart	46.0%	41.7%	12.3%
KANAWHA	38,685	14,117	19,411	5,157	Mondale	36.5%	50.2%	13.3%
LEWIS	3,494	1,653	1,552	289	Hart	47.3%	44.4%	8.3%
LINCOLN	6,895	1,525	5,134	236	Mondale	22.1%	74.5%	3.4%
LOGAN	11,960	3,239	7,483	1,238	Mondale	27.1%	62.6%	10.4%
MCDOWELL	9,537	2,275	5,811	1,451	Mondale	23.9%	60.9%	15.2%
MARION	15,755	5,983	8,452	1,320	Mondale	38.0%	53.6%	8.4%
MARSHALL	7,800	3,135	4,121	544	Mondale	40.2%	52.8%	7.0%
MASON	5,182	1,845	3,125	212	Mondale	35.6%	60.3%	4.1%
MERCER	12,850	4,394	6,939	1,517	Mondale	34.2%	54.0%	11.8%
MINERAL	3,399	1,490	1,704	205	Mondale	43.8%	50.1%	6.0%
MINGO	8,193	1,687	5,946	560	Mondale	20.6%	72.6%	6.8%
MONONGALIA	13,376	4,803	7,256	1,317	Mondale	35.9%	54.2%	9.8%
MONROE	2,844	1,145	1,483	216	Mondale	40.3%	52.1%	7.6%
MORGAN	1,603	789	718	96	Hart	49.2%	44.8%	6.0%
NICHOLAS	5,585	2,114	3,084	387	Mondale	37.9%	55.2%	6.9%
OHIO	9,161	4,182	4,132	847	Hart	45.7%	45.1%	9.2%
PENDLETON	1,682	656	936	90	Mondale	39.0%	55.6%	5.4%
PLEASANTS	1,968	870	975	123	Mondale	44.2%	49.5%	6.3%
POCAHONTAS	2,299	1,027	1,118	154	Mondale	44.7%	48.6%	6.7%
PRESTON	4,316	1,687	2,344	285	Mondale	39.1%	54.3%	6.6%
PUTNAM	5,748	2,392	2,918	438	Mondale	41.6%	50.8%	7.6%
RALEIGH	15,673	4,702	8,870	2,101	Mondale	30.0%	56.6%	13.4%
RANDOLPH	6,749	3,177	2,951	621	Hart	47.1%	43.7%	9.2%
RITCHIE	1,379	607	670	102	Mondale	44.0%	48.6%	7.4%
ROANE	2,243	1,032	1,061	150	Mondale	46.0%	47.3%	6.7%
SUMMERS	3,973	1,628	2,011	334	Mondale	41.0%	50.6%	8.4%
TAYLOR	3,184	1,518	1,447	219	Hart	47.7%	45.4%	6.9%
TUCKER	2,227	866	1,228	133	Mondale	38.9%	55.1%	6.0%
TYLER	1,336	573	672	91	Mondale	42.9%	50.3%	6.8%
UPSHUR	2,453	1,117	1,090	246	Hart	45.5%	44.4%	10.0%
WAYNE	11,052	3,580	6,754	718	Mondale	32.4%	61.1%	6.5%
WEBSTER	3,138	1,202	1,712	224	Mondale	38.3%	54.6%	7.1%
WETZEL	4,968	2,205	2,367	396	Mondale	44.4%	47.6%	8.0%
WIRT	1,037	498	467	72	Hart	48.0%	45.0%	6.9%
WOOD	11,776	5,240	5,580	956	Mondale	44.5%	47.4%	8.1%
WYOMING	8,088	2,390	5,172	526	Mondale	29.5%	63.9%	6.5%
TOTAL	370,659	137,866	198,776	34,017	Mondale	37.2%	53.6%	9.2%
Certified Totals	369,245	137,866	198,776	32,603	Mondale	37.3%	53.8%	8.8%

WEST VIRGINIA REPUBLICAN

1984

County	Total Vote	Reagan	Stassen	Winner	Percentage of Total Vote: Reagan	Percentage of Total Vote: Stassen
BARBOUR	1,659	1,487	172	Reagan	89.6%	10.4%
BERKELEY	4,533	4,274	259	Reagan	94.3%	5.7%
BOONE	984	907	77	Reagan	92.2%	7.8%
BRAXTON	839	775	64	Reagan	92.4%	7.6%
BROOKE	1,300	1,181	119	Reagan	90.8%	9.2%
CABELL	6,980	6,419	561	Reagan	92.0%	8.0%
CALHOUN	574	528	46	Reagan	92.0%	8.0%
CLAY	553	486	67	Reagan	87.9%	12.1%
DODDRIDGE	1,589	1,417	172	Reagan	89.2%	10.8%
FAYETTE	1,570	1,407	163	Reagan	89.6%	10.4%
GILMER	577	540	37	Reagan	93.6%	6.4%
GRANT	2,668	2,464	204	Reagan	92.4%	7.6%
GREENBRIER	1,681	1,564	117	Reagan	93.0%	7.0%
HAMPSHIRE	715	667	48	Reagan	93.3%	6.7%
HANCOCK	1,985	1,825	160	Reagan	91.9%	8.1%
HARDY	568	535	33	Reagan	94.2%	5.8%
HARRISON	7,278	6,621	657	Reagan	91.0%	9.0%
JACKSON	3,710	3,384	326	Reagan	91.2%	8.8%
JEFFERSON	1,190	1,099	91	Reagan	92.4%	7.6%
KANAWHA	15,564	14,430	1,134	Reagan	92.7%	7.3%
LEWIS	2,452	2,177	275	Reagan	88.8%	11.2%
LINCOLN	1,424	1,328	96	Reagan	93.3%	6.7%
LOGAN	993	922	71	Reagan	92.8%	7.2%
MCDOWELL	638	595	43	Reagan	93.3%	6.7%
MARION	4,371	3,921	450	Reagan	89.7%	10.3%
MARSHALL	3,630	3,255	375	Reagan	89.7%	10.3%
MASON	3,959	3,417	542	Reagan	86.3%	13.7%
MERCER	3,356	3,222	134	Reagan	96.0%	4.0%
MINERAL	2,403	2,215	188	Reagan	92.2%	7.8%
MINGO	613	574	39	Reagan	93.6%	6.4%
MONONGALIA	5,389	4,841	548	Reagan	89.8%	10.2%
MONROE	1,437	1,359	78	Reagan	94.6%	5.4%
MORGAN	1,810	1,688	122	Reagan	93.3%	6.7%
NICHOLAS	1,421	1,301	120	Reagan	91.6%	8.4%
OHIO	5,304	4,859	445	Reagan	91.6%	8.4%
PENDLETON	605	580	25	Reagan	95.9%	4.1%
PLEASANTS	938	877	61	Reagan	93.5%	6.5%
POCAHONTAS	1,026	951	75	Reagan	92.7%	7.3%
PRESTON	4,162	3,704	458	Reagan	89.0%	11.0%
PUTNAM	2,761	2,587	174	Reagan	93.7%	6.3%
RALEIGH	2,714	2,539	175	Reagan	93.6%	6.4%
RANDOLPH	1,460	1,346	114	Reagan	92.2%	7.8%
RITCHIE	2,134	1,968	166	Reagan	92.2%	7.8%
ROANE	1,827	1,678	149	Reagan	91.8%	8.2%
SUMMERS	564	534	30	Reagan	94.7%	5.3%
TAYLOR	1,674	1,489	185	Reagan	88.9%	11.1%
TUCKER	918	851	67	Reagan	92.7%	7.3%
TYLER	2,140	1,940	200	Reagan	90.7%	9.3%
UPSHUR	3,135	2,873	262	Reagan	91.6%	8.4%
WAYNE	2,910	2,756	154	Reagan	94.7%	5.3%

WEST VIRGINIA REPUBLICAN

1984

County	Total Vote	Reagan	Stassen	Winner	Percentage of Total Vote: Reagan	Stassen
WEBSTER	380	338	42	Reagan	88.9%	11.1%
WETZEL	1,233	1,131	102	Reagan	91.7%	8.3%
WIRT	641	600	41	Reagan	93.6%	6.4%
WOOD	8,987	8,363	624	Reagan	93.1%	6.9%
WYOMING	1,070	1,001	69	Reagan	93.6%	6.4%
TOTAL	136,996	125,790	11,206	Reagan	91.8%	8.2%

WEST VIRGINIA DEMOCRATIC

1988

County	Total Vote	Dukakis	J. Jackson	Other	Winner	Percentage of Total Vote: Dukakis	J. Jackson	Other
BARBOUR	2,891	2,215	318	358	Dukakis	76.6%	11.0%	12.4%
BERKELEY	5,407	3,901	756	750	Dukakis	72.1%	14.0%	13.9%
BOONE	7,001	5,361	748	892	Dukakis	76.6%	10.7%	12.7%
BRAXTON	4,154	3,106	520	528	Dukakis	74.8%	12.5%	12.7%
BROOKE	6,272	4,744	629	899	Dukakis	75.6%	10.0%	14.3%
CABELL	15,526	11,218	2,760	1,548	Dukakis	72.3%	17.8%	10.0%
CALHOUN	1,875	1,341	266	268	Dukakis	71.5%	14.2%	14.3%
CLAY	2,526	1,893	281	352	Dukakis	74.9%	11.1%	13.9%
DODDRIDGE	778	538	108	132	Dukakis	69.2%	13.9%	17.0%
FAYETTE	11,817	9,113	1,555	1,149	Dukakis	77.1%	13.2%	9.7%
GILMER	2,205	1,534	294	377	Dukakis	69.6%	13.3%	17.1%
GRANT	557	433	57	67	Dukakis	77.7%	10.2%	12.0%
GREENBRIER	6,479	4,694	791	994	Dukakis	72.4%	12.2%	15.3%
HAMPSHIRE	2,690	1,963	212	515	Dukakis	73.0%	7.9%	19.1%
HANCOCK	8,186	6,364	871	951	Dukakis	77.7%	10.6%	11.6%
HARDY	2,693	1,973	204	516	Dukakis	73.3%	7.6%	19.2%
HARRISON	17,186	13,314	1,880	1,992	Dukakis	77.5%	10.9%	11.6%
JACKSON	4,048	3,071	550	427	Dukakis	75.9%	13.6%	10.5%
JEFFERSON	3,764	2,483	603	678	Dukakis	66.0%	16.0%	18.0%
KANAWHA	37,923	28,380	6,669	2,874	Dukakis	74.8%	17.6%	7.6%
LEWIS	3,372	2,409	452	511	Dukakis	71.4%	13.4%	15.2%
LINCOLN	6,322	4,837	618	867	Dukakis	76.5%	9.8%	13.7%
LOGAN	12,095	8,906	1,478	1,711	Dukakis	73.6%	12.2%	14.1%
MCDOWELL	7,341	5,196	1,501	644	Dukakis	70.8%	20.4%	8.8%
MARION	14,492	11,153	1,721	1,618	Dukakis	77.0%	11.9%	11.2%
MARSHALL	7,563	5,309	1,164	1,090	Dukakis	70.2%	15.4%	14.4%
MASON	4,995	3,830	612	553	Dukakis	76.7%	12.3%	11.1%
MERCER	11,446	8,465	1,525	1,456	Dukakis	74.0%	13.3%	12.7%
MINERAL	3,208	2,497	273	438	Dukakis	77.8%	8.5%	13.7%
MINGO	7,577	5,837	974	766	Dukakis	77.0%	12.9%	10.1%

WEST VIRGINIA DEMOCRATIC

1988

County	Total Vote	Dukakis	J. Jackson	Other	Winner	Percentage of Total Vote: Dukakis	J. Jackson	Other
MONONGALIA	12,959	9,850	1,838	1,271	Dukakis	76.0%	14.2%	9.8%
MONROE	2,303	1,702	261	340	Dukakis	73.9%	11.3%	14.8%
MORGAN	1,224	900	158	166	Dukakis	73.5%	12.9%	13.6%
NICHOLAS	5,252	4,064	636	552	Dukakis	77.4%	12.1%	10.5%
OHIO	7,915	5,739	1,171	1,005	Dukakis	72.5%	14.8%	12.7%
PENDLETON	1,952	1,375	181	396	Dukakis	70.4%	9.3%	20.3%
PLEASANTS	1,524	1,166	163	195	Dukakis	76.5%	10.7%	12.8%
POCAHONTAS	690	139	224	327	J. Jackson	20.1%	32.5%	47.4%
PRESTON	4,018	2,880	588	550	Dukakis	71.7%	14.6%	13.7%
PUTNAM	6,206	4,812	769	625	Dukakis	77.5%	12.4%	10.1%
RALEIGH	16,100	12,376	2,416	1,308	Dukakis	76.9%	15.0%	8.1%
RANDOLPH	6,587	4,911	732	944	Dukakis	74.6%	11.1%	14.3%
RITCHIE	1,411	1,023	171	217	Dukakis	72.5%	12.1%	15.4%
ROANE	2,164	1,526	359	279	Dukakis	70.5%	16.6%	12.9%
SUMMERS	3,744	2,853	378	513	Dukakis	76.2%	10.1%	13.7%
TAYLOR	2,716	2,097	302	317	Dukakis	77.2%	11.1%	11.7%
TUCKER	1,869	1,382	249	238	Dukakis	73.9%	13.3%	12.7%
TYLER	1,162	836	158	168	Dukakis	71.9%	13.6%	14.5%
UPSHUR	2,542	1,875	391	276	Dukakis	73.8%	15.4%	10.9%
WAYNE	8,950	7,016	966	968	Dukakis	78.4%	10.8%	10.8%
WEBSTER	2,642	1,979	361	302	Dukakis	74.9%	13.7%	11.4%
WETZEL	4,446	3,054	628	764	Dukakis	68.7%	14.1%	17.2%
WIRT	902	670	125	107	Dukakis	74.3%	13.9%	11.9%
WOOD	10,717	7,961	1,328	1,428	Dukakis	74.3%	12.4%	13.3%
WYOMING	7,713	6,025	845	843	Dukakis	78.1%	11.0%	10.9%
TOTAL	340,097	254,289	45,788	40,020	Dukakis	74.8%	13.5%	11.8%

Note: Results are listed as certified, although the Pocahontas County vote is extremely low and may not have been reported correctly.

WEST VIRGINIA REPUBLICAN

1988

County	Total Vote	Bush	Dole	Other	Winner	Percentage of Total Vote: Bush	Dole	Other
BARBOUR	1,994	1,512	250	232	Bush	75.8%	12.5%	11.6%
BERKELEY	3,569	2,909	357	303	Bush	81.5%	10.0%	8.5%
BOONE	943	751	85	107	Bush	79.6%	9.0%	11.3%
BRAXTON	894	726	97	71	Bush	81.2%	10.9%	7.9%
BROOKE	1,418	1,080	175	163	Bush	76.2%	12.3%	11.5%
CABELL	7,681	6,047	737	897	Bush	78.7%	9.6%	11.7%
CALHOUN	641	515	61	65	Bush	80.3%	9.5%	10.1%
CLAY	718	563	84	71	Bush	78.4%	11.7%	9.9%
DODDRIDGE	1,587	1,217	171	199	Bush	76.7%	10.8%	12.5%
FAYETTE	1,687	1,293	172	222	Bush	76.6%	10.2%	13.2%

WEST VIRGINIA REPUBLICAN

1988

County	Total Vote	Bush	Dole	Other	Winner	Percentage of Total Vote Bush	Dole	Other
GILMER	564	451	62	51	Bush	80.0%	11.0%	9.0%
GRANT	2,621	2,111	246	264	Bush	80.5%	9.4%	10.1%
GREENBRIER	1,985	1,575	201	209	Bush	79.3%	10.1%	10.5%
HAMPSHIRE	895	685	108	102	Bush	76.5%	12.1%	11.4%
HANCOCK	2,161	1,628	236	297	Bush	75.3%	10.9%	13.7%
HARDY	626	501	60	65	Bush	80.0%	9.6%	10.4%
HARRISON	6,806	5,081	761	964	Bush	74.7%	11.2%	14.2%
JACKSON	3,710	2,838	450	422	Bush	76.5%	12.1%	11.4%
JEFFERSON	1,139	889	139	111	Bush	78.1%	12.2%	9.7%
KANAWHA	17,723	13,355	2,194	2,174	Bush	75.4%	12.4%	12.3%
LEWIS	2,540	1,837	333	370	Bush	72.3%	13.1%	14.6%
LINCOLN	1,418	1,262	61	95	Bush	89.0%	4.3%	6.7%
LOGAN	1,070	847	95	128	Bush	79.2%	8.9%	12.0%
MCDOWELL	528	410	43	75	Bush	77.7%	8.1%	14.2%
MARION	4,181	2,947	552	682	Bush	70.5%	13.2%	16.3%
MARSHALL	3,766	2,851	452	463	Bush	75.7%	12.0%	12.3%
MASON	3,232	2,480	388	364	Bush	76.7%	12.0%	11.3%
MERCER	3,461	2,764	306	391	Bush	79.9%	8.8%	11.3%
MINERAL	2,719	2,075	278	366	Bush	76.3%	10.2%	13.5%
MINGO	883	703	83	97	Bush	79.6%	9.4%	11.0%
MONONGALIA	5,542	4,060	722	760	Bush	73.3%	13.0%	13.7%
MONROE	1,104	898	138	68	Bush	81.3%	12.5%	6.2%
MORGAN	1,772	1,436	165	171	Bush	81.0%	9.3%	9.7%
NICHOLAS	1,478	1,117	180	181	Bush	75.6%	12.2%	12.2%
OHIO	4,970	3,872	549	549	Bush	77.9%	11.0%	11.0%
PENDLETON	719	587	74	58	Bush	81.6%	10.3%	8.1%
PLEASANTS	887	713	89	85	Bush	80.4%	10.0%	9.6%
POCAHONTAS	1,009	774	134	101	Bush	76.7%	13.3%	10.0%
PRESTON	3,963	2,950	528	485	Bush	74.4%	13.3%	12.2%
PUTNAM	3,771	2,930	391	450	Bush	77.7%	10.4%	11.9%
RALEIGH	3,596	2,836	324	436	Bush	78.9%	9.0%	12.1%
RANDOLPH	1,549	1,215	163	171	Bush	78.4%	10.5%	11.0%
RITCHIE	2,455	1,979	241	235	Bush	80.6%	9.8%	9.6%
ROANE	2,061	1,693	177	191	Bush	82.1%	8.6%	9.3%
SUMMERS	631	538	44	49	Bush	85.3%	7.0%	7.8%
TAYLOR	1,590	1,169	180	241	Bush	73.5%	11.3%	15.2%
TUCKER	1,001	747	112	142	Bush	74.6%	11.2%	14.2%
TYLER	1,845	1,334	250	261	Bush	72.3%	13.6%	14.1%
UPSHUR	3,883	3,023	425	435	Bush	77.9%	10.9%	11.2%
WAYNE	3,554	3,074	203	277	Bush	86.5%	5.7%	7.8%
WEBSTER	375	281	40	54	Bush	74.9%	10.7%	14.4%
WETZEL	1,282	1,002	130	150	Bush	78.2%	10.1%	11.7%
WIRT	689	527	72	90	Bush	76.5%	10.4%	13.1%
WOOD	9,024	7,044	938	1,042	Bush	78.1%	10.4%	11.5%
WYOMING	1,230	1,003	94	133	Bush	81.5%	7.6%	10.8%
TOTAL	143,140	110,705	15,600	16,835	Bush	77.3%	10.9%	11.8%

WEST VIRGINIA DEMOCRATIC

1992

County	Total Vote	Brown	Clinton	Other	Winner	Percentage of Total Vote Brown	Clinton	Other
BARBOUR	2,985	266	2,365	354	Clinton	8.9%	79.2%	11.9%
BERKELEY	5,430	591	3,667	1,172	Clinton	10.9%	67.5%	21.6%
BOONE	6,754	671	5,509	574	Clinton	9.9%	81.6%	8.5%
BRAXTON	3,681	328	2,932	421	Clinton	8.9%	79.7%	11.4%
BROOKE	4,969	740	3,381	848	Clinton	14.9%	68.0%	17.1%
CABELL	13,109	2,408	9,013	1,688	Clinton	18.4%	68.8%	12.9%
CALHOUN	1,913	229	1,418	266	Clinton	12.0%	74.1%	13.9%
CLAY	2,212	147	1,765	300	Clinton	6.6%	79.8%	13.6%
DODDRIDGE	698	77	506	115	Clinton	11.0%	72.5%	16.5%
FAYETTE	9,470	1,239	7,181	1,050	Clinton	13.1%	75.8%	11.1%
GILMER	1,795	158	1,344	293	Clinton	8.8%	74.9%	16.3%
GRANT	387	29	286	72	Clinton	7.5%	73.9%	18.6%
GREENBRIER	5,930	600	4,253	1,077	Clinton	10.1%	71.7%	18.2%
HAMPSHIRE	2,693	210	1,869	614	Clinton	7.8%	69.4%	22.8%
HANCOCK	7,647	1,044	5,165	1,438	Clinton	13.7%	67.5%	18.8%
HARDY	2,504	160	1,830	514	Clinton	6.4%	73.1%	20.5%
HARRISON	14,586	1,341	11,098	2,147	Clinton	9.2%	76.1%	14.7%
JACKSON	4,378	750	3,224	404	Clinton	17.1%	73.6%	9.2%
JEFFERSON	4,100	471	2,479	1,150	Clinton	11.5%	60.5%	28.0%
KANAWHA	34,072	4,760	25,353	3,959	Clinton	14.0%	74.4%	11.6%
LEWIS	2,415	244	1,800	371	Clinton	10.1%	74.5%	15.4%
LINCOLN	5,604	647	4,345	612	Clinton	11.5%	77.5%	10.9%
LOGAN	10,437	1,297	8,267	873	Clinton	12.4%	79.2%	8.4%
MCDOWELL	6,736	347	5,700	689	Clinton	5.2%	84.6%	10.2%
MARION	13,798	1,579	10,324	1,895	Clinton	11.4%	74.8%	13.7%
MARSHALL	6,141	904	4,361	876	Clinton	14.7%	71.0%	14.3%
MASON	4,814	578	3,806	430	Clinton	12.0%	79.1%	8.9%
MERCER	8,385	753	6,229	1,403	Clinton	9.0%	74.3%	16.7%
MINERAL	2,856	350	2,055	451	Clinton	12.3%	72.0%	15.8%
MINGO	8,281	655	6,739	887	Clinton	7.9%	81.4%	10.7%
MONONGALIA	11,138	1,719	7,506	1,913	Clinton	15.4%	67.4%	17.2%
MONROE	2,368	230	1,767	371	Clinton	9.7%	74.6%	15.7%
MORGAN	1,201	118	852	231	Clinton	9.8%	70.9%	19.2%
NICHOLAS	4,991	523	3,836	632	Clinton	10.5%	76.9%	12.7%
OHIO	7,219	1,173	4,731	1,315	Clinton	16.2%	65.5%	18.2%
PENDLETON	1,633	90	1,264	279	Clinton	5.5%	77.4%	17.1%
PLEASANTS	1,480	193	1,071	216	Clinton	13.0%	72.4%	14.6%
POCAHONTAS	1,714	164	1,263	287	Clinton	9.6%	73.7%	16.7%
PRESTON	3,536	340	2,572	624	Clinton	9.6%	72.7%	17.6%
PUTNAM	6,557	892	4,867	798	Clinton	13.6%	74.2%	12.2%
RALEIGH	13,031	1,339	10,148	1,544	Clinton	10.3%	77.9%	11.8%
RANDOLPH	5,873	668	4,229	976	Clinton	11.4%	72.0%	16.6%
RITCHIE	1,207	113	926	168	Clinton	9.4%	76.7%	13.9%
ROANE	2,135	249	1,693	193	Clinton	11.7%	79.3%	9.0%
SUMMERS	2,856	296	2,171	389	Clinton	10.4%	76.0%	13.6%
TAYLOR	3,010	262	2,287	461	Clinton	8.7%	76.0%	15.3%
TUCKER	1,718	132	1,272	314	Clinton	7.7%	74.0%	18.3%
TYLER	1,130	150	756	224	Clinton	13.3%	66.9%	19.8%
UPSHUR	2,319	301	1,675	343	Clinton	13.0%	72.2%	14.8%
WAYNE	8,803	1,021	6,860	922	Clinton	11.6%	77.9%	10.5%

WEST VIRGINIA DEMOCRATIC

1992

County	Total Vote	Brown	Clinton	Other	Winner	Percentage of Total Vote Brown	Clinton	Other
WEBSTER	2,467	184	1,990	293	Clinton	7.5%	80.7%	11.9%
WETZEL	3,936	529	2,812	595	Clinton	13.4%	71.4%	15.1%
WIRT	1,014	97	812	105	Clinton	9.6%	80.1%	10.4%
WOOD	10,230	1,672	6,846	1,712	Clinton	16.3%	66.9%	16.7%
WYOMING	6,520	477	5,345	698	Clinton	7.3%	82.0%	10.7%
TOTAL	306,866	36,505	227,815	42,546	Clinton	11.9%	74.2%	13.9%

WEST VIRGINIA REPUBLICAN

1992

County	Total Vote	Buchanan	Bush	Fellure	Winner	Percentage of Total Vote Buchanan	Bush	Fellure
BARBOUR	1,738	262	1,380	96	Bush	15.1%	79.4%	5.5%
BERKELEY	3,451	473	2,873	105	Bush	13.7%	83.3%	3.0%
BOONE	674	81	567	26	Bush	12.0%	84.1%	3.9%
BRAXTON	612	63	518	31	Bush	10.3%	84.6%	5.1%
BROOKE	1,006	208	744	54	Bush	20.7%	74.0%	5.4%
CABELL	6,105	896	4,887	322	Bush	14.7%	80.0%	5.3%
CALHOUN	547	70	444	33	Bush	12.8%	81.2%	6.0%
CLAY	589	66	481	42	Bush	11.2%	81.7%	7.1%
DODDRIDGE	1,540	178	1,293	69	Bush	11.6%	84.0%	4.5%
FAYETTE	1,232	150	1,028	54	Bush	12.2%	83.4%	4.4%
GILMER	506	61	414	31	Bush	12.1%	81.8%	6.1%
GRANT	2,644	337	2,176	131	Bush	12.7%	82.3%	5.0%
GREENBRIER	1,789	197	1,507	85	Bush	11.0%	84.2%	4.8%
HAMPSHIRE	789	126	645	18	Bush	16.0%	81.7%	2.3%
HANCOCK	2,089	470	1,504	115	Bush	22.5%	72.0%	5.5%
HARDY	593	47	518	28	Bush	7.9%	87.4%	4.7%
HARRISON	5,567	773	4,557	237	Bush	13.9%	81.9%	4.3%
JACKSON	3,506	603	2,704	199	Bush	17.2%	77.1%	5.7%
JEFFERSON	1,433	243	1,128	62	Bush	17.0%	78.7%	4.3%
KANAWHA	14,960	1,984	12,360	616	Bush	13.3%	82.6%	4.1%
LEWIS	1,823	364	1,354	105	Bush	20.0%	74.3%	5.8%
LINCOLN	1,027	54	933	40	Bush	5.3%	90.8%	3.9%
LOGAN	690	114	540	36	Bush	16.5%	78.3%	5.2%
MCDOWELL	409	66	323	20	Bush	16.1%	79.0%	4.9%
MARION	3,168	556	2,438	174	Bush	17.6%	77.0%	5.5%
MARSHALL	3,550	658	2,698	194	Bush	18.5%	76.0%	5.5%
MASON	2,895	424	2,271	200	Bush	14.6%	78.4%	6.9%
MERCER	2,274	326	1,874	74	Bush	14.3%	82.4%	3.3%
MINERAL	2,457	412	1,936	109	Bush	16.8%	78.8%	4.4%
MINGO	584	50	502	32	Bush	8.6%	86.0%	5.5%

WEST VIRGINIA REPUBLICAN

1992

County	Total Vote	Buchanan	Bush	Fellure	Winner	Percentage of Total Vote Buchanan	Bush	Fellure
MONONGALIA	4,141	693	3,239	209	Bush	16.7%	78.2%	5.0%
MONROE	1,343	137	1,158	48	Bush	10.2%	86.2%	3.6%
MORGAN	1,889	282	1,532	75	Bush	14.9%	81.1%	4.0%
NICHOLAS	1,474	215	1,163	96	Bush	14.6%	78.9%	6.5%
OHIO	4,694	887	3,638	169	Bush	18.9%	77.5%	3.6%
PENDLETON	762	59	677	26	Bush	7.7%	88.8%	3.4%
PLEASANTS	852	93	722	37	Bush	10.9%	84.7%	4.3%
POCAHONTAS	878	127	724	27	Bush	14.5%	82.5%	3.1%
PRESTON	3,631	510	2,882	239	Bush	14.0%	79.4%	6.6%
PUTNAM	3,840	426	3,050	364	Bush	11.1%	79.4%	9.5%
RALEIGH	2,403	341	1,977	85	Bush	14.2%	82.3%	3.5%
RANDOLPH	1,274	170	1,051	53	Bush	13.3%	82.5%	4.2%
RITCHIE	2,130	285	1,738	107	Bush	13.4%	81.6%	5.0%
ROANE	1,695	235	1,365	95	Bush	13.9%	80.5%	5.6%
SUMMERS	501	48	435	18	Bush	9.6%	86.8%	3.6%
TAYLOR	1,577	272	1,218	87	Bush	17.2%	77.2%	5.5%
TUCKER	770	106	637	27	Bush	13.8%	82.7%	3.5%
TYLER	2,058	375	1,542	141	Bush	18.2%	74.9%	6.9%
UPSHUR	3,429	483	2,736	210	Bush	14.1%	79.8%	6.1%
WAYNE	2,338	269	1,955	114	Bush	11.5%	83.6%	4.9%
WEBSTER	377	60	292	25	Bush	15.9%	77.5%	6.6%
WETZEL	1,062	182	828	52	Bush	17.1%	78.0%	4.9%
WIRT	728	84	596	48	Bush	11.5%	81.9%	6.6%
WOOD	9,108	1,309	7,437	362	Bush	14.4%	81.7%	4.0%
WYOMING	956	107	805	44	Bush	11.2%	84.2%	4.6%
TOTAL	124,157	18,067	99,994	6,096	Bush	14.6%	80.5%	4.9%

WEST VIRGINIA DEMOCRATIC

1996

County	Total Vote	Clinton	LaRouche	Winner	Percentage of Total Vote Clinton	LaRouche
BARBOUR	2,766	2,420	346	Clinton	87.5%	12.5%
BERKELEY	5,537	4,662	875	Clinton	84.2%	15.8%
BOONE	6,816	5,882	934	Clinton	86.3%	13.7%
BRAXTON	3,332	2,850	482	Clinton	85.5%	14.5%
BROOKE	5,398	4,619	779	Clinton	85.6%	14.4%
CABELL	12,565	10,850	1,715	Clinton	86.4%	13.6%
CALHOUN	1,669	1,392	277	Clinton	83.4%	16.6%
CLAY	2,565	2,109	456	Clinton	82.2%	17.8%
DODDRIDGE	553	478	75	Clinton	86.4%	13.6%
FAYETTE	9,823	8,522	1,301	Clinton	86.8%	13.2%

WEST VIRGINIA DEMOCRATIC

1996

County	Total Vote	Clinton	LaRouche	Winner	Percentage of Total Vote: Clinton	Percentage of Total Vote: LaRouche
GILMER	1,606	1,337	269	Clinton	83.3%	16.7%
GRANT	451	386	65	Clinton	85.6%	14.4%
GREENBRIER	6,503	5,526	977	Clinton	85.0%	15.0%
HAMPSHIRE	2,465	2,013	452	Clinton	81.7%	18.3%
HANCOCK	7,872	6,691	1,181	Clinton	85.0%	15.0%
HARDY	2,197	1,762	435	Clinton	80.2%	19.8%
HARRISON	14,509	12,932	1,577	Clinton	89.1%	10.9%
JACKSON	3,871	3,443	428	Clinton	88.9%	11.1%
JEFFERSON	3,204	2,893	311	Clinton	90.3%	9.7%
KANAWHA	30,556	26,746	3,810	Clinton	87.5%	12.5%
LEWIS	2,738	2,340	398	Clinton	85.5%	14.5%
LINCOLN	4,600	4,502	98	Clinton	97.9%	2.1%
LOGAN	9,932	9,234	698	Clinton	93.0%	7.0%
MCDOWELL	6,973	6,254	719	Clinton	89.7%	10.3%
MARION	13,943	12,417	1,526	Clinton	89.1%	10.9%
MARSHALL	6,402	5,437	965	Clinton	84.9%	15.1%
MASON	4,671	4,033	638	Clinton	86.3%	13.7%
MERCER	8,682	7,135	1,547	Clinton	82.2%	17.8%
MINERAL	2,174	1,861	313	Clinton	85.6%	14.4%
MINGO	7,693	6,636	1,057	Clinton	86.3%	13.7%
MONONGALIA	12,076	10,392	1,684	Clinton	86.1%	13.9%
MONROE	2,205	1,942	263	Clinton	88.1%	11.9%
MORGAN	1,175	1,031	144	Clinton	87.7%	12.3%
NICHOLAS	4,854	4,090	764	Clinton	84.3%	15.7%
OHIO	6,959	6,121	838	Clinton	88.0%	12.0%
PENDLETON	1,799	1,550	249	Clinton	86.2%	13.8%
PLEASANTS	1,561	1,318	243	Clinton	84.4%	15.6%
POCAHONTAS	1,787	1,551	236	Clinton	86.8%	13.2%
PRESTON	3,961	3,279	682	Clinton	82.8%	17.2%
PUTNAM	6,810	5,648	1,162	Clinton	82.9%	17.1%
RALEIGH	12,249	10,313	1,936	Clinton	84.2%	15.8%
RANDOLPH	6,167	5,170	997	Clinton	83.8%	16.2%
RITCHIE	954	833	121	Clinton	87.3%	12.7%
ROANE	1,955	1,746	209	Clinton	89.3%	10.7%
SUMMERS	2,585	2,192	393	Clinton	84.8%	15.2%
TAYLOR	2,816	2,415	401	Clinton	85.8%	14.2%
TUCKER	1,581	1,353	228	Clinton	85.6%	14.4%
TYLER	961	832	129	Clinton	86.6%	13.4%
UPSHUR	2,117	1,877	240	Clinton	88.7%	11.3%
WAYNE	7,848	6,731	1,117	Clinton	85.8%	14.2%
WEBSTER	2,514	2,173	341	Clinton	86.4%	13.6%
WETZEL	3,493	2,909	584	Clinton	83.3%	16.7%
WIRT	930	761	169	Clinton	81.8%	18.2%
WOOD	9,771	8,268	1,503	Clinton	84.6%	15.4%
WYOMING	5,927	5,230	697	Clinton	88.2%	11.8%
TOTAL	297,121	257,087	40,034	Clinton	86.5%	13.5%

WEST VIRGINIA REPUBLICAN

1996

County	Total Vote	Buchanan	Dole	Other	Winner	Percentage of Total Vote: Buchanan	Dole	Other
BARBOUR	1,706	276	1,202	228	Dole	16.2%	70.5%	13.4%
BERKELEY	5,114	867	3,415	832	Dole	17.0%	66.8%	16.3%
BOONE	689	127	479	83	Dole	18.4%	69.5%	12.0%
BRAXTON	622	98	438	86	Dole	15.8%	70.4%	13.8%
BROOKE	1,235	250	770	215	Dole	20.2%	62.3%	17.4%
CABELL	6,791	986	4,880	925	Dole	14.5%	71.9%	13.6%
CALHOUN	507	64	395	48	Dole	12.6%	77.9%	9.5%
CLAY	618	94	451	73	Dole	15.2%	73.0%	11.8%
DODDRIDGE	1,079	183	743	153	Dole	17.0%	68.9%	14.2%
FAYETTE	1,446	223	1,021	202	Dole	15.4%	70.6%	14.0%
GILMER	483	76	348	59	Dole	15.7%	72.0%	12.2%
GRANT	2,474	522	1,680	272	Dole	21.1%	67.9%	11.0%
GREENBRIER	2,110	293	1,515	302	Dole	13.9%	71.8%	14.3%
HAMPSHIRE	928	186	624	118	Dole	20.0%	67.2%	12.7%
HANCOCK	1,953	418	1,204	331	Dole	21.4%	61.6%	16.9%
HARDY	541	95	384	62	Dole	17.6%	71.0%	11.5%
HARRISON	5,273	851	3,536	886	Dole	16.1%	67.1%	16.8%
JACKSON	3,058	495	2,142	421	Dole	16.2%	70.0%	13.8%
JEFFERSON	1,435	230	957	248	Dole	16.0%	66.7%	17.3%
KANAWHA	15,494	1,956	10,961	2,577	Dole	12.6%	70.7%	16.6%
LEWIS	1,902	344	1,270	288	Dole	18.1%	66.8%	15.1%
LINCOLN	1,324	169	1,029	126	Dole	12.8%	77.7%	9.5%
LOGAN	646	100	463	83	Dole	15.5%	71.7%	12.8%
MCDOWELL	400	64	297	39	Dole	16.0%	74.3%	9.8%
MARION	3,520	752	2,160	608	Dole	21.4%	61.4%	17.3%
MARSHALL	3,309	670	2,007	632	Dole	20.2%	60.7%	19.1%
MASON	3,085	587	2,115	383	Dole	19.0%	68.6%	12.4%
MERCER	2,717	543	1,844	330	Dole	20.0%	67.9%	12.1%
MINERAL	2,113	548	1,307	258	Dole	25.9%	61.9%	12.2%
MINGO	569	80	428	61	Dole	14.1%	75.2%	10.7%
MONONGALIA	4,872	744	3,169	959	Dole	15.3%	65.0%	19.7%
MONROE	1,205	144	941	120	Dole	12.0%	78.1%	10.0%
MORGAN	1,924	366	1,315	243	Dole	19.0%	68.3%	12.6%
NICHOLAS	1,379	216	979	184	Dole	15.7%	71.0%	13.3%
OHIO	4,758	652	3,217	889	Dole	13.7%	67.6%	18.7%
PENDLETON	700	103	533	64	Dole	14.7%	76.1%	9.1%
PLEASANTS	859	125	606	128	Dole	14.6%	70.5%	14.9%
POCAHONTAS	782	140	523	119	Dole	17.9%	66.9%	15.2%
PRESTON	3,683	726	2,396	561	Dole	19.7%	65.1%	15.2%
PUTNAM	4,609	688	3,306	615	Dole	14.9%	71.7%	13.3%
RALEIGH	3,076	497	2,208	371	Dole	16.2%	71.8%	12.1%
RANDOLPH	1,351	191	973	187	Dole	14.1%	72.0%	13.8%
RITCHIE	1,632	301	1,121	210	Dole	18.4%	68.7%	12.9%
ROANE	1,535	195	1,104	236	Dole	12.7%	71.9%	15.4%
SUMMERS	487	62	368	57	Dole	12.7%	75.6%	11.7%
TAYLOR	1,405	279	946	180	Dole	19.9%	67.3%	12.8%
TUCKER	794	165	532	97	Dole	20.8%	67.0%	12.2%
TYLER	1,538	265	1,054	219	Dole	17.2%	68.5%	14.2%
UPSHUR	3,145	540	2,161	444	Dole	17.2%	68.7%	14.1%
WAYNE	2,452	438	1,725	289	Dole	17.9%	70.4%	11.8%

WEST VIRGINIA REPUBLICAN

1996

County	Total Vote	Buchanan	Dole	Other	Winner	Percentage of Total Vote Buchanan	Dole	Other
WEBSTER	321	68	215	38	Dole	21.2%	67.0%	11.8%
WETZEL	1,000	175	652	173	Dole	17.5%	65.2%	17.3%
WIRT	549	114	371	64	Dole	20.8%	67.6%	11.7%
WOOD	9,323	1,453	6,352	1,518	Dole	15.6%	68.1%	16.3%
WYOMING	934	134	702	98	Dole	14.3%	75.2%	10.5%
TOTAL	127,454	20,928	87,534	18,992	Dole	16.4%	68.7%	14.9%

WISCONSIN

If Virginia can claim to be the "mother of presidents," then Wisconsin could boast that it is the "mother of presidential primaries." It was from the progressive agenda of Wisconsin's legendary Robert M. La Follette that presidential primaries got a major boost, and Wisconsin initiated one of the first in 1912.

For more than a half-century afterwards, the Badger State was a necessary stop for candidates traveling the primary route to their party's nomination. But the recent proliferation of primaries, especially early ones, has robbed Wisconsin's contest of much of its luster.

In 1968, Wisconsin voted second after New Hampshire. But in 1996, there were 20 states that held primaries in between the two, even though Wisconsin had moved its primary that year from April to mid-March. Still, in the realm of presidential primaries, few states have as rich a heritage as Wisconsin or as distinctive a voting process—the state's long-standing open primary rules make it effortless to vote in either party's primary.

Wisconsin has gained an image as an outpost of Midwestern liberalism. But that is based largely on just two Democratic primaries—Eugene McCarthy's victory in 1968 and George McGovern's in 1972. Both were fueled by opposition to the Vietnam War.

The list is longer of liberal contenders who needed a breakthrough win in Wisconsin, and failed to get it. Democrats Morris Udall in 1976, Jerry Brown in 1980 and Jesse Jackson in 1988, as well as Republican John Anderson in 1980, all made Wisconsin either the cornerstone of their campaigns or viewed it as a major target of opportunity. Yet all four lost the Wisconsin primary.

It would be closer to the mark to say that Wisconsin has a soft spot for outsiders. George Wallace bolted onto the national scene in 1964 by taking one-third of the Democratic primary vote in Wisconsin after campaigning against the pending civil rights bill. Jimmy Carter's dark-horse candidacy also was pushed along by a Wisconsin victory in 1976 (over Udall). Gary Hart edged Walter Mondale in the 1984 Democratic pri-

Recent Wisconsin Primary Results

Wisconsin held its first presidential primary in 1912.

	DEMOCRATS			REPUBLICANS		
Year	Turnout	Candidates	%	Turnout	Candidates	%
1996 (March 19)	356,168	BILL CLINTON*	98	576,575	BOB DOLE	52
					Pat Buchanan	34
1992 (April 7)	772,596	BILL CLINTON	37	482,248	GEORGE BUSH*	76
		Jerry Brown	34		Pat Buchanan	16
		Paul Tsongas	22			
1988 (April 5)	1,014,782	MICHAEL DUKAKIS	48	359,294	GEORGE BUSH	82
		Jesse Jackson	28			
		Al Gore	17			
1984 (April 3)	635,768	GARY HART	44	294,813	RONALD REAGAN*	95
		Walter Mondale	41			
1980 (April 1)	629,619	JIMMY CARTER*	56	907,853	RONALD REAGAN	40
		Edward Kennedy	30		George Bush	30
		Jerry Brown	12		John Anderson	27
1976 (April 6)	740,528	JIMMY CARTER	37	591,812	GERALD FORD*	55
		Morris Udall	36		Ronald Reagan	44
		George Wallace	12			
1972 (April 4)	1,128,584	GEORGE McGOVERN	30	286,444	RICHARD NIXON*	97
		George Wallace	22			
		Hubert Humphrey	21			
		Edmund Muskie	10			
1968 (April 2)	733,002	EUGENE McCARTHY	56	489,853	RICHARD NIXON	80
		Lyndon Johnson*	35		Ronald Reagan	10

Note: All candidates are listed that drew at least 10 percent of their party's primary vote. The names of winning candidates are capitalized. An asterisk (*) indicates an incumbent president.

mary (a nonbinding primary that year by national party fiat). And Brown nearly beat Bill Clinton in the state in 1992.

Brown had focused on Wisconsin early, knowing its terrain and proclivities well from his 1980 run. He carried a swath of counties on the eastern side of the state, from Racine through the Milwaukee suburbs north to Brown County (Green Bay). But Brown was hurt badly by his inability to win decisively in Dane County (Madison), home to the University of Wisconsin and a legion of liberal activists. McCarthy, McGovern and Udall had all carried Dane County by more than 20,000 votes; Brown won it by barely 2,000.

That enabled Clinton to win with a coalition of city and countryside. He carried Milwaukee County, source of nearly one-quarter of the Democratic primary vote, and swept the vast majority of counties in rural Wisconsin.

Clinton's winning 37 percent share of the primary vote was more than double the total that his fellow Southerner, Al Gore, had drawn in Wisconsin four years earlier. Looking for a post-Super Tuesday toehold in the Frost Belt, Gore came to Wisconsin calling for higher dairy price supports. But he finished third statewide, although he did leapfrog Jesse Jackson for second place in a number of rural counties.

Wisconsin's Democratic primary is usually where the action has been over the years. Only twice since 1956—in 1980 and 1996—have more votes been cast on the Republican side of the ballot. The reason in 1996 was obvious; there was no contest in the Democratic primary. Pat Buchanan took advantage of the situation to win his second-highest vote share of the primary season (33.8 percent—just one-tenth of a percentage point behind his showing the same day in Michigan). But Buchanan could carry only one small county in Wisconsin, and was unable to crack 40 percent of the vote in any of the more populous ones.

The more compelling Republican primary was in 1980. Stakes were high for John Anderson, who had lost the primary in his home state of Illinois two weeks earlier. But Ronald Reagan won the Wisconsin vote comfortably, giving Anderson a final nudge out of the GOP race and reducing George Bush's already slim prospects for that year's GOP nomination.

Bush ran virtually even with Reagan in the Milwaukee area and in prosperous Republican farm country in the south-central part of Wisconsin. But Reagan won almost everywhere else, including most of the smaller industrial centers. Anderson carried only three counties, all containing a branch of the University of Wisconsin.

WISCONSIN DEMOCRATIC

1968

County	Total Vote	Johnson	McCarthy	Other	Winner	Percentage of Total Vote Johnson	McCarthy	Other
ADAMS	1,231	347	670	214	McCarthy	28.2%	54.4%	17.4%
ASHLAND	3,683	1,571	1,890	222	McCarthy	42.7%	51.3%	6.0%
BARRON	5,235	1,289	3,371	575	McCarthy	24.6%	64.4%	11.0%
BAYFIELD	2,460	846	1,355	259	McCarthy	34.4%	55.1%	10.5%
BROWN	25,465	5,568	17,728	2,169	McCarthy	21.9%	69.6%	8.5%
BUFFALO	1,841	404	1,127	310	McCarthy	21.9%	61.2%	16.8%
BURNETT	1,468	493	729	246	McCarthy	33.6%	49.7%	16.8%
CALUMET	3,715	602	2,666	447	McCarthy	16.2%	71.8%	12.0%
CHIPPEWA	6,600	1,667	4,115	818	McCarthy	25.3%	62.3%	12.4%
CLARK	4,405	938	2,799	668	McCarthy	21.3%	63.5%	15.2%
COLUMBIA	5,826	1,419	3,665	742	McCarthy	24.4%	62.9%	12.7%
CRAWFORD	2,749	628	1,729	392	McCarthy	22.8%	62.9%	14.3%
DANE	59,467	15,006	40,522	3,939	McCarthy	25.2%	68.1%	6.6%
DODGE	10,126	2,684	6,204	1,238	McCarthy	26.5%	61.3%	12.2%
DOOR	3,113	651	2,021	441	McCarthy	20.9%	64.9%	14.2%
DOUGLAS	10,510	4,213	5,269	1,028	McCarthy	40.1%	50.1%	9.8%
DUNN	3,606	929	2,174	503	McCarthy	25.8%	60.3%	13.9%
EAU CLAIRE	10,127	3,409	5,946	772	McCarthy	33.7%	58.7%	7.6%
FLORENCE	512	179	228	105	McCarthy	35.0%	44.5%	20.5%
FOND DU LAC	11,989	3,612	7,065	1,312	McCarthy	30.1%	58.9%	10.9%
FOREST	1,456	518	736	202	McCarthy	35.6%	50.5%	13.9%
GRANT	5,579	1,018	3,639	922	McCarthy	18.2%	65.2%	16.5%
GREEN	3,414	558	2,447	409	McCarthy	16.3%	71.7%	12.0%
GREEN LAKE	2,426	555	1,473	398	McCarthy	22.9%	60.7%	16.4%
IOWA	2,556	513	1,689	354	McCarthy	20.1%	66.1%	13.8%
IRON	2,103	679	1,139	285	McCarthy	32.3%	54.2%	13.6%
JACKSON	1,934	527	1,110	297	McCarthy	27.2%	57.4%	15.4%
JEFFERSON	8,052	2,187	4,726	1,139	McCarthy	27.2%	58.7%	14.1%
JUNEAU	2,689	637	1,731	321	McCarthy	23.7%	64.4%	11.9%
KENOSHA	18,784	7,417	9,567	1,800	McCarthy	39.5%	50.9%	9.6%
KEWAUNEE	2,753	413	1,941	399	McCarthy	15.0%	70.5%	14.5%
LA CROSSE	11,212	3,750	6,758	704	McCarthy	33.4%	60.3%	6.3%
LAFAYETTE	2,445	437	1,662	346	McCarthy	17.9%	68.0%	14.2%
LANGLADE	3,077	992	1,704	381	McCarthy	32.2%	55.4%	12.4%
LINCOLN	3,751	1,142	2,141	468	McCarthy	30.4%	57.1%	12.5%
MANITOWOC	14,642	3,967	9,260	1,415	McCarthy	27.1%	63.2%	9.7%
MARATHON	17,341	5,165	10,236	1,940	McCarthy	29.8%	59.0%	11.2%
MARINETTE	6,481	2,085	3,725	671	McCarthy	32.2%	57.5%	10.4%
MARQUETTE	1,104	256	663	185	McCarthy	23.2%	60.1%	16.8%
MENOMINEE	200	67	75	58	McCarthy	33.5%	37.5%	29.0%
MILWAUKEE	206,753	103,215	90,780	12,758	Johnson	49.9%	43.9%	6.2%
MONROE	3,911	761	2,703	447	McCarthy	19.5%	69.1%	11.4%
OCONTO	3,817	888	2,321	608	McCarthy	23.3%	60.8%	15.9%
ONEIDA	4,697	1,457	2,559	681	McCarthy	31.0%	54.5%	14.5%
OUTAGAMIE	18,222	4,253	12,738	1,231	McCarthy	23.3%	69.9%	6.8%
OZAUKEE	7,163	2,091	4,305	767	McCarthy	29.2%	60.1%	10.7%
PEPIN	1,246	224	826	196	McCarthy	18.0%	66.3%	15.7%
PIERCE	3,559	742	2,188	629	McCarthy	20.8%	61.5%	17.7%
POLK	3,462	792	2,015	655	McCarthy	22.9%	58.2%	18.9%
PORTAGE	9,123	3,299	4,567	1,257	McCarthy	36.2%	50.1%	13.8%

WISCONSIN DEMOCRATIC

1968

County	Total Vote	Johnson	McCarthy	Other	Winner	Percentage of Total Vote Johnson	McCarthy	Other
PRICE	2,818	872	1,573	373	McCarthy	30.9%	55.8%	13.2%
RACINE	27,085	9,076	15,688	2,321	McCarthy	33.5%	57.9%	8.6%
RICHLAND	2,437	543	1,646	248	McCarthy	22.3%	67.5%	10.2%
ROCK	17,398	5,056	10,363	1,979	McCarthy	29.1%	59.6%	11.4%
RUSK	2,552	695	1,516	341	McCarthy	27.2%	59.4%	13.4%
ST. CROIX	4,700	1,065	2,795	840	McCarthy	22.7%	59.5%	17.9%
SAUK	5,835	1,155	3,885	795	McCarthy	19.8%	66.6%	13.6%
SAWYER	1,635	540	947	148	McCarthy	33.0%	57.9%	9.1%
SHAWANO	3,848	890	2,482	476	McCarthy	23.1%	64.5%	12.4%
SHEBOYGAN	17,940	7,370	9,073	1,497	McCarthy	41.1%	50.6%	8.3%
TAYLOR	3,162	760	1,990	412	McCarthy	24.0%	62.9%	13.0%
TREMPEALEAU	3,035	666	1,868	501	McCarthy	21.9%	61.5%	16.5%
VERNON	3,676	972	2,303	401	McCarthy	26.4%	62.6%	10.9%
VILAS	2,028	705	1,080	243	McCarthy	34.8%	53.3%	12.0%
WALWORTH	7,422	1,881	4,424	1,117	McCarthy	25.3%	59.6%	15.0%
WASHBURN	1,840	579	992	269	McCarthy	31.5%	53.9%	14.6%
WASHINGTON	8,391	2,442	4,914	1,035	McCarthy	29.1%	58.6%	12.3%
WAUKESHA	33,835	11,699	19,431	2,705	McCarthy	34.6%	57.4%	8.0%
WAUPACA	4,477	1,001	2,942	534	McCarthy	22.4%	65.7%	11.9%
WAUSHARA	1,687	418	1,021	248	McCarthy	24.8%	60.5%	14.7%
WINNEBAGO	17,626	5,392	11,104	1,130	McCarthy	30.6%	63.0%	6.4%
WOOD	11,495	2,859	7,426	1,210	McCarthy	24.9%	64.6%	10.5%
TOTAL	733,002	253,696	412,160	67,146	McCarthy	34.6%	56.2%	9.2%

WISCONSIN REPUBLICAN

1968

County	Total Vote	Nixon	Reagan	Other	Winner	Percentage of Total Vote Nixon	Reagan	Other
ADAMS	872	658	65	149	Nixon	75.5%	7.5%	17.1%
ASHLAND	1,809	1,466	138	205	Nixon	81.0%	7.6%	11.3%
BARRON	4,252	3,576	353	323	Nixon	84.1%	8.3%	7.6%
BAYFIELD	1,432	1,085	138	209	Nixon	75.8%	9.6%	14.6%
BROWN	17,334	13,805	2,406	1,123	Nixon	79.6%	13.9%	6.5%
BUFFALO	1,541	1,254	126	161	Nixon	81.4%	8.2%	10.4%
BURNETT	1,122	880	100	142	Nixon	78.4%	8.9%	12.7%
CALUMET	3,026	2,468	301	257	Nixon	81.6%	9.9%	8.5%
CHIPPEWA	4,183	3,427	311	445	Nixon	81.9%	7.4%	10.6%
CLARK	3,360	2,588	268	504	Nixon	77.0%	8.0%	15.0%
COLUMBIA	4,810	3,735	297	778	Nixon	77.7%	6.2%	16.2%
CRAWFORD	2,003	1,594	214	195	Nixon	79.6%	10.7%	9.7%
DANE	24,151	16,735	1,853	5,563	Nixon	69.3%	7.7%	23.0%
DODGE	8,701	7,053	737	911	Nixon	81.1%	8.5%	10.5%
DOOR	3,415	2,846	320	249	Nixon	83.3%	9.4%	7.3%

WISCONSIN REPUBLICAN

1968

County	Total Vote	Nixon	Reagan	Other	Winner	Percentage of Total Vote Nixon	Reagan	Other
DOUGLAS	4,268	3,329	369	570	Nixon	78.0%	8.6%	13.4%
DUNN	2,991	2,530	183	278	Nixon	84.6%	6.1%	9.3%
EAU CLAIRE	7,127	6,215	324	588	Nixon	87.2%	4.5%	8.3%
FLORENCE	423	327	59	37	Nixon	77.3%	13.9%	8.7%
FOND DU LAC	10,241	8,578	930	733	Nixon	83.8%	9.1%	7.2%
FOREST	934	763	98	73	Nixon	81.7%	10.5%	7.8%
GRANT	5,520	4,410	528	582	Nixon	79.9%	9.6%	10.5%
GREEN	3,341	2,643	238	460	Nixon	79.1%	7.1%	13.8%
GREEN LAKE	2,978	2,381	347	250	Nixon	80.0%	11.7%	8.4%
IOWA	2,127	1,568	157	402	Nixon	73.7%	7.4%	18.9%
IRON	961	737	86	138	Nixon	76.7%	8.9%	14.4%
JACKSON	1,567	1,198	193	176	Nixon	76.5%	12.3%	11.2%
JEFFERSON	6,697	5,349	564	784	Nixon	79.9%	8.4%	11.7%
JUNEAU	2,354	1,793	203	358	Nixon	76.2%	8.6%	15.2%
KENOSHA	10,196	8,069	1,159	968	Nixon	79.1%	11.4%	9.5%
KEWAUNEE	2,309	1,847	257	205	Nixon	80.0%	11.1%	8.9%
LA CROSSE	9,705	7,901	1,196	608	Nixon	81.4%	12.3%	6.3%
LAFAYETTE	2,067	1,655	147	265	Nixon	80.1%	7.1%	12.8%
LANGLADE	2,261	1,830	238	193	Nixon	80.9%	10.5%	8.5%
LINCOLN	2,911	2,343	239	329	Nixon	80.5%	8.2%	11.3%
MANITOWOC	8,239	6,620	886	733	Nixon	80.3%	10.8%	8.9%
MARATHON	11,051	8,861	900	1,290	Nixon	80.2%	8.1%	11.7%
MARINETTE	4,523	3,717	548	258	Nixon	82.2%	12.1%	5.7%
MARQUETTE	1,424	1,110	126	188	Nixon	77.9%	8.8%	13.2%
MENOMINEE	43	28	11	4	Nixon	65.1%	25.6%	9.3%
MILWAUKEE	104,800	82,492	12,797	9,511	Nixon	78.7%	12.2%	9.1%
MONROE	3,645	2,976	347	322	Nixon	81.6%	9.5%	8.8%
OCONTO	3,333	2,657	431	245	Nixon	79.7%	12.9%	7.4%
ONEIDA	3,388	2,802	312	274	Nixon	82.7%	9.2%	8.1%
OUTAGAMIE	16,096	13,700	1,558	838	Nixon	85.1%	9.7%	5.2%
OZAUKEE	6,931	5,365	893	673	Nixon	77.4%	12.9%	9.7%
PEPIN	805	622	81	102	Nixon	77.3%	10.1%	12.7%
PIERCE	2,808	2,329	231	248	Nixon	82.9%	8.2%	8.8%
POLK	2,642	2,158	217	267	Nixon	81.7%	8.2%	10.1%
PORTAGE	4,011	3,292	323	396	Nixon	82.1%	8.1%	9.9%
PRICE	2,003	1,614	168	221	Nixon	80.6%	8.4%	11.0%
RACINE	16,262	12,611	2,144	1,507	Nixon	77.5%	13.2%	9.3%
RICHLAND	2,476	1,854	204	418	Nixon	74.9%	8.2%	16.9%
ROCK	15,761	13,069	1,229	1,463	Nixon	82.9%	7.8%	9.3%
RUSK	1,530	1,223	132	175	Nixon	79.9%	8.6%	11.4%
ST. CROIX	3,267	2,514	364	389	Nixon	77.0%	11.1%	11.9%
SAUK	4,745	3,488	375	882	Nixon	73.5%	7.9%	18.6%
SAWYER	1,452	1,165	132	155	Nixon	80.2%	9.1%	10.7%
SHAWANO	5,239	4,301	616	322	Nixon	82.1%	11.8%	6.1%
SHEBOYGAN	11,555	9,297	931	1,327	Nixon	80.5%	8.1%	11.5%
TAYLOR	1,826	1,357	184	285	Nixon	74.3%	10.1%	15.6%
TREMPEALEAU	2,440	2,013	189	238	Nixon	82.5%	7.7%	9.8%
VERNON	3,136	2,452	380	304	Nixon	78.2%	12.1%	9.7%
VILAS	1,957	1,623	165	169	Nixon	82.9%	8.4%	8.6%
WALWORTH	9,217	7,569	912	736	Nixon	82.1%	9.9%	8.0%

WISCONSIN REPUBLICAN

1968

County	Total Vote	Nixon	Reagan	Other	Winner	Percentage of Total Vote: Nixon	Reagan	Other
WASHBURN	1,352	1,053	120	179	Nixon	77.9%	8.9%	13.2%
WASHINGTON	6,827	5,454	689	684	Nixon	79.9%	10.1%	10.0%
WAUKESHA	28,305	22,270	3,673	2,362	Nixon	78.7%	13.0%	8.3%
WAUPACA	6,108	4,928	745	435	Nixon	80.7%	12.2%	7.1%
WAUSHARA	2,540	2,075	264	201	Nixon	81.7%	10.4%	7.9%
WINNEBAGO	17,032	14,406	1,749	877	Nixon	84.6%	10.3%	5.1%
WOOD	8,095	6,667	559	869	Nixon	82.4%	6.9%	10.7%
TOTAL	489,853	390,368	50,727	48,758	Nixon	79.7%	10.4%	10.0%

WISCONSIN DEMOCRATIC

1972

County	Total Vote	Humphrey	McGovern	Muskie	Wallace	Other	Winner	Percentage of Total Vote: Humphrey	McGovern	Muskie	Wallace	Other
ADAMS	2,455	571	578	186	734	386	Wallace	23.3%	23.5%	7.6%	29.9%	15.7%
ASHLAND	5,289	1,664	983	1,038	1,130	474	Humphrey	31.5%	18.6%	19.6%	21.4%	9.0%
BARRON	7,584	2,040	2,416	559	1,693	876	McGovern	26.9%	31.9%	7.4%	22.3%	11.6%
BAYFIELD	3,480	1,130	665	503	837	345	Humphrey	32.5%	19.1%	14.5%	24.1%	9.9%
BROWN	39,149	5,549	11,311	3,547	9,902	8,840	McGovern	14.2%	28.9%	9.1%	25.3%	22.6%
BUFFALO	3,076	824	883	205	699	465	McGovern	26.8%	28.7%	6.7%	22.7%	15.1%
BURNETT	2,426	823	439	221	728	215	Humphrey	33.9%	18.1%	9.1%	30.0%	8.9%
CALUMET	6,093	920	2,138	473	1,500	1,062	McGovern	15.1%	35.1%	7.8%	24.6%	17.4%
CHIPPEWA	10,922	2,533	3,079	1,088	2,308	1,914	McGovern	23.2%	28.2%	10.0%	21.1%	17.5%
CLARK	6,548	1,145	1,836	819	1,878	870	Wallace	17.5%	28.0%	12.5%	28.7%	13.3%
COLUMBIA	9,517	1,876	2,795	645	2,471	1,730	McGovern	19.7%	29.4%	6.8%	26.0%	18.2%
CRAWFORD	4,259	1,043	1,283	298	1,075	560	McGovern	24.5%	30.1%	7.0%	25.2%	13.1%
DANE	81,989	12,912	35,197	5,053	11,112	17,715	McGovern	15.7%	42.9%	6.2%	13.6%	21.6%
DODGE	16,337	3,164	5,033	1,074	4,135	2,931	McGovern	19.4%	30.8%	6.6%	25.3%	17.9%
DOOR	5,232	963	1,294	461	1,432	1,082	Wallace	18.4%	24.7%	8.8%	27.4%	20.7%
DOUGLAS	13,047	4,909	2,931	1,654	2,254	1,299	Humphrey	37.6%	22.5%	12.7%	17.3%	10.0%
DUNN	6,947	1,772	2,717	403	1,247	808	McGovern	25.5%	39.1%	5.8%	18.0%	11.6%
EAU CLAIRE	18,485	5,621	5,934	1,167	3,154	2,609	McGovern	30.4%	32.1%	6.3%	17.1%	14.1%
FLORENCE	981	185	238	80	340	138	Wallace	18.9%	24.3%	8.2%	34.7%	14.1%
FOND DU LAC	19,754	3,701	5,521	1,568	4,307	4,657	McGovern	18.7%	27.9%	7.9%	21.8%	23.6%
FOREST	2,545	549	330	242	1,074	350	Wallace	21.6%	13.0%	9.5%	42.2%	13.8%
GRANT	8,956	1,421	3,687	738	1,992	1,118	McGovern	15.9%	41.2%	8.2%	22.2%	12.5%
GREEN	5,498	1,056	1,625	359	1,536	922	McGovern	19.2%	29.6%	6.5%	27.9%	16.8%
GREEN LAKE	3,699	494	957	371	1,189	688	Wallace	13.4%	25.9%	10.0%	32.1%	18.6%
IOWA	4,123	603	1,555	244	1,060	661	McGovern	14.6%	37.7%	5.9%	25.7%	16.0%
IRON	2,670	814	300	423	725	408	Humphrey	30.5%	11.2%	15.8%	27.2%	15.3%
JACKSON	3,712	924	886	180	1,045	677	Wallace	24.9%	23.9%	4.8%	28.2%	18.2%
JEFFERSON	13,809	3,006	4,121	852	3,421	2,409	McGovern	21.8%	29.8%	6.2%	24.8%	17.4%
JUNEAU	4,173	765	1,200	390	1,268	550	Wallace	18.3%	28.8%	9.3%	30.4%	13.2%
KENOSHA	29,425	5,905	7,700	5,238	6,462	4,120	McGovern	20.1%	26.2%	17.8%	22.0%	14.0%

WISCONSIN DEMOCRATIC

1972

County	Total Vote	Humphrey	McGovern	Muskie	Wallace	Other	Winner	Percentage of Total Vote Humphrey	McGovern	Muskie	Wallace	Other
KEWAUNEE	4,688	664	1,539	377	1,271	837	McGovern	14.2%	32.8%	8.0%	27.1%	17.9%
LA CROSSE	20,445	4,414	5,618	1,223	5,649	3,541	Wallace	21.6%	27.5%	6.0%	27.6%	17.3%
LAFAYETTE	4,565	926	1,487	320	1,136	696	McGovern	20.3%	32.6%	7.0%	24.9%	15.2%
LANGLADE	4,306	906	1,259	442	1,129	570	McGovern	21.0%	29.2%	10.3%	26.2%	13.2%
LINCOLN	6,622	1,737	1,629	645	1,586	1,025	Humphrey	26.2%	24.6%	9.7%	24.0%	15.5%
MANITOWOC	21,604	4,849	6,825	2,599	3,873	3,458	McGovern	22.4%	31.6%	12.0%	17.9%	16.0%
MARATHON	25,024	5,786	6,551	4,365	5,417	2,905	McGovern	23.1%	26.2%	17.4%	21.6%	11.6%
MARINETTE	9,027	1,707	1,967	946	2,832	1,575	Wallace	18.9%	21.8%	10.5%	31.4%	17.4%
MARQUETTE	2,055	317	541	172	686	339	Wallace	15.4%	26.3%	8.4%	33.4%	16.5%
MENOMINEE	303	40	136	46	38	43	McGovern	13.2%	44.9%	15.2%	12.5%	14.2%
MILWAUKEE	289,957	64,262	78,388	39,363	54,197	53,747	McGovern	22.2%	27.0%	13.6%	18.7%	18.5%
MONROE	6,598	1,544	1,678	395	1,833	1,148	Wallace	23.4%	25.4%	6.0%	27.8%	17.4%
OCONTO	6,354	1,026	1,450	656	2,092	1,130	Wallace	16.1%	22.8%	10.3%	32.9%	17.8%
ONEIDA	7,107	1,997	1,264	591	2,103	1,152	Wallace	28.1%	17.8%	8.3%	29.6%	16.2%
OUTAGAMIE	29,502	4,782	10,056	2,136	6,601	5,927	McGovern	16.2%	34.1%	7.2%	22.4%	20.1%
OZAUKEE	14,351	2,160	4,444	1,054	3,870	2,823	McGovern	15.1%	31.0%	7.3%	27.0%	19.7%
PEPIN	1,878	491	625	131	385	246	McGovern	26.1%	33.3%	7.0%	20.5%	13.1%
PIERCE	6,181	1,635	2,411	514	1,019	602	McGovern	26.5%	39.0%	8.3%	16.5%	9.7%
POLK	6,082	2,002	1,606	505	1,394	575	Humphrey	32.9%	26.4%	8.3%	22.9%	9.5%
PORTAGE	15,511	3,944	4,163	3,879	1,780	1,745	McGovern	25.4%	26.8%	25.0%	11.5%	11.3%
PRICE	3,614	840	725	471	1,042	536	Wallace	23.2%	20.1%	13.0%	28.8%	14.8%
RACINE	43,582	7,737	11,834	3,454	13,224	7,333	Wallace	17.8%	27.2%	7.9%	30.3%	16.8%
RICHLAND	3,581	664	1,196	167	1,040	514	McGovern	18.5%	33.4%	4.7%	29.0%	14.4%
ROCK	29,441	6,290	9,321	3,225	6,924	3,681	McGovern	21.4%	31.7%	11.0%	23.5%	12.5%
RUSK	4,128	931	1,258	440	998	501	McGovern	22.6%	30.5%	10.7%	24.2%	12.1%
ST. CROIX	7,950	2,302	2,626	760	1,478	784	McGovern	29.0%	33.0%	9.6%	18.6%	9.9%
SAUK	9,327	1,732	3,042	549	2,352	1,652	McGovern	18.6%	32.6%	5.9%	25.2%	17.7%
SAWYER	2,629	664	457	334	921	253	Wallace	25.3%	17.4%	12.7%	35.0%	9.6%
SHAWANO	6,948	1,205	1,484	593	2,524	1,142	Wallace	17.3%	21.4%	8.5%	36.3%	16.4%
SHEBOYGAN	26,457	6,247	9,993	2,023	3,998	4,196	McGovern	23.6%	37.8%	7.6%	15.1%	15.9%
TAYLOR	4,366	904	1,315	488	1,100	559	McGovern	20.7%	30.1%	11.2%	25.2%	12.8%
TREMPEALEAU	5,692	1,480	1,361	489	1,411	951	Humphrey	26.0%	23.9%	8.6%	24.8%	16.7%
VERNON	6,220	1,513	1,451	277	1,931	1,048	Wallace	24.3%	23.3%	4.5%	31.0%	16.8%
VILAS	3,555	833	454	238	1,442	588	Wallace	23.4%	12.8%	6.7%	40.6%	16.5%
WALWORTH	12,669	2,087	3,742	1,130	3,481	2,229	McGovern	16.5%	29.5%	8.9%	27.5%	17.6%
WASHBURN	3,108	910	716	314	871	297	Humphrey	29.3%	23.0%	10.1%	28.0%	9.6%
WASHINGTON	16,023	2,613	5,024	1,111	4,015	3,260	McGovern	16.3%	31.4%	6.9%	25.1%	20.3%
WAUKESHA	56,458	9,718	16,439	4,122	14,264	11,915	McGovern	17.2%	29.1%	7.3%	25.3%	21.1%
WAUPACA	7,507	1,467	1,923	465	2,329	1,323	Wallace	19.5%	25.6%	6.2%	31.0%	17.6%
WAUSHARA	3,304	575	852	251	1,138	488	Wallace	17.4%	25.8%	7.6%	34.4%	14.8%
WINNEBAGO	30,760	5,147	11,116	2,496	6,465	5,536	McGovern	16.7%	36.1%	8.1%	21.0%	18.0%
WOOD	16,276	3,818	3,930	1,976	4,039	2,513	Wallace	23.5%	24.1%	12.1%	24.8%	15.4%
TOTAL	1,127,935	233,748	333,528	115,811	248,586	196,262	McGovern	20.7%	29.6%	10.3%	22.0%	17.4%
Certified Totals	1,128,584	233,748	333,528	115,811	248,676	196,821	McGovern	20.7%	29.6%	10.3%	22.0%	17.4%

WISCONSIN REPUBLICAN

1972

County	Total Vote	Nixon	Other	Winner	Percentage of Total Vote Nixon	Percentage of Total Vote Other
ADAMS	630	625	5	Nixon	99.2%	0.8%
ASHLAND	1,082	1,048	34	Nixon	96.9%	3.1%
BARRON	2,721	2,651	70	Nixon	97.4%	2.6%
BAYFIELD	885	853	32	Nixon	96.4%	3.6%
BROWN	9,825	9,569	256	Nixon	97.4%	2.6%
BUFFALO	974	949	25	Nixon	97.4%	2.6%
BURNETT	830	781	49	Nixon	94.1%	5.9%
CALUMET	1,745	1,709	36	Nixon	97.9%	2.1%
CHIPPEWA	2,377	2,329	48	Nixon	98.0%	2.0%
CLARK	1,819	1,757	62	Nixon	96.6%	3.4%
COLUMBIA	3,300	3,219	81	Nixon	97.5%	2.5%
CRAWFORD	1,423	1,376	47	Nixon	96.7%	3.3%
DANE	15,637	15,036	601	Nixon	96.2%	3.8%
DODGE	5,454	5,343	111	Nixon	98.0%	2.0%
DOOR	2,699	2,622	77	Nixon	97.1%	2.9%
DOUGLAS	2,065	1,958	107	Nixon	94.8%	5.2%
DUNN	1,811	1,770	41	Nixon	97.7%	2.3%
EAU CLAIRE	4,069	3,963	106	Nixon	97.4%	2.6%
FLORENCE	340	320	20	Nixon	94.1%	5.9%
FOND DU LAC	6,216	6,071	145	Nixon	97.7%	2.3%
FOREST	528	510	18	Nixon	96.6%	3.4%
GRANT	4,614	4,535	79	Nixon	98.3%	1.7%
GREEN	2,693	2,648	45	Nixon	98.3%	1.7%
GREEN LAKE	1,841	1,775	66	Nixon	96.4%	3.6%
IOWA	1,533	1,484	49	Nixon	96.8%	3.2%
IRON	556	538	18	Nixon	96.8%	3.2%
JACKSON	1,025	1,007	18	Nixon	98.2%	1.8%
JEFFERSON	4,356	4,259	97	Nixon	97.8%	2.2%
JUNEAU	1,412	1,353	59	Nixon	95.8%	4.2%
KENOSHA	6,887	6,666	221	Nixon	96.8%	3.2%
KEWAUNEE	1,361	1,327	34	Nixon	97.5%	2.5%
LA CROSSE	6,350	6,215	135	Nixon	97.9%	2.1%
LAFAYETTE	2,402	2,365	37	Nixon	98.5%	1.5%
LANGLADE	1,115	1,088	27	Nixon	97.6%	2.4%
LINCOLN	2,196	2,157	39	Nixon	98.2%	1.8%
MANITOWOC	4,468	4,351	117	Nixon	97.4%	2.6%
MARATHON	6,053	5,886	167	Nixon	97.2%	2.8%
MARINETTE	2,832	2,744	88	Nixon	96.9%	3.1%
MARQUETTE	863	837	26	Nixon	97.0%	3.0%
MENOMINEE	37	34	3	Nixon	91.9%	8.1%
MILWAUKEE	49,941	47,770	2,171	Nixon	95.7%	4.3%
MONROE	2,294	2,246	48	Nixon	97.9%	2.1%
OCONTO	2,219	2,145	74	Nixon	96.7%	3.3%
ONEIDA	2,080	2,012	68	Nixon	96.7%	3.3%
OUTAGAMIE	9,423	9,076	347	Nixon	96.3%	3.7%
OZAUKEE	4,755	4,518	237	Nixon	95.0%	5.0%
PEPIN	515	498	17	Nixon	96.7%	3.3%
PIERCE	1,879	1,812	67	Nixon	96.4%	3.6%
POLK	2,101	2,042	59	Nixon	97.2%	2.8%
PORTAGE	2,278	2,204	74	Nixon	96.8%	3.2%

WISCONSIN REPUBLICAN

1972

County	Total Vote	Nixon	Other	Winner	Percentage of Total Vote: Nixon	Other
PRICE	910	897	13	Nixon	98.6%	1.4%
RACINE	9,016	8,758	258	Nixon	97.1%	2.9%
RICHLAND	1,503	1,475	28	Nixon	98.1%	1.9%
ROCK	9,708	9,472	236	Nixon	97.6%	2.4%
RUSK	858	838	20	Nixon	97.7%	2.3%
ST. CROIX	2,389	2,302	87	Nixon	96.4%	3.6%
SAUK	3,474	3,382	92	Nixon	97.4%	2.6%
SAWYER	780	764	16	Nixon	97.9%	2.1%
SHAWANO	3,138	3,068	70	Nixon	97.8%	2.2%
SHEBOYGAN	6,668	6,476	192	Nixon	97.1%	2.9%
TAYLOR	1,035	992	43	Nixon	95.8%	4.2%
TREMPEALEAU	1,731	1,712	19	Nixon	98.9%	1.1%
VERNON	2,051	2,010	41	Nixon	98.0%	2.0%
VILAS	1,304	1,274	30	Nixon	97.7%	2.3%
WALWORTH	6,000	5,805	195	Nixon	96.8%	3.3%
WASHBURN	1,045	1,004	41	Nixon	96.1%	3.9%
WASHINGTON	4,611	4,471	140	Nixon	97.0%	3.0%
WAUKESHA	14,576	14,155	421	Nixon	97.1%	2.9%
WAUPACA	3,912	3,836	76	Nixon	98.1%	1.9%
WAUSHARA	1,505	1,456	49	Nixon	96.7%	3.3%
WINNEBAGO	8,935	8,724	211	Nixon	97.6%	2.4%
WOOD	4,786	4,679	107	Nixon	97.8%	2.2%
TOTAL	286,444	277,601	8,843	Nixon	96.9%	3.1%

WISCONSIN DEMOCRATIC

1976

County	Total Vote	Carter	Udall	Wallace	Other	Winner	Percentage of Total Vote: Carter	Udall	Wallace	Other
ADAMS	2,211	930	553	461	267	Carter	42.1%	25.0%	20.9%	12.1%
ASHLAND	3,540	863	1,394	606	677	Udall	24.4%	39.4%	17.1%	19.1%
BARRON	5,381	2,182	1,602	650	947	Carter	40.6%	29.8%	12.1%	17.6%
BAYFIELD	2,809	636	1,023	435	715	Udall	22.6%	36.4%	15.5%	25.5%
BROWN	24,743	11,527	8,063	2,640	2,513	Carter	46.6%	32.6%	10.7%	10.2%
BUFFALO	2,062	809	676	287	290	Carter	39.2%	32.8%	13.9%	14.1%
BURNETT	1,883	642	438	309	494	Carter	34.1%	23.3%	16.4%	26.2%
CALUMET	4,450	2,346	1,132	443	529	Carter	52.7%	25.4%	10.0%	11.9%
CHIPPEWA	8,515	3,996	2,738	957	824	Carter	46.9%	32.2%	11.2%	9.7%
CLARK	5,245	2,153	1,222	1,147	723	Carter	41.0%	23.3%	21.9%	13.8%
COLUMBIA	6,942	2,608	2,691	770	873	Udall	37.6%	38.8%	11.1%	12.6%
CRAWFORD	2,862	1,238	791	388	445	Carter	43.3%	27.6%	13.6%	15.5%
DANE	65,124	15,075	38,570	3,268	8,211	Udall	23.1%	59.2%	5.0%	12.6%
DODGE	9,999	4,070	3,042	1,467	1,420	Carter	40.7%	30.4%	14.7%	14.2%
DOOR	3,428	1,572	867	501	488	Carter	45.9%	25.3%	14.6%	14.2%

WISCONSIN DEMOCRATIC

1976

County	Total Vote	Carter	Udall	Wallace	Other	Winner	Percentage of Total Vote Carter	Udall	Wallace	Other
DOUGLAS	9,907	2,295	4,934	1,166	1,512	Udall	23.2%	49.8%	11.8%	15.3%
DUNN	4,133	1,258	1,855	413	607	Udall	30.4%	44.9%	10.0%	14.7%
EAU CLAIRE	12,832	4,757	5,563	896	1,616	Udall	37.1%	43.4%	7.0%	12.6%
FLORENCE	654	258	145	144	107	Carter	39.4%	22.2%	22.0%	16.4%
FOND DU LAC	12,574	5,199	3,974	1,259	2,142	Carter	41.3%	31.6%	10.0%	17.0%
FOREST	1,648	737	303	385	223	Carter	44.7%	18.4%	23.4%	13.5%
GRANT	5,322	2,274	1,630	574	844	Carter	42.7%	30.6%	10.8%	15.9%
GREEN	4,112	1,772	1,499	438	403	Carter	43.1%	36.5%	10.7%	9.8%
GREEN LAKE	2,284	1,021	571	353	339	Carter	44.7%	25.0%	15.5%	14.8%
IOWA	3,195	1,358	1,146	295	396	Carter	42.5%	35.9%	9.2%	12.4%
IRON	1,914	688	487	388	351	Carter	35.9%	25.4%	20.3%	18.3%
JACKSON	2,532	1,264	567	431	270	Carter	49.9%	22.4%	17.0%	10.7%
JEFFERSON	8,074	3,187	2,625	1,137	1,125	Carter	39.5%	32.5%	14.1%	13.9%
JUNEAU	3,272	1,460	829	593	390	Carter	44.6%	25.3%	18.1%	11.9%
KENOSHA	20,279	7,285	7,312	2,595	3,087	Udall	35.9%	36.1%	12.8%	15.2%
KEWAUNEE	3,191	1,588	717	539	347	Carter	49.8%	22.5%	16.9%	10.9%
LA CROSSE	10,636	3,939	3,354	1,234	2,109	Carter	37.0%	31.5%	11.6%	19.8%
LAFAYETTE	2,553	1,053	833	308	359	Carter	41.2%	32.6%	12.1%	14.1%
LANGLADE	3,346	1,292	802	755	497	Carter	38.6%	24.0%	22.6%	14.9%
LINCOLN	4,459	1,643	1,355	881	580	Carter	36.8%	30.4%	19.8%	13.0%
MANITOWOC	13,795	6,694	4,103	1,212	1,786	Carter	48.5%	29.7%	8.8%	12.9%
MARATHON	17,089	5,301	6,031	3,636	2,121	Udall	31.0%	35.3%	21.3%	12.4%
MARINETTE	5,657	2,824	1,206	948	679	Carter	49.9%	21.3%	16.8%	12.0%
MARQUETTE	1,749	746	488	284	231	Carter	42.7%	27.9%	16.2%	13.2%
MENOMINEE	196	103	40	16	37	Carter	52.6%	20.4%	8.2%	18.9%
MILWAUKEE	182,637	60,618	62,499	24,121	35,399	Udall	33.2%	34.2%	13.2%	19.4%
MONROE	4,285	2,136	979	613	557	Carter	49.8%	22.8%	14.3%	13.0%
OCONTO	4,883	2,634	1,020	748	481	Carter	53.9%	20.9%	15.3%	9.9%
ONEIDA	4,629	1,783	1,195	1,012	639	Carter	38.5%	25.8%	21.9%	13.8%
OUTAGAMIE	18,325	8,840	5,805	1,775	1,905	Carter	48.2%	31.7%	9.7%	10.4%
OZAUKEE	8,688	3,360	2,677	1,027	1,624	Carter	38.7%	30.8%	11.8%	18.7%
PEPIN	1,217	399	367	160	291	Carter	32.8%	30.2%	13.1%	23.9%
PIERCE	4,047	1,411	1,269	369	998	Carter	34.9%	31.4%	9.1%	24.7%
POLK	4,750	1,297	1,431	521	1,501	Udall	27.3%	30.1%	11.0%	31.6%
PORTAGE	9,885	3,469	4,269	966	1,181	Udall	35.1%	43.2%	9.8%	11.9%
PRICE	2,774	960	731	658	425	Carter	34.6%	26.4%	23.7%	15.3%
RACINE	25,109	8,459	9,497	3,663	3,490	Udall	33.7%	37.8%	14.6%	13.9%
RICHLAND	2,595	1,260	734	308	293	Carter	48.6%	28.3%	11.9%	11.3%
ROCK	18,713	6,389	8,173	2,135	2,016	Udall	34.1%	43.7%	11.4%	10.8%
RUSK	3,165	1,418	903	459	385	Carter	44.8%	28.5%	14.5%	12.2%
ST. CROIX	4,965	1,495	1,592	472	1,406	Udall	30.1%	32.1%	9.5%	28.3%
SAUK	6,520	2,371	2,657	659	833	Udall	36.4%	40.8%	10.1%	12.8%
SAWYER	1,806	654	528	406	218	Carter	36.2%	29.2%	22.5%	12.1%
SHAWANO	4,557	2,082	990	1,020	465	Carter	45.7%	21.7%	22.4%	10.2%
SHEBOYGAN	17,999	9,376	5,430	1,094	2,099	Carter	52.1%	30.2%	6.1%	11.7%
TAYLOR	3,218	1,204	792	850	372	Carter	37.4%	24.6%	26.4%	11.6%
TREMPEALEAU	3,400	1,564	969	465	402	Carter	46.0%	28.5%	13.7%	11.8%
VERNON	3,639	1,356	1,035	639	609	Carter	37.3%	28.4%	17.6%	16.7%
VILAS	2,128	769	474	597	288	Carter	36.1%	22.3%	28.1%	13.5%
WALWORTH	8,442	3,467	2,753	1,124	1,098	Carter	41.1%	32.6%	13.3%	13.0%

WISCONSIN DEMOCRATIC

1976

County	Total Vote	Carter	Udall	Wallace	Other	Winner	Percentage of Total Vote Carter	Udall	Wallace	Other
WASHBURN	2,268	653	698	495	422	Udall	28.8%	30.8%	21.8%	18.6%
WASHINGTON	9,920	3,725	3,173	1,451	1,571	Carter	37.6%	32.0%	14.6%	15.8%
WAUKESHA	35,862	12,943	11,861	4,799	6,259	Carter	36.1%	33.1%	13.4%	17.5%
WAUPACA	4,607	2,201	1,187	730	489	Carter	47.8%	25.8%	15.8%	10.6%
WAUSHARA	2,548	1,210	615	465	258	Carter	47.5%	24.1%	18.2%	10.1%
WINNEBAGO	16,968	6,356	6,980	1,624	2,008	Udall	37.5%	41.1%	9.6%	11.8%
WOOD	11,382	4,718	3,317	1,826	1,521	Carter	41.5%	29.1%	16.0%	13.4%
TOTAL	740,528	271,220	263,771	92,460	113,077	Carter	36.6%	35.6%	12.5%	15.3%

WISCONSIN REPUBLICAN

1976

County	Total Vote	Ford	Reagan	Other	Winner	Percentage of Total Vote Ford	Reagan	Other
ADAMS	1,533	857	666	10	Ford	55.9%	43.4%	0.7%
ASHLAND	2,223	1,236	965	22	Ford	55.6%	43.4%	1.0%
BARRON	4,872	2,608	2,231	33	Ford	53.5%	45.8%	0.7%
BAYFIELD	1,922	1,017	888	17	Ford	52.9%	46.2%	0.9%
BROWN	23,379	9,307	13,972	100	Reagan	39.8%	59.8%	0.4%
BUFFALO	1,905	993	906	6	Ford	52.1%	47.6%	0.3%
BURNETT	1,406	702	695	9	Ford	49.9%	49.4%	0.6%
CALUMET	4,048	2,281	1,761	6	Ford	56.3%	43.5%	0.1%
CHIPPEWA	4,858	2,346	2,482	30	Reagan	48.3%	51.1%	0.6%
CLARK	4,168	1,890	2,263	15	Reagan	45.3%	54.3%	0.4%
COLUMBIA	5,747	3,805	1,930	12	Ford	66.2%	33.6%	0.2%
CRAWFORD	2,679	1,333	1,336	10	Reagan	49.8%	49.9%	0.4%
DANE	29,210	19,836	9,222	152	Ford	67.9%	31.6%	0.5%
DODGE	10,741	6,823	3,872	46	Ford	63.5%	36.0%	0.4%
DOOR	4,085	2,460	1,597	28	Ford	60.2%	39.1%	0.7%
DOUGLAS	4,111	2,454	1,639	18	Ford	59.7%	39.9%	0.4%
DUNN	3,197	1,590	1,594	13	Reagan	49.7%	49.9%	0.4%
EAU CLAIRE	8,136	4,710	3,363	63	Ford	57.9%	41.3%	0.8%
FLORENCE	620	346	262	12	Ford	55.8%	42.3%	1.9%
FOND DU LAC	14,447	9,612	4,784	51	Ford	66.5%	33.1%	0.4%
FOREST	1,102	465	634	3	Reagan	42.2%	57.5%	0.3%
GRANT	6,150	3,257	2,893		Ford	53.0%	47.0%	
GREEN	4,491	2,701	1,769	21	Ford	60.1%	39.4%	0.5%
GREEN LAKE	3,357	1,857	1,488	12	Ford	55.3%	44.3%	0.4%
IOWA	2,517	1,562	943	12	Ford	62.1%	37.5%	0.5%
IRON	1,240	515	722	3	Reagan	41.5%	58.2%	0.2%
JACKSON	2,268	1,040	1,225	3	Reagan	45.9%	54.0%	0.1%
JEFFERSON	8,713	4,804	3,879	30	Ford	55.1%	44.5%	0.3%
JUNEAU	2,951	1,691	1,253	7	Ford	57.3%	42.5%	0.2%
KENOSHA	14,675	7,690	6,891	94	Ford	52.4%	47.0%	0.6%

WISCONSIN REPUBLICAN

1976

County	Total Vote	Ford	Reagan	Other	Winner	Percentage of Total Vote Ford	Reagan	Other
KEWAUNEE	2,879	1,319	1,551	9	Reagan	45.8%	53.9%	0.3%
LA CROSSE	15,139	8,229	6,821	89	Ford	54.4%	45.1%	0.6%
LAFAYETTE	2,342	1,319	1,020	3	Ford	56.3%	43.6%	0.1%
LANGLADE	2,748	1,575	1,160	13	Ford	57.3%	42.2%	0.5%
LINCOLN	3,973	2,228	1,742	3	Ford	56.1%	43.8%	0.1%
MANITOWOC	10,128	5,243	4,823	62	Ford	51.8%	47.6%	0.6%
MARATHON	12,425	7,080	5,303	42	Ford	57.0%	42.7%	0.3%
MARINETTE	5,224	2,696	2,503	25	Ford	51.6%	47.9%	0.5%
MARQUETTE	1,674	986	579	109	Ford	58.9%	34.6%	6.5%
MENOMINEE	92	35	57		Reagan	38.0%	62.0%	
MILWAUKEE	110,344	61,293	48,594	457	Ford	55.5%	44.0%	0.4%
MONROE	4,725	2,394	2,322	9	Ford	50.7%	49.1%	0.2%
OCONTO	4,691	2,217	2,462	12	Reagan	47.3%	52.5%	0.3%
ONEIDA	4,276	1,965	2,292	19	Reagan	46.0%	53.6%	0.4%
OUTAGAMIE	18,233	10,496	7,684	53	Ford	57.6%	42.1%	0.3%
OZAUKEE	11,053	6,078	4,929	46	Ford	55.0%	44.6%	0.4%
PEPIN	819	393	420	6	Reagan	48.0%	51.3%	0.7%
PIERCE	3,078	1,856	1,190	32	Ford	60.3%	38.7%	1.0%
POLK	3,641	1,977	1,620	44	Ford	54.3%	44.5%	1.2%
PORTAGE	4,409	2,582	1,804	23	Ford	58.6%	40.9%	0.5%
PRICE	1,986	1,002	976	8	Ford	50.5%	49.1%	0.4%
RACINE	21,713	10,158	11,450	105	Reagan	46.8%	52.7%	0.5%
RICHLAND	2,713	1,663	1,042	8	Ford	61.3%	38.4%	0.3%
ROCK	16,458	8,699	7,694	65	Ford	52.9%	46.7%	0.4%
RUSK	1,888	818	1,053	17	Reagan	43.3%	55.8%	0.9%
ST. CROIX	4,093	2,259	1,794	40	Ford	55.2%	43.8%	1.0%
SAUK	5,196	3,393	1,785	18	Ford	65.3%	34.4%	0.3%
SAWYER	1,861	772	1,078	11	Reagan	41.5%	57.9%	0.6%
SHAWANO	5,519	2,907	2,585	27	Ford	52.7%	46.8%	0.5%
SHEBOYGAN	13,231	8,581	4,604	46	Ford	64.9%	34.8%	0.3%
TAYLOR	2,199	1,164	1,025	10	Ford	52.9%	46.6%	0.5%
TREMPEALEAU	3,250	1,642	1,597	11	Ford	50.5%	49.1%	0.3%
VERNON	4,327	2,146	2,170	11	Reagan	49.6%	50.2%	0.3%
VILAS	2,789	1,223	1,555	11	Reagan	43.9%	55.8%	0.4%
WALWORTH	11,061	6,263	4,676	122	Ford	56.6%	42.3%	1.1%
WASHBURN	1,914	1,007	884	23	Ford	52.6%	46.2%	1.2%
WASHINGTON	11,425	6,773	4,610	42	Ford	59.3%	40.4%	0.4%
WAUKESHA	39,153	20,548	18,409	196	Ford	52.5%	47.0%	0.5%
WAUPACA	6,458	3,791	2,652	15	Ford	58.7%	41.1%	0.2%
WAUSHARA	3,171	1,680	1,473	18	Ford	53.0%	46.5%	0.6%
WINNEBAGO	19,266	10,890	8,295	81	Ford	56.5%	43.1%	0.4%
WOOD	9,497	5,741	3,718	38	Ford	60.5%	39.1%	0.4%
TOTAL	591,812	326,869	262,126	2,817	Ford	55.2%	44.3%	0.5%

WISCONSIN DEMOCRATIC

1980

County	Total Vote	Brown	Carter	E. Kennedy	Other	Winner	Percentage of Total Vote Brown	Carter	E. Kennedy	Other
ADAMS	1,867	164	1,056	603	44	Carter	8.8%	56.6%	32.3%	2.4%
ASHLAND	3,061	224	1,703	1,071	63	Carter	7.3%	55.6%	35.0%	2.1%
BARRON	5,627	241	4,134	1,174	78	Carter	4.3%	73.5%	20.9%	1.4%
BAYFIELD	2,402	216	1,434	732	20	Carter	9.0%	59.7%	30.5%	0.8%
BROWN	21,962	4,086	10,633	6,839	404	Carter	18.6%	48.4%	31.1%	1.8%
BUFFALO	1,932	178	1,231	500	23	Carter	9.2%	63.7%	25.9%	1.2%
BURNETT	1,791	53	1,300	400	38	Carter	3.0%	72.6%	22.3%	2.1%
CALUMET	3,434	446	1,791	1,128	69	Carter	13.0%	52.2%	32.8%	2.0%
CHIPPEWA	7,237	754	3,869	2,438	176	Carter	10.4%	53.5%	33.7%	2.4%
CLARK	4,265	430	2,769	991	75	Carter	10.1%	64.9%	23.2%	1.8%
COLUMBIA	5,717	640	3,192	1,783	102	Carter	11.2%	55.8%	31.2%	1.8%
CRAWFORD	2,508	152	1,731	603	22	Carter	6.1%	69.0%	24.0%	0.9%
DANE	48,464	10,617	21,761	15,453	633	Carter	21.9%	44.9%	31.9%	1.3%
DODGE	8,053	944	4,364	2,609	136	Carter	11.7%	54.2%	32.4%	1.7%
DOOR	3,016	406	1,797	760	53	Carter	13.5%	59.6%	25.2%	1.8%
DOUGLAS	6,146	536	3,209	2,315	86	Carter	8.7%	52.2%	37.7%	1.4%
DUNN	4,371	619	2,541	1,135	76	Carter	14.2%	58.1%	26.0%	1.7%
EAU CLAIRE	10,526	1,473	5,551	3,242	260	Carter	14.0%	52.7%	30.8%	2.5%
FLORENCE	642	33	407	186	16	Carter	5.1%	63.4%	29.0%	2.5%
FOND DU LAC	9,958	1,483	5,091	3,172	212	Carter	14.9%	51.1%	31.9%	2.1%
FOREST	1,590	96	1,025	445	24	Carter	6.0%	64.5%	28.0%	1.5%
GRANT	5,301	427	3,294	1,529	51	Carter	8.1%	62.1%	28.8%	1.0%
GREEN	3,937	349	2,569	952	67	Carter	8.9%	65.3%	24.2%	1.7%
GREEN LAKE	2,001	245	1,166	556	34	Carter	12.2%	58.3%	27.8%	1.7%
IOWA	2,694	321	1,507	821	45	Carter	11.9%	55.9%	30.5%	1.7%
IRON	1,524	120	816	571	17	Carter	7.9%	53.5%	37.5%	1.1%
JACKSON	2,334	193	1,602	493	46	Carter	8.3%	68.6%	21.1%	2.0%
JEFFERSON	6,648	731	3,905	1,909	103	Carter	11.0%	58.7%	28.7%	1.5%
JUNEAU	2,638	259	1,498	817	64	Carter	9.8%	56.8%	31.0%	2.4%
KENOSHA	19,023	1,447	10,233	6,851	492	Carter	7.6%	53.8%	36.0%	2.6%
KEWAUNEE	2,085	288	1,052	713	32	Carter	13.8%	50.5%	34.2%	1.5%
LA CROSSE	9,712	1,163	6,323	2,081	145	Carter	12.0%	65.1%	21.4%	1.5%
LAFAYETTE	2,604	188	1,508	860	48	Carter	7.2%	57.9%	33.0%	1.8%
LANGLADE	2,698	206	1,666	771	55	Carter	7.6%	61.7%	28.6%	2.0%
LINCOLN	3,757	257	2,448	996	56	Carter	6.8%	65.2%	26.5%	1.5%
MANITOWOC	11,843	1,669	6,110	3,785	279	Carter	14.1%	51.6%	32.0%	2.4%
MARATHON	15,473	1,359	9,561	4,309	244	Carter	8.8%	61.8%	27.8%	1.6%
MARINETTE	5,221	523	2,904	1,670	124	Carter	10.0%	55.6%	32.0%	2.4%
MARQUETTE	1,369	141	797	399	32	Carter	10.3%	58.2%	29.1%	2.3%
MENOMINEE	234	18	69	146	1	E. Kennedy	7.7%	29.5%	62.4%	0.4%
MILWAUKEE	162,615	17,272	89,504	51,862	3,977	Carter	10.6%	55.0%	31.9%	2.4%
MONROE	3,766	528	2,470	730	38	Carter	14.0%	65.6%	19.4%	1.0%
OCONTO	3,921	471	2,205	1,167	78	Carter	12.0%	56.2%	29.8%	2.0%
ONEIDA	4,278	308	2,671	1,181	118	Carter	7.2%	62.4%	27.6%	2.8%
OUTAGAMIE	14,286	1,816	8,294	3,916	260	Carter	12.7%	58.1%	27.4%	1.8%
OZAUKEE	6,726	779	4,075	1,757	115	Carter	11.6%	60.6%	26.1%	1.7%
PEPIN	1,019	162	525	299	33	Carter	15.9%	51.5%	29.3%	3.2%
PIERCE	3,463	161	2,201	1,034	67	Carter	4.6%	63.6%	29.9%	1.9%
POLK	4,395	157	3,178	1,030	30	Carter	3.6%	72.3%	23.4%	0.7%
PORTAGE	9,965	1,387	4,694	3,809	75	Carter	13.9%	47.1%	38.2%	0.8%

WISCONSIN DEMOCRATIC

1980

County	Total Vote	Brown	Carter	E. Kennedy	Other	Winner	Percentage of Total Vote Brown	Carter	E. Kennedy	Other
PRICE	2,189	153	1,401	574	61	Carter	7.0%	64.0%	26.2%	2.8%
RACINE	20,330	2,064	12,182	5,742	342	Carter	10.2%	59.9%	28.2%	1.7%
RICHLAND	2,423	330	1,511	550	32	Carter	13.6%	62.4%	22.7%	1.3%
ROCK	13,667	1,180	7,808	4,505	174	Carter	8.6%	57.1%	33.0%	1.3%
RUSK	2,731	249	1,683	736	63	Carter	9.1%	61.6%	26.9%	2.3%
ST. CROIX	5,364	243	3,540	1,489	92	Carter	4.5%	66.0%	27.8%	1.7%
SAUK	5,062	611	2,893	1,438	120	Carter	12.1%	57.2%	28.4%	2.4%
SAWYER	1,631	105	1,094	409	23	Carter	6.4%	67.1%	25.1%	1.4%
SHAWANO	3,247	388	1,805	970	84	Carter	11.9%	55.6%	29.9%	2.6%
SHEBOYGAN	13,642	1,639	7,157	4,604	242	Carter	12.0%	52.5%	33.7%	1.8%
TAYLOR	2,610	221	1,690	657	42	Carter	8.5%	64.8%	25.2%	1.6%
TREMPEALEAU	3,741	366	2,293	1,043	39	Carter	9.8%	61.3%	27.9%	1.0%
VERNON	3,323	278	2,458	548	39	Carter	8.4%	74.0%	16.5%	1.2%
VILAS	2,144	150	1,347	568	79	Carter	7.0%	62.8%	26.5%	3.7%
WALWORTH	6,790	747	4,017	1,919	107	Carter	11.0%	59.2%	28.3%	1.6%
WASHBURN	1,977	109	1,336	509	23	Carter	5.5%	67.6%	25.7%	1.2%
WASHINGTON	8,079	1,105	4,492	2,319	163	Carter	13.7%	55.6%	28.7%	2.0%
WAUKESHA	29,351	3,620	17,445	7,858	428	Carter	12.3%	59.4%	26.8%	1.5%
WAUPACA	4,032	501	2,488	958	85	Carter	12.4%	61.7%	23.8%	2.1%
WAUSHARA	1,968	202	1,207	523	36	Carter	10.3%	61.3%	26.6%	1.8%
WINNEBAGO	14,891	2,383	8,129	4,134	245	Carter	16.0%	54.6%	27.8%	1.6%
WOOD	10,328	1,116	6,252	2,874	86	Carter	10.8%	60.5%	27.8%	0.8%
TOTAL	629,619	74,496	353,662	189,520	11,941	Carter	11.8%	56.2%	30.1%	1.9%

WISCONSIN REPUBLICAN

1980

County	Total Vote	Anderson	Bush	Reagan	Other	Winner	Percentage of Total Vote Anderson	Bush	Reagan	Other
ADAMS	2,324	528	642	1,080	74	Reagan	22.7%	27.6%	46.5%	3.2%
ASHLAND	3,072	1,094	520	1,395	63	Reagan	35.6%	16.9%	45.4%	2.1%
BARRON	5,191	1,186	1,066	2,751	188	Reagan	22.8%	20.5%	53.0%	3.6%
BAYFIELD	2,747	932	446	1,301	68	Reagan	33.9%	16.2%	47.4%	2.5%
BROWN	38,685	6,648	8,872	22,765	400	Reagan	17.2%	22.9%	58.8%	1.0%
BUFFALO	2,179	414	454	1,261	50	Reagan	19.0%	20.8%	57.9%	2.3%
BURNETT	1,634	379	260	907	88	Reagan	23.2%	15.9%	55.5%	5.4%
CALUMET	6,289	1,294	2,197	2,712	86	Reagan	20.6%	34.9%	43.1%	1.4%
CHIPPEWA	7,174	1,388	2,072	3,553	161	Reagan	19.3%	28.9%	49.5%	2.2%
CLARK	5,246	959	1,347	2,819	121	Reagan	18.3%	25.7%	53.7%	2.3%
COLUMBIA	8,876	2,730	3,075	2,857	214	Bush	30.8%	34.6%	32.2%	2.4%
CRAWFORD	2,548	493	637	1,364	54	Reagan	19.3%	25.0%	53.5%	2.1%
DANE	65,119	36,721	15,770	11,385	1,243	Anderson	56.4%	24.2%	17.5%	1.9%
DODGE	14,789	2,818	6,146	5,682	143	Bush	19.1%	41.6%	38.4%	1.0%
DOOR	5,811	1,119	1,685	2,918	89	Reagan	19.3%	29.0%	50.2%	1.5%

WISCONSIN REPUBLICAN

1980

County	Total Vote	Anderson	Bush	Reagan	Other	Winner	Percentage of Total Vote: Anderson	Bush	Reagan	Other
DOUGLAS	6,044	2,441	1,304	2,124	175	Anderson	40.4%	21.6%	35.1%	2.9%
DUNN	5,241	1,495	1,143	2,452	151	Reagan	28.5%	21.8%	46.8%	2.9%
EAU CLAIRE	10,998	2,794	3,832	4,154	218	Reagan	25.4%	34.8%	37.8%	2.0%
FLORENCE	801	134	213	440	14	Reagan	16.7%	26.6%	54.9%	1.7%
FOND DU LAC	19,284	3,121	8,233	7,614	316	Bush	16.2%	42.7%	39.5%	1.6%
FOREST	1,335	165	332	819	19	Reagan	12.4%	24.9%	61.3%	1.4%
GRANT	8,738	2,135	2,118	4,115	370	Reagan	24.4%	24.2%	47.1%	4.2%
GREEN	6,376	1,798	1,698	2,653	227	Reagan	28.2%	26.6%	41.6%	3.6%
GREEN LAKE	4,183	520	1,655	1,934	74	Reagan	12.4%	39.6%	46.2%	1.8%
IOWA	3,561	1,055	1,221	1,199	86	Bush	29.6%	34.3%	33.7%	2.4%
IRON	1,357	284	196	862	15	Reagan	20.9%	14.4%	63.5%	1.1%
JACKSON	2,834	473	791	1,518	52	Reagan	16.7%	27.9%	53.6%	1.8%
JEFFERSON	11,702	2,968	3,708	4,750	276	Reagan	25.4%	31.7%	40.6%	2.4%
JUNEAU	4,096	1,050	1,088	1,859	99	Reagan	25.6%	26.6%	45.4%	2.4%
KENOSHA	19,585	5,129	5,388	8,583	485	Reagan	26.2%	27.5%	43.8%	2.5%
KEWAUNEE	4,068	455	918	2,649	46	Reagan	11.2%	22.6%	65.1%	1.1%
LA CROSSE	18,553	4,813	4,713	8,692	335	Reagan	25.9%	25.4%	46.8%	1.8%
LAFAYETTE	3,480	920	923	1,507	130	Reagan	26.4%	26.5%	43.3%	3.7%
LANGLADE	3,627	702	1,182	1,647	96	Reagan	19.4%	32.6%	45.4%	2.6%
LINCOLN	5,322	1,182	1,683	2,336	121	Reagan	22.2%	31.6%	43.9%	2.3%
MANITOWOC	14,712	2,421	5,739	6,310	242	Reagan	16.5%	39.0%	42.9%	1.6%
MARATHON	19,274	4,818	5,692	8,270	494	Reagan	25.0%	29.5%	42.9%	2.6%
MARINETTE	8,134	1,093	2,366	4,495	180	Reagan	13.4%	29.1%	55.3%	2.2%
MARQUETTE	2,444	524	804	1,064	52	Reagan	21.4%	32.9%	43.5%	2.1%
MENOMINEE	100	24	25	47	4	Reagan	24.0%	25.0%	47.0%	4.0%
MILWAUKEE	189,249	59,607	62,543	63,381	3,718	Reagan	31.5%	33.0%	33.5%	2.0%
MONROE	5,570	1,148	1,452	2,821	149	Reagan	20.6%	26.1%	50.6%	2.7%
OCONTO	6,247	745	1,524	3,902	76	Reagan	11.9%	24.4%	62.5%	1.2%
ONEIDA	6,092	1,549	1,707	2,680	156	Reagan	25.4%	28.0%	44.0%	2.6%
OUTAGAMIE	28,261	7,867	8,359	11,626	409	Reagan	27.8%	29.6%	41.1%	1.4%
OZAUKEE	18,272	4,292	7,081	6,598	301	Bush	23.5%	38.8%	36.1%	1.6%
PEPIN	866	159	176	484	47	Reagan	18.4%	20.3%	55.9%	5.4%
PIERCE	3,837	1,313	690	1,671	163	Reagan	34.2%	18.0%	43.5%	4.2%
POLK	4,245	1,161	728	2,132	224	Reagan	27.3%	17.1%	50.2%	5.3%
PORTAGE	9,568	3,688	2,966	2,760	154	Anderson	38.5%	31.0%	28.8%	1.6%
PRICE	2,494	542	695	1,195	62	Reagan	21.7%	27.9%	47.9%	2.5%
RACINE	33,130	8,873	9,276	14,345	636	Reagan	26.8%	28.0%	43.3%	1.9%
RICHLAND	3,319	786	1,086	1,361	86	Reagan	23.7%	32.7%	41.0%	2.6%
ROCK	23,172	6,126	5,438	11,185	423	Reagan	26.4%	23.5%	48.3%	1.8%
RUSK	2,559	407	762	1,329	61	Reagan	15.9%	29.8%	51.9%	2.4%
ST. CROIX	5,673	1,880	1,077	2,460	256	Reagan	33.1%	19.0%	43.4%	4.5%
SAUK	7,667	2,382	2,423	2,651	211	Reagan	31.1%	31.6%	34.6%	2.8%
SAWYER	2,315	523	408	1,322	62	Reagan	22.6%	17.6%	57.1%	2.7%
SHAWANO	6,721	1,011	1,815	3,783	112	Reagan	15.0%	27.0%	56.3%	1.7%
SHEBOYGAN	20,345	5,878	7,896	6,186	385	Bush	28.9%	38.8%	30.4%	1.9%
TAYLOR	3,185	564	954	1,588	79	Reagan	17.7%	30.0%	49.9%	2.5%
TREMPEALEAU	4,165	796	920	2,373	76	Reagan	19.1%	22.1%	57.0%	1.8%
VERNON	4,861	1,002	1,071	2,674	114	Reagan	20.6%	22.0%	55.0%	2.3%
VILAS	3,685	770	780	2,060	75	Reagan	20.9%	21.2%	55.9%	2.0%
WALWORTH	14,434	3,542	3,749	6,812	331	Reagan	24.5%	26.0%	47.2%	2.3%

WISCONSIN REPUBLICAN

1980

County	Total Vote	Anderson	Bush	Reagan	Other	Winner	Percentage of Total Vote Anderson	Bush	Reagan	Other
WASHBURN	2,189	562	429	1,142	56	Reagan	25.7%	19.6%	52.2%	2.6%
WASHINGTON	17,508	3,868	6,053	7,211	376	Reagan	22.1%	34.6%	41.2%	2.1%
WAUKESHA	64,849	15,670	23,557	24,454	1,168	Reagan	24.2%	36.3%	37.7%	1.8%
WAUPACA	9,571	1,540	2,543	5,339	149	Reagan	16.1%	26.6%	55.8%	1.6%
WAUSHARA	3,745	478	1,278	1,914	75	Reagan	12.8%	34.1%	51.1%	2.0%
WINNEBAGO	28,410	5,554	10,413	12,096	347	Reagan	19.5%	36.7%	42.6%	1.2%
WOOD	14,116	3,123	4,161	6,520	312	Reagan	22.1%	29.5%	46.2%	2.2%
TOTAL	907,853	248,623	276,164	364,898	18,168	Reagan	27.4%	30.4%	40.2%	2.0%

WISCONSIN DEMOCRATIC

1984

County	Total Vote	Hart	Mondale	Other	Winner	Percentage of Total Vote Hart	Mondale	Other
ADAMS	1,870	876	796	198	Hart	46.8%	42.6%	10.6%
ASHLAND	4,308	1,746	2,086	476	Mondale	40.5%	48.4%	11.0%
BARRON	5,229	2,339	2,434	456	Mondale	44.7%	46.5%	8.7%
BAYFIELD	3,374	1,344	1,584	446	Mondale	39.8%	46.9%	13.2%
BROWN	23,190	12,076	8,376	2,738	Hart	52.1%	36.1%	11.8%
BUFFALO	1,829	842	798	189	Hart	46.0%	43.6%	10.3%
BURNETT	2,110	895	995	220	Mondale	42.4%	47.2%	10.4%
CALUMET	4,099	2,258	1,364	477	Hart	55.1%	33.3%	11.6%
CHIPPEWA	7,310	3,402	3,150	758	Hart	46.5%	43.1%	10.4%
CLARK	4,158	2,170	1,557	431	Hart	52.2%	37.4%	10.4%
COLUMBIA	6,238	3,440	2,086	712	Hart	55.1%	33.4%	11.4%
CRAWFORD	3,516	1,873	1,306	337	Hart	53.3%	37.1%	9.6%
DANE	40,427	18,801	13,818	7,808	Hart	46.5%	34.2%	19.3%
DODGE	10,403	5,625	3,725	1,053	Hart	54.1%	35.8%	10.1%
DOOR	2,640	1,372	893	375	Hart	52.0%	33.8%	14.2%
DOUGLAS	7,459	2,181	4,641	637	Mondale	29.2%	62.2%	8.5%
DUNN	4,281	1,959	1,857	465	Hart	45.8%	43.4%	10.9%
EAU CLAIRE	10,196	4,362	4,531	1,303	Mondale	42.8%	44.4%	12.8%
FLORENCE	567	269	242	56	Hart	47.4%	42.7%	9.9%
FOND DU LAC	9,808	5,007	3,549	1,252	Hart	51.1%	36.2%	12.8%
FOREST	1,653	828	668	157	Hart	50.1%	40.4%	9.5%
GRANT	6,141	3,637	1,931	573	Hart	59.2%	31.4%	9.3%
GREEN	2,898	1,697	857	344	Hart	58.6%	29.6%	11.9%
GREEN LAKE	2,140	1,110	786	244	Hart	51.9%	36.7%	11.4%
IOWA	2,346	1,325	760	261	Hart	56.5%	32.4%	11.1%
IRON	1,829	725	961	143	Mondale	39.6%	52.5%	7.8%
JACKSON	3,622	1,930	1,347	345	Hart	53.3%	37.2%	9.5%
JEFFERSON	6,366	3,225	2,371	770	Hart	50.7%	37.2%	12.1%
JUNEAU	2,619	1,385	981	253	Hart	52.9%	37.5%	9.7%
KENOSHA	20,065	7,565	10,629	1,871	Mondale	37.7%	53.0%	9.3%

WISCONSIN DEMOCRATIC

1984

County	Total Vote	Hart	Mondale	Other	Winner	Percentage of Total Vote Hart	Mondale	Other
KEWAUNEE	2,650	1,307	1,051	292	Hart	49.3%	39.7%	11.0%
LA CROSSE	15,537	7,147	6,925	1,465	Hart	46.0%	44.6%	9.4%
LAFAYETTE	2,437	1,400	821	216	Hart	57.4%	33.7%	8.9%
LANGLADE	3,246	1,713	1,191	342	Hart	52.8%	36.7%	10.5%
LINCOLN	3,342	1,542	1,397	403	Hart	46.1%	41.8%	12.1%
MANITOWOC	10,723	5,155	4,497	1,071	Hart	48.1%	41.9%	10.0%
MARATHON	13,119	5,889	5,573	1,657	Hart	44.9%	42.5%	12.6%
MARINETTE	4,151	2,041	1,689	421	Hart	49.2%	40.7%	10.1%
MARQUETTE	1,109	551	424	134	Hart	49.7%	38.2%	12.1%
MENOMINEE	386	165	123	98	Hart	42.7%	31.9%	25.4%
MILWAUKEE	157,439	56,010	69,812	31,617	Mondale	35.6%	44.3%	20.1%
MONROE	4,098	2,066	1,616	416	Hart	50.4%	39.4%	10.2%
OCONTO	3,663	1,775	1,497	391	Hart	48.5%	40.9%	10.7%
ONEIDA	4,578	2,267	1,788	523	Hart	49.5%	39.1%	11.4%
OUTAGAMIE	17,286	9,163	5,977	2,146	Hart	53.0%	34.6%	12.4%
OZAUKEE	6,147	3,052	2,165	930	Hart	49.7%	35.2%	15.1%
PEPIN	866	404	378	84	Hart	46.7%	43.6%	9.7%
PIERCE	3,481	1,577	1,497	407	Hart	45.3%	43.0%	11.7%
POLK	4,843	2,018	2,406	419	Mondale	41.7%	49.7%	8.7%
PORTAGE	8,319	3,430	3,817	1,072	Mondale	41.2%	45.9%	12.9%
PRICE	3,274	1,463	1,495	316	Mondale	44.7%	45.7%	9.7%
RACINE	19,559	7,919	8,375	3,265	Mondale	40.5%	42.8%	16.7%
RICHLAND	2,056	1,138	641	277	Hart	55.4%	31.2%	13.5%
ROCK	16,350	7,562	6,589	2,199	Hart	46.3%	40.3%	13.4%
RUSK	2,960	1,365	1,318	277	Hart	46.1%	44.5%	9.4%
ST. CROIX	5,802	2,483	2,745	574	Mondale	42.8%	47.3%	9.9%
SAUK	4,936	2,678	1,649	609	Hart	54.3%	33.4%	12.3%
SAWYER	2,306	1,107	882	317	Hart	48.0%	38.2%	13.7%
SHAWANO	5,345	2,862	1,823	660	Hart	53.5%	34.1%	12.3%
SHEBOYGAN	11,882	5,581	5,092	1,209	Hart	47.0%	42.9%	10.2%
TAYLOR	2,335	1,123	956	256	Hart	48.1%	40.9%	11.0%
TREMPEALEAU	4,111	1,943	1,799	369	Hart	47.3%	43.8%	9.0%
VERNON	4,674	2,258	1,978	438	Hart	48.3%	42.3%	9.4%
VILAS	2,700	1,478	888	334	Hart	54.7%	32.9%	12.4%
WALWORTH	5,611	2,821	1,945	845	Hart	50.3%	34.7%	15.1%
WASHBURN	1,855	747	915	193	Mondale	40.3%	49.3%	10.4%
WASHINGTON	8,139	4,140	2,917	1,082	Hart	50.9%	35.8%	13.3%
WAUKESHA	32,187	14,383	12,228	5,576	Hart	44.7%	38.0%	17.3%
WAUPACA	4,588	2,394	1,653	541	Hart	52.2%	36.0%	11.8%
WAUSHARA	2,022	1,011	809	202	Hart	50.0%	40.0%	10.0%
WINNEBAGO	14,305	6,966	5,429	1,910	Hart	48.7%	38.0%	13.4%
WOOD	8,660	4,077	3,525	1,058	Hart	47.1%	40.7%	12.2%
TOTAL	635,768	282,435	261,374	91,959	Hart	44.4%	41.1%	14.5%

WISCONSIN REPUBLICAN

1984

County	Total Vote	Reagan	Other	Winner	Percentage of Total Vote	
					Reagan	Other
ADAMS	788	767	21	Reagan	97.3%	2.7%
ASHLAND	1,359	1,268	91	Reagan	93.3%	6.7%
BARRON	2,452	2,416	36	Reagan	98.5%	1.5%
BAYFIELD	1,273	1,202	71	Reagan	94.4%	5.6%
BROWN	12,163	11,569	594	Reagan	95.1%	4.9%
BUFFALO	808	804	4	Reagan	99.5%	0.5%
BURNETT	924	913	11	Reagan	98.8%	1.2%
CALUMET	2,324	2,248	76	Reagan	96.7%	3.3%
CHIPPEWA	2,711	2,602	109	Reagan	96.0%	4.0%
CLARK	1,829	1,798	31	Reagan	98.3%	1.7%
COLUMBIA	3,368	3,289	79	Reagan	97.7%	2.3%
CRAWFORD	1,722	1,704	18	Reagan	99.0%	1.0%
DANE	11,490	10,527	963	Reagan	91.6%	8.4%
DODGE	6,276	6,034	242	Reagan	96.1%	3.9%
DOOR	2,058	2,030	28	Reagan	98.6%	1.4%
DOUGLAS	1,612	1,532	80	Reagan	95.0%	5.0%
DUNN	1,775	1,652	123	Reagan	93.1%	6.9%
EAU CLAIRE	4,285	4,000	285	Reagan	93.3%	6.7%
FLORENCE	322	321	1	Reagan	99.7%	0.3%
FOND DU LAC	5,722	5,275	447	Reagan	92.2%	7.8%
FOREST	668	663	5	Reagan	99.3%	0.7%
GRANT	3,461	3,397	64	Reagan	98.2%	1.8%
GREEN	1,960	1,938	22	Reagan	98.9%	1.1%
GREEN LAKE	1,640	1,624	16	Reagan	99.0%	1.0%
IOWA	1,120	1,087	33	Reagan	97.1%	2.9%
IRON	613	592	21	Reagan	96.6%	3.4%
JACKSON	1,635	1,624	11	Reagan	99.3%	0.7%
JEFFERSON	3,524	3,419	105	Reagan	97.0%	3.0%
JUNEAU	1,790	1,771	19	Reagan	98.9%	1.1%
KENOSHA	6,491	6,249	242	Reagan	96.3%	3.7%
KEWAUNEE	1,185	1,174	11	Reagan	99.1%	0.9%
LA CROSSE	8,430	8,086	344	Reagan	95.9%	4.1%
LAFAYETTE	1,275	1,249	26	Reagan	98.0%	2.0%
LANGLADE	1,436	1,423	13	Reagan	99.1%	0.9%
LINCOLN	1,631	1,604	27	Reagan	98.3%	1.7%
MANITOWOC	4,319	4,054	265	Reagan	93.9%	6.1%
MARATHON	5,173	4,898	275	Reagan	94.7%	5.3%
MARINETTE	2,468	2,421	47	Reagan	98.1%	1.9%
MARQUETTE	678	659	19	Reagan	97.2%	2.8%
MENOMINEE	53	49	4	Reagan	92.5%	7.5%
MILWAUKEE	56,531	52,396	4,135	Reagan	92.7%	7.3%
MONROE	1,988	1,946	42	Reagan	97.9%	2.1%
OCONTO	2,183	2,147	36	Reagan	98.4%	1.6%
ONEIDA	2,209	2,172	37	Reagan	98.3%	1.7%
OUTAGAMIE	11,235	10,644	591	Reagan	94.7%	5.3%
OZAUKEE	4,920	4,671	249	Reagan	94.9%	5.1%
PEPIN	284	275	9	Reagan	96.8%	3.2%
PIERCE	1,433	1,349	84	Reagan	94.1%	5.9%
POLK	2,060	2,019	41	Reagan	98.0%	2.0%
PORTAGE	2,204	2,054	150	Reagan	93.2%	6.8%

WISCONSIN REPUBLICAN

1984

County	Total Vote	Reagan	Other	Winner	Percentage of Total Vote Reagan	Other
PRICE	1,450	1,443	7	Reagan	99.5%	0.5%
RACINE	8,459	7,999	460	Reagan	94.6%	5.4%
RICHLAND	1,143	1,118	25	Reagan	97.8%	2.2%
ROCK	7,992	7,496	496	Reagan	93.8%	6.2%
RUSK	1,158	1,140	18	Reagan	98.4%	1.6%
ST. CROIX	2,220	2,170	50	Reagan	97.7%	2.3%
SAUK	2,939	2,871	68	Reagan	97.7%	2.3%
SAWYER	1,335	1,287	48	Reagan	96.4%	3.6%
SHAWANO	3,856	3,690	166	Reagan	95.7%	4.3%
SHEBOYGAN	5,739	5,430	309	Reagan	94.6%	5.4%
TAYLOR	903	888	15	Reagan	98.3%	1.7%
TREMPEALEAU	1,688	1,675	13	Reagan	99.2%	0.8%
VERNON	2,561	2,523	38	Reagan	98.5%	1.5%
VILAS	1,945	1,945		Reagan	100.0%	
WALWORTH	4,216	4,081	135	Reagan	96.8%	3.2%
WASHBURN	806	796	10	Reagan	98.8%	1.2%
WASHINGTON	5,535	5,333	202	Reagan	96.4%	3.6%
WAUKESHA	23,123	22,007	1,116	Reagan	95.2%	4.8%
WAUPACA	3,477	3,413	64	Reagan	98.2%	1.8%
WAUSHARA	1,550	1,517	33	Reagan	97.9%	2.1%
WINNEBAGO	8,542	8,058	484	Reagan	94.3%	5.7%
WOOD	4,318	4,123	195	Reagan	95.5%	4.5%
TOTAL	294,813	280,608	14,205	Reagan	95.2%	4.8%

Note: The votes for Reagan were cast for a ballot line designated "Ronald Reagan YES." Of the votes cast for "Other," 14,047 were for a ballot line designated "Ronald Reagan NO."

WISCONSIN DEMOCRATIC

1988

County	Total Vote	Dukakis	Gore	J. Jackson	Other	Winner	Percentage of Total Vote Dukakis	Gore	J. Jackson	Other
ADAMS	3,047	1,486	695	639	227	Dukakis	48.8%	22.8%	21.0%	7.4%
ASHLAND	3,966	2,007	648	1,053	258	Dukakis	50.6%	16.3%	26.6%	6.5%
BARRON	8,235	4,122	1,042	2,589	482	Dukakis	50.1%	12.7%	31.4%	5.9%
BAYFIELD	3,916	1,844	530	1,303	239	Dukakis	47.1%	13.5%	33.3%	6.1%
BROWN	37,427	20,354	6,793	7,812	2,468	Dukakis	54.4%	18.1%	20.9%	6.6%
BUFFALO	2,860	1,260	662	768	170	Dukakis	44.1%	23.1%	26.9%	5.9%
BURNETT	2,420	1,294	146	795	185	Dukakis	53.5%	6.0%	32.9%	7.6%
CALUMET	6,389	3,185	1,563	1,241	400	Dukakis	49.9%	24.5%	19.4%	6.3%
CHIPPEWA	9,993	4,931	2,040	2,500	522	Dukakis	49.3%	20.4%	25.0%	5.2%
CLARK	6,603	3,053	1,676	1,425	449	Dukakis	46.2%	25.4%	21.6%	6.8%
COLUMBIA	7,712	3,812	1,581	1,718	601	Dukakis	49.4%	20.5%	22.3%	7.8%
CRAWFORD	2,923	1,283	523	790	327	Dukakis	43.9%	17.9%	27.0%	11.2%
DANE	90,478	39,716	12,975	30,496	7,291	Dukakis	43.9%	14.3%	33.7%	8.1%
DODGE	11,429	5,414	2,383	2,687	945	Dukakis	47.4%	20.9%	23.5%	8.3%
DOOR	5,792	2,814	1,146	1,375	457	Dukakis	48.6%	19.8%	23.7%	7.9%

WISCONSIN DEMOCRATIC

1988

County	Total Vote	Dukakis	Gore	J. Jackson	Other	Winner	Percentage of Total Vote: Dukakis	Gore	J. Jackson	Other
DOUGLAS	9,618	5,634	1,316	1,965	703	Dukakis	58.6%	13.7%	20.4%	7.3%
DUNN	6,971	3,247	1,059	2,243	422	Dukakis	46.6%	15.2%	32.2%	6.1%
EAU CLAIRE	18,819	8,848	3,375	5,576	1,020	Dukakis	47.0%	17.9%	29.6%	5.4%
FLORENCE	792	428	133	167	64	Dukakis	54.0%	16.8%	21.1%	8.1%
FOND DU LAC	13,548	6,823	2,815	2,935	975	Dukakis	50.4%	20.8%	21.7%	7.2%
FOREST	1,744	914	372	338	120	Dukakis	52.4%	21.3%	19.4%	6.9%
GRANT	7,056	3,443	1,099	1,645	869	Dukakis	48.8%	15.6%	23.3%	12.3%
GREEN	4,883	2,253	1,028	1,122	480	Dukakis	46.1%	21.1%	23.0%	9.8%
GREEN LAKE	3,109	1,490	785	599	235	Dukakis	47.9%	25.2%	19.3%	7.6%
IOWA	3,453	1,442	780	896	335	Dukakis	41.8%	22.6%	25.9%	9.7%
IRON	1,476	854	213	284	125	Dukakis	57.9%	14.4%	19.2%	8.5%
JACKSON	3,525	1,535	988	833	169	Dukakis	43.5%	28.0%	23.6%	4.8%
JEFFERSON	9,309	4,381	1,827	2,437	664	Dukakis	47.1%	19.6%	26.2%	7.1%
JUNEAU	3,884	1,727	1,123	713	321	Dukakis	44.5%	28.9%	18.4%	8.3%
KENOSHA	25,594	13,956	2,525	6,470	2,643	Dukakis	54.5%	9.9%	25.3%	10.3%
KEWAUNEE	4,512	2,354	1,004	831	323	Dukakis	52.2%	22.3%	18.4%	7.2%
LA CROSSE	18,990	8,543	4,035	4,787	1,625	Dukakis	45.0%	21.2%	25.2%	8.6%
LAFAYETTE	3,061	1,475	625	638	323	Dukakis	48.2%	20.4%	20.8%	10.6%
LANGLADE	4,800	2,330	1,139	923	408	Dukakis	48.5%	23.7%	19.2%	8.5%
LINCOLN	5,054	2,286	1,014	1,298	456	Dukakis	45.2%	20.1%	25.7%	9.0%
MANITOWOC	17,132	9,282	3,883	3,006	961	Dukakis	54.2%	22.7%	17.5%	5.6%
MARATHON	24,639	11,537	4,636	6,474	1,992	Dukakis	46.8%	18.8%	26.3%	8.1%
MARINETTE	7,002	3,786	1,441	1,385	390	Dukakis	54.1%	20.6%	19.8%	5.6%
MARQUETTE	2,285	1,039	568	482	196	Dukakis	45.5%	24.9%	21.1%	8.6%
MENOMINEE	501	136	52	295	18	J. Jackson	27.1%	10.4%	58.9%	3.6%
MILWAUKEE	261,642	115,817	37,084	94,952	13,789	Dukakis	44.3%	14.2%	36.3%	5.3%
MONROE	6,259	2,618	1,993	1,279	369	Dukakis	41.8%	31.8%	20.4%	5.9%
OCONTO	6,461	3,323	1,424	1,266	448	Dukakis	51.4%	22.0%	19.6%	6.9%
ONEIDA	7,146	3,600	1,391	1,569	586	Dukakis	50.4%	19.5%	22.0%	8.2%
OUTAGAMIE	27,883	14,316	6,130	5,373	2,064	Dukakis	51.3%	22.0%	19.3%	7.4%
OZAUKEE	11,964	5,789	2,301	3,104	770	Dukakis	48.4%	19.2%	25.9%	6.4%
PEPIN	1,337	650	215	391	81	Dukakis	48.6%	16.1%	29.2%	6.1%
PIERCE	5,549	2,842	431	1,865	411	Dukakis	51.2%	7.8%	33.6%	7.4%
POLK	6,833	3,158	473	2,845	357	Dukakis	46.2%	6.9%	41.6%	5.2%
PORTAGE	12,145	6,239	2,116	2,912	878	Dukakis	51.4%	17.4%	24.0%	7.2%
PRICE	3,485	1,564	765	865	291	Dukakis	44.9%	22.0%	24.8%	8.4%
RACINE	34,472	17,006	5,652	9,755	2,059	Dukakis	49.3%	16.4%	28.3%	6.0%
RICHLAND	3,780	1,558	897	977	348	Dukakis	41.2%	23.7%	25.8%	9.2%
ROCK	24,180	12,251	4,351	5,859	1,719	Dukakis	50.7%	18.0%	24.2%	7.1%
RUSK	3,892	1,851	870	910	261	Dukakis	47.6%	22.4%	23.4%	6.7%
ST. CROIX	8,955	4,782	535	3,105	533	Dukakis	53.4%	6.0%	34.7%	6.0%
SAUK	8,121	3,552	1,932	1,959	678	Dukakis	43.7%	23.8%	24.1%	8.3%
SAWYER	2,598	1,278	407	726	187	Dukakis	49.2%	15.7%	27.9%	7.2%
SHAWANO	6,703	2,980	1,474	1,348	901	Dukakis	44.5%	22.0%	20.1%	13.4%
SHEBOYGAN	22,056	10,767	4,270	5,764	1,255	Dukakis	48.8%	19.4%	26.1%	5.7%
TAYLOR	4,031	1,757	951	1,033	290	Dukakis	43.6%	23.6%	25.6%	7.2%
TREMPEALEAU	5,414	2,262	1,492	1,296	364	Dukakis	41.8%	27.6%	23.9%	6.7%
VERNON	4,574	1,997	1,196	1,039	342	Dukakis	43.7%	26.1%	22.7%	7.5%
VILAS	3,424	1,662	680	863	219	Dukakis	48.5%	19.9%	25.2%	6.4%
WALWORTH	11,011	5,521	1,723	2,609	1,158	Dukakis	50.1%	15.6%	23.7%	10.5%

WISCONSIN DEMOCRATIC

1988

County	Total Vote	Dukakis	Gore	J. Jackson	Other	Winner	Percentage of Total Vote: Dukakis	Gore	J. Jackson	Other
WASHBURN	2,726	1,466	317	729	214	Dukakis	53.8%	11.6%	26.7%	7.9%
WASHINGTON	13,912	6,607	2,972	3,272	1,061	Dukakis	47.5%	21.4%	23.5%	7.6%
WAUKESHA	51,855	26,120	9,915	12,566	3,254	Dukakis	50.4%	19.1%	24.2%	6.3%
WAUPACA	6,399	3,124	1,470	1,321	484	Dukakis	48.8%	23.0%	20.6%	7.6%
WAUSHARA	3,381	1,595	850	687	249	Dukakis	47.2%	25.1%	20.3%	7.4%
WINNEBAGO	23,496	11,695	5,132	5,236	1,433	Dukakis	49.8%	21.8%	22.3%	6.1%
WOOD	14,151	7,107	3,065	2,987	992	Dukakis	50.2%	21.7%	21.1%	7.0%
TOTAL	1,014,782	483,172	176,712	285,995	68,903	Dukakis	47.6%	17.4%	28.2%	6.8%

WISCONSIN REPUBLICAN

1988

County	Total Vote	Bush	Other	Winner	Percentage of Total Vote: Bush	Other
ADAMS	1,171	985	186	Bush	84.1%	15.9%
ASHLAND	1,377	1,095	282	Bush	79.5%	20.5%
BARRON	3,444	2,697	747	Bush	78.3%	21.7%
BAYFIELD	1,291	995	296	Bush	77.1%	22.9%
BROWN	11,898	9,840	2,058	Bush	82.7%	17.3%
BUFFALO	1,084	886	198	Bush	81.7%	18.3%
BURNETT	752	515	237	Bush	68.5%	31.5%
CALUMET	2,750	2,365	385	Bush	86.0%	14.0%
CHIPPEWA	2,620	2,056	564	Bush	78.5%	21.5%
CLARK	2,237	1,696	541	Bush	75.8%	24.2%
COLUMBIA	3,112	2,502	610	Bush	80.4%	19.6%
CRAWFORD	1,126	817	309	Bush	72.6%	27.4%
DANE	18,342	14,596	3,746	Bush	79.6%	20.4%
DODGE	6,351	5,268	1,083	Bush	82.9%	17.1%
DOOR	3,099	2,666	433	Bush	86.0%	14.0%
DOUGLAS	2,195	1,451	744	Bush	66.1%	33.9%
DUNN	2,223	1,653	570	Bush	74.4%	25.6%
EAU CLAIRE	5,967	4,818	1,149	Bush	80.7%	19.3%
FLORENCE	326	272	54	Bush	83.4%	16.6%
FOND DU LAC	6,569	5,464	1,105	Bush	83.2%	16.8%
FOREST	568	487	81	Bush	85.7%	14.3%
GRANT	3,201	2,487	714	Bush	77.7%	22.3%
GREEN	2,747	2,233	514	Bush	81.3%	18.7%
GREEN LAKE	2,085	1,656	429	Bush	79.4%	20.6%
IOWA	1,202	925	277	Bush	77.0%	23.0%
IRON	500	434	66	Bush	86.8%	13.2%
JACKSON	1,119	854	265	Bush	76.3%	23.7%
JEFFERSON	4,124	3,367	757	Bush	81.6%	18.4%
JUNEAU	1,971	1,581	390	Bush	80.2%	19.8%
KENOSHA	7,421	6,089	1,332	Bush	82.1%	17.9%

WISCONSIN REPUBLICAN

1988

County	Total Vote	Bush	Other	Winner	Percentage of Total Vote	
					Bush	Other
KEWAUNEE	1,372	1,147	225	Bush	83.6%	16.4%
LA CROSSE	7,005	5,521	1,484	Bush	78.8%	21.2%
LAFAYETTE	1,204	957	247	Bush	79.5%	20.5%
LANGLADE	2,234	1,818	416	Bush	81.4%	18.6%
LINCOLN	1,857	1,504	353	Bush	81.0%	19.0%
MANITOWOC	4,261	3,476	785	Bush	81.6%	18.4%
MARATHON	8,170	6,640	1,530	Bush	81.3%	18.7%
MARINETTE	3,125	2,669	456	Bush	85.4%	14.6%
MARQUETTE	1,013	840	173	Bush	82.9%	17.1%
MENOMINEE	61	46	15	Bush	75.4%	24.6%
MILWAUKEE	73,788	62,780	11,008	Bush	85.1%	14.9%
MONROE	2,340	1,798	542	Bush	76.8%	23.2%
OCONTO	2,726	2,281	445	Bush	83.7%	16.3%
ONEIDA	3,195	2,642	553	Bush	82.7%	17.3%
OUTAGAMIE	12,531	10,610	1,921	Bush	84.7%	15.3%
OZAUKEE	8,271	7,171	1,100	Bush	86.7%	13.3%
PEPIN	340	253	87	Bush	74.4%	25.6%
PIERCE	1,828	1,235	593	Bush	67.6%	32.4%
POLK	1,873	1,278	595	Bush	68.2%	31.8%
PORTAGE	2,795	2,336	459	Bush	83.6%	16.4%
PRICE	1,322	1,064	258	Bush	80.5%	19.5%
RACINE	11,607	9,464	2,143	Bush	81.5%	18.5%
RICHLAND	1,892	1,431	461	Bush	75.6%	24.4%
ROCK	8,948	7,167	1,781	Bush	80.1%	19.9%
RUSK	1,154	896	258	Bush	77.6%	22.4%
ST. CROIX	3,012	2,028	984	Bush	67.3%	32.7%
SAUK	3,614	2,921	693	Bush	80.8%	19.2%
SAWYER	1,096	831	265	Bush	75.8%	24.2%
SHAWANO	3,072	2,488	584	Bush	81.0%	19.0%
SHEBOYGAN	7,817	6,521	1,296	Bush	83.4%	16.6%
TAYLOR	1,352	1,126	226	Bush	83.3%	16.7%
TREMPEALEAU	1,710	1,302	408	Bush	76.1%	23.9%
VERNON	1,768	1,285	483	Bush	72.7%	27.3%
VILAS	1,858	1,580	278	Bush	85.0%	15.0%
WALWORTH	7,069	5,858	1,211	Bush	82.9%	17.1%
WASHBURN	1,073	783	290	Bush	73.0%	27.0%
WASHINGTON	7,171	5,982	1,189	Bush	83.4%	16.6%
WAUKESHA	28,955	24,450	4,505	Bush	84.4%	15.6%
WAUPACA	3,721	3,174	547	Bush	85.3%	14.7%
WAUSHARA	1,712	1,407	305	Bush	82.2%	17.8%
WINNEBAGO	10,620	8,998	1,622	Bush	84.7%	15.3%
WOOD	5,890	4,787	1,103	Bush	81.3%	18.7%
TOTAL	359,294	295,295	63,999	Bush	82.2%	17.8%

WISCONSIN DEMOCRATIC

1992

County	Total Vote	Brown	Clinton	Tsongas	Other	Winner	Percentage of Total Vote Brown	Clinton	Tsongas	Other
ADAMS	2,533	691	1,215	411	216	Clinton	27.3%	48.0%	16.2%	8.5%
ASHLAND	3,394	1,348	1,343	434	269	Brown	39.7%	39.6%	12.8%	7.9%
BARRON	4,740	1,386	2,005	1,001	348	Clinton	29.2%	42.3%	21.1%	7.3%
BAYFIELD	2,940	1,227	902	480	331	Brown	41.7%	30.7%	16.3%	11.3%
BROWN	31,983	12,394	11,687	6,436	1,466	Brown	38.8%	36.5%	20.1%	4.6%
BUFFALO	1,886	579	815	355	137	Clinton	30.7%	43.2%	18.8%	7.3%
BURNETT	2,083	516	926	394	247	Clinton	24.8%	44.5%	18.9%	11.9%
CALUMET	5,226	1,956	1,818	1,107	345	Brown	37.4%	34.8%	21.2%	6.6%
CHIPPEWA	6,833	2,242	2,629	1,534	428	Clinton	32.8%	38.5%	22.4%	6.3%
CLARK	4,562	1,397	1,910	905	350	Clinton	30.6%	41.9%	19.8%	7.7%
COLUMBIA	6,264	1,927	2,695	1,265	377	Clinton	30.8%	43.0%	20.2%	6.0%
CRAWFORD	2,772	672	1,274	478	348	Clinton	24.2%	46.0%	17.2%	12.6%
DANE	78,061	28,131	25,918	18,377	5,635	Brown	36.0%	33.2%	23.5%	7.2%
DODGE	8,674	2,956	3,414	1,863	441	Clinton	34.1%	39.4%	21.5%	5.1%
DOOR	3,971	1,292	1,508	961	210	Clinton	32.5%	38.0%	24.2%	5.3%
DOUGLAS	8,611	3,209	3,219	1,494	689	Clinton	37.3%	37.4%	17.3%	8.0%
DUNN	5,032	1,713	1,962	982	375	Clinton	34.0%	39.0%	19.5%	7.5%
EAU CLAIRE	11,848	4,606	3,762	2,710	770	Brown	38.9%	31.8%	22.9%	6.5%
FLORENCE	1,132	309	493	224	106	Clinton	27.3%	43.6%	19.8%	9.4%
FOND DU LAC	9,242	3,354	3,138	2,322	428	Brown	36.3%	34.0%	25.1%	4.6%
FOREST	1,689	380	940	256	113	Clinton	22.5%	55.7%	15.2%	6.7%
GRANT	5,545	1,396	2,473	1,055	621	Clinton	25.2%	44.6%	19.0%	11.2%
GREEN	3,234	869	1,443	728	194	Clinton	26.9%	44.6%	22.5%	6.0%
GREEN LAKE	2,082	627	868	402	185	Clinton	30.1%	41.7%	19.3%	8.9%
IOWA	2,876	857	1,255	513	251	Clinton	29.8%	43.6%	17.8%	8.7%
IRON	1,216	396	476	218	126	Clinton	32.6%	39.1%	17.9%	10.4%
JACKSON	2,267	620	974	513	160	Clinton	27.3%	43.0%	22.6%	7.1%
JEFFERSON	7,836	2,735	2,990	1,711	400	Clinton	34.9%	38.2%	21.8%	5.1%
JUNEAU	3,162	836	1,594	489	243	Clinton	26.4%	50.4%	15.5%	7.7%
KENOSHA	20,852	7,459	7,959	4,174	1,260	Clinton	35.8%	38.2%	20.0%	6.0%
KEWAUNEE	4,101	1,342	1,809	656	294	Clinton	32.7%	44.1%	16.0%	7.2%
LA CROSSE	14,777	4,887	5,351	3,513	1,026	Clinton	33.1%	36.2%	23.8%	6.9%
LAFAYETTE	2,614	608	1,341	421	244	Clinton	23.3%	51.3%	16.1%	9.3%
LANGLADE	2,731	789	1,297	474	171	Clinton	28.9%	47.5%	17.4%	6.3%
LINCOLN	4,120	1,370	1,682	817	251	Clinton	33.3%	40.8%	19.8%	6.1%
MANITOWOC	14,178	4,807	5,351	3,251	769	Clinton	33.9%	37.7%	22.9%	5.4%
MARATHON	17,679	6,835	6,365	3,576	903	Brown	38.7%	36.0%	20.2%	5.1%
MARINETTE	6,099	1,834	2,614	1,198	453	Clinton	30.1%	42.9%	19.6%	7.4%
MARQUETTE	1,748	498	809	298	143	Clinton	28.5%	46.3%	17.0%	8.2%
MENOMINEE	306	88	126	69	23	Clinton	28.8%	41.2%	22.5%	7.5%
MILWAUKEE	181,924	60,589	71,083	39,211	11,041	Clinton	33.3%	39.1%	21.6%	6.1%
MONROE	5,117	1,410	2,237	1,078	392	Clinton	27.6%	43.7%	21.1%	7.7%
OCONTO	5,233	1,616	2,432	839	346	Clinton	30.9%	46.5%	16.0%	6.6%
ONEIDA	5,180	1,418	1,947	1,342	473	Clinton	27.4%	37.6%	25.9%	9.1%
OUTAGAMIE	20,531	8,184	6,457	4,647	1,243	Brown	39.9%	31.5%	22.6%	6.1%
OZAUKEE	10,038	3,537	2,679	3,440	382	Brown	35.2%	26.7%	34.3%	3.8%
PEPIN	1,150	341	498	187	124	Clinton	29.7%	43.3%	16.3%	10.8%
PIERCE	3,612	1,123	1,405	730	354	Clinton	31.1%	38.9%	20.2%	9.8%
POLK	4,828	1,300	2,092	900	536	Clinton	26.9%	43.3%	18.6%	11.1%
PORTAGE	10,745	4,451	3,917	1,854	523	Brown	41.4%	36.5%	17.3%	4.9%

WISCONSIN DEMOCRATIC

1992

County	Total Vote	Brown	Clinton	Tsongas	Other	Winner	Percentage of Total Vote Brown	Clinton	Tsongas	Other
PRICE	2,525	766	1,057	479	223	Clinton	30.3%	41.9%	19.0%	8.8%
RACINE	25,079	10,031	8,333	5,275	1,440	Brown	40.0%	33.2%	21.0%	5.7%
RICHLAND	2,615	816	1,194	419	186	Clinton	31.2%	45.7%	16.0%	7.1%
ROCK	18,026	5,111	8,163	3,303	1,449	Clinton	28.4%	45.3%	18.3%	8.0%
RUSK	3,148	961	1,343	585	259	Clinton	30.5%	42.7%	18.6%	8.2%
ST. CROIX	4,551	1,391	1,654	1,095	411	Clinton	30.6%	36.3%	24.1%	9.0%
SAUK	6,143	1,988	2,637	1,146	372	Clinton	32.4%	42.9%	18.7%	6.1%
SAWYER	1,784	628	702	298	156	Clinton	35.2%	39.3%	16.7%	8.7%
SHAWANO	4,711	1,647	1,863	930	271	Clinton	35.0%	39.5%	19.7%	5.8%
SHEBOYGAN	15,996	5,909	5,438	3,630	1,019	Brown	36.9%	34.0%	22.7%	6.4%
TAYLOR	2,961	898	1,301	566	196	Clinton	30.3%	43.9%	19.1%	6.6%
TREMPEALEAU	3,967	1,140	1,787	749	291	Clinton	28.7%	45.0%	18.9%	7.3%
VERNON	3,762	1,013	1,713	711	325	Clinton	26.9%	45.5%	18.9%	8.6%
VILAS	2,892	701	1,035	958	198	Clinton	24.2%	35.8%	33.1%	6.8%
WALWORTH	8,900	3,053	3,313	2,002	532	Clinton	34.3%	37.2%	22.5%	6.0%
WASHBURN	2,264	678	933	413	240	Clinton	29.9%	41.2%	18.2%	10.6%
WASHINGTON	11,691	4,344	3,716	3,008	623	Brown	37.2%	31.8%	25.7%	5.3%
WAUKESHA	44,041	16,605	12,122	12,713	2,601	Brown	37.7%	27.5%	28.9%	5.9%
WAUPACA	5,047	1,700	1,850	954	543	Clinton	33.7%	36.7%	18.9%	10.8%
WAUSHARA	2,723	790	1,222	441	270	Clinton	29.0%	44.9%	16.2%	9.9%
WINNEBAGO	18,444	6,489	6,219	4,300	1,436	Brown	35.2%	33.7%	23.3%	7.8%
WOOD	12,069	4,441	4,664	2,351	613	Clinton	36.8%	38.6%	19.5%	5.1%
TOTAL	772,596	266,207	287,356	168,619	50,414	Clinton	34.5%	37.2%	21.8%	6.5%

WISCONSIN REPUBLICAN

1992

County	Total Vote	Buchanan	Bush	Other	Winner	Percentage of Total Vote Buchanan	Bush	Other
ADAMS	1,434	224	1,019	191	Bush	15.6%	71.1%	13.3%
ASHLAND	1,921	307	1,465	149	Bush	16.0%	76.3%	7.8%
BARRON	3,103	538	2,304	261	Bush	17.3%	74.3%	8.4%
BAYFIELD	1,495	287	1,075	133	Bush	19.2%	71.9%	8.9%
BROWN	21,587	4,256	15,872	1,459	Bush	19.7%	73.5%	6.8%
BUFFALO	1,153	188	842	123	Bush	16.3%	73.0%	10.7%
BURNETT	1,342	198	973	171	Bush	14.8%	72.5%	12.7%
CALUMET	3,948	752	2,902	294	Bush	19.0%	73.5%	7.4%
CHIPPEWA	3,424	705	2,444	275	Bush	20.6%	71.4%	8.0%
CLARK	2,531	589	1,667	275	Bush	23.3%	65.9%	10.9%
COLUMBIA	4,339	540	3,530	269	Bush	12.4%	81.4%	6.2%
CRAWFORD	1,733	264	1,315	154	Bush	15.2%	75.9%	8.9%
DANE	30,858	4,027	23,954	2,877	Bush	13.1%	77.6%	9.3%
DODGE	7,431	1,123	5,866	442	Bush	15.1%	78.9%	5.9%
DOOR	3,382	493	2,655	234	Bush	14.6%	78.5%	6.9%

WISCONSIN REPUBLICAN

1992

County	Total Vote	Buchanan	Bush	Other	Winner	Percentage of Total Vote: Buchanan	Bush	Other
DOUGLAS	3,592	775	2,566	251	Bush	21.6%	71.4%	7.0%
DUNN	2,994	592	2,114	288	Bush	19.8%	70.6%	9.6%
EAU CLAIRE	6,226	1,057	4,701	468	Bush	17.0%	75.5%	7.5%
FLORENCE	798	83	660	55	Bush	10.4%	82.7%	6.9%
FOND DU LAC	7,599	1,525	5,654	420	Bush	20.1%	74.4%	5.5%
FOREST	1,035	99	851	85	Bush	9.6%	82.2%	8.2%
GRANT	3,892	523	3,012	357	Bush	13.4%	77.4%	9.2%
GREEN	2,136	295	1,686	155	Bush	13.8%	78.9%	7.3%
GREEN LAKE	2,345	380	1,607	358	Bush	16.2%	68.5%	15.3%
IOWA	1,763	208	1,366	189	Bush	11.8%	77.5%	10.7%
IRON	721	90	555	76	Bush	12.5%	77.0%	10.5%
JACKSON	1,344	259	955	130	Bush	19.3%	71.1%	9.7%
JEFFERSON	6,419	997	4,803	619	Bush	15.5%	74.8%	9.6%
JUNEAU	2,846	495	2,127	224	Bush	17.4%	74.7%	7.9%
KENOSHA	10,049	1,427	7,789	833	Bush	14.2%	77.5%	8.3%
KEWAUNEE	2,604	482	1,875	247	Bush	18.5%	72.0%	9.5%
LA CROSSE	10,048	1,661	7,626	761	Bush	16.5%	75.9%	7.6%
LAFAYETTE	1,923	258	1,522	143	Bush	13.4%	79.1%	7.4%
LANGLADE	2,065	236	1,651	178	Bush	11.4%	80.0%	8.6%
LINCOLN	2,504	273	2,101	130	Bush	10.9%	83.9%	5.2%
MANITOWOC	8,136	1,695	5,796	645	Bush	20.8%	71.2%	7.9%
MARATHON	9,873	1,408	7,796	669	Bush	14.3%	79.0%	6.8%
MARINETTE	4,695	792	3,474	429	Bush	16.9%	74.0%	9.1%
MARQUETTE	1,316	183	961	172	Bush	13.9%	73.0%	13.1%
MENOMINEE	134	25	94	15	Bush	18.7%	70.1%	11.2%
MILWAUKEE	92,991	14,632	70,661	7,698	Bush	15.7%	76.0%	8.3%
MONROE	4,099	567	3,197	335	Bush	13.8%	78.0%	8.2%
OCONTO	3,649	682	2,610	357	Bush	18.7%	71.5%	9.8%
ONEIDA	3,246	340	2,492	414	Bush	10.5%	76.8%	12.8%
OUTAGAMIE	15,065	2,398	11,661	1,006	Bush	15.9%	77.4%	6.7%
OZAUKEE	10,813	1,717	8,587	509	Bush	15.9%	79.4%	4.7%
PEPIN	638	143	438	57	Bush	22.4%	68.7%	8.9%
PIERCE	2,389	439	1,732	218	Bush	18.4%	72.5%	9.1%
POLK	3,061	615	2,132	314	Bush	20.1%	69.7%	10.3%
PORTAGE	3,753	568	2,877	308	Bush	15.1%	76.7%	8.2%
PRICE	1,418	231	1,058	129	Bush	16.3%	74.6%	9.1%
RACINE	14,754	2,654	10,637	1,463	Bush	18.0%	72.1%	9.9%
RICHLAND	2,006	291	1,567	148	Bush	14.5%	78.1%	7.4%
ROCK	10,712	1,449	8,191	1,072	Bush	13.5%	76.5%	10.0%
RUSK	1,850	302	1,369	179	Bush	16.3%	74.0%	9.7%
ST. CROIX	3,051	598	2,219	234	Bush	19.6%	72.7%	7.7%
SAUK	4,827	597	3,873	357	Bush	12.4%	80.2%	7.4%
SAWYER	1,317	237	910	170	Bush	18.0%	69.1%	12.9%
SHAWANO	3,830	683	2,848	299	Bush	17.8%	74.4%	7.8%
SHEBOYGAN	10,859	1,775	8,418	666	Bush	16.3%	77.5%	6.1%
TAYLOR	2,067	405	1,454	208	Bush	19.6%	70.3%	10.1%
TREMPEALEAU	2,033	291	1,551	191	Bush	14.3%	76.3%	9.4%
VERNON	2,408	475	1,719	214	Bush	19.7%	71.4%	8.9%
VILAS	2,464	235	1,990	239	Bush	9.5%	80.8%	9.7%
WALWORTH	8,733	1,198	7,023	512	Bush	13.7%	80.4%	5.9%

WISCONSIN REPUBLICAN

1992

County	Total Vote	Buchanan	Bush	Other	Winner	Percentage of Total Vote: Buchanan	Bush	Other
WASHBURN	1,413	255	997	161	Bush	18.0%	70.6%	11.4%
WASHINGTON	11,545	2,233	8,545	767	Bush	19.3%	74.0%	6.6%
WAUKESHA	40,937	7,607	30,379	2,951	Bush	18.6%	74.2%	7.2%
WAUPACA	4,666	733	3,414	519	Bush	15.7%	73.2%	11.1%
WAUSHARA	2,560	403	1,820	337	Bush	15.7%	71.1%	13.2%
WINNEBAGO	14,745	2,257	10,931	1,557	Bush	15.3%	74.1%	10.6%
WOOD	7,611	1,197	5,982	432	Bush	15.7%	78.6%	5.7%
TOTAL	482,248	78,516	364,507	39,225	Bush	16.3%	75.6%	8.1%

WISCONSIN DEMOCRATIC

1996

County	Total Vote	Clinton	Other	Winner	Percentage of Total Vote: Clinton	Other
ADAMS	1,944	1,896	48	Clinton	97.5%	2.5%
ASHLAND	1,611	1,571	40	Clinton	97.5%	2.5%
BARRON	2,185	2,142	43	Clinton	98.0%	2.0%
BAYFIELD	1,384	1,345	39	Clinton	97.2%	2.8%
BROWN	12,176	11,888	288	Clinton	97.6%	2.4%
BUFFALO	913	889	24	Clinton	97.4%	2.6%
BURNETT	991	969	22	Clinton	97.8%	2.2%
CALUMET	2,145	2,082	63	Clinton	97.1%	2.9%
CHIPPEWA	2,280	2,220	60	Clinton	97.4%	2.6%
CLARK	2,090	2,027	63	Clinton	97.0%	3.0%
COLUMBIA	2,600	2,559	41	Clinton	98.4%	1.6%
CRAWFORD	1,562	1,537	25	Clinton	98.4%	1.6%
DANE	33,423	32,325	1,098	Clinton	96.7%	3.3%
DODGE	3,522	3,452	70	Clinton	98.0%	2.0%
DOOR	1,253	1,223	30	Clinton	97.6%	2.4%
DOUGLAS	2,833	2,790	43	Clinton	98.5%	1.5%
DUNN	2,043	1,976	67	Clinton	96.7%	3.3%
EAU CLAIRE	5,999	5,865	134	Clinton	97.8%	2.2%
FLORENCE	366	356	10	Clinton	97.3%	2.7%
FOND DU LAC	2,703	2,629	74	Clinton	97.3%	2.7%
FOREST	977	958	19	Clinton	98.1%	1.9%
GRANT	1,890	1,842	48	Clinton	97.5%	2.5%
GREEN	1,109	1,089	20	Clinton	98.2%	1.8%
GREEN LAKE	868	850	18	Clinton	97.9%	2.1%
IOWA	1,095	1,078	17	Clinton	98.4%	1.6%
IRON	903	881	22	Clinton	97.6%	2.4%
JACKSON	1,191	1,177	14	Clinton	98.8%	1.2%
JEFFERSON	2,109	2,066	43	Clinton	98.0%	2.0%
JUNEAU	1,165	1,140	25	Clinton	97.9%	2.1%
KENOSHA	10,283	10,048	235	Clinton	97.7%	2.3%

WISCONSIN DEMOCRATIC

1996

County	Total Vote	Clinton	Other	Winner	Percentage of Total Vote Clinton	Other
KEWAUNEE	1,352	1,321	31	Clinton	97.7%	2.3%
LA CROSSE	7,442	7,279	163	Clinton	97.8%	2.2%
LAFAYETTE	1,249	1,230	19	Clinton	98.5%	1.5%
LANGLADE	1,160	1,134	26	Clinton	97.8%	2.2%
LINCOLN	1,611	1,571	40	Clinton	97.5%	2.5%
MANITOWOC	5,006	4,907	99	Clinton	98.0%	2.0%
MARATHON	6,077	5,967	110	Clinton	98.2%	1.8%
MARINETTE	2,999	2,921	78	Clinton	97.4%	2.6%
MARQUETTE	819	803	16	Clinton	98.0%	2.0%
MENOMINEE	174	168	6	Clinton	96.6%	3.4%
MILWAUKEE	112,304	109,533	2,771	Clinton	97.5%	2.5%
MONROE	2,822	2,763	59	Clinton	97.9%	2.1%
OCONTO	2,201	2,169	32	Clinton	98.5%	1.5%
ONEIDA	2,398	2,338	60	Clinton	97.5%	2.5%
OUTAGAMIE	8,367	8,166	201	Clinton	97.6%	2.4%
OZAUKEE	2,859	2,781	78	Clinton	97.3%	2.7%
PEPIN	473	467	6	Clinton	98.7%	1.3%
PIERCE	1,747	1,731	16	Clinton	99.1%	0.9%
POLK	2,343	2,288	55	Clinton	97.7%	2.3%
PORTAGE	3,628	3,558	70	Clinton	98.1%	1.9%
PRICE	1,071	1,046	25	Clinton	97.7%	2.3%
RACINE	12,395	12,097	298	Clinton	97.6%	2.4%
RICHLAND	1,168	1,163	5	Clinton	99.6%	0.4%
ROCK	8,458	8,302	156	Clinton	98.2%	1.8%
RUSK	1,106	1,084	22	Clinton	98.0%	2.0%
ST. CROIX	2,302	2,242	60	Clinton	97.4%	2.6%
SAUK	2,062	2,006	56	Clinton	97.3%	2.7%
SAWYER	1,397	1,352	45	Clinton	96.8%	3.2%
SHAWANO	1,422	1,398	24	Clinton	98.3%	1.7%
SHEBOYGAN	5,734	5,662	72	Clinton	98.7%	1.3%
TAYLOR	1,297	1,259	38	Clinton	97.1%	2.9%
TREMPEALEAU	1,808	1,775	33	Clinton	98.2%	1.8%
VERNON	1,873	1,831	42	Clinton	97.8%	2.2%
VILAS	2,035	1,975	60	Clinton	97.1%	2.9%
WALWORTH	4,289	4,156	133	Clinton	96.9%	3.1%
WASHBURN	1,096	1,069	27	Clinton	97.5%	2.5%
WASHINGTON	4,324	4,220	104	Clinton	97.6%	2.4%
WAUKESHA	15,518	15,172	346	Clinton	97.8%	2.2%
WAUPACA	2,204	2,141	63	Clinton	97.1%	2.9%
WAUSHARA	1,272	1,244	28	Clinton	97.8%	2.2%
WINNEBAGO	5,980	5,830	150	Clinton	97.5%	2.5%
WOOD	4,713	4,640	73	Clinton	98.5%	1.5%
TOTAL	356,168	347,629	8,539	Clinton	97.6%	2.4%

WISCONSIN REPUBLICAN

1996

County	Total Vote	Buchanan	Dole	Other	Winner	Percentage of Total Vote Buchanan	Dole	Other
ADAMS	2,504	879	1,332	293	Dole	35.1%	53.2%	11.7%
ASHLAND	1,699	502	950	247	Dole	29.5%	55.9%	14.5%
BARRON	3,304	1,098	1,812	394	Dole	33.2%	54.8%	11.9%
BAYFIELD	1,597	486	880	231	Dole	30.4%	55.1%	14.5%
BROWN	25,708	7,339	14,469	3,900	Dole	28.5%	56.3%	15.2%
BUFFALO	1,410	377	848	185	Dole	26.7%	60.1%	13.1%
BURNETT	1,295	441	680	174	Dole	34.1%	52.5%	13.4%
CALUMET	4,844	1,618	2,485	741	Dole	33.4%	51.3%	15.3%
CHIPPEWA	4,267	1,719	2,082	466	Dole	40.3%	48.8%	10.9%
CLARK	3,798	1,486	1,890	422	Dole	39.1%	49.8%	11.1%
COLUMBIA	5,323	1,829	2,869	625	Dole	34.4%	53.9%	11.7%
CRAWFORD	2,043	804	949	290	Dole	39.4%	46.5%	14.2%
DANE	40,721	11,292	22,257	7,172	Dole	27.7%	54.7%	17.6%
DODGE	8,714	3,254	4,583	877	Dole	37.3%	52.6%	10.1%
DOOR	3,438	898	1,983	557	Dole	26.1%	57.7%	16.2%
DOUGLAS	2,620	914	1,354	352	Dole	34.9%	51.7%	13.4%
DUNN	3,160	1,100	1,581	479	Dole	34.8%	50.0%	15.2%
EAU CLAIRE	8,928	2,704	5,015	1,209	Dole	30.3%	56.2%	13.5%
FLORENCE	722	238	397	87	Dole	33.0%	55.0%	12.0%
FOND DU LAC	9,117	3,284	4,768	1,065	Dole	36.0%	52.3%	11.7%
FOREST	1,262	398	689	175	Dole	31.5%	54.6%	13.9%
GRANT	4,116	1,568	1,917	631	Dole	38.1%	46.6%	15.3%
GREEN	2,627	805	1,525	297	Dole	30.6%	58.1%	11.3%
GREEN LAKE	2,368	788	1,305	275	Dole	33.3%	55.1%	11.6%
IOWA	1,901	576	1,065	260	Dole	30.3%	56.0%	13.7%
IRON	1,040	313	599	128	Dole	30.1%	57.6%	12.3%
JACKSON	1,788	620	970	198	Dole	34.7%	54.3%	11.1%
JEFFERSON	6,684	2,429	3,392	863	Dole	36.3%	50.7%	12.9%
JUNEAU	2,558	999	1,292	267	Dole	39.1%	50.5%	10.4%
KENOSHA	12,847	4,824	6,208	1,815	Dole	37.5%	48.3%	14.1%
KEWAUNEE	2,670	914	1,382	374	Dole	34.2%	51.8%	14.0%
LA CROSSE	11,774	3,307	6,927	1,540	Dole	28.1%	58.8%	13.1%
LAFAYETTE	2,104	722	1,090	292	Dole	34.3%	51.8%	13.9%
LANGLADE	2,059	650	1,153	256	Dole	31.6%	56.0%	12.4%
LINCOLN	2,968	1,042	1,560	366	Dole	35.1%	52.6%	12.3%
MANITOWOC	8,455	3,110	4,198	1,147	Dole	36.8%	49.7%	13.6%
MARATHON	11,162	3,744	5,905	1,513	Dole	33.5%	52.9%	13.6%
MARINETTE	6,069	2,045	3,231	793	Dole	33.7%	53.2%	13.1%
MARQUETTE	1,782	709	884	189	Dole	39.8%	49.6%	10.6%
MENOMINEE	119	33	68	18	Dole	27.7%	57.1%	15.1%
MILWAUKEE	107,782	40,477	51,746	15,559	Dole	37.6%	48.0%	14.4%
MONROE	4,907	1,648	2,712	547	Dole	33.6%	55.3%	11.1%
OCONTO	4,255	1,397	2,301	557	Dole	32.8%	54.1%	13.1%
ONEIDA	4,597	1,363	2,524	710	Dole	29.6%	54.9%	15.4%
OUTAGAMIE	17,680	5,338	9,493	2,849	Dole	30.2%	53.7%	16.1%
OZAUKEE	12,229	3,659	6,881	1,689	Dole	29.9%	56.3%	13.8%
PEPIN	569	186	321	62	Dole	32.7%	56.4%	10.9%
PIERCE	2,268	649	1,306	313	Dole	28.6%	57.6%	13.8%
POLK	2,925	870	1,645	410	Dole	29.7%	56.2%	14.0%
PORTAGE	5,148	1,861	2,575	712	Dole	36.1%	50.0%	13.8%

WISCONSIN REPUBLICAN

1996

County	Total Vote	Buchanan	Dole	Other	Winner	Percentage of Total Vote Buchanan	Dole	Other
PRICE	1,688	621	863	204	Dole	36.8%	51.1%	12.1%
RACINE	22,831	8,604	11,357	2,870	Dole	37.7%	49.7%	12.6%
RICHLAND	2,469	835	1,270	364	Dole	33.8%	51.4%	14.7%
ROCK	13,055	3,996	7,250	1,809	Dole	30.6%	55.5%	13.9%
RUSK	1,769	814	774	181	Buchanan	46.0%	43.8%	10.2%
ST. CROIX	3,891	976	2,298	617	Dole	25.1%	59.1%	15.9%
SAUK	4,869	1,619	2,588	662	Dole	33.3%	53.2%	13.6%
SAWYER	2,452	755	1,387	310	Dole	30.8%	56.6%	12.6%
SHAWANO	4,303	1,417	2,410	476	Dole	32.9%	56.0%	11.1%
SHEBOYGAN	12,293	4,138	6,023	2,132	Dole	33.7%	49.0%	17.3%
TAYLOR	2,786	1,154	1,313	319	Dole	41.4%	47.1%	11.5%
TREMPEALEAU	2,322	777	1,255	290	Dole	33.5%	54.0%	12.5%
VERNON	3,261	1,203	1,658	400	Dole	36.9%	50.8%	12.3%
VILAS	3,777	917	2,326	534	Dole	24.3%	61.6%	14.1%
WALWORTH	10,253	3,113	5,870	1,270	Dole	30.4%	57.3%	12.4%
WASHBURN	1,554	512	850	192	Dole	32.9%	54.7%	12.4%
WASHINGTON	14,885	5,744	7,350	1,791	Dole	38.6%	49.4%	12.0%
WAUKESHA	52,662	18,158	27,639	6,865	Dole	34.5%	52.5%	13.0%
WAUPACA	5,841	1,791	3,303	747	Dole	30.7%	56.5%	12.8%
WAUSHARA	2,793	1,024	1,477	292	Dole	36.7%	52.9%	10.5%
WINNEBAGO	14,189	4,208	7,769	2,212	Dole	29.7%	54.8%	15.6%
WOOD	8,707	3,051	4,550	1,106	Dole	35.0%	52.3%	12.7%
TOTAL	576,575	194,733	301,628	80,214	Dole	33.8%	52.3%	13.9%

WYOMING

Although presidential primaries are much in vogue in the rest of the country, they have not caught on in Wyoming. But in a sense, the traditional caucus fits the old-fashioned style of the state's politics. There is no major media market and Wyoming has been likened to one town "spread over miles and miles."

Neither party's caucuses draw more than several thousand voters statewide. But while GOP voters in the heavily Republican state can be found all over, Democrats are concentrated in the southern tier. More than a century ago, immigrant laborers came to southern Wyoming to build the Union Pacific rail line; the state's first coal miners followed. Like their counterparts in other states, most of these working men were drawn to the Democratic Party.

But the hearty band of Wyoming Democrats is hardly a liberal club. Democratic caucus-goers provided Bill Clinton with his first win outside the South in 1992 and gave Al Gore his initial victory anywhere in 1988. Four years earlier, Wyoming Democrats voted overwhelmingly for regional favorite son, Gary Hart of Colorado.

In recent years, Wyoming's Democratic caucuses have traditionally been held in early March on the eve of Super Tuesday. In 1988, the result was something of a split decision. Michael Dukakis ran ahead in the head count of caucus participants, but in the vote that mattered most—the election of delegates to the state convention—Al Gore won by a narrow margin. Gore thus gained a measure of momentum going into the Super Tuesday events, which would be the high-water mark of his candidacy that year.

In Wyoming two factors worked in Gore's favor. He was seen as a moderate Democrat, and he had the support of popular former Democratic Gov. Ed Herschler. Gore carried Natrona County (Casper), the second most populous in the state, as well as much of rural Wyoming.

Republicans in the Cowboy State are as conservative as their GOP brethren in other Rocky Mountain states, but they do not always move in lockstep with them.

In 1952, the Wyoming delegation divided evenly between Dwight Eisenhower and Robert Taft when most other states in the region were overwhelmingly for Taft. In 1976, though a majority of Wyoming's delegation was for Ronald Reagan, President Gerald Ford won more delegates in Wyoming than any other Rocky Mountain state.

Still, one thing has remained constant about Wyoming and that is its bit role in the presidential nominating process. The last time that Wyoming took center stage was at the 1960 Democratic convention. With John Kennedy on the verge of victory, Wyoming's divided delegation regrouped to vote as a bloc and dramatically put Kennedy over the top near the end of the first roll call.

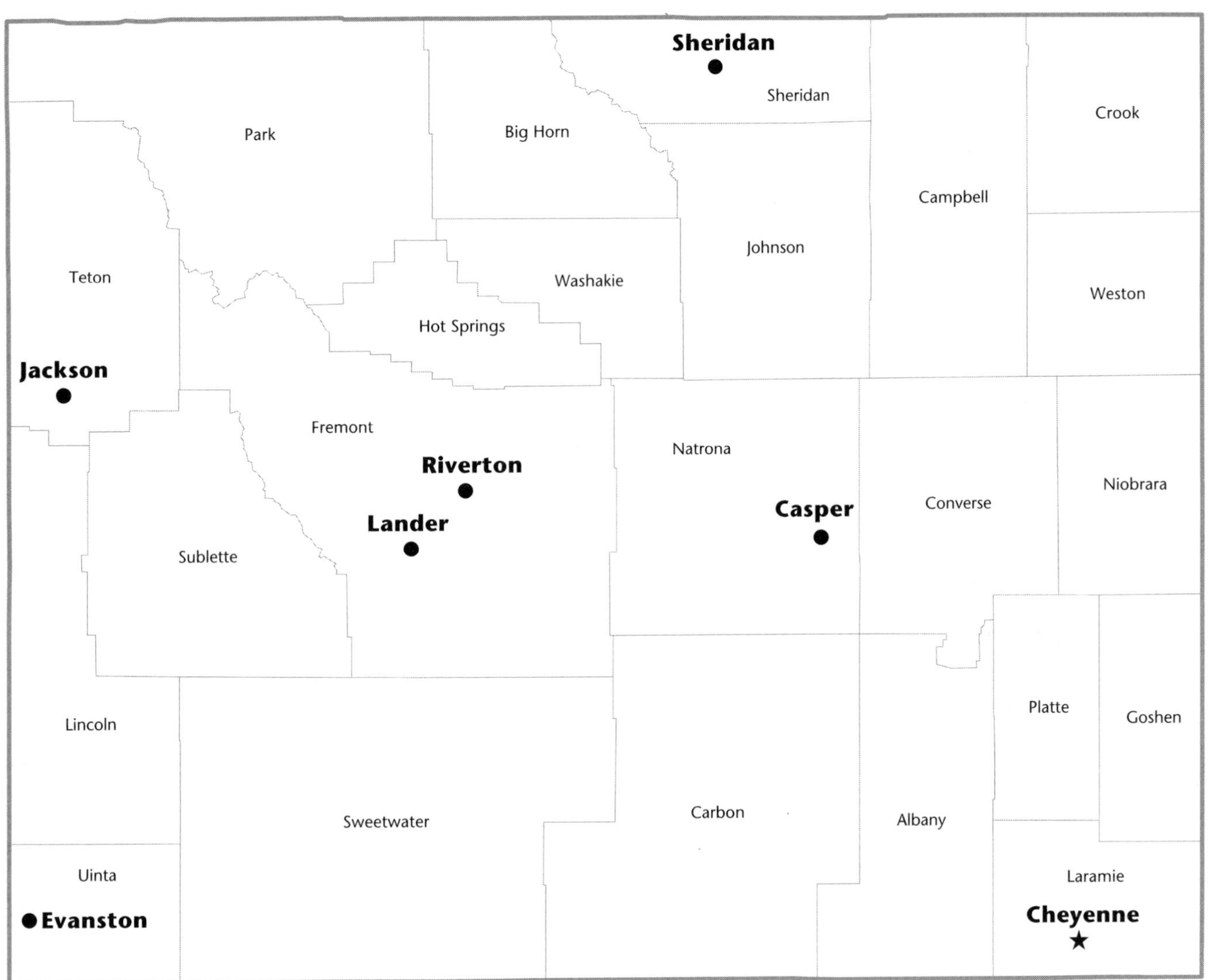
Sheridan
Sheridan
Park
Big Horn
Crook
Campbell
Johnson
Teton
Washakie
Weston
Hot Springs
Jackson
Fremont
Natrona
Riverton
Niobrara
Casper
Converse
Lander
Sublette
Platte
Goshen
Lincoln
Carbon
Albany
Sweetwater
Uinta
Laramie
Evanston
Cheyenne